KIM&BOOK

꿈을 향한 도전,
김앤북이 함께 합니다!

「김앤북」은 **편입** 교재 외에 **컴퓨터/IT** 관련 교재,
전기/소방, 미용사/사회복지사 등 전문 **자격 수험서**까지
다양한 분야의 도서를 출간하는 **종합 출판사**로 성장하고 있습니다.

편입수험도서
출판전문

✕

취업실용도서
출판전문

김앤북
KIM&BOOK

대학편입은 김영, 편입수험서는 김앤북!
편입수험서 No.1 김앤북

김영편입 영어 시리즈

| 어휘시리즈 | | 기출 1단계(문법, 독해, 논리) | | 워크북 1단계(문법, 독해, 논리) |

| 기출 2단계(문법, 독해, 논리) | | 워크북 2단계(문법, 독해, 논리) | | 기출 3단계(연도별 기출문제 해설집) |

김영편입 수학 시리즈

1단계 이론서(미분법, 적분법, 선형대수, 다변수미적분, 공학수학)

| 2단계 워크북(미분법, 적분법, 선형대수, 다변수미적분, 공학수학) | | 3단계 기출문제 해설집 |

축적된 **방대한 자료**와 **노하우**를 바탕으로 **전문 연구진**들의 교재 개발,
실제 시험과 **유사한** 형태의 문항들을 개발하고 있습니다.
수험생들의 **합격을 위한 맞춤형 콘텐츠**를 제공하고자 합니다.

내일은 시리즈 (자격증/실용 도서)

자격증

정보처리기사 필기, 실기

컴퓨터활용능력 1급, 2급 실기

빅데이터분석기사 필기, 실기

데이터분석 준전문가(ADsP)

GTQ 포토샵 1급

GTQi 일러스트 1급

리눅스마스터 2급

SQL개발자

실용

코딩테스트

파이썬

C언어

플러터

SQL

자바

코틀린(출간예정)

스프링부트(출간예정)

머신러닝(출간예정)

전기/소방 자격증

2024 전기기사 필기
필수기출 1200제

2025 소방설비기사 필기 공통과목
필수기출 400제

2025 소방설비기사 필기 전기분야
필수기출 400제

김앤북의 가치

도전 신뢰

끊임없이 개선하며 **창의적인 사고**와 **혁신적인 마인드**를 중요시합니다.
정직함과 **도덕성**을 갖춘 사고를 바탕으로 회사와 고객, 동료에게 **믿음**을 줍니다.

함께 성장

자신과 회사의 발전을 위해 **꾸준히 학습**하며, 배움을 나누기 위해 노력합니다.
학생, 선생님 **모두 만족**시킬 수 있는 **최고의 교육 콘텐츠**와 **최선의 서비스**를
위해 노력합니다.

독자 중심

한 명의 독자라도 **즐거움**과 **만족**을 느낄 수 있는 책, 많은 독자들이 함께 **교감**하는
책을 만들기 위해 노력합니다. **분야를 막론**하고 **독자들의 마음속**에 오래도록 깊이
남는 **좋은 콘텐츠**를 만들어가겠습니다.

김앤북은 메가스터디 아이비김영의 다양한 교육 전문 브랜드와 함께 합니다.

김영편입   김영평생교육원   미대편입 **Changjo**

UNISTUDY   더조은아카데미   메가스터디아카데미

메가스터디교육그룹 **아이비원격평생교육원**   엔지니어랩

합격을 완성할 단 하나의 선택

김영편입
영어

기출문제 해설집

문제편

PREFACE

편입영어, 점수가 곧 실력이다!

편입영어 시험은 영어를 잘하는 수험생을 선발하는 것이 아니라, 시험 성적이 우수한 학생을 선발하는 것입니다. 어찌 보면 영어를 잘하는 수험생이 편입영어 시험 성적도 높겠지만, 많은 이론을 알고 있다고 해도 실전에 적용하지 못한다면 점수를 올리는 데 한계가 있습니다.

이에 대비하기 위해서는 기출문제를 통해 문제 유형과 난이도를 파악하고, 짧은 제한시간 안에 시간안배를 적절히 하여 문제를 푸는 요령을 터득해야 합니다. 그리고 문제를 푸는 것으로 끝나는 것이 아니라 수험생이 지원하는 대학의 주요 평가요소에 맞춰 효율적으로 학습목표를 설정하는 것이 중요합니다.

『김영편입 영어 2025학년도 대비 기출문제 해설집』은 28개 대학교 46개 유형의 문제를 수록했습니다. 편입 수험생이 2024학년도 편입영어 시험에 출제된 문제를 통해 출제경향과 난이도를 파악하여 실전에 대비할 수 있도록 구성했습니다. 지문 해석뿐만 아니라 선택지 해석, 어휘, 문제 풀이 분석 및 오답에 대한 설명을 제공하여 편입 시험에 도전하는 수험생을 위하여 기출문제에 대한 자신감을 갖도록 기획했습니다.

또한, 영어 시험을 준비하는 자연계 수험생을 위해 인문계 문제 중 자연계에서 공통으로 출제되는 영어 문제에 대해서는 해당 문제 옆에 별도 표기를 하여 계열별 기출 문제를 쉽게 확인할 수 있도록 구성했습니다.

끝으로 바쁘신 와중에도 해설 원고 집필에 도움을 주셨던 김영편입 김응석, 배장현, 오수원, 윤상환 교수에게 감사의 마음을 전합니다.

김영편입 컨텐츠평가연구소

HOW TO STUDY

기출문제집에 수록된 모든 대학의 문제를 풀어보자!

기출문제는 각 대학별로 파트별 출제비율, 문제의 난이도, 문항 수, 제한시간 등은 다르지만 다양한 대학의 기출문제를 통해 실전감각을 익히는 데 도움이 될 것입니다. 처음부터 문제의 난이도가 높은 대학의 문제를 풀기보다는 본인의 수준에 맞는 문제를 통해 그동안 익혔던 이론을 실전에 대입해 보고 점차 난이도를 높여가는 것이 필요합니다.

실제 시험과 동일한 환경에서 풀어보자!

편입시험은 제한된 시간에 많은 문제를 풀어야 하기 때문에 시간안배가 중요합니다. 또한 문항별 배점이 다른 대학의 경우 배점이 높은 문제를 먼저 풀어 부족한 시간에 대비하는 것도 필요합니다. 실제 시험장에서 긴장하지 않고 시험환경에 얼마나 잘 적응할 수 있느냐가 고득점의 필수요건이므로, 기출문제집을 통해 이에 대비해야 합니다.

풀어본 문제는 해설과 함께 다시 한 번 확인하여 정리하자!

기출문제 해설집에는 지문 해석뿐만 아니라 문제의 해석, 분석, 어휘, 오답에 대한 설명 등이 상세하게 수록됐습니다.

어휘는 기출어휘에서 출제되는 경향이 높으므로 표제어뿐만 아니라, 선택지에 제시된 어휘를 잘 정리해서 암기해야 합니다. 『김영편입 영어 2025학년도 대비 기출문제 해설집』은 출제된 어휘를 상세하게 수록하여 사전의 도움 없이 어휘 학습이 가능하도록 구성했습니다.

문법은 문제별 출제 포인트를 제시하고, 해설과 문제에 적용된 문법 사항을 정리하여 문제를 쉽게 이해할 수 있도록 했습니다. 오답 노트를 만들어 취약한 부분을 정리하는 것이 필요하며, 해설이 이해가 안 되는 경우 문법 이론서를 통해 해당 문법 사항을 반드시 이해하고 넘어가야 합니다.

논리완성은 문제를 풀기 위해서 문장을 정확히 분석하는 능력을 키우는 동시에 다량의 어휘를 숙지하고 있어야 합니다. 『김영편입 영어 2025학년도 대비 기출문제 해설집』은 문제에 대한 정확한 해석뿐만 아니라 글이 어떻게 구성되어 해당 어휘가 빈칸에 적절한지에 대한 상세한 분석이 돼 있습니다. 또한 문제 및 선택지에 출제된 어휘도 상세히 수록하여 어휘 학습을 병행하는 데 도움이 되도록 구성했습니다.

독해는 편입시험에서 가장 비중이 높은 영역입니다. 지문 해석뿐만 아니라 선택지도 해석이 돼 있어 편입을 처음 접하는 학생들도 쉽게 이해할 수 있도록 구성했으며 오답에 대한 설명을 수록하여 문제의 이해도를 높였습니다.

CONTENTS

해설편

대학명		문법			어휘			논리완성	독해	생활영어	총 문항 수
		G/S, W/E	정문, 비문	재진술	동의어, 숙어	반의어	유추			대화문	
가천대 [인문계 A형]	문항 수	5			8			9	18		40
	백분율	12.5			20			22.5	45		100
가천대 [인문계 B형]	문항 수	3			8			11	18		40
	백분율	7.5			20			27.5	45		100
가톨릭대 [인문계]	문항 수	5						15	20		40
	백분율	12.5						37.5	50		100
건국대 [인문·예체능계]	문항 수	4			6			16	14		40
	백분율	10			15			40	35		100
건국대 [자연계]	문항 수	2			3			6	7	2	20
	백분율	10			15			30	35	10	100
경기대 [일반, 학사편입]	문항 수	10						10	10	10	40
	백분율	25						25	25	25	100
경찰대 [일반대학생 전형]	문항 수	2	2		5				30	1	40
	백분율	5	5		12.5				75	2.5	100
경희대 [인문체육계열]	문항 수				5			9	26		40
	백분율				12.5			22.5	65		100
경희대 [한의학과(인문)]	문항 수				10			9	31		50
	백분율				20			18	62		100

대학명		문법			어휘			논리완성	독해	생활영어	총 문항 수
		G/S, W/E	정문, 비문	재진술	동의어, 숙어	반의어	유추			대화문	
고려대 [세종 인문·자연계]	문항 수	8			5			7	20		40
	백분율	20			12.5			17.5	50		100
광운대 [인문계 1교시, 2교시]	문항 수		11					12	16	1	40
	백분율		27.5					30	40	2.5	100
단국대 [인문계 오전, 오후]	문항 수	10			10				20		40
	백분율	25			25				50		100
단국대 [자연계 오전, 오후]	문항 수	6			8				16		30
	백분율	20			26.7				53.3		100
덕성여대 [1교시]	문항 수	7			6			6	14		33
	백분율	21.2			18.2			18.2	42.4		100
덕성여대 [2교시]	문항 수	8			7			5	14		34
	백분율	23.5			20.6			14.7	41.2		100
명지대 [인문계]	문항 수	5			3			7	15		30
	백분율	16.7			10			23.3	50		100
서강대 [1차, 2차]	문항 수	4						6	20		30
	백분율	13						20	67		100
서울시립대 [인문계]	문항 수	2			2	1		7	28		40
	백분율	5			5	2.5		17.5	70		100
서울시립대 [자연계 II]	문항 수	1			1			4	14		20
	백분율	5			5			20	70		100

대학명		문법			어휘			논리완성	독해	생활영어	총 문항 수
		G/S, W/E	정문, 비문	재진술	동의어, 숙어	반의어	유추			대화문	
서울여대 [오전, 정오]	문항 수	10			5			11	14		40
	백분율	25			12.5			27.5	35		100
성균관대 [인문계]	문항 수	5			5			10	30		50
	백분율	10			10			20	60		100
성균관대 [자연계]	문항 수	2			3			5	15		25
	백분율	8			12			20	60		100
세종대 [인문계]	문항 수	30					5	10	15		60
	백분율	50					8.3	16.7	25		100
숙명여대 [A형]	문항 수	5			3			8	17		33
	백분율	15			9			24	52		100
숙명여대 [B형]	문항 수	4			3			9	17		33
	백분율	12			9			27	52		100
숭실대 [인문계]	문항 수	2			4			4	40		50
	백분율	4			8			8	80		100
숭실대 [자연계]	문항 수	2			4			4	15		25
	백분율	8			16			16	60		100
아주대 [인문계]	문항 수	9						5	36		50
	백분율	18						10	72		100
아주대 [자연계]	문항 수	4						3	18		25
	백분율	16						12	72		100

대학명		문법			어휘			논리완성	독해	생활영어	총 문항 수
		G/S, W/E	정문, 비문	재진술	동의어, 숙어	반의어	유추			대화문	
이화여대 [인문계 유형 1]	문항 수	4			5	5		20	16		50
	백분율	8			10	10		40	32		100
인하대 [인문계]	문항 수								40		40
	백분율								100		100
중앙대 [인문계]	문항 수	3			7			14	14	2	40
	백분율	7.5			17.5			35	35	5	100
한국공학대 [인문계]	문항 수	9			5			11	15		40
	백분율	22.5			12.5			27.5	37.5		100
한국외대 [T1, T2-1]	문항 수	4	2	2	9			4	29		50
	백분율	8	4	4	18			8	58		100
한국항공대 [인문계]	문항 수	2			5			10	13		30
	백분율	6.7			16.7			33.3	43.3		100
한성대 [인문계]	문항 수							11	34	5	50
	백분율							22	68	10	100
한양대 [서울 인문계]	문항 수				8			7	20		35
	백분율				23			20	57		100
홍익대 [서울 인문계]	문항 수	8			10			10	12		40
	백분율	20			25			25	30		100
홍익대 [서울 자연계]	문항 수	7			9			3	6		25
	백분율	28			36			12	24		100

ANALYSIS②

서강대학교

일반편입 / 인문계 / 30문항·60분

출제경향 및 난이도 분석

▶▶ 서강대는 1차(일반편입(인문))와 2차(학사편입(인문), 일반[학사]편입(자연))로 구분해 두 차례 편입영어 시험이 시행됐다. 지난해와 마찬가지로 30문항·60분으로 진행됐으며, 각 문제 당 차등배점을 부여했는데 난이도가 높은 독해 문제의 배점이 높았다. 서강대의 경우 매년 유형별 문항 수가 조금씩 바뀌는데 지난해와 달리 어휘는 출제되지 않았고, 문법의 비중이 감소했으며, 논리완성과 독해의 비중이 증가했다.

2022~2024학년도 서강대 영역별 문항 수 비교

구분	어휘	문법	논리완성	독해	합계
2022학년도	2	4	11	23	40
2023학년도	2	6	4	18	30
2024학년도	-	4	6	20	30

2024 서강대 영역별 분석

문법

구분	2022	2023	2024
W/E	-	4	2
G/S	4	2	2
합계	4/40 (10%)	6/30 (20%)	4/30 (13%)

▶▶ 대화문에서 어법상 옳지 않은 것을 고르는 유형 2문제와 밑줄 친 부분 중 어법상 옳지 않은 것을 고르는 Written Expression 유형 2문제가 출제됐다. 대화문에서 어법상 옳지 않은 것을 고르는 문제의 경우 올해 새롭게 출제된 문법 유형이기는 했지만, 기본적인 문법사항이 출제되어 정답을 고르는 데 어려움은 없었을 것이다. 출제된 문법사항으로는 명확한 과거를 나타내는 표현과 함께 쓰지 못하는 현재완료시제, 분사를 정동사의 역할을 할 수 있는 과거시제 동사로 고치는 문의 구성, 명사를 수식하는 형용사 등이 있었다.

논리완성

구분	2022	2023	2024
문항 수	11/40 (27.5%)	4/30 (13.3%)	6/30 (20%)

▶▶ 총 6문제가 출제됐는데 기존에 출제되었던 multi-blank 유형의 문제는 출제되지 않았고, one-blank 유형의 문제만 출제됐다. 토마스 모어가 불멸의 고전을 출판하여 잠시 '중단(abeyance)'된 문학의 유토피아가 되살아난 배경에 관한 문제, 절망이 자신을 압도하도록 내버려 두지 않는 상태를 나타낼 수 있는 'composure(평정)'를 고

르는 문제, 불변성과 반대되는 의미를 내포하고 있는 'malleable(유연한)'을 고르는 문제, 담배의 포장에 불쾌한 색상을 사용하고 병든 장기의 이미지를 동반하는 의도가 무엇인지 고르는 문제, 'comprehensive overview(포괄적인 개요)'와 유사한 의미를 나타낼 수 있는 'aggregate(종합하다)'를 고르는 문제 등이 출제됐다. 지난해에 비해 장문의 논리완성 문제의 비중이 증가했지만, 빈칸을 전후로 빈칸을 추론할 수 있는 단서가 비교적 명확히 제시되었으며 선택지의 단어도 기출어휘로 구성되어 문제의 내용을 제대로 이해했다면 정답을 고르기 어렵지 않았다.

독해

구분	2022	2023	2024
지문 수	9	8	9
문항 수	23/40 (57.5%)	18/30 (60%)	20/30 (67%)

▶▶ 문제의 난이도와 출제 유형은 지난해와 큰 차이가 없었다. 출제된 유형을 살펴보면 글의 제목, 글의 요지, 내용일치, 내용추론, 동의어, 문맥상 적절하지 않은 단어 고르기, 문장배열 등 편입시험에 자주 출제되는 유형이 골고루 출제됐다. 특히 글의 제목, 동의어, 문맥상 적절하지 않은 단어 고르기 등의 문제의 비중이 높았다. 출제된 지문의 내용을 살펴보면 건축에서 장식의 중요성, 브루투스의 혈통이 암살 음모에 대한 대응에 미친 영향, 인간이 포스트휴먼이 되고 있는 상황, 셰익스피어의 저작자 논란, '디지털'이라는 용어의 기원과 현재까지의 사용, 언어와 추상적 사고의 관계에 대한 철학적 개념, 범죄자에 대한 처벌에 초점을 맞추는 대신 치료와 갱생을 지향할 것을 주장하는 칼 메닝거 박사의 견해, 영국 식민지 호텔 바의 인종차별 등 다양한 주제의 지문이 문제로 출제됐다.

2025
서강대 대비
학습 전략

▶▶ 서강대는 문제 유형이 매년 조금씩 변경된다. 2023학년도 문제와 비교했을 때, 2024학년도의 경우 어휘가 출제되지 않았고 문법은 General Structure 유형이 출제되지 않고 대화문을 읽고 문법적으로 틀린 부분을 고르는 새로운 유형의 문제가 출제됐다. 문제 유형이 자주 바뀌는 대학임을 감안할 때 올해 출제되지 않은 문제가 다시 출제될 수 있으므로 최소 3~5개년의 서강대 기출문제를 풀고 출제된 모든 유형에 대한 대비가 필요하다. 그리고 독해의 출제 비중과 배점이 높으므로 다양한 주제의 고급 독해지문을 학습하여 독해력 향상에 힘써야 한다.

성균관대학교

일반·학사편입 / 인문계 / 50문항·90분

출제경향 및 난이도 분석

▶▶ 성균관대 편입영어 시험은 50문항·90분으로 진행됐으며, 영역별로 차등배점이 부여됐다. 특히 독해의 경우 30문항이 출제되어 전체 시험에서 가장 큰 비중을 차지했고, 다른 영역에 비해 문항 당 배점이 높아서 독해 영역이 시험의 당락을 좌우했을 것으로 보인다.

2022~2024학년도 성균관대 영역별 문항 수 비교

구분	어휘	문법	논리완성	독해	합계
2022학년도	5	5	10	30	50
2023학년도	5	5	9	31	50
2024학년도	5	5	10	30	50

2024 성균관대 영역별 분석

어휘

구분	2022	2023	2024
문항 수 (동의어)	5/50 (10%)	5/50 (10%)	5/50 (10%)

▶▶ 밑줄 친 어휘와 의미가 가장 가까운 것을 고르는 동의어 유형 5문제가 출제됐다. 출제된 어휘에는 sedentary(=desk-bound), skimp on(=cut back on), decommission(=deactivate), thriftness(=frugality), trenchant(=incisive)가 있었다. 제시어와 선택지가 대부분 기출어휘였지만 혼동을 줄 수 있는 어휘를 선택지로 제시하여 제시어의 의미를 정확히 알지 못한 수험생들은 정답을 고르기 어려웠을 것이다.

문법

구분	2022	2023	2024
문항 수 (W/E)	5/50 (10%)	5/50 (10%)	5/50 (10%)

▶▶ 밑줄 친 부분 중 어법상 옳지 않은 것을 고르는 Written Expression 유형 5문제가 출제됐다. 출제된 문법 사항으로는 if가 생략된 가정법 과거완료, 능동태와 수동태의 구분, 복수 명사와 호응하는 부정관사, 관계대명사 that/what의 구분, 단수 대명사와 복수 대명사의 구분, 전치사의 목적어로 쓰이는 명사, 동격을 나타내는 접속사 that 등이 있었다. 암기 위주의 문법사항을 물어보기보다 문장의 구조를 파악해야 풀 수 있는 문제가 주로 출제됐다.

논리완성

구분	2022	2023	2024
문항 수	10/50 (20%)	9/50 (18%)	10/50 (20%)

▶▶ 한 단락 길이의 지문에서 빈칸에 적절한 어구를 고르는 유형으로 10문제가 출제됐다. 문제를 풀 수 있는 결정적인 단서가 빈칸 앞뒤로 제시되어 있었지만, 일부 문제는 다의어가 출제되어 정답을 고르는 데 어려움을 주었다. 예를 들어, '법정'이라는 뜻으로 알고 있는 court가 '얻으려고 애쓰다'는 뜻으로도 쓰일 수 있고, '고자질쟁이'라는 뜻으로 알고 있는 telltale이 '숨길 수 없는'이라는 뜻으로도 쓰일 수 있음을 알아야 풀 수 있는 문제들이었다. 문제의 내용을 살펴보면 동남아시아가 추구하는 개발 전략, 석유의 기원과 관련한 소련 기술자들의 견해, 불발로 끝난 감옥 탈출 시도, 임금 인상과 물가 인상의 악순환, 고귀한 목표 추구에 헌신한 사람에 대한 경의, BTS 군 면제와 관련한 루머, 'man'이 갖고 있는 여러 가지 뜻, 선과 악의 이원론, 다양한 민족과 종교로 이루어져 있는 미국, 연쇄살인범을 둘러싼 집단 공포 등 다양한 내용의 글이 논리완성 문제로 활용됐다.

독해

구분	2022	2023	2024
지문 수	16	17	16
문항 수	30/50 (60%)	31/50 (62%)	30/50 (60%)

▶▶ 『The Economist』, 『The New York Times』, 『The Guardian』 등과 같은 대중매체뿐 아니라, 유발 노아 하라리의 『사피엔스(Sapiens)』 같은 베스트셀러에서 발췌한 수준 높은 글이 독해지문으로 출제됐다. 출제된 유형을 살펴보면 문맥상 적절하지 않은 단어 고르기, 글의 요지, 글의 제목, 내용파악, 내용일치, 지시대상, 부분이해, 글의 어조, 빈칸완성, 단락 나누기 등 지난해와 비슷한 유형의 문제가 출제됐다. 지문의 내용을 살펴보면 부자 감세로 인한 낙수 효과, 영어에 미치는 미국의 영향력, 생성형 인공지능의 비즈니스 활용, ChatGPT의 장단점, 중국의 패권주의, 인공지능을 활용한 해커 전술, 매력적인 국가로 만들려는 노력의 한계, 모나리자가 신비롭게 보이는 이유, 감시자본주의와 사생활 침해, 화가들에게 매력적인 동굴, 우주 팽창과 관련된 에드윈 허블의 업적, 커피 수요증가의 원인 등이 출제됐다.

2025 성균관대 대비 학습 전략

▶▶ 성균관대는 유형의 변화가 크지 않으므로 기출문제를 통해 평가 요소를 확인하고 학습 목표를 설정하는 것이 중요하다. 어휘는 기출어휘를 중심으로 학습하고, 문법은 문장의 구조와 관련된 문제가 주로 출제되므로 이에 대한 훈련이 필요하다. 논리완성은 한 단락 길이의 지문에서 문제가 출제되므로 빈칸을 추론할 수 있는 단서를 찾고 빈칸 앞뒤에 제시된 연결어나 지시어를 활용해 문제를 풀 수 있는 능력을 키우는 것이 중요하다. 독해는 현재 사회적으로 이슈가 되고 있는 다양한 분야의 영어 원문과 대중매체의 글을 자주 접하는 것이 도움이 될 것이다.

이화여자대학교

일반·학사편입 / 인문계 유형 1 / 50문항·100분

출제경향 및 난이도 분석

▶▶ 이화여대 편입영어 시험은 반의어 문제와 20지 선택형 논리완성 문제를 매년 출제하고 있다. 특히 20지 선택형 논리완성 문제의 경우 20개의 선택지 중에서 10개의 선택지를 정답으로 골라야 하며, 한 번 정답으로 고른 것은 다른 문제의 정답이 될 수 없으므로 주의해야 한다. 전체적으로 문제의 난이도는 높지만, 편입시험이 50문항·100분간 진행되어 문제 대비 제한시간이 적지 않으므로 서두르지 말고 차분하게 문제를 풀어야 한다.

2022~2024학년도 이화여대 영역별 문항 수 비교

구분	어휘	문법	논리완성	독해	합계
2022학년도	10	4	20	16	50
2023학년도	10	4	20	16	50
2024학년도	10	4	20	16	50

2024 이화여대 영역별 분석

어휘

구분	2022	2023	2024
동의어	4	5	5
반의어	6	5	5
합계	10/50 (20%)	10/50 (20%)	10/50 (20%)

▶▶ 동의어 유형 5문제와 반의어 유형 5문제가 출제됐다. 동의어 문제에는 pedagogical(=educational), convert(=transform), abject(=utter), inadvertently(=unpremeditatedly), decomposition(=breakdown) 이 출제됐으며, 반의어 문제에는 rampant(↔restrained), woeful(↔promising), salient(↔insignificant), polymath (↔ignoramus), detriment(↔advantage)가 출제됐다. 전체적으로 제시어와 선택지의 어휘 수준은 기출어휘를 꼼꼼히 공부한 수험생들이 어렵지 않게 해결할 수 있는 정도였다.

문법

구분	2022	2023	2024
W/E	4	4	4
G/S	–	–	–
합계	4/50 (8%)	4/50 (8%)	4/50 (8%)

▶▶ 밑줄 친 부분 중 어법상 옳지 않은 것을 고르는 Written Expression 유형 4문제가 출제됐는데, 문장구조 파악에 중점을 둔 문제가 대부분이었다. 앞에 제시된 not only를 보고 and를 but으로 고치는 상관접속사 문제 (not only A but also B), 여성의 글을 여성의 '표현으로' 장려한다는 의미가 되도록 전치사 to를 as로 고치는 문제 (promote A as B), 전체 시제인 현재시제에 맞춰 과거완료를 현재완료로 고치는 문제, 명사를 수식하는 품사는 부사가 아니라 형용사이므로 부사를 형용사로 고치는 문제가 출제됐다.

논리완성

구분	2022	2023	2024
문항 수	20/50 (40%)	20/50 (40%)	20/50 (40%)

▶▶ one-blank 유형 3문제, two-blank 유형 7문제, 20지 선택형 10문제가 출제됐다. 문제의 내용을 살펴보면, '면밀히 분석했다(carefully parsed)'와 의미적으로 유사한 '자세히 조사하는(scrutinizing)'을 고르는 문제, 시장의 변동성이 기업들에게 번영뿐 아니라 '역경(adversity)'도 초래할 수 있음을 고르고, 이런 시장의 변동성이 장단점이 있으므로 반드시 환영받는 '상황(state of affairs)'이 아님을 고르는 문제, edutainment가 education과 entertainment의 '혼성어(portmanteau)'임을 고르고, 수업을 게임화해서 즐거움을 '가져다준다(bring)'를 고르는 문제, 아티스트의 음반이 '걸작으로 칭찬받았다(was lauded as a tour de force)'는 내용을 통해 아티스트의 경력을 '되살려놓았다(revitalizing)'를 고르고, 이와 대조적인 양보절에서는 '쇠락해간다(waning)'를 고르는 문제 등 단순 어휘형 문제부터 전체적인 글의 흐름을 통해 빈칸의 내용을 유추해야 하는 논리형 문제까지 골고루 출제됐다.

독해

구분	2022	2023	2024
지문 수	7	7	7
문항 수	16/50 (32%)	16/50 (32%)	16/50 (32%)

▶▶ 독해에서 총 16문제가 출제됐다. 출제된 유형을 살펴보면 문장배열, 내용추론, 내용일치, 빈칸완성 등 독해 지문의 전체적인 내용을 정확하게 파악해야 풀 수 있는 문제들이 나왔는데, 그중에서도 빈칸완성 문제의 출제 비중이 높았다. 출제된 지문의 내용을 살펴보면 가스라이팅 가해자가 피해자에게 미치는 영향, 선충이라는 벌레를 먹고 사는 부생생물의 사냥법, 웹을 통한 독서가 이해력 저하를 일으키는 이유, 외국어로 배우는 영어 교육 분야에서의 형성적 평가, 체질량지수의 신뢰성에 대한 회의적인 시각, 철학자 임마누엘 칸트(Immanuel Kant)가 말하는 자유 의지, 세계주의자와 보호주의자의 경제관련 현격한 시각 차이 등이 출제됐다.

2025
이화여대 대비
학습 전략

▶▶ 이화여대는 어휘의 출제 비중이 높으며, 동의어와 반의어 문제가 함께 출제되므로 동의어뿐 아니라 반의어도 함께 학습해야 한다. 문법 문제의 경우 전체적인 문장구조 파악을 묻는 문제가 출제되므로, 평소 지문의 내용을 읽을 때 문장구조 파악 연습도 함께 해야 한다. 20지 선택형 논리완성 문제의 경우 정답으로 고른 어휘를 20지 선택지에서 소거해 나가야 같은 어휘를 다시 정답으로 고르는 것을 피할 수 있다. 독해의 경우 빈칸완성 문제의 출제 비중이 높으므로, 기출문제 풀이를 통해 빈칸을 전후로 제시된 단서가 무엇인지 정확하게 파악하는 연습이 요구된다.

중앙대학교

일반편입 / A형 / 40문항·60분

출제경향 및 난이도 분석

▶▶ 중앙대 편입영어 시험은 40문항·60분으로 진행됐으며, 영역별 차등배점이 부여됐다. 작년과 마찬가지로 관용어구를 알아야 풀 수 있는 생활영어 문제, No error 보기가 들어가 있는 문법 문제, 그리고 복잡한 구조와 긴 지문이 특징인 독해 문제가 출제됐다.

2022~2024학년도 중앙대 영역별 문항 수 비교

구분	어휘&생활영어	문법	논리완성	독해	합계
2022학년도	8	3	15	14	40
2023학년도	9	3	14	14	40
2024학년도	9	3	14	14	40

2024 중앙대 영역별 분석

어휘&생활영어

구분	2022	2023	2024
동의어	6	7	7
생활영어	2	2	2
합계	8/40 (20%)	9/40 (22.5%)	9/40 (22.5%)

▶▶ 동의어 유형 7문제와 생활영어 유형 2문제가 출제됐다. 밑줄 친 어휘와 의미가 가장 가까운 것을 고르는 동의어 문제에서는 lurch(=stagger), crockery(=dish), reprehend(=fulminate), vitiate(=invalidate), brackish(=saline), victual(=food), parturition(=delivery)이 출제됐는데, 제시어와 선택지 모두 고급어휘가 출제되어 단어의 정확한 의미를 알지 못했던 수험생들은 문제를 풀기 어려웠을 것이다. 대화의 흐름상 적절하지 않은 보기를 고르는 생활 영어 문제는 관용어구의 이해도를 평가하는 것이 특징이다. pull down(허물어버리다), phase out(단계적으로 폐기하다), cut to the chase(시간 낭비 말고 본론으로 직행하다), pull up one's socks(분발하다), fall head over heels about(~에게 홀딱 반하다), knockout(굉장한 미녀) 등이 출제됐다.

문법

구분	2022	2023	2024
문항 수 (W/E)	3/40 (7.5%)	3/40 (7.5%)	3/40 (7.5%)

▶▶ 문장의 밑줄 친 부분 중 문법적으로 적절하지 않은 보기를 고르는 Written Expression 유형이 3문제 출제됐다. 중앙대 문법 문제에서는 문장의 밑줄 친 부분이 문법적으로 모두 옳은 경우 No error를 고르는 문제가

꾸준히 출제되고 있어서, 신중하게 정답을 골라야 했다. 이번 시험에서는 현재분사와 과거분사의 구분, 정관사 용법, 동사 measure와 명사 measurement를 구분하는 문제가 출제됐다. 특히 정관사 용법을 묻는 문제에서는 '1970년대에(in the 1970s)'와 같이 연도 앞에 정관사가 붙고 그 뒤에는 복수형으로 s가 온다는 사실을 알고 있어야 정답을 고를 수 있었다.

논리완성

구분	2022	2023	2024
문항 수	15/40 (37.5%)	14/40 (35%)	14/40 (35%)

▶▶ 한 문장으로 이루어진 짧은 문장에서 빈칸을 완성하는 어휘형 빈칸완성 8문제와 단락 길이의 문제에서 빈칸을 완성하는 논리형 빈칸완성 6문제가 출제됐다. 단문의 어휘형 논리완성 문제는 빈칸 전후로 단서가 비교적 명확하게 제시되어 있어서 빈칸에 들어갈 의미를 유추하는 것이 어렵지 않았지만, 선택지로 고급어휘가 제시되어 정답을 푸는 데 어려움이 있었을 것이다. 예를 들어 panegyric(칭찬)과 유사한 의미를 정답으로 고르는 문제가 출제됐는데, 선택지에 anecdote(일화), stipend(봉급, 급료), encomium(칭찬), homily(설교)가 제시되어 선택지의 뜻을 정확히 모를 경우 정답을 고르기 힘들었을 것이다. 논리형 빈칸완성 문제에서는 아이아이 원숭이의 환경 적응, 인상주의의 특징, 17세기의 의료 관행, 복잡한 육지 생태계를 제공해주는 다양한 식물, 언어가 의사소통에 영향을 미치는 방법, 체내에서 과잉염분을 배출해주는 바닷물고기의 특수세포 등의 내용이 출제됐고, two-blank 논리완성 문제에서는 '이유'를 나타내는 접속사 since, 진술된 내용을 '부연 설명'할 때 쓰는 부사 indeed(사실) 등의 연결사를 통해 글의 흐름에 적절한 내용을 정답으로 골라야 했다.

독해

구분	2022	2023	2024
지문 수	9	9	8
문항 수	14/40 (35%)	14/40 (35%)	14/40 (35%)

▶▶ 랄프 왈도 에머슨(Ralph Waldo Emerson)의 『자연(Nature)』, 말콤 글래드웰(Malcolm Gladwell)의 『티핑포인트(The Tipping Point)』, 케이트 크로퍼드(Kate Crawford)의 『The Atlas of AI』 등 문학과 비문학에서 발췌한 수준 높은 글이 독해 지문으로 출제됐다. 출제된 유형을 살펴보면 단락배열, 문장삽입, 내용추론, 내용일치, 글의 제목, 글의 주제, 빈칸완성, 글의 흐름상 적절치 않은 보기 고르기 등이 나왔는데, 글의 전체 내용을 전반적으로 파악해야 정답을 고를 수 있었다. 출제된 지문의 내용을 살펴보면 인간과 자연의 심오한 관계, 대기의 제일 아래층을 형성하는 대류권, 생물학 혁명이 시작되는 미래, 교정시설에서의 정신건강 치료, 찰스 라이엘(Charles Lyell)의 작품과 생애, 인공지능을 지적 시스템으로 이해하는 방법, 유전학의 하위분야인 후생유전학(epigenetics) 소개 등이 출제됐다.

2025
중앙대 대비
학습 전략

▶▶ 동의어, 생활영어, 논리완성 문제의 경우, 고급어휘와 관용어구가 주로 출제되므로 이에 대한 대비를 해야 한다. 문법은 특정 품사의 용법보다는 전체적인 문장구조 파악에 중점을 두고 문제가 출제되므로, 기출문제나 모의고사 등을 통해 문제에 대한 응용력을 길러야 한다. 그리고 독해는 긴 지문에 비해 문항수가 적어 시간이 부족할 수 있으므로 속독 훈련이 요구되며, 장문의 수준 높은 지문이 문제로 출제되므로 서강대, 성균관대, 한양대 등 상위권 대학의 기출문제를 비롯해 각종 과학저널과 다양한 에세이에 관심을 갖고 배경지식을 습득하는 것이 중요하다.

한국외국어대학교 서울 일반편입 인문계 / T1 A형 / 50문항·60분

출제경향 및 난이도 분석

▶▶ 한국외대 편입영어 시험은 50문항·60분으로 진행됐다. 한국외대 기출문제를 살펴보면, 지난 5년 동안 유형별 문항 수가 동일하고 난이도 또한 비슷한 수준으로 출제되고 있음을 확인할 수 있다. 따라서 기출문제를 중심으로 시험에 대비해야 한다. 그리고 제한시간 대비 독해 문제의 출제비중이 높으므로 시간안배에 특히 신경 써야 한다.

2022~2024학년도 한국외대 영역별 문항 수 비교

구분	어휘	문법&재진술	논리완성	독해	합계
2022학년도	9	8	4	29	50
2023학년도	9	8	4	29	50
2024학년도	9	8	4	29	50

2024 한국외대 영역별 분석

어휘

구분	2022	2023	2024
동의어	5	5	5
문맥상 동의어	4	4	4
합계	9/50 (18%)	9/50 (18%)	9/50 (18%)

▶▶ 동의어 5문제와 문맥상 동의어 4문제, 총 9문제가 출제됐다. 동의어 문제에서는 despondent(=morose), precarious(=insecure), grandiose(=eminent), composure(=poise), auspicious(=fortunate)가 출제됐는데, 제시어와 선택지 모두 출제 빈도가 높은 기출어휘로 구성되어 있었다. 그리고 문맥상 동의어 문제에서는 slate(=schedule), term(=termination), irregular(=unofficial), lost(=engrossed)가 출제됐는데, 네 개의 제시어는 모두 여러 가지 뜻을 갖고 있는 다의어로 제시어가 가진 다양한 의미가 선택지로 제시됐다. 따라서 주어진 문장에서 해당 제시어가 의미하는 바를 문맥을 통해 파악한 후 정답을 골라야 했다.

문법&재진술

구분	2022	2023	2024
G/S	2	2	2
W/E	2	2	2
정비문	2	2	2
재진술	2	2	2
합계	8/50 (16%)	8/50 (16%)	8/50 (16%)

▶▶ 빈칸에 알맞은 문법사항을 선택지에서 고르는 '문장 완성하기' 유형, 문법적으로 적절하지 않은 보기를 문장에서 고르는 '문장 내 오류 찾기' 유형, 그리고 문법적으로 틀린 문장을 고르는 '비문 고르기' 유형이 출제됐다. 출제된 문법사항으로는 'lest ~ should (~할까 봐)' 구문의 올바른 어순, 문의 구성, 타동사의 목적어, 대명사의 수 일치, 한정적 용법으로만 쓰이는 형용사 utter를 서술적 용법으로 쓰이는 형용사 perfect로 고치는 문제, 주어로 쓰일 수 없는 '절(he said)'을 '명사절(what he said)'로 고치는 문제 등이 출제됐다. 편입시험에 자주 나오는 문법사항이 주로 출제됐지만, 문장의 구조 및 문법사항에 대한 응용력이 요구되는 문제의 비중이 높았다. 또한 제시된 문장과 같은 의미로 쓰인 문장을 고르는 재진술 유형이 2문제 출제됐다. 'broken(고장난)'을 'not operable(작동하지 않는)'로 'still hang(그대로 머물러 있다)'을 'linger(머물러 있다)'로 바꾸어 표현할 수 있는지를 묻는 문제와 'doubt+that절(~라는 것을 의심하다, 믿지 않다)'과 'suspect that절(~라고 의심하다, 수상쩍게 생각하다)'의 뜻을 명확하게 알고 구분할 수 있는지를 묻는 문제가 출제됐다. 특히 doubt와 suspect의 미묘한 의미 차이를 모르는 수험생은 정답을 고르는 데 어려움이 있었을 것이다.

논리완성

구분	2022	2023	2024
문항 수	4/50 (8%)	4/50 (8%)	4/50 (8%)

▶▶ 단문의 어휘형 논리완성 4문제가 출제됐다. 문제의 내용을 살펴보면, 축구선수가 자신의 목소리를 싫어했다는 내용을 통해 공공장소에서 '말수가 적은(laconic)' 사람이라는 것을 고르는 문제, 과학자가 저명한 연구팀에 합류할 수 있는 기회를 여러 번 놓쳤다는 것을 통해 협업에 있어 '완고한(refractory)' 입장에 있다는 것을 고르는 문제, 'get rid of(제거하다)'와 유사한 의미인 'jettison(버리다, 포기하다)'을 고르는 문제, 'ingratiate oneself with(~의 환심을 사다)'의 구문을 묻는 문제가 출제됐다. 문장의 구조가 복잡하지 않고, 이유를 나타내는 접속사(because, for)나 'not only A but also B(A뿐만 아니라 B)' 구문 등 빈칸의 단서가 명확하게 제시되어 있어 쉽게 문제를 풀 수 있었다.

독해

구분	2022	2023	2024
지문 수	12	12	12
문항 수	29/50 (58%)	29/50 (58%)	29/50 (58%)

▶▶ 12지문에서 총 29문제가 출제됐다. 한국외대의 경우 지문의 수가 많고 제한시간이 짧아 문제를 제한시간 안에 풀기 위해서는 속독 능력이 요구된다. 출제된 유형을 살펴보면 글의 주제 및 제목, 빈칸완성, 내용일치, 내용추론, 지시대상, 부분이해 등이 출제됐다. 특히 글의 주제 및 제목, 내용일치, 내용추론 등 지문의 전체 내용을 파악해야 풀 수 있는 문제의 출제 비중이 높았다. 출제된 지문의 내용을 살펴보면 온라인 패션업체에서의 빅데이터 활용, '슈링크플레이션(shrinkflation)'의 정의와 이유, 형제자매가 개인의 삶에 미치는 영향, 심리사회적 현상으로서 활동 연속의 주요 특징들, 미루는 버릇과 주의력 결핍 과잉 행동 장애(ADHD)의 상관관계, ChatGPT의 등장으로 인한 학술 에세이의 표절과 이를 피하는 방법, 좋아하는 노래의 통증 차단 효과, '스탠드 유어 그라운드 법(Stand Your Ground Law)'의 합법성, '디지털 디톡스(digital detox)'라는 용어의 출현 및 관련 신조어, '바넘 효과(Barnum effect)'라는 용어의 유래와 응용, "어"와 "음"을 사용하는 언어 패턴 등이 출제됐다. 최근 사회적으로 이슈가 되는 주제와 관련된 지문의 출제 비중이 높았다.

2025
한국외대 대비
학습 전략

▶▶ 한국외대는 문제 유형과 난이도가 대체로 일관되게 유지되는 경향이 있다. 따라서 다년간의 기출문제를 통해 유형별 특징을 파악하고 시험에 대비하는 것이 중요하다. 어휘는 기출어휘 중심으로 학습하고, 문맥상 동의어 문제는 문장의 문맥을 통해 단어의 뜻을 유추하는 습관을 들이는 것이 도움이 될 것이다. 재진술 문제는 주요 관용표현을 숙지하고 문장구조를 파악하는 연습이 필요하다. 문법은 편입시험에 자주 출제되는 문법사항 위주로 숙지하고 다양한 문제를 풀어봄으로써 문제 응용력을 길러야 한다. 독해는 제한시간 대비 지문의 수가 많으므로 시간을 정해놓고 지문을 속독하는 훈련을 해야 한다. 그리고 최신 시사 관련 지문이 많이 출제되고 있으므로 대중매체를 통해 사회적으로 이슈가 되고 있는 주제의 지문을 많이 읽어보는 것이 중요하다.

한양대학교

일반·학사편입 / 서울 인문계 A형 / 35문항·60분

**출제경향 및
난이도 분석**

▶▶ 한양대 편입영어 시험은 인문계 시험의 경우 35문항·60분으로 진행됐는데, 작년 시험(40문항·70분)과
달리 문항 수 및 제한시간에 변화가 있었다. 작년까지 출제된 문법 문제가 올해는 출제되지 않았으며, 논리완
성 문제의 비중도 크게 감소했다.

2022~2024학년도 한양대 영역별 문항 수 비교

구분	어휘	문법	논리완성	독해	합계
2022학년도	1	2	14	23	40
2023학년도	6	1	16	17	40
2024학년도	8	-	7	20	35

**2024 한양대
영역별 분석**

어휘

구분	2022	2023	2024
문항 수(동의어)	1/40 (2.5%)	6/40 (15%)	8/35 (23%)

▶▶ 동의어 유형 8문제가 출제됐다. 출제된 어휘에는 exacerbation(=aggravation), perspicacity(=sagacity),
intractable(=stubborn), nefarious(=malevolent), impetus(=inducement), pejorative(=denigratory), abtruse
(=recondite), veracity(=honesty)가 있었고, 제시어와 선택지 모두 편입시험에서 출제 빈도가 높은 기출어휘여서
기출어휘를 꼼꼼히 익힌 수험생들은 어렵지 않게 문제를 풀 수 있었을 것이다.

논리완성

구분	2022	2023	2024
문항 수	14/40 (35%)	16/40 (40%)	7/35 (20%)

▶▶ 전체 문항 수 대비 논리완성의 비중이 크게 감소했다. 문제의 내용을 살펴보면, A의 정의가 B이고, B의 정
의가 A라는 내용을 통해 '순환정의(circular definition)'를 묻는 문제, 그의 말투가 통렬하고 신랄했다는 내용
을 통해 그가 내세운 주장이 '거칠었다(asperity)'를 고르는 문제, 'not A; indeed B(A가 아니라 B)' 구문을 활
용해 '두드러진(distinctive)'과 상반된 표현인 '지엽적인(peripheral)'을 고르는 문제, 책을 읽을 때 그냥 넘기
지 못하고 다 읽어버린다는 내용을 통해 '건너뛰지 못하고 읽는 사람(a poor skipper)'임을 고르는 문제, 연주
를 즉흥적으로 하고 여러 장르를 흡수했다는 내용을 통해 '다양성과 혁신을 포용하고(embrace diversity and
innovation)' 있음을 고르는 문제, 나와 의견이 다른 사람을 무지몽매하게 여긴다는 내용을 통해 이런 성향이

'갈등을 조장할(fuels conflicts)' 수 있음을 고르는 문제 등 단문의 어휘형 논리완성 문제부터 전체적인 글의 흐름을 통해 빈칸에 적절한 내용을 고르는 중·장문의 논리완성 문제까지 골고루 출제됐다.

독해

구분	2022	2023	2024
지문 수	13	13	16
문항 수	23/40 (57.5%)	17/40 (42.5%)	20/35 (57%)

▶▶ 지문의 전체적인 내용을 파악해야 풀 수 있는 글의 요지, 글의 제목, 단락배열, 내용일치, 빈칸완성 등 편입영어 시험의 일반적인 유형이 출제되었을 뿐 아니라, 수능 영어 시험에서 주로 출제되는 '글에 드러난 저자의 심경변화' 유형도 올해 새롭게 출제됐다. 출제된 지문의 내용을 살펴보면, 불완전성에 의해 유지되는 사회, 능력주의 조직과 관료주의 조직의 차이, 삶을 의미 있게 살 수 있도록 해주는 죽음의 가치, 문서로 거의 남아있지 않은 역사의 한계, 우리가 경험하는 방식에 영향을 미치는 감정, 로마제국과 함께 성장한 건축기술, 캐리커처가 '표현주의적'이라고 묘사되는 이유, 현대 문명에 기여한 피타고라스의 업적, 양자물리학을 이해하기 위한 조건, 계급을 나타내는 중요 지표가 되는 식단, 오랫동안 간과된 균형감각의 재발견, 거짓기억현상의 이해, 멸종위기에 처한 양서류의 생존전략 등이 『What Is History?』, 『The Philosophy of Ownership』, 『The Culture of the New Capitalism』, 『The Aesthetic Brain: How We Evolved to Desire Beauty and Enjoy Art』 등과 같이 다양한 분야의 전문서적에서 출제됐다.

2025
한양대 대비
학습 전략

▶▶ 한양대 편입영어 시험은 올해 문항 수 및 제한시간에 변화가 있었지만, 문제의 유형과 난이도는 비슷하게 출제됐다. 따라서 과년도 기출문제를 통해 한양대에서 큰 비중을 차지하는 독해 문제에 대비해야 한다. 독해지문의 내용을 살펴보면 철학, 역사, 생물 등 인문학과 자연과학을 총망라하는 수준 높은 문제가 출제됨을 알 수 있으므로, 전문서적을 통해 다양한 분야의 배경지식을 쌓아두는 것이 필요하다.

2024학년도 대학별 문항 수 및 제한시간

대학명	계열	과목 및 문항 수	제한시간
가천대	인문계	영어 40	60분
	자연계	수학 25	60분
가톨릭대	인문계	영어 40	90분
	자연계	영어 20, 수학 20	90분
건국대	인문·예체능계	영어 40	60분
	자연계	영어 20, 수학 20	60분
경기대	인문·예체능계	영어 40	60분
	자연계	영어 25, 수학 20	100분
경찰대	일반대학생 전형	영어 40	60분
경희대	인문체육계열	영어 40	90분
	한의학과 인문	영어 50	90분
	자연계	수학 30	90분
고려대[세종]	인문·자연계	영어 40	60분
광운대	인문계	영어 40	60분
	자연계	영어 공통, 수학 30	수학 60분
단국대	인문계	영어 40	60분
	체육교육/산업경영(야)	영어 30	60분
	자연계	영어 30, 수학 20	120분
덕성여대	인문·자연계	1교시 33, 2교시 34	50분
명지대	인문계	영어 30	60분
	자연계	영어 공통, 수학 25	수학 60분
서강대	인문계	영어 30	60분
	자연계	영어 공통, 수학 20	수학 60분
서울시립대	인문계	영어 40	60분
	자연계 I	수학 30	90분
	자연계 II	영어 20, 수학 20	90분
서울여대	인문·자연계	영어 40	70분
성균관대	인문계	영어 50	90분
	자연계	영어 25, 수학 20	90분
세종대	인문계	영어 60	100분
	자연계	수학 25	100분
숭실대	인문계	영어 50	90분
	자연계	영어 25, 수학 25	90분
아주대	인문계	영어 50	90분
	자연계	영어 25, 수학 25	90분
이화여대	인문계	영어 50	100분
	자연계	수학 30	100분
인하대	인문계	영어 40	80분
	자연계	영어 20, 수학 30	영어 50분·수학 70분
중앙대	인문계	영어 40	60분
	공학계열(수학과 포함)	수학 30	60분
한국공학대	인문계	영어 40	60분
	자연계	수학 25	60분
한국외대	인문계	영어 50	60분
	자연계	영어 25, 수학 20	90분
한국항공대	인문계	영어 30	60분
	자연계	영어 20, 수학 20	90분
한성대	인문계	영어 50	90분
	자연계	영어 25, 수학 20	90분
한양대	인문계	영어 35	60분
	자연계	영어 공통, 수학 25	130분
홍익대	인문계	영어 40	70분
	자연계	영어 25, 수학 15	70분

* 자연계 시험의 경우 대학별 학과에 따라 전형방법이 상이하오니 지원하는 대학의 모집요강을 반드시 참고하시기 바랍니다.

가천대학교   2024학년도 인문계 A형
▶▶ 40문항·60분

[문항별 배점: 01-08 1.2점/ 09-13 2.1점/ 14-21 2.4점/ 22-31 3.1점/ 32-40 3.3점]

[01-08] Choose the one that is closest in meaning to the underlined part.

01 One likely explanation for Grubbe's neglect is that his initial success with X-ray treatments may have given him false confidence about his understanding of how radiation affects tissues. He was working under a false premise, but his <u>arrogance</u> made him bold, with regard to his patients' health and with his own.

① conceit   ② homage

③ fiat   ④ compunction

02 The textile collection amassed by Bess has traditionally been seen as a <u>conspicuous</u> attempt to display her wealth and position herself at the top of Tudor society. But the latest project suggests the reality is more nuanced: the researchers say the textiles represent an expression of Bess's creative ingenuity.

① salient   ② sanguine

③ reticent   ④ tangential

03 One focused on calling out what many viewers see as <u>egregious</u> age erasing: the promotion of women age 58, 57, 54 and 53 as paragons of mature beauty whose years have seemingly been smoothed from their faces.

① prepossessing
② prodigious
③ flagrant
④ magnanimous

04 Those creators will have a harder time bringing cases against systems that were trained on their work yet don't closely imitate it. A judge's recent decision dismissing part of a copyright lawsuit brought by comedian Sarah Silverman and others against Meta <u>bears</u> this <u>out</u>.

① vindicates
② nullifies
③ conjugates
④ prostrates

05 As if I were an excited child on a weekend outing with my father, I clambered up to the top deck for a better view, <u>sheepishly</u> claiming the front seat with its unobscured prospect.

① breathlessly
② ponderingly
③ timorously
④ covertly

06 The National Trust, which owns or manages hundreds of country estates and great country houses, was established a century ago on the rising nostalgia for a lost rural paradise. Because so many properties are great houses, it can <u>pander to</u> a sense of deference to the great landed families.

① abate
② indulge
③ swerve
④ exacerbate

07 Today, migrants are the producers of an enormous digital <u>almanac</u> of the trek to the United States, documenting the route and its pitfalls in such detail that, in a few stretches, people can find their way on their own, without smugglers.

① contents
② itinerary
③ yearbook
④ diagram

08 In 1927, the British novelist Elinor Glyn published a short story in *Cosmopolitan* magazine that would define the then-<u>nascent</u> culture of celebrity. Glyn's story explored the concept of It: the mysterious, indescribable, possibly magical quality that stars and other screen luminaries have and ordinary people don't.

① epicurean　　　　　　② inimical

③ spendthrift　　　　　④ burgeoning

[09-11] Choose the one that is grammatically INCORRECT.

09 The success of modern advertising, its penetration into every corner of American life, ①<u>reflects</u> a culture that has itself chosen illusion ②<u>over</u> reality. At a time when political candidates all have professional image-makers ③<u>attach</u> to their staffs, and the President of the United States can be an actor who once sold shirt collars, all the cultural signs are pointing to more illusions in our lives rather than ④<u>fewer</u>.

10 Netflix ①<u>credits</u> its large subscriber base and its recommendation algorithm ②<u>as</u> the reasons that a 22-year-old show like "Six Feet Under" or a once forgotten basic cable legal drama like "Suits" can become a hit on ③<u>their</u> service. Mr. Sarandos said that the company doesn't have a division for licensing original series ④<u>nor does he</u> see any reason to set one up.

11 But even in January there are bulbs ①<u>pushing</u> up through the soil of my neighbors' gardens. I feel a new kind of gratitude ②<u>at</u> the unfolding of the English spring, incremental and reassuring, with ③<u>what was</u> yesterday the bare branches of the weeping willow today gently ④<u>gauzed</u> with new leaf: a swipe of yellow ocher, cadmium green, cerulean blue.

[12-14] Choose the most appropriate word or phrase for each blank.

12 Sheriff Clark in Selma, Ala., cannot be dismissed as a total monster; I am sure he loves his wife and children and likes to get drunk. One has to assume that he is a man like me. But he does not know what drives him to use the club, to menace with the gun and to use the cattle prod. Something awful _____ to a human being to be able to put a cattle prod against a woman's breasts. What happens to the woman is ghastly. What happens to the man who does it is in some ways much, much worse.

① must have happened
② could not happen
③ should have happened
④ will not happen

13 The Oscar-winning *Nomadland* observes an America _____ ignored, or never seen in the first place. The film redirects attention to where the cinematic gaze is usually fleeting, and often made by those inured to passing over service work, alternative living situations, older people, women in general, and particularly older single women uninterested in stagnation, cordiality or disappearance.

① far more forgotten than
② as well forgotten as
③ no less forgotten than
④ not so much forgotten as

14 Gender attitudes do not affect economic reality, but rather _____. The rise of women is not the result of any ideology or political movement; it is a result of the widespread realization, sometime after the Second World War, that families in which women work are families that prosper. And countries in which women work are countries that prosper.

① part of the other way
② the way of leaning in
③ the other way around
④ on their own ways

[15-22] Choose the most appropriate word or phrase for each blank.

15 It is widely assumed that the British form a relatively homogeneous society with a strong sense of identity, but it is an assumption that requires considerable _____. For example, in his famous *Dictionary of Modern English Usage*, Fowler wrote: 'It must be remembered that no Englishman, or perhaps no Scotsman, calls himself a Briton without a sneaking sense of the ludicrous, or hears himself referred to as a BRITISHER without squirming.'

① proficiency   ② commiseration

③ munificence   ④ qualification

16 Even when a first-class author has enjoyed immense success during his lifetime, the majority have never appreciated him so sincerely as they have appreciated second-rate men. He has always been reinforced by the ardour of the passionate few. And in the case of an author who has emerged into glory after his death the happy sequel has been due solely to the _____ of the few. They could not leave him alone; they would not. They kept on savouring him, and talking about him, and buying him.

① capricious appreciation

② objective conjecture

③ intermittent interest

④ obstinate perseverance

17 Visitors to Takasakiyama threw caramels wrapped in paper to the monkeys — a common practice in Japanese zoos, but one the Takasakiyama macaques had never before encountered. In the course of play, some young monkeys discovered how to unwrap the caramels and eat them. The habit was passed on successively to their playmates, their mothers, and the dominant males and finally to the subadult males. The process of the _____ took about three years.

① transplant   ② acculturation

③ evolution   ④ inheritance

18 If you absolutely must have that sugary drink, try to consume it with a meal, or in one sitting rather than _____ it all day, Dr. Quinonez said: "I would rather you're a gulper not a sipper." Drinking water after you've finished eating can also help swish out any sugars, she added.

① nestling   ② postponing

③ devouring   ④ contemplating

19 As Haidt, a psychologist, has written, the mere presence of a smartphone in our field of vision is a(n) _____ on our focus. Even a locked phone in our pocket or on the table in front of us screams silently for the shattered fragments of our divided attention.

① spot   ② image

③ drain   ④ gambit

20 It is well documented that the Incan people developed domesticated plants and animals that helped them form large settlements. They undertook a tremendous amount of effort to transform dry mountain terrain into land suitable for _____ life.

① apathetic   ② sedentary

③ unwonted   ④ pioneer

21 A recast is a form of corrective feedback and is more subtle than other forms of feedback. Although there were many cases of recasts found in the data, they did not appear to be particularly effective. This makes recasts a somewhat _____ concept to deal with, and research often produces mixed results.

① luculent   ② locative

③ elusive   ④ myopic

22 Prior to 2020, the seasonal interplay of mobility and weather conditions existed in a delicate balance manifesting in a winter surge of respiratory bugs. However, this _____ was knocked out of whack by the COVID pandemic, resulting in winter bugs all year long and a change in viral dynamic which the researchers say "may never be the same again."

① equilibrium ② vagary

③ conundrum ④ upheaval

[23-40] Read the following passages and answer the questions.

New brain research has shed light on the function of sleep. Scientists have observed that interstices in the brain expand during sleep, widening pathways through which toxins can be expelled. These spaces form a plumbing system of sorts, known as the glymphatic system, which is what allows cerebrospinal fluid to flow throughout the brain. Slumber effectively opens up this network of channels and crevices, allowing the fluid to clear out toxic materials much more quickly than it does during waking hours. This indicates that sleep functions as kind of protective measure against damage and deterioration.

23 Which of the following is NOT true of the passage?

① The brain system clears out toxic substances more quickly during sleep.

② Sleep widens the crevices in the brain so that toxins can be effectively expelled.

③ Cerebrospinal fluid helps to dispose of toxic materials.

④ Sleep floods the brain with fluids that widen the spaces between brain cells.

Is it possible to think of any examples of mutually respectful onscreen romantic relationships between a working-class woman and a middle-class man? Or ones where the working-class woman is physically strong and the man is shy, slightly-built and Ⓐ_____? These comparisons show how conventional notions of masculinity and femininity have been reinforced by class power dynamics. Femininity is often associated with refinement and classiness, embodied by those with capital. While a "real man" is "big and strong", a "gentleman" doesn't have to be Ⓑ_____: he has cultural capital and so doesn't need conventionally masculine physical strength.

24 **Which of the following is most appropriate for the blanks Ⓐ and Ⓑ?**
① bold — puny
② demure — beefy
③ reserved — scrawny
④ impudent — brawny

Social media profiles have become founts of information for recruiters vetting job candidates. Although employers cannot demand access to a job candidate's social media profiles, employers are within their right to view what is publicly available. There are justifiable reasons to Ⓐ_____ people based on their social media activities. For example, an employer can disqualify someone found to be posting racist jokes.

25 **Which of the following is most appropriate for the blank Ⓐ?**
① weave out
② weep away
③ wash up
④ weed out

The mayor of Nice was slapped with an indictment complaint yesterday by diverse nonprofit groups. The complainants said that the mayor betrayed the public's trust and breached some laws of the city. His Ⓐ_____ allege that the mayor is not doing his job of preserving peace and order in the city. The City Council, being in charge of investigating the complaint, should immediately determine if the mayor has indeed been Ⓑ_____ in his duties because the public's confidence in the government is at stake.

26 Which of the following is most appropriate for the blanks Ⓐ and Ⓑ?

① revilers — negligent

② detractors — composed

③ renegades — remorseful

④ apostles — conscientious

In the 1940s a movie genre was invented by American filmmakers, which would eventually earn the Ⓐappellation "film noir." The films of this genre are characterized by the use of high-contrast lighting and flashbacks Ⓑrecounted by omniscient narrators. The heroes of film noir movies are morally ambiguous and cynical about the actions of the people around them. Today, six decades after the introduction of the genre, the popularity of film noir has yet to completely Ⓒwane. Many recent movies have Ⓓpaid no heed to noir techniques, in particular period pieces that evoke an earlier decade.

27 Which of the following underlined Ⓐ, Ⓑ, Ⓒ, and Ⓓ is NOT appropriately used?

① Ⓐ   ② Ⓑ

③ Ⓒ   ④ Ⓓ

28-29

New Age Travellers, one of the crucial sub-cultures, reject urban life, forming communities and moving around the countryside in caravans, to live a natural and simple life. They are the Ⓐ_____ of the 1960's Hippies. Their transient lifestyle has made them unpopular with the more conservative population. From 1985 they were engaged in repeated Ⓑ_____ with the police who were strongly encouraged by the Conservative government to make life hard for them. The trouble they caused, largely accusations of the pilfering and leaving litter were either untrue or greatly exaggerated. Yet while denounced as 'unwashed scroungers', the New Age Travellers have had a profound influence on the whole country. For their supposedly 'cranky' views about an imperiled ecology acquired growing acceptance in the 1990s as the population at large began to appreciate the madness of destroying countryside for the sake of yet more cars.

28 **Which of the following is most appropriate for the blanks Ⓐ and Ⓑ?**

① inheritors — conspiracy

② descendants — confrontations

③ offshoots — liaison

④ precursors — skirmishes

29 **Which of the following is NOT true of "New Age Travellers"?**

① Conservative people repudiated their vagrant and insanitary lives.

② They were charged with stealing things, which proved groundless or amplified.

③ Their idea of ecological crisis was once considered eccentric.

④ Their cranky way of life was eventually absorbed into the mainstream.

30-31

Is inflation bad? It depends on the circumstances. Fast price increases Ⓐ_____ trouble, but moderate price gains can lead to higher wages and job growth.

How does inflation affect the poor? Inflation can be especially hard to Ⓑ_____ for poor households because they spend a bigger chunk of their budgets on necessities like food, housing and gas.

Can inflation affect the stock market? Rapid inflation typically means trouble for stocks. Ⓒ_____ assets in general have historically fared badly during inflation booms, while tangible assets like houses have held their value better.

30   Which of the following is most appropriate for the blank Ⓐ?

① deter   ② spell

③ rescind   ④ survey

31   Which of the following is most appropriate for the blanks Ⓑ and Ⓒ?

① beat — Social

② dodge — Real

③ shoulder — Financial

④ proclaim — Fixed

According to The Framers, intellectual property rights exist to "promote the progress of science and useful arts." The latest marvels in coding and computing have introduced unseen forms of creation to humanity. But by producing works faster and cheaper, they could reduce demand for human-painted portraits. That, Ⓐ_____, could lead to a decline in artistic progress.

A broader thinking of copyright, inspired by what some AI companies are already doing, could ensure that human creators get some recompense when AI consumes their work, processes it and produces new material based on it in a manner current law doesn't contemplate. But such a shift shouldn't be so punishing that the AI industry has no room to grow. That way, these tools, Ⓑ_____ human creators, can push the progress of science and useful arts far beyond what the Framers could have imagined.

32 Which of the following is most appropriate for the blank Ⓐ?

① nevertheless

② in comparison

③ in turn

④ if not

33 Which of the following is most appropriate for the blank Ⓑ?

① in return for

② in concert with

③ on behalf of

④ for all

34-35

Between 1995 and 2002, the incidence of peanut allergies in young children increased, according to studies by medical allergists. Ⓐ The increase in peanut and other food allergies in adolescents led scientists and doctors to look for possible causes and contributing factors. Ⓑ In a home environment, due to the use of antibacterial soaps and sprays, the area is kept largely sterile. Ⓒ Therefore, the body does not learn to recognize and later combat some harmful viruses and bacteria. Ⓓ The absence of germs to fight, some theorize, leads the immune system to begin focusing on other, more Ⓔ_____ substances such as peanuts, milk, and eggs.

34 Where would the below sentence best fit?

One idea gaining support is the "hygiene hypothesis," which suggests that the human immune system requires contact with a wide range of environmental pathogens in order to strengthen itself.

① Ⓐ   ② Ⓑ

③ Ⓒ   ④ Ⓓ

35 Which of the following is most appropriate for the blank Ⓔ?

① innocuous   ② punitive

③ conjugal   ④ inquisitive

The effects of meaningful labor during imprisonment demonstrate marked benefits to both the prisoner and society. Some of these benefits take the forms of reduced recidivism, increased job skills and employability, and improved quality of life. In fact, corporations have hired jails to have their inmates perform work from manufacturing to telemarketing. Ⓐ_____, some critics argue that prisoners who work are little more than bonded slaves, earning nothing for their labor and forced to do work that may be beyond their physical or mental capacity. Others are more concerned about the economic factors of noncompetitive labor or issues involved in giving inmates responsibility for critical components of products.

36 Which of the following is most appropriate for the blank Ⓐ?

① That is

② For example

③ Similarly

④ However

37 Which of the following can be inferred from the passage?

① Employment might counteract the dire conditions prisoners experience.

② Prisoners can make a living while working in correctional facilities.

③ Employment in jails is detrimental to economic competitiveness of a society.

④ Enhancing the inmate labor model would enhance the penal system.

In the 1950s, scholars believed that the mediated and one-sided nature of parasocial relationships Ⓐ_____ the possibility of mutual give-and-take. Any reciprocal relationship with a television or radio personality could only be "suggested". At best, viewers could attempt to reach the media personality through the occasional fan mail or by calling in to a TV/radio station.

The internet, and particularly social media, has added another dimension to this dynamic. A celebrity's Instagram profile or an influencer's YouTube channel often speak directly to those that follow or subscribe to them. The follower or subscriber can reply to their posts and expect a reciprocal reply, even if rarely. These reciprocal encounters Ⓑ_____ the boundaries that separate the real and parasocial, 'friend' and 'celebrity' and Ⓒ_____ the illusion that fans are involved in a celebrity or media personality's life.

The potential for reciprocity may lead fans to not just believe that the celebrity or media personality is a friend who they "know" in a personal capacity, but also to expect some semblance of accountability. Against this expectation, revelations that contradict the celebrity's perceived image can produce shock, disappointment, or anger, and in extreme cases, end with fans publicly denouncing their 'parasocial friend'. In Mulaney's case, a departure from the super-relatable wife guy image prompted fans to *wonder* not just "how could he do this to her" but also "how could he do this to us?"

38 Which of the following is most appropriate for the blank Ⓐ?
① facilitated   ② precluded
③ calculated   ④ concealed

39 Which of the following is most appropriate for the blanks Ⓑ and Ⓒ?
① unsettle — dare
② redraw — efface
③ erode — perpetuate
④ sustain — circulate

40 Which of the following CANNOT be inferred from the passage?

① Mulaney fans find themselves distraught, disappointed, and weirdly offended at his choices.

② When people feel invested in a person, they tend to develop intimacy even at a distance.

③ Nowadays, media users can easily form a parasocial bond with celebrities.

④ Only isolated, mentally-vulnerable people fall for the lure of parasocial relationships.

가천대학교   2024학년도 인문계 B형
▶▶ 40문항·60분

[문항별 배점: 01-08 1.2점/ 09-13 2.1점/ 14-21 2.4점/ 22-31 3.1점/ 32-40 3.3점]

[01-08] Choose the one that is closest in meaning to the underlined part.

01 Merchandise is important. It's important for fans who can express their fandom. It's important for artists and other rightsholders who use it as an extra <u>revenue</u> stream.

① clientele   ② proceeds

③ broadcast   ④ referendum

02 Weary of <u>extravagant</u> product claims and irrelevant associations, consumers trained by years of advertising to distrust what they hear seem to be developing an immunity to commercials.

① outrageous   ② rapacious

③ enthusiastic   ④ fraudulent

03 In step with an energetic breed of charter school advocates nationally, the reformers who descended on New Orleans were convinced that progressive pedagogy and discipline had an especially sorry record in low-income districts, where many children faced more than their share of disorder and violence. Chaotic classrooms, the newcomers argued, were a major reason schools <u>failed</u>.

① quelled   ② invoked
③ foundered   ④ convoked

04 Although his disease put up barriers to his ability to pursue these purposes, he always found the <u>mettle</u> to circumvent these obstacles rather than be impeded by them.

① expertise   ② strategy
③ fortitude   ④ prerogative

05 I inhabited house of two storeys stood at the blind end, detached from its neighbours in a square ground. The other houses of the street, conscious of decent lives within them, gazed at one another with brown <u>imperturbable</u> faces.

① irascible   ② impious
③ laconic   ④ placid

06 She is privileged enough to benefit from both Black and white culture, dipping in and out of it when it's convenient and profitable. That is the biggest issue with her <u>foray</u> into hip-hop.

① instigation   ② portal
③ clash   ④ pillage

07 The increasingly <u>fraught</u> and emotional dialogue pits the progressive ideals of inclusion not just against historical business practices but also the definition of acting itself.

① political   ② representative
③ charged   ④ antagonistic

08 Life itself, then, could <u>insult</u> and ridicule and even torment the provocateur: the mocker brutally mocked by personal reality.

① adulate   ② eulogize

③ affront   ④ euphemize

[09-11] Choose the one that is grammatically INCORRECT.

09 Thatcher's belief that 'monetarism' alone could produce the revolution she sought proved ①<u>ill-found</u>. The resulting surge in unemployment dramatically increased public expenditure. Social welfare spending rocketed ②<u>to deal with</u> the rise in unemployed and prematurely retired people. But even without this result from their own policies, the Conservatives ③<u>would have found</u> the task of reducing public expenditure insuperable. ④<u>Whatever</u> savings could be made did not offset increased costs from less avoidable factors.

10 I now preferred the bus to the Tube, at least ①<u>if</u> I could spare the time for a slower journey. Riding through London this way ②<u>gave</u> me the geography lesson that the convenience of the Underground ③<u>had spared</u> me. It taught me how the city's circulatory system ④<u>flowing</u>, and it illuminated the centuries of transformation of a place like the Hampstead Road.

11 False memories do exist, but their construction appears to begin much later in life. A study presented children with fictitious events to see if they ①<u>could mislead into</u> remembering these non-existent events, yet the children almost universally ②<u>avoided</u> the bait. As for why adults begin to fill in gaps in their memories ③<u>with</u> invented details, she pointed out that memory is a fundamentally constructive activity: We use it to build understanding of the world, and that sometimes ④<u>requires</u> more complete narratives than our memories can recall by themselves.

[12-14] Choose the most appropriate word or phrase for each blank.

12 Striking Hollywood writers this summer worried that streaming services would rely on AI to churn out bingeable rom-coms. The writers won that negotiation, putting their crisis on pause. But individual creators won't always be able to win concessions from employers planning to use artificial intelligence — _____ to win them from makers of large language models with whom they have no relationship.

① still more   ② much less
③ furthermore   ④ as if

13 Marketers spend a lot of time and money trying to hold the attention of their target audiences, especially Gen Z. Creating specific content and keeping it short, all while being authentic, are some of the things that appeal to this demographic. _____, it should not be surprising that TikTok has really taken off with Gen Z.

① However   ② Given this
③ Alternately   ④ Notwithstanding

14 Further studies report on some patients learning that they have been given placebos _____ clinically tested and approved drugs, thus breaching the trust established in their physicians in some cases and inducing the reverse "nocebo" effects to occur in others. This exacerbates further a patient's medical state and occasionally accelerates causes leading to death.

① in reference to   ② in line with
③ in place of   ④ in accordance with

[15-22] Choose the most appropriate word or phrase for each blank.

15 Other hip hop artists, like Public Enemy and Queen Latifa, are explicitly progressive in their critiques of the socio-political systems that surround them. They further _____ the black prophetic tradition by urging listeners to awaken to new levels of political and spiritual consciousness, to read, and to prepare to take forthright action in a far-downfallen world.

① recant   ② map out
③ tap into   ④ disparage

16 The love of the country-cottage look and the old-fashioned dress style of the upper class, says much about the way the British perceive themselves. Because the past is glorious for the British, they prefer its reassurance to the uncertainty of the future. Speaking of fashion, Charlotte Du Cann notes the price the British pay for their nostalgia: "Those who come to Britain want to buy what we sell with conviction: our cosy comforting past. The hand-crafted nostalgia that we market so desperately _____ contemporary design of its rebellious energy."

① ascertains   ② enmeshes
③ divests   ④ refines

17 Most literary critics agree that few American writers have _____ their generation to the same degree as F. Scott Fitzgerald, whose novels and short stories captured the spirit of the Jazz Age, a time when young Americans upturned traditional social mores.

① epitomized   ② provoked
③ assuaged   ④ snubbed

18 The protagonist's nobility is unequivocally proven by the fact that he stands up for groups he doesn't belong to. In other words, minorities, who aren't very prevalent in the novel at all, are used as _____ for a white character's development.

① obstacles   ② props
③ collapses   ④ masks

19 A W.H.O. agency has classified aspartame, an artificial sweetener widely used in diet drinks and low-calorie foods, as possibly carcinogenic to humans. It is the first time the prominent body has _____ publicly on the effects on aspartame, which has been a contentious ingredient for decades.

① handed over　　　　　② bowed out
③ come by　　　　　　④ weighed in

20 Since the 1980s, there has been a strong interest in the role that assessment can have during the learning process, rather than just at the end of it. The work of Black and Wiliam in particular, and the 'Assessment for Learning movement' more generally, has had a great deal of impact on many educational systems around the world. While most externally mandated testing is summative, Black and Wiliam focused on _____ assessment.

① formative　　　　　② diagnostic
③ placement　　　　　④ aptitude

21 The minister's _____ did not have any significant impact on the freshmen students who were disobedient. The freshmen students continued to smoke cigarettes and blow their smoke in his face while he spoke.

① progeny　　　　　　② recess
③ denomination　　　　④ fulmination

22 In the last few years, almost against his will, since he had spent decades resolutely trying to put the whole business behind him, he had become fascinated with the event, in a mellow, non-obsessive kind of way, since he was of a calm, _____, even contemplative, temperament.

① phlegmatic　　　　　② frenetic
③ eclectic　　　　　　④ esoteric

[23-40] Read the following passages and answer the questions.

As a consequence of poor planning and disorder, the research team postponed attacking the root of the problem until there was little Ⓐ_____ left to them. They were obliged to implement a Ⓑ_____, last-minute solution to the problem. They were able to temporarily avoid the problem, but decided to find ways to better organize their plans and prevent the issue from reoccurring.

23 Which of the following is most appropriate for the blanks Ⓐ and Ⓑ?

① reimbursement — prescient

② alternative — premeditated

③ recourse — desperate

④ option — measured

Class and gender stereotypes make it much less socially acceptable to portray bookish, nerdy working-class girls. Risks and repercussions are also much greater for working-class girls who Ⓐ_____ social boundaries. All this being said, I'm really glad to see screen time given to a subjective experience of class crisis, something still felt by many of us who supposedly have seamlessly Ⓑ_____ our class backgrounds.

24 Which of the following is most appropriate for the blanks Ⓐ and Ⓑ?

① overcome — emulated

② defy — impersonated

③ confront — portended

④ breach — transcended

A baby experiencing constant anxiety can wind up producing high levels of the hormone cortisol, which could lead to a stress-response system that is over-prepared to fight back. Experiencing Ⓐ<u>undue</u> stress as an infant may damage the development of the prefrontal cortex, Ⓑ<u>facilitating</u> the set of skills known as executive functions, which comprise working memory, self-regulation, and cognitive flexibility. Professor Smith, citing several neuroscientists, calls these skills "the developmental building blocks — the neurological Ⓒ<u>infrastructure</u> — Ⓓ<u>underpinning</u> non-cognitive abilities like resilience and perseverance." The damage to the prefrontal cortex can lead to behavioral problems that are self-defeating.

25 **Which of the following underlined Ⓐ, Ⓑ, Ⓒ, and Ⓓ is NOT appropriately used?**

① Ⓐ   ② Ⓑ

③ Ⓒ   ④ Ⓓ

The charge has often been made against American writers that they do not describe society, and have no interest in it. They only describe individuals in opposition to it, or isolated from it. Of course, what the American writer is describing is his own situation. But what is *Anna Karenina* describing if not the tragic fate of the isolated individual, Ⓐ_____ her time and place? The real difference is that Tolstoy was describing an old and dense society in which everything seemed — to the people in it, though not to Tolstoy — to be fixed forever. And the book is a masterpiece because Tolstoy was able to Ⓑ_____, and make us see, the hidden laws which really governed this society and made Anna's doom inevitable.

26 **Which of the following is most appropriate for the blanks Ⓐ and Ⓑ?**

① on behalf of — dissect

② regardless of — camouflage

③ in compliance with — pervert

④ at odds with — fathom

It's not uncommon for people to Ⓐ_____ the importance of demonstrating their competence and power, often at the expense of demonstrating their warmth. I think it's especially common for people striving for leadership positions — in politics, business, law, medicine. Too many people try to be the smartest guy in the room — the alpha — and that's not actually how you become persuasive or become a good leader. It's a mistake. People judge trustworthiness before competence. They make inferences of trustworthiness and warmth before competence and power. And the reason is that it answers the question, "Is this person friend or foe?" With a stranger, you first want to know what their intentions are toward you, and then you want to know, "Can they carry out those intentions?" You have to connect with people and build trust before you can influence or lead them.

27 **Which of the followings is most appropriate for the blank Ⓐ?**
① retort ② overvalue
③ intersperse ④ play down

28-29

For years, entertainment company executives happily licensed classic movies and television shows to Netflix. Both sides enjoyed the Ⓐ_____: Netflix received popular content like "Friends" and Disney's "Moana," which satisfied its ever-growing subscriber base, and it sent bags of cash back to the companies.

But around five years ago, executives realized they were "selling nuclear weapons technology" to a powerful rival, as Disney's chief executive, Robert A. Iger, put it. Studios needed those same beloved movies and shows for the streaming services they were building from scratch, and Ⓑ_____ Netflix's rise was only hurting them. Immediately, the content faucets were, in large part, Ⓒ_____.

28 Which of the following is most appropriate for the blanks Ⓐ and Ⓑ?

① investment — reporting

② deviation — interrupting

③ spoils — fueling

④ variation — endorsing

29 Which of the following is most appropriate for the blank Ⓒ?

① let loose   ② set up

③ turned off   ④ within limits

30-31

This heartfelt movie-musical of *The Color Purple* sugars the pill and softens the blow, planing down the original's barbed and knotty surfaces, taking away some of the shock of violence and tragedy and Ⓐ_____ the experience more towards female solidarity and triumph over adversity. But that's perhaps part of a creatively emollient process that began in 1985 with Steven Spielberg's powerful if Ⓑ<u>bowdlerised</u> screen version of the Alice Walker novel; the film was then transformed into a hit Broadway musical in 2005, which is now the Ⓒ_____ for this new adaptation.

30 Which of the following is most appropriate for the blanks Ⓐ and Ⓒ?

① tilting — template

② distorting — model

③ elevating — script

④ revolving — origin

31 Which of the following is closest in meaning to the underlined Ⓑ<u>bowdlerised</u>?

① intensified   ② oscillated

③ inflated   ④ edited

32-33

The mimic octopus is a creature whose survival abilities are as unique as they are Ⓐ_____. Ⓑ It imitates toxic fish to avoid being eaten itself, and it can imitate a predatory sea snake to scare off trespassers. Ⓒ Many species exist that survive in part by resembling sticks, leaves, or other animals. Ⓓ Scientists have suggested that, within these species, members showing adaptive coloring or designs were overlooked by predators while the differently marked members were consumed. Ⓔ The survivors were then left to mate and to pass on their beneficial forms as a natural defense.

32 Which of the following is most appropriate for the blank Ⓐ?

① mundane   ② versatile

③ diurnal   ④ verdant

33 Where would the below sentence best fit?

This talented cephalopod is capable of imitating several different species of creatures found in its environment, and it does so for different purposes.

① Ⓑ   ② Ⓒ

③ Ⓓ   ④ Ⓔ

34-35

One of the most influential music theorists of the 20th century, John Cage is remembered for being to music what Marcel Duchamp was to art — someone who constantly questioned what defined music. One of his best-known interests was in removing the creator from music and instead creating music based on natural patterns and chance. One of his famous works involved music created by laying musical bars over astrological maps and assigning notes based on the location of the stars and planets. His stated goal was to remove personal agency and purpose from music and let music act as a reflection of the natural Ⓐchaos of the world, rather than as an effort to organize and improve nature.

34 According to the passage, which of the following best paraphrases John Cage's philosophy of music?

① Music is a reflection of the one who creates music and ambience.
② Music should be inherently different from meaning of creation.
③ Music should derive from nature rather than personal influence.
④ Music should be based on our current notions of musical theory.

35 Which of the following is closest in meaning to the underlined Ⓐchaos?

① trinket   ② bedlam
③ apparition   ④ panegyric

36-37

Mercury is employed to create the massive telescopes used in observatories. These instruments have traditionally included large parabolic mirrors made of glass that redirect incoming light in a way that magnifies distant objects. The problem is that the glass mirrors are Ⓐprohibitively expensive to produce. However, with a slight modification to the design of the telescope, mercury can serve as an inexpensive alternative because it is highly reflective in its liquid state. When a large pool of mercury is spun rapidly, it forms a smooth, curved surface that functions in a manner similar to the Ⓑ_____.

36 Which of the following is closest in meaning to the underlined Ⓐprohibitively?

① exorbitantly   ② engagingly
③ exasperatingly   ④ effervescently

37 Which of the following is most appropriate for the blank Ⓑ?

① liquid solvent
② glass mirrors
③ telescopic image
④ magnified objects

As Alexis de Tocqueville wrote in his monumental study, *Democracy in America*: 'when all privileges of birth and fortune are abolished, when all professions are accessible to all, and a man's own energies may place him at the top of any one of them, an easy and unbounded career seems open to his ambition.... But this is an erroneous notion. For when men are nearly alike, and all follow the same track, it is very difficult for any one individual to walk quick and cleave a way through the same throng which surrounds and presses him.'

A century and a half ago, Tocqueville recognized that the Ⓐ_____ of democratic societies breeds a desire for social distinction, a yearning to rise above the crowd. But given the fact that those who do make it to the top in socially mobile societies have often risen from the lower ranks, they still look like everyone else. In the socially immobile societies of aristocratic Europe, generations of fixed social conditions produced Ⓑ_____. The accent of one's voice, the shape of one's nose, or even the set of one's chin immediately communicated social status. Aside from the nasal bray and uptilted head of the Boston Brahmin, Americans do not have any native sets of personal status signals. If it weren't for his Mercedes-Benz and Manhattan townhouse, the Ⓒparvenu Wall Street millionaire often couldn't be distinguished from the man who tailors his suits. Hence, the demand for status symbols, for the objects that mark one off as a social success, is particularly strong in democratic nations.

38 **Which of the following is most appropriate for the blank Ⓐ?**
① inherent privileges
② demand for professionals
③ career boundaries
④ competitive nature

39 **Which of the following is most appropriate for the blank Ⓑ?**
① distinctive class flexibility
② headstrong behavior
③ unrevealing appearances
④ subtle class signals

40 Which of the following is closest in meaning to the underlined ©<u>parvenu</u>?

① upstart
② exemplar
③ liberal
④ conservative

가톨릭대학교

2024학년도 인문계 A형
▶▶ 40문항·90분

자연계
▶▶ 영어 20문항, 수학 20문항·90분
인문·자연계 공통 영어문제 별도 * 표시

[01-05] 빈칸에 들어갈 가장 적절한 표현을 고르시오.

01* Plenty of people feel a moral obligation to _____ their own greenhouse gas emissions to mitigate climate change.

① tout   ② curb
③ ignite   ④ expedite

02 The museum is in a financially _____ position due to a sharp decline in visitor numbers and reduced government funding.

① precarious   ② precocious
③ preposterous   ④ presumptuous

03* Studies show that some personality traits are fairly stable but others are _____ enough to go through some changes as we age.

① inherent   ② malleable
③ provocative   ④ versatile

04 Pointing fingers at each other or gesticulating angrily provokes more _____, and the ensuing emotional violence envelops you both in a dance of destruction.

① elation   ② groove
③ animosity   ④ serenity

05* As an independent third party, the Pope would, on occasion, be asked to _____ disputes between kingdoms.

① proliferate   ② deliberate
③ obliterate   ④ arbitrate

[06-10] 빈칸에 들어갈 어법에 맞는 표현을 고르시오.

06* Established politicians may find it necessary to embrace data-driven campaigning strategies _____ favor messages echoing the existing conviction of voters.

① what   ② which
③ where   ④ whose

07 A study found that learners who stop and ask themselves if they are going about goal pursuit in the most efficient way possible _____ greater progress toward their goals.

① reports   ② reported
③ to report   ④ reporting

08 Recent studies have shown that pesticides can affect human brainwave activity and _____, loss of memory, and inability to concentrate.

① irritate   ② irritability
③ cause irritability   ④ cause of irritability

09* Ecology is not a single domain but rather a synthesis of various ecological subfields and specialties _____ from different scientific disciplines, all of which share the common goal of understanding the interactions between organisms and their environments.

① stem   ② stems
③ stemming   ④ stemmed

10 In less than a century, once-thriving ecosystems have become deserts, and consequently, cod, one of the world's favorite fish, _____ extinction; in fact, at the collapsed fishery in Newfoundland, up to 810,000 tons of cod that were historically caught each year _____ missing.

① nearing — go

② was near — went

③ has neared — is gone

④ is nearing — have gone

[11-20] 빈칸에 들어갈 가장 적절한 표현을 고르시오.

11 Enclosure refers to the division or consolidation of communal fields, meadows, pastures, and other arable lands in western Europe. This process transforms the lands into meticulously outlined farm plots that are individually owned and managed — like in the modern times. Before enclosure, much farmland existed in the form of numerous, dispersed strips under the control of individual cultivators only during the growing season and until harvesting was completed for a given year. Thereafter, and until the next growing season, the land was _____. To enclose land was to put a hedge or fence around a portion of this open land and thus prevent the exercise of common grazing and other rights over it.

① left fallow to rejuvenate the soil for the next planting season

② preserved for private uses of landowners with exclusive rights to it

③ carefully managed for farmland wildlife restoration and habitat conservation

④ at the disposal of the community for grazing by village livestock and other purposes

12 All leaders are directed and inspired as much by their readings as they are by their closest advisers. Thus, the book choices a leader makes can be crucial. As with all things touching on leadership, the books that work for one leader may not work for another. Failing to make conscious choices about what to read is one of the worst things a leader can do. It's far better for leaders to make their own mistakes than it is to permit best-seller lists, editors, or literary critics to make leaders' choices for them. No leaders worth their salt would let outsiders choose their chief lieutenants for them, and by the same token leaders shouldn't let someone else choose their books. In reading, as in so many other areas, _____ is an essential prerequisite for effective leadership and for avoiding the most pernicious and lasting forms of failure.

① cultivating one's ability to empathize
② maintaining one's intellectual independence
③ educating oneself about a wide variety of topics
④ allowing others to get involved in decision-making

13 Many fathers and mothers express a sense of betrayal, feeling let down by their children's perceived lack of availability or responsiveness, particularly when they've provided a life they see as enviable compared with their own childhoods. Parents expect a reciprocal bond of kinship in which their years of parenting will be repaid with later closeness. However, this expectation of reciprocity often goes unmet in a time when _____. If providing shelter, food, and clothing is deemed sufficient, then gratitude to parents seems warranted, regardless of how one's life unfolds. On the other hand, if parents are expected to cultivate the happiness of their adult children, the latter may, justly or not, hold their parents accountable for any unhappiness they experience.

① the parameters of parenting are ambiguous
② economic hardships hinder forming personal bonds
③ generational gap has driven parents and children apart
④ family value is regarded as the most important social virtue

14* Singapore is now the communications and financial hub of Southeast Asia as well as a thriving high-tech manufacturing center. The Singaporean government has played an active role in the development process but has also allowed market forces freedom to operate. Singapore has encouraged investment by multinational companies (especially those involved in technology) and has itself invested heavily in housing, education, and some social services. This system _____. The government is able to manipulate the election process, ensuring that the opposition never holds more than a few seats in parliament. While many Singaporeans object to such a situation, others counter that the system has brought fast growth as well as a clean, safe, and remarkably corruption-free society.

① is far from fully democratic
② pursues inclusive governance
③ seeks transparency in election
④ is resistant to political regulation

15* Public eye behavior in the U.S. is considerably more restricted than in other parts of the world. In the U.S., staring openly at someone in a public place is considered rude and an infringement on his or her privacy. Instead, Americans practice what Erving Goffman refers to as "civil inattention," a very subtle practice whereby people give others just enough eye contact to _____ their presence but at the next moment withdraw that eye contact so they are not singled out as an object of particular _____. When two people are walking toward each other, civil inattention permits eye contact up to approximately eight feet before the eyes are cast downward as they pass — as Erving Goffman puts it, "a kind of dimming of light."

① feel — resistance
② reveal — attention
③ impose — interest
④ acknowledge — curiosity

16 Why does man create art? Surely one reason is an irresistible urge to adorn himself and decorate the world around him. Art is, however, much more than decoration, for it is laden with meaning. Art enables us to communicate our understanding in ways that cannot be expressed otherwise. Truly a picture is worth a thousand words, not only in its descriptive value but also in its symbolic significance. In art, man _____. We must think of art not in terms of everyday prose but as poetry, which is free to rearrange conventional vocabulary and syntax in order to articulate novel, often multiple meanings and moods. A painting likewise suggests much more than it states. And like a poem, the value of art lies equally in what it says and how it says. It does so partly by implying meanings through allegory, pose, facial expressions and the like or by evoking them through the visual elements: line, form, color, and composition.

① is subject to the burden of his genius and personality
② works with materials that have little or no shape of their own
③ is an inventor of symbols who conveys complex thoughts in new ways
④ demonstrates his unique power of finding the hidden aspects of nature

17* Much powerful writing is rooted in firsthand experience. Drawing on personal experience gives a special, authentic touch to the discussion of larger issues. When we read about gender roles or the immigrant experience, we assume that the writer knows the subject at first hand. While reading about affirmative action, we want to know whether the author can say: "I was there" — as a target, a beneficiary, a witness, or a close, caring observer. We want to see what theories or statistics mean to the lives of people the author has known or observed. Words are just words until _____.

① we can relate them to the experience of someone involved
② we can see their relevance in the broader scope of society
③ they align with our own perspectives and understanding
④ we interpret their meanings in the context of authentic history

18 In the realm of urban planning, there is an ongoing and intricate discourse about the most effective approach to shaping the development of cities. Advocates for a laissez-faire model contend that cities should grow organically based on market demands, allowing market forces to guide the evolution of urban landscapes. However, urban experts hold a contrasting view, arguing that such an approach is not without pitfalls. For instance, the rapid expansion of metropolitan areas like Beijing and Mumbai, where uncontrolled urban sprawl, driven solely by market forces, has resulted in infrastructural challenges, environmental degradation, and unequal access to resources. This exemplifies how spontaneous urban growth _____.

① may lead to homogenization of the city's cultural landscapes
② often results in developments that fall short of meeting market needs
③ ensures equitable distribution of resources and promotes sustainability
④ might lead to unintended consequences and hinder sustainable development

19 Platforms have become an arena for viral anonymous speech. This type of speech spreads partly through "bots", automated programs that communicate directly with users, which lowers the accountability costs for sharing false information and manipulated content. It deprives voters of valuable information to judge the credibility of the messages directed at them. Platforms gather an unprecedented amount of intrusive data on people's backgrounds, interests, and choices, which allows campaigns to "microtarget" advertising, such as by sending one set of messages to older white male voters and another to young African American women. The practice drives profits for the platforms, but _____. Political operatives may deploy microtargeting for negative messaging intended to depress voter turnout. The platforms' design may encourage extremism and offer voters additional worrisome content similar to what they or their social media friends have chosen. Those who can control platform content may help one candidate and hurt another.

① it fails to reach a wider circle of citizens
② it can also fuel polarization and political manipulation
③ it may result in unintended discrimination against minority groups
④ it hardly brings like-minded people together for election campaigns

20 By the turn of the 20th century, summertime became further embedded in American popular culture as advertisers used the season as a way of promoting their products, often with themes of nostalgia and romance. For example, Kodak attracted customers with a campaign that solidified their cameras as essential tools for telling "the story of a summer vacation." In addition, the rise of unionization combined with overcrowded cities led urban planners to begin developing leisure activities for the working class. For example, in New York City, Coney Island and Jones Beach became popular spots for urban workers, who benefited from changes won by labor unions for "8 hours for work, 8 hours for sleep, 8 hours for what we will." Yet, even when summer excursions to the beach began making waves through American culture, many working-class black people traveled to the nation's growing beach resorts _____. As reported by *The Chicago Defender*, the number of black men and women traveling as wait-staff, butlers, and porters was high.

① for social status advancement
② to diversify their vacation hubs
③ to satisfy their longing for nature
④ as employees rather than as guests

[21-30] 다음 글을 읽고 물음에 답하시오.

Victorians linked cleanliness to ideas of morality and respectability. The new science of microbes only intensified the Victorian preoccupation with tackling germs, which they now knew could lurk out of sight. Ⓐ <u>In September 1888, the Aberdeen Evening Express reported that 13 people had been poisoned by carbolic acid in one incident — five died.</u> Ⓑ <u>Chemical cleaning products to eradicate dirt and disease were heavily advertised and highly effective, but their toxic ingredients, like carbolic acid, were contained in bottles and packages that were indistinguishable from other household products.</u> Ⓒ <u>Only in 1902 did the Pharmacy Act make it illegal for bottles of dangerous chemicals to be similar in shape to ordinary liquids.</u> Ⓓ <u>Boxes of caustic soda and baking powder could easily be mistaken.</u>

21 Which order works best for the flow of the passage?

① Ⓐ — Ⓑ — Ⓒ — Ⓓ
② Ⓐ — Ⓑ — Ⓓ — Ⓒ
③ Ⓑ — Ⓒ — Ⓐ — Ⓓ
④ Ⓑ — Ⓓ — Ⓐ — Ⓒ

Research has made it clear that the effectiveness of helping is an essential reinforcer. For example, take a study that asked participants to donate to one of two different charities: UNICEF and Spread the Net. The UNICEF appeal was relatively general and abstract, because UNICEF is a large organization that funds a variety of children's health-care initiatives. While a donation to UNICEF would clearly benefit children in need, it was unclear to donors exactly who would benefit and how. The Spread the Net appeal, in contrast, was more concrete and descriptive. It explained that it would use the funds to buy bed nets to stop the spread of malaria in regions of the world where it was endemic. The study suggests that potential donors are more inclined to help when they can clearly see the tangible results their efforts will bring.

22* What is the main implication of the passage?

① People tend to donate more when they see the immediate impact of their contributions.
② Spread the Net is more effective than UNICEF in using donations for children in need.
③ When making a donation, it is important to research and understand the charity's cause.
④ It is crucial for all charities to maintain transparency in their management of donations.

Sometimes adults think that certain children don't care about learning or doing well, particularly in school. However, it is important to verify that the children have the competence to do what is asked. Sometimes children want to follow instructions but lack the ability. Ross Greene, a clinical child psychologist, pointed out that kids do well if they can, but many adults believe that kids only do well if they want to. Thus, there is a common belief that if kids are doing poorly, it is because they lack motivation and don't want to do well rather than because they lack necessary skills. This leads adults to reward and punish rather than teach. They may say that the children just want attention, want their own way, have a bad attitude, and are not motivated. Greene listed things that children might have trouble with such as understanding instruction, handling transitions, keeping track of time, and maintaining focus. Rather than punishing them for something they cannot do, it would be better to figure out what the problem is.

23 What is the main idea of the passage?
① Improving children's school performance begins with assessing their essential skills.
② Determining the aptitude of each child is crucial for customized education.
③ Rewards, not punishments, are more effective in shaping children's behavior.
④ Motivating children is an essential prerequisite for their continued learning.

Whales and dolphins, collectively known as cetaceans, are very social animals like humans. In the wild, generally coastal waters or the open sea, they live in loosely to highly structured groups known as pods. Typically, the pods are composed of nuclear and extended family members with whom they interact for prolonged periods of time or for life. For example, orcas, the largest members of the dolphin family, live in tightly knit maternal groups consisting of the mother, her adult sons, her adult daughters, and her daughters' offspring, all of whom bond for life. These relationships are so exacting that each pod has its own distinct dialect by which it communicates. Some researchers believe the orca may be the most socially bonded species on the planet. When individual orcas are captured, the entire social pattern of the group is destroyed. Often members not targeted for capture are either injured or killed in the process. Placing newly acquired specimens in confinement with more seasoned residents results in a totally abnormal and artificial social structure.

24* According to the passage, which of the following is NOT true?

① Orcas form close-knit maternal pods with multiple generations of family.

② There are distinct dialects used by different orca families.

③ Capturing an individual orca can pose risks to non-targeted pod members.

④ Introducing newly acquired orcas to existing captives improves social integration.

In grocery stores and drugstores, it's common to encounter an aisle filled with various "air freshener" products. From scented candles to "fresh-smelling" sprays and "natural" plug-in air diffusers, marketing encourages us to use these products to mask unpleasant odors and create a pleasant home fragrance. Ⓐ However, a significant issue arises as these products typically contain a range of chemicals that, when released, may directly impact our health, including our brain health. Ⓑ Air freshening products are loaded with molecules known as "volatile organic compounds" or VOCs, which are potent air pollutants and include recognized carcinogens like formaldehyde and benzene. Ⓒ In a 30-year-old study, researchers showed that plants could cut down VOCs in small airtight containers, which led consumers to overestimate the value of their houseplants. Ⓓ Furthermore, scented candles and aerosol sprays may release elevated levels of particulate matter, known as a brain toxin. If you opt to freshen your air, consider simmering spices and herbs in water on your stove. Additionally, seek out unscented cleaning supplies and candles.

25* Which of the following should be deleted for the flow of the passage?

① Ⓐ 　　　　　② Ⓑ

③ Ⓒ 　　　　　④ Ⓓ

Scientific studies have revealed that the drive to play is a biologically hard-wired tool, common to nearly all mammals. Play triggers the activation of the brain's reward centers, leading to the release of feel-good chemicals such as dopamine and oxytocin, as well as powerful neural growth factors that support learning and mental flexibility. It induces a drop in stress hormones, uplifts mood, and brings about an energizing effect. An often underestimated aspect of play is its impact on cognition. Researchers have observed that animals engaged in play go through a sequence of actions that are frequently more random, chaotic, and variable than serious real-life events. This dynamic activity requires improvisation, creativity, and adaptability in the face of uncertainty. In essence, play serves as a training ground, preparing individuals to expect the unexpected and adapt with aplomb.

26* **What is the main point of the passage?**

① Play is a universal trait found in almost all mammals.

② Play enhances cognitive abilities as well as emotional well-being.

③ Play helps the brain to release chemicals which facilitate neural growth.

④ The impact of play on brain health has been a controversial topic in science.

Botanists caution that the surge in demand for succulents, particularly in Asia, poses a threat to crucial and rare species. Dr. Cornelia Klak, highlighting the insatiable appetite for these plants in the Asian market, expresses concern about the collecting mania that has intensified during lockdowns, jeopardizing succulent populations that can thrive for up to a century. What's alarming is the indiscriminate uprooting of these plants, with local collectors neglecting their age and depleting entire populations, including the venerable, long-standing ones. Given that South Africa harbors approximately one-third of the world's succulent species, experts warn that this trend may lead to irreversible losses of these natural wonders. The spike in houseplant demand during the peak of the COVID-19 pandemic further exacerbated the situation, with indoor gardening driving a remarkable 500% sales increase for plant retailers in the U.K.

27 What is the best title for the passage?

① Succulents Lead a Global Boom of Indoor Gardening

② Causes of Plant Sales Spike in the Times of COVID-19

③ Succulent Mania: Rising Appetite and Conservation Concerns

④ Asian Succulent Craze: A Boon for South African Economy

Games offer players the chance to make quick decisions in low-risk settings, allowing them to see the impact of their choices and try again if needed, fostering valuable life skills. Teachers can incorporate role-playing games in the classroom to help students inhabit different perspectives within holistic systems of thought, prompting students to think about their own agency as they weigh possibilities and contemplate alternative plans of action. In the virtual game "Alba: A Wildlife Adventure," for example, players launch mini-missions where they discover and protect species of endangered animals. Though students might not consider themselves conservationists or adventurers during gameplay, the low-risk setting can encourage them to reflect on the larger-scale impacts they could have in the real world. As a follow-up activity, students could conduct further research on animals they encountered or even take local nature walks to identify smaller ecosystems of local wildlife.

---

28 What is the topic of the passage?

① Tech-driven approaches to enhancing environmental awareness among students

② Advantages and challenges of implementing games in educational settings

③ Beneficial impact of role-playing games on students' intellectual growth

④ Various educational game types and their unique learning benefits

Some people think of marketing management as finding enough customers for the company's current output. But this view is too limited. Marketing management is not concerned with serving all customers in every way. Instead, marketers want to serve selected customers that they can serve well and profitably. A company has a desired level of demand for its products. At any point in time, there may be no demand, adequate demand, irregular demand, or too much demand. Marketing management must find ways to deal with these different demand states. It may be concerned not only with finding and increasing but also with changing or even reducing demand. For example, Yosemite National Park is badly overcrowded in the summer. Poor companies sometimes have trouble meeting demand during peak usage periods. In these cases of excess demand, demarketing may be required to reduce the number of customers. Thus, marketing management seeks to affect the types of customers served and the level, timing, and nature of their demand in a way that helps companies achieve their objectives.

29* **What is the main point of the passage?**

① Demarketing strategies are particularly useful in times of recession.

② Marketing management should broadly cover management of demand changes.

③ Marketing success depends on targeting the right consumer segment for a product.

④ Attracting additional customers should be the top priority in an ever-evolving market.

Sudan faces some of the most daunting political issues in North Africa. Some cut across religious divides while others seem to focus more on ethnic and racial differences within the country. A Sunni Islamist state since a military coup in 1989, Sudan imposed Islamic law across the country and in the process antagonized moderate Sunni Muslims as well as the nation's large non-Muslim (mostly Christian and animist) population in the south. A long civil war between the Muslims north and the Christian and animist south also proved disastrous, producing more than 2 million casualties, mostly in the south, in the past 20 years. Although the carnage in the south has lessened since 2001 (a tentative peace agreement was signed in 2004), a newer conflict erupted in the Darfur region in the western portion of the country. Ethnicity, race, and control of territory seem to be at the center of the struggle in the largely Muslim region as a well-armed Arab-led militia group has attacked hundreds of black-populated villages, killing over 200,000 people and driving 2.5 million more from their homes.

30 According to the passage, which of the following is NOT true?

① The causes of conflict in Sudan are complex beyond religious issues.

② The severity of damage has been stronger in the south than in the north.

③ Casualties increased in the south due to a conflict in the Darfur region.

④ An Arab-led militia group is responsible for the massive killings of blacks.

[31-32] 다음 글을 읽고 물음에 답하시오.

Reversing climate change requires massive societal change. Most often, we look to two sources to drive these large-scale behavioral changes — top-down levers created and enforced by regulatory bodies or bottom-up actions voluntarily engaged in and promoted by individual consumers. Both of these methods have severe limitations related to large-scale changes. For a recent example, consider the controversy over plastic straws. In order to eliminate this waste from consumption, policy makers could ban the use of straws in restaurants and retail environments. These bans are slow and controversial. Another option would be social marketing initiatives focused on discouraging use at the consumer level. Each consumer could be educated on the impact of the choice related to the affected sea life and amount of waste, and each time confronted with the option to resist its use. This type of consistent action _____ due to "drop in the bucket" perceptions and puts the responsibility each time on the consumer in the face of choice overload and competing motivations. Alternatively, meso-level initiatives, such as voluntary brand responses, can drive societal change more effectively. Numerous brands like Starbucks, Alaska Airlines, and McDonald's voluntarily ceased to offer disposable straws. While each level has its pros and cons, brand-level action is certainly more scalable than the individual level and more flexible and innovative than the policy level.

31* What is the best expression for the blank?

① is arduous and demotivating

② can be laborious but rewarding

③ often goes unnoticed and unappreciated

④ may appear minor but is surely impactful

32* **What is the best title for the passage?**

① How Does Sustainability Increase Brand Value?

② Green Business: How the Environment Impacts Business

③ Small Actions Can Make Big Differences on Climate Change!

④ Unique Role of For-Profit Brands: Bridging the Gap in Climate Action

[33-35] 다음 글을 읽고 물음에 답하시오.

A group of multi-national scientists have used gene-splicing techniques to create an extraordinary tomato. It contains levels of antioxidants 200 percent higher than unmodified tomatoes. When fed to highly cancer-susceptible mice, the tomatoes significantly extended the mice's lifespan. These studies have received wide attention, but an equally momentous achievement of genetic modification has been largely ignored for almost a decade. That innovation is Golden Rice, a collection of new rice varieties that is bio-fortified, or enriched, by genes that express beta-carotene, the precursor of vitamin A, which is converted in the body, as needed, to the active form.

In developing countries, 200-300 million children are at risk of vitamin A deficiency, which can be devastating and even fatal. It increases susceptibility to common childhood infections such as measles and diarrhoeal diseases, and is the single most important cause of childhood blindness in developing countries. Golden Rice could save hundreds of thousands of lives every year and enhance the quality of life for millions more.

But one aspect of this shining story is _____. Intransigent opposition by anti-science, anti-technology activists Greenpeace, Friends of the Earth, and a few other groups has spurred already risk-averse regulators to adopt an overly cautious approach that has _____ approvals.

Nine years after its creation, despite its vast potential to benefit humanity, Golden Rice remains hung up in regulatory red tape, with no end in sight. There is absolutely nothing about Golden Rice that should require endless case-by-case reviews and bureaucratic dithering. By contrast, plants constructed with less precise techniques generally are subject to no government scrutiny or requirements (or opposition from activists) at all. The Golden Rice story makes it clear that we do not yet have the will and the wisdom to make that happen.

33* **What are the best expressions for the blanks?**

① veiled — withheld

② tarnished — stalled

③ distorted — prompted

④ overestimated — triggered

34* **What is the best title for the passage?**

① Leaders of the New Green Revolution

② Are Genetically Modified Food Safe?

③ A Squandered Golden Opportunity

④ New Wrinkles in Plant Research

35* **According to the passage, which of the following is true?**

① Golden Rice has been recognized as widely as genetically modified tomatoes.

② Golden Rice is a newly developed grain that has the potential to help cure cancers.

③ The approval of Golden Rice is imminent due to accumulating evidence of safety.

④ Golden Rice's potential is being hamstrung by misguided legislation and backward thinking.

The Goth subculture first took root in the U.K. in the 1980s, when bands such as The Cure and Bauhaus became increasingly popular. It soon evolved to become more than a musical movement. Goths typically favoured black clothes and dark, often crimped hair; many sported long coats, corsets and chokers. What connection do these Goths have to the people who helped forge medieval Europe? Those historical Goths were a Germanic people who migrated across the continent, building kingdoms and sometimes fighting against established powers such as the Romans. Today, ancient Goths are seen as the archetype of anti-classicalism. When the Gothic leader Alaric I sacked Rome in AD 410, it was a hugely symbolic moment in the fall of the classical world. The word 'Gothic' has been a label for the non-classical ever since. The modern Goth subculture also leans on that symbolic frame of reference of the 'other'. The word 'vandal', the name of another Germanic tribe that spread across Europe from the fifth century, has also been co-opted by today's Goths, though 'vandal' has such specific connotations that no one wants to use that term to describe themselves. Goth counterculture is not inherently destructive — there's no throwing around bins or breaking windows. Being a Goth is just a determined choice to be 'other'. In that sense, modern Goth culture is almost an extension of the symbolic and metaphorical legacy of the ancient Goths.

36 What is the topic of the passage?

① Symbolic connection from ancient Goths to modern counterculture
② Unveiling the etymological roots of popular modern Goth terms
③ New insights into ancient conflicts between Romans and Goths
④ Musical traditions inherited by the Gothic subculture

37 According to the passage, which of the following is NOT true?

① The ancient Goths' conquest of Rome marked the decline of classical influence.
② Modern Goths have adopted 'vandal' as a self-identifying label.
③ Modern Goths typically distance themselves from historical Gothic associations.
④ The modern Goth subculture embraces a sense of otherness as a distinctive choice.

The New York State Office for the Aging recently announced plans to distribute 'robot companions' to more than 800 older adults in the state. The plan aims to battle social isolation by providing older adults with robots Ⓐthat can initiate conversations, play games and provide general support. Social isolation can be a problem for some people as they get older and experience reduced mobility or live away from family members and friends. For some, the COVID-19 pandemic has exacerbated experiences of isolation and loneliness. At the forefront of the innovative approach to Ⓑresolving these issues is ElliQ, a smart speaker with a moving 'head' that turns to face the human speaker and lights up when talking. Featuring artificial intelligence, ElliQ is designed to provide support for older adults living alone. ElliQ also has a proactive ability to engage users in small talk. It appears to show 'empathy', can suggest activities and reminds people Ⓒto take medication or attend appointments. It's accompanied by a touchscreen that allows video calls to friends and family. While the New York State Office for the Aging highlights the positive impact of ElliQ, acknowledging approximately 20 daily interactions between users and the robot, the introduction of robotic companionship _____. Some people worry about replacing human love and care with robot 'care'. Others worry that robot companions might deceive people about the fact that they are merely machines, not conscious beings. Additionally, privacy concerns emerge as the use of social robots involves the collection of personal data, Ⓓraise questions about the balance between technological advancements and safeguarding individual privacy.

38 Which of the following is NOT grammatically correct?

① Ⓐ ② Ⓑ

③ Ⓒ ④ Ⓓ

39 What is the best expression for the blank?

① sparks a debate on its ethical implications

② spurs much enthusiasm and positive reception

③ leads to debates on its practicality and necessity

④ provokes unanimous rejection and moral outrage

40 According to the passage, which of the following is NOT true about ElliQ?

① It can engage in verbal conversations with humans.

② It is designed to help people cope with the challenges of social isolation.

③ It can help its users to remember their appointment times.

④ It has yet to reach a stage of development where it can make video calls.

KONKUK
UNIVERSITY

건국대학교

2024학년도 인문·예체능계 A형
▸▸ 40문항·60분

[문항별 배점: 01-20 2점/ 21-40 3점]

[01-06] 밑줄 친 어휘와 의미가 가장 가까운 것을 고르시오.

01 The <u>endorsement</u> of our native powers of making sense of our experience according to our own standards of rationality should also make it possible for us to acknowledge the ubiquitous contributions made by sense perception to the tacit components of articulate knowledge.

① dissociation   ② ratification   ③ equilibrium
④ incongruity   ⑤ alienation

02 The main difference between a <u>fictitious</u> mathematical entity, like a complex number, and a fantastic character like Sherlock Holmes, lies in the greater hold which the latter has on our imagination.

① veritable   ② spurious   ③ legitimate
④ detrimental   ⑤ tangible

03 Lucy's roommate, a classical music major, found Lucy's love of hip-hop totally <u>repugnant</u>.

① rampant ② rude ③ repulsive
④ raw ⑤ regressive

04 The archaeological 'record' is not a record at all, but made, not given, 'data'. 'The past' is gone and lost, and *a fortiori*, through the <u>equivocality</u> of things and the character of society, never existed as a definitive entity 'the present' anyway.

① stability ② agility ③ fragility
④ ambiguity ⑤ specificity

05 The people in that city are <u>congenial</u>, and any visitor who stays more than a day or two soon catches the spirit.

① shy ② mean ③ eccentric
④ easygoing ⑤ cold-hearted

06 The child was so spoiled by her <u>indulgent</u> parents that she pouted and became grumpy when she did not receive all of their attention.

① lenient ② ingenuous ③ discreet
④ unfathomable ⑤ precarious

[07-16] 빈칸에 들어갈 가장 적절한 단어를 고르시오.

07 The word *incongruous* contains three key word parts. *In-* here means 'not'; *con-* means 'together'; *gru-* means to 'move or come'. *Incongruous* behavior, therefore, is behavior that _____ someone's usual behavior.

① can not support ② is not followed by ③ disagrees with
④ does not bring ⑤ is not related with

08 Bored by the _____ prose of the typical Victorian novelist, he was attracted by the terse prose of the young American writer.

① tranquil ② obtuse ③ verbose
④ partial ⑤ inconsistent

09 Finding themselves existentially homeless in the real world, many have found the experience of community online, especially in the form of social networks. The influence of online communities has drastically increased with the _____ of digital connectivity afforded by smartphones.

① ubiquity   ② concentration   ③ convenience
④ authenticity   ⑤ unification

10 If you describe someone as _____, you mean that they hold the older and more traditional ideas of their religion or party.

① degraded   ② orthodox   ③ shabby
④ cynical   ⑤ radical

11 If workers are _____, they are told by their employers to leave their job, usually because there is no more work for them to do.

① laid off   ② put up with   ③ called upon
④ fallen apart   ⑤ pulled down

12 She is a(n) _____, as disinclined to base her future on impractical dreams as she would be to build a castle on shifting sand.

① optimist   ② skeptic   ③ idealist
④ pessimist   ⑤ pragmatist

13 We often hear the expression "music is the _____ language." By this people mean that even if two people do not speak each other's language, they can at least appreciate music together. But like so many popular sayings, this one is only partially true. Although all people do have the same physiological mechanisms for hearing, what a person actually hears is influenced by his or her culture.

① clandestine   ② hedonistic   ③ taciturn
④ authentic   ⑤ universal

14 In a revolutionary development in technology, some manufacturers now make
_____ forms of plastic; some plastic trash bags, for example, gradually decompose
exposed to sunlight.

① inexpensive   ② biodegradable   ③ endurable

④ transparent   ⑤ multi-functional

15 The medical researchers defend their new treatment by saying that it follows
accepted, standard practices. What, therefore, must have been the critics' _____
about the treatment? They must have alleged it was nonstandard, violating
acceptable medical practices.

① suggestion   ② accusation   ③ provision

④ conclusion   ⑤ justification

16 Frequently, the test makers attempt to _____ you by using familiar words in
an unfamiliar way. Suppose you have found one answer choice that perfectly fits
the meaning of the sentence as a whole but can not find a second answer that
seems exactly right. Reread the sentence, substituting that perfect answer choice
for the blank, and then take a fresh look at the other answer choices.

① relieve   ② persuade   ③ invalidate

④ mislead   ⑤ enlighten

The shift from a teacher-centered, high-art focus to a more egalitarian, student-centered orientation highlights several issues about musical and educational values. In the past, musical values were typically rooted in the widespread music conservatory system, and the music curriculum was implemented by classically trained music teachers. In the context of early twenty-first century education, musical values in education are increasingly motivated by multiple sources-political democracy, cultural policies, mass media, art advocacy, social justice campaigns, school communities, and not least the individual musical preferences of teachers and students. The presence of these various sources is indicative of the breakdown of monolithic value systems, the demise of cultural hegemony, and the emergence of a world-view that acknowledges diverse ways of being musical. The goodness and value of individual music cultures are acknowledged in the multiple ways in which music functions _____, whether it is their quest for freedom, celebration of rites of passage, rebellion against social injustice, gratitude for divine intervention, or transmission of cultural heritage in the telling of a story.

17 윗글의 주제로 가장 적절한 것은?

① Music education for social justice

② How to train classical music teachers

③ Importance of democracy in education

④ Changes of musical values in education

⑤ Breakdown of music education in schools

18 빈칸에 들어갈 말로 가장 적절한 것은?

① for teaching the value of justice

② in the everyday lives of people

③ for student-centered education

④ in the whole school curriculum

⑤ for improving students' freedom

[19-20] 다음 글을 읽고 물음에 답하시오.

The English Gothic style of the 13th-15th centuries is characterized by pointed arches and increasingly ornate designs for the vault. Windows were tall and narrow in the Early English period (13th century), and later, in the Decorated period, had tracery (= lace-like patterns) at the top. In the Perpendicular period (15th century), they were greatly increased in size and filled with stained glass showing pictures of saints. Ceilings with elaborate fan vaults (= curved strips of stone spreading out from a point) are supported by flying buttresses that lean at an angle from the wall and form an arch. Salisbury Cathedral is a characteristic Early English building. Exeter Cathedral dates mainly from the Decorated period and Gloucester Cathedral with its fan vaults is typical of the Perpendicular period.

19 윗글의 제목으로 가장 적절한 것은?

① Sub-types of English Gothic Style
② Typical Structure of English Cathedrals
③ The Origin of Stained Glass in England
④ Arch and Vault: Two Fundamental Elements
⑤ The History of English Architecture

20 윗글의 내용과 일치하는 것은?

① Early English 시기 특징은 창문 위쪽의 레이스 모양 장식이다.
② Decorated 시기의 창문들은 길고 넓은 모양을 띠고 있다.
③ Perpendicular 시기에 창문들이 작아지고 스테인드글라스로 장식되었다.
④ 15세기로 갈수록 둥근 천정(vault) 디자인의 장식적 요소가 줄어들고 단순해졌다.
⑤ Gloucester Cathedral과 Salisbury Cathedral의 건축은 약 2세기의 시차가 있다.

21 Aesthetic designs are more effective at fostering positive attitudes than unaesthetic designs, and make people more Ⓐ<u>tolerant</u> of design problems. For example, it is common for people to name and develop feelings toward designs that have fostered positive attitudes (e.g., naming a car), and Ⓑ<u>rare</u> for people to do the same with designs that have fostered negative attitudes. Such personal and positive relationships with a design Ⓒ<u>evoke</u> feelings of affection, loyalty, and patience — all significant factors in the long-term usability and overall success of a design. These positive relationships have implications for Ⓓ<u>what</u> effectively people interact with designs. Positive relationships with a design result in an interaction that helps Ⓔ<u>catalyze</u> creative thinking and problem solving.

① Ⓐ   ② Ⓑ   ③ Ⓒ
④ Ⓓ   ⑤ Ⓔ

22 Timber is a challenging material because architects and engineers must understand Ⓐ<u>how</u> nature designed it as well as what they are trying to do with it. Wood itself has evolved over millions of years to withstand the forces it encounters in nature while also being able to transport water and nutrients and Ⓑ<u>performs</u> functions necessary for the tree's survival. Engineers are concerned with predicting the strength and stiffness of wood, a prediction Ⓒ<u>which</u> involves accounting for knots, grain structure, moisture content, species, deviations in grade, etc. Such deviations are commonly referred to as defects. These "defects" serve a purpose for the tree and are intrinsic to Ⓓ<u>its</u> structure. As trees are harvested from the forest, humankind seeks to reformulate or re-engineer wood Ⓔ<u>to fulfill</u> a new purpose.

① Ⓐ   ② Ⓑ   ③ Ⓒ
④ Ⓓ   ⑤ Ⓔ

23 Those speakers of creole languages Ⓐ<u>who</u> had access to education Ⓑ<u>were</u> duly Ⓒ<u>convincing</u> that their speech Ⓓ<u>was</u> wrong, and they often tried to make it more similar to the Ⓔ<u>standard</u>.

① Ⓐ   ② Ⓑ   ③ Ⓒ
④ Ⓓ   ⑤ Ⓔ

24 Then, since no discussion Ⓐ<u>of</u> pragmatics can proceed without a basic understanding of semantics and the Ⓑ<u>proposed</u> theoretical bases Ⓒ<u>for</u> distinguishing Ⓓ<u>between</u> the two fields, the remainder of the chapter will be devoted to Ⓔ<u>sketch</u> the domains of semantics and pragmatics.

① Ⓐ   ② Ⓑ   ③ Ⓒ
④ Ⓓ   ⑤ Ⓔ

[25-30] 빈칸에 들어갈 가장 적절한 단어를 고르시오.

25 There are several similarities between auditory and visual perception. One is the problem of perceptual _____. Both systems manage to deal with widely varying sensory information, and give us remarkably stable perceptions. For example, when you see a person walking towards you, you correctly conclude that the person is not growing in size, even though the retinal image could simplistically be interpreted in such a way.

① dependency   ② constancy   ③ abstruseness
④ dissonance   ⑤ parsimony

26 One unspoken truth about creativity — it isn't about wild talent so much as it is about _____. To find a few ideas that work, you need to try a lot that don't. It's a pure numbers game. Geniuses don't necessarily have a higher success rate than other creators; they simply do more — and they do a range of different things. They have more successes and more failures. That goes for teams and companies too. It's impossible to generate a lot of good ideas without also generating a lot of bad ideas. The thing about creativity is that at the outset, you can't tell which ideas will succeed and which will fail. So the only thing you can do is try to fail faster so that you can move onto the next idea.

① disparity   ② productivity   ③ propensity
④ equanimity   ⑤ serendipity

27 In one psychological study of confirming-evidence bias, two groups read two reports of carefully conducted research on the effectiveness of the death penalty as deterrent to crime. One report concluded that the death penalty was effective; the other concluded it was not. Despite being exposed to solid scientific information supporting counter-arguments, the members of both groups became even more convinced of the _____ of their own position after reading both reports. They automatically accepted the supporting information and dismissed the conflicting information.

① nature   ② characteristic   ③ validity

④ aspect   ⑤ deficiency

28 Intelligent technology can help us overcome many cultural and societal obstacles. If we build them correctly, artificially intelligent machines can become mediators and arbiters, providing communal guidance we can rely upon to be _____. A group of politically neutral programmers have formed a coalition to build a "truth machine." Thirty of the biggest and most influential tech companies have authored the Digital Geneva Accord, subscribing to a set of principles that commits them not to assist any governments to mount cyber-attacks against "innocent civilians or enterprises from anywhere."

① powerful   ② impartial   ③ efficient

④ communicative   ⑤ innovative

29 Licensing grants individuals formal or legal permission to practice their profession. Licenses are granted by states or even local agencies. The licensing authority provides the licensee with a set of rules to follow to keep the license. If the rules are violated, the authority may have the right to _____ the licensee or recall the license. Clearly a license is a privilege, not a right, and if licensees want to maintain that privilege, they must follow the prescribed code.

① probate   ② incarcerate   ③ sanction

④ infuriate   ⑤ procrastinate

30 A very large body of work in AI begins with the assumptions that information and knowledge should be represented in first-order logic and that reasoning is theorem proving. On the face of it, this seems _____ as a model for people. It certainly doesn't seem as if we are using logic when we are thinking, and if we are, why are so many of our thoughts and actions so illogical? In fact, there are psychological experiments that purport to show that people do not use logic in thinking about a problem.

① irreversible ② inconsiderate ③ implausible
④ imperative ⑤ irreducible

[31-32] 밑줄 친 Ⓐ~Ⓔ 가운데 문맥상 자연스럽지 않은 것을 고르시오.

31 For nonscientific short articles where a term would be used only once, Ⓐavoid jargon altogether. There is little benefit to introducing new vocabulary or notation if you will not be using it again. And for nonstatisticians, equations full of Greek symbols, subscripts, and superscripts are more likely to Ⓑreawaken math anxiety than to promote effective communication. The same logic applies to introductory or concluding sections of scientific papers. Using a new word means that you must Ⓒdefine it, which takes attention away from your main point. If you will not be using that term again, Ⓓpreclude other ways to describe numeric facts or patterns. Replace complex or unfamiliar words, acronyms, or mathematical symbols with their everyday equivalents, and rephrase complicated concepts into more Ⓔintuitive ones.

① Ⓐ ② Ⓑ ③ Ⓒ
④ Ⓓ ⑤ Ⓔ

32 There is a widespread belief that creativity is best served through inner peace, stillness, and calmness. One of my colleagues was convinced that her own creative writing was best when she had no Ⓐdistractions, quietly sipping tea in a peaceful setting. However, after three months of such Ⓑlanguid writing days, she produced nothing that she was proud of. Shortly thereafter, her first baby was born and her schedule went from long, open, peaceful, Ⓒunstructured days to tightly orchestrated, minute-by-minute slots, punctuated by extreme activity. The result? She became prolifically Ⓓproductive. In her words, she was "wired." The way she put it to me was, "I have ninety minutes when Sam is napping, and I run to the computer and write like crazy. I'm totally focused." Turns out, my colleague is onto something. In fact, it is better to be ⒠reposed when attempting to think creatively.

① Ⓐ   ② Ⓑ   ③ Ⓒ

④ Ⓓ   ⑤ Ⓔ

[33-34] 다음 글을 읽고 물음에 답하시오.

All phobias are learned, usually by children watching a parent's reaction to certain things. Children take their cues as to what is dangerous in life from the adults closest to them. If your child sees you focusing on an object or situation in an unhealthy way, they will be more likely to focus on that object or situation in a similar fashion. One classic psychology study involved mothers and their twelve-month-old babies. Each mother was with her baby throughout the study, but the mothers were divided into two groups, A and B. Both groups A and B were exposed to the same situation, the only difference being that group B mothers had to positively encourage their baby to continue playing with the things in front of them, whereas the mothers in group A just had to be themselves in response to what their baby was playing with.

What were these babies playing with? An extremely large but tame python. The study went as follows: the children from group A were placed on the floor so the python could slither among them. As the fear of snakes is _____ in humans but isn't activated until approximately the age of two, these babies saw the python as a large toy. As the group A babies started playing with the live python, they looked up to see what their mothers were doing. The mothers, who were told to be themselves, naturally looked horrified. Seeing the fear on their mothers' faces, the babies burst into tears. When it was group B's turn, as instructed the mothers laughed and encouraged their babies to keep playing with the python. As a result, these babies were grabbing and chewing on the python, all because their mothers were supportive of their new toy.

33 빈칸에 들어갈 말로 가장 적절한 것은?

① tractable   ② arbitrary   ③ cryptic

④ innate   ⑤ inconsequential

34 윗글의 내용과 일치하지 <u>않는</u> 것은?

① 아이들의 공포증은 대개 부모의 반응을 통해 학습된다.

② 12개월 된 아기들이 심리학 연구에 참여했다.

③ 집단 A의 어머니들은 아기들이 잘 놀도록 격려했다.

④ 아기들은 길들인 큰 비단뱀을 가지고 놀았다.

⑤ 집단 B의 어머니들은 비단뱀을 보고 웃었다.

[35-36] 다음 글을 읽고 물음에 답하시오.

Social domain theory views emotions and moral judgments as reciprocal processes that cannot be disentangled. This view differs from emotivist or intuitionist approaches to morality, which give priority to emotional and implicit processes while avoiding reasoning as largely post hoc rationalizations. From the social domain perspective, this treatment of emotions and reasoning as distinct and opposing influences represents a false dichotomy. Rather, this theory assumes that _____ experiences are an important component of moral judgments and that the latter involves a complex integration of thoughts, feelings, and experiences. To borrow from Kant's famous saying, moral reasoning without emotion is empty; emotions without reasoning are blind. Children's _____ experiences influence their understanding, encoding, and memory of moral violations and are part of a complex evaluative process.

35 빈칸에 공통으로 들어갈 말로 가장 적절한 것은?

① strong   ② mutual   ③ satisfactory

④ confident   ⑤ affective

36 윗글의 주제로 가장 적절한 것은?

① Importance of social domain theory

② Kant's theory of moral reasoning and emotion

③ Role of moral judgment in children's development

④ Reciprocity of emotions and moral judgments

⑤ Difference between social domain theory and emotivist approaches

[37-38] 다음 글을 읽고 물음에 답하시오.

We are not naturally prosocial, which is evident from the fact that both religious and nonreligious authorities constantly have to command us to fulfill our obligations. ⒜ We are forever reminding children to share their toys, and adults to stick to the socially agreed rules of behaviors. ⒝ In reality, in the absence of social and religious warnings, prosocial behavior is largely confined to close family and friends. ⒞ Many ethnographic studies demonstrate that aid is usually freely given to family and friends without expectation of return. ⒟ The demands of living in super-large communities have made it necessary to impose demands of generosity — or at least neutrality — in our interactions with those with whom we live. ⒠ It would help prevent crime and delinquency from bursting the fragile bonds that hold our communities together.

37 윗글의 내용과 일치하지 <u>않는</u> 것은?

① 인간이 천성적으로 친사회적인 것은 아니다.
② 친족이나 친구들과 잘 지내기 위해서는 관용이 필요하다.
③ 범죄와 비행은 우리 공동체의 취약한 유대감을 파괴할 수 있다.
④ 종교적·비종교적 권위자들은 우리에게 의무를 수행하라고 명령해야 한다.
⑤ 사회적·종교적 경고가 없다면, 인간은 주로 가까운 친족이나 친구에게만 친사회적 행동을 보일 것이다.

38 글의 흐름상 다음 문장이 들어가기에 가장 적절한 곳은?

It is given to those outside this magic circle of a few hundred people only on the explicit agreement to return or repay the favour.

① Ⓐ   ② Ⓑ   ③ Ⓒ
④ Ⓓ   ⑤ Ⓔ

[39-40] 다음 글을 읽고 물음에 답하시오.

Many species have languages; birds and baboons can warn others in their group of the approach of predators. But animal languages can share only the simplest of ideas, almost all of them linked to what is immediately present, a bit like mime. Several researchers have tried to teach chimps to talk, and chimps can, indeed, acquire and use vocabularies of one or two hundred words; they can even link pairs of words in new patterns. But their vocabularies are small and they don't use syntax or grammar, the rules that allow us to generate a huge variety of meanings from a small number of verbal tokens. Their linguistic ability seems never to exceed that of a two- or three-year-old human, and that is not enough to create today's world. And here's where the butterfly flapped its wings. Human language crossed a subtle linguistic threshold that allowed utterly new types of communication. _____, human languages let us share information about abstract entities or about things or possibilities that are not immediately present and may not even exist outside of our imagination.

39 빈칸에 들어갈 말로 가장 적절한 것은?

① Unfortunately   ② Hopefully   ③ Above all
④ Nonetheless   ⑤ By the way

40 윗글의 내용과 일치하는 것은?

① 침팬지는 단어들을 연결하여 새로운 어구 패턴을 만들 수 있다.
② 침팬지의 언어능력은 두세 살짜리 어린아이보다 우월하다.
③ 침팬지의 언어는 어휘가 수천 개에 이를 정도로 매우 풍부하다.
④ 새들은 포식자가 접근해도 동료 집단에게 경고할 수 없다.
⑤ 침팬지는 인간처럼 통사 혹은 문법구조를 이용한다.

건국대학교   2024학년도 자연계 A형
▶▶ 영어 20문항, 수학 20문항 · 60분

[문항별 배점: 01-20 2점]

[01-03] 밑줄 친 어휘와 의미가 가장 가까운 것을 고르시오.

01 During the first few months we lived in our house, we suffered one <u>calamity</u> after another; first the furnace exploded; then the washing machine stopped working; then the roof began to leak.

① disaster   ② diameter   ③ diagnosis
④ disease   ⑤ difficulty

02 It was religion, not <u>secular</u> thought, that advanced the view that nature is founded on a deep rationality.

① worldly   ② separate   ③ guarded
④ awkward   ⑤ profound

03 They lived in the <u>dreary</u> little town in the Midwest.

① peaceful and calm
② rural and pastoral
③ dull and depressing
④ warlike and fiery
⑤ cozy and comfortable

[04-08] 빈칸에 들어갈 가장 적절한 단어를 고르시오.

04 The doctor paid _____ attention to his patients; he made careful notes of even tiny changes in their illnesses.

① cool   ② rare   ③ passionate
④ meticulous   ⑤ sincere

05 When an underwater object is seen from outside the water, its appearance becomes _____. This is because refraction changes the direction of the light rays that come from the object.

① disposed   ② distorted   ③ dismissed
④ distressed   ⑤ discharged

06 When photography came along in the nineteenth century, painting was put in crisis. The photograph, it seemed, did the work of imitating nature better than the painter ever could. Some painters made _____ use of the invention. There were Impressionist painters who used a photograph in place of the model or landscape they were painting.

① imaginable   ② pragmatic   ③ illogical
④ moderate   ⑤ independent

07 A: You're not eating your spaghetti correctly.
B: I'm not?
A: You're supposed to put your spaghetti in the spoon and twirl it with the fork.
B: (laughs)
A: Why are you laughing?
B: Why do you want _____?
A: What do you mean?
B: I was born in Italy!

① to add insult to injury
② to have the right chemistry
③ to go home and kick the dog
④ to teach a fish how to swim
⑤ to mend the barn after the horse is stolen

08 A: Have you seen Sue's new car?

   B: Yeah. It looks good, but she's had nothing but problems with it.

   A: That's too bad. It sounds like she got a real _____.

   B: She sure did! No sooner did she drive it home from the dealer's than it proved defective and started breaking down.

   ① parasite   ② bread   ③ deal
   ④ duck   ⑤ lemon

[09-10] 밑줄 친 Ⓐ~Ⓔ 중 어법상 적절하지 않은 것을 고르시오.

09 Laughter Ⓐ<u>resulting</u> from humor shows Ⓑ<u>itself</u> when people find themselves in an unfavorable situation, Ⓒ<u>for</u> which they generally Ⓓ<u>would</u> have felt anger and/or fear, and the detection of incongruent elements allows Ⓔ<u>themselves</u> to watch it from a different perspective.

   ① Ⓐ   ② Ⓑ   ③ Ⓒ
   ④ Ⓓ   ⑤ Ⓔ

10 We are often told that there is no innovation without competition, Ⓐ<u>what</u> is absurd Ⓑ<u>given</u> that most of the greatest innovations in science and technology Ⓒ<u>have</u> resulted from the sharing of research Ⓓ<u>across</u> academic silos, national borders, and language barriers. In truth, no great innovations Ⓔ<u>occur</u> in isolation.

   ① Ⓐ   ② Ⓑ   ③ Ⓒ
   ④ Ⓓ   ⑤ Ⓔ

[11-13] 빈칸에 들어갈 말로 가장 적절한 것을 고르시오.

11 If you cannot retrieve a fact or idea, stay with it until the memory appears. Don't give up assuming it's lost. When a memory doesn't surface the moment we want, the default response is to assume it is forgotten. You likely didn't forget. You just need to give the brain a moment to shuffle through the mental forest. The key is not to force the memory, but instead, to relax and let it come. If you are stuck for an extended period, try recalling anything. Then use the power of _____ to steer toward the information. For example, if you are struggling to recall the earlier chapters of a book, start with the middle or later chapters, or any part that comes easy.

① concentration   ② association   ③ continuation
④ internalization   ⑤ reconciliation

12 It is well known that the ancient Greeks, Indians and Chinese produced vast bodies of sophisticated knowledge, ranging over mathematics, medicine, and astronomy. Indeed, much of this knowledge was appropriated and reworked by the Muslims and Christian scholars who are normally credited with having initiated the scientific project. So why then should we not also call these antique sages "scientists"? The simple but generally applicable answer is that their societies did not assign a specific social role to the scientist. What we would now recognize as _____ was always done in service of something else, not as an end in itself. That "something else" may be leisure or statecraft, each in its own way forcing science to operate within a rigid framework that allowed for considerable innovation but never autonomy.

① science   ② knowledge   ③ project
④ religion   ⑤ creativity

13　The most disastrous activities of humans included hunting with firearms, ranching activities, and the building of beach resorts. There is little doubt that the Nene's near-extinction was hastened after shotguns were brought to Hawaii. It seems reasonable to assume that many more Nene were killed when guns became common. _____, as people moved further inland on the islands they began to open more and more land for the development of ranches and beach resorts. These developments forced the geese out of their natural nesting and breeding ranges. As these ranches and resorts became more and more plentiful, the Nene population accordingly decreased.

① As a result
② To recapitulate
③ On the other hand
④ In a similar fashion
⑤ In a notable contrast

14　다음 글의 제목으로 가장 적절한 것은?

The devastation began on May 18, when an explosion, estimated at 500 times the force of the atomic bomb that destroyed the Hiroshima, ripped off the top 1,200 feet of the 9,700-foot volcano. In less than seven days, a cloud of volcanic gas containing some toxic chemicals and minute particles of radioactive substances spread over the nation. Scientists say that within several months the cloud — invisible to the naked eye in most regions — will cover the Northern Hemisphere in the stratosphere above 55,000 feet. It is expected to last about two years before completing its fall to earth. The environmental effects are considerable. The greatest economic impact is expected to be to the agriculture and timber industries in the country.

① Atomic Energy: Merits and Demerits
② Nuclear Umbrella: Causes and Effects
③ Exploding Volcano: Full Impact Yet To Come
④ Environmental Crisis: Some Novel Immense Disasters
⑤ Global Warming: Rationales and Immediate Consequence

[15-16] 다음 글을 읽고 물음에 답하시오.

A carbon sink is a natural feature that absorbs or stores more carbon than it releases. $\boxed{A}$ The value of carbon sinks is that they can help create equilibrium in the atmosphere by removing excess CO_2. $\boxed{B}$ One example of a carbon sink is a large forest. Its mass of plants and other organic material absorb and store tons of carbon. However, the planet's major carbon sink is its oceans.

Since the Industrial Revolution began in the eighteenth century, CO_2 released during industrial processes has greatly increased the proportion of carbon in the atmosphere. $\boxed{C}$ Carbon sinks have been able to absorb about half of this excess CO_2, and the world's oceans have done the major part of that job. They absorb about one-fourth of humans' industrial carbon emissions, doing half the work of all Earth's carbon sinks combined.

Like kitchen sinks, the ocean sinks can fill up, though. The Southern Ocean, the strongest ocean sink, has taken in about 15 percent of the world's excess CO_2. $\boxed{D}$ Clearly, the oceans do not have an infinite capacity to absorb carbon. $\boxed{E}$ As their absorption capacity weakens, the buildup of CO_2 and other so-called greenhouse gases in the atmosphere increases, the result being a worldwide warming of the climate.

15 윗글의 제목으로 가장 적절한 것은?

① Oceans: Earth's Major Carbon Sink
② Increase of Greenhouse Gases
③ CO_2: The Cause of Climate Warming
④ Equilibrium: What Carbon Sinks Make
⑤ Overflow of The Southern Ocean

16 글의 흐름상 다음 문장이 들어가기에 가장 적절한 곳은?

However, a multinational scientific survey completed in 2007 has shown that this ocean is reaching its carbon saturation point.

① $\boxed{A}$ ② $\boxed{B}$ ③ $\boxed{C}$
④ $\boxed{D}$ ⑤ $\boxed{E}$

[17-18] 다음 글을 읽고 물음에 답하시오.

Smart cities are definitely nudging the world toward some sustainability goals, and smart technologies are visibly improving city services within some fast-growing economies, most notably China. But Ⓐincrementally improving the management of electrical grids, pollution and waste, transportation, and city services can take the world only a short distance toward global sustainability. Smart city technologies do very little to alter and can even worsen problems such as wasteful consumption, feelings of alienation, income inequality, and inequality of services. The positive discourse of smart cities can also obscure the ways that the political and economic structures of cities themselves have Ⓑlong been a cause of global environmental degradation.

Ecologist William Rees, who coined the term "ecological footprint," reminds us of the complex ways that cities and the accompanying suburban sprawl draw down global resources and harm distant ecosystems. Urban economics, as he demonstrates, Ⓒtends to exaggerate the value of urbanization for sustainability by underestimating the global environmental damage from the rising consumption of city residents. Most cities rely on land, food, fresh water, natural resources, and energy far beyond their borders. And they rely on externalizing the cost of waste into distant lands, the global commons, and future generations. ⒹMeasured locally, the ecological footprint of the residents of a smart city may seem to be declining. But taking into account the shadows of consumption in faraway lands, this footprint looks very different, with deep social and environmental costs for Ⓔmarginalizing peoples and fragile ecosystems.

17 윗글의 주제로 가장 적절한 것은?

① Causes of global environmental degradation

② Use of smart technologies for sustainable future

③ Environmental crises for residents of a smart city

④ Reduction of the cost of waste for future generations

⑤ Negative effects of smart cities on global sustainability

18 밑줄 친 Ⓐ~Ⓔ 가운데 어법상 옳지 <u>않은</u> 것은?

① Ⓐ   ② Ⓑ   ③ Ⓒ

④ Ⓓ   ⑤ Ⓔ

[19-20] 다음 글을 읽고 물음에 답하시오.

Gypsies are a people scattered through many countries. The name Gypsy comes from the word 'Egyptian' because Gypsies were once thought to have come from Egypt. Some people now believe that they originally came from India. In the US Gypsies are called Roma, and in Britain they are known as Romanies or travellers. Roma or Romanies, like many other minority groups, have a strong sense of pride in their identity. Gypsies have always been associated with fortune-telling. They can be found at fairgrounds predicting people's future by reading their palm or looking into a crystal ball. Because of the mystery associated with their origins and their magical powers, Gypsies have a popular romantic image that _____ the reality of families living on dirty caravan sites and being moved on by council officials or the police. Americans have little contact with Gypsies and think of the Roma only as exciting, mysterious people who wear brightly colored clothes and gold jewellery and have unusual powers.

19 빈칸에 들어갈 말로 가장 적절한 것은?

① results from   ② depends on   ③ conflicts with
④ coincides with   ⑤ accounts for

20 Gypsy에 대한 윗글의 내용과 일치하는 것은?

① 고대 이집트에서부터 기원한 민족이다.
② 일정한 곳에 머무르지 않아 정체성 인식이 약하다.
③ 주술적 능력 때문에 대체로 두려운 존재로 여겨진다.
④ 미국인은 빈번한 접촉을 통해 그들을 흥미롭다고 생각한다.
⑤ 영국에서는 이들을 Romany 혹은 '여행자'라고 부른다.

KYONGGI UNIVERSITY

경기대학교   2024학년도 일반편입 A형 (인문·사범·예체능계)
▶▶ 40문항·60분

[문항별 배점: 01-10 2점/ 11-30 2.5점/ 31-40 3점]

[01-10] Choose the option that best completes each dialogue.

01   A: Was I too harsh on Amy for coming in late?
B: No. She needed to be _____.

① deferred   ② salvaged
③ reprimanded   ④ provoked

02   A: I can't believe that I fell for that scam.
B: It's not your fault. Anyone could have been _____.

① spoiled   ② deceived
③ infected   ④ offended

03   A: Many of my plants died due to the cold spell!
B: Maybe you should get some that are known to be quite _____, like pansies.

① hardy   ② canny
③ serene   ④ brazen

04 A: I'd like to have this skirt shortened, please.

B: OK. The _____ can be done in an hour.

① exchange　　　　　② variation

③ substitute　　　　 ④ alteration

05 A: I appreciate this award for my charitable work, but I don't feel that I've earned it.

B: You have. Your dedication to charity is _____.

① inscrutable　　　　② prosperous

③ commendable　　　④ opportunistic

06 A: I've decided to give up volunteer coaching.

B: Quitting is of course your _____, but I wish you'd reconsider.

① prerogative　　　　② rectitude

③ arraignment　　　　④ endowment

07 A: Did you manage to talk Beth into working on the project?

B: I tried to _____ her, but no amount of sweet talk could convince her.

① condone　　　　　② appease

③ endorse　　　　　④ cajole

08 A: Will your trip to Spain be a long one?

B: No, I'm only planning on a brief _____.

① lapse　　　　　　② jaunt

③ streak　　　　　　④ breach

09 A: I'm sorry your proposal got rejected.

B: Well, my efforts proved _____ this time, but I'll try again later!

① baleful　　　　　　② extant

③ forlorn　　　　　　④ futile

10   A: Don't be too hard on yourself. You tried your best in the tennis tournament.

B: Thanks. But in _____, I should have practiced more.

① hindsight   ② aftermath

③ remission   ④ prognosis

[11-20] Choose the option that best completes each sentence.

11   The man spoke with such _____ that it was hard not to believe him, even when he was wrong.

① reclusiveness   ② conviction

③ reliance   ④ inclination

12   ForReal photo-editing software offers a 30-day money back guarantee, so there is no _____ to pay if you are unsatisfied!

① extension   ② allegation

③ obligation   ④ intrusion

13   Building a house is a very complicated process, and you are likely to _____ several unexpected expenses.

① incur   ② enhance

③ enact   ④ induce

14   The recent leak of classified information has led Jackson Corp. to _____ strict security measures.

① delude   ② impose

③ enclose   ④ relegate

15   Because of a heavy downpour, the district has been _____ with water, and most residents have left their homes.

① exasperated   ② inundated

③ proliferated   ④ tranquilized

16 A 2,000-year-old ceramic bowl was recently discovered in nearly _____ condition, with only a few scratches on its underside.

① pristine   ② sparse
③ archaic   ④ tranquil

17 Even after being pressed by the authorities, the journalist refused to _____ the name of his confidential source.

① obscure   ② rescind
③ expunge   ④ divulge

18 The judge's failure to uphold proper legal procedures led to accusations that the criminal conviction represented a(n) _____ of justice.

① umbrage   ② amnesty
③ travesty   ④ ravage

19 The wedding photographer asked guests to ignore her presence so that she could capture _____ rather than posed photos.

① dormant   ② cordial
③ nimble   ④ candid

20 While the prosecutor argued that the defendant's DNA was the most important evidence in the case, the defense lawyer minimized its importance, calling it _____.

① recondite   ② obdurate
③ peripheral   ④ obtrusive

[21-30] Choose the option that best completes each sentence.

21 By the time the boy _____ at school, the first class had finished.
① would arrive   ② arrived
③ is arriving   ④ has arrived

22 Many young people enjoy _____ the night sky using simple telescopes.
① observing   ② to observe
③ observed   ④ observe

23 The company has come under fire for _____ many regard as blatantly anti-competitive business practices.
① that   ② which
③ whose   ④ what

24 The entrepreneur struggled for many years _____ investors to put money into his AI startup.
① attracting   ② attracted
③ to attract   ④ having attracted

25 _____ you encounter any problems during your stay at the Windsor Hotel, please do not hesitate to contact the front desk for assistance.
① Would   ② Should
③ Could   ④ May

26 During the school performance, the child _____ in the middle of the front row stood out for her beautiful voice.
① sung   ② to sing
③ singing   ④ sang

27 The doctor recommended that his patient _____ in the hospital overnight for observation.

① remain
② remains
③ remained
④ would remain

28 The high cost of raising children _____ as one of the main reasons for declining birth rates in many countries.

① have cited
② have been cited
③ has cited
④ has been cited

29 Scientists often travel to remote locations _____ search of undiscovered animal species.

① in
② to
③ on
④ from

30 Despite _____ for a down payment, the young couple considered applying for a mortgage.

① they had saved not enough up yet
② they had not yet saved up enough
③ having not yet saved up enough
④ having saved up enough not yet

[31-40] Read the passage, question(s), and options. Then, based on the given information, choose the option that best answers each question.

Sunscreen use is vital for protecting against skin cancer. Unfortunately, many people are wary about using sunscreen due to concerns about the chemicals that some of the products contain. Some experts hope that a new generation of sunscreens developed using natural compounds can assuage these consumers' fears. The compounds were discovered in algae and were found to protect coral reefs from harsh UV light. The compounds could serve as the basis for new sunscreens that could then be marketed as nature-based alternatives to current chemical sunscreens. The new sunscreens might also have the added benefit of being less damaging to marine habitats.

31 What is the main idea of the passage?

① Scientists have identified potentially harmful health impacts of certain sunscreens.

② The creation of plant-based sunscreens might reduce consumer fears about sunscreen use.

③ The concerns about sunscreen use are leading to negative health outcomes.

④ Consumers are increasingly worried about the environmental impact of sunscreens.

Livestock, particularly cattle, are a significant source of greenhouse gas emissions. Cows release large amounts of methane, which is a natural byproduct of their digestive process. Researchers are investigating approaches to reducing these methane emissions. One possibility is to feed cattle more corn instead of grass, as digesting grass-based feed produces more methane. Another option is to use additives. For example, adding probiotics to cattle feed has been shown to reduce methane production during digestion of regular feed.

32 What is the passage mainly about?

① The impact of livestock on climate change

② Why methane is more harmful than other gases

③ How livestock farming is becoming more sustainable

④ Strategies for lowering methane emissions from cattle

In the 2nd century AD, the Roman emperor Antoninus Pius ordered the construction of a defensive barrier across the isle of Britain as a way to secure the northwestern frontier of his empire. Dubbed the Antonine Wall, it was meant to supercede Hadrian's Wall, which was 160 kilometers to the south. Unlike its stone-built predecessor, the Antonine Wall was constructed primarily of turf and wood. Consequently, it has not been as well preserved. There may have been plans to add stone ramparts, but the wall was abandoned shortly after its completion, and these improvements were never implemented.

33 Which of the following is correct about the Antonine Wall?

① It was built to the south of Hadrian's Wall.

② It was composed mainly of a combination of stone and wood.

③ It has aged poorly compared with Hadrian's Wall.

④ It was abandoned before construction was completed.

AlphaGo is the first computer program to defeat a human professional at the abstract strategy game called Go. This program is touted as an example of artificial intelligence (AI), as its knowledge of Go was acquired through a process known as machine learning. This process involves the computer program analyzing large amounts of data to develop its own rules or algorithms. In the case of AlphaGo, the program independently learned to identify the best possible moves in the game, simply by playing a large number of games against human and computer-based opponents. Subsequent versions of the program — AlphaGo Master and Zero — were even more powerful than the original.

---

34 What is the best title for the passage?

① The AI That Figured Out How to Best Humans at Go

② AI Teaches Humans How to Play Go Better

③ AI Is No Match for Top-Ranked Go Player

④ New AI Beats Its Predecessor at Go

35-36

An insect called the spotted wing drosophila, or SWD, has wreaked havoc on fruit growers in the United States. Having appeared from Southeast Asia, the insect is invasive and has destroyed cherry and raspberry crops. It is a vinegar fly, the same family from which the common fruit fly comes, but unlike its relative, it does not favor damaged fruit. Instead, it uses a sharp appendage to penetrate the skin of fruits and deposit eggs inside. Affected fruits are ruined gradually from within, so unsuspecting farmers are often shocked to discover that seemingly perfect harvests are in fact worthless.

SWD are vulnerable to insecticides, which are the first line of defense for farmers. The pest can also be controlled by promptly harvesting ripened fruits and by planting fruit tree varieties that ripen before the insect's peak season in mid-summer.

35 Which of the following is correct about the SWD?

① It spread from the United States to Southeast Asia.

② It is related to the fruit fly but not to the vinegar fly.

③ It deposits its eggs on the surface of fruits.

④ It has not developed resistance to insecticides.

36 What can be inferred about the SWD from the passage?

① It mostly infests recently harvested fruits.

② It feeds primarily on other fly species.

③ Its control measures have so far been ineffective.

④ Its infestation is difficult to detect in its early stages.

37-38

Until the 19th century, reports of mysterious objects passing across the skies had mainly involved comets or meteors, and these celestial phenomena had generally been interpreted as divine portents.

Then, in response to rapid technological progress, the public discourse surrounding unidentified flying objects (UFOs) shifted. In the late 19th century, when people reported unfamiliar objects in the skies, they often described exotic flying machines. The public was generally amused by these sightings and often assumed that the machines were the work of eccentric inventors.

In the early 20th century, as war loomed over Europe, discussion of UFO sightings again shifted. Fearing a German attack, many in Europe and North America blamed UFO sightings on German technology, pointing specifically to the recently developed Zeppelin, a large, gas-filled airship. These reports surged at the outset of World War I.

As time passed, new technologies continued to influence UFO reports and the public's reaction to these reports. After the Nazis' defeat in World War II, UFOs were often connected with Soviet rocket tests. Then, in the 1950s, as the Cold War deepened paranoia, the now-familiar notion that UFOs are alien technologies took hold of the public imagination.

37 What is the best title for the passage?

① UFOs No Longer Eliciting the Fear That They Once Did
② UFOs Described in Strikingly Consistent Way throughout History
③ UFO Reports and Public's Reactions Shift with Technology and the Times
④ UFO Sightings Drastically Increased with Advent of New Technologies

38 Which of the following is correct according to the passage?

① Religious interpretations of UFOs had declined by the end of the 19th century.
② Reports of flying machines initially resulted in public panic.
③ UFO sightings were generally connected to German rocket tests.
④ The idea that UFOs were alien technologies became common prior to the Cold War.

Many of the behavioral changes associated with adolescence are widely attributed to the release of reproductive hormones during puberty. However, it has been difficult for scientists to disentangle the influence of puberty from that of adolescence on young people. While the two terms overlap significantly, they are also distinct. Puberty refers specifically to the process by which individuals develop reproductive functions, a process that occurs during adolescence. Adolescence, meanwhile, is a broad term that encompasses not only puberty-related changes but also a host of physical and psychological changes marking the transition from childhood to early adulthood.

In order to isolate specifically puberty-related changes from general adolescence-related ones, researchers devised a carefully constructed experiment involving Siberian hamsters. These small rodents undergo puberty at different ages depending on when during the year they are born. Those born when daylight hours are long enter puberty at a younger age than those born when daylight hours are shorter. By controlling the amount of light that newborn hamsters received, the researchers bred two groups of hamsters: one that underwent puberty at around 30 days of age and another that did so at around 100 days of age. The researchers then observed whether behavioral changes occurred in response to the rodents approaching physical maturity or to the release of reproductive hormones during puberty.

The researchers were specifically interested in whether the former group showed the shift from play to social dominance behaviors earlier than the latter group. Researchers found that the transition happened at the same age in both groups, independently of puberty. This led to the conclusion that reproductive hormones are unlikely to be the cause of at least some of the behavioral changes associated with adolescence.

39 **Which of the following is correct according to the passage?**

① The definition of puberty encompasses that of adolescence.

② The puberty timing of Siberian hamsters can be controlled.

③ Domineering behavior indicates prepuberty in Siberian hamsters.

④ The study suggests that reproductive hormones are responsible for behavioral changes.

40   What can be inferred from the passage?

① Siberian hamsters breed at different times of the year.

② Puberty significantly precedes adolescence in most mammals.

③ Reproductive hormones tend to increase after puberty.

④ Adult Siberian hamsters generally enjoy playing with peers.

2024학년도 학사편입 A형(인문·예체능계)
▶▶ 40문항·60분

자연계(일반편입)
▶▶ 영어 25문항, 수학 20문항·100분

인문·자연계 공통 영어문제 별도 * 표시

[문항별 배점: 01-10 2점/ 11-30 2.5점/ 31-40 3점]

[01-10] Choose the option that best completes each dialogue.

01* A: We've been walking around for hours. I really need to rest.

B: Good idea. All the sightseeing we've done today has really _____ my energy.

① sapped   ② hoisted

③ plucked   ④ precluded

02* A: The reviews for that new movie *Squadron* vary widely.

B: Yeah. I was surprised by how mixed the _____ has been.

① admission   ② conception

③ endurance   ④ reception

03* A: Are communications on this mobile application secure?

B: Yes, all messages are _____, so they can't be viewed by hackers.

① circulated   ② encrypted

③ unravelled   ④ deciphered

04 A: Please _____ your bag in the overhead compartment, sir.

B: OK, I will. Just let me get something out of it first.

① stow   ② beset

③ ascend   ④ stock

05 A: This shrub is everywhere. Is it invasive?

B: No, it's actually _____ to this area.

① intolerant   ② domestic

③ hereditary   ④ indigenous

06 A: I get seasick quite easily.

B: Me, too. Even short journeys by boat make me feel very _____.

① barren   ② queasy

③ peevish   ④ drowsy

07 A: Why did Jacky look so happy before leaving work today?

B: Her manager _____ her request for an overseas transfer!

① empowered   ② allocated

③ granted   ④ committed

08 A: Did your boss change her mind about giving you a raise?

B: No. She was _____ that the company can't afford to.

① capricious   ② diffident

③ intrepid   ④ adamant

09 A: My sister always assumes the worst about people.

B: There's nothing wrong with being a little _____.

① lenient   ② reticent

③ cynical   ④ tenuous

10 A: Are you prepared for the ups and downs of starting a business?

B: Yes, I've planned for every possible _____.

① contingency   ② hyperbole

③ deference   ④ propensity

[11-20] Choose the option that best completes each sentence.

11* By making a list of tasks, employees can see which are less or more important and _____ the work accordingly.

① prioritize ② conserve

③ transform ④ formulate

12* The farmer trained his dog to round up livestock that had _____ too far from the herd.

① strayed ② wavered

③ fluttered ④ trembled

13* The company _____ environmental regulations by shipping waste out of the state.

① ensnared ② swindled

③ abducted ④ circumvented

14 The dancer _____ gracefully across the stage, her dress spinning with each movement.

① jumbled ② twirled

③ wriggled ④ fumbled

15* The professor's tendency to _____ about a variety of topics made it difficult for students to follow the logic of his lectures.

① ramble ② tamper

③ whimper ④ snivel

16 As part of its commitment to environmental sustainability, the hedge fund _____ itself of all assets related to fossil fuel production.

① deposed ② divulged

③ divested ④ desisted

17 *Don Quixote*'s humor arises from the _____ between the protagonist's fantastic expectations and mundane reality.

① tantrums   ② retributions

③ incongruities   ④ ramifications

18 The newly discovered evidence completely _____ the defendants, establishing their innocence beyond any doubt.

① retaliated   ② exonerated

③ repudiated   ④ ameliorated

19* Having mastered the violin by the age of ten, Maria was acknowledged as a musical _____.

① culprit   ② patron

③ prodigy   ④ surrogate

20 Excessive monitoring of employee performance can result in a highly _____ workplace culture, undermining employee creativity and enthusiasm.

① extenuating   ② unwitting

③ tantalizing   ④ stultifying

[21-30] Choose the option that best completes each sentence.

21 The couple went in search of a venue _____ they could hold an outdoor wedding.

① that   ② when

③ where   ④ which

22* In response to the earthquake, neighboring countries offered _____ humanitarian aid to those affected.

① provide   ② provided

③ providing   ④ to provide

23* The mayor promised _____ a solution to Greenville's housing crisis.

① to stop nothing to find at

② nothing to stop to find at

③ to stop at nothing to find

④ nothing to stop at to find

24 Two factions of city council are engaged in a bitter dispute _____ the cost of public services.

① over
② from
③ across
④ among

25 Several employees _____ with huge workloads confronted their boss about the problem.

① to struggle
② struggling
③ struggled
④ struggle

26* The woman _____ as a waitress when she was discovered by a talent agency and offered a modeling job.

① has worked
② will have worked
③ was working
④ has been working

27* The space capsules _____ astronauts descend from space to Earth are designed to withstand intense heat and pressure.

① that
② which
③ in that
④ in which

28 The teacher demanded that the student _____ in a respectful manner.

① behave
② behaves
③ will behave
④ would behave

29* _____ on the northwest corner of Central Park, Excalibur Tower gives residents unparalleled views of the city.

① Situated
② Situating
③ To be situated
④ Having situated

30 A recession is almost certain to occur, should the economic stimulus measures currently being debated by Congress _____.

① vote down
② be voted down
③ have voted down
④ have been voted down

[31-40] Read the passage, question(s), and options. Then, based on the given information, choose the option that best answers each question.

When modern dental floss was introduced in the early 19th century, many people resisted using the product. Some disliked the idea of putting their fingers in their mouths and preferred to use toothpicks. Others simply found dental floss difficult to use. In the early 1800s, the product consisted of unwieldy spools of silk thread, which people had to cut with a knife. It was not until the late 19th century, when Asahel Shurtleff invented the now-familiar dispenser with a U-shaped prong for cutting the thread, that dental floss became easier to use and thus more widely embraced by consumers.

31* What is the passage mainly about?

① Why flossing did not become immediately popular
② How inventors improved on the original version of dental floss
③ Why early versions of dental floss were relatively ineffective
④ How interest in using dental floss increased and decreased over time

Plants have evolved to disperse seeds in numerous ways. Some plants do so through structures, typically seedpods, that have a natural line of weakness. When this weak point breaks open, pressure within the seedpod causes the seeds to be forcefully ejected. This process is known as explosive dehiscence. Often, the ejection of seeds is triggered by inadvertent contact between animals and the seedpod. However, sometimes explosive dehiscence results from natural development of pressure within the plant, causing the plant to break open spontaneously.

32* What is the main purpose of the passage?

① To outline different methods of seed dispersal

② To explain the process of explosive dehiscence

③ To analyze the role of animals in seed dispersal

④ To contrast explosive dehiscence with other seed dispersal methods

---

When England's Bodiam Castle was constructed in 1385, it was surrounded by an extensive system of waterworks. With the exception of the most prominent of these features — the castle's wide quadrangular moat — these have all been lost to time. Bodiam's moat currently surrounds its walls on all sides. It is spanned only by modern wooden bridges, which would have been drawbridges at the time of the castle's construction. Moats are normally defensive structures, but Bodiam's was designed as more of a landscape feature, to make the castle appear grander against its surroundings.

---

33 Which of the following is correct about Bodiam Castle?

① It is currently surrounded by many waterworks.

② Its moat no longer completely encircles its walls.

③ The original bridges across its moat have disappeared.

④ The primary purpose of its moat was originally to defend castle residents.

The theory of the uncanny valley was introduced by roboticist Masahiro Mori to explain humans' apparent aversion to certain humanoid robots. According to Mori, as robots become more human-like in appearance, they come to be viewed more favorably by humans. However, there comes a point at which robots become nearly but not fully human-like in nature. At this point, where the uncanny valley begins, the robots elicit an unsettling feeling from humans. When robots become indistinguishable from humans, they are once again viewed in a positive light.

34* What is the main topic of the passage?

① The role of robots' appearance in shaping human-robot interactions

② A possible link between robots' appearance and humans' response to those robots

③ An attempt to update Masahiro Mori's theory of the uncanny valley

④ The effect of human discomfort with human-like robots on robot development

35-36

In 2018, a group of researchers discovered a 1,230-year-old Heldreich's pine in Italy's Pollino National Park, where the species is relatively common. The pine tree, subsequently dubbed *Italus*, is more than a century older than the tree previously thought to be the oldest in Europe — a 1,075-year-old pine in Greece.

When the researchers found *Italus* sticking out from a cliff face, a large portion of the trunk had rotted away, and the innermost rings were mostly gone. The tree's poor condition made it difficult for the researchers to determine its age, as the inner rings of trees have important information about their age. At least 20 centimeters of the tree's innermost rings were gone, potentially representing decades worth of information.

Ultimately, the researchers conducted radiocarbon dating on exposed parts of the tree's roots. This dating method enabled the researchers to figure out when the tree germinated. Given that roots produce rings at a different rate than the trunk, the researchers also cross-dated the ring patterns of the remaining trunk with those of the roots. By doing so, they were able to determine that the tree was 1,230 years old.

35 Which of the following is correct about *Italus*?

① It is a species of pine tree that is rare in Pollino National Park.

② It is a few years older than the tree previously thought to be Europe's oldest.

③ Its surviving trunk rings measured only 20 cm in diameter.

④ Its roots and trunk exhibited different rates of ring growth.

36 Why did the researchers have difficulties determining *Italus*'s age?

① They found it hard to get access to its location.

② The radiocarbon dating analysis yielded inconclusive results.

③ They could not obtain any samples from its roots.

④ A significant part of its trunk was badly decomposed.

37-38

Polish-French physicist Madame Marie Curie, who discovered the radioisotopes polonium and radium, made notable contributions to the Allied effort during World War I. When the conflict broke out, she discontinued her research and decided to help her country win the fight by saving lives. X-rays, discovered in 1895 by Wilhelm Roentgen, Curie's fellow Nobel laureate, had quickly led to the development of X-ray machines. These devices were desperately needed to treat wounded soldiers on the battlefields, but most X-ray machines were available only at large hospitals.

Curie saw this problem and took it upon herself to find a solution, inventing a radiological car equipped with an X-ray machine. The car also contained a photographic darkroom where X-ray images could be developed as well as an electric generator that enabled the car's engine to power the X-ray machine. When the French military delayed giving her the funding needed to produce the car, Curie turned to the Union of Women of France, from which she successfully obtained the money. Her invention of the radiological car greatly helped treat wounded soldiers during the First Battle of the Marne, the decisive battle that stopped the Germans from invading Paris in 1914.

37* **Which of the following is correct about the radiological car?**

① It contained both an X-ray machine and a darkroom.

② It could not power the X-ray machine on its own.

③ It was produced in large numbers with French military funding.

④ It was completed after the end of the First Battle of the Marne.

38* **What prompted Marie Curie to invent the radiological car?**

① She was commissioned by a women's organization to create a mobile X-ray machine.

② She received military support to study military applications for X-rays.

③ She recognized the lack of direct access to X-ray machines on the battlefield.

④ She was concerned by the lack of hospital space for wounded soldiers.

In 1986, Mexico hosted what was to become one of the most memorable soccer World Cups. Most recall the tournament for the performance of the Argentinean player Diego Maradona — in particular, two goals that he scored against England. The first of these goals resulted from flagrant cheating, with Maradona deflecting the ball into the net with his hand. The second goal involved a remarkable display of skill, with Maradona weaving his way through several English players. While the majority of pundits backed Brazil to win the tournament, Maradona's performance carried his team all the way to the final, where they defeated West Germany 3-2 to take home the trophy.

Mexico's success as host was impressive, given that they were stand-ins for Colombia, who backed out for economic reasons three years before the tournament began. Soccer body FIFA decided on Mexico as host despite rival stand-in bids from the US, Canada, and Brazil. This decision came much to the chagrin of the US, which claimed FIFA's choice smacked of corruption. Others also questioned Mexico's viability, even though the country had successfully hosted a World Cup before. There were also calls to relocate when, eight months before the tournament began, Mexico was hit with a devastating earthquake. However, FIFA decided against a second relocation.

39 According to the passage, who were the favorites to win the 1986 World Cup?
① Brazil
② Mexico
③ England
④ West Germany

40 Which of the following is correct about the 1986 World Cup?
① Colombia was forced to step down as host by FIFA.
② The US criticized the choice of Mexico as the new host nation.
③ It was Mexico's debut as a World Cup host nation.
④ It was moved to a new venue due to an earthquake.

KOREAN NATIONAL POLICE UNIVERSITY

경찰대학　　　2024학년도 일반대학생 전형
▶▶ 40문항·60분

[01-05] 밑줄 친 단어의 뜻과 가장 가까운 것을 고르시오.

01 The cruel dictator <u>abased</u> his people, forcing them to live in poverty and fear.

① degraded ② prosecuted ③ relieved
④ rejuvenated ⑤ sabotaged

02 The writer <u>embellished</u> the story with details that were not true, such as the hero's bravery and the villain's evilness.

① refuted ② hoaxed ③ exaggerated
④ added ⑤ invented

03 They moved with a minimum of effort and noise, and knew how to sit, walk and run in the most <u>agile</u> and efficient manner.

① nimble ② invasive ③ fashionable
④ tricky ⑤ dubious

04 One must not <u>soak</u> bran nor grind it, but may put it in a sieve or in a basket.

① flavor ② manipulate ③ bake
④ drench ⑤ snitch

05 Now the fertility of first crosses between species, and of the hybrids produced from them, is largely governed by their systematic <u>affinity</u>.

① management   ② kinship   ③ coordination
④ communication   ⑤ mutation

06 다음 대화의 빈칸에 들어갈 말로 가장 적절한 것은?

A: Did you hear about the latest climate change report? It's really alarming.
B: Yeah, I did. It says that we have less than 10 years to take action to prevent the worst effects of climate change.
A: That's not a lot of time. I'm starting to feel really worried about the future.
B: I know. It's hard to know what to do.
A: I think we all need to do our part to reduce our carbon footprint. We can start by making small changes, like driving less, eating less meat, and recycling more.
B: Yeah, that's a good idea. We can also support organizations that are working to fight climate change.
A: I'm going to volunteer for a local environmental organization. I think it is important to _____.
B: That's great. I'm going to make some changes to my lifestyle. I will bike to work more often and eat less meat.
A: That's awesome! It's important to do what we can, even if it's just small changes.

① support those who are fighting climate change
② collect scientific evidence for climate change
③ reduce our carbon footprint
④ get involved and make a difference
⑤ make people aware of climate change

Adoption in the United States has become increasingly difficult, especially for infants. International adoptions have ⒜ plummeted/augmented in recent years due to stricter policies in other countries and a Hague Convention treaty designed to encourage domestic adoptions. Domestically, ⒝ fewer/more young mothers are voluntarily giving up their babies, and private adoption has become a costly waiting game. Fostering to adopt is now a common option, but it can also be a long process due to legal requirements to give birth parents a chance before terminating their rights. Intervention has emerged as a new way for prospective adopters to ⓒ speed up/slow down the process and have more of a say in whether the birth family should be reunited.

07

	⒜	⒝	ⓒ

① plummeted — fewer — speed up

② plummeted — more — speed up

③ augmented — fewer — slow down

④ augmented — more — slow down

⑤ augmented — fewer — speed up

The ⒜ amazing/worrisome thing about spiders is that they bite. A few, such as Black Widows and Brown Recluses, are actually dangerous. In backyards, Black Widows might be found beneath pieces of wood or trash lying on the ground; Brown Recluses are more often found inside homes, especially on floors behind furniture. In other words, unless your backyard is particularly ⒝ clean/trashy, you probably don't have to worry too much about any really dangerous spiders. Moreover, both of these ⓒ venomous/innocuous species have striking field marks making them easy to identify. If you acquire a spider field guide, the first thing you need to do is to look up these two species, notice the widow's "red hour-glass," and the recluse's "violin," and henceforward keep your distance from spiders with those marks.

08

	⒜	⒝	ⓒ

① amazing — clean — innocuous

② amazing — trashy — venomous

③ amazing — clean — venomous

④ worrisome — trashy — venomous

⑤ worrisome — trashy — innocuous

[09-10] 밑줄 친 부분 중 어법상 옳지 않은 것을 고르시오.

09 DNA is a natural part of our diet ①being present in foods which either retain or are derived from whole cells (fruits, vegetables, meat, etc.). ②This being the case it would be expected that we would also digest the DNA from GE foods without any health problems. It would therefore appear that the mere presence of genetic material in GE food only poses a danger in certain special cases as, for example, ③where antibiotic resistance genes persist in a product. However, the main hazards that result from the use of genetic engineering in food production ④stemming from the fact that genetic engineering brings about combinations of genes that would never occur naturally and, in the case of plants and animals, genetic engineering is an imprecise technology ⑤resulting in the random incorporation of the new genes into the host DNA.

10 Before some of the greatest explorers in history were born, Vikings ①had already navigated their way around the world. But with no compasses, satellites or radios, how did these tribes of Scandinavians manage ②to map the globe so impressively? The answer is simpler than you might expect — experience. Rather than ③relying on devices, Viking travellers trusted nature to guide them. They would study the positions of the stars and Sun, and even the colour of the sea and movement of the waves would give them an indication of how close they were to land. Once a journey was complete, sailors would recount their voyage to others who ④wished to make the same journey. This ancient wisdom would be passed through generations. The only tools Viking sailors needed ⑤relating to the Sun. For example, a Sun-shadow board would be used at noon to check whether the ship was on course.

11 다음 중 어법상 옳지 <u>않은</u> 것은?

① Policy experts have long argued that the coordination costs associated with inter-organizational arrangements often exceed the benefits.

② Educational reforms in history teaching confirm the existence of the vital relation between current social interests and the learning process.

③ At that period, it prevailed in all the schools a most extraordinary reverence for the writings of Aristotle, the preceptor of Alexander the Great.

④ With the interest of people being focused on the event, it seems timely to post my findings about it.

⑤ If we could obtain information regarding all the earth's surface, we should discover that the earth is almost always undergoing shocks.

12 다음 중 어법상 옳은 것은?

① Records of cranes keeping in captivity by Chinese nobility date back more than two thousand years.

② The food industry spends billions of dollars each year to develop products, packaging, advertising and marketing techniques that entice us to buy more food.

③ When there comes to the effects of global warming on weather trends, there is more agreement among the growing number of meteorologists.

④ Being asked what he was master, he replied that he was simply a "philosopher," that is, a "lover of wisdom."

⑤ No matter what well ventilated the nursery may be, all children more than six weeks old need unmodified outside air.

[13-14] 빈칸 Ⓐ, Ⓑ, Ⓒ에 들어갈 낱말로 가장 적절한 것을 고르시오.

Humanity is on course to Ⓐ_____ multiple global "tipping points" that could lead to irreversible instability or the complete collapse of ecological and institutional systems, a United Nations report warned Wednesday. The third annual Interconnected Disaster Risks report from the U.N. University's Institute for Environment and Human Security in Bonn, Germany, found that drastic changes will occur if urgent actions are not taken around six problems when sociological systems are no longer able to Ⓑ_____ risks. The tipping points include several issues that California is confronting head-on — groundwater depletion, rising insurance costs, extreme heat and species extinction. The other threats are melting glaciers and space debris. According to U.N. officials, "when one system tips, other systems may also be pushed over the Ⓒ_____."

13

       Ⓐ   Ⓑ   Ⓒ

① traverse — outreach — edge

② traverse — outreach — center

③ transgress — buffer — edge

④ transgress — outreach — center

⑤ transmit — buffer — edge

Now we can begin to understand that we live in proportion as we breathe. The activity of the child is in close relation to the strength of its lungs, and so, too, is the calmness, dignity and power of a man in proportion to the depth and tranquility of his Ⓐ_____. If the lungs are strong and active, there is courage and boldness. If Ⓑ_____, there is cowardice and debility. To be out of spirits is to be out of breath. To be animated and joyous is to be full of breath. Breathing is an actual vivifying act, and the need of breath as felt is a real life-hunger and a proof that without the continual charging of the blood-column with the proper force, all the other vital organs would soon Ⓒ_____ and cease action altogether.

14

           Ⓐ   Ⓑ   Ⓒ

① perspiration — feeble — endure

② perspiration — energetic — endure

③ respiration — feeble — stagnate

④ respiration — energetic — stagnate

⑤ inspiration — feeble — endure

[15-16] 글의 흐름으로 보아 주어진 문장이 들어가기에 가장 적절한 곳을 고르시오.

15

> So, how many muscles make up this vast system of tissue, strength and mobility?

The human body is a wondrous thing, especially when you consider how intricate and efficient each bodily system is. (①) For instance, an adult's blood vessels could encircle the earth 2.5 times if connected end to end; the human nose is capable of recognizing more than a trillion different scents; and a human heart beats more than 3 billion times in an average lifespan. (②) But among the most impressive systems of the body are the musculoskeletal system and all its muscles, ligaments, bones, tendons and connective tissue. (③) This system allows us to move about freely starting with climbing out of bed each morning and then getting to school, work or play, followed by all the countless activities and movements that follow. (④) It turns out the answer is not as straightforward as one might think, says James Smoliga, DVM, Ph. D. (⑤) "The numbers vary," he explains, with some experts saying the body has close to 600 muscles and others saying it may be as many as 840. He says this discrepancy exists because "anatomists have different ways of deciding whether a given muscle is one muscle with multiple parts or if it should be considered multiple distinct muscles."

16

Kings and queens competed to build the tallest, most magnificent monuments, but this came at a cost — huge amounts of stone were needed to build them, not to mention the costs of labour.

In the early days of Ancient Egypt, pharaohs and other wealthy members of society were buried in mastabas. These were flat-roofed, rectangular structures with sloping sides, which helped to protect the grave from scavenging animals and thieves. (①) But during the Third Dynasty, an architect named Imhotep came up with the idea of stacking multiple mastabas on top of each other, creating a much taller structure composed of a number of 'steps'. (②) This would act as a staircase, allowing the deceased to ascend to the heavens. (③) The first was called the Pyramid of Djoser, and it was built around 2680 BCE. (④) Over the next few hundred years, pyramids became the norm for pharaonic burials, and eventually the sides became smooth rather than stepped. (⑤) Pyramids were also easy targets for gravediggers. By the time of the Seventh Dynasty, it was much more common for pharaohs to be buried in tombs carved deep into the rock.

[17-18] 주어진 글 다음에 이어질 글의 순서로 가장 적절한 것을 고르시오.

17

Hospitals and health systems around the country have been rolling out flavors of "acute hospital care at home" programs as part of a national movement to not only boost the patient experience but to reduce hospital overcrowding and bed shortages, problems that are expected to intensify as more and more baby boomers advance into their senior years.

Ⓐ If the answer is yes, and the patient is on board, they are "transferred" home, where they're met by a professional who sets up everything they need to be monitored on their own turf.

Ⓑ This may include a 4G-enabled tablet for video visits with a virtual care team accessible 24/7 at the push of a button; a phone that immediately connects to that team; a wearable device that continually tracks their vital signs; a blood pressure cuff; a pulse oximeter; an emergency alert necklace; and so on.

C Exactly how a program works can vary from hospital to hospital and state to state, based on regulatory issues. But generally, a patient lands in the ER or other inpatient unit and is screened to see if they'd be a good fit.

① A — C — B   ② B — A — C   ③ B — C — A
④ C — A — B   ⑤ C — B — A

18

According to Family Voices, an advocacy group, more than 12 million children in the United States have some medical problem, from asthma to cerebral palsy.

A But they receive little recognition and few supports. While the president has tipped his rhetorical hat to family caregivers, proposed legislation to help ease some of the burden still languishes in Congress, and no one expects any relief soon.

B In many instances, a family member is the primary caregiver. This is a national issue. More than 25 million Americans are family caregivers taking care of spouses and parents as well as children.

C The U.S. Department of Health and Human Services counts about 4 million children with special needs, including 2 million with mental retardation and developmental disabilities. Who takes care of all these children?

① A — C — B   ② B — A — C   ③ B — C — A
④ C — A — B   ⑤ C — B — A

[19-20] 다음 글에서 전체 흐름과 관계없는 문장을 고르시오.

19

The Black Death spread throughout Europe in the 14th century, killing an estimated 50 million people. It changed society for ever. ①One of these changes, it's been argued, was the breakdown of the feudal system. ②As the number of peasants dwindled, there were fewer people to work the land — the main source of wealth and power for the lords, and the foundation of the feudal system. ③Nevertheless the feudal system serves as an analogy for the imbalanced structure of Medieval society. ④Those who survived the deadly disease seized their chance to get richer — from lands left by the dead and by demanding higher wages in return for labour. ⑤More money meant the lower classes could afford to dress like their social superiors and a law was passed in 1363 in a bid to stop this trend. The law put restrictions on the clothes and diets of people at every level of society, but it was impossible to enforce and it's been suggested that this led to the emergence of a middle class.

20

The distinction between natural science and history begins at the point where we seek to convert facts into knowledge. ①Here we observe that the one seeks to formulate laws, the other to portray events. In the one case thought proceeds from the description of particulars to the general relations. ②In the other case it clings to a genial depiction of the individual object or event. For the natural scientist the object of investigation which cannot be repeated never has, as such, value. ③It serves his purpose only so far as it may be regarded as a type or as a special instance of a class from which the type may be deduced. The natural scientist considers the single case only so far as he can see in it the features which serve to throw light upon a general law. ④On the other hand, a historian should find the single exact cause which brought about a historical event. For the historian the problem is to revive and call up into the present, in all its particularity, an event in the past. ⑤His aim is to do for an actual event precisely what the artist seeks to do for the object of his imagination. It is just here that we discern the kinship between history and art, between the historian and the writer of literature. It is for this reason that natural science emphasized the abstract; the historian, on the other hand, is interested mainly in the concrete.

[21-26] 다음 글의 빈칸에 들어갈 말로 가장 적절한 것을 고르시오.

Though Glinda the Good Witch from *The Wizard of Oz* and the Sanderson sisters in *Hocus Pocus* had colorful wardrobes, the base of the standard witch costume is typically a black dress, cloak or robe. "Historically, healing women and others who would later be called witches would wear what everyone else in their village community did — homemade clothes that were made to be functional," says Katherine Walker, an assistant professor of English at the University of Nevada, Las Vegas. "In the medieval period and beyond, these clothes would feature cloaks or hoods. So it's very likely that, in terms of dress, witches at first were not _____." It didn't take long, however, for these garments to be affiliated with witches. "The connection with a black dress in particular is probably the result of the association of the color black with the devil and 'black magic' throughout the Renaissance," Walker explains.

21 ① visually distinct from their neighbors
　　② susceptible to their neighbors' criticism
　　③ meant to be harmful to their neighbors
　　④ considered as frugal as their neighbors
　　⑤ identical with their neighbors in costumes

Only in the twentieth century did non-European cultures adopt a truly global vision. This was one of the crucial factors that led to the collapse of European hegemony. Thus in the Algerian War of Independence (1954-62), Algerian guerrillas defeated a French army with an overwhelming numerical, technological and economic advantage. The Algerians prevailed because they were supported by a global anti-colonial network, and because they worked out how to harness the world's media to their cause — as well as public opinion in France itself. The defeat that little North Vietnam inflicted on the American colossus was based on a similar strategy. These guerilla forces showed that even superpowers could be defeated if _____.

22 ① their strategy was exposed to the enemy
　　② no lessons were learned from previous invasions
　　③ they didn't have a well-trained, elite unit
　　④ they engaged the adversary in fierce combat
　　⑤ a local struggle became a global cause

When you're inside the walls of high tech, whether for an interview or for a temporary work assignment, there's one thing you should keep in mind. You'll be judged largely on your attitude. High-tech people like others who are enthusiastic and show it. If that sounds corny, sorry, but it's true. A positive attitude, a smile, a sense of humor — these can do wonders for you when you come in. When you're interviewing for a position, you'll not only see the hiring manager, you'll be interviewed by three to six others, usually people who would be your future associates if you get the job. Each of these people is going to judge you mainly by something called "fit." Yes, you have to be smart, demonstrate that you understand the job and can perform it. But you can do all that and still strike out on the question of "fit." Your attitude and demeanor during the interviews will, it's hoped, settle the question of _____.

23 ① how well you'll perform in your future job
② how politely you'll respond to your supervisors
③ how humorous you are in the workplace
④ how enthusiastic you are towards demanding tasks
⑤ how well you'll fit into the group

We have a tendency to imagine that life can not exist under conditions other than terrestrial, and that the other worlds can only be inhabited on the condition of being similar to our own. But terrestrial nature itself demonstrates to us the error of this way of thinking. We die in the water: fishes die out of the water. Again, short-sighted naturalists affirm categorically that life is impossible at the bottom of the sea: first, because it is in complete darkness; second, because the terrible pressure would burst any organism; third, because all motion would be impossible there, and so on. There is no light in these depths: they make it with their own phosphorescence. Other inquirers visit subterranean caverns, and discover animals and plants whose organs have been transformed by _____.

24 ① enormous pressure of water
② adaptation to their gloomy environment
③ interbreeding tendencies across different species
④ natural inclination of marine lives
⑤ sudden environmental changes

What Ptolemy saw in the movements of the stars led him to the conclusion that they were bright points attached to the inside of a tremendous globe. The movements of this globe were only compatible with the supposition that the earth occupied its center. The obvious fact that the sun, the moon, and the stars rose day by day, moved across the sky in a glorious never-ending procession, and duly set when their appointed courses had been run, demanded some explanation. The circumstance that the fixed stars preserved their mutual distances from year to year, and from age to age, appeared to Ptolemy to prove that the sphere which contained those stars, and on whose surface they were believed by him to be fixed, revolved completely around the earth once every day. He would thus account for all the phenomena of rising and setting consistently with the supposition that _____.

25 ① the constellation of stars affects our globe
② our globe was stationary
③ the sun is the center of the universe
④ our globe revolves around the sun
⑤ our globe was dynamic

Perhaps the most serious obstacle impeding the evolution of a land ethic is the fact that our educational and economic system is headed away from, rather than toward, an intense consciousness of land. People today are separated from the land by many middlemen, and by innumerable physical gadgets. They have no vital relation to it; to them it is the space between cities on which crops grow. Turn them loose for a day on the land, and if the spot does not happen to be a golf links or a 'scenic' area, they are bored stiff. If crops could be raised by hydroponics (water culture) instead of farming, it would suit them very well. Synthetic substitutes for wood, leather, wool, and other natural land products suit them better than the originals. In short, land is _____.

26 ① the model they aspire to copy
② something they have outgrown
③ the spot for their organic products
④ something profitable to them in any case
⑤ what they cultivate with the assistance of mediators

27 다음 글의 주제로 가장 적절한 것은?

It is difficult to find an issue that more exemplifies the dysfunction of American government today than immigration. In the past year, more than a million people have entered the United States through the southern border, overflowing shelters and straining public services. Most of the newcomers claim asylum, a status that allows them to be in the country legally but leaves them in limbo. They often must wait years for their cases to be heard, and it can be a lengthy process to obtain legal permission to work. This nation has long drawn strength from immigration, and providing asylum is an important expression of America's national values. But Congress has failed to provide the necessary resources to welcome those who are eligible and to turn away those who are not. Instead, overwhelmed immigration officials allow nearly everyone to stay temporarily, imposing enormous short-term costs on states and cities that the federal government hasn't done enough to mitigate.

① how hard new immigrants obtain a new citizenship

② why so many immigrants cross the southern border

③ who should be blamed for the recent immigration problems

④ what makes asylum processes so difficult and lengthy

⑤ why US government becomes unwelcome to immigrants

28 다음 글의 내용과 일치하는 것은?

Ozone molecules are constantly being destroyed by natural compounds containing nitrogen, hydrogen, and chlorine. The nitrogen comes from soils and the ocean, the hydrogen comes mostly from atmospheric water vapor, and the chlorine comes from the oceans. Ozone is also continuously being destroyed when it absorbs ultraviolet light. This process produces atomic oxygen (O) that reacts with molecular oxygen (O_2) to form another ozone molecule (O_3). With creative and destructive forces balanced, the average amount of ozone in the stratosphere since Earth's current atmosphere developed is believed to have remained fairly constant. The scientific and public policy issue now surrounding stratospheric ozone arises as a result of concern that ozone destruction resulting from releases of chlorofluorocarbons and halons may be upsetting the natural balance.

① The nitrogen and the hydrogen come from the same sources.
② Ultraviolet light has nothing to do with the amount of ozone.
③ Ozone is produced by the reactions of atomic oxygen.
④ Creative forces are greater than destructive ones, making the amount of ozone constant.
⑤ The breakdown of the natural balance of ozone is a great concern.

29 다음 글의 제목으로 가장 적절한 것은?

Poor listeners are inexperienced in hearing difficult, expository material. Good listeners apparently develop an appetite for hearing a variety of presentations difficult enough to challenge their mental capacities. Perhaps the one word that best describes the bad listener is "inexperienced." Although he spends 40 percent of his communication day listening to something, he is inexperienced in hearing anything tough, technical, or expository. He has for years painstakingly sought light, recreational material. The problem he creates is deeply significant, because such a person is a poor producer in factory, office, or classroom. Inexperience is not easily or quickly overcome. However, knowledge of our own weakness may lead us to repair it. We need never become too old to meet new challenges.

① How to Use Light Listening Material

② What Inexperienced Listeners Should Do

③ Pleasure of Being a Good Listener

④ Don't Reveal the Weak Points of Your Listening

⑤ Time Needed to Be a Good Listener

30 다음 글의 요지로 가장 적절한 것은?

Most rockets are made up of several stages, which are detached, as the craft travels into space. The largest, most expensive part of the rocket is the first stage, that might account for some 80% of the launch price. So far, the expensive rocket stages have been dumped into the ocean after one mission, making aerospace activities so expensive that space tourism has been impossible. But now, engineers have allowed the rockets to steer safely down the atmosphere and land on a platform to be reused. One of them is the New Shepard rocket that will fly into space and detach a manned capsule. The six paying tourists will experience four minutes in a state of weightlessness and see Earth's bend, before the capsule will once again head towards Earth carried by parachutes. The rocket's first stage will slow down shortly before contact with Earth, landing softly to be readied for a new launch.

① Recycling makes space tourism more affordable.

② Future space travel has a long way to go.

③ Reused rockets are good for the environment.

④ The pricey rocket stages were thrown into the sea.

⑤ Engineers figured out how to reduce rocket velocity before landing.

31 다음 글의 내용과 일치하지 <u>않는</u> 것은?

Most of us rely on expiration dates to know whether our groceries are still fresh. But as British-based industrial designer Solveiga Pakštaite learned when she interviewed blind people for a project on public transportation, if you can't see, you can't read those dates. The revelation inspired the 23-year-old to design the Bump Mark, a series of raised bumps coated with a layer of gelatin on food packaging. As the gelatin protein decays, the bumps become tangible. That's when you know the food is past its prime. This works because gelatin — made from animal hooves — rots at roughly the same rate as a steak, fish fillet, or bag of salad. The potential for this technology is even greater than what you might think. Printed dates are just guidelines, not true indicators of food spoilage, so we waste a lot of perfectly good food. (In the U.K., grocery stores and consumers throw away a total of 12 million tons of food every year.) Because the Bump Mark measures real rates of decay, the invention could help fix that. Pakštaite is now doing market research, studying manufacturing, and running lab tests to increase the accuracy of the gelatin-to-food decay rate. From a fresh idea, fresh food.

① For a project on public transit, Pakštaite spoke with blind persons.
② Food packaging bearing the Bump Mark features a number of raised bumps covered in gelatin.
③ The bumps become noticeable when the food has lost its freshness.
④ The rate of deterioration of gelatin is faster than that of a steak.
⑤ Printed dates are only recommendations rather than accurate indicators of food degradation.

[32-33] 다음 글을 읽고 물음에 답하시오.

My colleague Jonathan Rothwell and I reported hundreds of places that exceed commonly held expectations in Brookings's recently released Black Progress Index, an interactive tool and report developed in partnership with the NAACP that provides a means to understand the health and well-being of Black people and the conditions that shape their lives. Instead of comparing Black people to white people, we examine life expectancy differences among the Black population in different places. This method reveals the locales where Black people are thriving.

Researchers often Ⓐ_____ compare rates of home ownership, educational attainment, income and mortality without attending to past and present discrimination that intended to create disparities. Consequently, broad national averages void of context policy and local contexts camouflage the very real progress that's occurring across the country.

Still, in places like Jefferson County, Ohio, the average Black person lives 33 fewer years than Manassas Park, Va. and Weld County, Colo. That gap is roughly equivalent to 100 years of progress in living standards, medical science, and public health.

Black people are not a(n) Ⓑ_____. They have widely different outcomes in very different places. Local contexts matter as Black people do. Lower life expectancy in counties and metro areas across the country suggests that people are losing battles against racism. But geographic areas where Black people are thriving offer more than hope: People's civic actions are delivering positive change.

32 윗글의 요지로 가장 적절한 것은?

① Black people's well-being needs to be scientifically studied.

② Black people's well-being is clearly represented in figures of national averages.

③ Black people's well-being depends on their local contexts.

④ Black people's well-being lags far behind that of white people.

⑤ Black people's well-being is irrelevant to their civic actions.

33 빈칸 Ⓐ, Ⓑ에 들어갈 말로 짝지은 것 중 가장 적절한 것은?

Ⓐ   Ⓑ

① sharply — monolith

② sharply — assortment

③ sharply — colossus

④ sloppily — monolith

⑤ sloppily — assortment

[34-35] 다음 글을 읽고 물음에 답하시오.

Although most people in the United States no longer live on farms, the ideal of home ownership is just as strong in the twentieth century as it was in the nineteenth. When U.S. soldiers came home after World War II, Ⓐ_____, they dreamed of buying houses and starting families. So there was a tremendous boom in home building. The new houses, typically in the suburbs, were often small and nearly identical, but they satisfied a deep need. Many saw the single-family house as the basis of their way of life.

For the new suburbanites of the 1950s and 1960s, Ⓑ_____, life inside their small houses was very different from life on a farm. First, the family spent much less time together in the house. The father frequently drove, or *commuted*, as much as an hour to work each morning. The children went to school all day and played after school with neighborhood children. The suburb itself was sometimes called a *bedroom community* because people used their houses basically for sleeping. Second, the suburb frequently was not a stable community: families moved frequently as the fathers sought *upward mobility* — better-paying jobs and bigger houses. Although the idea of home was still as precious as always, it had taken on a different meaning.

In the seventies and eighties, as more women entered the labor force, the family spent even less time together. But the picture is changing: people can now *telecommute*, or work at home, while being linked to the office by means of their computer. More and more people can now stay at home. So the old expression could change from "Home, sweet home" to "Home, sweet office," but the emphasis on the cherished home will most likely stay the same.

34 윗글의 제목으로 가장 적절한 것은?

① Life on a Farm and in the Suburbs

② The Evolving Notion of Home

③ Building Homes in America

④ Theoretical Analysis of Demography

⑤ Women Employment and Social Mobility

35 빈칸 Ⓐ, Ⓑ에 들어갈 말로 가장 적절한 것은?

           Ⓐ   Ⓑ

① in addition — however

② in addition — similarly

③ for example — however

④ on the contrary — however

⑤ on the contrary — similarly

There have been sightings of strange things in the sky since ancient times, but it was only in the middle of the 20th century they acquired the name 'unidentified flying object', or UFO. During the 1940s and 1950s, there was a huge surge in sightings around the world, often described as disc-shaped craft or 'flying saucers'. The timing of this first great UFO wave was significant, coming at a period of widespread public paranoia caused by the nuclear arms race. The most common theory in the early days was that UFOs were advanced military aircraft that had been developed in total secrecy.

Within a few years public perceptions changed, thanks in part to Hollywood. Suddenly UFOs were no longer assumed to originate on Earth, but from another planet. Since then, the situation has been complicated by other alleged evidence for extraterrestrial visitation, from rumours that governments are concealing information about their dealings with UFO occupants to apparent memories of alien abduction recalled under hypnosis. Although these cases have little or no direct connection to strange objects seen in the sky, the term UFO still tends to be applied to them. Last year, for example, a UK newspaper carried the headline 'UFO hunter spots alien lizard on Mars', even though no flying object was involved.

The fact is that the terminology has become hopelessly confused. To some people, particularly in official circles, 'unidentified flying object' means just that: an airborne object that hasn't been identified. To many ordinary people, however, UFO means 'alien spacecraft'. For this reason, the US military has started using the term UAP, for unidentified aerial phenomena, to avoid appearing to talk about extraterrestrials every time they say they've seen something they can't explain. And UAP has another advantage, because UFOs may not always be literal 'flying objects'. As you'll see, some may be mirages, unusual weather effects or even astronomical bodies. Therefore 'aerial phenomena' is a much more appropriate term in these cases.

UFO and UAP do have one letter in common, and that's U, for unidentified. But it's important not to read too much into this. It doesn't automatically mean that what's been spotted came from another planet, or defies the known laws of physics. In the case of a photograph or video, for example, the resolution simply may not be good enough to work out what it shows. With a fleeting eyewitness report, even by a trained observer like a pilot or police officer, if they had no firm idea of the size or distance of the object, it might have been anything from a person's drone to an alien starship. And electronic systems such as radar are designed to pick up particular types of known objects, so anything falling outside the expected parameters is likely to be classed as 'unidentified'.

36   윗글의 제목으로 가장 적절한 것은?

① The Shifting Language of Skybound Mysteries: UFO to UAP

② The Shift in Public Opinion Regarding UFO

③ A Scientific Approach to the Issue of Alien Life

④ UAP: A New Hypothesis toward Its Identity

⑤ Unraveling the Mystery of UAP: Mere Optical Illusions

37   윗글의 내용과 일치하는 것은?

① People haven't reported seeing unusual objects in the sky until modern times.

② Advances in technology allow aviation experts to accurately identify fast flying objects.

③ The term UAP was first used by a group of civilians interested in UFO.

④ UAP refers only to mysterious flying objects from other planets.

⑤ Hollywood played a role in changing public attitudes towards UFO.

Having distinguished two different arguments against commodification, I now turn to one hotly contested case, that of commercial surrogacy. Contracts for "surrogate motherhood," as the practice is commonly known, typically involve a couple unable to conceive or bear a child, and a woman who agrees, in exchange for a fee, to be inseminated with the sperm of the father, to carry the child to term, and to give it up at birth.

A I would like to consider both of those analogies. Each can help clarify the moral status of commercial surrogacy. As is often the case with reasoning by analogy, however, we may find that the intuitions that constitute our moral starting point do not emerge unscathed. Reflecting on the rights and wrongs of surrogacy may lead us to revise our initial views about the moral status of baby-selling and of sperm-selling.

B Some argue that commercial surrogacy represents an objectionable kind of commodification. How can such claims be assessed? Many arguments about commodification proceed by way of analogy. Those who oppose contracts for surrogate motherhood argue that they are morally tantamount to baby-selling. With commercial surrogacy as with baby-selling, a woman is paid a fee (typically $10,000 in the surrogacy market), in exchange for relinquishing a child.

C Defenders of commercial surrogacy must either resist the analogy or defend both practices. Those who dispute the analogy argue that commercial surrogacy is more like selling sperm than selling a baby; when a woman agrees to undergo a pregnancy for pay, she does not sell a preexisting child but simply allows another couple to make use of her reproductive capacity. And if it is morally permissible for men to sell their reproductive capacity, this argument goes, why is it not morally permissible for women to sell theirs?

38 주어진 글 다음에 이어질 글의 순서로 가장 적절한 것은?

① A — C — B
② B — A — C
③ B — C — A
④ C — A — B
⑤ C — B — A

39 윗글의 제목으로 가장 적절한 것은?

① How Has Surrogacy Been Developed?

② The Ugly Facets of Surrogacy

③ Two Views on Commercial Surrogacy

④ Why Do We Stop Commodification of Motherhood?

⑤ When Do We Permit Commercial Surrogacy?

40 윗글의 내용과 일치하는 것은?

① For those who oppose surrogate motherhood, it is like sperm-selling.

② Supporters of surrogate motherhood argue that it is equivalent to baby-selling.

③ It is generally agreed that commercial surrogacy is more like selling sperm than selling a baby.

④ Analogy is used only for those who defend surrogate motherhood.

⑤ Contemplation on the ethics of surrogacy may change our initial view on it.

KYUNGHEE
UNIVERSITY

경희대학교   2024학년도 인문·체육계열
▶▶ 40문항·90분

[01-05] Choose the answer that is closest in meaning to the underlined word in the sentences below.

01 This suggests human blood in particular was chosen for another, presumably ritual, reason. Being picked as the donor of this blood may well have been an honour, though that is impossible to tell. But given many pre-Columbian peoples' <u>proclivity</u> for human sacrifice, rather than mere bloodletting, it might not have been an honour that was highly sought after. 1.7점

① appreciation   ② conventions   ③ phobia
④ concerns   ⑤ predisposition

02 In recent years, efforts to enact gun-safety measures have <u>floundered</u> in Maine. An expert in gun laws believes that Maine has been slow to enact gun control in part because residents tend to see the state as safe. 1.7점

① uncovered   ② augmented   ③ emerged
④ faltered   ⑤ sprouted

03 Despite the recent <u>setbacks</u> on the battlefield, the general does not intend to give up fighting or to sue for any kind of peace. On the contrary, his belief in the country's ultimate victory over the enemy has hardened into a form that worries some of his advisers. 1.7점

① oppositions   ② sacrifices   ③ obstacles
④ collisions   ⑤ advances

04 A lifelong bachelor, who saw out his days on an estate outside Oslo, his greatest attachment was to his work. When he died, aged 80, he gave thousands of items and his personal papers to his hometown. It is at last doing justice to his <u>munificence</u> and his genius. 1.7점

① magnanimity   ② commitment   ③ connoisseurship
④ ingenuity   ⑤ extravagance

05 Shane Campbell-Staton, a biologist at Princeton University, studies how animals adapt to human creations like cities and pollution. His interest was <u>piqued</u> by a film about the tuskless female elephants of Gorongosa National Park, in Mozambique. 1.7점

① conceived   ② provoked   ③ represented
④ disseminated   ⑤ upheld

[06-14] Choose the most appropriate word to fill in the blanks.

06 Culture is not _____; it comprises a variety of cultural practices that people engage in across a range of social configurations they participate in. 1.7점

① ethnocentric   ② consistent   ③ esoteric
④ monolithic   ⑤ inherited

07 Psychologists have developed a theory of how people explain, make excuses about, and justify their behaviors. It postulates that people are motivated to _____ their own or other people's behavior to either internal or external causes, depending on the circumstances of an event. 1.7점

① tout   ② attribute   ③ account
④ appraise   ⑤ recount

08 Although some claim that technology is racially neutral, others argue that the use of technology in the United States has _____ the racial and class divisions by allowing those with resources to benefit from technology and those who are poor to be denied access. 1.7점

① alleviated   ② prevented   ③ exacerbated
④ confounded   ⑤ nullified

09 In Mesoamerica, which roughly corresponds to the location of modern-day Central America and southern Mexico, the first significant society _____ around 1,200 B.C. and flourished for centuries before eventually declining a little more than half a millennium later. 1.7점

① ended   ② released   ③ transferred
④ broke   ⑤ emerged

10 Obesity is a common, serious, and costly chronic disease, _____ more than 40% of U.S. adults and almost 20% of children. 1.7점

① substantiating   ② attracting   ③ nettling
④ afflicting   ⑤ taunting

11 What makes him _____ is being considered changeable, frivolous, effeminate, cowardly, and irresolute; from these qualities a prince must guard himself as if from a reef, and he must strive to make everyone recognize in his actions greatness, spirit, dignity, and strength; and concerning the private affairs of his subjects, he must insist that his decision be irrevocable. 2점

① allured   ② collaborative   ③ despised
④ maudlin   ⑤ optimistic

12 The human understanding when it has once adopted an opinion draws all things else to support and agree with it. And though there be a greater number and weight of instances to be found on the other side, yet these it either neglects and despises, or else by some distinction sets aside and rejects; in order that by this great and pernicious predetermination the authority of its former conclusions may remain _____. 2점

① inviolate   ② vilified   ③ indefinite
④ cryptic   ⑤ assessed

13 In a democracy, conservatism relies on equality of opportunity. The race of life, in which only some get prizes, is seen as illegitimate unless everybody gets a fair start. But in the past four decades the starting line has become more uneven, as the successful have _____ resources for their children, and wealth had become more regionally concentrated. 2점

① depleted   ② publicized   ③ hoarded
④ marred   ⑤ overseen

14 The mysteriousness, the eeriness, the ancient _____ of the great depths have led many people to suppose that some very old forms of life — some "living fossils" — may be lurking undiscovered in the deep ocean. Some such hope may have been in the minds of the *Challenger* scientists. The forms they brought up in their nets were weird enough, and most of them had never before been seen by man. But basically they were modern types. There was nothing like the trilobites of Cambrian time or the sea scorpions of the Silurian, nothing reminiscent of the great marine reptiles that invaded the sea in the Mesozoic. 3점

① ephemerality   ② unchangingness   ③ homogeneity
④ variety   ⑤ manifoldness

[15-17] Read the following passage and answer the questions.

There's a sense, once a whisper, that's growing louder every day. Glaciers are melting, children are being slaughtered, hatred runs <u>rampant</u>. Sometimes it feels like the world's approaching a nadir. Or like you are.

The antidote to any despair might be hope, experts say. A It's one of the most powerful human mindsets, and possible to achieve even when it feels out of reach. B Being hopeful doesn't mean engaging in wishful thinking or blind optimism. C Rather, it's the belief or the expectation that the future can be better, and that more importantly, we have the capacity to pursue that future. The opposite of hope, therefore, is not pessimism, but rather apathy, with its loss of motivation. D While wishing is passive, hope is about taking action to get one step closer to what you wish for.

Being hopeful is associated with an array of benefits. Research suggests that people with more hope throughout their lives have fewer chronic health problems; are less likely to be depressed or anxious; have stronger social support; and tend to live longer. E

15 The underlined word, "<u>rampant</u>," is closest in meaning to _____. 2점

① prevalent ② restrained ③ punctilious
④ continuous ⑤ tenacious

16 Choose the <u>most</u> appropriate place to insert the following sentence. 3점

People who are high in hope do not remain passive but always work toward at least one goal that's intrinsically meaningful.

① A ② B ③ C
④ D ⑤ E

17 Which of the following is NOT true according to the passage? 3점

① A hopeful person is not characterized as being indifferent to life.
② Hope entails doing something to work toward the desired outcome.
③ During times of adversity, we can turn to hope to overcome despair.
④ The adversities around us sometimes make us feel that we are at a low point.
⑤ Having apathetic feelings is likely to result in rapid deterioration of one's health condition.

[18-19] Read the following passage and answer the questions.

Some researchers contend that sleep plays no role in the consolidation of declarative memory (i.e., memory involving factual information). These researchers note that people with impairments in rapid eye movement (REM) sleep continue to lead normal lives, and they argue that if sleep were crucial for memory, then these individuals would have apparent memory deficits. Yet the same researchers acknowledge that the cognitive capacities of these individuals have never been systematically examined, nor have they been the subject of studies of tasks on which performance reportedly depends on sleep. Ⓐ_____ such studies were done, they could only clarify our understanding of the role of REM sleep, not sleep in general.

These researchers also claim that improvements of memory overnight can be explained by the mere passage of time, rather than Ⓑ_____ sleep. But recent studies of memory performance after sleep, including one demonstrating that sleep stabilizes declarative memories from future interference caused by mental activity during wakefulness, make this claim unsustainable. Certainly there are memory consolidation processes that occur across periods of wakefulness, some of which neither depend on nor are enhanced by sleep. But when sleep is compared with wakefulness, and performance is better after sleep, then some benefit of sleep for memory must be acknowledged.

18 **Which of the following best fits into Ⓐ and Ⓑ?** 3점
① If — modulated by
② Since — confounded by
③ While — explained by
④ Even if — attributed to
⑤ Even though — deprived by

19 Which of the following is NOT true according to the passage? 3점

① People with impairments to REM sleep continue to lead normal lives.

② Cognitive abilities of individuals with impairments to REM sleep must be examined systematically to confirm the effect of sleep on declarative memory.

③ Improvements of memory that occur overnight might be explained merely by the passage of time.

④ Some research findings demonstrate the role of sleep in stabilizing declarative memory.

⑤ There is sufficient evidence to conclude that sleep plays no role in the consolidation of declarative memory.

[20-21] Read the following passage and answer the questions.

Racial discrimination and bias are painful realities and increasingly recognized as detrimental to the health of adults and children. These stressful experiences may also appear to be Ⓐ_____ from mother to child during pregnancy, altering the strength of infants' brain circuits. A recent study demonstrated that infants of mothers who experience discrimination generally had weaker connections between their amygdala and prefrontal cortex. The amygdala is an area of the brain associated with emotional processing that is altered in many mood disorders. It also appears to be involved in ethnic and racial processing, such as differentiating faces. The findings of the study suggest that the connectivity changes that researchers found may reduce infants' ability to regulate their emotions and Ⓑ_____ risk for mental health disorders.

20 Which of the following best fits into Ⓐ and Ⓑ? 2점

① mandated — remove

② bestowed — offset

③ inherited — decrease

④ transmitted — increase

⑤ adopted — facilitate

21 **Which of the following CANNOT be inferred from the passage?** 3점

① How we treat and interact with people matters, especially during pregnancy.

② The experience of discrimination during pregnancy can have profound ramifications on offspring.

③ Greater cultural inclusivity is necessary for increasing the birth rate.

④ The same region of the brain deals with both emotional and racial processing.

⑤ The amygdala is sensitive to prenatal stress.

[22-23] Read the following passage and answer the questions.

Our diets are filled with iconic duos. Peanut butter and jelly. Eggs and bacon. Cookies and milk. But there's one duo that takes the cake: salt and pepper. Nearly every savory recipe calls for salt and pepper, from pasta to salad dressing, to soups and tacos. It is sometimes considered the bare minimum seasoning blend for every dish.

There has always been chatter about salt's impact on our bodies, particularly for issues like high blood pressure. But what about its counterpart, pepper? Is black pepper good for you, or should excess amounts be avoided, like with salt? While black pepper contains compounds like antioxidants which have a wide range of health benefits, there is still insufficient data that suggests black pepper is an effective treatment for any ailments or that it helps prevent the development of illness or disease.

However, black pepper may help in the prevention or treatment of disease if you use it as a substitute for other spices. Excess sodium Ⓐ_____ can lead to a condition called hypertension or high blood pressure. Those with high blood pressure are advised to limit their sodium consumption to prevent cardiovascular complications like heart attack and stroke. This can be difficult, because food with less salt might not taste as good. This is where spices like black pepper can make a huge difference because they can bring flavor without the health consequences. Black pepper can turn an Ⓑ_____ bland dish into something with a very mild kick.

22 Which of the following is the <u>most</u> appropriate title for the passage? 2점

① Try Black Pepper as a Substitute

② The Best Seasoning Blend: Salt and Pepper

③ Black Pepper Contains Antioxidants

④ Black Pepper Prevents Illness

⑤ The Strong Flavor of Black Pepper

23 Which of the following best fits into Ⓐ and Ⓑ? 3.3점

① digestion — oddly

② intake — otherwise

③ extraction — awfully

④ nibbling — original

⑤ indulgence — overly

24 Put the following story into a logical order. 3점

Ⓐ Consequently, the 1950s saw a growing number of women engaged in farm labor, even though rhetoric in the popular media called for the return of women to domestic life.

Ⓑ But in agriculture, unlike other industries where women were viewed as temporary workers, women's employment did not end with the war in agriculture.

Ⓒ Instead, the expansion of agriculture and a steady decrease in the number of male farmworkers combined to cause the industry to hire more women in the postwar years.

Ⓓ Most scholarship on women's employment in the United States recognizes that the Second World War dramatically changed the role of women in the workforce.

Ⓔ These studies also acknowledge that few women remained in manufacturing jobs once men returned from the war.

---

① Ⓔ-Ⓓ-Ⓑ-Ⓒ-Ⓐ

② Ⓔ-Ⓓ-Ⓒ-Ⓑ-Ⓐ

③ Ⓓ-Ⓔ-Ⓑ-Ⓒ-Ⓐ

④ Ⓓ-Ⓑ-Ⓒ-Ⓐ-Ⓔ

⑤ Ⓓ-Ⓔ-Ⓒ-Ⓑ-Ⓐ

[25-27] Read the following passage and answer the questions.

The people of southern Madagascar are in peril. More than 1.1 million of them are going hungry, according to the U.N. That means more than 500,000 children under the age of five are at risk of being acutely malnourished. Many families are eking out their meager diets with cactus.

This calamity has several causes, and the U.N. emphasizes climate change. Man-made climate change has certainly affected the world's fourth-largest island. Southern Madagascar has long suffered from erratic rains. Droughts are common, and famines were recorded in 1903, 1910, 1916, 1921, and 1943 among other years. Yet of late the rains have become even less regular; today's drought is the worst in 40 years. The harvest of cassava, a staple, is expected to be 60-90% less than in normal years. The price of rice is soaring.

In addition, Covid-19 has made people poorer. Madagascar's economy shrank by 4.2% last year, despite a fast-growing population. The island has all but shut itself off from the outside world, causing its main source of hard currency, tourism, to collapse. The well-heeled foreigners who used to trek through its rainforests in search of lemurs stayed at home. The 1.5 million people who depend on them lost their livelihoods.

Donors should pitch in to prevent people from starving. Children, especially, need enough nutrients if they are to avoid growing up with stunted bodies and minds. At the same time, the current disaster should be a wake-up call for Madagascar's government. If successive regimes had not mismanaged the economy so badly for so long, the Malagasy would be prosperous enough to cope better with shocks.

25 The underlined word, "well-heeled," is closest in meaning to _____. 3점
① extroverted   ② adventurous   ③ affluent
④ energetic   ⑤ well-cultured

26 Which word best describes the tone of the underlined sentence? 2점
① dejected   ② critical   ③ sympathetic
④ bewildered   ⑤ sarcastic

27 Which of the following CANNOT be inferred from the passage? 3점

① Cactus has been the preferred staple food in southern Madagascar for a long time.

② Irregular rain is not an unexpected event in southern Madagascar.

③ Malnourishment is likely to yield critical health consequences.

④ The tourism industry must get back on its feet in order for Madagascar's economy to revive.

⑤ The poverty of Madagascar is in part due to its recent economic crisis.

[28-29] Read the following passage and answer the questions.

The myth of woman plays a considerable part in literature; but what is its importance in daily life? To what extent does it affect the customs and conduct of individuals? In replying to this question it will be necessary to state precisely the relations this myth bears to reality.

There are different kinds of myths. This one, the myth of woman, sublimating a Ⓐmutable aspect of the human condition — namely, the "division" of humanity into two classes of individuals — is a Ⓑstatic myth. It projects into the realm of Platonic ideas a reality that is directly experienced or is conceptualized on the basis of experience; in place of fact, value, significance, knowledge, Ⓒempirical law, it substitutes a transcendental Idea, timeless, unchangeable, necessary. This idea is Ⓓindisputable because it is beyond the given: it is endowed with absolute truth. Thus, as against the dispersed, Ⓔcontingent, and multiple existences of actual women, mythical thought opposes the Eternal Feminine, unique and changeless. If the definition provided for this concept is contradicted by the behavior of flesh-and-blood women, it is the latter who are wrong: we are told not that Femininity is a false entity, but that _____. The contrary facts of experience are impotent against the myth.

28 Out of the underlined Ⓐ~Ⓔ, which is not likely to fit into the context? 3.3점

① Ⓐ   ② Ⓑ   ③ Ⓒ

④ Ⓓ   ⑤ Ⓔ

29 Choose the <u>most</u> appropriately inferred phrase to fill in the blank. 3.3점

① some women are not intellectual

② the women concerned are not feminine

③ women are fellow human beings

④ women are multiple existences

⑤ women are generally not belligerent

[30-31] Read the following passage and answer the questions.

A young woman holds up a book and smiles. "This is day one of me reading 'The Song of Achilles'," she says. The video jumps forward. "And this," she moans, her face stained with tears, "is me finishing it." Another clip, entitled "Books that will make you SOB," offers written notes on how assorted stories got readers to cry, such as "I can't think about it without bawling" and "ended up crying sm [so much]. I had to change my shirt." A This is BookTok, as the literary wing of the app TikTok is known. Imagine the emotional pitch of a Victorian melodrama, add music, and you have the general idea. B

BookTok is passionate. It is also profitable — at least for publishers. Bloomsbury, a publishing house based in Britain, recently reported record sales and a 220% rise in profits, which Nigel Newton, its boss, put down partly to the "absolute phenomenon" of BookTok. On Amazon, BookTok is so influential that it has leapt into the titles of books themselves. The novel "It Ends With Us," for instance, is now listed as "It Ends With Us: TikTok made me buy it!" C Evidently TikTok did a good job: the romance is riding high in the top 100 in both Britain and America.

The medium is not quite as gushy as it might seem. Much of the overdone emotion is ironic, and some of the videos are very funny — particularly those with the hashtag #writtenbymen, which poke fun at the male gaze. D Nonetheless, many would make mainstream book reviewers tut. E Until fairly recently, their perspective was marginalized in both fiction and criticism. White men dominated both — even though most novel-readers are female.

30 Which of the following is the <u>most</u> appropriate title for the passage? 2점

① BookTok is popularizing the romance genre.

② A new form of literary criticism is boosting sales of books.

③ Young women are reviving the appetite for reading fiction.

④ Young women's sentimentalism is a recent syndrome.

⑤ BookTok is changing the traditional way of bookselling.

31 Choose the <u>most</u> appropriate place to insert the following sentence. 3.3점

But why should the young women who are BookTok's stars care about what old-fashioned literary types think of them?

① A   ② B   ③ C

④ D   ⑤ E

The French eat foie gras, the Icelandic devour *hakarl*(fermented fish with an aroma of urine), Americans give thanks by baking tinned pumpkin in a pie. The range of human foods is not just a source of epicurean joy but a reflection of ecological and anthropological variety — the consequence of tens of thousands of years of parallel yet independent cultural evolution.

And yet, as choice has proliferated in other ways, diets have been squeezed and standardized. Even Parisians eventually let Starbucks onto their boulevards. Dan Saladino, a food journalist at the BBC, reminds readers of what stands to be lost. In "Eating to Extinction" he travels far and wide to find "the world's rarest foods." These include the murnong, "a radish-like root with a crisp bite and the taste of sweet coconut"; for millennia it was a primary food for Australia's Aboriginals, before almost vanishing.

Evident is Ⓐ_____ over the past century. Inside the stomach of a man who died 2,500 years ago, and whose body was preserved when it sank into a Danish peat bog, researchers found the remains of his last meal: "a porridge made with barley, flax and the seeds of 40 different plants." In east Africa, the Hadza, one of the last remaining hunter-gatherer tribes, "eat from a potential wild menu that consists of more than 800 plant and animal species." By contrast, most humans now get 75% of their calorie intake from just eight foods.

Even within each of those food groups there is Ⓑ_____. Decades of selective breeding and the pressures of global food markets mean that farms everywhere grow the same varieties of cereals and raise the same breeds of livestock.

32 **Which of the following best fits into Ⓐ?** 3.3점

① the rapid decline in the diversity of human foods

② the anthropological evidence of human food variety

③ increasing of human appetites by rarest foods

④ globalization of local foods to retain human legacy

⑤ necessity to ameliorate chosen foods

33 **Which of the following best fits into Ⓑ?** 3.3점

① hybridization　　　② differentiation　　　③ homogenization

④ degeneration　　　⑤ mutation

[34-35] Read the following passage and answer the questions.

From the conditions of frontier life came intellectual traits of profound importance. The works of travelers along each frontier from colonial days onward describe certain common traits, and these traits have, while softening down, still persisted as survivals in the place of their origin, even when a higher social organization succeeded. The result is that to the frontier the American intellect owes its striking characteristics. That coarseness and strength combined with acuteness and inquisitiveness; that practical, inventive turn of mind, _____; that masterful grasp of material things, lacking in the artistic but powerful to effect great ends; that restless, nervous energy; that dominant individualism, working for good and for evil, and withal that buoyancy and exuberance which comes with freedom — these are traits of the frontier, or traits called out elsewhere because of the existence of the frontier. Since the days when the fleet of Columbus sailed into the waters of the New World, America has been another name for opportunity, and the people of the United States have taken their tone from the Ⓐincessant expansion which has not only been open but has even been forced upon them. He would be a Ⓑprudent prophet who should assert that the expansive character of American life has now entirely Ⓒceased. ⓄMovement has been its Ⓔdominant fact and, unless this training has no effect upon a people, the American energy will continually demand a wider field for its exercise.

34 Choose the <u>most</u> appropriately inferred phrase to fill in the blank. 3.3점

① aspiring for sedentary occupations

② indulgent in austere life

③ jealous of communal spirit

④ faithful to traditionalism

⑤ quick to find expedients

35 Out of the underlined Ⓐ~Ⓔ, which is NOT likely to fit into the context? 3.3점

① Ⓐ   ② Ⓑ   ③ Ⓒ

④ Ⓓ   ⑤ Ⓔ

[36-37] Read the following passage and answer the questions.

Steve Neale, in his article on genre, makes two useful distinctions which are helpful in understanding the work of the referent in genre films. Ⓐ First he distinguishes between verisimilitude and realism. These terms refer in significantly different ways to the work of the referent. Ⓑ Realism is today the more familiar term through which we judge whether a fiction constructs a world we recognize as like our own; but, as we have seen, realism is a highly problematic category. Ⓒ Steve Neale, therefore, revives a concept from literary history, to underline the fact that, in fiction, 'reality' is always constructed. Ⓓ Neale then distinguishes between cultural verisimilitude and generic verisimilitude. In order to be recognized as a film belonging to a particular genre — a western, a musical, a horror film — it must comply with the rules of that genre: in other words, genre conventions produce a second order verisimilitude — what ought to happen in a western or soap opera — by which the credibility or truth of the fictional world we associate with a particular genre is guaranteed. Ⓔ Whereas generic verisimilitude allows for considerable play with fantasy inside the bounds of generic credibility (e.g. singing about your problems in the musical; the power of garlic in gothic horror movies), cultural verisimilitude refers us to the norms, mores, and common sense of the social world outside the fiction.

36 **Which of the following is NOT true of generic verisimilitude?** 3.3점

① It gives credibility to fantasy within generic bounds.

② It secures the truth of the fictional world in a particular genre.

③ It must follow the rules of a genre.

④ It is a kind of second-order verisimilitude.

⑤ It makes us judge whether a fiction constructs a life-like world.

37 **Choose the <u>most</u> appropriate place to insert the following sentence.** 3.3점

Verisimilitude, he argues, refers not to what may or may not actually be the case but rather to what the dominant culture believes to be the case, to what is generally accepted as credible, suitable, proper.

① Ⓐ   ② Ⓑ   ③ Ⓒ

④ Ⓓ   ⑤ Ⓔ

[38-40] Read the following passage and answer the questions.

Antonie Van Leeuwenhoek, a 17th-century Dutch businessman and scientist, was inordinately proud of his clean teeth. Every morning he scrubbed them with salt before rinsing his mouth with water. After eating, he carefully cleaned his teeth with a toothpick. Few people of his age, he remarked in a letter in 1683, had such clean and white teeth. Yet when he looked closely, he found "there remains or grows between some of the molars and teeth a little white matter" — now called dental plaque.

As an expert microscopist who had observed tiny organisms in water a few years earlier, van Leeuwenhoek wondered whether Ⓐthey might also be present in this white matter. A microscope showed that it did indeed contain "many very Ⓑsmall living animals, which moved very prettily".

Few people suspected that such Ⓒmicro-organisms might cause diseases. At the time, doctors followed the doctrine of Hippocrates, believing diseases were caused by an imbalance of the "humours" within the body (blood, phlegm, yellow bile and black bile). Epidemic diseases, meanwhile, were attributed to Ⓓmiasma, the "bad air" given off by swamps or decomposing matter. Suggestions that disease might be transmitted by Ⓔtiny living things were rejected by doctors.

The notion that tiny organisms caused diseases, now known as germ theory, was only embraced in the second half of the 19th century. The key obstacle was not intellectual but cultural. Doctors were conservative and regarded new, experiment-based findings as a challenge to their professional identity. While astronomers rushed to adopt telescopes, which transformed their understanding of the universe, doctors _____ to win them from makers of large language models with whom they have no relationship. to the new worlds revealed by the microscope.

38 Out of the underlined Ⓐ~Ⓔ, which one refers to a different thing? 2점

① Ⓐ
② Ⓑ
③ Ⓒ
④ Ⓓ
⑤ Ⓔ

39 Which is the best phrase to fill in the blank? 2점

① turned a blind eye

② resorted

③ turned their attention

④ put their place down

⑤ made way

40 Which of the following CANNOT be inferred from the passage? 3점

① No awareness of germs was made until the advent of the microscope.

② Diseases were once attributed to bodily fluids.

③ The earlier initiation of germ theory was deterred by miasmic theory.

④ Identifications of germs dated back much earlier than medical cautions against them.

⑤ Pioneers of germ theory would be the doctors who were well-acquainted with microscopy.

KYUNGHEE
UNIVERSITY

경희대학교　　2024학년도 한의학과(인문)
▶▶ 50문항·90분

[01-10] Choose the answer closest in meaning to the underlined word or phrase.

01 Joan was born to a well-off family whose fortune was <u>squandered</u> by her dissolute father. 1점

① conserved　　　　② wasted　　　　③ amassed
④ secured　　　　　⑤ renounced

02 In today's hi-tech culture, one may imagine that human memories, once properly stored, could be <u>retrieved</u> from the mind as faithfully as computer files are downloaded from a disk. 1점

① recovered　　　　② relinquished　　　③ reimbursed
④ reverberated　　　⑤ reiterated

03 In an effort to motivate their employees and to create a more <u>conducive</u> work environment, a growing number of organizations are introducing new workplace designs. 1점

① facile　　　　　　② mandatory　　　　③ inimical
④ helpful　　　　　⑤ obnoxious

04 Plutonium is radioactive. The pure metal first delivered to the laboratory displayed varying densities, and the molten state was so reactive that it <u>corroded</u> almost every container it contacted. 1점

① ignited   ② vaporized   ③ eroded

④ exacerbated   ⑤ consolidated

05 Ecotourism is a new model of tourism to <u>alleviate</u> the impact of ordinary tourism on the ecosystem. 1점

① assuage   ② aggravate   ③ provoke

④ spur   ⑤ probe

06 He ordered two coffees from one of the circling waiters, and for a while we watched the people on the beach from our shady seclusion, their bare bodies <u>smudged</u> by the haze of heat, so that they looked somehow primordial, lying or moving slowly, half naked, along the shore. 1점

① plastered   ② cleared   ③ smeared

④ mutated   ⑤ cloned

07 A society, almost necessarily, begins every success story with the chapter that most advantages itself, and in America, these <u>precipitating</u> chapters are almost always rendered as the singular action of exceptional individuals. "It only takes one person to make a change," you are often told. This is a myth. 1점

① repulsive   ② propitious   ③ provoking

④ obtrusive   ⑤ ominous

08 In October 2021, *Forbes* anointed Bankman-Fried the richest 20-something in the world. But last November, fears mounted on social media that Bankman-Fried's empire has a lot less money than it <u>let on</u>. When panicked customers withdrew billions of dollars in deposits from FTX, it turned out that Bankman-Fried did not have the funds to pay them back. 1점

① revenued   ② refunded   ③ retributed

④ restored   ⑤ revealed

09 State-of-the-art medical robotic technologies feature high-resolution 3D magnification systems and instruments that can <u>maneuver</u> with far greater precision than the human wrist and fingers. 1점

① contrive   ② drill   ③ outperform
④ manage   ⑤ stratify

10 The founders of the American meritocracy believe they were destroying a <u>nascent</u> class system and building a fluid, mobile society. In retrospect, this was vainglorious — you can't undermine social rank by setting up an elaborate process of ranking.

① burgeoning   ② full-blown   ③ retreating   1점
④ subliminal   ⑤ withering

[11-15] Choose the best answer for the blank.

11 Despite the customs officers' abiding efforts, large amounts of drugs are _____ into the country annually. 1.3점

① indicted   ② ordained   ③ thrived
④ yielded   ⑤ smuggled

12 A genetically engineered dietary supplement permanently disabled more than 5,000 Americans with a fatal blood disorder before it was _____ by the Food and Drug Administration. 1.3점

① recalled   ② plundered   ③ confounded
④ taunted   ⑤ coordinated

13 Happiness and misery play a role in evolution only to the extent that they encourage or discourage survival and reproduction. Perhaps it's not surprising, then, that evolution has moulded us to be neither too miserable nor too happy. It enables us to enjoy a momentary rush of pleasant sensations, but these never last for ever. Sooner or later they _____ and give place to unpleasant sensations. 1.3점

① substitute   ② subside   ③ suspect
④ subsist   ⑤ subsidize

14 For now, this is what we know of matter: A handful of types of elementary particles, which vibrate and fluctuate constantly between existence and non-existence and swarm in space even when it seems that there is nothing there, combine together to _____ like letters of a cosmic alphabet to tell the immense history of galaxies, of the innumerable stars, of sunlight, of mountains, woods and fields of grain, of the smiling faces of the young at parties, and of the night sky studded with stars. 1.3점

① infinity   ② indifference   ③ insolence
④ inception   ⑤ indefiniteness

15 If Manhattan is an island defined by its street grid, Barbados is an island where plantations function in much the same way. In Bridgetown, a plaque identifying the spot where a slave cage once sat hangs on the exterior of a bank. Sugar-mill smokestacks and windmills _____ the countryside. The past is present almost everywhere, acknowledged or not. 1.3점

① emphasize   ② interrupt   ③ punctuate
④ immobilize   ⑤ accentuate

[16-17] Choose the best answer for the blank.

16 The notion of the wounded healer, which dates back to antiquity, is in common currency. It means that the therapist's own _____ can paradoxically serve as a source of his healing capacities. 2.7점

① needs and desires
② fitness and well-being
③ composure and equanimity
④ impulse and preoccupation
⑤ suffering and vulnerability

17 When we _____ against a disease, we are injecting a weakened strain of the disease into the body, which is then stimulated to develop antibodies for the disease. 2.7점

① censor   ② inoculate   ③ afflict
④ grapple   ⑤ disseminate

[18-19] Choose the best answer for the blanks.

18 The amount of human intelligence, Elon Musk noted, was Ⓐ_____, because people were not having enough children. Meanwhile, the amount of computer intelligence was going up Ⓑ_____, like Moore's Law on steroids. 2.7점

① taking off — unprecedentedly
② putting off — outrageously
③ leveling off — exponentially
④ turning off — disproportionately
⑤ rounding off — alarmingly

19 When confronting stagflationary shocks, a central bank must Ⓐ_____ its policy stance even as the economy heads toward a recession. The situation today is thus fundamentally different from the global financial crisis or the early months of the pandemic, when central banks could Ⓑ_____ monetary policy aggressively in response to falling aggregate demand and deflationary pressure. The space for fiscal expansion will also be more limited this time, public debts becoming unsustainable. 1.3점

① tighten — aggravate
② ease — tighten
③ tighten — differentiate
④ ease — loosen
⑤ tighten — ease

[20-21] Read the passage and answer the questions.

Whether by accident or unconscious design, 2023 has been the year of the movie wife. In Bradley Cooper's *Maestro*, Sofia Coppola's *Priscilla*, even Christopher Nolan's *Oppenheimer* and Michael Mann's *Ferrari* — those last two made by male directors who aren't exactly known for exploring the experiences of women — the movie wife has come barging in from the sidelines in all her glory. She may not be the main character, but she's _____ about taking up space in the frame.

20 Choose the best answer for the blank. 1.3점

① reserved   ② resultant   ③ repulsive

④ regressive   ⑤ resolute

21 Choose the best title for the passage. 2.7점

① Roles of Women in Popular Movies

② Rights of Actresses as Movie Wives

③ The Rise of Movie Wives This Year

④ The Year of Awakening Male Directors

⑤ Portrayal of Wives in Box Office Movies

[22-23] Read the passage and answer the questions.

As lay-offs roiled the tech industry in the late 2022, Blind — an online forum for verified but _____ professionals — became the de facto channel for communication amid the tumult. At the time, more than 95% of Twitter employees were among Blind's 8 million users, whose numbers grew by 2 million last year. Those users, many of whom work in tech, discuss everything from visa issues and mental health to unethical practices, make it a vital platform for industry whistle-blowers. Blind monetizes by summarizing user sentiment and suggesting changes to criticized companies.

22 **Choose the best answer for the blank.** 1.3점

① disgruntled ② anonymous ③ legitimate
④ scrupulous ⑤ distinguished

23 **How does Blind support itself?** 2.7점

① by charging membership fees to subscribers
② by soliciting professional advisers and donors
③ by promoting its service to the public online
④ by seeking those who grudge over their jobs
⑤ by selling problems and solutions to companies

[24-25] Read the passage and answer the questions.

When we feel genuinely overwhelmed and anxious because of stress, it's our body's way of telling us to recalibrate and rebalance. Nobody is truly limitless. When we heed our internal cues and acknowledge our <u>fallibility</u>, we emerge more focused and healthier overall — and also less stressed and anxious.

Anxiety can be a healthy, helpful emotion that is a constructive aspect of human life. It can foster emotional connection when we convey our vulnerable feelings to others. And in the form of stress, it can serve as an internal barometer to remain balanced and healthy. It's about time _____.

24 **Choose the answer closest in meaning to the underlined word, 'fallibility'.** 1.3점

① disposition to err
② state of indeterminacy
③ propensity to perfection
④ proposition to difference
⑤ penchant for connectivity

25 **Choose the best answer for the blank.** 2.7점

① we mind our own business

② we start putting it to good use

③ we endure bad feelings for good

④ we are completely free from anxiety

⑤ we figure out ways to dismiss anxiety

[26-27] Read the passage and answer the questions.

Educators must be proficient in some special skill. But, in addition to this, there is a general outlook which it is their duty to put before those whom they are instructing. They should exemplify the value of intellect and of the search for knowledge. They should make it clear that what at any time passes for knowledge may, in fact, be erroneous. They should _____ an undogmatic temper, a temper of continual search and not of comfortable certainty. They should try to create an awareness of the world as a whole, and not only of what is near in space and time.

Through the recognition of the likelihood of error, they should make clear the importance of tolerance. They should remind the student that those whom posterity honors have very often been unpopular in their own day; and that, on this ground, social courage is a virtue of supreme importance. Above all, every educator who is engaged in an attempt to make the best of the students to whom he speaks must regard himself as the servant of truth and not of this or that political or sectarian interests.

26 **Choose the most appropriate answer for the blank.** 1.3점

① inculcate   ② preclude   ③ eliminate

④ eradicate   ⑤ mitigate

27 **Which is NOT true about educators?** 3점

① They should eschew any sectarian interests.

② They should hold a macro-vision of the world.

③ They should vindicate the search for knowledge.

④ They should be convinced of the infallibility in knowledge.

⑤ They should present a general perspective to their students.

[28-29] Read the passage and answer the questions.

Surveillance capitalism unilaterally claims human experience as free raw material for translation into behavioral data. Although some of these data are applied to product or service improvement, the rest are declared as a proprietary behavioral surplus, fed into advanced manufacturing processes known as "machine intelligence," and fabricated into prediction products that anticipate what you will do now, soon, and later. Finally, these prediction products are traded in a new kind of marketplace for behavioral predictions that I call "behavioral futures markets". Surveillance capitalists have grown immensely wealthy from these trading operations, for many companies are eager to lay bets on our future behavior.

28 Choose the answer closest in meaning to the underlined word, 'proprietary'. 1.3점

① conjoint　　　② mutual　　　③ public

④ exclusive　　　⑤ communal

29 Which is NOT true about surveillance capitalism? 3점

① It turns human experience into predictive data.

② It compels companies to be keen on prediction products.

③ It is predicated on consumers' behaviors for future marketing.

④ Its marketing relies on correct analyses of all existing data.

⑤ It produces wealthy individuals who sell surplus behavioral data.

[30-31] Read the passage and answer the questions.

Acupuncture combined with deep learning and artificial intelligence rehabilitation robots is also the hotspot of future research. The existing clinical research on acupuncture revolves around acupuncture methods such as Electro-acupuncture and dry needling and focuses on the rehabilitation of stroke sequelae, mainly by manual manipulation and supplemented by tools. In case of another emergency like the pandemic in the future, combining material technology with engineering to explore the development of acupuncture robots of artificial intelligence may contribute to rehabilitating neurological and motor functions in patients with post-stroke sequelae. Currently, there are upper limb exoskeleton robots, including the design and development of remote rehabilitation robots. The acupuncture robots will be equipped with various sensors, such as mechanical and electrical sensors, to reduce the pain of needle injections. Furthermore, the design included a study protocol for acupoint positioning, mechanical stimulation, and detection of deqi, for which strategies have been developed.

*deqi: needle sensation or response, sequelae: after-effect

30 **Choose the best title for the passage.** 2.7점

① Incorporation of Various Sensors & Protocols into Acupuncture Robots
② Post-Stroke Rehab Innovation in Acupuncture via AI & Material Tech
③ Review of Current Research on Acupuncture & Robots
④ Fastest Ways to Reduce Post-stroke Effects of Acupuncture
⑤ Clinical Focus on Stroke Rehabilitation in Acupuncture

31 **Which of the following can be inferred from the passage?** 3점

① Acupuncture robots are in use for remote treatment.
② Acupuncture robots are versatile in treating all post-effects of treatment.
③ Using robots in acupuncture has not been fully accepted in general.
④ More research on AI rehab robots can help reduce patients' pain during and after acupuncture treatment.
⑤ Stroke rehabilitation through current acupuncture methods is done manually and ineffectively.

[32-33] Read the passage and answer the questions.

For Mary Anne Hitt, policy and advocacy is at the core of the climate crisis. Her experience with the Sierra Club, Appalachian Voices, and now with Climate Imperative highlights that changing climate policy allows women to change the world. In her essay "Beyond Coal", she recounts her experience as director of Beyond Coal, a campaign by Sierra Club to eliminate fossil fuels, and promotes a full transition to renewable and sustainable energy. In her time on the campaign, over 300 coal plants were retired. As a woman from West Virginia, she understood that this was a difficult transition for governments and individuals to make because some families have built their lives on the coal industry.

Her argument in her essay and behind the Beyond Coal was that coal is, "simply _____ in the twenty-first century." Coal plants are almost always placed in low-income, minority communities where they do not have access to the health care they need in order to combat the effect of the coal emissions. The coal plants were uneconomic and unprofitable compared to renewable alternatives. By educating individuals and governments about the harmful effects of these plants and the economic, social, and long-term benefits they would see from retiring or transitioning the plants to renewable energy. Again, this example shows how a feminist climate leader made an extremely influential change in the climate movement, and how women can be an integral part of the movement.

32 **Choose the best answer for the blank.** 2.7점

① defensible   ② unremitting   ③ unrelenting

④ untenable   ⑤ indisputable

33 **Which is NOT true about Mary Anne Hitt?** 3점

① She had a strong commitment to using policy and advocacy in addressing the climate crisis.

② She showcased the impact of strategic initiatives, which resulted in closing down coal plants.

③ She highlighted adverse effects of coal on marginalized communities' health and environment.

④ She modeled how women's engagement in climate policy can drive significant global change.

⑤ She demonstrated the superiority of feminist leadership in climate action in the future.

[34-35] Read the passage and answer the questions.

The strong economic pressures to adopt the most efficient systems mean that humans are incentivized to cede more and more power to AI systems that cannot be controlled, putting us on a pathway toward being supplanted as the earth's dominant species. There are no easy solutions to our Ⓐ_____. A possible starting point would be to address the remarkable lack of regulation of the AI industry, which currently operates with little Ⓑ_____, much of the research taking place in the dark. The problem, however, is that competition within and between nations pushes against any common-sense safety measures. As the race toward powerful AI systems quickens, corporations and governments are increasingly incentivized to reach the finish line first. The future of humanity is closely intertwined with the progression of AI. It is thus a disturbing realization that natural selection may have more sway over it than we do. But as of now, we are still in command. It is time to take this threat seriously. Once we hand over control, we will not get it back.

34 **What is the author's attitude toward AI?** 2.7점

① resigned   ② apprehensive   ③ celebratory

④ restive   ⑤ maudlin

35 **Choose the best answer for Ⓐ and Ⓑ, respectively.** 2.7점

① predicament — oversight

② feat — consideration

③ dilemma — autonomy

④ evasion — procedure

⑤ inertia — motivation

[36-38] Read the passage and answer the questions.

The ethics of care, which has extended to moral inquiries in diverse spheres, private and public, including education, child care, health service, politics and global civility, was originally conceived as a feminist psychological theory. A Carol Gilligan first vindicated the care perspective as an alternative, but equally legitimate form of moral reasoning obscured by masculine liberal justice traditions. B Virginia Held argues that the ethics of care is a moral theory distinct from the established moral approaches such as Kantian ethics or utilitarianism. C Unlike the dominant moral theories, the ethics of care emphasizes care as a key moral value that forms the foundation of interpersonal relation and social institution. D The ethics of care considers the human condition fundamentally _____. E It presupposes the relational self as ontologically and epistemologically basic. It thus presents a critique of traditional liberalism, which espouses the concept of a rational, autonomous and self-sufficient individual.

36 **Choose the best place to insert the following sentence.** 2.7점

Subsequent theorists took a cue from and further developed the polemic.

① A   ② B   ③ C

④ D   ⑤ E

37 **Choose the best answer for the blank.** 1.3점

① exclusive   ② egocentric   ③ interdependent

④ antagonistic   ⑤ instrumental

38 **Which is NOT true about care ethics?** 3점

① It concerns a range of fields, private and public.

② It stemmed from a feminist moral theory.

③ It is opposed to traditional moral approaches.

④ It accentuates justice as a prime moral value.

⑤ It calls into question traditional liberalism.

[39-41] Read the passage and answer the questions.

It is true that Lincoln did not seek immediate abolition: Neither was he a radical egalitarian. A He was, rather, a gradual emancipationist who wanted to compensate slave owners. B The antislavery Lincoln was born in, and came to lead, a nation in which anti-Black prejudice was a fact of life. C There was hardly a mighty current of sentiment in the land to emancipate the enslaved and extend citizenship to the newly freed in a Promised Land of radical and civil equality. D He did not waver from a morally informed insistence that slavery be put on a path to "ultimate extinction." E He maintained this position to his political detriment throughout the 1850s — he won no major office between a single term in the U.S. House and his election to the presidency in 1860. _____, he refused to retreat from his antislavery commitment during the crisis over secession in 1860~61 — a time when a purely political man might have done — and he stood by emancipation after 1862, declining to give in to pressure for a negotiated peace with the Confederacy in order to end a devastating war. He campaigned on an abolitionist constitutional amendment in 1864.

39 **Choose the best place to insert the following sentence.** 3점

Yet to depict Lincoln as only a reluctant warrior against slavery fails to do him justice.

① A ② B ③ C

④ D ⑤ E

40 **Choose the best answer for the blank.** 2.7점

① Vitally ② Marginally ③ Relatedly

④ Nominally ⑤ Abruptly

41 **Which is NOT true about Lincoln?** 3점

① Lincoln initially did not advocate for immediate abolition but rather leaned toward a gradual emancipationist approach.

② Though not a radical abolitionist, Lincoln was against the expansion of slavery and insisted on its ultimate extinction.

③ Despite political setbacks due to his anti-slavery stance, he was able to hold major offices but refused to compromise for political gains.

④ Lincoln resisted pressure for a negotiated peace and fought for emancipation during his 1864 campaign.

⑤ Lincoln's stance on slavery evolved from his moral convictions and unwavering commitment to the gradual abolition.

[42-44] Read the passage and answer the questions.

If you have lived in one house from birth to maturity, you will find the house Ⓐ_____ your psyche. The house where I spent most of my younger years was unusually beautiful. Not just aesthetically pleasing; much more than that. The architect's artistic standard was very high. Everything around us indoors, every surface and area, was nobly proportioned, handsome and generous in material and workmanship. A house, so Ⓑ_____ planned and intended to give pleasure, must have an influence on a person living in it, and most of all, on a child, because for a child the house is pretty much the world.

Ⓐ Such daily experience will have the same power over the mind as music or poetry.

Ⓑ If that world has been deliberately made beautiful, a familiarity with and expectation of beauty, on the human scale and in human terms, may develop in a child.

Ⓒ To a child living in it, the experience of the presence of a house is permanent and inclusive.

Ⓓ But the experience of music or poetry is brief and occasional.

42 **Choose the best answer for Ⓐ.** 2.7점

① disillusioned with   ② incompatible with   ③ detached from

④ fraught with   ⑤ entangled with

43 **Choose the best answer for Ⓑ.** 1.3점

① temporarily   ② carefully   ③ hazardously

④ arbitrarily   ⑤ indolently

44 **Put the sentences above into a logical order.** 3점

① A — C — D — B

② B — A — D — C

③ B — D — C — A

④ C — B — D — A

⑤ B — A — C — D

[45-47] Read the passage and answer the questions.

In 1828, Nikolai Gogol set off for St. Petersburg, the capital of Czarist Russia. Failing at first to find employment there, he <u>embezzled</u> his mother's mortgage payment to finance a trip to Germany. Afterwards, he obtained a bureaucratic position, which he soon left. In 1836, he published a comic play satirizing the Russian bureaucracy, which caused such a scandal that he left Russia to live in Rome for six years. In Italy he wrote his most famous novel, *Dead Souls*. He also became increasingly religious with his piety turning morbid. Obsessed with his own sinfulness, he burnt his manuscripts and starved himself. Gogol is the _____ figure of modern Russian fiction, who proved immensely influential on later writers. Discarding the conventions of eighteenth-century literature, he presented a bleakly comic vision of everyday life. Critics often credit his stories for introducing the antihero in modern literature — a type of protagonist utterly lacking in heroic qualities like courage, strength or idealism.

45 **Which is closest in meaning to the underlined word, 'embezzled'?** 1.3점

① repaid   ② swapped   ③ compensated

④ accumulated   ⑤ misappropriated

46 **Choose the best answer for the blank.** 2.7점

① seminal   ② elusive   ③ eccentric

④ repulsive   ⑤ affected

47 **Which is NOT true about Gogol?** 3점

① He lived in exile abroad.

② He became a religious fanatic.

③ He depicted ordinary people with their foibles.

④ He departed from eighteenth-century literature.

⑤ He made an enduring career with a bureaucratic job.

[48-50] Read the passage and answer the questions.

In Poland, an unexpected surge of voters has <u>ousted</u> a populist coalition government in favor of a pro-E.U. party, which won the most parliamentary seats. Once in place, the new government will work on making the changes its leaders have promised, and the E.U. has called for. In particular, it will move to restore the political independence of the judiciary and media _____ E.U. rules. These reforms, in turn, will help Poland access as much as possible of the €35 billion that Poland can claim as the funds which the E.U. set aside for member states to help with pandemic recovery. The E.U. withheld that money from the previous government in response to its bid to bring judges and journalists under government control. For the past several years, a populist government in Warsaw has boosted its popularity by demonizing the union, its rules on democracy, and its social policy. It has turned state-media outlets into a tool of government propaganda and stacked the country's courts with political cronies.

48 **Choose the best answer for the blank.** 2.7점

① at odds with   ② on account of   ③ in want of

④ in line with   ⑤ in lieu of

49 **Which is closest in meaning to the underlined word, 'ousted'?** 1.3점

① ushered   ② triggered   ③ incited

④ enticed   ⑤ expelled

50 **Which is NOT true regarding Poland?** 3점

① The voters have brought about a political shift.

② The new government will go against the E.U. rules on democracy.

③ A source of division between Poland and the E.U. is now on its way out.

④ The previous populist government has exploited state media for self-serving aims.

⑤ The E.U. has strategically withheld the funds for Poland to pressure Poland's government for change.

KOREA
UNIVERSITY

고려대학교 세종   2024학년도 인문·자연계
▶▶ 40문항·60분

[01-04] Choose the one that is grammatically <u>incorrect</u>. 각 1.5점

01 A single ant or bee ①<u>are</u> not smart, ②<u>but</u> ant and bee colonies are. The reason, as writer Peter Miller ③<u>discovers</u>, is something ④<u>called swarm</u> intelligence.

02 The human digestive system is a complex mechanism, ①<u>which</u> allows us to transform food into nutrients ②<u>that</u> are used throughout the body. It requires the coordination of various organs in the body, each ③<u>of which</u> plays a part in breaking down food into fuel. It begins in the mouth, ④<u>which</u> saliva starts the process of digestion.

03 In recent years, the industrialized world has ①<u>found itself</u> in the grips of an energy crisis. The fact that limited supplies of fossil fuel are being depleted ②<u>becomes</u> more evident with each passing day. ③<u>Given</u> the current global rate of consumption, in a short time, there will not be enough fuel to supply the growing demand. A temporary solution to this problem involves drilling for oil in areas that are currently protected as wildlife preserves for ④<u>its</u> pristine wilderness.

04 The boy wanted to do something to help the people of Central America who were less fortunate than ①he. There was a little girl ②in a blue dress who sold flowers with her blind grandmother. The girl was only about six years old, and she seemed frail, even though she always smiled. He bought flowers from them often, and brought the flowers ③home to give to his mother and sisters. He was most aware of the poverty ④when he and his parents would go out to eat in restaurants.

[05-08] Choose the one that is grammatically correct for each blank. 각 1.5점

05 One effect of climate change is that some areas of the Earth are getting warmer. As temperature averages _____, there will be an increase in extreme weather and natural disasters.

① continue to be risen
② continue being risen
③ continue to rise
④ continue being rising

06 As we acknowledge the basic truth that every one of us lives by causing some harm, we can consciously amend our behavior to reduce the amount of practical damage we might do, without _____ needless feelings of guilt.

① being drawing into
② being drawn into
③ having drawn into
④ having drawing into

07 "Multi-tasking" strategies are not as effective _____. It takes anywhere from fifteen minutes to an hour to get one's mind around a difficult problem, and to establish the conditions to develop a worthwhile solution. If one switches too soon and too often from one task to the next, it is likely that what the mind will come up with is going to be superficial, if not trivial.

① as widely believed
② as widely believing
③ as are widely believing
④ as having widely believed

08 Gore lost the 2000 election by just five electoral votes. He demanded a hand recount of ballots from Florida. However, when the case went to the U.S. Supreme Court, the justices declared that the manner _____ in violation of the United States Constitution.

① where the recount has been conducted were

② in which the recount was conducting has been

③ in which the recount was being conducted was

④ where the recount was being conducted have been

[09-13] Choose the one that is closest in meaning to the underlined word. 각 1.5점

09 The role of a cybersecurity expert is to <u>ensure</u> the safety and privacy of personal information collected by institutions such as universities and banks.

① sustain   ② process

③ respect   ④ guarantee

10 The conference allowed attendees to <u>collaboratively</u> engage with industry leaders from around the world, effectively expanding their knowledge and networks.

① interactively   ② ethically

③ directly   ④ presumably

11 The champions' dedication and skill on the field were <u>unequaled</u>, earning them the admiration and respect of all who witnessed their unmatched prowess.

① aggressive   ② unfair

③ excessive   ④ incomparable

12 Many people believe there are differences in the way that males and females use language. Is it true that men are more <u>confident</u> than women and communicate more directly?

① extroverted   ② talkative

③ assured   ④ objective

13 Bed bugs feed on human blood and live inside bedding. They generally spread in luggage and can survive for several months without feeding. They can also lay eggs inside luggage or furniture. These eggs — which can lay <u>dormant</u> for several years — will then hatch when they are moved to a new location.

① insolent   ② invisible
③ inactive   ④ insistent

[14-20] Choose the most appropriate one for each blank.

14 Researchers studying animals in extremely cold environments discovered that tiny snailfish are full of antifreeze proteins, a special type of protein that _____ their bodies from freezing in icy waters. 2점

① strengthens   ② helps
③ prevents   ④ distracts

15 The majority of people in Korea are literate. As most are able to read newspapers and magazines, they generally have opinions on important matters. In addition, they are quite _____ and therefore able to state their ideas clearly to their superiors. 2점

① figurative   ② articulate
③ submissive   ④ obscure

16 When the girl moved to the city she frequently got _____ if she went out alone. She could never remember which direction she had come from; she was unable to _____ herself to her new surroundings. 2.5점

① secured — satisfy
② exhausted — locate
③ isolated — detect
④ lost — orient

17 Despite being a best-selling writer, Georgette Heyer continuously _____ to engage in any form of publicity for her publications after the success of her novel *These Old Shades*. She believed that her private life was _____ to the success of her novels. As a result, her fans didn't even learn of her married name until after her death. 2.5점

① refused — irrelevant

② consented — inappropriate

③ abhorred — agreeable

④ attempted — favorable

18 While there has been some evidence that nostalgia is associated with mental health _____, it is important to remember that there are different types of nostalgia and that some can be highly destructive. A recent study found that conscious acts of extreme nostalgia have positive effects, while smaller and momentary, more unconscious nostalgic experiences can result in _____ mental health effects, such as anxiety and fear. 2.5점

① problems — terrible

② benefits — negative

③ risks — critical

④ cares — significant

19 What is considered an unnecessary bother in the U.S., or too much of a fuss, is considered fundamental in Japan. Owners of American shops might find giving personal attention to customers to be beneath them. But this is not considered _____ in Japan. On the contrary, personal attention is considered one of the necessary ingredients for business success. 3점

① decent   ② demanding

③ decorative   ④ demeaning

20 Hula dancing has been an important Hawaiian tradition for hundreds of years. Fairly _____, hula dances originally honored gods and chiefs and were used to pass down stories that explained all manners of natural phenomena. To recognize the full significance of hula dancing, audience members must have a strong familiarity with the history and stories behind it. Therefore, those with extensive knowledge of hula dancing generally prefer hula to other forms of artistic expression. 3점

① enchanting and amusing
② spiritual and meaningful
③ exquisite and fascinating
④ sacred and passionate

21 Which of the underlined words is <u>not</u> appropriate for the context? 3점

In 1829, the statesman Sir Robert Peel established London's first organized, citywide police force. Peel's police force was based on successful military units with civil-policing duties. And Peel introduced several concepts that are ①<u>central</u> to modern policing. These "Peelian Principles" essentially established the standard of "serve and ②<u>enslave</u>." Peel believed a police force should maintain law and order, but in service of the public and with their consent and cooperation. The use of force was a last resort, and Peel expected his men to earn respect through ③<u>devotion</u> to duty and proper conduct. And although much has changed in policing, the basic call to protect citizens rather than ④<u>control</u> them remains central to the mission of the department to this day.

22 **Which of the following is true about dogs and cats?** 3점

How many differences between dogs and cats can you spot? In fact, the differences between dogs and cats may not be as easy to spot as you think. During the day, your dog is active and playful. While it may take an occasional nap, it prefers being at your side. A cat, on the other hand, sleeps away much of the daylight hours, preferring to jump into turbo time right before you jump into bed. Cats are more playful in the evenings, but there are many cats who make time for their pet parents during the day. A routine helps get your cat more on your schedule.

One major difference between dogs and cats is the way they sound. Your dog will bark, howl, or growl, whereas a cat meows or snarls. When giving warning signals, cats will often arch their back and the hair on their back may stand up. Dogs will show warning by baring their teeth and staring. Both animals will usually make sounds, such as growling or snarling, when warning another animal or human to keep their distance.

Behavior is tough to compare too closely, because, like humans, dog and cat behavior and personality can vary greatly. Some cats are extroverts while some dogs are introverts. Species and breed only determine behavior so much. The rest is left to their individual personality and the environmental factors that they are raised in every day.

① Dogs and cats have similar activity patterns during the day.
② Routine is needed more for dogs than it is for cats.
③ Dogs and cats have different ways of expressing warning.
④ Behaviors and personalities of dogs are more diverse than those of cats.

23 **Which of the following is true about the red berry described in the passage?** 3점

A new fad has been making its way around trendy circles in New York in recent years — parties in which the star attraction is a small red berry called the "miracle fruit." The berries, which are as safe as any common fruit, are native to West Africa. A European explorer discovered the berries in 1725, but they are hard to grow in other climates. In the 1970s, people hoped that the berry could be the source of a sugar substitute. But in 1974, the U.S. Food and Drug Administration (FDA) declared that the berry's active chemical substance, a protein called miraculin, was a food additive. Food additives, unlike fruits, are heavily regulated. This meant that getting the berry to market in the form of a sugar substitute would be a long, costly process.

To attend the miracle fruit parties, guests pay the average cost of a meal. As they arrive, the host hands each one a miracle fruit, which they are instructed to chew and roll around on their tongue for two minutes. The berry has a mild, bland taste, but after only a few moments, it has worked its miracle.

With their tongues well coated, the guests are turned loose on a buffet of specially chosen finger foods. Now, the exclamations of surprise and delight begin. What is all the fuss about? Miraculin binds to the taste buds and blocks a person's ability to taste sour flavors. The result is a topsy-turvy food experience in which sour things taste sweet and sweet things taste even sweeter. Lemons, for example, taste like lemon drops. Hot sauce tastes like spicy sugar syrup. Goat cheese tastes like cheesecake.

① Its chemical substance is modified when combined with other foods.
② Its chemical substance causes it to influence the way that certain foods taste.
③ Its sugary and appetizing taste motivates people to enjoy some foods at a party.
④ Its potential for sugar addiction caused it to be regulated as a food additive.

24 **Which of the following is <u>not</u> a role or a function of the water in the Red River Gorge?** 4점

The critical fact about water, wherever you find it in the Red River Gorge, is motion. Moving, it is gathering. All the little seeps and trickles of the slopes, the tiny streams heading up near the ridgetops and leaping and tumbling down the steep ravines — all are moving toward their union in the river. And in the movement of its waters the place also is in motion; not to the human eye, nor to the collective vision of human history, but within the long gaze of geologic time the Gorge is moving within itself, deepening, changing the outline of its slopes; the river is growing into it like a great tree, steadily incising its branches into the land. For however gentle it may appear in certain seasons, this network of water known in sum as the Red River moves in its rocky notches as abrasive as a file.

How the river works as maker of the landscape, arm of creation will always remain to some degree unknown, for it works with immeasurable leisure and patience, and often it works in turmoil. Although its processes may be hypothesized very convincingly, every vantage point of the country is also a point of speculation, a point of departure from the present surface into the shadowy questions of origin and of process.

① a fertilizing force that causes nearby trees and plants to grow in abundance
② a unifying force that converges various forms of water into the Red River
③ an agent for meditation that leads one to ponder over its origin and process
④ a change agent that steadily transforms water and its surroundings

25 Which of the following is <u>not</u> a reason for honey being used for medicinal remedies or skin products? 3점

Honey is the only food product that humans eat that is made by an insect. In addition, even with all our technical abilities — sending humans into space, designing computers, and creating 3-D printers — no one has figured out how to make artificial honey. There's really no substitute for what bees have always known how to do.

In addition to its many uses as a sweetener, honey has been used for centuries as a medicinal remedy. Because it's very difficult for any kind of bacteria to survive in honey, it makes for a perfect barrier on cuts and can prevent infection. Honey is also an effective remedy to soothe a sore throat. It has even been found to be as effective in suppressing coughs in children as an over-the-counter cough suppressant.

Another use for this remarkable natural substance is in skin and hair products. People have long known that honey is a humectant, which means that it attracts and retains moisture, in addition to being antimicrobial. This makes it a perfect ingredient in lotions, soaps, lip balms, and shampoos. You can purchase many personal products containing honey, or you can try your hand at making your own.

① its ability to absorb and hold moisture
② its potential for infection prevention
③ its non-artificial production process
④ its capacity for preventing bacteria growth

26 Which of the following is the author's intention for quoting the underlined sentence? 3점

Many people say Shakespeare's writing is old, boring, and difficult to read. However, that is simply not true. Even though Shakespeare wrote during the 1500s and 1600s, his themes are still relevant today, and his writing is actually easy to understand if you take the time to break it down.

Shakespeare wrote many plays and poems that had excitement, suspense, comedy, romance, and human drama. Shakespeare's writing also shows that people faced the same challenges and emotions in the Renaissance era as they do today. For example, he wrote about a young man who had to prove to his father that he was responsible.

Shakespeare's language is not too difficult to figure out if you have patience and focus on the words as metaphors. For example, think about this quote: "Let every eye negotiate for itself" (from *Much Ado About Nothing*). You know what all of those words mean individually, but you may not understand what they mean together. That is because he sometimes used words in a nonliteral way. Basically, Shakespeare is saying "Let each person decide for himself or herself." He is saying that everyone should be able to make his or her own choices or judgments. This message is as relevant today as it was when it was written long ago. Whether you like comedy or tragedy, action or romance, you may find that you can relate to Shakespeare's stories more than you think.

① to indicate that the underlying ideas in Shakespeare's works can resonate with present-day readers
② to prove that the language used in Shakespeare's writing is not outdated and conventional
③ to demonstrate that the nonliteral style of Shakespeare's writing can limit readers' comprehension
④ to show that various meanings are implied and alluded to in the expressions of Shakespeare's works

27 **Which of the following is <u>not</u> an adverse effect of taking aspirin?** 3점

Everyone has suffered from a cold at one time or another. While we wait for a cold cure to be developed, most people simply end up taking some form of over-the-counter medication. The scary thing is that some of the medicines taken to treat cold symptoms may actually be counterproductive. For example, aspirin appears to be the perfect drug to take to fight headaches and throat inflammation, but the truth is that it can actually have adverse effects on us.

Some researchers believe that using aspirin to treat colds can increase the amount of virus you shed through nasal secretions. This means you could potentially infect a lot more people with the virus when you blow your nose near them. Another problem is that aspirin may suppress some of our immune responses and cause our noses to become even stuffier.

Some studies have also linked aspirin to the development of a condition called Reye's syndrome when used to treat children between the ages of three and twelve. It often affects the brain or liver, causing major organ damage and, in very severe cases, death. Doctors, therefore, recommend that aspirin not be given to anyone under nineteen who is suffering from a viral illness, including the common cold.

Colds themselves may not harm us permanently, but the way we treat cold symptoms could. That means you should avoid aspirin if you are under nineteen, and if you are unsure about any other medication, you should consult a doctor.

① Aspirin may do serious harm to some internal body parts of young children.
② Aspirin may cause more virus from the nose to spread when blowing one's nose.
③ Aspirin may intensify the stuffed-up feeling inside one's nose.
④ Aspirin may abruptly increase the extent to which one's nose is running.

28   **Which of the following is true about the fungus called _yartsa gunbu_?** 3점

High on a plateau near the Himalayas, 15,000 feet above sea level, Silang Yangpi and his wife, Yangjin Namo, crawl along steep mountain slopes, searching for a tiny fungus that is believed to have incredible healing powers. They are looking for a thin brown stalk that grows a few inches out of the soil. This stalk is attached to the head of a bright yellow caterpillar. For some, the caterpillar fungus looks like an odd mushroom, but for Silang and Yangjin, it represents a significant portion of their annual income. Caterpillar fungi have transformed the rural economy, leading to a modern-day gold rush.

The fungus is called _yartsa gunbu_. This means "summer grass, winter worm," although it is technically neither grass nor worm. It is formed when certain caterpillars are infected by a parasitic fungus called _Ophiocordyceps sinensis_. The fungus eats the inside of the caterpillar, killing the creature, but leaving its exterior intact. In spring, the fungus blooms in the form of a brown stalk that erupts from the caterpillar's head. Though the process occurs underground, as the fungus flowers, it pushes its way out of the ground. This happens only in the fertile meadows high up in the Himalayan mountains. Although people have tried to farm the fungus, all attempts to do so have failed.

① It is not difficult for people to grow _yartsa gunbu_ in rural areas.
② _Yartsa gunbu_ has led a rural area to undergo a change in its economy.
③ _Yartsa gunbu_ is formed after some caterpillars eat a particular fungus.
④ The blooming process of _yartsa gunbu_ happens only outside the soil.

Which of the following is the most appropriate for the blank? 3점

As the sun heats the humid air in Accra — the capital city of Ghana — a terrible-smelling black smoke begins to rise above the Agbogbloshie Market. Past the vegetable merchants is a scrap market filled with piles of old and broken electronics equipment. This scrap — consisting of broken TVs, computers, and monitors — is known as "e-waste." Further beyond the scrap market are many small fires. Fueled by old car tires, they are burning away the plastic covering from valuable wire in the e-waste. People walk through the poisonous smoke with their arms full of brightly colored computer wire. Many of them are children.

E-waste is being produced on a scale never seen before. Computers, cell phones, and other electronic equipment become obsolete in just a few years, leaving consumers with little choice but to buy newer models to keep up. Each person in the world discards, on average, over six kilograms of e-waste every year.

Sadly, in most of the world, the bulk of all this waste ends up in landfills. There it poisons the environment: e-waste contains a variety of substances that are toxic, such as lead, mercury, and arsenic. Recycling is, in many ways, the ideal solution to the problem: e-waste contains significant amounts of valuable metals such as silver, gold, and copper. In theory, recycling gold from old computers is far more efficient — and less environmentally destructive — than digging it up from the earth. The problem is that a large percentage of e-waste dropped off for recycling in wealthy countries is diverted to the developing world — to countries like Ghana. As the quantity of e-waste increases worldwide, _____.

① it leads people living in the developing world to have a positive attitude toward e-waste
② it provides people living in the developing world with business opportunities to make them rich
③ it poses an increasing threat to the health of people living in the developing world
④ it causes people living in the developing world to collect more valuable metals from e-waste

30 **Which of the following is the purpose of the passage?** 3점

Water is one of our most valuable resources, but like many natural resources, it is becoming scarce. The World Health Organization reports that globally three out of ten people do not have access to safe, clean water at home and 2.7 billion people find water scarce for at least one month a year. Water scarcity is caused by various issues, including drought, pollution, overuse, and sometimes from conflicts such as war and dictatorial governments. Many of us who don't face water shortages often take this resource for granted; we do not understand or appreciate the vast amount of water we use and depend on daily.

Some innovative ideas are being implemented worldwide to deal with water scarcity. One solution being carried out in rural India is to use solar power to make dirty water clean. Solar-powered pumps filter undrinkable water and make it useable. However, this solution is complex and costly, and villagers must buy the clean water in order to pay for the cost of the solar power technology. Another solution is the use of Fog Catchers. Fog Catchers are large nets or screens that are set up across a mountainside; they catch the morning fog which then drips into collection trays. In contrast to the previous solution, the water is free, but it is limited in quantity and would not supply enough water for a larger village or for irrigation. Finally, and unlike any other solution, some scientists in Belgium have created a solar-powered machine that turns urine into drinkable water!

While all of these solutions are promising and address the problem, they may not produce enough water to make them viable. In addition, their implementation would require massive amounts of money and resources. Therefore, the most sustainable and practical solutions are the ones that call for changes that we can make on a daily basis. These include taking shorter showers, turning off the water while washing your hands and brushing your teeth, and reusing your pasta or rice water for watering plants. Educating ourselves and the people around us about water usage and practicing ways we can conserve water in our communities are essential steps.

① to address the water scarcity problem and propose solutions that the author believes are the best

② to analyze the water scarcity problem and explore the critical causes that result in the problem

③ to discuss advantages and disadvantages of various solutions to the water scarcity problem

④ to describe the water scarcity problem and explain how its potential solutions work

[31-32] **Read the following passage and answer the questions.** 각 4점

Often our children don't appreciate the sacrifices we make, and that can really hurt us. This isn't because they're insensitive. They are, in fact, very sensitive. They can discern the underlying motives behind our generosity — motives that are so unconscious that they often escape our immediate awareness.

When we give and give until we're exhausted, usually it's because we feel that this is the only way others will accept us or maintain a relationship with us. We may fear that if we stop giving, our children will stop loving us, seeing us just for what we can give, rather than seeing us for who we truly are. We believe this because we have such little trust in our own value — in our own selves.

On the deepest level, we fear we're lacking in some aspects of being a good parent. Without our grandiose gestures of self-sacrifice, we are afraid that our children, our spouse, our neighbors, and even our own parents, might see through us to only our flaws or what we lack. So, we aren't giving our children what they need, rather we are giving them what will shield them from seeing, we believe, our deficiencies. Thus, we center our lives around our children, tolerate abuse, and keep giving.

31 Which of the following is the author's perspective on parents' grandiose gestures of self-sacrifice?

① Parents' self-sacrifices are essential qualities for good parenting.
② Parents' continual acts of giving cover up their true love for their children.
③ Parents' self-sacrifices can nurture a loving parent-child relationship.
④ Parents' self-sacrifices are driven by the need to hide their own insufficiencies.

32 Which of the following is the topic of the passage?

① The sensitivity of children towards parental sacrifices
② The necessity of self-sacrifice in relationships
③ The fear-driven dynamics of parental sacrifices
④ The pursuit of self-identity through sacrificial acts

[33-34] Read the following passage and answer the questions. 각 3점

Planning to work in the same field or industry for your entire working life just is not practical anymore. One reason for this is technology. Skills you learn today will be obsolete very soon. And then what will you do? Work hard? Win the lottery? Hope for the best or pray? You might get lucky. These strategies might bring you a nice, comfy life, working at a job you like and retiring while you are still young and healthy enough to enjoy it. But most of us working today have to look beyond the little box of "career."

If you think you can work eight hours a day and build a career, think again. If you think you can't be replaced by artificial intelligence or have your job outsourced, you are wrong. An employer can always replace you or find someone who can do your job more cheaply. One way to protect yourself is to take what you do at the office and do it on your own as a freelancer for a limited time without a contract. You may even find that you make more money as a freelancer and are able to quit your full-time job.

Another strategy is to find something to do besides what you are doing and keep finding a smarter way to do it. That could be turning a hobby into a small business or using your skills to create products and services that you can sell. In other words, think like an <u>entrepreneur</u>. Find someone who is willing to help you make your idea a reality. You will need money, organization, workers, and a lot of energy. You will need to be a risk taker, an innovator, a problem solver, and a hard worker. Being an <u>entrepreneur</u> is not an 8-hour-a-day job; it is a 24-hour-a-day job. And when things go well, you have your rewards.

33 **Which of the following is the reason that the author introduced the underlined word?**

① to urge readers to take a business idea and turn it into reality

② to urge readers to learn about business through trial and error

③ to urge readers to run different businesses simultaneously

④ to urge readers to gather important information about business

34 Which of the following is the author's intention?

① to encourage readers to think of new ways to earn a living in today's fast-changing workplaces

② to explain how artificial intelligence or other workers may replace you at some point in your career

③ to give readers advice on what they should do after losing their full-time jobs

④ to give readers instructions on how to find a secure job that may allow them to earn more money

[35-36] Read the following passage and answer the questions. 각 3점

In *How Smart Are Animals?*, author Gita Simonsen discusses the problems scientists face in assessing animal intelligence. The first problem is defining animal intelligence. Too often, our tests of animal intelligence are based on how well animals can imitate human behavior. This method does not recognize other elements of intelligence that animals use in their own lives that humans may not possess.

Another method that scientists use with mammals is brain weight as a proportion of total weight. This measurement finds dolphins high in intelligence. However, since human intelligence is linked to language, and we can't communicate with dolphins, or other animals, it is not possible to fully assess their intelligence.

A further problem of animal intelligence testing, especially when comparing intelligence across species, is the assumption that humans must be smarter than any other animal. In a study where bees outperformed human babies, scientists reassessed the test itself. They concluded that the test must have been flawed and that the bees came out on top because of instinct, not intelligence.

A new method of assessment involves studying animals' neural networks and trying to figure out what traits they are designed to allow. This helps scientists to identify traits they had not even thought about. Nevertheless, the tiny size of some animal brains makes this method very challenging.

Simonsen concludes by quoting Gro Amdam, a professor at Arizona State University, who states, "Scientists need to develop better tools, methods, and theories for comparing the brain skills in different species, but <u>we are well on our way</u>."

35 **Which of the following best describes the meaning of the underlined sentence?**

① We are concentrating our efforts on the search for better ways to test animal intelligence.

② We are comparing the existing methods of testing animal intelligence and selecting better ones.

③ We are trying to get rid of the problems with existing methods of testing animal intelligence.

④ We are making good progress in developing more appropriate ways to assess animal intelligence.

36 **Which of the following is <u>not</u> mentioned in the passage as a problem of testing animal intelligence?**

① The definition of animal intelligence has been set up based on elements of human intelligence.

② The testing is designed in a way that makes it easier to elicit more intelligent behaviors from animals.

③ It is impossible for humans to communicate with animals by using language.

④ Some animals have such small brains that it is difficult to examine the animals' neural system.

[37-38] Read the following passage and answer the questions. 각 3점

The great advance in rocket theory 60 years ago showed that liquid-fuel rockets were far superior in every respect to the skyrocket with its weak solid fuel, the only kind of rocket then known. However, in the 1960s, large solid-fuel rockets with solid fuels about as powerful as liquid fuels made their appearance, and it is a favorite layperson's question to inquire as to which one is better. The question is meaningless; one might as well ask whether a gasoline or a diesel engine is better. It all depends on the purpose.

A liquid-fuel rocket is complicated, but has the advantage that it can be controlled beautifully. The burning of the rocket engine can be stopped completely or it can be reignited when desired. In addition, the thrust can be made to vary by adjusting the speed of the fuel pumps. A solid-fuel rocket, on the other hand, is rather simple in construction, though hard to build when a really large size is desired.

But once you have a solid-fuel rocket, it is ready for action on very short notice. A liquid-fuel rocket has to be fueled. However, once a solid-fuel rocket has been ignited, it will keep burning. It cannot be stopped and reignited whenever desired (it could conceivably be stopped and reignited after a precalculated time of burning has elapsed) and its thrust cannot be varied. Because a solid-fuel rocket can be kept ready for a long time, most military missiles employ solid fuels, but human-piloted spaceflight needs the fine adjustments that can only be provided by liquid fuel. It may be added that a liquid-fuel rocket is an expensive device; a large solid-fuel rocket is, by comparison, cheap. But the solid fuel, pound for pound, costs about 10 times as much as the liquid fuel. So you have, on the one hand, an expensive rocket with a cheap fuel, and on the other hand, a comparatively cheap rocket with an expensive fuel.

37 Which of the following is <u>not</u> a feature of a liquid-fuel rocket?

① It can be stopped or reignited as needed.

② Its fuel is cheaper than solid fuel.

③ It is rather complicated in construction.

④ It is cheap to build and maintain.

38 Which of the following can be inferred from the passage?

① The fundamental purpose of liquid-fuel rockets and solid-fuel rockets determines how they are built.

② After fueling, liquid-fuel rockets can be reignited soon, but solid-fuel rockets can be placed on standby for a long time.

③ Application fields of liquid-fuel rockets and solid-fuel rockets rely on the cost of construction and fuel.

④ The superiority of liquid-fuel rockets over solid-fuel rockets lies in their capability of orbiting heavy rockets.

Not all wildfires are started by humans. Lightning storms are a frequent cause. In addition, conditions, particularly in the American West, often create the perfect atmosphere for fires that burn out of control. Firefighters refer to the fire triangle, which are the three ingredients necessary for a wildfire: fuel, oxygen, and a heat source. Although wildfires occur all over the country, they are most common in the West. Frequent droughts and dry weather create brittle, dry trees, leaves, branches, and vegetation that go up quickly in flames. When forest fires get very large, the intense heat can even change local weather conditions — basically creating its own weather!

Firefighters have several ways of slowing and stopping the spread of a wildfire, although some fires take weeks to get under control. Spraying the fire and the surrounding vegetation with water and with flame retardants is one step. Another vital element is creating a fireline or firebreak, which deprives a fire of the fuel it needs to continue burning. A firebreak is created by clearing a strip of land of brush and vegetation, often with a tool called a pulaski. When the fire reaches the firebreak, the hope is that it will burn itself out for lack of fuel.

Firefighters also rely on the help of planes and helicopters. They can drop water or chemicals on the fire from above in an attempt to put out the blaze. The benefit of using airborne assistance is that it can cover relatively large distances in short periods of time. In addition, firefighters sometimes set <u>controlled burns</u>. They intentionally light fires to clear vegetation and again deprive a wildfire of its fuel.

Although wildfires are enormously destructive — to both natural and human-made habitats — they do serve some purposes in nature. A wildfire returns nutrients to the soil when decaying matter burns. A wildfire can remove layers of thick undergrowth that tend to block sunlight from reaching the forest floor. This allows new growth to receive the light it needs. In addition, fires rid the forest of plants that are diseased, as well as bugs that are harmful and destructive. The cost may not be worth the benefit, but like nearly everything in nature, wildfires have a job to do, too.

39 Which of the following is <u>not</u> mentioned in the passage?

① beneficial effects of wildfires on natural habitats

② some natural conditions for accelerating wildfires

③ effects of wildfires on the health of firefighters

④ attempts to block and impede the spread of wildfires

40 Which of the following is the main function of <u>controlled burns</u>?

① to create enough space to use airborne assistance

② to eliminate an ingredient that sustains wildfires

③ to restore the fertility of the forest floor by scorching it

④ to prevent in advance the fire's heat from becoming intense

KWANGWOON
UNIVERSITY

광운대학교

2024학년도 인문계 1교시 A형
▶▶ 40문항·60분

[01-02] 빈칸에 들어가기에 가장 적절한 것은? 각 1.9점

01 A: Are you saying I'm not qualified for the task?
B: _____

① No, I just wanted to say it's very challenging.
② Yes, you'll be okay this time.
③ No, wish me great luck.
④ Yes, just take it or leave it.
⑤ No, that's not a big deal.

02 Yuka fell and cut her leg really badly when she was hiking, but she's _____ now.

① on the run   ② up in arms   ③ on the mend
④ on the ropes   ⑤ under the weather

[03-10] 빈칸에 공통으로 들어가기에 가장 적절한 것은? 각 1.9점

03 He lay _____ with half-closed eyes.
The president has to operate within an _____ political system.

① intricate   ② improper   ③ insignificant
④ impertinent   ⑤ inert

04 When she hit a deer on a rural road, her _____ car insurance covered the extensive damage to her vehicle.

The professor provided a _____ overview of the course on the first day of class.

① compound   ② compatible   ③ comparable

④ comprehensive   ⑤ comprehensible

05 It would be the most _____ remark for those politicians.

The offer could not have come at a more _____ moment.

① amenable   ② opportune   ③ plenary

④ nebulous   ⑤ blatant

06 A rich _____ of humor runs through the book.

In a similar _____, the sequel mirrors the original movie's humor and charm.

① vein   ② way   ③ facet

④ dimension   ⑤ manner

07 He had broken the law _____, but still he had broken it.

We hope to rectify the mistakes made _____ in the past.

① unanimously   ② inexorably   ③ unwittingly

④ infallibly   ⑤ unfavorably

08 The engineer monitored the _____ to check the steam pressure in the pipes.

The teacher used the test results to _____ the students' understanding of the topic.

① gauge   ② judge   ③ screen

④ appraise   ⑤ benchmark

09 The job _____ a wide range of responsibilities.

This area of London _____ Piccadilly to the north and St. James's Park to the south.

① evacuates   ② confiscates   ③ insinuates

④ encompasses   ⑤ derails

10 Trust is a(n) _____ aspect of any strong relationship.

The user experience is _____ to the way libraries measure their performance.

① practical ② integral ③ plausible

④ appealing ⑤ functional

[11-14] 어법상 가장 적절한 것은? 각 1.9점

11 ① I wish you feel better soon.

② I insisted that he apologizes.

③ You ought to have not come.

④ What do you suggest we do?

⑤ Anne said me goodbye and left.

12 ① He is the man whose brother I went to school with.

② It rained a lot, what we hadn't expected.

③ We stayed at the hotel where you recommended.

④ He tried on three jackets, none of them fitted him.

⑤ Is there anything I can do it for you?

13 ① This was the place of which we first met.

② She's one of the kindest people who I know.

③ The valley in that town lies is heavily populated.

④ The check, across which Mike came in a field, was fake.

⑤ Whichever one of you broke the window must pay for it.

14 ① I've never done it and I will never.

② I won't probably see you again.

③ My friends are all eating out tonight.

④ We felt tired and also were hungry.

⑤ The weather was fairly perfect.

[15-21] 어법상 가장 적절하지 않은 것은? 각 2.3점

15 ① The company will cover any travel expenses.

② Prices are subject to be changed.

③ Let's reconsider before making a decision.

④ Please be invited to the opening night party.

⑤ It will be less expensive for us to send the order by ship.

16 ① I'm always going away in the beginning of January.

② There is a small shop on the corner of the street.

③ The players shook hands at the end of the game.

④ I will see you at the entrance to the building.

⑤ The hotel is on a small island in the middle of a lake.

17 ① I'll be making the trip to Lisbon alone.

② I was just beginning to wonder where you were.

③ The piece can also be played on piano.

④ We're so sorry we made a mistake with your order.

⑤ The trade conference will be held on February 10th.

18 ① I've lived here all my life.

② Has it stopped raining already?

③ He has never driven a car before.

④ Have you heard anything from Ben recently?

⑤ I haven't seen Tom since last year.

19 ① We have decided to change our policy on invoicing.

② She spoke French so that the children wouldn't understand.

③ It was the first time that I heard her sing.

④ Her husband was sitting in the front of the car.

⑤ He was reading a book about the moon.

20 ① I can't remember when I last felt so content with the world.

② You have to accept that Jane's gone and won't be coming back.

③ She can't bear it when people criticize her work, and she gets very upset.

④ We always enjoy when the whole family gathers for the barbecue.

⑤ He owed it to his mentor to complete the research they had started together.

21 ① There were a large number of candidates for the job.

② There might be drinks if you wait for a bit.

③ I'm ready to do anything but work on a farm.

④ Nobody will ever know what happened to him.

⑤ Travelers from other countries should contact its travel agents directly.

[22-24] 빈칸에 들어가기에 가장 적절한 것은? 각 2.3점

22 Compared with other fields, nutritional science is _____. That is partly because it is hard to do well. Randomized controlled trials, used to test drugs, are tricky. Few people want to stick to an experimental diet for years. Instead, most nutritional science is based on observational studies that try to establish associations between particular foods or nutrients and diseases. They cannot be used to definitively prove a causal connection between a disease and a particular contributing factor in a diet.

① overstated ② understudied ③ well-received

④ underfunded ⑤ undercharged

23 The story of NASA started a little more than half a century ago in a desolate region of what is now called Kazakhstan. Because it was from there that the Soviet Union launched Sputnik, the first artificial satellite, Americans were _____. The Soviets had taken the lead in a race for which we were not yet fully prepared.

① compensated ② envisaged ③ unconvinced

④ preoccupied ⑤ dumbfounded

24 Fine art, such as painting, sculpture, music and poetry, is categorized as something which only has a(n) _____ function. This point was made over a thousand years ago by the Greek philosopher Aristotle, who wrote: "The aim of art is to represent not the outward appearance of things but their inward significance." He noted that artists produced objects, drama and music which reflected their emotions and ideas, rather than just trying to capture a true image of nature.

① personal and social
② atheistic and theoretical
③ abstract but creative
④ aesthetic or conceptual
⑤ immaterial but objective

25 글의 제목으로 가장 적절한 것은? 2.9점

Korea's first domestically developed lunar orbiter successfully settled into the moon's orbit, enabling the country to step closer to its goal of becoming a global powerhouse in the space economy. The Korea Aerospace Research Institute (KARI) said Wednesday that the Danuri, also known as the Korea Pathfinder Lunar Orbiter, was stably captured by the moon's gravity a day earlier to rotate 100 kilometers above its surface every two hours. As a result, Korea became the seventh country in the world to explore the moon, following Russia, the U.S., Japan, the European Union, China and India.

① A Growing Need for Exploring the Space
② The Difficulty of Developing a Lunar Orbiter
③ Korea Becomes 7th Nation to Explore the Moon
④ Danuri's Epic Journey to the Moon
⑤ The Bright Side of Exploring the Moon

26 Anorexia nervosa, a condition in which patients continually seek to lower their body weight, is medically the most serious and least understood of all the eating disorders. Some anorexics attempt to control their body weights through a number of different strategies such as compulsive hyperactivity. _____, they would jog five hours per day, then come home, wash, and go on an exercycle for another hour to burn off all calories that they consumed. Other anorexics indulge in a significant degree of self-starvation. They intake as few calories as possible and become progressively desperate if they fail to keep their weight down.

① After all
② For example
③ In fact
④ On the other hand
⑤ In addition

27 John Paul Getty Jr., the U.S.-born benefactor, lavished Britain with his philanthropic gifts. He was knighted for giving away more than $200 million to many U.K. charities, including the National Gallery in London, the British Film Institute and to the families of striking coal miners. Getty even used his inheritance to purchase masterpieces for British museums so that the Getty Museum, established by his father, wouldn't be able to purchase them. In part, this was an act of _____ and a show of his deep love for the sanctuary Britain gave him.

① greed to collect as many works of art as possible
② brinkmanship that made him the world's richest man
③ consideration to preempt family arguments among his sons
④ violence as a means to resolve political crisis
⑤ defiance against his estranged relationship with his father

[28-31] 글의 내용과 가장 잘 부합하는 것은? 각 2.9점

The sun produces large amounts of visible light during the day. The problematic light is ultraviolet light. It contains more energy than visible light and it is this light that causes suntan, sunburn and even skin cancer. Recently the amount of ultraviolet light reaching the earth has increased, especially around the North and South Poles. In the past there was a thick ozone layer, but as man-made pollutants have reduced the layer, more and more ultraviolet light has been reaching the earth.

28
① Visible sunlight causes minor skin problems such as suntan and sunburn.
② Man-made pollutants are the only cause of thinning the ozone layer.
③ The amount of ultraviolet light we get has increased.
④ Both visible light and ultraviolet light are harmful.
⑤ The amount of ultraviolet light produced by the sun has increased.

Drones are also assisting emergency organizations after natural disasters. In 2015, for example, a powerful cyclone destroyed thousands of buildings in the Pacific island nation of Vanuatu. Around 75,000 people lost their homes, and at least 15 died. After the storm, drones photographed the damage. These surveys helped emergency workers assess the situation quickly and answer important questions: Which areas were hardest hit? Were crops damaged? What roads were affected? Emergency workers used the data to create a detailed map of the affected area. They were then able to transport aid to the people who needed it most.

29
① Drones helped to identify storm damage.
② Drones could deliver medical supplies after a disaster.
③ Drones could analyze weather conditions.
④ Emergency workers should be able to manipulate drones.
⑤ Emergency workers are knowledgeable about geology.

By the early 20th century, the movie studios kept the names of the actors and actresses anonymous to keep them from acquiring their own place in a competitive market. As the public's demand for motion pictures increased, however, so did the public's preference for certain actors and actresses. In order to combat fear that public recognition would result in a demand by the stars for higher salaries, producers went to great lengths to keep the identity of the actors anonymous by various different means, including demanding the use of pseudonyms.

30　① Most movie stars did not earn much money in the early 20th century.

② Producers promoted the real name of their actors to advertise their films.

③ Movie stars were not willing to use different names.

④ The actors' names were kept unknown for the film makers' benefit.

⑤ The public preferred film stars who used pseudonyms.

When I returned with the rum, they were already seated on either side of the captain's breakfast-table — Black Dog next to the door and sitting sideways so as to have one eye on his old shipmate and one, as I thought, on his retreat. He bade me go and leave the door wide open. "None of your keyholes for me, sonny," he said; and I left them together and retired into the bar. For a long time, though I certainly did my best to listen, I could hear nothing but a low gattling; but at last the voices began to grow higher, and I could pick up a word or two, mostly oaths, from the captain.

31　① The speaker was ready to get away at any time.

② Black Dog used to be subordinate to the captain.

③ The speaker was not anxious to understand what the two seamen said.

④ The captain and his old shipmate talked quietly so as not to be overheard.

⑤ Black Dog wouldn't let the speaker eavesdrop on his conversation with the captain.

[32-40] 다음 글을 읽고 물음에 답하시오.

32-33

Many would argue that Bell and McBride's "all gasoline, no brakes, and no steering wheel" analogy is a gross oversimplification of teenage brain development. In fact, according to research conducted by Casey and Caudle (2013), adolescents are actually better able to regulate impulses than adults under certain circumstances. During a series of laboratory experiments, Somerville et al. (2011) showed test subjects the images of positive, negative, and neutral facial expressions and measured their ability to regulate their responses. When no emotional information was present (i.e., the facial expression was neutral), teenagers performed as well as adults, if not better. However, when emotional cues were present, either positive or negative, adolescents were far less able to suppress their response. This diminished ability was not observed in adults or children, who find it equally difficult to regulate control whether emotional cues are present or not. This seems to contradict the oversimplification that teenagers are generally unable to act rationally or make good decisions. While this may be true in heated or stressful situations, perhaps because they tend to rely on the amygdala — the part of the brain that guides instinct — rather than the prefrontal cortex, in neutral situations adolescents are actually better equipped to control impulses and make rational decisions than adults.

32 제목으로 가장 적절한 것은? 2.9점

① Questioning the Stereotype

② How to Make Sensible Decisions

③ Brain Development over Lifetime

④ Unstoppable Adolescent Impulsivity

⑤ Peak Performance and Rapid Decline

33 밑줄 친 Somerville et al. (2011)의 내용으로 가장 적절한 것은? 3.1점

① Feeling positive can help teens make better decisions.

② Teens are better at regulating their emotions than adults.

③ Teenagers lack the ability to navigate their actions and choices.

④ Stress can force teens into the use of the amygdala in their brains.

⑤ Children tend to lose their ability to make wise decisions in the neutral state.

I pulled the stick out and laid the fish in the grass beside the kid's bicycle. I took out the knife. "Right here?" I said. The kid nodded. I started cutting down into him. I came to his guts and turned him over and stripped everything out. I kept cutting until there was only a flap of skin on his belly holding him together. I took the halves and tore him in two.

I handed the kid the tail part.

"No," he said, shaking his head. "I want that half."

I said, "They're both the same! Now watch it, _____."

"I don't care," the boy said, "If they're both the same, I'll take that one. They're both the same, right?"

"They're both the same," I said. "But I think I'm keeping this half here. I did the cutting."

"I want it," the kid said. "I saw him first."

"Whose knife did we use?" I said.

"I don't want the tail," the kid said.

I looked around. There were no cars on the road and nobody else fishing. There was an airplane droning, and the sun was going down. I was cold all the way through. The kid was shivering hard, waiting.

"I got an idea," I said. I opened my creel and showed him a trout. "See? It's a green one. It's the only green one I ever saw. So whoever takes the head, the other guy gets the green trout and the tail part. Is that fair?"

"I guess so," he said. "Okay, I guess so. You take that half. I got more meat on mine."

"I don't care," I said.

---

34 빈칸에 들어가기에 가장 적절한 것은? 3.1점

① please be my guest

② you're as tired as I am

③ I'm not thinking about it

④ you should have helped me

⑤ I'm going to get mad in a minute

35 글의 내용과 가장 잘 부합하는 것은? 3.1점

① Two boys threaten each other with violent actions.

② Two boys find compromises to resolve a conflict over a desired object.

③ Two boys tease each other about sharing a single fish between them.

④ Two boys get into trouble in an attempt to steal other people's property.

⑤ Two boys eventually fail to reach an agreement.

36-37

During the last ten years, Dr. O'Keefe has conducted several studies focusing on running and its impact on health and longevity. His research involved analyzing data from about 5,000 European adults, aged between 20 and 92. The findings revealed that those who ran 1 to 2.4 hours weekly at a slow or moderate pace experienced the most significant decrease in mortality rates, even more so than runners who ran longer distances at higher speeds. This conclusion _____ other studies, like a 15-year research project involving over 55,000 Americans aged 18 to 100. This study found that running for just 5 to 10 minutes daily at less than six miles per hour substantially reduced the risk of death from all causes and extended life expectancy.

Dr. Duck-Chul Lee emphasizes the most notable health and longevity benefits of running are seen at lower levels of the activity. Even running less than a mile several times a week can significantly improve cardiovascular health and lifespan. The physiological advantages of running are partly due to *exerkines,* molecules released by various organ systems in response to exercise. Although research in this area is relatively new, studies have linked *exerkines* to decreased inflammation, new blood vessel formation, and cellular mitochondria regeneration, as explained by Dr. Lisa Chow. While more research is needed, short bursts of intense exercise, like brief runs, are known to activate some of these benefits related to *exerkines.*

Additionally, running has mental health benefits. A review of research on exercise and depression showed that adults engaging in 2.5 hours of moderate physical activity weekly had a 25% lower risk of depression than inactive individuals. Even those who exercised for half this recommended duration still had an 18% lower risk. Karmel Choi, a psychologist at Massachusetts General Hospital, notes that starting to run even once or twice a week can significantly enhance mental health compared to not exercising at all.

36 빈칸에 들어가기에 가장 적절한 것은? 3.1점

① aligns with   ② gives rise to   ③ calls for

④ deviates from   ⑤ questions

37 글을 읽고 유추할 수 있는 내용으로 가장 적절한 것은? 3.7점

① *Exerkines* are produced less at lower levels of an activity.

② Americans are likely to run more often than Europeans.

③ Intense exercise can exacerbate the symptoms of depression.

④ Intense running can damage internal organ systems.

⑤ Frequent running contributes to health improvement.

38-40

Genetic modification is not <u>novel</u>. Humans have been altering the genetic makeup of plants for millennia, keeping seeds from the best crops and planting them in following years, breeding and crossbreeding varieties to make them taste sweeter, grow bigger, last longer. In this way we've transformed the wild tomato, *Lycopersicon*, from a fruit the size of a marble to today's giant, juicy beefsteaks. From a weedy plant called teosinte with an "ear" barely an inch long has come our foot-long (0.3-meter-long) ears of sweet white and yellow corn.

However, the technique of genetic engineering is new, and quite different from conventional breeding. Traditional breeders cross related organisms whose genetic makeups are similar. In so doing, they _____. By contrast, today's genetic engineers can transfer just a few genes at a time between species that are distantly related or not related at all.

Genetic engineers can pull a desired gene from virtually any living organism and insert it into virtually any other organism. They can put a rat gene into lettuce to make a plant that produces vitamin C or splice genes from the cecropia moth into apple plants, offering protection from fire blight, a bacterial disease that damages apples and pears. The purpose is the same: to insert a gene or genes from a donor organism carrying a desired trait into an organism that does not have the trait.

38 밑줄 친 <u>novel</u>의 뜻으로 가장 적절한 것은? 3.7점

① difficult or impossible to define or explain
② not likely to offend or upset anyone
③ easily or clearly seen or understood
④ different from anything known before
⑤ that must be respected and not attacked or destroyed

39 빈칸에 들어가기에 가장 적절한 것은? 3.7점

① transfer none of the genes at all
② insert each gene one after another
③ transfer tens of thousands of genes
④ insert the target genes only
⑤ transfer previously altered genes

40 글의 내용과 부합하지 <u>않는</u> 것은? 3.7점

① Conventional breeding only allows crossbreeding between genetically similar organisms.
② Genetic engineering allows people to protect apple and pear trees from any kinds of diseases.
③ Conventional breeding allows people to grow plants that are larger or sweeter than their previous generations.
④ Genetic engineering allows people to alter the genetic makeup of an organism.
⑤ Conventional breeding allows people to combine various traits between species that are closely related.

KWANGWOON
UNIVERSITY

광운대학교

2024학년도 인문계 2교시 A형
▶▶ 40문항·60분

[01-02] 빈칸에 들어가기에 가장 적절한 것은? 각 1.9점

01 A: How are you feeling about the new job?

B: I'm a mix of excited and nervous. It's a whole new field for me.

A: It's always good to try new things. You'll _____ in no time and find your groove.

① go belly up

② face the music

③ bend the rules

④ get your feet wet

⑤ get a friendly fire

02 We might get time to visit the zoo while we're in New York, but we'll have to play it by _____.

① hand   ② nose   ③ eye

④ ear   ⑤ heart

03 Unable to _____ his excitement, he shared the news of his promotion with everyone he met.
The patients were in a _____d area of the hospital, designated for highly infectious diseases.

① confide   ② confine   ③ release
④ degrade   ⑤ reverse

04 She hoped to _____ at least some of her losses.
After an exhausting few weeks I needed some time to _____.

① recuperate   ② lacerate   ③ fraternize
④ surmise   ⑤ undermine

05 When she proposed a new marketing strategy, I immediately _____ed her idea.
She checked her exam results and found her name _____ to the last, just above her best friend's.

① clear   ② render   ③ adhere
④ second   ⑤ prompt

06 He struggled to understand the _____ concept presented in the advanced physics lecture.
The new policy significantly affected the status of _____s seeking permanent residency in the country.

① sage   ② expertise   ③ alien
④ migrant   ⑤ intent

07 The new restaurant _____ for a wide range of tastes.
The online platform _____ to freelance workers, providing them with tools to manage their projects efficiently.

① orients   ② diverges   ③ directs
④ charges   ⑤ caters

08   They secured a victory in the face of overwhelming _____.
He's always at _____ with his father over politics.

① times   ② ones   ③ losses
④ odds   ⑤ bottoms

09   You _____ my name on the list of winners.
She _____ on a trip to the seaside because she was ill.

① mixed up   ② moved on   ③ missed out
④ made out   ⑤ messed up

10   The cereal brand will lose some of its _____ colors by 2024.
He was the _____ intellectual, remarkably detached from the real world.

① impeccable   ② quintessential   ③ subsidiary
④ intoxicating   ⑤ provisional

[11-14] 어법상 가장 적절하지 않은 것은? 각 1.9점

11   ① We are pleased to announce our upcoming lecture.
② Her father was in hospital during the summer.
③ If you have any questions, feel free to ask me.
④ Each of the answers are worth three points.
⑤ The competition is open to both teams and individuals.

12   ① There was a smoking cigarette end in the ashtray.
② His proposal that the system should be fixed rejected.
③ His grandmother didn't have a very nice personality.
④ She's taking that medicine whether she likes it or not!
⑤ Everybody told me I must stop worrying.

13
① It is still too early to judge your proposal.
② You won't find smaller memory sticks than ours.
③ His charge was to obtain specific informations.
④ The conference was attended by hundreds of people.
⑤ Our dresses were the same except mine was red.

14
① Green apples often taste better than red.
② Make sure you insure your camera against loss or damage.
③ Banks actively encourage people to borrow money.
④ We have a team of eight working on product development.
⑤ The milk was so good that we couldn't stop drinking it.

[15-21] 어법상 가장 적절하지 않은 것은? 각 2.3점

15
① The damage is reported to be extensive.
② Very little got known about the woman.
③ We climbed over the wall without being seen.
④ The postcard might have been sent to the wrong address.
⑤ I've been offered the job, but I don't think I will accept it.

16
① The first design was much more to my taste.
② I'll be out of contact for a business trip abroad.
③ Her version of events were accepted without question.
④ Do you offer a variety of shipping options?
⑤ In Sweden it is against the law to hit a child.

17
① Since coming out of hospital, I have been to the gym every day.
② Before taking the back off the computer, make sure it is unplugged.
③ Before changing last year, the speed limit in the downtown area was 60km/h.
④ After leaving Oxford University in 1983, he spent a year teaching at a local school.
⑤ While welcoming the new policy, I think it should have been introduced a month ago.

18

① Luckily I was feeling in a good mood.

② There were a whole lot of people I didn't know.

③ Too much bureaucracy represses creativity and initiative.

④ She watched a quite interesting film last night.

⑤ We were questioned by the immigration officer.

19

① The teenagers envied him his lifestyle.

② Melanie dared her friend to try the spicy dish.

③ The judges awarded both finalists equal points.

④ You don't object to working late tonight, do you?

⑤ The police warned to stay inside with the windows closed.

20

① Photography of the plant is strictly forbidden.

② I would like to remind you all about the office dress code.

③ We have transferred the funds as requested.

④ The tension and excitement built gradually all day.

⑤ They had their hands tie behind their backs.

21

① All the furniture was destroyed in the fire.

② Displayed on the board was the exam results.

③ Neither of the Korean scholars has won this year.

④ Either the station or the cinema is a good place to meet.

⑤ Over the last few years there have been many changes.

[22-24] 빈칸에 들어가기에 가장 적절한 것은? 각 2.3점

22 Scientists believe overfishing, pollution and rising water temperatures due to climate change may be making the reefs more vulnerable to yellow-band disease. The disease's impact cannot be reversed, unlike the effects of coral bleaching. The loss of corals could have a devastating impact on the ecosystem — the reef is "like a forest, _____ massive amounts of life, and its death could eventually impact humans too," she added.

① dismantling ② attempting ③ investigating
④ sustaining ⑤ contaminating

23 New species are generally found rather than awakened. And they are typically discovered in remote places like rainforests or Antarctic plateaus. But not so a species of bacterium described in a paper just published in *Extremophiles*. As Russell Vreeland and Heng-Lin Chui, the paper's authors, point out, the bug is new to science. But it is not new to Earth. In fact, the microbe may have been _____ for millions of years before being awakened by an industrial disaster.

① squirming ② forged ③ simmering
④ encountered ⑤ slumbering

24 Dolphins are excellent _____ and are highly social, even clever. In one famous instance, a dolphin named Kelly managed to trick her trainers into giving her extra treats. She was rewarded each time she gave them a piece of trash she found in her enclosure. One day, she hid a paper bag under a rock, tearing off small pieces one at a time and getting a new reward for each piece.

① problem-solvers ② treasure hunters ③ mind-readers
④ peacemakers ⑤ freedom fighters

25 글의 제목으로 가장 적절한 것은? 2.9점

Korea's first domestically developed lunar orbiter successfully settled into the moon's orbit, enabling the country to step closer to its goal of becoming a global powerhouse in the space economy. The Korea Aerospace Research Institute (KARI) said Wednesday that the Danuri, also known as the Korea Pathfinder Lunar Orbiter, was stably captured by the moon's gravity a day earlier to rotate 100 kilometers above its surface every two hours. As a result, Korea became the seventh country in the world to explore the moon, following Russia, the U.S., Japan, the European Union, China and India.

① A Growing Need for Exploring the Space
② The Difficulty of Developing a Lunar Orbiter
③ Korea Becomes 7th Nation to Explore the Moon
④ Danuri's Epic Journey to the Moon
⑤ The Bright Side of Exploring the Moon

[26-27] 다음 글을 읽고 물음에 답하시오. 각 2.9점

Various studies have also found a correlation between intelligence and crime. Moffitt et al. found that men with a lower IQ went on to commit two or more crimes by the age of twenty. Denno (1994) also tested the intelligence of nearly 1,000 children at different points in their life and found a consistent negative correlation between IQ and criminal behavior. However, others, such as Menard and Morse have claimed that the association is too weak to be considered statistically significant. Yet regardless of the extent to which intelligence affects propensity toward criminal behavior, it does appear to be a factor, which raises another question — are we born intelligent, and by extension, _____? Researchers at the University of Queensland found that only up to a maximum of 40% of intelligence is inherited and the rest is determined by environmental factors.

26 빈칸에 들어가기에 가장 적절한 것은?

① law-abiding   ② circumstantial   ③ bad-tempered
④ ingenious   ⑤ thought-provoking

27 밑줄 친 <u>Denno (1994)</u>의 내용으로 가장 적절한 것은?

① Criminality is inherited.

② Criminal behavior is not related to intelligence.

③ The younger the child, the more crimes committed.

④ Those with low IQ were likely to commit more crimes.

⑤ Negative labels given to an individual encourage deviant behavior.

[28-31] 글의 내용과 가장 잘 부합하는 것은? 각 2.9점

A common misconception is that dyslexia is a disease. Another misconception is that a person with dyslexia is less intelligent. Both of these ideas are false. In fact, research shows no link between intelligence and dyslexia. Many people with dyslexia go on to achieve highly in their fields of choice. Having dyslexia means reading is hard for you, not that you're incapable or lazy. Finding techniques to help manage dyslexia is critical to successful learning and self-esteem.

28 ① Limited intelligence accounts for dyslexia.

② Individuals with dyslexia may read very slowly.

③ Dyslexia is a clinically recognized mental disorder.

④ A person with dyslexia tends to have high self-esteem.

⑤ Dyslexia helps people to adopt an easy-going approach to life.

About 3 percent of people in the world have food allergies, causing hives, nausea or, in rare cases, potentially fatal anaphylactic shock. Dozens of people die each year from eating peanuts. Soy allergies are prevalent in Asian countries, where soy is a staple. Genetically engineered crops are the result of the effort to reduce food allergies. Nonallergenic crops could be used for special products, like soy formula for babies allergic to soy. With nonallergenic crops, the overall level of allergens in the food supply may fall enough to limit the risks of accidental exposure.

29　① Genetic engineering is used to reduce food allergies.

　② Peanuts are the most common food to cause allergies.

　③ Most people are vulnerable to food allergies.

　④ Babies with allergies are fed with soy formula.

　⑤ Allergies are sometimes fatal to infants.

　　While eco-buildings may be good for the environment, there are practical problems with their affordability. They are often too costly to become a large-volume method of construction. As for their long-term efficiency, not much energy can be realistically generated by solar panels in places which do not have large amounts of sunlight, and not every location has access to a natural water source. To produce an affordable eco-building, compromises have to be made. The building will have to be smaller or made of less durable materials and with technology which uses more energy. These compromises can be easier to make for schools, where ideas about conservation are useful for education, or for businesses where ecologically aware features are a useful marketing tool.

30　① The amount of renewable energy tends to be limited.

　② Green buildings turned out to be detrimental to nature.

　③ Eco-buildings seem to value function more than beauty.

　④ Schools can afford the environmentally friendly buildings.

　⑤ Eco-buildings are more spacious than traditional buildings.

　　When I returned with the rum, they were already seated on either side of the captain's breakfast-table — Black Dog next to the door and sitting sideways so as to have one eye on his old shipmate and one, as I thought, on his retreat. He bade me go and leave the door wide open. "None of your keyholes for me, sonny," he said; and I left them together and retired into the bar. For a long time, though I certainly did my best to listen, I could hear nothing but a low gattling; but at last the voices began to grow higher, and I could pick up a word or two, mostly oaths, from the captain.

31 ① The speaker was ready to get away at any time.

② Black Dog used to be subordinate to the captain.

③ The speaker was not anxious to understand what the two seamen said.

④ The captain and his old shipmate talked quietly so as not to be overheard.

⑤ Black Dog wouldn't let the speaker eavesdrop on his conversation with the captain.

[32-40] 다음 글을 읽고 물음에 답하시오.

32-33

Democratic Gov. Kathy Hochul signed legislation on Saturday to legalize natural organic reduction, popularly known as human composting, making New York the sixth state in the nation to allow that method of burial. Washington state became the first state to legalize human composting in 2019, followed by Colorado and Oregon in 2021, and Vermont and California in 2022.

The process goes like this: the body of the deceased is placed into a reusable vessel along with plant material such as wood chips, alfalfa and straw. The organic mix creates the perfect habitat for naturally occurring microbes to do their work, quickly and efficiently breaking down the body in about a month's time.

The end result is a heaping cubic yard of nutrient-dense soil amendment, the equivalent of about 36 bags of soil, that can be used to plant trees or enrich conservation land, forests, or gardens. For urban areas such as New York City where land is limited, it can be seen as a pretty attractive burial alternative.

Michelle Menter, manager at Greensprings Natural Cemetery Preserve, a cemetery in central New York, said the facility would "strongly consider" the alternative method. "It definitely is more in line with what we do," she added.

32 제목으로 가장 적절한 것은? 2.9점

① The Advantages of Green Burial

② New York Allows Human Composting

③ Living in an Environmentally Conscious Way

④ How to Employ a New Method of Burial

⑤ The Six States Legalizing Natural Organic Reduction

33 글의 내용과 부합하지 <u>않는</u> 것은? 3.1점

① There aren't plenty more land for burial of the deceased in New York City.

② Both California and Oregon are the states where green burial is allowed.

③ It takes around a month for natural organic reduction to be accomplished.

④ The manager at Greensprings Natural Cemetery Preserve is willing to introduce human composting.

⑤ At the end of natural organic reduction, remains of the departed are shipped their home for the last time.

34-35

There are questions about how climate-friendly cultivated meat, or lab-grown meat, really is. A study published earlier this year reported that, in some circumstances, cultivated meat could be more polluting than the conventional stuff. Industry advocates have retorted that the assumptions made around the type of growth-solution used are inaccurate. They say that the study assumes the use of resource-intensive and medical-grade ingredients, which the industry is moving away from.

But even fans of cultivated meat acknowledge that the technology will use a lot of energy. Another study published in January found that per kilogram of meat produced, tank-grown meat is likely to use much more energy than farm-grown protein. This is largely because the bioreactor needs a lot of power to control its temperature. Ⓐ_____, cultivated meat will only cut the carbon footprint of the meat industry if renewable energy is used in the production process. And even then, according to the study, it will only do so for pork and beef.

Whether all this effort can make lab-grown meat attractive and cheap enough to appeal to consumers remains to be seen. Ⓑ_____, many companies have decided to pursue a hybrid strategy, mixing relatively cheap plant protein with their cultivated animal cells. Some firms add just a small amount of animal-fat cells to plant-based protein to improve the taste of, say, a sausage. For others, the proportion of cultivated meat will be much higher.

34 ⓐ와 ⓑ에 들어가기에 가장 적절한 쌍은? 3.1점

① As a result — In the mean time

② As such — At a stark contrast

③ However — On the grounds

④ On the other hand — For instance

⑤ For the time being — Notwithstanding

35 글의 내용과 가장 잘 부합하는 것은? 3.1점

① Cultivated meat has a higher protein content, providing more energy.

② The addition of animal-fat cells applies only to the pork and beef flavors.

③ A number of companies are trying to avoid expensive and high-quality ingredients.

④ Cultivated meat satisfies customers' desire to reduce carbon emissions and protect the environment.

⑤ The measurement unit being controlled, cultivated meat does not necessarily require more energy.

36-37

Schwartz noted that beyond the functions served by the general process of gift exchange, the characteristics of the gift itself also act as a powerful statement of the giver's perception of the recipient. He also suggested that acceptance of a particular gift constitutes an acknowledgment and acceptance of the identity that the gift is seen to imply. Among children this may lead to lasting changes in self-perceptions, but presumably gifts have ⓐ_____ influence on the self-concept of an adult.

Nevertheless, the importance of this symbolic function of gift selection appears clear enough in a gift shop's recent advertisement, which asks, "Do you want your gifts to tell someone how creative you are, how thoughtful you are, or just how big your Christmas bonus was? Do you buy with a specific price or a specific personality in mind?" While the answers to such basic questions about gift selection may be personally ⓑ_____, the underlying behavioral questions have not been addressed by empirical research.

There can be little doubt that gift-giving is a pervasive experience in human life and consumer behavior, the present findings suggest that preference for cognitive balance is a concept which can go far toward explaining gift selection and evaluation.

36 ⓐ와 ⓑ에 들어가기에 가장 적절한 쌍은? 3.1점

① less — ineffable

② more — unaccountable

③ less — ambiguous

④ more — inevitable

⑤ less — evident

37 글의 내용과 가장 잘 부합하는 것은? 3.7점

① The acceptance of a gift may have great influence on children.

② Most people consider a gift as signifying their social status when they buy it.

③ Generous gifts make it easier for people to develop their social skills.

④ Explaining gift selection and evaluation can be done without a doubt.

⑤ The gift itself tends not to exhibit the giver's perception of the receiver.

38-40

Here we introduce our first attempt at tracking AI's impact on jobs. Using American data on employment by occupation, we single out white-collar workers. These include people working in everything from back-office support and financial operations to copy-writers. White-collar roles are thought to be especially vulnerable to generative AI, which is becoming ever better at logical reasoning and creativity.

However, there is as yet little evidence of an AI hit to employment. In the spring of 2020, white-collar jobs rose as a share of the total, as many people in service occupations lost their job at the start of the COVID-19 pandemic. The white-collar share is lower today, as leisure and hospitality have recovered. Yet in the past year the share of employment in professions supposedly at risk from generative AI has _____ by half a percentage point.

It is, of course, early days. Few firms yet use generative AI tools at scale, so the impact on jobs could merely be delayed. Another possibility, however, is that these new technologies will end up destroying only a small number of roles. While AI may be efficient at some tasks, it may be less good at others, such as management and working out what others need.

To see how it all shakes out, we will publish updates to this analysis every few months. But for now, a jobs <u>apocalypse</u> seems a way off.

38 빈칸에 들어가기에 가장 적절한 것은? 3.7점

① fluctuated ② been raised ③ fallen

④ been falling ⑤ risen

39 밑줄 친 <u>apocalypse</u>의 뜻으로 가장 적절한 것은? 3.7점

① emergence ② genesis ③ catastrophe

④ cacophony ⑤ dependence

40 글의 내용과 가장 잘 부합하는 것은? 3.7점

① The AI technologies have not affected blue-collar jobs.

② Companies are not yet using generative AI tools on a large scale.

③ The COVID-19 pandemic has accelerated the advent of generative AI.

④ Copy-writers have lost their jobs due to the development of generative AI.

⑤ The use of AI turned out to be inefficient at service jobs.

단국대학교

2024학년도 인문계 오전

▶▶ 40문항·60분

체육교육/산업경영(야)(영어 30문항·60분) 공통 영어문제 별도 * 표시

[문항별 배점: 01-30 2점/ 31-40 4점]

[01-10] 밑줄 친 부분과 뜻이 가장 가까운 것을 고르시오.

01* People who had committed crimes for or against apartheid could receive <u>amnesty</u> if they did one thing: tell the truth about their crimes.

① absolution   ② conviction

③ compensation   ④ execution

02* It has always been a dream of mine to <u>peregrinate</u> from one side of Europe to the other with nothing but a backpack.

① commute   ② investigate

③ traverse   ④ resonate

03* She always enjoyed the long bus ride very much because her seat companions usually turned out to be amiable, and if they did not, she took <u>vicarious</u> pleasure in gazing out at the almost unmitigated elegance along the fabulous street.

① artificial   ② genuine

③ substitute   ④ temporary

04 They appear to have at least a <u>rudimentary</u> understanding of the link between diet and health.

① primeval ② fundamental
③ truculent ④ superficial

05 Streaming and on-demand services have demonstrated <u>exponential</u> growth in recent years, largely due to the widespread availability of high-speed Internet connections and improved wireless connectivity.

① collateral ② expletive
③ remarkable ④ retardant

06 There are different theories about why women are so <u>underrepresented</u> in engineering, and in STEM in general.

① unspecified ② obviated
③ discomposed ④ underestimated

07 As perception of men and women continues to change in the United States, and as the job market <u>evolves</u>, it will be interesting to see if these trends continue or change.

① advances ② affiliates
③ ebbs ④ elicits

08 Attacking the individual, instead of their argument, is a <u>strategy</u> employed to block an argument.

① stigma ② discretion
③ tactic ④ camouflage

09 Most waste-water is simply injected back into <u>porous</u> rock formations via disposal wells or released into river systems, jeopardizing aquatic ecosystems.

① frangible ② igneous
③ sedimentary ④ spongy

10   Because flowing water continues to move, this creates an <u>inexhaustible</u> amount of energy that can be stored and used when the demand is highest.

① improbable   ② boundless

③ minimum   ④ explicit

[11-15] 어법상 빈칸에 가장 적절한 것을 고르시오.

11*   While volunteering for an environmental nonprofit during his probation period, he found the cause _____ he would dedicate much of his life.

① of what   ② as

③ to which   ④ why

12*   A leaked Amazon memo from 2022 revealed that the company had to change its expansion plans because, _____ its high turnover rate, it would simply run out of people within a few years.

① given   ② giving

③ be given   ④ have been given

13*   He has faced multiple ethnics probes, all of _____ appear to have been dropped.

① them   ② those

③ which   ④ whom

14   Despite his disability he tried to lead _____ as possible.

① as a normal life   ② a normal life

③ as normal as a life   ④ as normal a life

15   Winston looked up again at the portrait of Big Brother who was the colossus that straddled the world and the rock _____ the hordes of Asia dashed themselves in vain.

① which   ② against which

③ for which   ④ under which

[16-20] 밑줄 친 부분 중 어법에 맞지 않은 것을 고르시오.

16 When I didn't really understand ①<u>where</u> my career was going because I was just kind of winging it, I would do ②<u>licensing</u> deals with a lot of different companies that would contradict ③<u>itself</u>, like a cupcake brand ④<u>with</u> a weight-loss pill at the same time.

17 Andrew Weber, a former Assistant Secretary of Defense, says the Energy Department, ①<u>which</u> operates several national laboratories, ②<u>was</u> likely able to employ ③<u>sophisticating</u> scientific methods in order to make ④<u>its</u> conclusion about COVID-19.

18 He knows ①<u>that if</u> the rain forests of Samoa ②<u>continue</u> to disappear, ③<u>hundreds of</u> potential drugs ④<u>hiding</u> there may never be found.

19 The collapse of Silicon Valley Bank and the Biden Administration's unprecedented response, ①<u>guaranteeing</u> deposits and backstopping regional banks, have catalyzed an important and ②<u>necessary</u> national conversation over ③<u>what went</u> wrong, and ④<u>what can do</u> to prevent future crises.

20 ①<u>Though</u> a brother, he considered himself as my master, and me as his apprentice, and, accordingly, expected the same service from me ②<u>as</u> he would from ③<u>another</u>, while I thought he required too much ④<u>from</u> me, who from a brother expected more indulgence.

Every community of humans faces a life-or-death question: How do we distribute water? Some water has to be held as a community resource if a town, city, or even nation is to survive. Many early human settlements were based on irrigation systems. These exist because earlier people agreed where the water should flow and to whom. Wells in desert lands are protected by cultural traditions that make them a shared resource among traveling peoples. Many large lakes, such as Lake Michigan in the United States, are mostly reserved for public use, not for the people who own houses on their shores.

Water-use laws can prevent a few powerful people from gaining control over all available water. But water laws do not make water freely available in equal amounts to everyone. Farmers need huge amounts of it. So do many industries. Families, Ⓐ_____, do not need nearly that much. There is also the issue of pollution. Water laws must prevent careless pollution by some users before the water reaches all users.

Problems occur when government is not strong enough to make and enforce laws. Often, the water in dispute is an international (or interstate) resource. Ⓑ_____, the Mekong River in Southeast Asia starts in China and then winds through Laos, Cambodia, and Vietnam. The Vietnamese government, no matter how <u>conscientious</u> it is, has little control over how much of the Mekong water reaches Vietnam and what kind of condition it is in. The upstream nations, especially China, determine that. As upstream dams take more of the river, Vietnam has a greater need to negotiate an effective water-rights agreement with other governments. International agreements have worked elsewhere. We will see if they will work along the Mekong.

21* **Which is the most appropriate for the blanks Ⓐ and Ⓑ?**

① however — For example
② moreover — Therefore
③ for instance — Nevertheless
④ in contrast — On the other hand

22* **According to the passage, which is the closest in meaning to the underlined word "conscientious"?**

① strict   ② humble
③ meticulous   ④ negligent

23 Which is the best title of the passage?

① Sharing the Water

② Preventing Water Pollution

③ Facing Community Resources

④ Enforcing Laws on Water Use

[24-26] 다음 글을 읽고 물음에 답하시오.

Arthur Keith was one of those misbegotten researchers who have turned out to be wrong in many of the things they said. A prominent anatomist and anthropologist in the early 20th Century, he was a proponent of scientific racism and opposed racial mixing. At least Ⓐ_____ his racial views, he was convinced humans originated in Europe, not Africa as is now universally accepted.

Keith also described a notion that became known as the cerebral Rubicon. Noting that humans have larger brains than other primates, he argued that human intelligence only became possible once our brains reached a particular Ⓑ_____ size. For *Homo*, the genus to which we belong, he thought the minimum volume was around 600-750 cubic cm (37-46 cubic inches). For our species *Homo sapiens*, it was 900 cubic cm (55 cubic inches). He further argued that any smaller brain wouldn't have enough computational power to support human reasoning.

It's certainly true that *Homo sapiens*, as a species, have large brains. But what this means is increasingly murky. There is gathering evidence from genetics and neuroscience that brain size is far from the be-all and end-all of intelligence. Instead, changes to the brain's wiring diagram, to the shapes of neurons, and even to when and where certain genes are turned on, are all equally, if not more, important. Size, as we might have guessed, isn't everything.

The human brain contains around 86 billion specialized cells called neurons, which connect to each other and send signals back and forth. Many neuro-scientists suspect that changes to the pattern of connections are more important for the development of human cognition than anything as crude as the brain's volume.

24 Which is the most appropriate for the blank Ⓐ?

① mostly based on   ② partly since that

③ partly because of   ④ mostly due to

25* Which is the most appropriate for the blank ⑧?

① moderate   ② approximate

③ maximum   ④ threshold

26* According to the passage, which is NOT true?

① It is universally accepted that humans originated in Africa.

② Brain size does not matter for human intelligence.

③ Some researchers suggest that connections of brain cells are more important than the brain size for intelligence.

④ Arther Keith supported scientific racism and objected mixing different races.

[27-28] 다음 글을 읽고 물음에 답하시오.

If we put the stories of hockey players and the Beatles and Bill Joy and Bill Gates together, I think we get a more complete picture of the path to success. Joy and Gates and the Beatles are all undeniably talented. Lennon and McCarteney had a musical gift of the sort that comes along once in a generation, and Bill Joy had a mind so quick that he was able to make up a complicated algorithm on the fly that left his professors in awe. That much is obvious.

What truly distinguishes their histories is not their extraordinary talent but their extraordinary opportunities. The Beatles, for the most random of reasons, got invited to go to Hamburg. _____ Hamburg, the Beatles might well have taken a different path. "I was lucky," Bill Gates said at the beginning of our interview. That doesn't mean he isn't brilliant or an extraordinary entrepreneur. It just means that he understands what incredible good fortune it was to be at Lakeside in 1968.

All the outliers we've looked at so far were the beneficiaries of some kind of unusual opportunity. Lucky breaks don't seem like the exception with software billionaires and rock bands and star athletes. They seem like the rule.

27* Which is the most appropriate for the blank?

① In addition to   ② Thanks to

③ Apart from   ④ Without

28* According to the passage, which is true?

① Bill Gates was not very bright, but he was an excellent entrepreneur.
② Talent is the most important factor to be successful.
③ Bill Joy is a beneficiary of an unusual opportunity.
④ Since the Beatles were greatly gifted, they would have succeeded in any case.

[29-30] 다음 글을 읽고 물음에 답하시오.

There are a few different factors that need to come together for a pandemic to occur. First, in order for a virus or bacteria to cause a pandemic, it must be a relatively new version of that entity. If this is the case, it means that people as a whole have had little exposure to it and thus will not have any biological protection against it. The disease will not be easily recognized and rejected by our bodies. The disease, usually a virus or bacteria, forces entrance into some of the cells of the body. The virus or bacteria then uses these cells to replicate itself. A virus initiates this process by inserting its genetic code into the cells. This code then becomes briefly part of the cell's genetic sequence. The virus uses the cell to produce new viruses. A bacterium may initiate an analogous process, though by more indirect means. The end result is the same. New viruses or bacteria are produced within the cell. Eventually, there are too many entities for the host cell to contain and the cell breaks open, thus freeing these new viruses or bacteria to infect other cells.

For a virus or bacteria to cause a pandemic, there must be an easy mode of transmission from person to person. The most infectious organisms tend to infect the nose and lungs. This is because the mechanisms of the body's responses in those affected areas — coughing and sneezing — actually help to transmit the disease. The viral or bacterial entities are spread in the air and are easily passed on to successive victims. Besides being infectious, for a virus to truly start a pandemic it must have a sustainable rate of infection. This is the third factor that contributes to a pandemic. That is, an infection must be both very easy to pass on and also not immediately deadly. A virus or bacteria cannot kill its host too quickly. If people start to die before the virus can spread, the pandemic will collapse. The scope of the pandemic in the 14th century was devastating because it satisfied the above necessary requirements. The version of the disease was a new subtype that most people were not resistant to.

29 Which is the topic of the passage?

① How to protect human beings from a pandemic

② The mechanism in which a pandemic spreads

③ The importance of medical technology

④ Differences between a pandemic and other diseases

30 According to the passage, which is true?

① The viruses or bacteria of a pandemic are more aggressive than those of other diseases.

② The pandemic virus or bacteria prevents its cell from being replicated.

③ The easiest way in which a pandemic spreads is by rats and fleas.

④ The pandemic of the 14th century was easily passed and did not cause quick death.

[31-32] 다음 글을 읽고 물음에 답하시오.

Arguably, groupthink can be avoided with effective planning of the decision-making process. An environment needs to be created in which team members feel able to challenge decisions or opinions without fear of reprisal. The group also needs to be objective in its assessment of alternatives and the risks that each carries, before making a decision. Furthermore, they should be flexible enough to reconsider the alternatives should information come to light that challenges the validity of their original decision. So what measures can be taken to avoid groupthink? According to Janis, one method is to create the role of "Ⓐ＿＿＿＿ evaluator" within the group. This person essentially plays the role of devil's advocate, raising objections or doubts at all points during the decision-making process. The role of the leader is also key, as rather than taking a dominant role, he or she should aim to attend fewer meetings so that the group feels free to work how it wants without fear of judgement. The leader should also, if resources allow, set up several independent groups working on the same problem because this will allow for varying perspectives to emerge. Furthermore, outside experts should be frequently consulted so the group can gain a Ⓑ＿＿＿＿ perspective on their work.

31 **Which is the most appropriate for the blanks Ⓐ and Ⓑ?**

① dominant — impartial

② unfair — balanced

③ assertive — biased

④ critical — neutral

32 **According to the passage, which is NOT true?**

① An environment should be created where group members can dissent from opinions.

② The leader should attend meetings often in order to listen to varying opinions.

③ The group has to be unbiased in its assessment of alternatives and the risks.

④ The group should be supple enough to consider other options when encountering any validity issue of the original decision.

[33-35] 다음 글을 읽고 물음에 답하시오.

ChatGPT was released by the technology company OpenAI for public use on 30 November 2022. GPT-4, the large language model (LLM) underlying the most advanced version of the chatbot, and others, such as Google's Med-PaLM2, are poised to transform health care. The possibilities — such as LLMs producing clinical notes, filling in forms for reimbursement and assisting physicians with making diagnoses and treatment plans — have captivated both _____.

The first step in training an LLM involves feeding the model massive text-based data sets from the Internet, to produce a base model. This initial training period requires considerable engineering expertise and vast computing power. The pre-trained model is then trained further on higher-quality curated data sets, and specialists assess the model's output to ensure that it is accurate and aligns with relevant safety protocols and ethical norms.

Ⓐ Other work has shown that GPT-4 can pass examinations in some other specialist areas, such as neurosurgery and medical physics. Studies have also demonstrated the impressive abilities of LLMs in diagnosing challenging cases and in translating complex surgical consent forms into language that can be easily understood by patients.

Ⓑ In March last year, for example, Microsoft researchers described how GPT-4, which has no medical-specific training, can pass certain medical tests, including the United States Medical Licensing Examination. In July, we co-authored a study in which we found that clinicians often preferred clinical notes that were generated by GPT-4 to those generated by physicians.

Ⓒ This expert feedback can even be used to train the model further. For example, ChatGPT has been fine-tuned to give users the experience of having a human-like conversation. Some LLMs have shown impressive capabilities in the medical domain.

Yet, despite the promise of LLMs to improve the efficiency of clinical practice, enhance patients' experiences and predict medical outcomes, there are significant challenges around deploying them in health-care settings. LLMs often generate hallucinations — convincing outputs that are false. If circumstances change — for example, because a new virus emerges — it is not yet clear how a model's knowledge base (a product of its training data) can be upgraded without expensive retraining.

33 Which is the most appropriate for the blank?

① technology companies and health-care institutions

② health training and clinical centers

③ OpenAI and Google

④ public institutions and private companies

34 Which is the topic of the passage?

① Efficient training of large language models (LLMs) in health care

② Possibilities and challenges of applying generative AI to health care

③ Promising future of ChatGPT in health care business shown by Microsoft

④ Hallucinating outcomes produced by ChatGPT applied in health care

35 Which is the most appropriate order for Ⓐ, Ⓑ, and Ⓒ?

① Ⓐ — Ⓑ — Ⓒ

② Ⓒ — Ⓑ — Ⓐ

③ Ⓐ — Ⓒ — Ⓑ

④ Ⓒ — Ⓐ — Ⓑ

Wolves and dogs are similar in their social and aggressive behavior. Both species were group hunters. They had to hunt as a team to kill larger animals. Wolves have a leader, and all the other wolves follow him. The leader of a wolf pack is usually stronger than the others in the pack. If another wolf tries to take over, that wolf can be removed from the pack. Wolves must travel and hunt in packs in order to survive. This is called social order. Without social order, wolves will fight each other. Wolves need to work together in the wild; _____, they will not be able to survive.

Dogs have a similar social order in their families. The mother and father are the leaders, and the pups have to follow them. The same social order can also be seen with sled dogs. The strongest dog in the group is the leader and pulls the sled in the front. The leader gives instructions to the other dogs pulling the sled. Teamwork is the only way to pull the sled, so the other dogs must follow the leader.

Territory is another important factor for wolves and dogs. Both animals will fight to protect their territory. They will even kill other animals that threaten their territory. Humans have been able to train dogs to use this behavior. Dogs are trained to protect their homes from strangers and to be guard dogs. Today's modern dogs do not howl like wolves. But dogs still show the same signs of aggression when angered. Like wolves, dogs will show their teeth when they are ready to fight and when they see a threat.

36ˆ **According to the passage, which is NOT true?**

① Both wolves and modern dogs show their teeth as a sign of aggression.

② Dogs may kill other animals when their territory is threatened.

③ Both wolves and modern dogs howl in order to protect their territory.

④ The strongest wolf is the leader of the pack in social order.

37ˆ **Which is the most appropriate for the blank?**

① otherwise   ② thus

③ nonetheless   ④ finally

[38-40] 다음 글을 읽고 물음에 답하시오.

In the 15 years since its inception, Airbnb has become the travel industry's bread and butter. But once regarded as the Ⓐ_____ option, Airbnb prices began creeping up as the platform became more popular. Airbnb's average global price rose from $110 per night in 2020 to $137 in 2021, according to All The Rooms, which catalogs vacation-rental properties. In February, Airbnb cited its average daily rate (ADR) as $153 for the last quarter of 2022. Meanwhile, in the fourth quarter of 2022, Hilton reported an ADR of $151.81, and InterContinental Hotel Group reported $125.58. While costs are up across the board, the gap between hotels and Airbnb is closing.

A spokesperson of Airbnb says that "Airbnb often provides more space and more amenities" and that its prices remain below those of some major hotel chains. But for travelers looking for one or two nights away, Airbnb's narrowing price advantage, plus the lack of certain hotel luxuries like reception and regular cleaning, are Ⓑ_____.

As hotels begin to offer better deals than independent rentals, here's how to find a great place to stay that doesn't dent the pocketbook too much.

38* **Which is the best summary for the passage?**

① The collapse of lower priced Airbnb begins.

② As Airbnb prices rise, hotels may draw more attention from people.

③ Hotel chains start to offer reasonable rate for short-term travelers.

④ You can find the best rental place using All The Rooms.

39* **Which is the most appropriate for the blanks Ⓐ and Ⓑ?**

① creative — flaws

② reasonable — benefits

③ affordable — drawbacks

④ economical — advantages

40 **Which is the most appropriate topic that could follow the passage?**

① How to find good amenities in hotels

② How to travel with limited budget

③ How to run Airbnb with better service

④ How to book great hotels smarter

단국대학교   2024학년도 인문계 오후
▸▸ 40문항·60분

[문항별 배점: 01-30 2점/ 31-40 4점]

[01-10] 밑줄 친 부분과 뜻이 가장 가까운 것을 고르시오.

01   According to a study, roughly a third of the world's population is at risk from water scarcity, and population growth is only <u>exacerbating</u> the issue.

① mitigating   ② edifying

③ oscillating   ④ aggravating

02   Aphids, grasshoppers, and gall wasps appeared in the Cretaceous, and another important insect to evolve was the eusocial bee, which was <u>integral</u> to the ecology and evolution of flowering plants.

① additional   ② prosperous

③ essential   ④ counterproductive

03   Her pluck was rewarded with thanks from the new president in probably his only <u>magnanimous</u> gesture of the day.

① indulgent   ② spectacular

③ magnificent   ④ conformed

04 At such times the talk might be rambling but it was always <u>erudite</u> and sparkling with ideas.

① teeming   ② strait
③ scholarly   ④ loquacious

05 The chess player looked <u>pensive</u> as he was trying to decide which piece to move.

① panic   ② redolent
③ inflated   ④ musing

06 It's unlikely that the vehicle could avoid the kind of collisions with micrometeoroids that leave space junk <u>riddled</u> with craters over time.

① consorted   ② filled
③ depurated   ④ proliferated

07 From its origin, through the height of the Tang Dynasty, and to the slow <u>demise</u>, the Silk Road played a unique role in foreign relations.

① manifestation   ② niche
③ shroud   ④ quietus

08 Most nineteenth-century signatures were written with <u>indelible</u> ink, while in the twentieth century they were often embroidered.

① impermeable   ② erasable
③ inexpungible   ④ murky

09 Too much mercury that becomes concentrated in fish can make adult eagles <u>sterile</u> when they eat fish.

① intoxicated   ② unprolific
③ amorphous   ④ dislocated

10 He sees the main problem as being the lack of <u>empirical</u> data and argues that more thorough surveys are very important.

① reliable   ② theoretical
③ observed   ④ qualitative

11 With the advent of photography in the nineteenth century came the prospect that the subjectivity inherent in using words or drawings to capture _____ observed might be overcome.

① what is   ② which was
③ are being   ④ that was being

12 It's getting dark, and by the time he arrives in LA, she _____ tidying up their newly moved house there.

① has finished   ② will finish
③ will have finished   ④ would have finished

13 John was eight years older than she and for many years he paid her scanty attention though he took it for granted that eventually they would marry; the betrothal papers had been signed while he was yet a child and Judith _____ a baby.

① not more than   ② no more than
③ not less than   ④ no less than

14 Even _____ the poetic faculty, of which, as far as we can judge, he was utterly destitute, the want of a language would have prevented him from being a great poet.

① had he possessed   ② if he possessed
③ were he possessed   ④ did he possess

15 _____ that she had no consciousness of being observed, and one emotion after another crept into her face.

① So engrossing Jenny was
② So engrossing was Jenny
③ So engrossed Jenny was
④ So engrossed was Jenny

[16-20] 밑줄 친 부분 중 어법에 맞지 <u>않은</u> 것을 고르시오.

16 Mark Twain ①<u>invested in</u> ventures that lost ②<u>a number of</u> money, and ③<u>in the wake of</u> this financial setback he ④<u>filed for</u> protection from his creditors via bankruptcy.

17 It ①<u>leaves</u> traces only in very peculiar cases, like the skin of a thirty-thousand-year-old mammoth ②<u>stalls</u> in Siberian permafrost or the famous prehistoric iceman, a five-thousand-year-old mummy naturally ③<u>preserved</u> in an alpine glacier ④<u>on</u> the Italian-Austrian border.

18 Fifteen people with brain damage ①<u>took part in</u> the study, ②<u>which</u> was performed by some university researchers, and the fifteen people with brain damage were more willing than other people ③<u>taking risks</u>, that is, the brain-damaged people did not ④<u>feel frightened</u> when their attempt failed.

19 During the American Civil War ①<u>horse-drawing</u> wagons served as ambulances to carry wounded soldiers from the battlefield to what we ②<u>would call</u> a hospital, and even ③<u>by the standards</u> of the time some military doctors and "hospitals" were ④<u>much worse</u> than others.

20 Hundreds of years ①<u>passed</u> since ②<u>the Black Death</u> but the special genre of art that ③<u>rose</u> form that era is still famous today, and works of art, including oil paintings, musical pieces, and others, ④<u>remind us that</u> artists can create beauty out of anything, even death.

The _____ of microcosm and macrocosm — that is the most ancient principle of universal harmony, and it was for a long time the most commanding. The human world reflects the physical world, proclaims this principle; further, the same patterns marshal the connections between things at every level of being: physical, chemical, biological, psychological, and theological; on earth as it is in heaven, among angels as it is among men.

A taste of this view's strange charm — a single pattern imposing itself at every level — still lingers today in the fascination with fractals. Many examples of these geometrical figures contain smaller embedded images of themselves, which then contain smaller embedded images still, and so on <u>ad infinitum</u>. Look into a well-known fractal, the triangle described by the Polish mathematician Waclaw Sierpinski in 1915. You will see that within the outer triangular boundary, each of the three next largest triangles is an exact copy of the whole. Thus, the same triangular structure repeats itself at every scale, high and low, macro and micro. There is no smallest triangle: an infinity of ever more diminutive shapes is generated by simple three-sided iteration and miniaturization. It is a most elegant way to make a universe. Once upon a time, this was considered not merely a mathematical curiosity but the secret to all creation.

21 **Which is the most appropriate for the blank?**

① conspectus ② inheritance

③ consonance ④ initialside

22 **Which is the closest meaning to the underlined word "ad infinitum"?**

① incessantly ② intermittently

③ transcendentally ④ transitorily

23 **According to the passage, which is NOT true?**

① The most ancient principle of universal harmony can be seen in fractals.

② The harmonious relation between microcosm and macrocosm was considered the secret to all creation.

③ The principle of universal harmony has fascinated people since the ancient time.

④ Waclaw Sierpinski justified the principle of universal harmony by presenting one circular figure.

[24-25] 다음 글을 읽고 물음에 답하시오.

The University of Michigan law school, like many other US educational institutions, uses a policy of affirmative action when it comes to applicants from disadvantaged backgrounds. Around 10 percent of the students Michigan enrolls each fall are members of racial minorities, and if the law school did not significantly relax its entry requirements for those students — admitting them with lower than everyone else — it estimates that percentage would be less than 3 percent. Furthermore, if we compare the grades that the minority and non-minority students get in law school, we see that the white students do better. That's not surprising: if one group has higher undergraduate grades and test scores than the other, it's almost certainly going to have higher grades in law school as well. This is one reason that affirmative action program recently went all the way to the US Supreme Court. For many people it is troubling that an elite educational institution lets in students who are less qualified than their peers.

A few years ago, however, the University of Michigan decided to look closely at how the law school's minority students had fared after they graduated. They looked at everything that could conceivably be an indication of real-world success. And what they found surprised them.

"We knew that our minority students, a lot of them, were doing well," says Richard Lempert, one of the authors of the Michigan study. "I think our expectation was that we would find a half- or two-thirds of them had not done as well as the white students but nonetheless a lot were quite successful. But we were completely surprised. We found that they were doing every bit as well. There was no place where we saw any serious _____." What Lempert is saying is that by the measure that a law school really ought to care about — how well its graduates do in the real world — minority students aren't less qualified. They are just as successful as white students.

24 According to the passage, which is the most appropriate for the blank?

① abuse 　　　　　　② discrepancy

③ improvement 　　　④ extortion

25 According to the passage, which is true?

① A half- or two-thirds of minority students of Michigan law school had not done as well as the white students.

② Due to a policy of affirmative action, 10 percent of the students Michigan enrolls each fall are racial minorities.

③ Those who engage in college education agree on the idea of a policy of affirmative action.

④ Michigan law school did not significantly relax its entry requirements for racial minorities.

[26-28] 다음 글을 읽고 물음에 답하시오.

On the subject of physical health and medical research, there are thousands of amazing websites where people can get information. However, when does the amount of available information affect its validity and health benefit? The Internet is greatly influencing people's attitudes about their own healthcare: probably, this worldwide cultural trend improves global health. Because computer users can look up almost any topic of interest to them, they become their own researchers. In the busy modern world, doctors don't always take the time to explain illnesses and possible remedies to their patients; they may not give scientific details in words that are easy to understand, either. _____, many hopeful people take advantages of Internet resources to find the facts they need for good medical decisions. But are the beliefs of "experts" always completely accurate or real? Are they helpful to everyone that needs advice on a specific medical condition? The health products or books that seem the most wonderful are often the most fraudulent — that is dishonest or false. Do sick or worried people expect too much when they look for clear, easy answers to difficult health questions or problems on the computer?

26 Which is the topic of the passage?

① Advantages of the Internet for health problems

② Effects of research on global health

③ Validity of medical decisions by experts

④ Benefits and costs of the Internet for people's health

27 Which is the most appropriate for the blank?

① However   ② For example

③ For this reason   ④ In other words

28 According to the passage, which is NOT true?

① The Internet is a significant factor that affects people's attitudes toward their healthcare.

② Some medical information available on the Internet might be inaccurate or dishonest and could be dangerous.

③ People can look up any topics of interest to them on the Internet and try to find easy answers to difficult health questions.

④ Doctors are too busy to help their patients and recommend them to use the Internet resources for medical decisions.

[29-30] 다음 글을 읽고 물음에 답하시오.

Why have we been unable to bridge the gap and prepare workers for the jobs of the future, or even the jobs of today? The answer lies in both the job market and our educational system. The job market is changing more quickly than ever before. Many of the jobs that companies need to fill today did not exist when current job applicants were in school, making it difficult for educational programs to keep up with the demands of the market. Nevertheless, many business leaders argue that schools are not doing enough to provide the technical training that many jobs demand. For example, only a quarter of all schools in the United States teach computer science. Most schools and universities continue to offer the same type of education that they have provided in the past. As a result, many students graduate with degrees that do not prepare them for the jobs that are available. Given this mismatch between the education system and the job market, many labor experts say we cannot and perhaps should not depend on traditional schooling to close the skills gap and should instead find alternative solutions.

29 According to the passage, which is true?

① There is no gap between the education system and the job market in the US.

② The IT training is demanded to follow numerous education programs.

③ The education system of schools has not changed a lot.

④ Companies provided job applicants with technical training.

30 Which is the topic of the passage?

① Cause of the skills gap

② Choosing the skill-training program

③ Job market bright for IT

④ Careers in the future

[31-33] 다음 글을 읽고 물음에 답하시오.

Europeans first settled in what is now South Africa in the 1600s. These colonists set up a government and lived apart from native African. Even after South Africa became a self-ruling country in 1910, white people remained firmly in control. From 1948 to 1994, the nation was ruled under a system known as apartheid. Apartheid kept blacks and whites apart: separate schools, separate neighborhoods, separate rights. No black person had right to vote or take part in the government. In a nation of 32 million black people and 6 million whites, no black person had Ⓐ_____. Black South African and others who tried to fight this system were silenced quickly and sometimes violently. Thousands were thrown in prison. Hundreds were tortured and murdered by the police. White South African leaders looked away, even though these acts were against the law. They wanted white people to stay in power.

Apartheid could not last forever. After a long struggle, South Africa held its first open election in 1994. Once black citizens had Ⓑ_____, they used it. They elected Nelson Mandela the country's first black president. He had spent 27 years in prison for fighting for black equality. As white rule came to an end, many whites feared that blacks would seek revenge for the cruelties of apartheid. So the white government and Mandela's new government made a deal. Mandela and others felt that for South Africa's newborn democracy to grow strong, its people needed to face their ugly past.

31 Which is the topic of the passage?

① Segregation rule toward the blacks in South Africa

② Background and birth of democracy in South Africa

③ History of white European settlement in South Africa

④ Acute racial conflicts in modern South Africa

32 Which is the most commonly appropriate for the blanks Ⓐ and Ⓑ?

① a voice ② a law

③ a nation ④ a dream

33 According to the passage, which is true?

① When South Africa became a self-ruling country, black people took over the power.

② After the election, many whites subjected to the black power represented by Nelson Mandela.

③ Nelson Mandela was the first black president elected through the policy called apartheid.

④ People who fought against apartheid were brutally treated and killed, which was against the law.

The acceptance of sex-role stereotypes not only limits the individual, but also has bad effects on society generally. Sex-role stereotypes have been costly to society. They have prevented a number of people from assuming more productive roles and have resulted in the expenditure of substantial resources on emotional and physical problems generated by these stereotypes. Ⓐ In the past two decades, millions of Americans have begun to change their ideas about the "naturalness" of sex roles. Traditional discriminations are coming to be perceived as an irrational system that threatens women with lifelong inferiority and wasted potential and restricts men to the role of always being competitive, aggressive, and emotionally insensitive.

If men and women achieve sexual equality in our society, what will be the effects? One obvious answer is that society's supply of talent in every segment of the work force would _____. Ⓑ Breaking down the occupational barriers that separate women and men would also help them relate to each other as equals. Some feminists and social scientists have urged that men and women be socialized to be flexible in their role playing and to express themselves as human beings rather than in traditional feminine or masculine ways. Ⓒ This idea is called "androgyny," from *andro* (male) and *gyne* (female). The notion is to have people explore a broad range of role-playing possibilities and to choose to express emotions and behaviors without regard to sex-role stereotypes. Ⓓ If a male wants to be a nurse or a kindergarten teacher and a female wants to be a soldier or a firefighter — and they're good at it — then it is functional for society if both develop their talents and are allowed to achieve everything they're capable of.

34 **Which is the topic of the passage?**

① Benefits of having a job with sex-role stereotypes

② Controversial issues between feminists and socialists

③ Reasons to preserve the traditional concept of sex-role

④ Changes in the traditional sex-role stereotypes

35 **Which is the most appropriate for the blank?**

① harmonize ② deteriorate

③ increase ④ combine

36 Which is the best place for the sentence below?

People thus are encouraged to pursue tasks and careers at which they are most competent and with which they are most comfortable and to express the attitudes and emotions they really feel.

① A
② B
③ C
④ D

[37-38] 다음 글을 읽고 물음에 답하시오.

For the Earth to be overpopulated, there needs to be insufficient food, water, and space for humans to live. Indian economist Raj Krishna estimates that India alone is capable of increasing crop yields to the point of providing the entire world's food supply. The World Food Programme confirms that there is sufficient food grown to feed the world and there is the same amount of fresh water on the planet now as there was 10,000 years ago; it has simply been redistributed. So how is it possible that the number of people in the world is impacting on our planet?

It is not an increase in population that is a dire threat. It is an increase in consumption. Materialism and overconsumption are facts of life for everybody in the western world, as possessions reflect a person's status in society and people strive to obtain happiness through owning the latest fashionable goods. Not only that, but waste is a widespread occurrence which has a huge impact on our resources. In addition, our current consumption is imbalanced, unsustainable, and estimated to be 30% higher than the Earth can regenerate. It is a sad truth that 80% of the world's resources are currently used by just 20% of the world's population, which means that a fifth of us use four-fifths of the world's food and energy.

37 Which is true about the view of Raj Krishna?

① India alone is not able to supply sufficient food for the world.
② The crop yields can increase to the point of providing the world's food supply.
③ In the future, the food will be less sufficient than water and space for humans.
④ The lack of water supply will be no more a problem in India than in the world.

38 According to the passage, which is true?

① An increase in population is the most serious problem the world has in common.

② Materialism is not a critical fact of life for everyone in the western world.

③ A fifth of the world's population uses 80% of the world's food and energy.

④ A desire to follow trends cannot be the measure of a person's status and happiness.

[39-40] 다음 글을 읽고 물음에 답하시오.

There are many factors to consider when exploring career options. Job setting, working with a specific group of people, geographic location, and earnings are just a few occupational characteristics that you may consider. Be open-minded. Consider occupations related to your initial interests. For example, you may be interested in health care, and certain qualities of nursing may appeal to you, such as patient care and frequent public contact. Exploring other health occupations that share these characteristics — including doctors, respiratory therapists, and emergency medical technicians — may stimulate your interest in a health field other than nursing.

Don't eliminate any occupation or industry before you learn more about it. Some occupations and industries invoke certain positive or negative images.

Ⓐ For some people, fashion designers produce a glamorous image, while production occupations in manufacturing industries bring to mind a less attractive image.

Ⓑ For example, the opportunity to travel makes a flight attendant's job seem exciting, but the work is strenuous and tiring; flight attendants stand for long periods and must remain friendly when they are tired and passengers are unpleasant.

Ⓒ However, jobs often are not what they first appear to be, and misconceptions are common. Exciting jobs may have dull aspects, while less glamorous occupations may interest you once you learn about them.

On the other hand, many people consider automotive assembly work dirty and dull; however, production worker in the motor vehicle manufacturing industry are among the highest paid in the nation.

39 Which is the most appropriate order for the sentence Ⓐ, Ⓑ, and Ⓒ?

① Ⓐ — Ⓒ — Ⓑ

② Ⓑ — Ⓒ — Ⓐ

③ Ⓒ — Ⓐ — Ⓑ

④ Ⓐ — Ⓑ — Ⓒ

40 Which is the main idea of the passage?

① When hunting jobs, earnings should be considered earlier than interests.

② Understanding working conditions in detail is the essential part of job-searching.

③ When exploring career options, consider payment and people who work together.

④ When choosing an occupation, you should take into account its various aspects.

DANKOOK UNIVERSITY

단국대학교

2024학년도 자연계 오전
▶▶ 영어 30문항, 수학 20문항·120분

[문항별 배점: 01-25 3점/ 26-30 5점]

[01-08] 밑줄 친 부분과 뜻이 가장 가까운 것을 고르시오.

01 After forgetting their anniversary, Rob bought his wife a magnificent bunch of flowers as a <u>conciliating</u> gesture.

① exonerating   ② soothing
③ clarifying   ④ flaring

02 Sophie's family were in an <u>exultant</u> mood after her success in the competition.

① triumphant   ② furious
③ amiable   ④ lethargic

03 That human rights are <u>infringed</u> is unacceptable in a civilized society.

① ingrained   ② eradicated
③ oppressed   ④ infracted

04 Every society holds certain groups of people in high esteem while <u>condemning</u> others, whether on the basis of their skills, accent, gender, religion, or skin color.

① oppressing   ② criticizing
③ praising   ④ judging

05 The most <u>absurd</u> customs and the most ridiculous ceremonies are everywhere excused by an appeal to the phrase, *but that's the tradition*.

① irresistible   ② sensible

③ preposterous   ④ hilarious

06 If we had carried out a fair assessment of our strengths and decided upon our value, another's suggestion that we were <u>inconsequential</u> would not wound us.

① arrogant   ② insignificant

③ disparaged   ④ overestimated

07 An old Soviet joke used to say that under capitalism people lived under a system of <u>exploitation</u> of man by man but under communism it is the other way round.

① unfair use   ② pure speculation

③ total employment   ④ instant gratification

08 Although he usually plays quite <u>flamboyant</u> people, his character in this play is rather an ordinary person.

① elusive   ② outgoing

③ exaggerating   ④ colorful

[09-11] 어법상 빈칸에 가장 적절한 것을 고르시오.

09 Scientists have researched what conditions are like beyond Earth's atmosphere and what effects space travel _____ on the human body.

① has   ② is

③ does   ④ having

10 Although the exact process by which memories are coded and retrieved _____ a mystery, there is no doubt that eating the right food can help us make the best use of our brains' ability.

① is remained as   ② remain as

③ remains   ④ are remained

11 Had I _____ that a very important message was included, I would have thrown away the letter.

① not been told   ② not be told

③ not told   ④ was not told

[12-14] 밑줄 친 부분 중 어법에 맞지 않은 것을 고르시오.

12 Before ①considering some present-day instances of utilitarian thinking, it is ②worth to ask whether Bentham's philosophy is objectionable, and ③if so, ④on what grounds.

13 Accordingly, the possession of ①a great many material goods becomes desirable ②not principally because such goods provide ③any objective or subjective pleasure ④because they confer honor.

14 By necessaries I understand not only ①the commodities indispensably necessary for the support of life, but whatever ②the custom of the country renders ③them indecent for ④creditable people to be without.

[15-16] 다음 글을 읽고 물음에 답하시오.

We should not consume more water than we actually need. If we do, we won't have enough water in the future. However, just how much is too much? If we remove more fresh water than nature replaces, we have taken too much.

Many cities run campaigns to get people to stop wasting water. They show them ways they can cut back on water use. They also increase water bills for people who use too much. Ⓐ_____, they fund programs that reduce water use. For example, they give people shower heads and toilets that use less water. Ⓑ_____, they make laws limiting the amount of water people can use.

Another threat to our water supply is pollution. When our sources of fresh water get polluted, we can no longer use this water. This also endangers the animals that rely on the water. There are several things we can all do to conserve water. We can save lots of water by not letting the tap run while we brush our teeth.

15 Which is the most appropriate for the blanks Ⓐ and Ⓑ?

① However — Generally   ② Therefore — Initially

③ In addition — Finally   ④ Moreover — Overall

16 According to the passage, which is NOT true?

① One of the major threats to our water supply is water pollution.

② If people use too much water, they pay increased water bills in many cities.

③ There are lots of movements to raise awareness of dangers of wasting water.

④ In order to save fresh water, the government should cut off water supply.

[17-18] 다음 글을 읽고 물음에 답하시오.

In the latest study, researchers measured biomarkers in blood plasma that are associated with a higher risk of developing Alzheimer's, particularly amyloid beta 40 and 42. Half of the 108 participants were told to try to bring themselves to a place of calm by imagining a serene scene, listening to relaxing sounds, and closing their eyes — essentially, mindfulness meditation. The goal was to decrease their heart rate oscillations, encouraging their heart rate to have a steadier, more consistent beat.

Although no definitive single cause has been identified for causing Alzheimer's, clumps of amyloid beta protein known as plaques have been found to be one of key features of the disease. Certain types of this protein can be particularly toxic when they clump together inside brain cells, causing them damage that affects their normal function and causes Ⓐ<u>them</u> to die.

Mather and her team hadn't expected the levels of amyloid beta to be "affected so robustly." And it wasn't just for older adults who already might have been more susceptible to having higher levels of amyloid beta. "The effects were significant in both younger and older adults," Mather says. "This is an intriguing finding because, in healthy adults, lower plasma levels of amyloid beta are associated with lower risk of getting Alzheimer's disease later," she says. "Slow-paced breathing might have benefits not only for emotional well-being — but also for improving biomarkers associated with Alzheimer's disease."

The researchers aren't sure why, exactly, Ⓑ<u>this</u> might be. But one hypothesis is that slow, deliberate breathing may mimic some of the benefits of deep sleep, which research has found might clear neuro-toxic waste products from the brain and nervous system at a faster rate. The build-up of these waste products seems to play a role in the development of Alzheimer's.

17 What does the underlined word "<u>them</u>" in Ⓐ refer to?

① Alzheimer's patients

② brain cells

③ certain types of protein

④ plaques

18 What does the underlined word "<u>this</u>" in Ⓑ refer to?

① that slow breathing might mimic some of the benefits of deep sleep

② that emotional well-being might clear neuro-toxic waste products

③ that slow-paced breathing might have benefits for emotional well-being

④ that slow-paced breathing has benefits for improving biomarkers related to Alzheimer's disease

[19-20] 다음 글을 읽고 물음에 답하시오.

Like many nineteenth-century reformers, Thomas Carlyle dreamt not of a world in which everyone would financially equal, but of one in which high and low alike would come by their inequalities honestly. "Europe requires a real aristocracy," he wrote, "only it must be aristocracy of talent. False aristocracies are insupportable." What he was imagining was a system _____ had not been coined: a meritocracy.

The new ideology of meritocracy competed with two alternative notions of social organization: the egalitarian principle, calling for absolute equality in the distribution of goods among all members of society; and the hereditary principle, endorsing the automatic transfer of titles and posts from the wealthy to their children. Like aristocrats of old, meritocrats were prepared to tolerate a great deal of inequality, but like radical egalitarians, they favored (if only for a transitional phase) complete equality of opportunity. If everyone received the same education and had the same chance to enter any career, they argued, subsequent differences in income and prestige would be justified by reference to individuals' particular talents and weaknesses. Consequently, there would be no need artificially to equalize salaries or assets; hardships would be merited no less than privileges.

19 Which is the most appropriate for the blank?

① whose name   ② whose source

③ which term   ④ which result

20 According to the passage, which is NOT true?

① Carlyle dreamt of a social system where both the lower and the upper classes can obtain inequalities in an honest way.

② Like aristocrats of old, meritocrats were willing to accept inequality of opportunity.

③ In the egalitarian system, it is required that goods should be absolutely equally distributed.

④ In the meritocratic system, salaries and assets do not have to be artificially equalized.

[21-23] 다음 글을 읽고 물음에 답하시오.

Learn how to draw inferences in order to understand your reading better, and to be able to respond to it more accurately. An inference is an expectation about something you don't know directly, based on information you have. It is similar to a guess or Ⓐ_____.

Inferences are affected by circumstances, by interpretations, and by assumptions you make. First, think about how circumstances can affect your inferences. For example, imagine you are in a biology class and the teacher announces there will be a quiz. You will infer that the quiz will be about biology, not history or English (even though the teacher didn't say directly what it would be about!) If the teacher announces the quiz loudly and angrily, you might infer that your teacher is giving the quiz because the class hasn't studied enough, or the teacher is angry with the students for some reason. Your own beliefs affect the inferences you make, too. For example, if you believe biology is the hardest class you have, you might infer that Ⓑ_____. Language also plays an important role in inferences. The writer can lead the reader to certain inferences through Ⓒ_____. In order to understand the role of language in inferences, consider where you are getting your inference as you read.

21 Which is the title of the passage?

① Teacher's Role in Class

② How to Prepare for a Test Well

③ Using Inference for Better Understanding

④ Ways of Improving Language Skills

22 Which is the most appropriate for the blanks Ⓐ and Ⓒ?

① creation — rhetoric

② imagination — meaning

③ prediction — word choice

④ suspicion — storyline

23 Which is the most appropriate for the blank Ⓑ?

① the teacher will push me to take extra classes

② the teacher will help me with the test

③ the test will make a great result

④ the test will be extremely hard

[24-25] 다음 글을 읽고 물음에 답하시오.

There are clear characteristics that determine whether an animal is a mammal. The offspring of mammals develop in their mothers' wombs. When mammals are born, they are alive. Female mammals produce milk to feed their babies. Mammals have hair or fur to keep themselves warm in cold weather. Mammals can grow teeth as they mature, and they also have arms and hands.

Birds are different from mammals. Birds have feathers and wings. An animal does not have to be able to fly to be considered a bird. But birds must have feathers. Pigeons, turkeys, chickens, and ducks are birds because they all have feathers. Birds lay eggs and take care of the eggs until they hatch. Birds need more _____ because they need to fly for long periods of time. So they have more complex respiratory systems.

Bats nurse their young with the milk they produce. Bats have fur and use their hands to catch food. People saw that bats did not have feathers but still called them birds. People used to think that bats were birds just because they could fly. But now we know that there is no such thing as a featherless bird. Even a penguin has feathers. Penguins are big fat birds, but they cannot fly. Penguins can swim, but that does not make them fish. So even though bats can fly, they are not birds. Bats are the only mammals that can fly.

24 Which is the most appropriate for the blank?

① energy   ② oxygen
③ feathers   ④ water

25 According to the passage, which is true?

① Bats and birds are similar in that they use their hands to catch food.
② A penguin is classified as a bird because it can fly.
③ All that has feathers is not birds.
④ Mammals grow their hair to protect themselves from cold weather.

[26-27] 다음 글을 읽고 물음에 답하시오.

Although there may be debate as to specifics, there is no doubt the last few decades have shown increasing changes in our climate. With each passing year, the need for global action and intervention becomes clearer. From increased extreme weather and flooding to the failing of many plant and animal species, _____. One example is in the Great Barrier Reef around Australia. The Great Barrier Reef is a collection of coral reef that stretches over 2,300km. This living underwater ecosystem provides a home to hundreds of species of different kinds of other water animals, fish, and birds. Unfortunately, the Great Barrier Reef, like all coral reefs, is sensitive to changes in water temperature. Thus, the increased ocean temperatures that are part of global warming have seriously impacted the Great Barrier Reef. Coral reefs are delicate systems. They contain tiny living organisms within them, a kind of algae. These organisms not only give the corals their different beautiful colors, but also help create a living under water ecosystem. These algae produce food which they pass on to the coral. This, in turn, allows the coral to grow and spread, providing homes and food for other water animals. Unfortunately, increases in temperature cause coral reefs to kick out algae from their structures. This disrupts the entire ecosystem and results in a loss of color in the corals. Any non-living coral becomes a washed-out white in color. If not given the chance to recover, the damage could become permanent. A recent scientific survey found that fully two-thirds of the Great Barrier Reef has now changed to this washed-out white color.

26 Which is the most appropriate for the blank?

① people contributed to solving the problems

② living ecosystem failed

③ international legislation should be passed on

④ nothing is unaffected

27 According to the passage, which is NOT true?

① When corals are dead, their color changes into washed-out white.

② Increased ocean temperature can lead to a loss of color in the Great Barrier Reef.

③ Algae in the Great Barrier Reef are provided help such as homes and food.

④ Australia has a collection of coral reef which is long enough to be around 2,300km.

[28-30] 다음 글을 읽고 물음에 답하시오.

To discern the geometry of a snowflake, you need a microscope and good cold temperatures — the canonical six-sided flake forms only below -15 degrees Celsius, or 5 degrees Fahrenheit. Work on examining and depicting snowflakes began seriously in the seventeenth century in Robert Hooke's famous compendium of microscopic observations and continued through the next two hundred years as better microscopes resulted in ever more intricate illustrations of their six-sided symmetry.

Whereas Hooke's flakes are a little uncouth, the resplendent forms drawn by the Arctic explorer William Scoresby in 1820 exhibit exemplary symmetry. Scoresby saw God imparting his own perfection to his creation.

Are snowflakes really quite so immaculate? Scoresby drew them that way, but other snowflake scientists' reports might prompt second thoughts.

During one particularly brutal winter freeze in 1855, the British meteorologist James Glaisher sketched snowflakes and handed them on to an illustrator to provide the finishing touches. The drawings were lovely, each flake flawless in its own six-sided way. As Glaisher remarked, _____, the ideal was not perceived but rather inferred: the sketches had none of it. The illustrator had assumed the symmetry of the flakes in order to round out the finished pictures.

28 Which has the closest meaning to the underlined word "immaculate"?

① immodest
② immune
③ immanent
④ impeccable

29 Which is the most appropriate for the blank?

① furthermore
② however
③ nevertheless
④ moreover

30 According to the passage, which is true?

① The six-sided snowflakes can be seen with the naked eye.
② The observations of snowflakes set to work seriously in the nineteenth century.
③ The snowflakes do not form at less than -15 degrees Celsius, or 5 degrees Fahrenheit.
④ The symmetry was assumed for rounded flakes by an illustrator.

DANKOOK
UNIVERSITY

단국대학교   2024학년도 자연계 오후
▶▶ 영어 30문항, 수학 20문항·120분

[문항별 배점: 01-25 3점/ 26-30 5점]

[01-08] 밑줄 친 부분과 뜻이 가장 가까운 것을 고르시오.

01   Many Korean analysts say that the detailed guidelines for <u>subsidies</u> for electric vehicles under the IRA are not much different from what they expected.

① accessories   ② fixtures
③ grants   ④ securities

02   Observational studies that track disease <u>incidence</u> in different populations suggest that garlic use in the diet may act as a cancer-fighting agent, particularly for prostate and stomach cancer.

① anticipation   ② control
③ impediment   ④ occurrence

03   If you put a <u>rusty</u> nail in soda, the acid in the soda will react with the rust on the nail.

① dyed   ② corroded
③ lumbered   ④ stooped

04 Stephen Suomi at the National Institute of Child Health and Human Development works with rhesus monkeys that possess the same genetic <u>predisposition</u> to shyness that affects humans.

① alteration   ② extortion

③ heredity   ④ inclination

05 With no stable source of income, H. M. <u>panhandles</u> all day long with uncertainty, never knowing whether he will have a bite to eat this day.

① begs   ② hurtles

③ plods   ④ rampages

06 His <u>weary</u> face brought tears to my eyes when his frail body walked into my room.

① peppy   ② fatigued

③ robust   ④ scowled

07 He was giving me the same treatment which he used to whip horses into submission, and I suffered a lifelong sense of <u>resentment</u>.

① compensation   ② wretchedness

③ indignation   ④ sacrifice

08 You thought it would be quite simple; it is extraordinarily complicated. You thought it would be terrible; it is merely <u>squalid</u> and boring.

① filthy   ② splendid

③ monotonous   ④ wrathful

[09-11] 어법상 빈칸에 가장 적절한 것을 고르시오.

09 Students of her class were assured that _____ questions they asked would be answered as soon as possible.

① any of ② every
③ whose ④ whichever

10 When Mary saw the picture in the art gallery, she realized that it was exactly what she _____.

① has been searching for
② has searched for
③ had been searching for
④ is searching for

11 Wu Wenguang's daughter, Wu Ye is carrying on the family tradition of playing the instrument and is keen _____ new music for it.

① to compose ② on composing
③ composed ④ to be composed

[12-14] 밑줄 친 부분 중 어법에 맞지 않은 것을 고르시오.

12 When my father left ①to drive home to Connecticut after the party, he assumed I ②will join, ③offering to drop me at the apartment I ④shared with my friend Kristina in Village.

13 Inevitably, these companies don't trust their frontliners to do ①a good job, and they design the jobs for interchangeable ②pairs of hands ③rather than humans with brains, wasting so ④many talent and potential along the way.

14 The 38-year-old serial entrepreneur has lately become known ①for talking ②up the risks of AI, but he is most animated ③in talking about ④their possibilities.

[15-16] 다음 글을 읽고 물음에 답하시오.

Just as *Brown V. Board of Education** resulted in the desegregation of more than just public schools, legal experts say, the affirmative action cases the court is considering now are bound to set a new precedent that calls into question any place in American life where laws or policies protect, boost or deny people based on racial representation.

"Today, we're ostensibly talking about education. But there is a spillover effect, for example, in government contract set-asides for minority businesses because they exclude whites who want to participate. It's an example of Ⓐ_____. So we need to review and overturn all public contracts. Same thing with employment. A white plaintiff says, 'Well, yeah, I didn't get the job. You're considering race and that's Ⓑ_____.' I see a whole onslaught of more emboldened plaintiff's articulating Ⓒ_____ claims," University of Howard's Powell says.

There'll also be a certain amount of excess caution on the parts of private businesses and public entities that, say, provide scholarships exclusively to specific racial groups. "There will be negative repercussions for things like financial aid and for scholarships that are given out with a race-conscious component to them," the University of Maryland's Park says. Whether the Supreme Court goes as far in scrubbing race preferences from American life as so many legal experts predict remains, of course, an open question until a decision comes down.

* 흑인 학교 분립은 불법이라는 연방 대법원의 판례

15 Which is the topic of the passage?

① Racial problems and their solutions in a society
② Racial prejudice in college admission in America
③ Controversial issues on affirmative action in America
④ Positive effects of affirmative action in a society

16 Which is the most commonly appropriate for the blanks Ⓐ, Ⓑ, and Ⓒ?

① minority to priority
② democratic action
③ race-conscious admission
④ reverse discrimination

Plane crashes rarely happen in real life the same way they happen in the movies. Some engine part does not explode in a fiery bang. The rudder doesn't suddenly snap under the force of takeoff. The typical commercial jetliner — at this point in its stage of development — is about as dependable as a toaster. Plane crahses are much more likely to be the result of _____ of minor difficulties and seemingly trivial malfunctions.

In a typical crash, for example, the weather is poor — not terrible, necessarily, but bad enough that the pilot feels a little bit more stressed than usual. In an overwhelming number of crashes, the plane is behind schedule, so the pilots are hurrying. In 52 percent of crashes, the pilot at the time of the accident has been awake for twelve hours or more, meaning that he is tired and not thinking sharply. And 44 percent of the time, the two pilots have never flown together before, so they're not comfortable with each other. Then the errors start — and it's not just one error. The typical accident involves seven consecutive human errors. One of the pilots does something wrong that by itself is not a problem. Then one of them makes another error on top of that, which combined with the first error still does not amount to catastrophe. But then they make a third error on top of that, and then another and another and another *and another*, and it is the combination of all those errors that leads to disaster.

These seven errors, furthermore, are rarely problems of knowledge or flying skill. It's not that the pilot has to negotiate some critical technical maneuver and fails. The kinds of errors that cause plane crashes are invariably errors of teamwork and communication. One pilot knows something important and somehow doesn't tell the other pilot. One pilot does something wrong, and the other pilot doesn't catch the error.

17 **Which is the most appropriate for the blank?**

① an exaggeration

② a distinction

③ an arrangement

④ an accumulation

18 According to the passage, which is true about airplane crashes?

① Disastrous plane crashes are mostly due to serious mechanical problems of jetliners.
② The weather condition is the most influential cause for a typical crash.
③ Seven successive human errors can cause a plane crash.
④ The two pilots who are so comfortable with each other could cause a plane crash.

[19-21] 다음 글을 읽고 물음에 답하시오.

There is little information available about the legendary blues guitarist Robert Johnson, and the information that is available is as much rumor as fact. What is undisputable, however, is Johnson's impact on the world of rock and roll. Some consider Johnson the father of modern rock; his influence extends to artists from Muddy Waters to Led Zeppelin, from the Rolling Stones to the Allman Brothers Band. Eric Clapton, arguably the greatest living rock guitarist, has said that "Robert Johnson to me is the most important blues musician who ever lived.... I have never found anything more deeply soulful than Robert Johnson." While the impact of Johnson's music is evident, the genesis of his remarkable talent remains Ⓐ_____ in mystery.

For Johnson, born in 1911 in Hazelhurst, Mississippi, music was a means of escape from working in the cotton fields. As a boy he worked on the farm that belonged to Noel Johnson — the man rumored to be his farther. He married young, at age 17, and lost his wife a year later in childbirth. That's when Johnson began traveling and playing the blues.

Initially Johnson played the harmonica. Later, he began playing the guitar, but apparently he was not very good. He wanted to learn, however, so he spent his time in blues bars watching the local blues legends Son House and Willie Brown. During their breaks, Johnson would go up on stage and play. House reportedly thought Johnson was so bad that he repeatedly told Johnson to get lost. Finally, one day, he did. For six months, Johnson mysteriously Ⓑ_____. No one knew what happened to him. When Johnson returned half a year later, he was suddenly a first-rate guitarist. He began drawing crowds everywhere he played.

19 Which is the most appropriate purpose of the passage?

① To demonstrate a detailed description of Johnson's music style

② To explain how much Johnson's music affected modern blues musician

③ To demonstrate the mystery of the popularity of blues

④ To provide a brief overview of Johnson's life and influence

20 Which is the most appropriate for the blanks Ⓐ and Ⓑ?

① shrouded — disappeared

② exceptional — transgressed

③ veiled — remained

④ entrapped — disclosed

21 According to the passage, which is true about Johnson?

① He was frustrated because he had a serious breakdown.

② He started playing the harmonica after learning how to play the guitar.

③ He became popular when he returned after six months of absence.

④ He could go up on stage in local blues bars whenever he wanted.

[22-23] 다음 글을 읽고 물음에 답하시오.

Language frequently serves as an ethnic boundary marker. The native language of an individual is the primary indicator of ethnic group identity in many areas of the world. Like language, religion may serve as an ethnic boundary marker. The major world religions such as Christianity, Islam, and Buddhism encompass numerous distinct ethnic groups, so that religious affiliation does not always indicate ethnic affiliation. But in many cases, religion and ethnic group more or less correspond. The Jews may be categorized as either a religious or an ethnic group. Ⓐ_____, the Sikhs in India constitute both a religious and an ethnic group. In still other situations, religious differences may be the most important marker of ethnic identity. For example, the Serbs and Croats speak the same language; the most important distinction between these two groups is that the Serbs are Eastern Orthodox and the Croats are Catholic. Ⓑ_____, the Chinese ethnic identity transcends religious differences; a person is still Chinese whether he or she is a Muslim, Christian, Buddhist, Taoist, or Marxist atheist.

22 Which is the most appropriate for the blanks Ⓐ and Ⓑ?

① Similarly — Conversely

② For example — Therefore

③ In addition — Consequently

④ Nevertheless — However

23 Which is the topic of the passage?

① Ethnic identity combined with language and religion

② Ethnic features of language and religion

③ Language and religion as ethnic boundary markers

④ Uniqueness of language and religion in one ethnic group

[24-25] 다음 글을 읽고 물음에 답하시오.

The Clovis people were a prehistoric Paleoindian group that first appeared in North America around 13,500 years ago at the end of the last ice age. How the Clovis people arrived in North America and where they came from is still highly debated. One theory proposes that they originated in the Alaskan region and migrated south in pursuit of prey. Another hypothesis argues that the ancestors of the Clovis came from South America. Scholars point to pre-Clovis sites in Brazil and Chile which share similar traits with the Clovis culture. A more recent idea is that the Clovis came from Europe to North America by boat, keeping close to the edges of ice sheets that spanned from Greenland to New York. However, none of these theories has been fully accepted by archaeologists.

A variety of well-preserved artifacts provide a glimpse into the Clovis way of life. Evidence unearthed at various sites includes fluted stone points now dubbed Clovis points. They were probably attached to a type of spear and used for hunting big game. The length of most Clovis points found at the sites ranges from one to five inches. Larger points were necessary to hunt big game such as the monstrous mastodon and mammoth. These giant animals were preferred because meat from a single animal could provide sufficient food for a large tribe for about a month. Besides the meat, the Clovis also used the bones, tusks, and hides to make shelters and fashion, cooking utensils, tools, and other weapons. It is likely that the Clovis used ambush-hunting techniques as their prey congregated at marshy watering locations. The soft terrain would have hindered the movement of the animals.

24 What is the topic of the passage?

① The rise and fall of the Clovis people

② How the Clovis people hunted big game

③ The migration patterns of the Clovis people

④ The origins and way of life of the Clovis people

25 According to the passage, which is true about the Clovis?

① Recent theories show that Greenland is their origin.

② Some scholars say that their ancestors lived in Brazil and Chile.

③ Some scholars say that they used bridges to reach North America.

④ The Clovis point was used as an arrow in hunting big game.

[26-27] 다음 글을 읽고 물음에 답하시오.

An avalanche is the sudden sliding or movement of a large area of earth down a mountain. It consists of a mixture of materials, such as snow, ice, rock, and soil. Avalanches are usually triggered by changes in temperature, sound vibrations, or vibrations in the earth. The size and force of most avalanches pose serious dangers for both life and property and account for many lives lost each day.

In order to understand how avalanches occur, it is important to understand the Ⓐ_____ of snow that enable tons of snow to descend down a mountainside. The most important of the Ⓑ_____ is the shape of the snow crystals. Depending on humidity, temperature, or other atmosphere conditions, snow crystals can appear in many different shapes. The most common shape, and the one that creates the most stable snow layer, is the hexagon. However, the shape of a snow crystal can change due to temperature gradation, or variances in temperature, within an accumulated amount of snow or snowpack. Snow crystals that are closer to the ground's residual heat form facets, or rounded area, which reduce a snow crystal's ability to form a strong layer. Heavily faceted crystals, located deep in the snowpack, make the snow highly unstable, leading to avalanches.

---

26 Which is the most commonly appropriate for the blanks Ⓐ and Ⓑ?

① commonalities

② quantities

③ assets

④ properties

27 According to the passage, which is true?

① An avalanche consists only of snow, ice, and soil.

② The size and force of snow crystals do not change due to temperature.

③ Weather conditions of a mountain can affect the shape of a snow crystal.

④ Snow crystals that are deeply located in the snowpack make the snow strong.

Memory is not perfect. Most people have experienced forgetting the answer on a test before. People who like to multi-task also tend to forget things more readily. In addition, as people get older, memory capabilities start to <u>increase</u>, and it can become harder to store and recall information. Furthermore, brain damage or medical diseases can cause memory problems. In extreme circumstances, people can <u>lose</u> their memory completely.

Ⓐ_____, there are ways to teach the brain how to remember better and reach its maximum potential via memory techniques. One way to improve memory (other than repetition) is to involve the senses in an experience: seeing, hearing, feeling, tasting, and touching. The more senses that are involved in an experience, the better the brain is able to recall the experience. Ⓑ_____, if a student reads a book while listening to the audio version of that book at the same time, the brain will better understand and recall the contents of that particular book. Another way to improve memory is to use mnemonic <u>devices</u>. These are memory techniques one uses to help remember information. One type of mnemonic is called a music mnemonic, wherein words are put to a song. An example of a popular music mnemonic is the alphabet song in which the letters of the alphabet are sung to help children remember the letter names as well as the order of the letters. Another type of mnemonic is a name mnemonic. For example, knowing HOMES helps to remember the names of the US Great Lakes because each lake starts with one of the letters in HOMES (Huron, Ontario, Michigan, Erie, and Superior).

One of the best ways to improve one's memory is to take care of the brain. Studies have shown that exercising regularly, sleeping well, and eating a balanced diet all play an important <u>role</u> in the quality of a person's memory.

28 Which is the most appropriate for the blanks Ⓐ and Ⓑ?

① Conversely — However

② In addition — Moreover

③ Similarly — In contrast

④ Nevertheless — For example

29 Which underlined word is NOT appropriate in the context?

① <u>increase</u>　　　　② <u>lose</u>

③ <u>devices</u>　　　　④ <u>role</u>

30 According to the passage, which is true about memory?

① People who have good memory usually have excellent senses.

② Repetition is the best way to remember information better at a given time.

③ The quality of one's memory is dependent on health and condition of the brain.

④ A name mnemonic is a way of remembering the information by putting it into a song.

DUKSUNG
WOMEN'S
UNIVERSITY

덕성여자대학교

2024학년도 1교시
▶▶ 33문항·50분

[01-03] Select the word that has the same meaning as the word in capital letters.

01 **DETER** 2점

① halt ② steer

③ trace ④ hinder

02 **CAUCUS** 3점

① corpse ② meeting

③ partnership ④ dispersal

03 **LIAISON** 3점

① permission ② laziness

③ remedy ④ association

[04-06] Choose the answer that has the closest meaning to the underlined word.

04 Excavations at Pompeii have continued <u>sporadically</u>. 3점

① vigorously ② cautiously

③ constantly ④ occasionally

05 France had an absolute <u>monarchy</u> until the Revolution. 2점

① imperialism   ② empire

③ stronghold   ④ monologue

06 The court ordered a drunk driving offender to pay high <u>redress</u> to the victims of the car crash. 3점

① compensation   ② evidence

③ property   ④ significance

[07-12] Choose the best answer to complete each question.

07 A system of education should be _____ by the _____ of students it turns out, for quality is preferred to quantity. 3점

① controlled — intelligence

② justified — number

③ examined — wealth

④ judged — caliber

08 We seldom feel _____ when we are allowed to speak freely, but any _____ of our free speech brings anger. 2점

① angry — defense

② blessed — restriction

③ scholarly — understanding

④ enslaved — misuse

09 Because of her _____ nature, Sam often acts purely on impulse. 2점

① stoic   ② reflective

③ passionate   ④ wistful

10 The candidate's inability to connect with middle-class voters was his greatest _____. 2점

① shortcoming   ② virtue

③ extinction   ④ performance

11 The auditor discovered a significant financial _____ in the company's records, prompting an immediate investigation by the finance department to identify the inconsistencies before the annual report was finalized. 4점

① infusion
② discrepancy
③ complacency
④ cohesion

12 After completing the inventory count, the warehouse manager had to _____ the total number of products to ensure accurate stock levels. 4점

① merge
② skew
③ collide
④ tally

[13-17] Choose the best answer to make each sentence grammatically correct.

13 If you _____ to me, you would have been safe. 4점

① had listened
② listened
③ listen
④ will listen

14 The _____ produced at our factory in Seoul. 3점

① good are
② goods are
③ goods is
④ good is

15 A colleague congratulated me _____ my performance in the exam. 2점

① for
② on
③ to
④ with

16 Before the Civil War, one-eighth of the residents of the United States _____ slaves.

① is
② was
③ were
④ have been

3점

17 The professor, known for her erudition and _____ teaching style, captivates students and fosters a deep appreciation for the subject matter. 3점

① pedagogical
② pedagogically
③ pedagogue
④ pedagogy

[18-19] Identify the part where the English grammar is <u>incorrect</u> in the following paragraphs.

18 After years of dreaming about it, Amanda finally decided to pursue her passion for photography. She <u>bought a new camera and enrolled in a photography course</u>. On the first day of class, she was excited but nervous. The instructor handed out the syllabus and explained the assignments, <u>emphasizing the importance of paying attention to the details</u>. Amanda was determined to excel, so she carefully read <u>through the instructions and begun working on her first assignment</u>. She set about the task by using her keen eye for detail and creativity. <u>Little did she know that the challenge awaiting her</u> would test not only her technical skills but also her ability to capture the essence of the subjects in a unique way. 4점

① bought a new camera and enrolled in a photography course
② emphasizing the importance of paying attention to the details
③ through the instructions and begun working on her first assignment
④ Little did she know that the challenge awaiting her

19 <u>As a child</u>, I spent most of my free time messing around with computers. I supposed <u>it wouldn't have been too hard</u> to foresee my career as a computer programmer. It has afforded me a stable job that <u>pays well and lets me enjoy my work</u>. However, I do wish I had <u>spent more my time hang out</u> with other people. 3점

① As a child
② it wouldn't have been too hard
③ pays well and lets me enjoy my work
④ spent more my time hang out

[20-33] Read the following passages and answer the questions.

When we learn in history that great Roman leaders like Julius Caesar and Marc Anthony loved the great Egyptian queen Cleopatra, we assume that Cleopatra used her great beauty as a strategy to put Egypt on a more favorable footing with Rome. This is how her life is always portrayed in movies. However, we don't know whether _____. Instead, some evidence seems to suggest that she was not. A set of coins from the reign of Cleopatra depicts her as having an enormous neck and hawk-like features.

20　Which of the following best completes the passage? 3점

① Cleopatra was truly beautiful

② she was truly loved by Caesar

③ Cleopatra was truly the queen

④ she was a truly honest queen

21-23

As recently as the 1860s, most people believed that the earth, and humanity with it, was created a mere 6,000 to 7,000 years ago. For centuries, beautifully worked flints were regarded as the work of elves, a notion once far more plausible than the idea that humans roamed the world's wildernesses in small bands long before the days of the Greek and Roman Empires. Even when these stones were accepted as man-made tools, they were attributed to the Romans or Early Britons.

Today, we think in wider terms, but the older ideas about humanity's beginnings faded slowly. _____ the late eighteenth and early nineteenth centuries, excavators, mainly enthusiastic amateurs, began to associate fossil remains of men and extinct animals with the stone tools. Still, most geologists continued to think in Biblical terms, maintaining that these associations were merely coincidental. They believed the Flood had mixed the bones of ancient animals with the tools and remains of recent humans. These theories finally crumbled as archaeologists began to find bones and tools together in unflooded, undisturbed deposits, including a number of important sites on the banks of the Sommes River in France. British investigators, who came to check the French deposits, were convinced that the bones and tools had not collected as a result of flooding, and they announced their conclusions in 1859.

This was the same year that Darwin published *On the Origin of Species*, the date that marks the beginning of modern research into human evolution.

21 Which of the following words should be used to fill in the blank in the passage?

① During   ② Although   3점

③ While   ④ Whenever

22 All of the following types of archaeological evidence were mentioned except

_____. 3점

① carbon dating

② fossils

③ extinct animals remains

④ man-made objects

23 The turning point in scientific theories about the age of humanity's existence on earth was _____. 4점

① exclusively related to the publication of Darwin's *On the Origin of Species* in 1859

② the discovery of the remains of extinct animals and humans together in an unflooded area in France

③ the development of theological research of the Bible

④ the growth of new theories about the Flood and its effects on humanity

24-26

Like snakes, lizards, and crocodiles, turtles are reptiles. The earliest fossils recognized as turtles are about 200 million years old and date from the time when dinosaurs roamed Earth. Unbelievably, turtles have changed little in appearance since that time.

There are many different types of turtles in many different climates around the world. In contrast to other reptiles, whose populations are confined largely to the tropics, turtles are most abundant in southeastern North America and southeastern Asia. They live in lakes, ponds, salt marshes, rivers, forests, and even deserts. The sizes of turtles vary. Bog or mud turtles grow no larger than about 4 inches (10 centimeters) long. At the other end of the spectrum is the sea-roving leatherback turtle, which may be more than 6.5 feet (2 meters) in length and weigh more than 1,100 pounds (500 kilograms).

Turtles live longer than most other animals, but reports of turtles living more than a century are questionable. Several kinds, however, have lived more than 50 years in captivity. Even in natural environments, box turtles and slider turtles can reach ages of 20 to 30 years. The ages of some turtles can be estimated by counting the growth rings that form each year on the external bony plates of the shell.

24 The author mentions dinosaurs in the first paragraph to _____. 3점
① illustrate the age of the turtle fossils
② uncover the mystery of turtle origins
③ show that turtles may become extinct
④ bring the life of the turtle into focus

25 Turtles are different from other reptiles because they _____. 3점
① have changed a lot over time
② have adapted themselves only to North America
③ are desert dwellers
④ live in different climates

26 When the author discusses the theory that turtles may live to be more than 100, the tone can best be described as _____. 3점
① respectful　　　　② ridiculing
③ interested　　　　④ skeptical

27-29

Alone in the room, he threw his head back in the chair, and his glance happened to rest upon a bell, a disused bell, that hung in the room and communicated, for some purpose now forgotten, with a chamber in the highest floor of the building. It was with great astonishment, and with a strange <u>inexplicable</u> dread, that, as he looked, he saw this bell begin to swing. Soon it rang out loudly, and so did every bell in the house.

This was succeeded by a clanking noise, deep down below as if a person were dragging a heavy chain over the casks in the wine merchant's cellar. Then he heard the noise much louder on the floors below; then coming up the stairs; then coming straight toward his door.

It came in through the heavy door, and a specter passed into the room before his eyes. And upon its coming in, the dying flame leaped up, as though it cried, "I know him! Marley's ghost!"

27 **The word <u>inexplicable</u> means _____.** 3점
① explaining in simple terms
② not able to be taken out of
③ without an expressed reason
④ explaining in complex terms

28 **The bell that began ringing _____.** 4점
① was the only bell in the house
② did so by itself
③ could be rung from another room
④ was attached to every bell in the house

29 **The man who was listening to the bell _____.** 3점
① dragged a chain across the wine casks
② was with his family
③ was apparently very frightened
④ was Marley's ghost

30-32

What is a cord of wood? Some people say the cord is the most <u>elastic</u> unit of measure ever devised by the mind of humans. A "standard" cord is a pile of stacked wood 4 × 4 × 8 feet; that's 128 cubic feet. How much of this actually contains wood? That depends on what kind of wood, the size and straightness of the sticks, and who does the piling. Small crooked sticks, cut from hardwood limbs and piled by one of those cordwood artists who know how to make air spaces, may contain less than 30 cubic feet of solid wood per cord. Smooth, round wood such as birch or spruce, in sizes eight inches and larger, will average 100 cubic feet or more per cord. That's with the bark on. Removing the bark will make 10 to 12 percent more cubic volume in the same sized stack.

The heating value of wood varies enormously with the kind of tree. Black locust, white oak, hickory, black birch, and ironwood are the best. A cord of any of these woods, when seasoned, is worth approximately a ton of coal. Beech, yellow birch, sugar maple, ash, and red oak are next. White birch, cherry, soft maple, sycamore, and elm are comparatively poor fuel woods, with basswood, butternut, poplar, and the softwoods at the bottom of the scale.

30 **Which title best expresses the main idea of this selection?** 3점

① Fuels

② The Value of a Cord of Wood

③ Kinds of Trees

④ Standard Measures

31 **Which word has the closest meaning to the underlined word <u>elastic</u> in the passage?**

① flexible   ② plausible   2점

③ obsolete   ④ rigid

32 **Which of the following is NOT true?** 4점

① Peeling the bark off decreases the cubic volume of wood in a cord.

② Butternut and poplar have a low heating value.

③ The cubic feet of wood depends upon who does the piling.

④ The amount of heat supplied by the wood depends upon the type of tree from which the wood came.

Morality may be a hard concept to grasp, but we acquire it fast. A preschooler will learn that it's not all right to eat in the classroom because the teacher says it's not. If the rule is lifted and eating is approved, the child will happily comply. But if the same teacher says it's also acceptable to push another student off a chair, the child hesitates. He'll respond, "No, the teacher shouldn't say that," says psychologist Michael Schulman, co-author of *Bringing Up a Moral Child*. In both cases, somebody taught the child a rule, but the rule against pushing has a stickiness about it, one that resists coming unstuck even if someone in authority countenances it. That's the difference between a matter of morality and one of mere social convention, and Schulman and others believe kids feel it innately.

33 **What is the main point of the passage?** 4점

① Preschoolers acquire morality faster than social conventions.
② Teachers play a crucial role in shaping children's morality.
③ Morality has a stickiness that distinguishes it from social conventions.
④ Michael Schulman is the sole author of *Bringing Up a Moral Child*.

DUKSUNG WOMEN'S UNIVERSITY

덕성여자대학교　2024학년도 2교시
▶▶ 34문항·50분

[01-05] Choose the best answer to complete each question.

01 The author's writing style was characterized by its _____, using vivid and expressive language. 3점

① ambiguity　　　　② clarity

③ perplexity　　　　④ vagueness

02 The bright, sunny day brought a feeling of _____ to the children as they began their summer break. 3점

① ambivalence　　　② desolation

③ jubilation　　　　④ melancholy

03 The artist's abstract painting was open to various _____, allowing viewers to interpret it in different ways. 3점

① connotations　　　② pretexts

③ fallacies　　　　　④ opacities

04 The chef's _____ interpretation of the traditional recipe brought out subtleties of flavor that had eluded previous cooks. 3점

① palatable　　　　② standard

③ reticent　　　　　④ ingenious

05 The speaker's _____ tone conveyed a sense of urgency and importance. 3점

① passive   ② pensive

③ resolute   ④ quizzical

[06-12] Choose the one which is closest in meaning to the underlined part.

06 The movie had a <u>profound</u> impact on the audience. 2점

① superficial   ② sarcastic

③ deep   ④ joyous

07 The diplomat's <u>nuanced</u> approach to negotiations allowed for a delicate resolution to the international conflict. 2점

① straightforward   ② subtle

③ rigid   ④ impulsive

08 Her cheerful <u>demeanor</u> brightened everyone's day. This uplifting effect was evident as her kindness positively influenced the mood of everyone she interacted with.

① attitude   ② appearance   3점

③ behavior   ④ cognition

09 The economic downturn resulted in a <u>surge</u> in unemployment. It had a significant impact on households, with many individuals experiencing financial hardships. 3점

① decline   ② spike

③ stability   ④ reduction

10 The artist's work is known for being <u>esoteric</u>. It is quite niche and only appeals to a small group of enthusiasts who are really into this kind of art. 3점

① mainstream   ② obscure

③ popular   ④ universal

11 The climber's ascent up the mountain was arduous, requiring immense physical endurance and mental <u>fortitude</u>. 3점

① tenacity   ② resistance

③ dominance   ④ breakdown

12 The novel presented an <u>intricate</u> storyline. It demanded careful attention from readers to unravel its depth and nuances. 3점

① simple   ② heavy

③ elaborate   ④ clear

[13-20] Choose the best answer to complete each question.

13 _____ to a speed of over 100km per hour, the truck skidded out of control and spun off the road. 3점

① To accelerate

② Having accelerated

③ It accelerated

④ Been accelerating

14 Strategically placed _____ the majestic fireplace, the antique painting added a touch of elegance to the room. 3점

① up

② among

③ between

④ beside

15 The committee, composed of experts from various fields, _____ finalizing its recommendations, which they believe _____ crucial for the upcoming conference.

① is — is   3점

② is — are

③ are — is

④ are — are

16 My parents are finally going to get _____ a car so I won't have to drive them around anymore. 3점

① on their own
② their
③ them
④ themselves

17 Considering the recent developments, it is apparent that the team _____ have completed the project sooner if they _____ been more proactive in addressing the initial challenges. 3점

① must — might
② would — should
③ could — had
④ might — had

18 My cousin shared his lunch with me, _____ was very kind of him. 3점

① that
② who
③ what
④ which

19 When he _____ from the company where he _____ for 20 years, he felt devastated. 3점

① has been fired — has worked
② fired — had worked
③ fired — worked
④ was fired — had been working

20 The principal requested the teachers to avoid the subject of religion with children, _____ confuse them with ideas that conflict with how they are being raised.

① so as not to
3점
② so as to not
③ not to as so
④ not so as to

21-22

> Language experts choosing the Oxford Word of the Year 2023 were dazzled by a bright young thing, selecting a relative newcomer, "rizz," for the top spot. Derived from the word "charisma," "rizz" refers to a person's ability to attract a romantic partner through "style, charm, or attractiveness," dictionary publisher Oxford University Press(OUP) said in its announcement. The word received more than 32,000 votes from the public. While Word of the Year contenders do not need to be new words, they must have a significance to the year in question. OUP said its 2023 shortlist was chosen to "Ⓐ_____ the mood, ethos, or preoccupations of the year."

21 Choose the most appropriate word for blank Ⓐ. 3점

① delineate
② emulate
③ manifest
④ reflect

22 According to this passage, what can be inferred about the selection criteria for the Word of the Year? 3점

① The voting process involves an exclusive decision from language experts.
② The public plays a significant role in contributing to the selection.
③ College students are specifically included in the voting process.
④ The entire voting process takes place internally within Oxford University Press.

23-24

In the fast-paced and interconnected world of today, technology stands as a ubiquitous force shaping the dynamics of communication and social interactions. While technological advancements have undeniably revolutionized the way individuals connect and share information, there is an escalating concern about the potential detrimental effects on face-to-face social interactions. The advent of smartphones, social media platforms, and instant messaging applications have brought people closer virtually, transcending geographical barriers. Friends and family members separated by vast distances can now easily communicate and share experiences in real-time. However, this ease of connectivity raises questions about the quality of these interactions and their impact on in-person relationships.

23 **What is the role of technology in the contemporary world, according to the passage?**

① It plays a major role in communication and social interactions. 3점

② It doesn't really affect communication.

③ It doesn't impact the way individuals connect.

④ It improves the quality of face-to-face social interactions.

24 **From the passage, what concern does the author express regarding the impact of technological advancements on social interactions?** 3점

① The author views technological advancements as having solely positive effects on social interactions.

② The author emphasizes the negligible impact of technology on the dynamics of communication.

③ The author is concerned about the potential negative consequences of technology on face-to-face interactions.

④ The author suggests that technology has not changed the way individuals connect in the contemporary world.

Climate change is the greatest threat that humanity is facing today, and whether we choose to close our eyes to our impending doom or not, it's on its way. That is, unless we start making some fundamental changes in the way that we live. Governments around the globe need to start making more forceful moves to encourage their citizens to buy into green living. The average citizen can't impact every aspect of climate change, but if the government pressures people to make real changes in their everyday lives, the summative impact would be immense. One way that the government can affect change is by applying more strict taxes on gas-guzzling vehicles and providing monetary incentives for citizens who choose hybrid and electric vehicles. In some countries, citizens have to pay a large fee just for the right to own a vehicle, a fee that contributes to the development of new, more efficient public transit. This may be an audacious move for the American government, but dire situations require <u>drastic</u> action.

The American government can also pass legislation to ban harmful products, including plastic bags, straws, and other plastic materials that have turned our oceans into garbage dumps. Something as simple as using a reusable bag made of biodegradable materials when you shop for groceries would make a huge difference, and it really doesn't force people to make a huge sacrifice.

25 **In the second paragraph, the underlined word <u>drastic</u> most nearly means _____.**

3점

① rash and unplanned

② naïve and thoughtless

③ aggressive and controlling

④ quick and impactful

26 **What is the main message of the passage?** 3점

① Average citizens can impact every aspect of climate change.

② Governments should work with citizens to make a positive impact on climate change.

③ Governments should play a sole role in climate change through stricter laws.

④ Governments should not interfere with the lives of citizens regarding climate change.

27 Which of the following is NOT mentioned in the passage as governments' action against climate change? 3점

① Governments should pressure people to make major changes in their everyday lives.
② Governments should apply more taxes to gas powered cars.
③ Governments should encourage people to use biodegradable materials instead of plastic.
④ Governments should offer incentives for solar powered homes.

28-30

Although competition is inherent in human nature, its role is secondary to the crucial themes of bonding, care, and cooperation, which are fundamental for survival. Mary Clark, a cultural anthropologist, emphasizes the necessity of expanded social bonding beyond immediate family ties, especially crucial for protecting vulnerable infants in early human societies.

The enduring importance of social bonding persists in modern society, as emphasized by Robert Putnam in his study on Italian regional governments. Even though the regional governments had similar ways of organizing, they worked differently in how well they got things done. This difference was because they were in diverse social, economic, and cultural situations.

Putnam introduced the concept of social capital, highlighting the significance of strong civil society bonds. Regions with high voter turnout and active participation in various community activities, such as newspapers, choral societies, literary clubs, and soccer clubs, demonstrated highly developed social capital. These rich networks of nonmarket relationships fostered trust and reciprocity, notably improving the efficiency of human interactions.

In contemplating your community, consider comparing local enterprises to corporate establishments. Reflect on local food sources, leisure activities, banking options, and asset ownership, as these elements serve as predictors of local prosperity and relationship quality, both influenced by the strength of social bonds.

28 What term does the passage use to describe the nonmarket relationships enhancing human connections? 3점

① competitive tendencies   ② crucial themes
③ social capital   ④ immediate family bonds

29 What specific activities were mentioned as indicators of strong social capital in localities according to Putnam's study? 3점

① voting and club activities

② economic policies

③ similar organizational structures

④ newspaper readership

30 What can we infer about the role of social capital from the passage? 3점

① Social capital doesn't affect how well communities work.

② Social capital only depends on government structures.

③ Good social capital helps communities work better.

④ Social capital causes problems in communities.

31-34

Microaggressions refer to subtle, often unintentional expressions, behaviors, or environmental cues that convey hostile attitudes toward culturally marginalized groups. Initially coined in 1970 by Chester M. Pierce to describe insults directed at African Americans, the term has broadened its scope to encompass various marginalized groups like the LGBTQ+ community, economically disadvantaged individuals, and those with disabilities.

Psychologist Derald Wing Sue defines microaggressions as brief, everyday exchanges that subtly communicate denigrating messages based on an individual's group membership. These actions, while not consciously <u>malicious</u>, are delivered by individuals who may be unaware of the harm their words or behaviors cause to others.

Despite their seemingly innocuous nature, microaggressions accumulate to create an environment of exclusion and invalidation for marginalized communities, eroding their sense of belonging. Acknowledging the pervasive impact of these subtle interactions is vital in fostering inclusive environments and promoting empathy and understanding.

Recognizing, addressing, and educating individuals about the inadvertent harm caused by microaggressions are critical steps in fostering respect and appreciation for diverse identities and experiences.

31 **What is the distinguishing factor about microaggressions, as mentioned in the text?**

① They are consciously intended to harm. 3점

② They convey negative messages subtly.

③ They are always overt and direct.

④ They are exclusively targeted towards economically disadvantaged individuals.

32 **How do microaggressions impact socially marginalized groups, according to the text?** 3점

① By empowering them to voice their opinions

② By validating their experiences

③ By creating an environment of exclusion and invalidation

④ By reinforcing a sense of belonging

33 **Why is understanding the impact of microaggressions considered crucial?** 3점

① Because it fosters respect for diverse identities and experiences.

② Because it reinforces societal power dynamics.

③ Because it is harmless and inconsequential.

④ Because it only affects specific cultural norms.

34 **In the second paragraph, the word <u>malicious</u> means _____.** 3점

① evil

② exclusive

③ favorable

④ intentional

MYONGJI
UNIVERSITY

명지대학교

2024학년도 인문계
▶▶ 30문항·60분

자연계
▶▶ 영어 공통, 수학 25문항·60분

[문항별 배점: 01-05 2점/ 06-15 3점/ 16-24 4점/ 25-26 5점/ 27-30 3.5점]

[01-03] Choose the one that has the closest meaning to the underlined word.

01 It is important to record that there was little, if any, <u>discernible</u> pattern to the distribution of these discursive strategies by age, gender or ethnicity.

① revelatory
② negative
③ obvious
④ perceptible

02 The team's remarkable <u>prowess</u> was a testament to their determination, skill, and exceptional teamwork.

① expertise
② persistence
③ camaraderie
④ achievement

03 She pleaded for the clinic to make an exception but the clinic director remained <u>adamant</u> and would not perform the procedure.

① unyielding
② pliable
③ ingenious
④ vehement

[04-05] Choose the one that best fills in the blank.

04 In the span of just over a century, cruel practices such as the killing of witches and the persecution of heretics were suddenly _____, quickly passing from the unexceptionable to the unthinkable.

① emancipated
② abolished
③ superimposed
④ wrangled

05 The explorers faced extreme _____ in cold weather, where the air was thin and freezing.

① fervor
② adversity
③ rigidity
④ indulgence

[06-10] Choose the part that is <u>not</u> grammatically acceptable.

06 Matter, as we know it — atoms, stars, planets, trees, rocks and us — ①<u>accounts for</u> less than 5% of the known universe. The rest remains somewhat of a mystery. A dark one. Astronomers and cosmologists think around 25 percent of our universe ②<u>is made of</u> something called dark matter, and the remainder — around 70 percent — is ③<u>that's known</u> as dark energy. Dark matter doesn't interact with light, so we can't see it. The only reason we know there's something out there ④<u>beyond what</u> we can directly see is because it interacts with gravity.

07 Under the Mongol emperors, China developed one of the most enduring and successful luxury products in the history of the world — a product ①<u>which spread</u> in a matter of centuries from grand palaces to simple parlours all over the world: a Chinese blue and white porcelain. We now think of blue and white ②<u>as quintessentially Chinese</u>, but that is not how it began. This archetypal Chinese aesthetic in fact comes from Iran. Thanks to the long Chinese habit of writing on objects, we know exactly ③<u>which gods the vases offered to</u>, ④<u>who commissioned</u> them, and indeed the very day on which they were dedicated.

08 Vaccination, as the Jenner procedure became known after the Latin *vacca* for cow, ①proved to be safe and was subsequently taken up globally. Jenner received many honours and awards, and the work led to the eventual eradication of smallpox in 1976. Every medical student around the world now learns about Jenner. Even Blossom, the cow who provided the original cowpox material for Jenner's experiment, is remembered. ②Her hide sits in St George's Hospital Medical School. But Wortley Montagu, whose pioneering work ③laid the groundwork for Jenner's experiments, is forgotten. Whether her work would be remembered ④has she been a gentleman physician, rather than a lady socialite, can only be guessed at.

09 Today the theory of evolution is about ①as much open to doubt as the theory that the earth goes round the sun, but the full implications of Darwin's revolution ②have yet to be widely realized. Zoology is still a minority subject in universities, and even those who choose to study it often make ③its decision without appreciating its profound philosophical significance. Philosophy is still taught almost as if Darwin ④had never lived. No doubt this will change in time.

10 The miscalculations by countless Native American leaders ①deceived by Europeans were due to the fact that no living inhabitants of the New World had been to the Old World, so of course they ②could have had no specific information about the Spaniards. Even so, we find it hard to avoid the conclusion that Inca emperor Atahuallpa ③should be more suspicious, if only his society had experienced a broader range of human behavior. Pizarro too arrived at Cajamarca with no information about the Incas other than what ④he had learned by interrogating the Inca subjects he encountered in 1527. However, while Pizarro himself was illiterate, he belonged to a literate tradition. From books, the Spaniards knew of many contemporary civilizations remote from Europe.

[11-15] Choose the one that best fills in the blank.

11 Many universities have learned the hard way that parents and students equate the quality of education with the price of tuition. To increase enrollment and address complaints about the rising costs of education, many boards of trustees reduce tuition. This, _____, invariably results in a decrease, not an increase, in student enrollment. Reducing the price of tuition decreases both the perceived quality of the education offered by the school and the prestige of the school itself, which correspondingly decreases demand. Conversely, when universities increase the price of tuition, student enrollment increases.

① however ② for example
③ therefore ④ in addition

12 After the mid-Victorian years the British found it difficult to think of themselves as inevitably progressive. Instead, they began worrying about the degeneration and corruption of their culture, their institutions, their racial "stock." George Bernard Shaw sharp-wittedly contends that Britain is "_____." Much of the literary culture of the period expresses similar views. The decadent movements offer sinister analogies to Roman imperial decline and fall, while realist novelists paint gloomy pictures of contemporary society.

① in an advanced state of rottenness
② in the heyday of its power
③ nothing but an arrogant fledgling
④ recovering its past glory

13 The central focus of modern-day biological theories about supposedly innate sexually mandated patterns of thought and behavior is the notion that _____. The egg strategy mandates that women be more picky in choosing a mate, have fewer mates, and expend more care and effort than men on nurturing infants and children. Sperm strategy obliges men to seek to mate with a lot of different females and to spend less care and effort than women on nurturing infants and children. These two opposed strategies, in turn, reflect the differences between the size and quantity of eggs and sperm. Women have a fixed supply of eggs. Once pregnant, they cannot have another baby until at least eighteen months go by. Males, in contrast, produce sperm by the tens of millions. Since it is the female whose body devotes itself to the task of nurturing the fetus, it is to the reproductive advantage of the males to go about impregnating one female after another in rapid succession.

① men and women have completely distinct genetic mechanisms

② both sexes, by nature, are in competition with each other

③ the survival strategies employed by the two sexes are very different

④ men and women, by nature, have distinct reproductive strategies

14 Americans now use singular verbs with the noun the United States. However, in the early days of the country, they referred to the United States using the plural form. This little usage difference has long been a fascination for historians. Many have suspected that the cause was the Civil War. In fact, James McPherson, a renowned historian, noted bluntly: "The war marked a transition of the United States to a singular noun." _____. Using big data, researchers could see how frequently American books used the phrase "The United States are . . ." vs. "The United States is . . ." for every year in the country's history. The transformation was a little more gradual than McPherson claimed and didn't accelerate until well after the Civil War ended. Fifteen years after the Civil War, there were still more uses of "The United States are . . ." than "The United States is . . ."

① And it turns out that McPherson was absolutely right

② But it turns out that McPherson wasn't entirely correct

③ However, McPherson's claim proved to be preposterous

④ However, nobody believed McPherson's claim

15 In 2008, Barack Obama was running as the first African-American presidential nominee of a major party, and the polls suggested that race was not a factor in how Americans voted. _____, Gallup conducted numerous polls before and after Obama's first election. Their conclusion? American voters largely did not care that Barack Obama was black. Shortly after the election, two well-known professors at the University of California, Berkeley pored through other survey-based data and reached a similar conclusion. And so, during Obama's presidency, this became the conventional wisdom in many parts of the media and in large swaths of the academy.

① In short
② For example
③ In hindsight
④ On the contrary

16 Which question <u>cannot</u> be answered about the Mary Celeste?

The mystery of the Mary Celeste remains an enigmatic maritime tale. In November 1872, the Mary Celeste, a merchant ship, was discovered adrift in the Atlantic Ocean. The vessel was intact, fully provisioned, and seaworthy, yet completely devoid of its crew. Not a soul was on board. The ship's log indicated that it had set sail from New York for Genoa with a cargo of industrial alcohol. A month later, a passing British ship found the Mary Celeste floating aimlessly near Portugal. The crew of the rescuing vessel were baffled as they boarded the ship to find everything seemingly undisturbed — meals partially eaten, personal belongings left behind, and a lifeboat missing. The fate of the crew remains a maritime mystery. There were no signs of struggle or foul play. Speculation swirled, proposing theories of piracy, mutiny, or an attack by a giant sea creature. However, no definitive explanation emerged. The truth behind the crew's disappearance aboard the Mary Celeste remains a haunting and unsolved mystery.

① Where was the Mary Celeste found adrift?
② What cargo was the Mary Celeste carrying?
③ Who was the captain of the Mary Celeste?
④ What were some theories about the disappearance of the Mary Celeste's crew?

17 Which of the following can be correctly inferred from the passage?

We may never know exactly when human language arose. However, deduction suggests that it has most likely existed for about 150,000 years. Archaeological and fossil remains of human beings suggest that some feature possessed by Homo sapiens beyond simple brain size was crucial in enabling this species to speak language and take over the world. While the brains of earlier species of the genus Homo, such as habilis and erectus, became increasingly larger over the millennia, no cultural development accompanied this increase in brain size. Only with Homo sapiens do we see an abrupt cultural explosion: symbolic artifacts buried in graves, evidence of nomadic lifestyles following game instead of maintaining one home base, and a major turn in the intricacy of tools.

① Brain size was crucial for the development of language.
② Homo habilis and Homo erectus did not speak language.
③ Homo habillis and Homo erectus moved around following game.
④ Homo habilis and Homo erectus did not use tools.

18 Which of the following is <u>not</u> a way to overcome depression?

Depression can pull you into a vortex of sadness, fatigue, and apathy. Alex Korb, neuroscientist, demystifies the intricate brain processes that cause depression and offers a practical and effective approach to getting better.

Here are some practical tips and tricks:

A. Focus on making one small positive change at a time, such as incorporating a short exercise routine into your day.

B. Seek out opportunities to connect with others, whether it's joining a club or volunteering for a cause you care about. Building meaningful relationships can have a profound impact on your mood.

C. Create a relaxing bedtime routine, minimize exposure to electronic devices before bed, and create a comfortable sleep environment to improve the quality of your sleep.

D. When negative thoughts arise, question their validity and look for evidence to the contrary. Reframe your perspective to focus on the positive aspects of a situation.

① take a short walk everyday

② volunteer for a cause you care about

③ avoid using your smartphone for too long before bed

④ ignore negative thoughts whenever they arise

19 Choose the sentence that does <u>not</u> belong to the passage.

Growing up usually leads to marked reversals of some or all innate infantile taste aversion. The Chinese love their tea scalding hot and bitter. ①Gauchos have their equivalent bitter drink, maté, sucked up hot from a communal cup. Americans savor their morning grapefruit chilled and cut into bite-size pieces. ②Germans take their meat with dollops of bitter horseradish. Sourness also abounds in world cuisine; sour milk, sour cream, sauerkraut, sourdough, and sour apple. ③Not to mention vinegar used to pickle meat, fish and vegetables. Most remarkable, perhaps, is the reversal of the infantile aversion to peppery foods. In much of China, Central America, India and Africa, people expect to experience a tingling, burning, mouth-watering fulsomeness of fiery, hot condiments at every meal. ④Take away the chili pepper, and they will be ecstatic with joy. What babies abhor, children and adults learn to crave.

20 Which of the following best summarizes the main idea of the passage?

Having well-educated people run the government is generally desirable, provided they possess sound judgment. But history shows little connection between prestigious academic credentials and practical wisdom. One of the most ruinous examples of credentialism gone awry is described in David Halberstam's classic book *The Best and the Brightest*. It shows how John F. Kennedy assembled a team with glittering credentials who, for all their technocratic brilliance, led the United States into the folly of the Vietnam War. Alter saw a similarity between Kennedy's team and Obama's, who "shared the Ivy League as well as a certain arrogance and a detachment from the everyday lives of most Americans." As things turned out, Obama's economic advisors contributed to a folly of their own, less lethal than Vietnam but consequential nonetheless for the shape of American politics. Insisting on a Wall Street-friendly response to the financial crisis, they bailed out the banks without holding them to account, discredited the Democratic Party in the eyes of many people, and helped pave the way to Trump.

① The correlation between education and sound judgments is uncontroversial.

② The government does not need to be run by well-educated people.

③ According to history, academic credentials and practical wisdom do not always go together.

④ Credentialism is responsible for most follies of the Kennedy and Obama administrations.

21   Which of the following is the passage mainly about?

Scientists have studied past climate changes to understand the factors that can cause the planet to warm or cool. The big ones are changes in solar energy, ocean circulation, volcanic activity, and the amount of greenhouse gases in the atmosphere. However, the warming is best explained by rising greenhouse gas concentrations. Greenhouse gases have a powerful effect on climate. And since the Industrial Revolution, humans have been adding more of them to the atmosphere, primarily by extracting and burning fossil fuels like coal, oil, and gas, which releases carbon dioxide. The rapid increases in greenhouse gases have caused the climate to warm abruptly. But greenhouse gases aren't the only climate-altering compounds people put into the air. Burning fossil fuels also produces pollution that reflects sunlight and cools the planet.

① how humans cause climate change

② how bad the effects of greenhouse warming are

③ whether climate change is real

④ whether scientists agree about the causes of climate change

22   Which of the following is true about Nostradamus?

Nostradamus was a 16th-century seer. He and his prophecies are still well known today and continue to be the subject of debate. Nostradamus was born in France in 1503. He first worked as a physician and began his medical practice in the 1530s, although he did so without a medical degree. He began making prophecies in about 1547, and he published his prophecies in a book entitled *Centuries* (1555). Nostradamus gained notoriety during his lifetime when some of his predictions appeared to have come true. Nostradamus's predictions, which are written in a cryptic and vague manner, tended to be about general types of events like natural disasters and conflict-related events that tend to occur regularly as time goes on. Some people believe that his prophecies have predicted actual events, such as the French Revolution, the rise of Adolf Hitler, and the 9/11 attacks. Others maintain that because his prophecies tend to be about general types of events that occur frequently throughout history, it's possible to find one that seems to match almost any event that has occurred.

① He was a doctor with a medical degree before he began making prophecies.
② It was only after his death that he became famous.
③ His predictions were primarily about some specific events in history.
④ His prophecies were written in an obscure and ambiguous style.

23 Choose the best order after the sentences in the box.

> The scientists conducted an experiment to test the effects of fertilizer on plant growth. The aim of the study was to unravel the mysteries of plant nourishment.

A The experiment unveiled the potent effects of the unique fertilizer formula, highlighting its power in augmenting plant growth and vitality. The experiment proved the effectiveness of the formula in enhancing plant development.

B Over the course of the next few weeks, they diligently monitored the plants' progress, noting every growth spurt, every budding leaf, and every hint of vibrancy. They observed significant differences between the two groups. The results were astounding: the plants receiving the special solution exhibited faster growth and brighter, healthier leaves.

C For this goal, they selected a diverse range of plants, varying from sturdy shrubs to delicate blossoms. Then, they divided the plants into two groups, giving one group regular water and the other group water mixed with a special fertilizer.

① C — A — B
② C — B — A
③ B — C — A
④ B — A — C

24 Choose the best title for the passage.

> Every time Mithilesh turns on her stove to cook, her eyes begin to burn. The small home the 29-year-old housewife shares with her husband, daughter, son and elderly in-laws in the slums of the Indian capital Delhi quickly fills up with smoke, making it hard for anyone to see. She often has difficulty breathing and experiences uncontrolled bouts of coughing. But even when she steps outside her home, there is little respite. Delhi, the world's second largest megacity, has some of the worst outdoor air quality in the world. One recent study published by the Energy Policy Institute at the University of Chicago warned that the lives of residents in India's capital are being cut short by up to 11.9 years compared to if air pollution was reduced to levels recommended by the WHO. Mithilesh and her family are an extreme example of something happening globally. Although almost everyone in the world now breathes air that is polluted in some way, those who are worst hit are also the least able to protect themselves or escape from it. The story of air pollution is one of environmental inequality.

① The Wealth Gap Issue in India
② Delhi, the City with the Worst Outdoor Air Quality
③ Clean Air, a Luxury that Many Can't Afford
④ Air Pollution, a Scourge on Planet Earth

25　Which of the following is <u>not</u> consistent with the result of the underlined 'study'?

In a series of surveys conducted in Western Europe, including the UK and the Netherlands, a team of social psychologists found that college-educated respondents have more bias against less-educated people than they do against other disfavored groups. The researchers surveyed the attitudes of well-educated Europeans toward a range of people who are typically victims of discrimination — Muslims, people of Turkish descent living in Western Europe, people who are poor, obese, blind, and less educated. They found that the poorly educated were disliked most of all. In a similar study conducted in the United States, the researchers offered a revised list of disfavored groups, including African Americans, the working class, and people who are poor, obese, and less-educated. The American respondents also ranked the less-educated at the bottom.

Beyond showing the disparaging views that college-educated elites have of less-educated people, the authors of the <u>study</u> offer several intriguing conclusions. Most of all, they challenge the familiar notion that educated elites are morally more enlightened than people with less education, and therefore more tolerant. The authors conclude that well-educated elites are no less biased than less-educated folk; "it is rather that their targets of prejudice are different." Moreover, the elites are unembarrassed by their prejudice. They may denounce racism and sexism but are unapologetic about their negative attitudes toward the less-educated.

① The poorly educated are the most disfavored group among college-educated elites both in Western Europe and in America.
② It challenges the familiar notion that educated elites are more tolerant than people with less education.
③ Well-educated elites are more biased than less-educated folk.
④ Well-educated elites are not ashamed of their prejudice against the less-educated.

26 **Which of the following best summarizes the main idea of the passage?**

In *Still Connected* (2011), the sociologist Claude Fischer reviewed forty years of surveys that asked people about their social relationships. "The most striking thing about the data," he noted, "is how consistent Americans' ties to family and friends were between the 1970s and 2000s. We rarely find differences of more than a handful of percentage points either way that might describe lasting alterations in behavior with lasting personal consequences. Yes, Americans entertained less at home and did more phone calling and emailing, but they did not change much on the fundamentals." Though people have reallocated their time because families are smaller, more people are single, and more women work, Americans today spend as much time with relatives, have the same median number of friends and see them as often, and remain as satisfied with the number and quality of their friendships as their counterparts in the decade of Gerald Ford. Users of the Internet and social media have more contact with friends, and they feel that the electronic ties have enriched their relationships. Fischer concluded that human nature rules: "People try to adapt to changing circumstances so as to protect their most highly valued ends, which include sustaining the volume and quality of their personal relationships — time with children, contact with relatives, a few sources of intimate support."

① Despite the decline of large families and changes in lifestyle, Americans' ties to family and friends have not changed much since the 1970s.

② Due to the Internet and social media, Americans are much lonelier today than before.

③ The Internet and social media are playing a great role in preventing Americans from feeling isolated and alienated.

④ The decline of large families and changes in lifestyle are alienating and isolating Americans more and more.

[27-28] Read the passage below and answer the questions that follow.

In English, when you do something "to death," it signifies doing it excessively, repeatedly, or until you're completely worn out. It's a phrase commonly used informally to stress the idea of overdoing something. Interestingly, there have been instances where people literally 'danced themselves to death.'

In 1518, a 'dance plague' saw citizens of French city Strasbourg reportedly dancing uncontrollably for days on end — with fatal results. On a sweltering summer's day in July 1518, a woman called Frau Troffea stepped into a square in Strasbourg and begun to dance. At first, those around her only watched, curiosity piqued by this unusual public display. They watched a woman who would not, could not, stop.

She danced for nearly a week, fell occasionally due to exhaustion but largely undaunted by the body's other warning signs: pain, hunger, shame. She kept up her solo dance-a-thon, and before long, some three-dozen other Strasbourgeois joined in. By August, the dancing epidemic had claimed as many as 400 dancing victims. They danced as if compelled, feet bloodied and limbs twitching, and many of them danced themselves to death.

The Strasbourg dancing plague might sound like the stuff of legend, but it's well documented in 16th-century historical records. It's also not the only known incident of its kind. Similar manias took place in Switzerland, Germany and Holland, though few were as large — or deadly — as the one in 1518.

_____. According to historian John Waller, the explanation most likely concerns St. Vitus, a Catholic saint who pious 16th-century Europeans believed had the power to curse people with a dancing plague. Other theories have suggested the dancers were members of a religious cult, or even that they accidentally ingested ergot, a toxic mold that produces spasms and hallucinations. Scientists and historians, however, still aren't sure what led people in Strasbourg to dance themselves to death.

27 **Which of the following best fits the blank?**

① Why did St. Vitus curse the people with a dancing plague?

② What could have led people to dance themselves to death?

③ How did religious cults lead people to dance themselves to death?

④ How did the horrors of disease and famine trigger a dancing plague?

28 **Which of the following is true according to the passage?**

① Frau Troffea danced alone for nearly a week in the cold winter of 1518.

② 400 victims died during the dancing epidemic in Strasbourg.

③ The 'dance plague' in Strasbourg was not very well documented.

④ Some theories linked the 'dance plague' to hallucinations.

[29-30] Read the passage below and answer the questions that follow.

Everyone knows examples of apparently irrational food habits. In some countries people like dog meat but despise cow milk; we like cow milk but we won't eat dogs; some tribes in Brazil relish ants but despise venison. And so it goes around the world.

A̲ The half of the riddle that pertains to pig haters is well known to Jews, Muslims, and Christians. The god of the ancient Hebrews went out of his way to denounce the pig as unclean, a beast that pollutes if it is tasted or touched. About 1,500 years later, Allah told his prophet Mohammed that the status of swine was to be the same for the followers of Islam. Among millions of Jews and hundreds of millions of Muslims, the pig remains an abomination, despite the fact that it can convert grains and tubers into high-grade fats and protein more efficiently than any other animal.

B̲ The riddle of the pig strikes me as the best example. It presents the challenge of having to explain why certain people should hate, while others love, the very same animal.

C̲ Less commonly known are the traditions of the fanatic pig lovers. The pig-loving center of the world is located in New Guinea and the South Pacific Melanesian islands. To the village-dwelling horticultural tribes of this region, swine are holy animals that must be sacrificed to the ancestors and eaten on all important occasions, such as marriages and funerals. In many tribes, pigs must be sacrificed to declare war and to make peace. The tribesmen believe that their departed ancestors crave pork. So overwhelming is the hunger for pig flesh among both the living and the dead that from time to time huge feasts are organized and almost all of a tribe's pigs are eaten at once. For several days in a row, the villagers gorge on great quantities of pork. When it is all over, the pig herd is so reduced in size that years of painstaking husbandry are needed to rebuild it. No sooner is this accomplished than preparations are made for another gluttonous orgy. And so the bizarre cycle of apparent mismanagement goes on.

29 Choose the best order after the passage in the box.

① B — C — A   ② B — A — C

③ A — B — C   ④ A — C — B

30 Which of the following is <u>not</u> true according to the passage?

① Both Jews and Muslims hate pigs since they are useless animals.

② Pigs are considered sacred in New Guinea.

③ Many tribes in the South Pacific Melanesian islands sacrifice pigs to declare war.

④ People in the South Pacific Melanesian islands sometimes organize a huge feast of gorging on pigs.

서강대학교

2024학년도 1차
▶▶ 30문항·60분

[01-06] Choose the answer that best completes the sentence.

01 The literary utopias had fallen into _____ since St. Augustine's era some thousand years earlier, but the publication of Sir Thomas More's enduring classic revived the fortunes of the genre, becoming the fountain for the outpouring of what we now call utopias. 2점

① distinction　　　　② location　　　　③ affluence
④ abeyance　　　　⑤ aberration

02 The enraged mob _____ the government building, leaving a trail of broken glass and scattered files in their wake. 2점

① ransacked　　　　② goldbricked　　　　③ barracked
④ bushwhacked　　　　⑤ leapfrogged

03 Even in the face of tragedy, she exuded an air of quiet _____, refusing to let despair overwhelm her. 2점

① foreclosure　　　　② conjecture　　　　③ composure
④ imposture　　　　⑤ discomfiture

04 Psychologists and anthropologists assure us that the human psyche is _____, contrary to the popular conception that states "a leopard can't change its spots."

① alchemical   ② omniscient   ③ monolithic   2점

④ ostentatious   ⑤ malleable

05 Years of government research prove conclusively that young people are drawn to cigarette smoking by the image the product portrays through its packaging. Over the years, tobacco companies have spent billions of dollars on aggressive advertising associating their brand image with positive and successful lifestyles. Activists, realizing this, lobbied the government to require that cigarette packaging be made as unattractive as possible. Ultimately, to _____ smoking in the eyes of the young, laws were enacted forcing tobacco companies to package cigarettes as unattractively as possible, using off-putting colors and accompanied by images of diseased organs. 3점

① disenthrall   ② disparage   ③ disinterest

④ disincline   ⑤ disinherit

06 The economist analyzed the data from various sources to assess the overall economic performance of the region. Despite fluctuations in individual sectors, the figures revealed a stable growth trend. Understanding the importance of studying diverse data sets side by side, the researcher aimed to present potential investors with a comprehensive overview of the region's economic landscape. By _____ information from different sources, a clearer picture emerged, which facilitated more informed decisions regarding his client's future investment strategies. 3점

① propagating   ② abnegating   ③ variegating

④ aggregating   ⑤ denigrating

[07-08] Choose the line in each dialog that is incorrect or awkward.

07   A: How are things going with your thesis? 3점

　① B: Great. I've finished it up just last week.

　② A: That's wonderful! You're really ahead of schedule.

　③ B: Not really. I've fallen behind in my other classes.

　④ A: No worries. I'm sure you'll catch up before long.

　⑤ B: I know I will, but right now it feels impossible.

08   A: Have you heard? Bus fare is going up again. 3점

　① B: No way! Wasn't it raised just six months ago?

　② A: Yes. Every public transportation was increased.

　③ B: But this time it's just the bus fare. Oh, this is terrible!

　④ A: Oh, well. It's the times. Things are getting tougher.

　⑤ B: I know, but I don't know how I'll keep up with it.

[09-10] Read the following passage and answer the questions.

Adolf Loos, an Austrian architect, made ornamentation sound like something practiced only by primitive peoples or criminal deviants. But even a <u>cursory</u> glance at history demonstrates that ornament has always played a role in architecture, whether on ancient Greek temples, Gothic cathedrals, Renaissance palazzos, or the Capitol in Washington DC. Indeed, it is often the nature of the ornament that distinguishes different historical periods.

The reason for the persistence of ornamentation in architecture is that, far from being superfluous, it performs several useful functions. With ornament, an architect could give meaning to a building not only by incorporating specific references to what goes on inside but also by simply dialing the intensity of its ornamentation up or down. For instance, the main entrance of the Philadelphia Board of Education Building is not merely larger than the service entrance, it is more elaborately decorated, topped by two winged female figures and a medallion containing what looks like a coat of arms. Without distinctive ornamentation, a building risks being less nuanced, but without meaningful ornament, it risks becoming meaningless.

09 Which word is the best synonym for the underlined <u>cursory</u>? 3점

① intangible   ② superficial   ③ genuine

④ wonted   ⑤ contriving

10 Which of the following is correct according to the passage? 3점

① Adolf Loos was enthusiastic about the use of ornamentation in architecture.

② Ornamentation in architecture is always indicative of primitive culture.

③ The US Capitol is known for its ornamental entrances and exits.

④ Architectural ornamentation is becoming less and less fashionable.

⑤ The abandonment of ornamentation in architecture causes needless confusion.

[11-12] Which of the underlined is grammatically NOT correct?

11 The arrival of the Spanish in Mexico in 1521 marked the beginning of the transformation of the region's cuisine, as the introduction of livestock — specifically cattle and pigs — Ⓐ<u>precipitating</u> the decline of the region's traditional plant-centered diet. Ⓑ<u>To reconnect with</u> their roots, a growing number of Mexicans and Mexican Americans are Ⓒ<u>readopting</u> traditional "plant-forward" eating habits. For example, one-time staples like maize, beans, and squash — known as the Three Sisters — Ⓓ<u>now feature</u> more prominently in everyday family meals. With such cooking making a resurgence, revivalists feel they are reclaiming a culinary tradition and Ⓔ<u>pushing back</u> against colonialism by bringing back a narrative of heritage and sustainability. 3점

① Ⓐ   ② Ⓑ   ③ Ⓒ

④ Ⓓ   ⑤ Ⓔ

12 The capitalist ideology of abundance Ⓐ<u>was helping to</u> create a new cultural space, although several strong voices Ⓑ<u>had emerged to</u> contest it. It was an arena Ⓒ<u>being filled with</u> commercial iconography and catchy slogans, with visions of goods and Ⓓ<u>endlessly consumption</u>, with fashion shows and gaudy shop windows, with huge electrical billboards and mechanized displays Ⓔ<u>towering over</u> city streets. 3점

① Ⓐ   ② Ⓑ   ③ Ⓒ

④ Ⓓ   ⑤ Ⓔ

[13-14] Read the following passage and answer the questions.

Marcus Junius Brutus's decision to join the plot to assassinate Julius Caesar cannot be divorced from the legacy etched in his very bloodline. From his illustrious ancestor, Lucius Junius Brutus, flowed a fierce current of republican ideals and unflinching opposition to tyranny. This founding father of the Roman Republic played a pivotal role in expelling the last king and establishing a system built on freedom and shared power. The oath he instituted among senators, swearing to uphold these values and forbid the rise of another monarch, echoed through generations, resonating deeply within the soul of his descendant.

Therefore, the act of joining the conspiracy against Caesar, far from being a betrayal of Rome, was, for Brutus, a desperate but necessary defense of the Roman Republic and the freedom it had long upheld. He did not strike down a friend, but a potential tyrant, his hand guided by the ghosts of liberty-fighters and the whispers of his proud lineage. In that fateful moment, Brutus wasn't just acting for himself, but for the very spirit of Rome at its best, echoing the oath coined by his forefather centuries ago, to never allow a dictator to regain control over the Republic to enslave its free and independent people.

13   **What is the passage mainly about?** 4점

① Key differences between the Roman Kingdom and the Roman Republic

② The effect of Brutus's lineage on his response to the assassination plot

③ The threat Julius Caesar's rule posed to the ideals of the Roman Republic

④ Reasons Brutus was considered just as much a tyrant as Caesar

⑤ The long-term effects of Caesar's assassination on the Roman Empire

14   **Which is correct according to the passage?** 4점

① Brutus saw the plot to assassinate Caesar as a betrayal of the Empire.

② Brutus and Caesar were founding fathers of the Roman Republic.

③ Brutus was a descendant of a founding father of the Roman Republic.

④ Brutus was motivated to assassinate Caesar for personal reasons.

⑤ Brutus hoped to become the emperor of Rome by assassinating Caesar.

[15-16] Read the following passage and answer the questions.

Though science fiction prizes reason, it fears rationality that has lost its grounding in the human; in other words, rationality that no longer arises from within human cognition. In science fiction films that feature supercomputers — such as Skynet in the *Terminator* films (1984-2009) or Arnim Zola in *Captain America: The Winter Soldier* (2014) — the human is in danger of being replaced with the technological, and the computer represents the super-storehouse or ultimate embodiment of knowledge. Yet this, albeit writ large, reflects life in the "real" world as it is lived today. As information grows more and more disembodied, humans must, by necessity, interface with machines in order to function. Consequently, traditional notions of "the human" fall into obsolescence as people become "posthuman." This means that being human is defined in terms of a new context — our interaction with artificially intelligent machines. In the posthuman world, humans have become less distinguishable from cyborgs or computers. In the contemporary landscape of computers, the Internet, and cyberspace, science fiction has become less and less fictional.

15 **Which word is the best synonym for the underlined obsolescence?** 3점

① deficiency　　　　② evolution　　　　③ redundancy

④ resurgence　　　　⑤ perpetuity

16 **Which is the best title for the passage?** 4점

① Sources of Cultural Anxieties: Cyborgs and Computers

② The Fear of Rationality: Science Fiction as Cultural Doomsayer

③ Human versus Animal: Humanity versus Artificial Intelligence

④ Reality and Fantasy in Science Fiction: The Newest Frontiers

⑤ Science Fiction Fulfilled: How We Have Become Posthuman

[17-18] Read the following passage and answer the questions.

Conspiracy theorists dismiss "the Man from Stratford" as an imposter. They suppose that he was an Ⓐilliterate actor mouthing some nobler man's words, somehow able to memorize lines despite his ignorance. The truth of the Authorship Controversy is that it is an Ⓑoffshoot of the cult of Shakespeare that emerged with the Romantic movement of the late eighteenth and early nineteenth centuries. Before that time, no one had any doubts about Shakespeare's identity as the author of the plays of William Shakespeare. However, once he had been turned into a god, sects and heretics naturally emerged, eager to pull him down.

In point of fact, however, William Shakespeare was neither a fabulous aristocrat nor a Ⓒflamboyant double agent. Indeed, he came from a Ⓓprovidential town in middle England where he attended grammar school. As he grew, his primary concern became keeping out of trouble and bettering himself and his family. Perhaps that he came from a perfectly unremarkable background is the most remarkable thing of all. Maybe it was because Shakespeare was a nobody that he could become everybody. He speaks to every nation in every age because he understood what it is to be human. He didn't lead the life of a Ⓔpampered aristocrat. He was a working craftsman who had to make his daily living and face the problems working people face every day. His life was ordinary; it was his mind that was extraordinary. His imagination leaped to distant lands and ages past, through fantasy and dream, yet it was always rooted in the real.

17 Which of the underlined words is NOT consistent with the passage? 3점

① Ⓐ   ② Ⓑ   ③ Ⓒ

④ Ⓓ   ⑤ Ⓔ

18 Which is the best title for the passage? 4점

① The Relationship Between Shakespeare and the Romantic Movement

② The Cult of Shakespeare: A Myth of Authorship

③ The Importance of Being a Good Actor: Tips from the Bard

④ The Reason Why We Should or Should Not Respect Shakespeare

⑤ Shakespeare Authorship Controversy: Extraordinary Everyman

[19-21] Read the following passage and answer the questions.

In the twenty-first century, we tend to associate the word "digital" with computation, but its origins ⒶhHark back to ancient times. The term derives from *digitus* in classical Latin, meaning "finger," and later from *digit*, which refers to whole numbers less than ten as well as to fingers or toes. Digital procedures long Ⓑpostdate the development of electronic computers, as we might understand a number of earlier devices or systems as operating using digital principles. For instance, the abacus is a simple digital calculator dating from 300 BCE; furthermore, Morse code and Braille represent more recent digital practices. What each of these examples has in common is their use of the word "digital" to refer to discrete elements or separate numbers. This focus on the discrete and the separate is central to the functioning of today's digital electronics, which, at a basic level, operate by distinguishing between two values: zero and one.

While the digital anticipated computation, today the two terms are closely linked, and the adjective "digital" is typically a Ⓒshorthand for the binary systems that Ⓓunderpin computation. Thus we are living through a "digital revolution," are at risk of an increasing "digital divide," and are plugged into "digital devices" that play "digital audio" and store our "digital photographs." Some of us even practice "digital humanities." The Ⓔslippage between the digital and computation seems so complete that it is easy to assume that the two terms are and always have been synonymous.

19 **Which of the underlined words is NOT correct?** 3점

① Ⓐ hark back to

② Ⓑ postdate

③ Ⓒ shorthand for

④ Ⓓ underpin

⑤ Ⓔ slippage between

20 **What is the main idea of the passage?** 4점

① The term digital is quickly becoming obsolete.

② Electronic computers will soon surpass digital systems.

③ The origin of computing dates back to the abacus.

④ The sense of the term digital has changed over time.

⑤ Digital binary systems arose alongside electronic computers.

21 **Based on the passage, what can be inferred about the future of "digital" as a term?** 4점

① It will continue to be associated with computing.

② It will once again be used to refer to fingers and toes.

③ It will take on a new significance as technology advances.

④ It will fall into disuse and fade from people's vocabularies.

⑤ It will develop a fixed meaning and cease evolving.

[22-24] Read the following passage and answer the questions.

John Searle, the eminent American philosopher of language, introduced the concept of "the principle of expressibility," which posits the fundamental nature of human thought in its relationship to language. This principle asserts that any thought capable of being articulated in one language can be expressed just as <u>succinctly</u> in any other. At its core, this concept proposes that thought transcends the limitations of specific languages and operates within an abstract, universal realm.

Searle's notion challenges the boundaries imposed by linguistic determinism, suggesting that beneath the multitude of spoken languages lies a common substrate of thought — a universal language of the mind that operates independently of words. This language of thought is purely conceptual, residing in the abstract realm of ideas and concepts, devoid of the constraints imposed by linguistic structures.

From Searle's perspective, the languages we speak serve as vehicles that embody and carry our thoughts. They act as tools to convey the rich tapestry of abstract ideas formulated within the language of thought. Thus, while the language of thought itself remains inaccessible and <u>ineffable</u>, our spoken languages serve as conduits through which we attempt to convey and articulate the vast complexities of our internal mental landscapes.

22 **Which is the best synonym for the underlined <u>succinctly</u>?** 3점
　① profoundly　　　　② abstractly　　　　③ indifferently
　④ perfunctorily　　　⑤ efficiently

23 **What is the passage mainly about?** 4점
　① The quest for the universal language from which all languages arose
　② Why certain ideas and concepts are better expressed in one language than another
　③ The philosophical concept that abstract thought underlies all languages
　④ How language is able to bridge the gap between abstraction and concrete ideas
　⑤ Translating the language of thought into a clearer expression of truth

24 **Which phrase best conveys the meaning of the underlined <u>ineffable</u>?** 4점

① able to be thought in words

② communicable without words

③ unable to be expressed in words

④ fundamental to all words

⑤ clearly expressible in words

[25-26] Read the following passage and answer the questions.

Dr. Karl Menninger, a pioneering psychiatrist and authority on criminal psychology, proposes upending the traditional "punishment for crime" model underlying criminal justice in America. Unlike the retributive justice system which emphasizes punishment, Menninger proposed focusing on the offender, advocating for treatment and rehabilitation instead of simply fitting the punishment to the offense.

Driven by a holistic view of well-being that posits total health as the way to true rehabilitation, Menninger championed humane therapy and rejected labeling individuals as "insane." In his book *The Crime of Punishment*, he condemned all forms of punishment, including imprisonment and capital punishment, as cruel and ineffective. He believed punishment fails both individuals and society, specifically by neglecting the mental health needs of prisoners.

Menninger's approach resonates with inmates and continues to inform calls for criminal justice reform. Instead of rigid punishment based solely on the crime, his philosophy pushes for individualized treatment and rehabilitation plans, promoting empathy and understanding over vengeance. This shift in perspective challenges us to rethink how we handle crime, prioritizing rehabilitation and the unique needs of each individual involved.

25 **Which is the best title for the passage?** 4점

① Rethinking Retribution: How the Punishment Already Fits the Crime

② Beyond Punishment: Why Criminals Need Treatment, Not Vengeance

③ Retributive Justice: Menninger's Return to the Fundamentals

④ Unlocking Human Potential: Empowering Criminal Insanity

⑤ An Eye for an Eye: What Needs to Be Done Indeed Must Be Done

26 **What can be inferred from the passage?** 4점

① Menninger's approach to criminal justice is unpopular with inmates.

② Menninger's philosophy is currently considered mainstream.

③ Menninger's program doesn't help offenders overcome mental illness.

④ Menninger's proposal has challenged the current justice system.

⑤ Menninger's reputation has suffered due to his theories.

[27-29] Read the following passage and answer the questions.

In the late eighteenth and early nineteenth centuries, European-style grand hotel bars, such as those at Colombo's Galle Face and Singapore's Raffles hotels, played an important role in British colonial life. In their heyday these establishments strove to offer their guests a taste of home. Today, however, we can look back and see in them a microcosm of the broader imperial narrative, one that reflected the changing times in which such hotel bars thrived.

At that time, traditional gender norms were giving way to the shifting social dynamics then underway in Britain and the western world. For example, the debut of the "Singapore Sling" cocktail at Raffles Hotel — a seemingly small change — disrupted the tradition of the colonial bar as a male-only space. For, as cocktails were then considered drinks appropriate for women yet unsuitable for men, this change was likely instituted in anticipation of welcoming female patrons into bars in defiance of longstanding social taboos.

Furthermore, the bars in colonial grand hotels revealed the state of racial tensions in the colonial period. Despite a veneer of inclusion — and, in fact, being owned and operated by Arab, Jewish, and Arminian entrepreneurs — the maintenance of race-based distinctions, while complicated, was upheld in colonial hotel bars. For, while superficially welcoming a diverse clientele and claiming no restrictions, the grand hotel barrooms nevertheless discreetly adhered to longstanding racial hierarchies. In other words, racial restrictions were not overtly imposed, but covertly. For instance, Eurasian patrons were typically subjected to subtle forms of segregation, such as in seating or in quality of service.

In conclusion, colonial hotels, being progressive yet exclusionary, integrated yet discriminatory, encapsulated the paradoxes and hypocrisies of their times. They endure as historical witnesses, revealing the then ongoing struggles over gender norms and racial divisions in existence at a time when the world was in the process of slowly changing.

27 **Which is the best title for the passage?** 4점

① Mixing Cultures, Mixing Drinks: Celebrating Colonial Diversity

② Rituals and Refinement: A Taste of Colonial Hotel Barrooms

③ Progress Amid Exclusion: British Colonial Hotel Bars

④ Cheers to Social Change: Gender Roles and Cocktail Culture

⑤ Grand Hotels: The Way of the Past or a Dream for the Future?

28 **Which is NOT correct according to the passage?** 4점

① British colonial hotel barroom culture spearheaded social progress in Britain.

② Colombo's Galle Face and Singapore's Raffles hotels were styled as "grand hotels."

③ Colonial grand hotel bars attempted to disguise their discriminatory practices.

④ The "Singapore Sling" was likely not intended initially for male bar-goers at Raffles.

⑤ Colonial grand hotels participated in the pattern of social change in their times.

29 **What can be inferred from the passage?** 4점

① The "Singapore Sling" cocktail was created solely to increase profits.

② Eurasians in Colombo and Singapore protested the racism of hotel bars.

③ Cocktails were not as unpopular with men in Britain as they were in the colonies.

④ The change embraced by British colonial bars produced mixed results.

⑤ A return to the grand hotel system would likely help society progress.

30 Reorder the following sentences in the best way to form a coherent passage. 4점

Ⓐ But there's no actual written record of a city named Berlin until the 1240s.

Ⓑ Furthermore, it didn't become a capital until 1701, when Prussian King Frederick the First declared it so and built the Charlottenburg Palace.

Ⓒ Whatever the case, the city has seen its fair share of history and been a center point of German culture for the greater part of a millennium.

Ⓓ Berlin is currently the capital of Germany, but no one quite knows when it was first settled.

Ⓔ There is evidence of a few buildings having existed there as far back as the late 1100s.

① Ⓓ-Ⓔ-Ⓐ-Ⓑ-Ⓒ　　　② Ⓓ-Ⓐ-Ⓒ-Ⓑ-Ⓔ　　　③ Ⓔ-Ⓐ-Ⓑ-Ⓒ-Ⓓ

④ Ⓔ-Ⓑ-Ⓒ-Ⓐ-Ⓓ　　　⑤ Ⓔ-Ⓓ-Ⓐ-Ⓒ-Ⓑ

서강대학교   2024학년도 2차
▸▸ 30문항·60분

[01-04] Choose the answer that makes the best sense grammatically.

01 A: What did the teacher discuss at the beginning of today's class?
B: She explained _____, so we'd understand exactly what's required. 2점

① us the presentation project
② presentation the project to us
③ the presentation project to us
④ us the presentation to project
⑤ the project to presentation to us

02 Historian Caroline Ware argued in her book *Greenwich Village* that American culture _____ a major transformation by 1915. 2점

① is undergone   ② undergo   ③ is undergoing
④ had undergone   ⑤ be undergoing

03 While it was clear that an explosion had taken place in the library's basement, no one was sure _____ it happened, there being no clues anywhere to be found.

① that   ② which   ③ why   2점
④ whenever   ⑤ what

04 It is required that all employees _____ in their uniforms by 6:30 a.m., prepared to begin work. 2점

① are dressing   ② will be dressed   ③ be dressed

④ dressing   ⑤ having dressed

[05-10] Choose the answer that best completes the sentence.

05 If the Earth were to suddenly spin much faster than at its current rate, there would be some _____ changes in store. For starters, speeding up the planet's rotation by even one mile per hour would cause water to migrate from the poles, raising sea levels around the equator by a few inches. 3점

① replicable   ② adhesive   ③ squelchy

④ drastic   ⑤ exonerating

06 Popular culture depicts medieval warhorses as _____ creatures — tall, muscular, and powerful, with shining knights atop. But new research shows that the steeds of the Middle Ages were likely much smaller than we might expect. 3점

① minuscule   ② majestic   ③ infinitesimal

④ imbalanced   ⑤ slight

07 While the police were initially certain that the suspect was guilty, _____ information, which came in the form of an eyewitness, caused them to lose confidence and look further. 3점

① recumbent   ② subordinate   ③ inordinate

④ consequent   ⑤ subsequent

08 The research team _____ the existence of a new particle based solely on observed anomalies, still lacking tangible evidence of the particle itself. 3점

① presumes   ② resumes   ③ subsumes

④ plumes   ⑤ consumes

09 Among experts in conservation, the consensus opinion concerning wildlife-friendly grape farming is that _____. This flies in the face of the conventional wisdom of farmers which teaches that any over-growth of weeds and brambles on the borders of fields encourages pests and thereby poses a threat to vulnerable grapes and, ultimately, to yields. The practice of certain grape-growers in New Zealand, however, reveals that untended rows in vineyards are beneficial, encouraging the activity of a helpful butterfly that thrives in disorderly spaces. A similar type of "untidiness," employed by a growing number of Swiss grape growers, supports birds that provide natural pest control to otherwise vulnerable grapes. 3점

① sacrificing yields for the environment is now a necessity
② controlled untidiness in vineyards can prove beneficial
③ organic pest control is a distressing issue for farmers
④ sustainability is only practical in particular regions
⑤ many grape varieties will soon be going extinct

10 The mountaineers reached a point where the path became increasingly dangerous, with loose rocks and narrow ledges becoming more and more frequent. Despite their experience, they felt uneasy as they navigated the treacherous terrain, knowing that one wrong step could result in a fatal fall. Assessing the situation, they decided to proceed cautiously, taking every possible safety measure in the face of the difficult conditions. Eventually, they successfully navigated the _____ route, and they were relieved to have reached safer ground. 3점

① presumptuous   ② precocious   ③ pretentious
④ propitious   ⑤ precipitous

11 **Reorder the following sentences in the best way to form a coherent passage.** 4점

Ⓐ This innovation of creating such multidimensional stages allowed audiences to vicariously inhabit these theatrical spaces.

Ⓑ Once he learned about light and color, the dramatization of spaces and objects, and the forging of atmospheres, he then brought these to the interior décor of other consumer institutions.

Ⓒ Along with other prominent American stage designers, Joseph Urban reconceived the stage as an integrated three-dimensional space.

Ⓓ To achieve these modern effects, he dispensed with painted scenery and instead emphasized colored light, spot-lighting, and indirect lighting.

Ⓔ Rejecting the crowded stage "realism" of the late nineteenth century, he introduced a streamlined "modernity" which had theatrical depth, dramatic sweep, and more expressive stage atmospheres.

① Ⓐ, Ⓑ, Ⓓ, Ⓒ, Ⓔ   ② Ⓒ, Ⓑ, Ⓐ, Ⓓ, Ⓔ   ③ Ⓔ, Ⓐ, Ⓓ, Ⓑ, Ⓒ
④ Ⓒ, Ⓔ, Ⓑ, Ⓓ, Ⓐ   ⑤ Ⓒ, Ⓐ, Ⓔ, Ⓓ, Ⓑ

[12-13] Read the following passage and answer the questions.

1660 marks a pivotal year in English theater. Not for a groundbreaking play or a renowned playwright, but for a woman named Margaret Hughes. Her revolutionary act? Stepping onto the professional stage as Desdemona in Shakespeare's *Othello*. This wasn't simply casting against type; it was a tectonic shift in a world where for ages, female roles had been the domain of men and boys.

This, however, wasn't entirely uncharted territory. Women had long graced stages, captivating crowds in private household productions and intimate gatherings. They embodied queens, whispered sonnets, and breathed life into characters forbidden to them in the public sphere. These "amateur" performances, far from frivolous, were the fertile ground where female artistry grew, waiting to bloom on the grander stage.

Hughes's bold move wasn't just a performance; it was a challenge. It defied the rigid conventions that confined women to the sidelines of artistic expression. Her Desdemona wasn't just a character; she was a symbol of progress, pushing open the doors of professionalism and paving the way for generations of women to follow. The echo of her footsteps would resound across English theater, shattering barriers and claiming a rightful place in the spotlight.

12 **Which best describes the author's overall tone in the text?** 4점

① indifferent and disinterested

② exuberant and enthusiastic

③ accusatory yet forgiving

④ critical yet charmed

⑤ cynical and satirical

13 **Which is the best title for the passage?** 4점

① From Drawing Rooms to Footlights: Women Claim the English Stage

② The Case for Cross-Dressing: Why Men Sometimes Make Better Women

③ Shakespeare for All: Democratizing the Bard for the Masses to Enjoy

④ All the Stage is a World: Shakespeare's Inclusive Vision for the Theater

⑤ The Rise and Fall of Margaret Hughes: A Cautionary Tale

[14-16] Read the following passage and answer the questions.

The frequency and skill with which modern Americans dissect their own and others' psychologies is a fascinating historical development. They draw on a relatively young science of the mind — psychology — which offers novel ways of imagining the self. For example, at the turn of the twentieth century, Sigmund Freud defined the psychological concept of "sublimation" as "the diverting of a sordid impulse into an acceptable channel." It is a concept that educated Americans still apply to each other's behavior and that historians apply to people who lived long before Freud. One might wonder, however, whether sublimation existed before 1900; in other words, was it discovered or invented?

Some psychological conditions, or at least discussion of them, have come and gone over time. In the nineteenth century, doctors commonly diagnosed troubled middle-class women with "neurasthenia"; in the twentieth century, women in a similar state were said to have suffered a "nervous breakdown." Both syndromes, at least in the United States, had periods of being in vogue and then, seemingly just as suddenly as they arrived, disappearing. The same is true with the "melancholic" personality diagnosis, which appeared in antebellum America, swept the nation, and then, just as quickly, vanished.

Americans have learned psychology in school — millions took college psychology courses in the 1990s alone — and from the mass media, on such programs as *Dr. Joyce Brothers* and *Dr. Phil*. It should come as no surprise, then, that Americans are alert to clinical pathologies in themselves and others. Regardless of the accuracy or inaccuracy of such "diagnoses," the profusion of psychological ideas and discussions taking place among both professionals and lay people means that there exists a history of talk about mentality.

14 According to the passage, how has the media influenced the public's understanding of psychology? 3점

① By creating a platform for professional debate
② By popularizing psychological ideas and discussions
③ By tracing the history of psychological concepts
④ By providing accurate scientific information
⑤ By focusing only on severe mental illnesses

15 **What does the shift from "neurasthenia" to "nervous breakdowns" imply?** 3점

① A decline in mental health awareness

② A societal shift in understanding mental health issues

③ A growing antipathy towards methods of medical diagnosis

④ A lack of interest in psychological conditions

⑤ A mistrust of psychological practices

16 **What can be inferred about "sublimation" from the passage?** 4점

① It has misled people into undervaluing self-diagnosis.

② It has always existed as a concept yet remained unnamed until Freud.

③ Its role in the future of psychology remains unknown.

④ It was discovered accidentally by Freud in his study of Americans.

⑤ Its existence still has implications in mental health discourse.

[17-18] Read the following passage and answer the questions.

Heart disease is a leading killer around the world and the top cause of death in the United States. It killed an estimated 17.9 million people in 2019, representing 32% of all deaths globally, according to the World Health Organization. But not all heart disease is the same. It can affect the blood vessels to the heart or brain, heart muscles and valves, and other areas of the body. Cardiovascular diseases can require long-term treatment, or they can come on suddenly and seriously. For example, Lisa Marie Presley, daughter of Elvis Presley, died at the age of 54 after going into cardiac arrest and being rushed to a hospital. Likewise, Buffalo Bills safety Damar Hamlin, 24, went into cardiac arrest and collapsed on the field during a game between the Bills and the Cincinnati Bengals. It is not clear what <u>triggered</u> either Presley's or Hamlin's cardiac arrest. However, there is a way to know if you are at risk of heart problems — by contacting your doctor and scheduling a complete physical examination.

17 **Which word is the best synonym for the underlined <u>triggered</u>?** 3점

① precipitated   ② transpired   ③ recuperated

④ invigorated   ⑤ summoned

18 Which of the following is NOT correct according to the passage? 4점

① Heart disease was the top cause of death in the US in 2019.

② Lisa Marie Presley died at the age of 54 due to a heart attack.

③ Damar Hamlin experienced cardiac arrest during a football game.

④ Cardiovascular diseases always come on suddenly and seriously.

⑤ It is unknown what caused Presley's and Hamlin's heart attacks.

[19] Read the following passage and answer the question.

> In any language, a "sign" — meaning the group of sounds used by speakers of that language to refer to objects or concepts in the world — is, by necessity, <u>arbitrary</u>. In other words, there is no natural connection between a word and what it is used to refer to. For example, the large plant growing on your lawn, which English speakers refer to by using the word "tree," could just as easily be "*arbol*," which, in Spanish, it is.

19 Which word is the best synonym for the underlined <u>arbitrary</u>? 3점

① methodical　　② immutable　　③ conciliatory

④ sagacious　　⑤ accidental

[20-21] Read the following passage and answer the questions.

Within the context of postwar America's pervasive optimism and celebratory atmosphere, the plays of Tennessee Williams stand out as a distinct counterpoint. While the nation reveled in its hard-won victory in World War 2, entertaining visions of endless prosperity, Williams's dramatic works turned their focus to the often-overlooked experiences of the marginalized, ostracized, and emotionally adrift.

The distance between the prevailing social exuberance and Williams's chosen thematic terrain raises questions about the relationship between art and its historical context. Despite the apparent distance between the era's dominant optimism and the pessimism of Williams's plays, the dramas clearly resonated with audiences, who turned the shows into smash Broadway hits. Figures like Blanche DuBois in *A Streetcar Named Desire* and Laura Wingfield in *The Glass Menagerie*, wrestling with being outsiders on the verge of being utterly displaced, connected with audiences because their experiences resonated with universal human concerns, even amidst the outward hopefulness of the postwar boom.

This seemingly unexpected identification speaks to the enduring power of art to transcend the narratives of a specific historical moment to connect with the fundamental human desire for empathy, understanding, and a sense of shared humanity. Williams's characters, grappling with internal demons and navigating a hostile-to-indifferent world, offered a mirror to audiences who, beneath the surface of their being "winners," recognized their own insecurities and yearnings for belonging, acceptance, and wholeness.

20 **What does the passage mainly say about Tennessee Williams?** 4점

① His plays helped to give rise to the optimism of postwar America.

② His characters appeal mainly to ostracized defeatists and outcasts.

③ His plays resonate with audiences due to their universal themes.

④ His theories on art and its historical context were groundbreaking.

⑤ His exuberance helped theatergoers find solace in hard times.

21 **What can be inferred from the passage?** 4점

① Underlying America's 1940s exuberance was a current of worry and despair.

② Tennessee Williams was critical of the way the Allies won World War 2.

③ A play needed to be downbeat and depressing to succeed in the 1940s.

④ Tennessee Williams's plays became much less influential in the 1950s.

⑤ American postwar playwrights avoided war themes unless optimistic.

[22-23] Read the following passage and answer the questions.

Following the atomic bombings of Hiroshima and Nagasaki that brought World War 2 to a close, a chilling silence descended over the media, muffling public awareness of the full scope of atomic weaponry's power to devastate. Initially, details of the aftereffects of the bombings were scarce, choked by deliberate obfuscation ginned up by various actors, not least of which being the American media. Even the esteemed *New York Times*, always prolific and hard-hitting in its war coverage, remained silent on the unfolding horror of radiation sickness among civilians. Emerging information, though irrefutable, was carefully filtered or suppressed, and this with the aim of crafting a narrative intended to shield the public from the gruesome reality of the bomb's aftermath.

News coverage of Nagasaki saw a grudging shift in this policy, however. The *New York Times*, for example, finally acknowledged the fact that radiation was an issue, but obliquely and while downplaying its significance. Yet, the truth, undeniable and irrefutable, began to seep through the cracks. The haunting reality of survivors' suffering, the specter of radiation sickness, and the grim fate of the radiation-exposed pierced through the censorship, forcing public awareness to confront the catastrophic consequences of atomic warfare.

22   **What is the passage mainly about?** 4점

① The abrupt end of World War 2 following the atomic bombing of Japan

② The grim discovery of the devastating power of radioactive fallout

③ The cover-up of the aftereffects of radiation exposure by the US media

④ The *New York Times*' hard-hitting coverage of the atomic bomb detonations

⑤ The role of the media in exposing high-level government corruption

23   **What can be inferred from the text?** 4점

① The *New York Times* embraced bias and narrative-crafting as part of their ethos.

② The mainstream media is generally unbiased and objective during times of war.

③ The *New York Times* was shamed for its suppression of facts about the bombings.

④ The relativity of "truth" means that all depictions of an event are equally valid.

⑤ The *New York Times* attempted to portray the U.S. in a negative light with its coverage.

[24-25] Read the following passage and answer the questions.

Universities should tolerate no disruption or intimidation; but as far as speech alone goes, they must cease to see its supervision as within their <u>remit</u>. They should protect the rights of students to have nonpolitical spaces on campus (like libraries and dorms) and should remember that the opportunity to study and work in the absence of political intrusions is a great part of what the university exists to provide. They should promote faculty and evaluate students without respect to demography or ideology, seeking to abide not just by the letter, but the spirit of our nondiscrimination laws, including the recent Supreme Court ruling on affirmative action; and if the fact that in a liberal-democratic society it is deeply corrosive for powerful institutions to find ways around aspects of the law they happen to disagree with is not compelling enough reason to do so, then they should remember that these discriminatory policies are deeply unpopular across all racial groups.

24 **What is the best synonym for the underlined <u>remit</u>?** 4점

① purview　　　　② expanse　　　　③ surfeit

④ apogee　　　　⑤ nadir

25 **Which is the main purpose of the article?** 3점

① To promote increased supervision of on-campus activities

② To suggest the enforcement of on-campus disciplinary regulations

③ To emphasize the importance of social pressure on university policies

④ To advocate for the idea that university campuses are political spaces

⑤ To affirm the university's stance on free speech and diversity on campus

[26-28] Read the following passage and answer the questions.

Greenwashing, a concerning practice in the corporate world, involves companies misleadingly showcasing commitments to issues like decarbonization and biodiversity loss. It's a facade that conceals unethical practices while claiming sustainability efforts, undermining trust, and stalling real progress toward environmental goals. Companies often resort to greenwashing when facing pressure to display ethical responsibility without compromising profits. This practice allows them to _____ genuine sustainability efforts by presenting misleading claims about their environmental impact.

Examples of greenwashing abound, with some companies opting for superficial changes, like replacing plastic straws with seemingly eco-friendly alternatives that actually generate more waste. Others create their own watered-down standards or seek out weak certifications to appear compliant while neglecting true sustainability practices. Even within the investment sector, accusations of greenwashing arise, casting doubt on the authenticity of sustainable investment initiatives.

However, it's crucial to distinguish cases accurately. Sometimes, accusations of greenwashing might not align with the reality of a company's efforts. In one instance Baillie Gifford, an investment company, faced criticism for its ties to the fossil fuel industry, yet its actual investment in such sectors was notably lower than the industry average. This highlights the need for balanced judgment when labeling actions as greenwashing.

Tackling greenwashing requires vigilant scrutiny and exposing clear instances of misleading claims. Consumers play a pivotal role by questioning and supporting genuinely committed companies that prioritize environmental responsibility over mere marketing strategies. A collective effort to unveil greenwashing practices is essential in fostering trust and propelling genuine strides toward a sustainable future.

26 Which word best completes the sentence? 3점

① lockstep   ② backtrack   ③ sidetrack

④ sidestep   ⑤ claptrap

27 **What does the passage mainly say about "greenwashing"?** 4점

① It is a serious issue that must be discerned carefully.

② It is a pervasive issue tainting nearly every industry.

③ It is working to protect the earth from further damage.

④ It is dependent upon the government for funding.

⑤ It is an unavoidable reality in our modern economy.

28 **What can be inferred from the passage?** 4점

① The media fail to promote good corporate behavior.

② Companies hire public relations experts to stop greenwashing.

③ The corrupt media attack compliant companies.

④ Companies use environmental commitment as advertising.

⑤ The public prefers greenwashing to paying higher prices.

There was widespread scientific belief during the mid-twentieth century that the subjective experience of psychosis and the state of mind induced by psychedelic drugs were similar enough to warrant further study. However, in the 1960s a moral panic related to psychedelic drugs took hold. Simultaneously, requirements for evidence in medicine were becoming more rigorous, further erecting barriers against psychedelic research. Funding, access, and permissions for research related to psychedelic drugs slowly _____, and research into these substances was largely forgotten by psychiatry. In the proceeding decades, however, research related to psychosis and psychedelics has returned and proceeds unfettered, albeit having somewhat changed direction. Gone is much of the mainstream interest in detailed descriptions of the experience of psychosis that psychoanalytically trained psychiatrists sought through the application of psychedelic drugs. Instead, research on psychosis and psychedelics shares with the rest of psychiatry an often singular focus on neurobiological and genetic research.

29 **Which expression best completes the sentence?** 4점

① surged up　　　② dug up　　　③ dried up
④ plunged into　　⑤ buzzed up

30 **What is the passage mainly about?** 4점

① The similarities between psychosis and the psychedelic experience
② The results of research on psychosis and psychedelic drugs
③ The increased demands for evidence and its impact on research
④ The changed role of psychedelic drugs in psychiatric research
⑤ The moral dilemma still plaguing research into psychedelics

서울시립대학교   2024학년도 인문계
▶▶ 40문항·60분

[01-02] 다음 글에서 문법적으로 어색한 것을 고르시오.

01 How Shakespeare won over America in the early nineteenth century is ①<u>something of a mystery</u>. The absence of rivals had ②<u>a good dealing to do with</u> it. ③<u>So too did</u> the growing familiarity with his works. Actors from Britain toured the land with a repertory ④<u>rich in Shakespeare</u> while schoolbooks featured his famous speeches.

02 Western leaders have agreed to "de-risk" global supply chains linked to China. This means maintaining trading ties and being open to cooperation with Beijing in multiple areas such as climate change while also giving government support and protection to essential homegrown industries. But ①<u>when it comes to</u> clean energy, the difficulty of successfully de-risking ②<u>with respect to</u> China has not been adequately understood by Western leaders. The West needs a more refined approach, and the answer cannot be subsidies alone. If Western governments begin an all-out subsidy war against each other, ③<u>that will</u> only shift investment to the highest bidder. ④<u>Nor subsidies would</u> achieve their purpose. Attempting to compete with China on cost in every sector would likely waste taxpayer money and lead to greater damage from climate change.

03 다음 밑줄 친 "woke"의 의미와 가장 가까운 것을 고르시오.

Oscar-winning filmmaker Sharmeen Obaid-Chinoy has been linked to directing an upcoming *Star Wars* film, making her the first woman to be at the helm of a film in the iconic franchise — but right-wing critics are blasting the movie as "woke" after Obaid-Chinoy said it's "about time" a woman directed a *Star Wars* installment.

① mediocre
② sexist
③ too boring
④ politically progressive

[04-08] 다음 글에서 빈칸에 들어갈 단어로 가장 적절한 것을 고르시오.

04 The International Court of Justice made a ruling clarifying the meaning of its prior judgment on a territorial dispute over the Temple of Preah Vihear between Thailand and Cambodia. The ruling suggests that the current court is willing to engage in significant efforts to fill in interpretive gaps where the language of prior judgment lacks clarity. At the same time, the reluctance of the court to _____ on the location of the frontier to the north and west of the temple shows its caution and necessitates further negotiation.

① head
② opine
③ hinge
④ preclude

05 *Guy Ritchie's The Covenant* follows U.S. Army Sergeant John Kinley (Jake Gyllenhaal) and Afghan interpreter Ahmed (Dar Salim). After an ambush, Ahmed goes to Herculean lengths to save Kinley's life. When Kinley learns that Ahmed and his family were not given safe passage to America as promised, he must repay his debt by returning to the war zone to _____ them before the Taliban hunts them down first.

① trap
② retrieve
③ forgive
④ sacrifice

06 *Fountain* is a landmark of twentieth-century art because it marks a radically new approach to the task of making art. No artistic skill was involved to render it an artwork; Duchamp was not a ceramicist but an erstwhile painter, and all he did was add a bogus signature. The factory-made object exists because of its functionality, not its beauty. And yet by elevating it onto a pedestal and placing it in an art gallery, Duchamp gave it the status of art. His decision to do this — his _____, if you will — is the real work of art, and in that sense, seeing a photograph of it is as good as seeing the real thing.

① concept
② objection
③ obstinacy
④ commitment

07 Even as check use has rapidly declined over the past couple of decades, check fraud has risen sharply, particularly since the pandemic. The con artists may start with stealing pieces of paper, but they _____ technology and social media to commit fraud on a grander scale, banking insiders and fraud experts said.

① forge
② encrypt
③ impersonate
④ leverage

08 Hotels often lag in implementing digital transformation and AI due to a combination of factors. Key among these is the perception of high costs and complexity, which can be daunting, especially for smaller establishments. There's also a strong adherence to traditional methods rooted in the hospitality industry's emphasis on personal, human touch, leading to a(n) _____ to adopt seemingly impersonal technology.

① impeccability
② disposition
③ inclination
④ reluctance

09 빈칸에 들어갈 단어로 가장 적절한 것을 고르시오.
One way to take the pulse of global cities is to use real-time _____ indicators. *The Economist* has constructed an "exodus index" using Google data on visits to sites of retail and recreation, public transport, and workplaces.

① mobility
② visibility
③ diversity
④ sustainability

10 밑줄 친 apologists와 가장 유사한 의미를 지닌 단어를 고르시오.

As well as ruling an immense and diverse country, Cleopatra was a city planner who made Alexandria into one of the most vibrant cities of the ancient world, a skillful military strategist and diplomat, a gifted linguist, and even the author of treatises on medicine. Despite these accomplishments, the story of this remarkable woman has been shaped by <u>apologists</u> for Roman imperial expansion, men such as Plutarch, who described her romantic and political involvement with two figures he wrote about: Julius Caesar and Mark Antony.

① critics   ② proponents
③ opportunists   ④ insurgents

11 밑줄 친 말의 반대말을 고르시오.

US Energy Secretary <u>extolled</u> oil executives for boosting output and lauded the industry's creative visionaries in an attempt to ease tensions between the Biden administration and fossil-fuel producers.

① demoted   ② disseminated
③ blamed   ④ acclaimed

12 Ⓐ와 Ⓑ에 들어갈 가장 적절한 표현을 순서대로 고르시오.

In the United States, the great replacement conspiracy theory has been supercharged over the past decade by social media and the backlash to the election of President Barack Obama. The theory holds that there is an ongoing Ⓐ＿＿＿＿ of white people and culture as part of a deliberate strategy by Jews and liberal elites. The great replacement theory's spread was Ⓑ＿＿＿＿ by the terrorist strategy known as accelerationism, an effort to foment cataclysmic violent chaos as a means to seize power.

① emigration — revealed
② diffusion — rejuvenated
③ concentration — derided
④ diminution — abetted

13 다음 글에 이어질 내용을 글의 흐름상 가장 적절하게 배열한 것을 고르시오.

H. G. Wells may not have been an expert in any particular scientific field, but he believed wholeheartedly in the idea of science, especially when it came to the rational government of human beings.

Ⓐ At different times, he called this virtuous elite the New Republicans, the Samurai, and the Open Conspiracy; it can be thought of as an idealized version of the Fabian Society, the elite socialist group to which Wells briefly belonged.

Ⓑ In book after book, novels and nonfiction alike, Wells hammered home the message that humanity could improve its lot only by entrusting power to a self-selected caste of enlightened technicians, who would rule according to the dictates of science.

Ⓒ "The dominant men of the new time," he writes, will "all be artists in reality, with a passion for simplicity and directness and an impatience of confusion and inefficiency," dedicated to creating the "future world state to which all things are pointing."

Ⓓ He first described this caste in *Anticipations*, the 1901 book he called "the keystone to the main arch of my book."

① Ⓑ — Ⓐ — Ⓓ — Ⓒ
② Ⓐ — Ⓑ — Ⓓ — Ⓒ
③ Ⓑ — Ⓐ — Ⓒ — Ⓓ
④ Ⓐ — Ⓑ — Ⓒ — Ⓓ

14 다음 글에서 전체 흐름과 가장 <u>관계없는</u> 문장을 고르시오.

In addition to building emotional resilience, cli-fi also helps readers connect emotionally to the climate crisis, which is perhaps its most important achievement. ① <u>Studies show that a lack of emotional connection to their future selves prevents people from taking actions in the present that may help them in the future.</u> ② <u>Connecting with characters who are experiencing the effects of climate change can help readers connect with their future selves potentially experiencing similar effects.</u> ③ <u>The genre as a whole shows the range of potential consequences of climate change, as each work imagines the consequences differently.</u> ④ <u>In this way, cli-fi narratives may be more effective at driving action compared to scientific literature alone.</u>

15 다음 글의 주제로 가장 적합한 것을 고르시오.

Through photographs, each family constructs a portrait-chronicle of itself — a portable kit of images that bears witness to its connectedness. It hardly matters what activities are photographed so long as photographs get taken and are cherished. Photography becomes a rite of family life just when, in the industrializing countries of Europe and America, the very institution of the family starts undergoing radical surgery. As that claustrophobic unit, the nuclear family, was being carved out of a much larger family aggregate, photography came along to memorialize, to restate symbolically, the imperiled continuity and vanishing extendedness of family life. Those ghostly traces, photographs, supply the token presence of the dispersed relatives. A family's photograph album is generally about the extended family — and, often, is all that remains of it.

① Rapid changes in family systems have created demand for family photos.
② Photography reflected the impact of the shift from extended to nuclear family life.
③ Photos have been useful in remembering lost relatives and family members.
④ The growing importance of the family in industrialized countries was one reason for the development of photography.

16 다음 글의 내용과 가장 거리가 <u>먼</u> 것을 고르시오.

Almost a decade ago, a price war broke out between petrostates in the Persian Gulf and the frackers in America, whose innovative drilling techniques gave rise to the shale revolution. Some even called this new economics of oil "Sheikhs v shale".

For much of the interim period the petrostates and the hardscrabble shale producers remained critical to this new oil order, though their tussle unfolded in strange ways. In 2016, the OPEC producers' cartel joined forces with Russia to create OPEC+ which its autocratic masterminds hoped would let them control oil prices in order to benefit their regimes. Yet instead of responding by dousing the world in oil, the frackers unexpectedly developed OPEC-like self-restraint. Under pressure from investors to improve profits, they kept a tight rein on drilling activity even when crude surged above $100 a barrel.

That unusual discipline continued until 2023, when American producers awoke from their slumber. Record shale output allowed America to extract more oil than any country in history, offsetting desperate efforts by OPEC+ to curtail production in order to prop up prices. Some experts call it "the great rebalancing" — a historic shift of oil production away from the Gulf and towards the western hemisphere.

① For a long time, petrostates in the Persian Gulf have had significant influence on the oil market.

② For several years before 2023, shale producers tried to maximize their profits by restraining their production.

③ American frackers pumped an unprecedented amount of oil in 2023.

④ For the last decade, key players in the oil market have intimately coordinated their oil productions.

On the first day of class, Jerry Uelsmann, a professor at the University of Florida, divided his film photography students into two groups. Everyone on the left side of the classroom, he explained, would be in the "quantity" group. They would be graded solely on the amount of work they produced. On the final day of class, he would tally the number of photos submitted by each student. One hundred photos would rate an A, ninety photos a B, eighty photos a C, and so on. Meanwhile, everyone on the right side of the room would be in the "quality" group. They would be graded only on the excellence of their work. They would only need to produce one photo during the semester, but to get an A, it had to be a nearly perfect image.

At the end of the term, he was surprised to find that all the best photos were produced by the Ⓐ_____ group. During the semester, these students were busy taking photos, experimenting with compositions and lighting, testing out various methods in the darkroom, and learning from their mistakes. In the process of creating hundreds of photos, they honed their skills. Meanwhile, the Ⓑ_____ group sat around speculating about perfection. In the end, they had little to show off for their efforts other than unverified theories and one mediocre photo.

It is easy to get bogged down trying to find the optimal plan for change: the fastest way to lose weight, the best program to build muscle, the perfect idea for a side hustle. We are so focused on figuring out the best approach that we never get round to taking action. As Voltaire once wrote, Ⓒ"_____"

17 Ⓐ와 Ⓑ에 들어갈 단어들을 순서대로 고르시오.

① quantity — quantity

② quantity — quality

③ quality — quality

④ quality — quantity

18 Ⓒ에 가장 알맞은 문장을 고르시오.

① The best is the enemy of the good.

② Common sense is not so common.

③ Judge a man by his questions rather than his answers.

④ Optimism is the madness of insisting that all is well when we are miserable.

[19-20] 다음 글을 읽고 문제에 답하시오.

With an environment devoid of oxygen and high in methane, for much of its history Earth would not have been a welcoming place for animals. The earliest life forms we know of were microscopic organisms (microbes) that left signals of their presence in rocks about 3.7 billion years old.

A When cyanobacteria evolved, they set the stage for a remarkable transformation. They became Earth's first photo-synthesizers, making food using water and the Sun's energy, and releasing oxygen as a result. This catalyzed a sudden, dramatic rise in oxygen, making the environment less hospitable for other microbes that could not tolerate oxygen.

B Something revolutionary happened as microbes began living inside other microbes, functioning as organelles for them. Mitochondria, the organelles that process food into energy, evolved from these mutually beneficial relationships. Also, for the first time, DNA became packaged in nuclei. The new complex cells boasted specialized parts playing specialized roles that supported the whole cell.

C These clusters of specialized, cooperating cells eventually became the first animals. Sponges were among the earliest animals. By about 580 million years ago (the Ediacaran Period) there was a proliferation of other organisms, in addition to sponges. However, about 541 million years ago, most of the Ediacaran creatures disappeared.

D The Cambrian Period witnessed a wild explosion of new life forms. A shift also occurred towards more active animals, with defined heads and tails for directional movement to chase prey.

However, despite all the changes that were to come, by the end of the Cambrian Period nearly all existing animal types or phyla were established.

19 글의 흐름에 맞게 배열하시오.

① A — B — C — D
② B — C — A — D
③ C — A — D — B
④ D — A — B — C

20 밑줄 친 내용에 해당하는 두 가지를 고르시오.

(a) The great oxidation event

(b) Extinction of non-avian dinosaurs

(c) Disappearance of the Neanderthals

(d) Appearance of multicellular lives

① a, b   ② b, c

③ c, d   ④ a, d

[21-22] 다음 글을 읽고 문제에 답하시오.

Quantum Information Science and Technology, which includes quantum computing, networking, sensing, and metrology, leverages the fundamental properties of matter to generate new information technologies. For example, quantum computers can, in principle, use the unique properties of atoms and photons to solve certain types of problems exponentially faster than a conventional computer can. Over many decades, harnessing quantum aspects of nature has produced critical technologies.

Quantum Information Science and Technology will bring new capabilities for both civilian and military purposes. Prior examples of quantum-related technologies include semiconductor microelectronics, photonics, the global positioning system, and magnetic resonance imaging. Future scientific and technological discoveries in quantum may be even more impactful.

Aside from their potential benefits, quantum technologies can also pose national security challenges. With further advancements in coming years, a large-scale quantum computer could potentially allow for the decryption of most commonly used cybersecurity protocols, putting at risk the infrastructure protecting today's economic and national security communications. In short, whoever wins the race for quantum computing supremacy could potentially compromise the communications of others. Without effective mitigation, the impact of adversarial use of a quantum computer could be <u>devastating</u> to national security systems and the nation.

21 밑줄 친 <u>devastating</u>과 가장 유사한 의미를 지닌 단어를 고르시오.

① shattering   ② susceptible

③ vulnerable   ④ appealing

22 위 글을 읽고 유추하기 가장 <u>어려운</u> 것을 고르시오.

① Quantum-related technologies have been conducive to some innovations in medical and automotive industries.

② A state with quantum technology inferior to its adversary's may be exposed to national security breaches.

③ Quantum computers decisively outperform conventional computers.

④ Quantum Information Science and Technology has been prohibited from civilian uses.

[23-24] 다음 글을 읽고 문제에 답하시오.

In the days immediately after the United States dropped atomic bombs on Hiroshima and Nagasaki, radiation was largely a mystery to the Japanese public; men and women had survived the explosion but were succumbing to a new illness — an "evil spirit," as a national newspaper put it.

Nine years later, Japan had another encounter with nuclear technology: on March 1, 1954, the U.S. tested what was the world's most powerful hydrogen bomb on Bikini Atoll, in the Pacific. The blast was more than twice the size that engineers had predicted, and a shower of radioactive ash reached far enough to envelop a voyaging Japanese tuna boat named the Lucky Dragon No. 5. The twenty-three crew members had no idea what had dusted them — "I took a lick; it was gritty but had no taste," one wrote later — but by the time they returned to shore they were burned, blistered, and in the early stages of acute radiation sickness. Their contaminated tuna was sold at the market before anyone stopped it.

The ordeal caused a panic in Japan; a petition against future hydrogen-bomb tests secured the signature of one in every three citizens. It was the start of what became known as Japan's "nuclear _____." In less than a year, Japanese filmmakers had released *Godzilla*, about a creature mutated by American atomic weapons. "Mankind had created the Bomb," the film's producer, Tomoyuki Tanaka, said of his monster, "and now nature was going to take revenge." Godzilla's radioactive breath and low-budget special effects were campy to the rest of the world but not to the Japanese, who watched the film in silence and left theatres in tears.

23 빈칸에 들어갈 표현으로 가장 적절한 것을 고르시오.

① infatuation   ② addiction

③ allergy   ④ worship

24 위 글의 내용과 가장 거리가 <u>먼</u> 것을 고르시오.

① The Japanese film *Godzilla* was not well-received by international audiences partly owing to its substandard special effects.

② The crew of Lucky Dragon No. 5 did not realize the nature of the substance that engulfed them until later.

③ The Japanese audience expressed their disapproval of the movie *Godzilla*'s political message with silence.

④ After the atomic bombings of Hiroshima and Nagasaki, it took some years before Japanese people recognized the nature of radiation.

[25-26] 다음 글을 읽고 문제에 답하시오.

If the conscious mind is like a general atop a platform who sees the world from a distance and analyzes things linearly and linguistically, the unconscious mind is like a million little scouts. The scouts career across the landscape, sending back a constant flow of signals and generating instant responses. They maintain no distance from the environment around them, but are immersed in it. They scurry about, interpenetrating other minds, landscapes, and ideas. These scouts coat things with emotional significance. They come across an old friend and send back a surge of affection. They descend into a dark cave and send back a surge of fear. Contact with a beautiful landscape produces a feeling of sublime elevation. Contact with a brilliant insight produces delight while contact with unfairness produces righteous anger. Each Ⓐ_____ has its own flavor, texture, and force, and reactions loop around the mind in a stream of sensations, impulses, judgments, and desires. These signals don't control our lives, but they shape our interpretation of the world and they guide us, like a spiritual GPS, as we Ⓑ_____ our courses. If the general thinks in data and speaks in prose, the scouts crystallize with emotion, and their work is best expressed in stories, poetry, music, image, prayer, and myth.

25 Ⓐ, Ⓑ에 들어갈 가장 적절한 표현을 순서대로 고르시오.

① perception — chart
② conception — figure
③ reception — flip
④ inception — plan

26 위 글의 내용과 가장 거리가 <u>먼</u> 것을 고르시오.

① It is our unconscious mind that makes us pleased when we encounter an exceptional insight.

② The conscious mind is inferior to the unconscious mind as the latter controls our lives.

③ The unconscious mind predominantly colors our reactions with emotions.

④ The workings of the unconscious mind are best conveyed in narratives and paintings.

[27-28] 다음 글을 읽고 문제에 답하시오.

The debate over whether companies should allow flexible work-from-home (WFH) arrangements versus mandating their employees to return to the office continues to divide the US workforce.

But the booming South Korean office market may Ⓐ<u>undermine</u> arguments that it is better for employees to head back to the office — at least for those watching the US's struggling commercial-real-estate sector. In Seoul, over 98% of grade-A offices are occupied thanks to white-collar workers returning to the office. The increase in competition for office space has led to a roughly 15% rise in rental prices over the last year, Bloomberg reported. As COVID-19 restrictions have Ⓑ<u>eased</u>, the number of jobs allowing employees to work from home has declined.

In addition to the strong demand in the Korean office market, there has been a general shortage of office space since 2021 due to government restrictions on redevelopment and the pandemic's disruption of construction. The Korean economy has also seen steady growth, bolstering both international and domestic investment.

But US business districts have struggled because of the rise in popularity of working from home and many employees' reluctance to start Ⓒ<u>commuting</u> five days a week again. Goldman Sachs found that the share of US workers who work from home at least some of the workweek has Ⓓ<u>stabilized</u> this year to around 20% to 25%, below a pandemic peak of 47% but above the pre-pandemic average of 2.6%. Almost 30% of employees also now use a hybrid work model, *Forbes* reported. Commercial landlords have seen tenants cut space or move out completely amid the new remote-work culture, and office vacancies were at a 30-year high of 18.2% in the US in the second quarter, according to CBRE research.

27 밑줄 친 단어 중 문맥상 가장 <u>적절치 않은</u> 것을 고르시오.

① Ⓐ undermine   ② Ⓑ eased

③ Ⓒ commuting   ④ Ⓓ stabilized

28 위 글에 이어질 내용으로 가장 적절한 것을 고르시오.

① The Biden administration recently announced plans to incentivize developers to convert empty offices into apartments to help alleviate the US office market crisis.

② The Biden administration recently encouraged companies to provide workers with more flexibility to activate the US office market.

③ Surveys showed that Gen Z and Class of 2023 graduates want in-person work.

④ US commercial landlords need to develop more spacious workplaces to entice US companies which look for vacant workplaces.

[29-30] 다음 글을 읽고 문제에 답하시오.

Ⓐ It's clear that prioritizing the development of _____ strategies is vital in the face of volatility and uncertainty. But what exactly do leaders need to prepare for? And what should be prioritized to make _____ operations a reality?

Ⓑ But these disruptions aren't happening in isolation. We're seeing a ripple effect on multiple industries and individuals, with those less prepared to weather such challenges taking the biggest hit.

Ⓒ No matter where you are in the world right now, economies are struggling. Geopolitical tensions, rising inflation and interest rates, and many other external factors continue to impact businesses across the globe.

Ⓓ The UK, for instance, just reached the country's highest interest rates since the 2008 financial crisis. And this news follows on from higher-than-expected inflation data which continues to remind us of the challenges businesses are facing today.

---

29 빈칸에 공통적으로 들어갈 가장 적절한 말을 고르시오.

① rigid   ② resilient

③ transparent   ④ autonomous

30 위 문단들을 논리적 순서에 맞게 배열하시오.

① A — B — C — D   ② C — A — D — B

③ A — D — C — B   ④ C — D — B — A

[31-32] 다음 글을 읽고 문제에 답하시오.

Electric vehicle (EV) markets are still showing great strength across the board, breaking new records as sales surge. A total of 14% of all new cars sold were electric in 2022, up from around 9% in 2021 and less than 5% in 2020.

Despite surging EV sales, the transition has really only just begun. This means that demand should continue to soar on the back of subsidies and future phase-out targets and regulations for internal combustion engine (ICE) vehicles. When total costs of EV ownership are _____ with those of ICE vehicles (and even begin to drop below them) in the second half of the decade, we can expect an extra upswing.

As the demand for EVs rises rapidly, so does the demand for the minerals inside their batteries. The rapid increase in electric vehicle sales during the Covid-19 pandemic has exacerbated concerns over China's dominance in lithium battery supply chains. Meanwhile, the ongoing war in Ukraine has pushed prices of raw materials — including cobalt, lithium, and nickel — to record highs.

The dependence on specific suppliers is not the only concern. Batteries make up a big part of an EV's total cost and typically account for 30% to 40% of their value, but this proportion increases with larger battery sizes.

Europe is currently pushing hard to develop its battery supply chain, but this takes time and sourcing dependencies remain. The EU's Critical Raw Materials Act is the bloc's attempt to secure supply chains and boost European autonomy to ensure the EU has access to materials needed to meet the bloc's target of moving to net-zero greenhouse gas emissions by 2050.

31 빈칸에 들어갈 가장 적절한 표현을 고르시오.

① at risk   ② on the rise

③ in comparison   ④ on a par

32 위 글을 읽고 유추할 수 <u>없는</u> 것을 고르시오.

① Europe currently makes efforts to strengthen EV battery supply chains.

② EVs are increasing the number of small car parts suppliers.

③ China's dominance in EV battery metal poses challenges to the EV industry.

④ EV sales are expected to continue to surge.

[33-34] 다음 글을 읽고 문제에 답하시오.

The new trend, known as "tang ping", is described as a(n) Ⓐ_____ to society's pressures to find jobs and perform well while working long shifts. China has a shrinking labour market and young people often work more hours. The term "tang ping" is believed to have originated in a post on a popular Chinese social media site. "Lying flat is my wise movement," a user wrote in a since-deleted post on the discussion forum Tieba, adding: "Only by lying down can humans become the measure of all things." The comments were later discussed on Sina Weibo, another popular Chinese microblogging site, and the term soon became a Ⓑ_____. The idea behind "tang ping" — not overworking, being content with more attainable achievements, and allowing time to unwind — has been praised by many and inspired numerous memes. It has been described as a spiritual movement.

33 Ⓐ와 Ⓑ에 들어갈 적절한 말을 순서대로 고르시오.

① toxin — trend

② remedy — anonymity

③ antidote — buzzword

④ venom — catchphrase

34 위 글을 읽고 유추하기 가장 <u>어려운</u> 것을 고르시오.

① "Tang ping" is a response to societal pressures regarding job search and high performance during long working hours.

② Through "tang ping", Chinese youth have begun to engage in active political participation.

③ The discussion on Sina Weibo indicates the rapid spread of the trend through online discourse.

④ The concept of "lying flat" as a wise movement suggests a rejection of overworking and a desire for a more relaxed and balanced lifestyle.

Digital humanities is not a unified field but an array of Ⓐ_____ practices that explore a universe in which: a) print is no longer the exclusive or the normative medium in which knowledge is produced and/or disseminated; instead, print finds itself absorbed into new, multimedia configurations; and b) digital tools, techniques, and media have altered the production and dissemination of knowledge in the arts, human and social sciences. Digital humanities seeks to play an inaugural role with respect to a world in which, no longer the sole producers, stewards, and disseminators of knowledge or culture, universities are called upon to shape natively digital models of scholarly discourse for the newly emergent public spheres of the present era (the www, the blogosphere, digital libraries, etc.), to model excellence and innovation in these domains, and to facilitate the formation of networks of knowledge production, exchange, and dissemination that are, at once, global and local.

The first wave of digital humanities work was Ⓑ_____, mobilizing the search and retrieval powers of the database, automating corpus linguistics, stacking hypercards into critical arrays. The second wave is qualitative, interpretive, experiential, emotive, and generative in character. It harnesses digital toolkits in the service of the humanities' core methodological strengths: attention to complexity, medium specificity, historical context, analytical depth, critique and interpretation. Such a crudely drawn dichotomy does not exclude the emotional, even sublime potentiality of the quantitative any more than it excludes embeddings of quantitative analysis within qualitative frameworks. Rather it imagines new couplings and scalings that are facilitated both by new models of research practice and by the availability of new tools and technologies.

35 Ⓐ, Ⓑ에 들어갈 가장 적절한 단어를 순서대로 고르시오.

① convergent — quantitative

② divergent — subjective

③ interdisciplinary — descriptive

④ intensified — statistical

36 위 글을 읽고 가장 유추하기 <u>어려운</u> 것을 고르시오.

① The transformative nature of digital humanities extends beyond traditional boundaries, fostering global and local networks for knowledge production, exchange, and dissemination.

② Digital humanities is characterized as a diverse set of practices exploring a transformed universe where print is no longer the exclusive medium for knowledge dissemination.

③ Digital humanities, built upon the advancements in digital technology, is evolving by harnessing big data and prioritizing quantitative methods over qualitative approaches.

④ The evolving landscape of research practice and technological advancements contributes to the ongoing development and integration of digital methods in the humanities.

[37-38] 다음 글을 읽고 문제에 답하시오.

Cities can make us Ⓐ_____. They always have — diseases spread more easily when more people are close to one another. And disease is hardly the only ill that accompanies urban density. Cities have been demonized as breeding grounds for vice and crime from Sodom and Gomorrah on. But cities have flourished nonetheless because they are humanity's greatest invention, indispensable engines for creativity, innovation, wealth, and connection, the loom on which the fabric of civilization is woven.

But cities now stand at a crossroads. During the global COVID crisis, cities grew silent as people worked from home — if they could work at all. The normal forms of socializing ground to a halt. How permanent are these changes? Advances in digital technology mean that many people can opt out of city life as never before. Will they? Are we on the brink of a post-urban world?

City life will Ⓑ_____, but individual cities face terrible risks, argue Edward Glaeser and David Cutler, and a wave of urban failure would be absolutely disastrous. In terms of intimacy and inspiration, nothing can replace what cities offer. Great cities have always demanded great management, and our current crisis has exposed fearful gaps in our capacity for good governance. It is possible to drive a city into the ground, pandemic or not. Glaeser and Cutler examine the evolution that is already happening and describe the possible futures that lie before us: What will distinguish the cities that will flourish from the ones that won't? In America, they argue, deep inequities in health care and education are a particular blight on the future of our cities; solving them will be the difference between our collective good health and a downward spiral to a much darker place.

37 Ⓐ, Ⓑ에 들어갈 가장 적절한 단어를 순서대로 고르시오.

① fragile — stumble

② robust — flourish

③ wholesome — persist

④ sick — survive

38 위 글의 주제로 가장 적합한 것을 고르시오.

① If the current urban crisis is not addressed, the sustainability of the city could be jeopardized.

② Cities, as the central places of modern civilization, continually lead humanity worldwide to prosperity.

③ After the COVID-19 pandemic crisis, humanity worldwide should abandon cities and return to a rural way of life.

④ For the future development of cities, local initiatives led by regional governments are crucial.

[39-40] 다음 글을 읽고 문제에 답하시오.

Plato describes love in such a way that constancy is not an important feature of it, let alone a logically necessary condition. At the lowest stage of Plato's ladder of love, x loves y because y is physically beautiful. This kind of love will not be constant (we might think) because physical beauty fades with time, sometimes very quickly. But this is not exactly why, for Plato, love at this lowest stage is not constant. For Aristotle, if x loves y because y is pleasant or useful to x, x's love will not endure precisely because y's being pleasant or useful is not something that lasts. ⒶThus, in Aristotle, we find the claim that because x loves y for P, x will no longer love y when P is gone. But in Plato, x's love for y, when it is based on y's physical beauty, is not constant for a different reason: x Ⓑinitially realizes not only that the physical beauty possessed by y is also possessed by many other people but also that physical beauty does not hold a candle to other kinds of beauty.

There is no hint in Plato that x's love for y, when it is based on y's physical beauty, ends exactly when y's beauty fades. Rather, x's love for y ends even Ⓒbefore that beauty fades. The lover, ideally, recognizes that y's beauty will fade and hence that this sort of beauty is inferior to other kinds. Thus x, not wanting to become overly attached to lesser beauty — since happiness does not lie here — progresses to the next level of Plato's ladder, at which a more substantial beauty provides the basis of love: moral virtue and intellectual excellence. Again, however, x realizes that even this superior type of beauty or goodness is not what x is yearning for. It, too, is widespread and fades with time (even if slowly). People die, taking their mental beauty with them, so that sort of beauty is perishable and hence inferior. Love can be constant, for Plato, only when its object is Ⓓperfectly beautiful or good. This means not that its object is a kind of thing that could change, even if as a matter of fact it never does change, but that it is a kind of thing for which all change is impossible. This is Plato's "Absolute Beauty," that which x all along had desired and which is accessible only at the highest level of the "Ascent." Platonic love is, in this regard, the pagan version of the human love for the Christian God.

39 다음 중 문맥상 <u>어색한</u> 단어를 고르시오.

① Ⓐ Thus
② Ⓑ initially
③ Ⓒ before
④ Ⓓ perfectly

40 위 글에서 유추할 수 있는 가장 적절한 것을 고르시오.

① For Plato, there is only one type of love.
② Plato was a Christian thinker.
③ Aristotle's theory of love is the same as Plato's.
④ For Aristotle, love has a cause.

서울시립대학교   2024학년도 자연계 II
▶▶ 영어 20문항, 수학 20문항·90분

01 다음 중 문법적으로 <u>어색한</u> 것을 고르시오. 2점

Taylor Swift is one of ①<u>the most influential singer and songwriter</u> of her era. ②<u>Born in</u> 1989, she released her first album in 2006 and toured the United States with country music performances, then gradually ③<u>shifted to</u> pop music. Swift has released 14 albums, and her net worth soared to $1.1 billion ④<u>following</u> 2023's wildly popular Eras Tour.

02 아래 밑줄 친 단어와 문맥상 의미가 가장 가까운 단어를 고르시오. 2점

The Avengers, which brought together the superheroes that Marvel had established across four years of blockbuster movies, already looked like it was going to be a huge worldwide hit. It was the culmination of a decade of work by Marvel's producers and executives, including Kevin Feige, the president of Marvel Studios. It was also a sign that Marvel had placed a winning bet when, emerging from bankruptcy, the company had mortgaged the rights to its own characters to secure a line of credit from a Wall Street bank. The studio had <u>staked</u> its entire future on that loan, which financed the first movies Marvel Studios made.

① gambled   ② secured
③ predicted   ④ ruined

[03-04] 빈칸에 들어갈 말로 가장 적절한 것을 고르시오.

03 In 2024, patent expirations are _____. Medicines worth $38 billion in sales, including many biotech drugs, will meet competition from cheaper generics. 3점

① dissipating   ② mounting

③ discrediting   ④ encouraging

04 Unexpected economic trends _____ predictions in 2023. In a surprising turn of events, the expected recession in 2023 never materialized, and inflation rates, which peaked in late 2022, continued to decline throughout 2023. Economies, contrary to predictions, remained generally robust. 2점

① defied   ② supported

③ appraised   ④ contributed to

[05-06] 빈칸에 들어갈 말로 가장 적절한 것을 순서대로 고르시오.

05 AI allows for easier and more comprehensive data aggregation, which in turn empowers nefarious actors to undertake Ⓐ_____ cyberattacks, including spearphishing attacks targeting specific individuals or organizations. When this is combined with high-quality AI-generated content, even the most Ⓑ_____ of Internet users may be vulnerable. 3점

① ardent — relentless

② customized — ingenuous

③ tailored — vigilant

④ random — prudential

06 The ability to maintain, cope, and withstand is about Ⓐ_____, whereas the ability to recover or bounce back is about Ⓑ_____. So, for instance, taking an industry-level unit of analysis, during the COVID-19 pandemic, most organizations providing health care and education services withstood difficulties whereas those in the travel and tourism industries suffered and then recovered. An example at a business level of analysis is the taxi industry. Traditional taxi companies were resilient when their performance degraded at first with the lockdowns but then recovered as volume returned. Local disability-specialized taxi companies were robust and somewhat insensitive. These examples reflect that they are different concepts and demonstrate that the mechanisms driving these outcomes are different. 2점

① vulnerability — flexibility
② adaptability — anti-fragility
③ durability — tenacity
④ robustness — resilience

[07-08] 다음 글을 읽고 문제에 답하시오.

When violators are less likely to be punished through domestic judicial action, the power of the courts to bring governments into line with international law decreases. The law-and-economics literature often adopts a statistical terminology and refers to occasions on which a violator of law is not prosecuted as type II errors. A higher likelihood of type II error creates a lower incentive for actors to obey the law because there is a lower probability that they would face a penalty for not doing so.

A Therefore, courts face important information asymmetries with respect to enforcing international commitments on the other branches of government. Legislatures and executives often violate legal commitments and have an incentive to keep these violations hidden.

B Information is crucial to the reduction of type II errors. Enforcement mechanisms depend on effective monitoring mechanisms. Violators cannot be punished unless their transgressions are observed. While courts have strong enforcement powers, they have relatively weak monitoring powers.

C This is the reason why courts depend on other actors to bring information to them regarding alleged violations of international commitments. Overcoming information asymmetries through fire alarm mechanisms is therefore a crucial component of effective enforcement of international commitments by domestic courts.

07 글의 흐름에 맞게 위 문단의 순서를 배열하시오. 3점

① A — B — C
② B — A — C
③ C — B — A
④ C — A — B

08 위 글에서 유추할 수 있는 내용으로 가장 거리가 <u>먼</u> 것을 고르시오. 3점

① When it comes to the court rulings, lack of information may cause 'false negative' results.
② With sufficient information, courts can have substantial impact on a state's commitment to international treaties.
③ It is easy for courts to prove government violations of international commitments.
④ For effective implementation of international commitments, domestic courts need other actors to monitor governments.

[09-10] 다음 글을 읽고 문제에 답하시오.

117 job applications are submitted on LinkedIn every second. That equates to more than ten million job applications each day. Factor in other job search engines like Indeed, Glassdoor and ZipRecruiter, all of which make applying for a job as simple as a few clicks on your keyboard, and you can see how recruiters are being inundated with resumes.

Ⓐ The concept behind the automated video interview, or AVI is quite simple. Chosen applicants are invited to engage with a hiring platform to record and submit video responses to written questions that appear on applicants' screens. AI algorithms analyze the video responses, looking for things like the applicant's facial expressions, use of key words and tone of voice. A transcript of the responses along with a report summarizing the candidate's performance are then provided to the recruiter who decides if the candidate Ⓐ_____ to the next phase of the interview process.

Ⓑ However, the process is also fraught. AI recruitment platforms have been criticized for building bias into their algorithms. And job candidates find AVIs confusing because the format is relatively new, stress-inducing because of the time constraints imposed on responses, and unsettling because of the lack of transparency around how they will ultimately be assessed.

Ⓒ There are obvious advantages to this type of interview. Employers gain efficiencies by screening significantly more applicants using significantly fewer human resources. And, in theory, AVIs remove implicit bias making the interview process more objective. Applicants appreciate the flexibility of being able to choose when they conduct the interview and the convenience of being able to do so in a comfortable location of their choice.

Ⓓ It's not surprising then that companies in search of the most qualified candidates are seeking more efficient ways to sift through this flood of applicants. And so, a new and rapidly growing trend has Ⓑ_____, the use of AI in the recruitment process. A surprisingly large number of companies — *Harvard Business Review* estimates as many as 86% of all employers — are now limiting or eliminating human involvement in the initial stages of the interview process and replacing the interviewer with artificial intelligence.

09 다음 Ⓐ와 Ⓑ에 들어갈 말을 순서대로 고르시오. 2점

① drops out — materialized

② advances — emerged

③ proceeds — changed

④ falls — shifted

10 글의 흐름에 맞게 위 문단의 순서를 배열하시오. 3점

① A — B — C — D

② D — C — B — A

③ A — D — C — B

④ D — A — C — B

[11-12] 다음 글을 읽고 문제에 답하시오.

Naturally, almost any mammal species that is sufficiently large is capable of killing a human. People have been killed by pigs, horses, camels, and cattle. Nevertheless, some large animals have much nastier dispositions and are more incurably dangerous than are others. Tendencies to kill humans have disqualified many otherwise seemingly ideal candidates for domestication.

One obvious example is the grizzly bear. Bear meat is an expensive delicacy, grizzlies weigh up to 1,700 pounds, they are mainly herbivores (though also formidable hunters), their vegetable diet is very broad, they thrive on human garbage (thereby creating big problems in Yellowstone and Glacier National Parks), and they grow relatively fast. If they would behave themselves in captivity, grizzlies would be a fabulous meat production animal. The Ainu people of Japan made the experiment by routinely rearing grizzly cubs as part of a ritual. For understandable reasons, though, the Ainu found it prudent to kill and eat the cubs at the age of one year. Keeping grizzly bears for longer would be suicidal; I am not aware of any adult that has been _____.

Another otherwise suitable candidate that disqualifies itself for equally obvious reasons is the African buffalo. It grows quickly up to a weight of a ton and lives in herds that have a well-developed dominance hierarchy, a trait whose virtues will be discussed below. But the African buffalo is considered the most dangerous and unpredictable large mammal of Africa. Anyone insane enough to try to domesticate it either died in the effort or was forced to kill the buffalo before it got too big and nasty. Similarly, hippos, as four-ton herbivores, would be great barnyard animals if they weren't so dangerous. They kill more people each year than do any other African mammals, including even lions.

11 문맥상 빈칸에 들어갈 단어로 가장 적절한 것을 고르시오. 2점

① tamed　　　　② sane

③ captured　　　④ crazy

12 위 글의 제목으로 가장 적절한 것을 고르시오. 3점

① How to Raise Violent Animals
② Animals That Are Difficult to Domesticate
③ The Brutality of Grizzly Bears and African Buffalos
④ Animals That Kill People

[13-14] 다음 글을 읽고 질문에 답하시오.

The Sierra Club's Equity Language Guide discourages using the words *stand*, *Americans*, *blind*, and *crazy*. The first two fail at inclusion because not everyone can stand and not everyone living in this country is a citizen. The third and fourth, even as figures of speech ("Legislators are blind to climate change"), are insulting to the disabled. The guide also rejects *the disabled* in favor of *people living with disabilities*, for the same reason that *enslaved person* has generally replaced *slave*: to affirm, by the tenets of what's called "people-first language," that "everyone is first and foremost a person, not their disability or other identity."

The guide's purpose is not just to make sure that the Sierra Club avoids obviously derogatory terms, such as *welfare queen*. It seeks to cleanse language of any trace of privilege, hierarchy, bias, or exclusion. In its zeal, the Sierra Club has clear-cut a whole national park of words. *Urban*, *vibrant*, *hardworking*, and *brown bag* all crash to earth for subtle racism. *Y'all* supplants the patriarchal *you guys*, and *elevate voices* replaces *empower*, which used to be uplifting but is now condescending. *The poor* is classist; *battle* and *minefield* disrespect veterans; *depressing* appropriates a disability; *migrant* — no explanation, it just has to go.

Equity-language guides are proliferating among some of the country's leading institutions, particularly nonprofits. The American Cancer Society has one. So do the American Heart Association, the American Psychological Association, the American Medical Association, the National Recreation and Park Association, the Columbia University School of Professional Studies, and the University of Washington.

Although the guides refer to language "evolving," these changes are a revolution from above. They haven't emerged organically from the shifting linguistic habits of large numbers of people. They are handed down in communiqués written by obscure "experts" who purport to speak for vaguely defined "communities," remaining unanswerable to a public that's being morally coerced. A new term wins an argument without having to debate. When the San

Francisco Board of Supervisors replaces *felon* with *justice-involved person*, it is making an ideological claim — that there is something illegitimate about laws, courts, and prisons. If you accept the change — as, in certain contexts, you'll surely feel you must — then you also acquiesce in the argument.

13 위 글에서 유추할 수 있는 내용으로 가장 거리가 <u>먼</u> 것을 고르시오. 3점

① Equity-language guides discourage using potentially derogatory words such as *urban* because of its implicit racism.

② Equity-language guides tend to morally coerce the public by the standards they have arbitrarily set up.

③ According to the Sierra Club's Equity Language Guide, *empower* is a word to avoid due to its connotation of superiority.

④ One of the main assumptions of the Sierra Club's Equity Language Guide is that one's identity needs to be prioritized.

14 위 글의 주제에 대해 저자가 취하는 관점으로 가장 적합한 것을 고르시오. 2점

① petulant   ② critical

③ approving   ④ expository

Stress isn't inherently bad. Stressing your muscles through weight training, for example, leads to beneficial changes. In addition, short-term stress in healthy people typically isn't a hazard. But if stress is continuous, especially in older or unhealthy individuals, the long-term effects of the response to stress may lead to significant health issues.

Stress occurs when you face a new, unpredictable or threatening situation, and you don't know whether you can manage it successfully. When you're physically or emotionally stressed, your body snaps into fight-or-flight mode. Cortisol rushes through your system, signaling your body to release glucose. Glucose, in turn, provides energy to your muscles so that you are better prepared to fight off a threat or run away. During this cortisol rush, your heart rate may rise, your breathing may become rapid, and you may feel dizzy or nauseated.

If you truly needed to fight or flee a predator, your cortisol levels would drop back down once the conflict was over. When you're chronically stressed, however, those levels stay elevated. Remaining in that heightened state is no good since high levels of cortisol can exacerbate health conditions such as cardiovascular disease, diabetes and chronic gastrointestinal problems. Stress can also cause or contribute to anxiety, irritability, poor sleep, substance abuse, chronic distrust or worry, and more.

_____, there are many ways to combat stress. Keep a daily routine, get plenty of sleep, eat healthy foods, and limit your time following the news or engaging in social media, recommends the World Health Organization. It also helps to stay connected with others and to employ calming practices such as meditation and deep breathing. One of the most successful tools, though, is physical activity.

15 빈칸에 들어갈 적절한 말을 고르시오. 2점

① Unfortunately　　② In contrast

③ Luckily　　④ In sum

16 위 글에서 유추할 수 있는 내용으로 가장 거리가 먼 것을 고르시오. 2점

① Short-term stress can produce constructive changes.

② If stress is continuous, the level of cortisol would stay heightened.

③ Engaging in social media is recommended to combat stress.

④ With an elevated level of cortisol, an individual's breathing may become rapid.

[17-18] 다음 글을 읽고 문제에 답하시오.

The defining question about global order in the decades ahead will be: can China and the US escape Thucydides's trap? The historian's metaphor reminds us of the dangers two parties face when a rising power rivals a ruling power — as Athens did in 5th century BC and Germany did at the end of the 19th century. Most such challenges have ended in war. Peaceful cases required huge adjustments in the attitudes and actions of the governments and the societies of both countries involved.

The rapid emergence of any new power disturbs the Ⓐ_____. In the 21st century, as Harvard University's Commission on American National Interests has observed about China, "a diva of such proportions cannot enter the stage without effect".

If we were betting on the basis of history, the answer to the question about Thucydides's trap appears Ⓑ_____. In 11 of 15 cases since 1500 where a rising power emerged to challenge a ruling power, war occurred. Think about Germany after unification as it overtook Britain as Europe's largest economy. In 1914 and in 1939, its aggression and the UK's response produced world wars.

Uncomfortable as China's rise is for the US, there is nothing unnatural about an increasingly powerful China demanding more say and greater sway in relations among nations. Americans, particularly those who lecture Chinese about being "more like us", should reflect on our own history.

17 밑줄 친 부분에 들어갈 말을 순서대로 고르시오. 2점

① disequilibrium — apparent
② disequilibrium — obscure
③ status quo — ambivalent
④ status quo — obvious

18 위 글의 내용과 가장 거리가 먼 것을 고르시오. 3점

① Although the conflict between the United States and China is sharp, it is likely that an anticipated war will be averted.

② The ongoing shift in the dynamics of international relations highlights the need for a comprehensive strategy to address the challenges posed by a more influential China.

③ The historical patterns strongly support the idea that conflicts have arisen when rising powers confront ruling ones.

④ In many cases since 1500 where a rising power emerged to challenge a ruling power, war occurred.

[19-20] 다음 글을 읽고 문제에 답하시오.

The leading science journal, *Nature*, has _____ a controversial paper claiming the discovery of a superconductor — a material that carries electrical currents with zero resistance — capable of operating at room temperature and relatively low pressure.

This year's report by Dias and Salamat is the second significant claim of superconductivity to crash and burn in 2023. In July, a separate team at a start-up company in Seoul described a crystalline purple material dubbed LK-99 — made of copper, lead, phosphorus and oxygen — that they said showed superconductivity at normal pressures and at temperatures up to at least 127°C (400 Kelvin). There was much online excitement and many attempts to reproduce the results, but researchers quickly reached a consensus that the material was not a superconductor at all.

Superconductors are important in many applications, from magnetic resonance imaging machines to particle colliders, but their use has been limited by the need to keep them at extremely low temperatures. For decades, researchers have been developing new materials with the dream of finding one that exhibits superconductivity without any refrigeration.

Specialists in the field have been sceptical since this year's Dias and Salamat paper was published, says Lilia Boeri, a physicist at the Sapienza University of Rome. This, she says, is in part because of controversies swirling around the team and in part because the latest paper was not written to what she considers a high standard.

19 빈칸에 들어갈 가장 적절한 말을 고르시오. 3점

① extracted   ② contracted

③ retracted   ④ detracted

20 위 글의 내용과 가장 거리가 <u>먼</u> 것을 고르시오. 3점

① Specialists in the field have been sceptical since the publication of Dias and Salamat's paper.

② The LK-99 claim garnered much online excitement, but researchers quickly reached a consensus that the material was not a superconductor.

③ The report by Dias and Salamat terminated the controversy surrounding the discovery of a superconductor.

④ Doubts about superconductor-related papers seem to stem from controversies surrounding the team and the quality of the latest paper.

서울여자대학교　　2024학년도 오전 A형
　　　　　　　　　　▶▶ 40문항·70분

[문항별 배점: 01-10 2점/ 11-30 2.5점/ 31-40 3점]

[01-05] Choose the one that is closest in meaning to the underlined expression.

01　We only went to the party to <u>oblige</u> some old friends who especially asked us to be there.

① obey　　　　　　　　　② repay
③ salute　　　　　　　　 ④ indulge

02　The real <u>thrust</u> of the film is its examination of San Francisco's Haight-Ashbury.

① shock　　　　　　　　 ② point
③ content　　　　　　　　④ weakness

03　*How Far Can You Go?* (1980) examines the impact of a secular, <u>permissive</u> society on the personal relationships of British Catholics.

① liberal　　　　　　　　② inventive
③ persevering　　　　　　④ encouraging

04 The <u>remnants</u> of the Roman Empire can be found in many countries in Asia, Europe, and Africa.

① profiles
② remains
③ delicacies
④ adaptations

05 The books on the shelf were arranged <u>haphazardly</u>.

① deliberately
② skillfully
③ carelessly
④ linearly

[06-10] Choose the one that best completes the sentence.

06 The exhibition will _____ more than 170 artworks, including miniature paintings going back to the mid-16th century.

① brace
② uplift
③ advance
④ feature

07 Today more and more teenagers are overweight than before, and the main _____, nutritionists say, is increasing reliance on fast food.

① culprit
② arbiter
③ plaintiff
④ prosecutor

08 Since none of the polls had predicted the winner, everyone was _____ by the results of the election.

① disguised
② astounded
③ confronted
④ evaporated

09 It can be _____ to your health to eat decayed food.

① eligible
② gratifying
③ detrimental
④ intermittent

10 There was quite a _____ when the employees were asked to take pay cuts.

① jest
② clamor
③ windfall
④ diversion

[11-15] Identify the one underlined word or phrase that should be corrected or rewritten.

11 ①Jennifer's and David's car ②broke down again, but ③luckily they knew ④how to fix it.

12 In the ①year 500, ancient Greece was reaching its highest ②level of civilization, with great achievements in the fields of ③artistic, architecture, politics, ④and philosophy.

13 It was our public school system ①that allowed me, an immigrant girl from India ②who arrived as a child ③not knowing a word of English, ④becoming a reporter for *The Wall Street Journal*.

14 Political views ①held by newspaper owners on current topics can ②usually be found in press editorials, ③as well as in the selection and coverage of news stories, and it is often discussed ④what extent these influence readers.

15 Jerome was not so much ①upset about the concert cancellation ②but disappointed ③that he ④would be unable to spend the day with old friends.

[16-20] Choose the one that best completes the sentence.

16 We are indebted to the Arabs not only for reviving Greek works but also _____ useful ideas from India.

① for introducing   ② they introduced

③ introducing   ④ to introduce

17 When a human being gets hurt, the brain excretes _____ enkephalin to numb the pain.

① a chemical calling

② a chemical called

③ calling a chemical

④ called a chemical

18 Those were the soldiers _____ to save the city.

① their responsibility was

② whose was the responsibility

③ whose responsibility it was

④ from whom the responsibility was

19 _____ 925 public statues in Britain, only 158 are women standing on their own.

① Of ② With

③ About ④ For

20 Plastic has become a necessity of modern life, its unique combination of lightness, durability and low cost _____ undeniable utility and a high level of convenience.

① provide ② provides

③ provided ④ providing

[21-26] Choose the one that best completes the sentence.

21 Can we rely on Artificial Intelligence (AI) to give us unbiased information? Is it safe to let AI control machinery or drive our cars? And the big question — will it take our jobs away? There's no denying that technology makes a difference. Often, it is transformative. And it's natural for people to fear change. To worry about job security. To worry about the future, about climate change and social inequality. These aren't abstract issues. They are genuine fears for many of us, but here's the twist: _____.

① technology may also be our best bet in addressing them

② we are overwhelmed by more urgent and significant problems

③ AI will take over the repetitive, tedious, labour-intensive tasks

④ we cannot measure how much technology is impacting our daily lives

22 Cognitive neuroscience and its neighboring disciplines have for decades investigated human behavior and its neural correlates. By far, most of this research has conceived of mental states as "internal" — states that exist inside the heads of individuals. This approach has led to many important findings, yet has also had to confront important challenges. One such problem is that the cognitive concept of mind has been historically defined and investigated context-free — even excluding the rest of the body, of which the brain is one part. However, every feeling, thought and behavior _____, and thus it is intuitive that embodied experience may impact our mental processing and sense of self, and vice versa.

① occurs in the context of the body
② has its root in enduring mental states
③ constitutes what we normally call "self"
④ is a subjective as well as historical phenomenon

23 Environmental changes are a story shared across every species on the planet. The effects vary across locations and ecosystems, but the many significant problems tend to come back to one source: _____. Nature moves and evolves on its own, and it would likely have continued doing so if humans were never here at all. The reality, however, is that we are here — so even natural shifts occur on a playing board of our own design. "We're seeing the consequences of our actions play out in real time," says Shane. "Species are going extinct at an incredible rate. Natural ecosystems worldwide are being uprooted. Animal populations are being reshuffled around the globe — intentionally and unintentionally — and bringing new challenges for native species."

① natural selection
② divine purpose
③ ecological adjustment
④ human impact

24 Harlow separated newborn monkeys from their mothers and reared them in cages containing two artificial mothers. One "mother" was made of wire with a rubber nipple from which the infants could get milk. It provided food, but no physical comfort. The other artificial mother had no nipple but was made of soft, comfortable terrycloth. If attachments form entirely because caregivers provide food, the infants would be expected to prefer the wire mother. In fact, they spent most of their time with the terrycloth mother. And when they were frightened, the infants immediately ran to their terrycloth mother and clung to it. Harlow concluded that the monkeys _____. The terrycloth mother provided feelings of softness and cuddling, which were things the infants needed when they sensed danger.

① liked terrycloth better than a nipple
② were not hungry when they were afraid
③ were motivated by the need for comfort
④ showed disturbance when caregivers were unavailable

25 In our modern society, it's difficult to get enough sleep. We lead busy, overworked lives and often have to forgo sleep to get everything done. Round-the-clock television shows tempt us to stay up late. And if we do manage to get a full night's sleep or grab a nap, we run the risk of being labeled "unmotivated" or "lazy" by the go-getters around us. Yet research suggests that _____. Studies indicate that sufficient sleep is as important to health as regular exercise and a nutritious diet. It may even make us smarter.

① babies and children need more sleep than adults do
② sleep-deprived people have trouble learning new skills
③ those who insist on getting their rest are the wisest of all
④ we need to view a good night's rest as an unnecessary luxury

26 Plato mourned the invention of the alphabet, worried that the use of text would threaten traditional memory-based arts of rhetoric. In his "Dialogues," Plato claimed the use of this more modern technology would create "forgetfulness in the learners' souls, because _____," that it would impart "not truth but only the semblance of truth" and that those who adopt it would "appear to be omniscient and will generally know nothing." If Plato were alive today, would he say similar things about ChatGPT, a conversational artificial intelligence program released by OpenAI?

① they will know nothing
② they will not use their memories
③ they will not bother to seek truth
④ they will be interested in the alphabet

[27-40] Read the following passages and answer the questions.

27-28

The fate of nearly all living organisms — over 99.9 percent of them — is to compost down to nothing. When your sparkle is gone, every molecule you own will be nibbled off you or sluiced away to be put to use in some other system. That's just the way it is. Even if you make it into the small pool of organisms, the less than 0.1 percent, that don't get devoured, the chances of being fossilized are very small. In order to become a fossil, several things must happen. First, you must die in the right place. Only about 15 percent of rocks can preserve fossils, so it's no good kneeling over on a future site of granite. In practical terms the deceased must become buried in sediment, where it can leave an impression, like a leaf in wet mud, or decompose without exposure to oxygen, permitting the molecules in its bones and hard parts to be replaced by dissolved minerals, creating a petrified copy of the original. Then as the sediments in which the fossil lies are carelessly pressed and folded and pushed about by Earth's processes, the fossil must somehow maintain an identifiable shape. Finally, but above all, after tens of millions or perhaps hundreds of millions of years hidden away, it must be found and recognized as something worth keeping.

* compost: 썩다

27 Which of the following is NOT included among conditions of fossilization?

① Dying in sediment

② Composting down to nothingness

③ Decomposing without exposure to oxygen

④ Sediments being pressed and folded

28 Which of the following CANNOT be inferred from the passage?

① It is not easy to become a fossil.

② Some fossils are from tens of millions of years ago.

③ Granite is an optimal environment for fossilization.

④ Having a recognizable shape is important for a fossil to be found.

29-30

Biologists classify organisms into species. Animals are said to belong to the same species if they tend to mate with each other, giving birth to fertile offspring. Horses and donkeys have a recent common ancestor and share many physical traits. But they show little sexual interest in one another. They will mate if induced to do so — but their offspring, called mules, are sterile. Mutations in donkey DNA can therefore never cross over to horses, or vice versa. The two types of animals are consequently considered two distinct species, moving along separate evolutionary paths. By contrast, a bulldog and a spaniel may look very different, but they are members of the same species, sharing the same DNA pool. They will happily mate and their puppies will grow up to pair off with other dogs and produce more puppies.

Species that evolved from a common ancestor are bunched together under the heading 'genus' (plural genera). Lions, tigers, leopards and jaguars are different species within the genus *Panthera*. Biologists label organisms with a two-part Latin name, genus followed by species. Lions, for example, are called *Panthera leo*, the species *leo* of the genus *Panthera*. Genera in their turn are grouped into families, such as the cats (lions, cheetahs, house cats), the dogs (wolves, foxes, jackals) and the elephants (elephants, mammoths, mastodons). All members of a family trace their lineage back to a founding matriarch or patriarch. All cats, for example, from the smallest house kitten to the most ferocious lion, share a common feline ancestor who lived about 25 million years ago.

29 Which of the following is NOT true according to the passage?

① Mules pair off with donkeys to reproduce.

② Mutations in bulldog DNA can cross over to spaniels.

③ House kittens and cheetahs belong to the same family.

④ Horses and donkeys are not naturally attracted to each other.

30 Which of the following is true according to the passage?

① Mating is a sufficient condition for belonging to the same species.

② Genera that belong to a family share a common founding ancestor.

③ The two-part Latin name of an organism consists of species and family.

④ Sharing physical traits is a necessary condition for being members of the same species.

31-32

During their wedding planning, Hunter Kane's future wife, Ashley Kane, tried out the sound of her first name with his original last name, Snyder — and was not loving Ⓐit. That was when he realized they had more than one name option to consider. Once he and Ms. Kane discussed the possibility of his taking her name, "it felt pretty comforting," he said. It helped that Mr. Kane had never had a "strong connection" to his original last name, and also was extremely close to Ms. Kane's parents and sister. "It felt like if my last name didn't mean that much, then why wouldn't we take hers, when I already feel like such a big part of their family?" he said. At their 2022 wedding, the couple chose to surprise guests with Ⓑthe news by displaying a neon sign reading "The Kanes" at the reception. They enjoyed hearing guests' reactions, even if it did cause a bit of chaos. "We heard stories from people running back and changing the last name on a card, or people worrying about a check not clearing," Mr. Kane said.

31 **Which of the following does the underlined Ⓐ refer to?**

① Hunter Kane ② Ashley Kane

③ Hunter Snyder ④ Ashley Snyder

32 **Which of the following does the underlined Ⓑ refer to?**

① That Hunter took the bride's family name

② That the Kanes did not want to accept checks

③ That Ashley and Hunter decided to get married

④ That Hunter became so close to Ashley's family

33-34

West European countries and the United States have both found it necessary to shift workers from one place to another because of changes in labor market conditions. This labor mobility can, in the two geographical areas referred to, be distinguished by a difference in approach rather than degree. In the United States, the use of labor relocation to bring about a satisfactory manpower adjustment has, for the most part, been limited to the movement of workers among different plants of the same enterprise. Conversely, most programs for the relocation of workers in Western Europe have been implemented on an inter-firm basis. This difference has meant that in the United States support for geographical mobility has largely been left to private resources, while in Western Europe the government has taken the initiative — and has accepted a major share of the financial burden in the movement of labor from one location to another.

33   Which of the following is true of West European programs for labor mobility?

① They have been dependent on personal resources.

② They have aimed at limiting the migration of labor.

③ They have permitted workers to move without changing employers.

④ They have had the same motivation as labor relocation in the US.

34   Which of the following is true of labor relocation in the US?

① Labor problems have been regarded as insignificant.

② Private firms basically have paid most of the costs.

③ The government has played a major role in geographical mobility.

④ The US workers have had more opportunities than West European workers.

The deeds of Benjamin Franklin in just one of half a dozen areas could make men living normally busy lives feel like lazy do-nothings. Unschooled, he learned to stumble around in five languages and mastered natural science, diplomacy, and economics. Born in poverty, he prospered so well as a printer, shopkeeper, and publisher that he was able to retire at the age of forty-two. His inventions are legion. He established a university and a public library and practically invented the Philadelphia municipal government. As a diplomat, legislator, and architect of the United States government, Franklin did the work not of one founding father but of a dynasty.

35 **Which of the following is NOT mentioned as a field of Franklin's accomplishments?**

① Law ② Education

③ Foreign affairs ④ Architecture

36 **Which of the following is NOT true of Franklin's life?**

① He educated himself.

② He succeeded in his business.

③ He was undisciplined.

④ He lived an unusually active life.

It is not too much of an exaggeration to say that almost nobody in Britain drank tea at the beginning of the eighteenth century, and nearly everybody did by the end of it. Official imports grew from around six tons in 1699 to eleven thousand tons a century later, and the price of a pound of tea at the end of the century was one-twentieth of the price at the beginning. Furthermore, those figures do not include smuggled tea, which probably doubled the volume of imports for much of the century until the duty levied on tea was sharply reduced in 1784. Another confounding factor was the widespread practice of adulteration, the stretching of tea by mixing it with ash, willow leaves and more dubious substances often colored and disguised using chemical dyes. Tea was adulterated in one way or another at almost every stage along the chain from leaf to cup, so that the amount consumed was far greater than the amount imported.

Black tea began to become more popular, partly because it was more durable than green tea on long voyages, but also as a side effect of this adulteration. Many of the chemicals used to make fake green tea were poisonous, whereas black tea was safer, even when adulterated. As black tea started to displace the smoother, less bitter green tea, the addition of sugar and milk helped to make it more palatable.

37 What is the passage mainly about?

① Popularity of black tea in Britain

② Britain's peculiar enthusiasm for tea

③ Various methods of tea adulteration

④ Differences between green tea and black tea

38 Which of the following is true of the 18th century Britain?

① Green tea was safer than black tea when adulterated.

② It was mainly in the stage of leaves that tea was adulterated.

③ The amount of smuggled tea doubled that of imported tea until 1784.

④ Sugar and milk began to be added to lessen the bitterness of green tea.

"Flight shame" has been gathering pace in Europe. The term speaks of the guilt of taking flights at a time when the world needs to dramatically cut greenhouse gas emissions. This growing resistance to aviation has reinvigorated rail travel. It is also changing our ideas of how, why and where we travel. Although "shame" is a negative term, the goals are positive — for people who take part in the movement as well as for the environment. It is less about "shaming" other people who fly than changing your own travel patterns. What's more, the aim of many promoting less flying is by no means to discourage people from exploring the world. The movement is instead about revelling in the slow, deliberate journeys that are possible without aviation. One of the obvious choices is train travel, which has one-10th the emissions of flying.

It's easy to forget that a plane is not always the fastest option, as train travel typically brings you from the center of one city to that of another. In particular, high-speed trains have huge potential as an alternative: new high-speed lines have been shown to reduce aviation transport on the same routes by as much as 80%. _____. Roger Tyers is a climate sociologist who recently returned from a "no-flying fieldtrip" to China, which took him two weeks by train each way. It might sound like a daunting expedition, but he is glowing about his trip. "I've seen some incredible things that you just wouldn't see getting on a plane." He lists a lot of other advantages: digital detox, no jetlag, talking to different people, and "just appreciating the size of our planet and how diverse it is."

39 Which of the following best fits in the blank?

① Slow travel needn't be limited to short distances, either
② The no-flying movement is also gaining popularity elsewhere
③ After all, flying is probably the most carbon-intensive activity you can do
④ The flight shame movement is about rediscovering the diversity of the earth

40 Which of the following is true according to the passage?

① High-speed trains emit more carbon than slow-speed trains.
② The round-trip journey by Roger Tyers took him two weeks.
③ Using the term "shame" for climate action is not a good idea.
④ The no-flying movement aims to urge people to alter their travel habits.

SEOUL WOMEN'S UNIVERSITY

서울여자대학교

2024학년도 정오 A형
▶▶ 40문항·70분

[문항별 배점: 01-10 2점/ 11-30 2.5점/ 31-40 3점]

[01-05] Choose the one that is closest in meaning to the underlined expression.

01 Caves are often formed by selective <u>wearing away</u> of cliffs by the sea.

① erosion ② evasion
③ congestion ④ conjunction

02 The students were instructed to remain <u>stationary</u> during the experiment to ensure accurate results.

① impartial ② invariable
③ immobile ④ irrelevant

03 The elusive snow leopard can be <u>spotted</u> in the mountainous regions of Central Asia.

① tamed ② sighted
③ captured ④ trapped

04 There were at least five hundred protesters outside the courthouse, angrily denouncing the jury's <u>lenient</u> sentence.

① merciful   ② rigorous
③ restrained   ④ insignificant

05 It is hard to <u>fathom</u> how the ancient Egyptians built the pyramids without modern machinery.

① overlook   ② anticipate
③ brood over   ④ comprehend

[06-10] Choose the one that best completes the sentence.

06 Meaningful collaboration between people and machines must not _____ human creativity.

① refine   ② instill
③ complement   ④ subvert

07 Spain's parliament recently passed a resolution _____ legal rights to apes.

① halving   ② granting
③ converting   ④ ascribing

08 The natural disaster caused a massive _____ in the small town, leaving many people homeless and without basic necessities.

① upheaval   ② aberration
③ consensus   ④ tranquility

09 In times of crisis, it's important for people to come together and show _____ to those who are most affected.

① conformity   ② detachment
③ inquisitiveness   ④ solidarity

10   The drunk man became _____ and started picking fights with other customers.

    ① submissive   ② conscientious

    ③ belligerent   ④ apathetic

[11-15] Identify the one underlined word or phrase that should be corrected or rewritten.

11   ①Financial planners usually recommend that an individual ②saves two to six ③months' income for ④emergencies.

12   Plastic is one of the biggest threats ①our oceans face today, ②causing untold harm to ecosystems, ③and posing a potential health threat to more than three billion people ④depend on seafood.

13   ①More than thirty thousand Americans took their own lives last year, ②men mostly, ③and the highest rate being ④among those older than sixty-five.

14   ①Even though I have been gardening for over a decade, I haven't found a way to prevent rodents from stealing ②many of my produce: last year, they ③made off with ④most of my beans.

15   ①A significant number of essays ②selected by readers ③has been rejected by the editorial staff ④as unworthy of publication.

[16-20] Choose the one that best completes the sentence.

16   _____ able to weigh up legal evidence and moral questions of right and wrong has been devised by computer scientists.

    ① Software is   ② Software that is

    ③ That is software   ④ That software is

17 I agreed to the terms and conditions, certifying that I wouldn't hold _____.

① the responsible company

② the company responsible

③ responsible the company

④ company the responsible

18 Many of us stay up far too late _____ the night texting friends or scrolling through social media.

① into   ② for

③ at   ④ on

19 Popular culture represents the triumph of a democratic aesthetic, _____ Mark Twain approved of a hundred years ago when he insisted that he wrote for the millions.

① so   ② but

③ that   ④ one

20 It is now over a month since the Korean movie _____ in Berlin.

① first released

② released first

③ was first released

④ has first been released

[21-26] Choose the one that best completes the sentence.

21 Several centuries ago, before the industrial revolution, men and women shared the provider role. Men were responsible for providing food, either by hunting or by farming, and shelter, perhaps by building it themselves. But women, too, were expected to be providers. They provided food, in such activities as growing a garden, milling flour, and cooking. They were responsible for other kinds of providing as well, such as producing clothing by spinning, weaving, and sewing it. In short, men and women shared the provider role. In an agricultural society, _____, for men were not off in factories while women remained at home.

① they shared time and space as well

② their roles became far more divided

③ a man was in competition with other men

④ the provider role for men was a source of strain

22 The Titanic struck an iceberg on the night of April 14, 1912 and sank in the North Atlantic waters in the wee hours of the following morning. In many ways, the sinking of the Titanic can be seen as the perfect, tragic end to an era of seemingly boundless technological innovation as well as decadent lifestyles built on vast inequalities of wealth. As has been popularly remembered, many people believed that "God himself cannot sink this ship." People truly believed that the technological innovations surrounding shipbuilding and other industries had made the Titanic invincible. When she did sink, on her maiden voyage, _____. Ensuing investigations would search for an explanation that would allow them to reassert their confidence, but in the end they came up empty-handed.

① collective fascination with the disaster began

② this confidence in human innovation was shaken

③ it symbolized the end of the era of wealthy gentlemen

④ it was by no means the greatest at-sea catastrophe in western history

23 Let's face it; people tend to be much braver hiding behind an online persona. You are much more likely to say something online that you would never say in person. The anonymity provided by the Internet caused a rampant cyberbullying problem as well. It's easier to say terrible things to someone when you may not be held accountable for your actions. In the worst cases, some of the things people say online might even be deadly. Youth suicides are on the rise, and _____.

① technology addiction is becoming more widespread
② online bullying may be one of the primary causes
③ therapists should be ready to provide online consultations
④ this shows how harmful uncontrolled access to social media can be

24 Distinctions between free persons and slaves, between whites and blacks, between rich and poor are rooted in fictions. Yet it is an iron rule of history that every imagined hierarchy disavows its fictional origins and claims to be natural and inevitable. For instance, many people who have viewed the hierarchy of free persons and slaves as natural and correct have argued that _____. Hammurabi saw it as ordained by the gods. Aristotle argued that slaves have a "slavish nature" whereas free people have a "free nature." Their status in society is merely a reflection of their innate nature.

① slavery is an imagined order
② slavery is not a human invention
③ slaveholders are rewarded for their merits
④ slaves deserve every perk free people enjoy

25 The word we use is "microplastics." It is a broad category, accommodating any piece of plastic less than five millimeters in length. We have known for a while now that they are causing harm to fish. In a study published in 2018, fish exposed to microplastics were shown to have lower levels of growth and reproduction; their offspring, even when they were not themselves exposed, were observed as also having fewer young, suggesting that _____. In 2020, another study demonstrated that microplastics alter the behavior of fish.

① the contamination lingers through the generations
② microplastics are capable of accumulating in the brains of fish
③ higher levels of exposure can result in changing the behavior of fish
④ microplastic ingestion causes fish to become more vulnerable to infection

26   A recent UNESCO report draws attention to the counterintuitive gendering of the field of computer technology. In Arab countries, and indeed in India, there is a far higher proportion of women studying computer science than in the west. It is those countries where _____ that have the greatest imbalance of male over female students of computer science and, consequently, of software developers.

① gender equality is most advanced

② gender biases are still commonly witnessed

③ programming is not popular among women

④ women's participation in higher education is not guaranteed

[27-40] Read the following passages and answer the questions.

27-28

Scholars once proclaimed that the Agricultural Revolution was a great leap forward for humanity. They told a tale of progress fueled by human brain power. Evolution gradually produced ever more intelligent people. Eventually, people were so smart that they were able to decipher nature's secrets, enabling them to tame sheep and cultivate wheat. As soon as this happened, they cheerfully abandoned the grueling, dangerous and often spartan life of hunter-gatherers, settling down to enjoy the pleasant, satiated life of farmers.

That tale is a fantasy. There is no evidence that people became more intelligent with time. Foragers knew the secrets of nature long before the Agricultural Revolution, since their survival depended on an intimate knowledge of the animals they hunted and the plants they gathered. Rather than heralding a new era of easy living, the Agricultural Revolution left farmers with lives generally more difficult and less satisfying than those of foragers. Hunter-gatherers spent their time in more stimulating and varied ways, and were less in danger of starvation and disease. The Agricultural Revolution certainly enlarged the sum total of food at the disposal of human-kind, but the extra food did not translate into a better diet or more leisure. Rather, it translated into population explosions and pampered elites. The average farmer worked harder than the average forager, and got a worse diet in return.

27   Which of the following came along with the Agricultural Revolution?

① Better diet   ② More intelligence

③ More leisure   ④ Population growth

28 Which of the following is NOT true according to the passage?

① Foragers were less in danger of starvation than farmers.
② Hunter-gatherers deciphered nature's secrets for survival.
③ The Agricultural Revolution is a great leap for humanity.
④ The Agricultural Revolution brought benefits to some elites.

29-30

Should cash be used to spur children to do better on reading and math tests? Suzanne Windland, a homeowner raising three children in a placid enclave of eastern Queens, doesn't think so. Her seventh grader, Alexandra, had perfect scores last year. But she doesn't want New York City's Department of Education to hand her $500 in spending cash for that achievement. That's what Alexandra would earn if her school was part of a pilot program that will reward fourth and seventh graders with $100 to $500, depending on how well they perform on 10 tests in the next year. Mrs. Windland wants Alexandra to do well for all the timeless reasons — to cultivate a love of learning, advance to more competitive schools and the like. She has on occasion bought her children toys or taken them out for dinner when they brought home pleasurable report cards, but she does not believe in Ⓐdangling rewards beforehand. "It's like giving kids an allowance because they wake up every morning and brush their teeth and go off to school. That's what they're supposed to be doing."

29 Which of the following is true according to the passage?

① Alexandra benefited from the program last year.
② All students in New York City are eligible for the program.
③ To receive $500, one must have perfect scores in 10 subjects.
④ Mrs. Windland wants Alexandra to study hard to advance to a selective school.

30 Which of the following does the underlined Ⓐ refer to?

① Perfect scores
② Good report cards
③ Monetary incentives
④ Competitive schools

What is the cause of chronic fatigue syndrome? Past research has suggested a link to the Epstein-Barr virus, but now many scientists are questioning that connection. New findings suggest that the Epstein-Barr virus is not a primary cause, but it may still trigger the illness. The symptoms may be due to a variety of things, rather than just one. Still some researchers are sticking with the idea of the Epstein-Barr virus causing the illness. They say that it is premature to make such a judgment.

Chronic fatigue syndrome has been dubbed the "yuppie disease" by some since it is often diagnosed in professional women in their twenties and thirties. It may be the result of never recovering completely from illnesses such as the flu. Though the cause is not clear, the symptoms are. To be called a chronic fatigue sufferer, one must have the debilitating illness for more than six months and must exhibit at least eight of the eleven symptoms, including sore throat, mild fever, and muscular aches.

31 What is the passage mainly about?

① Diseases affecting professional women
② How to diagnose chronic fatigue syndrome
③ Symptoms caused by the Epstein-Barr virus
④ Causes and symptoms of chronic fatigue syndrome

32 Which of the following is true according to the passage?

① The cause of the illness is not agreed upon.
② It is not very difficult to recover from the illness.
③ The illness is more common among men than women.
④ The Epstein-Barr virus has nothing to do with the illness.

33-34

A huge ancient city has been found in the Amazon, hidden for thousands of years by lush vegetation. The discovery changes what we know about the history of people living in the Amazon. The houses and plazas in the Upano area in eastern Ecuador were connected by an astounding network of roads and canals. The area lies in the shadow of a volcano that created rich local soils but also may have led to the destruction of the society. While we knew about cities in the highlands of South America, like Machu Picchu in Peru, it was believed that people only lived nomadically or in tiny settlements in the Amazon. "This is older than any other site we know in the Amazon. We have a Eurocentric view of civilization, but this shows we have to change our idea about what is culture and civilization," says Prof. Stephen Rostain, director of investigation at the National Center for Scientific Research in France, who led the research. "It changes the way we see Amazonian cultures. Most people picture small groups, probably naked, living in huts and clearing land — this shows ancient people lived in complicated urban societies," says co-author Antoine Dorison.

33　According to the passage, which of the following is to be called in question?

① People only lived nomadically or in tiny settlements in the Amazon.

② Ancient people in the Amazon may have lived in a complicated urban society.

③ The volcano near the Upano area may have led to the destruction of its society.

④ The houses and plazas in the Upano area were connected by a network of roads and canals.

34　What would be the best title of the passage?

① The History of Amazonian Cultures

② The Europeans in the Ancient Amazon

③ A Travel to Machu Picchu and the Amazon

④ An Ancient City in the Middle of the Amazon

35-36

Travelers in 2024 don't need convincing that they have an important role to play in addressing the climate crisis. This awareness is reflected in an ever-increasing array of studies finding that more than three-quarters of global travelers want to travel more sustainably over the coming year, and that 90% of consumers look for sustainable options when traveling. With other sustainable tourism studies finding that an intention-behavior gap remains, destinations investing in sustainability — in the tourism sector and beyond — can help to bridge it. Mindful travel to places recovering from unrest or disaster, meanwhile, can also help to support a more sustainable future for these destinations.

35 According to the passage, travelers of today _____.

① should avoid destinations that are recovering from disaster

② are largely looking for ways of traveling more sustainably

③ have little awareness of their role in addressing the climate crisis

④ mostly do not practice sustainable tourism because it costs more money

36 According to the passage, "an intention-behavior gap" in sustainable tourism may be overcome by _____.

① developing cheap local tour courses to attract global travelers

② spending money to make destinations more environment-friendly

③ constantly reminding travelers of the necessity of sustainable tourism

④ providing information on whether a destination has sustainable options

Plagiarism is one of academia's oldest crimes, but Claudine Gay's resignation as Harvard University's president following plagiarism allegations has sparked a fresh online debate: about _____. Some academics are even advocating for a more streamlined publishing model in which researchers can copy more and write less — so long as the source of the information is clear. The notion that all researchers must compose their own sentences remains a bedrock principle for many, but that view might encounter new resistance in a world with essentially limitless access to information and increasingly sophisticated artificial intelligence (AI) algorithms that can reproduce language with eerie accuracy. "I think the idea that one should never ever copy somebody else's words is a bit outdated," says Lior Pachter, a computational biologist at the California Institute of Technology in Pasadena, adding that the key is to ensure that information is properly sourced. Academia has larger problems, he says, including data fabrication.

37 **Which of the following best fits in the blank?**

① how politics is involved in academic matters

② when copying text should be a punishable offense

③ why a renowned scholar ever commits such a crime

④ why plagiarism is still a crime in the information age

38 **Lior Pachter argues that _____.**

① any kind of plagiarism should be punished as severely as data fabrication

② using AI algorithms in writing an academic paper is to be strictly prohibited

③ copying others' words should be allowed more broadly insofar as the source is clear

④ the very concept of plagiarism is useless when AI can reproduce language with accuracy

39-40

Autonomous vehicles will _____. Cars are among the most expensive things most people own, yet they sit idle, on average, 96% of the time. That is justified by the convenience of having access to a car whenever you need it. These days, however, you can summon a car at will using a smartphone app for a taxi service, car-sharing scheme or rental provider. Google reckons that shared, self-driving taxis could have utilization rates of more than 75%. If so, a much smaller number of cars would be needed to move the same number of people around. "There will be fewer cars on the road — perhaps just 30% of the cars we have today," predicts Sebastian Thrun, a computer scientist at Stanford University and a former leader of Google's self-driving-car project. The idea that autonomous vehicles will be owned and used much as cars are today is a "tenuous assumption", says Luis Martinez of the International Transport Forum. Fleets of self-driving vehicles could, he says, replace all car, taxi and bus trips in a city, providing as much mobility with far fewer vehicles. Research by Dan Fagnant of the University of Utah, drawing on traffic data for Austin, Texas, found that an autonomous taxi with dynamic ride-sharing could replace ten private vehicles.

39 **Which of the following best fits in the blank?**

① challenge the notion of car ownership
② transform the industry of car insurance
③ be a fatal blow to the transportation industry
④ be held to a higher standard than human drivers

40 **Which of the following is true according to the passage?**

① The average utilization rates of the cars we have today are 96%.
② Autonomous vehicles will be purchased and used much as cars are today.
③ The value of automobile manufacturing will shift from services to products.
④ As many as ten privately-owned cars could be replaced by a self-driving taxi.

성균관대학교　　2024학년도 인문계
▶▶ 50문항·90분

[01-05] Choose one that is closest in meaning to the underlined expression.

01 Making healthy lifestyle choices can help e-sports players stay fit and reduce the risk of developing a <u>sedentary</u> lifestyle. 1.9점

① desk-bound　　② lustful　　③ innocent
④ hypnotizing　　⑤ bewitching

02 Some Uber drivers said they might <u>skimp on</u> the New Year feast to save money as they feared losing their livelihood in 2024. 1.9점

① reinforce　　② grumble　　③ skip
④ cut back on　　⑤ pile up

03 Although the Nanaimo bunker was <u>decommissioned</u> in the 1990s, the Department of National Defence has not yet determined what it intends to do with the bunker structure itself following the soil remediation. 1.9점

① introduced　　② deactivated　　③ free of charge
④ gratuitous　　⑤ purposeless

04 Germany's environment minister once used Christmas as an opportunity to show off her housewifely <u>thriftiness</u> by being pictured ironing soon-to-be-reused sheets of wrapping paper. 1.9점

① rationality ② image ③ frugality
④ indiscretion ⑤ generosity

05 For over four decades, the late Robert Heinecken was a <u>trenchant</u> observer of social politics. 1.9점

① dominant ② dull ③ fallible
④ nebulous ⑤ incisive

[06-10] Choose one that is either ungrammatical or unacceptable.

06 ①<u>All</u> of this would ②<u>have</u> been more tolerable had ③<u>it</u> been ④<u>applying</u> with ⑤<u>some</u> degree of consistency. 1.8점

07 Robert Brown is one ①<u>of</u> a small ②<u>numbers</u> of social scientists ③<u>who</u> can write effectively ④<u>both</u> to specialists and to the general ⑤<u>reading</u> public. 1.8점

08 ①<u>That</u> happened in the second ②<u>half</u> of the twentieth century has been ③<u>described</u> ④<u>rather</u> dismissively ⑤<u>as</u> the cola-colonization of the world. 1.8점

09 ①<u>During</u> the long period that baseball was ②<u>developing</u> from a gentleman's recreation to the national pastime, ③<u>another</u> sport was ④<u>shaping</u> up to challenge ⑤<u>their</u> unquestioned preeminence. 1.8점

10 ①<u>Since</u> many odd languages were of military ②<u>significant</u> during World War II, the anthropological linguist had a chance ③<u>to</u> introduce his method of ④<u>working</u> directly ⑤<u>with</u> the native informant. 1.8점

11 Over the last half century in much of East and Southeast Asia, national leaders have pursued a development strategy that has rescued hundreds of millions of people from poverty, _____ foreign investment to construct export-oriented industry. Farmers gained greater incomes through factory work, making basic goods like textiles and clothing before evolving into electronics, computer chips and cars.

① obstructing ② occluding ③ courting 1.9점

④ arraigning for ⑤ denouncing for

12 Soviet engineers often found hydrogen not because they wanted it but because they had a different theory of how petroleum originates. They believed it was generated from inorganic matter rather than crunched-up dinosaur bones. On this view, carbon from the earth's mantle would interact with hydrogen deep underground to produce hydrocarbons(the chief component of petroleum), so it made sense to look for hydrogen as a _____ sign of petroleum. 1.9점

① restricted ② telltale ③ sensitive

④ spurious ⑤ underhand

13 Jack pressed on, reached the railway and waited for a train. When it came, he hurled himself aboard and burrowed in among the empty coal bags. After he escaped, his fellow prisoners covered for him, stuffing a dummy under his blankets and pretending he was asleep. _____, Jack had booked a haircut and shave from a Boer barber for the next morning and forgotten to cancel it. His absence was noticed by the barber. Later, the barber was offered a hefty reward for Jack's recapture. 1.9점

① Favorably ② Thankfully ③ Unfortunately

④ Fortuitously ⑤ Gracefully

14 What's more dubious about Pill's story is that he attributes this zero-sum jockeying for position to an attempt to avoid an inevitable decline in real income, brought on largely by _____. Although he was careful to include price hikes by firms as well as wage demands in his discussion, this is still basically the classic wage-price-spiral story. In that story, workers see a rise in their cost of living, say, because of surging energy prices, and demand wage increases to offset these losses — but firms then raise prices to reflect higher labor costs, and off we go.

① higher energy prices   1.9점
② prosperity of the company
③ protection of the private sector
④ uncompromising negotiation
⑤ cultural change

15 Still, think how much grimmer the world would be if there were no prizewinners to announce, if we didn't take a moment to celebrate those who have dedicated their lives to the pursuit of some noble or beautiful goal. But what about those who do not win prizes? This much larger group may not be all Mozarts, but they do suggest the essential meaning and tension in winning a prize: For every winner, there are many, many others who go unrecognized. We should take care to assign prizes their proper weight, to neither _____. A prize is a wonderful thing, but it is the work, and the artist's commitment to it, that matters. 1.9점

① remember them momentarily nor permanently
② celebrate them officially nor secretly
③ nominate them based on the dedication nor luck
④ mistake them for meaning too much nor too little
⑤ value them for the collaborative work nor fortune

[16-20] Choose one that is most appropriate for the blank.

16 For months it was rumored that the government might allow the members of BTS to skip the military service, on the basis they had already served their country by earning it billions of dollars, and it would be more beneficial to allow them to carry on doing so. But in October, the members of BTS announced they were all planning to enlist, with Jin, as the oldest, going first. _____, the reports he was being sent to the front line surprised some fans, who had assumed he would be given a less risky role. 2.1점

① Even so ② As usual ③ Even now
④ And thus ⑤ In summary

17 I have considerable admiration for scientists in general, and evolutionists and ethologists in particular, and though I think they have sometimes gone astray, it has not been purely through prejudice. Partly it is due to sheer semantic accident — the fact that "man" is a(n) _____ term. It means the species; it also means the male of the species. If you begin to write a book about man or conceive a theory about man you cannot avoid using this word. You cannot avoid using a pronoun "he" as a substitute for the word. 2.1점

① impartial ② technical ③ traditional
④ ambiguous ⑤ admirable

18 Today the secular world doesn't need Satan. Good and evil, however, are in great demand. The old Iranian dualism of good versus evil is entirely an arbitrary one, but it's effective for maintaining social order. In US history, the good/evil dualism was projected onto _____. The undiscovered countries of Africa and North America were cast in the role of evil, conveniently enough, as they were both un-Christian and ripe for exploration and exploitation in a way that much of seventeenth century Asia was not. 2.1점

① the continent itself
② its mysterious history
③ the segregation of the society
④ its socioeconomic structure
⑤ the racial discrimination

19 Lakshmi, an Indian-American immigrant, closed her speech by paying tribute to the participants of the conference, saying they "build a truer mosaic of what America looks like today. While our nation is far from perfect, full of contradictions and hypocrisy in its policies, it can still show the world, that a country needn't consist of only people from the same ethnicity or religion," she said. "It can be built, with all of us who see the best possible America, and help it lurch forward, stumbling often along the way, towards a future, where we will share the same rights and hopefully, _____." 2.1점

① America comes first
② nobody is perfect
③ we need more volunteers
④ no more foreign workers
⑤ all are welcome

20 In the mid-1980s a collective fear — initiated and fueled by law enforcement and the media — gripped the world, and _____. If one were to believe all the hype, a monster was lurking at every turn, just waiting to destroy another life. The FBI even went so far as to state that their numbers showed 500 serial killers on the loose in the US at any given time (the actual number is probably much closer to 50). Supposed experts and authors came out of the woodstock and have ridden this wave of hysteria in the way of badly researched (and in many cases, fabricated) quickie true-crime books and dubious hypotheses and theories. 2.1점

① people started watching more thrillers
② the story of apocalypse was spreading
③ superstition replaced the scientific beliefs
④ the myth of the serial killer was born
⑤ people wanted the more strict law enforcement

[21-22] Choose the one that is inappropriate for the whole context.

21 Tax cuts for the wealthy have long drawn support from conservative lawmakers and economists who argue that such measures will Ⓐ"trickle down" and eventually boost jobs and incomes for everyone else. But a new study says 50 years of such tax cuts have only helped one group — the rich. The new paper examines 18 Ⓑunderlineddeveloped countries — from Australia to the United States — over a 50-year period from 1965 to 2015. The study compared countries that passed tax cuts in a specific year, such as the U.S. in 1982 when President Ronald Reagan slashed taxes on the wealthy, with those that didn't, and then examined their economic outcomes. Per capita gross domestic product and unemployment rates were nearly identical after five years in countries that Ⓒslashed taxes on the rich and in those that didn't, the study found. But the analysis discovered one major change: The incomes of the rich grew much faster in countries where tax rates were Ⓓlowered. Instead of trickling down to the middle class, tax cuts for the rich may not accomplish much more than help the rich keep more of their riches and Ⓔreduce income inequality, the research indicates. 2.1점

① Ⓐ   ② Ⓑ   ③ Ⓒ
④ Ⓓ   ⑤ Ⓔ

22 For the immediate future and perhaps for longer, Ⓐby far the most powerful influence on world English is likely to be the United States. But this influence may be Ⓑdecreasingly challenged in time. Sardonic rumors that the 'native speaker is dead' have circulated since a book of that title was published by Thomas Paikeday in Canada in 1985. But we must regard such reports as grossly Ⓒ'exaggerated'. In view of the claim that native speaker 'owns' the language, a more appropriate heading might be 'The Ⓓtoppling of the native speaker'. In the future, the native speaker may not automatically be regarded as the Ⓔauthority to whom non-native speakers defer in determining what is correct in the language. 2.1점

① Ⓐ   ② Ⓑ   ③ Ⓒ
④ Ⓓ   ⑤ Ⓔ

23 The main point of the following passage would be '_____'. 2.1점

Many generative AI tools will be easier to access than previous technologies. This is not like the advent of personal computers or smartphones, where employers needed to buy lots of hardware, or even e-commerce, where retailers needed to set up physical infrastructure before they could open an online storefront. Yet not all businesses will be enthusiastic adopters. Although the technology promises to do away with drudgery, some people worry that it may ultimately replace them. A survey by a consultancy finds that frontline workers are more likely to be concerned, and less likely to be optimistic, about AI than managers or leaders are. In some cases, unions may act to slow the adoption of the technology; some may go as far as the writers' guild in Hollywood, which was on strike for much of 2023, in part because of concerns about AI's impact on jobs.

① Managers in the public sector may feel no impulse to innovate.
② Using AI is less valuable than previous approachable technologies.
③ AIs are prone to hallucinations or fake news.
④ Many of the companies are using AI to build a tool to help rich managers.
⑤ AI holds much promise for businesses but we should not expect the adoption overnight.

24 The one which has the different opinion from others is _____. 2.1점

> ⓐ When students type questions for an assignment on ChatGPT, the latter responds with explanations and examples. It provides students with an alternative way of answering assignment questions.
>
> ⓑ ChatGPT can speak out the responses for students with sight impairments. It can also summarize the topics or concepts from a course for students with learning disabilities.
>
> ⓒ ChatGPT can understand students' learning styles, providing a personalized learning experience. It can analyze students' academic performance and structure the course to meet their requirements.
>
> ⓓ Using ChatGPT in higher education can assist professors in multiple ways. For example, it can develop a comprehensive lesson plan for a course. It can also provide access to links containing additional educational resources for a course.
>
> ⓔ Using ChatGPT for writing assignments will only promote cheating and plagiarism. Since ChatGPT generates responses quickly, it will decrease students' abilities to brainstorm, think critically, and be creative with their answers.

① ⓐ   ② ⓑ   ③ ⓒ

④ ⓓ   ⑤ ⓔ

25 The underlined "<u>this evaluation</u>" would mean that _____. 2.1점

China disagrees with <u>this evaluation</u>. The Chinese are calling for an end to "hegemonism" — the Chinese and Russian codeword for domination of the world by a single power. Yet all the signs are that China is positioning itself to be the next great hegemon. China has been recruiting nations in South America, the Middle East, and Asia for what it has specifically told each of them will be the "new world order," one that will put an end to the "gunboat diplomacy," "neo-colonialism," and the "hegemonism" of an unnamed rival power. That unnamed power is the United States.

① China's future is not bright
② China will face technological challenges
③ China will be next super power
④ China will give up one-child policy
⑤ China would never be equal to the United States

26 The best title of the following passage would be _____. 2.0점

Perhaps the most effective weapon in a hacker's arsenal is "spear phishing" — using personal information gathered about an intended target to send them an individually tailored message. An email seemingly written by a friend, or a link related to the target's hobbies, has a high chance of avoiding suspicion. This method is currently quite labor intensive, requiring the would-be hacker to manually conduct detailed research on each of their intended targets. However, an AI similar to chatbots could be used to automatically construct personalized messages for large numbers of people using data obtained from their browsing history, emails and tweets.

① Enhancing Hacker Tactics with AI
② How to Identify Spam Mails
③ Avoiding the Targets of Hackers
④ Emails Can Be Dangerous
⑤ Personalized Message Produced by AI

27 Which one is true of the passage? 2.0점

> Most rabbits have, in their skill set, the ability to pretend that they're healthy even when they're quite sick. It's sort of the inverse of playing possum, but done for the same purpose, namely, to deflect attention from predators, who would consider a sick rabbit easy pickings. As a result of this playacting, rabbits often die suddenly — or what appears to be suddenly — when, in fact, they've been sick for a while.

① Rabbits may die without being sick.
② It's not easy to keep rabbits as a pet.
③ Rabbits pretend to be dead before the predators.
④ In fact, rabbits are smarter than the possums.
⑤ It's not surprising for a rabbit to die all of a sudden.

[28-30] Read the following passage and answer the questions.

> Imagine that when you are very young, the map of the world you use to guide your immature self is correspondingly underdeveloped, like a child's drawing of a house: always straight and centered, portraying only the front; always with a door and two windows; always with a square for the outside wall and a triangle for the roof; always with a chimney and smoke. This is a very low-resolution representation of a house. Ⓐ<u>It is more hieroglyph than drawing</u>. It is something that represents the idea of house, or perhaps home, generically, like the words "house" or "home" themselves. However, it is almost always enough: The child who drew the picture knows it is a house, and the other children and the adults who see the picture know it is a house. Ⓑ<u>It is a good-enough map</u>. But all too often appalling events occur within houses. These are not so easy to represent. A few squares, a triangle, a smattering of flowers, and a benevolent solar orb offer only an inadequate representation of the horrors characterizing such a dwelling place. Maybe what is happening inside the house is beyond understanding. But how can what is terrifying be beyond both tolerability and understanding? How can trauma even exist without comprehension? These are great mysteries. But everything is not experienced at the same level of conception. We have all been petrified by the unknown even though that seems a contradiction in terms. But the body knows what the mind does not yet grasp. And it remembers. And it demands that understanding be established. And there is simply no escaping that demand.

28   The underlined Ⓐ"It is more hieroglyph than drawing" means that it is more '_____'. 2.0점

① contradictory than confirming

② biased than impartial

③ conceptual than graphic

④ appalling than peaceful

⑤ established than temporary

29   The underlined Ⓑ"It is a good-enough map" may suggest that the drawing by children '_____'. 2.0점

① locates the exact place

② fulfills its purpose

③ characterizes a terrifying moment

④ is more vivid than the picture

⑤ is actually very creative yet controversial

30   According to the above passage, the author thinks that the understanding of old memories is, in some sense, '_____'. 2.0점

① an exaggeration of the reality

② the unchanging fact

③ a prerequisite to experience itself

④ the contradiction of the reality

⑤ the benevolent solar orb

[31-33] Read the following passage and answer the questions.

Mr. Diouf was among the lucky ones: He made it to the Canary Islands alive. But the whole experience was dreadful, he said. He was imprisoned and deported to Senegal. Upon his return, together with two other repatriates, he set up his nonprofit, known as AJRAP, or the Association of Young Repatriates, whose mission is persuading Senegal's youth to stay. In his quest, Mr. Diouf has sought the help of some high-profile allies: He wrote a letter to the country's president, Macky Sall, but never got an answer. He even tried to go to Brussels to speak with the authorities of the European Union but was denied a visa. But that has not held him back. When it has the funds, AJRAP organizes vocational training in baking, poultry breeding, electricity and entrepreneurship, to provide alternatives to embarking on a pirogue. Mr. Diouf also speaks to young people in local schools to rectify the overly rosy picture of Europe often painted by those who made it there. But he is painfully aware of his limitations. "We know that the European Union sent funds to Senegal to create jobs," he said with quiet resignation in his voice. "But we have not seen any of this money." After the initial peak of 2006-2007, the number of people trying to cross the Atlantic Ocean decreased in the following years. But recently, the route has seen a resurgence in popularity, especially among young people struggling to find jobs, and fishermen affected by their ever-shrinking catch.

31 The underlined part "he is painfully aware of his limitations" may suggest that _____. 2.0점

① most people in Senegal choose to migrate anyway
② Senegal is the safest country in Africa
③ Europe is too dangerous to live
④ only young authorities are aware of the danger
⑤ people with low incomes may pay higher tax than the rich

32 According to the passage, Mr. Diouf _____. 2.0점

① did not experience a disastrous voyage at sea
② concedes that it is getting easier to make his case
③ is fighting an uphill battle against emigration
④ has become an accomplice in his colleagues' deaths
⑤ thinks that Senegal has all different kinds of jobs which are scarce in Europe

33   **What kind of attitude does Mr. Diouf have?** 2.0점

① optimistic   ② buoyant   ③ indifferent

④ adamant   ⑤ pliable

[34-35] Read the following passage and answer the questions.

All the many species of hominids that preceded us had prominent browridges, but we Homo sapience gave them up in favor of our small, active eyebrows. _____. One theory is that eyebrows are there to keep sweat out of the eyes, but what the eyebrows do really well is convey feelings. Think how many messages you can send with a single arched eyebrow, from "I find that hard to believe" to "Watch your step." One of the reasons the Mona Lisa looks enigmatic is that she has no eyebrows. In one interesting experiment, subjects were shown two sets of digitally doctored photographs of well-known people: one with the eyebrows eliminated and the other with the eyes themselves taken away. Surprisingly, but overwhelmingly, volunteers found it harder to identify the celebrities without eyebrows than without eyes.

34   **The best expression for the blank would be _____.** 2.2점

① It makes sense

② It's not easy to say why

③ It is out of the question

④ There is no rule without exception

⑤ A picture is worth a thousand words

35   **According to the experiment, the best way to disguise oneself would be _____.**

① to wear full make-up   2.2점

② to hide your mouth

③ to put on sunglasses

④ to dye one's hair

⑤ to cover eyebrows

[36-38] Read the following passage and answer the questions.

The "invasion of privacy" is now a predictable dimension of social inequality, but it does not stand alone. It is the systematic result of a "pathological" division of learning in society in which surveillance capitalism knows, decides, and decides who decides. Demanding privacy from surveillance capitalists or lobbying for an end to commercial surveillance on the internet is like asking Henry Ford to make each Model T by hand. So here is what is at stake: Surveillance capitalism is profoundly antidemocratic, but its remarkable power does not originate in the state, as has historically been the case. Its effects cannot be reduced to or explained by technology or the bad intentions of bad people; they are the consistent and predictable consequences of an internally consistent and successful logic of accumulation. Surveillance capitalism rose to dominance in the US under conditions of relative lawlessness. From there it spread to Europe and it continues to make inroads in every region of the world.

Surveillance capitalist firms, beginning with Google, dominate the accumulation and processing of information. They know a great deal about us, but our access to their knowledge is sparse: hidden in the shadow text and read only by the new priests, their bosses, and their machines. The unprecedented concentration of knowledge produces an equally unprecedented concentration of power: _____ that must be understood as the unauthorized privatization of the division of learning in society. This means that powerful private interests are in control of the definitive principle of social ordering in our time, just as Durkheim warned of the subversion of the division of labor by the powerful forces of industrial capital a century ago.

36 **The author believes that _____.** 2.0점
   ① surveillance capitalism cannot be explained by our knowledge itself
   ② the division of learning in society has been hijacked by surveillance capitalism
   ③ the processing of information is detrimental to the surveillance capitalist corporations
   ④ the bosses of the company are not aware of the accumulation of information
   ⑤ people in the powerful forces of industrial capital are less likely to be affected by surveillance capitalism

37 According to the author, lobbying for an end to commercial surveillance on the internet is _____. 2.0점

① inconceivable   ② confidential   ③ sequential
④ persuasive   ⑤ attainable

38 The most appropriate expression for the blank is _____. 2.0점

① asymmetries   ② equal rights   ③ laws
④ requirements   ⑤ illusions

[39-40] Read the following passage and answer the questions.

The bear hug between capital and politics has had far-reaching implications for the credit market. The amount of credit in an economy is determined not only by purely economic factors such as the discovery of a new oil field or the invention of a new machine, but also by political events such as regime changes or more ambitious foreign policies. After the Battle of Navarino, British capitalists were more willing to invest their money in risky overseas deals. They had seen that if a foreign debtor refused to repay loans, the British army would get their money back. This is why today a country's credit rating is far more important to its economic well-being than are its Ⓐ_____. Credit ratings indicate the probability that a country will pay its debts. In addition to purely economic data, they take into account political, social and even cultural factors. An oil rich country cursed with a despotic government, endemic warfare and a corrupt judicial system will usually receive a low credit rating. As a result, it is likely to remain relatively poor since it will not be able to raise the necessary capital to make the most of its oil bounty. A country devoid of natural resources, but which enjoys peace, a fair judicial system and a free government is likely to receive a high credit rating. Ⓑ_____, it may be able to raise enough cheap capital to support a good education system and foster a flourishing high-tech industry.

39 According to the passage, which one is NOT relevant to others? 2.0점

① political instability
② indigenous warfare
③ a dictatorial government
④ a dishonest judicial system
⑤ a harmonious society

40 The most appropriate words for the blanks Ⓐ and Ⓑ are _____. 2.0점

	Ⓐ	Ⓑ
①	natural resources	As such
②	free government systems	Conversely
③	judicial systems	In the end
④	overseas deals	In conclusion
⑤	education systems	However

[41-42] Read the following passage and answer the questions.

The attraction of caves as art studios and galleries does not stem from the fact that they were convenient for the artists. In fact, there is no evidence of continuous human habitation in the decorated caves, and certainly none in the deepest, hardest-to-access crannies reserved for the most spectacular animal paintings. Cave artists are not to be confused with "cavemen."

Nor do we need to posit any special affinity for caves, since the art they contain came down to us through a simple process of _____: outdoor art, such as figurines and painted rocks, is exposed to the elements and unlikely to last for tens of thousands of years. Paleolithic people seem to have painted all kinds of surfaces, including leather derived from animals as well as their own bodies and faces, with the same kinds of ochre they used on cave walls. The difference is that the paintings on cave walls were well enough protected from rain and wind climate change to survive for tens of millennia. If there was something special about caves, it was that they are ideal storage lockers.

41 The most appropriate expression for the blank would be _____. 2.0점
① invisible hand
② golden ratio
③ accident fallacy
④ vicious circle
⑤ natural selection

42 Which is true of the above passage? 2.0점

① Cavemen showed the great artistry.

② Cavemen used caves for their art exhibition.

③ Paleolithic people drew pictures of animals they hunted.

④ Cave paintings are found even in the uninhabitable caves.

⑤ Paleolithic artists used the different kinds of colors on human bodies.

[43-45] Read the following passage and answer the questions.

A light-footed doe peaked out of the edge of the woods and stopped to look at me. She was about fifteen feet away. I froze. Not because I had any conscious objection to killing, not even in the odd mutuality of that single beat, as we both stood there trying to figure out how to respond. I just did not know what to do. And then she was gone. I don't remember how I explained it to my father. Just the silence as we drove home. Ⓐ As well as being a poor deer hunter, I was _____. There were a couple of years when, bored and cold, fiddling with my gun, I accidentally squeezed off a shot. Ⓑ If I had not later done the same thing in my parents' basement while playing with a loaded handgun, I would say that the unanticipated sound of a high-powered rifle in the woods is the loudest sound that I have ever heard. Ⓒ I always lied about the reason. "My gun went off by accident" was not an acceptable hunting story. Nor, really, was "I saw a huge buck and took aim but missed." Ⓓ And so I settled on wild dogs. Three different years, I came in from the woods with a tale of shooting at a dog. Ⓔ One year, I somehow found a tuft of hair, perhaps from a squirrel, which I passed around as evidence that I had managed to graze one. Another year, standing in a long line of hunters at the edge of a field as another group walked through the woods to drive the deer toward us, my gun went off when I was trying to catch a falling snowflake in my mouth.

43 The most appropriate expression for the blank would be _____. 2.2점

① contagious　　② dangerous　　③ immature

④ brave　　⑤ curious

44 If the given passage is divided into three paragraphs, the best boundary would be _____. 2.2점

① Ⓐ and Ⓒ   ② Ⓐ and Ⓓ   ③ Ⓑ and Ⓓ

④ Ⓑ and Ⓔ   ⑤ Ⓒ and Ⓔ

45 It appears that the author _____. 2.2점

① didn't want to kill the animals

② missed target on purpose

③ didn't know how to tell a lie

④ was clumsy with firearms

⑤ never made the same mistake again

[46-48] Read the following passage and answer the questions.

In 1929 astronomer Edwin Hubble was studying the light spectra of galaxies and announced that his observations showed that many galaxies were redshifting — they were in fact moving away from us. But what he'd actually discovered was the expansion of the universe. Those galaxies weren't just speeding away on their own, the very fabric of space-time itself was ballooning outward. He didn't believe this was evidence of expansion; it would take another seventy years before scientists realized that not only was the universe expanding — the expansion was speeding up.

Nearly a decade before Hubble took to the telescope, Albert Einstein proposed a theory called the cosmological constant in tandem with his theory of general relativity. The idea being that the universe was a static place and the density remained constant. When Einstein saw Hubble's news about the redshifting galaxies he threw his theory away, except <u>Einstein was sort of right</u>, go figure. The universe is not a static place — we know it's expanding rapidly, but the density in the universe still remains constant. Think of it like this, imagine you're in your living room with a table and TV and some books and a cup of coffee. Now imagine if that room began to expand like a balloon and got bigger and bigger. The objects in your living room would not increase in density — they are what they are. This is the same with our universe, as it balloons out the density remains the same, hence, your cup of coffee is the cosmological constant.

46 Edwin Hubble _____. 2.0점

① thought the universe was expanding

② wanted to prove Albert Einstein's theory

③ didn't realize that his finding showed the expansion of the universe

④ inspired Einstein to think about the theory of the cosmological constant

⑤ found something that made Einstein give up his theory of general relativity

47 What does the underlined "Einstein was sort of right" mean? 2.0점

① Even Einstein could be wrong

② Einstein's idea was partially correct

③ Einstein's theory is too ambiguous

④ Einstein knew finally he could prove everything

⑤ It was wise for Einstein to admit that he was wrong

48 In the above passage, the universe is compared to _____. 2.0점

① TV set

② some books

③ a table

④ living room

⑤ a cup of coffee

[49-50] Read the following passage and answer the questions.

Analysts expect China's growing thirst for coffee to be a key driver of future demand for the beans as coffee shops expand beyond Beijing and Shanghai to dozens of mid-sized cities where young professionals have warmed to the beverage. China's rising coffee demand is an opportunity for international chains like Starbucks and Tim Hortons that are investing heavily in China, though they face a steep challenge from rapidly expanding local brands. Data from the International Coffee Organization sent to Reuters show coffee consumption in China grew 15% in the year-long season ended in September from the previous cycle to 3.08 million bags. "The Chinese consumer is increasingly adopting Western lifestyles and coffee is obviously one of the beverages that represent that," said the managing director of market research firm.

The number of branded coffee shops in China grew a staggering 58% in the last 12 months to 49,691 outlets, according to Alegra Group, a company that tracks growth of coffee chains. There is harsh competition between the local chains and international chains, said Matthew Barry, a beverages analyst for Euromonitor. Each one is trying to grab as big a share as they can of the growing market, he said. Alegra Group estimates China's Luckin Coffee added 5,059 stores in the last 12 months, while another Chinese chain, Cotti Coffee, opened 6,004 outlets in the period. "The scale of the opportunity is such that both (local and international chains) will have to be very aggressive in <u>facing off against the other</u> and I think that should ensure a very dynamic marketplace in the next few years," Barry said. Chinese coffee consumption still pales when compared to top consumers, the United States and Brazil, that use more than 20 million bags per year. But the growing demand signals China is undergoing a cultural change similar to other tea-loving Asian countries including Japan and South Korea.

49 **What is true of the above passage?** 2.0점
① China's coffee shops cannot eventually expand beyond Beijing.
② There will be no more growing demand for coffee in China.
③ China's new thirst for coffee spurs cut-throat cafe competition.
④ China's coffee consumption surpasses that of Japan and South Korea.
⑤ There is no competition between local and international chains in terms of coffee shops.

50 The underlined "<u>facing off against the other</u>" means that they are '_____'. 2.0점

① encountering dynamic cultural change

② competing with each other

③ deliberately purchasing the affordable coffee

④ moderately tracking the growth of new coffee chains

⑤ overweighing international chains like Starbucks over local ones

SUNGKYUNKWAN
UNIVERSITY

성균관대학교   **2024학년도 자연계**
▶▶ 영어 25문항, 수학 20문항·90분

[01-02] Choose one that is either ungrammatical or unacceptable.

01   The click and flow of a word processor can be ①<u>seductive</u>, and you may find yourself ②<u>adding</u> a few unnecessary words or even a whole passage just ③<u>to experience</u> the pleasure of running your fingers over the keyboard and ④<u>watching</u> your words ⑤<u>appeared</u> on the screen. 1.8점

02   The patrol ①<u>emerged from</u> the wire, and the young marines ②<u>climbing</u> slowly up the slope of the new fire support base, ③<u>bent over</u> with fatigue, ④<u>picking</u> their way around shattered stumps and dead trees that ⑤<u>gave</u> no shelter. 1.8점

[03-05] Choose one that is closest in meaning to the underlined expression.

03   Mr. Putin has turned the exits of major Western companies into a <u>windfall</u> for Russia's loyal elite and state itself. 1.9점

     ① loss   ② bonanza   ③ shortfall
     ④ disaster   ⑤ disadvantage

04 Exchanges of missile and artillery fire between Israel and Hezbollah, a Lebanese Shia militia allied with Iran, <u>presage</u> a possible second front. 1.9점

① explain   ② prevent   ③ escalate

④ foretell   ⑤ follow

05 According to one research study, labor market performances of the subjects, who were <u>in utero</u> during the worst time of the Korean War (1950-1953), were significantly lower in 1990. 1.9점

① child   ② unborn   ③ active

④ ill   ⑤ refugee

[06-10] Choose one that is most appropriate for the blank.

06 A tea pavilion — _____, almost austere in expression, with thin walls, flat roof and empty walls — is only a background for the careful practice of preparing and sharing the drink between the host and the guests. Focus on subtle, sensual experience is a celebration of transient beauty of objects and careful gestures.

① a fully occupied space   2.1점

② an extravagant building

③ the most impressive building

④ a pretty and luxurious flat

⑤ an extremely modest building

07 Here is an anecdote. Prince George's (PG) County, a Maryland county next to Washington, DC, used to have a large white majority. After the _____ of a large black middle class made the county much more diverse (although whites were still in the majority), PG voters passed a law called TRIM in 1978. TRIM puts a legal ceiling on the property tax rate, a binding constraint on the main source of revenue for school financing. 2.1점

① influx   ② induction   ③ emigration

④ protest   ⑤ prosperity

08 Like diversity, the post-pandemic spread of remote work brings benefits while raising coordination costs. Running a workforce virtually imposes what management organization scholars call "management overhead". Even when the network connection is not patchy and people don't forget to unmute themselves, virtual meetings _____ lots of signals, such as eye contact and gestures. 2.1점

① allow   ② let out   ③ strip out
④ promote on   ⑤ pass under

09 When a disaster such as a hurricane strikes a region, many goods experience an increase in demand or a decrease in supply, putting upward pressure on prices. Policymakers often object to these price hikes. They argue that businesses and economists should pay more attention to our shared social values. "During a time of crisis, it's time for all of us to _____, it's not time for us to grab." 2.2점

① throw in   ② take out   ③ pull over
④ pitch in   ⑤ persevere

10 On January 15, 2000, *The New York Times* reported that in the first week of the new millennium local hospitals had recorded an astonishing 50.8% more deaths than in the last week of 1999. *The Times* suggested that this phenomenon was due to infirm people willing themselves to stay alive long enough to witness the dawning of the new age. Apparently, the anticipation of _____ events can motivate people to live longer. 2.2점

① trivial   ② obscure   ③ mundane
④ momentous   ⑤ insignificant

The media often seem to thrive on superlatives, and we, their audience, are confused as to whether the price increases we have recently seen in the stock market are all that unusual. Data that suggest that we are setting some new record (or at least close to doing so) are regularly stressed in the media, and if reporters look at the data in enough different ways, they will often find something that is close to setting a record on any given day. In covering stock market, many writers mention "record one-day price changes" — measured in points on the Dow rather than percentage terms, so that records are much more likely. Although the media have become increasingly _____ about reporting in terms of points on the Dow in recent years, the practice still persists among some writers.

This record overload — the impression that new and significant records are constantly being set — only adds to the confusion people have about the economy. It makes it hard for people to recognize when something truly and importantly new really is happening. It also, with its deluge of different indicators, encourages an avoidance of individual assessment of quantitative data — a preference for seeing the data interpreted for us by experts.

11 **What is most appropriate for the blank?** 2.0점

① reckless ② persistent ③ enlightened
④ encouraged ⑤ enthusiastic

12 **What is NOT true of the above passage?** 2.0점

① The media often confuse people by their record overload.
② Record overload causes something new to go unrecognized.
③ The media often suggest that we are setting new record in the stock market.
④ Record overload encourages people to ignore opinions by the expert.
⑤ Measuring stock price changes in points rather than percentage terms makes setting new records more likely.

[13-15] Read the following passage and answer the questions.

The health risk from bedbugs is minor: itchy bites and a small risk of allergies and secondary infections. Mosquitoes spread malaria, dengue fever and yellow fever. But no human pathogen is known to use bedbugs as a vector. As the present panic suggests, the bigger impact (of bedbugs) tends to be psychological. Mosquitoes, leeches, and other parasites are unpleasant, but do not colonize your home. If a traveler brings bedbugs back from their holidays, they can start an infestation that can be very difficult to shift.

The insects thrive in warm environments with plenty of dark places to hide. Cities, and crowded blocks of flats, are ideal. The bugs shelter in the crannies of furniture, in mattress seams or in cracks in walls, coming out to feed at night. Warm, centrally heated homes accelerate their life-cycles, making the problem worse — as does a warming climate.

The introduction and widespread use of insecticide such as DDT in the aftermath of the second world war came close to eliminating the bugs from most rich-world houses. But that chemical assault exerted a powerful evolutionary pressure on the insects to develop resistance to the poisons. Just as bacteria have evolved resistance to many of the antibiotics once used to kill them, modern bedbugs are almost invulnerable to at least some insecticides. That growing resistance has been boosted by a depleting arsenal of chemicals to hurl against them. Fumigants such as hydrogen cyanide, sulphur dioxide and DDT itself are now regarded in most places too toxic to use. Pyrethroids, which are the active ingredients in many commercially available insecticide sprays, are safer, but become less effective every year.

13 Health risk of bedbugs is relatively lower than that of other insects because bedbugs _____. 2.0점

① only thrive in warm climate
② do not colonize your home
③ only come out to feed at night
④ are relatively easy to kill
⑤ do not carry diseases around

14 According to the passage, _____ is <u>NOT</u> a reason for the spread of bedbugs.

① poor hygiene   1.9점

② global warming

③ frequent travel

④ ineffective insecticides

⑤ centrally heated homes

15 Fumigants such as hydrogen cyanide, sulphur dioxide, and DDT are no longer used to kill bedbugs because _____. 2.1점

① Fumigants have become less effective

② Bedbugs are invulnerable to most fumigants

③ Fumigants are harmful even to human body

④ Commercially available insecticides use Pyrethroids

⑤ Fumigants such as DDT are too costly to use

The world has forgotten _____. We analyzed data from the Fraser Institute, a free-market think-tank, which measures "economic freedom" on a ten-point scale. We considered cases where a country improves by 1.5 points or more — a quarter of the gap between Switzerland and Venezuela — within a decade, indicating that bold, liberalizing reforms have been undertaken. In the 1980s and 1990s such "daredevil economics" was common, as countries left the Soviet Union, and many deemed unreformable, such as Ghana and Peru, proved they were in fact reformable. Politicians changed foreign-trade rules, fortified central banks, cut budget deficits and sold state-owned firms. In recent years just a handful of countries, including Greece and Ukraine, have implemented reforms. By the 2010s reforms have ground to a halt.

Daredevil economics has declined in popularity in part because there is less need for it. Although in recent years economies have become less liberal, the average one today is 30% freer than it was in 1980s. There are fewer state-run companies. Tariffs are lower. But the decline of daredevil economics also reflects a widely held belief that liberalization failed. In the popular imagination, terms such as "structural-adjustment plan" or "shock therapy" conjure up images of impoverishment in Africa, the creation of mafia states in Russia and Ukraine, and human-right abuses in Chile. Books such as Joseph Stiglitz's "Globalization and its Discontents" fomented opposition to the free-market Washington consensus. In Latin America, "neoliberal" is now a term of abuse; elsewhere, it is rarely used as an endorsement.

16 **What is most appropriate for the blank?** 2.0점

① how to reform

② how to overcome inequality

③ how to run central banks

④ how to protect human rights

⑤ how to oppose to the free market

17 According to the passage, which one is <u>NOT</u> associated with the "daredevil economics"? 2.0점

① promoting free market
② lowering import tax
③ promoting economic freedom
④ pursuing market liberalization
⑤ increasing state-run companies

[18-20] Read the following passage and answer the questions.

The banning of menthol cigarettes, the mint-flavored products that have been aggressively marketed to Black Americans, has long been an elusive goal for public health regulators. But Covid-19 and the Black Lives Matter movement have put new pressure on Congress and the White House to reduce racial health disparities. And there are few starker examples than this: Black smokers smoke less but die of heart attacks, strokes and other causes linked to tobacco use at higher rates than white smokers do. About 85 percent of Black smokers use *Newport*, *Kool* and other menthol brands that are easier to become addicted to and harder to quit than plain tobacco.

Menthol is a substance found in mint plants, and it can also be synthesized in a lab. It creates a cooling sensation in tobacco products and _____ the harshness of the smoke, making it more tolerable. Some studies have shown that menthol also acts as a mild anesthetic. Back in 1953, when menthol was not widely used, a Philip Morris Co. survey revealed that 2 percent of white smokers preferred a menthol brand, while 5 percent of Black smokers did. "The industry looked at that and said, 'We're missing an opportunity,' and consciously targeted the African-American community," said Matthew L. Myers, president of the Campaign for Tobacco-Free Kids.

Tobacco companies have targeted Black communities with menthol cigarettes for decades. They distributed free samples, offered discounts and sponsored countless concerts and special events, among them the famous *Kool Jazz Festival*. Tobacco companies also gained good will by advertising in newspapers and magazines geared to a Black readership — and by donating money to civil rights organizations. The companies have also been frequent donors to Black political candidates.

18 **What is most appropriate for the blank?** 1.9점

① does　　　　　　② masks　　　　　　③ reveals

④ emphasizes　　　⑤ sets aside

19 **According to the passage, which one is <u>NOT</u> a tactic that tobacco companies use to target Black smokers with menthol cigarettes?** 2.0점

① offering price discounts

② distributing free samples

③ advertising in Black newspapers

④ donating to civil rights organization

⑤ reducing cigarette tax for Black smokers

20 **According to the passage, banning menthol cigarettes will _____.** 2.1점

① bankrupt the cigarette industry

② make white smokers consume more menthol cigarettes

③ increase the demand for menthol cigarettes

④ decrease racial health disparities

⑤ reduce the quality of menthol cigarettes

[21-22] Read the following passage and answer the questions.

Beyond animosity toward particular groups, there is another possible cause of discrimination, called statistical discrimination. It is based on the assumption that employers have imperfect information about possible employees. If some relevant but unobservable employee characteristic happens to be correlated with an otherwise irrelevant but observable characteristic, then employers may rely on the observable characteristic when making hiring decisions.

Some employers, for instance, prefer not to hire workers with criminal records. The simplest way to avoid doing so is to ask job applicants whether they have criminal records, and many employers do. Some U.S. states, however, have passed "ban the box" laws that prohibit employers from asking. (The "box" refers to the place on the job application that a person would check to signal a clean record.) The goal of these laws is to help ex-offenders find jobs and thus reenter society as law-abiding citizens.

Despite the noble intent of these laws, one unintended consequence is that they foster statistical discrimination. Statistics show that black men are more likely to have served time in prison than white men. If employers are aware of this fact, those who care about criminal records but are prohibited from asking about them may avoid hiring black men. As a result, black men without a criminal past would suffer from discrimination because of their group's average characteristics. Some studies have compared states with and without "ban the box" policies and have found that these laws significantly reduce employment for young black men without college degrees. These results suggest that policymakers should look for ways to help ex-offenders that do not inadvertently promote statistical discrimination.

21 **Employers use statistical discrimination in hiring decisions because they _____.**

① have a good knowledge of statistics   2.0점
② do not have enough information about applicants
③ can simply ask job applicants about criminal records
④ want to satisfy the demand of their customers
⑤ do not use the observable characteristic when making hiring decisions

22 The objective of the "ban the box" laws is _____. 2.0점

① to ban hiring employees with certain beliefs

② to reduce the burden of applicants in the job market

③ to help employers hire the best possible job applicants

④ to better screen the job candidates with criminal records

⑤ to protect ex-offenders from being discriminated in the job market

[23-25] Read the following passage and answer the questions.

Fifteen years ago, Easterly and Levine published "Africa's Growth Tragedy", highlighting the disappointing performance of Africa's growth, and the toll it has taken on the poor. Since then, growth has picked up, averaging 5-6 percent a year, and poverty is declining at about one percentage point a year. The statistical tragedy is that we cannot be sure this is true. Take economic growth, which is measured in terms of growth in GDP. GDP in turn is measured by national accounts. While there has been some progress, today, only 35 percent of Africa's population lives in countries that use the 1993 UN System of National Accounts; the others use earlier systems, some dating back to the 1960s.

The proximate causes of the problem with statistics are: weak capacity in countries to collect, manage and disseminate data; inadequate funding; diffuse responsibilities; and fragmentation, with many diffuse data collection efforts. But I would submit that the underlying cause is that statistics are _____. Take the poverty estimates. They assess whether people are better off today than they were five years ago. If the estimate takes place during an election year, there is a strong tendency to keep the results under wraps. Worse still, there is a tendency to drag their feet in completing the survey. And the raw data of household surveys are almost never publicly available (so there is little chance of being able to replicate them).

There is another aspect to the statistical tragedy. After a lot of bad experiences, the international community has decided that African countries should develop their own National Statistical Development Strategies (NSDS), and that all statistical activities should be consistent with the NSDS. The tragedy is that donors, including the World Bank, undertake statistical activities without ensuring that they are consistent with the NSDS. Why? Because they need data for their own purpose — to publish reports — and this means getting it faster, with little time to strengthen the countries' statistical capacity.

23 **What is most appropriate for the blank?** 1.9점

① inherently opaque

② inherently equitable

③ fundamentally political

④ economically efficient

⑤ unreasonably misleading

24 **What is the best title of the passage?** 2.0점

① Africa's statistical tragedy

② Africa's unreliable poverty data

③ Africa's disappointing growth performance

④ Africa's National Statistical Development Strategies (NSDS)

⑤ Guideline to Africa's data gathering practice for international organizations

25 **What is <u>NOT</u> the problem with statistics in Africa?** 2.1점

① lack of funding

② Africa's electoral system

③ scattered data collection efforts

④ low ability to collect and manage data

⑤ inconsistency between NSDS and donors' statistical activities

세종대학교 　　2024학년도 인문계 A형
　　　　　　　▶▶ 60문항·100분

[문항별 배점: 01-10 2.8점, 오답 -0.7점/ 11-15 3.8점, 오답 -0.95점/ 16-30 3.2점, 오답 -0.8점/
31-45 2.8점, 오답 -0.7점/ 46-60 4.2점, 오답 -1.05점]

[01-10] 주어진 문장의 빈칸에 들어갈 가장 알맞은 단어를 고르시오.

01 Because facial expressions for the six emotions used in this study appear to be influenced very little by cultural differences, it is possible to conclude that they must be _____, meaning biologically hard-wired in the brain at birth.

① cognate　　　　　　　　② affectionate
③ innate　　　　　　　　　④ erudite

02 The company accounted for over 30% of the country's GDP and hired over 250,000 employees at the _____ of its expansion.

① siege　　　　　　　　　② zealot
③ stake　　　　　　　　　④ zenith

03 In basic psychological theory, two forces determine our behavior in a given situation: our internal, _____ factors (i.e., who we are) and the influences of the situation in which we are behaving.

① intransitive　　　　　　② dispositional
③ sequential　　　　　　　④ contractive

04 The team's _____ will be tested next week when it faces a rivalry game against the #1 ranked team at the sold-out stadium packed with hostile fans.

① recitation   ② dusk
③ proximity   ④ mettle

05 Children with autism find social communication difficult. Their language use is often _____, using some words in their own unusual ways.

① conventional   ② organic
③ idiosyncratic   ④ existential

06 The culture of the ancient Hebrews ascribed holiness to the name by silence declaring it _____. That is, indescribable and unspeakable.

① indomitable   ② ineffable
③ unbendable   ④ unpalatable

07 Retrograde _____ refers to the loss of memory for events occurring before the event in which the brain was damaged.

① memoir   ② nostalgia
③ amnesia   ④ memorial

08 The January 6th attack on the U.S. Capitol is widely described as a(n) _____, as it is viewed as a rebellious act against the U.S. government.

① annexation   ② insurrection
③ deportation   ④ colonization

09 We have no idea what the first language was like. Some words might have been _____, which means they sound like the things they refer to. For example, "cuckoo" sounds like the call of the bird.

① onomatopoeic   ② avian
③ piscine   ④ lexical

10 The life-force known as Chi that _____ the Universe created an upwelling of life, but then receded, resulting in the extinction of countless species.

① permeated   ② waned

③ permitted   ④ waxed

[11-15] 보기와 같이 주어진 단어 쌍과 가장 유사한 관계를 가진 단어 쌍을 고르시오.

[보기]

night : moon ::

① shadow : light   ② moon : star

③ day : sun   ④ ray : laser

정답은 ③번입니다.

---

11 herbivore : plants ::

① carnivore : meat   ② omnivore : insects

③ predator : species   ④ scavenger : herbs

12 marathon : endurance ::

① sprint : speed   ② javelin throw : sharpness

③ hurdle : obstacle   ④ pole vault : weight

13 microscope : magnify ::

① telescope : dignify   ② binoculars : purify

③ periscope : rectify   ④ stethoscope : amplify

14 book : chapter ::

① poem : song   ② play : scene

③ rhyme : lyric   ④ movie : prose

15 export : import ::

① examine : inspect   ② extraordinary : remarkable

③ extinct : extant   ④ exaggerate : embellish

[16-30] 주어진 문장의 빈칸에 들어갈 가장 알맞은 표현을 고르시오.

16 This will _____ demonstrates curiosity, imagination, and a desire to learn.

① be benefited for any child whom
② benefit from all child that
③ benefit any child who
④ be benefited every child whoever

17 The violin is _____ member of the string family.

① the smallest and highest-pitched
② smallest, highest-pitched
③ the smallest, highest-pitch
④ smallest and the highest-pitch

18 Even if you are very strong, _____ the newspaper against high air pressure this way.

① you're difficult to lift
② it's difficult for you lift on
③ you're difficult for it to lift up
④ it's difficult to lift

19 A pianist can produce magnificent music _____ of an orchestra.

① both alone or the accompaniment
② both the alone and accompaniment
③ either alone or with the accompaniment
④ either the alone and with accompaniment

20 The gravity of a black hole is _____, not even light.

① too strong that anything can't escape it
② so strong that nothing can escape it
③ too strong nothing to escape
④ so strong to that anything can escape

21 Why _____ some words that sound alike?

① do different languages have you think

② have different languages do you think

③ have you think different languages do

④ do you think different languages have

22 To Jacques's surprise and dismay, _____, the *Trieste* came to a stop.

① at about 340 feet below the surface

② about at 340 foot the surface below

③ below the surface about at 340 foot

④ 340 about feet below at the surface

23 _____, artists always insist that they create their art to please themselves.

① When questioned

② When they having questioned

③ Having been questioning them

④ Being questioning

24 This made _____ to punch a hole.

① stiff the straw enough

② the straw enough stiff

③ the straw stiff enough

④ enough stiff the straw

25 While _____ everywhere, there may be slight differences based on the country where you're streaming.

① many of our content available are

② many our contents will available

③ much our contents available is

④ much of our content will be available

26 The more she learned about the case, _____.

① the more became she suspicious

② she became the more suspicious

③ the more suspicious she became

④ she became suspicious the more

27 I'd _____ out tonight.

① not go rather

② not rather go

③ go rather not

④ rather not go

28 This is _____, but it is not sufficient.

① an appropriately suggestion entire

② an entirely appropriate suggestion

③ a suggestion appropriately entire

④ a suggestion entire appropriate

29 Using this special software, you can find the history of _____.

① any most building

② almost any building

③ most all of any buildings

④ almost of buildings

30 She _____ there was no more she could do.

① reached the conclusion that

② reached to a conclusion which

③ reaches at conclusions that

④ reaches the conclusions which

[31-45] 다음 밑줄 친 부분 중 틀린 것을 고르시오.

31 The ①narrative presents a ②hypothetical scenario of a company that is considering a ③variety of promotions to increase its ④sell volume.

32 Opponents ①counter that the project would ②lock in decades of additional greenhouse gas emissions, the main ③driven of climate change, and threaten the ④fragile ecosystem of the gulf.

33 The ①housing market saw a bump in October even ②as if mortgage rates hit 8%, suggesting that recent lower rates could ③keep the ④rally going.

34 The state has launched what ①is it a ②first-in-the-nation program to provide legal assistance, case management, and ③other services for ④new arrivals.

35 For ①businesses that rely on products, ②keeping track of analytics is one of the ③most critical thing that you can do ④to ensure continuity of revenue.

36 Inflation has been ①fallen steadily since it ②peaked in the summer of 2022 ③at 9.1%, measured by the consumer price ④index.

37 The newspaper has ranked 24 diets ①based on input from ②a panel of health experts and identified ③those that are best for people concerned about ④joint healthy.

38 ①A small study published in a reputable journal in 2017 found that ②study participants who received intensive ③training in deep breathing had better attention levels and better emotions ④comparing to the control group.

39 Most stocks pay dividends ①quarterly, but ②handful of quality ③public companies distribute their dividends ④on a monthly basis.

40 The district enrolled 46,829 students, a slight dip of ①more than 250. The ②decline would have been ③more stark had it not been for an increase in ④migrate students.

41 Since it is an essential ①guide to what ②matter most, you'll get full ③access to ④a wealth of independent reporting and global analysis.

42 The report shows major cities are home ①to large shares of people ②experiencing homelessness, with nearly 1 ③in 4 members of the country's total homeless population ④founded in New York City.

43 Doctors ①struggling with trauma or ②depression avoided seeking treatment due to ③fear what they might have to ④disclose it in the future, according to physician groups.

44 ①Jagging and bumpy, the walls of the tunnel ②barely resemble ③underpasses made by modern-day ④machinery.

45 Thanks ①in large part ②for a generation of musicians devoted to ③preserving it, a renaissance of the language is ④underway.

[46-60] 주어진 글을 읽고 물음에 가장 알맞은 답을 고르시오.

46-49

I have been asked on numerous occasions about the political makeup of our college campus. Typically, my response is something along the lines of: "We have very passionate advocates at both ends of the spectrum, but many people fall somewhere in the middle."

There are two main reasons for this. On the one hand, some students simply do not care about political issues. On the other, students often feel as though it is not worth the persistence, frustration and exhaustion that inevitably comes with addressing political discord. We should recognize, however, that there is an important distinction between genuine political Ⓐ_____ and the choice to avoid political conversations that require extensive time and energy to initiate and navigate successfully.

When college students voice their preference to avoid talking about politics, I cannot blame them. The United States political landscape has reached an Ⓑ<u>inflection point</u>. More tension, hatred and turmoil exists in our political system now than ever before. Right now, we must decide whether we have what it takes to heal our democratic system and more importantly, to learn how to talk to each other.

I am often told that our generation is the country's only hope. First, let me say that I am sure that this experience is not unique to me. As a collective group of current and soon-to-be twenty-somethings, we often feel the weight of safeguarding a two-hundred-and-something-year-old system on our shoulders. It is therefore easy to fall into the mindset that our individual efforts are trivial. It is a fair question: What can you do to change our country's trajectory?

I am here to tell you that at this Ⓑ<u>inflection point</u>, healing and progress are possible, but only with your help. When we reject political conversations simply because they are difficult, we fail the future generations of American citizens who will have to work ten times harder to preserve what will be left of our democracy. The time is now and the implications are severe.

46 Which of the following words is most suitable for the blank Ⓐ?

① apathy　　　　　　　　② empathy

③ sympathy　　　　　　　④ homeopathy

47 According to the passage, which of the following best describes the meaning of Ⓑ?

① the highest point in a political system

② the average point of a given period or era

③ a point when a significant change occurs

④ a linear point at which turning back is not possible

48 Which of the following best describes the author of this passage?

① a prospective college dean who is interested in creating a bipartisan faculty group on campus

② a hypocritical political pundit who is criticizing the lack of political enthusiasm on campus

③ an enthusiastic college professor who is conducting research about administrative policy on campus

④ a concerned college student who is promoting more political discourse on campus

49 According to the passage, which of the following can <u>NOT</u> be assumed as the author's opinion of the political landscape of the United States?

① The political chasm between the opposing sides is deep nationwide.

② The political system has begun to recuperate, and more involvement has expedited the process.

③ While some are truly indifferent about politics, many simply refrain from political dialogue.

④ Postponing difficult political discussions will exacerbate the political quarrel.

On November 21st, 2016, a line of thunderstorms swept through Victoria, Australia, leading to an unprecedented health crisis. Over 3,000 people were hospitalized as a powerful downdraft carried a thick layer of allergenic particles through Melbourne, causing a fatal asthma epidemic that overwhelmed emergency services and claimed at least ten lives.

Weather and climate risks are not always localized events like this sudden asthma outbreak but are intricate interactions influenced by factors such as location and demographics. Complexities in these mechanisms can amplify impacts, as seen in the 2016 storm. Gradual climate changes may trigger sudden and unforeseeable consequences when crossing certain thresholds. The interplay of various factors, such as weather patterns conducive to allergenic grass growth, can turn seemingly ordinary events into catastrophic incidents.

A high likelihood of drought and crop failures; changes to regional climate that upset whole economies; storms more destructive in both their winds and their rains: what is known about the impacts of climate change is already worrying enough. The known unknowns add to the anxiety. It is not just the question of the ice sheets, an uncertainty massive enough to weigh down a continent. There are other tipping points, too, which could see ocean currents shift, or deserts spread. And in the spaces between all these troubles are the unknown unknowns, as surprising, and deadly, as a thunderstorm that kills through pollen.

In essence, what we consider rare extremes today may become commonplace disruptions tomorrow, and new extremes may emerge, bringing additional uncertainties and dangers. The urgency to address climate change lies not only in understanding the known risks but also in preparing for the unpredictable and potentially lethal unknowns that may lie ahead.

50 What unexpected consequence occurred in Victoria, Australia, on November 21st, 2016, due to the thunderstorms?

① Unprecedented air pollution resulted in respiratory issues.

② A swarm of locusts overwhelmed the local healthcare system.

③ The sudden rise in temperatures caused a widespread fever outbreak.

④ A powerful earthquake shook the region and caused significant damage.

51 In the context of climate change, what analogy is used to convey the potential impact of unknown unknowns?

① A calm before the storm
② A thunderstorm that kills through pollen
③ Known risks becoming commonplace disruptions
④ The weight of uncertainty on a continent

52 According to the passage, what does the interplay of various factors during a storm reveal about climate change impacts?

① Predictability of consequences resulting from climate change
② Complexity and unpredictability when crossing certain thresholds
③ Limited impact on human beings causing chaos
④ Decreased intensity of weather events such as lethal thunderstorms

53 How does the passage describe the intricacies of weather and climate risks?

① They are exclusively influenced by economic factors.
② Demographics play a justifiable role in weighing down a continent.
③ Their complexities can be intensified by factors such as location and demographics.
④ The impact of climate risks is partially determined by technological advancements.

One day, four boys were walking in the grounds of Lascaux, an old mansion in southwest France. When their dog fell through a crack in some rocks, the boys went to rescue it and found that the hole led to a cavern. Ⓐ<u>It</u> would prove to be one of the most exciting archaeological discoveries of the 1900s.

News of the discovery traveled fast. People were soon flocking to explore the caves. In all, they found seven underground chambers connected by narrow passageways, with paintings and engravings on the ceilings and walls. A team of top archaeologists soon arrived at the caves. They were amazed by the sensational finding— the paintings dated from around 15000 B.C.E. and were perfectly preserved. The paintings of prehistoric animals captured the world's imagination. They offer us a glimpse of the lives of our ancestors in the distant past. Archaeologists were worried about what to do with the caves. Europe was involved in World War I, so there was no spare money to spend on developing and protecting the site. They decided to seal the caves until after the war.

The caves were opened to the public in 1948, and thousands of people visited them. But Ⓑ<u>it</u> soon became clear that the visitors were having a harmful effect. The gases and water vapor in their breath dampened the cave walls and damaged the precious paintings. Attempts were made to protect them, but in 1963 Ⓒ<u>it</u> was decided to close the caves. Twenty years later a life-size replica of the biggest cave was opened nearby.

54 According to the passage, which of the following is <u>NOT</u> true about the paintings of the caves?

① They depicted an old mansion in southwest France.
② They dated from around 15000 B.C.E.
③ They were well preserved when found.
④ They showed the lives of our ancestors in the distant past.

55 Which of the following can be inferred from the last paragraph of the passage?

① The precious paintings were successfully recovered from the damage.
② The cave had a harmful effect on the gases and water vapor in people's breath.
③ The copy of the cave minimized the damage to the original.
④ The caves will be opened twenty years later.

56 Which of the following is true about the underlined <u>it</u>?

① Ⓐ refers to a cavern.
② Ⓑ refers to a harmful effect.
③ Ⓒ refers to a life-size replica.
④ All three refer to the biggest cave.

'Flying car', 'roadable aircraft', 'dual-mode vehicle' and other terms are used to describe the all-purpose vehicle that can fly like an airplane and drive on the highway like an automobile. Make it amphibious and we have the perfect all-purpose vehicle! $\boxed{A}$ Nevertheless, this might be taking our ideas a bit too far.

It has long been the dream of aviation and automobile enthusiasts to have a vehicle that will bring them the best of both worlds. Many drivers stuck in rush hour traffic have fantasies about being able to push a button and watch their car's wings unfurl as they lift above the stalled cars in front of them. Just as many pilots who have been grounded at an airport far from home by Ⓐ_____ weather have wished for some way to wheel their airplane out onto the highway and drive home. $\boxed{B}$

A designer of a flying car will encounter many obstacles, including conflicting regulations for aircraft and automobiles. As an automobile, such a vehicle must be able to fit within the width of a lane of traffic and pass under highway overpasses. $\boxed{C}$ It must be able to keep up with normal highway traffic and meet all safety regulations. It must also satisfy vehicle exhaust emission standards for automobiles. These regulations are easier to meet if the vehicle could be officially classed as a motorcycle. Therefore, the wings must be able to fold or retract and the tail or canard surfaces may have to be stowable. $\boxed{D}$ The emission standards and crashworthiness requirements will add weight to the design. The need for an engine/transmission system that can operate in the stop and go environment of the automobile will also add system complications and weight.

57 According to the passage, which of the following is **NOT** true?

① There are multiple terms referring to an all-purpose vehicle that can drive and fly.
② Many drivers who are stuck in traffic have fantasies that their cars can fly.
③ A flying car needs to satisfy the exhaust emission regulations for automobiles.
④ Motorcycles have higher emission standards than cars.

58 Which of the following is most suitable for the blank Ⓐ?

① representative   ② reciprocal
③ inclement   ④ implement

59 What is the author's main purpose in writing this passage?

① to show that a flying car is a practical and readily available all-purpose vehicle

② to convey the feelings of pilots who have been grounded at an airport

③ to explain the difficulties lying ahead in designing a flying car

④ to investigate the complicated structure and weight of a dual-motor vehicle

60 Which is the most appropriate place for the sentence below?

This yearning has resulted in many designs for roadable aircraft since as early as 1906.

① Ⓐ

② Ⓑ

③ Ⓒ

④ Ⓓ

SOOKMYUNG WOMEN'S UNIVERSITY

숙명여자대학교   2024학년도 A형
▶▶ 33문항·60분

[01-03] 밑줄 친 부분과 가장 비슷한 의미의 표현을 고르시오. 각 2.5점

01 The Industrial Revolution marked a significant shift in human history, transforming <u>agrarian</u> societies into industrial ones. Factories emerged, powered by steam engines, leading to increased production and urbanization.

① urban   ② remote   ③ underdeveloped
④ intuitive   ⑤ agricultural

02 The two sides completed the release of Israeli hostages and detained Palestinians and looked <u>poised</u> to free more as the pause in fighting was extended by two days.

① composed   ② interested   ③ concerned
④ excited   ⑤ flustered

03 Love for outdoors should correspond with more <u>considerate</u> behavior, safety awareness, critics say.

① joyful   ② independent   ③ brave
④ adventurous   ⑤ mindful

[04-16] 빈칸에 들어갈 가장 적절한 표현을 고르시오. 각 2.5점

04 The English tutoring robots will aid students _____ brushing up their English language knowledge, conversation skills and pronunciation.

① from   ② to   ③ away
④ in   ⑤ instead

05 The audience, eager for the concert to begin, _____ quietly in their seats.

① are waiting   ② waiting   ③ waits
④ has waited   ⑤ are waited

06 The committee, composed of experts in their respective fields, _____ a series of recommendations that _____ carefully examined by policymakers before any implementation.

① have drafted — should be
② will draft — are
③ drafts — will be
④ drafting — would be
⑤ would have drafted — must be

07 Sanchez compared his promises to expand on women's and workers' rights, health and housing services, as well as adapting to climate change, _____ he called the reactionary and negationist agenda of the Popular Party and Vox.

① for which   ② with what   ③ in which
④ when   ⑤ for whom

08 A task of religion is to help us live peacefully and even joyously with the realities _____ there are no easy explanations.

① that   ② from which   ③ for what
④ how   ⑤ for which

09 Ukraine is building a formidable military. But it will face huge difficulties sustaining it, given that the war has wrecked the country's economy. So, Ukraine _____ an economic ward of the West, with Washington and its allies funding the country's defense for the foreseeable future.

① was there as　　　② had been as　　　③ kept remaining

④ will likely remain　　⑤ will haven't remained

10 Kennedy emphasized the importance of _____ between the two adversaries. One step in this direction is the proposed arrangement for a direct line between Moscow and Washington, to avoid on each side the dangerous delays, misunderstandings, and misreadings of other's actions which might occur at a time of crisis.

① indirect negotiations

② careful considerations

③ tentative cease-fire

④ economic relationship

⑤ direct communications

11 The World Resources Institute called efforts to fight climate change "_____," failing on 41 of its 42 performance metrics.

① woefully inadequate　② very impressive　　③ narrowly miss

④ slightly dangerous　　⑤ still optimistic

12 China, in my view, is not the grave threat that is portrayed everyday by the US. China is an ancient civilization of 1.4 billion people that aims for high living standards and technological excellence like other successful countries. We will best solve our global problems not by vainly _____ China, but by cooperating, negotiating, trading, and also competing economically, with China.

① attempt to eliminate

② providing various options to

③ promoting the past

④ organizing effective

⑤ trying to contain

13 Despite facing numerous setbacks, the group members exhibited remarkable resilience and perseverance, proving their _____ in the face of adversity.

① aptitude ② tenacity ③ proclivity

④ complacency ⑤ equivocation

14 The diplomat's nuanced negotiation skills were not only instrumental in resolving the protracted international conflict but also showcased his _____ understanding of diplomatic intricacies.

① ersatz and superficial

② perspicacious and discerning

③ obtuse and perfunctory

④ ostentatious and grandiloquent

⑤ fortuitous and serendipitous

15 The historian's research unveiled a hitherto _____ perspective on ancient civilizations, challenging prevailing notions about their societal structures and historical development.

① arcane and cryptic

② ubiquitous and pervasive

③ didactic and pedantic

④ cacophonous and dissonant

⑤ banal and trite

16 The playwright's dialogue was replete with _____ expressions, capturing the zeitgeist of the era in which the play was set and evoking a sense of nostalgia among the audience.

① anachronistic and outdated

② mellifluous and sonorous

③ ubiquitous and omnipresent

④ poignant and evocative

⑤ prosaic and commonplace

17-18

> We want to develop a system that can signal to people who are nearing their personal thermal thresholds for safety, so we need to collect all these Ⓐ_____ inputs to see how they correlate. Developed by French medical company BodyCap, the pill houses a small battery, a temperature sensor and a transmitter to Ⓑ_____ the data.

17 Which are the most suitable expressions for Ⓐ and Ⓑ?

① physiological — communicate
② safe — deliver
③ stable — interpret
④ negative — collect
⑤ medical — earn

18 Which title can best describe the passage?

① The Importance of Electronic Safety
② French Medical Company's Status in the Personal Safety
③ The Importance of Data in Personal Safety
④ The Relationship between Safety and Thermal Thresholds
⑤ Electronic Pills for Next-Generation Tech

19-20

Generations of Black people have suffered discrimination in every imaginable sphere of life — housing, education, politics, employment, healthcare, in the criminal justice system and more. Reparations of some kind are in order for Black Californians today, and most Californians seem to agree and support cash reparations as well as other types of reparations. The state's lawmakers Ⓐ_____ the difficult process of grappling with these recommendations. What they should not do is put this report on a shelf and forget about it. It is past time to address the systemic Ⓑ_____ of racism for centuries. California is an excellent place to start.

19 Which are the most suitable expressions for Ⓐ and Ⓑ?

① must start — atrocities

② put aside — weakness

③ will avoid — violence

④ worry about — sacrifice

⑤ can deliver — structure

20 Which of the following can best describe the passage?

① Black people's reparations will be forgotten by the lawmakers.

② A promise to free Black slaves was finally fulfilled.

③ Financial compensation for victims of injustices is common.

④ Reparations for the descendants of slaves are overdue.

⑤ Black slavery was one of the worst crimes against humanity in history.

21-22

The leaders at the Paris summit recognized the urgent need for a massive expansion of official development financing from the multilateral development bank (MDBs), meaning the World Bank, the African Development Bank, the Asian Development Bank and others. Yet to expand their lending by the amounts needed, the MDBs will require more paid-in capital from the US, Europe and other major economies. Yet the US Congress Ⓐ_____ investing more capital in the MDBs and the US Ⓑ_____ is so far blocking global action for climate change.

21 Which are the most suitable expressions for Ⓐ and Ⓑ?
① makes — agreement
② opposes — opposition
③ costs — financing
④ accelerates — disagreement
⑤ delays — earning

22 Which title can best describe the passage?
① The Relationship between France and the US
② The Landscape of World Banks
③ Major Economies and World Banks
④ US Foot-dragging in Fighting Climate Change
⑤ Massive Expansion of World Banks and Lack of the US Capital

Jared Diamond, a renowned biologist and geographer, has made significant contributions to our understanding of the intricate relationship between geography, the environment, and the development of human societies. His seminal work, "Guns, Germs, and Steel," is a comprehensive exploration that challenges traditional notions of determinism by emphasizing the pivotal role of environmental factors in shaping the course of history. In this groundbreaking work, Diamond delves into the geographical distribution of domesticable plants and animals, arguing that these factors have been instrumental in influencing the rise and fall of civilizations. The availability of these resources, he posits, is not a result of inherent superiority or inferiority but rather a product of environmental conditions. Diamond's approach challenges deterministic perspectives by highlighting the nuanced interplay between human societies and their ecological surroundings.

23 **What does Jared Diamond's work "Guns, Germs, and Steel" primarily focus on?**

① The inherent superiority or inferiority of civilizations

② The universal nature of historical development in the rise and fall of civilization

③ The overall insignificance of environmental factors

④ The inevitability of ecological surroundings challenged by the deterministic perspective

⑤ The interplay among geography, environment, and the development of human societies

24 **How does Diamond's approach challenge deterministic perspectives?**

① By asserting the dominant nature of history

② By reemphasizing the irrelevancy of environment

③ By highlighting the nuanced interplay between human societies and their ecological surroundings

④ By suggesting the inevitability of historical outcomes as a result of inherent superiority or inferiority

⑤ By disregarding the role of geography in the development of civilizations

25-26

In philosophy, the concept of the object serves as a fundamental cornerstone, referring to entities with distinct boundaries and properties. Object-oriented ontology, as proposed by contemporary philosophers, posits that all entities, whether human or non-human, possess equal ontological status. According to this perspective, understanding the agency and existence of objects is crucial for a comprehensive philosophical understanding that goes beyond anthropocentrism. Objects, in this philosophical framework, contribute to the intricate fabric of reality, challenging traditional perspectives that may prioritize human experience over non-human entities. By recognizing the inherent agency of objects, object-oriented ontology offers a more inclusive and expansive worldview that encompasses the diverse manifestations of existence.

25 What is the fundamental concept in philosophy that refers to entities with distinct boundaries and properties?

① Subject　　　　　② Object　　　　　③ Predicate
④ Abstract　　　　　⑤ Concept

26 According to object-oriented ontology, what is crucial for a comprehensive philosophical understanding?

① Ignoring the agency of objects
② Focusing solely on human entities
③ Disregarding the existence of non-human entities
④ Understanding the agency and existence of objects
⑤ Rejecting the fabric of reality beyond anthropocentrism

27-28

Absurdism, a philosophical outlook associated with thinkers like Albert Camus, contends that the search for inherent meaning or purpose in life is futile. Camus argues that the human condition is characterized by an "absurd" clash between the human desire for meaning and the apparent meaninglessness of the universe. In the face of the absurd, Camus suggests embracing life's uncertainties and creating one's own meaning through rebellion and the pursuit of individual values. This perspective stands in contrast to existentialism, which also grapples with questions of meaning but often proposes that individuals must create their own purpose.

27 According to Absurdism, why is the search for inherent meaning futile?

① Because inherent meaning is readily available through human desires.

② Because individuals must create their own meanings.

③ Because the human condition is characterized by an absurd clash.

④ Because existentialism provides definitive answers.

⑤ Because meaning is predetermined by external factors.

28 How does Camus suggest individuals respond to the absurd?

① By accepting the inherent meaninglessness of the universe

② By searching for a predetermined purpose to embrace life's uncertainties

③ By dissenting from the absurd and creating one's own meaning

④ By relying on external factors to determine meaning

⑤ By rebelling against questions of meaningful life altogether

James Joyce, a luminary of modernist literature, wielded language with unprecedented precision to craft narratives that explored the intricate recesses of human consciousness. His magnum opus, "Ulysses," stands as a testament to the profound use of stream-of-consciousness narration, inviting readers to navigate the labyrinthine minds of its characters.

29 How does James Joyce's use of stream-of-consciousness narration in his magnum opus, "Ulysses," contribute to the exploration of human consciousness in modernist literature?

① By simplifying the complexity of human consciousness
② By circumventing the intricate recesses of human consciousness
③ By presenting an indirect narrative structure to explore reader's mind precisely
④ By inviting readers to steer for the complex minds of its characters.
⑤ By avoiding the exploration of human unconsciousness altogether.

Evolution, the guiding force of biological processes, extends its tendrils into the realms of sociology and politics. The concept of survival of the fittest, originating in biology, is mirrored in political ideologies where power structures vie for dominance. Societal structures evolve as a response to internal and external pressures, embodying the principle of adaptation. However, in the face of the ecological crisis, the very essence of survival is at stake, prompting a reevaluation of societal paradigms and questioning the sustainability of current political trajectories.

30 How does the concept of survival of the fittest mirror in political ideologies, according to the passage?

① Political ideologies have no connection to the concept of survival of the fittest.
② Power structures in politics struggle for ascendancy, embodying the principle of survival of the fittest.
③ Survival of the fittest applies to biological evolution.
④ Political ideologies prioritize equality over the concept of survival of the fittest through social structures.
⑤ Societal structures have no impact on the adaptation principle in politics.

A myth, therefore, is true because it is effective, not because it gives us factual information. If, however, it does not give us new insight into the deeper meaning of life, it has failed. If it works, that is, if it forces us to change our minds and hearts, gives us new hope, and compels us to live more fully, it is a valid myth. A myth is essentially a guide; it tells us what we must do in order to live more richly. If we do not apply it to our situation and make the myth a reality in our own lives, it will remain as incomprehensible and remote as the rules of a board game, which often seem confusing and boring until we start to play.

31 Which of the following can be most correctly inferred from the statement above?

① Mythology gives us rich sense of living even if it remains incomprehensible.

② We are often confused and bored with a myth because it does not give us factual information.

③ Mythology will only transform us if we follow its directives.

④ We will be more compelled to lead a rich and full life due to fact of a myth.

⑤ The validity of myth depends on the power of human hearts and minds.

Nearly 30 years into global negotiations to address climate change, efforts to control the problem are lagging, reflecting stalled progress toward creating a sustainable trajectory more broadly. Each year of delay adds to the urgency of the problem, and of the need to maintain Earth's resilience against the most severe effects of global warming. Now, a similar expert consensus is emerging around water security.

32 **Which of the following inferences is best supported by the statement made above?**

① Most countries seem to understand that neglecting water could undo the progress made on other fronts.

② We are facing a global water crisis that warrants the same level of attention and action as the climate crises.

③ The link between climate and water crises points to a broader issue of Earth's ability of maintaining resilience.

④ We have to choose either climate or water for its urgent need of protection before it is too late.

⑤ The severe effects of global warming will be delayed by the critical condition of water security in a near future.

In the intricate tapestry of literature and the artistic symphony of storytelling, the examination of unreliable narrators becomes a literary odyssey into the dance between truth and perception. Literary analyses, reminiscent of narrative sonnets, delve into characters whose narratives intentionally mislead, inviting readers to question the boundaries of reality and fiction. As literary scholars navigate classic novels and contemporary works, the question of whether unreliable narrators serve as mere plot devices or profound explorations of human subjectivity permeates discussions. The allure of narratives crafted with intentional ambiguity raises considerations about the nature of truth in storytelling and the dynamic relationship between authors, characters, and readers.

33 What role does intentional ambiguity play in the considerations about the nature of truth in storytelling as discussed in the passage?

① Intentional ambiguity has no impact on considerations about the nature of truth in storytelling.

② Considerations about the nature of truth in storytelling are irrelevant to intentional ambiguity.

③ In the passage, intentional ambiguity raises considerations about the nature of truth in storytelling within the expansive milieu of literature.

④ Literary analyses, enriched by narrative sonnets, emphasize the role of intentional ambiguity in the nature of truth in storytelling.

⑤ The intricate dance between truth and perception is accentuated by intentional ambiguity in the passage.

SOOKMYUNG WOMEN'S UNIVERSITY

숙명여자대학교　　2024학년도 B형
▶▶ 33문항·60분

[01-03] 밑줄 친 부분과 가장 비슷한 의미의 표현을 고르시오. 각 2.5점

01 Deconstruction involves examining the ways in which binary oppositions in texts are constructed and then <u>destabilizing</u> these oppositions, revealing the complexities and fluidity of meaning.

　① decreasing　　　② undermining　　　③ reshuffling
　④ allocating　　　⑤ cultivating

02 A new analysis from researchers suggests that the distressing <u>disparity</u> in outcomes for black and white colon cancer patients could narrow if hospitals simply treated all patients with the same level of high-quality care.

　① incongruity　　　② similarity　　　③ consistency
　④ likeness　　　⑤ balance

03 In the US, the inclusion of race as a factor in college admissions was always controversial. But it was also repeatedly deemed <u>constitutional</u>.

　① illicit　　　② unauthorized　　　③ social
　④ legal　　　⑤ illegitimate

[04-16] 빈칸에 알맞은 가장 적절한 표현을 고르시오. 각 2.5점

04 The commercial interests of many industries, including alcohol, tobacco and fossil fuels, _____ comparable with the public interest or human health.

① will serve   ② are against   ③ go against
④ don't work   ⑤ aren't always

05 _____ affecting sea levels, coastal erosion will be one of the subjects leaders will address when they meet for COP28 in Dubai in December.

① In global warming
② To global warming
③ With global warming
④ Global warming for
⑤ Global warming in

06 There is no such thing as absolute freedom within a society. Different freedoms must be balanced against each other, and any reasoned discussion among typical Americans would inevitably conclude that the right to an AR-15 is _____ sacred than others' right to live.

① more significantly   ② slightly more   ③ far more
④ not more   ⑤ far less

07 There's evidence from a 2013 survey of employers by the Association of American College and Universities that some employers favor students with a strong liberal arts background _____ degrees in "practical" fields such as business.

① with whom   ② to those with   ③ with whose
④ for whom   ⑤ from whose

08 The immediate focus must be saving lives. Using Islamophobic and racist tropes, _____, in ways that silence debate, on a public stage, prevents that from happening — both in Gaza and in the US.

① even accidentally   ② perhaps intentionally   ③ more critically
④ absolutely politically   ⑤ only desperately

09 The team was tasked with _____ the intricacies of the proposed policy, carefully weighing its potential impact on diverse stakeholder groups.

① mitigating   ② obfuscating   ③ intimidating

④ juxtaposing   ⑤ elucidating

10 Duncan, who speaks _____ Korean, said he was only able to do it because he did his undergraduate in Korean history at a Korea university.

① impeccable   ② broken   ③ imperfect

④ receptive   ⑤ rudimentary

11 The avant-garde artist's unconventional approach to sculpture pushed the boundaries of _____ art, challenging traditional norms and conventions.

① iconoclastic   ② derivative   ③ ostentatious

④ ubiquitous   ⑤ placid

12 Korean language has grown with the country's "Cool Korea" image that emerged from a combination of _____. The image has taken root around the world, including the US.

① DMZ and military power

② low birth rate and youth unemployment

③ gap between the rich and the poor

④ high suicide rate among older people

⑤ K-pop and high-tech

13 The entrepreneur's innovative business model not only disrupted traditional markets but also served as a testament to her _____ for pioneering strategies and groundbreaking ideas.

① penchant and inclination

② proclivity and disparity

③ propensity and unconsciousness

④ aversion and antipathy

⑤ innovation and breaker

14 All foreign nationals residing in Korea for more than six months are _____ to enroll in the National Health Insurance program and pay monthly premium based on their income and assets.

① invited   ② suggested   ③ exempted
④ required   ⑤ waived

15 The artist's use of color is not merely decorative; each hue is a deliberate _____, conveying subtle emotions and contributing to the overall narrative and thematic richness.

① milieu and ambiance
② panacea and solution
③ modicum and smattering
④ confluence and amalgamation
⑤ nuance and delicacy

16 All members of the crowd have valuable and necessary insights that add to our collective wisdom. However, _____ we take the information diet and literacy of the crowd seriously, we will continue to shortchange our ability to make difficult and complex decisions. Advocates for a more representative, just, and equal democracy ought to recognize the need to become champions of literacy.

① for a time being
② within the limit
③ more or less
④ without limitation
⑤ unless and until

17-18

Hundreds of thousands of Americans travel across the Mexican border every year to the tiny town of Los Algodones, in search not of sun and sand, but root canals and veneers. Around 600 dentists cram the four main streets at just a fraction of the cost of dentists in the United States. Los Algodones is better known to Americans as "Molar city," a nickname that spread by Ⓐ_____ long before the internet made shopping around for health care Ⓑ_____.

17 Which are the most suitable expressions for Ⓐ and Ⓑ?

① news — available

② word of mouth — easier

③ car — meaningful

④ newspaper advertisements — less expensive

⑤ travelers — average

18 Which title can best describe the passage?

① Mexico has longer history of dental care and service.

② Americans and Mexicans compete for better dentistry.

③ Mexican people are given higher quality of dental service.

④ Mexico has larger number of dentists than that of the US.

⑤ Americans seek cheaper dentistry in a Mexico city.

19-20

The lead author of the US Constitution, James Madison, was an ardent enthusiast of Locke. He was born into slave-owning wealth and was interested in protecting wealth from the masses. Madison feared Ⓐ_____, in which the people participate in politics directly, and championed representative government, in which the people elect representatives who supposedly represent their interests. Madison feared local government because it was too close to the people and too likely to favor wealth redistribution. Madison therefore championed a Ⓑ_____ in a far-off capital.

19 **Which are the most suitable expressions for Ⓐ and Ⓑ?**

① direct democracy — federal government
② direct saving — strong constitution
③ voting right — direct investment
④ media criticism — financial support
⑤ casting votes — strong government

20 **Which title can best describe the passage?**

① The weakness of democracy
② How to promote wealth
③ The nature of US politics
④ Representatives of the people
⑤ Political campaigns in the local government

21-22

Resonance, explored extensively in aesthetics and music, serves as a multifaceted concept with profound implications. In aesthetics, resonance manifests when an artwork or idea evokes emotional or intellectual responses, creating a meaningful connection with the audience. In the realm of music, resonance involves the amplification and prolongation of sound, enriching the auditory experience and evoking emotional depth. The phenomenon of resonance transcends the boundaries of individual perception, fostering a shared experience that resonates across diverse audiences. It is through resonance that art and music become powerful conduits for emotional expression, creating a bridge between the creator and the observer or listener.

21 **Where is resonance often explored as a concept?**

① In politics   ② In ethics   ③ In aesthetics

④ In metaphysics   ⑤ In epistemology

22 **What does resonance involve in the context of music?**

① Restriction of sound

② Amplification and prolongation of sound

③ Elimination of emotional depth

④ Disconnection from the audience and observer creativity

⑤ Reduction of auditory experience

23-24

After taking stock of AI's current limitations, I don't think that artists and other inventors are in danger of Ⓐ_____ anytime soon. To my mind and to many theorists, critics and media lovers, the most compelling artistic expressions contain some sort of original idea that reflects a lived human experience, and contemporary AI models lack exactly this capacity. Even if AI bots can create passable text blocks and captivating graphic designs, they cannot fabricate the sort of Ⓑ_____ art that speaks to our humanity.

23 **Which are the most suitable expressions for Ⓐ and Ⓑ?**

① survival — vivid

② thriving — primitive

③ extinction — genuine

④ recreation — impressive

⑤ imagination — complex

24 **Which title can best describe the passage?**

① AI's current limitations will be overcome in a near future.

② AI and humanity are competing for the highest level of art.

③ AI can put the artists and inventors into a danger.

④ AI can't reproduce wonders of original human creativity.

⑤ AI bots are typically imitating human experiences and ideas.

Game theory, a branch of mathematics and economics, analyzes strategic interactions between rational decision-makers. It explores situations where the outcome for each participant depends not only on their own choices but also on the choices of others. Game theorists use models to predict and understand how individuals or entities might behave in competitive or cooperative scenarios. The Prisoner's Dilemma, a classic example in game theory, illustrates the tension between individual and collective rationality. It highlights situations where individuals, acting in their self-interest, may collectively result in a suboptimal outcome.

25 **What does game theory analyze?**

① Individual choices between self-interest and collective outcome

② Strategic interactions between rational decision-makers

③ Cooperative scenarios and participant competitiveness

④ Competitive scenarios for the collective rationality

⑤ Non-rational decision-making and a suboptimal outcome

26 **What does the Prisoner's Dilemma illustrate?**

① The inevitability of cooperative outcomes

② The harmony between individual and collective rationality

③ The tension among actors in making rational decisions

④ The absence of suboptimal outcomes in collective rationality

⑤ The predictability of individual choices

27-28

Epistemological pluralism, a perspective within philosophy of knowledge, contends that there are multiple ways of knowing and understanding the world. Unlike epistemological monism, which asserts a single, universal method of acquiring knowledge, epistemological pluralists argue for the legitimacy of diverse epistemic approaches. This perspective recognizes that different cultures, disciplines, and modes of inquiry may offer valuable and distinct insights into the nature of reality. Epistemological pluralism encourages an open-minded exploration of various knowledge systems.

27 **What does epistemological pluralism contend?**

① There is a single, universal method of acquiring knowledge.
② There should be multiple ways that lead us to knowledge of the world.
③ Diverse epistemic approaches are illegitimate for plural cultures and societies.
④ Different cultures provide identical insights into the nature of reality.
⑤ Epistemological monism is a valid approach in a philosophical knowledge.

28 **What does epistemological pluralism encourage?**

① A close-minded exploration of knowledge systems
② A rejection of epistemic approaches
③ A reliance on an exclusive method of acquiring knowledge
④ An open-minded exploration of various knowledge systems
⑤ Ignoring the insights of different cultures

Quantum mechanics introduces the uncertainty principle, formulated by Werner Heisenberg, which posits that certain pairs of properties — such as position and momentum — cannot simultaneously be precisely known. This inherent limit to precision challenges classical notions of determinism, highlighting the fundamental probabilistic nature of quantum systems. The uncertainty principle underscores the limits of our ability to precisely measure certain physical attributes.

29 **What does the uncertainty principle in quantum mechanics assert about certain pairs of properties?**

① Their static nature of quantum mechanics

② The impossibility of simultaneous precision

③ The certainty of determinism

④ The uncertainty of quantum systems

⑤ The inherent limit to probability of the uncertainty principle

As governments gather in Dubai in the United Arab Emirates for this year's climate conference in early December, two things are painfully clear. First, we are already in a climate emergency. Second, the richer countries, and especially the US, continue to turn their back on the poorer countries. The US will no doubt deny such accountability. It will claim that paying around $60 billion a year for past and current emissions would be far too costly. In fact, with the annual US gross domestic product of around $26 trillion, a levy of $60 billion per year would amount to just 0.2 percent of the US gross domestic product, a sum that is easily within reach.

30 Which of the following conclusions can most properly be drawn?

① The US should be responsible for the worst part of climate disaster since they are the richest country.

② There should be agreement on the rate of warming that would cause the climate crisis based on each country's CO_2 emissions.

③ Every country needs to participate in solving out the problem of climate change as soon as possible.

④ The United Arab Emirates, the largest oil producer, and the US, the superpower, shall work more closely to solve out the climate crisis.

⑤ This year's debate will therefore focus on climate justice and financing.

Think of the recent summit meeting between the Chinese and American presidents as two boxers clinching during a long bout. The Chinese leader wasn't throwing any punches, happily, but he might be saving his strength for later rounds. China's President Xi Jinping has used the clinch metaphor to characterize the state of Sino-American relations, according to intelligence reports described by US officials. And it's probably an apt summary of where the two superpowers stand now.

---

31 Which of the following inferences is best supported by the statement made above?

① The two leaders did not fight against each other according to their intelligence report developed by each government.

② China-US relationship cannot be thrown away because of their fierce competition for military prowess.

③ China had to employ boxers' strategies of sharing punches with their American counterpart.

④ The two leaders were in a tactical pause during what might be protracted competition.

⑤ The two presidents put their priority on the competition for economic as well as military strengths.

As Israel suffered its own version of 9/11, on Oct. 7, when Hamas launched a surprise attack on Israel, US President Joe Biden urged Israel not to make the mistakes they made when they were similarly attacked, while providing all the moral, political and military support he could. His advice went unheeded, and Israel now finds itself condemned by friends and enemies alike. As was true for the US in 2001, Israel has reacted to Hamas attack with seemingly legitimate fury directed at their Gaza homeland. While such rage may provide momentary catharsis, it nearly always results in outsize destruction.

32 **Which of the following assumptions can most properly be drawn?**

① Israel and the US should've worked more closely for the moral, political, and military cooperation.

② Israel's reaction to Hamas attack was differently performed than that of the US after the 9/11, 2001.

③ Israel and the US did lack the armed response to the attack they suffered from in a similar way.

④ Israel after Oct. 7 should've taken a different path from that of the US.

⑤ Israel and the US could've made same mistake right after they were attacked.

In the dystopian tapestry of ecological crisis and the impending specter of global warming, the fragility of the planet becomes a haunting narrative where humanity grapples with its own undoing. Sociological reflections, reminiscent of dystopian epics, unravel the threads of human activities that weave the fabric of environmental decay. As the world stands on the brink of ecological catastrophe, political ideologies clash in a desperate struggle for solutions, mirroring the survival instincts ingrained in the human psyche. The question of whether humanity can overcome its self-destructive trajectory looms large, casting a shadow over the possibilities of a sustainable future.

33 How does the fragility of the planet become a haunting narrative in the passage?

① The fragility of the planet becoming a haunting narrative has reinforced the community of global resistance against the false hope of regaining.

② Becoming a haunting narrative prioritizes the fragility of the planet over ecological crisis through sociological reflection.

③ The fragility of the planet becomes a haunting narrative due to ecological crisis and the impending global warming.

④ Dystopian epics dismiss the fragility of the planet in sociological reflections.

⑤ The ecological catastrophe can be overwhelmed by political Ideologies and human instincts.

SOONGSIL
UNIVERSITY

숭실대학교   2024학년도 인문계
▶▶ 50문항·90분

[문항별 배점: 01-10 1점/ 11-20 1.5점/ 21-35 2점/ 36-45 2.5점/ 46-50 4점]

[01-02] Choose the one that is grammatically NOT correct.

01   Early in the COVID-19 pandemic, doctors ①noticed that for what was originally ②described as a respiratory virus, SARS-CoV-2 ③seemed to have a strong effect on the brain, ④caused everything from loss of taste and smell and brain fog to, in serious cases, stroke.

02   With so many of us ①living longer, there is a ②posing problem for many aging societies. Especially, the recruitment of ③nursing staff has not ④keeping pace with the rapid rise in the elderly population.

[03-06] Choose the most appropriate word for the blank.

03   Salesforce says it derives its benchmarks for online traffic and spending from data flowing through its Commerce Cloud e-commerce service, which it says _____ a window into the behavior of 1.5 billion people in 60 countries traversing thousands of e-commerce sites.

    ① provides   ② eliminates

    ③ interprets   ④ alleviates

04 Generative AI technology can create more jobs than it is expected to eliminate even as its ability to _____ the job market has been discussed widely on social media sites.

① boost   ② wreck

③ merge   ④ proliferate

05 Within the Ursa Minor constellation lies an extraordinary planetary system that defies conventional expectations. Halla, a planet found in close proximity to the red giant star Baekdu, _____ despite being situated at a distance that is deemed impossible for its survival.

① exhausts   ② exists

③ exonerates   ④ extorts

06 Drug developers have long needed to _____ clinical trials to improve the safety, efficacy, and adoption of new therapies among historically underrepresented groups.

① diversify   ② exclude

③ impede   ④ scour

[07-10] Choose the expression closest in meaning to the underlined.

07 Holiday shoppers in the U.S. are seeking out the best deals and strategically <u>nabbing</u> the deepest discounts ahead of Cyber Monday, according to data from retailer websites aggregated by third parties.

① disposing   ② grabbing

③ overhauling   ④ spreading

08 Global household wealth fell last year for the first time since the financial crisis in 2008, as inflation and the <u>appreciation</u> of the US dollar wiped some $11.3 trillion off assets.

① default   ② mean

③ strength   ④ participation

09 A series of detailed investigation could not provide any information on his <u>spurious</u> claims.

① deceitful   ② genuine

③ ossified   ④ vehement

10 Sean used to make <u>facetious</u> remarks even in serious circumstances.

① arid   ② funny

③ inadequate   ④ placid

[11-13] Read the following passage and answer the questions.

I was raised in one of those university-based, liberal elite families that politicians like to ridicule. In my childhood, every human being — regardless of gender — was exactly alike Ⓐ<u>under the skin</u>, and I mean exactly, barring his or her different opportunities. My parents wasted no opportunity to bring this point home. One Christmas, I received a Barbie doll and a softball glove. Another brought a green enamel stove, which baked tiny cakes by the heat of a lightbulb, and also a set of steel-tipped darts and competition-quality dartboard. Did I mention the year of the chemistry set and the ballerina doll?

It wasn't until I became a parent — I should say, a parent of two boys — I realized I had been fed a line and swallowed it like a sucker (barring the part about opportunities, which I still believe). This dawned on me during my older son's dinosaur phase, which began when he was about two-and-a half. Oh, he loved dinosaurs, all right, but only the blood-swilling carnivores. Plant-eaters were wimps and losers, and he refused to wear a T-shirt marred by a picture of a stegosaur. I looked down at him one day, as he was snarling around my feet and doing his toddler best to gnaw off my right leg, and I thought: This goes a lot deeper than culture.

Raising children tends to bring on Ⓑ<u>this kind of politically incorrect reaction</u>. Another friend came to the same conclusion watching a son determinedly bite his breakfast toast into the shape of a pistol with which he hoped would blow away — or at least terrify — his younger brother. Once you get past the guilt part — Did I do this? Should I have bought him that plastic allosaur with the oversized teeth? — such revelations can lead you to consider the far more interesting field of gender biology, where the questions take different shape: Does love of carnage begin in culture or genetics, and which drives which? Do the gender roles of our culture reflect an underlying biology, and, in turn, does the way we behave influence that biology?

11 The underlined Ⓐ in the sentence means _____.

① if not unfairly discriminated

② despite the racial differences

③ beneath apparent differences

④ at the moment of one's birth

12 The underlined Ⓑ refers to _____.

① the parents' unusual sense of gender equality

② the boy's infatuation with the blood-swilling carnivores

③ the son's violent behavior being something more than culture

④ a son's biting his toast into the shape of a pistol

13 Which of the following is NOT true about the author?

① We don't know whether she loved a Barbie doll when a kid.

② Her older son hated a stegosaur because it is a plant-eater.

③ She bought her son a plastic allosaur.

④ She is now confused about the driving force of the gender roles.

[14-15] Read the following passage and answer the questions.

China's youth are seen as key to growth in the country's huge consumer market. ⒶBut as the economy struggles post-Covid and companies pull back on hiring, the jobless rate for those aged 16 to 24 hit a record 22% in June before authorities halted the data, amplifying concerns the real number could be even higher. But rather than pulling back on spending, Gen Z consumers are instead re-evaluating their priorities. Many are splashing out on relatively affordable experiences rather than scooping up big-ticket items like gadgets or working toward longer-term financial goals, such as building up savings or buying a home. Overseas travel is out of reach for many, but domestic hotspots are booming. ⒷSo is China's box office, which is setting records.

The number of Chinese Gen Zs who want to drop out of the rat race — a movement known as "lying flat" — has grown in the past 18 months as a response to the ultra-competitive job market, said Zak Dychtwald, founder of trend research company Young China Group. People are still spending in traditional sectors. Consumption data was strong in the first half of 2023, and Ⓒeven if retail sales undershoot expectations, companies are likely to top margin estimates for the second half given leaner cost structures and reduced inventory burdens, according to Bloomberg Intelligence. ⒹTherefore, retailers with large youth customer bases in China have either voiced concerns over the uncertainties surrounding China's recovery, or are relying on discounts and promotions to support sales. When they do shop, some young Chinese are being more cautious than they have in stronger economic times.

14 Which of the following is NOT appropriate?

① Ⓐ   ② Ⓑ

③ Ⓒ   ④ Ⓓ

15 Which of the following is NOT true?

① The jobless rate for people aged 16 to 24 may be higher than 22%.

② Most Gen Z consumers are more interested in domestic hotspots than overseas travel.

③ The number of employment has steadily increased during the post-Covid.

④ Some retailers expect sales increase with discounts and promotions.

[16-18] Read the following passage and answer the questions.

The study of acquired aphasia has been an important area of research in understanding the relationship between the brain and language. Aphasia is the neurological term for any language disorder that results from brain damage caused by disease or trauma. In the second half of the nineteenth century, significant scientific advances were made in localizing language in the brain based on the study of people with aphasia. In the 1860s, the French surgeon Paul Broca proposed that language is localized in the left hemisphere of the brain, and more specifically in the front part of the left hemisphere (now called Broca's area). At a scientific meeting in Paris, he claimed that we speak with the left hemisphere. Broca's claim was based on a study of his patients who suffered language deficits after brain injury to the left frontal lobe. A decade later, Carl Wernicke, a German neurologist, described another variety of aphasia that occurred in patients with lesions in areas of the left temporal lobe, now known as Wernicke's area. Lateralization is the term used to refer to the localization of function to one hemisphere of the brain. Language is lateralized to the left hemisphere, and the left hemisphere appears to be the language hemisphere from infancy on.

Most aphasics do not show total language loss. Rather, different aspects of language are selectively impaired, and the kind of impairment is generally related to the location of the brain damage. Because of this damage-deficit correlation, research on patients with aphasia has provided a great deal of information about how language is organized in the brain. Patients with injuries to Broca's area may have Broca's aphasia, as it is often called today. Broca's aphasia is characterized by labored speech and certain kinds of word-finding difficulties, but it is primarily a disorder that affects a person's ability to form sentences with the rules of syntax. Unlike Broca's patients, people with Wernicke's aphasia produce fluent speech with good intonation, and they may largely adhere to the rules of syntax. However, their language is often semantically incoherent.

16 **Which of the following is best for the title?**

① Acquired Aphasia　　　② Lateralization

③ Aphasic Phases　　　④ Brain Plasticity

17 **Which of the following is NOT mentioned about Broca's aphasia?**

① semantic inconsistency　　　② word retrieval difficulties

③ agrammatic sentence　　　④ non-fluent speech

18 Which of the following is NOT true?

① Aphasia may result from either disease or trauma.

② The study of Broca's area preceded to that of Wernike's area.

③ Broca's area and Wernicke's area are the same lobe of the brain.

④ Most aphasics show selective impairment of different aspects of language.

[19-20] Read the following passage and answer the questions.

There are some major differences between the supermarket and a traditional marketplace. The cacophony of a traditional market has given way to programmed, innocuous music, punctuated by enthusiastically intoned commercials. A stroll through a traditional market offers an array of sensuous aromas; if you are conscious of smelling something in a supermarket, there is a problem. The life and death matter of eating, expressed in traditional markets by the sale of vegetables with stems and roots and by hanging animal carcasses, is purged from the supermarket, where food is processed somewhere else, or at least trimmed out of sight.

But the most fundamental difference between a traditional market and the places through which you push your cart is that in a modern retail setting nearly all the selling is done without people. The product is totally dissociated from the personality of any particular person selling it — with the possible exception of those who appear in its advertising. The supermarket purges sociability, which slows down sales. It allows manufacturers to control the way they present their products to the world. It replaces people with packages.

Packages are an inescapable part of modern life. They are omnipresent and invisible, deplored and ignored. During most of your waking moments, there are one or more packages within your field of vision. Packages are so ubiquitous that they slip beneath conscious notice, though many packages are designed so that people will respond to them even if they're not paying attention.

Once you begin pushing the shopping cart, it matters little whether you are in a supermarket, a discount store, or a warehouse club. The important thing is that you are among packages: expressive packages intended to engage your emotions, ingenious packages that make a product useful, informative packages that help you understand what you want and what you're getting. Historically, packages are what made self-service retailing possible, and in turn such stores increased the number and variety of items people buy. Now a world without packages is unimaginable.

19 Which of the following is far from the line of demarcation between the supermarket and a traditional marketplace?

① auditory experience
② olfactory experience
③ public hygiene
④ packaging

20 Which of the following is true?

① Packages are ubiquitous and literally invisible.
② Packages are deceptive as well as informative.
③ Packages are expressive and humble.
④ Packages enabled self-service retailing.

[21-23] Read the following passage and answer the questions.

Proteins are produced in tiny factories inside the cells of the body. Biologists call them ribosomes. These factories get going when they receive a message that "tells" them to make a certain protein. Each such message is generated using DNA. A DNA sequence that corresponds to the relevant protein sequence is copied onto another molecule, appropriately called a "messenger," which transmits a form of the sequence to the ribosomes. The messenger molecules, called messenger RNA (ribonucleic acid), are another kind of nucleic acid sequence. The DNA sequences are therefore a kind of template, a specific sequence of nucleotides that can be transcribed to produce the message that is then translated into an amino-acid sequence when the protein is made. That process is called "gene expression." This terminology gives the impression that the whole process is implicit in the gene, or at least in the information that the gene holds, which simply needs to be "expressed."

But it is a little Ⓐ_____ to say, as we often do, that the DNA sequence "determines" the protein. In fact, the DNA just sits there, and occasionally the cell reads off from it a sequence that it needs, in order to get some protein produced. This looks very much like my hi-fi equipment reading the digital information on a CD to generate the real "action": the music. So the first step in the reductionist chain of cause and effect is not a simple causal event at all. When a sequence is read off, that is an important event, which initiates a whole series of subsequent events. These are physical events. True. But it is the process of reading that matters, as well as the object that is read.

This process involves certain systems of proteins. If we wish to identify an agent of the action, it must be those systems. They "read" the DNA code. DNA does nothing outside the context of a cell containing these protein systems, just as the CD can do nothing without the CD reader. So, we have the paradox that proteins are required for the machinery to read the code to produce the proteins.

21 What is the most suitable option to fill in the blank Ⓐ?

① odd   ② rude

③ natural   ④ succinct

22 What is the role of messenger RNA in the process of gene expression?

① It codes for amino acids directly.

② It reads the DNA code.

③ It folds DNA threads in the nucleus.

④ It transmits DNA sequences to ribosomes.

23 Which is the best title for the text?

① Unraveling the Genetic Tapestry of Disease: Exploring Mechanisms and Challenges in Medical Research

② Revolutionizing Genetics: Recombinant DNA Technology and Gene Editing in the 21st Century

③ Decoding the Symphony of Gene Expression: Proteins, Ribosomes, and the Intricacies of DNA

④ Genetic Determinism, Personal Traits, and the Influence of Environment: Navigating the Complex Landscape of Human Identity

[24-26] Read the following passage and answer the questions.

A few days later I found two of the black yearlings at another carcass. One grabbed a piece of meat, tossed it in the air, then leaped up and caught it in his jaws. He dropped it and pounced on it like it was alive and trying to get away. After that he ran off with the meat, threw it up again, and caught it on the run. I later began a list of games young wolves play and called this the tossing game.

Another black yearling ran in and chased the first one. The lead brother dropped the meat and the other black grabbed it. When he ran off with it, the first yearling chased him. They reversed the chase and the second black pursued the first. Then the lead black suddenly stopped and lay down in tall grass. As the other wolf ran in, the one hiding in the grass jumped up and wrestled him to the ground. I called that the ambush game.

Later, as the two stood side by side, one brother suddenly ran off. That looked like a dare for his brother to chase him. The other black accepted the challenge and went after him at top speed. The two took turns chasing each other in straight lines and in zigzag patterns, a game of catch me if you can. They ran, pranced, and twirled around in front of each other. It did not matter who chased whom, the point of all that playing was not to win, it was to have fun. The best word to describe the behavior of the yearlings was Ⓐexuberant. As I watched them, I had a thought: they loved being wolves.

All that play served a purpose. I later saw a cow elk chase one of the yearlings. Although she could outrun the wolf in a straight-out race, he zigzagged back and forth so nimbly that she soon gave up in frustration. The vigorous play chasing had prepared him to outmaneuver the cow. At times the yearlings actively invited elk to chase them. I saw them do play bows in front of elk to get them to initiate a pursuit, then easily get away using the tricks they had perfected during their play sessions. It was like they were showing off.

24 Which of the following is closest in meaning to Ⓐ?

① abject

② animated

③ lugubrious

④ apathetic

25 Which game is NOT introduced in the text?

① the stalking game

② the tossing game

③ the ambush game

④ the catch-me-if-you-can game

26 What purpose did the vigorous play chasing serve for the yearlings?

① to win against other wolves

② to showcase their strength

③ to stay healthy

④ to learn how to run away from attackers

[27-29] Read the following passage and answer the questions.

This report from the dying days of the nineteenth century is cited by the *Oxford English Dictionary* as the earliest example of the secondary meaning of the word "drugs" — today, perhaps, its primary meaning — "a substance with intoxicating, stimulant or narcotic effects used for cultural, recreational or other non-medical purposes." Prior to this point, "drugs" had referred generally to all medications. Over the previous decades, intoxicating or mind-altering drugs had often been grouped together, but a qualifying adjective such as "poisonous," "inebriating," "dangerous" or "addictive" had been required to make the meaning clear. With the twentieth century, the single word "drugs" came to incorporate all these meanings implicitly. "Drugs" became a shorthand for a collection of substances that, when not used under appropriate medical supervision, carried the risk of self-poisoning, addiction or mental illness. The only official objection to the new meaning of "drugs" came from the American Pharmaceutical Association, who were concerned that their legitimate trade was being tarnished. But the new usage of "drugs" caught on, and was soon freighted with meanings and associations that extended far beyond the pharmaceutical trade.

The new century saw the rising tide of what became known as the Progressive Era, a dynamic vision of modernity in which the benefits and risks of drugs were sharply recalibrated. The hallmarks of the new movement were the expansion of government, the growth of citizen and community activism, and the replacement of laissez-faire politics and economics with state intervention and regulation. Despite its name, the great successes of the Progressive Era were achieved by mobilising coalitions from across the political spectrum, uniting progressive and conservative interests against a shared enemy: the overweening might of industry, empire and plutocracy. Alcohol prohibition in the United States, perhaps the era's most ambitious project, was a case in point, achieved by an alliance of progressive forces — temperance campaigners, the women's movement, working men's societies, labour unions and the medical profession — with the conservative voices of the churches and the old Puritan elites. For some, it was a campaign for social justice against the breweries and distillers who were eroding the social fabric for private profit; for others, it was a moral crusade to rid society of the evils of drink. Behind both lay the shared conviction that intoxication, whether by alcohol or other drugs, was running out of control, and threatening the civilised society of the future.

27 What was the primary meaning of the word "drugs" before the late nineteenth century?

① intoxicating substances for recreational purposes
② medications in general
③ narcotic substances used for medical purposes
④ mind-altering drugs with specific adjectives for clarity

28 Who opposed the casual use of terms like "drug evil" and "drug habit," and why?

① the government, due to concerns about public health
② the American Pharmaceutical Association, concerned about their trade
③ the Progressive Era activists, aiming for social justice
④ the alcohol and tobacco conglomerates, protecting their interests

29 What marked the Progressive Era's approach to drugs and alcohol?

① laissez-faire politics and economic policies
② strict state intervention and regulation
③ opposition from the pharmaceutical industry
④ isolationist attitudes towards global trade

[30-32] Read the following passage and answer the questions.

An early version of Mickey Mouse may soon be everywhere: on shirts, in movies, onstage making crude remarks and shaking his hips in little white trousers. As of Monday, the iteration of Mickey Mouse from the 1928 movie *Steamboat Willie* — the mischievous rodent who uses a goose as a trombone — is available in the public domain in America.  Later depictions of the character are still under copyright. But the change is a major moment that Disney fought hard to postpone.

In 1998, Congress extended copyright periods for a range of works. The Copyright Term Extension Act — sometimes called the "Mickey Mouse Protection Act" due to Disney's role in lobbying Congress — lengthened the period of copyright for many materials published before 1978 to 95 years. That law "transferred wealth to a tiny subset of rights owners," Jennifer Jenkins, a clinical law professor at Duke University and the director of Duke's Center for the Study of the Public Domain, told me in an email, and "stymied" the public's ability to access and build on American cultural heritage.

Disney itself has a complicated relationship with copyright: Although the company has a vested interest in retaining the rights to its inventions, it has also benefited greatly from public-domain works. Some of its hits are based on existing intellectual property; think of the fairy tales underlying major movies, or the *Hamlet* plotlines in the *Lion King* franchise. Its movies draw on sources including Lewis Carroll, the Brothers Grimm, Victor Hugo, and Hans Christian Andersen, Jenkins explained. A spokesperson for Disney told me, "We will, of course, continue to protect our rights in the more modern versions of Mickey Mouse and other works that remain subject to copyright, as well as work to safeguard against consumer confusion caused by unauthorized uses of Mickey and our other iconic characters."

A purpose of copyright laws is to stimulate the creation of new works, Paul Heald, a law professor and an expert on copyright at the University of Illinois, told me. Copyright laws assure artists that if they create something, they can enjoy exclusive rights to it for a period of time after its release. But the length of that period is a balancing act. If copyright laws are too restrictive, Heald said, that can curb creative expression. More works being in the public domain is not only good for creativity, he told me — "it's part of the plan of the Framers of the Constitution."

30 According to Jennifer Jenkins, what impact did the Copyright Term Extension Act have on the public's access to cultural heritage?

① It increased access to cultural heritage.

② It had no impact on access to cultural heritage.

③ It thwarted the public's ability to access cultural heritage.

④ It transferred wealth to cultural heritage.

31 What is mentioned as a complication in Disney's relationship with copyright?

① Disney has no interest in retaining the rights to its inventions.

② Disney has never benefited from public-domain works.

③ Disney's hits are not based on existing intellectual property.

④ Disney has benefited from public-domain works but wants to protect its inventions.

32 What is a consequence of works entering the public domain, according to Paul Heald?

① increased control by big companies

② limitation of creative expression

③ enrichment of public domain that benefits creativity

④ a loss of copyright protection for artists

[33-35] Read the following passage and answer the questions.

Solar and wind power hit a new record this year, generating more U.S. power than coal for the first five months of 2023, according to preliminary data from the Energy Information Administration (EIA). It's the first time on record that wind and solar have out-produced coal for five months, according to industry publication, *E&E News*, which first calculated the Ⓐ_____. Official EIA data, which is released with a Ⓑ_____, shows wind and solar energy out-producing coal for January, February and March, while real-time figures "indicate that same trend continued in April and May," EIA spokesperson Chris Higginbotham said in an email.

When hydroelectric power is counted among the renewable mix, that record stretches to over six months, with renewables beating out coal starting last October, according to the EIA. "From a production-cost perspective, renewables are the cheapest thing to use — wind and solar. So, we're going to see more and more of these records," said Ram Rajagopal, a professor of civil and environmental engineering at Stanford University.

The figure marks a new high for clean power and a steep decline in coal-fired power generation, which as recently as 10 years ago made up 40% of the nation's electricity. And while the monthly figures are preliminary and could be revised in the coming months, according to the EIA, more renewables in the pipeline mean that coal power is set to keep falling. "We expect that the United States will generate less electricity from coal this year than in any year this century," EIA Administrator Joe DeCarolis said in May. "As electricity providers generate more electricity from renewable sources, we see electricity generated from coal decline over the next year and a half."

For years, coal power has been declining, pushed out by increasingly cheap natural gas — also a fossil fuel — driven by a hydraulic fracturing boom. But coal saw a brief resurgence last year when natural gas prices shot up in the wake of Russia's invasion of Ukraine, leading some utilities in the U.S. and Europe to sign on coal-powered generators. Globally, coal use reached a new high in 2022, however, its bounceback has been short-lived in the U.S., as coal plants in the country retire at a steady pace. Six coal-fueled generating units have been closed so far this year.

33 What is the most suitable option for Ⓐ and Ⓑ?

① figures — contest

② sanctions — lag

③ sanctions — contest

④ figures — lag

34 When does the EIA expect the United States to generate less electricity from coal than in any year this century?

① by the end of the next century

② by the end of 2022

③ by the end of 2023

④ within the next 10 years

35 What led to a brief resurgence of coal power last year?

① the closure of coal-fueled generating units

② a decline in renewable energy production

③ a boom in hydroelectric power

④ the increase in natural gas prices following Russia's invasion of Ukraine

It's a disarmingly simple description of a pop star: *a cool person who gives off an amazing vibe*. But it's an image he's been chasing for a long time. As a teenager, Jungkook decided to join BTS because he was so impressed by the English-speaking and rap skills of the group's leader, RM. He used to upload covers of his favorite pop songs on SoundCloud, and regularly gushes about the likes of Justin Bieber, Usher, and Ariana Grande. The first time I saw him perform live, he flew through a stadium, suspended by a cable over tens of thousands of fans, his vocals so stable you'd think he was reclining on a chaise. But underpinning this desire for coolness is an equally old obsession with excellence. The title of *Golden* immediately evokes Jungkook's best-known nickname: the golden *maknae*. Coined by RM, it refers to his status as the youngest ("*maknae*," in Korean) member, who seems to be preternaturally talented at everything he does. Not only is Jungkook a powerful dancer and a strong vocalist, but he also excels at drawing, painting, songwriting, archery, wrestling, sprinting, swimming — a compilation of him simply *being good at stuff* has more than 18 million views on YouTube. When it comes to his main job as a performer, he's a known Ⓐ_____ who is exacting about his work. So expectations have been high for *Golden,* the release of which was preceded by two singles, the U.K. garage track "Seven (feat. Latto)," which set a Spotify record for the fastest song to reach 1 billion streams, and the early-2000s throwback "3D (feat. Jack Harlow)." But I wasn't prepared for the stunning main track, "Standing Next to You," which brings to mind Parliament-Funkadelic and Michael Jackson. It's not quite like any song that Jungkook or BTS have done before.

36 **Which option is best for Ⓐ?**

① sloth   ② perfectionist

③ assistant   ④ easy-goer

37 **Which statement among the following is NOT true?**

① In his teens, Jungkook joined BTS impressed by RM's English and rap skills.

② Jungkook regularly shared pop song covers on SoundCloud, admiring artists like Justin Bieber.

③ Jungkook excels at dancing, singing, drawing, painting, songwriting, archery, wrestling, sprinting, and swimming.

④ "Standing Next to You" follows a similar vein as Jungkook's and BTS's prior works.

[38-39] Read the following passage and answer the questions.

AI was at the center of the dispute that ground Hollywood to a halt this summer, when both writers and actors took to the picket lines in a historic double strike. When writing tools like ChatGPT and AI image-generation tools like Midjourney emerged, Hollywood creatives became worried that AI was going to take their jobs. After months of negotiations, the guilds representing each profession carved out protections against a future version of Hollywood created mostly via AI. But some filmmakers worry that those protections aren't robust enough. Earlier this year, ChatGPT gained usage in Hollywood writers' rooms, especially to generate new pilot ideas for new shows more cheaply. In response, the Writers Guild of America demanded — and eventually secured — protections against studios using AI to write or edit scripts, or creating scripts with ChatGPT and then paying writers a lower wage to adapt them. The contracts won't prohibit the use of ChatGPT in script writing: Writers can choose to use AI as a tool for research or ideas generation. But crucially, the writers will always be compensated for their work, and remain at the center of the process. Meanwhile, actors became similarly worried that studios wanted to replace them with "digital replicas." Instead of paying actors, studios could scan their bodies, pay them for a day's work, and then fill out scenes using AI technology. After a months-long stalemate, the producers eventually agreed to a consent-based model in which actors must unambiguously opt in to being scanned and creating a digital likeness of themselves. The actors will also be entitled to full residuals for the digital replica's appearances. However, some actors are still calling for outright bans of synthetic performers, and worry that the contract they signed contains loopholes to allow AI to increasingly encroach on their jobs.

38 Which of the following is best for the title?

① AI and the Hollywood Strikes

② Hollywood Taken Over by AI

③ AI and Computer Graphics

④ The Battle for Intellectual Property

39 **Which of the following is NOT true?**

① Some filmmakers are still not satisfied with the protections against AI.

② Writers are worried about receiving lower wage due to the scripts generated by AI.

③ The new contracts will ban the use of AI in script writing and editing.

④ The producers will need actors' approval of the use of digital replicas.

[40-42] Read the following passage and answer the questions.

For the Greeks, beauty was a virtue: A kind of excellence. Persons then were assumed to be what we now have to call — lamely, enviously — *whole* persons. If it did occur to the Greeks to distinguish between a person's "inside" and "outside," they still expected that inner beauty would be matched by beauty of the other kind. The well-born young Athenians who gathered around Socrates found it quite paradoxical that their hero was so intelligent, so brave, so honorable, so seductive — and so ugly. One of Socrates' main pedagogical acts was to be ugly — and teach those innocent, no doubt splendid-looking disciples of his how full of Ⓐ_____ life really was.

They may have resisted Socrates' lesson. We do not. Several thousand years later, we are more wary of Ⓑthe enchantments of beauty. We not only split off — with the greatest facility — the "inside" (character, intellect) from the "outside" (looks); but we are actually surprised when someone who is beautiful is also intelligent, talented, good.

It was principally the influence of Christianity that deprived beauty of the central place it had in classical ideals of human excellence. By limiting excellence (*virtus* in Latin) to moral *virtue* only, Christianity set beauty adrift — as an alienated, arbitrary, superficial enchantment. And beauty has continued to lose prestige. For close to two centuries it has become a convention to attribute beauty to only one of the two sexes: The sex which, however Fair, is always Second. Associating beauty with women has put beauty even further on the defensive, morally.

A beautiful woman, we say in English. But a handsome man. "Handsome" is the masculine equivalent of — and refusal of — a compliment which has accumulated certain demeaning overtones, by being reserved for women only. That one can call a man "beautiful" in French and in Italian suggests that Catholic countries — unlike those countries shaped by the Protestant version of Christianity — still retain some vestiges of the pagan admiration for beauty. But the difference, if one exists, is of degree only. In every modern country that is Christian or post-Christian, women *are* the beautiful sex — to the detriment of the notion of beauty as well as of women.

40 Which of the following best fits in Ⓐ?

① ambiguities ② dangers

③ blessings ④ paradoxes

41 The underlined Ⓑ suggests from the context that _____.

① visual attraction has an amazing power of love

② physical beauty can be quite deceptive and misleading

③ only those who have beautiful minds can be trusted

④ intelligent people hardly take care of their looks

42 Which of the following best captures the author's attitude toward the association of beauty with women in modern times?

① It is a fair sign of female empowerment.

② It shows that the Greek notion of beauty is now restored.

③ It shows that women's beauty mirrors their moral excellence.

④ It undermines the dignity of women and the notion of beauty.

[43-45] Read the following passage and answer the questions.

A political concept of resistance implies a struggle against a force of power and violence by those who suffer under it, that is, it includes an analysis and recognition of the superiority of that power, and the aim to dismantle that power. Much of what today goes by the name of resistance, however, is retaliation against the enemy, a counter-move in what is seen as Ⓐ_____ of (violent) action and reaction, attack and counter-attack between designated opponents. The aim is not to dismantle power, the aim is victory over the enemy, that is, gathering enough power on one's own side to overpower the other side.

Hence the crucial question is less what Ⓑ_____ are than where the consideration of history begins, that is, which is the "original" action to which the second is but a counter-move. Thus it was reported in the news that Palestinians were throwing stones and Israeli settlers were shooting, "but it is unclear as yet who began." That is, the concept of "resistance" becomes part of the ideologizing structure of justifying one's own action (or the actions of those with whom the subject identifies), where the other's action preceding ours is said to be the cause of — or to have given us cause for — violent action on our part.

It is why every military force in the world is called a "defence" force, governed by a civil ministry of defence that explains what the current military action is a defence against. Thus a British Falklands war is a defensive war, and sinking the Argentinian warship *General Belgrano* a defensive action against its hostile change of course, just as bombing Iraq is but retaliation in defence of an already attacked Kuwait and a justified response to Sadam Hussein's failure to respond to the UN's ultimatum. In fact, Ⓒ_____ history, we will find that there never has been an aggressive move in the world, since there always was some previous action or event considered by one or the other party to have been the "cause" for "retaliation."

43 Which of the following best fits in Ⓐ?

① the chronological sequence
② the diplomatic clashes
③ the military strategies
④ the mutual destructions

44 Which of the following best fits in ⑧?

① the diplomatic gestures

② the human instinct

③ the power relations

④ the international politics

45 Which of the following best fits in ⓒ?

① demystifying   ② viewing

③ recognizing   ④ consulting

[46-47] Read the following passage and answer the questions.

If it is essential that a teacher like his pupils, it is also important that he know them. A teacher must not expect the young to be like himself nor the people he knows. He must learn the pattern of their thoughts and emotions. If he does this, he will understand many of the strange things they do and will be able to forget some of the unpardonable actions of his students.

How can a teacher know his students thoroughly? Mainly by close Ⓐ_____ with them. He can give them a party occasionally or play games with them. Listen to them when they think you are doing something else, and try to discover how their emotions and minds really function. You can also learn a great deal about them by remembering your own youth. The more you can remember of the earliest days of your life, the better you can understand the young.

Some of the least successful teachers of general subjects are men and women who, even when they were boys and girls, studied very much and seldom played rough or silly games. Often they enjoyed themselves the most when they tried to be like the teachers. Such young people often receive good grades and then hesitate to go into rude world to earn a living by adventurous competition. They enter the teaching profession, and are surprised when they dislike so much of it. Sometimes they are extremely effective with bright, hard-working boys and girls who remind them of themselves. They Ⓑ_____ all their ambitions on such pupils, training them to win prizes of money for future education and to pass difficult examinations. But they seldom work well with ordinary pupils, who fill the average class, because they themselves have never been either ordinary or young.

46 Which of the following best fits in Ⓐ and Ⓑ?

① association — project ② cooperation — endow

③ observation — fathom ④ orchestration — underscore

47 Which of the following is NOT true?

① Loving students and knowing them should go together in education.

② Your childhood memories can help you understand students.

③ Some teachers have troubles working with ordinary students.

④ Good teachers try their hardest to be a perfect role-model.

[48-50] Read the following passage and answer the questions.

The origins of many regional dialects of American English can be traced to the people who settled in North America in the seventeenth and eighteenth centuries. Because they came from different parts of England, these early settlers already spoke different dialects of English, and these differences were carried to the original thirteen American colonies. By the time of the American Revolution, there were three major dialect regions in the British colonies: the Northern dialect spoken in New England and around the Hudson River, the Midland dialect spoken in Pennsylvania, and the Southern dialect. These dialects differed from one another and from the English spoken in England in systematic ways. Some of the changes that occurred in British English spread to the colonies; others did not. Ⓐ

How dialects develop is illustrated by the pronunciation of words with an *r* in different parts of United States. As early as the eighteenth century, the British in southern England were dropping their *r*'s before consonants and at the ends of words. Ⓑ By the end of the eighteenth century, *r*-drop was a general rule among many of the early settlers in New England and the southern Atlantic seaboard. Close commercial ties were maintained between the New England colonies and London, and Southerners sent their children to England to be educated, which reinforced the *r*-drop rule. The *r*-less dialect is still spoken today in Boston, New York, and Savannah, Georgia. Ⓐ_____, later settlers came from northern England, where the *r* had been retained; as the frontier moved westward, so did the *r*. Ⓒ Pioneers from all three dialect areas spread westward. The mingling of their dialects leveled many of their dialect differences, which is why the English used in large sections of the Midwest and the West is similar. Ⓓ

48 Which one is the best place for the following sentence?

The words *card* and *cod* are homophones in the Bostonian version of that dialect.

① Ⓐ   ② Ⓑ

③ Ⓒ   ④ Ⓓ

49 Which of the following best fits in Ⓐ?

① However   ② Furthermore

③ Accordingly   ④ Consequently

50 Which of the following is NOT true?

① Different dialects of British English from early settlers resulted in three major dialects in American English by the end of the eighteenth centuries.

② Sound changes in American English tended to spread to British English.

③ The *r*-drop is still observed in Boston and New York today.

④ People in the Midwest and the West share the general linguistic rule, including *r*-retention.

숭실대학교   2024학년도 자연계
▶▶ 영어 25문항, 수학 25문항·90분

[문항별 배점: 01-10 1점/ 11-20 2.5점/ 21-25 3점]

[01-02] Choose the one that is grammatically NOT correct.

01   Strong online traffic on Black Friday ①<u>demonstrating</u> a notable pattern of shoppers ②<u>putting</u> time and effort into ③<u>selecting</u> the lowest-cost, best-value merchandise, said Rob Garf, vice president and general manager for retail at Salesforce, which tracks data ④<u>flowing</u> through its Commerce Cloud e-commerce service.

02   A simple definition of the new historicism is ①<u>what</u> it is a method ②<u>based</u> on the parallel ③<u>reading</u> of literary and non-literary texts, usually ④<u>of</u> the same historical period.

[03-06] Choose the most appropriate word for the blank.

03 When Thomas Hobbes described life in a state of nature as "solitary, poor, nasty, brutish and short," he _____ one of the most celebrated sentences in English language.

① accumulated   ② penned
③ theorized   ④ waded

04 The emergence of AI applications, such as OpenAI's ChatGPT chatbot, has _____ the integration of AI into everyday life, leading to heightened public awareness and discussion.

① avoided   ② demoted
③ mitigated   ④ propelled

05 Singapore and Zurich surpassed New York to become the world's most _____ cities to live in this year, according to a new global survey. The sky-high cost of car ownership, pricey alcohol and rising grocery prices saw Singapore pull ahead of the US city.

① exertive   ② expensive
③ expletive   ④ extraneous

06 Poverty in developing countries is increasing just as the population of urban areas around the globe continues to _____ as well.

① accommodate   ② enumerate
③ increase   ④ expound

[07-10] Choose the word(s) closest in meaning to the underlined.

07 In a groundbreaking case in Britain regarding whether AI can possess patent rights, a U.S. computer scientist faced a <u>setback</u> on Wednesday, when the UK Supreme Court ruled that AI cannot be considered a patent inventor.

① failure   ② knack

③ overrule   ④ victory

08 Consumers are being very strategic, wanting to maximize their shopping when they think they'll get the best discounts. The online retail sector is one of the few where the consumer <u>is in the driver's seat</u>, particularly with toys and seasonal holiday merchandise.

① goes in his favor   ② is in charge

③ is his interest   ④ loses the control

09 The resulting export surplus will be settled by an inflow of <u>bullion</u>, primarily gold and silver.

① precious metal   ② rich resources

③ exchangeable values   ④ mining products

10 That was the most serious <u>aspersion</u> that he had received in years.

① advice   ② benediction

③ coercion   ④ slander

[11-13] Read the following passage and answer the questions.

Native North American language speakers number 372,000. Most of these speakers (237,000) live in an American Indian or Alaska Native area (AIANA). People spoke Navajo more often than any other Native North American language. Over 169,000 people spoke this language nationally. Most of these Navajo speakers (112,000) lived in an AIANA. Navajo speakers numbered nearly 9 times larger than the second and third most commonly spoken languages of Yupik and Dakota, with both languages having approximately 19,000 speakers. While 84.5 percent of Yupik speakers lived in an AIANA, 51.5 percent of Dakota speakers did. Although the majority of Native North American language speakers resided in an AIANA, only a small percentage of the people living in these areas actually spoke a Native North American language.

Of people living in an AIANA, 5.4 percent spoke a Native North American language, and this percentage did not vary greatly across age groups. Among those who Ⓐ_____ as American Indian or Alaska Native alone, older people reported speaking a Native North American language more often than younger people. Over 1 in 5 of these people aged 65 and over spoke such a language, while about 1 in 10 people aged 5 to 17 did so. Among those who Ⓐ_____ as American Indian or Alaska Native in combination, people aged 65 and over were slightly less likely than other people to speak a Native North American language, although people aged 5 to 17 and people aged 18 to 64 were not significantly different from each other.

Speakers of Native North American languages concentrated most heavily in the states of Alaska, Arizona, and New Mexico. Sixty-five percent of Native North American language speakers lived in these three states. Just nine counties within these states contained half of the nation's Native North American language speakers. Apache County in Arizona had 37,000 speakers of a Native North American language, making it the highest in the nation. McKinley County, New Mexico, had the second most speakers, 33,000. Together, about 20 percent of all Native North American language speakers in the nation lived in these two counties.

11 Which of the following best fits in Ⓐ?

① identified   ② disguised

③ established   ④ nominated

12 Which of the following is NOT mentioned?

① the number of speakers of Native North American languages

② the use of Native North American languages by age groups

③ the use of Native North American languages mandated by state policy

④ the number of speakers of Native North American languages by county

13 Which of the following is NOT true?

① Navajo is the mostly spoken Native North American language.

② Among the people of American Indian or Alaska Native in combination, older people were more likely than younger people to speak a Native North American language.

③ More than a half of Native North American language speakers lived in the states of Alaska, Arizona, and New Mexico.

④ Apache County in Arizona had the highest number of speakers of a Native North American language in the nation.

[14-15] Read the following passage and answer the questions.

We do not know how art began any more than we know how language started. If we take art to mean such activities as building temples and houses, making pictures and sculptures, or weaving patterns, there is no people in all the world without art. If, on the other hand, we mean by art some kind of beautiful luxury, something to enjoy in museums and exhibitions or something special to use as a precious decoration in the best parlour, we must realize that this use of the word is a very recent development and that many of the greatest builders, painters or sculptors of the past never dreamed of it. We can best understand this difference if we think of architecture. We all know that there are beautiful buildings and that some of them are true works. But there is scarcely any building in the world which was not erected for a particular purpose. Those who use these buildings as places of worship or entertainment, or as dwellings, judge them first and foremost by standards of utility. But apart from this, they may like or dislike the design or the proportion of the structure, and appreciate the efforts of the good architect to make it not only practical but "right." In the past the attitude to paintings and statues was often similar. They were not thought of as mere works of art but as objects which had a definite function. He would be a poor judge of houses who did not know the requirements for which they were built. Ⓐ_____, we are not likely to understand the art of the past if we are quite ignorant of the aims it had to serve. The further we go back in history, the more definite but also the more strange are the aims which art was supposed to serve.

14 Which of the following best fits in Ⓐ?
① Conversely　　　　② Alone
③ Ironically　　　　④ Similarly

15 The thematic emphasis of the paragraph is placed on _____.
① the mysterious origin of language and art
② the essential difference between paintings and sculptures
③ the function and practicality of art in the past
④ the transformative power of art today

[16-18] Read the following passage and answer the questions.

Eugenics, the selection of desired heritable characteristics in order to improve future generations, typically in reference to humans, was coined as a term in 1883 by British explorer and natural scientist Francis Galton. Influenced by Charles Darwin's theory of natural selection, Galton advocated for a system that would provide "the more suitable races or Ⓐstrains of blood a better chance of prevailing speedily over the less suitable." Social Darwinism, the popular theory in the late 19th century that life for humans in society was ruled by "survival of the fittest," helped advance eugenics into serious scientific study in the early 1900s. By World War I many scientific authorities and political leaders supported eugenics. However, it ultimately failed as a science in the 1930s and '40s, when the assumptions of eugenicists became heavily criticized and the Nazis used eugenics to support the Ⓑextermination of entire races.

Although eugenics as understood today dates from the late 19th century, efforts to select matings in order to secure offspring with desirable traits date from ancient times. Plato's *Republic* depicts a society where efforts are undertaken to improve human beings through selective breeding. Later, Italian philosopher and poet Tommaso Campanella, in *City of the Sun* (1623), described a utopian community in which only the socially elite are allowed to Ⓒprocreate. Galton, in *Hereditary Genius* (1869), proposed that a system of arranged marriages between men of distinction and women of wealth would eventually produce a gifted race. In 1865 the basic laws of heredity were discovered by the father of modern genetics, Gregor Mendel. His experiments with peas demonstrated that each physical trait was the result of a combination of two units (now known as genes) and could be passed from one generation to another. However, his work was largely ignored until its rediscovery in 1900. This fundamental knowledge of Ⓓheredity provided eugenicists — including Galton, who influenced his cousin Charles Darwin — with scientific evidence to support the improvement of humans through selective breeding. For eugenicists, nature was far more contributory than nurture in shaping humanity.

16 Who is credited with the discovery of the basic laws of heredity in 1865, providing scientific evidence to support eugenics?

① Charles Darwin

② Tommaso Campanella

③ Gregor Mendel

④ Francis Galton

17 Which of the following statements is NOT true?

① The term "eugenics" was first used by Francis Galton.

② Galton believed a structured union between distinguished men and affluent women would yield a generation endowed with exceptional abilities.

③ Eugenics faced its downfall in the 1930s and '40s when the underlying assumptions were heavily criticized, and the Nazis exploited it to justify the extermination of entire races.

④ According to eugenicists, the influence of nature is almost identical with that of nurture in molding the characteristics of humanity.

18 Which word definition is the most accurate?

① Ⓐ strain: a type, variety, breed, etc., of an animal

② Ⓑ extermination: the act of taking for granted, or supposing a thing without proof

③ Ⓒ procreate: to render a representation of something, using words, sounds, images, or other means

④ Ⓓ heredity: a process of gradual change in a given system, subject, product, etc., especially from simpler to more complex forms

[19-20] Read the following passage and answer the questions.

The Twenty-seventh Amendment, ratified in 1992, stands as an amendment to the Constitution of the United States. It specifically stipulates that any alteration to the rate of compensation for members of the U.S. Congress must take effect only after the subsequent election in the House of Representatives. Commonly known as the Congressional Compensation Act of 1789, the Twenty-seventh Amendment was actually the second of 12 amendments proposed by the first Congress in 1789, 10 of which would be ratified and became the Bill of Rights. Absent a time period for ratification by the states, the expiration of which would render the amendment inoperable, it remained dormant for almost 80 years after only six states voted for ratification. In 1873 Ohio ratified the amendment as an expression of dissatisfaction with then-current attempts by Congress to increase the salaries of its members. The amendment once again lay dormant, but in 1978 another state, Wyoming, ratified it. In 1982, after an undergraduate research paper written by Gregory Watson, then a student at the University of Texas in Austin, became the foundation for a movement to curtail political corruption by ratifying the amendment, efforts picked up steam. By May 5, 1992, the requisite 38 states had ratified the amendment (North Carolina had re-ratified it in 1989), and it was certified by the archivist of the United States as the Twenty-seventh Amendment on May 18, 1992, more than 202 years after its original proposal.

19 Which state ratified the Twenty-seventh Amendment, expressing dissatisfaction with attempts to increase congressional salaries?

① North Carolina ② Ohio

③ Texas ④ Wyoming

20 What event in 1982 led to increased efforts to ratify the Twenty-seventh Amendment?

① a movement against political corruption

② the archivist's certification

③ the Congressional Compensation Act

④ the expiration of the ratification time period

Statistically, there's a good chance you know somebody who has experienced Long COVID, the name for chronic symptoms including fatigue, brain fog, and pain following a case of COVID-19. About 14% of U.S. adults report having had Long COVID at some point, according to federal data. ⒶBut many people don't realize that other viruses, even very common ones, can trigger similarly long-lasting and debilitating symptoms. A study published Dec. 14 in *The Lancet Infectious Diseases* focuses on the risk of developing "Long flu" after a severe case of influenza.

Al-Aly and his colleagues used records from the U.S. Department of Veterans Affairs to compare the long-term health outcomes of about 11,000 people hospitalized with influenza from 2015 to 2019 with those of about 81,000 people hospitalized with COVID-19 from 2020 to 2022. The researchers tracked how many people went on to develop any of 94 health risks associated with the two viruses in the year and a half after they were hospitalized. Relative to influenza survivors, people who had had COVID-19 were at increased risk of 64 of the identified complications, including fatigue, mental-health problems, and pulmonary, gastrointestinal, and heart issue. They were also more likely to die during the study period, in keeping with other research comparing the long-term outcomes of the two illnesses. Influenza survivors, Ⓑconsequently, were at increased risk of only six health problems, most of them related to the respiratory and cardiovascular systems. "COVID is still more serious than the flu," Al-Aly says, noting that it affects numerous organ systems while influenza is mostly a respiratory illness. ⒸBut long-term health problems were common in both groups during the 18 months of follow-up. The researchers recorded about 615 health issues per 100 people in the COVID-19 group, compared with about 537 per 100 people in the influenza group. Those numbers reflect the fact that some people experience numerous chronic symptoms after an infection, Al-Aly says. It's important to note that the people included in the study were all hospitalized, meaning they were very sick during the acute phases of their illnesses. The study population was also overwhelmingly male and older, with an average participant age of 70. ⒹTherefore, the results may not translate to the entire population.

21 Which of the following is NOT appropriate from the context?

① Ⓐ   ② Ⓑ

③ Ⓒ   ④ Ⓓ

22 Which of the following is NOT mentioned?

① the range of participants

② the cases of symptom

③ the process of treatment

④ the limitation of research

23 Which of the following is NOT true?

① Long COVID refers to the long-lasting and debilitating symptom after a case of COVID-19.

② About 14% of U.S. adults may have experienced fatigue, mental-health problems, and heart issue.

③ The COVID-19 group tended to have fewer long-term health issues than the influenza group during the same research period.

④ The results of the study may not apply to all the age groups.

[24-25] Read the following passage and answer the questions.

The past 18 months have been filled with setbacks for a sector that had until recently been coasting on a decade-plus of frenzied growth. According to Layoffs.fyi, a site that tracks job losses in tech, nearly 260,000 workers have been laid off so far this year, compared with 165,000 last year. These numbers are particularly notable in a year that has seen a mostly-hot labor market. The good news is that, although tech layoffs are elevated far above where they were in early 2022, these numbers are still way lower than they were at the beginning of the year. In January, some 90,000 workers were laid off across 276 companies, Layoffs.fyi found. Last month, the total was closer to 8,000. But the broader tech environment, especially for start-ups, is brutal: Erin Griffith reported in *The New York Times* last week that about 3,200 venture-backed companies were wiped out in 2023.

The long tail of over-hiring during the flush early days of the pandemic is the main factor driving current layoffs in tech, Roger Lee, the creator of Layoffs.fyi, told me. As my colleague Derek Thompson wrote in January, "When interest rates were low, investors valued growth narratives, and tech companies had a monopoly on these narratives . . . When inflation and interest rates increased, the companies that were making long-term promises were most at risk, and they got clobbered." Tech firms are still correcting for the reams of workers they hired when it seemed like the party would never end. And now AI is adding to some tech companies' problems, threatening their core operations. Many companies' projections got hammered by interest rates remaining higher this year than executives had hoped, so some that have already laid off employees "are going back to the well and making further cuts," Lee explained.

Some of this timing is cyclical. The end of the year is historically a popular time for layoffs. It marks the final stretch of the fiscal year for many organizations; companies are taking stock of that year's performance, and planning ahead for the next one. In the short term, we may continue to see trends such as cuts continue, Lee said. Inflation has moderated, and some economists are cautiously predicting that the Federal Reserve may lower rates in 2024; that would make investing in companies cheaper and could spur growth in the tech sector next year, Nick Bunker, the economic-research director at Indeed Hiring Lab, told me. But he doesn't predict rapid gains in tech hiring, in part because companies may have learned a thing or two from the over-hiring spree of 2021. Tech executives have been chastened by the blows of the past few years. Many are being more disciplined in their approach to hiring, Lee said, and "they are focusing more on efficiency, rather than growth at all costs."

24 Which statement among the following is NOT true?

① According to Layoffs.fyi, 260,000 workers in the tech sector have been laid off so far this year.

② 3,200 venture-backed companies were wiped out in 2023.

③ Over-hiring during the early days of the pandemic is the main factor driving current layoffs in the tech sector.

④ According to Roger Lee, tech firms are still undergoing layoffs due to economic downturn.

25 Which statement among the following is true?

① The end of the year is a popular time for layoffs because employees demand year-end bonuses.

② About tech hiring in the near future, Roger Lee predicts continuous layoffs.

③ It is highly probable that the Federal Reserve will keep interest rates steady due to inflation in 2024.

④ As mentioned in the text, growth at all costs is the approach of many tech executives toward hiring.

AJOU
UNIVERSITY

아주대학교   2024학년도 인문계
▶▶ 50문항·90분

[01-05] Choose the word that best completes the sentence.

01 In 1961, renowned German novelist Günter Grass openly criticized communist East Germany for building the Berlin Wall ostensibly to prevent West Germans from infiltrating the country. In reality, the wall was more effective at preventing East Germans from _____. 0.8점

① defecting   ② exploring   ③ interfering
④ revolting   ⑤ unifying

02 Imagine brain scanning technology improves greatly in the coming decades to the point that we can observe how each individual neuron talks to other neurons. Then, imagine we can record all this information to create a _____ of someone's brain on a computer. This is the concept behind mind uploading — the idea that we may one day be able to transition a person from her biological body to a synthetic hardware. 0.8점

① bank   ② design   ③ map
④ network   ⑤ simulation

03 While most people are willing to do the right thing when they are fully informed of the consequences of their actions, this willingness is not always because people care for others. A part of the reasons why people act altruistically is due to societal pressures as well as their desire to view themselves in a good light. Since being righteous is often _____, demanding people to give up their time, money, and effort, ignorance offers an easy way out. 0.8점

① beneficial   ② costly   ③ ethical

④ ridiculous   ⑤ strenuous

04 The evolution of eye color in cats has been mapped for the first time, and researchers found that one unusual ancestor is responsible for the feline family's dazzling variety of peepers, from yellow-eyed tigers to blue-eyed snow leopards. In the new study, scientists identified different eye colors in living cats and used a computer model to predict where they _____ on the feline family tree. Their model found that the ancestor of all cats must have had gray and brown eyes, and the gray enabled other colors to later emerge. 0.8점

① arranged   ② distributed   ③ evolved

④ transferred   ⑤ transcended

05 Technology is the key to a better way of life. Our ancient ancestors knew that, so they shaped stone tools to craft, cut, and harvest. They observed the destructive power of nature and learned to cook with fire. Then, we moved on wheels until we flew with wings. We channeled electricity into glass bulbs and shined light into the darkness. Our greatest scientists learned to divide atoms, but they still are trying to fuse them. Each of these _____ has made humanity more remarkable over time. 0.8점

① advancements   ② benefits   ③ ideas

④ movements   ⑤ transitions

[06-10] Choose the expression that best completes the sentence.

06 Marketers for luxury brands such as Prada, Gucci, Cartier, and Louis Vuitton manage lucrative franchises that have endured for decades _____ now a $270 billion industry. 1.1점

① in what some believe is
② in what is some believe
③ what is some believe in
④ what some believe in is
⑤ what some believe is in

07 Another example shows how difficult it can be to get even small reforms on the farm. Only recently _____ they'd been demanding for years: that they be allowed to fill tomato baskets to the brim. 1.0점

① won farm workers a concession
② did win farm workers a concession
③ farm workers did win a concession
④ did farm workers win a concession
⑤ farm workers win a concession

08 As Richard Whatmore reminds us in his new book, "sometimes the present prevents us from understanding the past." We risk thinking that the philosophers of the 18th century were answering our questions instead of their own, when in fact it is the fundamental weirdness of their ideas _____. 1.0점

① that makes so interested
② that makes them so interesting
③ which is made so interested
④ which is made them so interesting
⑤ so interesting that makes them

09 Journalists serve to reinforce a conceptual model and discourse defined by aggression, and ultimately help to maintain marketing as a male-defined practice. It is because of these far-reaching consequences that business publications should _____ and the corporate discourse on which they report. 1.0점

① be themselves emancipated from their readers' perceived agenda
② emancipate from their readers' perceived agenda
③ emancipate themselves from their readers' perceived agenda
④ emancipate their readers' perceived agenda from
⑤ be their readers' perceived agenda emancipated from

10 U.S. households are increasingly fragmented — the traditional family of four with a husband, wife, and two kids makes up _____ total households than it once did. 1.0점

① much smaller percentage of
② much fewer percentage of
③ a much fewer percent of
④ a much smaller percent of
⑤ a much smaller percentage of

[11-14] Choose the underlined word or phrase that must be changed for the sentence to be correct.

11 Nowadays, we ①are bombarded with messages about excellence, distinction, and success, and we hear voices ②telling us you should be a top student, a winner, a leader, or preferably all three. And it's what made me think a little bit more about ③what's going on here. How do we manage this? Because all of this leads to a profound sense of what the philosopher Alain de Botton ④has called status anxiety. And for me, this is a kind of anxiety that ⑤arouses through our constant worry about not being good enough or always needing to be someone better or to have something better. 1.0점

12 A growing body of research in psychology and related fields suggests that winter brings some profound changes in how people think, feel, and behave. ①While it's one thing to identify seasonal tendencies in the population, ②it's much trickier to try to untangle why they exist. Some of winter's effects have been tied to cultural norms and practices while others likely reflect our bodies' innate biological responses to ③be changed meteorological and ecological conditions. The natural and cultural changes that come with winter often occur simultaneously, ④making it challenging to tease apart the causes ⑤underlying these seasonal swings. 1.0점

13 ①Caring for green spaces improves the mental health of ②those who live near those spaces. In the child maltreatment study, the researchers noted that one potential explanation for the association between micro-neighborhood greening and reduced child maltreatment ③may be the effect that micro-neighborhood greening has on parents' stress. Stress is strongly associated with child maltreatment. Youth engagement may also be key to these programs' success ④at reduced crime and a benefit in itself. Six organizations doing greening work were interviewed around the country, and participants said that centering on youth voices ⑤was essential. 1.0점

14 ①Nowhere is the need for social norms more important than in the area of lobbying. On the one hand, members of the worlds' second-oldest profession ②do play an important role in our political process. The expansion of state functions ③has made it all but impossible for any elected representative ④to keep up with all the issues she is required to vote on, and lobbyists can help fill in the information gaps. "Lobbyists are, in many cases, expert technicians," admitted then-senator John F. Kennedy ⑤while advocated limits to their power. 1.0점

[15-18] Choose the number with the correct set of statements that can be restated or inferred from the original text.

15   Today, at a time when New York is at the center of an enormous and diversified metropolitan area, it is easy to forget the significance of the set of skills that immigrants like the Borgenichts brought to the New World. From the 19th century through the mid-20th century, the garment trade was the largest and most economically vibrant industry in the city. More people worked making clothes in New York than at anything else, and more clothes were manufactured in New York than in any other city in the world. The distinctive buildings that still stand on the lower half of Broadway in Manhattan — from the big ten- and fifteen-story industrial warehouses in the twenty blocks below Times Square to the cast-iron lofts of SoHo and Tribeca — were almost all built to house coat makers and hatmakers. 1.1점

Ⓐ Lower Broadway in Manhattan had distinctive buildings built mainly for coat makers and hatmakers.

Ⓑ The largest and most economically dynamic industry in New York was the garment trade in the 19th century.

Ⓒ The Borgenichts, immigrants to the New World, first brought crucial garments to New York.

Ⓓ New York led the world in the garment trade, with more clothes being manufactured than in any other city.

---

① Ⓐ & Ⓑ   ② Ⓐ & Ⓒ   ③ Ⓑ & Ⓒ

④ Ⓐ, Ⓑ & Ⓓ   ⑤ Ⓑ, Ⓒ & Ⓓ

16 People care not only about their absolute status but also about their status relative to other people's status. Statistics on the income gap — the divergence between the income of the top one percent and that of the rest — abound. This divergence is often attributed to corporate greed. But unfortunately, the problem is much broader than this. I say "unfortunately," because if it were just the result of corporate greed, it would be easier to fix. To appreciate better the nature of this divergence, we may find it helpful to watch a golf tournament. Even on the links, not everybody is paid the same. Tiger Woods and the greenskeepers receive very different wages. This difference is what we economists call *skill premium*. 1.1점

Ⓐ Individuals' concern with both their absolute and relative status is evident in income gap statistics.

Ⓑ Corporate greed, often linked to the income gap, is a broader and more challenging issue to address.

Ⓒ Income divergence is compared to a golf tournament, illustrating the concept of the *skill premium* among individuals.

Ⓓ The wage gap between Tiger Woods and greenskeepers results from the different degrees of passion.

---

① Ⓐ & Ⓑ   ② Ⓐ & Ⓒ   ③ Ⓑ & Ⓓ

④ Ⓐ, Ⓑ & Ⓓ   ⑤ Ⓑ, Ⓒ & Ⓓ

17 Researchers found the difference between how long American men and women live increased to 5.8 years in 2021, the largest since 1996. This is an increase from 4.8 years in 2010, when the gap was at its smallest in recent history. The COVID-19 pandemic, which took a disproportionate toll on men, was the biggest contributor to the widening gap from 2019-2021, followed by unintentional injuries, poisonings (mostly drug overdoses), accidents, and suicides. "There's been a lot of research into the decline in life expectancy in recent years, but no one has systematically analyzed why the gap between men and women has been widening since 2010," said the first author of the research. 1.1점

Ⓐ The life expectancy gap is consistent across all age brackets.

Ⓑ There has been a lack of systematic analysis into the reasons for the widening gap between American men and women's life expectancy.

Ⓒ Unintentional injuries including drug overdoses, accidents, and suicides have played a role in the declines in the life expectancy of men and women.

Ⓓ The COVID-19 pandemic disproportionately affected American men, contributing significantly to the widening gap between American men and women's life expectancies from 2019 to 2021.

① Ⓐ & Ⓑ   ② Ⓑ & Ⓒ   ③ Ⓑ & Ⓓ

④ Ⓐ, Ⓑ & Ⓓ   ⑤ Ⓑ, Ⓒ & Ⓓ

18 Meerkats live in family groups, known as mobs, of up to 50 individuals and are led by a female matriarch, who dominates up to 80% of breeding to maintain her control. If a subordinate female attempts to breed, she is evicted from the social group and any offspring are killed. Subordinates of both sexes assist in rearing, enabling dominant females to breed multiple times a year and often live longer than subordinates. 1.1점

Ⓐ An extreme reproductive skew in female meerkats can be found.

Ⓑ Meerkats live in family groups or mobs led by a dominant female matriarch.

Ⓒ Social status becomes a cause of longevity in male meerkats.

Ⓓ A dominant female holds significant control over breeding, limiting the breeding attempts of subordinate females.

① Ⓐ & Ⓑ   ② Ⓑ & Ⓒ   ③ Ⓐ, Ⓑ & Ⓓ

④ Ⓐ, Ⓒ & Ⓓ   ⑤ Ⓑ, Ⓒ & Ⓓ

[19-50] Read each passage and answer the corresponding questions for each.

19-22

A Starbucks opened in Seattle in 1971 at a time when coffee consumption in the United States had been declining for a decade and rival brands used cheaper coffee beans to compete on price. Starbucks's founders decided to experiment with a new concept: a store that would sell only the finest imported coffee beans and coffee brewing equipment. (The original store didn't sell coffee by the cup, but only beans.)

B Howard Schults came to Starbucks in 1982. While in Milan on business, he had walked into an Italian coffee bar and had an epiphany: "There was nothing like this in America. It was an extension of people's front porch. It was an emotional experience." To bring this concept to the United States, Schults Ⓐset about creating an environment for Starbucks coffee houses that would reflect Italian elegance melded with U.S. informality. He Ⓑenvisioned Starbucks as a "personal treat" for its customers, a "Third Place", a comfortable, sociable gathering spot bridging the workplace and home.

C Starbucks's expansion throughout the United States was carefully planned. All stores were company-owned and operated, ensuring complete control over an Ⓒunparalleled image of quality. In a "hub" strategy, Starbucks's coffee houses entered a new market in a clustered group. Although this deliberate saturation often Ⓓcannibalized 30 percent of one store's sales by introducing a store nearby, any drop in revenues was offset by efficiencies in marketing and distribution costs, and the enhanced image of convenience. A typical customer would stop by Starbucks about 18 times a month. No U.S. retailer had had a higher frequency of customer revisits.

D Part of Starbucks's success undoubtedly lies in its products and services, and its Ⓔrelentless commitment to providing the richest possible sensory experiences. (1)_____. Schults believed that to exceed customer's expectations, it is first necessary to exceed employees'. Since 1990, Starbucks has provided comprehensive healthcare to all employees, including part-timers. Health insurance now costs the company more each year than coffee. A stock option plan called Bean Stock allows employees to participate in its financial success. Schults also believed Starbucks's operations should run in a respectful, ethical manner, making decisions with a positive impact on communities and the planet.

19 Which of the following would be the best title for the above passage? 1.1점

① The Rise of Italian Coffee Business in America

② Starbucks: A Journey from Declining Brands to Unprecedented Success

③ Howard Schults's Impact on Starbucks's Global Expansion

④ The Evolution of Starbucks: From Beans to Brews to Social Responsibility

⑤ Competitive Strategies in the Coffee Industry

20 Which of the following would best fit in blank (1) in paragraph Ⓓ? 1.1점

① But another key is its enlightened sense of responsibility, manifested in a number of different ways.

② Starbucks has partnered with Conservation International to ensure that coffee it purchases is responsibly grown and ethically traded.

③ The employees volunteer community service hours for causes big and small such as rebuilding New Orleans after Hurricane Katrina.

④ It took Starbucks 10 years of development to create the world's first recycled beverage cup made of 10 percent postconsumer fiber.

⑤ Its primary focus is supporting literacy programs for children and families in the United States and Canada.

21 Which of the following pairs includes an expression that CANNOT replace the underlined expression in the above passage? 0.8점

① Ⓐ set about, began

② Ⓑ envisioned, pictured

③ Ⓒ unparalleled, exceptional

④ Ⓓ cannibalized, reduced

⑤ Ⓔ relentless, outstanding

22 According to the above passage, which of the following is NOT true? 1.1점

① The inaugural Starbucks store specialized in selling only the highest quality imported coffee beans and brewing equipment.

② Starbucks spends more money on employees' health insurance than on coffee.

③ Howard Schults joined Starbucks in 1982 after a business trip to Paris.

④ Starbucks employed a "hub" strategy for its expansion in the United States.

⑤ Starting from 1990, Starbucks has offered comprehensive healthcare coverage to all employees, including those working part-time.

23-26

A Over the course of the fifth century, the Western Roman Empire fragmented into a series of post-Roman kingdoms largely dominated by 'barbarian' rulers. As a result, Ⓐin order to come to terms with the longer-term impact of Christianity on the Roman Empire, we need to shift our focus eastwards, to the so-called Eastern Roman Empire ruled from Constantinople and the world of Byzantium.

B Around the year 312, Emperor Constantine had adopted Christianity as his favored cult. Ⓑ**Only in 380 did Theodosius I declare** Christianity to be the official religion of the Roman state — the instincts of Constantine had been largely tolerant in matters of religion. The fusion of Christian faith and Roman political identity would only really culminate in Constantinople in the sixth and seventh centuries between the accession of the emperor Justinian (527) and the death of Heraclius (641). Christianity brought into the religious life of the Roman Empire much greater intolerance of Ⓒ**what was deemed** to be religious error (heresy) and deviance. Justinian, in particular, turned the Roman Empire into a much more persecutory state. Whereas previous emperors had attempted to ban pagan sacrificial acts, for example, Justinian made it illegal to even be a pagan and introduced the death penalty for those caught making false conversions. (1)_____. Anti-Jewish measures would further intensify under Heraclius, whose court presented the Christian Roman Empire as a 'New Israel'.

C At the same time, Christianization also led to much greater concern for the poor and needy Ⓓ**than had characterized** traditional Roman ideology, with emperors helping to fund hospitals and orphanages. Justinian's legislation revealed unprecedented concern for the interests of vulnerable women, children, and the disabled. The Christianization of the Roman Empire, thus ultimately, served to make Roman political culture at once much more socially cohesive and integrated as well as ever more exclusive and persecutory.

D On the face of it, one might expect that Christianity would have brought immediate changes to the social landscape of the Roman Empire in the fourth century. Ⓔ**Giving the apostle Paul's view** that 'all are equal in Christ', it would seem the natural course. But things did not turn out that way. Where slavery was concerned, for example, the earliest Christians were less interested in abolishing it than in seeing enslaved people as a model of devoted service that Christians should imitate as 'slaves of Christ'. In the later Empire, things changed, but only a little. Christian bishops worked to free captives who had been sold into slavery by pirates and barbarians, yet Christian clergy continued to own slaves.

23 Which of the following would be the best title for the above passage? 1.0점

① The Complexity of Christianity in the Western Roman Empire
② Social Exclusion and Development in Christianization
③ Christianity's Role in the Roman Empire
④ Christianity's Impact on the Shift to the East
⑤ Contrasting Effects of Christianity on Roman Social Dynamics

24 Which of the following would best fit in blank (1) in paragraph B? 1.1점

① Under him, steady downward pressure was applied on the legal status and civil rights of heretics, Samaritans, and Jews.
② Christianity made significant long-term changes, but its impact was more limited in the couple of centuries after it started receiving imperial support.
③ Nonetheless, the physical landscape did change, with grand churches being built.
④ The growth of Christianity and the Church did contribute to the decline of traditional paganism, especially public rites such as animal sacrifice.
⑤ Pagan emperors had always been closely associated with the divine and this continued with the Christian God.

25 According to the above passage, which of the following is NOT true? 1.1점

① Christianity in the Roman Empire led to immediate abolition of slavery in the fourth century.
② Theodosius I adopted Christianity as the official religion of the Roman state.
③ Justinian's laws demonstrated a high level of care for vulnerable women.
④ Christian clergy in the later Empire kept their slaves, while bishops endeavored to liberate captives sold into slavery.
⑤ The merging of Christian faith and Roman political identity was achieved in Constantinople during the sixth and seventh centuries.

26 Choose the underlined word or phrase that must be changed for the sentence to be correct. 0.8점

① Ⓐ in order to come to terms with
② Ⓑ Only in 380 did Theodosius I declare
③ Ⓒ what was deemed
④ Ⓓ than had characterized
⑤ Ⓔ Giving the apostle Paul's view

Ⓐ Each passing week there seems to be a strengthening in the evidence that air pollution harms our health. Now research in Rome has revealed the impact of air pollution on our mental health. Dr. Federica Nobile of the department of epidemiology of the Lazio Regional Health Service explained what led to the research. "Recent studies have linked air pollution to the development of psychiatric disorders, including depression, anxiety, and psychotic episodes. However, all these associations have been mainly investigated in small groups, making their results challenging to generalize."

Ⓑ Nobile's team started with census data on more than 1.7 million adults that were living in Rome in 2011 and matched these with medical and public health insurance records. Health records were scanned for the next eight years for new cases of mental health problems, including people admitted to a hospital or those with new repeat prescriptions for antipsychotics, antidepressants, and mood stabilizers. These were compared with air pollution data and traffic noise where people lived as well as other societal factors that may affect mental health including poverty, unemployment, education, and marital status.

Ⓒ They found that people living in areas with higher particle pollution had a greater chance of developing schizophrenia, depression, and anxiety disorders. This was matched by an analysis of drug prescriptions, where people Ⓐ_____ 30 and 64 had the clearest association with air pollution. Using data from the study, it is possible to predict the benefits from improving the city's air. Reducing Rome's average particle pollution by 10 percent could reduce these common mental health conditions by 10-30 percent. (1)_____.

Ⓓ Prof. Francesco Forastiere of Italy's National Research Council said: "Our discovery underscores the critical importance of implementing stringent measures to reduce human exposure to air pollutants. These are crucial not only for safeguarding against physical ailments but also for preserving mental wellbeing." Understanding of these issues Ⓑ_____. Seventy-one years ago, London's great smog of 1952 led to the deaths of about 12,000 people, mainly from breathing problems, heart attacks, and strokes. Research from the 1990s added lung cancer to the list of air pollution impacts but the effects on brain health were overlooked. A study on pet dogs in Mexico in 2002 helped lead to conclusions that air pollution exposure added to the risk of dementia later in life. And it was observations of the association between living in an urban area and the greater risk of schizophrenia that led researchers to investigate air pollution as a possible cause.

27 Which of the following would be the best title for the above passage? 1.0점

① From London's Smog to Rome's Insight

② Unravelling the Link Between Air Pollution and Mental Health

③ The Growing Evidence of Air Pollution's Influence in Rome

④ Preserving Minds and Bodies: The Danger of Addressing Air Pollution

⑤ The Untouched Threat: Air Pollution's Impact on Society

28 Which of the following would best fit in blank (1) in paragraph C? 1.1점

① Dr. Ioannis Bakolis, of King's College London said: "The large-scale study in Rome provides much-needed evidence."

② It increases our confidence on the link between air pollution and psychiatric disorders, augmenting previous findings from the UK, U.S., and Denmark.

③ Rome residents' average exposure to annual PM2.5 is more than three times higher than what the WHO suggests.

④ Even greater improvements would be achieved by meeting the European Commission's proposed air pollution limits for 2030 and the World Health Organization guidelines.

⑤ Other studies found that air pollution also had a role in severity and relapse in people with psychiatric disorders.

29 Which of the following pairs would best fit in blanks Ⓐ and Ⓑ to make the flow of the argument acceptable? 0.8점

① aged between — has been slowly improving

② aged between — have been slowly improving

③ aged of — has been slowly improved

④ aged between — have been slowly improved

⑤ aging of — has slowly improved

30 According to the above passage, which of the following is NOT true? 1.1점

① Dr. Nobile's research team used census data on more than 1.7 million adults living in Rome in 2011.

② Prof. Forastiere stated that the effects of air pollution on brain health were recognized and addressed in the 1990s.

③ Dr. Nobile said that the link between air pollution and the development of psychiatric disorders has been investigated mainly in small-scale studies.

④ The research on pet dogs in Mexico in 2002 found that exposure to air pollution increased the likelihood of developing dementia later in life.

⑤ Dr. Nobile's research indicated that a 10% decrease in the average particle pollution in Rome could result in a 10-30% decline in prevalent mental health conditions.

A We are constantly reminded about how exercise benefits our bone and muscle health or reduces fat. However, there is also an increasing interest in one element of our Ⓐanatomy that is often overlooked: our fascia. Fascia is a thin casing of connective tissue, mainly made of collagen — a rope-like structure that provides strength and protection to many areas of the body. It surrounds and holds every organ, blood vessel, bone, nerve fiber, and muscle in place. ❶ And scientists increasingly recognize its importance in muscle and bone health.

B It is hard to see fascia in the body, but you can Ⓑget a sense of what it looks like if you look at a steak. ❷ Fascia provides general and special functions in the body, and is arranged in several ways. The closest to the surface is the superficial fascia, which is underneath the skin between layers of fat. Then we have the deep fascia that covers the muscles, bones, and blood vessels. The link between fascia, muscle, and bone health and function Ⓒis reinforced by recent studies that show the important role fascia has in helping the muscles work, by assisting the Ⓓcontraction of the muscle cells to generate force, and affecting muscle stiffness. ❸ Each muscle is wrapped in fascia. These layers are important as they enable muscles that sit next to or on top of each other to move freely without affecting each other's functions.

C Fascia also assists in the transition of force through the musculoskeletal system. An example of this is our ankle where the achilles tendon transfers force into the plantar fascia. ❹ This sees forces moving vertically down through the achilles and then transferred horizontally into the bottom of the foot — the plantar fascia — when moving. Similar force transition is seen from muscles in the chest running down through to groups of muscles in the forearm. There are similar fascia connective chains through other areas of the body. When fascia doesn't function properly, such as after injury, the layers become less able to Ⓔfacilitate movement over each other or help transfer force. ❺ Injury to fascia takes a long time to repair, probably because it possesses similar cells to tendons (fibroblasts), and has a limited blood supply.

D Recent studies discovered that fascia, particularly the layers close to the surface, have been shown to have the second-highest number of nerves after the skin. The fascial linings of muscles have also been linked to pain from surgery to musculoskeletal injuries from sports, exercise, and aging. Up to 30% of people with musculoskeletal pain may have fascial involvement or fascia may be the cause.

31 Which of the following would be the best title for the above passage? 1.0점

① Fascia Finally Starting to Receive Attention

② Examining Fascia in the Body: A Comparison with Steak

③ The Rising Awareness of Nerves in Fascia and Its Link to Pain

④ The Slow Healing Process of Fascia and Its Limited Blood Supply

⑤ The Overlooked Importance of Collagen in Bone and Muscle Health

32 According to the above passage, which of the following is true? 1.1점

① Fascia is primarily responsible for reducing fat in the body and transferring force into the major body organs.

② Fascia surrounds and supports various structures in the body, playing a crucial role in musculoskeletal health.

③ The deep fascia is located underneath the skin between layers of fat in the human body, covering muscles, bones, and blood vessels.

④ Musculoskeletal pain is rarely associated with fascial involvement according to recent studies.

⑤ The layers of fascia have been demonstrated to possess the highest quantity of nerves.

33 The following sentence is removed from the above passage. In which part may it be inserted to support the argument made by the author? 1.0점

> It is the thin white streaks on the surface or between layers of the meat.

① ❶   ② ❷   ③ ❸

④ ❹   ⑤ ❺

34 Which of the following pairs includes an expression that CANNOT replace the underlined expression in the above passage? 0.8점

① Ⓐ anatomy, study of the structure of living things

② Ⓑ get a sense of, discern

③ Ⓒ is reinforced, is strengthened

④ Ⓓ contraction, dilation

⑤ Ⓔ facilitate, ease

A Dopamine is famous for the role it plays in reward processing, an idea that dates back at least 50 years. Dopamine neurons monitor the difference between the rewards you thought you would get from a behavior and what you actually got. Neuroscientists call this difference a reward prediction error.

B Eating dinner at a restaurant that just opened and looks likely to be nothing special shows reward prediction errors in action. If your meal is very good, that results in a positive reward prediction error, and you are likely to return and order the same meal in the future. Each time you return, the reward prediction error shrinks until it eventually reaches zero when you fully expect a delicious dinner. But if your first meal is terrible, that results in a negative reward prediction error, and you probably won't go back to the restaurant.

C Dopamine neurons communicate reward prediction errors to the brain through their firing rates and patterns of dopamine release, which the brain uses for learning. They fire in two ways. Phasic firing refers to rapid bursts that cause a short-term peak in dopamine. This happens when you receive an unexpected reward or more rewards than anticipated. Phasic firing encodes reward prediction errors. By contrast, tonic firing describes the slow and steady activity of these neurons when there are no surprises; it is background activity interspersed with phasic bursts. Phasic firing is like mountain peaks, and tonic firing is the valley floors between peaks.

D Tracking information used in generating reward prediction errors is not all dopamine does. About 15 years ago, reports started coming out that dopamine neurons respond to aversive events — think brief discomforts like a puff of air against your eye, a mild electric shock or losing money — something scientists thought dopamine did not do. These studies showed that some dopamine neurons respond only to rewards while others respond to both rewards and negative experiences, leading to the hypothesis that there might be more than one dopamine system in the brain.

35 According to the above passage, which of the following is NOT true? 1.1점

① Dopamine neurons monitor the difference between anticipated rewards and the actual rewards received.

② Dopamine neurons communicate reward prediction errors through patterns of dopamine release.

③ Some dopamine neurons also respond to aversive events or negative experiences such as mild discomfort or monetary loss.

④ Recent studies contradicted the previous belief that dopamine neurons only responded to rewards.

⑤ The findings on phasic firing lead to the hypothesis that there might be more than one dopamine system in the brain.

36 According to the above passage, which of the following is true about "tonic firing"?

① It involves rapid bursts of dopamine neuron activity. 1.0점

② It refers to steady activity in the absence of surprises.

③ It encodes information about the unexpectedness of rewards.

④ It occurs when an individual receives more rewards than anticipated.

⑤ It facilitates learning by signaling deviations from predicted outcomes.

37 Which of the following would be the best title for the first 3 paragraphs of the passage? 1.0점

① Dopamine's Influence on Neurons

② The Impact of Dopamine on Dining Habits

③ Dopamine's Reaction to Negative Events

④ Dopamine's Role in Reward Processing and Learning

⑤ The Evolution of Dopamine's Functions

38 Which of the following is examined in the above passage? 1.1점

① The biological or neurological mechanisms behind dopamine neuron firing patterns

② A theoretical framework of dopamine firing patterns and their relationship to reward prediction errors

③ The effects of different dopamine firing patterns on learning, memory, or cognitive processes over extended periods

④ A cause-and-effect relationship between dopamine firing patterns and specific behaviors

⑤ Dopamine's involvement in disorders like Parkinson's disease or schizophrenia

A Plato's *Symposium* (written around 385 BCE) portrays an evening party among close male associates and friends. The dramatic date of the gathering within *Symposium* is 416 BCE, identifiable from the historical record of the tragic poet Agathon's victory in Athens' annual drama competition, to which the play alludes. The comedian Aristophanes is recognizable from his *Clouds* — staged several years prior to the party, in 423 BCE in which Socrates is caricatured. Plato's *Symposium* is populated by historical figures of Athens, though the dialogue is a work of the author's imagination (he would have been only 11 years old in the year 416 BCE).

B A symposium ("drinking together") was a social gathering of high-status male guests. The party represented in Plato's *Symposium* is on the small side — symposia could be gatherings of as many as thirty. Partygoers would have been used to singing songs and hymns in honor of various gods — drinking songs of this sort have survived from antiquity until today. Symposiasts might expect to be entertained by song, dance, poetry, and even rhetoric — but not rigorous philosophical debate.

C The topic of discussion among the symposiasts in this text is Eros or love — but above all love containing the element of desire, as opposed to the type of love one might have for family or friends. The partygoers of *Symposium* would not have recognized the type of language and categories we now use to describe sexuality and sexual orientation. "The lover" and "the beloved" are more useful categories for understanding the relative status of sex partners in ancient Greece. Desire, therefore, might be expressed for women or younger males in ways that were not exclusive; younger men, whatever their feelings may have been, were not supposed to exhibit desire for older men.

D Among the real-life characters in the dialogue, the most problematic is Alcibiades (451-404 BCE), an enduring figure of controversy for disciples of Socrates (such as Plato), critics of Socrates, and the Athenian public. A brilliant politician (or, perhaps, manipulator) and military general, Alcibiades rose to superstar prominence and power early. Precocious, handsome, wealthy, persuasive — even seductive — Alcibiades attracted both praise and censure from the Athenian public. His association with Socrates posed a major moral question. Alcibiades was part of a group, including several other associates of Socrates, accused of mutilating the city's protective statues (known as "herms") and mocking sacred rites in advance of an invasion of Sicily for which he himself had advocated. Implicit in this accusation was that Alcibiades was attempting to undermine Athens' democracy.

39 Which of the following is NOT true about Plato's *Symposium* according to the above passage? 1.1점

① The party depicted in Plato's *Symposium* is set to have taken place in 416 BCE.

② Plato's *Symposium* features actual historical figures.

③ Plato's *Symposium* is written around 385 BCE.

④ Plato's *Symposium* is a record of historical events.

⑤ The participants of the party in Plato's *Symposium* have a discussion on Eros.

40 Which of the following is NOT a common expectation of a symposium according to the passage? 0.8점

① Entertainment through song, dance, poetry, and rhetoric

② Relaxed and enjoyable atmosphere

③ Social gathering of high-status male guests

④ Rigorous philosophical debate

⑤ Songs and hymns honoring various gods

41 Which of the following is LEAST likely to be inferred from paragraph C? 1.1점

① The concept of Eros in the discussion encompasses desire.

② The ancient Greeks did not use our contemporary terminology to describe sexual orientations.

③ Women were not considered as objects of male affection among the high-status males in the ancient Greek society.

④ There were social norms that discouraged younger men from exhibiting desire for older men in their relationship in ancient Greek society.

⑤ In ancient Greek society, the framework for understanding relationships was based more on the roles of the lover and the beloved rather than specific sexual orientations.

42 Which of the following is LEAST likely to be inferred about Alcibiades from the passage? 1.1점

① He had an association with Socrates.

② He was against an invasion of Sicily.

③ He rose to prominence early in his career.

④ He was both admired and criticized by the Athenian public.

⑤ He was accused of being part of a group involved in the mutilation of the city's protective statues (herms).

43-46

A People generally get together to form groups precisely because they are similar. For example, they are all interested in playing poker, listening to rock and roll, or passing a chemistry test. And groups tend to fall apart because the group members become dissimilar and thus no longer have enough in common to keep them together.

B Although similarity is critical, it is not the only factor that creates a group. Groups have more underentitativity when the group members have frequent interaction and communication with each other. Interaction is particularly important when it is accompanied by interdependence — the extent to which the group members are mutually dependent upon each other to reach a goal. In some cases, and particularly in working groups, interdependence involves the need to work together to successfully accomplish a task. When group members are interdependent, they report liking each other more, tend to cooperate and communicate with each other to a greater extent, and may be more productive.

C Still another aspect of working groups, whose members spend some time working together and that makes them seem "groupy," is that they develop group structure — the stable norms and roles that define the appropriate behaviors for the group as a whole and for each of the members. The relevant social norms for groups include customs, traditions, standards, and rules as well as the general values of the group. These norms tell the group members what to do to be good group members and give the group more entitativity. Effective groups also develop and assign social roles (the expected behaviors) to group members. For instance, some groups may be structured such that they have a president, a secretary, and many different working committees.

D Although cognitive factors such as perceived similarity, communication, interdependence, and structure are often important parts of what we mean by being a group, they do not seem to be sufficient. Groups may be seen as groups even if they have little interdependence, communication, or structure. Partly because of this difficulty, an alternative approach to thinking about groups, and one that has been very important in social psychology, makes use of the affective feelings that we have toward the groups that we belong to. Social identity refers to the part of the self-concept that results from our membership in social groups. Generally, because we prefer to remain in groups that we feel good about, the outcome of group membership is a positive social identity — our group memberships make us feel good about ourselves.

43 Which of the following is the best title for the passage? 1.0점

① Beyond Similarity and Interaction

② Understanding Group Spirit

③ Factors Shaping Entitativity within Groups

④ Exploring Group Interdependence

⑤ The Role of Social Identity in Group Formation

44 Which of the following is CLOSEST in meaning to "entitativity" in the passage?

① affection　　　　② community　　　　③ consistency　　　　1.0점

④ similarity　　　　⑤ unity

45 Which of the following is the best example supporting the argument in paragraph
A? 1.1점

① An individual talks positively about her group to others.

② Members frequently collaborate, communicate ideas, and rely on each other's
contributions to complete tasks.

③ Individuals volunteer to work together in a non-profit organization focused on
environmental conservation.

④ In a volunteer organization, the group establishes specific roles such as a president,
treasurer, and committee members.

⑤ In a book club when new members join with vastly different literary tastes, the common
ground that initially united the group weakens.

46 Which of the following is LEAST likely to be inferred from the passage? 1.1점

① Initial group formation often occurs due to shared interests, characteristics, or goals.

② Interdependent groups tend to exhibit higher cooperation, closer relationships amongst
members, and potentially higher productivity.

③ Working groups tend to develop stable norms, roles, customs, traditions, and rules that
define appropriate behaviors for the entire group and individual members.

④ Emotional attachment derived from group membership contributes more significantly
to an individual's positive self-concept than cognitive factors.

⑤ Emotional ties and positive feelings toward the group play an important role in group
cohesion and individual satisfaction.

A Have you ever encountered a Ⓐsubpar hotel breakfast while on holiday? You don't really like the food choices on offer, but since you already paid for the meal as part of your booking, you force yourself to eat something anyway rather than go down the road to a cafe. Economists and social scientists argue that such behavior can happen due to the "sunk cost fallacy" — an inability to ignore costs that have already been spent and can't be recovered. In the hotel breakfast example, the sunk cost is the price you paid for the hotel package. At the time of deciding where to eat breakfast, such costs are unrecoverable and should therefore be ignored.

B Similar examples range from justifying finishing a Ⓑbanal, half-read book (or half-watched TV series) based on prior time already "invested" in the activity, to being less likely to quit exclusive groups such as sororities and sporting clubs, which often took more effort to complete the initiation ritual. While these behaviors are not rational, they're all too common, so it helps to be aware of this tendency. In some circumstances, you might even use it for your benefit.

C While the examples above may seem relatively trivial, they show how common the sunk cost fallacy is. And it can affect decisions with much higher stakes in our lives. Imagine that Bob previously bought a house for $1 million. Subsequently, there's a nationwide housing market crash. All houses are now cheaper by 20% and Bob can only sell his house for $800,000. Bob's been thinking of upgrading to a bigger house (and they are now cheaper!), but will need to sell his existing house to have funds for a downpayment. However, he refuses to upgrade because he perceives a loss of $200,000 relative to the original price he paid of $1 million. Bob is committing the sunk cost fallacy by letting the original price influence his decision making — only the house's current and projected price should matter. Bob might be acting irrationally, but he's only human. Part of the reason we may find it difficult to ignore such losses is because losses are psychologically more Ⓒsalient relative to gains — this is known as loss Ⓓaversion.

D While most of the evidence for the sunk cost fallacy comes from individual decisions, it may also influence the decisions of groups. In fact, it is sometimes referred to as the Concord Fallacy because the French and British governments continued funding the doomed supersonic airliner long after it was likely it would not be commercially Ⓔviable.

47 Which of the following pairs includes an expression that CANNOT replace the underlined expression in the above passage? 0.8점

① Ⓐ <u>subpar</u>, inferior
② Ⓑ <u>banal</u>, trite
③ Ⓒ <u>salient</u>, lucrative
④ Ⓓ <u>aversion</u>, disinclination
⑤ Ⓔ <u>viable</u>, feasible

48 Which of the following is NOT true about Bob in paragraph Ⓒ? 1.0점

① Bob decides not to upgrade based on rational judgment about the future house prices.
② Bob is letting the sunk cost (the initial $1 million purchase price) unduly influence his decision-making.
③ Bob is aware that the value of his house has dropped from $1 million to $800,000.
④ Bob refuses to upgrade because he perceives a loss of $200,000 compared to the initial purchase price ($1 million).
⑤ Bob's reluctance to upgrade is influenced by psychological attachment to the initial investment.

49 Which of the following is suggested in the passage to counteract or mitigate the effects of the sunk cost fallacy? 1.1점

① Check if you are justifying behavior due to the costs you paid in the past.
② Stop making rational judgments about costs that have already incurred.
③ If it is difficult to overcome the sunk cost fallacy, have others make decisions for you.
④ Do not force yourself to ignore costs that have already been spent.
⑤ Stay committed to long-term relationships even through challenges or difficulties.

50 Which of the following is LEAST likely to be inferred from the above passage?

1.1점

① People tend to continue investing resources in situations where further investment is not beneficial.

② The sunk cost fallacy applies to groups, organizations, or governments.

③ People tend to overvalue past expenditures when making current decisions.

④ People may be more prone to clinging onto sunk costs because the psychological impact of losses is greater than gains.

⑤ People may persist in an investment due to the enjoyment derived from the continued investment.

아주대학교

2024학년도 자연계
▶▶ 영어 25문항, 수학 25문항 · 90분

[01-03] Choose the word that best completes the sentence.

01 I am a man who has been filled with a profound conviction that the easiest way of life is the best. Hence, though I belong to a profession proverbially energetic and nervous, even to turbulence, at times, yet nothing of that sort have I ever suffered to invade my peace. I am one of those unambitious lawyers who never addresses a(n) _____, or in any way draws down public applause; but in the cool tranquility of a snug retreat, do a snug business among rich men's bonds and mortgages and title-deeds. 0.8점

① ailment　　　　　② betrayal　　　　　③ coalition
④ jury　　　　　　⑤ speech

02 Since 2012, The World Happiness Report has ranked the average life satisfaction of more than 150 nations. In the past four years, the top slot has been taken by one country: Finland. Surprising is the fact that as the country has ascended to the top of the well-being charts, its economic development has remained remarkably flat. This seeming _____ confirms what many people have long suspected — that our traditional focus on economic growth doesn't translate into greater well-being. 0.8점

① ambiguity　　　　② contradiction　　　③ discord
④ proposition　　　⑤ revelation

03   Scientists have created _____ human embryos using stem cells in a groundbreaking advance that sidesteps the need for eggs or sperm. Scientists say these model embryos, which resemble those in the earliest stages of human development, could provide a crucial window on the impact of genetic disorders and the biological causes of recurrent miscarriages. However, the work also raises serious ethical and legal issues as the lab-grown entities fall outside current legislation in the UK and most other countries. 0.8점

① benign   ② ingenuine   ③ synthetic
④ tedious   ⑤ vertical

[04-05] Choose the expression that best completes the sentence.

04   Increasingly many New Yorkers tune out the city by tuning in to iPods and cellphones, adding an extra layer of personal sound to the public sound of the city. Yet through it all, the democratic ear takes it all in — there is no neat flap of skin like the eyelid to turn the sound on or off. Never _____ as a New York eardrum. 1.0점

① was overworked an organ so there
② was an organ overworked there
③ was there so overworked organ
④ was there so overworked an organ
⑤ there was so an organ overworked

05   Suppose the former employer informs you of instances of misconduct which could prompt you to reject the individual for employment. _____ the applicant based on this bad reference, the previous employer may be liable for the tort of intentional interference with employment contract. 0.8점

① Should refuse you to hire
② You should refuse hiring
③ You should refuse to hire
④ Should refuse you hiring
⑤ Should you refuse to hire

[06-07] Choose the underlined word or phrase that must be changed for the sentence to be correct.

06 In Wesley Medical Center, and in most hospitals today, the people ①<u>monitoring patients' heart rhythms</u>, blood pressure, or respiratory functions are not nurses ②<u>who interact with them</u>. They are "telemetry" technicians who are supposed to ③<u>alert those nurses to meaningful changes</u> in the vital signs transmitted by electronic devices ④<u>hooking up to the patients</u>. The technicians in telemetry units typically watch screens showing heart rhythms and numbers for many patients at a time — sometimes dozens — and often sit in a room ⑤<u>far from the patients</u> they are watching. 1.0점

07 In these early days, many have been content playfully ①<u>exploring</u> AI's possibilities. However, as these AI tools begin to unlock rapid advancements across all sectors of our society, more ②<u>fine-grained</u> control over who governs these foundational technologies will become increasingly important. In 2024, we will likely ③<u>to see</u> future-focused leaders ④<u>incentivizing</u> the development of their sovereign capabilities through ⑤<u>increased</u> research and development funding, training programs, and other investments. 1.0점

[08-09] Choose the number with the correct set of statements that can be restated or inferred from the original text.

08 The old-line Wall Street law firms had a very specific idea about what it was that they did. They were corporate lawyers. They represented the country's largest and most prestigious companies, and "represented" meant they handled the taxes and the legal work behind the issuing of stocks and bonds and made sure their clients did not run afoul of federal regulations. They did not do litigations; that is, very few of them had a division dedicated to defending and filing lawsuits. As Paul Cravath, one of the founders of Cravath, Swaine, and Moore, the very whitest of the white-shoe firms, once put it, the lawyer's job was to settle disputes in the conference rooms, not in the courtroom. 1.1점

Ⓐ Old-line Wall Street law firms specialized in corporate law, managing taxes, and overseeing stock and bond issuances for major companies.

Ⓑ Old-line Wall Street law firms rarely handled litigation, lacking dedicated divisions for lawsuits.

Ⓒ Corporate lawyers in Wall Street firms focused on ensuring regulatory compliance, with emphasis on litigation.

Ⓓ Paul Cravath asked lawyers at prestigious firms to aim to resolve disputes in conference rooms, not in courtrooms.

① Ⓐ & Ⓑ   ② Ⓐ & Ⓒ   ③ Ⓒ & Ⓓ
④ Ⓐ, Ⓒ & Ⓓ   ⑤ Ⓐ, Ⓑ, Ⓒ & Ⓓ

09 It's one of the great paradoxes of evolution. Humans have demonstrated that having large brains is key to our evolutionary success, and yet, such brains are extremely rare in other animals. Most get by on tiny brains, and don't seem to miss the extra brain cells (neurons). Why? The answer that most biologists have settled on is that large brains are costly in terms of the energy they require to run. And, given the way natural selection works, the benefits simply don't exceed the costs. 1.1점

Ⓐ Not all species require large brains to thrive.

Ⓑ Larger brains cause higher cognitive abilities or survival benefits.

Ⓒ While large brains have been evolutionarily advantageous for humans, they might not confer the same benefits across all species or environmental contexts.

Ⓓ If the energy expended on maintaining a larger brain doesn't significantly increase an organism's chances of survival and reproduction, it might not be favored by natural selection.

① Ⓐ & Ⓑ   ② Ⓑ & Ⓒ   ③ Ⓑ & Ⓓ
④ Ⓐ, Ⓒ & Ⓓ   ⑤ Ⓑ, Ⓒ & Ⓓ

[10-25] Read each passage and answer the corresponding questions for each.

10-13

A Most established companies focus on incremental innovation, entering new markets by tweaking products for new customers, using variations on a core product to stay on top of the market, and creating interim solutions for industry-wide problems. When Scott Paper Ⓐcouldn't compete with Fort Howard Paper Co. on price for the lucrative institutional toilet tissue market, it borrowed a solution from European companies: a dispenser that held bigger rolls. Scott made the larger rolls of paper and provided institutional customers with free dispensers, Ⓑlater did the same thing with paper towels. ❶ Scott not only won over customers in a new market: it became less vulnerable to competitors, such as Fort Howard, which could lower prices but weren't offering the larger rolls or tailor-made dispensers.

B Newer companies create disruptive technologies that were cheaper and more likely to alter the competitive space. ❷ Established companies can be slow to react or invest in these disruptive technologies because they threaten their investment. Then they suddenly find Ⓒthemselves facing formidable new competitors, and many fail. To avoid this trap, incumbent firms must carefully monitor the preference of both customers and non-customers and uncover evolving, difficult-to-articulate customer needs.

C What else can a company do? In a study of industrial products, a new-product specialist named Cooper found that the number one success factor is a unique, superior product. Such products succeed 98 percent of the time, Ⓓcompared to products with a moderate advantage (58 percent success) or minimal advantage (18 percent success). Another key factor is a well-defined product concept. ❸ Other success factors are technological and marketing synergy, quality of execution in all stages, and market attractiveness.

D Cooper also found that products designed solely for domestic markets tend to show a high failure rate, low market share, and low growth. ❹ Those designed for the world market achieve significantly more profits at home and abroad. Yet only 17 percent of the products in his study were designed with an international orientation. ❺ The implication is that companies should consider adopting an international perspective in designing and developing new products, Ⓔeven if only to sell in their home market.

10 Which of the following would be the best title for the above passage? 1.0점

① Critical Success Factors in Industrial Product Development

② The Dangers of Disruptive Technologies for New Companies

③ Strategies to Overcome Global Market Challenges

④ The Importance of a Domestic Perspective in Product Design

⑤ The Impact of Social Media on New Product Development

11 The following sentence is removed from the above passage. In which part may it be inserted to support the argument made by the author? 1.1점

> The company carefully defines and assesses the target market, product requirements, and benefits before proceeding.

① ❶   ② ❷   ③ ❸

④ ❹   ⑤ ❺

12 Choose the underlined word or phrase that must be changed for the sentence to be correct. 0.8점

① Ⓐ couldn't compete with

② Ⓑ later did the same thing

③ Ⓒ themselves facing formidable new competitors

④ Ⓓ compared to

⑤ Ⓔ even if only to sell

13 According to the above passage, which of the following is NOT true? 1.1점

① Newer companies need to attentively observe the preferences of both existing customers and potential customers to combat novel competitors.

② Key factors contributing to success include the excellence of a product and a well-defined product concept.

③ Scott provided institutional customers with a free dispenser for larger rolls of paper towels.

④ Established companies typically prioritize incremental innovation, approaching new markets by adjusting products for new customers.

⑤ Only 17 percent of the products in Cooper's study were designed with an international perspective.

A The spread of false narratives around three recent extreme weather events in Latin America shows how climate change misinformation in Spanish and Portuguese can Ⓐunderline efforts to address and mitigate the effects of global warming in the region, according to a new study. Environmental organizations Roots and Friends of the Earth, which are part of the Climate Action Against Disinformation Coalition, Ⓑcommissioned the progressive research firm Purpose to analyze how cyclone floods in Brazil and Peru as well as wildfires in Chile became Ⓒfertile grounds for misinformation to flourish online.

B Online posts in Brazil, Peru, and Chile falsely attributed the events to dam breakages, arson, and climate research centers that study the atmosphere, sowing confusion, Ⓓdeflecting conversations about extreme weather preparedness, and politicizing climate action, the study concluded. The new research points to "a troubling cycle," Max MacBride, counter-disinformation lead at Roots, said in a statement. A cyclone Ⓔbattered the state of Rio Grande do Sul in southern Brazil in September. The storm's unusually heavy rains and wind gusts caused intense flooding and landslides that killed more than 30 people and severely damaged countless homes. While news sources online reported on the flooding in the context of a climate catastrophe, (1)_____.

C The false narrative began circulating a couple of days after the storm as center-right local leadership in the region publicly inquired about the "opening of the gates" to the company operating the dams, as stated in a media release, according to the study. The company responded, saying there was no evidence suggesting the dams had influenced the flooding. The Brazilian state's environmental department then confirmed the floods were caused by the cyclone and had no connection to the dams, but the false narrative kept spreading online.

D The study examined 66,800 posts, including posts on the social media site X and news portal comments about the floods and cyclone. A small number of them (1,800 posts) were found to also discuss the dam gates. But this small portion reached a significantly larger audience of over 5.2 million people, suggesting how social media algorithms can boost misinformation. "We won't be able to protect people in Latin America from climate change if professional disinformers keep manipulating weather disasters by gaming social media algorithms," Michael Khoo, the climate disinformation program director at Friends of the Earth, said in a statement.

14 Which of the following would be the best title for the above passage? 1.0점

① False Narratives are Under the Radar of the Platform's Content Moderation Policies

② False Narratives About Renewable Energy are Adapted to Different Languages

③ Arson is Blamed as the Single Cause of Forest Fires

④ A Few Conspiracy Theory Posts Have Little Reach Online

⑤ Climate Change Misinformation in Latin America Threatens Efforts to Combat It

15 According to the above passage, which of the following is true? 1.1점

① Roots and Friends of the Earth analyzed false narratives about cyclone floods in Brazil and Peru, and wildfires in Chile.

② The study reveals that misinformation had little impact on efforts to address global warming in Latin America.

③ The study examined 66,800 posts, most of which contained misinformation regarding dam gates.

④ Aligning with authorities confirming natural causes, false narratives about a cyclone in southern Brazil persisted online.

⑤ False narratives in Brazil, Peru, and Chile falsely attributed extreme weather events to dam breakages, arson, and climate research centers.

16 Which of the following pairs includes an expression that CANNOT replace the underlined expression in the passage? 0.8점

① Ⓐ undermine, weaken

② Ⓑ commissioned, incentivized

③ Ⓒ fertile, productive

④ Ⓓ deflecting, turning away

⑤ Ⓔ battered, damaged

17 Which of the following would best fit in blank (1) in paragraph B? 1.1점

① disinformation spreaders were falsely claiming the floods were the result of three dams' gates being opened.

② parts of cities in the central and southern regions experienced more than 400 forest fires amid extreme heat and drought.

③ wildfires at the time were mainly caused by a combination of factors.

④ some social media companies have implemented content moderation guidelines to curb climate change misinformation on their platforms.

⑤ this helped steer the online conversation away from the impact of climate change and how it can exacerbate flooding.

18-21

A Why would people simply hand over something precious or valuable when they could use it themselves? To me as an anthropologist, this is an especially powerful question because giving gifts likely has ancient roots. And gifts can be found in every known culture around the world. Gifts serve lots of purposes. Some psychologists have observed a "warm glow" — an intrinsic delight — that's associated with giving presents. ❶ Theologians have noted how gifting is a way to express moral values such as love, kindness, and gratitude in Catholicism, Buddhism, and Islam. And philosophers ranging from Seneca to Friedrich Nietzsche regarded gifting as the best demonstration of selflessness. It's little wonder that gifts are a central part of Hanukkah, Christmas, Kwanzaa, and other winter holidays. ❷ But of all the explanations for why people give gifts, the one I find most convincing was offered in 1925 by a French anthropologist named Marcel Mauss.

B Like many anthropologists, Mauss was puzzled by societies in which gifts were extravagantly given away. For example, along the northwest coast of Canada and the United States, indigenous peoples conduct potlatch ceremonies. In these days-long feasts, hosts give away immense amounts of property. ❸ Mauss sees potlaches as an extreme form of gifting. Yet, he suggests this behavior is totally recognizable in almost every human society. ❹

C Mauss observed that gifts create three separate but inextricably related actions. Gifts are given, received, and reciprocated. The first act of giving establishes the virtues of the gift giver. They express their generosity, kindness, and honor. ❺ The act of receiving the gift, in turn, shows a person's willingness to be honored. This is a way for the receiver to show their own generosity that they are willing to accept what was offered to them. The third component of gift giving is reciprocity, returning in kind what was first given. In this way, gifting becomes an endless loop of giving and receiving, giving and receiving.

D This last step — reciprocity — is what makes gifts unique. Unlike buying something at a store, in which the exchange ends when money is traded for goods, giving gifts builds and sustains relationships. This relationship between the gift giver and receiver is bound up with morality. Gifting is an expression of fairness because each present is generally of equal or greater value than what was last given. And gifting is an expression of respect because it shows a willingness to honor the other person. In these ways, gifting tethers people together. It keeps people connected in an infinite cycle of mutual obligations.

18 Which of the following is NOT true about gift giving according to the above passage? 1.1점

① Gifts serve various purposes, including expressing moral values such as love, kindness, and gratitude.

② Some psychologists associate giving presents with an intrinsic delight or "warm glow."

③ Gift giving can be found in every known culture around the world.

④ Philosophers, such as Seneca and Friedrich Nietzsche, regarded gifting as the best demonstration of selflessness.

⑤ Giving gifts aligns with economic or evolutionary rationality, so it remains a prevalent practice in various cultures.

19 The following sentence is removed from the above passage. In which part may it be inserted to support the argument made by the author? 1.1점

Consider a famous potlatch in 1921, held by a clan leader of the Kwakwaka'wakw Nation in Canada who gave community members 400 sacks of flour, heaps of blankets, sewing machines, furniture, canoes, gas-powered boats, and even pool tables.

① ❶   ② ❷   ③ ❸
④ ❹   ⑤ ❺

20 Which of the following is NOT true about Marcel Mauss' observations on gift giving?

1.1점

① Mauss suggests that gift giving establishes virtues, such as generosity and kindness in the gift giver and shows the receiver's willingness to be honored.

② Mauss's perspective implies that the practice of giving and receiving gifts is a widespread phenomenon found in various societies and cultures.

③ According to Mauss, the process of giving and receiving gifts is tied to moral values and social connections.

④ Mauss observes that giving gifts forms an endless loop of mutual obligations between the gift giver and receiver.

⑤ Mauss suggests that the cycle of giving, receiving, and reciprocating transfers the value of social solidarity to future generations.

21 Which of the following is the LEAST relevant keyword for Mauss' observations on gift giving? 1.0점

① contemporary context

② cultural practices

③ human society

④ psychological aspects

⑤ reciprocity

22-25

A Our ability to process verbal language is not based solely on semantics, i.e. the meaning and combination of linguistic units. Other parameters come into play, such as prosody, which includes pauses, accentuation, and intonation. Affective bursts "Aaaah!" or "Oh!", for example, are also part of this, and we share these with our primate cousins. They contribute to the meaning and understanding of our vocal communications. When such a vocal message is emitted, these sounds are processed by the frontal and orbitofrontal regions of our brain. The function of these two areas is, among other things, to integrate sensory and contextual information leading to a decision.

B Are they activated in the same way when we are exposed to the emotional vocalizations of our close cousins — the chimpanzees, macaques, or bonobos? Are we able to differentiate between them? A research team sought to find this out by exposing a group of 25 volunteers to various human and simian vocalizations. "The participants were placed in an MRI scanner and were given headphones. After a short period of familiarization with the different types of vocalizations, each participant had to categorize them, i.e. identify to which species they belonged," explains Leonardo Ceravolo, first author of the study.

C These vocalizations were of the affiliative type, i.e. linked to a positive interaction, or of the agonistic type, i.e. linked to a threat or distress. The results show that for macaque and chimpanzee vocalizations, the frontal and orbitofrontal regions of the participants were activated in a similar way to human vocalizations. The participants were able to differentiate between them easily.

D On the other hand, when confronted with the "sounds" of bonobos, also close cousins of humans, the involved cerebral areas were much less activated, and categorization was at chance level. "It was thought that kinship between species — the 'phylogenetic distance' — was the main parameter for having the ability, or not, to recognize these different vocalizations. We thought that the closer we were genetically, the more important this ability was," explains Didier Grandjean, who led the study. "Our results show that a second parameter comes into play: acoustic distance. The further the dynamics of the acoustic parameters, such as the frequencies used, are from those of humans, the less certain frontal regions are activated. Bonobo calls are very high-pitched and can sound like those of certain birds. This acoustic distance in terms of frequencies, compared with human vocalizations, explains our inability to decode them, despite our close phylogenetic proximity."

22 Which of the following is NOT a method of data collection of the research described in the passage? 1.1점

① Volunteers are exposed to various types of vocalizations from both humans and different species of primates.

② The researchers systematically controlled the sequence and presentation of vocalizations by randomizing or structuring the order.

③ The participants are placed in an MRI scanner while exposed to these vocalizations.

④ Before the categorization task, the participants are given a short period to familiarize themselves with the different types of vocalizations.

⑤ Participants are required to identify to which species (human, chimpanzee, macaque, or bonobo) each vocalization belongs.

23 Which of the following is the LEAST relevant keyword for the research? 1.0점

① Acoustic Variations

② Brain Activation

③ Cognitive Ability

④ Genetic Proximity

⑤ Vocalization

24 Among the following questions, to which does the study NOT provide an answer? 1.1점

① Can humans differentiate between these simian vocalizations?

② Are humans capable of identifying the different emotional aspects of affiliative or agonistic vocalizations emitted by a bonobo?

③ Are the frontal and orbitofrontal regions of the brain activated similarly when exposed to simian and human vocalizations?

④ What role does phylogenetic proximity versus acoustic distance play in the brain's response to and recognition of vocalizations among different primate species?

⑤ What factors influence the ability of humans to distinguish between the simian sounds?

25 Which of the following is LEAST likely to be inferred from paragraph ☐D? 1.1점

① The acoustic divergence makes it challenging for humans to decode or categorize bonobo vocalizations.

② Despite bonobos being close cousins of humans in terms of genetic relatedness, participants had difficulty categorizing bonobo vocalizations.

③ The acoustic properties of bonobo vocalizations create a significant acoustic difference from human vocalizations.

④ The study reveals that phylogenetic proximity is not the factor influencing our ability to identify the simian sounds but the acoustic proximity is a determining factor.

⑤ It was believed that the ability to recognize vocalizations was primarily linked to the genetic closeness or phylogenetic proximity between the species.

이화여자대학교   2024학년도 인문계 유형 1
▸▸ 50문항·100분

[01-05] Choose the <u>synonym</u> of the underlined word.

01 Depending on each student's learning style, <u>pedagogical</u> methods can encourage either engagement or disinterest.

① elemental   ② invitational   ③ educational

④ artificial   ⑤ conventional

02 The term 'photosynthesis' refers to the process by which green plants and some organisms <u>convert</u> light into energy.

① transfer   ② transform   ③ transit

④ transpire   ⑤ transmit

03 Though it ended in <u>abject</u> failure, her experiment taught her an all-important lesson about the significance of uncontrolled variables.

① unremarkable   ② utter   ③ abrupt

④ glorious   ⑤ qualified

04 The environmental educator noted that without an inclusive approach, bans could <u>inadvertently</u> harm those who are already among the most vulnerable in society, such as individuals who require plastic straws to eat and drink.

① calculatedly   ② consciously   ③ deliberately

④ unpremeditatedly   ⑤ voluntarily

05 Chemical reactions involve both the synthesis and <u>decomposition</u> of compounds.

① breakaway   ② breakwater   ③ breakdown

④ break-in   ⑤ breakneck

[06-10] Choose the <u>antonym</u> of the underlined word.

06 A combination of <u>rampant</u> economic inequality, slowing growth, and some of the most patriarchal social dynamics in the developed world managed to turn gender equality into a polarizing election issue.

① remained   ② regained   ③ retrained

④ restrained   ⑤ retained

07 Although a record 57 women were elected to parliament in the last election, they still make up a <u>woeful</u> 19% of lawmakers.

① proportionate   ② proposed   ③ propelled

④ prosaic   ⑤ promising

08 One of the most <u>salient</u> dimensions of comparatist ecocritical analysis, obviously, is its attention to the role of linguistic and cultural differences in communities' engagement with global ecological crises that range from toxification to biodiversity loss and climate change.

① indicative   ② innovative   ③ intelligent

④ informative   ⑤ insignificant

09 The word 'algorithm' takes its origin from the name of a renowned Muslim <u>polymath</u> named al-Khwarizmi, often described as the founder of algebra.

① intellectual   ② linguist   ③ ignoramus
④ libertine   ⑤ impresario

10 A truly egalitarian society aims to eradicate all forms of stratification, irrespective of any <u>detriment</u> to individual prestige.

① adherence   ② admonition   ③ addiction
④ advantage   ⑤ adeptness

11 Choose the most logical order for the following sentences.

Ⓐ Gaslighting should be considered a serious issue as such, for victims require the acknowledgement and reassurance of those around them to once again trust themselves. Ⓑ At first, this can lead to the victim simply experiencing moments of confusion, anxiety, and self-doubt. Ⓒ Gaslighting is a form of psychological manipulation in which an individual is made to question their reality, memory, or sanity. Ⓓ However, gaslighting can ultimately erode self-confidence and mental well-being, leading to dependency on the gaslighter's version of reality and isolation from support networks. Ⓔ Imagine a scenario where someone is repeatedly told events that in fact happened did not, or that they occurred differently from how they remember them.

---

① Ⓒ — Ⓔ — Ⓐ — Ⓑ — Ⓓ
② Ⓐ — Ⓑ — Ⓓ — Ⓒ — Ⓔ
③ Ⓒ — Ⓔ — Ⓑ — Ⓓ — Ⓐ
④ Ⓔ — Ⓒ — Ⓑ — Ⓓ — Ⓐ
⑤ Ⓒ — Ⓔ — Ⓑ — Ⓐ — Ⓓ

[12-21] Fill in the blanks with the best-fitting option.

12 Plastic usage in the U.S., even when recycled, has also _____ other countries. Millions of tons of plastic waste, often collected from recycling plants, are shipped to low-income countries that don't have the infrastructure to _____ pollution caused by plastic entering waterways or being incinerated.

① harmed — prevent
② helped — preclude
③ damaged — produce
④ harnessed — procure
⑤ harassed — propel

13 The human rights group _____ organizes demonstrations at U.N. climate meetings to draw attention to the connection between global warming and human rights, and to call for _____ action to reduce fossil fuel consumption.

① routinely — swifter
② unusually — heavier
③ remotely — smarter
④ regrettably — more serious
⑤ exceptionally — quicker

14 Market fluctuations can lead to both prosperity and _____ for businesses, which is why market stability is not always a welcome state of _____.

① adherence — repair
② inflexibility — grace
③ advantage — matter
④ insecurity — mind
⑤ adversity — affairs

15 Significant social movements often have a _____ impact upon civilizations; for instance, a political revolution may bring about either dramatic reforms or debilitating _____ within the political landscape.

① dramatic — improvement
② seismic — stagnation
③ minuscule — enervation
④ chaotic — enrichment
⑤ beneficent — bounty

16 Although it may _____ a multitude of more precisely worded ethical peccadilloes, the term 'plagiarism' most commonly refers to the act of using someone else's work or ideas without proper _____.

① surround — payment
② exclude — acknowledgement
③ include — transfer
④ encompass — credit
⑤ mean — reimbursement

17 A _____ of the words 'education' and 'entertainment,' edutainment seeks to _____ enjoyment to the classroom through the use of engaging media and the gamification of lesson objectives.

① mishmash — curb
② portmanteau — bring
③ mismatch — convey
④ portrayal — cater
⑤ mashup — limit

18 Though intended to be the _____ artist's kiss-off, the album was lauded as a tour de force for its innovative fusion of musical genres, _____ her career and bringing renewed attention to her catalog.

① fading — jeopardizing
② up-and-coming — invigorating
③ waning — revitalizing
④ tired — standardizing
⑤ fruitful — rejuvenating

19 Under tremendous pressure, the team of lawyers carefully parsed each line of the document, _____ the legal ramifications of the proposed legislation.

① scrutinizing   ② gormandizing   ③ elegizing
④ energizing   ⑤ atomizing

20 Human emotions as we understand them exhibit a broad _____ from euphoria to dysphoria, reflecting varying states of mind.

① inspection   ② compilation   ③ sputum
④ compendium   ⑤ spectrum

21 The result of countless studies on the issue, there is now a well-established _____ between sleep patterns and cognitive function.

① collaboration   ② collation   ③ codification
④ correlation   ⑤ commodification

[22-25] Choose the faulty expression among the five choices.

22 More print-based than the sciences and social sciences, the humanities are experiencing the effects of digital technologies. At the epicenter of change are the Digital Humanities. The Digital Humanities have been ①around since at least the 1940s, but it was not until the Internet and World Wide Web that they ②came into their own as emerging fields with ③their own degree programs, research centers, scholarly journals and books, and a growing body of expert practitioners. Nevertheless, many humanities scholars remain ④not only vaguely aware of the Digital Humanities ⑤and lack a clear sense of the challenges they pose to traditional modes of inquiry.

23 Feminism is less a unified school than a social and intellectual movement and a space ①of debate. On the one hand, feminist theorists champion the identity of women, demand rights for women, and promote women's writings ②to representations of the experience of women. On the other hand, feminists ③undertake a theoretical critique of the heterosexual matrix that ④organizes identities and cultures in terms ⑤of the opposition between man and woman.

24 The Myers-Briggs Type Indicator (MBTI) is a popular tool for understanding personality types. However, the MBTI has several clear drawbacks. The test's reliability and validity ①had often faced scrutiny, with concerns about the inconsistency of results and its classification system ②lacking empirical evidence. Additionally, the test's tendency to place individuals into distinct boxes ③might lead to stereotyping or bias, potentially ④affecting decision-making processes in hiring or personal relationships. Still, the MBTI provides a framework that helps individuals gain insights into their preferences, behaviors, and potential career paths. It also encourages self-reflection and promotes better understanding of how different personality types interact, ⑤fostering improved communication in various settings.

25 Numerous efforts have been made to save bee populations from colony collapse syndrome (CCS) due to the ①<u>critical</u> role bees play in pollination and ecosystems. Scientists, conservationists, and beekeepers have united ②<u>globally</u> to combat this threat. Research initiatives focus on identifying the causes behind CCS, such as pesticide exposure, habitat loss, pathogens, and climate change. One ③<u>crucially</u> approach involves advocating for more sustainable agricultural practices, promoting the reduction of pesticide usage and adopting bee-friendly alternatives. Conservation efforts emphasize creating and restoring bee-friendly habitats, ensuring ④<u>diverse</u> and ⑤<u>abundant</u> foraging grounds with ample floral resources.

[26-27] Answer the questions after reading the passage below.

In most circumstances, *Arthrobotrys oligospora* is saprotrophic, meaning it consumes decaying organic matter like dead leaves. However, scientists have found that nutritional deprivation can cause the fungi to undergo molecular changes, enabling it to become Ⓐ_____ preying on unsuspecting worm species called nematodes.

Fungi cannot pursue its prey in the hot-on-the-heels manner that other predators do, and a study published last month outlined how the fungi have evolved a trickier, more sinister way to predate.

When *A. oligospora* senses a nearby nematode, it relies on pheromones to lure nematodes to its mycelium, the underground network of microscopic threads that make up a fungus. *A. oligospora* likely evolved the means to use olfactory mimicry to attract its nematode prey through the olfactory neurons in nematodes. This means that the fungus secretes food cues and sex pheromones to Ⓑ_____ the worm in question.

Nematodes produce small molecules called ascarosides, which regulate their behavior and development. Fungi like *A. oligospora* are thought to "eavesdrop" and detect the signals made by these ascarosides, which create a molecular pattern that fungi can recognize. As the trap is thought to be a very energy-consuming process, *A. oligospora* only forms it when prey are near.

26 **Which expression best completes Ⓐ?**

① carnivorous   ② carnal   ③ credulous

④ herbivorous   ⑤ versatile

27 **Which expression best completes Ⓑ?**

① choke   ② digest   ③ hide

④ seduce   ⑤ transform

[28-29] Answer the questions after reading the passage below.

Why should hypertext, and web reading in general, lead to poorer comprehension? The answer lies in the relation of working memory (i.e., the contents of consciousness) to long-term memory. Material is held in working memory for only a few minutes, and the capacity of working memory is severely limited.

For example, I find that if I repeat phone numbers out loud several times so they occupy working memory to the exclusion of other things, I can retain them long enough to punch in the number.

For retention of more complex matters, the contents of working memory must be transferred to long-term memory, preferably with repetitions to facilitate the integration of the new material with existing knowledge schemas.

The small Ⓐ_____ involved with hypertext and web reading — clicking on links, navigating a page, scrolling down or up, and so on — increase the cognitive load on working memory and thereby reduce the amount of new material it can hold. With linear reading, Ⓑ_____ the cognitive load is at a minimum, precisely because eye movements are more routine and fewer decisions need to be made about how to read the material and in what order. Hence the transfer to long-term memory happens more efficiently.

28 **Which expression best completes Ⓐ?**

① distractions　　② disadvantages　　③ displacements
④ disinterests　　⑤ distensions

29 **Which expression best completes Ⓑ?**

① at least　　② by contrast　　③ by definition
④ by the way　　⑤ by and large

[30-32] Answer the questions after reading the passage below.

Formative assessment stands as a valuable tool in the field of English as a Foreign Language (EFL) education, offering several advantages that aid both students and educators alike. Firstly, it provides ongoing feedback that helps learners grasp their strengths and weaknesses in real-time, enabling them to identify areas needing improvement. This Ⓐ_____ guidance allows for personalized learning experiences tailored to individual needs, fostering a more effective learning process.

This customizability is a boon for teachers as well since formative assessment in EFL classrooms allows educators to adapt their teaching methods dynamically. By gaining insight Ⓑ_____ students' ongoing performance, teachers can modify lesson plans and instructional approaches to better cater to diverse learning styles and needs. This adaptability ensures that students receive the support necessary for their language development.

A final advantage is that formative assessment encourages active student engagement. It prompts learners to take ownership of their progress by regularly reflecting on their learning goals and adjusting their strategies accordingly. This process of self-assessment enhances motivation and autonomy in language learning, promoting a deeper understanding of the English language.

30 What <u>cannot</u> be inferred from the passage?
① Formative assessment allows educators to change lessons to match students' achievements.
② Formative assessment provides students opportunities for self-reflection.
③ Formative assessment is useful in EFL classrooms.
④ Formative assessment primarily aids students.
⑤ Formative assessment lets students know how they are performing.

31 Which expression best completes Ⓐ?
① continuous ② sporadic ③ curious
④ furious ⑤ cumulus

32 Which expression best completes Ⓑ?
① of ② in ③ for
④ on ⑤ into

[33-34] Answer the questions after reading the passage below.

For decades, health specialists have Ⓐ_____ whether the Body Mass Index (BMI) is truly a reliable way to measure health risks. The widely-used metric, which calculates people's weight in relation to their height, has long faced criticism over its inaccuracies and oversimplification. For instance, some experts point out that, for people of significantly shorter- or taller-than-average height, BMI scores are at times misleading. What's more, as the system is primarily based on 19th-century data from a narrow demographic of White European men, many question its relevance to women and to people of other racial and ethnic groups.

What further complicates the matter are global variations in how overweight and obese individuals are defined. For instance, whereas Europe and the Americas tend to set higher thresholds, with a BMI of 25 to 30 typically considered overweight, countries in the Asia-Pacific region, including Korea, tend to view a BMI of 23 to 24.9 as overweight and 25 or above as obese. This different standard reportedly addresses higher risks of various metabolic diseases among Asians at lower BMI levels indicated in some studies. Accordingly, the UK's National Health Service has different BMI cut-offs for Black and Asian people. Nonetheless, the need for these adjustments adds fuel to an ongoing debate about the index's global relevance and reliability.

33 **Which expression cannot complete Ⓐ?**

① considered ② contemplated ③ pondered

④ wandered ⑤ wondered

34 **Which does not indicate a criticism of the BMI mentioned in the passage?**

① its reliance on racially specific data

② inaccurate standards for people from Europe and the Americas

③ the need for different standards globally

④ its inapplicability to people of below-average height

⑤ its potential lack of relevance to women

[35-37] Answer the questions after reading the passage below.

According to philosopher Immanuel Kant, free will arises when we make the rational choice to act in Ⓐ_____ with moral principles. In other words, it is our ability to make choices based on reason, independent of external factors, that determines our autonomy.

Consider a situation where someone is faced with the decision to act honestly despite the potential for personal gain. For instance, imagine you were mistakenly given too much change when buying something at a store. From Kant's point of view, your rational decision to return the Ⓑ_____ money, driven by your adherence to the moral principle of honesty, is an example of free will in action.

In this case, free will isn't just about the immediate desire for more money or the fear of getting caught. Instead, it's about making a rational decision to act in keeping with morality — in this instance, honesty. Despite the temptation to keep the extra cash, they choose to return it because they recognize it as the morally right thing to do, guided by their own rational judgment rather than external pressures.

35 Which expression best completes Ⓐ?

① allowance ② insistence ③ indifference
④ affordance ⑤ accordance

36 Which expression best completes Ⓑ?

① recess ② regress ③ redress
④ express ⑤ excess

37 Which statement is true according to the passage?

① Kant believes that succumbing to external pressures demonstrates our free will.
② Returning the money is an irrational act.
③ Kant claims that an example of free will is the act of returning the money.
④ Kant holds all morality to be relative.
⑤ Kant believes that the temptation to keep the money is an indication of free will.

[38-40] Answer the questions after reading the passage below.

Since the paralyzing effect of the pandemic devastated economies worldwide, there has been much discussion about the future of the globalized economy. While some believe that a return to the status quo is in order now that the worst of the crisis has passed, others have called for significant reforms to supply chains and economic engagement to ensure that such an economic crisis never happens again. Your own thoughts on this issue will likely differ significantly whether you Ⓐ_____ more with globalist or protectionist views.

On the one hand, globalists tend to prioritize interconnected economies and open trade. As such, their views on supply chains advocate for increased collaboration between nations, aiming for cost-effective production and access to diverse markets. For instance, consider the production of a simple T-shirt. Its cotton might come from India, manufactured into fabric in China, dyed in Bangladesh, assembled in Vietnam, and finally sold globally. This process highlights the intricate web of global connections.

Protectionists, however, prioritize domestic industries by imposing tariffs or trade barriers. They argue that these ways of shielding local businesses from foreign competition preserve jobs and industries within their country. For instance, a protectionist policy might involve imposing tariffs on imported goods to incentivize domestic production, protecting local industries but potentially limiting access to international markets.

38 Which statement is not true according to the passage?

① Protectionist policies may make it difficult to sell goods to other countries.
② Globalists favor affordability.
③ Protectionists want to incentivize foreign competition.
④ Tariffs protect local jobs according to protectionists.
⑤ The pandemic brought economic chaos.

39 Which of the following indicates a globalist view?

① international competition
② multinational partnerships
③ prioritizing local jobs
④ increased tariffs
⑤ barriers to trade

40 Which expression best completes Ⓐ?

① align   ② define   ③ design

④ resign   ⑤ decline

[41-50] Select <u>the most</u> appropriate item from the box below. Each item should be used only once.

① curtained	② unhinged	③ an inability to	④ outbreak
⑤ a gift for	⑥ an array of	⑦ in defense of	⑧ digressions
⑨ bluster	⑩ curtailed	⑪ a smidgeon of	⑫ dichotomies
⑬ outcry	⑭ euphemistic	⑮ bewildered	⑯ bedecked
⑰ luster	⑱ eugenic	⑲ in lieu of	⑳ unearthed

41 As the zero-waste movement lost much of its _____, more organizations started pushing for policies that make it easier for individuals to reduce their plastic usage.

42 Despite permission to protest, climate activists say their work has been _____ by a slew of rules and restrictions.

43 Plastic straws became a target for environmentalists after a viral video of a turtle with one lodged in its nose sparked a(n) _____.

44 Working alongside local authorities, the celebrated multinational team of archaeologists _____ a trove of artifacts dating back to the Bronze Age.

45 Perplexed by the student's justification of his unruly conduct, the school administrator stood _____.

46 Some of the most powerful and historically ancient beliefs about emotions are connected with _____ of gender, associating some mental states more with women, and others with men.

47 Ecocriticism and the environmental humanities form _____ new interdisciplinary areas that have emerged across the humanities and qualitative social sciences over the last two decades.

48 When the star lecturer fell ill, the academy offered recordings _____ live sessions.

49 The shrewd client saw through the agent's artfully _____ language and turned down the offer.

50 The would-be magician demonstrated _____ legerdemain, though his on-stage demeanor left much to be desired.

INHA UNIVERSITY

인하대학교

2024학년도 인문계
▶▶ 40문항·80분

자연계
▶▶ 영어 20문항·50분, 수학 30문항·70분

인문·자연계 공통 영어문제 별도 * 표시

[01-03] Choose the most appropriate one for each blank.

01* 1점

Allergies are very widespread. Every year more than 50 million people in America experience allergy symptoms including postnasal drip, coughing and fatigue with varying severity. People living with allergies may be prone to experiencing mental health disorders, such as anxiety and depression. The _____ of mental health disorders and allergies have received little attention but recent studies have shed light on the parallels that may improve treatment for patients. Allergies themselves can have a significant impact on a person's mental health. How can allergies affect mental health and vice versa?

① contributions   ② death rates   ③ best treatments
④ correlations   ⑤ medical expenses

02 * 2점

A recent paper published in *Nature Sustainability* on electric vehicles and their impact on the environment claims that electric vehicle (EV) buying incentives often fail to deliver on the government's investment. Not only do U.S. subsidies flow to the well-off, but it turns out tax credits (up to $7,500 in 2023) can incentivize the wrong buyers, leading many to increase their carbon footprint. According to the research, if you drive a fair amount, then you are likely well-suited to drive an electric vehicle. However, if you seldom drive and the vehicle is mostly going to sit in the garage, then you may counterintuitively be better off owning a gasoline-powered vehicle. This is because the batteries that power EVs are responsible for an outsize share of emissions during the manufacturing process. Because EVs are dirtier to build but cleaner to drive, _____. In the U.S., the typical non-luxury EV needs to run between 28,069 and 68,160 miles before netting a positive environmental impact.

① emissions are easy to control
② batteries are the essential component in EVs
③ gasoline-powered vehicles have become a thing of the past
④ public dollars spent as incentives are going to be worth the money
⑤ EVs must meet certain mileage thresholds before environmental advantages are realized

03 * 1.5점

Some people say robots will soon take over the world. Or will they? To celebrate the 100th anniversary of the coining of the word *robot*, by the Czech playwright Karel Čapek, we thought it would be fun to take a look at a list of AI's failed attempts to replace humans. Let's begin with face recognition. The Scottish soccer team Inverness Caledonian Thistle FC bypassed facial recognition in favor of ball recognition by replacing their human camera operators with AI-operated ball-tracking cameras. Now, cameras would always follow the action by automatically following the ball. Sounds great, except fans watching at home missed most of the scoring plays as the AI-operated cameras constantly mistook the referee's bald head for the soccer ball. Scores of viewers called the team to complain, one fan going so far as to suggest supplying the referee with a _____.

① small wig   ② right-sized ball   ③ better camera
④ pair of clean glasses   ⑤ sensor

04* Which of the following is the best title of the passage? 1점

As with any storm, bomb cyclones develop when drastically different air masses clash — typically, cold and dry air moving down from the north and warm, moist air coming up from the tropics. The warmer air rapidly rises, creating cloud systems, lowering air pressure and developing into a storm system that circulates counterclockwise around that center of low pressure. Rapid storm strengthening is a signal that increasing amounts of warm air are being drawn into a storm's circulation, spiraling toward its center and rising out its top. When more air escapes out the top of the storm than is being sucked inward, air pressure drops even further.

① What Prevents Bomb Cyclones?
② How Do Bomb Cyclones Form?
③ How Strong Is a Bomb Cyclone?
④ How Long Does a Bomb Cyclone Last?
⑤ Why Do People Call It a Bomb Cyclone?

05* How does the tone change from the first paragraph to the next one? 1.5점

The beach is a wonderful escape from daily life. It lends the sense that one is indeed on vacation, even if one is merely a short drive from home. While lying on the beach, to-dos and calendar invites and work-related notifications drift and disappear into the crashing waves; wine surreptitiously transported in a Gatorade container tastes like you imagine it does in photos of people on vacation in Hawaii; and you get the sense that, even with all the hardships, life may actually be beautiful. Then you have to leave.

The good vibes fade almost immediately upon leaving the beach, replaced instead with the distinct rage of finding that everything you own is now covered in one-hundred-million pieces of sand, sand that has since turned into an impossible-to-remove, glue-like substance. It covers your feet and your legs, it's on your neck and in your hair, it's on your phone and your keys and your bag and your magazine, it's all over your car, it's in your kitchen and your breakfast cereal somehow; it's most certainly in your bathroom, and now your feet are re-sanded after every subsequent shower. You say, "I'm never going back to the beach."

① delighted — sad
② excited — fearful
③ happy — annoyed
④ anxious — amazed
⑤ disappointed — joyful

06 * Which of the following <u>least likely</u> belongs to the underlined <u>explanations</u>? 2점

More than half of Americans routinely take prescription or over-the-counter drugs, but women tend to experience side effects at up to twice the rate of men, according to the U.S. Food and Drug Administration (FDA). The difference historically has been attributed to biological sex differences, but a new study published in *Social Science and Medicine* debunks that view, proposing instead a set of gender-based social factors that better explain observed disparities. "For a long time, the pattern in biomedical research has been to observe a sex disparity in outcomes, and to infer that this is due to biology," said Sarah Richardson, leader of the research team. "We would like to accelerate the consideration of social and other variables as factors in producing those disparities." The researchers used publicly available data from the FDA Adverse Event Reporting System, where people who are harmed by drugs can report incidents. Their gender hypothesis around the sex disparity in adverse drug events proposes a series of <u>explanations</u>.

① Women are more likely than men to engage in "health-seeking behaviors" as caretakers: for example, women more actively take prescription drugs or see a doctor.
② Women are more likely to face bias and discrimination in the clinic, negatively affecting the likelihood that they will be diagnosed with a condition or be treated properly.
③ Gender stereotypes, stigma, identities, and social norms influence how events are subjectively experienced, and women tend to take weight gain or hair loss as more serious adverse event than men do.
④ Genetic and hormonal differences between men and women contribute to many sex-specific illnesses and disorders, and treatments must take this into account.
⑤ Women are more likely than men to live in poverty, and to encounter sexual harassment and violence at home and work, all of which are associated with mental and physical health problems.

07[*] **Which of the following is stated or implied in the passage?** 1.5점

A soda lake is a lake with a pH value of more than the normal measure of 6 or 7, usually between 9 and 11. High carbonate concentration, especially sodium carbonate, is responsible for the alkalinity of the water. A soda lake may also contain a high concentration of sodium chloride and other salts making it saline or hypersaline lake. Soda lakes occur naturally in both arid and semi-arid areas. They are highly productive ecosystems compared to the freshwater lakes, and are therefore the most productive aquatic environment on Earth. Multicellular organisms such as brine shrimp and fish are found in plenty in the soda lakes. The microorganisms in these lakes are good sources of food for some of the animals including flamingos and other birds. Africa and Asia have the highest number of soda lakes since the two continents have vast desert conditions which are perfect for the formation of soda lakes. Lake Natron in Tanzania is one of the most outstanding soda lakes in Africa because of the high pH of water which is always about 12. The lake is a regular feeding ground for the majority of the 2.5 million East Africa's flamingos.

① The water of soda lakes has no sodium chloride.
② Soda lakes are likely to be formed in a dry climate.
③ The pH of the water in a soda lake is usually 6-7.
④ Freshwater lakes are better ecosystems than soda lakes.
⑤ Flamingos come to Lake Natron to seek alkalinity-free water.

08* Which of the following is stated or implied in the passage? 1.5점

Pink-haired Aitana Lopez is followed by more than 200,000 people on social media. While she posts selfies from concerts and her bedroom, brands have paid about $1,000 a post for her to promote their products on social media — despite the fact that she is entirely fictional. Aitana is a "virtual influencer" created using artificial intelligence tools, one of the hundreds of digital avatars that have broken into the growing $21 billion content creator economy.

Their emergence has made human influencers worry that their income is being shrunken due to digital rivals. The same concern is shared by people in more established professions that their livelihoods are under threat from generative AI-technology that can spew out human-like text, images and code in seconds.

Human influencers contend that their virtual counterparts should have to disclose that they are not real. "What freaks me out about these influencers is how hard it is to tell they're fake," said Danae Mercer, a content creator with more than 2 million followers. Many other markets are contending with the problem, with India being one country that forces virtual influencers to reveal their AI origins.

① Influencers are disrupting the market by overcharging.
② Brands are turning to AI-generated influencers for promotions.
③ Virtual influencers are becoming illegal in many countries.
④ Virtual influencers pose a threat to luxury brands.
⑤ Influencers have a lot of negative associations related to being fake or superficial.

09* Which of the following is <u>not</u> a fitting summary of the chef's tips to making the best pizza? 1.5점

A London-based pizza chef, Michele Pascarella, just won Global Pizza Maker of the Year. So what are his tips to making the best pizza in the world? Pascarella's restaurant rotates its menu throughout the year, using whatever ingredients are in season. "It's very important, because when you use seasonal ingredients, you pay less money and they're better," he says. Pascarella also believes the best pizzas only have a few ingredients. "When you do this kind of job, you learn to appreciate the simple ingredients," he said. "For good pizza chefs, the best plate is the simple one." If you're making it at home and don't have all the equipment a pizzeria has, he also has a tip for you: put a little more water in the dough. "If you use 1 kilogram flour, it's better to use 700 grams of water," he said. Interestingly, Pascarella says no fruit. "I don't really like pineapple on pizzas," he stresses. Sorry to all the pineapple-on-pizza fans. Lastly, "in this job, you never learn enough," he said. "Every day we can learn something." Pascarella said his goal is to keep making new pizza every day.

① Keep it simple
② Keep experimenting
③ Adjust for home cooking
④ Work with seasonal products
⑤ Believe in the power of fruits

10 Which of the following is <u>not</u> stated or implied in the passage? 2점

The Godzilla story began in 1954 with the release of the original film by Toho Studios. Since then, there have been 32 live-action films made in Japan and Hollywood, including "Godzilla vs. Kong." The first movie established that Godzilla was a dinosaur from the Jurassic period that lived in the Pacific Ocean and was mutated by American H-bomb testing in the South Pacific, becoming a monstrous and radioactive creature. The core narrative of the films had Godzilla attack Tokyo or other cities.

Then starting in the 1960's, Godzilla starts fighting other monsters that come from other islands in the South Pacific, emerge from the ocean, or invade from space. The subsequent movies follow a formulaic pattern: Godzilla fights other monsters, they destroy Japanese cities, and then Godzilla usually wins, making the world safe again. This has made Godzilla one of the most well-known icons globally, going from a dark and menacing presence to a heroic figure and protector.

① Godzilla films started out as a story of a national hero.
② Godzilla films have become popular outside Japan as well.
③ The image of Godzilla over time has changed substantially.
④ Almost always a Japanese city or two would get destroyed in a Godzilla movie.
⑤ There was an anti-American sentiment in the evolution of the Godzilla story.

11. Which of the following is the best place for the sentence in the box? 1점

For example, in ancient Greece the old year was represented by an old man, while a baby symbolized the upcoming new year.

One of the oldest and most universally observed traditions, New Year's Eve festivities are celebrated across a variety of social, cultural, and religious groups. A The earliest known records of New Year's celebrations can be traced back to the Babylonians and Assyrians of Mesopotamia about 2000 BCE. B Other ancient cultures celebrated the holiday with practices and symbols that are still used today. C Many cultures began to celebrate New Year's Eve on December 31 after the Gregorian calendar was established in 1582. D However, cultures that follow a lunar calendar celebrate the start of the new year at a different time, including February in Tibet and March or April in Thailand. E

① A   ② B   ③ C
④ D   ⑤ E

12* Which of the following does not fit in the passage? 1.5점

America has a new epidemic. It can't be treated using traditional therapies even though it has debilitating and even deadly consequences. The problem seeping in at the corners of our communities is loneliness. [A]Loneliness is detrimental to mental and physical health leading to an increased risk of heart disease, dementia, stroke and premature death. As researchers track record levels of loneliness, public health leaders are banding together to develop a public health framework to address the epidemic. [B]Loneliness occurs when the connections a person needs in life are greater than the connections he or she has. Some may experience psychological loneliness when they don't feel like they have anyone to confide in or trust. [C]Societal loneliness is feeling systemically excluded because of a group characteristic, including gender, race, or disability. Existential or spiritual loneliness comes from feeling disconnected from oneself. [D]Self-reported feelings of loneliness decreased to 34% in January 2023, and the problem is not as severe as it was during the pandemic. Loneliness is experienced throughout a person's lifespan and it can spiral as a result of trauma, illness and the effects of aging. [E]It can also be exacerbated by technology taking the place of human interaction, which helps explain why young people report the highest rates of loneliness.

① A   ② B   ③ C
④ D   ⑤ E

[13-14] Choose the best order for a passage starting with the given sentences in the box.

13* 1.5점

> Indigenous Peoples' Day is a holiday in the United States that takes place on the second Monday of October. The day honors the Indigenous peoples of the U.S. — American Indians, Native Alaskans, and Native Hawaiians, most of whom were violently uprooted and exploited beginning with the arrival of Europeans in the Americas. It celebrates diversity and also reflects on the historical mistreatment of Indigenous peoples.

A They have called attention to the violence that Columbus and his crew carried out against the Indigenous peoples. They have also noted the long-lasting impact of European colonization, which began with Columbus's voyages.

B In the 21ˢᵗ century many more states and cities have begun to observe Indigenous Peoples' Day on the second Monday in October, either in place of or in addition to Columbus Day.

C In recent decades, however, a growing number of Indigenous activists and their supporters have protested the holiday for ignoring the point of view of Indigenous Americans.

D Indigenous Peoples' Day arose as a response to Columbus Day, a holiday that commemorates the arrival of Christopher Columbus in the Americas in 1492. That holiday has celebrated the explorer for opening the New World to European settlement.

① B — A — C — D
② B — C — A — D
③ D — B — C — A
④ A — B — C — D
⑤ D — C — A — B

14* 2점

> As Gen Z grow up, their dollars matter more and more in the global economy. This generation, born between 1997 and 2012, represents an estimated $450 billion in spending power across the world — with $360 billion in the U.S. alone, according to some estimates.

Ⓐ Part of this choosiness is because of how much and how hard they're working to have discretionary income in the first place. Money is a daily concern for Gen Z, especially right now.

Ⓑ These young people not only have this money — experts say they're also willing to spend it, even amid a period of high financial anxiety. However, Gen Z's buying patterns are different than the generations that came before them.

Ⓒ They're not simply spending on whatever they want the moment they think of it; instead, they're being extremely deliberate with who gets their dollars, and when.

Ⓓ Not only are most of them still on entry-level salaries, but they are also having to stretch their paychecks during a period of spiking inflation and high cost-of-living.

① Ⓐ — Ⓑ — Ⓓ — Ⓒ
② Ⓓ — Ⓐ — Ⓒ — Ⓑ
③ Ⓑ — Ⓒ — Ⓐ — Ⓓ
④ Ⓒ — Ⓓ — Ⓐ — Ⓑ
⑤ Ⓑ — Ⓓ — Ⓐ — Ⓒ

[15-16] Read the passage and answer the questions.

Frederick Douglass was born into slavery in Maryland in 1818. The wife of Douglass' owner taught him to read and he began making contacts with educated free Blacks. He escaped to New York around age twenty and continued his self-education. In the early 1840s, the anti-slavery movement was gaining momentum. From 1841 to 1845, Douglass traveled extensively through the northern states, speaking on the injustice and brutality of slavery. Many Americans couldn't believe that such an eloquent and intelligent Black man had so recently been a slave. Douglass' *Narrative of the Life of Frederick Douglass*, written in 1845, recounts his own life experiences and emphasizes _____ as a significant means with which to bring down slavery. Douglass argues that slave owners — even those that present themselves as devout and pious — face a corruption of values that includes the effort to dehumanize enslaved people by keeping them illiterate and uneducated.

15* Which of the following is most appropriate for the blank? 1.5점

① law   ② labor   ③ religion
④ property   ⑤ education

16* Which of the following is <u>not</u> stated or implied about Frederick Douglass in the passage? 1.5점

① He ran away from his owner.
② He wrote an autobiographical book.
③ He made an anti-slavery public speech.
④ He was a slave from the moment he was born.
⑤ He supported devout and pious slave owners.

[17-18] Read the passage and answer the questions.

There are several possible explanations for why dairy fats may not be as harmful as previously thought — and may even be healthful. Among the various types of saturated fats that can be found in foods, dairy products contain certain ones that appear to be neutral or beneficial for health, including those linked to reduced risks of Type 2 diabetes and coronary heart disease. Milk fat is also naturally packaged in a unique structure called the milk fat globule membrane. Components of this structure can help bind cholesterol in the digestive tract, potentially improving blood cholesterol levels. It's also becoming clear that certain types of dairy foods may be better for you than others. _____, yogurt and cheese appear to be most associated with health benefits. This may be because both are fermented foods, which can supply good bacteria to your gut. They also contain other beneficial molecules made during fermentation, including vitamin K, which is linked to heart health. Harder cheeses like Cheddar and Parmesan also seem to result in a more gradual absorption of fats into the blood than softer cheeses and butter, which can help you feel fuller longer.

17* **Which of the following is most appropriate for the blank?** 1.5점
① However ② Rarely ③ For instance
④ Instead ⑤ Unfortunately

18* **Which of the following is stated or implied in the passage?** 1.5점
① Dairy fats can be beneficial for health.
② Low-fat milk is not better than whole milk.
③ Milk provides more beneficial bacteria than yogurt.
④ Harder cheeses are harmful to health.
⑤ Softer cheeses help us feel fuller longer.

[19-20] Read the passage and answer the questions.

Finding dead seals along California's coast is not new in itself. The marine mammals get sick, are stillborn or even wash ashore after being fatally struck by a boat. But decapitated seals? That was something new for North Coast ecologists. Again and again since 2015, the mysterious and gruesome deaths kept occurring, primarily involving harbor seal pups at MacKerricher State Park. Ecologist Frankie Gerraty started hearing about the decapitated harbor seals and tried to understand the phenomenon, only with clues, not any confirmation. "I went from domestic dogs to eagles... what is doing this?" he said. "It's my job to really be a(n) _____ and look into these carcasses and try to figure out what is going on with them." Actually, he had a hunch it could be coyotes because they spend a lot of time on beaches. But when he saw one of the headless seals up close, he thought the cut along the neck was too clean to be a coyote's work, and worried it might even be a human's. Then the video footage proved him wrong. A wildlife camera was set up near MacKerricher State Park, and Gerraty captured a coyote dragging a freshly killed seal into the camera view, proceeding to take its head off. So, researchers have finally solved the years-long mystery of the headless seals.

19 **Which of the following is most appropriate for the blank?** 1점

① artist   ② detective   ③ predator

④ priest   ⑤ undertaker

20 **Which of the following is stated or implied in the passage?** 1.5점

① Dogs killed harbor seal pups.

② Finding dead seals on the beach was an unusual event.

③ A coyote was on the researcher's list of potential culprits.

④ The head cut of the seals was done by a human.

⑤ A freshly killed coyote was captured in the video footage.

[21-24] Choose the most appropriate one for each blank.

21 1.6점

One of the ways we can rest is by _____. That means occasionally putting down the smartphone and closing up the laptop. Temporarily reducing our time in front of the screen, otherwise known as a digital detox, is good for our health. So in your free time, avoid the urge to check your work email every five minutes. If you're on a walk to the park or standing in line for a cup of coffee, avoid the temptation of pulling out your phone to check your social media pages. Just allow your mind to drift and see where it takes you.

① taking a short nap
② steering clear of the screen
③ avoiding a busy schedule
④ staying digitally connected
⑤ turning to the wilderness

22 2.2점

In the United States, cabbage will probably never be voted most popular vegetable — not even in winter when it's at its best. _____. The French like them so much that they call their sweethearts "petits choux," or little cabbages. In Greek mythology, cabbages sprang from the tears of Lycurgus, king of Thrace, after he was driven mad by Dionysus, god of wine; thus, they were considered a remedy for drunkenness. In Egypt cabbage was worshipped as a god and, to show their great respect for the vegetable, it was the first dish Egyptians touched at their banquets.

① Also, cabbages may be available year-round
② Yet cabbages are admired in other cultures
③ Likewise, cabbages vary in color and shape
④ There are a lot of nutritional benefits in cabbages
⑤ Few people like cabbages no matter how they are cooked

23 2.4점

The new world is dynamic and unpredictable. Old approaches will no more be efficient to meet the needs of the rising challenges. The research shows that currently, 21% of businesses have reported using their resources to _____ of their employees. Going forward, this can be the best possible time to learn new skills and adapt to the changing business environment. Despite the various challenges posed by emerging trends in business, the job seekers and graduates will have the necessary time to upgrade to these new skillsets that are highly in demand while going through the hiring process. However, one thing remains the same through all times: the commitment to lifetime learning.

① promote the re-skilling and up-skilling
② encourage the traditional knowledge
③ support the work-life balance
④ demand the lifetime loyalty
⑤ downsize the number

24 1.8점

When you hear stories of great warriors, typically they are stories about men. However, throughout history, there have been great women warriors who have Ⓐ_____ gender norms and fought for change in their communities. Fu Hao was a warrior from the Shang dynasty who lived during the 13th century BC. She was one of King Wu Ding's 64 wives and became the second most powerful person. From an early age, she had military training. One of Fu Hao's first battles was against the Tu Fang in Shang territory. Leading her troops into battle, she defeated the Tu Fang. Later she commanded the largest army in ancient Chinese history, with an estimated 13,000 men. She even had her own private troops. At the age of 33, she fell ill and died. Buried in the tomb with her are over 130 weapons that Ⓑ_____ her military strength.

	Ⓐ	Ⓑ
①	obeyed	refute
②	complied	prove
③	refused	contradict
④	shattered	demonstrate
⑤	authorized	bear witness to

25 Which of the following is the best title of the passage? 1.6점

When it comes to cold or COVID symptoms, there's something about a cough that can be very frustrating. A cough is uncomfortable, but it can also be disruptive when it just won't quit. A cough isn't necessarily something you should just shrug off. A simple way to ease a cough is with salt water. Salt can kill bacteria and it's also soothing. However, salt doesn't kill viruses, so it may not help you heal your cough faster. Ginger is well known for its power in calming an upset stomach. It can also work wonders for a cough. Pepcid, Prilosec, or other antacids can relieve acid reflux and mitigate any associated coughs. If you find it to be a chronic issue, making certain dietary changes may help, such as avoiding citrus, chocolate, high-fat foods and incorporating high-fiber foods into your diet, like brown rice, celery, and lettuce. You may also want to drink lots of water and keep your portions small at meals if your coughs are due to reflux.

① How To Eat Healthy
② Health Risks of a Cough
③ How To Get Rid of a Cough
④ Potential Triggers of a Cough
⑤ Differences between COVID and Cold

26 Which of the following is stated or implied in the passage? 2.2점

In 1888, the process of awarding the prestigious Bowdoin Prize began routinely: Harvard students anonymously submitted their best essays in hopes of receiving the honor and impressive sum of as much as $100. Contest judges also assessed essays submitted by female students at the University's "Annex" (later Radcliffe College), but the winners didn't receive University recognition or funds — an outside donor supplied an award of $30. The men's and women's papers were somehow submitted together that year, and a classics essay called "The Roman Senate Under the Empire" by E.B. Pearson received top prize. It was quickly discovered that Pearson was actually *Miss* E.B. Pearson. The faculty swiftly ruled out her piece for contention, and the runner-up (a man) received $75 in her stead. Pearson received the $30 Annex prize, "thus paying $70 outright for being a woman," according to a Boston Post newspaper article from the time.

① Pearson submitted the essay as an act of rebellion.
② In the 1888 contest, the first prize winner received $100 and the second $75.
③ Judges at first made a wrong assumption about the identity of the essay writer.
④ E.B. Pearson did not actually write "The Roman Senate Under the Empire."
⑤ The Boston Post newspaper article criticized the contest judges for awarding a woman too much money.

27 Which of the following best describes the mood of the passage? 2.2점

Danny got turned around with some difficulty and crawled back along the length of the concrete tunnel. He had just reached the end, the cold spill of light coming down from above when the snow did give in, a minor fall, but enough to powder his face and clog the opening he had wriggled down through and leave him in darkness. At the far end of the tunnel, Danny heard the stealthy crackle of dead leaves as something came for him on its hands and knees. At any moment he would feel its cold hand close over his ankle.

① relaxing   ② scary   ③ hilarious
④ boring   ⑤ depressing

28 **Which one refers to a different person from the others in the passage?** 1.8점

I donated a kidney to Ⓐa stranger. I can survive with just one so I didn't see any reason not to donate the other. People kept saying it was a crazy thing to do, or that it was too dangerous. Not everyone thinks like me, so not many people must be doing this, which made me more determined to help. I was in hospital for three days, sat on the sofa for one more, then got back to normal life. A month later, the hospital got an email from Ⓑa stranger, the person who received my kidney. "Hi, I'm the guy who has got your kidney," it said. You are told that whoever you donate to might not get in contact, so I wasn't expecting to hear from Ⓒhim but I was so happy that he was doing so well. We wrote a lot and got to know each other, I was fascinated to hear all about his life. My husband and I went down to meet him in Folkestone, where he was living with his wife, and we went for a swim in the sea and drank Champagne. I would have been happy for anyone to get my kidney, but it was the cherry on the top that it went to Ⓓthe nicest person and now we are good friends. In October, I ran the York marathon and Stuart came to support me and he met Ⓔmy dad, who now completely understands why I gave my kidney away.

① Ⓐ   ② Ⓑ   ③ Ⓒ

④ Ⓓ   ⑤ Ⓔ

29 **Which of the following is not stated about the wall in the passage?** 1.8점

The most massive construction project of Roman Empire in Britain was the huge northern frontier wall, started in AD 122 and some six years in the building. The great wall was the work of the emperor Hadrian, a patient and thorough man who spent half of his twenty-one-year reign systematically traveling the boundaries of his vast empire, sorting out problems. In Britain, Rome's problem was the warlike peoples in the north of the island whom the Roman army had found it impossible to subdue. Running seventy-three miles from the River Tyne on the east coast to the Solway Firth on the west, Hadrian's Wall was a huge stone-faced rampart with a succession of full scale frontier forts along its length.

① Who built it

② How it was built

③ How long it was

④ When it was built

⑤ Where it was located

30 What is mainly discussed in the passage? 1.6점

The symptoms of depression and burnout can be challenging to distinguish: both may cause you to sleep too much or too little, or to struggle to focus. But depression is a diagnosable medical condition, whereas burnout is not. With burnout, you might feel overwhelmed by unrelenting tasks at work, leading to feelings of cynicism, depletion and resentment of your job, which might cause a lack of energy for your hobbies. With depression, on the other hand, you might not find your hobbies enjoyable at all. Or you might isolate yourself or neglect your hygiene and physical health.

① How to overcome depression

② The physical signs of burnout

③ Steps to improve mental health

④ The effects of burnout on depression

⑤ Differences between burnout and depression

31 Which of the following is the best place in the passage for the sentence in the box? 2.2점

> The case with language is similar.

Imagine that you have stomachache and you go to the doctor. The doctor would ask you to describe your symptoms and also to describe the relevant background to your symptoms. You would probably be asked such questions as: When did the trouble start? Have you eaten anything that might have caused it? Has it affected your appetite? A By investigating the medical history relevant to your present state, the doctor can learn more about your stomachache. B I say relevant because obviously a doctor would not ask you such a question as: Has your big toe been hurting? C By investigating the history that is relevant to the present state of the English language, we can gain insight into the language, and we can begin to explain how it got to be as it is. D For example, we can explain why it is that we have such apparently crazy spelling; how it is that words come into existence; why it is that sometimes we seem to have a choice of words to express more or less the same thing; and so on. E By looking at how English has changed, and the factors that have influenced those changes, we can begin to answer questions like these.

① A   ② B   ③ C
④ D   ⑤ E

32 Which of the following does <u>not</u> fit in the passage? 2.4점

The response to the idea of work from home has been mixed among executives, with many claiming that less time in the office means less collaboration, weaker ties with colleagues, and fewer learning opportunities. It's an argument not without merit. According to a recent study called "The Power of Proximity to Coworkers," beneficial teamwork and important collaborations suffer when employees work from home. Moreover, younger employees, particularly women, may be hurt most by remote work. [A]<u>In the study, which focused on a group of software engineers at a Fortune 500 company, engineers working in the same building as all their teammates received a 23 percent more online feedback on their codes than engineers with distant teammates.</u> [B]<u>Young women engineers were especially more likely to ask follow-up questions when working in person, focusing on particular problems in their programming. In remote scenarios, that back-and-forth dynamic vanished.</u> [C]<u>The productivity of engineers working remote and away from the disruptions caused by co-workers nearby is surprisingly high which leads to more promotions, pay raises and top evaluations in the long run.</u> [D]<u>Their paper notes that going remote made engineers under 30 five times more likely to quit than when working in the same building as their co-workers, and female engineers four times more likely to quit.</u> [E]<u>The paper also identifies a tradeoff. For senior engineers, onsite work reduced coding output by 21 percent, possibly because more of their time was devoted to giving feedback to younger colleagues.</u>

① A   ② B   ③ C

④ D   ⑤ E

33 Which of the following is the best order for a passage starting with the given sentences in the box? 2.4점

> As social beings, humans are wired to forge strong bonds with groups that could help us survive against outside threats, research shows. It's a natural evolutionary impulse.

A For example, if someone sees a comrade in pain — a fellow member of one's group — the brain will react with empathy. "My brain would simulate the suffering of the other person by reactivating how I feel when I am feeling bad," Klimecki explains.

B But, instead, if it is an adversary experiencing pain, not only is the same empathetic region of the brain not as active, she says, "we also sometimes see more activation related to *schadenfreude*, that is, malicious joy."

C Olga Klimecki, a neurology researcher and lecturer at the University of Jena in Germany, says brain scans show how powerfully social identity can shape our emotional response to situations.

① A — B — C
② B — C — A
③ C — A — B
④ A — C — B
⑤ C — B — A

34 Which of the following is most appropriate for the blank? 1.6점

> Many professional window washers have some unusual stories to tell. A guy named Mirko working for Sunstruck Window Cleaning said about a time he was cleaning large panels of glass at an office that hadn't been cleaned for a long time: "When I had almost finished, one of the employees walked into the glass thinking there was nothing there, and broke his nose. It was funny and horrific at the same time. He was so embarrassed. To remedy the situation, I said to him: 'That's the best _____ you can give me.'"

① compliment   ② explanation   ③ advice
④ therapy   ⑤ offer

[35-36] Read the passage and answer the questions.

In a scene from the 1993 film *Jurassic Park*, two scientists who study fossils brush sand away from the skeleton of a Velociraptor. While the scene is full of iconic imagery, I would like to point out that it gets a few things wrong about what it's actually like to dig up dinosaurs. When you discover a dinosaur skeleton, you assess what material is already exposed. It would likely emerge that the skeleton is at least partially disarticulated, meaning that the various bones have been jumbled up and are not nicely assembled into a skeleton. It is highly unlikely that more than a small amount of the dinosaur's skeleton would even be preserved. When animals die, their soft tissue rots away, leaving behind a hard skeleton. However, <u>this leaves nothing behind to hold it together</u>. Scavenging animals, wind, and water move the bones around before they are covered with sediment and fossilized. The skeletons we find are almost never as neatly preserved as the Velociraptor in *Jurassic Park*.

35 **What is the writer most likely to be?** 1.6점

① an actor   ② a historian   ③ a park ranger

④ a film director   ⑤ a paleontologist

36 **What is the consequence of the underlined part?** 2.4점

① reinforcement   ② fossilization   ③ expedition

④ disarticulation   ⑤ arrangement

[37-38] Read the passage and answer the questions.

Boredom has a negative reputation for a reason. At work, it's often viewed as a counterproductive state that ignites discomfort, desperation for a new role, or perhaps simply a desire for the day to end. Boredom at work has been linked to risky decision-making, costly mistakes, and accidents triggered by inattention or lack of focus — and that's not to mention the fatigue that being bored can generate. Boredom can also incite other types of problematic behavior, such as "cyberloafing" (that is, non-work-related browsing) and childish emotional responses. Prolonged exposure to monotonous activities can even cause hallucinations. _____, one recent study found a linkage between boredom at work and burnout, as well as decreases in job satisfaction and increased desire to quit.

On the flip side, recent research shows that boredom — when handled constructively — has big "bright sides." Moments of boredom can offer a pause, or a short respite for your brain and body in a world designed to distract, overwhelm, and overstimulate. A sense of boredom can create the space to daydream, which can hatch creativity, new ideas, and innovation. Prolonged boredom can prompt you to reflect and ask yourself, "Am I on the right path? Am I doing the right thing?"

37 **Which of the following is most appropriate for the blank?** 2.4점
① In addition　　　② Otherwise　　　③ By contrast
④ Ironically　　　⑤ Regardless

38 **What is mainly discussed in the passage?** 1.8점
① The causes of workplace boredom
② The benefits of being bored at work
③ The problems of cyberloafing
④ The pros and cons of workplace boredom
⑤ The extent of monotony in workplace

[39-40] Read the passage and answer the questions.

> For the last 50 years or so, researchers have demonstrated that exposure to gas stoves can be harmful to humans. When you use a gas stove, it emits poisonous gases called nitrogen oxides, including nitrogen dioxide, a respiratory irritant thought to trigger asthma. A study published last year found that families who use gas stoves in homes with poor ventilation, or without range hoods, can blow past the national standard for safe hourly outdoor exposure to nitrogen oxides within just a few minutes; there are no agreed upon standards for nitrogen oxides in indoor air. Ⓐ Rates of nitrogen oxide emission levels were in direct proportion to the amount of gas the stove was burning. Ⓑ Another research suggested that gas-burning stoves may be linked to nearly 13 percent of childhood cases of asthma in the U.S. Ⓒ There's more data on how gas stoves affect children than there is on how they affect adults. The same research showed adults with asthma may also be susceptible to worsened symptoms. Ⓓ
>
> Experts say the average person should use caution with gas stoves, but these findings don't necessarily mean you will get sick. Some people may consider switching from a gas stove to an induction range when they are in the market for a new appliance. Ⓔ For those with a gas stove currently, here are a few simple ways to mitigate potential health risks.

39 **Which of the following is the best place in the passage for the sentences in the box?** 2.2점

In addition to asthma, there are other health dangers associated with gas stoves. Researchers who collected 234 samples of unburned natural gas from 69 homes around Boston found 21 toxic pollutants in the gas, including benzene.

① Ⓐ   ② Ⓑ   ③ Ⓒ
④ Ⓓ   ⑤ Ⓔ

40 Which of the following will be discussed right after the passage? 1.8점

① Results of exposure to gas stoves

② How to purchase kitchen appliances

③ Types of pollutants gas stoves emit

④ Merits of using an induction range

⑤ How to lower the health risks of gas stoves

CHUNG-ANG UNIVERSITY

중앙대학교   2024학년도 인문계 A형
▶▶ 40문항·60분

[01-07] 다음 문장의 밑줄 친 부분과 가장 가까운 의미를 지닌 것을 고르시오. 각 2점

01 As we walked together, she'd now and then <u>lurch</u> into me.

① stagger   ② jive

③ saunter   ④ glide

02 We manufacture in quality and, relatively speaking, in price the finest and best value <u>crockery</u> in the world.

① cutlery   ② dish

③ glassware   ④ silverware

03 If citizens respond in a negative way to what we are saying, we should be the last people to <u>reprehend</u> them.

① fulminate   ② approve

③ eulogize   ④ override

04 Development programs have been <u>vitiated</u> by the rise in population.

① vilified   ② accentuated

③ invalidated   ④ correctified

05 I am very happy to be able to provide you with this <u>victual</u>.

① ticket ② food

③ truce ④ freshet

06 The centurion found the wells in this area were <u>brackish</u>.

① gooey ② palatable

③ saline ④ soporific

07 The difficulties anticipated by the doctors at <u>parturition</u> did not materialize.

① diagnosis ② delivery

③ operation ④ postmortem

[08-09] 다음의 대화들 중 흐름이 가장 적절하지 <u>않은</u> 것을 고르시오. 각 2점

08 ① A: No one is likely to buy it anymore.

B: We'd better phase it out immediately.

② A: When are we going to open?

B: Christmas day. The schedule is tight, but we can pull this down.

③ A: Welcome to my office. How was the weather getting in?

B: I am in a hurry. Let's cut to the chase.

④ A: Is that pizza place legit?

B: Do you doubt it?

09 ① A: I have to wade through the hefty document.

B: That is right. You need to skim the surface of the subject.

② A: For her re-election, Sam must have pulled up her socks and decided to go the extra mile.

B: You bet. Every dog has its day.

③ A: I am sure I will hit the jackpot this time.

B: Wait. Don't count your chickens before they hatch.

④ A: He's fallen head over heels about her.

B: No wonder. She is a knockout.

10 For companies like FedEx, the ①<u>optimization</u> problem of efficiently ②<u>routing</u> holiday packages is so complicated that they often employ highly ③<u>specializing</u> software to find a solution. ④<u>No error</u>.

11 This concept was developed ①<u>in the 1970</u> by a group of Dutch women dissatisfied with ②<u>the increasing</u> importation of food and the decreasing number of farms and farmers in ③<u>their communities</u>. ④<u>No error</u>.

12 Lewis Rutherford ①<u>was educated</u> as a lawyer, and among his inventions ②<u>was a micrometer</u> for ③<u>the measure of</u> astronomical photographs. ④<u>No error</u>.

[13-20] 다음 빈칸에 가장 적합한 단어 및 구문을 고르시오. ^{각 2점}

13 He was sickened by _____ and panegyrics expressed by speakers who had previously been among the first to slander the man.

① anecdotes   ② stipends
③ encomiums   ④ homilies

14 Even though the king was a(n) _____ man, the sudden attack took him by surprise, and his resistance was short-lived.

① inane   ② germinal
③ congenial   ④ redoubtable

15 In 1633, the inquisition of the Roman Catholic Church forced Galileo Galilei to _____ his theory that the Earth moves around the Sun.

① recant   ② retard
③ beatify   ④ buttress

16 The cycles include a wide variety of factors that cause the economy to go from recession to _____ to recession over a period of years.

① anomaly
② obloquy
③ expansion
④ depression

17 The prominence of the independent filmmaker at this time underscores the fact that filmmaking largely remained an individual enterprise at the outset of the twentieth century, _____ the corporatist structure of film production that became synonymous with Hollywood and the studio system by the 1920s.

① removed from
② associated with
③ resulted from
④ collaborated with

18 Arriving in New Orleans days after Hurricane Katrina had passed and without an adequate number of vehicles of its own, the armed forces began to _____ any working form of transportation they could find.

① abrogate
② encumber
③ rehabilitate
④ commandeer

19 Some anthropologists contend that the ancient Egyptians switched from grain production to barley after excessive irrigation and salt accumulation made the soil _____ to grains.

① inhospitable
② acrimonious
③ evanescent
④ benignant

20 Because mercury has a variety of innocuous uses, including in thermometers and dental fillings, few people realize that it is one of the most _____ substances on the planet.

① congenital
② deleterious
③ antiquated
④ rudimentary

21 The government of Madagascar has recently designated portions of the territory and the surrounding islands as protected reserves for wildlife. Madagascar is home to a vast array of unique, exotic creatures. One such animal is the aye-aye. Initially categorized as a member of the order Rodentia, the aye-aye is more closely related to the lemur, a member of the primate order. Since the aye-aye is so different from its fellow primates, however, it was given its own family: Daubento-niidae. The aye-aye is perhaps best known for its large, round eyes and long, extremely thin middle finger. These _____ are quite sensible, allowing the aye-aye to be awake at night and retrieve grubs, which are one of its primary food sources, from deep within hollow branches.

① adaptations
② similitudes
③ prototypes
④ nomenclatures

22 By the late 1880s and early 1890s, Impressionism was a firmly established feature of the art landscape, familiar even outside France, and was continually attracting new followers. Its fate was that of every modern creative concept: on the one hand, traditionalists continued to combat the movement, accusing it of _____ aesthetic norms and, in the broadest of political terms, of undermining the existing order; on the other hand, Impressionism had itself become the target of newer movements with their own new scales of values. Any style is necessarily one-sided and will offer opponents a purchase if they choose to highlight its shortcomings. The Impressionists no longer saw any point in _____ with academic views in order to gain entry to the Salon. Indeed, certain aspects of the Impressionist programme had meanwhile _____ the art that was given official support.

① adhering to — aligning — mirrored
② embracing — opposing — contrasted
③ challenging — departing — superseded
④ abandoning — compromising — influenced

23 Medical practice at the beginning of the 17th century was still largely based on the system of medicine introduced by Hippocrates. This had been consolidated as a comprehensive theoretical system of treatment by Galen in the 2nd century. It was believed that disease was caused by the _____ of the body's four humours. Physicians examined their patients to determine which humour was in excess and prescribed accordingly. Many of the treatments involved bleeding, purgatives, diaphoretics and clysters (enemas) to rid the body of these _____ influences. It was not unusual for heroic treatment to further weaken an already weak patient, although presumably those of a more robust constitution took such medicine in their stride.

① proportion — neutral

② composition — natural

③ imbalance — noxious

④ alignment — beneficial

24 Microbes probably took root on land early in Earth history, but it is plants that changed the world, providing both food and physical structure for complex terrestrial ecosystems. Today, some 400,000 species of land plant account for half of Earth's photosynthesis and an estimated 80 percent of our planet's total biomass. Indeed, Earth's resplendent robe of green is such a _____ feature of our planet that it can be detected from space. In 1990, as NASA's Galileo spacecraft winged toward Jupiter, it trained its mechanical eyes on the distant Earth, revealing in our planet's reflected light a distinctive peak in the so-called Vegetation Red Edge. This signature arises because land vegetation strongly absorbs incoming visible radiation but reflects _____ wavelengths back to space. Visitors to the early Earth would have observed no such feature.

① lugubrious — radioactive

② clairvoyant — embellished

③ pervasive — infrared

④ indigenous — isotopic

25 The importance of language becomes evident when looking at names and terminology, which carry surprisingly strong meanings. For example, recent research shows that the language used to describe health threats can affect people's memory and risk perceptions. Furthermore, the words we choose can influence how well our listeners _____ new information. The use of figurative speech and metaphors, for example, can make abstract concepts easier to grasp.

① hand in   ② take in
③ give in   ④ barge in

26 Saltwater fish drink water through their gills, where it is _____ the bloodstream. Since seawater has a high level of salinity, saltwater fish are at risk of having too much salt in their system. This problem is overcome by using special cells in the gills and scales that excrete excess salt. The other main difficulty that saltwater fish face is that they dehydrate easily. The relative salinity of the seawater that surrounds them is much higher than the water inside their own body, so they are constantly _____ water through osmosis — the process by which water naturally goes from an area of low to high density. To make up for this, saltwater fish urinate infrequently, and in small and highly concentrated amounts.

① passed through — ensuring
② infiltrated in — inhaling
③ enlivened by — keeping
④ diffused into — losing

[27-28] 다음 글을 읽고 물음에 답하시오. 각 3점

To go into solitude, a man needs to retire as much from his chamber as from society. I am not solitary whilst I read and write, though nobody is with me. But if a man would be alone, let him look at the stars.

A The stars awaken a certain reverence, because though always present, they are inaccessible; but all natural objects make a kindred impression, when the mind is open to their influence. Nature never wears a mean appearance. Neither does the wisest man extort her secret, and lose his curiosity by finding out all her perfection. Nature never became a toy to a wise spirit. The flowers, the animals, the mountains, reflected the wisdom of his best hour, as much as they had delighted the simplicity of his childhood.

B When we speak of nature in this manner, we have a distinct but most poetical sense in the mind. We mean the integrity of impression made by manifold natural objects. It is this which distinguishes the stick of timber of the wood-cutter, from the tree of the poet. The charming landscape which I saw this morning, is indubitably made up of some twenty or thirty farms. Miller owns this field, Locke that, and Manning the woodland beyond. But none of them owns the landscape. There is a property in the horizon which no man has but he whose eye can integrate all the parts, that is, the poet. This is the best part of these men's farms, yet to this their warranty-deeds give no title.

C The rays that come from those heavenly worlds, will separate between him and what he touches. One might think the atmosphere was made transparent with this design, to give man, in the heavenly bodies, the perpetual presence of the sublime. Seen in the streets of cities, how great they are! If the stars should appear one night in a thousand years, how would men believe and adore; and preserve for many generations the remembrance of the city of God which had been shown! But every night come out these envoys of beauty, and light the universe with their admonishing smile.

27 위 글의 단락을 논리적 흐름에 맞게 순서대로 배열한 것으로 가장 적합한 것을 고르시오.

① B — A — C

② B — C — A

③ C — B — A

④ C — A — B

The layer of air next to the earth, which extends toward for about 10 miles, is known as the troposphere. On the whole, the troposphere makes up about 75% of all the weight of atmosphere. It is the warmest part of the atmosphere because most of the solar radiation is absorbed by the earth's surface, which warms the air immediately surrounding it. A steady decrease of temperature with increasing elevation is a most striking characteristic of this region, whose upper layers are colder because of their greater distance from the earth's surface and because of the rapid radiation of heat into space. Temperatures within the troposphere decrease about 3.5° per 1,000-foot increase in altitude. Within the troposphere, winds and air currents distribute heat and moisture. Strong winds, called jet streams, are located at the upper levels of the troposphere. These jet streams are both complex and widespread in occurrence. They normally show a wave-shaped pattern and move from west to east at velocities of 150 mph, but velocities as high as 400 mph have been noted. The influences of changing locations and strengths of jet streams upon weather conditions and patterns are no doubt considerable. Current intensive research may eventually reveal their true significance.

28 위 글을 통해 추론할 수 있는 것으로 가장 적합한 것을 고르시오.

① On average, the velocities in the jet streams within the troposphere are around 275 mph.

② The atmosphere is thicker than the remaining 25% of the troposphere for its proximity to the earth.

③ A jet plane will usually have its better rate of speed on its run from Seoul to Washington DC than the other way round.

④ At the top of Jungfrau, about 12,000 feet above the town of Interlaken in Switzerland, the temperature is usually 42° colder than on the ground.

While the 20th century was the century of physics, electronics, and communication, the years to come are considered to be mainly dominated by the biological revolution that already started in the second half of the 20th century as well as nanotechnology. It is an exciting new front that deals with minuscule nanometer-scaled assemblies and devices. Traditionally, miniaturization was a process in which devices became smaller and smaller by continuous improvement of existing techniques. Yet, we rapidly approach the limits of miniaturization using the conventional top-down fabrication tools. One of the key futuristic ways of making tiny machines will be to scale them up from _____. For that purpose, many lessons could be learned about the arrangement of nano-scale machines as occurs in each and every biological system. The living cell is actually the only place in which genuine functional molecular machines, as often described in futuristic presentations of nanotechnology, could actually be found. Molecular motors, ultrasensitive nano-scale sensors, DNA replication machines, protein synthesis machines, and many other miniature devices exist even in the very simple early pre-bacterial cells that evolved more than 3 billion years ago. When we climb higher on the evolution tree, the nanomachines of course become more sophisticated and powerful. Yet, only billions of years after life emerged, we are beginning to utilize the concepts of recognition and assembly that lead to the formation of nano-scale machines for our technological needs. On the other hand many principles and applications of nano-technology that were developed for non-biological systems could be very useful for immediate biological applications such as advanced sensors and molecular scaffolds for tissue engineering as well as long-term prospects such as *in situ* modifications at the protein and DNA levels.

While the fields of nanobiotechnology and bionanotechnology are very new, their prospects are immense. The marriage between biotechnology and nanotechnology could lead to a dramatic advancement in the medical sciences. It may well be a place in which many of the current diseases and human disorders will be eradicated. In a reasonable time-scale, cancer and AIDS may be regarded in the same way that polio and tuberculosis are being considered now. Genetic defects could be identified and corrected already even before birth. Nano-scale robots that may be inserted into our body could perform very complicated surgical tasks such as a brain surgery.

29 빈칸에 들어가기에 가장 적합한 것을 고르시오.

① the bacterial level　　② the physical level
③ the molecular level　　④ the atomic level

30 위 글을 통해 추론할 수 <u>없는</u> 것을 고르시오.

① The 21st century is dominated by biological revolution and nanotechnology, a shift from traditional sciences.

② Nanobiotechnology barely promises treatments for diseases such as cancer and AIDS, similar to the way cures were found for polio and tuberculosis.

③ Miniaturization approaches its limits; future technology focuses on nano-scale machine development.

④ Nano-scale robots and machines could revolutionize the medical technologies, performing intricate surgeries and cellular-level manipulations.

[31-32] 다음 글을 읽고 물음에 답하시오. 각 3.5점

In Baltimore, as in many communities with a lot of drug addicts, the city sends out a van stocked with thousands of clean syringes to certain street corners in its inner-city neighborhoods at certain times in a week. The idea is that for every dirty, used needle that addicts hand over, they can get a free clean needle in return. Ⓐ<u>In principle</u>, needle exchange sounds like a good way to fight AIDS, since the reuse of old HIV-infected needles is responsible for so much of the virus's spread. But, at least on first examination, it seems to have some Ⓑ<u>obvious limitations</u>. Addicts, for one, aren't the most organized and reliable of people. So what guarantee is there that they are going to be able to regularly Ⓒ<u>break into</u> the needle van? Second, most heroin addicts go through about one needle a day, shooting up at least five or six times — if not more — until the tip of the syringe becomes so blunt that it is _____. They need a lot of needles. How can a van, coming by once a week, serve the needs of addicts who are shooting up Ⓓ<u>around the clock</u>? What if the van comes by on Tuesday, and by Saturday night an addict has run out? To analyze how well the needle program was working, researchers at Johns Hopkins University began to ride along with the vans in order to talk to the people handing in needles.

31 빈칸에 들어가기에 가장 적합한 것을 고르시오.

① effective   ② useless

③ refined   ④ weighty

32 위 글에서 논지의 흐름상 가장 적합하지 <u>않은</u> 것을 고르시오.

① Ⓐ   ② Ⓑ

③ Ⓒ   ④ Ⓓ

The mental health movement in the United States began with a period of considerable enlightenment. Dorothea Dix was shocked to find the mentally ill in jails and almshouses and crusaded for the establishment of asylums in which people could receive humane care in hospital-like environments and treatment which might help restore them to sanity. By the mid 1800s, 20 states had established asylums, but during the late 1800s and early 1900s, in the face of economic depression, legislatures were unable to appropriate sufficient funds for decent care. A Asylums became overcrowded and prison-like. Additionally, patients were more resistant to treatment than the pioneers in the mental health field had anticipated, and security and restraints were needed to protect patients and others. Mental institutions became frightening and depressing places in which the rights of patients were all but forgotten.

These conditions continued until after World War II. At that time, new treatments were discovered for some major mental illnesses theretofore considered untreatable (penicillin for syphilis of the brain and insulin treatment for schizophrenia and depressions), and a succession of books, motion pictures, and newspaper exposés called attention to the plight of the mentally ill. B Improvements were made, and Dr. David Vail's Humane Practices Program became a beacon for today. But changes were slow in coming until the early 1960s. At that time, the Civil Rights movement led lawyers to investigate America's prisons, which were disproportionately populated by blacks, and they in turn followed prisoners into the only institutions that were worse than the prisons — the hospitals for the criminally insane. The prisons were filled with angry young men who, encouraged by legal support, were quick to demand their rights. C The young cadre of public interest lawyers liked their role in the mental hospitals. The lawyers found a population that was both passive and easy to champion. These were, after all, people who, unlike criminals, had done nothing wrong. And in many states, they were being kept in horrendous institutions, an injustice, which once exposed, was bound to shock the public and, particularly, the judicial conscience. Patients' rights groups successfully encouraged reform by lobbying in state legislatures.

Judicial interventions have had some definite positive effects, but there is growing awareness that courts cannot provide the standards and the review mechanisms that assure good patient care. D The details of providing day-to-day care simply cannot be mandated by a court, so it is time to take from the courts the responsibility for delivery of mental health care and assurance of patients rights and return it to the state mental health administrators to whom the mandate was originally given.

33 아래의 문장이 들어갈 위치로 가장 적합한 곳을 고르시오.

The hospitals for the criminally insane, by contrast, were populated with people who were considered "crazy" and who were often kept obediently in the place through the use of severe bodily restraints and large doses of major tranquilizers.

① Ⓐ   ② Ⓑ
③ Ⓒ   ④ Ⓓ

34 위 글의 제목으로 가장 적합한 것을 고르시오.

① Development of Mental Health Treatment in Correctional Facilities
② Reform of Asylums after the Civil Rights Movement
③ Long-term Care of the Mentally Ill for the Benefit of Community
④ Role of the Judicial Interventions in Improving the Mental Institutions

[35-36] 다음 글을 읽고 물음에 답하시오. 각 3.5점

By 1829 Lyell was beginning to formulate an idea that would occupy him all his life, namely that present day natural forces could explain all geological events and there was no need for catastrophes in the geologic past. Cuvier and Brongniart had published an important study of the sediments and fossils of the Paris basin in 1811. They saw that freshwater shells alternated with marine shells, and they interpreted this to be due to revolutions in Earth history, but Lyell thought the pattern could also be explained by slow alternation between freshwater and marine conditions. He saw a similarity between present-day Scottish lake sediments that he had studied earlier and the older Paris sediments, and saw no need to invoke Earth revolutions. His travels to volcanic areas in Italy led him to the same conclusion.

Lyell practiced law from 1825 to 1827 but poor eyesight suggested he needed a different career, and he chose geology. He was elected a fellow of the Geological Society in 1826. In 1828 he visited the Auvergne volcanic region in south-central France with Murchison. In 1831 he was appointed professor at King's College London where he lectured in geology, but did not remain there for long. His interests turned to publishing a book on geology, possibly for better financial gain compared to that of academia. He published the first edition of his most important work, *Principles of Geology*, in three volumes between 1830 and 1833; it was very popular among the general public and underwent twelve editions (the last edition being posthumous).

For Lyell, not only were presently operative causes able to explain past events, but _____. This made his book quite controversial, especially among catastrophists such as Sedgwick and Conybeare. Lyell also did not accept that the Earth was undergoing long-term cooling, which would have invalidated his uniformity of nature assumption. Lord Kelvin, the English physicist repeatedly pointed out that Lyell's view violated the second law of thermodynamics.

Charles Darwin and Lyell became good friends: "I saw more of Lyell than of any other man both before and after my marriage. His mind was characterized, as it appeared to me, by clearness, caution, sound judgment and a good deal of originality." Lyell welcomed Darwin's new theory on coral reefs but was much less enthusiastic about Darwin's natural selection theory in *Origin of the Species* (1859). For Lyell, the evolution of the species implied a progressive path which was inconsistent with his repetitive cyclic approach and his concept of uniformity in nature.

35 빈칸에 들어가기에 가장 적합한 것을 고르시오.

① he thought cataclysmic events played a significant role in the formation of the Earth's surface

② he implausibly maintained their intensity was the same as today

③ he firmly believed the laws that govern geologic processes had changed during Earth's history

④ he argued that the Earth had largely been shaped by sudden, short-lived, and violent events

36 위 글의 내용과 일치하지 <u>않는</u> 것을 고르시오.

① Lyell's view of constant past and present natural forces clashed with catastrophists and violated thermodynamics principles.

② Lyell argued that slow and continuous natural forces could explain Earth's geological history.

③ Lyell, initially a lawyer, became a renowned geologist and authored *Principles of Geology*.

④ Darwin and Lyell were close; Lyell admired Darwin's coral reef theory, agreeing with his concept of natural selection.

Let's ask the deceptively simple question, What is artificial intelligence? If you ask someone in the street, they might mention Apple's Siri, Amazon's cloud service, Tesla's cars, or Google's search algorithm. If you ask experts in deep learning, they might give you a technical response about how neural nets are organized into dozens of layers that receive labeled data, are assigned weights and thresholds, and can classify data in ways that cannot yet be fully explained.

A In 1978, when discussing expert systems, Professor Donald Michie described AI as knowledge refining, where "a reliability and competence of codification can be produced which far surpasses the highest level that the unaided human expert has ever, perhaps even could ever, attain." In one of the most popular textbooks on the subject, Stuart Russell and Peter Norvig state that AI is the attempt to understand and build intelligent entities. "Intelligence is concerned mainly with rational action," they claim. "Ideally, an intelligent agent takes the best possible action in a situation."

B What are the social and material consequences of including AI and related algorithmic systems into the decision-making systems of social institutions like education and health care, finance, government operations, workplace interactions and hiring, communication systems, and the justice system? There are a lot of issues on code and algorithms or the latest thinking in computer vision or natural language processing or reinforcement learning.

C Each way of defining artificial intelligence is doing work, setting a frame for how it will be understood, measured, valued, and governed. If AI is defined by consumer brands for corporate infrastructure, then marketing and advertising have predetermined the horizon. If AI systems are seen as more reliable or rational than any human expert, able to take the "best possible action," then it suggests that they should be trusted to make high-stakes decisions in health, education, and criminal justice.

D When specific algorithmic techniques are the sole focus, it suggests that only continual technical progress matters, with no consideration of the computational cost of those approaches and their far-reaching impacts on a planet under strain.

37 위 글에서 논지의 흐름상 가장 적합하지 <u>않은</u> 것을 고르시오.

① A ② B
③ C ④ D

38 위 글의 주제로 가장 적합한 것을 고르시오.

① The primary reason for focusing on AI's rational and intelligent action
② The various ways of defining and understanding AI as an intelligent system
③ The importance of human experts in managing AI systems
④ The computational impacts on AI's high-stakes decisions

It has been a long-held belief within the field of biology that our DNA is fixed and unchangeable. While environmental factors may cause us to gain weight, lose a limb, or contract a virus, our underlying genetic sequence will remain constant. ⒶHowever, this popular view among scientists is beginning to shift towards a more fluid definition of the human genome; a new subfield within genetics, epigenetics, is exploring how environmental factors can actually change the expression of our genetic code throughout the course of our lives.

Epigenetics is the study of heritable changes to the cellular phenotypes of the DNA sequence, changes that have occurred as a result of external environmental factors after conception. ⒷEnvironmental factors are able to stimulate a particular gene, switching it on or off or altering it in some way. Through cellular division, the changes to the gene then have the potential to be passed on as heritable traits in subsequent generations.

One way that scientists are delving into epigenetic inquiry is by studying heritability in animals. ⒸScientists have been able to show that when a rat is subjected to a stressful environment during pregnancy, epigenetic changes to the fetus can engender behavioral problems in the rat's progeny as they mature and reach adulthood.

Scientists are also using human twins to better understand epigenetics and a related process called DNA methylation. DNA methylation causes genes to be expressed either stronger or weaker. By testing DNA samples taken from identical twins, scientists are able to identify areas where DNA methylation has impacted the expression of a particular gene in the sequence. ⒹSince identical twins have identical DNA, creating a methylation profile for each twin allows scientists to account for any subtle to extreme differences in behavior, closing the window to understanding how epigenetic processes affect both our personalities and our genetic code.

Epigenetics is still in the nascent stages of its development as a field of biological study, but it is nonetheless an incredibly exciting and groundbreaking area. It throws a wrench into Darwin's theory of evolution since it demonstrates how evolutionary changes can occur within one generation instead of spanning thousands of years. The possibility of such rapid evolutionary changes has major implications for how we think of not only life on earth but also the power we have to impact it, for better or worse.

39 위 글의 흐름상 가장 적합하지 <u>않은</u> 것을 고르시오.

① Ⓐ   ② Ⓑ

③ Ⓒ   ④ Ⓓ

40 위 글의 내용과 일치하는 것을 고르시오.

① Epigenetics is a subfield of biological study focusing on the variability of heritability.

② Darwin's theory illustrates the way evolutionary changes go along with epigenetics.

③ DNA methylation profiles show where DNA structures have affected the environmental factors.

④ Biological changes are not determined by the function of DNA in both animals and humans.

한국공학대학교

2024학년도 인문계
▸▸ 40문항·60분

[별도 표기가 없는 문제는 2.5점]

[01-05] Choose the one that is closest in meaning to the underlined word(s).

01 The illustration had too much <u>redundant</u> detail. The artist should consider streamlining it to enhance its clarity and impact.
① deficient   ② superfluous
③ inadequate   ④ incompetent

02 Any attack by enemy soldiers will <u>hamper</u> the arrival of food rations for our troops.
① hinder   ② assist
③ facilitate   ④ decelerate

03 What others say and do is a <u>projection</u> of their reality and perception, not yours.
① scheme   ② operation
③ proposal   ④ manifestation

04 Today's business environment makes it impossible for organizations to afford to <u>squander</u> any resources. 3점
① dissipate   ② engender
③ assemble   ④ accumulate

05 North Americans often <u>hold off</u> a certain distance in conversation, which is about 21 inches apart found by studies. 2점

① cease   ② initiate

③ withdraw   ④ maintain

[06-08] Choose the one that best fills in the blank.

06 It's important for writers to avoid using excessive _____ in their work, as it can alienate readers who are not familiar with specialized terms.

① slang   ② jargon

③ parley   ④ altercation

07 In the midst of the intense pain, Maximilian's efforts to form coherent words were in vain; his unsteady movements led him to lean against the wall, fighting to remain upright. Maximilian tried to speak, but he could _____ nothing; he staggered, and supported himself against the wall.

① refer   ② verify

③ describe   ④ articulate

08 In a last-ditch effort, the suspect chose to _____ for mercy, hoping to avoid the maximum penalty.

① plead   ② require

③ demand   ④ litigate

[09-14] Choose the one that most grammatically completes the sentence.

09 An engineer wears a helmet of sensors — part of a brain scanner that requires _____.

① as almost much power as a nuclear submarine

② almost as much power as a nuclear submarine

③ as much almost as power as a nuclear submarine

④ as much as power as an almost nuclear submarine

10 I used to hold two assumptions: one, poor people are poor in part because they're uneducated and don't make good choices; two, they then need people like me to figure out what they need and get it to them. It turns out, the evidence says _____. Dozens of studies indicate that people use direct financial assistance to enhance their own lives in various ways, such as food, security, housing, healthcare, and education.

① besides   ② otherwise

③ likewise   ④ in the end

11 In 1989, 170 nations signed the Basel Convention to address the problem of the international trade in waste. The agreement required developed nations to notify developing nations of hazardous waste shipments coming into the country. Six years later, after pressure from environmental groups and developing nations, the Basel Convention _____ hazardous waste shipments to poor countries completely.

① modified banning

② was modified to ban

③ was to modify banning

④ was modified to be banned

12 _____ without loads of salt and butter, popcorn can be an excellent healthy snack that contains a surprising amount of nutrients.

① Preparing

② To prepare

③ When prepared

④ Unless you prepare

13 Predictive genetic testing poses ethical and practical dilemmas. Personally, I don't think knowing whether I have the potential to develop an incurable disease will, in any way, enhance the quality of my life, _____ interpret the genetic test results without the help of a medical professional.

① I nor would be able to

② nor would I be able to

③ nor I would be able to

④ I would nor be able to

14   Some British scientists suggest _____ a bottom-up method. This contrasts with their view of top-down approaches in the study of animal behavior.

① that they term
② which is termed
③ what they term
④ where they term

[15-16] Choose the one that is grammatically INCORRECT.

15   A few bones of Spinosaurus have been found in the deserts of Egypt and were described about 100 years ago by a German paleontologist. Unfortunately, ①all his Spinosaurus bones were destroyed in World War II. So all ②we're left with are just a few drawings and notes. From these drawings, we can see this creature, which lived about 100 million years ago, was very big and it had tall spines ③on its back, forming a magnificent sail, and it had long, slender jaws like a crocodile with conical teeth that ④may have used to catch slippery prey like fish.

16   I once worked with this woman who after 20 years of marriage and an extremely ugly divorce, was finally ready for her first date. Ten minutes into the date, the man stands up and says, "I'm not interested," and walks out. The woman was so hurt she couldn't move. All she could do ①was call a friend. Here's what the friend said: "Well, what do you expect? You have big hips, you have nothing interesting to say, ②why would a handsome, successful man like that ever go out with a loser like you?" Shocking, right, that a friend could be so cruel? But it would be much less shocking if I told you it wasn't the friend who said that. It's what the woman said to herself. We all start thinking of all our faults and all our shortcomings ③maybe not as harshly, but ④we all doing it. 3점

[17-25] Choose the one(s) that best complete(s) the sentence.

17   Apple first became the world's most valuable stock in 2011, when its market cap was under $340 billion and it comprised about 3.3% of the S&P 500. Since then, it has rarely _____ that title. It first reached $1 trillion in value in mid-2018, and it achieved a $2 trillion valuation in August 2020, making it the first US company to surpass that level.

① held   ② forfeited

③ waived   ④ involved

18   In this book, "everyday heroes" are not those that personify physical bravery. Though heroes such as firefighters are by no means less praiseworthy, I chose to feature passionate promoters of social justice and equality. Their work is humanitarian in nature. They are founders or leaders of successful nonprofits, representing a diverse range of _____ and people. Nearly all self-identify as social entrepreneurs.

① causes   ② cultures

③ sectors   ④ corporates

19   Many people fear failure and try to avoid it even when they have the opportunity to succeed. As a result, many people won't attempt something if they think they might fail. _____ their view so that failure is fine and nothing to worry about could be the key to opening new opportunities to be successful in life.

① Altering   ② Ignoring

③ Collecting   ④ Confirming

20   As K-pop continues its global ascendancy, it is expected to become even more diverse, with an increasing number of independent artists breaking into the scene. Despite the industry's rigid standards, K-pop artists are _____ norms through sophisticated subtexts and modern themes. 2점

① finding ways challenging

② to find ways challenging

③ finding ways to challenge

④ to find ways to be challenging

21 Most people around the world are right-handed. This fact also seems to have held true throughout history. According to studies, two right-handed parents have only a 9.5 percent chance of having a left-handed child, Ⓐ_____ two left-handed parents have a 26 percent chance. One simple idea suggests that people normally get right-handedness from their parents, and another common theory is that left-handed people suffer mild brain damage during birth. Ⓑ_____, if this theory were true, it would not explain why the percentage of left-handed people is so similar in every society. Whatever the reasons behind it, people's attitudes toward left-handedness changed a lot over the years.

① whereas — However
② yet — In addition
③ all the while — Therefore
④ because — On the other hand

22 Frequently, engineering students arrive at university armed with good qualifications. However, they are vague about the kind and quality of impact they can make on society when they leave three to four years later. One of the ways in which engineering education programs demonstrate _____ to society is in addressing pressing concerns, such as poverty alleviation and sustainable development in emerging nations. 3점

① relevance　　　　　② complexity
③ exclusivity　　　　④ profitability

23 Just what is a role model? First, let's recognize _____. It is not necessarily the smartest, strongest, or most successful person you know — although it could be. A role model is a person who has the characteristics you want for yourself and who can help you develop those traits.

① what it is
② what he is
③ what it is not
④ what he is not

24 Leo is immeasurably wise. He has so much knowledge and experience and is interested in so many _____ subjects, like Greek history, diamond mining, dinosaurs, and alternative medicine. Even though they are not related he enjoys them all. 2점

    ① diverse   ② academic

    ③ technical   ④ specialized

25 Modern Paris sits above limestone and gypsum. Over 2,000 years ago, the Romans were the first to mine these stones, leaving behind large holes in the ground and tunnels where the stones had been removed. In the beginning, these tunnels lay beyond the city limits, but as Paris grew, _____. In December 1774, a tunnel collapsed, swallowing houses and people.

    ① it dug deeper into them

    ② it was built around them

    ③ it spread out above them

    ④ more land was reclaimed

[26-40] Read the following passages and answer the questions.

Immortality has become commonplace. It has long departed the field of religion in which it appeared as the motive of the very first cults and therefore, the staple food of believers. In religious contexts, immortality often refers to the indefinite continuation of the soul or mind beyond physical death, a belief that has been a major point of focus and a source of comfort for many believers. However, immortality has acquired the dignity of a scientific subject, studied in laboratories attempting to understand the mechanisms of aging, hoping to control or neutralize them. It is now commonplace in the media to see explanations of the role of telomerase, the enzyme involved in the division of germ cells, to which the body turns for renewal. The opinion according to which senescence is a pathology that might soon be cured is increasingly pervasive — death is a simple disease that will be overcome with antioxidants and a careful diet. There is nothing natural about death, we hear, ever more frequently.

*senescence: 노쇠

26   **Which is the best title of the passage?**

① The Impact of Diet on Aging and Lifespan

② The Evolution of Immortality: From Religion to Science

③ The Path to Immortality: Antioxidants and Careful Diets

④ The Illusion of Death: How Science is Overcoming Aging

Medical practice was revolutionized by Hippocrates, the "father of Western medicine." Ⓐ He changed medicine in many ways. Ⓑ For example, he was an advocate for publishing medical knowledge, focusing on patient care rather than diagnosis, and demanding that physicians act professionally. Ⓒ That is, diet and living habits are linked to disease, and making modifications to them may help to reduce the occurrence or severity of certain diseases. Ⓓ Hippocrates' insights into the connections between environment, lifestyle, and health have had a lasting influence, laying the foundation for preventive medicine.

---

27   **Choose the most suitable position of the sentence below in the above passage.**

He also recognized that some diseases could be caused by the environment.

① Ⓐ   ② Ⓑ

③ Ⓒ   ④ Ⓓ

About a century ago, when General Motors had first proposed adding lead to petrol — in order to improve performance — scientists were alarmed. They urged the government to investigate the public health implications. Thomas Midgley, Jr., American engineer and chemist who discovered the effectiveness of tetraethyl lead as an antiknock additive for gasoline, breezily assured government officials that "the average street will probably be so free from lead that it will be impossible to detect it or its absorption," although he conceded that "no actual experimental data has been taken." General Motors funded a government bureau to conduct some research, adding a clause saying it had to approve the findings.

28 Which is implied in the passage about General Motors? 3점

① It was unaware of the potential dangers of lead in petrol.

② It actively suppressed evidence regarding the toxicity of lead in petrol.

③ It conducted thorough and unbiased research on the effects of lead in petrol.

④ It added a condition to research funding to approve findings before publication.

Toxicology is the science of adverse effects of chemical substances on living organisms. Living organisms include the algae in the sea, animals and people, all flora and fauna. There are no safe substances, all chemicals can be poisonous and cause injury or death. But they can be used safely: the effect depends on the dose and exposure. It is possible by limiting these to handle and benefit from the properties of chemical substances in an 'acceptably safe' way. Toxicological studies aim to assess the adverse effects related to different doses in order to find this 'acceptably safe' level.

---

29 Which is NOT suggested in the above passage?

① All chemicals can potentially cause poisoning and harm at certain doses.

② The effect of a chemical substance depends on the dose and exposure.

③ Toxicological studies aim to find an 'acceptably safe' level of chemical exposure.

④ Toxicology is the study of the beneficial effects of chemical substances on living organisms.

Artificial Intelligence (AI) is revolutionizing the way we live and work, with applications in various fields such as healthcare, education, and transportation. AI systems can learn, solve problems, and plan, imitating human intelligence and senses like visual perception and speech recognition. However, AI also presents challenges, such as the need to evaluate and recognize truth in the information it generates. As AI continues to evolve, it is crucial for individuals to develop critical thinking skills and learn how to verify the accuracy of information presented by AI systems. This will ensure that the benefits of AI are maximized while potential risks are minimized.

30 According to the passage, what should we do to utilize AI effectively?

① We should only use AI for simple, repetitive tasks and not for complex problem-solving.

② We should avoid using AI until it is perfected and can operate without any human oversight.

③ We should replace human decision-making with AI to ensure maximum efficiency in all sectors.

④ We should cultivate our ability to think critically and learn how to authenticate the information that AI systems provide.

Intellectual property rights (IPR) have been defined as ideas, inventions, and creative expressions based on which there is a public willingness to bestow the status of property. IPR provide certain exclusive rights to the inventors or creators of that property, in order to enable them to reap commercial benefits from their creative efforts or reputation. There are several types of intellectual property protection like patent, copyright, trademark, etc. IPR is prerequisite for better identification, planning, commercialization, rendering, and thereby protection of invention or creativity. Each industry should evolve its own IPR policies, management style, strategies, and so on depending on its area of specialty. Pharmaceutical industry currently has an evolving IPR strategy requiring a better focus and approach in the coming era.

---

31 What is the main purpose of IPR in the pharmaceutical industry?

① To restrict access to new drugs and treatments

② To promote sharing of all pharmaceutical innovations

③ To limit the types of intellectual property protection available

④ To enable inventors and creators to benefit commercially from their innovations

"From the time you're a baby to the time you die, you're an individual who wants to be recognized and respected," Hirami said. She says children start to understand this through their daily interactions with multiple age groups. This understanding shapes their social development and sense of self-worth throughout their lives.

32 **Which best explains the main idea of the above passage?** 2점

① A friend is known in necessity.

② Respect is a basic human need.

③ Empty vessels make the most sound.

④ Heaven helps those who help themselves.

While opinions differ wildly about what the ramifications for society will be if the human lifespan is extended, most ethicists agree that the issue should be discussed now, since it might be impossible to stop or control the technology once it's developed. "If this could ever happen, then we'd better ask what kind of society we want to get," Mike Callahan, an ethicist at Harvard University said, "We had better not go anywhere near it until we have figured those problems out."

33 **Which is implied in the passage?**

① The human lifespan will definitely be extended in the near future.

② The technology to extend the human lifespan is already developed and ready for use.

③ Most ethicists believe that the issue of extended human lifespan should be discussed now to avoid potential societal issues.

④ Mike Callahan believes that the technology to extend the human lifespan should be developed without considering the consequences.

34-35

Newspaper articles _____: some element of lying is inherent in all journalism because it is impossible for one article to include all the details of the story. Journalists may also manipulate the order in which they present information to achieve more drama or other effects in their writing. Choosing details and the order to describe them is considered proper and ethical behavior for journalists. Editors can even reflect their paper's political bias when writing opinion pieces about elections and politics.

34 **Which is true to the above passage?**

① Newspaper articles are always unable to convey the complete truth.
② All journalists are required to include every detail of a story in their articles.
③ Journalists are not allowed to manipulate the order of information in their writing.
④ Editors are prohibited from reflecting their paper's political bias in opinion pieces.

35 **Which is the most suitable for the blank?** 2점

① should try to be equitable
② should be read with scrutiny
③ can never tell the entire truth
④ can sometimes make fictitious stories

36-37

Scott's expedition brought back 40,000 scientific items, including almost 20 kilograms of rock. Of the 2,000 animal and plant species the expedition brought back, some 400 were new discoveries. The most important fossil, located next to Scott's body, was a tree from 250 million years ago. _____ running low on food, the explorers went in a different direction to enable them to find this fossil. The tree had only been found in Australia, Africa, and South America. So finding it in the Antarctic was proof that these countries and continents had all been joined together in the past.

36 Which is the most emphasized in the above passage?

① The role of teamwork in survival situations
② The physical hardships endured by Scott's team
③ The importance of scientific discovery in Scott's expedition
④ The significance of the tree fossil in proving continental drift

37 Which is the most suitable for the blank? 3점

① Under   ② Despite
③ At the cost of   ④ Instead of

38-40

[A] Moor has the essayist's gift for making new connections, the adventurer's love for paths untaken, and the philosopher's knack for asking big questions. With a breathtaking arc that spans from the dawn of animal life to the digital era, *On Trails* is a book that makes us see our world, our history, our species, and our ways of life anew.

[B] While thru-hiking the Appalachian Trail, Moor began to wonder about the paths that lie beneath our feet: How do they form? Why do some improve over time while others fade? What makes us follow or strike off on our own? Over the course of seven years, Moor traveled the globe, exploring trails of all kinds, from the miniscule to the massive. He learned the tricks of master trail-builders, hunted down long-lost Cherokee trails, and traced the origins of our road networks and the Internet. In each chapter, Moor interweaves his adventures with findings from science, history, philosophy, and nature writing.

[C] Throughout, Moor reveals how this single topic — the oft-overlooked trail — sheds new light on a wealth of age-old questions: How does order emerge out of chaos? How did animals first crawl forth from the seas and spread across continents? How has humanity's relationship with nature and technology shaped world around us? And, ultimately, how does each of us pick a path through life?

38 Choose the appropriate order of the paragraphs.

① [A] — [C] — [B]   ② [B] — [A] — [C]
③ [B] — [C] — [A]   ④ [C] — [A] — [B]

39 What did Moor explore during his seven-year journey?

① The history of the Appalachian Trail
② The techniques of master trail-builders
③ The origins of the Internet and road networks
④ The formation and evolution of trails and paths

40 Which is the best title of the passage?

① Trails: An Exploration of Paths and Life
② The Philosophy of Trails: A Global Exploration
③ The Evolution of Trails: From Ant Paths to the Internet
④ The Wisdom of Trails: A Journey Through Time and Space

HANKUK UNIVERSITY OF FOREIGN STUDIES

한국외국어대학교

2024학년도 T1 A형(서울 인문계 일반편입)
▶▶ 50문항·60분

[문항별 배점: 01-13 1점/ 14-17 1.5점/ 18-30 2점/ 31-40 2.5점/ 41-50 3점]

[01-04] Choose the one that best completes the sentence.

01 The soccer player is _____ in public because he doesn't like the sound of his own squeaky and annoying voice.
① bewildered
② laconic
③ affable
④ rubicund

02 The scientist's _____ approach to collaboration led to several missed opportunities to join a prominent research team.
① refractory
② buoyant
③ corporeal
④ miscellaneous

03 Not only should we _____ the junk that weighs us down, but we also need to get rid of anything that is not essential.
① atrophy
② emulate
③ jettison
④ subjugate

04 I did my utmost to _____ myself with her, for I knew that if anyone could obtain the information I required, she would do so.

① capitulate   ② ingratiate
③ apprehend   ④ conspire

[05-09] Choose the one that best replaces the underlined word.

05 They left the Arctic with an encouraging message to the world not to feel <u>despondent</u> about climate change but to take action.

① rapturous   ② spirited
③ opulent   ④ morose

06 He has somehow leapt to a higher plateau during the last few years — all the more amazing given his <u>precarious</u> health.

① boisterous   ② insecure
③ egregious   ④ exemplary

07 The queen's <u>grandiose</u> manner and regal bearing caused everyone in the room to fall silent the moment she entered.

① obsequious   ② courteous
③ erratic   ④ eminent

08 Most of us would have responded to the insult with outrage, but he understood that he must maintain his <u>composure</u> at all costs.

① eccentricity   ② poise
③ umbrage   ④ ferocity

09 The festival takes place during the warmest months of spring, which is considered the most <u>auspicious</u> time of the year.

① sinister   ② fortunate
③ strenuous   ④ formidable

10 The high court is <u>slated</u> to deliver its verdict later this month.

① criticized   ② covered

③ scheduled   ④ appointed

11 A maturity benefit is the amount you receive after your insurance policy reaches its <u>term</u>.

① semester   ② expression

③ agreement   ④ termination

12 Often the presence of <u>irregular</u> forces in conflict zones makes it difficult to differentiate soldiers from criminals.

① unofficial   ② discontinuous

③ asymmetrical   ④ nonconforming

13 As the sun dipped below the horizon, people strolled along the bustling streets, <u>lost</u> in the rhythm of urban life.

① stolen   ② defeated

③ squandered   ④ engrossed

[14-15] Choose the one that is closest in meaning to the given sentence.

14 The fan's being broken let the smoke hang still in the chamber.

① The fan malfunctioned as the smoke was let in the chamber.

② Only after the smoke had been let out of the chamber, the fan operated again.

③ The smoke lingered in the chamber because the fan was not operable.

④ It was not until the fan worked again that the smoke was let out.

15 I strongly doubt that the attorney is lying to save his client.

① Lying to save his client is something the attorney doubts, I feel.

② I suspect that the attorney is not telling the truth so he can save his client.

③ Telling a lie to save his client is not what the attorney is doing, I believe.

④ I think that the attorney knows that his client is not telling the truth.

[16-17] Choose the one that best completes the sentence.

16 There is always in the back of my mind _____ reach our enemies before we have won the battle.

① dread lest help should

② lest dread should help

③ lest should help dread

④ dread should help lest

17 It is well documented that this kind of infection is _____ from a fish.

① when contracted most severe

② severe when contracted most

③ most severe when contracted

④ contracted when most severe

[18-19] Choose the one that makes the sentence grammatically INCORRECT.

18 ①Engaging in interdisciplinary studies allows students ②to explore diverse ③fields of knowledge and may also ④prepare for the modern workforce.

19 ①Storm-scarred, the lighthouse softly ②whispers of wind and tide, ③their ancient skin ④bearing timeless tales.

[20-21] Choose the one that is grammatically INCORRECT.

20 ① When Sylvia broke off their relationship, he was visibly bereft.

② Kevin remains blissfully unaware that anything is amiss.

③ It is all a result of segregated communities where illiteracy is rife.

④ The standards for female beauty in Hollywood are utter.

21 ① I have not decided what I will do today to relieve my stress.

② What wrong you did in the past will always come back to haunt you.

③ Everyone agreed that he said was bordering on racism and politically incorrect.

④ I bet you would not criticize the painting if you knew that it cost a fortune.

[22-50] Read the following passages and answer the questions.

22-23

Big data is increasingly playing a role in trend forecasting and analyzing consumer behavior. Today, using big data is how brands build new strategies, by tailoring the online consumer experience and enabling the customer to lead the way. The fashion industry's major players are getting on the big data bandwagon. One front-runner is Amazon, which earlier this year made an attempt to determine how people measure up by asking for their sizes when they login for purchases. This massive collection of body types is basically a pool of big data, which is collected by Amazon in order to gain a better understanding of how bodies change over time. What this data can potentially do for online retailers is Ⓐ_____, especially since over 40 percent of returns happen just because the clothes don't fit. So, improving the chances that customers will have that much-desired "perfect fit" will make them more satisfied and drastically reduce the number of returns.

22 Which of the following is the major topic of the passage?

① Major front-runners in the fashion industry

② The application of big data in online fashion retail

③ Amazon's strategy for processing consumer complaints

④ The superiority of data-driven decisions in advertising

23 Which of the following best fits into Ⓐ?

① unprecedented

② obscure

③ aberrant

④ inconsequential

24-25

Understanding the process of simultaneous interpretation is a huge scientific challenge. Recently, however, a handful of researchers have taken up the task, and one region of the brain — the caudate nucleus — has caught their attention. The caudate nucleus isn't a specialist language area; neuroscientists know it for its role in processes like decision making and trust. It's like a(n) Ⓐ_____, coordinating activity across many brain regions to produce stunningly complex behaviors. This means the results of interpretation studies appear to tie into one of the biggest ideas to emerge from neuroscience over the past decade or two. It's now clear that many of our sophisticated abilities are made possible not by specialist brain areas dedicated to specific tasks, but by lightning-fast coordination between areas that control more general tasks, such as movement and hearing. Simultaneous interpretation, it seems, is a feat made possible by our interactive brains.

24 According to the passage, which of the following is NOT true?

① A few researchers are investigating the process of simultaneous interpretation.

② The caudate nucleus is involved in decision making and trust.

③ Movement and hearing are among the activities considered general tasks.

④ There is a specialist brain area dedicated to simultaneous interpretation.

25 Which of the following best fits into Ⓐ?

① orchestra conductor

② dedicated observer

③ neural surgeon

④ effective filter

"Shrinkflation" is the practice of reducing the size of a product while maintaining its sticker price. The "shrink" in shrinkflation relates to the change in product size, while the "-flation" part relates to inflation, the rise in the price level. Raising the price per amount is a strategy employed by companies, mainly in the food and beverage industries, to Ⓐ_____ boost profit margins or maintain them in the face of rising input costs. The primary reason for shrinkflation is the increase in production costs, including the commodity needed to make the product, fuel to run machinery, electricity to run the plant, and labor costs. Shrinkflation is basically a hidden form of inflation. Companies are Ⓑ_____ that customers will likely spot product price increases and so opt to reduce the size of their products instead, mindful that minimal shrinkage will probably go unnoticed. More money is squeezed out not by lifting prices but by charging the same amount for a package containing a bit less. Academic research has shown that consumers are more sensitive to explicit price increases than to package downsizing. However, this practice can result in negative consumer brand perceptions and intentions to repurchase the product and lead to static or declining unit sales volume over time.

26 Which of the following is the major topic of the passage?

① Definition and reasons for shrinkflation

② Signs of an economic slowdown

③ How companies invest profit margins

④ Academic research on shrinkflation

27 Which of the following ordered pairs best fits into Ⓐ and Ⓑ?

① explicitly — conscious

② stealthily — aware

③ slightly — oblivious

④ significantly — dubious

28-30

We don't choose our siblings the way we choose our partners and friends. Of course, we don't choose our parents either, but they usually make that up to us by sustaining us on the way to adulthood. Brothers and sisters are just sort of there. And yet, when it comes to our development, they can be more influential than parents. This holds whether they are older and cool, or younger and frustrating. Part of siblings' sway has to do with their sheer presence. Eighty-two percent of kids live with a sibling, a greater share than those who live with a father, and about 75 percent of 70-year-olds have a living sibling. For those of us who have brothers or sisters, our relationships with them will likely be the Ⓐ_____ of our life. Whether these relationships make our life better or worse is a more complicated question. On the upside, positive interactions with siblings during adolescence foster empathy, prosocial behavior, and academic achievement. When a sibling relationship is bad, however, it can make people more likely to be depressed and anxious in adolescence. Moreover, whether a person models herself after her siblings or tries to distinguish herself has particularly important consequences. One study found that siblings who felt positively about each other tended to achieve similar education levels, while those who spent unequal time with their dad and perceived unequal parental treatment had Ⓑ_____ educational fortunes.

28 Which of the following is the major topic of the passage?

① The anatomy of sibling dynamics at schools

② The influence of siblings on individuals' lives

③ The rivalry among siblings during adolescence

④ The relationship between siblings and parents

29 According to the passage, which of the following is true?

① Siblings are chosen in a manner similar to parents and friends.

② Sibling influence is usually attributed to their age and character.

③ The majority of 70-year-olds do not have siblings who are alive.

④ Siblings who felt negatively about each other tend to get anxious during adolescence.

30 Which of the following ordered pairs best fits into Ⓐ and Ⓑ?

① longest — diverging

② cornerstone — improved

③ disaster — unequal

④ enduring — fewer

31-32

Activity streaks are psycho-social phenomena. They require unchanging performance within temporal parameters, that is successful completion of a predetermined task within a specified time-frame. The person on a streak typically attributes their streak to their own volition and not outside pressure — although they may be competing with others to maintain their streak. If the person on the streak thinks the streak has not been broken and can also quantify its duration — i.e., can tell you how long the streak has been going on, then we can say they have an activity streak. Why is this important? Well, app designers have seized on this to establish a market presence and keep people using, and paying for, their apps. There are over 100 apps incorporating activity streaks. The app Duolingo, for example, counts the number of days in your language learning streak, but you set the standard for what counts as a "day" — 1 lesson, 15 minutes of study, or completing a level, it's up to you. Duolingo lets you compete with friends and follow others and it sends messages to your friends on major milestones such as a 100 day streak. Streaks are similar to habits but can be distinguished from them in that the former demands strategic planning and ceases if the behavior is not performed, while the latter relies on reflex-like responses to perform the task. Despite the appeal of habit-formation for minimizing thinking, streaks motivate individuals through the challenge of maintaining an unbroken sequence.

31 Which of the following is the major topic of the passage?

① How Duolingo keeps its customers

② The main characteristics of an activity streak

③ How predetermining your task demands strategic planning

④ The differences between streaks and motivation

32 According to the passage, which of the following is NOT true?

① Habits are similar to streaks but the latter is volitional.

② Duolingo allows you to set your streak's daily performance standard.

③ Competing with others is an essential element to streak formation.

④ Motivation to maintain an unbroken sequence keeps people using some apps.

33-34

You don't procrastinate because you are lazy, unorganized, or even stressed out. You procrastinate because you're unable to effectively regulate your own emotions — a trademark symptom of Attention Deficit Hyperactivity Disorder (ADHD). This is the finding from multiple research projects dedicated to studying procrastination. "To tell the chronic procrastinator to just do it is like telling a person with a clinical mood disorder to cheer up," say psychologists. Everyone procrastinates. People with ADHD aren't the only ones who stare at blank computer screens waiting for the keyboard to start typing automatically. Neurotypicals also stare into space and don't know how to begin. They, too, put off going to the dentist until their toothache is unbearable. They, too, push the tall stack of papers to the back of the desk. But those with ADHD are masters at task avoidance. While waiting for inspiration, they eat, binge-watch, scroll through social media and do other activities that soothe their aching soul. While everyone experiences the anguish of procrastination, the unfinished task may actually lead individuals with ADHD to experience physical and mental pain. Planning, prioritizing, motivating, organizing, and decision-making can cause a person with ADHD to become overwhelmed and shut down.

33 Which of the following is the major topic of the passage?

① Typical routines of people with ADHD

② Strategies for overcoming the habit of procrastination

③ Effects of procrastination on physical and mental health

④ The interrelation of procrastination and ADHD

34 According to the passage, which of the following is NOT true?

① Procrastination typically occurs when you are under stress.

② People that do not have ADHD also avoid beginning tasks.

③ Those with ADHD have difficulty controlling their emotions.

④ It is not helpful to tell the habitual procrastinator to get started.

35-37

If you've tried out ChatGPT, you'll surely have wondered what it will soon revolutionize — or, as the case may be, what Ⓐit will destroy. Among ChatGPT's first victims, holds one now-common view, will be a form of writing that generations have grown up practicing throughout their education, which has been the center of humanistic pedagogy for generations. If ChatGPT becomes able instantaneously to whip up a plausible-sounding academic essay on any given topic, what future could there be for the academic essay itself? "For years there have been programs that have helped professors detect plagiarized essays," says Noam Chomsky. "Now it's going to be more difficult, because it's easier to plagiarize. But that's about Ⓑits only contribution to education that I can think of." As the relevant technology now stands, Chomsky sees the use of ChatGPT as "basically high-tech plagiarism" and "a way of avoiding learning." He likens Ⓒits rise to that of the smartphone: many students "sit there having a chat with somebody on their iPhone. One way to deal with that is to ban iPhones; another way to do Ⓓit is to make the class interesting." That students instinctively employ high technology to avoid learning is a sign that the educational system is failing. Most technological disruptions leave both positive and negative effects in their wake. If the college essay is indeed unsalvageable, perhaps ChatGPT will finally bring about its replacement with something more interesting.

35 Which of the following is the best title for the passage?

① ChatGPT: High-Tech Plagiarism and How to Avoid it

② ChatGPT: Revolution in or Destruction of Education?

③ ChatGPT: Its Parallelism with the Advent of the iPhone

④ ChatGPT: Salvaging the Academic Essay

36 According to the passage, which of the following is NOT true?

① The academic essay has been regarded as vital to humanistic pedagogy for a long time.

② Many programs have been developed to detect writing that does not cite others' works properly.

③ Chomsky welcomes the rise of ChatGPT as it makes essay writing intriguing.

④ By using high technology, students tend to avoid learning, which indicates that the educational system is not working.

37 Which of the following is different from the others in what it refers to?

① Ⓐ   ② Ⓑ

③ Ⓒ   ④ Ⓓ

38-40

There is no doubt that music can soothe the soul for some, but it turns out that it could also be a temporary soother for physical pain. A small study invited 63 young adults to bring two of their favorite songs. The researchers also had the young adults pick one of seven songs that the team considered relaxing and were unfamiliar to the study participants. ⒶThey instructed the participants to stare at a monitor screen while listening to their favorite music and one of the seven relaxing instrumental songs. All the while, the researchers stuck a hot object on the participants' left inner forearms. When rating their experiences, people were more likely to report feeling less pain when listening to their favorite songs compared with hearing the unfamiliar relaxing song or silence. In order to determine which genre of favorite song reduced the pain the most, the researchers interviewed the participants about the favorite song Ⓑthey had brought and their rating of pain. The results showed that people who listened to bittersweet and moving songs felt less pain than when Ⓒthey listened to songs with calming or cheerful themes. People who listened to bittersweet songs also reported more chills — the thrill and shivers you get on your skin from listening to pleasurable music. This sensation was associated with lower ratings of unpleasantness elicited by the burning pain Ⓓthey felt in the experiment. While not thoroughly studied, the researchers said they thought those musical chills could be causing these pain-blocking effects. Still, there is nothing wrong with picking a more upbeat song if that is your preference. Music provides many other health benefits, including stress reduction and a good night's sleep.

38 Which of the following is the major topic of the passage?

① Different feelings between bittersweet and cheerful songs

② Numerous health benefits of upbeat songs

③ Pain-blocking effects of one's favorite song

④ Influence of musical chills on pleasantness

39 According to the passage, which of the following is true?

① Each participant was requested to listen to seven relaxing songs.

② The researchers stuck a hot object on the participants' right inner forearms.

③ Bittersweet songs generated thrills and shivers in the participants.

④ Calming songs were found to be the most effective soother for physical pain.

40 Which of the following is different from the others in what it refers to?

① Ⓐ   ② Ⓑ

③ Ⓒ   ④ Ⓓ

41-42

In the US, a "Stand Your Ground Law" is a law that allows people to protect themselves if they feel their lives are in danger, regardless of whether they could have safely exited the situation. A Stand Your Ground Law holds that ordinary people should not feel forced to leave premises they have every right to be in and allows them to use lethal force against a person if they feel that this other person is an imminent threat to their safety. The legality of a Stand Your Ground Law is rooted in home defense. For this reason, another name for it is the "Castle Doctrine," because the law allows people to do whatever they feel is necessary to protect themselves and their home, or "castle." This includes the use of deadly force, such as using a gun or knife to defend themselves, even if it results in a fatal injury. ⒶThis law protects those who choose to defend themselves and their property, even when there is a legitimate opportunity for a safe escape. While some US states limit a lethal response to situations when escape is impossible, states that uphold Stand Your Ground do not.

41 According to the passage, which of the following is true?

① Throughout the US, attempting to flee imminent danger is required before deadly force is permitted.

② A Stand Your Ground Law protects the rights of people who are in places they have no right to be in.

③ Deadly force is never permitted in states without a Stand Your Ground Law.

④ The underlying concept behind the Castle Doctrine is home defense.

42 According to the passage, which of the following can be inferred from Ⓐ?

① An intruder may legally shoot a homeowner who has shot at him.

② It is illegal for a homeowner to shoot if they can escape from an intruder.

③ A homeowner does not have to try to escape before shooting an intruder.

④ The homeowners prefer fleeing from an imminent threat to shooting.

43-44

According to the global news database Factiva, the first mention of "digital detox" was in 2006, but usage did not take off until 2010. In 2013, digital detox was added to the *Oxford Online Dictionary*, and by mid-2019, the total number of entries on digital detox in the database was rapidly approaching 9,000. The numbers and texts reflect that "smartphone overuse" and "restricting media use" have become talking points. The topic is discussed in social media, blogs, family gatherings, schools, and workplaces. New terms and aphorisms related to digital detox have enriched our vocabularies. FOMO has emerged as shorthand for a new condition: "Fear of Missing Out," a force presumably driving smartphone and social media use. JOMO is the opposite: "Joy of Missing Out," what digital detoxers strive for, a sense of enjoying life here-and-now and not through a screen. "Phubbing" is shorthand for mobile phone snubbing: using the phone to shut someone out. "Screen wall" is another way to say the same thing, and screen time is emerging as a central object of negotiation in families. Already in 2008, the UK Post Office was cited as saying that 13 million Britons suffered from "nomophobia" or "No Mobile Phobia," feeling stressed when their mobile was out of battery or lost. Digital detox is a relatively new term but stands in a long tradition of using medical vocabulary to talk about media use. Throughout history, media have been likened to infections, trash, and poison; digital detox is a metaphorical way to clean up.

43 Which of the following is the major topic of the passage?

① The origin of the concepts of digital detox and nomophobia

② The advent of the term digital detox and its related coinages

③ The process of metaphorical conceptualization of new medical terms

④ The need of restricting use of media and new terms among the young

44 According to the passage, which of the following is true?

① 13 million Britons suffered from JOMO in 2008, according to the UK Post Office.

② The use of the term digital detox reached its peak in 2010.

③ The term digital detox did not exist in the Oxford Online Dictionary in 2006.

④ FOMO is the primary motivation for reducing smartphone use.

45-47

The "Barnum effect" refers to the tendency to accept generic statements as accurate personal descriptions, particularly when they are flattering. The Barnum effect is named for the nineteenth-century US showman P.T. Barnum because it incorporates two of his famous dictums: "My secret of success is always to have a little something for everyone" and "There's a sucker born every minute." A typical Barnum-effect statement may be detailed or appear specific, but in fact will be vague, ambiguous, and even self-contradictory and thus, Ⓐ_____. Whether they are aware of it or not, the phenomenon is a major trick of astrologers, psychics, and fortune tellers. The effect was first demonstrated in 1949 in an experiment by US psychologist Bertram Forer, who gave college students personality profiles supposedly based on a test they had taken earlier. In fact, the profiles were composed of statements taken from astrology books, and all the subjects got the same list. Asked to rate on a scale of zero to five the degree to which the description reveals the basic characteristics of their personality, the subjects gave an average rating of more than four out of five, demonstrating the Barnum effect. However, knowing about the Barnum effect doesn't mean you can easily resist it. Yet, the best advice psychologists can offer is to be aware of the effect and try not to give in to flattery.

45 Which of the following is the major topic of the passage?

① The co-optation of the Barnum effect in flattery

② The origin of the term Barnum effect and its applications

③ The principle of the Barnum-effect statements by astrologers

④ The relationship between the Barnum effect and the entertainment industry

46 According to the passage, which of the following CANNOT be inferred?

① It would be difficult not to give in to flattery recognizing that the Barnum effect has been invoked.

② The participants in Forer's experiment suffered psychological damage from the experiment.

③ Fortune tellers tend to use typical Barnum-effect statements as they are pertinent to anyone.

④ The personality profile statement "You have a tendency to be generous" elicits the Barnum effect.

47 Which of the following best fits into Ⓐ?

① applicable to everyone

② useful for psychologists

③ unfavorable to astrologers

④ customized to the individual

Spoken "uhs" and "ums" have long intrigued psychologists and linguists, because people tend to say them without deliberation. Sigmund Freud pioneered the examination of speech errors for insight into a person's unconscious self; George Mahl, a psychiatrist, continued this tradition in the 1950s, tying the emotional states of patients to their "uhs," "ums," and other so-called disfluencies. Later, in the 1980s, psycholinguists began using disfluencies to study how the brain produces language. Now come data showing that uses of "uh" and "um" seem to be patterned along social lines. American linguist Mark Liberman reported that, according to his analysis of transcribed phone conversations, women say "um" 22 percent more frequently than men do, while men say "uh" more than twice as often as women do. In addition, dialectologist Jack Grieve made headlines. By mapping 600 million tweets, he found a preference for starting sentences with "um" in regions including New England and the upper Midwest; in an area stretching west to Arizona, "uh" was dominant. Grieve speculates that "um" may be somewhat more polite than "uh." If so, perhaps the northeastern preference for "um" is simply an expression of a regional formality. But at the same time, he admits this is a hunch. Herb Clark, a cognitive psychologist cautions that the stories big data tells about language are provisional. Data can show us what people are saying and writing, but not why. As data proliferate and computing becomes ever faster, we can expect more and more headlines about smaller and smaller grains of lexical sand. But only controlled experiments will explain what is behind the data and Ⓐ_____.

48 Which of the following is the best title for the passage?

① Unveiling Linguistic Patterns: "Uh" and "Um"
② Mapping Gender Linguistic Differences: From Freud to Big Data
③ Between the Lines: Introspective Aspects of Speech Disfluencies
④ How to Correct Unconscious Speech Disfluencies

49 According to the passage, which of the following is NOT true?

① Individuals often utter "uhs" and "ums" without conscious thought or intention.
② According to Grieve, "um" sounds politer than "uh."
③ Grieve found regional differences in Americans' use of "uhs" and "ums."
④ Big data enables us to elucidate the underlying reasons for what we say.

50 **Which of the following best fits into Ⓐ?**

① keep big data from ultimately becoming big noise

② prioritize speculative interpretations over rigorous analysis

③ decrease the frequency of speech errors

④ compensate for the shortcomings of brain studies

HANKUK
UNIVERSITY
OF FOREIGN STUDIES

한국외국어대학교

2024학년도 T2-1 B형(서울 인문계 학사편입/글로벌 인문계 일반·학사편입)
▶▶ 50문항·60분

T2-2(글로벌 자연계 일반·학사편입)
▶▶ 영어 25문항, 수학 20문항·90분

인문·자연계 공통 영어문제 별도 * 표시

[문항별 배점: 01-13 1점/ 14-17 1.5점/ 18-30 2점/ 31-40 2.5점/ 41-50 3점]

[01-04] Choose the one that best completes the sentence.

01 When voting for someone, what matters most is what he has done, not his illustrious political _____.

① pedigree　　　　② meritocracy
③ inquisitiveness　④ mediocrity

02* A confused defense left an attacker wide open for an easy goal — which felt, in some ways, _____ of the two teams' difference in caliber.

① enigmatic　　　② emblematic
③ systematic　　　④ pragmatic

03* Vines threatened to engulf the buildings in greenery, and grass to _____ on the flower plots.

① condense　　　② encroach
③ embark　　　　④ ponder

04* The malicious rumors were spread deliberately to _____ the band's reputation and harm their recording company's bottom line.

① ascertain
② debut
③ scathe
④ amputate

[05-09] Choose the one that best replaces the underlined word.

05* This adds <u>credence</u> to the argument that mastery of certain sentence structures is not wholly a function of age or language exposure.

① temerity
② scruple
③ imprudence
④ reassurance

06 The old woman's <u>effervescent</u> personality brought a warm spark to every room she entered.

① bubbly
② reserved
③ belligerent
④ impetuous

07* Looking at the new calendar, it's that time of year to <u>speculate</u> what awaits this tired world in the New Year.

① irradiate
② prognosticate
③ arraign
④ ameliorate

08 Eliminating monthly subscriptions, eating out less, and buying used items are tips for leading an <u>abstemious</u> life.

① indulgent
② prosperous
③ harmonious
④ spartan

09* The court personnel perceived that the presence of cameras in the courtroom made the participating attorneys' actions more <u>flamboyant</u> than usual.

① soporific
② refined
③ ostentatious
④ inconspicuous

10[*] Poor external rotation in the shoulder is a good <u>index</u> of whether or not the rotator cuff muscles need rehabilitation.

① list   ② sign

③ finger   ④ number

11[*] Until 1949, nearly everyone with a close connection to the United Kingdom was classified as a British <u>subject</u>.

① topic   ② citizen

③ proposition   ④ participant

12 The medical investigators made a special focus on injuries in victims of <u>blunt</u> object assault.

① curt   ② candid

③ brusque   ④ dull

13 The committee was <u>charged</u> with improving the current educational system.

① accused   ② lunged

③ entrusted   ④ loaded

[14-15] Choose the one that is closest in meaning to the given sentence.

14 A great deal of effort has been expended in trying to do what has proved to be impossible.

① People made a lot of effort but failed because the job could just not be done.

② A lot of effort has been made to improve the situation with regard to the trial.

③ People invested a lot of effort to understand the things that could be identified.

④ No effort has been put forth because people realized it was impossible to accomplish.

15 Hardly had they reached Edinburgh than they were ordered to return to London.

① As soon as they were told to come back to London, they had not reached Edinburgh.

② It was not long before they were ordered to return to London that they had left for Edinburgh.

③ Shortly after they were ordered to come back to London, they had to reach Edinburgh.

④ The moment they had arrived at Edinburgh, they had to come back to London.

[16-17] Choose the one that best completes the sentence.

16 Excessive engine oil burning is often the consequence of _____.

① a more severe engine performance issue

② more performance issue a severe engine

③ a severe issue engine more performance

④ performance issue a more severe engine

17 I _____ the boy tampering with the lock on the door to the storage room.

① noticed not to have pretended

② have noticed not pretended to

③ pretended not to have noticed

④ have not pretended to noticed

[18-19] Choose the one that makes the sentence grammatically INCORRECT.

18 I was not ①surprising that the writer was feeling ②discouraged after ③all the criticism he ④had received on his new novel.

19 The didactic nature of children's literature is something ①that scholars continue ②to study as the argument remains ③as to whether authors act more as teachers ④and artists.

[20-21] Choose the one that is grammatically INCORRECT.

20[*] ① At that time, my partner objected to taking the trash out.

② When it comes to playing computer games, he's the best.

③ Plastics are often used to making a wide range of materials.

④ What do you say to joining us for supper in a couple of days?

21 ① She didn't know how valuable it was.

② I'd forgotten what a difficult route it was.

③ That depends on how much we have to pay.

④ He didn't insist what progress they had made.

[22-50] Read the following passages and answer the questions.

22-23

Known as the "Sun King" for the magnificence of his fashions, Louis XIV made the wig an essential accessory at his court for men and women alike. Once established at court, wigs became standard among high-ranking professional groups, such as judges, priests, and the like. To meet growing demand, the number of master wigmakers boomed in France during Louis XIV's reign. In Paris, it increased from 200 in 1673 to 945 in 1771. In the provinces, journeyman wigmakers traveled around the country as well, and soon ordinary people began wearing wigs, to the consternation of the upper classes. At the heart of wig economics was the hair itself. Higher priced wigs used women's hair because of its length and the belief that it was of higher quality than men's. Traders at fairs would buy hair from peasant girls. Blond or silver-gray hair was often in high demand, followed by black. Naturally curly hair was the most valuable of all. With so many wigs to make, French artisans bought hair from all around Europe. This continued until the profound social changes that took place as a result of the French Revolution brought the fashion for wigs to an end.

22 According to the passage, which of the following is true?

① Louis XIV called for simpler hairstyles at court.

② In Paris, the number of journeyman wigmakers reached 945 in 1771.

③ Wealthy French women favored imported wigs with straight hair the most.

④ The upper classes disliked the fact that ordinary people began wearing wigs.

23 According to the passage, which of the following CANNOT be inferred?

① The price of wigs differed depending on hair color.

② Peasant girls could earn money by selling their hair.

③ The styles of wigs were different between men and women at court.

④ Attitudes toward wigs altered drastically after the French Revolution.

24-25

One of the most impressive differences across languages is the ways that they locate things in space. Some languages, like English, tend to prefer to use an egocentric frame of reference. For instance, if you're taking a tour of a model home, the realtor might motion toward the bay windows and say, "And on your right is one of the most delightful features of this home." The phrase "on your right" has to be interpreted from your perspective. If you were facing another way or if you were in another place, it would refer to a totally different region in space, which is why it's called egocentric. However, not all languages work like this. Some languages use geocentric systems, which don't refer to your position, for locating things in space. There are different types of geocentric systems; the cardinal directions we use (north, south, east, west) are one example, but others include "uphill" versus "downhill" or "uptown" versus "downtown."

24 Which of the following is the best title for the passage?

① How Languages Express Directions Differently

② Why Different Languages are Perspectivized Differently

③ How Geocentric Systems Work in Different Languages

④ Where Egocentric and Geocentric Systems Come From

25* According to the passage, which of the following is true?

① Egocentricity is the default system among languages.

② "Uphill" and "downhill" are examples of egocentric expressions.

③ Geocentric perspectives refer to different directions depending on your position.

④ Cardinal directions are one type of geocentric system that some languages use.

26-27

In recent decades, discussions about the shortcomings of traditional education have led to various reforms and alternative approaches. The advent of technology has further revolutionized schooling, through the integration of digital tools, online learning platforms, and personalized education plans. While the goals of schooling have remained Ⓐ_____ — to impart knowledge, foster critical thinking, and prepare individuals for societal roles, the methods and structures continue to Ⓑ_____. The ongoing dialogue surrounding education highlights the importance of adaptability and innovation in meeting the diverse needs of learners in the 21st century. Understanding the historical context of schooling systems provides insight into the challenges and opportunities faced by educators today. As we navigate the complexities of a rapidly changing world, the quest for effective and inclusive education remains a constant, driving force in shaping the future of schooling.

26* Which of the following is the best title for the passage?

① The Ceaseless Quest for Better Schooling

② A Historical Lens on School Educators

③ Integration of Technology in Education

④ The Revolution of Alternative Schooling

27* Which of the following ordered pairs best fits into Ⓐ and Ⓑ?

① versatile — reverse

② consistent — evolve

③ sterile — transform

④ static — stagnate

28-30

The famous French philosopher Denis Diderot lived nearly his entire life in poverty, but that all changed in 1765. Diderot was 52 years old and his daughter was about to be married, but he could not afford to pay the dowry. Despite his lack of wealth, Diderot's name was well-known because he was the co-founder and writer of *Encyclopédie*, one of the most comprehensive encyclopedias of the time. When Catherine the Great, the Empress of Russia, heard of Diderot's financial troubles, she offered to buy his library from him for £1000, which is approximately $50,000 US dollars. Suddenly, Diderot had money to spare. Shortly after this lucky sale, Diderot acquired a new scarlet robe. That's when everything went wrong. Diderot's scarlet robe was beautiful. So beautiful, in fact, that he noticed how out of place it seemed when surrounded by the rest of his common possessions. The philosopher soon felt the urge to buy some new things to match the beauty of his robe. He replaced his old rug with a new one from Damascus. He decorated his home with beautiful sculptures and a better kitchen table. He bought a new mirror to place above the mantle and a luxurious leather chair. These Ⓐ_____ purchases have become known as the "Diderot Effect." The Diderot Effect states that obtaining a new possession often creates a spiral of consumption which leads you to acquire more new things. As a result, we end up buying things that our previous selves never needed to feel happy or fulfilled.

28 Which of the following is the best title for the passage?

① How Sudden Wealth Improves your Life
② Coordination and Unity in Interior Design
③ How Buying Leads to More Buying
④ The Philosophical Meaning of Material Consumption

29 According to the passage, which of the following is true?

① Diderot became rich and famous by publishing an encyclopedia.
② The Empress of Russia bought Diderot's books, enabling him to pay the dowry.
③ Purchasing the beautiful scarlet robe made Diderot happy and content.
④ Diderot replaced his kitchen table with a new one from Damascus.

30 Which of the following best fits in Ⓐ?

① conventional   ② rational

③ premeditated   ④ reactive

31-32

Personal color analysis aims to assign individuals flattering colors that can inform their choices around clothing, makeup, and accessories based on their complexion and skin tone. The process can take 60 minutes, with color consultants draping hundreds of fabric swatches across clients' shoulders to carefully examine what makes their faces light up rather than emphasize dark circles or wrinkles. For decades, it's been used by politicians, chief executive officers, and the social elite as a way to put their best feet forward. Now, on the heels of a TikTok craze, it's sprouting up from California to New York, and Gen Z loyalists are increasingly making trips to Seoul with the procedure topping their bucket list. In the US, a session in Brooklyn, New York, can cost $545, whereas in Korea, most studios' rates hover from $80 to $160. In any event, clients emerge with personal, customized palette swatches, specific makeup recommendations, and suggestions for what kind of jewelry to buy. The craze around personal color was booming before Covid-19 hit South Korea. Now it's resurging along with international visitation. For Koreans, the tourism boom brings an added benefit: big retail spending. Customers often walk out with color swatches in hand and recommendations to buy specific skin-care and makeup products, along with an itch to overhaul their wardrobes. The boom may create jobs, too. As the spike in demand reveals a need for more practitioners, more and more color consulting workshops are available at Korean job fairs, and companies like the Korea Fashion Psychology Institute are offering certification programs for color consulting.

31 Which of the following is the major topic of the passage?

① Personal color analysis and its benefits for Korean industries

② The importance of personal color for politicians and executives

③ The ongoing development of post-Covid tourism in Korea

④ TikTok's role in fueling the personal color craze in Korea

32 According to the passage, which of the following is NOT true?

① A personal color analysis takes about an hour, using hundreds of swatches.

② Personal color analysis first became popular in Korea after Covid-19.

③ Korean studios charge less for a personal color analysis than those in New York.

④ More international customers are now visiting Korean studios.

33-34

Voting for a loser isn't just mentally taxing. The day before and the day of the 2008 general election, researchers gathered multiple saliva samples from voters. Ⓐ<u>Among men, but not women, who voted for a losing candidate, testosterone plummeted once the election results were announced, to a degree expected of actual contestants in a competition, rather than vicarious participants.</u> Backing a losing candidate can also damage Ⓑ_____. An analysis of surveys from 1964 to 2004 found that over time, voters who supported losers were less likely than others to see the electoral process as fair. They also tended to be less satisfied with democracy generally. Notably, in 2004, the loser's supporters rated their satisfaction with democracy 0.55 on a scale of 0 to 1, compared with the winner's supporters' 0.77 rating. This disaffection is magnified when voters are startled by a loss. Among voters who backed losing candidates in Canada's 1997 federal election, 72 percent of those who weren't surprised remained satisfied with democracy, versus just 57 percent of those who were surprised.

33* Which of the following is closest in meaning to Ⓐ?

① Men backing a losing candidate experienced a testosterone drop similar to active competitors.

② The testosterone levels of men and women increased to that of actual contestants.

③ The relationship between voters and candidates is similar to that of participants and observers of a competition.

④ After the election, voters' testosterone levels reached as high as those of contest observers.

34[*] **Which of the following best fits into Ⓑ?**

① the integrity as citizens in a democracy

② the satisfaction of voters with the candidate

③ voters' trust in the political system

④ the emotional health of the voters

35-37

Waiting in line is a scourge of modernity. According to David Andrews' book, *Why does the Other Line Always Move Faster?* it wasn't common until the Industrial Revolution synchronized workers' schedules, causing lines that gobbled up lunch hours and evenings. Given that Americans are estimated to collectively waste tens of billions of hours a year in lines, it's no wonder that some people try to cut, and others bitterly resent them. Yet jumping the queue without inviting violence is possible. Here are some pointers, based on social science. First, pick the right queue. It's virtually impossible to cut the line for a once-in-a-lifetime event — the Chicago Cubs playing the World Series, say. But in a repeating scenario like a security line, people are more likely to let you in, perhaps because they anticipate needing a similar favor someday. Using game theory to determine what conditions would make line-cutting socially permissible, researchers found that people queuing just once display little tolerance for line-cutting. But when the queue repeats, people let in intruders who claim an urgent need or who require minimal service time. Bribing can also work, and it may not even cost you. In one study, queuers were offered cash by an undercover researcher if they'd let the researcher cut. A majority agreed, but oddly, most of them then refused the cash. They appreciated the offer not out of greed, but because it proved the intruder's desperation. The person directly behind an intrusion usually gets to decide whether to allow it, according to a study co-authored by the psychologist Stanley Milgram. If that person doesn't object, other queuers tend to stay quiet. The experiment also found that two simultaneous intruders provoked greater ire than one — so if you're going to line-jump, Ⓐ＿＿＿＿.

35 Which of the following is the best title for the passage?

① How to Avoid Intruders in Lines

② The Historical Roots of Line-Waiting

③ Navigating the Art of Line-Cutting

④ A Social Analysis of Time Expenditure in Queuing

36 According to the passage, which of the following is NOT true?

① Queuing was not prevalent before the Industrial Revolution.

② It was found that people queuing once are less tolerant of line-cutting.

③ Most of the queuers in the study accepted cash and let the intruders in.

④ If the person behind the intruder gives permission, the other queuers usually do not complain.

37 Which of the following best fits into Ⓐ?

① travel solo

② apologize sincerely

③ pay for your impoliteness

④ cut in front of your friends

About five years ago, the Metropolitan Museum of Art (the Met) took a small step that has proved monumental: It stopped entreating visitors not to use their cellphones. The decision was driven by the recognition that cellphones are omnipresent in modern society, and fighting them is a losing battle. "People ask me what our biggest competition is," says Sree Sreenivasan, the Met's chief digital officer. "It's not the Guggenheim; Ⓐit's not the Museum of Natural History. It's Netflix. It's *Candy Crush*." Accepting that cellphones are here to stay has led museums to think about how they can work with the technology. One way is to design apps that allow visitors to seek out additional information. The Brooklyn Museum, for example, has an app through which visitors can ask curators questions about artworks in real time. Museums including the Guggenheim and the Met have experimented with beacon technology, which uses Bluetooth to track how visitors move through galleries and present them with additional information through an app. Beacons have the potential to offer detailed histories about works, and directions to specific paintings or galleries. Sreenivasan points out that once museum apps incorporate GPS technology, visitors will be able to plot their path through galleries just as they now plan their commute on Google Maps — no more getting lost in the Egyptian wing or staring at a paper map in search of a particular Monet sunrise.

38 Which of the following is the best title for the passage?

① Museums Invite you to Turn on your Phones

② Cellphones have Revolutionized Modern Art

③ Technology Connects Museums with Each Other

④ Museums Announce a Battle with Modern Distractions

39 According to the passage, which of the following is true?

① About a decade ago, the Met began allowing visitors to use their smartphones.

② The Museum of Natural History adopted beacon technology.

③ Visitors can ask curators questions through an app at the Brooklyn Museum.

④ Visitors plotted their way through the galleries using Google Maps.

40 Which of the following is closest to what Ⓐ refers to?

① The Guggenheim
② The biggest competitor
③ The Metropolitan Museum of Art
④ The chief digital officer

41-42

The battery pack of a Tesla Model S is a feat of intricate engineering. Thousands of cylindrical cells with components sourced from around the world transform lithium and electrons into enough energy to propel the car hundreds of kilometers, again and again, without tailpipe emissions. But when the battery comes to the end of its life, its green benefits fade and problems begin. If it ends up in a landfill, its cells Ⓐ_____, including heavy metals. And recycling the battery can be a hazardous business, warn materials scientists. If you cut too deep into a Tesla cell, or in the wrong place, it can short-circuit, combust, and release toxic fumes. That's just one of the many problems confronting researchers who are trying to tackle an emerging problem: how to recycle the millions of electric vehicle (EV) batteries that manufacturers expect to produce over the next few decades. Current EV batteries are really not designed to be recycled. That wasn't much of a problem when EVs were rare. But now the technology is taking off. Several carmakers have said they plan to phase out combustion engines within a few decades, and industry analysts predict at least 145 million EVs will be on the road by 2030, up from just 11 million last year. So, now people are starting to realize this is an issue.

41[*] According to the passage, which of the following is true?

① To make an EV battery requires predominantly locally sourced items.
② Last year, 11 million EV batteries were recycled.
③ Some car companies are planning to stop making combustion engines.
④ Slicing a Tesla cell open is a relatively safe process.

42* Which of the following best fits into Ⓐ?

① can be replaced with core materials

② will need recharging and repair

③ absorb pollutants from the landfill

④ can release problematic toxins

43-44

Art influences society by changing opinions, instilling values and translating experiences across space and time. Research has shown art affects the fundamental sense of self. Painting, sculpture, music, literature, and the other arts are often considered to be the repository of a society's collective memory. Art preserves what fact-based historical records cannot: how it felt to exist in a particular place at a particular time. Art in this sense is communication; it allows people from different cultures and different times to communicate with each other via images, sounds, and stories. Art is often a vehicle for social change. It can give voice to the politically or socially disenfranchised. A song, film, or novel can rouse emotions in those who encounter it, inspiring them to rally for change. Researchers have long been interested in the relationship between art and the human brain. For example, in 2013, researchers from Newcastle University found that viewing contemporary visual art had positive effects on the personal lives of nursing home-bound elders. Art also has Ⓐ<u>utilitarian influences</u> on society. For example, there is a demonstrable, positive correlation between schoolchildren's grades in math and literacy, and their involvement with drama or music activities. As the National Art Education Association points out, art is beneficial for the artist as an outlet for work. Art not only fosters the human need for self-expression and fulfillment; it is also economically viable. The creation, management and distribution of art employs many. So, what are you waiting for?

43 According to the passage, which of the following is NOT true?

① Art can inspire people to make a change in society.

② Interest in the connection between the brain and art is a new field of study.

③ Elderly nursing home patients benefited from viewing art.

④ Students who are involved in drama have higher grades in math.

44 **Which of the following is closest in meaning to Ⓐ?**

① practical benefits

② conservative effects

③ aesthetic values

④ theoretical implications

45-47

Sometimes we see things as human because we're lonely. In one experiment, people who reported feeling isolated were more likely than others to attribute free will and consciousness to various gadgets. Ⓐ_____, feeling kinship with objects can reduce loneliness. When college students were reminded of a time they'd been excluded socially, they compensated by exaggerating their number of Facebook friends — unless they were first given tasks that caused them to interact with their phone as if it had human qualities. The phone apparently stood in for real friends. At other times, we personify products in an effort to understand them. One US study found that three in four respondents cursed at their computer — and the more their computer gave them problems, the more likely they were to report that it had "its own beliefs and desires." When we personify products, they become harder to cast off. After being asked to evaluate their car's personality, people were less likely to say they intended to replace it soon. And anthropomorphizing objects is associated with a tendency to hoard. So how do people assign traits to an object? In part, we rely on looks. On humans, wide faces are associated with dominance. Similarly, people rated cars, clocks, and watches with wide faces as more dominant-looking than narrow-faced ones, and preferred them — especially in competitive situations. An analysis of car sales in Germany found that cars with grilles that were upturned like smiles and headlights that were slanted like narrowed eyes sold best. The purchasers saw these features as increasing a car's friendliness and aggressiveness, respectively.

45* **Which of the following is the major topic of the passage?**

① The importance of psychology in an industry

② The tendency of humans to personify objects

③ Positive effects of personification on marketing

④ The problems of people's attachment to products

46* According to the passage, which of the following is true?

① According to a study, those who experienced problems with computers were not likely to treat them as humans.

② After evaluating their cars' personalities, the owners decided to replace them.

③ People prefer narrow-faced products to wide-faced ones.

④ In Germany, cars with human-looking features sold the most.

47* Which of the following best fits into Ⓐ?

① In turn

② Otherwise

③ To make matters worse

④ This notwithstanding

48-50

James Madison, one of the Founding Fathers of the United States, asserted, "It is the reason, alone, of the public, that ought to control and regulate the government." However, the means for government officials to hear from the people are limited. Elected officials receive input either electronically or at town halls, and some agencies occasionally ask for public comments on complex regulations. Still, Americans express very low levels of confidence that they influence the policymaking process or that elected officials understand the views of the people. With developments in AI, this situation is growing worse. AI, Ⓐ_____ as citizens, can generate vast numbers of communications to policymakers. When the Federal Communications Commission took public comments on whether to retain the net neutrality policy, the New York Attorney General later found nearly 18 million of the 22 million comments were fabricated, using generated fake names, or real names without consent. The largest portion of fake messages was generated by the broadband industry, which wanted fewer regulations. Among the genuine comments, 98.5 percent favored retaining net neutrality. In addition, researchers recently sent 32,398 emails to legislative offices, some written by citizens, others generated by AI, which can deliver thousands of letters that sound genuine in seconds. The study found legislative offices could not discern which were fake. We are just seeing the beginning of what will become a flood of false input Ⓑ_____ genuine input and further undermining public confidence. So what can be done? It may be that the collapse of a flawed system requires not a superficial repair, but a major upgrade.

48 **What is the main purpose of the passage?**

① To describe how to discern AI fabrications from genuine input

② To warn about AI controlling public opinion

③ To ask Americans to use reason when voting

④ To demonstrate a potential problem with net neutrality

49 **According to the passage, which of the following is true?**

① AI was used by an industry to argue for more regulations.

② Over 20 million fake messages were sent to the Commission.

③ Americans have great faith that they influence their elected officials.

④ The majority of genuine comments to the Commission wanted net neutrality.

50 **Which of the following ordered pairs best fits into Ⓐ and Ⓑ?**

① regulating — generating

② masquerading — drowning

③ posing — highlighting

④ overcoming — overwhelming

KOREA AEROSPACE UNIVERSITY

한국항공대학교

2024학년도 인문계 (항공운항과, 항공교통물류학부, 경영학부)
▶▶ 30문항·60분

자연계
▶▶ 영어 공통, 수학 20문항·영어 60분, 수학 60분

[01-05] Choose the word that is closest in meaning to the underlined expression. 각 3.1점

01 The euro approached <u>parity</u> with the U.S. dollar for the first time in over a decade.
① paucity
② disparity
③ equality
④ division

02 As <u>ingenious</u> as we humans may be, the natural world is smarter.
① clever
② inept
③ inexperienced
④ opulent

03 She is not a big fan of social media because she does not like to draw <u>undue</u> attention to herself.
① poor
② excessive
③ green
④ fair

04 It is an austerity program, demonstrating how to get by while <u>scrimping</u>.
① skimping
② squandering
③ dissipating
④ enjoying

05 The circumstance leads one to consider the much-mooted question as to how far it may be accepted as <u>veracious</u> history.

① boundless   ② deceptive

③ factual   ④ quarrelsome

[06-10] Choose the one that best completes the sentence. 각 3.3점

06 Epistemologists argue about the exact nature of knowledge and understanding, but a few commitments are widely shared. One is that knowledge involves true beliefs, at least as a necessary (if not sufficient) condition. I can't know that humans have 30 chromosomes (because it isn't true). And if someone doesn't believe that humans evolved through natural selection, we wouldn't say that she knows it (even though it's true). A second common set of commitments is that understanding goes beyond knowledge in being more _____ (it requires seeing how different pieces of information fit together) and in being more functional (it requires being able to work with the information in some way). The authors use these common commitments to develop the following baseline definition of understanding: One understands a subject(issue, concept, theory, …) only if one grasps how a constellation of facts relevant to that subject are related to one another (causally, inferentially, explanatorily, etc.) in such a way as to be able to make new connections or draw new inferences with novel information. As a result, the object of understanding is always a body — and never a single piece — of information.

① diverse   ② implicit

③ physical   ④ holistic

07 In his new book, Goldfarb explains how roads and cars are changing the lives of wildlife all over the world — and how roadkill has created a crisis for biodiversity. For species like ocelots and Florida panthers and tiger salamanders, roadkill is a true existential threat. Roadkill is not only eliminating animals, it's in many cases eliminating those healthy animals that populations need to remain strong. _____ the issue of roadkill, highways are cutting off animals from their sources of food and their migration paths, while traffic noise drowns out their ability to communicate with each other. Amid these challenges, Goldfarb says, certain species have made remarkable adaptations. He notes that Chicago's coyotes allegedly look both ways before crossing the street and use crosswalks at red lights. We think about roads as these forces that are universally or exclusively harmful to animals, and certainly they're incredibly destructive. But wildlife is also incredibly adaptive and clever and they're finding ways to make a living in our midst.

① For ② Beyond
③ Lest ④ Albeit

08 The Federal Aviation Administration says it's steadily preparing for air taxi travel to become a reality — at least, at some point. In May, the agency released an updated blueprint for airspace and procedure changes to accommodate this type of aircraft. Joby Aviation bills itself as providing a "faster, cleaner, and smarter way to carry people through their lives," with "a green alternative to driving that's bookable at the touch of an app." But, experts say, that doesn't necessarily mean this kind of transportation is going to be available to just anyone who wants to spend less time in rush hour traffic. It's a great innovation for those with means. But, the industry faces challenges from noise to NIMBY concerns. There's also the optics: Rich people flying above the rest of us normal folks. Because this type of transportation will likely mainly be provided by private sector companies, there are concerns that it will exclude low-income people. _____ there will be funding mechanisms to make this an affordable option to all, integrating it into existing transit systems, it will not be accessible to all.

① Unless ② Once
③ Only if ④ Because

09 Exercise is an elixir. There's a solid body of evidence linking physical activity to improved moods. A previous study found that people who exercise regularly report fewer days of bad mental health. And a recent meta-analysis found that physical activity was more effective than medications in reducing symptoms of depression. Antidepressant medicines tend to be faster in treating an episode of depression. But physical exercise has more _____ effects than an antidepressant does. For some people, medication gives them a benefit in the beginning, but then it fades over time, whereas a lifestyle change can have a more permanent and lasting effect. Researchers use a range of evidence-based recommendations and tools, from medicines to therapy to behavioral approaches including fitness, nutrition, sleep and stress management, to help empower patients.

① acute　　　　　　　　　② durable
③ resilient　　　　　　　　④ inexpensive

10 After World War II, the focus of demographic scholars and policymakers shifted from worries about too few babies to fears of too many — specifically in poor countries. Many of these thinkers were based in the United States. In 1968, Paul R. Ehrlich published the best-selling book *The Population Bomb,* in which he warned that overpopulation would soon lead to mass starvation. Birth control became a cornerstone of aid policy. They were saying that we should focus aid on what they called 'the walking wounded' who could be saved. This way of thinking was very prevalent in the 1970s and that was the time when the Chinese leadership was considering its new population policy. _____, when China declared in 1980 that most Chinese families would only be permitted to have one child — and would be punished for violating the law — this was absolutely not occurring in a vacuum. When the one-child policy was unveiled, it didn't even face much international criticism. The program had a lot of apologists in the West. It was seen as not only acceptable but as pioneering.

① In contrast　　　　　　② What is worse
③ Instead　　　　　　　　④ In other words

[11-12] Choose the one that is either ungrammatical or unacceptable. 각 3.8점

11 As a species, who are we? Are humans innately hostile and violent toward people who belong to communities other than our own? Or are we inherently friendly and cooperative? These are difficult questions ①<u>to crack</u> open. Over the years, some researchers — primatologists, evolutionary biologists and others — have tried to make headway by looking to chimpanzees and bonobos, our closest living relatives, for insights. Now, in a study, two collaborators argue that wild bonobos — known ②<u>for</u> friendlier and more peaceful tendencies compared to chimpanzees — cooperate not just within their own ③<u>communal</u> group but also across other bonobo groups, with more cooperative individuals leading the charge. This paves the way for the broader groups to form social ties. The researchers say this suggests that warfare may not be humanity's inevitable evolutionary legacy. Cooperation and peace ④<u>may as well</u> be a deep part of who we are too. That is, both the capacity for war and the capacity for peace may live inside us, alongside one another.

12 If the United States were more like the rest of the world, a McDonald's Quarter Pounder might be known as the McDonald's 113-Grammer, John Henry's 9-pound hammer would be 4.08 kilograms, and any 800-pound gorillas in the room would likely weigh 362 kilos. One reason this country never adopted the metric system might be pirates. Here's what happened: In 1793, the brand new United States of America needed a standard measuring system because the states were using a hodgepodge of systems. For example, in New York, they were using Dutch systems, and in New England, they were using English systems. This made interstate commerce difficult. Thomas Jefferson knew about a new French system and thought it was just ①<u>what</u> America needed. He wrote to his pals in France, and the French sent a scientist named Joseph Dombey off to Jefferson carrying a small copper cylinder with a little handle on top. It was about 3 ②<u>inch</u> tall and about the same wide. This object was intended to be a standard for weighing things, part of a weights and measure system being developed in France, now known as the metric system. The object's weight was 1 kilogram. Crossing the Atlantic, Dombey ran into a giant storm. It blew his ship quite far south into the Caribbean Sea. And you know who was lurking in Caribbean waters in the late 1700s? Pirates. These pirates were basically water-borne criminals tacitly supported by the British government, and they were tasked with harassing enemy shipping. The pirates took Joseph Dombey prisoner on the island of Montserrat, hoping ③<u>to obtain</u> a ransom for him. The pirates weren't interested in the objects Dombey was carrying. They were auctioned off along with the rest of the contents of his ship. Would it really have made any difference if Dombey ④had been able to deliver his kilogram to Jefferson? We don't know for sure, but it seems like there was a missed opportunity there.

[13-17] Choose the best for the blank. 각 3.5점

13 Studying army ants for a living comes with certain occupational hazards. "They're very aggressive," says Isabella Muratore. "They have venom, so they will sting you and they will bite you. It's not that bad. It's just that you're usually getting stung by hundreds of them at once." The ants are fierce predators, devouring other insects — sometimes even frogs, lizards and birds. But what's even more remarkable about them is their _____. Muratore has been studying how army ants build bridges by linking their bodies, which could give scientists insights into controlling swarms of robots. Commonly found in Central America, South America and Africa, the ants scour forest floors in long foraging lines. When they encounter obstacles — like a gap between leaves or branches — they build a bridge, linking themselves together like a barrel of monkeys. The workers will string themselves across that gap, and then other workers will walk on top of them. Basically, they create shortcuts to make things easier for the other ants or just to allow them to traverse something that they otherwise couldn't.

① fatal virulence
② misdemeanor offense
③ architectural prowess
④ unconditional oblation

14 How our emotions such as fear influence our sense of time is a complex process that science only partially understands, says Ed Miyawaki, a neurologist; there is not a single place in the brain involved in timekeeping, but several. One place near the optic nerve tracks time, for example, which is how people sense time of day by daylight. Dopamine-rich networks in the brain teach us to anticipate rewards, he says, and the cerebellum, which allows us to time our movements, also has its own kind of clock. "There's an emotional clock, there's a memory clock, there are all these kinds of clocks," Miyawaki says. However, they aren't particularly synchronized; the brain has no master clock. There's just complex interplay among our senses that act on our sense of time. That's partly what gives variability to our sense of time — why new experiences, like traveling to a foreign land, seem to stretch the day out, or why hours seem to vaporize for a kid engrossed in a video game. Miyawaki, who is also a psychiatrist, says sometimes you can even see the differences in someone's internal sense of time. He's treated severely depressed patients who move extremely slowly, almost like sloths, because their emotional state has so altered their timing. "The idea that _____ is just wrong," says Miyawaki.

① time helps record memories
② time is just one monolithic thing
③ time depends on emotion
④ time gets twisted beyond recognition

15 Economists argue that much of the automation we've seen in recent years is excessive. Businesses are using machines to kill jobs without generating significantly lower production costs, while also imposing all the costs on society that comes with greater unemployment and lower wages. Businesses don't take into account these social costs when making the decision to automate away jobs (economists call these social costs "negative externalities"). They say it's not just business that's to blame. Companies may be guilty of excessively automating because they don't factor in all the social costs it creates. _____. In the U.S., the government, through the tax code, is actually giving companies extra encouragement to automate jobs. That's because it taxes capital at a lower rate than labor and provides all sorts of tax write offs for purchasing machines, software, and equipment.

① Accordingly, governments inevitably intervene
② But governments are also culpable
③ Thus aggressive tax policy emerges in no time
④ To the contrary, governments are not accountable

16 New research shows that if carbon emissions soar, we could end up with super-sized lobsters. But you'll have to strap that bib on fast; _____. A new study shows that if carbon dioxide emissions reach extreme levels, the changes in the world's oceans might result in lobsters 50 percent bigger than normal. Lobsters can take carbon from the water and use it to build their exoskeletons, says marine geologist Justin Ries. The theory is that lobsters are able to convert the extra carbon into material for building up their shells. His research team built several tanks to hold marine life, and simulated high-CO_2 environments at the rates predicted for 100 years from now, 200 years from now and beyond. Lobsters, crabs and shrimp did well in the environment, according to Ries, but other things didn't — corals and other "calcifiers" like clams, scallops and oysters, for example. Unlike the lobsters, these species' shells grew thinner in the increased CO_2 environments. "Actually, six of these species began to dissolve under the highest CO_2 level," Ries says. And that's why those giant lobsters might want to stay trim. Clams and other species are part of the lobster's diet. If thinner shells make them easier prey, the lobsters' food source won't last long — not good news for the predators. Even though lobsters are building stronger shells, their populations would probably be sure to follow.

① the jumbo lobsters would be inedible
② carbon emissions would decrease quickly
③ there would be no predator for the jumbo lobsters
④ the jumbo lobsters probably wouldn't last for long

17 A long time ago, in between undergrad and grad school, I had a job as a New York City foot messenger. It was pretty cool. I got to know the subway system with startling accuracy. I delivered stuff to Annie Leibovitz's studio weekly. And I got to peer into the lives of many working for investment banks. But the best part of the job was the elevators — those long, high-speed elevator rides. Being a physics student, I knew about Albert Einstein's famous recognition that riding on an upwardly accelerating elevator would be the same as feeling the force of gravity while being stationary on a planet's surface. It was this equivalence that led him to key parts of the General Theory of Relativity. Being the dork that I was, I kept a red ball with me — so that every time I got on an elevator, I could toss it upwards at the exact moment the elevator accelerated upwards or downwards. If I caught it just right, the ball would seem to hang in the air for a moment, like _____. Everyone else in those workday elevators thought I was nuts — but it always blew my mind.

① space-time had been warped by gravity

② a perfect harmony of natural law had been met

③ gravity had been canceled

④ Einstein had recognized gravity

[18-30] Read the following passages and answer the questions. 각 3.3점

18-19

Studies sought to explain the complicated relationship that people and animals have with salt, also known as sodium chloride. We are happy to drink sodas, sports drinks, and even tap water that contain a little salt. But if you imagine a very high concentration of sodium like ocean water, you really hate it. This aversion to super salty foods and beverages holds unless your body is really low on salt, something that's pretty rare in people these days. But experiments with mice found that when salt levels plummet, the tolerance for salty water goes up. Animals start liking ocean water. The reason for this change involves at least two different interactions between the body and brain. When the concentration of sodium in the bloodstream begins to fall below healthy levels, a set of neurons in the back of the brain respond by dialing up an animal's craving for salt. If you stimulate these neurons, then animals run to a sodium source and start eating. _____, a different set of neurons in the front of the brain monitors the saltiness of any food or water the mice are consuming. And usually, these neurons will set an upper limit on saltiness. But when salt levels get extremely low, the body sends a signal that overrides these salt-limiting neurons. That allows mice to tolerate the saltiness of sea water. The scientists were able to mimic this phenomenon in the lab by stimulating these neurons.

18 **What can be inferred from the passage above?**

① Brain cells play a role in altering salt tolerance.
② Our body knows why we are never thirsty for ocean water.
③ Animals need only a tiny amount of sodium in their diet.
④ Salt overconsumption can raise the risk for heart disease and stroke.

19 **Choose the words that best fill in the blank.**

① Arguably   ② Meanwhile
③ Not to mention   ④ Above all

The typical assumption is when prices fall people buy more. This seems obvious, but why? Economists identify two factors. First is the "substitution effect:" if the price of apples fall relative to oranges people will substitute away from oranges toward apples, and the demand for apples rises. Second is the "income effect:" if you were buying apples before their price went down, and your money income is constant, a lower price for apples raises your overall purchasing power. Some of this additional purchasing power will be spent on apples, so the demand for apples goes up. This is all perfectly sensible for individual goods, considered in isolation. But what happens in the aggregate? If the prices of all goods and services fall (including wages) due to a generalized insufficiency of aggregate demand, then there is no substitution effect, since the price of everything is going down. Furthermore, one person's spending is someone else's income, so if the price of everything is falling, so are money incomes. Thus, the income effect disappears when we aggregate. Things can get much more complicated. There are some channels for price adjustment that are stabilizing and some that are destabilizing.

20 What can be inferred from the passage above?

① The logic of micro demand cannot be easily extended to the whole system.

② Falling prices would not be a cure for inflation.

③ Wage and price adjustment may solve the macro problem of under-utilized resources.

④ Natural price adjustment will solve the deflation problem in the long term.

21-22

We've all heard of people who have encyclopedic memories, and a lot of us probably assume that'd be a great thing to have. But I argue that it's actually not, because a lot of memories contain details that are irrelevant to living our daily lives. In fact, I would argue they're not just irrelevant, _____ they can be detrimental to living our daily lives. An interesting case comes from this old study by a Russian neuropsychologist Luria, who had this patient, Patient S., who he reported was able to memorize basically everything from his life. But Patient S. was actually at a disadvantage, because he had trouble identifying the commonalities, the patterns in the world. And those commonalities, those patterns are what actually allow us to make intelligent decisions. If you see a dog off leash, barking at you, and previously you've been bitten by a dog barking at you off leash, you probably want to avoid that dog, even if it doesn't look exactly like a previous dog you've seen. It doesn't matter that it doesn't have brown spots or a white tail. What matters is that it has those features that indicate it's one of those broad categories of aggressive dogs. Our memories ultimately are there to help us make decisions, to act in the world in an intelligent manner. Evolution doesn't care if you can remember who hit the home run in the 1968 World Series. Evolution cares about whether or not you are an individual who's making appropriate decisions in the environment to maximize your chances of survival.

21 Choose the words that best fill in the blank.

① whether   ② although

③ once   ④ but

22 What would be the best title of the passage above?

① Danger of messing with short-term memory

② Brains rewrite memories

③ Best memory system could be one that forgets

④ Never fading memories could help with evolution

Most people are focused on the present: today, tomorrow, maybe next year. A Fixing your flat tire is more pressing than figuring out if you should use an electric car. Living by the beach is a lot more fun than figuring out when your house will be underwater because of sea level rise. That basic human relationship with time makes climate change a tricky problem. "I consider climate change the policy problem from hell because you almost couldn't design a worse fit for our underlying psychology, or our institutions of decision-making," says a climate expert. B Those institutions — including companies and governments that ultimately have the power to dramatically reduce greenhouse gas emissions — can be even more obsessed with the present than individuals are. C Many companies are focused on quarterly earnings and growth. That helps drive short-term behavior, such as leasing new land to drill for fossil fuels, that makes long-term climate change worse. Fortunately, our collective focus on the present also offers hints about how to harness that hyperfocus on the present to inspire action. D In the political realm, that could mean that an elected official gets more votes because they support policies that reduce emissions. The promise of a benefit in the next election may be more galvanizing than the goal of protecting future generations, even if the latter has more moral weight. The benefits that we get today are more salient, and we want them more than benefits that may be larger, but will accrue in the future.

23 **Find the best place for the following sentence.**

For example, there are ways to highlight the quick payoff for addressing climate change.

① A　　　　　　　　　② B
③ C　　　　　　　　　④ D

24 **What would be the best title of the passage above?**

① How our perception of time shapes our approach to climate change
② Our obsession with the future obscures the present
③ Extreme weather starts to catch our policy-makers' attention
④ Why the public is skeptical that climate activism will make changes

Economies happen in places, and they have an effect on the physical form of places. If the next American economy will be export-oriented, lower-carbon, and innovation-driven, as Larry Summers has posited, what kind of landscape will result? The short answer: denser and better connected. An export-oriented economy will need a robust port infrastructure, which the U.S. more or less has, but also a freight network, guided by an intelligent, coordinated freight strategy, which the U.S. sorely lacks, so American manufactured goods can make it to the ports as fast as possible. A lower-carbon economy will also increase the value of denser places, where transit makes sense, and where a detached single-family home isn't the only residential option. But what's jaw-dropping to me is how much innovation also relies on density — measured in blocks, not miles. Ed Glaeser and others, going as far back as Alfred Marshall in 1890, have noted the gains from agglomeration, or geographically clustered activities. But they've generally looked at agglomeration at the metropolitan scale, and metros tend to be quite far-flung places, stretching across several counties. A couple of papers have described how dramatically the benefits of innovation and agglomeration fall off once people spread out beyond walking distance. Some researchers found that the intellectual spillovers that drive innovation and employment drop off dramatically as firms and people move more than a mile apart. As they note, "Information spillovers that require frequent contact between workers may dissipate over a short distance as walking to a meeting place becomes difficult or as random encounters become rare." These effects are staggering. As you move out beyond just one mile, the power of intellectual ferment to create another new firm or even another new job drops to one-tenth or less of what it is closer in, or as the economists say in their inimitable prose: _____. The initial attenuation is rapid, with the effect of own-industry employment in the first mile up to 10 to 1000 times larger than the effect two to five miles away. Obviously walk-ability isn't the sine qua non of innovation. The greater Boston area's innovation hub is actually named for a highway (Route 128), and Silicon Valley and Austin are both car-dependent. But you have to wonder how many ideas we've missed because people were driving, not walking.

25 Choose the best for the blank.

① Agglomeration economies attenuate with distance

② Idea-generating benefits of agglomeration are inversely related to psychological distance

③ Speed and direction of agglomeration matter

④ Agglomeration mediates exponential growth of employment

26 What can be inferred from the passage above?

① Physical proximity is the first and foremost prerequisite to sharing economy.

② Investment is tied to innovation, which stimulates job growth.

③ Geographically clustered activities should be analyzed in the metropolitan level.

④ The next American economy will depend on humans actually spontaneously talking.

Arsenii Alenichev typed a sentence like "Black African doctors providing care for white suffering children" into an artificial intelligence program designed to generate photo-like images. His goal was to see if AI would come up with images that flip the stereotype of white saviors or the suffering Black kids. "We wanted to invert your typical global health tropes." In his small-scale exploration, here's what happened: _____ his specifications, the AI program almost always depicted the children as Black. As for the doctors, he estimates that in 22 of over 350 images, they were white. For this experiment, they used an AI site called Midjourney. Alenichev didn't just put in one phrase to see what would happen. He brainstormed ways to see if he could get AI images that matched his specifications, collaborating with anthropologists. They realized AI did fine at providing on-point images if asked to show either Black African doctors or white suffering children. It was the combination of those two requests that was problematic. So they decided to be more specific. They entered phrases that mentioned Black African doctors providing food, vaccines or medicine to white children who were poor or suffering. They also asked for images depicting different health scenarios like "HIV patient receiving care." Try as they might, the team was unable to get Black doctors and white patients in one image. Out of 150 images of HIV patients, 148 were Black and two were white. "You didn't get any sense of modernity in Africa" in the images, Alenichev says. "It's all harking back to a time that it never existed, but it's a time that exists in the imagination of people that have very negative ideas about Africa." Generally, AI programs that create images from a text prompt will draw from a massive database of existing photos and images that people have described with keywords. The results it produces are, in effect, remixes of existing content. And there's a long history of photos that depict suffering people of color and white Western health and aid workers. Uganda entrepreneur Teddy Ruge says that the idea of the "white savior" is a remnant of colonialism, a time when the Global North put forth the idea of "white expertise over the savages." To compensate for decades of white savior imagery, Ruge says, Africans and people from the Global South "have to contribute largely to changing the databases and overwhelming the databases, so that we are also visible."

27 Choose the words that best fill in the blank.

① According to   ② Despite

③ On top of   ④ Without

28 What can be inferred from the passage above?

① Global community needs to have conversations about who should be held accountable when AI generates biased images.

② AI comes up with on-point images as long as we provide detailed specifications.

③ We should insist on understanding AI as something apolitical, because it is.

④ AI-generated images can propagate stereotypes.

Although our modern rules of war can be traced back to ancient civilizations and religions, it was Henri Dunant, the founder of the Red Cross, who began the process of codifying these customs into international humanitarian law. In 1864, he helped establish the first Geneva Convention, an international treaty that required armies to care for the sick and wounded on the battlefield. It was adopted by 12 European countries. Over the next 85 years, diplomats debated and adopted additional amendments and treaties to address the treatment of combatants at sea and prisoners of war — not just combatants on battlefields. In 1949, after the horrors of World War II, diplomats gathered again in Geneva to adopt four treaties that reaffirmed and updated the previous treaties and expanded the rules to protect civilians. They're now collectively known as the Geneva Conventions of 1949 and contain the most important rules of war. Since then, the rules of war have been ratified by 196 states. They protect people who are not fighting in the conflict and curb the brutality of war by setting limits on the weapons and tactics that can be employed. They're also used in domestic and international courts to determine if a government or non-governmental militant group is guilty of a war crime. If a warring party is accused of violating international humanitarian law — whether by an individual, group, country or observer — countries are obligated to investigate. The U.N. Security Council, a group of 15 countries at the U.N. charged to maintain international peace and security, may also impose sanctions — like a travel ban or an arms embargo — as an incentive for warring parties to comply with the rules of war. Although there are many rules contained in the Conventions, here are several crucial principles that are relevant to ongoing conflicts. Intentionally targeting civilians, buildings such as schools or houses and infrastructure like water sources or sanitation facilities is a war crime. Killing or injuring a person who has surrendered or is no longer able to fight is also prohibited, as is punishing someone for an act that another person, even a family member, has committed. Attacks should only be directed at military objectives, and military targets such as bases and stockpiles should not be placed in or near populated areas. If the expected incidental civilian damage of an attack is excessive and disproportionate to the anticipated military gain, then the attack legally cannot be carried out. There is one caveat: a civilian structures, for example a school, _____ if it is being used for specific military operations — as a base to launch attacks, for example, or a weapons storehouse.

29 Choose the best for the blank.

① can be disguised

② must be registered beforehand

③ may become a legitimate target

④ can avoid ratifying the rules of war

30 What can be inferred from the passage above?

① It is debatable that any retaliation must be proportionate during the war.

② Enforcing the rules of war can be difficult because unanimous consent is required by the warring countries.

③ The rules of war help guarantee safe passage for civilians to flee violence.

④ The Geneva Conventions allow exceptions to harm soldiers incapacitated in combat.

HANSUNG UNIVERSITY

한성대학교

2024학년도 인문계 A형
▶▶ 50문항·90분

자연계
▶▶ 영어 25문항, 수학 20문항·90분

인문·자연계 공통 영어문제 별도 * 표시

[01-05] Choose the best expression for the blank in each dialogue.

01* A: You promised you'd go to the library to study. I don't believe you did that. It seems you played soccer with your friends instead.

B: What are you talking about? I went to the library. I studied very hard for many hours.

A: Oh, _____! Look at the grass stains on your pants, and you're still wearing your sweaty jersey. Do I need more proof that you're lying?

B: OK, OK! I played a little, but then I went to the library. I swear. 2.5점

① give off it ② iron it out
③ come off it ④ break it on

02* A: I am surprised Conrad is your friend. To tell you the truth, nobody else likes him.

B: I find that hard to believe. He's a very nice guy.

A: A nice guy doesn't constantly _____.

B: He's never like that with me. I'm sure those other people deserved it! 1.5점

① laugh people at ② put people down
③ calm people down ④ back people down

03[*] A: My older sister is awesome. She's 20 kilos overweight, but she's determined to run a full marathon in a couple of months.

B: That sounds quite impossible! If she's serious about it, she'd better _____ on hardcore training right now.

A: She's on it! She's been dieting and running ten kilometers a day for a couple of weeks. She's starting to look healthier and fitter already.

B: If that's the case, I think she'll finish her marathon. 2점

① set up   ② set out
③ run off   ④ run down

04[*] A: I've been working for this company for ten years, but I've never gotten a raise. Not even a penny!

B: That's not right. Why don't you discuss this with your boss?

A: I'm terrified of how she'd react, so I've never _____ the nerve to talk to her.

B: You have to do it. You'll never get what you want unless you ask for it. 2점

① hung up   ② caught up
③ broken out   ④ worked up

05[*] A: I really don't know what to do about my son. He's wasting his life endlessly playing games and checking things on Instagram and TikTok. If he keeps this up, he'll never graduate.

B: My daughter was exactly like that, but I found a way to _____.

A: Really? What did you do? Tell me. I'm desperate.

B: It's simple. I stopped giving her money and didn't give her any until she changed her ways. 1.5점

① lead her on
② wipe her out
③ sort her down
④ straighten her out

[06-16] Choose the best word for each blank.

06[*] Out of the 9 million deaths worldwide _____ to air pollution in 2019, 62 percent were caused by cardiovascular disease. A study carried out recently in China informed that even a very short exposure to micro-dust pollutants in the air might provoke acute coronary syndrome, which means reduced blood flow to the heart. The syndrome often results in a fatal heart failure. 1.5점

① adjusted　　　　　② attributed

③ accustomed　　　④ admonished

07[*] You can often hear people complaining about the way they were raised. They claim their parents have messed them up. Focusing on parents' Ⓐ_____ has a certain magnetism in that one doesn't have to scrutinize one's own deficiencies. Seeing things as the parents' fault Ⓑ_____ one of personal responsibility. By blaming one's parents, one can sit back and comfortably wallow in misery without having to work hard on improving one's life. 1.5점

① flaws — absolves

② perfection — sentences

③ admiration — presents

④ achievements — rewards

08 Tipping functions as an additional "thank you" for a good service, but it can also serve as a "sorry." The majority of tips are given in circumstances where it appears that workers are less fortunate than the customers. The urge to tip is explained by some psychologists as the need to repent for the guilt involved in the unequal relationship. Skeptical people, however, scoff at this view and perceive tipping as nothing more than a very convenient way for the employer to _____ payment responsibilities onto others. 2점

① foist　　　　　② avoid

③ collect　　　　④ require

09 In the middle of intensifying climate crisis, the Toronto International Airport has recently made a great progress toward realizing its ESG — environmental, social and governance — goals. The airport's triumphs in this field have contributed to its outstanding _____ when confronted with life-threatening weather events that have become quite frequent in recent years. All airport employees work together to cope quickly and adequately with unanticipated weather disruptions. 2점

① infirmity   ② resilience

③ negotiation   ④ preoccupation

10 Some legendary, award-winning movie actors claim that their best performance is always the first take because it is the most spur-of-the-moment, honest and genuine. Copious takes _____ that spontaneity. The viewers instinctively feel whether the actor's thoughts, feelings and reactions come from the heart, or whether the actor's delivery is merely a skillful reciting of the lines. 1.5점

① ruin   ② derive

③ comprise   ④ embellish

11 The Argumentative Theory of Reasoning argues that reasoning has developed not to help people discern truth and make better judgments, but rather to win arguments. The theory posits that reasoning is a purely _____ phenomenon. It helps us convince others and be careful when others try to convince us. 1.5점

① social   ② useless

③ unequivocal   ④ unidirectional

12 Studies have shown that when people's mental health improves, they're more likely to Ⓐ_____ in their relationships and careers and adopt healthier habits. When they feel mentally well, people become more productive, find meaning in everyday experiences, and are better equipped to cope with change and Ⓑ_____.

① fail — opinions   2점

② thrive — adversity

③ digress — safety

④ flourish — luck

13 Technology will continue to _____ AI governance as regulatory efforts by governments falter, tech companies remain largely unconstrained, and far more powerful AI models and tools spread beyond the control of governments. 2점

① follow
② outstrip
③ reinforce
④ denounce

14 Milk is not an _____ part of the human diet. Far Eastern cultures and the native cultures of the Americas and of parts of Africa never use milk. Many Asians actually have lactose intolerance, rare in northern Europeans. The Hong Kong Chinese say that Westerners have a weird smell because of their dairy diet. 2점

① integral
② inessential
③ antiquated
④ unconventional

15 When a topic is entered in a search engine, websites about that topic are displayed in a certain order, according to an algorithm. Most search engines give priority to websites that the user has visited often. If users go more often to websites appearing on top, as most people do, then they are bound to visit websites that support their views rather than the views of others. Many are not even mindful that algorithms can _____ them into echo chambers. 2점

① initiate
② propagate
③ manipulate
④ incorporate

16 Stalin was infamously paranoid about everyone, but he detested geneticists in particular because they seemed to go against the communist party line by promoting the popularized idea of the survival of the fittest. He saw this as an inherently American capitalist idea, a _____ for those with superior skills or intelligence to amass wealth while workers lived in poverty. 2점

① tribute
② reference
③ sympathy
④ justification

[17-19] Read the following and answer the questions.

Diseases that devastate crops are spreading very fast. A variety of fungus is poised to make a dustbowl out of most of the world's fertile land. It has been spreading like wildfire across the globe, from Latin America and Africa to Bangladesh in Asia. Not only does it cause wheat blast, but yearly the same fungus wipes out the amount of rice that could feed dozens of millions of people. Potatoes are destroyed by potato blight, a water mold, causing a financial damage of up to $10bn annually. Spuds are also wrecked by blackleg, a bacterial disease, and potato virus "Y." Such Ⓐ_____ bring pandemonium to a food system already weakened by war and climate change. A plant pandemic can thrust the world toward mass hunger. Chances of that happening in 2024 are more likely than ever. Most agriculturalists depend on monocultures, which are efficient but fragile. Only one infected plant may lead to the annihilation of the whole crop. Global warming also increases the range of Ⓑ_____ by diminishing previously adverse conditions for their survival.

17   Choose the best title. 2점

① The Devastation of Wheat

② Adverse Climate Conditions

③ Plant Diseases Spreading Fast

④ The Vulnerability of Monocultures

18   Choose the best word for Ⓐ and Ⓑ. 2점

① genes

② lectins

③ pathogens

④ endorphins

19   Which statement is true? 2.5점

① Food system is not destabilized yet.

② The same fungus destroys wheat, rice and potatoes.

③ Global warming gets in the way of plant diseases.

④ Potatoes are destroyed by mold, bacteria, and a virus.

[20-22] Read the following and answer the questions.

Russia's invasion of Ukraine has been going on much longer than any experts predicted. Its impact on the military, economy, and diplomacy has been Ⓐ_____ for nearly two years now. However, there are many other Ⓑ_____ costs of the war, such as the psychological scars left on everyone involved. As Ukraine and its allies are making long-term strategies for the country's restoration, the Ukrainian government is also looking for policy solutions for the care of its soldiers. ⓒIt will also need assistance on a much larger scale to provide care for all who need it. Ukraine has many groups that are experiencing a variety of traumas. ⒹLet's also not forget internally and externally displaced persons. ⒺFollowing the combatants, there are health-care providers and first responders who have witnessed horrific scenes, which left them deeply traumatized. ⒻIn the first place, there's the largest and most affected group — millions of soldiers. ⒼFinally, the last group is prisoners of war. All four groups will have to be taken care of.

20* **Choose the best words for Ⓐ and Ⓑ.** 2점

① instant — innovative
② evident — unseen
③ surprised — insignificant
④ hampered — reassigned

21* **What does ⓒIt refer to?** 2.5점

① the war
② Ukraine's restoration
③ the aid from the allies
④ the Ukrainian government

22* **What is the correct ordering of Ⓓ, Ⓔ, Ⓕ, and Ⓖ?** 2점

① Ⓓ — Ⓕ — Ⓖ — Ⓔ
② Ⓓ — Ⓔ — Ⓕ — Ⓖ
③ Ⓕ — Ⓔ — Ⓓ — Ⓖ
④ Ⓕ — Ⓖ — Ⓓ — Ⓔ

[23-25] Read the following and answer the questions.

Modern adults are plagued by an Ⓐexcess of seriousness. We've denied our natural play drive, and that's creating all kinds of issues — for ourselves, our children, and our planet. Psychologists assert that Ⓑthe opposite of play isn't work; Ⓒits depression. Play in adulthood Ⓓmay looks frivolous, but recent studies imply that it may be Ⓔso crucial as the need to sleep. Scientists found that the play instinct originates in our brain stem, which is one of our oldest parts in terms of evolutionary development. Through play, young animals learn to control their bodies and their habitats, and once they accomplish this, they become adults and most stop playing. However, some animals never stop playing, including humans. Only now, scientists are attempting to work out why. One possibility is that useful discoveries come out of play. No doubt, many of humanity's greatest inventions, artworks, and scientific breakthroughs have been brought about by the need to play.

23   **Which word has the opposite meaning to Ⓐexcess?** 2점

① abuse   ② deficit
③ concern   ④ pretense

24   **Which one is grammatically correct?** 1.5점

① Ⓑ   ② Ⓒ
③ Ⓓ   ④ Ⓔ

25   **Which statement is not true?** 2.5점

① Play inspires human imagination and creativity.
② Some animals continue to play in adulthood.
③ Inhibiting the urge to play in adulthood has grave consequences.
④ Researchers figured out why adult play is important a long time ago.

[26-28] Read the following and answer the questions.

> Seventeen years after she started her extraordinary rise to superstardom, Taylor Swift has never had more economic, cultural and political clout than today. This year she soared to No. 5 on the Forbes' World's 100 Most Powerful Women — quite a jump from No. 79 in 2022! The so-called Taylor Swift Effect actually means an astonishing financial ripple effect. Just two nights of her touring in Denver added approximately $140 million to Colorado's GDP thanks to fans spending an average of $1,300 each on merch, hotels, and restaurants. She performed three nights in Philadelphia in May, making that month the strongest month for the city's hotel revenues since before the pandemic. It is estimated by the U.S. Travel Alliance that, overall, her U.S. concert tour swelled Ⓐthe state coffers by more than $5bn. She is practically a whole conglomerate whose presence is felt in many aspects of the economy. Although often taken lightly for her very young and very female audience, she is in fact Ⓑ_____.

26 **Choose the best title.** 2점

① Taylor Swift Jumps to No. 5

② Taylor Swift Fills Stadiums Across America

③ Taylor Swift Brings Hope to Hospitality Industry

④ Taylor Swift Becomes an Economic Powerhouse

27 **What does Ⓐthe state coffers mean?** 2점

① the state budget

② the financial plan

③ the bank accounts

④ the financial statement

28 **Choose the best expression for Ⓑ.** 2.5점

① a total fraud

② going back to her roots

③ a force to be reckoned with

④ making her long-awaited comeback

[29-31] Read the following and answer the questions.

The political situation in Latin America has always been volatile. In the early 2000s, most power belonged to the left-wing political parties. In the 2010s came the period of the right-wing Ⓐ_____ in Argentina and Brazil. Then again, by 2023, 12 out of 19 countries were Ⓑ_____ by progressive, left-wing politicians. Things seem to be changing again! The change started with Argentinians choosing Javier Milei as their new president, making him the first libertarian president in the history of Latin America. He's been stirring the stagnant waters of Argentinian left-wing populism, with its big government and big social handouts. Unlike his predecessor, Milei champions right-wing populism which upholds "anarcho-capitalist" free market economy and small government. People call him Argentinian Trump because, like Trump, he has gained popularity as a political outsider and a former TV personality. He also speaks in plain language and promises radical changes in almost all aspects of economy and politics. Among them, the most drastic ones are dollarizing the economy, Ⓒannihilating the central bank, and reducing the number of government ministries from 18 to 8 to slash public spending. How many of his election promises he'll keep remains to be seen.

29 **Choose the best words for Ⓐ and Ⓑ.** 2점
① reign — governed
② hermit — ruled
③ empire — ousted
④ downfall — banned

30 **Which word has the opposite meaning to Ⓒannihilating?** 2점
① shielding ② deferring
③ persisting ④ dissolving

31 **Which statement is not true?** 2.5점
① The political situation in Latin America has been erratic.
② Milei is popular because he is not part of the political establishment.
③ Latin American left-wing populism is characterized by big government handouts.
④ As a libertarian president, Milei promises to make marginal changes to the government.

[32-34] Read the following and answer the questions.

What should firms do to improve the diversity of their workforce? Partly out of fear of being called out for prejudice, corporate America rushed to embrace diversity, equity and inclusion (DEI) schemes. By 2022, three quarters of the S&P 500 had a chief diversity officer.

Now many think the pendulum has swung too far. The resignation of Claudine Gay, a black woman, as president of Harvard University, has ignited a broader debate about merit and identity. Bill Ackman and Elon Musk, two billionaires, have criticized DEI for itself being discriminatory.

As America's culture wars rage on, bosses are being caught in the middle. Progressives argue that DEI enables companies to do their bit to tackle America's entrenched Ⓐ_____. Conservatives see it as an attack on Ⓑ_____. One side ignores the costs of many DEI schemes, while the other ignores the real benefits of diversity. As with so many areas touched by the culture wars, it is disappointing that the thinking on DEI has also become muddled. It is truly worrisome that the clear, simple argument for diversity is being drawn out.

32 **Choose the best words for Ⓐ and Ⓑ.** 2점

① equalities — meritocracy

② equalities — humanitarianism

③ inequalities — meritocracy

④ inequalities — humanitarianism

33 **How does the author feel about the muddled thinking on DEI?** 2점

① hostile

② indifferent

③ aggressive

④ apprehensive

34 **Which statement is true?** 2.5점

① Opinions on DEI are influenced by one's political persuasion.

② The tension between DEI supporters and its opponents has diminished.

③ America's culture wars make it easier for business leaders to uphold DEI.

④ As of 2022, the majority of corporate America did not have a chief diversity officer.

[35-37] Read the following and answer the questions.

Philanthropy in Asia is very different from its Western counterpart including America. Most research into philanthropy defines it as formal financial gifts to registered charities and, by that definition, America is the most generous nation on earth. But a lot of philanthropy in Asia — and the rest of the developing world — is Ⓐ_____. According to surveys by the Charities Aid Foundation, a British group, Indonesia is the world's most generous country in terms of the number of people who donate money, spend time Ⓑvolunteering and lend strangers a helping hand. Such small-scale, informal generosity continues Ⓒto provide vital assistance within poor communities across the region.

A more strategic sort of giving, involving philanthropy professionals, is gradually emerging. By any measure, however, Ⓓorganized philanthropy across Asia is on a much smaller scale than in the West. Indeed, total private giving in India came to about $13bn in the 2022 financial year, and total giving in China was about $21bn in 2020. By contrast, in America, even after the post-COVID decline in philanthropy, total giving Ⓔcome to almost $500bn in 2022.

35 **Choose the best title.** 2점

① The Cause of Philanthropy

② The Benefits of Philanthropy

③ The Philanthropy in Asia and America

④ The Decline of Philanthropy Across Countries

36 **Choose the best word for Ⓐ.** 2점

① informal   ② organized

③ invalidated   ④ indiscriminate

37 **Which one is <u>not</u> grammatically correct?** 1.5점

① Ⓑ   ② Ⓒ

③ Ⓓ   ④ Ⓔ

[38-40] Read the following and answer the questions.

When Walt Disney first released the animated short film *Steamboat Willie* in November 1928, it was groundbreaking. Being one of the first animations to use synchronized sound, it would become one of the most critically acclaimed and popular animated films.

The Walt Disney Co. has fought to keep its copyright of the cartoon character as long as possible, lobbying the U.S. government to extend copyright protection beyond its expiration due in 1984. Many lawmakers agreed, and in 1976 the law was changed to allow owners to retain copyright protection for the lifetime of the author, plus an additional 50 years. In 1998, Disney once again successfully lobbied along with other entertainment companies to extend copyright protections to the life of the author plus 70 years, for a maximum of 95 years from the creation of the copyrighted material.

In January Ⓐ_____, the copyright on *Steamboat Willie* officially expired, and Mickey Mouse finds himself in the public domain. This means that anyone in the U.S. can use the *Steamboat Willie* version of the Mickey Mouse character without fear of copyright Ⓑ<u>infringement</u>.

38 Choose the correct year for Ⓐ. 2점
① 2014   ② 2024
③ 2034   ④ 2044

39 Which word has the same meaning as Ⓑ? 2점
① violation   ② protection
③ indulgence   ④ divergence

40 Which statement is <u>not</u> true? 2점
① The copyright on *Steamboat Willie* was originally supposed to expire in 1984.
② *Steamboat Willie* was one of the first animations to use synchronized sound.
③ The Walt Disney Co. has endeavored to extend the copyright on *Steamboat Willie*.
④ The *Steamboat Willie* version of the Mickey Mouse character cannot be used by everyone in the U.S.

[41-44] Read the following and answer the questions.

We are not as good Ⓐat reasoning as we would like to think. We need to learn how to do better. Psychological studies also show us why we need to work on Ⓑour skills. In some of the experiments, the question is whether an argument is valid; logically it is not possible for its premises to be true while its conclusion is false. The results show that many people assess an argument Ⓒas valid because they want its conclusion to be true. Consider this argument: 'If the referees are unfair, then Manchester United will lose. But the referees will be fair, so Manchester United will win.' Many Manchester United fans will probably believe that this argument is valid. This belief is incorrect, however, because its premises are true but its conclusion is false if the referees are fair but Manchester United loses anyway. It is possible for Manchester United to lose whether the referees are fair or not. The fans' mistake results Ⓓfrom their reluctance to imagine the possibility of their team Ⓔ_____, which they want to avoid. That is why fans of rivals of Manchester United make this mistake less often. They are willing to entertain the possibility of Manchester United Ⓕ_____ regardless Ⓖwith the fairness of the referees. Of course, that does not mean that they are smarter or more logical than Manchester United fans, because they will make the same mistake about their own favorite team. Ⓗ_____.

41 Which one is not grammatically correct? 1.5점

① Ⓐ   ② Ⓒ   ③ Ⓓ   ④ Ⓖ

42 What kind of skills are meant by Ⓑour skills? 2점

① our betting skills   ② our football skills
③ our reasoning skills   ④ our emotional skills

43 Choose the best words for Ⓔ and Ⓕ. 2점

① losing — losing   ② losing — winning
③ winning — losing   ④ winning — winning

44 Which statement is the most suitable for Ⓗ? 2.5점

① Both sides engage in wishful thinking
② Neither side engages in faulty reasoning
③ Both sides engage in valid argumentation
④ Neither side engages in illogical processes

In the ancient world, chickens Ⓐwere reared mainly for cock-fighting, a vicious betting game which relied on their extreme rage when Ⓑis roused. The winning and therefore reproducing birds were easily infuriated, especially by anything colored red. From this, cocks acquired their reputation for cockiness. Their ferocity could scare off ghosts.

Chickens in pre-industrial times were mainly used as alarm clocks — the Greek word is *alektryones* 'awakener' — while geese Ⓒwere utilized primarily as watch animals. The modern domestic chicken Ⓓis descended from a jungle fowl, a territorial ground-dwelling non-migratory bird. As powerful short-range flyers, they roosted in trees to escape predators at night, and modern domestic chickens still urgently need to roost as the sun goes down.

Chickens in Egyptian religion had a role as sacrificial birds and as markers of time. Roman knowledge of chicken-rearing probably stemmed from Egypt; fourth-century B.C. Greek records state that the Egyptians had mastered both poultry husbandry and the artificial incubation of chicks: their incubators were capable of hatching up to 15,000 eggs at a time. Historically, there is no doubt that the egg came before the chicken as a food for human beings. However, common sense meant that hens too old to Ⓔ_____ were eaten, along with roosters too old to do their jobs.

45 Which one is <u>not</u> grammatically correct? 1.5점
① Ⓐ   ② Ⓑ
③ Ⓒ   ④ Ⓓ

46 Choose the best expression for Ⓔ. 2점
① tell time   ② lay eggs
③ roost in trees   ④ participate in cock-fighting

47 Which statement is <u>not</u> true? 2.5점
① In ancient Egypt, chickens were not farmed.
② The ancestor of the modern-day chicken did not migrate.
③ In ancient times, chickens were well-recognized as fierce animals.
④ Before the industrial age, geese mainly served a different purpose from chickens.

[48-50] Read the following and answer the questions.

Self-control is one of those cognitive abilities you do not appreciate until you lose it. Its source is the prefrontal cortex. Often called the brain's executive center, it stops you from making counter-productive or dangerous mistakes.

Self-control countermands the nucleus accumbens that tempts us to gamble, the visual cortex that sees a mirage in the desert, and the amygdala that makes us jump at noises in the dark. It is the space between a thought and an action, Ⓐ_____. Without self-control, we would all be in prison or dead.

Some people have more self-control than others, and by studying these variations, researchers have shown how crucial this trait is throughout our lives. One test of self-control is the famous marshmallow experiment, in which researchers give four- to six-year-old children a marshmallow and tell them they can either eat it right away or wait until the researcher returns and receive more marshmallows. Some children ate the marshmallow immediately, while others waited ten and even fifteen minutes without giving in to the temptation. Children who ate the marshmallow right away were more likely to struggle in school, find it hard to pay attention, and have difficulty maintaining friendship.

48 **Choose the best topic.** 2.5점
① the importance of self-control
② various cognitive features of our brain
③ ways of gaining self-control in childhood
④ pitfalls of exercising too much self-control

49 **Choose the best expression for Ⓐ.** 2점
① the rise before the fall
② the look before the leap
③ the mind before the matter
④ the carriage before the horse

50 **Which one is the visual cortex responsible for?** 2점
① anxiety   ② insomnia
③ hallucination   ④ hyperactivity

한양대학교

2024학년도 서울 인문계 A형
▶▶ 35문항·60분

자연계
▶▶ 영어 공통, 수학 25문항·130분
인문·자연계 공통 영어문제 별도 * 표시

[01-08] 밑줄 친 단어의 뜻과 가장 가까운 것을 고르시오.

01 Unsubstantiated claims often suggest that internet memes related to psychiatric symptoms visually depict and promote aversive behaviour (e.g., self harm), leading to an <u>exacerbation</u> of symptoms. 2점

① abatement ② alleviation ③ aggravation
④ ambivalence ⑤ amelioration

02 The diplomat's <u>perspicacity</u> in navigating complex international negotiations was complimented. His keen insight to discern underlying intentions and nuances proved invaluable in securing advantageous agreements. 2점

① obtuseness ② sagacity ③ ineptitude
④ credence ⑤ verboseness

03 For most of the twentieth century, the evolutionary origin of feathers had been a classic but <u>intractable</u> problem. Decades of efforts to explain feathers as adaptations for flight derived from elongated scales had failed to yield any significant empirical support. 2점

① stubborn ② enervating ③ debilitating
④ preventable ⑤ counterproductive

04 The company's <u>nefarious</u> activities were eventually exposed, revealing a series of unethical and illegal practices. These actions, under the guise of legitimacy, had caused significant harm to customers and the environment. 2점

① mundane   ② sedentary   ③ altruistic

④ subversive   ⑤ malevolent

05 The industrialization of food in the nineteenth century was a major <u>impetus</u> for the introduction of salt into human diets. The dramatic expansion of the vegetable and fruit canning industry in the late nineteenth and early twentieth centuries saw the increasing use of salt, and sugar, for their preservative qualities. 2점

① disclosure   ② dealbreaker   ③ inducement

④ impediment   ⑤ compromise

06 Advocates of reducing animal agriculture have proposed the names "slaughter-free," "cruelty-free," "animal-free" and "clean meat." But traditional meat producers have rejected these as <u>pejorative</u> to conventional products. 2점

① abrogative   ② denigratory   ③ congenial

④ dispassionate   ⑤ inviolable

07 The professor's lectures were known for their <u>abstruse</u> content, often delving into subjects that were obscure and beyond the comprehension of the average student. His expertise in these arcane topics, while impressive, sometimes alienated those not well-versed in the field. 2점

① recondite   ② malicious   ③ flamboyant

④ substantive   ⑤ pedagogical

08 Her penchant for <u>veracity</u> made her a standout journalist. Her dedication to the truth was unwavering, ensuring that her reports were always factual and reliable.

① mendacity   ② honesty   ③ artifice   2점

④ falsity   ⑤ erudition

09 Isaac Newton defined the mass of a body as 'the quantity of matter' it contains, which begs the question of what matter is or how its 'quantity' can be measured. The problem is that, though we can define some quantities in terms of more fundamental quantities (e.g. speed in terms of distance and time), some concepts are so fundamental that any such attempt leads to a(n) _____ definition like that just stated. To escape from this, we can define such quantities 'operationally', by which we mean that we describe what they do — i.e. how they operate — rather than what they are. 3점

① figurative   ② empirical   ③ circular
④ hypothetical   ⑤ lexical

10 In the heated debate, his arguments were marked by _____. Each point was delivered with a harshness and severity that seemed to go beyond mere disagreement. His tone was not just critical, but also biting and caustic, indicating a deep-seated frustration and irritability with the opposing viewpoints, which added a layer of tension to the discussion. 3점

① languor   ② geniality   ③ asperity
④ subterfuge   ⑤ contrition

11 Today we live with calendars at hand but, at the same time, we live with the feeling that everything in history occurs without particular regard for its chronology, and that even music is a sort of warehouse of samples, whose shelf life — whose relative permanence or oblivion, whose chronological placement — is ultimately _____ because, when we get down to it, it can be pushed around according to our inner needs and desires as listeners, performers, and composers.

① irrelevant   ② elucidating   ③ miscellaneous   3점
④ circumscribed   ⑤ self-explanatory

12 Throughout the entire Charlie Chan film series one finds a constant return to the problems and solutions posed by modern technology, such that Chan's solving of the mystery in film after film depends on his ability to utilize (or else uncover the criminal use of) technological devices: microscopes, phonographs, picture wires, photoelectric cells, radiographs, laboratory experiments, ultraviolet film projection, and so on. It is important to note here that these moments of gadgetry are not _____ to the narratives; indeed, they routinely constitute the most distinctive parts of each film. 3점

① intrinsic   ② favorable   ③ conducive
④ peripheral   ⑤ consequent

13 Though I have read so much, I am a bad reader. I read slowly and I am _____. I find it difficult to leave a book, however bad and however much it bores me, unfinished. I could count on my fingers the number of books that I have not read from cover to cover. 3점

① an efficient scroller
② a choosy bibliophile
③ a poor skipper
④ a rapid peruser
⑤ a thoughtful perceiver

14 The evolution of jazz music, from its roots in the early 20th century to its myriad contemporary forms, reflects the dynamic nature of this genre. Originating within African American communities, jazz combined elements of blues, ragtime, and European music to create a unique and expressive sound. Improvisation is a defining characteristic of jazz, allowing musicians to spontaneously create and vary melodies, harmonies, and rhythms during performances. This element of improvisation makes each jazz performance a unique experience. Over the decades, jazz has evolved to include influences from other genres such as funk, rock, and even classical music. The enduring appeal of jazz lies in its ability to _____. 3점

① embrace diversity and innovation
② sustain a connection to its socio-political origins
③ selectively exclude contemporary components of music
④ explore commercial trends while retaining its essence
⑤ adhere to traditional components of African American music

15 We have a tendency to think that people who agree with us are brilliant and insightful, and that those who disagree with us could use a little help in seeing reality for what it is. As George Carlin put it, "Have you ever noticed that anybody driving slower than you is an idiot, and anyone going faster than you is a maniac?" This propensity to believe that we see the world accurately, while anyone who has a different opinion is benighted, _____. As psychologist Lee Ross has argued, if I see the world as it is and you disagree with me, then I have only a few possible interpretations of your behavior: You might be incompetent, you might be irrational, or you might be mistaken. Whatever the case, I can't reason with you.

① fuels conflicts   3점
② relieves stress
③ minimizes risk
④ inspires action
⑤ triggers delusions

16 다음 글에 드러난 'I'의 심경 변화로 가장 적절한 것은? 2점

After years of meticulous research and relentless fieldwork, the discovery I had been chasing seemed to elude me. I sat in my office surrounded by piles of data, the red numbers on the digital clock glaring at me, a reminder of another day slipping by. The weight of expectation bore down on my shoulders, my ambition turning into an oppressive shadow. My breathing was shallow, my focus scattered. The university had invested heavily in my work, and here I was about to admit that my theory was incorrect. I decided to take a walk to clear my head. As I wandered through the empty campus, the words of my mentor came to mind: "Science is not a pursuit of affirmation, but an exploration of the unknown. Each wrong turn is a step towards the truth." Suddenly, it all made sense. The pressure dissipated as I realized that my "failure" was actually a valuable finding. A sense of liberation replaced the anxiety. With renewed vigor, I understood that acknowledging my theory's flaws would contribute to the greater body of knowledge. I returned to my office not with a sense of defeat, but with the satisfaction of contributing a piece to the ever-expanding puzzle of science.

① hopeful → disillusioned
② frustrated → enlightened
③ confident → hesitant
④ impatient → contented
⑤ curious → resigned

17 다음 글의 요지로 가장 적절한 것은? 4점

Organized work, and the customs, practices and institutions, along with the tightly woven affective fabric of wishes, dreads and ambitions, that sustain it, provides the means for societies to maintain themselves continuously in being, maintaining themselves through the maintenance of exertion itself. Societies may project aims for themselves through five-year plans and vaguer ambitions for ever-greater dominion over the natural and human world, but this imperial expansiveness is not really projective in that it must in fact remain open and incomplete, since completion of a society's aim would produce exhaustion, inertia and dissipation. Societies bound by the mythos of work as collective striving grow in order to remain the same, or not to decay and disappear. By the same token, they remain in being through exerting themselves. Work always aims at some kind of completion, cessation or remission: keeping a society 'working' in the way that projects of work do aims at ongoing incompletion, or the work only of keeping itself at work in being.

① Societies are sustained by the open-ended incompletion of work.
② The importance of work-life balance cannot be overemphasized.
③ Civilization was achieved thanks to myths about the value of work.
④ Goals must be set realistically to minimize overexertion and burnout.
⑤ A productive society accounts for the long-term effects of its polices.

18 주어진 글 다음에 이어질 순서로 가장 적절한 것은? 4점

In craftsmanship we are able to judge how well someone performs by looking at the concrete results of their labors. To displaced or discarded workers, those results at least make legible why they have been cast aside; the quality of Indian software programs and Chinese manufactured goods are solid facts.

A But in fact the bureaucratic machinery chases after something quite intangible; one can quantify what kinds of work seem autonomous, for example, but not what specifically an autonomous act is. Craftsmanship requires mastering and owning a particular domain of knowledge; this new version of talent is not content-specific or content-determined.

B Cutting-edge firms and flexible organizations need people who can learn new skills rather than cling to old competencies. The dynamic organization emphasizes the ability to process and interpret changing bodies of information and practice.

C It might seem that the meritocracy machinery of testing and on-the-job evaluation is equally solid. The measures, after all, are standardized, with numbers often taking the place of names on tests to assure objectivity.

① A — C — B
② B — A — C
③ B — C — A
④ C — A — B
⑤ C — B — A

[19-20] 다음 글의 제목으로 가장 적절한 것을 고르시오.

We should see death as it really is: the limit that gives form to our lives. It's both wrong and unhelpful to see death as a confinement, as an unfair stoppage of our projects. Things that go on endlessly lose their value. An Epicurean tip for getting through difficulties is to remember that pain comes to an end. Well, death is "this too shall pass" taken to its logical conclusion. Another Epicurean tip for getting through tough times is to remember the goods of life, like friendship and conversation. Well, death provides the shapeliness to time that makes these pleasures substantial. The sooner we stop thinking of death as a mere transition and come to terms with it as an absolute end, the sooner we can start enduring our temporary bouts of suffering and enjoying our precious encounters with beauty. Without a container, life could never be full, let alone overflowing. 3점

19 ① Why Death is the Great Equalizer
② Strategies to Reduce Anxiety about Death
③ Embrace the Grim Reaper: Death Improves Life
④ How to Cope with the Meaninglessness of Life
⑤ Lessons from Epicure: The Beauty of Uncertainty

The difficulty in discussing ownership as one of the major factors of human existence and experience is that little data exist. Most of those who have examined economics, whether they were concerned philosophically with man, or materialistically with property, have had many of their thoughts molded by written history. But written history does not encompass the experience of man. At best, it plunges into the past only briefly. The written record is confined to the last five or six thousand years of human experience. By the time we find learned men examining property and property relationships, we are in the historic period and these men are dealing with the findings of the historians. Nearly all the early historians were men who looked at government and war as the major factors which mold human social order. They entered the story at a point where the fundamental guidelines were disappearing in a welter of working relationships already aged and warped with custom. 3점

20 ① The Epic Saga of Property Wars
② Oral Histories of Ownership: Tales of Social Order
③ The Illusion of Ownership: How History Shapes Economic Thought
④ Ownership: A Historical Perspective Limited by Written Records
⑤ An Interdisciplinary Approach to Ownership Through the Ages

[21-26] 다음 글의 내용과 가장 가까운 것을 고르시오.

Emotions have a big influence on how we process the information coming in through our senses. We all have the experience of being in a good mood and noticing sunny skies and chirping birds, or being in a bad mood and noticing dark clouds and pigeon crap all over the place. Our emotions color what we notice and how we experience them. Emotions are housed deep in the brain below its surface. These regions are called limbic areas. The limbic brain is responsible for our joys and fears, our happiness and sadness, our delights and disgusts. It is closely linked with the autonomic nervous system. This part of the brain is "autonomic" because it does its work tirelessly behind the scenes without our even being aware that it is humming along. The autonomic nervous system controls our heart rate and blood pressure and sweating responses, and links our brain and body in emotional experiences.

3점

21
① Positive moods highlight the unpleasant darker aspects of things.

② Sweating responses are mainly controlled by the conscious part of the brain.

③ The limbic areas of the brain are located on the outer layer of the brain.

④ The limbic system in the brain is primarily responsible for logical reasoning.

⑤ The autonomic nervous system regulates responses like heart rate in relation to emotional experiences.

The city of Rome first became the seat of a republic governed by a senate with members drawn from notable families and by elected magistrates or consuls. As the Roman armies conquered more and more of Italy and beyond, the populace struggled to maintain a governmental system that could administer efficiently and that could satisfy both the landed aristocracy (patricians) and the general class of free citizens (plebs). A crisis eventually arose in the first century B.C.E. that resulted in the assumption of dictatorial power by the military leader Julius Caesar. Although he was assassinated, his rule ushered in the Roman Empire and a succession of emperors beginning with Augustus Caesar in 27 B.C.E. The breadth and complexity of the Empire demanded new construction practices capable of producing very large buildings relatively quickly and economically. 3점

22
① The Roman Empire started immediately after the city of Rome was founded.

② The Roman Republic was initially led by a senate, elected consuls and the common plebeians.

③ The Roman Republic successfully managed the needs of both patricians and plebeians throughout its expansion without much internal conflict.

④ After Julius Caesar's assassination, there was a long period without an emperor before the Roman Empire began.

⑤ Roman architecture evolved as their political system changed from a republic to an empire.

Van Gogh was right in saying that the method he had chosen could be compared to that of the caricaturist. Caricature had always been 'expressionist', for the caricaturist plays with the likeness of his victim, and distorts it to express just what he feels about his fellow man. As long as these distortions of nature sailed under the flag of humour nobody seemed to find them difficult to understand. Humorous art was a field in which everything was permitted, because people did not approach it with the prejudices they reserved for Art with a capital A. But the idea of a serious caricature, of an art which deliberately changed the appearance of things not to express a sense of superiority, but maybe love, or admiration, or fear, proved indeed a stumbling block as Van Gogh had predicted. Yet there is nothing inconsistent about it. It is the sober truth that our feelings about things do colour the way in which we see them and, even more, the forms which we remember. Everyone must have experienced how different the same place may look when we are happy and when we are sad. 3점

23 ① Van Gogh claimed that his method was entirely distinct from that of a caricaturist.
② Van Gogh had anticipated that serious caricature was readily accepted without much skepticism.
③ Caricature, according to Van Gogh, strictly adheres to realistic portrayals without distortion.
④ Caricature is described as 'expressionist' because it distorts likenesses to express the artist's feelings.
⑤ Van Gogh believed that altering appearances in art to convey emotions like love or fear was generally accepted without controversy.

My principal objection to the refusal to call history a science is that it justifies and perpetuates the rift between the so-called 'two cultures'. The rift itself is a product of this ancient prejudice, based on a class structure of English society which itself belongs to the past; and I am myself not convinced that the chasm which separates the historian from the geologist is any deeper or more unbridgeable than the chasm which separates the geologist from the physicist. But the way to mend the rift is not, in my view, to teach elementary science to historians or elementary history to scientists. This is a blind alley into which we have been led by muddled thinking. After all, scientists themselves do not behave in this way. I have never heard of engineers being advised to attend elementary classes in botany. 3점

24 ① The rift between history and science, in the author's view, can be bridged by incorporating more science into history education.

② The division between 'two cultures' for the author is a product of the contemporary class structure of English society.

③ According to the author, the gap between historians and geologists is significantly greater than that between geologists and physicists.

④ The author argues that the refusal to recognize history as a science reinforces an outdated divide between history and science.

⑤ The author's main objection to classifying history as a science is that it would create a larger divide between different academic disciplines.

Pythagoras, as everyone knows, said that "all things are numbers." This statement, interpreted in a modern way, is logically nonsense, but what he meant was not exactly nonsense. He discovered the importance of numbers in music, and the connection which he established between music and arithmetic survives in the mathematical terms "harmonic mean" and "harmonic progression." He thought of numbers as shapes, as they appear on dice or playing cards. We still speak of squares and cubes of numbers, which are terms that we owe to him. He also spoke of oblong numbers, triangular numbers, pyramidal numbers, and so on. These were the numbers of pebbles required to make the shapes in question. He presumably thought of the world as atomic, and of bodies as built up of molecules composed of atoms arranged in various shapes. In this way he hoped to make arithmetic the fundamental study in physics as in aesthetics. 3점

---

25 ① Pythagoras's statement "all things are numbers" aligns perfectly with modern logical interpretations.

② Pythagoras believed that numbers had no practical application beyond their mathematical properties.

③ Pythagoras's view of the atomic structure of the world suggested that bodies were composed of molecules arranged in various shapes.

④ The idea of shaping numbers into oblong, triangular, and pyramidal forms was developed by mathematicians after Pythagoras.

⑤ Pythagoras's teachings primarily targeted philosophical concepts, leaving arithmetic's integration into physics and aesthetics to others.

The greatest minds in the physics community are probably those working on the unresolved problem of how quantum physics can be applied to the extremely powerful forces of gravity that are believed to exist inside black holes, and which played a vital part in the early evolution of our universe. However, the fundamental ideas of quantum physics are really not rocket science: their challenge is more to do with their unfamiliarity than their intrinsic difficulty. We have to abandon some of the ideas of how the world works that we have all acquired from our observation and experience, but once we have done so, replacing them with the new concepts required to understand quantum physics is more an exercise for the imagination than the intellect. Moreover, it is quite possible to understand how the principles of quantum mechanics underlie many everyday phenomena, without using the complex mathematical analysis needed for a full professional treatment. 4점

26　① The principles of quantum mechanics cannot be understood without complex mathematical analysis.

② Quantum physics has little relevance to the powerful gravitational forces in black holes and the early universe.

③ The greatest minds in physics focus mainly on the application of quantum physics to everyday phenomena.

④ Quantum physics is about the intellectual challenge usually associated with complex scientific theories like "rocket science."

⑤ Quantum physics is less about complexity and more about reimagining familiar concepts.

27 다음 글의 내용과 거리가 가장 <u>먼</u> 것은? 3점

One of the things that made most Italians finally accept that they were unified, and gradually made them feel as if they belonged to the same people, was that they began eating the same thing. It was a process in which pasta — and to some extent pizza — played a central role. In the mid-1800s, pasta and pizza were mostly regional specialties, poor man's food from Naples and the surrounding area. After Italy's unification, immigrants from the country's poor south flocked to cities in the north searching for work. They took their favorite food with them — and poor man's food soon became everyone's favorite. As John Dickie writes in his book *Delizia*, one of the most remarkable traits of the Italians' love of food today is how democratic it is. In the past, the rich and the poor, the people living in the cities and the countryside, lived on completely different diets; today it's likely that their children and grandchildren share the same knowledge and appreciation of tasty cooking. Everyone dreams about the same bowl of pasta, although the sauce varies slightly from region to region.

① Food was crucial to the formation of Italian national identity.
② Pasta and pizza were once associated with specific regions.
③ Pasta went national when rural labor moved to the cities.
④ Diet remains an important marker of class origin in Italy.
⑤ Local differences in pasta sauces can still be found across Italy.

The sense of balance was ignored in the treatises of antiquity, as well as in the dozens of Renaissance and Baroque representations and allegories of the senses. For centuries the body's relationship to the world was thought to be mediated only by our ability to smell, see, hear, taste or touch. The claim that we have five senses, and only those, was prevalent in Europe, America, and much of Asia. This is partly owing to the fact that the distinction between up and down and right and left seems so obvious to us that we appreciate its importance only when we feel dizzy or lose ground. As with friends we speak of well only after they are dead, we recognize the goodness of our more integrative senses when we miss them. We do not do so <u>on a whim</u>, but because the regulating principle of our vital clock, like that of our internal compass, cannot be perceived except through the intervention of a dissonance, through the natural or artificial production of an unbalancing bodily phenomenon.

From the beginning of the nineteenth century, theories of perception began to deal with sensory qualities other than the classical senses. The sensation of pain, for example, which later became known as nociception, was associated with the sense of touch, while thirst, hunger and the urge to urinate were some of the subjects of endocrinology. To some extent, medicine and physiology began to distinguish between ways of accessing the outside world and the perception of processes occurring, as it were, from the skin inwards. However, when it came to the sense related to the passage of time or that of equilibrium it was not very clear to what extent these sensations referred to 'the outside' or 'the inside.' Nor did it seem obvious that they were purely individual sensations, or that they could vary according to habit or custom.

28 윗글의 내용과 가장 거리가 먼 것은? 4점

① For centuries, theories of perception focused on the five senses.

② The sense of balance was an object of study since the Renaissance and Baroque periods.

③ Theories of perception advanced qualitatively at the beginning of the nineteenth century.

④ Nineteenth-century theorists drew connections between the sense of touch and the sensation of pain.

⑤ Nineteenth-century theorists were unsure whether sensations related to the sense of balance were completely individual.

29 밑줄 친 "<u>on a whim</u>"의 뜻과 가장 가까운 것은? 3점

① to make ends meet
② as food for thought
③ once in a blue moon
④ off the top of one's head
⑤ by the skin of one's teeth

[30-31] 다음 글을 읽고 물음에 답하시오.

The phenomenon of false memories, a captivating subject in cognitive psychology, explores the fallibility and malleability of human memory. This concept, popularized by Elizabeth Loftus's groundbreaking research, demonstrates that our memories are not always accurate reflections of reality. False memories refer to the psychological instances where people recall events differently from the way they happened or, in some cases, recall events that never occurred at all. Loftus's experiments, particularly the "Lost in the Mall" technique, revealed how suggestible memories can be. In these experiments, subjects were implanted with false memories of being lost in a shopping mall as children. Astonishingly, many subjects recalled this fabricated event with vivid details, demonstrating the ease with which false memories can be created. This research has profound implications, particularly in the legal field, where eyewitness testimonies can be crucial. The formation of false memories involves complex cognitive processes. Factors such as suggestion, social pressure, and the malleability of memory during recall contribute to this phenomenon. These memories can be as detailed and vivid as true memories, making them indistinguishable from actual experiences in the mind of the individual. False memory research highlights the _____ nature of memory. Rather than being a passive storage of facts, memory is an active and dynamic process, susceptible to distortion. This understanding has significant implications for various fields, including psychology, legal studies, and even history, where the reliability of memory is of paramount importance.

30 윗글의 내용과 가장 거리가 <u>먼</u> 것은? 3점

① The phenomenon of false memories indicates the potential for memories to be distorted or fabricated.

② Memory is a dynamic process that can be influenced by factors like suggestion and social pressure.

③ False memories can be as detailed and graphic as true memories.

④ Loftus's "Lost in the Mall" experiment involved implanting people with fabricated memories of childhood events.

⑤ Loftus's research confirmed the reliability of eyewitness testimonies in many legal scenarios.

31 빈칸에 들어갈 가장 적절한 것은? 3점

① stable
② reflective
③ submissive
④ replicated
⑤ reconstructive

[32-33] 다음 글을 읽고 물음에 답하시오.

Over 8,000 frog and toad species hop and croak around the globe. They are masters of adaptation and have a range of unique survival strategies. However, according to the IUCN Red List, amphibians are the second most threatened group on our planet and undisputedly the most threatened vertebrate class with 40.7% of threatened species. Ongoing habitat loss, climate change and the pandemic chytrid disease are some of the main drivers that contribute to the threat to amphibians. However, why some species are more vulnerable than others remains largely unknown. Frogs and toads are not always brown and green, but exhibit an incredible range of colours, patterns and even textures that did not develop by chance. Some species blend in seamlessly with their surroundings not to be detected, while others use <u>conspicuous</u> colours and patterns (aposematism) as a warning signal to shout: "Don't touch me, I'm poisonous and inedible!" But colour does not only function as a visual signal as they show.

Beyond camouflage and aposematism, colour and particularly the melanisation measured as lightness plays a crucial role in regulating body temperature. Colour-based thermoregulation is increasingly supported for insect groups, which, like anurans, depend on absorbing sunlight to heat up and maintain their body temperature. The relationship between colour lightness, physiology and distribution is conceptualized in the thermal melanism hypothesis stating that darker coloured organisms are favoured to live in colder regions as they heat up faster whereas lighter coloured ones benefit from the prevention of overheating in warmer regions.

32 밑줄 친 "<u>conspicuous</u>"의 뜻과 가장 가까운 것은? 2점

① implicit   ② unnoticeable   ③ unique

④ evident   ⑤ vague

33 윗글의 내용과 가장 거리가 <u>먼</u> 것은? 3점

① Amphibians are the most threatened vertebrate group on Earth.

② The coloring of frogs and toads serves purposes beyond just being a visual cue.

③ Frogs and toads possess a variety of strategies for survival.

④ The reason why certain species are more susceptible to threats than others is still largely a mystery.

⑤ The thermal melanism hypothesis suggests that the colour of mammal groups plays a significant role in their ability to regulate body temperature.

Foundation models are large, pre-trained models that act as the basis or initial point for diverse machine learning tasks. These models undergo training on extensive datasets to acquire patterns, features, and representations beneficial for a broad array of downstream applications. Technologically speaking, foundation models are not novel as they rely on self-supervised learning and deep neural networks, concepts that have been around for years. However, the very large scale and scope of foundation models in recent years have pushed the boundaries regarding what is achievable. Their potency stems from scale that requires advancements in computer hardware, and accessibility of a significantly larger pool of training data. This led them to an exceptional level of homogenization. Indeed, researchers and developers can exploit the knowledge acquired by foundation models and adapt it to a diverse range of tasks without training from scratch, thanks to different approaches of transfer learning. Certainly, their robustness to domain shifts and out-of-distribution data remains questionable. Foundational models are transforming the fields of natural language processing and computer vision by exhibiting zero-shot and few-shot generalization capabilities. This can extend their applicability to tasks that go beyond what they were exposed to during their training. When these models are scaled up and trained with vast text datasets, their zero- and few-shot performances match, and in some instances, even surpass that of fine-tuned models.

34 윗글의 내용과 가장 거리가 <u>먼</u> 것은? 4점

① Foundation models serve as a starting point for various machine learning tasks.

② The mechanisms of foundation models are new, and recent advancements in scale and scope have significantly expanded their capabilities.

③ The effectiveness of foundation models is attributed to their extensive training on large datasets and advancements in computer hardware.

④ Foundation models are altering natural language processing by showcasing zero-shot and few-shot generalization capabilities.

⑤ The very large scale and scope of foundation models allow researchers to apply the knowledge gained from these models to a diverse range of tasks.

35 윗글의 제목으로 가장 적절한 것은? 3점

① The Evolution and Impact of Foundation Models in Machine Learning
② Exploring the Impact of Fine-tuned Models
③ Can Traditional Methods Surpass Foundation Models?
④ The Declining Significance of Large Datasets in Advanced Machine Learning
⑤ Superiority of Zero- and Few-shot Performances in Unsupervised Models

홍익대학교

2024학년도 서울 인문계 A형
▶▶ 40문항·70분

[01-10] Choose the one that is closest in meaning to the underlined word.

01 Explaining the meticulous, self-consciously Flaubertian style of these early works, Bellow acknowledged that he had been timid and felt the incredible <u>effrontery</u> of announcing myself to the world as a writer and an artist.

① congestion   ② circumspection

③ uncouth   ④ insolence

02 The prophets <u>fulminated</u> against their contemporaries who thought their temple worship was sufficient.

① lauded   ② inveighed

③ mistrusted   ④ consoled

03 To compound the farce, following the verdicts the coup leader, General Min Aung Hlaing, issued a partial pardon and <u>magnanimously</u> cut Ms. Suu Kyi's outrageous four-year sentence in half.

① ferociously   ② coltishly

③ chivalrously   ④ callously

04 This is not to say, as some analytically minded philosophers might, that one never trails off in silent aporia or <u>prattles</u> on in search of the right word.

① scrutinizes   ② impleads

③ enunciates   ④ blathers

05 Marcuse rejected the prevailing political judgment of the anti-communist revolutionary Left that the social democratic and communist historic compromises with capitalism were due, chiefly, to the <u>perfidy</u> of opportunist party and trade union leadership.

① treachery   ② alliance

③ despotism   ④ clique

06 If some philosophical theories are really unintelligible, the nonsense must be heavily disguised, requiring <u>sedulous</u> argumentation to unmask.

① enticing   ② condoning

③ feculent   ④ punctilious

07 In 1947, Wittgenstein resigned from his professorship at Cambridge because he wanted to write and because he felt his teaching did not have a good effect, and so he went to live in Ireland, away from the disintegrating and <u>putrefying</u> English civilization.

① elutriating   ② gangrening

③ configurating   ④ recalescing

08 In fact, given the <u>opprobrium</u> attached to most kind of lying, leaders who think that they have good reason to deceive another state or their own public usually prefer spinning and concealment to lying.

① decency   ② chastity

③ vilification   ④ abidance

09 In Trinh's work, the exclusionary principle of deconstruction is <u>insouciantly</u> transgressed, so much so, in fact, that a work like *Woman, Native, Other* could be considered hostile to deconstruction and, as such, considered to be deconstruction's Other.

① staggerily   ② tremendously

③ blenchingly   ④ equanimously

10 While Cantor's constructions and formulations may seem <u>jejune</u> to us now with our familiarity with set theory and topology, one has to strive, for a hermeneutic interpretation, to see how difficult it once would have been to achieve basic, especially founding, conceptualizations and results.

① puerperal   ② puerile

③ clairaudient   ④ cardiant

[11-18] Choose one that is either ungrammatical or unacceptable.

11 ①<u>Economics</u> is ②<u>a disgrace</u>, according to Claudia Sham, ③<u>the former Federal Reserve researcher</u>, who has chosen to no longer identify as ④<u>an economist</u>.

12 Approximately ①<u>half Americans</u> who make ②<u>too little</u> to file ③<u>federal tax returns</u> ④<u>do not</u> own a computer.

13 Yet ①<u>this undecidability</u> is ②<u>in reality</u> a deep-structural rather than a political one; and it explains ③<u>what</u> so many commentators on Utopia ④<u>should have emitted</u> contradictory assessments on the matter.

14 It ①<u>has often been observed</u> that we need to distinguish between the Utopian form and the Utopian wish: between the written text or genre and something ②<u>that</u> a Utopian impulse ③<u>detectable in</u> daily life and ④<u>its practices</u> by a specialized hermeneutic or interpretive method.

15 Though there was only a single, communal "I," there was also, so to speak, ①a manifold and variegated "us," an observed company of very diverse personalities, each of ②whom expressed creatively his own unique contribution to the whole enterprise of cosmical exploration, while all were ③binding together in a tissue of ④subtle personal relationships.

16 At this point the expression of the Utopian impulse has come ①as closely to the surface of reality ②as it can without turning into a conscious Utopian project and ③passing over into ④that other line of development we have called the Utopian program and Utopian realization.

17 ①Inasmuch as the practice of the genre ②necessarily includes a generic reference to More's foundational text, ③history and the succession of Utopian generations become themselves interiorized within the later Utopias and variously ④incorporated the Utopian argument.

18 That impression of uncanniness would ①be stronger if less time ②had elapsed between his ③exclamation and the untoward event, or if he had ④been able to produce innumerable similar coincidences.

[19-28] Choose the one that is most suitable for the blank.

19 Any blemishes on the _____ of a career were forgivable if accompanied by substantial achievements in the service of the cause.

① escutcheon   ② escalope

③ escuage   ④ escritoire

20 Britain is working out how best to manage the presence of coronavirus, which has been possible only because a quick and well-targeted vaccine roll-out has kept deaths at European rather than American levels, _____ public concern.

① impersonating   ② deteriorating

③ dampening   ④ impassioning

21 A Trotskyist, James's view of *droits de l'homme*, instead, seems to have been as the wordy promises of eloquent phrasemakers who, driven by their true economic motor of history to _____, were in the end only willing to give up the aristocracy of the skin at the point of the insurgent's gun.

① perorate   ② gregarine
③ sporulate   ④ excise

22 Tabby wore her pink uniform out to Dunkin' Donuts and called the cops when the drunks who came in for coffee got _____.

① unflappable   ② spruce
③ snazzy   ④ obstreperous

23 Dissenting voices such as Milan Kundera and Harold Bloom have alleged that *Nineteen Eighty-Four* is actually a bad novel, with thin characters, humdrum prose and an implausible plot, but even they couldn't _____ its importance.

① acquiesce   ② gainsay
③ swoon   ④ tress

24 The second conflict that came to a head in 1925 was located in the quite different atmosphere of the agricultural sector, and a Presbyterian missionary named Sam Higginbotham was at the center of this _____.

① plight   ② pledger
③ pleonexia   ④ plinth

25 The ridicule enflamed the views of already hostile liberal journalists, whose _____ at government officials whetted appetites for more critical political news.

① temblor   ② scrooch
③ froth   ④ jeering

26 Just as campfires leave traces in the soil, so the needs of speech call forth tiny changes in the skeleton: nothing so dramatic as the hollow bony box in the throat with which the howler monkeys of the South American forests amplify their _____ voices, but still telltale signs such as one might hope to detect in a few fossils.

① scrummy   ② stentorian
③ spiteful   ④ stately

27 The growing proletarianization of modern man and the increasing formation of masses are two aspects of the same process: fascism attempts to organize the newly created proletarian masses without affecting the property structure which the proletarian masses strive to _____.

① eliminate   ② consume
③ ingest   ④ supplant

28 I hastened to leave the narrow street at the next turning but after having wandered about for a while without being _____, I suddenly found myself back in the same street, where my presence was now beginning to excite attention.

① disoriented   ② directed
③ mislaid   ④ attenuated

[29-31] Read the following passage and answer the questions.

The word 'model,' in its usual scientific sense, is quite different from the sense in which it is used in logic. For example, the Newtonian model of the physics of moving bodies employs the concepts of mass and force, velocity and acceleration, and posits relationships between those concepts in the form of Newton's laws of mechanics as they apply to idealized bodies of matter. A more up-to-date example is provided by the Watson-Crick helix model of DNA and its role in cell replication and other biological processes. Some scientific models are very speculative, such as cosmological ones that describe the evolution of the universe from the Big Bang to its final collapse or, alternatively, its endless expansion, or models that hypothesize continuously bifurcating universes. Roughly speaking, then, scientific models are theories that represent, in idealized form, various kinds of objects in the world and their (possibly dynamic) interrelationships in order to explain actual phenomena.

For logicians, models are the realizations of axiom systems that are given by interpreting their basic notions in one way or another. One of the simplest examples of an axiom system is that for an ordering relation 'x is smaller than y.' The axioms are *transitivity* (for any x, y, and z, if x is smaller than y and y is smaller than z, then x is smaller than z), *asymmetry* (for any x and y, it cannot be true at the same time that both x is smaller than y and y is smaller than x), and *compatibility* (for any x and y, if x is not equal to y, then either x is smaller than y or y is smaller than x). Examples of models of these axioms are given by the integers and by the real numbers, both with their usual ordering relations. The real numbers also form a model of the statement of *density* (for any x and y, if x is smaller than y then there should be a z such that x is smaller than z and z is smaller than y). That statement is false for the integers. Being considered a possible axiom, Ⓐthe assumption of density is both *consistent with* and *independent of* the basic axioms for an ordering relation 'x is smaller than y.'

29 Which of the following can be inferred from the passage?

① Biological phenomena, such as heredity via DNA, cannot be understood through a scientific model.

② Not the integers, but the real numbers, can be a model of the 'smaller than' ordering relation because the axiom of density does not hold for them.

③ Scientific models should be concrete enough to exclude ideas based on speculations without any tangible evidence.

④ With respect to the above mentioned axioms, any two different real numbers can be ordered in terms of the 'smaller than' ordering.

30 According to the passage, the axiom of density is <u>not</u> true for the integers because
_____.

① the integers cannot be a model representing interrelationships between actual objects

② unlike the real numbers, only the integers satisfy the ordering relation

③ sometimes there cannot be any third integer between two integers, as in 1 and 2

④ any two different integers must be in the 'smaller than' relation

31 According to the passage, why does the author say Ⓐ?

① Because the axiom of density is contradictory with the axiom of transitivity but not with the axiom of asymmetry.

② Because the axiom of density can be, but need not be, added to other basic axioms for the 'smaller than' ordering.

③ Because you can always find a number between two different numbers if they are in the 'smaller than' ordering.

④ Because only the integers can describe the phenomena in the actual world and represent them.

[32-34] Read the following passage and answer the questions.

Aestheticism is dominated by the idea of expression which would hold that the work of art materializes and delivers the inner subjective feelings of the artist to a beholder who presumably experiences the same emotions in its presence. In aestheticism, art remains alienated from discourse and maintains no epistemological status. In contemporary art, this model has been largely displaced by a critical anti-aesthetic tradition of representationalism (although there are signs of aestheticism's re-emergence in line with the 'affective turn' taking place in the humanities and social sciences). According to representationalism, the work of art is an inessential conduit for a truth or a political ideology. Once the work's message has been received, the concrete materiality of the work is rendered redundant. Central to the representational model is the idea that the work of art is a product of a self-conscious logical argument, always prior to the fabrication of the work. Of course, these constitute extreme positions that rarely see the light of day within the specialized field of contemporary art discourse. In non-specialized art commentary, however, one often encounters a fusion of both positions: where art might be seen as both the beautiful product of artistic expression and the provider of a message. Yet, even within the more specialized fields of critical art discourse, representationalism and aestheticism tend to govern thinking on art from a distance.

More than any other thinker, Martin Heidegger sets out a way of thinking the work of art outside of the modern Cartesian framework to which both of these arguments essentially belong. He wishes to preserve an autonomous power for art which is not held hostage to the vague and ineffable experience of aesthetics or the instrumental thinking of representationalism. In Heidegger's conception of the encounter with the work of art, knowing is associated with both willing resoluteness and a non-willing letting, where the act of artistic creation is thought more as an event in which phenomena are 'let' to emerge, rather than a strictly voluntary act whether that act is spontaneous or calculated. Heidegger retrieves the Greek terms *technē* and *poiēsis* which link the production of art to an ontological-phenomenological, epistemological, modality prior to a productionist conception of the work of art (and a productionist interpretation of being). Art, in Heidegger's view, constitutes a kind of letting (*Lassen*) that is prior to, and counter to, the metaphysical idea of production (the forming of matter in accordance with a preconceived idea, or image, in the mind). In accordance with this view, making art, rather than being thought as 'creation,' is thought in terms of letting something already existing emerge from out of concealment. In a very broad sense, Heidegger's thinking on art would seem to be amenable to an autopoietic mode of production.

32 According to the passage, aestheticism views the work of art as _____.

① a creature influenced by discourse which artists and beholders participate in

② an independent realization of the artist's own inner feelings and emotions

③ an object which holds a specific position in the beholder's epistemological view

④ a deliverer of some messages representing the artist's political ideology

33 Which of the following can be inferred from the passage?

① Both aestheticism and representationalism are under the influence of Cartesian thought which Heidegger argued against.

② In contemporary art, aestheticism has already replaced representationalism in accordance with the 'affective turn.'

③ In contemporary critical art discourse, critics tend to obviously make a choice between aestheticism and representationalism.

④ Critics standing for representationalism generally disregard the importance of logical arguments for the work of art.

34 According to the passage, which of the following is <u>not</u> likely to be Heidegger's thought of art?

① Art has an autonomous power, and is not subject to subjective aesthetic experience or instrumental thinking.

② Strictly speaking, the creation of art is not due to the artist's volition, but a kind of event that is let to emerge.

③ Making art is actually not an act of making something but just of revealing something from where it is hidden.

④ The productional understanding of the work of art is actually correlated to the autopoietic understanding of art.

Jeremy Bentham's Panopticon is the architectural figure that assures the automatic functioning of modern power. We know the principle on which it was based: at the periphery, an annular building; at the centre, a tower; this tower is pierced with wide windows that open onto the inner side of the ring; the peripheric building is divided into small cells, each of which extends the whole width of the building; they have two windows, one on the inside, corresponding to the windows of the tower; the other, on the outside, allows the light to cross the cell from one end to the other. All that is needed to secure the order, then, is to place a supervisor in a central tower and to shut up in each cell a madman, a convict, a patient, a condemned man, etc. By the effect of backlighting, one can observe from the tower, standing out precisely against the light, the small captive shadows in the cells of the periphery. They are like so many cages, so many small theatres, in which each actor is alone, perfectly individualized and constantly visible. The panoptic mechanism this way arranges spatial unities that make it possible to see constantly and to recognize immediately. In short, it reverses the principle of the dungeon; or rather of its three functions — to enclose, to deprive of light and to hide — it preserves only the first and eliminates the other two. Full lighting and the eye of a supervisor capture better than darkness, which ultimately protected. Visibility is a trap.

To begin with, this made it possible — as a negative effect — to avoid those compact, swarming, howling masses that were to be found in places of confinement, those painted by Goya or described by Howard. Each individual, in his place, is securely confined to a cell from which he is seen from the front by the supervisor; but the side walls prevent him from coming into contact with his companions. He is seen, but he does not see; he is the object of information, never a subject in communication. The arrangement of his room, opposite the central tower, imposes on him an axial visibility; but the divisions of the ring, those separated cells, imply a lateral invisibility. And this invisibility is a guarantee of order. If the inmates are convicts, there is no danger of a plot, an attempt at collective escape, the planning of new crimes for the future, bad reciprocal influences; if they are patients, there is no danger of contagion; if they are madmen there is no risk of their committing violence upon one another. The crowd, a compact mass, a locus of multiple exchanges, individualities merging together, a collective effect, is abolished and replaced by a collection of separated individualities. From the point of view of the guardian, it is replaced by a multiplicity that can be numbered and supervised; from the point of view of the inmates, by a sequestered and observed solitude. Hence in Panopticon, the surveillance is permanent in its effects, even if it is discontinuous in its action; that the perfection of power should tend to render its actual exercise Ⓐ_____; that this architectural apparatus should be a machine for creating and sustaining a power relation independent of the person who exercises it; in short, that the inmates should be caught up in a power situation of which they are themselves the bearers.

35 Which of the following is most appropriate for Ⓐ?

① necessary   ② unnecessary

③ unintentional   ④ intentional

36 Which of the following can be inferred from the passage?

① Full lighting system in Panopticon eventually increases the risk of the inmates' committing violence upon one another.

② Bentham's Panopticon aims at enclosing the swarming mass of people and depriving them of light entirely.

③ Bentham's Panopticon divides the architectural space into the small units which help the modern form of power function more automatically.

④ The collective power of the inmates in Bentham's Panopticon could be abolished due to the increased numbers of guardians.

37 Which of the following is most likely to be the main purpose of the writing?

① To inform readers how the new form of power has been achieved through spatial mechanism of Panopticon

② To inform readers how the danger of contagion or violence can be avoided in prison cells

③ To inform readers how the concepts of modern power and individuality have been replaced by the collective man power in the contemporary era

④ To inform readers how the functioning of modern power is derived from discontinuous and impermanent surveillance system

[38-40] Read the following passage and answer the questions.

Native-speakerism is defined as a pervasive ideology within English language teaching (ELT), characterized by the belief that 'native-speaker' teachers represent a 'Western culture' from which spring the ideals both of the English language and of English language teaching methodology. This bias is based on the spurious, poorly-defined, and ideologically constructed concepts of 'native speaker' and 'non-native speaker,' and has been seen to produce numerous negative consequences for English language teachers who are defined as 'non-native speaker teachers.' The fact that such an ideology is at play, based on spurious and ill-defined terms, is particularly problematic when we consider the fact that such individuals make up the majority of English language teachers worldwide, with conservative estimates at around 80%.

Holliday coined the term 'native-speakerism' which seeks to deal with the issues of culture and politics in ELT in a more overarching way by including discussions of culturism and Orientalism. In his book, Edward Said, a professor of English in Columbia University, described Orientalism as "the corporate institution for dealing with the Orient — dealing with it by making statements about it, describing it, by teaching it, settling it, ruling over it: in short Orientalism as a Western style for dominating, restructuring, and having authority over the Orient."

Said described orientalism as reductive in the sense that it essentializes complex systems, cultures, and groups and explains them in simplistic ways, lacking in nuance. The 'Orient' as a construct reflects this, with the simplicity of the terminology highlighting the reductive nature of the discourse. Susser provides a clear example of Orientalism at work in ELT through an examination of materials offering advice to foreign teachers entering Japan, and research into cross-cultural learning styles. Susser found that the texts were grounded in assumptions, stereotypes, platitudes, and errors, which seemed intended to legitimize the authority of Western teachers over local teachers, students, and educational institutions by 'othering' them and attempting to solve problems that have been constructed by the writers from stereotypical images of the Japanese.

A clear example of this given by Susser is a statement by Dadour and Robbins concerning Japanese students, in which they claim that student preferences is to passively absorb information provided by teachers. This is a common stereotypical depiction of students in Japan, China, and other East Asian nations, and one which has not only been questioned on theoretical grounds, but has also been shown to be incorrect in research on student attitudes. The ways in which structures and systems with western-centric biases have used discourses in ELT to dominate the profession has led to a number of undesirable consequences for 'non-native speaker' professionals.

38 Which of the following <u>cannot</u> be inferred from the passage?

① Native-speakerism tends to affect employment practices, tipping the scale in favor of 'native-speakers', particularly, though not limited to settings where English is a foreign language.

② ELT remains a field dominated by Western 'native-speaker' voices.

③ The concept of native-speakerism is over-deterministic, underplaying the role of agency and how non-native speaker teachers exercise choice.

④ One aspect of the concept of native-speakerism is an ideological discourse that uses 'othering' to marginalize non-Western cultures.

39 Which of the following is the purpose of the passage?

① To describe the relation between native speakerism and orientialism

② To explain how native speakerism has resulted in stereotypical images of the Japanese

③ To inform the reader of the negative effect of ideologically constructed concept of native speakerism

④ To provide examples for problematic discourse of native speakerism that commonly includes western-centric biases

40 Which of the following <u>cannot</u> be a good example of "undesirable consequences for 'non-native speaker' professionals"?

① Student preferences for Western models of English

② 'Non-native speaker' teachers being portrayed as less authentic

③ ELT materials having a positive orientation towards 'native speaker' teachers over non-native counterparts

④ Mediatized discourses highlighting the reductive nature of the native-speakerist discourse

HONGIK
UNIVERSITY

홍익대학교   2024학년도 서울 자연계 A형
▶▶ 영어 25문항, 수학 15문항·70분

[01-09] Choose the one that is closest in meaning to the underlined word.

01   The author used his inhuman, yet all too human narrator to gaze upon the theological <u>heft</u> of human lives and to call its bluff in his dystopian novel.

    ① insignificance   ② fragility

    ③ weight   ④ meagerness

02   Most of his recent novels are narrated in accents of punishing <u>blandness</u>; all of them make plentiful use of techniques such as cliché, banality, and evasion.

    ① objectivity   ② particularity

    ③ dullness   ④ impartiality

03   The directives which the captions give to those looking at pictures in magazines soon become even more explicit and more <u>imperative</u> in the film where the meaning of each single picture appears to be prescribed by the sequence of all preceding ones.

    ① precise   ② essential

    ③ implicit   ④ eccentric

04 The film responds to the <u>shriveling</u> of the aura with an artificial build-up of the personality outside the studio and the cult of the movie star, fostered by the money of the film industry, preserves not the unique aura of the person but the spell of the personality.

① burgeoning   ② bustling
③ flushing   ④ dwindling

05 This class of morbid anxiety would then be no other than what is uncanny, <u>irrespective</u> of whether it originally aroused dread or some other affect.

① impertinent   ② irreverent
③ regretful   ④ regardless

06 An accident or a death will rarely take place without having cast its shadow before on their minds and for the reason they are in the habit of mentioning this state of affairs in the most modest manner, saying that they have <u>presentiment</u> which usually comes true.

① tranquility   ② foreboding
③ composure   ④ hostility

07 The Houthis had refrained from directly confronting U.S. forces, even as the Biden administration took the lead in announcing the formation of a maritime <u>coalition</u> to confront the Yemeni militants.

① alliance   ② summation
③ arbitration   ④ lien

08 A predominant ideology of internationalization in higher education today is instrumentalism, with the goal to enrich the labor force and consolidate the economic <u>prowess</u> of a country.

① reliance   ② capacity
③ compassion   ④ diffidence

09 Other research on immigrants reveals the importance of their ties to their country of emigration and to their new identities as transnationals and as people who shuttle between communities, rather than as <u>acculturating</u> newcomers.

① affirming　　　　　② assimilating
③ acceding　　　　　④ abbreviating

[10-15] Choose one that is either ungrammatical or unacceptable.

10 One can follow the swarming activity of these procedures that, far from ①<u>being</u> regulated or eliminated by government's administration, ②<u>have</u> reinforced themselves in a ③<u>proliferating</u> illegitimacy and combined in accord with unreadable but stable tactics to the point of ④<u>being constituted</u> everyday regulations and surreptitious creativities.

11 That object-choice has ①<u>effected</u> on a narcissistic basis, so that the object-cathexis, when obstacles come in this way, can regress to narcissism. The narcissistic identification with the object then becomes a substitute for the erotic cathexis, the result of ②<u>which</u> is that ③<u>in spite of</u> the conflict with the loved person the love-relation need not ④<u>be</u> given up.

12 It is true that the operations of ①<u>walking on</u> can be ②<u>traced</u> on city maps in such a way as to ③<u>transcribing</u> their paths and their trajectories but these thick or thin curves only refer, like words, ④<u>to</u> the absence of what has passed by.

13 One would be tempted ①<u>to</u> regard these cases as non-psychogenic, if it ②<u>were</u> not for the fact that the psycho-analytic method has succeeded ③<u>in</u> arriving ④<u>for</u> a satisfactory solution.

14 Security of supply is ①<u>of concern</u> in a ②<u>politically unstable</u> world, and new demands for ③<u>imported</u> oil from China and other growing economies are ④<u>stressing in</u> markets.

15   All require some form either ①<u>of land use</u>, ②<u>with</u> its attendant disruption of the associated ecosystems, or of extraction, ③<u>in which</u> can be disruptive for fossil fuels, though ④<u>less so</u> for nuclear ones.

[16-19] Choose the one that is most suitable for the blank.

16   Foucauldian discipline may be identified neither with an institution nor with an apparatus since it is a type of power, a _____ for its own exercise, comprising a whole set of instruments, techniques, procedures, levels of application; it is an anatomy of power, a technology.

① modality   ② modicum
③ molt   ④ mood

17   Many adults still retain their apprehensiveness in this respect, and no bodily injury is so much dreaded by them _____ an injury to the eye.

① for   ② with
③ as   ④ through

18   In 1997, the Asian financial crisis struck, _____ the need for an economic bailout from the International Monetary Fund.

① threatening   ② precipitating
③ chagrining   ④ mobilizing

19   *Chogi yuhak* (early study-abroad) even worked as a disadvantage in some cases as returnees reported experiencing tremendous stress in _____ in English in the workplace.

① performing   ② exploiting
③ exploring   ④ bringing

In the twentieth century a number of philosophers have begun to be concerned about what they take to be the fateful consequences of holding human knowledge of the world to be analogous to visual perception. John Dewey argued in 1929, Ⓐ_____, that Western philosophy since Plato and Aristotle has been dominated by a "spectator theory of knowledge" in which the theory of knowing is modeled after what was supposed to take place in the act of vision, and he criticized philosophy's corresponding insistence on the importance of unclouded observation and accurate representation of reality — on *seeing* the world clearly — for reinforcing the traditional depreciation of practical activity on the part of the intellectual class. In Dewey's judgment, the spectator theory of knowledge reflects the profound conviction (or prejudice) prevalent among Western philosophers that the aim of philosophical or scientific inquiry is to come to know reality — as we seem to do in vision — without in any way interfering with it or modifying it through practical activity. He claims, further, that the main consequence of this search for the accurate, undistorted representation of what is independently real has been the familiar, but in his view needless and fruitless, dispute between philosophers over which objects are in fact the most certain and most real — physical, mathematical, or logical objects — and over which kind of object genuine knowledge should seek to conform to.

As an alternative to the spectator theory of knowledge Dewey himself proposes a practical, participatory conception of knowledge based on the idea of experimentation. According to this model, the inquirer does not seek a purely theoretical understanding of the world through endeavoring to bring his thoughts into conformity with a reality which is assumed to be independent of human activity, but rather operates on the objects of study (for example, through adding chemicals to one another or through changing the soil in which plants grow) and so participates in generating the things that are known. If all genuine knowledge is understood according to this model of experimentation, Dewey maintains, the object of knowledge will not be thought of as something fixed with antecedent existence or essential being, but will be seen to reside in the consequences of directed action in whatever field we are working, be it physics, chemistry, sociology, or psychology. As a result, no single object of knowledge can be held up as the most real, because all the things we know will be understood to be the products of specific practical operations on objects in the world which are designed to deal with specific, equally pressing problems.

20 Which of the following is the most appropriate for Ⓐ?

① for example ② however
③ therefore ④ then

21 According to the passage, which of the following is <u>not</u> likely to be the characteristics of the "spectator theory of knowledge"?

① How people acquire knowledge is, and should be, modeled based on how they see and observe the actual reality.

② Philosophical theories should describe in a correct way what is real in the actual world.

③ Practical aspects had better be ignored in doing philosophy because they are not related to understand the actual reality.

④ Disputes on what is certain and what is real are not significant because they do not contribute to our actual lives.

22 Which of the following can be inferred from the passage?

① Philosophers cannot see what is real because they build their theories based on what and how they can see.

② According to Dewey, people can acquire knowledge on the unchanging reality only based on the experimentation.

③ For Dewey, what is important is not the fixed reality but the result of actions, through which we can gain knowledge.

④ Plato and Aristotle wrote works on practical issues and therefore they can be said to be respectful to the experimental knowledge.

Real numbers are called 'real' because they seem to provide the magnitudes needed for the measurement of distance, angle, time, energy, temperature, or of numerous other geometrical and physical quantities. However, the relationship between the abstractly defined 'real' numbers and physical quantities is not as clear-cut as one might imagine. Real numbers refer to a mathematical idealization rather than to any actual physically objective quantity. The system of real numbers has the property of density, for example, that between any two of them, no matter how close, there lies a third. It is not at all clear that physical distances or times can realistically be said to have this property. If we continue to divide up the physical distance between two points, we would eventually reach scales so small that the very concept of distance, in the ordinary sense, could cease to have meaning. It is anticipated that at the 'quantum gravity' scale of 10^{20}th of the size of a subatomic particle, this would indeed be the case. But to mirror the real numbers, we would have to go to scales indefinitely smaller than this: 10^{200}th, or 10^{2000}th, for example. It is not at all clear that such absurdly tiny scales have any physical meaning whatever. A similar remark would hold for correspondingly tiny intervals of time.

The real number system is chosen in physics for its mathematical utility, simplicity, and elegance, together with the fact that it accords, over a very wide range, with the physical concepts of distance and time. It is not chosen because it is known to agree with these physical concepts over all ranges. One might well anticipate that there is indeed no such accord at very tiny scales of distance or time. It is commonplace to use rulers for the measurement of simple distances, but such rulers will themselves take on a granular nature when we get down to the scale of their own atoms. This does not, in itself, prevent us from continuing to use real numbers in an accurate way, but a good deal more sophistication is needed for the measurement of yet smaller distances. We should at least be a little suspicious that there might eventually be a difficulty of fundamental principle for distances on the tiniest scale. As it turns out, Nature is remarkably kind to us, and it appears that the same real numbers that we have grown used to for the description of things at an everyday scale or larger retain their usefulness on scales much smaller than atoms — certainly down to less than one-hundredth of the 'classical' diameter of a sub-atomic particle, say an electron or proton — and seemingly down to the 'quantum gravity scale', twenty orders of magnitude smaller than such a particle! This is a quite extraordinary extrapolation from experience. The familiar concept of real-number distance seems to hold also out to the most distant quasar and beyond, giving an overall range of at least 10^{42}, and perhaps 10^{60} or more. The appropriateness of the real number system is not often questioned, in fact. Why is there so much confidence in these numbers for the accurate description of physics, when our initial experience of the relevance of such numbers lies in a comparatively limited range?

23 According to the passage, why is the real number system used in physics?

① Because of its concreteness and intuitiveness

② Because of its exhaustive and total accordance with reality

③ Because of its mathematical elegance and usefulness

④ Because of its applicability to indefinitely small subatomic scales

24 Which of the following <u>cannot</u> be inferred from the passage?

① Physical phenomena can be mathematically idealized by using real numbers.

② A physical quantity always corresponds to a certain real number in a meaningful way.

③ Real numbers can be used to express infinitesimal as well as enormous quantities.

④ The density of real numbers may not be useful in measuring physical quantities.

25 Which of the following is most likely to <u>follow</u> the passage?

① The reason why the real number system is so confidently used in many areas of physics

② The reason why the real number system is different from other number systems

③ The reason why the rulers for the measurement cannot be used in physics

④ The reason why the mathematical utility, simplicity, and elegance are physically crucial

MEMO

MEMO

MEMO

합격을 완성할 단 하나의 선택

김영편입
영어

기출문제 해설집

해설편

CONTENTS

교재의 내용에 오류가 있나요?
www.**kimyoung**.co.kr ➡ 온라인 서점 ➡ 정오표 게시판
정오표에 반영되지 않은 새로운 오류가 있을 때에는 교재 오류신고
게시판에 글을 남겨주세요. 정성껏 답변해 드리겠습니다.

해설편

합격을 완성할 단 하나의 선택

김영편입 영어
2025학년도 대비
기출문제 해설집

해설편

01 ①	02 ①	03 ③	04 ①	05 ③	06 ②	07 ③	08 ④	09 ③	10 ③
11 ③	12 ①	13 ④	14 ③	15 ④	16 ④	17 ②	18 ①	19 ③	20 ②
21 ③	22 ①	23 ④	24 ②	25 ④	26 ①	27 ④	28 ②	29 ④	30 ②
31 ③	32 ③	33 ②	34 ②	35 ①	36 ④	37 ①	38 ②	39 ③	40 ④

01 동의어 ①

likely a. 그럴듯한 neglect n. 태만 confidence n. 자신감 radiation n. 방사선; 방사선 치료 tissue n. (세포들로 이뤄진) 조직 premise n. (주장의) 전제 arrogance n. 오만함(= conceit) with regard to ~와 관련해 patient n. 환자 homage n. 경의, 존경 fiat n. 명령, 지시 compunction n. 죄책감

그루베(Grubbe)가 태만해지게 된 한 가지 그럴듯한 설명은 그가 엑스레이 치료에서 거둔 처음의 성공이 방사선 치료가 인체 조직에 어떤 영향을 미치는지에 관한 그의 이해에 잘못된 자신감을 불어넣었을지도 모른다는 것이다. 그는 전제가 잘못된 채 일하고 있었지만, 그의 오만함이 환자의 건강과 자신의 건강과 관련해 그를 대담하게 만들었다.

02 동의어 ①

textile n. 직물, 옷감 collection n. 소장품 amass v. 모으다, 수집하다 conspicuous a. (남의) 이목을 끄는, 두드러진(= salient) display v. 드러내다; 과시하다 position v. (특정한 위치에) 두다 Tudor n. 튜더 왕조의 nuance v. ~에 미묘한 차이를 주다 ingenuity n. 독창성, 창의력 sanguine a. 낙관적인 reticent a. 말을 잘 안 하는 tangential a. 거의 관계없는

베스(Bess, Elizabeth의 애칭)가 수집한 직물 소장품은 그녀의 재산을 과시하고 그녀 자신을 튜더 왕조의 최상부에 올려놓기 위한 두드러진 시도라고 전통적으로 여겨져 왔다. 그러나 최근의 프로젝트는 현실은 이보다 더 미묘한 차이를 보여준다는 것을 시사한다. 즉 연구원들은 직물이 베스의 창의적인 독창성의 표현을 나타낸다고 주장한다.

03 동의어 ③

call out 불러내다, 소집하다, 출동시키다 egregious a. 악명 높은; 지독한(= flagrant) erase v. (완전히) 지우다 paragon n. 모범, 전형 mature a. 성숙한 seemingly ad. 겉보기에 smooth v. 매끈하게 하다, 반듯하게 펴다 prepossessing a. (외모가) 매력적인 prodigious a. 엄청난 magnanimous a. 너그러운

사람들은 많은 시청자들이 악명 높은 나이 지우기라고 여기는 것을 동원하는 일에, 즉 겉으로 보기에 나이의 흔적들이 얼굴에서 사라진 58세, 57세, 54세, 그리고 53세의 여성들을 성숙미의 전형이라고 선전하는 일에 집중했다.

04 동의어 ①

bring a case[lawsuit] against ~을 상대로 소송을 제기하다 closely ad. 밀접하게 imitate v. 모방하다 dismiss v. (소송을) 기각하다 copyright n. 저작권 bear something out ~이 사실임을 증명하다 (= vindicate) nullify v. 무효화하다 conjugate v. (동사를 수·인칭·시제에 따라) 변화시키다 prostrate v. (특히 예배를 보기 위해) 엎드리다

그 창작자들은 자신들의 작품으로 훈련되었지만 그 작품을 아주 비슷하게 모방하지는 않은 시스템을 상대로 소송을 제기하느라 보다 힘든 시간을 보내게 될 것이다. 코미디언 사라 실버맨(Sarah Silverman) 등이 메타(Meta)를 상대로 제기한 저작권 소송 중 일부를 기각한 재판관의 최근 결정은 이것이 사실임을 증명한다.

05 동의어 ③

outing n. 나들이 clamber up 기어오르다 deck n. (배의) 갑판; (이층 버스의) 층 sheepishly ad. 소심하게(= timorously) claim v. 차지하다 unobscured a. 은폐되지 않은 prospect n. 전망 breathlessly ad. 헐떡이면서 ponderingly ad. 숙고하여 covertly ad. 은밀히

마치 아버지와 주말 나들이에 나선 신나는 아이인 것처럼, 나는 더 좋은 전망을 보기 위해 2층으로 올라간 다음, 전망이 가리지 않는 앞좌석을 소심하게 차지했다.

06 동의어 ②

The National Trust 내셔널 트러스트(명승지 보존을 위한 민간단체) estate n. (보통 시골 지역에 정원 등이 있는 대규모) 사유지 country house (특히 유명 가문의) 시골 저택 nostalgia n. 옛날을 그리워함; 향수(鄕愁) rural a. (도시에 대하여) 시골의, 지방의 property n. 부동산; 건물 pander to (욕망에) 영합하다, 방조하다, 만족시키다(= indulge) deference n. 존경 landed a. 많은 토지를 소유한 abate v. 약화시키다 swerve v. (특히 자동차가 갑자기) 방향을 바꾸다 exacerbate v. 악화시키다

수백 개의 시골 사유지와 시골의 큰 저택을 소유하거나 관리하는 내셔널 트러스트(National Trust)는 잃어버린 시골 낙원에 대한 향수(鄕愁)가 높아짐에 따라, 100년 전에 설립되었다. 너무나 많은 부동산이 큰 저택이기 때문에, 내셔널 트러스트는 대지주 가문에 대한 (사람들의) 존경심에 영합할 수 있다.

07 동의어 ③

migrant n. 이주자 almanac n. 연감(= yearbook)(어떤 분야에 관하여 한 해 동안 일어난 경과, 사건 등을 수록하는 간행물) trek n. (특히 힘든) 여행, 여정 document v. (상세한 내용을) 기록하다 route n. 경로 pitfall n. (눈에 잘 안 띄는) 위험, 함정 stretch n. (한 연속의) 시간, 일, 노력 on one's own 스스로 smuggler n. 밀수범 itinerary n. 여행 일정표 diagram n. 도표, 도해

오늘날 이주자들은 미국으로 가는 여정을 기록한 엄청난 디지털 연감을 생산하고 있는데, 그 경로와 거기에 있는 위험을 아주 상세하게 기록하고 있어서, 사람들은 몇 번만 들여다보면 밀수업자의 도움 없이도 스스로 길을 찾을 수 있다.

08 동의어 ④

novelist n. 소설가 short story 단편소설 nascent a. 발생기의, 초기의(= burgeoning) celebrity n. 유명인, (유명) 연예인 indescribable a. 형언할[말로 다 할] 수 없는 screen n. 영화 luminary n. 권위자, 선각자 epicurean a. 쾌락주의적 inimical a. ~에 해로운 spendthrift a. 돈을 헤프게 쓰는

1927년, 영국의 소설가 엘리너 글린(Elinor Glyn)은 『코스모폴리탄』 잡지에 단편소설을 발표했는데, 이 소설은 유명인들이 당시에 향유했던 초기 문화를 정의해주었다. 글린의 단편소설은 '그것(유명인의 명성)'의 개념을 탐구했는데, 그것은 신비스럽고, 형언할 수 없는, 아마도 유명인들과 영화 권위자들은 갖고 있지만, 일반인들은 갖고 있지 않는 마법 같은 자질이다.

09 동사와 과거분사의 구분 ③

At a time이 이끄는 관계부사절에서 5형식 동사 have의 목적보어가 목적어와의 관계에서 잘 쓰였는지를 묻고 있다. 이미지 메이커들은 스스로 '배속하는 주체'가 아니라, 정치 후보들에 의해 참모진으로 '배속되는 객체'이다. 따라서 목적보어로 동사원형이 아니라 '과거분사'가 와야 하므로, ③을 attached로 고쳐야 한다.

penetration n. 침투 reflect v. 반영하다 illusion n. 환상 attach v. 소속[배속]시키다 staff n. 직원; (군대의) 참모 collar n. (윗옷의) 칼라, 깃

미국인의 삶 구석구석에 침투한 현대 광고의 성공은 현실보다는 환상을 선택한 문화를 반영한다. 정치 후보들이 모두 전문 이미지 메이커들을 참모진으로 두고 있고 미국의 대통령도 한때 셔츠 칼라를 팔았던 배우일 수 있는 시대에, 모든 문화적인 징후들은 우리 삶에서 환상을 줄이기보다 환상을 늘리는 쪽으로 향하고 있다.

10 대명사 their와 its의 구분 ③

③에서 their가 가리키는 대상은 Netflix로 단수대명사인 its가 되어야 하므로, ③을 its로 고쳐야 한다.

credit A as B A를 B라고 믿다 subscriber n. 구독자 hit n. 인기작품 division n. (조직의) 분과[부, 국] license v. (공적으로) 허가하다 set up 설립하다

넷플릭스는 넷플릭스의 대규모 구독자 기반과 추천 알고리즘을 '식스 핏 언더(Six Feet Under)' 같이 방영한 지 무려 22년이나 지난 프로그램이나 '슈츠(Suits)' 같이 한때 잊혀버린 케이블TV 기본형의 법정 드라마가 넷플릭스 인기작이 될 수 있는 이유라고 여긴다. 서랜도스(Sarandos)씨는 넷플릭스는 오리지널 시리즈 라이선스 부서를 따로 두지 않으며, 그도 그런 부서를 만들어야 할 이유를 발견하지 못한다고 말했다.

11 관계대명사절의 수일치 ③

관계대명사 what이 이끄는 절에서 what이 be동사의 주어인 경우 '보어인 명사가 단수인지 복수인지'에 따라 단수와 복수를 정한다. 따라서 ③에 관계대명사 what이 be동사 was의 주어가 되고, 보어가 the bare branches로 복수이므로, ③의 what was를 what were로 고쳐야 한다.

bulb n. (양파 등의) 구근(球根) gratitude n. 고마움, 감사 unfold v. 펼쳐지다 incremental a. 서서히 증가하는 reassuring a. 안심시키는 branch n. 가지 weeping a. (나무의) 가지를 늘어뜨린 willow n. 버드나무 gauze v. (상처에 붙이는) 거즈로 덮다 swipe n. 일격 ocher n. 황토색

그러나 심지어 1월에도 이웃집 정원의 흙을 뚫고 올라오는 구근들이 있다. 어제까지만 해도 앙상한 가지를 늘어뜨린 버드나무였는데, 오늘 보니 옐로우 오커, 카드뮴 그린, 세룰리안 블루가 한데 어우러진 새로운 잎들이 가지에 덮임에 따라 영국의 봄이 서서히 안심되게 시작되는 것에 일종의 감사한 마음이 생긴다.

12 조동사+have+p.p. ①

조동사 must를 이용한 He must be crazy to do such a thing 은 '그런 짓을 하다니 그는 미쳤음에 틀림없다'는 뜻인데, 이 글은 빈칸 문장을 제외하고 모두 현재 시제로 되어 있다. 현재 벌어지고 있는 보안관의 악행은 그는 한 인간에게 먼저 일어난 일의 결과인 것이다. 따라서 과거의 일에 대한 강한 추측을 나타낼 때는 must have p.p.를 사용하므로, ①의 must have happened가 빈칸에 적절하다.

sheriff n. 보안관 dismiss v. 묵살하다, 치부하다 get drunk 취하다 assume v. 추정하다 drive v. (사람을 특정한 방식의 행동을 하도록) 만들다 club n. 곤봉 menace with ~로 협박하다 cattle prod 소몰이 막대(전류가 흐름) awful a. 끔찍한 ghastly a. 섬뜩한

앨라배마(Alabama) 주 셀마(Selma)에 있는 보안관 클라크(Clark)를 완전한 괴물로 치부할 수는 없다. 나는 그가 아내와 아이들을 사랑하고 술에 취하는 것을 좋아한다고 확신한다. 그도 나와 같은 남자라고 생각해야 한다. 그러나 무엇이 그로 하여금 곤봉을 사용하고 총으로 협박하고 소몰이 막대를 사용하게 만드는지를 그는 알지 못한다. 여성의 가슴에 소몰이 막대를 찌를 수 있다니 한 인간에게 어떤 끔찍한 일이 일어났음에 틀림없다. 그 여성에게 일어나는 일은 너무나 섬뜩하다. 그런 짓을 하는 그 남자에게 일어나는 일은 어떠한 면에서는 훨씬 더 섬뜩하다.

13 not so much A as B ④

forgotten(잊혀진)과 ignored(무시된, 간과된)가 병치된 구문인데, 알고 있던 것을 잊어버린 것이 아니라 못 보고 지나쳤, 간과된 것이라고 forgotten을 부정하고 ignored를 긍정하는 의미는 ④의 not so much forgotten as ignored만이 갖고 있어서 ④가 빈칸에 적절하다. (far) more forgotten than ignored는 반대로 ignored를 부정하고 forgotten을 긍정하는 의미이며, as ~ as나 no less ~ than은 둘 모두를 긍정하는 의미이다.

Oscar-winning a. 오스카상을 수상한(미국의 아카데미상을 받은) observe v. 관찰하다 redirect v. ~의 방향을 바꾸다 cinematic a. 영화(제작)의 gaze n. 응시, (눈여겨보는) 시선 fleeting a. 잠깐 동안의 inured to ~에 단련된[익숙한] pass over something ~을 무시하다 alternative a. 대안적인 stagnation n. 불경기 cordiality n. 진심; 온정 disappearance n. 소멸, 실종

오스카상을 수상한 '노매드랜드(Nomadland)'라는 영화는 잊혔다기보다 오히려 무시되거나 처음에는 결코 눈에 띄지 않는 미국을 관찰한다. 이 영화는 영화의 시선이 보통 잠깐밖에 머무르지 않는 곳으로, 그리고 영화의 시선이 종종 서비스직, 대안적 거주환경, 노인, 일반 여성, 특히 불경기, 온정, 실종에 관심 없는 노인 독신 여성들을 무시하는 데 익숙한 사람들에 의해 만들어지는 곳으로 관심을 돌린다.

14 논리완성 ③

여성의 지위 향상이 이념 때문이 아니라, 여성이 일하는 가정이 번영한다는 인식 때문이라고 했는데, 이것은 성별을 대하는 태도가 경제적 현실에 영향을 주는 것과 영향의 방향이 정반대인 상황이므로, 빈칸에는 rather와 함께 쓰여 오히려 그 '반대이다'가 되도록 ③의 the other way around(경제적 현실이 성별을 대하는 태도에 영향을 준다)가 적절하다.

gender n. 성(性), 성별 rise n. 성공, 출세, 지위 향상 ideology n. 이념 prosper v. 번영하다 the other way around 반대로, 거꾸로

성별을 대하는 태도는 경제적 현실에 영향을 주지 않으며, 오히려 그 반대이다.(경제적 현실이 성별을 대하는 태도에 영향을 준다.) 여성의 지위 향상은 이념이나 정치운동의 결과가 아니라, 제2차 세계대전 이후, 여성이 일하는 가정이 번영하는 가정이라는 인식이 널리 확산된 결과이다. 그래서 여성이 일하는 국가들이 번영하는 국가이다.

15 논리완성 ④

빈칸이 들어있는 문장의 but 앞에서 영국인들이 동질적인 사회를 형성하고 있다는 가정이 널리 퍼져 있다는 '긍정적인' 내용이 왔으므로, but 다음에 온 빈칸에는 이와 상반된 '부정적인' 내용이 와야 한다. 빈칸 다음에, 잉글랜드 사람도 스코틀랜드 사람도 자신을 영국인이라고 부르거나 남이 그렇게 부르는 것을 들으면 반드시 터무니없다고 생각하고 어색해한다고 했으므로, 영국이 동질적인 사회를 형성하고 있다는 가정에는 상당한 '수정'이 필요할 것이다. 따라서 빈칸에는 ④의 qualification이 적절하다.

homogeneous a. 동질적인 Englishman n. 잉글랜드 사람 Scotsman n. 스코틀랜드 사람 Briton n. 영국인 sneaking a. (감정을) 남몰래 품고 있는 ludicrous a. 터무니없는 refer to A as B A를 B로 여기다 Britisher n. 영국인 squirm v. 몹시 어색해 하다 proficiency n. 숙달, 능숙 commiseration n. (특히 시합에서 진 사람에 대한) 위로의 표현 munificence n. 아낌없이 줌 qualification n. 자격; 수정

영국인들이 강력한 정체성 의식을 가진 비교적 동질적인 사회를 형성하고 있다는 가정이 널리 퍼져 있지만, 그런 가정에는 상당한 수정이 필요하다. 예를 들어, 파울러(Fowler)는 그의 유명한 『현대영어 용법 사전』에서 "잉글랜드 사람도 스코틀랜드 사람도 자신을 영국인이라고 부르면 반드시 남몰래 터무니없다고 생각하게 되고, 자신이 영국인이라고 일컬어지는 것을 들으면 반드시 몹시 어색해 하게 된다는 것을 기억해야 한다."고 썼다.

16 논리완성 ④

이류 작가들과는 달리 일류 작가는 높이 평가받지 못했다고 했으며, 일류 작가의 경우 열정적인 소수의 열의에 의해 더욱 강해졌다고 한 다음, 등위접속사 and로 연결되었으므로, 사후에 일류 작가라는 영광을 얻은 저자의 경우도 마찬가지로, '열정적인 소수의 열의'에 의해 그러했을 것이다. 따라서 '열의, 열정'에 해당하는 ④의 '끈질긴 인내심'이 빈칸에 적절하다.

first-class a. 최고급의, 일류의 immense a. 엄청난 appreciate v. 높이 평가하다 second-rate a. 썩 훌륭하지는 못한, 이류의 ardour n. 열정 glory n. 영광, 명예 sequel n. (책이나 영화의) 속편 be due to ~때문이다 solely ad. 오로지 leave someone alone ~를 내버려두다 keep on 계속하다 savour v. 음미하다[즐기다] capricious a. 변덕스러운 objective a. 객관적인 conjecture n. 추측 intermittent a. 간헐적인 obstinate a. 끈질긴 perseverance n. 인내심

심지어 일류 작가가 일생 동안 엄청난 성공을 거두었을 때에도, 대다수는 이류 작가들을 높이 평가하는 만큼 일류 작가를 그렇게 진심으로 높이 평가하지 않았다. 그는 항상 열정적인 소수의 열의에 의해 더욱 강해졌다. 그리고 사후에 (일류 작가의) 영광을 얻은 작가의 경우, 그 행복한 속편은 오로지 소수의 끈질긴 인내심 덕분이었다. 그들은 그를 혼자 내버려 둘 수 없었고, 내버려 두려고도 하지 않았다. 그들은 계속해서 그가 쓴 책을 음미했고, 그가 쓴 책에 관해 이야기했으며, 그가 쓴 책을 샀다.

17 논리완성 ②

다카사키야마 동물원의 원숭이들은 캐러멜 껍질을 벗겨 먹는 법을 몰랐지만, 놀이 과정에서 터득하게 되었고, 캐러멜 껍질을 벗겨 먹는 이 습관이 원숭이 사회 안에서 새끼들의 또래집단으로부터 어른 집단으로까지 전해졌는데, 이것은 다른 집단(새끼 집단)과의 지속적인 접촉을 통해 그 집단(어른 집단)의 문화가 변화되는 문화변용에 해당하므로 빈칸에는 ②의 acculturation이 적절하다.

throw v. 던지다 wrap v. ~을 싸다[포장하다] practice n. 관행 macaque n. 마카크, 짧은 꼬리 원숭이 unwrap v. (포장지 등을) 벗기다 pass something on to somebody ~을 …에게 전하다 successively ad. 연속적으로 playmate n. 놀이 친구 dominant a. 지배적인 male n. 남성 subadult a. 거의 어른이 다 된 transplant n. (생체 조직

등의) 이식; 이식된 장기조직 acculturation n. 문화변용, 사회화 evolution n. 진화 inheritance n. 상속; 유전

다카사키야마 (동물원) 방문객들이 종이에 싼 캐러멜을 원숭이에 던졌는데, 이것은 일본의 동물원에서는 흔한 관행이지만, 다카사키야마 동물원의 짧은 꼬리 원숭이들한테는 이전에 한 번도 마주친 적이 없던 일이었다. 놀이 과정에서, 일부 어린 원숭이들이 캐러멜 껍질을 벗겨 먹는 법을 터득했다. 이 습관은 그들의 놀이 친구, 그들의 엄마 원숭이, 지배하는 수컷 원숭이, 그리고 마침내 거의 어른이 다 된 원숭이들한테까지 연속적으로 전해졌다. 이 문화변용 과정은 대략 3년이 걸렸다.

18 논리완성 ①

A rather than B 구조가 쓰였다. A에 해당하는 것이 'in one sitting'이고, B에 해당하는 것이 '빈칸+it all day'이며, it은 sugary drink(설탕이 든 음료수)를 가리킨다. 설탕이 든 음료수를 한꺼번에 마시는 것과 하루 종일 마시는 것을 비교하고 있음을 알 수 있는데, 하루 종일 마신다는 것은 '벌컥벌컥 마시는' 것이 아니라 하루 종일 '갖고 있으면서 홀짝 거리며 마시는' 것을 말한다. 이렇게 하루 종일 '갖고 있는' 것에 해당하는 표현으로 '둥지를 품듯이 안고 있다'는 뜻을 갖고 있는 ①의 nestling이 빈칸에 적절하다.

absolutely ad. 정말로 sugary a. 설탕이 든 meal n. 식사, 끼니 in one sitting 한번에 gulp v. 벌컥벌컥 마시다 sip v. (음료를) 홀짝이다, 조금씩 마시다 swish v. 베어내다, 자르다 nestle v. 편안하게 안고 있다, 따뜻이 감싸다, 껴안다 postpone v. 연기하다, 미루다 devour v. (몹시 배가 고파서) 걸신들린 듯 먹다 contemplate v. 심사숙고하다

만일 당신이 설탕이 든 음료수를 꼭 마셔야 한다면, 식사할 때 같이 마시도록 하며, 아니면 하루 종일 그것을 갖고 있으면서 마시기보다 한번에 마시도록 해야 한다고 퀴노네즈(Quinonez) 박사가 말했다. "당신이 홀짝거리며 마시는 사람이 아니라 벌컥벌컥 마시는 사람이었으면 합니다." 당신이 식사를 마친 후 물을 마시는 것 또한 (입안에 남아있는) 설탕을 제거하는 데 도움을 줄 수 있다고 그녀가 덧붙여 말했다.

19 논리완성 ③

빈칸 다음 문장에서, 우리 눈앞의 테이블에 올려둔 잠금 상태의 스마트폰은 우리의 주의력을 산산이 부숴버린다고 했다. 따라서 스마트폰이 시야에 있다는 것, 즉 눈에 보인다는 것만으로도 우리의 집중력이 '고갈될' 것이므로, ③의 drain이 빈칸에 적절하다.

mere a. 단지 ~만의 presence n. (특정한 곳에) 있음, 존재 field of vision 가시 범위, 시야 scream v. 소리치다 shattered a. 산산이 부서진 fragment n. 조각, 파편 spot n. 얼룩; 장소 drain n. (정력 따위의) 소진, 고갈 gambit n. (대화 등의 초반에 우세를 확보하기 위한) 수; 계략

심리학자 하이트(Haidt)가 글에서 밝혔듯이, 스마트폰이 우리의 시야에 있다는 것만으로도 우리의 집중력을 고갈시킨다. 심지어 호주머니에 넣어 두었거나 우리 눈앞의 테이블에 올려둔 잠금 상태의 스마트폰도 우리의 분산된 주의력을 산산이 부숴버리기 위해 무언으로 소리치고 있다.

20 논리완성 ②

잉카인이 대규모 '정착지'를 형성했다고 했으므로, 빈칸에는 건조한 산악 지형을 '한 곳에 머물기에, 정주하기에' 적합한 곳으로 바꾸었다고 해야 한다. 따라서 ②의 sedentary가 적절하다.

Incan a. 잉카 사람의 domesticate v. (동물을) 사육하다; (작물을) 재배하다 settlement n. 정착지 undertake v. ~에 착수하다 transform v. 탈바꿈시키다 terrain n. 지형 suitable for ~에 적합한 apathetic a. 냉담한 sedentary a. 한 곳에 머물러 사는, 정주하는 unwonted a. 특이한 pioneer a. 선구적인

잉카인들이 식물을 재배하고 동물을 사육했다는 것은 기록에 잘 남아있는데, 이런 활동이 대규모 정착지를 형성하는 데 도움을 주었다. 잉카인들은 건조한 산악 지형을 정주 생활에 적합한 땅으로 바꾸기 위해 엄청난 노력을 기울였다.

21 논리완성 ③

교정 피드백의 한 형태인 리캐스트는 다른 형태의 피드백보다 포착하기가 힘들다고 했으며, 그다지 효과적인 것 같지도 않다고 했다. 따라서 빈칸에도 같은 맥락으로 리캐스트에 대한 '부정적인' 내용이 들어가야 하므로, '포착하기 힘든'과 비슷한 '파악하기 힘든'이라는 뜻의 ③의 elusive가 적절하다.

corrective a. (이전에 잘못된 것을) 바로잡는[교정의] n. 교정하는 것 subtle a. 미묘한, 포착하기 힘든 deal with ~을 다루다[처리하다] mixed a. (의견·생각 등이) 엇갈리는 luculent a. (설명 등이) 명쾌한 locative a. 위치를 나타내는 elusive a. 파악하기 어려운 myopic a. 근시안적인

리캐스트는 교정 피드백의 한 형태로 다른 형태의 피드백보다 포착하기가 더 힘들다. 비록 데이터에서 발견된 많은 리캐스트 사례들이 있었지만, 그 사례들은 특별히 효과적인 것 같지는 않았다. 이것은 리캐스트를 다소 파악하기 힘든 개념으로 만들며, 연구는 종종 엇갈린 결과를 내놓는다.

22 논리완성 ①

2020년 이전에는 사회적 유동성과 기상 조건의 계절적 상호작용은 '세심한 균형'을 이루어 겨울철에만 유행성 호흡기 질병이 급증했다고 한 다음, 역접부사 however가 왔다. 이런 '균형'이 코로나바이러스감염증-19로 깨어지게 되었다는 내용이 되어야 하므로, ①의 equilibrium이 빈칸에 적절하다.

prior to ~전에 seasonal a. 계절적인 interplay n. 상호작용 mobility n. 사회적 유동성 delicate a. 세심한; 미묘한 manifest v. 나타내다 surge n. 급증, 급등 respiratory a. 호흡 기관의 bug n. (가벼운) 유행성 질병 knock out ~을 나가떨어지게 하다 whack n. 강타 pandemic n. 전 세계적인 유행병 viral a. 바이러스성의 dynamic n. 역학; 원동력 equilibrium n. 균형 (상태) vagary n. 변덕; (날씨의) 예측할 수 없는 변화 conundrum n. 수수께끼 upheaval n. 격변, 대변동

2020년 이전에는 사회적 유동성과 기상 조건의 계절적 상호작용은 세심한 균형 속에 존재하여 겨울철에만 유행성 호흡기 질병이 급증했다. 그러나 이러한 균형 상태는 코로나바이러스감염증-19라는 세계적인 유행병의 강타로 깨어져, 그 결과, 겨울철 유행병이 1년 내내 존재하며, '결코 다시는 예전과 같아지지 않을 것'이라고 연구원들이 말하는 바이러스 역학에서의 변화가 초래되었다.

23 내용일치 ④

글림프 시스템으로 알려진 배수 시스템은 뇌척수액이 뇌 전체에 흐르게 해 독성 물질을 제거해주는데, 비수면 상태보다 수면 상태에서 이 청소하는 속도가 더 빠르다고 했을 뿐, 수면이 뇌세포 사이의 공간을 넓혀주는 체액을 뇌에 넘치게 한다는 내용은 본문과 관련 없으므로, ④가 정답이다.

shed light on ~을 밝혀주다   interstice n. 틈새, 빈틈   pathway n. 통로, 경로   toxin n. 독소   expel v. (공기나 물을) 배출하다   plumbing n. 배관; 급배수   glymphatic system 글림프 시스템(뇌에서 생산되는 노폐물을 씻어내는 시스템)   cerebrospinal fluid 뇌척수액   slumber n. 잠, 수면   channel n. 수로; 경로   crevice n. 틈   clear out 청소하다   toxic a. 독성이 있는   measure n. 조치   deterioration n. 악화, 저하   dispose of ~을 없애다   flood -v. 침수시키다

새로운 뇌 연구가 수면의 기능을 밝혀냈다. 과학자들은 수면 중에 뇌 안의 빈틈들이 확대되어 독소가 배출될 수 있는 통로가 넓어지는 것을 관찰했다. 이 공간들은 글림프 시스템이라고 알려진 일종의 배수 시스템을 형성하는데, 글림프 시스템은 뇌척수액이 뇌 전체에 흐르도록 해준다. 수면은 이런 배수로와 빈틈의 네트워크를 효과적으로 열어주어 뇌척수액이 독성 물질을 깨어있을 때보다 훨씬 더 빨리 제거하게 해준다. 이것은 수면이 손상과 악화로부터 일종의 보호조치 기능을 한다는 것을 보여준다.

이 글에 따르면, 다음 중 옳지 않은 것은?
① 뇌 시스템은 수면 중에 보다 빠른 속도로 독성 물질을 제거한다.
② 수면은 독소가 효과적으로 배출될 수 있도록 뇌의 틈을 넓혀준다.
③ 뇌척수액은 독성 물질을 없애도록 도와준다.
④ 수면이 뇌세포 사이의 공간을 넓혀주는 체액을 뇌에 넘치게 한다.

24 빈칸완성 ②

빈칸 Ⓐ 앞에 등위접속사 and가 있으므로, 빈칸 Ⓐ의 내용은 and 앞의 내용과 같은 맥락이어야 한다. 따라서 남자가 수줍음이 많고, 체격이 가냘프다고 했으므로, 이런 남자에게 어울리는 demure(얌전한)가 Ⓐ에 적절하다. while이 이끄는 부사절과 주절의 내용은 상반된 내용을 담고 있는데, 부사절에서 진짜 남자는 덩치가 크고 힘이 세다고 했으므로, 빈칸 Ⓑ에는 이와 상반되게 '덩치가 크고 힘이 셀 필요가 없다'고 해야 적절하므로, Ⓑ에는 beefy(우람한)가 적절하다.

mutually ad. 상호간에   respectful a. 존중하는   onscreen a. (텔레비전·영화) 화면의   romantic relationship 연인 관계   middle-class a. 중산층의   slightly-built a. 가냘픈 체격인   conventional a. 전통적인, 종래의   masculinity n. 남성성, 남자다움   femininity n. 여성성, 여성다움   refinement n. 고상함   classiness n. 세련됨   embody v. (사상·특질을) 상징[구현]하다; 포함하다   physical strength 체력

노동자 계급 여성과 중산층 남성 사이에 상호 존중하는 연인 관계가 영화나 TV 화면에 나온 예들을 생각할 수 있는가? 아니면 노동자 계급 여성이 신체적으로 힘이 세고 남성은 수줍음 많으면서 체격은 가냘프며 성격은 얌전한 예들을 생각할 수 있는가? 이런 비교는 남성다움과 여성다움에 대한 전통적인 개념들이 계급 권력 역학에 의해 어떻게 강화되어 왔는지를 보여준다. 여성다움은 종종 자본을 가진 사람들이 구현하는 고상함과 세련됨과 관련이 있다. '진짜 남자'는 '덩치가 크고 힘이 센' 반면, '신사'는 우람할 필요가 없다. 그는 문화 자본을 갖고 있으므로, 전통적으로 남성적인 체력을 필요로 하지 않는다.

다음 중 빈칸 Ⓐ와 Ⓑ에 들어가기에 가장 적절한 것은?
① 대담한 ― 작고 연약한
② 얌전한 ― 우람한
③ 내성적인 ― 뼈만 앙상한
④ 무례한 ― 건강한

25 빈칸완성 ④

사람들의 소셜 미디어 활동에 근거해 그 사람들을 어떻게 할 때 정당한 이유가 있는지를 묻고 있다. 빈칸 다음의 예시문에서 고용주는 인종차별적인 농담을 게시한 입사 지원자를 부적격으로 처리할 수 있다고 했으므로, 빈칸에도 같은 맥락으로 '부적격으로 처리'하거나 '걸러내는' 의미가 적절하다. 따라서 빈칸에는 '걸러내다'는 뜻인 ④가 정답이다.

profile n. (사진과 함께 싣는) 인물 소개, 프로필   fount n. 샘, 분수; 원천   vet v. 상세히 조사하다   job candidate 입사 지원자, 구직자   justifiable a. 정당한   disqualify v. 실격시키다; 부적격으로 처리하다   post v. 게시하다   racist a. 인종차별적인

소셜 미디어 프로필은 구직자들을 조사하는 고용주들에게 정보의 원천이 되어왔다. 비록 고용주들이 입사 지원자의 소셜 미디어 프로필 접속을 요구할 수는 없지만, 공개적으로 이용 가능한 정보를 볼 권리는 있다. 소셜 미디어 활동에 근거해 사람들을 걸러내는 데는 정당한 이유가 있다. 예를 들어, 고용주는 인종차별적인 농담을 게시한 것으로 드러난 누군가를 부적격으로 처리할 수 있다.

다음 중 빈칸 Ⓐ에 가장 적절한 것은?
① 엮어서 만들다
② 울며 보내다
③ 설거지를 하다
④ 걸러내다

26 빈칸완성 ①

시장이 자신의 직무를 이행하지 않고 있다고 주장하는 사람들은 그에 대해 안 좋게 '비방하는' 사람들일 것이므로, Ⓐ에는 '비방하는 사람들'이라는 뜻인 revilers나 detractors가 적절하다. 그리고 고발한 내용 중에는 시장이 '직무를 제대로 이행하지 않고 있다'는 주장이 있으므로, 이 고발을 조사하는 시의회 역시 시장이 '직무를 태만하게 하는지'를 판결해야 할 것이다. 따라서 Ⓑ에는 negligent(태만한)가 적절하므로, 두 빈칸에 모두 적절한 ①이 정답이다.

mayor n. 시장 slap v. 혹평하다, 모욕하다, (벌금을) 부과하다; ~을 (행정 명령 등으로) 단속하다 indictment n. 고발, 기소 complaint n. 고발; (민사의) 고소 nonprofit group 비영리 단체 complainant n. 원고, 고소인 betray v. (원칙 등을) 저버리다 breach v. (합의나 약속을) 위반하다 allege v. (증거 없이 혐의를) 주장하다 order n. 질서 city council 시의회 be in charge of ~을 담당하다 at stake 성패가 달려 있는, 위태로운

니스(Nice)의 시장이 어제 다양한 비영리 단체들로부터 기소 고발당하는 굴욕을 겪었다. 고발인들은 시장이 대중의 신뢰를 저버렸고 시의 몇 가지 법규를 위반했다고 말했다. 그를 비방하는 사람들은 도시의 평화와 질서를 유지하는 직무를 시장이 이행하지 않고 있다고 주장한다. 고발 조사를 맡은 시의회는 정부에 대한 국민의 신뢰가 걸린 만큼 시장이 직무를 태만하게 했는지를 즉시 판결해야 한다.

다음 중 빈칸 Ⓐ와 Ⓑ에 들어가기에 가장 적절한 것은?
① 비방하는 사람 ― 태만한
② 비방하는 사람 ― 침착한
③ 배신자 ― 후회하는
④ 사도 ― 양심적인

27 글의 흐름상 적절하지 않은 표현 고르기 ④

누아르 영화라는 장르는 누가 만들었는지, 이 장르의 특징은 무엇이고, 이 장르의 주인공들은 어떠한 모습인지 등 누아르 영화에 대해 전반적으로 소개하는 글이다. 누아르 영화라는 장르가 도입된 지 60년이 지난 오늘날 이 장르의 인기가 완전히 '시들지(wane)' 않았다고 했는데, 시들지 않고 있다면, 많은 최근 영화들도 누아르 영화 기법을 '도입했다'고 해야 글의 흐름상 자연스러울 것이다. 따라서 Ⓓ의 paid no heed to(~를 전혀 신경 쓰지 않았다)를 incorporated(도입했다)로 고쳐야 한다.

genre n. (예술 작품의) 장르 filmmaker n. 영화제작자 appellation n. 명칭 film noir 누아르 영화(암울한 암흑가·범죄 영화의 총칭) be characterized by ~가 특징이다 high-contrast a. 고대비의[선명한] lighting n. (어떤 장소의) 조명 flashback n. (영화·연극 등에서) 플래시백(과거 장면으로의 순간적 전환) recount v. (특히 자기가 경험한 것에 대해) 이야기하다 omniscient narrator 전지적 시점의 화자 hero n. (소설·영화 등의) 남자 주인공 ambiguous a. 애매모호한 cynical a. 냉소적인 have yet to do 아직 ~하지 않았다 wane v. 약해지다, 시들어지다 pay heed to ~에 신경 쓰다 period piece 시대물(연극·영화 등) evoke v. (감정·기억·이미지를) 떠올려 주다

1940년대에, 미국의 영화제작자들이 영화 장르를 하나 만들었는데, 이 장르는 결국 '누아르 영화'라는 명칭을 얻게 되었다. 이 장르의 영화들은 고대비 조명과 전지적 화자가 이야기하는 플래시백 사용이 특징이다. 누아르 영화의 주인공들은 도덕적으로 모호하며, 주변 인물들의 행동에 냉소적이다. 이 장르가 도입된 지 60년이 지난 오늘날에도, 누아르 영화의 인기는 아직 완전히 시들지 않았다. 많은 최근 영화들, 특히 과거 연대를 연상시키는 시대극 영화들이 누아르 기법을 <전혀 신경 쓰지 않았다.>

28-29

중요한 하위문화들 중 하나인 뉴에이지주의자들은 자연스럽고 소박한 삶을 살기 위해 도시의 삶을 거부하고, 공동체를 형성해 카라반을 타고 시골 지역을 돌아다닌다. 그들은 1960년대 유행했던 히피의 후예들이다. 단기 체류하는 그들의 생활방식으로 그들은 보수적인 사람들에게 평판이 좋지 못했다. 1985년부터 그들은 그들의 삶을 어렵게 만들라는 보수적인 정부의 부추김을 강력하게 받은 경찰들과 반복적으로 대립했다. 그들이 일으킨 문제 — 대체로 좀도둑질과 쓰레기 버리기 같은 혐의들 — 는 사실이 아니거나 크게 과장된 것이었다. 하지만 '씻지도 않고 물건을 슬쩍하는 사람들'로 비난받긴 했지만, 뉴에이지주의자들은 국가 전체에 중대한 영향을 미쳤다. 왜냐하면 더 많은 자동차 길을 내기 위해 시골 지역을 파괴하는 광기를 일반 국민들이 인식하기 시작한 1990년대에 위태로운 생태계에 관한 그들의 '괴팍한' 견해가 점차 받아들여졌기 때문이었다.

New Age travellers 뉴에이지주의자(현대 사회의 가치를 거부하고 이동 주택을 타고 이동해 다니며 사는 사람들) crucial a. 중대한 sub-culture n. 하위문화 caravan n. 카라반, 이동식 주택(승용차에 매달아 끌고 다님) descendant n. 후손, 후예 Hippie n. 히피(서구 기성 사회생활 양식을 거부하는 사람) transient a. 단기 체류의 conservative a. 보수적인 accusation n. 혐의; 비난 pilfer v. 좀도둑질을 하다 litter n. (공공장소에 버려진) 쓰레기 exaggerate v. 과장하다 denounce v. 비난하다 scrounge v. 슬쩍 훔치다 supposedly ad. 추정상, 아마 cranky a. 기이한 imperil v. 위태롭게 하다 ecology n. 생태계 at large 전체적인 for the sake of ~를 위해서

28 빈칸완성 ②

빈칸 앞의 They는 뉴에이지주의자들로 '영국에서 현대 사회의 가치를 거부하고 이동 주택을 타고 이동해 다니며 사는 사람들'을 가리키며, 히피들은 '서구 기성 사회생활 양식을 거부하는 사람들'이라는 뜻으로 두 집단의 성격이 비슷하며, 시대적으로 1985년 이후 활동한 뉴에이지주의자들과 비교해, 히피들은 1960년대 활동한 세대이므로, 뉴에이지주의자들이 히피의 '후예'라고 해야 문맥상 적절하다. 그리고 뉴에이지주의자들은 보수적인 사람들에게 평판이 좋지 못하다고 했으므로, 보수적인 정부가 강력하게 부추긴 경찰들과 반복적인 '대립'에 휘말렸다고 해야 적절하므로, ②가 정답이다.

다음 중 빈칸 Ⓐ와 Ⓑ에 들어가기에 가장 적절한 것은?
① 상속인 ― 음모
② 후예 ― 대립
③ 파생물 ― 연락
④ 선구자 ― 소규모 충돌

29 내용파악 ④

위태로운 생태계에 관한 그들의 견해는 괴팍하게 여겨졌지만 1990년대에 점차 받아들이게 되었다고 했을 뿐, 그들의 괴팍한 생활방식이 주류에 흡수되었는지는 이 글에서 알 수 없으며, 오히려 경찰들과 대립을 일으킨 부분이 강조되므로, ④가 정답이다.

다음 중 '뉴에이지주의자들'과 일치하지 않는 것은?
① 보수적인 사람들은 그들의 정처 없이 떠돌아다니고 비위생적인 삶을
거부했다.
② 그들은 물건을 슬쩍하는 혐의를 받고 있는데, 근거가 없거나 과장된
것으로 밝혀졌다.
③ 생태계 위기에 대한 그들의 생각은 한때 괴팍한 것으로 여겨졌다.
④ 그들의 괴팍한 생활방식은 결국 주류에 흡수되었다.

30-31

인플레이션(물가상승)은 나쁜 것인가? 그것은 상황에 따라 다르다. 가파른
물가 상승은 문제를 초래하지만, 적당한 인플레이션은 임금 인상과 일자리
증가로 이어질 수 있다.
인플레이션은 가난한 사람들에게 어떤 영향을 미치는가? 인플레이션은
가난한 가족이 감당하기 특히 힘들 수 있는데, 왜냐하면 가난한 가족은
예산의 상당부분을 식료품, 주택, 그리고 휘발유 같은 생필품에 지출하기
때문이다.
인플레이션은 주식시장에 영향을 미칠 수 있는가? 가파른 인플레이션은
보통 주식에 골칫거리를 의미한다. 금융 자산들은 일반적으로 인플레이션
호황기일 때 역사적으로 좋지 않은 성적을 거두었던 반면, 주택 같은 유형
자산들은 그들의 가치를 잘 유지해 왔다.

inflation n. 인플레이션, 물가상승 depend on ~에 달려 있다 spell
v. ~의 (보통 나쁜) 결과를 초래하다 moderate a. 온건한; 적당한 lead
to ~로 이어지다 wage n. 임금 shoulder v. 감당하다, 짊어지다, 떠맡다
household n. 가정, 가족 chunk n. 상당히 많은 양 budget n. 예산
necessities n. 필수품 stock market 주식시장 trouble n. 골칫거리
asset n. 자산 fare badly 잘못 되어가다 boom n. 갑작스런 대유행,
붐, 호황 tangible asset 유형 자산

---

30 빈칸완성   ②

빈칸 Ⓐ 다음에 역접의 접속사 but이 왔다. but 다음에 '적당한 인플레이
션은 임금 인상과 일자리 증가로 이어진다'는 긍정적인 내용이 왔으므
로, but 앞의 빈칸에는 부정적인 내용이 와야 한다. 따라서 문제를 '초래
하다'는 뜻이 되도록 ②의 spell이 빈칸에 적절하다.

다음 중 빈칸 Ⓐ에 들어가기에 가장 적절한 것은?
① 단념시키다
② 초래하다
③ 폐지하다
④ 점검하다

---

31 빈칸완성   ③

빈칸 Ⓑ 다음에 이유를 나타내는 접속사 because가 와서 인과관계가 쓰
였음을 알 수 있다. 가난한 가족은 생필품에 그들이 가진 돈의 많은 부분
을 써야 한다고 했으므로, 그 결과 인플레이션은 가난한 사람들이 '감당
하기에' 특히 더 힘들 수 있을 것이다. 따라서 Ⓑ에는 shoulder가 적절하
고, 주식은 '금융' 자산에 해당하므로, Ⓒ에는 Financial이 적절하다.

다음 중 빈칸 Ⓑ와 Ⓒ에 들어가기에 가장 적절한 것은?
① 이기다 ― 사회의
② 기피하다 ― 실물의
③ 감당하다 ― 금융의
④ 선포하다 ― 고정의

32-33

미국 헌법을 만든 사람들에 따르면, 지적재산권은 "과학과 유용한 예술의
발전을 촉진하기 위해" 존재한다고 한다. 코딩과 컴퓨팅 분야에서의 최근
의 경이로움은 보이지 않는 형태의 창조물을 인류에게 소개했다. 그러나
저작물들을 보다 빠르고 저렴하게 생산하면, 인간이 그리는 초상화에 대한
수요가 줄어들 수 있다. 그것은 결과적으로 예술적 발전에 있어서 쇠퇴로
이어질 수 있다.
일부 AI(인공지능) 기업들이 이미 하고 있는 관행에 자극받아 저작권의
범위를 보다 폭넓게 고려할 경우, AI가 인간 창작자들의 작품을 소비하고,
가공하고, 현행법이 고려하지 않는 방식으로 그들의 작품으로 새로운 작품
을 만들 때 인간 창작자들이 어느 정도 보상을 받도록 보장할 수 있을
것이다. 그러나 그러한 변화가 AI 산업이 성장할 여지가 없을 정도로 극도
로 처벌적이어서는 안 된다. 그렇게 해야, 이들 AI 도구들이 인간 창작자들
과 협력하여, 헌법을 만든 사람들이 상상할 수 없었을 정도로 과학과 유용
한 예술의 발전을 추진할 수 있을 것이다.

intellectual property rights 지적재산권 marvel n. 놀라운 일, 경이
humanity n. 인류 portrait n. 초상화 in turn 그다음에는, 또한, 결국,
결과적으로 copyright n. 저작권 ensure v. 보장하다 recompense
n. 보상, 배상 in a manner ~의 방식으로 contemplate v. 고려하다
shift n. (입장의) 변화 room n. 여지 in concert with ~와 협력하여

---

32 빈칸완성   ③

빈칸 앞은 '저작물들을 보다 빠르고 저렴하게 생산하면, 인간이 그리는
초상화에 대한 수요가 줄어들 수 있다'는 내용이고, 빈칸 다음은 예술적
발전이 쇠퇴할 수 있다는 내용으로, 빈칸을 전후로 순차적인 일들의 인
과관계를 나타내고 있다. 따라서 '결과적으로'라는 뜻의 ③ in turn이 빈
칸에 적절하다.

다음 중 빈칸 Ⓐ에 가장 적절한 것은?
① 그럼에도 불구하고
② ~와 비교하여
③ 결과적으로
④ 그렇지 않다면

---

33 빈칸완성   ②

빈칸 Ⓑ 앞의 That way는 '그렇게 해야'라는 뜻으로, 앞 문장인 "인간 창
작자들이 어느 정도 보상을 받게 하자는 변화조치가 AI 산업이 성장할
여지가 없을 정도로 극도로 처벌적이어서는 안 된다."는 문장을 가리키
고 있다. 따라서 인간 창작자들도 보상을 받되 AI가 성장할 수 없을 정
도로까지 차단하지만 않는다면, AI 도구들이 인간 창작자들과 '협력하
여' 발전을 이뤄낼 수 있을 것이다. 따라서 ②의 in concert with가 정답
이다.

다음 중 빈칸 ⓑ에 가장 적절한 것은?
① ~에 대한 보답으로
② ~와 협력하여
③ ~을 대신하여
④ ~에도 불구하고

34-35

알레르기 전문의들의 연구에 따르면, 1995년에서 2002년 사이에, 어린 아이들 사이에서 땅콩 알레르기 발병률이 증가했다고 한다. 청소년들 사이에서 땅콩과 다른 식품 알레르기가 증가함에 따라 과학자들과 의사들은 가능성 있는 원인들과 기여 요인들을 찾게 되었다. <지지를 받는 한 가지 개념은 바로 '위생 가설'인데, 위생 가설은 인간의 면역체계가 스스로 강해지기 위해서는 매우 다양한 환경의 병원균과 접촉해야 한다는 것을 시사해준다.> 가정환경에서 항균 비누와 스프레이를 사용하기 때문에, 가정환경은 대체로 멸균 상태를 유지한다. 따라서 신체는 해로운 바이러스와 세균을 인식하는 법을 배우지 못해서 나중에 이들과 싸우지 못하게 된다. 싸울 세균이 없기 때문에, 우리 몸의 면역체계가 땅콩, 우유, 그리고 계란과 같이 보다 무해한 다른 물질들에 집중하기 시작한다는 이론을 일부 사람들은 제시한다.

incidence n. 발생률, 발병률 peanut n. 땅콩 allergist n. 알레르기 전문 의사 adolescent n. 청소년 contributing factor 기여 요인 hygiene n. 위생 hypothesis n. 가설 immune system 면역체계 pathogen n. 병원균 antibacterial a. 항균성의 soap n. 비누 sterile a. 살균의 germ n. 세균 theorize v. 이론을 제시하다 innocuous a. 무해한, 위험하지 않은 substance n. 물질

34 문장삽입   ②

제시문은 "지지를 받는 한 가지 개념은 바로 '위생 가설'인데, 위생 가설은 인간의 면역체계가 스스로 강해지기 위해서는 매우 다양한 환경의 병원균과 접촉해야 한다는 것을 시사해준다."라는 뜻이다. 따라서 제시문은 그 앞에 이 '위생 가설' 개념이 나오게 된 배경에 대한 설명이 있고, 그다음에 '위생'과 관련한 멸균상태의 생활환경이 '위생 가설' 설명의 시작으로 제시되어 있는 ⓑ에 들어가는 것이 적절하다.

35 빈칸완성   ①

땅콩 알레르기 발병률이 청소년들 사이에서 증가했다고 한 다음, 그 이유로 위생 가설을 제시했다. 위생 가설에 따르면, 우리가 멸균 환경에 살다보니 병원균과 접촉할 기회가 없어서 병원균과 싸우지 못하게 되는 결과를 초래했다는 것이다. 따라서 세균과 싸우는 우리 몸의 면역체계는 싸울 세균이 없는 관계로 땅콩, 우유, 계란과 같이 다른 물질에 집중하게 됐다는 것인데, 이것들은 모두 우리 몸에 '무해한' 물질이므로, ①의 innocuous가 빈칸에 적절하다.

다음 중 빈칸 ⓔ에 가장 적절한 것은?
① 무해한
② 징벌의
③ 부부관계의
④ 호기심이 많은

36-37

수감 기간 동안 의미 있는 노동이 주는 영향은 수감자와 사회 둘 모두에 현저한 이익이 됨을 보여준다. 이런 이익들 중 일부는 재범률 감소, 직무 기술 및 고용가능성 증가, 그리고 삶의 질 향상이라는 형태를 취한다. 실제로, 기업들은 교도소 수감자들이 제조업에서부터 텔레마케팅에 이르기까지 다양한 일을 수행하도록 교도소들을 고용해 왔다. 그러나 일부 비평가들은 일하는 수감자들이 자신이 일하는 것에 대한 어떠한 보상도 받지 못하고 있으며, 신체 및 정신 능력 범위를 넘어서는 일을 하도록 강요받는 종속 노예와 마찬가지라고 주장한다. 또 다른 사람들은 비경쟁 노동이라는 경제적 요인들이나 수감자들에게 제품의 중요 부품에 대한 책임을 부여하는 것과 관련한 문제들에 대해 더 우려하고 있다.

meaningful a. 의미 있는 imprisonment n. 수감, 감금 marked a. 두드러진, 현저한 prisoner n. 죄수, 수감자 recidivism n. 상습적 범행, 재범 employability n. 고용가능성 corporation n. 기업, 법인 jail n. 교도소, 감옥 inmate n. 수감자, 재소자 little more than ~와 마찬가지인 bonded slave 종속 노예 capacity n. 용량; 능력 component n. (구성) 요소, 부품

36 빈칸완성   ④

빈칸 ⓐ 앞에서는 수감기간 동안 노동하는 것의 '긍정적인' 영향에 대해 이야기한 반면, ⓐ 다음에는 수감기간 동안 노동하는 것의 '부정적인' 영향에 대해 언급하고 있어, 빈칸 앞뒤로 상반된 내용을 보여주고 있다. 따라서 빈칸에는 역접부사인 ④ However가 정답이다.

다음 중 빈칸 ⓐ에 가장 적절한 것은?
① 다시 말하면
② 예를 들어
③ 마찬가지로
④ 그러나

37 내용추론   ①

수감기간 동안 노동이 주는 영향으로 직무 기술 증가, 고용가능성 증가, 삶의 질 향상이 있다고 했다. 따라서 수감자들이 겪는 끔찍한 상황을 어느 정도 '상쇄해' 줄 수 있을 것이므로, ①이 정답이다. ② 수감자들이 일하는 것에 대한 어떠한 보상도 받지 '못한다고' 했다. ③ 교도소에서의 고용이 사회의 경제적 경쟁력에 해롭다고 볼 수는 없다. ④ 수감자 노동 모델 강화와 형벌제도 강화의 관련성을 본문에서 찾을 수 없다.

다음 중 이 글에서 추론할 수 있는 것은?
① 고용은 수감자들이 겪는 끔찍한 상황을 상쇄해 줄지도 모른다.
② 수감자들은 교정시설에서 일하는 동안 생활비를 벌 수 있다.
③ 교도소에서의 고용은 사회의 경제적 경쟁력에 해롭다.
④ 수감자 노동 모델을 강화하면 형벌제도를 강화시킬 것이다.

38-40

1950년대에, 학자들은 준사회적 관계의 간접적이고 일방적인 성격이 상호 교류 가능성을 가로막는다고 믿었다. TV나 라디오 유명인사와의 어떤 상호적인 관계는 단지 '제안될' 수 있을 뿐이었다. 기껏해야, 시청자들은

가끔 보내는 팬레터나 TV와 라디오 방송국에 전화를 거는 행동을 통해 대중매체의 유명인사에게 다가가려고 시도할 수 있는 정도였다.

인터넷, 그리고 특히 소셜 미디어가 이런 역학관계에 다른 차원을 제공했다. 유명 연예인의 인스타그램 프로필이나 인플루언서의 유튜브 채널은 종종 그들을 팔로우하거나 그들의 채널을 구독하는 사람들에게 말이 직접 전달된다. 팔로워나 구독자는 그들의 게시물에 댓글을 달 수 있고 비록 드물더라도 상호 댓글을 기대할 수 있다. 이런 상호적인 만남은 진짜 관계와 준사회적 관계를 구분해주는 경계, 그리고 '친구'와 '유명인'을 구분해주는 경계를 서서히 무너뜨리며, 팬이 유명 연예인이나 미디어 유명인사의 삶에 관여하고 있다고 영구적으로 착각하게 만든다.

상호주의의 잠재력은 팬들로 하여금 유명 연예인이나 미디어 유명인사가 그들이 개인적으로 '알고 지내는' 친구라고 믿을 뿐 아니라, 어느 정도 책임감 비슷한 것을 기대하게 만들 수도 있다. 이런 기대에 반하여, 유명 연예인에 대해 갖고 있던 이미지와 모순되는 사실이 밝혀지면 충격, 실망, 분노를 유발할 수 있으며, 극단적인 경우, 그들은 '준사회적 친구'를 공개적으로 비난하며 관계를 끝낼 수 있다. 멀레이니(Mulaney)의 경우, 매우 공감 가는 아내 남자(아내에 대한 게시물 콘텐츠로 유명해진 남자) 이미지에서 벗어나는 바람에 팬들은 "어떻게 그가 그녀에게 그럴 수 있어?"뿐 아니라, "어떻게 그가 우리에게 그럴 수 있어?"라고 '생각하게' 되었다.

scholar n. 학자 mediated a. 중재된, 간접적인 one-sided a. 일방적인 parasocial relationship 준사회적 관계(한 개인이 유명인과 친밀감과 애착을 형성하는 일방적이고 비호혜적인 관계) preclude v. 방해하다, 가로막다 mutual a. 상호적인 reciprocal a. 상호간의 personality n. 유명인, 유명인사 at best 기껏해야 call in (특히 직장에) 전화를 하다 dimension n. 차원, 관점 subscribe to ~에 구독하다 erode v. (서서히) 무너뜨리다 perpetuate v. 영구화하다 illusion n. 착각; 환상 be involved in ~에 관련되다 potential n. 잠재력 reciprocity n. 상호[호혜]주의 semblance n. 유사, 비슷한 것 accountability n. 책임 revelation n. 폭로된 사실, 뜻밖의 새 사실 contradict v. (사실·진술이) 모순되다 perceive v. 인지하다, 인식하다 denounce v. 비난하다 departure n. 벗어남[일탈]; 배반 super-relatable a. 매우 공감 가는 prompt v. ~하도록 촉발하다

---

38 빈칸완성 ②

준사회적 관계가 간접적이고 일방적이라고 했다. 따라서 그런 성격이 상호 교류 가능성을 '가로막는다'고 해야 적절하므로, ②의 preclude가 빈칸에 적절하다.

다음 중 빈칸 Ⓐ에 가장 적절한 것은?
① 용이하게 하다
② 가로막다
③ 계산하다
④ 감추다

---

39 빈칸완성 ③

준사회적 관계는 일방적이어서 상호 교류할 수가 없는데, 유명인의 말이 직접 전달되고 드물더라도 상호 답글을 받을 수 있다는 가능성은 진짜 관계와 준사회적 관계를 구분해주는 경계와 친구와 유명인을 구분해주는 경계를 '서서히 무너뜨릴' 수 있을 것이다. 따라서 빈칸 Ⓑ에는 erode가 적절하고, 같은 맥락에서 서로 교류가 되면서 마치 팬이 유명

인들의 삶에 직접적으로 관여하고 있다는 착각을 '영구화시킬' 수 있을 것이다. 따라서 빈칸 Ⓒ에는 perpetuate가 적절하므로, ③이 정답이다.

다음 중 빈칸 Ⓑ와 Ⓒ에 가장 적절한 것은?
① 불안하게 하다 ― 모험적으로 해보다
② 변경하다 ― 지우다
③ 서서히 무너뜨리다 ― 영구화하다
④ 지탱하게 하다 ― 순환시키다

---

40 내용추론 ④

준사회적 관계는 팬이 자신이 좋아하는 유명인들에 대해 친밀감과 애착을 느끼는 일방적인 관계를 말하는데, 이 준사회적 관계를 형성하는 사람이 오직 고립되거나 정신적으로 취약한 사람들이라고 단정 지을 수는 없으므로, ④가 정답이다.

다음 중 이 글에서 추론할 수 없는 것은?
① 멀레이니 팬들은 그의 선택에 대해 몹시 당황하고, 실망하고, 기묘하게도 불쾌해 한다.
② 사람들이 한 사람에 대해 애착을 느낄 때, 떨어져 있어도 친밀함이 생기는 경향이 있다.
③ 오늘날, 미디어 사용자들은 유명 연예인들과 준사회적 관계를 쉽게 형성할 수 있다.
④ 오직 고립되고 정신적으로 취약한 사람들만 준사회적 관계의 유혹에 넘어간다.

2024 가천대학교(인문계 B형)

01 ②	02 ①	03 ③	04 ③	05 ④	06 ④	07 ③	08 ③	09 ①	10 ④
11 ①	12 ②	13 ②	14 ④	15 ③	16 ③	17 ①	18 ②	19 ④	20 ①
21 ④	22 ①	23 ③	24 ④	25 ①	26 ④	27 ②	28 ②	29 ③	30 ①
31 ④	32 ②	33 ①	34 ③	35 ②	36 ①	37 ②	38 ④	39 ④	40 ①

01 동의어 ②

merchandise n. 상품, 제품 revenue n. 수익, 수입(= proceeds) clientele n. 소송 의뢰인; 고객; 환자 broadcast n. 방송 referendum n. 국민 투표

상품은 중요하다. 그것은 팬덤을 표현할 수 있는 팬들에게 중요하다. 그것은 추가 수익원으로 그것을 사용하는 아티스트와 기타 권리 소유자들에게 중요하다.

02 동의어 ①

weary of ~에 싫증이 난 extravagant a. 낭비하는, 사치스러운; 터무니없는, 지나친(= outrageous) distrust v. 믿지 않다 immunity n. 면제; 면역(성) rapacious a. 탐욕스러운 enthusiastic a. 열렬한, 열광적인 fraudulent a. 사기를 치는

과도한 제품 관련 주장과 관련 없는 연관성에 싫증이 난 소비자들은 그들이 듣는 것을 믿지 않도록 수년간의 광고에 의해 훈련되어 광고에 대한 면역성을 키워가고 있는 것처럼 보인다.

03 동의어 ③

in step with ~와 보조를 맞추어, ~와 일치하여, 협조하여 charter school 차터 스쿨(공적 자금을 받아 교사·부모·지역 단체 등이 설립한 학교) advocate n. 지지자, 옹호자 descend v. 내려가다[오다]; 갑자기 습격하다; (불시에) 몰려가다 pedagogy n. 교육학 discipline n. 훈련, 훈육 chaotic a. 혼돈된; 무질서한, 혼란한 fail v. 실패하다(= founder) quell v. 진압[진정]하다; 억누르다 invoke v. 빌다, 기원하다; 호소하다 convoke v. 소집하다

전국적으로 활발한 차터 스쿨 지지자들과 마찬가지로, 뉴올리언스에 갑자기 몰려온 개혁가들은 많은 아이들이 그들의 몫 이상의 무질서와 폭력에 직면한 저소득 지역에서는 진보적인 교육학과 훈육이 특히 안 좋은 기록을 가지고 있다고 확신했다. 새로 온 사람들은 혼란스러운 교실이 학교가 실패한 주요 원인이라고 주장했다.

04 동의어 ③

barrier n. 장벽, 장애 mettle n. 기개, 용기(= fortitude) circumvent v. (곤란·문제점 등을) 교묘히 회피하다 obstacle n. 장애(물), 방해(물) impede v. 방해하다 expertise n. 전문적 기술[지식, 의견] strategy n. 전략 prerogative n. 특권

비록 그의 질병이 이러한 목적을 추구하는 그의 능력에 장벽이 되었지만, 그는 항상 이러한 장애물에 방해받기 보다는 장애물을 피하는 용기를 발휘했다.

05 동의어 ④

inhabit v. 살다, 거주하다 blind a. 막다른 detached a. 분리된, 떨어져 있는 decent a. (복장·집 등이) 버젓한, 알맞은, 품위 있는 gaze at ~을 응시하다 imperturbable a. 쉽게 동요하지 않는, 침착한(= placid) irascible a. 화를 잘 내는, 성마른 impious a. 불경한 laconic a. 간결한

나는 막다른 골목에 세워진 2층집에 살았는데, 그 집은 광장에 있는 이웃들과 떨어져 있었다. 거리의 다른 집들은 그 안에서의 품위 있는 삶을 의식하며 갈색의 침착한 얼굴로 서로를 응시했다.

06 동의어 ④

privilege v. 특권[특전]을 주다 foray n. 침략, 약탈; (전문 분야 이외로의) 진출(= pillage) instigation n. 선동 portal n. 정문, 입구 clash n. 충돌

그녀는 흑인 문화와 백인 문화의 혜택을 모두 누릴 수 있는 특권이 있다. 편리함과 유익함을 따라 그 문화에 발을 들여놓기도 하고 빼기도 한다. 그것이 그녀가 힙합에 진출하는 데 있어 가장 큰 문제다.

07 동의어 ③

fraught a. 난처한, 걱정하는, 긴장된(= charged) pit v. (사람·지혜·힘 등을) 경쟁시키다(against) inclusion n. 포함, 포괄 political a. 정치의 representative a. 대표적인 antagonistic a. 적대적인

점점 더 긴장되고 감정적인 대화는 포용의 진보적인 이상을 역사적인 비즈니스 관행과 맞서게 할 뿐 아니라 행동 그 자체의 정의와도 맞서게 한다.

08 동의어 ③

insult v. 모욕하다(= affront) ridicule v. 비웃다, 조롱하다 torment v. 괴롭히다 provocateur n. 선동가 mocker n. 조롱하는[놀리는] 사람 brutally ad. 잔인하게 mock v. 조롱하다, 놀리다 adulate v. 아첨하다 eulogize v. 칭송하다, 칭찬하다 euphemize v. 완곡하게 말하다

그렇다면 삶 자체가 선동가를, 즉 개인적인 현실에 의해 잔인하게 조롱당하는 조롱하는 사람을, 모욕하고 비웃고 심지어 괴롭힐 수도 있다.

09 2형식 동사의 보어 ①

prove는 2형식 동사로서 명사 상당어구나 형용사 상당어구가 보어로 와야 한다. 따라서 prove 다음에 형용사가 와야 하는데 의미상 find(발견하다)가 아니라 found(근거를 두다)의 과거분사가 적절하다. 그러므로 ① ill-found를 ill-founded(근거 없는)로 고친다.

monetarism n. 통화주의 ill-founded a. 근거 없는 surge n. 급증, 급등 public expenditure 공공 지출 rocket v. 치솟다, 급증[급등]하다 prematurely ad. 너무 이르게 insuperable a. 이겨내기 어려운, 극복할 수 없는 offset v. 상쇄하다

'통화주의'만으로도 그녀가 추구하는 혁명을 일으킬 수 있다는 대처(Thatcher)의 믿음은 근거가 없는 것으로 드러났다. 그 결과 초래된 실업의 급증은 공공 지출을 극적으로 증가시켰다. 실업자와 조기 퇴직자의 증가에 대처하기 위해 사회 복지 지출이 급증했다. 그러나 그들 자신의 정책으로 인한 이러한 결과가 없었더라도 보수당은 공공 지출을 줄이는 과제가 극복할 수 없다는 것을 알았을 것이다. 할 수 있는 그 어떤 절감도 더 불가피한 요소들로 인한 비용 증가를 상쇄하지 못했다.

10 문의 구성 ④

'teach+목적어+의문사절'의 형태로 쓰인 문장으로 의문사절은 '의문사+주어+동사'의 어순을 따른다. how 뒤에 the city's circulatory system이 주어인데 동사가 시제가 없는 형태이므로 ④ flowing을 시제를 가진 동사의 형태로 고쳐야 한다. 과거시제 동사 flowed로 고친다.

spare v. (시간·돈 등을) 할애하다; 면하게 하다 illuminate v. 조명하다, 비추다 transformation n. 변화

나는 이제 적어도 느린 여행을 할 시간을 낼 수 있다면 지하철보다 버스를 선호했다. 버스를 타고 런던을 지나가는 것이 지하철의 편리함이 내게 면하게 했던 지리학 수업을 제공해주었다. 그것은 도시의 순환 체계가 어떻게 흐르는지 내게 가르쳐 주었고, 햄스테드 로드와 같은 장소의 수세기 동안의 변화를 조명해주었다.

11 수동태 ①

'mislead A into B' 구문에서 A가 주어로 앞에 나간 것으로, they는 mislead하는 행위의 주체가 아닌 대상이므로 수동태가 되어야 한다. 따라서 ① could mislead into를 could be misled into로 고친다.

fictitious a. 허구의 mislead v. 오도하다 non-existent a. 존재하지 않는 bait n. 미끼, 유혹(물) invent v. 발명하다; 날조하다

거짓 기억은 존재하지만, 그것들의 구성은 인생에서 훨씬 늦게 시작되는 것처럼 보인다. 한 연구는 아이들에게 허구의 사건을 제시하여 아이들이 이러한 존재하지 않는 사건을 기억하도록 오도될 수 있는지 알아보았지만, 아이들은 거의 보편적으로 함정을 피했다. 어른들이 날조된 사항들로 기억의 공백을 메우기 시작하는 이유에 대해 그녀는 기억이 근본적으로 구성적인 활동이라고 지적했다. 우리는 그것을 세계에 대한 이해를 구축하기 위해 사용하고, 그것은 때때로 우리의 기억이 스스로 기억할 수 있는 것보다 더 완전한 이야기를 필요로 한다.

12 논리완성 ②

인공지능을 사용하려는 고용주들로부터 양보를 얻어내는 것보다 아무런 관계가 없는 대형 언어 모델 제작자들로부터 양보를 얻기가 더 힘들 것이다. 따라서 부정문에서 '하물며[더구나] ~은 더더욱 아니다'는 뜻인 ② much less가 빈칸에 적절하다.

striking a. 파업 중인 churn out 대량 생산하다 bingeable a. (폭식·폭음) 하기 쉬운, 흥청망청하기에 좋은 rom-com n. 로맨틱 코미디 pause n. (일시적인) 중지, 휴지 concession n. 양보 still more 더구나, 하물며 much less 하물며[더구나] ~은 더더욱 아니다 furthermore ad. 게다가 as if 마치 ~인 것처럼

올 여름 파업 중인 할리우드 작가들은 스트리밍 서비스가 AI(인공지능)에 의존하여 탐닉하기 쉬운 로맨틱 코미디를 대량으로 만들어 낼 것이라고 우려했다. 작가들은 그 협상에서 승리하여 위기를 일시 중지시켰다. 하지만 개인 창작자들은 인공지능을 사용하려는 고용주들로부터 항상 양보를 얻어낼 수 있는 것은 아니며, 더구나 그들과 아무런 관계가 없는 대형 언어 모델 제작자들로부터 양보를 얻는 것은 더더욱 불가능할 것이다.

13 논리완성 ②

마케팅 담당자가 Z세대의 관심을 끌기 위해 특정 콘텐츠를 만들고 영상을 짧게 유지한다고 했는데 이런 상황을 고려하면 짧은 동영상을 제작·공유할 수 있는 플랫폼인 틱톡이 Z세대에게 유행하는 것은 당연하다는 것이다. 따라서 '~을 고려하면'의 뜻인 ② Given this가 빈칸에 적절하다.

authentic a. 진정한, 진짜의 demographic a. 인구 통계학의 take off 급격히 인기를 얻다[유행하다] given a. [전치사적 또는 접속사적] ~이라고 가정하면, ~을 고려하면 alternately ad. 번갈아, 교대로 notwithstanding ad. 그럼에도 불구하고

마케팅 담당자는 목표 고객, 특히 Z세대의 관심을 끌기 위해 많은 시간과 돈을 소비한다. 특정 콘텐츠를 만들고 모두 진실하면서도 그것을 짧게 유지하는 것은 이 인구 통계학적 집단에게 매력적인 요소 중 일부다. 이런 점을 감안할 때 틱톡(TikTok)이 실제로 Z세대에게 큰 인기를 얻고 있는 것은 놀랄 일이 아니다.

14 논리완성 ③

위약(placebo)과 임상적으로 승인된 약물은 서로 대비되는 대상이므로 '~대신에'의 뜻인 ③ in place of가 빈칸에 적절하다.

placebo n. 위약 clinically ad. 임상적으로 breach v. (법률·약속 등을) 어기다, 위반하다, 파기하다 induce v. 야기하다, 유발하다 reverse a. 반대의 exacerbate v. 악화시키다 accelerate v. 가속하다, 촉진시키다 in reference to ~에 관하여 in line with ~에 따라 in place of ~대신에 in accordance with ~에 따라서

추가 연구는 일부 환자들이 임상적으로 시험을 거치고 승인된 약물 대신에 위약을 투여 받았다는 사실을 알게 되어, 어떤 경우에는 의사에 대한 확립된 신뢰가 깨어졌고 다른 경우에는 반대로 '노시보' 효과가 발생하게 되었다고 보고한다. 이것은 환자의 의학적 상태를 더욱 악화시키고 때때로 사망에 이르는 원인을 가속화시킨다.

15 논리완성 ③

힙합 아티스트들이 사회 정치적인 시스템에 대한 비판에 진보적이라고 했으므로, 그들이 음악을 통해 사회적·정치적 의식을 갖도록 촉구하는 것은 흑인의 예언적 전통과 일치하는 것이라 유추할 수 있다. 따라서 이 전통을 '활용하다'는 뜻인 ③ tap into가 빈칸에 적절하다.

explicitly ad. 명백하게 progressive a. 진보적인 critique n. 비평, 비판 prophetic a. 예언의, 예언적인 awaken v. 자각시키다, 깨닫게 하다 forthright a. 솔직한; 똑바른 downfallen a. 몰락한 recant v. (신앙·주장 등을) 취소하다, 철회하다 map out ~을 계획하다 tap into ~을 활용하다 disparage v. 깔보다, 얕보다

퍼블릭 에너미(Public Enemy)와 퀸 라티파(Queen Latifa)와 같은 다른 힙합 아티스트들은 그들을 둘러싼 사회 정치적인 시스템에 대한 비판에서 명백하게 진보적이다. 그들은 듣는 사람에게 새로운 정치적·정신적 의식 수준으로 깨어나고, 읽고, 그리고 멀리 몰락한 세계에서 직접적인 행동을 취할 준비를 하도록 촉구함으로써 흑인의 예언적 전통을 더욱 활용한다.

16 논리완성 ③

영국인들의 과거에 대한 사랑을 패션을 예로 들어 이야기하고 있는데, 이런 과거의 패션에 대한 선호는 현대적 디자인이 무언가를 박탈당하게 할 것이다. 따라서 'divest A of B'의 형태로 쓰여 '~에게서 …을 빼앗다[박탈하다]'의 뜻인 ③ divest가 빈칸에 적절하다.

old-fashioned a. 구식의 glorious a. 영광스러운 reassurance n. 안심, 안도; 확신 nostalgia n. 향수 conviction n. 확신, 신념 cosy a. 아늑한 comforting a. 위로가 되는 hand-crafted a. 수공예인, 수제의 contemporary a. 현대의, 당대의 rebellious a. 반항적인 ascertain v. 확인하다 enmesh v. (곤란 등에) 말려들게 하다, 빠뜨리다 divest v. 빼앗다, 박탈하다 refine v. 정제하다; 세련되게 하다

컨트리-코티지(시골풍의) 패션과 상류층의 구식 드레스 스타일에 대한 사랑은 영국인들이 자신을 인식하는 방식에 대해 많은 것을 말해준다. 과거는 영국인들에게 영광스러운 것이기 때문에, 그들은 미래의 불확실성보다 과거의 확신을 선호한다. 패션에 대해 말하면서, 샬롯 두 캔

(Charlotte Du Cann)은 영국인들이 그들의 향수에 대해 지불하는 가격에 주목한다. "영국에 오는 사람들은 우리가 확신을 가지고 판매하는 것, 즉 아늑하고 위로가 되는 우리의 과거를 사고 싶어 합니다. 우리가 매우 필사적으로 판매하는 수공예 향수는 현대 디자인에서 반항적인 에너지를 박탈합니다."

17 논리완성 ①

F. 스콧 피츠제럴드를 문학 작품에서 재즈 시대의 정신을 가장 잘 표현한 미국 작가로 이야기하고 있다. 따라서 F. 스콧 피츠제럴드는 그들의 세대를 대표한다고 할 수 있으므로 '~의 전형이다, 전형적으로 보여주다'는 뜻인 ① epitomized가 빈칸에 적절하다.

capture v. (사진·문장 등에) 담다[표현하다] upturn v. 뒤집다 mores n. (사회의) 관례, 관습 epitomize v. ~의 전형이다, 전형적으로 보여주다; 요약하다 provoke v. (감정 등을) 일으키다; 화나게 하다 assuage v. 누그러뜨리다 snub v. 무시하다

대부분의 문학 비평가들은 F. 스콧 피츠제럴드(F. Scott Fitzgerald)와 같은 정도로 그들의 세대를 전형적으로 보여주는 미국 작가는 거의 없다는 데 동의하는데, 그의 소설과 단편 소설은 젊은 미국인들이 전통적인 사회적 관습을 뒤집은 시기인 재즈 시대의 정신을 포착했다.

18 논리완성 ②

주인공은 다른 집단을 옹호하는 모습을 통해 자신의 고귀함을 드러낸다고 했으므로 소설 속에서 소수 집단의 주인공이 다수 집단인 백인의 발전을 위한 소품(버팀대)으로 쓰인다면 주인공의 고귀함은 드러날 것이다. 따라서 '소품'이나 '버팀대'의 뜻인 ② props가 빈칸에 적절하다.

protagonist n. 주인공 nobility n. 고귀함, 고결함 unequivocally ad. 모호하지 않게, 명백히 stand up for 옹호하다, 지지하다 belong to ~에 속하다 minority n. 소수; 소수 집단[민족] prevalent a. 널리 퍼진, 일반적인 obstacle n. 장애(물), 방해(물) prop n. 소품, 지주, 버팀대 collapse n. 붕괴; (희망·계획 등의) 좌절 mask n. 가면, 복면

주인공의 고귀함은 그가 속하지 않은 집단을 옹호한다는 사실로 명백히 입증된다. 다시 말해, 소설 속에서 그다지 일반적이지 않은 소수 집단은 백인 등장인물의 발전을 위한 소품으로 사용된다.

19 논리완성 ④

WHO 기관이 수십 년 동안 논쟁 중인 성분인 아스파탐의 발암 가능성에 대해 공개적으로 의견을 제시한 것에 대해 이야기하고 있다. 따라서 논쟁에 관여하거나 의견을 제시한다는 뜻인 ④ weighed in이 빈칸에 적절하다.

artificial sweetener 인공 감미료 carcinogenic a. <의학> 발암성의 prominent a. 현저한, 두드러진; 저명한 contentious a. 논쟁을 좋아하는, 이론의 여지가 있는 ingredient n. (혼합물의) 성분, 재료 publicly ad. 공공연하게, 공개적으로 hand over 이양하다, 양도하다 bow out ~에서 물러나다; 사직하다 come by 들르다 weigh in (논의·언쟁·활동 등에) 끼어들다[관여하다], 의견을 제시하다

세계보건기구(WHO) 기관은 다이어트 음료 및 저칼로리 식품에서 널리 사용되는 인공 감미료인 아스파탐을 인간에게 발암 가능성이 있는 것으로 분류했다. 이 저명한 단체가 수십 년 동안 논쟁의 여지가 있는 성분이었던 아스파탐의 효과에 대해 공개적으로 의견을 제시한 것은 이번이 처음이다.

---

20 논리완성 ①

양보의 접속사 While이 왔으므로 summative와 반대되는 의미의 표현이 와야 한다. 학습 과정이 끝난 다음에 성취 여부를 종합적으로 평가하는 것은 총괄적(summative)인 반면, 학습 과정 중에 성과를 평가하고 학습을 개선하는 것은 '형성적'이라 할 수 있다. 그러므로 '형성적인'의 뜻인 ① formative가 빈칸에 적절하다.

assessment n. 평가 externally ad. 외부적으로, 외부에서 mandated a. 위임 통치를 받고 있는, 권한을 가진 summative a. 부가적인, 누적적인 formative a. 형성의, 발달의 diagnostic a. 진단의 placement n. 놓기, 배치; 취직 알선 aptitude n. 소질, 적성

1980년대 이후 평가가 학습 과정이 끝나고 나서가 아니라 학습 과정 중에 할 수 있는 역할에 대한 관심이 높아졌다. 특히 블랙(Black)과 윌리엄(Wiliam)의 연구, 그리고 더 일반적으로 '학습 운동을 위한 평가'는 전 세계의 많은 교육 시스템에 큰 영향을 미쳤다. 대부분의 외부 위임 테스트는 총괄적이지만, 블랙과 윌리엄은 형성적 평가에 중점을 두었다.

---

21 논리완성 ④

신입생들이 계속해서 담배를 피웠다고 했으므로 목사가 학생들에게 담배를 피우지 말라고 나무랐지만 소용이 없었다는 것이다. 따라서 '격렬한 비난, 질책'의 뜻인 ④ fulmination이 빈칸에 적절하다.

minister n. 성직자, 목사 disobedient a. 복종하지 않는, 반항적인 blow v. 내뿜다 progeny n. 자손; 결과, 소산 recess n. 휴식, 휴회 denomination n. 명칭; 종파; 액면 금액 fulmination n. 맹렬한 비난, 질책

목사의 질책은 반항적인 신입생들에게 그 어떤 큰 영향도 미치지 않았다. 신입생들은 그가 말하는 동안 계속해서 담배를 피우며 그의 얼굴에 연기를 내뿜었다.

---

22 논리완성 ①

그의 성격을 나타내는 표현이 와야 하는데 mellow, non-obsessive, calm, contemplative 등의 표현에서 그의 성격을 유추할 수 있다. 그는 침착하고 냉정한 기질을 가진 사람이므로 '침착한, 냉정한'의 뜻인 ① phlegmatic이 빈칸에 적절하다.

resolutely ad. 단호히, 결연히 fascinate v. 매혹하다 mellow a. 온화한, 원숙한, 원만한 calm a. 침착한, 차분한 contemplative a. 명상적인 temperament n. 기질 phlegmatic a. 침착한, 냉정한 frenetic a. 발광한; 열광적인 eclectic a. 절충적인 esoteric a. 비밀의; 심원한, 난해한

거의 그의 의지에 반하여, 단호하게 모든 일을 뒤로 미루려고 수십 년 노력한 후 지난 몇 년 동안, 그는 침착하고, 냉정하고, 심지어 명상적인 기질이 있었기 때문에 원숙하면서도 비강박적인 방식으로 그 사건에 매료되었다.

---

23 빈칸완성 ③

Ⓐ 연구팀이 문제를 해결할 대안이나 수단, 선택 사항이 거의 없을 때까지 문제 해결을 최대한 미뤘다는 것이므로 alternative, recourse, option이 적절하다. Ⓑ 최후의 해결책을 시행해야 했다고 했으므로 last-minute(마지막 순간의, 최후의)와 유사한 표현으로 '필사적이고 절실함'을 뜻하는 desperate가 적절하다. 따라서 상기 두 조건을 모두 만족시키는 ③이 정답이다.

disorder n. 무질서, 혼란 postpone v. 연기하다, 미루다 root n. (곤란 등의) 근원, 원인 be obliged to do ~할 의무가 있다 last-minute a. 마지막 순간의, 막바지의 temporarily ad. 일시적으로

허술한 계획과 무질서의 결과로 연구팀은 그들에게 남은 수단이 거의 없을 때까지 문제의 근원을 공격하는 것을 미루었다. 그들은 그 문제에 대한 필사적이고 최후의 해결책을 시행해야 했다. 그들은 일시적으로 문제를 피할 수는 있었지만 계획을 더 잘 세우고 문제가 재발하지 않도록 막는 방법을 찾기로 결정했다.

다음 중 빈칸 Ⓐ와 Ⓑ에 들어가기에 가장 적절한 것은?
① 상환 — 선견지명이 있는
② 대안 — 계획적인
③ 수단 — 필사적인
④ 선택 — 신중한

---

24 빈칸완성 ④

계급과 성별에 대한 고정 관념으로 인해 노동자 계급의 소녀들이 사회적 경계나 계급 배경을 넘는 것이 사회적으로 덜 용인되고 있다는 것이다. 그런 사회에서는 계급이나 성별 사이의 사회적 경계에 저항하거나 깨뜨리는 것이 더 위험한 일이므로 빈칸 Ⓐ에는 defy나 breach가 적절하고, 자신이 속한 계급과 다른 계급 안에서 느끼는 계급 위기 감정은 계급 배경을 초월하여 구애받지 않는 사람도 주관적으로 경험하게 되는 것이어서 빈칸 Ⓑ에는 '넘다, 초월하다'는 transcend가 적절하다. 따라서 ④가 정답이다.

stereotype n. 고정 관념 acceptable a. (사회적으로) 용인되는[받아들여지는] bookish a. (활동적이거나 실용적인 것보다) 책[학문]을 좋아하는 nerdy a. 괴짜인 repercussion n. (보통 pl.) (사건·행동의 간접적인) 영향, 반향 screen time 스마트폰 화면을 보는 시간 supposedly ad. 추정상, 아마 seamlessly ad. 이음매가 없이, 균일하게

계급과 성별에 대한 고정 관념은 책을 좋아하고 괴짜인 노동자 계급의 소녀들을 묘사하는 것을 훨씬 덜 사회적으로 용인하게 만든다. 위험과 반향은 또한 사회적 경계를 깨뜨리는 노동자 계급의 소녀들에게 훨씬 더 크다. 이렇긴 해도, 나는 계급 위기의 주관적 경험을 볼 수 있는 시간이 주어져서 정말 기쁜데, 이는 계급 배경을 매끄럽게 초월한 것으로 추정되는 우리 중 많은 사람들이 여전히 느끼는 것이다.

다음 중 빈칸 Ⓐ와 Ⓑ에 들어가기에 가장 적절한 것은?
① 극복하다 ― 모방하다
② 무시하다 ― 흉내 내다
③ 직면하다 ― ~의 전조가 되다
④ 위반하다 ― 초월하다

다음 중 빈칸 Ⓐ와 Ⓑ에 들어가기에 가장 적절한 것은?
① ~을 대신하여 ― 분석하다
② ~에 상관없이 ― 위장하다
③ ~에 따라 ― 왜곡하다
④ ~와 대립하여 ― 헤아리다

25 문맥상 적절하지 않은 단어 고르기   ②

아기가 과도한 스트레스를 경험하면 전전두엽 피질이 손상되며 이로 인해 나타나는 문제에 대해 이야기하고 있다. 따라서 작업 기억, 자기 조절, 그리고 인지 유연성 등의 실행 기능을 촉진하는 것이 아니라 방해한다고 해야 적절하므로 Ⓑ는 hampering이 되어야 한다.

wind up ~ing 결국 ~하게 되다 lead to ~로 이어지다 undue a. 지나친, 과도한 prefrontal cortex 전전두엽 피질 building block 구성 요소 infrastructure n. (단체 등의) 하부 조직[구조], (경제) 기반 underpin v. 뒷받침하다 resilience n. 회복력; 탄성 perseverance n. 인내, 인내력 self-defeating a. 자멸적인

지속적인 불안을 경험하는 아기는 결국 높은 수준의 코르티솔 호르몬을 생산하게 되고, 이는 반격할 준비가 너무 지나치게 되어있는 스트레스 반응 시스템을 초래할 수 있다. 유아기에 과도한 스트레스를 경험하면 전전두엽 피질의 발달을 손상시켜, 작업 기억, 자기 조절, 그리고 인지 유연성을 포함하는 실행 기능으로 알려진 일련의 기술을 <촉진할> 수 있다. 스미스(Smith) 교수는 몇몇 신경과학자들의 말을 인용해 이러한 기술을 "회복력과 인내력과 같은 비인지적 능력을 뒷받침하는 발달적 구성 요소 즉, 신경학적 기반이라고 부른다." 전전두엽 피질의 손상은 자멸적인 행동 문제로 이어질 수 있다.

26 빈칸완성   ④

Ⓐ 개인의 시간과 장소는 개인이 존재하는 사회를 말하고 고립된 개인은 사회로부터 고립된 것이고 비극적 운명은 이 개인이 사회와 사이가 좋지 않게 불화를 빚고 있다는 것이므로 at odds with가 적절하다. Ⓑ the hidden laws가 빈칸 동사와 see의 목적어인데, 숨겨진 법칙을 우리에게 보여주려면 먼저 그것이 어떤 것인지 헤아려 파악해야 할 것이므로 '헤아리다'는 뜻의 fathom이 적절하다.

in opposition to ~에 반대하여 isolated a. 고립된 tragic a. 비극적인 fate n. 운명 dense a. 밀집한 masterpiece n. 걸작, 명작 doom n. 파멸 inevitable a. 불가피한, 필연적인

미국 작가들이 사회를 묘사하지 않고 사회에 관심이 없다는 비난이 종종 제기되어 왔다. 그들은 단지 사회에 반대하거나 사회로부터 고립된 개인들만을 묘사한다. 물론 미국 작가가 묘사하고 있는 것은 그 자신의 상황이다. 그러나 『안나 카레니나(Anna Karenina)』가 묘사하고 있는 것이 그녀의 시간과 장소와 불화한 고립된 개인의 비극적 운명이 아니면 무엇인가? 진정한 차이점은 톨스토이(Tolstoy)는 모든 것이 톨스토이에게는 아니지만 그 안에 있는 사람들에게는 영원히 고정된 것처럼 보이는 오래되고 밀집한 사회를 묘사하고 있었다는 것이다. 그리고 이 책이 걸작인 이유는 톨스토이가 이 사회를 실제로 지배하고 안나(Anna)의 파멸을 불가피하게 만든 숨겨진 법칙들을 헤아리고 우리에게 보여줄 수 있었기 때문이다.

27 빈칸완성   ②

사람들은 따뜻함보다 능력과 힘을 중요하게 생각한다는 의미가 되어야 하므로 빈칸에는 at the expense of와 반대되는 표현이 와야 한다. 따라서 '과대평가하다'는 뜻의 ② overvalue가 빈칸에 적절하다.

uncommon a. 드문 competence n. 능력, 역량 at the expense of ~을 희생하여 strive for ~을 얻으려고 노력하다 persuasive a. 설득력 있는 trustworthiness n. 신뢰성, 신뢰[신용]할 수 있음

사람들이 종종 자신의 따뜻함을 보여주는 것을 희생하면서 자신의 능력과 힘을 보여주는 것의 중요성을 과대평가하는 것은 드문 일이 아니다. 나는 그것이 특히 정치, 사업, 법률, 의학 분야에서 지도자 지위를 얻으려고 노력하는 사람들에게 흔한 일이라고 생각한다. 너무 많은 사람들이 이 방에서 가장 똑똑한 사람, 즉 일류의 사람이 되려고 노력하지만, 그것이 실제로 설득력을 얻거나 좋은 지도자가 되는 방법은 아니다. 그것은 실수이다. 사람들은 능력보다 신뢰성을 먼저 판단한다. 그들은 능력과 힘보다는 신뢰성과 따뜻함을 먼저 추론한다. 그리고 그 이유는 그것이 "이 사람은 친구인가 적인가?"라는 질문에 답하기 때문이다. 낯선 사람에게 당신은 먼저 당신에 대한 그들의 의도가 무엇인지 알고 싶어 하고, 그다음에 "그들이 그 의도를 수행할 수 있는가?"를 알고 싶어 한다. 사람들에게 영향을 미치거나 이끌기 전에 사람들과 관계를 맺고 신뢰를 쌓아야 한다.

다음 중 빈칸 Ⓐ에 들어가기에 가장 적절한 것은?
① 대꾸하다
② 과대평가하다
③ 배치하다
④ 경시하다

28-29

수년 동안, 엔터테인먼트 회사 경영진들은 넷플릭스에 고전 영화와 텔레비전 프로그램의 라이선스를 기꺼이 제공했다. 양측 모두 성과를 누렸다. 넷플릭스는 "프렌즈"와 디즈니의 "모아나" 같은 인기 있는 콘텐츠를 받았고, 그것은 계속 늘어나는 구독자 기반을 만족시켰고, 엔터테인먼트 회사에 많은 돈을 돌려주었다.
그러나 약 5년 전, 엔터테인먼트 회사 경영진들은 그들이 디즈니의 최고 경영자인 로버트 아이거(Robert A. Iger)가 말한 것처럼 강력한 경쟁자에게 "핵무기 기술을 팔고 있다"는 것을 깨달았다. 스튜디오들은 그들이 처음부터 무에서 구축하고 있던 스트리밍 서비스를 위해 (넷플릭스에 공급하던 것과) 동일한 사랑받는 영화와 프로그램이 필요했고, 넷플릭스의 상승을 부추기는 것은 그들을 해칠 뿐이었다. 즉시 콘텐츠 공급이 대부분 차단되었다.

executive n. 경영간부, 임원, 이사 license v. ~에게 면허를 주다, 인가[허가]하다 ever-growing a. 계속 늘어나는 subscriber n. 기부자; 구독자 bags of 다량의, 다수의 from scratch 처음부터, 무(無)에서 faucet n. (통·수도의) 꼭지, 주둥이 in large part 대부분

28 빈칸완성   ③

Ⓐ 넷플릭스는 인기 있는 콘텐츠를 통해 구독자를 만족시켰고, 콘텐츠를 제공한 회사는 많은 돈을 벌었다고 했으므로 양측 모두 성과를 얻었다고 할 수 있다. 따라서 '(노력 따위의) 성과'의 뜻인 spoils가 적절하다.
Ⓑ 스튜디오에 좋지 않은 영향을 미치고 즉시 넷플릭스에 콘텐츠 제공을 중단했다고 했으므로 넷플릭스의 성장이 스튜디오에 해를 끼쳤다는 의미가 되어야 한다. 따라서 '부추기다'는 뜻인 fueling이 적절하다.

다음 중 빈칸 Ⓐ와 Ⓑ에 들어가기에 가장 적절한 것은?
① 투자 ― 보고하는 것
② 탈선 ― 방해하는 것
③ 성과 ― 부추기는 것
④ 변화 ― 지지하는 것

29 빈칸완성   ③

스튜디오들이 넷플릭스에 콘텐츠를 공급하는 것이 그들에게 해를 끼칠 뿐이라는 사실을 알고 콘텐츠 공급을 중단했을 것이라 추론할 수 있다. 따라서 '(전기·가스·수도 등을) 끄다'는 뜻의 ③ turned off가 빈칸에 적절하다.

다음 중 빈칸 Ⓒ에 들어가기에 가장 적절한 것은?
① 마음대로 하게 하다
② 설립하다
③ 끄다
④ 어느 한도 내에서

30-31

"The Color Purple"의 이 감동적인 뮤지컬 영화는 불쾌감을 덜고 충격을 완화하며, 원작의 가시 돋치고 매듭 있는 표면을 평평하게 만들고, 폭력과 비극의 충격을 일부 제거하며, 그 경험을 여성들의 단결과 역경에 대한 승리 쪽으로 더 많이 기울어지게 한다. 하지만 그것은 아마도 1985년에 앨리스 워커(Alice Walker)의 소설을 스티븐 스필버그(Steven Spielberg)가 강력하면서도 불온한 부분을 삭제한 스크린 버전으로 만들어서 시작된 창조적 완화 과정의 일부일 수 있다. 그리고 나서 이 영화는 2005년에 인기 있는 브로드웨이 뮤지컬로 변모했고, 이것은 지금 이번에 새로 나온 각색본의 본보기다.

heartfelt a. 진심 어린, 감동적인 sugar the pill 불쾌한 것을 완화시키다; 싫은 것을 좋게 보이게 하다 soften the blow 충격을 완화하다 plane v. 평평하게 하다 barbed a. (말이) 가시가 돋친, 신랄한 knotty a. 매듭이 있는 take away 제거하다 solidarity n. 연대, 단결 triumph n. 승리 adversity n. 역경, 불운 emollient a. 부드럽게 하는, 완화하는 bowdlerize v. (책·연극 등에서) 충격적인[불온한] 부분을 삭제하다 transform v. 변형시키다, 변모시키다 adaptation n. 각색; 적응

30 빈칸완성   ①

Ⓐ 여성들의 단결과 역경에 대한 승리의 경험을 주로 다루었다는 의미가 되어야 하므로' (의견·상황 등이 어느 한쪽으로) 기울어지게 하다'는 뜻

의 tilting이 적절하다. Ⓒ 뮤지컬 영화 "The Color Purple"은 2005년에 브로드웨이 뮤지컬로 각색되었고, 이것을 본떠 이번에 새로 나온 각색본을 만들었다는 의미로 '모범, 본보기'의 뜻의 template, model이 적절하다. 따라서 상기 두 조건을 모두 만족시키는 ①이 정답이다.

다음 중 빈칸 Ⓐ와 Ⓒ에 들어가기에 가장 적절한 것은?
① 기울어지게 하다 ― 본보기
② 왜곡하다 ― 모범
③ 승진시키다 ― 대본
④ 회전시키다 ― 기원

31 동의어   ④

bowdlerize는 '(책·연극 등에서) 충격적인[불온한] 부분을 삭제하다'하다는 의미이므로 ④ edited가 동의어로 적절하다.

다음 중 밑줄 친 Ⓑbowdlerized와 의미가 가장 가까운 것은?
① 격렬하게 하다
② 진동[동요]시키다
③ 부풀리다
④ 편집하다

32-33

흉내 문어는 생존 능력이 다재다능한 만큼 독특하기도 한 생물이다. <이 유능한 두족류 동물은 자신의 환경에서 발견되는 여러 종의 생물을 모방할 수 있으며, 다양한 목적으로 그렇게 한다.> 그것은 자신이 잡아먹히는 것을 피하기 위해 독성 물고기를 모방하며, 침입자들에게 겁을 주기 위해 포식성 바다뱀을 모방할 수 있다. 막대기, 잎, 또는 다른 동물을 닮아 일부 생존하는 많은 종들이 존재한다. 과학자들은 이 종들 내에서 적응 변색이나 디자인을 보여주는 개체들은 포식자들이 못 보고 지나쳤지만, 다르게 표시된 개체들은 잡아먹혔다고 말했다. 그 후 생존자들은 남겨져 짝짓기를 하고 그들의 자연 방어로서 유익한 형태를 물려주었다.

mimic octopus 흉내 문어 cephalopod n. 두족류의 동물(문어·오징어 등) imitate v. 모방하다, 흉내 내다 toxic a. 유독한, 독성의 predatory a. 포식성의 sea snake 바다뱀 sacre off ~에게 겁을 주다 trespasser n. 불법 침입자, 침해자 adaptive a. 적응할 수 있는, 적응성의 overlook v. 못 보고 넘어가다, 간과하다 predator n. 포식자, 포식 동물 mate v. 짝짓기를 하다 pass on 물려주다

32 빈칸완성   ②

흉내 문어는 잡아먹히는 것을 피하기 위해 독성 물고기를 모방하거나 침입자들에게 겁을 주기 위해 포식성 바다뱀을 모방하는 등 다양한 목적으로 생존할 수 있는 생물이다. 따라서 '다재다능한'의 뜻의 ② versatile이 빈칸에 적절하다.

다음 중 빈칸 Ⓐ에 들어가기에 가장 적절한 것은?
① 평범한
② 다재다능한
③ 주행성의
④ 신록의

33 문장삽입

제시문은 "이 유능한 두족류 동물은 자신의 환경에서 발견되는 여러 종의 생물을 모방할 수 있으며, 다양한 목적으로 그렇게 한다."라고 했다. ⑧ 다음에서 다양한 목적으로 모방하는 예로 잡아먹히는 것을 피하거나 침입자들에게 겁을 주기 위해 독성 물고기와 포식성 바다뱀을 모방하는 것에 대해 이야기하고 있으므로 제시문은 ⑧에 들어가야 적절하다.

34-35

20세기의 가장 영향력 있는 음악 이론가 중 한 명인 존 케이지(John Cage)는 마르셀 뒤샹(Marcel Duchamp)이 미술에 했던 것을 음악에 했던 것으로 유명하다. 그는 음악을 정의하는 것이 무엇인지 끊임없이 의문을 제기했다. 그의 가장 잘 알려진 관심사 중 하나는 음악에서 창작자를 제거하고 대신 자연스러운 패턴과 우연을 기반으로 음악을 만드는 것이었다. 그의 유명한 작품 중 하나는 점성술 지도 위에 음악 세로줄의 마디를 긋고 별과 행성의 위치에 따라 음표를 지정하여 만든 음악과 관련된 것이었다. 그의 명백한 목표는 음악에서 개인적인 작용과 목적을 제거하고 음악이 자연을 조직하고 개선하려는 노력으로서가 아니라 세계의 자연스러운 혼란을 반영하는 것으로서 작용하게 하는 것이었다.

be remembered for ~으로 기억되다[유명하다] based on ~에 근거하여, ~을 기반으로 하여 astrological a. 점성술[학]의 note n. 음표 stated a. 정해진; 명백히 규정된 reflection n. 반영

34 내용파악 ③

마지막 문장에서 존 케이지의 음악 철학을 이야기하고 있는데 음악에서 개인적인 작용과 목적을 제거하고 자연의 자연스러운 혼란을 반영하는 것이라고 했다. 따라서 존 케이지는 음악에서 개인적인 영향보다는 자연의 반영을 중시했다고 할 수 있으므로 ③이 적절하다.

이 글에 따르면, 다음 중 존 케이지의 음악 철학을 가장 잘 표현한 것은?
① 음악은 음악과 분위기를 만드는 사람의 반영이다.
② 음악은 창작의 의미와 본질적으로 달라야 한다.
③ 음악은 개인적인 영향보다는 자연에서 파생되어야 한다.
④ 음악은 음악 이론에 대한 현재의 이론에 기초해야 한다.

35 동의어 ②

chaos는 '혼란, 혼돈'의 의미이므로 ② bedlam이 동의어로 적절하다.

다음 중 밑줄 친 ⒶChaos와 의미가 가장 가까운 것은?
① 자질구레한 장신구
② 혼란
③ 유령
④ 찬사

36-37

수은은 천문대에서 사용되는 거대한 망원경을 만드는 데 사용된다. 이 기구들은 들어오는 빛의 방향을 멀리 있는 물체를 확대하는 방식으로 바꾸는

대형 포물면 유리 거울을 전통적으로 포함하고 있었다. 문제는 유리 거울을 제작하는 데 비용이 엄청나게 많이 든다는 것이다. 그러나 망원경의 설계를 약간 수정하면, 수은은 액체 상태에서 반사성이 높기 때문에 저렴한 대안으로 사용될 수 있다. 대량의 수은을 빠르게 회전시키면 그것은 유리 거울과 비슷한 방식으로 작동하는 매끄러운 곡면을 형성한다.

mercury n. 수은 observatory n. 관측소, 천문대, 기상대 parabolic a. 포물선(모양)의 redirect v. ~의 방향을 바꾸다 magnify v. 확대하다; 과장하다 slight a. 약간의, 조금의 modification n. (부분적) 변경, 수정 alternative n. 대안 reflective a. 반사하는 spin v. 회전시키다

36 동의어

prohibitively는 '엄두를 못낼 만큼, 엄청나게'의 의미이므로 ① exorbitantly가 동의어로 적절하다.

다음 중 밑줄 친 ⒶProhibitively와 의미가 가장 가까운 것은?
① 터무니없이, 엄청나게
② 매력적으로
③ 분통이 터지게
④ 거품이 일어

37 빈칸완성 ②

수은을 빠르게 회전시키면 매끄러운 곡면을 형성한다고 했는데 이 곡면이 둘째 문장에 나온 포물면 유리 거울과 같은 것이므로, 이것이 비용이 많이 드는 유리 거울을 대신할 수 있다는 것이다. 따라서 빈칸에는 ②의 '유리 거울'이 적절하다.

다음 중 빈칸 ⑧에 들어가기에 가장 적절한 것은?
① 액체 용제
② 유리 거울
③ 망원경 영상
④ 확대된 물체

38-40

알렉시 드 토크빌(Alexis de Tocqueville)이 그의 기념비적인 연구서인 『미국의 민주주의(Democracy in America)』에서 썼듯이, '출생과 재산의 모든 특권이 폐지되고, 모든 직업이 모든 사람에게 접근 가능하며, 한 사람이 자신의 힘으로 그 직업들 중 어느 하나에서 최고의 위치에 오를 수도 있을 때, 쉽고 무한한 경력이 그의 야망에 열려있는 것처럼 보인다... 그러나 이것은 잘못된 생각이다. 왜냐하면 사람들이 거의 같고 모두가 같은 길을 따라갈 때, 어느 한 개인이 빨리 걸어서 그를 둘러싸고 압박하는 같은 군중을 헤치고 나아가는 것은 매우 어렵다.'
1세기 반 전 토크빌은 민주주의 사회의 경쟁적 성향이 사회적 뛰어남에 대한 욕구, 즉 군중보다 더 높아지려는 열망을 키운다는 것을 깨달았다. 그러나 사회적으로 이동 가능한 사회에서 정상에 오르는 사람들이 종종 하위 계급에서 상승했다는 사실을 감안할 때, 그들은 여전히 다른 모든 사람들과 같아 보인다. 사회적으로 이동할 수 없는 귀족적인 유럽 사회에서는, 여러 세대에 지속된 고정된 사회적 조건들이 미묘한 계급 신호를 만들어냈다. 목소리의 억양, 코의 모양, 심지어 턱의 생김새는 즉시 사회적 지위를 전달했다. 보스턴 브라민(Boston Brahmin)의 콧소리와 위로 올라

간 머리를 제외하면, 미국인들은 그 어떤 고유한 개인적인 지위 신호도 가지고 있지 않다. 만약 그의 메르세데스 벤츠와 맨해튼 타운하우스가 아니라면, 벼락부자인 월스트리트의 백만장자는 종종 그의 양복을 만들어주는 사람과 구별될 수 없을 것이다. 따라서 지위 상징에 대한 요구, 즉 사회적으로 성공한 자임을 나타내주는 물건에 대한 요구는 민주주의 국가에서 특히 강하다.

monumental a. 기념비적인 abolish v. 폐지하다 unbounded a. 무한한 ambition n. 야망 erroneous a. 잘못된 alike a. 서로 같은, 비슷한 cleave a way through ~을 헤치고 나아가다 breed v. 일으키다, 야기하다 distinction n. 구별, 차별, 탁월함, 뛰어남 yearning n. 동경, 열망 rise above ~을 초월하다 aristocratic a. 귀족의 aside from ~을 제외하고 nasal a. 코의; 콧소리의; 비음의 bray n. 나귀의 울음소리; 시끄러운 소리[잡담] uptilt v. 위로 기울이다 Boston Brahmin 보스턴 브라민(보스턴의 전통적인 상류층 엘리트) parvenu n. 벼락부자, 벼락출세자 millionaire n. 백만장자 tailor v. (양복을) 짓다 mark ~ off ~을 구별[표시]하다

다음 중 밑줄 친 ⓒparvenu와 의미가 가장 가까운 것은?
① 벼락부자
② 모범
③ 자유주의자
④ 보수주의자

---

38 빈칸완성   ④

사회적으로 이동이 가능한 민주주의 사회에서는 출신이나 재산과 관련된 특권이 없고, 직업에 대한 제한이 없으며, 자신의 힘으로 최고의 위치에 오를 수 있다. 따라서 이런 사회에서 사람들은 경쟁에서 이겨서 높은 자리에 오르고 싶은 욕구가 클 수 있다. 따라서 경쟁적 성향이 있다는 의미의 ④ competitive nature가 빈칸에 적절하다.

다음 중 빈칸 ⓐ에 들어가기에 가장 적절한 것은?
① 고유의 특권
② 전문가에 대한 수요
③ 직업 경계
④ 경쟁적 성향

---

39 빈칸완성   ④

빈칸 다음 문장에서 사회적으로 이동할 수 없는 계급사회에서는 목소리의 억양, 코의 모양, 심지어 턱의 생김새만으로도 그 사람의 사회적 지위를 알 수 있다고 했다. 따라서 귀족적인 유럽 사회에서는 자신의 신분을 나타낼 수 있는 미묘한 계급 신호가 만들어졌다는 의미로 ④ subtle class signals가 빈칸에 적절하다.

다음 중 빈칸 ⓑ에 들어가기에 가장 적절한 것은?
① 독특한 계급 유연성
② 완고한 행동
③ 겉으로 드러나지 않는 모습
④ 미묘한 계급 신호

---

40 동의어   ①

parvenu는 '벼락부자, 벼락출세자'의 의미이므로 ① upstart가 동의어로 적절하다.

2024 가톨릭대학교(인문계 A형)

01 ②	**02** ①	**03** ②	**04** ③	**05** ④	**06** ②	**07** ②	**08** ③	**09** ③	**10** ④
11 ④	**12** ②	**13** ①	**14** ①	**15** ④	**16** ③	**17** ①	**18** ④	**19** ②	**20** ④
21 ④	**22** ①	**23** ①	**24** ④	**25** ③	**26** ②	**27** ②	**28** ③	**29** ②	**30** ③
31 ①	**32** ④	**33** ②	**34** ③	**35** ④	**36** ①	**37** ②	**38** ④	**39** ①	**40** ④

01 논리완성 ②

기후변화를 완화하려면 온실가스 방출을 억제해야 한다. curb가 가장 적절하다.

obligation n. 의무 mitigate v. 완화하다 tout v. 홍보하다, 장점을 내세우다 curb v. 억제하다, 제한하다 ignite v. 불붙이다, 점화하다 expedite v. 촉진시키다, 신속히 처리하다

많은 사람들은 기후변화를 완화하기 위해 자신의 온실가스 방출량을 억제해야 할 도덕적 의무를 느끼고 있다.

02 논리완성 ①

방문객이 줄고 정부 지원금이 줄어들면 재정적으로 위태로워질 것이다. precarious가 가장 적절하다.

financially ad. 재정적으로, 경제적으로 precarious a. 불확실한, 불안정한, 위태로운 precocious a. 조숙한 preposterous a. 터무니없는 presumptuous a. 주제넘은, 건방진

그 박물관은 방문객 수의 급감과 정부 지원금의 감소로 인해 재정적으로 위태로운 입장에 있다.

03 논리완성 ②

또 다른 성격 특징들은 변화를 겪는다고 했으니 stable의 반대인 '유연하고 변하기 쉽다'는 뜻의 낱말이 와야 한다. malleable이 가장 적절하다.

stable a. 안정적인 inherent a. 내재적인, 원래 있는 malleable a. 유연한 provocative a. 자극적인, 도발적인 versatile a. 다재다능한, 다용도의, 다목적의

연구 결과에 따르면, 일부 성격 특징들은 아주 안정적이지만 또 다른 특징들은 나이가 들면서 일부 변화를 겪을 만큼 유연하다고 한다.

04 논리완성 ③

손가락질과 화난 몸짓이 자극하는 것은 부정적인 감정이므로 적대감을 나타내는 animosity가 가장 적절하다.

point fingers at ~에게 손가락질을 하다 gesticulate v. 몸짓[손짓]으로 가리키다 ensue v. 뒤따르다, 이어지다 elation n. 우쭐한 감정 groove n. 홈, 리듬 animosity n. 반감, 적대감 serenity n. 고요함, 평정심

서로에게 손가락질을 하는 것이나 화난 몸짓을 하는 것은 더 많은 반감을 자극하며, 이어지는 감정적 폭력이 당신들 두 사람을 모두 감싸 파괴의 춤을 추게 만든다.

05 논리완성 ④

제3자는 양 당사자 사이에서 분쟁을 중재할 수 있다. 중재한다는 뜻의 arbitrate가 가장 적절하다.

a third party 제3자 on occasion 이따금씩, 때때로 dispute n. 분쟁 proliferate v. 확산시키다; 증식[번식]하다 deliberate v. 신중히 생각하다 obliterate v. 없애다, 지우다 arbitrate v. (분쟁을) 중재하다

독립적인 제3자로서, 교황은 이따금씩 왕국들 사이의 분쟁을 중재해 달라는 요청을 받곤 했다.

06 관계대명사 ②

data-driven campaigning strategies 뒤에 이것을 수식하는 관계절이 와야 하는데, favor가 동사로 나와 있으므로 주격의 관계대명사 which가 적절하다.

embrace v. 포용하다 data-driven a. 데이터 기반의, 증거 기반의 favor v. 지지하다 echo v. 그대로 되풀이하다 conviction n. (사실에 입각한) 확신, 신념

기성 정치가들은 유권자들이 갖고 있는 기존의 확신을 되풀이하는 메시지를 지지하는 데이터 기반 유세 전략을 포용하는 것이 필요하다고 여길 것이다.

07 문의 구성 ②

that절에서 who부터 possible까지가 관계절로 주어인 learners를 수식하므로, 빈칸에는 주어 learners에 대한 동사가 필요하다. 과거시제 동사 reported가 가장 적절하며, 관계절 안의 동사들이 현재시제인 것

은 늘 그렇게 한다는 일반적 사실을 나타내며 report 동사가 과거시제인 것은 연구가 밝혀낸 그때 그랬다는 뜻이다.

go about 열심히 하다 pursuit n. 추구 efficient a. 능률적인, 효율적인 progress n. 진전, 진척

한 연구 결과, 멈추어 서서 자신이 가능한 한 가장 효율적인 방식으로 목표를 추구하고 있는지 자문하는 학습자들이 목표를 향한 더 큰 진전을 보고한 것으로 밝혀졌다.

08 병치   ③

can 다음의 동사원형 affect와 병치를 이루는 동사원형으로 cause가 와야 하고, cause의 목적어로 빈칸 다음의 두 명사와 병치를 이루는 명사 irritability가 와야 한다. 따라서 ③이 가장 적절하다.

pesticide n. 살충제 inability n. 무능함, 불능 irritate v. 자극하다, 짜증나게 하다, 화나게 하다 irritability n. 성급함

최근 연구들이 보여준 바에 따르면, 살충제는 인간의 뇌파활동에 영향을 끼치며, 성급함과 기억 상실과 집중 불능을 유발할 수 있다.

09 현재분사   ③

빈칸 이하는 subfields and specialties를 수식하는 형용사 기능을 해야 하므로 현재분사 stemming이 필요하다.

ecology n. 생태학 domain n. 분야, 영역 subfield n. 하위분야 specialty n. 전문분야, 전공 stem from ~에서 유래하다

생태학은 단일한 영역이 아니라, 다양한 과학 학문에서 유래한 다양한 생태학 하위분야들과 전문 분야들을 종합한 영역이다. 이 분야들은 모두 유기체와 환경 사이의 상호작용을 파악한다는 공통 목표를 공유하고 있다.

10 시제 / 동사의 태   ④

have become의 결과로 현재완료나 현재시제가 와야 하므로 첫 번째 빈칸에는 has neared와 is nearing 모두 가능하다. 두 번째 빈칸에서 is gone은 '지나갔다'는 뜻으로 쓰이긴 하지만, 주어인 810,000 tons와 수 일치에 어긋나고 뒤에 2형식동사 go의 보어로 missing이 있으므로 수동태 is gone이 될 수 없고 have gone이 맞다.

thriving a. 번성하는, 번영하는 consequently ad. 그래서, 그 결과 cod n. <어류> 대구 extinction n. 멸종, 소멸 near v. 접근하다, 가까이 가다 go missing 사라지다

100년도 채 안 되어 한때 번성하던 생태계가 사막이 되어버렸고, 그 결과 세계에서 가장 즐겨 먹는 생선 중 하나인 대구가 멸종에 가까워지고 있다. 사실, 뉴펀들랜드의 붕괴된 어장에서는 과거 매년 최대 81만 톤이나 잡히던 대구가 사라져버렸다.

11 논리완성   ④

enclosure는 토지의 사유화에 관한 이야기이므로, 사유화 이전의 공적 사용에 관한 이야기가 나와야 한다. 빈칸 바로 뒤 마지막 문장에도 common grazing 정보가 나온다. 따라서 ④가 가장 적절하다.

enclosure n. 울타리치기, 인클로저 consolidation n. 통합, 합병 pasture n. 초지, 목초지 arable a. 경작 가능한 meticulously ad. 꼼꼼히, 세심하게 outline v. 구획하다 dispersed a. 흩어진, 분산된 strip n. 길고 좁은 땅, 조각 exercise n. 실천, (권리의) 행사 grazing n. 방목 fallow a. 땅을 놀리는, 휴한지의 at the disposal of ~의 뜻대로, ~의 마음대로, ~의 처분대로

인클로저는 서유럽에서 있었던 공동의 밭과 초원과 목초지와 또 다른 경작 가능한 땅의 분할이나 통합을 가리킨다. 이 과정은 토지를 꼼꼼히 구획하여 현대에서처럼 개개인이 소유하고 관리하는 농지들로 바꾸어놓는다. 인클로저 전에는, 많은 농경지가 작물의 생장기 동안만 그리고 그해 추수가 끝날 때까지만 개별 경작자들이 통제하는 수많은 산재한 땅뙈기의 형태로 존재했다. 그 후 그리고 다음 해 작물의 생장기가 올 때까지는 해당 토지가 마을의 가축을 방목하거나 또 다른 목적을 위해 공동체의 뜻대로 사용되었다. 땅을 인클로즈하는 것은 이 넓은 빈 땅의 일정 부분 주위에 울타리나 담을 쳐서 공동 방목이나 그 땅에 대한 또 다른 권리 행사를 하지 못하게 하는 것이었다.

① 다음 작물 파종기에 맞게 흙을 되살리기 위해 휴한지로 방치되었다
② 그 땅에 대한 독점권을 가진 지주들이 사적으로 쓰도록 보존되었다
③ 농경지의 야생동물 회복과 서식처 보존을 위해 세심하게 관리되었다
④ 마을의 가축을 방목하거나 또 다른 목적을 위해 공동체의 뜻대로 사용되었다

12 논리완성   ②

지도자가 해야 할 선택을 남에게 맡기지 말라는 것이므로 지도자의 선결요건은 독립성 유지라는 것을 알 수 있다. 그러므로 ②가 가장 적절하다.

adviser n. 조언자, 고문, 자문 crucial a. 중요한 touch on ~에 관해 언급하다, ~에 관련되다 literary critic 문학 비평가 worth one's salt 밥값을 하다 chief lieutenant 부사령관 prerequisite n. 선결요건 pernicious a. 치명적인

모든 지도자들은 가장 가까운 조언자들에게서만큼이나 독서에서도 지도를 받고 영감을 받는다. 따라서 지도자가 하는 책의 선택은 중요할 수 있다. 리더십에 관한 모든 것들과 마찬가지로 책도 한 지도자에게 효과가 있는 책이 다른 지도자에게는 효과가 없을 수도 있다. 무엇을 읽을지에 대해 의식적으로 선택하지 못하는 것은 지도자가 할 수 있는 최악의 일 중의 하나다. 지도자 자신이 실수를 하는 것이 베스트셀러 목록이나 편집자나 문학 비평가들에게 지도자가 해야 할 선택을 대신 하도록 허용하는 것보다 훨씬 낫다. 지도자다운 지도자 중에 자기 부사령관을 외부인에게 대신 선택하게 하는 자는 없으며, 마찬가지로 지도자들은 책의 선택도 다른 사람이 대신 해서는 안 된다. 다른 많은 분야에서처럼 독서에서도, 지적 독립성을 유지하는 것이 효과적인 리더십을 위한, 그리고 가장 유해하고 지속적인 형태의 실패를 피하기 위한, 필수적인 선결요건이다.

① 공감 능력을 기르는 것
② 지적 독립성을 유지하는 것
③ 광범위한 주제에 관해 독학하는 것
④ 타인들이 의사결정에 관여하도록 허용하는 것

13 논리완성 ①

빈칸 이하에서 부모노릇이 providing shelter, food, and clothing까지인지 to cultivate the happiness of their adult children까지인지에 따라 부모에 대한 자녀의 태도가 달라져 부모의 기대 충족이 달라짐을 설명했으므로 '부모노릇의 한계(parameter)가 불분명하다'고 한 ①이 정답이다.

betrayal n. 배신 let down 실망시키다 availability n. 쓸모 있음, 소용에 닿음 responsiveness n. 반응, 즉각적인 대응 enviable a. 선망할 만한, 부러워 할 만한 reciprocal a. 상호간의 kinship n. 친밀관계 parenting n. 부모노릇하기, 자녀양육 repay v. 갚다, 보답하다 unmet a. 충족되지 않는 gratitude n. 감사 warrant v. 보증하다, 정당화하다 accountable a. 책임이 있는

많은 부모들은 자녀들이 자신에게 쓸모없다거나 반응하지 않는다고 인식하여 실망을 느끼고 배신감을 표현하는데, 자신이 어렸을 때에 비하면 부러워할 만하다고 여겨지는 삶을 자녀에게 제공했을 때 특히 그렇다. 부모들은 부모노릇을 한 세월이 나중에 (자녀와의) 친밀함으로 보상받게 될 상호적인 친밀관계의 결속을 기대한다. 그러나 이러한 상호성에 대한 기대는 부모노릇의 한계가 불분명한 시대에는 종종 충족되지 못한다. 만일 의식주를 제공하는 것으로 부모노릇을 충분히 했다고 여겨진다면 부모에 대한 감사는 자식의 삶이 어떻게 펼쳐지는가에 상관없이 보장되는 것 같다. 반면에 부모가 성인이 된 자녀의 행복을 키워줄 것으로 자녀가 기대한다면, 옳든 그르든, 자녀는 그들이 경험하는 그 어떤 불행에 대해서도 부모가 책임이 있다고 생각할지 모른다.

① 부모노릇의 한계가 불분명한
② 경제적 어려움이 대인관계 결속을 방해하는
③ 세대 간 격차가 부모와 자녀를 떼어놓은
④ 가족의 가치가 가장 중요한 사회적 미덕이라고 여겨지는

14 논리완성 ①

빈칸 이하에서 정부가 선거 과정을 조종한다고 했고 의회에서 야당은 항상 소수이도록 되어있다고 했으므로, 싱가포르의 체제가 민주적이지 않음을 알 수 있다. 따라서 정답은 ①이다.

hub n. 중심 manipulate v. (사람·여론 등을) 조종하다; (시장·시가 등을) 조작하다 opposition n. 야당 parliament n. 의회, 국회 object to ~에 반대하다 corruption-free a. 부정부패가 없는 far from ~와 거리가 먼, ~가 아닌 transparency n. 투명성

싱가포르는 현재 번영하는 첨단기술 제조의 중심지일 뿐 아니라 동남아시아 통신 및 금융의 중심지이다. 싱가포르 정부는 발전 과정에서 적극적 역할을 수행해왔고 시장의 힘들이 자유롭게 작동하도록 허용했다. 싱가포르는 다국적 기업(특히 기술 관련 기업들)의 투자를 독려했고, 스스로도 주택, 교육, 그리고 일부 사회복지에도 크게 투자해왔다. 이런 체제는 결코 충분히 민주적이지 않다. 정부는 선거 과정을 조종할 수 있고, 야당이 의회

에서 소수의 의석 이상은 절대 차지하지 못하도록 보장되어있다. 많은 싱가포르인들이 이런 상황에 반대하지만 또 다른 싱가포르인들은 이런 체제가 깨끗하고 안전하며 놀라울 정도로 부패가 없는 사회 뿐 아니라 빠른 성장도 가져다주었다고 반론을 제기한다.

① 결코 충분히 민주적이지 않다
② 포괄적 지배를 추구한다
③ 선거의 투명성을 추구한다
④ 정치 규제에 저항한다

15 논리완성 ④

빈칸이 있는 문장의 대명사 their와 they는 모두 상대방인 others를 가리킨다. 상대방을 너무 안 보는 것은 상대방이 거기 있음을 무시하는 셈이며 너무 오래 보는 것은 상대방을 호기심에 찬 눈길로 보는 셈이다. 따라서 정답은 ④이다. attention이나 interest도 괜찮지만 첫 빈칸의 단어 reveal과 impose가 적절치 않다.

eye behavior 눈 행동, 시선 처리 restricted a. 제한된 stare at ~을 응시하다 rude a. 무례한 infringement on ~의 침해, 위반 civil inattention 시민적 무관심, 예의바른 무관심 subtle a. 미묘한 single out 골라내다, 집어내다 cast downward 아래로 던지다 dim v. 흐려지다

미국에서는 사람들 앞에서의 눈 행동이 세계 다른 나라에서보다 상당히 더 제한되어 있다. 미국에서는 공공장소에서 남을 빤히 응시하는 것은 무례하며 사생활 침해인 것으로 간주된다. 대신 미국인들은 어빙 고프만이 "시민적 무관심"이라고 부르는 행동을 실천하는데, 사람들이 남들에게 그들의 존재를 인정할 정도로만 시선 접촉을 해주고 다음 순간에는 시선 접촉을 거두어 그들이 특별한 호기심의 대상으로 뽑히지 않도록 해주는 아주 미묘한 관행이다. 두 사람이 서로를 향해 걸어갈 때, 시민적 무관심은 약 8피트 정도까지는 시선 접촉을 허용하다가 서로 지나갈 때 눈길을 아래로 던진다. 이를 어빙 고프만은 "일종의 밝기 낮추기"라고 말한다.

① 느끼다 ─ 저항
② 드러내다 ─ 주의
③ 부과하다 ─ 관심
④ 인정하다 ─ 호기심

16 논리완성 ③

예술의 가치는 상징적 중요성이 있다고 했으므로 예술가인 인간은 상징을 만든다는 내용이 들어가야 한다. 따라서 정답은 ③이다.

irresistible a. 저항할 수 없는 decorate v. 장식하다 laden with ~가 가득 실린 otherwise ad. 다른 식으로, 다르게 significance n. 의미, 의의; 중요성 rearrange v. 재배열하다 novel a. 새로운 allegory n. 우화 evoke v. 불러일으키다, 환기하다 composition n. 구도, 구성

인간은 왜 예술을 창조하는가? 확실히, 이유 중의 하나는 자신과 자기 주변 세계를 장식하고픈 저항할 수 없는 욕망이다. 그러나 예술은 장식에 그치지 않고 훨씬 그 이상이다. 왜냐하면 예술에는 의미가 가득 실려 있기 때문이다. 예술은 우리로 하여금 달리는 표현될 수 없는 방식으로 우리의 이해를 전달할 수 있게 해준다. 진정, 그림은

천 마디 말의 가치가 있는데, 묘사적 가치에서만이 아니라 상징적 중요성에서도 그러하다. 예술에서 인간은 복잡한 생각을 새로운 방식으로 전달하는 상징의 발명가이다. 우리는 예술을 일상적인 산문의 관점에서 생각할 것이 아니라 시로 생각해야 하는데, 시는 새롭고, 종종 다중적인 의미와 분위기를 분명히 나타내기 위해 전통적인 어휘와 문법을 자유롭게 재배열한다. 그림도 마찬가지로 그것이 말하는 것보다 훨씬 더 많은 것을 암시한다. 그리고 시처럼 예술의 가치도 그것이 말하는 내용과 말하는 방식에 똑같이 존재한다. 예술은 우화, 포즈, 얼굴표정 등을 통해 의미를 암시하거나 선과 형태와 색채와 구도라는 시각적 요소를 통해 의미를 불러일으킴으로써 말을 한다.

① 자신의 천재성과 인성이라는 짐을 지게 된다
② 그 자체의 형태가 거의 없거나 아예 없는 재료로 작업한다
③ 복잡한 생각을 새로운 방식으로 전달하는 상징의 발명가이다
④ 자연의 숨겨진 측면들을 발견하는 고유한 힘을 보여준다

17 논리완성   ①

첫 문장에서 글이 경험에 뿌리를 두고 있다고 한 다음, 그 이하 내용이 우리는 글을 읽을 때 직접 관여한 사람의 경험을 알고 싶어 한다는 것이므로 ①이 가장 적절하다.

firsthand a. 직접적인   gender role 성별 역할   immigrant n. 이민자   at first hand 직접적으로   affirmative action 소수자 우대 정책   beneficiary n. 수혜자, 혜택 받는 사람

많은 강력한 글은 직접 경험에 뿌리를 두고 있다. 개인적인 경험을 이용하는 것은 큰 이슈에 대한 논의에 특별하고 진정성 있는 느낌을 더해준다. 성(性)역할이나 이민자 경험에 대한 글을 읽을 때 우리는 작가가 그 주제를 직접적으로 알고 있다고 가정한다. 소수자 우대 정책에 관해 읽는 동안 우리는 저자가 대상자로서나, 수혜자로서나, 목격자로서나, 가까운 애정 어린 관찰자로서 "내가 거기 있었다"라고 말할 수 있는지 알고 싶어 한다. 우리는 저자가 알고 지내왔거나 관찰해온 사람들의 삶에 이론이나 통계가 무엇을 의미하는지 알고 싶어 한다. 우리가 글을 관여자의 경험과 연관지을 수 있을 때까지는 글은 그냥 글에 불과하다.

① 우리가 글을 관여자의 경험과 연관 지을 수 있을 때까지
② 우리가 글의 의미를 더 넓은 사회적 범위에서 볼 수 있을 때까지
③ 글이 우리 자신의 시각 및 이해와 일치될 때까지
④ 우리가 글의 의미를 진정한 역사의 맥락에서 해석할 때까지

18 논리완성   ④

마지막 문장의 주어 This는 앞 문장에서 언급된 '베이징과 뭄바이의 도시 팽창이 여러 부정적인 결과를 초래한 것'을 가리키므로, 빈칸을 포함한 how절에도 시장의 수요, 시장의 힘에 따른 도시 팽창이 가져다주는 부정적 결과의 내용이 와야 한다. 따라서 정답은 ④이다. ② 시장의 힘에 따른 도시 팽창은 곧 시장의 필요에 따른 도시 팽창이다.

realm n. 영역, 분야   ongoing a. 진행 중인   intricate a. 복잡한   discourse n. 담론, 언설   advocate n. 옹호자, 주창자   laissez-faire n. 자유방임주의   demand n. 수요   pitfall n. 함정, 위험   sprawl n. 무질서하게 뻗어나감   solely ad. 오로지   degradation n. 저하, 퇴화   spontaneous a. 자동적인

도시계획 분야에서는 가장 효과적인 도시 발전 접근법에 대한 복잡한 담론이 진행되고 있다. 자유방임 모델의 옹호자들은 도시는 시장의 수요에 바탕을 두고 유기적으로 성장해야 하고, 시장의 힘이 도시 풍경의 진화를 인도하도록 허용해야 한다고 주장한다. 그러나 도시 전문가들은 이와 반대되는 견해를 갖고, 이런 접근법에는 함정이 없지 않다고 주장한다. 가령, 베이징과 뭄바이 같은 거대도시 지역의 급속한 팽창은 통제되지 않은 도시 팽창이 오로지 시장의 힘으로만 추진되어 결국 기간시설의 어려움, 환경 악화, 그리고 자원에 대한 불평등한 접근이라는 결과를 초래했다고 주장한다. 이것은 저절로 발생하는 도시의 성장이 의도치 않은 결과를 초래해 지속 가능한 발전을 방해한다는 점을 예증한다.

① 도시의 문화 풍경의 동질화를 초래할 수 있다
② 대개 시장의 필요를 충족시키지 못하는 발전을 초래한다
③ 자원의 평등한 분배를 보장해 지속 가능성을 촉진시킨다
④ 의도치 않은 결과를 초래해 지속 가능한 발전을 방해한다

19 논리완성   ②

플랫폼이 거짓 정보가 퍼지는 장이 된다고 했으므로 그 결과는 부정적인 내용이 되어야 하겠는데, 백인과 흑인에게 따로 정보를 보낸다고 했으니 '양극화와 거짓 조작'이 들어간 ②가 빈칸에 적절하다.

arena n. 각축장, 원형 경기장   anonymous a. 익명의   bot n. 보트(특정 작업을 반복 수행하는 프로그램)   automated a. 자동화된   manipulate v. 조작하다   intrusive a. 침해하는, 침입적인   operative n. 정보원   turnout n. 투표자 수

플랫폼은 바이러스처럼 퍼지는 익명의 말이 각축을 벌이는 무대가 되었다. 이런 유형의 말은 부분적으로는 "보트"를 통해 퍼지는데, 보트는 사용자들과 직접 소통하는 자동화된 프로그램으로, 거짓 정보와 조작된 내용을 공유하는 것의 책임 비용을 낮추어준다. 이는 유권자들에게서 그들을 향한 메시지의 신뢰성을 판단하기 위한 귀중한 정보를 빼앗는다. 플랫폼들은 사람들의 배경, 관심사, 선택에 대한 유례없는 많은 양의 침입적인 정보를 모으며, 이는 나이 많은 백인 남성 유권자들에게는 특정 메시지를 보내고 젊은 흑인 여성들에게는 또 다른 메시지를 보내는 것과 같은 "세분화된 표적" 광고 유세를 가능하게 해준다. 이런 관행은 플랫폼의 이익을 키워주지만 또한 양극화와 정치적 조작을 부추길 수 있다. 정치 정보원들은 유권자들의 투표를 저하시킬 의도의 부정적인 메시지 작업을 위해 세분화된 표적을 이용할 수 있다. 플랫폼의 설계는 극단주의를 부추기고 유권자들에게 그들 자신이나 소셜 미디어 친구들이 선택한 것과 비슷한 우려스러운 추가 정보를 제공한다. 플랫폼 내용을 통제할 수 있는 이들은 특정 후보자를 돕고 다른 후보자에게 해를 끼칠 수 있다.

① 더 넓은 범위의 시민들에게 접근하지 못한다
② 또한 양극화와 정치적 조작을 부추길 수 있다
③ 소수 집단들에 대한 의도치 않은 차별을 초래할 수 있다
④ 같은 의견의 사람들을 선거 유세를 위해 함께 모이게 거의 하지 못한다

20 논리완성   ④

마지막 문장에서 휴가철 휴가지에 흑인들이 간 것은 '웨이터나 집사나

짐꾼'으로서 간 것이라 했으므로, 손님이 아니라 고용인으로 갔다고 해야 한다. 따라서 정답은 ④이다.

embedded in ~에 새겨진   promote v. 홍보하다   nostalgia n. 향수   solidify v. 굳히다, 강화하다   unionization n. 노조 결성, 노동조합화   overcrowded a. 인구 과밀의   excursion n. 소풍, 외유   resort n. 휴양지

20세기가 되면서, 광고주들이 여름을 종종 향수와 낭만을 주제로 한 상품 홍보 방법으로 사용함에 따라 여름이 미국의 대중문화에 더 깊이 새겨졌다. 가령, 코닥(Kodak)은 그들의 카메라를 "여름휴가 이야기"를 들려주기 위해 꼭 필요한 도구로 고정시키는 광고로 고객들을 끌어들였다. 게다가 인구 과밀 도시와 결합된 노조 결성의 증가는 도시 계획자들로 하여금 노동자 계층을 위한 여가 활동을 개발하기 시작하도록 유도했다. 가령, 뉴욕 시에서 코니아일랜드와 존스 비치는 도시 노동자들에게 인기 있는 휴가지가 되었는데, 이들은 "8시간 노동, 8시간 수면, 8시간 여가"를 위해 노조가 얻어낸 변화로부터 이득을 본 셈이다. 그러나 해변으로 가는 여름 소풍이 미국 문화에 흐름을 만들기 시작하긴 했는데도, 많은 노동자 계급 흑인들은 손님이 아니라 고용인으로 미국의 늘어나는 해변 휴양지로 갔다. 『시카고 디펜더』지에 보도되었듯이, 웨이터, 집사, 짐꾼으로 간 흑인 남녀들의 숫자가 많았다.

① 사회적 지위 향상을 위해
② 휴가 중심지를 다각화하기 위해
③ 자연에 대한 열망을 충족시키기 위해
④ 손님이 아니라 고용인으로

21 문장배열   ④

글의 제시된 부분 마지막에서 '미생물(세균)이 보이지 않는 곳에 숨어 있을 수 있다는 것을 알게 되었다'고 했으므로, 보이지 않는 세균을 없앨 수 있는 화학 청소용품에 대해 언급한 ⑧가 먼저 오고, ⑧의 마지막에서 '다른 가정용품과 구별되지 않는 병과 포장상자에 들어있었다'고 한 것의 예로 ⑩가 오고, 이로 인한 피해 사례를 소개한 ⓐ가 그다음에 오고, 이를 시정하기 위한 법제정에 관한 ⓒ가 마지막으로 와야 한다. 따라서 정답은 ④이다.

link A to B A를 B와 연결 짓다   respectability n. 훌륭함   microbe n. 미생물   intensify v. 강화하다, 증대하다   lurk v. 잠복하다, 숨어 있다   eradicate v. 제거하다   poison v. 중독시키다   carbolic acid 석탄산   indistinguishable a. 구분할 수 없는   toxic a. 유독한   caustic soda 가성소다(독극물)

빅토리아 시대 사람들은 청결을 도덕성과 훌륭함과 연계시켰다. 미생물에 대한 새로운 과학은 미생물과 싸우는 일에 대한 빅토리아 시대 사람들의 강박을 더욱 강화시켰다. 이들은 이제 미생물이 보이지 않는 곳에 숨어 있을 수 있다는 것을 알게 된 것이다. ⑧ 먼지나 질병을 제거하기 위한 화학 청소용품들이 크게 광고되고 아주 효과적이었지만, 석탄산 같은 이 용품의 독성 성분들은 다른 가정용품과 구별되지 않는 병과 포장상자에 들어있었다. ⑩ 가성소다와 베이킹파우더 상자가 쉽게 혼동되었다. ⓐ 1888년 9월, 『에버딘 이브닝 프레스』지는 한 사건에서 13명이 석탄산에 중독되어 5명이 사망했다고 보도했다. ⓒ 1902년이나 되어서야 제약법이 위험한 화학물질을 담은 병을 평범한 액체 병과 비슷한 모양으로 만드는 일을 불법화했다.

22 내용파악   ①

기부자들은 기부 결과가 생생하고 구체적일 때 더 기부를 많이 한다는 것이 주제다. 유니세프나 모기장 보내기 운동 본부 이야기는 사례이므로 주요 함의로는 부족하다. 따라서 정답은 ①이다.

reinforcer n. 자극 요인, 강화요인   donate v. 기부하다   charity n. 자선; 자선 단체   fund v. 자금 지원을 하다   initiative n. 계획   appeal n. 호소력   spread n. 확산   tangible a. 생생한, 손에 잡힐 듯한, 구체적인

연구가 명확히 밝힌 바에 따르면, 도움의 효과는 도움을 강화시키는 데 필수적인 것이다. 가령, 기부 참여자들에게 유니세프와 모기장 보내기 운동 본부라는 두 자선 기관 중 한 곳에 기부하라고 요청한 연구를 보자. 유니세프는 아이들의 건강 돌봄 계획을 다양하게 지원하는 큰 단체이기 때문에 유니세프의 호소력은 비교적 일반적이고 추상적이었다. 유니세프 기부는 분명 가난한 아이들에게 도움을 주지만, 기부자들에게는 누가 정확히 혜택을 입는지 어떻게 입는지가 불분명했다. 반면 모기장 보내기 운동 본부의 호소력은 더 구체적이고 묘사적이었다. 이 본부는 자기네가 지원금을 이용하여 모기장을 사서 말라리아 풍토병이 있는 세계의 지역에서 말라리아의 확산을 중단시키겠다고 설명했다. 이 연구는 잠재적 기부자들이 자신의 기부가 가져올 구체적 결과를 분명히 볼 수 있을 때 도움을 제공하는 경향이 더 크다는 것을 시사한다.

이 글의 주된 함의는 무엇인가?
① 사람들은 자기 기부의 즉각적 영향을 볼 때 기부를 더 많이 하는 경향이 있다.
② 모기장 보내기 운동 본부가 유니세프보다 가난한 아이들을 위한 기부금을 이용함에 있어 더 효과적이다.
③ 기부를 할 때는 자선 단체의 대의명분을 찾아보고 이해하는 것이 중요하다.
④ 모든 자선 단체들이 기부금 운영에 투명성을 유지하는 것이 중요하다.

23 글의 요지   ①

아이들이 학습이 안 되는 이유는 동기나 욕구가 없어서가 아니라 기량이 부족하기 때문이라고 했으므로 정답은 ①이다.

verify v. 입증하다   instruction n. 지시   clinical a. 임상의   motivation n. 동기   reward v. 보상하다   transition n. 이행, 과도(기), 변화   keep track of ~을 확인하다

때때로 어른들은 어떤 아이들은 특히 학교에서 배우는 것이나 학교생활을 잘 하는 것에 대해 관심이 없다고 생각한다. 그러나 아이들이 요구되는 것을 할 능력을 갖추고 있다는 것을 입증하는 것이 중요하다. 때때로 아이들은 지시를 따르고 싶어 하지만 능력이 모자란다. 임상 아동심리학자인 로스 그린은 아이들은 할 수 있으면 잘하지만, 많은 어른들은 아이들이 잘하고 싶을 때만 잘한다고 생각한다고 지적했다. 따라서 아이들이 제대로 못하면 그건 그들에게 필요한 기술이 없어서가 아니라 동기가 부족해서 그리고 잘하고 싶지 않아 해서라고 생각하는 통념이 있다. 이 때문에 어른들은 가르치기보다 보상과 처벌을 하게 된다. 어른들은 아이들이 그저 관심 받기를 원하며 제 맘대로 하기를 원하며 나쁜 태도를 갖고 있고 동기가 없다고 말할 수도 있다. 그린은 아이들이 어려움을 겪는 것들을 열거했는데, 지시를 이해하는 것, 변화를 다루는 것, 시간 가는 줄을 알고 있는 것, 집중을

유지하는 것 등이다. 아이들이 할 수 없는 것 때문에 아이들을 처벌하기보다는 문제가 무엇인지 파악하는 것이 더 낫다.

이 글의 요지는 무엇인가?
① 아이들의 학업성취도 향상은 그들의 필수적 기술을 평가하는 것으로 시작된다.
② 각 아동의 적성을 결정하는 것이 맞춤식 교육에 중요하다.
③ 처벌이 아니라 보상이 아이들의 행동을 형성하는 데 더 효과적이다.
④ 아이들에게 동기를 부여하는 것은 그들의 지속적 학습에 꼭 필요한 선결요건이다.

---

24 내용일치   ④

마지막 문장에서 새로 데려온 고래를 원래 있던 고래와 함께 두면 비정상적 관계가 생긴다고 했으므로 ④가 잘못된 진술이다.

cetacean n. 고래목 동물 loosely ad. 느슨하게 highly structured 고도로 조직화된 pod n. 무리, 떼 orca n. 범고래 offspring n. 자식 dialect n. 방언 targeted a. 표적이 된 capture v. 붙잡다, 포획하다 specimen n. 견본, 표본

고래와 돌고래는 다 합쳐서 고래목 동물로 알려져 있는데, 인간처럼 매우 사교적인 동물이다. 야생의 바다, 일반적으로 해안 바다나 망망대해에서 이들은 pod(떼)라 알려진 구조가 느슨한 집단에서 고도화된 집단까지 집단을 이루어 살아간다. 대체로 pod는 그들이 장기간이나 평생 동안 함께 상호작용하는 핵가족 구성원이나 대가족 구성원으로 이루어져 있다. 가령, 돌고랫과 중 가장 큰 범고래들은 암컷어미와 성체 수컷새끼들과 성체 암컷새끼들과 암컷새끼의 새끼들로 이루어진 단단한 모계 집단에서 살아가며 모두가 평생 결속을 이룬다. 이런 관계는 매우 엄격하기 때문에 각 pod는 의사소통하는 나름의 별개의 방언을 갖고 있다. 일부 연구자들은 범고래가 지구상에서 가장 사회적으로 결속이 강한 종일 것으로 생각한다. 범고래 개체들이 포획되면 집단의 전체 사회 패턴이 붕괴된다. 종종 포획 과정에서 포획 표적이 되지 않은 구성원들이 부상을 입거나 죽는다. 새로 획득한 견본 고래를 더 노련한 원래 있던 고래들과 같이 가두어두면 완전히 비정상적이고 인위적인 사회 구조가 만들어진다.

이 글에 의하면, 다음 중 사실이 아닌 것은?
① 범고래는 다수의 세대들과 함께 결속 강한 모계 pod를 형성한다.
② 서로 다른 범고래 가족들이 쓰는 별개의 방언들이 있다.
③ 범고래 한 개체를 포획하면 표적이 되지 않은 pod 구성원들도 위험해질 수 있다.
④ 새로 획득한 범고래를 기존의 포획된 범고래들에게로 끌어들이면 사회 통합이 개선된다.

---

25 글의 흐름상 적절하지 않은 문장 고르기   ③

ⓒ는 "30년 된 연구에서 연구자들은 식물이 작은 밀폐 용기에서 휘발성 유기화합물을 줄일 수 있다는 것을 보여주었고, 이는 소비자들로 하여금 이 실내 식물의 가치를 과대평가하게 만들었다."라는 뜻으로 방향제의 독성과 이를 막는 방법이 주제인 글에 어울리지 않는다. 따라서 정답은 ③이다.

---

encounter v. 만나다 air freshener 방향제 odor n. 악취 fragrance n. 향기 release v. 방출하다 pollutant n. 오염입자 carcinogen n. 발암물질 cut down 줄이다 airtight container 기밀용기, 밀폐용기

식료품점과 잡화점에서는 다양한 "방향제" 제품으로 가득 찬 통로를 발견하는 일이 흔하다. 방향 양초부터 "냄새가 신선한" 스프레이와 "천연" 플러그인 공기 확산기까지 마케팅은 우리에게 이런 제품을 써서 불쾌한 악취를 가리고 쾌적한 집안 향기를 만들라고 독려한다. 그러나 이런 제품에는 보통 공기 중으로 방출되면 뇌 건강을 비롯해 우리 건강에 직접 영향을 끼칠 수 있는 일군의 화학물질들이 들어있다. 방향제 제품들에는 "휘발성 유기화합물", 즉 VOC라는 분자가 가득 들어있다. 이 물질은 강력한 공기 오염입자이며 포름알데히드와 벤젠 같은 공인된 발암물질을 함유하고 있다. <30년 된 연구에서 연구자들은 식물이 작은 밀폐 용기에서 휘발성 유기화합물을 줄일 수 있다는 것을 보여주었고, 이는 소비자들로 하여금 이 실내 식물의 가치를 과대평가하게 만들었다.> 게다가 방향 양초와 에어로졸 스프레이는 뇌 독소로 알려진 높은 수치의 입자를 방출할 수 있다. 공기를 신선하게 하기로 한다면 난로 위에 올려놓은 물에 향신료나 풀을 넣어 끓이는 걸 고려해보라. 그뿐 아니라 향이 없는 청소 제품이나 양초도 찾아보라.

---

26 글의 요지   ②

놀이가 기분을 증강시키는 정서적 효과를 언급한 후 인지에 미치는 영향도 언급하므로 글의 요지로는 ②가 적절하다.

drive n. 욕망 hard-wired a. 내장된, 선천적인 activation n. 활성화 release n. 방출 factor n. 요인 flexibility n. 유연성 uplift v. 증강시키다 go through 겪다, 경험하다 cognition n. 인지 improvisation n. 즉흥적 행동 adaptability n. 적응능력 uncertainty n. 불확실성 aplomb n. 침착함

과학 연구는 놀려는 욕망이 생물학적으로 타고난 도구로, 거의 모든 포유류에 공통점이라는 것을 밝혔다. 놀이는 뇌의 보상 중추의 활성화를 초래하여, 학습과 정신적 유연성을 뒷받침하는 강력한 신경 성장 요인일 뿐 아니라 도파민과 옥시토신 같이 기분을 좋게 만드는 화학물질이 방출되게 만든다. 놀이는 스트레스 호르몬의 감소를 유발하고, 기분을 증강시키며, 에너지를 강화하는 효과를 낸다. 놀이의 종종 과소평가되는 측면은 인지에 끼치는 영향이다. 연구자들은 놀이를 하는 동물들이 진지한 실세계 사건들보다 대개 더 무작위적이고 혼란스러우며 가변적인 많은 일련의 행위들을 거친다고 말했다. 이런 역동적 활동은 불확실성 앞에서 즉흥성, 창의력, 적응능력을 요구한다. 본질적으로 놀이는 훈련장으로 기능함으로써 개체들이 예상치 않은 것을 예상하고 침착하게 적응하도록 준비시켜준다.

이 글의 요지는 무엇인가?
① 놀이는 거의 모든 포유류에서 발견되는 보편적인 특징이다.
② 놀이는 정서적 행복뿐 아니라 인지 능력도 향상시킨다.
③ 놀이는 뇌가 신경 성장을 촉진시키는 화학물질을 방출하게 돕는다.
④ 놀이가 뇌 건강에 끼치는 영향은 과학에서 논란이 되는 주제였다.

---

27 글의 제목   ③

다육식물이 수요 폭증으로 위험하다는 경고가 있다는 것을 알리는 글이므로 정답은 ③이다.

botanist n. 식물학자 caution v. ~에게 조심시키다, 경고하다 surge n. 급증, 급등 succulent n. 다육식물(선인장 등) pose a threat 위협하다 highlight v. 강조하다 insatiable a. 탐욕스러운 lockdown n. 봉쇄 neglect v. 무시하다 deplete v. 고갈시키다 irreversible a. 돌이킬 수 없는 exacerbate v. 악화시키다

식물학자들은 특히 아시아 지역에서의 다육식물의 수요 급증이 중요하고 귀한 종(種)에 위협을 제기한다고 경고한다. 코넬리아 클라크 박사는 아시아 시장에서의 이 식물에 대한 탐욕스러운 욕구를 강조하면서 봉쇄 동안 강화된 집단 열광에 대해 우려를 표명한다. 이러한 열광이 최대 100년간 번성할 수 있는 다육식물들의 개체수를 위험에 빠뜨린다는 것이다. 놀라운 점은 이 식물들이 무차별적으로 뿌리 뽑힌다는 것인데, 지역 수집가들이 식물의 나이를 무시하고 오래된 유서 깊은 식물을 비롯하여 전체 개체수를 고갈시키고 있는 것이다. 남아프리카가 전 세계 다육식물 종의 약 3분의 1을 보유한다는 것을 고려할 때, 전문가들은 이런 추세가 이 자연의 경이로운 식물들의 돌이킬 수 없는 손실을 가져올 수 있다고 경고한다. 코로나 팬데믹 절정 동안 실내식물 수요의 급증은 상황을 더욱 악화시켰고, 실내 원예는 영국의 식물 소매업자들에게 500% 판매 신장이라는 놀라운 기록을 가져다주었다.

이 글의 제목으로 가장 적절한 것은?
① 다육식물이 실내 원예의 전 세계적 증가를 일으키다
② 코로나-19 시기에 있었던 식물 판매 급증의 원인들
③ 다육식물 열광: 늘어나는 욕구와 보존상의 우려
④ 아시아 다육식물 열풍: 남아프리카 경제에 주는 혜택

28 글의 주제 ③

게임이 학생들에게 실세계에 적용 가능한 순기능을 한다는 긍정적 평가의 글이다. 따라서 정답은 ③이다. ① 예를 든 것에 불과하다. ② 난점에 대한 언급은 없다. ④ 다양한 유형의 게임이 제시되지 않았다.

low-risk a. 위험이 낮은 impact n. 영향 foster v. 길러주다, 육성하다 incorporate v. 통합시키다 inhabit v. ~에 살다, 존재하다 holistic a. 전체론의, 전체론적인 prompt v. 촉진시키다 reflect on 곰곰이 생각하다 conservationist n. 환경보호론자 follow-up n. 후속조치 conduct v. 실행하다

게임은 플레이어들에게 위험이 낮은 환경에서 빠른 결정을 내릴 기회를 제공함으로써 이들이 자신의 선택의 영향을 보고 필요하면 다시 시도하도록 해주어 귀중한 생활기술을 키워준다. 교사들은 역할분담 게임을 수업 시간에 통합시켜 넣어 학생들이 사고의 전체론적인 시스템 내에서 상이한 관점을 갖도록 도와주고, 그럼으로써 학생들이 여러 가능성들을 비교해보고 대안적 행동 계획을 숙지하면서 자신의 행위주체성에 대해 생각하도록 촉진시킬 수 있다. 예를 들어, 가상 게임 "알바: 야생동물 모험"에서 플레이어들은 멸종 위기에 처한 동물들을 발견해 보호하는 작은 미션들을 시작한다. 학생들은 게임을 하는 동안 스스로를 환경보존운동가나 모험가라 생각하지 않을지 모르지만, 위험이 낮은 환경은 이들에게 자신이 현실 세계에 끼칠 수 있는 더 큰 영향을 생각해볼 수 있도록 격려한다. 후속 활동을 통해 학생들은 자신들이 만난 동물을 더 찾아볼 수 있고 심지어 지역 야생동물의 더 작은 생태계를 알아보기 위해 지역의 자연을 산책해 볼 수도 있다.

이 글의 주제는 무엇인가?
① 학생들 사이에 환경 의식을 향상시키기 위한 기술 주도적 접근
② 교육 환경에서 게임을 실행하는 일의 이점과 난점
③ 역할분담 게임이 학생들의 지적 성장에 끼치는 이로운 영향
④ 다양한 교육 게임의 유형과 이들의 고유한 학습 장점들

29 글의 요지 ②

마케팅의 핵심은 고객을 줄이는 것까지 포함하여 수요 변화에 적응해 이윤을 내는 것이라 했으므로 정답은 ②이다.

current a. 현재의 output n. 생산량, 생산물 demand n. 수요 demarketing n. 고객을 일부러 줄이는 마케팅 objective n. 목적 overcrowded a. 지나치게 붐비는

일부 사람들은 마케팅 관리가 회사의 현 생산물을 위한 충분한 고객을 찾는 일이라고 생각한다. 그러나 이런 관점은 지나치게 제한적이다. 마케팅 관리는 모든 방식으로 모든 고객에게 서비스하는 것이 아니다. 오히려 마케팅 전문가들은 자신들이 이윤을 내면서 잘 서비스할 수 있는 선별된 고객에게 서비스를 제공하고 싶어 한다. 기업에게는 제품에 대한 원하는 수준의 수요가 있다. 어느 시점에서든, 수요가 아예 없을 수도 있고 충분할 수도 있으며 불규칙하거나 너무 많을 때도 있다. 마케팅 관리는 이 상이한 수요 상태에 대처할 방안을 찾아야 한다. 마케팅 관리는 수요를 찾아내고 늘리는 일뿐 아니라 변화시키고 줄이기까지 하는 일도 관여해야 한다. 예를 들어, 요세미티 국립공원은 여름이면 끔찍하게 붐빈다. 형편없는 기업들은 최고 이용 시기에 수요를 맞추느라 때때로 곤란을 겪는다. 이런 과잉 수요의 경우에 디마케팅이 고객 수를 줄이는 데 필요할 수 있다. 따라서 마케팅 관리는 서비스를 받는 고객의 유형과 수요의 수준, 시기 및 성질에 영향을 끼치고자 하되, 기업이 목적을 이루도록 도움이 되는 방식으로 영향을 끼치고자 한다.

이 글의 요지는 무엇인가?
① 디마케팅 전략은 불황기에 특히 유용하다.
② 마케팅 관리는 수요 변화 관리를 넓게 포괄해야 한다.
③ 마케팅 성공은 제품에 맞는 올바른 고객 타겟팅에 달려 있다.
④ 추가 고객을 끌어들이는 것이 계속 진화하는 시장의 최우선 고려사항이 되어야 한다.

30 내용일치 ③

다르푸르 지역의 갈등은 남쪽이 아니라 서쪽이다. 따라서 정답은 ③이다.

daunting a. 위협적인 cut across 가로지르다, ~에 해당되다 divide n. 분열, 구분선 impose v. 강요하다, 부과하다 antagonize v. 적으로 돌리다 civil war 내전 disastrous a. 비극적인, 재앙의 casualties n. 사상자 tentative a. 잠정적인

수단은 북아프리카에서 가장 위협적인 정치 쟁점들 중 일부를 마주하고 있다. 일부 쟁점들은 종교적 분파들에 두루 관련이 있고 다른 것들은 수단 내의 종족 및 인종 차이에 관한 것이다. 1989년 군사 쿠데타 이후 수니파 이슬람 국가인 수단은 이슬람교 법을 전국에 강제했고 그 과정에서 온건파 수니 이슬람교도들과 남부의 많은 비이슬람교도(대개 기독교도와 정령신앙 신도들)를 적으로 돌렸다. 북쪽 이슬람교도들과 남쪽 기독교도 및 정령신앙 신도들 간의 긴 내전 또한 재난이었고, 지난 20년 동안 주로 남부에서 200만 명 넘는 사상자를 냈다. 남부의 살육은 2001년(2004년 잠정 평화 협정이 체결되었다)

이후 줄어들었지만 수단 서부의 다르푸르 지역에서 새로운 갈등이 분출했다. 아랍인이 이끄는 잘 무장한 민병대가 수백 곳의 흑인 주민 마을들을 공격해 20만 명이 넘는 이들을 살해하고 250만 명의 주민을 집에서 내쫓으면서, 종족, 인종, 영토 통제가 이슬람교도가 대다수인 이 지역에서 분쟁의 중심에 있는 듯하다.

이 글에 의하면, 다음 중 사실이 **아닌** 것은?
① 수단 갈등의 원인은 종교 쟁점을 넘어 복잡하다.
② 피해의 심각성은 북부보다 남부가 더 컸다.
③ 다르푸르 지역의 갈등으로 인해 남부의 사상자가 늘었다.
④ 아랍인이 이끄는 민병대가 흑인들의 대량 학살에 책임이 있다.

31-32

기후변화를 뒤집으려면 거대한 사회 변화가 필요하다. 대체로 우리는 이 대규모 행동 변화를 추진하기 위한 두 가지 원천을 본다. 규제 조직이 만들어 집행하는 하향식 수단이거나 아니면 개별 소비자들이 자발적으로 참여해 촉진시키는 상향식 행동들이다. 이 두 방법 모두 대규모 변화와 관련해 심각한 한계가 있다. 최근의 사례로, 플라스틱 빨대에 대한 논쟁을 생각해보자. 이 쓰레기를 소비자로부터 제거하기 위해 정책 입안자들은 식당과 소매점에서 빨대 사용을 금지할 수 있다. 이 금지는 느리고 논란이 된다. 또 다른 선택은 소비자 수준에서 빨대 사용을 좌절시키는 데 집중된 사회 마케팅 계획이다. 각 소비자는 자신의 선택이 해양 생명체와 쓰레기양에 끼치는 영향과 관련해 교육을 받을 수 있고, 매번 빨대 사용에 저항하라는 선택에 직면할 수 있다. 이런 유형의 지속적인 행동은 "새 발의 피"라는 인식 때문에 힘들고 의욕을 꺾으며, 선택의 과부하와 서로 경합하는 동기들 앞에서 책임을 매번 소비자에게 전가시킨다. 다른 한편, 중간 수준의 계획, 가령 자발적인 브랜드 대응 같은 계획은 사회 변화를 더욱 효과적으로 추진할 수 있다. 스타벅스, 알래스카 항공, 그리고 맥도날드 같은 수많은 브랜드들은 자발적으로 1회용 빨대 제공을 중단했다. 물론 각 수준마다 장단점은 있지만 브랜드 수준의 행동은 개인 수준의 행동보다 규모 측정이 더 가능하고, 정책 수준보다 더 유연하고 혁신적이다.

reverse v. 뒤집다 massive a. 거대한, 대규모의 societal a. 사회의 top-down a. 하향식의 bottom-up a. 상향식의 plastic straw 플라스틱 빨대 initiative n. 계획, 추진력 impact n. 영향 consistent a. 일관된, 지속적인 confronted with ~에 직면하는 alternatively ad. 그 대신, 그렇지 않으면 scalable a. 저울로 잴 수 있는 flexible a. 유연한 a drop in the bucket 새 발의 피, 언 발에 오줌 누기

31 빈칸완성 ①

기업 수준의 환경운동이 좋다는 흐름이므로, 개인 차원의 운동이 나쁘다는 쪽으로 가되, 앞에는 새 발의 피라는 하찮은 효과가 언급되고, 뒤에는 책임 전가의 내용이 나오므로, '힘들고 의욕도 꺾는다'는 ①이 적절하다.

빈칸에 들어가기에 가장 적절한 표현은?
① 힘들고 의욕을 꺾는다
② 힘들지만 보람 있다
③ 대개 주목도 못 받고 인정도 못 받는다
④ 사소해보이지만 분명히 영향이 크다

32 글의 제목 ④

하향식 금지 조치는 느리고 논란이 된다고 했고 소비자 수준에서의 자발적 참여는 힘들고 의욕이 꺾인다고 한 반면, 브랜드의 환경보존 활동은 효과가 가장 좋다고 했으므로 제목으로는 ④가 적절하다.

이 글의 제목으로 가장 적절한 것은?
① 지속 가능성은 어떻게 브랜드 가치를 증가시키나?
② 녹색 사업: 환경이 어떻게 사업에 영향을 끼치는가
③ 작은 행동이 기후변화에 큰 차이를 만들어낼 수 있다!
④ 영리 브랜드의 고유한 역할: 기후 행동의 격차 메꾸기

33-35

다국적 과학자 집단은 유전자 접합 기술을 이용하여 특별한 토마토를 만들어냈다. 이 토마토는 유전자 변형을 하지 않은 천연 토마토보다 200퍼센트 더 높은 항산화제를 함유하고 있다. 암에 매우 취약한 생쥐에게 먹였더니 이 토마토는 생쥐의 수명을 크게 늘렸다. 이 연구들은 널리 주목을 받았지만 유전공학의 똑같이 중요한 업적 하나는 거의 10년 동안 대체로 무시당했다. 그 혁신은 황금쌀인데, 이것은 비타민 A의 전구물질인 베타카로틴을 표명하는 유전자로 성분을 강화한 새로운 쌀 품종이며, 베타카로틴은 몸속에서 필요할 때 활성화된다.

개발도상국에서는 2-3억 명의 아이들이 비타민 A 결핍의 위험에 처해있다. 비타민 A의 결핍은 파괴적이고 심지어 치명적일 수 있다. 그것은 홍역과 설사 질환 같은 흔한 아동기 질환에 대한 취약성을 증가시키고, 개발도상국 아동기 시력상실의 가장 중요한 단일 원인이다. 황금쌀은 수십만 명의 생명을 매년 구할 수 있고 수백만 명의 삶의 질을 개선할 수 있다. 그러나 이 빛나는 이야기의 한 가지 측면은 변색되어 있다. 과학과 기술을 반대하는 활동가들인 그린피스와 지구의 친구들과 소수의 또 다른 단체들에 의한 비타협적인 반대가 이미 위험을 싫어하던 규제 당국으로 하여금 과도하게 신중한 접근법을 채택하게 함으로써 이 작물의 승인을 정체시켰던 것이다.

황금쌀은 만든 지 9년이 지나고 인류에게 이익이 될 어마어마한 잠재력이 있는데도 아직 규제당국의 요식절차에 걸려 있고, 이는 끝이 보이지 않는다. 황금쌀에는 끝없이 사례별로 검토해야 하고 관료들이 머뭇거려야 할 게 전혀 없다. 반면, 정확하지도 않은 기술로 만들어진 식물들은 대개 그 어떤 정부의 감시나 요구(혹은 환경단체의 반대)를 받지도 않는다. 황금쌀의 이야기는 우리가 아직 그것을 실현시킬 의지도 지혜도 없다는 것을 명확히 보여준다.

gene-splicing n. 유전자 접합 antioxidant n. 항산화제 unmodified a. 유전자 변형이 안 된 feed v. 먹이다, 공급하다 extend v. 연장시키다 momentous a. 중대한 bio-fortify v. 생체 강화하다 precursor n. 전구물질, 전 물질 devastating a. 파괴적인 dithering n. 머뭇거림, 꾸물거림 red tape n. 관청의 불필요한 요식절차

33 빈칸완성 ②

황금쌀의 정책 추진이 잘 되지 못하는 이유에 대한 내용이 이어지므로, 이 빛나는 이야기의 한 가지 측면은 '변색되어' 있다고 하는 게 적절하고, 승인이 잘 안 되는 관료제의 폐해는 이 작물의 승인을 '정체시켰다'고 하는 게 적절하다. 따라서 정답은 ②이다.

빈칸에 들어가기에 가장 적절한 표현은?
① 가려져 있는 ─ 철회시키다
② 변색된 ─ 정체시키다
③ 왜곡된 ─ 촉진시키다
④ 과대평가된 ─ 초래하다

34 글의 제목 ③

유전자 조작 식품을 활용하지 못하는 세태를 비판하는 글이므로 부정적 뉘앙스가 담긴 ③이 정답이다.

이 글의 제목으로 가장 적절한 것은?
① 새로운 녹색 혁명의 지도자들
② 유전자 조작 식품은 안전한가?
③ 낭비되는 황금 기회
④ 식물 연구의 신기원

35 내용일치 ④

황금쌀의 가능성이 관료제의 요식절차 때문에 방해받는다는 것이 주제이므로 ④가 정답으로 적절하다.

이 글에 의하면, 다음 중 사실인 것은?
① 황금쌀은 유전자 조작 토마토만큼 널리 인정받았다.
② 황금쌀은 암 치료에 도움이 될 가능성이 있는 새로 개발된 곡물이다.
③ 황금쌀의 승인은 안선성에 대한 증거가 축적되어 곧 임박했다.
④ 황금쌀의 가능성은 잘못된 입법과 후진적 사고 때문에 방해받고 있다.

36-37

고스 하위문화는 1980년대 영국에서 처음 뿌리를 내렸다. 당시 더 큐어와 바우하우스 같은 밴드는 점점 더 인기를 끌었다. 고스 문화는 곧이어 음악 운동 이상의 것으로 진화했다. 고스들은 대개 검은 옷과, 대개 머리 인두질을 한 검은 머리를 선호했다. 많은 이들은 긴 코트를 입었고 코르셋과 목에 꽉 끼는 목걸이를 착용했다. 이 고스들은 중세 유럽을 만드는 데 도움을 주었던 사람들과 어떤 관련이 있을까? 역사적인 고스족은 대륙을 넘어 이주하여 왕국을 세우고 때로는 로마 같은 기존 세력들과 싸운 게르만족이었다. 오늘날, 고대 고스족은 (그리스 로마 문명에 반대한) 반고전주의의 원형으로 간주된다. 고스족의 지도자 알라리크 1세가 서기 410년로 로마를 약탈했을 때, 그것은 고대 세계의 몰락을 알리는 상징성이 큰 순간이었다. '고딕'이라는 단어는 그 이후 비고전적인 것을 나타내는 꼬리표였다. 현대 고스 하위문화는 또한 '다른 편'의 그 상징적인 준거기준에 의지한다. 5세기부터 유럽으로 퍼져나간 다른 게르만족의 이름인 '반달'이라는 단어도 또한 오늘날의 고스들이 흡수했지만, '반달'은 너무 구체적인 함의가 있어서 누구도 그 용어를 자신을 묘사할 때 쓰고 싶어 하지 않는다. 고스 반문화는 원래부터 파괴적인 것은 아니어서 쓰레기를 아무 데나 버리거나 창문을 깨는 행위는 없다. 고스 사람이라는 것은 그저 '다른 편'이 되는 확고한 선택일 뿐이다. 그런 의미에서 현대 고스 문화는 고대 고스족의 상징적, 은유적 유산의 확장에 가깝다.

goth n. 고스(1980년대에 유행한 록 음악의 한 형태. 가사가 주로 세상의 종말, 죽음, 악에 대한 내용을 담음); 고스 음악 애호가(검은 옷을 입고, 흰색과 검은색으로 화장을 함) take root 뿌리 내리다 crimped a. 고데한, 인두질로 머리를 꾸불꾸불하게 구부린 sport v. 입다, 착용하다 choker n. 목에 끼는 목걸이 forge v. 만들다 medieval a. 중세의 Germanic a. 게르만 족의 anti-classicism n. 고대 로마와 그리스에 대한 반발 sack v. 약탈하다 vandal n. 반달족, 공공기물 파손자 connotation n. 함축의미 extension n. 확장 legacy n. 유산

36 글의 주제 ①

고대 고스족이 고대 그리스 로마 고전주의의 반대편, 즉 다른 편에 있었던 것과 마찬가지로 오늘날의 고스 문화도 비고전적인 것이라는 꼬리표를 달고 있어서 고대 고스족의 상징적 유산의 확장이라고 설명한다. 따라서 ①이 주제로 적절하다.

이 글의 주제는 무엇인가?
① 고대 고스족으로부터 현대 반문화로의 상징적 연결성
② 대중적인 현대 고스 용어들의 어원 밝히기
③ 로마인과 고스족 사이의 고대 갈등에 대한 새로운 통찰들
④ 고스 하위문화가 물려받은 음악 전통

37 내용일치 ②

현대 고스가 반달이라는 이름을 원하지 않는다는 내용이 나오므로 ②가 옳지 않은 진술이다.

이 글에 의하면, 다음 중 사실이 아닌 것은?
① 고대 고스족의 로마 정복은 고대 영향력의 쇠퇴의 계기였다.
② 현대 고스들은 '반달'을 자기 정체성의 이름으로 채택했다.
③ 현대 고스들은 대개 역사적 고스 연관성으로부터 거리를 둔다.
④ 현대 고스 하위문화는 '다른 편임'을 고유한 선택지로 포용한다.

38-40

뉴욕 주 고령화 사무국은 최근 '로봇 친구'를 주 내의 800명 이상의 노인들에게 배포할 계획을 발표했다. 이 계획의 목적은 노인들에게 대화를 시작하고 게임을 하고 일반적인 지원을 제공할 로봇을 제공함으로써 사회적 고립과 싸우는 것이다. 사회적 고립은 나이가 들어 활동이 줄거나 가족과 친구들로부터 멀리 떨어져 살 때 일부 사람들에게 문제가 될 수 있다. 일부에게 코로나-19 팬데믹은 고립과 고독의 경험을 악화시켰다. 이런 문제를 해결하는 혁신적 접근법의 최전선에 엘리Q가 있는데, 이것은 움직이는 '머리'로 인간을 마주보고 말할 때 불이 켜지는 스마트 대화이다. 인공지능을 탑재한 엘리Q는 독거노인들에게 지원을 제공하려 설계되었다. 엘리Q는 또한 일상적 대화에 사용자들을 참여시키는 주도적 능력도 있다. '감정이입'을 보이는 듯하고, 활동을 제안할 수 있으며 사람들에게 약을 먹거나 약속에 가라고 일깨워줄 수도 있다. 터치스크린이 달려 있어 친구나 가족에게 화상전화도 할 수 있다. 뉴욕 주 고령화 사무국은 엘리Q의 긍정적 영향을 강조하면서 로봇과 사용자들 사이에 매일 약 20건의 교류가 있었다고 알리고 자랑하지만, 로봇 친교를 도입하는 일은 그 윤리적 함의에 대한 논쟁을 촉발시킨다. 일부 사람들은 인간의 애정과 돌봄을 로봇의 '돌봄'으로 대신하는 일에 관해 우려한다. 다른 이들은 로봇 친구가

이들이 의식 있는 존재가 아니라 기계에 불과하다는 사실에 대해 사람들을 기만할 수 있다고 우려한다. 게다가 사교적 로봇의 사용이 개인 정보 수집을 포함하게 되면서 사생활 우려도 등장하며, 기술 진보와 개인 사생활 보호 간의 균형에 대한 문제를 제기하고 있다.

distribute v. 배포하다 companion n. 동료, 친구 battle v. 싸우다 isolation n. 고립 initiate v. 시작하다 support n. 지원 loneliness n. 고독, 외로움 forefront n. 맨 앞, 최전방 empathy n. 공감, 감정이입 appointment n. 만날 약속 interaction n. 교류, 상호작용 deceive v. 속이다 emerge v. 등장하다 safeguard v. 지키다, 보호하다

---

38 어법상 적절하지 않은 표현 고르기   ④

마지막 문장이 privacy concerns가 주어이고 동사는 emerge인데 뒤에 등위접속사가 없으니 분사구문이 되도록 ⓓ raise를 현재분사 raising으로 바꾸어야 한다.

---

39 빈칸완성   ①

로봇 친구 도입이 가져올 부정적 여파를 적어야 한다. 그러나 사생활, 인간과 기계의 문제는 실용적인 문제가 아니라 윤리적 문제이므로 정답은 ①이다. ④는 윤리는 있지만 만장일치라는 단어에 대한 언급이 없다.

빈칸에 들어가기에 가장 적절한 표현은?
① 로봇의 윤리적 함의에 대한 논쟁을 촉발시킨다
② 많은 열의와 긍정적 수용을 촉발시킨다
③ 로봇의 실용성과 필요성에 대한 논쟁을 초래한다
④ 만장일치의 거부와 도덕적 분노를 촉발한다

---

40 내용파악   ④

엘리Q가 화상 통화도 터치스크린으로 가능하다고 했으므로 ④는 옳지 않은 진술이다.

이 글에 의하면, 다음 중 엘리Q에 관해 사실이 아닌 것은?
① 그것은 인간과 말로 대화를 할 수 있다.
② 그것은 사람들이 사회적 고립의 문제에 대처하는 걸 돕도록 설계되었다.
③ 그것은 사용자들이 약속 시간을 기억하도록 도울 수 있다.
④ 그것은 아직 화상 통화를 만들 수 있는 발전 단계까지는 도달하지 못했다.

2024 건국대학교(인문·예체능계 A형)

01 ②	02 ②	03 ③	04 ④	05 ④	06 ①	07 ③	08 ③	09 ①	10 ②
11 ①	12 ⑤	13 ⑤	14 ②	15 ②	16 ④	17 ④	18 ②	19 ①	20 ⑤
21 ④	22 ②	23 ③	24 ⑤	25 ②	26 ②	27 ②	28 ②	29 ③	30 ③
31 ④	32 ⑤	33 ④	34 ③	35 ⑤	36 ④	37 ②	38 ④	39 ①	40 ①

01 동의어 ②

endorsement n. 시인, 승인; 보증(= ratification) make sense of ~을 이해하다 rationality n. 순리성, 합리성 ubiquitous a. 어디에나 있는, 아주 흔한 tacit a. 암묵적인, 무언의 articulate a. (생각 등이) 명확히 표현된, (논리) 정연한 dissociation n. 분리, 분리 작용; 분리 상태 equilibrium n. 평형 상태, 균형 incongruity n. 부조화, 모순, 부적합 alienation n. 소원하게 하기, 멀리하기, 불화

우리 자신의 합리성 기준에 따라 우리의 경험을 이해하는 우리의 타고난 능력이 보증된다면 우리는 또한 감각 인식이 명확한 지식의 암묵적 구성요소에 미치는 편재적 기여를 인정할 수 있을 것이다.

02 동의어 ②

fictitious a. 허구의, 지어낸(= spurious) mathematical a. 수학(상)의, 수리적(數理的)인 complex number 복소수(複素數) hold n. 지배력, 위력, 영향력 veritable a. 진정한 legitimate a. 정당한; 합법적인 detrimental a. 해로운 tangible a. 분명히 실재하는, 유형(有形)의

복소수와 같은 허구적인 수학적 실체와 셜록 홈스(Sherlock Holmes)와 같은 기이한 등장인물 사이의 주요 차이점은 후자가 우리의 상상력에 더 큰 영향력을 갖는다는 데 있다.

03 동의어 ③

repugnant a. (대단히) 불쾌한[혐오스러운](= repulsive) rampant a. 걷잡을 수 없는, 만연[횡행]하는 rude a. 무례한, 저속한 raw a. 익히지 않은, 날것의; 가공되지 않은 regressive a. 퇴행[퇴보]하는

클래식 음악을 전공한 루시(Lucy)의 룸메이트는 루시의 힙합 사랑을 완전히 불쾌하게 여겼다.

04 동의어 ④

archaeological a. 고고학의 a fortiori ad. 한층 더한 이유로, 더욱더 equivocality n. 다의성, 모호, 의심스러움(= ambiguity) stability n. 안정, 안정성[감] fragility n. 부서지기 쉬움, 무름; 허약 specificity n. 특별함, 특수함

고고학적인 '기록'은 전혀 기록이 아니며, 주어진 '자료'가 아니라 만들어진 '자료'이다. '과거'는 모두 지나간 것이고 잃어버린 것이며, 더욱이 사물의 모호성과 사회의 특성을 통해, 여하튼 결정적인 실체인 '현재'로서 존재하지 않았다.

05 동의어 ④

congenial a. 마음이 맞는, 기분 좋은, 즐거운; 친절한(= easygoing) shy a. 수줍은 mean a. 인색한; 심술궂은 eccentric a. 괴짜인, 별난, 기이한 cold-hearted a. 냉담한, 인정 없는

그 도시의 사람들은 마음씨 좋으며, 하루나 이틀 이상 머무르는 방문객은 누구나 곧 그 기운을 받게 된다.

06 동의어 ①

spoil v. (아이를) 응석받이로[버릇없게] 키우다 indulgent a. (자기) 하고 싶은 대로 다 하게 놔두는; 너그러운, 관대한(= lenient) pout v. (못마땅해서) 입을 삐쭉 내밀다; 토라지다 grumpy a. 성미 까다로운, 심술난 ingenuous a. 순진한, 천진한 discreet a. 신중한, 조심스러운 unfathomable a. 불가해한 precarious a. 불안정한, 위태로운

그 아이는 관대한 부모 때문에 너무 버릇없이 자라서 부모의 전적인 관심을 전혀 받지 못하면 토라지고 심술궂게 군다.

07 논리완성 ③

세 개의 핵심 부분이 포함된 incongruous에서 in은 '부정, 반대'의 뜻을 의미하는 접두어이고, con-은 '함께'라는 의미이며, gru-는 '이동하거나 움직이는' 것을 의미한다고 했다. 이를 종합해 보면 '함께 움직이지 않는다'는 의미이다. 따라서 Incongruous behavior란 누군가의 일반적인 행동과 '일치하지 않는다'는 의미이므로, 빈칸에는 ③이 적절하다.

incongruous a. 조화하지 않는; 어울리지 않는 key a. 가장 중요한, 핵심적인, 필수적인 support v. 지지[옹호, 재청]하다 disagree with 일치하지 않다, ~에게 안 맞다 be related with ~와 관계가 있다

'incongruous(어울리지 않는)'라는 단어에는 세 개의 핵심 부분이 포함되어 있다. 여기서 In-은 '아니오'를 의미하고, con-은 '함께'를 의미하며, gru-는 '이동하거나 움직이는' 것을 의미한다. 따라서 '부조리한' 행동은 누군가의 평소 행동과 일치하지 않는 행동이다.

08 논리완성 ③

빅토리아 시대 작가의 어떤 점이 그를 싫증이 나게 했는지에 대한 내용이 빈칸에 적절한데, 주절에서 그가 젊은 작가의 간결한 산문에 매료되었다고 했다. 따라서 빈칸에는 terse와 반대되는 의미의 ③ verbose가 와야 문맥상 적절하다.

attract v. (주의·흥미 따위)를 끌다, 유인하다 terse a. (문체·표현이) 간결한, 간명한 tranquil a. 간결한, 간단한 obtuse a. 둔한, 둔감한 verbose a. 장황한 partial a. 부분적인 inconsistent a. 내용이 다른, 부합하지 않는

전형적인 빅토리아 시대 소설가의 장황한 산문에 싫증이 난 그는 젊은 미국 작가의 간결한 산문에 매료되었다.

09 논리완성 ①

온라인 커뮤니티의 영향력은 스마트폰에 의해 디지털 연결이 '어디에서나 가능해짐'에 따라 증가하게 된 것이므로, 빈칸에는 ① ubiquity가 적절하다.

existentially ad. 실존(주의)적으로 afford v. ~할 수 있다, ~할 여유가 있다 ubiquity n. (동시에) 도처에 있음, 편재(遍在) concentration n. 정신 집중, 전념 convenience n. 편의, 편리 authenticity n. 확실성, 신뢰성 unification n. 통일, 단일화

현실 세계에서 실존적으로 자신을 노숙자라고 생각하는 많은 사람들은 온라인 커뮤니티, 특히 사회 관계망에서의 경험을 찾아왔다. 온라인 커뮤니티의 영향력은 스마트폰에 의해 디지털 연결이 어디에서나 가능해짐에 따라 급격히 증가했다.

10 논리완성 ②

누군가가 종교나 정당에 대한 더 오래되고 전통적인 생각을 가지고 있다는 것은 그들의 신앙이나 신념에 있어 '정통파'라는 것을 의미하므로, 빈칸에는 ② orthodox가 적절하다.

degraded a. 타락[퇴화]한, 모욕을 당한 orthodox a. 정통의, 전통적인 shabby a. 다 낡은[해진], 허름한 cynical a. 냉소적인; 부정적인 radical a. 근본적인, 철저한

만약 당신이 누군가를 정통파라고 설명한다면, 당신은 그들이 종교나 정당에 대한 더 오래되고 더 전통적인 생각을 가지고 있다는 것을 의미한다.

11 논리완성 ①

빈칸에 들어갈 적절한 구동사를 고르는 문제이다. 더 이상 할 일이 없어 고용주로부터 직장에서 해고당하는 상황과 관련된 용어는 lay off이므로, 정답은 ①이다.

lay somebody off (일감이 부족하여) ~를 해고[정리 해고]하다 put up with 참다, 참고 견디다 call upon (연설 등을) ~에게 청하다; 요구하다 fall apart (물건이) 산산이 부서지다; (조직·체제·관계 등이) 무너지다

pull down 허물다; 좌절시키다

만약 근로자가 해고되면, 그들은 대개 더 이상 할 일이 없기 때문에 그들의 고용주로부터 직장을 그만두라는 지시를 받는다.

12 논리완성 ⑤

비현실적인 꿈을 바탕으로 미래를 설계하는 것을 꺼리는 사람은 실생활의 행동과 결과를 중시하는 '실용주의자'라고 볼 수 있다.

disinclined a. 내키지 않는, 꺼리는 impractical a. 터무니없는, 비현실적인 shifting a. 이동하는; 변하는; (바람·방향 따위) 변하기 쉬운 optimist n. 낙천주의자, 낙관론자 skeptic n. 회의론자, 의심 많은 사람 idealist n. 이상가, 이상주의자 pessimist n. 비관주의자 pragmatist n. 실용[실익]주의자, 실무가

그녀는 움직이는 모래 위에 성을 쌓는 것처럼 비현실적인 꿈을 바탕으로 미래를 설계하는 것을 꺼리는 실용주의자이다.

13 논리완성 ⑤

두 번째 문장은 첫 번째 문장을 부연 설명하고 있는데, 첫 번째 문장에서 두 사람이 서로의 언어를 사용하지 않더라도, 함께 음악을 감상할 수 있다고 했다. 이는 음악의 '보편성'에 대한 특징이므로, 빈칸에는 ⑤가 적절하다.

physiological a. 생리학(상)의; 생리적인 clandestine a. 비밀리에 하는, 은밀한 hedonistic a. 쾌락주의(자)의 taciturn a. 말 없는, 말이 적은, 과묵한 authentic a. 진본[진품]인, 진짜인 universal a. 일반적인; 보편적인

우리는 종종 "음악이 보편적인 언어다."라는 표현을 듣는다. 이것은 비록 두 사람이 서로의 언어를 사용하지 않더라도, 적어도 음악을 함께 감상할 수는 있다는 것을 의미한다. 그러나 많은 유명한 격언들이 그러하듯이, 이것은 단지 부분적으로만 사실이다. 비록 모든 사람들이 청각에 대한 동일한 생리적 기제를 가지고는 있지만, 한 개인이 실제로 듣는 것은 그 사람의 문화에 의해 영향을 받는다.

14 논리완성 ②

첫 문장의 예를 세미콜론 이하에서 설명하고 있는데, 일부 쓰레기봉투는 햇빛에 노출되면 분해된다고 했으므로, 일부 제조업체들이 생산하고 있는 형태의 플라스틱은 '생분해되는' 특성을 가지고 있다고 볼 수 있다. 따라서 ② biodegradable이 정답이다.

decompose v. 분해[부패]되다 inexpensive a. 값싼, 비싸지 않은 biodegradable a. 생분해[자연분해]성의(박테리아에 의해 무해 물질로 분해되어 환경에 해가 되지 않는) endurable a. 참을 수 있는, 견딜 수 있는 transparent a. 투명한; 속이 뻔히 들여다보이는, 명백한 multi-functional a. 다기능의

기술의 획기적인 발전으로 일부 제조업체에서는 현재 생분해되는 형태의 플라스틱을 생산하고 있다. 예를 들어, 일부 플라스틱 쓰레기봉투는 햇빛에 노출되면 점차 분해된다.

15 논리완성 ②

첫 번째 문장은 새로운 치료법을 옹호하는 의학 연구원의 입장이고, 두 번째 문장은 비판자들이 이 치료법을 비난한 이유가 무엇이었는지에 대한 질문이다. 세 번째 문장은 두 번째 문장에 대한 답변으로 비판자들이 새로운 치료법을 비난하는 주장이다. 따라서 빈칸에는 ② accusation (비난)이 적절하다.

defend v. 방어하다; 옹호하다 allege v. (증거 없이) 혐의를 제기하다, 주장하다 suggestion n. 제안 accusation n. 혐의 (제기), 비난; 고발 provision n. 공급, 지급, 제공 conclusion n. 결론, (최종적인) 판단 justification n. 타당한[정당한] 이유

의학 연구원들은 새로운 치료법이 널리 받아들여지는 표준 관행을 따른다고 말함으로써 그들의 새로운 치료법을 옹호한다. 따라서 그 치료에 대한 비판자들의 비난은 무엇이었음에 틀림 없는가? 그들은 그것이 기준에 맞지 않으며 허용할 수 있는 의료 관행을 위반했다고 주장했음에 틀림 없다.

16 논리완성 ④

시험 출제자가 두 개의 정답을 골라야 하는 문제를 출제할 때 익숙한 단어를 익숙하지 않은 방식으로 사용한다는 것은 응시자에게 혼란을 주어 정답을 선택하는 것을 더 어렵게 만드는 것을 목표로 한다고 볼 수 있다. 따라서 mislead가 적절하다. 세 번째 문장은 이런 문제의 함정에 대한 해결책이라고 볼 수 있다.

relieve v. 없애[덜어] 주다; 완화하다 persuade v. 설득하다, 납득시키다 invalidate v. 틀렸음을 입증하다 mislead v. 오해하게 하다, 현혹시키다 enlighten v. 이해시키다

종종 시험 출제자는 익숙한 단어를 익숙하지 않은 방식으로 사용하여 응시자를 현혹시키려 한다. 문장 전체의 의미에 완벽하게 맞는 하나의 답을 찾았지만, 정확하게 맞는 것처럼 보이는 또 하나의 답을 찾을 수 없다고 가정해 보자. 문장을 다시 읽고, 빈칸에 그 완벽한 답을 대입한 다음, 다른 선택지들을 새로운 시각으로 살펴보라.

17-18

교사 중심의 고급 예술을 강조하는 것에서 더욱 평등주의적이며 학생 중심적인 방향으로의 변화는 음악과 교육의 가치에 대한 여러 문제를 부각시킨다. 과거에는, 음악의 가치가 일반적으로 널리 보급되어 있는 음악 학교라는 제도에 뿌리를 두었고, 음악 교육 과정은 전통적인 방식으로 교육을 받은 음악 교사에 의해 이루어졌다. 21세기 초반의 교육 상황에서는, 교육에서 음악의 가치가 정치적 민주주의, 문화 정책, 대중 매체, 예술 옹호, 사회 정의 운동, 학교 공동체, 그리고 특히 교사와 학생의 개인적인 음악적 선호도 등과 같은 다양한 요인들에 의해 점점 더 영향을 받는다. 이러한 다양한 요인들의 존재는 획일적 가치 체계의 붕괴, 문화적 패권의 종말과 음악이라는 것의 다양한 방식을 인정하는 세계관의 등장을 보여 준다. 개인적 음악 문화의 이점과 가치는 자유를 향한 추구이든, 통과 의례에 대한 축하이든, 사회적 불평등에 대한 저항이든, 신의 중재에 대한 감사이든, 이야기를 통한 문화유산의 전달이든, 음악이 사람들의 일상생활 속에서 역할을 하는 다양한 측면에서 인정된다.

egalitarian a. 평등주의의 orientation n. (목표하는) 방향, 지향; 경향 conservatory n. 음악[미술, 예술] 학교 implement v. 시행[이행]하다 monolithic a. 단일체의; 획일적이고 자유가 없는 hegemony n. 주도권, 지배권, 패권 diverse a. 다양한 quest n. 탐색, 탐구, 찾음, 추구 rite n. 의식, 의례 passage n. 통과 rebellion n. 반란, 모반 gratitude n. 고마움, 감사 divine a. 신[하느님]의, 신성한 intervention n. 사이에 듦, 개재; 조정 transmission n. 전파, 전달

17 글의 주제 ④

이 글에서는 '교육에서의 음악 가치가 과거에는 음악 학교라는 제도에 뿌리를 두었는데, 21세기에 와서는 다양한 요인들의 영향을 받는다'고 그 변화를 설명하고 있으므로, ④가 글의 주제로 적절하다.

윗글의 주제로 가장 적절한 것은?
① 사회정의를 위한 음악 교육
② 클래식 음악 교사를 양성하는 방법
③ 교육에서 민주주의의 중요성
④ 교육에서 음악 가치의 변화
⑤ 학교에서 음악 교육의 실패

18 빈칸완성 ②

음악은 자유를 표현하고, 전통을 기념하고, 불의에 항의하고, 신에게 감사를 표하고, 문화유산을 전달하는 등 사회 내에서 다양한 기능을 수행한다. 따라서 사람들의 일상생활에서 음악이 수행하는 역할의 포괄적이고 다각적인 특성을 포착하는 표현이 빈칸에 적절하므로 ②가 정답이다.

빈칸에 들어갈 말로 가장 적절한 것은?
① 정의의 가치를 가르치기 위한
② 사람들의 일상생활에서
③ 학생 중심의 교육을 위한
④ 전체 학교 교육과정에서
⑤ 학생들의 자유를 향상하기 위해

19-20

13~15세기의 영국의 고딕 양식은 끝이 뾰족한 아치와 점점 더 화려한 둥근 지붕 디자인이 특징이다. 초기 영국의 건축양식 시기(13세기)에는 창문이 높고 좁았으며, 이후 장식기에는 창문의 윗부분에 트레이서리(레이스 모양의 무늬 장식)가 있었다. 수직 양식의 시기(15세기)에는 창문의 크기가 많이 커졌고, 성인들의 그림이 들어간 스테인드글라스로 채워졌다. 정교한 부채꼴 모양의 둥근 천장(한 지점에서 펼쳐져 있는 곡선형을 이룬 돌 조각)은 벽에서 일정 각도로 비스듬히 기울어져 아치를 형성하는 플라잉 버트레스에 의해 지지된다. 솔즈베리 대성당은 전형적인 초기 영국 건축물이다. 엑서터 성당은 주로 장식기부터 시작된 것이고 부채꼴 둥근 천장이 있는 글로스터 대성당은 수직 시대의 건축물을 대표한다.

pointed a. (끝이) 뾰족한[날카로운] ornate a. (특히 아주 작거나 복잡한 디자인으로) 화려하게 장식된 vault n. 아치형 지붕[천장], 둥근 천장 Early English 초기 영국의 건축 양식(12~13세기의 초기 고딕 양식) decorated a. <건축> (종종 D-) 장식식(式)의 tracery n. 트레이서리(교

회 창문 윗부분의 돌에 새긴 장식 무늬) perpendicular a. 수직 양식의 (14~15세기 잉글랜드에서 많이 쓰인 건축 양식) flying buttress 플라잉 버트레스(대형 건물 외벽을 떠받치는 반 아치형 벽돌 또는 석조 구조물)

19 글의 제목 ①

이 글은 13~15세기 영국에서 유행한 고딕 건축양식의 각 시기별 하위 유형의 특징에 대해 주로 논하고 있으므로, ①이 제목으로 적절하다.

윗글의 제목으로 가장 적절한 것은?
① 영국 고딕 양식의 하위 유형
② 영국 성당의 전형적인 구조
③ 영국에서 스테인드글라스의 기원
④ 아치와 둥근 천장: 두 기본 요소
⑤ 영국 건축사

20 내용일치 ⑤

솔즈베리 대성당은 전형적인 초기 영국 고딕 양식의 건물이라고 했으므로 13세기의 건물이라고 볼 수 있으며, 글로스터 대성당은 15세기 수직 양식 시기의 대표 건축물이라고 했다. 따라서 두 성당의 건축 양식에는 약 2세기의 시차가 있다고 볼 수 있으므로, ⑤가 정답이다.

윗 글의 내용과 일치하는 것은?
① Early English 시기 특징은 창문 위쪽의 레이스 모양 장식이다.
② Decorated 시기의 창문들은 길고 넓은 모양을 띠고 있다.
③ Perpendicular 시기에 창문들이 작아지고 스테인드글라스로 장식되었다.
④ 15세기로 갈수록 둥근 천장(vault) 디자인의 장식적 요소가 줄어들고 단순해졌다.
⑤ Gloucester Cathedral과 Salisbury Cathedral의 건축은 약 2세기의 시차가 있다.

21 의문부사 ④

ⓓ의 what은 의문 대명사나 의문 형용사로 쓰이므로 부사인 effectively를 수식할 수 없다. 따라서 what을 부사를 수식할 수 있는 의문부사 how(얼마나)로 고쳐야 한다. 그 경우에 '의문사+부사+주어+동사'의 간접 의문절 구문이 된다.

aesthetic a. 심미적, 미학적 foster v. 조성하다, 발전시키다 tolerant a. 관대한, 아량 있는 evoke v. (감정·기억·이미지를) 떠올려 주다[환기시키다] implication n. 영향; 함축, 암시 catalyze v. 촉진시키다

미학적 디자인은 미가 결핍된 디자인보다 긍정적인 태도를 기르는 데 더 효과적이며, 사람들을 디자인 문제에 대해 더 관대하게 만든다. 예를 들어, 사람들이 긍정적인 태도를 조성해온 디자인에 이름을 붙이고 그것에 대한 감정을 키우는 것은 흔한 일이지만(예: 차에 이름을 붙여주기), 사람들이 부정적인 태도를 조성해온 디자인에 대해 이와 같은 행동을 하는 경우는 드물다. 디자인과의 이러한 개인적이고 긍정적인 관계는 애정, 충성심, 인내심을 불러일으킨다. 이들 모두는 디자인의 장기적인 유용성과 전반적인 성공에 있어 중요한 요소이다. 이러한 긍정적인 관계는 사람들이 디자인과 얼마나 효과적으로 상호 작용하는지에 영향을 끼친다. 디자인에 대한 긍정

적인 관계는 창의적인 사고와 문제 해결을 촉진하는 데 도움이 되는 상호 작용을 초래한다.

22 to부정사의 병치 ②

두 번째 문장의 동사 performs는 to transport와 병치를 이루어야 하므로, ②는 원형동사 perform이 되어야 한다.

timber n. 목재, 재목 challenging a. 도전적인; 자극적인 withstand v. 견디어 내다 encounter v. 맞닥뜨리다, 접하다 stiffness n. 단단함; 딱딱함 knot n. 매듭; 옹이 grain n. (목재·천·암석 등의) 결 deviation n. 편차 intrinsic a. 고유한, 본질적인 harvest v. 수확하다, 거둬들이다

목재는 까다로운 재료인데, 건축가와 기술자가 그들이 그 목재로 무엇을 하려고 하는지 뿐 아니라 자연이 목재를 어떻게 디자인했는지도 이해해야 하기 때문이다. 나무 자체는 수백만 년에 걸쳐 진화해 오면서 자연에서 맞닥뜨리는 힘을 견뎌 내면서도 동시에 물과 영양분을 운반하고 나무의 생존에 필요한 기능을 수행할 수 있었다. 기술자들은 나무의 내구력과 단단함을 예측하는 데 관심을 가지는데, 이 예측에는 옹이, 결의 구조, 수분 함량, 종, 등급의 편차 등을 고려하는 것이 포함된다. 그러한 편차는 흔히 결점이라고 불린다. 이러한 "결점"은 나무의 목적에 이바지하며 나무의 구조에 내재되어 있다. 나무가 숲에서 수확됨에 따라, 인류는 나무를 재구성하거나 재설계하여 새로운 목적을 달성하려고 한다.

23 감정 및 심리 유발 동사의 분사의 태 ③

감정동사는 사물을 수식 또는 서술하면 현재분사, 사람을 수식 또는 서술하면 과거분사를 사용한다. 크레올 언어를 구사하는 사람들이 '확신시키다(convince)'의 대상이므로, ⓒ는 과거분사 convinced가 되어야 한다.

creole n. 크리올어(유럽의 언어와 특히 서인도 제도 노예들이 사용하던 아프리카어의 혼성어로서 모국어로 사용되는 언어) duly ad. 적절한 절차에 따라, 예상대로

교육을 받을 수 있던 크리올 언어를 구사하는 사람들은 그들의 언어가 잘못되었다는 것을 예상대로 확신했고, 그들은 종종 그 언어를 사람들이 인정할 수 있는 표준에 더 가깝게 만들려고 노력했다.

24 be devoted to ~ing ⑤

be devoted to는 '~에 헌신하다'는 의미로, to는 to부정사의 to가 아니라 전치사 to이다. 전치사의 목적어로 동사가 오는 경우 그 형태는 동명사여야 한다. 따라서 ⓔ는 동명사 sketching이 되어야 한다.

pragmatics n. 화용론(話用論)(언어·기호 따위를 사용자 입장에서 연구하는 것) semantics n. 의미론 sketch v. 개요를 제시하다

그렇다면 화용론(話用論)에 대한 그 어떤 논의도 의미론에 대한 기본적인 이해와 두 분야를 구별하기 위해 제안된 이론적 기반 없이는 진행될 수 없으므로, 이 장의 나머지 부분은 의미론과 화용론 영역을 기술하는 데 할애될 것이다.

25 논리완성 ②

빈칸 다음 문장에서 '두 체계는 매우 다양한 감각 정보를 처리하고 우리에게 놀라울 정도로 안정된 지각을 제공한다'고 했는데, 그 다음 예의 경우, 다가오는 사람의 크기가 커지는 망막상의 감각 정보를 처리하면서도 실제 그 사람의 크기는 불변인 것으로 지각하여 안정된 지각을 제공한다는 것이다. 따라서 빈칸에는 '안정성, 불변성'을 의미하는 ② constancy가 적절하다.

auditory a. 청각의 visual a. 시각의 perception n. 지각 (작용), 지각력; 인식(력) perceptual constancy 지각항등성 remarkably ad. 두드러지게, 현저하게 retinal a. (눈의) 망막의 interpret v. (의미를) 설명[해석]하다 dependency n. 의존, 종속 constancy n. 불변성, 항구성 abstruseness n. 난해함, 심오함 dissonance n. 불협화음, (의견) 충돌 parsimony n. (돈에 지독히) 인색함

청각적 지각과 시각적 지각 사이에는 몇 가지 유사점이 있다. 한 가지는 지각 불변성의 문제이다. 두 체계는 매우 다양한 감각 정보를 처리하고 우리에게 놀라울 정도로 안정된 지각을 제공한다. 예를 들면, 어떤 사람이 당신을 향해 걸어오는 것이 당신 눈에 보일 때, 망막상의 이미지는 단순히 그렇게(몸집이 커지고 있다고) 해석될 수 있음에도 불구하고, 당신은 그 사람의 몸집이 커지고 있지 않다고 정확하게 결론을 내릴 수 있다.

26 논리완성 ②

대시 이하에서 'not A so much as B(A라기 보다는 오히려 B이다)'의 구문이 사용되었으며, A가 wild talent이므로 B에는 wild(=uncontrolled) talent(재능이 마구 방종하게 발휘되는 것)와 반대되어야 한다. 따라서 창의성은 효과 없는 아이디어를 시도한 끝에 효과 있는 아이디어를 발견하는 데 있어, 마지막 문장에서 언급했듯이, 더 빨리 실패를 끝내고 더 빨리 성공하려는 생산성(효율성)의 문제라고 할 수 있으므로 빈칸에는 ② productivity가 적절하다.

unspoken a. 입 밖에 내지 않은, 무언의, 언외의 numbers game 숫자놀음 necessarily ad. 어쩔 수 없이, 필연적으로 go for ~에 해당되다 generate v. 발생시키다, 만들어 내다 outset n. 착수, 시초, 최초, 발단 disparity n. 차이, 격차 propensity n. 경향, 성향 equanimity n. 침착, 평정 serendipity n. 우연히 발견하는 능력, 행운

창의성에 관해 말해지지 않은 한 가지 사실은 그것이 방종한 재능에 관한 것이라기보다는 오히려 생산성에 관한 것이라는 점이다. 효과 있는 몇 가지 아이디어를 발견하기 위해서 당신은 효과 없는 많은 아이디어를 시도해야 한다. 그것은 순전히 숫자놀음이다. 천재들이 반드시 다른 창조자들보다 성공률이 더 높은 것이 아니라, 그저 더 많은 것을 하는데, 다양한 일들을 한다. 그들은 더 많은 성공을 하고 더 많은 실패를 한다. 그것은 팀과 회사에도 해당된다. 형편없는 아이디어를 많이 만들어 내지 않고는 좋은 아이디어를 많이 만들어낼 수 없다. 창의성에 대해 중요한 것은, 어느 아이디어가 성공하고 어느 아이디어가 실패할 것인지를 처음에는 알 수 없다는 것이다. 그래서 당신이 할 수 있는 유일한 것은 다음 아이디어로 넘어갈 수 있도록 더 빨리 실패하려고 하는 것이다.

27 논리완성 ③

두 집단의 구성원들은 자신들의 신념과 일치하는 정보는 받아들이고 상충하는 정보는 무시했다고 했으므로, 반론을 뒷받침하는 확실한 정보에도 불구하고 자신이 가지고 있는 견해의 타당성을 더 확신했다고 볼 수 있다. 따라서 빈칸에는 ③ validity가 적절하다.

psychological a. 심리학의[을 사용한] conduct v. 수행하다, 처리하다 effectiveness n. 유효(성), 효과적임 deterrent n. 단념하게 하는 것, 억지[제지]물 expose v. 드러내다; 노출시키다; 접하게[경험하게] 하다 solid a. 단단한; 확실한; 믿음직한 counter-argument n. 반론, 반박 automatically ad. 자동적으로; 무의식적으로 dismiss v. 묵살[일축]하다 validity n. 유효함, 타당성 aspect n. 측면, 양상 deficiency n. 결핍; 결점

확증-증거 편향을 다룬 한 심리학 연구에서, 두 집단은 범죄 억제책으로서의 사형제도의 효과에 대해 신중하게 실시된 연구에 대한 두 편의 보고서를 읽었다. 한 보고서는 사형제도가 효과적이라고 결론 내렸고, 다른 보고서는 그렇지 않다고 결론 내렸다. 반론을 뒷받침하는 확실한 과학적 정보를 접했음에도, 두 집단의 구성원들은 두 보고서를 모두 읽은 후 자신들이 가진 견해의 타당성을 훨씬 더 확신하게 되었다. 자동적으로 그들은 지지하는 정보는 받아들였고 상충하는 정보는 무시했다.

28 논리완성 ②

인공 지능 기계를 올바르게 만든다면, 그 기계는 조정자와 중재자가 될 수 있다고 했다. 조정자와 중재가 되기 위해서는 판단이 편파적이지 않고 공정해야 하고, 정치적으로 중립이라는 것도 공정성을 의미하므로, 빈칸에는 ② impartial이 적절하다.

overcome v. 극복하다 obstacle n. 장애 mediator n. 중재인, 조정관 arbiter n. 중재인, 조정자 communal a. 공동의, 공용의 rely upon ~에게 의존하다 neutral a. 중립적인 coalition n. 연합체, 연합 author v. (서적 따위를) 쓰다, 저술하다 commit v. 저지르다; (엄숙히) 약속하다 assist v. 돕다, 도움이 되다 mount v. 시작하다 impartial a. 공정한 communicative a. 말을 잘 하는, 의사 전달의 innovative a. 획기적인

지능형 기술은 우리가 많은 문화적, 사회적 장애를 극복하는 데 도움이 될 수 있다. 인공 지능 기계를 올바르게 만든다면, 그 기계는 조정자와 중재자가 되어, 우리가 공정을 기하기 위해 믿을 수 있는 공동 지침을 제공할 수 있다. 일단의 정치적으로 중립적인 프로그래머들이 '진실 기계'를 만들기 위해 연합을 결성했다. 가장 크고 영향력 있는 기술 기업 중 30개 회사는 디지털 제네바 협정을 입안하여, '어디에서든지 무고한 민간인 혹은 기업'에 대한 사이버 공격을 시작하는 정부는 돕지 않기로 하는 일련의 원칙에 동의했다.

29 논리완성 ③

규칙을 위반하면, 그 기관은 면허를 취소할 권리를 가질 수 있다고 했으므로, or 앞도 이와 비슷한 의미의 동사가 적절하다. 따라서 면허받은 사람에게 '제재를 가한다'라는 의미의 ③ sanction이 적절하다.

grant v. 승인[허락]하다 permission n. 허락, 허가, 승인 practice v. (의사·변호사 등이) 개업하다, 영업하다 licensee n. (무엇의 생산·사용) 인가를 받은 사람[기업] recall v. 취소하다, 철회하다 privilege n. 특전, 특권 prescribed a. 규정된, 미리 정해진 probate v. (유언장을) 공증하다 incarcerate v. 감금[투옥]하다 sanction v. 처벌하다, 제재를 가하다 infuriate v. 극도로 화나게 만들다 procrastinate v. 미루다, 질질 끌다

면허 발부는 개인에게 개업을 할 수 있는 공식적 혹은 법적인 허가를 해주는 것이다. 면허는 국가나 심지어 지방의 기관에서 발부된다. 면허를 관리하는 당국은 면허를 받은 사람에게 그 면허를 유지하기 위해 지켜야 할 일련의 규칙을 제공한다. 그 규칙을 위반하면, 그 기관은 면허를 받은 사람에게 제재를 가하거나 면허를 취소할 권리를 가질 수 있다. 분명히 면허는 특혜이지, 권리가 아니며, 면허를 받은 사람이 그 특혜를 유지하기 위해서는 규정된 법규를 따라야 한다.

30 논리완성   ③

인공지능과 달리 사람들은 생각할 때 논리를 사용하지 않는다고 했으므로, 인공지능식 사고는 사람들을 위한 모델로서 타당해 보이지 않는다고 볼 수 있다. 따라서 ③ implausible이 적절하다.

theorem n. (특히 수학에서의) 정리(定理) purport v. 주장하다[칭하다] irreversible a. (이전 상태로) 되돌릴[철회할] 수 없는, 취소[번경]할 수 없는 inconsiderate a. 사려 깊지 못한 implausible a. 믿기 어려운, 타당해 보이지 않는 imperative a. 반드시 해야 하는, 긴요한, 필수적인 irreducible a. 더 이상 줄일[단순화할] 수 없는

인공지능의 많은 작업은 정보와 지식이 1차 논리로 표현되어야 한다는 가정과 추론은 정리 증명이라는 가정에서 시작된다. 표면적으로 이것은 사람들을 위한 모델로서는 타당해 보이지 않는 것 같다. 우리가 생각할 때 논리를 사용하는 것 같지는 않은 것이 확실한데, 만약 논리를 사용한다면 왜 그렇게 많은 우리의 생각과 행동이 그토록 비논리적이겠는가? 사실, 사람들이 문제에 대해 생각할 때 논리를 사용하지 않는다는 것을 보여주는 심리학 실험이 있다.

31 문맥상 적절하지 않은 단어 고르기   ④

비과학적인 글에서는 전문적인 수학 용어 대신 이를 대체할 수 있는 일반적인 언어를 사용하라고 했으므로, 수와 관련된 사실이나 패턴을 설명할 다른 방법을 '배제하는' 것이 아니라 '찾아야' 할 것이다. 따라서 ⑩를 find로 고쳐야 한다.

jargon n. (특정 분야의 전문·특수) 용어 notation n. 표시[표기]법, 기호법 subscript n. 아래에 적은 문자[숫자, 기호] superscript n. 어깨글자 reawaken v. (어떤 감정·기억을) 다시 불러일으키다 promote v. 촉진[고취]하다 preclude v. 배제하다; 가로막다 acronym n. 두문자어 equivalent n. (~에) 상당[대응]하는 것, 등가물 rephrase v. (뜻을 더 분명히 하기 위해) 바꾸어 말하다 intuitive a. 직감[직관]에 의한; 이해하기 쉬운

한 용어가 한 번만 사용될 짧은 비과학적인 글을 위해서는 특수 용어를 완전히 피해야 한다. 다시 사용하지 않을 것이라면, 새로운 어휘 또는 표기를 도입하는 것은 거의 도움이 되지 않는다. 그리고 통계학자가 아닌 사람

들에게는 그리스 기호와 아래쪽 숫자와 어깨 숫자로 가득한 방정식이 효과적인 의사소통을 촉진하기보다는 수학에 대한 불안을 환기시킬 가능성이 높다. 과학 논문의 서론과 결론 부분에도 똑같은 논리가 적용된다. 새로운 단어를 사용하는 것은 당신이 그것을 정의해야 한다는 것을 의미하는데, 그것은 당신이 말하려는 요점에서 주의를 멀리 돌려놓는다. 만약 당신이 그 용어를 다시 사용하지 않을 작정이라면, 수와 관련된 사실이나 패턴을 설명할 수 있는 다른 방법을 <배제하라>. 복잡하거나 익숙하지 않은 단어, 두문자어, 또는 수학적 기호를 일상에서 사용하는 일반적인 언어로 대체하고, 복잡한 개념을 더 이해하기 쉬운 것으로 바꾸어 쓰라.

32 문맥상 적절하지 않은 단어 고르기   ⑤

창의력은 평온, 고요함과는 달리 긴장되어 있는 상태에서 가장 잘 발휘된다는 글이다. 마지막 문장은 결론이므로 창의적으로 생각하려고 시도할 때는 '평온한(reposed)' 것이 아니라 이와 반대인 'aroused(흥분된, 각성된)' 상태인 게 낫다는 흐름이 되어야 한다.

creativity n. 창조성; 독창력 stillness n. 고요, 정적 convinced a. (전적으로) 확신하는 distraction n. (주의) 집중을 방해하는 것 sip v. (음료를) 홀짝이다[거리다], 조금씩 마시다 languid a. 힘없는, 나른한 unstructured a. 체계가 없는, 조직화되지 않은 orchestrate v. 편성[조직화]하다; 조정하다 punctuate v. 간간이 끼어들다 wired a. 신경이 날카로워진 be onto something 무언가를 알아내다 reposed a. 평온한, 침착한

창의력은 내면의 평화, 고요함, 평온함 등을 통해 가장 잘 발휘된다는 믿음이 널리 퍼져 있다. 내 동료 중 한 명은 집중을 방해하는 것이 전혀 없는 조용한 환경에서 조용히 차를 마실 때, 창의적인 글이 가장 잘 나온다고 확신했다. 그러나 그렇게 나른하게 글을 쓴 지 석 달이 지났지만, 그녀는 스스로 자랑스러워할 만한 것을 전혀 쓰지 못했다. 그 직후 그녀의 첫 아이가 태어났고, 그녀의 일정은 지루하고, 한가하고, 평화롭고, 체계가 없는 나날을 보내는 것에서 분 단위로 빈틈없이 짜여 돌아가는 중에 간간이 매우 격한 활동이 끼어 있는 것으로 바뀌었다. 그 결과는? 그녀는 다작 면에서 생산성이 높아졌다. 그녀의 말로 하자면 그녀는 '신경이 곤두서' 있었다. 그녀가 내게 그것을 표현한 대로 하자면, "샘(Sam)이 낮잠을 자고 있으면 내게는 90분이 주어진 것이어서, 나는 컴퓨터로 달려가 미친 듯이 글을 써. 나는 완전히 집중되어 있어."라고 말했다. 알고 보니 내 동료는 무언가를 알아낸 것이다. 사실 창의적으로 생각하고 시도할 때는 <평온해져 있는> 것이 더 낫다는 것이다.

33-34

모든 공포증은 일반적으로 아이들이 특정한 것들에 대한 부모의 반응을 지켜봄으로써 학습된다. 아이들은 자신들에게 가장 가까이 있는 어른들로부터 삶에서 위험한 것이 무엇인지에 대한 실마리를 얻는다. 만약 당신의 자녀가 당신이 한 사물이나 상황에 불건전하게 집중하고 있는 것을 본다면, 그들은 이와 비슷한 방식으로 그 사물이나 상황에 초점을 맞출 가능성이 더 클 것이다. 한 대표적인 심리학 연구는 어머니들과 그들의 12개월 된 아기들을 참여시켰다. 각각의 어머니는 연구가 이루어지는 동안 아기와 함께 있었지만, 그 어머니들은 A와 B 두 집단으로 나뉘었다. A와 B 두 집단 모두 같은 상황에 노출되었는데, 유일한 차이는 집단 B의 어머니들은 자녀가 그들 앞에 있는 것들을 계속 가지고 놀도록 긍정적으로 격려해야 했지만, 집단 A의 어머니들은 자신들의 아기가 놀고 있는 것에 반응하여 평소대로 행동해야 했다.

이 아기들은 무엇을 가지고 놀고 있었을까? 몸집이 아주 크지만 길들여진 비단뱀이었다. 연구는 다음과 같이 진행되었다. 집단 A에 속한 아이들은 바닥에 놓여서 그들 사이로 비단뱀이 미끄러져 갈 수 있었다. 뱀에 대한 두려움이 인간에게 선천적이지만 대략 두 살까지는 활성화되지 않기 때문에 이 아기들은 비단뱀을 큰 장난감으로 보았다. 집단 A 아기들은 살아있는 비단뱀과 놀기 시작하면서, 자신들의 어머니가 무엇을 하고 있는지를 살피기 위해 올려다보았다. 그 어머니들은 평소대로 행동하도록 말을 들었기 때문에 당연히 겁에 질린 표정이었다. 자신들 어머니의 얼굴에 나타난 무서움을 보았을 때 그 아기들은 갑자기 울음을 터뜨렸다. 집단 B의 차례가 되었을 때, 지시를 받은 대로 그 어머니들은 웃으며 자신들의 아기들을 비단뱀과 계속 놀도록 격려했다. 그 결과 이 아기들은 비단뱀을 붙잡고 깨물고 있었는데, 순전히 그들의 어머니들이 그들의 새 장난감을 지지했기 때문이었다.

phobia n. 공포증 cue n. 신호, 임시, 단서 divide v. 나누다 expose v. 드러내다; 노출시키다 encourage v. 격려[고무]하다, 용기를 북돋우다 be oneself (남의 영향을 받지 않고) 평소의[정상적인] 자기 모습 그대로이다 tame a. 길들여진 python n. 비단뱀 slither v. (매끄럽게) 스르르 나아가다[기어가다] horrified a. 겁에 질린, 충격 받은 burst into tears 와락 울음을 터뜨리다 supportive a. 지원하는, 도와주는, 힘을 주는

---

33 빈칸완성   ④

뱀에 대한 두려움이 두 살까지는 활성화되지 않는다고 했다. 사람들은 뱀을 본질적으로 무서워하고 있지만 두 살까지는 발현되지 않는다는 의미이므로, 인간에게 뱀에 대한 두려움은 선천적이라고 볼 수 있다.

빈칸에 들어갈 말로 가장 적절한 것은?
① 유순한
② 임의적인
③ 수수께끼 같은
④ 선천적인
⑤ 중요하지 않은

---

34 내용일치   ③

연구에 참여한 집단 A의 어머니들은 평소대로 행동하라는 말을 들었기 때문에 자녀들이 뱀과 함께 놀 때 겁에 질린 표정을 보였다고 했다. 따라서 ③이 글의 내용과 일치하지 않는다.

윗글의 내용과 일치하지 않는 것은?
① 아이들의 공포증은 대개 부모의 반응을 통해 학습된다.
② 12개월 된 아기들이 심리학 연구에 참여했다.
③ 집단 A의 어머니들은 아기들이 잘 놀도록 격려했다.
④ 아기들은 길들인 큰 비단뱀을 가지고 놀았다.
⑤ 집단 B의 어머니들은 비단뱀을 보고 웃었다.

35-36

사회영역이론은 감정과 도덕적 판단을 뗄 수 없는 상호적 과정으로 간주한다. 이 견해는 도덕성에 대한 감정주의적 또는 직관론적 접근법들과는 다른데, 그러한 접근법들은 대체로 사후(事後) 합리화로서의 추론을 피하면

서 감정적, 암묵적 과정을 우선시한다. 사회적 영역 관점에서 보면, 이렇게 감정과 추론을 별개의 대립되는 영향력으로 다루는 것은 거짓 이분법에 해당한다. 오히려, 이 이론은 정서적인 경험이 도덕적 판단의 중요한 요소이며 후자는 사고, 감정, 그리고 경험의 복합적인 통합을 수반한다고 가정된다. 칸트의 유명한 말을 빌리자면, 감정이 없는 도덕적 추론은 공허하고, 추론이 없는 감정은 맹목적이다. 아이들의 정서적인 경험은 도덕적 위반에 대한 그들의 이해와 부호화와 기억에 영향을 미치며, 복잡한 평가 과정의 일부분이다.

reciprocal a. 상호간의 disentangle v. ~의 얽힌 것을 풀다; (얽힘·혼란 따위로부터) ~을 해방시키다 give priority to ~에게 우선권을 주다, ~을 우선으로 하다 post hoc a. 먼저 있었던 사건을 이유로 드는, 전후 인과의 dichotomy n. 이분법, 양단법 integration n. 통합 evaluative a. 평가하는, 가치[양]를 어림[감정]하는

---

35 빈칸완성

빈칸 앞의 this theory는 사회영역이론을 가리킨다. 이 이론은 감정과 추론을 별개의 대립되는 영향력으로 보지 않으며, 감정과 도덕적 판단이 상호적 관계에 있는 것으로 보는데, 뒤의 that절에서 the latter(도덕적 판단)를 주어로 하므로 빈칸에는 감정이 주어가 되어 상호적인 관계를 나타내도록 ⑤ affective가 적절하다.

빈칸에 공통으로 들어갈 말로 가장 적절한 것은?
① 강한
② 상호간의
③ 만족스러운
④ 자신감 있는
⑤ 정서적인

---

36 글의 주제

이 글은 ⑤처럼 사회영역이론과 감정주의적 접근법을 대등하게 비교한 것이 아니고, ① 사회영역이론이 중요한 이유를 설명한 것도 아니고, 사회영역이론이 어떤 이론인지를 설명한 글인데, 사회영역이론은 감정과 도덕적 판단을 분리할 수 없는 상호작용 과정으로 간주하는 이론이므로 ④가 주제로 적절하다.

윗글의 주제로 가장 적절한 것은?
① 사회영역이론의 중요성
② 칸트의 도덕적 추론과 감정에 관한 이론
③ 아동 발달에 있어서 도덕적 판단의 역할
④ 감정과 도덕적 판단의 상호성
⑤ 사회영역이론과 감정주의적 접근의 차이

37-38

우리는 천성적으로 친사회적이지는 않은데, 이는 종교 관계자와 비종교 관계자들이 끊임없이 우리에게 의무를 이행하라고 명령한다는 사실에서 확실히 명백하다. 우리는 언제나 아이들에게는 장난감을 (다른 아이들과) 함께 사용할 것을, 그리고 어른들에게는 사회적으로 합의된 행동 규칙을 지킬 것을 상기시킨다. 실제로 사회적 경고와 종교적 경고가 없다면 친사회적 행동은 대개 가까운 가족과 친구로 한정된다. 많은 민족지학적 연구

에 따르면 도움은 대개 친족과 친구에게 대가를 기대하지 않고 아낌없이 주어진다고 한다. <몇백 명 정도로 이루어진 이 마법의 원 밖에 있는 사람들에게는 도움이 호의를 갚거나 보답하겠다는 명시적인 동의가 있을 때만 제공된다는 것을 많은 민족지학 연구가 증명한다.> 초대형 공동체에서 살아야할 필요로 인해, 우리가 함께 사는 사람들과 갖는 상호작용에 관한 — 혹은 적어도 중립성 — 의 요건을 부과해야 할 필요가 있게 되었다. 그것은 범죄와 비행이 우리 공동체를 하나로 묶어주는 취약한 유대관계가 깨지는 것을 방지하는 데 도움이 될 것이다.

prosocial a. 친사회적인, 사회에 이로운 command v. 명령하다, 지시하다 in the absence of ~이 없을 때에, ~이 없어서 ethnographic a. 민족지(誌)의; 민족지학의 impose v. 도입하다; 부과하다 generosity n. 관대한 행위; 후한 행동 neutrality n. 중립 interaction n. 상호작용, 상호의 영향 delinquency n. (특히 청소년의) 비행[범죄] burst v. 폭발하다, 파열하다

---

37 내용일치 ②

친사회적 행동은 대개 가까운 가족과 친구로 한정되며, 도움은 대개 친족과 친구에게는 대가를 기대하지 않고 아낌없이 주어진다고 했다. 따라서 이를 통해 친족과 친구들 사이에는 관용이 자연스럽게 존재한다고 볼 수 있으므로, 관용이 필요하다고 한 ②가 본문의 내용과 일치하지 않는다.

윗글의 내용과 일치하지 않는 것은?
① 인간이 천성적으로 친사회적인 것은 아니다.
② 친족이나 친구들과 잘 지내기 위해서는 관용이 필요하다.
③ 범죄와 비행은 우리 공동체의 취약한 유대감을 파괴할 수 있다.
④ 종교적·비종교적 권위자들은 우리에게 의무를 수행하라고 명령해야 한다.
⑤ 사회적·종교적 경고가 없다면, 인간은 주로 가까운 친족이나 친구에게만 친사회적 행동을 보일 것이다.

---

38 문장삽입 ④

제시된 문장의 this magic circle이 문제를 풀 수 있는 단서이다. 이 마법의 원은 친족과 친구에 해당하므로, "많은 민족지학적 연구에 따르면 도움은 대개 친족과 친구에게 대가를 기대하지 않고 아낌없이 주어진다고 한다."고 한 다음에 제시문이 삽입되어야 한다. 따라서 제시문의 위치로 적절한 곳은 Ⓓ이다.

39-40

많은 종(種)들은 언어를 가지고 있다. 새와 개코원숭이는 자신들의 집단에 있는 다른 개체들에게 포식자의 접근에 대해 경고할 수 있다. 하지만 동물의 언어는 가장 단순한 생각만을 공유할 수 있으며, 이런 생각들 대부분은 다소 무언극 비슷하게 지금 당장 존재하는 것과 연관되어 있다. 몇몇 연구자들은 침팬지에게 말하는 법을 가르치려고 노력해 왔는데, 침팬지는 실제로 100~200개의 단어의 어휘를 습득하고 사용할 수 있으며, 심지어 새로운 어구 패턴을 만들 수도 있다. 하지만 침팬지의 어휘는 규모가 작고, 구문이나 문법, 즉 우리로 하여금 적은 수의 음성 언어적 기호들(tokens)로부터 매우 다양한 의미를 만들어 낼 수 있게 해 주는 규칙을 사용하지 않는다. 이들의 언어 능력은 두세 살짜리 인간의 언어 능력을 결코 능가하

지 못하는 것 같은데, 그것으로는 오늘날의 세상을 만들기에 충분하지 않다. 그리고 여기가 나비가 날개를 퍼덕인 곳이다. 인간의 언어는 완전히 새로운 형태의 의사소통을 가능하게 하는 미묘한 언어적 임계점(한계)을 넘었다. 무엇보다도, 인간의 언어는 추상적인 실체에 대한 정보나 지금 당장 존재하지 않고, 심지어 우리의 상상력 밖에도 존재하지 않을 수도 있는 사물이나 가능성에 대한 정보를 우리로 하여금 공유하게 한다.

baboon n. 개코원숭이 predator n. 포식자, 포식 동물 immediately ad. 즉시, 즉각 mime n. 무언극 syntax n. 구문론, 통사론 verbal a. 언어[말]의 subtle a. 미묘한, 감지하기 힘든 threshold n. 한계, 임계점 abstract a. 추상적인

---

39 빈칸완성 ③

인간의 언어는 완전히 새로운 형태의 의사소통을 가능하게 하는 미묘한 언어적 한계점을 넘었다고 했고, 빈칸 다음의 문장은 인간의 언어가 동물의 언어와는 차원이 다른 새로운 의사 소통(추상적인 존재 또는 사물이나 가능성에 대한 정보 공유)을 가능하게 한다는 것을 강조하고 있다. 이어지는 문장이 이전 문장의 의미를 더 강조하고 있으므로, ③ Above all이 빈칸에 적절하다.

빈칸에 들어갈 말로 가장 적절한 것은?
① 불행히도
② 희망적으로
③ 무엇보다도
④ 그럼에도 불구하고
⑤ 그런데

---

40 내용일치 ①

몇몇 연구자들은 침팬지에게 말하는 법을 가르치려고 노력해 왔는데, 침팬지는 실제로 100~200개의 단어를 습득하고 사용할 수 있으며, 이 단어를 조합하여 어구를 만들 수도 있다고 했으므로 ①이 글의 내용과 일치한다.

윗글의 내용과 일치하는 것은?
① 침팬지는 단어들을 연결하여 새로운 어구 패턴을 만들 수 있다.
② 침팬지의 언어능력은 두세 살짜리 어린아이보다 우월하다.
③ 침팬지의 언어는 어휘가 수천 개에 이를 정도로 매우 풍부하다.
④ 새들은 포식자가 접근해도 동료 집단에게 경고할 수 없다.
⑤ 침팬지는 인간처럼 통사 혹은 문법구조를 이용한다.

01 ①	02 ①	03 ③	04 ④	05 ②	06 ②	07 ④	08 ⑤	09 ⑤	10 ①
11 ②	12 ①	13 ④	14 ③	15 ①	16 ④	17 ⑤	18 ⑤	19 ③	20 ⑤

01 동의어   ①

calamity n. 재난(= disaster); 참화, 재해 furnace n. 가마, 화덕; 용광로; 난로 explode v. 폭발하다 leak v. 새다, 새어나오다 diameter n. 직경, 지름 diagnosis n. 진단 disease n. 질병 difficulty n. 어려움, 곤란

우리 집에 살던 처음 몇 달 동안, 우리는 차례로 재난을 겪었다. 처음에는 아궁이가 터졌고, 그다음에는 세탁기가 작동을 멈췄고, 그다음에는 지붕이 새기 시작했다.

02 동의어   ①

secular a. 세속적인(= worldly), 비종교적인 be founded on ~을 토대로 하고 있다 rationality n. 합리성 separate a. 분리된; 독립된 guarded a. 보호되어 있는; 감시 받고 있는 awkward a. 서투른; 거북한, 어색한 profound a. 뜻깊은, 심원한

자연이 깊은 합리성을 바탕으로 하고 있다는 관점을 발전시킨 것은 세속적인 사상이 아니라 종교였다.

03 동의어   ③

dreary a. 황량한, 음산한; 따분한, 울적한(= dull and depressing) rural a. 시골의, 지방의 pastoral a. 목가적인, 전원의 warlike a. 전쟁의; 호전적인 fiery a. 불타는; 열렬한 cozy a. 아늑한, 포근한

그들은 중서부의 황량한 작은 마을에 살았다.

04 논리완성   ④

'환자들의 병에서 발생하는 작은 변화까지도 면밀하게 기록했다.'고 했는데, 이것은 환자들에게 '세심한' 주의를 기울인 것에 대한 부연설명이라 할 수 있다.

tiny a. 작은, 조그마한 cool a. 냉정한, 침착한 rare a. 드문 passionate a. 열렬한, 열의에 찬 meticulous a. 지나치게 세심한, 매우 신중한 sincere a. 성실한; 성심성의의

그 의사는 환자들에게 세심한 주의를 기울였는데, 환자들의 병에서 발생하는 작은 변화까지도 면밀하게 기록했다.

05 논리완성   ②

굴절로 인해 물체에서 나오는 광선의 방향이 바뀐다면, 그 물체는 원래의 모습이 아닌 다른 모습으로 '왜곡돼서, 일그러져서' 보일 것이다.

object n. 물체, 사물 refraction n. 굴절 disposed a. 배치된 distorted a. 일그러진, 왜곡된 dismissed a. 해고된 distressed a. 고뇌에 지친; 가난한 discharged a. 방출된

물 밖에서 수중의 물체를 보면 그 모습이 일그러진다. 이는 굴절이 물체에서 나오는 광선의 방향을 바꾸기 때문이다.

06 논리완성   ②

모델이나 풍경 대신에 사진을 놓고 그림을 그렸다는 것은 사진을 '실용적인' 용도로 사용한 것으로 볼 수 있다.

crisis n. 위기, 난국 imitate v. 모방하다 invention n. 발명; 발명품 in place of ~을 대신해서 landscape n. 풍경 imaginable a. 상상할 수 있는, 상상의 pragmatic a. 실용적인, 현실적인 illogical a. 비논리적인 moderate a. 절제하는; 적당한 independent a. 독립한, 자주의

19세기에 사진술이 등장했을 때, 그림은 위기에 처했다. 사진은 자연을 모방하는 작업을 그때껏 화가가 할 수 있었던 것보다 더 잘 해내는 것처럼 보였다. 어떤 화가들은 그 발명을 실용적으로 사용했다. 그들이 그리고 있는 모델이나 풍경 대신에 사진을 사용한 인상주의 화가들이 있었다.

07 생활영어   ④

스파게티의 본고장인 이탈리아에서 태어난 B에게 A가 스파게티를 올바로 먹는 방법을 지적하고 있으므로, B에게는 이런 상황이 번데기 앞에서 주름을 잡고 있는 상황, 혹은 공자 앞에서 문자를 쓰고 있는 상황으로 느껴졌을 것이며, 이에 해당하는 영어 표현은 teach a fish how to swim이다.

twirl v. 빙빙 돌리다 add insult to injury 설상가상, 엎친 데 덮친 격 have the right chemistry 찰떡궁합이다 go home and kick the dog 종로에서 뺨 맞고 한강 가서 눈 흘긴다 teach a fish how to swim 공자 앞에서 문자 쓴다, 번데기 앞에서 주름 잡는다 mend the barn after the horse is stolen 소 잃고 외양간 고친다

A: 스파게티를 올바로 못 먹는구나.
B: 내가?
A: 원래 스파게티는 숟가락에 담고 나서 포크로 돌려야 해.
B: (웃음)

A: 왜 웃니?
B: 넌 왜 공자 앞에서 문자를 쓰고 싶어 하니?
A: 무슨 뜻이야?
B: 나는 이탈리아에서 태어났어!

08 생활영어   ⑤

결함이 있는 것으로 드러나고 고장이 나기 시작했다는 것은 차에 하자가 있다는 것이다. 따라서 '불량품'이라는 뜻을 가진 ⑤가 빈칸에 들어가야 한다.

defective a. 결함이 있는, 하자가 있는   break down (기계 따위가) 고장나다   parasite n. 기생생물, 기생충   deal n. 거래   lemon n. <구어> (결함 있는 자동차 따위의) 불량품

A: 수(Sue)의 새 자동차 봤니?
B: 그래. 차는 좋아 보이지만, 그녀에게는 문제만 생긴 차였어.
A: 참 안 됐어. 그녀가 진짜 불량품을 산 것 같아.
B: 정말 그랬어. 대리점에서 운전해서 집에 오자마자 결함이 있는 것으로 드러나고 고장이 나기 시작했어.

09 대명사   ⑤

재귀대명사는 주어의 동작이나 행위가 주어 자신을 대상으로 하는 경우에 쓴다. ⓒ에는 문맥상 to watch하는 행위를 할 수 있는 것이 와야 하므로 앞에서 언급된 people을 가리키는 대명사가 와야 한다. 주어의 행위가 주어 자신에게 향하는 경우가 아니므로 ⓒ는 them이어야 한다.

unfavorable a. 형편이 나쁜, 불리한; 바람직하지 못한   detection n. 발견, 간파, 탐지   incongruent a. 일치[조화]하지 않는   element n. 요소, 성분   perspective n. 전망, 시각, 견지

유머로부터 나오는 웃음은 사람들이 대개 분노, 그리고/또는, 두려움을 느꼈을 좋지 않은 상황에 있을 때 나오며, 그 일치하지 않는 요소를 감지함으로써, 사람들은 그것을 다른 관점에서 바라볼 수 있다.

10 관계대명사   ①

'most of ~ language barriers'가 given that 다음의 절이므로, what이 이끌고 있는 명사절 what is absurd의 동사가 없는 상태다. 따라서 Ⓐ를 관계대명사 which로 고쳐야 한다. which의 선행사는 앞의 절 there is no innovation without competition이다.

innovation n. 혁신   competition n. 경쟁   absurd a. 불합리한; 터무니없는   given that ~임을 고려하면   silo n. 저장고, (미사일 등의) 사일로   border n. 국경   barrier n. 장벽   in isolation 고립되어

우리는 경쟁 없이는 혁신이 없다는 말을 흔히 듣는데, 과학 기술의 가장 위대한 혁신의 대부분이 (구별되는) 학문 영역, 국경, 언어 장벽을 넘어 연구를 공유하는 것에서 비롯되었다는 점을 고려할 때 그것은 터무니없는 말이다. 사실, 위대한 혁신들은 고립된 채로 일어나지 않는다.

11 논리완성   ②

빈칸에 들어갈 단어의 예를 그 다음 문장에서 제시하고 있는데, 예를 들어 '어떤 책의 앞 장(章)들을 떠올리기 위해 중간 장이나 뒷장에서 시작하는 것'은, 앞 장의 내용과 중간 장이나 뒷장의 내용이 연관되어 있으므로 시작하는 곳의 한 개념이 앞 장의 다른 개념을 불러일으켜 기억나게 하는 '연상(聯想, association)' 작용을 이용하는 것이다. 따라서 ②가 정답이다.

retrieve v. 만회하다, 회수하다; 생각해내다, 상기하다   assume v. 추정하다, 가정하다   surface v. 나타나다, 표면화되다   default n. 불이행, 태만; 디폴트, 초기 설정   shuffle v. 발을 질질 끌다, 이리저리 움직이다   relax v. 마음을 풀다, 긴장을 풀다   stuck a. (~에 빠져) 움직일 수 없는[꼼짝 못하는]; (불쾌한 상황·장소에) 갇힌   extended a. (기간을) 연장한, 장기적인   recall v. 생각해내다, 상기하다   concentration n. 집중, 전념   association n. 연합, 관련; 연상   continuation n. 계속, 지속, 존속   internalization n. 내면화, 내재화   reconciliation n. 조정; 화해

만약 어떤 사실이나 아이디어를 상기해낼 수 없다면, 기억이 날 때까지 상기하기를 계속하라. 그것을 완전히 잊어버렸다고 가정하고서 포기해버리지 마라. 우리가 원하는 순간에 기억이 떠오르지 않을 때, 기본적인 반응은 그것을 잊어버렸다고 가정하는 것이다. 아마도 잊어버리지는 않았을 것이다. 단지 뇌가 정신의 숲을 뒤적일 수 있는 잠깐의 시간을 줄 필요가 있을 뿐이다. 핵심은 기억을 강요하는 것이 아니라, 오히려 그 대신, 긴장을 풀고 기억이 나게 하는 것이다. 만약 장시간 동안 기억해내지 못하고 막혀 있는 상태라면, 어떤 것이든 떠올려 보라. 그런 다음 연상(聯想)의 힘을 이용하여 정보를 향해 나아가라. 예를 들어, 어떤 책의 앞 장(章)들을 떠올리기 위해 애쓰고 있다면, 중간 장이나 뒤에 나오는 장에서, 혹은 쉽게 떠오르는 아무 부분에서라도 시작하라.

12 논리완성   ①

빈칸을 포함한 문장 이하는 왜 고대의 현자(賢者)들을 '과학자'로 부를 수 없는지를 설명하는데, 과학이 그 자체 하나의 목적으로서 행해지는 것이 아니라 다른 것을 위해 행해졌고, 그 '다른 것'이 과학이 자주성을 갖지 못하게 하여 과학이 독자적인 영역이 되지 못하다 보니 과학을 하는 사람도 과학자라고 부를 수 없었던 것이다. 그러므로 빈칸에는 '과학'이 들어가야 한다.

sophisticated a. 정교한, 복잡한   astronomy n. 천문학   appropriate v. 전유(專有)하다, 자기 것으로 하다, 사사로이 쓰다   be credited with ~한 공로를 인정받다, 공적을 인정받다   initiate v. 시작하다, 개시하다   sage n. 현인(賢人), 철인(哲人)   applicable a. 적용[응용]할 수 있는, 들어맞는, 적절한   assign v. 할당하다; 부여하다, 주다   specific a. 특정한   recognize v. 인지하다, 인식하다   statecraft n. 경륜(經綸), 국정 운영 기술   rigid a. 엄격한, 엄정한   framework n. 하부구조, 골조, 뼈대   innovation n. 혁신   autonomy n. 자주성, 자율성   science n. 과학   knowledge n. 지식   project n. 프로젝트   religion n. 종교   creativity n. 창의성

고대 그리스인, 인도인 그리고 중국인이 수학, 의학, 천문학 등에 걸친 방대한 양의 고도로 발달된 지식을 만들어냈다는 사실은 잘 알려져 있다. 실제로, 이 지식의 상당 부분은 중세 시대에 과학 활동을 시작한 공이 있는 것으로 일반적으로 여겨지고 있는 이슬람교와 기독교 학자들에 의해

전용되고 재가공되었다. 그렇다면 왜 우리가 이 고대의 현자(賢者)들도 '과학자'라고 부르면 안 되는가? 단순하면서도 일반적으로 적절한 대답은 그들이 속했던 사회들이 과학자에게 특정한 사회적 역할을 부여하지 않았다는 것이다. 우리가 오늘날 과학으로 인정하는 것은 그 자체 목적으로서가 아니라 항상 다른 것을 위해 행해졌다. 그 '다른 것'은 여가 혹은 국정운영 기술일 수도 있는데, 각각은 나름의 방식으로 상당한 혁신을 허용했으나 (과학의) 자주성은 절대 허용하지 않은 고정된 체제 내에서 과학이 운용되도록 했다.

13 논리완성 ④

인간들이 자연에 해를 끼치는 활동으로 사냥, 목장경영, 해변 리조트 건설을 소개하고 있다. 빈칸 앞까지는 총기의 보급으로 인한 하와이 기러기의 멸종위기를 설명하고 있으며, 빈칸 뒤에는 목장과 해변 리조트 개발로 인한 하와이 기러기 개체수의 감소를 소개하고 있다. 하와이 기러기를 멸종에 이르게 하는 행위는 다르지만, 같은 결과를 초래하는 것이므로 빈칸에는 ④가 적절하다.

firearm n. 화기, 총 ranching n. 목장경영 nene n. 하와이 기러기 (= Hawaiian goose) hasten v. 빠르게 하다, 촉진하다 force ~ out of ~을 내쫓다 nesting n. 보금자리, 둥우리 breeding n. 번식

인간들이 가장 끔찍한 재난을 불러일으키는 활동에는 총기를 가지고 하는 사냥, 목장경영, 해변 리조트 건설 등이 있다. 엽총을 하와이에 들여온 이후에 하와이 기러기의 멸종이 촉진되었다는 것은 의심의 여지가 거의 없다. 총이 보편화됨에 따라 더욱더 많은 하와이 기러기들이 죽임을 당했다고 추정하는 것은 합리적인 것처럼 보인다. 이와 유사하게, 사람들이 섬에서 내륙으로 더 들어감에 따라 그들은 목장과 해변 리조트를 개발하기 위해 점점 많은 토지를 개간하기 시작했다. 이러한 개발들로 인해 하와이 기러기들은 자연 서식지와 번식지로부터 내쫓겼다. 이런 목장과 리조트들이 더욱 많아졌고, 하와이 기러기의 개체수는 그에 따라 줄어들었다.

① 그 결과
② 요약하자면
③ 반면에
④ 이와 유사하게
⑤ 매우 대조적으로

14 글의 제목 ③

'독성 화학물질과 방사성 입자가 포함된 화산 가스 구름이 성층권에 머물러 있음으로 인해 향후에 입게 될 환경과 경제의 피해가 엄청날 것으로 예상된다'는 내용이므로, 글의 제목으로는 ③이 가장 적절하다.

devastation n. 황폐, 파괴; 참화 explosion n. 폭발 estimate v. 어림잡다, 추정하다, 추단하다 rip off 뜯어내다, 파괴하다 volcanic a. 화산의 toxic a. 독성의, 유독한 chemical n. 화학물질 minute a. 미세한 particle n. 미립자, 분자 radioactive a. 방사성의, 방사능의 substance n. 물질 invisible a. 눈에 보이지 않는 the naked eye 육안, 맨눈 the Northern Hemisphere 북반구 stratosphere n. 성층권 considerable a. 상당한 agriculture n. 농업 timber n. 목재

참화는 5월 18일에 시작되었는데, 히로시마를 파괴한 원자폭탄의 힘의 500배로 추정되는 폭발로 인해 9,700피트 높이의 화산의 상부 1,200피트가 부서져 날아가 버렸다. 7일이 채 못 돼서, 일부 독성 화학물질과 미세한 방사성 물질 입자가 포함된 화산 가스 구름이 전국으로 퍼져나갔다. 과학자들은 몇 달 안에 그 구름 — 대부분의 지역에서 육안으로 보이지 않는 — 이 55,000피트 이상의 성층권에서 북반구를 뒤덮을 것이라고 말하고 있다. 그 구름은 지상으로 완전히 떨어질 때까지 약 2년 동안 지속될 것으로 예상된다. 환경에 미치는 영향은 상당하다. 가장 큰 경제적 영향은 그 나라의 농업과 목재 산업에 미칠 것으로 예상된다.

다음 글의 제목으로 가장 적절한 것은?
① 원자력: 장점과 단점
② 핵우산: 원인과 결과
③ 폭발하는 화산: 완전한 충격은 아직 오지 않았다
④ 환경 위기: 몇 가지 새로운 거대한 재난
⑤ 지구 온난화: 근본적인 이유와 즉각적인 결과

15-16

탄소 싱크는 배출하는 양보다 더 많은 탄소를 흡수하거나 저장하는 천연 지형이다. 탄소 싱크의 가치는 잉여 이산화탄소를 제거함으로써 대기 안의 평형 상태를 만드는 데 도움을 줄 수 있다는 데 있다. 탄소 싱크의 한 예는 거대한 숲이다. 그 안의 수많은 식물 및 기타 유기 물질은 많은 양의 탄소를 흡수하고 저장한다. 하지만, 지구에서 가장 중요한 탄소 싱크는 바다이다.

18세기에 산업혁명이 시작된 이래로, 산업 공정 중에 배출된 이산화탄소는 대기의 탄소 비율을 크게 증가시켰다. 탄소 싱크는 이러한 잉여 이산화탄소 중 거의 절반을 흡수할 수 있었는데, 지구의 바다가 그 일에 있어서 주된 역할을 해왔다. 바다는 인간의 산업으로 인한 탄소 배출물의 약 1/4을 흡수하여, 지구의 모든 탄소 싱크를 합친 것이 하는 일의 절반을 하고 있다.

하지만, 부엌의 싱크대와 마찬가지로 바다의 (탄소) 싱크대도 가득 찰 수 있다. 바다의 가장 강력한 (탄소) 싱크대인 남극해는 전 세계 잉여 이산화탄소의 대략 15퍼센트를 흡수해왔다. <그러나 2007년에 완료된 다국적 과학 조사 결과, 이 바다가 탄소 포화점에 이르고 있다는 것이 드러났다.> 분명히, 바다는 탄소를 흡수하는 무한한 능력을 갖추고 있지 않다. 바다의 흡수 능력이 약해지면서 대기 중의 이산화탄소와 기타 소위 온실가스의 축적이 증가하며, 그에 따른 결과는 전 세계적인 기후온난화이다.

carbon sink 탄소 싱크(탄소를 함유하는 유기 화학물질을 축적하고 저장할 수 있는 천연 또는 인공 저장소) feature n. 지세, 지형 absorb v. 흡수하다 store v. 저장하다, 비축하다 equilibrium n. 평형상태, 균형 atmosphere n. 대기 remove v. 제거하다, 없애다 excess n. 과잉, 잉여 organic a. 유기체의 proportion n. 비율; 조화, 균형 emission n. (빛·열·가스 등의) 배출; (대기 속의) 배출물, 배기가스 infinite a. 무한한

15 글의 제목 ①

본문에서는 잉여 이산화탄소를 흡수하고 저장하는 역할을 하는 데 있어서 바다가 매우 큰 몫을 담당하고 있다는 사실을 주로 이야기하고 있으므로, 글의 제목으로는 ①이 가장 적절하다.

윗글의 제목으로 가장 적절한 것은?
① 바다: 지구에서 가장 중요한 탄소 싱크
② 온실가스의 증가
③ 이산화탄소: 기후온난화의 원인
④ 평형상태: 탄소 싱크가 만들어내는 것
⑤ 남극해의 범람

16 문장삽입 ④

주어진 문장은 '그러나 2007년에 완료된 다국적 과학 조사 결과, 이 바다가 탄소 포화점에 이르고 있다는 것이 드러났다.'라는 의미이므로, 특정 바다의 탄소 흡수 능력을 언급하고 있는 부분의 뒤에 위치해야 한다. 그러므로 남극해가 전 세계 잉여 이산화탄소의 대략 15퍼센트를 흡수해왔음을 언급한 내용 다음인 Ⓓ에 들어가는 것이 적절하다.

17-18

스마트 도시는 확실히 세계가 몇몇 지속가능성 목표를 향해 나아가도록 자극하고 있으며, 스마트 기술은 특히 중국과 같이 일부 급성장하는 국가 내에서 도시 서비스를 눈에 띄게 개선하고 있다. 그러나 전력망, 오염 및 폐기물, 운송, 도시 서비스의 관리를 점진적으로 개선하는 것은 세계가 범지구적인 지속가능성을 향하여 단지 짧은 거리만 나아가도록 할 수 있다. 스마트 도시 기술은 낭비적인 소비, 소외감, 소득 불평등, 서비스 불평등 등과 같은 문제를 바꾸는 데 있어 할 수 있는 것이 거의 없으며, 심지어 문제를 악화시킬 수도 있다. 스마트 도시에 관한 긍정적인 담론은 또한 도시의 정치 및 경제 구조 자체가 오랫동안 지구 환경 악화의 원인이 되어 온 방식들을 감춰 버릴 수도 있다.
'생태 발자국'이라는 용어를 만든 생태학자 윌리엄 리즈(William Rees)는 도시와 그것이 수반하고 있는 교외의 불규칙한 팽창이 전 세계의 자원을 고갈시키고 멀리 떨어진 생태계를 훼손하는 복잡한 방식을 우리에게 상기시킨다. 그가 보여주고 있듯이, 도시경제학은 도시 주민들의 소비 증가로 인한 지구 환경의 훼손을 과소평가함으로써 지속가능성을 위한 도시화의 가치를 과장하는 경향이 있다. 대부분의 도시는 (도시의) 경계 훨씬 너머에 있는 땅, 식량, 담수, 천연자원, 에너지에 의존하고 있다. 그리고 그 도시들은 폐기물 비용을 멀리 있는 땅, 전 세계의 공유지, 그리고 미래 세대에게로 외부화하는(외부에 떠넘기는) 것에 의존하고 있다. 국부적으로 측정하면, 스마트 도시 주민들의 생태 발자국은 감소하고 있는 것처럼 보일 수도 있다. 그러나 소비가 멀리 떨어져 있는 땅에 미치는 영향을 고려하면, 주변화된(낙후된) 민족들과 손상되기 쉬운 생태계에 대한 막대한 사회적, 환경적 비용으로 인해 이 생태 발자국은 매우 다르게 보인다.

nudge v. 조금씩 밀다; 자극하다 sustainability n. 지속[유지] 가능성, 환경 파괴 없이 지속될 수 있음 notably ad. 현저하게; 그 중에서도 특히 incrementally ad. 증가하여, 점진적으로 alter v. 바꾸다, 변경하다 consumption n. 소비 alienation n. 소외 discourse n. 담론 obscure v. 어둡게 하다; 가려서 감추다 degradation n. 좌천, 강등; 타락, 저하 ecologist n. 생태학자, 환경운동가 coin v. (신어·신표현을) 만들어 내다 term n. 용어 accompanying a. 수반하는 sprawl n. 불규칙하게[모양 없이] 퍼짐; (도시 등의) 스프롤 현상 ecosystem n. 생태계 demonstrate v. 증명하다, 설명하다 exaggerate v. 과장하다 underestimate v. 과소평가하다 border n. 경계, 국경 externalize v. 외면화하다, 외부화하다 common n. 공유지, 공용지 take ~ into account ~을 고려하다 marginalize v. 사회[집단]의 주변적인 지위로 내쫓다, 사회의 주류에서 몰아내다 fragile a. 허약한, 망가지기 쉬운

17 글의 주제 ⑤

위 글은 스마트 도시 기술이 도시 서비스와 관리에 일부 개선을 제공하긴 하지만 낭비적인 소비, 불평등, 환경 파괴와 같은 문제를 악화시킬 수 있다는 점을 다루고 있으므로, 스마트 도시가 전 세계의 지속가능성에 기여하는 데 있어서의 한계를 강조하고 있다고 할 수 있다. 그러므로 ⑤가 정답이다.

윗글의 주제로 가장 적절한 것은?
① 전 세계의 환경 악화 원인
② 지속가능한 미래를 위한 스마트 기술의 활용
③ 스마트 도시 거주자들의 환경위기
④ 미래 세대를 위한 폐기물 비용 절감
⑤ 스마트 도시가 전 세계의 지속가능성에 미치는 부정적 영향

18 어법상 옳지 않은 표현 고르기 ⑤

막대한 사회적, 환경적 비용은 '주변화된' 민족들이 입게 되는 것이므로, Ⓔ는 수동을 나타내는 과거분사로 써야 한다. marginalized로 고친다.

19-20

집시들은 많은 나라에 흩어져 있는 민족이다. 집시라는 이름은 "이집트인"이라는 단어로부터 왔는데, 이는 집시들이 한때 이집트에서 왔다고 여겨졌었기 때문이다. 현재 일부 사람들은 그들이 원래 인도에서 왔다고 믿고 있다. 미국에서 집시들은 로마(Roma)라고 불리고, 영국에서 그들은 로마니(Romanies) 혹은 여행자로 알려져 있다. 로마 혹은 로마니는 다른 많은 소수 집단들과 마찬가지로 그들의 정체성에 대해 강한 자부심을 가지고 있다. 집시들은 항상 점을 치는 것과 결부되어져 왔다. 그들은 축제마당 같은 곳에서 손금을 읽거나 수정 구슬을 들여다봄으로써 사람들의 미래를 예측해 준다.
그들의 기원과 마법 같은 힘에 신비스러움이 결부돼 있기 때문에 집시들은 대중적으로는 낭만적인 이미지를 가지고 있는데, 이는 가족들이 더러운 이동주택(캠핑카) 주차장에서 살면서 의회 공무원이나 경찰에 의해 이리 저리로 옮겨가는 현실과는 상충된다. 미국인들은 집시들과 거의 접촉하지 않고 로마를 밝은 색의 옷과 황금 장신구를 착용하고 특이한 힘을 가진 흥미진진하고 신비로운 사람들로만 여기고 있다.

scatter v. 뿔뿔이 흩어버리다; 산재시키다 identity n. 정체성, 독자성 fortune-telling n. 길흉[운세] 판단, 점(占) fairground n. 장터, 축제장소, 박람회장 predict v. 예언하다 palm n. 손바닥 council n. 회의, 협회; 지방의회 jewellery n. 보석류; 장신구

19 빈칸완성 ③

낭만적인 이미지와 공권력에 의해 이리저리로 쫓기는 것은 서로 어울리지 않으므로 빈칸에는 '~와 상충되다[양립하지 않는다]'라는 의미의 ③이 적절하다. ① ~에 기인하다 ② ~에 달려 있다 ④ ~와 일치하다 ⑤ ~을 설명하다

20 내용일치 ⑤

"영국에서 그들은 로마니(Romanies) 혹은 여행자로 알려져 있다."라고
돼 있으므로, ⑤가 일치하는 진술이다.

Gypsy에 대한 윗글의 내용과 일치하는 것은?
① 고대 이집트에서부터 기원한 민족이다.
② 일정한 곳에 머무르지 않아 정체성 인식이 약하다.
③ 주술적 능력 때문에 대체로 두려운 존재로 여겨진다.
④ 미국인은 빈번한 접촉을 통해 그들을 흥미롭다고 생각한다.
⑤ 영국에서는 이들을 Romany 혹은 '여행자'라고 부른다.

01 ③	02 ②	03 ①	04 ④	05 ③	06 ①	07 ④	08 ②	09 ④	10 ①
11 ②	12 ③	13 ①	14 ②	15 ②	16 ①	17 ④	18 ③	19 ④	20 ③
21 ②	22 ①	23 ④	24 ③	25 ②	26 ③	27 ①	28 ④	29 ①	30 ③
31 ②	32 ④	33 ③	34 ①	35 ④	36 ④	37 ③	38 ①	39 ①	40 ①

01 생활영어 ③

자신이 에이미에게 너무 엄하게 한 거 아니냐는 A의 말에 B가 그렇지 않다고 대답했으므로, B는 에이미에게 엄하게 대한 것이 옳다고 생각하고 있는 것이다. 따라서 빈칸에는 be harsh on의 의미를 내포하고 있는 표현이 들어가야 할 것이므로 '질책하다', '호되게 꾸짖다'라는 의미의 ③이 정답이 된다.

harsh a. 호된, 모진, 가혹한 defer v. 연기하다; 경의를 표하다 salvage v. (해난·화재 따위로부터) 구조하다; (악화된 사태로부터) 구하다, 지키다 reprimand v. 견책하다; 호되게 꾸짖다 provoke v. 성나게 하다

A: 내가 에이미한테 늦게 들어온 거에 대해 너무 심하게 한 거야?
B: 아니. 걔는 호되게 꾸짖어야 해.

02 생활영어 ②

사기를 당한 것에 자책하고 있는 A에게 B가 네 잘못이 아니라고 위로하고 있으므로, 누구든지 그런 일을 당했을 수 있었을 거라는 흐름으로 이어져야 한다. 사기를 당한다는 것은 누군가에 '속는' 것이라 할 수 있으므로 빈칸에는 ②가 들어가야 한다.

fall for ~에 속다, ~에 사기당하다 scam n. 사기 spoil v. 망쳐놓다, 못쓰게 만들다 deceive v. 속이다, 기만하다 infect v. 감염시키다, 전염시키다 offend v. 성나게 하다, 불쾌하게 하다

A: 내가 그런 사기를 당했다는 게 믿어지지 않아.
B: 네 잘못이 아냐. 누구든지 속을 수 있었을 거야.

03 생활영어 ①

자신이 키우던 식물이 추위 때문에 죽었다는 말을 하는 A에게 B가 해줄 수 있는 조언으로는 좀 더 '추위에 강한' 식물을 선택하게 하는 것이 될 것이다.

cold spell (평상시보다 기온이 낮은) 한동안의 추위 hardy a. 강건한, 튼튼한, 내한성의 canny a. 신중한; 검약한, 검소한 serene a. 고요한 brazen a. 놋쇠로 만든; 철면피의

A: 한파 때문에 내 식물들이 많이 죽었어!
B: 너는 아마도 팬지처럼 꽤 추위에 잘 견딘다고 알려진 것들을 구해야 할 것 같아.

04 생활영어 ④

A가 원하고 있는 '스커트의 길이를 줄이는 것'을 지칭할 수 있는 표현이 B의 대답 속 빈칸에 들어가야 하므로, '수선', '(기성복의) 치수 고치기'의 의미를 가진 ④가 정답이 된다.

shorten v. 짧게 하다, ~의 치수를 줄이다 exchange n. 교환 variation n. 변화, 변동 substitute n. 대리; 대용품 alteration n. 변경; 개조; (기성복의) 치수 고치기

A: 이 스커트 좀 줄여주세요.
B: 알겠습니다. 1시간 안에 수선이 가능합니다.

05 생활영어 ③

상을 받을 자격이 되는지 모르겠다면서 겸손해하는 A에게 B가 그럴 만한 자격이 된다고 말했으므로, 그의 자선행위는 '칭찬받아 마땅하다'는 말이 이어지는 것이 자연스럽다.

appreciate v. 평가하다; 감상하다; 고맙게 여기다 award n. 상(賞), 수상(授賞); 상품 charitable a. 자비로운; 자선의 earn v. (감사·보수 등을) 받을 만하다, ~을 할 만한 값어치가 있다 dedication n. 헌신 charity n. 자선 (행위) inscrutable a. 불가사의한, 수수께끼 같은 prosperous a. 번영하는, 번창하고 있는 commendable a. 칭찬할 만한, 훌륭한 opportunistic a. 기회[편의]주의적인

A: 나의 자선 활동에 대해 이 상을 준 것은 고맙지만, 내가 받을 만했던 것 같진 않아.
B: 넌 받을 만했어. 자선 사업에 대한 너의 헌신은 칭찬받을 만해.

06 생활영어 ①

자원봉사 지도 활동을 그만두기로 했다는 A의 말에 B가 재고할 것을 권하고 있는데, 앞에 but이 있으므로 그 앞 문장은 그런 판단을 존중한다는 내용이 되는 것이 자연스럽다. 그러므로 그만두는 결정은 본인의 고유한 권한이라는 내용을 만드는 ①이 정답으로 적절하다.

volunteer a. 자발적인, 지원의 reconsider v. 다시 생각하다, 재고하다 prerogative n. 특권, 특전 rectitude n. 정직, 청렴 arraignment n. (법정으로의) 소환, 심문; 비난, 규탄 endowment n. 기증, 기부

A: 저는 자원봉사 지도 활동을 그만두기로 했어요.
B: 그만두는 것은 당연히 당신의 특권이지만, 다시 생각해 보셨으면 좋겠어요.

A: 너무 자신을 나무라지 마. 너는 테니스 대회에서 최선을 다했잖아.
B: 고마워. 그래도 돌이켜보니, 내가 연습을 더 많이 했어야 했어.

07 생활영어　　　　④

B의 '아무리 달콤한 말을 해도 설득시킬 수 없었다'라는 말을 통해, 빈칸에도 설득시키거나 구슬리는 것과 관련된 표현이 들어가야 함을 알 수 있다. 그러므로 ④가 정답으로 적절하다.

talk ~ into … ~를 설득해서 …하게 하다　work on ~에 종사하다　convince v. ~에게 납득시키다, 설득하여 ~하게 하다　condone v. 용서하다, 너그럽게 봐주다　appease v. 달래다, 진정시키다　endorse v. 배서하다; 찬성하다　cajole v. 부추기다; 구워삶다, 감언으로 속이다

A: 베스(Beth)를 설득해서 그 프로젝트에 종사하게 했나요?
B: 그녀를 꼬드기려 했지만, 아무리 달콤한 말을 해도 설득할 수 없었어요.

08 생활영어　　　　②

스페인으로 긴 여행을 떠날 것이냐는 A의 질문에 그렇지 않다고 B가 대답한 상황이므로, 결국 B는 짧은 여행을 계획하고 있는 것이 된다. 그러므로 '소풍', '짧은 여행'이라는 의미를 가진 ②가 정답이다.

lapse n. (시간의) 경과, 흐름, 추이; (과거의 짧은) 기간, 시간　jaunt n. 짧은 여행, 소풍　streak n. 줄, 선; 연속　breach n. 위반, 불이행

A: 너의 스페인 여행은 오래 걸릴까?
B: 아니, 나는 그저 짧은 여행을 계획하고 있어.

09 생활영어　　　　④

B의 제안이 거절당한 상황이므로 이는 결국 B의 노력이 아무런 성과를 얻지 못한 것이다.

reject v. 거절하다　baleful a. 재앙의, 해로운　extant a. 현존하는, 잔존하는　forlorn a. 고독한, 쓸쓸한　futile a. 무익한, 헛된

A: 당신의 제안이 거절당한 것을 유감스럽게 생각합니다.
B: 음, 이번에는 제 노력이 헛수고가 되었지만, 나중에 다시 도전해볼게요!

10 생활영어　　　　①

B의 '내가 연습을 더 많이 했어야 했어.'라는 말은 뒤늦은 깨달음에 해당하므로, 빈칸에는 ①이 적절하다. in hindsight는 '지나고 나서 보니까', '돌이켜보니'의 의미를 갖고 있다.

be hard on ~에게 심하게[모질게] 굴다　hindsight n. (일이 다 벌어진 뒤에) 사정을 다 알게 됨, 뒤늦은 깨달음　in hindsight 지나고 나서 보니까, 돌이켜보니　aftermath n. (전쟁·재해 따위의) 결과, 여파, 영향　remission n. 용서, 사면; 경감　prognosis n. 예후(豫後)

11 논리완성　　　　②

'such ~ that …' 구문은 원인과 결과의 문장을 만든다. 그가 틀렸을 때조차도 그의 말을 믿지 않는 것이 어려웠던 것의 원인으로는 '그가 매우 확신에 차서 말했던 것'이 적절하다.

recluseveness n. 은둔　conviction n. 신념, 확신　reliance n. 의지, 의존　inclination n. 경향, 성향

그 남자는 너무나 확신 있게 말해서 그가 틀렸을 때조차도 그의 말을 믿지 않기가 어려웠다.

12 논리완성　　　　③

30일간 사용해 본 뒤 마음에 들지 않으면 환불을 받을 수 있다는 것이므로, 이 경우에는 돈을 지불해야 할 '의무'가 전혀 발생하지 않는다고 할 수 있다.

guarantee n. 보증; 보증서　unsatisfied a. 불만족의　extension n. 연장; 확대　allegation n. 주장; 진술　obligation n. 의무　intrusion n. 강요; 방해

ForReal 사진편집 소프트웨어는 30일 환불 보증을 제공하므로, 만족하지 못하시는 경우에는 돈을 지불할 의무가 없습니다!

13 논리완성　　　　①

'예기치 못한 지출'은 내가 입게 되는 손실에 해당하므로, '(부채·손실 따위를) 입다[지다]', '(비용을) 물게 되다'라는 의미의 ①이 빈칸에 들어가기에 가장 적절하다. ④ you가 아니라 집을 짓는 것이 예기치 않은 경비 지출을 유발하는 것이므로 induce(유발하다)는 부적절하다.

complicated a. 복잡한　unexpected a. 예기치 않은, 뜻밖의　expense n. 지출, 비용　incur v. (좋지 못한 상황을[에]) 초래하다[처하게 되다]; (비용을) 발생시키다[물게 되다]　enhance v. 향상시키다　enact v. (법률을) 제정하다　induce v. 권유하다, 꾀다, 유발하다

집을 짓는 것은 매우 복잡한 과정이며, 따라서 여러 가지 예기치 못한 지출을 겪게 될 가능성이 높다.

14 논리완성　　　　②

기밀 정보가 밖으로 새어나갔다면, 재발 방지를 위해 엄격한 보안 조치를 '도입'하거나 '시행'하게 됐을 것이다.

leak n. (비밀의) 누설; 누설된 비밀　classified a. 기밀의　strict a. 엄격한　delude v. 미혹시키다, 속이다　impose v. (새로운 법률·세금 등을) 도입[시행]하다; (힘들거나 불쾌한 것을) 부과하다　enclose v. 둘러싸다, 에워싸다　relegate v. 퇴거를 명하다; 좌천시키다

최근에 기밀 정보가 누설되어서 잭슨(Jackson)사(社)는 엄격한 보안 조치를 시행하게 됐다.

15 논리완성 ②

Because of 뒤에는 원인에 해당하는 내용이 오고, 주절에는 결과에 해당하는 내용이 온다. 폭우가 가져올 결과로는 빗물에 의해 사는 곳이 '침수되는' 것이 가장 자연스럽다.

downpour n. 폭우, 호우 district n. 지역, 지구 resident n. 거주자, 주민 exasperate v. 화나게 하다; 악화시키다 inundate v. 범람시키다, 침수시키다 proliferate v. 증식하다, 급격히 늘다 tranquilize v. 진정시키다, 고요하게 하다

폭우로 인해 그 지역은 침수됐고, 주민들 대부분이 집을 떠났다.

16 논리완성 ①

아주 오래된 도자기가 약간의 흠집만 있는 상태라면 '거의 원래 상태로' 잘 보존된 것이라 할 수 있다.

pristine a. 원래의; 자연[원래] 그대로의 sparse a. 성긴, 드문드문한; (인구가) 희박한 archaic a. 낡은, 고풍스러운 tranquil a. 고요한

최근에 2,000년 된 도자기 그릇 한 개가 아랫면에 약간의 흠집만 있는 거의 원래 상태로 발견되었다.

17 논리완성 ④

기밀 사항에 대해 당국이 압박을 가하는 이유로는 그것을 '발설하게' 하려는 것이 적절하다.

press v. 압박하다, 괴롭히다 refuse v. 거부하다 confidential a. 기밀의 obscure v. 어둡게 하다; 덮어서 감추다, 가리다 rescind v. (법률·행위 등을) 폐지하다; (계약 등을) 무효로 하다, 취소하다 expunge v. 지우다, 삭제하다 divulge v. (비밀을) 누설하다, 밝히다; 폭로하다

그 언론인은 심지어 당국의 압박을 받은 후에도 자신의 비밀 정보원의 이름을 누설하길 거부했다.

18 논리완성 ③

판사가 법적 절차를 제대로 유지하지 않고 왜곡되게 했다면 그러한 절차에서 나온 유죄판결은 왜곡되고 우스꽝스럽게 일그러진 모습의 정의가 될 것이다. 이것을 정의의 희화화라 할 수 있으므로 빈칸에는 ③이 가장 적절하다. ④ 법적 절차를 완전히 없앤 것이 아니므로 정의를 파괴한 것은 아니다.

uphold v. 지지하다, 변호하다; 유지하다, 관리하다 proper a. 적절한 legal a. 법적인, 법률이 요구하는 procedure n. 순서, 수순; 절차 accusation n. 비난, 규탄 criminal a. 범죄의; 형사상의 conviction n. 신념, 확신; 유죄판결 umbrage n. 불쾌, 노여움 amnesty n. 사면,

특사 travesty n. 졸렬한 모방[모조품], 희화화 ravage n. 파괴, 황폐

판사가 적절한 법적 절차를 유지하지 못한 것은 그 형사(刑事) 유죄판결이 정의의 희화화를 나타내는 것이라는 비난으로 이어졌다.

19 논리완성 ④

rather than 전후에는 서로 상반되는 의미의 표현이 와야 하므로 빈칸에는 posed와 반대되는 의미를 가진 ④가 들어가야 한다.

presence n. 존재 posed a. 포즈를 취한 dormant a. 동면의; 잠복한 cordial a. 충심으로부터의, 성심성의의 nimble a. 재빠른, 민첩한 candid a. 정직한; <사진> 포즈를 취하지 않은, (사진이) 자연스러운 모습 그대로 찍은

그 웨딩사진 작가는 포즈를 취한 사진보다는 자연스러운 모습을 담은 사진을 찍을 수 있도록 하객들에게 자신의 존재를 무시해 달라고 부탁했다.

20 논리완성 ③

calling 이하는 앞 부분을 부연하여 설명하는 역할을 하고 있다. 중요성을 최소화했다는 것은 '지엽적인' 것으로 다루었다는 말이므로 빈칸에는 ③이 들어가야 한다.

prosecutor n. 검찰관, 기소자 defendant n. 피고 evidence n. 증거 minimize v. 최소화하다; 경시하다 recondite a. 심원한, 난해한, 잘 이해받지 못하는 obdurate a. 완고한, 고집 센 peripheral a. (중요하지 않은) 주변적인, 지엽적인 obtrusive a. 강요하는, 주제넘게 나서는

검사는 피고인의 DNA가 사건에서 가장 중요한 증거라고 주장한 반면, 피고인측 변호인은 그것은 지엽적인 것이라면서 그 중요성을 최소화했다.

21 시제 ②

by the time은 'by the time 주어+과거 동사, 주어+had+p.p.', 'by the time 주어+현재 동사, 주어+will+have+p.p.'의 형태로 쓴다. 주어진 문장의 경우, 주절에 과거완료 동사가 왔으므로 빈칸에는 과거 동사가 들어가야 한다.

소년이 학교에 도착했을 때는 이미, 첫 번째 수업은 이미 끝난 상태였다.

22 동명사를 목적어로 취하는 타동사 ①

enjoy는 동명사를 목적어로 하는 타동사이므로 빈칸에는 ①이 들어가야 한다.

observe v. 관찰하다, 관측하다

많은 젊은이들이 간단한 망원경을 사용하여 밤하늘을 관측하는 것을 즐긴다.

23 선행사를 포함하는 관계대명사 what ④

전치사 for의 목적어가 되는 명사절을 이끄는 역할과 자신이 이끄는 절 안에서 타동사 regard의 목적어가 되는 역할을 동시에 할 수 있는 표현이 필요하므로, 빈칸에는 선행사를 포함하는 관계대명사인 what이 들어가야 한다.

blatantly ad. 노골적으로, 뻔뻔스럽게

그 회사는 많은 사람들이 노골적으로 반(反)경쟁적인 사업 관행으로 간주하는 것으로 인해 비난을 받게 되었다.

24 to부정사 ③

투자자들을 끌어들이는 것이 그 기업가가 고군분투한 이유에 해당하므로, 빈칸에는 목적을 나타낼 수 있는 to부정사가 들어가야 한다.

entrepreneur n. 실업가, 기업가 struggle v. 노력하다, 분투하다 investor n. 투자자 startup n. 스타트업, 신생 창업기업

그 기업가는 자신의 인공지능 스타트업에 돈을 투자하도록 투자자들을 끌어들이기 위해 수년간 고군분투했다.

25 가정법 미래 ②

가능성이 희박한 미래를 가정하는 '가정법 미래'는 'If+주어+should+동사원형, 주어 will[can, may, would, should, could, might]+동사원형'의 형태를 취하는데, 이때 주절에 명령문이 오는 것도 가능하다. 주어진 문장이 바로 그러한 경우에 해당하며, 여기서 종속절의 If를 생략하면 도치가 일어나서 'Should+주어+동사원형'의 형태가 된다. 따라서 ②가 정답이다.

encounter v. ~와 우연히 만나다, 조우하다 hesitate v. 주저하다 contact v. 접촉하다, 연락하다 assistance n. 도움, 조력

윈저(Windsor) 호텔에 머무르시는 동안 문제가 발생하면 주저하지 말고 프런트에 연락하여 도움을 요청하십시오.

26 현재분사의 용법 ③

주절의 동사는 stood out이므로 빈칸에는 주어 the child를 수식하는 역할을 할 수 있는 준동사가 들어가야 한다. the child는 노래하는 행위의 주체이므로, 능동을 나타내는 현재분사 singing으로 수식하는 것이 적절하다.

row n. 열, 줄; (극장 따위의) 좌석의 줄 stand out 눈에 띄다, 두드러지다

학교 공연 중에 앞줄 가운데에서 노래를 부르던 아이는 목소리가 아름다워서 눈에 띄었다.

27 주장·제안 동사가 이끄는 that절 속의 동사 형태 ①

주장, 제안의 타동사가 이끄는 that절 속의 동사는 주어의 수와 시제와 상관없이 'should+동사원형'이어야 하며, 이때 should는 생략이 가능하다. 그러므로 ①이 정답이다.

overnight ad. 밤새도록; 하룻밤 사이에 observation n. 관찰, 관측

의사는 주의 깊게 지켜볼 수 있도록 밤새 병원에 남아 있을 것을 그의 환자에게 권고했다.

28 동사의 수일치 / 동사의 태 ④

주어인 The high cost가 3인칭 단수이므로 조동사로는 have가 아닌 has가 적절하며, 또한 이것은 cite하는 행위의 주체가 아닌 대상이므로 수동태로 표현해야 한다. 따라서 ④가 정답이다.

decline v. 감소하다, 감퇴하다 cite v. 인용하다, 예증하다

자녀 양육에 드는 높은 비용은 많은 국가에서 출산율이 감소하고 있는 주된 원인 중의 하나로 인용되어 왔다.

29 in search of ①

'~을 찾아서'는 in search of로 표현한다.

undiscovered a. 발견되지 않은, 미지의 species n. 종(種), 종류

과학자들은 종종 아직 발견되지 않은 동물 종(種)을 찾아 외딴 곳으로 여행한다.

30 문의 구성 ③

전치사 Despite 뒤에는 절이 아닌 동명사가 와야 하고, not yet은 have 동사와 과거분사 사이에 위치하므로 ③이 정답으로 적절하다.

down payment 계약금 mortgage n. (담보) 대출

그 젊은 부부는 아직 계약금을 낼 만큼의 돈을 모으지 못했음에도 불구하고, 담보대출을 신청하는 것을 고려했다.

31 글의 요지 ②

'일부 제품에 들어 있는 화학 물질 때문에 많은 사람들이 자외선 차단제 사용을 꺼리고 있지만, 천연 합성물을 사용하여 개발한 자외선 차단제가 이러한 소비자들의 두려움을 완화시킬 수 있을 것'임을 이야기하고 있는 내용이다. 그러므로 ②가 정답으로 적절하다.

vital a. 지극히 중요한, 필수적인 chemical n. 화학 제품[물질] expert n. 전문가 compound n. 합성물, 혼합물 assuage v. 진정시키다, 완화시키다 consumer n. 소비자 algae n. 조류(藻類, 수중에 생육하는 부유 식물의 총칭) coral reef 산호초 alternative n. 대안 benefit n. 이익, 이득 habitat n. 서식지

자외선 차단제의 사용은 피부암 예방을 위해 필수적이다. 불행하게도, 많은 사람들은 일부 제품에 들어 있는 화학 물질에 대한 염려 때문에 자외선 차단제 사용에 대해 경계심을 갖고 있다. 일부 전문가들은 천연 합성물을 사용하여 개발된 새로운 세대의 자외선 차단제가 이러한 소비자들의 두려움을 완화시킬 수 있기를 희망한다. 그 합성물은 조류(藻類)에서 발견되었고 거친 자외선으로부터 산호초를 보호하는 것으로 밝혀졌다. 그 합성물은 새로운 자외선 차단제의 기초로서의 역할을 할 수 있을 것이며, 그 경우에는 현재의 화학적 자외선 차단제에 대한 자연을 기반으로 한 대안으로 시판될 수 있을 것이다. 그 새로운 자외선 차단제는 해양 서식지에 피해를 덜 끼친다는 추가적인 이점도 가질 수 있을 것이다.

위 글의 요지는 무엇인가?
① 과학자들은 특정 자외선 차단제가 건강에 잠재적으로 해로운 영향을 미친다는 사실을 확인했다.
② 식물성 자외선 차단제의 개발은 자외선 차단제 사용에 대한 소비자의 우려를 줄여줄 수 있을 것이다.
③ 자외선 차단제 사용에 대한 우려는 건강에 대한 부정적인 결과로 이어지고 있다.
④ 자외선 차단제가 환경에 미치는 영향에 대해 소비자들의 우려가 커지고 있다.

32 글의 주제 ④

소의 소화 과정에서 자연적으로 발생하는 부산물인 메탄의 배출을 줄이기 위한 방법들을 소개하고 있는 내용이다.

livestock n. 가축 significant a. 상당한; 중요한 emission n. (빛·열·가스 등의) 배출; (대기 속의) 배기가스 byproduct n. 부산물 digestive a. 소화의 investigate v. 조사하다, 연구하다 reduce v. 줄이다, 감소시키다 feed n. 먹이, 사료 additive n. 첨가제 probiotic n. 활생균(숙주의 건강에 유익한 효과를 나타내는 미생물 또는 그 성분)

가축, 특히 소는 온실가스 배출의 중대한 원천이다. 소는 매우 많은 양의 메탄을 방출하는데, 메탄은 소의 소화 과정에서 자연적으로 발생하는 부산물이다. 연구원들은 이러한 메탄의 배출을 줄이기 위한 해법을 연구하고 있다. 한 가지 가능한 수단은 소에게 풀 대신 옥수수를 더 많이 먹이는 것인데, 풀을 바탕으로 하는 사료를 소화시키는 과정에서 더 많은 메탄이 발생하기 때문이다. 또 다른 선택은 첨가제를 사용하는 것이다. 예를 들어, 소의 사료에 활생균을 첨가하면 통상적인 사료를 소화시키는 동안 메탄의 생성이 감소하는 것으로 나타났다.

위 글은 주로 무엇에 관한 것인가?
① 가축이 기후변화에 미치는 영향
② 왜 메탄이 다른 가스보다 더 해로운가
③ 축산업이 더 지속가능해질 수 있는 방법
④ 소의 메탄 배출을 낮추기 위한 전략

33 내용파악 ③

'돌로 쌓은 하드리아누스 장벽과는 달리, 안토니누스 장벽은 주로 토탄(土炭)과 나무로 축조되었고, 그 결과, 이 장벽은 잘 보존되지 못했다.'라는 내용이 있으므로, ③이 옳은 진술이다. ① 남쪽으로 160킬로미터 떨어진 곳에 있던 하드리아누스 장벽을 대신하기 위한 것이므로, 하드리아누스 장벽의 북쪽에 지어진 것이다.

barrier n. 울타리, 방벽 isle n. 섬 frontier n. 국경, 국경지방 dub v. ~라고 칭하다 supercede v. 대신하다 predecessor n. 전임자, 선배 construct v. 건조하다, 건설하다, 축조하다 turf n. 잔디, 이토(泥土); 토탄(土炭) consequently ad. 따라서, 그 결과로서 preserve v. 보전하다, 유지하다; 보존하다 rampart n. 성벽 abandon v. 버리다; 단념하다 implement v. 이행하다, 실행하다

서기 2세기에 로마 황제 안토니누스 피우스(Antoninus Pius)는 자신의 제국의 북서쪽 국경을 확고히 하기 위해 브리튼 섬을 가로지르는 방어 장벽을 건설할 것을 명령했다. 안토니누스 장벽이라고 불린 이 장벽은 남쪽으로 160킬로미터 떨어진 곳에 있던 하드리아누스 장벽을 대신하기 위한 것이었다. 돌로 쌓은 이전 장벽과는 달리, 안토니누스 장벽은 주로 토탄(土炭)과 나무로 축조되었다. 그 결과, 이 장벽은 잘 보존되지 못했다. 돌로 쌓은 성벽을 추가하려는 계획이 있었을지도 모르지만, 이 장벽은 완공 직후에 버려졌고, 이러한 개선은 결코 실행되지 않았다.

다음 중 안토니누스 장벽에 관해 옳은 것은?
① 그것은 하드리아누스 장벽의 남쪽에 지어졌다.
② 그것은 주로 돌과 나무의 조합으로 이루어져 있었다.
③ 그것은 하드리아누스 장벽에 비해 시간이 지남에 따라 상태가 나빠졌다.
④ 그것은 완공 이전에 버려졌다.

34 글의 제목 ①

프로 바둑 선수를 꺾은 인공지능 프로그램 알파고와 그것의 학습 방법을 이야기하고 있는 내용이므로, 제목으로는 ①이 적절하다.

defeat v. 쳐부수다, 이기다, 패배시키다 abstract a. 추상적인, 관념적인 strategy n. 전략 Go n. 바둑 tout v. 극구 칭찬[선전]하다 artificial intelligence 인공지능 acquire v. 얻다, 획득하다 involve v. 수반하다, 포함하다 analyze v. 분석하다 independently ad. 자주적으로, 자유롭게 identify v. 확인하다, 인지하다 move n. <체스·바둑·장기> 말의 움직임, 말 쓸 차례, 수 subsequent a. 차후의

알파고는 바둑이라 불리는 추상적인 전략 게임에서 인간 프로 선수를 이긴 최초의 컴퓨터 프로그램이다. 이 프로그램은 기계 학습으로 알려진 과정을 통해 바둑에 대한 지식을 얻었기 때문에 인공지능(AI)의 표본으로 선전되고 있다. 이 과정은 컴퓨터 프로그램이 많은 양의 데이터를 분석하여 자신만의 규칙이나 알고리즘을 개발하는 것을 수반한다. 알파고의 경우, 그 프로그램은 단순히 인간과 컴퓨터 기반의 상대들과 많은 게임을 하는 방법을 통해 바둑에서 가능한 최고의 수를 찾아내는 법을 독자적으로 학습했다. 그 프로그램의 후속 버전인 알파고 마스터와 알파고 제로는 원형보다 훨씬 더 강력했다.

위 글의 제목으로 가장 적절한 것은?
① 바둑에서 인간을 이기는 방법을 알아낸 인공지능
② 인공지능이 인간에게 바둑을 더 잘 두는 방법을 가르치다
③ 인공지능은 최상위 바둑 선수에게는 적수가 못 된다
④ 새로운 인공지능이 바둑에서 이전의 인공지능을 능가하다

35-36

점박이 날개 초파리 혹은 SWD라 불리는 곤충이 미국의 과일 재배업자들에게 큰 피해를 입혔다. 동남아시아에서 출현한 이 곤충은 침입성이

강해서 체리와 라즈베리 작물을 파괴했다. 그것은 보통의 초파리(과일파리)가 속해있는 것과 똑같은 과(科)인 초파리(초산파리)이지만, 친척뻘 되는 다른 초파리(과일파리)와는 달리, 손상된 과일을 좋아하지 않는다. 대신에, 그것은 날카로운 부속기관을 사용하여 과일의 껍질을 뚫은 다음 그 안에 알을 낳는다. 그 초파리의 알이 침범한 과일들은 안에서부터 서서히 파괴되기 때문에, 의심하지 않는 농부들은 겉보기에 아무 문제가 없어 보이는 수확물이 사실은 아무 쓸모가 없다는 것을 알게 되고는 종종 충격을 받는다.

SWD는 농민들의 제1 방어선인 살충제에 취약하다. 또한 익은 과일을 신속하게 수확하고, 그 곤충이 가장 많이 들끓을 때인 한여름이 오기 전에 다 익는 과수 품종을 심음으로써 그 해충을 방제할 수 있다.

spotted wing drosophila 점박이 날개 초파리   wreak havoc on ~을 혼란시키다; ~을 파괴하다, 파멸시키다 invasive a. 침입하는, 침략적인 crop n. 수확; 농작물, 곡물 fruit fly 과일파리, 초파리 relative n. 친척, 친족 favor v. 편애하다 appendage n. 부속물 penetrate v. 꿰뚫다, 침입하다 skin n. 피부; (과일 따위의) 껍질 deposit v. (특정한 장소에) 놓다, 두다; (알을) 낳다 affected a. 영향을 받은; (병 따위에) 걸린, 침범된 ruin v. 망치다 unsuspecting a. 의심하지 않는, 수상히 여기지 않는 vulnerable a. 상처를 입기 쉬운; 약점이 있는 insecticide n. 살충제 pest n. 해충 promptly ad. 신속히 ripen v. 익다, 원숙하다

---

35 내용파악 ④

두 번째 문단 첫 번째 문장에서 '살충제에 취약하다'라고 했으므로 ④가 옳은 진술이다. ② SWD가 곧 초산파리이다.

다음 중 SWD에 관해 옳은 것은?
① 그것은 미국에서 동남아시아로 퍼져나갔다.
② 초파리(과일파리)와는 동족에 속하지만 초산파리와는 그렇지 않다.
③ 그것은 과일 표면에 알을 낳는다.
④ 그것은 살충제에 대한 내성이 발달하지 않았다.

---

36 내용추론 ④

"그것은 과일의 껍질을 뚫은 다음 그 안에 알을 낳으며, 그 과일들은 안에서부터 서서히 파괴되기 때문에, 의심하지 않는 농부들은 겉보기에 아무 문제가 없어 보이는 수확물이 사실은 아무 쓸모가 없다는 것을 알게 되고는 종종 충격을 받는다."는 내용을 통해 초기 단계에서는 그것이 들끓고 있는지의 여부를 발견하기 어려움을 추론할 수 있다.

위 글에서 SWD에 대해 추론할 수 있는 것은?
① 그것은 주로 최근에 수확한 과일에 들끓는다.
② 그것은 주로 다른 종(種)의 파리를 먹고 산다.
③ 그것의 방제 조치는 지금까지 효과가 없었다.
④ 그것이 들끓는 것은 초기 단계에서 발견하기 어렵다.

37-38

19세기까지, 하늘을 가로지르는 신비한 물체에 대한 보고는 주로 혜성이나 유성에 관한 것이었고, 이러한 천체 현상은 일반적으로 신성한 징조로 해석되었다.
그 후 기술이 급속도로 발전함에 따라 미확인 비행 물체(UFO)를 둘러싼

대중의 담론도 바뀌었다. 19세기 후반, 사람들이 하늘에 있는 낯선 물체를 알려왔을 때, 그들은 종종 색다른 비행 기계를 묘사했다. 대중들은 이러한 것을 목격하는 것을 대체로 즐겼고 종종 그 기계들이 괴짜 발명가들의 작품일 것이라 추측했다.
20세기 초, 유럽 도처에 전쟁이 다가오면서 UFO 목격에 대한 논의가 다시 바뀌었다. 독일의 공격을 두려워한 유럽과 북미의 많은 사람들은 UFO의 목격을 독일의 기술 탓으로 돌리면서, 특히 바로 얼마 전에 개발된 체펠린 비행선, 즉 가스로 가득 차 있는 대형 비행선을 지목했다. 이러한 보고는 1차 세계대전이 시작되면서 급증했다.
시간이 흘러가면서, 새로운 기술들이 UFO 관련 보고와 이 보고들에 대한 대중의 반응에 계속해서 영향을 미쳤다. 나치가 2차 세계대전에서 패배한 후, UFO는 소련의 로켓 실험과 종종 연결 지어졌다. 그러다가 1950년대에 냉전이 편집증을 심화시키면서 UFO가 외계의 기술이라는 이제는 친숙해진 개념이 대중의 상상력을 사로잡았다.

comet n. 혜성 meteor n. 유성 celestial a. 천체의 phenomenon n. 현상; 사건 interpret v. 해석하다, 설명하다 divine a. 신의, 신성한 portent n. 징조, 전조 discourse n. 담화, 이야기 unidentified a. 확인되지 않은, 미확인의, 정체불명의 exotic a. 외래의, 이국적인; 색다른 sighting n. 관찰하기; (UFO나 항공기 따위의) 관찰[목격] 사례 assume v. 추정하다, 추측하다 eccentric a. 별난, 괴상한 loom v. 어렴풋이 나타나다; (위험·근심 등이) 불안하게 다가오다 specifically ad. 명확히, 분명히; 특히 surge v. (물가가) 급등하다, 급격히 오르다 outset n. 착수, 시작 deepen v. 깊게 하다, 깊어지다 paranoia n. 편집병, 망상증 alien a. 외국의, 외계의 take hold of 붙잡다

---

37 글의 제목 ③

본문은 UFO에 대한 사람들의 인식과 반응이 시대상황과 기술발전에 따라 변해왔음을 이야기하고 있는 내용이므로, 제목으로는 ③이 적절하다.

위 글의 제목으로 가장 적절한 것은?
① 더 이상 예전처럼 공포를 자아내지 못하고 있는 UFO
② 유사 이래로 현저하게 일관된 방식으로 묘사된 UFO
③ 기술과 시대에 따른 UFO의 보고와 대중의 반응 변화
④ 신기술의 등장으로 급격히 증가한 UFO 목격

---

38 내용일치 ①

"19세기까지는 하늘을 가로지르는 신비한 물체들을 신성한 징조로 해석했지만, 기술이 급속도로 발전함에 따라 19세기 후반에는 사람들이 하늘에 있는 낯선 물체를 알려왔을 때, 그들은 종종 색다른 비행 기계를 묘사했다."고 돼 있다. 그러므로 19세기 후반에는 UFO를 종교적으로 해석하는 것이 줄어들었다고 할 수 있다.

위 글에 의하면 다음 중 옳은 것은?
① UFO에 대한 종교적인 해석은 19세기 말 무렵에 줄어들었다.
② 비행 기계에 대한 보고가 처음에는 대중의 공포를 초래했다.
③ UFO의 목격은 일반적으로 독일의 로켓 실험과 연결 지어졌다.
④ UFO가 외계인의 기술이라는 생각은 냉전시대 이전에 널리 퍼지게 되었다.

39-40

청소년기와 관련된 많은 행동 변화들은 사춘기 동안의 생식 호르몬 분비에 크게 기인한다. 그러나, 과학자들은 사춘기가 젊은이들에게 미치는 영향을 청소년기가 젊은이들에게 미치는 영향과 구분 짓기가 어려웠다. 두 용어가 상당히 중첩되긴 하지만, 그것들은 또한 뚜렷이 다르기도 하다. 사춘기는 개인이 생식 기능을 발달시키는 과정을 특히 지칭하는데, 이것은 청소년기 동안 일어나는 과정이다. 한편, 청소년기는 사춘기와 관련된 변화뿐만 아니라 유년기에서 초기 성년기로의 이행을 나타내는 많은 신체적, 심리적 변화를 포괄하는 광범위한 용어이다.

특별히 사춘기와 관련된 변화를 청소년기와 관련된 일반적인 변화로부터 분리하기 위해, 연구원들은 시베리아 햄스터를 포함시키는 면밀하게 구성된 실험을 고안했다. 이 작은 설치류는 연중 언제 태어났는지에 따라 서로 다른 나이에 사춘기를 겪는다. 낮 시간이 길 때 태어난 시베리아 햄스터는 낮 시간이 짧을 때 태어난 것들보다 더 어린 나이에 사춘기에 들어간다. 연구원들은 새로 태어난 햄스터가 받는 빛의 양을 조절함으로써 두 그룹의 햄스터를 사육했는데, 생후 30일 무렵에 사춘기를 겪은 그룹과 생후 100일 무렵에 사춘기를 겪은 그룹이었다. 그런 다음 연구원들은 행동 변화가 그 설치류가 신체적 성숙에 가까워지는 것에 반응하여 일어나는지 아니면 사춘기 동안 생식 호르몬이 분비되는 것에 반응하여 일어나는지를 관찰했다.

연구원들은 놀이에서 사회적 지배 행동으로의 전환을 전자(前者)의 그룹이 후자(後者)의 그룹보다 더 일찍 보여주는지에 특히 관심이 있었다. 연구원들은 그러한 전환이 사춘기와 무관하게 두 그룹 모두에서 같은 나이에 일어났다는 사실을 발견했다. 이를 통해 청소년기와 관련된 행동 변화들 중 적어도 일부는 생식 호르몬이 원인이 아닐 가능성이 높다는 결론에 이르렀다.

adolescence n. 청소년기, 청년기 attribute v. (~의) 탓으로 하다, (~의) 행위로[소치로, 업적으로] 하다 reproductive a. 생식의 puberty n. 사춘기 disentangle v. (혼란스러운 주장·생각 등을) 분리해내다, 구분하다; (얽매고 있는 것에서) 풀어 주다 term n. 용어 overlap v. 부분적으로 겹치다 significantly ad. 상당히, 크게 distinct a. 별개의, 다른 specifically ad. 특히 encompass v. 포함하다, 에워싸다 a host of 많은, 다수의 transition n. 변이, 변천 isolate v. 고립시키다 devise v. 궁리하다, 고안하다 rodent n. 설치류 동물 undergo v. (영향·변화 따위를) 받다; 경험하다, 겪다 breed v. 기르다, 양육하다; 번식시키다 observe v. 관찰하다, 관측하다 maturity n. 성숙 dominance n. 우세, 우월, 지배 independently of ~와 관계없이[별개로]

---

39 내용일치 ②

"시베리아 햄스터는 연중 언제 태어났는지에 따라 서로 다른 나이에 사춘기를 겪는데, 새로 태어난 햄스터가 받는 빛의 양을 조절함으로써 생후 30일 무렵에 사춘기를 겪은 그룹과 생후 100일 무렵에 사춘기를 겪은 그룹을 연구원들이 만들어냈다."는 내용을 통해 ②가 옳은 진술임을 알 수 있다.

위 글에 의하면 다음 중 옳은 것은?
① 사춘기의 정의는 청소년기의 정의를 포함한다.
② 시베리아 햄스터의 사춘기 시기는 조절이 가능하다.
③ 지배 행동은 시베리아 햄스터의 사춘기 전(前) 시기를 나타낸다.
④ 그 연구는 생식 호르몬이 행동 변화의 원인임을 시사한다.

---

40 내용추론 ①

"이 작은 설치류는 연중 언제 태어났는지에 따라 서로 다른 나이에 사춘기를 겪는다."라는 말에는 번식 시기가 연중 다양하다는 의미가 내포돼 있다.

위 글에서 추론할 수 있는 것은?
① 시베리아 햄스터는 연중 서로 다른 시기에 번식한다.
② 사춘기는 대부분의 포유류에서 청소년기보다 시기적으로 훨씬 앞선다.
③ 생식 호르몬은 사춘기 이후에 증가하는 경향이 있다.
④ 다 자란 시베리아 햄스터들은 일반적으로 또래들과 노는 것을 즐긴다.

01 ①	**02** ④	**03** ②	**04** ①	**05** ④	**06** ②	**07** ③	**08** ④	**09** ③	**10** ①
11 ①	**12** ①	**13** ④	**14** ②	**15** ①	**16** ③	**17** ③	**18** ②	**19** ③	**20** ④
21 ③	**22** ④	**23** ③	**24** ①	**25** ②	**26** ④	**27** ④	**28** ①	**29** ③	**30** ②
31 ①	**32** ②	**33** ③	**34** ②	**35** ④	**36** ④	**37** ①	**38** ③	**39** ①	**40** ②

01 생활영어　　　　　　　　　　　　　　　①

쉬어야 한다는 A의 말에 B가 동의한 상황이므로, B 또한 무척 지쳐 있다고 할 수 있다. 이는 곧 힘이 고갈되거나 빠져 있는 상태에 있는 것이므로, 빈칸에는 '약화시키다', '활력을 빼앗다'라는 의미의 ①이 적절하다.

sap v. (세력·체력·신앙 따위를) (서서히) 약화시키다, 해치다; 기력을 빼앗다 hoist v. (무거운 것을) 천천히 감아올리다; 높이 올리다 pluck v. 뜯다, 잡아 뽑다 preclude v. 제외하다; 방해하다

A: 우리는 몇 시간째 돌아다니고 있어. 난 정말 쉬어야 해.
B: 좋은 생각이야. 우리가 오늘 한 관광 때문에 나도 정말 힘이 빠졌어.

02 생활영어　　　　　　　　　　　　　　　④

신작 영화에 대한 논평이 다양하다는 A의 말에 B가 공감한 상황인데, 논평이 다양하다는 것은 '반응'이 서로 엇갈린다는 말로 달리 나타낼 수 있으므로 ④가 정답이 된다.

vary v. 변화하다, 바뀌다; 다양하다 mixed a. 뒤섞인, 잡다한, 혼성의 admission n. 입장, 입학; 허가 conception n. 개념작용; 파악, 이해 endurance n. 인내, 참을성 reception n. 받아들임; (평가되는) 반응, 인기, 평판

A: 저 신작 영화 "Squadron"에 대한 논평이 매우 다양해.
B: 그래. 반응이 너무 엇갈려서 놀랐어.

03 생활영어　　　　　　　　　　　　　　　②

어플의 보안이 확실하냐는 A의 물음에 B가 그렇다고 대답했는데, 해킹이 불가능한 것은 통신 내용이 '암호화'되기 때문으로 보는 것이 가장 타당하다.

circulate v. 순환시키다; (소문 등을) 유포시키다 encrypt v. 암호화하다 unravel v. (엉클어진 실·짠 것 등을) 풀다; 해명하다 decipher v. (암호문 등을) 해독하다

A: 이 모바일 애플리케이션으로 하는 통신은 안전한가?
B: 그래, 모든 메시지가 암호화되기 때문에 해커가 볼 수 없어.

04 생활영어　　　　　　　　　　　　　　　①

'짐칸 등에 물건을 집어넣다'라는 의미를 가진 표현이 들어가야 자연스러우므로 ①이 정답이 된다.

overhead a. 머리 위의, 천장에 매달린 compartment n. (기차 안의 칸막이를 한) 객실; (가구 등의 물건 보관용) 칸 stow v. 집어넣다; 가득 채워 넣다; 싣다 beset v. 포위하다, 에워싸다 ascend v. (오르막길·사다리 따위를) 올라가다, 오르다 stock v. (점포에 물품을) 사들이다; 비축하다, 갖추다

A: 선생님, 가방은 머리 위 짐칸에 넣어주세요.
B: 네, 그렇게 하겠습니다. 먼저 가방에서 뭐 좀 꺼낼게요.

05 생활영어　　　　　　　　　　　　　　　④

급속히 퍼지는 성질을 가진 침입종이냐는 A의 질문에 B가 그렇지 않다고 대답했으므로, 이와 대조되는 의미, 즉 '토착의', '그 고장에 고유한'이라는 의미를 가진 ④가 빈칸에 들어가기에 적절하다.

shrub n. 키 작은 나무, 관목(灌木) invasive a. 침입하는, 급속히 퍼지는 intolerant a. 아량이 없는, 편협한 domestic a. 가정의; 국내의, 자국의 hereditary a. 세습의; 유전에 의한 indigenous a. 토착의; 그 고장에 고유한

A: 이 관목이 사방에 널려 있네. 침입종이야?
B: 아니, 그것은 사실 이 지역의 토착종이야.

06 생활영어　　　　　　　　　　　　　　　②

A와 B 모두 쉽게 뱃멀미를 한다고 했는데, 뱃멀미는 배를 타고 이동하는 경우에 '속이 메스꺼워지는 것'이므로 빈칸에는 ②가 적절하다.

seasick a. 뱃멀미가 난, 뱃멀미의 barren a. (땅이) 불모의, 메마른; 불임의 queasy a. 메스꺼운, 느글거리는 peevish a. 성마른, 안달하는 drowsy a. 졸음이 오는, 졸리게 하는

A: 난 뱃멀미를 잘 해.
B: 나도 그래. 배를 타고 짧은 여행을 해도 속이 너무 메스꺼워져.

07 생활영어 ③

재키가 기분이 좋았던 것은 자신의 해외 파견 요청을 부장이 '허락'했기 때문일 것이다.

request n. 요구, 의뢰 overseas a. 해외의, 외국으로 가는 transfer n. 이동, 이전; (다른 대학·부서·부대로의) 이적 empower v. ~에게 권력[권한]을 주다 allocate v. 할당하다, 배분하다 grant v. 주다, 부여하다; 승낙하다 commit v. 위임하다, 위탁하다

A: 오늘 퇴근하기 전에 재키(Jacky)는 왜 그렇게 행복해 보였을까?
B: 부장님이 그녀의 해외 파견 요청을 허락했거든!

08 생활영어 ④

사장이 임금을 올려주기로 마음을 바꿨냐는 A의 물음에 B는 그렇지 않다고 대답했다. 이는 임금을 인상해 줄 여력이 없다는 회사의 입장을 사장이 '단호히' 고수하고 있는 것이다.

raise n. 임금 인상 can't afford to ~할 여유가 없다 capricious a. 변덕스러운 diffident a. 자신 없는, 사양하는, 수줍은 intrepid a. 두려움을 모르는 adamant a. 요지부동의, 단호한, 강경하게 주장하는

A: 사장님이 너에게 임금 인상을 해주는 것에 대해 (해주기로) 마음을 바꿨니?
B: 아니야. 사장님은 회사가 그렇게 할 형편이 안 된다고 강경하게 주장했어.

09 생활영어 ③

사람들에 대해 최악을 가정한다는 것은 기본적으로 사람들을 비하하거나 업신여기는 마음이 내재해 있는 것이다. 그러므로 빈칸에는 '냉소적인'이라는 의미의 ③이 들어가는 것이 가장 자연스럽다.

assume v. (사실일 것으로) 추정[상정]하다; (권력·책임을) 맡다; (특질·양상을) 띠다[취하다] lenient a. 관대한; 인정 많은 reticent a. 과묵한 cynical a. 냉소적인 tenuous a. 희박한; 엷은; 미약한; 보잘것없는

A: 나의 언니는 항상 사람들에 대해 최악을 가정해.
B: 조금 냉소적인 게 잘못된 건 아냐.

10 생활영어 ①

사업을 시작하면서 겪게 될 우여곡절에 대비하고 있는지를 묻는 A에게 B가 그렇다고 대답하면서 그에 부연해서 이야기하고 있는 상황이므로, 빈칸에는 미래에 겪게 될 '우여곡절'과 유사한 의미 혹은 그러한 의미를 내포하고 있는 표현이 들어가야 한다. 따라서 '만일의 사태'라는 뜻의 ①이 이러한 의미에 가장 가깝다.

ups and downs 우여곡절, (삶의) 굴곡 contingency n. 우연, 우발사건, 만일의 사태 hyperbole n. 과장, 과장어법 deference n. 복종, 존경 propensity n. 경향, 성질

11 논리완성 ①

어떤 일이 덜 중요하고 어떤 일이 더 중요한지를 알게 되면, 먼저 해야 할 일과 그렇지 않은 일을 구별할 수 있을 것이고 이에 따라 일의 우선순위를 매길 수 있게 될 것이다.

task n. (일정한 기간에 완수해야 할) 일, 임무 employee n. 직원, 종업원 accordingly ad. (그것에) 따라서, 그에 맞게 prioritize v. (계획·목표)에 우선순위를 매기다 conserve v. 보존하다, 보호하다 transform v. 변형시키다 formulate v. 공식화하다

직원들은 업무 목록을 작성함으로써 어느 것이 덜 중요하고 어느 것이 더 중요한지를 알 수 있고 그에 따라 업무의 우선순위를 정할 수 있다.

12 논리완성 ①

찾아서 모으는 행위는 흩어져 있거나 떨어져 있는 것을 대상으로 한다. 그러므로 빈칸에는 이와 같은 의미 혹은 속성을 지닌 ①이 들어가야 한다.

round up ~을 (찾아) 모으다 livestock n. 가축류 herd n. 짐승의 떼 stray v. 길을 잃다, 옆길로 빗나가다, 일행에서 처지다[탈락하다]; 헤매다 waver v. 망설이다, 주저하다 flutter v. 퍼덕거리다 tremble v. 떨다, 전율하다

농부는 무리로부터 너무 멀리 벗어난 가축들을 찾아 모으도록 자신의 개를 훈련시켰다.

13 논리완성 ④

폐기물을 외부로 반출한 것은 환경 규제를 '피하기' 위함이었을 것이다.

environmental a. 주위의, 환경의 regulation n. 규칙, 규정 ensnare v. 함정에 빠트리다, 유혹하다 swindle v. 속이다, 사취하다 abduct v. 유괴하다 circumvent v. 선수를 쓰다; 회피하다

그 회사는 폐기물을 주(州) 밖으로 수송함으로써 환경 규제를 피했다.

14 논리완성 ②

무용수의 동작에 맞춰 그녀가 입고 있는 옷도 똑같은 움직임을 보였을 것이므로, 빈칸에는 spin과 유사한 의미를 가진 표현이 들어가야 한다. 따라서 ②가 정답이 된다.

spin v. (팽이 따위가) 돌다, 뱅뱅 돌다 jumble v. 뒤범벅이 되다, 뒤섞이다 twirl v. 빙빙 돌다 wriggle v. 몸부림치다, 꿈틀거리다 fumble v. 더듬어 찾다; 만지작거리다

그 무용수는 무대를 가로질러 우아하게 빙빙 돌았는데, 동작을 취할 때마다 그녀의 드레스도 돌았다.

15 논리완성 ①

학생들이 그의 강의를 따라가기 어려웠던 이유로는 여러 주제에 대해 '횡설수설하거나 두서없이 이야기한 것'이 적절하다.

lecture n. 강의 ramble v. 이리저리 거닐다; 두서없이 이야기하다 tamper v. 참견하다, 간섭하다 whimper v. 훌쩍이다, 울먹이다 snivel v. 콧물을 흘리다, 코를 훌쩍이다

그 교수는 다양한 주제에 대해 두서없이 이야기하는 경향이 있었기 때문에 학생들이 그가 하는 강의의 논리를 따라가기가 어려웠다.

16 논리완성 ③

환경의 지속가능성과 화석연료의 생산은 양립할 수 없는 관계에 있으므로, 전자를 추구하는 경우에는 후자를 배제하거나 줄여야 한다. 그러므로 빈칸에는 '박탈'의 의미를 가진 동사인 ③이 정답이다.

commitment n. 범행; 위임; 공약, 서약, 헌신, 참여 sustainability n. 지속[유지] 가능성, 환경 파괴 없이 지속될 수 있음 asset n. 자산, 재산 fossil fuel 화석연료 depose v. (고위층 사람을) 면직[해임]하다, (권력의 자리에서) 물러나게 하다 divulge v. (비밀을) 누설하다, 밝히다; 폭로하다 divest v. (지위·권리 등을) 빼앗다; 처분하다, 없애다 desist v. 그만두다, 중지하다

환경의 지속가능성에 대한 헌신의 일환으로 그 헤지펀드는 화석연료 생산과 관련된 모든 자산을 처분했다.

17 논리완성 ③

fantastic expectations과 mundane reality는 서로 상반되는 개념이므로 이를 나타낼 수 있는 ③이 정답으로 적절하다.

arise v. (문제·사건·기회 등이) 일어나다; 발생하다, 생기다 protagonist n. 주역, 주인공 fantastic a. 환상적인, 공상적인, 기상천외의 mundane a. 현세의; 일상적인 tantrum n. 울화, 언짢은 기분 retribution n. 보답; 징벌 incongruity n. 부조화 ramification n. (흔히 pl.) 파생된 문제, 부차적 영향, 파급 효과

『돈키호테』의 유머는 주인공의 공상적인 기대와 일상적인 현실 사이의 부조화에서 발생한다.

18 논리완성 ②

새로운 증거가 피고인들의 무죄를 확고히 하였다면 그들은 '혐의에서 완전히 벗어날 수' 있었을 것이다.

evidence n. 증거 defendant n. 피고 establish v. 설립하다; 제정하다; 확고히 굳히다, 확립하다 innocence n. 결백, 무죄 retaliate v. 보복하다, 앙갚음하다 exonerate v. ~의 결백을[무죄를] 증명하다; ~의 혐의를 벗겨주다 repudiate v. 거부하다, 부인하다 ameliorate v. 개선하다, 개량하다

새롭게 발견된 증거는 의심할 여지없이 피고인들의 무죄를 확고히 하여 그들의 혐의를 완전히 벗겨주었다.

19 논리완성 ③

어린 나이에 바이올린을 통달했다는 것은 마리아가 '재주가 남달리 뛰어난 아이'라는 것이므로, 빈칸에는 '신동'이라는 뜻의 ③이 들어가야 한다.

acknowledge v. 인정하다, 승인하다 culprit n. 죄인, 범죄자 patron n. (사업·예술 따위의) 보호자, 후원자; (상점·여관 따위의) 고객, 단골손님 prodigy n. 천재, 신동 surrogate n. 대리, 대리인

10살의 나이에 이미 바이올린에 정통하게 된 마리아(Maria)는 음악의 신동으로 인정받았다.

20 논리완성 ④

창의성과 열의를 저해하는 것과 관련이 깊은 표현이 필요하므로, ④가 정답으로 적절하다.

excessive a. 과도한, 지나친 undermine v. (명성 따위를) 음험한 수단으로 훼손하다 enthusiasm n. 열심, 열광 extenuating a. 죄를 가볍게 하는, 참작할 수 있는 unwitting a. 모르는, 부지불식간의 tantalizing a. 애타게 하는, 감질나게 하는 stultifying a. 멍청하게 만드는, 무력하게 만드는, (의욕·열정 등을) 없애는

직원의 업무수행에 대한 과도한 감시는 매우 무기력한 직장 문화를 초래하여, 직원의 창의성과 열의를 저해할 수도 있다.

21 관계부사 ③

빈칸 뒤에 완전한 절이 주어져 있으므로 접속사와 부사의 역할을 동시에 할 수 있는 관계부사로 두 문장을 연결시킬 수 있다. 선행사가 장소의 명사이므로 관계부사 where가 정답이 된다.

venue n. (경기·회의 등의) 개최지

그 커플은 야외 결혼식을 올릴 수 있는 장소를 찾아 나섰다.

22 부정사를 목적어로 취하는 타동사 ④

offer는 부정사를 목적어로 하는 타동사이므로 빈칸에는 ④가 들어가야 한다.

in response to ~에 응하여[답하여] neighboring a. 이웃의, 인접해 있는 humanitarian a. 인도주의적인 affected a. 영향을 받은; (병 따위에) 걸린, 침범된

지진에 대응해서, 주변 국가들은 피해를 입은 사람들에게 인도적 지원을 제공하겠다고 말했다.

23 promise+to부정사 / 타동사의 목적어 ③

promise는 부정사를 목적어로 취하며 타동사 find 뒤에는 전치사 없이 바로 목적어가 온다.

mayor n. 시장 stop at nothing (원하는 것을 얻기 위해) 어떤 일도 서슴지 않다 solution n. 해법, 해답

시장은 그린빌의 주택 위기에 대한 해결책을 찾기 위해 어떤 일도 서슴지 않겠다고 약속했다.

24 전치사 over ①

the cost of public services는 dispute의 주제나 내용에 해당하므로 빈칸에는 '~에 관해서[대해서]'의 의미를 가진 전치사 over가 들어가는 것이 적절하다.

faction n. 당파, 파벌 council n. 협의회; 지방의회 dispute n. 토론; 논쟁

시의회의 두 정파가 공공서비스 비용을 놓고 치열한 논쟁을 벌이고 있다.

25 현재분사의 용법 ②

주절의 동사는 confronted이므로 주어 Several employees를 수식하는 역할을 할 수 있는 준동사가 들어가야 한다. Several employees는 고군분투하는 행위의 주체이므로, 능동을 나타내는 현재분사로 수식하는 것이 적절하다.

employee n. 직원, 종업원 workload n. 업무량, 작업량 confront v. 대항하다, 맞서다

엄청난 업무량에 고군분투하고 있던 몇몇 직원들이 그 문제에 대해 상사에게 맞섰다.

26 시제 ③

종속절에 과거를 명확하게 나타내주는 과거시제의 when절이 있으므로 현재완료시제와 미래완료시제는 주절에 올 수 없다. 그러므로 과거진행시제인 ③이 정답이 되며, 과거진행시제는 과거의 특정 시점이나 기간 중에 이뤄진 동작이나 상태 등을 나타낸다.

talent agency 탤런트 양성[배출] 기관 offer v. 제공하다, 제안하다

그 여성은 탤런트 양성 기관에 발견되어 모델 일을 제안 받았을 때 웨이트리스로 일하고 있었다.

27 전치사+관계대명사 ④

문장의 주어는 The space capsules이고 동사는 are이다. 그러므로 astronauts descend from space to Earth는 주어를 수식하는 역할을 해야 하겠는데, 이것이 완전한 절이므로 그 앞에는 관계부사 where이

올 수 있다. 한편, 관계부사 where는 in which로 바꿔 표현할 수 있으므로 ④가 정답이 된다.

astronaut n. 우주비행사 descend v. 내려오다 withstand v. 저항하다; 견디다 intense a. 심한, 격렬한

우주비행사들이 우주공간에서 지구로 타고 내려오는 우주 캡슐은 극심한 열과 압력을 견딜 수 있도록 설계돼 있다.

28 주장·제안 동사가 이끄는 that절 속의 동사 형태 ①

주장, 제안의 타동사가 이끄는 that절 속의 동사는 주어의 수와 시제에 상관없이 'should+동사원형'이어야 하며, 이때 should는 생략이 가능하다. 그러므로 ①이 정답이다.

demand v. 요구하다 behave v. 행동하다 respectful a. 공손한

선생님은 그 학생에게 공손한 태도로 행동할 것을 요구했다.

29 수동 분사구문 ①

분사구문의 주어가 생략돼 있다는 것은 이 분사구문의 주어가 주절의 주어와 같다는 것을 의미한다. 주절의 주어인 Excalibur Tower가 situate하는 행위의 주체가 아닌 대상이므로 수동의 분사구문이 되는 것이 적절하며, 따라서 과거분사인 ①이 정답이다. ③의 경우, '센트럴 파크의 북서쪽 모퉁이에 위치해 있기 위해서는'라는 의미가 돼서 어색하다.

resident n. 거주자, 주민 unparalleled a. 비할 데 없는, 견줄 데 없는

센트럴 파크의 북서쪽 모퉁이에 위치해 있기 때문에, 엑스칼리버 타워는 주민들에게 비할 데 없는 도시 전망을 제공한다.

30 수동태 ②

콤마 다음의 should the economic stimulus measures는 if the economic stimulus measures should에서 if가 생략되면서 도치가 일어난 것이다. the economic stimulus measures는 부결하는 행위의 주체가 아닌 대상이므로 수동태가 되어야 하며, 따라서 ②가 정답이 된다.

recession n. 경기후퇴, 불황; 물러남 stimulus measures 경기부양책 currently ad. 현재, 지금 vote down (투표를 통해) ~을 부결[거부]하다

현재 의회에서 논의되고 있는 경기부양책이 부결된다면 경기침체가 발생할 것이 거의 확실하다.

31 글의 주제 ①

본문은 '치실이 도입되었을 때 사람들이 거부감과 불편함을 느껴 인기를 얻지 못하다가 19세기 후반에 개선된 제품이 나와서 사용하기가 편해지자 비로소 널리 사용되게 되었다'는 내용이다.

dental floss 치실 introduce v. 소개하다, 도입하다 resist v. 저항하다 toothpick n. 이쑤시개 consist of ~로 이루어져 있다 unwieldy a. 다루기 힘든 spool n. (실을 감아놓는 데 쓰는) 실패, 얼레 thread n. 실, 무명실 dispenser n. 디스펜서(휴지·종이컵 등을 빼내어 쓰게 된 장치) prong n. 갈퀴, 포크 모양의 물건 embrace v. 받아들이다, 채택하다

19세기 초에 현대식 치실이 소개되었을 때, 많은 사람들은 그 제품을 사용하는 것에 저항했다. 어떤 사람들은 입에 손가락을 넣는다는 생각을 싫어하여 이쑤시개를 사용하는 것을 선호했다. 다른 사람들은 단순히 치실을 사용하는 것이 어렵다고 생각했다. 1800년대 초 그 제품은 다루기 힘들도록 실크 실을 실패에 감아놓은 것으로 이루어져 있어서 사람들은 그것을 칼로 잘라야 했다. 아셀 셔틀레프(Asahel Shurtleff)가 지금은 익숙해져 있는, 실을 자르는 용도의 U자 형태의 갈퀴가 있는 디스펜서를 발명한 19세기 후반에 와서야, 치실은 사용하기 쉬워져서 소비자들에게 더 널리 받아들여졌다.

위 글은 주로 무엇에 관한 것인가?
① 치실이 곧바로 인기를 끌지 못한 이유
② 발명가들이 치실의 최초 버전을 어떻게 개선했는가
③ 치실의 초기 버전이 상대적으로 효과가 없었던 이유
④ 치실의 사용에 대한 관심이 어떻게 해서 시간이 지남에 따라 늘어나고 줄어들었는가

32 글의 목적   ②

씨앗 꼬투리 안의 압력으로 인해 씨앗이 강제로 분출되는 과정인 '폭발성 열개(裂開)'에 대해 주로 설명하는 글이므로, 글의 목적으로는 ②가 적절하다.

evolve v. 진화하다 disperse v. 흩뜨리다, 흩어지게 하다 line n. 종류 seedpod n. (콩 등의) 꼬투리 eject v. 내뿜다, 분출하다 explosive a. 폭발하기 쉬운, 폭발성의 dehiscence n. <식물> 열개(裂開), 터짐; <의학> (봉합의) 터져 벌어짐 trigger v. (일련의 사건·반응 등을) 일으키다, 유발하다 inadvertent a. 부주의에 의한; 무심코 저지른, 우연의 spontaneously ad. 자발적으로

식물은 다양한 방법으로 씨앗을 흩뜨리도록 진화해 왔다. 어떤 식물들은 자연적인 종류의 약한 경계선을 가진 구조물 — 일반적으로 씨앗 꼬투리 — 을 통해 그렇게 한다. 이 약한 부분이 열릴 때, 씨앗 꼬투리 안의 압력으로 인해 씨앗이 강제로 분출된다. 이러한 과정은 폭발성 열개(裂開)로 알려져 있다. 종종, 씨앗의 분출은 동물과 씨앗 꼬투리 사이의 우연한 접촉에 의해 유발된다. 그러나 때때로 폭발성 열개는 식물 안에서 압력이 자연적으로 생겨남으로 인해 발생하여, 식물이 저절로 쪼개져서 열리게 한다.

위 글의 주된 목적은 무엇인가?
① 씨앗을 퍼트리는 다양한 방법을 개략적으로 설명하기 위해
② 폭발성 열개(裂開)의 과정을 설명하기 위해
③ 씨앗을 퍼트리는 데 있어서의 동물의 역할을 분석하기 위해
④ 폭발성 열개(裂開)를 씨앗을 퍼뜨리는 다른 방법들과 대조하기 위해

33 내용파악   ③

해자에 현대식 나무다리만 걸쳐져 있다고 했으므로, ③이 옳은 진술이

다. ① 시간이 지나면서 해자 외에는 모두 사라졌다. ② 현재 그 성의 벽을 사방으로 둘러싸고 있다. ④ 경관을 돋보이게 하는 성격이 더 강했다.

construct v. 건설하다, 축조하다 extensive a. 광범위하게 미치는; 광대한, 넓은 waterworks n. 급수시설, 상수도 with the exception of ~은 예외로 하고, ~을 제외하고, ~외에 prominent a. 현저한, 두드러진 feature n. 특징, 특색; 지형, 지세 quadrangular a. 사각형의 moat n. (도시나 성곽 둘레의) 해자(垓子) span v. (강·계곡 따위에) 걸치다, 걸리다 drawbridge n. 도개교(跳開橋), 옛날 성의 해자에 걸쳐 놓은 들어 올리는 방식의 다리)

영국의 보디엄(Bodiam) 성이 1385년에 건설되었을 때, 그것은 광범위한 수로로 둘러싸여 있었다. 이러한 특징들 중 가장 두드러진 것들 — 그 성의 넓은 사각형 해자(垓子) — 을 제외하면, 이 모든 것들은 시간이 지남에 따라 모두 사라졌다. 보디엄 성의 해자(垓子)는 현재 그 성의 벽을 사방으로 둘러싸고 있다. 그 해자에는 현대식 나무다리만 걸쳐져 있는데, 성이 건설됐을 당시에는 다리가 도개교(跳開橋)였을 것이다. 해자는 대개 방어용 구조물이지만, 보디엄 성의 해자는 경관을 나타내는 특징이 보다 강하도록 설계되었으며, 그 결과 주변에 비해 성이 더 웅장해 보인다.

다음 중 보디엄 성에 관해 옳은 것은?
① 그것은 현재 많은 수로들로 둘러싸여 있다.
② 그것의 해자는 더 이상 벽을 완전히 에워싸고 있지 않다.
③ 그것의 해자를 가로지르는 원래의 다리는 사라지고 없다.
④ 그것의 해자가 가진 주된 목적은 본래 성의 주민들을 보호하는 것이었다.

34 글의 주제   ②

'로봇이 인간과 비슷하게 생겼을수록 호감도가 높아지다가 일정 수준에 다다르면 오히려 불쾌감을 느끼게 되며, 로봇이 인간과 구분이 되지 않을 만큼 완전히 똑같으면 그 불쾌감이 사라진다'는 '불쾌한 골짜기 이론'에 대한 내용이다. 그러므로 ②가 정답으로 적절하다.

uncanny a. 초자연적인, 초인적인; 기괴한, 기분 나쁜 apparent a. 명백한; 겉치레의 aversion n. 혐오, 반감 humanoid a. 인간을 닮은 appearance n. 외모, 겉보기 favorably ad. 호의적으로, 우호적으로 elicit v. (진리·사실 따위를 논리적으로) 이끌어 내다; (대답·웃음 따위를) 유도해 내다 unsettling a. 마음을 산란하게 하는 indistinguishable a. 분간[구별]할 수 없는 positive a. 긍정적인 light n. 견해, 양상

로봇공학자 모리 마사히로(Masahiro Mori)의 불쾌한 골짜기 이론은 인간을 닮은 특정 로봇에 대한 인간의 혐오를 설명하기 위해 도입되었다. 모리에 따르면, 로봇의 외형이 인간과 점점 더 비슷해질수록 인간은 로봇을 더 호의적으로 바라보게 된다. 그러나 로봇이 거의 인간과 유사하지만 더할 나위 없이 완전히 유사하지는 않은 지점이 도래한다. 그러나 불쾌한 골짜기가 시작되는 이 지점에서, 로봇은 인간들로부터 불안한 느낌을 이끌어낸다. 로봇이 인간과 구분이 되지 않게 되면, 다시금 긍정적인 시각에서 로봇을 바라보게 된다.

위 글의 주제는 무엇인가?
① 인간과 로봇의 상호작용을 형성하는 데 있어서 로봇의 외모가 가진 역할
② 로봇의 외모와 그 로봇에 대한 인간의 반응 사이의 가능한 연관성
③ 모리 마사히로의 불쾌한 골짜기 이론을 새롭게 하려는 시도
④ 인간과 유사한 로봇에 대한 인간의 불쾌함이 로봇 개발에 미치는 영향

35-36

2018년에 한 연구팀이 이탈리아의 폴리노(Pollino) 국립공원에서 1,230년 된 헬드라이히 소나무를 발견했는데, 그 공원에서는 이 품종의 소나무를 비교적 흔히 찾아볼 수 있다. 이후에 이탈루스(Italus)라 칭하게 된 이 소나무는 이전에 유럽에서 가장 오래된 것으로 여겨졌던 그리스의 1,075년 된 소나무보다 한 세기 이상 더 오래되었다.

연구원들이 이탈루스가 절벽 면에서 튀어나온 것을 발견했을 때, 줄기의 많은 부분이 썩어서 없어진 상태였고, 가장 안쪽의 고리들은 대부분 사라져 있었다. 나무의 안쪽 고리들이 나이에 대한 중요한 정보를 가지고 있기 때문에, 그 나무의 열악한 상태는 연구원들이 그 나무의 나이를 알아내기 어렵게 만들었다. 나무의 가장 안쪽 고리들 중 적어도 20센티미터가 사라져 있었는데, 이는 잠재적으로 수십 년의 가치가 있는 정보가 사라졌다는 것을 의미했다.

궁극적으로, 연구원들은 노출된 뿌리 부분에 방사성탄소 연대측정을 실시했다. 이 연대측정 방법을 통해 연구원들은 나무가 언제 싹이 텄는지를 알아낼 수 있었다. 뿌리가 줄기와는 다른 속도로 고리를 만들어낸다는 점을 고려하여, 연구원들은 또한 남은 줄기의 고리 패턴과 뿌리의 고리 패턴에 대해 교차 연대측정을 실시했다. 그렇게 함으로써, 그들은 그 나무가 1,230살이라는 것을 알아낼 수 있었다.

species n. 종, 종류 relatively ad. 상대적으로 subsequently ad. 그 후, 계속해서 dub v. (새 이름·별명을) 주다[붙이다], ~라고 칭하다 stick out 튀어나오다, 돌출하다 portion n. 일부, 부분 trunk n. (나무의) 줄기 rot away 썩다, 썩어 없어지다 innermost a. 가장 안쪽의 potentially ad. 잠재적으로; 어쩌면 conduct v. 집행하다, 처리하다, 관리하다 radiocarbon dating 방사성탄소 연대측정 exposed a. 노출된 germinate v. 싹이 트다, 자라기 시작하다 given that ~임을 고려[감안]하면

---

35 내용파악 ④

"뿌리가 줄기와는 다른 속도로 고리를 만들어낸다는 점을 고려했다."는 내용을 통해 ④가 옳은 진술임을 알 수 있다. ① 비교적 흔히 찾아볼 수 있다고 했다. ② 한 세기 이상 더 오래 됐다. ③ 나무의 가장 안쪽 고리들 중 적어도 20센티미터가 사라져 있었다고 했다.

다음 중 이탈루스에 관해 옳은 것은?
① 그것은 폴리노 국립공원에서는 보기 드문 소나무 종(種)이다.
② 그것은 이전에 유럽에서 가장 오래된 나무로 여겨졌던 것보다 몇 년 더 오래된 것이다.
③ 남아있는 그것의 줄기에 있는 고리는 지름이 20cm밖에 되지 않았다.
④ 그것의 뿌리와 줄기는 고리의 성장 속도가 서로 달랐다.

---

36 내용파악 ④

"줄기의 많은 부분이 썩어서 없어진 상태였고, 가장 안쪽의 고리들은 대부분 사라져 있었다. 나무의 안쪽 고리들이 나이에 대한 중요한 정보를 가지고 있기 때문에, 그 나무의 열악한 상태는 연구원들이 그 나무의 나이를 알아내기 어렵게 만들었다."라는 내용을 통해 ④가 정답임을 알 수 있다.

연구원들이 이탈루스의 나이를 파악하는 데 어려움을 겪은 이유는 무엇인가?

① 그들은 그것의 위치에 접근하는 데 어려움을 겪었다.
② 방사성탄소 연대측정 분석에서 결정적이지 않은 결과가 나왔다.
③ 그들은 뿌리에서 샘플을 전혀 얻을 수 없었다.
④ 줄기의 상당 부분이 심하게 썩어 있었다.

37-38

방사성 동위원소인 폴로늄과 라듐을 발견한 폴란드계 프랑스인 물리학자 마리 퀴리(Marie Curie) 부인은 1차 세계대전 동안 연합군의 활동에 주목할 만한 공헌을 했다. 전쟁이 발발했을 때, 그녀는 자신이 하던 연구를 중단하고 사람들의 목숨을 구함으로써 조국이 싸움에서 승리하는 것을 돕겠다고 결심했다. 퀴리의 동료 노벨상 수상자인 빌헬름 뢴트겐(Wilhelm Roentgen)이 1895년에 발견한 X선은 빠르게 X선 기계의 개발로 이어졌다. 이러한 장치는 전쟁터에서 부상당한 군인들을 치료하기 위해 절실히 필요했지만, 대부분의 X선 기계는 대형 병원에서만 이용이 가능했다. 이러한 문제를 알게 된 퀴리는 해결책을 찾는 일에 자청하고 나서서, X선 기계가 설비돼 있는 방사선 자동차를 발명했다. 그 자동차에는 엔진이 X선 기계에 동력을 공급할 수 있게 하는 발전기뿐만 아니라 X선 사진을 현상할 수 있는 암실도 갖추고 있었다. 프랑스 군부가 그 자동차를 생산하는 데 필요한 자금의 지급을 미루자, 퀴리는 프랑스 여성연합에 의지했고, 그곳에서 성공적으로 자금을 확보했다. 그녀의 방사선 자동차 발명은 1914년 독일이 파리를 침공하는 것을 막는 데 결정적인 역할을 했던 전투인 1차 마르네(Marne) 전투 동안 부상당한 군인들을 치료하는 데 큰 도움을 주었다.

radioisotope n. 방사성 동위원소 notable a. 두드러진, 현저한; 유명한 contribution n. 기여, 공헌 conflict n. 전투, 분쟁 break out (전쟁·화재 따위가) 일어나다, 발발하다 discontinue v. 그만두다, 중지하다 laureate n. 계관 시인, 수상자 device n. 장치 desperately ad. 필사적으로, 절실하게 wounded a. 상처 입은, 부상당한 take it upon oneself to 자청해서 ~하다, 자기마음대로 ~하기로 결정하다 radiological a. 방사선의 equip v. 설비하다, 장비하다 generator n. 발전기 delay v. 지연시키다, 연기하다 obtain v. 얻다, 획득하다 invade v. 침입하다

---

37 내용파악 ①

"X선 기계가 설비돼 있는 방사선 자동차에는 발전기뿐만 아니라 X선 사진을 현상할 수 있는 암실도 갖추고 있었다."라고 돼 있으므로 ①이 정답이다. ② 발전기를 갖추고 있었다. ③ 군부는 자금 지원을 지연시켰다. ④ 마르네 전투에서 부상당한 군인들을 치료하는 데 도움을 주었으므로 발명된 것은 마르네 전투 이전이다.

다음 중 방사선 자동차와 관해 옳은 것은?
① 그것은 X선 기계와 암실을 모두 갖추고 있었다.
② 그것은 X선 기계에 자체적으로 전원을 공급할 수 없었다.
③ 그것은 프랑스 군부의 자금 지원으로 대량 생산되었다.
④ 그것은 1차 마르네 전투가 끝난 후에 완성되었다.

---

38 내용파악 ③

"X선 장치는 전쟁터에서 부상당한 군인들을 치료하기 위해 절실히 필요했지만, 대부분의 X선 기계는 대형 병원에서만 이용이 가능했던" 상황 때문에 이러한 장치를 갖추고 있는 자동차를 발명하게 되었다.

마리 퀴리가 방사선 자동차를 발명하게 된 계기는 무엇인가?
① 그녀는 한 여성단체로부터 이동식 X선 기계를 만들어 달라는 의뢰를 받았다.
② 그녀는 X선의 군사적 응용 방안을 연구하기 위해 군사적 지원을 받았다.
③ 그녀는 전쟁터에서 X선 기계에 대한 직접적인 접근이 부족하다는 것을 인식했다.
④ 그녀는 부상당한 군인들을 위한 병원 공간이 부족하다는 사실이 걱정스러웠다.

39-40

1986년, 멕시코는 가장 기억에 남는 월드컵 중의 하나가 된 대회를 개최했다. 대부분의 사람들은 아르헨티나 선수 디에고 마라도나(Diego Maradona)의 활약, 특히 그가 영국을 상대로 넣은 두 골로 인해 그 대회를 기억한다. 이 골들 중 첫 번째 골은 마라도나가 공을 자신의 손으로 골대 안으로 굴절시켜 넣는 악명 높은 부정행위로 인한 것이었다. 두 번째 골에서는 마라도나가 여러 명의 영국 선수들을 헤집고 들어가는 놀라운 기술을 선보였다. 대부분의 전문가들이 브라질이 대회에서 우승하는 쪽에 걸었지만, 마라도나의 활약으로 그의 팀은 결승까지 진출했고, 그들은 서독을 3-2로 꺾고 고국으로 우승 트로피를 가져갔다.
대회 시작 3년 전에 재정적인 이유로 개최를 철회한 콜롬비아를 멕시코가 대신한 것이었다는 점을 고려하면, 개최국으로서의 멕시코의 성공은 인상적이었다. 미국, 캐나다, 브라질이 서로 대신 개최하겠다고 경쟁적으로 나섰음에도 불구하고, 축구 기구인 FIFA는 멕시코를 개최국으로 결정했다. 이러한 결정은 미국을 매우 분하게 만들었으며, 미국은 FIFA의 선택에 부패가 개입한 낌새가 있다고 주장했다. 다른 국가들 또한 멕시코가 이전에 월드컵을 성공적으로 개최한 적이 있었음에도 불구하고 멕시코의 성공적인 개최 가능성에 의문을 제기하기도 했다. 대회 시작 8개월 전에 멕시코에 엄청난 지진이 발생했을 때에도 개최지를 이전하라는 요구가 있었다. 그러나 FIFA는 두 번째 개최지 이전을 하지 않기로 결정했다.

host v. 주최하다, 개최하다 memorable a. 기억할 만한, 잊지 못할 recall v. 상기시키다 flagrant a. 극악무도한, 언어도단의, 악명 높은 deflect v. 피하다; 굴절시키다 remarkable a. 주목할 만한, 현저한 weave v. 이리저리 빠져 나가다, 누비며 가다 pundit n. 전문가, 박식한 사람 back v. (경마 등에) 돈을 걸다 impressive a. 인상적인, 감동을 주는 given that ~임을 감안[고려]하면 stand-in n. 대리인(잠시 남의 일을 대신하는 사람); (영화에서 배우의) 대역 back out (하기로 했던 일에서) 빠지다, 철회하다 chagrin n. 유감, 억울함, 분함 smack of ~한 낌새가 있다 corruption n. 부패 viability n. 실행가능성 relocate v. 다시 배치하다, 이전시키다 devastating a. 파괴적인, 황폐화시키는

39 내용파악   ①

대부분의 전문가들이 브라질이 대회에서 우승하는 쪽에 걸었다고 했으므로 ①이 정답이다.

위 글에 의하면, 1986년 월드컵 우승 후보는 어느 팀이었는가?
① 브라질
② 멕시코
③ 잉글랜드
④ 서독

40 내용파악   ②

"FIFA가 멕시코를 개최국으로 정한 것은 미국을 매우 분하게 만들었으며, 미국은 FIFA의 선택에 부패가 개입한 낌새가 있다고 주장했다."라는 내용을 통해 ②를 정답으로 선택할 수 있다. ① 재정난으로 스스로 물러났다. ③ 이전에 월드컵을 성공적으로 개최한 적이 있다 ④ 지진에도 불구하고 개최지가 옮겨지지 않았다.

다음 중 1986년 월드컵에 관해 옳은 것은?
① 콜롬비아는 FIFA에 의해 개최국 자리에서 물러날 수밖에 없었다.
② 미국은 멕시코를 새로운 개최국으로 선택한 것을 비판했다.
③ 그 대회는 멕시코가 월드컵 개최국이 된 첫 무대였다.
④ 그 대회는 지진으로 인해 새로운 장소로 옮겨졌다.

2024 경찰대학(일반대학생 전형)

01 ①	02 ③	03 ①	04 ④	05 ②	06 ④	07 ①	08 ④	09 ④	10 ⑤
11 ③	12 ②	13 ③	14 ③	15 ④	16 ⑤	17 ④	18 ⑤	19 ③	20 ④
21 ①	22 ⑤	23 ⑤	24 ②	25 ②	26 ②	27 ③	28 ③	29 ②	30 ①
31 ④	32 ③	33 ④	34 ②	35 ③	36 ①	37 ⑤	38 ③	39 ③	40 ⑤

01 동의어 ①

cruel a. 잔인한, 무자비한 abase v. (지위·품격을) 떨어뜨리다, 비하(卑下)하다(= degrade) prosecute v. 기소[고발]하다; 수행하다 relieve v. (불쾌감·고통 등을) 없애[덜어] 주다 rejuvenate v. 다시 젊어 보이게 하다 sabotage v. (항의의 표시로 장비·운송 시설·기계 등을 고의로) 파괴하다

그 무자비한 독재자는 국민의 품격을 떨어뜨려, 가난과 두려움 속에서 살도록 강요했다.

02 동의어 ③

embellish v. 장식하다, 윤색하다; (이야기를) 과장을 섞어 재미있게 하다(= exaggerate) bravery n. 용기, 용감함 villain n. (이야기·연극 등의 중심인물인) 악당[악한] evilness n. 악, 불선(不善), 사악 refute v. 논박[반박]하다 hoax v. (특히 불쾌한 일에 대해) 거짓말[장난질]을 하다(= trick, deceive) invent v. 발명하다; (사실이 아닌 것을) 지어내다[날조하다](create or make up something, such as a story in order to trick people)

그 작가는 주인공의 용기와 악당의 사악함 같은 사실이 아닌 세부 내용들로 이야기를 윤색했다.

03 동의어 ①

minimum n. 최소한도; 극히 적은 양 agile a. (움직임이) 날렵한, 민첩한(= nimble) invasive a. 급속히 퍼지는, 침습성의 fashionable a. 유행하는 tricky a. (다루기) 까다로운, 힘든; 교묘한 dubious a. 의심하는; 수상쩍은

그들은 최소한의 노력과 소음으로 움직였으며, 가장 민첩하고 효율적인 방식으로 앉고, 걷고, 달릴 줄 알았다.

04 동의어 ④

soak v. (액체 속에) 담그다(= drench) bran n. (쌀·보리 등의) 겨, 밀기울 grind v. (곡식 등을 잘게) 갈다 sieve n. 체(가루·물 등을 거르는 데 쓰는 부엌 도구) flavor v. (음식물에) 풍미를 더하다 manipulate v. 조종하다 bake v. (음식을) 굽다 snitch v. (아이가 부모님·선생님에게) 일러바치다, 고자질하다

밀기울은 물에 담그거나 갈아서는 안 되지만 체나 바구니에 담아둘 수는 있다.

05 동의어 ②

fertility n. 번식력, 생산성 hybrid n. 잡종 govern v. 지배[좌우]하다 systematic a. 체계적인; <생물> 분류법의, 분류학상의 affinity n. 친족 관계, 유사성(= kinship)(a similarity of characteristics) management n. 경영, 관리 coordination n. 조직(화), 조화 communication n. 의사소통; 통신 mutation n. 돌연변이; 변화

이제 종(種) 간의 최초 교배와 이들로부터 생산된 잡종의 번식력은 그들의 분류학적 유사성에 의해 주로 좌우된다.

06 생활영어 ④

'탄소 배출량을 줄이기 위해 작은 변화부터 시작하자'라는 대화의 주된 취지를 고려할 때, A가 지역 환경단체에서 자원봉사를 하려는 것 역시 '참여를 통해 변화를 이루어 내려는' 의도임을 추론할 수 있다. 한편, ① 은 앞서 B가 한 말인 '기후 변화에 맞서 싸우기 위해 노력하는 조직을 지원하자'는 내용을 반복하는 것이므로 적절하지 않다. ②는 '지역 환경단체의 자원봉사자'가 할 수 있는 일이라기보다는 전문 과학자들의 영역이라고 볼 수 있으므로 적절하지 않다. ③은 앞서 언급된 내용이기도 하고, 굳이 '지역 환경단체의 자원봉사자'가 되지 않더라도 일상생활에서 실천할 수 있는 내용이므로 적절하지 않다. ⑤의 경우, '지역 환경단체'가 벌이는 캠페인의 일환으로 볼 수도 있겠지만, B의 '지역 환경단체를 위한 자원봉사'와 직접 연결하기에는 근거가 부족하다.

alarming a. 걱정스러운, 두려운 take action ~에 대해 조치를 취하다, 행동에 옮기다 footprint n. (무엇이) 차지하는 공간, 영향 carbon footprint 탄소 발자국(온실 효과를 유발하는 이산화탄소의 배출량) volunteer v. 자원하다, 자원봉사하다 get involved 관여하다, 참여하다 make a difference 변화를 가져오다, 영향을 주다

A: 최신 기후 변화 보고서에 대해 들었어? 정말 걱정스러워.
B: 그래, 나도 들었어. 기후 변화로 인한 최악의 영향을 막기 위해 조치를 취할 수 있는 시간이 10년도 채 안 남았다고 해.
A: 시간이 많지 않아. 나는 정말 미래가 걱정되기 시작해.
B: 동감이야. 무엇을 해야 할지 모르겠는 걸.
A: 탄소 배출량을 줄이기 위해 모두가 각자의 역할을 다해야 한다고 생각

해. 운전을 줄이고, 고기를 덜 먹고, 재활용을 늘리는 등, 작은 변화부터 시작할 수 있을 거야.

B: 그래, 그거 좋은 생각이야. 우리는 또 기후 변화에 맞서 싸우기 위해 노력하는 조직을 지원할 수도 있어.

A: 나는 지역 환경단체에서 자원봉사를 할 거야. 참여해서 변화를 이루어 내는 것이 중요하다고 생각해.

B: 훌륭해. 나는 내 생활 방식에 약간의 변화를 줄까 해. 더 자주 자전거를 타고 출근하고, 고기 먹는 걸 줄일 거야.

A: 정말 멋져! 작은 변화라도 우리가 할 수 있는 일을 하는 것이 중요하지.

① 기후 변화에 맞서 싸우는 사람들을 지지하다
② 기후 변화에 대한 과학적 증거를 수집하다
③ 탄소 배출량을 줄이다
④ 참여해서 변화를 이루어 내다
⑤ 사람들에게 기후 변화를 인식시키다

07 문맥상 적절한 표현 고르기 ①

Ⓐ '입양이 점점 더 어려워졌다'는 진술에 비추어 볼 때 해외 입양 역시 '급감했다'고 추론할 수 있다. Ⓑ 입양이 점점 더 어려워진 것은 입양하려는 부모들에 비해 아기를 포기하려는 엄마들의 숫자가 '줄어들기' 때문이라고 추론할 수 있다. Ⓒ 조정 절차는 예비 입양 부모들에게 '더 많은 발언권을 가질 수 있게' 한다고 한 것과 마찬가지로 입양하려는 부모들에게 유리하도록, 입양 절차의 속도도 '높여서' 입양 대기 기간을 줄여줄 것으로 추론할 수 있다.

adoption n. 입양 infant n. 유아 plummet v. 급락하다, 수직으로 떨어지다 augment v. 늘리다, 증가시키다 strict a. 엄격한 treaty n. 조약 domestic a. 국내의 voluntarily ad. 자발적으로 costly a. 많은 돈이 드는 waiting game 대기 전술[정책](행동을 취하지 않고 상황 전개를 지켜보는 것) foster v. (수양부모로서) 아이를 맡아 기르다, 위탁 양육하다 birth parent 친부모, 생부모 terminate v. 끝내다, 종료하다 intervention n. 조정, 중재 prospective a. 장래의, 장차의 have a say 발언권이 있다 reunite v. 재결합하다

미국에서의 입양은 점점 더 어려워졌는데, 특히 유아의 경우 더욱 그렇다. 최근 몇 년간 해외 입양은 다른 나라들의 더 엄격해진 정책과 국내 입양을 장려하려는 헤이그 협약으로 인해 급감했다. 국내적으로는, 자발적으로 아기를 포기하는 젊은 엄마들의 수가 줄어들고 있으며, 사설 기관을 통한 입양은 비용이 많이 드는 지구전이 되어버렸다. 이제 입양 전 위탁 양육이 일반적 선택이지만, 친권이 종결되기 전 친부모에게 기회를 주어야 한다는 법률적 요건으로 인해 이 역시 기나긴 과정이 될 수 있다. 조정 절차는 예비 입양 부모들이 입양 과정의 속도를 높이고 친가족의 재결합 여부에 대해 더 많은 발언권을 가질 수 있는 새로운 방법으로 등장했다.

08 문맥상 적절한 표현 고르기 ④

Ⓐ '위험한 거미가 사람을 문다'고 한다면 이는 사람들을 '걱정스럽게 만드는' 일이다. Ⓑ 두 가지 위험한 거미가 자주 발견되는 '나무 조각이나 쓰레기 등이 놓여있는' 공간은 '어지러운, 난잡한' 상태라고 표현할 수 있다. Ⓒ 이 두 가지 '위험한' 거미들은 '독이 있는' 거미들이라 할 수 있다.

worrisome a. 걱정스럽게 만드는, 걱정스러운 trashy a. 쓰레기 같은, 난잡한; (밭이) 먼저 작물의 마른 잎 따위로 뒤덮인 venomous a. 독이 있는 striking a. 눈에 띄는 identify v. (신원·정체를) 알아보다 field mark (식물·조류·곤충 등의 식별에 활용되는) 특징적 색깔과 무늬 field guide (식물·조류 등의) 휴대용 도감 hour-glass n. 모래시계, 수은시계 henceforward ad. 이후, 향후 innocuous a. 무해한, 위험하지 않은

거미에게 있는 걱정스러운 점은 그들이 사람을 문다는 것이다. 검은과부거미와 갈색은둔거미와 같은 몇몇 거미들은 실제로 위험하다. 뒷마당의 땅에 놓여있는 나무 조각이나 쓰레기 아래에서 검은과부거미를 발견할 수 있다. 갈색은둔거미는 집안에서, 특히 가구 뒤편 바닥에서 더 자주 발견된다. 다시 말해서, 뒷마당이 특별히 난잡하지 않다면 위험한 거미들에 관해 너무 걱정할 필요는 없을 것이다. 더욱이, 이 두 종류의 독거미들은 눈에 띄는 색깔과 무늬가 있기에 쉽게 식별할 수 있다. 만약 휴대용 거미 도감을 가졌다면, 가장 먼저 해야 할 일은 이 두 종을 찾아보고 검은과부거미의 "빨간 모래시계", 갈색은둔거미의 "바이올린" 같은 특징적 무늬를 확인한 다음, 앞으로 그런 무늬가 있는 거미들과는 거리를 두는 것이다.

09 문의 구성 ④

④가 들어있는 문장에서 the main hazards부터 food production까지가 that 관계대명사절의 수식을 받는 명사 주어이므로 그다음에는 시제를 가진 동사가 필요하다. 따라서 ④ stemming은 stem이 되어야 한다. 그리고 the fact와 동격인 that절 안에는 두 개의 절이 and로 연결되어 있다. ① being present는 분사구로서 앞서 나온 명사 a natural part of our diet를 수식하고 있는데, being은 생략 가능하다. ② If this is the case라는 절에서 접속사 if가 생략되고 is가 현재분사 being으로 변하여 분사구문이 되었는데, 주절의 주어와 다른 주어인 This는 남게 된 독립 분사구문이다. ③ where는 '~경우에'라는 의미의 '상황' 접속사이며 앞의 as는 '~처럼'이라는 의미의 '양태' 접속사이다. 양태 접속사 뒤에는 '주어+동사'가 생략되고 '전치사+명사구'(as in the city: 도시에서처럼)나 종속접속사의 부사절이 올 수 있는데, 여기서는 as it does(=the mere presence ~ poses a danger) where절에서 it does가 생략된 것이다. Sometimes the hole widens to let more light in, as when we enter a shadowy room.(어두운 방에 들어갈 때처럼 때때로 [눈의] 구멍이 넓어져서 더 많은 빛이 들어오게 한다.)도 같은 예다. ⑤ 명사 technology를 수식하는 분사구이고, 자동사이므로 과거분사가 아닌 현재분사로 표현한 것은 적절하다.

diet n. 식사, 음식, 식단 retain v. 보유하다 be derived from ~에서 유래하다 digest v. 소화하다 GE a. 유전적으로 조작된(= genetically engineered) antibiotic resistance (세균의) 항생 물질에 대한 내성, 항생제 내성 persist v. 집요하게 계속되다 hazard n. 위험 genetic engineering 유전공학 stem from ~에 기인[유래]하다 in the case of ~에 관하여는, ~에 관하여 말하면 imprecise a. 부정확한, 애매한 random a. 무작위의 incorporation n. 합체, 결합, 합동

DNA는 (과일, 채소, 고기 등과 같이) 온전한 세포들을 유지하는 식품이나 온전한 세포들로부터 유래하는 식품에 존재하는 우리 식단의 자연적인 부분이다. 그렇다고 한다면 우리는 GE(유전자 조작) 식품의 DNA도 아무런 건강상의 문제 없이 소화할 것으로 예상될 것이다. 따라서 GE 식품 내에 유전 물질이 단순히 존재한다는 것은, 예를 들어, 항생제 내성 유전자가 제품(식품) 내에 남아 있는 경우처럼 특수한 경우에만 위험이 되는 것으로 여겨질 것이다. 그러나, 식품 생산에 유전공학을 사용함으로써 발

생하는 주요 위험은, 유전공학이 자연적으로는 절대 발생하지 않을 유전자 조합을 만들어내고, 식물과 동물의 경우 유전공학은 새로운 유전자가 숙주 DNA 속으로 무작위적으로 통합되는 결과를 초래하는 부정확한 기술이라는 사실에서 비롯된다.

10 문의 구성 ⑤

The only tools라는 문장의 주어를 목적격 관계대명사 that이 생략된 관계절 Viking sailors needed가 수식하고 있다. 따라서 그다음에는 시제를 가진 동사가 필요하므로 ⑤ relating to는 were related to가 되어야 한다. ① were born이라는 과거 시점보다 더 앞선 시점의 사건을 나타내므로 대과거로 나타내었다. ② manage to do는 '~을 그럭저럭 해내다, 곧잘 ~하다'는 의미를 가진다. ③ rather than이라는 전치사구 다음에 동명사 형태가 적절하게 사용되었다. ④ 시제의 일치에 따라 과거 시제로 표현하였고, wish to do는 '~하기를 원하다, ~하고 싶어 하다'는 의미이다.

explorer n. 탐험가 navigate v. (바다·강 등을) 항해하다 compass n. 나침반 satellite n. (인공) 위성 radio n. 무선 장치 map v. ~의 지도를 만들다[그리다] indication n. 지시, 암시 recount v. (특히 자기가 경험한 것에 대해) 이야기하다[말하다] voyage n. 항해, 항행 sun-shadow board 태양-그림자판(바이킹들이 햇빛과 그림자를 활용하여 선박의 현재 위치를 예측하고 항로를 조절하는 데 사용했던 도구)

역사상 가장 위대한 탐험가들이 태어나기 전, 바이킹들은 이미 전 세계를 항해했다. 하지만 나침반도, 위성도, 무선 장치도 없었던 이 스칸디나비아 부족들은 어떻게 지구의 지도를 그토록 인상적으로 만들었는가? 대답은 예상보다 간단한데, 그것은 바로 경험이었다. 바이킹 항해자들은 장치에 의존하기보다 자연이 그들을 안내해 줄 것이라고 믿었다. 그들은 별과 태양의 위치를 연구했고, 바다의 색깔과 파도의 움직임을 통해 그들이 육지와 얼마나 가까이 있는지를 파악했다. 항해가 끝난 뒤 그들은 같은 여행을 하고 싶어 하는 사람들에게 자신들의 항해에 관한 이야기를 들려주었다. 이처럼 오래된 지혜가 여러 세대를 거치며 전해진 것이었다. 바이킹 선원들에게 필요한 유일한 도구는 태양과 관련된 것이었다. 예를 들어, 정오에는 태양-그림자판을 이용해 배가 항로를 따라 잘 가고 있는지를 확인했다.

11 정비문 ③

On the desk lies a book.처럼 장소 부사어가 문두에 오고 완전자동사이면 주어와 동사가 도치된다. 여기서 문두에 유도부사 There를 사용하면 장소 부사어는 주어 뒤로 가서 There lies a book on the desk.가 된다. ③에서 prevailed가 lies와 같은 완전자동사이고 in all the schools가 장소 부사어이고 이하 전부가 주어인데, 주어가 길어서 뒤로 간 것이다. 따라서 it을 there로 고쳐야 한다. ① associated는 과거분사로 수동의 의미를 갖고 that절의 주어 costs를 적절히 수식하고 있다. that절의 본동사는 exceed이다. ② 주어 reforms, 타동사 confirm, 타동사의 목적어 the existence로 구성된 문장이다. 한편, 전치사구 between A and B 형태의 수식을 명사 relation이 받고 있다. ④ 'with+목적어+보어'의 부대상황 분사구문에서 보어에 해당하는 분사구 being focused가 적절히 사용되었다. ⑤ 이 문장에서 should는 법조동사로서 '(아마, 틀림없이) ~일 것이다'는 의미로 예상·추측을 나타낸다.

coordination n. 조직(화), 조정, 조화 arrangement n. 준비; 합의, 협의 exceed v. 넘다, 초과하다 reform n. 개혁 confirm v. 사실임을 보여주다 vital a. 생명에 필수적인 prevail v. 만연[팽배]하다, 보급되다 extraordinary a. 비범한, 대단한 reverence n. 숭상, 공경 preceptor n. 지도 교사, 스승 timely a. 시기적절한, 때맞춘 regarding prep. ~에 관하여[대하여] undergo v. (특히 변화·안 좋은 일 등을) 겪다[받다]

① 정책 전문가들은 조직간 합의와 관련된 조정 비용이 종종 이익을 초과한다고 오랫동안 주장해 왔다.
② 역사 교육 분야의 교육 개혁은 현재의 사회적 관심과 학습 과정 사이에 매우 중요한 관계가 존재한다는 것을 확실히 해준다.
③ 그 시절, 알렉산더 대왕의 스승인 아리스토텔레스의 저술에 대한 매우 특별한 경외심이 모든 학파에 널리 퍼져 있었다.
④ 사람들의 관심이 그 사건에 집중되고 있어서, 그것에 관한 나의 조사 결과를 게시하는 것이 시기적절해 보인다.
⑤ 지표면 전체에 관한 정보를 얻을 수 있다면, 지구가 거의 언제나 충격을 받고 있다는 사실을 발견하게 될 것이다.

12 정비문 ②

spend 동사는 '어떤 일을 하는 데에[어떤 일에, ~하기 위해] 돈, 시간, 노력 등을 쓴다'는 의미를 가지고 있다. 여기서 '돈, 시간, 노력 등'은 spend 동사의 목적어로 표현되고 '어떤 일을 하는 데에'는 '(in) ~ing'로, '어떤 일(것)에'는 'on 명사'로, '~하기 위해'는 'to 동사원형'으로 표현된다. '~하기 위해'의 경우로 to develop ~로 표현되었으므로 ②는 어법상 옳은 문장이다. ① cranes는 '길러진'이라는 수동의 의미로 수식되어야 하므로 현재분사 keeping을 과거분사 kept로 바꾸어야 한다. ③ when it comes to는 '~라면, ~에 대해서[관해서]라면'이라는 의미를 갖는다. 그러므로 When there comes to the effects의 there를 it으로 바꾼다. ④ be master of가 '~에 정통하다'라는 의미의 표현이므로 master 다음에 of를 넣어야 한다. ⑤ well이라는 부사를 수식하려면 what이 아닌 부사 how여야 하므로 No matter how로 바꾸어야 한다.

crane n. 학, 두루미 keep v. (동물을) 기르다[치다] captivity n. 감금, 억류 nobility n. 귀족 entice v. 유도하다 when it comes to ~라면, ~에 대해서[관해서]라면 meteorologist n. 기상학자 ventilate v. 환기하다 nursery n. 탁아소, 놀이방, 보육원 unmodified a. 수정되지 않은

① 중국 귀족들에 의해 감금되어 길러진 학들에 대한 기록은 2000년 이상 전으로 거슬러 올라간다.
② 식품 산업은 우리로 하여금 더 많은 음식을 구매하도록 유혹하는 제품, 포장, 광고 및 마케팅 기술을 개발하기 위해 매년 수십억 달러를 쓴다.
③ 지구 온난화가 날씨 추세에 미치는 영향에 관해서라면, 점점 더 많은 기상학자들 사이에 더 많은 동의가 이루어지고 있다.
④ 그가 무엇에 정통한지에 대해 질문을 받았을 때 그는 자신은 단지 "철학자" 즉, "지혜를 사랑하는 사람"일 뿐이라고 답했다.
⑤ 탁아소의 환기가 아무리 잘 되더라도 생후 6주가 넘은 모든 어린이에게는 조절되지 않은(자연 상태 그대로의) 외부 공기가 필요하다.

13 빈칸완성 ③

Ⓐ traverse는 단순히 '~을 가로지르다(move across ~)'인 의미인 반면, transgress는 '~의 한계를 넘어서다(go beyond the limits of ~)'는 의미이다. 문맥상 일종의 '(수용 가능한) 한계점'인 '티핑포인트[임계점]'를 '넘어서다'는 의미가 필요하므로 transgress가 적절하다. Ⓑ 문맥상 '~ 위험을 완충하다(to lessen the harmful effects of ~)'는 의미가 필요하므로 buffer가 들어가는 것이 적절하다. Ⓒ push ~ over the edge가 '~로 하여금 한계에 이르게 하다(= make ~ reach ~'s limit), 더 이상 버틸 수 없게 하다'는 의미의 표현이므로 edge가 적절하다.

tip v. (어떤 것이 어느 방향으로 가도록) 살짝 건드리다 tipping point 티핑포인트(작은 변화들이 어느 정도 기간을 두고 쌓여, 이제 작은 변화 하나만 더 일어나도 갑자기 큰 영향을 초래할 수 있는 상태가 된 단계) irreversible a. (이전 상태로) 되돌릴[철회할] 수 없는 collapse n. 붕괴 drastic a. 과감한; 급격한 urgent a. 긴급한 buffer v. (충격을) 완화하다, 완충하다(to lessen the harmful effects of ~) confront v. 정면으로 부딪치다 head-on ad. 정면으로 groundwater n. 지하수 depletion n. 고갈 debris n. 잔해, 쓰레기 official n. 공무원

인류는 이미 돌이킬 수 없는 불안정성, 즉 생태적, 제도적 시스템의 완전한 붕괴를 초래할 수 있는 세계적인 다중적 "티핑포인트(임계점)"를 넘어서는 과정에 있다고 유엔 보고서가 수요일 경고했다. 독일 본(Bonn)에 있는 유엔 대학교 환경 및 인간 안보 연구소의 3차 연례 상관적 재난 위험 보고서는 사회학적 시스템이 더 이상 위험을 완충할 수 없을 때, 6가지 문제에 대하여 긴급한 조치를 취하지 않으면 급격한 변화가 일어날 것이라는 것을 발견했다. 캘리포니아가 정면으로 직면하고 있는 티핑포인트들에는 지하수 고갈, 보험 비용 상승, 극심한 더위, 생물 종(種) 멸종 등, 여러 문제들이 포함돼 있다. 나머지 위협으로는 녹고 있는 빙하, 우주 잔해가 있다. UN 관계자에 따르면, "한 시스템이 무너지면 다른 시스템들도 더 이상 버틸 수 없게 될지도 모른다."

14 빈칸완성 ③

Ⓐ 필자는 폐의 활동이 강한가 혹은 약한가에 관해 이야기하고 있는데, 이는 곧 '호흡(respiration)'을 가리킨다. Ⓑ 호흡이 '강하고 활동적인(strong and active)' 것과 대조되는 상태를 기술하고 있으므로 '아주 약한(feeble)'이라는 표현이 필요하다. Ⓒ 혈액이 힘찬 호흡을 통해 지속적으로 '충전(charge)'되지 않는다면 신체의 기관들은 산소 공급이 부족해져 '정체될(stagnate = not be active)' 것이다.

lung n. 폐, 허파 calmness n. 고요, 평온, 침착 dignity n. 위엄, 품위 in proportion to ~와 비례하여 tranquility n. 평온함, 차분함, 평정 respiration n. 호흡 boldness n. 배짱, 대담 feeble a. 아주 약한 debility n. 쇠약 out of spirits 기가 죽어, 맥없이 out of breath 숨이 가쁜 animate v. 생기를 불어넣다 joyous a. 아주 기뻐하는 vivify v. ~에 생기를 주다 proof n. 증거 charge v. 충전하다; ~으로 채우다 column n. 기둥, 원주 organ n. (인체 내의) 장기[기관] stagnate v. 침체되다(= become stagnant) perspiration n. 발한 (작용); 땀; 노력 inspiration n. 영감 energetic a. 정력적인, 활기에 찬 endure v. 견디다, 인내하다

이제부터 우리는 호흡에 비례해 살아간다는 것을 이해할 수 있게 된다. 어린이의 활동은 폐의 힘과 밀접한 관계가 있으며, 어른의 침착함, 위엄, 힘은 그의 호흡의 깊이와 평온함에 비례한다. 폐가 강하고 활동적이면 용기와 배짱이 생긴다. 호흡이 약하면 비겁해지고 쇠약해진다. 기운이 없다는 것은 숨이 가쁘다는 것이다. 활력이 넘치고 즐겁다는 것은 호흡이 충만하다는 것이다. 호흡은 실제로 생기를 주는 행위이며, 느껴지는 호흡에 대한 욕구는 실제 생명에 대한 갈망이며, 적절한 힘으로 혈관을 지속적으로 충전하지 않는다면 다른 모든 중요한 기관들이 바로 정체되어 버리고, 완전히 활동을 중단할 것이라는 증거이다.

15 문장삽입 ④

주어진 문장에서 '이 방대한 조직, 근력 및 이동성의 시스템(this vast system of tissue, strength and mobility)'은 '근골격계'를 가리키고 있다. 따라서 주어진 문장은 근골격계를 일반적으로 소개하는 내용 다음에 있으면서, 근육의 개수에 대해 구체적으로 진술하는 내용 바로 앞에 들어가는 것이 적절하다. 특히 ④ 다음에 나오는 '그 대답(the answer)'이 가리키는 것은 주어진 문장에서 던지는 근육 개수 질문에 대한 대답임을 알 수 있다.

wondrous a. 경이로운, 경탄스러운 intricate a. 복잡한 blood vessel n. 혈관 encircle v. 둘러싸다[두르다] trillion n. 1조 scent n. 냄새, 향기 billion n. 10억 lifespan n. 수명 musculoskeletal a. 근골격의, 근육과 골격의[에 관한] ligament n. 인대 tendon n. 힘줄, 건(腱) connective tissue 결합 조직 countless a. 무수한, 셀 수 없이 많은 mobility n. 이동성, 기동성 straightforward a. 간단한 DVM 수의학 박사(= Doctor of Veterinary Medicine) discrepancy n. (같아야 할 것들 사이의) 차이[불일치] anatomist n. 해부학자 distinct a. 뚜렷이 다른, 별개의

인체는 경이로운 것이다. 특히 각 신체 시스템이 얼마나 복잡하고 효율적인지 고려할 때 더욱 그렇다. 예를 들어, 성인 한 사람의 혈관을 끝에서 끝까지 모두 연결하면 지구 둘레를 2번 반이나 에워쌀 수 있다. 인간의 코는 1조가 넘는 다양한 냄새를 인식할 수 있다. 인간의 심장은 평생 30억 번 이상 박동한다. 그러나 신체의 시스템 중에서도 가장 인상적인 것은 근골격계와 그것을 구성하는 근육, 인대, 뼈, 힘줄 및 결합 조직들이다. 이 근골격계 덕분에 우리는 매일 아침 침대에서 일어나 학교로, 일하러 가거나 놀러 갈 수 있고 그에 수반되는 무수히 많은 활동과 동작을 자유롭게 행할 수 있다. <그렇다면 이 방대한 조직, 근력 및 이동성의 시스템을 구성하는 근육은 모두 몇 개인가?> 수의학 박사인 제임스 스몰리가(James Smoliga)는 그 대답이 사람들의 생각만큼 간단하지 않다는 것이 밝혀지고 있다고 말한다. 일부 전문가는 신체에 600개에 가까운 근육이 있다고 말하고, 다른 전문가는 840개라고 말하는 등, "근육의 숫자는 다양합니다."라고 그는 설명한다. "특정 근육을 여러 부분으로 구성된 하나의 근육으로 보아야 할지, 여러 개의 서로 다른 근육으로 보아야 할지를 판단하는 방식이 해부학자들마다 다르기" 때문에 이러한 불일치가 존재한다고 그는 말한다.

16 문장삽입 ⑤

'마스타바 → 피라미드 → 바위 무덤'으로 변화했던 이집트 권력자들의 무덤 양식의 변화를 기술하고 있는 글이다. 주어진 문장은 '엄청난 비용과 석재 조달의 어려움'이라는 기념물(피라미드) 건설의 단점을 밝히고

있으므로, 또 다른 단점인 쉽게 도굴될 수 있다는 점을 언급한 문장 앞인 ⑤에 들어가는 것이 적절하다. 그 경우에는, 이런 단점들로 인해 피라미드보다는 '바위를 파서 매장하는 대안적 양식의 무덤들이 더 흔해졌다'는 진술에 잘 연결된다.

mastaba n. 고대 이집트의 석실 분묘, 마스타바(돌·벽돌로 만든 귀인의 분묘) scavenge v. (먹을 것 등을 찾아) 쓰레기 더미를 뒤지다 come up with ~을 제시[제안]하다 stack v. 쌓다[포개다] ascend v. 오르다, 올라가다 BCE 기원전(= before the Common Era) magnificent a. 웅장한 monument n. 기념물 not to mention ~은 말할 것도 없고[물론이고] gravedigger n. 도굴꾼

고대 이집트 초기, 파라오들과 사회의 다른 부유한 구성원들은 마스타바(석실 분묘)에 묻혔다. 이 마스타바는 경사진 측면을 가진 지붕이 평평한 직사각형 구조였는데, 시신을 훼손하는 동물들이나 도둑으로부터 무덤을 보호하는 데 도움이 되었다. 그러나 제3왕조 시대 임호텝(Imhotep)이라는 건축가는 다수의 마스타바를 층층이 쌓아 여러 개의 '계단들'로 이루어진 훨씬 더 높은 구조물을 만들어 내는 아이디어를 생각해 냈다. 이것은 사자(死者)가 하늘로 올라갈 수 있도록 계단 역할을 하는 것이었다. 이렇게 만들어진 첫 번째 구조물이 조세르의 피라미드(Pyramid of Djoser)라고 불리는 것으로서 기원전 2680년경에 지어졌다. 그 후 수백 년 동안 피라미드는 파라오 무덤의 표준이 되었고, 결국 측면은 계단식으로 남아 있지 않고 매끄러워지게 되었다. <왕들과 왕비들은 가장 높고 가장 웅장한 기념물들을 건설하기 위해 경쟁했지만, 비용이 많이 들었다. 기념물들을 짓기 위해서는 엄청난 노동 비용은 물론이고 어마어마한 양의 돌이 필요했다.> 피라미드들은 또한 도굴꾼들의 손쉬운 표적이었다. 제7왕조 시대가 되면, 파라오들은 바위를 깊이 파서 만든 무덤에 묻히는 일이 더 흔해졌다.

---

17 단락배열 ④

'가정 내 응급 병원 치료' 프로그램의 개요를 설명하는 글이다. 이 프로그램이 작동하는 개념을 기술하고 있으므로 그다음에 C 환자의 병원 이송 및 판정 → A (가정 내 응급 병원 치료 대상으로 판정되면) 집으로 이송되어 전문가와 만남 → B '가정 내 응급 병원 치료'에 활용되는 장비들 소개"의 순서로 이어지는 것이 적절하다. 다시 말해, 제시된 글에서 언급된 program에 대해 정확하게 설명한 C, 그다음에 C 끝의 if they'd be a good fit에 대한 긍정적인 답의 경우를 설명한 A, 그다음에 A 끝부분의 everything they need에 해당하는 것을 구체적으로 밝혀 설명한 B로 이어지게 된다.

roll something out (반죽 같은 것을) 밀어서 펴다; (신상품을) 출시하다 flavor n. (독특한) 풍미; (물건·사람의) 특징, 특색; 특정 형태나 종류의 것들 overcrowding n. 과밀 intensify v. 심해지다 baby boomer n. (특히 2차 세계대전 후의) 베이비 붐 세대의 사람 regulatory a. 규정하는, 단속하는 ER n. (병원의) 응급실(= emergency room) inpatient n. 입원환자 unit n. (특히 병원의) 부서[과] screen v. (적절한지) 확인하다[거르다] on board 탑승한 monitor v. 추적 관찰하다 turf n. (자신의 집·직장이 있는) 자기 지역, 근거지 24/7 a. 연중무휴의 ad. 하루 24시간 1주 7일 동안, 1년 내내, 언제나 cuff n. (혈압 측정기의) 가압대(加壓帶) pulse oximeter 펄스옥시미터(혈액의 산소포화도를 비혈관적으로 측정하는 기기)

전국의 병원과 의료 시스템은 다양한 특색의 "가정 내 응급 병원 치료" 프로그램들을 선보이고 있는데, 이는 환자들의 경험을 개선하고, 베이비붐

세대가 노년에 접어들면서 점점 더 심화할 것으로 예상되는 병원 과밀 및 병상 부족 현상을 줄이기 위한 전국적 캠페인의 일환이다.
C 프로그램의 정확한 작동 방식은 규제 문제에 기초하여 병원마다, 주마다 다를 수 있다. 그러나 일반적으로, 환자가 응급실 또는 입원환자 병동에 도착하면 (가정 내 응급 병원 치료에) 적합한지를 검사받는다.
A 만약 적합하다면, 환자는 차에 태워져 집으로 "이송"되는데, 환자의 주거지역에서 환자를 추적 관찰하는 데 필요한 모든 것을 설치해 주는 전문가를 만나게 된다.
B 여기에는 버튼 하나만 누르면 연중무휴 24시간 지원되는 원격 진료팀의 영상 문진용 4세대 이동통신 태블릿, 진료팀과 직접 연결되는 전화, 생체 신호 추적용 착용 장비, 혈압 체크용 가압대, 펄스옥시미터, 비상경보용 목걸이 등등이 포함된다.

---

18 단락배열 ⑤

주어진 문장에서 '의학적 문제를 가진 아동'이라고 했던 내용이 C에서 '특별한 도움이 필요한 아동'으로 재진술 및 상술(詳述)되고 있다. C에서 제기된 이 아동들에 대한 돌봄, 즉 '간병인'의 문제가 상술되는 B가 그 뒤에 이어지고, 이들 '가족 간병인'에 대한 지원이 거의 이루어지지 않는 현실을 지적하는 A가 마지막에 오는 것이 적절하다.

advocacy group (특정 운동의) 활동 그룹, 시민 단체 asthma n. 천식 cerebral palsy 뇌성 마비 retardation n. 지연, 지체 caregiver n. 간병인, (병자·불구자·아이들을) 돌보는 사람 tip one's hat to 모자를 조금 올려 ~에게 인사하다, 경의를 표하다 rhetorical a. 미사여구식의 legislation n. (의회에서 통과되는) 제정법 languish v. 약화되다, (진전이) 시들해지다 relief n. (고통·불안 등의) 경감[완화, 제거]

시민 단체인 Family Voices에 따르면, 미국 내에서 1,200만 명이 넘는 아동이 천식에서부터 뇌성 마비에 이르는 의학적 문제를 갖고 있다고 한다.
C 미국 보건복지부에서는 정신 지체 및 발달 장애를 가진 2백만 명을 포함, 특별한 도움이 필요한 아동의 숫자가 약 400만 명에 달하는 것으로 추산한다. 이 아이들을 누가 다 돌보는가?
B 많은 경우에, 가족 식구가 일차적인 간병인이다. 이는 국가적 문제다. 2,500만 명 이상의 미국인들이 배우자, 부모, 자녀를 돌보는 가족 간병인이다.
A 하지만 그들은 인정도, 지원도 거의 받지 못한다. 대통령이 미사여구를 동원해 가며 가족 간병인들에게 경의를 표했지만, 그들의 부담을 얼마간 줄이는 데 도움을 줄 법률제정은 여전히 의회에서 지지부진하며, 조만간 그런 지원이 있을 것을 기대하는 이는 아무도 없다.

---

19 문맥상 적절하지 않은 문장 고르기 ③

흑사병으로 인한 대규모 인구 감소로 인해 노동력의 가치가 치솟자 봉건 영주들의 부와 권력, 나아가 체제 전체가 붕괴하고 그 와중에 중산층이 출현하였다는 내용이 소개되고 있다. 그런데 '봉건 제도가 중세 사회의 불균형 구조에 대한 유추적 역할을 제공한다'는 ③의 진술은 글 전체의 흐름과 무관하다.

Black Death 흑사병 breakdown n. 고장, 파손; 붕괴 feudal a. 봉건 제도의 peasant n. 소작농 dwindle v. (점점) 줄어들다 work the land 땅을 경작하다 analogy n. 비슷함; 유추 medieval a. 중세의

in a bid to do ~하기 위하여, ~을 겨냥하여 diet n. 식사, 식습관 emergence n. 출현, 발생

14세기에 흑사병이 유럽 전역으로 퍼져 나가 약 5천만 명이 사망했다. 이 일로 사회는 영원히 변했다. 이러한 변화들 중 하나가 봉건 체제의 붕괴라고 주장되어왔다. 농민의 수가 점점 줄어들면서 영주들의 부와 권력의 주요 원천이자 봉건 체제의 토대였던 땅을 경작할 사람들의 숫자도 줄어들었다. <그럼에도 불구하고 봉건제도는 중세 사회의 불균형 구조에 대한 유추적 역할을 한다.> 그 치명적인 질병에서 살아남은 사람들은 죽은 자들이 남기고 간 땅으로부터, 그리고 노동의 대가로 더 높은 임금을 요구함으로써, 부자가 될 기회를 잡았다. 돈이 많아진 하층 계급이 사회의 상류 계급처럼 옷을 입을 수 있게 되자 1363년에 이러한 추세를 막기 위한 법률이 나왔다. 이 법은 사회 각계각층의 의복과 식습관을 제한하였지만 강제할 방법이 없었으며, 이로 인해 중산층이 출현하게 되었다는 지적이 있다.

20 문맥상 적절하지 않은 문장 고르기 ④

필자는 사물의 일반성(보편성), 추상성에 관심을 갖는 '자연과학자'와 사건의 특수성, 구체성에 관심을 갖는 '역사가' 사이의 연구 대상의 차이를 대조적으로 기술하고 있다. ④의 진술은 '역사가는 어떤 특정한 역사적 사건을 초래한 단 하나의 보편적, 절대적 원인을 찾는다'는 의미이다. 이는 본문의 취지를 고려해볼 때 역사가가 아니라 오히려 자연과학자의 목적에 가까우므로 전체 문맥에 부적절하다.

convert v. 전환시키다 proceed v. 진행하다 particular n. 개개의 일, 사항, 조목 genial a. 친절한, 다정한 deduce v. 연역하다, 추론하다 kinship n. 친족 관계, 혈족 관계; 유사(성)

자연과학과 역사의 구별은 사실을 지식으로 전환하려는 지점에서 시작된다. 여기서 우리는 전자는 법칙을 정립하려 하고, 후자는 사건들을 묘사하려 한다는 것을 알 수 있다. 전자의 경우에는 사고(思考)가 세부 사항에 대한 기술(記述)로부터 일반적 관계로 나아간다. 후자의 경우에는 개별 사물이나 사건에 대한 온화한 서술을 고수한다. 자연과학자에게는 반복될 수 없는 연구의 대상은 그 자체로 가치가 없다. 하나의 유형으로 간주될 수 있거나, 이러한 유형이 추론될 수 있는 어떤 부류의 특수한 사례로 간주될 수 있는 경우에 한해서만 연구의 대상은 자연과학자의 목적에 부합한다. 자연과학자는 일반 법칙을 밝히는 데 도움이 되는 특징들을 단일 사례 안에서 관찰할 수 있는 한에서만 단일 사례를 고려한다. <이에 반하여, 역사가는 어떤 역사적 사건을 초래한 단 하나의 정확한 원인을 찾아야 한다.> 역사가의 과제는 과거의 어떤 사건을 최대한 상세하게 되살려 내어 현재에 소환하는 것이다. 역사가의 목표는 예술가가 상상의 대상을 위해 하고자 하는 바로 그것을 실제 사건을 위해 행하는 것이다. 바로 여기에서 우리는 역사와 예술, 역사가와 문학 작가 사이의 유사성을 인식하게 된다. 자연과학이 추상적인 것을 강조하고 이에 반해 역사가는 주로 구체적인 것에 관심을 갖는 것은 바로 이러한 이유 때문이다.

21 빈칸완성 ①

오늘날 마녀를 떠올릴 때 자동적으로 연상되는 검은색 드레스와 망토 등 이른바 '마녀의 표준 복장'은 나중에 검은색이 악마, '흑마법'을 연상시킴으로 인한 편견의 결과일 뿐, 처음에는 복장으로 그들을 일반들과 구별하기는 쉽지 않았을 것이라고 말하는 글이다. 구체적으로 빈칸

다음의 진술이 "그러나 이런 옷들이 마녀와 연관되기까지 오랜 시간이 걸리지 않았다."인데, '그러나'로 연결된 점에 주목하면 정답을 추론할 수 있다. 한편, 빈칸 앞에 부정을 나타내는 not이 있으므로 ⑤는 정답이 될 수 없다.

witch n. 마녀 wardrobe n. (한 개인이 가지고 있는) 옷 costume n. 의상, 복장 cloak n. 망토(소매가 없이 어깨 위로 걸쳐 둘러 입도록 만든 외투) robe n. 가운, 길고 헐거운 겉옷 functional a. 기능 위주의 hood n. 두건, (외투 등에 달린) 모자 garment n. 의복, 옷 affiliate v. 연계되다 association n. 연관, 연상

『오즈의 마법사(The Wizard of Oz)』의 착한 마녀 글린다(Glinda)와 『호커스 포커스(Hocus Pocus)』의 샌더슨(Sanderson) 자매는 화려한 옷들을 갖고 있었지만, 마녀의 표준 복장은 일반적으로 검은 드레스, 망토 또는 가운이다. "역사적으로, 여성 치유사들, 그리고 나중에 마녀로 불리게 될 또 다른 사람들은 마을 공동체의 모든 사람들이 입던 것과 같은 옷, 즉 기능성을 강조한 수제 옷들을 입곤 했습니다."라고 라스베가스 소재 네바다 대학 영어과 조교수인 캐서린 워커(Katherine Walker)는 말한다. "중세 시대나 그 이후에, 이들 옷의 특징은 망토나 후드였습니다. 그러므로 마녀들이 처음에는 복장 면에서 이웃 사람들과 시각적으로 구별되지 않았을 가능성이 매우 높습니다." 그러나 이런 옷들이 마녀와 연관되기까지 오랜 시간이 걸리지 않았다. "특히 검은색 드레스와의 연관성은 검은색이 악마 및 '흑마법'을 연상시킨 결과일 것입니다."라고 워커는 설명한다.

① 이웃 사람들과 시각적으로 구별되다
② 이웃 사람들의 비판에 취약하다
③ 이웃 사람들에게 해를 끼치려는 의도이다
④ 이웃 사람들만큼 검소하다고 여겨지다
⑤ 이웃 사람들과 의상이 동일하다

22 빈칸완성 ⑤

알제리, 북베트남과 같은 비유럽 약소민족이 프랑스, 미국 같은 범유럽 계열의 초강대국들을 상대로 승리할 수 있었던 것은 모두 비유럽 민족들의 자주독립을 위한 '지역적 투쟁(a local struggle)'이 '반식민주의적인 공감대와 지지' 속에서 '세계적 대의(a global cause)'로 확장될 수 있었기 때문이라고 말하는 글이다. 따라서 빈칸에는 범유럽 계열 초강대국들의 패배의 조건이 들어가야 하므로 '지역적 항쟁이 세계적 대의가 되다'는 내용이 들어가는 것이 적절하다. 이 글에서 cause는 '대의명분', 즉 '어떤 일을 꾀하는 데 내세우는 합당한 구실이나 이유'를 뜻한다.

hegemony n. 패권, 지배권 prevail v. 승리하다, 이기다 anti-colonial a. 반식민주의의 work out ~을 이해하다, 만들어내다 harness v. 이용하다 cause n. (정치·사회적 운동) 대의명분, 이상 inflict v. (괴로움 등을) 가하다, 안기다 colossus n. 거인, 거대한 것

20세기가 되어서야 비로소 비유럽 문화권들은 세계적 시각을 채택하였다. 이는 유럽의 패권을 붕괴시킨 결정적인 요인들 가운데 하나였다. 알제리 독립전쟁(1954~62)에서 알제리 게릴라들은 압도적인 수적, 기술적, 경제적 우위를 점하고 있었던 프랑스군을 격파하였다. 알제리인들이 승리할 수 있었던 것은 전 세계적인 반식민주의 네트워크의 지원을 받았고, 자신들의 대의를 위해 프랑스 자체의 여론은 물론 세계의 미디어를 활용하는 방법을 강구해냈기 때문이다. 작은 북베트남이 미국이라는 거인에게 안겼던 패배 역시 유사한 전략에 기초한 것이었다. 이들 게릴라 세력들은 지역적 항쟁이 세계적 대의가 되면 초강대국도 패배할 수 있음을 보여주었다.

① 그들의 전략은 적에게 노출되었다
② 이전 침략으로부터 교훈을 얻지 못했다
③ 그들에게는 잘 훈련된 엘리트 부대가 없었다
④ 그들은 치열한 전투에서 적과 교전했다
⑤ 지역적 항쟁이 세계적 대의가 되었다

23 빈칸완성   ⑤

(취업) 면접에서 지원자는 '직무에 대한 이해도와 업무 수행 능력을 증명'하는 것도 중요하지만 태도와 표정, 유머 감각 등 이른바 '품행/품성(demeanor)'을 통해 그 직장 사람들과 얼마나 '잘 어울릴지', 얼마나 '적합할지'를 보여주는 것이 중요하다고 말하는 글이다. 따라서 ⑤가 빈칸에 적절하다. 한편, 본문 앞부분에서 언급된 '열정(enthusiastic)'은 일반적인 '품성'의 영역에 속한다. 그런데 ④는 그러한 일반적인 품성에 대해 '까다로운 일 앞에서도 얼마나 열정적인가'라는 특수한 경우로 한정시켜 진술하는 오류를 범하고 있다. 반면, ③은 일반적 품성의 한 특수한 예인 '유머 감각'을 너무 일반화하는 오류를 범하고 있다.

temporary a. 일시적인 assignment n. 배정, 배치 enthusiastic a. 열정적인 associate n. (사업·직장) 동료 strike out (어떤 목표나 기회를) 실패하다, 놓치다 demeanor n. 처신, 거동, 몸가짐, 품행

면접을 위해서건, 일시적인 업무 배정을 위해서건 당신이 첨단기술 직장에 발을 들여놓는다면, 한 가지 명심해야 할 것이 있다. 당신은 주로 당신의 태도에 따라 평가받을 것이라는 점이 그것이다. 첨단기술 종사자들은 열정적이고 열정적임을 드러내 보이는 사람을 좋아한다. 이런 얘기가 진부하게 들린다면 미안하지만, 그건 사실이다. 긍정적인 태도, 미소, 유머 감각 이런 것들은 당신이 그런 직장에 들어갈 때 경이롭게 작용한다. 당신이 어떤 일자리를 위해 면접을 할 때, 당신은 채용 담당자뿐만 아니라 세 명 내지 여섯 명의 다른 사람들도 함께 만나게 될 것인데, 그들은 보통 당신이 채용된다면 함께 일할 미래의 동료들이다. 이들은 주로 "적합성"이라는 것으로 당신을 판단할 것이다. 물론, 당신은 똑똑해야 하고, 당신이 직무를 이해하고 그것을 수행할 수 있다는 것을 증명해야 한다. 그러나 그 모든 것을 잘 해내더라도 "적합성" 문제로 실패할 수 있다. 면접에서 당신이 보이는 태도와 품행으로 '당신이 그 집단에 얼마나 잘 적합할 것인가'라는 문제를 해결하게 될 것으로 기대된다.

① 당신이 미래의 직장에서 얼마나 잘 수행할 것인지
② 당신이 당신의 상사에게 얼마나 정중하게 대응할 것인지
③ 당신이 직장에서 얼마나 유머러스한지
④ 당신이 까다로운 일에도 얼마나 열정적인지
⑤ 당신이 그 집단에 얼마나 잘 적합할 것인지

24 빈칸완성   ②

이 글은 지구 이외의 다른 행성이나 지구 안의 극한 환경에서 생명체가 존재할 가능성에 대해 말하고 있다. 인간의 편견과 제한된 지식으로 인해 이른바 극한의 환경 속에서 생명체가 존재할 가능성 자체를 부정하는 것은 잘못되었다는 주장을 함축하고 있다. 빈칸을 포함한 문장은 '지하 동굴처럼 빛이 없는 극한의 어두운 환경에서도 적응하여 생존하기 위해 신체(기관)를 변화시킨 동물과 식물이 발견되고 있다'는 내용이 되어야 이러한 글 전체의 요지를 뒷받침할 수 있다. 따라서 ②가 빈칸에 적절하다.

terrestrial a. 지구의; 육생(陸生)의 short-sighted a. 근시안적인 naturalist n. 자연주의자; 박물학자 affirm v. 단언하다 categorically ad. 단정적으로, 절대적으로 motion n. 운동, 동작 phosphorescence n. 인광(燐光)(을 발함), 푸른 빛 inquirer n. 탐구자 subterranean a. 지하의 cavern n. 동굴 gloomy a. 어두운, 어둑어둑한 interbreed v. 이종 교배하다 marine a. 바다의, 해양의 inclination n. 성향, 경향

우리는 생명이 지구 외의 다른 조건에서는 존재할 수 없으며, 다른 세계에서는 오직 우리 자신의 세계(지구)와 유사한 조건에서만 생명체가 서식할 수 있다고 상상하는 경향이 있다. 하지만 지구의 자연 그 자체가 이러한 생각이 잘못되었음을 우리에게 보여준다. 인간은 물속에서 죽지만 물고기는 물 밖에서 죽는다. 또한, 근시안적인 자연주의자들은 바다 밑바닥에서는 생명체가 살 수 없다고 단정적으로 확인한다. 첫째는 완전히 어둡기 때문이고, 둘째는 엄청난 압력이 어떤 생명체라도 터뜨려버리기 때문이며, 셋째는 모든 움직임이 그곳에서는 불가능하기 때문이라는 등의 이유를 든다. 이 정도 깊은 곳에는 빛이 없다. 생물들은 자신의 인광(燐光)으로 빛을 만들어낸다. 다른 연구자들은 지하 동굴을 탐험하는데, 어두운 환경에 대한 적응에 의해 변형된 기관을 가진 동물과 식물들을 발견한다.

① 엄청난 수압
② 어두운 환경에 대한 적응
③ 이종 교배 경향
④ 해양 생물의 자연스러운 성향
⑤ 갑작스러운 환경 변화

25 빈칸완성   ②

이 글은 프톨레마이오스의 천동설을 소개하고 있는데, '별들은 거대한 구체 내부에 붙어 있는 빛나는 점들이다', '구체의 움직임은 지구가 그 중심에 있다는 가정과 일치한다', '태양, 달, 별들이 지정된 경로를 따라 이동한 뒤 적절한 시기에 진다', '고정된 별들이 상호 간의 거리를 유지한다', '별들을 담고 있는 구체가 지구 주변을 하루에 한 번 공전한다'는 내용들은 모두 '지구는 구체(우주)의 중심에 있으면서 정지한(stationary) 상태에 있다'는 가정과만 양립할 수 있는 설명들이다. 따라서 ②가 빈칸에 적절하다.

Ptolemy n. 프톨레마이오스(기원 2세기의 Alexandria의 천문·지리·수학자, 천동설을 주장) tremendous a. 엄청난, 굉장한 compatible a. 양립될 수 있는, 모순이 없는 supposition n. 추정, 가정, 가설 glorious a. 장엄한 procession n. 행진, 행렬 course n. 항로 duly ad. 적절한 때에, 때를 맞춰 account for ~을 설명하다 consistently ad. 일관되게 constellation n. 별자리

프톨레마이오스(Ptolemy)는 별들의 움직임을 관찰하고 그 별들은 거대한 구체(球體) 내부에 붙어 있는 빛나는 점들이라는 결론을 내렸다. 이 구체의 움직임은 지구가 그 중심에 있다는 가정과만 양립할 수 있었다. 태양, 달 및 별들은 매일 떠오르고, 장엄하게 끝없이 이어지는 행렬을 이루며 하늘을 가로질러 이동하고, 지정된 경로를 따라 다 이동했을 때 때맞추어 진다는 이 명백한 사실에 대해 어떤 설명이 필요했다. 고정된 별들이 해마다, 시대마다 상호 간의 거리를 유지한다는 이 상황은 프톨레마이오스에게는 그 별들을 포함하고 있고, 그 표면 위에 그 별들이 고정되어 있다고 그가 믿었던 그 구체가 하루에 한 번 지구 주위를 완전히 한 바퀴 돈다는 것을 증명하는 것처럼 보였다. 이렇게 하여 그는 일관되게 뜨고 지는 그 모든 현상을 우리 지구가 정지해 있다는 가정으로 설명하곤 했다.

① 별들의 별자리가 우리 지구에 영향을 미친다
② 우리 지구는 정지해 있다
③ 태양이 우주의 중심이다
④ 우리 지구는 태양을 중심으로 공전한다
⑤ 우리 지구는 역동적이다

26 빈칸완성

이 글은 우리의 교육 및 경제 체제가 토지에 대한 의식 부족으로 인해 토지 윤리의 발전을 방해하고 있다는 문제점을 다루고 있다. 또한, 사람들이 토지와 직접적인 연관성이 없어지면서 토지에 대한 관심이 줄어들고, 이를 대체하는 인공적인 제품들이 등장하면서 토지의 가치가 저하되고 있다고 주장한다. outgrow는 타동사로서 '(옷 등에 비해 사람의 몸 등이) 너무 커져 맞지 않게 되다,' '~보다 더 커지다[많아지다]'는 의미도 있지만 본문에서는 '성장하여 벗어나다'는 의미이다.

impede v. 지연시키다, 방해하다, 훼방 놓다 head v. (특정 방향으로) 향하다 intense a. 치열한, 열정적인 middleman n. 중간 상인, 중개인 innumerable a. 셀 수 없이 많은, 무수한 gadget n. 도구, 장치, 기구 vital a. 필수적인; 생명 유지와 관련된 turn loose ~를 자유롭게 해주다 scenic a. 경치가 뛰어난 stiff ad. 몹시, 매우 hydroponics n. 수경 재배 synthetic a. 합성의, 인조의 substitute n. 대체물 outgrow v. 성장하여 벗어나다, (세월이 흐르면서) ~을 그만두다(to stop being interested in or involved with (something or someone) because you have changed as you have grown older) mediator n. 중재인, 조정자

토지 윤리의 발전을 가로막는 가장 심각한 장애물은 아마도 우리의 교육 및 경제 체제가 토지에 대한 강렬한 의식을 향해있기보다는, 오히려 그런 의식을 외면하고 있다는 사실일 것이다. 오늘날 사람들은 많은 중개인들과 무수한 물리적 도구들에 의해 토지와 분리되어 있다. 요즘 사람들은 토지와 필수적인 어떤 관계도 맺지 않는다. 그들에게 토지는 도시들 사이에서 작물들이 자라는 어떤 공간일 뿐이다. 사람들을 토지 위에 하루 동안 풀어놓으면, 어쩌다가 그곳이 골프장이나 '경치가 빼어난' 지역인 경우가 아니면 그들은 매우 지루할 것이다. 만약 농작물들이 농사가 아닌 수경 재배로 길러질 수 있다면, 그것이 요즘 사람들과 잘 어울릴 것이다. 목재, 가죽, 모직물 그리고 여타 토지에서 생산되는 천연 제품들을 대체하는 합성 제품들이 원래 제품들보다 (현대인들에게는) 더 잘 맞는다. 간단히 말해, 토지는 사람들이 성장 발전하여 이제는 벗어나버린 것이다.

① 사람들이 모방하기를 열망하는 모범
② 사람들이 성장 발전하여 벗어나버린 것
③ 유기농 제품을 위한 곳
④ 어떤 경우에도 사람들에게 이익이 되는 것
⑤ 중재자의 도움을 받아 사람들이 재배하는 것

27 글의 주제

필자는 미국의 이민(자) 문제는 '미국 의회의 실패', '이민국 관리들의 무분별한 체류 허가', '미국 연방 정부의 적절한 조치 부재' 등, 미국 정부 여러 부문의 잘못(기능 장애)이 중첩되어 생긴 일이라는 점을 강조하고 있다. 따라서 '미국이 현재 겪고 있는 이민(자) 문제의 책임은 미국 의회와 행정부에 있다'고 주장하는 글로서, 글 전체의 주제는 ③ '최근 이민 문제의 책임은 누구에게 있는가'가 적절하다.

exemplify v. 전형적인 예가 되다 dysfunction n. 기능 장애, 고장 immigration n. 이민 border n. 국경 overflow v. (사람들로) 넘쳐나다 shelter n. 보호소, 대피소 strain v. 혹사하다, 무리하게 사용하다 newcomer n. 신입자, 신참자 asylum n. 망명 in limbo 불확실한 상태로 lengthy a. 너무 긴, 장황한 hear v. (법정에서) 심리[공판]를 갖다 case n. 사건 permission n. 허락, 허가, 허용 eligible a. 적격의, 자격이 있는 turn away 물리치다 overwhelm v. 어쩔 줄 모르게 만들다 temporarily ad. 일시적으로 mitigate v. 완화시키다

오늘날 미국 정부의 기능 장애를 이민 문제보다 더 잘 보여주는 문제를 찾기란 어렵다. 지난 한 해 동안 100만 명 이상의 사람들이 남부 국경을 통해 미국에 입국해, 보호소는 넘쳐나고 공공 서비스의 부담은 가중되었다. 대부분의 신규 이민자들은 망명을 신청하는데, 이는 그들이 합법적으로 미국에 머물 수 있도록 허용하되 그들을 불확실 상태의 지위에 머무르게 만든다. 그들은 자신의 사건이 심리(審理)되기까지 수년씩 기다려야 하는 경우가 많으며, 합법적인 취업 허가를 받기까지 오랜 시간이 걸릴 수 있다. 이 나라는 오랫동안 이민을 통해 힘을 키워왔으며, 망명을 허용하는 것은 미국의 국가적 가치의 중요한 표현이다. 그러나 미국 의회는 자격 있는 자들을 맞이하고 자격 없는 자들을 물리치는 데 필요한 자원들을 제공하는 데 실패했다. 그 대신, 압도되어버린 이민국 관리들은 거의 모든 사람들이 일시적으로 머물 수 있도록 허용함으로써, 여러 주와 도시에 막대한 단기적 비용을 부담 지우지만, 연방 정부는 이 비용 부담을 완화하기 위해 충분한 조치를 취하지 않았다.

다음 글의 주제로 가장 적절한 것은?
① 새로운 이민자들이 새 시민권을 얼마나 어렵게 획득하는가
② 왜 그토록 많은 이민자들이 남쪽 국경을 넘는가
③ 최근 이민 문제의 책임은 누구에게 있는가
④ 무엇이 망명 절차를 그토록 어렵고 오래 걸리도록 만드는가
⑤ 왜 미국 정부는 이민자들을 환영하지 않는가

28 내용일치

'오존이 파괴되면서 자연적인 균형이 깨질지 모른다는 우려가 있고, 그 결과 성층권 오존을 둘러싼 과학적, 정책적 이슈들이 생겨나고 있다'고 하였으므로 ⑤가 본문의 내용과 일치한다. ① '질소는 토양에서 생기고, 수소는 대부분 대기 중의 수증기에서 나온다'고 했으므로 잘못된 진술이다. ② '오존이 자외선을 흡수할 때 계속 파괴된다'고 하였는데, 이는 자외선이 증가하면 오존이 파괴되어 오존량이 줄어들고, 자외선이 감소하면 파괴되는 오존이 줄어들어 오존량은 증가할 것으로 판단할 수 있는 근거가 되므로, 잘못된 진술이다. ③ '산소 원자(O)가 산소 분자(O_2)와 반응하여 또 다른 오존 분자(O_3)를 형성한다'고 하였으므로 잘못된 진술이다. ④ '창조와 파괴의 힘이 균형을 이루어 오존량이 대체로 일정하게 유지된다'고 하였으므로 잘못된 진술이다.

molecule n. 분자 compound n. 화합물 nitrogen n. 질소 hydrogen n. 수소 chlorine n. 염소 water vapor 수증기 ultraviolet a. 자외선의 stratospheric a. 성층권의 release n. (가스·화학 물질 등의) 방출[유출] chlorofluorocarbon n. 클로로플루오르카본, 프레온 가스(순환성 냉매(冷媒), 발포제, 용제로서 쓰이며 오존층 파괴의 문제를 유발함) halon n. 할론(탄소와 할로겐으로 구성된 가스) upset v. 어긋나게 하다, 망치다

오존 분자는 질소, 수소, 염소를 함유한 천연 화합물에 의해 지속적으로 파괴되고 있다. 질소는 토양과 바다에서 생기고, 수소는 대부분 대기 중의

수증기에서, 염소는 바다에서 생긴다. 또한 오존은 자외선을 흡수할 때도 계속해서 파괴되고 있다. 이 과정에서 산소 원자(O)가 생성되어 산소 분자(O₂)와 반응하여 또 다른 오존 분자(O₃)를 형성한다. 창조와 파괴의 힘이 균형을 이루면서, 현재의 대기가 생성된 이후 평균적인 오존량은 대체로 일정하게 유지되어 온 것으로 믿어진다. 프레온 가스와 할론의 방출로 인해 오존이 파괴되면서 자연적인 균형이 깨질지 모른다는 우려의 결과로, 이제는 성층권 오존을 둘러싼 과학적, 정책적 이슈들이 생겨나고 있다.

다음 글의 내용과 일치하는 것은?
① 질소와 수소는 같은 근원에서 나온다.
② 자외선은 오존의 양과 아무런 관련이 없다.
③ 오존은 산소 원자의 반응에 의해 생성된다.
④ 창조적인 힘이 파괴적인 힘보다 더 커서 오존의 양을 일정하게 만든다.
⑤ 오존의 자연적인 균형이 무너지는 것은 크게 우려할 만한 일이다.

29 글의 제목   ②

이 글은 경청자의 태도와 역량에 대해 다루고 있으며, 경청할 내용에 대한 이해력 부족이나 어려움을 겪는 경우 이를 극복하기 위한 노력이 필요하다는 점을 강조하고 있다. 또한, 경청 능력을 향상시키기 위해서 다양한 주제와 어려운 내용을 듣는 연습이 필요하다고 제안하고 있다. 따라서 이 글은 소통 및 협업에 있어서 중요한 요소인 '경청에 대한 인식과 훈련의 필요성'을 '미숙한 경청자들'에게 강조하는 것이라고 볼 수 있으므로 가장 적절한 제목은 ②이다.

inexperienced a. 미숙한 expository a. 설명적인 apparently ad. 보아하니; 명백히 appetite n. 식욕; 욕구 technical a. (특정 주제와 관련된) 전문적인 painstakingly ad. 힘들여, 고생고생해서 light a. 가벼운, 무겁지 않은 recreational a. 오락 삼아 하는 일의

서툰 경청자는 어렵고 설명적인 자료를 듣는 데 미숙하다. 좋은 경청자는 자신의 정신 능력에 도전할 만큼 충분한 난이도를 가진 다양한 설명을 듣고자 하는 욕구를 발달시키는 것 같다. 아마도 나쁜 경청자를 가장 잘 묘사하는 단어는 "미숙한"일 것이다. 그런 사람은 의사소통하는 하루의 40%를 무언가를 경청하는 데 쓰지만, 어려운 전문적인, 또는 설명적인 내용을 듣는 데는 미숙하다. 그는 가볍고 오락적인 내용을 여러 해 동안 힘써 찾아왔다. 공장, 사무실 또는 교실에서 그런 사람의 생산성은 형편없기 때문에 그런 사람이 만들어 내는 문제는 매우 중요하다. 미숙함은 쉽게, 신속히 극복되지 않는다. 그러나 우리 자신의 약점을 아는 것이 우리로 하여금 그 약점을 고치게 만들지 모른다. 우리는 나이가 너무 많아 새로운 도전에 대처할 수 없게 될 필요는 전혀 없다.

다음 글의 제목으로 가장 적절한 것은?
① 가벼운 경청 자료의 활용법
② 미숙한 경청자들이 해야 할 일
③ 좋은 경청자가 되는 즐거움
④ 경청에 약점이 있음을 드러내지 말라
⑤ 좋은 경청자가 되는 데 필요한 시간

30 글의 요지   ①

이 글은 로켓의 재활용에 대한 최근의 혁신적인 기술에 대해 소개하고 있다. 기존에는 로켓의 각 단계가 일회용으로 사용되어 비용이 많이 들

었는데, 이제는 일부 로켓이 대기권 내에서 제어되어 지상에 착륙하여 재사용될 수 있게 되었다고 한다. 이로 인해 우주 탐사 또는 우주 관광 산업에서의 비용 절감 효과가 기대되고 있다고 말한다. 따라서 이 글의 요지로는 ①이 가장 적절하다. 한편, ③, ④, ⑤의 내용은 본문의 내용과 일치, 또는 추론 가능한 내용이지만, 글 전체의 요지가 될 수는 없다.

detach v. 분리하다 craft n. 우주선 account for ~을 차지하다 dump v. 버리다 mission n. 임무 aerospace n. 항공우주 산업 steer v. 조종하다 manned a. 승무원이 탄, 유인의 weightlessness n. 무중력 bend n. 굽기, 굴곡, 만곡 parachute n. 낙하산 launch n. 발사 affordable a. (가격 등이) 알맞은, 감당할 수 있는 velocity n. 속도

대부분의 로켓은 다단계로 구성되며, 우주선이 우주로 이동하면서 분리된다. 로켓에서 가장 크고 비싼 부분은 1단계로, 발사 가격의 약 80%를 차지할 수 있다. 지금까지 이 비싼 로켓 단계들은 단 한 번의 임무를 마친 후 바다에 버려져, 항공우주 활동의 비용을 너무나 증가시켜서 우주 관광을 불가능하게 만들었다. 하지만 이제 엔지니어들은 로켓이 안전하게 대기권 아래로 내려와 플랫폼에 착륙하여 재사용할 수 있게 하고 있다. 그중 하나가 뉴 셰퍼드(New Shepard) 로켓으로, 우주로 날아가 유인 캡슐을 분리할 예정이다. 여섯 명의 유료 관광객들이 4분간 무중력 상태를 경험하고 지구의 굴곡을 보고난 후, 캡슐은 다시 낙하산에 실려 지구로 돌아올 것이다. 1단계 로켓은 지구와 접촉하기 직전에 속도를 늦추면서 부드럽게 착륙하여 새 발사를 준비할 것이다.

다음 글의 요지로 가장 적절한 것은?
① 재사용이 우주 관광을 더욱 (비용적으로) 감당할 만한 것으로 만들어준다.
② 미래의 우주여행은 아직 갈 길이 멀다.
③ 재사용 가능한 로켓은 환경에 좋다.
④ 비싼 다단계 로켓들이 바다에 던져졌다.
⑤ 엔지니어들은 착륙 전 로켓의 속도를 줄이는 방법을 알아냈다.

31 내용일치   ④

'젤라틴은 스테이크, 생선 살 또는 봉지에 들어 있는 샐러드와 거의 비슷한 속도로 부패한다'라고 하였으므로 ④는 잘못된 진술이다.

expiration n. 만료, 만기, 종결 grocery n. 식료품 및 잡화 industrial designer 산업 디자이너 revelation n. 폭로; 드러냄 inspire v. 고무하다; 영감을 불어넣다 bump n. 융기, 혹 layer n. 층, 켜, 겹 gelatin n. 젤라틴 packaging n. 포장재, 포장 protein n. 단백질 decay v. 부패하다 tangible a. 유형(有形)의; 만질 수 있는 prime a. (품질 등이) 최고[최상등급]의 n. 한창때, 전성기 hoof n. (말 등의) 발굽 (pl. hooves) rot v. 썩다, 부패하다 fillet n. 살코기 potential n. 가능성, 잠재력 guideline n. 지침, 가이드라인 indicator n. 지표 spoilage n. 부패 bear v. (눈에 보이게) 있다[지니다] feature v. 특별히 포함하다, 특징으로 삼다 degradation n. 저하, 악화

대부분의 사람들은 식료품이 여전히 신선한지의 여부를 알기 위해 유통기한에 의존한다. 그러나 영국에서 활동하는 산업 디자이너 솔베이가 팍슈타이테(Solveiga Pakštaite)가 대중교통 프로젝트를 위해 시각 장애인들을 인터뷰하면서 알게 되었듯이, 만약 볼 수 없다면 이러한 날짜를 읽을 수 없는 것이다. 그 깨달음은 이 23살 청년으로 하여금 젤라틴층으로 덧입힌 일련의 코팅된 돌기들인 돌기 표기(Bump Mark)를 식품 포장재에 디자인하게끔 고무시켰다. 젤라틴 단백질이 부패함에 따라 돌기는

점점 더 도드라지면서 만져지게 된다. 바로 그때 당신은 식품이 최상의 상태가 지났음을 알게 된다. 이것은 동물 발굽으로 만들어진 젤라틴이 스테이크, 생선살 또는 봉지에 들어 있는 샐러드와 거의 비슷한 속도로 부패하기 때문에 가능한 것이다. 이 기술의 잠재력은 생각보다 더 대단하다. (식품에 표기된) 인쇄된 날짜는 식품 부패의 진정한 지표가 아니라 단지 지침에 불과한 것인데, (이 날짜를 따르다 보니) 우리는 온전한 식품을 많이 버리고 있다. (영국의 식료품점들과 소비자들은 매년 총 1,200만 톤의 음식물을 버리고 있다.) 돌기 표기는 실제 부패 속도를 나타내기 때문에, 이 발명은 그것(낭비)을 바로잡는 데 도움이 될 수 있다. 이제 팍슈타이테는 시장 조사와 함께 제조를 연구하며, 젤라틴-식품 부패 속도의 정확도를 높이기 위해 실험실 테스트를 실행하고 있다. 신선한 아이디어에서 신선한 식품이 나온다.

다음 글의 내용과 일치하지 않는 것은?
① 팍슈타이테는 대중교통 프로젝트를 위해 시각 장애인들과 인터뷰를 진행했다.
② 돌기 표기가 적용된 식품 포장에는 여러 개의 돌기가 있으며, 그 위에는 젤라틴이 덮여 있다.
③ 식품의 신선도가 떨어지면 돌기가 눈에 띄게 된다.
④ 젤라틴의 부패 속도는 스테이크보다 빠르다.
⑤ 인쇄된 날짜는 식품 부패의 정확한 지표라기보다는 권장 사항에 불과하다.

32-33

나의 동료 조나단 로스웰(Jonathan Rothwell)과 나는 최근 브루킹스 연구소에서 발표한 미국 흑인 발전 지표(Black Progress Index)에서 일반적으로 예상되는 수준을 초과하는 수백 지역들을 발표했는데, 이 지표는 미국 흑인 인권 단체인 전미 유색인 지위 향상 협회(NAACP)와 제휴하여 개발한 대화형 도구이자 보고서로, 흑인들의 건강과 복지, 그리고 그들의 삶을 형성하는 조건들을 이해할 수 있는 수단을 제공한다. 우리는 흑인들과 백인들을 비교하는 대신, 다양한 지역의 흑인 인구집단 사이의 평균 수명 차이를 분석했다. 이 방법은 흑인들이 번영하고 있는 지역들을 보여준다. 연구자들은 종종 차이를 조장하기 위해 의도된 과거와 현재의 (인종) 차별에 주의를 기울이지 않은 채 주택 소유율, 교육 성취도, 수입, 사망률 등을 대충 비교하는 것에 그치고 만다. 결과적으로 지역 상황 정책 및 지역적 상황이 결여된 개괄적인 전국 평균값들이 전국에서 일어나고 있는 실질적 진전을 가려버린다.
그럼에도 불구하고, 오하이오 주 제퍼슨 카운티(Jefferson County)와 같은 일부 지역의 흑인 평균 수명은 버지니아 주 매나사스 파크(Manassas Park)와 콜로라도 주 웰드 카운티(Weld County)보다 33년이나 짧다. 이러한 격차는 생활수준, 의학, 공중 보건 측면에서 약 100년의 발전에 해당하는 것이다.
흑인은 하나의 동질적 통일체가 아니다. 그들은 서로 다른 장소에서 다양한 결과를 낳는다. 흑인들이 중요한 것처럼 지역적 상황도 중요하다. 미 전역의 군(郡)과 대도시 지역에서 흑인들의 평균 수명이 낮다는 것은 인종차별과의 싸움에서 우리가 패배하고 있다는 것을 시사한다. 그러나 흑인이 번영하고 있는 지리적 지역들은 희망 이상의 단서를 제공한다. 사람들의 시민적 행동이 긍정적인 변화를 가져다준다는 것이다.

exceed v. 넘다, 초과하다 release v. (대중들에게) 공개하다, 발표하다 NAACP n. 전미 유색인 지위 향상 협회(= National Association for the Advancement of Colored People) interactive a. 상호적인, 서로 작용하는 in partnership with ~와 제휴[협력]하여 well-being n. 행복, 안녕, 복지 life expectancy 기대수명, 평균수명 locale n. 현장, 장소

thrive v. 번창하다, 번영하다; 성공하다 sloppily ad. 엉성하게, 대충 discrimination n. 차별; 차이 disparity n. (특히 한쪽에 불공평한) 차이 broad a. 개괄적인 void of ~이 결여된, ~가 없는 context n. 맥락, 전후 사정, 상황 camouflage v. 위장하다, 감추다 county n. 군(郡)(주(州)(state) 바로 밑의 행정 단위) equivalent a. 동등한[맞먹는] monolith n. 거대한 돌기둥[거석]; (변화가 느리고 개개인에게 무관심한) 거대한 단일 조직[사회], 완전한 통일체 civic a. 시의; 시민의 assortment n. (같은 종류의 여러 가지) 모음, 종합 colossus n. 대단히 중요한 사람[것]; 거인, 거대한 것

32 글의 요지 ③

필자는 흑인 복지를 연구할 때 전국 평균 지표들(주택 소유율, 교육 수준 등)은 '지역 상황 정책과 지역적 상황들(context policy and local contexts)이 결여된' 전국 평균에 불과한 것으로, 지역 곳곳에서 벌어지고 있는 '실질적 진전들을 가려(camouflage) 보이지 않게 한다'고 지적한다. 같은 흑인이라 해도 그가 '어떤 지역에서 살고 있는가?', '그 지역의 상황은 어떠한가?', '그 지역의 상황을 반영한 정책이 존재하는가?', '그 지역에는 흑인들의 적극적인 시민 참여가 있는가?' 등, 흑인 복지 연구를 위해서는 '지역적 특수성과 상황'을 고려하는 것이 가장 중요함을 강조하고 있다. 따라서 이 글의 요지는 ③이 가장 적절하다고 볼 수 있다.

윗글의 요지로 가장 적절한 것은?
① 흑인 복지는 과학적으로 연구되어야 한다.
② 흑인 복지는 전국 평균 수치로 명확하게 표현된다.
③ 흑인 복지는 지역적 상황에 달려 있다.
④ 흑인 복지는 백인의 복지에 비해 훨씬 뒤처져 있다.
⑤ 흑인 복지는 그들의 시민적 행동과 무관하다.

33 빈칸완성 ④

Ⓐ 만약 어떤 연구자들이 '차이를 조장하기 위해 의도된 과거와 현재의 (인종) 차별에 주의를 기울이지 않는다'거나, '개괄적인 평균값만을 비교해 전국에서 일어나고 있는 실질적 진전을 보지 못한다'면 그 연구자들이 '엉성하게, 대충대충(sloppily)' 비교하는 것이라고 표현할 수 있을 것이다. Ⓑ 필자는 미국 전역에 존재하는 흑인들을 '하나의 동질적인 통일체'로 이해하는 것에 반대하고 있다. monolith는 흔히 '(변화가 느리고 개개인에게 무관심한) 거대한 단일 조직[사회](a very large and powerful organization that acts as a single unit)'를 못마땅하게 (disapprovingly) 칭하는 말이다.

34-35

미국 대부분의 사람들이 더 이상 농장에서 살지는 않지만, 19세기와 마찬가지로 20세기에도 주택 소유에 대한 이상은 여전히 강력하다. 예를 들어, 제2차 세계대전이 끝난 뒤 미국으로 돌아온 군인들은 집을 사서 가정을 꾸리는 꿈을 꾸었다. 그 결과 주택 건설 부문에 엄청난 붐이 일어났다. 일반적으로 교외 지역에 위치한 새 집들은 대개 작고 거의 똑같았지만 (주택 소유에 대한) 깊은 욕구를 충족시켜 주었다. 많은 사람들이 단독주택을 자신들의 삶의 방식의 토대로 보았다.
그러나 1950년대와 1960년대의 새로운 교외 지역 거주민들에게 작은 주택 안에서의 생활은 농장에서의 삶과는 아주 달랐다. 먼저, 집에서 가족

이 함께 보내는 시간이 훨씬 줄어들었다. 아버지는 매일 아침 직장까지 한 시간이나 걸려 운전하거나 통근하는 일이 잦았다. 아이들은 온종일 학교에 가고 방과 후에는 동네 아이들과 놀았다. 때때로 교외 지역은 침실 공동체라고 불렸는데, 이는 사람들이 기본적으로 잠자는 용도로만 그들의 집을 사용했기 때문이다. 두 번째로, 교외 지역은 종종 안정적인 공동체가 아니었는데, 아버지들이 더 나은 급여와 더 큰 집과 같은 사회경제적 지위 상승을 추구함에 따라 가족들이 자주 이사했기 때문이다. 비록 가정의 개념은 여전히, 언제나처럼 소중한 것이었지만, 그것의 의미는 달라졌다. 70년대와 80년대에는 더 많은 여성들이 노동력에 진입함에 따라 가족이 함께 보내는 시간이 더욱 적어졌다. 그러나 그러한 양상은 변화하고 있는데, 사람들이 컴퓨터를 통해 사무실과 접속된 상태로 집에서 일할 수 있게 되면서 원격근무 즉, 재택근무를 할 수 있기 때문이다. 점점 더 많은 사람들이 집에 머무를 수 있게 된 것이다. 그러므로 "집, 아늑한 집"이라는 오래된 표현이 "집, 편안한 사무실"로 바뀔 수는 있겠지만, 소중한 집의 중요성은 여전히 유지될 것이다.

ownership n. 소유, 소유권; 소유자임   tremendous a. 엄청난, 굉장한   suburb n. 교외(도심지를 벗어난 주택 지역)   identical a. 동일한, 똑같은   single-family house 단독주택   suburbanite n. (도시) 교외 거주자   commute v. 통근하다   upward mobility 경제적[사회적] 상태의 상승   telecommute v. (컴퓨터 등의) 통신 시설을 이용하여 재택[원격] 근무하다   cherish v. 소중히 여기다   demography n. 인구 변동, 인구 통계학   in addition 게다가, 덧붙여   on the contrary 그와는 반대로   similarly ad. 비슷하게, 마찬가지로

---

34 글의 제목 　　　　　②

이 글은 제2차 세계대전 이후 늘어난 교외 지역의 단독주택 중심의 주거생활, 최근의 재택근무 증가에 이르는, 미국인들의 집에 대한 관심과 이와 연관된 생활 패턴의 변화를 기술하고 있다. 다시 말해, 20세기 미국에서 집의 개념이 시간이 흐름에 따라 변화하고 진화하는 과정을 보여주고 있는 글이므로, 가장 적절한 제목은 ②이다. 한편, '농장에서의 삶(생활)'을 집중 조명하면서 '농장에서의 생활'과 '교외에서의 생활'을 비교하는 글은 아니므로 ①이 제목이 될 수는 없다.

윗글의 제목으로 가장 적절한 것은?
① 농장과 교외에서의 생활
② 집에 대한 개념의 진화
③ 미국에서 주택 짓기
④ 인구통계의 이론적 분석
⑤ 여성 고용과 사회이동

---

35 빈칸완성 　　　　　③

Ⓐ '주택 소유에 대한 이상이 강력하다'는 진술은 추상적이고 일반적이다. 따라서 예시(例示)를 통해 구체화하는 것이 필요한데, 바로 뒤에서 '제2차 세계대전 후 전역한 군인들의 주택 소유에 대한 열망'이 구체화되고 있으므로, 빈칸에는 예시의 연결어 for example이 적절하다. Ⓑ 첫 번째 단락에서 '19세기와 마찬가지로 20세기에도 주택 소유에 대한 이상은 여전히 강력하다'고 하였다. 또한 주거의 형태가 농장에서 교외 지역의 단독주택으로 바뀌기는 했지만, 그 형태가 어떻든지 간에 여전히 집은 미국인들의 '삶의 토대'라고 하였다. 그런데 두 번째 단락에서는 '교

외 지역 거주민들의 삶과 농장에서의 삶은 아주 달랐다'는 역접(逆接: 앞에서 서술한 사실과 상반되는 사태 또는 그와 일치하지 않는 사태가 뒤에서 성립함을 나타내는 일)의 내용이 자세히 기술되고 있으므로, 첫 번째 단락과 두 번째 단락 사이에는 이러한 역접의 연결어 however가 들어가는 것이 적절하다.

36-37

고대로부터 하늘에서 이상한 물체들이 목격되었지만, 20세기 중반에야 비로소 그것들은 '미확인 비행 물체', 즉 UFO라는 이름을 얻었다. 1940년 대와 1950년대에는 세계 각지에서 디스크 모양의 우주선이나 '비행접시'로 묘사되는 목격 사례들이 크게 늘어났다. 이러한 첫 번째 대규모 UFO 목격 사례의 급증은 그 시기가 의미심장했는데, 때마침 핵무기 경쟁으로 인해 대중의 공포가 널리 퍼져 있던 시기에 일어났던 것이다. 초기에는 UFO가 비밀리에 개발된 첨단 군사 항공기라는 이론이 가장 일반적이었다. 몇 년 안에 대중들의 인식은 변했는데, 이는 부분적으로 할리우드 때문이었다. 갑작스레 UFO는 더 이상 지구에서 생겨난 것으로 여겨지지 않고, 다른 행성에서 온 것으로 여겨지게 되었다. 그 이후로 정부가 UFO 탑승자들과 행한 거래에 관한 정보를 숨기고 있다는 소문으로부터 최면 상태에서 회상된 외계인에 의한 납치에 대한 분명한 기억에 이르기까지, 외계인 방문에 대한 또 다른 추정적 증거들이 제시되면서 상황은 한층 더 복잡해졌다. 하늘에서 목격되는 이상한 물체와 이들 사건은 직접적인 연관성이 전혀 없거나, 거의 없음에도 불구하고 UFO라는 용어가 이들 사건에 여전히 적용되는 경향이 있다. 예를 들어, 작년에 영국의 어느 신문에는 "UFO 연구자가 화성에서 외계의 도마뱀을 발견했다"라는 표제를 단 기사가 실렸는데, 그 어떤 비행 물체와도 상관없는 내용이었다.

사실은, 용어가 절망적으로 혼란스러워졌다. 어떤 사람들, 특히 관변(官邊) 인사들에게 '미확인 비행 물체'란 글자 그대로 식별되지 않은 공중 물체를 의미한다. 그러나 많은 일반인들에게 UFO는 '외계 우주선'을 의미한다. 이러한 이유로 미 국방부는 그들이 설명할 수 없는 무언가를 보았을 때마다 외계인에 관해 이야기하는 것처럼 비치지 않도록 미확인 공중 현상의 약어인 UAP라는 용어를 사용하기 시작했다. 그리고 UAP라고 하면 또 다른 이점이 있는데, UFO가 항상 글자 그대로 '비행 물체'가 아닐 수도 있기 때문이다. 알다시피, 일부 UFO는 신기루, 특이한 기상 현상 또는 심지어 천체일 수도 있다. 따라서 이런 경우에는 '공중 현상'이라는 용어가 훨씬 더 적합하다.

UFO와 UAP는 한 글자가 공통되는데, 그것은 미확인을 의미하는 U이다. 하지만 여기에 너무 많은 의미를 부여하지 않는 것이 중요하다. 그것이 목격된 것이 다른 행성에서 왔다거나 자명한 물리 법칙을 거스른다는 것을 자동적으로 의미하지는 않는다. 예를 들어, 사진이나 동영상의 경우, 그것이 보여주는 내용을 파악하기에는 해상도가 충분히 좋지 않을지도 모른다. 파일럿이나 경찰관과 같이 훈련된 관찰자에 의한 보고도, 그것이 순간적 목격에 관한 보고이다 보니, 그들이 물체의 크기나 거리를 확실히 알지 못하면, 그 물체는 어떤 사람의 드론에서부터 외계의 우주선까지 그 모든 것이었을 수 있다. 레이더와 같은 전자 시스템은 특정 유형의 알려진 물체들을 감지하도록 설계되어 있으므로 예상되는 범위를 벗어난 모든 것들이 '미확인'으로 분류될 가능성이 있다.

sighting n. (특히 특이한 것·잠깐밖에 볼 수 없는 것) 목격(함)   craft n. 우주선   saucer n. 받침, 접시 모양의 물건   wave n. (특정한 활동의) 급증   paranoia n. 편집증(偏執症), 망상증; (근거 없는) 심한 불신[의심]   race n. 경주; 경쟁   military a. 군사의, 무력의   secrecy n. 비밀 유지   originate v. 비롯되다   complicated a. 복잡한   allege v. (증거 없이) 혐의를 제기하다[주장하다]   extraterrestrial a. 지구 밖 생물체의, 외계의   n. 외계인   conceal v. 감추다, 숨기다   dealings n. 거래 관계

occupant n. (주택·방·건물 등의) 사용자[입주자]; (특정 시간에 차량·의자 등에) 타고[앉아] 있는 사람 apparent a. (명사 앞에서 사용되었을 때) ~인 것처럼 보이는[여겨지는](seeming to be true but possibly not true) abduction n. 납치 hypnosis n. 최면 headline n. (신문 기사, 특히 제1면 머리기사의) 표제 hunter n. (특정한 것을) 찾아다니는 사람 spot v. 발견하다 lizard n. 도마뱀 Mars n. 화성 terminology n. (어떤 개념을 나타내는) 용어들 hopelessly ad. 절망적으로 circle n. (관심·직업 등으로 연결된 사람들의) ~계[사회] official circles 관변(官邊: 정부나 관청 쪽. 또는 그 계통) airborne a. 비행 중인, 하늘에 떠 있는 aerial a. 공중의 phenomenon n. 현상(pl. phenomena) mirage n. 신기루 astronomical a. 천문학적인 defy v. (권위·법률·규칙 등에) 반항[저항, 거역]하다 physics n. 물리학 resolution n. 해상도 work out 이해하다, 알아내다 fleeting a. 순식간의, 잠깐 동안의 electronic a. 전자의 parameter n. (보통 pl.) (일정하게 정한) 한도 –bound (복합형) ~으로 갇힌; ~행(行)의(skybound 천상(天上) 행의) optical illusion 착시(錯視)

36 글의 제목   ①

첫 번째 단락에서 UFO라는 용어가 등장한 과정이 다루어진다. 두 번째 단락에서는 UFO가 대중들의 인식 속에서 '외계인의 존재'와 직결됨(문제점)을 지적하였다. 세 번째 단락에서는 UFO라는 용어가 초래하는 혼란과 그에 대한 대안으로 등장한 UAP라는 용어가 UFO보다 훨씬 더 다양한 현상들을 더 정확하게 기술할 수 있음을 조명하였다. 마지막으로 네 번째 단락에서는 '미확인(unidentified)'이라는 용어를 외계인과 자동적으로 결부시키지 말 것을 다시금 강조하고 있다. 따라서 이 글은 처음에는 UFO로 불리다가 이후 UAP로 불리게 되는(또는 그렇게 불러야 한다는) 용어의 변화 및 그 필요성을 중점적으로 기술하고 있다고 볼 수 있으므로 ①이 제목으로 가장 적절하다.

윗글의 제목으로 가장 적절한 것은?
① 하늘의 수수께끼를 칭하는 용어의 변화: UFO에서 UAP로
② UFO에 대한 여론의 변화
③ 외계생명체 문제에 대한 과학적 접근
④ UAP: 그 정체성에 대한 새로운 가설
⑤ UAP의 수수께끼를 풀다: 단순한 착시

37 내용일치   ⑤

두 번째 단락에서 '몇 년 안에 (UFO에 대한) 대중들의 인식은 변했는데, 이는 부분적으로 할리우드 때문이었다'고 하였으므로 ⑤가 본문의 내용과 일치한다. ① '고대로부터 하늘에서 이상한 물체들이 목격되었다'고 하였으므로 잘못된 진술이다. ② 네 번째 단락에서 '사진과 동영상의 해상도 문제', '레이더와 같은 전자 시스템의 한계', '파일럿, 경찰관과 같이 훈련된 관찰자들의 한계' 등이 언급되고 있으므로 잘못된 진술이다. ③ 세 번째 단락에서 '미 국방부가 UAP라는 용어를 처음 사용했다'고 했으므로 잘못된 진술이다. ④ 세 번째 단락에서 '신기루, 특이한 기상 현상 또는 심지어 천체들'까지 UAP로 불릴 수 있다고 했으므로 잘못된 진술이다.

윗글의 내용과 일치하는 것은?
① 사람들은 현대에 와서야 비로소 이상한 물체들을 하늘에서 목격했다고 보고한다.
② 기술 발전으로 인해 항공 전문가들은 빠르게 비행하는 물체를 정확하게 식별할 수 있다.
③ UAP라는 용어는 UFO에 관심이 있는 민간인 집단에 의해 처음 사용되었다.
④ UAP는 다른 행성에서 온 신비한 비행 물체만을 가리킨다.
⑤ 할리우드는 UFO에 대한 대중의 태도를 바꾸는 데 어느 정도의 역할을 했다.

38-40

상품화를 반대하는 두 가지 서로 다른 주장을 구별 지었으므로, 이제 나는 뜨거운 논란이 벌어지고 있는 사례인 상업적 대리모에 대해 살펴보겠다. 일반적으로 알려진 "대리모" 계약은 아이를 임신하거나 낳을 수 없는 부부와, 수수료를 받고 아버지의 정자를 받아 임신해 만삭까지 임신을 유지하여 출산한 후 아이를 포기하기로 동의하는 여성이 관련된 것이다.

B 어떤 사람들은 상업적 대리모는 바람직하지 않은 유형의 상품화를 대표한다고 주장한다. 그러한 주장을 어떻게 평가할 수 있을까? 상품화에 대한 많은 논쟁은 유추를 통해 진행된다. 대리모 계약을 반대하는 사람들은 그것이 도덕적으로 아기를 파는 것과 같다고 주장한다. 아기를 파는 경우와 마찬가지로 상업적 대리모의 경우에도, 여성은 아이를 포기하는 대가로 수수료(일반적으로 대리모 시장에서 10,000달러 정도)를 받는다.

C 상업적 대리모 옹호자들은 이러한 유추에 저항하거나, 두 가지 관행 모두를 방어해야 한다. 그러한 유추에 반박하는 사람들은 상업적 대리모는 아기를 파는 것보다는 정자를 파는 것과 더 비슷하다고 주장한다. 돈을 받고 임신하기로 동의한 여성은 이미 있는 아이를 파는 것이 아니라 단순히 자신의 생식 능력을 이용하도록 다른 부부에게 허락하는 것일 뿐이라는 것이다. 그리고 남성이 자신의 생식 능력을 파는 것이 도덕적으로 허용된다면, 여성이 자신의 생식 능력을 파는 것이 도덕적으로 허용되지 않을 이유가 없다는 것이 이 주장의 논거이다.

A 나는 이 두 가지 유추를 모두 고려하고자 한다. 두 가지 유추 모두 상업적 대리모의 도덕적 상태를 명확히 하는 데 도움이 될 수 있다. 그러나 유추에 의한 추론이 흔히 그렇듯이, 우리의 도덕적 출발점을 구성하는 그런 직관들이 상처를 입게 된다. 대리모의 옳고 그름을 곰곰이 생각해 보면, 아기 판매와 정자 판매의 도덕적 상태에 대한 우리의 초기 견해를 수정하게 될 수도 있다.

commodification n. 상품화 contested a. 논쟁의 대상인, 이론(異論)이 있는 surrogacy n. 대리모 (행위); 대리모 제도 surrogate a. 대리의, 대용의 motherhood n. 어머니인 상태 conceive v. (아이를) 가지다[임신하다] fee n. 수수료 inseminate v. 수정(受精)시키다 sperm n. 정자 carry a baby to term 달이 찰 때까지 아기를 배고 있다 objectionable a. 불쾌한; 반대할 만한 assess v. 평가하다 proceed v. 진행하다, 나아가다 analogy n. 유추 tantamount to (나쁜 효과가) ~와 마찬가지의[~에 상당하는] relinquish v. 포기하다 dispute v. 반박하다 undergo v. 겪다 pregnancy n. 임신 preexist v. 이전부터 존재하다 reproductive a. 생식의 clarify v. 명확하게 하다 status n. 상태, 상황; 지위, 자격 intuition n. 직관력; 직감 constitute v. ~을 구성하다 unscathed a. 다치지 않은, 아무 탈 없는 revise v. 변경하다 equivalent a. 동등한, 맞먹는 contemplation n. 고찰, 심사숙고

⑤ 대리모 윤리에 대한 고찰은 이에 대한 우리의 초기 견해를 바꾸어놓을 수도 있다.

38 단락배열 ③

첫 번째 단락에서 필자는 '상품화를 반대하는 두 가지 서로 다른 주장'을 구별 지은 후, 이제 '상업적 대리모에 대한 논란'을 살펴보겠다고 하였으므로 바로 다음에는 그러한 논란의 한 쪽 주장이 나올 것으로 예상할 수 있다. 따라서 먼저 '상업적 대리모 반대자들'의 주장이 소개되는 B 단락이 나오고 이어서 C 단락에서 '상업적 대리모 옹호자들'의 주장이 소개된다. 마지막으로 A 단락에서 이 두 입장에 대한 일종의 변증법적 '종합'이 기술되고 있다. '반대'와 '옹호' 두 가지 주장의 논거가 되는 유추들을 인용하되, 그러한 '직관적인 유추'들은 윤리적 논의에서 어떤 한계가 있음을 확인하는 것이다. 한편, B 단락과 C 단락의 연결 부분을 볼 때 C → B → A로 이어질 수 없는 이유는 분명하다. 즉 C 단락 첫 번째 문장에서 '상업적 대리모 옹호자들은 이러한 유추에 저항한다'라고 했는데, '이러한 유추(the analogy)'는 곧 B 단락에서 언급된 '상업적 대리모 반대자들'이 이용하는 유추이기 때문이다.

39 글의 제목 ③

이 글은 상업적 대리모 관행에 대한 찬·반 양론이 각각 활용하는 유추 (analogy)적 논거를 소개한 다음, 그러한 유추적 논의가 대리모 관행의 윤리적 상태를 판단하는 데 유용성과 한계를 동시에 가진다고 평가하고 있다. 따라서 이 글의 제목으로는 ③이 가장 적절하다고 볼 수 있다.

윗글의 제목으로 가장 적절한 것은?
① 대리모는 어떻게 발전해 왔는가?
② 대리모의 추악한 면
③ 상업적 대리모에 대한 두 가지 견해
④ 우리는 왜 모성의 상품화를 중단하는가?
⑤ 상업적 대리모는 언제 허용되는가?

40 내용일치 ⑤

A 단락에서 '대리모의 옳고 그름을 곰곰이 생각해 보면, 아기 판매와 정자 판매의 도덕적 상태에 대한 우리의 초기 견해를 수정하게 될 수도 있다'고 하였으므로 ⑤가 본문의 내용과 일치한다. ① 대리모 관행은 '정자를 파는 것과 같다'는 논거를 사용하는 이들은 '대리모 옹호자들'이다. ② 대리모 관행이 '아기를 파는 것과 같다'고 주장하는 이들은 '대리모 반대자들'이다. ③ '상업적 대리모는 정자를 파는 것과 같다'는 논거는 '대리모 옹호자들'의 주장이고 '상업적 대리모는 아기를 파는 것과 같다'는 주장은 '대리모 반대자들'의 주장이다. 본문에서는 이 두 주장이 대조적으로 소개되었을 뿐이지 어느 쪽 견해가 '더 일반적으로 받아들여지고 있다'는 비교의 내용은 없다. ④ '아기를 파는 것과 같다'(반대자들) 또는 '정자를 파는 것과 같다'(옹호자들)는 식의 유추는 양측이 모두 사용하고 있다.

윗글의 내용과 일치하는 것은?
① 대리모 반대자들에게 그것은 정자를 파는 것과 같다.
② 대리모 옹호자들은 그것이 아기를 파는 것과 같다고 주장한다.
③ 상업적 대리모는 아기를 파는 것이라기보다는 정자를 파는 것과 더 비슷하다는 것이 더 일반적으로 받아들여진다.
④ 유추는 대리모를 옹호하는 사람들에게만 사용된다.

2024 경희대학교(인문·체육계열)

01 ⑤	02 ④	03 ③	04 ①	05 ②	06 ④	07 ②	08 ③	09 ⑤	10 ④
11 ③	12 ①	13 ③	14 ②	15 ①	16 ④	17 ⑤	18 ④	19 ⑤	20 ④
21 ③	22 ①	23 ②	24 ①	25 ③	26 ②	27 ①	28 ①	29 ②	30 ⑤
31 ⑤	32 ①	33 ③	34 ⑤	35 ②	36 ①	37 ④	38 ④	39 ①	40 ⑤

01 동의어 ⑤

proclivity n. 성향, 기질, 경향(= predisposition) sacrifice n. 희생, 제물 bloodletting n. <의학> 사혈(瀉血) appreciation n. 진가 알기, 감사, 가치의 상승 convention n. 관습, 집회, 협정 phobia n. 공포증 concern n. 관심사

이것은 특히 인간의 피가 또 다른, 아마도 의식적인 이유로 선택되었음을 암시한다. 알 수 없는 일이지만, 이 피의 기증자로 선택되는 것은 영광이었을 것이다. 그러나 콜럼버스 이전의 많은 종족들이, 단순한 사혈(瀉血: 피를 뽑는 것)이 아니라, 인간 제물을 바치는 성향을 가졌음을 감안하면, 그것은 열렬히 추구된 영예는 아니었을지도 모른다.

02 동의어 ④

enact v. 법을 제정하다 gun-safety measures 총기 안전 법안 flounder v. 허둥대다, 실수하다(= falter) uncover v. 폭로하다, 밝히다 augment v. 증대시키다 emerge v. 등장하다 sprout v. 싹트다, 생기다

최근 몇 년 동안 Maine주에서는 총기 안전 법안을 제정하려는 노력이 실패로 돌아갔다. 한 총기 법 전문가는 주민들이 Maine주를 안전하다고 생각하는 경향이 있기 때문에 Maine주가 총기규제 법을 제정하기 위한 조치가 느렸다고 말한다.

03 동의어 ③

setback n. 좌절, 차질, 방해(= obstacle) sue for 청하다 harden v. 굳어지다 opposition n. 반대, 반발 sacrifice n. 희생 collision n. 충돌 advance n. 발전, 진보

최근 전장에서의 좌절에도 불구하고 장군은 전투를 포기하거나 그 어떤 종류의 평화도 청할 생각이 없다. 오히려 국가가 적에게 궁극적 승리를 거둘 것이라는 그의 믿음은 일부 참모들을 걱정하게 만드는 형태로 굳어졌다.

04 동의어 ①

see out 끝까지 견뎌내다[살다, 지켜보다] attachment n. 애착, 집착 do justice to 공정하게 평가하다[다루다] munificence n. 후함, 아낌없이 줌(= magnanimity) commitment n. 몰입, 약속, 전념, 헌신; 책무

connoisseurship n. 감식안 ingenuity n. 창의력, 재간 extravagance n. 낭비, 사치

평생 독신으로 오슬로 외곽의 저택에서 여생을 보냈던 그는 자신의 일에 가장 큰 애착을 가졌다. 80세의 나이로 세상을 떠났을 때 그는 수천 개의 물품과 개인 서류를 고향에 기증했다. 이제 마침내 그의 고향이 그의 관대함과 그의 천재성을 공정하게 평가하고 있다.

05 동의어 ②

pique v. 자극하다, 화나게 하다(= provoke) tusk n. 엄니, 상아 conceive v. 마음에 품다, 상상하다 represent v. 대표하다, 표현하다 disseminate v. 살포하다, 퍼뜨리다 uphold v. 떠받치다, 지지하다

프린스턴 대학의 생물학자인 Shane Campbell-Staton은 동물들이 도시와 공해와 같은 인간의 창조물(환경)에 어떻게 적응하는지를 연구한다. 그의 관심은 모잠비크에 위치한 Gorongosa 국립공원의 엄니 없는 암컷 코끼리에 관한 영화로부터 자극 받았다.

06 논리완성 ④

문화가 '사람들이 참가하는 다양한 사회적 구성체들 전체에서 행하는 다양한 문화적 관행으로 구성된다.'라고 다양성을 강조한 것에서 문화가 단일하고 획일적인 것이 아님을 추론할 수 있다.

comprise v. 구성하다 engage in 관여하다 configuration n. 구성, 배치 ethnocentric a. 자민족중심주의의 consistent a. 일관된, 일치하는 esoteric a. 비밀의, 난해한, 심오한 monolithic a. 획일적인, 단일결정의 inherit v. 물려받다, 상속되다

문화는 단일한 것이 아니다: 문화는 사람들이 참가하는 다양한 사회적 구성체들 전체에서 행하는 다채로운 문화적 관행으로 구성된다.

07 논리완성 ②

사람들이 자신의 행동을 객관적으로 직시하기보다는, 자신의 행동을 설명하고, 변명하고, 정당화하고자 한다는 단서로부터, 사람들이 항상 자신의 행동의 원인을 내부적 혹은 외부적 원인 탓으로 돌리고자 한다는 것을 추론할 수 있다.

postulate v. 가정하다, 요구하다 tout v. 권유하다, 조르다 attribute v. ~탓으로 생각하다[여기다] account v. 설명하다, 책임지다 appraise v. 평가하다 recount v. 상술하다, 이야기하다

심리학자들은 사람들이 자신의 행동을 설명하고, 변명하고, 정당화하는 방식에 대한 이론을 발전시켰다. 이 이론에서는 사람들은 사건의 상황에 따라 자신이나 다른 사람의 행동을 내부적 또는 외부적 원인 탓으로 돌리도록 동기 부여된다고 가정한다.

---

08 논리완성   ③

Although는 역접의 연결사다. 따라서 Although가 이끄는 종속절의 내용과 주절의 내용은 서로 반대가 되어야 한다. 종속절에서 기술의 중립성을 주장했으므로, 주절에는 기술이 중립적이지 않고 기술의 비대칭이 인종적, 계급적 분열을 악화시킨다는 내용이 와야 한다. 그러므로 빈칸에는 ③이 와야 한다.

class n. 계급 division n. 분열 access n. 접근 alleviate v. 경감하다, 덜다 prevent v. 막다, 방해하다 exacerbate v. 악화시키다 confound v. 혼동하다, 당황케 하다 nullify v. 무효로 하다

비록 일부 사람들은 기술이 인종적으로 중립적이라고 주장하지만, 다른 사람들은 미국에서 기술의 사용이 자원이 있는 사람들로 하여금 기술의 혜택을 누리게 하고, 가난한 사람들로 하여금 (기술의 혜택에의) 접근을 거부당하게 함으로써 인종과 계급 분열을 악화시켰다고 주장한다.

---

09 논리완성   ⑤

문명이 번성하고 쇠퇴하기 위해서는, 먼저 그 문명이 출현해야 한다. 그러므로 빈칸에는 ⑤가 와야 한다.

Mesoamerica n. 중앙아메리카 correspond to 해당하다 flourish v. 번성하다 millennium n. 천년 release v. 발표하다, 출시하다, 해방하다 transfer v. 넘겨주다, 옮기다

오늘날의 중앙아메리카와 멕시코 남부에 해당하는 메소아메리카에서는 기원전 1,200년경에 처음으로 중요한 사회가 등장하여 수세기 동안 번성하다가, 500년 조금 더 지난 후 결국 쇠퇴했다.

---

10 논리완성   ④

비만이라는 만성 질병이 환자들에게 주는 것은 고통이다. 따라서 빈칸에는 ④가 와야 한다.

obesity n. 비만 chronic disease 만성 질환 afflict v. 괴롭히다 substantiate v. 구체화하다 nettle v. 안달 나게 하다 taunt v. 비웃다

비만은 흔하고 심각하면서도 비용이 많이 드는 만성 질환으로, 미국 성인의 40% 이상과 어린이의 거의 20%가 앓고 있다.

---

11 논리완성   ③

변덕, 경박함, 여성스러움, 비겁함, 우유부단이라는 자질들로부터 군주

가 자신을 보호해야 한다는 것은 이것들이 군주의 바람직하지 못한 자질이라는 말이므로 군주를 경멸받게 만들 것이다. 따라서 빈칸에는 ③이와야 한다.

frivolous a. 경솔한 effeminate a. 여자 같은, 나약한 cowardly a. 비겁한 irresolute a. 우유부단한 reef n. 암초 subject n. 신하, 가신, 신민 irrevocable a. 취소할 수 없는, 돌이킬 수 없는 allured a. 매혹하는 collaborative a. 협력적인, 합작의 despised a. 경멸하는 maudlin a. 감상적인 optimistic a. 낙천적인

그를 경멸받게 만드는 것은 변덕이 심하고, 경박하고, 여성스럽고, 비겁하고, 결단력이 없는 것으로 여겨지는 것이다. 군주는 마치 암초로부터 자신을 보호하듯이 이러한 (부정적인) 자질들로부터 자신을 보호해야 한다. 군주는 자신의 행동에서 모든 사람이 위대함과 정신과 존엄함과 힘을 알아차리도록 만들려고 애써야 한다. 그리고 군주는 신하들의 사적인 일에 관해서는, 자신의 결정이 되돌릴 수 없다고 주장해야 한다.

---

12 논리완성   ①

인간의 이해력은 자신이 선택한 이론 — 일종의 편견 — 을 벗어날 수 없다는 것이 이 글의 논지다. 자신이 선택한 의견과 반대되는 수많은 사례에도 불구하고 인간은 자신의 편견을 고집하고 심지어는 신성시하며 어떤 경우에도 그 편견을 포기하지 않는다. 그러므로 빈칸에는 ①이 와야한다.

adopt v. 채택[채용]하다 neglect v. 무시하다 despise v. 경멸하다 distinction n. 구별, 차별 set aside 제쳐두다 pernicious a. 해로운, 파멸적인 predetermination n. 사전에 결정[운명]짓기 inviolate a. 침범되지 않은, 신성한 vilify v. 비방하다, 중상하다 indefinite a. 애매한, 불명확한 cryptic a. 비밀의, 수수께끼 같은 assess v. 평가하다, 가늠하다

인간의 이해력은, 어떤 의견을 일단 채택하고 나면, 다른 모든 의견들을 그 의견을 지지하고 그 의견과 일치하게 만든다. 그리고 반대편에서 더 많고 더 중요한 사례들이 발견된다 할지라도, 인간의 이해력은 이것들을 무시하고 경멸하거나, 아니면 어떤 차별을 통해, 옆으로 제쳐두고 거부하는데, 그것은 이 크고 해로운 예정을 통해, 인간의 이해력이 먼저 내린 결론의 권위가 침해되지 않도록 하기 위해서이다.

---

13 논리완성   ③

'부의 지역적 집중이 심화되면서 출발선은 더욱 불균등해졌다.'라는 단서로부터 성공한 사람들이 자신들의 자녀를 위해 자원을 '축적하고' 있음을 추론할 수 있다.

conservatism n. 보수주의 illegitimate a. 불법의, 서출의 deplete v. 고갈하다 publicize v. 알리다, 공개하다 hoard v. 저장하다 mar v. 훼손하다, 망쳐놓다 oversee v. 감독하다, 두루 살피다

민주국가에서, 보수주의는 기회의 평등에 기반을 둔다. 만일 모든 사람이 공평하게 출발하지 않으면, 일부만이 상을 움켜쥐는 인생의 레이스는 불공정한 것으로 간주된다. 그러나 지난 40년 동안 성공한 사람들이 자녀를 위해 자원을 축적하고, (그에 따라) 부의 지역적 집중이 심화되면서 출발선은 더욱 불균등해졌다.

14 논리완성   ②

많은 사람들이 심해에 '아주 오래된 형태의 생명체, 즉 '살아있는 화석'이 아직 발견되지 않은 채 숨어 있을지도 모른다고 생각하게 되었다.'라는 단서로부터, 사람들이 심해의 생명체가 고대로부터 지금까지 '변함 없이' 존재해온 것으로 생각하고 있다는 것을 알 수 있다.

eeriness n. 무시무시함, 섬뜩함 great depths 심해 luck v. 잠복하다 trilobites n. 삼엽충 Cambrian a. <지질> 캄브리아기의 Silurian n. <지질> 실루리아기 Mesozoic n. <지질> 중생대 ephemerality n. 단명(短命), 덧없음 unchangingness n. 불변 homogeneity n. 동질성, 균질성 variety n. 다양성 manifoldness n. 복합적임, 다양함

심해의 신비함, 섬뜩함, 고대로부터의 불변성 때문에, 많은 사람들은 아주 오래된 형태의 생명체, 즉 '살아있는 화석'이 심해에 아직 발견되지 않은 채 숨어 있을지도 모른다고 생각하게 되었다. (해저 탐사선) '챌린저'호 과학자들의 마음속에는 그런 희망이 얼마간 있었을지도 모른다. 그들이 그물로 건져 올린 생명체들은 충분히 기괴했고, 그 대부분은 인류가 본 적이 없는 것들이었다. 하지만 기본적으로 그 생명체들은 현대에 속하는 유형의 것이었다. 캄브리아기의 삼엽충이나 실루리아기의 바다 전갈처럼 중생대에 바다를 침범한 거대한 해양 파충류를 연상시키는 것은 없었다.

15-17

한때는 속삭임이었던 어떤 느낌이 날마다 더 커지고 있다. 빙하가 녹고, 아이들이 학살당하고, 증오가 만연한다. 때로는 세상이 절망의 밑바닥에 가까워지고 있는 것처럼 느껴진다. 아니 당신들도 그렇게 되고 있는 것 같다. 절망에 대한 해독제가 희망일 수 있다고 전문가들은 말한다. 희망은 인간이 가진 가장 강력한 사고방식 중 하나이며, 손이 닿지 않는다고 느껴질 때조차도 획득할 수 있다. 희망을 갖는다는 것은 소망적인 사고나 맹목적인 낙관주의를 갖는 것을 의미하지 않는다. 오히려 희망은 미래가 더 나아질 수 있다는 믿음 또는 기대이며, 더 중요하게는 우리에게 그러한 미래를 추구할 수 있는 능력이 있다는 믿음 또는 기대이다. 따라서 희망의 반대는 비관주의가 아니라 오히려 동기를 상실한 무관심이다. <높은 희망을 가진 사람들은 계속 수동적으로 있지 않고 본질적으로 의미 있는 하나 이상의 목표를 향해 항상 노력을 경주한다.> 소망이 수동적인 반면, 희망은 소망하는 것에 한 걸음 더 다가가기 위해 행동하는 것이다.
희망을 갖는 것은 다양한 이점과도 관련이 있다. 연구에 따르면, 일생 동안 많은 희망을 가진 사람은 만성적인 건강 문제가 적고, 우울하거나 불안해할 가능성이 적으며, 사회적 지지도 강하고, 더 오래 사는 경향이 있다고 한다.

whisper n. 속삭임 glacier n. 빙하 slaughter v. 학살하다 rampant a. 만연한 nadir n. 천저(가장 낮은 곳) antidote n. 해독제 engage in 참여하다 wishful thinking 소망적 사고(바라는 대로 이뤄질 것이라고 생각하는 것) blind a. 맹목적인 pursue v. 추구하다 apathy n. 무관심 take action 조치를 취하다 an array of 다수의 chronic a. 만성적인 depressed a. 우울한

15 동의어   ①

rampant는 '만연한'이라는 뜻이므로 ①의 prevalent가 정답이다.

밑줄 친 단어 "rampant"와 가장 가까운 의미를 가진 것은?
① 만연한

② 삼가는
③ 꼼꼼한
④ 계속되는
⑤ 끈질긴

16 문장삽입   ④

주어진 문장, 즉 '높은 희망을 가진 사람들은 계속 수동적으로 있지 않고 본질적으로 의미 있는 하나 이상의 목표를 향해 항상 노력을 경주한다.'는 높은 희망을 가진 사람들은 수동적이지 않고 능동적이라는 특징을 설명하고 있다. 그런데 ⒟ 다음에 오는 문장이 '소망이 수동적인 반면, 희망은 원하는 것에 한 걸음 더 다가가기 위해 행동하는 것이다.'라는 뜻으로 희망의 능동성을 말하고 있다. 따라서 주어진 문장은 ⒟에 들어가는 것이 논리적으로 적절하다.

17 내용일치   ⑤

마지막 단락에서 '희망을 가진 사람은 만성적인 건강 문제가 적다.'고 했지만 그렇다고 희망의 반대인 냉담이 건강을 급격히 악화시킨다고까지 말할 수는 없으므로 ⑤가 본문의 내용과 일치하지 않는다. ① 희망의 반대는 무관심이라 했다. ② 두 번째 단락 마지막 문장에서 언급되었다. ③ 절망의 해독제가 희망일 수 있다고 했다. ④ 첫 단락에서 세상도 당신들도 절망의 밑바닥에 가까워지고 있는 것처럼 느껴진다고 했다.

다음 중 이 글의 내용과 일치하지 않는 것은?
① 희망이 있는 사람은 삶에 무관심하지 않다.
② 희망은 원하는 결과를 얻기 위해 무언가를 하는 것을 수반한다.
③ 역경의 시기에는 희망을 통해 절망을 극복할 수 있다.
④ 우리 주변의 역경은 때때로 우리가 바닥을 치고 있다고 느끼게 한다.
⑤ 냉담한 감정을 가지면 건강 상태가 급격히 악화될 가능성이 높다.

18-19

일부 연구자들은 수면이 선언적 기억(사실, 정보와 관련된 기억)을 강화하는 데 아무런 역할을 하지 않는다고 주장한다. 이 연구자들은 급속 안구 운동(REM) 수면 장애가 있는 사람들이 정상적인 생활을 계속하고 있다고 지적한다. 그리고 이 연구자들은 수면이 기억에 중요한 역할을 한다면, 이 사람들에게 명백한 기억손상이 있을 것이라고 주장한다. 그러나 (동시에) 같은 연구자들은 이러한 개인들의 인지 능력이 체계적으로 조사된 바가 없으며, 이러한 개인들은 수행 능력이 수면에 의존하는 것으로 알려진 과제에 대한 연구의 대상도 된 적이 없다는 점 또한 인정한다. (더 나아가) 이러한 연구들이 이루어진다고 하더라도, 그 연구들은 일반적인 수면이 아니라, 렘수면의 역할에 대한 이해를 명확히 할 수 있을 뿐이다.
이 연구자들은 또한 하룻밤 사이에 기억력이 향상되는 것은 수면으로 인한 것이 아니라 단순한 시간의 흐름으로 인한 것으로 설명할 수 있다고 주장한다. 그러나 수면이 깨어 있는 동안의 정신 활동으로 인한 미래의 간섭으로부터 선언적 기억을 안정화시킨다는 것을 보여주는 연구를 포함하여, 수면 후 기억력에 대한 최근의 연구는 이러한 주장을 지속 가능하지 않게 만든다. 물론 깨어 있는 동안에도 기억 강화 과정이 일어나며, 그 중 일부는 수면에 의존하지도 않고 수면에 의해 향상되지도 않는다. 그러나 수면과 깨어 있는 상태를 비교했을 때, 수면 후 수행 능력이 더 좋다면 수면이 기억력에 미치는 일부 이점은 인정되어야 한다.

consolidation n. 통합, 합동 declarative memory 선언적 기억(의식적으로 회상하고 "선언"할 수 있는 사실이나 사건에 대한 기억) note v. 지적하다 impairment n. 손상, 감손 rapid eye movement 급속 안구운동(REM) memory deficits 기억 손상 performance n. 수행능력

---

18 빈칸완성　　　　　　　　　　　④

빈칸 Ⓐ는 주절이 연구 효과가 제한적임을 지적하는 부정적인 내용이므로 '연구들이 이루어진다고 하더라도'라는 의미가 되게 양보의 접속사 Even if나 Even though가 적절하다. 한편, 하룻밤 사이에 기억력이 향상되는 것은 수면에 기인하는 것이거나 혹은 단순한 시간의 흐름에 기인하는 것이다. 따라서 빈칸 Ⓑ에는 '~에 기인하다'라는 의미의 attributed to가 와야 한다.

다음 Ⓐ와 Ⓑ에 들어갈 말로 가장 적절한 것은?
① 만일 ― 조절하다
② ~때문에 ― 틀렸음을 입증하다
③ ~동안에 ― 설명하다
④ 비록 ~일지라도 ― 기인하다
⑤ 비록 ~일지라도 ― 박탈하다

---

19 내용일치　　　　　　　　　　　⑤

'하지만 수면과 깨어 있는 상태를 비교했을 때, 수면 후 수행 능력이 더 좋다면 수면이 기억력에 미치는 일부 이점은 인정되어야 한다.'라는 마지막 문장의 단서로부터 ⑤가 본문의 내용과 일치하지 않는다는 것을 알 수 있다. 또 첫 문장에서 이렇게 주장한 연구자들은 램 수면장애자도 정상생활을 한다고 지적하지만 그 이하에서 연구조사가 아직 이루어지지 않았다고 한 점으로 볼 때 충분한 증거가 있다고는 할 수 없다. ③ 두 번째 단락 첫 문장의 '하룻밤 사이에 발생하는 기억력 향상은 수면으로 인한 것이 아니라 단순한 시간의 흐름으로 인한 것으로 설명할 수 있다'라는 주장은 그 다음 문장에서 '수면 후 기억력에 대한 최근의 연구는 이러한 주장을 지속 가능하지 않게 만든다'고 하여 그 타당성이 부정되었는데, 부정되면 수면으로 인한 것일 수도 있고 단순한 시간의 흐름으로 인한 것일 수도 있다는 말이 되므로 글의 내용과 일치한다.

다음 중 이 글의 내용과 일치하지 않는 것을 고르시오?
① 렘수면 장애가 있는 사람도 정상적인 생활을 계속할 수 있다.
② 수면이 선언적 기억에 미치는 영향을 확인하기 위해서는 렘수면 장애가 있는 개인의 인지 능력이 체계적으로 검사되어야 한다.
③ 하룻밤 사이에 발생하는 기억력 향상은 단순히 시간의 흐름으로 설명할 수 있다.
④ 일부 연구 결과들은 선언적 기억을 안정시키는 데 있어서 수면의 역할을 입증해준다.
⑤ 수면이 선언적 기억의 통합에 아무런 역할을 하지 않는다는 결론을 내릴 수 있는 충분한 증거가 있다.

20-21

인종 차별과 편견은 고통스러운 현실이며 성인과 어린이의 건강에 해로운 것으로 점점 더 많이 인식되고 있다. 이러한 스트레스 경험은 임신 중에 산모로부터 아이에게 전달되어 유아의 뇌 회로의 강도를 변화시키는 것으로 보인다. 최근 연구에 따르면, 차별을 경험한 산모의 유아는 일반적으로 편도체와 전전두엽 피질 사이의 연결이 약하다고 한다. 편도체는 감정 처리와 관련된 뇌 영역으로, 많은 기분 장애에서 변화된 모습을 보인다. 또한 편도체는 얼굴을 구별하는 것과 같은 민족 및 인종적 처리에도 관여하는 것으로 보인다. 이 연구 결과는 연구자들이 발견한 연결성 변화가 유아의 감정 조절 능력을 감소시키고 정신 건강 장애의 위험을 증가시킬 수 있음을 시사한다.

discrimination n. 차별 detrimental a. 유해한 pregnancy n. 임신 brain circuit 뇌 회로 strength n. 강도, 내구력 amygdala n. 편도체 prefrontal cortex 전전두엽 피질

---

20 빈칸완성　　　　　　　　　　　④

빈칸 Ⓐ는 '최근 연구에 따르면 차별을 경험한 산모의 유아는 일반적으로 편도체와 전전두엽 피질 사이의 연결이 약하다고 한다.'라는 단서로부터 차별에 따른 스트레스의 경험이 산모에게서 유아에게로 '전달'됨을 추론할 수 있다. 빈칸 Ⓑ는 유아의 감정 조절 능력을 감소한다는 것은 유아의 정신 건강 장애의 위험이 '증가'한다는 것을 의미한다.

다음 중 Ⓐ와 Ⓑ에 들어갈 말로 가장 적절한 것은?
① 명령하다 ― 제거하다
② 수여하다 ― 상쇄하다
③ 유전하다 ― 감소하다
④ 전달하다 ― 증가하다
⑤ 채택하다 ― 용이하게 하다

---

21 내용추론　　　　　　　　　　　③

이 글 어디에도 출산율과 관련된 내용은 보이지 않는다. 그러므로 이 글에서 추론할 수 없는 것은 ③ '출산율을 높이려면 문화적 포용성을 높여야 한다.'이다. ④ 편도체를 가리킨다.

다음 중 이 글로부터 추론할 수 없는 것은?
① 특히 임신 중에는 사람들을 대하고 사람들과 상호작용하는 방식이 중요하다.
② 임신 중 차별의 경험은 자녀에게 심각한 영향을 미칠 수 있다.
③ 출산율을 높이려면 문화적 포용성을 높여야 한다.
④ 뇌의 동일한 영역이 감정과 인종 처리를 모두 처리한다.
⑤ 편도체는 태아기 스트레스에 민감하다.

22-23

우리의 식단은 상징적인 듀오(짝)로 가득하다. 땅콩버터와 젤리. 계란과 베이컨. 쿠키와 우유. 하지만 그 중에서도 단연 돋보이는 듀오가 있으니, 바로 소금과 후추다. 파스타부터 샐러드 드레싱, 수프와 타코에 이르기까지 거의 모든 맛좋은 요리법에는 소금과 후추가 필요하다. 때로 소금과 후추는 모든 요리를 위한 최소한의 향신료 혼합으로 여겨지기도 한다.
소금이 우리 몸에 미치는 영향, 특히 고혈압과 같은 문제에 대해 항상 논란이 있어 왔다. 하지만 이에 대응되는 후추는 어떨까? 후추도 건강에 좋을까, 아니면 소금과 마찬가지로 과다 섭취를 피해야 할까? 후추에는 다양한 건강상의 이점이 있는 항산화제와 같은 화합물이 포함되어 있지만, 후추가 질병의 효과적인 치료법이나 질병의 발병을 예방하는 데 도움이

된다는 데이터는 아직 충분하지 않다.

그러나 후추를 다른 향신료 대신 사용하면 질병 예방이나 치료에 도움이 될 수 있다. 과도한 나트륨 섭취는 고혈압증 또는 고혈압이라는 질환을 유발할 수 있다. 고혈압 환자는 심장마비나 뇌졸중과 같은 심혈관 합병증을 예방하기 위해 나트륨 섭취를 제한하는 것이 좋다. 소금이 적은 음식은 맛이 떨어질 수 있기 때문에 이는 어려울 수 있다. 이때 후추와 같은 향신료는 건강에 영향을 주지 않으면서도 풍미를 더할 수 있기 때문에 큰 도움이 될 수 있다. 후추는 후추가 아니면 밋밋할 수 있는 요리를 아주 부드러운 맛으로 바꿔줄 수 있다.

iconic a. 상징적인 take the cake 단연 뛰어나다 savory a. 맛있는, 즐거운 recipe n. 요리법 seasoning blend 조미료 혼합 chatter n. 수다, 논란 excess n. 과도한 antioxidant n. 항산화제 ailment n. 질병 development n. 발병 substitute n. 대체, 대용품, 예비품 hypertension n. 고혈압 sodium n. 나트륨 consumption n. 섭취 cardiovascular a. 심장 혈관의 complications n. 합병증 stroke n. 뇌졸중 make a huge difference 도움이 되다 bland a. 밋밋한

22 글의 제목 ①

식단의 대표적인 듀오인 소금과 후추에 대해 이야기하면서, 소금은 건강상의 문제를 일으킬 수 있는 반면, '후추는 다른 향신료 대신 사용하면 질병 예방이나 치료에 도움이 될 수 있고, 건강에 영향을 주지 않으면서도 풍미를 더할 수 있음'을 말하고 있는 내용이다. 그러므로 제목으로는 ①이 가장 적절하다.

다음 중 이 글의 제목으로 가장 적절한 것은?
① 후추를 대용품으로 사용해보세요.
② 최고의 조미료 블렌드(혼합): 소금과 후추
③ 후추는 항산화 성분을 함유하고 있다
④ 후추는 질병을 예방한다.
⑤ 후추의 강한 풍미

23 빈칸완성 ②

빈칸 Ⓐ는 나트륨의 과도한 섭취가 고혈압을 불러온다는 단서로부터 '섭취하다' 정도의 표현이 와야 함을 추론할 수 있다. 빈칸 Ⓑ의 경우, 후추를 음식에 넣으면 음식 맛이 살아나므로 음식의 맛이 밋밋해진다는 것은 후추를 음식에 넣지 않은 경우라는 것을 추론할 수 있다. 따라서 빈칸 Ⓑ에는 '그렇지 않으면'이 와야 한다.

다음 중 Ⓐ와 Ⓑ에 들어갈 말로 가장 적절한 것은?
① 소화 — 이상하게
② 섭취 — 그렇지 않으면
③ 추출 — 몹시, 지독히
④ 한입, 한입 물어뜯기 — 독창적인
⑤ 탐닉, 방종 — 지나치게

24 문장배열 ③

이 문제를 푸는 단서는 두 가지이다. 그 하나는 이 글이 역사적 사실을 연대기적으로 기술하고 있다는 것이고 다른 하나는 이 글의 구조가 인과

논리에 기대고 있다는 것이다. 그러므로 이 글은 제 2차 대전 중 미국 여성들의 노동시장 참여에서 시작하여 1950년대의 여성들의 농업 노동시장에 대한 설명으로 마무리된다. 즉, 2차 대전으로 인한 여성 고용의 변화라는 주제를 곧바로 언급한 Ⓓ가 먼저 오고, Ⓓ에서 여성 역할의 변화를 인정한 것에 이어 제조업에 여성이 거의 없었음을 인정한 Ⓔ가 그다음에 오고, 농업 분야에서는 여성 고용이 계속되었음을 언급한 Ⓑ가 그다음에 오고, 농업 분야에서 여성을 더 많이 고용하게 되었다고 한 Ⓒ가 그다음에 오고, 그 결과 1950년대에도 농업에서의 여성 고용이 늘어났다는 Ⓐ가 마지막에 오는 것이 적절한 순서이다.

scholarship n. 학문, 연구 workforce n. 노동력 manufacturing job 제조업 temporary worker 임시직 노동자 engage in 종사하다 rhetoric n. 수사, 수사학

Ⓓ 미국의 여성 고용에 관한 대부분의 연구들은 2차 세계대전으로 인해 노동력에서 여성의 역할이 극적으로 변화했음을 인정한다. Ⓔ 이 연구들은 또한 남성들이 전쟁에서 돌아온 후에, 제조업 일자리에 남아있는 여성은 거의 없었다는 사실을 인정한다. Ⓑ 그러나 여성을 임시직으로 여겼던 다른 산업과 달리, 농업 분야에서의 여성 고용은 전쟁과 함께 끝나지 않았다. Ⓒ 대신, 농업의 확장과 남성 농업 노동자의 꾸준한 감소라는 현상이 결합된 결과, 농업업계에서는 전후 몇 년 동안 더 많은 여성을 고용하게 되었다. Ⓐ 결과적으로, 1950년대에는 여성을 가정으로 복귀시켜야 한다는 대중매체의 수사에도 불구하고 농업 노동에 종사하는 여성의 수는 증가했다.

25-27

마다가스카르 남부의 주민들이 위험에 처해 있다. 유엔에 따르면 110만 명 이상이 기아에 허덕이고 있다. 이는 5세 미만 어린이 50만 명 이상이 심각한 영양실조 위험에 처해 있다는 것을 의미한다. 많은 가정이 선인장으로 빈약한 식단을 채우고 있다.

이러한 재난에는 여러 가지 원인이 있으며, 유엔은 기후 변화를 강조한다. 인간이 초래한 기후 변화는 확실히 세계에서 네 번째로 큰 이 섬에 영향을 미쳤다. 마다가스카르 남부는 오랫동안 불규칙한 비로 고통받아왔다. 가뭄은 흔하고 1903년, 1910년, 1916년, 1921년, 1943년에는 기근이 기록되기도 했다. 하지만 최근에는 비가 더욱 불규칙해져 40년 만에 최악의 가뭄을 겪고 있다. 주식인 카사바의 수확량은 평년보다 60~90% 감소할 것으로 예상된다. 쌀 가격도 치솟고 있다.

게다가, 코로나19는 사람들을 더욱 가난하게 만들었다. 빠르게 증가하는 인구에도 불구하고, 마다가스카르의 경제는 작년에 4.2% 감소했다. 마다가스카르는 외부 세계로부터 거의 담을 쌓아 주요 수입원인 관광업이 붕괴되었다. 여우원숭이를 찾아 열대우림을 트레킹하던 부유한 외국인들은 이제 집에 머물러 있다. 이들에게 의존하던 150만 명의 주민들은 생계 수단을 잃었다.

기부자들은 사람들이 굶주리지 않도록 힘을 보태야 한다. 특히 어린이들은 성장단계에서 몸과 마음이 발육부진상태로 되지 않으려면 충분한 영양분이 필요하다. 동시에 현재의 재난은 마다가스카르 정부에 경각심을 불러일으키는 계기가 되어야 한다. 만일 역대 정권이 그토록 오랫동안 경제를 잘못 관리하지만 않았었다면, 마다가스카르는 (지금) 충격에 더 잘 대처할 수 있을 만큼 번영했을 것이다.

malnourished a. 영양실조의 eke out 보충하다, ~의 부족분을 채우다 meager a. 빈약한 cactus n. 선인장 calamity n. 재난 erratic a. 불규칙한 cassava n. 카사바나무(여러 가지 방법으로 요리하거나 가루로도 빻아서 식용함) staple n. 주식 all but 거의 shut oneself off from ~로부터 담을 쌓다, 단절하다 lemur n. (마다가스카르산) 여우원숭

이 stunted a. 발육[성장]을 저해당한 wake-up call 사람들의 주의를 촉구하는 일 well-heeled a. 부유한, 돈이 많은

---

25 동의어 ③

well-heeled는 '유복한', '부유한'이라는 의미이므로, ③이 정답이다.

밑줄 친 단어 "well-heeled"와 가장 가까운 의미를 갖고 있는 것은?
① 외향적인
② 모험심이 넘치는
③ 부유한
④ 활력이 넘치는
⑤ 교양 있는

---

26 글의 어조 ②

'만일 역대 정권이 그토록 오랫동안 경제를 잘못 관리하지만 않았었다면, 마다가스카르는 (지금) 충격에 더 잘 대처할 수 있을 만큼 번영했을 것이다.'라는 밑줄 친 문장은 역대정권의 실정을 비판하는 톤을 담고 있다. 따라서 밑줄 친 문장의 톤은 ② '비판적'이다.

다음 중 밑줄 친 문장의 어조를 가장 잘 묘사하고 있는 것은?
① 낙담한
② 비판적인
③ 동정적인
④ 당황한
⑤ 냉소적인

---

27 내용추론 ①

많은 가정이 선인장으로 빈약한 식단을 채우고 있다고 한 것과 주식인 카사바의 수확량은 평년보다 60~90% 감소할 것으로 예상된다고 한 것에서 선인장은 모자라는 식량을 보충하는 것이고 주식은 카사바임을 알 수 있으므로 ①이 추론할 수 없는 것이다. ⑤ 마다가스카르는 외부 세계로부터 거의 담을 쌓아 주요 수입원인 관광업이 붕괴되어서 주민들이 생계 수단을 잃은 것은 최근의 경제 위기가 이들의 빈곤의 부분적인 원인임을 말해준다.

다음 중 이 글로부터 추론할 수 없는 것은?
① 선인장은 오랫동안 마다가스카르 남부에서 선호되는 주식이었다.
② 불규칙한 비는 마다가스카르 남부에서 예상치 못한 사건이 아니다.
③ 영양실조는 건강에 중대한 영향을 미칠 가능성이 높다.
④ 마다가스카르 경제가 살아나려면 관광산업이 다시 일어서야만 한다.
⑤ 마다가스카르의 빈곤은 부분적으로 최근의 경제 위기로 인한 것이다.

28-29

여성의 신화(여성을 신화화하는 것)는 문학에서 상당한 부분을 차지한다. 하지만 일상생활에서 그것은 얼마나 중요한가? 그것은 개인의 관습과 행동에 어느 정도로 영향을 미치는가? 이 질문에 대답하려면 이 신화가 현실과 맺고 있는 관계를 정확하게 기술할 필요가 있을 것이다.
신화에는 다양한 종류가 있다. 인간 조건의 <가변적인> 측면 — 즉 인류를

두 계층의 개인으로 "분할"하는 것 — 을 승화시키는 이 여성의 신화는 정적인 신화이다. 그것은 직접 경험되거나 경험에 기초하여 개념화되는 현실을 플라톤의 이데아 영역에 투사한다. 사실, 가치, 의미, 지식, 경험적 법칙 대신에, 그것은 시간을 초월하고 불변하며 필수적인 초월적 이데아로 대체한다. 이 이데아는 주어진 것 너머에 있기 때문에 논란의 여지가 없다. 그것은 절대적인 진리를 부여받았다. 따라서 실제 여성의 분산되고, 우연적이고, 다중적인 존재에 반대하는 것처럼, 신화적 사유는 유일하고 불변하는 영원한 여성성에도 반대한다. 이 개념에 대해 제공된 정의가 살과 피를 지닌 평범한 여성의 행동과 모순된다면, 틀린 것은 후자이다. 우리는 여성성이 거짓 실체라는 말을 듣게 되는 것이 아니라, 관련된 여성이 여성적이지 않다는 말을 듣게 된다. 경험의 반대되는 사실들은 신화에 맞서 무력하다.

considerable a. 상당한 bear v. 맺다 sublimate v. 승화하다 project v. 투사하다 Platonic ideas 플라톤의 이데아 in place of ~대신에 significance n. 의미 substitute v. 대체하다 transcendental Idea (현실을 넘어서는) 초월적인 이데아 endow v. 부여하다 dispersed a. 분산된 contingent a. 우발적인, 불의의 contradict v. 모순되다 flesh-and-blood n. (평범한·정상적인) 인간 impotent a. 무력한

---

28 문맥상 적절하지 않은 단어 고르기 ①

인류를 두 계층의 개인으로 "분할"하는 인간의 조건이란 것의 의미는, 인간이 남자와 여자로 나누어져 있다는 것이다. 인간이 남자와 여자로 분할된다는 것은 변할 수 없는 불변적인 인간의 조건이다. 그러므로 Ⓐ mutable을 immutable로 고쳐야 한다.

---

29 빈칸완성 ②

이 글은 시몬드 보부아르 『제 2의 성』의 일부이다. 여기서 여성의 신화는 고대의 신화가 아니라 우리 사회가 여성에 대해 갖고 있는 여성에 대한 편견이다. 마지막 문장에서 '경험의 반대되는 사실은 신화에 맞서 무력하다.'고 했는데, 이것은 여성에 대한 우리의 편견이 아주 견고하다는 것이다. 따라서 여성이 우리의 편견에서 벗어나는 언행을 하게 되면, 편견에 사로잡힌 우리는 그러한 언행을 '여성적이지 않다'라고 판단한다.

빈칸에 들어가기에 가장 적절하게 추론된 문구를 고르시오.
① 어떤 여성들은 지적이지 않다
② 관련된 여성은 여성적이지 않다
③ 여성은 동료 인간이다
④ 여성은 다중적 존재다
⑤ 여성은 일반적으로 호전적이지 않다

30-31

한 젊은 여성이 책을 들고 미소를 짓는다. "오늘이 내가 'The Song of Achilles'를 읽는 첫날입니다."라고 그녀가 말한다. 영상이 앞으로 넘어간다. "그리고 이렇게 나는 이 책을 끝냅니다." 눈물로 얼룩진 얼굴로 그녀는 신음한다. "당신을 흐느끼게 만들 책"이라는 제목의 또 다른 영상에서는 "울지 않고는 생각할 수 없다", "결국 너무 많이 울었다. (너무 울어서) 셔츠를 갈아입어야 했다" 등 다양한 이야기가 어떻게 독자들을 울게 만들었는지에 대한 메모 글을 제공한다. 이것은 TikTok 앱의 문학 부문으로 잘 알려진 BookTok이다. 빅토리아 시대 멜로드라마의 감정적 피치를 상상하고, 여기에 음악을 추가하면, 당신은 (BookTok에 대한) 일반적인 아이디어

를 얻게 된다.

BookTok은 열정적이다. 그것은 적어도 출판사에게는 수익성이 있다. 영국에 본사를 둔 출판사인 Bloomsbury는 최근 기록적인 매출과 220%의 이익 증가를 보고했는데, 이 회사의 사장인 Nigel Newton은 (이런 이익의 증가가) 부분적으로는 BookTok의 "절대 현상"에 기인한 것이라고 말했다. Amazon에서 BookTok은 너무나 영향력이 커서 책 제목 자체에 뛰어들었다. 예를 들어, 소설 "It Ends With Us,"는 이제 "It Ends With Us.: 틱톡 때문에 이 책을 사게 되었어요!"로 목록에 실린다. 분명히 TikTok은 좋은 일을 했다. 이 로맨스(소설)는 영국과 미국 모두에서 상위 100위 안에 들었다.

이 매체(BookTok)는 보기만큼 지나치게 감정적이지는 않다. 과장된 감정의 대부분은 아이러니하고, 일부 동영상은 매우 재미있으며, 특히 남성의 시선을 조롱하는 해시태그 #writtenbymen이 있는 동영상은 매우 웃기다. 그럼에도 불구하고 (BookTok의) 많은 동영상들은 주류 서평가들로 하여금 경멸의 말을 하게 할 것이다. <그런데 왜 BookTok의 스타인 젊은 여성들이, 구시대 문학가들이 자신들을 어떻게 생각하는지에 관심을 가져야 하는 가?> 상당히 최근까지도 이들(여성들)의 관점은 소설과 비평 모두에서 소외되었다. 대부분의 소설 독자가 여성임에도 불구하고 백인 남성이 두 분야를 모두 지배했다.

moan v. 신음하다 stained a. 얼룩진 sob v. 흐느끼다 assorted a. 선별된, 잡다한 bawl v. 외치다, 울다 put down to ~탓으로 돌리다 leap into ~에 이르다 gushy a. 지나치게 감정적인, 과장된 말을 하는 poke fun at 조롱하다 male gaze (여성을 성적으로 바라보는) 남성의 시선 tut n. 쯧[체](하고 혀를 차기: 경멸이나 모욕을 나타냄)

---

30 글의 제목 ⑤

이 글은 최근 젊은 여성들 사이에서 선풍적인 인기를 얻고 있는 새로운 형태의 독서 경험 발표 방식이자 서적 판매 방식이기도 한 BookTok을 다루고 있다. 따라서 적절한 제목은 ⑤이다.

다음 중 이 글의 제목으로 가장 적절한 것은?
① BookTok은 로맨스 장르를 대중화하고 있다.
② 새로운 형태의 문학 비평이 도서 판매를 촉진하고 있다.
③ 젊은 여성들이 소설 읽기에 대한 욕구를 되살리고 있다.
④ 젊은 여성들의 감상주의는 최근 유행하는 신드롬이다.
⑤ BookTok이 전통적인 서적 판매 방식을 바꾸고 있다.

---

31 문장삽입 ⑤

주어진 문장은 '그런데 왜 BookTok의 스타인 젊은 여성이 구시대 문학가들이 자신들을 어떻게 생각하는지에 관심을 가져야 하는가?'이다. 이 문장의 핵심은 구시대의 문학가들과 BookTok의 스타들과의 관계이다. 이 글에서 이 둘 사이의 관계가 언급되는 것은 이 글의 마지막 부분이다. 따라서 주어진 문장이 들어갈 곳은 Ⓔ이다. Ⓔ 앞 문장의 '(BookTok의) 많은 동영상들'은 BookTok의 동영상에 나오는 스타인 젊은 여성들을 가리키고 '주류 서평가들'은 구시대 문학가들에 해당한다.

32-33

프랑스인은 푸아그라, 아이슬란드인은 '하칼'(소변 향이 나는 발효 생선)을 먹으며, 미국인은 통조림 호박을 파이에 넣어 구워 감사의 마음을 전한다.

인간이 먹는 다양한 음식은 미식의 즐거움일 뿐만 아니라 생태학적, 인류학적 다양성을 반영한다. 이는 수만 년에 걸쳐 진행된 평행하면서도 독립적인 문화적 진화의 결과다.

그러나 선택이 (다양화가 아닌) 다른 방식으로 확산됨에 따라 식단이 압축되고 표준화되었다. 심지어 파리 사람들도 결국 스타벅스가 자신들의 도로에 들어서는 것을 용인했다. BBC의 음식 저널리스트인 Dan Saladino는 독자들에게 잃어버릴 수 있는 것이 무엇인지 상기시켜 준다. "Eating to Extinction(먹다가 죽기)"에서 그는 '세계에서 가장 희귀한 음식'을 찾기 위해 먼 곳을 여행한다. 여기에는 "아삭한 식감과 달콤한 코코넛 맛을 지닌 무와 같은 뿌리"인 무르농(Murnong)이 포함된다. 거의 사라지기 전까지, 수천 년 동안 그것(무르농)은 호주 원주민의 주요 음식이었다.

지난 세기 동안 인간 식품의 다양성이 급속히 쇠퇴했다는 것은 분명하다. 연구자들은, 덴마크의 토탄 습지에 가라앉았을 때 시신이 보존된 2,500년 전에 사망한 한 남성의 뱃속에서 (그 남자가 먹었던) 마지막 식사의 잔해를 발견했다. 그것은 "보리와 아마와 40가지 식물의 씨앗으로 만든 죽"이었다. 동부 아프리카에 남아 있는 마지막 수렵 채집 부족 중 하나인 Hadza족은 "800종 이상의 식물과 동물로 구성된 강력한 야생 메뉴를 먹는다." 이와 대조적으로, 대부분의 (현대) 인간은 이제 단 8가지 음식에서 칼로리 섭취량의 75%를 얻는다.

심지어 이들 각 식품군 내에서도 균질화가 존재한다. 수십 년간의 선택적 육종(번식)과 세계 식품 시장의 압박으로 인해 모든 농장에서는 동일한 품종의 곡물을 재배하고 동일한 품종의 가축을 기른다.

foie gras 푸아 그라(거위 간으로 만든 파테(pâté)) hakarl n. 하칼(아이슬란드 전통 음식) fermented a. 발효한 aroma n. 향 urine n. 소변 tinned a. 통조림으로 된 epicurean a. 식도락의 proliferate v. 증식하다, 풍부해지다 boulevard n. 대로 radish n. 무 Aboriginal n. 오스트레일리아 원주민의 peat bog 이탄 늪 porridge n. 죽 barley n. 보리 flax n. 아마 breeding n. 육종, 번식

---

32 빈칸완성 ①

빈칸 이하에서 "2,500년 전에 사망한 한 남성은 보리와 아마와 40가지 식물의 씨앗이라는 다양한 것들을 먹었는데, 대부분의 현대 인간은 이제 단 8가지 음식을 먹는다"고 했으므로, 빈칸에는 ① '인간 음식 다양성의 급격한 쇠퇴'가 들어가는 것이 적절하다.

다음 중 Ⓐ에 들어갈 말로 가장 적절한 것은?
① 인간 음식 다양성의 급격한 쇠퇴
② 인간 음식 다양성에 대한 인류학적 증거
③ 희귀한 음식으로 인한 인간의 식욕 증가
④ 인류의 유산을 보존하기 위한 향토음식의 세계화
⑤ 선택한 음식을 개선할 필요성

---

33 빈칸완성 ③

마지막 문장, 즉 ' 수십 년간의 선택적 육종(번식)과 세계 식품 시장의 압박으로 인해 모든 농장에서는 동일한 품종의 곡물을 재배하고 동일한 품종의 가축을 기른다.'라는 단서로부터 빈칸에 ③이 와야 함을 추론할 수 있다.

다음 중 ⓑ에 들어갈 말로 가장 적절한 것은?
① 혼성화
② 차이
③ 동질화
④ 타락
⑤ 돌연변이

34-35

개척지 생활의 조건에서 매우 중요한 (미국의) 지적 특성이 생겨났다. 식민지 시대부터 각 개척지를 따라 여행한 사람들의 작품에는 몇 가지 공통된 특성이 묘사되어 있다. 그리고 이러한 특성은 약화되기는 했지만 더 높은 사회 조직이 성공한 후에도 여전히 그것이 생겨난 곳에서 살아남아 지속되고 있다. 그 결과 미국의 지성은 개척지에 힘입어 눈에 띄는 고유한 특징을 갖게 되었다. 그 특징들이란 예민함과 호기심이 결합된 난폭함과 강인함; 실용적이고 창의적인 성향, 편법을 찾아내는 재빠름; 예술적인 면은 부족하지만 큰 목적을 달성하는 데는 강력한 물질적인 것에 대한 뛰어난 이해력; 불안하고 신경질적인 에너지; 선한 쪽으로도 악한 쪽으로도 작용하는 지배적인 개인주의, 그리고 동시에 자유에서 오는 활력과 충만함 ─ 이러한 것들이 개척지의 특성들 또는 개척지의 존재로 인해 다른 곳에서 소환되는 특성들이다. 콜럼버스 함대가 신대륙의 바다로 항해해 들어온 시절부터, 미국은 기회의 다른 이름이었다. 그리고 미국인들은 개방적일 뿐만 아니라 심지어 강요되어 온 끊임없는 확장으로부터 그들의 어조를 취했다. 그는 미국인의 삶의 팽창적인 성격이 이제 완전히 종식되었다고 주장해야 하는 <신중한> 예언자가 될 것이다. 운동(팽창)은 그것(미국인의 삶)의 지배적인 사실이었다. 그리고 이러한 훈련이 국민에게 아무런 영향을 미치지 않으면, 미국의 에너지는 그것이 발휘되기 위한 더 넓은 영역을 계속 요구할 것이다.

frontier n. 개척지, 변경 striking a. 두드러진 coarseness n. 난폭함, 조야함 acuteness n. 날카로움 inquisitiveness n. 호기심 turn of mind 성향, 기질 masterful a. 능수능란한 grasp n. 움켜 쥠, 이해 withal ad. 동시에 buoyancy n. 부력, 기력, 명랑, 활력 exuberance n. 넘쳐흐름, 충만, 풍요 fleet n. 함대 incessant a. 끊임없는, 그칠 새 없는 prudent a. 신중한, 분별 있는 rash a. 경솔한, 무분별한, 성급한

---

34 빈칸완성　　　　　　　　　　⑤

빈칸에 들어갈 표현은 빈칸 앞에 있는 표현과 순접관계에 있다. 따라서 빈칸에 들어갈 표현은 빈칸 앞에 있는 표현, 즉 '실용적이고 창의적인 성향'과 연관되어 있어야한다. 보기들 중에서 '실용적이고 창의적인 성향'과 의미가 통하는 표현은 ⑤이다.

빈칸을 채우기 위해 가장 적절하게 추론된 문구를 고르시오.
① 정주하는 직업을 열망하는
② 금욕적인 삶을 탐닉하는
③ 공동체 정신을 질투하는
④ 전통주의에 충실한
⑤ 편법 찾기에 재빠른

---

35 문맥상 적절하지 않은 단어 고르기　　②

마지막 문장의 '그리고 이러한 훈련이 국민에게 아무런 영향을 미치지 않으면 미국의 에너지는 그것이 발휘되기 위한 더 넓은 영역을 계속 요

구할 것이다.'로부터 '미국인의 삶의 팽창적 성격이 이제 완전히 종식되었다'는 주장이 신중한 주장이 아니라 성급하고 조급한 주장임을 알 수 있다. 그러므로 ⓑ prudent를 rash로 고쳐야 한다.

36-37

Steve Neale은 장르에 관한 그의 글에서, 장르 영화에서 기준이 되는 작품(표준적인 영화)을 이해하는 데 도움이 되는 두 가지 유용한 구분을 제시한다. 먼저 그는 핍진성(그럴듯함)과 리얼리즘(사실주의)을 구분한다. 이 용어들은 기준이 되는 작품을 상당히 다른 방식으로 지칭한다.
리얼리즘은 오늘날 더 친숙한 용어로서, 우리는 이를 통해 픽션(허구)이 우리가 우리 자신의 세계처럼 인식하는 세계를 구성하는지 여부를 판단한다. 그러나 앞서 살펴본 바와 같이 리얼리즘은 매우 문제가 많은 범주다. 따라서 Steve Neale은 픽션(허구)에서 '리얼리티'는 항상 구성된다는 사실을 강조하기 위해 하나의 개념을 문학사에서 되살려낸다. <그는 핍진성(그럴듯함)이란 실제로 사실일 수도 있고 아닐 수도 있는 것을 의미하지 않고, 지배적인 문화가 사실이라고 믿는 것, 일반적으로 믿을만하고 적합하며 적절하다고 받아들여지는 것을 의미한다고 주장한다.> Neale은 문화적 핍진성과 일반적 핍진성을 구분한다. 어떤 영화가 서부극, 뮤지컬, 공포영화 등 특정 장르에 속하는 영화로 인정받기 위해서, 영화는 해당 장르의 규칙을 준수해야 한다. 달리 말해, 장르의 관습은 서부극이나 연속극에서 일어나야 할 일이라는 2차적 핍진성을 만들어내며, 이를 통해 우리가 특정 장르와 연관시키는 픽션(허구)의 세계의 신뢰성 또는 진실성이 보장된다. 일반적 핍진성은 일반적인 신뢰성의 범위 내에서 판타지를 이용하는 것을 상당히 허용하는 반면(예: 뮤지컬에서 자신의 문제를 노래하는 것, 고딕 공포 영화에서 마녀의 힘), 문화적 핍진성은 우리로 하여금 픽션(허구) 바깥의 사회 세계의 규범, 관습, 상식을 참조하게 한다.

referent n. 지시대상, 관계항 verisimilitude n. 그럴듯함, 핍진성(진실에 가깝다고 여겨지는 정도) term n. 용어 construct v. 구성하다 generic a. 일반적인, 포괄적인 comply with 따르다, 지키다 genre conventions 장르의 관습[관행] soap opera 연속극 make play with 효과적으로 이용하다 credibility n. 신뢰성 mores n. 관습, 습속

---

36 내용파악　　　　　　　　　　⑤

'리얼리즘은 오늘날 더 친숙한 용어로서, 우리는 이를 통해 픽션(허구)이, 우리가 우리 자신의 세계처럼 인식하는 세계를 구성하는지 여부를 판단한다.'라는 단서로부터 ⑤는 일반적 핍진성과 무관하고 리얼리즘에 관한 진술임을 알 수 있다.

다음 중 일반적 핍진성과 관련하여 사실이 아닌 것은?
① 그것은 일반적인 범위 내에서 판타지에 신뢰성을 부여한다.
② 그것은 특정 장르에서의 픽션(허구)세계의 진실성을 확보한다.
③ 그것은 장르의 규칙을 따라야 한다.
④ 그것은 일종의 2차적 핍진성이다.
⑤ 그것은 우리로 하여금 픽션이 실제와 같은 세계를 구성하는지 판단하게 만든다.

---

37 문장삽입　　　　　　　　　　④

주어진 문장, '그는 핍진성(그럴듯함)이란 실제로 사실일 수도 있고 아닐 수도 있는 것을 의미하지 않고, 지배적인 문화가 사실이라고 믿는 것,

일반적으로 믿을만하고 적합하며 적절하다고 받아들여지는 것을 의미한다고 주장한다.'은 핍진성이란 용어를 설명하고 있다. 따라서 이 문장은 핍진성을 본격적으로 논하는 내용이 시작되는 ⓓ에 위치해야 한다.

38-40

17세기 네덜란드의 사업가이자 과학자였던 Antonie Van Leeuwenhoek는 자신의 깨끗한 치아에 대한 자부심이 대단했다. 그는 매일 아침 소금으로 이를 문지른 다음 물로 입을 헹궜다. 식사 후에는 이쑤시개로 치아를 조심스럽게 닦았다. 그는 1683년 편지에서 그 나이 또래의 사람들 중 이렇게 깨끗하고 하얀 치아를 가진 사람은 거의 없다고 말했다. 하지만 그가 자세히 살펴보았을 때, 그는 "일부 어금니와 치아 사이에 약간의 하얀 물질이 남아 있거나 자라는 것"을 발견했다 ― 이를 현재는 치태라고 부른다.

몇 년 전에 물속에서 작은 생물체를 관찰한 경험이 있는 현미경 전문가인 van Leeuwenhoek은 이 하얀 물질에도 그것들이 존재할 수 있는지 궁금해 했다. 현미경으로 관찰해보니, 실제로 그것에는 "매우 예쁘게 움직이는 아주 작은 살아있는 동물들"이 많이 포함되어 있었다.

이러한 미생물이 질병을 일으킬 수 있다고 의심하는 사람은 거의 없었다. 당시 의사들은 히포크라테스의 교리를 따랐고, 질병은 체내 '체액'(혈액, 가래, 황담즙, 흑담즙)의 불균형에 의해 발생한다고 믿었다. 한편, 전염병은 늪이나 썩은 물질이 내뿜는 '나쁜 공기'인 미아스마가 원인으로 여겨졌다. 질병이 작은 생물체에 의해 전염될 수 있다는 제안은 의사들에 의해 거부되었다.

현재 세균 이론으로 알려진, 작은 유기체가 질병을 일으킨다는 개념은 19세기 후반에야 받아들여졌다. 핵심적인 장애물은 지적인 문제가 아니라 문화적 문제였다. 의사들은 보수적이었고 실험에 기초한 새로운 발견을 자신들의 직업적 정체성에 대한 도전으로 여겼다. 천문학자들이 우주에 대한 이해를 변화시킨 망원경을 서둘러 도입한 반면, 의사들은 현미경으로 밝혀진 새로운 세계에 눈을 감아버렸다.

inordinately ad. 지나치게, 과도하게　scrub v. 씻다, 문지르다　toothpick n. 이쑤시개　molar n. 어금니　dental plaque 치태, 치면세균막　humour n. 체액　phlegm n. 가래　yellow bile 황담즙　black bile 흑담즙　attribute to ~탓이다　miasma n. (지저분한·불쾌한) 공기 [기운, 냄새]　decompose v. 부패하다, 변질하다　germ theory 세균 이론　embrace v. 받아들이다

38 지시대상　　　　　　　　④

ⓔ miasma는 미생물이 아니라 '늪이나 썩은 물질이 내뿜는 나쁜 공기'이다. 다른 보기들은 모두 작은 유기체, 즉 세균을 가리킨다.

39 빈칸완성　　　　　　　　①

빈칸이 들어 있는 마지막 문장에서 'while'은 역접의 접속사다. 따라서 의사들은, 우주에 대한 이해를 변화시킨 망원경을 서둘러 도입한 천문학자들과 정반대의 행동을 했음을 추론할 수 있다. 즉 의사들은 '현미경으로 밝혀진 새로운 세계'를 외면했다. 따라서 빈칸에는 ① '눈을 감아버렸다, 못 본 체했다'가 와야 한다.

다음 중 빈칸을 채우기에 가장 적절한 구는?
① 눈을 감아버렸다, 못 본 체했다
② 의존했다

③ 관심을 돌렸다
④ 양보했다
⑤ 길을 만들었다

40 내용추론　　　　　　　　⑤

'현재 세균 이론으로 알려진, 작은 유기체가 질병을 일으킨다는 개념은 19세기 후반에야 받아들여졌다. 의사들은 보수적이었고 실험에 기초한 새로운 발견을 자신들의 직업적 정체성에 대한 도전으로 여겼다.'라는 내용으로부터 ⑤ '세균 이론의 선구자는 현미경에 정통한 의사들이었을 것이다.'는 추론할 수 없다는 것을 알 수 있다.

다음 중 이 글로부터 추론할 수 없는 것은?
① 현미경이 등장하기까지는 세균에 대한 인식이 전혀 이루어지지 않았다.
② 질병은 한때 체액에 기인한다고 여겨졌다.
③ 세균 이론의 초기 시작은 나쁜 공기 이론에 의해 저지되었다.
④ 세균에 대한 식별은 세균에 대한 의학적 경고보다 훨씬 이전으로 거슬러 올라갔다.
⑤ 세균 이론의 선구자는 현미경에 정통한 의사들이었을 것이다.

01 ②	**02** ①	**03** ④	**04** ③	**05** ①	**06** ③	**07** ②	**08** ⑤	**09** ④	**10** ①
11 ⑤	**12** ①	**13** ②	**14** ①	**15** ③	**16** ⑤	**17** ②	**18** ③	**19** ⑤	**20** ⑤
21 ③	**22** ②	**23** ⑤	**24** ①	**25** ②	**26** ①	**27** ④	**28** ④	**29** ④	**30** ③
31 ④	**32** ④	**33** ⑤	**34** ②	**35** ①	**36** ②	**37** ③	**38** ④	**39** ④	**40** ①
41 ③	**42** ⑤	**43** ②	**44** ②	**45** ⑤	**46** ①	**47** ⑤	**48** ④	**49** ⑤	**50** ②

01 동의어 ②

well-off a. 유복한, 부유한 fortune n. 재산, 운 dissolute a. 방탕한, 타락한 squander v. 낭비하다(= waste) conserve v. 보존하다, 절약하다 amass v. 축적하다 secure v. 확보하다, 보호하다 renounce v. 포기하다, 부인하다

조안(Joan)은 부유한 집안에서 태어났지만, 집안의 재산은 그녀의 방탕한 아버지가 탕진해버렸다.

02 동의어 ①

retrieve v. 회수하다(= recover) relinquish v. 포기하다 reimburse v. 상환하다 reverberate v. 반향하다 reiterate v. 되풀이하다, 다시 행하다

오늘날의 하이테크 문화에서, 인간의 기억은, 일단 적절하게 저장되면, 컴퓨터 파일을 디스크에서 다운로드하는 것처럼 충실하게 정신으로부터 회수될 수 있다고 사람들은 생각할지 모른다.

03 동의어 ④

conducive a. 도움이 되는, 기여하는(= helpful) facile a. 용이한; 유창한 mandatory a. 명령의, 의무의, 강제적인 inimical a. 해로운, 적대적인 obnoxious a. 불쾌한, 싫은

직원들에게 동기를 부여하고 보다 도움이 되는 작업 환경을 조성하기 위해, 점점 더 많은 조직들이 새로운 업무현장 디자인을 도입하고 있다.

04 동의어 ③

radioactive a. 방사능의 density n. 밀도, 농도, 조밀도 molten state 용융상태 corrode v. 부식하다, 침식하다(= erode) ignite v. 불을 붙이다, 점화시키다 vaporize v. 증발하다 exacerbate v. 악화시키다 consolidate v. 강화하다, 통합하다

플루토늄은 방사성 물질이다. 실험실에 처음 전달된 그 순수 금속(플루토늄)은 다양한 밀도를 보였으며, 용융(액화) 상태에서는 반응성이 너무나 강해 접촉하는 거의 모든 용기를 부식시켰다.

05 동의어 ①

ecotourism n. 생태관광 alleviate v. 경감하다; 완화하다(= assuage) aggravate v. 악화시키다 provoke v. 도발하다 spur v. 자극하다 probe v. 조사하다

생태관광은 일반 관광이 생태계에 미치는 영향을 완화하기 위한 새로운 관광 모델이다.

06 동의어 ③

order v. 주문하다 seclusion n. 한거(閑居), 격리 bare a. 벌거벗은, 노출된 smudge v. 얼룩을 내다, 손상하다(= smear) haze n. 안개, 혼탁 primordial a. 최초의, 근본의, 원시의 plaster v. 회반죽을 바르다, 메우다 clear v. 분명히 하다, 맑게 하다 mutate v. 돌연변이 시키다 clone v. 복제하다

그는 돌아다니는 웨이터들 중 한 명에게서 커피 두 잔을 주문했고, 잠시 동안 우리는 그늘진 곳에서 해변의 사람들을 지켜보았는데, 그들은 이글거리는 열기에 더러워진 몸을 드러내고 있어서 해변을 따라 반나체로 누웠다가 천천히 움직이는 모습이 어떻게든 원시적으로 보였다.

07 동의어 ②

advantage v. 유리하게 하다 precipitating a. (무언가의 도래를) 재촉하는(= propitious 상서로운, 길조의) render v. 표현하다, 되게 하다 repulsive a. 혐오감을 일으키는, 매정한 provoking a. 자극적인, 성가신, 부아가 나는 obtrusive a. 주제넘게 나서는, 돌출한 ominous a. 불길한

사회는 거의 필연적으로 모든 성공 스토리를 자신에게 가장 유리한 장(章)으로 시작하며, 미국에서는 이러한 성공의 도래를 재촉하는 상서로운 장들이 거의 항상 뛰어난 개인의 단 한 번의 행동으로 표현된다. 당신은 "변화를 만드는 데는 한 사람만 있으면 된다."는 말을 자주 듣는다. 이것은 근거 없는 통념(거짓)이다.

08 동의어 ⑤

anoint v. 선정하다, 기름을 부어 신성하게 하다 mount v. 쌓이다

let on 폭로하다, 누설하다(= reveal) panic v. 공황상태에 빠지다, 당황하게[허둥대게] 하다 withdraw v. 인출하다 deposit n. 예치금, 예금 FTX 가상화폐 거래소(Futures Exchange의 약자) revenue n. 매출, 세입, 수입 refund v. 환불하다 retribute v. 되돌려주다 restore v. 회복하다, 복원하다

2021년 10월, 『포브스』는 Bankman-Fried을 세계에서 가장 부유한 20대로 선정했다. 그러나 지난 11월, 소셜 미디어에서는 Bankman-Fried의 제국이 스스로 발표한 것보다 훨씬 적은 돈을 보유하고 있다는 우려가 커졌다. 당황한 고객들이 FTX에서 수십억 달러의 예금을 인출하자, Bankman-Fried에게는 그들에게 되돌려 줄 자금이 없다는 사실이 곧 드러났다.

---

09 동의어 ④

state-of-the-art a. 최첨단의, 최신 기술의 high-resolution a. 고해상도의 magnification n. 확대, 확대율 maneuver v. 조종하다, 교묘히 다루다(= manage) precision n. 정확, 정밀 contrive v. 고안하다, 궁리하다 drill v. 구멍을 뚫다; 훈련하다 outperform v. 능가하다 stratify v. 계층별로 분류하다

최첨단 의료 로봇 기술은 사람의 손목과 손가락보다 훨씬 더 정밀하게 조종할 수 있는 고해상도 3D 확대 시스템과 기구를 특징으로 한다.

---

10 동의어 ①

meritocracy n. 능력주의 nascent a. 발생기의, 초기의(= burgeoning) vainglorious a. 자만심[허영심]이 강한 full-blown a. 활짝 핀, 만개한 retreating a. 철수하는 subliminal a. 잠재의식의 withering a. 활기를 잃게 하는, 괴멸적인

미국 능력주의의 창시자들은 초기 계급 제도를 파괴하고 유동적이고 이동성 있는 사회를 구축하고 있었다고 믿는다. 돌이켜보면 이는 자만심이 강한 시도였다 ─ 정교한 등급화 과정을 수립함에 의해 사회적 등급을 약화시킬 수는 없다.

---

11 논리완성 ⑤

역접·양보의 의미를 갖는 전치사 'Despite'로부터 빈칸에 세관의 지속적인 노력이 실패했다는 의미를 갖는 표현이 와야 함을 추론할 수 있다. 그러므로 빈칸에는 ⑤ '밀반입되는'이 와야 한다.

customs officer 세관 abiding a. 지속적인 smuggle v. 밀수하다 indict v. 기소하다, 비난하다 ordain v. 명하다, 정하다 thrive v. 번성하다 yield v. 굴복하다, 생산하다

세관 당국의 지속적인 노력에도 불구하고, 매년 많은 양의 마약이 국내로 밀반입되고 있다.

---

12 논리완성 ①

유전자 조작 건강보조식품이 5천명에 달하는 미국인에게 영구적인 장애를 일으켰다는 것은 미국 식약청이 이 건강 보조 식품을 회수할 수밖에 없다는 것을 말하므로 빈칸에는 ①이 적절하다.

dietary supplement 건강보조식품 blood disorder 혈액질환 recall v. 회수[리콜]하다 plunder v. 약탈하다 confound v. 당황하게 하다, 혼동시키다 taunt v. 비웃다 coordinate v. 조정하다; 협력하다

어떤 유전자 조작 건강보조식품은 5,000명 이상의 미국인에게 치명적인 혈액 질환을 동반한 영구적인 장애를 초래하고 나서야, 미국 식품의약청(FDA)에 의해 회수되었다.

---

13 논리완성 ②

빈칸이 있는 문장 바로 앞 문장에서 '진화는 우리로 하여금 순간적으로 밀려오는 기분 좋은 감각을 즐길 수 있게 해주지만, 그 기분 좋은 감각은 영원히 지속되지는 않는다.'라고 했으므로 기분 좋은 감각은 금방 '가라앉는다'고 하는 것이 적절하다.

misery n. 고통, 불행 reproduction n. 번식 mould v. 주조하다 substitute v. 대신하다 subside v. 가라앉다, 진정되다 suspect v. 의심하다, 알아채다 subsist v. 부양하다, 생존하다 subsidize v. 보조하다, 원조하다

행복과 불행은 진화에 있어서 생존과 번식을 장려하거나 방해하는 정도로만 역할을 한다. 그렇다면 진화가 우리를 너무 비참하지도, 너무 행복하지도 않게 만들어놓았다는 것은 어쩌면 놀랍지 않을 것이다. 진화는 우리로 하여금 순간적으로 밀려오는 기분 좋은 감각을 즐길 수 있게 해주지만, 그 기분 좋은 감각은 영원히 지속되지는 않는다. 조만간 이러한 감각은 가라앉고 불쾌한 감각에게 자리를 내주게 된다.

---

14 논리완성 ①

몇몇 종류에 불과한 기본 입자들을 우주의 알파벳 문자들에 비유하여, 알파벳이 결합하여 어휘와 문장을 만들어내는 것처럼 기본 입자들이 결합하여 우주 안의 수많은 것들을 만들어낸다는 것이다. 무한히 많은 것들을 만들려면 무한히 많이 결합해야 할 것이므로 빈칸에는 'to infinity(무한히)'가 되게 ①이 적절하다.

elementary particle 소립자 vibrate v. 진동하다 fluctuate v. 불규칙하게 변동하다 studded a. 점점이 박혀 있는, 많은 infinity n. 무한대, 무한성 indifference n. 무관심, 냉담, 개의치 않음 insolence n. 오만, 무례 inception n. 시작, 초기 indefiniteness n. 불확정, 부정(不定)

현재로서는 이것이 우리가 물질에 대해 알고 있는 것인데, 존재와 비존재 사이에서 끊임없이 진동하고 변동하며 아무 것도 없는 것 같을 때에도 우주를 가득 채우고 있는 몇몇 종류의 기본 입자들이 우주의 알파벳 문자들처럼 무한히 결합하여, 은하, 무수한 별, 햇빛, 산과 숲과 곡식밭, 파티에서 젊은이들의 웃는 얼굴, 그리고 별이 가득한 밤하늘 등의 거대한 역사를 말해준다는 것이다.

---

15 논리완성 ③

마지막 두 문장을 비교하면, '제당공장 굴뚝과 풍차'가 The past에 해당

하고 '시골'은 장소로서 almost everywhere에 해당하므로, 빈칸에는 is present에 해당하는 '있다, 존재하다'는 의미의 단어가 들어가야 한다. 그런데 punctuate는 dot(점을 찍다)과 마찬가지로 '구두점을 찍다'는 뜻 이외에도 '~에 흩어져 있다'는 뜻도 있다. 따라서 빈칸에는 ③이 적절하다.

grid n. 격자; 바둑판 plaque n. 명판; 치석 hang on 달려있다 exterior n. 외부, 외면 sugar-mill 제당소(공장) smokestack n. (공장의) 높은 굴뚝 punctuate v. 여기저기에 위치하다 emphasize v. 강조하다 interrupt v. 방해하다 immobilize v. 움직이지 않게 하다, 고정시키다 accentuate v. 강조하다, 두드러지게 하다

맨해튼이 거리의 격자(격자 모양의 거리)로 정의되는 섬이라면, 바베이도스는 대형 집단농장이 이와 매우 같은 방식으로 기능하는 섬이다. 브리지타운에는 한때 노예 우리였던 곳을 알려주는 명판이 은행 외벽에 걸려 있다. 제당 공장의 굴뚝과 풍차가 시골에 흩어져 있다. 과거를 인정하든지 인정하지 않든지, 과거는 거의 모든 곳에 존재한다.

16 논리완성   ⑤

치료자는 상처를 낫게 하는 사람인데, 빈칸 뒤에서 '역설적으로'라 했으므로 빈칸에는 치료자 자신의 '상처'와 관련된 말이 적절하다. 그러므로 빈칸에는 ⑤ '고통과 취약성'이 와야 한다.

in common currency (공용 통화) 널리 통용되는 antiquity n. 고대, 태고 needs and desires 필요와 욕망 fitness and well-being 건강과 행복 composure n. (마음의) 평정 equanimity n. 격식, (특히 힘든 상황에서의) 침착, 평정 impulse n. 충동, 자극 preoccupation n. 심취, 몰두 suffering n. 고통 vulnerability n. 취약성, 상처받기 쉬움

고대로까지 거슬러 올라가는 상처 입은 치료자라는 개념이 널리 통용되고 있다. 그것은 치료자 자신의 고통과 취약성이 역설적으로 치유 능력의 원천이 될 수 있음을 의미한다.

17 논리완성   ②

주절이 '그 질병의 약화된 변종(백신)을 신체에 주입하여 그 질병에 대한 항체가 형성되도록 자극한다.'는 예방접종의 원리를 설명하고 있으므로, 빈칸에는 이와 관련된 ② '예방접종하다'가 들어가야 한다.

inoculate v. 예방접종하다 strain n. 종류, 유형, 변종 antibody n. 항체 censor v. 검열하다 afflict v. 학대하다, 괴롭히다 grapple v. 극복하려고 노력하다, 겨루다 disseminate v. 전파하다, 유포하다

어떤 질병에 대한 예방 접종을 할 때, 우리는 그 질병의 약화된 변종을 신체에 주입하고 있는데, 그러면 신체가 그 질병에 대한 항체를 발생시키도록 자극받는다.

18 논리완성   ③

'아이를 충분히 낳지 않기 때문에'라고 했으므로, 인간 지능의 총량은 늘지 않고 있다(일정 수준에 머물러 있다)고 해야 할 것이다. 따라서 빈칸 ④에는 leveling off가 적절하다. 한편, 마지막의 '강력한 무어의 법칙'이

성능이 급증하는 것을 의미하므로, 빈칸 ⑧에는 exponentially(기하급수적으로, 급격히)가 적절하다. 빈칸 ⑧의 경우는 다른 보기들도 엄청나게 큰 증가를 의미하는 것으로 적절하다.

Moore's Law 무어의 법칙(반도체의 집적회로의 성능이 24개월마다 2배로 증가한다는 법칙) on steroids 강력한, 극단적인 take off 이륙하다; 유행하다 unprecedentedly ad. 전례가 없을 만큼, 미증유로 put off 미루다, 연기하다 outrageously ad. 엄청나게, 터무니없게 level off 변동 없게 되다 exponentially ad. 기하급수적으로 turn off (길을) 벗어나다; (전기·가스·수도 등을) 끄다 disproportionately ad. 불균형적으로 round off 마무리 짓다; 다듬다 alarmingly ad. 놀랄 만큼

일론 머스크는 사람들이 아이를 충분히 낳지 않아서 인간 지능의 양이 일정 수준에 머물고 있다고 지적했다. 다른 한편, 컴퓨터 지능의 양은 무어의 법칙처럼 기하급수적으로 증가하고 있었다.

19 논리완성   ⑤

빈칸 ④의 경우, '경기 침체에도 불구하고'라는 첫 번째 문장의 단서와 '이번에는 재정 확대의 여지가 더 제한되고 공공 부채도 지속불가능해질 것이다.'라는 마지막 문장의 단서로부터 정부가 통화정책을 엄격히 관리해야 함을 추론할 수 있으므로 tighten이 적절하다. 빈칸 ⑧는 통화정책을 엄격히 관리해야 하는 현재의 상황이 과거와 다르다는 단서로부터, 과거에는 통화정책을 공격적으로 완화했음을 추론할 수 있으므로 ease가 적절하다.

stagflationary a. 스태그플레이션의(경기침체 하의 인플레이션) policy stance 정책기조 recession n. 경기침체 monetary policy 통화정책 aggregate demand (일정 기간의 상품 및 서비스의) 총수요 fiscal expansion 재정확대 unsustainable a. 지속 불가능한 tighten v. 엄하게 하다, 강화하다 aggravate v. 악화시키다 ease v. 완화하다 differentiate v. 구별하다 loosen v. 늦추다, 느슨하게 하다; 완화하다

스태그플레이션 충격에 직면한 중앙은행은 경제가 경기 침체로 향하더라도 정책기조를 강화해야 한다. 따라서 오늘날의 상황은 총수요 감소와 디플레이션 압력에 대응하여 중앙은행이 통화정책을 공격적으로 완화할 수 있었던 글로벌 금융위기나 팬데믹 초기와는 근본적으로 다르다. 이번에는 재정 확대의 여지가 더 제한되고 공공 부채도 지속불가능해질 것이다.

20-21

우연이든, 무의식적 설계이든, 2023년은 영화 속 아내의 해였다. Bradley Cooper 감독의 "Maestro", Sofia Coppola 감독의 "Priscilla", 심지어 Christopher Nolan 감독의 "Oppenheimer" 그리고 Michael Mann 감독의 "Ferrari" — 마지막 두 편의 영화는 여성의 경험을 탐구하는 것으로는 잘 알려지지 않은 남성 감독의 작품이다 — 에서 영화 속에 등장하는 아내는 방관자적 모습에서 벗어나 영광을 누리며 영화의 중심으로 불쑥 들어온다. 그녀는 주인공은 아닐지 몰라도 (영화의) 프레임 속에서 공간을 차지하는 것에 대해서는 단호하다.

by accident 우연히 barge in 불쑥 끼어들다 from the sidelines 방관자적 입장에서

20 빈칸완성 ⑤

'영화 속에 등장하는 아내는 방관자적 모습에서 벗어나 영광을 누리며 영화의 중심으로 불쑥 들어온다.'라는 단서로부터 최근에 개봉된 많은 신작 영화 속에서 아내인 인물들이 주연이 아님에도 불구하고 영화 속에서 확고한 입지와 존재감을 보여주고 있음을 추론할 수 있다.

빈칸에 들어가기에 가장 적절한 정답을 선택하시오.
① 남겨 둔, 예약한
② 그 결과에 따른(그에 따른)
③ 혐오감을 불러일으키는, 냉담한
④ 퇴행하는
⑤ 단호한, 확고한

21 글의 제목 ③

글에서 강조하고 있는 것은 2023년 개봉된 주요 영화들 속에서 아내의 존재감이, 주연 여부와 무관하게 부각되었다는 것이다. 이러한 위 글의 내용을 가장 잘 요약하고 있는 제목은 ③ '올해 개봉된 영화 속에서 아내라는 존재의 부상'이다. 열거된 4편의 영화들이 흥행작인지 여부를 알 수 없으므로 ⑤는 부적절하다.

이 글의 가장 적절한 제목을 고르시오.
① 인기 있는 대중영화 속에서 여성들의 역할
② 영화 속의 아내로서 여배우들의 권리
③ 올해 개봉된 영화 속에서 아내라는 존재의 부상
④ 남성 감독들이 깨어나는 해
⑤ 흥행 영화들 속에서의 아내들에 대한 묘사

22-23

2022년 말, 해고 사태가 기술 업계를 뒤흔들었을 때, Blind — 능력이 검증되었지만 익명인 전문가들을 위한 온라인 포럼 — 는 이러한 혼란 속에서 사실상의 의사소통 채널이 되었다. 당시 95% 이상의 트위터 직원이, 사용자가 800만에 달하는 Blind에 가입해 있었는데, Blind의 사용자는 지난해에 200만 명 증가했다. 기술 업계 종사자가 대부분인 이 사용자들은 비자 문제와 정신 건강부터 비윤리적 관행에 이르기까지 모든 것을 논의했고, 이를 통해 Blind는 업계 내부 고발자들에게 중요한 플랫폼이 되었다. Blind는 사용자의 정서를 요약하고, 비판을 받은 기업에 변화를 제안함으로써 수익을 창출한다.

lay-off n. 일시적 정리해고 roil v. 요동치게 만들다 verify v. 확인하다, 입증하다 de facto 사실상, 실제로 tumult n. 소동, 혼란; 심란함 whistle-blower n. 내부 고발자 monetize v. 화폐로 정하다, 돈을 벌다

22 빈칸완성 ②

온라인 포럼이라 했으므로 Blind를 사용하는 전문가들은 익명으로 사용했을 것으로 추론할 수 있다.

빈칸에 들어가기에 가장 적절한 정답을 선택하시오.
① 불만인, 언짢은
② 익명의, 무명의
③ 정당한, 합법의
④ 양심적인, 신중한
⑤ 뛰어난, 저명한

23 내용파악 ⑤

위 글의 마지막 문장, 즉 'Blind는 사용자의 정서를 요약하고, 비판을 받은 기업에 변화를 제안함으로써 수익을 창출한다.'라는 단서로부터 ⑤ '기업에 문제와 해결책을 판매함으로써'가 정답임을 알 수 있다.

Blind는 어떻게 스스로를 재정적으로 뒷받침하는가?
① 가입자에게 회비를 부과하여
② 전문적인 조언자와 기부자를 모집하여
③ 온라인으로 대중에게 서비스를 홍보함으로써
④ 자신의 직업에 대해 원망하는 사람들을 찾아서
⑤ 기업에 문제와 해결책을 판매함으로써

24-25

스트레스로 인해 정말로 압도당하고 불안을 느낄 때, 그것은 우리의 몸이 우리에게 재조정하고 균형을 다시 잡으라는 신호다. 아무도 진정으로 무한한 존재가 아니다. 내면의 신호에 귀를 기울이고 자신이 실수하기 쉬운 성향임을 인정할 때, 우리는 전반적으로 더 집중하고 더 건강해질 뿐만 아니라 스트레스와 불안도 덜 느끼게 된다.
불안은 건강하고 도움이 되는 감정으로서 인간의 삶의 건설적인 측면일 수 있다. 불안은 우리가 다른 사람에게 우리의 상처받기 쉬운 감정을 전달할 때 그들과의 정서적 연결을 촉진할 수 있다. 또한 스트레스의 형태로서 불안은 균형과 건강을 유지하기 위한 내적 지표 역할을 할 수도 있다. 이제 우리가 그것(불안)을 잘 활용하기 시작할 때가 되었다.

recalibrate v. 재조정하다 cue n. 단서 fallibility n. 잘못하기 쉬움 vulnerable a. 상처받기 쉬운 barometer n. 지표

24 동의어 ①

fallibility는 '잘못하기 쉬움'이라는 뜻이므로, ①이 정답이다.

밑줄 친 단어 'fallibility'에 가장 가까운 의미를 가진 정답을 고르시오.
① 실수하기 쉬운 성향
② 불확정성의 상태
③ 완벽을 추구하는 성향
④ 차이에 대한 명제 혹은 제안
⑤ 연결성에 대한 선호

25 빈칸완성 ②

빈칸이 들어있는 문장은 이 글의 주제를 포함하고 있다. 글의 주제는 얼핏 보았을 때 부정적인 것으로 여겨지는 스트레스와 그로 인한 불안이, 잘 관리하고 조절하기만 한다면, 우리의 정신 건강에 도움이 된다는 것이다. 이러한 주제를 품고 있는 것은 ② '우리는 그것을 잘 활용하기 시작한다.'이다.

빈칸에 들어가기에 가장 적절한 정답을 선택하시오.
① 우리는 우리 자신의 일에 집중한다
② 우리는 그것을 잘 활용하기 시작한다
③ 우리는 선을 위해 나쁜 감정을 견뎌낸다
④ 우리는 불안으로부터 완전하게 자유롭다
⑤ 우리는 불안감을 해소하는 방법을 알아낸다

26-27

교육자들은 어떤 특별한 기술에 능숙해야 한다. 그러나 이것 외에도, 교육자들이 가르치는 사람들 앞에서 보여줘야 할 일반적인 관점이 있다. 그들은 지성과 지식 탐구의 가치를 모범적으로 보여 주어야 한다. 그들은 어느 때는 지식으로 여겨지고 있는 것이 사실은 잘못된 것일 수 있음을 분명히 알려주어야 한다. 그들은 독단적이지 않은 성품, 즉 편안한 확신이 아니라 끊임없는 탐구의 성품을 심어주어야 한다. 그들은 시공간적으로 가까운 것뿐만 아니라, 세계 전체에 대한 인식을 형성하려고 노력해야 한다. 오류의 가능성을 인식함으로써 그들은 관용의 중요성을 분명히 해야 한다. 그들은 후손들이 존경하는 사람들이 당대에는 인기가 없는 경우가 많았으며, 이 땅에서 사회적 용기가 가장 중요한 덕목이라는 점을 학생들에게 상기시켜야 한다. 무엇보다도, 자신이 가르치는 학생들에게 최선을 다하려는 모든 교육자들은 그들 자신을 이쪽이나 저쪽의 정치적 또는 종파적 이해관계에서 벗어난, 진리의 종으로 여겨야 한다.

proficient a. 능숙한 erroneous a. 잘못된 undogmatic a. 비독단적인 temper n. 기질, 성품 likelihood n. 개연성 tolerance n. 관용 sectarian interests 정파적[종파적] 이해관계

26 빈칸완성 ①

이 글은 시종일관 교육자가 학생들을 대하는 바람직한 태도와 올바른 교육 방식에 대해 열거하고 있다. 빈칸이 있는 문장도 마찬가지다. 교육자는 학생들에게 독단적이지 않은 성품을 '심어주어야' 할 것이므로, 빈칸에는 ①이 적절하다.

빈칸에 들어가기에 가장 적절한 정답을 선택하시오.
① 심어주다
② 배제하다
③ 제거하다
④ 박멸하다
⑤ 완화하다

27 내용파악 ④

'그들은 지식으로 여겨지는 것이 사실은 잘못된 것일 수 있음을 분명히 알려주어야 한다.'라는 단서로부터 ④가 본문과 일치하지 않음을 알 수 있다.

다음 중 교육자들과 관련해서 사실이 아닌 것은?
① 그들은 어떠한 정파적 이해관계도 회피해야 한다.
② 그들은 세계에 대한 거시적 시각을 가지고 있어야 한다.
③ 그들은 지식에 대한 탐구를 옹호해야 한다.
④ 그들은 지식의 무오류성을 확신해야 한다.
⑤ 그들은 학생들에게 일반적인 관점을 제시해야 한다.

28-29

감시 자본주의는 인간의 경험이 행동 데이터로 변환할 공짜 원재료라고 일방적으로 주장한다. 이러한 데이터 중 일부는 제품이나 서비스의 개선에 적용되지만, 나머지는 독점적인 행동 잉여로 선언된 후, '기계 지능'으로 알려진 첨단 제조 공정에 공급되어, 당신이 지금, 곧, 그리고 나중에 무엇을 할 것인지 예측하는 예측 상품으로 가공된다. 마지막으로, 이러한 예측 상품은 내가 '행동 선물(先物) 시장'이라고 부르는 새로운 종류의 행동 예측 시장에서 거래된다. 감시 자본가들은 이러한 거래를 통해 막대한 부를 축적하고 있는데, 이는 많은 기업이 우리의 미래 행동에 베팅하기를 열망하고 있기 때문이다.

surveillance capitalism 감시 자본주의 unilaterally ad. 일방적으로 raw material 원재료 proprietary a. 독점권을 가진 behavioral surplus 고객 행동에 관한 잉여 정보 feed into ~에 넣다 fabricate v. 제조하다 lay a bet on 내기를 걸다

28 동의어

proprietary는 '독점적인'이라는 뜻이므로, ④가 정답이다.

밑줄 친 단어 'proprietary'에 가장 가까운 의미를 가진 정답을 고르시오.
① 결합하는
② 상호간의
③ 대중의
④ 독점적인
⑤ 공동의

29 내용파악 ④

두 번째 문장에서 "이러한 데이터 중 나머지는 독점적인 행동 잉여로 선언된 후, '기계 지능'으로 알려진 첨단 제조 공정에 공급되어, 예측 상품으로 가공된다"고 했는데, 이것은 데이터를 정확하게 분석하는 것이 아니라 데이터를 소비자의 행동을 예측할 수 있는 데이터로 상품화하여 거래한다 것을 의미하므로 ④가 사실이 아닌 진술이다.

다음 중 감시 자본주의에 대해 사실이 아닌 것은?
① 그것은 인간의 경험을 예측 가능한 데이터로 바꾼다.
② 그것은 기업들로 하여금 예측 제품에 열중하도록 강요한다.
③ 그것은 미래의 마케팅을 위한 소비자의 행동에 근거한다.
④ 그것의 마케팅은 기존의 모든 데이터에 대한 정확한 분석에 의존한다.
⑤ 그것은 잉여 행동 데이터를 판매하는 부유한 개인을 생산한다.

30-31

딥러닝 및 인공지능 재활 로봇과 결합한 침술은 미래 연구의 핫스팟(뜨거운 관심 영역)이다. 기존의 침술 임상 연구는 전침, 건침과 같은 침술 방법을 중심으로 돌아가고 있으며, 수작업을 주로 하며 도구로 보충되는 방식으로 뇌졸중 후유증의 재활에 초점을 맞추고 있다. 향후 팬데믹과 같은 또 다른 응급 상황이 발생할 경우, 소재 기술과 공학을 결합한 인공지능 침술 로봇 개발 연구는 뇌졸중 후유증 환자의 신경 및 운동 기능 재활에 기여할 수 있다. 현재, 상지(上肢) 외골격 로봇이 있는데, 이 로봇은 원격 재활 로봇의 설계 및 개발을 포함하고 있다. 침술 로봇에는 기계 센서와 전기 센서 등 다양한 센서를 장착해, 침을 놓을 때의 통증을 줄일 수 있게

될 것이다. 더 나아가, 경혈 위치 설정, 기계적 자극, 기혈 감지를 위한 연구 프로토콜(관찰기록)을 설계에 포함시켰으며, 이를 위한 전략도 개발되었다.

acupuncture n. 침술 rehabilitation n. 재활, 회복 hotspot n. 활동의 중심지; 인기 있는 유흥장소 electro-acupuncture n. 전자 침술 dry needling 건침 stroke n. 뇌졸중 sequela n. 후유증 motor function 운동기능 exoskeleton n. 외골격 injection n. 주사, 주입 protocol n. (실험의) 관찰기록 acupoint n. 침놓는 자리(혈) deqi (sensation) 득기감(침을 맞거나 놓을 때 느끼는 시린 느낌, 마비된 느낌 등의 감각)

---

30 글의 제목 ③

이 글은 최첨단 신기술이라고 할 수 있는 침술로봇의 활용과 발전 방향 및 전망에 대해서 기술하고 있다. 따라서 제목으로는 ③ '침술 및 로봇에 대한 현재 연구의 검토'가 적절하다. 다른 보기들은 제목이 되기에는 너무 지엽적이다.

이 글의 가장 적절한 제목을 고르시오.
① 침술 로봇에 다양한 센서 및 프로토콜 통합
② AI 및 소재 기술을 통한 침술 분야의 뇌졸중 후 재활 혁신
③ 침술 및 로봇에 대한 현재 연구의 검토
④ 침술을 통한 뇌졸중 후유증을 줄이는 가장 빠른 방법
⑤ 침술의 뇌졸중 재활에 대한 임상적 초점

---

31 내용추론 ④

끝에서 두 번째 문장에서 '침술 로봇에 센서가 장착되어 침을 놓을 때의 통증을 줄일 수 있게 될 것이다'라고 했으므로 ④를 추론할 수 있다. ① 원격 치료가 아니라 원격 재활 로봇이며 사용 중이 아니라 개발 중이다. ② 모든 후유증이 아니라 뇌졸중 후유증의 재활이다. ③ 침술 로봇 사용에 대한 반대 의견이 제시되지 않았으므로 일반적으로 받아들여져 왔다고 할 수 있다. ⑤ 수작업을 주로 하므로 수동적이긴 하겠지만 비효율적이라는 언급은 없다.

다음 중 위 글에서 추론할 수 있는 것은?
① 침술로봇은 원격 치료에 사용된다.
② 침술 로봇은 치료의 모든 후유증을 치료하는 데 다용도로 사용할 수 있다.
③ 침술에 로봇을 사용하는 것은 일반적으로 충분히 받아들여지지 않고 있다.
④ AI 재활 로봇에 대한 더 많은 연구는 침술 치료 중과 치료 후 환자의 통증을 줄이는 데 도움이 될 수 있다.
⑤ 현재의 침술 방법을 통한 뇌졸중 재활은 수동적이고 비효율적으로 이루어진다.

32-33

Mary Anne Hitt에게 정책과 옹호는 기후 위기의 핵심이다. Sierra Club, Appalachian Voices, 그리고 지금 Climate Imperative와 함께하는 그녀의 경험은, 기후 정책을 바꾸면 여성이 세상을 바꿀 수 있다는 것을 강조한다. 그녀의 에세이 "Beyond Coal"에서, 그녀는 화석 연료를 없애고 재생 가능하고 지속 가능한 에너지로의 완전한 전환을 촉진하기 위한 Sierra

Club의 캠페인인, Beyond Coal의 디렉터로서의 자신의 경험을 이야기한다. 그녀가 캠페인을 진행하는 동안, 300개가 넘는 석탄 발전소가 폐쇄되었다. 웨스트버지니아 출신의 여성으로서 그녀는, 석탄 산업을 기반으로 삶을 일궈온 일부 가정들이 있다는 것을 알기 때문에, 정부와 개인이 (석탄 산업을 벗어나는) 전환이 어려운 일이라는 것을 이해하고 있었다. 그녀의 에세이와 Beyond Coal 캠페인의 배경이 된 그녀의 주장은 석탄이 "21세기에는 더 이상 옹호될 수 없다"는 것이었다. 석탄 발전소는 거의 항상, 석탄 배출이 야기하는 (악)영향에 대처하는 데 필요한 의료 서비스를 이용할 수 없는 저소득, 소수 민족 커뮤니티에 배치된다. 석탄 발전소는 재생 가능한 대안에 비해 비경제적이고 수익성이 떨어진다. 이러한 발전소의 유해한 영향과 발전소를 폐쇄하거나 재생 에너지로 전환함으로써 얻을 수 있는 경제적, 사회적, 장기적 이점에 대해 개인과 정부를 교육함으로써 (개선이 가능한 일이다). 또한, 이 사례는 페미니스트 기후 운동 리더가 어떻게 기후 운동에 매우 영향력 있는 변화를 가져왔는지, 그리고 여성이 어떻게 기후 운동의 필수적인 부분이 될 수 있는지를 보여준다.

recount v. 진술하다 renewable a. 재생 가능한 sustainable a. 지속 가능한 retire v. 퇴직[퇴역, 은퇴]시키다 alternative n. 대안 integral a. 필수적인

---

32 빈칸완성 ④

빈칸 이하에서 석탄이 저소득 지역 사람들의 건강을 해친다는 점, 석탄이 비경제적이고 수익성이 떨어진다는 점 등, 석탄의 단점이 열거되므로 빈칸에는 부정적인 의미의 ④가 적절하다.

빈칸에 들어가기에 가장 적절한 정답을 선택하시오.
① 방어할 수 있는
② 끊임없는
③ 확고부동한
④ 옹호될 수 없는
⑤ 명백한

---

33 내용파악 ⑤

비록 이 글의 마지막 문장에서 '또한, 이 사례는 페미니스트 기후 운동 리더가 어떻게 기후 운동에 매우 영향력 있는 변화를 가져왔는지, 그리고 여성이 어떻게 기후 운동의 필수적인 부분이 될 수 있는지를 보여준다.'라고 하여 기후 운동에 있어서 여성 리더의 중요성을 역설하고는 있지만 그것이 ⑤에서 언급하고 있는 '페미니스트 리더십의 우월성'이라고 해석할 수는 없다.

다음 중 Mary Anne Hitt에 대하여 사실이 아닌 것은?
① 그녀는 기후 위기 해결을 위해 정책과 옹호 활동을 이용하겠다는 강한 의지를 가지고 있었다.
② 그녀는 석탄 발전소 폐쇄를 이끌어낸 전략적 이니셔티브의 영향력을 보여주었다.
③ 그녀는 석탄이 소외된 지역사회의 건강과 환경에 미치는 악영향을 강조했다.
④ 그녀는 기후 정책에 대한 여성의 참여가 어떻게 중요한 글로벌 변화를 이끌어낼 수 있는지를 모범으로 보여주었다.
⑤ 그녀는 미래의 기후 행동에서 페미니스트 리더십의 우월성을 보여주었다.

34-35

가장 효율적인 시스템을 채택해야 한다는 강력한 경제적 압력은, 인간이 통제될 수 없는 인공지능 시스템에 점점 더 많은 권한을 넘겨주게 되고, 결국 우리가 지구의 지배적인 종(種)으로서 (인공지능에 의해) 대체되는 길로 접어들게 된다는 것을 의미한다. 우리가 처한 곤경에 대한 쉬운 해결책은 없다. 한 가지 가능한 출발점은, 현재 거의 감독 없이 운영되고 있는 탓에 대부분의 연구가 암흑 속에서 진행되고 있는 AI 산업에 대한 현저하게 부족한 규제 문제를 해결하는 것이다. 그러나 문제는 국가 내의, 그리고 국가 간의 (AI) 경쟁으로 인해 상식적인 안전 조치조차 무시하게 하고 있다는 점이다. 강력한 AI 시스템을 향한 경쟁이 가속화됨에 따라, 기업과 정부는 결승선에 먼저 도달하라는 인센티브를 점점 더 많이 받고 있다. 인류의 미래는 AI의 발전과 밀접하게 얽혀 있다. 따라서 AI에 대한 지배력을 자연선택이 우리보다 더 많이 갖고 있을지도 모른다는 것은 우리를 불안하게 하는 깨달음이다. 그러나 현재로서는 우리가 여전히 주도권을 쥐고 있다. 이제 이 위협을 심각하게 받아들여야 할 때이다. 일단 통제권을 넘겨주고 나면 우리는 그것을 다시는 되찾을 수 없다.

adopt v. 채택하다   incentivize v. 인센티브를 주어 장려하다   cede v. 마지못해 양도하다   supplant v. 대신[대체]하다   address v. 다루다, 처리하다   common-sense n. 상식, 양식   safety measure 안전조치   intertwine v. 뒤얽히다   disturbing a. 불안한   realization n. 깨달음, 실현   hold sway over 지배하다, 마음대로 하다

---

34 저자의 태도 ②

이 글을 통해서 필자는 인공지능이 인간을 대체하는 새로운 지배 종으로 등장하게 될지도 모른다는 전망에 대해서 불안감을 드러내면서 그에 대한 대책을 촉구하고 있다. 그러므로 인공지능에 대한 필자의 태도는 ② '우려하는' 태도이다.

AI에 대한 글쓴이는 태도는?
① 체념하는
② 우려하는
③ 축하하는
④ 반항적인
⑤ 감상적인

---

35 빈칸완성 ①

빈칸 Ⓐ는 빈칸 앞의 문장, 즉 '가장 효율적인 시스템을 채택해야 한다는 강력한 경제적 압력은, 인간이 통제될 수 없는 인공지능 시스템에 점점 더 많은 권한을 넘겨주게 되고, 결국 우리가 지구의 지배적인 종으로서 인공지능에 의해 대체되는 길로 접어들게 된다는 것을 의미한다.'라는 단서로부터 우리 인류가 AI로 인해 '곤경'에 처해있음을 추론할 수 있다. 따라서 predicament나 dilemma가 적절하다. 한편, 빈칸 Ⓑ는 AI와 관련된 대부분의 연구가 '암흑 속에서 진행되고 있다'는 단서로부터 AI에 대한 '감시'가 부족하다는 것을 유추할 수 있다. 따라서 oversight가 적절하다.

빈칸 Ⓐ와 빈칸 Ⓑ 각각에 들어가기에 가장 적절한 정답을 선택하시오.
① 곤경 ― 감시
② 위업 ― 고려

---

③ 진퇴양난 ― 자율
④ 회피 ― 절차
⑤ 관성 ― 동기부여

36-38

교육, 보육, 의료 서비스, 정치, 그리고 글로벌 시민성 등 공적인 것과 사적인 것을 아우르는 다양한 영역에서의 도덕적 탐구로 확장된 돌봄의 윤리는 원래 페미니스트 심리학 이론으로 고안된 개념이었다. Carol Gilligan은 남성적 자유주의 정의 전통에 의해 가려진, 대안적이지만 동등하게 정당한 도덕적 추론 형식으로서의 돌봄의 관점을 처음으로 옹호했다. <뒤이은 이론가들은 이 논쟁에서 힌트를 얻어 논쟁을 더욱 발전시켰다.> Virginia Held는 돌봄의 윤리가 칸트 윤리나 공리주의와 같은 기존의 도덕적 접근 방식과는 구별되는 도덕 이론이라고 주장한다. 지배적인 도덕 이론들과 달리, 돌봄의 윤리는 대인 관계와 사회 제도의 기초를 형성하는 핵심적인 도덕 가치로서 돌봄을 강조한다. 돌봄의 윤리는 인간의 조건을 근본적으로 상호 의존적인 것으로 여긴다. 그것은 관계적 자아를 존재론적으로 그리고 인식론적으로 기본된 것으로 전제한다. 따라서 그것은 합리적이고 자율적이며 자족적인 개인이라는 개념을 지지하는 전통적인 자유주의에 대한 비판을 제시한다.

ethics of care 돌봄의 윤리   conceive v. 상상하다, 마음에 품다   indicate v. 나타내다, 가리키다   Kantian ethics 칸트의 윤리학(의무의 윤리학)   utilitarianism n. 공리주의   presupposes v. 추측[예상]하다   relational self 관계적 자아(독단적 자립적 자아의 반대)   ontologically ad. 존재론적으로   epistemologically ad. 인식론적으로   espouse v. 신봉하다(= support)   autonomous a. 자율적인, 자치의

---

36 문장삽입 ②

주어진 문장은 '뒤이은 이론가들은 이 논쟁에서 힌트를 얻어 논쟁을 더욱 발전시켰다.'인데, '뒤이은 이론가들'이 앞에 어떤 이론가가 있음을 암시하므로 주어진 문장은 Carol Gilligan에 대한 언급이 끝난 다음인 Ⓑ에 들어가는 것이 적절하다. 첫 문장에서 돌봄의 윤리가 원래 페미니스트 심리학 이론으로 고안되었다고 했는데, 이것을 부연 설명하여 Carol Gilligan이 '남성적' 자유주의 정의 전통에 대한 대안으로서의 (페미니스트적인) 돌봄의 관점을 처음으로 옹호했다고 한 것이다.

---

37 빈칸완성 ③

돌봄의 윤리가 관계적 자아를 '존재론적으로 인식론적으로 기본된 것으로 전제한다. 따라서 합리적이고 자율적이며 자족적인 개인이라는 개념을 지지하는 전통적인 자유주의에 대한 비판을 제시한다.'라는 단서로부터 돌봄의 윤리의 핵심이 인간의 상호의존적인 속성임을 알 수 있다.

빈칸에 들어가기에 가장 적절한 정답을 선택하시오.
① 독점적인
② 자기중심적인
③ 상호의존적인
④ 적대적인
⑤ 유익한

38 내용파악 ④

돌봄의 윤리가 강조하는 것은 인간의 관계성과 상호의존성이다. 그리고 이 글에서는 바로 그 점을 시종일관 옹호하고 있다. 그러므로 ④ '그것은 정의를 주된 도덕적 가치로서 강조한다.'는 돌봄의 윤리학의 강조점이 아니다.

다음 중 돌봄의 윤리학에 관하여 사실이 <u>아닌</u> 것은?
① 그것은 민간 및 공공의 다양한 분야와 관련이 있다.
② 그것은 여성주의 도덕 이론에서 비롯되었다.
③ 그것은 전통적인 도덕적 접근법들에 반대한다.
④ 그것은 정의를 주된 도덕적 가치로서 강조한다.
⑤ 그것은 전통적인 자유주의에 의문을 제기한다.

39-41

링컨이 즉각적인 노예제 폐지를 추구하지 않은 것은 사실이다. 그는 급진적 평등주의자도 아니었다. 그는 오히려 노예 소유주에게 보상을 하고자 했던 점진적 노예 해방론자였다. 링컨은 반(反)흑인 편견이 일상화된 나라에서 태어났고, 그 나라를 이끌게 된 노예제 반대론자였다. 급진적인 시민적 평등을 약속하는 땅(이상화된 미국)에서 노예를 해방하고 새로 해방된 사람들에게 시민권을 확대하려는 강력한 정서의 흐름이 이 땅(현실적인 미국)에는 거의 없었다. <그러나 링컨을 노예제도에 반대하는 망설이는 전사로만 묘사하는 것은 그를 공정하게 다루는 것이 아니다.> 그는 노예제도가 "궁극적인 소멸"의 길로 나아가야 한다는 도덕적 정보에 근거한 주장을 굽히지 않았다. 그는 1850년대 내내 정치적 손해를 감수하면서까지 이 입장을 유지했으며, 하원 의원 한 번을 제외하고는 1860년 대통령에 당선될 때까지 주요 공직에 당선되지 못했다. 매우 중대하게, 1860~61년(남부 주들의 연방) 탈퇴를 둘러싼 위기 상황에서도 ― 순전히 정치인이라면 그랬을 수도 있는 ― 반(反) 노예제 공약에서 후퇴하지 않았다. 그리고 그는 1862년 이후 노예해방을 지지하며, 파괴적인 전쟁(남북전쟁)을 끝내기 위해 남부 연방과 평화 협상을 추진하라는 압력에도 굴복하기를 거부했다. 그는 1864년 노예제 폐지 헌법 개정 운동을 벌이기도 했다.

abolition n. (법률·제도·조직의) 폐지 egalitarian a. 평등주의의 emancipationist n. 노예 해방론자 Promised Land (성서에 나오는) 약속의 땅(미국의 이상) waver v. 흔들리다, 꺾이다 insistence n. 주장, 단언 extinction n. 절멸 detriment n. 손해, 손실 the U.S. House 미 하원 constitutional amendment 헌법개정

39 문장삽입 ④

'그러나 링컨을 노예제도에 반대하는 망설이는 전사로만 묘사하는 것은 그를 공정하게 다루는 것이 아니다.'라는 주어진 문장 다음에는 흑인노예해방을 위해 단호히 행동하는 링컨의 모습을 설명하는 내용이 와야 한다. 그러한 링컨의 모습이 등장하는 것이 Ⓓ 이후이다. 따라서 주어진 문장은 Ⓓ에 들어가는 것이 적절하다.

40 빈칸완성 ①

링컨이 남부 주들의 연방탈퇴를 둘러싼 위기 상황에서도 반(反) 노예제 공약에서 후퇴하지 않은 것과 파괴적인 전쟁(남북전쟁)을 끝내기 위해 남부 동맹과 평화 협상을 추진하라는 압력에도 굴복하기를 거부한 것은 개인적으로나 역사적으로 '매우 중대한' 사실이다.

빈칸에 들어가기에 가장 적절한 정답을 선택하시오.
① 매우 중요하게
② 미미하게
③ 관련하여
④ 명목상으로
⑤ 갑자기

41 내용파악 ③

'그는 1850년대 내내 정치적 손해를 감수하면서까지 이 입장을 유지했으며, 하원 의원 한 번을 제외하고는 1860년 대통령에 당선될 때까지 주요 공직에 당선되지 못했다.'라는 단서로부터 ③ 중에 '주요 직책을 맡을 수 있었다.'고 한 것은 본문의 내용과 일치하지 않음을 알 수 있다. ⑤ his moral conviction은 본문 중의 a morally informed insistence에 근거한 것이다.

다음 중 링컨과 관련하여 사실이 <u>아닌</u> 것은?
① 링컨은 처음에는 즉각적인 노예제 폐지를 주장하지 않고 점진적인 노예 해방론자의 접근 방식을 지지했다.
② 급진적인 노예제 폐지론자는 아니었지만 링컨은 노예제 확대에 반대했고 노예제의 궁극적인 소멸을 주장했다.
③ 노예제 반대 입장으로 인해 정치적 좌절을 겪었지만 주요 직책을 맡을 수 있었다. 그러나 정치적 이익을 위해 타협하는 것을 거부했다.
④ 링컨은 1864년 캠페인 기간 동안 협상된 평화를 위한 압력에 저항하고 노예 해방을 위해 싸웠다.
⑤ 노예제도에 대한 링컨의 입장은 도덕적 신념과 점진적 노예제 폐지에 대한 확고한 의지에서 비롯된 것이었다.

42-44

만일 당신이 태어나서 성인이 될 때까지 한 집에서 살았다면 당신은 그 집이 당신 자신의 정신과 얽혀 있다는 것을 알게 될 것이다. 내가 어린 시절의 대부분을 보낸 집은 유난히 아름다웠다. 단순히 미적으로만 아름다운 것이 아니라 그 이상이었다. 건축가의 예술적 기준이 매우 높았다. 우리를 둘러싼 실내의 모든 표면과 공간은 건축자재와 솜씨 면에서 고상하게 균형 잡혀 있었고 멋스러우면서도 공간적으로 여유가 있었다. 세심하게 계획되고 즐거움을 주기 위해 의도된 집은, 그 안에 사는 사람, 무엇보다도 아이에게 영향을 미치기 마련인데, 아이에게 집은 거의 세상과 같기 때문이다.
Ⓑ 만일 그 세상이 의도적으로 아름답게 만들어졌다면, 아이는 인간적인 척도와 인간적인 관점에서 아름다움에 대한 친숙함과 기대감을 갖게 될 수 있다.
Ⓐ 그러한 일상적인 경험은 음악이나 시와 마찬가지로 마음을 움직이는 힘이 있다.
Ⓓ 하지만 음악이나 시의 경험은 짧고 가끔씩 하는 것이다.
Ⓒ 그 안에 사는 아이에게 집이 있다는 경험은 영구적이고 포괄적인 것이다.

maturity n. 성숙 aesthetically ad. 미학적으로 proportioned a. 균형이 잡힌 handsome a. 멋진 generous a. 공간적으로 여유가 있는 material n. 건축 자재 workmanship n. 솜씨, 장인의 기량

set off ~를 향해 출발하다 embezzle v. 횡령[착복]하다 mortgage payment 주택담보대출 satirize v. 풍자하다 morbid a. 병적인 bleakly ad. 몹시 침울해진 credit v. (행위·공적을) (남에게) 돌리다 antihero n. 반(反)영웅

---

42 빈칸완성 ⑤

태어나서 성인이 될 때까지 한 집에서 살았다면 그 집의 모든 것을 속속 들이 알고 있고 느끼고 있을 것이므로 그 집과 그 사람의 정신은 분리될 수 없게 하나로 얽혀 있을 것이다. 따라서 빈칸에는 ⑤가 적절하다.

빈칸 Ⓐ에 들어가기에 가장 적절한 정답을 선택하시오.
① 환멸을 느끼다
② 양립할 수 없다
③ 분리하다
④ 넘쳐난다
⑤ 뒤엉켜 있다

---

43 빈칸완성 ②

집이 그 집에 사는 사람에게 반드시 영향을 미치게 되어 있다면 좋은 영향, 바라는 영향을 미치도록 집 짓는 사람이 세심하게 계획하여 지을 것이므로 빈칸에는 ② '세심하게'가 적절하다.

빈칸 Ⓑ에 들어가기에 가장 적절한 정답을 선택하시오.
① 일시적으로
② 세심하게
③ 위험하게
④ 독단적으로
⑤ 게으르게

---

44 문장배열 ②

앞에 주어진 글이 '아이에게 집은 거의 세상(the world)과 같기 때문이다'로 끝났으므로 that world로 받고 있는 Ⓑ가 가장 먼저 오고, Ⓑ에서 '아이는 아름다움에 대한 친숙함을 갖게 될 수 있다'고 한 것이 아이가 집에서 아름다움을 일상적으로 친숙하게 경험하는 것을 의미하므로 그러한 일상적 경험(Such daily experience)으로 시작하는 Ⓐ가 그 다음에 오고, Ⓐ에 나온 음악이나 시의 경험의 단점을 말한 Ⓓ가 그다음에 오고, 집의 경험의 장점을 말한 Ⓒ가 마지막에 오는 것이 적절한 순서이다.

45-47

1828년 니콜라이 고골은 짜르(러시아 황제)의 수도 상트페테르부르크를 향해 갔다. 처음에 그곳에서 일자리를 구하지 못한 그는 어머니의 주택 담보 대출금을 횡령해 독일 여행 경비를 마련했다. 그 후 그는 관료직을 얻었지만 곧 그만두었다. 1836년에 그는 러시아 관료제를 풍자하는 희극을 발표하여 스캔들을 일으켰고, 결국 러시아를 떠나 6년 동안 로마에서 살게 되었다. 이탈리아에서 그는 가장 유명한 소설인 『죽은 영혼』을 썼다. 그는 또한 점점 더 종교적이 되어갔고, 그의 경건함은 병적으로 변했다. 그 자신의 죄 많음에 사로잡힌 그는 원고를 불태웠고 끝내 굶어 죽었다. 고골은 현대 러시아 소설의 중요한 인물로 후대 작가들에게 막대한 영향을 끼쳤다. 그는 18세기 문학의 관습을 버리고 일상적인 삶에 대한 암울하고 희극적인 비전을 제시했다. 비평가들은 종종 그의 이야기가 현대 문학에 반(反)영웅을 도입했다는 점을 공로로 인정하는데, 반(反)영웅은 용기, 힘, 이상주의와 같은 영웅적 자질이 전혀 없는 주인공 유형이다.

---

45 동의어 ⑤

embezzle는 '횡령하다'는 뜻이므로, ⑤가 정답이다.

밑줄 친 단어 'embezzled'에 가장 가까운 의미를 가진 정답을 고르시오.
① 갚다
② 교환하다
③ 보상하다
④ 축적하다
⑤ 횡령하다

---

46 빈칸완성 ①

고골이 후대 작가들에게 막대한 영향을 끼쳤고, 18세기 문학의 관습을 버리고 일상적인 삶에 대한 암울하고 희극적인 비전을 제시했으며, 비평가들은 종종 그의 이야기가 현대 문학에 안티히어로를 도입했다는 점을 공로로 인정한다는 등의 단서로부터 그가 중요하고 영향력 있는 작가임을 알 수 있다.

빈칸에 들어갈 말로 가장 적절한 것을 고르시오.
① 중요한
② 파악하기 어려운
③ 기묘한
④ 혐오감을 불러일으키는
⑤ 영향을 받은

---

47 내용파악 ⑤

'그 후 그는 관료직을 얻었지만 곧 그만두었다. 1836년에 그는 러시아 관료제를 풍자하는 희극을 발표하여 스캔들을 일으켰고, 결국 러시아를 떠나 6년 동안 로마에서 살게 되었다.'라는 단서로부터 ⑤ '그는 관료로서 오랜 경력을 쌓았다'가 본문의 내용과 일치하지 않음을 알 수 있다.

다음 중 고골과 관련하여 사실이 아닌 것은?
① 그는 해외에서 망명생활을 했다.
② 그는 종교적 광신자가 되었다.
③ 그는 연약함을 지닌 평범한 사람들을 묘사했다.
④ 그는 18세기 문학으로부터 벗어났다.
⑤ 그는 관료로서 오랜 경력을 쌓았다.

48-50

폴란드에서는, 예상치 못한 유권자의 급증으로 포퓰리즘 연립 정부가 축출되고 친(親)유럽연합 정당이 의회 의석의 대부분을 차지했다. 일단 들어서고 나면, 새 정부는 (새 정부의) 지도자들이 약속하고 EU가 요구한 변화를 이루기 위해 노력할 것이다. 특히, 새 정부는 EU 규정에 따라 사법부와 언론의 정치적 독립성을 회복하기 위해 노력할 것이다. 이러한 개혁은 또

한 EU가 (회원국의) 팬데믹 복구를 지원할 목적으로 회원국을 위해 챙겨둔 350억 유로에 달하는 기금을 폴란드가 최대한 많이 이용할 수 있게 도움을 줄 것이다. EU는 판사와 언론인을 정부 통제 하에 두려는 이전 정부의 시도에 대한 대응으로 해당 자금을 보류해왔다. 지난 몇 년 동안, 바르샤바의 (극우) 포퓰리즘 정부는 노조, 민주주의에 의거한 통치, 사회 정책을 악화하여 인기를 높여왔다. 포퓰리즘 정부는 국영 언론 매체를 정부 선전의 도구로 전락시키고 법원을 정권의 측근으로 채웠다.

surge n. 급증 oust v. 축출하다 coalition government 연립정부
judiciary n. 사법부 claim v. 차지하다, 요구하다 set aside 챙겨두다
bid n. 시도 boost v. 부양하다, 활성화시키다 state-media outlets
국영언론매체 propaganda n. 정치선전 stack v. 채우다

---

48 빈칸완성   ④

새로이 들어설 정부가 그 지도자들이 약속하고 EU가 요구한 변화를 이루기 위해 노력할 것이다, 라는 단서로부터 빈칸에 보기 ④ '~ 와 함께, ~에 따라'가 와야 함을 추론할 수 있다.

빈칸에 들어갈 말로 가장 적절한 것을 고르시오.
① ~와 불화하는
② ~때문에
③ ~이 필요한
④ ~에 따라
⑤ ~대신에

---

49 동의어   ⑤

oust는 '내쫓다, 축출하다'는 뜻이므로, ⑤가 정답이다.

밑줄 친 단어 'ousted'에 가장 가까운 의미를 가진 정답을 고르시오.
① 안내하다
② 야기하다
③ 자극하다
④ 유혹하다
⑤ 추방하다

---

50 내용파악   ②

'새 정부는 (새 정부의) 지도자들이 약속하고 EU가 요구한 변화를 이루기 위해 노력할 것이다. 특히, 새 정부는 EU 규정에 따라 사법부와 언론의 정치적 독립성을 회복하기 위해 노력할 것이다.'라는 단서로부터 ② '새 정부는 민주주의에 관한 유럽연합의 규칙을 어길 것이다.'가 본문의 내용과 일치하지 않음을 알 수 있다.

다음 중 폴란드와 관련하여 사실이 아닌 것은?
① 유권자들이 정치적 변화를 가져왔다.
② 새 정부는 민주주의에 관한 유럽연합의 규칙을 어길 것이다.
③ 폴란드와 유럽연합 사이의 분열의 근원이 이제 사라지고 있다.
④ 이전 포퓰리즘 정부는 사리사욕을 채우기 위해 국영 미디어를 악용했다.
⑤ 유럽연합은 폴란드 정부에 변화를 촉구하기 위해 전략적으로 폴란드에 대한 자금 지원을 보류했다.

01 ①	02 ④	03 ④	04 ①	05 ③	06 ②	07 ①	08 ③	09 ④	10 ①
11 ④	12 ③	13 ③	14 ③	15 ②	16 ④	17 ①	18 ②	19 ④	20 ②
21 ②	22 ③	23 ②	24 ①	25 ③	26 ①	27 ④	28 ②	29 ③	30 ①
31 ④	32 ③	33 ①	34 ①	35 ④	36 ②	37 ④	38 ②	39 ③	40 ②

01 주어와 동사의 수일치   ①

a single ant or bee 뒤에는 단수 동사 is가 와야 한다. 따라서 정답은 ①이다.

single a. 하나의 colony n. 군락지 swarm intelligence 떼지능, 군집지능

한 마리의 개미나 벌은 똑똑하지 않지만 개미와 벌 집단은 똑똑하다. 피터 밀러라는 작가가 발견한 바대로 그 이유는 군집지능이라 불리는 것이다.

02 관계부사   ④

mouth라는 선행사가 뒤의 관계절에서 '입 안에서는 침이 ~'라는 의미의 장소 부사어로 쓰이고 있다. 따라서 ④는 관계부사 where나 '전치사+관계대명사'의 형태인 in which로 고쳐야 한다.

digestive a. 소화의 complex a. 복잡한 transform v. 변형시키다 nutrient n. 영양분 coordination n. 조화, 조율 break down 분해하다 fuel n. 연료 saliva n. 타액, 침

인간의 소화계는 복잡한 메커니즘이며, 그것은 우리가 음식을 몸 전체에서 사용되는 양분들로 바꾸게 해준다. 그것은 몸속 다양한 기관들의 조율을 요구하며, 기관 각각은 음식을 연료로 분해할 때 역할을 한다. 그것은 입에서 시작되는데, 입 안에서는 침이 소화 과정을 시작한다.

03 대명사의 수일치   ④

④의 대명사 its가 가리키는 것은 areas이므로 복수 대명사 their로 고쳐야 한다. 따라서 정답은 ④이다.

industrialized a. 산업화된 grip n. 손아귀, 지배 fossil fuel 화석연료 deplete v. 고갈시키다 evident a. 명백한, 분명한 current a. 현재의 temporary a. 일시적인 drill v. 구멍을 뚫다

최근에 산업화된 세계는 에너지 위기에 사로잡혀 있었다. 화석연료의 제한된 공급량이 고갈되고 있다는 사실은 하루하루 지남에 따라 더욱 명백해진다. 현재의 세계 소비량을 감안하면 머지않아 늘어나는 수요를 충당할 연료가 부족해질 것이다. 이 문제에 대한 일시적 해결책은 그 자연 그대로의 야생성 때문에 현재 야생 보존구역으로 보호받고 있는 지역들에서 원유를 시추하는 것을 포함한다.

04 비교구문   ①

첫 문장의 비교구문인 who were less fortunate than he는 who were less fortunate than he was fortunate에서 온 것인데, 이때 fortunate는 반드시 생략해야 하고 was는 생략할 수도 있으나 그대로 두는 것이 더 자연스럽다. 따라서 ①을 he was로 고친다. ② '어떤 옷을 입은'의 뜻으로 옷 앞에는 전치사 in을 쓴다. ③ home은 '집으로'라는 뜻의 부사이고 to give는 '주기 위해서'의 부사적 용법의 부정사이다. ④ 때를 나타내는 종속접속사 when으로 최상급 most aware와 상응하여 동일인의 여러 때를 비교하여 특정한 때에 가장 aware하다는 의미이다.

fortunate a. 운 좋은 frail a. 약한, 부서지기 쉬운 aware of ~을 아는, 인식하는 poverty n. 빈곤, 가난

소년은 그보다 더 불행한 중앙아메리카 사람들을 돕기 위해 뭔가를 하고 싶었다. 눈 먼 할머니와 꽃을 파는 파란 옷을 입은 어린 소녀가 있었다. 이 소녀는 여섯 살밖에 안 되었고, 늘 웃고 있긴 했지만 너무 약해 보였다. 그는 소녀와 할머니에게서 자주 꽃을 사서 어머니와 누나들에게 주기 위해 집으로 가져갔다. 그는 그와 부모님이 식당에서 외식을 하러 나갈 때 그 가난을 가장 많이 느꼈다.

05 동사의 태   ③

동사 continue는 to부정사와 동명사를 모두 취할 수 있으므로 ③의 continue to rise와 continue rising이 모두 가능하다. rise는 자동사이므로 수동태가 불가능해서 ①과 ②는 틀린 표현이다. rise가 진행이 가능하지만 동명사 진행형인 ④는 쓰이지 않고 to부정사 진행형인 continue to be rising은 가능하다. 따라서 정답은 ③이다.

effect n. 영향, 효과 temperature n. 온도, 기온 natural disaster 자연재해 rise v. 오르다

기후 변화의 한 가지 영향은 지구상 일부 지역의 온도가 더 높아진다는 것이다. 기온 평균이 계속 오름에 따라 기상이변과 자연재해가 증가할 것이다.

06 전치사의 목적어 / 태   ②

전치사 without 다음에 '죄의식으로 끌려들어간다'는 의미의 수동태가 필요하므로 정답은 ②이다.

acknowledge v. 인정하다 cause harm 해를 끼치다 amend v. 수정하다 reduce v. 줄이다 needless a. 불필요한 feelings of guilt 죄의식

우리 모두가 어느 정도의 해를 끼치면서 살아간다는 근본적인 진실을 인정할 때, 우리는 우리가 저지를 수도 있는 실질적 해악의 양을 줄이려고 의식적으로 행동을 고치면서도, 불필요한 죄의식에 빠져들지 않을 수 있다.

---

07 비교 ①

as effective 뒤에 "널리 생각되는 만큼"이라는 뜻의 수동태 표현이 와야만 앞의 strategies라는 주어와 의미가 맞다. 따라서 정답은 ①이다. as effective as they are widely believed to be effective에서 they are와 to be effective가 생략된 것이다.

strategy n. 전략 get one's mind around ~을 이해하다 worthwhile a. 가치 있는 likely a. 가능한 superficial a. 피상적인 trivial a. 하찮은

"멀티태스킹" 전략은 널리 생각되는 만큼 효과적이지 않다. 어려운 문제를 이해한 다음 가치 있는 해결책을 개발할 조건을 확립하는 데 15분에서 1시간가량 시간이 걸린다. 한 가지 과제에서 다른 과제로 너무 금방 너무 자주 넘어가면 머리가 생각해낼 것이 하찮지는 않다 해도 피상적이게 될 것이다.

---

08 관계대명사절 / 시제 ③

the manner는 '방법'에 해당하므로 수식하는 관계절은 where절이 아니라 in which절이며, 재검표는 '시행되는' 것이므로 수동태여야 하고, 주어인 the manner가 단수이고 declared가 과거시제이므로 과거 단수 수동인 was이다. 따라서 정답은 ③이다.

electoral vote 선거인단 투표 recount n. 다시 세기, 재검표 ballot n. 투표용지 constitution n. 헌법 conduct v. 실행하다

고어는 2000년 대선에서 고작 선거인단 5명 차이로 졌다. 그는 플로리다 투표 결과를 수작업으로 재검표해야 한다고 요구했다. 그러나 이 사건이 미국 대법원으로 갔을 때 판사들은 재검표가 실행되는 방식이 미국 헌법 위반이라고 판결했다.

---

09 동의어 ④

cybersecurity n. 사이버 보안 expert n. 전문가, 숙련가 ensure v. 보장하다(= guarantee) privacy n. 사생활, 프라이버시 institution n. 기관 sustain v. 유지[지탱]하다 process v. 가공[처리]하나

사이버 보안 전문가의 역할은 대학 및 은행 같은 기관이 수집하는 개인정보의 안전과 비밀을 보장하는 것이다.

---

10 동의어 ①

conference n. 회의 collaboratively ad. 협력적으로(= interactively) engage with ~와 협력하다 expand v. 확대하다 ethically ad. 윤리적으로 presumably ad. 아마도, 추정컨대

회의는 참석자들로 하여금 전 세계에서 온 산업계 지도자들과 협조하도록 해주었고, 그럼으로써 그들의 지식과 네트워크를 효과적으로 확대하도록 해주었다.

---

11 동의어 ④

unequaled a. 비할 데 없는(= incomparable) admiration n. 경탄 witness v. 목격하다 prowess n. 솜씨, 기량 aggressive a. 공격적인 unfair a. 불공정한 excessive a. 과도한, 과잉의

우승자들의 그 분야에서의 헌신과 역량은 비할 데 없이 뛰어났고, 그로 인해 그들은 그들의 최고 기량을 목격한 모든 사람들의 경탄과 존경을 받았다.

---

12 동의어 ③

confident a. 자신감 있는, 확신하는(= assured) extroverted a. 외향적인 talkative a. 수다스러운 objective a. 객관적인

많은 사람들은 남성과 여성이 언어를 사용하는 방식에 차이가 있다고 생각한다. 남성들이 여성들보다 더 자신 있고 더 직접적으로 소통한다는 것은 사실일까?

---

13 동의어 ③

feed on ~을 먹고 살다 bedding n. 침구류 spread v. 퍼지다, 미치다 dormant a. 잠자는, 움직임이 없는(= inactive) hatch v. 알을 까고 나오다, 부화하다 insolent a. 무례한 invisible a. 보이지 않는 insistent a. 고집하는 지속되는

빈대는 인간의 피를 빨아먹으며 침구류 속에 살고 있다. 이들은 대개 집 속에서 퍼져나가며 먹지 않고도 여러 달을 생존할 수 있다. 이들은 또한 집이나 가구 속에 알을 낳는다. 이 알들은 몇 년 간 움직임이 없다가 새로운 장소로 옮겨질 때 알에서 깨어난다.

---

14 논리완성 ③

결빙방지 단백질이 동물의 몸을 얼지 않게 막아준다는 표현이 필요하므로 전치사 from과 어울리는 prevents가 빈칸에 들어가야 한다.

tiny a. 아주 작은 snailfish n. 꼼치 antifreeze protein 결빙방지 단백질 strengthen v. 강화하다 prevent v. 막다, 방지하다 distract v. 주의를 딴 데로 돌리다

극도로 추운 환경에서 동물을 연구하는 학자들은 매우 작은 꼼치들이 결빙방지 단백질로 가득 차 있다는 것을 발견했다. 이 결빙방지 단백질은 얼음 가득한 바다에서 이들의 몸이 얼지 않도록 방지해주는 특수 유형의 단백질이다.

15 논리완성 ②

뒤에서 able to state their ideas clearly(생각을 분명히 말할 수 있다)라고 했으므로 빈칸에는 articulate(생각·감정을 잘[명확히] 표현할 수 있는)가 적절하다.

literate a. 글을 읽고 쓸 줄 아는 figurative a. 비유적인 articulate a. 발음이 분명한; (사람이) (생각·감정을) 잘[명확히] 표현할 수 있는 submissive a. 복종하는 obscure a. 애매모호한, 불분명한

대한민국 대다수의 사람들은 글을 읽고 쓸 줄 안다. 대부분의 사람들이 신문과 잡지를 읽을 수 있으므로 한국인들은 대개 중요한 문제에 대한 의견을 갖고 있다. 그뿐 아니라 그들은 생각을 명확히 표현할 수 있기 때문에 자신의 상사나 윗사람, 연장자들에게 자기 생각을 분명히 말할 수 있다.

16 논리완성 ④

새로 이사 간 도시에서 혼자 외출을 한다면 길을 잃게 될 것이므로 첫 번째 빈칸에는 lost가 적절하고, 그 경우에는 새로운 환경에 적응할 수 없을 것이므로 orient oneself to(~에 적응하다)의 orient가 두 번째 빈칸에 적절하다.

surroundings n. 환경 locate v. 위치를 찾다 isolated a. 고립된 orient v. 방향 짓다 orient oneself to ~에 적응[순응]하다

그 소녀는 도시로 이사했을 때 혼자 밖으로 나가면 길을 자주 잃었다. 그녀는 자신이 어느 방향에서 왔는지 절대로 기억하지 못했고, 새로운 환경에 적응할 수 없었다.

17 논리완성 ①

Despite 다음의 긍정적인 정보와 대조를 이루어야 하므로, 출판물과 관련해 유명세를 '거부했다'는 말이 와야 하고, 작가가 유명세를 거부했다면 그 작가는 자신의 사생활이 유명해진 소설과 '무관하다'고 생각했을 것이다. 따라서 refused와 irrelevant가 정답이다.

publicity n. 유명세 refuse v. 거부하다 irrelevant a. 무관한, 무의미한 consent v. 동의하다 inappropriate a. 부적절한 abhor v. 혐오하다 agreeable a. 동의할 수 있는, 쾌활한

조젯 하이어는 베스트셀러 작가였음에도 불구하고, 그녀의 소설 『These Old Shades』가 성공한 후 출간과 관련된 어떤 형태의 유명세에도 계속해서 관여하기를 거부했다. 그녀는 자신의 사생활이 자기 소설의 성공과 무관하다고 생각했던 것이다. 그 결과, 그녀의 팬들은 그녀가 죽을 때까지 그녀의 결혼 후의 성씨(姓氏)조차 알지 못했다.

18 논리완성 ②

향수가 파괴적이라는 내용이 이어지고 while은 대조를 나타내므로 첫 번째 빈칸에는 이점이라는 의미의 benefits가 적절하고, '불안과 공포 같은'이라 했으므로 두 번째 빈칸에는 부정적인 의미의 negative가 적절하다.

nostalgia n. 향수 destructive a. 파괴적인 positive a. 긍정적인 momentary a. 순간적인 result in ~을 초래하다 negative a. 부정적인 critical a. 중요한 significant a. 중요한

향수가 정신 건강상의 이점과 관련이 있다는 증거는 일부 있었지만, 향수에도 다양한 유형이 있다는 것, 그리고 일부 향수는 아주 파괴적일 수 있다는 점을 기억해야 한다. 최근 연구가 발견한 바에 따르면, 극단적인 향수의 의식적 행위는 긍정적 영향을 끼치는 반면, 더 작고 일시적이고 무의식적인 향수 경험은 불안과 공포 같은 부정적인 정신 건강상의 영향을 초래할 수 있다.

19 논리완성 ④

미국의 경우와 일본의 경우가 서로 대조를 이루어야 한다. 미국에서는 '손님에게 개인적인 관심을 쏟는 것(=this)'을 상점 주인이 하기에는 '자존심 상하는(be beneath them)' 일이라 했고, 일본의 경우는 반대인데, 빈칸 앞에 not이 있으므로 빈칸에는 '자존심 상하게 하는, 굴욕적인'이라는 의미의 demeaning이 적절하다.

unnecessary a. 불필요한 bother n. 성가심 fuss n. 호들갑, 법석 ingredient n. 성분, 요소, 재료 decent a. 품위 있는 demanding a. 부담이 큰 decorative a. 장식적인 demeaning a. 굴욕적인, 비하하는, 품위를 떨어뜨리는

미국에서 불필요한 성가심이나 지나친 야단법석으로 간주되는 것이 일본에서는 근본적이라고 여겨진다. 미국 상점 주인들은 고객들에게 개인적 관심을 쏟는 것이 자신의 품위에 어울리지 않는 것이라고 여길지 모른다. 그러나 일본에서는 이런 일이 굴욕적이라고 여겨지지 않는다. 오히려 개인적 관심은 사업 성공의 필수 요건 중 하나라고 간주된다.

20 논리완성 ②

신을 숭배했다(honored gods)고 했으므로 spiritual하다고 해야 하고, 온전한 의미(full significance)라 했으므로 meaningful하다고 해야 한다.

familiarity n. 친숙함 extensive a. 광범위한 enchanting a. 매력적인 spiritual a. 영적인 exquisite a. 절묘한, 매우 아름다운 fascinating a. 매력적인 sacred a. 성스러운, 신성한 passionate a. 열정적인

훌라춤은 수백 년 동안 하와이의 중요한 전통이었다. 매우 영적이면서도 의미심장한 훌라춤은 원래 신들과 추장을 경배했고, 온갖 자연현상을 설명해주는 이야기를 대대로 전하는 데 사용되었다. 훌라춤의 온전한 의미를 인식하려면 관객은 역사와, 그 뒤의 이야기들을 잘 알아야 한다. 따라서 훌라춤에 대한 광범위한 지식을 갖춘 사람들은 대개 다른 형식의 예술 표현보다 훌라춤을 더 좋아한다.

21 글의 흐름상 적절하지 않은 표현 고르기 ②

②의 enslave(노예화하다)는 'serve(봉사하다)', 'in service of the public and with their consent and cooperation'과 어울리지 않는다. 이것을 save(구조하다)나 protect(보호하다)나 cooperate(협력하다) 같은 긍정적 의미로 바꾸어야 한다.

statesman n. 정치가 citywide a. 시 전체의 civil-policing n. 치안 enslave v. 노예로 만들다 cooperation n. 협력 last resort 최후의 수단 call n. 요청, 요구 mission n. 소명

1829년 정치가인 로버트 필 경은 런던 최초의 조직화된 시 전체의 경찰을 설립했다. 필의 경찰은 시민 치안 의무를 지닌 성공적인 군 조직에 기반을 두고 있었다. 그리고 필은 현대 경찰 치안업무에 중심적인 여러 개념을 도입했다. 이 "필의 원칙"은 본질적으로 "봉사와 <노예화>의 기준을 확립했다. 필은 경찰이 치안을 유지하되 공중을 위해 그들의 동의와 협력을 얻어서 유지해야 한다고 믿었다. 무력 사용은 최후의 수단이었고 필은 자기 부하들이 의무에 대한 헌신과 올바른 행실을 통해 존경을 받기를 바랐다. 그리고 치안에 있어 많은 것이 바뀌긴 했지만, 시민을 통제하는 것이 아니라 보호해야 한다는 기본적인 요구는 오늘날까지 경찰의 소명에 중심으로 남아있다.

22 내용파악 ③

경고 신호를 줄 때 고양이는 대개 등을 둥글게 말고 등의 털이 곤두서는 반면, 개는 이를 드러내고 상대를 빤히 바라봄으로써 경고 신호를 보낸다고 했으므로 정답은 ③이다.

spot v. 찾아내다 playful a. 놀기 좋아하는 occasional a. 가끔씩의 howl v. 울부짖다 growl v. 으르렁거리다 meow v. 야옹야옹하다 snarl v. 이빨을 드러내고 으르렁대다 signal n. 신호 stare v. 빤히 보다

개와 고양이 사이의 차이를 얼마나 찾아낼 수 있을까? 사실 개와 고양이 사이의 차이는 찾기가 생각만큼 쉽지 않을지도 모른다. 낮 동안 당신의 개는 능동적이고 잘 논다. 가끔 낮잠을 자긴 하지만 개는 당신 옆에 있기를 더 좋아한다. 반면에 고양이는 낮 동안 대부분의 시간을 혼자 자고 당신이 침대로 뛰어들기 직전에 터보맨(장난감)처럼 신나게 노는 시간으로 돌입하기를 좋아한다. 고양이는 저녁에 더 활동적이지만 반려 부모를 위해 낮 동안에 시간을 내 주는 고양이도 많다. 일상 과정을 확립하는 것이 당신의 고양이로 하여금 당신의 스케줄대로 더 움직이도록 하는데 도움이 된다. 개와 고양이의 주요 차이는 이들이 소리를 내는 방식이다. 당신의 개는 짖거나 길게 울부짖거나 으르렁거리는 반면, 고양이는 야옹거리거나 이빨을 드러내며 으르렁댄다. 경고 신호를 줄 때 고양이는 대개 등을 둥글게 말고 등의 털이 곤두선다. 개는 이를 드러내고 상대를 빤히 바라봄으로써 경고 신호를 보낸다. 두 동물 모두 다른 동물이나 인간에게 다가오지 말라고 경고할 때 대개 으르렁거리는 소리를 낸다.

행동을 매우 면밀하게 비교하는 것은 어려운 일이다. 왜냐하면 인간처럼 개와 고양이의 행동과 성격 역시 개인차가 크기 때문이다. 일부 고양이는 외향적이고 일부 개는 내향적이다. 종과 품종은 딱 그 정도만큼 행동을 결정한다. 나머지는 개별 성격과, 매일 양육 받는 환경 요인에 달려있다.

다음 중 개와 고양이에 대해 옳은 것은?
① 개와 고양이는 낮 동안에 동일한 활동 패턴을 보인다.
② 일상 과정은 고양이보다 개에게 더 필요하다.
③ 개와 고양이는 경고를 표현하는 방법이 다르다.
④ 개의 행동과 성격이 고양이보다 더 다양하다.

23 내용파악 ②

미라큘린이라는 단백질이 미뢰에 붙어 신 맛을 보는 능력을 막아 음식 맛을 느끼는 감각을 변화시킨다고 봐야 하므로 정답은 ②이다. 화학물질이 변하는 게 아니라는데 유의한다. ④ 레드베리의 설탕 중독 가능성이 아니라 레드베리가 과일로서 설탕 대체품의 원료로 인정받지 못하고 미라큘린 단백질로 인해 설탕 대체품(=식품 첨가물)으로 규제받게 된 것이다.

fad n. 일시적 유행 trendy a. 최신 유행의 native to ~에 토종인 sugar substitute 설탕 대체물 food additive 식품 첨가물 regulate v. 규제하다 costly a. 비용이 많이 드는 instruct v. 지시하다, 알려주다 chew v. 씹다 bland a. 밋밋한, 단조로운 coat v. 막을 씌우다 turn someone loose ~을 자유롭게 풀어주다 exclamation n. 탄성 sour a. 신 topsy-turvy a. 뒤죽박죽인, 혼란스러운 spicy a. 매운 finger food 손으로 집어먹게 만든 음식, 핑거 푸드

새로운 유행 하나가 최근 몇 년 사이에 뉴욕의 최신 유행 서클 주변으로 들어왔는데, 그것인 "기적의 과일"이라 불리는 작은 레드베리가 스타 급 명물이 되어 있는 파티이다. 레드베리는 흔한 과일만큼 안전한데 서아프리카가 원산지다. 유럽의 한 탐험가가 1725년 레드베리를 발견했지만 다른 기후에서는 재배가 어려웠다. 1970년대 사람들은 레드베리가 설탕 대체품의 원료가 될 수 있기를 바랐다. 그러나 1974년 미국 식약청(FDA)은 레드베리의 활성 화학물질, 즉 미라큘린이라는 단백질이 식품 첨가물이라고 선언했다. 식품 첨가물은 과일과 달리 규제를 크게 받는다. 이것은 베리를 설탕 대체품의 형태로 시장에 내놓는 것이 길고 비용이 많이 드는 과정이 되리라는 뜻이었다.

이 기적의 과일 파티에 다니기 위해 손님들은 평균 밥값을 지불한다. 이들이 도착하면 주인이 각자에게 기적의 과일을 나누어준다. 이들은 이 과일을 씹어서 2분 간 혀 위에서 굴리라는 지시를 받는다. 레드베리는 부드럽고 밋밋한 맛이 나지만 불과 몇 분 후 기적을 일으켰다.

혀에 막이 씌워지면 손님들은 뷔페식으로 잘 골라 차려놓은 핑거 푸드를 마음대로 먹을 수 있다. 이제 놀라움과 기쁨의 탄성이 시작된다. 이 소동은 온통 어찌된 일인가? 미라큘린이라는 단백질이 미뢰에 들러붙어서 신 맛을 느끼는 능력을 막는다. 그 결과는 신 맛이 달게 느껴지고 단맛이 훨씬 더 달게 느껴지는 혼란스러운 경험이다. 가령 레몬은 레몬 사탕 맛이 난다. 매운 소스는 매운 설탕시럽 맛이 난다. 염소치즈는 치즈케이크 맛이 난다.

다음 중 본문에서 설명하고 있는 레드베리에 관해 옳은 것은?
① 레드베리의 화학물질은 다른 음식과 결합하면 변한다.
② 레드베리의 화학물질은 특정 음식의 맛이 느껴지는 방식에 영향을 끼친다.
③ 레드베리의 단맛과 입맛을 당기는 맛은 사람들로 하여금 파티의 특정 음식을 즐기게 만든다.
④ 레드베리의 설탕 중독 가능성은 그것을 식품 첨가물로 규제 받도록 만들었다.

24 내용파악 ①

인근 나무와 식물을 자라게 한다는 언급은 본문에 없으므로 정답은 ① 이다.

critical a. 중요한 slope n. 경사면 stream n. 시냇물 head up 위로 향하다 ridgetop n. 협곡 꼭대기 leap v. 도약하다, 뛰어오르다 tumble

down 굴러 떨어지다 trickle n. 조금씩 흐르는 액체 gorge n. 협곡
gaze n. 시선 geologic a. 지질학의 ravine n. 협곡 steep a. 가파른
incise v. 새기다 notch n. 새김눈, 눈금 abrasive a. 거친, 연마제의
file n. (쇠붙이를 가는) 줄 shadowy a. 그늘진, 어두운, 보이지 않는

(켄터키의) 붉은 강 협곡에서 물을 어디서 발견하건, 물과 관련한 중요한
사실은 물이 움직인다는 점이다. 물은 움직이면서 모여든다. 경사면의 스며
든 물과 조금씩 흘러 떨어지는 물, 협곡 꼭대기 주변으로 올라가는 작은
시내, 그리고 가파른 협곡을 도약하면서 굴러 떨어지듯 흐르는 모든 물은
움직여 강에서 하나로 합쳐진다. 그리고 협곡 물의 움직임 속에서 협곡이라
는 장소 또한 움직인다. 인간의 눈이나 인간 역사의 집단적 시각에는 보이
지 않지만, 지질학 시간이라는 긴 시선에서 보면 붉은 강 협곡은 그 자체
내에서 움직이고, 깊어지고, 경사면의 윤곽을 바꾸고 있다. 이 강은 거대한
나무처럼 자라고 있고, 자기 지류들을 땅으로 새겨 넣고 있다. 특정 계절에
이 강이 아무리 고요해 보인다 해도 다 합쳐서 붉은 강이라 불리는 이
물줄기망은 쇠를 다듬는 줄처럼 거친 주변 암석들의 틈을 파고 들어간다.
이 강이 풍경의 창조자, 창조의 파로서 어떻게 작용하는지는 언제나 어느
정도 알려지지 않은 채 남을 것이다. 왜냐하면 이 강은 상당히 편안하게
끈기 있게 작용하며, 종종 혼돈 속에서 작용하기 때문이다. 이 강의 작용
과정을 상당히 설득력 있게 추정할 수는 있겠지만, 이 풍광에 대한 모든
관찰점도 또한 추정점이고, 현재의 표면에서 나와 강의 기원과 과정이라는
어둑한 질문으로 들어가는 출발점이기도 하다.

다음 중 붉은 강 협곡의 물의 역할이나 기능으로 옳지 않은 것은?
① 인근의 나무와 식물을 풍부히 자라도록 비옥하게 만드는 힘
② 다양한 형태의 물을 붉은 강으로 수렴시키는 통합의 힘
③ 강 협곡의 기원과 과정을 숙고하게 만드는 명상의 요인
④ 물과 주변 환경을 꾸준히 변화시키는 변화의 요인

---

25 내용파악   ③

꿀을 인공적으로 생산할 수 없다고는 했지만 그 점이 꿀이 치료약이나
피부제품에 쓰이는 이유는 아니다. 따라서 정답은 ③이다.

substitute n. 대체물 sweetener n. 감미료 medicinal a. 약효가
있는 remedy n. 치료법 infection n. 감염 sore a. 아픈, 따끔거리는
suppress v. 억제하다 over-the-counter a. 처방전 없이 약국에서 살
수 있는 remarkable a. 놀라운 humectant n. 보습제 purchase
v. 사다, 구매하다

꿀은 인간이 먹는 음식물 중 곤충이 만든 유일한 음식물이다. 게다가 인간
의 기술력 — 인간을 우주로 보내고 컴퓨터를 설계하고 3D 프린터를 만드
는 기술 — 이 아무리 뛰어나도 인공 꿀을 만드는 방법은 아무도 알아내지
못했다. 벌이 늘 알아왔던 꿀 제조법을 대체할 것은 실제로 전혀 없다.
감미료로 많이 쓰일 뿐 아니라 꿀은 수백 년 동안 치료제로도 사용되어
왔다. 어떤 종류의 박테리아건 꿀 속에서 생존이 매우 어려우므로, 베인
상처에 완벽한 장벽을 만들고 감염을 예방할 수 있다. 꿀은 또한 목이 아픈
증상을 완화할 때도 효과적인 치료법이다. 꿀은 아이들의 기침을 억제하는
데 처방전 없는 일반약인 기침 억제제만큼 효과가 있는 것으로 밝혀졌다.
이 놀라운 자연물질의 또 한 가지 용도는 피부와 모발 제품이다. 사람들은
꿀이 항균성이 있을 뿐 아니라 습기를 끌어들이고 보유해주는 보습제라는
것도 오랫동안 알고 있었다. 이로 인해 꿀은 로션, 비누, 립 밤, 샴푸의
완벽한 성분이 된다. 당신은 꿀이 함유된 개인용 제품을 많이 구매할 수
있고 아니면 직접 만들기를 시도해 볼 수도 있다.

다음 중 꿀이 치료약이나 피부제품에 쓰이는 이유가 아닌 것은?
① 습기를 흡수해 보유하는 능력
② 감염 예방 가능성
③ 천연 생산 공정
④ 박테리아 생장을 막는 능력

---

26 부분이해   ①

밑줄 친 인용문에 대해 글 후반부에서 "이 메시지는 오래전에 쓰였던 때
에도 의미 있었지만 지금도 여전히 뜻깊다. 여러분이 희극을 좋아하건
비극을 좋아하건, 액션물을 좋아하건 로맨스를 좋아하건 여러분이 생각
하는 것보다 셰익스피어의 이야기에 공감할 수 있다는 것을 알게 될 것이
다."라고 했으므로, 밑줄 친 문장을 인용한 저자의 의도로는 ①이 가장
적절하다.

theme n. 주제 relevant a. 의미 있는 break down 분석하다 poem
n. 시 excitement n. 흥분, 흥미진진함 suspense n. 서스펜스, 스릴감
challenge n. 어려움 figure out 이해하다 negotiate v. 협상하다,
(일을) 타결 짓다 tragedy n. 비극

많은 사람들이 셰익스피어의 글은 오래되었고 지루하며 읽기 어렵다고
말한다. 그러나 그것은 사실이 아니다. 셰익스피어가 1500년대와 1600년
대에 작품 활동을 한 것은 맞지만 그의 주제는 오늘날에도 여전히 관련성이
있으며, 그의 글은 시간을 들여 분석만 하면 실제로 이해하기 쉽다.
셰익스피어는 흥미와 서스펜스와 코미디와 로맨스와 인간 드라마를 갖춘
희곡과 시를 많이 썼다. 셰익스피어의 글은 또한 사람들이 르네상스 시대나
지금이나 똑같은 어려움과 감정에 직면한다는 것을 보여준다. 예를 들어,
그는 아버지에게 책임이 있다는 것을 아버지에게 증명해보여야 하는 한
청년에 대해 썼다.
셰익스피어의 언어는 끈기를 갖고 어휘들을 은유로 보고 집중해 읽기만
하면 이해하기 그리 어렵지 않다. 예를 들어, 이 인용문을 생각해보라. "모
든 눈이 스스로 (일을) 타결 짓게 하라(희곡 『헛소동』 발췌)." 여러분은
이 단어들이 개별적으로 무엇을 뜻하는지는 다 알지만 합치면 무슨 뜻인지
모를 수 있다. 그것은 작가가 어휘를 비유적으로 쓸 때가 있기 때문이다.
기본적으로 셰익스피어가 하는 말은 "각 사람이 스스로 판단하게 내버려두
어라"라는 뜻이다. 그는 누구나 자신의 선택이나 판단을 내릴 수 있어야
한다고 말하고 있는 셈이다. 이 메시지는 오래전에 쓰였던 때에도 의미
있었지만 지금도 여전히 뜻깊다. 여러분이 희극을 좋아하건 비극을 좋아하
건, 액션물을 좋아하건 로맨스를 좋아하건 여러분이 생각하는 것보다 셰익
스피어의 이야기에 공감할 수 있다는 것을 알게 될 것이다.

밑줄 친 문장을 인용한 저자의 의도는 무엇인가?
① 셰익스피어 작품의 기저 사상은 현재의 독자들에게 울림이 있다는 것을
   보여주는 것
② 셰익스피어의 글에 쓰인 언어가 낡고 전통적인 것이 아니라는 점을
   입증하는 것
③ 셰익스피어의 비유적 문체가 독자들의 이해를 제약할 수 있음을 입증하
   는 것
④ 셰익스피어 작품의 표현에 다양한 의미가 암시되어 있음을 보여주
   는 것

27 내용파악 ④

아스피린은 콧물의 양이 아니라 코에서 분비물을 통해 나오는 바이러스의 양을 늘릴 수 있다. 따라서 틀린 내용은 ④이다.

over-the-counter a. 의사의 처방 없이 팔리는 adverse effect 역효과 scary a. 두려운 symptom n. 증상 counterproductive a. 역효과를 내는 inflammation n. 염증 shed v. 떨어버리다, 제거하다 nasal a. 코의 secretion n. 분비물 infect v. 감염시키다 stuffy a. 답답한, 막힌

누구나 어느 때든 감기를 앓았던 적이 있다. 우리는 감기 치료제가 개발되기를 기다리지만 대부분의 사람들은 그저 병원에도 가지 않고 약국에서 이런 저런 약을 사먹고 만다. 무서운 점은 감기 증상을 치료하려 먹은 약 중 일부가 실제로는 오히려 반대 효과를 낼 수 있다는 것이다. 예를 들어, 아스피린은 두통과 목의 염증을 퇴치하는 완벽한 약처럼 보이지만 진실은 이 약이 실제로 우리에게 역효과를 낼 수 있다는 것이다.
일부 학자들은 아스피린을 감기 치료제로 사용하면 코의 분비물을 통해 떨어뜨리는 바이러스의 양이 늘어날 수 있다고 생각한다. 이는 사람들 가까이에서 코를 풀 때 그들을 바이러스에 감염시킬 확률이 늘어난다는 뜻이다. 또 다른 문제는 아스피린이 우리의 면역 반응 일부를 억제해 코가 훨씬 더 막히게끔 만들 수 있다는 것이다.
일부 연구는 또한 아스피린이 3세에서 12세 사이의 아이들 치료에 쓰일 때 레이 증후군이라는 병의 원인이 될 수 있다고 주장해왔다. 아스피린은 종종 뇌나 간에 영향을 끼쳐 주요 장기손상을 일으킬 수 있고, 아주 심각한 경우에는 사망까지 초래할 수 있다. 따라서 의사들은 보통 감기를 비롯해 바이러스 질환을 앓고 있는 19세 미만의 사람에게는 아스피린을 주지 말아야 한다고 권고한다.
감기 자체는 우리에게 영구 손상을 입히지 않을 수 있으나 우리가 감기 증상을 치료하는 방법은 영구 손상을 입힐 수 있다. 19세 미만일 경우 아스피린을 피해야 한다는 뜻이고, 다른 어떤 약에 대해서도 확신이 없다면 의사를 찾아가야 한다는 뜻이다.

다음 중 아스피린 복용의 역효과가 <u>아닌</u> 것은?
① 아스피린은 어린 아동의 내부 장기 일부에 심각한 해악을 초래할 수 있다.
② 아스피린은 코를 풀 때 더 많은 바이러스가 코로부터 퍼져나가게 만들 수 있다.
③ 아스피린은 콧속의 답답한 느낌을 악화시킬 수 있다.
④ 아스피린은 콧물이 흐르는 양을 갑자기 늘릴 수 있다.

28 내용파악 ②

동충하초가 농촌 경제를 변모시켜 현대판 골드러시를 초래했다고 했으므로 옳은 내용은 ②이다. ③ 동충하초는 애벌레가 특정 균류에게 먹힌 후에 형성된다.

plateau n. 고원, 고지대 steep a. 가파른 slope n. 경사면 stalk n. 줄기, 식물의 대 caterpillar n. 애벌레 fungus n. 균류, 곰팡이류, 버섯류 significant a. 상당한 gold rush 골드러시(19세기 미국, 금광 발견 이후 사람들이 그쪽으로 모여든 현상) erupt v. 분출하다 farm v. 농장에서 재배하다

해발고도 15,000피트 히말라야 인근 고원 높은 곳에서 Silang Yangpi와 그의 아내인 Yangjin Namo는 가파른 산기슭을 기어 올라가 놀라운 치유력

이 있다고 여겨지는 아주 작은 균류(버섯)를 찾고 있다. 부부는 흙을 뚫고 밖으로 몇 인치 자라는 가느다란 갈색 줄기를 찾고 있다. 이 줄기는 밝은 노란색 애벌레의 머리에 붙어 있다. 일부 사람들에게 애벌레 균류(버섯)는 희한한 버섯처럼 보이지만 부부에게 이건 이들의 연간 수입의 큰 부분이다. 애벌레 버섯은 농촌 경제를 변모시켜 현대판 골드러시를 초래했다.
이 버섯은 박쥐나방 동충하초라 불린다. 뜻은 "여름 풀, 겨울 벌레(동충하초)"라는 뜻이나, 이건 엄밀히 말해서 풀도 아니고 벌레도 아니다. 이 버섯은 특정 애벌레가 Ophiocordyceps sinensis라는 기생균류에 감염되면 만들어진다. 이 버섯(기생균류)은 애벌레 내부에서 애벌레를 파먹어 죽이지만 외골격은 건드리지 않는다. 봄철에, 이 버섯은 애벌레의 머리에서 분출하는 갈색 줄기의 형태로 피어난다. 그 과정은 지하에서 일어나지만 버섯이 피어나면서 땅위로 밀고 나온다. 동충하초가 이렇게 피는 것은 히말라야 산맥 높은 곳의 비옥한 초원에서만 가능하다. 사람들은 이 버섯을 재배해보려 노력했지만 모든 시도가 실패했다.

다음 중 동충하초라는 균류에 대해 옳은 것은?
① 농촌에서 동충하초를 재배하기가 어렵지 않다.
② 동충하초는 농촌지역의 경제 변화를 이끌었다.
③ 동충하초는 애벌레가 특정 균류를 먹은 후 형성된다.
④ 동충하초가 피는 과정은 오직 흙 외부에서만 일어난다.

29 빈칸완성 ③

바로 앞에서 problem이라고 문제를 설명하는 부분이므로 마지막 부분에 부정적인 내용이 와야 한다. 부정적인 내용은 ③뿐이다.

humid a. 습한 scrap market 폐기물 시장 burn away 태워 없애다 covering n. 덮개, 피복 on a scale 규모로 keep up 뒤처지지 않다, 따라잡다 discard n. 폐기물 landfill n. 매립, 매립지 lead n. 납 mercury n. 수은 arsenic n. 비소 recycling n. 재활용 dig up 파내다, 발굴하다

태양이 가나의 수도인 아크라의 습한 공기를 덥히면서 끔찍한 악취가 나는 검은 연기가 아그보그블로시 시장 위로 올라가기 시작한다. 야채상들을 지나가면 폐기물 시장이 있다. 낡고 고장 난 전자 장비 더미로 가득한 곳이다. 망가진 TV, 컴퓨터와 모니터로 이루어진 이 폐기물은 "e-폐기물"이라 알려져 있다. 폐기물 시장을 넘어서 더 멀리 가면 작은 불들이 많다. 낡은 차량 타이어를 연료 삼아 이 불로 e-폐기물의 귀중한 전선에서 플라스틱 피복을 태워버리는 것이다. 사람들은 유독한 연기 사이로 두 팔에 밝은 색의 컴퓨터 전선을 가득 들고 걸어간다. 그 중 많은 사람들은 아이들이다.
e-폐기물은 이전에 본 적이 없는 규모로 생산되고 있다. 컴퓨터와 휴대폰과 다른 전자 장비는 몇 년만 지나면 낡아버려 소비자들은 뒤처지지 않으려 새 모델을 살 수밖에 없다. 세계적으로 사람마다 매년 평균적으로 6킬로그램이 넘는 e-폐기물을 버린다.
애석하게도, 세계 대부분의 지역에서 이 모든 쓰레기 더미는 결국 매립지로 간다. 매립지에서 폐기물은 환경을 독으로 오염시킨다. e-폐기물은 납과 수은과 비소 같은 다양한 유독물질을 함유하고 있다. 재활용은 많은 측면에서 이 문제에 대한 이상적인 해결책이다. e-폐기물에는 은과 금과 구리 등 가치가 높은 금속도 상당량 포함되어 있다. 이론상 낡은 컴퓨터에서 금을 재활용하는 것이 땅에서 금을 파내는 것보다 훨씬 더 효율적이고 환경적으로도 파괴가 덜하다. 문제는 부유한 나라에서 재활용을 위해 버려지는 e-폐기물의 대부분이 가나 같은 개발도상국으로 간다는 것이다. 전 세계 e-폐기물의 양이 늘어나면서 e-폐기물은 개발도상국에 사는 사람들의 건강을 점점 더 위협하고 있다.

다음 중 빈칸에 들어가기에 가장 적절한 것은?
① e-폐기물은 개발도상국에 사는 사람들이 e-폐기물에 긍정적 태도를 갖도록 만들고 있다
② e-폐기물은 개발도상국에 사는 사람들에게 부자가 될 사업 기회를 제공한다
③ e-폐기물은 개발도상국에 사는 사람들의 건강을 점점 더 위협한다
④ e-폐기물은 개발도상국에 사는 사람들이 e-폐기물에서 더 가치 있는 금속을 수집하게 해 준다

30 글의 목적 ①

마지막 문단에서 물 부족 해결을 위한 제일 좋은 해결책이 나오므로 저자의 의견이 있는 글이다. 그 의견을 표명한 정답은 ①이다. 다른 보기들의 내용은 본문에 있지만 제일 중요한 것은 저자의 제안, 권고라는 점에 유의해야 한다.

scarce a. 부족한 scarcity n. 부족 overuse n. 과대사용, 남용 take ~ for granted ~을 당연시하다 appreciate v. 감사하다 filter v. 거르다 drip v. 떨어지다 urine n. 소변 promising a. 전망이 좋은 viable a. 실행 가능한 sustainable a. 지속 가능한 water v. 물을 주다

물은 가장 귀중한 자원 중 하나이지만 다른 많은 천연자원처럼 물도 점점 귀해지고 있다. 세계보건기구의 보고에 따르면, 전 세계 열 명 중 세 명은 집에서 안전하고 깨끗한 물을 쓰지 못하고 있고, 27억 명의 사람들이 일 년에 최소한 한 달은 물 부족을 겪고 있다. 물 부족의 원인은 가뭄과 오염과 과소비와 때로는 전쟁과 독재 정부 같은 갈등 등 다양한 쟁점이다. 물 부족을 겪지 않는 많은 사람들은 대개 이 자원(물)을 당연시한다. 우리는 우리가 매일 사용하고 의지하는 어마어마한 양의 물을 이해하지도 못하고 그 물이 있음에 감사하지도 않는다.

물 부족에 대처하기 위해 전 세계적으로 일부 혁신적인 아이디어들이 실행되고 있다. 인도 농촌에서 실행 중인 해결책 하나는 태양열을 이용하여 더러운 물을 깨끗하게 바꾸는 것이다. 태양력 펌프가 마실 수 없는 물을 걸러서 사용 가능하게 만든다. 그러나 이 해결책은 복잡하고 비용도 많이 들어서 마을 사람들은 태양열 기술 비용을 지불하기 위해 깨끗한 물을 사서 써야 한다. 또 다른 해결책은 포그캐처의 사용이다. 포그캐처란 산비탈에 걸쳐 설치한 거대한 그물이나 스크린으로 아침 안개를 포집한다. 포집된 안개는 수집 상자로 떨어진다. 앞의 해결책과 달리 물은 공짜이지만 양이 제한적이라 큰 마을이나 관개용수로 공급이 충분치 않다. 마지막으로, 그리고 앞의 다른 해결책과 달리, 벨기에의 일부 과학자들은 소변을 식수로 바꾸는 태양열 기계를 만들었다!

이 해결책 전부가 전망이 밝고 문제를 해결하긴 하지만 실행 가능할 만큼 충분한 물을 생산하지는 못할 수 있다. 게다가 이들의 실행은 어마어마한 돈과 자원을 요구한다. 따라서 가장 지속 가능하고 실용적인 해결책은 우리가 매일 실천할 수 있는 변화를 요청하는 해결책이다. 여기에는 샤워 시간 줄이기, 손을 씻고 이를 닦는 동안에 물을 틀지 않기, 그리고 파스타나 쌀을 가열한 물을 식물에 물을 줄 때 재사용하는 것이 있다. 우리 자신과 주변 사람들에게 물 사용을 교육하는 것과 우리가 우리 공동체에서 물을 보존하는 방책들을 실천하는 것이야말로 필수적인 조치이다.

이 글의 목적은 무엇인가?
① 물 부족 문제를 다루고 저자가 최상이라고 여기는 해결책을 제안하는 것
② 물 부족 문제를 분석해서 문제의 중요한 원인을 탐색하는 것
③ 물 부족 문제에 대한 다양한 해결책의 장단점을 논하는 것
④ 물 부족 문제를 기술하고 가능한 해결책이 어떻게 작동하는지 설명하는 것

31-32

대개 우리 자녀들은 우리가 하는 희생을 감사하지 않고, 그 때문에 우리는 상처 받는다. 아이들이 우리에게 고마워하지 않는 것은 아이들이 둔감하기 때문이 아니다. 아이들은 사실 아주 예민하다. 자녀들은 우리의 관대함 뒤에 있는 숨은 동기를 식별할 수 있다. 이 동기는 너무 무의식적이라 우리조차 즉시 알아차리지 못할 때가 많다.

우리가 지칠 때까지 주고 또 줄 때, 대개 그것은 이렇게 하는 것만이 다른 사람들이 우리를 받아들이거나 우리와 관계를 유지하게 되는 유일한 방법이라고 우리가 생각하기 때문이다. 우리는 우리가 주기를 멈추면 자녀들이 우리를 더 이상 사랑하지 않고, 우리의 진짜 모습 때문에 우리를 보지 않고 단지 우리가 줄 수 있는 것 때문에 우리를 볼까봐 두려워한다. 우리가 이런 생각을 하는 이유는 우리가 우리 자신의 가치를, 우리 자신의 자아를 거의 신뢰하지 않기 때문이다.

가장 깊은 층위에서 우리는 자신에게 좋은 부모가 될 만한 측면이 부족할까 봐 두려워한다. 자기희생이라는 거창한 몸짓이 없으면, 우리는 자녀들이, 배우자가, 이웃들이, 심지어 우리 부모가, 우리 속의 결함이나 부족한 점만을 볼까봐 두려워한다. 따라서 우리는 자녀들에게 그들이 필요로 하는 것을 준다기보다 오히려 우리가 생각하는 우리의 결함을 자녀들이 보지 못하게 해줄 뭔가를 주는 것이다. 따라서 우리는 아이들 중심으로 살고 학대를 견디면서 계속해서 주고 또 준다.

appreciate v. 높이 평가하다, 감사하다 sacrifice n. 희생 hurt v. 상처 주다, 다치게 하다 insensitive a. 둔감한 discern v. 식별하다 underlying a. 근본적인 generosity n. 관대함 exhaust v. 지치게 하다, 고갈시키다 grandiose a. 너무 거창한 tolerate v. 참아주다 abuse n. 학대 deficiency n. 결함, 결핍 shield v. 보호하다, 방패막이가 되어주다 flaw n. 결함 self-sacrifice n. 자기희생

31 내용파악 ④

부모가 자녀에게 주기만 하는 것은 자신의 결함을 들킬까 싶어서라고 했으므로 정답은 ④이다.

부모의 자기희생이라는 거창한 몸짓에 대한 저자의 관점은 무엇인가?
① 부모의 자기희생은 좋은 부모노릇에 꼭 필요한 자질이다.
② 부모가 지속적으로 주는 행위는 자기 자녀들에 대한 진정한 사랑을 은폐한다.
③ 부모의 자기희생은 다정한 부모 자녀 관계를 만들 수 있다.
④ 부모의 자기희생은 자신의 부족함을 숨기려는 욕구에 의해 추진된다.

32 글의 주제 ③

부모가 자녀에게 희생하는 것은 자신의 결함을 들킬까 두려워 그것을 숨기기 위함이라는 게 글에서 말하고자 하는 핵심적인 내용이다. 따라서 정답은 ③이다.

이 글의 주제는 무엇인가?
① 부모의 희생에 대한 자녀들의 민감함
② 관계에서 자기희생의 필요성
③ 부모 희생의 공포 기반 역학
④ 희생을 통한 자기 정체성 추구

33-34

평생 동안 같은 분야나 업계에서 일할 계획을 세우는 것은 더 이상 실용성이 없다. 그런 이유 중 하나는 기술이다. 오늘 당신이 배우는 기술은 얼마 가지 않아 낡아버릴 것이다. 그러면 무엇을 할 것인가? 열심히 일한다? 복권 당첨? 그저 잘 되기를 바라거나 기도하기? 당신이 운이 따를지도 모른다. 이런 전략들은 당신에게 근사하고 안락한 삶을 가져다줄 수도 있다. 좋아하는 일을 하면서 여전히 젊고 건강해서 은퇴를 즐길 수 있을 때 은퇴하는 삶 말이다. 그러나 오늘날 일하는 우리는 대부분 "경력"이라는 작은 상자 너머를 봐야 한다.

하루 8시간 노동을 하면서 경력을 쌓을 수 있다고 생각한다면 다시 생각하라. 인공지능으로 대체되지 않거나 하청에 일자리를 빼앗기지 않을 수 있다고 생각한다면 오산이다. 고용주는 언제나 당신을 대체하거나 당신의 일을 더 싸게 할 수 있는 사람을 찾을 수 있다. 자신을 보호하는 한 가지 방법은 당신이 사무실에서 하는 일을 가져다 계약 없이 제한된 시간 동안 프리랜서로 직접 하는 것이다. 심지어 프리랜서로 돈을 더 벌 수도 있고 정규직 일을 그만둘 수 있다.

또 다른 전략은 지금 하는 일 이외에 할 일을 찾고 그 일을 할 수 있는 더 영리한 방법을 계속 찾는 것이다. 이로써 취미를 작은 사업으로 바꿀 수 있고 당신의 기술을 사용해 팔 수 있는 제품과 서비스를 만들 수 있다. 다시 말해 창업주처럼 사고하라. 당신의 아이디어를 현실로 만드는 데 도움을 줄 의지가 있는 사람을 찾아내라. 돈과 조직과 일꾼과 많은 에너지가 필요할 것이다. 위험을 감수하고 혁신하고 문제를 해결하고 열심히 일해야 할 수 있다. 창업주가 되는 것은 8시간 노동을 하는 일이 아니라 24시간 일하는 직업이다. 그리고 일이 잘 되면 보상을 얻을 수 있다.

obsolete a. 진부한, 유행에 뒤진 lottery n. 복권 strategy n. 전략 comfy a. 안락한, 편안한 retire v. 은퇴하다 outsource v. 하청주다 contract n. 계약 freelancer n. 프리랜서 full-time job 정규직 entrepreneur n. 창업주 innovator n. 혁신가 reward n. 보상, 보람

---

33 부분이해　　　　　　　　　　　①

주제가 사업을 직접 꾸려 생계를 도모하라는 것이므로, 창업주라는 단어를 쓴 이유는 사업을 해 보라는 것이다. 따라서 정답은 ①이다.

저자가 밑줄 친 단어를 소개한 이유는 무엇인가?
① 독자들에게 비즈니스 아이디어를 잡다 현실화하도록 촉구하려고
② 독자들에게 시행착오를 거쳐 비즈니스에 대해 배우도록 촉구하려고
③ 독자들에게 동시에 여러 다른 사업을 운영하도록 촉구하려고
④ 독자들에게 사업에 대한 중요한 정보를 수집하도록 촉구하려고

---

34 저자의 의도　　　　　　　　　　①

이 글의 주제는 창업주가 되는 것이다. 따라서 정답은 ①이다.

저자의 의도는 무엇인가?
① 독자들에게 급변하는 오늘날의 일터에서 생계를 유지하기 위해 새로운 방법을 생각해보라고 독려하는 것
② 인공지능이나 다른 노동자들이 직장 생활의 일정 시점이 되면 우리 자리를 대신할 수 있음을 설명하는 것
③ 독자들에게 정규직을 잃은 후 무엇을 해야 할지 조언을 제공하는 것
④ 독자들에게 돈을 더 벌 수 있게 해 주는 안정된 직장을 찾는 법을 알려주는 것

35-36

『동물은 얼마나 똑똑한가?』라는 책에서 저자 기타 시몬슨은 동물의 지능을 평가할 때 과학자들이 마주하는 문제를 논한다. 첫 번째 문제는 동물의 지능을 정의하는 문제이다. 지나치게 자주, 동물의 지능에 대한 우리의 기준은 동물이 인간의 행동을 얼마나 잘 모방할 수 있는가에 바탕을 두고 있다. 이런 방법은 동물이 인간과 다른 삶에서 사용하는 지능의 다른 요소들을 인정하지 않는다.

과학자들이 포유류에게 쓰는 다른 방법은 뇌의 무게와 몸 전체 무게의 비율을 따지는 것이다. 이런 측정법에 의하면 돌고래는 지능이 높다. 그러나 인간의 지능은 언어와 관련이 있고 인간은 돌고래나 다른 동물과 소통을 할 수 없기 때문에 이것은 동물의 지능을 온전히 평가할 수 있는 방안이 아니다.

동물 지능 측정의 또 다른 문제, 특히 종을 가로질러(다른 종들과) 지능을 비교할 때 생기는 문제는 인간이 다른 어떤 동물보다 더 지능이 높다고 가정하는 것이다. 꿀벌이 인간의 아기들보다 검사 성적이 더 좋게 나온 한 연구에서 과학자들은 검사 자체를 다시 평가했다. 이들의 결론은 이 검사는 결함이 틀림없이 있었고 벌들은 지능 때문이 아니라 본능 때문에 이긴 것이라는 점이었다.

새로운 평가 방법은 동물의 신경망을 연구해서 신경망이 어떤 특성을 허용하도록 설계되어 있는지 알아보는 것이다. 이렇게 하면 과학자들은 자신들이 생각조차 못했던 특징들을 알아낼 수 있다. 그럼에도 불구하고 일부 동물 뇌의 아주 작은 크기 때문에 이 방법은 매우 어려워진다.

시몬슨은 애리조나 주립대학교의 그로 암담 교수의 말을 인용해 결론을 맺는다. 암담 교수의 말에 따르면 "과학자들은 상이한 종들의 뇌의 역량을 비교하기 위한 더 나은 도구와 방법과 이론을 개발해야 합니다. 그러나 우리는 그 일을 잘 해 나가고 있습니다."

face v. 마주하다 assess v. 평가하다 imitate v. 모방하다 recognize v. 인정하다 proportion n. 비율, 크기 outperform v. 실적[성적]면에서 ~을 능가하다 flawed a. 결함이 있는 come out on top (시합·논쟁·선거에서) 이기다 neural network 신경망 challenging a. 어려운 be well on one's way 잘 해 나가다

---

35 부분이해　　　　　　　　　　　④

be well on one's way는 '일이 잘 진행되고 있다'는 뜻이므로 가장 적절한 것은 ④이다.

밑줄 친 부분의 의미로 가장 적절한 것은?
① 우리는 동물의 지능을 평가할 더 나은 방법을 찾는 데 노력을 집중하고 있다.
② 우리는 동물 지능을 검사하고 더 나은 지능을 고르는 기존 방법들을 비교하고 있다.
③ 우리는 동물 지능을 검사하는 기존 방법의 문제를 제거하려고 노력 중이다.
④ 우리는 동물 지능을 평가할 더 적절한 방법을 개발하는 일에서 진전을 보고 있는 중이다.

36 내용파악 ②

동물에게서 지능 행동을 끌어내기 쉬운 방식에 대해서는 언급하지 않았다. 따라서 정답은 ②이다.

동물 지능 검사의 문제로 이 글에서 언급되지 않은 것은?
① 동물 지능의 정의가 인간 지능의 요소에 바탕을 두고 설정되었다.
② 검사법이 동물로부터 더 지적인 행동을 끌어내기가 더 쉬워지도록 설계된다.
③ 인간이 언어를 써서 동물과 소통하기가 불가능하다.
④ 일부 동물들은 뇌가 너무 작아 동물의 신경계를 검사하기가 어렵다.

37-38

60년 전 로켓 이론의 큰 진보는, 액체 연료 로켓이 모든 면에서, 당시 알려진 유일한 종류의 로켓이었던 약한 고체 연료 로켓보다 훨씬 더 우월하다는 것을 보여주었다. 그러나 1960년, 액체 연료와 비슷하게 강력한 고체 연료가 장착된 대형 고체 연료 로켓이 나타났고, 이제 비전문가가 가장 좋아하는 질문이 어떤 로켓이 더 나은가 하는 것이다. 이 질문은 무의미하다. 차라리 가솔린 엔진과 디젤 엔진 중 무엇이 더 나은가라고 질문하는 게 낫다. 답은 목적에 달려 있기 때문이다.

액체 연료 로켓은 복잡하지만 통제가 잘 된다는 장점이 있다. 액체 연료 로켓 엔진의 연소는 완전히 중지시킬 수 있고 원할 때 재점화할 수 있다. 뿐만 아니라 추진력도 연료 펌프 속도를 조절하여 얼마든지 바꿀 수 있다. 반면, 고체 연료 로켓은 구조는 다소 단순하지만, 아주 큰 크기의 것이 필요할 때는 제작하기가 어렵다.

그러나 일단 고체 연료 로켓이 있으면 곧바로 작동 준비가 가능하다. 액체 연료 로켓은 연료를 공급해야 한다. 하지만 고체 연료 로켓은 일단 점화만 되면, 계속 탄다. 원할 때마다 멈추고 재점화할 수는 없다(아마 미리 계산한 연소 시간이 다 지난 후에 멈추고 점화할 수는 있을 것이다). 그리고 추진도 변화시킬 수 없다. 고체 연료 로켓은 오랫동안 준비상태가 유지되기 때문에 대부분의 군사용 미사일은 고체 연료를 쓰지만 인간이 탄 우주선은 미세 조정이 필요하고 이것을 제공할 수 있는 것은 액체 연료뿐이다. 그뿐 아니라 액체 연료 로켓은 비싼 장비이다. 대형 고체 연료 로켓은 이에 비해 싸다. 그러나 고체 연료는 파운드당으로 비교하면 액체 연료보다 약 10배는 비싸다. 따라서 한 편으로는 싼 연료를 쓰는 비싼 로켓이 있고, 다른 한편으로는 비싼 연료를 쓰는 비교적 싼 로켓이 있는 셈이다.

advance n. 진보 liquid-fuel n. 액체 연료 in every respect 모든 면에서 solid fuel 고체 연료 make one's appearance 출현하다, 나타나다 layperson n. 비전문가 inquire v. 문의하다, 묻다 ignite v. 점화하다 construction n. 건조, 구축, 건축 thrust n. 추진 on short notice 갑자기, 당장에, 급하게 vary v. 다르게 하다, 변화시키다, 다르다 adjustment n. 조정 comparatively ad. 비교적

37 내용파악 ④

액체 연료 로켓은 비싼 장비라고 했으므로 정답은 ④이다.

액체 연료 로켓의 특징이 아닌 것은?
① 필요할 때 멈추거나 재점화할 수 있다.
② 연료가 고체 연료보다 싸다.
③ 건조하는 것이 다소 복잡하다.
④ 제조와 유지하는 것이 싸다.

38 내용추론 ②

두 번째 단락에서 '액체 연료 로켓은 원할 때 다시 재점화할 수 있다'고 했고 세 번째 단락에서 '고체 연료 로켓은 미리 계산한 연소 시간이 다 지난 후에야 재점화할 수 있다'고 했으므로 재점화를 위해 오랫동안 대기해야 한다고 할 수 있다. 따라서 ②가 추론할 수 있는 것이다. ③ 세 번째 단락에서 '고체 연료 로켓은 오랫동안 준비상태가 유지되기 때문에 군사용 미사일은 고체 연료를 쓰지만, 액체 연료만이 점화의 미세 조정이 가능하므로 이를 필요로 하는 유인 우주선으로는 액체 연료 로켓이 쓰인다'고 했으므로, 액체 연료 로켓과 고체 연료 로켓의 사용은 제작과 연료의 비용이 아니라 필요로 하는 가능한 연료 점화 방식에 달려있다고 할 수 있다.

이 글에서 추론 가능한 것은?
① 액체 연료 로켓과 고체 연료 로켓의 근본 목적이 그들의 제작 방식을 결정한다.
② 연료 주입 후 액체 연료 로켓은 곧바로 재점화 가능하지만 고체 연료 로켓은 오랫동안 대기를 해야 한다.
③ 액체 연료 로켓과 고체 연료 로켓의 사용은 제작 및 연료의 비용에 달려 있다.
④ 액체 연료 로켓이 고체 연료 로켓보다 우월하다는 점은 액체 연료 로켓이 무거운 로켓을 궤도에 올릴 수 있기 때문이다.

39-40

모든 산불이 인간에 의해 시작되는 것은 아니다. 번개를 동반한 폭풍이 빈번한 원인이다. 게다가 특히 미국 서부의 조건은 대개 통제할 수 없이 타는 산불을 초래하는 데 완벽한 대기를 만들어낸다. 소방관들은 산불에 필요한 연료, 산소 그리고 열원 이 세 가지 요소를 가리켜 산불 삼각형이라 부른다. 산불은 전국에서 발생하지만 서부에서 가장 흔하다. 빈번한 가뭄과 건조한 날씨가 재빨리 불꽃에 휘말리는, 바스라지게 약하고 건조한 나무와 잎사귀와 가지와 풀을 만들기 때문이다. 산불의 규모가 매우 커지면 강력한 열은 심지어 지역의 날씨 조건까지 바꾸어 새로운 날씨를 만들 수도 있다!

소방관들이 산불의 확산을 늦추어 멈추는 방법은 여러 가지가 있지만, 일부 산불은 잡히는 데 몇 주일이 걸리기도 한다. 물과 방연제를 불과 주변 초목에 뿌리는 것이 한 가지 조치이다. 다른 중요한 요소는 방화선이나 방화대를 만들어 불이 계속 타는 데 필요한 연료를 박탈하는 것이다. 방화대는 관목과 초목이 있는 길고 좁은 구역에서 관목과 초목을 풀라스키(도끼의 일종)라 불리는 도구로 다 베어버리는 것이다. 불이 방화대에 도달하면 연료가 부족해서 혼자 타고 꺼지길 바라는 것이다.

소방관들은 또한 비행기와 헬리콥터의 도움에 의지한다. 이들은 활활 타는 불길을 끄기 위해 위쪽에서 물이나 화학물질을 떨어뜨릴 수 있다. 공중에서 (물이나 화학물질을 떨어뜨리는) 도움을 사용할 때의 이점은 짧은 시간 내에 비교적 넓은 거리까지 불길을 잡을 수 있다는 것이다. 게다가 소방관들은 때로는 통제된 화재를 내곤 한다. 일부러 불을 내서 초목을 없애 이번에도 산불의 연료를 박탈하는 것이다.

산불이 자연 서식처와 인간의 거주지에 엄청나게 파괴적이긴 하지만 자연의 일부 목적에 이바지하는 면이 있다. 산불은 부패하는 물질이 연소할 때 토양에 양분을 돌려준다. 산불은 햇빛이 숲 바닥에 도달하지 못하게 막는 두꺼운 관목 층들을 제거해준다. 이렇게 하면 새로 자라는 나무가 필요한 빛을 받을 수 있다. 게다가 산불은 숲에서 해롭고 파괴적인 벌레뿐 아니라 병든 식물을 제거해준다. 비용과 이점이 똑같지는 않겠지만 자연의 거의 모든 것과 마찬가지로 산불 역시 나름 할 일이 있다.

wildfire n. 산불   lightning n. 번개   out of control 통제되지 않는
ingredient n. 성분, 요소   drought n. 가뭄   brittle a. 부서지기 쉬운
flame n. 불꽃   intense a. 강렬한   under control 통제 하에 있는
burn itself out 다 타서 꺼지다   blaze n. 활활 타는 불   undergrowth
n. 관목   block v. 막다

---

39 내용파악   ③

산불이 소방관의 건강에 끼치는 영향은 언급되어 있지 않다. 따라서 정
답은 ③이다.

이 글에서 언급되지 않은 것은?
① 산불이 자연 서식처에 끼치는 이로운 영향
② 산불을 촉발하는 일부 자연 조건
③ 산불이 소방관의 건강에 끼치는 영향
④ 산불의 확산을 막으려는 시도들

---

40 부분이해   ②

산불이 초목을 다 태워 연료를 뺏는 것이 controlled burns의 목적이다.
따라서 정답은 ②이다.

controlled burns의 주요 기능은 무엇인가?
① 공중 원조를 사용할 충분한 공간을 만드는 것
② 산불을 지속시키는 요소를 제거하는 것
③ 불로 태워버림으로써 숲 바닥의 비옥함을 회복시키는 것
④ 산불의 열이 강력해지는 것을 미리 막는 것

01 ①	02 ③	03 ⑤	04 ④	05 ②	06 ①	07 ③	08 ①	09 ④	10 ②
11 ④	12 ①	13 ⑤	14 ③	15 ②	16 ①	17 ③	18 ②	19 ①	20 ④
21 ⑤	22 ②	23 ⑤	24 ④	25 ③	26 ②	27 ③	28 ③	29 ①	30 ④
31 ⑤	32 ①	33 ④	34 ⑤	35 ②	36 ①	37 ⑤	38 ④	39 ③	40 ②

01 생활영어 　　　　　　　　　　　　①

"제가 자격이 없다고 말하는 건가요?"라고 날카롭게 묻는 A의 질문을 통해 A가 기분이 상했음을 알 수 있다. 이런 A의 질문에 대해 B가 할 수 있는 대답은 "맞다, 당신은 자격이 없다."고 노골적으로 말하거나 그런 의도로 한 말이 아니고 "힘든 일이라서 그렇게 이야기한 거다."라고 A를 달래는 말이 와야 적절하므로, ①이 정답이다.

be qualified for ~의 자격이 있다　task n. (특히 하기 싫은) 일, 과제　wish somebody luck ~에게 행운을 빌다　take it or leave it 선택은 자유다, 싫으면 그만두고　not a big deal 별일 아니다

A: 지금 제가 그 일을 할 자격이 없다고 말하는 건가요?
B: 아뇨, 저는 그저 그것이 매우 힘든 일이라는 것을 말하고 싶었을 뿐이에요.

① 아뇨, 저는 그저 그것이 매우 힘든 일이라는 것을 말하고 싶었을 뿐이에요.
② 네, 이번에는 괜찮을 겁니다.
③ 아뇨, 저에게 행운을 빌어 주세요.
④ 네, 싫으면 그만둬도 됩니다.
⑤ 아뇨, 그건 별일 아니에요.

02 논리완성 　　　　　　　　　　　　③

넘어져서 다리를 몹시 다쳤다는 부정적인 내용이 온 다음 역접의 접속사 but이 왔다. 따라서 but 다음에는 '긍정적인' 내용이 와야 적절하므로, ③의 '좋아지고 있는'이 빈칸에 적절하다.

hike v. 하이킹하다, 도보여행하다　on the run 도망 다니는; 계속 뛰어다니는　up in arms 화가 난, 격분한　on the mend 좋아지고 있는, 호전되는　on the ropes 패배하기 직전의　under the weather 몸이 좀 안 좋은

유카(Yuka)는 하이킹할 때 넘어져서 다리를 몹시 다쳤지만, 지금은 좋아지고 있다.

03 논리완성 　　　　　　　　　　　　⑤

inert는 '무기력한'이라는 뜻으로 쓰일 수 있고, '타성에 젖은'이라는 뜻으로도 쓰일 수 있으므로, ⑤가 두 빈칸에 적절하다.

lie v. 눕다　with half-closed eyes 눈을 반쯤 감은 채　intricate a. 복잡한; 난해한　improper a. 부적절한　insignificant a. 중요하지 않은　impertinent a. 무례한; 관계없는

그는 눈을 반쯤 감은 채 무기력하게 누워 있었다.
대통령은 타성에 젖은 정치제도 안에서 일해야 한다.

04 논리완성 　　　　　　　　　　　　④

'종합적인' 자동차 보험, '전반적인' 강의 개요라는 표현을 완성시키는 ④의 comprehensive가 두 빈칸에 적절하다.

insurance n. 보험　cover v. (비용·손실 등을) 보상하다　extensive a. 광범위한　overview n. 개관, 개요　course n. 강의, 강좌　class n. 학급; 수업　compound a. 합성의; 복잡한　compatible a. 호환이 되는; 양립할 수 있는　comparable a. 비교할 만한　comprehensible a. 이해할 수 있는

시골길에서 사슴과 부딪쳤을 때, 그녀의 종합 자동차보험이 그녀의 차량에 대한 광범위한 피해를 보상해 주었다.
그 교수는 수업 첫날에 강의의 전반적인 개요를 제시했다.

05 논리완성 　　　　　　　　　　　　②

'적절한' 발언이라는 표현을 완성시키고, 순간이라는 말과 호응하여 '시의적절한'이라는 뜻으로 모두 쓰일 수 있는 ②의 opportune이 두 빈칸에 적절하다.

remark n. 발언　amenable a. 유순한, 말을 잘 듣는　plenary a. (회의 등이) 총회의; 제한 없는　nebulous a. 흐릿한, 모호한　blatant a. (나쁜 행동이) 노골적인

그것은 그 정치인들에게 가장 적절한 발언이 될 것이다.
그 제안은 이보다 더 시의적절한 순간에 나올 수 없었을 것이다.

06 논리완성 　　　　　　　　　　　　①

vein은 '기질'이라는 뜻으로, a vein of humor(유머 기질, 해학성)로 쓰일 수 있고, 또한 '맥락'이라는 뜻으로, in a similar vein(비슷한 맥락에서)으로도 쓰일 수 있으므로, ①이 정답이다.

rich a. 풍부한 run through ~에 가득하다 sequel n. 후속편 mirror v. 반사하다, 반영하다 charm n. 매력 way n. 방식 facet n. 측면, 양상 dimension n. 규모; 차원 manner n. 방식; 예의

풍부한 해학성이 그 책에 가득하다.
비슷한 맥락에서, 그 후속편은 첫 영화의 유머와 매력을 반영하고 있다.

---

07 논리완성   ③

첫 번째 빈칸 다음에 "그래도, 그는 법을 어긴 것이었다."라는 부정적인 내용이 왔다. 역접의 접속사 but이 있으므로 but 앞에는 이보다는 '긍정적인' 내용이 와야 한다. 따라서 첫 번째 빈칸에는 일부러 그런 것이 아니라는 의미가 되도록 '자기도 모르게' 법을 어겼다는 말이 되어야 적절하다. 두 번째 빈칸 역시 과거에 '자기도 모르게' 저지른 실수를 바로잡기를 희망한다는 말이 되어야 하므로, ③이 정답이다.

rectify v. (잘못된 것을) 바로잡다, 수정하다 unanimously ad. 만장일치로 inexorably ad. 냉혹하게, 가차없이 infallibly ad. 확실하게; 반드시 unfavorably ad. 불리하게

그는 자기도 모르게 법을 어겼지만, 그래도 그는 법을 어긴 것이었다.
우리는 과거에 자기도 모르게 저지른 실수를 바로잡기를 희망한다.

---

08 논리완성   ①

gauge는 '게이지, 계량기, 측정기'라는 뜻의 명사로 쓰일 수 있고, 이해력을 '측정하다'는 뜻의 동사로도 쓰일 수 있으므로, ①이 두 빈칸에 적절하다.

check v. 확인하다 steam pressure 증기압력 judge n. 판사, 심판 v. 판단하다 screen n. 화면 v. 차단하다; 보호하다 appraise v. 살피다; (업무를) 평가하다 benchmark n. 기준 v. 벤치마킹하다(경쟁력 신장을 위해 경쟁업체의 상품이나 운영과정을 연구하다)

그 기사는 파이프 안의 증기압력을 확인하기 위해 계량기를 감시했다.
그 교사는 그 주제에 대한 학생들의 이해력을 측정하기 위해 시험성적을 사용했다.

---

09 논리완성   ④

'포함하다'라는 뜻으로도 쓰이고, '둘러싸다'는 뜻으로도 쓰일 수 있는 ④의 encompasses가 두 빈칸에 적절하다.

evacuate v. 대피시키다, 철수하다 confiscate v. 몰수하다, 압수하다 insinuate v. (불쾌한 일을) 암시하다[넌지시 말하다] derail v. 탈선하다, 탈선시키다

그 일은 다양한 범주의 책임을 포함한다.
런던의 이 지역은 북쪽으로는 피카딜리(Piccadilly)와 남쪽으로는 세인트 제임스 공원(St. James's Park)을 둘러싸고 있다.

---

10 논리완성   ②

'무엇을 구성하는 구성요소로서의' 측면이라는 뜻으로도 쓰이고, '없어서는 안 되는, 필수적인'이라는 뜻으로도 쓰일 수 있는 ②의 integral이 두 빈칸에 적절하다.

practical a. 실질적인; 실현 가능한 plausible a. 타당한 것 같은, 그럴듯한, 이치에 맞는 appealing a. 매력적인; 호소하는 functional a. 기능 위주의; 직무상의

신뢰는 모든 강력한 관계를 구성하는 한 측면이다.
사용자 경험은 도서관이 도서관의 성과를 측정하는 방식에 필수적이다.

---

11 정비문   ④

① I wish 다음에 '목적어+to do'의 구문을 취해서 '~에게 …하기를 바라다'는 뜻으로 쓰일 수 있으므로, I wish you to feel better soon.으로 고쳐야 한다. 'wish 가정법'으로 보고 가정법 과거 I wish you felt better soon.으로 고치면 '사실은 곧 회복되지 않는다'는 뜻을 포함하여 의미가 부적절해진다. ② '주장'을 나타내는 동사 insist 다음에 오는 that절의 동사는 'should+동사원형'이나 '동사원형'이 와야 한다. 따라서 apologizes를 should apologize나 apologize로 고쳐야 한다. ③ ought to have p.p.는 '~했어야 했는데'라는 뜻으로 과거의 유감을 나타내는데, ought to have p.p.의 부정형은 ought not to have p.p.이다. 따라서 ③에서 ought to have not come을 ought not to have come으로 고쳐야 한다. ⑤ say는 4형식으로 못 쓰고 3형식만 가능한 동사이다. 따라서 said me goodbye를 said goodbye to me로 고쳐야 한다. 반면, ④는 원래 What do you suggest we should do?에서 suggest는 '제안'을 나타내는 동사이므로, should가 생략된 형태이다. 또한 이 문장은 원래 Do you suggest + what we do?에서 suggest와 같이 인식류 동사가 쓰인 경우, 의문사를 문두에 보내므로, What do you suggest we do?의 형태가 된 것이다.

apologize v. 사과하다 say goodbye to ~에게 작별인사를 하다

① 나는 네가 몸이 곧 회복되기를 바란다.
② 나는 그가 사과해야 한다고 주장했다.
③ 너는 여기에 오지 말았어야 했다.
④ 너는 우리가 무엇을 해야 한다고 제안하는가?
⑤ 앤(Anne)은 나에게 작별 인사를 하고 떠났다.

---

12 정비문   ①

① He is the man.과 I went to school with the man's brother.가 관계대명사 whose에 의해 합쳐진 형태이다. 이때 whose brother가 두 문장을 연결하고 있어서 with 다음에 목적어가 없다. ② what은 선행사를 포함하고 있는 관계대명사로, 선행사 없이 쓸 수 있긴 하지만, 앞 문장 전체를 받는 관계대명사는 what이 아니라 which이므로, ②에서 what을 which로 고쳐야 한다. ③ 타동사 recommend의 목적어가 없으므로 부적절하다. 따라서 recommend의 목적어가 선행사인 the hotel이 되도록 관계부사 where를 관계대명사 which로 고쳐야 한다. ④ He tried on three jackets.와 None of them fitted him.이라는 두 문장이 연결

사 없이 연결되어 부적절하다. 따라서 ④를 He tried on three jackets, and none of them fitted him.으로 고치거나 관계대명사 which를 써서 He tried on three jackets, none of which fitted him.으로 고쳐야 한다. ⑤ Is there anything + I can do it for you?에서 it이 관계대명사 that으로 바뀐 후 생략된 형태로, do의 목적어가 선행사 anything이 되므로, do 다음에 온 it은 불필요하다. 따라서 ⑤를 Is there anything I can do for you?로 고쳐야 한다.

try on ~을 입어보다   **fit** v. ~에게 잘 어울리다

① 그는 형이 내가 학교에 같이 다녔던 내 친구인 사람이다.
② 비가 많이 왔는데, 그것을 우리는 예상하지 못했다.
③ 우리는 네가 추천한 그 호텔에서 숙박했다.
④ 그는 재킷을 세 벌 입어봤지만, 세 벌 중에 어느 것도 그에게 잘 어울리지 않았다.
⑤ 내가 너를 위해 할 수 있는 것이 있을까?

---

13 정비문   ⑤

① of which와 같이 '전치사+관계대명사' 다음에는 완전한 절이 올 수 있지만, 선행사 the place와 호응하는 전치사는 in이므로, ①에서 of를 in으로 고쳐야 한다. ② 선행사가 the kindest와 같이 최상급에 의해 수식받는 경우 관계대명사 that을 사용하므로, who를 that으로 고쳐야 한다. ③ in that town lies가 관계절로 The valley를 수식하는데, '전치사+관계대명사'에서 관계대명사가 없으므로 which를 넣어 is 앞의 주어가 The valley in which that town lies로 되어야 한다. ④ 일반적으로 '전치사+관계대명사'의 형태가 가능하지만, come은 come across(자동사+전치사)의 형태로 쓰여야만 '~을 우연히 발견하다'는 뜻이 되므로, 즉 across는 come과 너무 관계가 깊으므로, across는 come과 떨어질 수 없다. 따라서 ④를 The check, which Mike came across in a filed, was fake.로 고쳐야 한다. 반면, ⑤에서 whichever는 관계형용사로 쓰였으며, Whichever one of you는 '너희들 중에 누구든 ~한 사람'이라는 의미로 쓰일 수 있으므로, ⑤가 문법적으로 올바른 형태이다.

heavily populated 인구밀도가 아주 높은   **check** n. 수표   **come across** ~을 우연히 발견하다   **fake** a. 가짜의, 위조의

① 이곳은 우리가 처음 만났던 장소였다.
② 그녀는 내가 알고 있는 가장 친절한 사람들 중 한 명이다.
③ 그 마을이 놓여있는 계곡은 인구밀도가 아주 높다.
④ 그 수표는 마이크(Mike)가 들판에서 우연히 발견한 것인데, 가짜였다.
⑤ 너희들 중에 누구든 창문을 깨뜨린 사람은 창문에 대해 배상해야 한다.

---

14 정비문   ③

① never를 포함한 빈도부사는 조동사 have나 will 다음에 오는데, I will never는 원래 I will never do it.에서 반복되는 do it을 생략한 형태이다. 이렇게 생략하면 never가 will 앞으로 가서 I never will이 되어야 하며 will에 강세가 가해진다. ② 부사 probably는 will 다음에 오지만 won't 보다는 앞에 온다. 따라서 won't probably see를 probably won't see나 will probably not see로 고쳐야 한다. ④ also는 be동사 다음에 오므로 were hungry를 were also hungry로 고쳐야 한다. ⑤ perfect는 '완

벽한'이라는 뜻이므로, fairly와 같은 정도부사의 수식을 받을 수 없다. 따라서 fairly를 삭제해야 한다. ③ all이 대명사나 형용사가 아니라 부사로 쓰일 때 여기서처럼 be동사 are 다음에 올 수도 있고 are 앞에 올 수도 있다. 물론 형용사 즉, 전치 한정사로 My friends 앞에 올 수도 있다. 옳은 문장이다.

eat out 외식하다   **fairly** ad. 꽤, 상당히

① 나는 그것을 결코 한 적이 없으며, 앞으로도 결코 하지 않을 것이다.
② 나는 아마도 당신을 다시 보지 않을 것이다.
③ 나의 친구들은 모두 오늘 밤 외식하고 있다.
④ 우리는 피곤함을 느꼈으며, 또한 배가 고팠다.
⑤ 날씨는 완벽했다.

---

15 정비문   ②

① any는 부정문 뿐 아니라 긍정문에도 쓰이는데, 긍정문에서 쓰일 경우 '어떠한 것이든'이라는 뜻으로 쓰인다. ③ Let's+do는 '~하자'는 뜻으로 쓰이는 청유문이며, 전치사 before 다음에 전치사의 목적어로 동명사 making이 온 형태이다. ④ please는 명령문 앞에 붙어서 정중하게 요청할 때 쓰는 표현으로 동사원형과 함께 쓰이며, be invited to는 '~에 초대되다'는 뜻인데, 명령문 행태로는 '초대합니다, 초대하니 참석해 주세요'라는 뜻으로 쓰인다. ⑤ it이 가주어, to send ~가 진주어로 쓰였으며, for us to send의 의미상 주어이다. 그리고 전치사와 교통수단이 같이 쓰일 경우, 'by+무관사+교통수단'으로 쓰이므로, by ship이 맞는 표현이다. 반면, ② be subject to는 '~하기 쉽다'는 뜻으로, 이때 to는 전치사이다. 전치사 다음에는 명사와 동명사만 올 수 있으므로, are subject to be changed를 are subject to change(이때 change가 명사)로 고치거나 are subject to being changed로 고쳐야 한다.

cover v. (경비를) 부담하다   **expense** n. 경비   **order** n. 주문, 주문품

① 회사가 어떠한 여행경비이든 부담할 것이다.
② 가격은 변경될 수 있다.
③ 결정을 내리기 전에 다시 생각해보자.
④ 개막식 밤 파티에 초대하니 부디 참석해 주시길 바랍니다.
⑤ 우리가 주문한 물건을 배로 보내는 것이 덜 비쌀 것이다.

---

16 정비문   ①

1월 초와 같이 '시작(beginning)'과 '끝(end)'을 나타내는 시점에는 전치사 at을 보통 쓰므로, ③의 at the end of는 맞는 표현이며, ①의 in the beginning of January는 at the beginning of January로 고쳐야 한다. always가 진행형과 함께 쓰인 것은 '걸핏하면 ~한다, ~하기 일쑤다'라는 뜻이다. ② '길 모퉁이에' 또는 '방 구석에'는 on the corner of the street/the room이다. ④ the entrance와 같은 특정 '지점'을 나타낼 때 전치사 at을 쓰며, entrance to는 '~로 들어가는 입구'라는 뜻으로 쓰인다. ⑤ '~의 가운데에'라는 의미를 나타낼 때 the middle과 함께 전치사 in을 쓴다.

go away (특히 휴가를 맞아) 집을 떠나다, 어디를 가다

① 나는 1월 초에는 집을 떠나 어디 가기 일쑤다.
② 그 거리 모퉁이에 작은 가게가 하나 있다.
③ 그 선수들은 게임이 끝났을 때 악수를 했다.
④ 나는 그 건물 입구에서 당신을 만날 것이다.
⑤ 그 호텔은 호수 한가운데 있는 작은 섬에 있다.

17 정비문 ③

① trip 다음에 방향을 나타내는 전치사 to가 쓰였다. ② 동사 wonder의 목적어로 간접의문절이 왔는데, 간접의문절의 어순은 '의문사+주어+동사'이므로 맞게 쓰였다. ④ sorry와 같은 감정형용사 다음에 that절이 올 수 있으며, 이때 접속사 that은 생략 가능하다. ⑤ 무역 회의는 '주체'가 아니라 '대상'이므로, 수동태가 쓰였으며, 특정 날짜 앞에는 전치사 on을 쓴다. 반면, play 다음에 악기가 와서 '악기를 연주하다'는 뜻으로 쓰일 경우, 일반적으로 악기 앞에 정관사 the를 붙인다. 따라서 ③에서 on piano를 on the piano로 고쳐야 한다.

wonder v. 궁금해 하다   piece n. 한 편의 작품   hold a conference 회의를 열다

① 나는 혼자 리스본(Lisbon)으로 여행갈 것이다.
② 나는 당신이 어디에 있는지 궁금해지기 시작했다.
③ 그 곡은 또한 피아노로 연주될 수 있다.
④ 귀하의 주문에 실수를 한 것을 너무 죄송스럽게 생각합니다.
⑤ 무역 회의는 2월 10일에 열릴 것이다.

18 정비문 ②

① for all one's life는 '평생 동안'이라는 뜻이며, 이때 전치사 for는 생략 가능하다. ③ 부사 before는 현재완료시제와 함께 쓰여 경험을 나타낼 수 있다. ④ something은 긍정문에, anything은 부정문과 의문문에 각각 쓰인다. recently는 have와 p.p. 사이에 올 수도 있고 문미에 올 수도 있다. ⑤ since 다음에는 과거의 특정시점이 오며, since 앞의 절에는 현재완료시제가 쓰인다. 반면, '이미, 벌써'라는 뜻의 부사 already는 긍정문에 쓰이고 의문문에 쓰일 수 없다. 의문문에 쓰일 수 있는 같은 뜻의 부사는 yet이므로, ②에서 already를 yet으로 고쳐야 하며, it은 비인칭주어이고 'stop+~ing'는 '~하는 것을 멈추다'는 뜻으로 쓰인다.

all one's life 평생 동안

① 나는 이곳에 평생 살아왔다.
② 비는 이미 그쳤나요?
③ 그는 전에 결코 자동차를 운전한 적이 없다.
④ 최근엔 벤(Ben)한테서 어떤 소식 들었니?
⑤ 나는 작년 이후 탐(Tom)을 본 적이 없다.

19 정비문 ①

② 'so that+주어+may/can/will+동사원형'은 '~하기 위해'라는 뜻으로 쓰인다. spoke와 wouldn't가 시제일치를 보여준다. ③ 지각동사 hear가 5형식으로 쓰일 경우, 'hear+목적어+동사원형'이나 'hear+목적어+~ing' 형태로 쓰인다. ④ in the front of the car는 '차 안에서 앞쪽에'의

뜻으로 적절하게 쓰였다. 만약 in front of the car라고 하면 '차 앞에'의 뜻이 되어 차 밖으로 나가 그 앞 도로에 앉아 있었다는 부적절한 의미가 된다. ⑤ moon과 같이 세상에 하나뿐인 명사 앞에는 정관사 the를 붙인다. ① policy on invoicing은 '송장작성에 관한 정책'이라는 뜻이지만, 실제로는 invoicing policy로 많이 쓰인다. 경제 정책을 경제에 관한 정책이라 하여 policy on economy로 쓸 수도 있겠지만 실제로는 주로 economic policy로 쓰는 것과 마찬가지이다. 따라서 our invoicing policy로 고쳐야 한다.

invoicing n. 송장작성

① 우리는 우리의 송장작성 정책을 바꾸기로 결정했다.
② 그녀는 아이들이 이해하지 못하도록 불어로 말했다.
③ 그녀가 노래를 부르는 것을 처음으로 내가 들었다.
④ 그녀의 남편은 자동차 안에서 앞쪽에 앉아있었다.
⑤ 그는 달에 관한 책을 읽고 있었다.

20 정비문 ④

① remember가 간접의문절인 when절을 목적어로 취하고 있다. ② accept가 that절을 목적어로 취하고 있다. ③ bear가 when절을 목적어로 취할 수 없으므로 when절은 부사절이고 it을 목적어로 취한다. ⑤ owe가 가목적어 it을 취하고 진목적어는 that절이나 to부정사가 가능한데, 여기서는 to부정사가 쓰였다. ④ enjoy가 when절을 목적어로 취할 수 없으므로 when절을 부사절로 봐도 enjoy의 목적어가 없다. enjoy 다음에 목적어 it을 넣어야 한다.

be content with ~에 만족하다   bear v. 참다   get upset 속상해 하다

① 마지막으로 내가 세상에 만족했던 때가 언제였는지 기억이 나지 않는다.
② 당신은 제인(Jane)이 이미 떠났고 돌아오지 않을 것이라는 것을 받아들여야 한다.
③ 사람들이 그녀의 일을 비판할 때, 그녀는 그것(비판)을 참을 수 없으며, 매우 속상해 한다.
④ 가족 전체가 바비큐 파티를 위해 모일 때 우리는 항상 그것(모임)을 즐긴다.
⑤ 그가 그들이 함께 시작한 연구를 완성한 것은 그의 멘토 덕분이었다.

21 정비문 ⑤

① a number of 다음에는 '복수명사+복수동사'가 온다. ② drink가 명사로 쓰였으며 a bit은 a minute처럼 for가 있어도 되고 없어도 된다. 즉, wait (for) a bit이고 wait (for) a minute이다. ③ '~외에는 어떤 일이든 하다'는 뜻인 'do+anything but+동사원형'이라는 원형부정사 관용구문이 쓰였다. ④ know의 목적어로 의문사 what으로 시작하는 간접의문절이 왔으며, Anybody will never가 아니라 부정어 Nobody가 문두에 온 Nobody will ever가 쓰여서 맞다. ⑤ its가 가리키는 대상은 travelers로 복수명사이므로, 대명사 역시 복수가 되어야 한다. 따라서 its를 their로 고쳐야 한다.

candidate n. 후보, 지원자 for a bit 잠시 동안, 조금만 travel agent 여행사 직원

① 그 직무에 지원하는 사람들이 많았다.
② 조금만 기다리면 음료가 나올지도 모른다.
③ 나는 농장에서 일하는 것 외에는 어떤 일도 할 준비가 되어 있다.
④ 그에게 무슨 일이 일어났는지 아무도 결코 알지 못할 것이다.
⑤ 다른 나라에서 온 여행자들은 그들의 여행사 직원들과 직접 연락해야 한다.

22 논리완성   ②

약물 테스트에 사용되는 무작위 대조 실험을 하기가 까다로우며, 몇 년 동안 실험 식단을 이행하기도 어려워서 영양학 연구를 잘하기 어렵다고 했다. 따라서 같은 맥락으로 영양학은 '연구가 제대로 이뤄지지 않고 있다(understudied)'는 내용이 되도록 하는 ②가 빈칸에 들어가야 한다.

nutritional science 영양학 randomized controlled trial 무작위 대조 실험 tricky a. (하기가) 까다로운 stick to ~을 (바꾸지 않고) 고수하다 association n. 연관성 nutrient n. 영양분 causal connection 인과 관계 overstate v. 과장하다 understudy v. 연구를 제대로 하지 못하다 well-received a. 좋은 평가를 받은 underfunded a. 예산 부족의 undercharge v. 제값보다 싸게 청구하다

다른 분야들과 비교했을 때, 영양학은 연구가 제대로 이뤄지지 않고 있다. 그 이유의 일부는 영양학 연구는 잘 하는 것이 어렵다는 것이다. 약물 테스트에 사용되는 무작위 대조 실험은 하기가 까다롭다. 몇 년 동안 실험 식단을 고수하고 싶어 하는 사람은 거의 없다. 대신, 대부분의 영양학은 특정 음식이나 영양분과 질병과의 연관성을 확립하려고 하는 관찰 연구들을 기반으로 한다. 그런 관찰 연구를 사용해서는 질병과 식단의 특정 기여 요인 간의 인과관계를 명확하게 입증할 수 없다.

23 논리완성   ⑤

소련이 최초의 인공위성인 스푸트니크를 발사한 것에 대한 미국인들의 반응이 무엇인지가 빈칸에 들어가야 한다. 빈칸 다음에서 미국인들이 완전히 준비하지 못한 경주에서 소련이 이미 선두를 차지했다고 했으므로, 이에 대해 미국인들은 '당황했을' 것이다. 따라서 이와 관련 표현인 ⑤의 dumbfounded가 빈칸에 적절하다.

desolate a. (장소가) 황량한 artificial satellite 인공위성 take the lead 선두를 차지하다 race n. 경주, 경쟁 compensate v. 보상하다 envisage v. (미래의 일을) 예상하다 unconvinced a. 납득하지 못하는 preoccupied a. 몰두한, 여념이 없는, 열중한 dumbfounded a. (놀라서) 어안이 벙벙한

나사(NASA) 이야기는 반세기 이상 전에 지금의 카자흐스탄(Kazakhstan) 이라 불리는 황량한 지역에서 시작되었다. 바로 거기서 소련이 최초의 인공위성인 스푸트니크를 발사했기 때문이었다. 미국인들은 어안이 벙벙했다. 우리가 아직 완전히 준비하지 못한 경주에서 소련이 이미 선두를 차지하고 있었다.

24 논리완성   ④

아리스토텔레스가 글에서 예술의 목적이 사물의 내적인 의미를 표현하는 것이며, 감정과 생각을 반영하는 작품을 만들어내는 것이라고 했다. 따라서 빈칸에는 '감정'을 반영하는 작품과 관련된 '미적인(aesthetic)' 과 '생각'과 관련된 '개념적인(conceptual)'이 언급된 ④가 들어가는 것이 적절하다.

fine art 미술, 순수예술(아리스토텔레스는 그림, 조각뿐만 아니라 시, 음악도 이 범주에 포함시켰다) painting n. (물감으로 그린) 그림, 회화 sculpture n. 조각, 조소 poetry n. (집합적으로) 시 categorize v. ~을 분류하다 make a point 주장을 밝히다 represent v. 표현하다 object n. 물건; 작품 reflect v. 반영하다 capture v. 정확히 담아내다

회화, 조각, 음악, 시 같은 순수예술은 미적이거나 개념적인 기능만을 갖고 있는 것으로 분류된다. 이런 주장은 천 년 남짓 전에 그리스의 철학자 아리스토텔레스가 했는데, 다음과 같이 글에서 밝혔다. "예술의 목적은 사물의 겉모습을 표현하는 것이 아니라 내적인 의미를 표현하는 것이다." 그는 예술가들이 그저 자연의 사실적인 이미지를 담아내려 하기보다 감정과 생각을 반영하는 작품, 드라마, 그리고 음악을 만들어냈다고 지적했다.

① 개인적이고 사회적인
② 무신론적이고 이론적인
③ 추상적이지만 창조적인
④ 미적이거나 개념적인
⑤ 무형적이지만 객관적인

25 글의 제목   ③

한국 최초의 국내에서 개발된 달 궤도선인 다누리호가 달 궤도에 안착함으로써 한국이 세계에서 7번째로 달을 탐사한 국가가 됐음을 이야기하고 있는 내용이므로 ③이 제목으로 적절하다. ④ 다누리호의 여정에 대해서는 구체적으로 이야기하고 있지 않다.

domestically ad. 국내적으로, 국내(실정)에 알맞게 lunar orbiter 달 궤도선 powerhouse n. 발전소; 유력[실세] 집단[기관]; 최강자 gravity n. 중력 rotate v. 선회하다, 회전하다

한국 최초의 국내 개발 달 궤도선이 달 궤도에 성공적으로 안착함으로써 한국은 우주 경제에서 글로벌 강국이 되겠다는 목표에 한 발짝 더 다가설 수 있게 됐다. 수요일에 한국 항공우주연구원(KARI)은 한국형 달 궤도선으로도 알려져 있는 다누리호가 하루 전날에 달의 중력에 안정적으로 포획되어 달의 지표면 100km 상공에서 2시간마다 한 번씩 돌고 있다고 밝혔다. 이로써 한국은 러시아, 미국, 일본, 유럽연합, 중국, 인도에 이어 세계에서 7번째로 달을 탐사한 국가가 됐다.

글의 제목으로 가장 적절한 것은?
① 우주 탐사에 대한 필요성 증대
② 달 궤도선 개발의 어려움
③ 한국이 달을 탐사한 7번째 국가가 되다
④ 달을 향한 다누리호의 장대한 여정
⑤ 달 탐사의 밝은 면

26 빈칸완성   ②

빈칸을 전후로, 빈칸 앞에는 식욕부진증 환자들이 체중을 조절하려고 시도한다는 내용이 나오고, 빈칸 다음에는 그런 시도와 관련된 구체적인 사례가 나오므로, 빈칸에는 '예시'를 나타내는 ②의 For example이 적절하다.

anorexia nervosa 신경성 식욕부진증, 거식증   condition n. (치유가 안 되는 만성) 질환   patient n. 환자   eating disorder 섭식 장애   anorexic n. 식욕부진증 환자   compulsive a. 강박적인   hyperactivity n. 과잉행동   exercycle n. 엑서사이클(페달을 밟기만 하는 실내 운동 기구)   burn off (운동으로 칼로리 등을) 태우다[연소시키다]   consume v. 섭취하다   indulge in ~에 빠져들다   self-starvation n. 자발적 기아 (飢餓)   progressively ad. 점차적으로   desperate a. 절망적인

환자가 지속적으로 체중을 줄이려고 노력하는 질환인 신경성 식욕부진증은 의학적으로 가장 심각하고 모든 섭식 장애 중에서 가장 이해하기 어려운 질환이다. 일부 식욕부진증 환자들은 강박적 과잉행동과 같이 서로 다른 여러 전략을 통해 체중을 조절하려고 시도한다. 예를 들어, 그들은 섭취한 모든 열량을 연소시키기 위해 하루에 5시간 조깅한 다음 집에 와서 씻고, 추가로 1시간 엑서사이클 페달을 밟는다. 또 다른 식욕부진증 환자들은 상당한 수준의 자발적 기아(飢餓) 상태에 빠진다. 그들은 가능한 한 적게 열량을 섭취하며, 그들이 체중을 계속해서 낮추지 못할 경우 점차 절망에 빠지게 된다.

빈칸에 들어가기에 가장 적절한 것은?
① 결국
② 예를 들어
③ 사실
④ 반면에
⑤ 게다가

27 빈칸완성   ⑤

빈칸에는 존 폴 게티 2세가 한 행동의 성격이 어떠했는지가 들어가야 한다. 그의 아버지가 설립한 미술관이 걸작들을 구입하지 못하도록 선수를 쳐서 걸작들을 구매했다고 했으므로, '그의 아버지와의 관계가 좋지 못함'을 짐작할 수 있다. 따라서 이와 관련된 내용인 ⑤가 정답이다.

benefactor n. (학교·자선단체 등의) 후원자   lavish v. 아낌없이 주다   philanthropic a. 자선의   knight v. 기사 작위를 수여하다   give away ~을 기부하다   charity n. 자선단체   striking a. 파업 중인   coal miner 광부   inheritance n. 상속재산, 유산   masterpiece n. 걸작   sanctuary n. 성역, 피난처, 안식처   greed n. 탐욕, 욕심   brinkmanship n. 벼랑 끝 전술   preempt v. 먼저 차지하다; (예상된 사태를) 선수를 쳐서 회피하다   defiance n. (공개적으로 하는) 반항   estranged a. (~와 사이가) 소원해진, 멀어진

미국 태생의 후원자인 존 폴 게티 2세(John Paul Getty Jr)는 자선적인 선물들을 영국에 아낌없이 주었다. 그는 런던의 국립미술관(National Gallery)과 영국영화협회(BFI) 등 영국의 많은 자선단체들과 파업 중인 광부들의 가족들에게 2억 달러 이상을 기부한 공로로 기사작위를 받았다. 게티는 그의 아버지가 설립한 게티 미술관(Getty Museum)이 걸작들을 구매하지 못하도록, 그의 상속재산을 사용하여 대영박물관을 위해 걸작들을 구입하기도 했다. 부분적으로, 이것은 그의 아버지와의 소원한 관계에

대한 반항적인 행동이었고, 영국이 그에게 준 안식처에 대한 깊은 애정의 표시이기도 했다.

빈칸에 들어가기에 가장 적절한 것은?
① 가능한 한 많은 예술작품들을 수집하려는 탐욕
② 그를 세계 최고의 부자로 만드는 벼랑 끝 전술
③ 그의 아들들 사이에 벌어지는 가족 간의 언쟁을 선수 쳐서 회피하기 위한 고려
④ 정치 위기를 해결하기 위한 수단으로서 폭력
⑤ 그의 아버지와의 소원한 관계에 대한 반항

28 내용일치   ③

오존층이 감소됨에 따라 더 많은 자외선이 지구에 도달하고 있다고 했으므로, ③이 정답이다.

visible light 가시광선   ultraviolet light 자외선   suntan n. (피부의) 햇볕에 그을음   sunburn n. 햇볕에 심하게 탐, 햇볕으로 입은 화상   skin cancer 피부암   pole n. (지구의) 극   ozone layer 오존층   man-made a. 사람이 만든, 인공의   pollutant n. 오염 물질, 오염원

태양은 낮 동안 많은 양의 가시광선을 만들어낸다. 문제가 되는 빛은 자외선이다. 자외선은 가시광선보다 더 많은 에너지를 갖고 있으며, 햇볕에 그을리고 햇볕에 화상 입고 심지어 피부암까지 생기게 하는 것이 바로 이 자외선이다. 최근에 지구에 도달하는 자외선의 양이 특히 북극과 남극 주변에서 증가해 왔다. 과거에는 두꺼운 오존층이 있었지만, 인간이 만들어낸 오염물질들이 오존층을 감소시키면서, 더 많은 자외선이 지구에 도달하고 있다.

글의 내용과 가장 잘 부합하는 것은?
① 가시광선은 햇볕에 그을리고 햇볕에 화상을 입는 것과 같은 사소한 피부문제를 일으킨다.
② 인간이 만들어낸 오염물질들이 오존층을 얇게 만드는 유일한 원인이다.
③ 우리가 받는 자외선의 양이 증가해왔다.
④ 가시광선과 자외선은 모두 해롭다.
⑤ 태양이 만들어낸 자외선의 양이 증가해 왔다.

29 내용일치   ①

드론으로 피해지역을 촬영하고 이 데이터를 이용해 긴급구조요원들이 지도를 만들고 구호물자를 피해지역에 수송할 수 있었다고 했으므로, ①이 정답이다.

natural disaster 자연재해   cyclone n. 사이클론(강한 회오리바람을 일으키는 인도양의 열대성 폭풍)   the Pacific 태평양   survey n. 측량   be hardest hit 가장 타격을 입다   crop n. 농작물

드론은 또한 자연재해가 발생한 후에 긴급구조 단체들을 돕고 있다. 예를 들어, 2015년에 강력한 사이클론이 바누아투(Vanuatu)라는 태평양 섬나라에서 수천 채의 건물들을 파괴했다. 대략 75,000명이 집을 잃었고, 최소 15명이 목숨을 잃었다. 폭풍이 지나간 이후, 드론으로 피해지역을 촬영했다. 이런 조사는 긴급구조요원들이 상황을 신속하게 파악하고 "어떤 지역이 가장 피해를 입었는가?", "농작물이 피해를 입었는가?", "어떤 길이 피해를 입었는가?"와 같이 중요한 질문들에 대답할 수 있게 도움을 주었다. 긴급구조대원들은 그 데이터를 이용하여 피해지역을 상세한 지도로 만들

수 있었다. 그러고 나서, 그들은 구호물자를 가장 필요로 하는 사람들에게 수송할 수 있었다.

글의 내용과 가장 잘 부합하는 것은?
① 드론이 폭풍 피해를 확인하는 데 도움을 주었다.
② 드론은 자연재해가 발생한 이후 의료물자를 배달할 수 있었다.
③ 드론이 날씨 상황을 분석할 수 있었다.
④ 긴급구조요원들이 드론을 조종할 수 있어야 한다.
⑤ 긴급구조요원들은 지질학에 정통해 있다.

---

30 내용일치   ④

대중 인지도가 커지면 유명 영화배우들의 고액 출연료 요구로 이어질 것이라는 두려움에 대처하기 위해 영화 제작사들은 배우들에게 가명 사용을 요구하는 것을 비롯해 다양한 수단으로 배우들의 신원을 익명으로 유지하도록 많은 노력을 기울였다고 했으므로, ④가 정답이다. ③ 가명이나 익명의 사용에 대한 유명 영화배우들의 반응에 대해서는 언급이 없다.

anonymous a. 익명의 competitive market 경쟁 시장 motion picture 영화 preference n. 선호도 public recognition 대중 인지도 demand n. 수요 go to great lengths (목적 달성을 위해서) 많은 노력을 기울이다 identity n. 신원, 신분 pseudonym n. 필명, 가명

20세기 초에, 영화 제작사들은 배우들이 경쟁 시장에서 자리 잡는 것을 막기 위해 배우들의 이름을 익명으로 했다. 그러나 영화에 대한 대중의 수요가 증가함에 따라, 특정 배우들에 대한 대중들의 선호도 역시 증가했다. 대중 인지도가 유명 영화배우들의 고액 출연료 요구로 이어질 것이라는 두려움에 대처하기 위해, 제작자들은 가명 사용을 요구하는 것을 비롯해 다양한 수단으로 배우들의 신원을 익명으로 유지하도록 많은 노력을 기울였다.

글의 내용과 가장 잘 부합하는 것은?
① 대부분의 유명 영화배우들은 20세기 초에 돈을 많이 벌지 못했다.
② 제작자들은 그들의 영화를 광고하기 위해 배우들의 실명을 홍보했다.
③ 유명 영화배우들은 다른 이름을 사용하길 꺼렸다.
④ 배우들의 이름은 영화제작자의 이익을 위해 비밀로 했다.
⑤ 대중은 가명을 사용한 유명 영화배우들을 선호했다.

---

31 내용일치   ⑤

"그(=블랙독)는 나가라고 하면서 문을 활짝 열어두라고 명령했다. '엿보면 안 돼! 이 녀석'이라고 그가 말했고 나는 두 사람을 남겨둔 채 술집으로 물러났다. 나는 좀 엿들어보려고 한참 동안 무진 애를 썼지만 소곤거리는 소리만 들을 수 있을 뿐이었다."라는 내용을 통해 ⑤가 정답임을 알 수 있다. ① 블랙독이 그런 것 같다고 화자에게 느껴진 것이다. ② 과거에는 선장과 동료였지만 지금은 부하이다. ③ 좀 엿들어보려고 한참 동안 무진 애를 썼다. ④ 엿듣지 못하게 일부러 조용히 대화한 것이 아니라는 것은 마침내 언성이 높아진 것에서 알 수 있다.

rum n. 럼주(酒)(사탕수수·당밀(糖蜜)로 만듦) sideways ad. 옆으로, 옆쪽으로 shipmate n. 동료 선원 retreat n. 퇴각, 퇴거 bid v. 명하다, 명령하다 sonny n. 얘야, 자네, 젊은이(나이 든 사람이 청년·소년을 부르는 말) oath n. 맹세, 서약; 저주, 욕설

내가 럼주를 가지고 돌아왔을 때, 그들은 벌써 선장의 아침식사 테이블에 마주 앉아 있었다. 블랙독(Black Dog)은 문 바로 옆에 비스듬하게 앉아 있었는데, 한쪽 눈으로는 옛 동료 선원을 보고 다른 쪽 눈으로는 내 생각에 도망칠 퇴로를 보고 있는 것 같았다. 그는 나에게 나가라고 하면서 문을 활짝 열어두라고 명령했다. "엿보면 안 돼! 이 녀석"이라고 그가 말했고, 나는 두 사람을 남겨둔 채 술집으로 물러났다. 나는 좀 엿들어보려고 한참 동안 무진 애를 썼지만 소곤거리는 소리만 들을 수 있을 뿐이었다. 하지만 마침내 언성이 점점 높아지기 시작해서, 나는 선장이 한 말을 한두 마디 알아들을 수 있었는데, 대부분 욕설이었다.

글의 내용과 가장 잘 부합하는 것은?
① 화자는 언제든 도망칠 준비가 되어 있었다.
② 블랙독은 예전에 선장의 부하였다.
③ 화자는 두 선원이 한 말을 알고 싶어 하지 않았다.
④ 선장과 그의 옛 동료 선원은 엿듣지 못하도록 조용히 이야기를 나눴다.
⑤ 블랙독은 자신이 선장과 나누는 대화를 화자가 엿듣지 못하게 했다.

32-33

많은 사람들은 "휘발유만 있고, 브레이크와 핸들은 없다."는 벨(Bell)과 맥브라이드(McBride)의 비유가 십대들의 두뇌 발달을 지나치게 단순화한 것이라고 주장할 것이다. 사실, 케이시(Casey)와 코들(Caudle)이 2013년 실시한 연구에 따르면, 특정 상황에서는 청소년들이 실제로 성인보다 충동을 더 잘 조절할 수 있다고 한다. 일련의 실험실 실험 기간 동안, 서머빌(Somerville) 등의 공동연구(2011년)는 실험 대상들에게 긍정적, 부정적, 그리고 중립적 얼굴 표정 이미지들을 보여준 다음, 반응을 조절하는 능력을 측정했다. 어떠한 감정 정보도 없을 때, (즉, 얼굴 표정이 중립적일 때) 십대들은 성인보다 더 잘 하진 않더라도 성인만큼은 반응을 잘 통제했다. 그러나 긍정적이든 부정적이든 감정적인 신호가 있을 때, 청소년들은 자신의 반응을 훨씬 덜 억제할 수 있었다. 이러한 감소된 능력은 성인이나 감정적인 신호가 있든 없든 통제 조절이 어려운 아이들에게는 관찰되지 않았다. 이것은 십대가 일반적으로 합리적으로 행동할 수 없거나 올바른 결정을 내릴 수 없다는 지나친 단순화와 모순되는 것처럼 보인다. 아마도 십대들이 전전두엽 피질보다는 본능을 안내하는 뇌 부위인 편도체에 의존하는 경향이 있을지도 모르기 때문에 흥분된 상황이나 스트레스가 많은 상황에서는 이것이 사실일지도 모르지만, 중립적인 상황에서는 청소년들이 어른보다 실제로 충동을 보다 더 잘 억제하고 합리적인 결정을 잘 내린다.

steering wheel (자동차의) 핸들 analogy n. 비유 gross a. (오해 등이) 심한, 엄청난 oversimplification n. 지나친 단순화 adolescent n. 청소년 impulse n. (갑작스러운) 충동 et al (특히 이름들 뒤에 써서) 외, 등 subject n. 연구[실험] 대상 neutral a. 중립적인 i.e. 즉, 다시 말하면 cue n. (무엇을 하라는) 신호 contradict v. 부정하다; ~와 모순되다 amygdala n. (소뇌의) 편도체 prefrontal cortex 전전두엽 피질 stereotype n. 고정 관념

---

32 글의 제목   ①

이 글은 특정 상황에서는 청소년들이 성인만큼 충동을 잘 조절할 수 있다는 주장을 하고 있는데, 이런 주장은 일반적으로 십대가 합리적으로 행동하거나 결정을 내릴 수 없다는 지나친 단순화와 모순된다는 내용을 다루고 있다. 따라서 ①이 제목으로 적절하다.

제목으로 가장 적절한 것은?
① 고정관념에 의문을 제기하기
② 분별 있는 결정을 내리는 방법
③ 평생 동안 이어지는 두뇌 발달
④ 제지할 수 없는 청소년의 충동성
⑤ 최고의 성과와 급격한 하락

33 부분이해 ④

십대가 합리적으로 행동할 수 없거나 올바른 결정을 내릴 수 없다는 주장은 흥분된 상황이나 스트레스가 많은 상황에서는 사실일 수 있는데, 십대들이 본능을 안내하는 뇌 부위인 편도체에 의존하는 경향이 있기 때문이라고 했다. 따라서 서머빌 등의 공동연구(2011)의 내용으로 ④가 적절하다. ⑤ 아이들은 중립이든 아니든 통제 조절이 어렵다고 했다.

밑줄 친 Somerville et al. (2011)의 내용으로 가장 적절한 것은?
① 긍정적으로 느끼는 것이 십대들이 더 나은 결정을 내리도록 도울 수 있다.
② 십대들은 성인들보다 감정 통제를 더 잘한다.
③ 십대들은 그들의 행동과 선택을 처리하는 능력이 부족하다.
④ 스트레스가 십대들이 그들의 두뇌에서 편도체 사용을 할 수밖에 없도록 만들다
⑤ 아이들은 중립적인 상태에서 현명한 결정을 내리는 능력이 부족한 경향이 있다.

34-35

나는 막대기를 뽑아내고 그 아이 자전거 옆의 풀밭에 물고기를 내려놓았다. 나는 칼을 꺼냈다. "바로 여기지?"라고 내가 말했다. 그 아이는 고개를 끄덕였다. 나는 생선 내부를 자르기 시작했다. 생선의 내장까지 처리한 다음 생선을 뒤집어서 완전히 껍질을 벗겨냈다. 생선의 형체를 유지시켜 주고 있던 배의 살갗이 한 겹만 있을 때까지 계속해서 잘랐다. 나는 반반씩 잡고 생선을 둘로 갈랐다.
나는 그 아이에게 꼬리 부분을 주었다.
"아니, 나는 그쪽 절반을 갖고 싶은데."라고 고개를 저으며 그 아이는 말했다.
"두개 다 똑같아! 지금 조심해라, 곧 화를 낼 것 같아."라고 내가 말했다.
"상관없어."라고 그 소년이 말했다. "만약 두 개가 똑같다면, 내가 그쪽 것을 가질게. 두 개가 모두 똑같다는 거잖아, 안 그래?"
"두 개가 모두 똑같지. 그러나 이쪽 절반을 내가 가져야 한다고 생각해. 내가 잘랐잖아."라고 내가 말했다.
"내가 그쪽 절반을 원한다고. 내가 생선을 먼저 봤잖아."라고 그 아이는 말했다.
"이 칼 주인은 누구더라?"라고 내가 말했다.
"나는 꼬리 부분을 원하지 않아."라고 그 아이가 말했다.
나는 주위를 둘러보았다. 길에는 차가 한 대도 지나가지 않았고, 아무도 낚시를 하고 있지 않았다. 비행기 하나가 윙윙 소리를 내며 지나가고 있었고, 해는 저물고 있었다. 나는 종일 추웠다. 그 아이는 몹시 떨며 기다리고 있었다.
"나한테 좋은 생각이 있어."라고 내가 말했다. 나는 내 통발을 연 다음, 그에게 송어를 보여주었다. "봤지? 이건 녹색 송어야. 내가 여태까지 본 유일한 녹색 송어지. 따라서 누가 이 생선의 대가리를 가져가든, 다른 사람이 녹색 송어와 꼬리부분을 가져가는 거야. 그럼 공평한 거지?"라고 내가 말했다.

"그런 것 같아. 좋아. 그런 것 같아. 네가 그쪽 절반을 가져가. 내 고기가 더 많아졌어."라고 그가 말했다.
"나는 상관없어."라고 내가 말했다.

stick n. 막대기 lay v. ~을 놓다, 눕히다 take out ~을 꺼내다 nod v. 머리를 끄덕이다 gut n. (동물의) 내장 turn over 몸[자세]을 뒤집다 strip v. 벗기다 flap n. 살이나 피부의 부분 belly n. 배, 복부 hold together 유지되게 하다 tear v. 찢다[째다] watch it 조심해(경고의 의미로 하는 말) be my guest 그러세요[그래라] drone v. 웅웅거리는 소리를 내다 shiver v. (추위·공포·흥분 등으로) 와들와들 떨다 creel n. (낚시꾼의) 고기 바구니, 통발 trout n. 송어

34 빈칸완성 ⑤

빈칸 전후의 내용은 생선을 반으로 자른 아이와 생선 자르는 것을 지켜보고 있던 아이 모두 같이 머리 쪽 반을 원하는 상황으로, 둘이 좋은 부분을 가져가겠다고 신경전을 벌이는 상황이다. 빈칸 바로 앞에 "조심해(Watch it)"라고 생선 자른 아이가 경고하였으므로, 같은 맥락으로 경고하며 '화를 내는' 내용이 와야 적절할 것이다. 따라서 ⑤가 정답이다.

빈칸에 들어가기에 가장 적절한 것은?
① 그러도록 해라
② 너도 나만큼 피곤하다
③ 나는 그것에 대해 생각하고 있지 않다
④ 네가 나를 도왔어야 했는데
⑤ 곧 화를 낼 것 같아

35 내용일치 ②

'두 소년이 생선 한 마리를 두고 서로 좋은 부분을 가져가겠다고 언쟁을 벌이다가, 해가 저물자 한 아이가 생선 꼬리 부분을 가지는 아이가 녹색 송어도 갖게 하자는 아이디어를 내서 두 소년이 합의점을 찾게 되는' 내용을 소개하고 있다. 따라서 ②가 정답이다.

글의 내용과 가장 잘 부합하는 것은?
① 두 소년은 난폭한 행동을 보이며 서로를 위협하고 있다.
② 두 소년은 원하는 부위를 두고 벌어진 갈등을 해결할 합의점을 찾는다.
③ 두 소년은 두 사람이 한 마리의 생선을 공유하는 것과 관련해 서로를 놀리고 있다.
④ 두 소년은 다른 사람들의 재산을 훔치려는 시도로 곤경에 처해있다.
⑤ 두 소년은 결국 합의에 이르지 못한다.

36-37

지난 10년 동안, 오키프(O'Keefe) 박사는 달리기가 건강과 장수에 미치는 영향에 초점을 맞춘 여러 가지 연구를 실시했다. 그의 연구에는 20~92세의 유럽의 성인 약 5,000명의 데이터를 분석하는 것이 포함됐다. 연구 결과에 따르면, 느리거나 적당한 속도로 일주일에 1시간에서 2.4시간 달렸던 사람들에게서 사망률이 가장 큰 폭으로 감소했으며, 심지어 더 빠른 속도로 더 먼 거리를 달렸던 사람들보다도 사망률이 더 크게 감소했다는 것을 보여주었다. 이러한 결론은 18~100세의 미국인 55,000명 이상이 참여한 15년간의 연구 프로젝트 같은 다른 연구들과도 일치한다. 이 연구는 매일 시간당 6마일 이하로 5분에서 10분 동안만 달려도 온갖 사망

위험이 상당히 감소되었고 기대수명이 늘어났다는 것을 발견했다.

이덕철 박사는 달리기의 가장 눈에 띄는 건강 및 장수 혜택이 보다 낮은 수준의 활동에서 나타난다고 강조한다. 심지어 1마일 이하로 일주일에 몇 차례 달리기만 해도 심혈관 건강과 수명이 크게 향상될 수 있다. 달리기의 생리학적인 이점은 부분적으로 운동에 반응하여 다양한 기관계에서 방출되는 분자인 '엑서킨' 덕분이다. 비록 이 분야에서의 연구가 상대적으로 생소하지만, 리사 초우(Lisa Chow) 박사가 설명한 바와 같이, 연구들은 '엑서킨'을 염증 감소, 새로운 혈관 형성, 그리고 세포 미토콘드리아 재생과 연관 지어 왔다. 더 많은 연구가 필요하지만, 짧게 달리는 것처럼, 짧고 격렬한 운동을 한바탕 하는 것이 '엑서킨'과 관련된 혜택들 중 일부를 활성화시키는 것으로 알려져 있다.

게다가, 달리기는 정신 건강에도 도움이 된다. 운동과 우울증에 대한 연구를 검토한 결과, 매주 2.5시간의 적당한 신체 활동을 하는 성인들이 비활동적인 성인들보다 우울증에 걸릴 위험이 25% 낮은 것으로 나타났다. 심지어 이 권장 기간의 절반 동안 운동한 사람들도 여전히 위험이 18% 낮았다. 매사추세츠(Massachusetts) 종합병원의 심리학자 카르멜 최(Karmel Choi)는 일주일에 한두 번이라도 달리기 시작하면 운동을 전혀 하지 않는 것보다 정신 건강이 크게 향상될 수 있다고 지적한다.

longevity n. 장수 pace n. (달리기의) 속도 moderate a. 보통의; 알맞은, 적당한 mortality rate 사망률 substantially ad. 상당히 life expectancy 기대수명 cardiovascular a. 심혈관의 lifespan n. 수명 physiological a. 생리학적인 molecule n. 분자 organ system 기관계 inflammation n. <병리> 염증 blood vessel 혈관 cellular a. 세포의 regeneration n. (잃은 부분의) 재생 burst n. (갑자기) 한바탕 ~을 함, 한바탕 몰두하기 intense a. 격렬한 activate v. 작동시키다, 활성화시키다 depression n. 우울증 engage in ~에 참여하다 duration n. (지속되는) 기간 general hospital 종합병원

---

36 빈칸완성 ①

유럽의 성인들을 대상으로 실시한 연구에 따르면, 느리거나 적당한 속도로 달렸던 사람들에게서 사망률이 큰 폭으로 감소했다고 한 다음, 미국인들을 대상으로 실시한 연구결과를 보여주었는데, 이 연구에서도 5~10분 달렸던 사람들한테서 사망위험이 줄어들었고 기대수명이 늘어났다고 했다. 즉, 두 연구결과의 방향이 일치하므로, 이와 관련된 표현인 ①의 aligns with(~와 일치하다)가 빈칸에 적절하다.

빈칸에 들어가기에 가장 적절한 것은?
① ~와 일치하다
② ~을 초래하다
③ ~을 요청하다
④ ~에서 일탈하다
⑤ ~에 의문을 제기하다

---

37 내용추론 ⑤

이 글은 느리거나 적당한 속도로 일주일에 1시간에서 2.4시간 달렸던 사람들한테서 사망률이 가장 큰 폭으로 감소했다고 했으며, 심지어 1마일 이하로 일주일에 몇 차례 달리기만 해도 심혈관 건강과 수명이 크게 향상될 수 있으며, 정신 건강에도 도움이 된다고 하는 등 전반적으로 자주 달리는 것이 건강에 도움이 된다는 내용을 다루고 있다. 따라서 ⑤가 정답이다.

글을 읽고 유추할 수 있는 내용으로 가장 적절한 것은?
① 엑서킨은 보다 낮은 수준의 활동에서 덜 생성된다.
② 미국인들이 유럽인들보다 더 자주 달리는 것 같다.
③ 격렬한 운동은 우울증 증상을 악화시킬 수 있다.
④ 격렬한 달리기는 체내의 기관계를 손상시킬 수 있다.
⑤ 자주 달리는 것이 건강 향상에 도움이 된다.

38-40

유전자 변형은 새로운 것이 아니다. 인간은 수천 년 동안 식물의 유전자 구성을 변경해 왔고, 최고의 농작물에서 나온 씨앗을 보관해 왔으며, 그 후 수년 동안 그 씨앗들을 심어 왔고, 품종들을 개량하고 이종 교배하여 더 맛있고, 더 크고, 더 오래 지속되도록 만들었다. 이러한 방식으로 우리는 야생 토마토인 '리코페르시콘'을 구슬 크기의 과일에서 오늘날의 거대하고 즙 많은 비프스테이크 토마토로 변형시켰고, 길이가 겨우 1인치에 불과한 '옥수수 알'이 달린 테오신트라는 잡초 식물에서 흰색과 노란색으로 된 1피트 길이(0.3미터 길이)의 달콤한 옥수수 알이 나오게 되었다.

그러나 유전 공학 기술은 새로운 것이며, 전통적인 교배방식과는 완전히 다르다. 전통적인 육종가들은 유전자 구성이 유사한 친척뻘 유기체들을 이종 교배한다. 그렇게 함으로써, 그들은 수만 개의 유전자들을 이동시킨다. 이와 대조적으로, 오늘날의 유전공학자들은 먼 친척인 종들이거나 아무런 관련 없는 종들 간에 한 번에 몇 개의 유전자만 이동시킬 수 있다. 유전공학자들은 거의 모든 생물에서 원하는 유전자를 추출해 거의 모든 생물에 삽입할 수 있다. 그들은 상추에 쥐 유전자를 넣어 비타민 C를 생산하는 식물을 만들거나 세크로피아 나방의 유전자를 사과 식물에 접합하여 사과와 배를 손상시키는 세균성 질병인 화상병으로부터 보호할 수 있다. 이렇게 하는 목적은 똑같다. 원하는 형질을 지닌 기증자 생물의 유전자나 유전자들을 그 형질이 없는 생물에 삽입하는 것이다.

genetic modification 유전자 변형 genetic makeup 유전자 구성 for millennia 수천 년 동안 crop n. 농작물 breed v. (품종을) 개량하다, 교배시키다 crossbreed v. 이종 교배하다 last v. 지속하다 marble n. (가지고 노는) 구슬 juicy a. 즙[수분]이 많은 weedy a. 잡초 같은 ear n. 옥수수 알 genetic engineering 유전 공학 conventional a. 전통적인, 종래의 genetic engineer 유전공학자 lettuce n. 상추 splice v. 접합하다 moth n. 나방 fire blight 화상병 pear n. 배 insert v. 삽입하다 donor n. 기증자 trait n. 특성; 형질

---

38 부분이해 ④

novel이 형용사일 때 '이전에 볼 수 없던 새로운'이라는 의미로 쓰이므로, ④가 정답이다.

밑줄 친 novel의 뜻으로 가장 적절한 것은?
① 정의 내리거나 설명하기 어렵거나 불가능한
② 어느 누구도 불쾌하게 하거나 속상하게 하지 않는
③ 쉽거나 분명하게 보이거나 이해되는
④ 이전에 알고 있는 어떤 것과도 색다른
⑤ 존중받아야 하고 공격당하거나 파괴되어서는 안 되다

---

39 빈칸완성 ③

유전 공학 기술이 전통적인 교배 방식과는 완전히 다르다고 했으므로,

대조를 나타내는 By contrast를 전후로 상반된 내용이 나와야 한다. By contrast 다음에서 '몇 개의 유전자만 이동시킬 수 있다'고 했으므로, By contrast 앞에는 '숫자'와 관련해 상반된 내용인 ③이 빈칸에 들어가야 한다.

빈칸에 들어가기에 가장 적절한 것은?
① 유전자들 중 어떤 것도 이동시키지 않는다
② 각각의 유전자를 차례로 삽입한다
③ 수만 개의 유전자들을 이동시킨다
④ 목표대상인 유전자들만 삽입한다
⑤ 이전에 변형된 유전자를 이동시킨다

---

40 내용일치

유전공학자들이 세크로피아 나방의 유전자를 식물에 접합하여 사과와 배를 손상시키는 화상병으로부터 보호해준다고만 했을 뿐, '모든 종류의 질병'으로부터 보호해주는 것은 아니므로, ②가 정답이다.

글의 내용과 부합하지 않는 것은?
① 전통적인 교배는 유전적으로 유사한 생물 간의 이종교배만을 허락한다.
② 유전공학은 사람들이 사과나무와 배나무를 모든 종류의 질병으로부터 보호하게 해준다.
③ 전통적인 교배는 이전 세대보다 더 크고 더 맛있는 식물이 자라도록 해준다.
④ 유전공학은 사람들이 생물의 유전자 구성을 변경할 수 있도록 해준다.
⑤ 전통적인 교배는 밀접하게 관련된 종들 간에 다양한 형질을 결합하도록 해준다.

01 ④	02 ④	03 ②	04 ①	05 ④	06 ③	07 ⑤	08 ④	09 ③	10 ②
11 ④	12 ②	13 ③	14 ①	15 ②	16 ③	17 ③	18 ④	19 ⑤	20 ⑤
21 ②	22 ④	23 ⑤	24 ①	25 ③	26 ①	27 ④	28 ②	29 ①	30 ④
31 ⑤	32 ②	33 ⑤	34 ①	35 ③	36 ⑤	37 ①	38 ⑤	39 ③	40 ②

01 생활영어 ④

B는 새 직장에서 생소한 분야의 일을 하게 된 상황이므로, A는 B에게 '곧 시작하고 나면 익숙해져 자신에게 맞는 천직임을 알게 될 것'이라는 덕담을 해주는 것이 자연스럽다.

nervous a. 소심한, 겁 많은, 불안한 groove n. (자기의 재능·흥미 따위에) 가장 알맞은 직업[생활양식 따위]; 적소(適所) go belly up 완전히 망하다 face the music (행동에 대해 용감히) 책임지다 bend the rules 규칙을 어기다, 편의대로 해석하다, 융통성 있게 적용하다 get one's feet wet 새로 시작하다, 새로운 활동이나 경험을 시작하고 처음부터 조금씩 익숙해지다 get a friendly fire 아군의 포격[총격]을 받다

A: 새 직장에 대해 어떻게 생각해?
B: 흥분과 불안이 뒤섞여 있어. 내게는 완전히 새로운 분야거든.
A: 새로운 것을 시도하는 건 항상 좋은 일이야. 곧 시작하고 나서 너의 천직임을 발견하게 될 거야.

02 논리완성 ④

'(사전 계획을 세우기보다) 그때그때 봐서[사정을 봐 가면서] 처리하다'라는 의미의 관용표현은 play it by ear이다.

play it by ear 그때그때 봐서 처리하다

뉴욕에 있는 동안 동물원을 방문할 시간이 생길 수도 있지만, 우리는 상황을 봐 가면서 해야 할 것이다.

03 논리완성 ②

만나는 사람 모두에게 승진 소식을 알린 것은 흥분된 마음을 자신에게만 '가둬놓을(confine)' 수 없었기 때문일 것이며, 매우 전염성이 강한 질병을 위해 지정돼 있던 곳은 전염병이 외부로 퍼지지 못하도록 '폐쇄돼(confined)' 있었을 것이다.

designate v. 지명하다, 지정하다 infectious a. 전염하는, 전염성의 confide v. (비밀 따위를) 털어놓다 confine v. 한정하다, 제한하다; 가두다 release v. 풀어놓다, 방출하다 degrade v. 지위를 낮추다, 좌천시키다, 격하하다 reverse v. 뒤집다, 뒤엎다

흥분을 마음속에 가둬 둘 수 없었기 때문에, 그는 자신이 만난 모든 사람들에게 승진 소식을 전했다.
그 환자들은 병원의 폐쇄 구역에 있었는데, 그곳은 매우 전염성이 강한 질병을 위해 지정돼 있던 곳이었다.

04 논리완성 ①

두 문장 모두 '만회', '복구', '회복'의 의미를 가진 동사가 필요하므로 ①이 정답으로 적절하다.

exhausting a. 소모적인; (심신을) 지치게 하는 recuperate v. (건강 따위를) 회복하다; (손실 따위를) 만회하다 lacerate v. 찢다, 잡아 찢다 fraternize v. 형제로서의 교제를 하다; 친하게 사귀다 surmise v. 추측하다, 짐작하다 undermine v. (명성 따위를) 음험한 수단으로 훼손하다, 몰래 손상시키다

그녀는 적어도 손실의 일부를 만회하기를 희망했다.
심신을 지치게 만드는 몇 주를 보낸 후에, 나는 회복할 시간이 필요했다.

05 논리완성 ④

second가 동사로 쓰이는 경우에는 '(동의·제안에) 찬성하다, 지지하다'라는 의미이며, 형용사로 쓰이는 경우에는 '두 번째의'라는 의미를 갖는다.

strategy n. 병법, 전략 clear v. 맑게 하다, 깨끗이 하다 a. 맑은, 투명한 render v. ~이 되게 하다; 주다, 갚다 adhere v. 고수하다, 집착하다 second v. 찬성하다, 지지하다 a. 두 번째의 prompt v. 자극하다, 격려하다, 고무하다 a. 신속한

그녀가 새로운 마케팅 전략을 제안했을 때, 나는 즉시 그녀의 아이디어에 찬성했다.
그녀는 시험 결과를 확인하고서 끝에서 두 번째에서 자신의 이름을 발견했는데, 가장 친한 친구의 이름 바로 위였다.

06 논리완성 ③

고급 물리학에서는 '이질적이거나 생소한(alien)' 개념이 제시됐을 것이며, 영주권을 얻으려 하는 사람들은 '외국인들(aliens)'이다.

concept n. 개념, 생각 physics n. 물리학 significantly ad. 상당히, 뚜렷하게 affect v. ~에 영향을 미치다 status n. (사회적) 지위, 자격; 신분 permanent residency 영주권 sage a. 슬기로운, 현명한 n. 현인(賢人), 철인(哲人) expertise n. (골동품·자료·미술품 등에 관한) 전문가의 의견; 전문적 기술 alien a. 외국인의; 이질적인; 생경한 n. 외국인, 외계인 migrant a. 이주(移住)하는 n. 이주자 intent a. 전념하고 있는, 열심인 n. 의향, 의도

그는 고급 물리학 강의에서 제시된 생소한 개념을 이해하기 위해 안간힘을 썼다.
새로운 정책은 그 나라의 영주권을 얻으려 하고 있던 외국인들의 지위에 상당한 영향을 미쳤다.

07 논리완성 ⑤

cater는 '음식물을 조달[장만]하다, 제공하다'와 '요구[분부]에 응하다'라는 의미를 함께 가지고 있다.

tool n. 도구, 공구; (어떤 목적을 이루기 위한) 수단[도구] efficiently ad. 능률적으로 orient v. 바른 방향에 놓다; (새로운 환경 따위에) 적응[순응]시키다 diverge v. 빗나가다, (진로 등을) 벗어나다; (의견 등이) 갈라지다, 다르다 direct v. (주의·노력 등을 어떤 방향으로) 돌리다, 향하게 하다; 지도하다 charge v. (의무·책임을) 지우다, 부담시키다; 충전하다 cater v. 음식물을 조달[장만]하다, 제공하다; 요구[분부]에 응하다

새로운 레스토랑은 다양한 맛을 제공한다.
온라인 플랫폼은 프리랜서 근로자들의 요구에 부응하여, 그들의 프로젝트를 효율적으로 관리할 수 있는 도구들을 제공한다.

08 논리완성 ④

odds에는 '역경', '곤란'이라는 의미가 있고, be at odds (with somebody) (over/on something)은 '(…을 두고) (~와) 불화하다, 뜻이 맞지 않다'라는 의미이다.

secure v. (특히 힘들게) 얻어 내다, 획득[확보]하다 in the face of ~에도 불구하고 overwhelming a. 압도적인, 저항할 수 없는 odds n. 어떤 일이 있을) 공산(가능성); 역경, 곤란 be at odds (with somebody) (over/on something) (…을 두고) (~와) 뜻이 맞지 않다, 불화하다

그들은 압도적인 역경에도 불구하고 승리를 손에 넣었다.
그는 정치에 대해 자기 아버지와 항상 다툰다.

09 논리완성 ③

miss out은 '~을 빠뜨리다[누락시키다]'라는 의미이며, miss out on은 '(참석하지 않음으로써 유익하거나 즐거운 것을) 놓치다'라는 뜻이다.

mix up 혼동하다 move on 계속 전진하다; 공격하다 miss out ~을 빠뜨리다[누락시키다] miss out on (참석하지 않음으로써 유익하거나 즐거운 것을) 놓치다 make out 이해하다, 알다 mess up (~을) 엉망으로 만들다[다 망치다]

너는 수상자 명단에서 내 이름을 누락시켰다.
그녀는 몸이 아파 바닷가 여행에서 빠졌다.

10 논리완성 ②

'현실 세계로부터 현저하게 동떨어져 있는 것'은 지식인의 전형적인 모습이라 할 수 있다. quintessential에는 '전형적인'이란 의미와 함께 '본질적인'이라는 의미도 있다.

intellectual n. 지식인 remarkably ad. 현저하게, 대단히 detach v. 떨어지게 하다, 분리하다 impeccable a. 결점[흠]이 없는, 나무랄 데 없는 quintessential a. 전형적인; 본질적인 subsidiary a. 부차적인, 종속적인 intoxicating a. 도취시키는 provisional a. 일시적인; 임시의

그 시리얼 브랜드는 2024년까지 본질적인 색상 중 일부를 잃게 될 것이다.
그는 현실 세계로부터 현저하게 동떨어져 있는 전형적인 지식인이었다.

11 정비문 ④

대명사 each는 단수 동사로 받는다. 따라서 ④는 Each of the answers is worth three points.가 되어야 한다.

upcoming a. 다가오는, 이윽고 나타날[공개될] lecture n. 강의, 강연 competition n. 경쟁; 경기대회

① 우리는 곧 있을 강연을 알리게 되어 기쁘다.
② 그녀의 아버지는 여름 동안 병원에 입원해 계셨다.
③ 궁금한 점이 있으면 저에게 마음껏 문의하십시오.
④ 그 답들 각각은 3점의 가치가 있다.
⑤ 그 대회는 팀과 개인 모두에게 열려 있다.

12 정비문 ②

②의 주어는 His proposal이고 that the system should be fixed는 주어와 동격을 이루는 that절이다. His proposal은 reject하는 행위의 주체가 아닌 대상이므로, 전체 문장은 수동태가 되어야 한다. 따라서 ②는 His proposal that the system should be fixed was rejected.가 되어야 한다.

cigarette end 담배꽁초 ashtray n. 재떨이 fix v. (생각·습관·제도 등을) 확립하다, 고치다 reject v. 거절하다, 각하하다 personality n. 개성, 성격

① 재떨이 안에는 연기를 내는 담배꽁초 하나가 있었다.
② 그 시스템이 고쳐져야 한다는 그의 제안은 거절당했다.
③ 그의 할머니는 성격이 별로 좋지 않았다.
④ 그녀는 좋든 싫든 그 약을 먹고 있다!
⑤ 모두가 내게 걱정을 그만해야 한다고 말했다.

to one's taste ~의 마음에 드는, ~의 취향인   abroad ad. 해외로
version n. (개인적 또는 특수한 입장에서의) 의견, 소견, 설명

① 첫 번째 디자인이 내 취향에 훨씬 더 맞았다.
② 해외 출장을 가야 해서 나에게서 연락이 끊길 것이다.
③ 사건에 대한 그녀의 설명이 이의 없이 받아들여졌다.
④ 다양한 배송 옵션을 제공하는가?
⑤ 스웨덴에서는 아이를 때리는 것이 법에 어긋난다.

13 정비문 ③

③에 쓰인 information은 불가산명사이므로 복수형으로 쓸 수 없다. 그러므로 ③은 His charge was to obtain specific information.이어야한다. ⑤ except 뒤에 that이 생략돼 있다.

proposal n. 제안, 제의   charge n. 책임, 의무   obtain v. 얻다, 획득하다   specific a. 일정한, 특정한   conference n. 회담, 회의   attend v. ~에 출석[참석]하다

① 너의 제안을 판단하기에는 아직 너무 이르다.
② 우리 것보다 더 작은 메모리 스틱은 찾지 못할 것이다.
③ 그의 책무는 구체적인 정보를 얻는 것이었다.
④ 그 회의에는 수백 명의 사람들이 참석했다.
⑤ 내 드레스가 빨간색이었다는 사실을 제외하면 우리의 드레스는 똑같았다.

14 정비문 ①

①에서 red 뒤에는 apples를 대신하는 대명사 ones가 있어야 한다. 그러므로 ①은 Green apples often taste better than red ones.가 되어야 한다.

insure v. 보험에 들다, 보험계약을 하다

① 녹색 사과는 종종 빨간 사과보다 맛이 더 좋다.
② 분실이나 파손에 대비해서 네 카메라를 반드시 보험에 가입하도록 해라.
③ 은행은 돈을 빌리라고 사람들에게 적극적으로 장려한다.
④ 우리는 제품 개발에 종사하는 8명으로 구성된 팀을 갖고 있다.
⑤ 그 우유는 너무나도 맛이 좋아서 우리는 그것을 마시는 것을 멈출 수가 없었다.

15 정비문 ②

know, believe, understand 등의 상태 동사는 'get+과거분사' 형태의 이른 바 동작수동에 쓰이지 않는다. 그러므로 ②는 Very little was known about the woman.이 되어야 한다.

① 피해 규모가 크다는 보고가 있다.
② 그 여자에 대해서는 알려진 것이 거의 없었다..
③ 우리는 들키지 않고 담을 넘었다.
④ 그 엽서는 잘못된 주소로 보내졌을 수도 있다.
⑤ 나는 그 직장을 제안받았지만, 받아들일 생각이 없다.

16 정비문 ③

③에서 주어가 Her version이므로 주어에 수를 일치시켜 단수 동사를 써야 한다. 그러므로 ③은 Her version of events was accepted without question.이 되어야 한다.

17 정비문 ③

③에서 changing의 의미상 주어는 주절의 주어인 the speed limit인데, 이것은 change하는 행위의 주체가 아닌 대상이므로 수동태로 나타내야 한다. 그러므로 ③은 Before being changed last year, the speed limit in the downtown area was 60km/h.가 되어야 한다.

gym n. 체육관   unplugged a. 플러그가 뽑혀 있는   policy n. 정책, 방침   introduce v. 소개하다; 도입하다

① 병원에서 나온 이후로 나는 매일 체육관에 다녀왔다.
② 컴퓨터의 뒷면을 떼어내기 전에 반드시 플러그가 뽑혀 있게 하라.
③ 작년에 변경되기 전에, 도심지역의 제한속도는 시속 60㎞였다.
④ 1983년에 옥스퍼드 대학교를 떠난 후, 그는 1년 동안 지역 학교에서 교편을 잡았다.
⑤ 새로운 정책을 환영하지만, 나는 그것이 한 달 전에 도입되었어야 했다고 생각한다.

18 정비문 ④

quite, such, what 등은 'quite/such/what+a(n)+형용사+명사'의 형태로 쓴다. 그러므로 ④는 She watched quite an interesting film last night.이 되어야 한다.

a whole lot of 아주 많은   bureaucracy n. 관료정치, 관료주의   repress v. 억누르다, 저지하다   creativity n. 창의성, 창조력   initiative n. 진취성; 결단력, 자주성   immigration n. 이주, 이민; 출입국 관리소

① 다행히도 나는 기분이 좋았다.
② 내가 모르는 사람들이 정말 많았다.
③ 지나친 관료주의는 창의성과 진취성을 억압한다.
④ 그녀는 어젯밤에 꽤 흥미로운 영화를 보았다.
⑤ 우리는 출입국 관리소 직원으로부터 질문을 받았다.

19 정비문 ⑤

⑤에 쓰인 동사 warn은 'warn+목적어+to부정사'의 형태로 쓴다. 그러므로 ⑤에서 warned 다음에 적절한 목적어를 첨가해야 한다. ⑤는 The police warned us to stay inside with the windows closed.가 되어야한다.

envy v. 부러워하다, 질투하다   dare v. (겁이 없음을 보여줄 수 있도록 힘들거나 곤란한 일을) 해 보라고 하다[부추기다]   spicy a. 양념 맛이 강한, 매운   award v. 수여하다, 주다   object to ~에 반대하다

① 십대들은 그의 생활방식을 부러워했다.
② 멜라니(Melanie)는 친구에게 그 매운 음식을 한번 먹어보라고 부추겼다.
③ 심사위원들은 두 결승진출자 모두에게 같은 점수를 주었다.
④ 너는 오늘밤 늦게까지 일하는 것에 반대하지 않지?
⑤ 경찰은 우리에게 창문을 닫은 채 안에 있으라고 경고했다.

20 정비문　　　　　　　　　　⑤

have가 사역동사로 쓰이는 경우, 목적어와 목적격 보어의 관계가 능동이면 목적격 보어 자리에 원형부정사를 쓰고, 목적어와 목적격 보어의 관계가 수동이면 목적격 보어 자리에 과거분사를 쓴다. ⑤에서 their hand는 tie하는 행위의 대상이므로 수동 관계이다. 그러므로 ⑤는 They had their hands tied behind their backs.가 되어야 한다. ② about 대신에 of를 쓸 수도 있으며 대명사 all은 you와 동격을 이루고 있다. ③ as 뒤에 we were가 생략돼 있다.

photography n. 사진술; 사진 촬영　strictly ad. 엄격히　forbidden a. 금지된　transfer v. 양도하다, 전달하다　request v. 요구하다, 청하다　gradually ad. 차차, 서서히

① 그 식물의 사진 촬영은 엄격히 금지돼 있다.
② 나는 여러분 모두에게 사무실 복장 규정에 대해 알려주고자 한다.
③ 우리는 요청한 대로 자금을 이체했다.
④ 긴장과 흥분이 하루 종일 조금씩 쌓였다.
⑤ 그들은 등 뒤로 손이 묶였다.

21 정비문　　　　　　　　　　②

②에서 주어는 the exam results이므로 복수 동사로 받아야 한다. 그러므로 ②는 Displayed on the board were the exam results.가 되어야 한다.

① 모든 가구(家具)가 화재로 파괴되었다.
② 게시판에 시험 결과가 게시돼 있었다.
③ 올해는 그 한국 학자 둘 중 아무도 수상을 하지 못했다.
④ 기차역이나 영화관은 만나기에 좋은 장소이다.
⑤ 지난 몇 년 동안 많은 변화가 있었다.

22 논리완성　　　　　　　　　　④

산호의 상실이 생태계에 파괴적인 영향을 미칠 수 있다는 것은 산호초가 많은 생명체를 먹여 살리는 중요한 역할을 하고 있기 때문일 것이다. 그러므로 빈칸에는 '떠받치다', '부양하다'라는 의미의 ④가 들어가는 것이 적절하다.

overfishing n. 남획　reef n. 암초(본문에서는 산호초(coral reef)의 의미로 쓰였다)　vulnerable a. 비난[공격]받기 쉬운, 약점이 있는; (유혹·설득 따위에) 약한　yellow-band disease 노란 띠 병(산호에 발생하는 질병)　reverse v. (방향·순서 따위를) 역으로 하다, 역으로 돌리다, 반대로 하다　coral bleaching 산호 백화 현상　devastating a. 황폐시키는, 파괴적인　ecosystem n. 생태계　dismantle v. (기계·구조물을) 분해[해체]하다; (조직·체제를) 해체하다　attempt v. 시도하다　investigate v. 조사하다, 연구하다　sustain v. (아래서) 떠받치다; 유지하다; 부양하다, 양육하다　contaminate v. 더럽히다, 오염시키다

과학자들은 남획, 오염, 그리고 기후변화로 인한 수온 상승이 산호초들을 노란 띠 질병에 더 취약하게 만들고 있을지도 모른다고 생각하고 있다. 산호 백화 현상과는 달리, 그 질병의 영향은 되돌릴 수 없다. 산호의 상실은 생태계에 파괴적인 영향을 미칠 수 있다. — 산호초는 "숲과 마찬가지로, 엄청나게 많은 생명체를 부양하고 있으며, 그것의 죽음은 결국 인간에게도 영향을 미칠 수 있습니다."라고 그녀는 덧붙였다.

23 논리완성　　　　　　　　　　⑤

본문에 소개되는 세균 종은 새로 생겨나 발견되는 것이 아니라 생긴 후 오랫동안 비활동 상태에 있다가 산업 재난의 비위생적 환경에 의해 활동성을 갖게 된 경우인데 이를 잠을 자고 있다가 깨어나게 되는 것에 비유하고 있다. '깨워지기' 전에는 그 세균이 '잠을 자고 있었다'고 할 수 있으므로 빈칸에는 ⑤가 적절하다.

species n. 종(種)　awaken v. (잠에서) 깨우다, 일으키다　typically ad. 전형적으로, 일반적으로　remote a. 먼, 먼 곳의; 외딴　rainforest n. 다우림, 열대 다우림　plateau n. 고원　bug n. 곤충, 벌레; 병원균　microbe n. 세균; 미생물　squirm v. (벌레처럼) 꿈틀거리다, 움직거리다　forge v. 날조하다, 위조하다　simmer v. (약한 불에) 부글부글[지글지글] 끓다　encounter v. 해후하다, 만나다, 마주치다　slumber v. (편안히) 자다; 선잠 자다

새로운 종(種)들은 일반적으로 깨어나게 되기보다 찾아내지게 된다. 그리고 그들은 전형적으로 열대 다우림이나 남극의 고원 같은 외딴 곳에서 발견된다. 그러나 『Extremophiles』에 막 발표된 한 논문에 기술돼 있는 박테리아 종은 그렇지 않다. 논문의 저자인 Russell Vreeland와 Heng-Lin Chui가 지적하고 있듯이, 그 병원균은 과학계에 새로운 것이다. 그러나 지구에게는 새로운 것이 아니다. 사실, 그 세균은 수백만 년 동안 잠을 잔 후 산업적인 재난에 의해 깨어나게 되었는지도 모른다.

24 논리완성　　　　　　　　　　①

돌고래 켈리가 쓰레기를 숨겨 두었다가 한 조각씩 가져다주면서 계속해서 보상을 받은 것은 창의적이고 계획적인 전략을 세운 것이며, 이것은 문제 해결 능력과 관련이 있다.

trick ~ into … ~을 속여 …하게 하다　treat n. 한턱, 한턱 냄　reward v. 보상하다　enclosure n. 울타리, 담　tear off 찢다　problem-solver n. 문제 해결사　treasure hunter 보물 사냥꾼　mind-reader n. 마음을 읽어내는 사람　peacemaker n. 조정자, 중재인　freedom fighter 자유의 투쟁자

돌고래는 뛰어난 문제 해결사이고 매우 사교적이며, 심지어 영리하기까지 하다. 유명한 한 사례에서, 켈리(Kelly)라는 이름의 돌고래는 조련사들을 속여 먹이를 추가로 더 주게 했다. 그녀는 자신의 울타리 안에서 발견한 쓰레기 조각을 조련사들에게 줄 때마다 보상을 받았다. 어느 날, 그녀는 종이봉지를 바위 아래에 숨겨놓고, 한 번에 하나씩 작은 조각을 찢어서 각각의 조각마다 새로운 보상을 받았다.

25 글의 제목 ③

한국 최초의 국내에서 개발된 달 궤도선인 다누리호가 달 궤도에 안착함으로써 한국이 세계에서 7번째로 달을 탐사한 국가가 됐음을 이야기하고 있는 내용이므로 ③이 제목으로 적절하다. ④ 다누리호의 여정에 대해서는 구체적으로 이야기하고 있지 않다.

domestically ad. 국내적으로, 국내(실정)에 알맞게 lunar orbiter 달 궤도선 powerhouse n. 발전소; 유력[실세] 집단[기관]; 최강자 gravity n. 중력 rotate v. 선회하다, 회전하다

한국 최초의 국내 개발 달 궤도선이 달 궤도에 성공적으로 안착함으로써 한국은 우주 경제에서 글로벌 강국이 되겠다는 목표에 한 발짝 더 다가설 수 있게 됐다. 수요일에 한국 항공우주연구원(KARI)은 한국형 달 궤도선으로도 알려져 있는 다누리호가 하루 전날에 달의 중력에 안정적으로 포획되어 달의 지표면 100km 상공에서 2시간마다 한 번씩 돌고 있다고 밝혔다. 이로써 한국은 러시아, 미국, 일본, 유럽연합, 중국, 인도에 이어 세계에서 7번째로 달을 탐사한 국가가 됐다.

글의 제목으로 가장 적절한 것은?
① 우주 탐사에 대한 필요성 증대
② 달 궤도선 개발의 어려움
③ 한국이 달을 탐사한 7번째 국가가 되다
④ 달을 향한 다누리호의 장대한 여정
⑤ 달 탐사의 밝은 면

26-27

여러 연구들에서도 지능과 범죄 사이의 상관관계가 드러났다. Moffitt et al.은 IQ가 더 낮은 남자들이 20살까지 두 건 이상의 범죄를 저지른다는 것을 발견했다. Denno(1994)는 또한 거의 1,000명의 아이들을 대상으로 다양한 시점에서 지능을 테스트하여 IQ와 범죄행동이 일관되게 음(陰)의 상관관계에 있음을 발견했다. 그러나 Menard와 Morse와 같은 다른 사람들은 그 연관성이 통계적으로 유의미하다고 간주되기에는 너무 약하다고 주장했다. 그러나 지능이 범죄행동 성향에 영향을 미치는 정도와는 상관없이, 지능은 실제로 (범죄행동의) 요인에 속하는 것으로 보이며, 이것은 또 다른 질문을 제기한다. 우리는 날 때부터 똑똑하게, 더 나아가, 법을 준수하도록 태어났는가? 퀸즐랜드 대학의 연구원들은 지능은 최대 40%만 부모로부터 물려받으며 나머지는 환경적인 요인에 의해 결정된다는 것을 발견했다.

various a. 가지가지의; 여러 가지의 correlation n. 상호관계, 상관관계 consistent a. 일치하는, 양립하는 negative a. 음(陰)의, 부정적인 claim v. 주장하다 association n. 연합, 관련 statistically ad. 통계적으로 regardless of ~와 관계[상관]없이 extent n. 정도; 범위 affect v. 영향을 미치다 propensity n. 경향, 성질 factor n. 요인, 요소 by extension 더 나아가 inherit v. 상속하다, 물려받다

26 빈칸완성 ①

지능이 범죄행동의 요인에 속하는 것으로 보인다면, 높은 지능은 범죄를 저지르지 않게, 즉 법을 잘 지키게 만들 것이므로, '지능은 선천적인 것인가? 그렇다면 법 준수 능력도 선천적인 것인가?'라는 질문이 제기될 것이다.

빈칸에 들어가기에 가장 적절한 것은?
① 법을 준수하는
② 상황에 의한
③ 성질이 나쁜
④ 창의력이 풍부한
⑤ 생각을 자극하는

27 부분이해 ④

"Denno(1994)는 또한 거의 1,000명의 아이들을 대상으로 다양한 시점에서 지능을 테스트하여 IQ와 범죄행동이 일관되게 음(陰)의 상관관계에 있음을 발견했다."라고 했는데, 음(陰)의 상관관계는 지능이 낮으면 범죄행동성이 높고 지능이 높으면 범죄행동성이 낮은, 서로 반대 방향의 상관관계를 말하므로 ④가 정답이다.

밑줄 친 Denno (1994)의 내용으로 가장 적절한 것은?
① 범죄성은 유전된다.
② 범죄행동은 지능과 관련이 없다.
③ 아이가 어릴수록 더 많은 범죄를 저지른다.
④ IQ가 낮은 사람들은 더 많은 범죄를 저지를 가능성이 있었다.
⑤ 개인에게 부여된 부정적인 꼬리표는 일탈적인 행동을 부추긴다.

28 내용일치 ②

"난독증이 있다는 것은 당신이 책을 읽는 것이 어렵다는 것을 의미한다."라는 내용을 통해 ②가 정답임을 알 수 있다.

misconception n. 오해, 그릇된 생각 dyslexia n. 난독증, 독서 장애 critical a. 결정적인, 중대한 self-esteem n. 자부심, 자존감

흔히 하는 오해 중의 하나는 난독증이 질병이라는 것이다. 또 다른 오해는 난독증이 있는 사람이 지능이 낮다는 것이다. 이 두 가지 생각은 모두 잘못됐다. 사실, 연구에 따르면 지능과 난독증 사이에는 어떠한 연관성도 없다. 난독증이 있는 많은 사람들이 자신이 선택한 분야에서 계속해서 크게 성공을 거두고 있다. 난독증이 있다는 것은 당신이 책을 읽는 것이 어렵다는 것을 의미할 뿐, 당신이 무능하거나 나태하다는 것을 의미하는 것은 아니다. 난독증 관리를 도와줄 기술을 찾는 것은 성공적인 학습과 자존감에 있어 매우 중요하다.

글의 내용과 가장 잘 부합하는 것은?
① 제한된 지능이 난독증의 원인이다.
② 난독증이 있는 사람들은 책을 읽는 속도가 매우 느릴 수 있다.
③ 난독증은 임상적으로 인정된 정신 질환이다.
④ 난독증이 있는 사람은 자존감이 높은 경향이 있다.
⑤ 난독증은 사람들이 삶에 대해 느긋한 접근 방식을 취하도록 도와준다.

29 내용일치 ①

"유전자조작 작물은 식품 알레르기를 줄이기 위한 노력의 결과이다."라는 내용을 통해 ①이 정답임을 알 수 있다. ④ 모든 알레르기가 아니라 콩 알레르기가 있는 아기의 경우에 그러하다.

hives n. 두드러기, 발진 nausea n. 메스꺼움 potentially ad. 잠재적으로 fatal a. 치명적인 anaphylactic shock 아나필락시스 쇼크, 과민성 쇼크 soy n. 콩, 대두 prevalent a. (널리) 보급된, 널리 행해지는; 유행하고 있는 staple n. 주요 산물; 주요 식품 genetically engineered 유전자 공학[조작]에 의해 생성된 crop n. 농작물 formula n. 유아용 유동식, 유아용 혼합 분유 accidental a. 우연한, 우발적인 exposure n. 노출

세계 인구의 약 3%가 식품 알레르기를 가지고 있으며, 이 식품 알레르기는 두드러기, 메스꺼움, 혹은 드문 경우에는, 잠재적으로 치명적인 아나필락시스 쇼크를 유발한다. 매년 수십 명의 사람들이 땅콩을 먹고 죽는다. 콩 알레르기는 콩을 주식으로 하는 아시아 국가에 널리 퍼져 있다. 유전자조작 작물은 식품 알레르기를 줄이기 위한 노력의 결과이다. 비(非)알레르기성 작물은 콩에 알레르기가 있는 아기를 위한 콩 혼합 분유와 같은 특수 제품에 사용될 수 있다. 비알레르기성 작물을 이용하면, 공급되는 식품에 들어 있는 알레르기 물질의 전반적인 수준이 충분히 내려가게 돼서, 우발적인 노출의 위험을 제한할 수 있게 된다.

글의 내용과 가장 잘 부합하는 것은?
① 유전공학은 식품 알레르기를 줄이는 데 이용된다.
② 땅콩은 알레르기를 일으키는 가장 흔한 식품이다.
③ 대부분의 사람들은 식품 알레르기에 취약하다.
④ 알레르기가 있는 아기에게는 콩 혼합 분유를 먹인다.
⑤ 알레르기는 때때로 유아에게 치명적이다.

30 내용일치 ④

'감당할 수 있는 비용의 친환경 건물을 만들기 위해서는, 타협이 이루어져야 한다'고 한 다음, '학교들의 경우에는, 이러한 타협이 더 쉽게 이루어질 수 있다'고 했으므로 학교는 (이러한 타협을 이루어) 친환경 건물을 감당할 수 있다고 할 수 있다. 따라서 ④가 글의 내용과 일치한다. ① '햇빛의 양이 많지 않은 장소', '자연적인 수원(水原)을 접할 수 없는 장소' 등, 재생 가능 에너지가 제한된 장소에서 친환경 건물의 장기적 효율성이 떨어진다는 말이 재생 에너지 양이 대체로 제한적인 경향이 있다는 말은 아니다. ③ 본문에서 전혀 언급되지 않았다.

affordability n. 구매 용이성, 경제성 costly a. 값이 비싼, 비용이 많이 드는 long-term a. 장기적인 efficiency n. 능률, 효율 generate v. 산출하다, 발생시키다 have access to ~에게 접근[출입]할 수 있다 affordable a. (가격 등이) 알맞은, 감당할 수 있는 compromise n. 타협, 양보 durable a. 튼튼한, 내구력 있는 conservation n. (자연·자원의) 보호, 관리; 보존 ecologically ad. 생태학적으로

친환경 건물은 환경에 유익할 수도 있지만, 경제성에 실제적인 문제가 있다. 친환경 건물은 종종 비용이 너무나도 많이 들어서 대규모의 건설 방법이 될 수는 없다. 친환경 건물의 장기적인 효율성에 대해 말하자면, 햇빛의 양이 많지 않은 장소에 있는 태양 전지판은 현실적으로 그다지 많은 에너지를 생산하지 못하며, 모든 장소가 자연적인 수원(水原)을 접할 수 있는 것은 아니다. 감당할 수 있는 비용의 친환경 건물을 만들기 위해서는, 타협이 이루어져야 한다. 건물 크기가 더 작아지거나, 내구성이 더 약한 재료로 그리고 더 많은 에너지를 사용하는 기술로 만들어져야만 할 것이다. 자원 보존에 대한 개념이 교육에 유용한 학교들이나 환경을 의식한다는 면모가 유용한 마케팅 도구가 되는 기업들의 경우에는, 이러한 타협이 더 쉽게 이루어질 수 있다.

① 재생 가능 에너지의 양은 제한되는 경향이 있다.
② 친환경 건물은 자연에 해가 되는 것으로 드러났다.
③ 친환경 건물은 아름다움보다 기능을 더 중요시하는 것 같다.
④ 학교는 친환경 건물을 감당할 수 있다.
⑤ 친환경 빌딩은 전통적인 빌딩보다 더 넓다.

31 내용일치 ⑤

"그(=블랙독)는 나가라고 하면서 문을 활짝 열어두라고 명령했다. '엿보면 안 돼! 이 녀석'이라고 그가 말했고 나는 두 사람을 남겨둔 채 술집으로 물러났다. 나는 좀 엿들어보려고 한참 동안 무진 애를 썼지만 소곤거리는 소리만 들을 수 있을 뿐이었다."라는 내용을 통해 ⑤가 정답임을 알 수 있다. ① 블랙독이 그런 것 같다고 화자에게 느껴진 것이다. ② 과거에는 선장과 동료였지만 지금은 부하이다. ③ 좀 엿들어보려고 한참 동안 무진 애를 썼다. ④ 엿듣지 못하게 일부러 조용히 대화한 것이 아니라는 것은 마침내 언성이 높아진 것에서 알 수 있다.

rum n. 럼주(酒)(사탕수수·당밀(糖蜜)로 만듦) sideways ad. 옆으로, 옆쪽으로 shipmate n. 동료 선원 retreat n. 퇴각, 퇴거 bid v. 명하다, 명령하다 sonny n. 얘야, 자네, 젊은이(나이 든 사람이 청년·소년을 부르는 말) oath n. 맹세, 서약; 저주, 욕설

내가 럼주를 가지고 돌아왔을 때, 그들은 벌써 선장의 아침식사 테이블에 마주 앉아 있었다. 블랙독(Black Dog)은 문 바로 옆에 비스듬하게 앉아 있었는데, 한쪽 눈으로는 옛 동료 선원을 보고 다른 쪽 눈으로는 내 생각에 도망칠 퇴로를 보고 있는 것 같았다. 그는 나에게 나가라고 하면서 문을 활짝 열어두라고 명령했다. "엿보면 안 돼! 이 녀석"이라고 그가 말했고, 나는 두 사람을 남겨둔 채 술집으로 물러났다. 나는 좀 엿들어보려고 한참 동안 무진 애를 썼지만 소곤거리는 소리만 들을 수 있을 뿐이었다. 하지만 마침내 언성이 점점 높아지기 시작해서, 나는 선장이 한 말을 한두 마디 알아들을 수 있었는데, 대부분 욕설이었다.

글의 내용과 가장 잘 부합하는 것은?
① 화자는 언제든 도망칠 준비가 되어 있었다.
② 블랙독은 예전에 선장의 부하였다.
③ 화자는 두 선원이 한 말을 알고 싶어 하지 않았다.
④ 선장과 그의 옛 동료 선원은 엿듣지 못하도록 조용히 이야기를 나눴다.
⑤ 블랙독은 자신이 선장과 나누는 대화를 화자가 엿듣지 못하게 했다.

32-33

민주당 주지사 캐시 호철(Kathy Hochul)은 일반적으로 인간 퇴비화(堆肥化)로 알려져 있는 자연적인 유기물 환원을 합법화하는 법안에 토요일 서명했는데, 이로써 뉴욕은 미국에서 그러한 매장 방법을 허용하는 6번째 주가 되었다. 워싱턴 주는 2019년에 인간 퇴비화를 합법화한 첫 번째 주가 되었고, 2021년에 콜로라도 주와 오리건 주가, 2022년에 버몬트 주와 캘리포니아 주가 그 뒤를 이었다.
퇴비화의 과정은 다음과 같다. 고인의 시신은 나무 조각, 자주개자리, 짚과 같은 식물성 재료와 함께 재사용 가능한 용기에 넣어진다. 그 유기 혼합물은 자연적으로 발생하는 미생물이 자기 일을 할 수 있는 완벽한 서식지를 만들어내어, 약 한 달 안에 빠르고 효율적으로 시신을 분해한다.
최종적인 결과물은 영양이 풍부한 1세제곱 야드의 토양개량제 더미인데, 이는 흙 약 36자루에 상당하는 것으로, 나무를 심거나, 보존구역 땅, 숲, 혹은 정원을 비옥하게 하는 데 사용될 수 있다. 땅이 제한돼 있는 뉴욕

시와 같은 도시 지역의 경우, 그것은 꽤 매력적인 매장의 대안으로 간주될 수 있다.

뉴욕 중심부에 있는 공동묘지인 Greensprings Natural Cemetery Preserve의 관리자인 미셸 멘터(Michelle Menter)는 우리 시설에서 그 대안적인 방법을 "강력하게 고려할 것"이라고 말했다. 그녀는 "그것은 확실히 우리가 하고 있는 일과 더 일치합니다."라고 덧붙였다.

legislation n. 입법, 법률제정 legalize v. 합법화하다 natural organic reduction 자연적인 유기물 환원(인체와 자연에서 발생하는 미생물에 의해 죽은 몸을 비료로 만드는 것) human composting 퇴비장(인체와 자연에서 발생하는 미생물에 의해 죽은 사람의 몸을 비료 상태로 만드는 것) burial n. 매장 the deceased 고인 vessel n. 용기, 그릇 alfalfa n. <식물> 자주개자리 habitat n. 서식지 microbe n. 세균, 미생물 heap v. 산더미가 되다, 쌓이다 nutrient-dense a. 영양이 풍부한 soil amendment 토양 개량제 equivalent n. 동등한 것, 등가물; 상당하는 것 enrich v. (토지를) 비옥하게 하다 alternative n. 대안, 선택 가능한 것 cemetery n. 공동묘지

32 글의 제목   ②

'뉴욕 시가 인간 퇴비화를 허용한 6번째 주가 되었음을 퇴비화의 과정 및 장점과 함께 이야기하고 있는 내용이므로 제목으로는 ②가 가장 적절하다.

제목으로 가장 적절한 것은?
① 친환경 매장(埋葬)의 장점
② 뉴욕이 인간 퇴비화를 허용하다
③ 환경을 생각하는 방식으로 살아가기
④ 새로운 매장 방법을 사용하는 방법
⑤ 자연적인 유기물 환원을 합법화하는 6개국

33 내용일치   ⑤

자연적인 유기물 환원이 완료된 후에 고인의 유해를 고향으로 보낸다는 내용은 언급돼 있지 않다.

글의 내용과 부합하지 않는 것은?
① 뉴욕 시에는 고인을 안장할 여분의 땅이 많지 않다.
② 캘리포니아 주와 오리건 주는 모두 친환경 매장이 허용되는 주들이다.
③ 자연적인 유기물 환원이 완료되는 데는 약 한 달이 걸린다.
④ Greensprings Natural Cemetery Preserve의 관리자는 기꺼이 퇴비장을 도입할 것이다.
⑤ 자연적인 유기물 환원이 끝나고 나면, 고인의 유해가 마지막으로 고향으로 보내진다.

34-35

배양육(培養肉), 즉 실험실에서 배양하여 만든 고기가 실제로 얼마나 기후 친화적인지에 대해서는 의문들이 있다. 올해 초에 발표된 한 연구에 의하면, 어떤 상황에서는, 배양육이 기존의 방법으로 만든 고기보다 환경오염을 더 많이 유발할 수 있다. 배양육 산업을 옹호하는 이들은 사용되는 배양 용액의 종류와 관련하여 세운 가정이 부정확하다고 반박했다. 그들은 그 연구가 (배양육 업계가) 자원 집약적이고 의학 급 수준인 원료들을

사용한다고 가정하고 있는데, 이는 업계가 멀리 하고 있는 원료들이라고 말한다.

그러나 배양육을 지지하는 사람들도 그 기술이 많은 에너지를 사용할 것이라는 것을 인정한다. 1월에 발표된 또 다른 연구에서는, 생산한 고기 1킬로그램 당, 탱크 속에서 키운 고기가 농장에서 키운 단백질(고기)보다 훨씬 더 많은 에너지를 사용할 가능성이 있다는 사실을 발견했다. 이것은 대체로 생물반응기가 온도를 조절하기 위해 많은 전기를 필요로 하기 때문이다. 결과적으로, 배양육은 생산 과정에서 재생 에너지를 사용하는 경우에만 육류 산업의 탄소 발자국을 줄일 것이다. 그리고 그 연구에 따르면, 심지어 그 경우에도 그것은 돼지고기와 쇠고기에만 해당될 것이다.

이 모든 노력이 실험실에서 키운 고기를 소비자들이 관심을 가지게 될 만큼 충분히 매력적이고 저렴하게 만들 수 있을지는 두고 봐야 할 일이다. 그 사이에, 많은 기업들은 자사의 배양된 동물 세포에 비교적 저렴한 식물성 단백질을 혼합하는 하이브리드 전략을 추구하기로 결정했다. 일부 기업에서는 가령 소시지의 맛을 개선하기 위해 식물성 단백질에 매우 적은 양의 동물성 지방세포만을 첨가한다. 다른 기업들은 배양된 고기의 비율이 훨씬 더 클 것이다.

climate-friendly a. 기후친화적인 cultivated meat 배양육, 재배 고기(동물의 줄기세포를 배양하여 만드는 고기) conventional a. 전통적인, 재래식의 advocate n. 옹호자; 주창자 retort v. 반박하다, 응수[대꾸]하다 assumption n. 가정, 억측, 가설 growth-solution n. 배양 용액 resource-intensive a. 자원집약적인 medical-grade a. 의료 등급의, 의학적 목적으로 사용할 수 있는 수준의 ingredient n. (혼합물의) 성분; 원료; (요리의) 재료 acknowledge v. 인정하다 bioreactor n. 생물반응기 carbon footprint 탄소 발자국(기업과 국가 등이 활동이나 상품을 생산하고 소비하는 과정을 통해 발생시키는 온실가스의 총량)

34 빈칸완성   ①

"배양육은 생산 과정에서 재생 에너지를 사용하는 경우에만 육류 산업의 탄소 발자국을 줄일 것이다."는 '배양육을 생산하는 것이 기존의 방식으로 고기를 생산하는 것보다 더 많은 에너지를 필요로 하는 것'의 결과에 해당하므로, 빈칸 Ⓐ에는 As a result가 적절하다. 한편, '많은 기업들이 자사의 배양된 동물 세포에 비교적 저렴한 식물성 단백질을 혼합하는 하이브리드 전략을 추구하기로 결정한 것'은 '실험실에서 키운 고기를 소비자들이 관심을 가지게 될 만큼 충분히 매력적이고 저렴하게 만들 수 있을지'가 아직 확정적이지 않은 상황에서 일어난 일이므로, 빈칸 Ⓑ에는 In the mean time이 적절하다.

Ⓐ와 Ⓑ에 들어가기에 가장 적절한 쌍은?
① 그 결과 — 그 동안[사이]에
② 그러한 것으로서 — 극명한 대조를 이루면서
③ 그러나 — 그 때문에
④ 반면에 — 예를 들면
⑤ 당분간은 — 그럼에도 불구하고

35 내용일치   ③

"많은 기업들은 자사의 배양된 동물 세포에 비교적 저렴한 식물성 단백질을 혼합하는 하이브리드 전략을 추구하기로 결정했다."라는 내용을 통해 ③이 정답임을 알 수 있다.

글의 내용과 가장 잘 부합하는 것은?
① 배양육은 단백질 함량이 더 높아서 더 많은 에너지를 제공한다.
② 동물성 지방 세포의 추가는 돼지고기와 쇠고기 맛에만 적용된다.
③ 많은 기업들이 값이 비싸고 품질이 뛰어난 원료를 피하려 하고 있다.
④ 배양육은 탄소 배출을 줄이고 환경을 보호하려는 고객의 욕구를 충족시켜준다.
⑤ 측정 단위가 통제되고 있는 상황에서 배양육이 반드시 더 많은 에너지를 필요로 하는 것은 아니다.

36-37

슈와르츠(Schwartz)는 선물 교환이라는 일반적인 과정이 하는 기능 이상으로, 선물 자체의 특성이 받는 사람에 대한 주는 사람의 인식을 강력하게 나타내는 것으로서의 역할도 한다고 지적했다. 그는 특정한 선물의 수용은 그 선물이 내포하고 있는 것으로 간주되는 정체성을 인정하고 수용하는 것이라는 의견을 제시했다. 아이들 사이에서는 이것이 자아 인식에 있어서의 지속적인 변화로 이어질 수 있지만, 아마도 선물은 성인의 자아 개념에는 영향을 덜 미칠 것이다.
그럼에도 불구하고, 선물 선택의 이러한 상징적 역할의 중요성은 최근 한 선물 가게의 광고에서 충분히 명확하게 드러난다. 그 광고는 이렇게 묻고 있다. "당신의 선물이 상대방에게 당신이 얼마나 창의적인지, 얼마나 사려 깊은지, 혹은 그저 당신의 크리스마스 보너스가 얼마나 많았는지를 말해주길 원하십니까? 특정 가격이나 특정 성격을 염두에 두고 구매하십니까?" 선물 선택에 대한 그러한 기본적인 질문들에 대한 답이 개인적으로는 분명할 수 있지만, 그 기저에 있는 행동적 질문들은 경험적 연구에 의해 다루어지지 않았다.
선물을 주는 것이 인간의 삶과 소비자의 행동에 만연한 경험이라는 데는 의심의 여지가 거의 없으며, 현재의 연구 결과는 인지적 균형을 선호하는 것이 선물 선택과 평가를 설명하는 데 크게 효과적일 수 있는 개념임을 시사한다.

characteristic n. 특질, 특색 perception n. 지각; 인식 recipient n. 수령인, 수용자 acceptance n. 받아들임; 수락 constitute v. 구성하다, 조직하다; ~의 구성요소가 되다 acknowledgment n. 승인; 고백, 자백 identity n. 일치, 동일성 imply v. 함축하다; 암시하다, 의미하다 lasting a. 영속하는, 영구적인, 오래가는 self-perception n. 자아 인식 presumably ad. 추측상; 아마 thoughtful a. 생각이 깊은, 신중한 specific a. 일정한, 특정한 evident a. 분명한, 명백한 underlying a. 기초가 되는, 근원적인 address v. (문제를) 역점을 두어 다루다 empirical a. 경험적인 pervasive a. (특히 좋지 않은 것이) 널리 퍼지는, 침투하는 preference n. 더 좋아함, 편애 cognitive a. 인식의, 인식력이 있는 evaluation n. 평가

36 빈칸완성 ⑤

빈칸 Ⓐ의 경우, "아이들 사이에서는 이것은 자아 인식에 지속적인 변화로 이어질 수 있다."는 내용 뒤에 but이 왔으므로, 선물이 성인의 자아 개념에는 영향을 덜 미친다는 의미가 되도록 less가 들어가는 것이 적절하다. 한편, 빈칸 Ⓑ의 경우, 주절에서 "그 기저에 있는 행동적 질문들은 경험적 연구에 의해 다루어지지 않았다."고 했는데, 연구가 이뤄지지 않았다는 것은 명쾌하게 밝혀지지 않았다는 것이므로, 대조를 이뤄야 하는 While절의 빈칸 Ⓑ에는 evident가 적절하다.

Ⓐ와 Ⓑ에 들어가기에 가장 적절한 쌍은?
① 더 적은 ― 말로 나타낼 수 없는
② 더 많은 ― 설명할 수 없는
③ 더 적은 ― 애매모호한
④ 더 많은 ― 불가피한
⑤ 더 적은 ― 명백한

37 내용일치 ①

"특정한 선물의 수용은 그 선물이 내포하고 있는 것으로 간주되는 정체성을 인정하고 수용하는 것이며, 아이들 사이에서는 이것이 자아 인식에 지속적인 변화로 이어질 수 있다."는 내용을 통해 ①이 정답으로 적절함을 알 수 있다.

글의 내용과 가장 잘 부합하는 것은?
① 선물의 수용은 아이들에게 큰 영향을 미칠 수 있다.
② 대부분의 사람들은 선물을 살 때 그것이 자신의 사회적 지위를 나타내는 것으로 생각한다.
③ 후한 선물은 사람들이 사회적 기술을 더 쉽게 발전시킬 수 있게 해준다.
④ 선물의 선택과 평가는 의심의 여지없이 설명될 수 있다.
⑤ 선물 자체는 받는 사람에 대한 주는 사람의 인식을 보여주지 않는 경향이 있다.

38-40

여기서 우리는 직업에 대한 인공지능의 영향을 추적하려는 우리의 첫 번째 시도를 소개한다. 직업별 고용에 대한 미국의 데이터를 사용하여 우리는 화이트칼라 직원을 선별한다. 화이트칼라 직원에는 백오피스 지원(배후에서의 업무지원)과 금융 업무에서부터 카피라이터에 이르는 다양한 분야에서 일하는 사람들이 포함된다. 화이트칼라 직원들의 역할은 논리적 추론과 창의력에 있어서 점점 더 향상되고 있는 생성형 AI에 특히 취약한 것으로 여겨지고 있다.
그러나 아직까지 AI가 고용에 타격을 입혔다는 증거는 거의 없다. 2020년 봄, 서비스 직종에 종사하는 많은 사람들이 코로나19 팬데믹이 시작되면서 일자리를 잃음에 따라 화이트칼라 일자리가 전체에서 차지하는 비중이 늘어났다. 지금은 화이트칼라 일자리의 비중이 (그때보다) 더 낮은데, 이는 레저 및 접대 관련 부문이 회복됐기 때문이다. 그러나 지난 한 해에는 AI로 인해 위험에 처해 있을 것으로 추정된 직업에서 고용 비중이 0.5 퍼센트 포인트 상승했다.
물론 아직은 초기 단계이다. 아직 생성형 AI 도구를 대규모로 사용하고 있는 기업은 거의 없기 때문에, 일자리에 대한 영향은 그저 지체되고 있는 것뿐일 수도 있다. 그러나 또 다른 가능성은 이 새로운 기술들이 소수의 직종들만을 파괴하는 것으로 끝날 것이라는 것이다. AI가 일부 업무에서는 효율적일 수 있지만, 관리와 타인이 필요로 하는 것을 해결하는 것과 같은 다른 업무들은 덜 능숙할 수도 있다.
이 모든 상황이 어떻게 전개되는지 알아보기 위해, 우리는 몇 달에 한 번씩 이 분석에 관한 최신 정보를 발표할 예정이다. 하지만 현재로서는 일자리의 파멸은 요원해 보인다.

introduce v. 소개하다; 도입하다 impact n. 영향 employment n. 고용 occupation n. 직업 single out 선발하다, 뽑아내다 vulnerable a. 상처를 입기 쉬운; 비난[공격]받기 쉬운, 약점이 있는 generative a. 발생의, 생성적인 pandemic n. 팬데믹, 전국적[대륙적, 세계적]으로 유행하는 병 hospitality n. 환대, 후한 대접 end up ~ing 결국에는 ~이

되다   efficient a. 능률적인, 효과적인   shake out 펼쳐지다, 결론이
나다   apocalypse n. (세계의) 파멸; (성서에 묘사된) 세상의 종말; 대재앙

---

38 빈칸완성 ⑤

문단의 첫 부분에서 'AI가 고용에 타격을 입혔다는 증거는 거의 없다'라
고 했고, 바로 앞에서 '지금은 화이트칼라 일자리의 비중이 (그때보다)
더 낮다'고 한 다음 Yet으로 연결되므로, 빈칸에는 "AI로 인해 위험에 처
해 있을 것으로 추정된 직업에서 고용 비중이 '상승했다'"라는 흐름으로
이어져야 한다. 따라서 ⑤가 정답이다.

---

39 동의어 ③

apocalypse는 '세상의 종말', '(넓은 범위에 미치는) 전면적인 파괴'라는
의미이므로 '파국', '파멸', '큰 재해'라는 뜻의 catastrophe가 동의어로
적절하다.

밑줄 친 apocalypse의 뜻으로 가장 적절한 것은?
① 출현
② 발생; 기원
③ 파멸
④ 불협화음
⑤ 의존

---

40 내용일치 ②

세 번째 문단 앞 부분에서 '아직 생성형 AI 도구를 대규모로 사용하고 있
는 기업은 거의 없다'고 했으므로 ②가 정답으로 적절하다.

글의 내용과 가장 잘 부합하는 것은?
① AI 기술은 블루칼라 일자리에 영향을 미치지 않았다.
② 기업들은 아직 생성형 AI 도구를 대규모로 사용하지 않고 있다.
③ 코로나19의 대유행으로 인해 생성형 AI의 등장이 가속화되었다.
④ 카피라이터는 생성형 AI의 발달로 일자리를 잃었다.
⑤ 서비스 직종에서는 AI 활용이 비효율적인 것으로 나타났다.

01 ①	**02** ③	**03** ③	**04** ②	**05** ③	**06** ④	**07** ①	**08** ③	**09** ④	**10** ②
11 ③	**12** ①	**13** ③	**14** ④	**15** ②	**16** ④	**17** ③	**18** ④	**19** ④	**20** ④
21 ①	**22** ③	**23** ①	**24** ④	**25** ④	**26** ②	**27** ④	**28** ③	**29** ②	**30** ④
31 ④	**32** ②	**33** ①	**34** ②	**35** ②	**36** ③	**37** ①	**38** ②	**39** ③	**40** ④

01 동의어 ①

apartheid n. 아파르트헤이트(남아프리카 공화국의 인종 차별 정책) amnesty n. 대사, 특사; 사면(= absolution) conviction n. 유죄 판결; 확신, 신념 compensation n. 보상, 배상; 보수 execution n. 사형 집행, 처형; 실행

아파르트헤이트에 찬성하거나 반대하는 범죄를 저지른 사람들은 그들이 한 가지 일을 한다면 사면을 받을 수 있었는데, 그것은 그들의 범죄에 대해 진실을 말하는 것이었다.

02 동의어 ③

peregrinate v. 여행하다, 횡단하다(= traverse) nothing but 오직; 그저[단지] ~일 뿐인 commute v. 통근하다 investigate v. 조사하다, 연구하다 resonate v. 울려 퍼지다, 반향하다

배낭 하나만 메고 유럽의 한쪽에서 다른 쪽으로 횡단하는 것은 항상 나의 꿈이었다.

03 동의어 ③

companion n. 동료; (우연한) 동행자 amiable a. 상냥한 vicarious a. 대리의(= substitute) gaze v. 가만히 보다, 응시하다 unmitigated a. 누그러지지 않은, 경감되지 않은; 순전한, 완전한 elegance n. 우아, 고상 fabulous a. 굉장히 좋은, 멋진 artificial a. 인공의, 인위적인 genuine a. 진짜의; 성실한 temporary a. 일시적인, 임시의

그녀는 항상 장시간 버스 타기를 매우 즐겼는데, 그녀와 좌석에 같이 앉는 사람들이 대개 상냥한 것으로 드러났기 때문이었으며, 만약 그런 사람이 아닌 것으로 드러나면, 그녀는 멋진 거리를 따라 거의 완벽하게 우아한 것을 내다보는 것에서 대리 만족을 누렸다.

04 동의어 ②

rudimentary a. 근본의, 기본의(= fundamental) primeval a. 초기의, 원시(시대)의 truculent a. 흉포한, 잔인한; 호전적인 superficial a. 피상적인, 천박한

그들은 식단과 건강 사이의 연관성에 대해 적어도 기본적인 이해는 하고 있는 것 같다.

05 동의어 ③

exponential a. 기하급수적인, 급격한(= remarkable) widespread a. 광범위한, 널리 퍼진 availability n. 유효성, 유용성, 이용도 collateral a. 부수[부차]적인, 이차적인 expletive a. 부가적인 retardant a. 더디게 하는; 저지하는

스트리밍 및 주문형 서비스는 최근 몇 년 동안 급격한 성장을 보였는데, 이는 대체로 고속 인터넷 연결의 광범위한 가용성과 향상된 무선 연결 덕분이다.

06 동의어 ④

underrepresented a. 불충분하게 표시[대표]된(= underestimated) STEM 과학·기술·공학·수학 융합교육(Science, technology, engineering, and mathematics) unspecified a. 명시되지 않은 obviate v. (위험·곤란 등을) 제거하다 discomposed a. 침착[평정]을 잃은

왜 여성들이 공학에서, 그리고 STEM(과학, 기술, 공학, 수학) 전반에서, 그렇게 소수인지에 대한 다양한 이론들이 있다.

07 동의어 ①

perception n. 지각 (작용); 인식; 지각력 evolve v. 진화하다, 발전하다(= advance) affiliate v. 가입하다; 제휴하다 ebb v. (조수가) 빠지다; (힘 따위가) 줄다, 쇠퇴하다 elicit v. (정보·반응을 어렵게) 끌어내다

미국에서 남성과 여성에 대한 인식이 계속 변화함에 따라, 그리고 취업 시장이 진화함에 따라, 이러한 추세가 지속되는지 아니면 변화하는지를 살펴보는 것은 흥미로울 것이다.

08 동의어 ③

strategy n. 전략(= tactic) block v. 막다, 방해하다 stigma n. 치욕, 오명 discretion n. (자유)재량; 분별, 신중 camouflage n. 위장

개인의 주장 대신에 개인을 공격하는 것이 주장을 막기 위해 사용되는 전략이다.

09 동의어 ④

inject v. 주입하다 porous a. 작은 구멍이 많은, 다공성의(= spongy) disposal well 주입정 jeopardize v. 위태롭게 하다 aquatic a. 수생의 frangible a. 부서지기 쉬운, 무른 igneous a. 화성의 sedimentary a. 침전물의; 퇴적성의

대부분의 폐수는 단순히 주입정을 통해 다공성의 암반층으로 도로 주입되거나 하천계로 방출되어 수생 생태계를 위태롭게 한다.

10 동의어 ②

inexhaustible a. 다 쓸 수 없는, 무진장의(= boundless) improbable a. 있을[일어날] 성 싶지 않은; 사실 같지 않은 minimum a. 최소[최저]의, 최소한도의 explicit a. 명백한; 솔직한

흐르는 물은 계속 움직이기 때문에, 이것이 무한한 양의 에너지를 생성하고, 이 에너지는 저장되어 수요가 가장 높을 때 사용될 수 있다.

11 전치사+관계대명사 ③

빈칸 뒤에 완전한 절이 왔으므로 빈칸에는 the cause를 선행사로 받는 '전치사+관계대명사'의 형태인 ③ to which가 적절하다. dedicate는 'dedicate+목적어+to+명사'의 형태로 쓰인다.

nonprofit a. 비영리적인 n. 비영리 단체 probation n. 보호 관찰 cause n. 대의, 목적

그는 보호 관찰 기간 동안 환경 비영리 단체에서 자진하여 일하면서 그의 생애의 대부분을 바칠 대의를 찾았다.

12 분사형 전치사 given ①

given은 전치사로 뒤에 명사나 that절과 결합하여 '~이 주어지면, ~을 감안하면'이라는 뜻으로 쓰인다. 따라서 빈칸에는 뒤의 명사 its high turnover rate를 목적어로 받을 수 있는 ① given이 적절하다. ② because절의 주어 it이 the company인데 회사가 높은 이직률을 주는 것이 아니므로 분사구문으로 부적절하다.

turnover n. (기업의 직원) 이직률 run out of ~을 다 써버리다

2022년 유출된 아마존 메모는 높은 이직률을 감안할 때 단지 몇 년 안에 인력이 고갈될 것이기 때문에 회사가 확장 계획을 변경해야 한다는 것을 보여주었다.

13 주격 관계대명사 ③

두 개의 절을 연결하는 접속사의 역할을 하면서 동사 appear 앞에서 주

어 역할을 하는 관계대명사가 필요하며 선행사는 probes(조사)로 사람이 아니다. 따라서 빈칸에는 ③ which가 적절하다.

multiple a. 다수의, 다양한 probe n. 정밀 조사; (불법행위·독직 등의) 적발 조사

그는 여러 차례의 인종 조사에 직면했는데, 그 모든 조사가 취하된 것으로 보인다.

14 'as ~ as' 구문에서의 올바른 어순 ④

'as ~ as' 원급비교 구문에 가산명사가 포함되는 경우에는 'as+형용사+a(n)+단수명사+as' 혹은 'as+형용사+복수명사+as'의 형태로 쓴다. 따라서 빈칸에는 단수명사가 왔으므로 ④ as normal a life가 적절하다.

disability n. (신체적·정신적) 장애

그의 장애에도 불구하고 그는 가능한 한 정상적인 삶을 살려고 노력했다.

15 전치사+관계대명사 ②

빈칸에는 the rock을 선행사로 하는 관계대명사가 들어가야 하는데, '바위에 부딪치다'가 dash oneself against the rock이므로 ② against which가 적절하다.

portrait n. 초상화 Big Brother 독재자 colossus n. 거상(巨像); 거인, 거대한 물건 straddle v. (활동 등이) ~에 걸쳐 있다, 미치다 dash v. 내던지다 in vain 헛되이

윈스턴(Winston)은 세계를 아우른 거대한 존재이자 아시아의 무리들이 헛되이 부딪친 바위인 독재자의 초상화를 다시 올려다보았다.

16 대명사의 수일치 ③

③이 가리키는 것은 a lot of different companies이므로 이것은 복수 대명사로 받아야 한다. 따라서 ③을 themselves로 고친다.

wing it 즉흥적으로 하다 contradict v. ~과 모순되다 at the same time 동시에

다소 즉흥적으로 하고 있었기 때문에 내 경력이 어디로(어떻게 되어) 가고 있는지 정말 이해하지 못했을 때, 나는 체중 감량 알약이 동시에 들어있는 컵케이크 브랜드처럼 서로 모순되는 많은 다른 회사들과의 거래를 허가하는 일을 하곤 했다.

17 현재분사와 과거분사의 구분 ③

scientific methods는 sophisticate하는(정교하게 하는) 행위의 주체가 아닌 대상이므로 수동관계를 나타내는 과거분사로 수식해야 한다. 따라서 ③을 sophisticated로 고친다.

assistant secretary of defense(ASD) 미 국방차관보 operate v. 경영하다, 운용하다 sophisticate v. 복잡[정교]하게 하다

전 국방부 차관보인 앤드류 웨버(Andrew Weber)는 에너지부가, 여러 국립 연구소를 운영하고 있어서, 코로나19에 대한 결론을 내리기 위해 정교한 과학적 방법을 사용할 수 있었을 것이라고 말한다.

18 현재분사와 과거분사의 구분　　　④

drugs는 hide하는(숨기는) 행위의 주체가 아닌 대상이므로 수동관계를 나타내는 과거분사로 수식해야 한다. 따라서 ④를 hidden으로 고친다.

rain forest 열대 우림　potential a. 잠재적인, 가능성 있는

그는 사모아의 열대 우림이 계속 사라지면, 그곳에 숨겨져 있는 수백 개의 잠재적인 약물이 결코 발견되지 않을 수도 있다는 것을 알고 있다.

19 수동태　　　④

do의 목적어가 주어져 있지 않고 행하는 것이 아니라 행해지는 것이므로 수동태가 적절하다. 따라서 ④를 what can be done으로 고친다.

collapse n. (내각·은행 등의) 붕괴　unprecedented a. 전례 없는 guarantee v. 보증하다, ~을 확실히 하다, 보장하다　deposit n. (은행) 예금　backstop v. 지지[보좌]하다　catalyze v. ~에 촉매 작용을 미치다, 촉진시키다

실리콘밸리은행(SVB)의 파산과 예금을 보장하고 지역은행을 지원하는 바이든 행정부의 전례 없는 대응은 무엇이 잘못되었고 미래의 위기를 막기 위해 무엇을 할 수 있는지에 대한 중요하고 필요한 국가적 대화를 촉진시켰다.

20 적절한 전치사　　　④

require가 'require+목적어+전치사+명사'의 형태로 쓰일 경우 사람 앞에 전치사는 of가 적절하다. 따라서 ④를 of로 고친다.

apprentice n. 도제, 견습생　indulgence n. 응석을 받음, 관대

비록 형이었지만, 그는 자신을 나의 주인으로, 나를 그의 견습생으로 여겼고, 따라서 그가 다른 사람에게 기대하는 것과 같은 시중을 나에게 기대했던 반면에, 나는 그가 형으로부터 더 많은 관대를 기대했던 나에게 너무 많은 것을 요구한다고 생각했다.

21-23

인간의 모든 공동체는 생사가 걸린 문제에 직면해 있다. 어떻게 물을 분배할 것인가? 만약 마을, 도시, 또는 심지어 국가가 생존하려면 일부 물은 지역사회 자원으로 보유해야 한다. 많은 초기 인간 정착은 관개 시스템에 기반을 두고 있었다. 이것들은 이전의 사람들이 물이 어디로 흘러가야 하고 누구에게 흘러가야 하는지에 대해 동의했기 때문에 존재한다. 사막 지역의 우물은 여행하는 사람들 사이에서 공유 자원이 되도록 하는 문화적 전통에 의해 보호받는다. 미국의 미시간 호수와 같은 많은 큰 호수는 대부분 호숫가에 집을 소유한 사람들을 위한 것이 아니라 공공 사용을 위해 비축된다.

물 이용에 관한 법은 소수의 강력한 사람들이 모든 이용 가능한 물을 지배하지 못하게 막을 수 있다. 그러나 수자원 법은 모든 사람에게 동일한 양의 물을 자유롭게 이용할 수 있게 해주지는 않는다. 농부들은 엄청난 양의 물을 필요로 한다. 많은 산업들도 그렇다. 그러나 가정에서는 거의 그만큼 많은 양이 필요하지 않다. 또한 오염 문제도 있다. 수자원 법은 물이 모든 사용자들에게 도달하기 전에 일부 사용자들에 의한 부주의한 오염을 방지해야 한다.

문제는 정부가 법을 제정하고 시행할 만큼 충분히 강하지 않을 때 발생한다. 종종 분쟁 중인 물은 국가들 간의 (또는 주들 간의) 자원이다. 예를 들어, 동남아시아의 메콩강은 중국에서 시작하여 라오스, 캄보디아, 베트남을 통과한다. 베트남 정부는 아무리 세심한 노력을 기울이더라도 베트남에 도달하는 메콩강 물의 양과 상태를 좌우할 수 있는 통제력이 거의 없다. 상류 국가들, 특히 중국이 그것을 결정한다. 상류의 댐들이 강을 더 많이 차지함에 따라 베트남은 다른 정부와 효과적인 수자원 권리 협정을 협상할 필요성이 더 커졌다. 국제 협정은 다른 곳에서도 효과를 발휘했다. 우리는 그 협정들이 메콩강을 따라서도 효과를 낼지 살펴볼 것이다.

life-or-death a. 생사[사활]가 걸린, 매우 중대한　distribute v. 분배하다, 배급하다　settlement n. 정착, 정주　irrigation n. 관개　well n. 우물　pollution n. 오염　careless a. 부주의한　interstate a. 각 주(州) 간의, 각 주 연합의　conscientious a. 양심적인, 성실한; 세심한, 공들이는　upstream a. 상류의

21 빈칸완성　　　①

Ⓐ 농부들과 많은 산업들에게는 많은 양의 물이 필요하지만 가정에서는 그만큼 많은 양이 필요하지 않다고 했으므로 역접의 의미를 가진 however와 in contrast가 적절하다. Ⓑ 분쟁 중인 물의 한 예로 동남아시아의 메콩강의 강물을 들고 있으므로 For example이 적절하다. 따라서 상기 두 조건을 모두 만족시키는 ①이 정답이다.

다음 중 빈칸 Ⓐ와 Ⓑ에 들어가기에 가장 적절한 것은?
① 그러나 ― 예를 들어
② 게다가 ― 그러므로
③ 예를 들어 ― 그럼에도 불구하고
④ 그에 반해서 ― 반면에

22 동의어　　　③

conscientious는 '세심한, 공들이는'이라는 의미이므로 '세심한, 꼼꼼한'의 의미인 ③이 동의어로 적절하다.

위 글에 의하면, 다음 중 밑줄 친 단어 "conscientious"와 의미가 가장 가까운 것은?
① 엄격한
② 겸손한
③ 세심한
④ 태만한

23 글의 제목　　　①

전 세계적으로 중대한 문제인 물 분배에 관한 글이다. 물은 한정된 자원

으로 일부 물은 지역사회의 공유 자원으로 보유해야 하며, 효과적인 물의 배분과 오염 방지를 위해 물 이용에 관한 법이 있으며, 국제적인 물 자원 문제 등에 대해 이야기하고 있다. 따라서 ①의 '물 공유하기'가 제목으로 적절하다.

다음 중 위 글의 제목으로 가장 적절한 것은?
① 물 공유하기
② 물 오염 방지하기
③ 지역사회 자원에 대처하기
④ 물 이용에 관한 법을 시행하기

24-26

아서 키스(Arthur Keith)는 그들이 말한 많은 것들에서 틀린 것으로 밝혀진 형편없는 연구자들 중 한 명이었다. 20세기 초 저명한 해부학자이자 인류학자인 그는 과학적 인종주의의 지지자였고 인종적 혼합에 반대했다. 적어도 부분적으로는 그의 인종적 견해 때문에, 그는 인간이 현재 보편적으로 받아들여지고 있는 아프리카가 아니라 유럽에서 기원했다고 확신했다.

키스는 또한 '뇌 루비콘'으로 알려지게 된 개념을 설명했다. 인간이 다른 영장류보다 더 큰 뇌를 가지고 있다는 점에 주목하면서, 그는 인간의 지능은 우리의 뇌가 특정한 임계 크기에 도달하고 나야만 가능해진다고 주장했다. 우리가 속한 속(屬)인 호모의 경우, 그는 최소 크기는 약 600-750 입방 cm(37-46 입방 인치)라고 생각했다. 우리 종인 호모 사피엔스의 경우, 그 크기는 900 입방 cm(55 입방 인치)이었다. 더 나아가 그는 더 작은 뇌는 인간의 추론을 뒷받침할 만큼 충분한 계산 능력을 갖지 못할 것이라고 주장했다.

호모 사피엔스가 한 종으로서 큰 뇌를 가지고 있다는 것은 확실하다. 그러나 이것이 의미하는 바는 점점 더 모호해지고 있다. 유전학과 신경과학에서 뇌의 크기가 결코 지능의 전부가 아니라는 증거가 늘어나고 있다. 대신 뇌 배선도의 변화, 뉴런 모양의 변화, 그리고 심지어 특정 유전자가 언제 어디서 작동하는지의 변화가 모두 (뇌 크기보다) 더 중요하지는 않다 해도 동일하게 중요하다. 우리가 짐작했던 대로 크기가 전부는 아니다.

인간의 뇌는 뉴런이라고 불리는 약 860억 개의 특수화된 세포를 가지고 있는데, 뉴런은 서로 연결되어 신호를 주고받는다. 많은 신경과학자들은 연결 패턴의 변화가 뇌의 크기만큼 조잡한 그 어떤 것보다 인간의 인지 발달에 더 중요할 것이라고 생각한다.

misbegotten a. (계획·생각 등이) 덜된, 엉터리의, 형편없는 prominent a. 현저한, 두드러진; 저명한 anatomist n. 해부학자 anthropologist n. 인류학자 proponent n. 지지자, 옹호자 mixing n. 혼합 originate v. 비롯되다, 유래하다 cerebral a. 대뇌의, 뇌의 Rubicon n. 루비콘 강, (결정을) 돌이킬 수 없는 지점 primate n. 영장류 genus n. <생물>(분류상의) 속(屬) computational a. 계산의 murky a. 흐린; (표현 따위가) 애매한 genetics n. 유전학 far from 전혀 ~이 아닌 the be-all and end-all 전부, 가장 중요한 것 wiring diagram 배선도 specialized a. 전문의; <생물> 분화된 crude a. 천연 그대로의; 조잡한

---

24 빈칸완성   ③

At least는 '적어도, 최소한'의 의미로 어떤 주장이나 논점의 일부를 나타내는 표현과 함께 쓰여야 자연스럽다. 따라서 '부분적으로'라는 의미의 partly가 와야 하고, 뒤의 명사 his racial views를 목적어로 취할 수 있는 것은 전치사이므로 because of가 적절하다.

---

25 빈칸완성   ④

인간이 지능을 갖기 위해서는 뇌가 특정 기준 크기에 도달해야 한다는 의미가 되어야 한다. threshold(임계)는 자극에 대해 반응하기 시작하는 '기준점'이나 '한계점'을 의미하는 단어로 빈칸에 적절하다.

다음 중 빈칸 ⑧에 들어가기에 가장 적절한 것은?
① 적당한
② 근사치인
③ 최대의
④ 임계의

---

26 내용일치   ②

인간이 지능을 갖는 데 있어 뇌의 크기 외에도 뇌 배선도의 변화, 뉴런 모양의 변화, 특정 유전자가 언제 어디서 작동하는지의 변화, 연결 패턴의 변화 등 다양한 이유가 있음을 이야기하고 있다. 뇌의 크기가 인간의 지능의 전부가 아니라고 했을 뿐 중요하지 않은 것은 아니므로 ②가 옳지 않다.

위 글에 의하면, 다음 중 옳지 않은 것은?
① 인간이 아프리카에서 기원했다는 것은 보편적으로 받아들여지고 있다.
② 뇌 크기는 인간의 지능에 중요하지 않다.
③ 일부 연구자들은 뇌 세포의 연결이 지능에 있어 뇌 크기보다 더 중요하다고 제안한다.
④ 아서 키스는 과학적 인종주의를 지지했고 다른 인종을 혼합하는 것에 반대했다.

27-28

만약 우리가 하키 선수들, 비틀즈, 빌 조이, 빌 게이츠의 이야기를 종합해보면 성공으로 가는 길을 좀 더 완벽하게 알 수 있다고 생각한다. 조이와 게이츠, 그리고 비틀즈는 모두 틀림없이 재능이 있다. 레논과 맥카트니는 한 세대에 한 번 나타나는 그런 음악적 재능을 가지고 있었고, 빌 조이는 머리의 회전이 아주 빨라서 그의 교수들을 경외에 빠지게 하는 복잡한 알고리즘을 즉석에서 만들 수 있었다. 거기까지는 분명하다.

그들의 이력을 진정으로 구별 짓는 것은 그들의 비범한 재능이 아니라 그들의 비범한 기회이다. 비틀즈는 가장 무작위적인 이유로 함부르크에 초대를 받았다. 함부르크가 없었다면, 비틀즈는 다른 길을 택했을지도 모른다. "저는 운이 좋았어요."라고 빌 게이츠는 인터뷰 초반에 말했다. 그렇다고 그가 뛰어나거나 비범한 기업가가 아니라는 뜻은 아니다. 그것은 그가 1968년에 레이크 사이드에 있었던 것이 얼마나 놀라운 행운이었는지를 이해한다는 것을 의미한다.

지금까지 살펴본 모든 특별한 인물들은 일종의 특이한 기회의 수혜자들이었다. 행운은 소프트웨어 억만장자, 록 밴드, 스타 운동선수들에게도 예외가 아닌 것 같다. 그들은 규칙인 것 같다.

undeniably ad. 틀림없이 talented a. 재능이 있는 come along (사람·사물·기회 등이) 나타나다, 등장하다 complicated a. 복잡한 on the fly 급히; 쉴 사이 없이, 몹시 분주하게 awe n. 경외, 두려움 extraordinary a. 비상한, 비범한 random a. 닥치는 대로의, 되는 대로의; 무작위의 entrepreneur n. 기업가 incredible a. 믿을 수 없는; 놀랄 만한, 엄청난 good fortune 행운 outlier n. 본체에서 분리된 물건; 국외자, 문외한 beneficiary n. 수혜자 lucky break 운, 행운

27 빈칸완성　　　　　　　　④

might well have taken이 있으므로 가정의 뜻을 나타내는 표현이 빈칸에 와야 한다. 함부르크에 초대를 받지 않았다면 비틀즈의 인생은 달라졌을지 모른다는 것이므로 '~이 없다면[없었다면]'의 의미를 가지는 Without이 빈칸에 적절하다.

다음 중 빈칸에 들어가기에 가장 적절한 것은?
① ~에 더하여
② ~덕분에[때문에]
③ ~을 제외하고
④ ~이 없다면

28 내용일치　　　　　　　　③

특별한 기회의 수혜자로 하키 선수들, 비틀즈, 빌 조이, 빌 게이츠 등을 이야기하고 있으므로 ③이 적절하다. ① 빌 게이츠가 함부르크로 가는 행운을 얻은 것은 사실이지만 그렇다고 그가 뛰어나거나 비범한 기업가가 아니라는 뜻은 아니다. ② 성공하는 데 있어 중요한 요소는 재능보다 기회. ④ 비틀즈가 재능이 있는 것은 사실이지만 어떤 경우에도 성공했을지의 여부는 위 글에서 알 수 없다.

위 글에 의하면, 다음 중 옳은 것은?
① 빌 게이츠는 그다지 똑똑하지는 않았지만 뛰어난 기업가였다.
② 재능은 성공하기 위한 가장 중요한 요소다.
③ 빌 조이는 특별한 기회의 수혜자이다.
④ 비틀즈는 엄청나게 재능이 있었기 때문에 어떤 경우에도 성공했을 것이다.

29-30

팬데믹이 발생하기 위해 함께 해야 하는 몇 가지 서로 다른 요소들이 있다. 첫째, 바이러스나 박테리아가 팬데믹을 일으키려면 그것은 비교적 신종 바이러스나 박테리아여야 한다. 이것이 사실이라면, 그것은 사람들은 전체적으로 그것에 거의 노출되지 않았기 때문에 그것에 대한 생물학적 보호를 받지 못할 것이라는 것을 의미한다. 이 질병은 우리 몸에서 쉽게 인식되고 거부되지 않을 것이다. 보통 바이러스나 박테리아인 이 질병은 신체의 일부 세포에 침입한다. 바이러스나 박테리아는 그런 다음 이 세포를 사용하여 자신을 복제한다. 바이러스는 유전자 코드를 세포에 삽입함으로써 이 과정을 시작한다. 이 코드는 그다음에 잠깐 사이에 세포의 유전자 서열의 일부가 된다. 바이러스는 세포를 사용하여 새로운 바이러스를 생성한다. 박테리아는 보다 간접적인 방법이긴 하지만 유사한 과정을 시작할 수 있다. 최종 결과는 동일하다. 새로운 바이러스나 박테리아가 세포 내에서 생성된다. 결국, 숙주 세포가 포함하기에는 너무 많은 개체가 있어서 세포가 파열되고, 이러한 새로운 바이러스나 박테리아가 다른 세포를 감염시킬 수 있게 된다.

바이러스나 박테리아가 팬데믹을 일으키려면 사람에서 사람으로 쉽게 전염되는 방법이 있어야 한다. 가장 전염성이 강한 유기체는 코와 폐를 감염시키는 경향이 있다. 이는 질병에 걸린 부위에서의 신체 반응의 메커니즘인 기침과 재채기가 실제로 질병을 전염시키는 데 도움이 되기 때문이다. 바이러스나 박테리아 개체는 공기 중에 퍼지고 잇따른 희생자에게 쉽게 전달된다. 전염성이 있는 것 외에도, 바이러스가 진정으로 팬데믹을 일으키기 위해서는 지속 가능한 감염률(감염속도)을 가져야 한다. 이것은 팬데

믹에 기여하는 세 번째 요인이다. 즉, 전염병이 전염되기 매우 쉽고 즉시 치명적이지 않아야 한다. 바이러스나 박테리아가 숙주를 너무 빨리 죽여서는 안 된다. 만약 바이러스가 퍼지기 전에 사람들이 죽기 시작하면, 팬데믹은 사라질 것이다. 14세기 팬데믹의 범위는 위에서 언급한 필수 요건을 충족시켰기 때문에 파괴적이었다. 그 질병의 변형은 대부분의 사람들이 저항력이 없는 신종 하위유형이었다.

come together (하나로) 합치다　pandemic n. 전국[세계]적인 유행병　relatively ad. 비교적　force an entrance into ~에 밀고[강제로] 들어가다　replicate v. 복제하다, 모사하다　initiate v. 시작하다　insert v. 삽입하다　analogous a. 유사한　break open 깨뜨려 열다, 부수어 열다　infect v. 감염시키다　transmission n. 전염　infectious a. 전염성의, 전염병의　organism n. 유기체; 생물　cough v. 기침하다　sneeze v. 재채기하다　spread v. 만연시키다, 퍼뜨리다　successive a. 연속적인, 연이은, 잇따른　sustainable a. 지속 가능한　contribute to ~에 기여하다　deadly a. 치명적인　devastating a. 파괴적인, 황폐시키는　subtype n. 아류형; 특수형　resistant a. 저항하는; 내성(耐性)이 있는

29 글의 주제　　　　　　　　②

팬데믹이 발생하기 위해 필요한 요건에 대해 이야기하고 있다. 바이러스나 박테리아가 팬데믹을 일으키려면 신종 바이러스나 박테리아여야 하고, 전염성이 있어야 하며, 감염속도가 지속 가능해야 한다고 했다. 이러한 요건이 모두 충족되었을 때 팬데믹이 발생한다는 것이므로 위 글의 주제로 ②가 적절하다.

다음 중 위 글의 주제는 무엇인가?
① 인간을 팬데믹으로부터 보호하는 방법
② 팬데믹이 확산되는 메커니즘
③ 의료 기술의 중요성
④ 팬데믹과 다른 질병의 차이점

30 내용일치　　　　　　　　④

14세기의 팬데믹은 세 번째 요인인 전염되기 매우 쉽고 즉시 치명적이지 않아야 한다는 조건을 충족한다고 했으므로 ④가 적절하다. ①, ③ 위 글에서 언급되어 있지 않다. ② 팬데믹 바이러스나 박테리아는 신체의 일부 세포에 침입한 다음 그 세포를 사용하여 자신을 복제한다고 했으므로 적절하지 않다.

위 글에 의하면, 다음 중 옳은 것은?
① 팬데믹의 바이러스나 박테리아는 다른 질병의 바이러스나 박테리아보다 공격적이다.
② 팬데믹 바이러스나 박테리아는 세포가 복제되는 것을 막는다.
③ 팬데믹이 퍼지는 가장 쉬운 방법은 쥐와 벼룩을 통한 것이다.
④ 14세기의 팬데믹은 쉽게 전파되었고 빠른 죽음을 초래하지 않았다.

31-32

아마 틀림없이, 집단 사고는 의사 결정 과정의 효과적 계획을 통해 피할 수 있을 것이다. 팀원들이 보복의 두려움 없이 결정이나 의견에 이의를 제기할 수 있다고 느끼는 환경이 조성될 필요가 있다. 집단은 또한 결정을 내리기 전에 대안과 각 대안이 수반하는 위험에 대한 평가에서 객관적이어

야 한다. 게다가, 그들은 그들의 원래 결정의 타당성에 이의를 제기하는 정보가 밝혀질 경우 대안을 재고할 수 있을 만큼 융통성이 있어야 한다. 그렇다면 집단 사고를 피하기 위해 어떤 조치를 취할 수 있을까? 재니스(Janis)에 따르면, 한 가지 방법은 집단 내에서 '비판적 평가자'의 역할을 할 사람을 만드는 것이다. 이 사람은 본질적으로 악마의 변호사 역할을 하고, 의사 결정 과정 동안 모든 지점에서 이의나 의심을 제기한다. 리더의 역할도 중요한데, 지배적인 역할을 하기보다는 집단이 판단의 두려움 없이 원하는 방식으로 자유롭게 일할 수 있도록 회의에 적게 참석하려고 노력해야 한다. 리더는 또한 자원이 허락한다면 동일한 문제에 대해 작업하는 여러 독립적인 집단을 구성해야 하는데, 왜냐하면 이는 다양한 관점이 나타날 수 있기 때문이다. 또한 외부 전문가와 자주 상담하여 집단이 자신의 업무에 중립적인 관점을 가질 수 있도록 해야 한다.

arguably ad. (충분히) 논증할 수 있는 일이지만, 아마[거의] 틀림없이 groupthink n. 집단 사고(집단 구성원의 토의에 의한 문제 해결법); 집단 순응 사고 challenge v. 도전하다; ~에 이의를 제기하다 reprisal n. 보복, 앙갚음 assessment n. 평가 alternative n. 대안 flexible a. 융통성 있는 come to light (사람들에게) 알려지다[밝혀지다] validity n. 정당성, 타당성; 유효성, 효력 essentially ad. 본질적으로 devil's advocate 악마의 변호인; 일부러 이의를 내세우는 사람 objection n. 이의, 반대 independent a. 독립적인, 독자적인 perspective n. 관점, 시각

---

31 빈칸완성 ④

Ⓐ devil's advocate는 논의가 활발하게 이뤄지도록 일부러 반대 입장을 취하는 사람으로 이러한 역할을 하는 사람은 '비판적'이라 할 수 있으므로 critical이 적절하다. Ⓑ '비판적 평가자'의 역할을 할 사람을 만들고, 동일한 업무에 여러 독립적인 집단을 구성하는 등 다양한 관점을 얻기 위해 노력한다고 했으므로 외부 전문가를 통해 '객관적이고 공정한' 평가를 얻는다고 할 수 있으므로 impartial, balanced, neutral이 적절하다. 따라서 상기 두 조건을 모두 만족시키는 ④가 정답이다.

다음 중 빈칸 Ⓐ와 Ⓑ에 들어가기에 가장 적절한 것은?
① 지배적인 — 공정한
② 불공평한 — 균형 잡힌
③ 단정적인 — 편견을 가진
④ 비판적인 — 중립적인

---

32 내용일치 ②

리더는 집단이 판단의 두려움 없이 원하는 방식으로 자유롭게 일할 수 있도록 회의에 적게 참석해야 한다고 했으므로 ②가 옳지 않다.

위 글에 의하면, 다음 중 옳지 <u>않은</u> 것은?
① 집단 구성원들이 의견에 이의를 제기할 수 있는 환경이 조성되어야 한다.
② 리더는 다양한 의견을 듣기 위해 회의에 자주 참석해야 한다.
③ 집단은 대안과 위험에 대한 평가에서 편견이 없어야 한다.
④ 집단은 원래 결정의 타당성 문제에 직면했을 때 다른 선택사항을 고려할 수 있을 만큼 유연해야 한다.

33-35

ChatGPT는 기술 회사인 OpenAI에 의해 2022년 11월 30일 대중에게 출시되었다. 챗봇의 최첨단 버전의 기초가 되는 대형 언어 모델(LLM)인 GPT-4와 또 다른 구글의 Med-PaLM2 같은 모델들은 의료 서비스를 탈바꿈시킬 태세를 갖추고 있다. LLM이 임상 기록을 작성하고, 상환 양식을 작성하고, 그리고 의사가 진단 및 치료 계획을 세우는 것을 돕는 등의 가능성은 기술 회사와 의료 기관 모두의 마음을 사로잡았다.

LLM을 훈련하는 첫 번째 단계는 그 모델에 인터넷에서 방대한 텍스트 기반 데이터 세트를 공급하여 기본 모델을 생성하는 것이다. 이 초기 훈련 기간에는 상당한 공학 전문 지식과 방대한 컴퓨터 사용 능력이 필요하다. 사전 훈련된 모델은 그런 다음 더 높은 품질의 선별된 데이터 세트에 대해 추가로 훈련되며, 전문가는 모델의 출력이 정확하고 관련된 안전 프로토콜 및 윤리적 규범과 일치하는지 확인하기 위해 모델의 출력을 평가한다. Ⓒ 이 전문가 피드백은 심지어 모델을 더 훈련시키는 데 사용될 수 있다. 예를 들어, ChatGPT는 사용자들에게 인간과 같은 대화를 하는 경험을 제공하기 위해 세부 조정되었다. 일부 LLM은 의료 분야에서 인상적인 능력을 보여주었다.
Ⓑ 예를 들어, 작년 3월에 마이크로소프트 연구원들은 의학 전문 훈련을 받지 않은 GPT-4가 어떻게 미국 의사면허 시험을 포함한 특정 의학 시험을 통과할 수 있는지 설명했다. 7월에 우리는 임상의들이 종종 의사에 의해 생성된 것보다 GPT-4에 의해 생성된 임상 기록을 선호한다는 것을 발견한 연구를 공동 집필했다.
Ⓐ 다른 연구에 따르면 GPT-4는 신경외과 및 의학 물리학과 같은 일부 다른 전문 분야의 시험을 통과할 수 있다. 연구는 또한 힘든 질병사례를 진단하고 복잡한 수술 동의서를 환자가 쉽게 이해할 수 있는 언어로 번역하는 데 있어 LLM의 인상적인 능력을 보여주었다.

그러나 임상 실습의 효율성을 개선하고 환자의 경험을 향상시키며 의료 결과를 예측하는 LLM의 장래성에도 불구하고, 그들을 의료 환경에서 사용하는 데 상당한 어려움이 있다. LLM은 종종 착각을 일으키는데, 이는 잘못된 설득력 있는 출력이다. 예를 들어, 새로운 바이러스가 발생하기 때문에 상황이 바뀌면 모델의 지식 기반(훈련 데이터의 산물)이 비용이 많이 드는 재훈련 없이 어떻게 업그레이드될 수 있는지 아직 명확하지 않다.

release v. 공개[발표]하다 underlie v. 기초가 되다, 근거에 있다 transform v. 변형시키다; 완전히 바꿔 놓다[탈바꿈시키다] poise v. (~의) 준비를 하다, (~할) 각오를 하다 clinical a. 임상(치료, 진찰)의 reimbursement n. 변제, 상환 diagnosis n. 진단 captivate v. ~의 마음을 사로잡다[매혹하다] initial a. 처음의, 최초의, 초기의 expertise n. 전문 지식[기술] curated a. 전문적인 식견으로 엄선한 specialist n. 전문가 assess v. 평가하다 output n. 출력 accurate a. 정확한; 정밀한 align v. 정렬하다 relevant a. (당면한 문제에) 관련된; 적절한 fine-tune v. ~을 (미세) 조정하다 impressive a. 인상적인 co-author v. 공동 집필하다 neurosurgery n. 신경외과(학) diagnose v. 진단하다 challenging a. 도전적인; 힘든 promise n. (밝은) 전망, 가망, 장래성 deploy v. 배치하다; 효율적으로 사용하다 hallucination n. 환각; 환영; 망상, 착각 circumstance n. (보통 pl.) 상황, 환경

---

33 빈칸완성 ①

LLM은 임상 기록을 작성하고, 상환 양식을 작성하고, 의사가 진단 및 치료 계획을 세우는 것을 도울 수 있다고 했으므로 의학 분야에서 활용할 수 있는 기술이다. 따라서 LLM을 만들어낸 기술 회사와 LLM을 이용하여 도움을 얻을 수 있는 의료 기관에서 관심을 보일 것이다.

다음 중 빈칸에 들어가기에 가장 적절한 것은?
① 기술 회사와 의료 기관
② 건강 교육과 임상 센터
③ OpenAI와 구글
④ 공공 기관과 사기업

34 글의 주제 ②

생성형 인공지능 모델인 LLM을 의료 분야에서 활용할 수 있는 여러 가지 가능성을 언급하고, 의료 분야에서 LLM를 사용하는 데 있어 잘못된 정보를 생성하거나 업그레이드 등의 문제에 대해 이야기하고 있다. 따라서 위 글의 주제로 ②가 적절하다.

다음 중 위 글의 주제는 무엇인가?
① 의료 분야에서 대형 언어 모델(LLM)의 효율적인 훈련
② 생성형 인공지능을 의료 분야에 적용하는 것의 가능성과 과제
③ 마이크로소프트가 보여주는 의료 사업에서 ChatGPT의 유망한 미래
④ 의료 분야에서 적용되는 ChatGPT에 의해 생성되는 환각 결과

35 단락배열 ②

전문가들이 LLM 모델을 평가하는 내용을 This expert feedback로 받고 있는 C가 가장 먼저 오고, LLM이 의료 분야에서 인상적인 능력을 보여주는 한 예로 마이크로소프트 연구원들의 연구를 설명한 B가 그다음에 오고, 이와 비슷한 결과를 보여주는 다른 연구의 사례를 들고 있는 A가 B 뒤에 와야 한다.

36-37

늑대와 개는 사회적이고 공격적인 행동이 비슷하다. 두 종 모두 집단 사냥꾼이었다. 그들은 더 큰 동물들을 죽이기 위해 팀을 이루어 사냥을 해야 했다. 늑대들은 리더가 있고, 다른 모든 늑대들은 그를 따른다. 늑대 무리의 리더는 보통 무리의 다른 늑대들보다 더 강하다. 만약 다른 늑대가 장악하려고 한다면, 그 늑대는 무리에서 제거될 수 있다. 늑대들은 살아남기 위해 무리를 지어 이동하고 사냥해야 한다. 이것을 사회적 질서라고 한다. 사회적 질서가 없으면 늑대들은 서로 싸울 것이다. 늑대들은 야생에서 협력해야 한다. 그렇지 않으면, 그들은 살아남을 수 없을 것이다.
개들은 그들의 가정에서 비슷한 사회적 질서를 가지고 있다. 엄마와 아빠가 리더이고, 새끼들은 그들을 따라야 한다. 동일한 사회적 질서는 썰매 끄는 개에서도 볼 수 있다. 무리에서 가장 강한 개가 리더이며 앞에서 썰매를 끈다. 리더는 썰매를 끄는 다른 개들에게 지시를 내린다. 팀워크가 썰매를 끄는 유일한 방법이므로 다른 개들은 리더를 따라야 한다.
영역은 늑대와 개에게 또 다른 중요한 요소다. 두 동물 모두 자신의 영역을 지키기 위해 싸울 것이다. 그들은 심지어 그들의 영역을 위협하는 다른 동물들을 죽일 것이다. 인간은 개들이 이런 행동을 하도록 훈련시킬 수 있었다. 개들은 낯선 사람들로부터 집을 보호하고 경비견이 되도록 훈련받는다. 오늘날의 현대의 개들은 늑대처럼 울부짖지 않는다. 그러나 개들은 화가 났을 때 여전히 같은 공격의 징후를 보인다. 늑대처럼, 개들은 싸울 준비가 되어있거나 위협을 감지할 때 이빨을 드러낼 것이다.

aggressive a. 침략적인, 공격적인 pack n. (사냥개·이리 등의) 떼, 무리 survive v. 살아남다, 생존하다 sled n. 썰매 give instructions to ~에게 명령하다 territory n. 영토, 영지; (행동·사상 등의) 영역, 분야

---

threaten v. 위협하다, 협박하다 guard dog 경비견 howl v. (개·늑대 따위가) 멀리서 짖다, 소리를 길게 뽑으며 짖다 aggression n. 공격, 침략; 공격성 anger v. 화나게 하다 threat n. 위협, 협박

36 내용일치 ③

현대의 개는 위협받을 때 공격의 징후로 이빨을 드러내긴 하지만 늑대처럼 울부짖지는 않는다고 했으므로 늑대와 개 모두 울부짖는다는 ③은 옳지 않다.

위 글에 의하면, 다음 중 옳지 않은 것은?
① 늑대와 현대의 개 모두 공격의 징후로 이빨을 드러낸다.
② 개들은 그들의 영역이 위협받을 때 다른 동물들을 죽일 수 있다.
③ 늑대와 현대의 개 모두 자신의 영역을 지키기 위해 울부짖는다.
④ 가장 강한 늑대는 사회적 질서에서 무리의 리더.

37 빈칸완성 ①

늑대는 살아남기 위해 무리를 지어 이동하고 사냥해야 하는 군거성 동물이라고 했는데, 빈칸 뒤에서 살아남을 수 없다고 했으므로 무리를 지어 협력하지 않는 반대의 경우를 가정하는 otherwise가 빈칸에 적절하다.

다음 중 빈칸에 들어가기에 가장 적절한 것은?
① 그렇지 않으면
② 따라서
③ 그럼에도 불구하고
④ 최후로

38-40

에어비앤비는 시작된 이후 15년 만에 여행 산업의 핵심이 되었다. 그러나 한때 저렴한 옵션으로 여겨졌던 에어비앤비의 가격은 플랫폼이 점점 더 인기를 얻으면서 서서히 오르기 시작했다. 공유 숙박 주거시설을 분류하는 All The Rooms에 따르면 에어비앤비의 전 세계 평균 가격은 2020년 1박에 110달러에서 2021년 137달러로 올랐다. 2월에 에어비앤비는 2022년 4분기 평균 일일 요금(ADR)을 153달러라고 말했다. 한편, 2022년 4분기에 힐튼은 ADR이 151.81달러, 인터컨티넨탈 호텔 그룹은 ADR이 125.58달러라고 보고했다. 가격은 전반적으로 상승하고 있지만 호텔과 에어비앤비 사이의 격차는 좁혀지고 있다.
에어비앤비의 한 대변인은 "에어비앤비는 종종 더 많은 공간과 편의시설을 제공하며" 그 가격은 여전히 일부 주요 호텔 체인의 가격보다 낮다고 말한다. 그러나 1박 또는 2박을 묵을 숙소를 찾는 여행자들에게 에어비앤비의 좁혀지고 있는 가격 우위와 리셉션 및 정기적인 청소와 같은 특정 호텔에서 누릴 수 있는 호사스러움의 부족은 단점이다.
호텔이 독립적인 임대보다 더 나은 거래를 제공하기 시작하므로, 재정 형편을 너무 나쁘게 하지 않는 훌륭한 숙박 장소를 찾는 방법을 이제 소개하겠다.

inception n. 처음, 시작, 개시 vacation-rental property 민박시설, 숙박시설 bread and butter 생계 (수단), 호구지책; 필수적인 것 creep up (양·가격 등이) 서서히 오르다 across the board 전반적으로, 일률적으로 spokesperson n. 대변인 amenity n. (pl.) 쾌적한 설비[시설], 문화적 설비 luxury n. 사치, 호사; 사치품; 즐거움, 쾌락 dent v. 움푹

들어가게 하다; 손상시키다, 약화시키다 pocketbook n. (개인·국가의) 재정 형편[경제 사정]

---

38 글의 주제

한때 저렴한 가격으로 인기를 얻었던 에어비앤비가 가격이 상승하면서 호텔 가격과 격차가 좁혀지면서 호텔에 사람들의 관심이 점점 더 커지고 있다는 것이 위 글의 주된 내용이다. 따라서 ②가 정답이다.

다음 중 위 글을 가장 잘 요약한 것은?
① 저가 에어비앤비의 붕괴가 시작된다.
② 에어비앤비 가격이 상승함에 따라 호텔이 사람들로부터 더 많은 관심을 끌 수 있다.
③ 호텔 체인들은 단기 여행자들에게 합리적인 요금을 제공하기 시작한다.
④ All The Rooms를 사용하여 최고의 공유 숙박 장소를 찾을 수 있다.

---

39 빈칸완성

Ⓐ 역접의 접속사 but이 있으므로 서로 반대되는 내용이 되어야 한다. 에어비앤비 가격이 오르고 있다고 했으므로 빈칸에는 가격이 '비싸지 않다'는 의미의 reasonable, affordable, economical이 적절하다. Ⓑ 에어비앤비가 가격이 오르면서 호텔 가격과 별로 차이가 나지 않고 호텔에서 누릴 수 있는 특급 서비스의 부족은 에어비앤비의 '단점'이라 할 수 있으므로 flaws, drawbacks가 적절하다. 따라서 상기 두 조건을 모두 만족시키는 ③이 정답이다.

다음 중 빈칸 Ⓐ와 Ⓑ에 들어가기에 가장 적절한 것은?
① 창조적인 ― 결점
② 비싸지 않은 ― 이익
③ 알맞은 ― 단점
④ 경제적인 ― 이점

---

40 뒷내용 추론

마지막 문장에서 재정적으로 너무 부담을 주지 않는 훌륭한 호텔을 찾는 방법이 있다고 하였으므로 위 글 다음에 올 수 있는 내용으로 ④ '훌륭한 호텔을 더 현명하게 예약하는 방법'이 적절하다.

다음 중 위 글 다음에 올 수 있는 가장 적절한 주제는 무엇인가?
① 호텔에서 좋은 편의시설을 찾는 방법
② 한정된 예산으로 여행하는 방법
③ 더 나은 서비스로 에어비앤비를 운영하는 방법
④ 훌륭한 호텔을 더 현명하게 예약하는 방법

2024 단국대학교(인문계 오후)

01 ④	02 ③	03 ①	04 ③	05 ④	06 ②	07 ④	08 ③	09 ②	10 ③
11 ①	12 ③	13 ②	14 ①	15 ④	16 ②	17 ②	18 ③	19 ①	20 ①
21 ③	22 ①	23 ④	24 ②	25 ②	26 ④	27 ③	28 ④	29 ③	30 ①
31 ②	32 ①	33 ④	34 ④	35 ③	36 ④	37 ②	38 ③	39 ①	40 ④

01 동의어 ④

at risk 위험에 처한   scarcity n. 부족, 결핍   exacerbate v. 악화시키다(= aggravate)   mitigate v. 완화시키다, 누그러뜨리다   edify v. 교화하다   oscillate v. 진동시키다; 동요시키다

연구에 따르면, 전 세계 인구의 약 3분의 1이 물 부족으로 위험에 처해 있으며, 인구 증가는 문제를 악화시키고 있을 뿐이다.

02 동의어 ③

aphid n. 진딧물   grasshopper n. 메뚜기   gall wasp 혹벌   Cretaceous n. (the C-) 백악기[층]   eusocial a. (곤충 등이) 완전히 사회성의, 진(眞)사회성의   integral a. 필수적인, 필요불가결한(= essential)   ecology n. 생태학; 생태 환경; 생태   flowering plant 현화식물   additional a. 부가적인, 추가의   prosperous a. 번영하는   counterproductive a. 역효과를 낳는

진딧물, 메뚜기, 그리고 혹벌은 백악기에 출현했고, 진화한 또 다른 중요한 곤충은 현화식물의 생태와 진화에 필수적인 사회성 벌이었다.

03 동의어 ①

pluck n. 용기, 결단, 결의   magnanimous a. 도량이 넓은, 관대한(= indulgent)   spectacular a. 구경거리의; 화려한   magnificent a. 장엄한   conform v. 따르다, 순응하다; 적합[순응]시키다

그녀의 용기는 새 대통령이 아마도 그 날의 그의 유일한 관대한 몸짓으로 보낸 감사의 보상을 받았다.

04 동의어 ③

rambling a. 산만한, 두서없는, 종작없는   erudite a. 학식 있는, 박식한(= scholarly)   sparkling a. 재기 넘치는, 번득이는   teeming a. 가득찬, 많은, 우글거리는   strait a. 좁은, 답답한; 엄중한   loquacious a. 말이 많은, 수다스러운

그러한 때에 이야기가 산만할 수도 있지만 이야기는 항상 박식했고 아이디어로 번득였다.

05 동의어 ④

pensive a. 생각에 잠긴, 수심 어린(= musing)   piece n. (장기·체스 따위의 졸 이외의) 말   panic a. (공포 따위가) 당황케 하는, 제정신을 잃게 하는   redolent a. 향기로운; ~을 생각나게 하는, 상기시키는   inflated a. 부푼, 팽창한; 과장된

체스 선수는 어떤 말을 움직일지 결정하려고 애쓰면서 생각에 잠긴 것처럼 보였다.

06 동의어 ②

vehicle n. 수송 수단(자동차·열차·선박·항공기·우주선 등)   collision n. 충돌   micrometeoroid n. 미소 유성체, 유성진(流星塵)   space junk 우주 쓰레기   riddled a. (~으로) 가득 찬(= filled)   crater n. 분화구; (달 표면의) 크레이터   consort v. 일치하다, 조화하다   depurate v. 정화하다   proliferate v. 증식하다; 급증하다

시간이 지남에 따라 우주 쓰레기를 크레이터로 가득 차게 만드는 그런 종류의 미소 유성체들과의 충돌을 우주선이 피할 수 있을 것 같지는 않다.

07 동의어 ④

height n. (the ~) 절정, 극치   demise n. 사망, 서거; 소멸, 종말(= quietus)   manifestation n. 명시, 표명   niche n. 적합한 지위, 적소; (시장의) 틈새   shroud n. 수의(壽衣); 덮개, 장막

그 기원부터 당나라 시대의 절정을 거쳐 서서히 소멸할 때까지 실크로드는 외교 관계에서 독특한 역할을 했다.

08 동의어 ③

indelible a. 지울 수 없는, 지워지지 않는(= inexpungible)   embroider v. 수를 놓다, 자수하다   impermeable a. 통과시키지 않는, 불침투성의   erasable a. 지울 수 있는   murky a. 어두운, 음침한; 흐린

대부분의 19세기 서명은 지워지지 않는 잉크로 쓰였지만 20세기에는 서명이 종종 수놓아졌다.

09 동의어　　②

mercury n. 수은　concentrated a. 집중된; 농축된　sterile a. 불임의, 새끼를 낳지 못하는(= unprolific)　intoxicated a. 술 취한; 흥분한, 들떠 있는　amorphous a. 무정형의　dislocate v. 탈구시키다; 혼란시키다

물고기에 농축되는 너무 많은 수은은 성체 독수리가 물고기를 먹을 때 성체 독수리를 불임이 되게 할 수 있다.

10 동의어　　③

empirical a. 경험적인, 경험[실험]상의(= observed)　thorough a. 철저한, 완전한　survey n. 조사, 검사　reliable a. 믿을[신뢰할] 수 있는　theoretical a. 이론적인　qualitative a. 질적인

그는 주요 문제를 경험적 자료의 부족인 것으로 간주하며, 보다 철저한 조사가 매우 중요하다고 주장한다.

11 선행사를 포함한 관계대명사 what　　①

inherent부터 observed까지 앞의 명사 the subjectivity를 수식하는 것으로 동사 capture의 목적어가 필요하다. capture의 목적어가 없으므로 선행사를 포함하는 관계대명사로 명사절을 이끄는 역할을 하는 what이 적절하다. 따라서 ① what is가 정답이다.

advent n. 출현, 도래　photography n. 사진술; 사진 촬영　prospect n. 전망　subjectivity n. 주관성　inherent a. 내재된, 고유의

19세기 사진술의 출현과 더불어, 관찰되는 것을 포착하기 위해 단어나 그림을 사용하는 것에 내재된 주관성이 극복될지도 모른다는 전망이 나왔다.

12 미래완료시제　　③

and 다음의 'by the time he(주어)+arrives(동사)'에서 arrives는 미래를 대신한 현재시제이므로 빈칸에는 미래완료시제가 와야 한다. 따라서 ③ will have finished가 정답이다.

tidy v. 정돈하다, 정리하다

날이 어두워지고 있고, 그가 LA에 도착할 때는 이미, 그녀는 그곳에서 새로 이사한 집을 정리하는 일을 마쳤을 것이다.

13 적절한 비교급 관용표현　　②

not more than(많아야=at most)과 not less than(적어도=at least)은 주로 수사 앞에서 쓰이므로 ①, ③을 먼저 정답에서 제외할 수 있다. 문맥상 아기에 불과하다는 의미로 a baby를 강조하여 수식하는 표현이 적절하므로 '단지 ~에 지나지 않다, ~일 뿐(= only)'의 뜻의 ② no more than이 정답이다. no less than은 '~와 같은, ~나 다름없는'의 뜻이다.

scanty a. 부족한, 불충분한　take ~ for granted ~을 당연한 일로 생각하다　betrothal n. 약혼

존(John)은 그녀보다 8살 더 많았고, 결국 그들이 결혼할 것이라고 당연하게 생각했지만 수년 동안 그녀에게 관심은 충분히 기울이지 않았는데, 그가 아직 아이였고 주디스(Judith)가 아기에 지나지 않았을 때 약혼 서류에 서명했던 것이다.

14 가정법 과거완료의 도치 구문　　①

주절의 동사가 'would+have+p.p.'인 것으로 보아 과거 사실에 반대되는 가정을 나타내는 가정법 과거완료 구문임을 알 수 있다. 따라서 if절은 'If+주어+had+p.p'가 되어야 하는데, If를 생략하면 'had+주어+p.p.'의 어순으로 도치된다. 따라서 ① had he possessed가 정답이다.

poetic a. 시적인　faculty n. 능력, 재능　utterly ad. 완전히　destitute a. ~이 없는　want n. 부족, 결핍

우리가 판단할 수 있는 한, 그가 완전히 결핍했던 시적인 재능을 그가 가지고 있었더라도, 언어 능력의 부족은 그가 위대한 시인이 되는 것을 막았을 것이다.

15 현재분사와 과거분사의 구분 / 'so ~ that' 도치 구문　④

'너무 ~해서 …하다'라는 의미의 'so ~ that' 구문인데 be동사의 보어인 'so ~'가 문두로 나갈 경우 주어와 동사가 도치된다. 그리고 engross와 같은 감정동사는 사람이 주어이거나 감정의 대상일 경우 과거분사를 쓰고, 사물이 주어이거나 감정을 유발하는 경우 현재분사를 쓴다. 주어가 사람으로 대상이므로 과거분사 형태인 engrossed가 적절하다. 따라서 상기 두 조건을 모두 만족시키는 ④ So engrossed was Jenny가 정답이다.

engrossed a. 몰두한, 열중한　consciousness n. 의식, 자각

제니(Jenny)는 너무 몰두해서 감시당하고 있다는 것을 의식하지 못했고 감정이 잇따라 그녀의 얼굴에 스며들었다.

16 수량형용사의 용법　　②

money는 불가산명사이므로 가산명사와 함께 쓰이는 a number of는 적절하지 않다. 따라서 불가산명사와 함께 쓰여서 '다량의, 많은'의 의미를 가지는 an amount of나 a great deal of로 고친다.

venture n. 모험; 투기적 사업[기업]　in the wake of ~에 뒤이어; ~의 결과로서　setback n. 좌절, 차질　file for ~을 신청[제기]하다　creditor n. 채권자　bankruptcy n. 파산

마크 트웨인(Mark Twain)은 사업에 투자해서 많은 돈을 잃었고, 이러한 재정적 차질 이후 그는 파산을 통한 채권자로부터의 보호를 신청했다.

17 문의 구성　　②

like는 '~처럼'이라는 뜻의 전치사로 뒤에 명사가 오는데 절의 형태가 와서 적절하지 않다. 따라서 ②의 stalls를 앞의 명사 mammoth를 수식할 수 있는 표현으로 고쳐야 하는데 mammoth는 stall하는 행위의 대상이므로 수동을 나타내는 과거분사 stalled가 적절하다.

permafrost n. 영구 동토층　stall v. 오도가도 못하게 하다　prehistoric a. 선사 시대의　alpine glacier 고산 빙하　mummy n. 미라

그것은 시베리아 영구 동토층에 갇힌 3만 년 된 매머드의 피부나 이탈리아-오스트리아 국경의 고산 빙하에 자연적으로 보존된 5천 년 된 미라인 유명한 선사 시대의 빙하 인간처럼, 매우 특이한 경우에만 흔적을 남긴다.

18 서술적 용법으로 쓰이는 형용사 willing　　③

형용사 willing은 '기꺼이 ~하는'의 뜻의 서술적 용법으로 쓰일 경우 뒤에 to부정사가 온다. 따라서 ③의 taking risks를 to take risks로 고친다.

brain damage 뇌 손상　be willing to do 기꺼이 ~하다　take a risk 위험을 무릅쓰다[감수하다]　frightened a. 두려움을 느끼는, 무서워하는

뇌 손상을 입은 15명의 사람들이 일부 대학 연구원들에 의해 수행된 연구에 참여했으며, 뇌 손상을 입은 그 15명의 사람들은 다른 사람들보다 기꺼이 위험을 감수했다. 즉, 뇌 손상을 입은 사람들은 시도가 실패했을 때 두려움을 느끼지 않았다.

19 복합분사의 형태　　①

명사, 형용사, 부사가 하이픈을 통해 분사와 결합하여 형용사처럼 쓰이는 복합분사에서 어떤 분사를 쓸 것인가는 수식받는 명사와의 관계에 의해 결정되는데, 수식받는 명사가 행위의 주체이면 현재분사를 쓰고 행위의 대상이면 과거분사를 쓴다. wagons는 draw하는 행위의 대상이므로 ①을 과거분사를 사용한 복합분사인 horse-drawn으로 고친다.

horse-drawn a. 말이 끄는　wagon n. 짐마차(보통 4륜으로 2마리 이상의 말이 끎)　battlefield n. 싸움터, 전장

남북전쟁 동안 말이 끄는 마차는 전장에서 부상당한 병사들을 우리가 병원이라고 부르는 곳으로 이송하는 구급차 역할을 했고, 당시의 기준으로도 일부 군의관과 '병원'은 다른 군의관과 병원보다 훨씬 열악했다.

20 현재완료시제　　①

'since+과거시점'이 있으므로 동사의 시제는 현재완료시제가 되어야 한다. 주어가 Hundreds of years로 복수이므로 동사의 수를 일치시켜 ①을 have passed로 고친다.

흑사병 이후 수백 년이 지났지만 그 시대에 등장한 특별한 예술 장르는 오늘날에도 여전히 유명하며, 유화, 악곡 등을 포함한 예술 작품들은 예술가들이 무엇에서든, 심지어 죽음에서도 아름다움을 창조할 수 있다는 것을 우리에게 상기시킨다.

21-23

가장 고대의 보편적 조화의 원리인 소우주와 대우주의 조화는 오랫동안 가장 위엄 있는 것이었다. 인간의 세계는 물리적 세계를 반영하고 이 원리를 분명히 나타낸다. 더 나아가, 동일한 패턴은 물리적, 화학적, 생물학적, 심리적, 신학적 등 존재의 모든 수준에서 사물 간의 관계를 열거한다. 하늘에서처럼 땅에서도 그러하며 인간 사이에서처럼 천사들 사이에서도 그러하다.

이 관점의 묘한 매력 — 단일한 패턴이 모든 수준에서 나타나는 것 — 의 맛은 오늘날에도 여전히 프랙탈의 매력에 남아 있다. 이러한 기하학적 도형의 많은 예는 그 자체의 더 작은 내장된 이미지가 포함되어 있으며, 이 이미지에는 여전히 더 작은 내장된 이미지가 포함되어 있고, 이런 식으로 무한히 반복된다. 잘 알려진 프랙탈인 1915년 폴란드 수학자 바츠와프 시에르핀스키(Waclaw Sierpinski)가 설명한 삼각형을 살펴보자. 바깥쪽의 삼각형 경계 내에서 다음으로 큰 세 개의 삼각형 각각이 전체의 정확한 사본이라는 것을 알 수 있다. 따라서 동일한 삼각형 구조는 높고 낮음, 크고 작음의 모든 규모에서 반복된다. 가장 작은 삼각형은 없다. 단순한 3면 반복과 소형화로 점점 더 작은 모양들이 무한히 생성된다. 그것은 우주를 만드는 가장 우아한 방법이다. 옛날에 이것은 수학적 호기심일 뿐 아니라 모든 창조의 비밀로 여겨졌다.

microcosm n. 소우주　macrocosm n. 대우주　commanding a. 지위하는; 위엄 있는　reflect v. 반영하다　proclaim v. 선언하다; 분명히 나타내다　marshal v. 늘어놓다, 열거하다; 정리하다　theological a. 신학적인　charm n. 매력　impose v. (자기 존재나 생각을) 내세우다[받아들이게 하다]　linger v. 남다, 좀처럼 없어지지 않다　fascination n. 매혹; 매력　fractal n. <수학·물리> 프랙탈, 차원 분열 도형(산의 기복·해안선 등 아무리 세분해도 똑같은 구조가 나타나는 도형)　geometrical a. 기하학(상)의, 기하학적인　embedded a. 내장된　triangular a. 삼각형의　repeat v. 되풀이하다, 반복하다　infinity n. 무한대　diminutive a. 작은, 소형의　iteration n. 되풀이, 반복　miniaturization n. 소형화

21 빈칸완성　　③

가장 고대의 보편적 조화의 원리라고 했으므로 harmony와 유사한 뜻의 단어가 빈칸에 와야 한다. 따라서 '조화'라는 뜻의 ③ consonance가 적절하다.

다음 중 빈칸에 들어가기에 가장 적절한 것은?
① 개요
② 상속
③ 조화
④ 시선

22 동의어　　①

ad infinitum은 '무한히, 끝없이'라는 의미이므로 ①이 동의어로 적절하다.

다음 중 밑줄 친 단어 "ad infinitum"과 의미가 가장 가까운 것은?
① 끊임없이
② 간헐적으로
③ 탁월하게; 초자연적으로
④ 일시적으로

23 내용일치 ④

바츠와프 시에르핀스키는 원형이 아니라 삼각형 즉, 프랙탈을 제시하여 보편적 조화의 원리를 정당화했다고 할 수 있다. 따라서 ④가 옳지 않다.

위 글에 의하면, 다음 중 옳지 않은 것은?
① 가장 고대의 보편적 조화의 원리는 프랙탈에서 볼 수 있다.
② 소우주와 대우주 사이의 조화로운 관계는 모든 창조의 비밀로 여겨졌다.
③ 보편적 조화의 원리는 고대부터 사람들을 매료시켰다.
④ 바츠와프 시에르핀스키는 하나의 원형 도형을 제시함으로써 보편적 조화의 원리를 정당화했다.

24-25

미시간 대학 로스쿨은 다른 많은 미국 교육기관과 마찬가지로 불리한 배경을 가진 지원자들에 대해 차별 철폐 조치 정책을 사용한다. 미시간 대학에 매년 가을 입학하는 학생 중 약 10퍼센트가 소수 인종의 구성원이며, 로스쿨이 그 학생들에 대한 입학 요건을 크게 완화하지 — 다른 모든 학생들보다 낮은 성적에 입학을 허가하지 — 않는다면 그 비율은 3퍼센트 미만이 될 것으로 추정하고 있다. 게다가, 우리가 로스쿨에서 소수 민족 학생들과 비소수 민족 학생들이 받는 성적을 비교해보면 백인 학생들이 더 잘한다는 것을 알 수 있다. 그것은 놀랍지도 않다. 한 집단이 다른 집단보다 학부 성적과 시험 성적이 높다면 로스쿨에서도 성적이 더 높을 것이 거의 확실하다. 이것이 차별 철폐 조치 프로그램이 최근 미국 대법원까지 가게 된 이유 중 하나다. 엘리트 교육 기관이 또래들보다 자격이 부족한 학생들을 입학시키는 것은 많은 사람들에게 마음 불편한 일이다.

그러나 몇 년 전 미시간 대학은 로스쿨의 소수 민족 학생들이 졸업 후 어떻게 일을 해냈는지 자세히 살펴보기로 결정했다. 그들은 실제 성공의 지표가 될 수 있는 모든 것을 살펴보았다. 그리고 그들이 발견한 것은 그들을 놀라게 했다.

"우리는 소수 민족 학생들 중 많은 학생들이 잘 하고 있다는 것을 알고 있었습니다."라고 미시간 연구의 저자 중 한 명인 리처드 렘퍼트(Richard Lempert)는 말한다. "저는 우리가 그들 중 절반 또는 3분의 2가 백인 학생들만큼 잘 하지는 못했다는 것을 발견할 것이라고 기대했지만, 그럼에도 불구하고 많은 학생들이 꽤 성공하였습니다. 하지만 우리는 완전히 놀랐습니다. 우리는 그들이 전적으로 잘 하고 있다는 것을 발견했습니다. 어디서도 심각한 차이를 찾아볼 수 없었습니다." 렘퍼트가 말하고자 하는 것은 로스쿨이 실제로 신경 써야 하는 기준 — 졸업생들이 실제 세계에서 얼마나 잘 하는지 — 에서 판단해 보면 소수 민족 학생들은 자격이 부족하지 않다는 것이다. 그들은 백인 학생들만큼 성공하고 있는 것이다.

affirmative action 차별 철폐 조치, 소수 민족 우대정책 when it comes to ~에 관한 한 applicant n. 지원자 disadvantaged a. 불리한 조건을 가진; (사회적·경제적으로) 혜택받지 못한 minority n. 소수 민족 [집단] significantly ad. 상당히, 크게 relax v. 완화하다 peer n. 동료, 또래 fare v. (사람이 잘·잘못) 살아가다, 지내다 conceivably ad. 생각되는 바로는, 상상으로는, 생각건대 every bit 전부, 모두; 어느 모로 보나, 전적으로 graduate n. 졸업생

24 빈칸완성 ②

미시간 대학의 연구자들은 소수 민족 학생들이 백인 학생들만큼 졸업

후에 성공하지 못할 것이라 예상했지만 연구 결과에 놀랐다고 했으므로 예상과 완전히 다른 결과가 나왔을 것이다. 따라서 소수 민족 학생들이 백인 학생들만큼 잘 해내고 있었다는 의미가 되어야 하므로 '차이가 없었다'는 것이 적절하다. 따라서 '불일치, 차이'라는 뜻의 ② discrepancy가 적절하다.

위 글에 의하면, 다음 중 빈칸에 들어가기에 가장 적절한 것은?
① 남용
② 차이
③ 개선
④ 강탈

25 내용일치 ②

소수 인종에 대한 입학 요건을 완화하여 미시간 대학에 매년 가을 입학하는 학생 중 약 10퍼센트가 소수 인종의 구성원이라고 했으므로 ②가 적절하다. ① 소수 민족 학생들은 백인 학생들만큼 잘 했고 둘 사이에 차이가 없었다. ③ 위 글에 언급되어 있지 않다. ④ 미시간 로스쿨은 입학 요건을 완화하여 다른 모든 학생들보다 낮은 성적을 가진 소수 인종 학생의 입학을 허가하고 있다.

위 글에 의하면, 다음 중 옳은 것은?
① 미시간 로스쿨의 소수 민족 학생들의 절반 또는 3분의 2는 백인 학생들만큼 잘 하지 못했다.
② 차별 철폐 조치 정책으로 인해 미시간 대학에 매년 가을 입학하는 학생 중 10퍼센트가 소수 인종이다.
③ 대학 교육에 종사하는 사람들은 차별 철폐 조치 정책의 생각에 동의한다.
④ 미시간 로스쿨은 소수 인종에 대한 입학 요건을 크게 완화하지 않았다.

26-28

신체 건강 및 의학 연구의 주제에 관해서 사람들이 정보를 얻을 수 있는 수천 개의 놀라운 웹사이트가 있다. 그러나 그 많은 사용 가능한 정보는 언제 그 타당성과 건강상의 이점에 영향을 미치는가? 인터넷은 자신의 건강 관리에 대한 사람들의 태도에 큰 영향을 미치고 있다. 아마도 이 세계적인 문화적 추세는 세계 보건을 향상시킨다. 컴퓨터 사용자는 자신이 관심 있는 거의 모든 주제를 찾아볼 수 있기 때문에 자신의 연구원이 된다. 바쁜 현대 세계에서 의사들은 항상 환자에게 질병과 가능한 치료법을 설명하기 위해 시간을 내지는 못한다. 그들은 과학적 세부 사항을 이해하기 쉬운 말로 제공하지 못할지도 모른다. 이러한 이유로 많은 희망에 찬 사람들은 좋은 의학적 결정에 필요한 사실을 찾기 위해 인터넷 자원을 활용한다. 하지만 '전문가'의 신념은 항상 완전히 정확하거나 진짜인가? 그들은 특정한 의학적 상태에 대한 조언이 필요한 모든 사람들에게 도움이 되는가? 가장 굉장한 것처럼 보이는 건강 제품이나 책이 가장 사기적일 때가 종종 있는데, 그것은 정직하지 않거나 거짓이다. 아픈 사람들이나 걱정하는 사람들이 어려운 건강 질문이나 문제에 대한 명확하고 쉬운 답변을 컴퓨터에서 찾을 때 그들이 너무 많은 것을 기대하는 것인가?

amazing a. 놀랄 만한, 굉장한 validity n. 정당성, 타당성; 유효성 healthcare n. 건강 관리 look up (사전·참고 자료·컴퓨터 등에서 정보를) 찾아보다 take advantage of 이용하다 accurate a. 정확한; 정밀한 fraudulent a. 사기의, 사기를 치는, 부정의 false a. 거짓의, 허위의

26 글의 주제 ④

인터넷에서 사람들이 건강 및 의학에 관한 많은 정보를 얻을 수 있게 됨에 따라 그로 인한 장단점을 이야기하고 있다. 자신이 직접 필요한 의학 정보를 찾을 수 있어서 의학적 결정을 내리는 데 도움을 받을 수 있지만 그 정보가 거짓일 수도 있어서 주의가 필요하다는 것이다. 따라서 위 글의 주제로 ④ '인터넷이 사람들의 건강에 미치는 이득과 손실'이 적절하다.

위 글의 주제는 무엇인가?
① 건강 문제에 대한 인터넷의 장점
② 연구가 세계 보건에 미치는 영향
③ 전문가에 의한 의학적 결정의 타당성
④ 인터넷이 사람들의 건강에 미치는 이득과 손실

27 빈칸완성 ③

빈칸 앞뒤로 원인과 결과를 나타낸다. 의사들이 항상 환자에게 질병과 가능한 치료법을 설명할 시간이 없고 질병에 대해 이해하기 쉬운 말로 이야기하지는 않으므로, 사람들이 의학적 결정에 필요한 정보를 직접 인터넷에서 찾는다고 할 수 있다. 따라서 '이러한 이유로'의 뜻의 ③ For this reason이 적절하다.

다음 중 빈칸에 들어가기에 가장 적절한 것은?
① 그러나
② 예를 들어
③ 이러한 이유로
④ 다시 말해서

28 내용일치 ④

바쁜 현대 세계에서 의사들은 항상 환자에게 질병과 가능한 치료법을 설명할 시간을 내지는 못하며 환자들이 의학적 결정에 필요한 사실을 찾기 위해 인터넷 자원을 활용한다고 했다. 하지만 의사들이 환자들에게 인터넷 자원을 사용할 것을 권고한다는 것은 언급되어 있지 않으므로 ④가 옳지 않다.

위 글에 의하면, 다음 중 옳지 않은 것은?
① 인터넷은 사람들의 건강 관리에 대한 태도에 영향을 미치는 중요한 요소다.
② 인터넷에서 사용할 수 있는 일부 의료 정보는 부정확하거나 부정직하며 위험할 수 있다.
③ 사람들은 인터넷에서 자신이 관심 있는 어떤 주제라도 찾아보고 어려운 건강 질문에 대한 쉬운 답을 찾으려 노력할 수 있다.
④ 의사들은 너무 바빠서 환자들을 도울 수 없고 그들에게 의료 결정을 위해 인터넷 자원을 사용할 것을 권고한다.

29-30

왜 우리는 격차를 메우고 노동자들에게 미래의 일자리, 심지어 오늘날의 일자리를 위해 준비시키는 일을 할 수 없었는가? 그 답은 취업 시장과 우리의 교육 시스템에 있다. 취업 시장은 그 어느 때보다 빠르게 변화하고

있다. 오늘날 기업이 채워야 할 일자리의 상당수는 현재의 구직자들이 재학 중일 때는 존재하지 않아 교육 프로그램이 시장의 요구를 따라잡기 어려웠다. 그럼에도 불구하고 많은 기업 리더들은 학교가 많은 직업이 요구하는 기술 교육을 제공하기 위해 충분한 일을 하지 않고 있다고 주장한다. 예를 들어, 미국의 모든 학교 중 4분의 1만이 컴퓨터 공학을 가르친다. 대부분의 학교와 대학은 과거에 제공한 동일한 유형의 교육을 계속 제공하고 있다. 결과적으로, 많은 학생들은 취업 가능한 직업에 대해 준비시켜주지 않는 학위를 갖고 졸업한다. 교육 시스템과 취업 시장 사이의 이러한 불일치를 고려할 때, 많은 노동 전문가들은 기술 격차를 좁히기 위해 전통적인 학교 교육에 의존할 수 없고 아마도 그렇게 해서는 안 되며 대신 대안적인 해결책을 찾아야 한다고 말한다.

bridge the gap 격차를 메우다 job applicant 구직자 keep up with ~에 뒤처지지 않다, 따라가다 degree n. 학위 given prep. ~을 고려해 볼 때 mismatch n. 부조화, 불일치 alternative a. 대안적인, 대체의

29 내용일치 ③

취업 시장은 빠르게 변화하고 있는데 학교는 전통적인 교육 방식을 고수하고 있어서 변화하는 노동 시장의 요구를 따라잡지 못하고 있다고 했으므로 ③이 적절하다. ① 미국의 교육 시스템과 취업 시장 사이의 격차를 좁히기 위해 전통적인 학교 교육에 의존하지 않고 대안적인 해결책을 찾아야 한다. ②, ④ 위 글에 언급되어 있지 않다.

위 글에 의하면, 다음 중 옳은 것은?
① 미국의 교육 시스템과 취업 시장 사이에는 격차가 없다.
② IT 교육은 수많은 교육 프로그램을 따르도록 요구된다.
③ 학교의 교육 시스템은 크게 변하지 않았다.
④ 기업들은 구직자들에게 기술 교육을 제공했다.

30 글의 주제 ①

우리가 미래의 일자리, 심지어 오늘날의 일자리에 대비하지 못하는 이유로 교육 시스템의 미비를 들고 있다. 취업 시장은 빠르게 변화하는데 학교는 전통적인 교육 시스템에 머물러 있어 기술 격차가 커지고 있다는 것이다. 따라서 위 글의 주제로 ① '기술 격차의 원인'이 적절하다.

위 글의 주제는 무엇인가?
① 기술 격차의 원인
② 기술 교육 프로그램 선택하기
③ IT에 밝은 취업 시장
④ 미래의 직업

31-33

유럽인들은 1600년대에 지금의 남아프리카에 처음 정착했다. 이 식민지 개척자들은 정부를 수립하고 아프리카 원주민들과 떨어져 살았다. 1910년 남아프리카 공화국이 자치 국가가 된 이후에도 백인들은 확고하게 지배권을 유지했다. 1948년부터 1994년까지, 이 국가는 아파르트헤이트로 알려진 제도 하에서 통치되었다. 아파르트헤이트는 흑인과 백인을 별도의 학교, 별도의 동네, 별도의 권리로 분리시켰다. 어떤 흑인도 투표하거나 정부에 참여할 권리가 없었다. 3,200만 명의 흑인과 600만 명의 백인으로 이루어진 국가에서, 어떤 흑인도 발언권이 없었다. 이 체제에 맞서 싸우

려던 남아프리카 흑인들과 다른 사람들은 신속하게 그리고 때로는 폭력에 의해 침묵 당했다. 수천 명이 감옥에 갇혔다. 수백 명이 경찰에 의해 고문당하고 살해당했다. 비록 이러한 행위들이 법에 어긋났음에도 불구하고, 남아프리카의 백인 지도자들은 외면했다. 그들은 백인들이 권력을 유지하기를 원했다.

아파르트헤이트는 영원히 지속될 수 없었다. 오랜 투쟁 끝에 남아프리카 공화국은 1994년에 첫 공개 선거를 치렀다. 일단 흑인 시민들이 투표권을 갖게 되자 그들은 그것을 사용했다. 그들은 넬슨 만델라(Nelson Mandela)를 그 국가의 최초의 흑인 대통령으로 선출했다. 그는 흑인 평등을 위해 싸운 죄로 27년을 감옥에서 보냈다. 백인 통치가 끝나자 많은 백인들은 흑인들이 아파르트헤이트의 잔인함에 대한 복수를 모색할 것을 두려워했다. 그래서 백인 정부와 만델라의 새 정부는 협상했다. 만델라와 다른 사람들은 남아프리카 공화국의 신생 민주주의가 강해지기 위해서는 남아프리카 공화국 사람들이 그들의 추악한 과거를 직시해야 한다고 느꼈다.

settle v. 정착하다   colonist n. 식민지 주민; 식민지 개척자[이주자]   live apart from ~과 떨어져 살다   self-ruling a. 자치의   apartheid n. 아파르트헤이트(남아프리카 공화국의 인종 차별 정책)   separate a. 갈라진, 분리된   take part in ~에 참여[참가]하다   silence v. 침묵시키다   torture v. 고문하다   murder v. 살해하다   look away 눈길을 돌리다, 외면하다   come to an end 끝나다   revenge n. 복수, 보복   cruelty n. 잔인함   newborn a. 갓 태어난; 신생의

---

31 글의 주제   ②

남아프리카 공화국은 아파르트헤이트의 체제 하에서 흑인들이 오랜 시간 인종 차별을 당했지만 오랜 투쟁 끝에 흑인들이 투표권을 갖고 넬슨 만델라를 대통령으로 선출하여 신생 민주주의가 탄생했다는 것이다. 따라서 위 글의 주제로 ② '남아프리카 공화국의 민주주의 배경과 탄생'이 적절하다.

위 글의 주제는 무엇인가?
① 남아프리카 공화국의 흑인에 대한 인종 차별 정책
② 남아프리카 공화국의 민주주의 배경과 탄생
③ 남아프리카 공화국의 백인 유럽 정착의 역사
④ 현대 남아프리카 공화국의 심각한 인종 갈등

---

32 빈칸완성   ①

투표하거나 정부에 참여할 권리를 나타내는 표현이 빈칸에 공통적으로 들어가야 한다. 따라서 '발언권, 투표권'이란 뜻의 ① a voice가 적절하다.

다음 중 빈칸 Ⓐ와 Ⓑ에 공통적으로 들어가기에 가장 적절한 것은?
① 발언권, 투표권
② 법률
③ 국가
④ 꿈

---

33 내용일치   ④

아파르트헤이트에 맞서 싸운 사람들은 고문당하고 살해당했는데, 남아

프리카의 백인 지도자들은 이러한 행위들이 법에 어긋남을 알고 있었지만 자신들의 권력을 유지하기 위해 외면했다고 했으므로 ④가 적절하다. ① 남아프리카 공화국이 자치 국가가 된 후에도 백인들이 지배권을 유지했다. ② 넬슨 만델라가 대통령이 된 후에 백인 정부는 흑인들이 복수할 것이 두려워서 만델라의 새 정부와 협상했다. ③ 넬슨 만델라는 흑인들이 투표권을 갖고 실시된 첫 공개 선거에서 선출된 대통령이었다.

위 글에 의하면, 다음 중 옳은 것은?
① 남아프리카 공화국이 자치 국가가 되었을 때, 흑인들이 권력을 장악했다.
② 선거 후, 많은 백인들이 넬슨 만델라로 대표되는 흑인 권력에 종속되었다.
③ 넬슨 만델라는 아파르트헤이트라는 정책을 통해 선출된 최초의 흑인 대통령이었다.
④ 아파르트헤이트에 맞서 싸운 사람들은 잔인하게 대우받고 살해당했는데, 이것은 법에 어긋나는 일이었다.

34-36

성 역할 고정관념의 수용은 개인을 제한할 뿐만 아니라 사회 전반에도 나쁜 영향을 미친다. 성 역할 고정관념은 사회에 큰 비용을 초래했다. 그들은 많은 사람들이 더 생산적인 역할을 맡는 것을 막았고 이러한 고정관념에 의해 발생하는 정서적, 신체적 문제에 상당한 자원을 지출하는 결과를 초래했다. 지난 20년 동안 수백만 명의 미국인들이 성 역할의 "자연스러움"에 대한 생각을 바꾸기 시작했다. 전통적인 차별은 평생의 열등감과 잠재력 낭비로 여성을 위협하고 남성을 항상 경쟁적이고, 공격적이며, 감정적으로 둔감한 역할로 제한하는 비합리적인 시스템으로 인식되고 있다. 만약 남성과 여성이 우리 사회에서 남녀평등을 이루면 어떤 영향이 있을까? 한 가지 분명한 대답은 노동력의 모든 부분에서 사회의 인재 공급이 증가할 것이라는 것이다. 여성과 남성을 구분하는 직업적 장벽을 허무는 것은 또한 그들이 동등한 사람으로서 서로 관계를 갖는 데 도움이 될 것이다. 일부 페미니스트들과 사회 과학자들은 남성과 여성이 유연하게 자신의 역할을 수행하고 전통적인 여성적이거나 남성적인 방식이 아닌 인간으로서 자신을 표현하도록 사회화되어야 한다고 촉구했다. 이 생각은 남성을 뜻하는 andro와 여성을 뜻하는 gyne에서 온 "androgyny(양성성)"라고 불린다. 이 개념은 사람들이 광범위한 역할 수행 가능성을 탐색하고 성 역할 고정관념과 상관없이 감정과 행동을 표현하는 것을 선택하도록 하는 것이다. <따라서 사람들은 그들이 가장 유능하고 가장 편안한 일과 직업을 추구하고 그들이 실제로 느끼는 태도와 감정을 표현하도록 권장된다.> 남성이 간호사나 유치원 교사가 되고 싶어 하고 여성이 군인이나 소방관이 되고 싶어 하고 그들이 그것을 잘한다면, 그들 둘 다 재능을 개발하고 그들이 할 수 있는 모든 것을 성취할 수 있도록 허용된다면 그것은 사회를 위해 제 기능을 하는 것이다.

stereotype n. 고정관념   costly a. 값이 비싼, 비용이 많이 드는; 희생이 큰   assume v. (책임·임무 등을) 떠맡다   expenditure n. 지출; 소비   substantial a. 상당한   naturalness n. 자연스러움; 타고남; 당연함   discrimination n. 차별   lifelong a. 일생의, 평생의   inferiority n. 열등, 하위   potential n. 가능성, 잠재력   restrict v. 제한[한정]하다   talent n. (타고난) 재능; 재주 있는 사람들, 인재   occupational a. 직업의   barrier n. 장벽, 장애물   relate v. 관계가 있다; (사람이) 사회적 관계를 갖다   equal n. 동등한 사람[것]   flexible a. 융통성 있는, 유연한   androgyny n. 양성성   without regard to ~을 고려하지 않고, ~에 상관없이   pursue v. 추구하다   kindergarten teacher 유치원 교사

34 글의 주제 ④

성 역할 고정관념이 개인뿐만 아니라 사회에 나쁜 영향을 미침에 따라 전통적인 성 역할에 대한 생각이 변화하고 있고 이로 인해 인재 공급이 증가하고 남녀가 동등한 사람으로서 서로 관계를 갖는 등 사회에 긍정적인 영향을 줄 수 있다는 것이다. 따라서 위 글의 주제로 ④ '전통적인 성 역할 고정관념의 변화'가 적절하다.

위 글의 주제는 무엇인가?
① 성 역할 고정관념을 가진 직업을 갖는 것의 이점
② 페미니스트와 사회주의자 사이의 논쟁적인 문제들
③ 성 역할의 전통적인 개념을 유지하는 이유
④ 전통적인 성 역할 고정관념의 변화

35 빈칸완성 ③

남녀평등이 이루어지면 남녀가 직업을 선택하는 데 제한이 없을 것이므로 노동력의 모든 부분에서 인재 공급은 늘어날 것이다. 따라서 '증가하다'는 뜻의 ③ increase가 적절하다.

다음 중 빈칸에 들어가기에 가장 적절한 것은?
① 조화하다
② 악화되다
③ 증가하다
④ 결합하다

36 문장삽입 ④

제시문은 전통적인 성 역할 고정관념에 상관없이 자신이 되고 싶은 직업을 자유롭게 선택하고 감정을 표현해야 한다는 것으로 "androgyny(양성성)", 즉 사람은 남성적 특성과 여성적 특성이 함께 있다고 보는 개념을 부연해서 설명하는 것이다. 따라서 Ⓓ에 들어가야 적절하다. Ⓓ 다음 문장이 주어진 문장의 내용을 예를 들어 좀 더 자세히 설명하고 있다.

37-38

지구가 인구 과잉이 되려면 식량, 물, 그리고 인간이 살 공간이 부족해야 한다. 인도의 경제학자 라즈 크리슈나(Raj Krishna)는 인도만으로도 전 세계 식량 공급을 제공할 정도로 작물 수확량을 늘릴 수 있다고 추정한다. 세계식량계획(WFP)은 세계를 먹여 살릴 만큼 충분한 식량이 재배되고 있고 지금 지구상에 10,000년 전과 같은 양의 담수가 있다는 것을 확인시켜준다. 그것은 단순히 재분배되었다. 그렇다면 어떻게 전 세계의 사람들의 수가 우리 행성에 영향을 미치고 있는 것이 가능한가?
긴박한 위협이 되는 것은 인구 증가가 아니다. 그것은 소비의 증가다. 물질주의와 과소비는 서구 세계의 모든 사람들에게 피할 수 없는 인생의 현실인데, 소유물은 사회에서 사람의 지위를 반영하고 사람들은 최신 유행 상품의 소유를 통해 행복을 얻기 위해 노력하기 때문이다. 그뿐만 아니라 낭비는 우리 자원에 큰 영향을 미치는 광범위한 현상이다. 게다가, 우리의 현재 소비는 불균형하고, 지속 불가능하며, 지구가 재생할 수 있는 것보다 30% 더 높은 수준인 것으로 추정된다. 현재 세계 인구의 20%만이 세계 자원의 80%를 사용하고 있다는 것은 슬픈 사실이며, 이는 우리 중의 5분의 1이 세계 식량과 에너지의 5분의 4를 사용한다는 것을 의미한다.

overpopulated a. 인구 과잉의 insufficient a. 불충분한, 부족한 yield n. 산출물; 수확량 sufficient a. 충분한 feed v. 먹이다, 먹여 살리다 redistribute v. 재분배[재구분]하다 impact v. 영향[충격]을 주다 dire a. 무서운; 긴박한, 극단적인 threat n. 위협, 협박 consumption n. 소비 fashionable a. 유행하는, 유행을 따른 waste n. 낭비, 허비 widespread a. 광범위한, 널리 퍼진 unsustainable a. 지속 불가능한 regenerate v. 재생하다

37 내용파악 ②

라즈 크리슈나는 인도만으로도 전 세계 식량 공급을 제공할 정도로 작물 수확량을 늘릴 수 있다고 했으므로 ②가 적절하다.

다음 중 라즈 크리슈나의 견해에 대해 옳은 것은?
① 인도만으로는 세계에 충분한 식량을 공급할 수 없다.
② 작물 수확량은 세계 식량 공급을 제공할 정도로 증가할 수 있다.
③ 미래에는 식량이 인간에게 물과 공간보다 덜 충분할 것이다.
④ 물 공급의 부족은 세계에서와 마찬가지로 인도에서도 문제가 되지 않을 것이다.

38 내용일치 ③

세계 인구의 20%만이 세계 자원의 80%를 사용하고 있다고 했으므로 ③이 적절하다. ① 가장 심각한 문제는 인구 증가가 아니라 소비의 증가다. ② 물질주의와 과소비는 서구 세계의 모든 사람들에게 피할 수 없는 인생의 현실이다. ④ 소유물은 사람의 지위를 반영하고 사람들은 최신 유행 상품의 소유를 통해 행복을 얻기 위해 노력한다고 했으므로 유행을 따르고자 하는 욕망이 사람의 지위와 행복의 척도라고 할 수 있다.

위 글에 의하면, 다음 중 옳은 것은?
① 인구 증가는 세계가 공통적으로 가지고 있는 가장 심각한 문제다.
② 물질주의는 서구 세계의 모든 사람들에게 삶의 중요한 사실이 아니다.
③ 세계 인구의 5분의 1이 세계 식량과 에너지의 80%를 사용한다.
④ 유행을 따르고자 하는 욕망이 사람의 지위와 행복의 척도가 될 수 없다.

39-40

직업 선택을 모색할 때 고려해야 할 많은 요소가 있다. 작업 환경, 특정 집단의 사람들과 함께 일하는 것, 지리적 위치 그리고 임금은 고려할 수 있는 몇 가지 직업적 특성에 불과하다. 열린 마음을 가져라. 초기 관심사와 관련된 직업을 고려하라. 예를 들어, 당신은 건강관리에 관심이 있을 수도 있고, 환자 치료와 빈번한 대중 접촉과 같은 간호의 특정 특성이 당신에게 매력적일 수도 있다. 이러한 특성을 공유하는 다른 건강 관련 직업들 ― 의사, 호흡기 치료사 및 응급 구조사를 포함하여 ― 을 모색하는 것은 간호 이외의 건강 분야에 대한 관심을 자극할 수 있다.
어떤 직업이나 산업도 더 알아보기 전에 성급하게 제외시키지 마라. 일부 직업과 산업은 특정한 긍정적인 이미지나 부정적인 이미지를 불러일으킨다.
Ⓐ 어떤 사람들에게는 패션 디자이너가 매력적인 이미지를 만들어내는 반면, 제조업의 생산직은 덜 매력적인 이미지를 떠올리게 한다.
Ⓒ 그러나 직업은 처음에 보이는 것과 같지 않은 경우가 많으며 오해가 일반적이다. 흥미로운 직업은 지루한 측면이 있을 수 있지만, 덜 매력적인 직업은 일단 그것에 대해 알게 되면 당신의 흥미를 끌 수 있다.

B 예를 들어, 여행할 수 있는 기회는 승무원의 직업을 흥미롭게 보이게 하지만, 일은 힘들고 피곤하다. 승무원은 오랫동안 서 있고 그들이 피곤하거나 승객이 불쾌할 때에도 친절해야 한다.

다른 한편, 많은 사람들은 자동차 조립 작업을 더럽고 지루하다고 생각한다. 그러나 자동차 제조업에서 생산직 근로자는 국내에서 가장 많은 임금을 받는 사람들 중 하나다.

explore v. 탐험하다; 탐구하다, 조사하다 earning n. (pl.) 소득, 수입 characteristic n. 특질, 특성, 특색 open-minded a. 마음이 넓은, 편견이 없는 initial a. 처음의, 초기의 frequent a. 잦은, 빈번한 nursing n. (직업으로서의) 간호(업무) appeal v. 관심[흥미]을 끌다, 매력적이다 respiratory a. 호흡의, 호흡 기관의 therapist n. 치료 전문가, 치료사 emergency medical technician 응급 구조사, 응급 구조 대원 eliminate v. 제거하다, 배제하다 invoke v. (느낌·상상을) 불러일으키다, 환기시키다 glamorous a. 매력이 넘치는, 매혹적인 bring to mind ~을 상기하다, 머리에 떠올리다 misconception n. 오해 dull a. 지루한, 따분한 strenuous a. 몹시 힘든, 격렬한

---

39 단락배열   ①

일부 직업과 산업은 긍정적인 이미지나 부정적인 이미지를 불러일으킨다고 했으므로, 긍정적인 이미지를 떠올리게 하는 예로 패션 디자이너를 부정적인 이미지를 떠올리게 하는 예로 제조업의 생산직을 들고 있는 A가 가장 먼저 와야 한다. 그다음에 역접을 나타내는 표현인 However가 와서 매력적인 직업이 지루할 수 있으며 덜 매력적인 직업이 흥미를 끌 수도 있다는 내용의 C가 오고, 그 예로 각각 승무원의 경우와 생산직 근로자의 경우를 들고 있는 B가 마지막에 와야 한다.

---

40 글의 요지   ④

직업 선택을 모색할 때 작업 환경, 특정 집단의 사람들과 함께 일하는 것, 지리적 위치 그리고 임금에 대해 알아보고 그 외에도 자신이 관심 있는 분야의 직업에 대해 처음에 보이는 것과 다를 수 있으므로 자세히 알아보고 선택할 것을 이야기하고 있다. 따라서 위 글의 요지로 ④가 적절하다.

위 글의 요지는 무엇인가?
① 일자리를 찾을 때는 관심사보다 소득을 먼저 고려해야 한다.
② 근로 조건을 자세히 이해하는 것은 구직활동의 필수적인 부분이다.
③ 직업 선택을 모색할 때는 보수와 함께 일하는 사람들을 고려하라.
④ 직업을 선택할 때는 다양한 측면을 고려해야 한다.

2024 단국대학교(자연계 오전)

01 ②	02 ①	03 ④	04 ②	05 ③	06 ②	07 ①	08 ④	09 ①	10 ③
11 ①	12 ②	13 ④	14 ③	15 ③	16 ④	17 ②	18 ④	19 ①	20 ②
21 ③	22 ③	23 ④	24 ②	25 ④	26 ④	27 ③	28 ④	29 ②	30 ④

01 동의어 ②

magnificent a. 장엄한, 훌륭한, 굉장한, 멋진 conciliating a. 달래는, 회유하는(= soothing) exonerate v. ~의 무죄를 입증하다; (의무·임무·일 따위에서) 면제[해제]하다 clarify v. 분명[명료]하게 하다 flaring a. 너울너울[활활] 타는, 번쩍번쩍 빛나는; 화려한

기념일을 잊어버린 후 롭(Rob)은 화해의 표시로 아내에게 멋진 꽃다발을 사 주었다.

02 동의어 ①

exultant a. 몹시 기뻐하는; 승리를 뽐내는, 의기양양한(= triumphant) furious a. 격노한; 맹렬한, 사나운 amiable a. 상냥한 lethargic a. 혼수 상태의; 무기력한

소피(Sophie)의 가족은 그녀가 대회에서 성공한 후 의기양양한 기분에 빠져 있었다.

03 동의어 ④

infringe v. 어기다, 침해하다(= infract) unacceptable a. 받아들일 수 없는, 용인[용납]할 수 없는 ingrain v. (습관 등을) 깊이 뿌리박히게 하다 eradicate v. 근절하다, 뿌리 뽑다 oppress v. 압박하다, 억압하다

인권이 침해되는 것은 문명사회에서 용납될 수 없다.

04 동의어 ②

hold somebody in high esteem ~를 높이 존경하다 on the basis of ~을 기준으로 하여, ~에 근거하여 condemn v. 비난하다(= criticize) oppress v. 압박하다, 억압하다 praise v. 칭찬하다 judge v. 판단하다

모든 사회는 기술, 억양, 성별, 종교, 피부색, 그 어느 것에 근거해서든, 다른 사람들을 비난하면서 특정 집단의 사람들을 높이 존경한다.

05 동의어 ③

absurd a. 터무니없는(= preposterous) ridiculous a. 웃기는, 우스꽝스러운 excuse v. 용서하다; 변명하다 irresistible a. 억누를 수 없는, 저항할 수 없는 sensible a. 분별 있는 hilarious a. 유쾌한, 즐거운

가장 터무니없는 관습과 가장 우스꽝스러운 의식은 어디에서나 '그러나 그것이 전통이다'라는 문구에 호소함으로써 용서된다.

06 동의어 ②

inconsequential a. 중요하지 않은, 하찮은(= insignificant) wound v. 상처를 입히다; (감정을) 해치다 arrogant a. 거만한, 오만한 disparage v. 깔보다, 얕보다; 비방[비난]하다 overestimate v. 과대평가하다

만일 우리가 우리의 강점을 공정하게 평가하고 우리의 가치를 결정했더라면, 우리가 중요하지 않다는 다른 사람의 제안은 우리에게 상처를 입히지 않을 것이다.

07 동의어 ①

capitalism n. 자본주의 exploitation n. 이기적 이용, 착취(= unfair use) communism n. 공산주의 the other way round 반대로[거꾸로]; 반대 (상황) pure speculation 순전한 추측 employment n. 고용 instant a. 즉시의, 즉각적인 gratification n. 만족감, 희열

옛 소련의 농담은 자본주의 하에서 사람들은 인간이 인간을 착취하는 체제 아래에서 살지만 공산주의 하에서는 정반대라고 말하곤 했다.

08 동의어 ④

flamboyant a. 현란한, 화려한(= colorful) ordinary a. 보통의, 일상적인; 평범한 elusive a. 파악하기 어려운; 이해하기 어려운 outgoing a. 사교적인 exaggerating a. 과장하는

그는 보통 꽤 화려한 사람들을 연기하지만, 이 연극에서 그의 역할은 오히려 평범한 사람이다.

09 문의 구성 ①

동사 have researched의 목적어로 what이 이끄는 의문사절이 두 개가 온 것으로 의문사절의 어순은 '의문사+주어+동사'이다. 따라서 빈칸에는 동사가 와야 하는데 '~에 영향을 미치다'는 표현은 have an effect on 이므로 ① has가 적절하다.

과학자들은 지구 대기권 너머에는 상황이 어떤지와 우주여행이 인체에 어떤 영향을 미치는지 연구해왔다.

10 2형식 동사 remain ③

by which ~ and retrieved가 주어 the exact process를 수식하는 것으로 빈칸에는 동사가 와야 하는데 remain은 2형식 동사로 뒤에 명사 상당어구나 형용사 상당어구가 보어로 온다. 명사 상당어구인 a mystery가 보어로 왔으므로 ③ remains가 적절하다.

exact a. 정확한 retrieve v. 생각해내다, 상기하다 there is no doubt that ~라는 것에 의심의 여지가 없다

기억을 암호화하고 생각해내는 정확한 과정은 미스터리로 남아있지만, 적절한 음식을 먹는 것이 우리가 뇌의 능력을 최대한 활용하는 데 도움을 줄 수 있다는 것은 의심의 여지가 없다.

11 가정법 과거완료의 도치 구문 ①

주절의 동사가 'would+have+p.p'인 것으로 보아 가정법 과거완료 문장임을 알 수 있다. 따라서 종속절은 'If+주어+had+p.p'의 형태가 와야 하는데 If를 생략할 경우 'had+주어+p.p'의 어순으로 도치된다. 그러므로 빈칸에는 ① not been told가 적절하다.

매우 중요한 메시지가 포함되어 있다는 말을 듣지 않았더라면 나는 그 편지를 버렸을 것이다.

12 worth+(동)명사 ②

worth는 전치사적 형용사로 뒤에 명사나 동명사를 목적어로 취한다. 따라서 to부정사는 목적어로 취할 수 없으므로 to ask를 동명사의 형태인 asking으로 고친다.

utilitarian a. 공리주의의 objectionable a. 이의가 있는, 반대할 만한 ground n. (종종 pl.) 근거, 이유

오늘날의 공리주의적 사고의 몇 가지 사례를 살펴보기 전에, 벤담(Bentham)의 철학이 반론의 여지가 있는지, 만약 그렇다면 어떤 근거에서 그러한지 질문해 볼 가치가 있다.

13 not because A but because B ④

'not because A but because B' 구문으로 앞에 not because가 있으므로 because 앞에 but이 와서 'A 때문이 아니라 B 때문이다'는 표현이 되어야 한다. 따라서 ④를 but because로 고친다.

desirable a. 바람직한, 호감 가는, 가치 있는 confer v. (상·학위·명예·자격을) 수여[부여]하다

따라서, 많은 물질적 재화의 소유는 주로 그러한 재화가 모든 객관적 또는 주관적 쾌락을 제공하기 때문이 아니라 명예를 부여하기 때문에 가치 있는 것이 된다.

14 가목적어-진목적어 구문 ③

5형식 구문에서 to부정사구가 목적보어 뒤로 후치된 경우에는 앞에 가목적어 it을 써야 하므로, ③의 them을 가목적어 it으로 고친다. 주어진 문장은 'render+가목적어(it)+목적보어(indecent)+진목적어(to be without)'의 구조를 가진 구문이며, for creditable people은 to be without의 의미상 주어이다. 그리고 복합관계대명사 whatever가 without의 목적어이다.

necessary n. (종종 pl.) 필수품 commodity n. 일용품, 필수품; 상품 indispensably ad. 반드시, 꼭 indecent a. 버릇없는, 품위 없는; 부당한 creditable a. 명예가 되는; 칭찬할 만한, 훌륭한; 신용할 수 있는

내가 이해하는 바로는, 필수품은 삶의 유지에 반드시 필요한 상품일 뿐 아니라 그 나라의 관습으로 인해 훌륭한 사람들이 가지지 않으면 꼴사나운 일이 되어버리는 모든 것이다.

15-16

우리는 실제로 필요한 것보다 더 많은 물을 소비해서는 안 된다. 그렇게 하면 미래에는 물이 충분하지 않을 것이다. 하지만, 얼마만큼이 너무 많은 것인가? 만약 우리가 자연이 대체하는 것보다 더 많은 담수를 제거한다면 우리는 너무 많이 가져간(소비한) 것이다.
많은 도시들은 사람들이 물을 낭비하는 것을 멈추게 하기 위해 캠페인을 벌인다. 그들은 그들에게 물 사용을 줄일 수 있는 방법을 보여준다. 그들은 또한 물을 너무 많이 사용하는 사람들에게 수도 요금을 인상한다. 게다가, 그들은 물 사용을 줄이는 프로그램에 자금을 지원한다. 예를 들어, 그들은 사람들에게 물을 덜 사용하는 샤워기와 화장실을 제공한다. 마지막으로, 그들은 사람들이 사용할 수 있는 물의 양을 제한하는 법을 제정한다.
우리의 물 공급에 대한 또 다른 위협은 오염이다. 우리의 담수 공급원이 오염되면, 우리는 더 이상 이 물을 사용할 수 없다. 이것은 또한 물에 의존하는 동물들을 위험에 빠뜨린다. 우리 모두가 물을 보존하기 위해 할 수 있는 몇 가지 일이 있다. 우리는 이를 닦는 동안 수도꼭지를 틀어놓지 않음으로써 많은 물을 절약할 수 있다.

consume v. 소비하다, 소모하다 replace v. 대신하다, 대체하다 waste v. 낭비하다 cut back on ~을 줄이다 fund v. 자금을 제공하다 threat n. 위협, 협박 pollution n. 오염 endanger v. 위험에 빠뜨리다, 위태롭게 하다 tap n. (수도 등의) 꼭지 brush v. ~을 닦다

15 빈칸완성 ③

Ⓐ 많은 도시들이 물 낭비를 멈추기 위해 벌이는 여러 가지 캠페인에 대해 언급하고 있는데 물 사용을 줄이는 프로그램에 자금을 지원하는 것은 그 일들 중에 하나이므로 '부가, 첨가'의 의미를 가지는 In addition, Moreover가 적절하다. Ⓑ 여러 가지를 언급할 때 마지막에 해당하므로 Finally가 적절하다. 따라서 상기 두 조건을 모두 만족시키는 ③이 정답이다.

다음 중 빈칸 Ⓐ와 Ⓑ에 들어가기에 가장 적절한 것은?
① 그러나 — 일반적으로
② 그러므로 — 처음에
③ 게다가 — 마지막으로
④ 게다가 — 종합적으로

16 내용일치

물을 너무 많이 사용하는 사람들에게 수도 요금을 인상하거나, 물 사용을 줄이는 프로그램에 자금을 지원하거나, 물의 양을 제한하는 법을 제정하는 등 물 사용을 줄이기 위한 다양한 캠페인을 벌이고 있지만 물 공급을 중단해야 한다고는 하지 않았으므로 ④가 옳지 않다.

위 글에 의하면, 다음 중 옳지 않은 것은?
① 우리의 물 공급에 대한 주요 위협 중 하나는 수질 오염이다.
② 사람들이 물을 너무 많이 사용하면, 그들은 많은 도시에서 인상된 수도 요금을 지불한다.
③ 물 낭비의 위험성에 대한 인식을 높이기 위한 많은 운동이 있다.
④ 담수를 절약하기 위해서, 정부는 물 공급을 중단해야 한다.

17-18

최근 연구에서, 연구자들은 알츠하이머 발병 위험이 높은 것과 관련된 혈장 내 바이오마커, 특히 아밀로이드 베타 40과 42를 측정했다. 108명의 참가자 중 절반은 고요한 장면을 상상하고, 편안한 소리를 듣고, 눈을 감음으로써 자신을 평온한 곳으로 이끌도록 노력하라는 지시를 받았는데, 이것은 본질적으로 마음 챙김 명상이다. 목표는 심박수의 진동을 줄여 심박수가 보다 안정되고 일관된 박동을 갖도록 촉진하는 것이었다.
알츠하이머병을 일으키는 결정적인 단일 원인은 확인되지 않았지만, 플라크로 알려진 아밀로이드 베타 단백질 덩어리가 이 질병의 주요 특징 중 하나로 밝혀졌다. 특정 유형의 이 단백질은 뇌세포 내에서 함께 뭉칠 때 특히 독성이 있을 수 있으며, 뇌세포의 정상적인 기능에 영향을 미치고 뇌세포를 죽게 하는 손상을 일으킬 수 있다.
매더(Mather)와 그녀의 연구팀은 아밀로이드 베타 수치가 "그렇게 강력하게 영향을 받을 것"이라고는 예상하지 못했다. 그리고 이미 아밀로이드 베타 수치가 높아지는 것에 더 취약했을 수도 있는 것은 노인들뿐만이 아니다. "그 영향은 젊은이와 노인 모두에게 상당했습니다."라고 매더는 말한다. "이것은 흥미로운 발견입니다. 왜냐하면 건강한 성인들의 경우 아밀로이드 베타의 혈장 수준이 낮으면 나중에 알츠하이머병에 걸릴 위험이 낮은 것과 관련이 있기 때문입니다."라고 그녀는 말한다. "느린 호흡은 정서적 건강뿐만 아니라 알츠하이머병과 관련된 바이오마커를 개선하는 데도 도움이 될 수 있습니다."
연구자들은 정확히 이것이 왜 그런지 확신하지 못한다. 그러나 한 가지 가설은 느리고 의도적인 호흡이 깊은 수면의 이점 중 일부를 모방할 수 있다는 것인데, 연구에 따르면 이것이 뇌와 신경계로부터 나오는 신경 독소 노폐물을 더 빠른 속도로 제거할 수 있다. 이러한 노폐물의 축적은 알츠하이머병의 발병에 역할을 하는 것으로 보인다.

measure v. 측정하다 biomarker n. 생물지표, 바이오마커 blood plasma 혈장 develop v. (병에) 걸리다 calm n. 고요, 평온 serene a. 고요한, 잔잔한, 조용한 relaxing a. 마음을 느긋하게 해 주는, 편한 mindfulness n. 마음 챙김 meditation n. 명상 oscillation n. 진동 steady a. 변함[변동]없는, 한결같은; 안정된 consistent a. 한결같은, 일관된 definitive a. 결정적인, 최종적인 identify v. 확인하다; 인지[판정]하다 toxic a. 유독한, 독성의 clump v. (세균 등이) 엉겨 붙다, 뭉치다 (together) robust a. 강건한, 튼튼한 susceptible a. ~의 영향을 받기 쉬운, 감염되기 쉬운 significant a. 중대한, 중요한; 상당한 intriguing a. 흥미[호기심]를 자아내는 emotional well-being 정서적 건강, 정서적 행복 hypothesis n. 가설, 가정 deliberate a. 고의의, 의도[계획]적인 mimic v. 흉내 내다, 모방하다 waste product (생산 과정에서 나오는) 폐기물; (몸의) 노폐[배설]물

17 지시대상

아밀로이드 베타 단백질이라는 특정 유형의 단백질이 뇌세포 내에서 뭉칠 때 독성이 있을 수 있다고 했으므로 이 단백질은 뇌세포에 손상을 가한다고 할 수 있다. 따라서 Ⓐ는 brain cells를 가리킨다.

밑줄 친 단어 Ⓐthem이 가리키는 것은 무엇인가?
① 알츠하이머병 환자
② 뇌세포
③ 특정 유형의 단백질
④ 플라크

18 지시대상

바로 앞 문장의 "느린 호흡은 정서적 건강뿐만 아니라 알츠하이머병과 관련된 바이오마커를 개선하는 데도 도움이 될 수 있습니다."는 것을 가리킨다. 그리고 느린 호흡이 알츠하이머병에 걸릴 위험을 낮추는 이유에 대한 한 가지 가설을 뒤에서 언급하고 있으므로 ④가 적절하다.

밑줄 친 단어 Ⓑthis가 가리키는 것은 무엇인가?
① 느린 호흡은 깊은 수면의 이점 중 일부를 모방할 수 있다
② 정서적 건강은 신경 독소 노폐물을 제거할 수 있다
③ 느린 호흡은 정서적 건강에 도움이 될 수 있다
④ 느린 호흡은 알츠하이머병과 관련된 바이오마커를 개선하는 데 도움이 된다

19-20

많은 19세기 개혁가들과 마찬가지로 토머스 칼라일(Thomas Carlyle)은 모든 사람이 경제적으로 평등한 세상이 아니라 높은 사람과 낮은 사람 모두가 정직하게 그들의 불평등을 얻는 세상을 꿈꿨다. 그는 "유럽은 진정한 귀족을 필요로 한다. 오직 재능 있는 귀족이어야 한다. 거짓 귀족은 견딜 수 없다."라고 썼다. 그가 상상하고 있던 것은 명명되지 않은 체제, 즉 능력주의였다.
능력주의의 새로운 이념은 사회 조직의 두 가지 대안적인 개념과 경쟁했다. 사회의 모든 구성원들 사이에서 상품의 분배에 있어 절대적인 평등을 요구하는 평등주의 원칙과 부자들로부터 그들의 자녀들에게로 직함과 직책이 자동적으로 이전되는 것을 지지하는 세습 원칙이다. 옛날의 귀족들처럼 능력자들은 많은 불평등을 견딜 준비가 되어 있었지만, 급진적인 평등주의자들처럼 그들은 (과도기적 단계에서만이라도) 완전한 기회의 평등을 선호했다. 만약 모든 사람이 동일한 교육을 받고 어떤 직업에도 들어갈 수 있는 동일한 기회를 가졌다면, 그들은 소득과 명성의 후속 차이는 개인의 특별한 재능과 약점과 관련지음으로써 정당화될 것이라고 주장했다. 결과적으로 급여나 자산을 인위적으로 동등하게 할 필요는 없을 것이다. 고난도 특권도 마찬가지로 겪거나 누릴 만한 (이유가 있는) 것일 것이다.

reformer n. 개혁가 financially ad. 재정적으로, 재정상 equal a. 동등한, 평등한 inequality n. 불평등, 불균등 honestly ad. 정직하게 insupportable a. 견딜[참을] 수 없는; 지지할 수 없는 meritocracy n. 실력[능력]주의 coin v. (신어·신표현을) 만들어 내다 compete v. 겨루다, 경쟁하다 alternative a. 대체 가능한, 대안적인 egalitarian a. 평등주의의 n. 평등주의자 principle n. 원칙, 원리 absolute a. 절대적인 distribution n. 분배, 배급 hereditary a. 세습의 endorse v. 지지하다, 보증하다 aristocrat n. 귀족 meritocrat n. 엘리트, 실력자

radical a. 급진적인, 과격한 transitional a. 변천하는; 과도적인, 과도기의 subsequent a. 뒤의, 차후의 prestige n. 명성, 위신 reference n. 참조, 참고 justify v. 정당화하다 equalize v. 평등[동등]하게 하다

---

19 빈칸완성 ①

coin이 '(신어·신표현을) 만들어 내다'라는 의미로 빈칸에는 "a system"인 meritocracy(능력주의)를 표현할 수 있는 명사가 와야 하므로 name이 적절하다. 참고로 term에도 '용어'라는 뜻이 있지만 which term이 a system을 가리키는데 a system을 용어라고 하기는 어렵다.

---

20 내용일치 ②

능력자들은 과도기적 단계에서라면 완전한 기회의 평등을 선호했다고 했으므로 기회의 불평등에 반대했다고 할 수 있다. 따라서 ②가 옳지 않다.

위 글에 의하면, 다음 중 옳지 않은 것은?
① 칼라일은 하층 계급과 상류 계급이 모두 정직한 방식으로 불평등을 얻을 수 있는 사회 체제를 꿈꿨다.
② 옛날의 귀족들처럼 능력자들은 기회의 불평등을 기꺼이 받아들였다.
③ 평등주의 체제에서는 상품은 절대적으로 균등하게 분배되어야 한다.
④ 능력주의 체제에서는 급여와 자산을 인위적으로 균등화할 필요가 없다.

21-23

읽기를 더 잘 이해하고 그것에 더 정확하게 대응할 수 있기 위해 추론하는 방법을 배워라. 추론은 당신이 가지고 있는 정보를 기초로 하여 당신이 직접적으로 알지 못하는 것에 대해 예상하는 것이다. 그것은 추측이나 예측과 비슷하다.
추론은 상황, 해석 및 당신이 내리는 가정에 의해 영향을 받는다. 먼저, 상황이 어떻게 당신의 추론에 영향을 미칠 수 있는지 생각해보라. 예를 들어, 여러분이 생물학 수업을 듣고 있고 선생님이 퀴즈가 있을 것이라고 발표한다고 상상해 보라. (선생님이 그것이 무엇에 관한 것인지 직접적으로 말하지는 않았지만!) 당신은 퀴즈가 역사나 영어가 아니라 생물학에 관한 것일 것이라고 추론할 것이다. 만약 선생님이 큰 소리로 화를 내며 퀴즈를 발표하면, 그 학급이 충분히 공부하지 않아서 선생님이 퀴즈를 내거나 선생님이 어떤 이유에서인지 학생들에게 화가 났다고 추론할 수 있다. 당신 자신의 신념도 당신이 하는 추론에 영향을 미친다. 예를 들어, 생물학이 당신이 듣는 가장 어려운 수업이라고 생각한다면, 당신은 시험이 매우 어려울 것이라고 추론할 수 있다. 언어는 또한 추론에서 중요한 역할을 한다. 작가는 단어 선택을 통해 독자를 특정한 추론으로 이끌 수 있다. 추론에서 언어의 역할을 이해하기 위해 읽을 때 추론을 어디서 얻고 있는지 고려해 보라.

inference n. 추론, 추리 accurately ad. 정확하게 expectation n. 예상, 기대 directly ad. 직접적으로 guess n. 추측 circumstance n. (보통 pl.) 상황, 환경 interpretation n. 해석, 설명 assumption n. 가정 infer v. 추론하다

---

21 글의 제목 ③

읽기를 더 잘 이해하기 위해 추론하는 방법에 대한 글로 추론은 상황, 해석 및 당신이 내리는 가정에 의해 달라질 수 있다고 했다. 따라서 ③ '더 나은 이해를 위한 추론 사용'이 제목으로 적절하다.

다음 중 위 글의 제목으로 적절한 것은?
① 수업에서 선생님의 역할
② 시험을 잘 준비하는 방법
③ 더 나은 이해를 위한 추론 사용
④ 언어 능력을 향상시키는 방법

---

22 빈칸완성 ③

Ⓐ guess와 유사한 의미의 표현이 와야 하는데 앞에서 추론은 직접적으로 알지 못하는 것에 대한 예상이라고 했으므로 '예측'이란 뜻의 prediction이 적절하다. ⓒ 언어가 추론에 중요한 역할을 한다고 했으므로 빈칸에는 언어와 관련된 내용이 와야 한다. 따라서 '단어 선택'이란 뜻의 word choice가 적절하다.

다음 중 빈칸 Ⓐ와 ⓒ에 들어가기에 가장 적절한 것은?
① 창조 — 수사법
② 상상 — 의미
③ 예측 — 단어 선택
④ 혐의 — 줄거리

---

23 빈칸완성 ④

신념이 추론에 영향을 미칠 수 있는 한 예로 생물학 수업을 제시하고 있는데 당신이 생물학 수업이 어렵다고 생각한다면 그 시험도 어렵게 생각할 것이다. 따라서 빈칸에는 ④가 적절하다.

다음 중 빈칸 Ⓑ에 들어가기에 가장 적절한 것은?
① 선생님은 나에게 추가 수업을 들으라고 강요할 것이다
② 선생님은 시험을 도와줄 것이다
③ 시험이 좋은 성과를 낼 것이다
④ 시험이 매우 어려울 것이다

24-25

동물이 포유류인지 아닌지를 결정하는 분명한 특징들이 있다. 포유류의 새끼는 어미의 자궁에서 자란다. 포유류가 태어나면 그들은 살아 있다. 암컷 포유류는 새끼에게 먹이를 주기 위해 모유를 생산한다. 포유류는 추운 날씨에 몸을 따뜻하게 하기 위해 머리털이나 털을 가지고 있다. 포유류는 성숙하면서 이빨이 자랄 수 있고, 팔과 손도 가지고 있다.
새는 포유류와 다르다. 새는 깃털과 날개를 가지고 있다. 동물이 새로 간주되기 위해 날 수 있어야 하는 것은 아니다. 하지만 새는 깃털을 가지고 있어야 한다. 비둘기, 칠면조, 닭, 오리는 모두 깃털을 가지고 있기 때문에 새이다. 새는 알을 낳고 알이 부화할 때까지 보살핀다. 새는 오랜 시간 동안 날아야 하기 때문에 더 많은 산소가 필요하다. 그래서 그들은 더 복잡한 호흡 체계를 가지고 있다.
박쥐는 그들이 생산하는 모유로 새끼를 키운다. 박쥐는 털을 가지고 있고

손을 사용해 먹이를 잡는다. 사람들은 박쥐가 깃털이 없는 것을 알았지만 여전히 그들을 새라고 불렀다. 사람들은 박쥐가 날 수 있다는 이유만으로 새라고 생각하곤 했다. 하지만 이제 우리는 깃털이 없는 새 같은 것은 없다는 것을 안다. 펭귄도 깃털이 있다. 펭귄은 크고 뚱뚱한 새이지만 날 수 없다. 펭귄은 수영을 할 수 있지만, 그렇다고 해서 물고기가 되는 것은 아니다. 그래서 박쥐는 날 수 있지만 새가 아니다. 박쥐는 날 수 있는 유일한 포유류이다.

characteristic n. 특질, 특성, 특징 mammal n. 포유동물 offspring n. 자식; (동물의) 새끼 womb n. 자궁 mature v. 성숙하다 hatch v. (알이) 부화하다 complex a. 복잡한 respiratory a. 호흡의, 호흡기관의 nurse v. ~에게 젖을 먹이다, 키우다, 양육하다 featherless a. 깃털이 없는

---

24 빈칸완성 ②

새들이 날기 위해서는 복잡한 호흡 체계를 가지고 있어야 한다고 했으므로 빈칸에는 호흡과 관련된 표현이 와야 한다. 호흡을 하는 데 산소가 필요하므로 ② oxygen이 적절하다.

다음 중 빈칸에 들어가기에 가장 적절한 것은?
① 에너지
② 산소
③ 깃털
④ 물

---

25 내용일치 ④

포유류는 추운 날씨에 몸을 따뜻하게 하기 위해 머리털이나 털을 가지고 있다고 했으므로 ④가 적절하다. ① 손을 사용해 먹이를 잡는 것은 박쥐에게만 해당된다. ② 펭귄은 새이지만 날 수 없다. ③ 새는 모두 깃털을 가지고 있어야 한다.

위 글에 의하면, 다음 중 옳은 것은?
① 박쥐와 새는 손을 사용해 먹이를 잡는다는 점에서 비슷하다.
② 펭귄은 날 수 있기 때문에 새로 분류된다.
③ 깃털을 가진 모든 것이 새는 아니다.
④ 포유류는 추운 날씨로부터 자신을 보호하기 위해 털을 기른다.

26-27

비록 세부사항에 대한 논쟁이 있을 수 있지만, 지난 수십 년간 우리의 기후에 증가하는 변화가 있었다는 것은 의심의 여지가 없다. 해가 지날수록 세계적인 행동과 개입의 필요성이 더욱 분명해진다. 증가한 극심한 날씨와 홍수에서부터 많은 동식물 종의 감소에 이르기까지 영향을 받지 않은 것은 없다. 한 예는 호주 주변의 그레이트 배리어 리프에 있다. 그레이트 배리어 리프는 2,300km 이상에 걸쳐 뻗어 있는 산호초 지역이다. 이 살아 있는 수중 생태계는 수백 종의 다양한 종류의 다른 수생 동물, 물고기 및 새에게 서식지를 제공한다. 불행하게도 그레이트 배리어 리프는 모든 산호초와 마찬가지로 수온 변화에 민감하다. 그러므로, 지구 온난화의 일부인 해수 온도의 상승은 그레이트 배리어 리프에 심각한 영향을 미쳤다. 산호초는 정교한 체계다. 그들은 그들 안에 일종의 조류(藻類)인 작은 생물체를 포함하고 있다. 이 유기체들은 산호에 다양한 아름다운 색깔을 줄

뿐만 아니라 수중 생태계 아래에서 생활하는 것을 돕는다. 이 조류는 산호에 전달하는 먹이를 생산한다. 이것은 결국 산호가 자라고 퍼지게 하여 다른 수중 동물에게 서식지와 먹이를 제공한다. 불행하게도, 온도 상승은 산호초가 그들의 체계에서 조류를 쫓아내게 한다. 이것은 전체 생태계를 붕괴시키고 산호의 색을 잃게 한다. 살아 있지 않은 산호는 색이 바랜 흰색이 된다. 회복할 기회가 주어지지 않으면 그 피해는 영구적이 될 수 있다. 최근의 한 과학적 조사는 그레이트 배리어 리프의 3분의 2가 이제 이 색이 바랜 흰색으로 변했다는 것을 발견했다.

specific n. (종종 pl.) 명세, 상세한 점 intervention n. 중재, 조정; 개입, 간섭 extreme weather 극심한 날씨, 기상이변 flooding n. 홍수, 범람 coral reef 산호초 stretch v. (~으로) 뻗어 있다, 펼쳐 있다 underwater a. 물속의, 수중의 ecosystem n. 생태계 algae n. 조류 (藻類: 물속에 사는 하등 식물의 한 무리) kick out ~를 쫓아내다 disrupt v. 붕괴시키다, 분열시키다 washed-out a. (빨아서) 색이 바랜 permanent a. 영속하는, 영구적인

---

26 빈칸완성 ④

지난 수십 년간 기후가 점점 더 변화함에 따라 날씨와 동식물에 영향을 미쳤다는 것이다. 빈칸 앞에 'from A to B'의 구문이 와서 '~에서부터 …에 이르기까지'의 의미이므로 극심한 날씨와 홍수에서부터 동식물 종의 감소에 이르기까지 모두 영향을 받았다는 내용이 되어야 한다. 따라서 빈칸에는 '영향을 받지 않은 것이 없다'는 의미의 ④가 적절하다.

다음 중 빈칸에 들어가기에 가장 적절한 것은?
① 사람들은 문제를 해결하는 데 기여했다
② 생물 생태계가 실패했다
③ 국제법이 통과되어야 한다
④ 영향을 받지 않은 것은 없다

---

27 내용일치 ③

조류는 산호에 전달하는 먹이를 생산하고, 이것이 산호가 자라고 퍼지게 하여 다른 수중 동물에게 서식지와 먹이를 제공한다고 했다. 따라서 조류가 서식지와 먹이를 제공받는 것이 아니라 제공하는 것이므로 ③이 옳지 않다.

위 글에 의하면, 다음 중 옳지 않은 것은?
① 산호가 죽으면, 그들의 색깔은 색이 바랜 흰색으로 변한다.
② 해수 온도의 상승은 그레이트 배리어 리프의 색상 손실을 유발할 수 있다.
③ 그레이트 배리어 리프의 조류는 서식지와 먹이와 같은 도움을 제공받는다.
④ 호주에는 약 2,300km에 달하는 긴 산호초 지역이 있다.

28-30

눈송이의 기하학적 구조를 식별하기 위해서는 현미경과 충분히 찬 온도가 필요하다. 표준 육면체의 눈송이는 섭씨 -15도 또는 화씨 5도 이하에서만 형성된다. 눈송이를 조사하고 묘사하는 작업은 17세기에 로버트 혹 (Robert Hooke)의 유명한 현미경 관찰 개론에서 진지하게 시작되었고, 보다 뛰어난 현미경으로 인해 육면 대칭의 더 복잡한 그림을 그릴 수 있게

됨에 따라 다음 200년 동안 계속되었다.

후크의 눈송이는 약간 투박하지만, 1820년에 북극 탐험가 윌리엄 스코어스비(William Scoresby)가 그린 화려한 형태는 모범적인 대칭을 보여준다. 스코어스비는 신이 자신의 창조물에 자신의 완벽함을 부여하는 것을 보았다.

눈송이가 정말로 그렇게 완벽한가? 스코어스비는 그것들을 그렇게 그렸지만, 다른 눈송이 과학자들의 보고서는 다시 생각해보게 할지도 모른다. 1855년 특히 혹독한 겨울 혹한 기간 동안, 영국의 기상학자 제임스 글레이셔(James Glaisher)는 눈송이를 스케치하여 그것들을 삽화가에게 맡겨 마무리 작업을 하게 했다. 그 그림들은 아름다웠고, 각각의 눈송이는 그 자체로 육면체로 완벽했다. 그러나 글레이셔가 말했듯이 이상은 인식되지 않고 오히려 추론되었다. 스케치에는 그것(인식된 이상)이 전혀 없었다. 삽화가는 완성된 그림을 마무리 짓기 위해 눈송이의 대칭을 가정했다.

discern v. 식별하다, 분간하다　geometry n. 기하학; 기하학적 구조　snowflake n. 눈송이　canonical a. 규범적인, 표준적인　compendium n. 대요, 요약, 개론　observation n. 관찰, 관측　intricate a. 복잡한　symmetry n. 대칭　illustration n. 삽화, 도해; 실례; 설명, 해설　uncouth a. 거친, 투박한　resplendent a. 눈부시게 빛나는, 화려한　Arctic a. 북극의　explorer n. 탐험가, 답사자　exemplary a. 모범적인, 전형적인　symmetry n. 대칭, 균형　impart v. 나누어 주다, 주다　perfection n. 완벽, 완전　immaculate a. 결점이 없는, 완전한　prompt v. 촉구하다, 유발하다　second thought 재고, 다시 생각함　brutal a. (기후가) 혹독한, 사나운　freeze n. 결빙; 혹한　flawless a. 흠 없는; 완벽[완전]한　round out 완성하다, 마무리 짓다

---

28 동의어　　　　　　　　　　④

immaculate는 '결점이 없는, 완전한'이라는 의미이므로 ④가 동의어로 적절하다.

다음 중 밑줄 친 단어 "immaculate"와 의미가 가장 가까운 것은?
① 조심성 없는
② 면역의
③ 내재하는
④ 결점이 없는

---

29 빈칸완성　　　　　　　　　②

완성된 스케치의 눈송이는 육면 대칭으로 완벽했지만 눈송이는 실제로는 그렇지 않았고 삽화가가 그림을 완성하기 위해 눈송이의 대칭을 가정해서 그린 것에 불과하다는 것으로 서로 대조되는 내용이므로 빈칸에는 역접의 접속부사인 ② however가 적절하다.

다음 중 빈칸에 들어가기에 가장 적절한 것은?
① 더욱이
② 그러나
③ 그럼에도 불구하고
④ 게다가

---

30 내용일치　　　　　　　　　④

삽화가가 그림을 완성하기 위해 눈송이의 대칭을 가정해서 그렸다고 했으므로 ④가 적절하다. ① 육면체의 눈송이는 인식되지 않고 추론된 것이다. ② 눈송이의 관찰은 19세기가 아니라 17세기에 로버트 훅의 현미경 관찰 개론에서 시작되었다. ③ 눈송이는 섭씨 -15도 또는 화씨 5도 이하에서만 형성된다.

위 글에 의하면, 다음 중 옳은 것은?
① 육면체의 눈송이는 육안으로 볼 수 있다.
② 눈송이의 관찰은 19세기에 진지하게 연구하기 시작했다.
③ 눈송이는 섭씨 -15도 또는 화씨 5도 이하에서 형성되지 않는다.
④ 삽화가는 둥근 눈송이의 대칭을 가정했다.

01 ③	02 ④	03 ②	04 ④	05 ①	06 ②	07 ③	08 ①	09 ④	10 ③
11 ②	12 ②	13 ④	14 ④	15 ③	16 ④	17 ④	18 ③	19 ④	20 ①
21 ③	22 ①	23 ③	24 ④	25 ②	26 ④	27 ③	28 ④	29 ①	30 ③

01 동의어 ③

guideline n. (국가가 제시한) 지침 subsidy n. (국가의) 보조금(= grant) IRA n. 인플레이션 감축법(Inflation Reduction Act) accessory n. 장신구 fixture n. 붙박이 설치물(변기 등 이사 때 이동할 수 없는 세간) security n. 보안; (pl.) 유가 증권

많은 한국의 분석가들은 인플레이션 감축법(IRA)에 따른 전기차 보조금 세부 지침이 그들의 예상과 크게 다르지 않다고 말한다.

02 동의어 ④

incidence n. 발생비율(= occurrence) population n. (특정 계층의) 사람들 garlic n. 마늘 diet n. 식사, 음식 cancer-fighting a. 항암의 agent n. (특정 효과를 위해 쓰이는) 물질 prostate n. 전립선 stomach n. 위, 복부 anticipation n. 예상, 기대 control n. 지배 impediment n. 방해, 장애

다양한 사람들의 질병 발병률을 추적하는 관찰 연구는 음식에 마늘을 사용하는 것이 특히 전립선암과 위암에 대해 항암제로 작용할지도 모른다는 것을 시사한다.

03 동의어 ②

rusty a. 녹슨(= corroded) nail n. 못 soda n. 탄산수 acid n. 산 dye v. 염색하다 lumber v. (육중한 덩치로) 느릿느릿 움직이다 stoop v. 몸을 굽히다

만약 당신이 녹슨 못을 탄산수에 넣는다면, 탄산수에 들어있는 산이 못의 녹에 반응할 것이다.

04 동의어 ④

rhesus monkey 붉은털원숭이 predisposition n. 성향; (병에 대한) 소인(= inclination) alteration n. 변경, 수정 extortion n. 금품 강요, 갈취 heredity n. 유전(적 특징)

국립 아동보건인간발달연구소의 스티븐 수오미(Stephen Suomi)는 인간에 영향을 주는 것과 똑같은 수줍음에 대한 유전적 소인을 갖고 있는 붉은 털원숭이를 대상으로 연구한다.

05 동의어 ①

panhandle v. 길거리에서 구걸하다(= beg) all day long 하루 종일 have a bite to eat 한 입 먹다 hurtle v. (화살·열차 등이) 휙 소리 내며 (날아) 가다 plod v. (지쳐서) 터벅터벅 걷다 rampage v. 미친 듯이 행동하다

안정적인 수입원이 없는 H. M.은 오늘 그가 먹게 될지를 전혀 알지 못한 채 불안한 마음으로 하루 종일 길거리에서 구걸한다.

06 동의어 ②

weary a. (몹시) 지친(= fatigued) bring tears to a person's eyes ~의 눈물을 짓게 하다 frail a. (체질이) 허약한 peppy a. 기운 넘치는 robust a. 원기 왕성한 scowl v. 노려보다

그가 허약한 몸으로 내 방에 들어왔을 때, 그의 지친 얼굴은 내 눈에 눈물이 나게 만들었다.

07 동의어 ③

whip v. 채찍질하다 submission n. 굴복 resentment n. 분개, 분노 (= indignation) compensation n. 보상; 보수 wretchedness n. 가엾음 sacrifice n. 희생

그는 말을 채찍질로 굴복시키기 위해 사용한 것과 똑같은 대우를 나에게 하여, 나는 평생 분개심을 느꼈다.

08 동의어 ①

extraordinarily ad. 엄청나게 squalid a. 추잡한(= filthy) splendid a. 정말 멋진 monotonous a. 단조로운 wrathful a. 몹시 성난

당신은 그것이 매우 간단할 것이라고 생각했지만, 그것은 엄청나게 복잡하다. 당신은 그것이 끔찍할 것이라고 생각했지만, 그것은 그저 추잡하고 지루할 뿐이다.

09 복합관계형용사 ④

assure와 같은 '확신'을 나타내는 동사는 'assure+목적어+that절'의 형태로 '~에게 …을 확신시키다'는 뜻을 나타낸다. 이를 수동태로 고칠 경우, 목적어가 문두로 나가 '주어+be동사+assured+that절'의 형태를 취한다. were assured 다음의 that절에서 빈칸부터 asked까지가 would의 주어가 되고 '빈칸+questions'가 asked의 목적어가 되므로 빈칸에는 명사를 수식하며 관계절을 이끄는 관계형용사 whichever나 whatever가 들어가야 한다. 따라서 ④의 whichever가 빈칸에 적절하다. ① any of 다음에 명사가 올 경우, 그 명사 앞에 한정사가 와서 any of the여야 한다. ② every 다음에는 단수명사가 와야 한다. ③ whose는 앞에 선행사가 있어야 한다.

assure v. 확신시키다 **as soon as possible** 가능한 한 빨리

그녀의 반 학생들은 그들이 어떤 질문을 하든 가능한 한 빨리 답변을 듣게 될 것이라고 확신했다.

---

10 과거완료진행형 ③

search for의 목적어가 관계대명사 what이 되며, 그녀가 깨달았던 시제가 과거이므로, 그녀가 '찾고 있었던' 시제는 과거보다 더 이전 시제인 '과거완료'나 '과거완료진행형' 시제가 되어야 한다. 따라서 ③의 had been searching for가 빈칸에 적절하다.

art gallery 미술관, 화랑

미술관에서 그 그림을 보았을 때, 메리(Mary)는 그것이 바로 자신이 찾고 있었던 것임을 깨달았다.

---

11 be keen on ②

be keen on은 '~에 열중하다'는 뜻의 관용적인 표현으로, 이때 전치사 on이 목적어를 받기 위해서는 동명사가 이어져야 한다. 따라서 ②의 on composing이 빈칸에 적절하다.

carry on 계속하다 **compose** v. 작곡하다

우웬광(Wu Wenguang)의 딸인 우예(Wu Ye)는 그 악기를 연주하는 가족 전통을 계속 이어나가고 있으며, 그 악기를 위한 새로운 음악을 작곡하는 일에 열중하고 있다.

---

12 시제일치 ②

he assumed I will join은 원래 he assumed that I will join에서 that이 생략된 형태로, 주절의 동사가 과거시제이므로, that절의 동사 역시 '과거시제'로 시제를 일치시켜야 한다. 따라서 ②의 will join을 would join으로 고쳐야 한다.

assume v. 생각하다 **drop** v. (어디로 가는 길에) 내려주다

파티가 끝난 후 코네티컷(Connecticut)에 있는 집으로 차를 몰고 가려고 파티 장소를 떠날 때, 아버지는 내가 같이 갈 것이라 생각해서, 내 친구 크리스티나(Kristina)와 같이 살고 있는 빌리지(Village)의 아파트에 내려주겠다고 제안하셨다.

---

13 many와 much의 구분 ④

talent는 '재능'이라는 뜻으로 불가산명사이다. 불가산명사와 쓸 수 있는 형용사는 many가 아니라 much이므로, ④를 much로 고쳐야 한다.

inevitably ad. 필연적으로 **frontliner** n. 일선 직원, 최전선에서 일하는 사람 **interchangeable** a. 교체할 수 있는 **along the way** 그 과정에서

필연적으로, 이 기업들은 일선 직원들이 일을 잘 해낼 것이라고 생각하지 않으며, 일자리를 똑똑한 사람들이 아니라 교체 가능한 사람들에게 맞게 설계하며, 그러는 중에 너무나 많은 재능과 잠재력을 낭비한다.

---

14 대명사의 수일치 ④

④의 their가 가리키는 대상이 risks가 아니라 AI로 단수이므로, ④를 its로 고쳐야 한다.

serial entrepreneur 연쇄창업가 **talk up** ~을 (실제보다 더) 좋게 말하다 **animated** a. 활기가 넘치는

38세의 그 연쇄창업가는 인공지능의 위험을 실제보다 좋게 이야기하는 것으로 최근에 유명해졌지만, 그는 인공지능의 가능성에 대해 말할 때 가장 활기가 넘친다.

15-16

브라운 대 교육위원회 재판(흑인 학교 분립은 불법이라는 연방 대법원의 판례)이 공립학교뿐 아니라 그 이상에서의 인종 차별 철폐를 초래했듯이, 법원이 현재 검토하고 있는 사회적 약자 우대 정책 관련 소송들은 법이나 정책이 인종적 대표성에 근거해 사람들을 보호하거나 격려하거나 부정하는 미국 생활의 모든 부분에 의문을 제기하는 새로운 선례를 틀림없이 만들 것이라고 법률 전문가들은 말한다.
"오늘날 우리는 표면적으로는 교육에 관해 이야기하고 있습니다. 그러나 예를 들어 소수인종 기업들을 위한 정부 계약 할당에는 계약에 참여하길 원하는 백인들을 배제하기 때문에 부작용이 있습니다. 그것은 역차별의 한 예입니다. 그래서 우리는 모든 공공 계약을 재검토하고 뒤집을 필요가 있습니다. 고용도 마찬가지입니다. 백인 원고 측은 '글쎄요, 저는 아직도 직장을 구하지 못했습니다. 당신은 인종을 고려하고 있지만, 그것은 역차별입니다.'라고 말합니다. 저는 더욱 대담해진 원고 측이 역차별 주장이라고 또렷한 목소리로 맹공을 퍼붓는 것을 보게 됩니다."라고 하워드 대학교의 파월(Powell)이 말한다.
또한, 이를테면, 특정 인종 집단에만 장학금을 제공하는 민간 기업들과 공공단체들 편에서는 어느 정도의 과도한 신중함이 있을 것이다. "인종을 의식한 부분이 있는 가운데 지급되는 재정 지원 같은 것들과 장학금의 경우에 부정적인 영향이 있을 것입니다."라고 메릴랜드 대학교의 파크(Park)가 말한다. 연방대법원이 미국 생활로부터 인종적 선호를 제거하는 데 있어 너무나 많은 전문가들이 예상하는 만큼의 성공을 거둘지는 물론 결정이 내려질 때까지는 미해결 문제로 남아 있다.

desegregation n. 인종 차별 철폐   affirmative action 사회적 약자 우대정책   be bound to do 틀림없이 ~할 것이다   set a precedent 선례를 만들다   call into question ~에 의문을 제기하다   ostensibly ad. 표면적으로는   spillover effect 부작용, 여파   contract n. 계약, 약정   overturn v. (판결 등을) 뒤집다   plaintiff n. (민사 소송의) 원고, 고소인   onslaught n. 맹공격   embolden v. 대담하게 하다   articulate v. 분명히 표현하다   scholarship n. 장학금   repercussion n. 영향, 파문   race-conscious a. 소수인종 우대의   Supreme Court 대법원   scrub v. 북북 문질러 없애다   open question 미해결 문제

15 글의 주제 ③

이 글은 사회적 약자 우대정책이 원래 의도한 취지와는 다르게, 백인들이 정부 계약에서 배제되고 취업에서도 불이익을 받는 등 역차별적인 현실에 대해 말하므로 글의 주제로 ③이 적절하다.

다음 중 글의 주제는?
① 사회에서의 인종 문제와 그 해결책
② 미국 대학 입학허가에서의 인종적 편견
③ 미국에서의 사회적 약자 우대 정책과 관련한 논란이 되는 문제들
④ 사회적 약자 우대 정책이 사회에 미치는 긍정적인 영향

16 빈칸완성 ④

affirmative action은 흑인 등 소수인종에게 가했던 차별을 철폐하고 이들에게 우선권을 제공하는 정책을 말하는데, 이로 인해 정부 사업을 따내는 데 있어서 흑인들에게 유리하게 작용해 백인들이 배제되는 상황을 이야기하고 있다. 이것은 백인이 역으로 차별받는 상황에 해당하므로, 빈칸 Ⓐ에 '역차별'이 적절하고, 백인이 취업을 못하고 있는데, 그게 인종을 고려하기 때문이라는 언급이 있으므로, 빈칸 Ⓑ 역시 백인에 대한 '역차별'이 적절하다. 그리고 더욱 대담해진 백인 원고 측이 맹공을 퍼붓는 주장이라고 했으므로, 마찬가지로 '역차별'이 빈칸 Ⓒ에 적절하다.

다음 중 빈칸 Ⓐ, Ⓑ, Ⓒ에 공통적으로 들어가기에 가장 적절한 것은?
① 소수집단 우선
② 민주적인 조치
③ 인종을 고려한 입학허가
④ 역차별

17-18

비행기 추락사고는 영화에서 일어나는 것과 같은 방식으로는 실제 인생에서는 거의 일어나지 않는다. (영화에서처럼) 어떤 엔진 부품이 화염에 휩싸이고 쾅 소리를 내며 폭발하지는 않는다. 비행기의 방향타는 이륙하는 힘을 받아 갑자기 툭하고 부러지지 않는다. 일반적인 상업용 제트기는 ― 현재 개발 단계에서는 ― 거의 토스터기 만큼이나 신뢰할 수 있다. 비행기 추락사고는 사소한 어려움과 겉보기에 대수롭지 않은 오작동이 누적된 결과일 가능성이 훨씬 높다.
예를 들어, 일반적인 추락사고에서는, 날씨가 나쁜데 ― 반드시 끔찍할 정도는 아니지만, 조종사가 평소보다 조금 더 스트레스를 받을 정도로 충분히 나쁘다. 압도적인 수의 추락사고에서는, 비행기가 일정보다 늦어져, 조종사가 서두르고 있다. 추락사고 중 52%에서, 사고 당시 조종사는 12시간 이상 깨어 있었는데, 이 말은 그가 피곤한 상태이며 민첩하게 생각하

지 못했음을 의미한다. 그리고 추락사고 중 44%에서, 두 명의 조종사는 이전에 같이 비행해 본 적이 없어서, 그들은 서로가 편하지 않은 상태이다. 그때 실수가 시작된다. 그리고 그 실수는 한 번의 실수에 그치지 않는다. 일반적인 사고에는 인간이 저지른 일곱 번의 연속적인 실수들이 포함된다. 조종사들 중 한 명이 잘못을 저지르는데, 그 자체로는 문제가 되지 않는다. 그다음에 그들 중 한 명이 거기에다가 또 하나의 실수를 저지르는데, 첫 번째 실수와 결합되지만, 여전히 재앙으로 이어지지는 않는다. 그러나 그다음에 그들은 거기에다가 세 번째 실수를 하고, 그다음에 네 번째, 다섯번째, 여섯 번째, 그리고 '일곱 번째' 실수를 하는데, 대참사를 일으키는 것은 이 모든 실수가 결합되어서이다.
게다가, 이 일곱 가지 실수들이 지식이나 비행기술의 문제인 경우는 드물다. 조종사들이 어떤 중대한 기술적인 동작을 잘 해내야 하는데 실패해서가 아니다. 비행기 추락사고를 일으키는 종류의 실수들은 예외 없이 팀워크와 소통의 실수이다. 조종사 한 명이 중요한 어떤 것을 알고 있지만, 어찌 된 일인지 다른 조종사에게 그것을 알려주지 않는다. 조종사 한 명이 잘못을 저지르고, 다른 조종사가 그 잘못을 알아채지 못하는 것이다.

crash n. 추락, 불시착   bang n. 쾅 (하는 소리)   rudder n. (비행기의) 방향타   snap v. 툭 (하고) 부러지다   takeoff n. (비행기의) 이륙   dependable a. 믿을 수 있는   trivial a. 사소한, 하찮은, 대수롭지 않은   malfunction n. 오작동   consecutive a. 연속적인   on top of that 거기에다   amount to (합계가) ~에 달하다   catastrophe n. 참사, 재앙   maneuver n. (조심해서 기술적으로 하는) 동작   invariably ad. 예외 없이   somehow ad. 어찌 된 일인지

17 빈칸완성 ④

비행기 추락사고가 '어떠한' 것의 결과인지가 빈칸에 들어가야 하는데, 이 문제의 단서가 빈칸 다음 단락에 나온다. 다음 단락의 마지막 부분에 "대참사를 일으키는 것은 이 모든 실수가 결합되어서이다."라고 했으므로, 빈칸에 적절한 것은 '결합'에 해당하는 ④의 an accumulation(누적)이다.

다음 중 빈칸에 가장 적절한 것은?
① 과장
② 차이
③ 준비
④ 누적

18 내용파악 ③

"일반적인 사고에는 인간이 저지른 일곱 번의 연속적인 실수들이 포함된다."고 했으며, "대참사를 일으키는 것은 이 모든 실수가 결합되어서이다."라고 했으므로 ③이 정답이다.

위 글에 의하면, 다음 중 비행기 추락에 관해 옳은 것은?
① 처참한 비행기 추락사고는 대부분 제트기의 심각한 기계적인 문제 때문이다.
② 기상 조건은 일반적인 비행기 추락사고의 가장 유력한 원인이다.
③ 인간이 저지른 일곱 번의 연속적인 실수가 비행기 추락사고를 일으킬 수 있다.
④ 두 명의 조종사가 서로 편할 경우 비행기 추락사고를 일으킬 수 있다.

19-21

전설적인 블루스 기타리스트인 로버트 존슨(Robert Johnson)에 관해 입수할 수 있는 정보는 거의 없으며, 입수할 수 있는 정보도 사실만큼이나 소문이 많다. 그러나 논쟁의 여지가 없는 것은 존슨이 로큰롤 세계에 미친 영향이다. 일각에서는 존슨을 모던 록의 아버지라고 여긴다. 그의 영향은 머디 워터스(Muddy Waters)에서 레드 제플린(Led Zeppelin)에 이르는, 그리고 롤링 스톤스(Rolling Stones)에서 올맨 브라더스 밴드(Allman Brothers Band)에 이르는 많은 아티스트들에게 미친다. 거의 틀림없이 현존하는 가장 위대한 록 기타리스트인 에릭 클랩튼(Eric Clapton)은 "저에게 로버트 존슨은 역사상 가장 중요한 블루스 뮤지션입니다. 저는 로버트 존슨보다 더 영혼이 깊은 뮤지션을 본 적이 없습니다."라고 말했다. 존슨의 음악이 미친 영향은 분명하지만, 그의 놀라운 재능의 기원은 미스터리에 싸여 있다.

미시시피(Mississippi) 주 헤이즐허스트(Hazelhurst)에서 1911년에 태어난 존슨에게, 음악은 목화밭에서 일하는 것으로부터의 탈출 수단이었다. 소년이었을 때, 그는 노엘 존슨(Noel Johnson) 소유의 농장에서 일했는데, 그 사람이 그의 아버지라는 소문이 돌았다. 그는 17세의 젊은 나이에 결혼했는데, 1년 뒤 출산으로 그의 아내를 잃었다. 존슨이 여행을 하고 블루스를 연주하기 시작한 때가 바로 그때였다.

처음에 존슨은 하모니카를 연주했다. 나중에, 그는 기타를 연주하기 시작했지만, 그는 그다지 능숙하지는 못했던 것 같다. 그러나 그는 배우고 싶어서, 블루스 바에서 그 지역의 블루스 전설인 선 하우스(Son House)와 윌리 브라운(Willie Brown)의 연주를 들으며 시간을 보냈다. 그들이 중간에 잠깐 쉴 때, 존슨이 무대 위로 올라와 연주했다. 소문에 의하면, 선 하우스는 존슨의 실력이 너무 형편없어서 존슨에게 당장 꺼져버리라고 반복적으로 말했다고 한다. 마침내, 어느 날, 존슨은 실제로 그렇게 했다. 6개월 동안, 존슨이 불가사의하게도 사라졌던 것이다. 그가 어떻게 되었는지 아무도 알지 못했다. 존슨이 6개월 뒤에 돌아왔을 때, 그는 갑자기 일류 기타리스트가 되어 있었다. 그는 연주하는 모든 곳에서 관중을 끌어모으기 시작했다.

legendary a. 전설의 arguably ad. 거의 틀림없이 genesis n. 기원, 발생 shroud v. (정보 등을) 감추다[가리다] escape n. 탈출, 도피 break n. (작업 중의) 휴식 (시간) reportedly ad. 소문에 의하면 get lost (씩) 꺼져버리다 first-rate a. 일류의 draw crowds 관중을 끌어 모으다

---

19 글의 목적 ④

이 글은 전설적인 블루스 기타리스트인 로버트 존슨의 생애와 그의 영향력에 대해 개략적으로 설명하고 있으므로, 글의 목적으로 ④가 가장 적절하다.

다음 중 글의 가장 적절한 목적은?
① 존슨의 음악 스타일을 자세하게 설명하기 위해
② 존슨의 음악이 현대 블루스 뮤지션에게 얼마나 많은 영향을 미쳤는지를 설명하기 위해
③ 블루스 인기의 미스터리를 설명하기 위해
④ 존슨의 생애와 영향력에 관해 개략적으로 설명하기 위해

---

20 빈칸완성 ①

역접의 접속사 while이 이끄는 절에서 존슨의 음악이 갖는 영향력은 '분명하다'고 했으므로, 이와 상반되는 주절에는 '분명하지 않다'는 내용이 와야 한다. 따라서 '가려져 있는'이라는 뜻의 shrouded나 '베일에 싸인'이라는 뜻의 veiled가 빈칸 Ⓐ에 적절하고, 선 하우스가 볼 때 존슨의 실력이 형편없어서 당장 꺼지라고 존슨에게 말했는데, 실제로 존슨이 '그렇게 했다(사라졌다)'고 했으므로, 빈칸 Ⓑ에는 이와 동일한 내용인 disappeared가 적절하다.

다음 중 빈칸 Ⓐ와 Ⓑ에 가장 적절한 것은?
① 가려진 — 사라지다
② 비범한 — 위반하다
③ 베일에 싸인 — 남아있다
④ 덫에 걸린 — 폭로하다

---

21 내용파악 ③

그가 6개월 동안 모습을 감춘 후 돌아왔을 때 그는 일류 기타리스트가 되어 관중을 끌어 모았다고 했으므로 ③이 정답이다. ① 그가 건강이 쇠약해졌는지는 이 글에서 알 수 없다. ② 그는 하모니카를 기타보다 먼저 연주했다. ④ 그는 지역의 블루스 전설들이 쉬는 동안에 무대에 오를 수 있었다.

위 글에 의하면, 다음 중 존슨에 관해 옳은 것은?
① 그는 건강이 심각하게 쇠약해져 좌절감을 느꼈다.
② 그는 기타를 연주하는 법을 배운 이후에 하모니카를 연주하기 시작했다.
③ 그는 6개월간의 부재를 끝내고 돌아왔을 때 인기를 끌었다.
④ 그는 원할 때마다 지역 블루스 바의 무대에 오를 수 있었다.

22-23

언어는 종종 민족의 경계 지표 역할을 한다. 개인의 모국어는 세계의 많은 지역에서 민족 집단의 정체성을 나타내는 주요 지표이다. 언어와 마찬가지로, 종교도 민족의 경계 지표 역할을 할지도 모른다. 기독교, 이슬람교, 불교 등 세계의 주요 종교는 수많은 별개의 민족 집단들을 포함하고 있어서, 어떤 종교에 속해있느냐가 어떤 민족에 속해있느냐를 항상 나타내지는 않는다. 그러나 많은 경우, 종교와 민족 집단은 어느 정도 일치한다. 유대인들은 종교 집단으로도 민족 집단으로도 분류될 수 있다. 마찬가지로, 인도의 시크교도들도 종교 집단과 민족 집단 둘 모두를 구성한다. 또 다른 상황에서, 종교적 차이는 민족적 정체성을 나타내는 가장 중요한 지표일지도 모른다. 예를 들어, 세르비아 사람들과 크로아티아 사람들은 같은 언어를 사용하지만, 두 집단의 가장 중요한 차이는 바로 세르비아 사람들은 동방 정교회 신자이고 크로아티아 사람들은 가톨릭 신자라는 것이다. 반대로, 중국의 민족적 정체성은 종교적 차이를 초월한다. 예를 들어, 어떤 사람이 이슬람교 신자이든, 기독교 신자이든, 불교 신자이든, 도교 신자이든, 마르크스주의의 무신론자이든 간에 그 사람은 여전히 중국인이다.

serve as ~의 역할을 하다 boundary marker 경계지표 native language 모국어 indicator n. 지표 identity n. 정체성 encompass v. ~을 포함하다 distinct a. 별개의, 전혀 다른 affiliation n. 소속 more or less 어느 정도 correspond v. 일치하다 categorize v. 분류

하다 constitute v. ~을 구성하다 Eastern Orthodox 동방 정교회
transcend v. 초월하다 Taoist n. 도교 신자 atheist n. 무신론자

22 빈칸완성 ①

"많은 경우, 종교와 민족 집단은 어느 정도 일치한다."라고 한 다음 그 예
로, 유대인들은 종교 집단으로도 민족 집단으로도 분류될 수 있으며, 인
도의 시크교도들도 종교 집단과 민족 집단 둘 모두를 구성한다고 했다.
따라서 두 예시가 '비슷한' 내용임을 알 수 있으므로, 빈칸 Ⓐ에는
Similarly(마찬가지로)가 적절하다. 반면, 빈칸 Ⓑ를 전후로는 상반된 내
용이 나오므로, 빈칸 Ⓑ에는 Conversely(반대로)가 적절하다.

다음 중 빈칸 Ⓐ와 Ⓑ에 가장 적절한 것은?
① 마찬가지로 — 반대로
② 예를 들어 — 따라서
③ 게다가 — 결과적으로
④ 그럼에도 불구하고 — 그러나

23 글의 주제 ③

이 글은 언어와 종교가 민족의 경계 지표 역할을 한다는 내용을 민족에
따라 유사점과 차이점으로 구분해 설명하고 있으므로 글의 주제로 ③이
적절하다.

다음 중 글의 주제는?
① 언어 및 종교와 결합된 민족적 정체성
② 언어와 종교의 민족적 특징
③ 민족의 경계 지표로서의 언어와 종교
④ 한 민족 집단에서 언어와 종교의 독특함

24-25

클로비스 사람들은 마지막 빙하기가 끝날 때인 대략 13,500년 전에 북아
메리카에 처음 출현한 선사시대의 팔레오인디언 집단이었다. 클로비스 사
람들이 어떻게 북아메리카에 도착했고 그들이 어디서 왔는지는 여전히
많은 논쟁이 있다. 한 이론은 그들이 알래스카 지역에서 왔으며, 먹이(사냥
감)를 찾아 남쪽으로 이동했다고 제안한다. 또 다른 가설은 클로비스 사람
들의 조상들이 남아메리카에서 왔다고 주장한다. 학자들은 클로비스 문화
와 유사한 특징을 공유하는 브라질과 칠레의 클로비스 이전 시대의 유적지
를 지적한다. 보다 최근의 가설은 클로비스 사람들이 그린란드에서 뉴욕에
이르는 빙상의 가장자리와 가까운 거리를 유지하며 배를 타고 유럽에서
북아메리카로 왔다는 것이다. 하지만 이러한 이론들 중 어느 것도 고고학
자들에 의해 완전히 인정되지는 않았다.
잘 보존된 다양한 인공물들은 클로비스 사람들의 생활방식을 엿볼 수 있게
해준다. 다양한 유적지에서 발굴된 증거에는 이제는 클로비스 촉이라 불리
는 세로로 홈이 새겨진 돌촉들이 있다. 이 돌촉들은 아마도 일종의 창에
부착되어 덩치가 큰 사냥감을 사냥하는 데 사용되었을지도 모른다. 그 유
적지에서 발견된 대부분의 클로비스 촉들의 길이는 1~5인치이다. 보다
큰 촉들은 무시무시하게 큰 마스토돈과 매머드 같은 거대한 사냥감을 사냥
하는 데 필수적이었다. 이렇게 거대한 동물들은 선호됐는데, 왜냐하면 하
나의 동물에서 나오는 고기가 큰 부족이 약 한 달 동안 먹고 살 수 있을
정도로 충분한 음식을 제공해 주었기 때문이다. 고기 외에도, 클로비스
사람들은 뼈, 상아, 가죽을 이용해 주거지, 옷, 요리기구, 도구, 그리고 기타

무기들을 만들었다. 클로비스 사람들은 그들의 먹이들이 물을 먹을 수 있
는 늪지대에 모이기 때문에, 매복 사냥 기술을 사용했을 가능성이 있다.
그 연한 지형이 동물들의 이동을 방해했을 것이다.

prehistoric a. 선사시대의 migrate v. 이주하다, 이동하다 prey n.
(사냥 동물의) 먹이[사냥감] hypothesis n. 가설 ancestor n. 조상
edge n. 끝, 가장자리 span v. (넓은 범위에) 걸치다 archaeologist
n. 고고학자 artifact n. (역사적 의미가 있는) 인공물 unearth v. (땅속
에서) 파내다 fluted a. 세로로 홈이 새겨진 dub v. ~을 …이라고 부르다
game n. 사냥감 monstrous a. 무시무시하게 큰 tusk n. (코끼리의)
엄니[상아] hide n. (짐승의) 가죽 shelter n. 주거지, 피신처 ambush
n. 매복 (공격) congregate v. 모이다 marshy a. 늪의, 습지의 terrain
n. 지형 hinder v. 방해하다

24 글의 주제 ④

이 글은 클로비스 사람들은 누구이며, 어디서 왔고, 어떻게 북아메리카
에 왔는지, 그리고 그들의 생활방식은 어떠한지에 관한 여러 가지 가설
에 대해 이야기하고 있다. 따라서 글의 주제로 ④가 적절하다.

다음 중 글의 주제는?
① 클로비스 사람들의 흥망성쇠
② 어떻게 클로비스 사람들은 거대한 사냥감을 사냥했는가
③ 클로비스 사람들의 이주 패턴
④ 클로비스 사람들의 기원과 생활방식

25 내용파악 ②

"또 다른 가설은 클로비스 사람들의 조상들이 남아메리카에서 왔다고
주장하며, 학자들이 클로비스 문화와 유사한 특징을 공유하는 브라질과
칠레의 유적지를 지적했다."라고 했으므로 ②가 정답이다. ① 가장 최근
의 가설은 클로비스 사람들이 유럽에서 왔다고 했다. ③ 그들이 '교량'이
아니라 '배'를 타고 왔을 수 있다고 했다. ④ 클로비스 촉은 '창'에 부착되
어 사용됐다고 했다.

위 글에 의하면, 다음 중 클로비스 사람들에 관해 옳은 것은?
① 최근의 이론들은 그린란드에서 그들이 왔다는 것을 보여준다.
② 일부 학자들은 그들의 조상들이 브라질과 칠레에 살았다고 말한다.
③ 일부 학자들은 그들이 교량을 사용해 북아메리카에 도착했다고 말한다.
④ 클로비스 촉은 거대한 사냥감을 사냥하는 데 활로 사용되었다.

26-27

눈사태는 넓은 지역의 땅이 갑자기 산 아래로 미끄러지거나 움직여 내려오
는 것을 말한다. 눈사태는 눈, 얼음, 바위, 흙과 같은 물질의 혼합물로 이루
어져 있다. 눈사태는 대개 온도 변화, 소리 진동, 또는 땅의 진동에 의해
유발된다. 대부분의 눈사태의 크기와 힘은 생명과 재산 모두에 심각한 위
험을 초래하고 매일 많은 생명을 잃게 한다.
눈사태가 어떻게 발생하는지 이해하기 위해서는 수 톤의 눈이 산비탈을
따라 내려올 수 있게 하는 눈의 특성을 이해하는 것이 중요하다. 특성
중 가장 중요한 것은 눈 결정의 모양이다. 습도, 온도 또는 또 다른 대기
조건에 따라 눈 결정은 다양한 모양으로 나타날 수 있다. 가장 일반적인
모양이자 가장 안정적인 눈 층을 만드는 모양은 육각형이다. 그러나 눈

결정의 모양은 쌓인 눈이나 눈더미 안의 온도 변화 또는 온도 차이로 인해 변할 수 있다. 지면의 잔열에 더 가까운 눈 결정은 작은 면들, 즉 둥근 면적을 형성하고 이 면들이 눈 결정의 강한 층을 형성할 수 있는 능력을 감소시킨다. 눈더미 깊숙한 곳에 있는, 작은 면이 심히 많이 난 결정들이 눈을 매우 불안정하게 만들어 눈사태를 일으킨다.

avalanche n. 눈사태 consist of ~로 구성되다, ~로 이루어져 있다 trigger v. 일으키다, 유발하다 vibration n. 진동 pose v. (위협·문제 등을) 제기하다 account for ~을 설명하다 descend v. 내려오다, 내려가다 mountainside n. 산비탈, 산허리 crystal n. <광물학·화학> 결정, 결정체 depending on ~에 따라 humidity n. 습도 hexagon n. 6각형 gradation n. 단계[점차]적 변화 variance n. 변화, 변동; 차이 residual heat 잔열 facet n. (다면체의) 면, (결정체·보석의) 작은 면

---

26 빈칸완성 ④

눈사태가 발생하는 이유로 눈 결정의 모양의 변화를 이야기하고 있다. 눈 결정의 모양은 눈이 가진 특성을 말하므로 두 빈칸에는 '어떤 사물에 존재하는 성질'을 뜻하는 ④ properties가 적절하다.

다음 중 빈칸 Ⓐ와 Ⓑ에 공통적으로 들어가기에 가장 적절한 것은?
① 공유성
② 양
③ 자산
④ 특성

---

27 내용일치 ③

습도, 온도 또는 또 다른 대기 조건에 따라 눈 결정은 다양한 모양으로 나타날 수 있다고 했으므로 ③이 정답이다.

위 글에 의하면, 다음 중 옳은 것은?
① 눈사태는 눈, 얼음, 흙으로만 이루어져 있다.
② 눈 결정의 크기와 힘은 온도에 의해 변하지 않는다.
③ 산의 기상 조건은 눈 결정의 모양에 영향을 줄 수 있다.
④ 눈더미 깊숙한 곳에 있는 눈 결정은 눈을 견고하게 만든다.

28-30

기억력은 완벽하지 않다. 대부분의 사람들은 이전에 시험에서 답을 잊어버린 경험이 있다. 여러 가지 일을 동시에 하는 것을 좋아하는 사람들은 또한 일을 더 쉽게 잊어버리는 경향이 있다. 게다가, 사람들이 나이가 들면서 기억력이 <증가하기> 시작하고, 정보를 저장하고 기억하는 것이 더 어려워질 수 있다. 더욱이, 뇌 손상이나 의학적 질병은 기억력 문제를 일으킬 수 있다. 극단적인 상황에서는 사람들이 기억력을 완전히 잃을 수 있다. 그럼에도 불구하고, 뇌에게 기억 기술을 통해 더 잘 기억하고 뇌의 최대 잠재력에 도달하는 방법을 가르치는 방법이 있다. 기억력을 향상시키는 (반복 이외의) 한 가지 방법은 보기, 듣기, 느끼기, 맛보기 및 만지기와 같은 감각들을 하나의 경험에 포함시키는 것이다. 경험에 포함된 감각이 더 많을수록 뇌는 경험을 더 잘 기억할 수 있다. 예를 들어, 학생이 책을 읽으면서 동시에 그 책의 오디오 버전을 듣는다면, 뇌는 그 특정한 책의 내용을 더 잘 이해하고 기억할 것이다. 기억력을 향상시키는 또 다른 방법은 기억 증진 장치를 사용하는 것이다. 이것들은 정보를 기억하는 데 도움

을 주기 위해 사용하는 기억 기술이다. 기억법의 한 유형은 음악 기억법이라 불리는데, 단어들을 노래에 넣는 것이다. 인기 있는 음악 기억법의 한 예는 알파벳 글자들을 노래로 불러 아이들이 글자 순서뿐만 아니라 글자 이름을 기억할 수 있도록 도와주는 알파벳 노래다. 기억법의 또 다른 유형은 이름 기억법이다. 예를 들어, HOMES를 아는 것은 각 호수가 HOMES (Huron, Ontario, Michigan, Erie, and Superior)의 글자 중 하나로 시작하기 때문에 미국 5대호의 이름을 기억하는 데 도움이 된다. 기억력을 향상시키는 가장 좋은 방법 중 하나는 뇌를 돌보는 것이다. 연구 결과, 규칙적으로 운동하고, 잘 자고, 균형 잡힌 식사를 하는 것이 모두 사람의 기억력의 질에 중요한 역할을 하는 것으로 밝혀졌다.

multi-task v. 한꺼번에 여러 일을 처리하다 furthermore ad. 더욱이, 게다가 brain damage 뇌 손상 extreme a. 극도의, 극단적인, 극심한 circumstance n. (보통 pl.) 상황, 환경 potential n. 가능성, 잠재력 repetition n. 반복, 되풀이 involve v. 포함하다 at the same time 동시에 mnemonic a. 기억을 돕는; 기억(술)의

---

28 빈칸완성 ④

Ⓐ 기억력을 잃을 수 있지만 기억 기술을 통해 기억력을 향상시킬 수 있다는 내용이다. 빈칸을 전후로 상반된 내용을 언급하고 있으므로 역접의 접속부사 Nevertheless가 적절하다. Ⓑ 기억력을 향상시키는 한 가지 방법인 경험에 감각을 포함시키는 것의 예로 책을 읽으면서 동시에 그 책의 오디오 버전을 듣는 것을 들고 있으므로 For example이 적절하다. 따라서 상기 두 조건을 모두 만족시키는 ④가 정답이다.

다음 중 빈칸 Ⓐ와 Ⓑ에 들어가기에 가장 적절한 것은?
① 반대로 ─ 그러나
② 게다가 ─ 더욱이
③ 마찬가지로 ─ 그에 반해서
④ 그럼에도 불구하고 ─ 예를 들어

---

29 문맥상 적절하지 않은 단어 고르기 ①

넷째 문장 첫머리에 In addition(게다가)이 있으므로 앞의 문장을 부연하는 내용이 와야 한다. 쉽게 잊어버리는 경향에 대해 이야기하고 있으므로 뒤에도 이와 유사한 내용이 이어져야 한다. 따라서 나이가 들면서 기억력은 감소하기 시작한다고 해야 적절하므로 ① increase(증가하다)를 decrease(감소하다)로 고쳐야 한다.

---

30 내용파악 ③

마지막 문단에서 기억력을 향상시키는 가장 좋은 방법 중 하나는 뇌를 돌보는 것이라고 언급하고, 연구 결과 규칙적으로 운동하고, 잘 자고, 균형 잡힌 식사를 하는 것이 기억력의 질에 중요한 역할을 하는 것으로 밝혀졌다고 했으므로 ③이 정답이다.

위 글에 의하면, 다음 중 기억력에 관해 옳은 것은?
① 기억력이 좋은 사람들은 대개 뛰어난 감각을 가지고 있다.
② 반복은 주어진 시간에 정보를 더 잘 기억하는 가장 좋은 방법이다.
③ 기억력의 질은 뇌의 건강과 상태에 달려 있다.
④ 이름 기억법은 노래에 정보를 넣어 기억하는 방법이다.

2024 덕성여자대학교(1교시)

01 ④	**02** ②	**03** ④	**04** ④	**05** ②	**06** ①	**07** ④	**08** ②	**09** ③	**10** ①
11 ②	**12** ④	**13** ①	**14** ②	**15** ②	**16** ③	**17** ①	**18** ③	**19** ④	**20** ①
21 ①	**22** ①	**23** ②	**24** ①	**25** ④	**26** ④	**27** ③	**28** ②	**29** ③	**30** ②
31 ①	**32** ①	**33** ③							

01 동의어 ④

deter v. 억지하다, 방해하다(= hinder) halt v. 멈추다 steer v. 조종하다 trace v. 추적하다

02 동의어 ②

caucus n. 간부회의(= meeting) corpse n. 시체 partnership n. 협력, 제휴 dispersal n. 분산

03 동의어 ④

liaison n. 연락, 연결(= association) permission n. 허가 remedy n. 구제 association n. 연합, 연상

04 동의어 ④

excavation n. 구멍파기, 굴착; 발굴 sporadically ad. 산발적으로, 이따금(= occasionally) vigorously ad. 열렬히 cautiously a. 조심스럽게

폼페이에서의 발굴은 산발적으로 계속되었다.

05 동의어 ②

monarchy n. 군주제; 군주국(= empire) absolute monarchy 절대 군주국 imperialism n. 제국주의(정책, 사상) stronghold n. 거점 monologue n. 독백

프랑스는 혁명 전까지 절대 군주국가를 갖고 있었다.

06 동의어 ①

court n. 법원 drunk driving offender 음주운전 가해자 redress n. 배상(= compensation) victim n. 희생자 car crash 교통사고 evidence n. 근거 property n. 자산 significance n. 중요성

법원은 음주운전 가해자에게 교통사고 피해자에 대한 고액의 배상금을 지급하라고 명령했다.

07 논리완성 ④

for절에서 양보다는 질이 선호된다고 했으므로 두 번째 빈칸에는 '질'이라는 의미의 caliber가 적절하고 이것은 교육 시스템에 대한 판단이나 평가의 기준이므로 첫 번째 빈칸에는 judged가 적절하다.

turn out 생산하다 quality n. 양 prefer v. 선호하다 quantity n. 질 caliber n. 질, 우수성

교육 시스템은 양보다 질이 더 선호되기 때문에 그 시스템이 배출하는 학생의 질로 판단되어야 한다.

08 논리완성 ②

자유롭게 말하도록 허용되어 있을 때는 그것이 얼마나 복된 것인지 모르지만, 그 자유가 제약되면 불편해져서 분노를 낳는다는 말이다. 역접의 접속사 but으로 연결되었으므로, 첫 번째 빈칸에는 anger와 반대되는 blessed가 적절하고 두 번째 빈칸에는 allowed와 반대되는 restriction이 적절하다.

blessed a. 복 받은 free speech 언론의 자유 restriction n. 제약 scholarly a. 학자의 enslaved a. 예속된 misuse n. 오용

언론의 자유가 허용될 때 우리는 행복을 거의 느끼지 못하지만, 언론의 자유가 제약되면 분노를 느낀다.

09 논리완성 ③

충동적으로 행동하는 사람은 열정적이고 성미가 급한 성격이라 할 수 있다.

act on impulse 충동적으로 행동하다 stoic a. 금욕적인 reflective a. 사색적인 passionate a. 열정적인, 성미 급한 wistful a. 그리워하는

그녀의 열정적인 성격 때문에 샘(Sam)은 종종 순전히 충동적으로 행동한다.

10 논리완성 ①

inability가 무능력이라는 의미이므로, 빈칸에는 사람에 대한 부정적인 의미인 shortcoming이 적절하다.

candidate n. 후보 shortcoming n. 단점 virtue n. 미덕 extinction n. 멸종 performance n. 업무수행

그 후보가 중산층 유권자들과 소통하지 못하는 무능력이 그의 가장 큰 단점이었다.

---

11 논리완성 ②

뒤에서 재무 부서에서 불일치가 무엇인지 확인했다고 하였으므로, 앞에서도 회계 감사원이 불일치에 상당하는 것을 발견해야 한다.

auditor n. 회계 감사관 financial a. 재무의 prompt v. 촉진하다 annual report 연간보고서 finalize v. 완성하다 infusion n. 주입 discrepancy n. 불일치 complacency n. 만족 cohesion n. 응집력

회계 감사관이 회사 기록에서 중요한 재무 불일치를 발견하여, 재무 부서에서 즉시 조사하여 연례 보고서가 완성되기 전에 불일치 사항을 확인했다.

---

12 논리완성 ④

재고품의 수를 다 헤아린 후 재고 수준을 정확하게 맞추려면 제품의 총수가 몇 개인지 계산해야 한다.

complete v. 끝내다 inventory n. 재고 warehouse manager 창고 관리자 ensure v. 보장하다 stock n. 재고 merge v. 병합하다 skew v. 기울이다 collide v. 충돌하다 tally v. 계산하다, 기록하다

재고품의 수를 다 헤아린 후 창고 관리자는 정확한 재고 수준을 보장하기 위해 제품의 총수를 계산해야 했다.

---

13 가정법 ①

주절의 동사의 형태가 '조동사의 과거형+have p.p.'이므로 가정법 과거완료의 문장임을 알 수 있다. 가정법 과거완료의 조건절의 형태는 'if+주어+had p.p.'이므로 ①이 빈칸에 적절하다.

네가 내 말을 들었더라면, 안전했을 텐데.

---

14 문의 구성 / 태 ②

produce라는 동사가 있으므로 주어가 필요한데, 상품은 사람에 의해 생산되는 것이므로, 수동태가 적합하다. 상품은 goods라는 복수형 명사로 복수 취급하므로 are가 동사로 적절하다.

그 상품은 서울에 있는 우리 공장에서 생산된다.

---

15 동사 ②

congratulate는 A on B 꼴로 사용하고, 'A에게 B에 대해서 축하하다'는 의미이다.

한 동료가 나에게 시험에서 좋은 성적을 거둔 것에 대해 축하해 주었다.

---

16 일치 / 시제 ③

분수와 같이 부분을 나타내는 명사는 그 뒤 전명구에 있는 명사의 수에 따라 단수와 복수가 정해진다. 여기서는 residents가 복수이므로 복수 동사가 필요하다. 남북전쟁 전은 과거 시점이므로 과거시제이다.

Civil War 남북전쟁 resident n. 거주민

남북전쟁 이전에는 미국 인구의 8분의 1이 노예였다.

---

17 형용사 ①

등위접속사 and로 연결되어 있고, 앞은 박식함이라는 명사, 뒤에는 강의 스타일이라는 명사가 있으므로 강의 스타일이라는 명사를 수식하는 형용사가 필요하다.

erudition n. 학식 pedagogical a. 교육적인 captivate v. 매혹하다 foster v. 키우다 appreciation n. 이해

학식과 교육적인 강의 스타일로 유명한 그 교수는 학생들을 매혹하고 주제에 대한 깊은 이해를 키워준다.

---

18 시제의 일치 ③

③ and로 연결되어 있는데 앞에서 과거 시제 동사 read이 쓰였으므로, 뒤에도 과거시제여야 한다. 따라서 begun을 began으로 고쳐야 한다.

pursue v. 추구하다 enroll v. 등록하다 nervous a. 긴장한, 초조한 instructor n. 강사 hand out 나누어주다 assignment n. 과제 pay attention to ~에 주의를 기울이다 excel v. 최선을 다하다 set about 착수하다 keen a. 날카로운 challenge n. 도전 capture v. 포착하다 subject n. 피사체

수년간 간절히 바란 끝에 마침내 아만다(Amanda)는 사진에 대한 열정을 추구해보기로 결심했다. 그녀는 새 카메라를 사서 사진 강좌에 등록했다. 수업 첫날, 그녀는 설레면서도 긴장했다. 강사는 강의 계획서를 나눠주고 과제를 설명하면서 세부 사항에 주의를 기울이는 것이 중요하다고 강조했다. 아만다는 남보다 잘할 결심이 서 있어서 지침을 주의 깊게 읽은 후 첫 번째 과제를 시작했다. 그녀는 디테일에 대한 예리한 안목과 창의력을 발휘하여 과제에 착수했다. 그녀는 자신을 기다리고 있는 도전이 기술적인 능력뿐만 아니라 피사체의 본질을 독특한 방식으로 포착하는 능력까지 시험하게 될 줄은 거의 알지 못했다.

---

19 한정사 / 동사의 용법 ④

more는 much의 비교급이다. much나 more는 all 같은 전치 한정사가 아니므로 한정사인 소유격 my 앞에 바로 올 수 없다. 의미는 '내 시간 중 더 많은 부분'이 되어야 하므로 전치사 of를 넣어야 '명사+명사'를 연결할 수 있다. 게다가 spend 동사는 'spend+목적어+on+명사' 혹은 'spend+목적어+(in) ~ing'의 형태로 사용해야 하므로, hang out도

hanging out으로 고쳐야 한다. 그래서 ④를 spent more of my time hanging out으로 고쳐야 한다.

mess around with 만지작거리다 foresee v. 예견하다 afford v. 제공하다 stable a. 안정된 pay well 보수가 좋다 hang out with 어울리다

어렸을 때 나는 여가시간 대부분을 컴퓨터를 만지작거리면서 보냈다. 내가 컴퓨터 프로그래머라는 직업을 갖게 되리라 예상하는 것이 그리 어렵지 않았을 것 같다. 그것으로 나는 보수도 좋고 즐겁게 일할 수 있는 안정적인 직업을 갖게 되었다. 하지만 다른 사람들과 어울리는 데 더 많은 시간을 보냈더라면 좋았을 텐데 하는 생각이 든다.

---

20 빈칸완성   ①

앞에서 클레오파트라의 미모를 이야기하고 있고, 뒤에서도 역시 외모와 관련된 이야기가 이어지고 있으므로, 외모라는 주제를 담고 있는 ①이 빈칸에 적절하다.

assume v. 가정하다 strategy n. 전략 footing n. 기반 portray v. 그리다 reign n. 통치 hawk n. 매

줄리어스 시저와 마크 안토니우스와 같은 위대한 로마 지도자들이 이집트의 위대한 여왕 클레오파트라를 사랑했다는 것을 역사에서 배울 때, 우리는 클레오파트라가 자신의 뛰어난 미모를 일종의 전략으로 이용해 이집트를 로마와의 좀 더 유리한 관계에 있게 했다고 가정한다. 그녀의 삶은 영화에서 항상 이렇게 묘사된다. 그러나 우리는 그녀가 정말로 아름다웠는지 모른다. 오히려 몇 가지 증거는 그녀가 그렇지 않았다는 것을 암시하는 듯하다. 클레오파트라의 통치 시기에 만들어진 동전 세트에는 그녀가 거대한 목과 매와 같은 이목구비를 가진 것으로 묘사되어 있다.

다음 중 이 글을 완성하기에 가장 적절한 것은?
① 클레오파트라는 정말 아름다웠다.
② 그녀는 진정으로 시저의 사랑을 받았다.
③ 클레오파트라는 정말로 여왕이었다.
④ 그녀는 진정으로 정직한 여왕이었다.

21-23

최근 1860년대까지만 해도 대부분의 사람들은 지구가, 그리고 지구와 더불어 인류도, 불과 6,000~7,000년 전에 만들어졌다고 믿었다. 수 세기 동안 아름답게 세공된 부싯돌은 요정이 만든 것으로 여겨졌는데, 이는 그리스와 로마 제국 시대 훨씬 이전에 인간이 작은 무리를 지어 세계의 황무지를 돌아다녔다는 생각보다 한때는 훨씬 더 그럴듯한 생각이었다. 이 돌이 인간이 만든 도구로 받아들여졌을 때도 로마인이나 초기 영국인이 만든 것으로 여겨졌다.
오늘날 우리는 더 넓은 관점에서 생각하고 있지만, 인류의 시작에 대한 오래된 생각은 서서히 사라졌다. 18세기 말과 19세기 초 동안, 주로 열성적인 아마추어 발굴가들이 인간과 멸종된 동물의 화석 유해를 석기 도구와 연관 짓기 시작했다. 하지만 지질학자 대부분은 이러한 연관성이 단지 우연일 뿐이라고 주장하면서 계속 성경적 관점에서 생각했다. 그들은 노아의 홍수로 인해 고대 동물의 뼈와 최근 인류의 도구와 유골이 섞였다고 믿었다. (하지만) 고고학자들이 프랑스 솜므강 유역 여러 주요 유적지를 비롯해 홍수에 휩쓸리지 않은 멀쩡한 퇴적층에서 뼈와 도구를 함께 발견하기 시작하면서 이러한 이론은 마침내 무너졌다. 프랑스 퇴적층을 확인하러 왔던 영국 조사관들은 뼈와 도구가 홍수로 인해 한데 모인 것이 아니라고 확신

하고 1859년에 그들의 결론을 발표했다. 이 해는 다윈이 『종의 기원(On the Origin of Species)』을 출간한 해로, 인류 진화에 관한 현대적 연구의 시작을 나타내는 연대이기도 했다.

flint n. 부싯돌 elf n. 요정 notion n. 통념 plausible a. 그럴듯한 roam v. 어슬렁거리다 attribute A to B A를 B의 탓으로 돌리다 excavator n. 발굴자 associate A with B ~A와 B를 연관시키다 extinct a. 멸종된 geologist n. 지질학자 coincidental a. 우발적인 Flood n. (the F~) 노아의 홍수 remains n. 유해 crumble v. 붕괴하다 archaeologist n. 고고학자 deposits n. 퇴적층 site n. 장소 be convinced 확신하다

---

21 빈칸완성   ①

주어는 excavators이므로, 빈칸에 18세기와 19세기라는 명사를 목적어로 받는 전치사 During이 필요하다. 나머지는 모두 접속사이다.

---

22 내용파악   ①

탄소 연대 측정법은 지금은 많이 사용되는 방법이지만 이 글에는 언급되어 있지 않다.

_____을 제외하고는 다음의 고고학적 증거들이 모두 언급되었다.
① 탄소 연대 측정법
② 화석
③ 멸종된 동물의 잔해
④ 인공물

---

23 내용파악   ②

비과학을 대표하는 입장은 성경에 입각한 해석이었다. 이 관점의 붕괴는 프랑스 고고학자들의 퇴적층 연구에서 비롯되었다고 하였다.

인류의 지구 존재 연대에 관한 과학 이론의 전환점은 _____이었다.
① 1859년 다윈의 『종의 기원』 출판과만 관련된 것
② 프랑스의 홍수가 없었던 지역에서 멸종된 동물과 인간의 유해가 함께 발견된 것
③ 성경에 대한 신학적 연구의 발전
④ 노아의 홍수와 그것이 인류에 미친 영향에 대한 새로운 이론의 발전

24-26

뱀, 도마뱀, 악어와 마찬가지로 거북이도 파충류이다. 거북이라고 알아볼 수 있는 최초의 화석은 약 2억 년 된 것으로, 공룡이 지구를 돌아다니던 시절의 것이다. 놀랍게도 그 이후로 거북의 겉모습은 거의 변하지 않았다. 거북은 전 세계 다양한 기후에 다양한 종류로 존재한다. 거북은 주로 열대에 국한되어 있는 다른 파충류와 달리 북미 남동부와 동남아시아에서 가장 많이 볼 수 있다. 거북은 호수, 연못, 염습지, 강, 숲, 심지어 사막에도 서식한다. 거북의 크기는 다양하다. 늪지 거북이나 진흙 거북은 길이가 약 4인치(10센티미터) 이하로 자란다. 반면에 크기로 볼 때 정반대에 있는 바다 거북은 몸길이가 6.5피트(2m)가 넘고 무게가 1,100파운드(500kg)가 넘을 수 있다.

거북은 다른 동물 대부분보다는 오래 살지만, 100년 이상 산다는 보고는 믿기 힘들다. 하지만 몇몇 종류는 갇혀 있는 상태에서도 50년 이상 살기도 한다. 자연환경에서도 상자 거북과 슬라이더 거북은 20~30년까지 살 수 있다. 일부 거북의 나이는 등딱지 외부 골판에 매년 형성되는 나이테를 세어 추정할 수 있다.

lizard n. 도마뱀 crocodile n. 악어 reptile n. 파충류 fossil n. 화석 confine v. 국한되다 tropics n. 열대 salt marsh 염습지 bog n. 늪지 rove v. 방황하다 leatherback turtle 장수거북 captivity n. 감금 box turtle 상자거북 slider turtle 슬라이더 거북 growth ring 나이테 bony plate 골판 ridiculing a. 조롱하는

24 내용파악 ①

"거북이라고 알아볼 수 있는 최초의 화석은 약 2억 년 된 것으로, 공룡이 지구를 돌아다니던 시절의 것이다."라는 내용을 통해 공룡과 거북은 동시대에 살았다는 것을 알 수 있다.

저자가 첫 번째 단락에서 공룡을 언급하는 이유는?
① 거북이 화석의 나이를 설명하기 위해
② 거북이의 기원에 대한 수수께끼를 밝히기 위해
③ 거북이가 멸종될 수도 있다는 것을 보여주기 위해
④ 거북이의 삶에 초점을 맞추기 위해

25 내용파악 ④

거북은 '주로 열대에 국한되어 있는 다른 파충류와'는 다르다고 하였다.

거북이는 다른 파충류와 어떤 점에서 다른가?
① 시간이 지남에 따라 많이 달라졌다.
② 북미에만 적응했다.
③ 사막에서 산다.
④ 다양한 기후에서 살고 있다.

26 내용파악 ④

"100년 이상 산다는 보고는 믿기 힘들다"라고 하였다. 믿기 힘들다는 것은 회의적인 어조를 말한다.

저자가 거북이 100년 이상 살지도 모른다는 이론을 논의할 때의 어조는 어떠하다고 가장 잘 설명될 수 있는가?
① 존중하는
② 조롱하는
③ 관심 있는
④ 회의적인

27-29

방에 홀로 남은 그는 의자에 앉아 고개를 뒤로 젖혔고, 그의 시선은 우연히 방에 매달려 지금은 잊혀진 어떤 목적 때문에 건물 가장 높은 층에 있는 방과 연락하는 데 사용되던, 이제는 사용하지 않는 종에 머물렀다. 쳐다보고 있는데, 이 종이 흔들리기 시작해서 그는 매우 놀랐고, 설명할 수 없는 묘한 두려움에 사로잡혔다. 곧 종소리가 크게 울렸고, 집 안의 모든 종도

덩달아 울리기 시작했다.

종소리에 이어 와인 상인의 지하실에서 어떤 사람이 무거운 쇠사슬을 와인 통 위로 끌어당기는 듯한 소리가 아래층 깊숙한 곳에서 들렸다. 그리고는 아래층에서 훨씬 더 큰 소음이 들렸고, 계단을 올라오더니, 곧바로 문 쪽으로 다가왔다.

소음은 무거운 문을 통해 들어오더니, 유령이 그의 눈앞에서 방 안으로 들어왔다. 그 유령이 들어오자마자, 죽어가던 불꽃이 "나는 그를 알아! 말리의 유령이야!"라고 외치듯이 타올랐다.

glance n. 시선 astonishment n. 놀라움 inexplicable a. 설명할 수 없는 clanking a. 철커덕하는 drag v. 끌다 cask n. 통 cellar n. 지하실 specter n. 유령

27 동의어 ③

inexplicable 은 '불가해한', '설명(해석)할 수 없는'이라는 의미이므로 ③이 정답으로 가장 적절하다.

inexplicable의 의미는 _____.
① 간단한 용어로 설명하는
② 꺼내질 수 없는
③ 분명한 이유가 없는
④ 복잡한 용어로 설명하는

28 내용파악 ②

쳐다보고 있는데, 종이 흔들리기 시작해서 곧 큰 소리로 울렸다고 하였으므로, 종은 혼자서 울렸다.

울리기 시작한 종은 _____.
① 집안의 유일한 종이었다
② 혼자 울렸다
③ 다른 방에서 울려질 수 있었다
④ 집안의 모든 종에 연결되어 있었다.

29 내용파악 ③

종소리를 듣고 있던 사람에게 이내 유령이 나타났으므로 그는 겁먹었을 것이다.

종소리를 듣고 있던 남자는 _____.
① 와인 통을 가로질러 쇠사슬을 끌었다
② 가족과 함께 있었다
③ 매우 겁을 먹은 것 같았다
④ 말리의 유령이었다

30-32

목재의 코드란 무엇일까? 목재의 코드는 인간이 고안한 가장 탄력적인 측정 단위라고 말하는 사람도 있다. '표준' 코드는 4×4×8피트의 목재를 쌓은 더미로, 128 입방피트에 해당한다. 이것 중 실제로 목재를 포함하고 있는 부분은 얼마일까? 이는 목재의 종류, 나무토막의 크기와 곧은 형태, 쌓는 사람에 따라 다르다. 단단한 나뭇가지에서 베어내고 공기가 통하는

공간을 만들 줄 아는 코드목재 장인이 쌓은 작고 구부러진 나무토막들에는 포함되는 원목이 코드 당 30 입방피트가 안 될 수 있다. 자작나무나 가문비나무 같이 8인치 이상 크기의 매끄럽고, 둥근 목재는 코드 당 평균 100 입방피트 이상을 채울 수 있다. 이는 나무껍질이 있는 상태이다. 나무껍질을 제거하면 같은 크기의 더미에서 10~12% 더 많은 부피가 만들어질 것이다.(나무껍질이 제거되면 같은 크기의 더미에 더 많은 나무가 들어갈 수 있다는 의미)

목재의 난방 가치(발열량)는 나무의 종류에 따라 엄청나게 달라진다. 아까시나무, 흰 떡갈나무, 히코리, 물박달나무, 아이언우드가 가장 좋다. 이러한 목재로 된 한 코드는, 제대로 말리면, 석탄 약 1톤의 가치가 있다. 너도밤나무, 황자작나무, 사탕단풍, 물푸레나무, 북가시나무가 그 다음으로 좋다. 흰자작나무, 벚나무, 연단풍나무, 플라타너스, 느릅나무는 비교적 열악한 땔감용 목재이며, 참피나무, 버터너트, 포플러, 연목은 가장 좋지 않다.

elastic a. 탄력적인 unit of measure 측정 단위 devise v. 고안하다 stacked a. 쌓인 cubic a. 평방의 straightness n. 곧음 crooked a. 구부러진 limb n. 나뭇가지 solid wood 원목 birch n. 자작나무 spruce n. 가문비나무 bark n. 나무껍질 black locust 아까시나무 black birch 물박달나무 season v. 건조하다 approximately ad. 대략 beech n. 너도밤나무 yellow birch 황자작나무 sugar maple 사탕단풍 ash n. 물푸레나무 red oak 북가시나무 White birch 흰자작나무 soft maple 연단풍 sycamore n. 플라타너스 elm n. 느릅나무 basswood n. 참피나무 butternut n. 버터너트 softwood n. 연목 plausible a. 설득력 있는 obsolete a. 낡아빠진 rigid a. 엄격한

30 글의 주제 ②

첫 번째 문단에서는 코드가 무엇인지를 설명하고 있고, 두 번째 문단에서는 목재의 종류에 따른 난방 가치(발열량)를 설명하고 있다. ②가 글의 요지를 가장 잘 나타내는 제목이다.

다음 중 이 글의 요지를 가장 잘 표현하는 제목은?
① 연료들
② 목재 코드의 가치
③ 나무의 종류들
④ 표준 척도

31 동의어 ①

탄력성이 있다는 것은 유연하고 융통성 있다는 의미이다.

다음 중 elastic과 가장 가까운 의미를 가진 단어는?
① 유연한
② 그럴듯한
③ 케케묵은
④ 엄격한

32 내용일치 ①

껍질을 벗겨내면 한 코드 안에 10~12% 더 많은 부피가 만들어진다고 했다.

다음 중 사실이 아닌 것은?
① 나무껍질을 벗겨내면 한 코드 안의 목재 부피가 줄어든다.
② 버터너트와 포플러는 난방 가치(발열량)가 낮다.
③ 목재의 입방피트는 누가 쌓는지에 따라 달라진다.
④ 목재의 열량은 목재의 원료인 나무의 종류에 따라 다르다.

33 글의 요지 ③

교실에서 음식을 먹어는 안 된다는 규칙은 쉽게 해제될 수 있는 사회적 관습의 규칙인 반면에 친구를 의자에서 밀어서는 안 된다는 규칙은 쉽게 해제될 수 없는 도덕성의 규칙이어서 후자는 권위자가 해제해주어도 어기기 어려운 점착성(엄격성)을 갖고 있어서 전자와 구별된다는 것이 이 글의 요지이므로 ③이 정답으로 적절하다.

grasp v. 이해하다 acquire v. 습득하다 preschooler n. 취학전 아동 lift v. 해제하다 approve v. 허용하다 comply v. 따르다 bring up 양육하다 sticky a. 끈적끈적한, 완고한 come unstuck 떨어지다 countenance v. 장려하다, 찬성하다, 묵인하다 social convention 사회적 관습 innately ad. 선천적으로

도덕성은 이해하기 어려운 개념일 수 있지만, 우리는 그것을 빠르게 습득한다. 미취학 아동은 교사가 교실에서 음식을 먹어서는 안 된다고 말하기 때문에 교실에서 음식을 먹으면 안 된다는 것을 배우게 된다. 규칙이 해제되고 음식을 먹는 것이 허용되면, 아이는 기꺼이 이를 따를 것이다. 하지만 같은 그 교사가 다른 학생을 의자에서 밀어도 괜찮다고 말하면, 그 아이는 주저한다. 아이는 "아니에요, 선생님은 그렇게 말하면 안 돼요"라고 대답할 것이라고 『도덕적인 아이 키우기(Bringing Up a Moral Child)』의 공동 저자인 심리학자 마이클 슐먼(Michael Schulman)은 말한다. 두 경우 모두에서, 누군가가 아이에게 규칙을 가르쳤지만, 밀어서는 안 된다는 규칙에는 점착성(엄격성)이 있는데, 이는 권위 있는 사람이 묵인한다 해도 규칙이 풀어지는(해이해지는) 것에 저항하는 점착성(엄격성)이다. 이것이 바로 도덕성의 문제와 단순한 사회적 관습의 문제 사이의 차이이며, 슐먼과 다른 연구자들은 아이들이 이러한 차이를 타고난 본능으로 느끼고 있다고 믿는다.

이 글의 요지는?
① 미취학 아동은 사회적 관습보다 도덕성을 더 빨리 습득한다.
② 교사는 아이들의 도덕성을 형성하는 데 중요한 역할을 한다.
③ 도덕성에는 사회적 관습과 구별되는 점착성(엄격성)이 있다.
④ 마이클 슐먼은 『도덕적인 아이로 키우기』의 유일한 저자이다.

01 ②	02 ③	03 ①	04 ④	05 ③	06 ③	07 ②	08 ①	09 ②	10 ②
11 ①	12 ③	13 ②	14 ④	15 ②	16 ④	17 ③	18 ④	19 ④	20 ①
21 ④	22 ②	23 ①	24 ③	25 ④	26 ②	27 ④	28 ③	29 ①	30 ③
31 ②	32 ③	33 ①	34 ①						

01 논리완성   ②

생생하고 표현이 풍부한 언어를 사용했다고 했으므로, 그 작가의 문체는 명료함 혹은 명확함을 특징으로 했을 것이다. 따라서 ②가 정답으로 적절하며, 나머지 보기는 '생생하고 표현이 풍부한 언어'와 호응하지 않는다.

characterize v. ~의 특색을 이루다 vivid a. 생생한, 활발한, 선명한 expressive a. 표현이 풍부한 ambiguity n. 모호함, 불명료함 clarity n. 명료, 명확 perplexity n. 당혹; 혼란 vagueness n. 막연함, 애매함

그 작가의 문체는 생생하고 표현이 풍부한 언어를 사용하여 명료한 것이 특징이었다.

02 논리완성   ③

방학이 시작되는데 날씨까지 좋았다면 아이들의 기분은 매우 들떴거나 기뻤을 것이다. 따라서 ③이 정답으로 적절하다.

break n. 휴식, 휴가 ambivalence n. (애증 따위의) 반대 감정 병존, (상반되는) 감정의 교차 desolation n. 쓸쓸함, 외로움 jubilation n. 환희; 기쁨 melancholy n. 우울; 울적함

밝고 화창한 날이 여름방학을 시작하는 아이들에게 기쁜 감정이 들게 했다.

03 논리완성   ①

보는 이가 서로 다르게 해석할 수 있다는 것은 그 그림이 '내포하고 있는 의미'가 다양하다는 것이다. 따라서 빈칸에는 ①의 '함축, 내포'가 적절하다.

abstract painting 추상화 various a. 여러 가지의, 가지각색의, 다양한 interpret v. 해석하다, 설명하다 connotation n. 함축된 의미; 언외(言外)의 의미 pretext n. 구실, 핑계 fallacy n. 그릇된 생각; 허위, 오류 opacity n. 불투명

그 화가의 추상화는 다양한 함축적 의미에 열려(의미로 볼 수) 있어서, 보는 이로 하여금 그 그림을 서로 다른 방식으로 해석할 수 있게 해주었다.

04 논리완성   ④

이전의 요리사들이 발견하지 못했다는 것은 전통적인 요리법 그대로 해서는 발견할 수 없다는 말이며 이것은 전통 요리법에 대한 그 셰프의 해석이 매우 독창적이었거나 기발했다는 것을 의미한다.

interpretation n. 해석, 설명; (자기 해석에 따른) 연출; 연기 recipe n. 조리법; 비법 subtlety n. 미묘함; 교묘함, 절묘함 flavor n. 맛, 풍미 elude v. 교묘히 피하다, 회피하다; ~의 눈을 피하다, ~에게 발견되지 않다 palatable a. (음식 등이) 입에 맞는, 맛난 standard a. 표준의; 모범적인 reticent a. 과묵한; 말이 적은 ingenious a. 기발한; 독창적인

전통적인 요리법에 대한 그 셰프의 기발한 해석은 이전의 요리사들이 발견하지 못했던 미묘한 맛을 이끌어냈다.

05 논리완성   ③

'절박함', '중요함'의 느낌을 전달한 연설가의 어조로는 '진지함', '단호함', '결연함' 등이 적절하다.

convey v. 전달하다; (의미·사상·감정 따위를) 전하다 urgency n. 긴급, 절박, 화급 passive a. 수동적인 pensive a. 시름에 잠긴 듯한, 구슬픈 resolute a. 결연한, 단호한 quizzical a. 놀리는, 조롱하는; 기묘한

그 연설자의 결연한 어조는 절박하고 중요하다는 느낌을 전달했다.

06 동의어   ③

profound a. (지식·이해 등이) 깊은[심오한]; (영향·느낌·경험 등이) 엄청난[깊은](= deep) impact n. 영향, 효과 audience n. 청중, 관중, 관객 superficial a. 피상적인 sarcastic a. 빈정거리는, 비꼬는 joyous a. 즐거운, 기쁜

그 영화는 관객들에게 깊은 영향을 미쳤다.

07 동의어   ②

diplomat n. 외교관 nuanced a. 미묘한(= subtle) negotiation n. 협상, 교섭 allow for 고려하다 delicate a. 섬세한 resolution n. 결심, 결의; 해결 straightforward a. 똑바른, 정직한, 솔직한 rigid a. 엄격한, 융통성 없는 impulsive a. 충동적인

협상에 대한 그 외교관의 미묘한 접근 방식은 국제 분쟁에 대한 섬세한 해결을 고려한 것이었다.

08 동의어 ①

demeanor n. 태도(= attitude) uplifting a. 희망[행복감]을 주는, 사기를 높이는 evident a. 분명한, 명백한 positively ad. 적극적으로, 긍정적으로 influence v. ~에 영향을 미치다 interact with ~와 상호작용[소통]하다 appearance n. 외관, 겉보기; 생김새, 풍채 behavior n. 행동 cognition n. 인식, 인지

그녀의 쾌활한 태도는 모든 사람의 하루를 밝게 만들었다. 이러한 기분 고조 효과는 그녀의 친절함이 그녀가 소통한 모든 사람의 기분에 긍정적인 영향을 미쳤을 때 분명했다.

09 동의어 ②

economic downturn 경기 침체 result in ~을 초래하다 surge n. 급상승, 급등(= spike) unemployment n. 실업 significant a. 중대한; 상당한 impact n. 영향 household n. 가족, 세대 hardship n. 고난, 고초, 곤란 decline n. (가격의) 하락; 저하 stability n. 안정성, 안정 reduction n. 감소

경기 침체로 실업이 급증했다. 그것은 가계에도 큰 영향을 미쳐, 많은 사람들이 금전적인 어려움을 겪었다.

10 동의어 ②

esoteric a. 소수만 이해하는[즐기는]; 비밀의, 난해한(= obscure) niche a. 소수의 사람들만을 대상으로 하는, 소수의 사람들만 관심 있는, 틈새시장의 성격이 있는 appeal to ~에 호소하다, ~에 매력적이다 enthusiast n. 열광자, 팬 be into ~에 관심이 많다[좋아하다], ~에 열중하고 있다 mainstream a. 주류의 popular a. 대중적인, 인기 있는 universal a. 보편적인

그 예술가의 작품은 난해하기로 유명하다. 그것은 소수의 사람만 좋아하는 것이어서 이런 종류의 예술에 정말로 관심이 있는 작은 애호가 집단에게만 매력적으로 다가간다.

11 동의어 ①

ascent n. 상승; (산에) 오름, 등반 arduous a. 힘든, 곤란한 immense a. 막대한 fortitude n. 용기, 불굴의 정신, 강한 참을성, 인내(= tenacity) resistance n. 저항, 반대 dominance n. 우세, 우월, 지배 breakdown n. 고장, 파손

등산가가 그 산을 오르는 것은 고된 일이어서, 엄청난 육체적 인내력과 정신적 참을성이 요구되었다.

12 동의어 ③

intricate a. 난해한, 복잡한(= elaborate) storyline n. 줄거리 unravel v. (엉클어진 것을) 풀다; 해결하다 depth n. 깊이 nuance n. 뉘앙스; 미묘한 차이 simple a. 단순한; 수수한 heavy a. 무거운; 힘이 드는 clear a. 분명한, 명확한

그 소설은 복잡한 이야기 줄거리를 보여주었다. 그 소설의 깊이와 뉘앙스를 풀어내기 위해서는 독자들의 세심한 주의가 요구되었다.

13 분사구문 ②

트럭이 도로를 이탈한 것은 과속의 결과이므로, 완료 분사구문을 만드는 ②가 정답으로 적절하다. ① '~하기 위해'라는 목적의 의미를 나타내게 되어 어색한 의미의 문장을 만들므로 부적절하다.

skid v. 미끄러지다 spin v. (팽이 따위가) 돌다, 뱅뱅 돌다 accelerate v. 가속하다

시속 100㎞가 넘는 속도로 가속했기 때문에, 그 트럭은 통제 불능 상태로 미끄러져 빙빙 돌다가 도로를 이탈했다.

14 문맥상 적절한 전치사 ④

전치사 between과 among 뒤에는 복수 명사가 오므로 빈칸에 적절하지 않고, up의 경우 전치사로 사용될 수 있기는 하나 '~의 위로'라는 '이동'의 뜻이고 '~의 위에/위쪽에'라는 의미로는 above를 써야 한다. 그러므로 '~의 옆에'라는 의미의 전치사인 ④가 정답으로 적절하다.

strategically ad. 전략적으로 majestic a. 장엄한, 위엄 있는 antique painting 고미술품 그림 touch n. 기운, 조금, 약간의 차 elegance n. 우아, 고상, 기품

장엄한 벽난로 옆에 전략적으로 배치된 고미술품 그림은 그 방에 약간의 우아함을 더해주었다.

15 주어와 동사의 수일치 ②

집합명사 committee가 '위원회'라는 하나의 단체를 의미하는 경우에는 단수로 취급하고, 그 구성원인 '위원들'이라는 의미로 쓰였을 경우에는 복수로 취급한다. 주어진 문장의 경우 전자에 해당하므로 첫 번째 빈칸에는 단수 동사 is가 적절하다. 한편, 관계대명사의 수는 선행사에 일치시키며, which의 선행사는 복수 명사 recommendations이므로, 두 번째 빈칸에는 복수 동사 are가 들어가야 한다. 빈칸 앞의 they believe는 삽입절이다.

committee n. 위원회, 위원 be composed of ~으로 구성되어 있다 expert n. 전문가 finalize v. 결말을 짓다[내다], (계획 등을) 완성시키다; 최종적으로 승인하다 recommendation n. 추천, 권고 crucial a. 결정적인, 중대한 upcoming a. 다가오는, 곧 있을, 이윽고 나타날 conference n. 회의, 회담

다양한 분야의 전문가들로 구성된 그 위원회는 그들이 다가오는 회의에 중요하다고 생각하는 권고안을 마무리 짓고 있다.

16 재귀대명사 ④

get이 '~에게 (물건을) 사서 주다'라는 의미의 4형식 수여동사로 쓰였으며, 부모님이 차를 사준 대상은 부모님 자신이다. 주어의 행위가 주어 자신에게로 향하는 경우 목적어로는 재귀대명사를 쓴다. 따라서 ④가 정답이다.

부모님이 드디어 차를 마련하실 것이므로 나는 더 이상 부모님을 태우고 다닐 필요가 없을 것이다.

17 가정법 과거완료 ③

가정법 과거완료는 'if+주어+had p.p, 주어+would/should/could/might+ have p.p.'의 형태를 취하며, if절과 주절은 순서가 바뀔 수 있다. 그러므로 두 번째 빈칸에는 had가 들어가야 하며, 첫 번째 빈칸의 경우, 문장의 의미상 앞의 '~임이 분명하다'와 잘 어울리는 것은 '가능'의 의미를 가진 could이다. '불확실한 추측'의 의미인 might는 '했을지도 모름이 분명하다'로 어색하다. 따라서 ③이 정답이다.

apparent a. 명백한 proactive a. (사람·정책이) 상황을 앞서서 주도하는, 사전 대책을 강구하는 address v. (문제를) 역점을 두어 다루다 initial a. 처음의, 최초의

최근의 진전을 고려하면, 그 팀이 초기의 난제를 해결하는 데 좀 더 선제적으로 나섰더라면 그 프로젝트를 더 빨리 완료할 수 있었을 것임이 분명하다.

18 절의 일부를 선행사로 취할 수 있는 관계대명사 which ④

빈칸에 들어갈 관계대명사의 선행사는 앞 절의 술부인데, 절의 일부를 선행사로 취할 수 있는 것은 which이므로 ④가 정답이다. 술부인 shared부터 me까지를 to부정사로 나타내면 to share his lunch with me이고 이것을 진주어로 하여 가주어 it을 사용하면 관계절은 it was very kind of him to share his lunch with me에서 만들어진 것이 된다.

내 사촌이 점심을 나와 나누었는데, 그가 이렇게 한 것은 매우 친절했다.

19 태 / 시제 ④

he가 해고하는 행위의 주체가 아닌 대상이므로 첫 번째 빈칸에는 fire 동사의 수동태가 필요하다. 그러므로 능동태 동사 fired가 제시돼있는 ②와 ③을 정답에서 먼저 제외할 수 있다. 그런데 주절의 동사가 과거시제이므로 when절의 동사도 과거인 was fired가 첫 빈칸에 적절하고, 그가 20년간 일했던 것은 그가 해고되기 이전에 있었던 일이므로, 두 번째 빈칸에는 과거완료나 과거완료 진행 시제가 적절하다. 따라서 ④가 정답이다.

fire v. 해고하다 devastate v. 황폐시키다; 망연자실하게 하다

20년간 몸담았던 회사에서 해고됐을 때 그는 망연자실했다.

20 so as to의 부정 ①

'~하기 위해'라는 의미의 so as to를 부정하는 경우, 부정어 not을 to 앞에 두어 so as not to로 나타낸다.

principal n. 교장 request v. 요청하다 confuse v. 혼란스럽게 하다 conflict with ~와 모순되다, 양립하지 않다

교장은 교사들에게 종교와 관련된 주제를 아이들을 대상으로 해서는 피할 것을 요청했는데, 이는 그들이 양육되고 있는 방식과 충돌되는 생각들로 그들을 혼란스럽게 하지 않기 위함이었다.

21-22

2023년 옥스퍼드 올해의 단어를 선정하는 언어 전문가들은 밝고 젊은 것에 마음이 이끌려, 상대적으로 새로 생긴 단어인 "rizz"를 1위로 선택했다. "charisma"라는 단어에서 파생된 "rizz"는 "스타일, 아름다운 용모, 또는 매력"을 통해 연애 상대를 끌어당길 수 있는 능력을 가리킨다고 사전의 발행사인 옥스퍼드 대학교 출판부(OUP)가 발표를 통해 밝혔다. 이 단어는 대중들로부터 32,000표 이상을 받았다. 올해의 단어를 놓고 경쟁하는 단어들이 새로운 단어일 필요는 없지만, 반드시 해당 연도에 중요한 의미를 가지고 있어야 한다. OUP는 2023년 최종 후보 단어 명단이 "그 해의 분위기, 기풍, 또는 주요 관심사를 반영하여" 선택됐다고 말했다.

expert n. 전문가 dazzle v. 현혹시키다, 감탄하게 하다 relative a. 상대적인 be derived from ~에서 파생하다 refer to 언급하다; 지칭하다 attract v. (주의·흥미 등을) 끌다; ~의 마음을 끌다, 매혹하다 charm n. 매력; 아름다운 용모 contender n. 경쟁자 significance n. 의의, 의미; 중요성 in question 문제의, 당해(當該)의 shortlist n. 최종 후보자[심사 대상자] 명단 ethos n. 사회 사조; 기풍 preoccupation n. 선입관, 편견; (중대) 관심사

21 빈칸완성 ④

"올해의 단어를 놓고 경쟁하는 단어들이 새로운 단어일 필요는 없지만, 반드시 해당 연도에 중요한 의미를 가지고 있어야 한다."라고 했으므로, 2023년 최종 후보 단어 명단도 그 해의 분위기, 기풍, 또는 주요 관심사를 '반영하여' 선택되었을 것이다. 반영한다는 것은 거울이 사물을 반사하듯이 그대로 보여준다는 말로, 올해의 단어가 사회 분위기 등을 반영할 경우에도 있는 그대로 보여주는 것이므로 적절하다. delineate(묘사하다)나 manifest(명백히 나타내다)는 이보다 더 적극적인 행위의 의미를 가진다. 그러므로 ④가 정답이다. ① 묘사하다 ② 흉내 내다 ③ 명백히 하다

22 내용추론 ②

"2023년 옥스퍼드 올해의 단어로 선정된 rizz가 대중들로부터 32,000 표 이상을 받았다."는 내용을 통해 ②를 추론할 수 있다.

위 글에 의하면, 올해의 단어의 선정 기준에 대해 무엇을 추론할 수 있는가?
① 투표 과정에는 언어 전문가들의 독점적인 결정이 포함된다.
② 선정에 기여하는 데 있어 대중의 역할이 상당하다.
③ 투표 과정에 대학생들은 명확히 포함되어 있다.
④ 모든 투표 과정은 옥스퍼드 대학교 출판부 안에서 진행된다.

23-24

속도가 빠르고 서로 연결돼 있는 오늘날의 세계에서, 기술은 어디에서나 의사소통과 사회적 상호작용의 동력을 만들어내는 힘이 되고 있다. 기술의 발전이 개인이 서로 연결하고 정보를 공유하는 방식을 혁명적으로 변화시켰음은 부인할 수 없지만, 대면 방식의 사회적 상호작용에 잠재적으로 부정적인 영향을 미칠 수 있다는 우려가 커지고 있다. 스마트폰, 소셜 미디어 플랫폼, 그리고 메신저 애플리케이션의 등장으로 인해, 사람들은 지리적 장벽을 뛰어 넘어 가상의 공간에서 더 가까워졌다. 이제는 멀리 떨어져 있는 친구와 가족이 실시간으로 쉽게 소통하고 경험을 공유할 수 있다. 그러나 이와 같은 연결의 용이성은 이러한 소통의 질(質)과 직접 만나는 관계에 미치는 영향에 대해 의문을 야기한다.

fast-paced a. (이야기 등이) 빨리 진행되는 ubiquitous a. (동시에) 도처에 있는 social interaction 사회적 상호작용 undeniably ad. 부인하기 어려울 정도로; 명백하게, 틀림없이 revolutionize v. 혁명[대변혁]을 일으키다 escalate v. 단계적으로 확대[증가]되다 potential a. 잠재적인 detrimental a. 유해한, 손해되는 advent n. 도래(到來), 출현 virtually ad. 사실상, 거의; (컴퓨터를 이용하여) 가상으로 transcend v. (경험·이해력 등의 범위·한계를) 넘다; 초월하다 geographical a. 지리학의; 지리적인 barrier n. 장벽, 장애물 connectivity n. 연결성 impact n. 영향

---

23 내용파악   ①

"속도가 빠르고 서로 연결돼 있는 오늘날의 세계에서, 기술은 어디에서나 의사소통과 사회적 상호작용의 동력을 만들어내는 힘이 되고 있다.", "기술의 발전이 개인이 서로 연결하고 정보를 공유하는 방식을 혁명적으로 변화시켰음을 부인할 수 없다."라는 내용을 통해 ①이 정답으로 적절함을 알 수 있다.

위 글에 의하면, 현대 세계에서 기술의 역할은 무엇인가?
① 의사소통과 사회적 상호작용에 중요한 역할을 한다.
② 의사소통에는 실제로 영향을 미치지 않는다.
③ 개인 간의 연결 방식에는 영향을 미치지 않는다.
④ 대면 방식의 사회적 상호작용의 질을 향상시킨다.

---

24 내용파악   ③

두 번째 문장의 주절에서 "대면 방식의 사회적 상호작용에 잠재적으로 부정적인 영향을 미칠 수 있다는 우려가 커지고 있다."고 했으므로 ③이 정답으로 적절하다.

위 글에서 저자는 기술 발전이 사회적 상호작용에 미치는 영향에 대해 어떤 우려를 표명하고 있는가?

① 저자는 기술 발전이 사회적 상호작용에 긍정적인 영향만을 미치는 것으로 보고 있다.
② 저자는 기술이 의사소통의 동력에 미치는 무시할만한 영향을 강조한다.
③ 저자는 기술이 대면 방식의 상호작용에 미칠 수 있는 잠재적인 부정적 영향에 대해 우려하고 있다.
④ 저자는 기술이 현대 세계에서 개인이 서로 연결하는 방식을 바꾸지 않았다고 말한다.

25-27

기후 변화는 인류가 오늘날 직면하고 있는 가장 큰 위협이며, 우리가 우리의 임박한 멸망을 무시하기로 하든 그렇지 않든, 그것은 다가오고 있다. 우리가 우리의 생활 방식에 근본적인 변화를 시작하지 않으면, 그것은 계속해서 다가올 것이다. 전 세계 정부들은 시민들이 친환경적인 생활을 신봉하고 받아들이도록 더 강력한 조치를 취하기 시작해야 한다. 일반 시민이 기후 변화의 모든 측면에 영향을 미칠 수는 없지만, 만약 정부가 사람들에게 일상생활에서 실질적으로 변하도록 압박을 가한다면, 그 누적적인 영향은 엄청날 것이다. 정부가 변화에 영향을 줄 수 있는 한 가지 방법은 연료를 많이 소비하는 차량에 엄격한 세금을 더 많이 부과하고 하이브리드 및 전기 차량을 선택하는 시민들에게 금전적 인센티브를 제공하는 것이다. 일부 국가에서는, 시민들이 차량을 소유할 수 있는 권리를 얻기 위해서는 많은 수수료를 지불해야 하며, 이 수수료는 새롭고 보다 효율적인 대중교통 개발에 기여하게 된다. 이것이 미국 정부로서는 뻔뻔스런 조치일 수 있지만, 상황의 심각성은 급진적인 조치를 요구하고 있다.
미국 정부는 또한 유해한 제품을 금지하는 법률을 통과시킬 수도 있다. 이러한 제품들에는 우리의 바다를 쓰레기 처리장으로 만들어버린 비닐봉지, 빨대 및 기타 플라스틱 소재가 포함된다. 장보기를 할 때 생분해성 소재로 만든 재사용 가능한 가방을 쓰는 것과 같은 간단한 조치도 큰 차이를 만들어내며, 이것은 사람들에게 큰 희생을 강요하지 않는다.

close our eyes to 무시하다 impending a. 임박한 doom n. 운명, 숙명 fundamental a. 기초의, 근본적인 buy into 완전히 믿다, 믿고 받아들이다 green a. 환경 친화적인 aspect n. 양상, 국면 summative a. 누적적인 impact n. 영향 immense a. 막대한, 무한한 affect v. ~에게 영향을 주다 strict a. 엄격한 gas-guzzling a. (자동차 엔진 등이) 연료를 많이 소비하는 vehicle n. 운송수단, 차량 monetary a. 화폐의, 통화의 contribute to ~에 기여하다 efficient a. 능률적인, 효과적인 audacious a. 대담한, 철면피의 drastic a. 과감한, 철저한 legislation n. 입법, 법률제정 ban v. 금지하다 garbage dump 쓰레기 처리장 biodegradable a. 미생물에 의해 무해한 물질로 분해할 수 있는, 생물 분해성의 material n. 재료, 원료 grocery n. 식료품류, 잡화류 sacrifice n. 희생

---

25 동의어   ④

drastic은 '과감한', '급진적인'이라는 의미이므로 ④가 정답으로 가장 적절하다.

두 번째 단락의 밑줄 친 단어 drastic의 의미에 가장 가까운 것은?
① 경솔하고 계획되지 않은
② 순진무구하고 분별없는
③ 공격적이고 통제적인
④ 신속하고 영향력이 강한

26 글의 주제   ②

"기후 변화가 인류에 큰 위협이 되고 있는 상황에서 우리가 살아가는 방식에 근본적인 변화를 시작하지 않는 한, 그것은 계속해서 위협이 될 것이므로, 전 세계 정부들이 시민과 함께 친환경적인 노력을 경주해야 한다."라는 메시지를 전달하고 있는 글이다. 따라서 ②가 정답이다. ③ sole이 잘못이다.

위 글에서 전달하고자 하는 주된 메시지는 무엇인가?
① 일반 시민들이 기후 변화의 모든 측면에 영향을 미칠 수 있다.
② 정부는 기후 변화에 긍정적인 영향을 미치기 위해 시민들과 함께 노력해야 한다.
③ 정부는 보다 엄격한 법을 통해 기후 변화에 있어 독점적인 역할을 수행해야 한다.
④ 정부는 기후 변화와 관련하여 시민들의 삶을 방해해서는 안 된다.

27 내용파악   ④

'태양광 발전 주택에 대한 인센티브 제공'은 본문 어디에서도 언급하고 있지 않다.

다음 중 기후 변화에 대한 각국 정부의 조치로 위 글에서 언급되지 <u>않은</u> 것은?
① 정부는 사람들이 일상생활에서 중대한 변화를 일으키도록 압박을 가해야 한다.
② 정부는 가솔린 동력 자동차에 더 많은 세금을 적용해야 한다.
③ 정부는 사람들이 플라스틱 대신 생분해성 물질을 사용하도록 권장해야 한다.
④ 정부는 태양광 발전 주택에 인센티브를 제공해야 한다.

28-30

경쟁은 인간 본성에 내재돼 있지만, 경쟁의 역할은 생존에 필수적인 유대감, 돌봄, 협력이라는 중대한 주제에 부차적인 것이다. 문화인류학자 메리 클라크(Mary Clark)는 직계가족을 넘어서는 확장된 사회적 유대의 필요성을 강조하는데, 이는 초기 인간 사회에서 취약한 유아를 보호하기 위해 특히 중요했던 것이다.
로버트 퍼트넘(Robert Putnam)이 이탈리아 지방정부에 대한 연구에서 강조한 바와 같이, 사회적 유대의 항구적인 중요성은 현대 사회에서도 지속되고 있다. 지방정부들이 유사한 조직 방식을 갖고 있었지만, 그들이 업무를 얼마나 잘 처리하는가에 있어서는 달랐다. 이러한 차이는 그들이 다양한 사회적, 경제적, 문화적 상황에 처해 있었기 때문이었다.
퍼트넘은 사회적 자본의 개념을 도입하면서, 강력한 시민 사회적 유대의 중요성을 강조하였다. 투표율이 높고 합창단, 문학 동아리, 축구 동아리 등과 같은 다양한 공동체 활동에 적극적으로 참여하는 지역은 고도로 발달된 사회적 자본을 보여주었다. 이러한 비(非)시장 관계의 풍부한 네트워크는 신뢰와 호혜성을 함양시켰고, 특히 인간 상호작용의 효율성을 향상시켰다.
지역사회를 고려할 때에는 지역 기업을 법인 기업체와 비교하는 것을 고려해보라. 지역 식량원, 여가활동, 은행의 다양한 금융서비스, 자산 소유 등에 대해 성찰해보라. 왜냐하면 이 요소들이 지역의 번영과 관계의 질을 예측하는 요소로 작용하며, 이 둘 모두가 사회적 유대의 강도에 영향을 받기 때문이다.

inherent a. 본래부터 가지고 있는, 고유의   secondary a. 부차적인, 종속적인   crucial a. 결정적인, 중대한   bonding n. 접속; 긴밀한 유대   cooperation n. 협력, 협동   fundamental a. 기초의, 기본의, 근본적인   anthropologist n. 인류학자   emphasize v. 강조하다   expand v. 확장하다, 확대하다   vulnerable a. 취약한   enduring a. 지속하는, 영속적인   persist v. 지속하다, 존속하다; 고집하다   diverse a. 다양한   introduce v. 소개하다; 도입하다   significance n. 중요성; 의미   voter turnout 투표율   choral society 합창단   demonstrate v. 증명하다, 논증하다; (밖으로) 드러내다   nonmarket n. 노동시장 외의   relationship n. 관계, 관련   foster v. 기르다, 양육하다; 촉진하다, 조장하다   reciprocity n. 상호성, 상호관계   notably ad. 현저하게; 명료하게   efficiency n. 능률   interaction n. 상호작용   contemplate v. 심사숙고하다   enterprise n. 기획; 기업   corporate establishment 기업체   reflect on 곰곰이 생각하다, 반성하다   asset n. 자산, 재산   predictor n. 예언자, 예보자   prosperity n. 번영, 번창   influence v. 영향을 미치다

28 내용파악   ③

"투표율이 높고 합창단, 문학 동아리, 축구 동아리 등과 같은 다양한 공동체 활동에 적극적으로 참여하는 지역은 고도로 발달된 사회적 자본을 보여주었다. 이러한 비(非)시장 관계의 풍부한 네트워크는 신뢰와 호혜성을 함양시켰다."라는 내용을 통해 ③이 정답임을 알 수 있다.

인간관계를 강화하는 비(非)시장 관계를 설명하기 위해 위 글에서 사용하고 있는 용어는 무엇인가?
① 경쟁적 경향
② 중대한 주제
③ 사회적 자본
④ 직계가족의 유대

29 내용파악   ①

"투표율이 높고 합창단, 문학 동아리, 축구 동아리 등과 같은 다양한 공동체 활동에 적극적으로 참여하는 지역은 고도로 발달된 사회적 자본을 보여주었다."라는 내용을 통해 ①이 정답으로 적절함을 알 수 있다.

퍼트넘의 연구에 따르면, 지역사회의 강력한 사회적 자본의 지표로 언급된 구체적인 활동은 무엇인가?
① 투표와 동아리 활동
② 경제 정책
③ 유사한 조직 구조
④ 신문 독자층

30 내용추론   ③

"다양한 공동체 활동에 적극적으로 참여하는 지역은 고도로 발달된 사회적 자본을 보여주었다. 이러한 비(非)시장 관계의 풍부한 네트워크는 신뢰와 호혜성을 함양시켰고, 특히 인간 상호작용의 효율성을 향상시켰다."라는 내용을 통해 ③을 유추할 수 있다.

위 글에서 사회적 자본의 역할에 대해 무엇을 유추할 수 있는가?
① 사회적 자본은 공동체가 얼마나 잘 운영되는지에 영향을 미치지 않는다.
② 사회적 자본은 정부 구조에만 의존한다.
③ 좋은 사회적 자본은 지역 사회가 더 잘 운영될 수 있도록 도와준다.
④ 사회적 자본은 지역사회에서 문제를 일으킨다.

31-34

미세공격은 문화적으로 소외된 집단에 대해 적대적인 태도를 전달하는 미묘하고 종종 의도하지 않은 표현, 행동 또는 환경적 신호를 가리킨다. 1970년 체스터 M. 피어스(Chester M. Pierce)가 아프리카계 미국인을 향한 모욕을 설명하기 위해 처음 만든 이 용어는 그 범위가 확장되어 성(性)소수자 집단, 경제적으로 불우한 개인들 및 장애인들과 같은 여러 소외된 집단을 포괄하게 되었다.

심리학자 데럴드 윙 수(Derald Wing Sue)는 미세공격을 개인의 집단 소속에 기초하여 폄하하는 메시지를 미묘하게 전달하는 짧고 일상적인 언쟁으로 정의한다. 이러한 행동들은 의식적으로 악의적인 것은 아니지만, 자신의 말이나 행동이 다른 사람들에게 해를 끼치는 것을 알지 못할 수도 있는 사람들에 의해 전달된다.

겉으로 보기에 무해한 성격에도 불구하고, 미세공격은 누적되면, 소외된 공동체를 배제하고 부정하는 환경을 조성하여 그들의 소속감을 약화시킨다. 이러한 미묘한 상호작용의 만연한 영향을 인식하는 것은 포용적 환경을 조성하고 공감과 이해를 촉진하는 데 있어 중요하다.

미세공격으로 인한 의도하지 않은 피해에 대해 인식하고 대처하고 그에 대해 개인들을 교육하는 것은 다양한 정체성과 경험에 대한 존중과 인정을 촉진하는 데 있어 매우 중요한 단계이다.

microaggression n. 미세공격(일상생활에서 이뤄지는 사회적 약자에 대한 미묘한 차별) subtle a. 미묘한, 포착하기 힘든 unintentional a. 고의가 아닌 marginalized a. 소외된 coin v. (신어·신표현을) 만들어내다 insult n. 모욕 direct v. (주의·노력 등을 어떤 방향으로) 돌리다, 향하게 하다 term n. 용어 scope n. 범위, 영역 encompass v. 포위하다; 포함하다 LGBTQ+ 성(性)소수자 economically disadvantaged 경제적으로 불우한[어려운] denigrate v. 모욕하다; (인격·명예 등을) 훼손하다 malicious a. 악의 있는, 심술궂은 innocuous a. 무해한 accumulate v. 쌓이다; (돈 등이) 모이다 exclusion n. 제외, 배제 invalidation n. 무효화 erode v. 좀먹다, 부식하다 acknowledge v. 인정하다, 승인하다 pervasive a. 널리 퍼지는, 만연한 interaction n. 상호작용 foster v. 촉진하다, 조장하다 empathy n. 공감, 감정이입

31 내용파악 ②

"미세공격은 문화적으로 소외된 집단에 대해 적대적인 태도를 전달하는 미묘하고 종종 의도하지 않은 표현, 행동 또는 환경적 신호를 가리킨다.", "심리학자 데럴드 윙 수(Derald Wing Sue)는 미세공격을 개인의 집단 소속에 기초하여 폄하하는 메시지를 미묘하게 전달하는 짧고 일상적인 언쟁으로 정의한다."라는 내용을 통해 ②가 정답임을 알 수 있다.

미세공격에 대한 구별 요인으로 위 글에서 언급하고 있는 것은 무엇인가?
① 의식적으로 해를 끼치려는 의도를 가지고 있다.
② 부정적인 메시지를 미묘하게 전달한다.
③ 항상 노골적이고 직설적이다.
④ 경제적으로 어려운 사람들만을 대상으로 한다

32 내용파악 ③

"겉으로 보기에 무해한 성격에도 불구하고, 미세공격은 누적되면, 소외된 공동체를 배제하고 부정하는 환경을 조성하여 그들의 소속감을 약화시킨다."라는 내용을 통해 ③이 정답임을 알 수 있다.

위 글에 의하면, 미세공격은 사회적으로 소외된 집단에 어떻게 영향을 미치는가?
① 그들이 의견을 낼 수 있도록 힘을 실어줌으로써
② 그들의 경험을 검증함으로써
③ 배제와 부정의 환경을 조성함으로써
④ 소속감을 강화함으로써

33 내용파악 ①

"미세공격으로 인한 의도하지 않은 피해에 대해 인식하고 대처하고 그에 대해 개인들을 교육하는 것은 다양한 정체성과 경험에 대한 존중과 인정을 촉진하는 데 있어 매우 중요한 단계이다."라는 내용을 통해 ①을 정답으로 선택할 수 있다.

미세공격의 영향을 이해하는 것이 중요하게 여겨지는 이유는 무엇인가?
① 그것이 다양한 정체성과 경험에 대한 존중을 키워주기 때문이다.
② 그것이 사회적 권력 역학을 강화하기 때문이다.
③ 그것이 무해하고 중요하지 않기 때문이다.
④ 그것이 특정 문화 규범에만 영향을 미치기 때문이다.

34 동의어 ①

malicious는 '악의 있는'이라는 뜻이므로 '사악한'이라는 의미의 evil이 동의어로 적절하다.

두 번째 단락의 밑줄 친 단어 malicious의 의미는 무엇인가?
① 사악한
② 배타적인
③ 형편이 좋은
④ 의도적인

01 ④	02 ④	03 ①	04 ②	05 ②	06 ③	07 ③	08 ④	09 ③	10 ③
11 ①	12 ①	13 ④	14 ②	15 ②	16 ③	17 ②	18 ④	19 ④	20 ③
21 ①	22 ④	23 ②	24 ③	25 ③	26 ①	27 ②	28 ④	29 ②	30 ①

01 동의어 ④

discernible a. 식별 가능한(= perceptible) distribution n. 분배, 분포 discursive a. 담론의; 종잡을 수 없는 strategy n. 전략 gender n. 성별 ethnicity n. 민족성 revelatory a. (모르던 것을) 알게 하는 negative a. 부정적인 obvious a. 분명한

연령, 성별, 민족성에 따른 이런 담론 전략들의 분포에는 식별 가능한 패턴이 혹 있다 해도 거의 없다고 기록하는 것이 중요하다.

02 동의어 ④

remarkable a. 놀라운 prowess n. 뛰어난 솜씨, 위업(= achievement) testament n. (존재·사실의) 증거 determination n. 투지 skill n. 기술, 기량 exceptional a. 우수한 expertise n. 전문적 기술[지식, 의견] persistence n. 고집 camaraderie n. 우정; 동지애

그 팀의 놀라운 위업은 그들의 투지, 기량, 그리고 우수한 팀워크를 보여주는 증거였다.

03 동의어 ①

plead for ~해달라고 탄원하다 clinic n. (전문 분야) 병원 make an exception 예외로 하다 adamant a. 요지부동의, 단호한(= unyielding) procedure n. 절차; 수술 pliable a. 유연한; 고분고분한 ingenious a. 독창적인 vehement a. 격렬한

그녀는 예외로 해달라고 병원에 탄원했지만, 병원장은 여전히 요지부동이었으며, 수술을 하려고 하지 않았다.

04 논리완성 ②

잔인한 관행이 이제는 상상도 할 수 없는 일로 변했다면, 이는 그런 잔인한 관행들이 이미 '폐지됐기' 때문일 것이다.

persecution n. 박해 heretic n. 이교도 unexceptionable a. 나무랄 데 없는 emancipate v. 해방하다 abolish v. 폐지하다 superimpose v. 덧붙이다, 첨가하다 wrangle v. 말다툼하다, 언쟁하다

불과 한 세기 조금 넘는 기간 사이에, 마녀 살해와 이교도 박해 같은 잔인한 관행이 갑자기 폐지되어서, 나무랄 데 없는 일에서 상상도 할 수 없는 일로 빠르게 변했다.

05 논리완성 ②

공기가 희박하고 추운 날씨는 탐험가들에게 극심한 '고난'에 해당하므로, 빈칸에는 ②의 adversity가 적절하다.

face v. 직면하다 thin a. (산소 등이) 희박한 freezing a. 몹시 추운 fervor n. 열정, 열렬 adversity n. 역경, 고난 rigidity n. 엄격성 indulgence n. 하고 싶은 대로 함, 방종

그 탐험가들은 공기가 희박하고 몹시 차가운 추운 날씨에 극심한 고난에 직면했다.

06 관계대명사 that과 what의 구분 ③

the remainder가 ③ 앞의 is의 주어이고, ③이 들어있는 that's known as dark energy가 is의 보어인데, 관계대명사 that 앞에 있어야 하는 선행사가 없다. 따라서 ③에서 that은 부적절하므로, that을 자체적으로 선행사를 갖고 있는 what으로 하여 ③을 what's known으로 고쳐야 한다.

atom n. 원자 account for 차지하다 the rest 나머지 astronomer n. 천문학자 cosmologist n. 우주론자 dark matter 암흑 물질(우주에 존재하는 물질 중 아무런 빛을 내지 않는 물질) remainder n. 나머지 interact with ~와 상호작용을 하다 gravity n. 중력

원자, 항성, 행성, 나무, 암석, 인간 등, 우리가 알고 있는 물질은 알려진 우주의 5%도 되지 않는다. 나머지는 다소 미스터리로 남아 있다. 암흑 미스터리이다. 천문학자들과 우주론자들은 우리 우주의 대략 25%가 암흑 물질이라 불리는 것으로 만들어져 있으며, 나머지 — 대략 70% — 는 암흑 에너지로 알려져 있는 것이라고 생각하고 있다. 암흑 물질은 빛과 상호작용하지 않아서, 우리는 암흑 물질을 볼 수가 없다. 우리가 직접 볼 수 있는 것 너머에 무언가가 있다는 것을 우리가 아는 유일한 이유는 바로 그것이 중력과 상호작용하기 때문이다.

07 능동태와 수동태의 구분 ③

항아리는 제공하는 주체가 아니라 제공되는 객체이다. 따라서 ③에서 능동태로 쓰인 offered를 수동태인 were offered로 고쳐서 ③을 which gods the vases were offered to로 고쳐야 한다. 참고로 which는 의문형용사로 쓰여 명사인 gods를 수식해 주고 있다.

emperor n. 황제 enduring a. 오래 지속되는 grand a. 웅장한 palace n. 궁전 parlour n. (주택의) 응접실[거실] blue and white porcelain

청화백자 quintessentially ad. 본질적으로 archetypal a. 전형적인 aesthetic n. 미학 commission v. (작품 등을) 의뢰하다, 주문하다 dedicate v. (책·음악 등을) 바치다

몽골 황제의 통치 아래, 중국은 세계 역사상 가장 오래 지속되고 성공적인 사치품들 중 하나를 개발했는데, 그것은 바로 웅장한 궁전에서 전 세계의 소박한 응접실에 이르기까지 수 세기에 걸쳐 퍼져나간 제품인 중국의 청화백자이다. 지금 우리는 청화백자를 본질적으로 중국의 것이라고 여기지만, 청화백자는 그렇게 시작된 것이 아니다. 이 전형적인 중국의 미학은 사실 이란에서 유래한 것이다. 물건에 글을 쓰는 중국의 오랜 관습 덕분에, 우리는 그 항아리들이 어떤 신에게 바쳤던 것이었는지, 누가 그 항아리들을 주문의뢰 했는지, 그리고 그것이 언제 바쳐졌는지를 정확히 알 수 있다.

08 if가 생략된 가정법   ④

④에서 도치형태인 has she been이 왔고, ④ 앞에서 'would+V'가 온 점을 통해 if가 생략된 가정법이 쓰였음을 알 수 있다. ④ 앞의 주절은 현재사실에 대한 반대상황을 나타내고, if절은 과거사실에 반대되는 가정을 나타내므로, 혼합가정법이 쓰인 것이다. 따라서 ④를 if she had been에서 if가 생략된 had she been으로 고쳐야 한다.

vaccination n. 백신 접종; 종두 subsequently ad. 그 이후 honours n. 훈장, 서훈 eradication n. 근절; 박멸 small pox 천연두 blossom n. (특히 과수의) 꽃; 전성기 cowpox n. 우두(사람에게도 옮을 수 있는, 소의 바이러스성 질병) hide n. (특히 가죽 제품에 쓰이는 짐승의) 가죽 pioneering a. 선구적인 lay the groundwork for ~의 토대를 마련하다 socialite n. 사교계 명사(名士)

제너(Jenner)의 종두법이 젖소를 뜻하는 라틴어 'vacca'를 따라 알려지게 되면서, 백신 접종은 안전한 것으로 입증되었고, 그 이후 전 세계적으로 채택되었다. 제너는 많은 훈장과 상을 받았고, 제너의 연구는 결국 1976년 천연두의 박멸로 이어졌다. 이제 전 세계 모든 의대생들이 제너에 대해 배운다. 심지어 제너의 실험에 쓰인 우두 물질을 제공했던 젖소인 블라섬(Blossom)도 기억된다. 그 젖소의 가죽은 세인트 조지(St George) 병원 의과대학에 있다. 그러나 선구적인 연구로 제너의 실험을 위한 토대를 마련했던 워틀리 몬태규(Wortley Montagu)는 기억에서 잊혀졌다. 만일 그녀가 여자 사교계 명사가 아니라 남자 의사였더라면, 그녀의 연구가 기억되고 있을지는 오직 짐작만 할 수 있을 뿐이다.

09 대명사의 수일치   ③

③에서 its가 가리키는 대상은 zoology가 아니라, those who choose to study it(동물학을 공부하기로 선택한 사람들)이다. 가리키는 대상이 복수이므로, ③에서 its를 their로 고쳐야 한다.

open to doubt 의문의 여지가 있는 implication n. 의미; 영향; 함축 revolution n. 혁명 realize v. 깨닫다; 실현하다 zoology n. 동물학 appreciate v. 충분히 인식하다 profound a. 심오한 no doubt 의심할 여지없이

오늘날 진화론은 지구가 태양 주위를 돈다는 이론과 거의 마찬가지로 의심의 여지가 없지만, 다윈(Darwin) 혁명의 완전한 의미는 아직 널리 실현되지 않았다. 동물학은 여전히 대학교에서 소수의 사람들이 수강하는 과목이며, 심지어 동물학을 공부하기로 선택한 사람들조차 동물학의 심오한 철학

적 중요성을 충분히 인식하지 못한 채 결정을 내리는 경우가 많다. 철학은 거의 마치 다윈이 이 세상에 살지 않았던 것처럼 아직도 가르쳐진다. 의심할 여지없이, 이것은 시간이 지나면 달라질 것이다.

10 가정법 과거완료   ③

③은 뒤의 if절 동사가 'had+과거분사'인데, 잉카제국 황제의 행동은 과거의 행동이므로 혼합가정법이 아니라 가정법 과거완료로 표현되어야 한다. 따라서 ③을 should have been으로 고쳐야 한다.

miscalculation n. 오산, 오판 countless a. 수많은 Native American (아메리카 대륙에 원래 살고 있던) 아메리카 인디언 deceive v. 속이다 inhabitant n. (특정 지역의) 주민 Spaniard n. 스페인 사람 other than ~외에 interrogate v. 심문하다, 추궁하다 subject n. 백성, 신하 encounter v. 만나다, 마주치다 illiterate a. 글을 (읽거나 쓸 줄) 모르는 literate a. 글을 읽고 쓸 줄 아는 contemporary a. 현대의

유럽인들에게 속은 수많은 아메리카 인디언 지도자들이 오판한 것은 신대륙에 살고 있는 주민들이 구대륙에 가본 적이 없었고, 그래서 당연히 스페인 사람들에 대한 구체적인 정보를 가질 수 없었을 것이라는 사실 때문이었다. 그래도, 잉카제국 황제인 아투아알파(Atahuallpa)는 그의 사회가 보다 광범위한 인간 행동을 경험하기만 했더라도 더 수상쩍게 여겼을 것이라는 결론을 우리는 내리지 않기가 어렵다. 피사로(Pizarro) 역시 1527년에 그가 마주친 잉카 사람들을 심문해서 알아낸 것 이외에는 잉카 사람들에 대한 정보가 전혀 없는 가운데 카하마르카(Cajamarca)에 도착했다. 그러나 피사로 본인은 글을 읽고 쓸 줄 몰랐지만, 그는 글을 읽고 쓸 줄 아는 전통에 속해 있었다. 책을 통해, 스페인 사람들은 유럽에서 멀리 떨어진 많은 현대 문명에 대해 알고 있었다.

11 논리완성   ①

'학생 등록을 늘리기 위해' 이사회들이 수업료를 낮췄다고 했으므로, 그 목적에 맞게 등록이 늘었다는 내용이 예상됐지만, 빈칸 다음에 '변함없이 학생 등록이 줄었다'는 내용이 왔다. 따라서 빈칸에는 역접의 의미를 가진 ①의 however(그러나)가 들어가야 한다.

learn (something) the hard way (불쾌한 경험 등을 통해) 비싼 교훈을 얻다 equate A with B A와 B를 동일시하다 tuition n. 교수, 수업; 수업료 enrollment n. 등록 address v. 해결하다 board of trustees 이사회 invariably ad. 변함없이 prestige n. 명성 correspondingly ad. 상응하여 demand n. 수요 conversely ad. 반대로

많은 대학들은 부모와 학생들이 교육의 질을 수업료와 동일시한다는 것을 어렵사리 알게 되었다. 학생 등록을 늘리고 교육비 상승에 대한 불만을 해결하기 위해 많은 이사회들이 수업료를 낮추고 있다. 그러나 이것은 변함없이 학생 등록을 줄이는 결과를 초래할 뿐, 늘리지는 못하고 있다. 수업료를 낮추는 것은 학교가 제공하는 교육의 질 뿐 아니라, 학교의 명성도 떨어뜨리며, 이에 상응해 수요도 감소한다. 반대로, 대학교가 수업료를 올리면, 학생 등록이 증가한다.

12 논리완성   ①

빈칸 앞에 언급된 문장에서, 영국인들이 '퇴보와 부패에 대해 걱정하기

시작했다'고 했으므로, 바로 다음에 온 빈칸에도 이와 유사한 내용이 들어가야 한다. 따라서 조지 버나드 쇼가 영국의 퇴보와 부패와 관련하여 "영국이 이제 '선진화된 부패 상태에' 있다고 주장했다."고 해야 같은 맥락이 되며, 재치 있는 표현도 된다. 따라서 ①이 정답이다.

mid-Victorian a. 영국 빅토리아 왕조 중기의 inevitably ad. 필연적으로 degeneration n. 타락; 퇴보 corruption n. 부패 institution n. 제도 stock n. 혈통; 종족 sharp-wittedly ad. 재치 있게 contend v. (강력히) 주장하다 literary a. 문학[문예]의 decadent a. 퇴폐적인 sinister a. 불길한 analogy n. 비유 imperial a. 제국의 decline n. 쇠퇴 realist a. 사실주의의 novelist n. 소설가 paint a picture ~을 묘사하다 gloomy a. (미래에 대해) 비관적인, 암울한 advanced state 선진국 rottenness n. 부패 heyday n. 전성기 nothing but 오직 fledgling n. (막 날기 시작한) 어린 새; 초보자 glory n. 영광

중기 빅토리아 시대 이후, 영국인들은 스스로를 필연적으로 진보적이라고 보기는 어렵다는 것을 알게 되었다. 대신, 그들은 그들의 문화, 그들의 제도, 그들의 인종적인 '혈통'의 타락과 부패에 대해 걱정하기 시작했다. 조지 버나드 쇼(George Bernard Shaw)는 영국이 "선진화된 부패 상태에" 있다고 재치 있게 주장한다. 이 시기의 대부분의 문학적 문화가 유사한 견해를 드러낸다. 퇴폐적인 운동들이 로마 제국의 쇠망과 불길하게 유사한 예를 제시하는 한편, 사실주의 소설가들은 현대 사회를 암울하게 묘사한다.

① 선진화된 부패 상태에
② 권력의 전성기에
③ 단지 거만한 애송이
④ 과거의 영광을 회복하는

---

13 논리완성   ④

현대 생물학 이론들의 중심 초점이 무엇인지를 묻고 있는데, 빈칸 다음에서 난자의 전략은 짝을 고를 때 더 까다로워야 하고 짝짓기 대상의 수도 줄일 것을 요구하는 반면, 정자의 전략은 남성이 많은 여성들과 짝짓기를 할 것을 요구한다고 했다. 이와 같이 남성과 여성이 번식에 있어 전략이 다르므로, '남성과 여성은 선천적으로 다른 번식 전략을 갖고 있다'라는 ④가 빈칸에 적절하다.

supposedly ad. 아마 innate a. 타고난, 선천적인 mandate v. 요구하다 notion n. 개념 by nature 선천적으로 distinct a. 다른, 별개의 reproductive a. 번식의 egg n. 난자 picky a. (사람이) 까다로운 mate n. 짝; 섹스 파트너 v. 짝짓기를 하다 expend v. (시간·에너지를) 쏟다 nurture v. 양육하다 infant n. 갓난아기, 유아 sperm n. 정자 in turn 결국 pregnant a. 임신한 go by (시간이) 흐르다 fetus n. (임신 9주 후의) 태아 to the advantage of ~에게 유리하게 go about 계속 ~을 (바삐) 하다 impregnate v. 임신시키다 in succession 연이어

성별(性別)에 따라 부여된 선천적인 사고와 행동 패턴에 관한 현대 생물학 이론들의 중심 초점은 아마도 남성과 여성이 선천적으로 다른 번식 전략을 갖고 있다는 개념일지도 모른다. 난자의 전략은 여성이 짝을 고를 때 더 까다로워야 하고 더 적은 수의 짝들을 만나야 하며, 영유아를 양육하는 데 남성보다 보살핌과 노력을 더 많이 기울일 것을 요구한다. 정자의 전략은 남성이 많은 수의 다른 여성들과 짝짓기하고, 영유아를 양육하는 데는 여성보다 보살핌과 노력을 덜 기울일 것을 요구한다. 이런 두 개의 상반된 전략은 결국 난자와 정자의 크기와 양의 차이를 반영하고 있다. 여성들은

난자 공급이 일정하다. 일단 임신하면, 여성은 최소 18개월이 지나기 전까지는 또 다른 아기를 가질 수 없다. 이와 대조적으로 남성은 수천만 개의 정자를 생산한다. 몸이 태아를 양육하는 일에 전념하는 것이 바로 여성이기 때문에, 빠르게 연이어 여러 여성들을 임신시키는 것이 남성의 번식에 유리하다.

① 남성과 여성이 완전히 다른 유전 메커니즘을 갖고 있다
② 남성과 여성이 모두 선천적으로 서로 경쟁한다
③ 남성과 여성이 사용하는 생존 전략은 매우 다르다
④ 남성과 여성이 선천적으로 다른 번식 전략을 갖고 있다

---

14 논리완성   ②

오늘날에는 the United States를 단수취급 하지만, 과거에는 복수취급 했다고 했는데, 이렇게 변한 이유로 많은 역사가들은 남북전쟁 때문이라고 했으며, 역사가 맥퍼슨 역시 "남북전쟁이 미국을 단수명사로 전환시키는 계기가 됐다"라고 언급했다. 그런데 빈칸 다음에는 남북전쟁이 끝난 직후나 15년이 지난 뒤에도 the United States를 단수취급보다 복수취급 하는 경우가 더 많았다고 했다. 이는 곧 단수와 복수를 혼용해 썼다는 것이므로, 맥퍼슨의 주장은 부분적으로 옳고 '완전히 옳지는 않은 것'이다. 따라서 ②가 정답이다.

singular a. 단수의 verb n. 동사 noun n. 명사 refer to 언급하다 plural a. 복수의 usage n. 어법 fascination n. 매혹하는 힘 suspect v. ~이 아닌가 생각하다 the Civil War 미국 남북전쟁 renowned a. 저명한 bluntly ad. 직설적으로 transition n. 과도기 phrase n. 표현; 관용구 transformation n. (완전한) 변화 accelerate v. 가속화되다 absolutely ad. 전적으로 preposterous a. 말도 안 되는

미국인들은 이제는 the United States라는 명사에 단수 동사를 사용한다. 그러나 건국 초기에는 the Unites States를 복수형을 사용해 언급했다. 이런 작은 어법의 차이는 오랫동안 역사가들을 매혹시켜 왔다. 많은 역사가들은 그 원인이 남북전쟁이라고 생각해왔다. 실제로, 저명한 역사가인 제임스 맥퍼슨(James McPherson)은 "남북전쟁이 미국을 단수명사로 전환시키는 계기가 됐다."라고 직설적으로 말했다. 그러나 맥퍼슨이 완전히 옳지는 않았던 것으로 드러났다. 연구원들은 빅데이터를 이용하여 미국의 책들이 "The United States are~"라는 표현과 "The United States is~"라는 표현을 미국 역사에서 매년 얼마나 자주 사용하는지를 확인해볼 수 있었다. (단수 동사로의) 변화는 맥퍼슨이 주장하는 것보다 조금 더 서서히 일어났으며, 남북전쟁이 끝나고 한참 지난 후까지 그 속도가 빨라지지 않았다. 남북전쟁이 끝난 지 15년이 지났지만, "The United States are~"가 "The United States is~"보다 여전히 더 많이 사용되고 있었다.

① 그리고 맥퍼슨이 전적으로 옳았음이 드러났다
② 그러나 맥퍼슨이 전적으로 옳지는 않았던 것으로 드러났다
③ 그러나 맥퍼슨의 주장은 터무니없는 것으로 입증되었다
④ 그러나 아무도 맥퍼슨의 주장을 믿지 않았다

---

15 논리완성   ②

앞 문장에 언급된 여론조사의 예로 빈칸 다음에서 갤럽 여론조사 결과를 제시하므로, 빈칸에는 ②의 For example이 적절하다.

run v. (특히 미국 선거에) 출마하다 presidential nominee 대선후보 poll n. 여론조사 race n. 인종 factor n. (어떤 현상의) 요소 conduct v. 실시하다 professor n. 교수 pore v. 자세히 조사하다 presidency n. 대통령 임기 conventional wisdom (대부분의 사람들이 가지고 있는) 일반적인 통념 swath n. (풀 베는 기계의) 한 번 벤 분량

2008년 버락 오바마(Barack Obama)는 주요 정당의 첫 아프리카계 미국인 대통령 후보로 출마했고, 여론조사는 미국인들이 투표를 하는 데 있어서 인종은 고려 요소가 아니라는 것을 시사해 주었다. 예를 들어, 갤럽(Gallup)은 오바마의 첫 대선 전후로 많은 여론조사를 실시했다. 여론조사의 결과는? 미국 유권자들은 버락 오바마가 흑인이라는 것을 대체로 상관하지 않았다. 대선 직후, UC 버클리의 저명 교수 둘은 다른 설문조사에 기초한 데이터를 면밀히 검토하여 비슷한 결론을 내렸다. 따라서 오바마 대통령의 임기 동안, 이것은 많은 언론과 많은 학계에서 일반적인 통념이 되었다.

16 내용파악 ③

① 지나가던 영국 선박이 포르투갈 인근에서 메리 셀러스트호를 발견했다고 했다. ② 메리 셀러스트호는 공업용 알코올을 싣고 있었다. ④ 해적질, 선상반란, 거대한 바다 생명체의 공격 등, 메리 셀러스트호의 미스터리를 둘러싸고 다양한 이론들이 무성했다고 했다. 반면, 메리 셀러스트호의 선장이 누구였는지는 이 글을 통해 알 수 없으므로, ③이 정답이다.

enigmatic a. 불가사의한 maritime a. 바다의, 해양의 tale n. 이야기 merchant ship 상선 adrift a. (배가) 표류하는 ad. 표류하여 the Atlantic Ocean 대서양 vessel n. (대형) 선박 intact a. 온전한, 손상되지 않은 provision v. (특히 특정 기간 동안 필요한 식량을) 공급하다 seaworthy a. 항해하기 적합한 devoid of ~이 없는 crew n. 승무원, 선원, 승조원 soul n. (특히 부정문에서) 사람 on board 승선한 log n. (특히 항해 등의) 일지[기록] set sail for ~을 향해 출항하다 cargo n. (선박의) 화물 passing a. 지나가는 float v. 떠다니다 aimlessly ad. 목적 없이, 정처 없이 baffled a. 당혹스러운 board v. 승선하다 undisturbed a. 그 누구도 손대지 않은 personal belongings 개인 소지품 missing a. 행방불명된 fate n. 운명, 숙명 foul play 살인 speculation n. 추측, 억측 swirl v. 소용돌이치다 piracy n. 해적 행위, 해적질 mutiny n. (특히 선원들의) 반란[폭동] definitive a. 결정적인, 명확한 haunting a. 좀처럼 잊을 수 없는 captain n. 선장

메리 셀러스트(Mary Celeste)호 미스터리는 여전히 불가사의한 해양 이야기로 남아있다. 1872년 11월, 상선 메리 셀러스트호는 대서양에서 표류 중인 채로 발견되었다. 그 배는 손상된 흔적이 없었고, 식량도 충분했으며, 항해하기에도 적합했지만, 선원들은 하나도 없었다. 배에 아무도 타고 있지 않았던 것이다. 메리 셀러스트호의 항해일지를 통해 그 배가 공업용 알코올을 싣고 뉴욕에서 출발하여 제노바로 출항했다는 것을 알 수 있었다. 한 달 뒤, 지나가는 영국 선박이 포르투갈 인근에서 방향을 잃고 떠다니는 메리 셀러스트호를 발견했다. 구조선의 선원들은 당혹스러워 했는데, 왜냐하면 그들이 메리 셀러스트호에 승선했을 때, 겉보기에는 그 누구도 손을 댄 흔적이 없었기 때문이었다. 음식도 일부만 먹었고, 개인 소지품도 남아 있었고, 구명정만 행방불명된 상태였다. 선원들의 운명은 여전히 해양 미스터리로 남아있다. 몸싸움이나 살인의 흔적은 전혀 없었다. 해적질, 선상반란, 또는 거대한 바다 생명체의 공격 등, 추측이 무성했다. 그러나 결정적인 설명은 나오지 않았다. 메리 셀러스트호에 탑승한 선원들의 실종 이면의 진실은 여전히 잊을 수 없는, 풀리지 않는 미스터리로 남아있다.

다음 중 메리 셀러스트호에 대해 대답할 수 없는 질문은?
① 어디서 메리 셀러스트호가 표류한 채 발견되었는가?
② 메리 셀러스트호는 무슨 화물을 싣고 있었는가?
③ 누가 메리 셀러스트호의 선장이었는가?
④ 메리 셀러스트호 선원의 실종과 관련한 이론들은 무엇이었는가?

17 내용추론 ②

세 번째 문장에서 '단순한 뇌 크기 이상의 호모 사피엔스가 갖고 있는 어떤 특징이 호모 사피엔스 종이 언어를 말할 수 있게 하는 데 결정적이었다'고 했는데, 이것은 호모 사피엔스가 이 특징을 갖고 있어서 언어를 말할 수 있었고 다른 종은 언어를 말할 수 없었다는 말이므로 ②가 정답이다. ① 뇌 크기가 아니라 호모 사피엔스가 가진 어떤 특징이 언어의 발달에 결정적이었다. ③ '호모 사피엔스가 등장해서야 비로소 한 곳에 정주하는 대신 사냥감을 쫓아가는 유목민의 생활방식의 증거 등, 문화가 폭발적으로 증가하는 것을 갑자기 보게 되었다'고 했으므로 두 종은 한 곳에 정주했다고 할 수 있다. ④ 호모 사피엔스에 와서 도구들이 복잡해졌다는 것을 감안할 때 두 종도 정교하지는 않더라도 도구를 사용했을 것으로 추론할 수 있다.

deduction n. 추론, 추정 archaeological a. 고고학의 fossil a. 화석의 remains n. 유적; 유해 Homo sapiens 호모 사피엔스, (현재 존재하는) 인류 species n. 종(種) Homo habilis 호모 하빌리스(도구를 만들어 쓴 초기 인류) Homo erectus 호모 에렉투스, 직립 원인(猿人) over the millennia 수천 년 동안에 explosion n. 폭발적인 증가 artifact n. (천연물에 대하여) 인공물 bury v. (시신을) 묻다, 매장하다 grave n. 무덤 nomadic a. 유목민의 game n. 사냥감 turn n. 전환, 변화 intricacy n. 복잡한 사항[내용]

인간의 언어가 언제 생겼는지 우리는 결코 정확히 알지 못할지도 모른다. 그러나 인간의 언어는 대략 15만 년 동안 존재해 왔던 것으로 추정된다. 인간의 고고학적 화석 유해는 단순한 뇌 크기 이상의 호모 사피엔스가 갖고 있는 어떤 특징이 호모 사피엔스 종이 언어를 말할 수 있게 하고 세상을 장악할 수 있게 하는 데 결정적이었다는 것을 시사해 준다. 호모 하빌리스와 호모 에렉투스 같은 호모 속(屬) 초기 종(種)들의 뇌는 수천 년 동안 점점 커졌던 반면, 어떤 문화적 발전도 뇌 크기 증가와 동반하지는 않았다. 호모 사피엔스가 등장해서야 비로소, 우리는 무덤에 매장된 상징적인 인공물들, 한 곳에 정주하는 대신 사냥감을 쫓아가는 유목민의 생활방식의 증거, 그리고 복잡해진 도구들의 주요 변화에 이르기까지 문화가 폭발적으로 증가하는 것을 갑자기 보게 되었다.

다음 중 위 글에서 올바르게 추론할 수 있는 것은?
① 뇌 크기는 언어의 발달에 결정적이었다.
② 호모 하빌리스와 호모 에렉투스는 언어를 말하지 않았다.
③ 호모 하빌리스와 호모 에렉투스는 사냥감을 쫓아 돌아다녔다.
④ 호모 하빌리스와 호모 에렉투스는 도구를 사용하지 않았다.

18 내용파악 ④

본문에서 우울증을 개선시키는 데 있어서의 몇 가지 실용적인 조언과 요령을 제시했는데, 매일 짧게 산책하는 것은 짧은 운동 루틴 추가에 해당되며, 당신이 관심 갖는 대의명분을 위해 자원봉사 하기, 취침 전에 전자기기 사용 피하기는 본문에 직접 언급되어 있다. 반면, 부정적인 생각

이 떠오르면 '무시하는' 게 아니라, 그것이 타당한지 의심해 보고 반대 증거를 찾아보라고 했으므로, ④가 정답이다.

depression n. 우울증 vortex n. 소용돌이 fatigue n. 피로 apathy n. 무관심 neuroscientist n. 신경과학자 demystify v. 이해하기 쉽게 해 주다 get better (병·상황 따위가) 좋아지다, 호전되다 tip n. 조언 trick n. 비결, 요령 at a time 한 번에 incorporate v. 포함하다, 편입시키다 cause n. 대의명분 care about ~에 관심을 가지다 electronic device 전자기기 validity n. 유효함; 타당성 to the contrary 그와 반대의 reframe v. 재구성하다 perspective n. 관점, 시각

우울증은 당신을 슬픔, 피로, 그리고 무관심이라는 소용돌이 속으로 빠뜨릴 수 있다. 신경과학자 알렉스 코브(Alex Korb)는 우울증을 유발하는 복잡한 뇌 과정을 이해하기 쉽게 설명해 주고, 우울증을 개선시키는 데 있어서의 실용적이고 효과적인 접근법을 제공해 준다.
여기에 몇 가지 실용적인 조언과 요령을 제시하고자 한다.
A. 짧은 운동 루틴을 당신의 하루일정에 추가하는 것과 같은 작은 긍정적인 변화를 한 번에 하나씩 만들어가는 데 주력해보자.
B. 클럽에 가입하는 것이든 관심 갖는 대의명분을 위해 자원봉사를 하는 것이든, 다른 사람과 연결될 수 있는 기회를 찾도록 해보자. 의미 있는 관계 구축은 당신의 기분에 중대한 영향을 미칠 수 있다.
C. 수면의 질을 높이기 위해 마음을 느긋하게 해주는 취침시간 루틴을 만들고, 자기 전의 전자기기 노출을 최소화하고, 편안한 수면환경을 조성해 보자.
D. 부정적인 생각이 떠오르면, 그것이 타당한지 의심해보고, 반대 증거를 찾아보도록 하자. 어떤 상황에서 긍정적인 측면에 집중하기 위해 당신의 관점을 재구성해보자.

다음 중 우울증을 극복할 수 있는 방법이 <u>아닌</u> 것은?
① 매일 짧게 산책하기
② 당신이 관심 갖는 대의명분을 위해 자원봉사 하기
③ 취침 전에 너무 오래 스마트폰을 사용하는 것을 피하기
④ 부정적인 생각이 떠오를 때마다 부정적인 생각을 무시하기

---

19 글의 흐름상 적절하지 않은 문장 고르기   ④

이 글은 어릴 적에 싫어하던 맛을 성장하면서 반대로 좋아할 줄 알게 된다는 내용이다. ④는 '음식에서 고추를 빼버리면, 그들은 즐거움으로 열광할 것이다'라는 의미인데, 앞 문장에서 사람들은 아주 매운 맛을 경험할 것으로 기대한다고 했으므로 매운 고추를 빼버리면 싫어할 것이다. 따라서 ④의 and 다음은 they will rise from the table in disgust(싫어서 식탁에서 일어날 것이다) 정도로 고쳐야 한다.

marked a. 현저한 reversal n. 뒤바뀜, 반전 innate a. 타고난, 선천적인 infantile a. 유아의, 어린 아이의 taste aversion 미각 혐오 scald v. (우유 등을) 비등점 가까이까지 가열하다 Gaucho n. 가우초(남미 대초원의 카우보이) equivalent a. (가치·의미·중요도 등이) 동등한 suck up 빨아들이다, 잘 흡수하다 savor v. 맛보다, 음미하다 grapefruit n. 자몽 chill v. 차갑게 하다 bite-size a. 한 입에 들어갈 만한 dollop n. (버터·진흙 등의) 덩어리; 조금, 소량 horseradish n. 서양고추냉이 take v. (음식·음료를) 먹다, 마시다 sourness n. 시큼함 abound v. 풍부하다, 충만하다 cuisine n. (음식점의) 요리 sauerkraut n. 사워크라우트(양배추를 싱겁게 절여서 발효시킨 독일식 김치) not to mention ~은 말할 것도 없고 vinegar n. 식초 pickle v. (채소 등을) 소금물[식초]에 절이다 peppery a. 얼얼하게 매운 tingling a. 얼얼하게 하는

burning a. 불타는; 화끈거리는 mouth-watering a. (음식이) 군침이 돌게 하는 fulsomeness n. (말씨 따위가) 역겨울 정도로 지나침 fiery a. (음식이나 음료가) 입안이 타는 것 같은[얼얼한] condiment n. 조미료, 양념 take away ~을 제거하다 chili pepper 고추 ecstatic a. 황홀해 하는, 열광하는 abhor v. 몹시 싫어하다, 질색하다 crave v. (특정 음식이) 먹고 싶다, 당기다

어른이 되면 보통 어릴 적에 갖고 있던 미각 혐오 중 일부 또는 전부가 현저하게 바뀐다. 중국인들은 뜨겁고 쓴 맛이 나는 차를 너무나 좋아한다. 가우초(Gaucho)들은 중국인들이 마시는 차에 해당하는 쓴 음료인 마테차를 마시는데, 뜨거울 때 공용 컵으로 마신다. 미국인들은 아침 자몽을 차갑게 한 다음 한 입에 먹을 수 있는 크기로 잘라 먹는다. 독일인들은 고기를 쓴 맛 나는 고추냉이와 함께 먹는다. 신 맛의 사워밀크, 사워크림, 사워크라우트, 사워도우, 그리고 사워애플 등 세계 요리에서 많이 볼 수 있다. 고기, 생선, 그리고 야채를 절이기 위해 사용되는 식초는 말할 것도 없다. 아마도 가장 놀라운 것은 유아기 때 얼얼하게 매운 음식을 싫어했던 것이 바뀐다는 것일지도 모른다. 중국, 중앙아메리카, 인도, 그리고 아프리카 대부분의 지역에서, 사람들은 모든 음식에서 입안이 타는 것 같고 아주 매운 양념이 주는 지나칠 정도의 얼얼하고, 화끈거리고, 군침 돌게 하는 것을 경험할 것으로 기대한다. <(음식에서) 고추를 빼버리면, 그들은 즐거움으로 열광할 것이다.> 아기들이 끔찍이 싫어하는 것을 아이들과 어른들은 간절히 원할 줄 안다.

---

20 글의 요지   ③

이 글에서는 '교육을 잘 받은 사람들이 건전한 판단력을 갖고 있다면 그들이 정부를 운영하는 것이 바람직하지만, 일류 학교의 성적증명서와 실질적인 지혜 간에 관련성이 거의 없다'면서, 그 예로 일류 학교의 성적증명서들로 채워진 케네디 정부와 오바마 정부가 저지른 어리석음에 대해 설명하고 있다. 따라서 글의 요지로는 ③이 적절하다.

desirable a. 바람직한 provided conj. (만약) ~라면 sound a. (신체·정신이) 건전한 prestigious a. 명망 있는, 일류의 credential n. 성적증명서 ruinous a. 파멸적인 credentialism n. (고용 때의) 자격[학력] 중시주의 go awry 실패하다 classic book 고전 best and brightest 엘리트 계급, 정예, 뛰어난 사람들 glittering a. 반짝이는; (경력이) 화려한 for all ~에도 불구하고 technocratic a. 테크노크라시(과학 기술 분야 전문가들이 많은 권력을 행사하는 정치 및 사회 체제의) brilliance n. 빛; 뛰어남, 총명 folly n. 어리석음, 어리석은 행동[생각] detachment n. 분리, 이탈, 거리를 둠 lethal a. 치명적인 consequential a. 중대한, 중요한 nonetheless ad. 그렇기는 하지만 bail out (경제적 위기에 처한 사람·회사 등을) 구제하다 hold somebody to account ~에게 책임을 묻다 discredit v. ~에 대한 평판을 나쁘게 하다 pave the way to ~을 위한 상황을 조성하다

교육을 잘 받은 사람들이 정부를 운영하는 것은 그들이 건전한 판단력을 갖고 있다면 일반적으로 바람직하다. 그러나 역사는 일류 학교의 성적증명서와 실질적인 지혜 간의 관련성을 거의 보여주지 않는다. 실패한 학력중시주의의 가장 파멸적인 사례들 중 하나는 데이비드 핼버스탬(David Halberstam)이 저술한 고전인 『The Best and the Brightest』에 설명되어 있다. 이 책은 어떻게 존 F. 케네디(John F. Kennedy) 대통령이 빛나는 성적증명서들을 가진 팀을 꾸렸는지를 보여준다. 이 팀은 과학기술분야의 뛰어난 전문가들로 구성되었음에도 불구하고, 미국을 어리석은 베트남전쟁으로 이끌었다. 앨터(Alter)는 케네디 정부 팀과 오바마(Obama) 정부 팀이 비슷하다는 것을 알게 되었다. 두 팀은 "어느 정도의 오만함과 미국인

들의 일상으로부터의 동떨어짐 뿐 아니라 아이비리그 출신이라는 점도 공유하고 있었다." 나중에 안 일이지만, 오바마 정부 경제고문들이 베트남 전쟁보다는 덜 치명적이지만 그래도 미국 정치 형태에 중대한 영향을 미친 어리석은 짓에 기여했다고 한다. 금융위기에 대해 월스트리트에 우호적인 대응을 주장하면서, 그들은 은행에게 책임을 묻지 않고 구제해 주었으며, 많은 사람들이 볼 때 민주당의 평판을 나쁘게 했으며, 트럼프 정부가 들어서도록 일조했다.

다음 중 글의 요지를 가장 잘 요약한 것은?
① 교육과 건전한 판단력간의 상관관계는 논란의 여지가 없다.
② 정부는 교육을 잘 받은 사람들에 의해 운영될 필요가 없다.
③ 학교 성적증명서와 실질적인 지혜가 항상 같이 가지 않는다는 것을 역사가 보여준다.
④ 학력중시주의는 케네디 행정부와 오바마 행정부가 저지른 대부분의 어리석은 행동의 원인이다.

21 글의 요지   ①

산업혁명 이후 인간이 화석연료를 연소하는 방식으로 대기에 온실가스를 추가해, 기후가 갑자기 따뜻해졌다고 한 다음, 기후변화를 일으키는 다른 오염물질도 인간이 만들어낸다고 하였으므로, ①의 "인간은 어떻게 기후변화를 일으키는가"가 글의 주제로 적절하다.

the planet 지구 solar a. 태양의[에 관한] ocean circulation 해양순환 volcanic a. 화산의 greenhouse gas 온실가스 concentration n. 집중; 농도; 농축 Industrial Revolution 산업혁명 extract v. 추출하다 burn v. (연료를) 태우다 fossil fuel 화석연료 coal n. 석탄 carbon dioxide 이산화탄소 compound n. (화학적) 화합물 pollution n. 오염; 오염물질 reflect v. 반사하다

과학자들은 지구가 따뜻해지거나 차가워지는 요인들을 이해하기 위해 과거에 있었던 기후변화를 연구해 왔다. 가장 큰 기후변화는 태양에너지, 해양순환, 화산활동, 그리고 대기 중 온실가스 양의 변화이다. 그러나 온난화는 온실가스 농도의 증가로 가장 잘 설명된다. 온실가스는 기후에 강력한 영향을 미친다. 그리고 산업혁명 이후, 인간은 주로 이산화탄소를 방출하는 석탄, 석유, 가스 같은 화석연료를 추출하고 연소시키는 방식으로 대기에 더 많은 온실가스를 추가했다. 온실가스의 급격한 증가로 기후가 갑자기 따뜻해졌다. 그러나 온실가스가 사람들이 대기에 배출하는 유일한 기후변화 화합물인 것은 아니다. 화석연료를 태우면 또한 햇빛을 반사하여 지구를 냉각시키는 오염물질이 생성된다.

다음 중 위 글은 주로 무엇에 관한 것인가?
① 인간은 어떻게 기후변화를 일으키는가
② 온난화의 영향은 얼마나 심각한가
③ 기후변화는 진짜인가
④ 기후변화의 원인에 대해 과학자들은 동의하는가

22 내용파악   ④

그의 예언은 아리송하고 애매한 방식으로 적혀 있었다고 했으므로, ④가 정답이다. ① 그는 의학 학위 없이 의료행위를 시작했다고 했다. ② 그는 평생 동안 악명을 떨쳤다고 했다. ③ 구체적인 사건들에 관한 예언이 아니라 일반적인 유형의 사건들에 관한 예언이었다.

seer n. 예언가 prophecy n. 예언 subject n. (논의 등의) 대상 physician n. 의사; 내과의사 degree n. 학위 entitled a. ~라는 제목의 gain notoriety 악명을 떨치다 cryptic a. 수수께끼 같은, 아리송한 maintain v. 주장하다 match v. 어울리다; 일치하다

노스트라다무스(Nostradamus)는 16세기의 예언가였다. 그와 그의 예언들은 오늘날에도 여전히 잘 알려져 있고 계속해서 논쟁의 대상이 되고 있다. 노스트라다무스는 1503년 프랑스에서 태어났다. 그는 처음에는 의사로 일했으며, 1530년대에 의학 학위 없이 의료행위를 시작했다. 그는 대략 1547년에 예언을 하기 시작했고 『백시선(百詩選, 1555년)』이라는 제목의 책에서 예언들을 발표했다. 노스트라다무스는, 그의 예언들 중 일부가 실현된 것처럼 보임에 따라, 평생 동안 악명을 떨쳤다. 노스타라다무스의 예언은 아리송하고 애매한 방식으로 적혀 있어서, 시간이 흐르면서 정기적으로 발생하는 자연재해와 분쟁 관련 사건들처럼 일반적인 유형의 사건에 관한 것인 경향이 있었다. 어떤 사람들은 그의 예언들이 프랑스혁명, 아돌프 히틀러(Adolf Hitler)의 등장, 그리고 9/11 공격과 같은 실제 사건들을 예언했다고 믿는다. 다른 사람들은 그의 예언들이 역사를 통틀어 자주 발생하는 일반적인 유형의 사건들을 다루는 경향이 있기 때문에, 발생한 거의 모든 사건들과 일치하는 것으로 보이는 예언을 찾는 것이 가능하다고 주장한다.

다음 중 노스트라다무스에 관해 옳은 것은?
① 그는 예언을 시작하기 전에 의학 학위를 가진 의사였다.
② 그가 죽고 난 다음에야 그는 유명해졌다.
③ 그의 예언들은 주로 역사상 일부 구체적인 사건들에 관한 것이었다.
④ 그의 예언들은 이해하기 힘들고 애매모호하게 적혀 있었다.

23 단락배열   ②

제시된 글에서, 과학자들이 실험을 실시했는데, 연구의 목표가 식물 영양의 미스터리를 푸는 것이라고 했다. 따라서 제시문 다음에 이어지는 문장으로, '이러한 목표를 달성하기 위해 과학자들이 어떻게 했는지를 다룬 ⓒ가 제일 처음 와야 하며, ⓒ에서 식물들을 두 집단으로 나눠서 한 집단에는 보통의 물을 주었고, 다른 집단에는 비료 섞인 물을 주었다고 했으므로, 두 집단 간에 차이가 있었다는 결과를 다룬 Ⓑ가 그다음에, 그리고 Ⓑ에서 특수 비료용액을 받은 식물들의 성장이 더 좋은 결과를 보였다고 했으므로, 결론적으로 비료가 식물성장에 효과가 있음을 입증했다는 Ⓐ로 마무리해야 자연스러운 흐름의 글이 된다.

fertilizer n. 비료 aim n. 목표 unravel v. (미스터리 등을) 풀다 nourishment n. 영양 sturdy a. 억센 shrub n. 관목 delicate a. 연약한 blossom n. (특히 유실수나 관목의) 꽃 over the course of ~동안 growth spurt 급성장 budding a. 싹트기 시작하는 hint n. 암시; 전조, 징후 vibrancy n. 활기 astounding a. 몹시 놀라게 하는 solution n. 용액 unveil v. 공개하다, 발표하다 potent a. 강력한 formula n. 조제법, 제조법 augment v. 증대시키다 vitality n. 활력

과학자들은 비료가 식물 성장에 미치는 영향을 시험하기 위해 실험을 실시했다. 연구의 목표는 식물 영양의 미스터리를 푸는 것이었다.
ⓒ 이러한 목표를 달성하기 위해, 그들은 억센 관목에서부터 연약한 꽃에 이르기까지 다양한 범주의 식물을 선정했다. 그다음에, 그들은 그 식물들을 두 집단으로 나누어 한 집단에는 보통의 물을 주었고, 다른 집단에는 특수 비료가 섞인 물을 주었다.
Ⓑ 그다음 몇 주 동안, 그들은 식물들의 진전 상황을 부지런히 추적 관찰했고, 급격한 성장이 있을 때마다, 새싹이 나올 때마다, 그리고 활기 띠는

징후가 보일 때마다 주목했다. 그들은 두 집단 간에 상당한 차이를 관찰했다. 결과는 놀라웠다. 특수 용액을 받은 식물들이 성장이 더 빠르고 더 밝고 건강한 잎들을 보여주었다.

Ⓐ 이 실험은 특수비료의 강력한 효과를 보여주었고, 식물의 성장과 활력을 증대시키는 데 있어서의 비료의 힘을 강조해 주었다. 이 실험은 식물 성장을 향상시키는 데 있어서의 비료의 효과를 입증해 주었다.

24 글의 제목   ③

인도의 빈민가에서 살고 있는 미틸레쉬의 거주 환경을 예로 들며, 많은 사람들이 실내외에서 나쁜 공기를 마시고 살 수 밖에 없는 환경적으로 불평등한 사회를 이야기하고 있는 글이다. 따라서 글의 제목으로는 ③이 적절하다.

turn on (가스 등을) 켜다 stove n. 가스레인지 burn v. 화끈거리다 elderly a. 나이가 지긋한 in-laws n. 인척(특히 시부모·장인과 장모) slum n. (도시) 빈민가 capital n. 수도 breathe v. 호흡하다 bout n. 한 판 승부; 한 차례의 일 cough v. 기침하다 respite n. (곤경·불쾌한 일의) 일시적인 중단 gap n. 격차 scourge n. 재앙, 골칫거리

미틸레쉬(Mithilesh)가 요리하기 위해 가스레인지를 켤 때마다, 그녀의 눈은 화끈거리기 시작한다. 인도의 수도 델리(Delhi)의 빈민가에서 29세의 주부인 미틸레쉬가 남편, 딸, 아들, 그리고 나이든 시부모님과 함께 사는 작은 집은 순식간에 연기로 가득 차 누구도 볼 수 없게 된다. 그녀는 종종 호흡 곤란을 겪고, 통제가 안 될 정도로 수차례 기침을 하게 된다. 그러나 심지어 그녀가 집 밖으로 나가서도, 이런 고통은 멈추지 않는다. 세계에서 두 번째로 큰 거대도시인 델리는 세계에서 실외 공기 질이 최악인 곳들 중 하나이다. 시카고 대학교 에너지 정책연구소가 발행한 한 최근의 연구는 인도 수도 주민들의 수명이 세계보건기구(WHO) 권고 수준으로 대기오염이 감소될 경우에 비해 11.9세나 짧아지고 있다고 경고했다. 미틸레쉬와 그녀의 가족은 전 세계적으로 일어나고 있는 극단적인 예이다. 이제 세계의 거의 모든 사람들이 어떤 식으로든 오염된 공기를 호흡하지만, 가장 큰 타격을 받는 사람들은 또한 자신을 보호하거나 그런 오염된 공기로부터 벗어날 수 없는 사람들이다. 이 대기오염 이야기는 환경 불평등의 이야기인 것이다.

글의 제목으로 가장 적절한 것을 고르시오.
① 인도의 부(富)의 격차 문제
② 델리, 최악의 야외 대기 질을 가진 도시
③ 맑은 공기, 많은 사람들이 가질 수 없는 사치
④ 대기 오염, 지구라는 행성의 재앙

25 부분이해   ③

본문에서 "고학력 엘리트들이 교육을 적게 받은 사람들과 '마찬가지로' 편견을 갖고 있다"고 했으므로, ③이 정답이다.

respondent n. 응답자 bias n. 편견, 선입관 disfavor v. 싫어하다 discrimination n. 차별 descent n. 혈통 obese a. 비만인 blind a. 시각장애인의 class n. 계급[계층] rank v. (등급·순위를) 매기다[평가하다] disparaging a. 우습게 여기는 intriguing a. 아주 흥미로운 enlightened a. 깨우친, 개화된 tolerant a. 관대한 no less ~ than ~와 마찬가지로 folk n. (일반적인) 사람들 denounce v. 비난하다 racism n. 인종차별 (주의) unapologetic a. 미안하다고 생각하지 않는

영국과 네덜란드 등, 서유럽에서 실시된 일련의 조사에서, 사회심리학자들로 구성된 팀은 대학교육을 받은 응답자들이 평소 싫어하는 다른 집단들에 대해 갖고 있는 편견보다 교육을 적게 받은 사람들에 대해 갖고 있는 편견이 훨씬 더 크다는 것을 발견했다. 연구원들은 이슬람교도, 서유럽 거주 터키계 사람들, 가난한 사람들, 비만인 사람들, 시각 장애인들, 그리고 교육을 적게 받은 사람들과 같이 일반적으로 차별 대상이 되는 다양한 사람들에 대해 고학력 유럽인들이 갖고 있는 태도를 조사했다. 그들은 교육을 거의 받지 못한 사람들을 가장 싫어한다는 것을 발견했다. 미국에서 실시된 유사한 연구에서, 연구원들은 싫어하는 집단의 개정된 목록을 제공했는데, 이 집단에는 아프리카계 미국인, 노동자, 가난한 사람들, 비만인 사람들, 그리고 교육을 적게 받은 사람들이 있었다. 미국인 응답자들도 교육을 적게 받은 사람들을 최하위로 평가했다.

연구 저자들은 대학교육을 받은 엘리트들이 교육을 적게 받은 사람들에 대해 우습게 여기는 견해들을 보여주는 것 외에도, 몇 가지 흥미로운 결론을 제시한다. 무엇보다도, 그들은 교육받은 엘리트들이 교육을 적게 받은 사람들보다 도덕적으로 훨씬 더 깨어있는 사람들이며, 따라서 보다 관대하다는 익숙한 개념에 이의를 제기한다. 연구 저자들은 고학력 엘리트들도 교육을 적게 받은 사람들과 마찬가지로 편견을 갖고 있다고 결론 내린다. "오히려 편견의 대상이 다르다는 것이다." 게다가, 엘리트들은 본인이 갖고 있는 편견에 대해 부끄러워하지도 않는다. 그들은 인종차별주의와 성차별주의를 비난할지도 모르지만, 교육을 적게 받은 사람들에 대해 갖고 있는 부정적인 태도에 대해서는 미안하게 생각하지 않는다.

다음 중 밑줄 친 연구의 결과와 일치하지 않는 것은?
① 교육을 거의 받지 못한 사람들이 대학교육을 받은 서유럽 및 미국의 엘리트들 사이에서 가장 싫어하는 집단이다.
② 이 연구는 교육을 받은 엘리트들이 교육을 적게 받은 사람들보다 더 관대하다는 익숙한 개념에 이의를 제기한다.
③ 고학력 엘리트들이 교육을 적게 받은 사람들보다 더 많은 편견을 갖고 있다.
④ 고학력 엘리트들은 교육을 적게 받은 사람들에 대해 갖고 있는 편견에 대해 부끄러워하지 않는다.

26 글의 요지   ①

이 글은 '1970년대부터 2000년대까지를 검토한 결과 가족이 대가족 수가 감소하고 생활방식도 많이 변화했지만, 그럼에도 불구하고 미국인들이 맺고 있는 가족과 친구들과의 관계는 큰 변화가 없었다'는 내용을 다루고 있다. 따라서 글의 요지를 가장 잘 요약한 것으로는 ①이 적절하다.

review v. 검토하다 striking a. 놀라운 consistent a. 한결같은, 일관된 tie n. 유대관계 a handful of 소수의, 소량의 either way (둘 중) 어느 쪽이든 lasting a. 지속적인 alteration n. 변화 entertain v. (손님을) 대접하다 median a. 중간값[중앙치]의 counterpart n. 대응 관계에 있는 사람[것] decade n. 10년 electronic a. 인터넷의[을 이용한], 온라인의 enrich v. 풍요롭게 하다 rule v. (값이) 그대로 유지되다 ends n. 목적, 목표 sustain v. 계속[지속]시키다 intimate a. 친밀한

『Still Connected(2011)』라는 책에서, 사회학자 클로드 피셔(Claude Fischer)는 사회적 관계에 대해 사람들에게 물었던 40년간의 설문조사들을 검토했다. "이 데이터에서 가장 놀라운 점은 1970년대와 2000년대 사이에 미국인들의 가족 및 친구 관계가 얼마나 일관되게 유지되었는가 하는 것입니다. 우리는 개인적으로 지속적인 영향을 미치는 행동에서 지속적인 변화를 설명해줄 수 있는 몇 퍼센트 이상의 차이를 거의 찾지 못합니

다. 그렇습니다. 미국인들은 집에서 손님 대접을 덜 하는 대신 전화통화를 더 많이 했고 이메일을 더 많이 보냈지만, 근본적으로는 변화가 크지 않았습니다."라고 그는 지적했다. 가족의 크기가 작아지고 독신이 많아지고 일하는 여성이 많기 때문에, 사람들은 주어진 시간을 재분배해 왔지만, 오늘날의 미국인들은 제럴드 포드(Gerald Ford) 대통령 재임시절 (1974~1977) 때만큼이나 친척들과 많은 시간을 보내고 똑같은 수의 친구들이 있고 그들과 자주 만나며, 그들과의 교우관계의 양과 질에 만족한다. 인터넷과 소셜 미디어 사용자들은 친구들과 더 많이 연락하고 있으며, 온라인에서의 관계가 그들의 관계를 풍요롭게 해줬다고 느낀다. 피셔는 인간의 본성은 그대로라고 결론짓는다. "사람들은 그들이 가장 소중히 여기는 목적을 지키기 위해 변화하는 환경에 적응하려고 노력하며, 그 목적에는 아이들과 보내는 시간, 친척들과의 교류, 그리고 몇 가지 친밀한 지지 원천 등, 그들의 개인적인 관계의 양과 질을 지속시키는 것이 포함된다."

다음 중 글의 요지를 가장 잘 요약한 것은?
① 대가족 수의 감소와 생활방식의 변화에도 불구하고, 미국인들이 맺고 있는 가족 및 친구와의 관계는 1970년대 이래 큰 변화가 없었다.
② 인터넷과 소셜 미디어로 인해, 미국인들은 이전보다 오늘날 더 외로워한다.
③ 인터넷과 소셜 미디어는 미국인들이 고립감과 서먹함을 느끼지 못하도록 하는 데 큰 역할을 하고 있다.
④ 대가족 수의 감소와 생활방식의 변화는 미국인들을 더욱 더 많이 소원하게 하고 고립시키고 있다.

27-28

영어에서, 당신이 어떤 것을 '죽도록' 한다고 할 때, '죽도록'이라는 말은 그것을 과도하게 반복적으로 완전히 녹초가 될 때까지 한다는 것을 의미한다. 이 '죽도록'이라는 말은 어떤 것을 무리하게 한다는 생각을 강조하기 위해 비공식적으로 흔히 사용되는 표현이다. 그런데 흥미롭게도, 글자 그대로 '죽도록 춤을 추다 죽은' 사례들이 있었다.

소문에 의하면, 1518년에 '댄스 전염병'이 돌아 프랑스의 도시 스트라스부르(Strasbourg) 주민들이 며칠 동안 계속 걷잡을 수 없을 정도로 춤을 춰서 치명적인 결과를 초래했다고 한다. 1518년 7월 어느 무더운 여름날, 트로페아 부인(Frau Troffea)이 스트라스부르 광장에 발을 내딛고는 춤을 추기 시작했다. 처음에, 그녀 주변에 있던 사람들은 쳐다보기만 했고, 이렇게 사람들 있는 데서 춤을 추는 보기 드문 광경에 호기심이 생겼다. 그들은 춤을 멈추려 하지 않고 멈출 수도 없는 이 여인을 지켜봤다.

그녀는 거의 일주일 동안 춤을 췄는데, 가끔 탈진해 쓰러졌지만, 통증, 배고픔, 수치심 같은 신체의 다른 경고신호에도 아랑곳하지 않았다. 그녀는 계속해서 홀로 '댄스 마라톤'을 이어나갔는데, 곧 대략 30명의 스트라스부르 주민들이 동참했다. 8월 무렵, 이 댄스 전염병으로 400명이나 되는 춤추는 사람들의 목숨이 희생되었다. 그들은 마치 강요받은 것처럼 춤을 추었고, 발은 피투성이가 되었으며, 팔과 다리는 경련이 일어났고, 많은 사람들이 춤을 추다 죽어갔다.

스트라스부르 댄스 전염병은 전설처럼 들릴 수 있지만, 이것은 16세기 역사 기록에 잘 기록되어 있다. 그것은 또한 그런 종류의 알려진 유일한 사건은 아니다. 이와 비슷한 광풍이 스위스, 독일, 네덜란드에서도 일어났지만, 1518년의 광풍만큼 대규모이거나 치명적인 것은 거의 없었다. 무엇이 사람들로 하여금 춤을 추다 죽게 만들 수 있었을까? 역사가 존 월러(John Waller)의 말에 따르면, 그에 대한 설명이 가톨릭 성인인 성 비투스(Vitus)와 관련 있을 가능성이 높다고 한다. 성 비투스는 댄스 전염병에 걸리게 사람들에게 저주를 내릴 수 있는 힘을 가졌다고 16세기의 독실한 유럽인들은 믿었다. 다른 이론들 중에는 춤추는 사람들이 사이비 종교 신자였다는 주장도 있었고, 춤추는 사람들이 발작과 환각을 일으킬

수 있는 맥각이라는 독성 곰팡이를 우연히 먹었다는 주장도 있었다. 그러나 과학자들과 역사학자들은 무엇이 스트라스부르 주민들을 죽도록 춤추다가 죽게 만들었는지에 대해서는 여전히 확신하지 못하고 있다.

to death 죽도록 signify v. 의미하다 worn out 녹초가 된 phrase n. 구절, 표현 stress v. 강조하다 literally ad. 글자[말] 그대로 plague n. 전염병 reportedly ad. 소문에 의하면 on end (어떤 기간 동안) 계속 fatal a. 치명적인 sweltering a. 무더운 Frau n. 부인, 여사 square n. 광장 pique v. (호기심을) 돋우다 exhaustion n. 탈진, 기진맥진 undaunted a. (곤경·실망 등에도) 끄떡없는 dance-a-thon n. 댄스 마라톤 epidemic n. 유행병 claim v. (목숨을) 빼앗다 compel v. 강요하다 bloodied a. 피투성이의 limbs n. 사지(四肢), 팔다리 twitch v. 씰룩거리다, 경련하다 deadly a. 치명적인 Catholic n. (로마) 가톨릭교도 saint n. 성인(聖人) pious a. 경건한, 독실한 curse v. 욕하다; 저주를 내리다 religious cult 사이비 종교 ingest v. (음식 등을) 먹다 ergot n. 맥각(지혈제) toxic mold 독성 곰팡이 spasm n. 발작 hallucination n. 환각

---

27 빈칸완성   ②

이 글은 '죽도록'이라는 표현을 언급하면서 흥미롭게도 실제로 죽도록 춤을 추다가 목숨을 잃은 사례가 역사적으로 있었다는 이야기를 하고 있다. 마지막 단락에서는 무엇 때문에 춤추는 사람들이 목숨을 잃게 되었는지에 대해서 여러 가지 설을 이야기하고 있으므로, 마지막 단락의 내용을 이끄는 질문으로 ②가 가장 적절하다.

다음 중 빈칸에 들어가기에 가장 적절한 것은?
① 왜 성 비투스는 댄스 전염병에 걸리게 사람들에게 저주를 내렸을까?
② 무엇이 사람들로 하여금 춤을 추다가 죽게 만들 수 있었을까?
③ 어떻게 사이비 종교 신자들이 사람들로 하여금 춤을 추다가 죽게 만들었을까?
④ 어떻게 질병과 기근에 대한 공포가 댄스 전염병을 촉발했을까?

---

28 내용일치   ④

① 트로페아 부인은 1518년 7월 어느 무더운 여름날에 춤을 추었다고 했다. ② 늦어도 8월까지 춤추다가 죽은 사람이 400명이나 된다고 했을 뿐, 그 후의 댄스 사망자 총 수는 알 수 없으며 또 400명은 400 dancing victims이지 400 victims가 아니다. ③ 스트라스부르 댄스 전염병은 전설처럼 들릴 수 있지만, 이것은 16세기 역사 기록에 잘 기록되어 있다고 했다. 반면, "춤추는 사람들이 발작과 환각을 일으킬 수 있는 맥각이라는 독성 곰팡이를 우연히 먹었다는 주장도 있었다."고 했으므로, ④가 정답이다.

위 글에 의하면 다음 중 옳은 것은?
① 트로페아 부인은 1518년 추운 겨울에 거의 일주일 동안 홀로 춤추었다.
② 스트라스부르에서 400명의 희생자들이 댄스 전염병 기간 동안 죽었다.
③ 스트라스부르에서의 '댄스 전염병'은 기록으로 잘 남아 있지 않았다.
④ 일부 이론들은 '댄스 전염병'을 환각과 연관 지었다.

29-30

겉으로 보기에 불합리한 식습관의 예들을 누구나 알고 있다. 몇몇 국가들에서는 사람들이 개고기를 좋아하지만, 우유는 싫어한다. 반면, 우리는 우유를 좋아하지만, 개는 먹지 않는다. 반면, 브라질에서 일부 부족들은 개미를 즐겨 먹지만, 사슴고기는 싫어한다. 그리고 이런 다양한 식습관은 전세계적으로 각각 다르다.

B 돼지 수수께끼가 가장 좋은 예라고 생각된다. 돼지 수수께끼는 똑같은 동물을 어떤 사람들은 싫어해야 하고 어떤 사람들은 좋아해야 하는 이유를 설명해야 하는 과제를 제시한다.

A 돼지를 싫어하는 사람들과 관련된 미스터리의 절반은 유대교도, 이슬람교도, 기독교도들에게 잘 알려져 있다. 고대 히브리인들이 믿는 신은 일부러 애써 나서서 돼지를 불결하다고 비난했는데, 먹거나 만지면 불결하게 만드는 짐승이라는 것이었다. 대략 1,500년이 지난 후, 알라신은 돼지의 지위가 이슬람교를 믿는 사람들에게도 이와 동일해야 한다고 예언자 마호메트(Mohammed)에게 말했다. 돼지가 다른 어떤 동물들보다도 곡물과 덩이줄기를 고급 지방과 단백질로 효과적으로 전환시킬 수 있다는 사실에도 불구하고, 돼지는 여전히 수백만 명의 유대교도들과 수억 명의 이슬람교도들에게 혐오 대상으로 남아있다.

C 일반적으로 더 적게 알려져 있는 것은 광신적인 돼지 애호가들의 전통이다. 돼지를 사랑하는 세계의 중심지는 뉴기니(New Guinea)와 남태평양 멜라네시아 제도(South Pacific Melanesian islands)에 위치해 있다. 이 지역 마을에 거주하는 원예 부족들에게, 돼지는 결혼식과 장례식 같이 중요한 행사가 있을 때마다 조상들에게 제물로 바친 다음 먹어야 하는 신성한 동물이다. 많은 부족들에게, 돼지는 전쟁을 선포하고 화해하기 위해 제물로 바쳐져야 한다. 그 부족들은 돌아가신 조상들이 돼지고기를 너무 먹고 싶어 한다고 믿는다. 살아있는 사람들과 죽은 사람들 사이에서 돼지고기를 먹고 싶어 하는 욕망이 너무나 압도적이어서 때때로 성대한 잔치를 열어 한 부족이 갖고 있는 거의 모든 돼지들을 한꺼번에 먹는다. 연달아 며칠 동안, 마을주민들은 엄청난 양의 돼지고기를 게걸스럽게 먹는다. 이런 잔치가 끝나면, 돼지 떼는 엄청나게 줄어들어, 다시 돼지 떼를 원상회복시키는 데 몇 년의 힘든 사육이 요구된다. 돼지 떼를 다시 원상회복시키자마자, 또 한 번 게걸스럽게 진탕 먹고 마시며 난잡하게 노는 잔치를 열기 위한 준비가 이루어진다. 따라서 이런 명백한 관리실패의 기괴한 순환이 계속된다.

apparently ad. 겉보기에는 irrational a. 불합리한 despise v. 혐오하다 relish v. (어떤 것을 대단히) 좋아하다 venison n. 사슴고기 riddle n. 수수께끼 strike A as B A에게 B라고 느끼게 하다 pertain to ~와 관련되다 Jew n. 유대인, 유대교도 ancient a. 고대의 Hebrew n. 유대인 go out of one's way 비상한 노력을 하다 denounce v. 비난하다 prophet n. 선지자, 예언자 status n. 신분, 지위 swine n. 돼지 abomination n. 혐오; 혐오감을 주는 것 grain n. 곡물 tuber n. (감자 따위의) 덩이줄기 protein n. 단백질 fanatic a. 광신적인 dwell v. 거주하다 horticultural a. 원예의 sacrifice v. 희생하다; 제물을 바치다 ancestor n. 조상 occasion n. (특별한) 행사[의식] marriage n. 결혼식 funeral n. 장례식 departed a. 세상을 떠난 crave v. ~을 (몹시) 원하다, 먹고 싶어 하다 pork n. 돼지고기 overwhelming a. 압도적인 feast n. 연회, 잔치 gorge on 잔뜩[실컷] 먹다 herd n. 가축의 떼, 무리 painstaking a. 힘든 husbandry n. 농업, 축산; 절약 rebuild v. 원상회복하다 gluttonous a. 게걸들린, 많이 먹는 orgy n. 진탕 먹고 마시며 난잡하게 노는 잔치 bizarre a. 기괴한

29 단락배열   ②

제시된 글은 개고기, 우유, 개미, 사슴고기를 예로 들며 나라마다 불합리한 식습관이 다 다르다고 설명하고 있다. 따라서 이런 불합리한 식습관과 관련된 예가 이어지는 것이 자연스러운데, 돼지를 예로 들어 나라마다 다르게 생각한다는 B가 먼저 오는 것이 자연스러우며, B에서 돼지 수수께끼가 어떤 사람들은 싫어하고 어떤 사람들은 좋아하는 이유를 설명하는 과제를 제시한다고 했으므로, 먼저 돼지를 싫어하는 이유를 제시하는 A가 그다음에 오고, 이보다 덜 알려진 경우로 돼지를 좋아하는 이유를 제시하는 C가 마지막으로 와야 글의 흐름상 자연스럽다.

30 내용일치   ①

유대교도들과 이슬람교도들은 돼지가 '쓸모없기' 때문이 아니라 '불결하기' 때문에 돼지를 싫어한다고 했으므로, ①이 정답이다.

위 글에 의하면 다음 중 옳지 않은 것은?
① 돼지가 쓸모없는 동물이기 때문에 유대교도들과 이슬람교도들은 돼지를 싫어한다.
② 돼지는 뉴기니에서 신성한 것으로 여겨진다.
③ 남태평양 멜라네시아 제도에 있는 많은 부족들은 전쟁을 선포하기 위해 돼지를 제물로 바친다.
④ 남태평양 멜라네시아 제도의 사람들은 때때로 돼지를 폭식하기 위해 성대한 잔치를 연다.

2024 서강대학교(1차)

01 ④	02 ①	03 ③	04 ⑤	05 ②	06 ④	07 ①	08 ②	09 ②	10 ⑤
11 ①	12 ④	13 ②	14 ③	15 ③	16 ⑤	17 ④	18 ⑤	19 ②	20 ④
21 ①	22 ⑤	23 ③	24 ③	25 ②	26 ④	27 ③	28 ①	29 ④	30 ①

01 논리완성 ④

but 이하에서 '되살려냈다(revived)'고 한 것은 반대로 그 이전에는 사멸이나 중단(abeyance) 상태에 있었다는 말이므로 빈칸에는 ④가 적절하다.

enduring a. 지속적인, 영속적인 fountain n. 분수; 원천, 근원 outpouring n. 흘러나옴, 유출 distinction n. 구별, 차별; 탁월 location n. 장소, 위치 affluence n. 풍부함, 풍요 abeyance n. 중지, 정지 fall[go] into abeyance (법률·규칙·제도 등이) 일시 정지되다 aberration n. 상궤를 벗어남, 탈선

문학의 유토피아는 수천 년 전 성(聖) 아우구스티누스 시대 이후 잠시 중단되었지만, 토마스 모어(Thomas More)경의 불멸의 고전이 출판되어 그 장르의 운명을 되살려 놓았고, 우리가 유토피아라고 부르는 것이 솟아나는 원천이 되었다.

02 논리완성 ①

유리가 부서지고 파일이 흩어진 것은 폭도들이 정부 건물을 약탈한(ransack) 데 따른 결과로 보는 것이 타당하다.

enraged a. 격분한 mob n. 폭도 trail n. 자국, 지나간 흔적 in one's wake ~의 여파로 ransack v. 샅샅이 뒤지다; 약탈하다 goldbrick v. 속이다 barrack v. 막사에 수용하다 bushwhack v. 덤불을 베어 헤치다 leapfrog v. 앞지르다, 뛰어넘다

격분한 폭도들이 정부 건물을 약탈했고, 그 여파로 부서진 유리와 흩어진 파일의 흔적만이 남아있었다.

03 논리완성 ③

절망이 자신을 압도하도록 내버려 두지 않았다는 것은 슬픔이나 좌절을 내비치지 않았다는 것이며, 이는 곧 냉정 혹은 평정(composure)의 태도를 보여주었다는 것이다.

tragedy n. 비극 exude v. 발산시키다 overwhelm v. 압도하다, 제압하다, 궤멸시키다 foreclosure n. 폐쇄, 폐지 conjecture n. 추측, 억측 composure n. 침착, 냉정 imposture n. 사기, 협잡 discomfiture n. 좌절; 당황

비극을 맞이해서도 그녀는 조용한 평정의 태도를 발산하여, 절망이 자신을 압도하도록 내버려 두지 않았다.

04 논리완성 ⑤

"표범은 자신의 얼룩무늬를 바꿀 수 없다"는 '고정 불변성'을 의미하는데, 앞에 contrary to가 있으므로 빈칸에는 '가변성'의 의미를 내포하고 있는 ⑤의 malleable(유연한)이 들어가야 한다.

anthropologist n. 인류학자 assure v. 납득시키다, 확신시키다; 보장하다 psyche n. 영혼, 정신 spot n. 반점, 얼룩 alchemical a. 연금술의 omniscient a. 무엇이든지 알고 있는 monolithic a. 이질적인 것이 없는, 획일적인 ostentatious a. 과시하는 malleable a. 적응성이 있는, 유연한

심리학자들과 인류학자들은 인간의 정신이 유연하다고 우리에게 확신시키는데, 이는 "표범은 자신의 얼룩무늬를 바꿀 수 없다"라는 일반적인 개념과 상반되는 것이다.

05 논리완성 ②

담배의 포장에 불쾌한 색상을 사용하고 병든 장기의 이미지를 동반하게 하는 것은 흡연을 깎아내리거나(disparage) 좋지 않게 보이도록 하는 의도를 가지고 있다고 봐야 한다.

portray v. 그리다, 묘사하다 associate v. 관련시키다, 결합하다 enact v. 법령화하다; (법률을) 제정하다 off-putting a. 혐오를 느끼게 하는 accompany v. ~에 동반하다 disenthrall v. 해방하다 disparage v. 헐뜯다, 나쁘게 말하다 disinterest v. ~에 무관심하게 하다 disincline v. 싫증나게 하다 disinherit v. 상속권을 박탈하다

수년간의 정부 연구는 제품이 포장을 통해 보여주는 이미지에 의해 젊은 사람들이 흡연에 이끌린다는 사실을 확실하게 증명한다. 수년에 걸쳐 담배 회사들은 그들의 브랜드 이미지를 긍정적이고 성공적인 라이프스타일과 연결시키는 공격적인 광고에 수십억 달러를 지출했다. 이를 깨달은 금연 운동가들은 담배 포장이 가능한 한 매력적이지 않게 만들어지도록 정부에 로비를 벌였다. 궁극적으로, 젊은 사람들에게 흡연이 좋지 않은 것으로 보이게 하기 위해, 담배 회사들로 하여금 불쾌한 색상을 사용하고 병든 장기의 이미지를 동반하게 하여 가능한 한 매력적이지 않게 담배를 포장하도록 강제하는 법이 제정되었다.

06 논리완성 ④

투자자들에게 그 지역의 경제 지형에 대한 포괄적인 개요를 제시하고자 한다면, 다양한 출처의 정보를 종합하여(aggregate) 상황을 보다 명확하게 파악해야 할 것이다.

analyze v. 분석하다 assess v. 평가하다, 사정하다 fluctuation n. 동요; 오르내림, 변동 reveal v. 드러내다, 밝히다 facilitate v. 용이하게 하다, 촉진하다 informed a. 정보에 근거한 propagate v. 번식시키다; 전파하다 abnegate v. 포기하다 variegate v. 얼룩덜룩하게 하다; 변화를 주다 aggregate v. 모으다, 집합시키다 denigrate v. 모욕하다

그 경제학자는 다양한 출처의 데이터를 분석하여 그 지역의 전반적인 경제 성과를 평가했다. 개별 부문에 변동이 있긴 했지만, 수치는 안정적인 성장 추세를 보여주었다. 다양한 데이터 세트를 나란히 연구하는 것이 중요하다고 이해하고 있었던 그 연구원은 잠재적인 투자자들에게 그 지역의 경제 지형에 대한 포괄적인 개요를 제시하는 것을 목표로 했다. 다양한 출처의 정보를 종합함으로써 상황 파악이 보다 명확하게 이뤄졌고, 이로 인해 그의 고객의 미래 투자 전략과 관련하여 보다 자세한 정보에 근거한 의사 결정을 원활히 내릴 수 있게 되었다.

업무용 출입구보다 더 클 뿐 아니라 보다 더 정교하게 장식돼 있는데, 날개 달린 두 여성의 조상(彫像)과 문장(紋章)처럼 보이는 것이 들어 있는 원형의 양각(陽刻)이 그 위에 놓여 있다. 독특한 장식이 없으면, 건물은 미묘한 차이가 드러나지 못할 위험이 더 크지만, 의미 있는 장식이 없으면, 무의미해질 위험이 있다.

architect n. 건축가 ornamentation n. 장식 deviant n. 비정상적인 사람, 괴짜; 이상 성격자 cursory a. 되는 대로의, 피상적인 palazzo n. 궁전, 전당 distinguish v. 구별하다 persistence n. 고집; 영속 far from 결코 ~이 아닌 superfluous a. 남는, 여분의; 불필요한 incorporate v. 통합하다; 구체화하다 reference n. 관계, 관련; 참조 intensity n. 강렬; 강도 elaborately ad. 정교하게 medallion n. 대형 메달; (초상화 등의) 원형의 양각 coat of arms 문장(紋章) distinctive a. 독특한, 특이한 nuance v. 미묘한 차이를 덧붙이다

07 어법   ①

현재완료시제는 last week 같은 명확한 과거를 나타내는 표현과는 함께 쓰지 못한다. 그러므로 ①에서 I've finished를 I finished로 고쳐야 한다.

A: 논문은 어떻게 되어가고 있니?
① B: 아주 좋아. 지난주에 마무리했어.
② B: 잘됐네! 예정보다 훨씬 빠르구나.
③ B: 그렇지는 않아. 다른 수업에서는 뒤쳐졌어.
④ B: 걱정하지 마. 조만간 따라잡을 수 있을 거야.
⑤ B: 그러겠지. 하지만 지금 당장은 불가능해 보여.

08 어법   ②

인상된 것은 대중교통의 요금으로 ②에서 Every public transportation을 Every public transportation fare로 고쳐야 한다.

A: 들었어? 버스 요금이 또 오르네.
① B: 말도 안 돼! 불과 6개월 전에 인상되었지 않니?
② A: 그랬어. 모든 대중교통 요금이 인상되었어.
③ B: 하지만 이번에는 버스 요금만이야. 아, 이건 끔찍한 일이야!
④ A: 아, 이것 참. 살기가 점점 힘들어지는 시대잖아.
⑤ B: 나도 알아. 하지만 어떻게 맞춰 나가야 할지 모르겠어.

09-10

오스트리아의 건축가 아돌프 로스(Adolf Loos)는 장식을 원시인들이나 정신이상 범죄자들만이 행하는 것처럼 여겨지게 만들었다. 그러나 역사를 대충 살펴봐도, 고대 그리스의 사원에서든, 고딕 양식의 대성당에서든, 르네상스 시대의 궁전에서든, 워싱턴 DC의 의사당에서든, 장식이 항상 건축에 중요한 역할을 해왔다는 것을 알 수 있다. 사실, 장식의 성격에 의해서 서로 다른 역사시대가 구분되는 경우가 많다.
건축에서 장식이 지속되는 이유는 장식이 불필요하기는커녕, 몇 가지 유용한 기능을 수행하기 때문이다. 장식이 있으면, 건축가는 건물 내부에서 일어나는 일들과의 명확한 관련성을 건축에 통합시킴으로써 뿐만 아니라 건물 장식의 강도를 단지 올리거나 내림으로써도 건물에 의미를 부여할 수 있을 것이다. 예를 들어, 필라델피아 교육위원회 건물의 주 출입구는

09 동의어   ②

cursory는 '되는 대로의', '피상적인'이라는 의미이므로 '깊이가 없는', '피상적인'이라는 뜻의 superficial이 동의어로 적절하다. ① 무형의 ③ 진짜의 ④ 일상의 ⑤ 고안하는

10 내용일치   ⑤

건축에서 장식은 몇 가지 유용한 기능을 수행하며 지속되고 있다고 했으므로 장식을 포기하면, 지금까지 익숙해져 있는 장식의 효과를 경험할 수 없게 되어 불필요한 혼란을 야기할 것이다. 따라서 ⑤가 옳은 진술이다. ① 장식을 원시인이나 정신이상 범죄자의 것으로 여겼다. ②, ④ 본문에 언급이 없다. ③ 미국 국회의사당이 아니라 필라델피아 교육위원회 건물이다.

위 글에 의하면 다음 중 옳은 것은?
① 아돌프 로스는 건축에서 장식을 사용하는 것에 대해 열광했다.
② 건축에서 장식은 항상 원시 문화를 나타낸다.
③ 미국 국회의사당은 장식이 돼 있는 출입구로 유명하다.
④ 건축의 장식은 점점 더 유행을 타지 않고 있다.
⑤ 건축에서 장식을 포기하는 것은 불필요한 혼란을 야기한다.

11 문의 구성   ①

ⓐ는 접속사 as가 이끄는 절의 동사인데, 분사는 정동사의 역할을 할 수 없으므로 ⓐ를 과거시제 동사 precipitated로 고쳐야 한다.

transformation n. 변형, 변화 cuisine n. 요리, 요리법 precipitate v. 재촉하다, 촉진시키다 staple n. 주요 산물, 중요 상품; 주요[기본] 식품 maize n. 옥수수 prominently ad. 두드러지게, 현저하게 resurgence n. 부활, 소생 revivalist n. 부흥운동가, 회복주의자 reclaim v. (분실하거나 빼앗긴 물건 등을) 되찾다[돌려 달라고 하다] culinary a. 요리의, 요리용의 push back against (잘못이라고 생각하는 것에 대해) 반박하다 heritage n. 유산, 세습재산 sustainability n. 지속가능성; (자원 이용이) 환경이 파괴되지 않고 계속될 수 있음

1521년에 스페인 사람들이 멕시코에 도착한 것은 그 지역의 요리법에 변화가 시작될 것임을 보여주는 것이었는데, 이는 가축, 특히 소와 돼지의 전래가 이 지역의 전통적인 채식 중심 식단의 쇠퇴를 촉진시켰기 때문이다. 자신들의 뿌리와 다시 연결되기 위해, 점점 더 많은 멕시코인들과 멕시코계 미국인들은 "채식을 지향하는" 전통적인 식습관을 다시 받아들이고 있다. 예를 들어, 예전에 주식으로 삼았던 — 세 자매로 알려져 있는 — 옥수수, 콩, 스쿼시가 이제 일상적인 가정의 식사에서 더 두드러지고 있다. 이러한 요리가 소생함에 따라, 회복주의자들은 그들이 전통적인 요리를 되찾고 있으며 유산과 지속 가능성에 대한 이야기를 상기시킴으로써 식민주의를 밀쳐내고 있다고 느낀다.

12 명사를 수식하는 형용사 ④

명사를 수식하는 역할을 하는 것은 부사가 아닌 형용사이므로 ⑩를 endless consumption으로 고쳐야 한다.

abundance n. 풍부, 부유 arena n. (고대 로마의) 투기장; (일반적) 경기장; 활동 장소 iconography n. 도해(법); 초상[조상(彫像)] 연구, 초상화(집) catchy a. 사람의 마음을 끄는, 매력 있는 consumption n. 소비 gaudy a. 화려한, 야한

비록 그것에 대항하는 몇몇의 강한 목소리들이 등장했었지만, 풍요라는 자본주의의 이념은 새로운 문화적 공간을 만들어내는 데 도움을 주고 있었다. 그것은 상업적인 상징들과 사람의 마음을 끄는 슬로건들로, 상품과 끝없는 소비라는 비전으로, 패션쇼와 화려한 상점의 진열장으로, 도시의 거리 위에 우뚝 솟아있는 거대한 전기 광고판과 기계화된 화면 등으로 가득 채워지고 있는 무대였다.

13-14

마르쿠스 유니우스 브루투스(Marcus Junius Brutus)가 율리우스 카이사르의 (Julius Caesar)의 암살 계획에 가담하기로 한 것은 그 자신의 혈통에 아로새겨져 있는 유산과 분리될 수 없다. 그의 뛰어난 조상이었던 루키우스 주니우스 브루투스(Lucius Junius Brutus)로부터 공화주의의 이상과 폭정에 대한 단호한 저항의 물결이 거세게 흘렀다. 이 로마 공화정의 창시자는 마지막 왕을 쫓아내고 자유와 공유된 권력에 기초한 체제를 구축하는 데 중추적인 역할을 했다. 그가 이런 가치관을 지키고 다른 군주의 등장을 허락하지 않겠노라고 맹세하며 원로원 의원들 사이에서 했던 서약은 여러 세대에 걸쳐 울려 퍼졌고, 그의 후손의 마음에도 깊은 울림을 남겼다. 따라서 카이사르에 대항하는 음모에 가담한 행위는 브루투스에게 있어서 결코 로마에 대한 배신이 아니었으며 로마 공화정과 그것이 오랫동안 지켜온 자유에 대한 필사적이지만 꼭 필요한 방어 행위였다. 자유를 위한 투사들의 혼령과 자랑스러운 그의 혈통의 속삭임에 이끌린 손으로, 그는 친구를 쓰러뜨린 것이 아니라 잠재적인 폭군을 쓰러뜨린 것이었다. 그 운명의 순간, 브루투스는 자신을 위해서가 아니라 가장 뛰어난 로마의 정신을 위해 행동하고 있었으며, 수세기 전에 자신의 조상이 독재자가 공화정의 통치권을 다시 갖게 되어 자유롭고 독립적인 국민들을 노예로 삼는 것을 결코 용납하지 않겠다며 만든 서약을 다시금 울려 퍼지게 하고 있었던 것이다.

assassinate v. 암살하다 divorce v. 이혼시키다; 분리시키다 legacy n. 유산, 물려받은 것 etch v. 뚜렷이 새기다[아로새기다] bloodline n. 혈통, 혈족 illustrious a. 뛰어난, 이름난, 저명한 unflinching a. 굽히지 않는, 움츠리지 않는, 단호한 tyranny n. 포학; 폭정, 전제정치 founding father 창시자 pivotal a. 중추적인, 중요한 expel v. 쫓아내

다; 추방하다 oath n. 맹세, 서약 senator n. 원로원 의원 swear v. 맹세하다, 선서하다 monarch n. 군주 resonate v. 공명하다, 울리다 descendant n. 자손, 후예 conspiracy n. 음모 betrayal n. 배신 forefather n. 조상, 선조 enslave v. 노예로 만들다

13 글의 주제 ②

브루투스가 카이사르의 암살에 가담한 것은 공화주의의 이상을 추구하고 폭정에 저항했던 그의 혈통, 즉 집안의 내력과 무관하지 않았음을 이야기하고 있는 내용이다.

위 글은 주로 무엇에 관한 것인가?
① 로마 왕정과 로마 공화정의 주된 차이점
② 브루투스의 혈통이 암살 음모에 대한 그의 대응에 미친 영향
③ 율리우스 카이사르의 통치가 로마 공화정의 이상에 제기한 위협
④ 브루투스가 카이사르만큼 폭군으로 여겨진 이유들
⑤ 카이사르 암살이 로마제국에 미친 장기적인 영향

14 내용일치 ③

브루투스는 로마 공화정의 창시자였던 루키우스 주니우스 브루투스의 후손이었으므로 ③이 옳은 진술이다.

위 글에 의하면 다음 중 옳은 것은?
① 브루투스는 카이사르를 암살하려는 음모를 제국에 대한 배신으로 여겼다.
② 브루투스와 카이사르는 로마 공화정의 창시자들이었다.
③ 브루투스는 로마 공화정의 창시자의 후손이었다.
④ 브루투스는 개인적인 이유로 카이사르를 암살할 동기를 가지고 있었다.
⑤ 브루투스는 카이사르를 암살함으로써 로마의 황제가 되기를 바랐다.

15-16

공상과학영화는 이성을 중시하지만, 인간에 기반을 두지 않은 합리성, 다시 말해 인간의 인식 안에서 더 이상 생겨나지 않는 합리성을 두려워한다. "터미네이터(1984~2009)"의 스카이넷이나 "캡틴 아메리카: 윈터 솔져(2014)"의 아르님 졸라와 같은 슈퍼컴퓨터가 등장하는 공상과학영화에서 인간은 과학기술로 대체될 위험에 처해 있으며, 컴퓨터는 지식의 초대형 저장소 혹은 지식의 궁극적인 구현체를 상징한다. 그러나 비록 분명하긴 해도, 이것은 오늘날 살아가는 "실제" 세계의 삶을 반영한다. 정보가 점점 더 인간이 아닌 것에서 나오게 됨에 따라, 인간이 역할을 다하기 위해서는 부득이 기계에 접속해야 한다. 그 결과, "인간"의 전통적인 개념은 사람들이 "포스트 인간"이 됨에 따라 쓸모없는 것이 되고 만다. 이것은 인간이라는 것이 인공지능 기계와의 상호작용이라는 새로운 맥락의 관점에서 정의된다는 것을 의미한다. 포스트휴먼 세계에서, 인간은 사이보그나 컴퓨터와 구별이 힘들게 되었다. 컴퓨터, 인터넷, 그리고 사이버 공간으로 이뤄진 현대의 풍경 속에서, 공상과학영화는 점점 덜 허구적인 것이 되었다.

prize v. 높이 평가하다, 존중하다 rationality n. 합리성 grounding n. 토대, 기초지식 cognition n. 인식, 인지 replace v. 대체하다 embodiment n. 구체화, 체현 writ large 뚜렷한, 역력한; 대대적인 disembodied a. 육체에서 분리된, 실체가 없는 interface v. 접속하다

obsolescence n. 노후화, 진부화 posthuman n. 포스트휴먼(인간과 로봇 및 기술의 경계가 사라져 현존하는 인간을 넘어선 신인류) define v. (성격·내용 따위를) 규정짓다, 정의하다 interaction n. 상호작용 distinguishable a. 구별할 수 있는 contemporary a. 동시대의; 현대의

---

15 동의어 ③

obsolescence는 '노후화', '쓸모없음'이라는 의미인데, 인간(human)이었던 사람들이 posthuman이 되고 나면 human은 이제는 쓸모없이 남아도는 여분의 것이 될 것이다. 따라서 '과잉', '여분'이라는 의미의 redundancy를 개념적 동의어로 선택할 수 있다. ① 결핍 ② 진화 ④ 부활 ⑤ 불멸

---

16 글의 제목 ⑤

인간이 부득이 기계에 접속해야만 하게 된 결과, 인간은 인공지능 기계와 상호작용하는 인간이라는 의미의 포스트휴먼이 되었고 이런 포스트휴먼 세계에서 공상과학영화는 점점 덜 허구적인 것, 즉 더욱 현실적인 것이 되었다고 했으므로 ⑤가 제목으로 적절하다.

위 글의 제목으로 가장 적절한 것은?
① 문화적 불안의 근원: 사이보그와 컴퓨터
② 합리성에 대한 두려움: 문화적 종말론자로서의 공상과학영화
③ 인간 대 동물: 인간 대 인공지능
④ 공상과학영화의 현실과 환상: 가장 새로운 미개척지
⑤ 실현된 공상과학영화: 우리는 어떻게 포스트휴먼이 되었는가

17-18

음모론자들은 "스트랫퍼드 출신의 그 남자"를 다른 사람의 행세를 하는 사기꾼으로 치부한다. 그들은 그가 어떤 더 고귀한 사람의 말을 그대로 떠들어댄 문맹의 배우였으며, 무식했지만 그럭저럭 대사를 외울 수 있었을 것으로 가정한다. 저자 진위 논쟁의 실체는 18세기 말과 19세기 초에 낭만주의 운동과 함께 등장한 셰익스피어 숭배의 파생물이다. 그 이전까지만 해도 윌리엄 셰익스피어의 희곡들의 저자로서의 셰익스피어의 정체에 대해 의심하는 사람은 아무도 없었다. 하지만 그가 신(神)으로 변하게 되자, 자연스럽게 그를 허물어뜨리고자 하는 종파와 이교도들이 등장하게 되었다.
하지만 사실대로 보자면, 윌리엄 셰익스피어는 대단한 귀족도 아니었고, 이중간첩 같은 화려한 두 가지 역할 수행자도 아니었다. 실제로, 그는 영국 중부의 <신의 뜻에 의한> 마을 출신이었고, 그는 거기서 문법학교를 다녔다. 자라면서, 그의 주된 관심사는 고생에서 벗어나서 자신과 가족을 더 나은 삶으로 이끄는 것이 되었다. 아마도, 그가 전혀 특별한 것이 없는 배경 출신이라는 점이 가장 특별한 점일 것이다. 셰익스피어가 모든 사람이 될 수 있었던 것은 그가 보잘것없는 사람이었기 때문일지도 모른다. 그는 인간이라는 것이 무엇인지를 이해하고 있었기 때문에, 모든 시대의 모든 종족들과 이야기한다. 그는 제멋대로 하는 귀족의 삶을 살지 않았다. 그는 일하는 장인(匠人)이었고, 매일 생계를 유지해야 했으며 일하는 사람들이 매일 마주치는 문제와 마주해야 했다. 그의 삶은 평범했으며, 그의 정신은 비범했다. 그의 상상력은 환상과 꿈을 통해 멀리 떨어진 나라와 지나간 시대로 비약했지만, 항상 현실에 뿌리를 두고 있었다.

---

conspiracy n. 음모 imposter n. (이름·주소·나이·직업 따위를) 사칭하는 사람, (다른 사람 행세를 하는) 사기꾼 mouth v. (소리는 내지 않고) 입 모양으로만 말하다; (실제 믿거나 이해하지 못하는 것을 입으로만) 떠들다 line n. (연극의) 대사 offshoot n. 파생물, 파생적인 결과 cult n. 예배, 제사, 숭배 sect n. 종파(宗派) heretic n. 이교도; 반대론자 pull down 허물어뜨리다, 떨어뜨리다 fabulous a. 전설적인; 엄청난, 대단한 aristocrat n. 귀족 flamboyant a. 화려한, 현란한 double agent 이중간첩 providential a. 섭리의, 신에 뜻에 의한 nobody n. 보잘것없는 사람, (특히 사회적으로) 이름 없는 사람 pampered a. 제멋대로 하는, 방자한 craftsman n. 장인(匠人)

---

17 글의 흐름상 적절하지 않은 단어 고르기 ④

ⓓ를 포함하고 있는 문장은 셰익스피어가 평범한 사람이었음 이야기하고 있으므로 '섭리의', '신에 뜻에 의한'이라는 의미의 providential은 적절하지 않다. 글의 흐름에 맞게 '지방의', '시골의'라는 의미의 provincial로 고치는 것이 자연스럽다.

---

18 글의 제목 ⑤

셰익스피어가 실제로는 다른 사람이었을 수도 있다는 저자 진위 논란에 대해, 그는 평범한 사람이었지만 비범한 정신을 가진 사람이었고, 그렇기에 위대한 작품들을 남길 수 있었다는 의견을 제시하고 있는 글이다. 그러므로 제목으로는 ⑤가 적절하다.

위 글의 제목으로 가장 적절한 것은?
① 셰익스피어와 낭만주의 운동과의 관계
② 셰익스피어 숭배: 저자 진위에 대한 사회적 통념
③ 훌륭한 배우가 되는 것의 중요성: 음유시인으로부터의 조언
④ 우리가 셰익스피어를 존경해야 하거나 혹은 존경하지 말아야 하는 이유
⑤ 셰익스피어의 저자 진위 논란: 비범한 보통 사람

19-21

21세기에, 우리는 "디지털"이라는 단어를 계산과 연관 짓는 경향이 있지만, 그 단어의 기원은 고대로 거슬러 올라간다. 그 용어는 고전 라틴어로 "손가락"을 의미하는 'digitus'에서 유래했으며, 나중에는 손가락이나 발가락뿐만 아니라 10 미만의 정수를 지칭하는 'digit'에서 유래되었다. 우리는 초기의 많은 장치나 시스템을 디지털 원리를 이용하여 작동한 것으로 이해할 수도 있기 때문에, 디지털 절차는 전자 컴퓨터의 개발보다 훨씬 더 <시기가 뒤진다.> 예를 들어, 주판은 기원전 300년에 만들어진 간단한 디지털 계산기이며, 뿐만 아니라 모스 부호와 점자는 보다 최근에 이뤄진 디지털 기술의 활용을 대표한다. 이러한 각각의 예들의 공통점은 별개의 요소들 혹은 분리된 숫자들을 나타내기 위해 "디지털"이라는 단어를 사용했다는 것이다. 분리되고 개별적인 것에 초점을 맞추는 것은 오늘날의 디지털 전자기기의 작동에서 가장 중요한데, 기본적인 수준에서, 이 기기들은 0과 1의 두 값을 구별함으로써 작동하기 때문이다.
디지털이 계산보다 먼저 있었지만, 오늘날 이 두 용어는 밀접하게 연결되어 있으며, 형용사 "디지털"은 일반적으로 계산의 토대가 되는 이진법 체계를 축약하여 표현하는 것으로 사용된다. 따라서 우리는 "디지털 혁명"을 겪으며 살고 있고, 늘어나는 "디지털 격차"의 위험에 처해 있으며, "디지털 오디오"를 재생하고 "디지털 사진"을 저장하는 "디지털 장치"에 연결되어

있다. 우리 중 일부는 심지어 "디지털 인문학"을 실천하기도 한다. 디지털과 컴퓨테이션이라는 두 용어 사이의 미끄러지듯 교차사용 되는 정도가 너무나도 완벽해 보여서(혼용되는 빈도가 매우 흔하다는 의미) 두 용어가 동의어이고 항상 동의어였던 것으로 추정하기가 쉽다.

computation n. 계산, 컴퓨터 사용[조작] hark back to ~을 상기하다[떠올리다]; ~로 거슬러 올라가다 derive from ~에서 유래[파생]하다 postdate v. (시간적으로) ~의 뒤에 오다 abacus n. 주판 discrete a. 별개의, 분리된 distinguish v. 구별[식별]하다 anticipate v. 예기하다, 예상하다; 앞지르다, 선수 치다, ~보다 앞서다 shorthand n. 속기, 약어(略語) binary system 이진법 체계 underpin v. 기초를 보강하다; ~을 떠받치다; ~에 근거를 주다 humanities n. 인문학 slippage n. 미끄러짐; 불이행 assume v. 추정하다, 가정하다 synonymous a. 동의어의, 같은 뜻의

---

19 글의 흐름상 적절하지 않은 단어 고르기 ②

ⓑ를 포함하고 있는 문장에서, 초기의 많은 장치들과 시스템들이 디지털 원리를 사용하여 작동한 것으로 이해할 수 있다면, 디지털 절차는 전자 컴퓨터의 개발보다 훨씬 '늦게' 일어난 게 아니라 훨씬 '먼저' 일어난 것이라 할 수 있다. 그러므로 ⓑ는 '(시기적으로) ~에 앞서다', '~보다 먼저 일어나다'라는 의미의 antedate여야 한다.

---

20 글의 주제 ④

본문에서는 "디지털"이라는 용어의 기원과 현재까지의 사용에 대해 주로 다루면서 "디지털"이라는 용어의 의미가 시간이 지남에 따라 변화해 왔음을 이야기하고 있다. 그러므로 ④가 정답으로 적절하다.

① 디지털이라는 용어는 빠르게 쓸모없어지고 있다.
② 전자 컴퓨터는 곧 디지털 시스템을 능가할 것이다.
③ 컴퓨팅의 기원은 주판까지 거슬러 올라간다.
④ 디지털이라는 용어의 의미는 시간이 지나면서 변화해 왔다.
⑤ 디지털 이진법 체계는 전자 컴퓨터와 함께 등장했다.

---

21 내용추론 ①

마지막 문장은 디지털이라는 용어와 계산이라는 용어의 경계가 모호해졌고 둘 사이의 차이나 구분이 희미해졌음을 이야기하고 있는데, 이를 통해 앞으로도 디지털이라는 용어와 계속해서 연관 지어질 것임을 추론할 수 있다.

위 글을 바탕으로, 용어로서의 '디지털'의 미래에 대해 추론할 수 있는 것은?
① 그것은 계산과 계속해서 연관 지어질 것이다.
② 그것은 다시금 손가락과 발가락을 지칭하는 데 사용될 것이다.
③ 그것은 기술이 발전함에 따라 새로운 의미를 갖게 될 것이다.
④ 그것은 사용되지 않게 되어 사람들이 쓰는 어휘에서 사라질 것이다.
⑤ 고정된 의미가 생겨나 점진적 변화를 중단할 것이다.

22-24

미국의 저명한 언어철학자인 존 설(John Searle)은 인간 사유의 근본적인 성격을 언어와의 관계에서 상정하는 "표현가능성의 원리"라는 개념을 도입했다. 이 원리에서는 한 언어로 표현될 수 있는 그 어떤 생각도 다른 언어로 똑같이 간결하게 표현될 수 있다고 주장한다. 이 개념의 핵심은 생각이 특정 언어의 제약을 초월하여 추상적이고 보편적인 영역에서 작동한다는 것이다.

설의 개념은 언어결정론이 강제하는 경계에 도전하며, 우리가 말하는 언어의 기저에 단어와는 별도로 작용하는 사고의 공통된 기반이 존재한다는 것을 시사한다. 이 생각의 언어는 순전히 개념적이며, 관념과 개념의 추상적 영역에 있어서 언어적 구조에 의해 강제된 제약이 없다.

설의 관점에서, 우리가 말하는 언어는 우리의 생각을 구체화하고 전달하는 수단의 역할을 한다. 그것들은 생각의 언어 안에서 형성된 추상적 관념의 풍부한 혼합물을 전달하는 도구로서의 역할을 한다. 따라서 생각의 언어 자체는 접근할 수 없고 설명할 수 없는 상태로 남아 있지만, 우리가 말하는 언어는 매우 복잡한 우리의 내적, 정신적 풍경을 전달하고 표현하고자 하는 통로의 역할을 한다.

eminent a. 저명한, 유명한 expressibility n. 표현할 수 있음, 표현가능성 posit v. (주장·논의의 근거로 삼기 위해 무엇을) 사실로 상정하다[받아들이다], 긍정적으로 가정하다 fundamental a. 기초의, 근본적인 assert v. 단언하다, 강력히 주장하다 articulate v. (생각·감정을) 분명히 표현하다[설명하다] succinctly ad. 간결하게, 간명하게 transcend v. (범위·한계를) 넘다; 초월하다 specific a. 일정한, 특정한 realm n. 영역 boundary n. 경계; 한계, 범위 impose v. 강제하다; 부과하다 linguistic a. 언어의, 언어학의 determinism n. 결정론 substrate n. 하층, 기저 independently of ~와는 별개로 reside v. 살다; 존재하다 devoid of ~이 없는[결여된] constraint n. 강제, 압박; 구속, 억제 vehicle n. 매개체 embody v. 구체화하다, 구현하다 tapestry n. 태피스트리(여러 가지 색실로 그림을 짜 넣은 직물), 벽걸이 융단 formulate v. 공식화하다; 명확하게 말하다 ineffable a. 말로 나타낼 수 없는, 이루 말할 수 없는 conduit n. 도관(導管); 수로

---

22 동의어 ⑤

succinctly는 '간결하게', '간단명료하게'라는 의미인데, 생각을 언어로 간결하게 표현한다는 것은 많은 말로 복잡하게 표현하는 것에 비해 적은 노력을 들인다는 말이므로 '효율적[능률적]으로'라는 의미의 efficiently를 개념적 동의어로 선택할 수 있다. ① 심오하게 ② 추상적으로 ④ 무관심하게

---

23 글의 주제 ③

본문은 한 언어로 표현된 생각이 다른 언어로도 동일하게 표현될 수 있다고 주장하는 존 설의 "표현 가능성의 원리"를 소개하면서 언어의 기저에 단어와는 별개로 작용하는 사고의 공통된 기반이 존재함을 이야기하고 있다. 그러므로 본문은 언어와 추상적 사고의 관계에 대한 철학적 개념을 다루고 있다고 할 수 있다.

위 글은 주로 무엇에 관한 것인가?
① 모든 언어가 생겨난 보편적인 언어에 대한 탐구
② 특정 관념과 개념이 한 언어에서 다른 언어에서보다 더 잘 표현되는 이유
③ 추상적인 생각이 모든 언어의 기저에 있다는 철학적 개념
④ 언어가 추상적인 개념과 구체적인 생각 사이의 간극을 어떻게 메울 수 있는가
⑤ 생각의 언어를 진실에 대한 보다 명확한 표현으로 옮기는 것

---

24 부분이해 ③

ineffable은 '말로 나타낼 수 없는', '이루 말할 수 없는'의 의미이므로 ③이 정답으로 적절하다.

다음 중 밑줄 친 ineffable의 의미를 가장 잘 전달하는 표현은?
① 말로 생각되어질 수 있는
② 말 없이 전달할 수 있는
③ 말로 표현할 수 없는
④ 모든 단어에 대해 근본적인
⑤ 말로 분명하게 표현할 수 있는

25-26

선구적인 정신의학자이자 범죄심리학의 권위자인 칼 메닝거 박사는 미국 형사 사법제도의 근간이 되는 전통적인 "범죄에 대한 처벌" 모델을 뒤집어 엎을 것을 제안한다. 범죄에 대한 처벌을 강조하는 보복적 형사 사법제도와 달리, 메닝거는 범죄자에 초점을 맞춰, 단순히 범죄에 맞는 처벌을 가하는 것 대신 치료와 갱생을 옹호했다.

메닝거는 총체적인 건강을 진정한 갱생의 길로 상정하는 전체론적 복지 관점에 이끌려, 인도적인 치료를 옹호했고 개인을 "정신이상"으로 낙인찍는 것을 거부했다. 자신의 저서 『처벌의 범죄』에서, 그는 투옥과 사형을 포함하는 모든 형태의 처벌을 잔인하면서도 비효과적이라고 비난했다. 그는 특히 처벌이 죄수들의 정신건강에 대한 요구를 무시함으로써, 개인과 사회 모두에게 도움이 되지 않는다고 믿었다.

메닝거의 접근법은 수감자들에게 반향을 일으키면서 형사 사법제도 개혁에 대한 요구를 지속적으로 알리고 있다. 그의 철학은 오로지 범죄에 근거한 경직된 처벌 대신, 개인에게 맞춰진 치료와 갱생 계획을 요구하며 복수심보다는 공감과 이해를 장려한다. 이러한 관점의 전환은 갱생 당사자 개인이 고유하게 필요로 하는 것을 우선시함으로써, 우리가 범죄를 다루는 방식을 다시 생각하게 만든다.

psychiatrist n. 정신병 의사, 정신의학자 upend v. (위아래를) 거꾸로 하다[뒤집다] punishment n. 형벌, 처벌 underlying a. 기초가 되는, 근원적인 retributive a. 보복의, 응보의 emphasize v. 강조하다 advocate v. 옹호하다; 주장하다 rehabilitation n. 사회 복귀; (범죄자 등의) 갱생 holistic a. 전체론적인 posit v. (주장·논의의 근거로 삼기 위해 무엇을) 사실로 상정하다[받아들이다] champion v. 옹호하다 humane a. 자비로운, 인도적인 label v. ~에 명칭을 붙이다, 분류하다 insane a. 미친, 발광한, 정신이상의 condemn v. 비난하다, 나무라다 imprisonment n. 투옥, 감금 capital punishment 사형 fail v. ~에게 쓸모가 없다 neglect v. 무시[경시]하다; 간과하다 resonate with ~에게 반향을 일으키다 inmate n. 수감자, 재소자 push for 요구하다 empathy n. 공감 vengeance n. 복수, 앙갚음 prioritize v. (계획·목표)에 우선순위를 매기다; 우선시키다

---

25 글의 제목 ②

본문은 "처벌을 강조하는 사법제도를 개선하여, 범죄자에 대한 처벌에 초점을 맞추는 대신 치료와 갱생을 지향할 것"을 주장하는 칼 메닝거 박사의 견해를 소개하는 내용이므로 제목으로는 ②가 적절하다.

위 글의 제목으로 가장 적절한 것은?
① 징벌에 대한 재고: 어떻게 처벌은 이미 범죄에 적합한가
② 처벌을 넘어서: 범죄자들에게 복수가 아닌 치료가 필요한 이유
③ 보복적 사법제도: 메닝거가 원칙으로 회귀하다
④ 인간 잠재력의 봉인 해제: 범죄자의 정신 이상에 권한을 부여하는 것
⑤ 눈에는 눈: 정말로 해야 할 일은 반드시 해야 한다

---

26 내용추론 ④

첫 문단의 "칼 메닝거(Karl Menninger) 박사는 미국 형사 사법제도의 근간이 되는 전통적인 '범죄에 대한 처벌' 모델을 뒤집어엎을 것을 제안한다."라는 내용을 통해 ④를 추론할 수 있다.

위 글에서 추론할 수 있는 것은?
① 형사 사법제도에 대한 메닝거의 접근방식은 수감자들에게 인기가 없다.
② 메닝거의 철학은 현재 주류로 간주되고 있다.
③ 메닝거의 프로그램은 범죄자들이 정신질환을 극복하는 데 도움이 되지 않는다.
④ 메닝거의 제안은 현행 형사 사법제도에 도전장을 던졌다.
⑤ 메닝거의 명성은 그의 이론으로 인해 타격을 입었다.

27-29

18세기 말과 19세기 초에, 콜롬보의 갈레 페이스(Galle Face)와 싱가포르의 래플스(Raffles) 호텔에 있는 것들과 같은 유럽 스타일의 고급 호텔의 바(bar)는 영국의 식민지 생활에서 중요한 역할을 했다. 전성기에 이 시설들은 손님들에게 본국의 맛을 제공하기 위해 노력했다. 그러나 오늘날 우리는 그들에게서 그러한 호텔 바(bar)가 번성했던 시대의 변화를 나타내는 보다 광범위한 제국주의 이야기의 축소판을 볼 수 있다.

당시에, 전통적인 성(性) 규범은 영국과 서구세계에서 진행 중이던 사회적 역학 관계 변화에 자리를 내주고 있었다. 예를 들어, 래플스 호텔에 ─ 겉으로 보기에는 작은 변화인 ─ "싱가포르 슬링" 칵테일이 등장함으로써 바(bar)는 남성전용 공간이라는 식민지의 전통이 깨지게 되었다. 당시에 칵테일은 여성에게는 적절하지만 남성에게는 어울리지 않는 음료로 여겨졌기 때문에, 이 변화는 아마도 오랜 사회적 금기를 무시하고 여성 고객을 바(bar)로 받아들이기 위한 기대로 도입되었을 것이기 때문이다.

나아가, 식민지의 고급 호텔에 있던 바(bar)는 식민지 시기의 인종적 긴장 상태를 드러나게 했다. 겉으로는 포용을 내세우고 있었지만, ─ 또한 실제로 아랍계, 유대계, 아르메니아계 기업가들이 소유와 운영을 맡고 있었지만 ─ 식민지의 호텔 바(bar)에서, 복잡한 양상인가 해도, 인종에 따른 차별은 지속되고 있었다. 왜냐하면, 표면적으로는 다양한 고객을 환영하고 아무런 제한도 주장하지 않았지만, 그럼에도 불구하고 고급 호텔의 바(bar)들은 조심스럽게 오랜 인종적 위계질서를 고수했기 때문이다. 다시 말해, 인종적인 제한은 노골적으로 가해진 것이 아니라 암암리에 이루어졌다. 예를 들어, 유라시아인의 고객들은 보통 좌석이나 서비스의 질 등에 있어서 대개 미묘한 형태의 차별을 받았다.

결론적으로, 식민지의 호텔들은 진보적이면서도 배타적이며, 인종 무차별

적이면서도 인종차별적이었으며, 그 시대의 역설과 위선을 압축해서 보여주었다. 이들은 역사의 목격자로서 존속하면서, 세계가 서서히 변화하던 시기에 존재하던 성(性) 규범과 인종적 분열을 둘러싼 당시의 지속적인 노력을 드러낸다.

heyday n. 전성기 establishment n. (사회) 시설, (공공 또는 사설의) 시설물 microcosm n. 소우주 norm n. 기준; 규범 underway a. (계획 따위가) 진행 중인 in defiance of ~을 무시하여 taboo n. 금기 veneer n. 겉치장, 허식 inclusion n. 포함, 포괄 entrepreneur n. 기업가 distinction n. 차별 superficially ad. 피상적으로 clientele n. 고객, 단골손님 restriction n. 제한, 한정 discreetly ad. 분별 있게, 신중하게 adhere to ~을 고수하다 hierarchy n. 계급제도 overtly ad. 명백하게, 공공연하게 impose v. 강제하다; 부과하다 covertly ad. 암암리에, 은밀하게 patron n. 고객, 단골손님; 후원자 segregation n. 분리, 격리, 차단; 인종차별(대우) exclusionary a. 배제의, 제외의 integrated a. 통합된; 인종 무차별 대우의 discriminatory a. 차별적인 encapsulate v. (사실·정보 따위를) 간약하다, 요약하다 hypocrisy n. 위선 ongoing a. 전진하는, 진행하는

---

27 글의 제목 ③

영국 식민지 호텔 바에서 여성을 받아들이는 노력을 하는 등 당시의 사회적 금기를 깨려는 노력을 하기도 했지만, 한편으로는 인종차별이 암암리에 남아있었음을 이야기하고 있다. 전자는 '진전' 후자는 '배제'로 표현할 수 있으므로, 제목으로는 ③이 적절하다.

위 글의 제목으로 가장 적절한 것은?
① 문화의 혼합, 술의 혼합: 식민지의 다양성 찬양
② 의식과 세련됨: 식민지 호텔 바의 스타일
③ 배제 속의 진전: 영국 식민지의 호텔 바
④ 사회 변화에 대한 환호: 성(性) 역할과 칵테일 문화
⑤ 고급 호텔: 과거의 길인가? 혹은 미래를 위한 꿈인가?

---

28 내용일치 ①

식민지의 호텔들은 세계가 서서히 변화하던 시기에 존재하던 성(性) 규범과 인종적 분열을 둘러싼 지속적인 당시의 노력을 드러냈을 뿐이며, 사회적 진보를 이끌어냈다는 것은 지나치다. 아무리 좋게 평가하더라도 식민지에서의 사회적 진보이지 영국의 사회적 진보를 이끌었다고는 결코 말할 수 없다.

위 글에 의하면 다음 중 옳지 않은 것은?
① 영국 식민지 시대의 호텔 바 문화는 영국의 사회적 진보를 이끌었다.
② 콜롬보의 갈레 페이스와 싱가포르의 래플스 호텔은 "고급 호텔"로 불렸다.
③ 식민지 시대의 고급 호텔의 바는 그들의 차별적인 관행을 감추려고 시도했다.
④ 처음에 "싱가포르 슬링"은 래플스의 바를 다니는 남성들을 위해 만들어진 것은 아니었을 것이다.
⑤ 식민지의 고급 호텔은 그 시대의 사회 변화 방식에 동참했다.

---

29 내용추론 ④

영국 식민지의 바에서 '싱가포르 슬링' 칵테일을 판매한 것은 바를 남성 전용 공간에서 벗어나게 하는 사회적 변화를 나타냈다. 그러나 표면적으로는 포용적인 것처럼 보이지만, 식민지 호텔 바에서는 여전히 인종적 긴장과 계급이 존재했다. 따라서 좋은 것과 나쁜 것이 뒤섞인 결과를 가져왔다고 볼 수 있다.

위 글에서 추론할 수 있는 것은?
① '싱가포르 슬링' 칵테일은 오로지 수익 증대를 위해 만들어졌다.
② 콜롬보와 싱가포르의 유라시아인들은 호텔 바의 인종차별에 항의했다.
③ 칵테일은 식민지에서처럼 영국에서도 남성들에게 인기가 없었다.
④ 영국 식민지의 바에서 받아들인 변화는 좋은 것과 나쁜 것이 뒤섞인 결과를 낳았다.
⑤ 고급 호텔 체제로의 회귀는 사회 발전에 도움이 될 것 같다.

---

30 문장배열 ①

베를린의 기원에 대한 불확실성을 소개한 ⑩, 초기의 역사적 증거와 기록이 부재한 것에 관한 내용인 ⑤와 ④, 베를린이 수도로 선정된 과정과 베를린의 역사적 중요성을 확인하는 ⑧와 ⓒ의 순서로 배열하는 것이 가장 자연스럽다.

declare v. 선언하다, 발표하다, 공표하다 millennium n. 천년간, 천년기 currently ad. 일반적으로, 널리; 현재 settle v. 정착시키다 evidence n. 증거

⑩ 베를린은 현재 독일의 수도이지만, 언제 처음 정착했는지는 아무도 알지 못한다.
⑤ 1100년대 후반까지 그 곳에 몇 개의 건물이 존재했었다는 증거가 있다.
④ 그러나 1240년대까지 베를린이라는 이름의 도시에 대한 실제 기록은 없다.
⑧ 게다가, 그것은 1701년에 프로이센의 프레데릭(Frederick) 1세가 수도로 선포하고 샬롯텐부르크 궁전을 건설하기 전까지는 수도가 되지 못했다.
ⓒ 어떤 경우든, 그 도시는 역사의 상당 기간 동안 존재했으며, 수백 년 동안 독일 문화의 중심지였다.

01 ③	02 ④	03 ③	04 ③	05 ④	06 ②	07 ⑤	08 ①	09 ②	10 ⑤
11 ⑤	12 ②	13 ①	14 ②	15 ②	16 ⑤	17 ①	18 ④	19 ⑤	20 ③
21 ①	22 ③	23 ①	24 ①	25 ⑤	26 ④	27 ①	28 ④	29 ③	30 ④

01 3형식 문형에 쓰이는 동사 explain ③

explain은 3형식 동사로 쓰이며, 'explain A to B'의 형태를 취해 'A를 B에게 설명하다'라는 의미를 나타낸다. 목적어 the presentation project에 to us가 이어진 ③이 적절하다.

A: 오늘 수업 시작 때 선생님이 무엇에 관해 이야기하셨니?
B: 우리가 정확히 무엇이 필요한지를 이해하도록 우리에게 발표 프로젝트를 설명해 주셨어.

02 시제 ④

by 1915 같은 'by 과거시점'은 과거완료와 함께 쓰인다. 따라서 과거완료 시제인 ④가 빈칸에 들어가야 한다.

transformation n. 변형, 변화 undergo v. (영향·변화·검사 따위를) 받다, 입다; (시련 등을) 경험하다, 겪다

역사학자 캐롤라인 웨어(Caroline Ware)는 자신의 저서 『그리니치 빌리지』에서 1915년에는 이미 미국 문화가 중요한 변화를 겪었다고 주장했다.

03 의문부사 why ③

be sure 다음에는 that절이나 간접의문절이 오는데, ① 빈칸 다음의 it이 an explosion을 가리키므로 '폭발이 일어난 것이 분명했다'고 한 다음 '폭발이 일어난 것을 아무도 확신하지 못했다'고 하는 것은 모순이다. ②, ⑤ 간접의문절이 되지만 it happened가 '주어+1형식동사'로 완결된 절을 이루므로 의문대명사 which와 what의 역할이 없어서 부적절하다. ④ 명사절이 아니라 부사절을 이루어 부적절하다. ③ 의문부사여서 완결된 절을 이끌 수 있으므로 정답이다.

explosion n. 폭발, 폭발음 basement n. 지하층, 지하실 clue n. 단서, 실마리

도서관 지하실에서 폭발이 일어난 것은 분명했지만, 왜 폭발이 일어났는지 아무도 확신하지 못했고, 어디에서도 단서를 찾을 수 없었다.

04 주장·요구의 동사가 이끄는 that절 속의 동사 형태 ③

주장·제안·요구의 동사가 이끄는 that절 속의 동사는 '(should) 동사원형'이어야 한다. require가 '요구'의 동사이므로 ③이 정답이 되며, 이때

be 앞에는 should가 생략돼 있다.

모든 직원들은 늦어도 오전 6시 30분까지는 유니폼을 입고 업무를 시작할 준비가 되어 있어야 한다.

05 논리완성 ④

두 번째 문장은 첫 번째 문장에 대한 부연설명에 해당하는데, '지구의 자전 속도가 시속 1마일만 빨라져도 물을 극지로부터 이동하게 만들어 적도 주변의 해수면을 상승시키는 것'은 '급격한' 변화의 예라 할 수 있으므로, 빈칸에는 ④가 적절하다.

for starters 우선 첫째로[먼저] in store ~에게 닥치려 하고 있는 rotation n. 회전, (지구의) 자전 migrate v. 이주하다, 이동하다 pole n. 극(極), 극지 equator n. 적도 replicable a. 반복 가능한; <유전학> 복제 가능한 adhesive a. 점착성의 squelchy a. 질척거리는 drastic a. 과감한, 극단적인; 급격한 exonerating a. 무죄임을 밝히는

만약 지구가 갑자기 현재 속도보다 훨씬 더 빨리 회전한다면, 몇 가지 급격한 변화가 닥쳐오게 될 것이다. 우선 먼저, 지구의 자전 속도가 시속 1마일만 빨라져도, 그로 인해 물이 극지(極地)로부터 이동하게 되어, 적도 주변의 해수면을 몇 인치 상승시킬 것이다.

06 논리완성 ②

바로 뒤에서 부연 설명하고 있는 '키가 크고, 근육이 발달돼 있으며, 힘도 센 모습과 호응하는 표현이 빈칸에 들어가야 할 것이므로, '장엄한', '위엄 있는'이라는 의미의 ②가 들어가는 것이 가장 자연스럽다.

medieval a. 중세의 warhorse n. 군마(軍馬); 노병 muscular a. 근육질의, 근육이 발달한 atop a. 꼭대기에, 정상에 steed n. 말, 군마(軍馬) minuscule a. 아주 작은, 하찮을 것 없는 majestic a. 장엄한, 위엄 있는 infinitesimal a. 극소의, 극미의 imbalanced a. 불균형한 slight a. 약간의, 작은; 사소한

대중문화는 중세 시대의 군마(軍馬)들을 번쩍이는 기사가 올라타고 있는 키 크고, 근육이 발달돼 있으며, 힘도 센 위풍당당한 동물로 그리고 있다. 하지만 새로운 연구는 중세 시대의 군마들이 아마도 우리가 기대하는 것보다 훨씬 더 작았을 것이라는 것을 보여준다.

07 논리완성 ⑤

경찰이 처음에는 용의자의 유죄를 확신했지만 자신감을 잃고 수사를 더 하기로 한 것은 '이후에' 용의자가 범인이 아닐 수도 있다는 정보가 입수됐기 때문일 것이다. 따라서 '처음에'와 반대되는 의미의 ⑤ '이후의'가 정답이다.

initially ad. 처음에, 시초에 suspect n. 용의자 confidence n. 확신, 자신감 recumbent a. 기댄, 가로누운 subordinate a. 종속하는 inordinate a. 과도한, 터무니없는 consequent a. 결과로서 일어나는 subsequent a. 차후의; 다음의, 계속해서 일어나는

경찰은 처음에는 용의자의 유죄를 확신했지만, 목격자의 형태로 들어온 이후의 정보로 인해 자신감을 잃고 더 수사해보기로 했다.

08 논리완성 ①

확실한 증거가 여전히 부족한 상태에서 새로운 입자가 존재한다고 보는 것은 '추정하는' 것에 불과하다.

particle n. 미립자, 분자 observe v. 관찰하다, 관측하다 anomaly n. 변칙, 이상; 변칙적[예외적]인 것[일] tangible a. 실체적인; 명확한, 확실한 presume v. 추정하다, 상상하다 resume v. 다시 차지하다, 다시 시작하다 subsume v. 포함하다 plume v. 자랑하다 consume v. 소비하다, 소모하다

그 연구팀은 관찰된 이상 현상에만 기초해 새로운 입자의 존재를 추정하고 있고, 입자 자체에 대한 확실한 증거는 여전히 부족하다.

09 논리완성 ②

뒤에서 언급한 "포도밭에 줄지어 선 포도나무를 돌보지 않은 채로 두는 것이 유익하다"와 호응하는 내용이 빈칸에 들어가야 하므로 ②가 정답으로 적절하다.

conservation n. (자연·자원의) 보호, 보존 consensus n. (의견·증언 따위의) 일치; 합의; 여론 fly in the face of (기존 통념에) 반대되다, 위배되다 conventional a. 전통적인; 인습적인, 관습적인 weed n. 잡초 bramble n. 가시나무, 들장미 pest n. 해충 pose a threat 위협이 되다 vulnerable a. 취약한, 약점이 있는 yield n. 산출; 수확(량) untended a. 간호[시중]받지 않는, 아무도 상관하지 않는 vineyard n. 포도밭 disorderly a. 무질서한 untidiness n. 단정하지 못함

자연보호 전문가들 사이에서 야생동물 친화적인 포도 재배에 관한 일치된 의견은 포도밭을 너저분한 상태로 통제하는 것이 유익한 것으로 드러날 수 있다는 것이다. 이는 밭의 경계에 잡초와 가시나무가 지나치게 자라면 해충을 불러들이게 돼서, 결과적으로 취약한 포도에게 위협이 되고, 궁극적으로는 수확량에 위협이 된다고 가르치는 농부들의 통념에 정면으로 위배된다. 그러나 뉴질랜드의 특정 포도 재배업자들의 관행은 포도밭에 줄지어 선 포도나무들을 돌보지 않은 채로 두는 것이 무질서한 공간에서 번성하는 유용한 나비의 활동을 촉진하여 유익하다는 것을 보여준다. 점점 더 많은 스위스 포도 재배업자들이 사용하는 유사한 종류의 "너저분함"은 그렇지 않으면 취약할 포도에 자연적인 해충 방제를 제공하는 새들을 먹여 살린다.

① 환경을 위해 수확량을 희생하는 것이 이제는 필수적이다
② 포도밭을 너저분한 상태로 통제하는 것이 유익한 것으로 드러날 수 있다
③ 유기농 해충 방제는 농부들에게 괴로운 문제이다
④ 지속가능성은 특정 지역에서만 실용적이다
⑤ 많은 포도 품종들이 곧 멸종될 것이다

10 논리완성 ⑤

'바위들이 널브러져 있고 바위 턱이 좁은 길', '위험한 지대' 등과 호응할 수 있는 표현이 필요하므로, 빈칸에는 ⑤의 '험한'이 들어가는 것이 적절하다.

ledge n. (절벽에서 튀어나온) 암붕(岩棚), 바위 턱 treacherous a. 믿을 수 없는, 방심할 수 없는; (안전한 것 같으면서도) 위험한 terrain n. 지대, 지세; 지형 assess v. 평가하다, 판단하다 relieve v. 안도하게 하다 presumptuous a. 주제넘은, 뻔뻔한 precocious a. 조숙한 pretentious a. 자만하는, 허세부리는 propitious a. 순조로운, 형편이 좋은 precipitous a. 험한, 가파른

그 등산가들은 널브러진 바위들과 좁은 바위 턱들이 점점 더 자주 나타나면서 길이 점점 더 위험해지는 지점에 도달했다. 경험에도 불구하고, 그들은 한 걸음만 잘못 디뎌도 치명적인 추락을 초래할 수 있다는 것을 알고 있었기에 그 위험한 지대를 지나가면서 불안함을 느꼈다. 상황을 평가한 그들은 어려운 여건에 맞서 가능한 모든 안전 조치를 취하면서 조심스럽게 나아가기로 결정했다. 마침내, 그들은 험한 길을 성공적으로 지나갔고, 더 안전한 땅에 도달하여 안도감을 느꼈다.

11 문장배열 ⑤

지시대명사나 인칭대명사가 없는 ⓒ가 가장 먼저 오고, ⓒ에서 언급한 무대를 통합된 '3차원 공간'으로 재인식한 것에 대해 '다차원 무대'라고 부연 설명하고 있는 Ⓐ가 그 뒤에 오고, 그 배경에 대한 설명인 Ⓔ가 그다음에 오고, Ⓔ에서 언급한 '현대성의 도입'에 대한 부연 설명인 Ⓓ가 그다음에, 이러한 개념을 다른 분야에 응용했다는 내용인 Ⓑ가 마지막에 오도록 하는 것이 가장 자연스러운 순서이다.

multidimensional a. 다차원의 vicariously ad. 대리로, 대리로서 inhabit v. ~에 살다, ~에 존재하다 theatrical a. 극장의, 연극의 forge v. 구축하다; 위조하다 décor n. 실내장식, 인테리어 prominent a. 현저한, 두드러진; 저명한 reconceive v. 새로운 방식으로 생각하다, 다시 생각하다 integrate v. 통합하다, 완전하게 하다 dispense with ~없이 지내다, ~을 배제하다 emphasize v. 강조하다 streamlined a. 능률화[간소화]된; 최신식의 dramatic sweep 극적인 전환(한 장면에서 다른 장면으로의 웅장한 전환) expressive a. 표현이 풍부한

ⓒ 미국의 다른 저명 무대 디자이너들과 함께, 조셉 어번(Joseph Urban)은 무대를 통합된 3차원 공간으로 재인식했다.
Ⓐ 그러한 다차원 무대를 창출해내는 이러한 혁신으로 인해 관객들은 이 극장 공간에 대리로 존재할 수 있게 되었다.
Ⓔ 그는 19세기 후반의 혼잡한 무대 "사실주의"를 거부하고, 연극적 깊이와 극적인 전환, 그리고 더욱 표현적인 무대 분위기를 가진 간소화된 "현대성"을 도입했다.

ⓒ 이러한 현대적인 효과를 얻기 위해 그는 그림으로 그린 무대배경을 배제하고 그 대신에 색깔 있는 조명, 스포트라이트, 간접 조명을 강조했다.
ⓓ 빛과 색, 공간과 사물의 극화, 분위기의 조성 등에 대해 알게 된 후 그는 이것들을 다른 소비자 시설의 실내 장식으로 가져왔다.

12-13

1660년은 영국 연극에 있어서 매우 중요한 해였다. 이는 획기적인 연극이나 유명한 극작가 때문이 아니라, 마가렛 휴스(Margaret Hughes)라는 이름의 여성 때문이었다. 그녀의 혁명적인 행위는 무엇이었을까? 그것은 바로 셰익스피어의 『오셀로』에서 데스데모나(Desdemona)역을 맡아 전문 배우로서 무대에 발을 내딛은 것이다. 이것은 단순히 전형적이지 않은 역할을 캐스팅한 것에 지나지 않는 것이 아니었으며, 여성의 역할이 오랫동안 남성과 소년들의 전유물이었던 세계에 지각변동을 일으킨 것이었다. 그러나 이것이 완전히 미지의 영역이었던 것은 아니었다. 오랫동안 여성은 사적인 가정 공연과 개인적인 모임에서 청중들을 매료시키며 무대를 빛내어왔다. 그들은 여왕을 구현했고, 소네트를 속삭였으며, 공적인 영역에서는 그들에게 금지돼 있던 등장인물에 생명을 불어넣었다. 이러한 "아마추어" 공연들은 시시하기는커녕, 여성의 예술적 수완이 자라나서 더 큰 무대에서 꽃피기를 기다리고 있던 비옥한 토대였다.
휴스의 대담한 움직임은 그저 공연에 그치는 것이 아니었다. 그것은 도전이었다. 그것은 예술 표현에서 여성들을 부차적인 역할에 국한시키는 엄격한 관행에 저항하는 것이었다. 그녀의 데스데모나는 등장인물에 그치지 않고 진보의 상징이 되었으며, 전문성의 문을 열고 여러 세대의 여성들이 따라 갈 길을 닦아주었다. 그녀의 발자취의 울림은 영국 연극계 전반에 퍼져나갔으며, 장벽을 깨고 스포트라이트를 받을 올바른 자리를 요구하게 되었다.

pivotal a. 중추적인, 중요한 groundbreaking a. 신기원을 이룬, 획기적인 renowned a. 유명한, 명성이 있는 playwright n. 극작가 tectonic shift 구조적인 변화 domain n. 영토, 영역 uncharted territory 미지의 영역, 미개척 영역 grace v. 우아하게 하다, 아름답게 꾸미다 captivate v. 매혹시키다, 현혹시키다 intimate a. 친밀한; 사사로운, 개인적인 far from 결코 ~이 아닌 frivolous a. 보잘것없는, 시시한 defy v. 도전하다, 반항하다 confine v. 제한하다 shatter v. 산산이 부수다, 박살내다 barrier n. 장벽, 울타리

---

12 저자의 어조 ②

저자는 마가렛 휴스를 영국 연극사에서 중요한 이정표를 남긴 인물로 긍정적으로 평가하고 있으며 그녀의 업적을 매우 열렬히 찬양하며 기술하고 있다. 그러므로 어조로는 ②가 적절하다.

다음 중 위 글의 저자의 전체적인 어조를 가장 잘 나타내는 것은?
① 무관심하고 흥미를 갖지 않는
② 열의가 넘치고 열정적인
③ 비난하면서도 책망하지 않는
④ 비판적이면서도 매혹된
⑤ 냉소적이고 풍자적인

---

13 글의 제목 ①

'오랫동안 여성은 가정 내에서의 공연과 개인적인 모임에서 연극 활동을 했는데, 마가렛 휴즈가 전문 배우로서 처음으로 무대에 오름으로써 여성들이 연극 무대에 오르게 되는 계기와 기틀을 마련했다'는 내용이므로 제목으로는 ①이 적절하다.

위 글의 제목으로 가장 적절한 것은?
① 거실에서 각광(脚光)까지: 여성들이 영국의 연극무대를 요구하다
② 여장(女裝)을 하는 근거: 남성이 때때로 여성의 역할을 더 잘하는 이유
③ 모두를 위한 셰익스피어: 대중이 즐길 수 있게 음유시인을 민주화하기
④ 모든 무대는 세상이다: 극장에 대한 셰익스피어의 포괄적인 비전
⑤ 마가렛 휴즈의 흥망성쇠: 경고를 들려주는 이야기

14-16

현대의 미국인들이 자신과 타인의 심리를 분석하는 빈도와 능력은 매우 흥미로운 역사적 발전이다. 그들은 상대적으로 새로운 마음의 과학인 심리학을 이용하고 있으며, 심리학은 자신을 상상하는 새로운 방법을 제공하고 있다. 예를 들어, 20세기로의 전환기에, 지그문트 프로이트(Sigmund Freud)는 "승화"의 심리학적인 개념을 "추악한 충동을 수용할 수 있는 경로로 방향 전환하는 것"이라 정의했다. 그것은 교육 받은 미국인들이 여전히 서로의 행동에 적용시키고 있고 또 역사가들이 프로이트보다 훨씬 이전에 살았던 사람들에게 적용시키고 있는 개념이다. 그러나, 사람들은 승화가 1900년 이전에도 존재했는지, 다시 말해, 그것이 발견된 것인지 아니면 만들어진 것인지를 궁금해 할지도 모른다.
어떤 심리적인 조건들, 또는 적어도 그것들에 대한 논의는 시간이 지나면서 나타났다가 사라졌다. 19세기에 의사들은 불안해하는 중산층 여성들을 흔히 "신경쇠약증"으로 진단했고, 20세기에는 비슷한 상태의 여성들을 "신경쇠약"을 앓았다고 말했다. 두 증후군 모두, 적어도 미국에서는, 유행한 시기가 있었고, 그런 다음 갑자기 나타났던 것처럼 갑자기 사라졌다. 미국에서 등장한 '우울한' 성격 진단도 똑같은데, 이것은 남북전쟁 전에 미국에서 등장하여 전국을 휩쓸었다가 마찬가지로 빨리 사라졌다.
미국인들은 학교에서 ― 1990년대에만 수백만 명이 대학 심리학 강좌를 들었다 ― 그리고 대중매체에서 '조이스 브라더스 박사(Dr. Joyce Brothers)'나 '필 박사(Dr. Phil)'와 같은 프로그램을 통해 심리학을 배웠다. 그렇다면, 미국인들이 자신과 타인의 임상병리에 대해 경각심을 갖고 있다는 것은 전혀 놀라운 일이 아닐 것이다. 그러한 "진단"의 정확성이나 부정확성과는 관계없이, 전문가들이나 일반인들 사이에 심리와 관련된 생각이나 논의가 풍부하게 일어나고 있다는 것은 정신 상태에 대해 이야기해 온 역사가 있다는 것을 의미한다.

frequency n. 빈번함; 횟수 dissect v. 해부하다; 분석하다 draw on (근원을) ~에 의존하다, ~에 의하여 얻다 relatively ad. 비교적, 상대적으로 novel a. 신기한, 새로운 define v. (성격·내용 따위를) 규정짓다; (말의) 정의를 내리다, 뜻을 밝히다 sublimation n. 승화 divert v. (딴 데로) 돌리다, (물길 따위를) 전환하다 sordid a. 더러운, 지저분한 impulse n. 자극, 충동 invent v. 발명하다; (이야기 따위를) 상상력으로 만들다 diagnose v. 진단하다 troubled a. 난처한, 당황한, 걱정스러운 neurasthenia n. 신경쇠약증 nervous breakdown 신경쇠약, 노이로제 syndrome n. 증후군 in vogue 유행하고 있는 melancholic a. 우울한, 우울증의 antebellum a. 전쟁 전의; 남북전쟁 전(前)의 alert a. 방심 않은, 정신을 바짝 차린 clinical a. 임상의 pathology n. 병리학 profusion n. 대량, 풍부 lay a. 속인의, 평신도의

14 내용파악   ②

"미국인들은 학교에서 심리학 강좌를 통해 그리고 대중매체에서 '조이스 브라더스 박사(Dr. Joyce Brothers)' '필 박사(Dr. Phil)'와 같은 프로그램을 통해 심리학을 배웠다."와 "전문가들이나 일반인들 사이에 심리와 관련된 생각이나 논의가 풍부하게 일어나고 있다"라는 내용을 통해 ②가 정답이 됨을 알 수 있다.

위 글에 의하면, 대중의 심리학 이해에 대중매체가 어떻게 영향을 미치는가?
① 전문적인 토론을 위한 플랫폼을 만듦으로써
② 심리학적 개념과 논의를 대중화함으로써
③ 심리학적 개념의 역사를 추적함으로써
④ 정확한 과학적 정보를 제공함으로써
⑤ 심각한 정신 질환에만 집중함으로써

15 내용파악   ②

본문에서 '신경쇠약증'에서 '신경쇠약'으로의 전환은 "어떤 심리적인 조건들이나 그것들에 대한 논의가 시간이 지나면서 나타났다가 사라졌다."는 언급에 대한 예로 제시됐다. 즉, 이것은 시간이 지남에 따른 정신건강 문제에 대한 사회적 이해의 변화를 나타낸다고 할 수 있다.

"신경쇠약증"에서 "신경쇠약"으로의 전환은 무엇을 의미하는가?
① 정신건강에 대한 인식의 감소
② 정신건강 문제에 대한 이해에 있어서의 사회적 변화
③ 의학적 진단 방법에 대한 반감 증가
④ 심리 상태에 대한 관심 부족
⑤ 심리학적 관행에 대한 불신

16 내용추론   ⑤

"'승화'의 심리학적인 개념은 교육 받은 미국인들이 여전히 서로의 행동에 적용시키고 있고 또 역사가들이 프로이트보다 훨씬 이전에 살았던 사람들에게 적용시키고 있는 개념이다.", "정신 상태에 대해 이야기해 온 역사가 있다"라는 내용을 통해 ⑤를 추론할 수 있다.

위 글에서 "승화"에 대해 추론할 수 있는 것은?
① 그것은 사람들로 하여금 자가 진단을 과소평가하도록 잘못 인도했다.
② 프로이트 이전까지 항상 하나의 개념으로 존재했지만 이름이 붙여지지 않은 채로 있어왔다.
③ 심리학의 미래에 있어서 그것의 역할은 아직 알려지지 않았다.
④ 프로이트가 미국인을 연구하는 과정에서 우연히 발견한 것이다.
⑤ 그 존재는 정신건강 담론에서 여전히 의미를 갖는다.

17-18

심장병은 전 세계의 주요 사망 원인이자 미국의 최대 사망 원인이다. 세계보건기구에 따르면, 2019년에 약 1,790만 명의 사람들이 심장병으로 목숨을 잃은 것으로 추정되는데, 이는 전 세계 사망자의 32%에 해당한다. 그러나 모든 심장병이 같은 것은 아니다. 그것은 심장이나 뇌로 가는 혈관, 심장 근육과 판막, 그리고 몸의 다른 부분에 영향을 줄 수 있다. 심혈관 질환은 장기간의 치료가 필요할 수도 있고, 갑작스럽고 심각하게 발생할 수도 있다. 예를 들어, 엘비스 프레슬리(Elvis Presley)의 딸인 리사 마리 프레슬리(Lisa Marie Presley)는 심정지 상태에 빠져 병원으로 급히 이송된 후 54세의 나이로 사망했다. 마찬가지로, 버팔로 빌스의 세이프티(최후방 수비수) 다마르 햄린(Damar Hamlin, 24세)은 빌스와 신시내티 벵골스의 경기 도중 심정지 상태에 빠져 경기장에서 쓰러졌다. 무엇이 프레슬리나 햄린의 심정지를 일으켰는지는 명확하지 않다. 그러나 심장 질환에 걸릴 위험이 있는지의 여부를 알 수 있는 방법이 있다. 그것은 의사에게 연락하여 완벽한 건강검진을 받도록 일정을 잡는 것이다.

estimate v. 어림잡다, 견적하다   affect v. ~에게 영향을 주다; ~에게 악영향을 미치다   valve n. <의학> 판막   cardiovascular disease 심혈관 질환   cardiac arrest 심장마비, 심정지   safety n. 세이프티(미식축구에서 상대 팀과 멀리 떨어져 있는 수비수)   collapse v. 무너지다, 붕괴하다; (사람이 과로·병 등으로) 쓰러지다[주저앉다]   trigger v. (일련의 사건·반응 등을) 일으키다, 유발하다   physical examination 건강검진

17 동의어   ①

trigger가 '(일련의 사건·반응 등을) 일으키다[유발하다]'라는 의미로 쓰였으므로 '(특히 나쁜 일을) 촉발시키다'라는 뜻의 precipitate가 동의어로 적절하다. ② 증발시키다 ③ (건강 따위를) 회복하다 ④ 원기[활기]를 돋구다 ⑤ 소환하다

18 내용일치   ④

"심혈관 질환은 장기간의 치료가 필요할 수도 있고, 갑작스럽고 심각하게 발생할 수도 있다."고 했는데, 장기간의 치료가 필요한 경우는 경미하게 시작한 후 서서히 악화되어 장기 치료가 필요한 경우를 말하므로 ④가 옳지 않은 진술이다.

위 글에 의하면 다음 중 옳지 않은 것은?
① 심장병은 2019년 미국에서 사망 원인 1위였다.
② 리사 마리 프레슬리는 심장마비로 54세의 나이로 사망했다.
③ 다마르 햄린은 축구 경기 도중에 심정지를 경험했다.
④ 심혈관 질환은 항상 갑작스럽고 심각하게 발생한다.
⑤ 프레슬리와 햄린의 심장마비의 원인은 무엇인지 알려지지 않았다.

19 동의어   ⑤

arbitrary가 '임의적인'이라는 의미로 쓰였으므로 '우연적인,' '우발적인'이라는 뜻의 accidental이 동의어로 적절하다. ① 질서정연한, 방법론적인 ② 불변의 ③ 회유적인 ④ 총명한

by necessity 필연적으로   arbitrary a. 임의의   lawn n. 잔디, 잔디밭

어떤 언어에서든, 그 언어의 사용자들이 세상의 물체나 개념을 지칭하기 위해 사용하는 소리의 집합을 의미하는 "기호"는 필연적으로 임의적이다. 다시 말해, 어떤 단어와 그 단어가 지칭하는 대상 사이에는 당연한 연관성이 전혀 없다. 예를 들어, 잔디밭에서 자라고 있는 큰 식물을 영어 사용자들은 "tree"라는 단어를 사용하여 지칭하지만, 스페인어로는 똑같이 쉽게 "arbol"이 될 수도 있는 것이다.

20-21

전후(戰後)의 미국이 낙관주의가 만연해 있고 축제 분위기에 젖어 있는 상황 속에서, 테네시 윌리엄스(Tennessee Williams)의 희곡 작품들은 이와 명확하게 정반대인 균형추로서 두드러진다. 나라가 2차 세계대전에서 힘겹게 얻어낸 승리를 한껏 즐기면서 끝없는 번영을 상상하고 있는 동안, 윌리엄스의 희곡 작품들은 주로 소외되고, 따돌림 받고, 감정적으로 표류하고 있던 사람들의 종종 간과되고 있던 경험들에 초점을 맞췄다.

사회 전반의 활기찬 분위기와 윌리엄스가 선택한 주제영역 사이의 거리는 예술과 그 역사적 상황 사이의 관계에 대해 의문을 제기한다. 이 시대의 지배적인 낙관주의와 윌리엄스의 희곡 작품이 가진 비관주의 사이에 분명한 거리가 있었음에도 불구하고, 이 드라마들은 의심의 여지없이 관객에게 반향을 일으켰고, 관객들은 그 작품들을 엄청난 브로드웨이 히트작으로 만들어주었다. 『욕망이라는 이름의 전차』의 블랑슈 뒤부아(Blanche DuBois)와 『유리 동물원』의 로라 윙필드(Laura Wingfield)와 같은 등장인물들은, 완전히 추방되기 직전에 국외자(局外者)가 된 것과 사투를 벌이고 있었지만, 관객들과 마음이 통했는데, 이는 전후의 호황이라는 겉보기에 희망찬 분위기 속에서도 그들의 경험이 보편적인 인간의 관심사에 반향을 일으켰기 때문이다.

이 겉으로 보기에 의외인 동일시는 특정한 역사적 순간의 서사를 초월하여 공감, 이해, 공유된 인간성 의식에 대한 근본적인 인간 욕구와 연결될 수 있는 예술의 지속적인 힘을 확증해준다. 내부의 악마와 싸우면서 적대적이고 무관심한 세계를 탐색하는 윌리엄스의 등장인물들은, 표면적으로는 "승자"처럼 보이지만 실제로는 자신의 불안, 그리고 소속, 수용, 온전함에 대한 갈망을 인식했던 관객들에게 거울이 되어주었다.

context n. 문맥; 배경, 상황 postwar a. 전후(戰後)의 pervasive a. 널리 퍼지는, 침투하는 optimism n. 낙관주의 celebratory a. 기념하는, 축하하는 distinct a. 별개의; 뚜렷한 counterpoint n. 평형추; 균형 revel in ~에 열중하다; ~을 한껏[대단히] 즐기다 marginalize v. 사회에서 소외하다, 사회적으로 무시하다 ostracize v. (사람을) 외면하다[배척하다] adrift a. 표류하여, 정처 없이 헤매어 prevailing a. 우세한, 주요한 exuberance n. 풍부, 윤택; 충일(充溢); 무성 thematic a. 주제의 terrain n. 지대, 지역 apparent a. 명백한; 외견상의, 겉보기에는 pessimism n. 비관주의 resonate with ~에게 반향을 일으키다 smash a. 대단한, 굉장한 on the verge of ~에 직면하여, 바야흐로 ~하려고 하여; ~직전에 displace v. 쫓아내다, 추방하다 connect with ~와 마음이 통하다, ~와 연결되다 identification n. 동일시, 일체화 transcend v. 초월하다 empathy n. 공감 grapple with 맞붙어 싸우다; 완수하려고 애쓰다, 해결하려고 고심하다 speak to ~을 확증하다

20 내용파악 ③

미국이 2차 세계대전에서의 승리를 즐기면서 끝없는 번영을 상상하고 있는 동안, 윌리엄스의 희곡 작품들은 주로 소외되고, 따돌림 받고, 감정적으로 표류하고 있던 사람들의 종종 간과되고 있던 경험들에 초점을 맞췄고, 그의 작품에 등장하는 인물들의 경험은 보편적인 인간 관심사에 대한 것으로 큰 반향을 일으켜서 관객들로부터 호응을 얻었다는 내용이다. 그러므로 ③이 정답으로 적절하다.

위 글은 테네시 윌리엄스에 대해 주로 무엇을 말하고 있는가?
① 그의 희곡 작품은 전후의 미국에 낙관주의를 낳는 데 도움이 되었다.
② 그의 등장인물들은 주로 배척당한 패배주의자들과 버림받은 사람들에게 호소한다.
③ 그의 희곡 작품들은 보편적인 주제로 인해 관객들에게 반향을 일으키고 있다.
④ 예술과 그 역사적 배경에 대한 그의 이론들은 획기적이었다.
⑤ 그의 활기는 연극 관람객들이 어려운 시기에 위안을 얻는 데 도움을 주었다.

21 내용추론 ①

"전후 미국 사회는 낙관주의가 만연해 있고 축제 분위기에 젖어 있었지만, 그런 가운데에서도 소외되고, 따돌림 받고, 감정적으로 표류하고 있던 사람들이 있었으며, 관객들 또한 불안, 그리고 소속, 수용, 온전함에 대한 갈망을 인식하고 있었다."는 내용을 통해 ①을 추론할 수 있다.

위 글에서 추론할 수 있는 것은?
① 1940년대 미국의 활기찬 분위기의 기저에는 걱정과 절망의 기류가 있었다.
② 테네시 윌리엄스는 연합국이 2차 세계대전에서 승리한 방식에 대해 비판적이었다.
③ 1940년대에 성공을 거두기 위해서는 희곡 작품이 비관적이고 우울해야 했다.
④ 테네시 윌리엄스의 희곡 작품은 1950년대에 훨씬 덜 영향력을 갖게 되었다.
⑤ 미국의 전후 극작가들은 낙관적이지 않으면 전쟁과 관련된 주제를 피했다.

22-23

히로시마와 나가사키에 원자폭탄이 투하되어 2차 세계대전이 막을 내리게 된 후, 언론에는 소름끼치는 침묵이 내려앉았고 원자 무기의 전체 파괴력에 대한 대중의 의식을 둔하게 했다. 처음에는, 원자폭탄 투하의 여파에 대한 상세한 보도가 거의 없었는데, 이는 다양한 행동가들에 의해 선동된 의도적인 혼란에 막혀버린 결과였으며, 특히 미국 언론이 그러했다. 항상 풍부하고 직설적인 전쟁 보도로 높은 평가를 받았던 『뉴욕타임스』조차도 민간인들 사이에 퍼지고 있던 방사능 질병의 공포에 침묵을 지켰다. 반박할 수 없는 새로운 정보는 조심스럽게 걸러지거나 억압되었으며, 이는 이야기를 만들어내려는 목적과 함께 원자폭탄의 여파라는 섬뜩한 현실을 대중이 접하지 못하게 하기 위한 것이었다.

그러나 나가사키에 대한 뉴스 보도에서는 이러한 정책에 마지못한 변화가 있었다. 예를 들어, 『뉴욕타임스』는 마침내 방사능이 문제라는 사실을 인정했다. 그러나 그것도 간접적으로 하는 한편, 그 중요성도 축소했다. 하지만 그 틈새로 부인할 수 없고 반박할 수 없는 진실이 새어 나오기 시작했다. 뇌리를 떠나지 않는 생존자들의 고통스러운 현실, 방사능 질병의 망령, 방사능에 노출된 사람들의 끔찍한 운명이 검열을 뚫고 나오면서, 대중들은 핵전쟁의 재앙적인 결과를 직시하게 되었다.

bring ~ to a close ~을 결판내다 chilling a. 냉랭한, 냉담한 descend v. 내리다, 내려가다[오다] muffle v. (소리를) 지우다, 둔탁하게 하다 devastate v. 유린하다, 황폐시키다 aftereffect n. 여파(餘波), 영향 choke v. 질식시키다, 숨 막히게 하다 deliberate a. 계획적인, 의도적인; 신중한 obfuscation n. 혼미, 혼동 gin up 선동하다, ~을 만들어내다 esteem v. 존경하다, 존중하다 prolific a. 다산의, (토지가) 비옥한; (작가가) 다작의; 풍부한 hard-hitting a. 직설적인 unfold v. (이야기·사태 따위가) 전개되다; (의중·생각 등을) 나타내다, 표명하다 radiation n. 방사선, 방사능 irrefutable a. 반박할 수 없는 suppress v. 억압하다;

억누르다, (증거·사실·성명 따위를) 감추다, 발표하지 않다 craft v. ~을 정교하게 만들다, 공들여 만들다 gruesome a. 소름끼치는, 섬뜩한 aftermath n. (전쟁·재해 따위의) 결과, 여파, 영향 grudging a. 인색한 acknowledge v. 인정하다, 승인하다 obliquely ad. 비스듬히, 완곡하게, 간접적으로 downplay v. ~을 중시하지 않다, 경시하다 seep v. 스며나오다, 새다 haunting a. 자주 마음속에 떠오르는, 뇌리를 떠나지 않는 specter n. 유령, 망령 grim a. 냉혹한, 엄한 pierce v. 꿰뚫다, 관통하다 censorship n. 검열 catastrophic a. 파국적인

22 글의 주제 ③

원자폭탄 투하에 따른 민간인의 피해와 고통에 대해 미국 주류 언론이 대체로 침묵하고 은폐하려는 행동을 했음을 이야기하고 있는 글이다.

위 글은 주로 무엇에 관한 것인가?
① 일본에 대한 원자폭탄 투하에 따른 2차 세계대전의 갑작스러운 종전
② 방사능 낙진의 파괴적인 힘에 대한 암울한 발견
③ 미국 언론의 방사선 피폭 후유증 은폐
④ 원자폭탄 폭발에 대한 뉴욕 타임스의 직설적인 보도
⑤ 정부 고위 당국자의 비리를 폭로하는 언론의 역할

23 내용추론 ①

"『뉴욕타임스』조차도 민간인들 사이에 퍼지고 있던 방사능 질병의 공포에 침묵을 지켰고, 반박할 수 없는 새로운 정보는 조심스럽게 걸러지거나 억압되었으며, 이는 이야기를 만들어내려는 목적과 함께 원자폭탄의 여파라는 섬뜩한 현실을 대중이 접하지 못하게 하기 위한 것이었다."라는 내용을 통해 ①을 추론할 수 있다.

위 글에서 추론할 수 있는 것은?
① 『뉴욕타임스』는 편견과 이야기 조작을 회사 내의 풍조로 받아들였다.
② 주류 언론은 전시(戰時)에 일반적으로 편견이 없고 객관적이다.
③ 『뉴욕타임스』는 원자폭탄 투하에 대한 사실을 은폐한 것에 대해 수치심을 느꼈다.
④ "진실"의 상대성은 사건에 대한 모든 기술이 똑같이 타당하다는 것을 의미한다.
⑤ 『뉴욕타임스』는 보도를 통해 미국을 부정적으로 묘사하려 했다.

24-25

대학은 그 어떤 방해나 위협도 용납해선 안 되지만, 다만 말에 관한 한, 그것에 대한 감시를 자신들의 소관 안에 있는 것으로 여기지 말아야 한다. 대학은 학생들이 (도서관이나 기숙사와 같은) 비정치적 공간을 가질 수 있는 권리를 보호해야 하며, 대학은 정치적 간섭 없이 공부하고 연구할 기회를 제공하는 것이 대학이 존재하는 이유 가운데 큰 부분을 차지한다는 것을 잊지 말아야 한다. 대학은 인구통계나 이념에 관계없이 교수진을 승진시키고 학생을 평가해야 하고, 최근에 있었던 차별철폐조치에 대한 대법원 판결을 비롯해서, 차별금지 법률의 내용과 정신을 준수하도록 노력해야 하며, 만약 자유민주주의 사회에서 (대학 같은) 강력한 기관이 그들이 어쩌다가 반대하는 법률의 측면들을 회피할 방법을 찾는 것이 매우 유해하다는 사실이 그렇게 하기에(차별금지 법률을 준수하기에) 충분히 설득력 있는 이유가 되지 않는다면, 그들은 이러한 차별적인 정책이 모든 인종 집단에서 매우 평판이 좋지 않다는 것을 기억해야 한다.

tolerate v. 관대히 다루다, 묵인하다 disruption n. 분열, 붕괴, 와해 intimidation n. 위협, 협박 supervision n. 감독, 감시 remit n. 소관 dorm n. 기숙사 intrusion n. 강요, 방해; 침입 faculty n. (대학의) 학부; 교수진 evaluate v. 평가하다 demography n. 인구(통계)학 abide by (약속·결의·규칙 등을) 지키다; (협정·결정·결과 따위에) 따르다 nondiscrimination n. 차별이 없음, 차별대우를 하지 않음 affirmative action 차별 철폐 조처 corrosive a. 부식성의; (정신적으로) 좀먹는, 유해한 compelling a. (너무나 흥미로워서) 주목하지 않을 수 없는[설득력 있는] discriminatory a. 차별적인

24 동의어 ①

remit가 '소관(所管, 맡아 관리하는 바, 또는 그 범위), 책임이나 권한의 영역'이라는 의미로 쓰였으므로 '범위', '권한'이라는 뜻의 purview가 동의어로 적절하다. ② 확대 ③ 과식, 과다 ④ 정점 ⑤ 최저점

25 글의 목적 ⑤

본문은 "대학이 학생들에게 정치적이지 않은 환경을 제공하고, 표현의 자유와 다양성을 존중해야 한다"는 주장을 제기하고 있다.

위 글의 주된 목적은 다음 중 무엇인가?
① 교내 활동에 대한 감독 강화를 추진하는 것
② 교내 징계규정의 시행을 제안하는 것
③ 대학 정책에 대한 사회적 압력의 중요성을 강조하는 것
④ 대학 캠퍼스가 정치적인 공간이라는 생각을 지지하는 것
⑤ 캠퍼스에서의 표현의 자유와 다양성에 대한 대학의 입장을 확인하는 것

26-28

재계의 우려스러운 관행인 그린워싱(greenwashing)은 기업들이 탈탄소화와 생물다양성 상실과 같은 문제에 대한 헌신을 오해의 소지가 있도록 보여주는 것이다. 그것은 한편으로는 지속가능성에 대한 노력을 주장하면서 다른 한편으로는 비윤리적인 관행을 은폐하는 허울에 불과해서, 신뢰를 훼손하고 환경 목표를 향한 실질적인 진전을 지연시킨다. 기업들은 이윤을 해치지 않으면서 윤리적인 책임을 보여줘야 한다는 압박에 직면할 때 종종 그린워싱에 의존한다. 이러한 관행은 그들이 환경에 미치는 영향에 대해 오해의 소지가 있는 주장을 제시함으로써 진정한 지속가능성 노력을 회피할 수 있도록 해준다.

그린워싱의 사례는 다양한데, 일부 기업은 실제로는 더 많은 폐기물을 발생시키지만 겉보기에는 친환경적인 대안으로 플라스틱 빨대를 대체하는 것 같은 피상적인 변화를 선택하고 있다. 다른 기업들은 진정한 지속가능성 관행을 무시하면서도 준수하는 것처럼 보일 수 있도록 자체적으로 희석시킨 기준을 만들거나 약한 인증을 찾아 나선다. 심지어 투자 부문 내에서조차 그린워싱에 대한 비난이 발생하면서, 지속가능한 투자 계획의 진정성에 의문을 제기하고 있다.

그러나 사례를 정확히 구분하는 것이 매우 중요하다. 때로는 그린워싱에 대한 비난이 기업의 실제 노력과 일치하지 않을 수도 있다. 한 예로, 투자 회사 Baillie Gifford는 화석연료 산업과 관련되어 있다는 비판을 받았지만, 그러한 분야에 대한 실제 투자는 업계 평균보다 현저히 낮았다. 이것은 행동을 그린워싱으로 분류할 때 균형 잡힌 판단이 필요하다는 것을 잘 나타내준다. 그린워싱에 대처하기 위해서는 주의 깊은 검토

와 함께 오해의 소지가 있는 주장의 명확한 사례를 공개하는 것이 요구된다. 소비자들은 단순한 마케팅 전략보다 환경적 책임을 우선시하는 진정으로 헌신적인 기업들에게 (그 진정성에) 의문을 제기하고 또 지지해줌으로써 매우 중요한 역할을 하고 있다. 신뢰를 높이고 지속가능한 미래를 향한 진정한 전진을 촉진하기 위해서는 그린워싱 관행을 밝혀내는 집단적 노력이 필수적이다.

greenwashing n. 그린워싱(실제로는 친환경적이지 않지만 마치 친환경적인 것처럼 홍보하는 '위장환경주의') showcase v. 전시[진열]하다; 두드러지게 나타내다 commitment n. 헌신; 약속 decarbonization n. 탄소제거, 탈(脫)탄소 biodiversity n. 생물 다양성 facade n. (건물의) 정면; (사물의) 겉, 외관 conceal v. 숨기다, 감추다 unethical a. 비윤리적인 sustainability n. (자원 이용이) 환경이 파괴되지 않고 계속될 수 있음, 지속가능성 undermine v. (명성 따위를) 음험한 수단으로 훼손하다, 몰래 손상시키다 stall v. 교묘하게 속여 지연시키다 resort to ~에 의지하다 compromise v. (명예·평판·신용 따위를) 더럽히다, 손상하다; 위태롭게 하다 abound v. (동물·물건·문제 등이) 많이 있다 superficial a. 피상적인 replace v. 대체하다 alternative n. 대안 watered-down a. 약화시킨 certification n. 증명, 보증 neglect v. 무시하다, 경시하다; 간과하다 accusation n. 비난 authenticity n. 확실성, 신빙성; 진정(眞正) crucial a. 결정적인, 중대한 vigilant a. 부단히 경계하고 있는; 방심하지 않는, 주의 깊은 scrutiny n. 조사, 감시, 감독 pivotal a. 중추적인 prioritize v. 우선시하다 unveil v. 정체를 드러내다, (비밀 따위를) 밝히다

26 빈칸완성 ④

"그린워싱은 지속가능성에 대한 노력을 주장하면서 다른 한편으로는 비윤리적인 관행을 은폐하는 허울에 불과해서, 신뢰를 훼손하고 환경 목표를 향한 실질적인 진전을 지연시킨다"라고 했으므로, 이러한 보여주기 식의 관행은 진정한 지속가능성 노력을 회피할 수 있게 해줄 것이다. 그러므로 '책임 따위를) 회피하다'라는 의미의 sidestep이 정답이다. ① (사람들이) 좁은 간격으로 발맞추어 걷기 ② 뒤를 쫓다 ③ 곁길로 빠지게 하다 ⑤ 허튼소리

27 내용파악 ①

본문에서는 그린워싱을 환경에 도움이 되지 않은 우려스러운 관행으로 평가하면서도 친환경을 지향한다는 기업의 태도나 실천을 섣불리 예단해선 안 된다고 추가적으로 언급하고 있다. 그러므로 이를 종합하고 있는 ①이 정답으로 적절하다.

위 글에서 "그린워싱"에 대해 주로 말하고 있는 것은?
① 그것은 신중하게 분별해야 할 심각한 문제이다.
② 그것은 거의 모든 산업을 부패시키고 있는 널리 퍼져 있는 문제이다.
③ 그것은 더 이상의 피해를 입지 않도록 지구를 보호하기 위해 노력하고 있다.
④ 그것은 자금 지원을 정부에 의존하고 있다.
⑤ 그것은 현대 경제에서 피할 수 없는 현실이다.

28 내용추론 ④

"기업들은 이윤을 해치지 않으면서 환경에 대한 윤리적인 책임을 보여줘야 한다는 압박에 직면할 때 종종 그린워싱에 의존한다."라고 했는데, 이는 곧 기업이 환경에 대한 노력을 자신들의 이미지 관리, 넓게 보면 홍보, 선전, 광고의 수단으로 사용하고 있다는 것이다.

위 글에서 추론할 수 있는 것은?
① 언론은 기업의 훌륭한 행동을 홍보하지 못하고 있다.
② 기업들은 그린워싱을 막기 위해 홍보 전문가를 고용하고 있다..
③ 부패한 언론이 규정을 준수하는 회사를 공격하고 있다.
④ 기업들은 환경에 대한 헌신을 광고로서 사용하고 있다.
⑤ 대중들은 더 높은 가격을 지불하는 것보다 그린워싱을 선호한다.

29-30

20세기 중반에는 주관적인 정신병 경험과 환각 약물로 인한 마음 상태가 추가적인 연구를 정당화시킬 만큼 유사하다는 과학적 신념이 널리 퍼져 있었다. 그러나 1960년대에는 환각 약물과 관련된 도덕적 공황상태가 확고히 자리를 잡았다. 동시에 의학의 증거 요건이 더욱 엄격해져, 환각제 연구에 대한 장벽이 더 높아졌다. 환각 약물과 관련된 연구를 위한 자금, 접근 및 허가가 서서히 줄어들면서 이러한 물질에 대한 연구는 대체로 정신의학에 의해 잊혀졌다. 그러나 그 이후 수십 년 동안 정신병과 환각제에 관련된 연구가 재개되었고, 비록 다소 방향이 바뀌긴 했지만 거의 방해받지 않은 채 진행되고 있다. 정신분석학 교육을 받은 정신과 의사들이 환각 약물을 통해 얻고자 했던 정신병 경험의 자세한 서술에 대한 주류의 관심도 많이 없어졌다. 대신, 정신병과 환각제에 관한 연구는 다른 나머지 정신의학과 함께 종종 신경생물학적ㆍ유전적 연구에 특별히 집중하고 있다.

psychosis n. 정신병, 정신이상 psychedelic a. 환각을 일으키는, 도취적인 warrant v. 보증하다, 정당화하다 rigorous a. 준엄한; 가혹한 psychiatry n. 정신병학, 정신의학 unfettered a. 속박 받지 않은, 제한 받지 않는, 규제가 없는 albeit conj. 비록 ~이지만 psychiatrist n. 정신병의사 neurobiological a. 신경생물학의 genetic a. 유전의

29 빈칸완성 ③

환각 물질에 대한 연구가 정신의학에 의해 잊혀진 것은 그 약물과 관련된 제반 여건이 좋지 않아졌기 때문일 것이므로, 빈칸에는 '자금, 접근 및 허가가 서서히 줄어들었다'는 의미를 만드는 ③이 정답으로 적절하다. ① 치솟다 ② 파내다 ④ 착수하다 ⑤ 윙윙거리다

30 글의 주제 ④

본문은 1960년대에 환각제에 대한 연구가 방해받았으나, 그 후 연구가 부활하고 그 방향이 조금 바뀌었다는 내용을 다루고 있다.

위 글은 주로 무엇에 관한 것인가?
① 정신병과 환각 경험 사이의 유사점
② 정신병과 환각제에 대한 연구 결과
③ 증거에 대한 요구 증가와 그것이 연구에 미치는 영향
④ 정신의학 연구에 있어서 환각제의 역할 변화
⑤ 여전히 환각제에 대한 연구를 괴롭히는 도덕적 딜레마

01 ②	**02** ④	**03** ④	**04** ②	**05** ②	**06** ①	**07** ④	**08** ④	**09** ①	**10** ②
11 ③	**12** ④	**13** ①	**14** ③	**15** ②	**16** ④	**17** ②	**18** ①	**19** ①	**20** ②
21 ①	**22** ④	**23** ③	**24** ③	**25** ①	**26** ②	**27** ①	**28** ①	**29** ②	**30** ④
31 ④	**32** ②	**33** ③	**34** ②	**35** ①	**36** ③	**37** ④	**38** ①	**39** ②	**40** ④

01 올바른 구동사 표현 ②

have something to do with ~는 '~와 관련이 있다'는 뜻이다. something 대신 a good deal, a great deal을 쓰게 되면 '~와 상당한 관련이 있다'는 의미를 가진다. 여기서 a good deal은 '다량, 상당량, 많음(a large amount)'을 뜻한다. dealing은 '거래, 매매'를 뜻하는 명사 이므로 문맥과 어울리지 않으며, 따라서 ②를 a good deal to do with로 바꿔야 한다. ① 'something of a+명사'는 '어느 정도의 ~, 다소의 ~'를 뜻하는 표현이다. ② 부사 So too이 문장 앞으로 선행하여 주어와 동사가 도치되면서 '~도 역시 마찬가지'를 뜻한다. 이때 did 는 대동사로서 앞서 나온 had a good deal to do with it을 가리킨다. ④ 앞서 나온 명사 a repertory를 뒤에서 수식하는데, 'a repertory (which was) rich in Shakespeare'에서 관계대명사와 be 동사가 생략된 것으로 볼 수 있다.

win over ~를 설득하다, ~를 자기편으로 끌어들이다 familiarity n. 익숙함, 친숙함 tour v. 순회하다 repertory n. 레퍼토리(특정한 극단이 몇 개의 연극을 교대로 공연하는 형식) feature v. 특별히 포함하다, 특징으로 삼다 speech n. (연극의) 대사

19세기 초, 셰익스피어가 미국을 매료시킨 경위는 어느 정도 미스터리이다. 그와 경쟁할 만한 상대가 없었다는 것이 그것과 상당한 관련이 있었다. 또한 그의 작품에 대한 (대중들의) 친숙도가 점점 높아졌다는 것도 상당한 관련이 있었다. 영국 배우들이 셰익스피어의 작품으로 가득 찬 레퍼토리로 미국을 순회 공연했으며, 교과서에는 그의 유명한 대사들이 수록되었다.

02 등위접속사 nor가 문두에 오는 경우의 도치 ④

④에 쓰인 nor는 등위접속사로서 부정의 의미를 담고 있기 때문에 문두에 왔을 때, 그 뒤에 오는 주어와 동사가 도치되어야 한다. 주어진 문장에서는 조동사 would가 있으므로 ④를 Nor would subsidies로 고쳐야 한다.

de-risk v. 위험을 제거하다 ties n. (강한) 유대[관계] multiple a. 많은; 다양한 homegrown a. 국내산의 when it comes to ~에 관한 한, ~에 대해서[관해서]라면 with respect to ~에 관하여 refined a. 세련된; 정제된 subsidy n. 보조금 all-out a. 총력을 기울인, 전면적인 bidder n. 가격 제시자; 응찰자 taxpayer n. 납세자

서구 지도자들은 중국과 연결된 글로벌 공급망의 "위험 제거"에 합의했다. 이는 중국과 교역 관계를 유지하고 기후 변화와 같은 다양한 분야에서 중국과 협력하는 동시에 국내 필수 산업에 정부의 지원과 보호를 제공하는

것을 의미한다. 그러나 청정에너지에 관한 한, 중국과 관련된 위험을 성공적으로 제거하는 것이 어렵다는 것을 서구 지도자들은 제대로 이해하지 못했다. 서구에는 좀 더 정교한 접근 방식이 필요하며, 보조금만으로는 답이 될 수 없다. 만약 서구 정부들이 서로에 대한 전면적인 보조금 전쟁을 시작하면, 그로 인해 투자는 최고 응찰자에게로 옮겨갈 뿐일 것이다. 보조금도 또한 그 목적을 달성하지 못할 것이다. 모든 부문에서 중국과 비용 경쟁을 시도하면 이는 아마도 세금 낭비로 이어지고 기후 변화로 인한 피해도 더 커질 것이다.

03 동의어 ④

woke는 형용사로 사용될 때 '사회적, 정치적 불의에 대해 깨어 있는 (alert to social and political injustice)'이라는 뜻을 가진다. 명사로 활용되면, 주로 '사회 불평등에 대해 깨어 있는 의식을 가진, 인종이나 성별 등 다양한 사회적 이슈에 민감한 사람들'을 가리키게 되었다. 따라서 가장 가까운 의미는 "politically progressive(정치적으로 진보적인)"이다. 한편, 이 표현은 과도한 정치적 올바름(PC: Politically Correct) 경향을 비판하는 우파 지식인들에 의해 그들을 폄하/비하하는 의도로 사용될 수 있다.

upcoming a. 다가오는, 곧 있을 helm n. (배를 조종하는) 키 at the helm (조직·사업 등을) 책임지고 있는 iconic a. ~의 상징[아이콘]이 되는, 우상의 franchise n. 독점 사업권 blast v. 혹평[맹비난]하다 it's about time (that) ~해야 할 때이다 installment n. (전집·연재물 등의) 1회분, 한 권 mediocre a. 보통 밖에 안 되는, 썩 좋지는 않은 sexist n. 성차별주의자 progressive a. 진보적인

오스카 수상 감독인 샤르민 오바이드-치노이(Sharmeen Obaid-Chinoy)가 앞으로 제작될 『스타워즈』를 감독할 것으로 알려지면서, 그녀는 이 상징적인 프랜차이즈 영화의 감독을 맡은 최초의 여성이 되었다. 그러나 오바이드-치노이가 이제는 여성들이 『스타워즈』 시리즈의 감독을 맡아야 할 때라고 말한 뒤, 우파 비평가들은 이 영화를 "의식 과잉"이라며 맹비난하고 있다.

04 논리완성 ②

영토 분쟁의 대상이 되는 사원이 어느 나라에 속하는 것인지를 판단하는 것은 곧 국경 위치를 확정하는 행위와 다름없으므로, 국제사법재판소가 이 문제를 신중하게 접근하고 있으며 나아가 명확한 의견 표명을 꺼리고 있다는 내용이다. 빈칸 뒤에 이어지는 '재판소가 (국경에 대한 발언을) 조심하고 있고 추가 협상이 필요하다'는 진술을 바탕으로 '재판소가 국

경에 대한 의견을 말하기(opine)를 꺼린다'는 것을 추론할 수 있다. opine은 '~에 관해 의견을 표명하다(to express an opinion about something)'는 의미이다.

ruling n. 판결 clarify v. 명확하게 하다 prior a. (다른 무엇·특정 시간보다) 사전의 territorial a. 영토의, 영토에 관한 engage in ~에 관여하다 interpretive a. 해석상의 reluctance n. 싫음, 마지못해 함, 꺼림, 마음 내키지 않음 opine v. 의견을 밝히다(to express an opinion about something) frontier n. 국경 caution n. 조심, 주의 negotiation n. 협상, 교섭 head v. (특정 방향으로) 가다[향하다] hinge on[upon] 전적으로 ~에 달려 있다 preclude v. (~로 하여금 …하지) 못하게 하다, (~가 ~하는 것을) 불가능하게 하다

국제사법재판소는 태국과 캄보디아 사이에 있는 프레아 비히어(Preah Vihear) 사원을 둘러싼 영토 분쟁에 대한 이전 판결의 의미를 명확히 하는 판결을 내렸다. 이번 판결은 현 재판소가 이전 판결에서 불분명했던 해석상의 공백을 메우기 위해 상당한 노력을 기울일 의향이 있음을 시사한다. 동시에, 재판소가 사원에서 북쪽과 서쪽으로 난 국경의 위치에 대해서는 의견을 말하기를 꺼린다는 것은 재판소가 조심하고 있음을 보여주고, 추가 협상이 필요함을 말해준다.

05 논리완성 ②

빈칸 앞에서 킨리는 자신의 목숨을 구하기 위해 헌신했던 아흐메드에게 '빚을 갚는다(repay his debt)'고 하였다. 따라서, 킨리는 아흐메드와 그의 가족이 탈레반으로부터 목숨을 잃을 위험에 처하자 그들을 그 위험으로부터 '구출하여 되찾아 오려' 할 것임을 추론할 수 있다.

covenant n. 약속[계약] Sergeant n. 병장 interpreter n. 통역사 ambush n. 매복 공격 Herculean a. 큰 힘이 드는, 대단히 곤란한; 헤라클레스와 같은, 힘이 장사인 length n. (무엇이 계속되는 긴) 시간[기간] go to Herculean lengths to do something (~하기 위해) 많은 애를 쓰다[어떤 고생도 마다하지 않다] passage n. (특정 지역에 대한) 통행[통과] 허가 retrieve v. (원래 있어야 할 자리로) 되찾아 오다, 회수하다 trap v. 가두다, (함정으로) 몰아 넣다

영화 『가이 리치스 더 커버넌트(Guy Ritchie's The Covenant)』는 미군 병장 존 킨리(제이크 질렌할)와 아프가니스탄 통역사 아흐메드(다르 살림)의 행로를 추적한다. 매복 끝에, 아흐매드는 킨리의 목숨을 구하기 위해 엄청난 고생을 한다. 아흐메드와 그의 가족이 미국으로의 안전한 통과를 약속대로 제공받지 못했다는 사실을 킨리가 알게 될 때, 그는 탈레반이 그들을 먼저 찾아내기 전에 전쟁 지역으로 돌아가 그들을 되찾아 옴으로써 그의 빚을 갚아야 한다.

06 논리완성 ①

예술 창작의 본질은 예술가의 '의도', '결심(결정)' 또는 '개념'에 있는 것이지, 어떤 물체 혹은 대상 그 자체에 있는 것이 아니라는 예술가 뒤샹의 급진적 사상을 소개하고 있는 글이다. 뒤샹은 '예술적 기교가 전혀 필요 없는' 공장에서 제작된 흔한 '세라믹 물건'을 단지 '받침대 위에 올려서 미술관 안에 두고' 거기에 '가짜 서명'을 덧붙임으로써, 그것을 예술 작품으로 간주하기로 '결정(decision)'했다. 뒤샹이 예술가로서 내린 이 '결정(decision)', 즉 그의 '개념(concept)'이 '실제 예술 작품'임을 선언한

것이다. 따라서 필자는 그 세라믹 물건을 사진으로 보든 실물로 보든 그 물건이 예술 작품이 아닌 것은 마찬가지'라고 한 것이다.

landmark n. 획기적 사건 render v. (어떤 상태가 되게) 만들다[하다] ceramicist n. 도예가 erstwhile a. 이전의, 지금까지의 bogus a. 가짜의 signature n. 서명 and yet 그럼에도 불구하고 elevate v. (들어) 올리다 pedestal n. (기둥·동상 등의) 받침대 gallery n. 화랑, 미술관 if you will 말하자면 objection n. 이의, 반대 obstinacy n. 아집, 완고함 commitment n. 약속; 헌신

『샘(Fountain)』은 예술 창작에 대한 새로운 급진적 접근 방식을 나타내기 때문에 20세기 미술의 기념비적인 작품이다. 그것을 예술 작품으로 만드는 데는 그 어떤 예술적 기교도 관여되지 않았다. 뒤샹(Duchamp)은 도예가가 아니라 전직 화가였으며, 그가 한 일이라곤 가짜 서명을 더한 것뿐이었다. 공장에서 만든 물건은 그 아름다움이 아니라 기능성 때문에 존재한다. 그러나 뒤샹은 그것을 받침대 위에 올려서 어떤 미술관 안에 둠으로써 그것에 예술의 지위를 부여했다. 이렇게 하기로 한 그의 결정 — 말하자면 그의 개념 — 이 실제 예술 작품이며, 그런 의미에서 그것의 사진을 본다 해도 실물을 보는 것과 마찬가지이다.

07 논리완성 ④

수표 사기꾼들이 '기술과 소셜 미디어를 금융 사기의 도구로 활용하고 있다'는 내용이다. leverage는 '지레의 작용'을 뜻하면서, 동사로 쓰면 '~을 (지렛대 삼아) 이용하다'는 뜻이다. 한편, forge, impersonate도 '사기 치다'와 밀접히 연관된 어휘이기는 하지만, 주어진 문장에서와 같이 '기술과 소셜 미디어'를 목적어로 삼는 것은 부적절하다.

fraud n. 사기 con artist n. 사기꾼 leverage v. ~에게 영향력을 미치다; ~을 (지렛대 삼아) 이용하다(to use ~ to achieve a desired result) grand a. (계획 등이) 매우 야심적인 forge v. (노력하여) 만들어내다; ~을 위조하다 encrypt v. (접근을 차단하기 위해 정보를) 암호화하다 impersonate v. (남을 속이기 위해 다른 사람인 척) 가장하다, 사칭하다

지난 몇십 년 동안 수표 사용이 급속히 감소했음에도 불구하고, 수표 사기는 특히 팬데믹 이후 급격히 증가했다. 은행 관계자들과 사기 전문가들은 사기꾼들이 종이조각을 훔치는 데서 시작하지만, 기술과 소셜 미디어를 활용하여 훨씬 더 큰 규모로 사기를 저지르고 있다고 말했다.

08 논리완성 ④

접대 산업인 호텔이 '개인적인 인간적 접촉을 강조하므로', '디지털로의 전환 및 AI 기술'을 '비인격적, 비인간적(impersonal) 기술'로 간주할 가능성이 크고, 이는 그런 방식으로의 전환을 호텔 산업이 '꺼리게' 만드는 결과를 초래할 것이라고 추론할 수 있다. 한편, impersonal이란 '개별 인간 또는 그들의 감정에 대해 관심이 없거나 관심을 드러내지 않고, 정서적인 따뜻함이 부족한(having or showing no interest in individual people or their feelings, lacking emotional warmth)' 것을 가리키는 말이다.

implement v. 시행하다 lag v. 뒤에 처지다, 뒤떨어지다 daunting a. 벅찬, 주눅이 들게 하는 adherence n. 고수; 집착 hospitality n. 환대, 후대, 접대 reluctance n. 꺼림, 마음 내키지 않음 seemingly ad. 외견상으로, 겉보기에는 impersonal a. 인간미 없는, 비인격적인

impeccability n. 완전무결함 disposition n. 기질, 성향 inclination n. 성향

호텔들은 여러 요인의 복합적인 작용으로 인해 디지털로의 전환 및 AI를 시행하는 것이 종종 지연된다. 핵심적인 요인은 비용이 많이 들고 복잡하다는 인식인데, 이는 특히 소규모 시설(호텔)의 경우 힘들 수 있다. 또한, 접대 산업은 개인적인 인간적 접촉을 강조한다는 것에 뿌리를 둔 전통적 방법을 강력히 고수하는 경향이 있어, 비인격적으로 보이는 기술을 채택하는 것을 꺼리게 된다.

09 논리완성   ①

도시 거주민들이 물건을 사기 위해(retail), 즐기기 위해(recreation), 일하러 가기 위해(workplace) "방문(visit)"하고, "이동(exodus)"하는 데이터를 이용해 만든 지표이므로, 이 지표는 "이동성(mobility)" 지표라고 부를 수 있을 것이다.

pulse n. 맥박; 고동 mobility n. 이동성, 기동성(ability to move quickly and easily) indicator n. 지표 exodus n. (많은 사람들이 동시에 하는) 탈출[이동] index n. 색인; 지표; 지수 retail n. 소매 visibility n. 가시성 sustainability n. 지속 가능성

세계 도시들의 활력을 측정하는 한 가지 방법은 실시간 이동성 지표를 사용하는 것이다. 『이코노미스트』지(紙)에서는 소매 및 유흥, 대중교통 및 직장으로의 방문을 보여주는 구글 데이터를 이용하여 "이동 지수"를 구축하였다.

10 동의어   ②

apologist는 '논쟁의 여지가 있는 어떤 것을 옹호하기 위해 주장을 펼치는 사람(a person who offers an argument in defense of something controversial)'을 가리키므로, '어떤 것을 주장하거나 지지하는 사람(person who argues for or supports something)'이라는 의미의 proponent가 가장 유사한 의미를 가진 단어이다.

immense a. 거대한 vibrant a. 활기찬 skillful a. 숙련된, 능숙한 military a. 군사의 diplomat n. 외교관 linguist n. 언어학자 treatise n. 논문 remarkable a. 탁월한 apologist n. 옹호자 imperial a. 제국의 romantic a. 연애[애정]의 critic n. 비평가 proponent n. (어떤 사상·행동 방침의) 지지자 opportunist n. 기회주의자 insurgent n. 반란[내란]을 일으킨 사람

클레오파트라는 거대하고 다양한 나라를 통치했을 뿐 아니라, 알렉산드리아를 고대 세계에서 가장 활기찬 도시 중 하나로 만들어낸 도시 계획가였으며, 숙련된 군사 전략가이자 외교관이었고, 재능 있는 언어학자였으며, 심지어 의학 논문들의 저자이기도 하였다. 이러한 업적들에도 불구하고, 이 탁월한 여성에 대한 이야기는 로마 제국의 확장을 옹호하는 사람들, 즉 플루타르크와 같은 남성들에 의해 만들어졌는데, 플루타르크는 자신이 쓴 두 인물, 율리우스 시저와 마르크 안토니우스와의 연애와 정치적 관련이라는 관점에서 그녀를 기술하였다.

11 반의어   ③

extol은 '극찬하다(to praise someone or something highly)'는 의미이므로 '비난하다; 잘못에 대한 책임이 ~에게 있다고 여기다(to say or think that a person or thing is responsible for something bad that has happened)'는 뜻의 blame이 반의어로서 가장 적절하다.

secretary n. 장관 executive n. 경영 간부, 임원, 중역 laud v. 칭찬하다 boost v. 신장시키다, 북돋우다 visionary n. 예언자, 공상가 ease v. 완화하다 administration n. 행정부 demote v. (흔히 처벌로) 강등[좌천]시키다 disseminate v. (정보·지식 등을) 퍼뜨리다[전파하다] acclaim v. 칭송하다

미국 에너지 장관은 생산량을 증가시킨 것에 대해 석유 기업 임원들을 극구 칭찬했고, 바이든 행정부와 화석 연료 생산업자들 사이의 긴장을 완화하려고 업계의 창의적 공상가들에게 찬사를 보냈다.

12 논리완성   ④

Ⓐ 흑인 대통령의 당선과 같은 유색인종의 지위 향상과 사회 진출에 "반발(backlash)"하는 의도에서 이 음모론이 증폭되고 있으므로, 이 음모론은 특정 세력(유대인, 진보 엘리트 등)이 백인의 우월한 지위와 세력을 "약화/감소"시킬 것을 기도(企圖)하고 있다고 믿게끔 만드는 것이라고 추론할 수 있다. Ⓑ 음모론의 본질은 '사회에 큰 반향을 일으킨 사건의 원인을 명확히 설명할 수 없을 때 그 배후에 거대한 권력이나 비밀스러운 조직이 있다고 여기며 유포되는 근거 없는 소문'이므로, 이러한 음모론을 퍼뜨리는 세력에게는 '남을 꾀거나 부추겨서 나쁜 짓을 하게 하려는' 즉 "나쁜 일을 부추기고 선동하려는" 의도가 있다고 추론할 수 있다.

replacement n. 대체 conspiracy n. 음모 supercharge v. (감정·긴장·에너지 등을) 지나치게 들이다 backlash n. 반발 ongoing a. 계속 진행 중인 diminution n. 축소, 감소 deliberate a. 고의의, 의도적인, 계획적인 liberal a. 진보적인 abet v. (나쁜 일을) 사주하다[교사하다] acceleration n. 가속(加速) foment v. (문제·폭력을) 조성[조장]하다 cataclysmic a. 대변동의; 대격동의 seize v. 장악하다 emigration n. (타국으로의) 이주, 이민 diffusion n. 발산; 보급 rejuvenate v. 다시 젊어지게 하다 deride v. 조롱하다

미국에서는 지난 10년 동안 소셜 미디어와 버락 오바마 대통령 당선에 대한 반발로 인해 거대 대체 음모론이 증폭되었다. 그 음모론은 유대인과 진보 엘리트들에 의한 의도적인 전략의 일환으로 백인과 그들의 문화가 지속적으로 축소되고 있다고 주장한다. 거대 대체 음모론의 확산은 권력 장악의 수단으로 대변동의 폭력적 혼란을 조장하려는 노력인, 가속주의로 알려진 테러리스트 전략에 선동된 것이었다.

13 단락배열   ①

주어진 문장의 핵심 내용인 "과학이라는 개념을 진심으로 믿었다", "인간을 합리적으로 통치한다"는 웰스의 사상을 상술(詳述)하는 내용이 필요하므로 Ⓑ가 이어지는 것이 가장 적절하다. Ⓑ에는 "인류가 자신의 운명을 개선하려면 과학 기술자들에게 권력을 맡겨야 한다"는 보다 구체적인 내용이 나오기 때문이다. Ⓐ에서 지칭되어진 "이 고결한 엘리트"는

앞서 Ⓑ에서 언급된 "기술자들로 이루어진 계급"임을 추론할 수 있다. 따라서 Ⓑ 다음에는 Ⓐ가 나와야 한다. 이어서 Ⓓ에서 이러한 새로운 엘리트 계급에 대해 웰스가 언급한 저서가 소개되고, 그 저서에서 이 엘리트 계급을 어떻게 언급했는지 상술하고 있는 Ⓒ가 마지막으로 나오는 것이 적절하다.

H. G. Wells H. G. 웰스(1866년~1946년), 영국 출신의 소설가 wholeheartedly ad. 진심으로, 성실하게 when it comes to ~에 관한 한, ~에 관해서라면 government n. 정부; 행정, 통치 hammer home (요점·생각 등을 충분히 이해하도록) 강조하다 lot n. 운명 entrust v. 맡기다 self-selected a. 자기 스스로 선택한 caste n. 세습적인 계급 enlightened a. 깨우친, 계몽된, 개화된 technician n. 기술자 dictate n. 명령; 요구; 규칙 virtuous a. 도덕적인, 고결한 conspiracy n. 음모, 음모단 idealize v. 이상화하다 keystone n. (아치 꼭대기의) 쐐기돌[이맛돌]; (계획·주장의) 핵심 dominant a. 지배적인 passion n. 열정 directness n. 단순명쾌함 impatience n. 참을 수 없음 confusion n. 혼란 inefficiency n. 비효율 dedicated to ~에 전념하는, 헌신하는

H. G. 웰스(H. G. Wells)는 특정 과학 분야의 전문가는 아니었을지 모르지만, 특히 인간에 대한 합리적 통치에 관한 한, 과학이라는 개념을 진심으로 믿었다.
Ⓑ 소설이든 비소설이든 연이어 쓴 책에서, 웰스는 과학의 명령에 따라 통치할 계몽된 기술자들의 스스로 선별한 계급에 권력을 맡김으로써만 인류는 자신의 운명을 개선할 수 있다는 메시지를 강조했다.
Ⓐ 때때로 그는 이 고결한 엘리트를 신공화주의자, 사무라이, 공개된 음모단이라고 불렀다. 이는 웰스가 잠시 소속되었던 엘리트 사회주의자 집단인 페이비언 협회(Fabian Society)의 이상화된 버전으로 생각될 수 있다.
Ⓓ 그는 "내 책으로 들어가는 주요 아치문의 초석"이라 불렸던 1901년의 저서 『예측(Anticipations)』에서 처음으로 이 계급에 대해 설명했다.
Ⓒ 그는 "새로운 시대의 지배자들은 모두 단순함과 명쾌함에 대한 열정을 지녔으며 혼란과 비효율을 견디지 못하는 사실상의 예술가들일 것이며," "만물이 가리키는 미래의 세계 국가"를 건설하는 데 헌신할 것이라고 쓰고 있다.

14 글의 흐름상 적절하지 않은 문장 고르기 ③

글 전체의 핵심 개념은 맨 첫 문장에서 언급된 기후 소설이 "독자로 하여금 기후 위기와 감정적/정서적 연결을 맺도록 하는" 기능이다. 이하에서 이 개념이 계속 이어지면서 상술되고 있는 반면에, 기후 소설이라는 장르가 "기후 변화에 따른 다양한 잠재적 결과들을 보여준다"는 ③의 진술은 이러한 "감정적/정서적 연결"과는 무관한 내용이다.

resilience n. (충격·부상 등에서의) 회복력 cli-fi n. 기후 소설(기후 변화를 주요 소재로 삼는 문학의 한 장르, climate fiction) potentially ad. 잠재적으로 genre n. (예술 작품의) 장르 narrative n. (특히 소설 속 사건들에 대한) 묘사[기술, 이야기]

감정적 회복력을 구축해 주는 것 외에도, 기후 소설은 독자로 하여금 기후 위기와 감정적으로 연결을 맺도록 돕는데, 이것이 아마도 기후 소설의 가장 중요한 공로일 것이다. 연구에 따르면 미래의 자신과 감정적 연결이 부족할 때 사람들은 미래의 자신에게 도움이 될 현재의 행동을 취하지 못한다고 한다. 기후 변화의 영향을 몸소 겪고 있는 등장인물들과 연결됨으로써, 독자들은 잠재적으로 유사한 영향을 겪고 있는 미래의 자신과 연결되는 데 도움을 받게 된다. <그 장르는 각 작품마다 결과를 다르게 상상하기 때문에, 장르 전체는 기후 변화에 따른 다양한 잠재적 결과들을 보여

준다.> 이러한 방식으로, 과학 문헌과 비교할 때 기후 소설은 행동을 유도하는 데 더 효과적일 수 있다.

15 글의 주제 ②

"유럽 및 미국과 같은 산업화 국가들에서 가족 제도 자체가 근본적인 수술을 받기 시작하는 바로 그 순간, 사진은 일종의 가족 의례가 된다"는 문장이 이 글 전체의 요지를 담고 있는 주제문이다. 이 문장 앞에 나온 내용과 뒤따르는 내용들은 이 주제문을 뒷받침하는 세부 사항들이다. 따라서 '대가족에서 핵가족으로 가족 체계가 변한 결과를 반영하는 가족사진'이 이 글 전체의 주제이므로, 이를 잘 담고 있는 ②가 정답이다. 한편, ①은 '가족 체계의 급격한 변화'라는 핵심 소재는 잘 담고 있으나 이것을 '가족사진에 대한 수요 창출'로 연결하는 것은 본문의 내용과 거리가 멀다.

portrait n. 초상화 chronicle n. 연대기 portable a. 휴대용의, 휴대가 쉬운 kit n. (특정한 목적용 도구·장비) 세트 bear witness to ~을 증언하다 matter v. 중요하다 so long as ~하는 동안은, ~하는 한은 cherish v. 소중히 여기다, 간직하다 rite n. 의식[의례] institution n. 제도; 기관 radical a. 근본적[기본적]인, 철저한 surgery n. 수술 claustrophobic a. 밀실 공포증을 앓는[느끼게 하는] nuclear a. 핵의 carve v. 조각하다, 깎아서 만들다 aggregate a. 집합적인, 군체를 이루는 come along 생기다, 나타나다 memorialize v. 기념하다 restate v. 다시 말하다 imperil v. 위태롭게 하다, 위험에 빠뜨리다 vanish v. 사라지다 ghostly a. 귀신 같은 token a. 증거가 되는 presence n. 존재 relative n. 친척; 동족 disperse v. (이리저리) 흩어지다

사진을 통해 각 가족은 자신들의 초상화 연대기, 즉 가족의 연결성을 증언하는 휴대용 이미지 세트를 구성하게 된다. 사진을 찍고 그 사진을 소중히 간직하는 한, 어떤 활동을 촬영하는지는 거의 중요하지 않다. 유럽 및 미국과 같은 산업화 국가들에서 가족 제도 자체가 근본적인 수술을 받기 시작하는 바로 그 순간, 사진은 일종의 가족 의례가 된다. 밀실 공포증을 느끼게 할 정도의 단위인 핵가족이 훨씬 더 큰 대가족 집합체에서 깎여 나오고 있었을 때, 사진이 등장해 가족생활의 위태로운 연속성과 사라져가는 확장성을 기념하고 상징적으로 다시 표현하게 되었다. 그 대가족의 유령과 같은 흔적인 사진은 흩어져버린 친척들의 존재 증거를 제공한다. 가족사진 앨범은 일반적으로 대가족에 관한 것이며, 또한 종종 대가족과 관련해 남아 있는 전부이기도 하다.

다음 글의 주제로 가장 적합한 것을 고르시오.
① 가족 체계의 급격한 변화로 인해 가족사진에 대한 수요가 창출되었다.
② 사진은 대가족 생활에서 핵가족 생활로의 전환의 영향을 반영하였다.
③ 사진은 헤어져 버린 친척과 가족을 기억하는 데 유용했다.
④ 산업화된 국가에서 가족의 중요성이 커지는 것이 사진이 발전하게 된 한 가지 이유였다.

16 내용일치 ④

"거의 10년 전 가격 전쟁이 발발했고, 그들의 싸움은 계속되었다"는 내용에 비추어 ④는 잘못된 진술이다. 구체적으로, 지난 10년 동안 OPEC는 러시아까지 끌어들여 석유 가격을 지배하려 하였고, 이러한 전략에 맞서 미국 셰일업체들은 극단적인 생산 자제를 통해 궁핍한 살림으로부터 오다가 2023년 결국 "기록적인 셰일오일 생산량으로 역사상 어느

나라보다 더 많은 석유를 추출하였고, 가격을 떠받치기 위해 생산량을 줄이려는 OPEC+의 필사적인 노력을 상쇄해버렸다"고 하였다. ① 첫 단락에서 언급된 "아랍 왕자 대 셰일"이라는 표현이라든지 두 번째 단락에서 언급된 OPEC 관련 내용들에 비추어 볼 때 타당한 진술이다. ② 두 번째 단락에 나오는 "셰일업체들은 OPEC과 같은 자제심을 발휘했다", "수익성을 개선하라는 투자자들의 압력을 받아 시추 활동을 엄격히 통제했다" 등의 내용에 비추어 타당한 진술이다. ③ 세 번째 단락에서 "기록적인 셰일오일 생산량으로 인해 미국은 역사상 어느 나라보다 더 많은 석유를 추출했다"고 하였으므로 타당한 진술이다.

break out 발발하다 petrostate n. 산유국 fracker n. 셰일오일 회사 (fracking n. 셰일가스 및 셰일오일 시추 기술. 석유 자원 채취를 위해 혈암층(shale beds)에 고압으로 액체를 주입하는 것으로 수압파쇄를 통해 셰일가스나 석유를 추출하는 기술) drilling n. 시추 shale n. 셰일, 이판암(얇은 층으로 되어 있어 잘 벗겨지는 퇴적암) sheikh n. (아랍 국가의) 왕자[족장, 가장, 촌장] interim a. 중간의, 임시의, 과도 기간의 hardscrabble a. 궁핍한, 먹고 살기도 힘든 tussle n. 몸싸움, 드잡이 unfold v. 펼쳐지다; 밝혀지다 cartel n. 카르텔, 기업 연합 autocratic a. 독재의; 독재적인 mastermind n. (뛰어난 두뇌로 흔히 범죄가 관련되는 복잡한 일을 계획하고) 지휘[조종]하는 사람 regime n. 정권 douse v. (무엇에 액체를 흠뻑) 붓다, 적시다 self-restraint n. 자제력 rein n. 고삐; 통솔력 crude n. 원유 barrel n. 한 통의 양, 배럴(석유 단위로 120~159리터) discipline n. 규율 slumber n. 잠 extract v. (화학적 과정 등을 거쳐) 뽑다, 추출하다 offset v. 상쇄하다 curtail v. 축소시키다 prop up 지원하다, 받쳐주다 hemisphere n. 반구 maximize v. 극대화하다 restrain v. 자제하다, 억제하다; 제지하다 pump v. 퍼올리다 unprecedented a. 전례 없는 intimately ad. 친밀하게

거의 10년 전, 페르시아 만의 산유국들과 혁신적인 시추 기술로 셰일 혁명을 일으킨 미국의 셰일오일 회사들 간의 가격 전쟁이 발발했다. 일부 사람들은 이 새로운 석유 경제를 "아랍 왕자 대 셰일"이라고 부르기까지 했다. 비록 그들의 싸움이 이상한 방식으로 전개되기는 했지만, 대부분의 과도기 동안 산유국들과 궁핍한 셰일 생산업체들은 이 새로운 석유 질서에 여전히 중요했다. 2016년 산유국 카르텔인 석유수출국기구(OPEC)는 러시아와 힘을 합쳐 OPEC+를 창설했고, OPEC+의 독재자들은 OPEC를 통해 자신들의 정권에 유리하도록 유가를 통제할 수 있기를 바랐다. 그러나 세계를 석유로 뒤덮는 방식으로 대응하는 대신, 셰일업체들은 뜻밖에도 OPEC과 같은 자제심을 발휘했다. 수익성을 개선하라는 투자자들의 압력을 받았던 그들은 원유 가격이 배럴당 100달러를 넘었을 때에도 시추 활동을 엄격히 통제했다.

이러한 이상한 규율은 미국 생산자들이 잠에서 깨어난 2023년까지 계속되었다. 기록적인 셰일오일 생산량으로 인해 미국은 역사상 어느 나라보다 더 많은 석유를 추출할 수 있었고, 가격을 떠받치기 위해 생산량을 줄이려는 OPEC+의 필사적인 노력을 상쇄해버렸다. 일부 전문가들은 이를 "거대한 재균형", 즉 걸프 만에서 서반구로 옮겨간 석유 생산의 역사적 이동이라고 부른다.

다음 글의 내용과 가장 거리가 먼 것을 고르시오.
① 오랫동안 페르시아 만의 산유국들은 석유 시장에 상당한 영향력을 행사해 왔다.
② 2023년 이전 몇 년 동안 셰일업체들은 생산을 억제하여 이익을 극대화하려고 노력했다.
③ 미국의 셰일업체들은 2023년에 전례 없는 양의 석유를 시추했다.
④ 지난 10년 동안 석유 시장의 핵심 주축들은 석유 생산을 긴밀하게 조정해 왔다.

17-18

플로리다 대학 교수인 제리 울스만(Jerry Uelsmann)은 강의 첫날에, 영화 사진 전공 학생들을 두 그룹으로 나누었다. 그는 교실 왼편에 있는 사람들은 모두 "수량" 그룹에 속할 것이라고 설명했다. 그들은 오로지 자신이 제작한 작품의 양에 따라 성적이 매겨질 것이다. 강의 마지막 날, 그는 학생들이 제출한 사진의 숫자를 집계할 것이다. 100장의 사진은 A등급, 90장은 B등급, 80장은 C등급 등으로 평가될 것이다. 한편, 교실 오른편에 있는 사람들은 모두 "품질" 그룹에 속하게 될 것이다. 그들은 오로지 그들 작품의 우수성에 의해서만 평가될 것이다. 그들은 학기 중에 오직 사진 한 장만 찍으면 되지만, A를 받으려면 거의 완벽한 이미지여야 했다. 학기 말, 그는 최고의 사진이 모두 수량 그룹에서 제작되었다는 사실을 알고 놀랐다. 학기 중에 이 학생들은 사진을 찍고, 구도와 조명을 실험하고, 암실에서 다양한 방법을 테스트하고, 실수로부터 배우기 바빴다. 수백 장의 사진을 만드는 과정에서 그들은 기술을 연마했다. 한편, 품질 그룹은 둘러앉아 완벽함에 대해 숙고했다. 결국 검증되지 않은 이론들과 보통 수준의 사진 한 장 외에는 그들의 노력을 뽐낼 만한 것이 거의 없었다. 변화를 위한 최적의 계획, 즉 가장 빠른 체중 감량 방법, 근육 강화를 위한 최고의 프로그램, 부업을 위한 완벽한 아이디어 등을 찾으려고 애쓰다가는 수렁에 빠지기 쉽다. 우리는 최고의 접근 방식을 찾는 데 너무 집중한 나머지 행동에 옮길 시간을 내지 못하고 만다. 볼테르는 일찍이 "최선(最善)은 선(善)의 적이다."라고 썼다.

grade v. 성적[학점]을 매기다 tally v. 기록하다; 총계를 내다 submit v. 제출하다 rate v. 평가하다 meanwhile ad. 한편 semester n. 학기 composition n. (그림·사진의) 구도 lighting n. 조명 darkroom n. (사진 현상·인화용) 암실 hone v. (특히 기술을) 연마하다 speculate v. 추측하다; 사색[숙고]하다 show off 으스대다, 자랑하다 unverified a. 증명되지 않은 mediocre a. 보통밖에 안 되는, 썩 좋지는 않은 bog down 교착 상태에 빠지다, 꼼짝 못하게 하다; 수렁에 빠지다 optimal a. 최적의 side hustle (본업 외에 추가적인 수입을 얻는) 부업 get round to ~을 할 시간[짬]을 내다

17 빈칸완성 ②

강의 마지막 날 교수는 "놀랐다"고 하였다. 놀랍지 않은 일반적인 예상은 최고 품질의 작품이 "품질" 그룹에서 나오는 것일 것이므로 놀라운 실제 결과는 "수량" 그룹에서 나왔다고 추론할 수 있다. 또한 빈칸 Ⓐ 다음에 나와 있는 내용들도 모두 "수량" 그룹에서 했을 만한 작업을 상술하고 있으므로 빈칸에는 "수량(quantity)"이 들어가는 것이 적절함을 알 수 있다. 이와 대조적으로 빈칸 Ⓑ 다음에는 완벽주의에 빠진 나머지 오히려 시원찮은 작품만 제출한 다른 그룹에 대한 내용이 나오고 있으므로 빈칸 Ⓑ에는 "품질(quality)"이 들어가야 함을 추론할 수 있다.

18 빈칸완성 ①

'기술을 습득하기 위해서는 최고, 최선만 고집하는 완벽주의의 함정에 빠지지 말고, 시행착오를 통해 배워라'가 글 전체의 요지이다. 세 번째 단락은 이러한 요지가 포함된 단락이고, 볼테르는 '완벽주의의 위험을 경고'하는 조언을 하였으리라고 추론할 수 있다.

① 최선(最善)은 선(善)의 적이다.
② 상식은 그다지 흔하지 않다.

③ 대답보다는 질문으로 사람을 판단하라.
④ 낙관주의는 우리가 비참할 때조차 모든 것이 괜찮다고 주장하는 일종의 광증(狂症)이다.

19-20

산소가 없고 메탄 농도는 높은 환경으로 인해, 지구 역사의 대부분 동안, 지구는 동물에게 환영받을 만한 장소는 아니었을 것이다. 우리가 알고 있는 최초의 생명체는 자신의 존재에 대한 신호를 약 37억 년 된 암석에 남긴 미세한 유기체(미생물)였다.

Ⓐ 시아노박테리아가 진화했을 때 그들은 놀라운 변화를 위한 발판을 마련했다. 그들은 지구 최초의 광합성자가 되어 물과 태양 에너지를 사용해 먹이를 만들고 그 결과 산소를 방출했다. 이는 산소의 갑작스럽고 급격한 증가를 촉발하여, 산소를 용납할 수 없는 다른 미생물에게는 환경이 살기 힘든 환경으로 되었다.

Ⓑ 미생물이 다른 미생물 내부에 살면서 그들을 위한 세포 소기관으로 기능하기 시작하면서 혁명적인 일이 일어났다. 먹이를 에너지로 처리하는 세포 소기관인 미토콘드리아는 이러한 상호 이익이 되는 관계로부터 진화했다. 그리고 처음으로 DNA가 핵 안에 담겼다. 이처럼 새로운 복합 세포는 전체 세포를 지탱하는 전문화된 역할을 수행하는 전문화된 부분들을 뽐냈다.

Ⓒ 이러한 전문화되고 협력하는 세포들의 덩어리는 결국 최초의 동물이 되었다. 해면동물은 이러한 최초의 동물 중 하나였다. 약 5억 8000만 년 전(에디아카라기)에는 해면동물들 외에 다른 생물들도 번성했다. 그러나 약 5억 4100만 년 전에 에디아카라기 생물의 대부분이 사라졌다.

Ⓓ 캄브리아기는 새로운 생명체가 폭발적으로 증가하는 시대였다. 또한 먹이를 뒤쫓기 위한 방향 이동을 위해 뚜렷한 머리와 꼬리를 갖춘, 보다 활동적인 동물들에게 변화가 나타났다.

그러나, 앞으로 일어날 모든 변화에도 불구하고 캄브리아기 말에는 거의 모든 기존 동물 유형이나 종족들이 확립되었다.

devoid of ~이 없는 microscopic a. 미세한, 현미경으로 봐야만 보이는 microbe n. 미생물 cyanobacteria n. 시아노박테리아, 청록색 세균 photosynthesize v. 광합성하다 catalyze v. (화학 반응을) 촉진시키다 hospitable a. 환대하는; 쾌적한 organelle n. 세포 소기관(小器官) mitochondria n. 미토콘드리아(진핵(眞核)생물의 세포질 속에 있는 호흡을 관장하는 소기관, 독자적인 DNA를 가지고 있음) package v. 포장하다 nucleus n. 세포핵(pl. nuclei) boast v. 자랑하다 cluster n. 무리, 다발 sponge n. 해면동물 Ediacaran a. (지질학 연대 중) 에디아카라기의 proliferation n. 급증, 확산 Cambrian a. 캄브리아기의, 캄브리아기 지층의 witness v. 목격하다 directional a. 방향의; 지향(성)의 define v. 윤곽[경계]을 분명히 정하다 chase v. 뒤쫓다, 추적하다 phylon n. 종족, 족(族)(pl. phyla) oxidation n. 산화(酸化)(a process in which a chemical substance changes because of the addition of oxygen) non-avian a. 조류가 아닌 multicellular a. 다세포의

---

19 단락배열 ①

주어진 첫 단락에서는 37억 년 전 지구상 최초의 생명체인 작은 미생물의 등장이 소개되고 있다. 이어서 Ⓐ 시아노박테리아의 출현으로 인한 지구 환경의 급격한 변화(산소의 급격한 증가. 그로 인해 다른 미생물 생존에 불리한 환경 조성됨) → Ⓑ (산소에 직접 노출되기보다는) 미생물이 다른 미생물 내부에 살기 시작함. 그 결과 세포 소기관이 생겨나고 DNA

가 핵 안에 담기는 등 전문화된 부분 세포를 가진 복합 세포가 최초로 등장함. → Ⓒ 이러한 전문화된 세포들의 덩어리는 최초의 동물(해면동물)로 진화하고 번성하다가 멸종함(에디아카라기) → Ⓓ 새로운 생물들이 폭발적으로 증가하고 보다 활동적인 동물 종들의 출현(캄브리아기)의 순서로 다루어지는 것이 자연스럽다. 아울러, 이러한 연결은 캄브리아기 말에 기존 동물 유형과 종족이 거의 결정되었다고 하는 마지막 단락과도 가장 잘 어울린다.

---

20 부분이해 ②

밑줄 친 부분은 "앞으로 일어날 모든 변화"라는 의미이므로 캄브리아기 말 '이후에' 일어날 변화를 가리킨다. 따라서 캄브리아기 말 '이전에' 일어난 일들을 선택지에서 걸러내고 남는 선택지들을 취합하는 이른바 '소거법'으로 접근할 필요가 있다. 산화는 '산소가 더해짐으로써 나타나는 화학적 변화'를 가리키므로 지구상에 산소가 대규모로 생성된 이후에 나타난 현상임을 추론할 수 있다. 따라서, (a) '대규모의 산화 사건'은 "산소의 갑작스럽고 급격한 증가"를 다룬 Ⓐ 단락에서 이미 언급된 것이니만큼, '캄브리아기 이전에 있었던 사건'에 해당한다. 또한, (d) '다세포 생물의 출현'에 관한 내용은 세포 소기관 및 복합 세포의 등장에 관해 언급하고 있는 Ⓑ 단락에서 이미 언급된 내용으로 이것 역시 '캄브리아기 이전에 있었던 사건'에 해당한다. (b) '비조류성 공룡의 멸종', (c) '네안데르탈인의 소멸'은 이 글에서는 언급된 적이 없는 내용이지만 고생물학적인 관점에서 볼 때 타당한 내용이다. 따라서 (a), (d)를 배제한 ②가 정답이다.

밑줄 친 내용에 해당하는 두 가지를 고르시오.
(a) 대 산화(酸化) 사건
(b) 비조류성 공룡의 멸종
(c) 네안데르탈인의 소멸
(d) 다세포생물의 출현

21-22

양자 컴퓨팅, 네트워킹, 감지 및 계측을 포함하는 양자 정보 과학기술은 물질의 기본 속성을 활용하여 새로운 정보 기술을 생성한다. 예를 들어, 양자 컴퓨터는 이론상으로 원자와 광자의 고유한 특성을 이용하여 기존 컴퓨터보다 기하급수적으로 더 빨리 특정 유형의 문제를 해결할 수 있다. 수십 년에 걸쳐 자연의 양자적 측면을 활용함에 따라 대단히 중요한 기술들이 생겨났다.

양자 정보 과학기술은 민간 및 군사적 용도에 모두 새로운 기능을 제공할 것이다. 양자 관련 기술의 이전 사례들로서는 반도체 초소형 전자공학, 포토닉스, 위성 위치 확인 시스템, 자기 공명 영상 등이 있다. 미래의 양자 분야 과학기술 발견들은 이보다 훨씬 더 큰 영향을 미칠 것이다.

잠재적인 이점들 외에도, 양자 기술은 국가 안보 문제를 제기할 수 있다. 향후 몇 년 동안 더욱 발전하면, 대규모의 양자 컴퓨터는 가장 흔히 사용되는 사이버 보안 프로토콜들의 암호를 해독해 오늘날의 경제 및 국가 안보 통신을 방어하는 공공 기반 시설들을 위험에 빠뜨릴 수 있을 것이다. 간단히 말해서, 양자 컴퓨팅 패권 경쟁에서 누가 승리하든, 상대방의 통신을 훼손시킬 잠재력을 갖게 될 것이다. 이를 효과적으로 완화시키지 못한다면, 양자 컴퓨터의 적대적 사용은 한 국가의 안보 체계 및 국가 전체에 엄청난 충격을 가져올 수 있다.

quantum n. 양자(量子)(the smallest amount of many forms of energy such as light) sensing n. (열·빛·연기 따위의) 감지(感知) metrology n. 계량학, 측량학 leverage v. ~에게 영향을 주다; ~을 활용하다 property n. 속성 in principle 이론상으로; 원칙적으로 atom n. 원자 photon n. 광자 exponentially ad. 기하급수적으로 harness v. 이용[활용]하다 critical a. 대단히 중요한[중대한] civilian a. 일반의, 민간의 military a. 군사의 prior a. (시간·순서가) 이전의, 선행하는 semiconductor n. 반도체 microelectronics n. 마이크로일렉트로닉스, 초소형 전자 공학[기술] photonics n. 포토닉스(빛을 사용한 정보 전달을 다루는 연구 분야) magnetic resonance 자기 공명 impactful a. 영향력이 강한, 인상이 강렬한 aside from ~외에도[뿐만 아니라] pose v. (위협·문제 등을) 제기하다 decryption n. (암호의) 해독 protocol n. 프로토콜, 통신 규약 infrastructure n. 사회[공공] 기반 시설 supremacy n. 패권, 우위 compromise v. ~을 위태롭게 하다 mitigation n. 완화, 경감 서로 adversarial a. 대립 관계에 있는, 적대적인 devastating a. 대단히 파괴적인, 엄청난 손상을 가하는; 엄청나게 충격적인 shattering a. 엄청나게 충격적인 susceptible a. 민감한; ~에 걸리기 쉬운 vulnerable a. 취약한, 연약한 appealing a. 매력적인; 호소하는 conducive to ~에 도움이 되는 adversary n. 상대방[적수] breach n. 위반; 파괴

---

21 동의어   ①

devastating은 '대단히 파괴적인', '엄청나게 충격적인'이라는 뜻을 가지고 있는데, 본문에서는 '엄청나게 충격적인'의 의미로 해석된다. 따라서 가장 유사한 의미를 지닌 단어는 shattering이다.

---

22 내용추론   ④

두 번째 단락에서 "양자 정보 과학기술은 민간 및 군사적 용도에 모두 새로운 기능을 제공할 것이다"고 하였으므로 ④는 잘못된 추론이다. ① 두 번째 단락에서 "양자 관련 기술의 이전 사례들로서는 반도체 초소형 전자공학, 포토닉스, 위성 위치 확인 시스템, 자기 공명 영상 등이 있다"고 하였는데, 이 중에서 위성 위치 확인 시스템은 자동차 산업의 혁신에 해당하고, 자기 공명 영상 기술은 의료 산업의 혁신과 관련 있는 내용으로 볼 수 있으므로, 타당한 추론이다. ② 세 번째 단락에서 "양자 컴퓨팅 패권 경쟁에서 누가 승리하든 상대방의 통신을 훼손시킬 수 있다"고 하였으므로 타당한 추론이다. ③ 첫 단락에서 "양자 컴퓨터는 기존 컴퓨터보다 기하급수적으로 더 빨리 특정 유형의 문제를 해결할 수 있다"고 하였으므로 타당한 진술이다.

위 글을 읽고 유추하기 가장 어려운 것을 고르시오.
① 양자 관련 기술은 의료 및 자동차 산업의 일부 혁신에 도움이 되었다.
② 양자 기술이 적대국보다 뒤처지는 국가는 국가 안보에 구멍이 뚫릴 수 있다.
③ 양자 컴퓨터는 기존 컴퓨터보다 성능이 뛰어나다고 단언할 수 있다.
④ 양자 정보 과학기술은 민간 이용이 금지되어 있다.

23-24

미국이 원자폭탄을 히로시마와 나가사키에 투하한 뒤 며칠 동안, 일본 대중에게 방사선은 대체로 하나의 수수께끼였다. 사람들은 폭발을 겪고도

살아남았지만 새로운 질병에 굴복하고 있었는데, 그것은 어떤 일본 국내 신문의 표현처럼 "악령"이었다.

9년 뒤, 일본은 원자력 기술과 또 한 번 맞닥뜨렸다. 1954년 3월 1일 미국은 태평양의 비키니 환초에서 세계에서 가장 강력한 수소폭탄을 실험했다. 폭발 규모는 엔지니어들이 예상한 것보다 두 배 이상 컸으며, 방사능재의 소나기가 멀리까지 날아가 항해 중이던 일본의 참치잡이 어선 제5후쿠류마루(第五福龍丸, Lucky Dragon No. 5)호를 뒤덮었다. 23명의 선원들은 자기들을 뒤덮은 것이 무엇인지 전혀 알 수 없었다. 나중에 한 선원은 "조금 핥아먹어 봤다. 모래알 씹는 것 같았고, 아무런 맛도 나지 않았다"고 썼다. 그러나 해안으로 돌아왔을 때, 그들은 화상을 입고 물집이 생겼으며, 급성 방사선 질환의 초기 단계에 접어든 상태였다. 그들의 오염된 참치들은 누군가 판매를 중단하기 전까지, 시장에서 팔려나갔다.

이 시련은 일본에 극심한 공포를 불러왔다. 미래의 수소폭탄 실험에 반대하는 청원서는 일본의 모든 시민 세 명 중 한 명꼴로 서명을 확보했다. 이 사건은 일본의 "원자력 알레르기"로 알려진 현상의 시작이었다. 그로부터 1년도 채 지나지 않아 일본의 영화제작자들은 미국의 핵무기로 인해 돌연변이가 일어난 생물에 관한 영화 『고질라(Godzilla)』를 개봉했다. 영화 제작자인 타나카 도모유키(Tomoyuki Tanaka)는 자신의 괴물에 관해 "인류가 원자폭탄을 만들었고," "이제 자연이 복수할 때가 되었다"고 말했다. 고질라가 숨 쉴 때 방사능이 나온다는 설정, 그리고 저렴한 특수효과들로 인해 해외에서는 우스꽝스럽게 여겨졌지만, 침묵 속에서 영화를 관람하고 눈물을 흘리며 극장을 나서는 일본인들에게는 그렇지 않았다.

radiation n. 방사선 succumb v. 굴복하다, 무릎을 꿇다 encounter n. 만남[접촉, 조우] atoll n. 환상(環狀) 산호도(가운데 해수 호수가 있는 고리 모양의 산호섬) Bikini Atoll 비키니 환초(環礁)(북태평양 Marshall 제도에 있으며, 1946년 원폭 실험 장소) hydrogen n. 수소 blast n. 폭발 radioactive a. 방사능의 envelop v. 감싸다, 뒤덮다 voyage v. 항해하다 dust v. (고운 가루를) 뿌리다 lick v. 핥아먹다 gritty a. 모래가 든, 모래 같은 blister v. 물집이 생기다 acute a. 급성의 ordeal n. 시련 panic n. 극심한 공포, 공황 petition n. 청원(서) secure v. 얻어내다, 확보하다 signature n. 서명 allergy n. 알레르기 mutate v. 돌연변이를 만들다 revenge n. 복수, 보복 low-budget a. 저예산의 campy a. 연극적인, 과장된 몸짓을 하는, 우스꽝스러운 infatuation n. (사랑의) 열병 addiction n. 중독 worship n. 예배, 숭배 engulf v. 완전히 뒤덮다, 감싸다 disapproval n. 반감, 못마땅함

---

23 빈칸완성   ③

세 번째 단락에서 참치잡이 어선 제5 후쿠류마루호 사건은 "일본에 극심한 공포를 불러왔다"고 하였고, "수소폭탄을 반대하는 청원에 일본의 모든 시민 세 명 중 한 명꼴로 서명했다"고 하였으므로 핵(원자력) 기술에 대한 일본인들의 태도는 "질색, 혐오, 반감"이었으리라고 추론할 수 있다. allergy는 '알레르기' 즉, '음식, 꽃가루, 먼지 등 신체가 과민하게 반응하는 일종의 손상된 면역 반응'을 가리키지만 비유적으로 '질색, 반감, 혐오(antipathy, a strong dislike)'를 뜻한다.

---

24 내용일치   ③

"해외에서는 우스꽝스럽게 여겨졌지만, 침묵 속에서 영화를 관람하고 눈물을 흘리며 극장을 나서는 일본인들에게는 그렇지 않았다"고 하였으므로 ③이 잘못된 진술이다. ① "저렴한 특수효과들로 인해 해외에서는

우스꽝스럽게 여겨졌다"고 하였으므로 본문의 내용과 일치한다. ② "자기들을 뒤덮은 것이 무엇인지 전혀 알 수 없었고," "해안으로 돌아왔을 때 급성 방사선 질환의 초기 단계에 접어든 상태였다"고 하였으므로 본문의 내용과 일치한다. ④ 첫 단락에서 "일본 대중에게 대체로 방사선은 하나의 수수께끼였다"고 하였고, 일본 국내 신문에서조차 방사선 피폭에 의한 질환을 "유령"으로 불렀다는 점에서 원자폭탄 투하 직후에는 방사선에 대한 이해가 일본 사회 전반적으로 부족했었다고 볼 수 있고, 이러한 인식이 바뀌게 된 결정적 계기가 그로부터 9년 뒤에 있었던 제5 후쿠류마루호 사건이므로 타당한 진술이라고 볼 수 있다.

위 글의 내용과 가장 거리가 먼 것을 고르시오.
① 일본 영화 『고질라(Godzilla)』는 부분적으로 수준 이하의 특수효과로 인해 해외 관객들로부터 호평을 받지 못했다.
② 제5 후쿠류마루호의 선원들은 자신들을 뒤덮은 물질의 성질을 나중에서야 깨달았다.
③ 일본 관객들은 영화 『고질라(Godzilla)』의 정치적 메시지에 대해 침묵으로 반감을 표시했다.
④ 히로시마와 나가사키의 원자폭탄 이후, 일본인들이 방사선의 본질을 인식하기까지는 몇 년이 걸렸다.

25-26

의식이 멀리 세상을 바라보며 상황을 선형적, 언어적으로 분석하는 단상 위의 장군과 같다면 무의식은 백만 명의 작은 정찰병들과 같다. 이 정찰병들은 풍경을 가로지르며 지속적인 신호의 흐름을 보내고, 즉각적인 응답을 생성한다. 그들은 주변 환경과 거리를 유지하지 않는다. 그들은 환경 속에 잠겨 있다. 그들은 분주히 이리저리 움직이면서 다른 사람의 마음, 풍경, 그리고 생각 속으로 침투한다. 이 정찰병들은 사물을 정서적 중요성으로 덧입힌다. 그들은 오랜 친구와 우연히 마주쳤을 때 밀려드는 사랑을 느끼게 한다. 어두운 동굴로 내려갈 때 두려움이 솟구치게 만든다. 아름다운 풍경을 보았을 때 숭고한 고양감을 자아낸다. 뛰어난 통찰력과 마주쳤을 때는 기쁨이 솟아나는 반면, 불공정함과 마주쳤을 때는 의로운 분노를 일으킨다. 각각의 지각 작용에는 고유한 풍미와 질감 그리고 힘이 있으며 감각과 충동, 판단과 욕망의 흐름을 따라 반응들이 우리의 마음 주변을 휘감으며 돌아간다. 이러한 신호들이 우리의 삶을 지배하지는 않지만, 세상에 대한 우리의 해석을 형성하고 우리가 인생행로를 정할 때 정신적인 GPS처럼 우리를 안내한다. 장군이 데이터로 생각하고 산문으로 말한다면 정찰병들은 감정으로 구체화되며 그들의 활동은 이야기, 시, 음악, 이미지, 기도 그리고 신화 속에서 가장 잘 표현된다.

atop prep. 꼭대기에, 맨 위에 linearly ad. 선형적으로 scout n. 정찰병, 척후병 career v. 달리다 immerse v. 담그다 scurry v. 종종걸음을 치다 interpenetrate v. 완전히 퍼지다, 서로 침투하다 come across ~을 우연히 발견하다 surge n. 급증, 급등 affection n. 애정 descend v. 내려가다 sublime a. 숭고한 elevation n. 고결, 고상 righteous a. (도덕적으로) 옳은 perception n. 지각, 자각; 인식 flavor n. 풍미 texture n. 질감, 감촉 loop v. 고리 모양으로 움직이다 stream n. 연속, 이어짐 sensation n. 감각 impulse n. 충동 chart v. (특정한 결과를 내기 위한 절차를 담은) 계획을 세우다 chart a course (배 등이) 진로를 계획하다[정하다] prose n. 산문 crystallize v. 구체화하다 conception n. (계획 등의) 구상; 이해, 신념; (난소의) 수정 figure v. 계산하다; 생각하다 reception n. 환영; 환영 연회 flip v. 툭 던지다; 탁 누르다 inception n. (단체·기관 등의) 시작[개시] exceptional a. 이례적일 정도로 우수한, 특출한

25 빈칸완성 ①

Ⓐ 어떤 일들이 주변에서 벌어지고 있음을 감각을 통해 받아들이고, 감정을 일으키며, 판단과 욕망의 흐름을 좇는 무의식적 반응에 대해 언급하고 있으므로 빈칸에는 '지각, 자각; 인식'을 뜻하는 perception이 들어가는 것이 적절하다. 한편, conception은 '구상(the process of forming an idea)'이라는 뜻이므로 적절치 않다. Ⓑ 문맥상 '진로를 정하다'는 뜻이 들어가는 것이 적절하므로 빈칸에는 chart, plan이 들어갈 수 있다. chart는 원래 '지도를 만들다', '기록하다'는 뜻을 가지지만 route, course 등을 목적어로 취하여 '(특정한 결과를 내기 위한 절차를 담은) 계획을 세우다'는 뜻을 가진다.

26 내용일치 ②

필자는 의식을 "단상 위의 장군"에, 무의식을 "백만 명의 작은 정찰병들"에 비유하면서 의식이 분석하고 판단하지만, 무의식은 감정을 통해 그러한 분석과 판단의 전제가 될만한 "정신적인 GPS" 역할을 한다고 하였다. 따라서 글 전체의 취지에 비추어 볼 때 의식과 무의식 간의 우열을 함부로 판단하는 것은 위험하며, 그러한 우열 판단의 근거가 될만한 구체적인 진술도 전혀 나와 있지 않다. 또한, 무의식이 주는 "신호들이 우리의 삶을 지배하지는 않는다"고 분명히 말하고 있으므로 ②는 분명히 잘못된 진술이다. ① "정찰병들(무의식)은 뛰어난 통찰력과 마주쳤을 때 기쁨이 솟아나게 한다"고 하였으므로 본문의 내용과 일치한다. ③ 무의식이라는 "정찰병들은 감정으로 구체화된다"고 하였으므로 타당한 진술이다. ④ "그들의 활동은 이야기, 시, 음악, 이미지, 기도 그리고 신화 속에서 가장 잘 표현된다"고 하였으므로 타당한 진술이다.

위 글의 내용과 가장 거리가 먼 것을 고르시오.
① 우리가 비범한 통찰력과 마주쳤을 때 우리를 기쁘게 하는 것은 우리의 무의식이다.
② 의식은 무의식에 비해 열등하며 무의식이 우리의 삶을 지배한다.
③ 무의식은 주로 우리의 반응을 감정으로 물들인다.
④ 무의식의 작용은 이야기와 그림으로 가장 잘 전달된다.

27-28

기업이 유연한 재택근무(WFH) 제도를 허용해야 하는지 아니면 직원들의 사무실 복귀를 의무화해야 하는지에 관한 논쟁에서 미국 근로자들의 의견은 계속 나뉜다.
그러나 한국의 사무실 임대 시장의 호황은, 적어도 미국 상업용 부동산 부문의 불황을 지켜보는 사람들에게는, 사무실 복귀가 더 낫다는 주장을 <약화시킬> 수 있다. 사무직 직원들의 사무실 복귀로 인해 서울의 A등급 사무실 98% 이상이 입주 상태이다. 블룸버그의 보도에 따르면 사무실 공간을 임대하려는 경쟁이 심화하면서 지난해 임대 가격이 약 15% 상승했다. 코로나19 제한이 완화되면서 재택근무를 허용하는 일자리의 수는 줄어들고 있다.
한국 사무실 임대 시장의 높은 수요에 더해, 정부의 재개발 규제와 코로나19로 인한 공사 차질로 인해 2021년부터 전반적으로 사무실 공간이 부족했다. 한국 경제도 꾸준히 성장함에 따라 국제 및 국내 투자 모두 강화되고 있다.
그러나 미국의 업무 지구들은 재택근무의 인기가 높아지고 많은 직원들이 주 5일 통근을 재개하는 것을 꺼리기 때문에 어려움을 겪고 있다. 골드만

삭스는 적어도 일주일 중 일부를 집에서 일하는 미국 근로자의 비율이 올해 약 20%~25%로 안정되었는데 이는 절정을 이루었던 팬데믹 당시의 47%보다는 낮지만, 팬데믹 이전 평균인 2.6%보다 높다는 것을 발견했다. 『포브스』지에 따르면 현재 직원 중 약 30%가 혼성 업무 모델을 활용 중이다. CBRE 조사에 따르면 상업용 건물주들은 새로운 원격 근무 문화 속에서 임차인들이 공간을 줄이거나 완전히 이사해 나가는 것을 목격하고 있으며, 2분기 미국의 사무실 공실률은 18.2%로 30년 만에 최고치를 기록했다고 한다.

arrangement n. 방식; 협의 versus prep. (소송·스포츠 경기 등에서) ~대(對) mandate v. 명령하다 workforce n. (한 국가·지역 내의) 노동 인구[노동력] booming a. 급속히 발전하는 undermine v. 약화시키다 head back to ~로 다시 향하다 struggling a. 발버둥이 치는; 기를 쓰는, 분투하는 argument n. 논거, 주장 real estate 부동산 white-collar a. 화이트칼라의, 사무직의 bolster v. 북돋우다, 강화하다 domestic a. 국내의 district n. 지구, 구역 reluctance n. 싫음, 마지못해 함, 꺼림, 마음 내키지 않음 commute v. 통근하다 stabilize v. 안정되다 hybrid n. 잡종, 혼성체 landlord n. 임대주, 임대 회사 tenant n. 세입자, 임차인 amid prep. ~가운데, ~중에 vacancy n. 빈 방, 공실 quarter n. 분기 incentivize v. 장려하다 convert v. 전환하다, 바꾸다 alleviate v. 완화하다 in-person a. 생생한, 직접의

---

27 문맥상 적절하지 않은 표현 고르기   ①

"미국 상업용 부동산 부문의 불황을 지켜보는 사람들"은 결국 미국의 사무실 임대 시장이 활성화되어 사무실 공실률이 낮아지는 것을 기대하는 사람들이다. 그러기 위해서는 지금보다 재택근무 비율을 줄이고, 사무실로 출퇴근하는 비율을 높여야 하는 것이므로, 한국 오피스 임대 시장의 호황은 '미국 근로자들의 사무실 복귀를 늘리자'는 주장의 논거, 즉 주장을 '뒷받침할 만한' 사례가 될 것이다. 따라서 ① undermine을 bolster 즉 '북돋우다, 강화하다'로 대체하는 것이 적절하다.

---

28 뒷내용 추론   ①

사무실 공실률이 높을수록 임대 회사들의 어려움이 커질 것이고, 이것이 부동산 시장 전반에 가져올 부정적 영향을 사전에 차단하기 위해 정부가 나설 것이라고 추론할 수 있다. 만약 애초에 사무실 용도로 지어진 공실(빈방)들을 사무실 용도가 아닌 주거용 목적의 아파트로 용도 전환하는 것을 정부가 정책적으로 허용한다면 부동산 업자(건물주, 임대 회사)들로서는 큰 도움이 될 것이다. 따라서 이 글 다음에 나올 내용으로 적절하다. ② "근로자들에게 더 많은 유연성을 제공한다"는 것은 사무실 출근과 재택근무를 근로자들이 자율적으로 결정하도록 한다는 것이다. 그러나 네 번째 단락의 내용에 따르면 미국 근로자들은 재택근무를 선호하므로, 만약 그렇게 한다면 사무실 공실률이 개선되기는커녕 오히려 악화할 것이므로 사무실 임대 시장의 불황을 부추길 뿐이다. 이러한 모순된 정책이 이 글 다음에 소개될 가능성은 거의 없다. ③ 근로자들이 재택근무와 출근(사무실) 근무를 선호하는 정도의 차이를 세대별로 비교하는 내용은 네 번째 단락에서 전혀 언급되지 않았으므로, 관련 내용이 바로 뒤에 다루어지는 것은 문맥상 적절하지 않다. ④ 네 번째 단락에 의하면 미국 사무실의 공실률이 높아지는 이유는 "새로운 원격 근무 문화 속에서 임차인들이 공간을 줄이거나 완전히 이사해 나가고" 있기 때문

이다. 다시 말해, 기업들이 사무공간을 비우고 나가는 이유가 기존의 사무공간이 좁아서는 아닌 것이다. 따라서 "사무공간을 더 널찍하게 만들어서 기업들을 유인한다"는 내용이 이 글 바로 다음에 다루어질 개연성은 거의 없다고 봐야 한다.

위 글에 이어질 내용으로 가장 적절한 것을 고르시오.
① 바이든 행정부는 최근 미국 사무실 임대 시장 위기의 완화에 도움이 되도록 개발업자들이 공실을 아파트로 전환하도록 장려하는 계획을 발표했다.
② 바이든 행정부는 최근 기업들이 미국 사무실 임대 시장 활성화를 위해 근로자들에게 더 많은 유연성을 제공하도록 장려했다.
③ 설문조사에 따르면 Z세대와 2023년 졸업생은 출근 근무를 원하는 것으로 나타났다.
④ 미국 상업용 건물주들은 비어 있는 사무공간을 찾는 미국 기업들을 유인하기 위해 더 널찍한 사무공간을 개발해야 한다.

29-30

Ⓒ 지금 세계 어느 곳이든 경제는 어려움을 겪고 있다. 지정학적 긴장, 높아지는 물가 상승률과 금리 그리고 다양한 외부 요인들이 전 세계 기업들에 계속 영향을 미치고 있다.
Ⓓ 예를 들어, 영국은 2008년 금융 위기 이후 최고 수준의 금리에 막 도달했다. 이 뉴스는 오늘날 기업들이 직면하고 있는 어려움을 계속 상기시켜주는 예상보다 높은 물가 상승률 데이터에서 생겨난 것이다.
Ⓑ 그런데 이러한 혼란은 고립적으로 발생하고 있는 것이 아니다. 우리는 그 파급효과가 여러 산업과 개인들에 미치는 것을 목격하고 있으며, 그러한 어려움을 견뎌낼 준비가 덜 된 사람들이 가장 큰 타격을 받고 있다. Ⓐ 변동성과 불확실성에 직면하여 탄력적인 전략 개발을 우선시하는 것이 필수적이라는 점은 분명하다. 그러나 리더는 정확히 무엇을 위해 준비해야 할까? 탄력적인 영업활동을 현실화하려면 무엇을 우선시해야 할까?

geopolitical a. 지정학(地政學)적인 inflation n. 인플레이션, 물가 상승률 interest rate 이자율, 금리 impact v. 영향을 미치다 follow on (남이 이미 가 있는 곳에) 뒤따라가다, ~의 결과로서 생기다 disruption n. 혼란, 붕괴 ripple effect 파급 효과 weather v. (역경 등을) 무사히 헤쳐 나가다[견디다] take a hit 타격을 입다, 손실을 보다 prioritize v. 우선순위를 매기다; ~을 우선시하다 resilient a. (충격·부상 등에 대해) 회복력 있는; 탄력적인 vital a. 필수적인 in the face of ~에도 불구하고; ~에 직면하여 volatility n. 휘발성; 변덕 operation n. 영업활동 rigid a. 엄격한, 융통성 없는 transparent a. 투명한; 명료한 autonomous a. 자율적인

---

29 빈칸완성   ②

Ⓑ, Ⓒ, Ⓓ에 언급된 경제적 혼란(disruptions)과 어려움(challenges, struggling)을 Ⓐ에서 '변동성과 불확실성'이라고 표현했는데, 이것에 직면해서는 변동이나 불확실성으로 인한 손실이나 피해를 신속히 회복하여 원래의 상태로 돌아가는 것이 중요할 것이므로, '탄력적인, 회복력 있는' 전략을 개발하고 그 전략에 따른 또 그런 영업활동을 실행하는 것을 우선시해야 할 것이다. resilient는 '나쁜 일 후에 다시 강해지고, 건강해지고, 성공할 수 있는 능력이 있는(able to become strong, healthy, or successful again after something bad happens)'이라는 뜻이다.

30 단락배열 ④

C 세계 경제의 어려움을 가장 일반적으로 진술 → D 경제적 어려움(위기)의 구체적인 예로 영국 사례를 제시 → B 그런데 이러한 혼란과 어려움이 파급효과를 미침을 언급 → A 이런 파급효과에 대해 탄력적인 전략과 영업활동을 실행하기 위한 리더의 역할론 제기와 같은 순서가 적절하다. 특히, B 문단의 첫 번째 문장에서 언급된 "이러한 혼란(these disruptions)"이 가리키는 것이 무엇인지를 확인하는 접근이 유효한데, 이는 D 문단에서 언급된 '영국 경제의 치솟는 금리', '예상을 뛰어넘는 높은 물가 상승률' 등을 지칭한다. 즉 C 와 D 는 for example에 의해, D 와 B 는 these disruptions에 의해 각각 연결되어 있다.

31-32

전기차(EV) 시장은 판매량이 급증하면서 신기록을 경신하며 여전히 전반적으로 큰 강세를 보이고 있다. 2022년 판매된 전체 신차 중 전기차의 비중은 14%로, 2021년 당시 약 9%, 2020년 당시 5% 미만이었던 것에서 증가한 수치이다.

전기차의 판매 급증에도 불구하고, 변화는 이제 막 시작된 것에 불과하다. 이는 (전기차에 대한) 보조금과 내연기관(ICE) 차량에 대한 단계적 폐지 목표 및 규제에 힘입어, 전기차의 수요가 계속 급증할 것이라는 의미이다. 향후 5년 안에 전기차 소유의 총비용이 내연기관 차량 소유 비용과 동등해지면 (그리고 심지어 그보다 아래로 내려가기 시작하면), 추가적인 상승도 기대된다.

전기차에 대한 수요가 급격히 증가함에 따라 배터리 내부의 광물질에 대한 수요도 급증하고 있다. 코로나19 팬데믹 기간에 전기차 판매가 급증하면서 리튬 배터리 공급망에서 중국이 차지하는 지배력에 대한 우려가 증폭되고 있다. 한편, 우크라이나 전쟁이 계속되면서 코발트, 리튬, 니켈을 포함한 원자재 가격은 사상 최고치를 기록하였다.

특정 공급국가에 대한 의존이 유일한 문제는 아니다. 배터리는 전기차의 총비용에서 큰 부분을 차지하고, 일반적으로 가격의 30~40%를 차지하지만, 배터리의 크기가 커질수록 이 비율은 더 증가하게 된다.

유럽은 현재 자체의 배터리 공급망 개발을 위해 애쓰고 있지만, 이는 시간이 걸리는 일이며 부품의 해외 구매 의존은 여전하다. 유럽연합의 핵심 원자재 법은 공급망을 안정적으로 확보하고 유럽의 자율성을 강화하여 늦어도 2050년까지 온실가스 순배출량을 제로로 만들겠다는 목표를 충족하는 데 필요한 소재들을 확보하기 위한 이 블록의 시도이다.

surge n. 급등, 급증 transition n. (다른 상태·조건으로의) 이행(移行)[과도(過渡)] soar v. 급증하다 on the back of ~의 결과로 subsidy n. 보조금 phase-out a. 단계적으로 폐지[중단]하는 combustion n. 연소 on a par with ~와 동등한[같은] upswing n. (어느 정도의 기간에 걸친) 호전[상승, 증가] mineral n. 광물(질) exacerbate v. 악화시키다 ongoing a. 계속 진행 중인 raw material 원자재, 원료, 소재 record high 사상 최고치를 기록하다 proportion n. 비율 sourcing n. (부품의) 대외구매: 흔히 외국으로부터의 구매 boost v. 신장시키다, 북돋우다 autonomy n. 자율성 net-zero emission 순(純)배출 제로(온실가스나 탄소 등의 물질을 배출하는 만큼 제거하여 존재하는 총량을 0으로 유지하는 것) at risk 위험한 상태에 있는 on the rise 증가하고 있는 in comparison 비교하여

31 빈칸완성 ④

빈칸을 포함한 문장에서는 전기차의 수요를 증가시키게 되는 '가격 유인 효과'를 언급하고 있다. 전기차가 아무리 친환경적이라 할지라도 구매 및 유지관리 비용이 내연기관 차량에 비해 비싸다면 수요는 한계가 있을 것이다. 따라서 전기차 구매 및 유지관리 비용이 내연기관 차량과 "같아지거나" 심지어 "더 싸게" 된다면 이는 전기차 수요를 증가시키는 강력한 유인 효과를 갖게 될 것이다. 그러므로 빈칸에는 "~와 같은(동등한)"이라는 의미의 ④가 들어가는 것이 적절하다.

32 내용추론 ②

전기차로 인해 소형차 부품 공급업체들의 수가 늘어나고 있는지를 알 수 있는 언급은 없으므로 ②는 추론할 수 없다. ① 다섯 번째 단락에서 "유럽은 현재 자체의 배터리 공급망 개발을 위해 애쓰고 있다"고 하였으므로 타당한 추론이다. ③ 세 번째 단락에서 "리튬 배터리 공급망에서 중국이 차지하는 지배력에 대한 우려가 증폭되고 있다"고 하였으므로 타당한 추론이다. ④ 첫 번째와 두 번째 단락에서 반복적으로 언급된 내용이다.

위 글을 읽고 유추할 수 없는 것을 고르시오.
① 유럽은 현재 전기차 배터리 공급망 강화를 위해 노력하고 있다.
② 전기차는 경차 부품 공급업체들을 늘려 가는 중이다.
③ 전기차 배터리 금속 부문에서 중국의 지배력은 전기차 산업에 도전 과제를 제기한다.
④ 전기차 판매는 계속해서 급증할 것으로 예상된다.

33-34

"탕핑(tang ping, 躺平)"으로 알려진 새로운 추세는 취업을 해서 장시간 교대 근무를 해가며 성과를 내는 사회적 압박으로부터의 해독제라고 설명할 수 있다. 중국의 노동 시장은 줄어들고 있고, 젊은이들은 종종 더 많은 시간을 일하고 있다. "탕핑"이라는 용어는 중국의 유명 소셜 미디어 사이트의 한 게시물에서 유래된 것으로 추정된다. 토론 포럼 티에바에 한 사용자는 지금은 삭제된 게시물에 "평평하게 몸을 누이는 것이 나의 현명한 운동"이라고 썼고 "인간은 누워야만 비로소 만물의 척도가 될 수 있다"고 덧붙였다. 이런 말들이 또 다른 유명 마이크로블로깅 사이트인 시나 웨이보에서 다루어지면서 이 용어는 금방 유행어가 되었다. "탕핑" 뒤에 숨어 있는 아이디어, 즉 과로하지 않고, 달성 가능한 더 많은 성취들에 대해서 만족하면서 긴장을 풀 수 있는 시간을 허용하자는 생각은 많은 사람들에게 칭송받으며 수많은 밈들에 영감을 제공했다. 이것은 일종의 정신 운동으로 묘사되고 있다.

antidote n. 해독제; 해결책 shift n. 교대 근무 (시간) shrink v. 줄어들다; 움츠러들다 originate v. 유래하다 microblogging n. 마이크로블로깅(짧막한 메시지나 영상 등을 인터넷에 정기적으로 올리는 활동) buzzword n. (언론 등에서 많이 사용되는) 유행어 attainable a. 이룰[달성할] 수 있는 unwind v. 긴장을 풀다 meme n. 밈(특정 메시지를 전하는 그림, 사진, 또는 짧은 영상으로 재미를 주는 것을 목적으로 함) toxin n. 독소 remedy n. 해결책; 치료(약) anonymity n. 익명성 venom n. (뱀 등의) 독; 앙심, 원한 catchphrase n. (특정 정치가나 연예인과 관련된) 유명 문구, 선전 구호 discourse n. 담론; 담화

33 빈칸완성 ③

Ⓐ "사회적 압박(society's pressures)"으로부터 벗어날 수 있게 해주는 방법이 있다면 그것은 일종의 "치유책, 해결책"이므로 remedy, antidote가 빈칸에 들어갈 수 있다. Ⓑ 이 용어는 "많은 사람들에게 칭송받으며 수많은 밈들에 영감을 제공했다"고 하였으므로 일종의 "유행어", "추세"가 되었다고 볼 수 있으므로 trend, buzzword, catchphrase가 빈칸에 들어갈 수 있다. 두 조건을 모두 만족시키는 ③이 정답이다.

34 내용추론 ②

본문의 내용에 따르면 "탕핑"은 "과로하지 않고, 달성 가능한 더 많은 성취들에 대해서 만족하면서 긴장을 풀 수 있는 시간을 허용하자"는 취지를 담고 있으므로 긴장과 갈등, 노력과 책임이 거의 필수적이라 할 "적극적 정치참여"와는 거리가 멀다. 따라서 ②는 추론할 수 없다. ① 첫 번째 문장에서 "탕핑은 취업을 해서 장시간 교대 근무를 해가며 성과를 내라는 사회적 압박으로부터의 해독제"라고 하였으므로 타당한 진술이다. ③ "유명 마이크로블로깅 사이트인 시나 웨이보에서 다루어지면서 이 용어는 금방 유행어가 되었다"고 하였으므로 타당한 진술이다. ④ "탕핑"이라는 말 속에는 "과로하지 않고, 달성 가능한 더 많은 성취들에 대해서 만족하면서 긴장을 풀 수 있는 시간을 허용하자는 생각"이 담겨 있다고 하였으므로 타당하다.

위 글을 읽고 유추하기 가장 <u>어려운</u> 것을 고르시오.
① "탕핑"은 취업 및 장시간 근무 중의 높은 업무성취와 관련된 사회적 압력에 대한 일종의 대응이다.
② 중국 청년들은 "탕핑"을 통해 적극적인 정치참여에 나서기 시작했다.
③ 시나 웨이보에 실린 토론은 온라인 담론을 통해 그 추세가 급속히 확산되고 있음을 보여준다.
④ 현명한 운동으로서의 "평평하게 눕는 것"의 개념은 과로에 대한 거부와 보다 편안하고 균형 잡힌 생활 방식에 대한 열망을 암시한다.

35-36

디지털 인문학은 하나의 통일된 분야가 아니라 경험세계(universe)를 탐구하는 일련의 수렴적 실천들인데, 이 경험세계에서는 첫 번째로, 활자는 지식이 생산되고/되거나 전파되는 독점적 혹은 규범적인 매체가 더 이상 아니고 그 대신, 활자는 새로운 멀티미디어 지형 속에 흡수된다. 두 번째로, 디지털적인 도구, 기술 및 미디어가 예술, 인문 과학 및 사회 과학 분야의 지식 생산 및 전파를 변화시켰다. 디지털 인문학은 더 이상 지식이나 문화의 유일한 생산자이자 관리자, 전파자가 아니게 된 대학들에게 새로이 등장하고 있는 현시대의 공공 영역들(월드와이드웹, 블로그 세상, 디지털 도서관 등)을 위해 태생적으로 디지털적인 학문적 담론을 형성하도록 요청하는 세상(world)과 관련하여 선도적인 역할을 수행하여, 이러한 영역들에서 수월성과 혁신을 모범적으로 구현하고, 세계적이면서 동시에 지역적인 지식을 생산, 교환 및 전파하는 네트워크들을 더욱 원활히 형성하고자 한다.
디지털 인문학의 첫 번째 추세는 정량(定量)적 작업으로서, 데이터베이스의 탐색 및 검색 기능을 동원하고, 자료 언어학을 자동화하며, 하이퍼카드들을 중요한 배열 속에 축적해 넣는다. 두 번째 추세는 정성(定性)적, 해석적, 경험적, 정서적, 생성적 성격을 띠고 있다. 그것은 복잡성에 대한 관심, 매체 특성성, 역사적 맥락, 분석적 깊이, 비평과 해석이라는 인문학의 핵심

방법론적 강점을 위해 디지털적 도구 세트를 활용한다. 이처럼 거친 이분법적 구별이라도 정성적 체계 내에 정량적 분석이 내장됨을 배제하지 않듯이, 정량적 접근의 정서적인, 심지어 숭고하기까지 한 잠재력을 배제하지 않는다. 오히려 그것은 새로운 연구 관행 모델과 새로운 도구 및 기술의 가용성에 의해 촉진되는 연결과 조절을 상상한다.

humanities n. 인문학 an array of 다수의, 죽 늘어선 universe n. (특정한 유형의) 경험 세계 convergent a. 한 점으로 향하는, 한데 모이는, 수렴의 exclusive a. 배타적인 normative a. 규범적인 medium n. 매체, 매개(물) disseminate v. (정보·지식 등을) 퍼뜨리다[전파하다] configuration n. 배열, 배치; 형상, 지형 inaugural a. 취임의; 첫 번째의 with respect to ~에 관하여 steward n. 관리인, 집사; 간사 scholarly a. 학자의; 학문적인 discourse n. 담론; 담화 sphere n. (활동·영향·관심) 영역 model v. ~의 모형을 만들다; ~을 모양으로 나타내다 domain n. 영역; 범위 facilitate v. 가능하게[용이하게] 하다 wave n. (특정한 활동의) 급증 quantitative a. 양적인, 정량(定量)적, 계량의 mobilize v. (물자·수단 등을) 동원하다 retrieval n. (정보의) 검색 corpus n. (자료 등의) 전부, 총체; 코퍼스 (컴퓨터로 읽을 수 있는 텍스트·예문 등의 집합체) corpus linguistics 자료 언어학 stack v. (깔끔하게 정돈하여) 쌓다 hypercard n. 하이퍼카드(여러 가지 하이퍼텍스트 개념의 구현에 필요한 정보 관리 도구를 이용자에게 제공하는 컴퓨터용 소프트웨어. 문자 데이터, 그래픽, 음성 및 영상을 수록할 수 있는 카드를 종류별로 쌓아 놓은 스택으로 구성됨) qualitative a. 성질상의, 질적인, 정성(定性)적 generative a. 생성의 harness v. 이용[활용]하다 toolkit n. 툴키트(단일 기능의 소프트웨어 도구 세트) core a. 핵심적인 methodological a. 방법론의, 방법론적인 critique n. 비평, 평론 crudely ad. 조잡하게, 투박하게 dichotomy n. 이분법 sublime a. 숭고한, 기품 있는 embed v. 끼워 넣다 embedding n. 내장, 내재 framework n. 틀; 체계 coupling n. 연결, 결합 scale v. 크기를 조절하다 divergent a. 분기(分岐)하는, 갈라지는 interdisciplinary a. 학제간의(여러 학문 분야가 관련된) descriptive a. 서술하는, 묘사하는 intensify v. 강화하다, 심화시키다 statistical a. 통계학적인 prioritize v. 우선순위를 매기다; ~을 우선시하다

35 빈칸완성 ①

Ⓐ 첫 단락에서 '디지털 인문학은 다중적인(다양한) 매체들, 즉 "멀티미디어"를 통한 지식 생산/교환/전파의 "네트워크들"을 형성한다'고 했는데, 이것은 다중매체상의 여러 정보, 데이터, 지식들이 네트워크를 타고 탐구자에게 수렴적(집중적)으로 전달되어 탐구자가 경험세계를 탐구하게 됨을 말하므로 빈칸에는 "집중하는" 또는 "수렴하는"이라는 의미의 convergent가 가장 적절하다. interdisciplinary(학제적인, 학문 간의)는 기존의 학문들에 대한 언급이 없어 부적절하다. Ⓑ 빈칸 바로 다음에 "데이터베이스의 탐색 및 검색 기능", "자료", "축적" 등의 개념이 집중적으로 언급되고 있으므로 빈칸에서는 "정량적"(quantitative) 작업이 언급되고 있음을 알 수 있다.

36 내용추론 ③

두 번째 단락에서 "이처럼 거친 이분법적 구별이라도 정성적 체계 내에 정량적 분석이 내장됨을 배제하지 않듯이, 정량적 접근의 정서적인, 심지어 숭고하기까지 한 잠재력을 배제하지 않는다"고 했고 "디지털 인문

학은 어느 한쪽 방법론보다는 서로의 "연결과 조절"을 중시한다"고 했다. 다시 말해 정량적 접근과, 정성적 접근 모두 중요한 것이라고 말하고 있으므로, ③의 진술은 잘못되었다.

위 글을 읽고 가장 유추하기 어려운 것을 고르시오.
① 디지털 인문학의 변형적 본성은 전통적 경계를 넘어 지식의 생산, 교환, 전파를 위한 글로벌 및 지역 네트워크를 조성한다.
② 디지털 인문학은 활자가 더 이상 지식 전파를 위한 독점적 매체가 아닌 변화된 세계를 탐구하는 다양한 실천들의 집합으로 특징지어진다.
③ 디지털 기술의 발전을 바탕으로 하는 디지털 인문학은 빅데이터를 활용하고 질적 접근보다 정량적 접근을 우선시하며 진화하고 있다.
④ 연구 관행과 기술이 발전하는 진화적 환경은 인문학의 디지털적 방법들이 지속적으로 개발되고 통합되는 것에 이바지한다.

37-38

도시는 우리를 아프게 할 수 있다. 도시는 언제나 그렇게 해왔는데, 더 많은 사람들이 서로 가까이 있을 때 질병이 더 쉽게 퍼지기 때문이다. 그리고 질병은 도시 밀도에 수반되는 유일한 병폐가 아니다. 소돔과 고모라 이후 줄곧, 도시는 악덕과 범죄의 온상으로 악마화되어 왔다. 그럼에도 불구하고 도시는 인류의 가장 위대한 발명품이자 창의성, 혁신, 부와 연결을 위한 필수 불가결한 엔진이자 문명의 구조를 짜는 직조기이기 때문에 번영을 누려왔다.
그러나 도시는 이제 기로(岐路)에 서 있다. 글로벌 코로나 위기 동안 사람들이 일할 수만 있으면 집에서 일하게 되면서 도시는 점점 조용해졌다. 정상적인 형태의 사교 활동들은 중단되었다. 이러한 변화는 얼마나 영구적일까? 디지털 기술의 발전은 많은 사람들이 예전과는 달리 도시 생활에서 벗어날 수 있음을 의미한다. 그들은 그렇게 할까? 우리는 탈(脫) 도시 세상의 문턱에 서 있는 것일까?
에드워드 글레이저(Edward Glaeser)와 데이비드 커틀러(David Cutler)는 도시 생활이 살아남기는 하겠지만, 개별 도시들은 끔찍한 위험에 직면할 것이며, 도시 실패의 급증은 절대적 재앙이 될 것이라고 주장한다. 친밀감과 영감의 측면에서, 도시가 제공할 수 있는 것들을 대체할 수 있는 것은 없다. 훌륭한 도시들은 언제나 훌륭한 관리를 요구해 왔으며, 우리가 겪는 현 위기로 인해 관리 역량의 현격한 차이가 드러났다. 팬데믹이건 아니건 간에 그 어떤 것이 도시 하나를 마비시키는 것은 가능하다. 글레이저와 커틀러는 이미 일어나고 있는 진화(사태 전개)를 검토하고, 우리 앞에 놓여 있는 있을 수 있는 미래를 설명한다. 번영할 도시와 그렇지 않은 도시를 어떻게 구별할 수 있을까? 그들은 미국에서 의료와 교육의 심각한 불평등이 특히 우리 도시의 미래에 어두운 그림자라고 주장한다. 이 문제의 해결 여부가 우리의 집단적 건강을 되찾느냐, 훨씬 더 어두운 곳으로 하향의 소용돌이로 치닫느냐의 차이를 만들 것이다.

density n. 밀도, 농도 accompany v. 동반하다, 수반하다 breeding ground 번식지, 온상 demonize v. 악마로 묘사하다 vice n. 악; 악덕 행위 flourish v. 번창하다 nonetheless ad. 그럼에도 불구하고 indispensable a. 없어서는 안 될, 필수적인 loom n. 베틀, 직기 fabric n. (사회·조직 등의) 구조 weave v. (wove-woven) 짜다[엮다], 짜서[엮어서] 만들다 crossroad n. 교차로, 기로, 갈림길 grind to a halt 서서히 (가다가) 멈추다 permanent a. 영구적인 opt v. (~을 하기로[하지 않기로]) 택하다 wave n. (특정한 활동의) 급증 intimacy n. 친밀감 inspiration n. 영감 governance n. 통치, 관리 into the ground 필요 이상으로; 쓰러질 때까지, 못 쓰게 되도록 blight n. (곡식의) 병충해; 장애, 어두운 그림자 collective a. 집단의 spiral a. 나선형의 fragile a. 부서지기 쉬운; 취약한 stumble v. 비틀거리다 robust a. 원기 왕성

한, 튼튼한 wholesome a. 건강에 좋은; 건전한 persist v. 고집스럽게 계속하다 address v. (문제·상황 등에 대해) 고심하다 jeopardize v. 위태롭게 하다 initiative n. 자주성; 주도권

37 빈칸완성   ④

Ⓐ 빈칸 다음에 "더 많은 사람들이 서로 가까이 있을 때 질병은 더 쉽게 퍼진다"고 하였으므로 도시로 인해 사람들이 "약해진다", "아프다" 또는 "병든다"는 의미가 필요하므로 fragile, sick이 가능하다. Ⓑ 빈칸 다음이 역접임에 주목한다. "도시 생활이 끔찍한 위험에 직면한다", "재앙" 등의 표현이 나오므로 ④의 '살아남기는 하겠지만 끔찍한 위험과 재앙에 직면한다'는 의미라고 보는 것이 가장 적절하다. 만약 stumble을 써야 한다면 '비틀거리기는 하겠지만 도시 생활은 나름대로 괜찮고, 버틸 만하다'는 식의 전개가 자연스러운 것이므로 정답이 될 수 없다. 한편, persist는 '평소, 예상 또는 정상적인 시간을 넘어서까지 계속 발생하거나 존재하다(to continue to occur or exist beyond the usual, expected, or normal time)'는 의미이므로 빈칸에 들어가게 되면 '도시가 예상 또는 정상적 시간을 넘어서까지 존속하다'는 뜻이 되어 정답이 될 수 없다.

38 글의 주제   ①

도시 생활은 "위기, 실패, 재앙"을 맞이할 수도 있고, 언제나 그래왔듯이 "훌륭한 관리를 통해 번영하는 훌륭한 도시"를 유지할 수도 있다. 이러한 글 전체의 요지를 맨 마지막 문장이 담고 있는데, 도시가 직면한 위기의 해결 여부에 따라 "집단적 건강을 회복할 수도 있고, 하향의 소용돌이로 치달을 수도 있다"고 하였으므로 가장 적절한 주제는 ①이라 할 수 있다.

위 글의 주제로 가장 적합한 것을 고르시오.
① 현재의 도시 위기를 해결하지 못하면 도시의 지속 가능성이 위태로워질 수 있다.
② 도시는 현대 문명의 중심지로서 전 세계 인류를 번영의 길로 지속적으로 이끌고 있다.
③ 코로나19 팬데믹 위기 이후 전 세계 인류는 도시를 버리고 농촌 생활 방식으로 돌아가야 한다.
④ 미래의 도시 발전을 위해서는 지방자치단체가 주도하는 지역 계획들이 중요하다.

39-40

플라톤은 불변성이 논리적으로 사랑의 필요조건은 말할 것도 없고 사랑의 중요한 특징도 아니라는 방식으로 사랑을 설명한다. 플라톤의 사랑의 사다리 중 가장 낮은 단계에서는, x는 y가 육체적으로 아름답기 때문에 y를 사랑한다. 육체적 아름다움은 시간이 지남에 따라, 때로는 매우 빨리 사라지기 때문에 (우리 생각에) 이런 종류의 사랑은 불변이 아니다. 그러나 플라톤이 보기에는, 이 가장 낮은 단계의 사랑이 불변이 아닌 이유는 그것 때문이 아니다. 아리스토텔레스가 보기에는, y가 x에게 즐겁거나 유용하기 때문에 x가 y를 사랑한다면, y가 주는 즐거움이나 유용성이 지속되지 않기 때문에 x의 사랑은 지속되지 않을 것이다. 따라서, 우리는 P로 인해 x가 y를 사랑하기 때문에, P가 사라지면 x는 더 이상 y를 사랑하지 않을 것이라는 주장을 아리스토텔레스에게서 발견하게 된다. 그러나 플라톤에게서는, y에 대한 x의 사랑이 y의 육체적 아름다움에 기초할 때, 이와 다른 이유로

그 사랑은 불변이지 않다. 즉, x는 y가 가진 육체적 아름다움을 다른 많은 이들도 갖고 있다는 것 뿐만 아니라, 육체적 아름다움이 다른 종류의 아름다움만큼 좋지는 못하다는 것도 <처음부터> 깨닫게 되기 때문이다.

플라톤의 경우, y에 대한 x의 사랑이 y의 육체적 아름다움에 기초할 때, 그 사랑은 정확하게 y의 아름다움이 사라질 때 끝난다는 암시는 없다. 오히려 y에 대한 x의 사랑은 그 아름다움이 사라지기 전에도 끝난다. 이 상적인 경우, 사랑하는 사람은 y의 (육체적) 아름다움이 사라질 것이고, 따라서 이러한 종류의 아름다움은 다른 종류의 아름다움에 비해 열등하다는 것을 인식한다. 따라서 덜 중요한 아름다움에 지나치게 집착하기 — 행복이 여기에 있지 않기에 — 를 원치 않는 x는 플라톤의 사다리에서 다음 단계로 나아간다. 그 단계에서는 좀 더 본질적인 아름다움, 즉 도덕적 미덕과 지적 수월성이 사랑의 토대를 제공한다. 그러나 x는 이 뛰어난 유형의 아름다움이나 선함조차도 x가 갈망하는 것이 아니라는 것을 다시 한 번 깨닫는다. 그러한 아름다움 역시 널리 퍼져 있으며 시간이 지남에 따라 (비록 느리기는 하지만) 사라진다. 사람들은 죽을 때 그들의 정신적 아름다움을 함께 가져가므로, 그러한 종류의 아름다움은 썩어 없어지는 것이고 따라서 열등한 것이다. 플라톤에 있어서 사랑의 대상이 완전히 아름답거나 선할 때에만 그 사랑은 불변일 수 있다. 이것은 그 대상이 비록 실제로는 변하지 않아도 변할 가능성이 있는 그런 종류의 것이라는 것을 의미하지 않고, 그 대상이 모든 변화가 불가능한 그런 종류의 것이라는 것을 의미한다. 이것이 플라톤의 "절대적 아름다움"이며, x가 항상 갈망했었고, "향상"의 가장 높은 수준에서만 접근할 수 있는 것이다. 이런 점에서 플라톤적 사랑은 그리스도교의 하느님에 대한 인간의 사랑의 이교(異敎)적 버전이다.

constancy n. 불변성 feature n. 특징 let alone ~커녕[~은 고사하고] necessary condition 필요조건 ladder n. 사다리; (지위 등의) 단계 fade v. 서서히 사라지다, 점점 희미해지다 endure v. 오래가다[지속되다] not hold a candle to somebody[something] ~만 못하다[~와 비교가 안 되다] lesser a. (크기·양·중요성이) 더 적은[작은], 덜한 progress v. 진전을 보이다, 진행하다 substantial a. 실질적인, 본질적인; (양·가치·중요성이) 상당한 perishable a. 썩기 쉬운; 죽을 운명의 ascent n. 상승, 향상 all along 내내, 죽, 항상 pagan n. 이교도; 비그리스도교도

---

39 문맥상 적절하지 않은 표현 고르기　②

플라톤은 사랑에 사다리(단계, 등급)가 있다고 본다. 가장 낮은 단계에 "육체적 아름다움으로 인한 사랑"이, 그 위에 "도덕적 미덕과 지적 수월성에 토대를 둔 사랑"이 있는데, 이들 모두 지속 시간의 차이는 있지만 유한하다(결국은 소멸된다). 반면 그보다 더 "향상"된 "완전히 아름답거나 선한", 즉 "절대적 아름다움"에 토대를 둔 사랑만은 불변이다. 따라서 플라톤은 사랑을 점점 더 높은 사다리(단계)를 오르며 고양되고 "향상" 되는 깨달음의 과정에서 바라보았고, "사랑의 불변성"은 사랑의 필요조건이 아니라 "절대적 아름다움"이라는 사랑의 대상이 갖는 속성이라고 보았다. 이와 같은 플라톤의 사랑론에서 사랑하는 이가 "처음부터 (initially)" "육체적 아름다움은 다른 많은 이들도 갖고 있고, 그 아름다움은 다른 종류의 아름다움만 못하다는 것을 깨닫는다"는 것은 사실상 불가능에 가깝다. 단계적으로 사다리(단계)를 오르며 "향상"되어야만 깨달을 수 있기 때문이다. 따라서, ⓑ initially를 '결국에는(finally, in the end) 또는 '나중에(later)' 혹은 '점차(gradually)', '조만간(soon, before long)'과 같은 표현들로 대체해야 한다.

---

40 내용추론　④

아리스토텔레스는 "즐거움"이나 "유용성"과 같은 것이 사랑의 원인이 된다고 보았으므로 ④가 적절한 진술이다. ① 플라톤은 사랑에 사다리(단계, 등급)가 있다고 보았으므로 오직 한 종류일 수가 없다. 본문에서는 최소한 "육체적 아름다움으로 인한 사랑," 그 위에 "도덕적 미덕과 지적 수월성에 토대를 둔 사랑," 그리고 가장 최상위에 그리스도교의 "하느님에 대한 사랑"에 필적하는 "절대적 아름다움"에 토대를 둔 사랑의 세 종류 사랑이 소개되고 있다. ② 맨 마지막 문장에서 플라톤을 pagan 즉 '이교도'라고 부른 데에서 그가 그리스도교와 무관한 사람임을 추론할 수 있다. ③ 아리스토텔레스는 "즐거움"이나 "유용성"과 같은 사랑의 이유가 유한하면 사랑도 유한하다(불변이 아니다)는 설명을 펼쳤다. 즉, 일종의 인과론으로 사랑을 설명하였다는 말이다. 이와는 달리 플라톤은 먼저 사랑에는 사다리(단계, 등급)가 있고, 깨달음의 단계(수준)에 따라 수반되는 사랑의 종류가 달라진다고 보았다.

위 글에서 유추할 수 있는 가장 적절한 것을 고르시오.
① 플라톤에게 사랑은 오직 한 종류뿐이다.
② 플라톤은 그리스도교 사상가였다.
③ 아리스토텔레스의 사랑론은 플라톤의 사랑론과 동일하다.
④ 아리스토텔레스에게 사랑에는 원인이 있다.

2024 서울시립대학교(자연계 Ⅱ)

| 01 ① | 02 ① | 03 ② | 04 ① | 05 ③ | 06 ④ | 07 ② | 08 ③ | 09 ② | 10 ④ |
| 11 ① | 12 ② | 13 ④ | 14 ② | 15 ③ | 16 ③ | 17 ④ | 18 ① | 19 ③ | 20 ③ |

01 one of+복수명사

one of 뒤에는 복수 가산명사가 온다. 그러므로 ①은 the most influential singers and songwriters가 되어야 한다. ④ '~에 이어', '~의 뒤에'라는 의미의 전치사로 쓰였다.

influential a. 영향력 있는 release v. (정보·레코드·신간 등을) 공개[발표, 발매]하다 gradually ad. 서서히, 차차 soar v. 높이 날다; (물가 등이) 치솟다

테일러 스위프트(Taylor Swift)는 동시대의 가장 영향력 있는 가수 겸 작곡가 중 한 명이다. 1989년생인 그녀는 2006년에 첫 앨범을 발표하고 컨트리음악 공연으로 미국을 순회했으며, 그런 다음에는 점차 대중음악으로 방향을 틀었다. 스위프트는 14개의 앨범을 발표했고, 2023년에 엄청난 인기를 끌었던 에라스 투어(Eras Tour) 이후 그녀의 순자산은 11억 달러로 치솟았다.

02 동의어 ①

stake v. (돈·생명 등을) 걸다(= gamble) establish v. 설립하다, 확립하다 culmination n. 최고점, 정상 executive n. 임원, 중역 bet n. 내기, 내기의 대상 emerge v. 나오다, 나타나다; (빈곤, 낮은 신분 등에서) 벗어나다, 빠져나오다 bankruptcy n. 파산, 도산 mortgage v. 저당 잡히다 secure v. 확보하다 predict v. 예언하다, 예보하다 ruin v. 파멸시키다, 망쳐놓다

마블이 4년간에 걸쳐 블록버스터 영화를 통해 구축한 슈퍼히어로들을 한데 모은 "어벤져스"는 이미 전 세계적으로 큰 성공을 거둘 것처럼 보였다. 그것은 마블 스튜디오의 사장인 케빈 파이기(Kevin Feige)를 비롯한 마블의 제작자들과 임원들이 10년 동안 해 온 작업의 정점이었다. 그것은 또한 파산에서 벗어난 마블이 월스트리트의 한 은행으로부터 일련의 융자금을 확보하기 위해 자사의 캐릭터들에 대한 권리를 저당 잡혔을 때, 그 회사가 성공적인 베팅을 했었음을 알려주는 것이기도 했다. 마블 스튜디오는 그 융자금에 회사의 모든 운명을 걸었으며, 그 융자금은 마블 스튜디오가 만든 첫 영화들에 제작 자금으로 공급되었다.

03 논리완성 ②

generics(제네릭 의약품, 일반 의약품)는 처음 개발되어 특허 받은 오리지널 의약품과 주성분 함량, 복용방법, 효능, 품질 등이 동일하게 만들어진 의약품으로, 오리지널 의약품의 특허가 만료된 후에 출시할 수 있다. 두 번째 문장의 주어로 나온 의약품은 오리지널 의약품으로, 이것이 제네릭 의약품과 경쟁하게 될 것이라는 것은 특허가 만료되는 오리지널

의약품들이 많아지고 있다는 말이며, 다시 말해 특허 만료가 '늘어나고' 있다는 것이다. 따라서 ②가 정답이다.

patent n. 특허, 특허권 expiration n. 만료, 만기 competition n. 경쟁 generic n. 상품 등록(특허)이 돼 있지 않은 제품, 일반 의약품 dissipate v. 사라지다, 흩어져버리다 mount v. (양이나 강도가) 증가하다, 늘다 discredit v. 믿지 않다, 의심하다 encourage v. 장려하다, 조장하다

2024년에 특허 만료가 늘어나고 있다. 많은 생명공학 의약품을 비롯해서, 판매 규모가 380억 달러에 달하는 여러 의약품들이 상표등록이 돼 있지 않은 보다 저렴한 일반 의약품과의 경쟁을 맞이하게 될 것이다.

04 논리완성

2024년에는 경기가 침체될 것으로 2023년에 내다봤으나 물가가 안정되고 전반적으로 경제가 안정된 모습을 보인 것은, 경제 동향이 예측을 '거스른' 행태를 나타낸 것이다.

unexpected a. 예기치 않은, 의외의, 뜻밖의 prediction n. 예언, 예보 recession n. 경기 후퇴 materialize v. 가시화(可視化)하다; 나타나다, 실현되다 peak v. 최고점[한도]에 달하다, 절정이 되다 decline v. 쇠하다, 감소[감퇴]하다 robust a. 강한, 건전한, 확고한 defy v. 문제시하지 않다, 허용하지 않다; (노력·해결 따위를) 거부하다, 저지하다, 물리치다 support v. 지지하다 appraise v. 평가하다, 인식하다 contribute to ~에 기여하다

예상치 못한 (2024년) 경제 동향이 2023년의 예측을 거스르고 있다. 상황이 뜻밖으로 전개되어, 2023년에 예상됐던 경기 침체는 전혀 나타나지 않았고, 2022년 말에 정점을 찍은 물가 상승률은 2023년 내내 하락세를 이어갔다. 경제는 예측과 달리 여전히 전반적으로 견고했다.

05 논리완성 ③

빈칸 Ⓐ의 경우, '특정 개인이나 조직을 대상으로 하는 스피어 피싱을 포함한다'는 내용을 근거로 '맞춤형의'라는 의미의 customized와 tailored가 들어갈 수 있음을 알 수 있다. 한편, 빈칸 Ⓑ의 경우, '고품질의 AI 생성 콘텐츠가 맞춤형 사이버 공격에 활용될 경우, 아무리 조심스러운 사용자라고 할지라도 피해를 입을 수 있다'는 흐름이 되어야 하므로 '경계심이 강한', '조심스러운'이라는 의미의 vigilant와 prudential이 들어갈 수 있다. 따라서 두 조건을 모두 만족시키는 ③이 정답이다.

comprehensive a. 포괄적인 aggregation n. 집합, 집성 empower v. ~에게 권한을 주다, ~할 수 있게 하다 nefarious a. 사악한 actor n. 배우; 행위자 undertake v. 착수하다; 떠맡다 spearphishing n.

스피어 피싱(특정한 개인들이나 회사를 대상으로 한 피싱 공격) specific a. 독특한; 특정한 AI-generated a. AI가 생성한[만들어낸] vulnerable a. 약점이 있는, 취약한 ardent a. 열렬한; 격렬한 relentless a. 가차 없는, 잔인한 customized a. 개개인의 요구에 맞춘 ingenuous a. 솔직한; 천진난만한 tailored a. (특정한 개인·목적을 위한) 맞춤의 vigilant a. 부단히 경계하고 있는; 방심하지 않는 random a. 되는 대로의, 임의의 prudential a. 신중한, 조심성 있는

AI는 더 쉽고 더 포괄적인 데이터 집계를 가능하게 하며, 이것은 다시 악의적인 행위자들로 하여금 특정 개인이나 조직을 대상으로 하는 스피어 피싱을 비롯한 맞춤형 사이버 공격에 착수할 수 있도록 해준다. 이것이 고품질의 AI 생성 콘텐츠와 결합되면, 가장 경계심이 강한 인터넷 사용자조차도 취약해질 수 있다.

---

06 논리완성 ④

택시 회사의 예를 통해, 어려움을 겪다가 본래 상태로 돌아오는 것은 '회복탄력성'과 관련돼 있고 처음부터 영향을 거의 받지 않은 것은 '견고성'과 관련돼 있음을 알 수 있다.

maintain v. 지속[유지]하다 cope v. 대처하다, 극복하다 withstand v. 저항하다; 잘 견디다 bounce back (병·곤경에서) 다시 회복되다 analysis n. 분석 pandemic n. 팬데믹 resilient a. 탄력 있는, 회복력 있는 degrade v. 지위가 떨어지다, 타락하다 lockdown n. 봉쇄, 락다운 disability-specialized a. 장애인 전문의 robust a. 튼튼한, 강건한 insensitive a. 영향을 받지 않는 vulnerability n. 취약성 flexibility n. 유연성, 융통성 adaptability n. 적응성 anti-fragility n. 반취약성 durability n. 영속성, 내구성 tenacity n. 고집, 끈기 robustness n. 견고성 resilience n. 회복력

유지하고 대처하며 견딜 수 있는 능력은 견고성에 관한 것인 반면, 회복하거나 반등하는 능력은 회복탄력성에 관한 것이다. 그래서 예를 들어, 산업 차원에서 분석해볼 때, 코로나19 팬데믹 기간 동안 의료 및 교육 서비스를 제공하는 대부분의 조직은 곤경을 견뎌냈지만, 여행 및 관광 산업은 어려움을 겪다가 회복했다. 사업 차원 분석에서의 한 예로 택시 사업을 들 수 있다. 전통적인 택시 회사는 봉쇄 조치로 처음에는 실적이 하락했지만 그 후 다시 이용량이 본래 상태로 돌아왔을 때 회복탄력성을 보여주었다. 지역의 장애인 전문 택시 회사는 견고했고 그래서 다소 아무런 영향을 받지 않았다. 이러한 예는 그들이 서로 다른 개념이며 이러한 결과를 이끌어내는 메커니즘이 서로 다른 것임을 나타낸다.

07-08

위반자가 국내 사법절차를 통해 처벌 받을 가능성이 적을 때에는, 법원이 정부를 국제법에 합치시킬 수 있는 힘이 줄어든다. 법-경제 관련 문헌은 통계 용어를 채택하는 경우가 많으며, 법 위반자가 불기소 처분을 받는 경우를 유형 II 오류라고 지칭한다. 유형 II 오류의 가능성이 높을수록 행위자가 법을 준수할 동기가 줄어드는데, 왜냐하면 법을 준수하지 않아도 처벌을 받게 될 확률이 더 낮기 때문이다.
B 정보는 유형 II 오류를 줄이는 데 있어서 매우 중요하다. 집행 메커니즘은 효과적인 감시 메커니즘에 좌우된다. 위반자는 그 위반행위가 목격되지 않는 한 처벌할 수 없다. 법원은 강력한 집행 권한을 가지고 있긴 하지만, 감시 권한은 상대적으로 약하다.
A 그렇기 때문에 법원은 정부의 나머지 부처에 국제적 의무를 강제하는

것과 관련해서 중요한 정보 비대칭에 직면한다. 입법부와 행정부는 종종 법적 의무를 위반하고 이러한 위반을 숨기려는 동기를 가지고 있다.
C 바로 이런 이유로 해서 법원은 다른 행위자들에게 의존하여 국제 의무 위반 혐의에 관한 정보를 제공받는다. 따라서 화재 경보 메커니즘을 통해 정보 비대칭을 극복하는 것은 국내 법원이 국제 의무 집행을 효과적으로 하는 데 있어서 중요한 요소이다.

violator n. 위반자, 위배자 punish v. 처벌하다 domestic a. 국내의, 가정의 judicial action 사법 처리 literature n. 문헌 statistical a. 통계의, 통계학의 terminology n. 전문용어 prosecute v. 기소하다 enforcement n. 집행; 강제 transgression n. 위반 observe v. 관찰하다; 보다, 목격하다 relatively ad. 상대적으로 asymmetry n. 불균형, 비대칭 commitment n. 의무, 책무 alleged a. 추정된 component n. 요소

---

07 단락배열 ②

주어진 글에서 언급한 유형 II 오류와 관련하여 정보의 중요성을 언급하고 있는 B 가 가장 먼저 오고, 법원은 이렇게 중요한 정보를 제대로 얻을 수 없는 정보 비대칭의 어려움에 처해 있음을 언급하고 있는 A 가 그다음에 오고, 이 정보 비대칭을 해결하기 위해 법원이 다른 주체로부터 정보를 얻어야 할 필요성에 대해 이야기하고 있는 C 가 마지막에 와야 한다.

---

08 내용추론 ③

본문에서는 법원이 정보 부족과 정보 비대칭으로 인해 정부의 국제 의무 위반을 발견하거나 입증하기가 어렵다는 취지로 이야기하고 있으므로 ③이 유추할 수 없는 진술이다. ① 아니라고 판정했지만 사실이어서 잘못 판정한 오류가 '부정 오류', 즉 '유형 II 오류'인데, 정보가 부족해서 법 위반자에게 유죄가 아니라고 잘못 판정하여 불기소 처분을 내리는 경우이다.

위 글에서 유추할 수 있는 내용으로 가장 거리가 먼 것을 고르시오.
① 법원 판결의 경우, 정보 부족으로 인해 '부정 오류'의 결과가 발생할 수 있다.
② 충분한 정보를 가지고 있는 경우, 법원은 국제 조약에 대한 국가의 의무에 상당한 영향을 미칠 수 있다.
③ 법원이 정부의 국제적 의무 위반을 입증하는 것은 쉬운 일이다.
④ 국제적 의무의 효과적 이행을 위해, 국내 법원은 정부를 감시할 다른 행위자가 필요하다.

09-10

링크드인(LinkedIn)에는 1초마다 117건의 입사지원서가 제출된다. 이는 매일 1,000만 건 이상의 입사지원서가 접수되고 있는 것과 같다. 모두가 몇 번의 키보드 클릭만으로 쉽게 입사 지원을 할 수 있는 Indeed, Glassdoor, ZipRecruiter와 같은 다른 구직 엔진들도 고려하면, 채용 담당자들에게는 이력서가 넘쳐나고 있다는 것을 알 수 있다.
D 그렇다면 가장 적임의 지원자를 찾는 기업들이 이렇게 엄청나게 많은 지원자들을 추려낼 보다 효율적인 방법을 모색하는 것은 놀라운 일이 아니다. 그래서 빠르게 늘어나고 있는 새로운 추세가 모습을 드러냈는데, 채용

과정에 인공지능을 활용하는 것이다. 놀랄 만큼 많은 기업들이 ─ 『하버드 비즈니스 리뷰』에서는 전체 고용주의 86%에 이르는 것으로 추정하고 있다 ─ 현재 면접 과정의 초기 단계에서 인간의 참여를 제한하거나 배제하고 면접관을 인공지능으로 대체하고 있다.

Ⓐ 자동화된 화상면접, 즉 AVI의 개념은 매우 간단하다. 선택된 지원자들은 채용 플랫폼에 참여하도록 초대받아 지원자들의 화면에 나타나는 서면 질문에 대한 화상 응답을 기록하여 제출하는 것이다. AI 알고리즘은 지원자의 표정, 주요 단어 사용 및 목소리 톤과 같은 것들을 찾으면서 화상 응답을 분석한다. 그런 다음 지원자의 성과를 요약한 보고서와 함께 응답의 사본이 지원자가 면접 과정의 다음 단계로 진출할지 여부를 결정하는 채용 담당자에게 제공된다.

Ⓒ 이런 면접 방식에는 분명한 이점이 있다. 고용주는 훨씬 적은 인력을 활용해 상당히 많은 지원자를 선별함으로써 효율성을 얻는다. 그리고 이론적으로는, AVI는 암묵적 편견을 배제하여 면접 과정을 보다 객관적으로 만든다. 지원자들은 자신들이 언제 면접을 볼지를 선택할 수 있는 유연성과 자신이 선택한 편한 장소에서 면접을 볼 수 있다는 편의성을 높이 평가한다.

Ⓑ 하지만 그 과정에도 위험 요소가 있다. 인공지능 채용 플랫폼은 그것의 알고리즘에 편견을 심어준다는 비판을 받아왔다. 구직자들은 AVI의 포맷이 비교적 새로운 것이기 때문에 AVI를 혼란스러워 하고, 응답에 대한 시간 제약으로 인해 스트레스를 받으며, 궁극적으로 어떻게 평가될지에 대한 투명성이 부족하여 불안을 느낀다.

application n. 신청, 지원, 지원서 submit v. 제출하다 equate v. 같게 하다 factor in ~을 고려하다 inundate v. 범람시키다, 가득하게 하다 resume n. 이력서 applicant n. 지원자 analyze v. 분석하다 facial expression 얼굴 표정 transcript n. 사본, 등본 summarize v. 요약하다 screen v. (원서·지원자를) 선발[심사]하다, (심사하여) 걸러내다 fraught a. ~을 내포한, ~으로 가득 찬; 위험한 relatively ad. 상대적으로 stress-inducing a. 스트레스를 유발하는 constraint n. 제약; 제한, 통제 impose v. (의무·세금·벌 따위를) 부과하다; 강요[강제]하다 unsettling a. 마음을 산란하게 하는, 동요시키는 transparency n. 투명, 투명성 assess v. 평가하다, 가늠하다 efficiency n. 효율성 significantly ad. 상당히, 뚜렷하게 implicit a. 은연중의; 무조건의 bias n. 편견 appreciate v. 평가하다; 진가를 인정하다 flexibility n. 융통성 qualified a. 자격 있는, 적임의 sift through 꼼꼼하게 살펴서 추려내다 eliminate v. 제거하다 replace v. 대체하다

09 빈칸완성 　　　　　　②

채용 담당자의 결정에 따라 지원자가 면접 과정의 다음 단계로 '나아가게' 되므로 Ⓐ에는 이러한 의미를 가진 advances와 proceeds가 가능하다. 한편, 지원자들을 추려낼 보다 효율적인 방법을 모색하는 경우, 새로운 방법이나 추세가 '나타나게' 됐을 것이므로, Ⓑ에는 이러한 의미를 가진 materialized나 emerged가 가능하다. 따라서 ②가 정답이다. ① 탈락하다 ─ 나타났다 ③ 나아가다 ─ 바뀌었다 ④ 탈락하다 ─ 변화했다

10 단락배열 　　　　　　④

주어진 글에서 '링크드인과 같은 구직 사이트를 이용하는 경우 손쉽게 입사지원을 할 수 있어서 채용 담당자들에게 이력서가 넘쳐나고 있음'을 이야기했으므로, 많은 지원자들을 추려낼 보다 효율적인 방법을 모

색한 결과 인공지능을 채용 과정에 활용하게 됐다는 내용의 Ⓓ가 다음에 와야 하고, 그에 대한 예로 자동화된 화상면접의 개념을 언급하고 있는 Ⓐ가 그다음에, 그리고 이러한 면접 방식의 장점과 단점에 대한 내용인 Ⓒ와 Ⓑ가 그 뒤에 이어져야 한다.

11-12

당연하게도, 충분히 큰 거의 모든 포유류 종(種)이 사람을 죽일 수 있다. 사람들은 돼지, 말, 낙타, 소 등에 의해 목숨을 잃어 왔다. 그럼에도 불구하고, 일부 대형 동물들은 다른 동물들보다 기질이 훨씬 더 난폭해서 구제불능일 정도로 더 위험하다. 인간을 죽이는 경향으로 인해, 만약 그렇지만 않았더라면 가축화하는 데 이상적으로 보였던 많은 동물들이 자격을 잃고 후보에서 밀려났다.

한 가지 분명한 예로 회색곰을 들 수 있다. 곰 고기는 값비싼 별미이고, 회색곰의 몸무게는 1,700 파운드까지 나가며, 그들은 (무시무시한 사냥꾼이기도 하지만) 주로 초식동물이며, 그들이 먹는 식물은 매우 광범위하고, 인간의 쓰레기를 먹고도 잘 자라며(그래서 옐로스톤과 글레이셔 국립공원에서 큰 문제를 일으키고 있다), 그리고 그들은 비교적 빨리 자란다. 만약 속박된 상태에서도 얌전하다면, 회색곰은 훌륭한 육류 생산 동물이 될 것이다. 일본의 아이누(Ainu)족 사람들은 의식의 일환으로 회색곰을 일상적으로 사육함으로써 그에 대한 실험을 해보았다. 하지만 이해할만한 이유로, 아이누족은 곰의 새끼를 한 살 때 죽여서 먹는 것이 현명하다는 것을 알게 되었다. 회색곰을 더 오래 두는 것은 자살 행위가 될 것이다. 나는 길들여진 성체 회색곰을 알지 못한다.

만약 그렇지 않았다면 적절했을 것이지만 똑같이 명백한 이유로 후보에서 밀려난 또 다른 동물은 아프리카 물소다. 아프리카 물소는 몸무게가 1톤이 될 때까지 빠르게 자라고, 잘 발달된 지배계급 체제의 무리에서 사는데, 이 특성의 장점에 대해서는 아래에서 논의할 것이다. 그러나 아프리카 물소는 아프리카에서 가장 위험하고 예측할 수 없는 대형 포유류로 여겨지고 있다. 물소를 길들이려고 할 만큼 제정신이 아닌 사람은 누구든 그렇게 하려다가 죽거나 아니면 물소가 너무 크고 난폭해지기 전에 죽여야 했다. 이와 유사하게, 4톤의 초식동물인 하마도 만약 그렇게 위험하지 않다면 농장의 마당에 키우기에 매우 좋은 동물이 됐을 것이다. 하마는 심지어 사자를 포함한 다른 어떤 아프리카 포유류보다 매년 더 많은 사람들을 죽인다.

mammal n. 포유류 동물 species n. 종(種), 종류 sufficiently ad. 충분한, 족한 nasty a. 불쾌한, 심술궂은, 난폭한 disposition n. 성질, 기질 incurably ad. 낫지 않을 정도로, 교정할 수 없을 만큼 disqualify v. ~의 자격을 박탈하다; 실격시키다; 적임이 아니라고 판정하다 domestication n. 길들이기; 교화 delicacy n. 섬세한 것, 우아함; 맛있는 것, 진미 herbivore n. 초식동물 formidable n. 무서운, 만만찮은 thrive v. 번창하다, 잘 자라다 garbage n. 쓰레기 relatively ad. 상대적으로 behave oneself 얌전하게 행동하다 captivity n. 감금, 속박 fabulous a. 엄청난, 굉장한 routinely ad. 일상적으로 rear v. 기르다, 사육하다 cub n. (곰·사자·호랑이 따위 야수의) 새끼 ritual n. 의식 prudent a. 신중한; 분별 있는, 현명한 suicidal a. 자살의 suitable a. 적당한, 알맞은 dominance hierarchy 지배계급(어느 정도의 지속성과 안정성을 갖는 관계로, 동물 집단의 구성원 상호 간에서 볼 수 있는 우위와 열위의 서열) trait n. 특색, 특성 insane a. 미친 barnyard n. 헛간의 앞마당; 농가의 안뜰

11 빈칸완성 ①

'회색곰을 사육해보려고 한 아이누족이 회색곰을 어렸을 때 죽여서 먹는 것이 현명하다는 것을 알게 되었으며, 회색곰을 더 오래 두는 것은 자살 행위가 될 것이다.'라는 말은 회색곰을 길들여 사육하는 것이 불가능에 가깝다는 의미이므로, 빈칸에는 '길들여진'이라는 의미의 ①이 적절하다. ② 제정신의 ③ 사로잡힌 ④ 미친

12 글의 제목 ②

풍부한 고기를 얻을 수 있음에도 길들여 사육할 수가 없어서 가축이 되지 못한 동물들에 대한 내용이므로, 제목으로는 ②가 적절하다.

위 글의 제목으로 가장 적절한 것을 고르시오.
① 난폭한 동물을 기르는 방법
② 가축으로 길들이기 어려운 동물들
③ 회색곰과 아프리카 물소의 잔혹성
④ 사람을 죽이는 동물들

13-14

시에라 클럽(Sierra Club)의 공정 언어 지침에서는 "stand", "Americans", "blind", "crazy"라는 단어를 사용하지 못하게 한다. 첫 두 단어가 공정 언어에 포함되지 못하는 것은 모두가 일어설 수 있는 것은 아니고 이 나라에 살고 있는 모든 사람이 시민인 것은 아니기 때문이다. 세 번째와 네 번째 단어는 비유적 표현("의원들은 기후 변화에 눈이 멀어 있다"인 경우에도 장애인들에게 모욕적이다. 이 지침은 또한 "장애인"이라는 말을 거부하고 "장애를 가지고 사는 사람들"이라는 말을 선호하는데, 이는 "노예가 된 사람"이 일반적으로 "노예"를 대체해온 것과 같은 이유에서다. 즉, 소위 "사람 우선 언어"라는 신조에 의해, "모든 사람은 장애나 다른 정체성이 아니라, 다른 무엇보다도 하나의 사람이다"라는 것을 확언하기 위함이다. 이 지침의 목적은 시에라 클럽이 "복지 여왕"과 같이 명백하게 경멸적인 용어를 반드시 피하게 하려는 것만이 아니다. 시에라 클럽은 그 어떤 특권, 위계질서, 편견 또는 배제의 흔적도 언어에서 말끔히 씻어내려고 한다. 열의에 찬 시에라 클럽은 엄청나게 많은 단어들을 모두 잘라내어 버렸다. "도시적인", "활기찬", "근면한", "갈색 가방"도 모두 미묘한 인종차별 때문에 땅으로 추락했다. "y'all(여러분)"이 가부장적인 "you guys(너희들)"을 대신하고, "발언권을 높여주다(elevate voices)"가 "권한을 주다(empower)"를 대체하는데, 이 단어가 이전에는 북돋워준다는 의미가 있었지만 이제는 거들먹거린다는 의미가 있기 때문이다. "가난한 사람들"은 계급주의적이고, "전투"와 "지뢰밭"은 퇴역군인들에게 실례가 되며, "우울한"은 장애를 도용한다. "이주자"는 설명할 것도 없이 그냥 사라져야 한다. 공정-언어 지침은 미국의 일부 주요 기관들, 특히 비영리 단체들 사이에서 확산되고 있다. 미국 암 협회도 지침을 가지고 있다. 미국 심장 협회, 미국 심리학 협회, 미국 의학 협회, 국립 레크리에이션 및 공원 협회, 콜롬비아 대학교 전문대학원 및 워싱턴 대학교도 마찬가지다.
이 지침들이 언어가 "진화"하고 있음을 가리키고 있긴 하지만, 이러한 변화들은 위로부터의 혁명이다. 이러한 변화들은 많은 사람들의 변하는 언어 습관에서 유기적으로 나타난 것이 아니다. 이러한 변화들은 모호하게 정의된 "공동체"를 대변한다고 칭하고 있는 잘 알려지지 않은 "전문가들"이 쓴 성명서에서 아래로 하달되며, 도덕적으로 강요당하고 있는 대중들에게는 여전히 아무 답변도 할 수 없는 변화들이다. 새로운 용어는 논의할 필요도 없이 논쟁에서 승리한다. 샌프란시스코 감독위원회가 "중범죄자"

를 "사법 집행 관련자"로 대신할 때, 그것은 법, 법원, 교도소에 뭔가 불법적인 것이 있다는 이념적 주장을 하고 있는 것이다. 만약 당신이 — 특정한 상황에서는, 당신이 받아들여야 한다고 틀림없이 생각할 것이듯이 — 그 변화를 받아들인다면, 그러면 당신은 그 논쟁을 묵인하고 있는 것이다.

equity n. 공평, 공정 discourage v. 방해하다, 저지하다 inclusion n. 포함 figures of speech 비유법 legislator n. 입법자, 법률제정자 insulting a. 모욕적인, 무례한 replace v. 대신하다, 대체하다 affirm v. 확인하다, 단언하다 tenet n. 교의, 신조 derogatory a. (명예·인격 따위를) 손상시키는 cleanse v. 정화하다, 깨끗하게 하다 privilege n. 특권, 특전 hierarchy n. 계급제도 bias n. 편견 exclusion n. 제외, 배제 vibrant a. 활기찬 racism n. 인종차별주의 supplant v. 대신하다 patriarchal a. 가부장적인 empower v. ~에게 권력[권한]을 주다 condescending a. 거들먹거리는, 잘난 체하는 classist a. 계급[계층] 차별주의, 계급적 편견을 가진 depressing a. 침울한 appropriate v. 전유하다; 착복하다 proliferate v. 증식하다, 급격히 늘다 nonprofit n. 비영리단체 linguistic a. 언어의, 언어학의 communiqué n. 공식 발표[성명] obscure a. 세상에 알려지지 않은, 무명의 purport v. (사실이 아닐 수도 있는 것을) 주장하다[칭하다] vaguely ad. 막연[애매]하게 define v. (성격·내용 따위를) 규정짓다, 한정하다 coerce v. 강요하다, 강제하다 felon n. 중죄인 illegitimate a. 불법의, 위법의 acquiesce in 묵묵히 따르다, 묵인하다

13 내용추론 ④

시에라 클럽은 소위 "사람 우선 언어"라는 신조에 의해, 모든 사람은 정체성이 아니라, 그저 한 명의 사람으로 평가받고 존중되어야 한다는 입장이다. 그러므로 ④는 본문에서 유추할 수 없는 내용이다.

위 글에서 유추할 수 있는 내용으로 가장 거리가 먼 것을 고르시오.
① 공정 언어 지침은 단어가 가진 암묵적인 인종차별 때문에 "도시적인"과 같이 잠재적으로 경멸적인 단어들을 사용하지 못하게 한다.
② 공정 언어 지침은 자신들이 임의로 설정한 기준에 의해 대중을 도덕적으로 강요하는 경향이 있다.
③ 시에라 클럽의 공정 언어 지침에 따르면 '권한을 주다'는 우월성을 내포하고 있기 때문에 피해야 할 단어이다.
④ 시에라 클럽의 공정 언어 지침의 주된 가정 중의 하나는 사람의 정체성을 우선시해야 한다는 것이다.

14 저자의 태도 ②

본문의 주제는 시에라 클럽의 공정 언어 지침에서 특정 단어들을 배제하고 있다는 것인데, 이에 대해 저자는 '공정 언어 지침이 대중을 도덕적으로 강요하고 있고, 일부 용어들의 교체에 특정 이념적 입장이 반영돼 있으며, 용어의 변경에 대중의 의견과 무관하게 몇몇 전문가들에 의해 결정되고 있다'고 지적하고 있다. 그러므로 저자는 주제에 대해 비판적인 입장을 취하고 있다고 할 수 있다.

위 글의 주제에 대해 저자가 취하는 관점으로 가장 적합한 것을 고르시오.
① 성마른
② 비판적인
③ 찬성하는
④ 설명적인

15-16

스트레스가 본질적으로 나쁜 것은 아니다. 예를 들어, 웨이트 트레이닝을 통해 근육에 스트레스를 주는 것은 유익한 변화로 이어진다. 또한 건강한 사람들에게 단기적인 스트레스는 일반적으로 위험하지 않다. 그러나 특히 나이가 많거나 건강하지 않은 사람들에게 스트레스가 지속된다면, 스트레스에 대한 반응의 장기적인 영향은 심각한 건강 문제로 이어질 수 있다. 스트레스는 당신이 새롭고, 예측할 수 없거나, 위협적인 상황에 직면할 때 발생하고, 당신이 그것을 성공적으로 관리할 수 있을지를 알지 못할 때 발생한다. 당신이 육체적으로 또는 감정적으로 스트레스를 받을 때, 당신의 몸은 곧바로 '투쟁이냐 도피냐'의 모드로 바뀐다. 코르티솔은 당신의 시스템 전체에 몰려들어, 당신의 몸이 포도당을 방출하도록 신호를 보낸다. 결국, 포도당은 당신이 위협과 싸우거나 도망칠 준비가 더 잘되도록 근육에 에너지를 공급한다. 이처럼 코르티솔이 몰려오는 동안, 당신의 심장박동 수가 늘어날 수 있고, 호흡이 빨라질 수도 있고, 어지럽거나 메스꺼움을 느낄 수도 있다.

만일 당신이 정말로 포식자와 싸우거나 도망쳐야 한다면, 당신의 코르티솔 수준은 그러한 갈등이 끝나면 다시 떨어질 것이다. 그러나 당신이 만성적으로 스트레스를 받을 때, 코르티솔 수준들은 높아진 채로 있을 것이다. 그렇게 높아진 상태로 있는 것은 좋지 않은데, 높은 수준의 코르티솔은 심혈관 질환, 당뇨병 및 만성 위장 질환과 같은 병을 악화시킬 수 있기 때문이다. 스트레스는 또한 불안, 짜증, 수면의 질 저하, 약물 남용, 만성적인 불신 또는 걱정과 그 이상의 것들을 유발하거나 그 원인이 될 수 있다. 다행히도, 스트레스와 싸울 수 있는 방법들이 많이 있다. 세계보건기구는 매일의 일과를 지키고, 충분한 수면을 취하고, 건강에 좋은 음식을 먹고, 뉴스를 보거나 소셜 미디어를 하는 시간을 줄일 것을 권장한다. 그것은 또한 다른 사람들과 계속 관계를 유지하고 명상과 심호흡과 같이 마음을 진정시키는 활동을 하는 것도 도움이 된다. 하지만, 가장 성공적인 도구들 중의 하나는 신체활동이다.

inherently ad. 본질적으로 beneficial a. 유익한 typically ad. 전형적으로 hazard n. 위험, 모험 unpredictable a. 예언[예측]할 수 없는 threatening a. 위협적인 glucose n. 포도당 dizzy a. 현기증 나는 nauseate v. 메스껍게 하다 flee v. 달아나다, 도망치다 predator n. 약탈자, 포식자 chronically ad. 만성적으로 elevated a. 높여진, 높은 exacerbate v. (병 등을) 악화시키다 cardiovascular disease 심혈관 질환 diabetes n. 당뇨병 gastrointestinal a. 위장의 contribute to ~에 기여하다, ~의 원인이 되다 substance abuse 약물 남용

---

15 빈칸완성 ③

스트레스의 폐해가 많은 상황에서 스트레스와 싸울 수 있는 방법들이 많이 있다는 것은 '다행스러운' 것이라 할 수 있다. 그러므로 빈칸에는 '다행스럽게도'라는 의미의 ③이 들어가야 한다. ① 불행하게도 ② 그와는 대조적으로 ④ 요컨대

---

16 내용추론 ③

마지막 문단에서 스트레스와 싸우는 방법으로 '소셜 미디어를 하는 시간을 줄일 것'을 권하고 있으므로, ③은 본문에서 유추할 수 없는 내용이다.

위 글에서 유추할 수 있는 내용으로 가장 거리가 먼 것을 고르시오.
① 단기적인 스트레스는 건설적인 변화를 일으킬 수 있다.
② 스트레스가 지속되면 코르티솔 수치가 높아진 채로 있을 것이다.
③ 스트레스를 극복하기 위해 소셜 미디어를 하는 것이 좋다.
④ 코르티솔의 수치가 높아지면, 개인의 호흡이 빨라질 수 있다.

17-18

앞으로 수십 년간의 세계질서에 관해 본질적인 의미를 규정하는 질문은 중국과 미국이 투키디데스(Thucydides)의 함정에서 벗어날 수 있는가? 하는 것일 것이다. 그 역사가의 은유는, 기원전 5세기에 아테네와 19세기 말에 독일이 그랬듯이, 신흥 강대국이 패권 국가와 경쟁할 때 두 당사자가 직면하는 위험을 우리에게 상기시켜 준다. 그러한 도전은 대부분 전쟁으로 끝났다. 평화적으로 끝난 사례들의 경우는 관련된 양국 정부와 사회의 태도와 행동에 엄청난 변화를 요구했다.

모든 신흥 강대국의 급속한 출현은 현재의 상황을 교란시킨다. 하버드 대학의 미국 국익 위원회가 중국에 대해 한 말과 같이, 21세기에 "그 정도 비중의 유명 여가수가 무대에 들어가서 아무런 결과물을 만들어내지 못하는 경우는 없다."

우리가 역사를 바탕으로 베팅한다면, 투키디데스의 함정에 대한 질문의 답은 분명해 보인다. 1500년 이후 신흥 국가가 등장하여 패권 국가에 도전했던 15건의 사례 가운데 11건에서 전쟁이 일어났다. 통일 이후 독일이 유럽 최대의 경제대국인 영국을 추월한 것을 생각해보자. 1914년과 1939년에 독일의 침략과 영국의 대응으로 세계대전이 일어났다.

중국의 부상이 미국에게 불편한 일이긴 하지만, 점점 더 강해지고 있는 중국이 국가 간의 관계에서 더 많은 발언권과 더 큰 영향력을 요구하는 것에는 부자연스러운 점이 전혀 없다. 미국인들, 특히 "우리와 더 닮아져야 한다"며 중국을 훈계하는 사람들은 우리 자신의 역사를 되돌아보아야 한다.

defining a. 본질적인 의미를 규정하는 Thucydides's trap 투키디데스의 함정(신흥 강국이 기존의 강대국을 위협할 때 전쟁을 유발하게 된다는 이론) metaphor n. 은유 observe v. 말하다; 관찰하다 diva n. 유명 여가수 proportion n. 비율; 정도; 규모 unification n. 통일 overtake v. 따라잡다, 추월하다 aggression n. 공격, 침략 sway n. 동요, 흔들림; 지배력, 영향력 lecture v. 강의하다; 훈계하다

---

17 빈칸완성 ④

"신흥 강대국과 패권 국가의 경쟁은 많은 경우에 전쟁으로 귀결됐고, 평화적으로 끝난 사례들의 경우에서도 양국 정부와 사회의 태도와 행동에 엄청난 변화를 요구했다."라는 내용을 통해 모든 신흥 강대국의 급속한 출현은 기존 질서에 큰 변화를 가져온다는 것을 알 수 있다. 그러므로 ⓐ에는 '현상(現狀)' '현재의 상황'이라는 의미의 status quo가 적절하다. 한편, 1500년 이후 신흥 국가가 등장하여 패권 국가에 도전했던 15건의 사례 가운데 11건에서 전쟁이 일어났다면, 투키디데스의 함정에 대한 질문의 답은 '전쟁'으로 결론이 날 가능성이 매우 높은 것이 명백하다고 할 수 있으므로, ⓑ에는 '명백한'이라는 의미를 가진 apparent와 obvious가 가능하다. 따라서 상기 조건을 모두 만족시키는 ④가 정답이다. ① 불균형 ─ 명백한 ② 불균형 ─ 불투명한 ③ 현재 상황 ─ 양면 가치의

18 내용일치 ①

본문은 미중 간의 갈등으로 인해 전쟁이 발생할 가능성이 매우 높다는 입장이므로 ①이 본문의 내용과 거리가 먼 진술이다.

위 글의 내용과 가장 거리가 먼 것을 고르시오.
① 미국과 중국의 갈등이 첨예하지만, 예상되는 전쟁은 피할 수 있을 것으로 보인다.
② 국제 관계의 역동성이 지속적으로 변화하고 있는 것은 보다 영향력 있는 중국에 의해 제기되는 문제를 해결하기 위한 포괄적인 전략의 필요성을 강조한다.
③ 역사의 양상은 신흥 강대국이 패권 국가와 대립할 때 분쟁이 발생했다는 생각을 강하게 뒷받침한다.
④ 1500년 이후 신흥강대국이 등장하여 패권 국가에 도전했던 많은 경우에 전쟁이 발생했다.

19-20

유력 과학저널 『네이처』는 상온과 상대적으로 낮은 기압에서 작동할 수 있는 초전도체 ─ 전기저항이 0인 상태에서 전류를 전달하는 물질 ─ 를 발견했다고 주장하는 논란의 여지가 있는 논문을 철회했다.
디아스(Dias)와 살라마트(Salamat)가 작성한 올해의 보고서는 초전도성을 주장했다가 폭망하고 만 2023년의 두 번째 주요 사례다. 7월에, 서울의 한 벤처기업의 이와 또 다른 팀은 LK-99라 불리는 보라색 결정질 물질 ─ 구리, 납, 인, 산소로 만들어진 ─ 에 대해 설명했는데, 그들은 이 물질이 상압과 적어도 127℃ (400 켈빈)까지의 기온에서 초전도성을 보였다고 말했다. 온라인은 흥분으로 들끓었고 결과를 재현하려는 많은 시도들이 있었지만, 연구원들은 이 물질이 초전도체가 전혀 아니라는 빠른 의견 일치에 도달했다.
초전도체는 자기 공명 영상 기기에서 입자 충돌기에 이르는 많은 응용 분야에서 중요하지만, 극도로 낮은 온도를 유지해야 한다는 점으로 인해 사용이 제한되어왔다. 수십 년 동안 연구원들은 냉동하지 않고도 초전도성을 보이는 물질을 찾겠다는 꿈을 갖고 새로운 물질을 개발해왔다.
로마 사피엔자(Sapienza) 대학의 물리학자 릴리아 보에리(Lilia Boeri)는 이 분야의 전문가들이 올해 디아스와 살라마트의 논문이 발표된 이후부터 회의적이었다고 말한다. 그녀의 말에 따르면, 이는 부분적으로는 그 연구팀을 둘러싸고 벌어지고 있는 논란 때문이기도 하고, 부분적으로는 최근의 그 논문이 자신이 높은 수준이라고 생각하는 기준에 맞게 작성되지 않았기 때문이기도 하다.

controversial a. 논의의 여지가 있는 superconductor n. 초전도체 electrical current 전류 resistance n. 저항 relatively ad. 상대적으로 significant a. 중대한, 중요한 superconductivity n. 초전도성 crash and burn 갑자기 완전히 망하다, 실패하다 crystalline a. 수정의, 투명한; 결정질의 dub v. ~라고 칭하다 lead n. <화학> 납 phosphorus n. <화학> 인(燐) reproduce v. 재생하다, 재현하다 consensus n. (의견·증언 따위의) 일치 magnetic resonance imaging machine 자기공명영상기기 particle collider 입자충돌기 refrigeration n. 냉동, 냉각 specialist n. 전문가 sceptical a. 회의적인 physicist n. 물리학자 swirl v. 소용돌이치다

19 빈칸완성 ③

많은 연구원들이 디아스(Dias)와 살라마트(Salamat)가 발견했다는 초전도체가 전혀 초전도체가 아니라는 데 의견이 일치하고 있고 논문도 높은 수준이 아니었다는 내용을 통해, 『네이처』가 그 논문을 철회했을 것임을 알 수 있다. 따라서 빈칸에는 '취소하다', '철회하다'라는 의미의 ③이 적절하다. ① 발췌하다 ② 계약하다 ④ 손상시키다

20 내용일치 ③

디아스와 살라마트의 보고서는 초전도체 발견을 둘러싼 논란을 종식시킨 것이 아니라 오히려 논란을 촉발시켰다고 볼 수 있다. 그러므로 ③이 정답이다.

위 글의 내용과 가장 거리가 먼 것을 고르시오.
① 디아스와 살라마트의 논문이 발표된 이후 그 분야의 전문가들은 회의적이었다.
② LK-99를 발견했다는 주장은 온라인에서 많은 흥분을 이끌어냈지만, 연구원들은 그 물질이 초전도체가 아니라는 빠른 의견 일치에 도달했다.
③ 디아스와 살라마트의 보고서는 초전도체 발견을 둘러싼 논란을 종식시켰다.
④ 초전도체 관련 논문에 대한 의구심은 연구팀과 최신 논문의 질을 둘러싼 논란에서 비롯된 것으로 보인다.

2024 서울여자대학교(오전 A형)

01 ④	02 ②	03 ①	04 ②	05 ③	06 ④	07 ①	08 ②	09 ③	10 ②
11 ①	12 ③	13 ④	14 ④	15 ②	16 ①	17 ②	18 ③	19 ①	20 ④
21 ①	22 ①	23 ④	24 ③	25 ③	26 ②	27 ②	28 ③	29 ①	30 ②
31 ④	32 ①	33 ④	34 ②	35 ④	36 ③	37 ②	38 ③	39 ①	40 ④

01 동의어 ④

oblige v. 강요하다; ~에게 은혜를 베풀다, ~을 기쁘게 해주다(= indulge) obey v. 복종하다 repay v. 은혜를 갚다, 보답하다 salute v. 인사하다, 경례하다

우리는 우리에게 참석해달라고 특별히 요청한 몇몇 옛 친구들을 기쁘게 해주기 위해 그 파티에 갔을 뿐이었다.

02 동의어 ②

thrust n. 밀기, 공격; 취지, 진의, 요지, 요점(= point) Haight-Ashbury 헤이트 애시베리(샌프란시스코의 한 지구, 60년대 히피와 마약 문화의 중심지) shock n. 충격, 충격적 사건 content n. 내용 weakness n. 약점

그 영화의 진짜 요점은 샌프란시스코의 헤이트 애시베리(Haight-Ashbury)를 고찰한 것이다.

03 동의어 ①

impact n. 충돌; 영향 secular a. 현세의, 세속적인 permissive a. 허용하는, 관대한, 관용의, 자유인(= liberal) inventive a. 발명의, 발명의 재능이 있는 persevering a. 참을성 있는, 끈기 있는 encouraging a. 장려하는, 고무하는

『How Far Can You Go?』(1980)는 세속적이고 자유방임적인 사회가 영국 가톨릭 신자들의 대인 관계에 미치는 영향을 고찰하고 있다.

04 동의어 ②

remnant n. 나머지, 잔여; 유물(= remain) profile n. 옆모습, 측면; 윤곽 delicacy n. 섬세함; 우아함 adaptation n. 적응, 순응

로마 제국의 유물은 아시아, 유럽, 아프리카의 여러 나라에서 찾아볼 수 있다.

05 동의어 ③

shelf n. 선반 arrange v. 배열하다, 정리하다, 정돈하다 haphazardly ad. 우연히, 되는 대로, 아무렇게나(= carelessly) deliberately ad. 신중히; 의도적으로 skillfully ad. 능숙능란하게, 교묘하게 linearly ad. 선으로, 연속적으로

선반 위의 책들이 아무렇게나 배열돼 있었다.

06 논리완성 ④

목적어인 170여 점의 작품은 전시회에서 전시될 대상에 해당하므로, 빈칸에는 '특징적으로 다루다', '특징으로 삼다', '두드러지게 하다'라는 의미의 ④가 들어가는 것이 자연스럽다.

exhibition n. 전람회, 전시회 miniature painting 세밀화(細密畵) brace v. 버티다, 떠받치다; 보강하다 uplift v. 들어 올리다; ~의 정신을 양양하다 advance v. 진전시키다; 촉진하다 feature v. 특별히 포함하다, 특징으로 삼다, 두드러지게 하다, 크게 다루다

그 전시회는 16세기 중반으로 거슬러 올라가는 세밀화(細密畵)를 비롯한 170여 점의 작품을 특징적으로 다룰 것이다.

07 논리완성 ①

영양학자들은 십대들이 과체중 상태가 된 것을 패스트푸드에 대한 의존도 증가 때문으로 보고 있다. 즉, 패스트푸드에 대한 의존도 증가가 십대들의 과체중이 초래된 원인인 것이다. 따라서 빈칸에는 '범인', '(문제를 일으킨) 장본인'이라는 의미의 ①이 적절하다.

nutritionist n. 영양학자 reliance n. 의지, 신뢰 culprit n. 범인; (문제를 일으킨) 장본인 arbiter n. 중재인 plaintiff n. 원고, 고소인 prosecutor n. 기소자, 고발자

오늘날 점점 더 많은 십대들이 이전보다 과체중이며, 영양학자들은 그 주된 원인이 패스트푸드에 대한 의존도 증가라고 말한다.

08 논리완성 ②

예측이 불가능했던 선거 결과에 대한 반응으로는 '놀라움', '경악' 등이 적절하다.

poll n. 투표, 투표결과; 여론조사 disguise v. 변장하다, 가장하다; 숨기다 astound v. 놀라게 하다, 경악시키다 confront v. ~에 직면하다, 맞서다 evaporate v. 증발시키다

어느 여론조사에서도 승자를 예측하지 못했기 때문에 모두가 선거 결과에 놀랐다.

09 논리완성 ③

부패한 음식의 섭취는 건강을 해치게 될 것이므로, 빈칸에는 '유해한'이라는 의미의 ③이 들어가야 한다.

decayed a. 썩은, 부패한 eligible a. 적격의, 적임의 gratifying a. 즐거운, 만족시키는 detrimental a. 유해한, 손해되는 intermittent a. 간헐적인

부패한 음식을 먹는 것은 당신의 건강에 해로울 수 있다.

10 논리완성 ②

직원들이 급여의 삭감을 요청받았다면 소란스러워졌거나 항의나 불만의 소리가 흘러나왔을 것이므로, 빈칸에는 ②가 들어가는 것이 적절하다.

jest n. 농담, 익살 clamor n. 소란; 소리 높은 불평[항의] windfall n. 예기치 않은 횡재 diversion n. 기분전환, 오락

직원들이 급여 삭감을 요청받았을 때, 상당히 큰 불평의 소리가 있었다.

11 명사의 소유격 ①

명사에 "-'s"를 붙여 소유격을 나타낼 수 있는데, 두 사람 각각의 소유를 나타낼 때는 각각의 명사에 "-'s"를 붙이고, 두 사람 공동의 소유를 나타낼 때는 뒤에 오는 명사에만 "-'s"를 붙인다. 주어진 문장은 각각의 명사에 "-'s"가 붙어 있으므로 뒤에 그들 각각이 소유한 자동차를 가리키는 대명사로 fix의 목적어가 them이어야 하는데 it이다. 이는 공동 소유의 자동차임을 말하는 것이므로 ①을 Jennifer로 고쳐야 한다.

break down (기계·차량이) 고장 나다

제니퍼(Jennifer)와 데이비드(David)의 차가 또 고장이 났지만, 다행히도 그들은 그 차를 수리하는 방법을 알고 있었다.

12 명사의 병치 ③

③은 이어지는 architecture, politics, philosophy와 함께 전치사 of의 목적어로 쓰였으므로, 이 역시 다른 것들과 마찬가지로 명사로 써야 한다. ③을 명사 art로 고친다.

civilization n. 문명 achievement n. 업적; 성취, 달성 architecture n. 건축술, 건축학

500년에, 고대 그리스는 예술, 건축학, 정치학, 철학 분야에서 위대한 업적을 남기며 최고 수준의 문명에 도달하고 있었다.

13 allow+목적어+to부정사 ④

allow가 5형식 문형으로 쓰이는 경우, 목적격 보어로는 to부정사가 온다. 그러므로 ④를 to become으로 고쳐야 한다. ① 강조 구문에 쓰인 that이다. ③ a child를 수식하는 현재분사이고 부정어인 not은 분사 앞에 붙인다.

immigrant a. (타국에서) 이주하는, 이민자의

영어를 한 마디도 알지 못하는 아이로 도착한 인도 출신 이민자 소녀인 내가 『월스트리트 저널』의 기자가 될 수 있게 해준 것은 바로 우리의 공립학교 제도였다.

14 extent와 함께 쓰는 전치사 ④

these influence readers가 '주어+동사+목적어'로 이뤄진 완전한 절의 형태이므로, what extent의 문법적인 역할이 없는 상태이다. 그런데 extent는 전치사 to와 함께 사용되어 '~ 정도로'의 뜻을 가지므로, what extent 앞에 전치사 to를 넣어야 한다.

editorial n. 사설 coverage n. 취재, 보도 extent n. 정도 influence v. 영향을 미치다

신문사 소유주들이 시사적인 주제에 대해 가지고 있는 정치적 견해는 대개 뉴스 기사의 선정과 취재에서 뿐만 아니라 언론사의 사설에서도 찾아볼 수 있으며, 이 견해가 독자에게 어느 정도로 영향을 미치는지에 관해 종종 논의가 이뤄지고 있다.

15 not so much A as B ②

'A라기보다는 B이다'라는 의미의 관용표현은 not so much A as B로 나타낸다. 그러므로 ②를 as로 고쳐야 한다.

upset a. 속상한, 마음이 상한 cancellation n. 취소 disappointed a. 실망한

제롬(Jerome)은 콘서트가 취소된 것에 대해 마음이 상했다기보다는 오랜 친구들과 하루를 보낼 수 없게 된 것에 실망했다.

16 병치 구조 ①

not only A but also B의 상관접속사 구문에서 A와 B의 자리에는 문법적인 구조나 역할이 동일한 표현이 온다. 주어진 문장에서 A의 자리에 '전치사+동명사' 형태인 for reviving이 왔으므로, B에 해당하는 빈칸에도 동일한 형태가 와야 한다. 따라서 ①이 정답이다.

be indebted to ~에게 신세를 지다, 은혜를 입다 revive v. 되살아나게 하다, 부활시키다 introduce v. 소개하다, 도입하다

우리가 그리스의 작품들을 되살린 것뿐 아니라 인도로부터 유용한 사상을 도입하게 된 것은 아랍인들의 덕택이다.

17 타동사의 목적어 / 수동을 나타내는 과거분사   ②

타동사 excrete의 목적어로 명사 a chemical이 적절하며, a chemical은 call하는 행위의 주체가 아닌 대상이므로 수동을 나타내는 과거분사로 수식해야 한다. 따라서 ②가 정답이다.

excrete v. 배설하다, 분비하다   enkephalin n. 엔케펄린(뇌하수체에서 만드는, 진통작용을 하는 물질)   numb v. 감각을 없애다, 마비시키다   chemical n. 화학제품, 화학물질

사람이 다치게 될 때, 뇌는 엔케펄린이라 불리는 화학물질을 분비하여 통증에 무감각하게 만든다.

18 관계대명사절   ③

문제와 보기에 2개의 동사가 제시돼 있으므로, 접속사 역할을 하는 관계대명사를 이용하여 두 문장을 연결해야 한다. 주어진 문장은 'Those were the soldiers. + It was the soldiers' responsibility to save the city.'로 파악할 수 있다. 두 번째 문장의 the soldiers'가 소유격 whose로 되고 whose responsibility가 It was 앞에 온 ③이 정답으로 적절하다.

저 사람들은 그 도시를 구하는 것을 책임으로 맡고 있던 군인들이었다.

19 부분을 나타내는 전치사   ①

'~중에서'와 같이 부분을 나타내는 전치사는 of이다.

statue n. 조각상, 조각물

영국에 있는 925개의 공공 조각물 중에서, 여성 혼자 서 있는 동상은 158개에 불과하다.

20 분사구문   ④

Plastic has become a necessity of modern life라는 절 뒤에 접속사 없이 빈칸 앞뒤로 두 개의 긴 명사구가 배치되어 있으므로 빈칸에는 분사구문을 만드는 현재분사인 ④가 적절하다. 그 경우에 빈칸 앞의 긴 명사구는 분사구문의 의미상 주어이고 빈칸 뒤의 긴 명사구는 목적어가 된다.

durability n. 내구성   undeniable a. 부인[부정]할 수 없는, 명백한; 흠잡을 데 없는, 더할 나위 없는   utility n. 유용, 유익   convenience n. 편리, 편의

플라스틱은, 그 특유한 경량성, 내구성, 저비용성의 결합으로 흠잡을 데 없는 효용성과 높은 수준의 편의성을 제공하여, 현대 생활의 필수품이 되었다.

21 논리완성   ①

twist가 '반전', '(사건·사태의) 예기치 않은 진전'의 의미로 쓰였다. AI가 초래할 것으로 예상되는 여러 문제들이 사람들을 두렵게 만들고 있는 상황에서의 반전은 'AI와 같은 기술을 이용하여 그 문제들을 해결하는 것'이 될 것이다. 그러므로 ①이 정답이다. ③은 우리의 일자리를 빼앗을 수 있는 것이기 때문에 부적절하다.

unbiased a. 선입관이 없는, 편견 없는   there's no ~ing ~하는 것은 불가능하다   transformative a. 변화시키는, 변화시키는 힘이 있는   inequality n. 불평등   genuine a. 진짜의; 진심에서 우러난   twist n. (사건·사태의) 예기치 않은 진전, 뜻밖의 전개, 반전

우리는 인공지능(AI)이 우리에게 편견 없는 정보를 제공해줄 것으로 믿을 수 있는가? AI로 하여금 기계를 제어하거나 자동차를 운전하게 해도 안전한가? 그리고 중요한 질문이 있는데, AI가 우리의 일자리를 빼앗을까? 기술이 중요하다는 것은 부인할 수 없다. 종종, 그것은 변화시키는 힘이 있다. 그리고 사람들이 변화를 두려워하는 것은 자연스러운 일이다. 직업의 안정성에 대해 걱정하는 것. 미래, 기후변화, 사회적 불평등에 대해 걱정하는 것. 이런 것들은 추상적인 문제가 아니다. 이것들은 우리 중 많은 사람들에게는 진심으로 두려운 것들이다. 하지만 여기에는 반전이 있다. 그것은 바로 기술이 이러한 문제들을 해결하는 데 있어서 우리가 할 수 있는 최선의 선택일 수도 있다는 것이다.

① 기술이 이러한 문제들을 해결하는 데 있어서 우리가 할 수 있는 최선의 선택일 수도 있다
② 우리는 보다 긴급하고 중대한 문제들에 압도당해 있다
③ AI가 반복적이고, 지루하고, 노동 집약적인 작업을 떠맡을 것이다
④ 우리는 기술이 우리의 일상생활에 얼마나 영향을 미치고 있는지를 측정할 수 없다

22 논리완성   ①

앞에서 '정신의 인지적인 개념이 신체를 배제한 채 맥락 없이 정의되고 연구돼 왔음'을 언급했는데, 그 뒤에 역접의 However가 왔으므로 빈칸을 포함하고 있는 절은 정신의 활동이 신체를 포함한 맥락 속에서 행해진다는 내용이 되어야 한다. 그러므로 빈칸에는 ①이 적절하다.

cognitive a. 인식[인지]의, 인식력 있는   neuroscience n. 신경과학   discipline n. 학과, 교과, (학문의) 분야   neural a. 신경의, 신경계의   correlate n. 서로 관계있는 사람[것], 상관물   conceive of 상상하다, 생각하다   define v. (성격·내용 따위를) 규정짓다; (말의) 정의를 내리다   context-free a. 맥락이 없는   exclude v. 제외하다, 배제하다   intuitive a. 직관적인   embody v. 구체화하다   impact v. 영향을 주다   vice versa 그 역[반대]도 마찬가지이다

인지신경과학과 그 주변 학문들은 수십 년 동안 인간의 행동과 그것의 신경적 상호연관성을 연구해왔다. 지금까지, 이 연구의 대부분은 정신의 상태를 개인의 머리 안에 존재하는 "내적인" 상태로 생각해왔다. 이러한 접근법은 많은 중요한 발견들로 이어졌지만, 또한 중요한 도전들에 직면해야만 했다. 그러한 한 가지 문제는 정신의 인지적인 개념이 역사적으로 맥락 없이 정의되고 연구되어 왔으며, 심지어 뇌가 일부를 이루고 있는 신체의 나머지 부분을 배제시키기까지 했다는 것이다. 그러나, 모든 감정, 생각 및 행동은 신체의 맥락에서 발생하며, 따라서 체화된 경험이 우리의 정신적 처리와 자아에 대한 이해에 영향을 미칠 수 있다는 것은 직관적인 것이며, 그 반대도 마찬가지이다.

① 신체의 맥락에서 발생한다
② 정신 상태를 지속하는 데 그 뿌리를 두고 있다
③ 우리가 대개 "자아"라고 부르는 것을 구성한다
④ 역사적인 현상일 뿐만 아니라 주관적인 현상이다

23 논리완성 ④

빈칸 이하에서는 인간으로 인해 생태계가 큰 피해를 입고 있음을 이야기하고 있다. 그러므로 이를 요약하는 ④가 빈칸에 들어가야 한다.

environmental a. 환경의 species n. 종(種), 종류 vary v. 변화하다, 가지각색이다 ecosystem n. 생태계 significant a. 중요한; 상당한 evolve v. 진화하다 consequence n. 결과; 중요성 extinct a. 멸종한, 절멸한 uproot v. 절멸하다 reshuffle v. 재편하다 intentionally ad. 의도적으로

환경 변화는 지구상의 모든 종(種)이 공유하는 이야기이다. 그 영향은 지역과 생태계마다 다르지만, 많은 중요한 문제들이 하나의 원천으로 귀결되는 경향이 있는데, 바로 인간의 영향이다. 자연은 스스로 움직이고 진화하며, 만약 인간이 전혀 이곳에 없다면 계속 그렇게 해왔을 것이다. 그러나 현실은 우리가 여기에 있다는 것이며, 그래서 심지어 자연의 변화조차 우리 자신이 설계한 놀이판 위에서 발생한다. "우리는 우리의 행동의 결과가 실시간으로 일어나는 것을 보고 있습니다."라고 쉐인(Shane)은 말한다. "종들은 믿을 수 없는 속도로 멸종되고 있습니다. 전 세계의 자연 생태계가 절멸하고 있습니다. 동물의 개체군들은 ― 의도적으로 그리고 의도치 않게 ― 전 세계에서 재편되고 있으며, 그 결과 토착종들에게 새로운 도전을 가져오고 있습니다."

① 자연 선택
② 신성한 목적
③ 생태학적 조정
④ 인간의 영향

24 논리완성 ③

면직물로 만든 인조 어미는 편안함을 제공했다고 했으므로, 두려움을 느끼게 됐을 때 새끼 원숭이들이 즉시 면직물로 만든 어미에게로 달려가 매달린 것은 편안함을 느끼고자 했기 때문일 것이다. 따라서 편안함의 필요가 달려가 매달리는 행동의 동기가 되었으므로 빈칸에는 ③이 적절하다.

rear v. 기르다 artificial a. 인조의, 인공의 nipple n. 젖꼭지 terrycloth n. 테리클로스(일반적으로 타월이라 불리는 면직물) attachment n. 애정, 애착 frighten v. 놀라게 하다, 두려워하게 하다 cuddle v. 꼭 껴안다

할로우(Harlow)는 갓 태어난 원숭이들을 어미로부터 분리시켜 두 마리의 인조 어미가 들어있는 우리에서 길렀다. 그 중 하나의 "어미"는 철사로 만들어져 있었는데, 거기에 고무 젖꼭지가 달려 있어서 새끼 원숭이들이 젖을 얻을 수 있었다. 그것은 먹을 것은 제공했지만 신체적인 편안함은 제공하지 않았다. 나머지 하나의 인공 어미는 젖꼭지가 없었지만 부드럽고 편안한 면직물로 만들어져 있었다. 만약 돌봄 제공자가 먹을 것을 제공한다는 이유만으로 애착이 형성되는 것이라면, 새끼 원숭이들은 철사로 만든 어미를 선호할 것으로 예상된다. 사실, 그들은 대부분의 시간을 면직물로 만든 어미와 함께 보냈다. 그리고 두려움을 느끼게 됐을 때, 새끼 원숭이들은 즉시 면직물로 만든 어미에게로 달려가 매달렸다. 할로우는 그 원숭이들이 편안함의 필요에 의해 동기부여가 되었다는 결론을 내렸다. 면직물로 만든 어미는 부드럽게 껴안는 느낌을 제공했는데, 이것은 원숭이 새끼들이 위험을 감지했을 때 필요한 것이었다.

① 젖꼭지보다 면직물을 더 좋아했다
② 두려움을 느꼈을 때 배가 고프지 않았다
③ 편안함의 필요에 의해 동기부여가 되었다
④ 돌봄 제공자가 부재중일 때 심적인 장애를 보았다

25 논리완성 ③

바로 앞 문장에서 충분한 수면과 낮잠에 대한 주변 사람들의 부정적인 시각을 언급했는데, 그 뒤에 Yet이 나왔으므로 빈칸에는 수면에 대한 긍정적인 시각의 일반적인 내용인 ③이 적절하다. ②는 '새로운 기술 학습'이 너무 특수한 내용이어서 이에 대한 근거가 본문에 없다.

overworked a. 혹사당하는 round-the-clock 24시간[밤낮 없이] 계속되는 grab a nap 잠깐 낮잠을 자다 run the risk of ~의 위험을 무릅쓰다 label v. (라벨을 붙여서) 분류하다; ~을 (…이라고) 부르다 unmotivated a. 동기 부여가 되지 않은 go-getter n. 진취적인 사람, 추진력 있는 사람, (특히 사업에서) 성공하려고 단단히 작정한 사람 indicate v. 나타내다 sufficient a. 충분한 nutritious a. 영양분이 있는

우리의 현대 사회에서, 충분한 수면을 취하는 것은 어려운 일이다. 우리는 바쁘고, 혹사를 당하는 삶을 살고 있으며 모든 것을 끝내기 위해 종종 잠을 포기해야 한다. 24시간 내내 방송되는 텔레비전은 우리를 늦게까지 깨어있도록 유혹한다. 그리고 밤에 충분한 수면을 취하거나 낮잠을 자게 되면, 우리는 주위에 있는 진취적인 사람들로부터 "동기부여가 돼 있지 않다"거나 "태만하다"고 불릴 위험이 있다. 하지만 연구에 따르면, 휴식을 고집하는 사람들이 가장 현명하다. 여러 연구는 충분한 수면이 규칙적인 운동과 영양가 있는 식단만큼이나 건강에 중요하다는 사실을 보여준다. 그것은 우리를 더 똑똑하게 만들어줄지도 모른다.

① 아기들과 아이들은 어른들보다 더 많은 잠을 필요로 한다
② 잠이 부족한 사람들은 새로운 기술을 배우는 데 어려움을 겪는다
③ 휴식을 고집하는 사람들이 가장 현명하다
④ 우리는 하룻밤 푹 자는 것을 불필요한 사치로 볼 필요가 있다

26 논리완성 ②

학습자들의 영혼에 '망각'을 불러일으킬 것이라 생각한 이유로는 그것이 '기억력을 사용하지 않게 만들 것'이라고 여긴 것이 적절하다.

mourn v. 슬퍼하다, 애도하다 threaten v. 협박하다, 위협하다 rhetoric n. 수사(修辭); 수사학; 웅변술 claim v. 주장하다 impart v. 주다, 전하다; 알리다 semblance n. 외형, 겉보기; 닮음 omniscient a. 전지(全知)의, 무엇이든지 알고 있는; 박식한 artificial intelligence 인공지능

플라톤은 글의 사용이 기억을 기반으로 하는 전통적인 수사(修辭) 기술을 위협할 거라 걱정하면서 알파벳의 발명을 한탄했다. 그가 쓴 『대화』에서, 플라톤은 이러한 보다 현대적인 기술을 사용하는 것은 그들(학습자들)이 자신들의 기억력을 사용하지 않을 것이기 때문에 "학습자들의 영혼에 망각을 불러일으킬 것이며, 그것은 "진실이 아니라 진실 비슷한 것만"을 전달할 것이고, 그것을 받아들이는 사람들은 "모든 것을 다 아는 것처럼 보이면서도

대체로 아무것도 모를 것이다."라고 주장했다. 만약 플라톤이 오늘날 살아 있다면, 그는 OpenAI가 공개한 대화형 인공지능 프로그램인 ChatGPT에 대해서도 비슷한 말을 할까?

① 그들은 아무것도 모를 것이다
② 그들은 자신들의 기억력을 사용하지 않을 것이다
③ 그들은 진리를 추구하려고 애쓰지 않을 것이다
④ 그들은 알파벳에 관심이 있을 것이다

27-28

99.9%가 넘는 거의 모든 생명체의 운명은 썩어서 사라지는 것이다. 당신에게서 생기가 사라지고 나면, 당신이 가지고 있는 모든 분자는 갉아 먹혀서 당신에게서 떨어져 나가거나 혹은 씻겨나가서 어떤 다른 조직체에서 이용될 것이다. 그건 그저 그렇게 될 수밖에 없다. 당신이 잡아먹히지 않는 0.1% 이하의 생물 무리에 성공적으로 들어간다 하더라도, 화석화될 가능성은 매우 낮다. 화석이 되기 위해서는 몇 가지 일들이 반드시 일어나야 한다. 먼저 적절한 장소에서 죽어야 한다. 화석을 보존할 수 있는 암석은 약 15%에 불과하기 때문에, 미래에 화강암이 될 자리에 쓰러지는 것은 아무 소용이 없다. 실제적으로 말하자면, (화석이 되기 위해서는) 죽은 사람은 젖은 진흙 속의 나뭇잎처럼 자국을 남길 수 있는 퇴적물 속에 묻히거나 산소에 노출되지 않은 채 분해되어, 뼈와 단단한 신체부위 속의 분자들이 용해된 광물로 대체되어 원본의 석화된 복사본이 만들어질 수 있어야 한다. 그 후에, 화석이 들어 있는 퇴적물이 지구의 과정에 의해 아무렇게나 눌리고 접히고 밀리게 되는 중에도, 화석은 어떻게든 식별 가능한 형태를 유지해야 한다. 끝으로, 그러나 가장 중요하게도, 수천만 년, 아마도 수억 년 동안 숨겨져 있었던 후에, 그것은 발견되어 보존할 가치가 있는 것으로 인정받아야 한다.

compost v. 썩다, 퇴비가 되다 sparkle n. 섬광; 생기, 활기 molecule n. 분자 nibble v. (짐승·물고기 등이) 조금씩 물어뜯다[갉아먹다] sluice v. (물줄기를 이용하여) 씻다 devour v. 게걸스럽게 먹다, 먹어치우다 fossilize v. 화석화하다 fossil n. 화석 preserve v. 보존하다 kneel over 갑자기 쓰러지다, 졸도하다 granite n. 화강암 deceased a. 죽은 sediment n. 침전물, 퇴적물 impression n. 인상, 감명; 자국, 흔적 decompose v. 분해하다, 부패하다 exposure n. 노출 replace v. 대신하다 dissolve v. 녹이다, 분해시키다 petrify v. 돌이 되게 하다, 경화시키다 identifiable a. 인식 가능한; 알아볼 수 있는

---

27 내용파악   ②

썩어서 사라지게 되면 화석이 될 수 없다. ①, ③, ④는 모두 본문에서 화석이 되기 위한 조건으로서 언급하고 있다.

다음 중 화석화 조건에 포함되지 <u>않는</u> 것은?
① 퇴적물 안에서 죽는 것
② 썩어서 사라지는 것
③ 산소에 노출되지 않고 분해되는 것
④ 퇴적물이 눌리고 접히는 것

---

28 내용추론   ③

화석이 되기 위해서는 진흙 속의 나뭇잎처럼 자국을 남길 수 있는 퇴적

물 속에 묻혀야 하며, 미래에 화강암이 될 자리에 쓰러지는 것은 아무 소용이 없다고 했다. 따라서 ③은 본문으로부터 추론할 수 없는 진술이다.

다음 중 위 글에서 추론할 수 <u>없는</u> 것은?
① 화석이 되는 것은 쉽지 않다.
② 어떤 화석들은 수천만 년 전의 것이다.
③ 화강암은 화석화에 있어 최적의 환경이다.
④ 화석이 발견되기 위해서는 알아볼 수 있는 모양을 가지고 있는 것이 중요하다.

29-30

생물학자들은 생물을 종(種)으로 분류한다. 동물들은 서로 짝짓기를 해서 새끼를 가질 능력이 있는 자손을 낳는다면 같은 종에 속한다고 한다. 말과 당나귀는 같은 조상으로부터 최근에 갈라져 나왔고 많은 신체적 특징을 공유한다. 그러나 그들은 서로에게 성적인 관심을 거의 보이지 않는다. 짝짓기를 하도록 유도하면 짝짓기를 하긴 하지만, 노새라 불리는 그들의 새끼는 자식을 낳지 못한다. 따라서 당나귀 DNA의 돌연변이는 절대 말에게 전달될 수 없고, 그 반대도 마찬가지다. 결과적으로 그 두 종류의 동물은 서로 다른 진화의 길을 가는 별개의 종으로 간주된다. 이와는 대조적으로, 불독과 스패니얼은 매우 다르게 보일 것이지만 같은 종에 속해서 DNA 풀을 공유한다. 그들은 즐겁게 짝짓기 할 것이고, 그들의 새끼들은 자라서 다른 개들과 짝을 이루어 더 많은 새끼를 낳을 것이다.

공통의 조상으로부터 진화한 종들은 '속(屬, genus)'(복수 형태는 genera이다)이라는 제목 아래 함께 묶인다. 사자, 호랑이, 표범, 재규어는 Panthera 속(屬) 안의 서로 다른 종(種)들이다. 생물학자들은 두 부분으로 된 라틴어 이름, 즉 속 뒤에 종이 오는 형식으로 생물에 이름을 붙인다. 예를 들어, 사자는 Panthera 속의 leo 종, 즉 Panthera leo라고 불린다. 속은 또한 고양이(사자, 치타, 집고양이), 개(늑대, 여우, 재칼), 코끼리(코끼리, 매머드, 마스토돈)와 같은 과(科)로 분류된다. 과에 속하는 모든 구성원은 그들의 혈통이 모계 시조(始祖)나 부계 시조로 거슬러 올라간다. 예를 들어, 가장 작은 집고양이에서부터 가장 사나운 사자에 이르는 모든 고양잇과 동물들은 약 2,500만 년 전에 살았던 공통의 고양이 조상을 공유한다.

organism n. 유기체, 생물체 species n. 종(種) give birth to ~을 낳다 fertile a. 비옥한; (사람·동물이) 새끼를 가질 수 있는 offspring n. 자식; (동물의) 새끼 donkey n. 당나귀 trait n. 특색, 특성 induce v. 유발하다 mule n. 노새 sterile a. 불모의; 자식을 못 낳는 mutation n. 돌연변이, 변종 vice versa 그 역[반대]도 마찬가지이다 evolutionary a. 진화의 bunch ~을 모으다, 엮다 genus n. 종류, 부류; <생물> 속(屬) label v. ~에 명칭을 붙이다, 분류하다 lineage n. 혈통, 계통 found v. 창시하다 matriarch n. 여가장 patriarch n. 가장, 족장 kitten n. 새끼 고양이 ferocious a. 사나운, 잔인한 feline a. 고양잇과의

---

29 내용일치   ①

말과 당나귀가 짝짓기 하여 낳은 새끼인 노새는 자식을 낳지 못한다고 했으므로 ①이 옳지 않은 진술이다.

위 글에 의하면, 다음 중 옳지 <u>않은</u> 것은?
① 노새는 당나귀와 짝을 지어 번식한다.
② 불독 DNA의 돌연변이가 스패니얼에게 전달될 수 있다.
③ 집고양이와 치타는 같은 과에 속한다.
④ 말과 당나귀는 선천적으로 서로에게 끌리지 않는다.

30 내용일치

과에 속하는 모든 구성원들은 그들의 혈통이 모계 시조(始祖)나 부계 시조로 거슬러 올라간다고 했는데, 속(屬)이 과(科)에 포함되는 것이므로 같은 과(科)의 속(屬)들은 공통의 시조를 공유한다고 할 수 있다. 따라서 ②가 옳은 진술이다. ① 짝짓기를 해서 새끼를 가질 능력이 있는 자손을 낳아야 한다. ③ 속과 종이다. ④ 그렇지 않다. 불독과 스패니얼은 생김새가 매우 다르지만 같은 종에 속한다.

위 글에 의하면, 다음 중 옳은 것은?
① 짝짓기는 같은 종에 속하기 위한 충분조건이다.
② 같은 과(科)의 속(屬)들은 공통의 시조를 공유한다.
③ 두 부분으로 된 생물의 라틴어 이름은 종과 과로 이루어져 있다.
④ 신체적 특성을 공유하는 것은 같은 종의 구성원이 되기 위한 필수 조건이다.

31-32

결혼을 준비하는 과정에서, 헌터 케인(Hunter Kane)의 예비 신부 애슐리 케인(Ashley Kane)은 그의 원래 성(姓)인 스나이더(Snyder)와 함께 자신의 이름을 발음해 보았는데, 그것이 마음에 들지 않았다. 그때 그는 자신들이 고려할 수 있는 선택지가 하나밖에 없는 것은 아니라는 것을 깨달았다. 그가 그녀의 성을 사용할 수도 있다는 것을 그와 케인 양이 논의하고 나자, "그것은 꽤 편안하게 느껴졌다."고 그는 말했다. 케인 씨가 그의 원래의 성에 대해 "강한 유대감"을 가져본 적이 없었고 또한 그가 케인 양의 부모님, 여동생과 매우 가까웠다는 사실도 도움이 되었다. 그는 "내 성이 그렇게 큰 의미가 있는 게 아니라면, 내가 이미 그들의 가족에게 큰 부분을 차지하고 있다고 느껴지는 상황에서 우리가 그녀의 성을 따르지 않을 이유는 없지 않겠어요?"라고 그는 말했다. 2022년 결혼식에서, 그 부부는 피로연에서 "케인즈 부부"라고 적힌 네온사인을 내걸어서 이 소식으로 하객들을 놀래주기로 했다. 그 상황은 정말로 약간의 혼란을 야기했지만, 그들은 하객들의 반응을 듣는 것을 즐겼다. "우리는 달려와 돌아가 카드에 있는 성을 바꾸는 사람들이나, 수표가 결제되지 않을 것을 걱정하는 사람들로부터 이야기를 들었습니다."라고 케인 씨가 말했다.

reaction n. 반응   chaos n. 혼돈, 무질서

31 지시대상   ④

미국에서는 부인이 남편의 성을 따르게 되는데, 애슐리 케인이 남편의 성 스나이더를 따르게 되면, 결혼 후에 그녀의 이름은 애슐리 스나이더가 된다.

다음 중 밑줄 친 Ⓐ가 가리키는 것은?
① 헌터 케인
② 애슐리 케인
③ 헌터 스나이더
④ 애슐리 스나이더

32 지시대상   ①

"스나이더 부부"가 아니라 "케인즈 부부"라고 적힌 네온사인을 내걸어

서 하객들에게 알려주고 싶어 했던 소식은 '헌터가 신부의 성을 따르기로 한' 사실이다.

다음 중 밑줄 친 Ⓑ가 가리키는 것은?
① 헌터가 신부의 성을 따른 것
② 케인즈 부부가 수표를 받고 싶지 않아 한 것
③ 애슐리와 헌터가 결혼하기로 결정한 것
④ 헌터가 애슐리의 가족과 너무 친해진 것

33-34

서유럽 국가들과 미국은 모두 노동시장의 여건 변화 때문에 한 곳에서 다른 곳으로 노동자를 이동시켜야 할 필요가 있다는 것을 알게 되었다. 이러한 노동력 이동은 언급된 두 지역에서 정도의 차이가 아닌 접근방식의 차이로 구별될 수 있다. 미국에서는, 만족스러운 인력 조정을 이끌어내기 위한 노동력 재배치의 활용이 대부분 동일한 기업의 서로 다른 공장들 간의 노동자 이동에 국한되어 왔다. 반대로, 서유럽의 노동력 재배치 프로그램 대부분은 기업 간에 시행되었다. 이러한 차이는 미국에서 지역적 이동에 대한 지원이 대부분 민간 자원에 맡겨졌던 반면, 서유럽에서는 정부가 주도권을 쥐고 노동력이 한 장소에서 다른 장소로 이동하는 데 드는 재정적 부담의 대부분을 받아들였다는 것을 의미한다.

mobility n. 이동, 이동성   distinguish v. 구별하다, 식별하다   relocation n. 재배치   enterprise n. 기획, 사업; 기업   conversely ad. 정반대로, 역으로   implement v. 이행하다, 실행하다   inter-firm a. 기업 간의   geographical a. 지리학의, 지리적인   initiative n. 주도권, 주도; 진취성

33 내용파악

"서유럽 국가들과 미국은 모두 노동시장의 여건 변화 때문에 한 곳에서 다른 곳으로 노동자를 이동시켜야 할 필요가 있다는 것을 알게 되었다." 라고 했으므로, 노동력 이동에 대한 동기는 서유럽 국가와 미국이 서로 같았다고 할 수 있다.

다음 중 서유럽의 노동력 이동 프로그램에 해당되는 것은?
① 민간 자원에 의존했다.
② 노동력의 이동을 제한하는 것을 목표로 했다.
③ 고용주의 변화 없이 노동자들이 이동하게 해주었다.
④ 미국의 노동력 재배치와 같은 동기를 가지고 있었다.

34 내용파악   ②

미국에서는 노동력의 지역적 이동에 대한 지원이 대부분 민간 자원에 맡겨져 있었다고 했으므로 ②가 정답으로 적절하다.

다음 중 미국의 노동력 재배치에 해당되는 것은?
① 노동력 문제가 대수롭지 않게 여겨졌다.
② 기본적으로 민간 기업이 대부분의 비용을 지불했다.
③ 지역적 이동에 있어 정부가 중요한 역할을 했다.
④ 미국 노동자들은 서유럽 노동자들보다 더 많은 기회를 가졌다.

35-36

벤자민 프랭클린의 행동은 여섯 분야 중 한 가지만으로도 평범한 삶을 사는 사람들로 하여금 자신들은 나태한 게으름뱅이라고 느끼게 할 수 있을 정도다. 정식 교육을 받지 않았지만, 그는 5개 국어를 익혀서 서투르게나마 말할 수 있었으며 자연과학, 외교술, 경제학을 통달했다. 가난 속에서 태어났지만, 그는 인쇄업자, 상인, 출판업자로서 큰 성공을 거둬서 42세의 나이에 은퇴할 수 있었다. 그의 발명품은 매우 많다. 그는 대학과 공공 도서관을 설립했으며, 필라델피아 시(市) 정부를 사실상 만들어냈다. 외교관, 법률제정자, 미국 정부의 설계자로서, 프랭클린은 한 명의 국부(國父)가 아니라 한 왕조의 일을 해냈다.

do-nothing n. 게으름뱅이, 무위도식자 unschooled a. 정식 교육[훈련]을 받지 않은 stumble v. 말을 더듬다; 우연히 만나다 diplomacy n. 외교, 외교술 prosper v. 번영하다, 성공하다 legion a. 많은, 무수한 municipal a. 시(市)의, 도시의, 자치 도시의, 시정(市政)의 diplomat n. 외교관 legislator n. 입법자, 법률제정자 architect n. 건축가; (사상·행사 등의) 설계자 founding father (국가·제도·시설·운동의) 창립자, 창시자

---

35 내용파악 ④

① 법률제정자, ② 대학과 공공 도서관의 설립자, ③ 외교관으로서의 업적은 언급됐지만, 건축 분야에서의 업적은 나타나 있지 않다. 그러므로 ④가 정답이다. architect of the United States government에서 architect는 '건축가'가 아니라 정부 수립의 '설계자'의 의미로 쓰인 것임에 유의한다.

다음 중 프랭클린의 업적 분야로 언급되지 않은 것은?
① 법
② 교육
③ 외무
④ 건축

---

36 내용파악 ③

그가 규율이 없었던 사람이라거나 그런 면모를 보여주는 일 등에 대해서는 전혀 언급돼 있지 않다.

다음 중 프랭클린의 삶에 해당되지 않는 것은?
① 그는 독학했다.
② 그는 사업에서 성공했다.
③ 그는 규율이 없었다.
④ 그는 매우 활동적인 삶을 살았다.

37-38

18세기 초 영국에서는 거의 아무도 차를 마시지 않았고 18세기 끝날 무렵에는 거의 모든 사람들이 차를 마셨다고 말해도 지나친 과장이 아니다. 공식 수입량은 1699년에 약 6톤에서 1세기 후에는 11,000톤으로 늘어났고, 18세기 말의 차(茶) 1파운드의 가격은 18세기 초 가격의 1/20이었다. 게다가 그 수치에는 밀수된 차가 포함되어 있지 않은데, 아마도 1784년에 차에 부과된 관세가 대폭 인하될 때까지 18세기 대부분의 기간 동안 밀수된 차가 수입량의 2배에 달했을 것이다. 또 다른 혼란스러운 요인은 섞음질을 하는 관행이 널리 퍼져있었다는 점이었는데, 이것은 차를 재, 버드나무 잎, 그리고 종종 화학염료를 사용해서 착색하고 위장한 보다 의심스러운 물질과 섞음으로써 차의 양을 늘리는 것이었다. 차는 잎에서부터 컵에 담겨지기까지 일련의 거의 모든 단계에서 이런저런 방법으로 섞음질이 이뤄졌고, 그 결과 소비된 양이 수입된 양보다 훨씬 많았다.

홍차가 보다 인기를 끌게 되기 시작한 것은 부분적으로는 긴 항해에서 녹차보다 더 오래 갔기 때문이기도 했지만, 이 섞음질의 부작용이기도 했다. 가짜 녹차를 만드는 데 사용된 많은 화학 물질들은 독성이 있었지만, 홍차의 경우는 섞음질을 했을 때조차도 더 안전했다. 홍차가 더 부드럽고 덜 쓴 녹차를 대체하기 시작하면서, 설탕과 우유의 첨가가 그것을 더 입맛에 맞게 만드는 데 도움을 주었다.

exaggeration n. 과장 smuggle v. 밀수하다 double v. ~을 두 배로 하다, ~에 같은 양을 보태다 levy v. (세금 따위를) 부과[징수]하다 confounding a. 어리둥절하게 하는, 당혹하게 만드는 factor n. 요인, 요소 adulteration n. 섞음질, 다른 것을 섞기 stretch v. (음식물·마약 등을) 묽게 하여 양을 늘리다 ash n. 재, 화산재 willow n. 버드나무 dubious a. 의심스러운, 수상한 substance n. 물질, 물체 disguise v. 변장하다, 가장하다 chemical a. 화학의, 화학상의 dye n. 염료 consume v. 소비하다, 소모하다 black tea 홍차 durable a. 오래 견디는, 튼튼한, 내구성이 있는 green tea 녹차 side effect 부작용 fake a. 가짜의, 위조의 poisonous a. 유독한, 유해한 displace v. 대신하다, 대체하다 addition n. 추가, 부가 palatable a. (음식 등이) 입에 맞는, 맛난

---

37 글의 주제   ②

본문은 18세기에 영국에서 차가 매우 인기를 끌게 되었음을 이야기하고 있다. 밀수나 섞음질을 해서 공급을 늘렸다는 것은 그만큼 수요가 많았다는 것이다.

위 글은 주로 무엇에 관한 것인가?
① 영국에서의 홍차의 인기
② 차에 대한 영국의 유별난 열의
③ 차를 섞음질하는 다양한 방법
④ 녹차와 홍차의 차이점

---

38 내용파악   ③

"1784년에 차에 부과된 관세가 대폭 인하될 때까지 18세기 대부분의 기간 동안 밀수된 차가 수입량의 2배에 달했을 것이다."라는 내용을 통해 ③이 정답임을 알 수 있다.

다음 중 18세기 영국에 해당되는 것은?
① 섞음질을 했을 때 녹차가 홍차보다 안전했다.
② 차에 섞음질을 한 것은 주로 잎의 단계에서 이루어졌다.
③ 1784년까지 밀수된 차의 양은 수입량의 2배에 달했다.
④ 녹차의 쓴맛을 줄이기 위해 설탕과 우유가 첨가되기 시작했다.

39-40

"플라이트 세임(비행 수치심)"이 유럽에서 속도를 내고 있다. 이 용어는 전 세계가 온실가스 배출을 극적으로 줄여야 하는 시기에 비행기를 타는 것에 대한 죄책감을 말하는 것이다. 이처럼 항공 여행에 대한 저항이 점점 커짐에 따라 철도 여행이 다시 활성화되었다. 그것은 또한 어떻게, 왜, 어디를 여행하는지에 대한 우리의 생각을 바꾸고 있다. 비록 "수치심"은 부정적인 용어이지만, 그 목표는 환경뿐만 아니라 그 운동에 참여하는 사람들에게도 긍정적이다. 그것은 비행기를 이용하는 다른 사람들을 수치스럽게 하는 것에 관한 것이라기보다는 당신 자신의 여행 방식을 바꾸는 것에 관한 것이다. 게다가, 비행기를 적게 탈 것을 장려하는 많은 사람들의 목표는 결코 사람들이 세계를 탐험하지 못하게 하는 것이 아니다. 이 운동은 그 대신 항공 여행을 하지 않고도 가능한 느리고 계획적인 여행을 한껏 즐기는 것에 관한 것이다. 확실한 선택 중의 하나가 기차 여행인데, 기차 여행에 따른 탄소배출량은 비행기를 타는 경우의 1/10에 불과하다. 기차 여행은 전형적으로 한 도시의 중심에서 다른 도시의 중심으로 당신을 데려오기 때문에, 비행기가 항상 가장 빠른 선택이 아니라는 점을 잊기 쉽다. 특히, 고속 열차는 대안으로서 큰 잠재력을 가지고 있다. 새로운 고속 열차 노선은 같은 경로의 항공 여행 수송을 80%나 감소시키는 것으로 나타났다. 느린 여행은 또한 단거리(여행)에 국한될 필요는 없다. 기후 사회학자인 로저 타이어스(Roger Tyers)는 최근에 중국으로 "무(無)비행 현지 출장"을 떠났다가 돌아왔는데, 기차를 타고 편도로 2주가 걸렸다. 힘든 여행이었을 것처럼 들릴지도 모르지만, 그는 그의 여행에 대해 기뻐하고 있다. "비행기를 타면 틀림없이 보지 못할 놀라운 것들을 보았습니다." 그는 디지털 해독, 시차 피로증세 없음, 다른 사람들과 이야기하기, 그리고 "지구의 크기와 그 다양성을 음미하는 것"과 같은 많은 다른 장점들도 열거한다.

gather pace 가속화되다, 빨라지다 emission n. 배출물, 배기가스 aviation n. 비행, 항공 reinvigorate v. 다시 활기를 띄게 하다, 소생시키다 negative a. 부정적인 term n. 용어 positive a. 긍정적인 shame v. 창피 주다, 망신시키다 revel in ~을 한껏 즐기다 deliberate a. 고의적인; 계획적인 potential n. 가능성, 잠재력 alternative n. 대안 fieldtrip n. 현장 견학[조사] 여행; (업무상의) 현지 출장 daunting a. (일 따위가) 벅찬, 힘겨운, 귀찮은, 어려운 expedition n. (탐험·전투 등 명확한 목적을 위한) 긴 여행, 탐험(여행), 원정 glow v. (감정이·기쁨이·분노가) 북받치다, (격정 따위로) 마음이 타오르다 digital detox 디지털 디톡스(스마트폰이나 컴퓨터 같은 디지털 기기에 중독된 상태에서 벗어나는 일) jetlag n. 비행기 여행의 시차로 인한 피로, 시차적응 appreciate v. 진가를 인정하다, 감상하다, 음미하다

39 빈칸완성 ①

바로 뒤의 "로저 타이어스가 기차를 타고 중국으로 현지 출장을 떠났다가 돌아왔고, 편도만 2주가 걸렸다."는 내용은 느린 여행을 중국으로의 먼 여행에서 해본 것이므로, "느린 여행은 단거리에 국한될 필요는 없다"라는 ①이 가장 자연스럽게 호응한다.

다음 중 빈칸에 들어가기에 가장 적절한 것은?
① 느린 여행은 또한 단거리에 국한될 필요는 없다
② 비행기 타지 않기 운동은 또한 다른 곳에서도 인기를 얻고 있다
③ 결국, 비행기를 타는 것이 아마도 당신이 할 수 있는 가장 탄소 집약적인 활동일 것이다
④ 플라이트 세임 운동은 지구의 다양성을 재발견하는 것이다

40 내용일치 ④

"플라이트 세임 운동은 비행기를 이용하는 다른 사람들을 수치스럽게 하는 것에 관한 것이라기보다는 당신 자신의 여행 방식을 바꾸는 것에 관한 것이다."라고 했으므로 ④가 옳은 진술이다. ①과 ③은 글의 내용과 무관하고 ②는 2주가 아니라 4주이다.

위 글에 의하면, 다음 중 옳은 것은?
① 고속 열차는 저속 열차보다 탄소를 더 많이 배출한다.
② 로저 타이어스의 왕복 여행은 그에게 2주가 걸렸다.
③ 기후 운동에 "수치심"이라는 용어를 사용하는 것은 좋은 생각이 아니다.
④ 비행기 타지 않기 운동은 사람들에게 여행 습관을 바꾸도록 촉구하는 것을 목표로 한다.

01 ①	02 ③	03 ②	04 ①	05 ④	06 ④	07 ②	08 ①	09 ④	10 ③
11 ②	12 ④	13 ③	14 ②	15 ③	16 ②	17 ②	18 ①	19 ④	20 ③
21 ①	22 ②	23 ②	24 ②	25 ①	26 ①	27 ④	28 ③	29 ④	30 ③
31 ④	32 ①	33 ①	34 ④	35 ②	36 ②	37 ②	38 ③	39 ①	40 ④

01 동의어 ①

cave n. 동굴 selective a. 선택적인, 선택성의 wearing away 닳아서 없어짐(= erosion 침식) cliff n. 절벽 evasion n. (책임·의무 등의) 회피; (질문에 대해) 얼버무림 congestion n. 혼잡, 붐빔 conjunction n. 결합, 연결

동굴은 종종 바다가 절벽을 선택적으로 닳아 없앰으로써 형성된다.

02 동의어 ③

instruct v. ~에게 지시하다, 명령하다 stationary a. 정지된, 움직이지 않는(= immobile) experiment n. 실험 ensure v. ~을 책임지다, 보장하다, 보증하다 impartial a. 공평한 invariable a. 불변의 irrelevant a. 부적절한, 무관계한

학생들은 정확한 결과를 보장하기 위해 실험 중에 계속 움직이지 않은 채로 있으라는 지시를 받았다.

03 동의어 ②

elusive a. (사람·동물 등이) 교묘히 잘 빠지는, 도망가기 쉬운 spot v. 탐지해내다, 발견하다(= sight) tame v. 길들이다 capture v. 붙잡다, 생포하다 trap v. 덫으로 잡다, 덫을 놓다

잡기 어려운 눈표범은 중앙아시아의 산악 지역에서 발견할 수 있다.

04 동의어 ①

protester n. 시위자 denounce v. (공공연히) 비난하다, 탄핵하다, 매도하다 jury n. 배심(원단) lenient a. 관대한(= merciful) sentence n. 판결, 선고 rigorous a. 가혹한, 엄격한 restrained a. 삼가는, 자제하는 insignificant a. 무의미한, 하찮은

법원 밖에서는 최소 500명의 시위자들이 배심원들의 관대한 판결을 성토하고 있었다.

05 동의어 ④

fathom v. (의미 등을) 헤아리다[가늠하다], 이해하다(= comprehend)

overlook v. 간과하다; 눈감아주다 anticipate v. 기대하다 brood over ~에 대해 곰곰이 생각하다

고대 이집트인들이 어떻게 현대적인 기계 없이 피라미드를 건설했는가는 이해하기 어렵다.

06 논리완성 ④

협업도 창의성도 모두 긍정적인 의미이고 must not은 금지의 의미를 나타내므로, 빈칸에는 부정적인 뜻을 가진 단어가 들어가야 한다. 그러므로 '파괴하다'라는 뜻을 가진 ④가 적절하다.

collaboration n. 협력, 제휴 refine v. 세련되게 하다, 품위 있게 하다 instill v. (사상 따위를) 스며들게 하다, 주입시키다 complement v. 보충하다, 보완하다 subvert v. (체제·권위 따위를) 뒤엎다, (국가·정부 따위를) 전복시키다, 파괴하다

사람과 기계의 의미 있는 협업이 인간의 창의성을 파괴시켜서는 안 된다.

07 논리완성 ②

권리는 부여, 소유, 행사의 대상이다. 보기 중에서 ②가 '부여'의 의미를 가지고 있으므로 빈칸에 들어가기에 적절하다.

parliament n. 의회 resolution n. 결심, 결의, 결의안 legal right 법적 권리 ape n. 원숭이, 유인원 halve v. 2등분하다 grant v. 주다, 부여하다 convert v. 전환하다, 바꾸다 ascribe v. (원인·동기 등을) ~에 돌리다, ~에 기인하는 것으로 하다

스페인 의회는 최근에 유인원에게 법적 권리를 부여하는 결의안을 통과시켰다.

08 논리완성 ①

'많은 사람들이 집을 잃고 생필품이 없는 상태'는 '격변'의 결과로 이해할 수 있다.

natural disaster 자연재해 massive a. 대규모의, 대량의 upheaval n. (사회적인) 대변동, 격변 aberration n. 일탈, 일탈적인 행동[일] consensus n. (의견·증언 따위의) 일치; 합의; 여론 tranquility n. 평온

자연재해가 그 소도시에 대규모의 격변을 일으켜 많은 사람들이 집을 잃고 생필품이 없는 상태가 되었다.

09 논리완성 ④

위기 상황에서 어려움에 처한 사람들에게 보여주어야 할 태도로는 '단결', '결속', '연대의식' 등이 적절하다.

affected a. 영향을 받은; (병 따위에) 걸린, 침범된 conformity n. (규칙·관습 등에) 따름, 순응 detachment n. 분리, 이탈; (세속·이해 따위로부터) 초연함 inquisitiveness n. 호기심이 많음 solidarity n. 연대, 결속, 단결

위기의 시기에는 사람들이 함께 모여 가장 큰 피해를 입은 사람들에게 단결력을 보여주는 것이 중요하다.

10 논리완성 ③

'다른 손님들에게 시비를 걸기 시작한' 행동과 관련 있는 태도로는 '호전적인'이라는 의미의 ③이 적절하다.

pick v. 계기를 만들다; (싸움을) 걸다 submissive a. 복종하는, 순종하는 conscientious a. 양심적인, 성실한 belligerent a. 호전적인, 적대적인 apathetic a. 냉담한

그 술 취한 남자는 호전적이 되어서 다른 손님들에게 싸움을 걸기 시작했다.

11 주장·제안 동사가 이끄는 that절 속의 동사 형태 ②

주장, 제안의 타동사가 이끄는 that절 속의 동사는 주어의 수와 시제와 상관없이 'should+동사원형'이어야 하며, 이때 should는 생략이 가능하다. 그러므로 ②를 save 혹은 should save로 고쳐야 한다.

financial planner 재무 설계자 income n. 소득, 수입 emergency n. 비상사태

재무 설계자들은 일반적으로 개인이 비상상황에 대비하여 2~6개월의 수입을 저축할 것을 권장한다.

12 문의 구성 ④

Plastic is one of the biggest threats our oceans face today 뒤에 2개의 분사구문 causing~과 posing~이 열거된 구조의 문장이다. ④의 앞에 이미 완전한 문장이 주어져 있는 상황이므로 ④의 자리에 정동사가 올 수 없고 관계절이나 분사구로 people을 수식해야 한다. 따라서 ④를 who depend on seafood나 depending on seafood로 고쳐야 한다.

threat n. 위협, 협박 untold a. 언급되어 있지 않은; 말로 다할 수 없는 ecosystem n. 생태계 pose v. (문제 등을) 제기하다 potential a. 잠재적인, 가능성 있는

플라스틱은 오늘날 우리의 바다가 직면한 가장 큰 위협들 중의 하나로, 생태계에 이루 말할 수 없는 해를 끼치고 있으며, 해산물에 의존하고 있는 30억 명 이상의 사람들에게 잠재적인 건강상의 위협을 가하고 있다.

13 분사구문 ③

분사구문은 접속사와 주어를 없애고 간략하게 표현하는 것인데 ③ 이하는 의미상 주어와 분사 being이 분사구문을 이루고 또 그 앞에 접속사 and가 있는 형태이다. 그러면 구태여 분사구문으로 하지 않고 being을 was로 하여 완전한 절을 만들거나, 아니면 접속사 and를 없애거나 전치사 with로 바꾸어 부대상황의 분사구문이 되게 해야 한다. ③을 삭제하거나 with로 고친다. ② 사실은 mostly men이 더 일반적이다.

take one's own life 자살하다 rate n. 비율

작년에 3만 명 이상의 미국인들이 스스로 목숨을 끊었는데, 대개 남성들이었고, 가장 높은 비율을 차지한 것은 65세 이상의 사람들이었다.

14 many와 much의 용법 구분 ②

many는 가산명사와 함께 쓰고 much는 불가산명사와 함께 쓴다. ③에 쓰인 produce는 '농산물[농작물]'이라는 의미의 불가산명사이므로 much와 함께 써야 한다. ②를 much of my produce로 고친다.

garden v. 정원을 손질하다, 원예를 하다 produce n. 농산물, 농작물 make off with ~을 가지고 도망가다

10년 넘게 원예를 해왔지만, 나는 설치류들이 내 농작물의 상당량을 훔쳐 가지 못하도록 할 방법을 찾지 못했다. 지난해에는 설치류들이 내 콩 대부분을 갖고 달아났다.

15 주어와 동사의 수일치 ③

주어는 essays이고 'A significant number of'와 '(which were) selected by readers'는 각각 앞뒤에서 주어를 수식하는 역할을 하고 있다. 주어인 essays가 복수이므로 동사인 ③을 have been rejected로 고쳐야 한다.

significant a. 중대한, 중요한; 상당한 reject v. 거절하다; 퇴짜놓다 editorial n. 사설, 논설 publication n. 발표, 간행, 출판

독자들에 의해 선정된 상당수의 에세이들이 출판할 가치가 없다는 이유로 편집진에 의해 거절되었다.

16 문의 구성 ②

has been 이하가 문장의 술부이므로 빈칸부터 right and wrong까지가 주어여야 한다. 과학자들에 의해 고안된 것은 물건인 명사이므로 that절인 ④가 아니라 that 관계절의 수식을 받은 명사인 ②가 빈칸에 적절하다.

weigh up 가늠하다 legal a. 법률의; 합법의 evidence n. 증거 moral
a. 도덕적인 devise v. 궁리하다, 고안하다, 발명하다

법적 증거와 옳고 그름에 대한 도덕적 질문을 따져볼 수 있는 소프트웨어
가 컴퓨터 과학자들에 의해 고안되었다.

---

17 hold ~ responsible 구문 ②

'hold+목적어+보어' 구문은 '~에게 책임을 묻다'는 뜻으로 'hold ~
responsible'로 표현한다. 그러므로 ②가 정답이다.

terms and conditions 계약조건 certify v. 증명하다, 보증하다

나는 계약조건에 동의하여, 회사에 책임을 묻지 않을 것임을 보증했다.

---

18 stay up late into the night ①

'밤늦게'는 late at night이고 '밤늦게까지'는 late into the night이다.
빈칸 뒤에 정관사를 수반한 'the night'이 주어져 있으므로 후자의 표현
으로 나타내야 한다. 따라서 ①이 정답이다. '너무 늦게'라는 뜻으로 too
가 late를 수식하며 too는 much나 far가 수식하므로 far가 too 앞에 있
다. late 대신 far를 쓴 far into the night도 '밤늦게까지'이고 until을 앞
에 붙인 until late at night도 '밤늦게까지'이다.

우리들 중 많은 사람들은 친구들에게 문자를 보내거나 소셜 미디어를 훑어
보면서 너무 밤늦게까지 깨어 있다.

---

19 'a/an+명사'를 대신하는 대명사 one ④

빈칸에는 바로 앞의 a democratic aesthetic과 동격을 이룰 수 있는 표
현이 들어가야 하겠는데, 'a+명사'는 대명사 one으로 받으므로 ④가 정
답이다.

represent v. 묘사하다, 그리다, 대표하다 triumph n. 승리, 대성공
aesthetic n. 미적(美的) 특질, 미학

대중문화는 100년 전에 자신은 수백만 명을 위해 글을 쓴다고 주장했을
때 마크 트웨인이 인정한 미학인 민주 미학의 승리를 대변한다.

---

20 시제 / 태 ③

'It is[has been] ~ since …'는 '…한 이래로[…한 지] ~이 된다'라는 의미
를 나타내는 표현이며, 이때 since 이하에는 과거시제가 원칙이다. 또한
since절의 주어인 the Korean movie는 release하는 행위의 대상이므
로 수동태가 되어야 한다. 그러므로 ③이 정답이다.

release v. (영화를) 개봉하다; (정보·레코드·신간 등을) 공개[발표, 발매]
하다

그 한국 영화가 베를린에서 최초로 개봉된 지 이제 한 달이 더 지났다.

---

21 논리완성 ①

산업혁명 이전의 농경사회에서는 아직 공장이 없던 때라, 남자가 집을
떠나는 일 없이 농사를 지으며 집에 여자와 함께 머물러 있었으므로, 남
녀는 시간과 공간도 공유했을 것이다.

shelter n. 은신처 spin v. (실을) 잣다, 방적하다 weave v. (직물·바구니
따위를) 짜다, 뜨다, 엮다 sew v. 바느질하다 agricultural a. 농업의

수세기 전, 산업혁명이 일어나기 전에, 남녀는 공급자 역할을 공유했다.
남자는 사냥을 하거나 농사를 지어서 식량을 공급하고 아마도 집을 손수
지어서 공급하는 책임을 졌다. 그러나 여자도 공급자가 될 것으로 기대되
었다. 그들은 정원을 가꾸고, 밀가루를 빻고, 요리를 하는 등의 활동을
통해 음식을 공급했다. 그들은 실을 잣고, 천을 짜고, 바느질하여 옷을
만들어내는 것과 같은 다른 종류의 공급에 대한 책임도 졌다. 간단히 말해,
남녀는 공급자의 역할을 공유했다. 농경사회에서, 그들은 시간과 공간도
공유했는데, 여자가 집에 있는 동안에 남자가 집을 떠나 공장에 있는 것이
아니었기 때문이었다.

① 그들은 시간과 공간도 공유했다
② 그들의 역할은 훨씬 더 나뉘게 되었다
③ 남자는 다른 남자들과 경쟁하고 있었다
④ 남자들의 공급자 역할은 긴장의 원천이었다

---

22 논리완성 ②

여러 산업 분야의 혁신을 통해 만들어졌기 때문에 타이타닉호는 절대로
침몰할 수 없다고 확신하고 있던 상황에서 그 배가 침몰해버렸다면, 앞
서 언급한 확신은 흔들리거나 꺾이게 되었을 것이다.

iceberg n. 빙산 sink v. 침몰하다, 침몰시키다 in the wee hours of
the following morning 다음날 한밤중에 boundless a. 무한한, 끝없는
decadent a. 퇴폐적인 maiden voyage 처녀항해 ensuing a. 다음의,
계속되는 investigation n. 조사, 연구 reassert v. 다시 주장하다;
(무엇이 사실임을) 재천명하다 confidence n. 신뢰; 확신 come up
empty-handed 허탕치다, 목표를 이루지 못하다

타이타닉(Titanic)호는 1912년 4월 14일 밤에 빙산에 부딪혔고 다음날
한밤중에 북대서양 바다에 침몰했다. 많은 면에서, 타이타닉호의 침몰은
엄청난 부(富)의 불평등에 기초하여 만들어진 퇴폐적인 생활방식뿐만 아
니라 무한해 보이는 기술혁신의 시대에 대한 완벽한 비극적 종말로 비춰질
수 있다. 널리 기억되어 왔듯이, 많은 사람들은 "신(神) 자신도 이 배를
침몰시킬 수 없다."고 믿었다. 사람들은 조선업과 다른 산업들을 둘러싼
기술혁신으로 인해 타이타닉호에게는 적(敵)이 없다고 진정으로 믿었다.
타이타닉호가 처녀항해에서 정말로 침몰해버렸을 때, 인간의 혁신에 대한
이러한 확신은 흔들렸다. 뒤이은 조사들을 통해 그들의 확신을 재천명할
수 있게 해 줄 설명을 찾으려 했지만, 결국 그들은 자신들의 목표를 이루지
못했다.

① 그 재난에 집단적으로 매료되기 시작했다
② 인간의 혁신에 대한 이러한 확신은 흔들렸다
③ 그것은 부유한 신사들 시대의 종말을 상징했다
④ 그것은 결코 서양 역사상 가장 큰 해상 재난이 아니었다

23 논리완성 ②

앞 문장의 '청소년 자살의 증가'는 그 앞에서 언급한 '사람들이 온라인상에서 하는 말 가운데 일부가 치명적일 수도 있다.'는 내용에 대한 예로 언급된 것이다. 그러므로 빈칸에는 '온라인상에서 이뤄지는 유해한 행위'를 그 원인으로 지목하는 내용이 들어가야 할 것이며, 따라서 ②가 정답으로 적절하다.

persona n. 페르소나, 외적 인격 in person 직접, 몸소 anonymity n. 익명, 익명성 rampant a. 만연하는, 대유행의 cyberbullying n. 사이버 폭력, 사이버 왕따 accountable a. 책임이 있는 deadly a. 치명적인 suicide n. 자살 on the rise 오르고 있는, 오름세에 있는

현실을 직시하자. 사람들은 온라인상의 인격 뒤에 숨어 있는 경우에 훨씬 더 용감한 경향이 있다. 당신이 결코 직접 말하지 않을 무언가를 온라인에서 말할 가능성은 훨씬 더 높다. 인터넷에 의해 제공된 익명성은 사이버 괴롭힘 문제가 만연하게 만들었다. 행동에 대해 책임을 지지 않게 될 수도 있을 때 누군가에게 끔찍한 말을 하기가 더 쉽다. 최악의 경우, 사람들이 온라인상에서 하는 말 가운데 일부는 심지어 치명적일 수도 있다. 청소년 자살이 증가하고 있는데, 온라인상의 괴롭힘이 주된 원인 중 하나일 수 있다.

① 기술 중독이 점점 널리 퍼지고 있다
② 온라인상의 괴롭힘이 주된 원인 중 하나일 수 있다
③ 치료 전문가들은 온라인 상담을 기꺼이 제공해야 한다
④ 이것은 소셜 미디어에 대한 통제되지 않은 접근이 얼마나 해로울 수 있는지 보여준다

24 논리완성 ②

빈칸이 포함된 문장을 다음 문장에서 부연하여 설명하고 있다. 다음 문장에서 "함무라비(Hammurabi)는 그것을 신(神)들이 정한 것으로 보았다."라고 했으므로, 이 내용과 호응하는 ②가 계급제도가 정당하다고 본 사람들의 생각으로 적절하다.

distinction n. 구별, 차별; 차이 be rooted in ~에 뿌리를 두고 있다 hierarchy n. 계급제도 disavow v. 부인하다, 거부하다 inevitable a. 불가피한; 필연의, 당연한 ordain v. (신·운명 등이) 정하다; (법률 등이) 규정하다, 제정하다 status n. 상태; 지위, 자격 innate a. 타고난, 선천적인

자유인과 노예, 백인과 흑인, 부자(富者)와 빈자(貧者) 사이의 구분은 허구에 뿌리를 두고 있다. 그러나 상상으로 만든 모든 계급제도가 그것의 허구적 기원을 부인하고 그것을 타당하고 필연적인 것이라고 주장하는 것이 역사의 철칙이다. 예를 들어, 자유인과 노예의 계급제도를 타당하고 올바른 것으로 여겼던 많은 사람들은 노예제도가 인간의 발명품이 아니라고 주장했다. 함무라비(Hammurabi)는 그것을 신(神)들이 정한 것으로 보았다. 아리스토텔레스(Aristotle)는 자유인들이 "자유로운 본성"을 가지고 있는 반면, 노예들은 "노예스러운 본성"을 가지고 있다고 주장했다. 사회에서의 그들의 지위는 그들의 타고난 본성의 반영일 뿐이라는 것이다.

① 노예제도는 상상에 의해 만들어진 체계다
② 노예제도는 인간의 발명품이 아니다
③ 노예 주인들은 그들의 공로에 대해 보상을 받은 것이다
④ 노예는 자유인들이 누리는 모든 특권을 누릴 자격이 있다

25 논리완성 ①

"미세 플라스틱에 노출된 물고기는 성장과 번식의 수준이 더 낮다는 것이 드러났고, 그들의 새끼 또한, 심지어 자신이 (미세 플라스틱에) 노출되지 않았을 때조차도, 새끼를 더 적게 낳는 것으로 관찰되었다."를 통해, '미세 플라스틱이 어미로부터 새끼에게로 전해져서 미세 플라스틱의 부작용이 대물림될 수 있음'을 추론할 수 있다. 그러므로 빈칸에는 이와 관련된 ①이 들어가는 것이 적절하다.

category n. 범주, 카테고리 accommodate v. 편의를 도모하다, 수용하다 expose v. (햇볕·바람·비 따위에) 쐬다, 맞히다, 노출시키다; (환경 따위에) 접하게 하다 reproduction n. 생식, 번식 offspring n. 자손, 후예; (동물의) 새끼 observe v. 관찰하다; 목격하다 demonstrate v. 증명하다, 논증하다 alter v. 바꾸다, 변경하다

우리가 사용하는 단어는 "미세 플라스틱"이다. 그것은 길이 5밀리미터 미만의 모든 플라스틱 조각을 수용하는 넓은 범주이다. 우리는 그것들이 물고기에게 해를 끼치고 있다는 사실을 이제껏 알고 있었다. 2018년에 발표된 한 연구에서, 미세 플라스틱에 노출된 물고기는 성장과 번식의 수준이 더 낮다는 것이 드러났고, 그들의 새끼 또한, 심지어 자신이 (미세 플라스틱에) 노출되지 않았을 때조차도, 새끼를 더 적게 낳는 것으로 관찰되었는데, 이는 오염이 대대로 지속된다는 사실을 시사한다. 2020년, 또 다른 연구에서는 미세 플라스틱이 물고기의 행동을 바꾼다는 것을 보여주었다.

① 오염이 대대로 지속된다
② 미세 플라스틱은 물고기의 뇌에 축적될 수 있다
③ 더 높은 수준의 노출은 물고기의 행동을 변화시키는 결과를 초래할 수 있다
④ 미세 플라스틱 섭취는 물고기가 감염에 더 취약해지도록 한다

26 논리완성 ①

첫 문장의 '직관에 반하는 성별화'가 두 번째 문장에서는 '서구보다 아랍 국가와 인도에서 여성 컴퓨터 공학도의 비율이 더 높다'는 말로 표현되었고, 이것이 세 번째 문장에서는 반대로 '여성 대비 남성의 수가 가장 불균형적으로 많은 것'으로 표현되었는데 이것이 직관에 반하려면 오히려 서구 선진국에 해당한다고 해야 한다. 따라서 빈칸에는 ①이 적절하다.

counterintuitive a. 직관에 반(反)하는, 직관에 어긋나는 gendering n. 성별화 proportion n. 비율 imbalance n. 불균형

최근의 한 유네스코 보고서는 컴퓨터 기술 분야의 직관에 반(反)하는 성별화에 관심을 쏟게 한다. 아랍 국가들과 인도에서는 서구에서보다 훨씬 더 높은 비율의 여성들이 컴퓨터 과학을 공부하고 있다. 컴퓨터 과학도들의, 그리고 결과적으로, 소프트웨어 개발자들의, 남녀 불균형이 가장 큰 것은 바로 양성평등이 가장 발달해 있는 국가들이다.

① 양성평등이 가장 발달해 있다
② 성 편견이 아직도 흔히 목격된다
③ 프로그래밍은 여성들 사이에서 인기가 없다
④ 여성의 고등교육 참여가 보장되지 않는다

27-28

한때, 학자들은 농업혁명이 인류에게 큰 발전을 가져왔다고 선언했다. 그들은 인간의 지적 능력에 힘입은 진보의 이야기를 전했다. 진화는 점차 더 똑똑한 사람들을 만들어냈다. 마침내, 사람들은 자연의 비밀을 해독할 정도로 똑똑해졌고, 이로 인해 양을 길들이고 밀을 재배할 수 있게 되었다. 이런 일이 일어나자마자, 그들은 수고롭고 위험하며 종종 엄격한 수렵채집인의 삶을 기쁜 마음으로 내던지고, 농부로서의 즐겁고 충분히 만족스러운 삶을 본격적으로 누리기 시작했다는 것이다.

그 같은 이야기는 환상이다. 시간이 지나면서 사람들이 더 똑똑해졌다는 증거는 존재하지 않는다. 수렵인들은 자연의 비밀을 농업혁명 훨씬 전부터 알고 있었는데, 이는 그들의 생존이 자신들이 사냥했던 동물과 채집했던 식물에 대한 정통한 지식에 달려 있었기 때문이다. 쉬운 삶을 살 수 있는 새로운 시대를 알리는 대신, 농업혁명은 농부들에게 수렵인들의 삶보다 대체로 더 힘들고 덜 만족스러운 삶을 남겨주었다. 수렵·채집인들은 더 활기차고 다양한 방식으로 시간을 보냈으며, 기근과 질병의 위험에도 덜 처해 있었다. 농업혁명은 확실히 인류가 마음대로 할 수 있는 식량의 총량을 늘어나게 했지만, 여분의 식량이 더 나은 식단이나 더 많은 여가로 이어지지는 못했다. 오히려, 그것은 인구폭발과 방자한 특권계층을 가져왔다. 평균적인 농부들은 평균적인 수렵인들보다 더 힘들게 일했지만, 그 대가로 얻은 것은 더 나빠진 식단이었다.

proclaim v. 선언하다, 공포하다 evolution n. 진화 decipher v. 해독하다 tame v. 길들이다 cultivate v. 재배하다 wheat n. 밀 grueling a. 녹초로 만드는 spartan a. 검소하고 엄격한 settle down to ~에 집중하기[본격적으로 ~하기] 시작하다 satiate v. 물리게 하다; (필요·욕망 따위를) 충분히 만족시키다 forager n. 수렵인 intimate a. 친밀한; (지식이) 깊은; 정통한 herald v. 알리다; 안내하다 stimulating a. 자극적인, 활기를 띠게 하는 varied a. 변화 있는, 다채로운 starvation n. 굶주림, 기아 at the disposal of ~의 뜻대로 되는 translate v. (결과로서) ~가 되다; 변화하다 pampered a. 제멋대로 하는, 방자한

---

27 내용파악 ④

마지막 문단에서 농업혁명이 "인구폭발과 방자한 특권계층을 가져왔다"라고 했으므로 ④가 정답이다.

다음 중 농업혁명과 함께 나타난 것은?
① 더 나은 식단
② 더 좋은 지능
③ 더 많은 여가
④ 인구 증가

---

28 내용일치 ③

첫 번째 문단의 '한때, 학자들은 농업혁명이 인류에게 큰 발전을 가져왔다고 선언했다'는 내용에 대해 두 번째 문단에서 그것이 환상이며, 왜 그러한지를 설명하고 있다. 그러므로 ③이 옳지 않은 진술이다.

위 글에 의하면, 다음 중 옳지 않은 것은?
① 수렵인들은 농부들보다 기아의 위험에 덜 처해 있었다.
② 수렵·채집인들은 생존을 위한 자연의 비밀을 해독했다.
③ 농업혁명은 인류에게 위대한 도약이다.
④ 농업혁명은 일부 특권 계층들에게 혜택을 가져왔다.

29-30

아이들이 읽기와 수학 시험을 더 잘 치르도록 자극하기 위해 돈을 사용해야 하는 걸까? 이스트 퀸즈(Queens)의 평온한 소수집단 거주지에서 세 자녀를 키우고 있는 집주인인 수잔 윈들랜드(Suzanne Windland)는 그렇지 않다고 생각한다. 7학년 학생인 그녀의 딸 알렉산드라(Alexandra)는 작년에 만점을 받았다. 하지만 그녀는 뉴욕시 교육부가 그 같은 성취에 대해 500달러의 현금을 지급하는 것을 원하지 않는다. 그 돈은 만약 알렉산드라의 학교가 내년에 10개 시험의 성적에 따라 4학년과 7학년 학생들에게 100달러에서 500달러를 포상으로 지급하는 시범 프로그램에 참여하는 경우에 받게 될 금액이다. 윈들랜드 부인은 알렉산드라가 배움에 대한 사랑을 기르고, 보다 경쟁력 있는 학교에 진학하는 것 등과 같이 시대를 초월한 보편적인 이유로 좋은 성적을 내길 원한다. 아이들이 흐뭇한 성적표를 집으로 가져왔을 때, 이따금씩 아이들에게 장난감을 사주거나 데리고 나가 저녁 식사를 하기도 했지만, 그녀는 미리 내건 보상을 신뢰하지 않는다. "그것은 매일 아침에 일어나 양치질을 하고 학교에 간다고 해서 아이들에게 용돈을 주는 것과 같습니다. 그것은 아이들이 해야 할 일입니다."

placid a. 평온한 enclave n. 타국 영토로 둘러싸인 지역[영토]; 고립된 장소; (타민족 속에 고립된) 소수민족 집단 reward v. 보상하다, 보답하다 timeless a. 영원한; 시간[시대]을 초월한; 특정한 시간에 한정되지 않는 cultivate v. 재배하다; 계발하다, 연마하다 and the like 기타 같은 종류의 것 on occasion 이따금, 때에 따라서 believe in ~의 존재를 믿다; ~을 좋다고[옳다고] 생각하다 dangle v. ~을 매달다; (마음이 동하도록) 언뜻 내비치다 beforehand ad. 미리, 사전에 allowance n. 용돈

---

29 내용일치 ④

"윈들랜드 부인은 알렉산드라가 배움에 대한 사랑을 기르고, 보다 경쟁력 있는 학교에 진학하는 것 등과 같이 시대를 초월한 보편적인 이유로 좋은 성적을 내길 원한다."라는 내용이 있는데, 여기서 '경쟁력 있는 학교'란 '(능력에 따라 학생을 뽑는) 선발제 학교'를 의미한다고 볼 수 있으므로 ④가 옳은 진술이다. ① 알렉산드라의 학교가 참여할 경우에 수혜를 입을 것이다. ② 프로그램에 참여한 학교의 학생들만이 자격이 있다. ③ 구체적인 점수는 언급하지 않았다.

위 글에 의하면, 다음 중 옳은 것은?
① 알렉산드라는 작년에 그 프로그램으로부터 수혜를 입었다.
② 뉴욕시의 모든 학생들은 그 프로그램의 자격이 된다.
③ 500달러를 받으려면 10개 과목에서 만점을 받아야 한다.
④ 윈들랜드 부인은 알렉산드라가 (능력에 따라 학생을 뽑는) 선발제 학교에 진학하기 위해 열심히 공부하기를 원한다.

---

30 지시대상 ③

밑줄 친 ⓐ는 '미리 내건 보상'이란 의미인데, 앞에서 뉴욕시 교육부가 좋은 성적을 받는 학생에게 금전적 보상을 하려는 프로그램에 대해 윈들랜드 부인이 부정적인 입장을 보인 것을 감안하면, ⓐ가 지칭하는 것으로는 ③이 적절하다.

다음 중 밑줄 친 Ⓐ가 가리키는 것은?
① 만점
② 좋은 성적표
③ 금전적 인센티브
④ 경쟁력 있는 학교

위 글에 의하면, 다음 중 옳은 것은?
① 그 병의 원인에 대해서는 의견이 일치되지 않고 있다.
② 그 병에서 회복하는 것은 그리 어려운 일이 아니다.
③ 그 병은 여성보다 남성에게 더 흔하다.
④ 엡스타인-바 바이러스는 그 병과 아무 관련이 없다.

31-32

만성피로증후군의 원인은 무엇일까? 과거의 연구에서는 엡스타인-바 (Epstein-Barr) 바이러스와의 연관성을 시사했지만, 지금 많은 과학자들은 그 관련성에 의문을 제기하고 있다. 새로운 연구 결과에서는 엡스타인-바 바이러스가 주된 원인은 아니지만, 여전히 그 질병을 유발할 수도 있음을 시사하고 있다. 증상이 단지 하나의 원인이 아니라 다양한 원인들 때문일 수 있다는 것이다. 그럼에도 불구하고 일부 연구원들은 엡스타인-바 바이러스가 그 질병을 유발한다는 생각을 고수하고 있다. 그들은 그러한 판단을 내리는 것이 시기상조라고 말한다.

일부에서는 만성피로증후군을 "여피(yuppie)족이 걸리는 병"으로 불러왔는데, 이는 만성피로증후군이 종종 20대와 30대의 전문직 여성에서 진단이 이뤄지기 때문이다. 그것은 독감과 같은 병에서 완전히 회복되지 못한 데 따른 결과일 수도 있다. 원인은 명확하지 않지만 증상은 명확하다. 만성피로증후군 환자로 불리기 위해서는 심신을 쇠약하게 하는 이 병이 6개월 이상 지속되어야 하며, 인후통, 미열, 근육통을 비롯한 11가지 증상 중 8가지 이상의 증상을 보여야 한다.

chronic fatigue syndrome 만성피로증후군 trigger v. (일련의 사건·반응 등을) 일으키다, 유발하다 symptom n. 징후; 증상 stick with ~에 충실하다; (이상(理想) 등을) 지키다 premature a. 조숙한; 너무 이른; 시기상조의 dub v. ~라고 칭하다, ~라는 별명으로 부르다 yuppie n. 여피족(도시에 사는 젊고 세련된 고소득 전문직 종사자) diagnose v. 진단하다 flu n. 인플루엔자, 독감 debilitating a. 쇠약하게 하는 sore throat 인후염 fever n. 발열; 열병 muscular ache 근육통

33-34

수천 년 동안 무성한 초목에 의해 숨겨져 있던 거대한 고대 도시가 아마존에서 발견되었다. 그 발견은 아마존에 살고 있는 사람들의 역사에 대해 우리가 알고 있는 것들을 바꾸고 있다. 에콰도르 동부의 우파노(Upano) 지역에 있는 집들과 광장들은 놀랍도록 잘 짜여진 도로와 운하로 연결되어 있었다. 그 곳은 그 지역의 토양을 비옥하게 만들었지만 그 사회를 파괴로 이끌었을지도 모르는 화산의 세력 범위 안에 놓여 있다. 우리는 페루의 마추픽추와 같은 남아메리카의 고지대의 도시들에 대해 알고 있지만, 사람들이 아마존에서 유목민으로만 살거나 혹은 작은 정착지에서만 살았다고 생각했다. "이곳은 우리가 아마존에서 알고 있는 그 어떤 다른 장소보다도 더 오래됐습니다. 우리는 문명에 대해 유럽 중심적인 관점을 가지고 있지만, 이것은 우리가 문화와 문명이 무엇인지에 대한 우리의 생각을 바꿔야 한다는 것을 보여줍니다."라고 연구를 이끈 프랑스 국립과학연구센터의 조사 책임자 Stephen Rostain 교수는 말한다. "그것은 우리가 아마존 문화를 보는 방식을 변화시킵니다. 대부분의 사람들은 오두막과 개간지에서 아마도 벌거벗은 채로 살고 있는 소규모 집단을 상상할 겁니다. (그러나) 이것은 고대인들이 복잡한 도시 사회에서 살았다는 것을 보여줍니다."라고 공동 저자인 Antoine Dorison은 말한다.

lush a. 푸르게 우거진, 무성한 vegetation n. 식물, 초목 plaza n. 광장 astounding a. 깜짝 놀랄만한, 대단한 canal n. 운하, 수로 nomadically ad. 유목생활을 하면서, 방랑 생활로 settlement n. 정착, 정착지 clearing land 개척지 complicated a. 복잡한 urban a. 도시의 co-author n. 공동 저자

31 글의 주제 ④

본문의 첫 문단에서는 만성피로증후군의 원인에 관해 다루고 있고, 두 번째 문단에서는 그 증상에 대해 다루고 있다.

위 글은 주로 무엇에 관한 것인가?
① 전문직 여성들이 걸리는 질병
② 만성피로증후군 진단 방법
③ 엡스타인-바 바이러스로 인한 증상
④ 만성피로증후군의 원인과 증상

33 내용파악 ①

대규모의 고대 도시가 아마존에서 새롭게 발견됨으로써 '사람들이 아마존에서 유목민으로만 살거나 혹은 작은 정착지에서만 살았을 것'이라는 기존의 통념이 의심받게 되었다. 그러므로 ①이 정답이다.

위 글에 의하면, 다음 중 이의가 제기될 수 있는 것은?
① 아마존에서 사람들은 유목민으로만 살거나 혹은 작은 정착지에서만 살았다.
② 아마존의 고대인들은 복잡한 도시 사회에서 살았을지도 모른다.
③ 우파노 지역 부근의 화산이 그 사회를 파괴로 이끌었을지도 모른다.
④ 우파노 지역의 집들과 광장들은 도로와 운하의 네트워크로 연결되어 있었다.

32 내용일치 ①

만성피로증후군의 원인에 대해 엡스타인-바 바이러스가 주된 원인이라는 의견과 다양한 다른 원인이 있을 수 있다는 의견이 공존하는 상황이다. 그러므로 ①이 옳은 진술이다. ② 최소 6개월은 지속되므로 회복이 쉽지 않다. ③ 본문에 관련된 언급이 없다. ④ 주된 원인이 아닐 수는 있어도 적어도 하나의 원인인 것은 맞다.

34 글의 제목 ④

무성한 초목에 의해 숨겨져 있던 거대한 고대 도시가 아마존에서 발견됐다는 사실과 그것이 갖는 의미에 대해 이야기하고 있는 글이므로, 제목으로는 ④가 적절하다.

위 글의 제목으로 가장 적절한 것은?
① 아마존 문화의 역사
② 고대 아마존의 유럽인들
③ 마추픽추와 아마존으로의 여행
④ 아마존 한가운데에 있는 고대 도시

35-36

2024년의 여행객들에게는 그들이 기후 위기에 대처하는 데 중요한 역할을 한다는 사실을 납득시킬 필요가 없다. 이러한 인식은 점점 더 많은 일련의 연구에서 나타나고 있으며, 글로벌 여행객의 3/4 이상이 내년에 보다 더 지속가능한 여행을 원한다는 것과 소비자의 90%가 여행할 때 지속가능한 선택지를 찾는다는 것이 드러났다. 지속가능한 관광에 대한 다른 연구에서는 의도와 행동 간의 간극이 남아있으며, 관광 부문과 그 이상의 분야에서 지속가능성에 투자하는 여행 목적지는 이 간극을 줄이는 데 도움을 줄 수 있는 것으로 나타났다. 한편, 사회적인 불안이나 재해로부터 복구 중에 있는 장소로의 주의 깊은 여행도 또한 이러한 목적지의 보다 더 지속가능한 미래를 지원하는 데 도움이 될 수 있다.

convince v. 설득시키다 address v. (문제를) 역점을 두어 다루다 sustainably ad. 환경을 파괴하지 않고 지속가능하게 consumer n. 소비자 destination n. 목적지, 행선지 unrest n. (사회적인) 불안 disaster n. 재해, 재난

---

35 내용파악 ②

"글로벌 여행객의 3/4 이상이 내년에 보다 더 지속가능한 여행을 원한다는 것과 소비자의 90%가 여행할 때 지속가능한 선택지를 찾는다는 것이 드러났다."고 했으므로 ②가 정답으로 적절하다.

위 글에 의하면, 오늘날의 여행객들은 _____.
① 재해로부터 복구 중에 있는 목적지를 피해야 한다
② 대체로 보다 더 지속가능한 여행을 할 수 있는 방법을 찾고 있다
③ 기후 위기를 해결하는 데 있어서의 자신들의 역할에 대해서는 거의 인식하지 못하고 있다
④ 돈이 더 많이 들기 때문에 대개 지속가능한 관광을 하지 않는다

---

36 내용파악 ②

"관광 부문과 그 이상의 분야에서 지속가능성에 투자하는 목적지는 이 간극을 줄이는 데 도움을 줄 수 있는 것으로 나타났다."라고 했으므로 ②가 정답이 된다. 지속가능성은 환경을 보존하는 가운데 개발이나 이용을 지속할 수 있는 가능성을 말하므로 지속가능하다는 말은 환경 친화적이라는 말과 같다.

위 글에 의하면, 지속가능한 관광에서 "의도-행동의 간극"은 _____을 통해 극복될 수 있을지도 모른다.
① 글로벌 여행객을 유치하기 위한 저렴한 현지 여행 코스 개발
② 목적지를 더 환경 친화적으로 만들기 위해 투자하는 것
③ 여행자들에게 지속가능한 관광의 필요성을 끊임없이 상기시키는 것
④ 목적지에 지속가능한 선택지가 있는지의 여부에 대한 정보 제공

37-38

표절은 학계에서 가장 오래된 범죄 중 하나이지만, 클로딘 게이(Claudine Gay)가 표절 혐의를 받은 뒤에 하버드 대학 총장직에서 사임한 것은 원전(原典)을 베끼는 것이 언제(어떤 경우에) 처벌 가능한 범죄가 되어야 하는가에 대한 논쟁을 온라인상에서 새롭게 촉발시켰다. 일부 교수들은 심지어 정보의 출처가 명확하기만 하면 연구자들이 더 많이 베끼고 더 적게 저술할 수 있는 보다 능률적인 출판 모델을 옹호하고 있다. 모든 연구자들이 자신의 문장을 구성해야 한다는 개념은 많은 사람들에게 기본 원리로 남아 있지만, 본질적으로 정보에 무제한적으로 접근할 수 있고 섬뜩할 정도의 정확성으로 언어를 재현할 수 있는 점점 더 정교해지고 있는 인공지능(AI) 알고리즘이 있는 세계에서는 이러한 견해가 새로운 저항에 직면할지도 모른다. 패서디나(Pasadena) 소재 캘리포니아 공과대학의 계산생물학자 리오르 패처터(Lior Pachter)는 "저는 다른 사람의 글을 절대 베껴서는 안 된다는 생각이 다소 시대에 뒤떨어졌다고 봅니다."라고 말하며, 정보의 출처를 반드시 올바르게 밝히도록 하는 것이 핵심이라고 덧붙였다. 그는 데이터 조작을 비롯한 더 큰 문제들이 학계에 있다고 말한다.

resignation n. 사직, 사임 plagiarism n. 표절 allegation n. (증거 없이 누가 부정한 일을 했다는) 혐의 academic n. 대학교수 advocate v. 옹호하다 streamlined a. 간소화 된 bedrock a. 밑바탕의; 공고한 sophisticated a. 정교한 eerie a. 섬뜩한 ensure v. 보증하다, 확실히 하다 source v. (인용문의) 출전(出典)을 명시하다 fabrication n. 위조

---

37 빈칸완성 ②

이어지는 "일부 교수들은 심지어 정보의 출처가 명확하기만 하면 연구자들이 더 많이 베끼고 더 적게 저술할 수 있는 보다 능률적인 출판 모델을 옹호하고 있다."라는 내용은 '특정 경우에는 표절이 범죄가 되지 않도록 해야 한다'라는 주장에 해당하므로, 빈칸에는 이와 관련된 ②가 들어가는 것이 적절하다.

다음 중 빈칸에 들어가기에 가장 적절한 것은?
① 정치가 학문적인 문제에 어떻게 관계되어 있는가
② 원전(原典)을 베끼는 것이 언제(어떤 경우에) 처벌 가능한 범죄가 되어야 하는가
③ 저명한 학자가 왜 그런 범죄를 저지르는가
④ 왜 표절은 정보화 시대에도 여전히 범죄인가

---

38 내용파악 ③

그는 다른 사람의 글을 절대 베껴서는 안 된다는 생각이 다소 시대에 뒤떨어진 것이라 여기고 있으며, 정보의 출처를 반드시 올바르게 밝히도록 하는 것을 가장 중요하게 여기고 있다. 그러므로 ③이 정답으로 적절하다.

리오르 패처터는 _____고 주장하고 있다.
① 어떤 종류의 표절이든 데이터 조작만큼 엄하게 처벌해야 한다
② 학술 논문을 작성하는 데 있어서 AI 알고리즘을 사용하는 것은 엄격하게 금지되어야 한다
③ 출처가 명확하기만 하다면 다른 사람의 글을 베끼는 것이 더 광범위하게 허용되어야 한다
④ 인공지능이 언어를 정확하게 재현할 수 있는 때에 표절이라는 개념은 쓸모가 없다

39-40

자율주행 자동차는 자동차 소유라는 개념에 도전하게 될 것이다. 자동차는 대부분의 사람들에게 가장 값비싼 소유물에 속하지만, 평균 96%의 경우에 아무 것도 하지 않는 채로 있다. 이것은 필요할 때마다 자동차를 이용할 수 있는 편리함에 의해 정당화된다. 그러나 요즘에는 택시 서비스, 차량 공유제도 혹은 렌트카 제공업체를 위한 스마트폰 앱을 이용하여 마음대로 차를 호출할 수 있다. 구글은 공유된 자율주행 택시가 75% 이상의 이용률을 가질 수 있을 것으로 추산하고 있다. 만약 그렇다면, 같은 수의 사람들을 이동시키기 위해 훨씬 더 적은 수의 자동차가 필요할 것이다. "도로에는 훨씬 적은 수의 자동차가 있게 될 것입니다. 아마 오늘날 우리가 가지고 있는 자동차의 30% 정도에 불과할 겁니다."라고 스탠포드 대학의 컴퓨터 과학자이자 구글의 자율주행 자동차 프로젝트의 전(前) 리더였던 세바스찬 스런(Sebastian Thrun)은 예측한다. 국제교통포럼의 루이스 마르티네즈는 자율주행 차량이 오늘날의 자동차만큼 소유되고 사용될 것이라는 생각을 "희박한 가정"이라고 말한다. 일단(一團)의 자율주행 자동차가 한 도시의 자동차, 택시 및 버스의 이동을 모두 대체할 수 있으며, 훨씬 더 적은 차량으로 동일한 이동성을 제공할 수 있다고 말한다. 텍사스 오스틴의 교통 데이터를 기반으로 한 유타 대학 댄 패그넌트(Dan Fagnant)의 연구에 따르면, 역동적인 승차 공유 기능을 갖춘 자율주행 택시 1대가 10대의 개인 차량을 대체할 수 있다.

autonomous a. 자율의 vehicle n. 차량, 탈것 own v. 소유하다 justify v. 정당화하다 convenience n. 편리, 편의 have access to ~에게 접근[출입]할 수 있다 summon v. 소환하다, 호출하다 reckon v. 간주하다, 판단하다, 평가하다 utilization n. 이용 tenuous a. 희박한; 가냘픈; 확실하지 않은, 막연한, 애매한 assumption n. 가정, 억측 replace v. 대체하다 draw on ~에 의지하다

---

39 빈칸완성 　　　　　　　　　　　　①

바로 다음 문장에서 '실제로 차를 이용하는 시간은 많지 않은데도 사람들은 필요할 때 편하게 사용할 수 있기 때문에 자동차를 소유한다'고 하여 현재의 자동차 소유에 대해 언급했으며, 앱을 통해 언제든지 자동차를 호출하여 이용할 수 있다면, 자동차 소유의 개념이 변하게 될 것이므로 빈칸에는 ①이 적절하다.

다음 중 빈칸에 들어가기에 가장 적절한 것은?
① 자동차 소유라는 개념에 도전하다
② 자동차 보험 산업을 변형시키다
③ 운수업계에 치명타가 되다
④ 인간 운전자보다 높은 수준에 있다

---

40 내용일치 　　　　　　　　　　　　④

본문 마지막 문장에서 '자율주행 택시 1대가 10대의 개인 차량을 대체할 수 있다'고 했으므로 ④가 정답이다. ① 4%이다. ③ 도로를 주행하는 자동차가 줄어들면 자동차 제품 생산의 가치는 낮아지고 자동차 공유 서비스 같은 서비스 제공의 가치는 높아져, 가치가 제품에서 서비스로 옮겨갈 것이다.

위 글에 의하면, 다음 중 옳은 것은?
① 오늘날 우리가 보유한 자동차의 평균 가동률은 96%이다.
② 자율주행 자동차는 오늘날 자동차만큼 구매되고 사용될 것이다.
③ 자동차 제조업의 가치가 서비스에서 제품으로 옮겨갈 것이다.
④ 10대나 되는 개인 소유의 자동차가 1대의 자율주행 택시로 대체될 수 있을 것이다.

2024 성균관대학교(인문계)

01 ①	02 ④	03 ②	04 ③	05 ⑤	06 ④	07 ②	08 ①	09 ⑤	10 ②
11 ③	12 ②	13 ③	14 ①	15 ④	16 ①	17 ④	18 ①	19 ⑤	20 ④
21 ⑤	22 ②	23 ⑤	24 ⑤	25 ③	26 ①	27 ⑤	28 ③	29 ③	30 ③
31 ①	32 ③	33 ④	34 ②	35 ⑤	36 ②	37 ①	38 ①	39 ⑤	40 ①
41 ⑤	42 ④	43 ②	44 ①	45 ④	46 ③	47 ②	48 ④	49 ①	50 ②

01 동의어 ①

stay fit 건강을 유지하다 sedentary a. 앉은 채 있는, 늘 (책상에) 앉아 있는(= desk-bound) lustful a. 정욕의 innocent a. 무고한; 순진한 hypnotizing a. 최면의, 매혹적인 bewitching a. 매혹적인

건강한 라이프스타일을 선택하면 e스포츠 선수는 건강을 유지하고 늘 앉아 있는 라이프스타일을 갖게 될 위험을 줄일 수 있다.

02 동의어 ④

skimp on 절약하다, 줄이다(= cut back on) feast n. 연회 reinforce v. 강화하다 grumble v. 불평하다 skip v. 빠뜨리다, 건너뛰다 pile up 축적하다

일부 우버(Uber) 운전자들은 2024년에 생계를 잃을까 두려워 돈을 아끼기 위해 새해 잔치를 줄일지도 모른다고 말했다.

03 동의어 ②

decommission v. 해체하다(= deactivate) structure n. 구조물 soil remediation 토양 정화 introduce v. 도입하다, 소개하다 free of charge 무료로 gratuitous a. 무료의, 불필요한 purposeless a. 무의미한, 무익한

나나이모(Nanaimo) 벙커는 1990년대에 해체되었지만, 국방부는 토양 정화 후에 벙커 구조물 자체를 어떻게 처리할지 아직 결정하지 않았다.

04 동의어 ③

minister n. 장관 show off 과시하다 thriftiness n. 절약(= frugality) iron v. 다림질하다 wrapping paper 포장지 rationality n. 합리성 indiscretion n. 무분별한 행동 generosity n. 너그러움

언젠가 독일 환경부 장관은 곧 재사용될 포장지를 다림질하는 모습이 사진으로 찍힘으로써 주부로서의 절약 정신을 과시하는 기회로 크리스마스를 이용한 적이 있다.

05 동의어 ⑤

trenchant a. 정곡을 찌르는, 신랄한(= incisive) dominant a. 지배적인 dull a. (날이) 무딘; 지루한 fallible a. 틀리기 쉬운 nebulous a. 모호한

고(故) 로버트 하이네켄(Robert Heinecken)은 40여 년 동안 사회 정치에 대한 예리한 관찰자였다.

06 수동태 ④

had 이하는 if it had been ~에서 if를 생략하고 주어와 had를 도치시킨 형태이다. apply는 '적용하다'는 뜻의 타동사이므로 '적용되다'는 의미로는 수동태여야 한다. 따라서 ④를 과거분사 applied로 고쳐야 한다. ③ all of this는 단수이므로 it이다. ⑤ a certain의 뜻의 some이다.

tolerable a. 참을 수 있는 apply v. 적용하다 consistency n. 일관성

이 모든 것이 어느 정도 일관성을 가지고 적용되었더라면 더 견딜 만했을 것이다.

07 명사의 수 ②

앞에 부정관사가 있으므로 ②에 쓰인 numbers를 number로 고쳐야 한다.

specialist n. 전문가 general reading public 일반 독자

로버트 브라운(Robert Brown)은 전문가들에게도 일반 독자들에게도 효과적으로 글을 쓸 수 있는 소수의 사회과학자 중 하나이다.

08 관계대명사 ①

①은 다음에 나오는 happen은 물론 has been의 주어도 되어야 한다. 따라서 선행사가 포함된 관계대명사 what으로 고쳐야 한다.

dismissively ad. 멸시하는 듯이 colonization n. 식민지화

20세기 후반에 일어난 것은 세계의 콜라 식민지화라고 다소 경멸적으로 기술되어 왔다.

09 대명사의 수일치　　　　　　　　⑤

⑤는 앞에 나온 명사 baseball을 가리키므로 단수 대명사 its로 고쳐야 한다.

recreation n. 오락　shape up 발전하다, 잘 되어 가다, 열심히 일하다　unquestioned a. 의심할 수 없는　preeminence n. 걸출, 탁월, 발군

야구가 신사들의 오락에서 국민 스포츠로 발전하는 오랜 기간 동안 또 다른 스포츠가 의문의 여지가 없는 그것의 우월성에 도전하기 위해 잘 되어가고 있었다.

10 전치사의 목적어　　　　　　　　②

②는 전치사 다음이므로 명사 significance로 고쳐야 한다. 앞의 of와 합쳐 of significance로 바꿔야 significant의 의미가 된다.

odd a. 이상한　anthropological a. 인류학적인　native a. 원주민의　informant n. 정보원

제2차 세계대전 당시 많은 이상한 언어들이 군사적으로 중요했기 때문에, 인류언어학자는 원어민 정보원과 직접 작업하는 자신의 방법을 소개할 기회를 가졌다.

11 논리완성　　　　　　　　③

산업을 구축하기 위해서는 외국인 투자를 받아야 하므로 빈칸에는 ③ court(= seek to gain)가 적절하다.

pursue v. 추구하다　strategy n. 전략　rescue v. 구하다　construct v. 구축하다　textile n. 직물　evolve v. 발전하다　obstruct v. 방해하다　occlude v. 막다　court v. 받고자 하다, 구애하다　arraign v. 기소하다　denounce v. 비난하다

지난 반세기에 걸쳐 동아시아 및 동남아시아의 많은 지역에서, 국가 지도 자들은 수출 지향 산업을 구축하기 위한 외국인 투자를 받으려고 하면서 수억 명의 사람들을 빈곤에서 구제한 개발 전략을 추구해왔다. 농부들은 공장 노동을 통해 더 많은 소득을 얻었고, 직물이나 의류와 같은 기본 상품을 만든 후, 전자제품, 컴퓨터 칩, 자동차 등으로 발전해갔다.

12 논리완성　　　　　　　　②

소련 엔지니어들은 탄소와 수소가 상호작용하여 석유를 만든다고 보았으므로 수소가 석유가 있음을 숨길 수 없이 보여주는 신호라고 생각했을 것이다. 따라서 빈칸에는 ②가 적절하다.

hydrogen n. 수소　petroleum n. 석유　inorganic matter 무기물　crunch v. 부러뜨리다　hydrocarbon n. 탄화수소　chief component 주성분　make sense 합리적이다　restrict v. 제한하다　telltale a. 숨길 수 없는　sensitive a. 민감한　spurious a. 거짓된　underhand a. 비밀의

소련 엔지니어들은 수소를 원해서가 아니라 석유가 어떻게 생성되는지에 대한 다른 이론을 가지고 있었기 때문에 수소를 발견한 경우가 많았다.

그들은 수소가 부서진 공룡 뼈가 아니라 무기물에서 생성되었다고 믿었다. 이 견해에 따르면 지구 맨틀에 있는 탄소가 지하 깊은 곳에서 수소와 상호 작용하여 탄화수소(석유의 주성분)를 생성한다. 따라서 석유의 숨길 수 없는 신호로서 수소를 찾는 것이 합리적이었다.

13 논리완성　　　　　　　　③

앞에서는 탈출이 성공한 내용이고, 뒤에는 문제가 있어 다시 잡혔다는 내용이다. 역접의 부사나 부정적인 의미의 연결사가 필요하다.

press on 서두르다　hurl v. 던지다　aboard ad. 탑승한　burrow in 굴을 파다　stuff v. 속에 집어넣다　dummy n. 인형　book v. 예약하다　cancel v. 취소하다　notice v. 알아채다　hefty a. 많은　unfortunately ad. 불행하게도　fortuitously ad. 우연히　gracefully ad. 우아하게

잭(Jack)은 서둘러서 철로에 다다랐고 기차를 기다렸다. 기차가 오자 그는 기차에 몸을 던져 빈 석탄 포대 사이로 몸을 숨겼다. 그가 탈출한 후 동료 죄수들이 그의 담요 아래에 인형을 넣어 그가 잠든 것처럼 보이게 만들어 그를 은폐해 주었다. 불행하게도, 잭은 보어(Boer)족 이발사에게 이발과 면도를 다음 날 아침으로 예약해두었는데 그것을 취소할 것을 잊어버렸다. 그의 부재는 이발사에게 들통이 났다. 나중에 이발사는 잭을 다시 체포한 대가로 거액의 포상금을 받았다.

14 논리완성　　　　　　　　①

임금-물가 스파이럴을 말하고 있다. 다음 문장에서 생계비가 늘어나는, 다시 말해 실질 소득이 감소하는 이유로 에너지 가격 상승을 말하고 있으므로 빈칸에는 ①이 적절하다.

dubious a. 의심스러운　zero-sum jockeying 제로섬 경쟁(서로의 이익 없이 서로 경쟁하는 것)　attribute A to B A를 B의 탓으로 돌리다　inevitable a. 불가피한　real income 실질 소득(인플레이션을 반영한 실제 구매력)　brought on largely by 주로 ~에 의해 야기된　price hike 가격 인상　wage demand 임금 인상 요구　wage-price spiral 임금-물가 스파이럴(노동조합의 임금 인상 요구 → 기업의 가격 인상 → 노동조합의 추가적인 임금 인상 요구라는 악순환)　surging a. 급등하는　offset v. 상쇄하다　loss n. 손실　reflect v. 반영하다　labor costs 노동 비용　off we go 여기부터 시작

필(Pill)의 이야기에서 더욱 의심스러운 점은 이러한 일자리를 위한 제로섬 경쟁을 대체로 에너지 가격 상승으로 인해 발생하는 불가피한 실질 소득 감소를 피하기 위한 노력 탓으로 돌리고 있다는 점이다. 그는 기업의 가격 인상과 노동조합의 임금 인상 요구 모두를 논의에 포함시키는 데 신중했지만, 이는 여전히 기본적으로는 고전적 임금-물가 스파이럴(악순환적 상승) 이야기이다. 이 이야기에서 노동자들은 이를 테면 에너지 가격 급등으로 인한 생활비 상승을 경험하고, 이러한 손실을 상쇄하기 위해 임금 인상을 요구한다. 하지만 기업들은 더 높아진 노동 비용을 반영하여 가격을 올리게 되고, 이 순환은 계속된다.

① 에너지 가격 상승
② 회사의 번영
③ 민간 부문 보호
④ 비타협적인 협상
⑤ 문화적 변화

15 논리완성 ④

to neither 앞의 comma는 일종의 부연 설명을 위한 콤마이다. '상에 적절한 중요성을 부여하는 것'을 부연 설명해야 한다. 'mistake A for B'는 'A가 B한다고 잘못 생각하다'라는 의미이므로 ④가 '상이 너무 많은 것을 의미한다고도 너무 적은 것을 의미한다고도 잘못 생각하지 않다'는 의미로 빈칸에 적절하다.

grim a. 더 암울한 prizewinner n. 수상자 announce v. 발표하다 celebrate v. 찬양하다 dedicate v. 헌신하다 tension n. 긴장, 노력 unrecognized a. 인정받지 못한 assign v. 부여하다 weight n. 중요성, 가치 commitment n. 헌신 momentarily ad. 일시적으로 officially ad. 공식적으로 nominate v. 지명하다 collaborative work 공동 작업

그럼에도 불구하고, 발표할 수상자가 없다면, 고귀하거나 아름다운 목표를 추구하는 데 자신의 인생을 바친 사람들을 찬양할 시간을 우리가 가지지 않는다면, 세상이 얼마나 더 암울해질지 생각해 보라. 하지만 수상하지 못하는 사람들은 어떤가? 훨씬 더 많은 이 사람들은, 모두가 모차르트인 것은 아니지만, 수상의 본질적인 의미와 긴장을 시사한다. 모든 수상자 각 한 명마다 훨씬 더 많은 수의 인정받지 못한 사람들이 있다. 우리는 상에 그 상의 적절한 중요성(가치)을 신중하게 부여하여, 그 상이 너무 많은 의미를 갖고 있다고도 너무 적은 의미를 갖고 있다고도 잘못 생각하지 말아야 한다. 상은 훌륭한 것이지만, 중요한 것은 작품과 예술가가 작품에 쏟는 헌신이다.

① 그들을 순간적으로도 영구적으로도 기억하지 않다
② 그들을 공식적으로도 은밀하게도 찬양하지 않다
③ 그들을 헌신에 기초해서도 행운에 기초해서도 수상자로 지명하지 않다
④ 그것들이 너무 많은 것을 의미한다고도 너무 적은 것을 의미한다고도 잘못 생각하지 않다
⑤ 그것들을 협업적 노력 때문에도 행운 때문에도 가치 있게 여기지 않다

16 논리완성 ①

BTS가 모두 군에 입대한다는 발표는 소문에 따라 면제를 기대했던 팬들로서도 어쩔 수 없이 받아들여야 했다. 군 입대는 어쩔 수 없는 일이라 해도 진이 최전방에 배치된다는 보도에 팬들은 놀랐다는 것이므로 빈칸에는 '그렇다 해도'라는 의미의 ①이 적절하다.

rumor v. 소문을 내다 skip v. 빼먹다 military service 군 복무 on the basis ~을 근거로 carry on doing so 계속해서 그렇게 하다 enlist v. 징집에 응하다, 입대하다 the front line 최전선 even so 그럼에도 불구하고 as usual 늘 그렇듯이

몇 달 동안 정부가 BTS 멤버들의 군 복무를 면제해줄지도 모른다는 소문이 돌았다. 그것은 그들이 이미 국가에 수십억 달러를 벌어다줌으로써 국가에 이바지했으며, 그들이 계속해서 그렇게 하도록 허용하는 것이 국가에 더 이익이 될 것이라는 것에 근거한 소문이었다. 하지만 10월, BTS 멤버들은 모두 군에 입대할 계획이라고 발표했으며, 맏형인 진이 먼저 가게 되었다. 그렇다 해도, 진이 최전방에 배치된다는 보도는 일부 팬들을 놀라게 했는데, 그들은 진이 덜 위험한 역할을 맡을 것이라고 생각했었다.

17 논리완성 ④

빈칸 다음에서 이 낱말은 이런 의미로도 쓰이고 저런 의미로도 쓰이는 낱말이라고 하였다. 따라서 '다의적인', '모호한'이라는 뜻의 ④가 빈칸에 적절하다.

admiration n. 존경 evolutionist n. 진화론자 ethologist n. 동물행동학자 go astray 잘못된 길로 가다 sheer a. 순전한 semantic a. 의미적인 species n. 종(種), 종류 conceive v. 생각하다 pronoun n. 대명사 cannot avoid ~ing ~할 수밖에 없다 impartial a. 공정한 ambiguous a. 모호한, 여러 가지 뜻으로 해석되는 admirable a. 감탄[칭찬]할 만한

나는 대체로 과학자들, 특히 진화론자들과 동물행동학자들을 상당히 존경한다. 그리고 그들이 때로는 엉뚱한 길로 빠지기도 한다고 생각하지만, 그것은 순전히 편견 때문인 것은 아니었다. 부분적으로 그것은 순전한 의미적인 사건, 즉 'man'이라는 단어가 다의적이라는 사실 때문이다. 이 단어는 사람 종(種)을 의미하기도 하고, 또한 사람 종의 수컷을 의미하기도 한다. 만약 '사람'에 대한 책을 쓰거나 '사람'에 대한 이론을 고안한다면, 이 단어를 사용하지 않을 수 없다. 또한 'man'이라는 단어 대신에 대명사 'he'를 사용할 수밖에 없다.

18 논리완성 ①

다음 문장에서 아시아의 대부분 지역과 아프리카와 북미의 미발견 국가들이 선/악 이원론으로 대조된다고 하였다. 이는 선/악 이원론이 대륙에 적용된 예라고 할 수 있으므로 ①이 정답이다.

secular a. 세속적인 demand n. 수요 dualism n. 이원론(두 가지 근본적인 원리가 서로 대립한다는 철학적 사상) arbitrary a. 자의적인 social order 사회 질서 project v. 투사하다 cast v. 캐스팅하다, (역을) 맡기다 convenient a. 이롭고 유리한 ripe a. 이용할 준비가 되어 있는 exploitation n. 착취

오늘날 세속 세계는 사탄이 필요하지 않다. 하지만 선과 악은 여전히 수요가 크다. 오래된 이란의 선 대 악이라는 이원론은 완전히 자의적인 것이지만, 사회 질서를 유지하는 데는 효과적이다. 미국 역사에서 선/악의 이원론은 대륙 자체에 투사되었다. 아프리카와 북미 대륙의 미발견 국가들은 비기독교 국가이고 17세기 아시아 대부분의 지역과 달리 탐험과 착취에 알맞았으므로 편리하게도 악의 역할을 맡게 되었다.

① 대륙 자체
② 미국의 신비로운 역사
③ 사회의 분리
④ 미국의 사회경제적 구조
⑤ 인종 차별

19 논리완성 ⑤

한 나라는 하나의 민족이나 종교를 가진 사람들로 이루어질 필요가 없으며, 모두가 같은 권리를 공유해야 한다는 말 다음에 올 수 있는 표현으로는 ⑤(모두가 환영 받는다)가 적절하다.

immigrant n. 이민자 tribute n. 찬사 participant n. 참가자, 참여자 metaphor n. 은유 far from 결코 ~이 아니다 contradiction n. 모순

hypocrisy n. 위선 ethnicity n. 민족성 consist of ~로 구성되다, 이루어지다 lurch forward 흔들리면서 앞으로 나아가다 stumble v. 비틀거리다 right n. 권리

인도계 미국인 이민자 라크쉬미(Lakshmi)는 회의 참가자들에게 찬사를 보내며 연설을 마무리했다. 참가자들이 "오늘날 현재 모습의 미국을 이루는 진정한 모자이크를 만들고 있습니다. 우리나라는 완벽하지 못하며 정책상 모순과 위선으로 가득 차 있지만, 여전히 세계에 한 국가가 같은 민족성이나 종교를 가진 사람들로만 구성될 필요가 없다는 것을 보여줄 수 있습니다."라고 그녀는 말했다. "그 국가는 가능한 최고의 미국을 바라보고 미국이 흔들리면서도 앞으로 나아가도록 도와주는 우리 모두가 도중에 종종 비틀거리면서도, 같은 권리를 공유하고 바라건대 모든 사람이 환영받는 미래를 향해 나아가는 가운데 세워질 수 있습니다."

① 미국이 가장 먼저다
② 완벽한 사람은 없다
③ 우리에게 더 많은 자원봉사자가 필요하다
④ 더 이상 외국인 근로자는 없어야 한다
⑤ 모두가 환영 받는다

---

20 논리완성 ④

다음 문장에서 또 다른 사람을 죽이려고 골목길에 숨어 기다리는 괴물이라고 한 것은 연쇄 살인범을 의미하고, FBI의 말도 연쇄 살인범에 대한 말이고, 마지막에서도 저질적인 실화 범죄 소설이라고 하여 이 글 전체가 연쇄 살인범에 대한 내용임을 알 수 있다. 그리고 과장된 보도, 과장된 FBI의 발표, 실화 범죄 소설이 형편없이 조사되고 많은 경우 날조되었음, 의심스러운 가설 및 이론 등은 실제와 다른 '신화, 허구'임을 말하고 있다. 따라서 빈칸에는 ④가 적절하다.

collective a. 집단적인 fuel v. 부채질하다 enforcement n. 집행 grip v. 꽉 붙잡다 myth n. 신화, 허구의 이야기 hype n. 과대광고 monster n. 괴물 lurking a. 숨어 기다리는, 잠복하는 serial killer 연쇄 살인범 loose a. 풀려 있는, 자유로운 expert n. 전문가 come out of the woodstock 예상치 못한 곳에서 나타나다 ride the wave 수혜를 입다 hysteria n. 과잉 반응 fabricated a. 조작된 quickie a. 빠른, 저질의 dubious a. 의심스러운

1980년대 중반, 법 집행 기관과 언론 매체에 의해 시작되고 부채질된 집단적인 공포가 세계를 휩쓸면서 연쇄 살인범 신화가 탄생했다. 과장된 보도를 모두 믿는다면, 모든 골목길마다 괴물이 숨어서 또 다른 사람의 생명을 빼앗으려고 기다리고 있었다. FBI는 자신들의 통계수치로 보면 미국에서는 어느 때든 500명의 연쇄 살인범이 돌아다니고 있다고 말하기까지 했다(실제 숫자는 아마 50명에 훨씬 더 가까울 것이다). 전문가와 저자로 추정되는 사람들이 난데없이 나타나 이 히스테리 물결을 타고, 형편없이 조사되고 (많은 경우 날조된) 저질적인 실화 범죄 소설과 의심스러운 가설 및 이론을 쏟아냈다.

① 사람들이 스릴러물을 더 많이 시청하기 시작했다
② 종말에 대한 이야기가 퍼지고 있었다
③ 미신이 과학적 믿음을 대체했다
④ 연쇄 살인범 신화가 탄생했다
⑤ 사람들은 더 엄격한 법 집행을 원했다

---

21 문맥상 적절하지 않은 단어 고르기 ⑤

부자들에 대한 세금 인하는 원했던 '낙수효과' 대신, 부자들은 더 부자가 되고 가난한 사람은 더 가난해지는 결과를 낳는다. 그렇다면 소득 불평등은 '감소'가 아니라 '악화'된다. 따라서 ⓒ reduce를 exacerbate로 바꿔야 한다.

tax cut 세금 인하 conservative lawmaker 보수 국회의원 trickle down 부유층에서 서민층으로 흘러가다 boost v. 촉진하다 income n. 소득, 수입 per capita gross domestic product 1인당 국내총생산 unemployment rate 실업률 income inequality 소득 불평등

부자들을 위한 세금 인하는 오랫동안 보수적인 입법자들과 경제학자들로부터 지지를 받아왔는데, 이들은 이러한 조치가 '낙수효과'를 일으켜, 결국 다른 모든 사람의 일자리와 소득을 촉진할 것이라고 주장한다. 그러나 새로운 연구에 따르면, 50년 동안의 이와 같은 부자들을 위한 세금 인하는 오직 한 집단, 즉 부자들에게만 도움이 되었다. 이 새로운 논문은 호주에서부터 미국에 이르는 18개의 선진국을 1965년부터 2015년까지 50년간 조사했다. 연구는 로날드 레이건 대통령이 부자들에 대한 세금을 대폭 인하한 1982년의 미국처럼 특정 연도에 부자들을 위한 세금 감면을 통과시킨 나라들을 그렇지 않은 나라들과 비교한 다음, 그들의 경제 결과를 조사했다. 연구 결과, 부자들에 대한 세금을 인하한 국가와 그렇지 않은 국가의 5년 후 1인당 국내총생산과 실업률은 거의 같았다. 그러나 분석 결과, 하나의 커다란 변화를 발견했는데, 부자들의 소득이 세율이 낮아진 국가에서 훨씬 더 빨리 증가한 것이었다. 부자들을 위한 세금 인하는 중산층으로까지 그 효과가 내려가지 않고, 부자들이 더 많은 부를 보존하도록 도와주고 소득 불평등을 <감소시키는> 정도의 성과밖에 내지 못할지 모른다는 것을 연구는 보여준다.

---

22 문맥상 적절하지 않은 단어 고르기 ②

세계 영어에 가장 강력한 영향을 미치고 있는 나라는 미국이라고 하고, 다음 문장은 '그러나'라고 시작했다. 앞에서 가장 강력하다고 했으므로 '그러나' 다음에는 그 강력함이 줄어들 수 있다고 해야 하고, 그러려면 영향력이 도전을 점점 더 크게 받을 것이라고 해야 한다. 따라서 ⑧ decreasingly를 increasingly로 바꿔야 한다.

immediate future 가까운 미래 be likely to ~할 가능성이 높다 sardonic a. 조롱하는, 냉소적인 rumor n. 소문 native speaker 원어민, 모국어 사용자 circulate v. 회자하다, 떠돌다 grossly exaggerated 지나치게 과장된 claim n. 주장 heading n. 제목 topple v. 비틀거리다, 와해하다, 흔들리다 automatically ad. 자동적으로 defer v. (의견에) 따르다, (의견·판단을) 맡기다 determine v. 결정하다

가까운 미래, 그리고 아마도 그보다 더 오랜 기간, 세계 영어에 가장 강력한 영향을 미칠 나라는 미국일 가능성이 크다. 그러나 이러한 영향력은 시간이 지남에 따라 <점점 덜> 도전받을 수도 있다. 1985년 캐나다에서 토마스 파이크데이(Thomas Paikeday)가 『원어민은 죽었다』라는 제목의 책을 출판한 이후, '원어민은 죽었다'라는 냉소적인 소문이 떠돌았다. 그러나 우리는 그러한 보고를 지나치게 '과장된' 것으로 간주해야 한다. 원어민이 언어를 '소유한다'는 주장을 고려해보면, 더 적절한 제목은 '원어민의 흔들림'일 것이다. 미래에는 원어민이 비원어민들이 그 언어에서 무엇이 옳은지 결정할 때 판단을 맡기는 권위자로 자동적으로 간주되지는 않을지도 모른다.

23 글의 요지   ⑤

AI는 과거의 기술보다 접근성이 좋다는 장점을 이야기한 후, 아직은 이 기술에 대한 우려가 많다고 이야기하고 있으므로 ⑤가 글의 요지로 적절하다.

generative AI 생성형 인공지능　access v. 접근하다　advent n. 도래, 출현　e-commerce n. 전자 상거래　retailer n. 소매상인　set up 세우다, 설립하다　physical a. 물리적인　infrastructure n. 기간시설, 사회적 생산기반　storefront n. 상점　enthusiastic a. 열렬한　adopter n. 채택자　do away with 제거하다　drudgery n. 힘들고 단조로운 일　survey n. 설문조사　consultancy n. 자문회사　frontline worker 최전선 노동자　manager n. 관리자　union n. 노동조합　Writers' guild 작가 협회　be on strike 파업하다　in part 부분적으로　impulse n. 충동　be prone to ~하는 경향이 있다　hallucination n. 환각　fake news 가짜 뉴스

많은 생성형 인공지능(AI) 도구가 이전 기술보다 쉽게 접근할 수 있게 될 것이다. 이는 고용주가 많은 하드웨어를 구매해야 했던 개인용 컴퓨터나 스마트폰의 출현, 또는 심지어 소매업체가 온라인 상점을 열기 전에 물리적 인프라를 구축해야 했던 전자 상거래의 출현과도 같지 않다. 그러나 모든 기업이 열렬하게 받아들이지는 않을 것이다. 이 기술이 힘들고 지겨운 업무를 없애주겠다고 약속하지만, 일부 사람들은 결국 인공지능이 자신들을 대체할 수 있다고 걱정한다. 컨설팅 회사의 조사에 따르면, 최전선 노동자들이 관리자나 리더보다 인공지능에 대해 더 우려하고, 낙관적이지 않다. 어떤 경우에는 노조가 이 기술의 도입 속도를 늦추기 위해 노력할 수도 있는데, 일부 노조는 인공지능이 일자리에 미칠 영향에 대한 우려를 부분적인 이유로 하여 2023년에 장기간 동안 파업을 벌였던 할리우드 작가 조합만큼이나 심한 행동을 보일지도 모른다.

글의 요지로 적절한 것은?
① 공공 부문의 관리자는 혁신 충동을 느끼지 못할 수 있다.
② 인공지능 이용은 이전의 접근 가능한 기술보다 가치가 떨어진다.
③ 인공지능은 환상이나 가짜 뉴스를 만들어내기 쉽다.
④ 많은 기업이 인공지능을 사용하여 부유한 관리자를 돕는 도구를 만들고 있다.
⑤ 인공지능은 비즈니스에 많은 가능성을 가지고 있지만 하루아침에 도입될 것으로 기대해서는 안 된다.

24 내용파악   ⑤

나머지는 모두 ChatGPT의 장점을 말하고 있지만, ⓔ는 단점을 이야기하고 있다.

assignment n. 과제　responses n. 답변　alternative n. 대안　sight impairment 시각 장애　learning disability 학습 장애　academic performance 학업 성취　multiple a. 다양한　comprehensive a. 포괄적인　access n. 접근　cheating n. 부정행위　plagiarism n. 표절　brainstorm v. 브레인스토밍하다

다음 중 다른 것과 다른 의견에 해당하는 것은?
ⓐ 학생이 ChatGPT에 과제에 관한 질문을 입력하면 ChatGPT는 설명과 예시로 응답한다. 그것은 학생들에게 과제 질문에 답하는 대안적인 방법을 제공한다.

ⓑ 시각 장애가 있는 학생들을 위해 ChatGPT는 응답을 크게 소리로 말해줄 수 있다. 그것은 학습 장애가 있는 학생들을 위해 강좌의 주제나 개념을 요약할 수도 있다.

ⓒ ChatGPT는 학생들의 학습 스타일을 이해하고 개인별 최적 학습 경험을 제공할 수 있다. 그것은 학생의 학업 성적을 분석하고 강좌를 학생의 요구 사항에 맞게 구성할 수도 있다.

ⓓ ChatGPT를 대학 교육에서 사용하는 것은 다양한 방식으로 교수들을 도울 수 있다. 예를 들어, 그것은 강좌를 위한 포괄적인 수업 계획을 개발할 수 있다. 그것은 또한 강좌를 위한 추가적인 교육 자료를 포함한 링크에 접근을 제공할 수도 있다.

ⓔ 글쓰기 과제에 ChatGPT를 사용하는 것은 부정행위와 표절을 촉진할 뿐일 것이다. ChatGPT는 빠르게 응답을 생성하기 때문에, 그것은 학생들이 고민하고 비판적으로 사고하며 창의적인 답변을 제시하는 능력을 감소시킬 것이다.

25 지시대상   ③

셋째 문장의 '징후'가 보여주는 바가 중국에 대한 외부의 평가인데, 패권 국가(hegemon)와 가장 가까운 낱말은 super power이다.

call for 요구하다　hegemonism n. 패권주의　codeword n. 암호　recruit v. 모집하다　specifically ad. 명확히　put an end to 종식시키다　gunboat diplomacy 포함선 외교(군사력을 배경으로 다른 국가에 압력을 행사하여 자국의 요구를 관철시키는 외교 정책)　neo-colonialism n. 신식민주의(정치적 지배는 없지만 경제적 힘을 이용하여 다른 국가를 지배하는 정책)　unnamed a. 이름이 밝혀지지 않은　rival a. 경쟁자의

중국은 이러한 평가에 동의하지 않는다. 중국은 단일 강대국이 세계를 지배하는 것을 의미하는 중국과 러시아의 암호인 '패권주의'의 종식을 요구하고 있다. 그러나 모든 징후는 중국이 차세대 패권국으로 자리매김하고 있다는 것을 보여준다. 중국은 남미, 중동, 아시아의 국가들을 중국이 "새로운 세계 질서"가 될 것이라고 그들 각각에 명확히 일러준 그 세계 질서를 위해 불러 모으고 있는데, 이것은 이름을 말하지 않은 라이벌 강대국의 '총칼 외교', '신식민주의', '패권주의'를 종식시킬 '세계 질서'이다. 그 이름을 말하지 않은 강대국이란 미국이다.

밑줄 친 'this evaluation'이 가리키는 것은?
① 중국의 미래는 밝지 않다.
② 중국은 기술적 도전에 직면할 것이다.
③ 중국은 차세대 초강대국이 될 것이다.
④ 중국은 한 자녀 정책을 포기할 것이다.
⑤ 중국은 결코 미국과 동등하게 되지 못할 것이다.

26 글의 제목   ①

AI는 맞춤형 메시지를 자동으로 구성하여 해커가 몸소 해야 하는 수고를 덜어줄 수 있으므로 해커의 전술을 향상시켜주는 셈이다.

arsenal n. 무기고　tailored a. 맞춤형의　suspicion n. 의심　labor intensive 노동 집약적인　would-be a. ~이 되고자 하는　manually ad. 수동으로, 몸소　detailed research 상세한 연구　automatically ad. 자동적으로　construct v. 구축하다　personalized a. 개인 맞춤형의　obtain v. 획득하다　browsing history 검색 기록

해커의 무기고에서 가장 효과적인 무기는 아마도 '스피어 피싱'일 것이다. 스피어 피싱이란 의도된 공격대상에 대해 수집한 개인 정보를 사용하여 개별적으로 맞춤화된 메시지를 보내는 것이다. 친구가 작성한 것처럼 보이는 이메일이나 공격대상의 취미와 관련된 링크는 의심을 피할 가능성이 크다. 이 방법은 현재 상당히 노동 집약적이다. 해커 지망자가 의도한 각각의 공격대상에 대한 상세한 조사를 몸소 행해야 하기 때문이다. 하지만 검색 기록, 이메일, 트윗에서 얻은 데이터를 사용하여 많은 사람을 위한 맞춤형 메시지를 자동으로 구성하는 데 챗봇과 유사한 인공지능이 사용될 수 있다.

글의 제목으로 가장 적절한 것은?
① AI로 해커 전술 강화하기
② 스팸 메일 식별 방법
③ 해커의 공격대상이 되길 피하기
④ 이메일은 위험할 수 있다
⑤ AI가 생성하는 개인 맞춤형 메시지

---

27 내용일치 ⑤

토끼가 갑자기 죽는 것처럼 보여도 사실은 오랫동안 아파 왔다는 내용이다. 그러므로 토끼가 갑자기 죽는다 해도 사실은 아파 왔다는 것을 아니까 놀라운 일이 아닌 게 된다. ③ 포식자 앞에서 죽은 척하는 것은 주머니쥐(possum)이다. 토끼는 건강한 척한다.

pretend v. ~인 척하다, 가장하다 inverse a. 반대의, 역(逆)의 possum n. 주머니쥐 playing possum 죽은 체하기 namely ad. 즉, 다시 말하자면 deflect v. 방향을 바꾸다[바꾸게 하다]; (관심·비판 등을) 피하다[모면하다] attention n. 주의 predator n. 포식자 pickings n. 먹잇감 playacting n. 연기

대부분의 토끼는 상당히 아픈데도 건강한 척할 수 있는 능력을 하나의 (생존)기술로 갖고 있다. 이는 죽은 체하기의 반대 개념이지만, 같은 목적을 위해, 즉 아픈 토끼를 쉬운 먹잇감으로 생각하는 포식자의 관심을 다른 데로 돌리기 위해 행해진다. 이러한 연기의 결과, 토끼는 실제로는 오랫동안 아파 왔는데도, 갑자기, 혹은 갑자기인 것처럼, 죽는 경우가 많다.

다음 중 사실에 부합하는 것은?
① 토끼는 아프지 않고 죽을 수도 있다.
② 토끼를 반려동물로 키우는 것은 쉽지 않다.
③ 토끼는 포식자 앞에서 죽은 척한다.
④ 사실 토끼는 주머니쥐보다 더 똑똑하다.
⑤ 토끼가 갑자기 죽는 것은 놀라운 일이 아니다.

28-30

아주 어릴 때, 미성숙한 자신을 인도하는 세상 지도는 마치 어린아이가 그린 집 그림처럼 발달되지 못했다는 것을 생각해보라. 그림 속의 집은 항상 똑바르고 중앙에 위치하며, 앞면만 표현되고, 항상 한 개의 문과 두 개의 창, 사각형의 외벽과 삼각형의 지붕, 그리고 굴뚝과 연기가 그려져 있다. 이것은 집에 대한 매우 저해상도의 표현이다. 이는 그림이라기보다는 상형문자에 가깝다. 그것은 일반적으로 "house"나 "home"이라는 단어들처럼 집이나 어쩌면 가정의 개념을 표현하는 것이다. 하지만 거의 언제나 그것으로 충분하다. 그림을 그린 아이는 그것이 집이라는 것을 알고, 그림을 보는 다른 아이들과 어른들도 그것이 집이라는 것을 안다. 그것은 충분히 좋은 지도이다. 하지만 너무도 자주 끔찍한 일들이 집 안에서 일어난다.

이러한 일들은 표현하기가 쉽지 않다. 몇 개의 사각형, 삼각형, 약간의 꽃, 그리고 자비로운 태양만 가지고는 그러한 집을 특징짓는 공포를 충분히 표현할 수 없다. 아마 집 안에서 일어나는 일은 이해할 수 없을지도 모른다. 그러나 끔찍한 것이 어떻게 견딜 수 없고 이해할 수 없는 것일 수 있는가? 트라우마(정신적 충격)는 어떻게 이해 없이 존재할 수조차 있는가? 이것들은 큰 미스터리이다. 하지만 모든 것이 같은 수준의 개념으로 경험되지는 않는다. 모순처럼 들리는 말이지만, 우리는 모두 미지의 것에 겁에 질린 적이 있다. 그러나 몸은 마음이 이해하지 못하는 것을 알고 있다. 그리고 몸은 기억한다. 그리고 몸은 이해가 이루어지도록 요구한다. 그리고 그 요구는 결코 피할 수 없다.

immature a. 성숙하지 않은, 치기 어린 correspondingly ad. 따라서 underdeveloped a. 발달하지 못한 straight a. 똑바른 resolution n. 해상도 representation n. 재현, 표현 hieroglyph n. 상형문자 generically ad. 일반적으로 adequate a. 적당한, 충분한 appalling a. 끔찍한 smattering n. 조금 benevolent a. 자애로운 orb n. 구체 inadequate a. 불충분한 tolerability n. 견딜 수 있는 정도 trauma n. 트라우마, 정신적 외상(外傷) comprehension n. 이해 petrify v. 망연자실하게 하다 contradiction n. 모순 grasp v. 이해하다, 파악하다 biased a. 편향적인 impartial a. 공정한

---

28 부분이해 ③

'more ~ than' 구문으로 그림보다는 상형문자에 가깝다는 말인데, 상형문자는 house나 home 같은 단어들처럼 집이나 가정 같은 사물의 개념을 표현하는 것이다. 따라서 ③이 정답이다.

밑줄 친 Ⓐ"It is more hieroglyph than drawing"은 무슨 의미인가?
① 확증적이라기보다 모순적이다
② 공정하다기보다 편향적이다
③ 사실적이라기보다 관념적이다
④ 평화롭다기보다 끔찍하다
⑤ 일시적이라기보다 확립된 것이다

---

29 부분이해 ②

아이들의 그림은 그것으로 충분하다는 말이다. 다음에는 그림을 그린 아이는 그것이 집이라는 것을 알고, 그림을 보는 다른 아이들과 어른들도 그것이 집이라는 것을 안다는 내용이 펼쳐진다. 따라서 그 그림은 그 그림이 가진 목적을 성취하고 있다고 보아야 한다.

밑줄 친 Ⓑ"It is a good-enough map"은 아이들의 그림에 대해 무엇을 시사하고 있는가?
① 정확한 장소의 위치를 가리킨다
② 그것의 목적을 달성한다
③ 끔찍한 순간을 특징짓는다
④ 그림보다 더 생생하다
⑤ 실제로 매우 창의적이지만 논란의 여지가 있다

---

30 내용파악 ③

집안에서 일어나는 끔찍한 일은 아마도 이해할 수 없을지도 모른다고

한 다음, 그러나 끔찍한 것이 어떻게 이해할 수 없는 것일 수 있는가? 트라우마는 어떻게 이해 없이 존재할 수조차 있는가?라고 의문을 던지는데, 이것은 과거 기억 속의 끔찍한 일에 대한 이해가 먼저 있어야 그 끔찍한 일이 가져다준 공포와 트라우마를 경험할 수 있는 것이 아닌가 하는 저자의 생각을 보여주는 것이다. 따라서 ③이 정답이다.

위 글에 의하면, 저자는 옛 기억에 대한 이해는 어떤 의미에서 '_____'이라고 생각한다.
① 현실에 대한 과장된 표현
② 변함없는 사실
③ 경험 그 자체를 위한 전제 조건
④ 현실의 모순
⑤ 자비로운 태양

31-33

디우프(Diouf) 씨는 운이 좋은 사람 중 하나였다. 그는 카나리아 제도에 살아서 도착했다. 하지만 그 모든 경험은 끔찍했다고 그는 말했다. 그는 투옥되었고 그리고 나서는 세네갈로 추방되었다. 귀국 후 그는 다른 두 명의 송환자와 함께 세네갈 젊은이들이 세네갈에 남도록 설득하는 비영리 단체인 젊은 송환자 협회(AJRAP)를 설립했다. 노력하는 중에 디우프 씨는 유명 인사들의 도움을 구했다. 예를 들어, 세네갈 대통령 마키 살(Macky Sall)에게도 편지를 썼지만 답장을 받지는 못했다. 심지어 그는 유럽연합 당국과 이야기를 나누기 위해 브뤼셀로 가려고까지 했지만, 비자를 거부당했다. 그래도 그는 꺾이지 않았다. 젊은 송환자 협회는 자금이 생기면 제빵, 가금류 사육, 전기, 경영 등 직업 훈련을 조직하여, 작은 배를 타고 세네갈을 떠나는 것에 대한 대안을 제시한다. 또한 디우프 씨는 유럽에 성공적으로 건너간 사람들에 의해 종종 그려진 유럽에 대한 지나친 장밋빛 그림을 바로잡으려고 현지 학교에서 젊은이들에게 연설한다. 하지만 그는 자신의 한계를 고통스럽게 인식하고 있다. "유럽연합이 세네갈에 일자리 창출을 위해 자금을 지원했다는 것은 알고 있습니다."라고 그는 조용히 체념한 듯한 목소리로 말했다. "하지만 우리는 이 돈을 전혀 보지 못했습니다." 대서양을 건너려는 사람들의 수는 2006~2007년에 정점을 찍은 후 몇 년 동안 감소했다. 그러나 최근에는 특히 일자리를 찾기 위해 애쓰는 젊은이들과 어획량 감소로 어려움을 겪는 어부들 사이에서 이 항로의 인기가 다시 살아나고 있다.

make it to ~에 도달하는 데 성공하다　dreadful a. 끔찍한　imprisoned a. 투옥된　deported a. 강제 퇴거된　repatriate n. 본국으로 송환된 사람　quest n. 추구　high-profile a. 유명한　ally n. 동맹　authority n. 당국, 관헌　vocational training 직업 훈련　poultry n. 가금류　entrepreneurship n. 경영　alternative n. 대안　embark on 착수하다　pirogue n. 피로그, 통나무배　rectify v. 정정하다　overly ad. 과도하게　rosy a. 장밋빛의, 낙관적인　resignation n. 포기　resurgence n. 부활　struggling a. 어려움을 겪고 있는　shrinking a. 수축하는　uphill a. 힘겨운　accomplice n. 공범

31 부분이해　①

디우프는 세네갈을 좋은 나라로 만들어 사람들이 유럽으로 불법 이주하지 않아도 되는 나라로 만들고 싶었다. 하지만 그의 노력에도 불구하고, 최근 대서양을 건너 유럽으로 가는 항로가 다시 인기를 얻고 있다고 했으므로, 그가 한계를 인식하고 있다는 것은 ①을 암시한다고 보아야 한다.

밑줄 친 부분 "he is painfully aware of his limitations"가 암시하고 있는 것은?
① 세네갈 사람 대부분은 어쨌든 이주를 선택한다.
② 세네갈은 아프리카에서 가장 안전한 국가이다.
③ 유럽은 살기에 너무 위험하다.
④ 젊은 당국자만이 위험을 인식하고 있다.
⑤ 저소득층이 부유층보다 더 높은 세금을 낼 수도 있다.

32 내용파악　③

디우프 씨가 세네갈을 유럽으로의 불법 이민을 감행하지 않아도 되는 나라로 만들려고 노력하지만, 한계를 절감하고 있다는 것은 그가 ③의 '어려운 싸움을 벌이고 있다'는 의미이다.

위 글에 따르면, 디우프 씨는 _____.
① 바다에서 비참한 항해를 경험하지 않았다
② 자신의 주장을 펼치는 것이 점점 더 쉬워지고 있음을 인정한다
③ 이민에 맞서 힘겨운 싸움을 벌이고 있다
④ 동료의 죽음에 공범이 되었다
⑤ 세네갈에는 유럽에 부족한 다양한 종류의 직업이 있다고 생각한다

33 태도　④

디우프 씨는 자신의 한계를 절감하고 체념 섞인 말도 하지만, 여러 가지 난관에 꺾이지 않고 세네갈을 젊은이들에게 좋은 나라로 만들기 위해 여전히 최선을 다하고 있다. 따라서 그의 태도는 '단호하다'라고 보아야 한다.

디우프 씨는 어떤 태도를 가지고 있는가?
① 낙관적인
② 자신에 찬
③ 무관심한
④ 단호한
⑤ 유연한

34-35

우리보다 앞서 살았던 많은 호미닌 종(種)들은 모두 눈썹 뼈가 도드라져 있었지만, 우리 호모 사피엔스는 작고 활동적인 눈썹을 위해 이 융기된 눈썹 뼈를 포기했다. 그 이유를 말하기는 쉽지 않다. 눈썹은 눈에 땀이 들어가지 못하게 하기 위해 거기 있다는 설(說)도 있지만, 눈썹이 정말 잘하는 일은 감정 전달이다. "믿기 어렵네요."에서 "발밑을 조심하세요."에 이르기까지 얼마나 많은 메시지를 아치형으로 구부린 눈썹 하나로 전달할 수 있는지 생각해보라. 모나리자가 신비롭게 보이는 이유 중 하나는 눈썹이 없기 때문이다. 한 흥미로운 실험에서 피실험자들에게 디지털로 조작된 유명인의 사진 두 세트(눈썹을 제거한 사진, 눈 자체를 제거한 사진)를 보여주었다. 놀랍지만 압도적으로 많은 지원자가 눈썹이 없는 유명인을 눈이 없는 유명인보다 식별하기를 더 어려워했다.

hominid n. 호미닌　precede v. 선행하다　browridge n. 눈썹 뼈　enigmatic a. 수수께끼 같은　subject n. 피실험자, 실험 대상　digitally doctored photograph 디지털 조작 사진　overwhelmingly ad. 압도적으로　celebrity n. 유명 인사　volunteer n. 지원자

34 빈칸완성 ②

다음 문장을 보면 '한 가지 이론은 ~이다'라고 한 다음 but으로 이어져서 그 이론이 신빙성이 없음을 암시하므로 앞에 언급한 문제가 설명하기 어려운 문제임을 알 수 있다. 따라서 빈칸에는 ②가 적절하다.

빈칸에 들어가기에 가장 적절한 표현은?
① 그것은 이치에 맞다
② 이유를 말하기가 쉽지 않다
③ 그것은 불가능하다
④ 예외 없는 규칙은 없다
⑤ 백문이 불여일견이다

35 내용파악 ⑤

마지막 문장에서 눈썹을 없앤 유명인들을 사람들은 알아보기 더 어려워했다고 했으므로, 변장을 잘하는 방법은 눈썹을 가리는 것이다.

실험에 의하면, 변장을 가장 잘하는 방법은?
① 풀 메이크업하기
② 입을 숨기기
③ 선글라스 착용하기
④ 머리 염색하기
⑤ 눈썹을 가리기

36-38

'사생활 침해'는 이제 예측가능한 사회적 불평등의 한 차원이지만, 그 자체로 홀로 존재하는 것은 아니다. 그것은 감시 자본주의가 알고, 결정하고, 누가 결정하는지를 결정하는 사회의 '병리적인' 학습 분업화의 체계적 결과이다. 감시 자본가들로부터 사생활을 요구하거나 인터넷에서의 상업적 감시를 중단하도록 로비를 벌이는 것은 헨리 포드(Henry Ford)에게 각각의 모델 T 자동차를 손으로 만들라고 요구하는 것과 같다. 문제의 관건은 이렇다. 감시 자본주의는 대단히 반민주적이지만, 그 놀라운 힘은 역사적으로 그래온 것처럼 국가에서 비롯되지는 않는다. 그 효과는 기술이나 나쁜 사람들의 나쁜 의도로 환원되거나 설명될 수 없으며, 그 효과는 내부적으로 일관되고 성공적인 축적 논리의 일관되고 예측가능한 결과이다. 감시 자본주의는 상대적 무법 상태였던 미국에서 등장하여 지배적인 지위를 획득했다. 이후 유럽으로 퍼져나가고 전 세계 모든 지역으로 계속해서 침투하고 있다.

구글을 시작으로 감시 자본주의 기업들은 정보의 축적과 처리를 지배하고 있다. 그들은 우리에 대해 많은 것을 알고 있지만, 그들의 지식에 우리가 접근하는 일은 극히 드물다. 사용자가 볼 수 없는 텍스트에 숨겨져 있고 새로운 사제(성역의 관리자)인, 기업의 사장과 기계만이 읽을 수 있다. 전례 없는 지식의 집중은 마찬가지로 전례 없는 권력의 집중을 낳는다. 이 비대칭성은 사회에서 학습 분업의 무단 사유화로 이해해야 한다. 이는 한 세기 전에 산업 자본의 강력한 힘에 의해 노동 분업이 전복될 것을 뒤르켐(Durkheim)이 경고했던 것처럼, 강력한 사적 세력이 우리 시대 사회 질서의 결정적인 원칙을 지배하고 있다는 것을 의미한다.

invasion of privacy 개인정보[사생활] 침해 dimension n. 차원 social inequality 사회적 불평등 pathological a. 병리학의, 병리상의; 병적인 surveillance capitalism 감시 자본주의(기업들이 개인 정보를 수집하고 분석하여 이를 이용하여 이윤을 창출하는 경제 시스템) what is at stake

관건 profoundly ad. 깊이; 엄청나게 antidemocratic a. 비민주적인 reduce v. 환원하다 consistent a. 일관성 있는 accumulation n. 축적 lawlessness n. 불법 inroad n. 침투 sparse a. 드문 shadow text 사용자가 볼 수 없는 텍스트 concentration of power 권력 집중 asymmetry n. 비대칭 privatization n. 사유화(공공 부문이나 공공 자산이 개인이나 민간 기업에 의해 소유되고 운영되는 것) private interest 사적 이해 subversion n. 파괴 division of labor 노동 분업 hijack v. 강탈하다, 납치하다 detrimental a. 해로운

36 내용파악 ②

두 번째 단락의 빈칸이 있는 문장에서 '사회에서 학습 분업의 무단 사유화로 이해해야 한다'고 했는데, 이것은 감시 자본주의가 학습의 분업을 무단으로 강탈하여 사유화하고 있음을 의미한다.

저자는 어떻게 믿고 있는가?
① 감시 자본주의는 우리의 지식 자체로는 설명할 수 없다.
② 사회에서의 학습 분업이 감시 자본주의에 의해 강탈당했다.
③ 정보 처리가 감시 자본주의 기업에 해롭다.
④ 회사의 상사가 정보 축적을 인식하지 못한다.
⑤ 산업 자본의 강력한 세력에 속하는 사람들은 감시 자본주의의 영향을 덜 받는다.

37 내용파악 ①

인터넷에서 상업적 감시를 종식시키기 위한 로비 활동은 자동 대량생산으로 유명한 포드에게 자동차를 모두 손으로 만들라는 말과 같다고 하였다. 이것은 상상할 수 없는 일이다.

저자에 따르면, 인터넷에서 상업적 감시를 종식시키기 위한 로비 활동은?
① 상상할 수 없는
② 기밀의
③ 순차적인
④ 설득력 있는
⑤ 달성할 수 있는

38 빈칸완성 ①

앞에서 모든 정보와 권력이 감시 자본주의 기업에 의해 독점되고 있다고 했으므로, 소수만 권력과 정보를 가지고 다수인 소비자들은 소외된다. 이를 비대칭성이라고 한다.

빈칸에 들어가기에 가장 적절한 표현은?
① 비대칭성
② 평등권
③ 법률
④ 필요조건
⑤ 환각

39-40

자본과 정치의 강한 결합은 신용 시장에 광범위한 영향을 미쳤다. 한 경제 국가에서의 신용의 정도는 새로운 유전의 발견이나 새로운 기계의 발명과 같은 순수한 경제적 요인뿐만 아니라 정권 교체나 야심에 찬 외교 정책과 같은 정치적 사건에 의해서도 결정된다. 나바리노(Navarino) 전투 이후 영국 자본가들은 위험한 해외 거래에 더욱 기꺼이 돈을 투자했다. 그들은 외국 채무자가 대출금 상환을 거부하면 영국군이 그들의 돈을 돌려받아줄 것이라고 알고 있었던 것이었다. 이것이 오늘날 한 나라의 경제적 안녕에 신용등급이 천연자원보다 훨씬 더 중요한 이유이다. 신용등급은 한 국가가 빚을 갚을 확률을 가리킨다. 신용등급은 순전히 경제적인 데이터 외에도 정치적, 사회적, 심지어 문화적 요인까지 고려한다. 독재 정부, 빈번한 지역 내 전쟁, 부패한 사법 시스템으로 저주받은 석유 부국은 대개 낮은 신용등급을 받을 것이다. 그 결과 그 나라는 석유의 풍요로움을 최대한 활용하는 데 필요한 자본을 조달할 수 없기에 상대적으로 빈곤한 상태를 유지할 가능성이 크다. 천연자원은 없지만, 평화, 공정한 사법 시스템, 자유로운 정부를 누리는 국가는 높은 신용등급을 받을 가능성이 크다. 그러한 국가로서, 그 국가는 훌륭한 교육 시스템을 지원하고, 번창하는 첨단 기술 산업을 육성하기에 충분한 저렴한 자본을 조달할 수 있을 것이다.

bear hug 힘찬 포옹 capital n. 자본 far-reaching a. 광범위한 implication n. 영향 credit market 신용 시장 oil field 유전 regime change 정권 교체 foreign policy 외교 정책 be willing to 기꺼이 ~하다 loan n. 대출 credit rating 신용등급 natural resources 천연자원 probability n. 개연성 take ~ into account ~을 고려하다 cursed a. 저주받은 despotic a. 독재적인 endemic a. 풍토병의 corruption n. 부패 judicial system 사법제도 high-tech industry 첨단 산업 raise capital 자금을 조성하다 bounty n. 풍부함 devoid of ~이 결여된 flourishing a. 번창하는 indigenous a. 토착의 dictatorial a. 독재의

② 자유로운 정부 시스템 — 반대로
③ 사법 시스템 — 결국
④ 해외 거래 — 결론적으로
⑤ 교육 시스템 — 그러나

41-42

화실과 화랑으로서의 동굴의 매력은 동굴이 화가들에게 편리했다는 사실에서 비롯되지 않는다. 사실, 벽화가 그려진 동굴에는 사람이 지속적으로 거주했다는 증거가 없으며, 가장 멋진 동물 그림만을 위한 가장 깊고 접근하기 어려운 틈새 동굴에도 그런 증거는 없다. 동굴 화가를 '동굴 주거인'과 혼동해서는 안 된다.
동굴에 특별한 애착을 가질 필요도 없다. 동굴에 담긴 예술은 단순한 자연선택 과정을 통해 우리에게 전해졌기 때문이다. 조각상이나 그림이 그려진 바위 같은 야외 예술은 비바람에 노출되어 수만 년 동안 지속될 가능성이 적다. 구석기시대의 사람들은 동굴 벽에 사용했던 것과 같은 종류의 황토로 자기 몸과 얼굴뿐만 아니라 동물 가죽을 비롯한 온갖 종류의 표면에 그림을 그렸던 것으로 보인다. 다른 점이 있다면 동굴 벽화 그림이 비바람의 기후 변화로부터 충분히 잘 보호되어 수만 년 동안 살아남을 수 있었다는 점이다. 동굴에 특별한 점이 있다면 동굴이 이상적인 보관함이라는 점이다.

stem from 비롯되다 cranny n. 구멍, 틈 spectacular a. 장관을 이루는 caveman n. 원시인 posit v. 가정하다 affinity n. 친근감 natural selection 자연선택 figurine n. 작은 입상(立像), 피규어 exposed a. 노출된 the elements 자연력; 비바람 paleolithic a. 구석기시대의 ochre n. 황토 climate change 기후 변화 accident fallacy 우연의 오류(fallacy of accident, 일반적인 원리나 규칙을 그것이 적용되지 않는 특수한 경우에 잘못 적용하여 저지르는 오류)

---

39 내용파악 ⑤

나머지는 모두 신용등급에 부정적인 영향을 미치는 요소이고, ⑤만 긍정적인 영향을 미치는 요소이다.

위 글에 의하면, 다음 중 다른 것들과 관련이 없는 것은?
① 정치적 불안정성
② 토착적인 지역 내 전쟁
③ 독재 정부
④ 부정직한 사법 시스템
⑤ 조화로운 사회

---

40 빈칸완성 ①

빈칸 Ⓐ 이하에서 '천연자원은 풍부한데, 정치, 사회, 문화적 측면에서 부정적인 요소를 갖고 있는 나라와 그 반대의 나라'를 비교하고 있으므로, 빈칸에는 natural resources가 적절하다. Ⓑ의 경우, 앞 문장에서 '높은 신용등급을 받을 가능성이 크다'고 했고 이하에서는 신용등급이 높은 국가로 할 수 있는 일을 설명하므로 '그러한 국가로서'라는 의미가 되게 As such가 적절하다.

빈칸 Ⓐ와 Ⓑ에 들어가기에 가장 적절한 단어는?
① 천연자원 — 그러한 것(사람)으로서

---

41 빈칸완성 ⑤

빈칸 이하에서 '야외 예술은 비바람에 노출되어 오래 지속되지 못한 반면, 동굴 예술은 비바람으로부터 보호되어 오래 살아남을 수 있었다'고 했으므로 빈칸에는 '자연선택'이 적절하다.

빈칸에 들어가기에 가장 적절한 표현은?
① 보이지 않는 손
② 황금 비율
③ 우연의 오류
④ 악순환
⑤ 자연선택

---

42 내용일치 ④

두 번째 문장에서 사람들이 거주한 증거가 없는 틈새 동굴에서 가장 멋진 동물 그림이 발견된다고 하였다. ① 동굴 화가들과 동굴 주거인들을 혼동해서는 안 된다. 위대한 예술성을 보여준 것은 동굴 화가들이었다. ② 동굴 주거인들은 그림과 관계없고 그림을 전시 목적으로 그렸다는 말도 찾아볼 수 없다. ③ 구석기시대 사람들은 동물 가죽에 그림을 그렸다고 했지, 사냥한 동물 그림을 그렸다는 말은 없다. ⑤ 다양한 색을 사용했다는 말도 없다. 오로지 황토만 나와 있다.

다음 중 위 글에 부합하는 것은?
① 동굴 주거인들은 위대한 예술성을 보여주었다.
② 동굴 주거인들은 예술 전시를 위해 동굴을 이용했다.
③ 구석기시대 사람들은 사냥한 동물 그림을 그렸다.
④ 사람이 살 수 없는 동굴에서도 동물 벽화가 발견된다.
⑤ 구석기시대 화가들은 인체에 다양한 색을 사용했다.

43-45

가벼운 발걸음의 암사슴 한 마리가 숲 가장자리 밖으로 불쑥 고개를 내밀고 멈추어 나를 바라보았다. 암사슴은 약 15피트 정도 떨어져 있었다. 나는 얼어붙었다. 죽이기를 의식적으로 반대해서는 아니었다. 우리 둘 모두 어떻게 대응해야 할지 알아내려 애쓰며 그곳에 서 있던 그 묘한 상호성의 한순간에도 죽이기를 반대할 생각은 들지 않았다. 그저 어떻게 해야 할지 몰랐을 뿐이었다. 그런 다음 암사슴은 가버렸다. 아버지께 어떻게 설명했는지 기억이 나지 않는다. 차를 몰고 집으로 돌아오는 길의 침묵만 기억난다.

A 나는 형편없는 사슴 사냥꾼인데다가 위험하기까지 했다. 지루하고 추울 때 내가 총을 만지작거리다가 실수로 총을 쏜 적이 여러 해에 있었다. 나중에 부모님의 지하실에서 장전된 권총을 가지고 놀다가, 똑같은 일을 저지르지 않았더라면, 숲에서 예상치 못한 고성능의 라이플총이 내던 소리가 내가 들어 본 소리 중에 가장 큰 소리일 것이다.

C 나는 항상 그 이유에 대해 거짓말을 했다. "총이 우연히 발사되었다."라는 말은 사냥 이야기로는 그럴듯하지 않았다. "큰 수사슴을 보고 조준했지만 빗나갔다."라는 말도 마찬가지였다. 그래서 나는 들개로 결정했다. 숲에서 돌아와 개를 쐈다고 이야기한 일이 세 해에 있었다. 어느 해에는 다람쥐 털인 것 같은 털 뭉치를 발견했는데, 그것을 나는 내가 다람쥐에게 풀을 뜯어 먹게 했다는 증거로 사람들에게 돌렸다. 또 다른 해에는 다른 그룹이 숲을 관통해 우리 쪽으로 사슴을 몰아온 동안, 나는 들판 가장자리에 길게 늘어선 사냥꾼 대열에 서서 입에 떨어지는 눈송이를 잡으려다가 총이 발사되었다.

light-footed a. 가볍게 발을 내딛는 doe n. 암사슴 peak v. 우뚝 솟다 edge n. 가장자리 mutuality n. 상호성 beat n. (심장) 박동, 박자, 한 번 흔들기 single beat 한 순간 figure out 이해하다 fiddle v. 만지작거리다 accidentally ad. 우연히 buck n. 수사슴 squeeze off a shot 총을 쏘다 basement n. 지하실 unanticipated a. 예상치 못한 take aim 겨냥하다 graze v. 방목하다, 풀을 뜯어 먹게 하다 tuft n. 솜털 snowflake n. 눈송이

---

43 빈칸완성 ②

빈칸 이하에서 '총을 만지작거리다가 실수로 총을 쏘았다', '장전된 권총을 가지고 놀다가, 똑같은 일을 저질렀다', '총이 우연히 발사되었다', '입에 떨어지는 눈송이를 잡으려다가 총이 발사되었다' 등의 언급을 보면 저자가 부주의로 총을 발사하는 위험한 인물임을 알 수 있다.

빈칸에 들어가기에 가장 적절한 표현은?
① 전염성의
② 위험한
③ 미성숙한
④ 용감한
⑤ 호기심 많은

---

44 단락 나누기 ①

A 앞의 이야기는 사슴을 놓친 에피소드이고, A에서 C까지의 이야기는 자기가 총을 잘 못 다루는 사람, 따라서 위험한 사람이었다는 설명이다. C 다음은 사고를 내고 저자가 늘어놓은 변명의 리스트이다. 개와 다람쥐 모두가 변명거리였다.

---

45 내용파악 ④

저자는 이 글에서만 벌써 세 번의 총기사고를 언급하고 있다. 따라서 총기 사용에 서툴렀다고 할 수 있다. ① 동물 살해를 의식적으로 반대하지는 않는다고 했다. ② 고의로가 아니라 어쩔 줄 모르다가 목표물을 놓쳤다. ③ 변명으로 거짓말을 계속하고 있다. ⑤ '부모님의 지하실에서 장전된 권총을 가지고 놀다가, 똑같은 일을 저지르지 않았더라면'이라고 가정법 과거완료로 말한 것은 사실은 같은 실수를 반복했다는 말이다.

저자는 어떤 사람이었던 것 같은가?
① 동물을 죽이기를 원하지 않았다.
② 고의로 표적을 놓쳤다.
③ 거짓말을 하는 방법을 몰랐다.
④ 총기 사용에 서툴렀다.
⑤ 다시는 같은 실수를 반복하지 않았다.

46-48

1929년 천문학자 에드윈 허블(Edwin Hubble)은 은하의 빛 스펙트럼을 연구하던 중 관측 결과 많은 은하가 적색편이를 보여주고 있다고 발표했다. 은하들은 실제로 우리에게서 멀어지고 있었다. 그러나 그가 실제로 발견한 것은 우주의 팽창이었다. 은하들이 혼자서 멀어지기보다는 시공간의 구조 자체가 바깥쪽으로 팽창하고 있었던 것이다. 그는 이를 팽창의 증거라고 믿지 않았다. 과학자들이 우주가 팽창하고 있을 뿐만 아니라 그 팽창 속도가 빨라지고 있다는 사실을 깨닫기까지는 70년이 더 걸렸다. 허블이 망원경을 사용하기 거의 10년 전에 알베르트 아인슈타인(Albert Einstein)은 일반 상대성 이론과 함께 우주 상수라는 이론을 제안했다. 우주는 정적인 공간이며 밀도는 일정하게 유지된다는 것이었다. 아인슈타인은 허블의 은하 적색편이 뉴스를 보고 자신의 이론을 버렸으나, 다만 이해하기 힘들지만 아인슈타인도 다소 옳은 면이 있었다. 우주는 정적인 공간이 아니다. 우주는 빠르게 팽창하고 있지만 우주의 밀도는 여전히 일정하게 유지되고 있다는 것을 우리는 알고 있다. 이렇게 생각해 보라. 거실에 테이블과 TV, 책 몇 권과 커피 한 잔이 놓여 있다고 상상해 보라. 이제 그 방이 풍선처럼 팽창하기 시작하여 점점 더 커진다고 상상해 보라. 거실에 있는 물건들의 밀도는 높아지지 않는다. 그대로 있을 것이다. 우리 우주도 마찬가지이다. 팽창해도 밀도는 똑같이 유지된다. 따라서 여러분의 커피 한 잔이 우주 상수이다.

astronomer n. 천문학자 light spectra 빛 스펙트럼 galaxy n. 은하 redshifting n. 적색편이(천체가 우리와 멀어지면서 빛이 빨갛게 편이되는 현상) expansion n. 확장 on one's own 혼자서 speed up 가속하다 cosmological constant 우주상수(아인슈타인이 제안한 우주의 정적인 상태와 밀도가 일정하게 유지되는 이론적 개념) in tandem with ~와 나란히 general relativity 일반 상대성 이론 static a. 정적인 density n. 밀도 go figure 이해가 안 된다 balloon v. (풍선처럼) 부풀다

46 내용파악 　　　　　　　③

허블은 처음에는 적색편이를 우주 팽창의 증거라고 깨닫지 못했다고 했다. ④ 아인슈타인이 허블보다 앞선 세대이다. 허블이 아인슈타인에게 영감을 주었다는 말은 없다. ⑤ 일반 상대성 이론이 아니라 우주가 팽창하지 않는 정적인 공간이라는 이론을 포기하게 했다.

에드윈 허블은 _____.
① 우주가 팽창하고 있다고 생각했다
② 알베르트 아인슈타인의 이론을 입증하고 싶었다
③ 자신의 발견이 우주의 팽창을 보여준다는 것을 깨닫지 못했다
④ 아인슈타인에게 영감을 줘서 우주 상수 이론에 대해 생각하게 된 계기가 되었다
⑤ 아인슈타인이 일반 상대성 이론을 포기하게 만든 무언가를 발견했다

47 부분이해 　　　　　　　②

sort of는 '다소, 조금은' 정도의 의미이다. 우주가 팽창하지 않는 정적인 공간이라는 생각은 틀렸지만, 밀도와 우주 상수가 일정하게 유지된다는 생각은 옳았다. 우주가 팽창하는데도 그 안의 물체의 밀도가 변함이 없다는 것은 이해하기 힘들다고 했다.

밑줄 친 "Einstein was sort of right"가 의미하는 것은?
① 아인슈타인도 틀릴 수 있다.
② 아인슈타인의 생각은 부분적으로 옳았다.
③ 아인슈타인의 이론은 너무 모호하다.
④ 아인슈타인은 마침내 모든 것을 증명할 수 있다는 것을 알았다.
⑤ 아인슈타인은 자신이 틀렸다는 것을 인정한 것이 현명했다.

48 내용파악 　　　　　　　④

우주를 거실에 비유하고, 거실이 팽창한다고 하였다. 나머지는 모두 거실 안의 물건들이다.

위 글에서 우주는 _____에 비유되고 있다.
① TV 세트
② 일부 책
③ 테이블
④ 거실
⑤ 커피 한 잔

49-50

분석가들은 커피 전문점이 베이징과 상하이를 넘어 젊은 직장인들이 커피를 즐기는 수십 개의 중소 도시로 확장되면서 중국의 커피에 대한 늘어나는 갈증이 향후 원두 수요의 주요 동력이 될 것으로 예상한다. 중국의 커피 수요 증가는 중국에 막대한 투자를 하는 스타벅스나 팀 홋튼스 같은 해외 체인점에게는 기회이지만, 이들은 또 빠르게 확장하는 현지 브랜드의 가파른 도전에 직면해 있다. 국제 커피 기구가 로이터 통신에 보낸 데이터에 따르면 중국의 커피 소비량은 지난 9월까지 1년 동안 전년 같은 기간 대비 15% 증가한 308만 봉지를 기록했다. "중국 소비자는 점점 더 서구적인 라이프스타일을 받아들이고 있으며 커피는 명백히 그런 라이프스타

일을 대표하는 음료 중 하나입니다."라고 시장 조사 회사의 전무이사는 말했다.

커피 체인점의 성장을 추적하는 회사인 알레그라 그룹(Alegra Group)에 따르면, 중국의 브랜드 커피숍 수는 지난 12개월 동안 무려 58% 성장하여 49,691개의 매장을 기록했다. 유로모니터의 음료 분석가인 매튜 배리(Matthew Barry)는 현지 체인점과 해외 체인점 간에 치열한 경쟁이 벌어지고 있다고 말했다. 각 업체는 성장하는 시장에서 최대한 많은 점유율을 차지하려고 노력하고 있다고 그는 말했다. 알레그라 그룹에 따르면, 중국의 루킨 커피는 지난 12개월 동안 5,059개의 매장을 추가했고, 또 다른 중국 체인점인 코티 커피는 같은 기간 동안 6,004개의 매장을 열었다. 배리는 "기회의 규모가 워낙 크기 때문에 (현지 및 해외 체인점) 모두 매우 공격적으로 상대방에 맞서야 할 것이며, 이로 인해 향후 몇 년 동안 매우 역동적인 시장이 될 것이라고 생각합니다."라고 말했다. 중국의 커피 소비량은 연간 2천만 봉지 이상을 소비하는 주요 소비국인 미국과 브라질에 비하면 여전히 미미한 수준이다. 하지만 이러한 수요 증가는 중국이 일본과 한국 등, 차를 좋아하는 다른 아시아 국가와 비슷한 문화적 변화를 겪고 있다는 신호이다.

thirst n. 갈증　demand n. 수요　bean n. 커피 원두　beverage n. 음료　steep a. 가파른　managing director 경영 이사　branded a. 브랜드화된　market research firm 시장 조사 기업　staggering a. 충격적인　track v. 추적하다　aggressive a. 공격적인; 적극적인　face off 대결할 준비를 하다　ensure v. 보장하다　pale v. 창백해지다

49 내용일치 　　　　　　　③

실제로는 글의 요지를 묻는 문제이다. 첫 번째 문장에서 커피에 대한 갈증이 커지며, 커피 전문점이 늘어나고 있다고 하였다. 이는 경쟁 심화를 의미한다. 따라서 ③이 본문의 내용에 부합한다.

다음 중 위 글에 부합하는 것은?
① 중국 커피숍은 결국 베이징을 넘어서는 확장이 불가능하다.
② 중국에서 커피 수요는 더 이상 증가하지 않을 것이다.
③ 커피에 대한 중국의 새로운 갈증이 치열한 카페 경쟁을 부추기고 있다.
④ 중국의 커피 소비량은 일본과 한국을 능가한다.
⑤ 커피 전문점 측면에서 현지 체인점과 해외 체인점 간의 경쟁이 없다.

50 부분이해 　　　　　　　②

face off는 '적과 대결하다'라는 의미인데 이것은 경쟁을 말한다.

밑줄 친 "facing off against the other"가 의미하는 것은?
① 역동적인 문화 변화를 만남
② 서로 경쟁함
③ 일부러 저렴한 커피를 구매함
④ 새로운 커피 체인점의 성장을 적당히 추적함
⑤ 현지 체인점보다 스타벅스와 같은 해외 체인점을 더 중시함

01 ⑤	02 ②	03 ②	04 ④	05 ②	06 ⑤	07 ①	08 ③	09 ④	10 ④
11 ③	12 ④	13 ⑤	14 ①	15 ③	16 ①	17 ⑤	18 ②	19 ⑤	20 ④
21 ②	22 ⑤	23 ③	24 ①	25 ②					

01 현재분사   ⑤

⑤는 지각동사 watch의 목적격 보어의 자리인데, appear는 자동사이므로 수동을 나타내는 과거분사로 쓸 수 없다. 그러므로 ⑤는 능동을 나타내는 원형동사나 현재분사여야 한다. ⑤를 appear나 appearing으로 고친다.

seductive a. 유혹하는 passage n. (책의) 구절; (음악의) 악절

워드프로세서의 클릭과 흐름은 유혹적일 수 있어서, 당신은 단지 키보드 위에서 손가락을 굴려 자신이 입력한 단어가 화면에 나타나는 것을 보는 즐거움을 경험하는 것만을 위해서도 불필요한 단어 몇 개나 심지어는 한 구절 전체를 추가하게 될지 모른다.

02 문의 구성   ②

②는 접속사 and 이하에 이어진 절의 정동사여야 하므로 과거시제 동사 climbed가 되어야 한다. ③과 ④는 주절에 이어지는 두 개의 분사구문이다.

patrol n. 순찰대, 정찰대 emerge v. 나오다, 나타나다, 모습을 드러내다 marine n. 해병대 slope n. 경사면, 비탈 fire support base 화력지원기지 bent a. 굽은, 구부러진, 뒤틀린 pick one's way 발 디딜 곳을 찾으며 조심스럽게 천천히 걸어가다 shatter v. 산산이 부수다, 박살내다 stump n. 그루터기 shelter n. 은신처, 피난 장소

정찰대는 철조망으로부터 모습을 드러냈고, 젊은 해병들은 피로로 인해 굽어진 몸으로 새로운 화력지원기지의 비탈길을 천천히 올라가면서, 몸을 피할 곳 없는 산산조각 난 그루터기와 죽은 나무들 주위로 길을 더듬어 나아갔다.

03 동의어   ②

windfall n. 우발적인 소득, 뜻밖의 횡재(= bonanza) loyal a. 충성스러운 loss n. 손실, 손해 shortfall n. 부족; 적자 disaster n. 재해, 재난 disadvantage n. 불리, 불이익

푸틴은 서방의 주요 기업들이 떠난 것을 러시아의 충성스러운 엘리트들과 국가 자체의 횡재로 바꾸어 놓았다.

04 동의어   ④

exchange n. 교환, 주고받기 artillery n. 포, 대포 militia n. 의용군, 민병대 ally v. 동맹[결연, 제휴]하게 하다 presage v. 전조가 되다, 예언하다(= foretell) front n. <군사> 전선(前線), 전선(戰線) explain v. 설명하다 prevent v. 막다, 방해하다 escalate v. 단계적으로 확대[증대, 강화, 상승]시키다 follow v. 따라가다; 따르다

이란과 동맹을 맺은 레바논 시아파 민병대인 헤즈볼라와 이스라엘 사이에 미사일과 포화가 오간 것은 제2의 전선이 형성될 가능성을 예고하고 있다.

05 동의어   ②

subject n. (논의 등의) 주제[대상, 화제], (다뤄지고 있는) 문제[사안] in utero 자궁 안에 있는, 아직 태어나지 않은(= unborn) significantly ad. 상당히, 현저히 active a. 활동적인; 활동 중인 refugee n. 난민

한 조사연구에 따르면, 한국전쟁(1950-1953)이라는 최악의 시기에 어머니 뱃속에 있었던 연구대상들의 노동시장 성과는 1990년에 현저히 더 낮았다.

06 논리완성   ⑤

'얇은 벽, 평평한 지붕, 비어 있는 벽 등, 밖으로 드러나는 것에 거의 꾸밈이 없다'는 것은 그 장소가 매우 수수하고 소박한 건물임을 알려주고 있다.

pavilion n. 큰 천막, 임시건물 austere a. 엄한; 꾸미지 않은, 간소한 subtle a. 미묘한 sensual a. (특히 육체적인 쾌락과 관련하여) 감각적인; 관능적인 celebration n. 축하; 의식 transient a. 일시적인; 순간적인

차를 마시는 임시건물 — 벽은 얇고, 지붕은 평평하고, 벽은 비어 있어서 외관상 거의 꾸밈이 없는 지극히 소박한 건물 — 은 음료를 준비하여 주인과 손님들이 함께 마시는 정성스런 관행을 위한 배경일 뿐이다. 미묘하고 감각적인 경험에 집중하는 것은 사물의 일시적인 아름다움과 정성스러운 몸짓을 칭찬하는 의식이다.

① 만석의 공간
② 호화로운 건물
③ 가장 인상적인 건물
④ 예쁘고 호화로운 아파트
⑤ 지극히 소박한 건물

07 논리완성 ①

백인이 대다수였던 카운티가 다양성을 갖게 된 것은 흑인들이 대규모로 그곳에 들어왔기 때문일 것이다.

anecdote n. 일화 diverse a. 다양한, 가지각색의 ceiling n. 천장; 상한선, 한계 property tax 소득세 binding a. 속박하는, 구속력 있는 constraint n. 강제, 압박; 억제 revenue n. 소득, 수입; 재원 financing n. 자금 조달 influx n. 유입(流入); (사람·사물의) 도래(到來), 쇄도 induction n. 끌어들임, 유도, 도입 emigration n. (타국으로의) 이주, 이민 protest n. 항의, 항변 prosperity n. 번영, 성공

여기 한 편의 일화가 있다. 프린스 조지(PG) 카운티는 워싱턴 DC 옆 메릴랜드 주에 위치한 카운티로, 백인이 대다수를 차지하고 있었다. 흑인 중산층이 대거 유입되면서 그 카운티가 훨씬 다양성을 갖게 된 후에 (백인들이 여전히 다수를 차지하고 있었지만), PG 유권자들은 1978년에 TRIM이라 불리는 법을 통과시켰다. TRIM은 재산세율에 법적 상한선을 두는데, 이는 학교에 자금을 조달하는 주요 재원에 대해 구속력 있는 제약을 가하는 것이다.

08 논리완성 ③

가상 회의는 실제로 직접 대면해서 하는 것이 아니므로, 눈맞춤과 제스처와 같은 신호들은 굳이 신경 쓰지 않아도 되는 것이 되어 사라지게 될 것이다.

diversity n. 다양성 post-pandemic a. 팬데믹 이후의 coordination n. 조정, 일치 virtually ad. 사실상, 실질적으로 impose v. 부과하다; 강제하다 management overhead 간접비 관리 patchy a. 누덕누덕 기운; 뒤죽박죽인 unmute v. 소리를 (껐다가) 켜다 virtual a. 가상의 allow v. 허락하다 let out (울음소리·신음소리 등을) 내다 strip out 완전히 제거하다 promote v. 홍보하다

다양성과 마찬가지로, 팬데믹 이후 원격 근무의 확산은 업무조정 비용을 높이는 한편 여러 가지 이점을 가져다준다. 가상(假想)의 방식으로 인력을 운영하는 것은 관리구조 학자들이 말하는 "간접비 관리"를 강제한다. 네트워크 연결이 부실하지 않고 사람들이 스스로 소리 내는 것을 잊지 않을 때에도, 가상 회의는 눈맞춤과 제스처와 같은 많은 신호들을 완전히 제거한다.

09 논리완성 ④

뒤에 나오는 동사 grab과 반대되는 의미를 가진 표현이 들어가야 하겠는데, grab(움켜잡다)이 재난으로 물자가 부족한 상황에서 자기만을 위하는 이기적인 태도를 나타내므로, (재난 극복에) '협력하다, 동참하다'라는 의미의 ④가 빈칸에 들어가기에 적절하다.

disaster n. 재해, 재난 policymaker n. 정책입안자 object to ~에 반대하다 hike n. (임금·가격) 인상 argue v. 주장하다 crisis n. 위기 grab v. 움켜잡다 throw in 던져 넣다, 덤으로 주다 take out 꺼내다; 데리고[가지고] 나가다; 취득하다 pull over (정차하거나 다른 차가 지나가도록) 길 한쪽으로 빠지다[차를 대다] pitch in 기여하다, 협력하다, 동참하다 persevere v. 참다, 견디다

허리케인과 같은 재난이 한 지역을 강타할 때, 많은 상품들은 수요의 증가 또는 공급의 감소를 겪게 되어, 가격 상승의 압박이 가해진다. 정책입안자들은 종종 이러한 가격 인상에 반대한다. 그들은 기업과 경제학자들이 우리의 공유된 사회적 가치에 더 많은 관심을 기울여야 한다고 주장한다. "위기의 시기 동안에는, 우리 모두가 협력해야 할 때이며, 움켜잡고 있어야 할 때가 아닙니다."

10 논리완성 ④

새천년의 시작은 매우 의미 있는 사건이라고 할 수 있으므로 빈칸에는 ④가 들어가는 것이 자연스럽다.

millennium n. 천년간, 천년기 astonishing a. 놀랄 만한, 놀라운 phenomenon n. 현상 infirm a. 허약한, 쇠약한 dawning n. 새벽, 여명; (새 시대 등의) 출현, 시작 apparently ad. 명백히; 외관상으로는 motivate v. ~에게 동기를 부여하다, 자극하다 trivial a. 하찮은; 사소한 obscure a. 불명료한 mundane a. 현세의, 세속적인 momentous a. 중요한 insignificant a. 무의미한, 하찮은

2000년 1월 15일, 『뉴욕타임스』는 지역 병원들이 새천년 첫 주에 1999년 마지막 주에 비해 놀랍게도 50.8% 더 많은 사망자를 기록했다고 전했다. 『타임스』는 이러한 현상이 새로운 시대의 시작을 목격할 수 있을 만큼 충분히 오래 생존하기를 원하는 병든 사람들 때문이라는 의견을 제시했다. 분명히 중대한 사건들에 대한 기대는 사람들에게 더 오래 살고자 하는 동기를 부여할 수 있다.

11-12

언론은 종종 최상급의 말을 즐기는 것 같고, 그들의 청중인 우리는 최근 주식시장에서 목격한 주가상승이 그렇게 이례적인 것인지에 대해 헷갈려 한다. 우리가 어떤 신기록을 세우고 있다는 (혹은 적어도 신기록에 가까이 있다는) 것을 암시하는 자료들은 언론에서 주기적으로 강조되며, 만약 기자들이 충분히 다른 방식으로 자료를 본다면, 그들은 그 어떤 특정한 날에라도 기록을 세우는 것에 가까운 무언가를 발견할 때가 많을 것이다. 주식시장을 보도할 때, 많은 기자들은 "기록적인 1일 가격 변동"을 언급하는데, 이것은 퍼센트가 아닌 다우존스 포인트로 측정한 것이어서 그것이 기록일 가능성이 훨씬 더 높아진다. 비록 최근 몇 년 동안 언론이 다우존스 포인트로 보도하는 것에 대해 점점 더 깨우쳐졌지만, 그 같은 관행은 일부 기자들 사이에서 여전히 지속되고 있다.
이러한 기록 과부하 ― 새롭고 중요한 기록들이 끊임없이 세워지고 있다는 인상 ― 는 사람들이 경제에 대해 가지고 있는 혼란을 가중시킬 뿐이다. 이것은 사람들로 하여금 진정으로 중요하고 새로운 것이 진짜로 일어나고 있는 때를 인식하기 어렵게 만든다. 서로 다른 지표들이 넘쳐나게 되면서, 또한 그것은 양적 자료에 대한 개인적인 평가를 회피하고 전문가들이 우리에게 해석해 준 자료를 보는 것을 선호하도록 조장한다.

thrive on 즐기다, 성공하다, 잘 해내다 superlative n. 최상급, 최상급의 말 stress v. 강조하다 persist v. 지속하다, 존속하다 overload n. 과부하 impression n. 인상, 감명 significant a. 중요한; 의미심장한 recognize v. 인식하다; 인지하다 deluge n. 대홍수, 호우, 범람; 쇄도 indicator n. 지표 assessment n. 평가, 판단 quantitative a. 양에 관한, 양적인 preference n. 선호 interpret v. 해석하다, 번역하다

11 빈칸완성 ③

Although가 이끄는 종속절과 주절의 내용이 대조를 이루어야 한다. 주절에서 '그 같은 관행이 일부 기자들 사이에서 여전히 지속되고 있다.'고 했으므로, 종속절에서는 '그러한 보도 관행이 잘못된 것임을 점점 더 깨우쳐가고 있다'라는 의미의 문장을 만드는 ③이 가장 적절하다.

빈칸에 가장 적절한 것은?
① 무모한
② 고집하는
③ 깨우친
④ 조장된
⑤ 열성적인

12 내용일치 ④

마지막 문장에서 "기록 과부하는 양적 자료에 대한 개인적인 평가를 회피하고 전문가들이 우리에게 해석해 준 자료를 보는 것을 선호하도록 조장한다."라고 했으므로, ④가 옳지 않은 진술이다.

위 글에 관해 옳지 않은 것은?
① 언론은 종종 기록 과부로 사람들을 혼란스럽게 한다.
② 기록 과부로 인해 새로운 것이 인식되지 못한 채 지나가게 된다.
③ 언론은 종종 우리가 주식시장에서 새로운 기록을 세우고 있다는 의견을 제시한다.
④ 기록 과부하는 사람들이 전문가의 의견을 무시하도록 부추긴다.
⑤ 주가 변화를 퍼센트가 아닌 포인트로 측정하면 새로운 기록 수립의 가능성이 높아진다.

13-15

빈대로 인한 건강상의 위험은 경미하다. 물린 후에 가려운 것, 알레르기와 이차 감염이 발생할 위험이 적게나마 있는 것 정도다. 모기는 말라리아와 뎅기열과 황열병을 퍼뜨린다. 그러나 빈대를 매개체로 사용하는 인간 병원체는 없는 것으로 알려져 있다. 현재의 공포감이 시사하듯이, (빈대의) 더 큰 영향은 심리적인 것인 경향이 있다. 모기, 거머리, 그리고 다른 기생충들은 불쾌하긴 해도, 여러분의 집에서 자리를 잡고 대량으로 서식하지는 않는다. 만일 여행자가 휴가를 갔다가 빈대를 데려온다면 빈대는 집에서 들끓기 시작할 수 있으며, 이 상황은 바꾸기 매우 힘들 수도 있다.

그 벌레들은 숨을 수 있는 어두운 장소가 많은 따뜻한 환경에서 잘 자란다. 도시, 그리고 사람들로 붐비는 아파트 건물들이 이상적이다. 그 벌레들은 가구의 틈새, 매트리스 솔기 혹은 벽의 갈라진 틈에 숨어 있다가 밤에 먹기 위해 밖으로 나온다. 따뜻한 중앙난방 방식의 집들은 기후온난화와 마찬가지로 그들의 수명 주기를 더 빠르게 만들어 문제를 더 악화시킨다. 2차 세계대전 직후에 DDT와 같은 살충제가 도입되어 광범위하게 사용됨으로써, 대부분의 부유한 국가 가정에서는 그 벌레들이 거의 제거되기에 이르렀다. 그러나 그러한 화학적 공격은 그 벌레들에게 강력한 진화적 압력을 가했고, 그 결과 그 벌레들은 독에 대해 저항력을 갖게 되었다. 박테리아가 한때 자신들을 죽이곤 했던 많은 항생제에 대해 저항력을 진화시켰듯이, 현대의 빈대는 적어도 일부 살충제에는 거의 취약하지 않다. 그 벌레에게 퍼부을 수 있는 화학물질의 비축량이 감소함에 따라 저항력은 더 커지게 되었다. 시안화수소, 이산화황, 그리고 DDT 자체와 같은 살충용 훈증제는 이제 대부분의 곳에서 사용하기에 독성이 지나치게 강한 것으로

간주되고 있다. 상업적으로 이용 가능한 많은 살충제 스프레이의 특효 성분인 피레트로이드는 더 안전하지만, 해마다 효과가 줄어든다.

bedbug n. 빈대 itchy a. 가려운 infection n. 감염, 전염 dengue fever 뎅기열 yellow fever 황열병 pathogen n. 병균균, 병원체 vector n. (병균의) 매개동물 leech n. 거머리 parasite n. 기생충, 기생생물 colonize v. 식민지로 만들다; 대량 서식하다 infestation n. 떼지어 해를 끼침, 들끓음, 횡행 thrive v. 번창하다 flat n. 아파트 shelter v. 숨다, 피난하다 cranny n. 벌어진[갈라진] 틈 crack n. 갈라진 틈, 균열 insecticide n. 살충제 aftermath n. (전쟁·재해 따위의) 결과, 여파, 영향; (전쟁 따위의) 직후의 시기 eliminate v. 제거하다 assault n. 습격, 강습, 공격 exert v. (힘·지력 따위를) 발휘하다, 쓰다 evolutionary a. 발전의; 진화의 resistance n. 저항력 antibiotic n. 항생물질, 항생제 invulnerable a. 상처 입지 않는, 공격에 견디는 deplete v. (세력·자원 따위를) 고갈[소모]시키다 arsenal n. 무기고; (일반적인) 축적, 재고 hurl v. 집어 던지다, 퍼붓다 fumigant n. (소독·살충용) 훈증약(燻蒸藥) hydrogen cyanide 시안화수소 sulphur dioxide 이산화황 toxic a. 유독한; 중독성의 pyrethroid n. 피레드로이드 active a. (약이) 특효 있는 ingredient n. 성분, 원료

13 내용파악 ⑤

'빈대로 인한 건강상의 위험은 경미하다. 모기는 말라리아와 뎅기열과 황열병을 퍼뜨린다. 그러나 빈대를 매개체로 사용하는 인간 병원체는 없는 것으로 알려져 있다.'라는 내용을 통해 ⑤가 정답으로 적절함을 알 수 있다.

빈대의 건강상의 위험은 다른 벌레들에 비해 상대적으로 낮은데, 왜냐하면 빈대가 _____ 때문이다.
① 온난한 기후에서만 잘 자라기
② 당신의 집에서 대량으로 서식하지 않기
③ 밤에만 먹으러 나오기
④ 비교적 죽이기 쉽기
⑤ 질병을 옮기지 않기

14 내용파악 ①

빈대가 확산되기 쉬운 환경에 대해 두 번째 문단에서 이야기하고 있는데, 불량한 위생 상태에 대해서는 언급하고 있지 않다.

위 글에 의하면, _____은 빈대 확산의 이유가 아니다.
① 위생 불량
② 지구 온난화
③ 잦은 여행
④ 효과가 없는 살충제
⑤ 중앙난방 방식의 집들

15 내용파악 ③

'시안화수소, 이산화황, 그리고 DDT 자체와 같은 살충용 훈증제는 이제 대부분의 곳에서 사용하기에 독성이 지나치게 강한 것으로 간주되고 있다.'는 내용을 통해 ③이 정답임을 알 수 있다.

시안화수소, 이산화황, DDT와 같은 훈증제는 더 이상 빈대를 죽이는 데 사용되지 않는데, 왜냐하면 _____ 때문이다.
① 훈증제의 효과가 떨어졌기
② 빈대는 대부분의 훈증제에 취약하기
③ 훈증제는 인체에도 해롭기
④ 상업적으로 구할 수 있는 살충제는 피레트로이드를 사용하기
⑤ DDT와 같은 훈증제는 너무 비싸서 사용할 수 없기

16-17

세계는 개혁하는 방법을 잊어버렸다. 우리는 자유시장 싱크탱크인 프레이저(Fraser) 연구소의 자료를 분석했는데, 이 연구소는 "경제적 자유"를 10점 척도로 측정하고 있다. 우리는 한 국가가 10년 안에 스위스와 베네수엘라의 격차의 1/4인 1.5점 이상 개선되는 경우들을 고려했는데, 이는 대담한 자유화의 개혁이 이루어졌음을 나타낸다. 1980년대와 1990년대에는, 여러 국가들이 소련을 떠났고, 가나와 페루와 같이 개혁이 불가능한 것으로 여겨졌던 많은 국가들이 실제로는 개혁이 가능한 것으로 입증됐기 때문에 이러한 "저돌적인 경제"가 일반적이었다. 정치인들은 대외무역 규정을 바꾸고, 중앙은행을 강화했으며, 예산 적자를 줄였으며, 국영기업을 매각했다. 최근 몇 년 동안에는, 그리스와 우크라이나를 비롯한 소수의 국가들만이 개혁을 시행했다. 2010년대 무렵에는 개혁이 완전히 멈췄다.

저돌적인 경제의 인기가 떨어진 것은 그것에 대한 필요성이 줄어든 이유도 일부 있다. 최근 몇 년 동안 경제가 덜 자유로워졌지만, 오늘날의 평균적인 경제는 1980년대에 비해 30퍼센트 더 자유롭다. 국영기업의 수는 더 적어졌고 관세는 더 낮아졌다. 하지만 저돌적인 경제의 쇠퇴는 또한 자유화가 실패했다는 널리 퍼져있는 믿음을 반영하기도 한다. 대중의 상상 속에서는, "구조조정 계획"이나 "충격 요법"과 같은 용어들은 아프리카의 빈곤, 러시아와 우크라이나의 마피아 국가 탄생, 칠레의 인권유린에 대한 이미지를 불러일으킨다. 조셉 스티글리츠(Joseph Stiglitz)의 『세계화와 그 불만들』과 같은 책들은 자유 시장을 추구하는 미국의 일치된 의견에 대한 반대 의견을 부추겼다. 라틴 아메리카에서 "신자유주의"는 이제 비난의 용어가 되었고, 다른 곳에서는 이 용어가 보증으로 거의 사용되지 않는다.

analyze v. 분석하다 indicate v. 가리키다, 보이다, 나타내다 bold a. 대담한 liberalize v. ~의 제약을 풀다; 자유주의화하다 reform n. 개혁 undertake v. 떠맡다; 착수하다 daredevil a. 무모한, 저돌적인 deem v. ~을 생각하다[간주하다] fortify v. 강화하다 budget n. 예산 deficit n. 적자 firm n. 회사 implement v. 이행하다, 실행하다 grind to a halt 완전히 멈춰서다 tariff n. 관세 structural-adjustment 구조조정 shock therapy 충격요법 conjure up 상기시키다 abuse n. 오용; 학대; 욕설 discontent n. 불평, 불만 foment v. (반란·불화 등을) 빚다, 조장하다 consensus n. 일치; 합의; 여론 endorsement n. 보증, 승인

16 빈칸완성 ①

첫 문단의 끝에서 '최근 몇 년 동안에는, 그리스와 우크라이나를 비롯한 소수의 국가들만이 개혁을 시행했다. 2010년대 무렵에는 개혁이 완전히 멈췄다.'라고 했으므로 빈칸에는 '개혁하는 방법'이라는 의미의 ①이 적절하다.

빈칸에 가장 적절한 것은?
① 개혁하는 방법
② 불평등을 극복하는 방법
③ 중앙은행을 운영하는 방법
④ 인권을 보호하는 방법
⑤ 자유 시장에 반대하는 방법

17 내용파악 ⑤

첫 번째 문단 후반부에서 저돌적인 경제의 결과물에 대해 이야기하고 있는데, '국영기업을 매각했다'고 했으므로, ⑤가 정답이다.

위 글에 따르면, 다음 중 "저돌적인 경제"와 관련이 없는 것은?
① 자유 시장을 촉진하는 것
② 수입세를 인하하는 것
③ 경제적 자유를 증진하는 것
④ 시장 자유화를 추구하는 것
⑤ 국영기업을 늘리는 것

18-20

미국 흑인들에게 적극적으로 판매되어 온 민트향 제품들인 멘톨 담배를 금지하는 것은 오랫동안 공중보건 규제기관들에게 도달하기 어려운 목표가 되어 왔다. 그러나 코로나 19와 '흑인의 생명도 소중하다' 운동은 의회와 백악관에 대해 인종 간의 건강 불균형을 줄여야 한다는 새로운 압박을 가했다. 게다가 이보다 더 두드러진 예는 거의 없는데, 바로 흑인 흡연자들은 담배를 덜 피우면서도, 백인 흡연자들보다 더 높은 비율로 심장마비, 뇌졸중, 그리고 그 밖의 담배 사용과 연관된 원인들로 인해 사망하고 있다는 것이다. 흑인 흡연자들 중 약 85퍼센트가 보통 담배보다 중독되기는 더 쉬우면서도 끊기는 더 어려운 Newport, Kool, 그리고 기타 멘톨 브랜드를 이용하고 있다.

멘톨은 박하에서 발견되는 물질로, 실험실에서도 합성이 가능하다. 멘톨은 담배 제품에서 시원한 느낌을 만들어내어 연기의 불쾌함을 가려주기 때문에, 연기를 더 참을 수 있게끔 한다. 일부 연구에서는 멘톨이 가벼운 마취제의 역할도 한다는 것을 보여주었다. 멘톨이 널리 사용되지 않았던 1953년에는, 필립모리스의 조사 결과, 백인 흡연자의 2퍼센트가 멘톨 브랜드를 선호한 반면 흑인 흡연자의 경우는 5퍼센트가 멘톨 브랜드를 선호했다. 어린이 금연 캠페인(Campaign for Tobacco-Free Kids)의 매튜 L. 마이어스 회장은 "담배업계는 그걸 보고 '우리가 기회를 놓치고 있다'고 말했고, 아프리카계 미국인 사회를 의식적으로 겨냥했다."고 말했다.

담배 회사들은 수십 년 동안 멘톨 담배로 흑인 사회를 겨냥해 왔다. 그들은 무료 샘플을 배포하고, 할인을 제공했으며, 수많은 콘서트와 특별 행사들을 후원했는데, 이 중에는 그 유명한 쿨 재즈 페스티벌(Kool Jazz Festival)도 포함돼 있다. 담배 회사들은 또한 흑인 독자층을 대상으로 한 신문과 잡지에 광고를 하고, 시민 권리 단체에 돈을 기부함으로써 호의를 얻었다. 그 회사들은 또한 흑인 정치 후보자들에게 자주 기부를 해왔다.

ban v. 금지하다 aggressively ad. 공격적으로, 적극적으로 elusive a. (교묘히) 도피하는; 달성하기 어려운 regulator n. 조정자, 단속자 racial a. 인종의, 민족의 disparity n. 불균형, 불일치 stark a. 뚜렷한, 두드러진 stroke n. 뇌졸중 addicted a. 중독된 plain a. 보통의, 평범한 substance n. 물질 synthesize v. 종합하다; <화학> 합성하다 tolerable a. 참을 수 있는 anesthetic a. 마취의; 무감각한 survey n. 조사, 검사 reveal v. 드러내다, 알리다 distribute v. 분배하다, 배포

하다 countless a. 무수한, 셀 수 없을 정도로 많은 gear v. (계획·요구 따위에) 맞게 하다, 조정하다 readership n. 독자 donate v. 기부하다 candidate n. 후보

---

18 빈칸완성 ②

뒤에 이어진 분사구문에서 '담배연기를 더 참을 수 있게 해준다'고 했는데, 이런 결과가 되려면 담배연기의 불쾌함이 덜 느껴져야 할 것이므로 '가리다'라는 뜻의 ②가 정답이 된다.

빈칸에 가장 적절한 것은?
① 행동하다
② 가리다
③ 드러내다
④ 강조하다
⑤ 따로 챙겨두다

---

19 내용파악 ⑤

마지막 문단에서 관련 내용을 다루고 있는데, '흑인 흡연자들을 위한 담뱃세 인하'는 언급하고 있지 않다.

위 글에 의하면, 다음 중 담배회사들이 멘톨 담배로 흑인 흡연자들을 겨냥하여 사용하는 전술이 아닌 것은?
① 가격 할인 제공
② 무료 샘플 배포
③ 흑색 신문에 광고하는 것
④ 민권 단체에 기부하는 것
⑤ 흑인 흡연자들을 위한 담뱃세 인하

---

20 내용파악 ④

인종 간의 건강 불균형의 예로 흑인 흡연자들이 백인보다 담배를 덜 피우면서도 더 많은 주요 질환을 겪고 있는 것을 들고 있는데, 이에 대한 원인을 많은 흑인 흡연자들이 보통 담배보다 중독되기 쉽고 끊기 어려운 멘톨 담배를 이용하고 있기 때문으로 보고 있다. 따라서 멘톨 담배를 금지시키면 흑인들이 주요 질환을 덜 겪게 될 것이고, 이는 나아가 건강 불균형이 해소되는 결과를 가져올 것이다.

위 글에 의하면, 멘톨 담배를 금지하는 것은 _____ 것이다.
① 담배 업계를 파산시킬
② 백인 흡연자들로 하여금 멘톨 담배를 더 많이 소비하게 할
③ 멘톨 담배에 대한 수요를 증가시킬
④ 인종 간의 건강 불균형을 감소시킬
⑤ 멘톨 담배의 품질을 떨어뜨릴

21-22

특정 집단에 대한 반감을 넘어, 통계적 차별이라고 불리는 또 다른 차별의 원인이 존재할 수 있다. 이는 고용주가 직원이 될 수 있는 사람들에 대해 불완전한 정보를 가지고 있다는 가정에 기초한다. 만약 관련이 있지만 관찰할 수는 없는 직원의 어떤 특성이 다른 식으로는 관련이 없지만 관찰할

수는 있는 특성과 우연히 상관관계가 있다면, 고용주는 고용 결정을 내릴 때 아마도 관찰할 수 있는 특성에 의존할 것이다.

예를 들어, 일부 고용주들은 전과가 있는 근로자들을 고용하지 않는 편을 선호한다. 그렇게 하는 것을 피할 수 있는 가장 간단한 방법은 구직자들에게 전과가 있는지를 물어보는 것이고, 많은 고용주들은 그렇게 하고 있다. 그러나 미국의 일부 주(州)들은 고용주들이 (전과 여부를) 물어보는 것을 금지하는 "확인란 금지"법을 통과시켰다. ("확인란"이란 어떤 사람이 전과가 없음을 알려주기 위해 체크할 수 있는 구직 신청서 상의 공간을 가리킨다.) 이 법들의 목적은 전과자들이 직업을 구하고 그럼으로써 법을 준수하는 시민으로서 사회에 다시 진출하는 것을 돕는 것이다.

이 법들의 고귀한 의도에도 불구하고, 한 가지 의도하지 않은 결과는 이 법들이 통계적 차별을 조장한다는 것이다. 통계에 따르면 흑인 남성이 백인 남성보다 교도소에서 복역했을 가능성이 더 높다. 고용주가 이러한 사실을 알고 있다면, 전과에 관심이 있지만 전과에 대해 묻는 것이 금지된 사람들은 흑인 남성을 고용하는 것을 피하려 할지도 모른다. 결과적으로, 전과 기록이 없는 흑인 남성은 자신이 속한 집단의 평균적인 특성 때문에 차별을 겪을 것이다. 일부 연구에서 "확인란 금지" 정책이 있는 주와 없는 주를 비교한 결과, 이 법이 대학 학위가 없는 젊은 흑인 남성의 고용을 상당히 감소시킨다는 사실을 발견했다. 이러한 결과는 정책입안자들이 부주의로 인한 통계적 차별을 조장하지 않는 방법을 찾아서 전과자들을 도와주어야 한다는 것을 시사한다.

animosity n. 반감, 적대감 discrimination n. 구별; 차별, 차별대우 statistical a. 통계의 assumption n. 가정, 억측, 가설 relevant a. 관련된, 적절한 unobservable a. 관찰할 수 없는 characteristic n. 특질, 특색 correlate v. 서로 관련시키다 applicant n. 응모자, 지원자 prohibit v. 금지하다 application n. 지원, 지원서 ex-offender n. 전과자 law-abiding a. 법을 준수하는, 준법의 intent n. 의향, 의도 unintended a. 의도하지 않은, 고의가 아닌 consequence n. 결과; 중요성 foster v. 조장하다, 조성하다 significantly ad. 상당히, 크게 inadvertently ad. 무심코, 부주의로

---

21 내용파악 ②

"특정 집단에 대한 반감을 넘어, 통계적 차별이라고 불리는 또 다른 차별의 원인이 존재할 수 있는데, 이는 고용주가 직원이 될 수 있는 사람들에 대해 불완전한 정보를 가지고 있다는 가정에 기초한다."라는 내용을 통해 ②가 정답임을 알 수 있다.

고용주들이 고용 결정을 하는 데 있어서 통계적 차별을 이용하는 것은 그들이 _____ 때문이다.
① 통계에 정통하기
② 지원자에 대한 충분한 정보를 가지고 있지 않기
③ 간단히 구직자들에게 범죄 기록에 대해 물어볼 수 있기
④ 그들의 고객의 수요를 만족시키고 싶기
⑤ 고용 결정을 내릴 때 관찰 가능한 특성을 사용하지 않기

---

22 내용파악 ⑤

"확인란 금지" 법은 고용주들이 구직자들에게 전과 여부를 물어보는 것을 금지하는 법인데, 이는 전과자들이 직업을 구하고 그럼으로써 법을 준수하는 시민으로서 사회에 다시 진출하는 것을 돕는 것, 즉 전과자라는 이유로 취업 시장에서 차별을 받는 일이 없도록 하기 위한 것이다.

"확인란 금지" 법의 목적은 _____이다.
① 특정 신념을 가진 직원들의 고용을 금지하는 것
② 취업 시장에서 지원자들의 부담을 줄이는 것
③ 고용주가 가능한 한 최고의 구직자를 고용하도록 돕는 것
④ 전과가 있는 구직 지원자를 더 잘 선별하는 것
⑤ 전과자들이 취업 시장에서 차별을 받지 않도록 보호하는 것

23-25

15년 전에, 이스털리(Easterly)와 레빈(Levine)은 아프리카의 성장의 실망스러운 성과와 그것이 가난한 사람들에게 끼친 피해를 강조하는 『아프리카의 성장 비극』을 출판했다. 그 이후, 성장은 회복되어 연평균 5~6%를 기록했고 빈곤은 1년에 약 1퍼센트 포인트씩 감소하고 있다. 통계적인 비극은 우리가 이것이 사실이라는 것을 확신할 수 없다는 것이다. GDP의 성장으로 측정되는 경제 성장을 예로 들어보자. GDP는 결국 국민계정으로 측정된다. 약간의 진전이 있었지만, 오늘날 아프리카 인구의 35%만이 1993년의 UN 국민계정체계를 사용하는 국가에 살고 있고, 나머지는 1960년대로 거슬러 올라가는 초기 체계를 이용하고 있다.
통계자료에 문제가 발생하는 가장 직접적인 원인은 데이터를 수집, 관리 및 배포할 수 있는 국가의 역량 부족, 자금 부족, 책임의 분산, 그리고 많은 데이터 수집 노력이 분산된 데 따른 분열 등이다. 그러나 나는 근본적인 원인은 통계자료가 본질적으로 정치적이기 때문이라고 말하고 싶다. 빈곤 추정치를 예로 들어보자. 그 추정치는 현재 사람들이 5년 전보다 더 잘 살고 있는지를 평가한다. 만약 추정하는 작업이 선거가 있는 해에 실시된다면, 그 결과를 비밀로 유지하려는 경향이 강하다. 더 심각한 문제는 조사를 완료하는 데 시간을 끄는 경향이 있다는 것이다. 그리고 가계조사의 미가공 데이터는 공개적으로 이용하는 것이 거의 불가능하다. (따라서 이 데이터를 복제할 수 있을 가능성은 거의 없다.)
그 통계적인 비극에는 또 다른 측면이 있다. 나쁜 일을 많이 겪고 난 후에, 국제 사회는 아프리카 국가들이 그들만의 국가통계 개발전략(NSDS)을 개발해야 하고, 모든 통계 활동이 NSDS와 일치해야 한다고 판단했다. 비극은 세계은행을 비롯한 기부자들이 그것이 확실히 NSDS와 일치하도록 하지 않은 채 통계활동을 시작한다는 것이다. 이유가 무엇일까? 왜냐하면 그들은 그들만의 목적을 위해 ― 보고서를 발표하기 위해 ― 데이터가 필요하기 때문이고, 이것은 그 국가들의 통계능력을 강화할 시간을 거의 주지 않은 채 데이터를 더 빨리 얻는 것을 의미한다.

take a toll (~에게) 큰 피해를[타격을] 주다, 희생자를 내다 pick up 회복되다[개선되다], 더 강해지다 statistical a. 통계의 tragedy n. 비극 proximate a. (시간·순서 따위가) (~에) 가장 가까운; (공간적으로) (~에) 아주 가까운, 인접한; (원인 따위가) 직접적인 statistics n. 통계, 통계자료 disseminate v. 널리 퍼뜨리다, 유포하다 inadequate a. 부적당한, 불충분한 diffuse a. 널리 퍼진, 분산된; 장황한 fragmentation n. 분열, 붕괴 submit v. 제출하다; 복종시키다; 공손히 아뢰다, 의견으로서 진술하다 underlying a. 기초가 되는, 근원적인 fundamentally ad. 근본적으로, 본질적으로 estimate n. 추정치, 추산 assess v. 평가하다 keep ~ under wraps 비밀로 해두다, 공개하지 않고 두다 drag one's feet 꾸물거리다 survey n. 조사, 검사 replicate v. 복제하다 aspect n. 양상; 국면; 견지 consistent a. 일치하는, 조화된 donor n. 기부자, 기증자 undertake v. 시작하다, 착수하다 ensure v. 책임지다, 보장하다, 보증하다

23 빈칸완성   ③

"빈곤 추정치를 추정하는 작업이 선거가 있는 해에 실시된다면, 그 결과를 비밀로 유지하려는 경향이 강하며, 더 심각한 문제는 조사를 완료하는 데 시간을 끄는 경향이 있다"는 것은 정치적인 입김이 작용한다는 것이므로, 빈칸에는 '본질적으로 정치적인'이라는 의미의 ③이 적절하다.

빈칸에 가장 적절한 것은?
① 본질적으로 불투명한
② 본질적으로 공평한
③ 본질적으로 정치적인
④ 경제적으로 효율적인
⑤ 터무니없이 오해의 소지가 있는

24 글의 제목   ①

아프리카의 통계를 신뢰할 수 없는 이유와 그 배경에 대해 이야기하고 있는 내용이므로, ①이 제목으로 적절하다. ② 빈곤 데이터는 예로 든 것이다.

위 글의 제목으로 가장 적절한 것은?
① 아프리카의 통계적 비극
② 아프리카의 신뢰할 수 없는 빈곤 데이터
③ 아프리카의 실망스러운 성장 성과
④ 아프리카 국가통계 개발전략(NSDS)
⑤ 국제기구를 위한 아프리카의 데이터 수집 관행에 대한 가이드라인

25 내용파악   ②

선거를 앞두고 통계자료를 숨기는 것이 잘못일 뿐, 선거 제도 자체는 문제가 되지 않는다.

아프리카 통계자료의 문제점이 아닌 것은?
① 자금 부족
② 아프리카의 선거 제도
③ 흩어져 있는 자료 수집 노력
④ 낮은 데이터 수집 및 관리 능력
⑤ NSDS와 기증자의 통계 활동 간의 불일치

01 ③	02 ④	03 ②	04 ④	05 ③	06 ②	07 ③	08 ②	09 ①	10 ①
11 ①	12 ①	13 ④	14 ②	15 ③	16 ③	17 ①	18 ④	19 ③	20 ②
21 ④	22 ①	23 ①	24 ③	25 ④	26 ③	27 ④	28 ②	29 ②	30 ①
31 ④	32 ③	33 ②	34 ①	35 ③	36 ①	37 ③	38 ④	39 ②	40 ④
41 ②	42 ④	43 ③	44 ①	45 ②	46 ①	47 ③	48 ④	49 ②	50 ①
51 ②	52 ②	53 ③	54 ①	55 ③	56 ①	57 ④	58 ③	59 ③	60 ②

01 논리완성　　　　　　③

빈칸에 들어갈 표현을 meaning 이하에서 부연 설명하고 있다. '태어날 때부터 뇌에 생물학적으로 내장돼 있다'는 것은 '선천적'이라는 것이므로 ③이 정답이다.

conclude v. 결론을 내리다, 추단하다 hard-wired a. 하드웨어에 내장된 cognate a. 조상이 같은, 동족의 affectionate a. 애정 깊은, 다정한 innate a. 타고난, 선천적인 erudite a. 박식한

본 연구에 사용된 6가지 감정에 대한 얼굴 표정들은 문화적 차이의 영향을 거의 받지 않는 것으로 보이기 때문에 그것들은 선천적인 것임에 틀림없다고 결론지을 수 있는데, 이는 태어날 때부터 뇌에 생물학적으로 내장돼 있다는 것을 의미한다.

02 논리완성　　　　　　④

매우 많은 직원을 고용한 것은 회사의 사세가 크게 확장됐던 시점에 있었던 일일 것이므로, 빈칸에는 '절정', '정점', '전성기'라는 의미를 가진 ④가 들어가야 한다.

account for 설명하다; (~의) 비율을 차지하다 employee n. 직원 expansion n. 확장, 확대 siege n. 포위 공격 zealot n. 열중하는 사람, 열광자 stake n. 말뚝, 막대기 zenith n. (성공·힘 등의) 정점, 절정, 전성기

그 회사는 그 나라 GDP의 30% 이상을 차지했으며, 사세 확장이 정점에 이르렀을 때는 25만 명 이상의 직원을 고용했다.

03 논리완성　　　　　　②

바로 앞의 internal과 호응할 수 있는 표현이 필요한데, internal은 '내적인', '정신적인'이라는 뜻이므로 '기질적인'이라는 뜻의 ②가 가장 잘 어울린다.

determine v. 결정하다 internal a. 내적인, 정신적인 factor n. 요소, 요인 influence n. 영향 behave v. 행동하다 intransitive a. <문법> 자동사의 dispositional a. 기질의, 성질의 sequential a. 연속되는, 일련의 contractive a. 줄어드는, 수축성의

기초 심리학 이론에서는, 주어진 상황에서 우리가 하는 행동을 두 가지 힘이 결정하는데, 그것은 우리의 내적, 기질적인 요소(즉, 우리의 됨됨이)와 우리가 행동하고 있는 상황의 영향이다.

04 논리완성　　　　　　④

1위 팀과의 대결에서 시험대에 오르게 될 것은 경기에 임하는 그 팀의 실력이나 자세가 될 것이다. 그러므로 빈칸에는 '기개'라는 의미의 ④가 들어가는 것이 적절하다.

packed with ~로 가득한 hostile a. 적개심에 불타는 recitation n. 낭독, 암송 dusk n. 땅거미, 황혼 proximity n. 근접, 가까움 mettle n. 기개, 혈기, 용기

입장권이 매진된 경기장에서 적대적인 팬들이 가득 들어찬 가운데 1위 팀과 라이벌전을 치를 다음 주에 그 팀의 기개는 시험대에 오를 것이다.

05 논리완성　　　　　　③

'일부 단어들을 그들만의 독특한 방식으로 사용한다.'는 것은 자폐증 아이들의 단어 사용이 일반적이지 않고 특이하다는 것을 의미한다.

autism n. 자폐증 conventional a. 전통적인, 관습적인 organic a. 유기적인; 유기체의 idiosyncratic a. 특유한, 색다른 existential a. 존재에 관한, 실존적인

자폐증을 가진 아이들은 사회적 의사소통을 어려워한다. 그들의 언어 사용은 종종 특이하며, 일부 단어들을 그들만의 독특한 방식으로 사용한다.

06 논리완성　　　　　　②

'That is'는 '다시 말해'라는 의미로 앞에 나온 내용을 부연해서 설명할 것임을 알려주는 역할을 한다. That is 이하에서 빈칸에 들어갈 표현을 indescribable and unspeakable로 설명했으므로, 빈칸에는 이와 유사한 의미의 ②가 들어가야 한다.

ascribe v. (원인·동기·기원 등을) ~에 돌리다; (성질·특징을) ~에 속하는 것으로 생각하다 declare v. 선언하다 indescribable a. 형언할 수 없는 indomitable a. 굴하지 않는, 완강한 ineffable a. 말로 나타낼

수 없는, 이루 말할 수 없는   unbendable a. 한결같은, 옹고집의
unpalatable a. 입에 맞지 않는, 맛없는

고대 히브리인들의 문화는 그 이름을 말로 나타낼 수 없는 것, 다시 말해
형언할 수 없고 말로 다 할 수 없다는 것이라고 선언하는 침묵에 의해
그 이름을 거룩한 이름으로 여겼다.

07 논리완성 ③

뇌가 손상된 사건 이전에 일어난 사건들에 대한 '기억 상실'을 일컫는다
는 내용을 통해, 빈칸에 '기억상실증'이라는 의미의 ③이 들어가야 함을
알 수 있다.

retrograde a. 퇴행성의, (건망증 따위가) 역행성의 memoir n. 회고록,
자서전 nostalgia n. 향수(鄕愁), 노스탤지어 amnesia n. 건망증, 기억
상실증 memorial n. 기념물, 기념비

역행성 기억상실증은 뇌가 손상된 사건 이전에 일어난 사건들에 대한 기억
상실을 일컫는다.

08 논리완성 ②

'반역' 행위로 간주되고 있다고 했으므로, '폭동', '반역'이라는 의미의 ②
가 가장 자연스럽게 호응한다.

Capitol n. 국회 의사당 describe v. 묘사하다 rebellious a. 반역하는,
반항적인 annexation n. 합병; 부가물 insurrection n. 반란, 폭동
deportation n. 국외추방, 강제 이송 colonization n. 식민지 건설

1월 6일의 미국 국회 의사당 습격은 미국 정부에 대한 반역 행위로 간주되
기 때문에 폭동으로 널리 묘사되고 있다.

09 논리완성 ①

빈칸 이하에서 '그 단어들이 그것이 가리키는 것과 비슷한 소리처럼 들
린다'고 했는데, 이것은 대상의 소리를 흉내 낸 말이라는 것이므로, 빈칸
에는 '의성어(擬聲語)의'라는 뜻의 ①이 적절하다.

cuckoo n. 뻐꾸기 onomatopoeic a. 의성어의 avian a. 조류의
piscine a. 어류의 lexical a. 사전의, 사전적인

우리는 최초의 언어가 어떠했는지를 전혀 알지 못한다. 어떤 단어들은 의
성어(擬聲語)였을지도 모르는데, 이는 그 단어들이 그것이 가리키는 것과
비슷한 소리처럼 들린다는 것을 의미한다. 예를 들어, "뻐꾸기"라는 단어는
그 새가 우는 소리처럼 들린다.

10 논리완성 ①

약해지기 이전에는 강하거나 많이 있는 상태였을 것이다. 그러므로 '~에
충만하다'라는 의미의 ①이 정답으로 적절하다. ④ 성장과 증대의 의미
가 있긴 하나, 이것은 자동사이므로 목적어를 취해야 하는 빈칸에는 들
어갈 수 없다.

upwelling n. (하층 해수의) 용승(湧昇) recede v. 물러나다; 감퇴하다,
줄다; 약해지다 extinction n. 멸종, 절멸 species n. 종류, 종(種)
permeate v. ~에 스며들다, 침투하다; ~에 충만하다 wane v. (달이)
이지러지다; 약해지다, 쇠약해지다 permit v. 허락하다, 허가하다 wax
v. 커지다, 증대하다

우주에 충만한 '기(氣)'라고 알려진 생명력이 생명체를 솟아나게 했으나,
그 후에는 약해지면서 수많은 종(種)의 멸종을 가져왔다.

11 단어 사이의 관계 유추 ①

초식동물(herbivore)은 식물(plants)을 먹고 살고, 육식동물(carnivore)
은 고기(meat)를 먹고 산다.

herbivore n. 초식동물 plant n. 식물, 초목 carnivore n. 육식동물
meat n. 고기 omnivore n. 잡식성 동물 insect n. 곤충 predator
n. 약탈자, 육식동물 species n. 종(種), 종류 scavenger n. 썩은 고기를
먹는 동물 herb n. 풀, 초본

12 단어 사이의 관계 유추 ①

마라톤(marathon)은 지구력(endurance)이 중요하고, 단거리 달리기
(sprint)는 스피드(speed)가 중요하다.

marathon n. 마라톤 endurance n. 인내력, 지구력 sprint n. 단거리
경주 speed n. 스피드, 속도 javelin throw 창던지기 sharpness
n. 날카로움 hurdle n. 장애물 경기 obstacle n. 장애, 방해물 pole
vault 장대 높이뛰기 weight n. 무게

13 단어 사이의 관계 유추 ④

현미경(microscope)은 작은 물체를 확대(magnify)하며 청진기
(stethoscope)는 작은 소리를 확대(amplify)한다.

microscope n. 현미경 magnify v. (렌즈 따위로) 확대하다; 크게 보이
게 하다 telescope n. 망원경 dignify v. 고상하게 하다 binoculars
n. 쌍안경 purify v. 깨끗이 하다, 순화하다 periscope n. 잠망경
rectify v. 개정하다, 고치다 stethoscope n. 청진기 amplify v. 확대하
다; 증폭하다

14 단어 사이의 관계 유추 ②

책(book)은 여러 개의 장(章, chapter)으로 이루어져 있고, 연극(play)
은 여러 개의 장면(scene)으로 이루어져 있다.

book n. 책 chapter n. (책·논문 따위의) 장(章) poem n. 시 song
n. 노래 play n. 희곡; 연극 scene n. (연극의) 장면; 희곡의 장(場)
rhyme n. 운(韻) lyric n. 서정시 movie n. 영화 prose n. 산문

15 단어 사이의 관계 유추 ③

수출(export)과 수입(import)은 서로 반의어 관계이며, 멸종한 (extinct)과 현존하는(extant)도 서로 반의어 관계이다.

export n. 수출 import n. 수입 examine v. 시험하다, 검사하다 inspect v. 조사하다, 검사하다 extraordinary a. 대단한, 비범한 remarkable a. 현저한, 주목할 만한 extinct a. 절멸한, 멸종한 extant a. 현존하는, 잔존하는 exaggerate v. 과장하다 embellish v. 윤색하다

16 동사의 태 / 관계대명사의 격 ③

타동사로 쓰인 benefit 뒤에 목적어 any child가 오고 이것을 선행사로 하는 주격 관계대명사 who가 제시돼 있는 ③이 정답이다.

demonstrate v. 증명하다, 논증하다; 드러내다 curiosity n. 호기심 benefit v. ~에게 이롭다; 이익을 얻다

이것은 호기심, 상상력, 학습 의욕을 보여주는 모든 아이들에게 이익이 될 것이다.

17 접속사 / 최상급 표현에 쓰이는 정관사 ①

두 개의 수식어가 하나의 명사를 수식할 때 그 두 수식어는 접속사로 연결되어야 하며, 형용사의 최상급 앞에는 정관사가 붙는다. 그러므로 ①이 정답이다.

string family 현악기 highest-pitched a. 음조가 가장 높은

바이올린은 현악기 중에서 가장 작으면서도 가장 음조가 높다.

18 사람을 주어로 쓰지 못하는 형용사 구문 / 동사의 종류 ④

difficult는 사람을 주어로 쓸 수 없으며 '가주어-진주어' 구문을 사용하여 표현한다. 또한 lift는 '~을 들어 올리다'라는 의미의 타동사로 쓰인 경우, 뒤에 전치사 없이 바로 목적어를 취한다. 그러므로 ④가 정답이다.

당신이 힘이 세더라도, 이렇게 높은 기압을 거슬러서 신문을 들어 올리는 것은 힘든 일이다.

19 병치구조 ③

both A and B, either A or B 등의 상관접속사 구문에서 A와 B의 자리에는 문법적인 구조나 역할이 같은 표현이 온다. 그러므로 either A or B 구문에서 부사 alone과 부사구 with the accompaniment가 병치돼 있는 ③이 정답으로 적절하다.

magnificent a. 훌륭한, 장엄한 accompaniment n. <음악> 반주

피아니스트는 혼자서 혹은 오케스트라의 반주와 함께 훌륭한 음악을 만들어 낼 수 있다.

20 'so ~ that …' 구문 ②

'너무 ~해서 …할 수 없다'는 'too+형용사(부사)+to부정사' 혹은 'so+형용사(부사)+that+부정의 주어+동사'의 형태로 나타낼 수 있다. 따라서 이를 만족시키는 ②가 정답이다.

gravity n. 중력 escape v. ~에서 달아나다

블랙홀의 중력은 너무나도 강해서 그 어떤 것도 블랙홀을 빠져나갈 수 없으며, 심지어 빛도 빠져나갈 수 없다.

21 간접의문문 ④

Do you think?와 Why do different languages have some words that sound alike?가 합쳐질 때 Why절은 간접의문절이 되어 'why+주어+동사'의 형태가 되는데, 주절 동사가 think일 때 의문사(why)가 문두로 가야 한다. 그러면 Why do you think different languages have some words that sound alike?가 되므로 ④가 정답이다.

왜 서로 다른 언어들이 비슷하게 들리는 단어들을 가지고 있다고 생각하나요?

22 수사의 위치 / 명사의 수 ①

척도를 나타내는 명사(feet)는 수사(340)의 뒤에 위치해야 하며 수사가 복수인 경우 이어지는 명사도 복수(feet)여야 한다. 이를 만족시키는 것은 ①뿐이다. about(대략)은 수사 바로 앞에 오며 전치사(at)가 그 앞에 온다.

dismay n. 당황, 낙담 come to a stop 멈추다, 정지하다

자크(Jacques)에게는 놀랍고 실망스럽게도, 트리에스테(Trieste) 호는 수면으로부터 약 340피트 아래에서 멈춰 섰다.

23 분사구문 ①

'그들(예술가들)이 질문을 받을 때'라는 의미가 적절하므로 수동태인 When they are questioned인데, 이것이 분사구문으로 되면 Being questioned이고, Being이 생략되고 접속사 When을 생략하지 않고 그래도 두면 When questioned가 된다. 따라서 ①이 정답이다. When they are questioned에서 they are가 생략된 것으로 볼 수도 있다.

질문을 받을 때, 예술가들은 항상 스스로를 만족시키기 위해 예술을 창작한다고 주장한다.

24 make+목적어+목적격 보어 / enough의 용법 ③

make가 5형식 문형에 쓰이는 경우, 'make+목적어+목적격 보어'의 형태로 쓰므로 the straw stiff이며, enough는 형용사나 부사를 뒤에서 수식하므로 the straw stiff enough가 된다. 그러므로 ③이 정답이다.

stiff a. 뻣뻣한, 딱딱한 straw n. 밀짚; 빨대

이것은 그 빨대를 구멍을 뚫을 수 있을 만큼 딱딱해지게 했다.

---

25 many, much / 조동사 ④

many는 복수명사와 호응하고 much는 단수명사와 호응한다. 그러므로 ①, ③을 정답에서 먼저 제외할 수 있다. 한편, 조동사 will 뒤에는 동사원형이 와야 하므로, will 뒤에 형용사 available이 온 ②도 빈칸에 들어갈 수 없다. 따라서 ④가 정답이 된다.

slight a. 근소한, 사소한 available a. 이용할 수 있는, 입수할 수 있는

우리의 많은 콘텐츠를 어디에서나 이용할 수 있을 것이지만, 스트리밍하는 국가에 따라 약간의 차이가 있을 수 있다.

---

26 'the more ~, the more …' 구문 ③

'~할수록 더욱 더 …하다'라는 의미의 'the more ~, the more …' 구문이 되어야 하며, the more 뒤에는 '주어+동사'가 온다.

그녀는 그 사건에 대해 알면 알수록 더 의심스러워졌다.

---

27 would rather의 용법 ④

would rather 뒤에는 동사원형이 오며, 부정어를 쓰는 경우에는 would rather 뒤에 위치시킨다.

나는 오늘밤에는 외출하고 싶지 않다.

---

28 수식어의 어순 ②

부사는 형용사를 수식하고 형용사는 명사를 수식한다. 그러므로 '부사(entirely)+형용사(appropriate)+명사(suggestion)'의 형태인 ②가 정답으로 적절하다.

sufficient a. 충분한 entirely ad. 전적으로, 아주 appropriate a. 적절한 suggestion n. 제안

이것은 전적으로 적절한 제안이지만 충분하지는 않다.

---

29 most, almost의 용법 / any+단수명사 ②

most 뒤에 가산명사가 오는 경우에는 복수명사가 오고, most는 all을 수식하지 못하며, almost는 전부를 의미하는 all, any, always 등을 수식한다. 상기 조건을 모두 만족시키는 ②가 정답으로 적절하다.

이 특별한 소프트웨어를 사용하면 거의 모든 건물의 역사를 찾을 수 있다.

---

30 타동사 / 동격절을 이끄는 접속사 ①

reach는 타동사이므로 그 뒤에 전치사 없이 목적어가 바로 와야 하며, 빈칸 뒤의 절을 동격절로 취하려면 접속사는 that이 필요하다.

그녀는 더 이상 할 수 있는 일이 없다는 결론에 도달했다.

---

31 소유격 대명사+명사 ④

소유격 대명사 뒤에는 명사 상당어구가 와야 하는데, its 뒤에 '동사(sell)+명사(volume)'의 형태가 온 점이 옳지 않다. 그러므로 ④를 명사 sales로 고쳐 volume과 함께 '판매량'이라는 의미의 복합명사를 이루도록 해야 한다.

present v. 제공하다 hypothetical a. 가설의, 가정의

그 서사(이야기)는 판매량을 늘리기 위해 다양한 프로모션을 고려하고 있는 한 기업의 가상 시나리오를 제시한다.

---

32 형용사+명사 ③

형용사 main 뒤에 과거분사 driven이 온 점이 옳지 않다. 형용사는 명사를 수식하는 역할을 하므로, ③을 '동인(動因)', '추진 요인'이라는 의미의 명사 driver로 고쳐야 한다.

counter v. 반박하다, 논박하다 lock in 가두다, 고정시키다 emission n. (빛·열·가스 등의) 배출; (대기 속의) 배출물, 배기가스 threaten v. 협박하다 fragile a. 무른, 망가지기 쉬운 ecosystem n. 생태계

반대론자들은 그 프로젝트가 기후변화의 주요 동인(動因)인 수십 년간의 온실가스 추가 배출을 고착시켜, 취약한 그 만(灣)의 생태계를 위협할 것이라고 반박하고 있다.

---

33 even as ②

even as는 접속사로 쓰여 '~하는 순간에도'라는 의미를 나타낸다. 그러므로 ②에서 if를 삭제해야 한다. as if가 '마치 ~처럼'이라는 의미로 쓰이기는 하나 even as if의 형태로는 쓰지 않는다.

bump n. 융기; 승진, 승급 mortgage rate 주택 담보대출 금리 rally n. <금융> (경기 따위의) 회복, 반등

주택담보대출 금리가 8%를 기록한 순간에도 10월 주택시장은 급등세를 보였다. 이는 최근에 더 낮아진 금리가 주택시장의 회복세를 지속시킬 수 있음을 시사한다.

---

34 문의 구성 ①

what부터 program까지는 has launched의 목적어가 되는 관계절인데, is의 주어가 what이고 보어가 a first-in-the-nation program이므로 it은 삭제해서 ①을 is로 고쳐야 한다.

launch v. 나서다, (사업 따위에 기세 좋게) 착수하다 legal a. 법률의
arrival n. 도착, 도착한 사람

그 주(州)는 새로 도착한 사람들에게 법률 지원, 사건 관리 및 기타 서비스
를 제공하는 전국 최초의 프로그램인 것을 시작했다.

---

35 one of+복수명사 ③

one of 뒤에는 복수 가산명사가 오므로 ③을 most critical things로 고
쳐야 한다.

keep track of ~을 놓치지 않도록 하다, 끊임없이 ~의 정보를 얻어내다
analytics n. 분석, 분석 정보 critical a. 대단히 중요한 ensure v.
~을 책임지다, 보장하다; 확실하게 하다 revenue n. 소득, 수익

제품에 의존하는 기업들에게는, 분석 정보를 끊임없이 얻는 것이 수익의
연속성을 보장하기 위해 할 수 있는 가장 중요한 일들 중의 하나다.

---

36 동사의 태 ①

fall은 '떨어지다'라는 의미의 자동사이므로 수동태 문장에 쓸 수 없다.
그러므로 ①을 능동을 나타내는 현재분사 falling으로 고쳐야 한다.

steadily ad. 꾸준히 peak v. 최고점에 달하다, 절정이 되다 consumer
price index 소비자 물가지수

인플레이션(물가상승)이 2022년 여름에 소비자 물가지수로 측정한 9.1%
에서 정점을 찍은 이후 꾸준히 떨어지고 있다.

---

37 전치사의 목적어 ④

전치사 뒤에는 명사 상당어구가 목적어로 온다. 그러므로 ④에 쓰인 형
용사 healthy를 명사 health로 고쳐야 한다. ③ those는 앞에 나온 diets
를 대신하고 있다.

input n. (일·사업 등을 성공시키기 위한) 조언[시간, 지식]; 입력 expert
n. 전문가 identify v. 확인하다, 인지하다 joint n. 관절

그 신문은 건강 전문가 패널의 조언을 바탕으로 24가지 식단에 순위를
매겼고, 관절 건강에 관심이 있는 사람들에게 가장 좋은 식단을 찾아냈다.

---

38 현재분사와 과거분사의 용법 구분 ④

현재분사에는 능동과 진행의 의미가 있고, 과거분사에는 수동과 완료의
의미가 있다. 주어진 문장에서 emotions는 compare하는 행위의 주체
가 아닌 대상이므로 수동 관계를 나타내는 과거분사로 수식해야 한다.
따라서 ④는 compared to가 되어야 한다.

reputable a. 평판이 좋은; 훌륭한, 존경할 만한 participant n. 참여자,
참가자 intensive a. 집중적인, 철저한 control group 대조군

2017년에 한 평판 좋은 학술지에 발표된 소규모 연구에서는 심호흡 집중
훈련을 받은 연구 참가자들이 대조군에 비해 주의력 수준이 우수하고 더

나은 감정 상태를 보인다는 사실을 발견했다.

---

39 a handful of   ②

'소수의'에 해당하는 표현은 명사 handful을 이용해서 a handful of로
나타낸다. 그러므로 ②를 a handful of로 고쳐야 한다.

stock n. 주식 dividend n. 배당금, 이익 배당 quarterly ad. 분기별로
distribute v. 분배하다, 배급하다

대부분의 주식은 분기별로 배당금을 지급하지만, 소수의 우량 공기업은
월별로 배당금을 배분한다.

---

40 형용사+명사 ④

④에 쓰인 migrate는 동사이므로 명사 students를 수식할 수 없다. 명
사를 수식하는 것은 형용사이므로 ④를 migrant로 고쳐야 한다.

district n. 지역, 지구 enroll v. 등록하다, 명부에 기재하다 slight
a. 약간의, 근소한 dip n. 하락 stark a. 극명한, 두드러진

그 지역은 46,829명의 학생을 등록했는데, 이는 250명 이상의 소폭 감소
를 기록한 것이다. 만약 이주 학생이 늘어나지 않았더라면, 감소폭은 더
두드러졌을 것이다.

---

41 동사의 수일치 ②

관계대명사 what은 관계절 다음에 be동사와 보어가 올 때 보어가 복수
명사일 경우에는 be동사가 복수형이기도 하지만, 그렇지 않은 경우에
는 단수로 취급한다. 따라서 ②를 matters로 고쳐야 한다.

access n. 접근, 출입 a wealth of 풍부한, 많은 analysis n. 분석

그것은 가장 중요한 것에 대한 필수 지침이기 때문에, 여러분은 많은 독립
적인 보고서 및 글로벌 분석을 충분히 접할 수 있게 될 겁니다.

---

42 find와 found의 의미 구분 ④

④는 '설립하다', '~의 기초를 두다'라는 의미를 가진 found의 과거분사
이므로 문장의 의미상 적절하지 않다. 이것을 '발견하다'라는 뜻의 find
의 과거분사인 found로 고쳐야 한다.

그 보고서는 주요 도시들이 노숙을 경험하는 상당 수 사람들의 본거지여
서, 미국 전체 노숙들이 가운데 거의 4명 중 1명이 뉴욕 시에서 발견된다는
것을 보여준다.

---

43 동격절을 이끄는 접속사 that ③

③ 앞의 to는 전치사이므로 fear는 명사이고, 그다음의 what절은 fear
의 내용을 나타내는 동격절이다. 동격절을 이끄는 접속사는 that이므로
③을 fear that으로 고쳐야 한다.

trauma n. 외상(外傷); 정신적 충격, 쇼크 depression n. 우울증
disclose v. 드러내다, 공개하다

의사단체들에 따르면, 정신적 충격이나 우울증으로 고생하고 있는 의사들이 향후에 이를 공개해야 할지도 모른다는 우려 때문에 치료를 기피했다.

44 올바른 형용사

①에는 bumpy와 유사한 의미를 가진 형용사가 와야 하겠는데, '삐죽삐죽한', '들쭉날쭉한'은 jagging이 아닌 jagged이므로, ①을 Jagged로 고쳐야 한다.

bumpy a. (길 따위가) 울퉁불퉁한 underpass n. 지하도

들쭉날쭉하고 울퉁불퉁한 터널의 벽은 현대의 기계가 만든 지하도를 거의 닮지 않았다.

45 thanks to

'~덕분에'는 thanks to로 나타내므로 ②를 to로 고쳐야 한다. 이때 in large part는 thanks와 to 사이에 삽입된 부사구임에 유의한다.

preserve v. 보존하다 underway a. (계획 따위가) 진행 중인

그 언어의 보존에 헌신한 한 세대의 음악가들에게 크게 힘입어, 그 언어의 르네상스가 진행되고 있다.

46-49

나는 우리 대학 캠퍼스의 정치적 성향의 구성에 대해 여러 차례 질문을 받아 왔다. 일반적으로, 나는 다음과 같이 대답했다. "우리는 정치적 스펙트럼의 양 극단에 매우 열정적인 지지자들을 가지고 있지만, 많은 사람들은 중도 성향에 해당됩니다."
여기에는 크게 두 가지 주된 이유가 있다. 한편으로, 일부 학생들은 정치적인 문제에 전혀 관심이 없다. 다른 한편으로, 학생들은 종종 마치 정치적인 불화를 해결하는 데 필연적으로 수반되는 끈기, 좌절, 소모 등을 겪을 가치가 없는 것처럼 느낀다. 그러나 우리는 진정한 정치적 무관심과 성공적으로 시작하고 진행하는 데 엄청난 시간과 에너지가 필요한 정치적 대화를 피하기로 하는 선택 사이에 중요한 차이가 있음을 인식해야 한다.
대학생들이 정치 이야기를 피하는 쪽을 더 선호한다고 말할 때, 내가 그들을 비난할 수는 없다. 미국의 정치 지형은 변곡점에 도달했다. 지금 우리의 정치 시스템에는 그 어느 때보다 더 많은 긴장과 증오, 혼란이 존재한다. 지금 당장 우리는 우리의 민주주의 시스템을 치유하는 데, 그리고 더 중요하게는 서로 대화하는 법을 배우는 데, 필요한 것을 우리가 가지고 있는지를 판단해야 한다.
나는 우리 세대가 이 나라의 유일한 희망이라는 말을 종종 듣는다. 우선, 말해두고 싶은 것은 이러한 경험을 나만 하는 것은 아니라는 확신이 든다는 것이다. 현재 그리고 곧 20대가 될 사람들의 집합체로서, 우리는 종종 200년이 더 된 체제를 수호해야 하는 부담을 어깨에 짊어지고 있다고 느낀다. 그러므로 우리 개인의 노력은 하찮다는 생각에 빠지기 쉽다. 다음과 같은 공정한 질문을 하나 던져보겠다. 여러분은 우리나라의 궤도를 바꾸기 위해 무엇을 할 수 있는가?
이 변곡점에서 치유와 진보는 여러분의 도움이 있어야만 가능하다는 것을 나는 이 자리에서 말하고자 한다. 어렵다는 이유만으로 정치적인 대화를

거부할 때, 우리는 우리의 민주주의에 남겨지게 될 것을 보존하기 위해 열 배 더 노력해야 할 미래 세대의 미국 시민들을 실망시키게 된다. 지금이 그 때이고 그것이 가진 의미는 막중하다.

passionate a. 열렬한 advocate n. 옹호자, 주창자 persistence n. 고집, 완고 frustration n. 좌절, 실패 exhaustion n. 소모, 고갈 inevitably ad. 불가피하게, 필연적으로 address v. (문제를) 역점을 두어 다루다 discord n. 불화, 불일치 recognize v. 인지하다, 인정하다 distinction n. 구별, 차별; 대조, 대비 genuine a. 진짜의; 진심에서 우러난 extensive a. 광대한, 광범위하게 미치는 initiate v. 시작하다, 개시하다 preference n. 더 좋아함, 편애 inflection point 변곡점 turmoil n. 소동, 혼란 safeguard v. 보호하다 trivial a. 사소한, 하찮은 trajectory n. 궤도, 탄도 reject v. 거절하다, 무시하다 preserve v. 보전하다, 보존하다 implication n. 내포, 함축

46 빈칸완성

빈칸을 포함하고 있는 문장은 'between A and B' 구문이 쓰였는데, A에는 앞의 On the one hand 이하에서 언급한 내용이 들어가야 하고, B에는 On the other 이하에서 언급한 내용이 들어가야 한다. On the one hand 이하에서 '일부 학생들은 정치적인 문제에 전혀 관심이 없다'라고 했으므로, 빈칸에는 '냉담', '무관심'이라는 의미의 ①이 적절하다.

다음 단어 중 빈칸 Ⓐ에 들어가기에 가장 적절한 것은?
① 무관심
② 공감
③ 동정
④ 동종요법

47 부분이해

inflection point는 '변곡점'이라는 의미인데, '중대한 전환점'이라는 뜻으로 흔히 쓰인다.

위 글에 의하면, 다음 중 Ⓑ의 의미를 가장 잘 설명한 것은?
① 정치 제도의 최고점
② 특정 기간이나 시대의 평균 시점
③ 중대한 변화가 일어나는 시점
④ 되돌아가는 것이 불가능한 직선상의 지점

48 내용파악

네 번째 문단의 "현재 그리고 곧 20대가 될 사람들의 집합체로서, 우리는 종종 200년이 더 된 체제를 수호해야 하는 부담을 어깨에 짊어지고 있다고 느낀다."라는 내용을 통해 글쓴이가 대학생임을 미루어 짐작할 수 있다.

다음 중 위 글의 저자를 가장 잘 설명하고 있는 것은?
① 대학에 초당적인 교수진 집단을 만드는 데 관심이 있는 예비 학장
② 대학의 정치적 열정 부족을 비판하는 위선적인 정치 전문가
③ 대학에 대한 행정정책에 관한 연구를 수행하고 있는 열성적인 교수
④ 대학에서 더 많은 정치적 담론을 장려하는 데 관심이 있는 대학생

49 내용파악 　　　　　　②

"지금 우리의 정치 시스템에는 그 어느 때보다 더 많은 긴장과 증오, 혼란이 존재한다."라는 내용을 통해 ②가 정답으로 적절함을 알 수 있다.

위 글에 의하면, 다음 중 미국의 정치 지형에 대한 저자의 견해로 상정할 수 없는 것은?
① 대립하는 양측 간의 정치적으로 벌어진 틈은 전국적으로 심각하다.
② 정치 체제가 회복되기 시작했고, 더 많은 참여가 그 과정을 진척시켰다.
③ 어떤 사람들은 정치에 대해 진정으로 무관심하지만, 많은 사람들은 단순히 정치적 대화를 자제한다.
④ 어려운 정치적 논의를 미루는 것은 정치적 논쟁을 악화시킬 것이다.

50-53

2016년 11월 21일, 일련의 폭풍우가 호주 빅토리아 주(州)를 휩쓸고 지나가면서, 전례 없는 보건 위기를 초래했다. 강력한 하강 기류가 멜버른 전역에 두꺼운 알레르기성 입자 층을 몰고 와서 3,000명이 넘는 사람들이 입원했고, 치명적인 천식 전염병이 발생하여 응급 구조대가 감당하지 못하는 가운데 최소 10명이 목숨을 잃었다.

날씨와 기후의 위험은 이러한 갑작스러운 천식 발병처럼 항상 국지적인 사건인 것은 아니며 위치와 인구 통계와 같은 요인의 영향을 받는 복잡한 상호 작용이다. 이러한 메커니즘의 복잡함은 2016년의 폭풍에서 볼 수 있듯이 영향을 확대시킬 수 있다. 점진적인 기후 변화는 특정 임계값을 넘을 때 갑작스럽고 예측할 수 없는 결과를 초래할 수 있다. 알레르기성 목초의 생장에 도움이 되는 기상 패턴과 같은 다양한 요인의 상호 작용은 겉으로 보기에는 평범한 사건을 재앙적인 사건으로 바꿀 수 있다.

가뭄과 흉작이 발생할 가능성이 높아진 것, 경제 전체를 뒤엎어 놓는 지역적인 기후 변화, 바람과 비가 모두 다 파괴적인 폭풍우 등, 기후 변화의 영향에 대해 알려져 있는 것들은 이미 충분히 우려스러운 수준이다. 알려진 무지(無知)(미리 알고 있는 것 중에 알지 못하는 부분)가 불안을 가중시킨다. 대륙을 짓누를 수 있을 정도로 거대한 불확실성인 빙상(氷床)의 문제만이 아니다. 해류가 이동하거나 사막이 확대되는 것을 볼 수 있는 다른 임계점들도 있다. 그리고 이 모든 문제들 사이의 공간에는 알려지지 않은 무지들(우리가 실제로 알지 못하는 것들)이 있으며, 이것들은 꽃가루를 통해 사망자를 발생시키는 폭풍우만큼 놀랍고 치명적이다.

본질적으로, 오늘 우리가 보기 드문 극단이라고 생각하는 것이 내일은 일상적인 혼란이 될 수 있고, 새로운 극단이 생겨 추가적인 불확실성과 위험을 가져올 수도 있다. 기후 변화를 시급히 해결하는 것은 알려진 위험을 이해하는 것뿐만 아니라 앞에 놓여 있을 수도 있는 예측할 수 없고 잠재적으로 치명적인 알려지지 않은 것들에 대비하는 것에도 달려 있다.

unprecedented a. 전례 없는, 미증유의 hospitalize v. 입원시키다 downdraft n. 하강 기류 allergenic a. 알레르기를 일으키는 fatal a. 치명적인 asthma n. 천식 epidemic n. 유행병, 전염병 overwhelm v. 압도하다, 제압하다 claim v. (병·재해 등이 인명을) 빼앗다 localize v. 한 지방에 그치게 하다, 국한하다 outbreak n. (소동·전쟁·유행병 따위의) 발발, 창궐 intricate a. 뒤얽힌 demographics n. 인구통계(자료) amplify v. 확대하다, 확장하다 trigger v. (일련의 사건·반응 등을) 일으키다, 유발하다 threshold n. 발단, 시초; 한계 interplay n. 상호 작용 conducive a. 도움이 되는 catastrophic a. 파멸적인 incident n. 사건 drought n. 가뭄 crop failure 흉작 tipping point 티핑 포인트, 임계점(작은 변화들이 어느 정도 기간을 두고 쌓여, 이제 작은 변화가 하나만 더 일어나도 갑자기 큰 영향을 초래할 수 있는 상태가 된 단계) pollen n. 꽃가루 urgency n. 긴급 lethal a. 죽음을 가져오는

50 내용파악 　　　　　　①

첫 문단에서 천식으로 인해 많은 인명피해가 발생했음을 언급하고 있는데, 천식은 호흡기 질환이므로 ①이 정답이다.

2016년 11월 21일, 호주 빅토리아 주에서 폭풍우로 인해 어떤 예상치 못한 결과가 발생하였는가?
① 전례 없는 대기 오염으로 인해 호흡과 관련된 문제가 발생했다.
② 메뚜기 떼가 지역 의료 시스템을 붕괴시켰다.
③ 갑작스러운 기온 상승으로 광범위하게 열병이 확산됐다.
④ 강력한 지진이 그 지역을 뒤흔들어 큰 피해를 입혔다.

51 내용파악 　　　　　　②

세 번째 문단 마지막 부분에서 "이것들은 꽃가루를 통해 사망자를 발생시키는 폭풍우만큼 놀랍고 치명적이다."라고 했으므로, ②가 정답이다.

기후 변화의 맥락에서, 알려지지 않은 무지의 잠재적 영향을 전달하기 위해 어떤 유추가 사용되는가?
① 폭풍 전의 고요함
② 꽃가루를 통해 인명을 빼앗는 폭풍우
③ 일상적인 혼란이 되어가는 알려진 위험
④ 대륙에 가해지는 불확실성의 무게

52 내용파악 　　　　　　②

두 번째 문단에서 "이러한 메커니즘의 복잡함은 영향을 확대시킬 수 있어서, 특정 임계값을 넘을 때 갑작스럽고 예측할 수 없는 결과를 초래할 수 있다."라고 했으므로 ②가 정답이다.

위 글에 의하면, 폭풍 동안 발생하는 다양한 요인들의 상호 작용은 기후 변화의 영향에 대해 무엇을 드러내는가?
① 기후 변화에 따른 결과의 예측 가능성
② 특정 임계값을 넘는 경우의 복잡성 및 예측 불가능성
③ 혼돈을 일으키는 인간에게 미치는 제한적인 영향
④ 치명적인 폭풍우와 같은 기상 현상의 강도 감소

53 내용파악 　　　　　　③

"날씨와 기후의 위험은 위치와 인구 통계와 같은 요인의 영향을 받는 복잡한 상호 작용이며, 이것은 겉으로 보기에는 평범한 사건을 재앙적인 사건으로 바꿀 수 있다."라고 했으므로 ③이 정답이 된다.

위 글에서는 날씨와 기후 위험의 복잡성을 어떻게 설명하고 있는가?
① 그것들은 전적으로 경제적 요인의 영향을 받는다.
② 인구 통계는 대륙을 짓누르는 데 타당한 역할을 한다.
③ 그것들의 복잡성은 위치와 인구 통계와 같은 요소들에 의해 심화될 수 있다.
④ 기후 위험의 영향은 부분적으로 기술 발전에 의해 결정된다.

54-56

어느 날, 네 명의 소년들이 프랑스 남서부에 있는 오래된 대저택인 라스코(Lascaux)의 땅을 걷고 있었다. 자신들의 개가 몇몇 바위 사이의 틈으로 떨어졌을 때, 소년들은 개를 구하러 갔고 그 구멍이 동굴로 이어진다는 사실을 알게 됐다. 그것은 1900년대의 가장 흥미로운 고고학적 발견 중 하나가 되었다.

그 발견에 관한 뉴스는 빠르게 전해졌다. 사람들은 곧 그 동굴을 탐험하기 위해 모여들고 있었다. 그들은 좁은 통로로 연결된 총 7개의 지하 방들을 발견했는데, 그 방의 벽과 천장에는 그림이 그려져 있고 새겨져 있었다. 최고의 고고학자들로 이루어진 한 팀이 곧 동굴들에 도착했다. 그들은 엄청난 발견에 — 그림들이 기원전 15,000년경의 것이고 완벽하게 보존돼 있다는 사실에 — 놀라움을 금치 못했다. 선사시대 동물들의 그림들은 세상 사람들의 상상력을 사로잡았다. 그 그림들은 우리로 하여금 먼 과거에 살았던 우리 조상들의 생활을 엿볼 수 있게 해준다. 고고학자들은 그 동굴들을 어떻게 해야 하는 지에 대해 걱정했다. 유럽은 1차 세계대전에 휩쓸린 상태였기 때문에, 그 장소를 개발하고 보호하는 데 돈을 쓸 여유가 없었다. 그들은 전쟁이 끝날 때까지 동굴들을 봉인하기로 결정했다.

그 동굴들은 1948년에 대중에게 공개되어 수천 명의 사람들이 방문했다. 그러나 방문객들이 해로운 영향을 미치고 있다는 사실이 곧 분명해졌다. 그들이 호흡하는 과정에서 발생하는 가스와 수증기가 동굴 벽을 축축하게 만들고 귀중한 그림들을 손상시켰다. 그것들을 보호하기 위한 시도들이 있었지만, 1963년에 동굴들을 폐쇄하는 결정이 내려졌다. 20년 후에 가장 큰 동굴을 실제 크기로 똑같이 본떠서 만든 동굴이 부근에서 공개되었다.

crack n. 갈라진 틈 cavern n. 동굴 archaeological a. 고고학적인 chamber n. 방, 침실 passageway n. 통로, 복도 engraving n. 조각, 조각술 preserve v. 보존하다, 보전하다 glimpse n. 흘끗 봄 ancestor n. 선조, 조상 cave n. 동굴 vapor n. 증기, 수증기, 김 dampen v. (물에) 축이다, 적시다 replica n. (실물을 모방하여 만든) 복제품

---

54 내용파악 ①

프랑스 남서부에 있는 오래된 대저택의 땅에서 동굴들과 동굴 속 그림이 발견된 것이지 그 그림들이 대저택을 묘사하고 있었던 것은 아니다.

위 글에 의하면, 다음 중 그 동굴들의 그림에 관해 옳지 않은 것은?
① 그것들은 프랑스 남서부에 있는 오래된 대저택을 묘사했다.
② 그것들은 기원전 15,000년경의 것이다.
③ 그것들은 발견되었을 때 잘 보존돼 있었다.
④ 그것들은 먼 과거에 살았던 우리 조상들의 생활을 보여주었다.

---

55 내용추론 ③

방문객들이 모형 동굴로 향하게 되면서, 보존을 위해 폐쇄한 원형 동굴은 그 피해를 최소화할 수 있게 됐을 것이다.

다음 중 위 글의 마지막 단락에서 추론할 수 있는 것은?
① 귀중한 그림들은 피해로부터 성공적으로 복구되었다.
② 동굴은 사람들의 호흡 속에 있는 가스와 수증기에 해로운 영향을 끼쳤다.
③ 모형 동굴은 원형 동굴의 손상을 최소화했다.
④ 동굴들은 20년 후에 개방될 것이다.

---

56 지시대상 ①

Ⓐ는 a cavern, Ⓑ는 that the visitors were having a harmful effect, Ⓒ는 to close the caves를 각각 가리킨다. 그러므로 ①이 정답이다.

57-60

'하늘비행 자동차', '도로주행 항공기', '듀얼 모드 차량'과 기타 용어들은 비행기처럼 하늘을 날 수 있고 자동차처럼 고속도로를 달릴 수 있는 다목적 차량을 묘사하는 데 쓰인다. 공륙(空陸) 양용으로 만들 수만 있다면 우리는 완벽한 다목적 차량을 갖게 되는 것이다! 그럼에도 불구하고, 이것은 우리로 하여금 다소 너무 지나친 생각을 하게 할지도 모른다.

항공과 자동차, 두 분야의 가장 좋은 점을 자신들에게 함께 가져다 줄 자동차를 갖는 것은 오랫동안 항공과 자동차 애호가들의 꿈이었다. 러시아워의 교통체증에 갇힌 많은 운전자들은 버튼을 누르면 차에서 날개가 펼쳐지면서 앞에서 오도 가도 못하고 있는 자동차들 위로 자신의 차가 떠오를 수 있게 되는 것을 상상한다. 집에서 멀리 떨어진 공항에서 악천후로 인해 이륙을 하지 못하게 된 많은 조종사들이 어떻게든 비행기를 고속도로로 몰고 가서 집으로 운전해 갈 수 있길 바랐던 것처럼 말이다. <이러한 열망은 일찍이 1906년부터 도로주행이 가능한 비행기에 대한 많은 설계를 낳았다.>

하늘비행 자동차의 설계자는 항공기와 자동차에 관한 상충되는 규정을 비롯한 많은 장애물과 마주칠 것이다. 이러한 차량은 자동차이기 때문에 차선의 폭 안에 꼭 맞아야 하며 고속도로의 고가도로 밑을 지나갈 수 있어야 한다. 그 차량은 정상적인 고속도로의 차량들을 따라갈 수 있어야 하며 모든 안전 규정을 충족해야 한다. 또한 그것은 자동차 배기가스 배출 기준을 충족해야 한다. 이러한 규정은 만약 그 차량을 공식적으로 오토바이로 분류할 수 있다면 더 쉽게 충족할 수 있다. 따라서 날개는 반드시 접거나 넣을 수 있어야 하며 꼬리 혹은 작은 날개 면은 집어넣을 수 있어야 할 수도 있다. 배출가스 기준과 충돌 내구성 요건은 설계를 더 무거워지게 할 것이다. 가다 서다를 반복하는 자동차 운행 환경에서 작동할 수 있는 엔진/변속기 시스템에 대한 필요성도 시스템을 더 복잡하면서도 더 무겁게 만들 것이다.

roadable a. 도로를 갈 수 있는; (비행기가) 자동차로 개조될 수 있는, 공륙(空陸) 양용의 vehicle n. 수송 수단, 탈것 amphibious a. 양서류(兩棲類)의; 수륙 양용의 aviation n. 비행, 항공 automobile n. 자동차 enthusiast n. 열광자, 팬 stuck a. (~에 빠져) 움직일 수 없는[꼼짝 못하는] stall v. (말·자동차·군대 등을) 오도가도 못 하게 하다 ground v. (배를) 좌초시키다; 이륙을 못하게 하다 encounter v. ~와 우연히 만나다, 마주치다 obstacle n. 장애물, 방해물 overpass n. 구름다리, 육교; 고가도로 keep up with ~을 따라잡다 exhaust n. (엔진의) 배기가스 emission n. (빛·열·가스 등의) 배출 fold v. 접다 retract v. (전에 한 말을) 철회[취소]하다; (일부분을) 집어넣다[오므리다] canard n. 카나드, 비행기의 동체 앞부분에 위치한 작은 날개 stowable a. 집어넣을 수 있는 crashworthiness n. 충돌 내구성 transmission n. (자동차의) 변속기 complication n. 복잡; 혼란

---

57 내용일치 ④

"하늘비행 자동차가 만들어지더라도 자동차 배기가스 배출 기준을 충족해야 한다. 이러한 규정은 만약 그 차량을 공식적으로 오토바이로 분류할 수 있다면 더 쉽게 충족할 수 있다."라는 내용을 통해 오토바이가

자동차보다 배출가스 기준이 낮음을 알 수 있다. 그러므로 ④가 옳지 않은 진술이다.

위 글에 의하면, 다음 중 옳지 <u>않은</u> 것은?
① 주행 및 비행이 가능한 다목적 차량을 지칭하는 용어는 다양하다.
② 교통체증에 빠진 많은 운전자들은 자신들의 차가 하늘을 날 수 있기를 상상한다.
③ 하늘을 나는 자동차는 자동차 배기가스 규정을 만족시켜야 한다.
④ 오토바이는 자동차보다 배출가스 기준이 높다.

---

58 빈칸완성

비행기의 운항을 불가능하게 하는 것은 악천후, 즉 '궂은 날씨'이므로 빈칸에는 '(날씨가) 험악한[궂은]'이라는 뜻의 ③이 적절하다.

다음 중 빈칸 Ⓐ에 들어가기에 가장 적절한 것은?
① 대표적인
② 상호간의
③ (날씨가) 험악한
④ 도구

---

59 글의 목적 ③

본문은 하늘비행 자동차를 설계하는 데 있어서의 애로사항에 대해 주로 이야기하고 있으므로 글을 쓴 목적으로는 ③이 적절하다.

저자가 이 글을 쓰는 주된 목적은 무엇인가?
① 하늘비행 자동차가 실용적이고 쉽게 이용할 수 있는 다목적 자동차라는 것을 보여주기 위해
② 공항에 이륙하지 못한 조종사들의 감정을 전달하기 위해
③ 하늘비행 자동차를 설계하는 데 있어서 앞에 놓여 있는 어려움들을 설명하기 위해
④ 이중 모터 자동차의 복잡한 구조와 무게를 조사하기 위해

---

60 문장삽입

주어진 문장은 "이러한 열망은 일찍이 1906년부터 도로주행이 가능한 비행기에 대한 많은 설계를 낳았다."라는 의미이므로, 도로주행이 가능한 비행기가 있었으면 좋겠다는 소망에 관한 내용 다음인 Ⓑ에 들어가는 것이 적절하다.

2024 숙명여자대학교(A형)

01 ⑤	**02** ①	**03** ⑤	**04** ④	**05** ①	**06** ③	**07** ②	**08** ⑤	**09** ④	**10** ⑤
11 ①	**12** ⑤	**13** ②	**14** ②	**15** ①	**16** ④	**17** ①	**18** ⑤	**19** ①	**20** ④
21 ②	**22** ④	**23** ⑤	**24** ③	**25** ②	**26** ④	**27** ③	**28** ⑤	**29** ④	**30** ②
31 ⑤	**32** ②	**33** ③							

01 동의어 ⑤

shift n. 변화, 이동, 전환 transform v. 변화시키다 agrarian a. 농경의 (= agricultural) emerge v. 등장하다 power v. 동력으로 삼다 steam engine 증기기관 urbanization n. 도시화 intuitive a. 직관적인

산업혁명은 인간 역사의 중요한 전환점으로, 농경사회를 산업사회로 변화시켰다. 증기기관을 동력으로 하는 공장이 등장하면서, 생산 증가와 도시화가 이루어졌다.

02 동의어 ①

release n. 석방 hostage n. 인질 detain v. 구금하다 poised a. 태세를 갖춘, 침착한(= composed) pause n. 중단 extend v. 연장하다 fluster v. 당황하다

양측은 이스라엘 인질과 구금된 팔레스타인인의 석방을 완료했으며, 전투 중단이 이틀 연장됨에 따라 더 많은 사람들을 석방할 준비를 침착하게 갖춘 것으로 보였다.

03 동의어 ⑤

correspond with 부합하다 considerate a. 사려 깊은(= mindful) awareness n. 의식 independent a. 독립적인 brave a. 용감한

야외에 대한 사랑은 더욱 사려 깊은 행동과 안전 의식에 부합해야 한다고 평론가들은 말한다.

04 전치사 ④

aid(돕다)는 '동사+목적어+(to) V' 구문 뿐 아니라 '동사+목적어+in ~ing' 구문으로도 쓰인다.

tutor v. 개인 교습하다 brush up 더욱 연마하다, 다시 공부하다

영어 과외 로봇은 학생들이 영어 지식, 회화 능력 및 발음을 더욱 연마하도록 도울 것이다.

05 주어와 동사의 수일치 ①

their (seats)를 통해 audience를 복수 명사로 취급하고 있다는 것을 알 수 있다. 따라서 ①이 정답이다. ② 동사가 필요한 자리인데, waiting은 분사이다. ③, ④ 단수 동사로 받고 있다. ⑤ wait는 자동사이므로 수동태가 될 수 없다.

eager for ~을 열망하는

콘서트가 시작되기를 열망하는 관객들은 조용히 자리에 앉아 있다.

06 명사 / 시제 ③

committee가 집합명사로 쓰였으므로 단수 동사로 받아야 한다. ① 동사의 수가 일치하지 않는다. ④ 분사 단독으로는 문장의 정동사가 될 수 없다. ⑤ 가정법 문장이 아니다. ② 의미상 권고 사항을 먼저 만들고(현재시제), 그다음에 정책 입안자들이 검토할(미래시제) 것이므로 시제가 뒤바뀌었다.

expert n. 전문가 respective a. 각각의 field n. 분야 policymaker n. 정책 입안자 implementation n. 시행

각 분야의 전문가로 구성된 위원회는 일련의 권고 사항 초안을 작성하고 이를 시행하기 전에 정책 입안자들이 신중하게 검토할 것이다.

07 전치사+관계대명사 ②

'비교하다'는 'compare A with B' 구문으로 쓰이므로 with가 있어야 한다. 전치사의 목적어인 관계절을 이끌면서 call이라는 동사의 목적어가 되는 관계사가 필요하므로, 관계사는 선행사를 포함하는 관계대명사 what이어야 한다.

expand v. 확대하다 right n. 권리 adapt to 적응하다 reactionary a. 반동적인, 극우적인 negationist n. 부정주의(사실이나 진실을 부정하는 태도)적인

산체스는 기후 변화에 적응할 뿐 아니라 여성과 노동자의 권리와 건강 및 주거 서비스를 확대하겠다는 자신의 공약을 그가 인민당과 복스당의 반동적이고 부정주의적인 의제라고 부른 것과 비교했다.

08 전치사+관계대명사　　⑤

'the realities에 대한 설명'은 'an explanation for the realities'이다. 따라서 ⑤의 for which가 정답이다.

joyously ad. 즐겁게

종교의 임무는 우리가 쉽게 설명할 수 없는 현실 여건들을 지니고 평화롭게, 심지어 즐겁게 살아가도록 돕는 것이다.

09 논리완성　　④

economic ward란 경제적으로 다른 나라에 의존하는 국가를 의미한다. 앞 문장에 '군대를 유지하기 힘들다'는 내용이 있고, 뒤 문장에 '미국과 동맹국들의 돈을 받게 될 것'이라는 내용이 있으므로, 우크라이나는 여전히 economic ward일 것이라는 말이 필요하다. ①, ②, ③은 시제부터 틀렸고 ⑤는 not의 위치도 will 다음에 있어야 한다.

formidable a. 막강한　sustain v. 유지하다　given that ~을 고려해볼 때　wreck v. 파괴하다　ward n. 병동　ally n. 동맹국　foreseeable a. 예측할 수 있는

우크라이나는 막강한 군대를 구축하고 있다. 그러나 전쟁으로 인해 국가 경제가 피폐해졌다는 것을 고려해볼 때, 우크라이나는 군대를 유지하는 데 큰 어려움을 겪을 것이다. 그래서 우크라이나는 서방의 경제적 피비호자로 남을 가능성이 크고, 미국 정부와 동맹국들은 당분간 국방비를 지원할 것이다.

10 논리완성　　⑤

다음 문장에서 direct line을 개통하자고 했으므로 이와 가장 유사한 ⑤ '직접적인 의사소통'이 적절하다.

adversary n. 적　step n. 단계　arrangement n. 준비　delay n. 지연　misreading n. 오독　crisis n. 위기　negotiation n. 협상　tentative a. 잠정적인　cease-fire n. 휴전

케네디는 두 적대국 사이에 직접적인 의사소통이 중요하다고 강조했다. 이러한 방향으로 가는 한 단계는 모스크바와 워싱턴 사이에 직통 전화선을 설치하여 위기 순간에 발생할 수 있는 양측의 위험한 지연, 오해, 상대방의 행동에 대한 오독을 피하자는 제안이다.

11 논리완성　　①

다음 문장에서 42개 중 41개에서 낙제했다고 했으므로, '형편없이 부족하다'라는 의미의 ①이 적절하다.

performance n. 성과　metrics n. 지표　woefully ad. 끔찍하게, 심히　inadequate a. 불충분한　optimistic a. 낙관적인

세계자원연구소는 기후 변화에 대응하기 위한 노력을 "심히 불충분하다"고 불렀는데, 42개 성과 지표 중 41개 지표에서 낙제점을 받았다.

12 논리완성　　⑤

'not A but B' 구문이므로 빈칸에는 뒤의 '협력, 협상' 등과 반대되는 의미의 표현이 필요하다. '억압하다, 제지하다'라는 의미의 contain이 포함돼 있는 ⑤가 정답으로 적절하다. ①은 문법적으로 attempting으로 고쳐야 하고, 고치더라도 eliminate는 완전히 없애는 것이므로 의미가 지나치게 과격하다.

grave a. 심각한　threat n. 위협　portray v. 묘사하다　living standard 생활수준　excellence n. 탁월성　vainly ad. 헛되이　cooperate v. 협력하다　negotiate v. 협상하다　contain v. 제지하다

내 생각에 중국은 미국이 매일 묘사하는 것처럼 심각한 위협이 아니다. 중국은 14억 인구를 보유한 오래된 문명으로 다른 성공한 국가들처럼 높은 생활수준과 기술적 탁월성을 목표로 하고 있다. 우리는 헛되이 중국을 억제하는 것이 아니라, 중국과 협력하고, 협상하고, 무역하고, 또 경제적으로 경쟁함으로써 우리의 전 세계적 문제를 가장 잘 해결할 수 있을 것이다.

13 논리완성　　②

resilience, perseverance와 관련된 표현은 ② tenacity이다.

setback n. 좌절　resilience n. 회복탄력성　perseverance n. 인내　in the face of ~에 직면하여　adversity n. 역경　aptitude n. 소질, 적성　tenacity n. 끈기　proclivity n. 성향　complacency n. 현실 안주　equivocation n. 얼버무리기

수많은 좌절에 직면했지만, 그 집단 구성원들은 놀라운 회복탄력성과 인내력을 보여주어, 역경에 맞선 그들의 끈기를 증명했다.

14 논리완성　　②

협상 기술이 뛰어난 외교관이라고 했고, 'not only ~ but also' 구문이므로, 뒤에도 마찬가지로 긍정적인 내용이 필요하다. 긍정적인 표현은 ② 밖에 없다.

diplomat n. 외교관　be instrumental in ~에 이바지하다　resolve v. 해결하다　protracted a. 오래 끈　showcase v. 보여주다　intricacy n. 복잡함　ersatz a. 모조품의　superficial a. 피상적인　perspicacious a. 명민한　discerning a. 안목이 있는　obtuse a. 둔감한　perfunctory a. 형식적인　ostentatious a. 과시하는　grandiloquent a. 호언장담하는　fortuitous a. 우연한　serendipitous a. 뜻밖의 발견을 할 수 있는

이 외교관의 미묘한 협상 기술은 장기화된 국제 분쟁 해결에 중요한 역할을 했을 뿐만 아니라, 외교적으로 복잡한 문제들에 대한 그의 통찰과 안목이 넘치는 이해를 보여주었다.

15 논리완성　　①

뒤의 분사구문에서 '지배적인 통념에 도전했다'고 하였으므로, 연구가 밝혀낸 관점은 새로 밝혀진, 이제까지는 비밀스럽게 숨겨져 있었던, 관점임을 알 수 있다. 따라서 ①이 적절하다.

unveil v. 밝히다 hitherto ad. 이제까지 perspective n. 관점, 시각 prevailing a. 지배적인 arcane a. 비밀의, 불가해한 cryptic a. 숨은, 신비의 ubiquitous a. 편재하는 pervasive a. 만연하는 didactic a. 교훈적인 pedantic a. 현학적인 cacophonous a. 귀에 거슬리는 dissonant a. 귀에 거슬리는 banal a. 진부한 trite a. 진부한

이 역사가의 연구는 고대 문명에 대한 이제껏 비밀스럽고 숨어있던 관점을 밝혀, 고대 문명의 사회 구조와 역사적 발전에 대한 지배적인 통념에 도전했다.

---

16 논리완성 ④

시대정신을 포착한다는 것은 '날카롭고 통렬한(poignant)' 표현임을 의미하며, 향수를 자아낸다는 것은 과거를 떠올리게 하는 '환기시키는(evocative)' 표현임을 의미한다. 따라서 ④가 정답이다.

be replete with ~으로 가득 차 있다 capture v. 포착하다 zeitgeist n. 시대정신 evoke v. 환기시키다 nostalgia n. 향수 anachronistic a. 시대착오적인 mellifluous a. 달콤한 sonorous a. 듣기 좋은 omnipresent a. 편재하는 poignant a. 통렬한 prosaic a. 따분한

그 극작가의 대사는 극의 배경이 된 당시의 시대정신을 포착하고 관객들에게 향수(鄕愁)를 불러일으키는 날카롭고 환기시키는 표현들로 가득했다.

17-18

우리는 안전을 위한 개인적인 열역학 임계값에 근접한 사람들에게 신호를 보낼 수 있는 시스템을 개발하기를 원하므로, 우리는 이 모든 생리적인 입력을 수집하여 상호 연관성을 확인해야 한다. 프랑스 의료 회사 BodyCap에서 개발한 이 알약에는 작은 배터리와 온도계와 데이터를 전달할 송신기가 들어가 있다.

signal v. 신호를 보내다 thermal a. 열의, 열량의 threshold n. 임계값 thermal threshold 열역학 임계값 house v. 수용하다 transmitter n. 송신기 physiological a. 생리적인 deliver v. 배달하다

---

17 빈칸완성 ①

사람의 열은 생리적인 현상이므로 빈칸 ⑧에는 physiological(생리적인)이 적절하고, transmitter(송신기)가 하는 일은 데이터를 전달하는 것이므로 빈칸 ⑧에는 communicate가 적절하다.

---

18 글의 제목 ⑤

이 글은 새롭게 개발된 '알약'의 기능을 설명하고 있으므로 ⑤가 제목으로 적절하다.

다음 중 이 글을 가장 잘 설명할 수 있는 제목은?
① 전자 안전의 중요성
② 개인 안전 분야에서 프랑스 의료 기업의 위상
③ 개인 안전에서 데이터의 중요성
④ 안전과 열역학 임계값의 관계
⑤ 차세대 기술로서의 전자 알약

19-20

여러 세대에 걸쳐 흑인들은 주택, 교육, 정치, 고용, 의료, 형사 사법 제도 등, 상상할 수 있는 모든 삶의 영역에서 차별을 겪어왔다. 오늘날 캘리포니아 주의 흑인들에게는 모종의 보상이 합당하며, 캘리포니아 주민 대부분은 현금 보상은 물론 다른 유형의 보상도 동의하고 지지하는 것으로 보인다. 캘리포니아 주 의원들은 이러한 권고사항들을 해결하는 어려운 과정을 바로 시작해야 한다. 그들이 하지 말아야 할 일은 이 보고서를 선반 위에 올려놓고 잊어버리는 것이다. 수 세기 동안 이어져 온 인종차별의 체계적인 잔학행위는 해결해야 할 때가 이미 지났다. 캘리포니아는 시작하기에 좋은 곳이다.

discrimination n. 차별 reparation n. 보상, 배상 be in order 합당하다 grapple v. 씨름하다, 해결하려고 고심하다 atrocity n. 잔학 행위 put aside 제쳐두다 sacrifice n. 희생 overdue a. 벌써 행해졌어야 할, 이미 늦어진

---

19 빈칸완성 ①

빈칸 ⑧의 경우, 다음 문장에서 뒤로 미루거나 잊어서는 안 된다고 했으므로, 어려운 문제라도 당장 착수해야 한다는 흐름이 되도록 must start가 적절하다. 빈칸 ⑧의 경우, 인종차별은 잔학한 행위이며 폭력 행위이므로 atrocities와 violence가 적절하다. 따라서 두 조건을 모두 만족시키는 ①이 정답이다.

---

20 내용파악 ④

마지막에서 두 번째 문장에서 '인종차별의 체계적인 잔학행위는 해결해야 할 때가 이미 지났다'고 했으므로 ④가 정답이다.

다음 중 이 글을 가장 잘 설명할 수 있는 것은?
① 흑인 보상 문제는 주 의원들이 잊을 것이다.
② 흑인 노예를 해방하겠다는 약속이 마침내 이루어졌다.
③ 불공정행위 피해자에 대해서는 금전적 보상이 일반적이다.
④ 노예의 후손들에 대한 보상은 이미 행해졌어야 했다.
⑤ 흑인 노예제도는 역사상 최악의 반인륜 범죄 중 하나였다.

21-22

파리 정상회의에 참석한 정상들은 세계은행, 아프리카개발은행, 아시아개발은행 등 다자개발은행(MDBs)의 공적 개발금융을 당장 대폭 확대해야 할 필요가 있다는 인식을 같이했다. 그러나 이 은행들이 필요한 만큼 대출을 확대하려면 미국, 유럽 및 기타 주요 경제권으로부터 더 많은 납입자본금이 필요할 것이다. 그러나 미국 의회는 더 많은 자본을 MDB들에 투자하기를 반대하며, 미국의 반대가 기후 변화에 대한 전 지구적 행동을 지금까지 가로막고 있다.

summit n. 정상회담 urgent a. 긴박한 massive a. 커다란 official a. 공적인 multilateral a. 다자간의 paid-in capital 납입자본 block v. 방해하다 accelerate v. 가속하다; 촉진하다 delay v. 연기하다 foot-dragging n. 망설임

21 빈칸완성 ②

앞 문장에서 더 많은 납입자본금을 필요로 할 것이라고 했다. 그런 다음에 시작하는 표현이 역접의 Yet이므로, 미국은 '납입자본금을 내지 않으려 한다, 투자에 반대한다'는 흐름을 만드는 oppose가 빈칸 Ⓐ에 적절하다. 뒤에도 이러한 '반대'가 방해물이 되고 있다고 해야 하므로 빈칸 Ⓑ에는 opposition이 들어가야 한다.

22 글의 제목 ④

마지막 문장이 주제문이다. 미국이 자본 투자를 반대하여 기후 변화에 맞서 싸우는 인류 전체의 노력에 방해가 되고 있다는 내용이므로, ④가 제목으로 적절하다.

다음 중 이 글을 가장 잘 설명할 수 있는 제목은?
① 프랑스와 미국의 관계
② 세계 은행들의 현황
③ 주요 경제국들과 세계 은행들
④ 기후 변화와 싸우는 데 있어서 미국의 지체함
⑤ 세계 은행들의 대규모 확장과 미국 자본의 부족

23-24

저명한 생물학자이자 지리학자 재레드 다이아몬드는 지리, 환경, 인간 사회 발전 사이의 복잡한 관계를 이해하는 데 크게 이바지했다. 그의 대표작 『총, 균, 쇠』는 역사의 흐름을 형성하는 데 있어 환경적 요인의 중추적인 역할을 강조함으로써, 전통적인 결정론적 통념에 도전하는 종합적인 연구이다. 이 획기적인 연구에서 다이아몬드는 작물로 재배 가능한 식물과 가축으로 사육 가능한 동물의 지리적 분포에 대해 탐구하며, 이러한 요소가 문명의 흥망성쇠에 영향을 미쳤다고 주장한다. 그는 이러한 자원의 이용가능성은 내재적인 우월성이나 열등성의 결과가 아니라 환경적 조건의 산물이라고 주장한다. 다이아몬드의 접근 방식은 인간 사회와 생태 환경 사이의 미묘한 상호작용을 강조함으로써 결정론적 관점에 도전하고 있다.

renowned a. 유명한 contribution n. 공헌 intricate a. 복잡한 seminal a. 중요한 comprehensive a. 종합적인 exploration n. 탐구 determinism n. 결정론 pivotal a. 중심이 되는 groundbreaking a. 획기적인 delve into 파고들다 distribution n. 분포 domesticable a. 가축화할 수 있는 be instrumental in ~에 공헌하다 availability n. 이용가능성 posit v. 주장하다 inherent a. 내재하는 interplay n. 상호작용 ecological a. 생태적인

23 내용파악 ⑤

첫 번째 문장과 마지막 문장에서 지리, 환경, 인간 사회 발전 사이의 상호작용에 초점을 맞추고 있음을 알 수 있다.

재레드 다이아몬드의 저서 『총, 균, 쇠』는 주로 무엇에 초점을 맞추고 있는가?
① 문명의 내재적 우월성 또는 열등성
② 문명의 흥망성쇠에서 역사 발전의 보편성
③ 환경적 요인의 전반적인 무의미성

24 내용파악 ③

마지막 문장에서 '인간 사회와 생태 환경 사이의 미묘한 상호작용을 강조함으로써'라고 했다.

다이아몬드의 접근 방식은 결정론적 관점에 어떻게 도전하는가?
① 역사의 지배적 성격을 주장함으로써
② 환경의 무관함을 다시 강조함으로써
③ 인간 사회와 생태 환경 간의 미묘한 상호작용을 강조함으로써
④ 내재적 우월성 또는 열등성으로 인한 역사적 결과의 불가피성을 제시함으로써
⑤ 문명의 발전에서 지리의 역할을 무시함으로써

25-26

철학에서 객체 개념은 뚜렷한 경계와 속성을 가진 독립체를 지칭하는 기본적인 주춧돌의 역할을 한다. 현대 철학자들이 제시하고 있는 객체 지향 존재론은 인간이든 비인간이든 모든 독립체는 동등한 존재론적 지위를 갖는다고 가정한다. 이 관점에 따르면, 객체의 작인과 존재의 이해는 인간 중심주의를 넘어서는 포괄적인 철학적 이해를 위해 매우 중요하다. 이 철학적 틀에서 객체는 현실의 복잡한 구조에 이바지하며, 비인간 독립체보다 인간의 경험을 우선시하는 전통적인 관점에 도전한다. 객체 지향 존재론은 객체에 내재하는 작인(作因)을 인정함으로써 존재의 다양한 표현을 포괄하는 보다 포괄적이고 확장된 세계관을 제시한다.

serve as ~의 역할을 하다 cornerstone n. 주춧돌 entity n. 독립체 property n. 자질 ontology n. 존재론 status n. 지위 perspective n. 관점, 전망 agency n. 작인(作因) crucial a. 결정적인, 중대한 anthropocentrism n. 인간중심주의 prioritize v. 우선시하다, 중요한 것부터 들다 expansive a. 포괄적인, 광범위한 encompass v. 포함하다 manifestation n. 징후, 표현

25 내용파악 ②

첫 문장이 '객체'라는 개념을 정의하고 있다.

뚜렷한 경계와 속성을 가진 독립체를 가리키는 철학의 기본 개념은 무엇인가?
① 주체
② 객체
③ 술어
④ 추상
⑤ 개념

26 내용파악 ④

세 번째 문장에서 '객체의 작인과 존재의 이해는 인간 중심주의를 넘어서는 포괄적인 철학적 이해를 위해 매우 중요하다'고 했으므로 ④가 정답이다.

객체 지향 존재론에 따르면, 포괄적인 철학적 이해를 위해 중요한 것은 무엇인가?
① 객체의 작인을 무시하는 것
② 인간 독립체에만 집중하는 것
③ 인간이 아닌 독립체의 존재를 무시하는 것
④ 객체의 작인과 존재를 이해하는 것
⑤ 인간 중심주의를 넘어선 현실의 구조를 거부하는 것

27-28

알베르 카뮈와 같은 사상가와 관련된 철학적 관점인 부조리주의는 삶에서 내재적 의미나 목적을 찾으려는 것은 쓸데없다고 주장한다. 카뮈는 인간의 조건은 의미에 대한 인간의 욕망과 우주의 명백한 무의미성 사이의 '부조리한' 충돌이라는 특징을 갖는다고 주장한다. 카뮈는 부조리에 맞서 삶의 불확실성을 받아들이고, 반항과 개인적 가치 추구를 통해 자신만의 의미를 창출하라고 제안한다. 이러한 관점은 실존주의와 대조를 이루는데, 실존주의도 의미의 문제를 가지고 씨름하지만, 개인이 자신의 목적을 창출해야 한다고 종종 주장한다.

absurdism n. 부조리주의 outlook n. 세계관 contend v. 주장하다 inherent a. 내재하는 futile a. 쓸데없는, 무익한 be characterized by ~라는 특징을 갖고 있다 clash n. 충돌 apparent a. 명백한 in the face of ~에 직면하여 embrace v. 받아들이다 rebellion n. 반역 existentialism n. 실존주의 stand in contrast to ~와 대조되다 grapple v. 씨름하다 readily ad. 쉽게, 순조롭게 definitive a. 확실한 predetermine v. 미리 결정하다 external a. 외적인

27 내용파악   ③

첫 번째 문장에서 내재적 의미를 찾으려는 것은 쓸데없다고 했고, 다음 문장에서 그 이유를 ③과 같이 설명하고 있다.

부조리주의에 따르면 내재적 의미를 찾는 것이 왜 쓸데없는가?
① 내재적 의미는 인간의 욕망을 통해 쉽게 얻을 수 있기 때문이다.
② 개인이 스스로 의미를 만들어야 하기 때문이다.
③ 인간의 조건은 부조리한 충돌을 특징으로 하기 때문이다.
④ 실존주의는 확실한 해답을 제공하기 때문이다.
⑤ 의미는 외부 요인에 의해 미리 결정되기 때문이다.

28 내용파악   ③

마지막에서 두 번째 문장에서 카뮈는 부조리한 현실에 맞서 반란을 일으키고, 우리의 행동과 가치를 통해 우리 자신의 의미를 창출해야 한다고 제안했다.

카뮈는 부조리에 대해 개인이 어떻게 대응하라고 제안하는가?
① 우주의 내재적인 무의미함을 받아들임으로써
② 이미 결정된 목적을 탐색하여 인생의 불확실성을 그대로 받아들임으로써
③ 부조리에 반대하고 자신만의 의미를 창조함으로써
④ 외부 요인에 의존하여 의미를 결정함으로써
⑤ 유의미한 삶이라는 문제에 대해 전적으로 반항함으로써

29 내용파악   ④

마지막 문장에서 '독자로 하여금 작중인물들의 미로 같은 마음속을 탐색하게 만든다'고 했다.

luminary n. 권위자 wield v. 휘두르다 unprecedented a. 전례 없는 craft v. 만들다 explore v. 탐구하다 recess n. 숨은 구석, 깊숙한 부분 magnum opus n. 걸작 testament n. 증거 profound a. 깊은, 심오한 stream-of-consciousness 의식의 흐름 navigate v. 항해하다, 항행하다 labyrinthine a. 미로와 같은 circumvent v. 우회하다 steer for 항해하다

모더니즘 문학의 거장 제임스 조이스는 전례 없이 정밀한 언어를 구사하여 인간 의식의 복잡한 심층을 탐구하는 서사(이야기)를 만들어냈다. 그의 걸작 『율리시스』는 의식의 흐름 서사 방식을 심오하게 활용한 하나의 증거로서, 독자로 하여금 작중인물들의 미로 같은 마음속을 탐색하게 만든다.

제임스 조이스가 그의 걸작 『율리시스』에서 의식의 흐름 서사 방식을 사용한 것은 모더니즘 문학에서 인간 의식의 탐구에 어떻게 기여하는가?
① 복잡한 인간 의식을 단순화함으로써
② 인간 의식의 복잡한 심층을 우회함으로써
③ 간접적인 서술 구조를 제시하여 독자의 마음을 정확하게 탐색하게 함으로써
④ 독자에게 작중인물들의 복잡한 마음속을 항해하도록 초대함으로써
⑤ 인간의 무의식에 대한 탐구를 완전히 피함으로써

30 내용파악   ②

두 번째 문장에 대한 재진술 문제이다. 생물학에서 시작된 적자생존 개념이 권력 구조가 지배권을 놓고 경쟁하는 정치 이데올로기에도 반영되어 있다는 말은, 생물학적 경쟁과 정치에서의 권력 경쟁에는 유사성이 있다는 말이다.

guiding force 원동력 tendril n. 영향력 realm n. 영역 mirror v. 비추다 vie for ~을 위해 경쟁하다 evolve v. 발전하다 embody v. 구현하다 at stake 위기에 처한 sustainability n. 지속 가능성 trajectory n. 궤도 ascendancy n. 지배 prioritize v. 우선시하다

생물학적 과정의 길잡이인 진화는 사회학과 정치학 영역으로 그 영향력을 확장하고 있다. 생물학에서 시작된 적자생존 개념은 권력 구조가 지배권을 놓고 경쟁하는 정치 이데올로기에도 반영되어 있다. 사회 구조는 내부 및 외부 압력에 대한 반응으로 발전하면서 적응 원리를 구현한다. 하지만 생태 위기에 직면한 지금, 생존의 본질 자체가 위태로워지면서 사회 패러다임에 대한 재평가를 촉진하고 현재 정치 궤도의 지속 가능성에 의문이 제기되고 있다.

이 글에 따르면 적자생존 개념은 정치 이데올로기에 어떻게 반영되어 있는가?
① 정치 이데올로기는 적자생존 개념과 아무런 관련이 없다.
② 정치 권력 구조는 지배를 위해 투쟁하며, 적자생존 원리를 구현하고 있다.
③ 적자생존은 생물학적 진화에도 적용된다.
④ 정치 이데올로기는 사회 구조를 통한 적자생존 개념보다 평등을 우선시한다.
⑤ 사회 구조는 정치의 적응 원칙에 영향을 미치지 않는다.

31 내용추론 ⑤

세 번째 문장이 신화가 타당한 경우를 설명하는데, '우리의 생각과 마음을 바꾸고 새로운 희망을 주며 더 온전히 살도록 만든다면'이라고 했으므로 ⑤ 신화의 타당성은 (긍정적으로 변화된) 생각과 마음의 힘에 달려 있다고 할 수 있다.

factual a. 사실에 기반을 둔, 사실을 담은 compel v. 강요하다 valid a. 타당한 incomprehensible a. 이해할 수 없는 boring a. 지겨운 directive n. 지시

따라서 신화는 사실적인 정보를 제공하기 때문이 아니라 효과적이기 때문에 사실이다. 하지만 신화가 우리에게 삶의 더 깊은 의미에 대한 새로운 통찰을 제공하지 못한다면 그것은 실패한 것이다. 신화가 효과가 있다면, 다시 말해서 우리의 생각과 마음을 바꾸고 새로운 희망을 주며 더 온전히 살도록 만든다면, 그것은 타당한 신화이다. 신화는 본질적으로 우리가 더 풍요롭게 살기 위해 무엇을 해야 하는지 알려주는 지침이다. 신화를 우리 상황에 적용하고 우리 삶에서 현실로 만들지 않으면, 신화는 게임을 시작하기 전까지는 혼란스럽고 지루해 보이는 보드게임 규칙처럼 이해하기 어렵고 먼 이야기로 남을 것이다.

다음 중 위 글에서 가장 정확하게 추론할 수 있는 것은?
① 신화는 이해할 수 없어도 우리에게 풍부한 삶의 감각을 준다.
② 신화는 사실적인 정보를 제공하지 않기 때문에 우리는 흔히 신화에 혼란스러워하고 지루해한다.
③ 신화는 우리가 그 지시를 따를 때만 우리를 변화시킬 것이다.
④ 우리는 신화의 사실로 인해 하는 수 없이 풍요롭고 온전한 삶을 살아야 한다.
⑤ 신화의 타당성은 인간의 마음과 정신의 힘에 달려 있다.

32 내용추론 ②

기후 변화를 통제하려는 노력이 정체 상태에 있으며, 이 문제는 급박하게 해결을 요한다는 문장에 더하여, 물 안보에도 비슷한 합의가 전문가들 사이에 이루어지고 있다고 이야기하며 끝을 맺고 있다. 따라서 지금의 기후 위기와 잠재적인 물 위기를 병치해서, 물에도 마찬가지 관심을 쏟아야 한다고 추론할 수 있다.

address v. 해결하다 lag v. 지체되다 stalled a. 정체된 sustainable a. 지속 가능한 trajectory n. 궤도 delay n. 지체 add to 더하다 urgency n. 급박성 resilience n. 회복 탄력성 global warming 지구 온난화 consensus n. 합의 security n. 보장 undo v. 망치다 front n. 분야

기후 변화를 해결하기 위한 전 지구적인 협상이 시작된 지 거의 30년이 지났지만, 문제를 통제하려는 노력은 더디게 진행되고 있으며, 이는 지속 가능한 폭넓은 궤도를 만들려는 진행이 지체되고 있다는 것을 반영하고 있다. 매년 지체가 쌓이면서 문제는 더욱 급박해지고 있으며, 지구 온난화의 가장 심각한 영향으로부터 지구의 회복력을 유지해야 할 필요성 역시 급박해지고 있다. 이제 물 안보에 대해서도 이와 비슷한 전문가들 사이의 합의가 형성되고 있다.

다음 추론 중 위의 문장에서 가장 적절하게 뒷받침하고 있는 것은?
① 대부분 국가가 물을 소홀히 하면 다른 분야에서 이룬 진전을 망칠 수 있다는 사실을 이해하는 것 같다.

② 우리는 기후 위기와 같은 수준의 관심과 행동으로 대처해야 할 전 지구적 물 위기에 직면해 있다.
③ 기후와 물 위기의 연관성은 지구의 회복력 유지 능력이라는 더 광범위한 문제를 가리킨다.
④ 더 늦기 전에 기후와 물 중 더 시급히 보호해야 할 것을 선택해야 한다.
⑤ 지구 온난화의 심각한 영향은 가까운 미래에 물 안보라는 중요한 상황으로 인해 지연될 것이다.

33 내용파악 ③

두 번째 문장과 마지막 문장에서 말하듯이 의도적인 모호성은 현실과 허구의 경계에 대해 질문하게 하고 이야기의 '진실'의 성격에 대해 생각하게 만든다.

unreliable narrator 믿을 수 없는 화자 odyssey n. 탐사, 여정 reminiscent a. 연상시키는 delve into 파고들다 navigate v. 항해하다 serve as ~의 역할을 하다 subjectivity n. 주체성 permeate v. 스며들다 allure n. 매력 craft v. 만들다 ambiguity n. 모호성 dynamic a. 역동적인 have an impact on 영향을 미치다 irrelevant a. 무관한 accentuate v. 강조하다

문학이라는 복잡한 태피스트리(장식용 직물)와 스토리텔링이라는 예술적 교향곡 속에서 믿을 수 없는 서술자에 대한 연구는 진실과 인식 사이의 춤으로의 문학적 모험여행(탐구)이 된다. 서사적 소네트(짧은 시)를 연상시키는 문학 분석은 의도적으로 오해를 불러일으키는 서사를 가진 등장인물을 탐구하여, 독자로 하여금 현실과 허구의 경계에 대해 질문하도록 유도한다. 문학 학자들이 고전 소설과 현대 작품을 탐색할 때, 믿을 수 없는 서술자가 그저 단순한 플롯 장치로 작동하는지, 아니면 인간의 주체성에 대한 심오한 탐구 역할을 하는지의 문제가 논의에 스며들게 된다. 의도적으로 모호하게 만들어진 서사의 매력은 스토리텔링에서 진실의 성격과 작가, 등장인물, 독자 간의 역동적인 관계에 대한 고찰을 불러일으킨다.

위 글에서 논의된 스토리텔링에서의 진실의 성격에 대한 고려에서 의도적인 모호성은 어떤 역할을 하는가?
① 의도적인 모호성은 스토리텔링에서 진실의 성격에 대한 고려에 영향을 미치지 않는다.
② 스토리텔링에서 진실의 성격에 대한 고려는 의도적인 모호성과는 무관하다.
③ 이 글에서 의도적인 모호성은 문학이라는 넓은 환경 속에서 스토리텔링에서의 진실의 성격에 대한 고찰을 제기한다.
④ 서사적 소네트에 의해 풍성해진 문학 분석은 스토리텔링에서 진실의 성격에서 의도적인 모호성의 역할을 강조한다.
⑤ 진실과 인식 사이의 복잡한 춤은 이 글의 의도적인 모호성으로 더욱 부각된다.

01 ②	02 ①	03 ④	04 ⑤	05 ③	06 ④	07 ②	08 ①	09 ⑤	10 ①
11 ①	12 ⑤	13 ①	14 ④	15 ⑤	16 ⑤	17 ②	18 ⑤	19 ①	20 ③
21 ③	22 ②	23 ③	24 ④	25 ②	26 ③	27 ②	28 ④	29 ②	30 ⑤
31 ④	32 ④	33 ③							

01 동의어

deconstruction n. 해체 examine v. 검토하다 binary opposition 이항대립 construct v. 구성하다, 구축하다 destabilize v. 불안정하게 만들다, 허물다(= undermine) reshuffle v. 개편[개각]하다 allocate v. 할당하다 cultivate v. 기르다, 육성하다

해체는 텍스트의 이항 대립이 구성되는 방식을 검토한 후 이런 대립을 허물어 의미의 복잡성과 유동성을 드러내는 일이다.

02 동의어 ①

disparity n. 불일치(= incongruity) outcome n. 결과 colon cancer 대장암 narrow v. 좁아지다 high-quality n. 고품질 consistency n. 일관성, 일치 likeness n. 유사성

연구자들의 새로운 분석은 흑인 및 백인 대장암 환자들의 결과가 드러내는 고통스러운 불일치가, 병원에서 모든 환자를 동일한 수준의 고품질 치료로 치료하기만 하면 좁혀진다는 것을 암시한다.

03 동의어 ④

factor n. 요인 admission n. 입학허가 controversial a. 논란이 되는 constitutional a. 헌법에 맞는, 합헌의(= legal) illicit a. 불법의 unauthorized a. 공인[승인]되지 않은 illegitimate a. 불법의

미국에서는 인종을 대학 입학에 있어서의 한 요소로 포함시키는 것이 늘 논란의 대상이 되었다. 그러나 그것은 또한 되풀이해서 합헌으로 간주되었다.

04 문의 구성 ⑤

The commercial interests가 주어이고 comparable이라는 형용사를 보어로 하는 동사가 필요하다. 따라서 2형식 동사 aren't와 부사 always로 된 ⑤가 정답이다. ①과 ④는 2형식 동사가 아니며 ②와 ③은 전치사 against 다음에 형용사 comparable이 이어질 수 없다.

commercial a. 상업의 comparable a. 비교할 만한, 비슷한, 필적할 만한 go against ~에 거스르다 serve v. 봉사하다; 복무하다

술과 담배와 화석연료를 비롯한 수많은 산업의 상업적 이해관계가 공적 이익이나 인간의 건강과 늘 비교될 수 있는 것은 아니다.

05 부대상황의 분사구문

주어 coastal erosion 앞에 '지구 온난화가 해수면에 영향을 끼치는 상황에서'라는 표현을 쓰려면 'with+명사+v~ing'의 부대 상황의 분사구문을 써야 한다. 따라서 정답은 ③이다.

affect v. 영향을 끼치다 coastal erosion 해안침식 address v. 다루다 COP28 제28차 유엔기후변화협약 당사국총회

지구 온난화가 해수면에 영향을 끼치는 가운데, 해안침식은 12월 두바이에서 COP28을 위해 지도자들이 만날 때 이들이 다루게 될 주제 중의 하나가 될 것이다.

06 논리완성

앞에서 절대적 자유는 없고 모든 자유는 서로 균형을 이루어야 한다고 한 것은 모든 자유의 가치가 같음을 말한다. AR-15 총기 소지권이란 내 생명을 지킬 나의 생명권을 말하며 이것이 다른 사람의 생명권과 똑같이 신성하다는 의미이므로 빈칸에는 같음을 나타내는 ④가 적절하다.

absolute a. 절대적인 reasoned a. 합리적인 typical a. 전형적인 inevitably ad. 불가피하게 sacred a. 신성한 significantly ad. 상당히 slightly ad. 약간 AR-15 n. 돌격소총

사회에 절대적 자유 같은 것은 없다. 서로 다른 자유들이 서로 균형을 이루어야 하며, 전형적인 미국인들 사이의 그 어떤 이성적인 논의도 AR-15 총기 소지권이 타인들의 생명권보다 더 신성하지는 않다는 결론을 반드시 내리게 될 것이다.

07 비교 구문 ②

빈칸 이하에 동사가 없어 관계절이 될 수 없으므로 관계사를 사용하지 않은 ②가 정답이다. 'favor A to B' 구문으로 students with a strong liberal arts background와 those with degree in practical fields가 병치를 이룬다.

favor v. 선호하다, 좋아하다 liberal arts 기초교양, 인문학 practical field 실용분야

2013년 미국대학협회가 고용주를 대상으로 조사해서 얻은 증거에 따르면 일부 고용주들은 경영 같은 "실용" 분야의 학위 소지자들보다 강력한 인문학 배경을 가진 학생들을 선호하는 것으로 나타났다.

08 논리완성 ①

두 번째 문장의 술부 prevents that happening이 '생명을 살리지 못하게 만든다'는 뜻이므로, 주어인 Using Islamophobic and racist tropes는 절대로 하지 말아야 할 행동이다. 강한 금지의 의미를 이루기에 적절한 부사어로는 ① '심지어 우발적으로라도'가 적절하다.

immediate a. 즉각적인, 즉시의 Islamophobic a. 이슬람교 혐오의 racist a. 인종차별의 trope n. 말의 수사(修辭); 비유적 용법 silence v. 침묵하게 하다 debate n. 논쟁

즉각적인 초점은 생명을 살리는 것이어야 한다. 이슬람교 혐오적이거나 인종차별적인 언어를 공개 석상에서 토론을 잠재우는 방식으로 심지어 우발적으로라도 사용하는 것은 가자 지구와 미국 모두에서 생명을 살리지 못하게 만든다.

09 논리완성 ⑤

어떤 정책의 복잡함은 이미 복잡한 것을 완화시킬 수는 없고 복잡한 면면들을 이해할 수 있게 명쾌하게 설명해야 할 필요가 있는 것이다. 따라서 ⑤ elucidating이 가장 적절하다.

task v. ~에게 과제를 맡기다 intricacy n. 복잡성, 복잡한 사항 weigh v. 저울질하다, 평가하다 potential a. 잠재적인, 가능한 stakeholder n. 이해관계 당사자 mitigate v. 완화하다 obfuscate v. 혼란을 주다 intimidate v. 위협하다 juxtapose v. 병치시키다 elucidate v. 명료히 설명하다, 자세히 설명하다

그 팀은 제안된 정책의 복잡성을, 그 정책이 다양한 이해집단에 끼치는 잠재적 영향을 세심하게 비교하여, 명료히 설명하는 과제를 부여받았다.

10 논리완성 ①

한국의 대학에서 한국사를 전공한 사람이라면 한국어 구사가 엉터리라거나 서툴거나 초보적이라기보다는 완벽할 것이다. 그러므로 ① impeccable이 정답이다.

impeccable a. 흠잡을 데 없는 broken a. 서투른 receptive a. 선뜻 받아들이는, 포용적인 rudimentary a. 기초의, 제대로 발달하지 못한

던컨은 한국어를 완벽하게 구사하는데, 단지 한국의 대학에서 한국사로 학부 과정을 이수했기 때문에 그렇게 할 수 있다고 말했다.

11 논리완성 ①

push the boundaries of(~의 경계를 밀어내다)는 '~의 영역을 확대하다'는 의미이고 전위 예술은 전통과 관습에 도전하므로, 빈칸에는 앞에 나온 unconventional과 같은 의미의 ① '인습타파적인'이 적절하다.

avant-garde n. 예술의 전위적인 사상이나 예술가들 boundary n. 경계 norm n. 규범 iconoclastic a. 우상이나 인습을 타파하는 derivative a. 다른 것을 본뜬, 새롭지 않은 ostentatious a. 과시하는, 호사스러운 ubiquitous a. 도처에 존재하는 placid a. 고요한, 평온한

그 전위 예술가의 조각에 대한 비관습적인 접근법은 전통적인 규범과 관습에 도전하면서 인습타파적인 예술의 영역을 확대해나갔다.

12 논리완성 ⑤

한국이 "훌륭한 코리아"라는 긍정적 명성을 얻으려면 결합된 것 두 가지가 모두 좋은 것이어야 한다. 따라서 빈칸에는 ⑤가 가장 적절하다.

emerge v. 나타나다, 출현하다 cool a. 훌륭한, 근사한 take root 뿌리를 내리다 DMZ n. 비무장지대 gap n. 격차

한국어는 K팝과 첨단기술의 결합으로부터 출현한 한국의 "훌륭한 코리아" 이미지와 더불어 성장했다. 이런 이미지는 미국을 비롯하여 전 세계에 뿌리를 내렸다.

13 논리완성 ①

혁신적인 사업가는 선구적인 전략과 획기적인 아이디어에 대한 '기호와 성향'을 가지고 있다는 흐름이 되는 것이 자연스럽다.

entrepreneur n. 사업가, 창업주 innovative a. 혁신적인 disrupt v. 혼란을 초래하다, 방해하다 testament n. 증거 pioneering a. 선구적인 groundbreaking a. 혁신적인, 획기적인 penchant n. 애호, 기호 inclination n. 성향 proclivity n. 애호 disparity n. 불일치 aversion n. 혐오 antipathy n. 반감 breaker n. 파괴자, 파쇄기

그 사업가의 혁신적 사업 모델은 전통 시장에 혼란을 초래했을 뿐 아니라 선구적인 전략과 획기적인 아이디어에 대한 그녀의 기호와 성향을 보여주는 증거로 기능했다.

14 논리완성 ④

All이라는 단어를 통해 대한민국 거주 외국인들 전체가 지켜야 하는 '의무사항'을 말하고 있음을 알 수 있다. 그러므로 정답으로는 ④가 적절하다.

national n. 시민, 국민 premium n. 보험료 income n. 소득 asset n. 자산 exempt v. ~을 면제시키다 require v. 요구하다 waive v. (권리 등을) 포기하다

대한민국에 6개월 이상 거주하는 모든 외국인은 국민건강보험에 등록하고 소득과 자산에 기초해 매달 보험료를 내야 한다.

15 논리완성 ⑤

빈칸 뒤에서 subtle emotions(미묘한 감정)이라고 한 것과 부합하게 각 색조가 신중한 뉘앙스와 섬세함을 지녔다는 흐름이 되도록 빈칸에는 ⑤가 들어가야 한다.

decorative a. 장식용의, 장식성의 hue n. 색조 deliberate a. 신중한
convey v. 전달하다 subtle a. 미묘한 contribute to ~에 기여하다
overall a. 전체적인, 전반적인 thematic a. 주제의 richness n. 풍성함
milieu n. 환경 ambiance n. 환경, 분위기 panacea n. 만병통치약
modicum n. 소량 smattering n. 소량 confluence n. 합류, 융합
amalgamation n. 결합, 혼합 nuance n. 미묘한 차이, 뉘앙스

그 화가의 색 사용은 장식적이기만 한 것은 아니다. 각 색조는 신중한
뉘앙스와 섬세함이어서, 미묘한 감정을 전달하고 전반적인 이야기와 주제
의 풍부함에 기여한다.

16 문의 구성　　　　　　　　　　　　　　　⑤

빈칸 이하에 두 개의 절이 이어져 있으므로 빈칸에는 부사절을 이끄는
접속사가 와야 함을 알 수 있다. 따라서 정답은 ⑤이다.

insight n. 통찰 shortchange v. ~에 못 미치다, 충족시키지 못하다
advocate n. 옹호자, 대변자 representative a. 대표하는 just a. 공정
한 literacy n. 문해력 for a time being 당분간 within the limit
테두리 내에서 more or less 대략, 거의 without limitation 제한 없이

집단의 모든 구성원은 우리의 집단지성을 증가시키는 가치 있고 필수적인
통찰력을 갖고 있다. 그러나 우리 집단의 정보 밥상과 문해력을 진지하게
받아들이지 않는다면 그리고 받아들일 때까지는, 우리는 어렵고 복잡한
결정을 내리는 능력을 계속 온전히 발휘하지 못하게 될 것이다. 대표성이
더 크고 공정하며 평등한 민주주의의 옹호자들은 문해력의 대변자가 될
필요성을 인식해야 한다.

17-18

수십만 명의 미국인들이 매년 멕시코 국경을 넘어 로스 알고도네스라는
작은 도시로 간다. 태양과 모래를 찾아서가 아니라 치근관과 치과용 라미
네이트를 찾아서 가는 것이다. 약 600명의 치과의사들이 네 개의 주요
거리에 꽉 들어차 있어서 미국 내 치과 비용의 일부만으로 치과 진료를
해준다. 로스 알고도네스는 미국인들에게 "어금니 도시"라고 더 잘 알려져
있다. 인터넷 덕분에 치료용 쇼핑이 더 쉬워지기 한참 전에 이미 입소문에
의해 퍼진 별명이다.

border n. 국경 tiny a. 아주 작은 canal n. 치근관, 이뿌리쪽 공간
veneer n. 치과용 라미네이트 cram v. 밀어 넣다 fraction n. 일부
molar n. 어금니

17 빈칸완성　　　　　　　　　　　　　　　　②

인터넷 덕분에 치료용 쇼핑이 더 쉬워지기 전부터 이미 입소문이 났었
다는 의미가 되는 것이 가장 자연스럽다. 따라서 정답은 ②가 된다.

빈칸 ⓐ와 ⓑ에 들어가기에 가장 적절한 표현은?
① 뉴스 ― 사용 가능한
② 입소문 ― 더 쉬운
③ 자동차 ― 의미있는
④ 신문광고 ― 덜 비싼
⑤ 여행자 ― 평균의

18 글의 제목　　　　　　　　　　　　　　　⑤

미국인들이 싼 치과 진료를 찾아 멕시코의 작은 도시로 간다는 내용이므
로 ⑤가 제목으로 적절하다.

이 글의 제목으로 가장 적절한 것은?
① 멕시코는 치과 치료와 서비스의 역사가 더 길다.
② 미국인과 멕시코인들은 더 나은 치과 의술을 두고 경쟁하고 있다.
③ 멕시코인들은 더 양질의 치과 진료를 받고 있다.
④ 멕시코는 미국보다 치과의사 수가 더 많다.
⑤ 미국인들은 멕시코의 한 도시에서 더 싼 치과 진료를 찾고 있다.

19-20

미국 헌법의 주요 저자였던 제임스 매디슨은 로크의 열렬한 지지자였다.
그는 노예를 소유한 부자 가문에 태어나 대중으로부터 부를 지키는 데
관심이 있었다. 매디슨은 국민이 정치에 직접 참여하는 직접 민주주의를
두려워했고 국민이 국민의 이익을 대변할 것으로 추정되는 대표를 선출하
는 대의제 정부를 옹호했다. 매디슨은 지방 정부를 두려워했는데, 지방
정부는 국민과 너무 가까워 부의 재분배를 지지할 가능성이 너무 컸기
때문이었다. 따라서 매디슨은 먼 수도에 있는 연방 정부를 주창했다.

ardent a. 열렬한 enthusiast n. 애호가, 지지자 mass n. 대중 fear
v. 두려워하다 champion v. 주창하다, 옹호하다 representative a.
대표하는, 대의제의 redistribution n. 재분배 far-off a. 멀리 떨어진
casting vote 캐스팅보트(합의체의 의결에서 가부가 동수인 경우에 의장
이 가지는 결정권)

19 빈칸완성　　　　　　　　　　　　　　　　①

국민이 정치에 직접 참여하는 체제는 '직접 민주주의'이고, 이것을 반대
한 매디슨이 옹호한 것은 수도의 중앙정부가 지방정부를 통제하는 '연
방 정부 체제'이다. 따라서 정답은 ①이다.

빈칸 ⓐ와 ⓑ에 들어가기에 가장 적절한 표현은?
① 직접 민주주의 ― 연방 정부
② 직접 구하기 ― 강력한 헌법
③ 투표권 ― 직접 투자
④ 미디어 비평 ― 금융 지원
⑤ 캐스팅보트 ― 강한 정부

20 글의 제목　　　　　　　　　　　　　　　③

미국 헌법의 창시자 매디슨의 정치관을 다루는 글로 건국 초 미국 정치
의 실상을 엿보게 하므로 제목으로는 ③ '미국 정치의 성격'이 적절하다.

위 글의 제목으로 가장 적절한 것은?
① 민주주의의 약점
② 부를 촉진하는 방법
③ 미국 정치의 성격
④ 국민의 대표들
⑤ 지방정부의 정치 유세

21-22

미학과 음악에서 광범위하게 탐구되고 있는 공명(共鳴)은 심오한 함의를 가진 다면적 개념으로 기능한다. 미학에서 공명은 예술작품이나 개념이 감정적 혹은 지적 반응을 불러일으켜 관객이나 독자와의 뜻깊은 연계를 창출할 때 나타난다. 음악 분야에서 공명은 소리의 확장과 연장을 포함함으로써 청각 경험을 풍요롭게 하고 정서적 심오함을 불러일으킨다. 공명 현상은 개인 지각의 경계를 초월하여 다양한 관객들 전체에 울림을 주는 공유된 경험을 길러준다. 미술과 음악이 정서적 표현의 강력한 전달자가 되어 창작자와 관중 혹은 감상자 사이에 다리를 만드는 것은 바로 공명을 통해서이다.

resonance n. 공명(共鳴) explore v. 탐색하다 extensively ad. 광범위하게 aesthetics n. 미학 multifaceted a. 다면적인 profound a. 심오한 implication n. 함의 manifest v. 드러나다 evoke v. 불러일으키다 realm n. 분야, 영역 conduit n. 관, 도관; 전달자

21 내용파악 ③

공명 개념은 미학과 음악에서 탐구가 광범위하게 이루어진다고 했으므로 정답은 ③이다.

개념으로서의 공명이 자주 탐색되는 분야는 어디인가?
① 정치
② 윤리학
③ 미학
④ 형이상학
⑤ 인식론

22 내용파악 ②

공명은 음악에서 소리의 확대와 연장을 포함한다고 했으므로 정답은 ② 이다.

공명은 음악의 맥락에서 무엇을 포함하는가?
① 음향의 제한
② 음향의 확대와 연장
③ 정서적 깊이의 제거
④ 관객과 관찰자 창의력으로부터의 분리
⑤ 청각 경험의 감소

23-24

현재 시점에서의 인공지능의 제약을 살펴본 후, 나는 예술가들과 다른 발명가들이 조만간 멸종 위기에 빠지리라고는 생각지 않는다. 내 생각에, 그리고 많은 이론가들과 비평가들과 미디어 애호가들의 생각에, 가장 설득력 있는 표현들은 살아있는 인간의 경험을 반영하는 어느 정도 독창적인 생각을 담고 있는데, 우리 시대 인공지능 모델에는 정확히 이 능력이 없다. 인공지능 보트가 꽤 괜찮은 텍스트 블록을 만들어내고 매력적인 그래픽 디자인을 만들어낼 수 있다 하더라도 이들은 우리의 인간성에 말을 거는 진정한 예술을 만들어낼 순 없다.

take stock of ~을 찬찬히 조사하다, 살피다 limitation n. 한계, 제약 inventor n. 발명가 extinction n. 멸종 theorist n. 이론가 critic

n. 비평가 compelling a. 강력한 lived a. 살아있는 contemporary a. 당대의, 현대의, 우리 시대의 bot n. 보트(특정 작업을 반복 수행하는 프로그램) passable a. 그런대로 괜찮은 captivating a. 매력적인 fabricate v. 만들어내다 speak to ~와 연결되다, ~에게 말을 걸다

23 빈칸완성 ③

인간의 능력을 따라잡는 인공지능은 아직 나오지 않았다는 내용이 주제이므로 인간 예술가들이 멸종(extinction)할 위험은 없다고 해야 한다. 그리고 진정한 예술은 인공지능과 반대인 인간에게 말을 거는 예술이어야 하므로 genuine이 들어가야 한다. 따라서 정답은 ③이다.

빈칸 Ⓐ와 Ⓑ에 들어가기에 가장 적절한 표현은?
① 생존 — 생생한
② 번영하는 — 원시적인
③ 멸종 — 진정한
④ 재창조 — 인상적인
⑤ 상상력 — 복잡한

24 글의 제목 ④

인공지능이 아직은 인간의 독창성을 따라잡지 못한다는 내용이 주제이므로 정답은 ④이다.

이 글의 제목으로 가장 적절한 것은?
① 인공지능의 현재 시점에서의 제약은 가까운 미래에 극복될 것이다.
② 인공지능과 인간은 가장 높은 수준의 예술을 놓고 경쟁 중이다.
③ 인공지능은 예술가와 발명가를 위험에 빠뜨릴 수 있다.
④ 인공지능은 독창적인 인간 창의력의 경이로움을 재현할 수 없다.
⑤ 인공지능 보트는 대개 인간 경험과 아이디어를 모방하고 있다.

25-26

게임이론은 수학과 경제학의 분과로, 합리적 의사결정자들 간의 전략적 상호작용을 분석한다. 게임이론은 각 참가자의 결과가 그들 각자의 선택뿐 아니라 상대의 선택에도 의존하는 상황을 탐색한다. 게임이론가들은 개인들이나 독립체들이 경쟁하거나 협력하는 시나리오에서 어떻게 행동할지 예측하고 파악하기 위한 모델을 사용한다. 죄수의 딜레마라는, 게임이론의 고전적 사례는 개인의 합리성과 집단의 합리성 간의 긴장을 잘 보여준다. 이 딜레마는 개인들이 자신의 이익을 위해 행동할 때 집단적으로는 최적이 아닌 결과를 초래하는 상황을 드러낸다.

interaction n. 상호작용 rational a. 합리적인 decision-maker n. 의사결정자 participant n. 참가자 entity n. 실체, 독립체 illustrate v. 예시하다 highlight v. 두드러지게 보여주다, 강조하다 suboptimal a. 최적이 아닌 cooperative a. 협력하는 competitive a. 경쟁하는

25 내용파악 ②

게임이론이 분석하는 것은 합리적 의사결정자들의 전략적 상호작용이다. 따라서 정답은 ②이다.

게임이론은 무엇을 분석하는가?
① 자기 이익과 집단적 결과 사이의 개인의 선택
② 합리적 의사결정자들 간의 전략적 상호작용
③ 협력 시나리오와 참가자 경쟁
④ 집단 합리성을 위한 경쟁 시나리오
⑤ 불합리한 의사결정과 최적이 아닌 결과

인식론적 다원주의는 무엇을 독려하는가?
① 지식 체계에 대한 폐쇄적 탐색
② 지식 접근법의 거부
③ 지식 탐색에 대한 배타적 방법에 대한 의존
④ 다양한 지식 체계에 대한 개방적 탐색
⑤ 상이한 문화의 통찰을 무시하는 것

26 내용파악 ③

죄수의 딜레마는 개인의 합리성과 집단의 합리성 간의 긴장을 보여준다고 했으므로 정답은 ③이다.

죄수의 딜레마는 무엇을 예시하는가?
① 협력적 결과의 불가피성
② 개인 합리성과 집단 합리성 간의 조화
③ 합리적 결정을 내릴 때 행위자들 간의 긴장
④ 집단 합리성 내의 최적이 아닌 결과의 부재
⑤ 개인 선택의 예측 가능성

27-28

인식론적 다원주의는, 지식 철학 내의 한 관점으로, 세상을 알고 이해하는 방식이 많다고 주장한다. 단일한 보편적 지식 습득 방법을 주장하는 인식론적 일원론과 달리, 인식론적 다원주의자들은 다양한 지식 접근법의 타당성을 옹호한다. 이 관점은 서로 다른 문화와 학문과 탐구 방식들이 현실의 성격에 대한 가치 있고 뚜렷한 통찰을 제공할 수 있다고 생각한다. 인식론적 다원주의는 다양한 지식 체계에 대한 개방적 탐색을 독려한다.

epistemological a. 인식론적인 pluralism n. 다원주의 perspective n. 견해, 관점, 시각 contend v. 주장하다 multiple a. 다수의 monism n. 일원론 assert v. 주장하다 legitimacy n. 타당성, 정당성 epistemic a. 지식의 discipline n. 학문 inquiry n. 탐구 distinct a. 뚜렷한, 분명한 open-minded a. 열린, 개방적인 exploration n. 탐색

27 내용파악 ②

인식론적 다원주의가 주장하는 바가 첫 문장의 that절에 표현되어 있다.

인식론적 다원주의는 무엇을 주장하는가?
① 지식을 습득하는 단일한 보편적 방법이 있다.
② 세계에 대한 지식으로 이끄는 다수의 방법이 있어야 한다.
③ 다양한 지식 접근법은 다수의 문화와 사회에 타당하지 않다.
④ 상이한 문화들은 현실의 성격에 대한 똑같은 통찰을 제공한다.
⑤ 인식론적 일원론은 철학 지식에서 유효한 접근법이다.

28 내용파악 ④

인식론적 다원주의는 다양한 지식체계에 대한 개방적 통찰을 독려한다고 했으므로 정답은 ④이다.

29 내용파악 ②

양자역학의 불확정성의 원리는 위치와 운동량(속도) 같은 특성의 특정한 쌍은 동시에 정확히 알 수 없다고 상정한다고 했으므로, 불확정성 원리의 주장은 동시 정확성의 불가능성이다. 따라서 정답은 ②이다.

quantum mechanics 양자역학(미시 물리학 분야) uncertainty principle 불확정성 원리 posit v. 상정하다, 받아들이다 inherent a. 내재하는 challenge v. 도전하다, 반대하다 determinism n. 결정론 highlight v. 강조하다, 돋보이게 하다 probabilistic a. 확률적인, 확률론적 underscore v. 강조하다

양자역학은 불확정성의 원리를 도입한다. 불확정성의 원리는 베르너 하이젠베르그가 공식화한 것으로, 위치와 운동량(속도) 같은 특성의 특정한 쌍은 동시에 정확히 알 수 없다고 상정한다. 정확성의 이 내재적 한계는 결정론이라는 고전적 개념에 도전을 가하며, 양자 체계의 근본적 확률성을 강조한다. 불확정성 원리는 특정한 물리적 속성을 정확히 측정하는 우리 능력의 한계를 강조한다.

양자역학의 불확정성 원리는 특정한 특성 쌍에 관해 어떤 주장을 하는가?
① 양자역학의 정적 성격
② 동시적 정확성의 불가능성
③ 결정론의 확실성
④ 양자 체계의 불확실성
⑤ 불확정성 원리의 확률의 내재적 한계

30 내용파악 ⑤

미국의 기후 분담금에 대한 갈등을 다루는 글이므로 결론은 이번 기후회의의 결론이 부유한 나라들의 산업발전으로 인한 기후 재난을 빈곤 국가들이 더 많이 당한다는 '기후 정의'와 기후 위기를 해결하기 위한 자금을 조달해야 하는 '재정 문제'라고 추론할 수 있다. 따라서 정답은 ⑤이다.
① 부유한 나라가 자기 책임을 다하지 않을 때 시정을 촉구할 수는 있으나 부유한 나라이기 때문에 책임을 져야 한다고 결론 내리는 것은 비논리적이다.

climate conference 기후회의 painfully ad. 고통스럽게 emergency n. 긴급사태, 위기 turn one's back on A A에 등 돌리다, 거부하다 deny v. 부인하다, 부정하다 accountability n. 책임 current a. 현재의 emissions n. 방출물, 배기가스, 배출 costly a. 비싼 gross domestic product 국내총생산(= GDP) levy n. 추가부담금 within reach 손이 닿는 곳에 있는, 힘이 미치는 곳에 (있는)

올해의 기후회의를 위해 12월 초 정부들이 아랍에미리트의 두바이에 모이면서 두 가지 고통스럽게 분명한 사실이 있다. 첫째, 우리는 이미 기후 위기에 처해있다. 둘째, 부유한 나라들, 특히 미국은 계속해서 가난한 나라들에게 등을 돌린다. 미국은 분명 이런 책임을 부정할 것이다. 미국은 과거

와 현재의 온실가스 방출에 대해 연간 600억 달러를 지불하는 것이 지나치게 비싸다고 주장할 것이다. 사실, 미국의 연간 GDP가 약 26조 달러인데 연간 600억 달러의 추가부담금은 미국 GDP의 0.2퍼센트에 불과하다. 이 정도는 이들이 쉽게 낼 수 있는 범위에 속한다.

위 글에 도출될 수 있는 결론으로 가장 적절한 것은?
① 미국은 가장 부유한 나라이므로 기후 재앙의 최악에 대해 책임을 져야 한다.
② 각국의 이산화탄소 배출량에 의거하여 기후 위기를 초래한 온난화 비율에 관해 합의가 있어야 한다.
③ 각국은 가능한 한 빨리 기후변화 문제를 해결하는 일에 참여해야 한다.
④ 아랍에미리트는 가장 큰 원유 생산국이고, 미국은 초강대국이므로 기후 위기를 해결하기 위해 더 가깝게 일할 것이다.
⑤ 따라서 올해의 토의는 기후 정의와 재정지원에 집중될 것이다.

---

31 내용추론 ④

두 지도자가 클린치하고 힘을 아껴 나중을 도모한다는 말로 보아 중미관계는 ④의 상태로 진술하는 것이 가장 적절하다.

summit meeting 정상회담 boxer n. 권투선수 clinch v. 권투선수들이 서로 끌어안다, 클린치하다 bout n. 시합 throw punches 펀치를 날리다 round n. 시합의 각 라운드 metaphor n. 은유 Sino-American relations 미중관계 intelligence report 정보보고서 official n. 공직자 apt a. 적절한 superpower n. 강대국

최근에 있었던 미중 정상의 회담을 두 권투선수가 긴 시합 동안 서로 끌어안고 클린치하는 것이라고 생각해보라. 중국의 지도자는 다행히 어떤 펀치도 날리지 않았지만 그는 나중 라운드를 위해 힘을 아껴두고 있는 것인지도 모른다. 미국 관료들이 묘사한 정보보고서에 따르면, 중국의 시진핑 주석은 클린치 은유를 사용해 미중관계의 특징을 묘사했다. 그리고 이는 두 강대국이 현재 서 있는 자리를 묘사하는 적절한 요약인 듯하다.

위의 진술이 가장 잘 뒷받침하는 추론은?
① 각 정부가 개진한 정보보고에 따르면 두 지도자는 서로 싸우지 않았다.
② 중미관계는 양국의 맹렬한 군사력 경쟁 때문에 버려질 수 없다.
③ 중국은 미국과 펀치를 공유하는 복서의 전략을 취해야 했다.
④ 양국 지도자들은 지연된 경쟁 동안 전략적 휴지기에 있었다.
⑤ 양국 지도자들은 군사력과 경제력을 위한 경쟁을 우선시했다.

---

32 내용추론 ④

미국 바이든 대통령이 이스라엘에게 미국이 9/11이후 했던 실수를 하지 말라고 촉구했는데, 그의 조언이 무시당했다고 했다. 이것은 이스라엘이 미국과는 다른 길을 갔어야 했는데 같은 길을 가버렸다는 말이므로 ④가 추론할 수 있는 내용이다.

launch v. 시작하다 surprise attack 기습공격 urge v. 촉구하다 unheeded a. 무시당한 condemn v. 비난하다 momentary a. 일시적인 catharsis n. 카타르시스 outsize a. 대형의, 특대의

하마스가 이스라엘에 기습공격을 한 지난 10월 7일, 이스라엘이 이스라엘판 9/11을 겪었을 때, 미 대통령 조 바이든은 이스라엘에게 미국이 (2001년 9월 11일) 비슷한 공격을 받았을 때 했던 실수를 저지르지 말라고 촉구했고, 그러면서도 모든 도덕적 정치적 군사적 지원은 할 수 있는 한

해주었다. 바이든의 조언은 무시당했고, 이스라엘은 현재 우방과 적 모두에게 비난을 받고 있다. 2001년 미국의 경우처럼, 이스라엘은 하마스의 공격에 하마스의 본거지인 가자지구를 겨냥한, 겉으로 보기에 타당한 분노로 대응했다. 이런 분노는 순간적인 카타르시스를 줄 수는 있으나 거의 항상 대규모 파괴를 일으킨다.

위 글에서 도출될 수 있는 가장 적절한 가정은?
① 이스라엘과 미국은 도덕적 정치적 군사적 협력을 위해 더 긴밀하게 협조했어야만 했다.
② 하마스의 공격에 대한 이스라엘의 대응은 2001년 9/11 테러 이후의 미국의 대응과 다르게 실행되었다.
③ 이스라엘과 미국은 그들이 겪었던 공격에 무장 대응을 하지 않았다는 점에서 비슷했다.
④ 이스라엘은 10월 7일 (기습공격) 이후 미국의 길과 다른 길을 갔어야만 했는데 그러지 않았다.
⑤ 이스라엘과 미국은 공격받은 이후 같은 실수를 할 수 있었을 텐데.

---

33 내용파악 ③

첫 문장에서 '생태계 위기와 임박한 지구 온난화의 유령이라는 디스토피아적 직조물에서 지구의 연약함은 인간이 스스로의 파괴와 씨름하는 잊을 수 없는 이야기가 된다'고 했으므로 정답은 ③이다.

dystopia n. 반이상향, 디스토피아 tapestry n. 태피스트리(여러 가지 색실로 그림을 짜 넣은 직물 또는 그런 직물을 제작하는 기술) ecological a. 생태적인, 생태계의 impending a. 임박한 specter n. 유령 fragility n. 연약함 haunting a. 자꾸 생각나는, 잊어지지 않는 undoing n. 원상회복, 파멸 thread n. 실, 가닥 decay n. 쇠락, 타락, 부패 catastrophe n. 재앙, 재난 psyche n. 심리, 마음, 정신 overcome v. 극복하다 trajectory n. 탄도, 궤적 loom large 크게 다가오다 sustainable a. 지속가능한 haunting a. 잊히지 않는, 잊을 수 없는 unravel v. 펼치다 cast a shadow over ~에 그림자를 드리우다

생태계 위기와 임박한 지구 온난화의 유령이라는 디스토피아적 직조물에서 지구의 연약함은 인간이 스스로의 파괴와 씨름하는 잊을 수 없는 이야기가 된다. 사회학적 성찰은 디스토피아적 서사시를 일깨우면서, 환경 파괴의 직물을 짜는 인간 활동의 실 가닥들을 펼쳐놓는다. 세상이 생태계 재앙에 직면함에 따라 정치 이데올로기들은 해결책을 향한 절박한 투쟁 속에서 충돌하는데, 이는 인간 심리에 뿌리박힌 생존본능을 반영한다. 인류가 자멸적인 길을 극복할 수 있느냐 없느냐의 문제가 점점 크게 다가오고 있으며, 이것이 지속가능한 미래의 가능성에 그림자를 드리운다.

위 글에 따르면 지구의 연약함은 어떻게 잊을 수 없는 이야기가 되는가?
① 지구의 연약함이 잊을 수 없는 이야기가 되는 것은 회복의 거짓 희망에 대항하는 전 세계적인 저항 공동체를 강화시켰다.
② 잊을 수 없는 이야기가 되는 것은 사회학적 성찰을 통해 생태계 위기보다 지구의 연약함을 우선시한다.
③ 지구의 연약함은 생태계 위기와 임박한 지구 온난화 때문에 잊을 수 없는 이야기가 된다.
④ 디스토피아 서사시는 사회학적 성찰에서 지구의 연약함을 무시한다.
⑤ 생태계의 재앙은 정치 이데올로기와 인간의 본능에 의해 압도될 수 있다.

2024 숭실대학교(인문계)

01 ④	02 ④	03 ①	04 ②	05 ②	06 ①	07 ②	08 ③	09 ①	10 ②
11 ③	12 ③	13 ③	14 ④	15 ③	16 ①	17 ①	18 ③	19 ③	20 ④
21 ①	22 ④	23 ③	24 ②	25 ①	26 ④	27 ②	28 ②	29 ②	30 ①
31 ④	32 ③	33 ④	34 ④	35 ④	36 ②	37 ④	38 ①	39 ③	40 ④
41 ②	42 ④	43 ①	44 ④	45 ④	46 ①	47 ④	48 ②	49 ①	50 ②

01 분사 ④

SARS-CoV-2가 뇌에 영향을 미칠 수 '있는 것 같다'는 내용으로, ④ 이하는 뇌와 관련된 구체적인 증상이다. SARS-CoV-2가 seemed의 주어이면서 caused의 주어가 되려면 접속사가 필요하다. 따라서 ④를 and it caused나 분사구문의 현재분사 causing으로 고쳐야 한다.

pandemic n. 팬데믹, 전 세계적 전염병 respiratory a. 호흡의 have an effect on ~에 영향을 미치다 brain fog 뇌 안개(집중력, 기억력, 사고력 저하를 특징으로 하는 인지 기능 장애) stroke n. 뇌졸중

코로나19 팬데믹 초기에 의사들은 원래 호흡기 바이러스라고 설명된 것 치고는 SARS-CoV-2가 뇌에 강력한 영향을 미치며, 미각과 후각 상실, 뇌 안개에서부터 심각한 경우 뇌졸중에 이르는 온갖 것들을 유발한다는 점에 주목했다.

02 현재완료의 형태 ④

현재완료는 'have+p.p.' 형태여야 하므로 ④를 kept로 고쳐야 한다.

pose v. 문제를 제기하다; 괴롭히다, 궁지에 빠뜨리다 recruitment n. 채용 staff n. 직원 keep pace with ~와 나란히 함께 가다

우리들 중 너무나도 많은 사람들이 더 오래 살게 되면서, 많은 고령화 사회에 한 가지 괴로운 문제가 있다. 특히 간호 인력 구인은 노인 인구의 급격한 증가에 보조를 맞추지 못했다.

03 논리완성 ①

'provide a window into ~'가 '~을 들여다 볼 수[이해할 수] 있게 하다'는 뜻의 표현이다.

derive v. 획득하다, 얻다 traverse v. 횡단하다 provide v. 제공하다 eliminate v. 제거하다 interpret v. 해석하다 alleviate v. 완화하다

세일즈포스(Salesforce)는 온라인 트래픽 및 지출을 위한 벤치마크를 자사의 커머스 클라우드(Commerce Cloud) 이커머스 서비스를 통해 도출된다고 말하는데, 이 데이터를 통해 60개국 15억 명의 사람들이 수천 개의 이커머스 사이트를 이용하는 행동을 파악할 수 있다고 설명한다.

04 논리완성 ②

even as는 역접의 접속사인데, even as 앞이 긍정적인 내용이므로 even as절에서는 일자리를 '없애다(eliminate)'와 같은 부정적인 내용으로 일자리 시장을 '파괴하다(wreck)'라고 하는 것이 적절하다.

even as 비록 ~이지만 boost v. 경기를 부양하다 wreck v. 파괴하다 merge v. 병합하다 proliferate v. 번창하다; 급격히 늘다

생성형 인공지능 기술이 일자리 시장을 파괴할 수 있다는 점이 소셜 미디어 사이트에서 널리 논의되어 왔지만, 실제로는 없앨 것으로 예상되는 것보다 더 많은 일자리를 창출할 수 있다.

05 논리완성 ②

역접의 전치사 despite로 연결되어 있는데, 뒤에서는 '생존이 불가능하다'라고 했으므로 앞에서는 '생존하고 있다(exists)'라고 해야 한다.

Ursa Minor constellation 작은곰자리 constellation n. 별자리 extraordinary a. 특이한 planetary system 행성계 defy v. 거부하다 conventional a. 전통적인 proximity n. 근접 red giant 적색거성 deem v. ~로 간주하다 exhaust v. 고갈시키다, 소모하다 exist v. 존재하다 exonerate v. 용서하다 extort v. 강탈하다

작은곰자리에는 통상적인 예상을 거스르는 특별한 행성계가 있다. 적색거성 백두와 매우 가까운 거리에서 발견되는 행성인 한라는 생존이 불가능하다고 여겨지는 거리에 위치해 있음에도 불구하고 존재하고 있다.

06 논리완성 ①

소외된 집단은 신약 개발자들의 새로운 치료법의 혜택을 오랫동안 누리지 못했다. 이들에게도 혜택이 가게 하려면 이들도 임상시험의 대상으로 포함하여 임상시험을 '다각화해야(diversify)' 할 것이다.

clinical trial 임상시험 efficacy n. 효능 underrepresented a. 불충분하게 대표된 diversity v. 다각화하다 exclude v. 배제하다 impede v. 방해하다 scour v. 닦다

약물 개발자들은 새로운 치료법의 안전성, 효능, 채택을 증진시키기 위한 임상시험을 역사적으로 소외된 집단 사이에 다각화할 것을 오랫동안 필요로 해왔다.

07 동의어 ②

seek out 찾다 strategically ad. 전략적으로 nab v. 붙잡다(= grab)
Cyber Monday 사이버 먼데이(미국에서 추수감사절 다음 날 월요일에 진행되는 온라인 쇼핑 할인 행사로, 블랙 프라이데이의 온라인 버전)
retailer n. 소매상 aggregate v. 모으다 third party 제3자, 타사
dispose v. 버리다 overhaul v. 정비하다 spread v. 펼치다; 퍼뜨리다

타사에서 집계한 소매업체 웹사이트의 데이터에 따르면, 미국의 명절 쇼핑객들은 사이버 먼데이를 앞두고 최고의 상품을 찾고 전략적으로 가장 큰 할인 혜택을 획득하고 있다.

08 동의어 ③

household n. 가계 financial crisis 금융위기 appreciation n. 가치 상승(= strength) wipe v. 쓸어버리다 asset n. 자산 default n. 채무불이행 mean n. 평균 participation n. 참가, 참여

인플레이션과 미국 달러화 가치 상승으로(강세로) 약 11조 3천억 달러의 자산이 사라지면서 전 세계 가계 자산이 지난해에 2008년 금융위기 이후 처음으로 감소했다.

09 동의어 ①

detailed a. 상세한 spurious a. 가짜의(= deceitful) genuine a. 진짜의; 성실한 ossified a. 뼈가 된 vehement a. 격렬한

일련의 세부 조사는 그의 허위 주장에 대한 어떠한 정보도 제공할 수 없었다.

10 동의어 ②

facetious a. 익살맞은(= funny) arid a. 건조한 inadequate a. 부적절한 placid a. 평온한

션(Sean)은 심각한 상황에서도 장난스러운 발언을 하곤 했다.

11-13

나는 정치인들이 조롱하길 좋아하는 대학 기반의 진보적인 엘리트 가정에서 자랐다. 내가 어렸을 때, 모든 인간은 성별과 상관없이 한 꺼풀 벗기면, 진정으로 말하건대, 단지 기회의 차이가 있다는 점만 제외하고는, 다 같았다. 부모님은 기회가 있을 때마다 이를 강조하셨다. 어느 해 크리스마스 날에 나는 바비 인형과 소프트볼 글러브를 선물로 받았다. 또 다른 해 크리스마스 날에는 전구의 열로 작은 케이크를 굽는 녹색 에나멜 스토브와 한 세트의 끝이 강철로 된 다트들과 대회용 다트판을 받았다. 내가 화학실험용품 세트와 발레리나 인형을 동시에 받은 해를 이야기했던가?
부모가 되고 나서야, 두 아들을 둔 부모가 되고 나서야, 나는 부모의 말을 맹신하며 컸다는 사실을 깨달았다(기회에 관한 말은 제외된다. 그런 말은 내가 지금도 믿고 있으니까). 큰아이가 두 살 반쯤 되었을 때 시작된 공룡기에 이런 생각이 들었다. 아, 큰아들은 공룡을 좋아했는데, 그건 괜찮지만, 피를 벌컥벌컥 마시는 육식공룡만 좋아했던 것이다. 초식공룡은 겁쟁이이

고 패배자라고 생각했고, 스테고사우루스(초식공룡) 그림이 그려져 있어서 보기가 싫게 된 티셔츠는 입기를 거부했다. 어느 날 내 발치에서 으르렁거리며 내 오른쪽 다리를 물려고 제 딴에는 최고로 애쓰는 녀석을 내려다보면서 이런 생각이 들었다. 이건 문화보다 훨씬 더 깊은 곳에 있는 문제구나. 아이를 키우다 보면 이런 종류의 정치적으로 올바르지 못한 반응을 초래할 때가 있다. 또 다른 친구는 아들이 단호한 마음으로 아침식사 토스트를 물어뜯어내어 권총 모양으로 만들어 동생을 날려버리거나 적어도 겁주려고 하는 것을 지켜보면서 나와 같은 결론에 도달했다. 내가 (어렸을 때) 이런 짓을 했나? 큰 이빨을 가진 플라스틱 알로사우루스를 사줬어야 했나? 와 같은 죄책감이 일단 지나가면, 훨씬 더 흥미로운 성(性) 생물학 분야를 고려하게 될 수 있는데, 이 분야에서는 질문의 형태가 다음과 같이 달라진다. 대량 학살을 좋아하는 것은 문화적인(후천적인) 것인가 아니면 유전적인(선천적인) 것인가, 그리고 어느 쪽이 어느 쪽을 주도하는가? 우리 문화에서 성 역할은 근본적인 생물학을 반영하는가? 그리고 또한 우리 행동방식이 그 생물학에 영향을 미치는가?

liberal a. 자유주의적인 ridicule v. 조롱하다 regardless of ~와는 상관없이 gender n. 성차 barring prep. ~을 제외하고 bring home 강조하다 be fed a line and swallow it like a sucker 빈말을 듣고 젖 빨듯이 삼키다, 맹신하다, 속다 dawn on 어렴풋이 떠오르다 dinosaur phase 공룡기(아이들의 성장기에 항문기, 남근기 등은 있는데 공룡기는 없는데 재미있으라고 만든 표현) blood-swilling a. 피를 벌컥벌컥 마시는 carnivore n. 육식성 동물 wimp n. 겁쟁이 mar v. 훼손하다 snarl v. 으르렁거리다 toddler n. 아장거리는 아이 gnaw v. 물어뜯다 bring on 초래하다 determinedly ad. 단호하게 blow away 날려버리다 terrify v. 무섭게[겁나게] 하다 allosaur n. 알로사우루스(육식공룡) oversized a. 너무 큰 carnage n. 대학살 culture n. 문화(후천적인 것) genetics n. 유전(선천적인 것)

11 부분이해 ③

under the skin은 '한 꺼풀 벗기면, 내면적으로는'의 뜻이므로 ③(외면적 차이 밑에, 즉 내면적으로)이 정답이다. skin은 인간의 외면을 비유하고 skin color는 인종차별을 비유한다.

문장에서 밑줄 친 ⒶⒶ는 _____을 의미한다.
① 부당한 차별이 아닌 경우
② 인종적 차이들에도 불구하고
③ 외면적 차이 밑에는
④ 태어나는 순간

12 부분이해 ③

여기서 reaction은 아이의 반응을 가리키고, politically correct하다는 것은 사회의 약자 층을 위한다는 의미로 이것을 문화적(후천적)인 것이라고 한다면 politically incorrect하다는 것은 약자를 위하지 않고 약육강식의 태도로 자신의 힘을, 심지어 폭력까지도 행사한다는 의미로 유전적, 본능적, 선천적인 것이라 할 수 있다. 따라서 아이가 본능적으로 보이는 폭력적 행동이라는 ③이 정답이다. 문화보다 더 깊은 내면의 것이므로 more than culture라 했다.

밑줄 친 ⑧는 _____을 가리킨다.
① 부모님의 남다른 양성평등 의식
② 피를 탐하는 육식동물에 대한 소년의 열광
③ 아들의 문화 이상의 것인 폭력적인 행동
④ 아들이 토스트를 물어뜯어 권총 모양으로 만드는 것

13 내용파악 ③

③ 죄의식을 언급한 부분에서 '알로사우루스를 사줬어야 했나?'라고 했다. 'should have pp'는 가정법 과거완료 표현으로 과거에 대한 반대의 의미이다. 따라서 저자는 아들에게 알로사우루스를 사 준적이 없다. ① 어렸을 때 바비 인형을 받았다고만 했지 좋아했는지 여부는 말하지 않았다. ② 아들이 초식공룡을 싫어했고 스테고사우루스 그림으로 훼손된 티셔츠를 입지 않으려고 했다는 것에서 스테고사우루스가 초식공룡임을 알 수 있다. ④ 마지막 문장에서 '생물학이 성 역할에 반영되어 주도하는가? 그리고 성 역할에 따른 행동방식이 또한 생물학에 영향을 미치고 주도하는가?'라고 했다.

다음 중 저자에 대해 옳지 않은 것은?
① 그녀가 어렸을 때 바비 인형을 좋아했는지 여부는 알 수 없다.
② 그녀의 큰아들은 스테고사우루스를 초식공룡이어서 싫어했다.
③ 그녀는 아들에게 플라스틱 알로사우루스를 사주었다.
④ 그녀는 성 역할의 원동력에 대해 지금 혼란스러워한다.

14-15

중국 젊은이들은 중국이라는 거대한 소비 시장에서 경제성장의 핵심으로 여겨지고 있다. 그러나 코로나 이후 경제가 어려움을 겪고 기업들이 고용을 줄이면서 16~24세의 실업률이 6월에 기록적인 22%를 보여주었는데, 그 후 당국이 데이터를 중단하여, 실제 수치는 더 높을 것이라는 우려가 증폭되고 있다. 하지만 Z세대 소비자들은 지출을 줄이는 대신 우선순위를 재평가하고 있다. 많은 이들이 기계장치 같은 고가의 제품을 구입하거나 저축이나 주택 구입과 같은 장기적인 재정 목표를 위해 노력하기보다는 상대적으로 저렴한 경험에 투자하고 있다. 해외여행은 엄두를 내지 못하지만 국내 인기 여행지는 호황을 누리고 있다. 기록을 세우고 있는 중국의 영화관람 수익도 마찬가지이다.
트렌드 리서치 회사인 영 차이나 그룹의 설립자 잭 다이크트왈드(Zak Dychtwald)는 지난 18개월 동안 경쟁이 치열한 취업 시장에 대한 대응으로 치열한 경쟁을 그만두기 — '바닥에 드러눕기(탕핑)'라고 알려진 추세 — 를 원하는 중국 Z세대의 수가 증가했다고 말했다. 사람들은 전통적인 분야에서는 여전히 소비를 하고 있다. 블룸버그 인텔리전스에 따르면 2023년 상반기 소비 데이터는 강세를 보였으며, 소매 판매가 예상치를 밑돌더라도, 비용 구조가 간소화되고 재고 부담이 줄어드는 것을 볼 때 하반기에는 기업들이 예상 마진을 상회할 가능성이 크다. <그러므로> 중국에 젊은 고객 기반을 크게 갖고 있는 소매업체들은 중국의 경기 회복을 둘러싼 불확실성에 대해 우려를 말해왔거나 할인 및 판매촉진 행사에 의존해 판매를 북돋우고 있다. 쇼핑을 할 때, 일부 젊은 중국인들은 경제가 호황일 때보다 더 신중하게 행동하고 있다.

pull back on 후퇴하다 jobless rate 실업률 authority n. 당국 halt v. 중단하다 amplify v. 증폭하다 concern n. 우려 priority n. 우선순위 splash out on 돈을 펑펑 쓰다 affordable a. 싼 scoop up 입수하다 big-ticket items 돈이 많이 드는 품목들 gadget n. 도구; 기계장치 domestic a. 국내의 hotspot n. 인기 여행지 booming a. 호황을

누리는 set record 기록을 세우다 rat race 치열한 경쟁 lying flat (중국의) 탕핑족(재물을 벌고 사회적 성취를 추구하라는 사회적 압력에서 벗어나 삶에 대해 열정이 없는 태도로 사는 생활방식을 추구하는 사람들) sector n. 분야 retail n. 소매 undershoot v. 못 미치다 be likely to ~할 것 같다 top v. 능가하다 margin estimate 예상 마진 cost structure 비용 구조 inventory burden 재고 부담

14 문맥상 적절하지 않은 단어 고르기 ④

앞 문장에서는 경제가 호황세로 돌아설 것이라고 했고, 다음 문장에서는 불확실하다고 했다. 빈칸 전후가 서로 반대의 의미이므로 역접의 접속사가 필요하다. However가 적절하다.

15 내용일치 ③

첫 문단에서 실업률이 늘어난다고 한 것은 고용이 감소한다는 말이다.

다음 중 옳지 않은 것은?
① 16~24세의 실업률은 22%보다 높을 수 있다.
② 대부분의 Z세대 소비자는 해외여행보다 국내 인기 여행지에 더 관심이 많다.
③ 코로나 이후에도 고용은 꾸준히 증가하고 있다.
④ 일부 소매업체는 할인 및 판매촉진 행사를 통해 매출이 증가할 것으로 기대한다.

16-18

후천성 실어증 연구는 뇌와 언어의 관계를 이해하는 중요한 연구 분야이다. 실어증은 질병이나 정신적 외상(外傷)으로 인한 뇌 손상으로 인해 일어나는 모든 언어 장애를 가리키는 신경학적 용어이다. 19세기 후반, 실어증 환자 연구를 바탕으로, 뇌에서 언어를 담당하는 곳을 찾아내는 데 상당한 과학적 진전이 이루어졌다. 1860년대 프랑스의 외과의 폴 브로카(Paul Broca)는 언어가 뇌의 좌반구, 더 구체적으로 좌반구의 앞부분(지금은 브로카 영역이라 불림)에 국한돼 있다는 의견을 제시했다. 파리에서의 한 과학 회의에서 그는 우리가 좌반구로 말을 한다고 주장했다. 브로카의 주장은 좌측 전두엽 뇌 손상 후 언어 장애를 겪은 환자들을 대상으로 한 연구에 근거한 것이었다. 10년 후, 독일 신경과학자 칼 베르니케(Carl Wernicke)는 지금은 베르니케 영역이라고 알려진 좌측 측두엽 부위가 손상된 환자에게서 발생하는 또 다른 유형의 실어증을 설명했다. 좌우 기능 분화는 뇌의 한 반구(半球)에 기능이 국한되는 것을 가리키는 용어이다. 언어는 좌반구에 분화되어 있으며, 좌반구가 유아기부터 언어 반구인 것 같다.
실어증 환자 대부분은 전면적인 언어 상실을 보이지 않는다. 오히려, 언어의 다양한 측면이 선택적으로 손상되며, 손상된 종류는 일반적으로 뇌 손상의 위치와 관련이 있다. 이러한 손상과 장애의 상관관계로 인해 실어증 환자 연구는 언어가 뇌에 구성되는 방식에 대한 많은 정보를 제공해왔다. 브로카 영역에 손상을 입은 환자는 오늘날 흔히 브로카 실어증이라고 불리는 실어증을 앓고 있을 수 있다. 브로카 실어증은 말을 무척 힘들게 하고 특정 종류의 단어를 찾는 데 어려움을 보이는 것이 특징이지만, 주로 문법에 따라 문장을 구성하는 능력에 영향을 미치는 장애이다. 브로카 실어증 환자와 달리 베르니케 실어증 환자는 근사한 억양으로 유창하게 말하며 문법을 대체로 준수할 수 있다. 하지만, 그들의 언어는 흔히 의미론적으로 일관성이 없다.

acquired a. 후천적인 aphasia n. 실어증 neurological a. 신경학적인 term n. 용어 language disorder 언어 장애 trauma n. 정신적 외상 make an advance 발전하다 localize v. 위치를 파악하다; 국한하다 surgeon n. 외과의사 hemisphere n. 반구(半球) language deficit 언어 장애 frontal lobe 전두엽 lesion n. 손상 temporal lobe 측두엽 lateralization n. 대뇌 좌우의 기능 분화 refer to 가리키다 impair v. 손상시키다 corelation n. 상관관계 be characterized by ~라는 특징을 갖고 있다 labored a. 힘드는; 굼뜬 affect v. 영향을 미치다 syntax n. 구문론, 문법 fluent a. 유창한 intonation n. 억양 adhere to ~을 고수하다 semantically ad. 의미론적으로 incoherent a. 일관성 없는 retrieval n. 불러오기

16 글의 제목 ①

첫 번째 문장에서 "후천성 실어증 연구는 뇌와 언어의 관계를 이해하는 중요한 연구 분야이다"라고 한 다음, 그 이하에서 브로카 실어증과 베르니케 실어증으로 나누어 설명하므로, 제목은 ①의 '후천성 실어증'이 적절하다. ③이 답이 되자면, 첫 번째 단계, 두 번째 단계 하는 식으로 실어증의 진행 '과정'이 설명되어야 한다.

다음 중 제목으로 가장 적절한 것은?
① 후천성 실어증
② 좌우 기능 분화
③ 실어증의 단계들
④ 뇌 가소성

17 내용파악 ①

마지막 세 문장을 참조한다. 의미론적 일관성 결여는 베르니케 실어증의 특징이다.

다음 중 브로카 실어증에 관해 언급되지 않은 것은?
① 의미론적 일관성 결여
② 단어를 생각해내는 어려움
③ 비문법적 문장
④ 유창하지 않은 말하기

18 내용일치 ③

브로카 실어증은 좌측 전두엽, 베르니케 실어증은 좌측 측두엽에 손상이 있을 때 일어난다고 하였다.

다음 중 옳지 않은 것은?
① 실어증은 질병이나 외상으로 인해 발생할 수 있다.
② 베르니케의 영역 연구보다 브로카의 영역 연구가 선행되었다.
③ 브로카 영역과 베르니케 영역은 뇌의 같은 엽이다.
④ 대부분의 실어증 환자는 언어의 다양한 측면에 선택적 장애를 보인다.

19-20

슈퍼마켓과 전통 시장에는 몇 가지 큰 차이가 있다. 전통 시장의 시끌벅적한 소리는 슈퍼마켓의 프로그램화된 무해한 음악에 자리를 내준다. 물론 거기엔 이따금 열광적인 억양의 상업광고가 끼어든다. 전통 시장을 거닐다 보면 다양한 감각적인 냄새를 맡을 수 있지만, 슈퍼마켓에서 무언가 냄새가 난다고 의식한다면 뭔가 문제가 있다는 것이다. 전통 시장에서 줄기와 뿌리가 있는 채소를 판매함으로써 그리고 동물의 사체를 걸어둠으로써 표현되는 먹는 것이 갖고 있는 삶과 죽음의 문제가 슈퍼마켓에서는 제거되는데, 거기에서는 식품이 다른 데서 가공되고, 최소한 눈에 띄지 않는 곳에서 다듬어진다.

그러나 전통 시장과 카트를 밀고 다니는 곳의 가장 근본적인 차이점은 현대 소매 환경에서는 거의 모든 판매가 사람 없이 이루어진다는 점이다. 제품은 그 제품을 판매하는 특정 사람의 개성과는 완전히 분리되어 있다. 물론 광고에 등장하는 사람은 예외이다. 슈퍼마켓은 판매를 늦추는 사교성을 제거한다. 그것은 제조업체가 제품을 세상에 선보이는 방식을 통제할 수 있게 한다. 그것은 사람을 포장으로 대체하고 있다.

포장은 현대 생활에서 피할 수 없는 부분이다. 포장은 어디에나 존재하며 눈에 보이지 않기도 하고, 개탄의 대상이 되기도 하고 무시되기도 한다. 깨어 있는 대부분의 순간 동안 시야에는 하나 이상의 포장이 들어와 있다. 포장은 어디에나 존재하기 때문에 의식적으로 지각하지 못하지만, 많은 포장은 사람들이 주의를 기울이지 않더라도 반응하게끔 디자인되어 있다. 일단 쇼핑 카트를 밀기 시작하면 슈퍼마켓, 할인점, 창고형 클럽 등, 쇼핑 장소는 크게 중요하지 않다. 중요한 것은 포장 안에 있다는 점이다. 감성을 자극하는 표현적인 포장, 제품을 유용하게 만들어 주는 기발한 포장, 원하는 것과 얻는 것을 이해하는 데 도움이 되는 유익한 포장 등등이다. 역사적으로 포장은 셀프 서비스 소매업을 가능하게 했고, 또 이에 따라 이러한 소매업 매장은 사람들이 구매하는 상품의 수와 다양성을 증가시켰다. 이제 포장이 없는 세상은 상상할 수 없다.

major a. 주요한 cacophony n. 불협화음 give way to ~에 자리를 내주다 innocuous a. 무해한 punctuate v. 간간이 끼어들다 intone v. 읊조리다, 영창하다 commercial n. 광고 stroll n. 산책 an array of 일련의 sensuous a. 감각적인 aroma n. 기분 좋은 향기 be conscious of 의식하다 stem n. 줄기 carcass n. 사체 purge v. 제거하다 process v. 가공하다 trim v. 다듬다 retail n. 소매 setting n. 환경 be dissociated from ~와 절연되어 있다 personality n. 인간적인 성격 sociability n. 붙임성 좋은 성격 manufacturer n. 제조업자 inescapable a. 피할 수 없는 omnipresent a. 편재하는 deplore v. 한탄[개탄]하다 ubiquitous a. 편재하는 slip v. 미끄러지다 pay attention 주목하다 warehouse club 창고형 매장 ingenious a. 기발한 unimaginable a. 상상도 할 수 없는 auditory a. 청각의 olfactory a. 후각의 hygiene n. 위생

19 내용파악 ③

음악과 냄새, 그리고 포장이 슈퍼마켓과 전통 시장을 구분하는 특징들로 열거되어 있다. 전통 시장이 비위생적이라는 말은 없다.

다음 중 슈퍼마켓과 전통 시장의 구분선에서 가장 멀리 떨어져 있는 것은?
① 청각적 경험
② 후각적 경험
③ 공중위생
④ 포장

20 내용일치   ④

① 세 번째 문단 두 번째 문장의 invisible은 네 번째 문장에 나와 있듯이 의식적으로 지각하지 못한다는 뜻이지, 말 그대로 눈에 안 보인다는 말이 아니다. ② 포장이 기만적이라는 말은 없다. ③ 포장이 겸손하다는 말은 없다. ④ 마지막에서 두 번째 문장이다.

다음 중 옳은 것은?
① 포장은 어디에나 존재하며 말 그대로 눈에 보이지 않는다.
② 포장은 정보를 제공할 뿐만 아니라 기만적이다.
③ 포장은 표현력이 풍부하고 겸손하다.
④ 포장을 통해 셀프 서비스 소매업이 가능해졌다.

21-23

단백질은 우리 몸의 세포 안에 있는 작은 공장에서 생산된다. 생물학자들은 이를 리보솜이라고 부른다. 이 공장은 특정 단백질을 만들라고 '명령하는' 메시지를 받으면 가동된다. 이러한 각각의 메시지는 DNA를 사용하여 생성된다. 관련 단백질 서열에 해당하는 DNA 서열은 '메신저'라는 적절한 이름으로 불리는 다른 분자에 복사되고, 이 분자가 리보솜에 한 형태의 서열을 전달한다. 메신저 RNA(리보핵산)라고 불리는 이 메신저 분자는 또 다른 종류의 핵산 서열이다. 따라서 DNA 서열은 일종의 템플릿, 다시 말해 복사되어 그 메시지를 만들 수 있는 특정한 뉴클레오타이드 서열이고, 그 메시지는 그다음에 아미노산 서열로 번역되어 단백질이 만들어진다. 이러한 과정을 '유전자 발현'이라고 한다. 이 용어는 전체 과정이 유전자나 적어도 유전자가 보유하고 있는 정보에 내재되어 있다가 단순히 '발현'되기만 하면 된다는 인상을 준다.
그러나 우리가 흔히 말하는 것처럼 DNA 서열이 단백질을 '결정한다'라는 말은 조금 이상하다. 사실, DNA는 그냥 그 자리에 있고, 때때로 세포가 어떤 단백질을 생산되게 하기 위해 자신에게 필요한 서열을 DNA로부터 읽어낸다. 이는 마치 하이파이 음향 기기가 CD의 디지털 정보를 읽어서 실제 '동작'인 음악을 생성하는 것과 매우 흡사하다. 따라서 환원주의적 인과율의 연쇄에서 첫 번째 단계는 단순한 인과율적 사건이 전혀 아니다. 서열이 읽어내질 때 그것은 하나의 전체 후속 사건 연쇄를 시작되게 하는 중요한 사건이다. 이는 물리적 사건들이다. 그렇다. 그러나 읽어지는 대상 뿐 아니라 읽는 과정도 중요하다.
이 과정에는 특정한 단백질 시스템이 관련된다. 우리가 이 동작의 주체를 파악하길 원한다면 그 주체는 이러한 시스템이어야 한다. 이 시스템은 DNA 코드(암호)를 '읽는다.' CD가 CD 리더기 없이는 아무것도 할 수 없는 것처럼, DNA는 이러한 단백질 시스템을 포함하고 있는 세포의 맥락 밖에서는 아무것도 하지 않는다. 따라서 기계적 시스템이 단백질을 생산하기 위한 암호를 읽으려면 단백질이 필요하다는 역설이 존재한다.

protein n. 단백질 tell v. 명령하다 generate v. 생산하다, 발생시키다 correspond to ~에 일치하다 relevant a. 적절한 molecule n. 분자 appropriately ad. 적절하게 transmit v. 송신하다 ribonucleic acid 리보핵산 nucleic a. 핵의 template n. 템플릿, 견본 nucleotide n. 뉴클레오타이드 transcribe v. 복사하다, 기록하다, 바꾸다 translate v. 번역하다, 옮기다 amino-acid n. 아미노산 gene expression 유전자 발현 terminology n. 용어 impression n. 인상 implicit a. 내재한 read off 읽다, 이해하다 reductionist n. 환원주의자 cause and effect 인과관계 causal a. 인과율의 initiate v. 착수시키다 tapestry n. 태피스트리(여러 가지 색실로 그림을 짜 넣은 직물. 또는 그런 직물을 제작하는 기술) recombinant a. 재조합형의 gene editing 유전자 편집 intricacy n. 복잡성

21 빈칸완성   ①

다음 문장에서 'DNA는 가만히 있고 세포가 단백질 생산에 필요한 서열을 DNA로부터 읽어낸다'고 했는데, 이것을 두고 DNA 서열이 능동적으로 단백질을 결정한다고 말하는 것은 '이상한' 말일 것이다.

빈칸 Ⓐ에 들어가기에 가장 적절한 것은?
① 이상한
② 무례한
③ 자연스러운
④ 간결한

22 내용파악   ④

첫 번째 문단 다섯 번째 문장에서 메신저 RNA는 DNA 서열을 리보솜에 보낸다고 하였다.

유전자 발현 과정에서 메신저 RNA의 역할은 무엇인가?
① 아미노산을 위해 직접 암호화한다.
② DNA 암호를 읽는다.
③ 핵에서 DNA 가닥을 꼰다.
④ DNA 서열을 리보솜으로 전송한다.

23 글의 제목   ③

첫 번째 문단에서 '유전자 발현'에 대해 설명한 다음, 이러한 '발현'에 대한 결정론적인 관점, 또는 환원주의적 관점을 비판하고, DNA의 복잡성과 더불어 단백질의 상대적 자율성을 설명하고 있는 글이다. 그러므로 ③이 정답으로 적절하다. 여기서 교향곡이란 복잡하게 많은 것들이 뒤섞여 있다는 의미이다. 이 글은 데니스 노블(Denis Noble)의 『The Music of Life: Biology Beyond Genes』이라는 책의 일부이다. 실제 책의 제목도 그렇지만, 문제가 출제된 본문에서도 음악에 대한 비유가 많은 것을 알 수 있다. 한편 ① 질병과 의학에 관한 이야기가 아니다. ② 21세기에 발견됐다는 내용은 없다. ④ 개인적 특성이나 환경, 인간 정체성에 관한 이야기가 아니다.

글의 제목으로 가장 적절한 것은?
① 질병의 유전적 태피스트리를 풀다: 의학 연구의 메커니즘과 도전 과제 탐구하기
② 유전학의 혁명: 21세기의 재조합 DNA 기술과 유전자 편집
③ 유전자 발현의 교향곡 해독하기: 단백질, 리보솜, 그리고 DNA의 복잡성
④ 유전적 결정론, 개인적 특성, 환경의 영향: 인간 정체성의 복잡한 풍경 탐색하기

24-26

며칠 후 나는 또 다른 사체에서 두 마리의 검은 새끼를 발견했다. 한 마리는 고기 한 조각을 집어 공중에 던지더니 뛰어올라 턱으로 물었다. 녀석은 고기를 떨어뜨리고 고기가 마치 살아서 도망치려는 것처럼 달려들었다. 그런 다음 그는 고기를 물고 뛰어가다가 다시 위로 던지고, 달리면서 물었다. 나는 나중에 어린 늑대들이 하는 게임 목록을 만들기 시작했는데, 이를

던지기 게임이라고 불렀다.

다른 검은 새끼가 달려들어 첫 번째 새끼를 쫓아갔다. 앞장선 녀석은 고기를 떨어뜨렸고 다른 검은 새끼가 고기를 물었다. 그가 고기를 들고 달아나자 첫 번째 새끼가 그 녀석을 쫓았다. 그러다가 쫓고 쫓기는 상황이 역전되어 두 번째 검은 녀석이 첫 번째 검은 녀석을 쫓았다. 그러다가 앞에 있던 검은 녀석이 갑자기 멈춰서 키 큰 풀밭에 누웠다. 다른 늑대가 뛰어들자, 풀숲에 숨어 있던 늑대가 뛰어올라 그 녀석을 땅바닥에 쓰러뜨렸다. 나는 그것을 매복 게임이라고 불렀다.

나중에 두 녀석이 나란히 서 있다가, 한 녀석이 갑자기 뛰어갔다. 마치 형에게 쫓아와 보라고 도전장을 내민 것처럼 보였다. 다른 검은 녀석은 도전을 수락하고 최고 속도로 동생을 쫓아갔다. 두 형제는 번갈아 가며 직선과 지그재그 패턴으로 서로를 쫓으며 '나 잡아 봐' 놀이를 했다. 그들은 서로 앞에서 달리고, 뛰어다니고, 빙글빙글 돌았다. 누가 누구를 쫓는지는 중요하지 않았고, 그 모든 놀이의 목적은 이기는 것이 아니라 재미있게 노는 것이었다. 녀석들의 행동을 묘사할 수 있는 가장 좋은 단어는 활기차다는 것이었다. 그 모습을 지켜보면서 이런 생각이 들었다. 그들은 늑대인 걸 좋아하는구나.

그 모든 놀이에는 목적이 있었다. 나는 나중에 암컷 엘크가 (늑대) 새끼 중 하나를 쫓는 것을 보았다. 직선 경주에서는 엘크가 늑대를 앞설 수 있었지만, 늑대는 너무도 민첩하게 앞뒤로 지그재그로 움직였기 때문에 엘크는 곧 좌절감에 포기했다. 활기찬 추격 놀이를 통해 어린 늑대는 엘크를 이길 준비가 되어있었다. 때때로 늑대새끼들은 엘크들에게 자기들을 추격하도록 적극적으로 도발했다. 나는 그들이 엘크 앞에서 머리를 조아리는 놀이를 하여 엘크로 하여금 추격을 시작하게 한 다음, 놀이 시간에 완벽하게 익힌 여러 기술을 이용해 쉽게 도망치는 것을 보았다. 그들은 마치 자랑해 보이고 있는 것 같았다.

yearling n. 한 살배기 동물 carcass n. 사체 grab v. 잡다 toss v. 던지다 leap v. 도약하다 jaw n. 턱 pounce v. 덮치다 get away 도망치다 on the run 달리면서 chase v. 추적하다 reverse v. 거꾸로 하다 lay down 눕다 ambush n. 매복 side by side 나란히 dare n. 도전 take turns 교대로[번갈아] 하다 prance v. 껑충거리며 뛰다 twirl v. 빙빙 돌다 exuberant a. 열의가 넘치는 elk n. 엘크 nimbly ad. 민첩하게, 재빠르게 frustration n. 좌절 vigorous a. 활력 있는 outmaneuver v. 술책으로 이기다 at times 때때로 initiate v. 시작하다 show off 과시하다

24 동의어   ②

exuberant는 '활력이 넘치는'이라는 뜻으로 animated(활기찬)가 의미상 가장 가깝다.

다음 중 ⓐ와 의미가 가장 가까운 것은?
① 비굴한
② 활기찬
③ 침울한
④ 냉담한

25 내용파악   ①

본문에서 몰래 접근하기 게임은 소개되지 않았다.

다음 중 본문에 소개되지 않은 게임은 무엇인가?
① 몰래 접근하기 게임
② 던지기 게임
③ 매복 게임
④ 나 잡아 봐라 게임

26 내용파악   ④

'그 모든 놀이에는 목적이 있었다'로 시작되는 마지막 문단의 내용을 통해서 정답을 찾을 수 있다. 놀이 시간에 완벽하게 익힌 여러 기술을 이용하여 새끼 늑대가 추격자로부터 쉽게 도망칠 수 있었다는 내용을 통해 ④가 정답으로 적절함을 알 수 있다.

활기찬 놀이 추격전은 새끼들에게 어떤 목적이 있었는가?
① 다른 늑대와의 대결에서 승리하기 위해
② 자신의 강점을 자랑하기 위해
③ 건강을 유지하기 위해
④ 공격자로부터 도망치는 방법을 배우기 위해

27-29

19세기 말의 이 보고서를 『옥스퍼드 영어 사전』은 '약물'이라는 단어가 이차적 의미(오늘날에는 아마도 그 주된 의미)인 '문화, 오락 또는 기타 비의학적 목적으로 사용되는 중독, 각성 또는 마약 효과가 있는 물질'이라는 의미로 쓰인 최초의 사례로 인용한다. 이때 이전에는 '약물'은 일반적으로 모든 약품을 지칭했다. 지난 수십 년 동안 중독성 또는 향정신성 약물도 흔히 함께 분류되었지만, 그 의미를 명확히 하기 위해 '유독한', '취하게 하는', '위험한' 또는 '중독성인'과 같은 수식하는 형용사가 필요했다. 20세기에 들어서면서 '약물'이라는 하나의 단어가 이 모든 의미를 암시적으로 포함하게 되었다. '약물'은 적절한 의학적 감독 아래 사용되지 않는다면 자가 중독, 중독 또는 정신 질환의 위험이 있는 물질을 통칭하는 약어가 되었다. '약물'의 새로운 의미에 대한 공식적인 유일한 반대는 미국 제약 협회에서 제기했는데, 이들은 자신들의 합법적인 거래가 훼손되지 않을까 우려했기 때문이다. 그러나 '약물'이라는 단어의 새로운 용법은 곧 인기를 끌었고, 제약 거래를 훨씬 넘어서는 의미와 연상을 갖게 되었다.

새로운 세기가 되어 진보의 시대라고 알려진 시대가 밀물처럼 들어왔다. 이는 근대성의 역동적인 관점에서 약물의 이점과 위험이 급격하게 재조정된 시대였다. 이 새로운 운동의 특징은 정부의 팽창, 시민 및 지역사회 운동의 성장, 자유방임주의 정치와 경제를 국가의 개입과 규제로 대체하는 것 등이었다. 이름과는 달리, 진보의 시대의 위대한 성공은 정치 스펙트럼 전반에 걸친 연합을 이루어, 압도적인 힘을 자랑하던 산업, 제국, 금권정치라는 공동의 적에 맞서 진보와 보수의 이해관계를 통합함으로써 달성되었다. 그 시대의 가장 야심 찬 프로젝트였던 미국 금주법이 딱 들어맞는 예였는데, 그것은 금주 운동가, 여성 운동, 노동자 단체, 노동조합, 의료계 등 진보적인 세력을 교회와 구(舊) 청교도 엘리트의 보수적인 목소리와 연합시킴으로써 달성되었다. 어떤 사람들에게는 금주법이 사적 이익을 위해 사회 구조를 좀먹는 양조장과 양조업자에 대항하는 사회 정의 캠페인이었고, 또 다른 사람들에게는 금주법이 술이라는 사회악을 제거하려는 도덕적 운동이었다. 이 두 가지의 이면에는 술에 의하든 다른 약물에 의하든, 취하는 것은 통제력이 저하되고, 미래의 문명사회를 위협하고 있다는 공통된 신념이 깔려 있었다.

cite v. 인용하다 intoxicating a. 취하게 하는 stimulant a. 자극적인 narcotic a. 중독의 prior to ~이전에 medication n. 약물, 의약품 mind-altering a. 향정신 작용성의 qualifying adjective 한정 형용사 inebriating a. 취하게 하는 incorporate v. 포함하다 implicitly ad. 암시적으로 shorthand n. 약칭(略稱); 속기 supervision n. 관리 pharmaceutical a. 제약의 legitimate a. 정당한, 합법적인 tarnish v. 손상시키다 catch on 인기를 끌다 freight v. 수송하다 rising tide 밀물 recalibrate v. 다시 측정하다 hallmark n. 특징 laissez-faire n. 자유방임주의 intervention n. 개입 regulation n. 규제 coalition n. 연합체; 연립 정부 overweening a. 자만하는 might n. 권력, 힘 plutocracy n. 금권정치 a case in point 적절한 사례 temperance n. 금주 brewery n. 양조장 distiller n. 증류주 생산업자, 양조업자 erode v. 부식하다 crusade n. 십자군 전쟁, 성스러운 운동

---

27 내용파악   ②

첫 문장에서 이 보고서가 '약물'이라는 단어가 이차적 의미로 쓰인 최초의 사례라고 했고, 이때 이전에 '약물'은 일반적으로 모든 약품을 지칭했다고 하였다.

19세기 후반 이전에 '약물'이라는 단어의 주된 의미는 무엇이었는가?
① 레크리에이션 목적의 중독성 물질
② 일반적인 약품
③ 의료 목적으로 사용되는 마약 물질
④ 명확히 하기 위한 특정 형용사를 가진 향정신성 약물

---

28 내용파악   ②

첫 단락의 끝에서 두 번째 문장에서 'drug'가 부정적인 의미로 쓰이는 것에 반대한 유일한 집단은 미국 제약 협회였다고 했으며, 그 이유는 자신들이 거래하는 일반적인 약품도 유해한 약물로 오해되어 그들의 거래가 훼손될까 우려했기 때문이라 했다.

'drug evil'이나 'drug habit'과 같은 용어를 일상적으로 사용하는 것에 반대한 것은 누구이며 그 이유는 무엇인가?
① 정부가, 공중 보건에 대한 우려로 인해
② 미국 제약 협회가, 그들의 거래에 대한 우려로 인해
③ 진보의 시대의 활동가들이, 사회 정의를 지향하고 있어서
④ 주류 및 담배 대기업이, 자신들의 이익을 지키고 있어서

---

29 내용파악   ②

두 번째 단락 두 번째 문장에서, '이 새로운 운동(진보의 시대의 접근 방식)의 특징은 자유방임주의 정치와 경제를 국가의 개입과 규제로 대체하는 것'이라고 했다.

약물과 술에 대한 진보의 시대의 접근 방식의 특징은 무엇인가?
① 자유방임주의 정치 및 경제 정책
② 엄격한 국가 개입 및 규제
③ 제약업계의 반대
④ 글로벌 무역에 대한 고립주의적 태도

거친 말을 하고 작은 흰색 바지를 입고 엉덩이를 흔들어 대는 미키 마우스의 초기 버전을 셔츠에서, 영화에서, 무대에서 어디서나 곧 볼 수 있을 것이다. 1928년 영화 "증기선 윌리"에서 거위를 트롬본 삼아 부는 장난꾸러기 설치류로 등장하는 미키 마우스가 월요일 현재 미국에서 공적 저작물로 이용할 수 있게 되었다. 그 캐릭터를 그 이후에 그려낸 것들은 여전히 저작권의 보호를 받는다. 하지만 이 변화는 디즈니가 그토록 늦추려고 애썼던 중요한 순간이다.

1998년, 의회는 다양한 저작물에 대해 저작권 기간을 연장했다. 디즈니의 의회 로비로 인해 '미키 마우스 보호법'이라고도 불리는 저작권 기간 연장법에 따라, 1978년 이전에 발표된 많은 자료의 저작권 기간이 95년간으로 연장되었다. 듀크 대학교 임상법 교수이자 듀크 공적 저작물 연구 센터 소장인 제니퍼 젠킨스(Jennifer Jenkins)는 이메일을 통해 이 법은 '극소수의 권리 소유자에게만 부를 이전했고', 미국의 문화유산에 대한 대중의 접근과 축적 능력을 '방해했다'라고 말했다.

디즈니 자체는 저작권과 복잡한 관계를 맺고 있다. 디즈니는 창작품에 대한 권리 보유에 있어 기득권을 가지고 있지만, 공적 저작물로부터도 많은 혜택을 받아왔다. 디즈니의 히트작 중 일부는 기존의 기적 재산에 기반을 두고 있다. 주요 영화의 바탕이 된 동화나 『라이온 킹』 프랜차이즈의 기반이 된 『햄릿』의 줄거리를 생각해보라. 디즈니 영화는 루이스 캐럴, 그림 형제, 빅토르 위고, 한스 크리스티안 안데르센 등의 원작을 바탕으로 제작된다고 젠킨스는 설명했다. 디즈니 대변인은 '물론 우리는 좀 더 현대적인 버전의 미키 마우스와 저작권이 남아 있는 다른 저작물에 대한 권리를 계속 보호할 것이며, 미키와 우리의 다른 상징적인 캐릭터의 무단 사용으로 인한 소비자 혼란을 방지하기 위해 노력할 것'이라고 말했다.

일리노이 대학교의 법학 교수이자 저작권 전문가 폴 힐드(Paul Heald)는 저작권법은 새로운 저작물의 창작 촉진이 그 목적이라고 말했다. 저작권법은 작가가 무언가를 창작하면 출시 후 일정 기간 배타적인 권리를 누릴 수 있도록 보장한다. 그러나 그 기간은 조정이 필요하다. 힐드는 저작권법이 너무 자유를 제한하는 경우 창의적인 표현을 억제할 수 있다고 말했다. 그는 더 많은 작품이 공적 저작물이 되는 것은 창의성에 도움이 될 뿐만 아니라 '헌법 초안 제정자들의 계획의 일부'라고 말했다.

crude a. 조잡한 as of ~현재 iteration n. 반복 mischievous a. 장난꾸러기의 rodent n. 설치류 public domain (저작권이 소멸된) 공적[자유 이용] 저작물, 공공 재산(특허·저작 등의 권리 소멸 상태) depiction n. 묘사 transfer v. 이전하다 subset n. 부분집합 clinical law 임상법 stymie v. 좌절시키다 access v. 접근하다 build on 축적하다 vested a. 기존의 retain v. 보유하다 intellectual property 지적 소유권 fairy tale 동화 franchise n. 독점 사업권, 프랜차이즈 spokesperson n. 대변인 safeguard v. 보호하다 iconic a. 상징적인 copyright law 저작권법 exclusive a. 배타적인 release n. 발매, 출시 balancing act (이해관계가 얽힌 개인·단체 사이의) 갈등 조정 (절차) restrictive a. (자유 등을) 제한[구속]하는 curb v. 억제하다

---

30 내용파악   ③

그녀는 저작권 기간 연장법이 미국의 문화유산에 대한 대중의 접근과 축적 능력을 '방해했다'라고 말했다.

제니퍼 젠킨스에 따르면, 저작권 기간 연장법이 대중의 문화유산 접근에 어떤 영향을 미쳤는가?
① 문화유산에 대한 접근성을 높였다.
② 문화유산에 대한 접근성에는 영향을 미치지 않았다.

③ 문화유산에 대한 대중의 접근성을 저해했다.
④ 부를 문화유산으로 이전했다.

---

31 내용파악 ④

디즈니가 저작권과 복잡한 관계를 가지고 있는 이유는 세 번째 문단에 설명되어 있다. 자신은 공적 저작물에서 이익을 얻으면서, 자기 창작물은 공적 저작물로 내놓지 않으려고 한다는 것이다.

디즈니의 저작권과의 관계에서 복잡한 점으로 언급되고 있는 것은 무엇인가?
① 디즈니는 자신의 창작품에 대한 권리를 보유하는 데 관심이 없다.
② 디즈니는 공적 저작물을 통해 이익을 얻은 적이 없다.
③ 디즈니의 히트작은 기존의 지적 재산에 기반하지 않는다.
④ 디즈니는 공적 저작물로부터 이익을 얻었지만, 자신의 창작물은 보호하고자 한다.

---

32 내용파악 ③

마지막 문단 마지막 문장에서 창의성에 도움이 된다고 하였다.

폴 힐드에 의하면, 작품이 공적 저작물이 되면 어떤 결과가 발생하는가?
① 대기업의 통제력 강화
② 창의적 표현의 제한
③ 창의성에 도움을 주는 공적 저작물의 풍요로움
④ 아티스트의 저작권 보호 손실

33-35

미국 에너지 정보국(EIA)의 예비 데이터에 따르면, 올해 태양광과 풍력 발전은 2023년 첫 5개월 동안 석탄보다 더 많은 전력을 생산하며 신기록을 세웠다. 수치를 처음 계산한 업계 간행물인 『E&E News』에 따르면, 풍력과 태양광이 5개월 동안 전력 생산에서 석탄을 앞지른 것은 기록상 처음이다. EIA 대변인 크리스 히긴보텀(Chris Higginbotham)은 이메일에서 시간이 지체되고 나서 발표되는 공식 EIA 자료에 따르면, 1월, 2월, 3월에 풍력과 태양광 에너지가 석탄의 에너지 생산량을 앞질렀지만, 실시간 수치는 "같은 추세가 4월과 5월에도 계속되었음을 보여줍니다."라고 말했다.
EIA에 따르면, 수력 발전을 재생에너지 믹스에 포함시킬 경우, 재생에너지가 지난 10월부터 석탄을 앞질러서 그 기록은 6개월 이상으로 늘어난다. "생산-비용 측면에서 볼 때 재생에너지는 풍력과 태양광이 사용하기에 가장 저렴합니다. 따라서 우리는 이러한 기록을 점점 더 많이 보게 될 것입니다."라고 스탠퍼드 대학교 토목 및 환경 공학 교수 람 라자고팔(Ram Rajagopal)은 말했다.
이 수치는 청정 전력의 새로운 최고 기록과 석탄 화력 발전의 급격한 감소를 나타내는데, 석탄 화력 발전은 최근 10년 전만 해도 미국 전력의 40%를 차지했었다. EIA에 따르면, 월간 수치는 예비 수치이며 향후 몇 달 내에 수정될 수 있지만, 재생에너지가 증가일로에 있다는 것은 석탄 발전량이 계속 감소할 것이라는 것을 의미한다. "올해 미국은 금세기 어느 해보다 석탄으로 만들어지는 전력이 적을 것으로 예상됩니다."라고 5월 EIA의 조 드캐롤리스(Joe DeCarolis) 국장이 말했다. "전기 공급업체들이 재생가능 에너지원에서 더 많은 전기를 생산함에 따라, 향후 1년 반 동안 석탄에서 생산되는 전기는 감소할 것으로 예상됩니다."

수년 동안 수압 파쇄 붐에 힘입어 또 하나의 화석 연료인 천연가스가 점점 더 저렴해짐에 따라, 석탄 발전은 감소하고 있다. 그러나 작년에 러시아의 우크라이나 침공 이후 천연가스 가격이 급등하면서 미국과 유럽의 일부 전력 회사들이 석탄 발전기를 이용했을 때 석탄이 잠시 부활했다. 전 세계적으로 석탄 사용량은 2022년에 최고치를 기록했지만, 미국에서는 석탄 발전소가 꾸준히 퇴역함에 따라 그 반등세가 오래가지 못했다. 올해 들어 지금까지 6개의 석탄 연료 발전소가 폐쇄됐다.

generate v. (전기·열 등을) 발생시키다 preliminary a. 예비의, 준비의 calculate v. 계산하다, 산정하다 release v. 발표하다 real-time n. 실시간 figure n. 수치 trend n. 추세 hydroelectric a. 수력 전기의 renewable a. 재생 가능한 stretch v. 뻗어가다 civil engineering 토목공학 steep a. 가파른 make up 구성하다 revise v. 수정하다 in the pipeline 진행 중인 set a. ~할 준비가 된 fossil fuel 화석연료 hydraulic fracturing 수압 파쇄 resurgence n. 부활 in the wake of ~이후에 invasion n. 침략 utility n. 공공시설 sign on 고용하다 bounceback n. 반등 retire v. 은퇴하다 at a steady pace 꾸준하게

---

33 빈칸완성 ④

빈칸 Ⓐ는 calculate의 목적어 자리이므로 수와 관련 있는 표현이 와야 하고, 빈칸 Ⓑ의 경우, 이어지는 내용에서, '보고서는 1, 2, 3월의 수치는 포함하고 있지만, 4월과 5월의 실시간 수치는 반영하지 못하고 있다'고 하였으므로, 데이터 발표에는 '시간의 지체'가 있다고 볼 수 있다.

다음 중 빈칸 Ⓐ와 Ⓑ에 들어가기에 가장 적절한 것은?
① 수치 — 경쟁
② 제재 — 지체
③ 제제 — 경쟁
④ 수치 — 지체

---

34 내용파악 ③

EIA는 미국이 금세기 올해(2023년)에 석탄으로부터 발전하는 전기량이 가장 적을 것으로 예상하고 있다.

EIA가 미국이 금세기 들어 석탄에서 전기를 가장 덜 생산할 것으로 예상하는 시기는 언제인가?
① 다음 세기 말까지
② 2022년 말까지
③ 2023년 말까지
④ 향후 10년 이내

---

35 내용파악 ④

작년에 러시아의 우크라이나 침공으로 인해 석탄 발전소 이용이 늘어났다고 하였다.

작년에 석탄 발전이 잠시 부활하게 만든 것은 무엇인가?
① 석탄 연료 발전소 폐쇄
② 재생에너지 생산량 감소
③ 수력 발전의 붐
④ 러시아의 우크라이나 침공에 따른 천연가스 가격 상승

36-37

'놀라운 분위기를 풍기는 멋진 사람'은 이 팝스타에 대한 천진하다 할 만큼 단순한 설명이다. 하지만 이는 그가 오랫동안 추구해온 이미지이다. 10대 시절, 정국이 BTS에 합류하기로 결심한 것은 그룹 리더 RM의 영어 구사력과 랩 실력에 깊은 인상을 받았기 때문이다. 그는 사운드클라우드에 자신이 좋아하는 팝송을 커버해서 올리곤 했고, 저스틴 비버, 어셔, 아리아나 그런데 등에 대해 신이 나서 말해대곤 했다. 내가 처음 그의 라이브 공연을 보았을 때, 그는 수만 명의 팬 위에서 케이블로 매달린 채 경기장을 날아다니면서도, 그의 보컬은 마치 소파에 누워 있는 듯 안정적이었다. 하지만 이러한 멋짐에 대한 열망의 밑바탕에는 탁월함에 대한 똑같이 오래된 집착이 깔려 있다. "골든"이라는 제목은 즉시 정국의 가장 잘 알려진 별명인 '황금 막내'를 떠올리게 한다. RM이 만든 이 별명은 멤버 중 가장 어린(우리말로 '막내') 멤버로서의 그의 지위를 가리키는데, 그는 그가 하는 모든 일에 초자연적으로 재능이 있어 보인다. 정국은 파워풀한 댄서일 뿐 아니라 강력한 보컬리스트이고, 드로잉, 그림, 작곡, 양궁, 레슬링, 단거리 달리기, 수영에서도 뛰어나다. '잘하는 것'만 모아놓은 영상이 유튜브에서 1,800만 뷰가 넘는 조회 수를 기록하고 있다. 본업인 가수에 관해서라면, 그는 자기 일에 대해 엄격한 완벽주의자로 알려져 있다. 그래서 "골든"에 대한 기대가 컸다. 이 음반이 발매되기 전에, 가장 빠르게 10억 스트리밍에 도달하여 스포티파이 신기록을 세운 영국 개러지 트랙 "Seven(라토 피처링)"과 2000년대 초반을 연상시키는 "3D(잭 할로우 피처링)"라는 두 싱글이 먼저 발매되었다. 그러나 나는 팔라먼트-펑카델릭과 마이클 잭슨을 떠올리게 하는 멋진 메인 트랙 "Standing Next to You"에 대해서는 전혀 예상하지 못했다. 정국이나 BTS가 이전에 했던 곡과는 전혀 다르다.

disarmingly ad. 무장 해제될 정도로, 천진스럽게 vibe n. 분위기, 느낌 chase v. 쫓다, 추적하다; 추구하다 gush about 자랑하다, 신나게 말하다 suspend v. 매달다 stable a. 안정된 recline v. 기대다, 눕다 chaise n. 소파 obsession n. 강박 underpin v. 받치다 evoke v. 연상시키다 status n. 지위 preternatural a. 초자연적인 archery n. 궁술 when it comes to ~에 관해 말하자면 release n. 발매 U.K. garage 영국에서 유래한 음악 장르 throwback n. 유사한 것 stunning a. 놀라운 Parliament-Funkadelic 미국의 펑크 음악 그룹

---

36 빈칸완성 ②

빈칸 다음에 자기 일에 '엄격한(exacting)' 사람이라는 말이 있다. 이런 사람을 가리켜 완벽주의자라고 한다.

빈칸 Ⓐ에 들어가기에 가장 적절한 것은?
① 게으름뱅이
② 완벽주의자
③ 조수
④ 태평한 사람

---

37 내용일치 ④

④ 마지막 문장에서 "Standing Next to You"는 예상하지 못했다고 하면서, 정국이나 BTS가 이전에 했던 곡과는 전혀 다르다고 하였다.

다음 중 옳지 않은 것은?
① 정국은 10대에 RM의 영어와 랩 실력에 감명을 받아 BTS에 합류했다.
② 정국은 저스틴 비버와 같은 아티스트를 동경하며 사운드클라우드에 팝송 커버곡을 자주 공유했다.
③ 정국은 춤, 노래, 드로잉, 그림, 작곡, 양궁, 레슬링, 단거리 달리기, 수영에 뛰어나다.
④ "Standing Next to You"는 정국과 BTS의 이전 작품들과 비슷한 맥락을 따르고 있다.

38-39

올여름 작가와 배우들이 역사적인 동시 파업으로 피켓 시위에 나섰을 때 할리우드를 멈추게 한 분쟁의 중심에는 AI가 있었다. ChatGPT와 같은 글쓰기 도구와 미드저니(Midjourney)와 같은 AI 이미지 생성 도구가 등장했을 때, 할리우드 창작자들은 AI가 자신들의 일자리를 빼앗을까 걱정하기 시작했다. 수개월 간의 협상 끝에 각 직업을 대표하는 협회들은 대부분 AI를 통해 만들어지는 미래 버전의 할리우드에 대한 보호책을 마련했다. 하지만 일부 영화 제작자들은 이러한 보호 장치가 충분히 튼튼하지 않다고 우려하고 있다. 올해 초, 할리우드 작가들의 작업실에서는 특히 새로운 작품의 새로운 파일럿 아이디어를 더욱 저렴하게 생성하기 위해 ChatGPT가 사용되기 시작했다. 이에 대한 대응으로, 미국작가협회는 스튜디오가 대본 작성이나 편집에 AI를 사용하거나, ChatGPT로 대본을 만든 다음 작가에게 낮은 임금을 지급하고 그것을 각색하게 하는 행위에 대한 보호를 요구했고, 결국 그러한 보호를 확보했다. 이 계약은 대본 작성에서의 ChatGPT 사용을 금지하지는 않을 것이다. 작가들은 AI를 연구나 아이디어 창출을 위한 도구로 사용할 수 있다. 그러나 결정적으로, 작가는 항상 자신의 작업에 대한 보상을 받고, 그 과정의 중심에 있을 것이다. 한편, 배우들도 스튜디오가 자신들을 '디지털 복제품'으로 대체하지 않을까 하는 비슷한 우려를 갖고 있었다. 스튜디오는 배우에게 돈을 지불하는 대신, 배우의 신체를 스캔하고 하루 일당을 지불한 다음, AI 기술을 사용하여 장면들을 채울 수 있다. 몇 달간의 교착 상태 끝에 제작자들은 결국 배우가 자신의 스캔과 디지털 복제본 제작에 명확하게 동의해야 하는 동의 기반 모델에 합의했다. 또한 배우들은 디지털 복제본의 출연에 대해 재방송료에 있어서도 완전한 권리를 갖게 된다. 하지만 일부 배우들은 여전히 합성 배우에 대한 전면적인 금지를 요구하고 있으며, 그들이 서명한 계약에 AI가 점점 더 많은 일자리를 잠식할 수 있는 허점이 포함되어 있지나 않을까 우려하고 있다.

dispute n. 분쟁 grind to a halt 멈춰 세우다 strike n. 파업 actor n. 배우 picket line 파업선 historic a. 역사적으로 중요한 double strike 동시 파업 carve out 노력하여 얻다 negotiation n. 협상 via prep. ~을 통하여 robust a. 강력한 guild n. 길드, 조합 Writers Guild of America 미국작가협회 secure v. 확보하다 adapt v. 각색하다 contract n. 계약서 prohibit v. 금지하다 crucially ad. 중요하게도 compensate for 보상하다 meanwhile ad. 한편 digital replica 디지털 복제품 stalemate n. 교착 상태 consent-based a. 동의를 기반으로 한 unambiguously ad. 분명하게 opt in to 동의하다 be entitled to ~에 대한 권리가 있다 residual n. (pl.) (영화·TV의 재방영·광고 방송 등에서 출연자에게 지불하는) 재방송료 call for 요구하다 outright a. 철저한, 완전한 ban n. 금지 synthetic performer 합성 배우, AI 배우 loophole n. 허점 encroach on 침해하다

38 글의 제목 ①

첫 번째 문장에서 이미 파업의 원인이 AI라고 지적하고 있으므로 제목으로는 ①이 적절하다. ② AI가 할리우드 영화제작 작업의 대부분을 맡아 하게 된 것은 아니며 파업 부분이 빠졌으므로 제목으로 부적절하다.

다음 중 제목으로 가장 적절한 것은?
① AI와 할리우드 파업
② AI에 점령당한 할리우드
③ AI와 컴퓨터 그래픽
④ 지적 재산권 쟁탈전

39 내용일치 ③

새로운 계약은 대본 작성에서의 AI 사용을 금지하지 않고 있다. 그러므로 ③이 정답이다.

다음 중 옳지 않은 것은?
① 일부 영화 제작자는 AI에 대응한 보호 조치에 여전히 만족하지 못하고 있다.
② 작가들은 AI가 생성한 대본으로 인해 낮은 임금을 받을까 걱정하고 있다.
③ 새로운 계약은 대본 작성 및 편집에 AI 사용을 금지한다.
④ 제작자는 디지털 복제본 사용에 대한 배우의 승인이 필요하다.

40-42

그리스인들에게 아름다움이란 하나의 미덕으로, 일종의 우수함이었다. 당시에는, 사람이란 오늘날이라면 — 자신이 없으면서도 부러워하며 — 전인적(全人的) 인간이라 해야 할 그런 존재로 여겨졌다. 그리스인들은 사람의 '내면'과 '외면'을 구분해야겠다는 생각이 들긴 했지만, 그래도 내면의 아름다움이 외면의 아름다움과 상응할 것이라고 기대했다. 소크라테스 주변에 모여들었던 아테네의 명문가 출신의 젊은이들은 자신들의 영웅이 그렇게도 지적이고, 용감하고, 존경스럽고, 매력적이면서, 동시에 그렇게도 추한 외모를 가졌다는 것이 대단히 모순적이라 생각했다. 소크라테스의 주된 교육적 가르침 가운데 하나는 자신이 추한 모습으로 있으면서, 틀림없이 멋진 외모를 가지고 있었던 저 순수한 제자들에게 인생이 실제로 얼마나 모순으로 가득 차 있는지를 가르쳐 준 것이었다.

그들은 소크라테스의 가르침에 반감을 느꼈을지 모른다. 그러나 우리는 그렇지 않다. 수천 년이 지난 지금, 우리는 아름다움의 매력에 대해 더욱 신중을 기한다. 우리는 인간의 '내면'(성격, 지성)을 '외면'(외모)으로부터 대단히 쉽게 분리시키는 것에 그치지 않고, 나아가 외모가 아름다운 사람이 지적이고 재능이 많고 선량하기까지 하면 실제로 놀라게 된다.

인간의 우수성에 대한 고전주의적 이상에서 아름다움이 차지하던 중심적 위치를 아름다움으로부터 박탈한 것은 주로 기독교의 영향이었다. 기독교는 우수성(라틴어로 비투스)을 도덕적 미덕으로만 제한해버림으로써 아름다움으로 하여금 소외되고 자의적이며 피상적인 매혹으로 표류하게 만들었다. 그리고 아름다움은 계속해서 명성을 잃어왔다. 거의 2세기 동안 아름다움을 두 성별 중 하나(여성)의 것으로만 여기는 것이 관습이 되었다. 그 성별(여성)은 아무리 아름다워도, 항상 제 2의 성이다. 아름다움을 여성과 연관 짓는 것은 아름다움을 도덕적으로 더욱 수세에 놓이게 만들었다. 우리는 영어로 여자는 아름답다고 하지만, 남자는 잘생겼다고 한다. '잘생겼다'는 아름답다는 말의 남성적 동의어이자, 동시에 여성에게만 하는 것

으로 되어있어서 비하적인 어조가 축적된 칭찬을 거부하는 것이기도 하다. 프랑스어와 이탈리아어로 남성을 '아름답다'라고 부를 수 있는 것은 개신교 기반의 국가와는 달리 이들 가톨릭 국가에는 여전히 아름다움에 대한 이교도적 찬양의 흔적이 남아 있음을 시사한다. 그러나 차이가 있다면 정도의 차이일 뿐이다. 기독교 국가이든 기독교 이후의 국가이든 모든 현대 국가에서 여성은 아름다운 성이며, 이것은 여성의 개념뿐 아니라 아름다움의 개념도 해치고 있다.

virtue n. 미덕 excellence n. 우수성 assume v. 가정하다 lamely ad. 자신 없게 occur to 떠오르다 well-born a. 잘난, 좋은 집안의 seductive a. 유혹적인 pedagogical a. 교육적인 paradox n. 모순, 역설 wary a. 조심하는, 경계하는 enchantment n. 매혹 split off 분리하다 facility n. 손쉬움 adrift a. 표류하는 arbitrary a. 자의적인, 변덕스러운 superficial a. 피상적인, 얄팍한 prestige n. 명성, 위신 convention n. 관례, 규칙 demeaning a. 비하하는 overtone n. 의미, 함축 vestige n. 흔적 pagan a. 이교도적인 detriment n. 손해 to the detriment of ~을 해치도록 notion n. 통념

40 빈칸완성 ④

전후에서 계속 이야기하고 있는 내용은 아름다움의 내면과 외면은 일치하지 않을 수 있다는 것이다. 이를 한 단어로 말하자면 paradox(모순)이다.

다음 중 빈칸 Ⓐ에 들어가기에 가장 적절한 것은?
① 모호성
② 위험
③ 축복
④ 모순

41 부분이해 ②

뒤 문장에서 지금의 우리는 내면과 외면을 구분하고 외면이 아름다워도 얼마든지 내면이 추할 수 있다고 생각하므로 어떤 사람에게서 이 둘이 일치하면 오히려 놀라게 된다고 했다. 그만큼 현대인은 '아름다운 외면에 속아 추한 내면을 못 볼 수 있다'는 것을 알고 있으므로 아름다운 외면이 가진 매력에 더욱 경계하는 것이다.

밑줄 친 Ⓑ은 문맥상 어떤 의미인가?
① 시각적 매력은 놀라운 사랑의 힘을 가지고 있다.
② 신체적 아름다움은 상당히 기만적이고 오해를 불러일으킬 수 있다.
③ 아름다운 마음을 가진 사람만이 신뢰받을 수 있다.
④ 지적인 사람들은 외모를 거의 관리하지 않는다.

42 내용파악 ④

마지막 문장에서 '여성은 아름다운 성이다'라고 한 것은 아름다움을 여성과 연관 지은 것인데, 이것이 여성의 개념뿐 아니라 아름다움의 개념도 해친다고 했으므로 ④가 정답이다.

다음 중 현대의 여성과 아름다움의 연관성에 대한 저자의 태도를 가장 잘 포착해낸 것은?

① 여성 권한 부여의 공정한 신호이다.
② 그리스인들이 가졌던 아름다움의 개념이 이제 회복되었음을 보여준다.
③ 여성의 아름다움은 도덕적 우수성을 반영한다는 것을 보여준다.
④ 여성의 존엄성과 아름다움의 개념을 훼손한다.

43-45

저항이라는 정치적 개념은 힘과 폭력에 시달리는 자들이 힘과 폭력에 맞서 투쟁하는 것을 의미한다. 다시 말해, 이는 그 힘의 우월성을 분석하고 인정하는 것과 그 힘을 해체하고자 하는 목표를 포함한다. 그러나 오늘날 '저항'이라는 이름으로 불리는 것 중 많은 것은 적에 대한 보복이며, 지정된 반대자들 사이의 (폭력적인) 행동과 반동, 공격과 반격의 시간적 연속으로 간주되는 것에 있어서의 대응조치이다. 목표는 힘을 해체하는 것이 아니라 적에 대한 승리이다. 다시 말해, 자기편에 충분한 힘을 모아 상대편을 압도하는 것이다.

따라서 중요한 질문은 힘의 관계가 무엇이냐가 아니라 역사의 고려가 어디에서 시작되느냐이다. 즉, 어느 쪽 행동이 두 번째 행동을 단순히 대응조치에 불과한 것으로 만드는 '최초의' 행동이냐 하는 것이다. 따라서 뉴스에서는 팔레스타인인은 돌을 던지고 이스라엘 정착민들은 총을 쏘았다고 보도되었지만, "누가 먼저 시작했는지는 아직 명확하지 않다." 다시 말해, '저항'이라는 개념은 자신의 행동(또는 자신이 동일시하는 사람들의 행동)을 정당화하는 이념화 구조의 일부가 되는데, 이 구조에서는 우리의 행동에 앞선 다른 편의 행동이 우리 편의 폭력적 행동의 원인이라거나 원인 제공을 우리에게 했다고 말해진다.

이러한 이유로 해서, 세계의 모든 군대는 현재의 군사 행동이 무엇에 대한 방어인지를 설명하는 민간 국방부에 의해 지배되는 '방어'군이라고 불린다. 따라서 영국의 포클랜드 전쟁은 방어 전쟁이며, 아르헨티나 전함 '제너럴 벨그라노(General Belgrano)'의 침몰도 적대적인 항로 변경에 대한 방어적 조치이다. 마찬가지로 이라크 폭격은 이미 공격받은 쿠웨이트를 방어하기 위한 보복이며, 사담 후세인이 유엔의 최후통첩에 대응하지 못한 것에 대한 정당한 대응이다. 사실, 역사를 살펴보면 세상에서 공격적인 조치는 전혀 없었다는 것을 알 수 있다. 왜냐하면 둘 중 어느 한 편이 '보복'의 '원인'이었다고 생각하는 앞선 행동이나 사건이 항상 있었기 때문이다.

resistance n. 저항 struggle n. 투쟁, 싸움 force n. 무력 recognition n. 인식 superiority n. 우월성 dismantle v. 해체하다, 분해하다 retaliation n. 보복, 앙갚음 counter-move n. 반격 designated a. 지정된 settler n. 정착민 justify v. 정당화하다 subject n. 주체 identify v. 동일시하다 ministry n. 부처, 장관 defence n. 방어 warship n. 전함 hostile a. 적대적인 bombing n. 폭격 aggressive a. 공격적인 ultimatum n. 최후통첩 consult v. 자문하다

43 빈칸완성 ①

다음 문장을 보면 공격이 있고, 반격이 있고, 다시 공격이 있고 반격이 있다고 했는데, 이는 사건들의 연속을 의미하고, 그다음 문단에서 어느 쪽에서 시작했느냐, 최초의 행동을 한 것이 어느 쪽이냐가 중요하다고 했는데, 이것은 시간과 관계된 것이다. 따라서 ①이 적절하다.

다음 중 빈칸 Ⓐ에 들어가기에 가장 적절한 것은?
① 시간적 연속
② 외교적 충돌
③ 군사 전략
④ 상호 파괴

44 빈칸완성 ③

그다음에 예로 든 이스라엘-팔레스타인 충돌에서 팔레스타인인들은 돌을 던지고 이스라엘 정착민들은 총을 쏘았다고 했는데, 이것이 힘에 있어서 이스라엘이 더 우세하다는 양측 사이의 힘의 관계를 의미하므로 ③이 적절하다.

다음 중 빈칸 Ⓑ에 들어가기에 가장 적절한 것은?
① 외교적 제스처
② 인간의 본능
③ 힘의 관계
④ 국제 정치

45 빈칸완성 ④

'역사를 살펴보면'은 '역사책이나 역사기록을 펼쳐서 관련 정보를 찾아보면'의 뜻이라 할 수 있다. 따라서 '(사전이나 책을) 찾아보다, 참고하다'는 뜻으로 쓰이는 동사 consult가 들어가는 것이 적절하다. view는 주로 '(경치나 전시물이나 영화를) 보다'의 뜻으로 쓰인다.

다음 중 빈칸 Ⓒ에 들어가기에 가장 적절한 것은?
① 신화를 벗기다
② 보다
③ 인식하다
④ 찾아보다

46-47

교사가 학생들을 좋아하는 것이 중요하다면, 그들을 알아야 하는 것도 마찬가지로 중요하다. 교사는 아이들이 교사 자신이나 교사가 아는 사람들과 같을 것이라고 기대해서는 안 되며, 그들의 생각과 감정의 패턴을 배워야 한다. 이를 통해 그는 학생들이 하는 많은 이상한 행동을 이해하고 학생들의 용서하기 어려운 행동 중 일부를 잊을 수 있다.

교사는 학생들을 어떻게 철저히 알 수 있을까? 주로 그들과의 밀접한 교제를 통해서이다. 그는 가끔 파티를 열거나 함께 게임을 할 수 있다. 학생들이 당신이 다른 일을 하고 있다고 생각할 때 그들이 하는 말을 귀담아듣고, 그들의 감정과 마음이 실제로 어떻게 작동하는지 알아내려 노력하라. 또한 당신 자신의 어린 시절을 기억함으로써 그들에 대해 많은 것을 배울 수 있다. 당신의 어린 시절을 더 많이 기억할수록, 아이들을 더 잘 이해할 수 있다.

일반교과목을 가장 못 가르치는 교사들 중 일부는 어렸을 때에도 공부는 많이 하고 거칠거나 유치한 놀이는 거의 하지 않은 사람들일 수 있다. 그들은 교사처럼 되려고 노력할 때 가장 즐거웠다. 그러한 젊은이들은 흔히 좋은 성적을 받고 나중에는 거친 세계로 들어가 모험적인 경쟁으로 생계를 유지하기가 망설여진다. 그들은 교직에 발을 들여놓는데, 교직 중에 마음에 들지 않는 부분이 아주 많아서 놀란다. 때로로 그들은 (어릴 적) 자신을 생각나게 하는 똑똑하고 부지런한 학생들에게는 대단히 효과적일 수 있다. 그들은 그러한 학생들에게 자신의 모든 야망을 투사하여, 그들을 미래 교육을 위한 상금을 획득하고 어려운 시험에 통과하도록 공부시킨다. 그러나 그들은 그들 자신이 평범하거나 미숙한 적이 없기 때문에 보통의 반을 가득 메우고 있는 평범한 학생들을 데리고는 거의 잘 해나가지 못한다.

essential a. 필수적인 pupil n. 학생 unpardonable a. 용서할 수 없는 thorough a. 철저한 association n. 교제 occasionally ad. 때때로 subject n. 과목 silly a. 바보 같은 grade n. 성적 rude a. 무례한 earn a living 생계를 유지하다 adventurous a. 모험적인 competition n. 경쟁 profession n. 직업 hard-working a. 부지런한

---

46 빈칸완성   ①

Ⓐ 다음 문장에서 '학생들을 위해 파티를 열고 학생들과 함께 게임을 한다'고 했으므로 '교제'라는 의미의 association이 적절하다. Ⓑ 어릴 적 자신을 생각나게 하는 똑똑하고 부지런한 학생들이라면 교사는 그들을 자신과 동일시하여 그들에게 모든 것을 쏟아 부을 것이다. 따라서 '쏟아 붓는다'와 유사한 '투사하다'는 뜻의 project가 적절하다.

다음 중 빈칸 Ⓐ와 Ⓑ에 들어가기에 가장 적절한 것은?
① 교제 — 투사하다
② 협력 — 기부하다
③ 관찰 — 헤아리다
④ 조화 — 강조하다

---

47 내용일치   ④

학생들에게 롤모델이 되기 위해 최선을 다하는 교사에 대한 언급은 없다.

다음 중 옳지 않은 것은?
① 학생을 사랑하는 것과 이해하는 것은 교육에서 병행되어야 한다.
② 어린 시절 기억이 학생을 이해하는 데 도움이 될 수 있다.
③ 평범한 학생들을 데리고 잘 헤나가는 데 어려움을 겪는 교사도 있다.
④ 좋은 교사는 완벽한 롤모델이 되기 위해 최선을 다한다.

48-50

미국 영어의 많은 지역 방언의 기원은 17세기와 18세기에 북미에 정착한 사람들로 거슬러 올라갈 수 있다. 이 초기 정착민들은 영국의 여러 다양한 지역에서 왔기 때문에 이미 영어의 여러 방언을 말했으며, 이러한 차이들은 최초의 13개 미국 식민지에 그대로 전달되었다. 미국 독립전쟁 때는 이미 영국식민지(미국)에 3개의 주요 방언 지역이 있었는데, 뉴잉글랜드와 허드슨강 주변에서 사용되는 북부 방언, 펜실베이니아에서 사용되는 중부 방언, 그리고 남부 방언이었다. 이러한 방언들은 서로 달랐고 영국의 영어와도 체계적으로 달랐다. 영국 영어에서 일어났던 일부 변화들은 식민지로 퍼졌고, 또 다른 변화들은 그렇지 않았다.
방언의 발전 방식은 미국의 다양한 지역에서의 r을 가진 단어들의 발음에 의해 설명될 수 있다. 일찍이 18세기에는 이미 남부 영국의 영국인들은 자음 앞과 단어 끝에서 r을 발음하지 않고 있었다. <card라는 단어와 cod라는 단어가 그 방언의 보스턴 버전에서는 동음이의어이다.> 18세기 말에 이미, 이 r음 삭제(r-drop)는 뉴잉글랜드와 남부 대서양 해안의 많은 초기 정착민들 사이에서 일반 규칙이 되었다. 뉴잉글랜드 식민지와 런던 사이에 밀접한 상업적 관계가 유지되고, 남부 사람들이 자녀를 영국으로 보내 교육하면서 r음 삭제 규칙을 강화하였다. r 없는 방언은 오늘날 보스턴, 뉴욕 및 조지아 주 서배너에서 아직도 사용되고 있다. 그러나 나중에 정착한 사람들은 r이 보존된 영국 북부에서 왔다. 서부 개척이 진행되면서 r도 서쪽으로 이동했다. 세 방언 지역의 개척자들도 서쪽으로 퍼져 나갔다.

이들의 방언이 섞이면서 방언 차이가 많이 평준화되었으며, 그런 이유로 해서 중서부 넓은 지역에서 사용되는 영어와 서부에서 사용되는 영어가 유사하다.

origin n. 기원, 출처 trace v. 추적하다 settler n. 정착민 dialect n. 방언 consonant n. 자음 seaboard n. 해안 지방 commercial a. 상업의 reinforce v. 강화하다 retain v. 유지하다 pioneer n. 개척자 mingling n. 혼합 level v. 평준화하다 section n. 구역

---

48 문장삽입   ②

주어진 문장의 card에서 r이 자음 d 앞에 있어서 발음되지 않으면 card가 cod와 같은 발음이 되어 동음이의어가 되므로 주어진 문장은 r이 자음 앞이나 단어 끝에서 발음되지 않고 있었다고 한 바로 다음인 Ⓑ에 들어가는 것이 적절하다. 주어진 문장에서 that dialect(그 방언)은 바로 앞 문장의 남부 영국의 영국인들이 r 없이 말했던 방언을 말하고, 이 방언이 미국 보스턴에 들어와 오늘날 보스턴 방언에서도 r 없이 말하여 card와 cod를 동일하게 발음하고 있다는 말이 된다. Ⓑ 앞뒤의 문장이 Ⓑ 없이 연결되어 그 이하 계속 r 없는 방언이 미국으로 들어와 여러 지역에 전파된 과정을 설명해갈 수 있었을 것인데, Ⓑ에서 잠깐 끼어들어 이렇게 r을 발음하지 않는 예는 오늘날 보스턴에서 찾아볼 수 있다고 예시한 것이며 뒤에 가서 보스턴뿐 아니라 뉴욕과 서배너에서도 사용된다고 언급한다.

---

49 빈칸완성   ①

앞 문장에서는 r-drop의 예가 나오고, 다음 문장은 r-보존을 이야기하고 있으므로, 접속사는 역접이 되어야 한다.

다음 중 빈칸 Ⓐ에 들어가기에 가장 적절한 것은?
① 그러나
② 또한
③ 따라서
④ 결과적으로

---

50 내용일치   ②

영국 영어가 미국 영어에 영향을 미쳤지, 그 반대는 사실이라고 할 수 없다. ① 미국 독립은 1776년이므로 18세기 말이라고 할 수 있다.

다음 중 옳지 않은 것은?
① 초기 정착민들의 다양한 영국식 영어 방언으로 인해 18세기 말에는 미국 영어에 세 가지 주요 방언이 생겼다.
② 미국 영어의 소리 변화는 영국 영어로 확산되는 경향이 있었다.
③ 오늘날에도 보스턴과 뉴욕에서 r음 삭제가 관찰되고 있다.
④ 중서부 사람들과 서부 사람들은 r음 유지를 비롯한 일반적인 언어 규칙을 공유한다.

2024 숭실대학교(자연계)

01 ①	02 ①	03 ②	04 ④	05 ②	06 ③	07 ①	08 ②	09 ①	10 ④
11 ①	12 ③	13 ②	14 ④	15 ③	16 ③	17 ④	18 ①	19 ②	20 ①
21 ②	22 ③	23 ③	24 ④	25 ②					

01 문의 구성   ①

①은 전체 문장의 동사가 위치해야 하는 자리이므로 시제를 가진 정동사가 와야 한다. ①을 과거시제 동사 demonstrated로 고친다. ② 전치사 of의 목적어로 쓰인 동명사이고 shoppers가 동명사의 의미상 주어이다. ③ 전치사 into의 목적어로 쓰인 동명사이다. ④ 앞의 명사 data를 수식하는 현재분사이다.

demonstrate v. 증명하다, 논증하다 notable a. 주목할 만한, 현저한 merchandise n. 상품

블랙 프라이데이의 강력한 온라인 트래픽은 쇼핑객들이 가장 저렴하고 가장 가치 있는 상품을 선택하는 데에 시간과 노력을 투입하는 현저한 패턴을 보여주었다고 Commerce Cloud 전자 상거래 서비스를 통해 유입되는 데이터를 추적하는 Salesforce의 부사장이자 소매 담당 총괄책임자인 롭 가프(Rob Garf)는 말했다.

02 접속사 that   ①

① 이하에 완전한 절이 주어져 있으므로 ①을 접속사 that으로 고쳐야 한다.

definition n. 정의(定義); 설명 historicism n. (가치 판단 등에 대한) 역사(중시)주의; 역사 결정론 parallel a. 평행의, 나란한

새로운 역사주의에 대한 간단한 정의는 그것은 대개 같은 역사적 시기의 문학적·비문학적 텍스트를 나란히 읽는 것에 기초한 방법이라는 것이다.

03 논리완성   ②

영어로 된 가장 유명한 문장 중의 하나에 자연 상태에서의 삶을 '고독하고, 가난하며, 불결하고, 잔인하고, 짧은' 것으로 묘사한 내용이 있는 것이므로, 빈칸에는 그러한 문장을 '썼다'는 의미로 ②가 들어가는 것이 적절하다.

describe v. 묘사하다, 기술하다 solitary a. 고독한, 외로운 nasty a. 불쾌한, 싫은; 불결한 brutish a. 잔인한 celebrated a. 유명한 accumulate v. (조금씩) 모으다; 축적하다 pen v. (편지 등을) 쓰다; (시·문장을) 쓰다 theorize v. 이론화하다 wade v. 걸어서 건너다

토마스 홉스(Thomas Hobbes)가 자연 상태에서의 삶을 "고독하고, 가난하며, 불결하고, 잔인하고, 짧은" 것으로 묘사했을 때, 그는 영어로 된 가장 유명한 문장 중 하나를 쓴 것이었다.

04 논리완성   ④

대중의 인식과 토론이 강화된 것은 AI 응용 프로그램의 등장이 AI가 일상생활에 통합되도록 '추진시킨' 데 따른 결과로 이해할 수 있으므로 빈칸에는 ④가 적절하다.

emergence n. 출현 application n. 응용; 응용 프로그램 chatbot n. 챗봇(문자 또는 음성으로 대화하는 기능이 있는 컴퓨터 프로그램 또는 인공 지능) integration n. 통합; 완성 public awareness 대중의 인식 avoid v. 피하다, 회피하다 demote v. ~의 지위를[계급을] 떨어뜨리다, 강등시키다 mitigate v. 누그러뜨리다, 완화하다 propel v. 추진하다, 나아가게 하다

OpenAI의 ChatGPT 챗봇과 같은 AI 응용 프로그램의 등장은 AI를 일상생활에 통합시키는 일을 추진시켰으며, 이로 인해 대중의 인식과 토론이 강화되었다.

05 논리완성   ②

두 번째 문장이 첫 번째 문장의 내용을 부연해서 설명하고 있다. "싱가포르가 천정부지의 자동차 소유 비용, 비싼 술, 식료품 가격 상승으로 미국 도시들을 앞질렀다."는 내용을 통해, 빈칸에 '생활비가 가장 많이 드는' 이라는 의미를 만드는 ②가 들어가야 함을 알 수 있다.

surpass v. ~보다 낫다, ~를 능가하다 survey n. 조사, 검사 sky-high a. 하늘을 찌를 듯한, 아주[너무] 높은 pricey a. 돈[비용]이 드는, 비싼 grocery n. 식료품류, 잡화류 pull ahead of ~을 앞서다 exertive a. 힘을 발휘하는; 노력[진력]하는 expensive a. 값비싼 expletive a. 부가적인 extraneous a. 외부로부터의; 무관계한

새로운 전 세계적 조사에 따르면, 싱가포르와 취리히가 뉴욕을 제치고 올해 세계에서 생활비가 가장 많이 드는 도시가 되었다. 싱가포르는 천정부지의 자동차 소유 비용, 비싼 술, 식료품 가격 상승으로 미국 도시들을 앞질렀다.

06 논리완성   ③

'~와 마찬가지로'라는 의미의 just as가 단서가 된다. 빈칸에는 just as 앞 부분과 마찬가지로 '증가'의 의미를 가진 단어가 들어가야 할 것이므로 ③이 정답이 된다.

poverty n. 가난, 빈곤 accommodate v. ~에 편의를 도모하다; ~의 수용력이 있다 enumerate v. 열거하다; 세다 increase v. 늘어나다, 증대하다 expound v. 상술하다, 해설하다

전 세계 도시 지역의 인구가 계속 증가하고 있는 것과 마찬가지로 개발도상국의 빈곤도 증가하고 있다.

---

07 동의어 ①

groundbreaking a. 신기원을 이룬, 획기적인 possess v. 소유하다 patent right 특허권 setback n. (진행 따위의) 방해; 좌절, 차질; 패배 (= failure) rule v. 판결하다 knack n. 숙련된 기술; 교묘한 솜씨 overrule v. (결정·의론·방침 따위를) 권한으로 뒤엎다, 파기[각하]하다 victory n. 승리

AI가 특허권을 가질 수 있는지와 관련된 영국의 한 획기적인 소송사건에서, 미국의 한 컴퓨터 과학자는 수요일에 미국 대법원이 AI를 특허 발명자로 볼 수 없다고 판결하자 좌절에 직면했다.

---

08 동의어 ②

consumer n. 소비자 strategic a. 전략의, 전략상 중요한 maximize v. 극대화하다; 최대한으로 활용하다 retail n. 소매(小賣) be in the driver's seat 책임자[경영자] 입장에 있다, 주도권을 가지고 있다(= be in charge) merchandise n. 상품, 제품 go in one's favor (소송이) 아무에게 유리하게 판결되다 lose the control 통제권을 잃다

소비자들은 매우 전략적인 태도를 취하고 있어서, 할인을 가장 많이 받을 거라고 생각할 때 쇼핑을 최대한으로 늘리려고 한다. 온라인 소매 부문은, 특히 장난감과 계절별 휴가 상품의 경우에, 소비자가 주도권을 쥐고 있는 몇 안 되는 부문 중의 하나이다.

---

09 동의어 ①

surplus n. 잉여; 흑자 inflow n. 유입, 유입물 bullion n. 금괴, 은괴; 귀금속(= precious metal) rich resource 풍부한 자원 exchangeable value 교환가능한 가치 mining product 채굴된 물질, 광물

그 결과로 초래된 수출 흑자는 주로 금과 은을 포함한 귀금속의 유입으로 해결될 것이다.

---

10 동의어 ④

aspersion n. 중상, 비방(= slander) advice n. 충고 benediction n. 기도; 축복 coercion n. 강제; 위압

그것은 그가 몇 년 동안 받았던 가장 심각한 비방이었다.

11-13

북아메리카 원주민 언어 사용자는 37만 2천명이다. 이들 중 대부분(23만 7천명)은 아메리카 인디언 혹은 알래스카 원주민 지역(AIANA)에 살고

있다. 사람들은 나바호(Navajo)어를 다른 어떤 북아메리카 원주민 언어보다 더 자주 사용했다. 전국적으로 이 언어를 사용한 사람은 16만 9천명 이상이었다. 이들 나바호어 사용자의 대부분(11만 2천명)은 AIANA에 살고 있었다. 나바호어의 사용자 수는 두 번째와 세 번째로 많이 사용되는 언어였던 유피크(Yupik)어와 다코타(Dakota)어 사용자 수보다 거의 9배 더 많았다. 이 두 언어는 약 1만 9천명의 사용자를 갖고 있었다. 유피어 사용자의 84.5%가 AIANA에 살고 있었던 반면, 다코타어 사용자의 경우는 51.5%가 그랬다. 북아메리카 원주민 언어 사용자의 대부분이 AIANA에 거주하고 있었지만, 이들 지역에 살고 있던 사람들 중 실제로 북아메리카 원주민 언어를 사용하는 사람은 극히 일부에 불과했다.

AIANA에 거주하는 사람 중 5.4%가 북아메리카 원주민 언어를 사용했으며, 이 비율은 연령대에 따라 크게 다르지 않았다. 자신을 아메리카 인디언 혹은 알래스카 원주민 중 하나에만 속한다고 밝힌 사람들 중에서, 나이가 많은 사람들이 젊은 사람들보다 북아메리카 원주민 언어를 더 자주 사용하는 것으로 전해졌다. 이들 중 65세 이상인 경우, 5명 중 1명 이상이 그러한 언어를 사용한 반면, 5~17세의 경우는 10명 중 1명 정도가 그랬다. 자신을 아메리카 인디언 혹은 알래스카 원주민을 합친 사람들에 속한다고 밝힌 사람들 가운데, 65세 이상인 사람들은 다른 사람들보다 북아메리카 원주민 언어를 사용하는 사람이 근소하게 적었던 반면, 5~17세 및 18~64세 사이의 사람들은 서로 큰 차이가 없었다.

북아메리카 원주민 언어 사용자들은 알래스카, 애리조나 및 뉴멕시코 주에 가장 집중돼 있었다. 북아메리카 원주민 언어 사용자의 65%가 이 3개 주에 살고 있었다. 이들 주 안의 불과 9개의 카운티에 전국 북아메리카 원주민 언어 사용자의 절반이 있었다. 애리조나 주의 아파치 카운티에 3만 7천명의 북아메리카 원주민 언어 사용자가 있어서 전국에서 가장 많았다. 뉴멕시코 주의 맥키니 카운티에는 두 번째로 많은 3만 3천명의 사용자가 있었다. 합치는 경우, 이 두 카운티에 전국의 북아메리카 원주민 언어 사용자의 약 20%가 살고 있었다.

approximately ad. 대략, 대강 reside v. 살다, 거주하다 vary v. 변화하다, 변하다; 다르다 slightly ad. 약간, 조금 significantly ad. 중대하게; 상당히, 뚜렷이 concentrate v. 집중하다; 한 점에 모이다 contain v. 내포하다, 포함하다

---

11 빈칸완성 ①

두 빈칸 뒤의 as American Indian or Alaska Native은 모두 자격 혹은 신분을 나타내고 있으므로, 빈칸에는 '(신원 등을) 확인하다[밝히다]'라는 의미의 ①이 적절하다. ② 연장[가장]하다 ③ 확립하다 ④ 지명하다

---

12 내용파악 ③

북미 원주민 언어의 사용을 주에서 정책적으로 의무화하고 있는지와 관련된 내용은 없다.

다음 중 언급되지 않은 것은?
① 북미 원주민 언어 사용자의 수
② 연령대에 따른 북미 원주민 언어의 사용
③ 주 정책에 의해 의무화된 북미 원주민 언어의 사용
④ 카운티에 따른 북미 원주민 언어 사용자의 수

13 내용일치 ②

"자신을 아메리카 인디언 혹은 알래스카 원주민을 합친 사람들에 속한다고 밝힌 사람들 가운데, 65세 이상인 사람들은 다른 사람들보다 북아메리카 원주민 언어를 사용하는 사람이 근소하게 적었다."고 했으므로 ②가 옳지 않은 진술이다.

다음 중 옳지 않은 것은?
① 나바호어는 가장 많이 사용된 북아메리카 원주민 언어이다.
② 아메리카 인디언 혹은 알래스카 원주민을 합친 사람들 중에서, 나이가 많은 사람들이 젊은 사람들보다 북아메리카 원주민 언어를 사용할 가능성이 더 높았다.
③ 북아메리카 원주민 언어 사용자의 절반 이상이 알래스카, 애리조나, 뉴멕시코 주에 살고 있었다.
④ 애리조나 주의 아파치 카운티는 미국에서 북아메리카 원주민 언어 사용자 수가 가장 많았다.

14-15

우리는 언어가 어떻게 시작되었는지 모르듯이 예술이 어떻게 시작되었는지도 모른다. 만약 우리가 예술의 의미를 사원과 집을 짓고, 그림과 조각품을 만들어 내거나, 문양을 짜내는 행위로 이해한다면, 예술이 없는 민족은 세상 어디에도 없다. 그와는 반대로, 만약 예술이 의미하는 바를 일종의 호화 사치품, 박물관과 전시회장에서 감상하는 어떤 대상이나 최고급 응접실의 진귀한 장식품으로 쓰이는 특별한 것이라고 한다면, 예술이라는 말을 이런 의미로 사용한 것은 최근에 들어서야 시작되었고 과거의 아무리 위대한 건축가, 화가, 조각가도 (예술을) 그런 의미로는 생각조차 해본 적이 없었다는 사실을 우리는 반드시 알아야 한다. 건축을 생각하면 이러한 차이를 가장 쉽게 이해할 수 있다. 우리 모두는 아름다운 건물이 있다는 것과 그 중 일부가 진정한 작품이라는 것을 알고 있다. 그러나 세상에 있는 건물 중에 특별한 목적 없이 지어진 것은 거의 없다. 이러한 건물들을 예배나 유흥의 장소, 혹은 주거지로 사용하는 사람들은 제일 먼저 효용성을 기준으로 그 건물들을 판단한다. 그렇지만 이 점을 제외하면, 그들은 건물의 디자인이나 비례를 따져 좋아하거나 싫어하는 경우가 있으며, 때로는 건축가의 노력을 평가하여 그가 실용적이면서도 "좋은" 건축물을 만들어냈다고 그에게 찬사를 보내기도 한다. 과거에는 그림과 조각품을 대하는 태도가 비슷했다. 그것들은 예술작품이라기 보다는 특정한 기능을 하는 대상으로 간주됐다. 건물들이 지어진 요건들을 모르는 사람이라면 건물을 제대로 평가하지 못할 것이다. 마찬가지로, 우리가 당시의 예술이 지향했던 목표를 알지 못한다면 과거의 예술을 온전히 이해하는 것은 어려운 일이다. 시대를 거슬러 올라갈수록 옛날의 예술이 목적했던 바는 그만큼 더 명확하지만 그 만큼 더 낯설기도 하다.

sculpture n. 조각, 조각 작품 weave v. 짜다, 뜨다, 엮다 exhibition n. 전람회, 전시회, 박람회 parlour n. 거실, 응접실 sculptor n. 조각가 architecture n. 건축술, 건축양식; 건조물 erect v. 똑바로 세우다; (건조물을) 건설[건립]하다 worship n. 예배, 참배 dwelling n. 주거; 주거지, 주택 foremost a. 일류의, 주요한 utility n. 유용, 유익 proportion n. 비율; 조화, 균형 appreciate v. 평가하다; 진가를 인정하다; 고맙게 여기다 architect n. 건축가 attitude n. 태도 definite a. 뚜렷한, 확실한 requirement n. 요구, 필요

14 빈칸완성 ④

'건물들이 지어진 요건을 모르는 사람이라면 건물을 제대로 평가하지 못할 것'이라는 내용과 '우리가 당시의 예술이 지향했던 바를 알지 못한다면 과거의 예술을 온전히 이해하는 것은 어려운 일이다.'라는 내용은 같은 맥락으로 이어지는 흐름이므로, 빈칸에는 '마찬가지로'라는 뜻의 ④가 들어가야 한다. ① 반대로 ② 단독으로 ③ 역설적이게도

15 내용파악 ③

과거에는 예술이 단순히 아름다움을 감상하는 데 사용되었던 것이 아니라, 특정 목적이나 기능을 수행하는 물건으로 간주되었음을 특히 글의 후반부에서 강조하고 있다.

위 글은 주제적 강조점을 _____에 두고 있다.
① 언어와 예술의 신비한 기원
② 회화와 조각의 본질적인 차이
③ 과거 예술의 기능과 실용성
④ 오늘날 예술의 변혁적인 힘

16-18

일반적으로 인간과 관련해 미래 세대를 향상시키기 위해 바람직한 유전적 특징을 선택하는 우생학은 1883년 영국의 탐험가이자 자연과학자인 프랜시스 골턴(Francis Galton)에 의해 하나의 용어로 만들어졌다. 찰스 다윈(Charles Darwin)의 자연선택설에 영향을 받은 골턴은 '보다 적합한 인종이나 혈통이 덜 적합한 인종보다 빠르게 우세할 수 있는 더 나은 가능성'을 제공하는 시스템을 지지했다. 사회에서 인간의 삶이 '적자생존'에 지배받는다는 19세기 후반에 인기를 끌었던 사회 다윈주의는 1900년대 초반에 우생학을 본격적인 과학연구로 발전시키는 데 도움을 주었다. 제1차 세계대전 무렵, 많은 과학 전문가들과 정치 지도자들이 우생학을 지지했다. 그러나 우생학자들의 가정은 혹독하게 비난받았고, 나치가 우생학을 이용해서 전체 인종의 몰살을 지지했던 1930년대와 1940년대에 우생학은 결국 과학으로서 실패했다.
오늘날 이해되는 이런 우생학은 19세기 후반부터 시작되었지만, 바람직한 특성을 가진 자손을 얻기 위해 짝짓기를 선택하려는 노력은 고대부터 시작되었다. 플라톤(Plato)의 『국가론(Republic)』은 선별적 품종개량을 통해 인간을 향상시키기 위해 노력하는 사회를 묘사한다. 나중에, 이탈리아의 철학자이자 시인인 톰마소 캄파넬라(Tommaso Campanella)는 『태양의 도시(City of the Sun, 1623)』에서 사회적으로 엘리트만 출산이 허용되는 유토피아 사회를 묘사했다. 『유전되는 천재(Hereditary Genius, 1869)』에서 골턴은 뛰어난 남성과 부유한 여성 간의 중매결혼 제도가 결국 재능 있는 인종을 만들어낼 것이라고 제안했다. 1865년 유전의 기본 법칙은 현대 유전학의 아버지인 그레고어 멘델(Gregor Mendel)에 의해 발견되었다. 완두콩을 대상으로 한 그의 실험은 물리적 특징이 두 개의 구성단위(오늘날 유전자라고 알려짐)가 결합된 결과이며 한 세대에서 다음 세대로 전해질 수 있다는 것을 입증했다. 그러나 그의 연구는 1900년에 그의 연구가 재발견될 때까지 대체로 무시되었다. 유전에 대한 이러한 기본적인 지식은 사촌인 찰스 다윈에게 영향을 미친 골턴 등 우생학자들에게 선별적 품종개량을 통한 인간의 향상을 뒷받침하는 과학적인 증거를 제공했다. 우생학자들에게, 자연은 인류 형성에 있어서 양육보다 훨씬 더 기여했다.

eugenics n. 우생학, 인종개량학　heritable a. 유전성의　in reference to ~와 관련하여　strain n. 혈통, 품종　prevail over ~보다 우세하다　extermination n. 몰살, 멸종　date from ~부터 시작하다　mating n. 교배, 짝짓기　offspring n. (사람·동물의) 자식, 자손　undertake v. 착수하다, 시작하다　breeding n. 품종 개량, 육종　procreate v. 아이[새끼]를 낳다　arranged marriage 중매결혼　of distinction 뛰어난, 탁월한　gifted a. 재능을 가진　genetics n. 유전학　pea n. 완두콩　be credited with ~한 것으로 여겨지다　distinguished a. 특히 뛰어난　affluent a. 부유한　yield v. (결과 등을) 초래하다　endowed with ~을 타고난　downfall n. 몰락　underlying a. 근본적인

---

16 내용파악 ③

본문에서 "유전의 기본 법칙은 현대 유전학의 아버지인 그레고어 멘델(Gregor Mendel)에 의해 발견되었다."라고 했으므로, ③이 정답이다.

1865년 유전의 기본 법칙을 발견해 우생학을 지지하기 위한 과학적인 증거를 제시한 사람은 누구인가?
① 찰스 다윈
② 톰마소 캄파넬라
③ 그레고어 멘델
④ 프랜시스 골턴

---

17 내용일치 ④

"우생학자들에게, 자연은 인류 형성에 있어서 양육보다 훨씬 더 기여했다."고 했으므로, ④가 정답이다.

다음 중 본문의 내용과 일치하지 않는 것은?
① '우생학'이라는 용어는 프랜시스 골턴에 의해 최초로 사용되었다.
② 골턴은 뛰어난 남자와 부유한 여성 간의 구조화된 결합이 선천적으로 능력이 뛰어난 세대를 만들 수 있다고 믿었다.
③ 우생학은 근본적인 가정이 혹독하게 비난받았고, 나치가 전체 인종의 말살을 정당화하기 위해 우생학을 이용했던 1930년대와 1940년대에 몰락했다.
④ 우생학자들에 따르면, 인간의 특성을 형성하는 데 있어서 자연의 영향은 양육의 영향과 거의 동일하다고 했다.

---

18 동의어 ①

strain은 '종류, 유형; 혈통, 품종'이라는 뜻으로 쓰이므로, ①이 단어에 대한 올바른 정의이다. 반면, ⑧의 뜻은 '몰살, 멸종'인데, assumption의 정의가 쓰였고, ⓒ의 뜻은 '출산하다'인데, depict의 정의가 쓰였으며, ⑩의 뜻은 '유전'인데, evolution에 대한 정의가 쓰여서 틀렸다.

어떤 단어의 정의가 가장 정확한가?
① Ⓐ strain: 동물의 유형, 종류, 품종 등
② Ⓑ extermination: 증거 없이 어떤 것을 지지하며 당연시하는 행위
③ Ⓒ procreate: 말, 소리, 이미지, 또는 그 밖의 다른 수단을 이용해 어떤 것을 묘사하는 것
④ Ⓓ heredity: 주어진 시스템, 대상, 제품 등이 특히 더 간단한 형태에서 복잡한 형태로 점진적으로 변화하는 과정

19-20

1992년에 비준된 미국 수정헌법 제27조는 미국 헌법의 수정조항이다. 미국 수정헌법 제27조는 미국 의원들에 대한 보수 비율의 어떠한 변경도 미 하원의 차기 선거 이후에 효력이 발생해야 한다고 구체적으로 규정하고 있다. '1789년 의원 보수 수정안'으로 흔히 알려진 미국 수정헌법 제27조는 사실 1789년 제1대 의회가 제안한 12개의 수정조항 중에 두 번째 조항이었는데, 그 중 10개만 비준되어 권리 장전이 되었다. 비준기한이 만료되면 수정헌법의 시행이 불가능해지지만, 각 주에서 비준해야 하는 기한이 없어서, 불과 6개 주만 비준에 서명한 이후 거의 80년 동안 휴면상태였다. 1873년에 오하이오 주가 의원들의 급여를 인상하려는 그 당시 통용되던 의회의 시도에 대한 불만의 표현으로 수정조항에 비준했다. 이 수정조항은 한 번 더 휴면상태가 되었지만, 1978년 또 다른 주인 와이오밍 주가 수정조항에 비준했다. 텍사스대학교 오스틴캠퍼스의 당시 학생이었던 그레고리 왓슨(Gregory Watson)이 작성한 대학생 연구논문이 수정조항을 비준하여 정치부패를 줄이자는 운동의 근간이 된 이후, 비준하려는 노력이 차츰 속도를 내었다. 1992년 5월 5일, 필수적인 38개 주가 수정조항에 비준했고(1989년 노스캐롤라이나 주가 다시 비준했다), 수정조항을 최초로 제안한지 202년 이상이 지난 1992년 5월 18일에 미국 기록문서 보관담당자에 의해 미국 수정헌법 제27조로 인증되었다.

amendment n. (미국 헌법의) 수정조항　ratify v. 비준하다, 재가하다　constitution n. 헌법　stipulate v. ~을 규정하다　alteration n. 변경, 수정　compensation n. 보수, 급여　Congress n. 의회, 국회　take effect 발효되다　subsequent a. 그다음의, 차후의　the House of Representative (미 의회의) 하원　congressional a. (미국) 의회의　act n. 법률, 법령　Bill of Rights 권리 장전　absent prep. ~없기 때문에　expiration n. (기한의) 만료, 만기　render v. (어떤 상태가 되게) 만들다　dormant a. 휴면상태인, 활동을 중단한　undergraduate a. (대학) 학부생, 대학생　corruption n. 부패　pick up steam (차량이) 차츰 속도를 내다　requisite a. 필수적인　certify v. (사실 등을) 인증하다　archivist n. 기록[문서] 보관 담당자

---

19 내용파악 ②

"1873년에 오하이오 주가 의원들의 급여를 인상하려는 그 당시 통용되던 의회의 시도에 대한 불만의 표현으로 수정조항에 비준했다."고 했으므로, ②가 정답이다.

어떤 주가 의회의 급여를 증가시키는 시도에 대해 불만을 표현하면서 수정헌법 21조에 비준했는가?
① 노스캐롤라이나
② 오하이오
③ 텍사스
④ 와이오밍

---

20 내용파악 ①

텍사스대학교 학생이던 그레고리 왓슨이 작성한 논문이 수정조항을 비준하여 정치부패를 줄이자는 운동의 근간이 되었고, 그 이후 비준하려는 노력이 속도를 내었다고 했으므로, ①이 정답이다.

1982년의 어떤 사건이 수정헌법 21조에 비준하는 노력을 증가시켰는가?
① 정치적 부패에 반대하는 운동
② 기록 보관 담당자의 인증
③ 의원 보수 수정안
④ 비준 기한 만기

21-23

통계적으로 볼 때, '장기 코로나바이러스감염증-19'를 앓은 적이 있는 사람을 당신이 알고 있을 가능성이 높은데, 장기 코로나바이러스감염증-19는 코로나바이러스감염증-19를 겪은 후의 피로감, 브레인 포그(뇌 안개), 그리고 통증 등 만성적인 증상을 가리키는 명칭이다. 연방 데이터에 따르면, 미국 성인의 약 14%가 어느 시점에 장기 코로나바이러스감염증-19를 앓은 적이 있다고 보고했다. 그러나 많은 사람들은 다른 바이러스들이, 심지어 매우 흔한 바이러스도, 이와 유사하게 오래 지속되는 쇠약해지는 증상을 유발할 수 있다는 것을 인식하지 못한다. 12월 14일자 『랜싯 전염병(The Lancet Infectious Diseases)』에 발표된 연구는 독감을 심하게 앓은 후 '장기 독감'에 걸릴 위험에 초점을 맞추고 있다.
알-알리(Al-Aly)와 그의 동료들은 미국 재향군인부의 기록을 이용해 2015년부터 2019년까지 독감으로 입원한 약 11,000명의 장기 건강 결과를 2020년부터 2022년까지 코로나바이러스감염증-19로 입원한 약 81,000명의 장기 건강 결과와 비교했다. 연구원들은 얼마나 많은 사람들이 입원 후 1년 반 동안 두 바이러스와 관련된 94가지 건강 위험 중 어떤 것에 계속 걸리는지를 추적했다. 독감 생존자들에 비해, 코로나바이러스감염증-19를 겪었던 사람들은 피로, 정신건강 문제, 그리고 폐, 위장, 그리고 심장 문제 등 확인된 합병증 중 64가지 위험이 증가했다. 그들은 또한 연구 기간 동안 사망할 가능성이 더 높았고, 이것은 두 질병의 장기 결과를 비교하는 다른 연구와도 일치했다. <결과적으로>, 독감 생존자들은 단지 6개의 건강 문제에만 걸릴 위험이 높았으며, 그 중 대부분은 호흡기와 심혈관계와 관련이 있었다. 알-알리는 독감이 주로 호흡기 질병인 반면, 코로나바이러스감염증-19는 수많은 장기에 영향을 미친다고 지적하며, "코로나바이러스감염증-19가 독감보다 훨씬 심각합니다."라고 말했다. 그러나 장기적인 건강 문제는 18개월의 추적 기간 동안 두 집단 모두에서 공통적으로 발생했다. 연구원들은 코로나바이러스감염증-19 집단에서 100명당 약 615건의 건강 문제를 기록했는데, 이에 비해 독감 집단에서는 100명당 약 537건의 건강 문제를 기록했다. 이 수치는 일부 사람들이 감염 후 수많은 만성적인 증상들을 겪는다는 사실을 반영한다고 알-알리는 주장한다. 연구에 포함된 사람들이 모두 입원했다는 점에 주목하는 것이 중요하며, 이는 질병의 급성 국면 동안 매우 아팠다는 것을 의미한다. 연구 집단은 또한 평균 참가자 연령이 70세로 남성과 노인이 압도적으로 많았다. 따라서 이 결과가 전체 집단으로까지는 해석되지 않을 수도 있다.

chronic a. 만성적인 fatigue n. 피로 brain fog 뇌 안개(머리가 멍해지면서 기억력을 비롯한 인지 기능과 집중력, 주의력 등이 저하되는 상태) federal a. 연방의 trigger v. 유발하다 long-lasting a. 오래 지속되는 debilitating a. 쇠약하게 하는 hospitalize v. ~을 입원시키다 relative to ~에 관하여; ~에 비하여 complication n. 합병증 pulmonary a. 폐의 gastrointestinal a. 위장의 in keeping with ~에 맞추어, ~와 일치하여 respiratory a. 호흡의, 호흡 기관의 cardiovascular system 심혈관계 follow-up n. 추적; 후속조치 acute a. (질병의) 급성의; 극심한 overwhelmingly ad. 압도적으로 translate v. 해석되다

21　글의 흐름상 적절하지 않은 표현 고르기　②

이 글은 독감 생존자들과 코로나바이러스감염증-19 생존자들을 비교하고 있는데, 코로나바이러스감염증-19 생존자들은 합병증 중 64가지 위험이 증가했다고 한 반면, 독감 생존자들은 6개의 건강 문제에만 걸릴 위험이 높다고 해서, 두 집단에서 '상반'된 결과를 보여주고 있다. 따라서 ®의 consequently는 인과관계를 나타내어 부적절하므로, ®를 '대조적인' 내용을 나타내는 meanwhile(다른 한편)로 고쳐야 한다.

22　내용파악　③

① 평균 참가자 연령이 70세로 남성과 노인이 압도적으로 많았다. ② 피로감, 뇌 안개, 그리고 통증이 언급되었다. ④ 연구 집단의 평균 참가자 연령이 70세로 노인이 압도적으로 많아서, 이 결과가 전체 집단으로까지는 해석되지 않을 수 있다고 했다. 반면, 치료 과정에 대해서는 본문에 언급되지 않았으므로, ③이 정답이다.

다음 중 본문에 언급되지 않은 것은?
① 참가자의 범위
② 증상의 사례들
③ 치료 과정
④ 연구의 한계

23　내용일치　③

연구원들은 2015년에서 2019년까지 독감으로 입원한 환자와 2020년에서 2022년까지 코로나바이러스감염증-19로 입원한 환자를 비교했으므로, '동일한 연구 기간'이 아니었다. 그리고 독감 생존자들은 단지 6개의 건강 문제에만 걸릴 위험이 높았던 반면, 코로나바이러스감염증-19 생존자들은 합병증 중 64가지 위험이 증가했다고 했다. 따라서 ③이 옳지 않은 진술이다.

다음 중 옳지 않은 것은?
① 장기 코로나바이러스감염증-19는 코로나바이러스감염증-19를 겪은 후, 오래 지속되는 쇠약해지는 증상을 가리킨다.
② 미국 성인의 약 14%가 피로, 정신 건강 문제, 그리고 심장 문제를 겪었을지도 모른다.
③ 코로나바이러스감염증-19 집단은 동일한 연구 기간 동안 독감 집단보다 적은 장기적인 건강 문제를 겪었던 경향이 있었다.
④ 연구의 결과는 모든 연령 집단에 적용되지는 않을지도 모른다.

24-25

지난 18개월은 최근까지 10여년의 열광적인 성장을 수월하게 이어온 어떤 한 부문에서 여러 가지 좌절을 겪은 시기였다. 기술 분야에서의 실직(失職)을 추적하는 사이트인 레이오프스(Layoffs.fyi)에 따르면, 165,000명이 정리해고 되었던 작년에 비해, 올해는 지금까지 거의 260,000명이 정리해고 되었다고 한다. 이 수치는 대체로 뜨거운 노동 시장을 경험한 해에 특히 주목할 만하다. 좋은 소식은 비록 기술 직군의 정리해고가 2022년 초보다는 훨씬 높지만, 여전히 올해 초보다는 훨씬 낮다는 점이다. 레이오프스는 1월에 대략 90,000명의 노동자가 276개의 기업에서 정리해고 되었다는 것을 발견했다. 지난달에는 총 8,000명에 근접했다.

그러나 보다 폭넓은 기술 직군의 환경은, 특히 창업기업에게는, 잔인하다. 에린 그리피스(Erin Griffith)는 대략 3,200개의 벤처 지원 기업들이 2023년에 사라졌다고 지난주 『뉴욕타임스(The New York Times)』에 말했다.

전 세계적인 유행병 초기의 돈이 넘치던 시기 동안 과잉채용의 긴 여파가 기술 분야에서 현재의 정리해고를 하도록 만든 주요 원인이라고 레이오프스의 창업자인 로저 리(Roger Lee)가 나에게 말했다. 나의 동료 데릭 톰슨(Derek Thompson)은 "금리가 낮았을 때, 투자자들은 성장 스토리를 높이 평가했고, 기술 기업들이 이런 성장 스토리를 독점했습니다. 인플레이션과 금리가 증가하자, 장기적인 약속을 하고 있던 기업들은 대부분 위험에 처했고, 그들은 엄청난 타격을 입었습니다."라고 1월에 쓴 글에서 밝혔다. 기술 기업들은 파티가 결코 끝나지 않을 것 같던 시기에 채용했던 수많은 노동자들을 대상으로 아직도 구조조정을 하고 있다. 그리고 지금 인공지능이 기술 기업의 문제를 가중시키고 있으며, 그들의 핵심 사업을 위협하고 있다. 금리가 경영진들이 바랐던 것보다 올해 더 높게 유지되고 있어서 많은 기업들의 예측은 타격을 받았고, 그래서 이미 직원들을 정리해고 했던 일부 기업은 "예전의 성공 방식으로 돌아가 추가적으로 감원을 하고 있다"고 로저 리는 설명했다.

이런 타이밍 중 일부는 주기적이다. 연말은 역사적으로 정리해고가 많이 일어나는 시기이다. 연말은 많은 조직의 회계연도의 마지막 기간을 의미한다. 그래서 기업들은 올해 실적을 검토하고 내년 실적을 미리 계획한다. 단기적으로는, 인력 감축과 같은 경향이 지속될지도 모른다고 로저 리가 말했다. 인플레이션이 완화되어, 일부 경제학자들은 2024년에 연방 준비제도 이사회가 금리를 낮출지도 모른다고 조심스럽게 예측하고 있다. 그리고 이런 금리 인하는 기업들이 투자를 보다 저렴하게 하도록 하며 내년도 기술 부문에서 성장에 박차를 가할 수 있다고 인디드 고용 연구소(Indeed Hiring Lab) 경제연구 책임자인 닉 벙커(Nick Bunker)가 나에게 말했다. 그러나 그는 기술업계의 채용이 급격하게 증가할 것으로 예상하지는 않는데, 이는 부분적으로 2021년 과잉채용을 하던 시기로부터 한두 가지 교훈을 얻었을지도 모르기 때문이다. 기술 기업의 경영진들은 지난 몇 년 동안의 타격으로 잘못을 깨달았다. 많은 경영진들은 채용 접근방식에서 보다 단련되어 있으며, "그들은 어떠한 희생을 치르더라도 성장에 초점을 맞추기보다 효율에 더 초점을 맞추고 있다."고 로저 리가 말했다.

setback n. 좌절, 차질 coast v. 순조롭게 나아가다, 수월하게 해 내다 frenzied a. 열광적인; 광적인 layoff n. (일시적) 정리해고 elevate v. 증가시키다 wipe out ~을 완전히 없애 버리다 flush a. (보통 잠깐 동안) 돈이 넘치는 drive v. (특정한 방식의 행동을 하도록) 만들다 interest rate 금리 narrative n. (실제의) 이야기 monopoly n. 독점 clobber v. 호된 손실을 가하다 reams of 무수히 많은 hammer v. 쳐부수다; 혼을 내다 executive n. 경영진 cyclical a. 순환하는 fiscal year 회계 연도 take stock of ~잘 검토하다 moderate v. 완화되다 the Federal Reserve 연방 준비제도 이사회 spur v. 박차를 가하다 spree n. (범행을) 한바탕 저지르기 chasten v. 잘못을 깨닫게 하다 blow n. (정신적인) 타격 discipline v. 단련하다 at all costs 어떤 희생을 치르더라도

---

24 내용일치 ④

기업들이 추가적으로 감원하고 있다고 로저 리가 말한 것은 맞지만, 그 이유가 경기침체 때문이 아니라 고금리 때문이라고 했으므로, ④가 정답이다.

다음 중 본문의 내용과 일치하지 않는 것은?
① 레이오프스에 따르면, 기술 부문의 260,000명의 노동자가 올해 지금까지 정리해고 되었다.
② 3,200개의 벤처 지원 기업들이 2023년에 사라졌다.
③ 전 세계적인 유행병 초기의 돈이 넘치던 시기 동안 이뤄진 과잉채용이 기술 분야에서 현재의 정리해고를 하도록 만든 주요 원인이다.
④ 로저 리에 따르면, 기술 기업들은 경기 침체로 정리해고를 여전히 겪고 있다.

---

25 내용일치

마지막 단락 넷째 문장에서 '단기적으로는, 인력 감축과 같은 경향이 지속될지도 모른다고 로저 리가 말했다.'고 했으므로 ②가 글의 내용과 일치한다. ③ 그다음 문장에서 '인플레이션이 완화되어, 일부 경제학자들은 2024년에 연방 준비제도 이사회가 금리를 낮출지도 모른다고 조심스럽게 예측하고 있다'고 했다. ④ 마지막 문장에서 '효율에 더 초점을 맞추고 있다'고 했다.

다음 중 본문의 내용과 일치하는 것은?
① 연말은 정리해고가 많이 일어나는 시기인데, 왜냐하면 직원들이 연말 보너스를 요구하기 때문이다.
② 가까운 미래에 기술 직군의 채용과 관련해 로저 리는 정리해고가 계속될 것으로 예측한다.
③ 2024년 인플레이션으로 인해 연방 준비제도 이사회가 금리를 안정적으로 유지할 가능성이 높다.
④ 본문에 언급된 바와 같이, 어떠한 희생을 치르더라도 성장에 초점을 맞추는 것이 많은 기술 기업의 경영진들이 고용과 관련한 접근 방식이다.

01 ①	02 ⑤	03 ②	04 ③	05 ①	06 ①	07 ④	08 ②	09 ③	10 ⑤
11 ⑤	12 ③	13 ④	14 ⑤	15 ④	16 ②	17 ③	18 ③	19 ④	20 ①
21 ⑤	22 ③	23 ⑤	24 ①	25 ①	26 ⑤	27 ②	28 ④	29 ①	30 ②
31 ①	32 ②	33 ②	34 ④	35 ⑤	36 ⑥	37 ④	38 ②	39 ④	40 ④
41 ③	42 ②	43 ③	44 ⑤	45 ⑤	46 ④	47 ③	48 ①	49 ①	50 ⑤

01 논리완성   ①

겉으로 보기에 서독인들이 동독에 들어가는 것을 막기 위해서였다면, 실제 의도나 효과는 그와 반대였을 것이므로, 동독인들이 나라를 탈출하는 데 더 효과적이었다는 흐름을 만드는 defecting이 빈칸에 적절하다.

renowned a. 유명한 ostensibly ad. 표면상으로는 infiltrate v. 침투하다 in reality 사실은 effective a. 효과적인 defect v. 도망하다, 탈주하다, 이탈하다 explore v. 개척하다 interfere v. 방해하다 revolt v. 반항하다 unify v. 통일시키다

1961년 독일의 저명한 소설가 귄터 그라스는 표면상으로 서독인의 침투를 막기 위해 베를린 장벽을 건설했다고 공산주의 동독을 공개적으로 비판했다. 사실, 장벽은 동독인들의 탈주를 막는 데 더 효과적이었다.

02 논리완성   ⑤

어떤 사람의 뇌의 모든 뉴런을 기록하고 복제하여 만든 그 사람의 뇌의 가상 복제품을 가리킬 수 있는 표현이 필요하므로 ⑤가 정답으로 적절하다.

brain scanning 뇌 스캐닝 to the point that ~할 정도로 neuron n. 신경세포 mind uploading 마인드 업로딩(정신 전송: 인간의 마음을 컴퓨터와 같은 인공물에 전송하는 것) transition v. 전이하다, 이동시키다 synthetic hardware 합성 하드웨어

뇌 스캐닝 기술이 향후 수십 년 안에 크게 발전하여 각각의 뉴런이 다른 뉴런과 어떻게 대화하는지 관찰할 수 있게 된다고 상상해 보라. 그런 다음, 이 모든 정보를 기록하여 컴퓨터로 누군가의 뇌의 시뮬레이션(복제품)을 만들 수 있다고 상상해 보라. 이것이 바로 마인드 업로딩의 기저 개념인데, 그것은 언젠가는 인간을 생물학적 신체에서 합성 하드웨어로 이동시킬 수 있다는 생각이다.

03 논리완성   ②

빈칸 다음에서 시간과 돈과 노력을 포기해야 한다고 했다. 따라서 빈칸에는 '비용이 많이 드는, 희생이 큰'이라는 의미의 costly가 적절하다. ⑤는 육체적으로 힘들다는 의미이므로 정답이 될 수 없다.

be willing to 기꺼이 ~하다 be informed of 알다 consequence n. 결과 care for 돌보다, 배려하다 altruistically ad. 이타적으로 be due to ~때문이다 societal pressure 사회적 압력 righteous a. 올바른, 정의로운 easy way out 쉬운 해결책 beneficial a. 이로운 costly a. 비용이 많이 드는 ethical a. 윤리적인 ridiculous a. 우스운, 어리석은 strenuous a. 정력적인, 열심인

대부분의 인간은 자기 행동이 어떤 결과를 초래할지 충분히 알고 있을 때 기꺼이 옳은 일을 하려고 하지만, 이러한 의지가 항상 타인을 배려하기 때문인 것은 아니다. 사람들이 이타적으로 행동하는 이유의 일부는 자신을 좋게 보고 싶어 하는 욕망뿐 아니라 사회적 압박 때문이기도 하다. 정의로워진다는 것은 종종 비용이 드는 일이며 사람들에게 자신의 시간, 돈, 노력을 포기하라고 요구하기 때문에, 모르고 있는 것이 쉬운 해결책이 된다.

04 논리완성   ③

빈칸 앞의 they는 '다양한 눈 색깔'을 가리킨다. 컴퓨터는 회색과 갈색 눈의 선조로부터 다양한 색깔이 어디서 어떻게 등장하게 되었는가를 예측해야 한다. 그러므로 '진화해서 나타났다'는 흐름을 만드는 evolved가 빈칸에 적절하다.

evolution n. 진화 map v. 지도를 만들다 be responsible for ~의 원인이 되다 feline a. 고양이의 dazzling a. 화려한 peeper n. 눈, 시력 family tree 가계도, 계보 emerge v. 나타나다 arrange v. 배열하다 distribute v. 분포하다 evolve v. 진화하다 transfer v. 수송하다 transcend v. 초월하다

고양이 눈 색깔의 진화가 처음으로 지도화되면서, 연구자들은 노란 눈 호랑이에서 파란 눈 눈표범에 이르기까지 고양잇과 동물의 놀라울 정도로 다양한 눈이 하나의 특이한 조상에 기인한다는 사실을 발견했다. 새로운 연구에서 과학자들은 살아있는 고양잇과 동물들의 다양한 눈 색깔을 확인하고 컴퓨터 모델을 사용하여 그 다양한 눈 색깔이 고양이 가계도상 어디서 진화했는지를 예측해 보았다. 그들의 모델에 따르면 모든 고양이의 조상은 회색과 갈색 눈을 가졌을 것이며, 회색이 나중에 다른 색이 나타날 수 있게 만들었다.

05 논리완성   ①

우리는 도구를 만들고, 불을 사용하고, 바퀴와 날개를 사용하는 등 많은 문명의 발전을 이루었으므로, 빈칸에는 advancements가 적절하다.

ancestor n. 조상, 선조   craft v. 만들다   channel v. 유도하다   glass bulb 유리 전구   fuse v. 융합하다   remarkable a. 놀라운, 주목할 만한   advancement n. 발전, 진보   transition n. 전이

기술은 더 나은 삶의 방식을 위한 관건이다. 고대 선조들은 이를 잘 알고 있었고, 그래서 그들은 만들고, 자르고, 수확할 수 있는 여러 모양의 돌 도구(석기)를 만들었다. 자연의 파괴적인 힘을 관찰하고 불로 요리하는 법을 배웠다. 그리고 우리는 바퀴로 이동하다가, 날개로 날기까지 했다. 유리 전구에 전기를 공급하여 어둠 속에 빛을 비췄다. 우리의 위대한 과학자들은 원자를 쪼개는 방법을 알게 됐지만, 아직도 원자를 융합하는 노력을 하고 있다. 이러한 발전은 각각 시간이 지나면서 인류를 더욱 놀라운 존재로 만들었다.

06 삽입절 ①

believe, think, suggest, think, feel 등의 의견을 나타내는 동사는 흔히 '주어+동사'의 꼴로 관계절 안에 삽입되어 쓰일 수 있다. 여기서는 'what is ~'라는 관계절 안에 'some believe(주어+동사)'가 삽입되어 what some believe is가 되는데, 빈칸 뒤의 industry는 is의 보어가 되어야 하고 전치가 in은 명사절인 what 관계절 앞에 와서 for decades 다음에 또 하나의 '전치사+명사구'로 이어져야 하므로, in what some believe is의 어순이 된다.

luxury brand 명품 브랜드   lucrative a. 수익성 있는   franchise n. 프랜차이즈   endure v. 지속하다

프라다, 구찌, 카르티에, 루이뷔통 같은 명품 브랜드의 마케팅 담당자들은 일부 사람들이 현재 2,700억 달러 규모에 이른다고 믿고 있는 산업에서 수십 년 동안 지속되어온 수익성 높은 프랜차이즈를 관리한다.

07 도치 ④

only가 있는 부사어가 문두에 올 때 주어와 동사는 도치되어야 한다. farm workers won a concession을 도치하면 ④의 did farm workers win a concession이 된다.

reform n. 개혁   brim n. 가장자리   concession n. 양보, 양해

또 다른 사례는 농장에서 작은 개혁이라도 이뤄내는 것이 얼마나 어려운 일인지 보여준다. 최근에서야 비로소 농장 노동자들은 수년 동안 요구해왔던 양보를 얻어냈는데, 그들이 토마토 바구니를 가장자리까지 가득 채워도 좋다는 양보였다.

08 강조구문 / 분사 ②

마지막 문장은 'it ~ that' 강조구문이고, when은 역접의 의미이다. ①과 ②가 강조구문의 that절이며, 강조되는 요소인 '그들의 사상의 근본적인 기이함'이 주어서서 목적어 them을 '철학자들'을 가리킨다. 그런데, 사람이 '흥미로운' 사람이 되려면 목적보어로 현재분사 interesting이 와야 한다. 따라서 정답은 ②이다.

risk v. 위험을 무릅쓰다   fundamental a. 근본적인   weirdness n. 이상함, 기이함

리처드 왓모어(Richard Whatmore)가 새 책에서 우리에게 상기시켜주듯이, "때로는 현재가 과거를 이해하는 데 방해가 된다." 사실은 18세기 철학자들을 그렇게도 흥미롭게 만드는 것이 그들의 사상의 근본적인 기이함인데도, 우리는 그들이 자신의 질문 대신 우리의 질문에 답하고 있다고 감히 생각해 버린다.

09 재귀대명사 / 병치 ③

that절에서 주어인 '기업 간행물들'이 ~에서 해방되려면 emancipate 가 타동사이므로 수동태 be emancipated from이나 재귀대명사 목적어를 사용한 emancipate themselves from이어야 한다. 따라서 ③이 정답이다. agenda와 discourse 두 명사가 and로 잘 병치되었다.

journalist n. 저널리스트, 신문 잡지 기자   serve to ~의 역할을 하다   reinforce v. 강화하다   conceptual model 개념적 모델   discourse n. 담론, 토론   aggression n. 공격, 침략; 공격성   ultimately ad. 궁극적으로, 결국   male-defined a. 남성으로 정의되는   practice n. 실행, 실천, 관행   far-reaching consequences 멀리 미치는 결과   business publication 비즈니스 출판물   emancipate v. 해방시키다   perceived agenda 인식된 의제   corporate discourse 기업 담론

신문 잡지 기자들은 공격성을 특징으로 하는 개념 모델과 담론을 강화하는 역할을 하며, 궁극적으로 마케팅을 남성적인 관행으로 유지하는 데 도움을 준다. 이러한 광범위한 결과 때문에 기업 간행물은 독자들이 인식하는 의제와 기자들이 보도하는 기업 담론에서 벗어나야 한다.

10 percent와 percentage의 용법 구분 ⑤

percent는 수와 함께 쓰고, 수가 없을 때는 percentage를 쓴다. 수식은 large/small로 한다. 가산명사이므로 a ~ percentage이다. 따라서 a much smaller percentage of가 정답이다.

household n. 가구   fragmented a. 파편화된   make up 구성하다

미국의 가족들은 점점 더 파편화되고 있다. 남편, 아내, 자녀 2명으로 구성된 전통적인 4인 가족이 전체 가구에서 차지하는 비율이 예전보다 훨씬 줄어들고 있다.

11 자동사와 타동사 ⑤

⑤에 쓰인 타동사 arouse(불러일으키다) 다음에 목적어가 없는 것이 옳지 않다. 따라서 이것을 자동사 arises로 고쳐야 한다.

bombard v. 폭격하다   excellence n. 우수함, 뛰어남   distinction n. 차별성, 특이성   preferably ad. 오히려, 되도록이면   status anxiety 지위 불안, 사회적 지위에 대한 불안   arouse v. 자는 사람을 깨우다; 자극하다   constant a. 지속적인, 끊임없는

오늘날 우리는 수월성, 차별성, 성공에 대한 메시지의 공세를 받고 있고, 우수한 학생, 승자, 리더가 되거나, 가능하면 세 가지 모두가 되어야 한다고 말하는 목소리를 듣는다. 그래서 나는 여기서 무슨 일이 벌어지고 있는가에 대해 조금 더 생각하게 되었다. 이걸 우리는 어떻게 하는가? 이 모든 것은 철학자 알랭 드 보통이 지위 불안이라고 불렸던 것을 절감하게 만들

기 때문이다. 내가 보기에 이것은 충분히 훌륭하지 못하거나, 항상 더 나은 사람이 되거나 더 나은 것을 가져야 한다는 끊임없는 걱정을 통해 일어나는 일종의 불안이다.

12 전치사 ③

③ 앞의 responses to가 '~에 대한 반응'을 의미하며 to가 전치사이다. 전치사 다음에는 원형동사 be가 올 수 없고 명사나 동명사가 와야 한다. be changed를 현재분사 changing(변화하는)으로 고치면 전치사 to의 목적어는 conditions라는 명사이고 changing은 conditions를 수식하여 옳은 표현이 된다.

related field 관련 분야 identify v. 확인하다, 식별하다 tricky a. 어려운, 까다로운 untangle v. 해명하다, 풀어내다 be tied to ~와 연결되다 cultural norms 문화적 관습 likely a. 아마, 가능성 있는 reflect v. 반영하다 innate a. 타고난, 본능적인 meteorological a. 기상학의 ecological a. 생태학적인 simultaneously ad. 동시에 challenging a. 도전적인, 어려운 tease apart 분리하다, 구분 짓다 underlying a. 근본적인, 밑에 숨겨진 seasonal swing 계절적인 변동

심리학 및 관련 분야의 늘어나는 연구에 따르면 겨울은 사람들의 사고, 감정, 행동 방식에 큰 변화를 가져온다. 사람들의 계절적 성향을 파악하는 것은 어렵지 않지만, 그런 성향이 존재하는 이유를 밝히는 것은 훨씬 더 까다로운 문제이다. 겨울이 미치는 일부 영향은 문화적 규범 및 관습과 관련지어졌지만, 또 다른 영향들은 기상 및 생태적 조건 변화에 대한 우리 몸의 타고난 생물학적 반응을 반영하는 것일 수 있다. 겨울과 함께 찾아오는 자연적, 문화적 변화는 흔히 동시에 일어나서, 이러한 계절적 변화의 근거가 되는 원인을 분리해내기 어렵게 만든다.

13 success in ~ing ④

'~하는 데 성공하다'가 succeed in ~ing이므로, '~함에 있어서의 성공'도 success in ~ing이다. 따라서 ④를 in reducing crime으로 고친다.

care for 돌보다, 관리하다 green space 녹지, 초록 공간 mental health 정신 건강 child maltreatment 어린이 학대 note v. 언급하다, 주목하다 association n. 관련성, 연관성 micro-neighborhood n. 소규모 동네, 마이크로 이웃 greening n. 녹지화 youth engagement 청소년 참여 center on 중심이 되다, 중점을 두다

녹지 공간 돌보기는 그 공간 근처에 사는 사람들의 정신 건강을 향상시킨다. 아동 학대 연구에서 연구진은 소규모 근린 녹지화와 아동 학대 감소 사이의 연관성에 대한 한 가지 가능한 설명은 소규모 근린 녹지화가 부모의 스트레스에 미치는 영향일 수 있다는 점에 주목했다. 스트레스는 아동 학대와 강한 연관성이 있다. 아동 참여 역시 이 프로그램이 범죄를 줄이는 데 성공하느냐에 핵심이며 그 자체로도 혜택이 될 수 있다. 전국에서 녹지화 사업을 하는 6개 단체를 인터뷰한 결과, 참가자들은 아동의 목소리에 중점을 두는 것이 필수적이라고 말했다.

14 분사 ⑤

⑤는 '그가 그들의 권한에 대한 제한을 옹호하면서도'라는 뜻의 종속절 while he advocated limits to their power을 분사구문으로 만들고 접

속사를 생략하지 않고 함께 쓴 것으로, 현재분사 advocating을 사용한 while advocating limits to their power로 고쳐야 한다.

social norms 사회적 규범, 사회적 표준 on the one hand 한편으로는 second-oldest profession 두 번째로 오래된 직업(여기서는 정치 로비스트를 가리킴) play a role 역할을 하다 expansion n. 확대, 증가 all but 거의 elected representative 선출 대표자, 선출된 대리인 keep up with ~에 발맞추다 technician n. 전문가, 기술자 senator n. 상원의원

로비 분야보다 사회 규범의 필요성이 더 중요한 곳은 없다. 한편으로는, 세계에서 두 번째로 가장 오래된 직업의 구성원은 우리의 정치 과정에서 중요한 역할을 하고 있다. 국가 기능의 확대는 선출된 대표가 모든 표결해야 하는 이슈에서 뒤처지지 않는 것을 거의 불가능하게 만들었으며, 로비스트는 그 정보 격차를 메우는 데 도움을 줄 수 있다. 당시 상원의원이었던 존 F. 케네디는 로비스트의 권한에 제한을 두는 것을 옹호하면서도 "로비스트는 많은 경우 전문 기술자이다."라고 인정했다.

15 추론 가능한 문장 고르기 ④

ⓒ 보르게니히트 부부는 미국에 의류 기술을 가져왔지, 중요한 의류를 가져왔다는 말은 없다.

enormous a. 엄청난 diversified a. 다양한 metropolitan area 대도시 지역 significance n. 중요성, 중요한 의미 immigrant n. 이민자 garment trade 의류 산업, 의복 산업 vibrant a. 활기찬 manufacture v. 생산하다 lower half 아랫부분 industrial warehouse 산업 창고 cast-iron a. 주철의 loft n. 다락방, 공간 house v. 수용하다 coat maker 외투 제조업자

뉴욕이 거대하고 다양한 대도시 지역의 중심에 있는 오늘날, 보르게니히트(Borgenichts) 부부와 같은 이민자들이 신대륙에 가져온 기술의 중요성을 잊어버리기 쉽다. 19세기부터 20세기 중반까지 의류 무역은 뉴욕에서 가장 크고 경제적으로 활기찬 산업이었다. 다른 어느 곳보다 많은 사람이 뉴욕에서 옷을 만드는 일을 했고, 전 세계 어느 도시보다 많은 옷이 뉴욕에서 만들어졌다. 타임스퀘어 아래 20블록에 있는 10층과 15층짜리 대형 산업 창고부터 소호와 트라이베카의 철제 공간에 이르기까지 맨해튼 브로드웨이의 아래쪽 지역에 여전히 남아 있는 독특한 건물들은 거의 모두가 코트 제작자와 모자 제작자를 수용하기 위해 지어졌다.

Ⓐ 맨해튼의 로어 브로드웨이에는 주로 코트 제작자와 모자 제작자를 위해 지어진 독특한 건물이 있었다.
Ⓑ 19세기 뉴욕에서 가장 크고 경제적으로 역동적인 산업은 의류 무역이었다.
ⓒ 신대륙으로 이민을 온 보르게니히트 부부가 처음으로 뉴욕에 중요한 의류를 가져왔다.
Ⓓ 뉴욕은 다른 어떤 도시보다 많은 의류가 생산되었고, 의류 무역에서 세계를 선도했다.

16 추론 가능한 문장 고르기 ②

Ⓐ 첫 번째 문장에서 개인들이 자신의 절대적 위치와 상대적 위치를 중요시한다고 하고, 다음 문장에서 소득 격차 통계를 말하고 있으니 이는 그런 위치를 나타내는 통계라고 보아야 한다. Ⓑ 기업의 탐욕이 소득 격

차와 연관되는 것은 사실이지만, 광범위하고 어려운 문제는 소득 격차이지 기업의 탐욕이 아니다. ⓒ 글의 요지이다. ⓓ 열정은 전혀 언급되지 않고 있다.

absolute status 절대적 지위 relative to ~에 비교하여, ~과의 상대적인 statistics n. 통계 income gap 소득 격차 divergence n. 이산, 격차 top one percent 상위 1% be attributed to ~의 탓으로 돌려지다 corporate greed 기업 탐욕 fix v. 고치다, 해결하다 links n. 골프장 greenkeeper n. 골프장 관리인 skill premium 기술 프리미엄, 기술 임금 차이

사람들은 자신의 절대적인 지위뿐만 아니라 다른 사람의 지위와 비교한 자신의 지위에도 관심이 있다. 소득 격차 — 상위 1%의 소득과 나머지 계층의 소득 격차 — 에 대한 통계는 수없이 많다. 이러한 격차는 종종 기업의 탐욕 탓으로 돌려진다. 하지만 안타깝게도 문제는 이보다 훨씬 더 광범위하다. 내가 '안타깝게도'라고 말하는 이유는 이것이 오로지 기업 탐욕의 결과라면 해결이 훨씬 쉽기 때문이다. 이러한 격차의 본질을 더 잘 이해하려면 골프 대회를 살펴보는 게 도움이 될 수 있다. 골프장에서도 모든 사람이 같은 돈을 받는 것은 아니다. 타이거 우즈와 골프장 관리인은 아주 다른 임금을 받는다. 이러한 차이를 경제학자들은 기술 프리미엄이라고 부른다.

Ⓐ 개인의 절대적 지위와 상대적 지위에 관한 관심은 소득 격차 통계에서 잘 드러난다.
Ⓑ 흔히 소득 격차와 연관되는 기업의 탐욕은 해결해야 할 더 광범위하고 어려운 문제이다.
Ⓒ 소득 격차를 골프 토너먼트에 비유하여 개인 간 기술 프리미엄의 개념을 설명하고 있다.
Ⓓ 타이거 우즈와 골프장 관리인 사이의 임금 격차는 열정의 차이에서 비롯된다.

17 추론 가능한 문장 고르기   ③

Ⓐ 모든 연령대를 비교하는 이야기는 없다. Ⓑ 마지막 문장에서 언급되고 있다. Ⓒ 의도하지 않은 부상과 중독, 사고, 자살 등이 모두 각각의 범주이다. 남녀 기대수명의 감소가 아니라 남녀 기대수명 격차의 확대에 역할을 했다. Ⓓ 남성에게 훨씬 더 큰 피해를 준 코로나19 팬데믹이 2019~2021년 격차 확대의 가장 큰 원인이라고 했다.

gap n. 차이, 격차 COVID-19 pandemic 코로나19 대유행 take a toll 사상자를 내다 disproportionate toll 불균형한 피해, 불균형한 영향 contributor n. 원인 unintentional injury 의도하지 않은 부상 poisoning n. 중독 drug overdose 약물 남용 suicide n. 자살 life expectancy 기대수명 systematically ad. 체계적으로 first author 제1 저자, 주저자

연구자들은 미국 남성과 여성의 기대수명 차이가 2021년에 5.8년으로 1996년 이후 가장 큰 차이라는 사실을 발견했다. 이는 최근 역사상 그 차이가 가장 작았던 2010년의 4.8년에서 늘어난 수치이다. 남성에게 훨씬 더 큰 피해를 준 코로나19 팬데믹이 2019~2021년 격차 확대의 가장 큰 원인이었으며, 의도하지 않은 부상, 중독(주로 약물 남용), 사고, 자살이 그 뒤를 이었다. "최근 몇 년간 기대수명 감소에 관한 많은 연구가 있었지만, 2010년 이후 남성과 여성의 격차가 확대되고 있는 이유를 체계적으로 분석한 연구는 없었다."라고 연구의 제1 저자는 말했다.

Ⓐ 기대수명 격차는 모든 연령대에서 일관성 있게 나타난다.

Ⓑ 미국 남성과 여성의 기대수명 격차 확대 이유를 밝히는 체계적인 분석이 부족했다.
Ⓒ 약물 남용, 사고, 자살 등 의도하지 않은 부상이 남성과 여성의 기대수명 감소에 어느 정도 역할을 했다.
Ⓓ 코로나19 팬데믹은 미국 남성에게 불균형적으로 영향을 미쳐 2019년부터 2021년까지 미국 남성과 여성의 기대수명 격차 확대에 크게 이바지했다.

18 추론 가능한 문장 고르기   ③

Ⓐ 우두머리 암컷만 번식하므로 극단적인 왜곡이다. Ⓒ 수컷 미어캣은 우두머리 암컷 새끼의 양육을 돕는다는 이야기만 있고, 다른 말은 없다.

known as ~라고 알려진 mob n. 무리 up to ~까지 matriarch n. 여성 가장 breeding n. 번식 subordinate n. 부하 evict v. 추방하다 offspring n. (동물의) 새끼 assist in ~에 도움을 주다 rearing n. 양육 skew n. 왜곡 longevity n. 장수

미어캣은 최대 50마리의 개체로 구성되는, 무리라고 알려진, 가족 집단에서 생활하며, 암컷 가장이 번식의 80%까지 지배하여 통제를 유지한다. 암컷 부하가 번식을 시도하면 사회적 무리에서 쫓겨나고, 새끼는 모두 죽임을 당한다. 암수 부하 모두가 양육을 돕기 때문에 우두머리 암컷은 1년에 여러 번 번식할 수 있고 부하보다 더 오래 사는 경우가 많다.

Ⓐ 암컷 미어캣의 극단적인 번식 왜곡을 발견할 수 있다.
Ⓑ 미어캣은 우두머리 암컷 가장이 이끄는 가족 집단 또는 무리를 이루어 생활한다.
Ⓒ 사회적 지위는 수컷 미어캣의 장수의 원인이 된다.
Ⓓ 우두머리 암컷이 번식에 대한 상당한 통제권을 가지고 있고, 암컷 부하의 번식 시도를 제한한다.

19-22

Ⓐ 스타벅스는 미국의 커피 소비량이 10년 동안 감소하고 경쟁 브랜드들이 값싼 원두를 사용해 가격 경쟁을 벌이던 1971년 시애틀에 문을 열었다. 스타벅스 설립자들은 새로운 개념을 실험해보기로 했다. 최고급 수입 원두와 커피 추출 장비만을 판매하는 매장이라는 개념이었다. (최초 매장에서는 커피를 잔 단위로 판매하지 않고 원두만 판매했다.)
Ⓑ 하워드 슐츠는 1982년 스타벅스에 입사했다. 밀라노에 출장 중이던 그는 이탈리아 커피 바에 들어갔다가 "미국에는 이런 곳이 없구나. 이곳은 집의 정면 현관을 확장한 것이구나. 감성적인 경험이야."라는 놀라운 깨달음을 얻었다. 슐츠는 이 개념을 미국에 도입하기 위해 스타벅스 커피하우스를 이탈리아의 우아함과 미국의 비격식성(편안함)이 어우러진 환경으로 조성하는 일에 착수했다. 그는 스타벅스를 고객들에게 '개인적인 대접을 하는 장소', 직장과 집을 연결하는 편안하고 사교적인 모임 장소인 '제3의 장소'로 상상했다.
Ⓒ 스타벅스의 미국 전역으로의 확장은 신중하게 계획되었다. 모든 매장은 회사 소유로 운영되어 최고의 품질 이미지를 완벽하게 관리할 수 있었다. 스타벅스의 커피 전문점은 '허브' 전략을 통해 새로운 시장에 집단적으로 진출했다. 이러한 의도적인 포화 상태는 (기존 매장) 인근에 매장을 개설해서 한 매장 매출의 30%를 잠식하는 경우도 흔했지만, 그 어떤 매출 감소도 마케팅 및 유통 비용의 효율성과 편리하다는 이미지의 제고에 의해 상쇄되었다. 일반적인 고객은 한 달에 18회 정도 스타벅스를 방문한다. 이보다 더 높은 빈도의 고객 재방문을 기록한 미국 소매업체는 없었다.
Ⓓ 스타벅스 성공의 일부는 의심의 여지 없이 제품과 서비스, 그리고 가능

한 한 가장 풍부한 감각적 경험을 제공하려는 끊임없는 노력에 있다. 하지만 또 다른 비결은 여러 가지 방식으로 나타나는 책임감의 깨달음이다. 슐츠는 고객의 기대를 뛰어넘으려면 먼저 직원의 기대를 뛰어넘어야 한다고 믿었다. 1990년부터 스타벅스는 파트타임 직원을 포함한 모든 직원에게 종합 의료 서비스를 제공하고 있다. 이제 회사는 건강보험에 커피보다 더 큰 비용을 매년 지출하고 있다. 빈 스톡(Bean Stock)이라는 스톡옵션 제도를 통해 직원들은 회사의 재정적 성공에 참여할 수 있다. 슐츠는 또한 스타벅스가 정중하고 윤리적인 방식으로 운영되어야 하며, 지역사회와 지구 전체에 긍정적인 영향을 미치는 결정을 내려야 한다고 믿었다.

founder n. 설립자 experiment v. 실험하다 on business 사업차 epiphany n. 깨달음 front porch 프론트 포치, 베란다 set about 착수하다 elegance n. 우아함 meld v. 섞다 envision v. 상상하다 ensure v. 보장하다 unparalleled a. 유례없는 hub n. 중심지, 중추 clustered a. 무리를 이룬 deliberate a. 의도적인 saturation n. 포화 cannibalize v. 동종업계의 시장을 침탈하다 revenue n. 수입 offset v. 상쇄하다 distribution cost 유통 비용 enhanced a. 향상된 stop by 들리다 retailer n. 소매점 revisit n. 재방문 relentless a. 끊임없는 commitment n. 헌신, 전념 exceed v. 능가하다 comprehensive a. 포괄적인 part-timer n. 아르바이트생 financial a. 재정적인 operation n. 운영 ethical a. 윤리적인 impact n. 영향 planet n. 행성 rise n. 등장 unprecedented a. 유례없는 postconsumer a. 최종 소비자가 사용 후에 버린 inaugural a. 최초의

19 글의 제목   ④

스타벅스가 성공한 비결은 무엇인지, 어떤 기업 철학을 가졌는지를 분석한 글이다. ④ 스타벅스의 발전과정으로 보면 제목으로 적절하다. ② 스타벅스가 쇠락하는 브랜드였다는 말은 아니다. ③ 슐츠가 중요한 역할을 하긴 했지만, 예를 들어, 최초의 개념, 제품의 초점 등 전 세계적 확장에 대해 더 많은 이야기를 하고 있다.

다음 중 위 글의 제목으로 가장 적절한 것은?
① 미국 내 이탈리아 커피 비즈니스의 부상
② 스타벅스: 쇠락하는 브랜드에서 전례 없는 성공으로 가는 여정
③ 스타벅스의 글로벌 확장에 대한 하워드 슐츠의 영향력
④ 스타벅스의 발전: 원두에서 제조를 거쳐 사회적 책임으로
⑤ 커피 산업의 경쟁 전략

20 빈칸완성   ①

빈칸 앞의 문장이 스타벅스의 성공 비결로 제품, 서비스, 감각적 경험 제공 등을 들고 있으므로 '또 다른 비결'이라고 명시하고 그 구체적 내용을 밝힌 ①이 빈칸에 적절하다.

다음 중 문단 D의 빈칸 (1)에 들어가기에 가장 적절한 것은?
① 하지만 또 다른 비결은 여러 가지 방식으로 나타나는 책임감의 깨달음이다.
② 스타벅스는 국제 자연 보호 단체인 국제 자연 보호 협회와 파트너십을 맺고 책임감 있게 재배되고 윤리적으로 거래되는 커피를 구매하고 있다.
③ 직원들은 허리케인 카트리나 이후 뉴올리언스 재건 등 크고 작은 지역 봉사활동에 자발적으로 참여하고 있다.

④ 스타벅스는 세계 최초로 최종 소비자가 사용 후 버린 섬유 10%가 포함된 재활용 음료 컵 개발에 10년이 걸렸다.
⑤ 스타벅스는 미국과 캐나다의 어린이와 가족을 위한 문해력 프로그램 지원에 중점을 두고 있다.

21 동의어   ⑤

relentless는 '끈질긴, 수그러들지 않는'의 의미이고, outstanding은 '아주 뛰어난, 인상적인'의 의미이므로 서로 다른 뜻이다.

22 내용일치   ③

슐츠가 스타벅스에 대한 깨달음을 얻었던 장소는 파리가 아닌 밀라노였다.

위 글에 의하면, 다음 중 옳지 않은 것은?
① 스타벅스 1호점은 최고급 수입 원두와 커피 추출 장비만을 전문적으로 판매하는 매장이었다.
② 스타벅스는 커피보다 직원들의 건강 보험에 더 많은 돈을 지출한다.
③ 하워드 슐츠는 1982년 파리 출장 후에 스타벅스에 입사했다.
④ 스타벅스는 미국 내 사업 확장을 위해 '허브' 전략을 채택했다.
⑤ 스타벅스는 1990년부터 파트타임 노동자를 포함한 모든 직원에게 종합 의료 보험을 제공하고 있다.

23-26

A 5세기 때 서로마 제국은 일련의 로마 후 왕국들로 분열하면서 대체로 '야만인' 통치자들에게 지배되었다. 그 결과, 기독교가 로마 제국에 미친 장기적인 영향을 이해하기 위해서는 우리의 관점을 동쪽으로 옮겨 콘스탄티노플과 비잔티움 세계에 의해 통치된 이른바 동로마 제국을 살펴보아야 한다.

B 서기 312년경에 콘스탄티누스 황제는 기독교를 그의 지지 종파로 받아들였다. 380년에야 비로소 테오도시우스 1세가 기독교를 로마 제국의 공식 종교로 선언했다. 콘스탄티누스 황제의 천성은 종교 문제에 있어서 대체로 관용적이었다. 기독교 신앙과 로마의 정치적 정체성의 융합은 유스티니아누스 황제 즉위(527년)와 헤라클레이우스 황제 사망(641년) 사이 6~7세기 콘스탄티노플에서 절정에 이르렀다. 기독교는 종교적 오류(이단)와 일탈이라 간주되는 것에 대한 훨씬 더 큰 불관용적 태도를 로마 제국의 종교 생활 속으로 가져왔다. 특히 유스티니아누스는 로마 제국을 훨씬 더 종교적으로 박해하는 국가로 만들었다. 예를 들어, 이전 황제들은 이교도 제사 행위를 금지하려 했던 반면, 유스티니아누스는 이교조차 불법으로 규정하고 거짓으로 개종하다 적발되면 사형에 처하는 제도를 도입했다. 그의 치하에서 이단자, 사마리아인, 유대인의 법적 지위와 시민권에 대한 지속적인 탄압이 가해졌다. 궁정에서 기독교 로마 제국을 '새 이스라엘'로 내세운 헤라클레이우스 황제 치하에서 반유대주의 조치는 더욱 강화되었다.

C 이와 동시에, 기독교화는, 황제들이 병원과 보육원에 자금을 지원하는 등, 가난하고 궁핍한 사람들에 대해, 전통 로마 이데올로기가 특징으로 보여준 것보다 훨씬 더 큰 관심을 쏟게 했다. 유스티니아누스 황제의 법안은 취약한 여성, 어린이, 장애인의 이익에 관한 전례 없는 관심을 드러냈다. 따라서 로마 제국의 기독교화는 궁극적으로 로마의 정치 문화를 훨씬 더 사회적으로 응집력 있고 통합적인 동시에 더욱 배타적이고 박해하는 문화로 만드는 역할을 했다.

D 표면적으로는, 기독교가 4세기 로마 제국의 사회 지형에 즉각적인 변화를 가져왔을 것이라고 예상할 수 있다. "그리스도 안에서는 모든 사람이 평등하다"라는 사도 바울의 견해를 고려하면 당연한 수순으로 보일 수 있다. 하지만 상황은 그렇게 되지 않았다. 예를 들어 노예제도를 살펴보자면, 초기 기독교인들은 노예제도 폐지보다는 노예를 '그리스도의 노예'로서 기독교인들이 본받아야 할 헌신적인 섬김의 모델로 보는 데 더 관심이 있었다. 후기 제국에서 상황은 변했지만 아주 조금만 변했을 뿐이다. 기독교 주교들은 해적과 야만인에게 잡혀 노예로 팔린 포로들을 해방하기 위해 노력했지만, 기독교 성직자들은 계속해서 노예를 소유했다.

over the course of ~동안 fragment v. 분열하다 barbarian n. 야만인 come to terms with 이해하다 shift v. 이동하다 so-called a. 소위 adopt v. 채택하다 cult n. 종파, 교파 tolerant a. 관대한, 포용적인 fusion n. 융합 culminate v. 절정을 이루다 accession n. 즉위 deem v. 간주하다 heresy n. 이단 deviance n. 비행 persecutory a. 박해적인 ban v. 금지하다 sacrificial a. 희생의 conversion n. 개종 fund v. 기금을 대다 orphanage n. 보육원 vulnerable a. 상처 입기 쉬운 the disabled 장애인 serve to ~의 역할을 하다 cohesive a. 응집력 있는, 통합된 integrated a. 통합된 exclusive a. 배타적인 turn out 밝혀지다 abolish v. 폐지하다, 철폐하다 devoted a. 헌신적인, 몰두하는 captive n. 포로, 사로잡힌 사람 pirate n. 해적

23 글의 제목   ⑤

기독교는 가난한 자들의 구제와 같이 긍정적인 영향과 더불어, 그 전에 비해 더 많은 박해와 같이 부정적인 영향을 모두 미쳤다는 내용이므로 ⑤가 제목으로 적절하다.

다음 중 위 글의 제목으로 가장 적절한 것은?
① 서로마 제국에서 기독교의 복잡성
② 기독교화의 사회적 배제와 발전
③ 로마 제국에서 기독교의 역할
④ 기독교가 동방으로의 이동에 미친 영향
⑤ 기독교가 로마의 사회 역학에 미친 대조적 영향

24 빈칸완성   ①

빈칸 앞에 유스티니아누스의 박해 이야기가 있고 빈칸 다음에는 유대인에 대한 박해로 반유대적 조치가 언급되었으므로, 'Under him(그의 통치 하에서)'이라고 하여 유스티니아누스를 가리키면서 유대인에 대한 탄압을 언급하고 있는 ①이 빈칸에 적절하다.

다음 중 문단 B의 빈칸 (1)에 들어가기에 가장 적절한 것은?
① 그의 치하에서 이단자, 사마리아인, 유대인의 법적 지위와 시민권에 대한 지속적인 탄압이 가해졌다.
② 기독교는 장기적으로 상당한 변화를 가져왔지만, 제국의 지원을 받기 시작한 후 몇 세기 동안은 그 영향력이 더 제한적이었다.
③ 그럼에도 불구하고 웅장한 교회가 세워지는 등 물리적 환경은 변화했다.
④ 기독교와 교회의 성장은 전통적인 이교주의, 특히 동물 희생과 같은 공적 의식의 쇠퇴를 낳았다.
⑤ 이교도 황제는 항상 신과 밀접한 관계를 가졌고, 이는 기독교의 신까지 이어졌다.

25 내용일치   ①

로마 제국 후기까지도 노예제도는 크게 바뀌지 않았다고 했다.

위 글에 의하면, 다음 중 옳지 않은 것은?
① 로마 제국의 기독교는 4세기에 노예제도를 즉각적으로 폐지했다.
② 테오도시우스 1세는 기독교를 로마의 국교로 채택했다.
③ 유스티니아누스의 법은 취약한 여성에 대한 높은 수준의 배려를 보여주었다.
④ 제국 후기 기독교 성직자들은 노예를 유지했지만, 주교들은 노예로 팔린 포로들을 해방하기 위해 노력했다.
⑤ 기독교 신앙과 로마의 정치적 정체성의 통합은 6~7세기 콘스탄티노플에서 성취되었다.

26 어법   ⑤

'~을 감안하면, ~을 감안해 볼 때'의 의미로 쓰이는 전치사적 용법의 형용사는 given이다. 따라서 ⓔ의 Giving을 Given으로 고쳐야 한다. ⓓ는 주격의 than 관계절로 선행사는 much greater concern이다.

27-30

A 매주 대기 오염이 건강에 해롭다는 증거가 강화되고 있는 것 같다. 이제 로마에서 진행된 연구에서 대기 오염이 정신 건강에 미치는 영향이 밝혀졌다. 라치오 지역 보건 서비스 역학과의 페데리카 노빌 박사는 이 연구의 배경을 다음과 같이 설명했다. "최근 연구에 따르면 대기 오염은 우울증, 불안, 정신병 증세를 포함한 정신 질환 발병과 관련이 있습니다. 하지만 이 모든 관련성은 주로 소규모 집단을 대상으로 조사되었기 때문에 그 결과를 일반화하기는 어렵습니다."
B 노빌 연구팀은 2011년 로마에 거주하는 170만 명 이상의 성인 인구조사 데이터에서 시작하여, 이를 의료 기록 및 공공 의료 보험 기록과 대조했다. 이후 8년 동안, 병원에 입원한 사람이나 항정신병약, 항우울제, 기분 안정제를 새롭게 반복 처방받은 사람을 포함해서, 새로운 정신 건강 발병 사례를 찾아보았다. 이를 이 사람들이 살고 있는 장소의 대기 오염 데이터 및 교통 소음은 물론, 빈곤, 실업, 교육, 결혼 여부 등 정신 건강에 영향을 미칠 수 있는 기타 사회적 요인과 비교해 보았다.
C 이들은 입자 오염이 심한 지역에 사는 사람들은 조현병, 우울증, 불안 장애에 걸릴 확률이 더 높다는 사실을 발견했다. 이는 약물 처방 분석 결과와도 일치했다. 이 분석에 따르면 30세에서 64세 사이 사람들이 대기 오염과 가장 뚜렷한 연관성을 보였다. 이 연구의 데이터를 사용하면 도시 대기 개선으로 인한 장점도 예측할 수 있다. 로마의 평균 입자 오염을 10퍼센트 줄이면 이 흔한 정신 건강 질병을 10~30퍼센트 줄일 수 있다. 유럽연합 집행위원회가 제안한 2030년 대기 오염 제한과 세계보건기구의 가이드라인을 충족함으로써 더 큰 개선을 이룰 수 있을 것이다.
D 이탈리아 국립 연구위원회의 프란체스코 포라스티에 교수는 이렇게 말했다. "우리의 발견은 인간의 대기 오염 물질 노출을 줄이는 엄격한 조치 시행이 얼마나 중요한지를 강조하고 있습니다. 이는 신체적 질병은 물론 정신적 건강을 지키는 데도 매우 중요합니다." 이러한 문제에 대한 이해는 서서히 개선되고 있다. 지금으로부터 71년 전 1952년 런던 대 스모그로 인해 약 12,000명이 주로 호흡기 질환, 심장마비, 뇌졸중으로 사망했다. 1990년대의 연구에서는 대기 오염 영향 목록에 폐암이 추가되었지만, 뇌 건강에 미치는 영향은 간과되었다. 2002년 멕시코의 한 애완견 연구는 대기 오염 노출이 만년에 치매 위험을 증가시킨다는 결론

을 도출하는 데 도움을 주었다. 그리고 도시 지역 거주와 조현병 위험 증가 사이의 연관성을 관찰한 결과, 연구자들은 대기 오염을 가능한 하나의 원인으로 조사하게 되었다.

epidemiology n. 역학, 전염병학 depression n. 우울증 census n. 인구조사 insurance n. 보험 prescription n. 처방 antipsychotics n. 항정신병약 antidepressant n. 항우울제 mood stabilizer 기분 안정제 particle pollution 입자 오염 schizophrenia n. 조현병 association n. 관계 underscore v. 강조하다 implement v. 실행[이행]하다 stringent a. 엄격한 safeguarding a. 보호하는 ailment n. 질병 stroke n. 뇌졸중 overlook v. 무시하다 dementia n. 치매 relapse n. 재발 prevalent a. 일반적인

27 글의 제목 ②

대기 오염이 정신 건강에 미치는 영향에 대해 Ⓐ 단락 둘째 문장에서 언급한 후 일관되게 설명해가고 있는 글이므로 ②가 제목으로 적절하다.

다음 중 위 글의 제목으로 가장 적절한 것은?
① 런던의 스모그에서 로마의 이해까지
② 대기 오염과 정신 건강의 연관성 밝혀내기
③ 로마에서 대기 오염의 영향에 대한 늘어나는 증거
④ 몸과 마음의 건강 지키기: 대기 오염 해결의 위험성
⑤ 아직 해결되지 않은 위협: 대기 오염이 사회에 미치는 영향

28 빈칸완성 ④

(1)의 앞에 '로마의 평균 입자 오염을 10퍼센트 줄이면 이 흔한 정신 건강 질병을 10~30퍼센트 줄일 수 있다.'는 내용이 있는데, 그 뒤에는 이와 관련된 내용을 부연하는 ④가 들어가는 것이 적절하다.

다음 중 문단 Ⓒ의 빈칸 (1)에 들어가기에 가장 적절한 것은?
① 킹스 칼리지 런던의 이오아니스 바콜리스 박사는 이렇게 말했다. "로마에서 진행된 대규모 연구는 절실히 필요한 증거를 제공합니다."
② 이 연구는 영국, 미국, 덴마크의 이전 연구 결과를 보강하여 대기 오염과 정신 질환 사이의 연관성에 대한 확신을 강화했다.
③ 로마 시민들의 연간 평균 미세먼지 노출량은 WHO가 제시한 수치보다 3배 이상 높다.
④ 유럽연합 집행위원회가 제안한 2030년 대기 오염 제한과 세계보건기구의 가이드라인을 충족함으로써 더 큰 개선을 이룰 수 있을 것이다.
⑤ 다른 연구에서도 대기 오염이 정신 질환 환자의 중증도 및 재발에 영향을 미친다는 사실이 밝혀졌다.

29 어법 ①

Ⓐ는 30세에서 64세 '사이'라는 의미이므로 (who are) aged between 이 필요하고, Ⓑ의 주어는 understanding으로 단수 취급하므로 ①, ③, ④ 중에서 단수 동사 has를 사용한 ①이 정답이다.

30 내용일치 ②

Ⓓ에서 1990년대에 대기 오염이 뇌 건강에 미치는 영향은 간과되었다고 했으므로 ②가 정답이다.

위 글에 의하면, 다음 중 옳지 않은 것은?
① 노빌 박사의 연구팀은 2011년 로마에 거주하는 170만 명 이상의 성인에 대한 인구조사 데이터를 사용했다.
② 포라스티에 교수는 대기 오염이 뇌 건강에 미치는 영향이 1990년대에 인식되고 다루어졌다고 말했다.
③ 노빌 박사는 대기 오염과 정신 질환 발병의 연관성은 주로 소규모 연구에서 조사되었다고 말했다.
④ 2002년 멕시코의 애완견을 대상으로 한 연구에 의해 대기 오염에 노출되면 만년에 치매에 걸릴 확률이 높아진다는 사실이 밝혀졌다.
⑤ 노빌 박사의 연구에 따르면 로마의 평균 미세먼지 오염도가 10% 감소하면 일반적인 정신 건강 질환이 10~30% 감소할 수 있다.

31-34

Ⓐ 우리는 운동이 어떻게 뼈와 근육 건강에 도움이 되고 지방을 줄이는지에 대해 끊임없이 듣는다. 하지만 흔히 간과되는 인체 해부적 구조의 한 요소인 근막(筋膜)에 관한 관심도 높아지고 있다. 근막은 주로 콜라겐으로 이루어진 얇은 결합 조직으로, 신체 여러 부위에 힘과 보호 기능을 제공하는 밧줄과 같은 구조이다. 근막은 모든 장기, 혈관, 뼈, 신경 섬유 및 근육을 둘러싸고 제자리에 붙잡아 놓는다. 그리고 과학자들은 근육과 뼈 건강에서 근막이 얼마나 중요한지 점점 더 많이 인식하고 있다.

Ⓑ 우리 몸에서 근막을 보기는 어렵지만, 스테이크를 보면 근막이 어떻게 생겼는지 짐작할 수 있다. <근막은 스테이크 표면이나 층 사이에 있는 얇은 흰색 줄무늬이다.> 근막은 신체에서 일반적 기능과 특수한 기능을 제공하며 여러 가지 방식으로 배열되어 있다. 표면에 가장 가까운 근막은 피부 아래 지방층 사이에 있는 얕은 근막이다. 그다음에는 근육, 뼈, 혈관을 덮고 있는 깊은 근막이 있다. 근막, 근육, 뼈 건강과 기능 사이의 연관성은 근막이 세포 수축을 도와 힘을 생성하고 근육 경직성에 영향을 미치는 등 근육 작동에 중요한 역할을 한다는 최근 연구에 의해 더욱 강조되고 있다. 각 근육은 근막으로 둘러싸여 있다. 이 층들은 옆으로나 아래위로 나란히 있는 근육들이 서로의 기능에 영향을 주지 않고 자유롭게 움직일 수 있게 해주기 때문에 중요하다.

Ⓒ 근막은 또한 근골격계를 통한 힘의 전달을 돕는다. 이것의 한 가지 예가 우리의 발목인데, 발목에서는 아킬레스건이 발바닥 근막으로 힘을 전달한다. 이 전달과정에서 힘은 아킬레스건을 통해 수직으로 아래로 내려간 다음, 움직일 때 발바닥인 족저근막으로 수평으로 전달된다. 가슴 근육에서 팔뚝 근육 무리들로까지 비슷한 힘의 이동을 볼 수 있다. 신체의 다른 부위에도 비슷한 근막 연결 사슬이 있다. 부상 후에서와 같이 근막이 제대로 기능하지 않으면, 근막 층이 서로의 움직임을 촉진하는 힘도 줄어들고, 힘 전달에도 도움이 줄어든다. 근막은 힘줄과 유사한 세포(섬유아세포)를 가지고 있고 혈액 공급이 제한적이기 때문에 아마도 부상을 회복하는 데 오랜 시간이 걸릴 것이다.

Ⓓ 최근 연구에서는 근막, 특히 표면과 가까운 층에 피부 다음으로 많은 수의 신경이 있다는 사실이 밝혀졌다. 근육의 근막 내벽은 스포츠, 운동, 노화로 인한 근골격계 손상에 대한 수술로 인한 통증과도 관련이 있다. 근골격계 통증이 있는 사람의 최대 30%는 근막과 연관이 있거나 혹은 근막이 원인일 수 있다.

exercise n. 운동 muscle n. 근육 anatomy n. 해부학 fascia n. 근막 casing n. 외피 connective tissue 결합 조직 collagen n. 콜라겐

organ n. 장기 nerve fiber 신경 섬유 hold in place 제자리에 유지하다 superficial a. 표면의 layer n. 층위 contraction n. 수축 generate v. 생산하다 stiffness n. 경직성 wrapped in ~에 싸인 transition n. 이행 musculoskeletal a. 근골격의 ankle n. 발목 tendon n. 힘줄 plantar a. 발바닥의 see v. 발생시키다 vertically ad. 수직으로 horizontally ad. 수평으로 forearm n. 전완 repair v. 수리하다 facilitate v. 용이하게 하다 fibroblast n. 섬유아세포 blood supply 혈액 공급 nerve n. 신경 aging n. 노화 up to ~까지 lining n. 내벽 musculoskeletal pain 근골격 통증 involvement n. 연관 discern v. 식별하다 dilation n. 확장

31 글의 제목   ①

근막은 무엇이고, 어떤 역할을 하는지에 대해 소개한 글이다. 글의 첫머리에서 '흔히 간과되는 근막에 관한 관심도 높아지고 있다'라는 말로 시작하면서 근막에 대해 설명하는 것을 통해, ①이 제목으로 가장 적절함을 알 수 있다.

다음 중 위 글의 제목으로 가장 적절한 것은?
① 드디어 주목받기 시작한 근막
② 몸 속의 근막 고찰하기: 스테이크와의 비교
③ 근막의 신경과 그것의 통증과의 연관성에 대한 인식 증가
④ 근막의 느린 치유 과정과 제한된 혈액 공급
⑤ 뼈와 근육 건강에서 간과되고 있는 콜라겐의 중요성

32 내용일치   ②

① 지방을 줄인다는 말은 없다. ③ 인체의 지방층 사이 피부 아래에 위치하는 것은 깊은 근막이 아니라 얕은 근막이다. ④ 관련이 있다고 ⑤에서 언급했다. ⑤ second-highest number이다.

위 글에 의하면, 다음 중 옳은 것은?
① 근막은 주로 체내 지방을 줄이고 주요 신체 기관에 힘을 전달하는 역할을 한다.
② 근막은 신체의 다양한 구조를 둘러싸고 지지하는 역할을 하며 근골격계 건강에 중요한 역할을 한다.
③ 깊은 근막은 인체의 피부 아래 지방층 사이에 위치하며 근육, 뼈, 혈관을 덮고 있다.
④ 최근 연구에 따르면 근골격계 통증은 근막 침범과 거의 관련이 없는 것으로 나타났다.
⑤ 근막층은 가장 많은 양의 신경을 보유하고 있는 것으로 입증되었다.

33 문장삽입   ②

스테이크는 근막을 쉽게 설명하고자 등장하는 비유인데 주어진 문장의 the meat가 스테이크를 말하므로, ⑧의 첫 문장 다음인 ❷에 들어가야 한다.

34 동의어   ④

contraction은 '수축'이고 dilation은 '확장'이므로 동의어가 아니라 반의어이다.

35-38

Ⓐ 도파민은 보상 처리에서의 역할로 유명한데, 보상 처리는 최소 50년 전으로 거슬러 올라가는 개념이다. 도파민 뉴런은 어떤 행동을 통해 얻으리라 생각한 보상과 실제로 받은 보상 사이의 차이를 감시한다. 신경 과학자들은 이 차이를 보상 예측 오류라고 부른다.
Ⓑ 막 개업하고 특별한 것 없어 보이는 레스토랑에서의 저녁 식사는 보상 예측 오류의 작동 방식을 보여준다. 식사가 매우 맛있었다면 이는 긍정적인 보상 예측 오류를 낳고, 당신은 나중에 돌아와 같은 식사를 주문할 가능성이 크다. 재방문할 때마다 보상 예측 오류는 줄어들고, 나중에 맛있는 저녁 식사를 기대할 때 보상 예측 오류는 0에 도달한다. 하지만 첫 번째 식사가 형편없으면 부정적인 보상 예측 오차를 낳고, 당신은 아마도 다시는 그 레스토랑을 찾지 않을 것이다.
Ⓒ 도파민 뉴런은 뇌가 학습에 사용하는 도파민 방출의 발화 속도와 패턴을 통해 보상 예측 오류를 뇌에 전달한다. 도파민 뉴런은 두 가지 방식으로 도파민 방출을 발화한다. 일시적 발화(phasic firing)는 도파민이 단기간에 최고조에 달하는 급격한 발화를 가리킨다. 이는 예상치 못한 보상을 받거나 예상보다 많은 보상을 받을 때 일어난다. 일시적 발화는 보상 예측 오류를 나타낸다. 이와는 대조적으로 지속적 발화(tonic firing)는 놀라움이라는 요소가 없을 때 일어나는 이러한 뉴런의 느리고 꾸준한 활동을 기술하며, 산재한 일시적인 발화들의 배경을 이루는 활동이다. 일시적 발화는 산의 봉우리와 같고 지속적 발화는 봉우리 사이의 하상(河床, 계곡 바닥)과 같다.
Ⓓ 보상 예측 오류 생성에 사용되는 정보를 추적하는 것이 도파민 역할의 전부인 것은 아니다. 약 15년 전, 도파민 뉴런이 혐오스러운 사건(눈에 연기가 들어오거나, 가벼운 감전 또는 돈을 잃는 것과 같은 짧은 불편함)에 반응한다는 보고가 나오기 시작했는데, 이는 과학자들의 생각에는 도파민의 역할이 아닌 것이었다. 이 연구에 따르면 일부 도파민 뉴런은 보상에만 반응하는 반면 다른 뉴런은 보상과 부정적인 경험 모두에 반응하는 것으로 나타나서, 뇌에 두 개 이상의 도파민 시스템이 있을 수 있다는 가설을 낳았다.

dopamine n. 도파민 play a role 역할을 하다 reward processing 보상 처리 date back 소급하다 neuron n. 신경세포 monitor v. 감시하다 reward prediction error 보상 예측 오차 shrink v. 수축하다 terrible a. 끔찍한, 형편없는 release n. 방출 anticipate v. 예상하다 encode v. 나타내다 by contrast 이와는 대조적으로 intersperse v. 사이사이에 배치하다 valley floor 하상(河床) track v. 추적하다 aversive a. 불쾌한 discomfort n. 불편 puff n. 연기 hypothesis n. 가설 cause-and-effect relationship 인과관계 schizophrenia n. 조현병

35 내용일치   ⑤

뇌에 둘 이상의 도파민 시스템이 있을 수 있다는 가설은 일시적 발화에 대한 연구 결과가 아니라 보상과 부정적인 경험 모두에 반응하는 도파민 뉴런의 발견이 낳은 것이다.

위 글에 의하면, 다음 중 옳지 않은 것은?
① 도파민 뉴런은 예상된 보상과 실제로 받은 보상 사이의 차이를 감시한다.
② 도파민 뉴런은 도파민 방출 패턴을 통해 보상 예측 오류를 전달한다.
③ 일부 도파민 뉴런은 가벼운 불편함이나 금전적 손실과 같은 혐오스러운 사건이나 부정적인 경험에도 반응한다.
④ 최근의 연구는 도파민 뉴런이 보상에만 반응한다는 기존의 믿음과 모순된다.
⑤ 일시적 발화에 대한 연구 결과는 뇌에 두 개 이상의 도파민 시스템이 있을 수 있다는 가설을 낳는다.

---

36 내용파악 ②

②를 제외한 나머지 모두는 phasic firing과 관련된 것이다.

위 글에 의하면, 다음 중 "tonic firing"에 대해 옳은 것은?
① 도파민 뉴런 활동의 급격한 폭발적 증가와 관련이 있다.
② 돌발 상황이 없는 상태에서 꾸준히 활동하는 것을 말한다.
③ 예상치 못한 보상에 대한 정보를 기록한다.
④ 개인이 예상보다 많은 보상을 받을 때 발생한다.
⑤ 예측 결과와의 편차를 신호로 알림으로써 학습을 촉진한다.

---

37 글의 제목 ④

관련된 중요 개념이 '도파민'과 '보상 처리'이므로 ④가 제목으로 적절하다. ① 너무 넓고, '보상 처리' 이야기가 없다. ③ 네 번째 단락에서 다루어지는 내용이다. ⑤ 도파민 기능이 어떤 식으로 발전하고 있다는 역사적인 맥락에 대한 내용은 없다.

다음 중 위 글의 첫 세 단락의 제목으로 가장 적절한 것은?
① 도파민이 뉴런에 미치는 영향
② 도파민이 식습관에 미치는 영향
③ 부정적인 사건에 대한 도파민의 반응
④ 보상 처리와 학습에서의 도파민의 역할
⑤ 도파민 기능의 진화

---

38 내용파악 ②

도파민 뉴런이 보상 예측 오류를 감시한다는 말로 시작하여 도파민 뉴런이 행하는 도파민 발화 패턴과 보상 예측 오류 사이의 관계를 이론적으로 설명하고 있으므로 ②가 정답이다. 다른 보기에는 보상 예측 오류에 대한 언급이 없다.

다음 중 위 글에서 살펴보고 있는 것은?
① 도파민 뉴런 발화 패턴 이면의 생물학적 또는 신경학적 메커니즘
② 도파민 발화 패턴과 보상 예측 오류와의 관계에 대한 이론적 틀
③ 장기간에 걸친 학습, 기억 또는 인지 과정에 대한 다양한 도파민 발화 패턴의 효과
④ 도파민 발화 패턴과 특정 행동 사이의 인과 관계
⑤ 파킨슨병이나 조현병 같은 질환에 대한 도파민의 관련성

39-42

Ⓐ 플라톤의 (기원전 385년경에 쓰인) 『향연』은 친한 남성 동료와 친구들 사이의 저녁 파티를 묘사하고 있다. 『향연』에 등장하는 모임의 극적인 날짜는 기원전 416년으로, 비극 시인 아가톤이 그 연극에도 언급된 아테네 연례 연극 경연대회에서 우승했다는 역사적 기록에서 확인할 수 있다. 희극작가 아리스토파네스는 파티가 열리기 몇 년 전인 기원전 423년 무대에 올려졌고, 소크라테스를 간략히 묘사했던 『구름』을 통해서 알아볼 수 있다. 플라톤의 『향연』에는 아테네의 역사적 인물들이 수도 없이 등장하지만, 대화는 작가의 상상력에서 나온 것이다 (기원전 416년 당시 플라톤의 나이는 11살에 불과했을 것이다).

Ⓑ 심포지엄('함께 술 마시기')은 지위가 높은 남성 손님들의 사교 모임이었다. 플라톤의 『향연』에 등장하는 파티는 작은 편에 속하는데, 심포지엄은 30명 정도가 모일 수도 있었다. 파티 참석자들은 다양한 신을 기리는 노래와 찬가를 부르는 데 익숙했을 것이며, 이런 종류의 음주 노래는 고대부터 오늘날까지 살아남아 있다. 심포지엄 참석자들은 노래, 춤, 시, 심지어 수사학까지 즐길 수 있기를 기대했지만 엄격한 철학적 논쟁은 기대하지 않았을 것이다.

Ⓒ 이 텍스트(『향연』)에서 심포지엄 참가자들의 토론 주제는 에로스 또는 사랑이지만, 무엇보다도 가족이나 친구에 대한 사랑과는 달리 욕망이라는 요소가 포함된 사랑이다. 『향연』에 참석한 사람들은 현재 우리가 섹슈얼리티나 성적 지향을 설명하며 사용하는 언어와 범주 유형을 인식하지 못했을 것이다. '사랑하는 사람'과 '사랑받는 사람'은 고대 그리스에서 성 파트너의 상대적 지위를 이해하는 데 더 유용한 범주이다. 따라서 욕망은 배타적이지 않은 방식으로 여성이나 젊은 남성에게 표현될 수 있었다. 하지만 젊은 남성은 자신의 감정이 어떠했든, 나이 든 남성에 대한 욕망을 드러내서는 안 되었다.

Ⓓ 대화에 등장하는 실존 인물 중 가장 문제적인 인물은 소크라테스의 제자들(플라톤 등)과 소크라테스의 비판자들과 아테네 대중에게 끊임없는 논란의 대상이 되었던 알키비아데스(기원전 451~404년)이다. 뛰어난 정치가(혹은 모략가)이자 군대의 장군이었던 알키비아데스는 일찌감치 권력을 잡고 스타의 반열에 올랐다. 조숙하고, 잘생기고, 부유하고, 설득력 있고, 심지어 유혹적이기도 했던 알키비아데스는 아테네 대중의 찬사와 비난을 동시에 받았다. 소크라테스와의 교류는 중요한 도덕적 질문을 제기하기도 했다. 알키비아데스는 ('헤르메스 주상'으로 알려져 있는) 아테네의 수호신상을 훼손하고 그 자신이 옹호했던 시칠리아 침공을 앞두고 행해진 신성한 의식을 조롱했다는 혐의로 고발된 무리의 일원이었는데, 그 무리에는 소크라테스의 다른 여러 동료도 포함되어 있었다. 이 고발에는 알키비아데스가 아테네의 민주주의를 훼손하려 했다는 혐의가 내포되어 있었다.

symposium n. 심포지엄 portray v. 그리다 associate n. 동료, 친구 annual a. 해마다 열리는 allude v. 언급하다 stage v. 무대에 올리다 caricature v. 풍자하다 populate v. 주거하다 high-status a. 지위가 높은 be used to ~ing ~에 익숙하다 antiquity n. 고대 entertain v. 즐겁게 하다 rhetoric n. 수사 enduring a. 지속적인 prominence n. 유명함 precocious a. 조숙한 seductive a. 유혹적인 manipulator n. 조종자 censure n. 비난 association n. 연관 mutilate v. 변형하다 statue n. 조각상 herm n. 헤르메스 주상(柱像: 두상 또는 흉상을 상부에 붙인 4면 주체(柱體)의 기념비) mock v. 조롱하다 sacred a. 신성한 rite n. 의식 invasion n. 침공 advocate v. 옹호하다 implicit a. 암시된 accusation n. 비난 undermine v. 약화시키다

39 내용파악 ④

④ 『향연』에는 역사적인 인물들이 등장하고, 실제 있었던 행사이지만, 그 속의 대화는 플라톤의 상상력에서 나온 것이라고 했으므로 a record 가 아니라 a fictitious record이다.

위 글에 의하면, 다음 중 플라톤의 『향연』에 대해 옳지 <u>않은</u> 것은?
① 플라톤의 『향연』에 묘사된 파티는 기원전 416년에 열렸던 것으로 설정되어 있다.
② 플라톤의 『향연』에는 실제 역사적 인물이 등장한다.
③ 플라톤의 『향연』은 기원전 385년경에 쓰였다.
④ 플라톤의 『향연』은 역사적 사건에 대한 기록이다.
⑤ 플라톤의 『향연』에서는 파티 참가자들이 에로스에 대해 토론하고 있다.

---

40 내용파악 ④

술을 마시며, 노래하고, 시를 읊으며 즐기는 분위기였으며, 엄격한 철학적 논쟁은 기대하지 않았다고 했다.

위 글에 의하면, 다음 중 심포지엄에서 일반적으로 기대되는 것이 <u>아닌</u> 것은?
① 노래, 춤, 시, 수사학을 통한 오락
② 편안하고 즐거운 분위기
③ 지위가 높은 남성 손님들의 사교 모임
④ 엄격한 철학적 논쟁
⑤ 다양한 신을 기리는 노래와 찬가

---

41 내용추론 ③

③ "욕망은 배타적이지 않은 방식으로 여성이나 젊은 남성에게 표현될 수 있었다."라고 하였으므로, 여성이 남성의 애정의 대상이 아니었던 것은 아니다.

다음 중 단락 ⓒ에서 가장 추론할 수 없는 것은?
① 토론에서 에로스의 개념은 욕망을 포괄한다.
② 고대 그리스인들은 성적 지향을 설명할 때 오늘날의 용어를 사용하지 않았다.
③ 고대 그리스 사회에서 지위가 높은 남성들 사이에서 여성은 남성의 애정의 대상으로 간주되지 않았다.
④ 고대 그리스 사회에서는 연하의 남성이 연상의 남성과의 관계에서 욕망을 드러내지 못하도록 하는 사회적 규범이 있었다.
⑤ 고대 그리스 사회에서 관계를 이해하는 틀은 특정한 성적 취향보다는 연인과 사랑하는 사람의 역할에 더 중점을 두었다.

---

42 내용추론 ②

ⓓ의 끝부분에서 an invasion of Sicily for which he himself had advocated(그 자신이 옹호했던 시칠리아 침공)이라 했으므로 ②는 추론할 수 없다.

다음 중 위 글로부터 알키비아데스에 대해 가장 추론할 수 <u>없는</u> 것은?
① 그는 소크라테스와 교류가 있었다.
② 그는 시칠리아 침공에 반대했다.
③ 경력 초기부터 두각을 나타냈다.
④ 그는 아테네 대중의 존경과 비난을 동시에 받았다.
⑤ 그는 도시의 보호상(헤르메스 주상) 훼손에 연루된 단체의 일원으로 기소되었다.

43-46

Ⓐ 사람들은 일반적으로 비슷하기 때문에 함께 모여서 그룹을 형성한다. 예를 들어, 이들은 모두 포커를 치거나 로큰롤을 듣거나 화학 시험에 합격하는 데 관심이 있다. 그리고 그룹 구성원들이 이질화되어 더 이상 그룹을 유지할 만큼의 공통점이 없어지면 그룹은 해체되는 경향이 있다.

Ⓑ 유사성은 매우 중요하지만, 유사성이 그룹을 만드는 유일한 요소는 아니다. 그룹 구성원들이 서로 자주 교류하고 소통할 때 그룹은 더 많은 집단 통일체 인식을 갖게 된다. 상호 작용은 그룹 구성원들이 목표를 달성하기 위해 서로 의존하는 정도인 상호 의존성을 동반할 때 특히 중요하다. 일부 경우에, 특히 작업 그룹에서 상호 의존성은 과제를 성공적으로 완수하기 위해 함께 협력해야 하는 필요성을 수반한다. 그룹 구성원들이 상호 의존적일 때, 서로를 더 좋아하고, 서로 더 많이 협력하고 소통하는 경향이 있으며, 더 생산적일 수 있다.

Ⓒ 구성원들이 함께 일하면서 시간을 보내며 그래서 더 '집단적'으로 보이는 작업 그룹의 또 다른 측면은 그룹 전체와 각 구성원에게 적절한 행동이 무엇인지를 정의하는 안정적인 규범과 역할이라 할 수 있는 그룹 구조를 발전시킨다는 점이다. 그룹과 관련된 사회적 규범에는 관습, 전통, 기준 및 규칙뿐만 아니라 그룹의 일반적인 가치가 포함된다. 이러한 규범은 그룹 구성원에게 좋은 그룹 구성원이 되기 위해 무엇을 해야 하는지 지시하고, 그룹에 더 많은 집단 통일체 인식을 부여한다. 또한 효과적인 그룹은 사회적 역할(기대되는 행동)을 개발하여 그룹 구성원에게 할당한다. 예를 들어, 일부 집단은 회장과 총무, 그리고 다양한 실무 위원회를 갖도록 구조화될 수도 있다.

Ⓓ 지각된 유사성, 의사소통, 상호의존성, 구조와 같은 인지적 요소는 흔히 우리가 생각하는 그룹의 의미의 중요한 부분이지만, 그것만으로는 충분하지 않은 것 같다. 그룹은 상호 의존성, 의사소통, 구조가 거의 없더라도 그룹으로 여겨질 수 있다. 부분적으로는 바로 이러한 어려움 때문에 집단에 대해 생각하는 대안적인 접근 방식이자, 사회 심리학에서 매우 중요하게 여겨지는 접근 방식은 우리가 속한 집단에 대해 갖는 정서적 감정을 활용한다. 사회적 정체성이란 사회 집단에 우리가 속해 있는 데서 비롯되는 자아 개념의 일부를 가리킨다. 일반적으로, 우리는 우리가 좋게 느끼는 집단에 머물러있기를 선호하기 때문에, 집단 소속의 결과는 긍정적인 사회적 정체성이다. 다시 말해, 우리의 집단 소속은 우리로 하여금 우리 자신에 대해 좋은 느낌을 갖게 한다.

fall apart 해체되다 dissimilar a. 다른, 닮지 않은 entitativity n. 집단 통일체 인식 interaction n. 상호작용 interdependence n. 상호의존 working group 작업 그룹 norm n. 규범 cognitive factor 인지 요인 social psychology 사회 심리학 affective a. 정서적인 social identity 사회적 정체성 outcome n. 결과 positive a. 긍정적인

---

43 글의 제목 ③

이 글은 집단의 결속성과 정체성에 이바지하는 여러 가지 요소들을 다루고 있는 글이다. 결국 지각된 유사성, 의사소통, 상호 의존성, 구조와 같

은 인지적 요소에 감정적 요소가 더해져야 우리는 집단 통일체 인식 (entitativity)을 갖고, 그런 집단에 속하는 것에 대해 좋은 느낌을 갖게 된다는 말이다. 따라서 'entitativity'가 이 글에서 가장 중요한 낱말이다. ① '집단'이 빠져 있다. ⑤ 사회적 정체성은 에서만 언급되었다.

다음 중 위 글의 제목으로 가장 적절한 것은?
① 유사성 및 상호 작용을 넘어서
② 그룹 정신의 이해
③ 그룹 내 집단 통일체 인식을 형성하는 요인
④ 그룹 상호 의존성 살펴보기
⑤ 그룹 형성에 있어서 사회적 정체성의 역할

---

44 동의어 ⑤

entitativity란 집단을 하나의 통일체로 보는 인식(the perception of a group as a unity)을 의미하므로 ⑤의 '통일성'이 의미적으로 가장 가깝다.

---

45 내용파악 ⑤

집단은 지각된 유사성으로 만들어지고, 그 유사성이 없어지는 순간 해체된다는 것이 의 내용이었다. ⑤가 취향이 같은 사람들이 모여 그룹을 만들고, 공통점이 약화될 때, 그룹도 약화된다는 말이다. ③은 유사성이 없어지는 순간 해체된다는 내용을 담고 있지 않으므로 ⑤에 비해 좋지 않다.

다음 중 단락 의 주장을 뒷받침하는 가장 좋은 예는 무엇인가?
① 개인이 다른 사람들에게 자기 그룹에 대해 긍정적으로 이야기한다.
② 구성원들은 자주 협업하고 아이디어를 전달하며 서로의 기여에 의존하여 과제를 마친다.
③ 개인이 환경 보호에 중점을 둔 비영리 단체에 자원하여 함께 일한다.
④ 자원봉사 단체에서 그룹은 회장, 총무, 실무 위원회 위원 등 구체적인 역할을 정한다.
⑤ 북클럽에서 문학 취향이 전혀 다른 새로운 회원이 가입했을 때, 처음에 그룹을 하나로 묶어주던 공통의 기반이 약해진다.

---

46 내용추론 ④

지각된 유사성, 의사소통, 상호의존성, 구조와 같은 인지적 요소는 흔히 우리가 생각하는 그룹의 의미의 중요한 부분이지만, 그것만으로는 충분하지 않기에, 인지적 요소에 더해 감정적인 요소가 필요하다는 것이지, 어느 것이 어느 것보다 더 중요하다는 말은 없다. 게다가 개인의 긍정적인 자아 개념에 어느 것이 더 크게 기여한다는 것도 나와 있지 않다.

다음 중 위 글을 통해 가장 추론할 수 없는 것은?
① 최초의 그룹 형성은 종종 공통의 관심사, 특성 또는 목표로 인해 발생한다.
② 상호 의존적인 그룹은 구성원 간의 협력과 관계가 더 긴밀하고 잠재적으로 더 높은 생산성을 보이는 경향이 있다.
③ 작업 집단들은 전체 그룹과 개별 구성원에게 적절한 행동을 정의하는 안정적인 규범, 역할, 관습, 전통 및 규칙을 개발하는 경향이 있다.
④ 집단 소속감에서 비롯된 정서적 애착은 인지적 요인보다 개인의 긍정적

인 자아 개념에 더 크게 기여한다.
⑤ 그룹에 대한 정서적 유대감과 긍정적인 감정은 그룹의 결속력과 개인의 만족도에 중요한 역할을 한다.

47-50

 휴가 중에 수준 이하의 호텔 아침식사를 경험한 적이 있는가? 제공되는 음식이 마음에 들지 않지만 이미 예약 때 식사비용을 냈기 때문에 길 건너 카페로 가는 대신 어쩔 수 없이 음식을 먹게 된다. 경제학자와 사회 과학자들은 '매몰 비용 오류' 때문에 이런 행동이 일어날 수 있다고 주장한다. 매몰 비용 오류란 이미 지출되어 회수할 수 없는 비용을 무시하지 못하는 것을 가리킨다. 호텔 아침식사의 예에서 매몰 비용은 호텔 패키지에 대해 지불한 값이다. 아침 식사 장소를 결정할 때 이 비용은 회수할 수 없으며 따라서 무시해야 한다.

B 비슷한 예들로는 이미 해당 활동에 '투자'한 시간을 근거로 반쯤 읽은 진부한 책(또는 반쯤 시청한 TV 시리즈)을 끝까지 다 읽는(보는) 것을 정당화하는 것에서부터 입회 의식을 끝내는 데 종종 더 많은 노력이 필요한 여학생 클럽이나 스포츠 클럽 같은 배타적인 집단을 그만둘 가능성이 더 적은 것까지 다양하다. 이러한 행동이 이성적인 것은 아니지만 너무도 흔한 일이기 때문에 이러한 경향을 알아두는 것이 도움이 된다. 일부 상황에서는 이를 자신의 이익을 위해 이용할 수도 있다.

C 위의 예는 비교적 사소해 보일 수 있지만 매몰 비용 오류가 얼마나 흔한지를 보여준다. 그리고 이 오류는 우리의 삶에서 훨씬 더 큰 이해관계가 걸린 결정에도 영향을 미칠 수 있다. 밥이 이전에 100만 달러에 집을 샀다고 가정해 보자. 그 후 전국적인 주택 시장 폭락이 있었다. 이제 모든 집값이 20%나 하락했고, 밥은 80만 달러에 집을 팔 수 밖에 없다. 밥은 더 큰 집으로 업그레이드할 생각이었지만(이제 더 싸졌으니까!) 계약금을 마련하려면 기존의 집을 팔아야 한다. 하지만 원래 낸 가격인 100만 달러에 비해 20만 달러의 손실이 있다고 생각하기 때문에 업그레이드를 거부한다. 주택의 현재 가격과 예상 가격만 중요시해야 하는데 원래 가격이 의사 결정에 영향을 미치게 함으로써 밥은 매몰 비용 오류를 범하고 있는 것이다. 밥은 비합리적으로 행동하고 있지만, 그는 결국 인간일 뿐이다. 우리가 이러한 손실을 무시하기 어려운 이유 중 하나는 손실이 이익보다 심리적으로 더 두드러지기 때문이다. 이를 손실 회피라고 한다.

D 매몰 비용 오류를 보여주는 증거의 대부분은 개인의 결정에서 찾을 수 있지만 이 오류는 집단의 결정에도 영향을 미칠 수 있다. 실제로 이 오류는 불운했던 콩코드 초음속 여객기가 상업적으로 실행 가능성이 없을 것으로 여겨진 후에도 오랫동안 프랑스와 영국 정부가 계속 자금을 지원했기 때문에 '콩코드 오류'라고 불리기도 한다.

encounter v. 마주치다 subpar a. 하위의 on offer 제공되어 있는 booking n. 예약 sunk cost fallacy 매몰 비용 오류 justify v. 정당화하다 banal a. 진부한 invested a. 투자한 sorority n. 여학생 클럽 initiation ritual 입단 의식 rational a. 합리적인 stake n. 이해관계 housing market crash 주택 시장 붕괴 downpayment n. 계약금 gain n. 이익, 이득 salient a. 현저한 aversion n. 회피 loss aversion 손실 회피 doomed a. 저주받은, 불운의 supersonic airliner 초음속 여객기 commercially viable 상업적으로 성공할 수 있는 feasible a. 실행 가능한

---

47 동의어 ③

salient는 '두드러진'이라는 의미이고, lucrative는 '수익이 되는'이라는 의미여서 두 단어는 아무런 관계가 없다.

48 내용파악 ①

밥이 주택 업그레이드를 포기한 이유는 매몰 비용 오류라는 '비합리적' 판단 때문이다.

다음 중 단락 ⓒ에서 밥에 대해 옳지 않은 것은?
① 밥은 미래 주택 가격에 대한 합리적인 판단에 따라 업그레이드하지 않기로 한다.
② 밥에게는 매몰 비용(초기 100만 달러의 구매 가격)이 의사 결정에 지나치게 영향을 미치고 있다.
③ 밥은 자기 집의 가치가 100만 달러에서 80만 달러로 떨어졌다는 사실을 알고 있다.
④ 밥은 초기 구매 가격(100만 달러)에 비해 20만 달러의 손실이 발생한다고 판단하여 업그레이드를 거부한다.
⑤ 밥이 업그레이드를 꺼리는 것은 초기 투자에 대한 심리적 애착의 영향을 받기 때문이다.

49 내용파악 ①

ⓑ의 끝부분에서 '이러한 행동(매몰 비용 오류의 행동)은 이성적인 것은 아니지만 너무도 흔한 일이기 때문에 이러한 경향을 알아두는 것이 도움이 된다'고 했으므로 자신의 행동을 확인해보라고 한 ①이 글에서 제안하고 있는 내용이다. ② 이성적인 판단을 내려야 한다. ③ 내용이 언급되어 있지 않다. ④ 무시해야 한다. ⑤ 장기적인 관계라는 말도 없다.

다음 중 매몰 비용 오류의 효과를 상쇄하거나 완화하기 위해 위 글에서 제안된 것은?
① 과거에 낸 비용으로 인해 행동을 정당화하고 있지는 않은지 확인하라.
② 이미 발생한 비용에 대해 이성적인 판단을 내리지 마라.
③ 매몰 비용 오류를 극복하기 어렵다면 다른 사람에게 의사 결정을 맡겨라.
④ 이미 지출한 비용을 억지로 무시하지 마라.
⑤ 도전과 어려움 속에서도 장기적인 관계에 열중하라.

50 내용추론 ⑤

① '콩코드 오류'가 그런 것이었다. ② 개인 차원의 예가 많긴 하지만, 집단적으로도 적용될 수 있다. ③ 매몰 비용 오류이다. ④ ⓒ의 마지막 문장에 제시되어 있다. ⑤ 글의 내용과 아무런 상관이 없는 문장이다.

다음 중 위 글로부터 가장 추론할 수 없는 것은?
① 사람들은 더 이상 투자해도 이득이 없는 상황에서도 자원을 계속 투자하는 경향이 있다.
② 매몰 비용 오류는 그룹, 조직 또는 정부에 적용된다.
③ 사람들은 현재의 의사 결정을 내릴 때 과거의 지출을 과대평가하는 경향이 있다.
④ 사람들은 이익보다 손실의 심리적 영향이 더 크기 때문에 매몰 비용에 집착하는 경향이 더 클 수 있다.
⑤ 사람들은 지속적인 투자에서 얻는 즐거움으로 인해 투자를 지속할 수 있다.

2024 아주대학교(자연계)

01 ④	02 ②	03 ③	04 ④	05 ⑤	06 ④	07 ③	08 ①	09 ④	10 ①
11 ③	12 ②	13 ①	14 ⑤	15 ⑤	16 ②	17 ①	18 ⑤	19 ③	20 ⑤
21 ④	22 ②	23 ③	24 ④	25 ④					

01 논리완성 ④

변호사가 하는 일과 관련 있는 표현이 들어가야 하므로, '배심원'이라는 의미의 ④가 정답으로 적절하다.

profound a. 심오한 conviction n. 확신 proverbially ad. 일반적으로 turbulence n. 격변, 변동 suffer 목적어 to V (묵묵히) ~하게 내버려두다 invade v. 침해하다 address jury 배심원단 앞에서 연설하다, 발언하다 draw down ~을 초래하다 applause n. 박수갈채 snug a. 아늑한 retreat n. 도피처 bond n. 채권 mortgage n. 담보 title-deed(s) n. 부동산 증서 ailment n. 질병 betrayal n. 배신, 누설

나는 인생의 가장 쉬운 길이 최상의 길이라는 심오한 확신으로 가득 차 살아온 인간이다. 그러므로 내가 대체로 정력적이고 예민한 직업에, 심지어 때로는 격변에, 속해 있긴 하지만, 그런 종류의 것이 나의 평온을 침해하게 내버려둔 적은 한 번도 없다. 나는 절대로 배심원단 앞에서 연설을 하거나 어떤 방식으로든 대중의 갈채를 끌어내는 짓을 하지 않는, 야심이라고는 하나도 없는 변호사 중 하나다. 오히려 아늑한 도피처의 냉정한 고요함 속에서, 부자들의 채권과 담보물과 부동산 권리증서 사이에서 아늑하게 업무를 보는 변호사이다.

02 논리완성 ②

행복 순위와 경제 발달의 상태가 반대되므로, '모순'이라는 의미의 ②가 정답으로 적절하다.

rank v. 순위를 매기다 slot n. 가늘고 긴 틈, 위치, 자리 as (대조) ~하지만, ~한 반면에 ascend v. 올라가다 flat a. 평평한, 단조로운, 활기 없는, 부진한, 불경기의 ambiguity n. 애매모호함 contradiction n. 모순 discord n. 불일치 proposition n. 명제 revelation n. 폭로

2012년 이후, 세계 행복 보고서는 150개가 넘는 국가의 평균적인 삶의 만족도에 순위를 매겨왔다. 지난 4년 동안 1등의 자리를 한 나라가 차지해왔는데, 핀란드이다. 놀라운 점은 핀란드가 행복차트의 최상위로 올라간 반면에, 그 나라의 경제 발전은 놀라울 정도로 계속 부진했다는 점이다. 이러한 겉으로 보이는 모순은 많은 사람들이 오랫동안 생각해왔던 것, 즉 경제 성장에 대한 우리의 전통적 관심 집중이 곧 행복의 증가로 해석되지는 않는다는 것을 입증해준다.

03 논리완성 ③

자연 난자나 정자의 필요를 회피하는, 즉 난자와 정자를 필요 없게 하는, 진보라 했으므로 인간 배아 세포를 인공적으로 합성했음을 추론할 수 있다. 따라서 정답은 ③이다.

sidestep v. 옆으로 비키다, 회피하다 window n. 관찰할 기회, 아는 수단, 창구 recurrent a. 재발하는 benign a. 이로운 ingenuine a. 진짜가 아닌 synthetic a. 합성의 tedious a. 지루한 vertical a. 수직의

과학자들은 난자나 정자의 필요성을 회피하는 혁신적인 진보 속에서 줄기세포를 이용하여 합성 인간 배아를 만들어왔다. 과학자들의 말에 따르면, 이 모델 배아는, 인간 발달의 가장 초창기의 배아를 닮은 것으로, 유전질환의 영향과 재발하는 유산의 생물학적 원인에 대해 알아볼 수 있는 중요한 수단을 제공할 수 있다. 그러나 이 연구는 또한 심각한 윤리적, 법적 문제를 제기하는데, 실험실에서 자란 실체들이 영국 및 다른 대부분의 국가들의 현재의 법망 바깥에 있기 때문이다.

04 도치 / so+형용사+a[an]+명사 ④

길거리 소음에 전자기기 소음까지 더해져 뉴욕시민의 고막이 고생을 한다는 내용이다. 문두에 부정어구 never가 있어서 주어와 동사 도치가 되어야 하므로 there was가 아니라 was there이며, 'so+형용사+a[an]+명사', 'such+a[an]+형용사+명사'이므로 so overworked an organ이어야 한다. 따라서 정답은 ④이다.

tune out 안 들리게 하다, 무시하다 tune in (채널을 ~에) 맞추다, 시청하다, 청취하다, 열심히 듣다 layer n. 층위 take in 받아들이다 flap n. 덮개 eardrum n. 고막 overworked a. 과로한

점점 더 많은 뉴요커들이 아이팟과 휴대폰에 귀를 기울여 들음으로써 도시의 소리를 안 들리게 하고 도시의 공적인 소리에 또 한 층의 개인적인 소리를 더하고 있다. 그러나 그 모든 것을 뚫고 민주적인 귀는 그 모든 것을 받아들인다. 소리를 켜거나 끌 수 있는 눈꺼풀 같은 깔끔한 피부덮개가 귀에는 없기 때문이다. 뉴욕에 사는 사람의 고막만큼 과로하는 기관은 전혀 없었다.

05 도치 ⑤

the previous employer may be ~가 주절이고 그 앞이 종속절인데, if절에서 if가 생략된 구문이므로 Should you로 도치가 되어야 한다. 따라서 정답은 ⑤이다.

inform A of B A에게 B를 알려주다 misconduct n. 비행, 불법행위 prompt v. 촉진시키다 applicant n. 지원자 reference n. 언급 liable for ~에 책임이 있는 interference n. 방해

전번의 고용주가 당신에게 어느 지원자의 불법행위 사례를 알려주어 당신이 그의 고용을 거부할 수 있도록 한다고 생각해보자. 만일 당신이 이 나쁜 언급을 근거로 그 지원자의 고용을 거부한다면 그 전번의 고용주는 고용 계약의 고의적 방해라는 불법행위의 책임이 있을 수 있다.

---

06 수동을 나타내는 과거분사 ④

electronic devices가 hook하는 행위의 주체가 아니라 대상이므로 과거분사의 수식을 받아야 한다. 따라서 ④를 hooked up to the patients로 고쳐야 한다.

monitor v. 모니터링하다 respiratory a. 호흡의 interact with 교류하다 telemetry n. 원격측정 alert A to B A에게 B를 경고해 알리다 vital sign 생체 신호 transmit v. 전송하다 hook up to ~에 연결하다

웨슬리 의료 센터에서, 그리고 오늘날 대부분의 병원에서, 환자의 심장박동, 혈압 혹은 호흡 기능을 모니터링하는 사람들은 환자들과 교류하는 간호사들이 아니다. 그들은 "원격측정" 기술자로, 환자들에게 연결되어 있는 전자 장치에 의해 전송되는 생체 신호의 유의미한 변화를 그 간호사들에게 알려야 한다. 이 원격측정 작업실에 있는 기술자들은 대개 많은 환자들(때로는 수십 명)의 심장박동과 수치들을 한꺼번에 보여주는 스크린을 지켜보며, 대개는 자신이 지켜보는 환자들로부터 멀리 떨어진 방에 앉아 있다.

---

07 조동사+동사원형 ③

조동사 will 뒤에 부사 likely가 오고 동사 원형이 바로 와야 하므로 to see를 see로 고쳐야 한다. be likely to V와 혼동하지 말아야 한다. 따라서 정답은 ③이다.

content a. 만족한 explore v. 탐색하다 unlock v. 풀다 fine-grained a. 미세한, 세밀한 incentivize v. 장려하다

이 초창기 시절에는, 많은 사람들이 인공지능의 가능성을 재미로 탐색하면서 만족했다. 그러나 이 인공지능 도구들이 우리 사회 전 부문에 걸쳐 급속한 진전을 보이기 시작함에 따라, 이 근본적인 기술을 지배하는 사람들에 대한 더욱 세밀한(세분화된) 통제가 점점 더 중요해질 것이다. 2024년에 우리는 아마 미래에 집중하는 리더들이 연구개발 자금지원, 훈련 프로그램 그리고 다른 투자들을 늘림으로써 자신들의 통치 능력 개발을 장려하는 것을 보게 될 것이다.

---

08 추론 가능한 문장 고르기 ①

Ⓐ 세 번째 문장 후반부에 언급되었다. Ⓑ 네 번째 문장에서 언급되었다. Ⓒ 소송을 강조했다는 내용은 본문의 내용과 정반대이므로 추론할 수 없다. Ⓓ 그의 로펌에서 변호사들이 법정이 아니라 회의실에서 분쟁을 조정했을 뿐 그가 그렇게 요구한 것은 아니었다. 따라서 정답은 ①이다.

old-line a. 보수적인 law firm 법률회사 represent v. 대변하다, 대표하다 prestigious a. 명망 높은 handle v. 다루다, 해결하다 issue v. 발행하다 stocks and bonds 주식 및 채권 run afoul 위반하다, 어기다 litigation n. 소송 white-shoe firm 화이트 슈 회사(아이비리그 대학 출신의 상류층 엘리트와 연관된 명망 있는 (법률) 회사) dispute n. 분쟁

보수적인 월스트리트의 로펌들은 자신들이 하는 일이 무엇인지 매우 구체적으로 알고 있었다. 이들은 기업 변호사들이었다. 이 변호사들은 이 나라의 가장 크고 가장 명망 높은 기업들을 대변했는데, 여기서 "대변했다"는 말의 의미는 이들이 주식과 채권을 발행하는 일 뒤에 있는 세금과 법률 업무를 처리함으로써 자기 고객들이 연방 법규를 어기지 않도록 보장했다는 뜻이었다. 이들은 소송을 하지 않았다. 다시 말해 이들 중에 법률 소송을 방어하고 소송을 제기하는 일을 전담하는 부서를 갖고 있는 로펌은 거의 없었다. 명망 있는 로펌 중에서도 가장 명망 있는 '크래버스, 스웨인 앤 무어'의 창립자 중 한 사람인 폴 크래버스가 한때 말했듯이, 변호사들의 업무는 법정이 아니라 회의실에서 분쟁을 조정하는 것이었다.

Ⓐ 보수적인 월스트리트 로펌들은 주요 기업들을 위해 기업법, 세금 관리, 그리고 주식 및 채권 발행 감독 업무를 했다.
Ⓑ 보수적인 월스트리트 로펌들은 법률소송 전담 부서가 없어 거의 소송을 다루지 않았다.
Ⓒ 월스트리트의 기업 변호사들은 소송을 강조하면서 규제 준수를 보장하는 일에 집중했다.
Ⓓ 폴 크래버스는 명망 높은 기업들을 상대로 하는 변호사들에게 분쟁을 법정이 아니라 회의실에서 해결하라고 요구했다.

---

09 추론 가능한 문장 고르기 ④

Ⓐ 대부분의 동물은 아주 작은 뇌로도 잘 살아간다고 했다. Ⓑ 큰 뇌가 비용이 크다고 했으므로 추론할 수 없다. Ⓒ 인간은 큰 뇌를 갖는 것이 진화의 성공의 핵심이라는 것을 입증해왔지만, 이런 뇌(진화를 성공시키는 큰 뇌)는 다른 동물에게서는 극히 드물다고 했다. Ⓓ 자연선택은 생존에 유리한 쪽으로 작동하는데, 큰 뇌가 생존 확률을 증가시키지 않는다면 뇌가 큰 쪽으로 자연선택이 이루어지지 않을 수 있다. 따라서 정답은 ④이다.

paradox n. 역설 demonstrate v. 보여주다, 입증하다 get by 잘해나가다 tiny a. 아주 작은 costly a. 비용이 큰 neuron n. 신경세포 natural selection 자연선택[도태] benefit n. 이점 exceed v. 능가하다 thrive v. 번성하다

그것은 진화의 큰 역설 중 하나다. 인간은 큰 뇌를 갖는 것이 진화의 성공의 핵심이라는 것을 입증해왔지만, 이런 뇌는 다른 동물에게서는 극히 드물다. 대부분의 동물들은 아주 작은 뇌로도 잘 살아가며 여분의 뇌세포(뉴런/신경세포)를 필요로 하지 않는 듯 보인다. 왜 그럴까? 대부분의 생물학자들이 내놓은 답은 큰 뇌가 그걸 가동하는 데 드는 에너지의 측면에서 비용이 너무 크다는 것이다. 그리고 자연선택이 작동하는 방식을 고려하면 큰 뇌의 이득은 큰 뇌의 비용을 결코 능가하지 못한다.

Ⓐ 모든 종이 번성하기 위해 뇌가 커야 하는 것은 아니다.
Ⓑ 큰 뇌는 더 높은 인지 능력이나 생존상의 이점을 초래한다.
Ⓒ 큰 뇌는 진화상으로 인간에게 이득이었지만 모든 종이나 환경 맥락 전체에서 동일한 이득을 제공하지는 않을 수 있다.
Ⓓ 큰 뇌를 유지하는 데 쓰이는 에너지가 동물의 생존 및 번식 확률을 크게 증가시키지 않는다면 자연선택이 큰 뇌를 선호하지 않을 수도 있다.

10-13

Ⓐ 대부분의 기존 회사들은 혁신을 서서히 증가시키는 데 초점을 맞추어, 새 고객들을 위해 상품을 수정하여 새로운 시장에 진입하고, 시장의 최정상에 머물기 위해 핵심 상품의 변종을 이용하며, 산업 전반의 문제에 임시방편의 해결책을 만들어낸다. 스콧페이퍼 사는 수익성 높은 기관용 저가 화장지 시장에서, 가격으로는 포트하워드페이퍼 사와 경쟁이 안 되자, 유럽 기업에서 해결책을 빌려왔다. 더 큰 두루마리가 달린 휴지 뽑는 기계였다. 스콧은 더 큰 두루마리 휴지를 만들어 기관 고객들에게 휴지 뽑는 기계를 무료로 제공했고 나중에 페이퍼타월(키친타월)도 똑같이 했다. 스콧페이퍼 사는 신규 시장 고객들을 얻었을 뿐 아니라 포트하워드 같은 경쟁자들에게도 덜 취약해졌다. 포트하워드 사는 가격을 낮출 수 있었지만 더 큰 두루마리 휴지나 맞춤식 휴지 뽑는 기계를 제공하지 못했기 때문이었다.

Ⓑ 신규 기업들일수록 더 싸고 경쟁 공간을 바꿀 가능성이 더 큰 파괴적 기술을 만든다. 기존 기업들은 이 파괴적 기술에 반응하거나 투자하는 데 느릴 수 있다. 그런 기술은 이들의 투자를 위협하기 때문이다. 그러다가 기존 기업들은 갑자기 자신들이 가공할 만한 새 경쟁사들을 마주하고 있다는 것을 발견하게 되고 결국 많은 기업들이 망한다. 이런 덫을 피하기 위해 현존 기업들은 고객들과 비 고객 둘 모두의 선호도를 주의 깊게 모니터링하고 진화하면서도 분명히 밝히기 어려운 소비자의 욕구를 알아내야 한다.

Ⓒ 기업은 다른 어떤 일을 할 수 있을까? 산업 제품 연구에서 쿠퍼라는 신제품 전문가는 제일가는 성공요인은 독특하고 우월한 상품이라는 점을 발견했다. 이런 제품은 온건한 이점이 있는 제품(58퍼센트 성공)이나 최소한의 이점이 있는 제품(18퍼센트 성공)에 비해 98퍼센트 성공한다. 다른 핵심 요인은 제품 콘셉트를 잘 정의하는 것이다. <기업은 (제품제작을) 진행하기 전에 표적 시장과 제품 요건 그리고 이익들을 세심하게 정의하고 평가한다.> 다른 성공 요인들로는 기술과 마케팅의 시너지, 모든 단계에서의 집행 품질, 그리고 시장의 매력이다.

Ⓓ 쿠퍼는 또한 오로지 국내 시장을 위해서만 설계된 제품은 실패율이 높고 시장 점유율이 낮고 성장률도 낮은 경향이 있다는 것을 발견했다. 세계 시장을 위해 설계된 제품은 국내에서 국외에서 모두 상당히 더 높은 이윤을 달성한다. 그러나 그가 연구한 제품들 중 17퍼센트만 국제적 지향점을 가지고 설계되었다. 이 함의는 기업들은 비록 자국 시장에서만 물건을 팔 생각이라 해도, 신제품을 설계하고 개발할 때 국제적 관점을 채택할 것을 고려해야 한다는 것이다.

established company 기존 기업 **incremental** a. 점증하는, 증가의 **innovation** n. 혁신 **tweak** v. 조정하다 **variation** n. 변종 **dispenser** n. 휴지 뽑는 기계(디스펜서) **threaten** v. 위협하다 **articulate** v. 분명히 표명하다 **moderate** a. 절제하는, 온건한 **implication** n. 함의, 속뜻 **international orientation** 국제적 지향

---

10 글의 제목 ①

제품 개발의 성공을 위해 해야 할 일들을 권고하는 글이므로 정답은 ① 이다.

다음 중 위 글의 제목으로 가장 적절한 것은?
① 산업 제품 개발의 중요한 성공 요인들
② 파괴적 기술이 신진 기업들에게 초래하는 위험들
③ 세계 시장의 난제를 극복할 전략들
④ 제품 설계 시 국내 관점의 중요성
⑤ 신제품 개발에 소셜 미디어가 끼치는 영향

---

11 문장삽입 ③

주어진 문장에서 '제품을 판매할 표적 시장과 제품 요건 그리고 제품 판매로 인한 이익들을 정의한다'고 했으므로 '성공의 다른 핵심 요인은 제품 콘셉트를 잘 정의하는 것이다'라고 한 다음인 ❸에 주어진 문장이 들어가는 것이 적절하다.

---

12 어법 ②

Ⓑ 앞에는 Scott를 주어로 하여 made와 provided로 시작하는 두 술부가 and로 연결되어 있는데, Ⓑ의 바로 앞에는 접속사가 없으므로 그 이하는 분사구문이 되어야 한다. 따라서 Ⓑ에서 did를 doing으로 고쳐야 한다.

---

13 내용일치 ①

새 기업들일수록 파괴적 기술(독특하고 새로운 상품)을 만든다 했지 고객들의 선호도를 주의 깊게 봐야 한다는 내용은 없다. 고객 선호도를 봐야 하는 것은 기업 일반이지 신진 기업이 아니다. 따라서 틀린 내용은 ① 이다. ③ 나중에 페이퍼타월도 두루마리 휴지와 똑같이 했다고 했다.

위 글에 의하면, 다음 중 옳지 않은 것은?
① 새 기업들일수록 기존 고객들과 잠재 고객들 모두의 선호도를 주의 깊게 관찰해야 새 경쟁자들과 싸울 수 있다.
② 성공에 기여하는 핵심 요인들로는 제품의 우수성과 잘 정의된 제품 콘셉트이다.
③ 스콧은 더 큰 두루마리 페이퍼타월을 위한 뽑는 기계를 무료로 기관 고객들에게 제공했다.
④ 기존 기업들은 대개 혁신을 천천히 할 것을 우선시하며 신진 시장에 진입할 때 신규 고객들을 위해 제품을 약간 조정한다.
⑤ 쿠퍼의 연구에서 제품의 17퍼센트만 국제적 관점으로 설계돼 있었다.

14-17

Ⓐ 새 연구에 따르면, 라틴아메리카에서 최근의 세 차례 극단적 날씨 사건을 둘러싸고 거짓 서사(이야기)가 확산된 것은, 스페인어와 포르투갈어로 된, 기후변화에 대한 거짓 정보가 이 지역 내 지구 온난화의 영향에 대처하고 이를 완화하려는 노력을 어떻게 망가뜨릴 수 있는지 보여준다. 환경단체 '루츠'와 '지구의 친구들'은 오보에 맞서는 기후행동 협력의 일환으로 진보적 연구 기업 Purpose에게 브라질과 페루의 사이클론 홍수와 칠레의 산불이 어떻게 온라인에서 거짓 정보가 번성하도록 하는 비옥한 땅이 되었는가를 분석해달라고 연구를 의뢰했다.

Ⓑ 연구의 결론에 따르면, 브라질과 페루와 칠레의 온라인 게시물들은 이런 기후 재난 사건들의 원인을 엉뚱하게 댐 파괴, 방화, 그리고 대기를 연구하는 기후연구 센터 탓으로 돌림으로써 혼란의 씨앗을 심고, 극단적 기후(기상이변) 대비에 대한 대화의 방향을 틀어지게 하며, 기후 행동을 양극화시켰다. 새로운 연구는 "난관의 순환"을 지적한다고, '루츠'의 오보 반대 운동의 주역 맥스 맥브라이드가 말했다. 지난 9월, 사이클론이 브라질 남부의 Rio Grande do Sul 주를 파괴했다. 이 폭풍의 이례적인 폭우와 돌풍은 엄청난 홍수와 산사태를 일으켜 30명 이상의 사망을 초래했고 수많은 가옥을 심각하게 손상시켰다. 온라인 뉴스 자료는 이 홍수를 기후 재앙의 맥락에서 보도했던 반면, 오보를 퍼뜨리는 자들은 홍수의 원인이

세 개의 댐 문을 개방했기 때문이라고 거짓 주장을 펼쳤다.

ⓒ 연구에 따르면, 거짓 서사(이야기)는 폭풍 이틀 후부터 돌기 시작했는데, 미디어 보도에서처럼, 중도 우파 성향의 이 지역 리더들이 댐을 운영하는 기업에 "댐 수문 개방"에 대해 공개적으로 문의하면서였다. 댐 운영 기업의 대답에 따르면 댐이 홍수에 영향을 끼쳤다는 증거는 전혀 없다는 것이었다. 그 다음 주 환경부도 홍수의 원인은 사이클론이며 댐과 아무 연관 없다고 확증해주었으나 거짓 서사는 온라인에서 계속 퍼져나갔다.

ⓓ 해당 연구는 소셜 미디어 X와 뉴스 포털 논평에서 홍수와 사이클론에 대한 66,800개의 포스트를 조사했다. 그 중 소수(1,800건)만 댐 수문을 논의한 것으로 발견되었다. 그러나 이 작은 비율의 뉴스가 520만 명이 넘는, 훨씬 더 큰 독자들에게 도달했고, 이는 소셜 미디어 알고리즘이 오보를 증폭시킬 수 있음을 시사한다. "전문 오보꾼들이 소셜 미디어 알고리즘을 갖고 장난을 쳐 기후 재난을 계속 조종한다면 라틴아메리카 사람들을 기후변화에서 지킬 수 없을 겁니다." 지구의 친구들 기후 오보 프로그램 디렉터 마이클 쿠카 한 말이다.

false narrative 거짓 서사, 거짓 내러티브 misinformation n. 오보, 틀린 정보 undermine v. 손상시키다, 약화시키다 mitigate v. 완화하다 commission v. 일을 의뢰[주문]하다 fertile a. 비옥한 deflect v. 굴절시키다, 방향을 딴 데로 돌리다 batter v. 때리다, 타격하다 wind gust 돌풍 landslide n. 산사태 inquire v. 묻다, 문의하다, 알아보다 center-right a. 중도우파 성향의 game v. 장난질하다

---

14 글의 제목 ⑤

글의 첫머리에서 '라틴아메리카에서 극단적 날씨 사건을 둘러싸고 거짓 이야기가 확산된 것은 기후변화에 대한 거짓 정보가 기후변화 영향을 완화하려는 노력을 어떻게 망가뜨릴 수 있는지 보여준다'고 했으므로 ⑤가 제목으로 적절하다.

다음 중 위 글의 제목으로 가장 적절한 것은?
① 거짓 서사는 플랫폼의 콘텐츠 완화 정책의 감시망 하에 있다
② 재생 에너지에 관한 거짓 서사는 상이한 언어들로 각색되고 있다
③ 방화는 산불의 단 하나 원인으로 비난받고 있다
④ 소수의 음모론 포스트가 온라인에서 별 주목을 받지 못하고 있다
⑤ 라틴아메리카 기후변화 관련 오보 때문에 기후변화와 싸우는 노력이 위협받고 있다

---

15 내용일치 ⑤

①에서 연구 단체는 루츠나 지구의 친구들이 아니라 Purpose라는 연구 단체이다. ②는 주제와 완전 반대이다. ③은 대부분이 아니라 소수만 댐 수문 관련 오보를 담고 있었다. ④는 온라인상의 거짓 서사는 당국과 맞지 않게 거짓을 계속 퍼뜨린다. ⓑ의 첫 문장에서 브라질과 페루와 칠레의 온라인 게시물들은 기후 재난 사건들의 원인을 댐 파괴, 방화, 그리고 대기를 연구하는 기후연구 센터 탓으로 돌렸다고 했으므로 ⑤가 정답이다.

위 글에 의하면, 다음 중 옳은 것은?
① 루츠와 지구의 친구들은 브라질과 페루의 사이클론 홍수, 그리고 칠레의 산불에 대한 거짓 서사를 분석했다.
② 연구가 밝힌 바에 따르면 오보는 라틴 아메리카 지구 온난화 대처 노력에 영향을 거의 끼치지 않았다.

③ 연구는 66,800 건의 포스트를 검토했고 대부분이 댐 수문에 대한 오보를 담고 있었다.
④ 자연적 원인을 확증하는 당국에 맞추어, 브라질 남부의 사이클론에 대한 거짓 서사는 온라인에서 지속되었다.
⑤ 브라질과 페루와 칠레의 거짓 서사는 극단적 날씨 사건들을 댐 붕괴, 방화, 그리고 기후연구 센터 탓으로 잘못 돌렸다.

---

16 동의어 ②

commission은 돈을 주고 작업을 의뢰한다는 뜻이고 incentivize는 인센티브를 주어 어떤 행동을 장려한다는 뜻이므로 commission을 대체할 수 없다. 나머지는 비유적으로 동의어로 볼 수 있다. 따라서 정답은 ②이다.

---

17 빈칸완성 ①

빈칸 앞의 While절에서 홍수를 제대로 다룬 온라인 뉴스 자료가 홍수를 기후재앙의 맥락에서 다루었다고 했으므로, 빈칸에는 이와 반대되게 거짓 서사에 해당하는 댐 관리 부실 때문이라고 한 ①이 가장 적절하다.

다음 중 단락 ⓑ의 빈칸 (1)에 들어가기에 가장 적절한 것은?
① 오보를 퍼뜨리는 자들은 홍수의 원인이 세 개의 댐 문을 개방했기 때문이라고 거짓 주장을 펼쳤다.
② 중남부 지역의 도시 일부가 혹서와 가뭄 한가운데서 400건 이상의 산불을 겪었다.
③ 당시 산불은 주로 여러 요인들에 의해 초래되었다.
④ 일부 소셜 미디어 기업들은 자기네 플랫폼의 기후변화 오보를 막기 위해 내용 조정 지침을 실행해왔다.
⑤ 이는 온라인 대화의 방향을 기후변화의 영향에서, 기후변화가 홍수를 어떻게 악화시킬 수 있는지에 관한 내용으로 틀어버렸다.

18-21

ⓐ 왜 사람들은 자신이 쓸 수 있는 귀중품이나 가치 있는 물건을 남에게 주어버리는 것일까? 선물을 주는 행위는 아마 고대에 뿌리가 있을 것이기 때문에 인류학자인 내게 이것은 특히 강력한 질문이다. 그리고 선물은 전 세계 알려진 모든 문화권에서 발견된다. 선물은 많은 목적에 이바지한다. 일부 심리학자들은 "따스한 만족감 — 내재적 기쁨 — 그것이야말로 선물을 주는 행위와 관련이 있다고 말했다. 신학자들은 선물을 주는 행위가 가톨릭교와 불교와 이슬람교에서 사랑과 친절과 감사와 같은 도덕적 가치를 표명하는 방법이라는 것에 주목해왔다. 그리고 세네카에서 프리드리히 니체에 이르는 철학자들은 선물 제공을 이타성을 입증하는 가장 좋은 증표라고 생각했다. 선물이 하누카, 크리스마스, 콴자와 또 다른 겨울 휴가의 중심 부분이라는 것은 거의 놀랍지 않다. 그러나 선물을 주는 이유에 대한 설명들 중에서 내가 가장 설득력 있다고 생각하는 것은 1925년 프랑스 인류학자 마르셀 모스가 제공한 것이다.

ⓑ 많은 인류학자들과 마찬가지로 모스는 선물이 과도하게 제공되는 사회를 보고 당혹스러워했다. 예를 들어, 캐나다와 미국의 북서쪽 해안지방을 따라 사는 토착 민족들은 포틀래치 의식을 시행했다. 며칠씩 지속되는 이 잔치에서 주인들은 어마어마한 양의 재산을 주어버린다. <캐나다 콰콰카와쿠 종족의 씨족장이 개최한 1921년의 유명한 포틀래치를 생각해보라. 그는 공동체 구성원들에게 400자루의 밀가루, 담요, 재봉틀, 가구, 카누,

휘발유 동력 배, 심지어 미니 당구대까지 주었다.> 모스는 포틀래치를 극단적 형태의 선물 주기라고 본다. 그러나 그는 이러한 행동이 거의 모든 인간 사회에서 완전히 알아볼 수 있다고 말한다.

C 모스는 선물이 따로따로이지만 밀접하게 연관된 세 가지 행위를 만들어낸다고 주장했다. 선물은 주어지고, 받아들여지고, 서로 교환된다는 것이다. 첫 번째 행위인 주는 것은 주는 사람의 미덕을 확립한다. 그는 자신의 관대함과 친절과 존경을 표현한다. 그다음, 선물을 받는 행위는 존중받고 싶은 의지를 보여준다. 이것은 받는 사람이 자신에게 제공되는 것을 받을 의지가 있다는 그들 자신의 관대함을 보여주는 방법이다. 선물 주기의 세 번째 요소는 호혜성, 즉 처음 주어진 것을 같은 것으로 돌려주는 것이다. 이런 식으로 선물하기는 주고받고 주고받기의 끝없는 고리가 된다.

D 마지막 단계인 이 호혜성은 선물을 독특하게 만드는 요소이다. 돈을 지불하고 물건을 손에 넣으면 교환이 끝나는 상점에서의 물건 구매와 달리, 선물을 주는 것은 관계를 구축하고 지속시킨다. 선물을 주는 자와 받는 자 간의 이 관계는 도덕성으로 묶여 있다. 각각의 선물이 일반적으로 지난번에 주어진 것과 같거나 더 큰 가치를 가진 것이기 때문에 선물하기는 공정함의 표현이다. 그리고 선물하기는 상대를 존중하려는 의지를 보여주기 때문에 존중의 표현이다. 이런 방식으로, 선물하기는 사람들을 한데 묶는다. 그것은 사람들을 상호 의무라는 무한 순환 속에서 서로 연결시켜 놓는다.

hand over 건네다, 주다 glow n. 빛, 따스함 intrinsic a. 내재적인 theologian n. 신학자 selflessness n. 이타성 convincing a. 설득력 있는 indigenous a. 토착의, 원주민의 potlatch n. 북미 인디언의 선물 행사, 포틀래치 feast n. 잔치 immense a. 거대한 reciprocate v. 서로 주고받다 honor n. 존경, 명예 loop n. 고리, 되풀이 tether v. 매다, 속박하다

18 내용파악   ⑤

선물을 주는 것이 경제적·진화적 이점과 관련이 있다는 말은 없다. 오히려 경제적으로 손실을 가져오는 것이다. 따라서 틀린 내용은 ⑤이다.

위 글에 의하면, 다음 중 선물 제공에 대한 내용으로 옳지 않은 것은?
① 선물은 사랑과 친절과 감사 같은 도덕적 가치를 표명하는 일을 비롯하여 다양한 목적에 이바지한다.
② 일부 심리학자들은 선물주기를 내재적 기쁨, 즉 "따스한 만족감"과 연관 짓는다.
③ 선물 주기는 전 세계의 알려진 모든 문화권에서 발견된다.
④ 세네카와 프리드리히 니체 같은 철학자들은 선물하기를 이타성의 최상의 증거라고 여겼다.
⑤ 선물을 주는 것은 경제적·진화적 합리성과 일치하므로 다양한 문화에 팽배한 관행으로 남아있다.

19 문장삽입   ③

주어진 문장은 포틀래치의 예를 든 문장이다. 캐나다 북서쪽 토착민들이 포틀래치를 한다는 일반 진술 뒤에 구체적 사례로 들어와야 하므로 주어진 문장의 자리는 ❸이 가장 적절하다.

20 내용파악   ⑤

모스의 주장에서 선물 주기가 미래 세대와 관련이 있다는 내용은 없다. 따라서 정답은 ⑤이다.

다음 중 선물 주기에 대한 마르셀 모스의 주장에 관해 옳지 않은 것은?
① 모스는 선물주기가 주는 사람에게 관대함과 친절 같은 미덕을 확립하고, 받는 사람의 존중받으려는 의지를 보여준다고 시사한다.
② 모스의 관점은 선물을 주고받는 관행이 다양한 사회와 문화권에서 발견되는 널리 확산된 현상이라는 것을 암시한다.
③ 모스에 따르면 선물을 주고받는 과정은 도덕적 가치와 사회적 관계와 묶여 있다.
④ 모스는 선물을 주는 것이 주는 사람과 받는 사람 간에 끝없는 상호 의무의 고리를 형성한다고 주장한다.
⑤ 모스는 선물을 주고받고 교환하는 순환이 사회 연대의 가치를 미래 세대에게 전달한다고 시사한다.

21 내용파악   ④

모스는 20세기 프랑스 인류학자로 1921년의 유명한 포틀래치를 관찰하고 자신의 주장을 펼친다. 20세기 학자로서 20세기의 현상을 연구한다는 것은 ①의 현대적 맥락을 말하는 것이고, 인류학자라는 것은 ②의 문화적 관행과 ③의 인간 사회가 관련됨을 의미하고(이러한 행동이 거의 모든 인간 사회에서 완전히 알아볼 수 있다고 했다) 그의 선물주기 행위의 세 번째 행위가 ⑤의 호혜성 행위이다. 그러나 따스한 만족감(내재적 기쁨)이라는 ④의 심리적 측면들은 심리학자들이 선물주기와 관련 있다고 파악한 것일 뿐 모스의 관련 핵심어는 아니다.

다음 중 선물 주기에 대한 모스의 주장에서 관련 핵심어로 가장 무관한 것은?
① 현대적 맥락
② 문화적 관행
③ 인간 사회
④ 심리적 측면들
⑤ 호혜성

22-25

A 음성언어를 처리하여 이해하는 우리의 능력은 의미론에만, 즉 언어학적 단위들의 의미와 결합에만, 기반을 두고 있지는 않다. 휴지기와 강세와 억양을 비롯한 운율 같은 다른 변수도 작동하게 된다. 예를 들어, "아!"나 "오!" 같은 감정 분출 어구들 또한 이러한 운율의 일부이며 우리는 이러한 특성을 영장류와 공유하고 있다. 이런 요소들은 우리의 음성적 의사소통의 의미와 이해에 기여한다. 이런 음성 메시지가 방출될 때 이런 소리들은 우리 뇌의 전두엽과 안와전두엽에 의해 처리된다. 뇌의 이 두 부위의 기능은 무엇보다 감각적 정보와 문맥적 정보를 통합하여 결정을 내리게 하는 것이다.

B 우리가 우리와 가까운 영장류 — 침팬지나 마카크 원숭이나 보노보 — 의 감정적 발성에 노출될 때도 이 부위들은 똑같은 방식으로 활성화될까? 우리는 이 발성들을 구별할 수 있을까? 한 연구팀은 25명의 지원자 집단을 다양한 인간 및 원숭이 발성에 노출시킴으로써 이 점을 알아보고자 했다. "참가자들에게 MRI 스캐너를 장착시키고 헤드폰을 주었습니다. 서로 다른 유형의 발성을 들려주어서 잠깐 익히게 한 후 각 참가자는 이

소리들을 분류해야 했어요. 다시 말해, 그 소리가 어느 종에 속하는지 식별하는 거죠." 이 연구의 첫 저자인 레오나르도 체라볼로의 설명이다.

C 이 발성들은 긍정적 교류와 연관된 친화 유형이거나, 아니면 위협이나 고통과 관련된 적대 유형이었다. 결과에 따르면, 마카크 원숭이와 침팬지의 발성에 대해서는 참가자들의 전두엽과 안와전두엽이 인간 발성에 반응하는 것과 동일한 방식으로 활성화되었다. 참가자들은 이들의 발성을 쉽게 구분할 수 있었다.

D 반면에, 마찬가지로 인간의 가까운 친척에 속하는 보노보의 "소리"를 마주했을 때 관련 뇌 부위는 활성화가 훨씬 덜 되었고 분류도 거의 우연 수준에 가깝게 잘 되지 않았다. "원래 종 사이의 친연성 — 즉 '계통발생적 거리' — 이 이런 서로 다른 발성을 구분하는 능력을 갖고 있느냐 없느냐의 주된 변수라고 생각했었죠. 우리는 유전적으로 가까울수록 이 능력이 중요해진다고 봤어요."라고 연구를 이끈 디디어 그랜진은 설명한다. "우리의 결과는 두 번째 변수가 작동한다는 것을 보여줍니다. 그것은 음향상의 거리죠. 사용된 주파수 같은 음향 변수의 역학이 인간의 음향 변수 역학과 거리가 멀수록 특정 전두엽 구역의 활성화도 덜 되었어요. 보노보의 소리는 피치가 높아서 특정 새소리처럼 들릴 수 있습니다. 주파수 관점에서의, 인간의 발성과 비교한, 이런 음향상의 거리는 우리가 계통상으로 가깝다 해도 보노보의 소리를 해석하지 못하는 이유를 설명해줍니다."

semantics n. 의미, 의미론 parameter n. 매개변수 come into play 작동하다 pause n. 휴지 accentuation n. 악센트 intonation n. 억양 prosody n. 운율 체계 affective a. 감정의 burst n. 폭발, 분출 primate n. 영장류 vocal a. 목소리의, 발성의 emit v. 분출하다 frontal region 전두부 orbitofrontal region 안와 전두부 sensory a. 감각의 activate v. 활성화하다 macaque n. 마카크 원숭이 bonobo n. 보노보, 난쟁이 침팬지 vocalization n. 발성 categorize v. 분류[범주화]하다 affiliative a. 친화적인, 제휴하는 agonistic a. 투쟁[논쟁]하는, 적대적인 distress n. 고통 cerebral area 뇌 부위 kinship n. 친족, 동류감 phylogenetic a. 계통 발생의 acoustic a. 음향의 high-pitched a. 소리가 높은 frequency n. 주파수

---

22 내용파악　　　　　　　　　　②

②에 대해서는 언급하지 않았다.

다음 중 위 글에서 설명한 연구의 데이터 수집 방법으로 옳지 않은 것은?
① 지원자들은 인간과 다른 종의 영장류, 둘 모두의 다양한 발성에 노출된다.
② 연구자들은 순서를 무작위로 바꾸거나 구조화함으로써 발성의 연속과 제시법을 체계적으로 통제했다.
③ 참가자들은 이 발성에 노출되는 동안 MRI 스캐너를 장착한다.
④ 분류 작업 전에 참가자들은 상이한 유형의 발성에 익숙해질 짧은 기간을 받는다.
⑤ 참가자들은 각 소리가 어떤 종(인간, 침팬지, 마카크 원숭이 혹은 보노보)에 속하는지 찾아내야 한다.

---

23 내용파악　　　　　　　　　　③

③ 인지 능력은 지식과 관련이 있으므로 음향을 구별하기만 하면 되는 실험과 무관하다.

다음 중 연구의 관련 핵심어로 가장 무관한 것은?
① 음향 차이
② 뇌 활성화
③ 인지 능력
④ 유전자 인접성
⑤ 발성

---

24 내용파악　　　　　　　　　　④

D에서 언급된 '서로 다른 발성을 구분하는 능력을 갖고 있느냐 없느냐의 주된 변수'가 곧 원숭이 종의 음향을 구별하는 인간의 능력에 영향을 끼치는 요인이라 할 수 있는데, 계통발생상의 인접성(거리)과 음향상의 거리가 이 요인에 해당하여 ⑤의 질문에 대한 답은 제공되고 있지만, '계통발생상의 인접성 대 음향상의 거리'라는 둘 사이의 비율이나 관계가 어떤 역할을 하는지에 대한 답은 제공되고 있지 않다. 따라서 ④가 정답이다.

아래의 질문 중 연구에 답이 제공되지 않는 것은?
① 인간은 이 원숭이류 발성들을 구별할 수 있는가?
② 인간은 보노보가 방출하는 친화적이거나 적대적 발성의 상이한 감정적 측면을 알아낼 수 있는가?
③ 뇌의 전두엽과 안와전두엽은 원숭이 발성과 인간 발성에 노출될 때 동일하게 활성화되는가?
④ 계통상의 인접성 대 음향상의 거리는 상이한 영장류의 발성에 반응하고 인식할 때 어떤 역할을 하는가?
⑤ 어떤 요인들이 원숭이 종의 음향을 구별하는 인간의 능력에 영향을 끼치는가?

---

25 내용추론　　　　　　　　　　④

계통상의 인접성과 음향상의 인접성(거리), 둘 모두 원숭이 음향을 알아보는 우리의 능력에 영향을 끼치는 요인이다. 따라서 틀린 정답은 ④이다. ⑤ 보노보의 "소리"를 마주하기 전까지는 종 사이의 친연성, 즉 '계통발생적 거리'가 발성을 구분하는 능력을 갖고 있느냐 없느냐의 주된 변수라고 생각했었는데, 보노보의 소리로 인해 두 번째 변수인 음향상의 인접성(거리)이 작동함을 알게 된 것이다.

다음 중 단락 D로부터 가장 추론할 수 없는 것은?
① 음향의 차이는 인간이 보노보의 발성을 해석하거나 분류하기 어렵게 만든다.
② 보노보가 유전 관계 면에서 인간과 가까운 친척임에도 불구하고 참가자들은 보노보 발성을 분류할 때 어려워했다.
③ 보노보 발성의 음향상 성질은 인간의 발성과 상당한 음향상의 차이를 만든다.
④ 연구에 따르면 계통상의 인접성은 원숭이 음향을 알아보는 우리의 능력에 영향을 끼치는 요인이 아니며 음향상의 인접성이 결정적 요소이다.
⑤ 발성을 알아보는 능력은 주로 종들 간의 유전적 인접성, 즉 계통상의 인접성과 관련이 있다고들 생각했다.

2024 이화여자대학교(인문계 유형 1)

01 ③	02 ②	03 ②	04 ④	05 ③	06 ④	07 ⑤	08 ⑤	09 ③	10 ④
11 ③	12 ①	13 ①	14 ⑤	15 ②	16 ④	17 ②	18 ③	19 ①	20 ⑤
21 ④	22 ④	23 ②	24 ①	25 ③	26 ①	27 ④	28 ①	29 ②	30 ④
31 ①	32 ⑤	33 ④	34 ②	35 ⑤	36 ⑤	37 ③	38 ③	39 ②	40 ①
41 ⑰	42 ⑩	43 ⑬	44 ⑳	45 ⑮	46 ⑫	47 ⑥	48 ⑲	49 ⑭	50 ⑤

01 동의어　③

depending on ~에 따라　pedagogical a. 교육의, 교육학의, 교수법의(= educational)　engagement n. 참여　encourage v. 독려[장려]하다　disinterest n. 무관심, 사심 없음　elemental a. 기본적인　invitational a. 초청의　artificial a. 인위적인　conventional a. 전통적인

각 학생의 학습 스타일에 따라 교수법은 참여를 독려할 수도 있고 무관심을 조장할 수도 있다.

02 동의어　②

photosynthesis n. 광합성　refer to ~을 가리키다　organism n. 유기체　convert v. 바꾸다, 개종하다, 전환하다(= transform)　transfer v. 전달하다　transit v. 통과하다 n. 수송, 환승　transpire v. 증산작용하다, 알고 보니 ~이다　transmit v. 전송하다

'광합성'이라는 용어는 녹색식물과 일부 유기체가 빛을 에너지로 바꾸는 과정을 지칭한다.

03 동의어　②

abject a. 극도로 비참한, 절망적인(= utter)　all-important a. 지극히 중요한　significance n. 의의, 의미, 중요성　uncontrolled a. 통제되지 않은　variable n. 변수　unremarkable a. 특별할 것 없는　abrupt a. 갑작스러운　glorious a. 영광스러운　qualified a. 자격이 있는

그녀의 실험은 완전한 실패로 끝나긴 했지만 그래도 그녀에게 통제되지 않은 변수의 중요성에 관해 지극히 중요한 교훈을 가르쳐주었다.

04 동의어　④

note v. 주목[주의]하다　inclusive a. 폭넓은, 포괄적인　ban n. 금지(법)　inadvertently ad. 우연히, 무심코(= unpremeditatedly)　harm v. 해롭게 하다, 손상하다　vulnerable a. 취약한, 연약한　plastic straw 플라스틱 빨대　calculatedly ad. 계획적으로, 고의적으로　consciously ad. 의식적으로　deliberately ad. 고의로, 의도적으로　voluntarily ad. 자발적으로

그 환경 교육가는 포괄적인 접근법이 없으면, 금지 조치가 먹고 마시기 위해 플라스틱 빨대를 꼭 필요로 하는 사람들 같은 이미 사회에서 가장 취약한 계층에 속한 사람들에게 무심코 해를 끼칠 수 있을 것이라는 데 주목했다.

05 동의어　③

chemical reaction 화학반응　synthesis n. 합성　decomposition n. 분해(= breakdown)　compound n. 화합물, 혼합물　breakaway n. 탈퇴　breakwater n. 방파제　break-in n. 침입　breakneck a. 정신없이 빠른, 빠르게 달리는

화학 반응은 화합물의 합성과 분해 둘 모두를 포함한다.

06 반의어　④

rampant a. 만연하는, 마구 퍼지는(↔ restrained a. 삼가는, 억제된)　patriarchal a. 가부장제의　dynamic n. 역학, 역동성　polarizing a. 양극화되는[하는]　regain v. 되찾다, 회복하다　retrain v. 재교육하다　retain v. 유지하다, 보유하다

선진국에서는 경제 불평등의 만연과 성장 둔화와 가장 가부장적인 사회 역학이 결합하여, 성 평등이 사회를 양극화시키는 선거 쟁점이 되었다.

07 반의어　⑤

woeful a. 통탄할, 슬픈(↔ promising a. 조짐이 좋은, 전도유망한)　record a. 기록적인　elect v. 선출하다　parliament n. 의회, 국회　election n. 선거　lawmaker n. 입법자, 국회의원　proportionate a. 비례하는　propel v. 몰고 가다, 나아가다　prosaic a. 평범한, 따분한

지난 선거에서 기록적으로 57명의 여성들이 국회의원으로 선출되었지만, 그들은 아직도 전체 국회의원 중에 슬프게도 19%를 구성한다.

08 반의어　⑤

salient a. 가장 중요한, 핵심적인, 두드러진(↔ insignificant a. 하찮은, 중요하지 않은)　comparatist a. 비교하는　ecocritical a. 생태비평의　obviously ad. 명백히　linguistic a. 언어의　engagement with ~에

대한 대응 range from A to B 범위가 A에서 B에 이르다 toxification
n. 독성화, 오염 biodiversity loss 생명 다양성 상실 indicative a.
~을 나타내는, 보여주는 informative a. 유용한 정보를 주는, 유익한

비교 생태 비평 분석의 가장 중요한 차원 중 하나는, 명백하게도, 독성화에
서 생명 다양성 상실과 기후변화에 이르는 전 지구적 생태 위기에 대처하
는 지역사회들의 노력에서 언어적 문화적 차이가 수행하는 역할에 관심을
기울이는 것이다.

---

09 반의어   ③

algorithm n. 알고리즘(문제 해결절차 및 방법) renowned a. 유명한
polymath n. 박식가, 박학다식한 사람(↔ ignoramus n. 무식한 사람)
algebra n. 대수, 대수학 libertine n. 난봉꾼 impresario n. 극장
등의) 기획자, (발레단이나 오페라단 극단의) 단장

'알고리즘'이라는 단어는 종종 대수학의 창시자라고 묘사되는 알콰리즈미
라는 유명한 이슬람교도 박식가의 이름에서 비롯된 것이다.

---

10 반의어   ④

egalitarian a. 평등주의(자)의 aim to do ~을 도모하다, 목표로 하다
eradicate v. 없애다, 근절하다 stratification n. 계층(화) detriment
n. 손상, 손해(↔ advantage 이익, 장점) prestige n. 명망, 명성, 위신
adherence n. 고수, 집착 admonition n. 책망 addiction n. 중독
adeptness n. 숙련

진정으로 평등주의적인 사회는 개인의 명망에 대한 손상과 무관하게 모든
형태의 계층을 근절하려고 한다.

---

11 문장배열   ③

ⓒ에서 가스라이팅의 정의를 내리고 ⓔ에서 가스라이팅의 사례를 든 다
음 ⓑ에서는 그 사례에 대한 서술로 가스라이팅의 첫 단계가, ⓓ에서는
최종적인 결과가 각각 설명되고 ⓐ에서 가스라이팅을 심각하게 봐야 하
는 이유를 말한다. 따라서 정답은 ③이다.

acknowledgement n. 인정 reassurance n. 안심 lead to ~을 초래하
다 at first 처음에는 self-doubt n. 자기의심 manipulation n. 조종
sanity n. 분별력, 제정신인 상태 ultimately ad. 최종적으로, 궁극적으
로 erode v. 잠식[침식]하다

ⓒ 가스라이팅이란 개인이 자신의 현실이나 기억이나 분별력을 의심하도
록 심리적으로 그를 조종하는 짓이다. ⓔ 누군가가 실제로 일어나지 않은
사건이 일어났다거나 그 사건이 그 누군가가 기억하는 것과 다르게 일어났
다는 말을 계속 듣는 시나리오를 상상해보라. ⓑ 처음에 이것은 피해자로
하여금 그저 혼란과 불안과 자기 의심의 순간들을 경험하도록 만든다. ⓓ
그러나 가스라이팅은 결국 피해자의 자기 확신과 정신적 안녕을 잠식해
그로 하여금 가스라이팅 가해자가 인식시키는 현실에 의존하게 만들고
지원 네트워크로부터 고립되게 만드는 결과를 초래한다. ⓐ 가스라이팅은
그 자체로 심각한 문제라고 간주해야 한다. 피해자가 다시 자신을 신뢰하
려면 주변 사람들이 인정해주고 안심을 시켜주는 노력을 기울여야 하기
때문이다.

---

12 논리완성   ①

even when recycled 뒤에는 재활용을 해도 부정적 측면이 있다는 내용
이 이어져야 할 것이므로 첫 번째 빈칸에는 부정적인 단어 harmed나
damaged가 적절하다. 한편, 저소득 국가들은 오염을 '방지할' 기반시
설이 없어 해를 입으므로 두 번째 빈칸에는 방지한다는 의미의 prevent
나 preclude가 와야 한다. 따라서 짝이 맞는 정답은 ①이다.

usage n. 사용 recycle v. 재활용하다 waste n. 폐기물 low-income
a. 저소득의 infrastructure n. 기반시설 waterway n. 수로, 항로
incinerate v. 소각하다, 태우다 harness v. 이용하다 harass v. 괴롭히
다, 희롱하다 preclude v. 막다 procure v. 획득하다, 조달하다 propel
v. 추진하다, 나아가다

미국의 플라스틱 사용은 플라스틱이 재활용될 때에도 다른 나라에 해를
끼쳤다. 수백만 톤의 플라스틱 폐기물은, 종종 재활용 공장에서 수집되기
도 하는데, 저소득 국가로 수송되지만 이런 저소득 국가들은 플라스틱이
수로로 들어가거나 소각됨으로써 초래되는 오염을 미연에 방지할 기반시
설이 없기 때문이다.

---

13 논리완성   ①

관심을 쏠게 하려면 시위가 늘 상시적으로 일어나야 하므로 첫 번째 빈
칸에는 routinely가 적절하고, 화석연료 소비를 줄이는 조치가 시급하
므로 두 번째 빈칸에는 swifter나 quicker가 적절하다. 따라서 정답은
①이다.

human right 인권 organize v. 조직하다 demonstration n. 시위
draw attention to ~에 주의를 끌다 call for 요청[요구]하다 routinely
ad. 일상적으로 swift a. 빠른, 신속한 unusually ad. 이례적으로

인권단체는 지구 온난화와 인권 간의 연계성에 관심을 쏠게 하고 화석연료
소비를 줄이기 위한 더욱 신속한 조치를 요청하기 위해 UN 기후회담 장소
에서 상시적으로 시위를 조직한다.

---

14 논리완성   ⑤

뒤에서 시장의 안정성이 반드시 좋은 것은 아니라고 했으므로 시장 변동
역시 늘 좋은 것은 아니라고 추론할 수 있으므로 첫 번째 빈칸에는
prosperity와 반대되는 adversity가 적절하고, 사태나 정세라는 의미
의 관용어는 state of affairs이므로 두 번째 빈칸에는 affairs가 적절하
다. 따라서 정답은 ⑤이다.

fluctuation n. 변동 prosperity n. 번영 adherence n. 고수
inflexibility n. 경직성 advantage n. 이득, 이익 insecurity n. 불안정
성 adversity n. 역경, 재난, 고난 repair n. 수리 state of affairs
일의 사태, 정세

시장 변동은 기업의 번영과 역경 둘 모두를 초래할 수 있다. 따라서 시장의
안정성이 항상 환영받는 사태인 것은 아니다.

15 논리완성   ②

정치 혁명이 극적인 개혁을 일으킨다고 했으니 사회 운동은 문명에 큰 영향을 끼친다고 해야 하므로 첫 번째 빈칸에는 dramatic이나 seismic이 적절하고, 두 번째 빈칸에는 debilitating과 어울리는 부정적 의미의 stagnation이 적절하다. 따라서 정답은 ②이다.

significant a. 중대한 seismic a. 지진의, 지각변동의, 어마어마한 stagnation n. 침체, 정체 minuscule a. 아주 작은 enervation n. 약화 chaotic a. 혼돈의 enrichment n. 강화, 비옥화 beneficent a. 이로운, 선을 베푸는 bounty n. 풍부함, 포상금

중요한 사회 운동은 종종 문명에 어마어마한 영향을 끼친다. 예를 들어, 정치 혁명은 정치 영역 내에 극적인 개혁을 초래할 수도 있고 쇠약하게 하는 침체를 초래할 수도 있다.

16 논리완성   ④

Although 절은 주절에 표현된 표절의 일반적인 의미와 다르게 세부적이고 지엽적인 의미를 '포함한다'고 해야 하므로 첫 번째 빈칸에는 include나 encompass가 적절하고, 표절이 남은 것을 그것에 가치를 더하는 공적에 대한 인정 없이 사용하는 것을 의미하므로 두 번째 빈칸에는 credit이 와야 한다. 따라서 정답은 ④이다.

a multitude of 다수의 worded a. 말로 된, 언어로 된 peccadillo n. 작은 과오, 사소한 잘못, 실수 plagiarism n. 표절 credit n. 신용; 칭찬; 공적, 인정, 명예 acknowledgement n. 인정 encompass v. 포괄하다 transfer n. 이동, 이전 reimbursement n. 변제, 상환

'표절'이라는 용어는, 더 정확한 말로 표현된 작은 윤리적인 잘못을 다수 포함할 수도 있지만, 가장 일반적으로는 다른 사람의 작품이나 아이디어를 타당한 공적 인정 없이 사용하는 행위를 가리킨다.

17 논리완성   ②

첫 번째 빈칸에는 두 단어의 혼성어를 뜻하는 portmanteau가 적절하고, 두 번째 빈칸에는 교실에 즐거움을 '가져온다'는 의미로 'bring ~ to 장소' 구문을 만드는 bring이 적절하다. 따라서 정답은 ②이다.

mishmash n. 뒤죽박죽 curb v. 막다 portmanteau n. 혼성어 mismatch n. 부조화 portrayal n. 묘사, 초상 mashup n. 매시업(여러 자료에서 요소를 따와 새로운 노래 등의 파일을 만든 것) curb v. 막다 convey v. 전달하다 cater v. (음식을) 공급[조달]하다; (욕구를) 충족시키다

'에듀케이션(교육)'이라는 단어와 '엔터테인먼트(오락)'라는 단어의 혼성어인 에듀테인먼트는 매력적인 미디어와 수업 목표의 게임화를 사용하여 교실에 즐거움을 도입하고자 한다.

18 논리완성   ③

주절에서 앨범이 칭송받았다고 했고 Though절에서 아티스트의 고별

음반이라고 했으므로 첫 번째 빈칸에는 아티스트를 부정적인 의미로 수식하는 '쇠락해가는'이라는 의미의 fading이나 waning이 적절하고, 두 번째 빈칸에는 주절의 긍정적인 의미에 부합하게 이 가수의 경력을 '다시 살려놓았다'는 의미로 revitalizing이 적절하다. 따라서 정답은 ③이다.

kiss-off n. 고별, 작별 laud v. 칭송하다 tour de force n. 역작, 걸작 fusion n. 융합 renewed a. 새로운 fade v. 사라지다 jeopardize v. 위험에 빠뜨리다, 위태롭게 하다 up-and-coming a. 떠오르는, 전도유망한 invigorate v. 활기를 띠게 하다 wane v. 시들어가다 revitalize v. 부활시키다 fruitful a. 생산적인, 유익한 rejuvenate v. ~을 다시 살리다, 쇄신하다

그 음반은 쇠락해가는 아티스트의 고별 음반이 되게 할 제작 의도에도 불구하고, 다양한 음악 장르들을 혁신적으로 융합한 것 때문에 역작으로 칭송받았고, 그녀의 경력을 되살려 놓았고 그녀의 음반목록에 대한 관심을 새롭게 불러일으켰다.

19 논리완성   ①

한 줄 한 줄 면밀히 분석했다고 했으므로 법률의 파급효과를 '면밀히 검토했다'는 표현이 적합하다. 따라서 정답은 ①이다.

tremendous a. 어마어마하게 큰 parse v. 분석하다 ramification n. 영향, 파급효과 scrutinize v. 자세히 조사하다 gormandize v. 폭식하다 elegize v. 슬픈 가락 조로[비가 조로] 읊다 energize v. 힘을 북돋다 atomize v. 원자화[세분화]하다

엄청난 압박 하에서 그 법률가 팀은 문서를 한 줄 한 줄 면밀히 분석하여, 제안된 법률의 법적인 파급효과를 자세히 조사했다.

20 논리완성   ⑤

인간의 감정을 '환희에서 불쾌함까지'라고 했으므로 빈칸에는 범위를 나타내는 spectrum이 와야 한다. 따라서 정답은 ⑤이다.

exhibit v. 보여주다 euphoria n. 환희 dysphoria n. 불쾌감 spectrum n. 범위, 스펙트럼 sputum n. 가래, 담 compilation n. 모음집, 편집, 편찬 inspection n. 점검, 조사 compendium n. 개요

우리가 이해하는바 인간의 감정은 환희에서 불쾌함까지 광범위한 스펙트럼을 보여주며, 시시각각 변하는 마음의 상태를 반영한다.

21 논리완성   ④

between sleep patterns and cognitive function 앞에는 둘 사이의 '상관관계'라는 단어가 와야 한다. 따라서 정답은 ④이다.

countless a. 수많은 well-established a. 확실히 정립된, 자리 잡은 cognitive a. 인지의 collaboration n. 협력 collation n. 대조 (조사) codification n. 부호화, 암호화, 코드화 correlation n. 상호 관계, 상관관계 commodification n. 상품화

이 문제에 대한 수많은 연구 결과, 현재 수면 패턴과 인지 기능 사이에는 잘 정립된 상관관계가 있다.

22 상관 구문 ④

Nevertheless 이하의 문장을 not only ~ but also … 구문으로 파악하고 ⑤를 but으로 고치는 것을 정답으로 하는 것을 생각할 수 있겠으나, 그럴 경우 병치구조가 만들어지지 않는다. 병치구조가 되려면 many humanities scholars not only remain vaguely aware of the Digital Humanities but also lack a clear sense of the challenges they pose to traditional modes of inquiry의 형태가 되어야 하기 때문이다. 따라서 ④에서 not을 삭제하여야 하며, 이 경우에 자연스러운 의미의 문장이 완성될 수 있다.

print-based a. 인쇄물 기반의 humanities n. 인문학 epicenter n. 진원지, 핵심 come into one's own 역량을 발휘하다, 인정받게 되다 emerge v. 출현하다 degree n. 학위 scholarly journal 학술지 practitioner n. 전문직 종사자 vaguely ad. 애매모호하게 pose v. 제기하다 inquiry n. 탐구

과학과 사회과학보다 더 인쇄물을 기반으로 하는 인문학은 디지털 기술의 영향을 겪고 있다. 변화의 중심에는 디지털 인문학이 있다. 디지털 인문학은 적어도 1940년대 이후부터 있었지만 인터넷과 월드와이드웹이 나오고 나서야 비로소 자체 학위 프로그램, 연구센터, 학술지와 단행본, 그리고 점증하는 현역 전문가들을 갖춘 신생 분야로 인정받게 되었다. 그럼에도 불구하고 많은 인문학자들은 디지털 인문학을 그저 애매모호하게 인식하고 있으며 또한 디지털 인문학이 전통적인 탐구 방식에 제기하는 도전에 대한 명확한 의식이 부족하다.

23 품사 ②

여성들의 글을 여성 경험의 표현으로서 장려한다는 의미가 되어야 하므로 ②에 쓰인 전치사 to를 as로 고쳐야 한다.

feminism n. 페미니즘 unified a. 통일된 school n. 학파 debate n. 논쟁 theorist n. 이론가 champion v. 옹호하다 promote v. 장려하다, 홍보하다, 고취하다 representation n. 재현 undertake v. 수행하다, 착수하다 critique n. 비평, 비판 heterosexual a. 이성애적인 matrix n. 모체, 기반 opposition n. 대립

페미니즘은 통일된 학파라기보다는 사회적이고 지적인 운동이자 논쟁의 공간이다. 한편으로, 페미니즘 이론가들은 여성의 정체성을 옹호하고 여성의 권리를 요구하며 여성의 글을 여성 경험의 표현으로서 장려한다. 다른 한편으로, 페미니스트들은 남녀 간 대립의 관점에서 정체성과 문화를 조직하는 이성애적 기반에 대한 이론적 비판도 수행한다.

24 시제 ①

글의 전체 시제가 현재시제이므로 ①의 과거완료시제를 현재완료시제인 have often faced로 고쳐야 한다.

indicator n. 지표 drawback n. 단점 reliability n. 신뢰성 validity n. 유효성 face v. 마주하다 scrutiny n. 감시, 꼼꼼한 점검 concern

n. 관심, 우려 inconsistency n. 비일관성 classification n. 분류 empirical a. 경험적인 distinct a. 다른 bias n. 편견 hiring n. 고용 preference n. 선호 self-reflection n. 자기성찰 promote v. 장려하다, 홍보하다 interact v. 상호작용하다 foster v. 조성하다, 기르다

마이어-브릭스 유형지표(MBTI)는 성격 유형을 파악하기 위한 인기 있는 도구이다. 그러나 MBTI는 몇 가지 분명한 단점을 갖고 있다. 이 검사는 결과의 비일관성에 대한 우려와 경험적 증거가 부족한 분류 체계로 인해 그 신뢰성과 타당성이 종종 면밀한 조사에 직면했다. 게다가 개인들을 별개의 상자에 넣는 이 검사의 경향은 고정관념이나 편견을 초래하여, 고용이나 대인관계에서의 의사결정 과정에 영향을 끼칠 수 있다. 그래도 MBTI는 개인들로 하여금 자신의 선호, 행동, 그리고 잠재적 경력진로에 대한 통찰을 얻도록 도움을 주는 틀을 제공한다. 그것은 또한 자기 성찰을 독려하고, 서로 다른 성격 유형들이 어떻게 상호작용하여 다양한 환경에서 개선된 공동체를 조성하는지를 더 잘 이해하게 해준다.

25 품사 ③

부사는 명사를 수식할 수 없고 형용사가 명사를 수식하므로 ③을 crucial로 고쳐야 한다.

numerous a. 수많은 colony collapse syndrome 군락지 붕괴 신드롬 critical a. 중요한 pollination n. 수분 conservationist n. 환경보호활동가 beekeeper n. 양봉가 threat n. 위협 initiative n. 계획 focus on ~에 초점을 맞추다 identify v. 확인하다, 밝히다 pesticide n. 살충제 exposure n. 노출 habitat n. 서식처 pathogen n. 병원균 crucial a. 중요한 advocate for ~을 옹호하다 sustainable a. 지속가능한 adopt v. 채택하다 bee-friendly a. 벌 친화적인 alternative n. 대안, 다른 선택지 abundant a. 풍부한 foraging n. 수렵채집 floral a. 식물의 ample a. 광대한, 풍만한

벌 개체군들을 군락지 붕괴 신드롬(CCS)에서 구하기 위해 수많은 노력이 이루어졌다. 꽃가루받이와 생태계에서 벌들이 행하는 중요한 역할 때문이었다. 과학자들과 환경보호활동가들과 양봉업자들은 힘을 모아 이 위협에 맞서 전 세계적으로 싸워왔다. 연구 계획은 살충제 노출과 서식처 상실과 병원균과 기후 변화 같은 CCS의 원인을 확인하는 것에 집중하고 있다. 한 가지 중대한 접근법은 더 지속 가능한 농업 관행을 옹호하고 살충제 사용 감소를 촉진시키고 벌 친화적인 대안들을 채택하는 일을 포함한다. 환경보호 노력들은 벌 친화적인 서식처를 만들고 회복시켜 풍부한 식물 자원을 갖춘 다양하고 풍부한 먹이(꿀) 채집 공간을 보장하는 것을 강조한다.

26-27

대부분의 상황에서 'Arthrobotryis oligospora'는 부생 생물이다. 이는 죽은 잎사귀처럼 썩어가는 유기물질을 먹는다는 뜻이다. 그러나 과학자들은 영양 결핍이 이 균류로 하여금 분자 변화를 겪게 해, 선충이라는 (자신이 잡아먹힐 거라고) 의심하지 않는 벌레를 먹고 사는 육식동물이 되도록 만들어준다는 것을 발견했다.

균류는 다른 포식자들처럼 맹렬한 방식으로 먹이를 쫓을 수 없고, 그래서 지난 달 발표된 한 연구는 이 균류가 어떻게 더 교묘하고 사악한 포식 방법을 진화시켰는지 개괄했다.

'A. oligospora'가 근처에 있는 선충을 감지하면 그것은 페로몬에 의지해, 균류를 구성하는 아주 작은 실가닥들의 지하 망인 균사체로 선충을 유혹해 끌어들인다. 'A. oligospora'는 아마도 후각 모방을 사용하여, 선충의 후각

신경세포를 통해 선충 먹이를 끌어들이는 수단을 진화시킨 듯하다. 이것은 균류가 먹이 신호와 성 페로몬을 분비해 이 벌레를 끌어들인다는 뜻이다. 선충은 아스카로사이드라는 작은 분자를 만들어낸다. 아스카로사이드는 선충의 행동과 발달을 조절한다. 'A. oligospora' 같은 균류는 이 아스카로사이드가 만드는 신호를 "엿듣고" 감지한다고 여겨진다. 이들은 균류가 알아볼 수 있는 분자 패턴을 만들어내기 때문이다. 이 덫의 생성은 매우 에너지 소모적인 과정이기 때문에 'A. oligospora'는 먹이가 가까이 있을 때만 덫을 만든다.

circumstances n. 상황 saprotrophic a. 부생생물의, 썩은 물질에 기대어 살아가는 decay v. 썩다, 부패하다 nutritional a. 영양의, 자양의 deprivation n. 박탈 fungus n. 균류, 곰팡이류 molecular a. 분자의 prey on ~을 먹고 살다 unsuspecting a. 의심하지 않는 nematode n. 선충 outline v. 개괄하다 tricky a. 교묘한 lure v. 꼬드기다, 유혹하다 mycelium n. 균사체 olfactory a. 후각의 mimicry n. 흉내 cue n. 신호 regulate v. 조절하다 trap n. 덫

---

26 빈칸완성 ①

균류가 영양이 결핍하면 worm을 먹는다고 했으므로 육식성이라는 단어가 들어가야 한다. 따라서 정답은 ①이다.

Ⓐ에 들어갈 가장 적절한 단어는?
① 육식성의
② 육체적인 욕망의
③ 남을 잘 믿는
④ 초식성의
⑤ 다재다능한

---

27 빈칸완성 ④

세 번째 문단은 이 균류가 먹이를 유인하는 과정을 다루므로 빈칸에는 '유혹하다'는 뜻의 seduce가 들어가야 한다. 따라서 정답은 ④이다.

Ⓑ에 들어갈 가장 적절한 단어는?
① 질식시키다
② 소화시키다
③ 숨기다
④ 유혹하다
⑤ 변형시키다

28-29

하이퍼텍스트와 일반적인 웹 읽기는 왜 이해력의 저하를 일으킬까? 그 답은 작업 기억(즉, 의식의 내용들)과 장기 기억 간의 관계에 있다. 읽은 내용은 작업 기억 속에 단 몇 분 동안만 보유되며 작업 기억의 역량이 대단히 제한되어 있다.
예를 들어, 전화번호를 큰 소리로 여러 차례 되풀이해 말해서 작업 기억이 다른 것들을 배제하고 전화번호만 기억하도록 만들면 그 번호를 숫자를 누르는 동안만큼은 기억할 수 있다.
더 복잡한 문제를 기억하려면 작업 기억의 내용을 장기 기억으로 옮겨야 하고 가급적 반복을 통해 새 재료가 기존의 지식 개요에 빨리 통합되도록 해야 한다.

하이퍼텍스트 및 웹 읽기와 관련된 작은 주의 산만 — 링크를 클릭한다거나 웹 페이지를 검색한다거나 스크롤을 오르락내리락하거나 등등의 작업 — 은 작업 기억에 인지 부하를 늘려서 작업 기억이 보유할 수 있는 새 정보량을 줄인다. 반면, 선형적 읽기의 경우는 인지 부하가 최소한이다. 눈의 움직임은 더 반복적이고 자료를 어떻게 읽어야 할지 어떤 순서로 읽어야 할지에 관해 결정을 크게 내리지 않아도 되기 때문이다. 따라서 장기 기억으로 옮겨가는 이동이 더 효율적으로 이루어진다.

hypertext n. 하이퍼텍스트(링크를 통해 웹상의 다른 문서나 멀티미디어 등으로 이동 가능하게 해 놓은 텍스트) comprehension n. 이해 working memory 작업 기억 severely ad. 심하게 to the exclusion of ~을 배제[제외]하고 retain v. 보유[유지]하다 retention n. 보유 preferably ad. 가급적 schema n. 개요, 윤곽 cognitive load 인지 부하[부담] at a minimum 최소한도인 transfer n. 이동

---

28 빈칸완성 ①

예문에 링크 클릭이나 웹 문서 검색 등이 나오므로 독서 중의 산만한 행동임을 알 수 있다. 따라서 정답은 ①이다.

Ⓐ에 들어갈 가장 적절한 단어는?
① 주의 산만
② 불이익
③ 이동
④ 무관심
⑤ 팽창

---

29 빈칸완성 ②

하이퍼텍스트와 일반적인 선형적 읽기 간의 차이를 대조하고 있으므로 적절한 연결어는 대조를 나타내는 표현이어야 한다. 따라서 정답은 ② 이다.

Ⓑ에 들어갈 가장 적절한 표현은?
① 최소한
② 반면에
③ 정의상
④ 그런데
⑤ 대체로

30-32

형성적 평가는 외국어로서의 영어(EFL) 교육 분야에서 귀중한 도구 역할을 하며 학생들과 교육자들 모두에게 도움이 되는 여러 이점을 제공하고 있다. 첫째, 형성적 평가는 학습자들이 실시간으로 자신의 강점과 약점을 파악하도록 도움으로써 이들이 개선을 필요로 하는 부분을 알아낼 수 있게 해 준다. 이러한 지속적 안내는 개인의 필요에 맞춘 개인화된 학습 경험을 가능하게 함으로써 더 효과적인 학습 과정을 발전시킨다.
이런 맞춤형 교육은 교사에게도 이득이다. 외국어로서의 영어(EFL) 교실에서의 형성적 평가는 교육자들이 환경에 맞추어 자신의 교육법을 역동적으로 조절하게 해주기 때문이다. 학생들의 진행 중인 학업성취에 대한 통찰을 얻음으로써 교사들은 수업 계획과 교육 접근법을 바꾸어 다양한 학습 방식과 필요를 더 잘 충족시킬 수 있게 된다. 이 적응 가능성을 통해 학생들

은 자신의 언어 발달에 필요한 지원을 확실히 받게 된다.

마지막 장점은 형성적 평가가 능동적인 학생 참여를 독려한다는 점이다. 형성적 평가는 학습자들이 정기적으로 자신의 학습 목표를 성찰해 그에 따라 전략을 조절함으로써 자신의 학습 진전에 대한 책임을 인정하도록 촉진시킨다. 이런 자기 평가 과정은 언어 학습의 동기와 자율성을 향상시켜 영어라는 언어를 더 깊이 이해하게 해준다.

formative assessment 형성적 평가 offer v. 제공하다 aid v. 돕다 grasp v. 파악하다 ongoing a. 진행 중인, 지속적인 personalize v. 개인화하다 customizability n. 맞춤식, 특별주문 boon n. 이득, 요긴한 것 performance n. 성적 take ownership of 책임을 인정하다 modify v. 바꾸다 foster v. 조성하다, 발전시키다 engagement n. 참여 reflect on ~를 성찰하다 adjust v. 조절하다 autonomy n. 자율성

---

30 내용추론   ④

형성적 평가는 교사와 학생 모두에게 도움이 된다고 했으므로 ④의 주로 학생을 돕는다는 내용은 적절치 않다.

이 글에서 추론할 수 없는 것은?
① 형성적 평가는 교육자가 학생의 성취에 맞추어 교육내용을 바꾸게 해준다.
② 형성적 평가는 학생들에게 자기 성찰의 기회를 제공한다.
③ 형성적 평가는 EFL 교실에서 유용하다
④ 형성적 평가는 주로 학생들을 돕는다.
⑤ 형성적 평가는 학생들이 자신의 학습수행 방식을 알게 해 준다.

---

31 빈칸완성   ①

형성적 평가는 지속적인 피드백(ongoing feedback)을 준다고 했으므로 빈칸에는 유사한 표현인 continuous가 적합하다. 따라서 정답은 ① 이다.

Ⓐ에 들어갈 가장 적절한 표현은?
① 지속적인
② 간헐적인
③ 호기심 많은
④ 분노에 찬
⑤ 누적

---

32 빈칸완성   ⑤

'~에 대한 통찰력'이라고 할 때는 insight into ~로 전치사는 into를 써야 한다. 따라서 정답은 ⑤이다.

33-34

수십 년 동안 보건 전문가들은 체질량지수가 건강상의 위험을 측정할 정말 믿을만한 방법인지 궁금히 여겨왔다. 사람들의 체중을 키와 관련해서 측정하는 널리 사용되는 체질량지수라는 측정 기준은 그 부정확성과 과도한 단순화 때문에 오랫동안 비판에 직면해왔다. 예를 들어, 일부 전문가들은

평균 신장보다 크게 작거나 큰 사람들에게 체질량지수는 때로 오해의 여지가 있다고 지적한다. 게다가 이 시스템이 주로 19세기 백인 유럽 남성들이라는 좁은 인구통계에서 나온 데이터를 기반으로 하기 때문에 많은 이들은 이것이 여성들, 그리고 다른 인종 및 종족 집단의 사람들에게 의미가 있는지 반문하고 있다.

문제를 더욱 복잡하게 만드는 것은 과체중과 비만인 사람들을 정의하는 방식이 전 세계적으로 차이를 보인다는 사실이다. 가령 유럽과 미국에서는 BMI 25-30까지를 과체중으로 간주하는 등 더 높은 문턱을 설정하는 반면, 한국 같은 아시아-태평양 국가들은 BMI 23-24.9까지를 과체중, 25 이상을 비만으로 본다. 이런 다른 기준은 보고에 따르면 일부 연구에서 드러나듯 BMI 수치가 더 낮은 아시아인들 사이에서 다양한 대사성 질환 위험이 더 높다고 이야기하는 문제를 유발한다. 따라서 영국의 국립보건당국은 흑인과 아시아인들에게는 다른 BMI 기준을 적용한다. 그럼에도 불구하고 이런 조정의 필요성은 체질량지수가 전 세계적으로 의미가 있는지 믿을만한지에 관한 논쟁을 더 부채질하고 있다.

specialist n. 전문가 Body Mass Index(BMI) 체질량지수 reliable a. 믿을 만한 widely-used a. 널리 쓰이는 metric n. 미터법, 측정규준 calculate v. 계산하다 significantly ad. 상당히 misleading a. 오해의 여지가 있는 demographic n. 인구 통계 relevance n. 타당성, 적절성 overweight a. 과체중의 metabolic disease 대사질환

---

33 빈칸완성   ④

whether절의 내용을 '깊이 생각해보거나 궁금하거나 의아하게 생각하다'는 뜻의 동사들은 적절하지만 '헤매다, 돌아다니다'는 뜻의 ④는 부적절하다.

Ⓐ에 들어갈 수 없는 표현은?
① 고려하다
② 생각하다
③ 숙고하다
④ 이리 저리 헤매다
⑤ 궁금해 하다

---

34 내용파악   ②

기존 BMI 기준의 통계 자료가 유럽 백인 남성들이라고 했으므로 ②의 유럽과 미국인들에게 부정확한 기준이라는 말은 정확치 않다. 오히려 여성과 다른 인종들에게 맞지 않는다고 해야 한다.

글에서 언급한 BMI의 비판을 보여주는 내용이 아닌 것은?
① 인종적으로 특정 데이터에 의존함
② 유럽과 미국의 사람들에게는 부정확한 기준임
③ 전 세계 기준을 달리해야 할 필요성
④ 평균 신장 이하의 사람들에게 적용할 수 없다는 점
⑤ 여성들에게 타당하지 않은 기준일 가능성

35-37

철학자 임마누엘 칸트에 따르면 자유의지는 우리가 도덕 원칙에 따라 행동하기로 이성적 선택을 할 때 발생한다. 다시 말해, 우리의 자율성을 결정하는 것은 바로 외부 요인과 무관하게 이성을 기반으로 선택할 수 있는 우리

의 능력이다.

누군가가 개인적 이득을 얻을 가능성이 있는데도 정직하게 행동하기로 한 결정에 직면해 있는 상황을 생각해보라. 예를 들어, 당신이 상점에서 뭔가를 사는데 거스름돈을 실수로 너무 많이 받았다고 상상해보라. 칸트의 관점에서 보면, 정직이라는 도덕 원칙을 고수하려고, 초과분의 돈을 돌려주기로 하는 당신의 이성적 선택은 자유의지가 작용하고 있다는 사례이다. 이 경우 자유의지는 정확히 말해 더 많은 돈에 대한 즉각적 욕망이나 발각될 것에 대한 두려움에 관한 것이 아니다. 오히려 자유의지는 도덕성 ─ 이 경우엔 정직함 ─ 에 맞게 행동하기로 이성적 결정을 내리는 것에 관한 것이다. 여분의 잔돈을 갖고 싶은 유혹에도 불구하고 사람들이 돈을 돌려주는 선택을 하는 이유는 외부의 압력이 아니라 자신의 이성적 판단에 의거해서, 그렇게 하는 것이 도덕적으로 옳은 일이라고 인식하기 때문이다.

arise v. 발생하다 rational a. 이성적인, 합리적인 in accordance with ~에 맞추어 autonomy n. 자율성 independent of ~와 관계없이 external a. 외부의 gain n. 이익, 이득 change n. 잔돈, 거스름돈 adherence n. 고수, 지킴 free will 자유의지 immediate a. 즉각적인 get caught 발각되다 temptation n. 유혹 extra cash 여분의 현금

---

35 빈칸완성　⑤

도덕 원칙에 '따라서, 일치하여'라는 표현은 in accordance with이므로 정답은 ⑤이다.

Ⓐ에 들어갈 가장 적절한 표현은?
① 허용량
② 고집
③ 무관심
④ 행위유도성
⑤ 일치

---

36 빈칸완성　⑤

초과분의 돈, 여분의 돈(extra money)의 뜻은 excess money이다. 따라서 정답은 ⑤이다.

Ⓑ에 들어갈 가장 적절한 표현은?
① 휴회
② 퇴행
③ 바로잡다
④ 표현하다
⑤ 초과분

---

37 내용일치　③

칸트가 말한 자유의지의 사례가 바로 초과분의 잔돈을 돌려주는 행위다. 따라서 맞는 내용은 ③이다.

다음 중 글의 내용과 일치하는 것은?
① 칸트는 외부 압력에 굴복하는 것이 우리의 자유의지를 보여준다고 생각한다.
② 돈을 돌려주는 것은 불합리한 행동이다.

③ 칸트는 자유의지의 사례가 돈을 돌려주는 행위라고 주장한다.
④ 칸트는 모든 도덕이 상대적이라고 생각한다.
⑤ 칸트는 돈을 가지려는 유혹이 자유의지를 보여준다고 생각한다.

38-40

팬데믹의 마비 효과가 전 세계 경제를 파괴시킨 이후 세계화된 경제의 미래에 대한 논의가 많았다. 일부 사람들은 이제 최악의 위기는 지나갔으므로 현 상태로 돌아가는 것이 합당하다고 생각하는 반면, 또 다른 사람들은 공급망과 경제 실행의 상당한 개혁을 통해 다시는 이런 경제 위기가 일어나지 않도록 확실히 해야 한다는 요구가 있었다. 이 문제에 대한 당신의 생각은 당신이 글로벌리즘 시각에 더 동조하는지 아니면 보호주의 관점에 더 동조하는지에 따라 달라질 수 있다.

한편으로 글로벌주의자들은 경제체제들의 상호연관성과 개방 무역을 우선시하는 경향이 있다. 그러한 사람들로서, 그들의 공급망에 대한 견해는 국가들 간의 협조를 증가시켜, 비용 효과적인 생산과 다양한 시장 접근을 목표로 할 것을 지지한다. 예를 들어, 간단한 티셔츠 생산을 생각해보라. 티셔츠용 면직물은 인도에서 와서 중국에서 직물로 제조되고 방글라데시에서 염색을 거쳐 베트남에서 만든 다음 마침내 전 세계로 팔려나간다. 이런 과정은 전 세계의 복잡한 연결망을 강조한다.

그러나 보호주의자들은 관세를 부과하거나 무역장벽을 부과함으로써 국내 산업을 중시한다. 이들은 이런 방식으로 지역 산업을 외국의 경쟁으로부터 보호하는 것이 자국 내 일자리와 산업을 보존한다고 주장한다. 예를 들어, 보호주의 정책은 국내 생산을 장려하기 위해 수입품에 관세를 매기지만, 국제 시장 접근을 제한하게 될 수 있다.

paralyzing a. 마비시키는 pandemic n. 팬데믹, 전국[전 세계]적인 유행병 devastate v. 파괴하다 status quo n. 현 상태 in order 정돈되어, 당연한, 합당한 protectionist n. 보호주의자 globalist n. 글로벌리즘 옹호자(자유무역 옹호자) prioritize v. 우선순위를 매기다; 우선시키다 collaboration n. 협력 aim for ~을 목표로 하다 access n. 접근 fabric n. 직물 intricate a. 복잡한 highlight v. 강조하다 tariff n. 관세 trade barrier 무역장벽 local a. 지역의, 국내의

---

38 내용일치　③

보호주의는 경쟁으로부터 자국 산업을 보호하므로 경쟁을 장려하지 않는다. 따라서 틀린 내용은 ③이다. ② affordability는 상품이나 원자재 등을 입수할 수 있는 가능성을 의미하는데, 글로벌리즘은 자유 무역을 통해 상품이나 원자재를 자유롭게 입수할 수 있는 것을 지지한다.

다음 중 글의 내용과 일치하지 않는 것은?
① 보호주의 정책은 다른 나라에 물건 파는 일을 어렵게 만들 수 있다.
② 글로벌리즘은 입수가능성을 지지한다.
③ 보호주의자들은 외국과의 경쟁을 장려하고 싶어 한다.
④ 보호주의자들에 의하면 관세는 국내 일자리를 보호한다.
⑤ 팬데믹은 경제 혼란을 초래했다.

---

39 내용파악　②

둘째 단락 첫 문장에서 '글로벌주의자들은 경제체제들의 상호연관성과 개방 무역을 우선시하는 경향이 있다'고 했으므로 ② '다국적 제휴'가 가장 적합하다. 따라서 정답은 ②이다. ① 두 번째 단락 두 번째 문장에서

'국가들 간의 협조를 증가시키는 것을 지지한다'고 했으므로 국제 경쟁이 아니라 국제 협조이다.

다음 중 글로벌리즘의 관점을 보여주는 것은?
① 국제 경쟁
② 다국적 제휴
③ 지역 일자리 중시
④ 관세 증가
⑤ 무역 장벽

40 빈칸완성 ①

보호주의와 글로벌리즘 시각 중 어디에 '동조하느냐'라는 표현이 와야 하는데, align with가 어떤 것에 동조하거나 일치한다는 뜻이므로 적절하다. 따라서 정답은 ①이다.

Ⓐ에 들어갈 가장 적절한 표현은?
① 동조하다
② 정의하다
③ 설계하다
④ 사임하다
⑤ 감소하다

41-50

① curtained a. 커튼을 친 ② unhinged a. 경첩을 뗀; 불안정한, 흐트러진 ③ an inability to ~에 대한 무능 ④ outbreak n. 시작, 개시, 발발 ⑤ a gift for ~에 대한 재능 ⑥ an array of 다수의 ⑦ in defense of ~을 방어하여 ⑧ digression n. 여담, 탈선, 딴 데로 새는 것 ⑨ bluster v. 고함치다, 엄포를 놓다 ⑩ curtail v. 축소[감축]하다 ⑪ a smidgeon of 미량의 ⑫ dichotomy n. 이분법, 이항대립 ⑬ outcry n. 아우성, 소란 ⑭ euphemistic a. 완곡어법의 ⑮ bewildered a. 당혹스러워하는, 어리둥절해 하는 ⑯ bedecked a. 장식한 ⑰ luster n. 윤택, 광 ⑱ eugenic a. 우생학의 ⑲ in lieu of ~ 대신, ~가 아니라(= instead of) ⑳ unearth v. 발굴하다, 파내다

41 논리완성 ⑰

쓰레기 완전 제거 운동이 광택, 빛, 즉 과거의 영광을 잃어서 완전 제거보다는 쉽게 줄이는 정책을 추진했다는 맥락이 되어야 하므로 lose luster가 어울린다. 따라서 정답은 ⑰이다.

push for 추진하다, 밀어붙이다 reduce v. 줄이다 zero-waste n. 쓰레기 완전 소거 운동

제로 폐기물(폐기물 완전 제거) 운동이 빛을 많이 잃음에 따라, 더 많은 조직들은 개개인이 플라스틱 사용을 더 쉽게 줄이도록 해줄 정책을 추진하기 시작했다.

42 논리완성 ⑩

시위가 허락되었으면 기후 활동가들의 활동이 자유로워야 하는데도 규

제 때문에 활동이 위축되었다는 의미이므로 curtailed가 적절하다. 따라서 ⑩이 정답이다.

permission n. 허가 protest n. 저항 activist n. 활동가 a slew of 많은, 다수의 restriction n. 규제

시위는 허락되었지만, 자신들의 활동이 수많은 규칙과 규제들에 의해 축소되었다고 기후 활동가들은 말한다.

43 논리완성 ⑬

코에 빨대가 꽂힌 거북이 모습은 인간의 환경파괴로 동물이 입은 참혹한 피해를 보여주므로 사람들의 분노를 불러일으킬 것이다. 따라서 정답은 '분노의 아우성'인 ⑬ outcry이다.

plastic straw 플라스틱 빨대 target n. 표적 environmentalist n. 환경운동가 viral a. 바이러스처럼 퍼지는 turtle n. 거북 lodged in ~에 꽂힌 spark v. 촉발시키다

코에 빨대가 꽂혀 있는 거북이 영상이 온라인으로 퍼져나가 분노의 아우성을 촉발시킨 후 플라스틱 빨대는 환경운동가들의 표적이 되었다.

44 논리완성 ⑳

주어가 '고고학자'이고 목적어가 '유물'이므로 동사로는 '발굴하다'가 적절하다. 따라서 정답은 unearthed인 ⑳이다.

authorities n. 당국 celebrated a. 유명한 multinational a. 다국적인 archaeologist n. 고고학자 artifact n. 유물, 공예품 Bronze Age 청동기 trove n. 발굴물, 발견물 date to 시기가 ~까지 거슬러 올라가다

그 유명한 다국적 고고학자 팀은 지역 당국과 함께 작업하는 가운데 청동기까지 거슬러 올라가는 유물을 발굴했다.

45 논리완성 ⑮

앞에서 무례한 행동의 정당화에 당혹스러워했다고 했으니 stand 뒤에도 비슷한 의미의 bewildered가 와야 한다. 따라서 정답은 ⑮이다.

perplex v. 당혹스럽게 하다 justification n. 정당화 unruly a. 무례한 conduct n. 행위 administrator n. 행정담당자

그 학생이 자신의 무례한 행동을 정당화하는 것에 당혹스러워진 학교 행정담당자는 그저 망연자실하게 서 있었다.

46 논리완성 ⑫

감정을 남녀로 분리해 연관 지으므로 둘로 나눔을 뜻하는 이분법이라는 단어, dichotomies가 와야 한다. 따라서 정답은 ⑫이다.

ancient a. 오래 된 emotion n. 감정 connected with ~와 연결된, 연관된 gender n. 성별, 젠더 associate A with B A를 B와 연관시키다

감정에 관한 가장 강력하면서도 역사적으로 오래된 믿음 중 일부는 몇몇
정신 상태들은 여성과 연관 짓고 또 다른 정신 상태들은 남성과 연관 짓는
성별 이분법과 관계되어 있다.

---

47 논리완성

form의 목적어로 '다수의' 분야라는 말이 되게 'an array of 복수명사'
형태로 만들어야 한다. 따라서 정답은 ⑥이다.

ecocriticism n. 환경 비평 environmental a. 환경의 humanities
n. 인문학 interdisciplinary a. 학제간의, 통섭의 emerge v. 출현하다
qualitative a. 질적인, 정성적인

환경비평과 환경 인문학은 지난 20년 동안 인문학과 정성적(질적) 사회
과학 전반에 걸쳐 출현한 다수의 학제적 분야들을 형성한다.

---

48 논리완성

생방송 강의 대신에 녹음을 제공한 것이므로 '대신에'라는 의미의 in lieu
of를 넣어야 한다.

lecturer n. 강사 fall ill 병들다 offer v. 제공하다 recording n. 녹음,
녹화 live a. 생방송의, 현장중계의, 실황의

그 스타 강사가 몸져눕자 학원은 현장 강의 대신 녹음을 제공했다.

---

49 논리완성

꿰뚫어볼 만한 언어는 교묘하게 완곡한 언어여야 한다. 겉으로 보기에
는 그럴 듯해도 속뜻이 맘에 안 들어 제안을 거절했다고 했기 때문이다.
따라서 정답은 euphemistic인 ⑭이다.

shrewd a. 민첩한, 영민한 see through ~을 꿰뚫어보다 artfully ad.
교묘하게 turn down 거절하다 offer n. 제안

그 영민한 고객은 그 에이전트의 교묘한 완곡어법의 말을 꿰뚫어보고 그의
제안을 거절했다.

---

50 논리완성 ⑤

뒤쪽이 though로 양보절인데 미진한 점이 많았다고 했으므로 주절에
는 재능이 있다는 의미가 와야 한다. 따라서 정답은 ⑤이다.

magician n. 마술사 demonstrate v. 실연하다, 직접 시연해보이다
legerdemain n. 날랜 손재주, 솜씨 on-stage a. 무대 위의 demeanor
n. 태도, 품행, 매너 leave much to be desired 미진한 점을 많이 남기다

그 마술사 지망자는 무대 매너는 미진한 점이 많았지만, 날랜 손재주의
재능을 보여주었다.

01 ④	02 ⑤	03 ①	04 ②	05 ③	06 ④	07 ②	08 ②	09 ⑤	10 ①
11 ③	12 ④	13 ⑤	14 ③	15 ⑤	16 ⑤	17 ③	18 ①	19 ②	20 ③
21 ②	22 ②	23 ①	24 ④	25 ①	26 ③	27 ②	28 ⑤	29 ④	30 ⑤
31 ③	32 ③	33 ③	34 ①	35 ⑤	36 ④	37 ①	38 ④	39 ④	40 ⑤

01 빈칸완성 ④

'최근의 연구들에서 정신건강 장애와 알레르기에서 유사점을 밝혀냈다'는 내용 앞에 but이 있으므로, 앞에서는 양자 사이의 관련성에 관심이 없었음을 언급해야 한다. 그러므로 빈칸에는 유사점을 보여주는 '상호관계'라는 의미의 ④가 들어가야 한다.

symptom n. 증상, 증세 postnasal drip 후비루(後鼻淚, 코와 목에서 분비하는 점액이 인두에 고이거나 목으로 넘어가는 느낌이 생기는 증세) cough v. 기침하다 fatigue n. 피로 varying a. (연속적으로) 바뀌는, 변화하는; 가지각색의 severity n. 엄격, 혹독함 be prone to ~하는 경향이 있다, ~하기 쉽다 disorder n. 장애, 질환 depression n. 우울증 shed light on 명확하게 밝히다, 해명하다 parallel n. 평행선; 유사점 significant a. 중요한; 상당한 impact n. 영향 affect v. ~에 영향을 미치다 vice versa 그 역[반대]도 마찬가지이다 contribution n. 기여, 공헌 death rate 사망률 treatment n. 치료, 치료법 correlation n. 상호관계 medical expense 의료비

알레르기는 매우 널리 퍼져 있다. 매년 미국에서 5천만 명 이상의 사람들이 후비루, 기침, 피로 등을 비롯한 알레르기 증상을 다양한 정도로 경험하고 있다. 알레르기가 있는 사람들은 불안과 우울증과 같은 정신건강 장애를 경험하는 경향이 있다. 정신건강 장애와 알레르기의 상관관계는 거의 관심을 받지 못했지만, 최근의 연구들은 환자들에 대한 치료 방법을 개선시켜 줄지도 모를 유사점들을 밝혀냈다. 알레르기 자체가 사람의 정신건강에 상당한 영향을 미칠 수 있다는 것이다. 어떻게 알레르기가 정신건강에 영향을 미칠 수 있고 그 반대도 마찬가지인가?

02 빈칸완성 ⑤

전기차는 배터리의 생산 과정에서 엄청난 양의 배출물을 유발한다고 했으므로, 차를 많이 운행하지 않는 사람이 전기차를 구입하면 전기차의 생산 과정에서 이미 발생된 배출물을 상쇄시키지 못할 것이다. 그러므로 '전기차는 어느 정도의 거리(임계 주행거리)를 주행한 후에야 비로소 환경에 기여하게 될 것'이라는 ⑤가 빈칸에 적절하다.

electric vehicle 전기차 deliver on (약속을) 지키다, (사람들의 기대대로 결과를) 내놓다[산출하다] subsidy n. 보조금 well-off a. 부유한 tax credit 세액공제 incentivize v. (인센티브를 주어) 장려하다 carbon footprint 탄소 발자국(개인 또는 기업, 국가 등의 단체가 활동이나 상품을 생산하고 소비하는 전체 과정을 통해 발생시키는 온실가스 총량) well-suited a. 적절한, 편리한 counterintuitively ad. 직관에 어긋나게 be better off 형편이 더 낫다, 부유하다 outsize a. 특대의;

특히 넓은; 지나치게 큰 emission n. 배출물, 배기가스 manufacture v. 제조하다, 생산하다 typical a. 전형적인, 대표적인 net v. 순이익을 얻다 positive a. 긍정적인; 건설적인

『Nature Sustainability』에 발표된 전기차와 그것이 환경에 미치는 영향에 관한 최근 논문에서는 전기차 구매 인센티브(유인책)가 종종 정부 투자에 걸맞은 성과를 이뤄내지 못한다고 주장하고 있다. 미국의 보조금이 부유층으로 흘러가고 있을 뿐만 아니라, 세액공제(2023년의 경우 최대 7,500달러)가 부적절한 구매자에게 인센티브를 주어서 많은 사람으로 하여금 온실가스 발생량을 증가시키게 할 수 있다는 것이 드러나고 있다. 그 연구에 따르면, 만약 꽤 많은 거리를 운행한다면, 전기차를 운전하기에 적합할 것이지만, 만약 운행을 거의 하지 않고 그 차량이 대부분 차고에 있을 거라면, 직관과는 반대로 가솔린 동력 차량을 소유하는 것이 더 나을 수 있다. 이것은 전기차에 동력을 공급하는 배터리가 생산 과정에서 엄청난 양의 배출물을 유발하기 때문이다. 전기차가 제조하는 데는 더 환경 파괴적이지만 운행하는 데는 더 청정하기 때문에, 전기차는 특정 임계 주행거리를 충족시킨 후에야 환경적 이점이 실현된다. 미국에서, 고급 대형 차량이 아닌 일반적인 전기차는 28,069마일에서 68,160마일 사이를 주행한 후에야 긍정적인 환경 영향이라는 순이익을 얻을 수 있다.

① 배출은 통제하기 쉽다
② 배터리는 전기차의 필수 구성요소이다
③ 가솔린 동력 자동차는 과거의 것이 되었다
④ 인센티브로 사용되는 공적 자금은 그 돈의 값어치를 하게 될 것이다.
⑤ 전기차는 특정 임계 주행거리를 충족시킨 후에야 환경적 이점이 실현된다

03 빈칸완성 ①

인공지능이 심판의 대머리를 축구공으로 착각함으로써 카메라가 공이 아닌 사람의 머리를 쫓아갔고, 그로 인해 시청자가 득점 장면을 놓치게 된 상황이므로, 해당 심판에게 가발을 씌움으로써 인공지능이 사람의 머리와 공을 명확하게 식별하게 한다면 이 문제를 해결할 수 있는 한 방편이 될 수 있을 것이다.

take over 인계 받다, 탈취하다, 장악하다 celebrate v. 기념하다, 축하하다 anniversary n. 기념일 coin v. (화폐를) 주조하다; (신어·신표현을) 만들어 내다 playwright n. 극작가 replace v. 대신하다, 대체하다 recognition n. 인식, 인지 bypass v. 회피하다; (단계를) 뛰어넘다 constantly ad. 항상, 빈번히 mistake A for B A를 B로 잘못보다 bald a. 대머리의 wig n. 가발

어떤 사람들은 로봇이 곧 세상을 장악할 것이라고 말한다. 아니, 로봇이 과연 그렇게 할까? 체코의 극작가 카렐 차페크(Karel Čapek)에 의해 '로봇'이라는 단어가 만들어진 지 100주년이 된 것을 기념하기 위해, 우리는 인간을 대체하려는 인공지능의 시도가 실패한 경우의 목록을 살펴보는 것이 흥미로울 거라 생각했다. 안면 인식부터 시작해보자. 스코틀랜드의 축구팀 Inverness Caledonian Thistle FC는 인간 카메라 기사들을 인공지능 작동 축구공 추적 카메라로 대체함으로써 안면 인식보다 축구공 인식을 우선시했다. 이제는 카메라가 항상 자동적으로 공을 따라감으로써 (선수들의) 동작을 추적할 것이다. 근사하게 들리지만, 가정에서 시청하는 팬들은 그렇지 못했는데, 인공지능 작동 카메라가 빈번히 심판의 대머리를 축구공으로 착각함에 따라 득점이 이뤄진 플레이의 대부분을 놓치게 됐기 때문이다. 수십 명의 시청자들이 그 팀에 전화를 해서 불평했고, 한 팬은 심판에게 작은 가발을 제공하는 것을 제안하기까지 했다.

04 글의 제목 ②

본문은 폭탄 사이클론이 어떤 과정을 통해 만들어지는지를 설명하고 있는 내용이므로, 제목으로는 ②가 적절하다.

drastically ad. 철저하게, 과감하게 the tropics 열대지방 lower v. 낮추다 circulate v. 순환하다, 순환시키다 counterclockwise ad. 시계 반대 방향으로 strengthen v. 강화하다; 강해지다 spiral v. 나선형으로 움직이다, 나선형을 그리다 suck v. 빨아들이다

여느 폭풍과 마찬가지로, 폭탄 사이클론도 서로 완전히 다른 기단(氣團)들 — 일반적으로는 북쪽에서 내려오는 차갑고 건조한 공기와 열대 지방에서 올라오는 따뜻하고 습한 공기가 충돌할 때 발생한다. 더 따뜻한 공기는 빠르게 상승하면서 구름체계를 만들어내고, 기압이 낮아지면서 저기압의 중심 주위를 시계 반대 방향으로 도는 폭풍전선으로 발전한다. 폭풍이 빠른 속도로 거세진다는 것은 점점 더 많은 양의 따뜻한 공기가 순환하는 폭풍 속으로 끌어들여져서, 중심을 향해 나선형으로 움직이면서 위쪽으로 솟아오르고 있다는 신호다. 안쪽으로 빨려 들어가고 있는 것보다 더 많은 공기가 폭풍의 위에서 빠져나갈 때 기압은 훨씬 더 떨어진다.

이 글의 제목으로 가장 적절한 것은?
① 폭탄 사이클론을 예방하는 것은 무엇인가?
② 폭탄 사이클론은 어떻게 형성되는가?
③ 폭탄 사이클론은 얼마나 강한가?
④ 폭탄 사이클론은 얼마나 오래 지속되는가?
⑤ 왜 사람들은 그것을 폭탄 사이클론이라고 부를까?

05 글의 어조 ③

첫 번째 문단에서는 해변을 찾는 데서 얻을 수 있는 즐거움과 행복을 느낄 수 있는 반면, 두 번째 문단에서는 해변을 떠난 후에 모래로 인해 겪는 불편함과 짜증을 엿볼 수 있다.

lend v. 주다, 제공하다; 부여하다 notification n. 통지, 통고; 통지서 surreptitiously ad. 몰래, 은밀히 transport v. 수송하다, 운반하다 hardship n. 고난, 고초 vibe n. 분위기, 기분 fade v. 흐릿해지다, 사라져가다 replace v. 대체하다 distinct a. 뚜렷한, 명백한 rage n. 격노 glue-like a. 접착제 같은 substance n. 물질, 물체, 본질 subsequent a. 뒤의, 차후의

해변은 일상으로부터 벗어날 수 있는 멋진 곳이다. 집에서 차로 금방 갈 수 있는 곳에 있는 것이라 하더라도, 해변은 사람들에게 정말로 휴가를 온 것 같은 느낌을 준다. 해변에 누워 있는 동안, 해야 할 일과 일정 초대, 업무 관련 통지는 부서지는 파도 속으로 떠내려가 사라지고, 게토레이 용기 안에 몰래 담아 온 와인은 하와이에서 휴가를 보내는 사람들의 사진 속 와인이 그럴 것처럼 풍미가 있다. 그리고 당신은 모든 고난에도 불구하고 산다는 것은 사실 아름다운 것일 수도 있다는 느낌을 받는다. 그런 다음에는 해변을 떠나야 한다.

좋은 기분은 해변을 떠나자마자 거의 즉시 사라지고, 그 대신 이제 당신이 갖고 있는 모든 것이 그 후 내내 제거할 수 없는 접착제 같은 물질로 변해버린 수 없이 많은 모래 알갱이들로 뒤덮여 있다는 것을 알게 되면서, 뚜렷한 분노가 자리하게 된다. 모래는 당신의 발과 다리를 뒤덮고 있고, 목에도 있고 머리카락 안에도 있다. 모래는 당신의 전화기와 열쇠, 가방과 잡지 위에도 있고, 자동차 위도 온통 뒤덮고 있다. 모래는 부엌에도 있고 어찌된 일인지 아침에 먹는 시리얼속에도 있다. 모래는 틀림없이 당신의 욕실에도 있고, 나중에 샤워를 할 때마다 발에 모래가 다시 묻어 나온다. 당신은 "해변에 다시는 가지 않을 거야."라고 말하게 된다.

첫 번째 단락에서 다음 단락으로 글의 어조가 어떻게 변하고 있는가?
① 기쁜 — 슬픈
② 흥분한 — 두려운
③ 행복한 — 짜증나는
④ 걱정스러운 — 깜짝 놀란
⑤ 실망한 — 즐거운

06 부분이해 ④

약으로부터 부작용을 겪는 비율이 여성이 남성에 비해 높은 원인에 대해 새로운 연구에서는 사회적 요인을 제시하고 있다. 나머지 보기는 모두 사회적 요인에 대한 내용인 것에 비해, ④는 생물학적 요인에 대한 내용이므로 ④가 정답으로 적절하다.

routinely ad. 일상적으로, 관례대로 prescription n. 처방전; 처방약 over-the-counter a. 처방전 없이 살 수 있는 over-the-counter drug 일반의약품 side effect 부작용 attribute v. (~의) 탓으로 하다, (~의) 행위로[소치로, 업적으로] 하다 debunk v. (생각·믿음 등이) 틀렸음을 드러내다[밝히다] gender-based a. 성별(性別)에 기반을 둔 disparity n. 차이, 불일치 infer v. 추론하다 accelerate v. 가속화하다 variable n. 변수 incident n. 사건 hypothesis n. 가정 adverse a. 불리한

미국 식품의약국(FDA)에 따르면, 미국인의 절반 이상이 일상적으로 처방약이나 일반약을 복용하고 있지만, 부작용을 겪는 비율은 여성이 남성에 비해 최대 2배에 이르는 경향이 있다. 역사적으로 그 차이는 생물학적 성별에 따른 차이에 의한 것으로 여겨졌지만, 『사회과학과 의학』에 발표된 새로운 연구에서는 그 견해가 잘못됐음을 밝히면서, 그 대신, 관찰된 차이를 보다 잘 설명해주는 성별(젠더)을 기반으로 한 사회적 요인을 제시하고 있다. "오랫동안, 생물의학 연구의 양상은 결과에서 나타나는 성별에 따른 차이를 관찰하고 이것이 생물학적 원인에 의한 것이라고 추론하는 것이었습니다."라고 연구팀의 리더인 사라 리차드슨(Sarah Richardson)은 말했다. "우리는 사회적 변수와 그 밖의 다른 변수들을 그러한 차이들을 만들어내는 요인들로 고려하는 것을 가속화하고 싶습니다." 그 연구원들은 FDA의 피해사례 보고시스템으로부터 공개적으로 이용 가능한 데이터를 이용했는데, 이 시스템에서는 약물로 인해 피해를 입는 사람들이 사고를 보고할 수 있도록 돼 있다. 약물 피해 사례에 있어서의 성별에 따른 차이를 둘러싼 그들의 성별(젠더) 가설은 일련의 설명들을 제시한다.

다음 중 밑줄 친 설명들에 해당될 가능성이 가장 적은 것은?
① 여성은 남성보다 "건강을 추구하는 행동"을 할 가능성이 높다. 예를 들어, 여성은 남성보다 더 적극적으로 처방약을 복용하거나 의사의 진료를 받는다.
② 여성은 진료실에서 편견과 차별에 직면할 가능성이 높아서 질병의 진단을 받거나 적절한 치료를 받을 가능성에 부정적인 영향을 미친다.
③ 성별 고정관념, 낙인, 정체성, 사회적 규범은 사건이 주관적으로 경험되는 방식에 영향을 미치며, 여성은 남성보다 체중 증가나 탈모를 더 심각한 피해 사례로 받아들이는 경향이 있다.
④ 남녀 간의 유전적, 호르몬적 차이는 남녀 각각에 고유한 많은 질병과 질환의 원인이 되며, 따라서 치료법은 이 점을 고려해야 한다.
⑤ 여성은 남성보다 가난하게 살 가능성이 높고, 가정과 직장에서 성희롱과 성폭력에 직면할 가능성이 높으며, 이는 모두 정신적, 신체적 건강 문제와 관련돼 있다.

07 내용추론　　②

'소다 호수는 건조 지역과 반건조 지역 모두에서 자연적으로 생겨난다.'라고 했으므로, 소다 호수는 건조한 기후에서 형성될 가능성이 높다고 할 수 있다.

carbonate n. 탄산염　concentration n. 농도　sodium carbonate 탄산나트륨　sodium chloride 염화나트륨　saline a. 소금의, 염분이 있는　semi-arid a. 반건조의, 비가 거의 오지 않는　productive a. 생산적인, 풍요로운　ecosystem n. 생태계　aquatic a. 수생(水生)의; 물의　multicellular organism 다세포 생물　brine n. 소금물　shrimp n. 새우　microorganism n. 미생물　continent n. 대륙　outstanding a. 걸출한

소다 호수는 pH값이 통상 수치인 6 또는 7 이상의, 대개 9에서 11 사이인 호수이다. 높은 탄산염 농도, 특히 탄산나트륨이 그 호수의 물을 알칼리성이 되게 한다. 소다 호수는 고농도의 염화나트륨과 기타 염류를 함유하고 있어, 염수(鹽水) 호수 혹은 초염수(超鹽水) 호수가 될 수도 있다. 소다 호수는 건조 지역과 반건조 지역 모두에서 자연적으로 생겨난다. 소다 호수는 담수(淡水) 호수에 비해 매우 생산적인 생태계이며, 따라서 지구상에서 가장 생산적인 수생(水生) 환경이다. 염수 새우와 물고기와 같은 다세포 생물이 소다 호수에서 많이 발견된다. 이들 호수에 있는 미생물들은 플라밍고와 그 밖의 새들을 비롯한 몇몇 동물들에게 훌륭한 먹이 공급원이 돼주고 있다. 아프리카와 아시아에 소다 호수가 가장 많이 있는데, 이는 그 두 대륙이 소다 호수 형성에 이상적인 광활한 사막 환경을 가지고 있기 때문이다. 탄자니아의 나트론(Natron) 호수는 항상 약 12인 높은 pH의 물이 담겨져 있기 때문에 아프리카에서 가장 두드러진 소다 호수에 속한다. 그 호수는 동아프리카에 있는 250만 마리의 플라밍고 대부분이 정기적으로 찾아와 먹이를 먹는 곳이다.

다음 중 이 글에 명시되거나 암시되어 있는 것은?
① 소다 호수의 물에는 염화나트륨이 없다.
② 소다 호수는 건조한 기후에서 형성될 가능성이 높다.
③ 소다 호수에 있는 물의 pH는 대개 6 ~ 7이다.
④ 담수 호수는 소다 호수보다 더 나은 생태계이다.
⑤ 플라밍고는 알칼리성이지 않은 물을 찾기 위해 나트론 호수로 온다.

08 내용추론　　②

브랜드들이 아이타나 로페즈(Aitana Lopez)라는 가상 인플루언서를

이용하여 제품을 홍보하고 있음을 언급하면서, 이와 관련된 시장이 매우 커지고 있음을 이야기했으므로, ②가 정답으로 적절하다.

post v. 게시하다, 공시하다　selfie n. 셀피(자기 모습을 스스로 찍은 사진을 일컫는 인터넷 속어), 셀카 사진　fictional a. 꾸며낸, 허구의; 소설적인　artificial intelligence 인공지능　break into 침입하다, 난입하다　emergence n. 출현, 발생　income n. 수입, 소득　shrink v. (천 등이) 오그라들다; (수량·가치 등이) 줄어들다　established a. 확립된, 기정[기성]의; 정평이 있는　livelihood n. 생계, 살림　under threat 위협 받고 있는　generative a. 발생의, 발생하는　spew out 토해내다, 뿜어내다　counterpart n. 상대물, 대응물　disclose v. 나타내다, 드러내다　freak out 기겁을 하게 만들다, 극도로 화나게 하다　fake a. 가짜의, 위조의　contend v. 주장하다　reveal v. 드러내다, 폭로하다

핑크색 머리의 아이타나 로페즈(Aitana Lopez)는 소셜 미디어에 20만 명 이상의 팔로워가 있다. 그녀가 콘서트와 그녀의 침실에서 찍은 셀카 사진을 올리는 동안, 브랜드들은 그녀가 소셜 미디어에 그들의 제품을 홍보하는 데 대해 게시물 한 개 당 약 1,000달러를 지불했다. 그녀가 완전히 허구의 인물임에도 불구하고 말이다. 아이타나는 인공지능 도구를 사용하여 만들어진 "가상 인플루언서"로, 점점 커지고 있는 210억 달러 규모의 콘텐츠 크리에이터 경제를 파고 들어온 수백 개의 디지털 아바타들 가운데 하나다.
그들의 출현으로 인해, 인간 인플루언서들은 디지털 경쟁자들 때문에 수입이 줄어들고 있다고 걱정하게 되었다. 인간이 만들어낸 것과 같은 텍스트, 이미지, 코드를 단 몇 초 만에 만들어낼 수 있는 생성형 인공지능 기술로 인해 생계가 위협을 받고 있다는 우려를 더 확고한 기성 직업에 종사하고 있는 사람들도 똑같이 하고 있다.
인간 인플루언서들은 가상 인플루언서들이 자신이 진짜가 아니라는 것을 드러내야 한다고 주장한다. "이 인플루언서들에 대해 저를 극도로 화나게 하는 것은 그들이 가짜라고 말하기가 매우 어렵다는 것입니다."라고 2백만 명 이상의 팔로워를 가진 콘텐츠 크리에이터 다나에 머서(Danae Mercer)가 말했다. 다른 많은 시장들이 이 문제와 싸우고 있으며, 인도는 가상 인플루언서들에게 인공지능으로 만든 것임을 반드시 밝히도록 하고 있는 국가들 중 하나다.

다음 중 이 글에 명시되거나 암시되어 있는 것은?
① 인플루언서들이 과도한 요금을 부과하여 시장을 교란시키고 있다.
② 브랜드들은 홍보를 위해 인공지능이 만들어낸 인플루언서들에게 의지하고 있다.
③ 가상 인플루언서는 많은 국가에서 불법이 돼 가고 있다.
④ 가상 인플루언서는 명품 브랜드에 위협이 되고 있다.
⑤ 인플루언서는 가짜이거나 천박하다는 것과 관련된 부정적인 의미를 많이 가지고 있다.

09 내용파악　　⑤

그는 파인애플을 피자 위에 올리는 것을 좋아하지 않았으므로, ⑤가 정답이다. ② 1년 내내 메뉴를 바꾼다고 한 것은 새로운 메뉴를 계속 실험적으로 시도한다는 말이다.

ingredient n. 원료; (요리의) 재료　in season 제철인　appreciate v. 평가하다; 고맙게 여기다　equipment n. 장비, 설비　pizzeria n. 피자 가게[판매점]　dough n. 반죽　stress v. 강조하다

런던에서 활동하고 있는 피자 요리사인 Michele Pascarella가 올해의 글로벌 피자 메이커 상을 방금 수상했다. 그렇다면, 세계 최고의 피자를 만들어내기 위한 그의 비결은 무엇일까? Pascarella의 레스토랑은 무슨 재료든 제철인 것을 사용하면서 1년 내내 메뉴를 바꾼다. "이 점은 매우 중요한데, 왜냐하면 여러분이 제철인 재료를 사용하면, 돈이 덜 들고 그런 재료가 더 낫기 때문입니다."라고 그는 말한다. Pascarella는 또한 최고의 피자에는 몇 가지 재료만 들어간다고 믿고 있다. "여러분이 이런 종류의 일을 하게 되면, 단순한 재료가 좋다는 것을 인정할 줄 알게 됩니다."라고 그는 말했다. "뛰어난 피자 요리사들에게 있어서 최고의 피자는 단순한 피자입니다." 만약 집에서 피자를 만들고 있는데 피자 가게에 있는 모든 장비를 가지고 있지 않은 경우에도, 그는 여러분에게 알려줄 비결이 있다. 바로 반죽에 물을 조금 더 넣는 것이다. "만약 여러분이 1킬로그램의 밀가루를 사용한다면, 700그램의 물을 사용하는 것이 더 좋습니다."라고 그는 말했다. 흥미롭게도, Pascarella는 과일은 이용하지 않는다고 말한다. "저는 피자 위에 파인애플을 올리는 것을 정말로 좋아하지 않습니다."라고 그는 강조한다. 파인애플을 올린 피자를 좋아하는 사람들에게는 유감스런 일이다. 끝으로, 그는 "이런 일에서는 아무리 배워도 부족하지요. 매일 우리는 무언가를 배울 수 있습니다."라고 그는 말했다. Pascarella는 그의 목표가 매일 새로운 피자를 계속 만드는 것이라고 말했다.

다음 중 최고의 피자를 만들기 위한 요리사의 비결을 적절하게 요약하지 않은 것은?
① 단순하게 하라
② 실험을 계속해라
③ 가정에서 요리하기에 알맞도록 조정하라
④ 제철 재료로 요리하라
⑤ 과일의 힘을 믿어라

10 내용추론 ①

태평양에 살고 있던 쥐라기 시대의 공룡인 고질라가 남태평양에서 실시한 미국의 수소폭탄 실험에 의해 돌연변이가 돼서 괴물 같은 방사능 생명체가 됐다는 것이 첫 번째 영화에서의 설정이었고, 고질라가 국민적인 영웅이 된 것은 한참 뒤의 일이다. 그러므로 ①이 정답이다. ⑤ 미국의 핵실험의 결과로 고질라가 괴물 같은 생명체가 됐고 그런 고질라가 일본의 도쿄나 다른 도시를 공격한다는 내용에서 반미 감정을 엿볼 수 있다.

establish v. 확립하다, 제정하다 dinosaur n. 공룡 mutate v. 변화하다, 돌연변이를 하다 monstrous a. 괴물 같은, 기괴한 radioactive a. 방사능의, 방사성의 emerge v. (물 속·어둠 속 따위에서) 나오다, 나타나다 invade v. 침입하다 subsequent a. 차후의 formulaic a. 정형화된 menacing a. 위협적인

고질라 이야기는 1954년 도호(Toho) 스튜디오가 원작을 발표하면서 시작됐다. 그 이후 "Godzilla vs. Kong"을 비롯해서, 일본과 할리우드에서 제작된 실사 촬영 영화가 32편에 이른다. 고질라는 태평양에 살고 있던 쥐라기 시대의 공룡으로, 남태평양에서 실시한 미국의 수소폭탄 실험에 의해 돌연변이가 돼서 괴물 같은 방사능 생명체가 됐다는 것이 첫 번째 영화에서의 설정이었다. 영화의 핵심적인 이야기는 고질라가 도쿄나 다른 도시를 공격하는 내용이었다.
그러고 나서 1960년대부터는, 고질라가 남태평양의 다른 섬들에서 오거나, 바다로부터 나오거나, 우주로부터 침입하는 다른 괴물들과 싸우기 시작한다. 후속 영화들은 정형화된 패턴을 따른다. 고질라가 다른 괴물들과 싸우고, 그 괴물들이 일본의 도시들을 파괴하고, 그 후에 대개 고질라가

승리하면서, 세상을 다시 안전하게 만든다는 것이다. 이로 인해, 어둡고 위협적인 존재에서 영웅적인 인물과 보호자로 변모하게 된 고질라는 세계적으로 가장 잘 알려진 아이콘들 중의 하나가 되었다.

다음 중 이 글에 명시되거나 암시되어 있지 않은 것은?
① 고질라 영화는 국민적인 영웅의 이야기로 시작했다.
② 고질라 영화는 일본 밖에서도 인기를 끌게 되었다.
③ 고질라의 이미지는 시간이 지나면서 상당히 달라졌다.
④ 거의 항상 일본의 한두 도시가 고질라 영화에서 파괴된다.
⑤ 고질라 이야기의 진화에는 반미 감정이 있었다.

11 문장삽입 ③

주어진 문장은 '예를 들어, 고대 그리스에서, 아기는 다가오는 새해를 상징했던 반면, 묵은해는 노인으로 나타내졌다.'라는 의미이므로, '상징'과 관련된 내용인 '다른 고대 문화들은 오늘날에도 여전히 사용되고 있는 의식들과 상징들로 그 축제일을 기념했다.'의 뒤에 오는 것이 적절하다.

represent v. 묘사하다, 나타내다; 대표하다 symbolize v. 상징하다 upcoming a. 다가오는 universally ad. 보편적으로 observe v. (명절·축일 따위를) 축하하다, 쇠다; (의식·제식을) 거행하다 celebrate v. (식을 올려) 경축하다; (의식·제전을) 거행하다 a variety of 다양한 be traced back to ~로 거슬러 올라가다 establish v. 제정하다; 확립하다 lunar calendar 음력

가장 오래되고 가장 보편적으로 지켜지는 전통들 중 하나인 새해 전야제는 다양한 사회, 문화, 종교 집단들에 걸쳐 거행되고 있다. 새해 기념행사들에 대해 알려져 있는 가장 오래된 기록은 기원전 2000년경 메소포타미아의 바빌로니아인들과 아시리아인들로 거슬러 올라갈 수 있다. 다른 고대 문화들은 오늘날에도 여전히 사용되고 있는 의식들과 상징들로 그 축제일을 기념했다. <예를 들어, 고대 그리스에서, 아기는 다가오는 새해를 상징했던 반면, 묵은해는 노인으로 나타내졌다.> 많은 문화들에서 1582년에 그레고리력이 제정된 후부터 12월 31일에 새해 전야를 기념하기 시작했다. 그러나 음력을 따르는 문화들은 티벳의 2월과 태국의 3월 또는 4월을 비롯한 다른 시간에 새해의 시작을 기념한다.

12 글의 흐름상 어색한 문장 고르기 ④

본문은 외로움이 갖는 심각성과 함께 이것이 점점 늘어나는 추세에 있다는 내용인 것에 반해, ⒟는 이것과 상반되는 내용이므로 글의 흐름상 적절하지 않다.

epidemic n. 유행병, 전염병 therapy n. 치료, 치료법 debilitating a. 쇠약하게 하는 deadly a. 치명적인 consequence n. 결과; 중요성 detrimental a. 해로운, 손해되는 dementia n. 치매 stroke n. 뇌졸중 premature death 조기 사망 band together 단결하다 framework n. 뼈대, 틀 address v. 역점을 두어 다루다 confide in 신용하다, 신뢰하다; 비밀을 털어놓다 exclude v. 배제하다, 배척하다 existential a. 존재에 관한, 실존의 pandemic n. 전국[전 세계]적인 유행병 lifespan n. 수명 spiral v. (착실히) 전진[증가]하다, 상승하다 trauma n. 정신적 외상, 쇼크, 트라우마 exacerbate v. 악화시키다 take the place of ~을 대신하다 interaction n. 상호작용

미국에는 새로운 전염병이 있다. 그것은 쇠약하게 만들고 심지어 치명적인 결과를 초래함에도 불구하고 전통적인 치료법을 사용하여 치료할 수 없다. 우리 사회의 구석구석에서 스며들고 있는 그 문제는 외로움이다. 외로움은 정신 및 신체 건강에 해로워서, 심장병, 치매, 뇌졸중 및 조기 사망의 위험 증가를 초래할 수도 있다. 연구자들이 기록적인 수준의 외로움을 추적함에 따라, 공중보건 분야의 지도자들은 그 전염병을 해결하기 위한 공중보건 체제를 발전시키기 위해 한데 뭉치고 있다. 외로움은 한 사람이 삶에서 필요로 하는 인간관계가 그 사람이 가지고 있는 인간관계보다 더 클 때 발생한다. 일부는 그들이 신뢰하거나 믿을 수 있는 사람이 없다고 느낄 때 심리적 외로움을 경험할 수도 있다. 사회적 외로움은 성별, 인종 혹은 장애를 비롯한 집단의 특성 때문에 체계적으로 배제되고 있다고 느끼는 것이다. 존재적 혹은 정신적 외로움은 자신과의 단절감에서 생겨난다. <외로움을 느낀다고 스스로 보고한 사례는 2023년 1월에 34%로 감소했으며, 이 문제는 팬데믹 기간만큼 심각하지 않다.> 외로움은 사람이 일생 동안 경험하는 것이며, 트라우마, 질병 및 노화 등으로 인해 차츰 증가할 수 있다. 외로움은 또한 인간의 상호작용을 대체하는 기술에 의해 악화될 수 있는데, 이러한 점은 젊은이들이 외로움을 보고하는 비율이 가장 높은 이유를 설명하는 데 도움이 된다.

13 단락배열 ⑤

제시문은 원주민의 날에 대해 언급하고 있으므로 이에 대한 부연 설명으로 원주민의 날이 콜럼버스의 날에 대한 대응으로 생겼다는 D가 그 뒤에 오고, 콜럼버스 날을 반대하는 사람들에 대해 이야기하고 있는 C가 그 뒤에 오고, 그들이 콜럼버스 날을 반대한 이유에 대해 언급하고 있는 A가 그 뒤에 오고, 이러한 이유로 21세기에는 콜럼버스의 날 대신 또는 추가로 원주민의 날을 기념하는 주와 도시가 늘어나기 시작했다는 B가 마지막에 와야 한다.

indigenous a. 토착의, 고유한, 원산의 uproot v. 뿌리째 뽑다; 몰아내다 exploit v. (부당하게) 이용하다; 착취하다 reflect on ~을 반성하다, 되돌아보다 mistreatment n. 학대, 혹사 commemorate v. 기념하다 long-lasting a. 오래 지속되는 colonization n. 식민지 건설, 식민지화

원주민의 날은 미국에서 10월 두 번째 월요일에 열리는 휴일이다. 그 날은 미국의 원주민인 아메리칸 인디언, 알래스카 원주민, 하와이 원주민들을 기리는데, 그들 대부분은 아메리카 대륙에 유럽인들이 도착하면서부터 격렬하게 뿌리 뽑히고 착취당했다. 그 날은 다양성을 기리고 또한 원주민들에 대한 역사적 학대를 되돌아본다.
D 원주민의 날은 1492년 크리스토퍼 콜럼버스(Christopher Columbus)가 아메리카 대륙에 도착한 것을 기념하는 휴일인 콜럼버스의 날에 대한 대응으로 생겼다. 그 휴일은 탐험가가 유럽 정착민들에게 신세계를 열어준 것을 기념했다.
C 그러나 최근 수십 년 동안 점점 더 많은 원주민 운동가들과 그들의 지지자들은 원주민 미국인들의 관점을 무시했다는 이유로 이 휴일에 반대했다.
A 그들은 콜럼버스와 그의 선원들이 원주민들을 상대로 행한 폭력에 주의를 환기시켰다. 그들은 또한 콜럼버스의 항해로 시작된 유럽 식민지화의 오래 지속되는 영향에 주목했다.
B 21세기에 더 많은 주와 도시들이 콜럼버스의 날 대신 또는 추가로 10월 두 번째 월요일에 원주민의 날을 기념하기 시작했다.

14 단락배열 ③

제시문은 Z세대의 소비력이 세계 경제에서 중요해지고 있음을 이야기하고 있다. B에서 These young people이 Z세대를 가리키므로 B가 제시문의 다음에 오고, 그들이 아무 생각 없이 소비하는 것이 아니라 신중하게 생각하고 소비하고 있음을 이야기하는 C가 그다음에 오며, 이런 까다로운 소비를 하는 이유에 대해 언급하는 A가 그 뒤에 오고, A에 대한 부연 설명으로 그들이 적은 급여를 받고 있고 물가와 생활비가 높은 시기에는 급여를 아껴서 오래 써야 한다는 내용의 D가 마지막에 와야 한다.

matter v. 중요하다 deliberate v. 숙고하다 choosiness n. 까다로움 discretionary income 재량 소득(가처분 소득에서 기본 생활비를 뺀 잔액) in the first place 우선 entry-level a. (직업이) 초보적인, 견습적인 paycheck n. 급료 지불 수표; 급료, 봉급 stretch one's paycheck 돈을 아껴서 더 오래 가게 하다

Z세대가 성장함에 따라, 그들의 부(富)가 세계 경제에서 점점 더 중요해지고 있다. 1997년에서 2012년 사이에 태어난 이 세대는 전 세계적으로 약 4,500억 달러의 소비력을 가지고 있으며, 일부 추정치에 따르면 미국에서만 3,600억 달러에 달한다.
B 이 젊은 사람들은 돈을 가지고 있을 뿐만 아니라, 전문가들은 높은 재정적 불안의 시기에도 이들은 기꺼이 돈을 쓸 것이라고 말한다. 그러나 Z세대의 구매 패턴은 이전 세대와는 다르다.
C 그들은 단순히 생각이 들자마자 무엇이든 그들이 원하는 곳에 돈을 쓰는 것이 아니라, 대신 누가 언제 그들의 돈을 받는지에 대해 매우 신중히 생각한다.
A 이런 까다로운 소비의 부분적인 이유는 우선 그들이 재량 소득을 갖기 위해 너무나 많이, 열심히 노력하고 있기 때문이다. 돈은 Z세대에게 매일의 관심사이며, 특히 지금 당장 그렇다.
D 그들 대부분은 여전히 초봉 수준의 급여를 받고 있을 뿐만 아니라 물가 상승과 생활비가 높은 시기에 급여를 아껴서 오래 써야 한다.

15-16

프레더릭 더글러스(Frederick Douglass)는 1818년 메릴랜드에서 노예로 태어났다. 더글러스 주인의 아내는 그에게 읽는 법을 가르쳤고 그는 교육받은 자유 흑인들과 접촉하기 시작했다. 그는 스무 살 무렵 뉴욕으로 도망쳐 독학을 계속했다. 1840년대 초, 노예제도 반대 운동이 힘을 얻고 있었다. 1841년부터 1845년까지 더글러스는 북부 주를 널리 여행하면서 노예제도의 부당함과 잔인함에 대해 연설했다. 많은 미국인들은 그렇게 말을 잘하고 똑똑한 흑인이 얼마 전까지만 해도 노예였었다는 것을 믿을 수 없었다. 더글러스는 1845년에 쓴 『프레더릭 더글러스의 삶에 대한 서술(Narrative of the Life of Frederick Douglass)』에서 자신의 삶의 경험을 이야기하고, 노예제도를 철폐하기 위한 중요한 수단으로서 교육을 강조한다. 더글러스는 노예 소유주들 — 스스로 독실하고 경건하다고 하는 사람들조차도 — 노예들을 문맹이고 교육 받지 못한 상태로 계속 둠으로써 비인간화하려는 노력을 포함하는 가치의 타락에 직면한다고 주장한다.

slavery n. 노예의 처지[신분]; 노예제도 educated a. 교육받은, 교양 있는 gain momentum 탄력을 받다 extensively ad. 광범위하게, 널리 injustice n. 부정, 불법, 부당 brutality n. 잔인성, 무자비 eloquent a. 웅변의, 능변인 slave n. 노예 recount v. 상술하다, 이야기하다 bring down 파멸[도산]시키다, 붕괴시키다 devout a. 독실한 pious a. 경건한 illiterate a. 문맹의 dehumanize v. ~의 인간성을 빼앗다

15 빈칸완성   ⑤

노예 소유주들이 노예가 된 사람들을 문맹이고 교육 받지 못한 상태로 계속 둠으로써 비인간화하려고 했다고 했으므로 빈칸에는 '교육'을 뜻하는 ⑤가 적절하다.

다음 중 빈칸에 들어가기에 가장 적절한 것은?
① 법
② 노동
③ 종교
④ 재산
⑤ 교육

16 내용파악   ⑤

마지막 문장에서 프레더릭 더글러스는 스스로 독실하고 경건하다고 하는 노예 소유주들조차도 노예들을 교육을 받지 못하게 함으로써 비인간화하려는 가치의 타락에 직면한다고 주장했으므로, ⑤는 옳지 않다.

다음 중 이 글에서 프레더릭 더글러스에 대해 명시되거나 암시되어 있지 않은 것은?
① 그는 주인에게서 도망쳤다.
② 그는 자전적인 책을 썼다.
③ 그는 노예제도 반대 공개 연설을 했다.
④ 그는 태어난 순간부터 노예였다.
⑤ 그는 독실하고 경건한 노예 소유주들을 지지했다.

17-18

유제품 지방이 이전에 생각했던 것만큼 해롭지 않을 수 있고 심지어 건강에 좋을 수도 있는 이유에 대한 몇 가지 가능한 설명이 있다. 식품에서 발견할 수 있는 다양한 종류의 포화 지방 중에서 유제품은 제2형 당뇨병과 관상 동맥 심장 질환의 위험 감소와 관련된 지방을 비롯한 건강에 중립적이거나 유익한 것으로 보이는 특정 지방을 포함하고 있다. 유지방은 또한 유지방구막이라고 불리는 독특한 구조에 자연 발생적으로 싸여 있다. 이 구조의 구성 요소는 소화관에서 콜레스테롤을 묶어두는 데 도움을 주어 잠재적으로 혈중 콜레스테롤 수치를 개선할 수 있다. 또한 특정 유형의 유제품이 다른 것보다 당신에게 더 좋을 수 있다는 것이 분명해지고 있다. 예를 들어, 요구르트와 치즈는 건강상의 이점과 가장 관련이 있는 것으로 보인다. 이는 둘 다 장에 좋은 박테리아를 공급할 수 있는 발효 식품이기 때문일 수 있다. 그들은 또한 심장 건강과 관련된 비타민 K를 포함하여 발효 중에 만들어진 다른 유익한 분자를 포함하고 있다. 체더 치즈나 파르메산 치즈 같은 단단한 치즈는 또한 부드러운 치즈나 버터보다 지방이 혈액에 더 점진적으로 흡수되는 것처럼 보이며, 이는 당신이 더 오랫동안 포만감을 느끼도록 도와줄 수 있다.

harmful a. 해로운, 유해한 healthful a. 건강에 좋은 saturated fat 포화 지방 dairy product 유제품 coronary a. 관상 동맥의 milk fat globule membrane 유지방구막 component n. 성분, 구성 요소 digestive tract 소화관 fermented food 발효 식품 gut n. 창자, 장; 소화관 fermentation n. 발효 (작용) gradual a. 점진적인; 완만한 absorption n. 흡수 full a. 배부른

17 빈칸완성   ③

특정 유형의 유제품이 다른 것보다 당신의 건강에 더 좋을 수 있다고 언급한 뒤에 그 예로 요구르트와 치즈를 들어 이야기하고 있다. 따라서 빈칸에는 '예를 들어'의 뜻의 ③이 적절하다.

다음 중 빈칸에 들어가기에 가장 적절한 것은?
① 그러나
② 드물게
③ 예를 들어
④ 대신에
⑤ 불행하게도

18 내용추론   ①

첫 번째 문장에서 유제품 지방이 이전에 생각했던 것만큼 해롭지 않을 수 있고 심지어 건강에 좋을 수도 있다고 언급한 뒤에 건강에 유익한 이유에 대해 설명하고 있으므로 ①이 적절하다. ② 저지방 우유와 전유에 대한 비교는 본문에 명시되어 있지 않다. ③ 유제품 중에서도 요구르트와 치즈가 건강상의 이점과 가장 관련이 있으며, 장에 좋은 박테리아를 공급한다고 했다. ④⑤ 단단한 치즈가 부드러운 치즈보다 지방이 혈액에 더 점진적으로 흡수되어 더 오랫동안 포만감을 느끼도록 도와준다고 했다.

다음 중 이 글에 명시되거나 암시되어 있는 것은?
① 유제품 지방은 건강에 유익할 수 있다.
② 저지방 우유는 전유보다 좋지 않다.
③ 우유는 요구르트보다 더 유익한 박테리아를 제공한다.
④ 단단한 치즈는 건강에 해롭다.
⑤ 부드러운 치즈는 우리가 더 오랫동안 포만감을 느끼도록 도와준다.

19-20

캘리포니아 해안에서 죽은 바다표범을 발견하는 것은 그 자체로 새로운 일이 아니다. 해양 포유류는 병에 걸리거나 사산(死産)되거나 심지어 배에 들이받혀 치명상을 입은 후에 해안으로 밀려온다. 하지만 목이 잘린 바다표범은? 그것은 북쪽 해안의 생태학자들에게 새로운 것이었다. 2015년 이후로 계속해서 신비롭고 섬뜩한 죽음이 발생했는데, 주로 멕케리처 주립 공원의 점박이 바다표범 새끼와 관련되어 있었다. 생태학자 프랭키 게라티(Frankie Gerraty)는 목이 잘린 점박이 바다표범에 대해 듣기 시작했고, 그 어떤 확증이 아니라 단서만 가지고 그 현상을 이해하려 애썼다. "집에서 기르는 개를 의심했다가 독수리로 넘어갔지만 …. 누가 이런 짓을 하는 걸까요?"라고 그는 말했다. "실제로 탐정이 되어서 이 시체들을 조사하고 그들에게 무슨 일이 일어나고 있는지 알아내는 것이 제 임무입니다." 사실 그는 코요테가 해변에서 많은 시간을 보내기 때문에 코요테일 수도 있다는 예감이 들었다. 하지만 그가 머리가 없는 바다표범 한 마리를 가까이서 보았을 때, 그는 목을 따라 절단된 부분이 너무 깨끗해서 코요테가 한 일이 아닐 것이라고 생각했고, 그것이 심지어 인간이 한 일일지도 모른다고 걱정했다. 그런 다음 비디오 영상이 그가 틀렸다는 것을 증명했다. 멕케리처 주립 공원 근처에 야생동물 카메라가 설치되었고, 게라티는 코요테가 갓 죽은 바다표범을 카메라 화면으로 끌고 들어가 그것의 머리를 절단하는 모습을 포착했다. 그래서 연구원들은 마침내 머리가 없는 바다표범의 수년간의 미스터리를 풀었다.

seal n. 바다표범, 물개 marine a. 바다의, 해양의 mammal n. 포유동물
stillborn a. 사산의 ashore ad. 해안에[으로] decapitate v. ~의 목을
베다, 참수하다 ecologist n. 생태학자 gruesome a. 소름끼치는, 섬뜩
한 harbor seal 점박이 바다표범 pup n. (여우·바다표범 따위의) 새끼
carcass n. (짐승의) 시체 figure out ~을 이해하다[알아내다] hunch
n. 예감, 육감, 직감 headless a. 머리가 없는

① 잠깐 낮잠을 자는 것
② 화면을 가까이 하지 않는 것
③ 바쁜 일정을 피하는 것
④ 디지털로 연결된 상태를 유지하는 것
⑤ 자연으로 향하는 것

19 빈칸완성　　②

빈칸에는 바다표범이 머리가 없는 이유에 대해 시체를 조사하고 무슨
일이 일어났는지 알아내는 일을 하는 사람이 들어가야 하므로 '탐정'을
뜻하는 ②가 정답으로 적절하다.

다음 중 빈칸에 들어가기에 가장 적절한 것은?
① 예술가
② 탐정
③ 포식자
④ 성직자
⑤ 장의사

20 내용추론　　③

코요테가 해변에서 많은 시간을 보내기 때문에 바다표범의 머리를 자른
것이 코요테일 수도 있다는 예감이 들었다고 했으므로 ③이 적절하다.
①④ 바다표범을 죽인 것은 코요테이다. ② 캘리포니아 해안에서 죽은
바다표범을 발견하는 것은 새로운 일이 아니라고 했다. ⑤ 코요테가 갓
죽은 바다표범의 머리를 절단하는 모습이 비디오 영상에 포착되었다.

다음 중 이 글에 명시되거나 암시되어 있는 것은?
① 개들이 점박이 바다표범 새끼들을 죽였다.
② 해변에서 죽은 바다표범을 발견하는 것은 이례적인 사건이었다.
③ 코요테는 연구원의 가능성 있는 범인 목록에 있었다.
④ 바다표범의 머리를 자른 것은 인간이 한 것이었다.
⑤ 갓 죽임을 당한 코요테가 비디오 영상에 포착되었다.

21 빈칸완성　　②

스마트폰을 내려놓고 노트북을 닫는 것, 즉 디지털 기기 사용을 멈추는
것을 의미하는 표현이 들어가야 한다. 따라서 빈칸에는 ②가 적절하다.

rest v. 쉬다, 휴식하다 steer clear of 피하다 temporarily ad. 일시적
으로 urge n. (강한) 충동 temptation n. 유혹 drift v. 표류하다,
떠돌다

우리가 휴식을 취할 수 있는 방법 중 하나는 화면을 가까이 하지 않는
것이다. 그것은 때때로 스마트폰을 내려놓고 노트북을 닫는 것을 의미한
다. 화면 앞에 있는 시간을 일시적으로 줄이는 것, 즉 디지털 디톡스는
우리 건강에 좋다. 따라서 여가 시간에 5분마다 업무 이메일을 확인하려는
충동을 피하라. 당신이 공원을 산책하거나 커피 한 잔을 마시기 위해 줄을
서 있다면, 소셜 미디어 페이지를 확인하기 위해 휴대폰을 꺼내고 싶은
유혹을 피하라. 그냥 마음이 표류하도록 내버려두고 마음이 당신을 어디로
데려가는지 보라.

22 빈칸완성　　②

빈칸 뒤에서 양배추를 좋아하는 프랑스, 그리스, 이집트 등에 대해 설명
하고 있다. 따라서 미국에서는 양배추가 인기가 없지만 프랑스나 이집
트 등의 다른 문화에서는 인기가 있다는 상반되는 의미가 되어야 한다.
그러므로 빈칸에는 ②가 적절하다.

sweetheart n. 연인, 애인 spring from ~로부터 일어나다, 야기하다,
~태생이다 drunkenness n. 술 취함, 취한 상태 worship v. 숭배하다
respect n. 존경, 경의 banquet n. (공식) 연회

미국에서 양배추는 아마도 가장 인기 있는 채소로 선정되지 않을 것이다.
심지어 그것이 가장 좋은 상태인 겨울에도 말이다. 그러나 양배추는 다른
문화에서는 존경받는다. 프랑스인들은 그것들을 너무 좋아해서 그들의 연
인을 "petits choux" 즉, 작은 양배추라고 부른다. 그리스 신화에서, 양배
추는 트라키아의 왕인 리쿠르고스(Lycurgus)가 와인의 신(神)인 디오니소
스(Dionysus)에게 미쳐버린 후, 그의 눈물에서 비롯되었다. 따라서 양배추
는 숙취 해소법으로 여겨졌다. 이집트에서 양배추는 신으로 숭배되었고,
그 채소에 대한 그들의 큰 존경을 보여주기 위해, 이집트인들이 그들의
연회에서 가장 먼저 손이 가는 음식이었다.

① 또한, 양배추는 일 년 내내 구할 수 있다
② 그러나 양배추는 다른 문화에서는 존경받는다
③ 마찬가지로, 양배추는 색깔과 모양이 다양하다
④ 양배추에는 많은 영양상의 이점이 있다
⑤ 어떻게 요리하든지 간에 양배추를 좋아하는 사람은 거의 없다

23 빈칸완성　　①

현재 기업은 새로운 세상에 대응하기 위한 방법으로 직원에게 새로운
기술을 배우고 변화하는 환경에 적응할 수 있는 교육을 하고 있다는 것
이 주된 내용이다. 리스킬링(재교육)과 업스킬링(향상 교육)이 이러한
직원들의 역량 개발을 위한 프로그램을 의미하므로 빈칸에는 ①이 적절
하다.

unpredictable a. 예측할 수 없는 adapt v. 적합[적응]시키다; (새로운
환경에) 순응하다 pose v. (문제 등을) 제기하다 emerging a. 최근
생겨난[만들어진] graduate n. 졸업생 commitment n. 헌신, 전념

새로운 세상은 역동적이고 예측할 수 없다. 오래된 접근방식은 증가하는
도전의 요구를 충족시키는 데 더 이상 효율적이지 않을 것이다. 연구에
따르면 현재 21%의 기업이 직원의 리스킬링(재교육)과 업스킬링(향상
교육)을 촉진하기 위해 자사의 자원을 사용하고 있다고 보고했다. 앞으로,
지금이 새로운 기술을 배우고 변화하는 비즈니스 환경에 적응할 수 있는
최적의 시기가 될 수 있다. 비즈니스의 최신 경향에 의해 제기되는 다양한
도전에도 불구하고, 구직자와 졸업생은 채용 과정을 거치면서 수요가 높은
이러한 새로운 기술을 향상시키는 데 필요한 시간을 가질 것이다. 그러나
한 가지는 항상 그대로인데, 바로 평생 학습에 대한 헌신이다.

① 리스킬링(재교육)과 업스킬링(향상 교육)을 촉진하다
② 전통지식을 장려하다
③ 일과 생활의 균형을 지지하다
④ 평생의 충성을 요구하다
⑤ 인원을 축소하다

24 빈칸완성 ④

'남자 전사들에 대한 이야기가 대부분이지만 사실은 여자 전사들도 있었음'을 언급하면서, 부호(Fu Hao)를 그 여자 전사의 한 인물로 이야기하고 있다. 이는 전사는 남자라는 성 규범에서 벗어나는 것이므로, 첫 번째 빈칸에는 refused나 shattered가 적절하다. 한편, 130개가 넘는 무기는 그녀의 군사력을 증명하는 것이므로 두 번째 빈칸에는 prove, demonstrate, bear witness to가 적절하다. 따라서 상기 두 조건을 모두 만족시키는 ④가 정답이다. ① 복종하다 ― 반박하다 ② 따르다 ― 증명하다 ③ 거부하다 ― 부정하다 ⑤ 권한을 주다 ― 증명하다

warrior n. 전사 shatter v. 산산이 부수다, 박살내다 dynasty n. (역대) 왕조 military training 군사 훈련 defeat v. 패배시키다, 물리치다 command v. 명령하다; 지휘하다 tomb n. 무덤 weapon n. 무기 demonstrate v. 증명하다, 논증하다

위대한 전사들의 이야기를 들을 때 일반적으로 남자에 대한 이야기이다. 그러나 역사를 통틀어 성(性) 규범을 깨뜨리고 지역사회의 변화를 위해 싸운 위대한 여자 전사들이 있었다. 부호(Fu Hao)는 기원전 13세기에 살았던 상(Shang) 왕조의 전사였다. 그녀는 무정(Wu Ding)왕의 64명의 아내 중 한 명이었고 두 번째로 강력한 인물이 되었다. 어릴 때부터 그녀는 군사 훈련을 받았다. 부호의 첫 번째 전투 중 하나는 상 지역에서의 토방(Tu Fang)과의 전투였다. 그녀는 자신의 군대를 이끌고 전투에 나서 토방을 물리쳤다. 나중에 그녀는 약 13,000명의 군인으로 이루어진 고대 중국 역사상 가장 큰 군대를 지휘했다. 그녀는 심지어 자신의 사병도 가지고 있었다. 33세의 나이에 그녀는 병에 걸려 죽었다. 그녀의 군사력을 보여주는 130개가 넘는 무기들이 그녀와 함께 무덤에 묻혔다.

25 글의 제목 ③

기침을 완화하는 방법으로 소금, 생강, 제산제, 식단 변화 등을 이야기하고 있다. 따라서 글의 제목으로는 ③이 적절하다.

when it comes to ~에 관해서라면 cough n. 기침 frustrating a. 좌절감을 낳게 하는, 초조하게[애타게] 하는 disruptive a. 분열[붕괴]시키는, 파괴적인 quit v. 그만두다, 그치다 shrug off 무시하다, 대수롭지 않게 취급하다 ease v. 완화하다 soothing a. 달래는, 진정시키는 ginger n. 생강 calm v. 진정시키다, 가라앉히다 upset stomach 배탈 do wonders 기적을 이루다; (약 등이) 굉장히 잘 듣다 antacid n. 제산제 relieve v. 경감하다, 완화하다 acid n. 산 reflux n. 역류 mitigate v. 완화하다, 진정시키다 chronic a. 만성의 citrus n. 감귤류

감기나 코로나 증상에 관해서라면, 기침에는 매우 낙심하게 만드는 점이 있다. 기침은 불편할 뿐만 아니라 멈추지 않을 때 방해가 될 수도 있다. 기침은 그저 대수롭지 않게 취급할 것이 아니다. 기침을 완화하는 간단한 방법은 소금물이다. 소금은 박테리아를 죽일 수 있고 진정시키기도 한다. 그러나 소금은 바이러스를 죽이지 않기 때문에 기침을 더 빨리 치료하는 데 도움이 되지 않을 수 있다. 생강은 배탈을 진정시키는 데 효험이 있는

것으로 잘 알려져 있다. 그것은 또한 기침에 놀라운 효과를 낼 수도 있다. 펩시드나, 프릴로섹이나, 또 다른 제산제는 위산 역류를 완화하고 관련된 기침을 완화할 수 있다. 만약에 그것이 만성적인 문제라고 생각된다면, 감귤류, 초콜릿, 고지방 식품을 피하고 현미, 셀러리, 상추와 같은 고섬유질 음식을 식단에 포함시키는 것과 같은 특정한 식단 변화를 하는 것이 도움이 될 수 있다. 만약 기침이 역류로 인한 것이라면 물을 많이 마시고 식사량을 적게 유지하는 것도 좋을 수 있다.

이 글의 제목으로 가장 적절한 것은?
① 건강하게 먹는 방법
② 기침의 건강상의 위험
③ 기침을 없애는 방법
④ 기침의 잠재적 유발 요인
⑤ 코로나와 감기의 차이점

26 내용추론 ③

E.B. 피어슨이 최고상을 받았지만 피어슨이 여자라는 사실이 밝혀지자마자 심사위원들은 재빨리 그녀의 작품을 경쟁에서 제외시켰다고 했다. 따라서 ③이 정답으로 적절하다. ② 75달러를 받은 차점자는 2등을 해서가 아니라 1등인 피어슨이 제외되어서 75달러를 그녀 대신 받은 것이다.

prestigious a. 명망 있는, 일류의 anonymously ad. 익명으로 submit v. 제출하다 in hopes of ~의 희망을 가지고, ~을 바라고 impressive a. 인상적인 assess v. 평가하다 annex n. 별관 donor n. 기증자, 기부자 faculty n. (학부의) 교수단 rule out 제외시키다, 배제하다 runner-up n. (경기·경쟁의) 차점자 stead n. 대신, 대리 outright ad. 완전히; 공공연히, 노골적으로

1888년, 명망 있는 모든 상을 수여하는 과정이 정기적으로 시작되었다. 하버드 학생들은 100달러에 달하는 인상적인 금액과 명예를 받기를 바라며 익명으로 최고의 에세이를 제출했다. 대회 심사위원들은 또한 대학의 _별관_(나중에 래드클리프 칼리지)에서 여학생들이 제출한 에세이를 평가했지만, (여학생) 수상자들은 대학의 인정이나 돈을 받지 못했다. 외부 기부자가 30달러의 상금을 제공했다. 그 해에 남녀의 논문이 어쨌든 함께 제출되었고, E.B. 피어슨(E.B. Pearson)의 고전 에세이 『제국 하의 로마 원로원(The Roman Senate Under the Empire)』이 최고상을 받았다. 피어슨이 실제로 미스 E.B. 피어슨이라는 사실이 금방 밝혀졌다. 교수진은 재빨리 그녀의 작품을 경쟁에서 제외시켰고, 차점자(남자)가 그녀를 대신하여 75달러를 받았다. 당시 보스턴 포스트 신문 기사에 따르면 피어슨은 30달러의 별관 상을 받았으며 "따라서 노골적으로 여자라는 이유로 70달러를 (벌금으로) 치른 셈이었다."

다음 중 이 글에 명시되거나 암시되어 있는 것은?
① 피어슨은 그 에세이를 반항의 행위로 제출했다.
② 1888년 대회에서, 1등 수상자는 100달러, 2등 수상자는 75달러를 받았다.
③ 심사위원들은 처음에 에세이 작성자의 신원에 대해 잘못된 가정을 했다.
④ E.B. 피어슨은 실제로 『제국 하의 로마 원로원』을 쓰지 않았다.
⑤ 보스턴 포스트 신문 기사는 대회 심사위원들이 여성에게 너무 많은 돈을 수여한 것을 비판했다.

27 글의 분위기   ②

무언가가 네 발로 그를 향해 다가오고 있었고, 화자의 발목 위로 그 무언가의 차가운 손이 닿는 것을 느낄 것이라고 했다. 이런 분위기는 '무서움'을 느끼게 하므로, 글의 어조로는 ②가 적절하다.

turn around 방향을 바꾸다   crawl v. 기어가다   clog v. 막다   opening n. 구멍, 틈   wriggle v. 꿈틀거리며 가다   stealthy a. 살며시[몰래] 하는   crackle n. 우지직 하는 소리   on one's hands and knees 네 발로 기어서   ankle n. 발목

대니(Danny)는 힘겹게 몸을 돌려 콘크리트 터널을 따라 기어갔다. 그가 터널 끝에 막 도달했을 때, 차가운 빛이 위에서 쏟아졌다. 그때 눈은 잦아들어 약간씩 내렸지만, 그래도 그의 얼굴을 덮어버리고 그가 꿈틀거리며 헤쳐 나왔던 틈을 막아버려 그를 어둠 가운데 두기에는 충분했다. 터널의 맨 끝에서, 대니는 무언가가 네 발로 그를 향해 다가옴에 따라, 낙엽이 살며시 부서지는 소리를 들었다. 어느 순간에라도 그의 발목 위로 그 무언가의 차가운 손이 와 닿는 것을 느낄 것이었다.

이 글의 전반적인 분위기는 무엇인가?
① 느긋한
② 무서운
③ 유쾌한
④ 지루한
⑤ 우울한

28 지시대상   ⑤

나머지 보기는 모두 신장을 기증한 낯선 사람을 가리키는 반면, ⑮의 경우 글의 저자가 신장 기증을 하는 이유를 완벽하게 이해하신 아버지를 가리키므로, ⑤가 정답이다.

donate v. (장기를) 기증하다   kidney n. 신장, 콩팥   fascinated a. 매료된   cherry on the top 금상첨화   give away 남에게 주다

나는 낯선 사람에게 신장을 하나 기증했다. 신장 하나로도 살 수 있어서 다른 신장을 기증하지 않을 이유가 없었다. 사람들은 신장 기증이 미친 짓이거나 너무 위험한 짓이라고 계속 이야기했다. 모두가 나처럼 생각하는 것은 아니며, 많은 사람들이 신장 기증을 하지 않음이 분명해서, 도움을 주고자 하는 나의 결심이 더욱 더 굳어졌다. 나는 3일 동안 병원에 있었고, 하루 이상 소파에 앉아 있은 다음, 일상으로 돌아갔다. 한 달 뒤, 병원은 낯선 사람에게서 이메일을 한 통 받았는데, 그 낯선 사람은 바로 나의 신장을 받았던 사람이었다. "안녕하세요. 저는 당신의 신장을 받은 사람입니다."라고 이메일에 적혀 있었다. 병원에서 해주는 말은 누구에게 기증하든 그 사람은 연락이 되지 않을 수 있다는 것이다. 그래서 나는 그에게서 소식을 듣게 될 거라고 기대하지는 않았지만, 그가 잘 지내고 있다니 너무 기분이 좋았다. 우리는 많은 이메일을 주고받았고, 서로를 알게 되었다. 그 사람이 살아온 인생 이야기를 모두 듣게 되어, 나는 매료되었다. 남편과 나는 포크스턴(Folkstone)에 있는 그를 만나러 갔는데, 그는 아내와 살고 있었고, 우리는 바다에 수영하러 갔으며 샴페인을 마셨다. 나는 나의 신장을 누가 받았더라도 너무 기분이 좋았을 테지만, 나의 신장이 가장 좋은 사람에게 갔다는 것이 금상첨화였고, 이제 우리는 친구가 되었다. 10월에 나는 요크(York) 마라톤에 나갔는데, 스튜어트(Stuart)가 나를 응원하러 와주었으며, 그는 내가 왜 내 신장을 남에게 주었는지를 이제 완벽하게 이해하신 나의 아버지를 만났다.

29 내용파악   ②

① 방벽은 로마 황제 하드리아누스의 작품이라고 했다. ③ 방벽은 길이가 73마일에 달한다고 했다. ④ 방벽은 서기 122년 건설이 시작되어 건설하는 데만 6년이 걸렸다고 했다. ⑤ 방벽은 타인 강에서부터 솔웨이 퍼쓰에 이르는 지역에 걸쳐있다고 했다. 반면, 방벽의 재질이 돌이라고 했을 뿐, 방벽의 축조방식에 관해서는 본문에 직접 언급되지 않았으므로, ②가 정답이다.

massive a. (육중하면서) 거대한   empire n. 제국   frontier n. 국경 (지역)   emperor n. 황제   thorough a. 철두철미한   reign n. (왕의) 통치 기간   sort out (문제를) 해결하다   warlike a. 호전적인   subdue v. 정복하다, 진압하다   run v. ~부터 …까지 이르다   rampart n. 방벽   a succession of 일련의   fort n. 요새

브리튼(Britain) 섬에서 로마 제국의 가장 거대한 건설 프로젝트는 거대한 북쪽 국경 방벽이었는데, 서기 122년에 시작되어 건설하는 데 대략 6년이 걸렸다. 이 거대한 방벽은 로마 황제 하드리아누스(Hadrian)의 작품이었다. 하드리아누스는 인내심이 강하고 철두철미한 사람으로, 그의 21년 통치 기간의 절반을 방대한 제국의 국경지역들을 계획적으로 돌아다니며 각종 문제들을 해결하는 데 보냈다. 브리튼 섬에서, 로마제국의 골칫거리는 로마군이 정복하기 불가능하다고 여겼던 브리튼 섬 북쪽의 호전적인 민족들이었다. 동쪽 해안의 타인(Tyne) 강에서부터 서쪽의 솔웨이 퍼쓰(Solway Firth)에 이르기까지 73마일에 달하는 하드리아누스 방벽은 그 방벽을 따라 일련의 대규모 국경 요새들로 이루어진 거대한 돌로 된 방벽이었다.

다음 중 이 글에서 하드리아누스 방벽에 관해 언급되지 않은 것은?
① 이 방벽은 누가 만들었는가
② 이 방벽은 어떻게 만들어졌는가
③ 이 방벽은 얼마나 긴가
④ 이 방벽은 언제 만들어졌는가
⑤ 이 방벽은 어디에 있는가

30 글의 주제   ⑤

이 글은 우울증과 번아웃의 증상들이 구별하기 힘들 수 있지만, 우울증은 진단할 수 있는 의학적인 질병인 반면, 번아웃은 그렇지 않다고 하면서 번아웃과 우울증을 구분해 설명하고 있으므로, 글의 주제로는 ⑤가 적절하다.

depression n. 우울증   burnout n. 번아웃, 극도의 피로   distinguish v. 구분[구별]하다   diagnosable a. 진단할 수 있는   medical condition 질병   overwhelmed a. 압도된   unrelenting a. 끊임없는   task n. (하기 싫은) 일, 과제   cynicism n. 냉소 (주의)   depletion n. 고갈, 소모   resentment n. 분노   isolate v. 고립시키다   neglect v. 소홀히 하다   hygiene n. 위생

우울증과 번아웃의 증상들은 구별하기 힘들 수 있다. 우울증과 번아웃은 모두 잠을 너무 많이 자게 하거나, 너무 적게 자게 하거나, 집중하는 데 어려움을 겪게 할 수도 있다. 그러나 우울증은 진단할 수 있는 의학적인 질병인 반면, 번아웃은 그렇지 않다. 번아웃의 경우, 당신이 직장의 끊임없는 업무에 압도되어, 냉소주의, 체력고갈, 직업에 대한 분노로 이어질 수 있으며, 이로 인해 당신의 취미 활동에 쏟을 에너지가 부족해질 수 있다.

반면, 우울증의 경우, 당신의 취미활동이 전혀 즐겁지 않을지도 모르며, 스스로를 고립시키거나 위생이나 신체건강을 소홀히 할지도 모른다.

이 글에서 주로 무엇이 논의되는가?
① 우울증을 극복하는 방법
② 번아웃의 신체적인 징후들
③ 정신건강을 향상시키는 조치들
④ 번아웃이 우울증에 미치는 영향
⑤ 번아웃과 우울증의 차이점

31 문장삽입   ③

제시문은 "언어의 경우도 비슷하다."라는 뜻으로, 제시문 뒤에는 언어와 관련된 내용이 시작되어야 하며, 제시문 앞에는 '언어가 아닌 다른 내용'이 와야 한다. ⓒ 앞에서 '병을 알기 위해서는 병력을 조사해 봐야 한다'고 했으며, ⓒ 뒤에서는 '언어를 알기 위해서는 언어의 역사를 조사해 봐야 한다'고 했으므로, 제시문은 ⓒ에 들어가는 것이 적절하다.

stomachache n. 복통 trouble n. 병, 통증 appetite n. 식욕 medical history 병력 present a. 현재의 big toe 엄지발가락 insight n. 통찰력 apparently ad. 겉보기에는

당신이 복통을 느껴서 병원에 간다고 상상해 보자. 의사는 당신에게 증상을 설명하고 증상과 관련된 배경도 설명하도록 요구할 것이다. 당신은 아마도 이런 질문들을 받게 될 것이다. 언제부터 복통이 시작됐습니까? 복통을 일으킬만한 것을 드신 적이 있습니까? 그것이 당신의 식욕에 영향을 주었습니까? 당신의 현재 상태와 관련된 병력을 조사함으로써, 의사는 당신의 복통에 관해 더 많은 것을 알 수 있다. 분명히 의사는 "엄지발가락이 아픈 적이 있습니까?"와 같은 질문을 당신에게 하지는 않을 것이기 때문에, 나는 '관련된'이라고 말하는 것이다. <언어의 경우도 비슷하다.> 영어의 현재 상태와 관련된 역사를 조사함으로써, 우리는 언어에 대한 통찰력을 얻을 수 있으며, 어떻게 영어가 현재의 영어가 되었는지를 설명하기 시작할 수 있다. 예를 들어, 왜 우리는 결함이 많아 보이는 철자법을 갖고 있는지, 어떻게 단어들이 존재하게 되었는지, 왜 때때로 우리는 다소 똑같은 것을 설명하기 위해서도 여러 단어들 중에서 하나를 골라서 쓰는 것 같은지, 등등을 우리는 설명할 수 있다. 영어가 어떻게 변화해 왔는지와 그러한 변화에 영향을 주었던 요인들을 살펴봄으로써, 우리는 이와 같은 질문들에 이제 대답할 수 있다.

32 글의 흐름상 적절하지 않은 문장 고르기   ③

이 글은 재택근무의 단점에 대해 다루고 있는 반면, ⓒ의 경우, 가까이에 있는 동료들로 인한 방해에서 떨어져 멀리 집에서 일하는 엔지니어들의 생산성이 높고 이것이 승진, 임금 인상 등으로 이어진다는, 전체적인 글의 흐름과 관련 없는 이야기를 언급하고 있으므로, ③이 정답이다.

executive n. 경영진 collaboration n. 공동 작업, 협업 tie n. 유대관계 merit n. 장점; 가치 proximity n. 가까움, 근접 suffer v. 악화되다 remote a. 원격의 follow-up n. 후속 back-and-forth 왔다 갔다 하는 dynamic n. 역동성 vanish v. 사라지다 disruption n. 붕괴; 중단; 혼란; 방해 in the long run 장기적으로 quit v. 그만두다 note v. 언급하다; 주목하다 tradeoff n. 상충관계, 모순적 관계, 균형점, 절충점 senior a. 선임의 onsite a. 현장의

재택근무라는 아이디어에 대한 반응은 경영진들 사이에서 엇갈렸는데, 많은 경영진들은 사무실에 있는 시간이 줄어든다는 것은 협업이 줄어들고, 동료들과의 유대관계가 약해지고, 학습기회가 줄어든다는 것을 의미한다고 주장했다. 그것은 장점이 없지 않은 주장이다. "동료와의 근접성의 힘"이라는 최근의 한 연구에 따르면, 유익한 팀워크와 중요한 협업은 직원들이 재택근무 할 때 어려워진다고 한다. 게다가, 젊은 직원들, 특히 여성들이 원격 근무로 가장 많은 타격을 받을지도 모른다. 어느 포춘 500대 기업에 다니는 소프트웨어 엔지니어들을 대상으로 한 연구에 따르면, 모든 팀원들과 같은 건물에서 일하는 엔지니어들이 먼 곳에 있는 팀원들을 둔 엔지니어들보다 코드와 관련한 온라인 피드백을 23% 더 받았다고 한다. 젊은 여성 엔지니어들은 직접 대면해 일할 때 프로그래밍의 특정 문제에 초점을 맞춰 후속 질문을 할 가능성이 특히 더 높았다. 원격 근무의 경우, 이런 피드백을 주고받는 역동성이 사라졌다. <가까이 있는 동료들로 인한 방해로부터 떨어져 멀리서(집에서) 일하는 엔지니어들의 생산성은 놀라울 정도로 높으며, 이것은 장기적으로 더 많은 승진, 임금 인상, 그리고 최고의 평가로 이어진다.> 원격 근무로 인해 30세 이하의 엔지니어들이 퇴사할 가능성이 동료들과 같은 건물에서 일할 때보다 5배 더 높아졌고, 여성 엔지니어들은 퇴사할 가능성이 네 배나 더 높아졌다고 그들의 연구논문은 주목한다. 논문은 상충관계도 확인한다. 선임 엔지니어들의 경우, 현장 근무로 코딩 생산량이 21% 줄었는데, 아마도 젊은 동료들에게 피드백을 주는 데에 더 많은 시간을 할애했기 때문일 것이다.

33 단락배열   ③

제시문에서 사회적 존재인 인간은 생존하는 데 도움을 줄 수 있는 집단과 유대를 형성한다고 했다. 따라서 제시문에 이어질 내용으로 사회적 존재와 관련된 '사회적 정체성', 유대관계와 관련된 '정서적 반응'을 언급한 ⓒ가 제일 먼저 와야 하며, 이 정서적 반응을 실제의 예로 소개한 Ⓐ가 그다음에, 그리고 동료들일 경우 어떻게 반응하는지를 소개한 Ⓐ와 대조적으로, 적일 경우에는 어떻게 반응하는지를 소개한 Ⓑ로 글을 마무리해야 문맥상 적절하다.

forge v. 구축하다 bond n. 유대관계 evolutionary a. 진화론적인 impulse n. 충동 neurology n. 신경학 identity n. 정체성 comrade n. 동료, 동지, 전우 fellow a. 같은 처지에 있는, 동료의 empathy n. 감정이입, 공감 reactivate v. 다시 작동시키다 simulate v. 흉내내다 adversary n. 적, 적대자 empathetic a. 감정 이입의[에 입각한] schadenfreude n. 남의 불행을 기뻐함 malicious a. 악의적인

사회적 존재로서, 인간은 외부의 위협으로부터 우리가 생존하는 데 도움을 줄 수 있는 집단과 강한 유대를 형성하게 되어 있다고 연구결과는 보여준다. 그것은 자연스러운 진화론적인 충동이다.
ⓒ 독일 예나대학교의 신경학 연구원이자 강사인 올가 클리메키(Olga Klimecki)는 사회적 정체성이 상황에 대한 우리의 정서적 반응을 얼마나 강력하게 형성할 수 있는지를 뇌 스캔을 통해 알 수 있다고 주장한다.
Ⓐ 예를 들어, 만일 누군가가 동지, 즉 한 집단의 동료가 고통스러워하는 모습을 본다면, 두뇌는 공감으로 반응할 것이다. "저의 두뇌는 기분이 안 좋을 때 제가 어떻게 느끼는지를 다시 작동시킴으로써 다른 사람의 고통을 흉내 낼 것입니다."라고 클리메키는 설명한다.
Ⓑ 그러나 고통을 느끼는 사람이 적이라면, 두뇌의 똑같은 공감 영역은 작동하지 않을 뿐 아니라, '샤덴프로이데(schadenfreude)', 즉 남의 불행에 대한 기쁨과 관련된 것이 더 많이 작동되는 것을 때때로 보게 됩니다."라고 그녀는 주장한다.

34 빈칸완성   ①

유리창 청소를 거의 끝마쳤을 무렵, 어떤 직원이 유리창이 있는데도 투명하니까 아무 것도 없는 줄 알고 유리창 쪽으로 걸어가다가 코가 깨지는 사고가 났다고 했다. 유리창에 부딪쳐 코가 깨졌다는 것은 유리창이 없는 줄 알 정도로 유리창이 너무 깨끗하다는 말로 생각될 수 있다. 따라서 유리창 청소부가 상황을 수습하기 위해 할 수 있는 말은 "그것(코가 깨지는 것)이 당신이 저에게 해줄 수 있는 최고의 '칭찬'입니다."가 적절하다. 따라서 ①이 정답이다.

unusual a. 특별한, 특이한 horrific a. 끔찍한 embarrassed a. 당황스러운 remedy v. 바로잡다 compliment n. 칭찬 therapy n. 치료법

많은 전문 유리창 청소부들은 들려줄 몇 가지 특별한 이야기들을 갖고 있다. Sunstruck Window Cleaning이라는 회사에 다니는 미르코(Mirko)라는 남자는 어떤 사무실에서 오랫동안 청소하지 않은 대형 유리 패널을 청소하던 날에 대해 이야기 해주었다. "제가 유리창 청소를 거의 끝마쳤을 무렵, 직원들 중 한 명이 아무 것도 없다고 생각하고 유리창으로 걸어가다가 코가 깨졌습니다. 그 장면이 너무 웃겼는데 동시에 끔찍했습니다. 그 사람은 너무 당황스러워 하더군요. 상황을 수습하기 위해, 그것이 당신이 저에게 해줄 수 있는 최고의 칭찬이라고 그에게 말해주었습니다."

35-36

1993년도 영화 "쥬라기 공원(Jurassic Park)"의 한 장면에서, 화석을 연구하는 두 명의 과학자가 벨로키랍토르의 뼈에 묻은 모래를 붓으로 털어낸다. 그 장면은 상징적인 장면들로 가득하지만, 나는 공룡을 발굴하는 것이 실제로 어떤 것인지에 대해 몇 가지 잘못 알고 있음을 지적하고 싶다. 당신이 공룡 골격을 발견하면, 그 어떤 물질이든 이미 노출된 물질을 평가하게 된다. 그 골격이 적어도 부분적으로 해체되어 있음이 아마도 드러날 것인데, 이것은 여러 뼈들이 뒤섞여서 하나의 골격으로 잘 조립되어 있지 않다는 것을 의미한다. 보존이라도 되어있을 공룡 골격은 소량에 불과할 가능성이 매우 높다. 동물이 죽으면 동물의 연한 조직은 썩어 없어지고, 딱딱한 골격만 남게 된다. 그러나 이렇게 되면 골격을 하나로 붙들어줄 아무 것도 남아 있지 않게 된다. 죽은 고기를 먹는 동물들, 바람, 그리고 물이 뼈들을 이리저리 옮겨놓고 난 후 뼈들은 퇴적물로 덮이고 화석화된다. 우리가 발견하는 골격들은 영화 "쥬라기 공원"에 나오는 벨로키랍토르만큼 깔끔하게 보존된 경우가 거의 전혀 없다.

fossil n. 화석 brush away ~을 털다 skeleton n. 뼈대, 골격 point out 지적하다 get something wrong (상황을) 오해하다 dig up 발굴하다 disarticulate v. 해체하다 jumble v. 뒤섞다 preserve v. 보존하다 tissue n. 조직 rot away 썩어 없어지다 hold together ~을 이어놓다 scavenge v. (직접 사냥한 것이 아닌) 죽은 고기를 먹다 sediment n. 침전물, 퇴적물 neatly ad. 깔끔하게 paleontologist n. 고생물학자

35 내용파악   ⑤

이 글의 저자는 공룡의 골격과 관련해 영화 "쥬라기 공원"에서 잘못 묘사된 점들을 지적하고 있다. 잘못된 점이 무엇인지 알고 이야기할 정도면 공룡과 같은 고생물을 잘 알고 있는 전문가일 가능성이 높으므로, ⑤의 '고생물학자'가 정답이다.

이 글의 저자의 직업은 무엇일 가능성이 가장 높은가?

① 배우
② 역사가
③ 공원 경비원
④ 영화 감독
⑤ 고생물학자

36 내용파악   ④

밑줄 친 부분은 "이렇게 되면 골격을 하나로 붙들어줄 아무 것도 남아 있지 않게 된다."라는 뜻이다. 골격을 붙들어주고 있던 연한 조직인 살이 썩어 없어져 남아 있지 않으면 골격은 흐트러져 해체될 것이므로, ④의 '해체'가 정답이다.

밑줄 친 부분의 결과는 무엇인가?

① 강화
② 화석화
③ 탐험
④ 해체
⑤ 배열

37-38

지루함이 부정적인 평판을 받는 데는 이유가 있다. 직장에서의 지루함은 불편함, 새로운 역할에 대한 절망, 또는 그저 하루가 끝나길 바라는 욕망을 유발하는 비생산적인 상태로 종종 간주된다. 직장에서의 지루함은 위험한 의사결정, 대가가 큰 실수, 그리고 부주의나 집중부족으로 촉발되는 사고와 관련되어 왔으며, 지루함으로 발생할 수 있는 피로감은 말할 것도 없다. 지루함은 또한 '사이버로핑(즉, 업무와 무관한 인터넷 검색)'과 유치한 감정 대응처럼 또 다른 유형의 문제 행동도 유발할 수 있다. 단조로운 활동에 장기간 노출되면 심지어 환각을 일으킬 수도 있다. 게다가, 최근의 한 연구는 직장에서의 지루함과 직업 만족도 저하, 퇴사 욕구 증가, 그리고 번아웃과의 관계를 발견했다.

반면, 최근의 연구는 지루함이 건설적으로 다뤄진다면, "긍정적인 면"도 크다는 것을 보여준다. 지루함을 느끼는 순간들은 주의를 산만하게 하고 압도하며 지나치게 자극하도록 설계된 세상에서 당신의 두뇌와 신체를 잠시 쉬게 해줄 수 있다. 지루한 감은 공상할 시간을 만들 수 있고, 이 공상이 창의력, 새로운 아이디어, 그리고 혁신을 만들어낼 수 있다. 장기적인 지루함은 당신으로 하여금 반성하고 스스로에게 이런 질문을 던지게 할 수 있다. "내가 올바른 길을 가고 있는가? 내가 잘 하고 있는가?"

boredom n. 지루함, 권태 reputation n. 평판 counterproductive a. 비생산적인, 역효과적인 ignite v. (사람의 감정을) 타오르게 하다 desperation n. 자포자기 decision-making n. 의사결정 costly a. 대가가 큰 trigger v. 촉발시키다 inattention n. 부주의 fatigue n. 피로 incite v. (분노·호기심을) 유발하다 cyberloafing n. 사이버로핑(근무자가 근무시간에 인터넷으로 시간을 보내거나 개인적인 것을 하기 위해 컴퓨터를 사용하는 것) that is 즉, 다시 말하면 browsing n. 브라우징(정보를 찾아 인터넷을 돌아다니기) childish a. 유치한 prolonged a. 장기적인 monotonous a. (지루할 정도로) 단조로운 hallucination n. 환각 on the flip side 반면 handle v. 다루다 respite n. (곤경·불쾌한 일의) 일시적인 중단 distract v. 산만하게 하다 daydream v. 공상에 잠기다 hatch v. 부화하다 prompt v. 촉발하다, 유도하다 reflect v. 되돌아보다 pros and cons 장점과 단점

37 빈칸완성 ①

빈칸을 전후로 모두 지루함에 대한 부정적인 내용이 연달아 이어지고 있으므로, '부연설명'이 이어질 때 쓰이는 부사인 ①이 빈칸에 적절하다.

다음 중 빈칸에 들어가기에 가장 적절한 것은?
① 게다가
② 그렇지 않으면
③ 대조적으로
④ 역설적이게도
⑤ 개의치 않고

38 글의 주제 ④

이 글은 직장에서의 지루함이 부정적인 결과를 많이 초래하지만, 지루함을 잘만 다룬다면 창의력도 생기고 자신을 되돌아 볼 시간을 갖게 되는 등 긍정적인 면도 제공한다고 했으므로, ④가 정답이다.

이 글에서 주로 무엇이 논의되는가?
① 직장에서 지루함의 원인
② 직장에서 지루함이 주는 혜택
③ 사이버로핑의 문제점
④ 직장에서의 지루함이 주는 장단점
⑤ 직장에서 단조로움의 정도

39-40

지난 50여 년 동안, 연구원들은 가스레인지에 노출되는 것이 인간에게 해로울 수 있다는 것을 증명해 왔다. 가스레인지를 사용할 때, 가스레인지는 천식을 유발하는 것으로 여겨지는 호흡기 자극물인 이산화질소와 같은 질소산화물이라 불리는 유독가스를 배출한다. 작년에 발표된 한 연구에 따르면, 환기가 잘 되지 않거나 레인지후드가 없는 가정에서 가스레인지를 사용하는 가족은 불과 몇 분 안에 질소산화물에 대한 안전한 시간당 실외 노출 국가표준을 넘어설 수 있으며, 실내 공기 중 질소산화물에 대한 합의된 기준은 전혀 없다고 한다. 질소산화물 배출 비율은 가스레인지가 연소하는 가스량에 정비례했다. 또 다른 연구는 가스를 연소하는 가스레인지가 미국에서 소아 천식 환자의 거의 13%와 관련 있을지도 모른다는 것을 시사해 주었다. 가스레인지가 어른에게 어떻게 영향을 미치는지에 관한 데이터보다 가스레인지가 아이들에게 어떻게 영향을 미치는지에 관한 데이터가 더 많다. 동일한 연구는 천식이 있는 어른들도 증상이 악화되기 쉬울 수도 있다는 것을 보여주었다. <천식 이외에도, 가스레인지와 관련된 다른 건강상의 위험들도 있다. 보스턴(Boston) 인근 69개의 가정에서 연소되지 않는 천연가스 샘플 234개를 수집한 연구원들은 가스에서 벤젠 등 21개의 유독성 오염물질을 발견했다.>
전문가들은 보통 사람들이 가스레인지를 주의해서 사용해야 한다고 말하지만, 이 연구결과가 반드시 당신이 병에 걸릴 것이라는 의미는 아니다. 사람들 중 일부는 새 가전제품을 사려고 할 때 가스레인지를 인덕션 레인지로 교체할 것을 고려할지도 모른다. 현재 가스레인지를 사용하는 사람들에게 말해줄, 잠재적인 건강상의 위험을 경감시킬 수 있는 몇 가지 간단한 방법이 있다.

gas stove (요리용) 가스레인지 emit v. 배출하다 nitrogen dioxide 이산화질소 nitrogen oxide 질소산화물 respiratory a. 호흡기의 irritant n. 자극물 asthma n. 천식 ventilation n. 환기 blow past

지나치다 agreed-upon a. 합의된 in direct proportion to ~에 정비례해서 be susceptible to ~을 하기 쉽다 toxic a. 유독성의 be in the market for ~을 사려고 하다 appliance n. 가전제품 mitigate v. 경감시키다

39 문장삽입 ④

제시문은 "천식 이외에도, 가스레인지와 관련된 다른 건강상의 위험들도 있다. 보스턴 인근 69개의 가정에서 연소되지 않는 천연가스 샘플 234개를 수집한 연구원들은 가스에서 벤젠 등 21개의 유독성 오염물질을 발견했다."라는 뜻이다. 따라서 제시문 앞에는 가스레인지가 천식에 미치는 영향이 나와야 하므로, "천식이 있는 어른들도 증상이 악화되기 쉬울 수도 있다."고 천식에 대한 언급을 마무리한 ⒟에 제시문이 들어가야 적절하다.

40 뒷내용 추론 ⑤

마지막 단락의 마지막 문장에서 "현재 가스레인지를 사용하는 사람들에게 말해줄, 잠재적인 건강상의 위험을 경감시킬 수 있는 몇 가지 간단한 방법이 있다."라고 했으므로, 이 글 다음에 이어질 내용으로 ⑤가 정답이다.

다음 중 이 글 다음에 오게 될 내용은 무엇인가?
① 가스레인지에의 노출이 낳는 결과
② 주방 가전제품을 구입하는 방법
③ 가스레인지가 배출하는 오염물질의 유형
④ 인덕션 레인지 사용의 장점
⑤ 가스레인지의 건강상의 위험을 낮추는 방법

01 ①	02 ②	03 ①	04 ③	05 ②	06 ③	07 ②	08 ②	09 ①	10 ③
11 ①	12 ③	13 ③	14 ④	15 ①	16 ③	17 ①	18 ④	19 ①	20 ②
21 ①	22 ④	23 ③	24 ③	25 ②	26 ④	27 ④	28 ③	29 ③	30 ②
31 ②	32 ③	33 ③	34 ①	35 ②	36 ④	37 ②	38 ②	39 ④	40 ①

01 동의어 ①

now and then 이따금씩 lurch v. 휘청거리다(= stagger) jive v. 자이브 음악에 맞춰 춤을 추다 n. 허튼소리 saunter v. 한가로이 거닐다 glide v. 미끄러지다

우리가 함께 걸어갈 때 그녀는 이따금씩 내 쪽으로 휘청거리곤 했다.

02 동의어 ②

manufacture v. 제조하다 crockery n. 그릇(도자기류, 오븐용)(= dish) cutlery n. 식기(날붙이 류, 쇠붙이 류) glassware n. 유리 제품, 유리 그릇 silverware n. 은식기

우리는 질 면에서 그리고, 상대적으로 말해, 가격 면에서도 세계에서 가장 뛰어나고 가장 가치 있는 그릇을 제조하고 있다.

03 동의어 ①

reprehend v. 꾸짖다, 나무라다, 비난하다(= fulminate) approve v. 승인하다 eulogize v. 칭송하다 override v. 기각[무시]하다

시민들이 우리가 하는 말에 부정적으로 대응한다고 해도 우리가 시민들을 비난해서는 안 된다.

04 동의어 ③

vitiate v. 가치를 떨어뜨리다, 무효로 하다(= invalidate) vilify v. 비난하다, 비방하다 accentuate v. 강조하다 correctify v. 고치다

개발 프로그램들은 인구 증가로 효과가 상실되었다.

05 동의어 ②

victual n. 양식, 음식(= food) truce n. 휴전 freshet n. 밀물의 흐름; 돌발홍수

당신에게 이 음식을 제공하게 되어 아주 기뻐요.

06 동의어 ③

centurion n. 100인 대장, 백부장(고대 로마 군대에서 병사 100명을 거느리던 지휘관) well n. 우물 brackish a. 염분이 있는(= saline) gooey a. 쫄깃한, 끈적거리는 palatable a. 맛좋은 soporific a. 최면성의, 잠들게 하는

그 백부장은 이 지역 우물물에 염분이 있다는 사실을 알게 됐다.

07 동의어 ②

anticipate v. 예상하다 parturition n. 분만(= delivery) materialize v. 실현되다 diagnosis n. 진단 operation n. 수술 postmortem n. 부검, 검시 a. 사후의

의사들이 분만 시 예상했던 어려움은 실현되지 않았다.

08 생활영어 ②

개장을 앞두고 준비하는 과정에 있는데 허물어뜨린다(pull down)는 말은 적절하지 않으므로 ②가 정답이다. pull this down 대신 pull this off라 해야 '잘 해낼 수 있다'는 말이 된다. ① phase it out은 점차적으로 없애가는 것을 말하며 immediately는 당장 phase it out하자는 말이다. ③ A는 찾아온 B를 환영하며 의례적으로 대화를 날씨 이야기로 시작하지만 B가 사정이 급해서 빨리 본론으로 들어가자고 하는 것은 A를 당황하게 할 수는 있어도 대화로서는 사정에 따라 할 수 있는 말이다.

phase out 단계적으로 폐기하다 pull something down 허물어뜨리다, 가치를 떨어뜨리다 cut to the chase 시간 낭비 말고 본론으로 직행하다 legit a. 믿을 만한

① A: 아무도 더 이상 그것을 사지 않을 것 같아.
   B: 즉시 그것을 점차적으로 없애는 게 낫겠어.
② A: 우리 언제 개장할 거지?
   B: 크리스마스 날이야. 스케줄이 빡빡하지만 우린 이것을 허물어뜨릴 수 있어.
③ A: 내 사무실에 잘 왔어. 올 때 날씨는 어땠어?
   B: 나 급해. 본론으로 바로 들어가자.
④ A: 이 피자집 믿을 만해?
   B: 의심하는 거야?

09 생활영어 ①

많은 분량의 문서를 다 읽어야 한다는 말에 옳다고 해놓고 겉만 훑어보라고 하는 것은 적절하지 않다. 따라서 정답은 ①이다.

wade through ~속을 걷다, 힘들여 해나가다 hefty a. 두둑한, 막대한 skim v. 겉만 훑어보다 pull up one's socks 정신 차리고 새로 시작하다, 분발하다 go the extra mile 여분의 노력을 더 기울이다, 특히 노력하다 Every dog has its day 쥐구멍에도 볕들 날 있다(참고 기다리면 좋은 날 온다) knockout n. 굉장한 것, 매력적인 미녀, 크게 히트한 상품 head over heels 곤두박이로, 깊이 빠져들어 fall head over heel about ~에 대해 넋이 나가다, 홀딱 반하다

① A: 이 묵직한 문서를 힘들여 다 봐야 해.
　 B: 맞아. 주제의 겉만 대충 훑어봐야 해.
② A: 그녀의 재선을 위해, 샘이 분발해서 더 열심히 하기로 결심했음에 틀림없어.
　 B: 맞아. 쥐구멍에도 볕들 날 있는 거지.
③ A: 이번에는 대박날 거야.
　 B: 기다려. 섣불리 단정 짓지 마.
④ A: 그가 그녀에게 푹 빠졌어.
　 B: 당연하지. 그녀가 굉장한 미녀잖아.

10 과거분사 ③

'고도로 전문화된'은 highly specialized로 쓰인다. 따라서 틀린 곳은 ③이다.

optimization n. 최적화 route v. 경로를 짜다; 전송하다, 보내다 specialized a. 전문화된

페덱스 같은 기업에게는 휴일 포장상품을 효과적으로 전송하는 일의 최적화 문제가 너무나 복잡해서, 해결책을 찾기 위해 고도로 전문화된 소프트웨어를 종종 사용한다.

11 정관사 ①

'1970년대에'라는 의미가 되려면 in the 1970s로 고치고, '1970년에'라는 의미면 in 1970로 고쳐야 한다. 이 경우에는 1970년 한 해만 가리킨다.

concept n. 개념 dissatisfied a. 불만이 있는 importation n. 수입

이 개념은 1970년대에, 식량 수입 증가와 그들의 지역사회의 농장과 농부들의 수 감소에 불만을 품은 네덜란드 여성들에 의해 개발되었다.

12 명사 ③

'~를 측정하기 위한'이나 '~의 측정을 위한'이라는 의미가 되려면 for 다음을 measuring이나 the measurement of로 바꾸어야 한다. 따라서 정답은 ③이다. measure는 명사라 해도 '치수, 척도, 수단, 조처'라는 의미이므로 부적절하다.

invention n. 발명, 발명품 micrometer n. 작은 길이 측정기, 마이크로미터 astronomical a. 천문학의

루이스 러더퍼드는 법률가로 교육을 받았고, 그의 발명품 중에는 천문 사진을 측정하기 위한 마이크로미터가 있었다.

13 논리완성 ③

순접의 접속사 and로 연결돼 있는 panegyrics와 같은 의미의 단어를 넣어야 한다. 따라서 정답은 '찬사'라는 뜻이 있는 ③이다.

sicken v. 역겹게 하다 panegyric n. 찬사, 칭찬 slander v. 중상[비방]하다 anecdote n. 일화 stipend n. 봉급, 급료 encomium n. 칭찬, 찬사 homily n. 설교, 훈계

그는 전에 그 사람을 비방하는데 앞장섰던 사람들이 그에게 칭찬과 찬사를 쏟아내는 것을 보고 역겨워졌다.

14 논리완성 ④

even though에 긍정적인 내용이 나와야 주절의 '왕의 저항이 오래가지 못했다'는 말이 논리적이게 된다. 그러므로 '가공할 만하다'는 의미의 redoubtable이 빈칸에 들어가야 한다.

inane a. 어리석은 germinal a. 미발달의, 새싹의 congenial a. 마음에 맞는 redoubtable a. 가공할 만한, 경외할 만한

왕은 가공할 만한 인간이었지만, 갑작스러운 공격은 왕을 놀라게 했고 왕의 저항은 오래가지 못했다.

15 논리완성 ①

앞에 '강요했다'는 단어가 나왔으므로 갈릴레오로서는 하기 싫은 일, 즉 자기 이론을 '철회하는' 일을 강제로 하게 했을 것이라 추론할 수 있다. 따라서 정답은 recant이다.

inquisition n. 종교재판 force v. 강요하다 recant v. 철회하다 retard v. 지연시키다 beautify v. 미화하다 buttress v. 지지하다, 받쳐주다

1633년, 로마 가톨릭교회의 종교재판소는 갈릴레오 갈릴레이로 하여금 지구가 태양 주위를 돈다는 그의 이론을 철회하도록 강요했다.

16 논리완성 ③

경제 용어로 cycle(주기)은 호황과 불황이 교호적으로 반복되는 것이므로, 불황 다음에는 불황의 반의어인 '호황'이 들어가야 한다. 따라서 정답은 expansion이다.

anomaly n. 변칙 obloquy n. 악평 expansion n. 호황 recession n. 불황 depression n. 불황

(경기) 주기는 경제가 불황에서 호황, 그리고 다시 불황으로 몇 년에 걸쳐서 옮겨가도록 만드는 광범위하고 다양한 요소를 포함한다.

수은은 온도계와 치아 충전재 등 무해한 용도가 다양하기 때문에, 수은이 지구상에서 가장 해로운 물질 중 하나라는 것을 아는 사람이 거의 없다.

17 논리완성 ①

independent filmmaker가 individual enterprise라고 했으므로 뒤의 corporatist structure와 반대가 되어야 한다. 따라서 '동떨어졌다'는 의미의 removed from이 정답이다.

prominence n. 명성; 탁월함 filmmaker n. 영화제작자 underscore v. 강조하다 outset n. 시초, 시작 corporatist n. 조합주의자, 기업식 synonymous a. 동의어의, 비슷한 removed from ~와 동떨어진 collaborated with ~와 협동한 associated with ~와 연관된 resulted from ~에서 초래된

이 시기에 독립 영화제작자들의 명성은 영화제작이 20세기 초에는 대개 개인 사업으로 남아있어, 1920년대 헐리우드 및 영화사 체제와 동의어가 된 기업식 영화 제작구조에서 동떨어져 있었다는 사실을 강조한다.

18 논리완성 ④

군대가 자체 차량이 충분치 않다고 했으므로 어떤 수송수단이건 '징발 했다'는 단어가 맞다. 따라서 정답은 commandeer이다.

adequate a. 충분한 vehicle n. 교통수단, 탈 것 armed forces 군대 abrogate v. 폐지하다 encumber v. 짐 지우다, 거추장스럽게 하다 rehabilitate v. 회복하다, 재활하다 commandeer v. 징발하다, 징용하다 transportation n. 운송[수송] 수단

허리케인 카트리나가 지나가고 며칠 후에, 충분한 자체 차량도 없이 뉴올리언스에 도착한 군대는 찾아낼 수 있는 온갖 형태의 수송수단을 모조리 징발하기 시작했다.

19 논리완성 ①

excessive irrigation과 salt accumulation으로 인해 토양이 어떻게 되어서 곡물 생산에서 보리로 바뀌어졌나를 생각하면 토양이 곡물에 '적합하지 않게' 되어서라고 할 수 있다. 따라서 정답은 inhospitable이다.

inhospitable a. 불친절한, (기후조건이) 유리하지 않은 acrimonious a. 말이 험악한, 신랄한 evanescent a. 덧없는 benignant a. 유익한, 다정한 contend v. 주장하다

일부 인류학자들은 고대 이집트인들이 과도한 관개와 염분 축적으로 인해 토양이 곡물에 적합하지 않게 되어버린 후에 곡물 생산에서 보리로 바꿨다고 주장한다.

20 논리완성 ②

수은의 용도가 긍정적인 것이라고 했으므로 수은에 대해 사람들이 잘 모르는 내용은 부정적인 내용이어야 한다. 따라서 innocuous와 반대로 '해로운'을 의미하는 단어 deleterious가 가장 적절하다.

innocuous a. 무해한 thermometer n. 온도계, 체온계 dental filling 치아 충전재 congenital a. 타고난, 선천적인 deleterious a. 해로운 antiquated a. 구식의 rudimentary a. 기초적인, 초보의, 미발달의

21 논리완성 ①

바로 앞에서 눈이 크고 둥글고 가운데 손가락이 길고 가늘다고 했고 그 것을 통해 음식을 찾을 수 있다고 했으므로 아이아이원숭이가 생존을 위해 환경에 맞게 '적응'했음을 알 수 있다.

designate v. 지정하다 reserve n. 보호구역 categorize v. 분류하다 order n. (생물분류) 목 Rodentia n. 쥐 aye-aye n. 아이아이원숭이(다람쥐원숭이) lemur n. 여우원숭이 primate n. 영장류 order n. <분류상의> 목(目) Daubento-niidae n. 아이아이과 retrieve v. 되찾다, 회수하다 grub n. 유충, 땅벌레, 음식 hollow a. 텅 빈 adaptation n. 적응 similitude n. 유사성 prototype n. 원형 nomenclature n. 명명법, 이름체계

마다가스카르 정부는 최근에 그 영토와 주변 섬들의 일부 구역을 야생동물 보호구역으로 지정했다. 마다가스카르는 아주 다양한 독특하고 이국적인 동물들의 서식처이다. 그런 동물 중 하나가 아이아이 원숭이다. 처음에는 쥐 목(目)의 구성원으로 분류되었던 아이아이 원숭이는 영장류 목(目)의 여우원숭이와 더 가깝다. 그러나 아이아이 원숭이는 동료 영장류와는 매우 다르기 때문에 자체 과(科)의 분류체계인 아이아이 과(科)를 따로 받았다. 아이아이원숭이는 아마도 크고 둥근 눈과 길고 아주 가느다란 가운데손가락으로 유명할 것이다. 이런 적응 상태는 아주 합리적이어서, 아이아이원숭이는 밤에 깨어나 주요 식량원들 중 하나인 벌레를 텅 빈 가지 속 깊은 곳에서 가져올 수 있다.

22 논리완성 ④

첫 번째 빈칸에는 전통주의자들이 인상파와 전쟁을 벌인다고 했으므로 규범을 '받아들이지 않는다'는 의미로 challenging이나 abandoning이 적절하고, 두 번째 빈칸에는 학계의 관점이 곧 전통적 관점이므로 인상파라는 새로운 사조는 그걸 따르는 데서 별 의미를 보지 못했다는 의미로 aligning이나 compromising이 적절하고, 마지막 빈칸에는 앞에서 인상주의자들이 학계의 전통주의자들의 견해와 타협하지 않는다고 했는데 사실은 오히려 타협하여 추종하는 것과 반대임을 밝히므로, 인상파 운동이 전통적인 공식 미술을 대체하거나 영향을 끼쳤다는 의미로 superseded나 influenced가 적절하다. 따라서 상기 조건을 모두 만족시키는 ④가 정답이다.

impressionism n. 인상파, 인상주의 firmly ad. 굳건히 feature n. 특징 fate n. 운명 accuse A of B A를 B라고 비난하다 norm n. 규범 undermine v. 기반을 약화시키다 highlight v. 부각시키다, 강조하다 shortcoming n. 단점 opponent n. 적, 상대 purchase n. 유리한 입장, 힘의 수단 gain entry to ~에 진입하다 align with ~에 맞추다 compromise with ~와 타협하다 supersede v. ~을 대신[대체]하다

1880년대 말과 1890년대 초 인상주의는 미술계에 굳건히 자리 잡은 특징이 되어 심지어 프랑스 밖에서도 잘 알려져 있었고 새로운 추종자들을 지속적으로 끌어들이고 있었다. 인상주의의 운명은 모든 현대 창작 개념의 운명이었다. 한편으로 전통주의자들은 인상파 운동과 계속 전쟁을 벌이면서, 인상파가 미학 규범을 버렸다고 비난했고, 가장 넓은 정치적 측면에서

는 기존 질서를 무너뜨렸다고 비난했다. 다른 한편으로 인상주의 자체도 그들 나름의 새로운 가치 척도를 가진 더 새로운 운동의 표적이 되었다. 어떤 양식이든 반드시 한쪽으로 치우쳐 있어서 적들이 그 양식의 단점을 부각시키기로 하면 적들에게 유리한 입장을 제공하기 마련이다. 인상주의 자들은 살롱 미술전에 진입하기 위해 학계의 견해와 타협하는 데서 더 이상 의미를 찾지 못했다. 사실은, 그 사이에 인상파 프로그램의 특정 측면들이 공식적 지지를 받고 있던 미술에 이미 영향을 끼치고 있었다.

23 논리완성 ③

첫 번째 빈칸은 그 다음 문장에서 체액이 과잉한 경우를 언급하므로 체액의 '불균형'이라고 해야 적절하고, 두 번째 빈칸은 몸에서 제거해야 할 것은 '해로운' 영향이므로 noxious가 적절하다.

consolidate v. 통합하다 comprehensive a. 포괄적인 four humours 4체액 in excess 과잉의, 너무 많은 prescribe v. 처방하다; 규정하다 accordingly ad. 그에 따라 bleeding n. 출혈, 방혈 purgative n. 설사약 diaphoretics n. 발한제 clyster n. 관장(灌腸) presumably ad. 아마도 robust a. 튼튼한, 건장한 constitution n. 체질 take A in one's stride A를 감당하다, 쉽게 해 치우다, 침착하게 대처하다

17세기 초의 의료 관행은 여전히 대체로 히포크라테스가 도입한 의학 체계에 기반을 두고 있었다. 이것은 2세기 때 갈레노스에 의해 이미 하나의 포괄적 치료 이론 체계로 통합되어 있었다. 당시에는 질병의 원인이 4체액의 불균형이라고들 생각했다. 의사들은 환자들을 검사해 어떤 체액이 과잉한지를 결정한 다음 그에 따라 처방을 했다. 치료 중 많은 것들에는 이 유독한 영향을 몸에서 제거하기 위해 방혈, 설사 유도, 발한, 관장이 포함되어 있었다. 용감무쌍한 이런 치료가 이미 약한 환자를 더 약하게 만드는 경우도 드물지 않았지만, 아마 더 튼튼한 체질인 사람들은 이런 약을 쉽게 감당해 냈을 것이다.

24 논리완성 ③

녹색 초목이 우주에서 보일 정도로 지구에 널리 '퍼져있다'는 의미이므로 첫 번째 빈칸은 pervasive가 적절하다. 한편, 태양의 가시광선을 흡수하고 반사하는 것은 가시광선 바깥의 적외선이거나 자외선일 것인데, Red Edge라 했으므로 '적외선의'라는 뜻의 infrared가 두 번째 빈칸에 적절하다.

microbe n. 미생물 take root on 뿌리 내리다 terrestrial a. 지상의 photosynthesis n. 광합성 biomass n. 생물량 resplendent a. 멋진, 찬란한, 눈부신 robe n. 망토 lugubrious a. 음울한 clairvoyant a. 예지력이 있는, 관통하는 눈을 지닌 pervasive a. 팽배한, 스며든 indigenous a. 토착의 embellish v. 장식하다 infrared a. 적외선의 isotopic a. 동위원소의 vegetation n. 초목 visible radiation 가시광선 reflect v. 반사하다 absorb v. 흡수하다 wing v. 날아가다 detect v. 발견하다, 감지하다, 찾아내다 train v. ~쪽으로 돌리다, 조준하다 Red Edge 레드에지(전자기 스펙트럼의 근적외선 범위에서 식생의 반사율이 빠르게 변화하는 영역)

미생물은 아마 지구 역사상 초창기에 땅에 뿌리를 내렸겠지만, 복잡한 육지 생태계에 식량 및 물질 구조를 제공함으로써 세상을 바꾸어놓은 것은 식물이다. 오늘날 약 40만 종의 육상식물이 지구 광합성의 절반을 차지하고, 우리 지구의 총 생물량의 80프로를 차지하는 것으로 추정된다. 사실,

지구의 찬란한 녹색 옷은 지구에 너무나 널리 퍼져있는 특징이어서 우주에서도 감지할 수 있다. 1990년, 미항공우주국의 갈릴레오 우주선이 목성으로 날아갈 때, 우주선은 그것의 기계 눈(센서)을 멀리 있는 지구 쪽으로 돌려, 소위 초목 레드에지의 특이한 봉우리를 지구의 반사된 빛 속에서 드러내 보여주었다. 이러한 특징적 현상이 발생하는 이유는 육지의 초목이 들어오는 태양 가시광선은 강하게 흡수하지만 적외선 파장은 우주로 반사하기 때문이다. 초창기 지구를 방문한 자들이 있었더라면 이런 특징을 전혀 보지 못했을 것이다.

25 논리완성 ②

새로운 정보를 '받아들인다'는 의미로 take in이 들어가야 개념을 grasp하기(이해하기) 쉽다는 말이 논리적으로 잘 이어진다. 따라서 정답은 ②이다.

evident a. 분명한, 눈에 띄는 terminology n. 전문용어 take in 받아들이다, 흡수하다 hand in 전하다, 건네다 give in 굴복하다 barge in 불쑥 들어가다, 끼어들다 abstract a. 추상적인 grasp v. 파악하다, 이해하다 figurative speech 비유적 표현 metaphor n. 은유(비유의 일종)

언어의 중요성은 이름과 전문용어를 보면 분명해지는데, 이름과 전문용어는 놀라울 만큼 강력한 의미를 전달한다. 예를 들어, 최근 연구에 따르면 건강상의 위험을 기술하는 데 쓰이는 언어는 사람들의 기억에 영향을 끼치고 인식을 위험에 빠뜨릴 수 있다. 게다가 우리가 선택하는 단어들은 우리의 말을 듣는 사람들이 새로운 정보를 얼마나 잘 받아들이느냐에도 영향을 끼칠 수 있다. 예를 들어, 비유표현과 은유의 사용은 추상적인 개념들을 이해하기 더 쉽게 만들어 줄 수 있다.

26 논리완성 ④

물이 아가미로 들어가 혈류 속으로 '퍼져 들어간다'는 의미로 첫 번째 빈칸에는 diffused into가 적절하다. 그리고 삼투압은 농도가 낮은 쪽에서 높은 쪽으로 물이 옮겨가는 현상이어서 염도나 낮은 물고기 몸속의 물이 몸 밖으로 빠져나가 탈수가 심해지니 물을 '잃는다'는 뜻이므로 두 번째 빈칸은 losing이 적절하다. 따라서 정답은 ④이다.

gill n. 아가미 scale n. 비늘 salinity n. 염도 excrete v. 배출하다, 분비하다 osmosis n. 삼투현상 infiltrate v. 침투하다 inhale v. 들이마시다 enliven v. 활기를 주다 diffuse v. 퍼져나가다, 확산되다 ensure v. 보장하다 urinate v. 소변보다 make up for ~을 벌충하다

바닷물고기는 아가미를 통해 물을 마시며, 아가미에서 물이 혈류 속으로 퍼져 들어간다. 바닷물은 염분이 높기 때문에 바닷물고기는 몸속에 지나치게 많은 소금이 있을 위험이 있다. 이런 문제를 극복하는 방법은 아가미와 비늘 속의 특수 세포를 이용하는 것이다. 이 세포들은 과잉 염분을 배출시키는 역할을 한다. 바닷물고기가 마주하는 또 하나의 중요한 어려움은 물고기의 탈수가 쉽게 일어난다는 것이다. 물고기를 둘러싼 바닷물의 상대적인 염도는 물고기 몸속의 물보다 훨씬 높아서 물고기는 삼투현상 — 물이 밀도가 낮은 곳에서 높은 곳으로 자연스레 가는 과정 — 을 통해 물을 계속 잃는다. 이것을 벌충하기 위해 바닷물고기는 소변 횟수가 극히 적고 소변 농도도 매우 높다.

27 단락배열 ④

첫 문단에 let him look at the stars라고 한 후에 ⒸBthose heavenly worlds(=stars)가 이어지고, 별을 경외와 경탄의 대상으로 보는 Ⓒ의 취지가 Ⓐ의 첫 문장으로 이어지고, Ⓐ의 나머지 부분에서 언급된 자연관을 Ⓑ의 첫 문장의 When절이 받아서 설명해나가는 순서로 배열되는 것이 가장 적절하다. 따라서 정답은 ④이다.

solitude n. 고독 retire v. 물러나다 chamber n. 방 reverence n. 경탄, 존경 inaccessible a. 접근 불가능한 delight v. 기쁨을 주다 poetical a. 시적인 manifold a. 여러 가지의 wood-cutter n. 나무꾼 integrate v. 통합하다 warranty-deed n. 보증서 adore v. 흠모하다, 사모하다 admonish v. 훈계하다, 충고하다, 책망하다 property n. 소유지 title n. 자격, 권리

고독 속으로 들어가려면, 사회로부터 물러나는 만큼 자기 방으로부터도 물러나야 한다. 책을 읽고 쓰는 동안은 아무도 나와 함께 있지 않아도 나는 고독하지 않다. 하지만 인간이 고독해지려고 한다면, 그로 하여금 별을 보게 하라.
Ⓒ 저 하늘에서 오는 빛은 그와 그가 만지는 것 사이를 갈라놓는다. 대기가 이런 설계로 투명하게 된 것은 숭고함의 영원한 존재를 저 천체들 속에서 인간에게 제시하기 위함이라고 생각할 수도 있겠다. 도시의 거리에서 보이는 저 하늘의 별들은 얼마나 크고 위대한가! 별들이 앞으로 수천 년 후 어느 날 밤 나타난다면 인간들은 어떻게 믿고 경탄하며, 우리에게 보여주었던 신의 도시에 대한 기억을 수 세대 동안 보존할까! 그러나 이 미(美)의 사절들(별들)은 매일 밤 나타나 훈계하는 미소로 우주를 밝힌다.
Ⓐ 별들은 경외감을 일깨운다. 늘 거기 존재하지만 접근할 수 없기 때문이다. 그러나 모든 자연물은 인간의 마음이 자연물의 영향에 열려있을 때 이와 비슷한 인상을 준다. 자연은 절대로 하찮을 수 없는 외양을 띠고 있지 않다. 아무리 지혜로운 사람도 자연의 비밀을 캐내지는 못하고, 자연의 완벽함을 모두 알아내어 호기심을 잃게 되지는 않는다. 자연은 지혜로운 영혼을 지닌 자에게는 절대로 장난감이 되지 않는다. 꽃과 동물과 산은 그의 소박한 어린 시절을 즐겁게 해주었던 만큼 그의 전성기의 지혜를 반영하기도 했다.
Ⓑ 자연에 대해 이런 식으로 말할 때 우리는 마음속에 독특하지만 가장 시적인 감각을 가진다. 이 감각은 다면적인 자연물이 만들어내는 온전한 인상을 의미한다. 나무꾼의 목재 막대기를 시인의 나무와 구별해주는 것이 바로 이것이다. 오늘 아침에 내가 본 매력적인 풍경은 약 20개 내지 30개 농장들로 구성되어 있다. 밀러는 이 들판을, 로크는 저 들판을, 그리고 매닝은 그 너머의 숲을, 소유하고 있다. 그러나 이들 중 누구도 풍경을 소유하지는 못한다. 그 모든 부분들을 통합할 수 있는 눈을 가진 사람, 즉 시인 외에는 아무도 갖지 못하는 소유지(풍경)가 지평선 안에 있다. 이것이 이 사람들의 농장들의 가장 좋은 부분이지만, 그들이 땅 문서를 가졌다고 해서 이것을 가질 자격이 있는 것은 아니다.

28 내용추론 ③

서울이 서쪽에 있고 워싱턴DC가 동쪽에 있으므로 서울에서 워싱턴DC로 가면 비행기가 서쪽에서 동쪽으로 흐르는 제트기류를 타고 가게 되므로, 반대 방향으로 가서 바람의 저항을 받을 경우보다 비행기 속도가 더 빨라질 수 있다. 따라서 정답은 ③이다. ① 제트기류의 평균 속도가 150mph이고 가장 높을 때가 400mph라고 했으므로 둘을 더해서 평균을 내는 방법은 옳지 않다. ④ 융프라우는 산봉우리로 인터라켄 마을

과 마찬가지로 지상이며 해발 고도의 차이가 약 12000피트일 뿐이다. 따라서 대류권인 하늘로 1000피트 올라갈 때마다 약 3.5도씩 기온이 낮아지므로 3.5도×12=42도라는 계산은 여기에 적용할 수 없다.

next to 옆에 있는 extend v. 뻗다, 넓히다, 확장되다, 연장되다 troposphere n. 대류권 make up 구성하다, 차지하다 solar radiation 태양 복사선 absorb v. 흡수하다 striking a. 놀라운 upper layer 상층부 rapid a. 빠른, 신속한 jet stream 제트기류 velocity n. 속도 considerable a. 상당한 significance n. 의미, 의의 mph n. 시속 마일(단위)

땅 바로 위의 공기층은 10마일 가량 위로 뻗어있는데 대류권이라 알려져 있다. 전체적으로 대류권은 대기 무게의 약 75%를 차지한다. 대류권은 대기 중에서 가장 따뜻한 부분이다. 태양복사의 대부분이 땅 표면에 의해 흡수되어 바로 위의 공기를 덥히기 때문이다. 높이가 올라갈 때마다 꾸준히 기온이 감소하는 현상은 대류권의 매우 놀라운 특징이다. 대류권의 상층부가 기온이 더 낮은 이유는 지표면에서 멀어지기 때문이기도 하고 열이 우주로 빨리 방출되기 때문이기도 하다. 대류권 내의 기온은 고도가 1000피트 상승할 때마다 약 3.5도씩 낮아진다. 대류권 내에서 바람과 기류는 열과 습기를 분포시킨다. 제트기류라 불리는 강력한 바람은 대류권 상층부에 위치해있다. 이 제트기류는 발생 양상이 복잡하고 광범위하다. 제트기류는 대개 파도 모양의 패턴을 보이며 서쪽에서 동쪽으로 시속 150마일의 속도로 움직이지만 시속 400마일 정도의 속도까지도 발견된 적이 있다. 제트기류의 변하는 위치와 강도가 기후 조건과 패턴에 끼치는 영향은 분명 상당하다. 현재 이루어지는 집중 연구는 결국 제트기류의 진정한 중요성을 밝혀줄 것이다.

위 글을 통해 추론할 수 있는 것으로 가장 적합한 것을 고르시오.
① 평균적으로 대류권 내의 제트기류의 속도는 시속 약 275마일이다.
② 대기는 대류권 위쪽의 25% 구역보다 75%구역이 땅과 가깝기 때문에 농도가 더 짙다.
③ 제트기는 서울에서 워싱턴DC로 갈 때 그 반대로 갈 때보다 대개 더 빠른 속도로 가게 될 것이다.
④ 스위스 인터라켄 마을에서 약 12000 피트 위에 있는 융프라우 꼭대기의 기온은 지면보다 대개 42도 더 낮다.

29-30

20세기는 물리학과 전자공학과 커뮤니케이션의 세기였지만 앞으로 올 세기는 주로 나노기술뿐 아니라 20세기 후반에 이미 시작된 생물학 혁명에 의해 지배받는다고 간주된다. 그것은 아주 미세한 나노미터 규모의 조립과 장치를 다루는 흥미진진한 새로운 전선이다. 전통적으로 소형화는 기존 기술의 지속적인 개선으로 장치들이 점점 더 작아지는 과정이었다. 그러나 우리는 전통적인 하향식 조립 도구를 사용하는 소형화의 한계에 급속히 다가가고 있다. 아주 작은 기계를 만드는 미래 지향적인 핵심 방법 중 하나는 기계를 분자 수준에서 쌓아올리는 것일 것이다. 그 목적을 위해, 모든 생체 시스템 각각에서 발생하는 배열과 같은 나노 규모 기계의 배열에 관해 많은 내용을 알아낼 수 있다. 생체 세포는 실제로 미래적인 나노기술의 제시에서 종종 묘사되는 것과 같은 진정한 기능적인 분자 기계가 발견될 수 있는 유일한 장소이다. 분자 모터, 초고감도 나노 규모 센서, DNA 복제 기계, 단백질 합성 기계, 그리고 다른 많은 소형 장치는 30억년도 더 전에 진화한 아주 단순한 초창기 박테리아 이전의 세포에서조차도 존재한다. 진화의 나무를 더 높이 올라가면 물론 나노기계는 더 정교하고 강력해진다. 그러나 생명체가 출현하고 수십억 년이 지나고 나서야 비로소 우리는 인식과 조립 개념을 활용하기 시작해 우리의 기술적 필요를 위해 나노 규모의 기계를 만들 것이다. 다른 한편으로, 비생물학적인 체계를

위해 개발된 나노 기술의 많은 원리와 응용들은 조직공학을 위한 첨단 센서와 분자 스캐폴드 같은 당장의 생물학 응용들뿐 아니라 단백질 및 DNA 층위에서의 원상태 변형 같은 장기적 전망에도 매우 유용할 수 있다. 나노생명기술과 생명나노기술 분야는 아주 새로운 분야지만, 이들의 가능성은 어마어마하다. 생명기술과 나노기술 간의 결합은 의학의 극적인 진보를 초래할 수 있다. 의학은 당연히 현재의 많은 질환이 근절될 장소가 될 것이다. 합리적인 기간 내에 암과 에이즈는 지금의 소아마비와 결핵처럼 간주될 것이다. 유전자 결함은 출산 전부터 이미 알아내서 고칠 수 있을 것이다. 우리 몸속에 삽입된 나노 규모의 로봇은 뇌수술 같은 아주 복잡한 수술도 실행할 수 있을 것이다.

physics n. 물리학 electronics n. 전자공학 dominate v. 지배하다 front n. 전선 minuscule a. 아주 작은, 초소형의 assembly n. 조립 miniaturization n. 소형화 top-down a. 하향식의 fabrication n. 제작, 조립, 만들기 molecular a. 분자의 futuristic a. 초현대식의, 미래지향적인 ultrasensitive a. 초고감도의 sensor n. 감지기, 센서 sophisticated a. 정교한 utilize v. 활용하다 eradicate v. 근절하다, 없애다 insert v. 삽입하다

29 빈칸완성 ③

The living cell is actually the only place in which genuine functional molecular machines could actually be found라는 내용을 통해, 기계를 이제 세포보다 더 작은 분자 층위에서 만든다는 것을 알 수 있다.

빈칸에 들어가기에 가장 적합한 것을 고르시오.
① 박테리아 층위
② 물리적 층위
③ 분자 층위
④ 원자 층위

30 내용추론 ②

나노생명기술로 암과 에이즈를 근절할 수 있을 것이라 했으므로 ②는 옳지 않은 진술이다.

위 글을 통해 추론할 수 없는 것을 고르시오.
① 21세기는 생물학 혁명과 나노기술, 즉 전통 과학으로부터의 변화에 지배를 받는다.
② 나노생명기술은 소아마비와 결핵을 치료했던 것처럼 암과 에이즈 같은 질병을 치료하겠다고 거의 약속해주지 못한다.
③ 소형화는 한계에 접근하고 있으며, 미래 기술은 나노 규모 기계개발에 집중하고 있다.
④ 나노 규모 로봇과 기계는 의료 기술을 혁명적으로 바꾸어 복잡한 수술과 세포 수준의 조종도 실행할 수 있다.

31-32

볼티모어에서는 마약 중독자가 많은 다른 많은 지역사회와 마찬가지로 일주일 특정 시간대에 도심 동네의 특정 길거리 모퉁이로 깨끗한 주사기 수천 개를 실은 밴이 보내진다. 중독자들이 더러운 헌 바늘을 건네주고 대신 깨끗한 주사바늘을 무료로 받을 수 있게 하려는 생각에서이다. 원칙

상 바늘 교체는 에이즈와 싸우는 좋은 방안처럼 들린다. HIV로 감염된 낡은 바늘을 재사용하는 탓에 바이러스가 널리 퍼지기 때문이다. 그러나 최소한 얼핏만 봐도 바늘 교체는 한계가 명백하다. 우선 먼저, 중독자들은 가장 계획성 있고 믿을 만한 사람들이 되지 못한다. 그러니까 이들이 바늘실은 밴을 규칙적으로 <침입할> 수 있을 것이라고 어떻게 장담하겠는가? 두 번째로, 대부분의 헤로인 중독자들은 하루에 대략 바늘 하나로 바늘 끝이 무뎌져 쓸모없어질 때까지 적어도 5-6회 — 더 많이는 아니라 해도 — 주사를 놓는다. 이들에게는 바늘이 많이 필요하다는 말이다. 일주일에 한 번 오는 밴 한 대가 하루 종일 주사를 맞는 중독자들의 필요를 어떻게 충족시킨단 말인가? 밴이 화요일에 오는데 토요일 밤에 이미 중독자의 주사기가 다되었다면? 바늘 프로그램이 얼마나 효과를 내는지 분석하기 위해, 존스홉킨스 병원 연구자들은 바늘을 제출하는 사람들과 이야기하기 위해 차를 타고 밴과 함께 가기 시작했다.

addict n. 중독자 stock v. ~을 갖추다 syringe n. 주사기 hand over 주다, 건네다 free a. 무료의 in return 보상으로, 보답으로, 교환해서 reuse n. 재사용 needle n. 바늘 be responsible for ~을 일으키다 limitation n. 한계 organized a. 짜임새 있는 around the clock 24시간, 하루종일 run out 다하다, 끝나다, 무일푼이 되다 hand in 제출하다

31 빈칸완성 ②

바늘을 5-6회 써서 끝이 무디어지면 쓸모없어진다. 따라서 정답은 useless이다.

빈칸에 들어가기에 가장 적합한 것을 고르시오.
① 효과적인
② 쓸모없는
③ 정제된
④ 무거운

32 글의 흐름상 적절하지 않은 표현 고르기 ③

밴이 와서 중독자들에게 바늘(주사기)을 무료로 나누어주는데, 나누어주는 사람들은 중독자가 와서 밴을 만나기를 바란다. 그런데 break into는 허락 없이 침입한다는 의미이므로 문맥상 적합하지 않다. 따라서 ③을 '만나다'라는 뜻의 meet up with로 고쳐야 한다.

33-34

미국의 정신건강 운동은 상당한 계몽의 기간으로 시작되었다. 도로시아 딕스는 정신질환자들이 감옥과 빈민구호소에 있는 것을 보고 충격을 받아, 정신병자 보호시설 설립 운동을 벌였는데, 그 시설은 사람들이 병원과 같은 환경에서 인간다운 치료와 돌봄을 받고 온전한 정신 상태로 돌아가도록 도움을 받을 수 있는 곳이었다. 1800년대 중반에는 이미 20개의 주가 정신병자 보호시설을 설립했다. 그러나 1800년대 말과 1900년대 초, 불황에 직면한 입법부들은 양질의 치료를 위한 충분한 지원금의 지출을 승인해줄 수 없었다. 정신병자 보호시설들은 과도하게 붐비어 감옥 같게 되었다. 게다가 환자들은 정신건강 분야의 선구자들이 예상했던 것보다 더 치료에 저항했고, 그래서 환자들과 또 다른 사람들을 보호하기 위한 안전조치와 제약이 필요했다. 정신병원들은 환자들의 권리가 거의 망각된 끔찍하고 우울한 장소가 되어버렸다.
이런 상태는 제2차 세계대전 이후까지 지속되었다. 당시, 이제껏 불치라

간주되던 일부 중증 정신질환을 치료할 새 치료법(뇌의 매독에는 페니실린, 조현병과 우울증에는 인슐린 치료)이 발견되었고, 연이은 책과 영화와 신문 폭로기사들이 정신병 환자들의 고통에 주의를 환기시켰다. 개선이 이루어졌고 데이비드 베일 박사의 인도주의 치료 프로그램은 오늘날을 위한 봉홧불이 되었다. 그러나 변화는 1960년대 초까지 느리게 진행되었다. 당시 민권운동은 변호사들로 하여금 미국의 교도소를 조사하도록 만들었는데, 당시 교도소에는 흑인들이 지나치게 많았다. 변호사들은 또한 재소자들을 따라 교도소보다 더 지독한 유일한 기관, 즉 정신질환 범죄자들을 위한 병원까지 가게 되었다. 교도소는 분노한 청년들로 가득 차 있었고, 이들은 법적 지원에 독려를 받아 재빨리 자신의 권리를 요구했다. <반면, 정신질환 범죄자들을 위한 병원에는 "미쳤다"고 간주되었던 사람들, 그리고 대개 심한 신체적 속박과 대량의 진정제 사용을 통해 순종적으로 갇혀 있는 사람들이 수용되어 있었다.> 젊은 공익변호사 집단은 정신병원에서 자신들이 맡은 역할을 좋아했다. 변호사들은 수동적이면서 변호하기 쉬운 인구집단을 발견했다. 이들은 결국 범죄자들과는 달리 아무 잘못도 저지르지 않은 사람들이었다. 그리고 많은 주에서 이들은 끔찍한 기관에 갇혀 있었는데, 이것은 일단 폭로되면 대중에게, 특히 사법부의 양심에, 충격을 줄 수밖에 없는 불의였다. 환자들의 권리 단체는 주 의회에서 로비를 하여 개혁을 성공적으로 독려했다.

사법부의 개입은 몇몇 확실한 긍정적인 영향을 끼쳤지만 법원이 양질의 환자 치료를 보장하는 표준과 평가 메커니즘을 제공할 수 없다는 인식이 늘고 있다. 일상의 돌봄을 제공하는 것에 대한 세부사항은 결코 법원이 명령할 수는 없기 때문에, 이제는 정신 건강 돌봄과 치료를 실행할 책임과 환자의 권리를 보장할 책임을 법원으로부터 거두어 원래 그 명령을 위임받은 정신 건강 담당 주 행정가들에게 돌려줄 때이다.

enlightenment n. 계몽 shock v. 충격을 주다 jail n. 교도소 almshouse n. 빈민구제소 crusade v. 운동을 벌이다 restore v. 회복시키다 sanity n. 멀쩡한 정신상태 asylum n. 정신병원 legislature n. 입법부 appropriate v. (의회가) ~의 지출을 승인하다 fund n. 자금 decent a. 적정한, 양질의 overcrowded a. 과도하게 붐비는 resistant a. 저항하는 pioneer n. 선구자 restraint n. 속박, 제약 frightening a. 끔찍한 beacon n. 봉홧불 disproportionately ad. 과도하게 injustice n. 불평등; 부당함 mandate v. 명령[지시]하다 n. 명령, 지시 administrator n. 행정가

---

33 문장삽입 ③

주어진 문장 안의 대조를 나타내는 by contrast로 보아 앞에는 교도소, 뒤에는 정신질환 범죄자 병원에 대한 내용이 있어야 한다. 따라서 적절한 자리는 ⓒ이다.

---

34 글의 제목 ①

이 글은 첫 단락에서는 감옥과 빈민구호소의 정신질환자들을 위한 정신병자 보호시설 설립 운동의 전개와 그런 시설들이 처한 열악한 상황과 느린 상황 개선을 설명했고, 두 번째 단락에서 1960년대 민권운동이 시작된 후 교도소와 정신질환 범죄자 시설에 수용된 환자들의 끔찍한 상황이 주목을 받고 그들의 치료와 처우에 대한 개혁이 본격적으로 진행되어 왔음을 설명했고, 세 번째 단락에서 현재 문제되고 있는 사법부 개입 문제에 대해 설명하므로 ① '교정 시설에서의 정신건강 치료의 발달'이 제목으로 적절하다. '발달'이 역사적 시대 과정에 따라 개선되어온 것을 의

미한다. ② 첫 단락이 제외되어 부적절하다. ③ 이 글에서는 공동체의 이익이 아니라 환자 개인의 권리와 인권과 복지가 주로 문제되고 있다.

위 글의 제목으로 가장 적합한 것을 고르시오.
① 교정 시설에서의 정신건강 치료의 발달
② 민권운동 후의 정신병자 보호시설 개혁
③ 공동체의 이익을 위한 정신질환자들의 장기적 치료
④ 정신병원 개선에서 사법부 개입이 하는 역할

35-36

1829년 무렵, 라이엘은 그를 평생 사로잡게 될 생각을 공식화하기 시작했다. 현재 존재하는 자연력은 모든 지질학적 사건을 설명할 수 있으며, 따라서 지질학적 과거의 격변은 필요가 전혀 없다는 생각이었다. 1811년에는 퀴비에와 브롱냐르가 파리 분지의 퇴적층과 화석에 대한 중요한 연구서를 앞서 출간했다. 이들은 민물의 조가비와 바닷물의 조가비가 교대로 나타났다고 보았고, 따라서 이들은 이것을 지구 역사의 급격한 변화 탓으로 해석했다. 그러나 라이엘은 이 패턴 또한 민물과 해양 환경 사이의 느린 교대 때문이라고 생각했다. 그는 자신이 과거에 연구했던 현재의 스코틀랜드 호수 퇴적층과, 옛 파리 퇴적층 간에 유사성이 있다고 보았기 때문에 지구의 혁명적 변화를 끌어들일 필요가 없다고 생각했다. 이탈리아의 화산지대로 그가 탐사를 갔던 일도 같은 결론이 났다.

라이엘은 1825년부터 1827년까지 법률가로 일했지만 시력이 나빠져서 다른 경력이 필요해졌고 그 때 그는 지질학을 선택했다. 그는 1826년 지질학회의 회원으로 선출되었다. 1828년에는 머친슨과 함께 프랑스 남중부에 있는 오베르뉴 화산지대를 방문했다. 1831년 그는 킹스칼리지 런던의 교수로 임명됐고 거기서 지질학을 강의했지만 오래 거기 있지는 않았다. 그의 관심은 지질학에 대한 책 출간으로 옮겨갔다. 아마 학계보다 재정적으로 이득이 더 되리라는 생각 때문이었을 것이다. 그는 그의 가장 중요한 저작 『지질학 원리』의 첫판을 세 권짜리로 1830년과 1833년 사이에 출간했다. 『지질학 원리』는 일반 대중 사이에서도 인기를 끌었고 12판을 찍었다(마지막 판은 사후에 나왔다).

라이엘에게는, 현재 작용하는 원인이 과거의 사건을 설명할 수 있었고, 뿐만 아니라, 그는 과거 사건들의 강도가 오늘날과 똑같다는 받아들이기 어려운 주장을 했다. 이 탓에 그의 책은 꽤 논란거리가 되었다. 특히 세지윅과 코니베어 같은 지각 격변설 주장자들에게 그랬다. 라이엘은 또한 지구가 장기적 냉각을 겪었다는 점도 받아들이지 않았다. 냉각 가설은 자신의 자연 가설의 불변성을 무효로 돌릴 것이기 때문이었다. 영국의 물리학자였던 켈빈 경은 라이엘의 견해가 열역학 제2법칙을 위반한 것이라고 반복해서 지적했다.

찰스 다윈과 라이엘은 좋은 친구가 되었다. "결혼 전과 후에 나는 다른 그 어떤 사람을 만난 것보다 라이엘을 더 많이 만났다. 그의 정신은 내가 보기에는 명료함, 신중함, 건전한 판단력과 독창성을 특징으로 하고 있었다." 라이엘은 다윈의 산호초에 대한 새 이론을 환영했지만 『종의 기원(1859년)』에 들어 있는 자연선택설에 대해서는 열의가 훨씬 덜했다. 라이엘이 보기에 종의 진화는 자신의 반복적인 순환적 접근법과 자연의 불변성 개념과 일치하지 않는 점진적 경로를 암시했기 때문이다.

formulate v. 공식화하다 occupy v. 점령하다, 사로잡다 namely ad. 즉 geological a. 지질학적 catastrophe n. 재난, 격변 sediment n. 퇴적층 fossil n. 화석 basin n. 분지 shell n. 조가비 marine a. 바다의, 해양의 invoke v. 적용하다, 들먹이다, 언급하다 volcanic region 화산지대 financial a. 재정의, 금융의 gain n. 이득 academia n. 학계 undergo v. 겪다, 경험하다 controversial a. 논란이 되는 thermodynamics n. 열역학 caution n. 신중함 enthusiastic a. 열의

가 있는 progressive a. 점진적인 inconsistent a. ~와 일치하지 않는 repetitive a. 반복적인, 되풀이하는 cyclic a. 순환적인, 주기적인, 순환하는 uniformity n. 획일성, 균질성

35 빈칸완성 ②

라이엘은 지구의 표면이 과거나 현재나 같으며 격변에 의해 지각이 형성된 게 아니라고 생각했다. 따라서 빈칸에는 ②가 들어가야 한다.

빈칸에 들어가기에 가장 적합한 것을 고르시오.
① 그는 지구의 대격변들이 지구 표면의 형성에 중대한 역할을 했다고 생각했다.
② 그는 그것들의 강도가 오늘날과 같다는 받아들이기 어려운 주장을 했다.
③ 그는 지각 과정을 지배하는 법칙들이 지구의 역사 동안 변했다고 굳게 믿었다.
④ 그는 지구가 대개 급격하고 짧고 격렬한 사건들로 형성되었다고 주장했다.

36 내용일치 ④

라이엘은 다윈과 가까운 친구였고 그의 산호초 이론에 동의했지만 자연선택설은 반대했다. 따라서 ④가 틀린 내용이다. ② 자연력은 모든 지질학적 사건을 설명할 수 있고 지질학적 과거의 격변은 필요가 전혀 없다고 했는데, '느리고 지속적인 자연력'은 격변 없이 작용하는 자연력과 같은 뜻이다.

위 글의 내용과 일치하지 않는 것을 고르시오.
① 과거 및 현재의 불변의 자연력에 대한 라이엘의 관점은 대격변론자들과 충돌했고 열역학 법칙도 위반했다.
② 라이엘은 느리고 지속적인 자연력으로 지구의 지질학 역사를 설명할 수 있다고 주장했다.
③ 라이엘은 원래 변호사였는데 유명한 지질학자가 되어 『지질학 원리』를 저술했다.
④ 다윈과 라이엘은 가까운 사이였다. 라이엘은 다윈의 산호초 이론에 감탄했고 그의 자연선택설에 동의했다.

37-38

간단해 보이지만 간단하지 않은 질문을 던져보자. 인공지능이란 무엇인가? 거리에서 보통 사람에게 이 질문을 던지면 사람들은 아마 애플의 시리, 아마존의 클라우드 서비스, 테슬라의 자동차 혹은 구글의 검색 알고리즘을 언급할지도 모른다. 딥 러닝 전문가들에게 물어보면 이들은 신경망이 어떻게 수십 개 층으로 조직되어 분류된 데이터를 받고 가중치와 기준치를 할당받아, 아직은 온전히 설명할 수 없는 방식으로 데이터를 분류하는지에 관해 전문적인 대답을 해줄 수도 있다. A 1978년 전문 시스템을 논하면서 도널드 미치 교수는 인공지능을 지식 정제라고 기술했다. 이렇게 인공지능이 정제한 지식에서는 "컴퓨터의 도움을 받지 않은 인간 전문가가 여태껏 성취했거나 앞으로 성취할 수 있는 가장 높은 수준을 훨씬 뛰어넘는 코드화의 신뢰성과 능력이 생산된다." 이 주제에 대한 가장 인기 있는 교과서 중 하나에서 스튜어트 러셀과 피터 노빙은 인공지능이 지능 실체를 이해하고 구축하려는 시도라고 말한다. "지능은 주로 합리적 행동에 관한 것이다."라는 게 그들의 주장이다. "이상

적으로, 지능이라는 행위주체는 특정 상황에서 가능한 최상의 행동을 취한다."라는 것이다.
B 인공지능과 관련 알고리즘 시스템을 교육 및 보건, 재정, 정부 운영, 직장 교류와 고용, 소통체계, 그리고 사법체제 같은 사회 제도의 의사결정 체제에 포함시킬 때 거기서 초래되는 사회적 물질적 결과는 무엇일까? 코드와 알고리즘, 혹은 컴퓨터 비전의 최신 사고, 혹은 자연 언어 처리나 강화 학습에 대한 수많은 쟁점들이 있다.
C 인공지능을 정의하는 각 방식은 정의 작업을 하면서, 인공지능이 앞으로 이해되고 측정되고 가치가 매겨지고 통치될 방식의 틀을 마련하고 있다. 만일 인공지능이 기업 인프라를 위한 소비자 브랜드에 의해 정의된다면 마케팅과 광고가 그 지평을 결정한다. 만일 인공지능이 어떤 인간 전문가보다 더 믿을 만하거나 합리적이며 "가능한 최상의 행위"를 할 수 있다고 간주된다면 이는 인공지능이 건강과 교육과 사법제도에서 중대한 이해관계가 걸린 결정을 내리도록 신뢰를 받아야 한다는 뜻이다.
D 구체적 알고리즘 기술이 (인공지능 정의의) 유일한 초점일 경우, 이는 오직 지속적인 기술적 진보만이 중요하며, 그 접근법의 전산상의 비용과 이들이 그 영향 하의 지구에 끼칠 지대한 영향은 전혀 고려하지 않는다는 뜻이다.

deceptively ad. 혹할 정도로 technical a. 전문적인 neural net 신경망 layer n. 층위 labeled a. 라벨이 붙은, 분류된 assign v. 할당하다 refining n. 정제 reliability n. 신뢰성 competence n. 역량, 능력 surpass v. 능가하다, 초과하다 unaided a. 도움 받지 않은 entity n. 실체, 존재 consequence n. 결과 decision-making n. 의사결정 reinforcement n. 강화 far-reaching a. 지대한 영향을 끼칠

37 글의 흐름상 적절하지 않은 단락 고르기 ②

위 글의 전체 주제는 인공지능을 정의하는 다양한 방법들인데, B는 인공지능을 사회 운영에 통합시켰을 때의 결과를 논하므로 전체 주제와 논리적으로 맞지 않다.

38 글의 주제 ②

문단별로 정리를 하면 인공지능을 정의하는 다양한 내용이 나온다. 따라서 정답은 ②이다.

위 글의 주제로 가장 적합한 것을 고르시오.
① 인공지능의 합리적 지적 행동에 초점을 맞추는 주된 이유
② 인공지능을 지적 시스템으로 정의하고 이해하는 다양한 방법들
③ 인공지능 시스템 관리에서 인간 전문가의 중요성
④ 인공지능이 내리는 중대한 결정에 대한 계산의 영향

39-40

생물학 분야 내에서 오랫동안 견지해온 믿음은 우리의 DNA가 고정되어 있고 불변이라는 것이다. 환경 요인은 우리의 몸무게를 늘리거나 팔다리를 잃게 만들거나 바이러스에 감염되게 만들 수 있지만 우리의 근본적인 유전자 배열은 일정하리라는 것이다. 그러나 과학자들 사이의 이러한 지배적 견해는 인간 유전체에 대한 더 유동적인 정의 쪽으로 바뀌기 시작하고 있다. 유전학 내의 새로운 하위분야인 후성유전학이 환경 요인이 우리 생애 동안 유전자 코드의 표현을 실제로 어떻게 바꾸어놓는지 탐색하고 있기 때문이다.

후성유전학은 DNA 염기서열 세포 표현형의 유전 가능한 변화, 즉 수정(受精) 이후 외부 환경 요인들의 결과로 발생한 변화를 연구한다. 환경 요인들은 특정 유전자를 자극하여, 해당 유전자를 켜거나 끌 수 있고 어떤 식으로든 바꿀 수 있다. 세포 분열을 통해 이제 유전자 변화는 유전 가능한 형질로서 뒤이은 세대들에게 전달될 가능성을 지니게 된다.

과학자들이 후성유전학을 연구하는 한 가지 방법은 동물의 유전 가능성을 연구하는 것이다. 과학자들은 쥐가 임신 기간 동안 스트레스 환경에 노출되면 태아의 후성유전적 변화가 쥐의 새끼가 성장해 성체가 되면 행동문제를 발생시킬 수 있음을 보여줄 수 있었다.

과학자들은 또한 인간 쌍둥이를 이용하여 후성유전학과 DNA 메틸화 반응이라는 관련 과정을 좀 더 잘 이해할 수 있다. DNA 메틸화 반응은 유전자를 더 강하거나 더 약하게 표현되도록 만든다. 일란성 쌍둥이에게서 채취한 DNA 견본을 검사함으로써 과학자들은 DNA 메틸화반응이 유전자 서열에서 특정 유전자의 표현에 영향을 미치는 영역을 알아낼 수 있다. 일란성 쌍둥이는 DNA가 같기 때문에, 쌍둥이 각자를 위한 메틸화 반응 윤곽을 만들면 과학자들은 행동의 미묘한 차이부터 극단적 차이까지 설명할 수 있어, 이를 통해 후생유전 과정이 우리의 성격과 유전자 코드에 어떤 영향을 끼치는지 파악할 수 있도록 창문을 <닫을> 수 있다.

후성유전학은 생물학 연구의 한 분야로서 아직 발전 초기 단계에 있지만, 그럼에도 불구하고 믿을 수 없을 만큼 흥미진진하고 혁신적인 분야이다. 후성유전학은 어떻게 진화상의 변화가 수천 년에 걸쳐서가 아니라 한 세대 내에서 발생할 수 있는지를 보여주기 때문에 다윈의 진화론을 방해한다. 이렇게 빠른 진화상의 변화의 가능성은 우리가 지구상의 생명체 뿐 아니라 좋든 나쁘든 우리가 그 생명체에게 끼칠 수 있는 영향력에 대해 어떻게 생각하는가에 대한 중요한 함의를 갖고 있다.

underlying a. 근본[근원]적인 epigenetics n. 후성유전학 delve into 캐다, 철저히 조사하다 methylation n. 메틸화 반응 progeny n. 자손 throw a wrench into ~에 초를 치다, 방해하다 fixed a. 고정된 factor n. 요인 limb n. 팔다리, 사지 underlying a. 근원적인 genetic sequence 유전자 서열 constant a. 일정한, 변함없는 heritable a. 유전되는 phenotype n. 표현형 cellular a. 세포의 alter v. 바꾸다 subsequent a. 이후의

③ DNA 메틸화 반응의 윤곽은 DNA 구조가 어디서 환경 요인에 영향을 끼쳤는지 보여준다.
④ 생물학적 변화는 동물과 인간 둘 모두에서 DNA의 기능에 의해 결정되지 않는다.

---

39 글의 흐름상 적절하지 않은 문장 고르기　④

새로운 후성유전학 연구로 과학자들이 행동의 미묘한 차이를 이해할 길을 '열었다'고 해야 하므로 ⓔ의 closing the window를 opening the window로 바꾸어야 한다.

---

40 내용일치　①

DNA를 통한 형질의 유전가능성이 고정불변이라는 것이 오래 지속되어 온 믿음이었지만 이제 후성유전학은 이 믿음과 반대되게 유전 가능성이 환경에 의해 어떻게 변할 수 있는가를 중점적으로 연구한다. 따라서 정답은 ①이다. ② 후성유전학은 다윈의 이론을 방해한다고 했고, ③ DNA 메틸화 반응은 환경에 영향을 끼치는 것이 아니라 받으며, ④ 생물학적 변화는 DNA의 기능과 관련이 깊다.

위 글의 내용과 일치하는 것을 고르시오.
① 후성유전학은 생물학의 하위 분야로, 유전 가능성의 가변성에 초점을 맞춘다.
② 다윈의 이론은 진화의 변화가 후성유전학에 동조하는 방식을 예시한다.

2024 한국공학대학교(인문계)

01 ②	02 ①	03 ④	04 ①	05 ④	06 ②	07 ④	08 ①	09 ②	10 ②
11 ②	12 ③	13 ②	14 ③	15 ④	16 ④	17 ②	18 ①	19 ①	20 ③
21 ①	22 ①	23 ③	24 ①	25 ③	26 ②	27 ③	28 ④	29 ④	30 ④
31 ④	32 ②	33 ③	34 ①	35 ③	36 ③	37 ②	38 ③	39 ④	40 ①

01 동의어

redundant a. 여분의, 과다한(= superfluous) streamline v. 합리화하다, 간소화하다 enhance v. 향상하다; (가치·능력·매력 따위를) 높이다 clarity n. 명료, 명확 impact n. 영향; 효과 deficient a. 부족한, 불충분한 inadequate a. 부적당한, 불충분한 incompetent a. 무능한

그 삽화는 세부묘사가 너무 과다했다. 화가는 그것의 명료성과 효과를 높이기 위해 그것을 간소화하는 것을 고려해야 한다.

02 동의어 ①

hamper v. 방해하다, 훼방하다(= hinder) ration n. 식량, 양식 troop n. 군대, 병력 assist v. 원조하다, 돕다 facilitate v. 용이하게 하다 decelerate v. 속력을 늦추다

적군의 그 어떤 공격도 우리 군대를 위한 보급 식량의 도착을 방해할 것이다.

03 동의어 ④

projection n. 투사, 투영(= manifestation 표현, 표시) perception n. 지각, 인식 scheme n. 계획, 기획 operation n. 운영, 경영 proposal n. 제안; 신청

다른 사람들이 하는 말과 행동은 당신의 현실과 인식이 아니라 그들의 현실과 인식의 투영이다.

04 동의어 ①

afford v. ~의 여유가 있다 squander v. 낭비[허비]하다(= dissipate) resource n. 자원 engender v. (상태 등을) 발생시키다, 야기시키다 assemble v. 모으다, 집합시키다 accumulate v. 모으다, 축적하다

오늘날의 사업 환경은 조직이 조금의 자원이라도 낭비할 여유를 허락하지 않는다.

05 동의어 ④

hold off (거리·간격 등을) 유지하다(= maintain) cease v. 그만두다,

그치다 initiate v. 시작하다 withdraw v. 철수하다, 회수하다

북미인들은 종종 대화할 때 일정한 거리를 유지하는데, 연구에 의해 그 서로 간의 거리가 약 21인치인 것으로 드러났다.

06 논리완성

as 이하는 앞 문장을 부연해서 설명하는 역할을 하고 있다. 빈칸에는 specialized terms의 의미를 가진 표현이 들어가야 할 것이므로 ②가 정답으로 적절하다.

excessive a. 과도한 alienate v. 소외하다, 따돌리다 specialized term 전문 용어 slang n. 속어 jargon n. (동업자·동일 집단 내의) 특수 용어; 은어 parley n. 회담; 교섭 altercation n. 언쟁

작가는 작품에서 특수 용어를 과도하게 사용하는 것을 피하는 것이 중요한데, 왜냐하면 그것이 전문 용어들을 잘 모르는 독자를 소외시킬 수 있기 때문이다.

07 논리완성

'극심한 고통 때문에 막시밀리안이 분명한 말들로 표현할 수 없었다'는 내용이므로 빈칸에는 ④가 들어가는 것이 적절하다.

coherent a. 일관성 있는, 논리 정연한 in vain 무익하게, 헛되이, 보람 없이 unsteady a. 불안정한, 건들거리는 upright a. 직립한, 똑바로 선 stagger v. 비틀거리다 refer v. 조회하다; 위탁하다, 맡기다 verify v. 입증하다 describe v. 묘사하다 articulate v. 똑똑히 발음하다

극심한 고통 속에서, 논리정연한 말을 하려는 막시밀리안(Maximilian)의 노력은 수포로 돌아갔고, 그의 몸이 불안정하게 움직였기 때문에 그는 벽에 기댄 채로 똑바로 서 있으려 애썼다. 막시밀리안은 말을 하려 했지만, 아무 것도 분명하게 말할 수 없었다. 그는 비틀거리며 벽에 몸을 기대고 있었다.

08 논리완성

최고형을 피하려는 마지막 노력이라면, 자비를 베풀어달라고 요구하는 것이 아니라 간청하기로 했을 것이다. 'plead for mercy'가 '자비를 베풀어달라고 간청하다'는 의미의 관용표현이다. require, demand는 전치사 for와 함께 쓰는 자동사가 아니기도 하다.

last-ditch a. (성공할 가망이 많지 않은데) 최후의 시도로 하는, 필사적인 suspect n. 용의자 plead for 간청하다 require v. 요구하다, 규정하다 demand v. 요구하다 litigate v. 법정에서 다투다, 소송하다

마지막 노력으로, 용의자는 최고형을 피할 수 있기를 바라면서 자비를 베풀어달라고 간청하기로 했다.

09 비교 구문 ②

원급비교로 '~만큼 많은 전력'은 as much power as ~인데, 부사 almost(거의)는 as 앞에 오므로, ②가 가장 적절한 어순이다.

엔지니어는 거의 핵잠수함만큼 많은 전력을 요구하는 뇌 스캐너의 일부인 감지장치 헬멧을 쓰고 있다.

10 부사 otherwise ②

빈칸 이하는 자신이 가지고 있었던 두 가지 가정을 뒤집는 연구 결과에 관한 내용이다. 그러므로 '증거는 그와 다르게(그렇지 않다고) 말한다'는 뜻이 되게 ②가 정답으로 적절하다.

assumption n. 가정, 억측 evidence n. 증거 indicate v. 표시하다, 나타내다 enhance v. 향상시키다 besides ad. 게다가 otherwise ad. 딴 방법으로, 그렇지 않고 likewise ad. 마찬가지로 in the end 마침내

나는 예전에 두 가지 가정을 하고 있었는데, 첫 번째는 가난한 사람들이 가난한 것은 부분적으로는 그들이 교육을 받지 못해서 좋은 선택을 하지 못하기 때문이라는 것이고, 두 번째는, 그러면 그들은 자신들이 필요로 하는 것을 알아내고 그것들을 그들에게 구해줄 나 같은 사람들이 필요하다는 것이다. 증거에 의하면 그렇지 않다는 것이 드러나고 있다. 수십 개의 연구에 따르면, 사람들은 식량, 안전, 주거, 의료, 교육 등, 다양한 방식으로 자신의 삶을 향상시켜줄 직접적인 재정적 지원을 사용하고 있다.

11 능동태와 수동태의 구분 ②

'가난한 나라로 유해 폐기물을 실어 보내는 것을 완전히 금지하도록' 바젤 협약이 개정되었다고 해야 올바른 내용이 된다. '개정되었다'는 수동태이고 빈칸 뒤에 동사 ban의 목적어가 있으므로 ban은 능동태인 to ban이어야 한다. 따라서 ②가 빈칸에 적절하다.

address v. (어려운 문제 등을) 다루다, 처리하다 agreement n. 협정, 조약 notify v. ~에게 통지하다 hazardous a. (특히 건강·안전에) 위험한 modify v. 수정하다 ban v. 금지하다

1989년, 국제 폐기물 거래의 문제점을 해결하기 위해 170개국이 바젤(Basel) 협약을 체결했다. 이 협약은 선진국들로 하여금 개발도상국에 그 국가로 들어오는 유해 폐기물 운송에 대해 통보하도록 규정하고 있었다. 6년 후, 환경 단체와 개발도상국들의 압력을 받은 뒤에, 바젤 협약은 가난한 국가로의 유해 폐기물 운송을 완전히 금지하도록 수정되었다.

12 분사구문 ③

주절의 주어가 popcorn이고 팝콘은 만들어지는 것이므로 수동태인 When it is prepared인데, 여기서 When은 생략하지 않고 남겨둔 채로 it이 삭제되고 being이 생략되면 When prepared가 된다. 따라서 ③이 정답이 된다.

contain v. 포함하다 nutrient n. 영양소

소금과 버터를 넣지 않고 만들어질 때, 팝콘은 엄청난 양의 영양소가 들어 있는 몸에 좋은 훌륭한 간식이 될 수 있다.

13 nor 뒤의 도치 ②

빈칸 앞에 I don't think로 시작하는 부정문이 왔다. 빈칸부터는 부정의 접속사 nor로 시작하는 절이 이어지는데, 하나의 절이 부정의 접속사 nor로 시작하면 그 뒤는 주어와 동사가 도치된다. 따라서 ②가 정답이다.

predictive a. 예언하는, 예보하는 genetic a. 유전의 pose v. (요구 따위를) 주장하다, (문제 등을) 제기하다 ethical a. 도덕상의, 윤리적인 potential n. 잠재력, 가능성 develop v. (병에) 걸리다 incurable disease 불치병 enhance v. 향상시키다 interpret v. 해석하다

예측 유전자 검사는 윤리적, 현실적 딜레마를 제기한다. 개인적으로, 나는 내가 불치병에 걸릴 가능성이 있는지를 아는 것이 어떤 식으로든 내 삶의 질을 향상시킬 것이라고 생각하지 않으며, 또한 전문 의료인의 도움 없이는 내가 그 유전자 검사의 결과를 이해할 수도 없을 것이다.

14 선행사를 포함한 관계대명사 what ③

앞에 선행사가 없으므로 ②와 ④는 빈칸에 들어갈 수 없다. 한편, term은 'term+목적어+목적격 보어'의 형태로 쓰는데, ①이 들어가는 경우 목적격 보어가 없는 상태가 되므로 ① 역시 정답이 될 수 없다. 따라서 선행사를 포함한 관계대명사 what이 들어있는 ③이 정답이며, 이때 what은 타동사 suggest의 목적어로서의 역할과 자신이 이끄는 절에서 term의 목적어가 되는 역할을 동시에 수행한다.

bottom-up a. 상향식의 contrast with ~와 대조를 이루다 top-down a. 하향식의 term v. 이름 짓다, 칭하다

일부 영국 과학자들은 그들이 상향식 방법이라 칭하는 것을 제안한다. 이것은 동물의 행동에 대한 연구에서 그들이 취하고 있는 하향식 접근법의 관점과 대조된다.

15 수동태 ④

④의 주어는 선행사인 conical teeth인데, 이빨은 '사용되는' 것이므로 동사 use는 수동태여야 한다. 따라서 ④를 may have been used to로 고쳐야 한다.

paleontologist n. 고생물학자 spine n. 등뼈; <동물> 가시 모양의 돌기 magnificent a. 장대한, 장엄한; 당당한 slender a. 홀쭉한, 가느다란 crocodile n. 악어 conical a. 원뿔의, 원뿔꼴의 slippery a. 미끄러운, 반들반들한

스피노사우루스의 뼈 몇 개가 이집트의 사막에서 발견되었으며 약 100년 전에 독일의 고생물학자에 의해 설명되었다. 불행하게도, 그의 모든 스피노사우루스의 뼈는 2차 세계대전 중에 파괴되었다. 그래서 우리에게 남은 것은 단지 몇 개의 그림과 메모뿐이다. 이 그림들로부터, 우리는 약 1억 년 전에 살았던 이 생물이 매우 컸고, 등에 가시 모양의 돌기가 나 있어서 웅장한 돛을 형성했으며, 악어처럼 원추형 이빨이 나 있는 길고 가느다란 턱을 가지고 있었으며 그 이빨은 물고기처럼 미끄러운 먹이를 잡는 데 사용됐을지도 모른다는 것을 알 수 있다.

16 문의 구성   ④

등위접속사 but 뒤에 절의 구조가 와야 한다. 따라서 ④는 we all do it이 되어야 옳다. ① 주어가 All, What, The only thing 등으로 시작하여 do 동사로 끝난 경우, be동사의 보어 자리에 원형부정사를 쓸 수 있다.

ugly a. 추한; 험악한 divorce n. 이혼 shortcoming n. 결점, 단점 harshly ad. 모질게, 가혹하게

나는 20년간의 결혼생활과 극도로 험악한 이혼 후에 마침내 첫 데이트에 나서는 이 여성과 함께 일한 적이 있다. 데이트 시작 10분 만에, 남자가 일어서더니 "전 관심이 없어요."라고 말하고는 걸어 나가고 만다. 그 여자는 너무나도 상처를 크게 받아서 움직일 수조차 없었다. 그녀가 할 수 있는 일이라곤 친구에게 전화하는 것뿐이었다. 친구가 한 말은 이렇다. "글쎄, 뭘 기대하는 거야? 너는 엉덩이도 크고, 흥미 있는 이야깃거리도 전혀 없어. 그렇게 잘생기고 성공한 남자가 왜 너 같은 패배자랑 데이트를 하려 하겠니?" 친구가 그렇게 잔인할 수 있다는 게 정말 충격적이지 않은가? 하지만 그 말을 한 게 친구가 아니었다는 말을 듣게 된다면 훨씬 충격이 덜 할 것이다. 그것은 그 여자가 스스로에게 한 말이었다. 우리는 모두 자신의 모든 잘못과 모든 결점에 대해 생각하기 시작한다. 이 만큼 가혹하게는 아닐지 몰라도, 우리는 모두 그렇게 하고 있다.

17 논리완성   ②

'애플 주식이 2011년 가장 가치 있는 주식 자리를 차지한 후 그 자리를 놓친 적이 거의 없다'는 내용이 되어야 하겠는데, 빈칸 앞에 부정어 rarely가 있으므로 '상실했다'라는 의미의 ②가 빈칸에 가장 적절하다.

market cap 시가 총액 comprise v. 포함하다, 구성하다 valuation n. 평가, 가치 판단 surpass v. 능가하다, 뛰어넘다 hold v. 유지하다, 간직하다 forfeit v. 상실하다, 몰수되다 waive v. 포기하다, 철회하다 involve v. 연루시키다

애플은 2011년 처음으로 세계에서 가장 가치 있는 주식이 되었는데, 이때 시가총액은 3,400억 달러 이하였고 S&P 500의 약 3.3%를 차지하고 있었다. 이후로, 애플은 그 타이틀을 거의 박탈당하지 않았다. 2018년 중반에 처음으로 1조 달러의 가치에 도달했고, 2020년 8월에 2조 달러의 가치를 달성하면서 처음으로 2조 달러를 돌파한 미국 기업이 되었다.

18 논리완성   ①

앞에서 언급한 정의, 평등, 인도주의 등은 모두 '대의(cause)'로 규정할 수 있다.

personify v. 구체화하다; 상징하다 praiseworthy a. 칭찬할 만한 feature v. 두드러지게 하다, 크게 다루다 humanitarian a. 인도주의의 nonprofit n. 비영리 단체 self-identify v. 스스로 신원을 규정하다 entrepreneur n. 실업가, 기업가 cause n. 주의, 주장; 대의 culture n. 문화 sector n. 분야 corporate n. 법인발행채권

이 책에서 "일상의 영웅"은 신체적 용기를 구현하는 사람들이 아니다. 소방관과 같은 영웅들이 칭찬받을 가치가 적은 것은 결코 아니지만, 나는 사회 정의와 평등을 열정적으로 추구하는 사람들을 주인공으로 삼기로 했다. 그들의 일은 본질적으로 인도주의적이다. 그들은 다양한 대의와 사람들을 대표하는 성공적인 비영리 단체의 설립자들이거나 리더들이다. 거의 모두가 자신을 사회적 기업가라고 밝힌다.

19 논리완성   ①

많은 사람들이 실패를 두려워해서 뭔가를 시도조차 하지 않는 상황에서, 실패가 괜찮은 것이며 걱정할 것이 전혀 아니게 되려면, 그들이 가지고 있던 기존의 견해나 관점을 바꿔야 할 것이다. 그러므로 빈칸에는 ①이 들어가는 것이 적절하다.

alter v. (모양·성질 등을) 바꾸다, 변경하다 ignore v. 무시하다 collect v. 모으다 confirm v. 확증하다, 확인하다

많은 사람들이 실패를 두려워하며 성공할 기회가 있을 때조차 실패를 피하려고 애쓴다. 그 결과, 많은 사람들은 실패할 수도 있다는 생각이 들면 뭔가를 시도하지 않으려 한다. 실패가 괜찮은 것이며 걱정할 것이 전혀 아니게 되도록 그들의 관점을 바꾸는 것이 인생에서 성공할 수 있는 새로운 기회를 여는 열쇠가 될 수 있다.

20 동격의 to부정사   ③

빈칸 앞의 be동사와 함께 진행형을 만드는 finding이 필요하며, way는 to부정사를 동격으로 취한다. 그러므로 ③이 정답이다.

ascendancy n. 우월, 우세 diverse a. 다양한, 가지각색의 rigid a. 엄격한 norm n. 기준; 규범 sophisticated a. 정교한; 고도로 세련된 subtext n. 서브텍스트(문학 작품의 텍스트 배후의 의미); 언외의 의미

K-pop이 그 우월적인 세계적인 위상을 지속하고 있어서, 점점 더 많은 독립적인 아티스트들이 그 현장에 들어오면서 K-pop은 훨씬 더 다양해질 것으로 예상된다. 업계의 경직된 기준에도 불구하고, K-pop 아티스트들은 매우 세련된 서브텍스트와 현대적인 테마를 통해 규범에 도전하는 방법을 모색해 나가고 있다.

21 논리완성   ①

빈칸 ⓐ의 경우, 전후에서 '부모가 모두 오른손잡이일 경우의 왼손잡이 자녀의 출생 비율'과 '부모가 모두 왼손잡이일 경우의 왼손잡이 자녀의

출생 비율'을 대조하고 있으므로 역접의 의미를 가진 whereas와 yet이 가능하다. 빈칸 ⓑ의 경우, 앞에서 제시한 '왼손잡이 가설'을 반박하는 내용을 시작하는 부분이므로 역접의 의미를 가진 However가 적절하다. On the other hand는 앞의 내용과 또 다른 면을 설명할 때 쓰이며 여기서처럼 앞의 내용과 결부지어 반박할 때는 부적절하다. 따라서 두 조건을 모두 만족하는 ①이 정답이다.

hold true 여전히 사실이다, 유효하다 mild a. 경미한 brain damage 뇌 손상

전 세계 대부분의 사람들은 오른손잡이다. 이 사실은 또한 역사를 통틀어서도 유효했던 것처럼 보인다. 연구에 따르면, 두 명의 오른손잡이 부모가 왼손잡이 아이를 가질 확률은 9.5%인 반면, 두 명의 왼손잡이 부모의 경우는 확률이 26%이다. 한 가지 단순한 견해는 사람들은 대개 부모로부터 오른손잡이 성향을 얻게 된다는 것이며, 또 다른 일반적인 이론은 왼손잡이 사람들이 태어날 때 가벼운 뇌 손상을 입는다는 것이다. 그러나 만약 이 이론이 사실이라면, 그것은 왜 모든 사회에서 왼손잡이 사람들의 비율이 그렇게 비슷한지 설명하지 못할 것이다. 이면에 자리하고 있는 이유가 무엇이든, 왼손잡이에 대한 사람들의 태도는 오랜 세월에 걸쳐 크게 바뀌어 왔다.

22 논리완성   ①

글의 앞부분은 공학 전공 대학생들이 사회에 미칠 수 있는 영향력의 종류와 특성에 대해 모호해한다는 내용이다. 빈칸을 포함하고 있는 문장에서는 이런 학생들이 사회와의 '관련성'을 보여줄 수 있는 방법에 관해 이야기하고 있다. 그러므로 빈칸에는 ①이 적절하다.

qualification n. 자격, 능력 vague a. 막연한, 애매한 demonstrate v. 증명하다, 논증하다; 설명하다 address v. (문제를) 역점을 두어 다루다, 처리하다 pressing a. 절박한, 긴급한 alleviation n. (고통의) 경감, 완화 sustainable a. (자원 이용이) 환경이 파괴되지 않고 계속될 수 있는; 지속가능한 relevance n. 관련성; 타당성 complexity n. 복잡성 exclusivity n. 배타성 profitability n. 수익성

공학 학생들은 우수한 자격을 갖춘 채 대학에 진학하는 경우가 많다. 하지만 그들은 3~4년 후에 학교를 떠날 때 자신들이 사회에 미칠 수 있는 영향의 종류와 질에 대해서는 잘 모르고 있다. 공학교육 프로그램이 사회와 관련 있음을 입증하는 방법 중의 하나는 신흥국의 빈곤완화와 지속가능한 발전과 같은 시급한 문제를 해결하는 것이다.

23 논리완성   ③

빈칸 다음의 문장에서 '롤모델이 반드시 이러저러할 필요는 없다'는 내용을 이야기하고 있으므로, 빈칸에는 '그것(롤모델)이 아닌 것'을 뜻하는 ③이 적절하다. 롤모델은 사람일 수도 있지만, 이 글에서는 시종일관 대명사 it으로 받고 있다는 점에 유의한다.

recognize v. 알아내다, 인지하다 characteristic n. 특질, 특색 trait n. 특색, 특성

롤모델이란 무엇인가? 우선, 롤모델이 아닌 것부터 알아보자. 롤모델은 당신이 아는 사람 중에 가장 똑똑하고, 가장 힘이 세고 혹은 가장 성공한 사람일 수도 있지만 반드시 그런 것은 아니다. 롤모델은 당신이 자신을

위해 원하는 특성을 가지고 있고, 그러한 특성을 발달시키도록 당신을 도와줄 수 있는 사람이다.

24 논리완성   ①

그리스 역사, 다이아몬드 채굴, 공룡, 대체 의학 등은 서로 간에 관련이 없는 '다양한' 주제들이라고 할 수 있다.

immeasurably ad. 헤아릴 수 없을 정도로; 매우, 대단히 dinosaur n. 공룡 alternative medicine 대체 의학 diverse a. 다양한, 가지각색의 academic a. 학구적인 technical a. 전문의, 특수한 specialized a. 전문적인

레오(Leo)는 대단히 지혜롭다. 그는 매우 많은 지식과 경험을 가지고 있으며, 그리스 역사, 다이아몬드 채굴, 공룡, 대체 의학과 같은 너무나 많은 다양한 주제에 관심이 있다. 비록 이들 주제는 서로 관련이 없지만, 그는 그 모두를 즐긴다.

25 논리완성   ③

처음에는 굴이 도시(파리) 경계 너머에 있었다고 했는데, 여기서 도시(파리)가 성장하면 면적도 더 넓어질 것이므로 도시 경계 너머의 굴들 위로 퍼져갔을 것이다. 따라서 빈칸에는 ③이 적절하다.

limestone n. 석회석 gypsum n. 석고 remove v. 옮기다, 움직이다; 제거하다 collapse v. 무너지다, 붕괴하다 swallow v. 삼키다

현대의 파리(Paris)는 석회암과 석고 위에 자리 잡고 있다. 2,000여 년 전에 로마인들이 최초로 이 돌들을 채굴하여, 땅에 큰 구멍을 남기고 돌들이 제거된 곳에 굴을 남겼다. 처음에는 이 굴들이 도시 경계 너머에 있었지만, 파리가 성장하면서 그 굴들 위로 퍼져나갔다. 1774년 12월에 굴 하나가 무너져서 집과 사람들을 삼켜버렸다.

① 파리는 굴 속으로 더 깊이 파고들었다
② 파리는 굴 주변에 지어졌다
③ 파리는 굴 위로 퍼져나갔다
④ 더 많은 땅이 개간되었다

26 글의 제목   ②

글의 앞부분에서는 종교적 견지에서 보는 불멸에 관해 설명하고 있고, 글의 뒷부분에서는 과학의 관점에서 "노화가 '산화방지제와 주의 깊은 식단으로 극복될 수 있는 질병'이 되었음"을 이야기하고 있으므로, ②가 제목으로 적절하다.

immortality n. 불멸 commonplace a. 평범한; 진부한 depart v. ~을 떠나다 staple food 주식(主食) context n. 문맥; (사건 등에 대한) 경위, 배경; 상황 indefinite a. 무기한의 neutralize v. 중화하다; 무효하게 하다 enzyme n. 효소 division n. 분열 germ cell 생식세포 turn to ~에 의지하다 renewal n. 부활; 재생 senescence n. 노쇠 pathology n. 병리학, 병리 pervasive a. 널리 퍼지는 antioxidant n. 산화방지제, 항산화제

불멸은 평범한 것이 돼버렸다. 불멸은 그것이 최초의 종교집단의 동기로서 나타나 그 결과 신자들의 주된 양식이 되었던 종교의 영역을 오래 전에 떠났다. 종교적 맥락에서, 불멸은 종종 영혼이나 정신이 육체적 죽음 이후에도 무한히 계속되는 것을 가리키는데, 이는 많은 신자들에게 중요한 관심의 초점이면서 위안의 근원이 되어 왔던 믿음이다. 그러나 불멸은 과학적 주제로서의 위엄을 갖게 되었으며, 노화를 통제하거나 무력화시킬 수 있게 되길 바라면서 그것의 메커니즘을 이해하려 하고 있는 실험실에서 연구되고 있다. 신체가 재생하는 데 필요한 생식세포의 분열에 관여하는 효소인 텔로머레이즈(telomerase)의 역할에 대한 설명을 언론에서 보게 되는 것은 이제 흔한 일이다. 노화가 곧 치료될 수 있는 병리 현상이며 죽음은 항산화제와 신중한 식단으로 극복될 수 있는 질병에 불과하다는 의견이 점점 보편화되고 있다. 죽음에 당연한 것은 없다는 말을 우리는 점점 더 자주 듣는다.

위 글의 제목으로 가장 적절한 것은?
① 식생활이 고령화와 수명에 미치는 영향
② 불멸의 진화: 종교에서 과학으로
③ 불멸로 가는 길: 항산화제와 신중한 식단
④ 죽음의 환상: 과학은 어떻게 노화를 극복하고 있는가

---

27 문장삽입 ③

주어진 문장은 '그는 또한 어떤 질병들은 환경에 의해 발생할 수 있다는 사실을 인식했다.'라는 의미이므로, 환경의 범주에 속하는 '식사법과 생활 습관'이 질병과 연관되어 있다는 내용이 뒤이어지는 Ⓒ에 오는 것이 적절하다.

revolutionize v. 혁명[대변혁]을 일으키다 advocate n. 옹호자, 주창자 diagnosis n. 진단 physician n. 내과의사 modification n. 수정, 변경 occurrence n. (사건 등의) 발생 severity n. 엄격, 가혹, 혹독 insight n. 통찰력 influence v. 영향을 미치다 foundation n. 기초, 토대 preventive a. 예방의, 예방하는

'서양 의학의 아버지'인 히포크라테스(Hippocrates)는 의술에 혁명을 일으켰다. 그는 많은 면에서 의학을 변화시켰다. 예를 들어, 그는 의학 지식을 출판하는 것과, 질병 진단보다는 환자 치료에 집중하는 것과, 의사에게 전문가답게 행동하도록 요구하는 것을 옹호한 인물이었다. <그는 또한 어떤 질병들은 환경에 의해 발생할 수 있다는 사실을 인식했다.> 즉, 식습관과 생활 습관은 질병과 연결돼 있으며, 이를 수정하는 것은 특정 질병의 발생이나 중증도를 낮추는 데 도움이 될 수 있다는 것이다. 환경, 생활방식과 건강 사이의 연관성에 대한 히포크라테스의 통찰력은 지속적인 영향을 미쳐 예방 의학의 토대를 마련했다.

---

28 내용추론 ④

학계의 반대가 있었음에도 불구하고 제너럴 모터스가 자신들이 유리하도록 연구결과를 승인해주는 쪽으로 은밀히 조종한 배경이 마지막 문장에 드러나 있다.

lead n. 납 petrol n. 가솔린, 휘발유 urge v. 재촉하다 implication n. 밀접한 관계, 영향; (예상되는) 결과 chemist n. 화학자 tetraethyl lead 테트라에틸납(휘발유 첨가제) antiknock a. 폭연(爆燃)을 방지하는, 엔진의 노킹을 억제하는 additive n. 첨가제 breezily ad. 쾌활하게, 가벼운 마음으로 assure v. 납득시키다, 확신시키다 detect v. 발견하다,

탐지하다, 감지하다 absorption n. 흡수 bureau n. 사무소; (미국 정부의) 부서[국] clause n. (조약·법률 등의) 조목, 조항 approve v. 시인하다; 승인하다

약 100년 전에, 제너럴 모터스(GM)가 — 성능 향상을 위해 — 휘발유에 납을 첨가할 것을 처음 제안했을 때, 과학자들은 깜짝 놀랐다. 그들은 공중 보건에 미치는 영향을 조사할 것을 정부에 촉구했다. 휘발유의 노킹 방지 첨가제로서 테트라에틸 납의 효과를 발견한 미국의 공학자이자 화학자인 토마스 미글리 주니어(Thomas Midgley, Jr.)는, "실제 실험 데이터는 수집되지 않았다."고 인정했음에도 불구하고, "아마도 보통의 거리에는 납이 너무나도 없기 때문에 납이나 납의 흡수를 탐지하는 것이 불가능할 것이다."라고 정부 관리들에게 가벼운 마음으로 확신시켰다. 제너럴 모터스는 정부 부서에 연구를 수행할 자금을 대면서, 정부가 조사 결과를 승인해야 한다는 조항을 추가했다.

위 글에서 제너럴 모터스에 대해 암시돼 있는 것은?
① 휘발유에 들어 있는 납의 잠재적 위험성에 대해 알지 못했다.
② 휘발유에 들어 있는 납의 독성에 관한 증거를 적극적으로 은폐하였다.
③ 휘발유에 들어 있는 납의 영향에 대해 철저하고 편견 없는 연구를 수행했다.
④ 연구비 지원에 조건을 달아서 연구 결과를 발표 전에 승인하도록 했다.

---

29 내용추론 ④

④의 '유익한'이 본문에서 언급하는 독물학의 정의, 즉 '살아있는 유기체에 대한 화학물질의 해로운 영향을 연구하는 학문'이라는 정의에 위배된다.

toxicology n. 독물학(毒物學) adverse effect 부작용 chemical substance 화학물질 organism n. 유기체, 생물 algae n. 조류(藻類) flora n. 식물군(植物群) fauna n. 동물군(動物群) poisonous a. 유독한, 유해한 injury n. 상해, 부상 dose n. 복용량 exposure n. 노출 property n. 특성, 성질 assess v. 평가하다

독물학(毒物學)은 살아있는 유기체에 대한 화학물질의 부작용에 관한 과학이다. 살아있는 유기체에는 바다의 조류(藻類), 동물과 사람, 모든 식물군과 동물군이 포함된다. 안전한 물질은 없으며, 모든 화학물질은 독성이 있을 수 있어서 부상이나 사망을 초래할 수 있다. 그러나 화학물질을 안전하게 사용할 수는 있으며, 그에 따른 영향은 복용량과 노출된 정도에 따라 달라질 수 있다. 그것은 '받아들일 수 있을 정도로 안전한' 방식으로 화학물질의 특성을 처리하고 이익을 얻을 수 있도록, 화학물질을 제한함으로써 가능하다. 독물학 연구는 이러한 '받아들일 수 있을 정도로 안전한' 수준을 찾기 위해 다양한 용량과 관련된 부작용을 평가하는 것을 목표로 한다.

위 글에서 시사하고 있지 않은 것은?
① 모든 화학물질은 특정 용량에서 중독과 손상을 일으킬 가능성이 있다.
② 화학물질의 영향은 용량과 노출된 정도에 따라 다르다.
③ 독물학 연구는 '받아들일 수 있을 정도로 안전한' 수준의 화학물질 노출의 수준을 찾는 것을 목표로 한다.
④ 독물학은 화학물질이 살아있는 유기체에 미치는 유익한 영향을 연구하는 학문이다.

30 내용파악 ④

'개인들은 비판적 사고 기술을 개발하고 AI 시스템이 제시하는 정보의 정확성을 입증할 방법을 배워야 한다'고 말하고 있으므로 우리가 AI를 효율적으로 사용하기 위해서 해야 할 일로는 ④가 적절하다.

Artificial Intelligence 인공지능 revolutionize v. 혁명[대변혁]을 일으키다 application n. 응용, 적용 transportation n. 운송, 수송; 교통기관 visual perception 시각 지각 speech recognition 음성 인식 evaluate v. 평가하다 recognize v. 알아보다, 인지하다 generate v. 산출하다, 발생시키다 evolve v. 진화하다 crucial a. 결정적인, 중대한 critical a. 비평의, 평론의 verify v. 입증하다 maximize v. 최대화하다, 극대화하다 potential a. 잠재적인 minimize v. 최소화하다

인공지능(AI)은 의료, 교육 및 교통과 같은 다양한 분야에서 응용되어 우리가 살고 일하는 방식에 혁명을 일으키고 있다. AI 시스템은 학습하고, 문제를 해결하고, 계획을 세울 수 있으며, 시각 지각과 음성 인식과 같은 인간의 지능과 감각을 모방할 수 있다. 그러나 AI는 그것이 생성하는 정보에서 진실을 평가하고 인식해야 할 필요성과 같은 과제도 제시한다. AI가 계속 발전함에 따라, 개인들이 비판적 사고 능력을 발전시키고 AI 시스템이 제시하는 정보의 정확성을 확인하는 방법을 배우는 것이 매우 중요해졌다. 이를 통해 AI의 혜택은 극대화하는 한편 잠재적인 위험은 최소화할 수 있을 것이다.

위 글에 의하면, AI를 효율적으로 활용하기 위해 우리는 무엇을 해야 하는가?
① 우리는 AI를 단순하고 반복적인 작업에만 사용해야 하고 복잡한 문제 해결에는 사용하지 말아야 한다.
② 우리는 AI가 완벽해져서 인간의 감시 없이 작동할 수 있을 때까지 AI를 사용하는 것을 피해야 한다.
③ 우리는 모든 부문에서 최대의 효율성을 보장하기 위해 인간의 의사 결정을 AI로 대체해야 한다.
④ 우리는 비판적으로 사고하는 능력을 배양하고 AI 시스템이 제공하는 정보의 진위를 확인하는 방법을 배워야 한다.

---

31 내용파악 ④

지적재산권(IPR)의 정의, 목적, 종류, 제약업계의 사례로 이어지는 글이다. 문제에서는 제약업계에서의 지적재산권 사용 목적을 묻고 있는데, 글 중반부의 지적재산권의 목적에 대한 설명 부분을 보면 in order to enable them to reap commercial benefits from their creative efforts or reputation이라는 내용이 명시되어 있다. 따라서 제약업계에서도 ④가 IPR의 주된 목적이다.

intellectual property right 지적재산권 define v. (성격·내용 따위를) 규정짓다, 한정하다; (말의) 정의를 내리다 bestow v. 주다, 수여하다, 부여하다 status n. 지위, 자격 exclusive a. 배타적인, 독점적인 reap v. 수확하다, 거둬들이다 commercial a. 상업의; 영리적인 reputation n. 명성, 신망 patent n. 특허 copyright n. 저작권 trademark n. 상표 prerequisite n. 선행조건, 필요조건 identification n. 동일하다는 증명[감정] commercialization n. 상업화, 상품화 render v. 제출하다, 교부하다; 표현하다 specialty n. 전문, 전공 pharmaceutical a. 제약의, 제약학의 currently ad. 일반적으로; 현재

지적재산권(IPR)은 재산의 지위를 부여하려는 대중의 의사가 있는 아이디어, 발명품, 창조적 표현으로 정의되어 왔다. 지적재산권은 그 재산의 발명가 혹은 창작자에게 일정한 배타적 권리를 제공하여, 그들이 자신들의 창조적인 노력이나 명성으로부터 상업적인 이익을 거둬들일 수 있도록 해준다. 지적재산 보호에는 특허, 저작권, 상표 등과 같은 여러 종류가 있다. IPR은 발명이나 창의성을 더 잘 식별하고, 계획하고, 상업화하고, 표현하고, 그럼으로써 더 잘 보호하기 위한 필수 조건이다. 각 산업은 전문 분야에 따라 고유한 지적재산권 정책, 관리 방법, 전략 등을 발전시켜야 한다. 현재 제약 산업은 지적재산권 전략이 발전하고 있으며, 그 전략에서는 다가오는 시대에 더 나은 집중과 접근을 요구하고 있다.

제약 산업에서 IPR의 주된 목적은 무엇인가?
① 새로운 약과 치료제에 대한 접근을 제한하는 것
② 모든 제약 혁신의 공유를 장려하는 것
③ 사용 가능한 지적재산권 보호 유형을 제한하는 것
④ 발명가와 창작자가 자신들의 혁신에서 상업적으로 이익을 얻을 수 있도록 하는 것

---

32 글의 요지 ②

인정받고 존중받고자 하는 욕구를 아이들은 일상의 상호작용을 통해 이해하기 시작하며, 이러한 이해는 일생 동안 그들의 사회적 발달과 자아 존중에 대한 인식을 형성한다는 내용이므로, 이를 통해 전달하고자 하는 것은 '존중 받는 것이 인간의 기본적인 욕구'라는 것이다.

recognize v. 인지하다, 인정하다 interaction n. 상호작용 self-worth n. 자아 존중감, 자부심

"당신이 아기일 때부터 죽을 때까지, 당신은 인정받고 존중받기를 원하는 개인입니다."라고 히라미(Hirami)는 말했다. 그녀는 아이들이 다양한 연령층 사람들과의 일상적인 상호작용을 통해 이것을 이해하기 시작한다고 말한다. 이러한 이해는 일생 동안 그들의 사회적 발달과 자아 존중에 대한 인식을 형성한다.

다음 중 위 글의 요지를 가장 잘 설명하는 것은?
① 친구는 궁핍함에 처해 있을 때 알 수 있다.
② 존중은 인간의 기본적인 욕구이다.
③ 빈 수레가 요란하다.
④ 하늘은 스스로 돕는 자를 돕는다.

---

33 내용추론 ③

이 글에서는 '수명 연장이 사회에 미치는 의미에 관해서는 의견이 다양할 수 있지만, 일단 그 기술이 개발되고 나면 멈추거나 통제하는 것이 불가능할 수 있으므로 그 문제에 대해 지금 논의가 이루어져야 한다'는 윤리학자들의 주장을 소개하고 있다. 마이크 캘러한이 주장하는 내용도 같다. 따라서 이 글에서 암시하는 것은 '많은 윤리학자들은 잠재적인 사회 문제를 피할 수 있도록 인간의 수명 연장 주제는 지금 논의되어야 한다고 믿는다'는 것이다.

ramification n. 부차적 영향, 파급 효과, 결과 lifespan n. 수명 extend v. 연장하다, 늘리다 ethicist n. 윤리학자

인간의 수명이 연장될 경우 사회에 어떤 영향을 미칠지에 대해 의견은 크게 다르지만, 대부분의 윤리학자들은, 일단 그런 기술이 개발되고 나면 멈추게 하거나 통제하는 것이 불가능할 수도 있기 때문에, 그 문제를 지금 논의해야 한다는 데 의견이 일치하고 있다. "만약 이런 일이 실제로 일어난다면, 우리는 어떤 종류의 사회를 원하는지를 물어보는 것이 좋을 겁니다."라고 하버드 대학의 윤리학자 마이크 캘러한(Mike Callahan)은 말했다, "우리는 그 문제들을 해결할 때까지는 그것과 멀리 떨어져 있는 것이 낫습니다."

다음 중 위 글에 암시되어 있는 것은?
① 인간의 수명은 가까운 미래에 틀림없이 연장될 것이다.
② 인간의 수명을 연장하는 기술은 이미 개발되어 사용할 준비가 되어 있다.
③ 대부분의 윤리학자들은 인간의 수명 연장 문제를 지금 논의해야 잠재적인 사회적 문제를 피할 수 있다고 생각한다.
④ 마이크 캘러한은 결과를 고려하지 않고 인간의 수명을 연장하는 기술을 개발해야 한다고 생각한다.

34-35

신문 기사는 결코 진실 전체를 말할 수 없다. 한 기사에 이야기의 모든 세부 사항을 포함시키는 것은 불가능하기 때문에, 어느 정도의 거짓말이 모든 저널리즘에 내재돼 있다. 기자들은 또한 정보를 제공하는 순서를 조작하여, 자신들의 글에 더 많은 극적 효과나 그 밖의 다른 효과를 얻을 수 있다. 세부 사항과 그것들을 기술하는 순서를 선택하는 것은 기자들에게 있어 적절하고도 윤리적인 행동으로 간주된다. 편집자들은 선거와 정치에 대한 의견 기사를 쓸 때, 심지어 그들의 신문이 갖고 있는 정치적 편향성을 반영할 수도 있다.

article n. (신문·잡지의) 기사, 논설 inherent a. 내재하는; 고유의 manipulate v. (사람·여론 등을) (부정하게) 조종하다; (시장·시가 등을) 조작하다 proper a. 적절한 ethical a. 윤리적인 editor n. 편집인 reflect v. 반영하다 bias n. 편견, 선입관 piece n. (신문·잡지에 실린 한 편의) 기사[글]

34 내용일치   ①

"한 기사에 이야기의 모든 세부 사항을 포함시키는 것은 불가능하기 때문에, 어느 정도의 거짓말이 모든 저널리즘에 내재돼 있다."고 했으므로 ①이 본문의 내용에 부합하는 진술이다.

다음 중 위 글의 내용에 부합하는 것은?
① 신문 기사가 항상 완전한 진실을 전달할 수 있는 것은 아니다.
② 모든 기자는 기사에 이야기의 모든 세부 사항을 포함시켜야 한다.
③ 기자들은 자신들의 글에서 정보의 순서를 조작하는 것이 허용되지 않는다.
④ 편집자들은 의견 기사에 그들의 신문이 갖고 있는 정치적 편향성을 반영하는 것이 금지돼 있다.

35 빈칸완성   ③

본문에서 이야기하는 것은 신문 기사는 그 기사를 쓰는 사람이 어떤 사건의 모든 세부 사항들을 다 포함할 수도 없고, 또 특정한 효과를 내기 위해 순서도 바꾸곤 하기 때문에 '신문 기사가 결코 완전한 진실을 전달할 수는 없다'는 것이다. 그러므로 ③이 정답으로 가장 적절하다. ④도 사실에 부합된 진술이긴 하지만, 빈칸 이하에서는 허구의 이야기를 만드는 것 뿐 아니라 이야기 순서 조작과 편집자의 정치적 편향성 반영까지 언급하므로, ④는 빈칸에 들어가기에 포괄적이지 못하다. 그리고 빈칸 이하에서 some으로 긍정하므로 빈칸에는 never ~ entire의 부분부정으로 표현하는 것이 콜론 이하가 그 앞을 풀어서 설명한 것이라는 것에 비추어 더 적절하다.

다음 중 빈칸에 들어가기에 가장 적절한 것은?
① 공정하기 위해 애써야 한다
② 음미하면서 읽혀야 한다
③ 결코 진실 전체를 말할 수 없다
④ 때때로 허구의 이야기를 만들 수 있다

36-37

스콧(Scott)의 탐험대는 거의 20킬로그램의 바위를 비롯한 40,000개의 과학적 물품들을 가지고 돌아왔다. 원정대가 가져온 2,000개의 동식물 종(種) 가운데 약 400개는 새로 발견한 것들이었다. 스콧의 시신 옆에 놓인 가장 중요한 화석은 2억 5천만 년 전의 나무였다. 식량이 고갈돼 가고 있었음에도 불구하고, 그 탐험가들은 다른 방향으로 나아가 이 화석을 발견할 수 있었다. 이 나무는 오스트레일리아, 아프리카, 남미에서만 발견된 적이 있었다. 따라서 남극에서 이것을 발견한 것은 이러한 국가들과 대륙들이 모두 과거에는 서로 연결되어 있었음을 입증하는 것이었다.

expedition n. 탐험, 원정; 탐험대, 원정대 fossil n. 화석 the Antarctic 남극 continent n. 대륙

36 내용파악   ③

이 글은 스콧(Scott)의 탐험대가 남극에서 매우 활발한 과학 탐사 활동을 벌였다는 것을 그들이 가져온 물건과 약 400 종의 새로운 발견, 특히 매우 오래된 나무 화석의 발견과 그 의미를 중심으로 이야기하고 있는 글이다. 따라서 ③이 정답이다. ④ 이 글이 스콧의 탐험을 배제하고 나무 화석의 과학적 중요성을 설명한 것은 아니다. 즉, 나무 화석이 대륙이동설을 입증해 주었다는 것을 강조하는 것이 아니라 그런 나무 화석 같은 과학적 발견을 스콧 탐험이 해내었다는 것을 강조하는 것이다.

위 글에서 가장 강조되고 있는 것은?
① 생존이 걸려 있는 위급상황에서의 팀워크의 역할
② 스콧의 탐험대가 견뎌낸 육체적인 어려움
③ 스콧의 탐험에서 이뤄낸 과학적 발견의 중요성
④ 대륙의 이동을 증명하는 데 있어 나무 화석이 가진 중요성

37 빈칸완성   ②

식량이 고갈돼 가고 있었던 상황과 화석을 찾기 위해 다른 방향으로 간 것(=탐사를 포기하지 않은 것)은 양보 관계에 있으므로, 빈칸에는 역접의 전치사 Despite가 적절하다.

38-40

B 애팔래치안 트레일(Appalachian Trail)을 장거리 도보여행으로 지나가는 동안, 무어(Moor)는 우리 발밑에 있는 길들이 궁금해지기 시작했다. 길은 어떻게 해서 생겨나는 걸까? 왜 어떤 길들은 시간이 지나면서 더 좋아지고 다른 것들은 사라지는 걸까? 무엇이 우리로 하여금 길을 따라가게 하거나 혹은 스스로 길을 개척하게 만드는 것일까? 7년 동안, 무어는 매우 작은 길에서 거대한 길에 이르는 온갖 종류의 길을 탐구하면서 전 세계를 여행했다. 그는 길을 잘 만드는 사람들의 비법을 익혔고, 오랫동안 잃어버렸던 체로키 트레일을 추적해서 찾아냈으며, 우리의 도로망과 인터넷의 기원을 추적했다. 각각의 장(章)에서, 무어는 자신의 모험을 과학, 역사, 철학, 자연 저술의 연구결과들과 함께 섞어 가며 이야기한다.

C 시종일관 무어는 어떻게 이 하나의 주제 — 종종 간과되어 왔던 길 — 가 예로부터 전해지는 많은 질문들을 새롭게 밝혀주는지를 보여준다. 그 질문들은 어떻게 혼돈 속에서 질서가 나타나는 것일까? 어떻게 동물들은 처음에 바다에서 기어 나와 대륙으로 퍼져 나갔을까? 인류의 자연 및 기술과의 관계가 어떻게 우리 주변의 세계를 형성해왔을까? 그리고, 궁극적으로, 우리 각자는 살아가면서 어떻게 길을 선택하는 것일까? 하는 것들이다.

A 무어는 새로운 관계를 맺는 수필가의 재능, 가보지 않은 길에 대한 모험가의 사랑, 그리고 중요한 질문을 던질 수 있는 철학자의 재주를 가지고 있다. 동물 생명의 여명기부터 디지털 시대까지를 놀랍게 아우르고 있는, 『On Trails』는 우리의 세계, 우리의 역사, 우리의 종(種), 그리고 우리의 삶의 방식을 새롭게 보게 해주는 책이다.

knack n. 숙련된 기술; 교묘한 솜씨 breathtaking a. 깜짝 놀랄 만한, 아슬아슬한 arc n. 호(弧), 호형(弧形) span v. (시간적으로) ~에 걸치다, ~에 미치다 species n. 종류, 종(種) thru-hike v. 장거리 도보여행[장거리 하이킹]을 하다   strike off 잘라내다, 베어내다 strike off[out] on one's own 새롭게 독자적인 길을 가기 시작하다 miniscule a. 극소의, 대단히 작은 massive a. 부피가 큰, 무거운 hunt down 추적해서 잡다 trace v. ~의 자국을 밟다, 추적하다 oft-overlooked a. 종종[자주] 간과된 trail n. 흔적; (황야나 미개지의) 오솔길 shed light on ~에 해결의 빛을 던지다; 새로운 정보를 주다; 해명[설명]하다 crawl v. 기다, 포복하다 continent v. 대륙

---

38 단락배열 ③

무어가 쓴 책 『On Trails』에 대한 리뷰이다. 책을 쓰게 된 계기와 과정에 대해 다루고 있는 B, 내용과 주제에 대해 다루고 있는 C, 책에 대한 최종 평가에 해당하는 A로 연결되는 것이 가장 자연스럽다.

---

39 내용파악 ④

"무어는 매우 작은 길에서 거대한 길에 이르는 온갖 종류의 길을 탐구하면서 전 세계를 여행했다."라고 했으므로 ④가 정답이다.

무어는 7년에 걸친 자신의 여행 동안 무엇을 탐구했는가?
① 애팔래치안 트레일의 역사
② 길을 잘 만드는 사람들의 비법
③ 인터넷과 도로망의 기원
④ 길의 형성과 발전

---

40 글의 제목 ①

『On Trails』라는 책에서 다루고 있는 '길과 인생의 전반적인 의미'를 리뷰하고 평가하는 글이므로, ①이 제목으로 적절하다.

위 글의 제목으로 가장 적절한 것은?
① 길: 길과 삶에 대한 탐구
② 길의 철학: 전 세계적인 탐험
③ 길의 진화: 개미 길에서 인터넷까지
④ 길의 지혜: 시공간을 가로지르는 여행

2024 한국외국어대학교(T1 A형)

01 ②	02 ①	03 ③	04 ②	05 ④	06 ②	07 ④	08 ②	09 ②	10 ③
11 ④	12 ①	13 ④	14 ③	15 ③	16 ①	17 ③	18 ④	19 ③	20 ④
21 ③	22 ②	23 ①	24 ④	25 ①	26 ①	27 ②	28 ②	29 ④	30 ①
31 ①	32 ③	33 ④	34 ①	35 ①	36 ③	37 ④	38 ③	39 ③	40 ①
41 ④	42 ③	43 ②	44 ③	45 ②	46 ②	47 ①	48 ④	49 ④	50 ①

01 논리완성 ②

그 축구 선수의 목소리가 날카롭고 듣는 사람들을 짜증나게 하는 목소리라고 했으므로, 그가 대중 앞에 섰을 때 보일 수 있는 행동은 자신의 목소리를 최대한 드러내지 않는 것이다. 따라서 정답은 ② '말수가 적은, 과묵한'이다.

squeaky a. 끼익[찍] 하는 소리가 나는, 날카로운 목소리의 annoying a. 짜증스러운 bewildered a. 어리둥절한 laconic a. 말수가 적은, 과묵한 affable a. 상냥한, 사근사근한 rubicund a. (문어) (얼굴 등이) 붉은, 불그레한, 홍조를 띤

그 축구 선수는 자신의 날카롭고 짜증나는 목소리가 싫어서 공공장소에서는 말수가 적다.

02 논리완성 ①

저명한 연구 팀에 합류할 수 있는 기회를 여러 번 놓쳤다고 했으므로 그 과학자의 성격은 사교적이지 못하고 완고하다는 것을 추론할 수 있다. 따라서 빈칸에는 ① '다루기 힘든, 고집 센'이 적절하다.

collaboration n. 공동작업 prominent a. 현저한, 유명한 refractory a. 다루기 힘든, 고집 센 buoyant a. 부력이 있는, 활황인, 자신감이 있는 corporeal a. 신체의, 형체를 가진 miscellaneous a. 여러 가지 종류의, 이것저것 다양한

그 과학자는 협업에 대한 완고한 접근 방식 때문에 저명한 연구팀에 합류할 수 있는 기회를 여러 번 놓쳤다.

03 논리완성 ③

not only절과 but also절이 나란히 병치되어 있다. the junk가 anything that is not essential과 상응하므로 빈칸에는 get rid of와 같은 ③ '버리다, 포기하다'가 와야 한다.

weigh down ~을 (마음·기분을) 짓누르다 atrophy v. 위축되다 emulate v. 모방하다 jettison v. 버리다, 포기하다 subjugate v. 예속시키다, 지배[통제]하에 두다

우리는 우리를 짓누르는 잡동사니를 버려야 할 뿐만 아니라 필수적이지 않은 것을 모두 제거해야 할 필요도 있다.

04 논리완성 ②

이유를 나타내는 for절에서 '그녀도 내가 요구하는 정보를 얻어낼 것이라는 것을 내가 알고 있었기 때문이었다'고 했으므로 나는 그녀의 환심을 사려고 최선을 다했을 것이다. 따라서 빈칸에는 '재귀대명사+with'와 함께 '~의 환심을 사다'라는 뜻의 표현을 만드는 ②가 적절하다.

capitulate v. (오랫동안 거부하던 것에) 굴복하다 ingratiate oneself with ~의 환심을 사다 apprehend v. 파악하다, 체포하다 conspire v. 음모[모의]를 꾸미다, 공모하다

나는 그녀에게 환심을 사기 위해 최선을 다했다. 왜냐하면 만약 누구든 내가 요구하는 정보를 얻을 수 있다면 그녀도 그렇게 할 것이라는 것을 내가 알고 있었기 때문이었다.

05 동의어 ④

Arctic n. 북극(권) despondent a. 낙심한, 풀이 죽은(= morose) rapturous a. 기쁨에 넘친, 황홀한 spirited a. 생기 있는, 혈기 넘치는 opulent a. 부유한, 풍요로운

그들은 기후변화에 낙담하지 말고 행동에 나서라는 격려의 메시지를 전 세계에 전하며 북극을 떠났다.

06 동의어 ②

plateau n. 고원, 대지 precarious a. 불안정한, 위험한(= insecure) boisterous a. 난폭하고 시끄러운 egregious a. 지독한, 어처구니없는 exemplary a. 본보기의, 전형적인

그는 지난 몇 년 동안 어떻게든 더 높은 단계로 도약했는데, 이는 불안정한 그의 건강 상태를 고려하면 더욱 놀라운 일이다.

07 동의어 ④

grandiose a. 웅장한, 장엄한(= eminent) regal a. 제왕의, 당당한 bearing n. 태도, 능력 obsequious a. 아부하는, 추종하는 courteous a. 예의바른, 정중한 erratic a. 별난, 괴짜의

여왕의 장엄한 태도와 위풍당당한 자태는 여왕이 입장하자마자 방 안의 모든 사람을 침묵하게 만들었다.

08 동의어 ②

composure n. 침착, 평정(= poise) at all costs 무슨 수를 써서라도 eccentricity n. 기이한 행동, 기벽 umbrage n. 불쾌, 분개 ferocity n. 잔인, 흉폭

우리들 대부분이었더라면 그 모욕에 분노로 대응했을 테지만, 그는 무슨 수를 써서라도 평정심을 유지해야 한다는 것을 이해하고 있었다.

09 동의어 ②

auspicious a. 길조의, 상서로운(= fortunate) sinister a. 불길한, 사악한 strenuous a. 분투하는, 정력적인 formidable a. 위협적인, 겁먹게 하는

그 축제는 일 년 중 가장 상서로운 시기로 여겨지는 가장 따뜻한 봄철에 열린다.

10 문맥상 동의어 ③

slate는 다의어로서 '후보자로 내세우다', '예정이다', '호되게 비판하다' 등의 의미를 가지고 있는데, 주어진 문장에서는 '예정하다'의 의미로 쓰였다.

high court 고등법원 slate v. 예정하다(= schedule) deliver v. (판결 등을) 선고하다 verdict n. 평결, 판결 criticize v. 비판하다, 비난하다 cover v. 씌우다, 포함하다 appoint v. 임명하다, 지정하다

고등법원은 이번 달 말에 판결을 내릴 예정이다.

11 문맥상 동의어 ④

term은 명사로서 '종결', '용어', '말투', '기간', '조건', '관계' 등의 다양한 의미를 가지고 있는데, 주어진 문장에서는 '종결'의 의미로 쓰였다.

maturity benefit 만기 급부 insurance policy 보험 증서 term n. 종결(= termination) semester n. 학기 expression n. 표현; 표정 agreement n. 합의, 동의

만기 지급 보험금은 보험이 종결된 후 받는 금액이다.

12 문맥상 동의어 ①

irregular는 '불규칙의', '비정상적인', '비정규의', '불안정한' 등의 의미를 가지고 있는 다의어인데, 주어진 문장에서는 '비정규적인'이란 의미로 쓰였다.

irregular a. 불규칙한; 비정규의(= unofficial) conflict zone 분쟁지대 discontinuous a. 불연속적인, 단속적인 asymmetrical a. 비대칭적인 nonconforming a. 관행[규범]을 따르지 않는, 국교를 신봉하지 않는

분쟁 지역에 비정규군이 존재하는 것이 군인과 범죄자를 구별하기 어렵게 만든다.

13 문맥상 동의어 ④

lost는 형용사로서 '분실한', '낭비한', '패배한', '열중하는', '자포자기의' 등의 뜻을 가지고 있는데, 주어진 문장에서는 '열중하는' 정도의 의미로 쓰였다.

dip below 밑으로 떨어지다 bustling a. 부산한, 북적거리는 lost a. 열중하는(= engrossed) stolen a. 훔친, 몰래 행해진 defeated a. 패배한 squander v. 낭비하다, 탕진하다

해가 지평선 아래로 내려가자, 사람들은 도시 생활의 리듬에 빠져 북적이는 거리를 거닐었다.

14 재진술 ③

주어진 문장에서 핵심적인 정보는 환풍기가 고장 났다는 것과, 그로 인해 방안에 연기가 머물러 있었다는 것이다. 주어진 문장과 같은 의미를 가진 문장은 ③이다.

fan n. 선풍기, 부채, 환풍기 chamber n. 방, 사무실 malfunction v. 제대로 작동하지 않다 operate v. 작동하다 linger v. 오래 남다, 머물다 let out 해방하다, 빠져 나가다

환풍기가 고장 나서 연기가 방 안에 그대로 머물러있었다.
① 연기가 방 안으로 유입되었을 때 환풍기가 제대로 작동하지 않았다.
② 연기가 방 밖으로 배출된 후에야 환풍기가 다시 작동했다.
③ 환풍기가 작동할 수 없었기 때문에 연기가 방 안에 머물러있었다.
④ 환풍기가 다시 작동하고 나서야 연기가 밖으로 배출되었다.

15 재진술 ③

주어진 문장에서 핵심적인 정보는 '나는 that절의 내용을 의심한다, 즉 that절의 내용이 사실이 아니라고 생각한다'는 것이고 that절 내용은 '변호사가 의뢰인을 구하기 위해 거짓말을 하고 있다'는 것이다. 결국 '변호사가 의뢰인을 구하기 위해 거짓말을 하고 있는 것은 아니라고 나는 믿는다'는 뜻이기 때문에 주어진 문장과 같은 의미를 가진 문장은 ③이다. doubt that절은 '~라는 것을 의심한다, 믿지 않는다'는 뜻이고 suspect that절은 '~라고 의심한다, 수상쩍게 생각한다'는 뜻이므로 ②는 suspect를 doubt로 고쳐야 주어진 문장과 같은 뜻이 된다.

attorney n. 변호사 client n. 의뢰인 suspect v. 의심하다, 알아채다, 생각하다

나는 변호사가 의뢰인을 구하기 위해 거짓말을 하고 있다는 것을 강하게 의심한다.
① 의뢰인을 구하기 위해 거짓말을 하는 것이 변호사가 의심하는 것이라고, 나는 생각한다.
② 나는 변호사가 의뢰인을 구하기 위해 진실을 말하지 않고 있다고 의심한다.
③ 의뢰인을 구하기 위해 거짓말을 하는 것은 변호사가 하고 있는 것이 아니라고, 나는 믿는다.
④ 나는 변호사가 그의 의뢰인이 거짓말을 하지 않고 있다는 것을 안다고 생각한다.

16 올바른 어순   ①

빈칸에 가장 먼저 올 단어는 There is 다음에 오는 명사이다. 따라서 여기서는 '두려움'이라는 뜻의 명사로 쓰인 dread가 먼저 오고, 그 다음은 종속접속사 lest와 '주어+조동사'인 help should가 와야 한다. lest ~ should는 '~할까 봐'라는 의미를 갖는 숙어적 표현이다.

dread a. 두려운, 무시무시한 lest ~ should ~할까 봐(= in case)(특정한 감정의 원인을 나타냄)

전투에서 우리가 승리하기도 전에 적에게 도움이 닿지 않을까 하는 두려움이 나의 마음 한구석에 항상 자리 잡고 있다.

17 올바른 어순   ③

2형식 동사 is의 주격보어로 최상급 형용사 most severe가 먼저 오고, 그 다음에는 '주어+be동사'인 it is가 생략된 when절인 when contracted가 이어져야 문장이 완성된다.

document v. 입증하다, 뒷받침하다 infection n. 전염병 contract v. 병에 걸리다 severe a. 심한

이런 종류의 전염병은 물고기로부터 감염될 때 가장 심각하다는 것은 잘 입증되어 있다.

18 타동사의 목적어   ④

이 문장은 동명사 Engaging부터 studies까지가 주어이고 allows로 시작하는 술부와 may로 시작하는 술부가 and로 연결되어 있는데, 두 번째 술부에서 prepare는 사람이 주어가 아니어서 타동사이므로 목적어가 있어야 한다. students를 가리키는 대명사 them을 목적어로 하여 ④를 prepare them for로 고쳐야 한다.

engage in 참여하다, 종사하다 interdisciplinary a. 다른 학문 분야와 제휴하는 field n. 분야

학제 연구에 참여하는 것은 학생들로 하여금 다양한 분야의 지식을 탐구할 수 있게 해주고, 또한 그들을 현대 노동력(노동시장)에 진입하게 준비시켜줄 수도 있다.

19 대명사의 수일치   ③

③ their가 가리키는 것은 단수 명사 the lighthouse이다. 그러므로 ③ their를 its로 고쳐야 한다.

storm-scarred a. 폭풍에 시달인 whisper v. 속삭이다 ancient skin 오래된 피부(표면) bear v. 품고 있다

폭풍에 시달린 등대는, 그 오래된 표면에 영원한 이야기를 담은 채, 바람과 조수에 대해 부드럽게 속삭인다.

20 정비문   ④

utter는 뒤의 명사를 수식하는 한정적인 용법으로만 쓰이는 형용사이므로 utter를 be동사의 보어로 서술적 용법으로 사용한 ④가 문법적으로 틀린 문장이다. utter를 같은 '완전한'이라는 뜻으로 서술적으로 쓰일 수 있는 perfect로 고쳐야 한다. ① 서술적으로 쓰인 형용사 bereft를 부사 visibly가 수식하고 있다. ② 서술적으로 쓰인 형용사 unaware를 부사 blissfully가 수식하고 있으며 amiss도 서술적으로만 쓰이는 형용사이다. ③ all은 '전적으로, 완전히'라는 뜻의 부사이고 rife는 서술적으로만 쓰이는 형용사이다.

break off 분리되다, 헤어지다 bereft a. 빼앗긴, 잃은, 상실감을 느끼는 visibly ad. 눈에 띄게, 역력히 blissfully ad. 행복에 넘쳐서 amiss a. 정상이 아닌, 잘못된 illiteracy n. 문맹 rife a. 많은, 풍부한, 만연한

① 실비아가 그들의 관계를 끊었을 때 그는 눈에 띄게 상실감을 느꼈다.
② 케빈은 행복하게도 아무런 잘못된 점도 알지 못한 채로 있다.
③ 그것은 전적으로 문맹이 만연한 분리된(인종차별적인) 공동체의 결과이다.
④ 할리우드에서 여성의 아름다움에 대한 기준은 완전하다.

21 정비문   ③

③은 접속사 that 다음에서 he said가 was의 주어가 될 수 없어 절을 이루지 못하므로 문법적으로 틀린 문장이다. 주어 자리에는 명사/명사구/명사절이 와야 하므로 he said를 명사절 what he said로 고쳐야 한다. ① today는 미래시제와 같이 쓰일 수 있고 what은 의문 대명사이다. ② wrong이 명사이고 What은 관계형용사이다. All wrong that you did …와 같다. ④ 가정법 과거여서 would not criticize와 knew이고 cost는 직설법적으로 과거시제 동사이다.

haunt v. 괴롭히다, 출몰하다 border on 어떤 상태에 가깝다 racism n. 인종주의 bet v. 확신하다 cost a fortune 엄청나게 비싸다

① 나는 오늘 스트레스를 해소하기 위해 무엇을 할지 아직 결정하지 않았다.
② 당신이 과거에 저지른 모든 잘못이 항상 되돌아와 당신을 괴롭힐 것이다.
③ 모든 사람은 그가 한 말이 인종 차별에 가깝고 정치적으로 올바르지 못하다는 데 동의했다.
④ 나는 당신이 그 그림이 비싼 값에 팔렸다는 걸 안다면, 그 그림을 비판하지 않을 것이라고 확신한다.

22-23

빅데이터는 트렌드 예측과 소비자 행동 분석에서 점점 더 중요한 역할을 하고 있다. 오늘날 브랜드는 빅데이터를 활용하여 온라인 소비자 경험을 맞춤화하고, 고객이 주도할 수 있도록 지원함으로써 새로운 전략을 수립하고 있다. 패션 업계의 주요 업체들은 빅데이터 열풍에 동참하고 있다. 선두 주자 중 하나인 Amazon은 올해 초 구매를 위해 로그인할 때, 사이즈를 물어봄으로써 고객의 신체 사이즈를 파악하려는 시도를 했다. 이 방대한 체형 데이터는 기본적으로 시간이 지남에 따라 체형이 어떻게 변화하는지를 더 잘 이해하기 위해 Amazon에서 수집하는 빅데이터 풀이다. 특히 반품의 40% 이상이 단지 옷이 맞지 않아서 발생하기 때문에, 이 데이터가 온라인 소매업체에 잠재적으로 줄 수 있는 유익은 전례 없을 정도로 많다. 따라서 고객이 원하는 '완벽한 핏'을 제공할 수 있는 가능성을 높이는 것은 고객들을 더욱 만족시키고 반품 건수를 크게 줄일 것이다.

forecast v. 예측하다   tailor v. 맞추다, 조정하다   get on bandwagon 시류에 편승하다   measure up 측정하다   perfect fit 몸에 꼭 맞는 옷   drastically ad. 급격하게

---

22 글의 주제 ②

이 글의 핵심적인 내용은 다양한 온라인 패션업체들이 빅데이터의 자료들을 활용하여 반품을 줄이고 고객의 만족도를 높이고 있다는 것이다. 따라서 이 글의 주제는 ② '온라인 패션 소매업에서의 빅데이터 활용'이다.

다음 중 이 글의 주제는?
① 패션업계의 주요 선두주자들
② 온라인 패션 소매업에서의 빅데이터 활용
③ 소비자 불만 처리를 위한 아마존의 전략
④ 광고에서 데이터에 따른 의사 결정의 우월성

---

23 빈칸완성 ①

단지 옷이 맞지 않아서 반품의 40%이상이 발생한다면, 고객의 체격에 관한 데이터를 미리 갖고 있으면 옷이 몸에 맞지 않아 발생하는 반품은 줄일 수 있어서 업체에 많은 유익을 줄 것이다. 따라서 빈칸에는 데이터가 업체에 해줄 수 있는 것(유익, 역할)이 전례 없을 정도로 많다는 의미로 ①의 '전례 없는'이 적절하다.

다음 중 Ⓐ에 들어가기에 가장 적절한 것은?
① 전례 없는
② 모호한
③ 정도에서 벗어난
④ 사소한

24-25

동시통역의 과정을 이해하는 것은 큰 과학적 도전이다. 하지만 최근 소수의 연구자들이 이 과제를 수행하면서, 뇌의 한 영역인 미상핵이 주목받고 있다. 미상핵이 언어를 전문으로 하는 영역은 아니지만, 신경과학자들은 의사 결정과 신뢰 같은 과정에서 미상핵이 하는 역할 때문에 미상핵을 잘 알고 있다. 그것(미상핵)은 여러 뇌 영역의 활동을 조율하여 놀랍도록

복잡한 행동을 만들어내므로 마치 오케스트라 지휘자 같다. 이것은 해석 연구들의 결과들이 지난 10~20년 동안 신경과학에서 나온 가장 큰 아이디어 중 하나와 연결되는 것처럼 보인다는 것을 의미한다. 이제 인간의 많은 정교한 능력은 특정 작업을 전담하는 특수한 뇌 영역이 아니라, 움직임과 청각 등 보다 일반적인 작업을 제어하는, 영역들 간의 빠른 조율에 의해 가능하다는 것이 분명해졌다. 동시통역은 우리의 상호작용하는 뇌에 의해 가능해진 위업인 것 같다.

simultaneous interpretation 동시통역   take up the task 일을 시작하다   caudate nucleus 미상핵(尾狀核)   coordinate v. 조율하다   stunningly ad. 깜짝 놀랄 정도로   sophisticated a. 정교한, 섬세한   dedicated to 전념하는, 헌신하는   lightning-fast a. 번개처럼 빠른   feat n. 위업   interactive a. 상호작용의

---

24 내용일치 ④

'동시통역은 우리의 상호작용하는 뇌에 의해 가능해진 위업인 것 같다.'는 단서로부터 ④ '동시통역을 전담하는 전문적인 뇌 영역이 있다.'라는 진술이 본문의 내용과 부합하지 않음을 알 수 있다.

본문에 따르면, 다음 중 사실이 아닌 것은?
① 몇몇 연구자들이 동시통역 과정을 연구하고 있다.
② 미상핵은 의사결정과 신뢰에 관여한다.
③ 움직임과 청각은 일반적인 과업으로 간주되는 활동 중 하나이다.
④ 동시통역을 전담하는 전문적인 뇌 영역이 있다.

---

25 빈칸완성 ①

빈칸 다음에 오는 진술, 즉 '(미상핵이) 여러 뇌 영역의 활동을 조율하여 놀랍도록 복잡한 행동을 만들어낸다.'라는 단서로부터 빈칸에는 ① '오케스트라 지휘자'가 와야 함을 추론할 수 있다.

다음 중 Ⓐ에 들어가기에 가장 적절한 것은?
① 오케스트라 지휘자
② 헌신적인 관찰자
③ 신경외과의
④ 효과적인 필터

26-27

"슈링크플레이션"은 표시가격을 그대로 유지하면서 제품의 크기를 줄이는 관행이다. 슈링크플레이션에서 '슈링크'는 제품 크기의 변화와 관련이 있고, '-플레이션' 부분은 물가 상승, 즉 인플레이션과 관련이 있다. 양에 의해 (양을 조절하여) 가격을 올리는 것은 주로 식음료 산업에서 기업이 투입 비용 상승에 직면하여 이익 마진을 은밀하게 높이거나 유지하기 위해 사용하는 전략이다. 슈링크플레이션의 주요 원인은 제품을 만드는 데 필요한 원자재, 기계 작동을 위한 연료, 공장 가동을 위한 전기, 그리고 인건비 등 생산 비용의 증가이다. 슈링크플레이션은 기본적으로 숨겨진 형태의 인플레이션이다. 기업들은 제품 가격 인상을 고객이 알아차릴 가능성이 높다는 것을 알고 있기 때문에, 최소한의 축소는 아마도 눈에 띄지 않을 것이라 생각하고 제품 크기를 줄이는 방법을 선택한다. (기업들은) 가격을 올리는 것이 아니라, 조금 더 적은 양을 담은 패키지에 동일한 금액을 청구함으로써 더 많은 수익을 쥐어짜낸다. 학계 연구에 따르면, 소비자는

패키지 축소보다 명시적인 가격 인상에 더 민감하게 반응하는 것으로 나타났다. 그러나 이러한 관행은 소비자의 브랜드 인식과 재구매 의도를 부정적으로 만들고, 시간이 경과함에 따라 판매량이 정체되거나 감소하는 결과를 초래할 수 있다.

shrinkflation n. 슈링크플레이션(제품의 가격은 그대로 두지만 크기나 중량을 줄여 가격을 인상하는 판매 전략) **sticker price** 표시가격 **boost** v. 신장시키다 **profit margin** 이윤 **in the face of** ~에 직면하여 **commodity** n. 원자재 **run** v. 운영하다 **spot** v. 알아차리다 **go unnoticed** 눈에 띄지 않고 넘어가다 **squeeze out** 쥐어짜다 **charge** v. 청구하다 **repurchase** v. 재구매하다

---

26 글의 주제   ①

이 글은 슈링크플레이션이 무엇인지를 정의를 내리고, 기업들이 슈링크플레이션을 시도하는 이유, 그리고 그 문제점 등을 포괄적으로 다루고 있다. 그러므로 이 글의 주제는 ① '슈링크플레이션의 정의와 이유'이다.

다음 중 이 글의 주제는?
① 슈링크플레이션의 정의와 이유
② 경제 침체의 신호들
③ 기업들이 이윤을 투자하는 방법
④ 슈링크플레이션에 대한 학계의 연구

---

27 빈칸완성   ②

Ⓐ 가격을 그대로 유지하면서 제품의 양을 줄이는 것은 본질적으로 고객의 눈을 속이기 위해 '은밀하게' 하는 행위이다. Ⓑ 기업들이 슈링크플레이션을 행하는 주된 이유는 고객들이 가격인상에 민감하게 반응한다는 것을 '알고 있기' 때문이다.

다음 중 Ⓐ와 Ⓑ에 들어가기에 가장 적절한 쌍은?
① 명시적으로 — 의식이 있는
② 은밀하게 — 알고 있는
③ 약간 — 망각의
④ 상당히 — 의심스러운

28-30

우리는 파트너와 친구를 선택하는 것과 같은 방식으로 형제자매를 선택하지 않는다. 물론 부모도 우리가 선택하지는 않지만, (부모는) 성인이 되는 과정에서 우리를 양육함으로써 우리에게 부모 역할을 해준다. 형제자매는 그냥 거기에 있는 것이다. 하지만 우리의 성장에 관해서라면, 그들은 부모보다 더 큰 영향을 미칠 수 있다. 이런 사실은 형제자매가 나이가 많고 멋있든, 어리고 답답하든 상관없이 마찬가지이다. 형제자매의 영향력 중 일부는 그들이 단지 존재한다는 것과 관련이 있다. 82%의 어린이가 형제자매와 함께 사는데, 이는 아버지와 함께 사는 어린이보다 더 많은 비율이며, 70세 노인의 약 75%는 살아있는 형제자매가 있다. 형제나 자매가 있는 사람들에게 형제나 자매와의 관계는 인생에서 가장 긴 시간이 될 가능성이 높다. 이러한 관계가 우리의 삶을 더 좋게 만드는지 아니면 더 나쁘게 만드는지는 좀 더 복잡한 문제이다. 긍정적인 측면에서, 청소년기에 형제자매와 긍정적인 상호작용을 하면 공감 능력, 친사회적 행동, 학업 성취도가 높아진다고 한다. 하지만 형제자매와의 관계가 나쁘면, 청소년기

에 우울증과 불안에 빠질 가능성이 높아질 수 있다. 더 나아가, 형제자매를 (자신의) 모델로 삼느냐 아니면 (형제자매로부터) 자신을 차별화하려고 노력하느냐 하는 것은 특히 중요한 영향을 미친다. 한 연구에 따르면, 서로에 대해 긍정적으로 생각하는 형제자매는 비슷한 교육 수준을 달성하는 경향이 있는 반면, (형제자매와 비교해) 아빠와 불평등하게 시간을 보내고 부모의 대우가 불평등하다고 인식하는 형제자매는 교육적 운명이 엇갈리는 것으로 나타났다.

sustain v. 지탱하다, 양육하다, 부양하다 **development** n. (아이의) 성장 **influential** a. 영향력이 있는 **cool** a. 멋진 **frustrating** a. 불만스러운, 좌절감을 주는 **sway** n. 장악, 지배, 영향 **sheer** a. 순전한, 순수한 **on the upside** 긍정적으로 생각해보면 **foster** v. 발전시키다, 키우다 **empathy** n. 공감 **prosocial** a. 친사회적인 **consequence** n. 결과

---

28 글의 주제   ②

이 글은 우리가 평생 동안 가장 긴 시간을 보내야 하는 형제자매란 존재가 우리의 삶에 미치는 긍정적인 영향과 부정적인 결과를 비교적 객관적인 시각에서 다루고 있다. 따라서 이 글의 적절한 주제는 ② '형제자매가 개인의 삶에 미치는 영향'이다.

다음 중 이 글의 주제는?
① 학교에서의 형제자매 역학 관계의 해부학
② 형제자매가 개인의 삶에 미치는 영향
③ 청소년기 기간 동안 형제자매 간의 라이벌 관계
④ 형제자매와 부모의 관계

---

29 내용일치   ④

'형제자매와의 관계가 나쁘면, 청소년기에 우울증과 불안에 빠질 가능성이 높아질 수 있다'고 했으므로 ④가 사실인 진술이다. ① 친구는 선택되지만 형제자매는 선택되지 않는다. ② 나이와 성격은 이 글에서 언급되지 않았다. ③ '70세 노인의 약 75%는 살아있는 형제자매가 있다'고 했는데 75%는 대다수라 할 수 있으므로 '살아있는 형제자매가 있다'고 해야 한다.

본문에 따르면, 다음 중 사실인 것은?
① 형제자매는 부모 및 친구와 비슷한 방식으로 선택된다.
② 형제자매의 영향력은 일반적으로 나이와 성격에 기인한다.
③ 70세 노인의 대다수는 살아 있는 형제자매가 없다.
④ 서로에 대해 부정적인 감정을 갖고 있는 형제자매들은 청소년기에 불안을 느끼는 경향이 있다.

---

30 빈칸완성   ①

Ⓐ '70세 노인의 약 75%는 살아있는 형제자매가 있다'라는 진술로부터 우리가 우리의 형제자매들과 우리의 인생에서 가장 긴 시간을 함께 보낸다는 사실을 알 수 있다. Ⓑ '서로에 대해 긍정적으로 생각하는 형제자매는 비슷한 교육 수준을 달성하는 경향이 있는' 단서로부터 그와 반대의 경우, 형제자매의 교육수준이 '분기되는' 즉 달라진다는 사실을 추론할 수 있다.

다음 중 Ⓐ와 Ⓑ에 들어가기에 가장 적절한 쌍은?
① 가장 긴 ― 분기되는
② 초석 ― 개선된
③ 재난 ― 불평등한
④ 지속되는 ― 더 적은

31-32

활동 연속은 심리사회적 현상이다. 이는 시간적 매개변수 내에서 변하지 않는 업무수행, 즉 지정된 시간 내에 미리 결정된 작업을 성공적으로 완료하는 것을 요구한다. 활동 연속 중인 사람은 일반적으로 자신의 활동 연속을 외부 압력이 아닌, 자신의 의지에 기인한다고 생각한다. 하지만 활동 연속을 유지하기 위해 다른 사람들과 경쟁할 수도 있다. 활동 연속 중인 사람이, 활동 연속이 깨지지 않았다고 생각하고 지속 시간을 수량화할 수도 있다면, 즉 활동 연속이 얼마나 오랫동안 지속되었는지 알 수 있다면, 우리는 그 사람이 활동연속을 하고 있다고 말할 수 있다. 이것이 왜 중요한 것일까? 글쎄, 앱 디자이너들은 시장의 입지를 구축하고 사람들이 앱을 계속 사용하고 비용을 지불하도록 하기 위해, 이를 활용해왔다. 활동연속을 포함하는 앱은 100개 이상 있다.

예를 들어, 듀오링고 앱은 언어 학습 일수를 계산하지만, 레슨 1회, 15분 학습, 레벨 완료 등 '하루'로 간주되는 기준을 사용자가 직접 설정할 수 있다. 듀오링고를 사용하면 친구들과 경쟁하고 다른 사람들을 따라갈 수 있다. 그리고 (학습자가) 100일 연속 학습과 같은 주요 이정표에 도달하면, 그것(듀오링고)은 (학습자의) 친구에게 메시지를 보내준다. 활동 연속은 습관과 유사하지만, 전자가 전략적인 계획을 요구하고 행동이 수행되지 않으면 중단되는 반면, 후자는 반사작용과 같은 반응에 의존하여 작업을 수행한다는 점에서, 습관과 구별될 수 있다. 사고의 최소화를 위한 습관 형성의 매력에도 불구하고, (습관 형성과 달리) 활동 연속은 중단되지 않는 순서를 유지해야 하는 도전을 통해 개인에게 동기를 부여한다.

streak n. 연속, 줄, 경향 performance n. 수행 temporal a. 시간의, 때의 parameter n. 매개변수 predetermined a. 미리 결정된 time-frame n. 시간 기간 volition n. 자유의지 quantify v. 수량화하다 seize on 이용하다, 포착하다 market presence 시장 입지 incorporating a. 결합하는 cease v. 끝나다 reflex-like a. 반사적인

본문에 따르면, 다음 중 사실이 아닌 것은?
① 습관은 활동연속과 비슷하지만 후자는 의지적이다.
② 듀오링고를 사용하면 활동 연속의 일일 성과 기준을 설정할 수 있다.
③ 타인과의 경쟁은 활동연속 형성에 필수적인 요소이다.
④ 깨지지 않는 순서를 유지하려는 동기는 사람들로 하여금 일부 앱을 계속 사용하도록 한다.

33-34

게으르거나 무조직적이어서, 심지어 스트레스를 받아서 당신이 (해야 할 일을) 미루는 것은 아니다. 당신이 (해야 할 일) 미루는 것은, 주의력 결핍 과잉 행동 장애(ADHD)의 대표적인 증상인 자신의 감정을 효과적으로 조절하지 못하기 때문이다. 이는 미루는 습관을 연구하는 여러 연구 프로젝트에서 밝혀진 결과이다. 심리학자들은 "만성적으로 미루는 사람에게 그냥 하라고 말하는 것은, 임상적 기분 장애를 가진 사람에게 기운을 내라고 말하는 것과 같습니다."라고 말한다. 누구나 미루는 것은 마찬가지다. 키보드가 자동으로 타이핑을 시작하기를 기다리며 빈 컴퓨터 화면을 응시하는 사람은 ADHD 환자만 있는 것이 아니다. 신경질환이 없는 사람도 허공을 응시하며 어떻게 시작해야 할지 모른다. 그들 또한 치통이 견딜 수 없어질 때까지 치과에 가는 것을 미룬다. 그들 또한 높은 서류 더미를 책상 뒤쪽으로 밀어 놓는다. 하지만 ADHD를 가진 사람들은 과제 회피의 달인이다. 영감을 기다리는 동안, 그들은 음식을 먹고, 빠른 시간에 여러 개의 TV 프로그램을 시청하고, 소셜 미디어를 스크롤하고, 아픈 영혼을 달래는 다른 활동을 한다. 누구나 미루는 것에 대한 괴로움을 경험하지만, 미완성된 작업은 실제로 ADHD 환자에게 신체적, 정신적 고통을 유발할 수 있다. 계획, 우선순위 정하기, 동기 부여하기, 조직하기, 의사 결정하기는 ADHD 환자를 압도하고 위축되게 만들 수도 있다.

procrastinate v. 꾸물거리다, 미루다 stress out 스트레스를 받다 regulate v. 조절하다 Attention Deficit Hyperactivity Disorder 주의력 결핍 과잉행동 장애(= ADHD) chronic a. 만성적인 clinical mood disorder 임상적 기분 장애 neurotypical n. 신경전형인, 신경질환이 없는 사람 stack n. 무더기 binge-watch v. 빠른 시간에 여러 개의 TV 프로그램을 보다 soothe v. 달래다 anguish n. 고통 shut down 멈추다, 정지하다

---

31 글의 주제   ②

이 글은 주로 활동 연속을 정의내리고 그 특징들과 활용들을 기술하고 있다. 따라서 이 글의 주제는 ② '활동 연속의 주요 특징들'이다.

다음 중 이 글의 주제는?
① 듀오링고가 고객을 유지하는 방법
② 활동 연속의 주요 특징들
③ 작업을 미리 결정하는 데 전략 계획이 필요한 이유
④ (활동) 연속과 동기의 차이

---

32 내용일치   ③

'하지만 활동 연속을 유지하기 위해 다른 사람들과 경쟁할 수도 있다.'라는 단서로부터 타인과의 경쟁은 활동연속의 필수적인 요소가 아님을 알 수 있다. 따라서 ③이 사실이 아니다.

---

33 글의 주제   ④

이 글은 해야 할 일을 미루는 습관이 나태나 게으름 혹은 성격의 문제가 아니라 Attention Deficit Hyperactivity Disorder (ADHD) (주의력 결핍 과잉행동 장애)에서 비롯되는 일종의 정신질환 증세라고 설명하고 있다. 따라서 이글의 주제는 ④ '미루는 버릇과 ADHD의 상관관계'이다.

다음 중 이 글의 주제는?
① ADHD 환자의 일반적인 일상
② 미루는 습관을 극복하기 위한 전략
③ 미루기가 신체적, 정신적 건강에 미치는 영향
④ 미루는 버릇과 ADHD의 상관관계

34 내용일치 ①

'게으르거나 무조직적이어서, 심지어 스트레스를 받아서 당신이 (해야 할 일을) 미루는 것은 아니다'라는 본문의 진술로부터 ① '미루는 일은 일반적으로 스트레스를 받을 때 발생한다.'가 본문의 내용과 일치하지 않는다는 것을 알 수 있다.

본문에 따르면, 다음 중 사실이 <u>아닌</u> 것은?
① 미루는 일은 일반적으로 스트레스를 받을 때 발생한다.
② ADHD가 없는 사람들도 일을 시작하는 것을 피한다.
③ ADHD가 있는 사람들은 자신의 감정을 조절하는 데 어려움을 겪는다.
④ 습관적으로 미루는 사람에게 시작하라고 말하는 것은 도움이 되지 않는다.

35-37

만일 당신이 ChatGPT를 사용해보았으면, 당신은 틀림없이 그것이 곧 무엇을 혁신하게 될지, 아니면 그럴 수도 있듯이, 무엇을 파괴하게 될지에 대해 궁금해졌을 것이다. 현재 공통적인 견해 중 하나에 의하면, 여러 세대에 걸쳐 인문주의 교육의 중심이었고, 여러 세대가 교육 전반에 걸쳐 실행하면서 성장해 온 글쓰기 형식이 ChatGPT의 첫 번째 희생자가 될 것이다. 만일 ChatGPT가 주어진 주제에 대해 그럴듯하게 들리는 학술 에세이를 즉각적으로 작성할 수 있게 된다면, 학술 에세이 자체에 어떤 미래가 있을까? 노암 촘스키는 "수년 동안 표절된 에세이를 발견하는 데 있어서 교수들에게 도움을 주는 프로그램들이 있어왔습니다."라고 말한다. "이제는 표절하기가 더 쉬워졌기 때문에 그것이(표절을 발견하는 것이) 더 어려워질 것입니다. 하지만 제가 생각할 수 있는 ChatGPT의 교육에 대한 기여는 그것뿐입니다." 현재 관련 기술이 발전한 상황에서 촘스키는 ChatGPT의 사용을 "기본적으로 첨단 기술적 표절"이자 "학습을 회피하는 방법"으로 보고 있다. 그는 ChatGPT의 등장을 스마트폰의 등장에 비유하고 있다. 많은 학생들이 "아이폰으로 누군가가 채팅을 하고 있습니다. 이를 해결하는 한 가지 방법은 아이폰을 금지하는 것이고, 그렇게 하는 또 다른 방법은 수업을 흥미롭게 만드는 것입니다."라고 말한다. 학생들이 본능적으로 학습을 회피하기 위해 첨단 기술을 사용한다는 것은 교육 시스템이 실패하고 있다는 신호이다. 대부분의 기술 혼란은 긍정적인 영향과 부정적인 영향을 모두 남긴다. 대학 에세이를 정말로 (표절로부터) 구해낼 수 없다면, ChatGPT가 마침내 대학 에세이를 더 흥미로운 것으로 대체시키는 결과를 가져올 것이다.

revolutionize v. 혁신하다 humanistic pedagogy 인문주의적인 교육 instantaneously ad. 동시에, 즉각적으로 whip up 잽싸게 만들다 plausible-sounding a. 그럴듯한 plagiarize v. 표절하다 relevant a. 관련 있는, 적절한, 관련된 disruption n. 붕괴 unsalvageable a. 구원할 수 없는

35 글의 제목 ①

이 글은 ChatGPT의 등장으로 인해 대학에서 학술 에세이의 표절이 일반화된 상황을 설명하고 표절을 막기 위한 방법으로 iPhone처럼 ChatGPT의 사용을 금지하는 것과, 그것이 불가능하면 표절의 표적이 되는 에세이를 다른 더 흥미로운 것으로 대체하는 것을 제시하므로 ①이 글의 제목으로 가장 적절하다. ② 학술 에세이의 표절이 제목에서 빠져 있다. ④ 표절이 일반화된 상황을 포착하지 못하는 제목이다.

다음 중 이 글의 가장 적절한 제목은?
① ChatGPT: 첨단 기술적 표절과 이를 피하는 방법
② ChatGPT: 교육의 혁명인가, 파괴인가?
③ ChatGPT: 아이폰의 출현과의 병행성
④ ChatGPT: 학술 에세이 구하기

36 내용일치 ③

'촘스키는 현재 관련 기술이 발전한 상황에서 ChatGPT의 사용을 "기본적으로 첨단 기술적 표절"이자 "학습을 회피하는 방법"으로 보고 있다.'라는 본문의 진술로부터 ③ '촘스키는 ChatGPT가 에세이 작성을 흥미롭게 만들므로 ChatGPT의 등장을 환영한다.'는 진술이 본문의 내용과 일치하지 않음을 알 수 있다.

본문에 따르면, 다음 중 사실이 <u>아닌</u> 것은?
① 학술 에세이는 오랫동안 인문학 교육에 필수적인 것으로 여겨져 왔다.
② 타인의 저작물을 적절하게 인용하지 않은 글을 탐지하기 위한 프로그램이 많이 개발되었다.
③ Chomsky는 ChatGPT가 에세이 작성을 흥미롭게 만들므로 ChatGPT의 등장을 환영한다.
④ 첨단 기술을 사용함으로써 학생들은 학습을 기피하는 경향이 있는데, 이는 교육 시스템이 제대로 작동하지 않음을 나타낸다.

37 지시대상 ④

다른 모든 it은 ChatGPT를 가리키지만 ⓓ의 its는 아이폰 사용 문제를 해결하는 것(dealing with that)을 나타낸다.

38-40

음악이 누군가의 영혼을 달래줄 수 있다는 것은 의심의 여지가 없다. 그러나 음악은 신체적 고통을 일시적으로 완화시켜주는 데도 도움이 될 수 있을 것으로 판명된다. 한 소규모 연구는 63명의 젊은 성인에게 자신이 좋아하는 노래 두 곡을 가져오도록 요청했다. 연구팀은 또한 청년들에게 7곡의 노래 중 하나를 선택하게 했는데, 이 노래들은 연구 참가자들에게는 생소했다. 그들은 참가자들에게 자신이 좋아하는 음악과 편안한 기악곡 7곡 중 하나를 들으면서 모니터 화면을 응시하도록 지시했다. 그 동안 연구진은 참가자의 왼쪽 안쪽 팔뚝에 뜨거운 물체를 붙였다. 참가자들은 자신의 경험을 평가할 때, 낯선 편안한 노래나 침묵을 들을 때보다 자신이 좋아하는 노래를 들을 때 고통을 덜 느낀다고 답했다. 어떤 장르의 좋아하는 노래가 통증을 가장 많이 감소시키는지를 알아보기 위해, 연구진은 가장 좋아하는 노래와 통증에 대한 평가에 대해 참가자들과 인터뷰를 했다. 그 결과, 괴롭고 즐거우며 감동적인 노래를 들은 사람들은 차분하거나 밝은 주제의 노래를 들었을 때보다 고통을 덜 느끼는 것으로 나타났다. 또한 괴롭고 즐거운 노래를 들은 사람들은 더 많은 오한을 보고했는데, 이런 전율과 떨림은 즐거운 음악을 들었을 때 당신이 피부로 느끼는 것이다. 이 감각은 그들이 실험에서 느낀 타는 듯한 통증으로 인한 불쾌감에 대한 낮은 평가와 관련이 있었다. 비록 철저하게 연구되지는 않았지만, 연구진은 이러한 음악적 오한이 통증 차단 효과를 유발할 수 있다고 생각한다고 말했다. 하지만 취향에 따라 더 경쾌한 노래를 선택하는 것이 잘못된 것은 아니다. 음악은 스트레스 감소와 숙면 등 다양한 건강상의 이점을 제공한다.

soother n. 달래는[위로하는] 사람[것] instruct v. 지시[명령]하다 instrumental a. 악기의, 도움이 되는 rate v. 평가하다 bittersweet a. 달콤 쌉쌀한, 괴롭고 즐거운 chill n. 오한 shiver n. 오한, 전율 elicit v. 이끌어내다, 유도하다 upbeat a. 경쾌한, 낙관적인

38 글의 주제 ③

이 글에서 주로 다루고 있는 것은 좋아하는 음악을 들으면 신체적 고통이 완화된다는 것이다. 그러므로 이 글의 주제는 ③ '좋아하는 노래의 진통효과'이다.

다음 중 이 글의 주제는?
① 괴롭고 즐거운 노래와 경쾌한 노래의 서로 다른 감정
② 신나는 노래의 수많은 건강상의 이점들
③ 좋아하는 노래의 통증 차단 효과
④ 음악적 오한이 쾌감에 미치는 영향

39 내용일치 ③

'괴롭고 즐거운 노래를 들은 사람들은 더 많은 오한을 보고 했는데, 이런 전율과 떨림은 즐거운 음악을 들었을 때 당신이 피부로 느끼는 것이다'라고 했다. 오한이 곧 전율과 떨림이므로 ③이 사실이다. ① 자신이 좋아하는 음악과 편안한 기악곡 7곡 중 하나를 들으라고 요구했다. ② 오른쪽 팔뚝 안쪽이 아니라 왼쪽 팔뚝 안쪽이다. ④ 신체적 고통을 달래주는 것은 진정시키는 노래가 아니라 좋아하는 노래이다.

본문에 따르면, 다음 중 사실인 것은?
① 각 참가자는 편안한 노래 7곡을 들어보라는 요청을 받았다.
② 연구자들은 참가자들의 오른쪽 팔뚝 안쪽에 뜨거운 물체를 붙였다.
③ 괴롭고 즐거운 노래는 참가자들에게 전율과 떨림을 불러일으켰다.
④ 진정시키는 노래는 신체적 고통을 달래는 데 가장 효과적인 것으로 밝혀졌다.

40 지시대상 ①

ⓐ They는 연구자들을 나타내고, 나머지 they는 피실험자를 나타낸다.

41-42

미국에서, 'Stand Your Ground Law(스탠드 유어 그라운드 법)'는 사람들이 안전하게 상황을 벗어날 수 있었는지 여부에 관계없이 생명이 위험하다고 느낄 때, 자신을 보호할 수 있도록 허용하는 법이다. 스탠드 유어 그라운드 법은 일반인이, 자신이 있을 권리가 있는 장소에서 강제로 나가야 한다고 느껴서는 안 되며, 다른 사람이 자신의 안전에 임박한 위협이 된다고 느끼는 경우, 그 사람에게 치명적인 무력을 사용할 수 있다고 주장한다. 스탠드 유어 그라운드 법의 합법성은 가정 방어에 뿌리를 두고 있다. 이런 이유 때문에, 이 법은 사람들이 자신과 자신의 집, 즉 "성(城)"을 보호하기 위해 필요하다고 생각하는 모든 행동을 할 수 있도록 허용하기 때문에, "캐슬 독트린"이라는 또 다른 이름으로 불린다. 여기에는 치명적인 부상을 초래하더라도 자신을 방어하기 위해 총이나 칼을 사용하는 등 치명적인 무력을 사용하는 것도 포함된다. 이 법은 안전한 탈출의 합법적인 기회가 있는 경우에도, 자신과 자신의 재산을 방어하기로 선택한 사람들을 보호한

다. 일부 미국 주에서는 치명적인 대응을 탈출이 불가능한 상황에 대한 반응으로 제한하고 있지만, 스탠드 유어 그라운드를 지지하는 주에서는 그렇지 않다.

premises n. 부지[지역], 구내 lethal a. 치명적인 imminent a. 임박한 legality n. 적법성, 정당함 fatal a. 치명적인 property n. 자산, 재산 legitimate a. 합법적인, 적법한

41 내용일치 ④

'스탠드 유어 그라운드 법의 합법성은 가정 방어에 뿌리를 두고 있고 이 법은 "캐슬 독트린"이라고도 불린다'고 했으므로 ④가 사실이다. ① '미국 전역에서'가 아니라 마지막 문장에서 언급된 '치명적인 대응을 제한하고 있는 일부 주에서' 그러하다. ② Stand Your Ground Law는 존재할 권리가 있는 장소에 있는 사람들을 보호하는 것이다. ③ Stand Your Ground Law가 없는 주의 경우, 탈출이 불가능한 상황에서는 치명적인 폭력이 허용된다.

본문에 따르면, 다음 중 사실인 것은?
① 미국 전역에서, 치명적인 무력이 허용되기 전에 임박한 위험을 피하려는 시도가 필요하다.
② Stand Your Ground Law는 존재할 권리가 없는 장소에 있는 사람들의 권리를 보호한다.
③ Stand Your Ground Law가 없는 주에서는 치명적인 폭력이 절대 허용되지 않는다.
④ 캐슬 독트린(Castle Doctrine)의 기본 개념은 가정 방어이다.

42 부분이해 ③

ⓐ '이 법은 안전한 탈출의 합법적인 기회가 있는 때에도, 자신과 자신의 재산을 방어하기로 선택한 사람들을 보호한다.'에서 '탈출의 기회가 있는 때에도'라는 것은 '탈출의 기회가 있어도 시도하지 않고'라는 말이고 '자신과 재산을 방어한다'는 것은 '침입자를 쏜다'는 말이므로 ⓐ의 내용을 가장 잘 설명하고 있는 것은 ③ '집주인은 침입자를 쏘기 전에 탈출을 시도할 필요가 없다.' 즉 먼저 탈출을 시도할 필요 없이 총을 쏠 수 있다는 말이다.

본문에 따르면, 다음 중 ⓐ로부터 추론할 수 있는 것은?
① 침입자는 자기에게 총을 쏜 집주인에게 합법적으로 총을 쏠 수 있다.
② 집주인이 침입자로부터 탈출할 수 있으면 총격을 가하는 것은 불법이다.
③ 집주인은 침입자를 쏘기 전에 탈출을 시도할 필요가 없다.
④ 집주인은 총격보다는 임박한 위협으로부터 도망치는 것을 선호한다.

43-44

전 세계적인 뉴스 데이터베이스 Factiva에 따르면, '디지털 디톡스'에 대한 첫 언급은 2006년에 이루어졌지만, 2010년이 되어서야 사용이 유행하기 시작했다. 2013년에 디지털 디톡스가 옥스퍼드 온라인 사전에 추가되었고, 2019년 중반에는 데이터베이스의 디지털 디톡스에 대한 총 항목 수가 9,000개에 육박했다. 이러한 수치와 텍스트는 "스마트폰 과다 사용"과 "미디어 사용 제한"이 논란거리가 되었음을 반영한다. 이 주제는 소셜 미디어, 블로그, 가족 모임, 학교, 직장에서 논의되고 있다. 디지털 디톡스와

관련된 새로운 용어와 경구는 우리의 어휘를 더욱 풍부하게 만들었다. FOMO는 스마트폰과 소셜 미디어 사용을 주도하는 것으로 추정되는 "Fear of Missing Out(소외의 두려움)"이라는 새로운 조건의 약칭으로 등장했다. JOMO는 그 반대이다. 디지털 디톡스 경험자가 추구하는 "Joy of Missing Out(소외의 즐거움)"은 화면이 아닌 지금 이 순간의 삶을 즐기는 감각이다. "Phubbing(퍼빙)"은 휴대전화를 차단하는 행위(휴대폰 차단)의 약어이다: 전화를 사용하여 누군가의 접근을 차단하는 것이다. Screen wall(스크린 월)은 같은 것을 다른 말로 표현한 것으로, 스크린 타임(전자기기 사용시간)이 가족 내 협상의 중심 대상으로 떠오르고 있다. 이미 2008년에 영국 우체국에서는 1,300만 명의 영국인이 휴대폰 배터리가 방전되거나 분실되었을 때 스트레스를 받는 "nomophobia(노모포비아)" 즉, "No Mobile Phobia(휴대폰 없는 공포증)"에 시달리고 있다고 밝혔다. 디지털 디톡스는 상대적으로 새로운 용어이지만 미디어 사용에 대해 이야기하기 위해 의학 용어를 사용하는 오랜 전통 위에 서 있다. 역사를 통틀어 미디어는 감염, 쓰레기, 독에 비유되었다. 디지털 디톡스는 이런 것들을 깨끗이 제거하는 은유적인 방법이다.

digital detox 디지털 디톡스, 디지털 거리 두기(디지털 기기 사용을 잠시 중단하고 휴식을 취하거나 디지털 기기 중독에서 벗어나는 일) take off 유행하다 entry n. 등재, 수록 talking point 논란거리 term n. 용어 aphorism n. 경구 shorthand n. 약칭 presumably ad. 아마도, 짐작건대 miss out 놓치다 phubbing Phone과 snubbing의 합성어로 스마트폰에 빠져 주변사람들에게 신경쓰지 않는 사람을 뜻함 snub v. 무시하다, 거부하다 screen time 스크린 타임(컴퓨터, 텔레비전 또는 게임기와 같은 장치를 사용하는 시간) nomophobia n. 노모포비아(휴대폰이 없을 때 불안을 느끼는 증상) metaphorical a. 은유적인

---

43 글의 주제 ②

이 글은 '디지털 디톡스'라는 용어가 출현하게 된 배경과 그 의미, 그리고 이와 관련된 다양한 신조어들을 설명하고 있다. 따라서 이 글의 주제는 ② '디지털 디톡스라는 용어의 출현 및 관련 신조어'이다.

다음 중 이 글의 주제는?
① 디지털 디톡스와 노모포비아 개념의 유래
② 디지털 디톡스라는 용어의 출현 및 관련 신조어
③ 새로운 의학용어의 은유적 개념화 과정
④ 청소년의 미디어 이용 제한 및 새로운 용어의 필요성

---

44 내용일치 ③

디지털 디톡스라는 용어가 옥스퍼드 온라인 사전에 추가된 것은 2013년이므로 ③이 사실이다. ① 1,300만 명의 영국인들은 JOMO가 아니라 "nomophobia(노모포비아)" 즉, "No Mobile Phobia(휴대폰 없는 공포증)로 고통 받았다. ② 디지털 디톡스라는 용어의 사용은 2010년에 유행이 시작된 것이고 계속 증가하고 있다. ④ FOMO는 스마트폰과 소셜 미디어 사용을 주도하는 것으로 추정되는 "Fear of Missing Out(실종에 대한 두려움)"이라는 새로운 조건의 약칭이다.

본문에 따르면, 다음 중 사실인 것은?
① 영국 우체국에 따르면, 2008년에 1,300만 명의 영국인이 JOMO로 고통 받았다고 한다.
② 디지털 디톡스라는 용어의 사용은 2010년에 정점에 이르렀다.

---

③ 2006년 옥스퍼드 온라인 사전에는 디지털 디톡스라는 용어가 존재하지 않았다.
④ FOMO는 스마트폰 사용을 줄이는 주요 동기이다.

45-47

'바넘 효과'는 일반적인 진술을, 특히 아첨하는 경우, 정확한 개인적 묘사(설명)로 받아들이는 경향을 말한다. 바넘 효과는 19세기 미국 쇼맨인 P.T. 바넘의 이름을 따서 명명되었는데, 그의 유명한 말(격언) 두 가지가 여기에 포함되어 있기 때문이다: "나의 성공 비결은 항상 모든 사람에게 작은 것을 주는 것이다."와 "매 순간마다 잘 속는 사람은 태어난다."이다. 전형적인 바넘 효과 문구는 상세하거나 구체적일 수 있지만, 실제로는 모호하고 애매하며 심지어 자기 모순적이기 때문에 모든 사람에게 적용될 수 있다. 그들이 알든 모르든, 이 현상은 점성술사, 심령술사, 점쟁이들의 주요 속임수이다. 이 효과는 1949년 미국 심리학자 버트람 포러(Bertram Forer)의 실험에서 처음 입증되었는데, 그는 대학생들에게 이전에 치른 테스트에 기초한 것으로 추정되는 성격 프로필을 주었다. 실제로 이 프로필은 점성술 책에서 발췌한 문장으로 구성되었으며, 모든 피실험자는 동일한 목록을 받았다. 성격 프로필의 설명이 자신의 성격의 기본 특성을 어느 정도 드러내는지를 0에서 5점까지의 척도로 평가하라는 요청을 받았을 때, 피실험자들은 평균적으로 5점 만점에서 4점 이상을 주며 바넘 효과를 입증했다. 하지만 바넘 효과에 대해 안다고 해서 (이 효과에) 쉽게 저항할 수 있는 것은 아니다. 하지만 심리학자들이 제공할 수 있는 최선의 조언은 이 효과를 인지하고 아첨에 굴복하지 않도록 노력하라는 것이다.

tendency n. 경향 generic a. 포괄적인 name for ~의 이름을 따서 붙이다 incorporate v. 포함하다, 창립하다 dictum n. 격언, 금언 sucker n. 잘 속는 사람 ambiguous a. 애매모호한 psychic n. 심령술사 demonstrate v. 입증하다, 설명하다 personality profile 성격 프로필 subject n. 피험자, 피실험자 flattery n. 아부, 아첨

---

45 글의 주제 ②

이 글은 바넘 효과의 의미가 무엇이고, 어떻게 유래했는지를 설명한 다음, 바넘 효과의 다양한 응용과 쓰임 및 그 효과의 증명 등에 대해 진술하고 있다. 그러므로 이 글의 주제로는 ② '바넘 효과라는 용어의 유래와 응용'이 적절하다.

다음 중 이 글의 주제는?
① 아첨에 바넘 효과의 적용(활용)
② 바넘 효과라는 용어의 유래와 응용
③ 점성가들에 의한 바넘 효과 진술의 원리
④ 바넘 효과와 엔터테인먼트 산업과의 관계

---

46 내용추론 ②

포러의 실험은 바넘 효과의 실효성을 실증적으로 입증했을 뿐 실험 참가자들에게 정신적 피해를 주지는 않았다.

본문에 따르면, 다음 중 추론할 수 없는 것은?
① 바넘 효과가 발현되었다는 사실을 인식하더라도 아첨에 굴복하지 않기는 어려울 것이다.
② 포러의 실험 참가자들은 실험으로 인해 정신적 피해를 입었다.

③ 점쟁이들은 누구에게나 관련이 있기 때문에 전형적인 바넘 효과 진술을 사용하는 경향이 있다.

④ "당신은 관대한 경향이 있다"라는 성격 프로필 진술은 바넘 효과를 이끌어낸다.

47 빈칸완성 ①

'전형적인 바넘 효과 문구는 상세하거나 구체적일 수 있지만, 실제로는 모호하며 애매하며 심지어 자기 모순적이다'라는 것은 바넘 효과 문구가 귀에 걸면 귀걸이, 코에 걸면 코걸이가 될 수 있다는 말이다. 따라서 빈칸에 들어갈 가장 적절한 표현은 ① '누구에게나 적용 가능한'이다.

다음 중 Ⓐ에 들어가기에 가장 적절한 것은?
① 누구에게나 적용 가능한
② 심리학자들에게 유용한
③ 점성술사에게 불리한
④ 개인에게 맞춤화된

48-50

"어"와 "음"이라는 말은 사람들이 심사숙고 없이 말하는 경향이 있기 때문에, 오랫동안 심리학자들과 언어학자들의 흥미를 끌었다. 지그문트 프로이트는 사람의 무의식적 자아에 대한 통찰을 위해 언어 오류 조사를 개척했으며, 정신과 의사인 George Mahl은 1950년대에 환자의 감정 상태를 "어", "음" 및 다른 소위 비유창성(눌변, 말더듬이)과 연관시켜 이러한 전통을 이어나갔다. 이후 1980년대에 심리언어학자들은 뇌가 언어를 생성하는 방식을 연구하기 위해 비유창성을 사용하기 시작했다. 이제 "어"와 "음"의 사용이 사회 계층에 따라 패턴화되는 것으로 보인다는 데이터가 나왔다. 미국의 언어학자 Mark Liberman은 녹취된 전화 대화를 분석한 결과(에 의거하여), 여성이 남성보다 "음"을 22% 더 자주 사용하는 반면, 남성은 "어"를 여성보다 2배 이상 더 자주 사용한다고 보고했다. 또한 방언학자 Jack Grieve의 연구도 화제가 되었다. 그는 6억 건의 트윗을 매핑하여 뉴잉글랜드와 중서부 지역을 포함한 지역에서는 "음"으로 시작하는 문장을 선호하는 반면, 서쪽에서 애리조나까지 이어지는 지역에서는 "어"가 지배적이라는 것을 발견했다. Grieve는 "음"이 "어"보다 다소 공손한 표현일 수 있다고 추측한다. 그렇다면 북동부 지역에서 "음"을 선호하는 것은 단순히 지역적 격식을 표현한 것일 수도 있다. 하지만 동시에 그는 이것이 직감일 뿐이라고 인정했다. 인지 심리학자인 Herb Clark은 빅데이터가 언어에 대해 알려주는 이야기는 잠정적인 것이라고 경고한다. 데이터는 사람들이 무엇을 말하고 쓰는지는 보여줄 수 있지만 그 이유를 알려주지는 못한다. 데이터가 급증하고 컴퓨팅 속도가 점점 빨라짐에 따라, 점점 더 작은 어휘 알갱이들에 대해 언급하는 헤드라인이 많아질 것으로 예상할 수 있다. 그러나 통제된 실험만이 데이터 뒤에 무엇이 있는지를 설명하고, 빅데이터가 궁극적으로 큰 소음이 되는 것을 막을 수 있다.

intrigue v. 흥미[호기심]를 불러일으키다 deliberation n. 숙고, 심사숙고 disfluency n. 눌변, 말더듬 psycholinguist n. 심리언어학자 transcribe v. 기록하다 dialectologist n. 방언학자 make headline 화제가 되다, 대서특필되다 map v. 지도를 만들다 speculate v. 추측하다 formality n. 격식 hunch n. 직감 provisional a. 잠정적인 lexical a. 어휘의

48 글의 제목 ①

이 글은 "어"와 "음"을 사용하는 언어 패턴에 대해 남녀별, 지역별로 그 양상을 보여주고 있다. 따라서 적절한 제목은 ① '언어 패턴 베일 벗기기: "어"와 "음"'이다.

다음 중 이 글의 가장 적절한 제목은?
① 언어 패턴 베일 벗기기: "어"와 "음"
② 성별 언어 차이 매핑: 프로이트에서 빅데이터까지
③ 행 사이: 언어 비유창성에 대한 성찰적 측면
④ 무의식적인 말의 비유창성을 교정하는 방법

49 내용일치 ④

'그러나 통제된 실험만이 데이터 뒤에 무엇이 있는지 설명하고, 빅데이터가 궁극적으로 큰 소음이 되는 것을 막을 수 있다.'라는 마지막 문장으로부터 ④ '빅데이터는 우리가 말하는 근본적인 이유를 밝힐 수 있게 해준다.'가 본문의 내용과 일치하지 않음을 알 수 있다.

본문에 따르면, 다음 중 사실이 아닌 것은?
① 개인은 의식적인 생각이나 의도 없이 "어"와 "음"을 말하는 경우가 많다.
② Grieve에 따르면, "um"은 "uh"보다 공손하게 들린다.
③ Grieve는 미국인들이 "uhs"와 "ums"를 사용하는 데 있어, 지역적 차이가 있음을 발견했다.
④ 빅데이터는 우리가 말하는 근본적인 이유를 밝힐 수 있게 해준다.

50 빈칸완성 ①

앞에서 '데이터는 사람들이 무엇을 말하고 쓰는지는 보여줄 수 있지만 그 이유를 알려주지는 못한다'고 했고 빈칸 앞에서는 '통제된 실험만이 데이터 뒤에 무엇이 있는지를 설명하고'라고 했는데, 이것이 통제된 실험이 데이터가 하지 못하는 부분을 보완해준다는 말이므로 빈칸에도 데이터에 도움이 되는 일을 한다는 내용인 ① '빅데이터가 궁극적으로 큰 소음이 되는 것을 방지하다.'가 와야 함을 추론할 수 있다.

다음 중 Ⓐ에 들어가기에 가장 적절한 것은?
① 빅데이터가 궁극적으로 큰 소음이 되는 것을 방지하다
② 엄밀한 분석보다 이론적인 해석을 우선시하다
③ 말실수의 빈도를 줄이다
④ 뇌 연구의 단점을 보완하다

2024 한국외국어대학교(T2-1 B형)

01 ①	02 ②	03 ②	04 ③	05 ④	06 ①	07 ②	08 ④	09 ③	10 ②
11 ②	12 ④	13 ③	14 ①	15 ④	16 ①	17 ③	18 ①	19 ④	20 ③
21 ④	22 ④	23 ③	24 ①	25 ②	26 ①	27 ②	28 ③	29 ②	30 ④
31 ①	32 ②	33 ①	34 ③	35 ③	36 ③	37 ①	38 ①	39 ③	40 ②
41 ③	42 ④	43 ②	44 ①	45 ②	46 ④	47 ①	48 ②	49 ④	50 ②

01 논리완성   ①

not A but B의 구문은 B, not A 구문으로 사용될 수 있으며 'A가 아니라 B이다'는 뜻이다. 따라서 what he has done(그가 이루어 온 일, 즉 업적)과는 반대되는 말이 빈칸에 적절한데, pedigree는 능력 또는 업적과 상관없는 후보자의 '혈통(가문)'을 의미하므로 빈칸에는 ①이 적절하다.

vote v. 투표하다 illustrious a. 걸출한, 저명한 pedigree n. (사람의, 특히 훌륭한) 가계, 혈통 meritocracy n. 실력[능력]주의; 실력자[엘리트]층 inquisitiveness n. 연구를 좋아함; 캐묻기 좋아함 mediocrity n. 보통, 평범

누군가에게 투표할 때, 가장 중요한 것은 그의 걸출한 정치적 혈통이 아니라 그가 이루어 온 일이다.

02 논리완성   ②

혼란스러운 수비로 공격수가 쉽게 골을 넣을 만한 상황이라면, 이는 두 팀의 역량 차이를 상징적으로 보여주는 것이다. 따라서 빈칸에는 ② emblematic이 적절하다.

confused a. 혼란한, 난잡한 defense n. 방어, 수비 caliber n. 도량, 재간, 역량 enigmatic a. 수수께끼 같은, 불가사의한 emblematic a. 상징적인, 전형적인 systematic a. 체계적인, 조직적인 pragmatic a. 실용적인

혼란스러운 수비로 공격수에게 쉽게 골을 허용했는데, 이는 어떤 면에서 두 팀의 역량 차이를 상징하는 것으로 느껴졌다.

03 논리완성   ②

덩굴 식물이 건물을 푸른 잎으로 뒤덮고 있는 상황은 식물이 제대로 관리되지 않는 상황이다. 그리고 등위접속사 and가 왔으며 grass 다음은 threatened가 생략된 것이므로 의미상 비슷한 상황을 만들기 위해서는 풀이 꽃밭을 잠식했다는 의미가 되어야 한다. 따라서 빈칸에는 ② encroach가 적절하다.

vine n. 포도나무; 덩굴 식물 threaten v. ~하겠다고 위협하다, ~할 우려가 있다, ~의 징후를 보이다(to do) engulf v. 완전히 에워싸다, 휩싸다 greenery n. 녹색 나뭇잎[화초] plot n. 작은 구획의 땅, 작은

토지[지구] condense v. 응축하다; 압축하다 encroach v. 침해하다, 잠식하다 embark v. (배에) 승선하다; 착수시키다 ponder v. 숙고하다, 곰곰이 생각하다

덩굴 식물이 건물을 푸른 잎으로 뒤덮을 기세였고, 풀이 꽃밭을 잠식할 기세였다.

04 논리완성   ③

악의적인 소문이 계획적으로 퍼졌다고 했으므로 밴드의 평판에 해가 되는 상황이다. 따라서 빈칸에는 부정적인 의미의 ③ scathe(해치다)가 적절하다.

malicious a. 악의적인, 적의 있는 deliberately ad. 고의로, 의도[계획]적으로 bottom line (계상된) 순익[손실], 경비 ascertain v. (옳은 정보를) 알아내다[확인하다] debut v. (청중 앞에서) 처음 연주[연기]하다; 신상품으로 소개하다 scathe v. 상처를 입히다, 해치다 amputate v. (수술로) 절단하다

악의적인 소문이 밴드의 평판을 훼손하고 음반사의 수익에 해를 끼치기 위해 계획적으로 퍼졌다.

05 동의어   ④

credence n. 신빙성(= reassurance) mastery n. 숙달, 통달 exposure n. 노출 temerity n. 무모함, 만용 scruple n. 양심, (양심의) 가책 imprudence n. 경솔, 무분별, 무모함

이것은 특정 문장 구조의 숙달이 전적으로 나이나 언어 노출의 함수인 것은 아니라는 주장에 신빙성을 더한다.

06 동의어   ①

effervescent a. 열광하는, 활발한(= bubbly) reserved a. 보류된; 내성적인 belligerent a. 적대적인, 공격적인 impetuous a. 성급한, 충동적인; 격렬한

그 노부인의 활발한 성격은 그녀가 들어간 모든 방에 따뜻한 생기를 불어넣었다.

07 동의어 ②

speculate v. 사색하다, 깊이 생각하다(= prognosticate) irradiate v. 비추다, 밝히다; 계몽하다 arraign v. (피고를) 법정에 소환하다; 나무라다 ameliorate v. 개선하다

새해 달력을 보니, 연중 이맘때가 이렇게 어려운 세상에서 새해에 어떤 일이 기다리고 있을지 깊이 생각해 볼 때이다.

08 동의어 ④

eliminate v. 없애다, 제거하다 subscription n. 구독료 abstemious a. (음식을) 절제하는; 검소한(= spartan) indulgent a. 멋대로 하게 하는, 관대한 prosperous a. 번영한, 번창한 harmonious a. 사이가 좋은, 조화로운

월 구독료를 없애고, 외식을 줄이고, 중고품을 구입하는 것은 검소한 삶을 위한 요령이다.

09 동의어 ③

perceive v. 감지[인지]하다 attorney n. 변호사 flamboyant a. 이색적인; 대담한(= ostentatious) soporific a. 최면의; 졸리는 refined a. 교양[품위] 있는, 세련된 inconspicuous a. 이목을 끌지 못하는, 눈에 잘 안 띄는

법원 직원들은 법정에 있는 카메라가 (재판에) 참여한 변호사들의 행동을 평소보다 더 대담하게 만든다는 것을 알아차렸다.

10 문맥상 동의어 ②

index는 '목록', '지표', '집게손가락(= index finger)', '지수' 등의 다양한 의미가 있는데, 어깨의 외회전이 안 좋다는 것은 재활이 필요하다는 것을 나타내는 지표가 될 것이다. 따라서 index의 문맥상 동의어로 적절한 것은 ② sign이다.

external rotation 외선(外旋), 외회전 rotator cuff muscle 회전근 rehabilitation n. 재건, 부흥; 복권, 복직

어깨의 외회전이 잘 안 되는 것은 회전근에 재활이 필요한지를 알 수 있는 좋은 지표이다.

11 문맥상 동의어 ②

subject는 '주제', '국민', '제안', '피험자' 등의 다양한 의미가 있는데, 영국이라는 한 국가와 밀접한 관계가 있는 사람이라면 그 국가의 '국민, 시민'일 것이므로, 문맥상의 동의어로는 ② citizen이 적절하다.

connection n. 관련성, 연관성 classify v. 분류[구분]하다

1949년까지만 해도 영국과 밀접한 관계가 있는 거의 모든 사람은 영국 시민으로 분류되었다.

12 문맥상 동의어 ④

blunt에는 '무뚝뚝한', '있는 그대로의', '솔직한', '무딘' 등의 뜻이 있는데, 피해자가 어떤 물건을 사용한 폭행에 의해 부상을 당한 것이므로, object를 수식하고 있는 blunt의 적절한 의미는 ④ dull(무딘)로 볼 수 있다.

curt a. 무뚝뚝한, 퉁명스런 brusque a. 무뚝뚝한, 퉁명스런

의료 수사관들은 둔기 폭행의 피해자가 입은 부상에 특별히 초점을 맞췄다.

13 문맥상 동의어 ③

charge는 '비난하다', '(짐을) 지우다', '(의무·책임을) 맡기다', '(세금을) 과하다', '채우다' 등의 다양한 의미를 가지고 있는데, 의원회가 현재 교육 시스템을 개선하는 임무를 맡은 것이므로, charged의 문맥상 동의어는 ③ entrusted(위임받은, 맡은)가 적절하다.

accuse v. 고발하다 lunge v. 찌르다, 돌진하다 load v. (짐을) 싣다

그 위원회는 현재의 교육 시스템을 개선하는 임무를 맡았다.

14 재진술 ①

제시문은 불가능하다고 입증되었음에도 불구하고 그것을 해내려고 많은 노력을 기울이는 상황을 설명하고 있다. 불가능하다고 입증되었다는 것은 이러한 노력이 실패로 끝났다는 것을 의미하므로, 이를 재진술한 문장으로 적절한 것은 ①이다.

put forth 노력하다, 힘쓰다 accomplish v. 완수하다, 성취하다

불가능한 것으로 판명된 일을 해내려 하는 데 많은 노력이 기울여졌다.
① 그 일은 도저히 행해질 수 없었기 때문에 사람들은 많은 노력을 했지만 실패했다.
② 그 시도와 관련하여 상황을 개선하기 위한 많은 노력이 이루어졌다.
③ 사람들은 확인될 수 있는 것들을 이해하기 위해 많은 노력을 기울였다.
④ 사람들은 그것을 성취하는 것이 불가능하다는 것을 깨달았기 때문에 어떤 노력도 기울이지 않았다.

15 재진술 ④

"Hardly[Scarcely]+had+S+p.p. ~ when[before]+S+V(과거시제)"는 '~하자마자 …하다'는 의미를 가진다. 제시된 문장은 "그들은 에든버러에 도착하자마자 런던으로 돌아오라는 명령을 받았다."는 의미가 된다. 따라서 그들이 에든버러에 도착한 직후 런던에 돌아와야 했던 것이므로 제시된 문장은 ④의 의미와 같다.

그들은 에든버러에 도착하자마자 런던으로 돌아오라는 명령을 받았다.
① 그들이 런던으로 돌아오라는 말을 들었을 때, 그들은 에든버러에 도착하지 못했다.
② 그들이 에든버러로 떠난 것은 런던으로 돌아오라는 명령을 받기 직전이었다.

③ 그들은 런던으로 돌아오라는 명령을 받은 직후, 에든버러에 도착해야 했다.

④ 그들은 에든버러에 도착하자마자 런던으로 돌아와야 했다.

16 형용사의 어순 ①

명사 수식어의 순서를 정할 때는 '한정사+형용사+명사'의 어순이 되어야 한다. 따라서 한정사인 a가 제일 앞에 와야 하며, 형용사 severe의 비교급인 more severe가 그다음에 오고, 합성명사 engine performance가 그다음에 오고, 마지막으로 핵심명사인 issue가 온 ①이 빈칸에 적절하다.

excessive a. 과도한 severe a. 심각한 performance n. (기계의) 성능, 효율

과도한 엔진오일 연소는 종종 더 심각한 엔진 성능 문제의 결과이다.

17 to부정사의 용법 ③

pretend는 to부정사를 목적어로 취하며, 부정사의 부정은 부정어 not을 to부정사 바로 앞에 둔다. '못 보는 척했다'가 아니라 '못 본 척했다'이므로, 본동사인 pretended보다 한 시제 앞선 완료 부정사 to have noticed가 적절하다. 이를 종합해 보면 ③이 정답이다.

tamper with (허락도 받지 않고 마음대로) 손대다[건드리다, 조작하다]

나는 그 소년이 창고 문에 달린 자물쇠를 건드리는 것을 못 본 척했다.

18 감정 타동사의 분사 ①

감정을 유발하는 경우에는 현재분사를 쓰고, 감정을 느끼게 되는 경우에는 과거분사를 쓴다. 주어인 내가 감정을 느끼게 되는 것이므로 ①은 surprised가 되어야 한다.

discouraged a. 낙담한, 낙심한 criticism n. 비판, 비난

나는 그 작가가 그의 새 소설에 대해 온갖 비판을 받은 후에 낙담하고 있다는 것에 놀라지 않았다.

19 whether A or B ④

whether는 whether A or B의 구문으로 사용하므로 ④는 or artists가 되어야 한다.

didactic a. 교훈적인, 설교하는

아동 문학의 교훈적인 성격은 작가가 교사의 역할을 더 많이 하는지 예술가의 역할을 더 많이 하는지에 대한 논쟁이 남아 있기 때문에 학자들이 계속해서 연구하고 있는 것(주제)이다.

20 정비문 ③

③ be used to ~ing는 '~에 익숙하다'는 의미이다. 따라서 "플라스틱이 다양한 재료를 만드는 데 익숙하다."라는 어색한 문장이 되었으므로, 'be used to+동사원형(~하는 데 사용되다)' 표현을 사용하여 "플라스틱은 다양한 재료를 만드는 데 자주 사용된다."라는 문장으로 고쳐야 한다. to making을 to make로 고친다. ① object to는 '~에 반대하다'는 의미로 to는 전치사이다. 따라서 동명사 taking은 적절하다. ② when it comes to에서 to는 전치사이므로, 동명사 playing은 적절하다. ④ what do you say to ~ing는 '~하는 게 어떻겠니?'라는 의미로 to는 전치사이므로, 동명사 joining은 적절하다.

① 그때 내 파트너는 쓰레기를 버리는 것에 반대했다.
② 컴퓨터 게임을 하는 것에 관해서는, 그가 최고이다.
③ 플라스틱은 다양한 재료를 만드는 데 자주 사용된다.
④ 며칠 후에 우리와 함께 저녁 식사를 하는 게 어떻겠니?

21 정비문 ④

자동사 insist가 목적어를 취하기 위해서는 전치사 on이 필요하다. 따라서 ④를 He didn't insist on what progress they had made.로 고쳐야 한다. ①, ③ how로 시작하는 간접의문절은 'how+형용사+S+V'의 구조로 사용된다. ② what으로 시작하는 간접의문절로서 'what+a+형용사+명사+주어+동사'로 사용된다.

① 그녀는 그것이 얼마나 가치 있는지 몰랐다.
② 나는 그것이 얼마나 어려운 경로인지 잊고 있었다.
③ 그것은 우리가 지불해야 하는 금액에 따라 달라진다.
④ 그는 그들이 어떤 진전을 이루었는지 굳이 강조하지 않았다.

22-23

그의 패션의 화려함으로 인해 "태양왕"으로 알려진 루이 14세(Louis XIV)는 가발을 그의 궁정에 있는 남녀 모두의 필수 액세서리로 만들었다. 궁정에서 가발이 자리 잡자, 가발은 판사, 성직자 등과 같은 고위직 직업군들 사이에서 표준이 되었다. 증가하는 수요를 충족시키기 위해, 루이 14세 통치 기간 동안 프랑스에서는 가발을 제작하는 장인의 수가 급증했다. 파리에서는 가발 제작자의 수가 1673년 200명에서 1771년 945명으로 증가했다. 지방에서도 도제 수습을 마친 가발 제작자들이 전국을 돌아다니며 가발을 팔았고, 상류층이 경악을 금치 못하게도 곧 평민들도 가발을 쓰기 시작했다. 가발 경제의 핵심은 머리카락 그 자체에 있었다. 고가의 가발에는, 길이가 길고 남성의 머리카락보다 품질이 높다는 믿음 때문에, 여성의 머리카락을 사용했다. 시장의 상인들은 시골 소녀들에게서 머리카락을 사고 했다. 금발이나 은회색 머리카락에 대한 수요가 높은 경우가 많았고, 검은색이 그 뒤를 이었다. 그중에서도 자연스런 곱슬머리가 가장 가치가 높았다. 만들어야 할 가발이 많았기 때문에 프랑스 장인들은 유럽 전역에서 머리카락을 구입했다. 이 유행은 프랑스 혁명으로 일어난 심각한 사회 변화가 가발의 유행을 종식시킬 때까지 계속되었다.

magnificence n. 장엄, 화려, 훌륭함 wig n. 가발 high-ranking a. 고위의, 중요한 reign n. (왕의) 통치 기간, 치세 province n. 주(州); 지방 journeyman n. (과거 도제 수업을 마치고 남 밑에서 일하던) 장인, 기능인 consternation n. 경악, 대경실색 fair n. 품평회; (대규모의)

박람회 peasant n. 소작농 artisan n. 장인, 기능 보유자 profound a. 엄청난, 심오한

22 내용일치   ④

"상류층이 경악을 금치 못하게도 곧 평민들도 가발을 쓰기 시작했다."고 했으므로, 상류층 사람들은 평민들이 가발을 쓰는 것을 원치 않았다고 볼 수 있다. 따라서 ④가 옳은 진술이다. ① 루이 14세의 패션이 화려하다고 했다. ② 1771년에 945명은 '도제 수습을 마친 가발 제작자(journeyman wigmaker)'의 수가 아니라 '가발을 제작하는 장인(master wigmaker)'의 수이다. ③ 자연스런 곱슬머리가 가장 가치가 높았다고 했다.

이 글에 따르면, 다음 중 옳은 것은?
① 루이 14세는 궁정에서 좀 더 소박한 헤어스타일을 요구했다.
② 파리에서 도제 수습을 마친 가발 제작자의 수가 1771년에 945명에 달했다.
③ 부유한 프랑스 여성들은 대개 직모의 수입 가발을 선호했다.
④ 상류층 사람들은 평민들이 가발을 쓰기 시작했다는 사실을 싫어했다.

23 내용추론   ③

루이 14세 궁정의 남녀 모두 가발을 착용했다고 언급되어 있지만, 성별에 따라 가발 스타일이 달랐는지는 이 글에 언급되어 있지 않다. 따라서 ③이 추론할 수 없다.

이 글에 따르면, 다음 중 추론할 수 없는 것은?
① 가발의 가격은 머리 색깔에 따라 차이가 있었다.
② 시골 소녀들은 머리카락을 팔아서 돈을 벌 수 있었다.
③ 궁정에서 가발 스타일은 남자와 여자가 달랐다.
④ 프랑스 혁명 이후 가발에 대한 사고방식이 크게 변했다.

24-25

언어들 사이의 가장 인상적인 차이점 중 하나는 공간에서 사물의 위치를 규정하는 방식이다. 영어와 같은 일부 언어는 자기중심적인 준거의 틀을 선호하는 경향이 있다. 예를 들어, 모델 하우스(견본 주택)를 둘러보는 중이라면 부동산 중개인이 돌출된 창문을 가리키며 "당신의 오른편에 이 집의 가장 멋진 특징이 있습니다."라고 말할 수도 있다. "당신의 오른편"이라는 표현은 당신의 관점에서 해석되어야 한다. 만약 당신이 다른 방향을 바라보고 있거나 다른 공간에 있다면, 그것은 공간상 전혀 다른 곳을 가리키며, 이 때문에 자기중심적이라고 불리는 것이다. 그러나 모든 언어가 이와 같은 것은 아니다. 일부 언어는 공간에서 사물의 위치를 규정하기 위해 당신이 있는 곳과 무관한 지구 중심적인 체계를 사용한다. 지구 중심적 시스템에는 다양한 유형이 있다. 우리가 사용하는 기본 방향(북, 남, 동, 서)은 하나의 예이지만, 다른 것들로는 "오르막길" 대 "내리막길" 또는 "주택지구" 대 "도심지" 등이 포함된다.

impressive a. 인상적인, 인상[감명] 깊은 egocentric a. 자기중심적인, 이기적인 frame of reference (개인의 판단과 이해를 지배하는) 준거 틀 realtor n. 부동산업자 bay window 돌출된 창, 퇴창 interpret v. (의미를) 설명[해석]하다 perspective n. 관점, 시각 geocentric a. 지구 중심적인 cardinal direction 기본방향(위)

24 글의 제목   ①

이 글은 언어마다 공간에서 사물의 위치를 정하는 방식이 어떻게 다른지를 설명하고 있다. 영어는 자기중심적인 준거의 틀을 가지고 있다고 했고, 일부 다른 언어는 지구 중심적인 체계를 사용하여 공간에서의 위치를 나타낸다고 했다. 따라서 글의 제목으로 가장 적절한 것은 ①이다.

다음 중 이 글의 제목으로 가장 적절한 것은?
① 언어가 방향을 다르게 표현하는 방법
② 언어마다 다른 관점을 갖게 되는 이유
③ 여러 언어에서 지구 중심적인 체계가 작동하는 방식
④ 자기중심적 체계와 지구 중심적 체계의 기원

25 내용일치   ④

우리가 사용하는 기본 방향(북, 남, 동, 서)이 지구 중심적인 체계의 하나의 예라고 했다.

이 글에 따르면, 다음 중 옳은 것은?
① 자기중심성은 언어의 기본 체계이다.
② 자기중심적인 표현의 예로는 "오르막길"과 "내리막길"이 있다.
③ 지구 중심적인 관점은 당신의 위치에 따라 다른 방향을 가리킨다.
④ 기본 방향은 일부 언어에서 사용하는 지구 중심적인 체계의 한 유형이다.

26-27

최근 수십 년 동안 전통적인 교육의 단점에 대한 논의로 인해 다양한 개혁과 대안적 접근 방식이 생겨났다. 기술의 등장은 디지털 도구, 온라인 학습 플랫폼 및 맞춤형 교육 계획의 통합을 통해 학교 교육에 더욱 혁명을 일으켰다. 학교 교육의 목표는 지식을 전달하고, 비판적 사고를 함양하며, 사회적 역할을 할 수 있도록 개인을 준비시키는 것 등으로 일관되게 유지되어 왔지만, 그 방법과 구조는 계속해서 발전하고 있다. 교육과 관련한 지속적인 논의는 21세기 학습자의 다양한 요구를 충족시키는 데 있어 적응성과 혁신의 중요성을 강조한다. 학교 교육 시스템의 역사적 맥락을 이해하면 오늘날 교육자들이 직면한 과제와 기회에 대한 통찰력을 얻을 수 있다. 우리가 급변하는 세계의 복잡성을 헤쳐 나가면서, 효과적이고 포괄적인 교육에 대한 탐구는 학교 교육의 미래를 형성하는 데 있어 여전히 변함없는 원동력이 된다.

shortcoming n. 결점, 단점 alternative a. 대체 가능한, 대안이 되는 approach n. 접근법, 처리 방법 revolutionize v. 혁명[대변혁]을 일으키다; 급격한 변화를 가져오다 integration n. 통합 impart v. (정보·지식 등을) 전하다 foster v. 조성하다, 발전시키다 diverse a. 다양한 inclusive a. (거의) 모든, 포괄적인

26 글의 제목   ①

이 글은 지식의 전달, 비판적 사고 함양, 그리고 사회적 역할을 할 수 있도록 개인을 준비시키는 등의 학교 교육의 목표를 강조하면서, 다양한 개혁, 대안적 접근 방식, 기술 통합을 통해 "교육을 개선하기 위한 지속적인 노력"에 대해 설명하고 있다. 따라서 ①이 글의 제목으로 적절하다.

다음 중 이 글의 제목으로 가장 적절한 것은?
① 더 나은 학교 교육을 위한 끊임없는 탐구
② 학교 교육자에 대한 역사적인 관점
③ 교육에 있어서의 기술의 통합
④ 대안 학교 교육의 혁명

27 빈칸완성 ②

지식의 전달, 비판적 사고 함양, 사회적 역할을 할 수 있도록 개인을 준비시키는 것은 학교 교육의 지속적인 성격을 나타낸다. 이러한 목표는 접근 방식의 변화에도 불구하고 일정하게 유지되고 있으므로 Ⓐ에는 consistent가 적절하다. 그리고 대조의 접속사 while이 있으므로, 학교 교육의 목표가 일정하게 유지되고 있지만, 교육의 방법과 구조는 지속적으로 발전하고 있다고 해야 문맥상 적절하다. 따라서 Ⓑ에는 evolve가 적절하다.

다음 중 Ⓐ와 Ⓑ에 들어가기에 가장 적절한 짝을 나열한 것은?
① 다재다능한 — 뒤집다
② 일관성 있는 — 진화하다
③ 무익한 — 변형시키다
④ 정적인 — 침체되다

28-30

프랑스의 저명 철학자 드니 디드로(Denis Diderot)는 거의 평생을 가난하게 살았지만, 1765년에 모든 것이 바뀌었다. 디드로는 52세였고 그의 딸은 결혼을 앞두고 있었지만, 지참금을 낼 여유가 없었다. 재력은 없었지만, 당시 가장 포괄적인 백과사전 중 하나인 "Encyclopédie"의 공동 창립자이자 저자였기 때문에 디드로의 이름은 잘 알려져 있었다. 러시아의 황후 예카테리나 대제(Catherine the Great)는 디드로의 경제적 어려움을 듣고 현재 미화로 약 5만 달러의 가치가 있는 1,000파운드에 그의 장서를 사주겠다고 제안했다. 갑자기 디드로에게는 여분의 돈이 생기게 되었다. 이렇게 운 좋게 매각한 직후, 디드로는 새로운 주홍색 가운을 구입했다. 그때 모든 것이 잘못되었다. 디드로의 주홍색 가운은 아름다웠다. 실제로 그 가운은 너무 아름다워서 그가 가지고 있는 나머지 것들에 둘러싸여 있을 때 그 가운이 얼마나 부적절해 보이는지 그는 깨닫게 되었다. 디드로는 곧 자신이 가지고 있는 가운의 아름다움에 걸맞은 새로운 물건을 사고 싶은 충동을 느꼈다. 그는 자신의 낡은 양탄자를 새로운 다마스쿠스 산 양탄자로 교체했다. 그는 자신의 집을 아름다운 조각품들과 더 나은 식탁으로 꾸몄다. 그는 벽난로 선반 위에 놓을 새로운 거울과 호화로운 가죽 의자를 샀다. 이러한 반응적인 구매(필요에 따른 자동적인 구매)는 "디드로 효과"로 잘 알려져 왔다. 디드로 효과는 새로운 소유물을 얻게 되면 더 많은 새로운 것을 구매하게 되는 소비의 악순환을 종종 야기한다는 것을 설명한다. 그 결과, 우리는 이전의 자신이 행복하거나 성취감을 느끼는 데 전혀 필요하지 않았던 물건을 구매하게 된다.

dowry n. 결혼 지참금 co-founder n. 공동 창립자 comprehensive a. 포괄적인, 종합적인 library n. 도서관, 서재, 장서 spare v. (여유가 있어서) 떼어두다 scarlet n. 주홍색 robe n. 옷, 가운 out of place 부적절한 rug n. 양탄자 mantle n. 벽난로 선반 spiral n. 나선, 악순환

28 글의 제목 ③

새로운 물건을 구입하게 되면 그 물건과 어울리는 다른 제품을 계속 구매하게 되는 현상인 '디드로 효과'를 설명하고 있다. 따라서 ③이 글의 제목으로 적절하다.

다음 중 이 글의 제목으로 가장 적절한 것은?
① 갑작스러운 부(富)가 당신의 삶을 어떻게 향상시키나
② 실내디자인의 조화와 통일성
③ 구매가 어떻게 더 많은 구매를 초래하나
④ 물질적 소비의 철학적 의미

29 내용일치 ②

러시아의 황후 예카테리나 대제(Catherine the Great)가 디드로의 경제적 어려움을 듣고 그의 장서를 사주어 디드로에게는 여분의 돈이 생기게 되었고 이것으로 결혼을 앞둔 딸의 지참금을 낼 수 있었으므로 ②가 글의 내용과 일치한다. ③ 디드로는 주홍색 가운을 아름답게 생각했지만, 주홍색 가운 구입 이후 그 물건과 어울리는 다른 제품을 계속 구매하게 되었으므로, 그 가운이 그를 행복하고 만족스럽게 해주었다고 보기는 어렵다. ④ 주방 식탁이 아니라 양탄자이다.

이 글에 따르면, 다음 중 옳은 것은?
① 디드로는 백과사전을 출판해서 부유하고 유명해졌다.
② 러시아의 황후가 디드로의 책을 사서 그로 하여금 지참금을 지불할 수 있게 했다.
③ 아름다운 주홍색 가운 구입이 디드로를 행복하고 만족스럽게 해주었다.
④ 디드로는 주방 식탁을 새로운 다마스쿠스 산 식탁으로 교체했다.

30 빈칸완성 ④

디드로의 제품 구매는 계획적이거나 합리적인 결정이 아니라, 주홍색 가운을 산 다음 그 가운의 아름다움과 어울리는 다른 물건에 대한 새로운 필요에 반응하여 구매를 계속 이어간 것이다. 하나의 구매가 연쇄적인 반응의 구매로 악순환된 것이므로, Ⓐ에는 ④ reactive가 적절하다.

다음 중 Ⓐ에 가장 적절한 것은?
① 관습[관례]적인
② 이성적인
③ 계획적인
④ 반응적인

31-32

퍼스널 컬러 분석은 개인의 안색과 피부 톤을 바탕으로 옷, 메이크업, 액세서리 선택에 도움을 줄 수 있는 개인을 돋보이게 하는 색상을 정해주는 것을 목표로 한다. 이 과정은 60분 정도 소요되며, 컬러 컨설턴트는 수백 개의 원단 견본을 고객의 어깨에 걸쳐놓고 다크서클이나 주름을 강조하는 것이 아니라 무엇이 얼굴을 화사하게 만드는지 면밀히 검토한다. 수십 년 동안 정치인, 최고 경영자(CEO), 사회 엘리트는 되도록 좋은 인상을 주려고 이 방법을 사용해 왔다. 현재 틱톡 열풍에 힘입어, 퍼스널 컬러 분석이 캘리포니아에서 뉴욕까지 생겨나기 시작하고 있으며, Z세대의 충성도 높

은 고객들은 퍼스널 컬러 분석 절차를 버킷리스트에 올려놓고 서울 여행을 하는 경우가 늘고 있다. 미국의 뉴욕주 브루클린에서는 퍼스널 컬러 분석 한 세션의 비용이 545달러인 반면, 한국의 대부분의 스튜디오의 비용은 80달러에서 160달러 사이이다. 아무튼 고객은 개인 맞춤형 팔레트 견본, 특정 메이크업 추천, 어떤 종류의 보석류를 구매할지를 제안 받게 된다. 코로나19가 한국을 강타하기 전에도 퍼스널 컬러에 대한 열풍이 불고 있었다. 이제 퍼스널 컬러 분석은 외국인 관광객의 방문과 함께 다시 급증하고 있다. 한국인에게 관광 열풍은 엄청난 소매 지출이라는 또 다른 혜택을 가져다준다. 고객은 그들의 옷을 점검받고 싶어 하는 동시에 종종 색상 견본을 손에 들고 특정 스킨 케어 및 메이크업 제품 구매에 대한 추천을 받는다. 이런 호황은 일자리를 만들 수도 있다. 수요 급증으로 더 많은 실무자의 필요성이 드러남에 따라 한국 취업박람회에서 컬러 컨설팅 워크숍이 점점 늘고 있으며, 한국패션심리연구원과 같은 단체에서는 컬러 컨설팅을 위한 자격증 프로그램을 제공하고 있다.

assign v. 할당하다, 배정하다, 부여하다 flattering a. 돋보이게 하는 complexion n. 안색 skin tone 피부색 drape v. (옷·천 등을 느슨하게) 걸치다[씌우다] swatch n. (직물의) 견본 light up (빛·색으로) 환하게 되다[만들다] put one's best foot toward 되도록 좋은 인상을 주려고 하다, 최선의 노력을 하다 on the heels of 아무의 뒤를 바짝 뒤따라서, ~에 잇따라서 craze n. (특히 일시적인) 대유행[열풍] sprout v. (무엇이, 특히 많은 수로) 생기다[나타나다] hover v. 맴돌다, 유지하다 in any event 아무튼, 좌우간 itch n. (~하고 싶어 몸이) 근질거림, 욕구

---

31 글의 주제 ①

퍼스널 컬러 분석이 많은 사람들 사이에서 큰 관심을 받고 있으며, 틱톡과 같은 소셜 미디어 플랫폼에서도 선풍적인 인기를 끌고 있다고 했다. 코로나19 이후 외국인 관광객의 방문에 힘입어 국내 산업에도 큰 영향을 미치고 있음을 소개하고 있으므로, 이 글의 주제로 적절한 것은 ①이다.

다음 중 이 글의 주제로 가장 적절한 것은?
① 퍼스널 컬러 분석과 그것이 한국 산업에 주는 이익
② 정치인과 기업인을 위한 퍼스널 컬러의 중요성
③ 코로나 이후 한국 관광의 지속적인 발전
④ 한국에서 퍼스널 컬러 열풍을 일으킨 틱톡의 역할

---

32 내용일치 ②

"코로나19가 한국을 강타하기 전에도 퍼스널 컬러에 대한 열풍이 불고 있었다."고 했으므로, 퍼스널 컬러 분석이 코로나19 이후 유행하게 된 것은 아니다. 따라서 ②가 정답이다.

이 글에 따르면, 다음 중 옳지 않은 것은?
① 퍼스널 컬러 분석은 수백 개의 견본을 사용하며, 약 1시간 정도 소요된다.
② 퍼스널 컬러 분석은 코로나19 이후 한국에서 처음으로 유행하게 되었다.
③ 한국 스튜디오는 뉴욕 스튜디오보다 퍼스널 컬러 분석 비용이 적게 든다.
④ 더 많은 해외 고객이 현재 한국 스튜디오를 방문하고 있다.

33-34

낙선한 후보에게 투표하는 것은 정신적으로만 부담이 되는 것이 아니다. 2008년 총선 전날과 당일, 연구자들은 유권자들로부터 여러 개의 타액 샘플을 수집했다. 낙선한 후보에게 투표한 여성을 제외한 남성의 경우, 선거 결과가 발표된 직후 테스토스테론 수치가 대리 참가자가 아닌 실제 경쟁자에게서 예상되는 정도까지로 떨어졌다. 낙선한 후보를 지지하면 정치 체제에 대한 유권자들의 신뢰도 떨어질 수 있다. 1964년부터 2004년까지 설문조사를 분석한 결과, 시간이 지남에 따라 낙선한 후보를 지지한 유권자들은 다른 유권자들보다 선거 과정이 공정하다고 생각하는 경향이 적었다. 그들은 또한 전반적으로 민주주의에 대한 만족도가 낮은 경향을 보였다. 특히 2004년에는 낙선한 후보의 지지자들은 민주주의에 대한 만족도를 1점 만점에 0.55점으로 평가한 데 반해, 당선된 후보들의 지지자들은 0.77점을 기록했다. 이러한 불만은 유권자들이 선거 패배에 놀랐을 때 더욱 커진다. 1997년 캐나다 연방 선거에서 낙선한 후보를 지지한 유권자들 중 놀라지 않은 유권자의 72%는 민주주의에 만족한 반면, 놀란 유권자는 57%에 그쳤다.

vote for ~에 (찬성) 투표하다, ~을 제안[제의]하다 taxing a. (육체적·정신적으로) 아주 힘든[부담이 큰] saliva n. 침, 타액 plummet v. 곤두박질치다, 급락하다 contestant n. (대회·시합 등의) 참가자 vicarious a. (느낌·경험이) 대리의[간접적인], 대행의 democracy n. 민주주의 disaffection n. 불평, (특히 정부에 대한) 불만, 민심 이탈 magnify v. 과장[확대]하다 startle v. 깜짝 놀라게 하다

---

33 부분이해 ①

낙선한 후보에게 투표한 남성에게서 관찰된 테스토스테론 수치 감소는 실제 경쟁자에게서 나타나는 수준으로까지 떨어졌다고 했다. 이는 낙선 후보를 지지한 남성들과 실제 선거에서 경쟁을 벌인 후보자가 비슷하다는 점을 설명하는 것이므로, Ⓐ가 의미하는 것과 가장 가까운 것은 ①이다.

다음 중 Ⓐ가 의미하는 것과 가장 가까운 것은?
① 낙선한 후보를 지지한 남성들은 실제 경쟁자들과 비슷한 테스토스테론 감소를 경험했다.
② 남성과 여성의 테스토스테론 수치가 실제 참가자의 수치보다 증가했다.
③ 유권자와 후보자의 관계는 경쟁의 참가자와 이를 지켜보는 사람들과의 관계와 유사하다.
④ 선거 후 유권자들의 테스토스테론 수치는 대회 참관인 수준에 도달했다.

---

34 빈칸완성 ③

낙선한 후보를 지지하는 유권자는 선거 과정을 공정하다고 생각할 가능성이 낮고, 민주주의 전반에 대한 만족도가 낮은 경향이 있다고 했다. 이는 낙선한 후보를 지지한 결과, 정치 시스템에 대한 신뢰가 하락했음을 시사하므로 ③이 빈칸에 적절하다.

다음 중 Ⓑ에 들어가기에 가장 적절한 것은?
① 민주주의에서 시민으로서의 성실성
② 후보에 대한 유권자들의 만족도
③ 정치 체제에 대한 유권자들의 신뢰
④ 유권자들의 정서적 건강

35-37

줄을 서서 기다리는 것은 현대의 재앙이다. 데이비드 앤드루스(David Andrews)의 저서 『왜 다른 줄이 항상 더 빨리 나아가는가?(Why does the Other Line Always Move Faster?)』에 따르면, 줄을 서는 것은 산업혁명이 노동자들의 스케줄을 시간적으로 통일시켜, 점심시간과 저녁시간에 몰려들어 줄이 생겨나기 전까지는 흔하지 않았다고 한다. 미국인들이 연간 수백억 시간을 줄 서기에 낭비하는 것으로 추정된다는 점을 감안하면, 새치기를 하려는 사람들이 있고, 그들에 대해 몹시 분개하는 사람들이 있다는 것은 당연한 일이다. 그러나 폭력을 유발하지 않고 새치기하는 것은 가능한 일이다. 다음은 사회 과학을 기반으로 한 몇 가지 조언이다. 우선 (새치기하기에) 적절한 줄을 골라라. 이를 테면, 시카고 컵스가 월드 시리즈를 치르는 것과 같이 일생에 한 번 있을 법한 경기에서 새치기를 하는 것은 사실상 불가능하다. 그러나 보안 검색대와 같이 반복적으로 일어나는 상황에서는 사람들이 당신을 끼워줄 가능성이 높은데 이는 아마도 언젠가 비슷한 호의가 (자신에게도) 필요할 것으로 예상하기 때문이다. 게임 이론을 사용하여 어떤 조건에서 끼어들기가 사회적으로 허용될 수 있는지 알아본 결과, 연구자들은 일회성 줄서기에서는 사람들이 끼어들기에 대한 관용을 거의 보이지 않는다는 사실을 발견했다. 그러나 줄서기가 되풀이될 때는, 긴급히 먼저 해야 할 필요가 있다고 주장하거나 서비스 시간을 최소한으로 짧게 끝내야 할 필요가 있는 새치기꾼들을 사람들은 들여보내준다. 뇌물도 효과가 있으며, 심지어 비용이 들지 않을 수도 있다. 한 연구에서는 정체를 숨긴 한 연구원이 줄서서 기다리는 사람들에게 자기가 새치기하도록 해주면 현금을 주겠다고 제안했다. 대다수가 동의했지만, 이상하게도 그들 대부분은 현금을 거절했다. 그들은 탐욕에서가 아니라 그 제안이 끼어들려고 하는 사람의 절박함을 증명했기 때문에 그 제안을 받아들였던 것이다. 심리학자 스탠리 밀그램(Stanley Milgram)이 공동 집필한 연구에 따르면 끼어드는 것을 허용할지는 보통 끼어드는 사람의 바로 뒤에 있는 사람이 결정한다고 한다. 그 사람이 반대하지 않으면 다른 대기자들은 조용히 있는 경향이 있다. 그 실험에서는 두 명이 동시에 끼어들면 한 명이 끼어들 때보다 더 큰 분노를 불러일으켰다는 사실도 발견했다. 따라서 새치기를 하려면 혼자서 하도록 하라.

scourge n. 재앙, 골칫거리 synchronize v. 동시에 발생하다[움직이다] gobble up 게걸스럽게 먹어 치우다 bitterly ad. 격렬히, 몹시 resent v. 분개하다, 원망하다 jump the queue 새치기하다 pointer n. (한 가지의) 충고[조언] cut the line 새치기하다 once-in-a-lifetime (아주 특별하여) 평생 단 한 번뿐인 undercover a. 비밀로 행해지는, 비밀의 appreciate v. 진가를 알아보다[인정하다]; 인식하다 out of greed 탐욕 때문에 intruder n. 불법 침입자 desperation n. 자포자기, 필사적임 simultaneous a. 동시의 ire n. 분노, 노여움

35 글의 제목 ③

이 글은 폭력을 유발하지 않으면서 효과적으로 새치기 할 수 있는 전략을 제공하고 있으므로, ③이 제목으로 적절하다.

다음 중 이 글의 제목으로 가장 적절한 것은?
① 기다리는 줄에 끼어드는 사람을 피하는 방법
② 줄서서 기다리는 것의 역사적 기원
③ 새치기 기술을 시행하기
④ 줄서서 기다리기에서의 시간 소비에 대한 사회적 분석

36 내용일치 ③

줄에 끼어드는 사람이 새치기의 대가로 기다리고 있는 사람에게 현금을 주겠다고 제안하면, 대다수의 사람은 현금은 거절하고 끼어들게 해주었다고 했다. 그 제안이 그들의 절박함을 증명했기 때문이라고 했다. 따라서 현금을 받고 끼어들게 해준 것이 아니므로, ③이 글의 내용과 일치하지 않는다.

이 글에 따르면, 다음 중 옳지 않은 것은?
① 산업혁명 이전에는 줄서서 기다리는 것이 일반적이지 않았다.
② 일회성의 줄을 서는 사람들은 새치기에 대해 덜 관대한 것으로 나타났다.
③ 연구에 참여한 줄서서 기다리는 사람들 대부분이 현금을 받고 침입자를 끼어들게 해주었다.
④ 끼어드는 사람의 뒤에 있는 사람이 허락하면, 다른 대기자들은 보통 불평하지 않는다.

37 빈칸완성 ①

두 명이 동시에 끼어들면 혼자서 끼어드는 것보다 더 큰 분노를 불러일으킨다고 했다. 따라서 새치기해야 할 상황이 생기면, 혼자서 끼어드는 것이 낫다고 할 수 있을 것이므로, 빈칸에는 ①이 적절하다.

다음 중 Ⓐ에 가장 적절한 것은?
① 혼자서 하라
② 진심으로 사과하라
③ 무례함에 대한 대가를 치러라
④ 친구 앞에 끼어들어라

38-40

약 5년 전, 메트로폴리탄 미술관(Met)은 기념비적인 것으로 증명된 작은 조치를 취했다. 즉, 방문객들에게 휴대폰을 사용하지 말라고 간청하는 것을 중단한 것이었다. 이 결정은 휴대폰이 현대 사회에서 어디에나 있으며, 휴대폰과 싸우는 것이 승산 없는 싸움이라는 인식에서 비롯된 것이다. 메트로폴리탄 미술관의 최고 디지털 책임자인 스리 스리니바산은 "사람들은 우리의 가장 큰 경쟁 대상이 무엇인지 묻습니다."라고 말한다. "경쟁자는 구겐하임 미술관이 아닙니다. 자연사 박물관도 아니고요. 넷플릭스입니다. '캔디크러쉬(게임)'이고요." 휴대폰이 메트로폴리탄 미술관에 머무르고 있다는 사실을 받아들이면서 박물관은 이 기술을 어떻게 활용할 수 있을지 생각하게 되었다. 한 가지 방법은 방문자가 추가 정보를 찾을 수 있는 애플리케이션을 만드는 것이다. 예를 들어, 브루클린 박물관에는 방문객들이 실시간으로 큐레이터에게 예술작품에 대해 질문할 수 있는 애플리케이션이 있다. 구겐하임 미술관과 메트로폴리탄 미술관을 비롯한 박물관에서는 비콘(어떤 신호를 알리기 위해 주기적으로 신호를 전송하는 기기) 기술을 실험했는데, 이 기술은 블루투스를 사용하여 방문자가 갤러리를 어떻게 이동하는지 추적하고 앱을 통해 추가 정보를 제공하는 것이다. 비콘 기술은 작품에 대한 자세한 이력과 특정 그림이나 갤러리에 대한 안내를 제공할 수 있는 잠재력을 가지고 있다. 스리니바산은 박물관 앱에 GPS 기술이 통합되면 사람들이 구글 지도에서 통근을 계획하는 것처럼 갤러리를 통해 경로를 계획할 수 있을 것이라는 점을 지적한다. 즉, 더 이상 이집트 문화관에서 길을 잃어버리거나 특정한 모네 일출(여러 개의 일출 그림이 있음)을 찾아 종이 지도를 확인하지 않아도 된다는 것이다.

take a step 조치를 취하다 entreat v. 간청[애원]하다 omnipresent a. 편재하는, 어디에나 있는 losing battle 승산 없는 싸움, 헛된 노력 seek out ~을 찾아내다 detailed a. 상세한, 세목에 걸친 point out 가리키다, 지적하다 plot v. (위치·항로 등을 지도에) 표시하다, (좌표를) 나타내다 commute n. 통근

38 글의 제목   ①

이 글은 박물관이 방문객들의 휴대폰 사용을 막는 대신 오히려 이를 수용하고 있으며, 블루투스 기술을 활용하여 방문객들에게 더욱 향상된 관람 경험을 제공하려는 시도에 대해 설명하고 있다. 따라서 글의 제목으로 ①이 적절하다.

다음 중 이 글의 제목으로 가장 적절한 것은?
① 박물관이 휴대폰을 켜도록 해준다
② 휴대폰이 현대 미술에 혁명을 가져왔다
③ 과학기술이 박물관을 서로 연결시켜준다
④ 박물관이 집중력을 산만하게 하는 현대물과의 싸움을 발표한다

39 내용일치   ③

"브루클린 박물관에는 방문객들이 실시간으로 큐레이터에게 예술작품에 대해 질문할 수 있는 애플리케이션이 있다."고 했으므로 ③이 정답이다. ① 5년 전이다. ② 비콘 기술을 채택한 곳은 구겐하임 미술관과 메트로폴리탄 미술관이다. ④ 구글 지도가 아니라 박물관의 자체 앱을 통해서 갤러리를 안내받을 수 있다.

이 글에 따르면, 다음 중 옳은 것은?
① 약 10년 전, 메트로폴리탄 미술관은 방문객들이 스마트폰을 사용할 수 있도록 허용하기 시작했다.
② 자연사 박물관은 비콘 기술을 채택했다.
③ 브루클린 박물관에서 방문객들은 앱을 통해 큐레이터에게 질문을 할 수 있다.
④ 방문객들은 구글 지도를 이용하여 갤러리 안에서 지나가는 길을 계획했다.

40 지시대상   ②

Ⓐ 앞 문장에서 "사람들은 우리의 가장 큰 경쟁 대상이 무엇인지 묻습니다."라는 언급이 있었고, 이에 대한 답변이 Ⓐ가 속한 문장이다. 따라서 Ⓐ it이 가리키는 것은 ② "The biggest competitor"라고 볼 수 있다. 메트로폴리탄 미술관의 가장 큰 경쟁자가 구겐하임 미술관이나 자연사 박물관 같은 다른 미술관이 아니라 넷플릭스나 캔디크러쉬 같은 휴대전화 기술이라고 해야 문맥상 적절하다.

다음 중 Ⓐ가 가리키는 것과 가장 가까운 것은?
① 구겐하임 미술관
② 가장 큰 경쟁자
③ 메트로폴리탄 미술관
④ 최고 디지털 책임자

41-42

테슬라 모델 S의 배터리 팩은 복잡한 공학기술의 위업이다. 전 세계에서 공급되는 부품들로 만들어진 수천 개의 원통형 셀(전지: 셀이 모여 배터리를 이룸)은 배기관을 통해 매연을 배출하지 않고 리튬과 전자를 수백 킬로미터 계속해서 자동차를 추진할 수 있는 충분한 에너지로 변환시킨다. 그러나 배터리의 수명이 다하면 환경적인 이점이 사라지고 문제가 발생한다. 만약 배터리가 매립지에 가게 된다면, 배터리 셀은 중금속을 포함한 문제가 되는 독소를 방출할 수 있다. 그리고 배터리를 재활용하는 것은 위험한 사업이 될 수 있다고 재료 과학자들은 경고한다. 당신이 테슬라 셀을 너무 깊게 자르거나 잘못된 곳을 자르게 되면, 그것은 누전을 일으키고, 연소하고, 유독 가스를 방출할 수 있다. 그것은 제조업체들이 향후 수십 년 동안 생산할 것으로 예상되는 수백만 개의 전기 자동차(EV) 배터리를 재활용하는 방법 등, 새로운 문제를 해결하려고 노력하는 연구자들이 직면한 많은 문제 중 하나일 뿐이다. 현재 전기 자동차 배터리는 실제로 재활용되도록 설계되지 않았다. 전기 자동차가 많지 않았을 때는 이것이 큰 문제가 되지 않았다. 그러나 이제 그 기술이 도약하고 있다. 몇몇 자동차 제조업체들은 수십 년 내에 내연기관 엔진을 점진적으로 폐지할 계획을 발표했으며, 업계 분석가들은 전기차가 지난해 1,100만 대에 불과했던 데서 증가하여 2030년에는 최소 1억 4,500만 대가 도로를 달릴 것으로 예측한다. 그래서 이제 사람들은 이것(배터리 재활용)이 문제라는 것을 인식하기 시작했다.

intricate a. (여러 부분·내용으로 되어 있어) 복잡한 cylindrical a. 원통[실린더]형의 component n. (구성) 요소, 부품 propel v. (몰거나 밀거나 해서) 나아가게 하다 tailpipe n. (자동차 등의) 배기관 emission n. (빛·열·가스 등의) 배출; 배기가스 fade v. 서서히 사라지다, 점점 희미해지다 landfill n. 쓰레기 매립지 hazardous a. 위험한 short-circuit v. 단락[쇼트]시키다; 누전시키다 combust v. 연소하기[시키기] 시작하다 toxic fume 유독 가스 tackle v. 씨름하다 phase out 단계적으로 폐지[삭감, 철거]하다

41 내용일치   ③

"몇몇 자동차 제조업체들은 수십 년 내에 내연기관 엔진을 점진적으로 폐지할 계획을 발표했다."고 했으므로 ③이 글의 내용과 일치한다.

이 글에 따르면, 다음 중 옳은 것은?
① 전기 자동차 배터리를 만들려면 주로 현지에서 조달된 부품이 필요하다.
② 작년에는 1,100만 개의 전기 자동차 배터리가 재활용되었다.
③ 일부 자동차 회사들은 내연기관 엔진을 만드는 것을 중단할 계획이다.
④ 테슬라 셀을 자르는 것은 비교적 안전한 과정이다.

42 빈칸완성   ④

만약 배터리가 매립지에 가게 된다면 위험한 이유에 대한 설명이 Ⓐ 다음에 이어지고 있다. 배터리를 재활용하는 것은 위험한 사업이 될 수 있다고 재료 과학자들은 경고한다고 했고 당신이 테슬라 셀을 너무 깊게 자르거나 잘못된 곳을 자르게 되면, 누전, 연소 그리고 유독 가스 방출을 일으킬 수 있다고 했다. 따라서 전기 자동차 배터리를 버리는 것은 문제가 되는 독소를 방출할 수 있다고 볼 수 있다.

다음 중 Ⓐ에 가장 적절한 것은?
① 핵심 소재로 대체 가능하다
② 충전 및 수리가 필요하다
③ 매립지에서 오염 물질을 흡수한다
④ 문제가 되는 독소를 방출할 수 있다

43-44

예술은 의견을 바꾸고, 가치를 심어주고, 경험을 여러 시공간으로 전함으로써 사회에 영향을 미친다. 연구는 예술이 근본적인 자아의식에 영향을 미친다는 것을 보여주었다. 그림, 조각, 음악, 문학 그리고 기타 예술은 종종 사회의 집단 기억(흔히 부모 세대에서 자식 세대로 전달되는 한 공동체의 기억)의 저장소로 간주된다. 예술은 사실에 기반한 역사적 기록이 보존할 수 없는 것을 보존하는데, 즉 특정한 시간 특정한 장소에 존재하는 것이 어떻게 느껴졌는지(살면서 느낀 감정)를 보존한다. 이러한 면에서 예술은 의사소통이다. 예술은 서로 다른 문화, 서로 다른 시대의 사람들이 이미지, 소리, 이야기를 통해 서로 소통할 수 있게 해준다. 예술은 종종 사회 변화를 위한 수단이 된다. 예술은 정치적으로나 사회적으로 소외된 사람들로 하여금 말하게 할 수 있다. 노래, 영화 혹은 소설은 그것을 접한 사람들에게 감정을 불러일으키며, 변화를 위해 이들이 결집하도록 영감을 줄 수 있다. 예를 들어, 2013년 뉴캐슬 대학의 연구원들은 현대 시각 예술을 감상하는 것이 요양원에 사는 노인들의 개인적인 삶에 긍정적인 영향을 미쳤다는 것을 확인했다. 예술은 또한 사회에 실용주의적인 영향을 미친다, 예를 들어, 학생들의 수학과 읽기·쓰기 성적과 연극이나 음악 활동 참여도 사이에 입증할 수 있는 긍정적인 상관관계가 있다. 국립미술교육협회(National Art Education Association)가 지적했듯이, 예술은 노력의 배출구로서 예술가에게 유익하다. 예술은 자기표현과 성취에 대한 인간적 욕구를 촉진할 뿐만 아니라, 경제적으로도 발전 가능성이 있다. 예술의 창작, 관리, 배포에 많은 사람이 고용된다. 그러니까 무엇을 기다리고 있는가?

instill v. 침투시키다, 스며들게 하다, 서서히 주입시키다 translate v. 바꾸다[옮기다], 바뀌다 repository n. 저장소[보관소], (지식·정보 등의) 보고(寶庫) preserve v. 지키다[보호하다]; 보존하다 disenfranchise v. ~으로부터 특권[권리, 권한]을 박탈하다 utilitarian a. 실용적인; 공리주의의 demonstrable a. 보여줄[입증할] 수 있는 outlet n. 발산[배출] 수단 fulfillment n. 이행, 수행, 완수; 실천 viable a. 실행 가능한, 발전 가능한, 생명력 있는 distribution n. 분배 (방식), 분포

43 내용일치 ②

2013년 뉴캐슬 대학의 연구원들은 현대 시각 예술을 감상하는 것이 요양원에 사는 노인들의 삶에 긍정적인 영향을 미쳤음을 확인했다. 이를 통해 뇌와 예술과 관련한 연구는 이전부터 있어 왔던 연구라고 볼 수 있다. 따라서 새로운 연구 분야라고 볼 수 없으므로 ②가 정답이다.

이 글에 따르면, 다음 중 옳지 않은 것은?
① 예술은 사람들이 사회를 변화시키도록 영감을 줄 수 있다.
② 뇌와 예술 사이의 관련성에 대한 관심은 새로운 연구 분야이다.
③ 노인 요양원 환자들은 예술 작품 감상으로 혜택을 받았다.
④ 연극을 하는 학생들이 수학 성적이 더 높다.

44 부분이해 ①

utilitarian은 '실용의, 실익의'라는 의미를 가지고 있는데, "예술은 또한 사회에 실용주의적인 영향을 미친다."고 한 다음 그에 대한 예를 Ⓐ 다음 문장에서 설명하고 있다. "학생들의 수학과 읽기·쓰기 성적과 연극이나 음악 활동 참여도 사이에 입증할 수 있는 긍정적인 상관관계가 있다."고 했는데, 이는 예술로 인한 실질적인 이점과 관련된 것이다. 따라서 Ⓐ가 의미하는 것으로 적절한 것은 ①이다.

다음 중 Ⓐ와 의미가 가장 비슷한 것은?
① 실질적인 이점
② 보수적인 효과
③ 미적 가치
④ 이론적 함의

45-47

때때로 우리는 외롭기 때문에 사물을 인간으로 생각한다. 한 실험에서 외로움을 느낀다고 보고한 사람들은 자유 의지와 의식이 다양한 장치의 속성이라고 생각할 가능성이 다른 사람들보다 더 높았다고 한다. 이번에는 또한, 사물과 친밀감을 느끼는 것이 외로움을 덜어줄 수 있다. 대학생들은 마치 휴대폰에 인간적인 특성이 있는 것처럼 휴대폰과 상호작용하도록 하는 과제를 먼저 부여받은 경우가 아니라면, 사회적으로 소외되었던 시절을 떠올리게 될 때, 페이스북 친구 수를 과장하는 것으로 보상했다. 전화기는 분명히 진정한 친구를 대신했다. 또 때때로, 우리는 제품들을 이해하기 위해 제품들을 의인화한다. 미국의 한 연구에 따르면 네 명의 응답자 중 세 명은 자신들의 컴퓨터에 대고 욕설을 내뱉었다. 그리고 컴퓨터가 그들에게 더 많은 골치를 썩일수록, 그들은 "컴퓨터가 그 자체의 신념과 욕구"를 갖고 있다고 보고할 가능성이 더 높았다. 제품을 의인화하면 그것을 버리기가 더 어려워진다. 자동차의 개성을 평가해 달라는 요청을 받은 사람들은 자동차를 곧 바꿀 의향이 있다고 답할 가능성이 적었다. 그리고 사물을 의인화하는 것은 물건을 비축하는 경향과 관련되어 있다. 그렇다면 사람들은 어떻게 사물에 특성을 부여하는가? 부분적으로 우리는 외모에 의존한다. 인간의 경우 큰 얼굴은 지배력과 관련이 있다. 마찬가지로 사람들은 특히 경쟁 상황에서 큰 모양의 자동차, 벽시계, 손목시계를 좁은 모양의 것들보다 더 월등히 높은 외관을 가지고 있다고 평가하고 이 제품들을 선호했다. 독일의 자동차 판매를 분석한 결과, 웃는 것처럼 위로 올라간 그릴과 가늘게 뜬 눈처럼 기울어진 헤드라이트를 가진 자동차가 가장 잘 팔리는 것으로 나타났다. 구매자들은 이러한 특징들이 각각 자동차의 친근함과 강한 특징을 증가시킨다고 보았다.

isolated a. 고립된, 외딴 attribute v. (~의 원인을) …에 귀착시키다; ~가 (…에게) 있다고 생각하다 gadget n. (작고 유용한) 도구, 장치 exclude v. 제외하다, 배제하다 stand in for ~를 대신하다 personify v. 의인화하다 curse v. 욕(설)을 하다 cast off ~을 (던져, 벗어) 버리다 anthropomorphize v. (신·동물을) 인격화하다, 의인화(擬人化)하다 hoard v. 비축[저장]하다 assign v. (일·책임 등을) 맡기다[배정하다, 부과하다] dominance n. 우월; 권세; 지배 competitive a. 경쟁을 하는 upturned a. 위로 향한; (아래위가) 거꾸로인[뒤집힌] slant v. 기울어지다, 비스듬해지다 respectively ad. 각자, 각각, 제각기

45 글의 주제 ②

사람들이 종종 기기, 컴퓨터, 자동차와 같은 사물을 의인화하는데, 이러한 경향이 외로움을 줄이거나 구매 결정에 영향을 미친다고 했다. 따라서 이 글의 주제로 적절한 것은 ②이다.

다음 중 이 글의 주제로 가장 적절한 것은?
① 산업에서 심리학의 중요성
② 사물을 의인화하는 인간의 경향
③ 의인화가 마케팅에 미치는 긍정적인 효과
④ 제품에 대한 사람들의 애착 문제

46 내용일치 ④

"독일의 자동차 판매를 분석한 결과, 웃는 것처럼 위로 올라간 그릴과 가늘게 뜬 눈처럼 기울어진 헤드라이트를 가진 자동차가 가장 잘 팔리는 것으로 나타났다."고 했으므로 ④가 이 글의 내용과 일치한다.

이 글에 따르면, 다음 중 옳은 것은?
① 한 연구에 따르면, 컴퓨터에 문제가 발생한 사람들은 컴퓨터를 의인화하지 않을 가능성이 높다.
② 자동차를 소유한 사람들은 자동차의 개성을 평가한 후 교체하기로 했다.
③ 사람들은 폭이 넓은 제품보다 좁은 제품을 선호한다.
④ 독일에서는 인간의 모습을 한 자동차가 가장 많이 팔렸다.

47 빈칸완성 ①

ⓐ 앞 문장에서 "외로움을 느낀다고 보고한 사람들은 자유 의지와 의식이 다양한 장치의 속성이라고 생각할 가능성이 다른 사람들보다 더 높았다."고 했는데, 이것은 외로움을 느끼는 것이 사물을 인간처럼 친밀하게 느끼게 만든 것을 말하며, ⓐ 다음에서 '사물과 친밀감을 느끼는 것이 외로움을 덜어줄 수 있다'고 했는데, 이것은 사물과의 친밀감이 외로움을 덜 느끼게 만든 것을 말한다. 즉, 'A는 B를 어떻게 하고, 이번에는 또한 B가 A(혹은 C)를 어떻게 한다'는 패턴의 문장 전개이다. 따라서 ① In turn이 빈칸에 적절하다.

다음 중 ⓐ에 가장 적절한 것은?
① 이번에는 또한
② 그렇지 않으면
③ 설상가상으로
④ 이런 점에도 불구하고

48-50

미국 건국의 아버지 중 한 명인 제임스 매디슨(James Madison)은 "정부를 통제하고 규제해야 하는 것은 바로 대중의 이성뿐이다."라고 주장했다. 그러나 공무원들이 국민들의 의견을 들을 수 있는 수단은 제한적이다. 선출직 공무원은 전자적(이메일)으로나 시청에서 국민의 의견을 받고, 일부 기관은 때때로 복잡한 규정에 대하여 대중의 의견을 구한다. 그래도, 미국인들은 자신들이 정책 입안 과정에 영향을 미친다는 것에 대해서나 선출직 공무원이 국민의 견해를 이해한다는 것에 대해 매우 낮은 신뢰도를 보인

다. 인공지능이 발전하면서 이런 상황은 더욱 악화되고 있다. 시민들로 위장한 인공지능은 정책 입안자들에게 방대한 양의 정보를 제공할 수 있다. 연방통신위원회(Federal Communications Commission)가 망 중립성 정책을 유지해야 할지에 대한 공개 의견을 받았을 때, 뉴욕 주 법무장관은 나중에 그 2,200만 개의 댓글 중 약 1,800만 개가 가짜 이름이거나 동의 없이 실명을 사용하여 조작된 것이라는 것을 발견했다. 가짜 메시지의 가장 큰 비중을 차지하는 것은 규제 완화를 원하는 브로드밴드 업계에서 만들어진 것이었다. 진짜인 댓글 중 98.5%가 망 중립성을 유지하는 것에 대해 찬성했다. 또한 연구원들은 최근 입법부 사무실에 32,398개의 이메일을 보냈는데, 일부는 시민이 직접 작성한 것이고, 일부는 몇 초 만에 진짜처럼 보이는 수천 개의 메일을 전달할 수 있는 인공지능으로 만들어진 것이다. 연구 결과에 따르면 입법부 사무실에서는 어느 것이 가짜인지 분간할 수 없었다고 한다. 우리는 가짜 의견이 넘쳐나서 진짜 의견을 압도하고 더 나아가 대중의 신뢰를 저해하게 될 사태의 시작을 목격하고 있을 뿐이다. 그래서 무엇을 할 수 있는가? 결함이 있는 시스템의 붕괴는 표면적인 복구 작업이 아니라 대대적인 업그레이드가 필요한 것인지도 모른다.

Founding Fathers (1787년의) 미국 헌법 제정자들 input n. (일·사업 등을 성공시키기 위한) 조언[시간, 지식 등](의 제공); 투입 confidence n. 신뢰; 자신(감) policymaking n. 정책 입안 retain v. 유지[보유]하다 net neutrality 망 중립성(통신망이 특정 사업자나 콘텐츠를 차별하지 않는 것) fabricate v. (거짓 정보를) 날조하다, 조작하다 consent n. 동의, 허락 discern v. 식별하다, 분간하다 overwhelm v. 압도하다 undermine v. 약화시키다 flawed a. 결함[결점]이 있는 superficial a. 깊이 없는, 피상적인

48 글의 목적 ②

이 글은 인공지능 발전이 대중의 의견을 압도하고 신뢰도 하락을 초래하고 있는 상황을 설명하고 있다. 망 중립성에 대한 의견 조사에서 발견된 조작된 댓글의 예와 같이 인공지능이 생성한 댓글이 국민의 의견(여론)과 정책 결정 과정에 영향을 미친 사례와 우려 사항에 대해 언급하고 있으므로, ②가 글의 목적으로 적절하다.

이 글의 주된 목적은 무엇인가?
① 인공지능으로 조작된 의견과 진짜 의견을 구별하는 방법을 설명하기 위해서
② 인공지능이 여론을 통제하는 것에 대해 경고하기 위해서
③ 미국인들에게 투표할 때 이성을 활용할 것을 요구하기 위해서
④ 망 중립성의 잠재적인 문제를 입증하기 위해

49 내용일치 ④

"위원회에게 보내진 진짜인 댓글 중 98.5%가 망 중립성을 유지하는 것에 대해 찬성했다."고 했으므로 ④가 정답이다.

이 글에 따르면, 다음 중 옳은 것은?
① 인공지능은 더 많은 규제를 주장하기 위해 업계에서 사용되었다.
② 2천만 건이 넘는 가짜 메시지가 위원회에 보내졌다.
③ 미국인들은 자신들이 선출된 공직자들에게 영향을 끼친다는 큰 믿음을 가지고 있다.
④ 위원회에게 보내진 진짜 의견의 대부분은 망 중립성을 원했다.

50 빈칸완성

Ⓐ 다음에서 망 중립성 정책에 대한 공개 의견 조사에서 일부는 인공지능에 의해 만들어졌다고 했으므로, 시민으로 '가장한' 인공지능이 방대한 양의 정보를 제공할 수 있다고 해야 문맥상 적절하다. 따라서 Ⓐ에는 masquerading이 적절하다. Ⓑ 앞에서 입법부는 어느 것이 인공지능에 의해 만들어진 것인지 분간할 수 없다고 했고, 대중의 신뢰를 저해하는 상황이라면, 진짜 의견이 가짜 의견으로 인해 압도되는 상황이라고 볼 수 있다. 따라서 Ⓑ에는 drowning 또는 overwhelming이 적절하다.

다음 중 Ⓐ와 Ⓑ에 들어가기에 가장 적절한 짝을 나열한 것은?
① 조절하다 ― 생성하다
② 가장하다 ― 익사시키다, 압도하다
③ 제기하다 ― 강조하다
④ 극복하다 ― 압도하다

2024 한국항공대학교(인문계)

01 ③	02 ①	03 ②	04 ①	05 ③	06 ④	07 ②	08 ①	09 ②	10 ④
11 ④	12 ②	13 ③	14 ②	15 ②	16 ④	17 ③	18 ①	19 ②	20 ①
21 ④	22 ③	23 ④	24 ①	25 ①	26 ④	27 ②	28 ④	29 ③	30 ③

01 동의어 ③

parity n. 동등, 동격; (다른 나라의 통화와의) 등가(等價)(= equality) paucity n. 소수, 소량, 결핍 disparity n. 부동(不同), 부등(不等), 불균형, 불일치 division n. 분할, 분배

유로화는 10여년 만에 처음으로 미국 달러화와의 등가(等價)에 근접했다.

02 동의어 ①

ingenious a. 발명의 재능이 풍부한, 창의력이 풍부한; 영리한(= clever) inept a. 부적절한; 서투른 inexperienced a. 경험이 없는, 미숙한 opulent a. 부유한, 풍족

우리 인간들이 영리할지도 모르지만, 자연의 세계는 더 똑똑하다.

03 동의어 ②

undue a. 지나친, 과도한(= excessive) attention n. 주의, 주목; 관심, 흥미 poor a. 빈약한 green a. 미숙한 fair a. 공평한, 공정한

그녀는 자신에게 지나친 관심을 끄는 것을 좋아하지 않기 때문에 소셜 미디어의 열렬한 애호가는 아니다.

04 동의어 ①

austerity n. 간소; 내핍, 긴축 demonstrate v. 증명하다, 논증하다 get by 그럭저럭 살아가다, 어떻게든 버텨내다 scrimp v. 절약하다, 아끼다(= skimp) squander v. (시간·돈 따위를) 낭비하다, 헛되이 쓰다 dissipate v. 흩뜨리다; 일소하다 enjoy v. 즐기다

그것은 긴축 프로그램으로, 절약을 하면서도 버텨나갈 수 있는 방법을 보여준다.

05 동의어 ③

much-mooted a. 많은 논란이 있는 veracious a. (사람이) 진실을 말하는, 정직한; (진술·보고 등이) 진실한(= factual) boundless a. 무한한, 끝없는 deceptive a. (사람을) 현혹시키는; 거짓의 quarrelsome a. 다투기를 좋아하는; 시비조의

그 상황은 그것이 어디까지 진실한 역사로 받아들여질 수 있는지에 대한 논란 많은 질문을 고려하게끔 한다.

06 논리완성 ④

'서로 다른 정보가 어떻게 조화를 이루는지 살펴본다'는 것은 '전체적인' 혹은 '총체적인' 성격과 관련이 있다.

epistemologist n. 인식론자 exact a. 정확한 commitment n. 공약, 서약, 약속 chromosome n. 염색체 evolve v. 진화하다 natural selection 자연선택 functional a. 기능의, 기능 본위의 baseline a. 기본적인 definition n. 정의; 설명 constellation n. 별자리; (관련 있는 생각·사물·사람들의) 무리, 기라성 relevant a. 관련된, 적절한 inferentially ad. 추론적으로, 추론에 의해 explanatorily ad. 설명하여, 설명적으로 inference n. 추리, 추론 novel a. 신기한, 새로운 diverse a. 다양한, 가지각색의 implicit a. 은연중의, 암시적인; 절대적인 physical a. 육체의; 실제의 holistic a. 전체론의, 전체론적인; 총체적인

인식론자들은 지식과 이해의 정확한 성격에 대해 논쟁하지만, 몇 가지 약속이 널리 공유되어 있다. 하나는 지식이 적어도 (충분조건은 아니더라도) 필요조건으로서 진정한 믿음을 포함한다는 것이다. 나는 인간이 30개의 염색체를 가지고 있다는 것을 알 수 없다 (왜냐하면 그것은 진실이 아니기 때문이다). 그리고 누군가가 인간이 자연선택을 통해 진화했다고 믿지 않는다면, 우리는 (비록 그것이 사실이라고 하더라도) 그녀가 그것을 안다고 말하지 않을 것이다. 공유하고 있는 두 번째 약속은 이해란 지식을 넘어 보다 더 총체적이고 (이를 위해서는 서로 다른 정보가 어떻게 조화를 이루는지 살펴 볼 필요가 있다) 또한 더 기능적이라는 (그것은 어떤 방식으로든 정보를 다룰 수 있어야 한다) 것이다. 저자들은 이러한 공유된 약속을 사용하여 이해에 대한 다음과 같은 기본적인 정의를 발전시킨다. 어떤 주제 (문제, 개념, 이론, …)를 이해한다는 것은 그 주제와 관련된 일련의 사실들이 새로운 연결을 만들어 내거나 새로운 추론을 이끌어낼 수 있는 방식으로 서로 어떻게 연관되어 있는지를 (인과적으로, 추론적으로, 설명적으로 등) 파악할 때에만 가능하다는 것이다. 결과적으로 이해의 대상은 항상 정보의 집단이며 결코 하나의 정보가 아니다.

07 논리완성 ②

'동물들을 식량원과 이동 경로로부터 차단하고 있는 한편, 교통 소음에 묻혀 서로가 의사소통을 할 수 없게 만들고 있는 것'은 고속도로가 로드킬 외에 추가적으로 초래하고 있는 문제점에 해당한다. 그러므로 빈칸에는 '(정도나 범위에 있어) ~를 넘어'라는 의미의 Beyond가 들어가는 것이 적절하다.

wildlife n. 야생동물 crisis n. 위기 biodiversity n. 생물 다양성 species n. 종(種), 종류 ocelot n. 오셀롯(중남미산(産)의 표범과 비슷한 스라소니) tiger salamander 호랑이도롱뇽 existential a. 존재에 관한, 실존의 threat n. 위협, 협박 eliminate v. 제거하다; 죽이다, 없애다 population n. 인구; 개체군 migration n. 이동, 이주 drown out (센 소리가 약한 소리 등을) 들리지 않게 하다, 압도하다, 몰아내다 remarkable a. 현저한 adaptation n. 적응, 순응 universally ad. 보편적으로 exclusively ad. 배타적으로 harmful a. 유해한

그의 새로운 책에서, 골드파브(Goldfarb)는 어떻게 도로와 자동차가 전 세계에 걸쳐 야생동물들의 삶을 바꾸고 있는지 그리고 어떻게 로드킬이 생물 다양성에 위기를 만들었는지를 설명한다. 오셀롯과 플로리다 표범 그리고 호랑이도롱뇽과 같은 종들에게 있어, 로드킬은 실존적 위협 그 자체다. 로드킬은 동물들을 죽이고 있을 뿐만 아니라, 많은 경우에 개체군이 강하게 유지되기 위해 필요로 하는 건강한 동물들을 죽이고 있다. 로드킬의 문제를 넘어, 고속도로는 동물들을 그들의 식량원과 이동 경로로부터 차단하고 있는 한편, 교통 소음에 묻혀 서로가 의사소통을 할 수 없게 만들고 있다. 이러한 난제들에 둘러싸인 가운데, 골드파브는 특정 종(種)들이 주목할 만한 적응을 했다고 말한다. 그는 시카고의 코요테들이 거리를 건너기 전에 양쪽 길을 살펴보고 빨간 신호등에서 횡단보도를 이용하는 것으로 전해지고 있다고 언급했다. 우리는 도로를 보편적으로 혹은 배타적으로 동물들에게 유해한 물리력이라고 생각하며, 그것들이 틀림없이 매우 파괴적이라고 생각한다. 그러나 야생동물들 또한 매우 적응력이 있고 영리하며, 그들은 우리 인간들 사이에서 살아나가는 방법을 찾아나가고 있다.

08 논리완성   ①

'모두가 에어 택시를 이용하는 것이 불가능하게 되는 것'은 '에어 택시를 모든 사람들이 감당할 수 있는 선택사항으로 만들고 기존의 공공여객운송 체계에 통합시키기 위한 자금조달 장치가 만들어지지 않은 경우'일 것이므로 빈칸에는 부정의 조건절을 이끄는 표현인 Unless가 적절하다.

steadily ad. 착실하게; 꾸준히 reality n. 실재, 실체 agency n. 대리; 대리점; (정부 따위의) 기관, 청(廳), 국(局) blueprint n. 청사진, 설계도, 면밀한 계획 procedure n. 절차; 방법; 수순 accommodate v. 편의를 도모하다; 수용하다 bill v. (~을 …로) 홍보하다 green a. 친환경의 alternative n. 달리 택할 방도, 대안 bookable a. (좌석 따위가) 예약할 수 있는 expert n. 전문가 transportation n. 운송, 수송; 교통기관 available a. 이용할 수 있는 means n. 재산, 재력 optic n. 눈 exclude v. 배제[제외]하다 affordable a. 줄 수 있는; 입수 가능한, (값이) 알맞은 integrate v. 통합하다 transit n. 운송; 공공 여객 운송 accessible a. 입수하기 쉬운, 이용할 수 있는

연방항공청은 에어 택시를 타고 다니는 것이 적어도 어느 시점에서는 현실이 될 수 있도록 꾸준히 준비하고 있다고 말하고 있다. 5월에 그 기관은 이러한 종류의 항공기를 수용하기 위한 공역(空域)과 절차 변경에 대해 업데이트된 청사진을 발표했다. 조비 항공(Joby Aviation)은 "앱 터치로 예약이 가능한 운전에 대한 친환경적인 대안"으로 "생활 속에서 사람들을 실어 보내는 더 빠르고, 더 깨끗하고, 더 똑똑한 방법"을 제공하고 있다고 홍보하고 있다. 그러나, 전문가들은 그것이 러시아워의 교통체증에서 더 적은 시간을 보내고 싶어 하는 누구나가 이러한 종류의 교통수단을 이용할 수 있다는 것을 의미하지는 않는다고 말한다. 그것은 재력이 있는 사람들에게는 훌륭한 혁신이다. 그러나 그 산업은 소음에서부터 님비(NIMBY)에 대한 우려에 이르는 어려움에 직면해 있다. 또한 보는 측면에서도 문제가

있는데, 바로 부유한 사람들이 우리와 같은 나머지 평범한 사람들의 머리 위를 날아다니는 광경이다. 이러한 종류의 교통수단은 주로 민간 기업에 의해 제공될 가능성이 높기 때문에, 그것이 저소득층 사람들을 배제하게 될 것이라는 우려가 있다. 이것을 모든 사람들이 감당할 수 있는 선택사항으로 만들고 기존의 공공여객운송 체계에 통합시키기 위한 자금조달 장치가 없는 한, 모두가 그것을 이용하는 것은 불가능할 것이다.

09 논리완성   ②

바로 뒤에서 "생활 습관의 변화는 보다 항구적이고 영속적인 효과를 줄 수 있다."라고 부연 설명하고 있으므로 빈칸에는 '지속적인'이라는 의미의 ②가 들어가야 한다.

elixir n. 묘약, 만병통치약 solid a. 견고한; 확실한, 믿을 수 있는 body of evidence 일련의 증거 meta-analysis n. 메타 분석(동일하거나 유사한 연구 주제로 실시된 많은 통계적 연구를 다시 통계적으로 통합하고 종합하는 문헌 연구의 한 방법) medication n. 약물 치료 symptom n. 증상, 증세 depression n. 우울증 antidepressant a. 항(抗)우울증의, 우울증을 치료하는 episode n. (재발성 질환의) 증상 발현(發現) nutrition n. 영양 empower v. 권한을 주다 acute a. 날카로운; 심각한; 급성의 durable a. 오래 견디는, 튼튼한; 영속성이 있는 resilient a. 탄력 있는 inexpensive a. 값싼

운동은 만병통치약이다. 신체 활동을 기분 개선과 연관 짓는 일련의 확실한 증거가 있다. 이전의 연구에서는 규칙적으로 운동하는 사람들이 정신 건강이 나쁜 날이 더 적다고 보고하는 것으로 드러났다. 그리고 최근의 메타 분석에서는 신체 활동이 우울증의 증상을 줄이는 데 약물치료보다 효과적이라는 것이 밝혀졌다. 우울증 치료제는 우울증의 발현을 보다 신속하게 치료하는 경향이 있다. 하지만 신체적 운동은 항우울제보다 더 지속적인 효과가 있다. 어떤 사람들에게는, 약물이 초기에는 효과가 있지만 시간이 지나갈수록 효과가 점점 약해진다. 반면에, 생활 습관의 변화는 보다 항구적이고 영속적인 효과를 줄 수 있다. 연구원들은 환자들에게 힘을 부여하기 위해 약물에서부터 치료, 그리고 신체단련, 영양, 수면 및 스트레스 관리를 포함한 행동적 접근법에 이르기까지, 증거를 기반으로 한 다양한 권장 사항과 도구를 이용한다.

10 논리완성   ④

빈칸 이하의 내용, 즉 "중국이 산아제한을 법으로 강제했던 것은 다른 나라들의 상황과 무관하게 일어나고 있던 일이 아니었다."는 앞 내용을 부연하는 것이다. 따라서 빈칸에는 '달리 말하면'이라는 뜻의 ④가 들어가야 한다.

demographic a. 인구학의 policymaker n. 정책입안자 specifically ad. 명확히; 특히 overpopulation n. 인구과잉 starvation n. 굶주림, 기아(飢餓) cornerstone n. 초석; 토대, 기초 wounded a. 상처 입은, 부상당한 prevalent a. (널리) 보급된, 널리 행해지는; 유행하고 있는 in a vacuum 진공상태에서 unveil v. 밝히다, 털어놓다 apologist n. 변호자, 옹호자

2차 세계대전 후, 인구학자들과 정책입안자들의 관심은 — 특히 빈곤 국가들에서 — 아이들이 너무 적은 것에 대한 걱정에서 아이들이 너무 많은 것에 대한 두려움으로 옮겨갔다. 이러한 사상가들 중 많은 사람들이 미국에 기반을 두고 있었다. 1968년에 폴 R. 얼리히(Paul R. Ehrlich)는 『인구

폭탄』이라는 베스트셀러를 출판했는데, 그 책에서 그는 인구 과잉은 곧 대량 기아로 이어질 것이라고 경고했다. 산아 제한은 원조 정책의 초석이 되었다. 그들은 우리가 구제가 가능한 이른 바 "걸어 다니는 부상자들"에 원조를 집중해야 한다고 말하고 있었다. 이러한 사고방식은 1970년대에 매우 만연해 있었고, 그 시기에 중국 지도부가 자국의 새로운 인구 정책을 고려하고 있던 때였다. 달리 말하자면, 중국이 1980년에 대부분의 중국 가정이 한 명의 아이만 갖도록 허용할 것이고 또한 법을 위반하는 경우에 처벌될 것이라고 선언했을 때, 이것이 진공상태에서(외부의 영향 없이) 일어나고 있는 것은 결코 아니었다. 한 자녀 정책이 발표되었을 때, 그것은 국제적인 비판에 많이 직면하지도 않았다. 서구에도 그 프로그램을 옹호하는 사람들이 많이 있었다. 그것은 수용할 수 있는 것일 뿐 아니라 선구적인 것으로 받아들여졌다.

① 그와는 대조적으로
② 설상가상으로
③ 그 대신에
④ 달리 말하자면

---

11 may well+동사원형 ④

④에 쓰인 may as well은 '~하는 편이 낫다'라는 의미이므로 주어진 문장의 흐름상 어색하다. 따라서 이것을 '아마 ~일 것이다', '~하는 것도 당연하다'라는 의미의 may well로 고쳐야 한다. ① 앞의 명사 questions를 수식하는 형용사적 용법의 to부정사이므로 questions를 가리키는 목적어 them이 crack 다음에 없는 것이 맞다. ② for 다음의 명사가 알려진(known) '이유'에 해당하므로 for이다.

species n. 종(種), 종류 innately ad. 선천적으로 hostile a. 적의 있는; 냉담한 inherently ad. 선천적으로; 본질적으로 cooperative a. 협력적인, 협조적인 crack open (사건 따위를) 해결하다, 폭로하다 primatologist n. 영장류동물학자 evolutionary biologist 진화생물학자 make headway (특히 서서히·어렵게) 나아가다[진전하다] relative n. 친척, 친족 insight n. 통찰력 collaborator n. 공동 연구자[저자] communal a. 자치단체의 lead the charge 먼저 책임을 지고 이끌다, 임무를 선도하다 pave the way for ~을 위해 길을 열다, ~에 대해 준비하다 inevitable a. 피할 수 없는, 불가피한 evolutionary a. 진화의, 진화론에 의한 legacy n. 유산

하나의 종(種)으로서의 우리는 누구인가? 인간은 우리 자신이 속한 공동체 이외의 공동체에 속한 사람들에게 선천적으로 적대적이고 폭력적인가? 아니면 본질적으로 우호적이고 협력적인가? 이것들은 답을 알아내기 어려운 질문들이다. 수년간에 걸쳐, 일부 연구자들 — 영장류동물학자들, 진화생물학자들 등등 — 은 통찰력을 얻기 위해 인간과 가장 가까운 살아있는 친척이라 할 수 있는 침팬지와 보노보들을 살펴봄으로써 진전을 이루려고 노력해왔다. 지금, 한 연구에서, 두 명의 공동 연구원들은 야생 보노보들 — 침팬지에 비해 더 친근하고 더 평화로운 성향으로 알려져 있음 — 이 자신들의 공동체 집단 내에서 뿐만 아니라 다른 보노보 집단들과도 협업하고, 보다 협력적인 개체들이 책임을 지고 이끈다고 주장한다. 이것은 보다 폭넓은 집단들이 사회적 유대를 형성할 수 있는 길을 열어준다. 연구자들은 이것이 전쟁이 인류의 피할 수 없는 진화론적 유산이 아닐 수도 있음을 시사하는 것이라고 말한다. 협력과 평화는 아마도 지금의 우리 안에 깊이 자리하고 있는 일부일 것이다. 즉, 전쟁을 위한 능력과 평화를 위한 능력 모두가 우리의 내면에서 서로 나란히 살아있는 것일지도 모른다.

---

12 명사의 수 ②

② 앞에 복수의 수사가 주어져 있으므로 ②는 복수 명사 inches여야 한다. ① 목적격의 관계대명사 what이다. ③ hope는 to부정사를 목적어로 취한다. ④ 과거사실의 반대를 가정하는 가정법 과거완료에서는 조건절의 동사로 had+p.p.를 쓴다.

the metric system 미터법 pirate n. 해적 hodgepodge n. 뒤범벅, 뒤죽박죽 interstate a. 주(州) 사이의 commerce n. 상업, 통상 pal n. 친구, 동료 weights and measures 도량형 run into ~와 우연히 만나다 lurk v. 숨다, 잠복하다 tacitly ad. 암암리에 task v. ~에 일을 부과하다 harass v. 괴롭히다, 애먹이다 take ~ prisoner ~을 포로로 잡아두다 ransom n. 몸값, 배상금 auction off 경매에 부치다

만약 미국이 나머지 다른 나라들과 더 비슷하다면, 맥도날드 쿼터파운더는 맥도날드 113그램 버거로 알려져 있을 것이고, 존 헨리의 9파운드 망치는 4.08킬로그램일 것이며, 방에 있는 800파운드의 고릴라라는 아마도 362킬로그램이 나갈 것이다. 미국이 미터법을 채택하지 않은 한 가지 이유는 해적 때문이었을 수도 있다. 발생한 일은 다음과 같다. 1793년, 미국이라는 완전히 새로운 나라는 측정 체계를 뒤죽박죽으로 사용하고 있었기 때문에 표준 측정 체계가 필요했다. 예를 들어, 뉴욕에서는 네덜란드의 체계를 사용하고 있었고, 뉴잉글랜드에서는 영국의 체계를 사용하고 있었다. 이것은 주(州)와 주(州) 사이의 거래를 어렵게 만들었다. 토마스 제퍼슨은 새로운 프랑스의 체계에 대해 알고 있었고 그것이 바로 미국이 필요로 하는 것이라고 생각했다. 그는 프랑스에 있는 친구들에게 편지를 썼고, 그 프랑스인들은 조셉 돔비(Joseph Dombey)라는 이름의 한 과학자를 제퍼슨에게 보냈는데, 그는 위에 작은 손잡이가 있는 작은 구리 원통을 가지고 있었다. 그것은 높이가 약 3인치였고 너비도 거의 같았다. 이 물체는 사물의 무게를 재는 표준으로 삼으려 했던 것으로, 프랑스에서 개발되고 있던 도량형 체계의 일부로 지금은 미터법으로 알려져 있는 것이었다. 이 물체의 무게는 1킬로그램이었다. 대서양을 건너던 돔비는 거대한 폭풍우를 만났다. 폭풍우는 그가 타고 있던 배를 멀리 남쪽의 카리브 해로 날려버렸다. 1700년대 후반에 누가 카리브해 바다에 숨어있었는지는 당신도 알지 않은가? 바로 해적들이다. 이 해적들은 기본적으로 배를 타고 돌아다니던 범죄자들이었는데, 영국 정부의 암묵적인 지원을 받아 적국의 선박을 괴롭히는 임무를 맡고 있었다. 해적들은 몸값을 받기를 희망하며 조셉 돔비를 몬세라트(Montserrat) 섬에 포로로 잡아두었다. 해적들은 돔비가 가지고 있던 물건들에는 관심이 없었다. 그것들은 그의 배에 실려 있던 나머지 물건들과 함께 경매에 부쳐졌다. 만약 돔비가 자신의 킬로그램(원통)을 제퍼슨에게 전달할 수 있었다면 정말로 어떤 변화가 있었을까? 우리는 확실히 모르지만, 거기서 기회를 놓친 것 같다.

---

13 논리완성 ③

뒤이어서 군대개미가 서로의 몸을 연결하여 다리를 만든다는 내용이 나오므로, 이와 관련된 ③이 정답으로 적절하다.

occupational a. 직업적인 hazard n. 위험, 위험요소 aggressive a. 공격적인, 적극적인 predator n. 포식자, 포식동물; 약탈자 devour v. 게걸스럽게 먹다, 먹어치우다 lizard n. 도마뱀 remarkable a. 주목할 만한, 현저한 insight n. 통찰력 swarm n. 떼, 무리 scour v. 샅샅이 뒤지다; 문질러 닦다 forage v. 마초를 찾아다니다; 식량징발에 나서다 encounter v. 우연히 만나다 obstacle n. 장애물, 방해물 a barrel of 다량의 shortcut n. 지름길 traverse v. ~을 건너다

생계를 위해 군대개미를 연구하는 것은 특정한 직업적 위험을 동반한다. "그 개미들은 매우 공격적입니다."라고 Isabella Muratore는 말한다. "그 개미들은 독을 가지고 있어서, 당신을 쏘고 깨물 겁니다. 그것은 그렇게 나쁘지 않습니다. 단지 대개 수백 마리의 그 개미들에게 한꺼번에 쏘이는 것일 뿐입니다." 군대개미는 다른 곤충들 — 때로는 개구리, 도마뱀, 새조차도 — 을 먹어치우는 사나운 포식자들이다. 그러나 그들에 대해 훨씬 더 놀라운 점은 그들이 가진 뛰어난 건축 솜씨다. Muratore는 군대개미가 어떻게 자신들의 몸을 연결함으로써 다리를 건설하는지를 연구해오고 있는데, 이것은 과학자들에게 로봇 무리를 통제하는 것에 대한 통찰력을 줄 수 있을 것이다. 중앙아메리카, 남아메리카, 아프리카에서 흔히 발견되는 군대개미는 먹을 것을 찾아다니는 긴 행렬을 이룬 채 숲의 바닥을 샅샅이 뒤진다. 나뭇잎과 가지 사이의 간격과 같은 장애물들을 만나면, 그들은 여러 마리의 원숭이처럼 서로를 연결하여 다리를 건설한다. 일개미들이 그 틈을 가로질러 자신들을 연결하고 나면, 다른 일개미들이 그 위를 걸어갈 것이다. 기본적으로, 그들은 다른 개미들의 상황을 더 쉽게 만들기 위해서나, 다른 개미들이 그렇지 않으면 건너갈 수 없는 것을 건널 수 있게 하기 위해서 지름길을 만든다.

① 치명적인 독성
② 경범죄
③ 건축 솜씨
④ 무조건적인 헌신

14 논리완성 ②

시간을 인지하는 것은 여러 요인의 영향을 받을 수 있다는 내용이 앞에 있으므로, 미야와키는 '시간이 획일적이다'라는 생각을 부정할 것이다.

partially ad. 부분적으로 neurologist n. 신경학자 optic nerve 시신경 cerebellum n. 소뇌(小腦) synchronize v. 동시에 진행시키다; (시계·행동 따위의) 시간을 맞추다 interplay n. 상호작용 variability n. 변하기 쉬움, 변화성 vaporize v. 증발하다, 기화하다 engrossed a. 몰두한, 전념한 psychiatrist n. 정신과의사 depressed a. 우울한 sloth n. 게으름, 나태; <동물> 나무늘보 alter v. 바꾸다, 변경하다

공포와 같은 우리의 감정이 우리의 시간 감각에 어떻게 영향을 미치는지는 과학이 부분적으로만 이해하고 있는 복잡한 과정이라고 신경학자 에드 미야와키(Ed Miyawaki)는 말하고 있는데, 왜냐하면 시간 기록에 관여하는 곳이 뇌에 하나만 있는 것이 아니라 여러 개이기 때문이다. 예를 들어, 시신경 부근의 한 곳이 시간을 추적하는데, 그것은 사람들이 일광으로 하루 중의 시간을 인지하는 방법이다. 뇌에 있는 도파민이 풍부한 조직은 우리에게 보상을 기대하도록 가르치며, 우리로 하여금 움직임의 시간을 측정할 수 있도록 해주는 소뇌에도 그 나름의 시계가 있다고 그는 말한다. 미야와키는 "감정과 관련된 시계도 있고, 기억과 관련된 시계도 있으며, 이러한 온갖 종류의 시계들이 있습니다."라고 말한다. 그러나, 이 시계들은 특별히 시간이 맞춰져 있지 않으며, 뇌에는 마스터 시계가 없다. 우리가 시간을 인지하는 데 영향을 미치는 복잡한 상호작용이 있을 뿐이다. 이것은 부분적으로 우리의 시간 인지에 가변성을 부여한다. 외국으로 여행하는 것과 같은 새로운 경험이 하루를 길게 늘어나게 만드는 것처럼 보이거나 또는 비디오 게임에 몰두한 아이에게 오랜 시간이 증발해버린 것처럼 보이는 것도 이 때문이다. 정신과의사이기도 한 미야와키는 당신이 때때로 심지어 누군가의 내적인 시간 인지의 차이를 볼 수 있다고 말한다. 그는 감정 상태가 그들의 시간 감각을 크게 바꿔놔서 거의 나무늘보처럼 극도로 느리게 움직이는 중증 우울증 환자들을 치료해 왔다. "시간이 획일적인 것일 뿐이라는 생각은 그저 잘못된 것입니다."라고 미야와키는 말한다.

① 시간은 기억을 기록하는 데 도움을 준다
② 시간은 획일적인 것일 뿐이다
③ 시간은 감정에 달려있다
④ 시간은 인식할 수 없을 정도로 뒤틀리게 된다

15 논리완성 ②

빈칸 이하는 "기업이 과도하게 자동화를 진행하게 된 것에는 정부가 부추긴 면도 없지 않다."는 내용이므로, ②가 빈칸에 들어가기에 적절하다.

excessive a. 과도한 generate v. (결과·상태·행동·감정 등을) 야기[초래]하다, 가져오다 significantly ad. 상당히, 의미심장하게 impose v. (의무·세금·벌 따위를) 지우다, 부과하다 wage n. 임금, 급료 take ~ into account ~을 고려하다 negative externality 부정적 외부효과 (어떤 경제 활동이 개인이나 기업 외부에 부정적인 영향을 미치는 경우) be to blame ~에 대하여 책임이 있다 factor in (특히, 예상·계획에서) ~을 계산에 넣다 tax code 세법 tax write off 세금 감면

경제학자들은 우리가 최근에 경험한 자동화의 많은 부분이 과도하다고 주장한다. 기업들이 기계를 사용함으로써 크게 낮은 생산 비용을 발생시키지 못하면서도 일자리는 없애고 있는 반면, 모든 비용은 사회에 전가하여 사회가 더 큰 실업과 더 낮은 임금을 떠안게 됐다는 것이다. 일자리를 자동화시키기로 결정할 때, 기업들은 이러한 사회적 비용을 고려하지 않는다(경제학자들은 이러한 사회적 비용을 "부정적 외부 효과"라고 부른다). 그들은 기업만 비난을 받아야 하는 것은 아니라고 말한다. 기업은 자신들이 만들어내는 모든 사회적 비용을 계산에 넣지 않음으로 인해 자동화를 과도하게 진행하는 데 대해 책임이 있는지도 모른다. 그러나 정부도 잘못이 있다. 미국에서, 정부는 세법을 통해 실제로 기업들에게 업무를 자동화하도록 추가적인 장려를 하고 있다. 이는 정부가 자본에 대해 노동보다 낮은 비율로 세금을 부과하고 기계, 소프트웨어, 장비를 구매하는 것에 대해 모든 종류의 세금을 감면해주기 때문이다.

① 이에 따라, 정부는 불가피하게 개입하게 된다
② 그러나 정부도 잘못이 있다
③ 따라서 공격적인 조세 정책이 지체 없이 등장한다
④ 그와는 반대로, 정부는 책임이 없다

16 논리완성 ④

탄소배출량이 늘어나는 경우, 랍스터는 그 탄소를 이용하여 몸집이 커질 수 있겠지만, 랍스터가 먹이로 삼는 생물들은 이산화탄소가 많은 환경에서 껍질이 얇아지거나 녹게 된다고 했다. 따라서 먹이가 줄어들게 되는 경우에 랍스터도 궁극적으로는 줄어들게 될 것임을 추론할 수 있다. 그러므로 빈칸에는 ④가 적절하다.

carbon emission 탄소 배출량 soar v. (물가 따위가) 급등하다 end up with 결국 ~하게 되다, 결국 ~을 가지게 되다 strap v. 끈으로 매다[묶다] bib n. 턱받이 carbon dioxide 이산화탄소 exoskeleton n. 외골격 marine geologist 해양지질학자 convert v. 전환하다, 바꾸다 simulate v. 가장하다; 흉내 내다; 모의실험하다 crab n. 게 shrimp n. 새우 coral n. 산호 calcifier n. 석회화 생물 clam n. 대합조개 scallop n. 가리비 oyster n. 굴 species n. 종(種), 종류 dissolve v. 녹다, 분해되다 trim a. 말쑥한, 깔끔한; (몸이) 홀쭉한, 군살 없는 predator n. 약탈자, 포식동물

새로운 연구는 만약 탄소 배출량이 급증한다면, 우리는 초대형 랍스터를 갖게 될 수도 있다는 것을 보여준다. 하지만 여러분은 랍스터용 턱받이를 서둘러 묶어야 할 것이다(가능하면 빨리 그 랍스터를 먹어야 할 것이다). 왜냐하면 초대형 랍스터는 아마도 오래 지속되지 못할 것이기 때문이다. 새로운 연구는 만약 이산화탄소 배출량이 극단적인 수준에 이른다면, 세계의 바다에 변화가 생김으로 인해 랍스터가 정상보다 50퍼센트 더 커질 수도 있다는 것을 보여준다. 해양지질학자 저스틴 라이즈(Justin Ries)는 랍스터가 물에서 탄소를 흡수하여 그것을 이용하여 그들의 외골격을 키울 수 있다고 말한다. 그 이론에 의하면, 랍스터들은 여분의 탄소를 그들의 껍질을 키울 수 있는 물질로 전환시킬 수 있다. 그의 연구팀은 해양생물들을 담아 둘 수 있는 여러 개의 탱크들을 만들었고, 지금으로부터 100년 후, 지금으로부터 200년 후, 그리고 그 이상까지 예측된 비율의 고농도 이산화탄소 환경을 모의실험했다. 라이즈에 따르면, 랍스터, 게, 새우는 그러한 환경에서 잘 살았지만, 산호와 그 외 다른 대합조개, 가리비, 굴과 같은 "석회화 생물들"은 그렇지 못했다. 랍스터들과는 달리, 이 종(種)들의 껍질은 이산화탄소가 증가한 환경에서 점점 더 얇아졌다. "실제로, 이 종들 중 6개는 가장 높은 이산화탄소 수준에서 녹기 시작했습니다."라고 라이즈는 말한다. 그리고 그런 이유로 대형 랍스터들은 늘씬한 상태로 있고 싶어 할 것이다. 대합조개와 기타 종들은 랍스터들의 먹이에 속하는 것들이다. 껍질이 얇아져서 더 손쉬운 먹이가 된다면, 랍스터의 먹이가 되는 원천은 오래 가지 못할 것이며, 이것은 포식자들에게 좋은 소식이 아니다. 비록 랍스터들이 더 강한 껍질을 키우고 있지만, 그들의 개체수는 아마도 반드시 먹이의 뒤를 따르게 될 것이다(마찬가지로 오래 가지 못할 것이다).

① 초대형 랍스터는 식용에 적합하지 않게 될 것이다
② 탄소배출량은 빠르게 감소할 것이다
③ 초대형 랍스터들의 포식자는 없게 될 것이다
④ 초대형 랍스터는 아마도 오래 지속되지 못할 것이다

---

17 논리완성   ③

'공이 땅에 떨어지지 않고 잠시 공중에 떠 있는 것'은 중력이 없는 경우에 가능한 일이므로, ③이 정답이다.

undergrad a. 대학생의 grad school 대학원 startling a. 놀라운, 깜짝 놀라게 하는 accuracy n. 정확도 stuff n. 재료, 물자; 물건 peer into 자세히 들여다보다 physics n. 물리학 recognition n. 인지, 인식 accelerate v. 빨라지다, 속력이 더해지다 stationary a. 움직이지 않는, 정지된 equivalence n. 같음; 등가(等價), 등치(等値); 등량(等量) the General Theory of Relativity 일반상대성이론 dork n. 유행에 뒤진[촌스러운] 사람; 바보, 얼간이 nuts a. 미친, 미치광이의 blow a person's mind 흥분시키다, 황홀하게 하다

오래 전에, 대학과 대학원 사이의 시기에, 나는 뉴욕시의 도보 배달원으로 일했다. 그 일은 꽤 괜찮았다. 나는 지하철에 대해 놀라울 정도로 정확하게 알게 되었다. 나는 애니 레보비츠(Annie Leibovitz)의 스튜디오로 매주 물건을 배달했다. 그리고 나는 투자은행에서 일하는 많은 사람들의 생활을 자세히 들여다보게 되었다. 하지만 그 일에서 가장 좋았던 부분은 엘리베이터, 즉 그 길고 빠른 엘리베이터를 타는 것이었다. 물리학과 학생이었던 나는 위쪽으로 가속하는 엘리베이터를 타는 것이 행성의 표면에 정지해 있는 동안 중력을 느끼는 것과 같다는 알버트 아인슈타인의 유명한 인식에 대해 알고 있었다. 그를 일반상대성이론의 핵심으로 이끈 것이 바로 이 등가성(等價性)이다. 당시에 나는 촌스런 사람이었기 때문에, 빨간 공을 가지고 있었다. 그래서 나는 엘리베이터에 탈 때마다, 엘리베이터가 위 혹은 아래로 가속하는 바로 그 순간에 그 공을 위로 던질 수 있었다. 만약

내가 그 공을 옳게 잡았다면, 그 공이 마치 중력이 사라진 것처럼, 잠시 공중에 떠 있는 것처럼 보였을 것이다. 그 작업용 엘리베이터에 있던 다른 사람들은 모두 내가 미쳤다고 생각했지만, 그것은 항상 나를 매우 황홀하게 했다.

① 시공간은 중력에 의해 뒤틀렸다
② 자연 법칙의 완벽한 조화가 이루어졌다
③ 중력이 사라졌다
④ 아인슈타인은 중력을 인식했다

18-19

여러 연구에서 사람들, 동물들과 염화나트륨이라고도 알려진 소금과의 복잡한 관계를 설명하려고 노력했다. 우리는 약간의 소금이 들어 있는 탄산음료, 스포츠 음료, 그리고 심지어는 수돗물을 마시는 것을 좋아한다. 그러나 만약 바닷물과 같이 매우 높은 농도의 소금을 상상한다면, 당신은 그것을 정말로 싫어한다. 매우 짠 음식과 음료에 대한 이러한 혐오는 당신의 몸에 매우 소금이 부족한 상태가 아니라면 지속되는데, 이런 상태는 오늘날의 사람들에게는 매우 드문 일이다. 그러나 쥐를 대상으로 한 실험의 결과, 나트륨의 수준이 급격히 떨어지면, 소금물에 대한 내성이 커진다는 사실이 드러났다. 이때에는 동물들이 바닷물도 좋아하기 시작한다. 이러한 변화가 일어나는 데는 몸과 뇌 사이에 최소한 두 가지의 서로 다른 상호작용을 수반한다. 혈류 속 나트륨의 농도가 건강한 수준 이하로 떨어지기 시작하면, 뇌의 뒤쪽에 있는 일련의 뉴런은 소금에 대한 동물의 갈망을 증가시키는 것으로 반응한다. 만약 당신이 이 뉴런들을 자극하면, 동물들은 나트륨 공급원으로 달려가서 먹기 시작한다. 그러는 동안, 뇌의 앞쪽에 있는 다른 일련의 뉴런은 쥐가 섭취하는 모든 음식이나 물의 염분을 모니터한다. 그리고 대개, 이 뉴런들은 염분에 대한 상한선을 정한다. 그러나 소금의 수준이 극도로 낮아지면, 신체는 염분을 제한하는 뉴런을 무시하도록 하는 신호를 보낸다. 그것은 쥐가 바닷물의 소금기를 견딜 수 있게 해준다. 과학자들은 이 뉴런들을 자극함으로써 실험실에서 이 현상을 모방할 수 있었다.

complicated a. 복잡한 sodium chloride 염화나트륨 tap water 수돗물 contain v. 포함하다 concentration n. 집중; 농축, 농도 sodium n. 나트륨 aversion n. 혐오, 반감 plummet v. 급락하다 tolerance n. 관용, 아량 interaction n. 상호작용 bloodstream n. 혈류 neuron n. 신경 단위, 뉴런 respond v. 응답하다, 반응하다 dial up 증가시키다, 고조시키다 craving n. 갈망, 열망 stimulate v. 자극하다 consume v. 소비하다, 소모하다; 다 먹어[마셔] 버리다 override v. 무시하다; 거절하다; (결정 따위를) 무효로 하다, 뒤엎다 mimic v. 모방하다, 흉내 내다 phenomenon n. 현상 lab n. 실험실

18 내용추론   ①

몸에 소금이 부족하게 되면 뇌 속의 뉴런이 관여하여 소금물에 대한 내성을 커지게 만든다는 내용을 통해 ①을 추론할 수 있다. ④는 의학적 상식의 측면에서는 옳을 수도 있으나 본문의 내용과는 상관이 없다.

위 글로부터 추론할 수 있는 것은?
① 뇌세포는 소금에 대한 내성을 바꾸는 데 일정한 역할을 한다.
② 우리 몸은 우리가 바닷물을 갈망하지 않는 이유를 알고 있다.
③ 동물들은 식단에 매우 적은 양의 나트륨만을 필요로 한다.
④ 소금의 과다 섭취는 심장병과 뇌졸중의 위험을 높일 수 있다.

19 빈칸완성 ②

빈칸 앞에서는 '뇌의 뒤쪽에 있는 일련의 뉴런의 작용'을 언급했고 빈칸 뒤에서는 이와 동시에 일어나는 '뇌의 앞쪽에 있는 다른 일련의 뉴런의 작용'을 언급하고 있으므로 빈칸에는 '그러는 동안, 그 사이에'라는 뜻의 ②가 적절하다.

빈칸에 들어가기에 가장 적절한 것을 고르시오.
① 아마도 틀림없이
② 그러는 동안
③ 두말할 필요도 없이
④ 무엇보다도

20 내용추론 ①

'가격이 하락할 때 사람들이 구매를 더 많이 한다'는 가정이 개별 상품에서는 맞아 떨어지지만, 모든 상품의 가격이 하락하는 경우에는 적용될 수 없고 상황은 훨씬 더 복잡해질 수 있다는 것이 본문에서 이야기하고 있는 내용이다. 이를 통해 ①의 내용을 추론할 수 있다.

typical a. 전형적인 assumption n. 인수, 수락; 가정, 억측 obvious a. 명백한 identify v. 확인하다; 인지하다, 판정하다 factor n. 요인 substitution n. 대체, 대용 relative a. 상대적인 demand n. 수요 income n. 소득, 수입 constant a. 일정한 purchasing power 구매력 additional a. 추가적인, 부가적인 sensible a. 분별 있는, 현명한; 합리적인 in isolation 별개로 in the aggregate 전체로서 wage n. 임금 generalized a. 전반적인 insufficiency n. 불충분, 부족 aggregate a. 집합한, 총계의 v. 모이다 complicated a. 복잡한 adjustment n. 조정, 조절 stabilize v. 안정시키다 destabilize v. 불안정하게 하다

전형적인 가정(假定)은 가격이 하락할 때 사람들이 구매를 더 많이 한다는 것이다. 이것은 분명해 보이지만 왜 그럴까? 경제학자들은 두 가지 요인을 확인한다. 첫째는, "대체효과"인데, 사과의 가격이 오렌지에 비해 하락하면, 사람들은 오렌지를 사과로 대체하게 되고, 그 결과 사과에 대한 수요는 증가하게 된다. 둘째는, "소득효과"이다. 만약 당신이 가격이 하락하기 전에 사과를 샀다면, 그리고 당신의 화폐 소득이 일정하다면, 더 낮은 사과 가격은 당신의 전체 구매력을 증가시킨다. 이러한 추가 구매력의 일부는 사과에 소비될 것이므로, 사과에 대한 수요는 증가한다. 분리해서 생각하는 경우, 이것은 개별 상품들에 대해서는 완벽하게 합리적이다. 그러나 전체적으로는 어떤가? 만약 (임금을 포함한) 모든 상품과 서비스의 가격이 전체 수요의 전반적인 부족으로 인해 하락한다면, 그 경우에는 모든 것의 가격이 하락하기 때문에 대체효과가 없다. 게다가, 한 사람의 지출은 다른 누군가의 소득이므로, 만약 모든 것의 가격이 하락한다면, 화폐 소득도 마찬가지로 하락한다. 따라서, 우리가 모든 것을 합치면, 소득효과는 사라진다. 상황은 훨씬 더 복잡해질 수 있다. 가격 조정을 위한 어떤 경로는 안정화 경로이고, 어떤 경로는 불안정화 경로이다.

위 글로부터 추론할 수 있는 것은?
① 미시적 수요의 논리를 전체 시스템으로 쉽게 확장할 수는 없다.
② 물가하락은 인플레이션의 해결책이 아닐 것이다.
③ 임금 및 가격 조정은 활용도가 낮은 자원의 거시적 문제를 해결할 수 있을 것이다.
④ 자연적인 가격 조정은 장기적으로 디플레이션 문제를 해결할 것이다.

21-22

우리는 모두 백과사전적인 기억력을 가지고 있는 사람들에 대해 들어본 적이 있으며, 우리 중 많은 사람들은 아마도 그러한 기억력을 가지기에 좋은 것으로 여길 것이다. 그러나 나는 실제로는 그렇지 않다고 주장하는데, 왜냐하면 많은 기억들이 우리가 일상생활을 살아가는 것과 무관한 지엽적인 것들을 포함하고 있기 때문이다. 사실, 나는 그것들이 관련이 없을 뿐만 아니라, 우리의 일상생활을 살아가는 데 해로울 수 있다고 주장한다. 러시아의 신경심리학자 루리아(Luria)의 이 오래된 연구에서 한 가지 흥미로운 사례를 얻을 수 있다. 루리아에게는 이러한 환자, 즉 환자 S.가 있었는데, 루리아의 보고에 의하면 그 환자는 자신의 삶에서 있었던 모든 일을 기억할 수 있었다. 하지만 환자 S.는 실제로는 불리한 입장에 있었는데, 그가 평범한 사건들, 즉 세상의 정형화된 양식들을 알아보는 데 어려움을 겪어왔기 때문이다. 그리고 그러한 평범한 사건들, 즉 그러한 세상의 정형화된 양식들이 우리로 하여금 실제로 지적인 결정을 내릴 수 있게 해준다. 만약 목줄이 풀려 있는 개가 당신에게 짖는 것을 보고 있고 이전에 당신이 목줄이 풀려 있는 개에게 물린 적이 있다면, 당신은 아마도 그 개를 피하고 싶을 것이다. 비록 그것이 당신이 본 이전의 개와 똑같이 생기지는 않았다고 하더라도 말이다. 갈색 점이나 흰 꼬리가 없다는 것은 중요하지 않다. 중요한 것은 그 개가 광범위한 범주의 공격적인 개들 중의 하나임을 나타내는 특징들을 가지고 있다는 점이다. 우리의 기억력이 가진 궁극적인 목적은 우리가 결정을 내리는 것을 돕고, 지적인 방식으로 세상에서 행동하도록 돕는 것이다. 진화는 당신이 1968년 월드시리즈에서 누가 홈런을 쳤는지를 기억할 수 있는지는 상관하지 않는다. 진화는 당신이 생존 가능성을 극대화하기 위해 환경에서 적절한 결정을 내리는 사람인지 아닌지에 관심을 갖는다.

encyclopedic a. 백과사전적인; 박학한 assume v. 추정하다, 가정하다; 당연한 것으로 여기다 contain v. 포함하다 irrelevant a. 부적절한; 무관계한 detrimental a. 유해한, 손해되는 neuropsychologist n. 신경심리학자 memorize v. 기억하다, 암기하다 identify v. 확인하다; 인지하다 commonality n. 공통성; 평범한[흔히 있는] 사건 leash n. 가죽끈; 사슬, 속박 bark v. (개·여우 따위가) 짖다 feature n. 특징, 특색 indicate v. 가리키다, 보이다 aggressive a. 공격적인, 적극적인 evolution n. 진화 appropriate a. 적절한 maximize v. 극대화하다

21 빈칸완성 ④

앞의 not just와 함께 'not just[only] ~ but (also) …' 구문을 이루어야 하므로, 빈칸에는 but이 들어가야 한다.

22 글의 제목 ③

본문은 일어난 모든 일들을 기억하는 것이 일상생활을 살아가는 데 해로울 수도 있음을 이야기하고 있다. 이는 망각이 일정 부분 중요한 역할을 한다는 것으로 달리 표현할 수 있을 것이므로, 제목으로는 ③이 적절하다.

위 글의 제목으로 가장 적절한 것은?
① 단기 기억을 방해할 위험성
② 뇌는 기억을 다시 쓴다
③ 최고의 기억 시스템은 망각하는 기억 시스템일 수 있다
④ 결코 약해지지 않는 기억력은 진화에 도움이 될 수 있다

23-24

대부분의 사람들은 현재, 즉 오늘, 내일, 아마도 내년에 집중한다. 당신의 펑크 난 타이어를 고치는 것이 당신이 전기차를 사용해야 할지를 알아내는 것보다 더 긴급한 일이다. 해변가에 사는 것은 해수면 상승 때문에 집이 언제 물에 잠길지를 알아내는 것보다 훨씬 더 재미있다. 인간과 시간과의 기본적인 관계가 기후 변화를 까다로운 문제로 만든다. "저는 기후 변화를 최악의 정책 문제라고 생각하는데, 왜냐하면 당신은 기후 변화 정책보다 더 우리의 근원적인 심리나 의사결정 기관에 적합하지 않은 정책을 거의 만들 수 없을 것이기 때문입니다."라고 한 기후 전문가는 말한다. 온실가스 배출을 극적으로 줄일 힘을 궁극적으로 가지고 있는 기업과 정부를 비롯한 기관들은 개인보다도 더 현재에 집착할 수 있다. 많은 기업들이 분기별 수익과 성장에 집중한다. 그것은 화석연료를 시추하기 위해 새로운 땅을 임대하는 것과 같은 단기적인 행동을 하도록 조장하며, 이로 인해 장기적인 기후 변화는 더 나빠지게 된다. 다행스럽게도, 우리가 집단적으로 현재에 집중하는 것은 또한 현재에 과도하게 집중하는 것을 활용하여 행동을 고취시킬 수 있는 방법을 암시해준다. <예를 들어, 기후 변화를 해결하는 데 대한 빠른 보상을 강조하는 방법들이 있다.> 정치적인 영역에서, 그것은 선출된 공무원이 배출물질을 줄이는 정책들을 지지하는 경우에 더 많은 표를 얻는다는 것을 의미할 수 있다. 다음 선거에서 이익이 될 거라는 기대는 미래 세대를 보호한다는 목표보다 더 고무적일 수 있다. 비록 후자가 도덕적으로는 더 중요하더라도 말이다. 우리가 오늘 얻는 이익이 더 두드러지며, 그래서 우리는 더 클지도 모르는 미래에 늘어날 이익보다는 오늘 얻는 이익을 더 원한다.

flat a. 평평한; (타이어가) 바람이 빠진, 펑크 난 pressing a. 절박한, 긴급한 figure out 이해하다; (문제를) 풀다, 해결하다 fit n. 적합, 적합성 underlying a. 기초가 되는, 근원적인 psychology n. 심리, 심리학 institution n. 협회, 기관; 제도 emission n. (대기 속의) 배출 물질, 배기가스 be obsessed with ~에 사로잡혀 있다 quarterly a. 연(年) 4회의, 철마다의 lease v. 빌리다, 임대[임차]하다 fossil fuel 화석 연료 harness v. (자연력을) 동력화하다, 이용하다 hyperfocus n. 과잉 집중 realm n. 범위, 영역 galvanizing a. 자극하는, 영감을 주는 moral a. 도덕적인 weight n. 중요성, 세력 salient a. 두드러진, 현저한 accrue v. 자연 증가로 생기다, (이익·결과가) (저절로) 생기다

---

23 문장삽입 ④

주어진 문장은 '예를 들어, 기후 변화를 해결하는 데 대한 빠른 보상을 강조하는 방법들이 있다'라는 의미이므로, 현재의 이익을 강조하여 행동을 이끌어내는 방법의 예에 해당한다. 따라서 ⓓ에 들어가는 것이 가장 적절하다.

---

24 글의 제목 ①

사람들이 현재에 집중하는 경향은 현재보다 미래에 영향을 더 크게 미치게 될 기후 변화를 등한시하게 하지만, 이런 성향을 이용하여 현재에 보상이 신속히 따르도록 하면 변화를 이끌어낼 수 있음을 이야기하고 있는 내용이다. 그러므로 ①이 제목으로 가장 적절하다.

위 글의 제목으로 가장 적절한 것은?
① 시간에 대한 우리의 인식이 기후 변화에 대한 우리의 접근방식을 어떻게 구체화시키나

② 미래에 대한 우리의 집착이 현재를 어둡게 하다
③ 극한의 날씨가 정책 입안자들의 관심을 끌기 시작하다
④ 왜 대중들은 기후 행동주의가 변화를 가져올 것이라는 데 회의적인가

25-26

경제는 여러 곳에서 발생하며, 장소의 물리적 형태에도 영향을 미친다. 만약 앞으로의 미국 경제가 래리 서머스(Larry Summers)가 가정한 것처럼 수출 지향적이고, 저탄소를 추구하며, 혁신 주도적이라면, 어떤 종류의 풍경이 연출될까? 간단한 답은 보다 밀도가 높아지고 연결성이 향상될 거라는 것이다. 수출 지향적인 경제를 위해서는 미국산 공산품이 최대한 빨리 항만에 도착할 수 있도록 미국이 어느 정도 확보하고 있는 견고한 항만 인프라뿐만 아니라 지능적이고 조직화된 화물운송 전략이 이끄는 화물운송 네트워크도 필요할 것인데, 미국은 이것이 심하게 부족하다. 저탄소 경제는 또한 밀도가 높은 지역의 가치를 끌어올릴 것인데, 이러한 곳은 사람들의 이동이 당연히 빈번하게 일어나고 멀리 떨어져 있는 단독주택이 유일한 주거 옵션이 아닌 곳이다. 하지만 나에게 매우 놀라운 점은 혁신이 밀도 — 마일이 아니라 블록 단위로 측정되는 — 에 매우 크게 의존하고 있다는 사실이다. 에드 글레이저(Ed Glaeser)와 1890년의 알프레드 마셜(Alfred Marshall)까지 거슬러 올라가는 다른 사람들은 집적, 혹은 지리적으로 밀집한 상태에서의 활동을 통해 얻는 이득에 주목했다. 하지만 이들은 대체로 대도시 규모에서의 집적(集積)을 살펴보는데, 대도시는 여러 군(郡)에 걸쳐 뻗어 있는 상당히 광범위한 장소인 경향이 있다. 일단 사람들이 걸어갈 수 있는 거리를 넘어서까지 퍼져나가고 나면, 혁신과 집적의 혜택이 얼마나 극적으로 감소하는지를 두어 편의 논문에서 기술했다. 일부 연구자들은 기업과 사람들이 움직여 1마일 이상 떨어지게 되면 혁신과 고용을 추진시키는 지적(知的) 파급효과가 크게 떨어진다는 사실을 발견했다. 그들이 주목한 바와 같이, "직원들 간의 빈번한 접촉을 요구하는 정보 파급효과는, 만나는 장소로 걸어가는 것이 어려워짐에 따라 혹은 무작위적인 만남이 드물어짐에 따라, 짧은 거리를 넘어가면 사라질 수도 있다." 이러한 효과는 엄청나다. 당신이 불과 1마일 밖으로만 이동해도, 또 다른 새로운 기업이나 심지어 또 다른 새로운 일자리를 창출할 수 있는 지적 발효의 힘은 더 가까운 곳에 있는 경우의 10분의 1 이하로 떨어지거나, 혹은 경제학자들이 그들의 독특한 산문에서 말하는 바와 같이, 집적(集積) 경제는 거리가 멀어질수록 약화된다. 최초의 약화는 빠르게 진행돼서, 첫 1마일 내에서의 자체 산업의 고용 효과는 2~5마일 떨어진 곳에서의 효과보다 10~1000배 더 크다. 분명히, 걸어갈 수 있다는 것이 혁신의 필수조건은 아니다. 보스턴 광역도시권의 혁신 허브는 실제로 고속도로(루트128)에서 이름을 가져왔으며, 실리콘밸리와 오스틴은 모두 자동차에 의존하고 있다. 그러나 당신은 사람들이 걸어가지 않고 자동차를 운전해 가기 때문에 우리가 얼마나 많은 아이디어를 놓쳤는지를 궁금하게 여겨야 한다.

posit v. 단정하다, 긍정적으로 가정하다 robust a. 튼튼한, 강한, 확고한 infrastructure n. 기간시설, 산업 기반, 인프라 freight n. 화물; 화물운송 coordinate v. 통합하다, 조정하다 sorely ad. 심하게, 몹시 dense a. 밀집한, 밀도가 높은 transit n. 수송; 운송, 운반 detached a. 떨어진, 분리된 jaw-dropping a. (놀라서) 입을 떡 벌리게 만드는 innovation n. 혁신 agglomeration n. 집적(集積), 응집 geographically ad. 지리적으로 clustered a. 군집(군생)한 far-flung a. 멀리 떨어진; 널리 퍼진 county n. <미국> 군(郡) spillover n. 여파, 파급효과 firm n. 회사 dissipate v. 사라지다, 흩어져 없어지다 staggering a. 어마어마한, 경이적인 ferment n. 효소; 발효; 동요 inimitable a. 흉내 낼 수 없는, 독특한 attenuate v. 가늘어지다; 약해지다 initial a. 처음의, 최초의, 시작의 sine qua non 필수조건

25 빈칸완성 ①

빈칸 앞의 '불과 1마일 밖으로만 이동해도, 또 다른 새로운 기업이나 심지어 또 다른 새로운 일자리를 창출할 수 있는 지적 발효의 힘은 더 가까운 곳에 있는 경우의 10분의 1 이하로 떨어진다'와 빈칸 뒤의 '1마일 내에서의 자체 산업의 고용 효과는 2~5마일 떨어진 곳에서의 효과보다 10~1000배 더 크다'는 모두 가까운 거리 안에 있는 것의 경제적 효과가 매우 크다는 것이므로, 이것을 반대로 '멀어질수록 약화된다'고 표현한 ①이 빈칸에 들어가기에 적절하다.

빈칸에 들어가기에 가장 적절한 것을 고르시오.
① 집적 경제는 거리가 멀어질수록 약화된다
② 아이디어를 창출해내는 집적의 이점은 심리적 거리와 반비례한다
③ 집적의 속도와 방향이 중요하다
④ 집적은 고용의 기하급수적 증가를 매개한다

26 내용추론 ④

본문은 가까운 거리 안에 있는 것이 사람들 간의 빈번한 접촉을 수반하여 혁신을 이끌어낸다는 것을 말하고 있는데, SNS 등 여러 통신 수단이 발달한 현 시점에서도 이러한 빈번한 접촉을 강조하는 것은 궁극적으로 서로 대면하여 자연스럽게 대화하는 것이 정보의 파급효과, 지적 파급효과를 누리는 데 있어 중요하다는 것을 의미한다고 볼 수 있다. 그러므로 ④가 본문에서 추론할 수 있는 내용으로 가장 적절하다. ①의 경우, 본문에서 물리적 근접성을 강조하고 있기는 하나, 공유경제와는 관련이 없다.

위 글로부터 추론할 수 있는 것은?
① 물리적 근접성은 공유경제의 가장 중요한 전제조건이다.
② 투자는 혁신과 맞물려 있으며, 이것은 일자리의 증가를 활발하게 만든다.
③ 지리적으로 밀집된 상태에서의 활동을 대도시 수준에서 분석해야 한다.
④ 앞으로의 미국 경제는 실제로 자연스럽게 대화하는 인간들에 달려있을 것이다.

27-28

아르세니 알레니체프(Arsenii Alenichev)는 사진 같은 이미지를 생성하도록 설계된 인공지능 프로그램에 "아픈 백인 아이들을 돌보고 있는 아프리카 흑인 의사들"과 같은 문장을 입력했다. 그의 목표는 인공지능이 백인 구원자들 혹은 아픈 흑인 아이들이라는 고정관념을 뒤집는 이미지들을 내놓을지를 알아보는 것이었다. "우리는 전 세계적으로 전형적인 건강 관련 수사(修辭)들을 뒤집고 싶었습니다." 그의 소규모 조사에서 일어난 일은 다음과 같다. 그의 상세한 기술(記述) 내용에도 불구하고, 인공지능 프로그램은 거의 항상 아이들을 흑인으로 묘사했다. 의사들에 관해서는, 그는 350개 이상의 이미지들 중 22개에서 의사가 백인이었던 것으로 추정한다. 이 실험을 위해, 그들은 미드저니(Midjourney)라고 불리는 인공지능 사이트를 이용했다. 알레니체프는 무슨 일이 일어날지 알아보기 위해 한 개의 문구만을 입력하진 않았다. 그는 인류학자들과 협력하면서, 그의 상세한 기술 내용과 일치하는 인공지능 이미지를 얻을 수 있는지를 알아보기 위한 방법들을 구상했다. 그들은 흑인 아프리카 의사들 또는 아픈 백인 아이들을 보여 달라고 요청하는 경우에는 인공지능이 딱 맞는 이미지들을 제공하는 것을 제대로 해냈다는 것을 깨달았다. 문제가 된 것

은 그 두 가지 요청을 조합하는 경우였다. 그래서 그들은 보다 더 구체적으로 기술하기로 결정했다. 그들은 가난하거나 아픈 백인 아이들에게 음식, 백신 또는 약을 제공하는 흑인 아프리카 의사들을 언급하는 문구들을 입력했다. 그들은 또한 "치료를 받는 HIV 환자"와 같이 건강과 관련된 다른 시나리오를 묘사하는 이미지들을 요청했다. 할 수 있는 대로 노력했지만, 그 팀은 흑인 의사들과 백인 환자들이 하나의 이미지에 있는 것은 얻을 수 없었다. HIV 환자들의 150개 이미지들 가운데, 148개는 흑인이었고 2개는 백인이었다. 알레니체프는 그 이미지들 속에서는 "아프리카의 현대적인 면모를 전혀 발견하지 못했습니다."라고 말한다. "그것은 모두 현대적인 면모가 전혀 존재하지 않았던 시대를 상기시키고 있지만, 그것은 아프리카에 대해 매우 부정적인 생각을 가진 사람들의 상상 속에 존재하는 시대입니다." 일반적으로, 텍스트 프롬프트로부터 이미지들을 만드는 인공지능 프로그램들은 사람들이 키워드로 설명해놓은 기존의 사진들과 이미지들의 거대한 데이터베이스로부터 가져올 것이다. 그 프로그램이 만들어내는 결과물은 사실상 기존 콘텐츠를 리믹스한 것이다. 그리고 아픈 유색인종과 백인 서양의 보건 및 구호단체 직원들을 묘사한 사진들은 역사가 오래됐다. 우간다의 사업가 테디 루지(Teddy Ruge)는 "백인 구세주"라는 개념은 (지구의 북반구에 위치한) 선진국들이 "백인의 전문 지식이 야만인들을 압도한다"라는 개념을 내놓았던 때인 식민주의의 잔재라고 말한다. 수십 년간 지속된 백인 구세주의 이미지를 상쇄시키기 위해, 아프리카인들과 제3세계 국가 사람들은 "우리도 눈에 보일 수 있도록, 데이터베이스를 바꾸고 데이터베이스를 압도하는 데 크게 기여해야 한다"고 루지는 말한다.

artificial intelligence 인공지능   generate v. 발생시키다, 야기하다   come up with 제시하다, 제안하다   flip v. 뒤집다, 뒤엎다   stereotype n. 고정관념   savior n. 구조자, 구세주   invert v. 거꾸로 하다, 역으로 하다, 뒤집다   typical a. 전형적인   trope n. 말의 수사(修辭); 비유적 용법; 수사 어구   specification n. 상술(詳述), 열거   depict v. 묘사하다, 서술하다   estimate v. 추정하다   collaborate v. 협력하다, 협동하다   anthropologist n. 인류학자   on-point a. 결함 없는, 완벽한   specific a. 일정한; 구체적인   get a sense of 발견하다   hark back to (말·사고 따위에서) (과거지사로) 되돌아가다, (~을) 상기하다   negative a. 부정적인   text prompt 프롬프트(컴퓨터가 조작자에 대하여 입력을 요구하고 있음을 나타내는 단말 화면상의 기호[글])   massive a. 육중한, 무거운; 대량의   entrepreneur n. 사업가, 기업가   remnant n. 나머지, 잔여   colonialism n. 식민주의, 식민지 정책   global north 주로 북반구의 유럽, 북아메리카 등에 위치한 선진국들   expertise n. 전문적인 기술[지식, 의견]   savage n. 야만인, 미개인   compensate for 보상하다, 벌충하다, 상쇄하다   global south 주로 남반구에 위치한 후진국들, 제3세계 국가들   overwhelm v. 압도하다

27 빈칸완성 ②

"아픈 백인 아이들을 돌보고 있는 흑인 의사들"과 같은 구체적인 기술을 한 것과 인공지능 프로그램이 거의 항상 아이들을 흑인으로 묘사한 것은 양보 관계에 있다. 그러므로 빈칸에는 '~에도 불구하고'라는 의미의 전치사 Despite가 들어가야 한다.

빈칸에 들어가기에 가장 적절한 것을 고르시오.
① ~에 의하면
② ~에도 불구하고
③ ~뿐만 아니라
④ ~없이

28 내용추론 ④

인공지능은 기존의 데이터베이스에서 얻은 정보를 가지고 사용자의 요구에 대응하기 때문에, 기존의 정보가 고정관념으로 치우쳐 있거나 편향된 것이라면 인공지능도 편향된 정보를 제공할 수밖에 없을 것임을 추론할 수 있다.

위 글에서 추론할 수 있는 것은?
① 인공지능이 편향된 이미지를 생성할 때 누구에게 책임을 물어야 하는지에 관해 국제 사회에서 대화를 나누어야 한다.
② 자세하고 구체적인 기술을 제공하기만 하면 인공지능은 딱 맞는 이미지를 제시한다.
③ 우리는 인공지능을 비정치적인 것으로 이해할 것을 요구해야 하는데, 왜냐하면 인공지능은 비정치적이기 때문이다.
④ 인공지능이 생성한 이미지는 고정관념을 전파할 수 있다.

29-30

우리의 현대적 전쟁 규칙들은 고대 문명들과 종교들로 거슬러 올라갈 수 있지만, 이러한 관습들을 국제 인도주의 법으로 성문화(成文化)하는 과정을 시작한 사람은 적십자의 설립자인 앙리 뒤낭(Henri Dunant)이었다. 1864년, 그는 최초의 제네바 협약의 제정에 기여했는데, 이것은 군대가 전장(戰場)의 환자들과 부상자들을 반드시 돌보도록 규정하는 국제조약이었다. 그것은 유럽의 12개국이 채택하였다. 그 후 85년에 걸쳐, 외교관들은 전장의 전투원들뿐만 아니라 해상의 전투원들과 전쟁 포로들에 대한 처우도 다루는 추가적인 개정들과 조약들을 논의하여 채택했다. 1949년, 2차 세계대전의 공포를 겪은 후에, 외교관들은 제네바에서 다시 모여 4개의 조약을 채택했는데, 그 조약들은 이전의 조약들을 재확인하고 갱신했으며 그 규칙을 민간인으로까지 확대했다. 그 조약들은 이제 한데 묶어서 1949년의 제네바 협약으로 알려져 있으며 가장 중요한 전쟁 규칙들을 포함하고 있다. 그 이후, 그러한 전쟁 규칙들은 196개 국가에 의해 비준되었다. 그 규칙들은 전투에서 싸우고 있지 않은 사람들을 보호하고 사용될 수 있는 무기들과 전술들에 제한을 둠으로써 전쟁의 잔혹성을 억제한다. 그 규칙들은 또한 국내·국제 법원에서 정부 혹은 비정부 전투 집단이 전쟁 범죄에 대해 유죄인지를 판단하는 데 사용되고 있다. 만일 교전 당사자가 국제 인도주의 법을 위반하여 — 개인, 단체, 국가에 의해서든, 관찰자에 의해서든 간에 — 기소된다면, 국가들은 조사할 의무가 있다. 국제 평화와 안전을 유지하는 임무를 맡고 있는 유엔 15개국으로 구성된 유엔 안전보장이사회는 교전 당사자들이 전쟁 규칙들을 준수하도록 하기 위한 유인책으로서 여행 금지 또는 무기 수출금지와 같은 제재들을 부과할 수도 있다. 그 협약에는 많은 규칙들이 포함되어 있지만, 계속되는 전투와 관련된 몇 가지 중요한 원칙들을 여기에 소개한다. 민간인들과, 학교나 가옥 같은 건물들과, 식수원이나 위생 시설 같은 기반 시설들을 의도적으로 표적으로 삼는 것은 전쟁 범죄이다. 항복했거나 더 이상 싸울 수 없는 사람을 죽이거나 다치게 하는 것 또한 금지돼 있으며, 다른 사람, 심지어 가족 구성원이 저지른 행위에 대해 누군가를 처벌하는 것도 마찬가지로 금지돼 있다. 공격은 군사 목표만을 향해야 하며, 기지와 비축물자와 같은 군사 목표물은 인구가 거주하는 지역이나 근처에 놓여서는 안 된다. 만일 공격에 따라 예상되는 민간인의 부수적인 피해가 과도하고 기대하는 군사적인 이득과 균형이 맞지 않는다면, 그 공격은 합법적으로 진행될 수 없다. 한 가지 단서가 있다. 예를 들어, 학교 같은 민간인 구조물들이 예를 들어, 공격을 시작하기 위한 기지나 무기 창고와 같은 특정 군사 작전을 위해 사용된다면, 합법적인 목표물이 될 수 있다.

founder n. 창립자, 설립자 codify v. 법전으로 편찬하다, 성문화하다 establish v. 설립하다, 창립하다; (법률 등을) 제정하다 treaty n. 조약 wounded a. 부상당한 diplomat n. 외교관 amendment n. 변경, 개선; (법안 등의) 수정안 address v. 역점을 두어 다루다 combatant n. 전투원 reaffirm v. 재확인하다 expand v. 확장하다, 확대하다 civilian n. 민간인 ratify v. 비준하다 conflict n. 싸움, 다툼, 전투 curb v. 억제하다, 구속하다 brutality n. 잔인, 무자비; 야만적 행위 tactics n. 전술, 병법 employ v. 쓰다, 사용하다 domestic a. 가정의; 국내의 warring a. 서로 싸우는, 적대하는 impose v. (의무 등을) 부과하다; 강제하다 sanction n. 인가; (pl.) 제재, 제재규약 arms embargo 무기 금수(禁輸) comply with ~을 따르다 crucial a. 결정적인, 중대한 relevant a. 관련된; 적절한, 타당한 ongoing a. 전진하는, 진행하는 intentionally ad. 의도적으로, 고의로 sanitation n. 위생 facilities n. 시설, 설비 surrender v. 항복하다, 굴복하다 prohibit v. 금지하다 objective n. 목표, 목적 stockpile n. 비축[축적], (자재 따위의) 재고 incidental a. 부차적인 excessive a. 과도한 disproportionate a. 불균형한 legally ad. 합법적으로 caveat n. 경고, 억제; 단서(但書)

29 빈칸완성 ③

'공격은 군사 목표만을 향해야 하며, 민간인의 피해가 과도하게 발생하는 상황이라면 그 공격은 합법적으로 진행될 수 없다.'라고 한 후에 한 가지 단서가 있다고 했는데, 그 단서는 곧 '이러이러한 경우에는 민간인에 대한 공격도 합법적일 수 있다'와 같은 것이 될 것이므로 빈칸에는 '합법적인 목표물이 될 수 있다'라고 한 ③이 적절하다.

빈칸에 들어가기에 가장 적절한 것을 고르시오.
① 위장될 수 있다
② 사전에 등록되어야 한다
③ 합법적인 목표물이 될 수 있다
④ 전쟁 규칙의 비준을 피할 수 있다

30 내용추론 ③

제네바 협약의 전쟁 규칙에서 전투와 직접적인 관련이 없는 민간인에 대한 공격을 전쟁 범죄로 규정하고 있으므로, 이것은 민간인의 통행과 안전의 보장에 도움이 될 것이다.

위 글에서 추론할 수 있는 것은?
① 전쟁 중에 행해지는 모든 보복은 비례를 이루어야 한다는 것은 논란의 여지가 있다.
② 전쟁 규칙의 시행은 참전국들의 만장일치가 필요하기 때문에 어려울 수 있다.
③ 전쟁 규칙은 민간인들이 폭력에서 벗어날 수 있는 안전한 통행을 보장하는 데 도움이 된다.
④ 제네바 협약은 전투 능력이 없는 군인에게 해를 입히는 예외를 인정하고 있다.

2024 한성대학교(인문계 A형)

01 ③	02 ②	03 ②	04 ④	05 ④	06 ②	07 ①	08 ①	09 ②	10 ①
11 ①	12 ②	13 ②	14 ①	15 ③	16 ④	17 ③	18 ③	19 ④	20 ②
21 ④	22 ③	23 ②	24 ①	25 ④	26 ②	27 ①	28 ③	29 ①	30 ①
31 ④	32 ③	33 ④	34 ①	35 ③	36 ①	37 ④	38 ②	39 ①	40 ④
41 ④	42 ③	43 ①	44 ①	45 ②	46 ②	47 ①	48 ①	49 ②	50 ③

01 생활영어 ③

도서관에 가서 열심히 공부했다는 B의 말에 A가 바지에 풀이 묻어 있고 셔츠가 땀에 젖어 있다는 증거를 지적하면서 하는 말은 '그런 거짓말 그만하라'는 말일 것이므로, 빈칸에는 ③이 적절하다.

stain n. 얼룩   sweaty a. 땀에 젖은   jersey n. (운동 경기용) 셔츠   swear v. 맹세하다   give off (냄새·빛 등을) 방출하다, 내뿜다   iron out 다림질하다; 원활하게 하다; (오해·장애물 등을) 없애다   come off it (거짓말이나 과장된 말을) 그만두다   break on ~에 부딪쳐 부서지다

A: 너는 공부하러 도서관에 가기로 약속했잖아. 네가 도서관에서 공부했다는 걸 나는 믿지 못하겠어. 대신 너는 친구들이랑 축구를 한 것 같은데.
B: 무슨 소리야? 난 도서관에 갔어. 여러 시간 열심히 공부했어.
A: 이런, 그딴 말 그만둬! 바지에 풀 묻은 거 좀 봐. 아직도 땀에 젖은 셔츠를 입고 있네. 네가 거짓말 하고 있다는 증거가 더 필요할까?
B: 알았어, 알았어! 조금 놀았지만, 그런 다음 도서관에 갔어. 맹세해.

02 생활영어 ②

A는 콘래드에 대해 좋지 않게 생각하는 입장이므로 부정적인 의미의 표현이 빈칸에 들어가야 한다. 그러므로 '~을 무시하다[깎아내리다]'라는 뜻의 put ~ down이 쓰인 ②가 정답이다. ①은 laugh at people인 경우에는 정답이 될 수 있다. '비웃다'라는 의미의 표현은 laugh at인데, 이때 목적어를 laugh와 at 사이에 둘 수 없다.

constantly ad. 항상, 변함없이   deserve v. ~할 만하다, 받을 가치가 있다   put ~ down (특히 다른 사람들 앞에서) ~를 바보로 만들다[깎아내리다]   calm down 진정시키다   back down 퇴각하다; 양보하다

A: 콘래드(Conrad)가 너의 친구라는 게 놀랍네. 솔직히 말하면, 다른 사람은 아무도 콘래드를 좋아하지 않아.
B: 믿기 어려운데. 그는 정말 좋은 사람이야.
A: 좋은 사람은 다른 사람들을 끊임없이 깎아내리지 않아.
B: 그가 나한테는 전혀 그렇지 않은데. 다른 사람들은 그럴 만했을 거야!

03 생활영어 ②

과체중인 사람이 마라톤 완주에 도전하려고 한다면, 그 사람에게는 마라톤에 대한 준비로 강한 훈련을 시작하라고 권할 것이다. '시작하다'라

는 의미의 ② set out이 정답이다.

be determined to ~하기로 마음먹다   fit a. 건강한, 튼튼한   be on something 무엇을 하는 중이다   set up 설립[수립]하다   set out (일·과제 등에) 착수하다[나서다]   run off 도망가다, 줄행랑치다   run down (건전지 등이) 다 되다, (기계 등이) 멈추다[정지하다]

A: 나의 언니는 대단해. 20킬로그램 과체중이지만, 몇 달 후에 마라톤 풀코스를 완주할 작정이야.
B: 그건 전혀 불가능해 보여! 언니가 진짜 그럴 거라면 지금 당장 강훈련을 시작하는 게 좋을 거야.
A: 언니는 지금 하고 있어! 몇 주 동안 다이어트를 하면서 하루 10킬로미터씩 달리고 있어. 벌써부터 더 건강하고 더 튼튼해 보여.
B: 그렇다면 내 생각에 언니는 마라톤을 완주할 것 같아.

04 생활영어 ④

사장이 어떤 반응을 보일지 겁이 났다면, 말을 꺼낼 용기를 내지 못했을 것이다. '용기를 내다'라는 의미의 표현은 work up the nerve이므로 ④가 정답이다.

raise n. 임금 인상   terrified a. 겁난, 놀란   work up the nerve 용기를 내다

A: 저는 이 회사에서 10년 동안 일했지만, 임금 인상을 한 번도 받지 못했어요. 단 한 푼도 말입니다!
B: 그건 옳지 않아요. 사장님과 이 일을 상의해보는 게 어때요?
A: 저는 사장님의 반응이 겁이 나서 사장님께 말을 꺼낼 용기를 내지 못했어요.
B: 꼭 해야 해요. 요구하지 않으면 원하는 것을 절대로 얻지 못할 거예요.

05 생활영어 ④

용돈을 주지 않은 것은 딸이 온종일 스마트폰만 하는 나쁜 습관을 바로 잡도록 하기 위한 것이었다.

desperate a. 필사적인; 자포자기의   lead on (사실이 아닌 호의·혜택·관심·애정 등을) 믿도록 만들다; 거짓으로 유혹하다   wipe out ~를 녹초로[기진맥진하게] 만들다   straighten out 바로잡다, 바르게 하다

A: 제 아들을 어떻게 해야 할지 정말 모르겠어요. 끝도 없이 게임을 하고 인스타그램이나 틱톡을 확인하면서 인생을 낭비하고 있어요. 계속 이러면 결코 졸업하지 못할 거예요.

B: 제 딸도 정확하게 그랬지만, 저는 딸을 바로 잡을 방법을 찾아냈죠.

A: 정말인가요? 어떻게 하셨어요? 말해주세요. 저는 간절합니다.

B: 간단해요. 용돈 주는 것을 중단했어요. 그래서 태도를 바꿀 때까지는 한 푼도 주지 않았어요.

---

06 논리완성 ②

빈칸 이하 2019까지가 deaths를 수식하여, '대기오염으로 인한 사망'이라는 말이 되는데, '~로 인한'이 attributed to ~이므로 빈칸에는 ② attributed가 적절하다.

cardiovascular disease 심혈관계 질환 exposure n. 노출, 맞힘 micro-dust n. 미세먼지 pollutant n. 오염물질 provoke v. 유발시키다 acute a. <의학> 급성의 coronary syndrome 관상동맥 증후군 fatal a. 치명적인 heart failure 심부전 adjust v. 조정하다, 조절하다 attribute v. (~의) 탓으로 하다, (~의) 행위로[업적으로] 하다 accustom v. 익숙하게 하다, 습관이 들게 하다 admonish v. 훈계하다, 타이르다

2019년에 대기오염으로 인한 전 세계 900만 건의 사망 중, 62%가 심혈관 질환에 의한 것이었다. 최근 중국에서 수행한 한 연구에 의해, 공기 중의 미세먼지 오염물질에 매우 짧은 시간 노출되더라도 급성 관상동맥 증후군이 유발될 수 있다는 사실이 알려졌다. 심장으로의 혈류 감소를 의미하는 이 증후군은 종종 치명적인 심부전을 초래한다.

---

07 논리완성 ①

부모가 자신들을 망쳐놨다고 주장하는 것은 부모의 잘못이나 결점에 초점을 맞추는 것이며, 이렇게 하는 경우, 자신은 책임에서 벗어날 수 있게 해준다.

mess up 망쳐놓다, 못쓰게 만들다 magnetism n. 자기(磁氣); 사람의 마음을 끄는 힘 scrutinize v. 자세히 조사하다, 음미하다 deficiency n. 결핍, 결여; 결함 sit back (특히 어떤 일에 관여하거나 안달내거나 하지 않고) 편히[가만히] 있다 wallow v. 탐닉하다, (주색 따위에) 빠지다 misery n. 불행, 고통 flaw n. 결점, 결함 absolve v. (~에 대해) 무죄임[책임 없음]을 선언하다 perfection n. 완벽 sentence v. 판결을 내리다, 선고하다 admiration n. 감탄, 칭찬 present v. 증정하다, 주다 achievement n. 성취, 달성 reward v. 보답하다

자신들이 길러진 방식에 대해 사람들이 불평하는 것을 종종 들을 수 있다. 그들은 부모가 자신들을 망쳐놨다고 주장한다. 부모의 결점에 초점을 맞추는 것은 자신의 결함을 살펴볼 필요가 없다는 점에서 어떤 매력이 있다. 상황을 부모의 잘못으로 간주하는 것은 자신에게 개인적인 책임을 면하게 해준다. 부모를 비난함으로써, 자신은 스스로의 삶을 개선하기 위해 열심히 노력할 필요 없이 가만히 있으면서 편안한 마음으로 불행을 탐닉할 수 있다.

---

08 논리완성 ①

고객이 주는 팁으로 직원들이 돈을 벌게 되는데, 이는 사실 고용주 직

원에게 해야 하는 일이다. 따라서 어떤 관점에서 보면, 팁은 결국 고용주가 자신이 해야 할 일을 다른 사람들(고객)에게로 떠맡기는 것이라 할 수 있다.

urge n. 충동 repent v. 후회하다, 뉘우치다, 유감으로 생각하다 skeptical a. 회의적인 scoff at 비웃다, 조롱하다 perceive v. 인식하다, 지각하다 foist v. 억지로 떠맡기다 avoid v. 피하다 collect v. 모으다 require v. 요구하다

팁은 좋은 서비스에 대해 추가적으로 "감사"를 표하는 기능을 하지만, 그것은 또한 "미안한 마음"을 표하는 역할을 할 수도 있다. 대부분의 팁은 일하는 사람들이 고객들보다 불행한 것처럼 보이는 상황에서 주어진다. 일부 심리학자들은 팁을 주고자 하는 충동을 그러한 불평등한 관계에 수반되는 죄책감에 대해 뉘우쳐야 할 필요성으로 설명한다. 그러나 회의적인 사람들은 이러한 견해를 비웃으면서 팁은 고용주가 지불 책임을 다른 사람들에게 억지로 떠맡기는 매우 편리한 방법에 불과한 것으로 인식하고 있다.

---

09 논리완성 ②

빈칸에 들어갈 표현에 대해 마지막 문장에서 부연해서 설명하고 있다. 공항의 직원들이 협력하여 예기치 않은 혼란에 대처한 것은 '어려운 상황에서 빠르게 회복하고 다시 일어날 수 있는 능력'을 보여준 것이라 할 수 있다.

intensify v. (정도·강도가) 심해지다[격해지다] governance n. 통치, 지배 triumph n. 승리, 성공 contribute v. 기여하다 outstanding a. 걸출한, 눈에 띄는, 현저한 cope with 대처하다 adequately ad. 충분히, 적절히 unanticipated a. 예기치 않은 disruption n. 분열, 와해; 혼란 infirmity n. 허약, 쇠약, 병약 resilience n. 탄성; 회복력 negotiation n. 협상 preoccupation n. 몰두, 열중

기후 위기가 심화되는 가운데 토론토 국제공항은 최근 그 공항의 ESG — 환경, 사회, 지배구조 — 목표를 실현하는 쪽으로 큰 진전을 이루었다. 이 분야에서 이뤄낸 그 공항의 성공은 최근 들어 매우 빈번해진 생명을 위협하는 기상이변에 직면했을 때 탁월한 회복력을 발휘하도록 하는 데 기여했다. 그 공항의 모든 직원들이 협력하여 예기치 않은 날씨로 인한 혼란에 대해 신속하고 적절하게 대처한다.

---

10 논리완성 ①

처음 시도한 연기가 가장 즉흥적이고, 꾸밈없고, 진정성 있다면, 여러 번 시도한 연기들에서는 그런 자연스러움이 나타나지 않을 것이다.

take n. <영화> 한 장면, 시도 spur-of-the-moment a. 즉석의, 충동적인 genuine a. 진짜의, 진심에서 우러난 copious a. 매우 많은, 풍부한 spontaneity n. 자발성, 무의식; 자연스러움 instinctively ad. 본능적으로 recite v. 암송하다, 낭송하다 line n. (연극 등의) 대사 ruin v. 망쳐놓다 derive v. 끌어내다; 획득하다 comprise v. 포함하다, ~로 이루어져 있다 embellish v. 아름답게 하다, 꾸미다; 윤색하다

상을 받은 일부 전설적인 영화배우들은 그들의 최고 연기는 항상 처음 시도한 연기라고 주장하는데, 이것은 가장 즉흥적이고, 꾸밈없고, 진정성 있게 한 연기이기 때문이라는 것이다. 여러 번 시도한 연기들은 그런 자연스러움을 훼손시킨다. 관객들은 배우의 생각, 감정, 반응이 마음에서 우러

나오는 것인지, 아니면 배우가 전달하는 것이 단지 대사의 능숙한 낭송인지를 본능적으로 느낀다.

11 논리완성 ①

빈칸을 포함하고 있는 문장을 마지막 문장에서 부연하고 있다. 마지막 문장에서, 추론은 '우리가 다른 사람들을 설득하고 다른 사람들이 우리를 설득하려고 할 때 주의를 기울이도록 돕는다'고 했는데, 다른 사람들과의 관계가 전제돼 있는 활동은 사회적인 것이므로 ①이 정답이 된다. 빈칸을 포함하고 있는 문장 앞의 to win arguments가 다른 사람들과의 관계와 관련돼 있는 것임을 통해서도 정답을 도출할 수 있다.

argumentative a. 논쟁적인 reasoning n. 추론, 추리 discern v. 분별하다, 식별하다 posit v. (주장·논의의 근거로 삼기 위해 무엇을) 사실로 상정하다[받아들이다] phenomenon n. 현상 convince v. 설득시키다 social a. 사회적인 useless a. 쓸모없는 unequivocal a. 명료한 unidirectional a. 단일 방향성의

논쟁적 추론 이론에서는 추론이 사람들이 진실을 분별하고 더 나은 판단을 하도록 도와주기 위해서가 아니라 논쟁을 이기기 위해 발전했다고 주장한다. 그 이론은 추론을 순전히 사회적 현상이라 상정한다. 추론은 우리가 다른 사람들을 설득하도록 돕고 다른 사람들이 우리를 설득하려 할 때는 조심하도록 돕는다.

12 논리완성 ②

첫 번째 빈칸을 포함한 부분은 and로 연결된 adopt healthier habits처럼 긍정적인 의미여야 하므로 thrive와 flourish가 가능하며, 대처해야 할 대상은 대개 어렵고 힘든 것이므로 두 번째 빈칸에는 adversity가 적절하다.

equip v. 갖추게 하다, 장비하다 cope with 대처하다 thrive v. 번성하다, 성공하다 adversity n. 역경, 불행 digress v. (이야기·의제 따위가) 옆길로 빗나가다, 본제를 벗어나다 flourish v. 번영하다, 번성하다

사람들은 자신들의 정신건강이 개선될 때, 그들의 인간관계와 직업에서 성공하고 보다 건강한 습관을 받아들일 가능성이 더 높다는 사실이 여러 연구에서 밝혀졌다. 정신적으로 건강하다고 느낄 때, 사람들은 더 생산적이 되고, 일상적인 경험들에서 의미를 찾고, 변화와 역경에 더 잘 대처할 수 있는 능력을 갖추게 된다.

13 논리완성 ②

as 이하는 모두 AI 거버넌스의 성공을 어렵게 하는 요인들에 해당한다. 이러한 환경에서는 기술이 계속해서 AI 거버넌스를 뛰어넘게 될 것이다.

AI governance AI 거버넌스(AI 도구와 시스템이 반드시 안전하고 윤리적이도록 보장하는 규제책: the guardrails that ensure AI tools and systems remain safe and ethical) regulatory a. 규제하는 falter v. 비틀거리다 unconstrained a. 구속받지 않는, 자유로운 follow v. 따르다 outstrip v. 앞지르다, 능가하다 reinforce v. 강화하다, 보강하다 denounce v. 비난하다, 탄핵하다

정부의 규제 노력이 흔들리고, 기술 기업들이 대체로 제약을 받지 않은 상태에 있고, 훨씬 더 강력한 AI 모델과 도구가 정부의 통제를 넘어 확산됨에 따라, 기술은 계속해서 AI 거버넌스를 능가할 것이다.

14 논리완성 ①

두 번째 문장 이하는 '우유를 기피하거나, 우유가 몸에 맞지 않거나, 우유의 냄새를 싫어하는 사람들도 있다'는 내용이다. 이는 곧 우유를 모든 사람이 먹고 있는 것은 아니라는 것, 다시 말해 식단에서 필수적인 부분은 아니라는 것이다.

lactose intolerance 유당분해효소결핍증(유당분해효소의 활성도가 연령에 따른 정상치보다 부족하여 유당을 소화시키지 못하는 질환) rare a. 드문 integral a. 완전한; 필수의 inessential a. 중요하지 않은, 없어도 되는 antiquated a. 낡아빠진, 노후한 unconventional a. 관습에 의하지 않은

우유는 인간의 식단에서 필수적인 부분이 아니다. 극동 문화권, 그리고 아메리카 대륙과 아프리카 일부 지역의 토착 문화권에서는 결코 우유를 사용하지 않는다. 많은 아시아인들은 실제로 북유럽 사람들에게는 드문 유당분해효소결핍증을 가지고 있다. 홍콩인들은 유제품 식단 때문에 서양인들에게서 이상한 냄새가 난다고 말한다.

15 논리완성 ③

사용자가 자신이 자주 방문한 웹사이트만을 지속적으로 방문하게 돼서, 그 결과 자신의 견해를 지지하는 웹사이트만을 방문하게 된다면, 같은 입장을 지닌 정보만을 되풀이해서 접하게 됨으로써 편견에 빠지게 될 것이며, 이는 곧 자신의 의지와는 무관하게 알고리즘에 의해 조종을 당하게 되는 것이다.

algorithm n. 알고리즘, 연산 priority n. 우선권 be bound to ~하지 않을 수 없다 mindful of ~을 염두에 두는[의식하는], ~에 유념하는 echo chamber 메아리방, 반향실(같은 입장을 지닌 정보만을 지속적으로 되풀이해서 편견에 빠지도록 하는 장소를 비유적으로 이르는 말) initiate v. 시작하다, 개시하다 propagate v. 선전하다, 보급하다 manipulate v. (사람·여론 등을) (부정하게) 조종하다 incorporate v. 통합하다

검색 엔진에 어떤 주제가 입력되면, 그 주제에 관한 웹사이트들이 알고리즘에 따라 일정한 순서로 제시된다. 대부분의 검색 엔진은 사용자가 자주 방문한 웹사이트에 우선권을 부여한다. 사용자가 대부분의 사람들이 그런 것처럼 상단에 나타나는 웹사이트를 더 자주 방문한다면, 그 경우에는 다른 사람들의 견해가 아니라 자신의 견해를 지지하는 웹사이트를 방문할 수밖에 없다. 많은 사람들은 알고리즘이 자신들을 반향실 안에 들어가도록 조종할 수 있다는 사실을 생각조차 할 수 없다.

16 논리완성 ④

공산주의와 자본주의는 대립하는 이념이므로, 공산주의 노선에 역행하는 개념은 곧 자본주의를 옹호하거나 합리화시키는 것으로 간주됐을 것이다.

infamously ad. 악명 높게 paranoid a. 편집증 환자의; 과대망상적인, 피해망상적인 detest v. 몹시 싫어하다, 혐오하다 geneticists n. 유전학자 communist party 공산당 the survival of the fittest 적자생존 inherently ad. 본질적으로 capitalist a. 자본주의의, 자본가의 amass v. 축적하다 tribute n. 공물, 조세; 찬사 reference n. 문의; 언급; 관련 sympathy n. 동정 justification n. 타당한[정당한] 이유, 합리화

스탈린(Stalin)은 모든 사람에 대해 피해망상을 갖고 있었던 것으로 악명이 높았지만, 특히 유전학자들을 혐오했는데, 이는 그들이 적자생존이라는 대중화된 개념을 내세워 공산당의 노선에 역행하는 것처럼 보였기 때문이다. 그는 이것을 본질적으로 미국 자본주의의 개념, 즉 노동자들은 빈곤 속에서 살아가는 반면 탁월한 기술이나 지능을 가진 사람들은 부를 축적하는 것을 합리화시키는 것으로 보았다.

17-19

농작물을 황폐화시키는 질병들이 급속도로 확산되고 있다. 다양한 진균류(眞菌類)가 세계의 비옥한 땅 대부분을 건조지대로 만들어버릴 태세다. 그것은 라틴 아메리카와 아프리카에서부터 아시아의 방글라데시에 이르는 전 세계에 들불처럼 퍼지고 있다. 그것은 밀 고사병을 일으킬 뿐만 아니라, 동일한 진균류가 매년 수천만 명을 먹일 수 있는 양의 쌀을 파괴하고 있다. 감자는 물 곰팡이인 감자 마름병에 의해 파괴되어, 매년 최대 100억 달러의 재정적 피해를 입히고 있다. 감자는 또한 박테리아성 질병인 흑반병(黑斑病)과 감자 바이러스 "Y"에 의해 파괴된다. 그러한 병원체들은 전쟁과 기후 변화로 인해 이미 약해진 식량 체계를 지옥으로 만든다. 농작물 팬데믹은 세계를 대량 기아 사태로 몰아갈 수 있다. 2024년에 그런 일이 일어날 가능성은 그 어느 때보다도 높다. 대부분의 농업인들은 단일경작에 의존하고 있는데, 단일경작은 효율적이기는 하지만 취약하다. 감염된 작물 단 하나가 전체 작물의 전멸을 초래할 수도 있다. 지구 온난화는 이전에는 병원체의 생존에 불리했던 환경을 줄임으로써 병원체가 미치는 범위를 또한 증가시키고 있다.

devastate v. 유린하다, 황폐화시키다 crop n. 농작물 fungus n. 버섯; 균류, 진균류(眞菌類) be poised to ~할 태세를 갖추고 있다, ~할 준비가 되다 dustbowl n. (가뭄·지나친 경작 등으로 생긴) 건조지대 fertile a. 비옥한 blast n. (식물의) 고사병; (전염병으로 인한) 재해, 피해 blight n. 마름병 mold n. 곰팡이 annually ad. 해마다, 매년 spud n. <구어> 감자 wreck v. 난파시키다; 파괴하다, 부수다 blackleg n. <식물> 흑반병(黑斑病) pandemonium n. 복마전; 지옥; 대혼란 pandemic n. 팬데믹, 전국적[대륙적, 세계적]으로 유행하는 병 agriculturalist n. 농업가, 농업 종사자 monoculture n. 단일경작, 일모작 infect v. 감염시키다 annihilation n. 전멸, 절멸 diminish v. (수량·크기·정도·중요성 따위를) 줄이다, 감소시키다 adverse a. 불리한, 해로운

17 글의 제목   ③

농작물을 황폐화시키는 질병들이 급속도로 확산되고 있음을 피해상황과 피해를 확산시키는 여건 등을 설명하면서 이야기하고 있는 글이다.

제목으로 가장 적절한 것을 고르시오.
① 밀의 황폐화
② 불리한 기후 조건
③ 급속도로 확산되고 있는 농작물 질병
④ 단일경작의 취약성

18 빈칸완성   ③

박테리아성 질병인 흑반병(黑斑病)과 감자 바이러스 "Y"는 '병원체'에 해당하며, 현재의 지구 온난화는 이러한 '병원체'가 더 확산될 수 있는 여건을 조성하고 있을 것이다.

Ⓐ와 Ⓑ에 들어가기에 가장 적절한 단어를 고르시오.
① 유전자
② 렉틴 단백질
③ 병원체
④ 엔도르핀

19 내용일치   ④

감자는 물 곰팡이인 감자 마름병, 박테리아성 질병인 흑반병, 감자 바이러스 "Y"에 의해 큰 피해를 입고 있다고 했다. 그러므로 ④가 옳은 진술이다. ② 감자는 해당되지 않는다.

다음 중 옳은 진술은?
① 식량 체계는 아직 불안정하게 되지 않았다.
② 동일한 진균류가 밀, 쌀, 감자를 파괴한다.
③ 지구 온난화는 작물 질병을 방해한다.
④ 감자는 곰팡이, 박테리아, 바이러스에 의해 파괴된다.

20-22

러시아의 우크라이나 침공은 그 어떤 전문가들이 예측한 것보다도 훨씬 더 오래 계속되고 있다. 그것이 군사, 경제 및 외교에 미치는 영향은 거의 2년 동안 분명하게 드러났다. 그러나 관련된 모든 사람들에게 남겨진 정신적 상처와 같이 그 전쟁으로 인한 보이지 않는 다른 손실이 많이 있다. 우크라이나와 동맹국들이 우크라이나의 복구를 위해 장기적인 전략을 세우고 있는 가운데, 우크라이나 정부 또한 자국의 군인들을 보살피기 위한 정책적 해결책을 모색하고 있다. 필요한 모든 사람들을 보살피기 위해서는 훨씬 더 큰 규모의 도움이 필요할 것이다. 우크라이나에서는 많은 집단들이 다양한 트라우마를 겪고 있다. Ⓕ 우선 먼저, 가장 규모가 크면서 가장 큰 피해를 입은 집단이 있는데, 바로 수백만 명의 군인들이다. Ⓔ 전투원들 다음으로, 끔찍한 장면을 목격한 의료진과 응급 의료요원들이 있는데, 이러한 장면들은 그들에게 트라우마를 깊게 남겼다. Ⓓ 또한 국내외의 난민들도 잊어선 안 된다. Ⓒ 끝으로, 마지막 집단은 전쟁 포로들이다. 우리는 네 개 집단 모두를 보살펴줘야 할 것이다.

diplomacy n. 외교, 외교술 scar n. 흉터; 상처 restoration n. 회복, 복구 assistance n. 도움, 원조, 지원 trauma n. 마음의 상처, 트라우마 displaced person 난민 combatant n. 전투원 first responder 응급 의료요원 traumatize v. 상처 입히다; 마음에 충격을 주다 affect v. 영향을 미치다; 충격을 주다

20 빈칸완성   ②

정신적 상처는 무형적 요소이므로 빈칸 Ⓑ에는 unseen이 적절하고, 빈칸 Ⓐ를 포함하고 있는 문장은 그 뒤 문장과 대조를 이루어야 하므로 빈칸 Ⓐ에는 unseen과 대비되는 evident가 적절하다.

ⓐ와 ⓑ에 들어가기에 적절한 단어들을 고르시오.
① 즉각적인 ― 혁신적인
② 명백한 ― 보이지 않는
③ 놀란 ― 무가치한
④ 방해받은 ― 재배정된

21 지시대상   ④

밑줄 친 ⓒ는 해당 문장 속의 'to provide care for all who need it'의 행위를 할 수 있는 주체이므로, 앞 문장의 the Ukrainian government 를 가리킨다고 보는 것이 가장 타당하다.

22 문장배열   ③

In the first place로 시작되는 ⑤가 가장 먼저 오고, ⑤에서 언급한 soldiers를 combatants로 받고 있는 ⑥가 그다음에, ⑥에 나오는 health-care providers and first responders 이외의 대상을 추가적으로 이야기하고 있는 ⑩가 그다음에, Finally로 시작되는 ⑨가 마지막에 오는 것이 자연스러운 순서다.

23-25

현대의 성인들은 과도한 진지함으로 인해 고통 받고 있다. 우리는 우리가 타고난 놀이 욕구를 부정해왔고, 그것이 우리 자신, 우리의 아이들, 그리고 우리의 지구에 온갖 종류의 문제들을 일으키고 있다. 심리학자들은 놀이의 반대는 일이 아니고 그것은 의기소침함이라고 주장한다. 어른이 돼서 하는 놀이가 경박해 보일 수도 있지만, 최근의 연구들은 그것이 잠을 자야 하는 것만큼이나 매우 중요할 수도 있다는 것을 암시한다. 과학자들은 놀이 본능이 진화적 발달의 관점에서 우리의 가장 오래된 부분들 중 하나인 우리의 뇌간에서 유래한다는 사실을 발견했다. 놀이를 통해, 어린 동물들은 그들의 몸과 서식지를 통제하는 법을 배우고, 이것을 달성하고 나면, 그들은 성체가 되고 대부분은 놀이를 멈춘다. 그러나 인간을 포함한 일부 동물들은 결코 놀이를 멈추지 않는다. 이제서야, 과학자들은 그 이유를 알아내려 하고 있다. 한 가지 가능성은 유용한 발견들이 놀이로부터 나온다는 것이다. 의심의 여지없이, 인류의 가장 위대한 발명품들, 예술작품들, 그리고 과학적인 돌파구들 중 많은 것들이 놀고자 하는 욕구에 의해 이루어졌다.

plague v. 괴롭히다, 귀찮게 하다 excess n. 과다, 과잉, 잉여 drive n. 충동, 본능적 욕구 assert v. 단언하다; 강력히 주장하다 opposite n. 정반대의 사람[사물] depression n. 의기소침; 우울증 frivolous a. 경솔한, 들뜬; 하찮은 imply v. 함축하다, 암시하다 crucial a. 결정적인, 중대한 originate v. 비롯하다, 생기다 in terms of ~의 관점에서 evolutionary a. 진화의 habitat n. 서식지 work out ~을 해결하다, (답을) 알아내다 breakthrough n. 돌파구; (과학·기술 등의) 획기적인 약진[진전, 발견] bring about 일어나게 하다, 초래하다

23 반의어   ②

excess는 '과다', '과잉'의 의미이므로 '부족', '결손'이라는 뜻의 deficit 이 반의어로 적절하다. ① 남용, 오용 ③ 관계, 관련 ④ 구실, 핑계

24 어법상 적절한 표현 고르기   ①

ⓒ 접속사의 역할을 하는 세미콜론 뒤에 왔으므로 절의 구조를 이루어야 한다. 그러므로 it's depression이 옳은 표현이다. ⓓ 조동사 may 뒤에 동사원형이 와야 하므로 may look이 되어야 한다. ⓔ 원급 비교의 'as ~ as' 구문은 앞에 부정어가 있는 경우에 'so ~ as'로 나타낼 수 있는데, 주어진 문장은 부정어가 없으므로 as crucial as여야 한다.

25 내용일치   ④

"어른이 돼서 하는 놀이가 경박해 보일 수도 있지만, '최근의' 연구들은 그것이 잠을 자야 하는 것만큼이나 매우 중요할 수도 있다는 것을 암시한다." "인간을 포함한 일부 동물들은 결코 놀이를 멈추지 않는다. '이제서야', 과학자들은 그 이유를 알아내려 하고 있다." 등에서, '최근의'와 '이제서야'를 통해 ④가 옳지 않은 진술임을 알 수 있다.

다음 중 옳지 않은 진술은?
① 놀이는 인간의 상상력과 창의력을 자극한다.
② 어떤 동물들은 어른이 되어서도 놀이를 계속 한다.
③ 성인기에 놀이를 하고 싶은 충동을 억제하는 것은 중대한 결과를 초래한다.
④ 연구원들은 성인에게 놀이가 중요한 이유를 오래 전에 밝혀냈다.

26-28

슈퍼스타의 반열에 놀랍게 등극하기 시작한 지 17년이 지난 지금, 테일러 스위프트(Taylor Swift)는 경제, 문화, 정치 등의 면에서 그 어느 때보다 큰 영향력을 발휘하고 있다. 올해 그녀는 포브스(Forbes)가 선정하는 세계에서 가장 영향력 있는 여성 100인에서 5위로 뛰어올랐는데, 이는 2022년의 79위에서 급등한 것이다. 소위 테일러 스위프트 효과는 실제로 놀라운 경제적 파급 효과를 의미한다. 그녀의 덴버 순회공연은 2박 3일에 불과했지만, 상품, 호텔, 레스토랑 각각에 평균 1,300 달러를 지출한 팬들 덕분에 콜로라도의 GDP는 대략 1억 4천만 달러 늘어났다. 5월에는 그녀가 필라델피아에서 3박 4일 동안 공연했는데, 그로 인해 그 달은 팬데믹 이전 이래로 그 도시의 호텔 수입이 가장 많았던 달이 되었다. U.S. Travel Alliance는 전체적으로 볼 때, 그녀의 미국 콘서트 투어가 국고를 50억 달러 이상 늘어나게 한 것으로 추정하고 있다. 그녀는 경제의 여러 측면에서 그 존재감을 느낄 수 있는 사실상 하나의 대기업이다. 비록 그녀의 매우 어리고 주로 여성인 청중들로 인해 종종 그녀가 가볍게 여겨지고 있지만, 그녀는 사실 무시할 수 없는 영향력을 가진 존재이다.

extraordinary a. 비범한, 엄청난 superstardom n. 슈퍼스타의 지위[신분] clout n. 영향력 soar v. 높이 날다; (물가 따위가) 급등하다, 치솟다 ripple effect 파급 효과 approximately ad. 대략, 대강, 얼추 merch n. 상품(= merchandise) revenue n. 소득; 재원 pandemic n. 전국적[대륙적, 세계적]으로 유행하는 병 estimate v. 어림잡다, 견적하다, 추단하다 overall ad. 전체적[종합적, 일반적]으로 (보면) swell v. 부풀다; (수량이) 증대하다; 커지다 the state coffers 국고(國庫) conglomerate n. 집성체, 집단; (거대) 복합기업 aspect n. 양상; 견지

26 글의 제목 ④

본문은 테일러 스위프트가 엄청난 파급 효과를 끼치고 있음을 특히 경제의 측면에서 구체적인 예를 통해 이야기하고 있는 내용이므로, 제목으로는 ④가 적절하다.

제목으로 가장 적절한 것을 고르시오.
① 테일러 스위프트가 5위로 뛰어오르다
② 테일러 스위프트가 미국 전역의 경기장을 가득 메우다
③ 테일러 스위프트가 환대 산업(숙박, 유흥 등의 서비스 산업)에 희망을 불어넣다
④ 경제 발전소(동력)가 된 테일러 스위프트

27 부분이해 ①

the state coffers는 '국고(國庫)'라는 뜻이므로 국가 예산(the state budget)을 의미한다고 할 수 있다. ② 재무 계획서 ③ 은행 계좌 ④ 재무제표

28 빈칸완성 ③

'그녀의 매우 어리고 주로 여성인 청중들로 인해 그녀는 종종 가볍게 여겨지고 있다'와 주절의 내용이 대조를 이루어야 한다. 그러므로 '가볍게 여겨질 수 없는 존재'의 의미를 가진 표현이 빈칸에 들어가야 할 것이다. 따라서 ③이 정답이 된다.

ⓑ에 들어가기에 가장 적절한 표현을 고르시오.
① 총체적인 사기극
② 그녀의 뿌리로 돌아가기
③ 무시할 수 없는 영향력을 가진 존재
④ 오랫동안 기다려온 그녀의 컴백

29-31

라틴 아메리카의 정치적 상황은 항상 불안정했다. 2000년대 초반에, 대부분의 권력은 좌파 정당에 속해 있었다. 2010년대에 아르헨티나와 브라질에서 우파가 집권하는 시기가 찾아왔다. 그리고 다시, 2023년까지, 19개국 중 12개국이 진보 좌파 정치인들에 의해 통치되고 있었다. 상황이 다시 바뀌고 있는 듯하다! 그러한 변화는 아르헨티나 국민들이 하비에르 밀레이(Javier Milei)를 새로운 대통령으로 선택하여, 그를 라틴 아메리카 역사상 최초의 자유주의 대통령으로 만들면서부터 시작되었다. 그는 큰 정부와 대규모 사회적 지원금을 내세우는 아르헨티나 좌파 포퓰리즘의 정체된 물을 휘젓고 있다. 전임자와 달리, 마일리는 "무정부적 자본주의" 자유시장 경제와 작은 정부를 지지하는 우파 포퓰리즘을 옹호한다. 그는 트럼프(Trump)처럼 정계의 아웃사이더이자 전직 TV 인기배우로 인지도를 올렸기 때문에 사람들은 그를 아르헨티나의 트럼프라고 부른다. 그는 또한 꾸밈이 없는 언어로 말하고 경제와 정치의 거의 모든 측면에서 급진적인 변화를 약속한다. 그 가운데 가장 과격한 것은 미국 달러화를 사용하는 경제를 만들고 중앙은행을 폐지하고 공공 지출을 줄이기 위해 정부 부처를 18개에서 8개로 줄이는 것이다. 그가 얼마나 많은 자신의 선거 공약을 지킬 것인지는 두고 볼 일이다.

political a. 정치적인 volatile a. 휘발성의; 폭발하기 쉬운; 변하기 쉬운; 변덕스러운 libertarian a. 자유 의지론을 주장하는; (특히 사상·행동의) 자유를 주장하는 stir v. 휘젓다, 뒤섞다 stagnant a. 정체된 handout n. (정부 등에서 주는) 지원금; (자료를 담아 배포하는) 인쇄물[유인물] predecessor n. 전임자 champion v. 옹호하다 uphold v. 지지하다 anarcho-capitalist a. 무정부적 자본주의의 personality n. 유명인사, 배우 plain a. 숨김없는, 솔직한, 있는 그대로의 radical a. 급진적인, 과격한 drastic a. 과감한; 극단적인, 급격한 dollarize v. (자국 통화를) 미국 달러로 전환하다 annihilate v. 전멸시키다; 폐지하다 slash v. (대폭) 삭감하다

29 빈칸완성 ①

첫 문장에서 라틴 아메리카의 정치적 상황이 불안정했음을 언급했으므로, 이어지는 문장들에서는 좌파와 우파의 집권이 계속 뒤바뀌면서 일어나는 상황을 이야기해야 한다. 그러므로 ⓐ에는 power(권력)과 관계된 reign이 적절하며, ⓑ에는 governed와 ruled가 가능하다. 따라서 두 조건을 모두 만족시키는 ①이 정답이다.

ⓐ와 ⓑ에 들어가기에 적절한 단어들을 고르시오.
① 통치 — 지배된
② 은둔자 — 통치된
③ 제국 — 축출된
④ 몰락 — 금지된

30 반의어 ①

annihilate는 '전멸시키다', '폐지하다'라는 의미이므로 '수호하다', '보호하다'라는 뜻의 shield가 반의어로 적절하다. ③은 자동사이므로 적절하지 않다. ② 연기하다 ③ 존속하다 ④ 해체하다

31 내용일치 ④

마일리는 과격하고 극단적인 변화를 약속하고 있으므로 ④가 본문의 내용과 일치하지 않는다.

다음 중 옳지 않은 진술은?
① 라틴 아메리카의 정치적 상황은 불규칙했다.
② 마일리가 인기가 있는 것은 그가 정치적 기득권층에 속해 있지 않기 때문이다.
③ 라틴 아메리카의 좌파 포퓰리즘은 정부의 지원금이 많다는 특징이 있다.
④ 자유주의 대통령으로서 마일리는 정부에 미미한 변화를 줄 것을 약속한다.

32-34

직원들의 다양성을 끌어올리기 위해 기업들은 무엇을 해야 할까? 미국 경제계는 서둘러 다양성, 형평성, 포용성 (DEI) 제도들을 수용하기 시작했는데, 이렇게 한 데는 편견을 가지고 있다는 비판을 받는 것을 두려워했던 이유도 일부 있었다. 2022년에는 이미, S&P 500 기업들 중 3/4이 다양성 담당 최고 관리자를 두고 있었다.

이제는 많은 사람들이 시계추가 너무 멀리까지 갔다(조치가 너무 지나쳐서 균형을 벗어났다)고 생각한다. 흑인 여성 클로딘 게이(Claudine Gay)가 하버드 대학의 총장에서 사임한 것은 능력과 정체성에 관한 보다 광범위한 논쟁에 불을 지폈다. 두 억만장자, 빌 애크먼(Bill Ackman)과 일론 머스크(Elon Musk)는 DEI 자체가 차별적이라고 비판했다.

미국의 문화전쟁이 계속해서 맹위를 떨치면서, 경영자들은 샌드위치 신세가 돼가고 있다. 진보주의자들은 DEI가 기업들로 하여금 미국의 고착화된 불평등을 해결하기 위해 제 역할을 다할 수 있게 해준다고 주장한다. 보수주의자들은 이것을 능력주의에 대한 공격으로 보고 있다. 한쪽은 많은 DEI 계획들의 비용을 무시하고 있는 반면, 다른 한쪽은 다양성이 주는 진정한 혜택을 무시하고 있다. 문화전쟁으로 인해 영향을 받은 매우 많은 분야들이 그러하듯이, DEI에 대한 생각 또한 혼란스러워진 것은 실망스러운 일이다. 다양성에 대한 명확하고 단순한 주장이 나오는 데 시간이 지체되고 있는 것은 참으로 우려스러운 일이다.

firm n. 회사 diversity n. 다양성 call out 비판적으로 지적하다 prejudice n. 편견 corporate a. 법인의, 회사의 embrace v. 받아들이다, 신봉하다 equity n. 공평, 공정 inclusion n. 포함, 포용 scheme n. 계획, 기획 pendulum n. (시계 따위의) 흔들리는 추 resignation n. 사직, 사임; 단념, 포기 ignite v. 불을 붙이다 merit n. 장점; 공로, 공적 identity n. 정체성 discriminatory a. 차별적인 be caught in the middle 샌드위치 신세가 되다, 가운데 끼다 tackle v. (일 따위에) 달라붙다, 착수하다 entrenched a. (권리·습관·생각 따위가) 확립된, 굳어버린 muddled a. 혼란스러워 하는, 갈피를 못 잡는 draw out (평상시보다 또는 필요 이상으로) ~을 길게 하다[끌다]

---

32 빈칸완성   ③

DEI가 다양성, 형평성, 포용성을 추구하는 것이므로, 이것은 기업들로 하여금 획일성, 불평등, 배타성을 해결하도록 만들 것이다. 그러므로 Ⓐ에는 이들 중의 하나인 inequalities가 들어가야 한다. 한편, 불평등을 해결하기 위해 평등을 지나치게 강조하면, 능력을 가진 사람들이 그에 맞는 대접을 제대로 받지 못할 수도 있다. 그러므로 Ⓑ에는 이와 관련된 meritocracy가 들어가야 한다.

Ⓐ와 Ⓑ에 들어가기에 적절한 단어들을 고르시오.
① 평등 ― 능력주의
② 평등 ― 인도주의
③ 불평등 ― 능력주의
④ 불평등 ― 인도주의

---

33 내용파악   ④

"DEI에 대한 생각 또한 혼란스러워진 것은 실망스러운 일이다. 다양성에 대한 명확하고 단순한 주장이 나오는 데 시간이 지체되고 있는 것은 참으로 우려스러운 일이다."라고 했으므로 ④가 정답으로 가장 적절하다.

DEI에 대한 혼란된 생각에 관해 저자는 어떻게 생각하고 있는가?
① 적대적인
② 무관심한
③ 공격적인
④ 걱정스러운

---

34 내용일치   ①

"진보주의자들은 DEI가 기업들로 하여금 미국의 고착화된 불평등을 해결하기 위해 자기들의 몫을 하도록 만든다고 주장하고 있고, 보수주의자들은 이것을 능력주의에 대한 공격으로 보고 있다."라는 내용을 통해 ①이 옳은 진술임을 알 수 있다.

다음 중 옳은 진술은?
① DEI에 대한 견해는 개인의 정치적 신조에 의해 영향을 받는다.
② DEI 지지자들과 반대자들 사이의 긴장이 줄어들었다.
③ 미국의 문화전쟁은 기업의 리더들이 DEI를 지지하기가 더 쉽게 해준다.
④ 2022년 현재, 대부분의 미국 기업에는 다양성 담당 최고 관리자가 없다.

35-37

아시아의 자선활동은 미국을 비롯한 서구의 자선활동과 매우 다르다. 자선활동에 대한 대부분의 연구에서는 등록된 자선단체에 공식적으로 금전적인 증여를 하는 것으로 자선활동을 정의하고 있으며, 그 정의에 따르면, 미국은 지구상에서 가장 너그러운 나라이다. 그러나 아시아와 나머지 개발도상국에서는 많은 자선활동이 비공식적이다. 영국의 단체인 Charities Aid 재단의 조사에 따르면, 돈을 기부하고, 자원봉사에 시간을 보내고, 낯선 사람에게 도움의 손길을 내미는 사람들의 숫자 면에서는 인도네시아가 세계에서 가장 너그러운 나라이다. 그러한 소규모의 비공식적인 너그러움은 그 지역 전체의 가난한 지역사회 안에서 필수적인 도움을 계속 제공하고 있다.

자선활동 전문가들이 관련되는 더 전략적인 유형의 기부가 점차 등장하고 있다. 그러나 어느 모로 보나 아시아 전역의 조직적인 자선활동은 서구보다 훨씬 작은 규모이다. 실제로 인도의 민간 기부 총액은 2022 회계 연도에 약 130억 달러에 달했고, 중국의 민간 기부 총액은 2020년에 약 210억 달러였다. 이와 대조적으로, 미국에서는 코로나 이후 자선활동이 감소한 후에도 2022년의 총 기부액이 거의 5,000억 달러에 달했다.

philanthropy n. 박애, 자선; 자선활동 counterpart n. 짝의 한 쪽; 상대물, 대응물 define v. (말의) 정의를 내리다, 뜻을 밝히다 formal a. 격식을 차린, 정중한; 공식적인 financial a. 금융의, 재무의 register v. 기록하다, 등록하다 charity n. 자선; 자선활동 definition n. 정의; 설명 generous a. 후한; 관대한, 아량 있는 survey n. 조사, 검사 in terms of ~의 관점에서 donate v. 기증하다, 기부하다 volunteer v. 지원하다, 자진하여 하다 strategic a. 전략적인 gradually ad. 차차, 서서히 organized a. 정리된, 조직화된 decline n. 감소, 하락

---

35 글의 제목   ③

아시아의 자선활동과 서구, 특히 미국의 자선활동이 공식적, 비공식적 자선활동의 측면에서 어떻게 다른가를 이야기하고 있는 내용이므로 ③이 제목으로 적절하다.

제목으로 가장 적절한 것을 고르시오.
① 자선활동의 원인
② 자선활동의 혜택
③ 아시아와 미국의 자선활동
④ 여러 국가 전역에서의 자선활동의 감소

36 빈칸완성 ①

등록된 자선단체에 '공식적으로' 금전적인 증여를 하는 자선활동의 측면에서는 미국이 가장 활발하다는 내용 뒤에 But이 왔으므로, 아시아에서는 '비공식적인' 자선활동이 많다는 내용이 이어지는 것이 자연스럽다.

Ⓐ에 들어가기에 가장 적절한 단어를 고르시오.
① 비공식적인
② 조직적인
③ 무효화된
④ 무차별적인

37 어법상 적절하지 않은 표현 고르기 ④

Ⓔ의 주어는 단수 명사 total giving이므로 come이 온 것은 옳지 않다. 과거의 상황에 대한 내용이므로 Ⓔ를 과거동사 came으로 고치는 것이 적절하다.

38-40

월트 디즈니가 1928년 11월에 처음으로 단편 애니메이션 "증기선 윌리(Steamboat Willie)"를 개봉했을 때, 그것은 획기적이었다. 동시녹음 사운드를 사용한 최초의 애니메이션 중 하나였던 "증기선 윌리"는 비평가들의 호평을 가장 많이 받은 가장 인기 있는 애니메이션 영화 가운데 하나가 되었다.
월트 디즈니사(社)는 그 만화의 캐릭터에 대한 저작권을 가능한 한 오랫동안 갖고 있기 위해 노력했고, 1984년으로 예정돼 있던 만료기한 이후까지 저작권 보호를 연장하기 위해 미국 정부에 로비를 벌였다. 많은 의원들이 동의해주었고, 1976년에 법이 변경되어 소유권자가 저자의 사후 50년까지 저작권 보호를 받을 수 있게 되었다. 1998년, 디즈니는 다른 엔터테인먼트 회사들과 함께 다시 한 번 성공적으로 로비를 벌여, 저작권 보호를 저자의 사후 70년까지, 저작권이 있는 자료가 만들어진 때로부터 최대 95년으로 연장했다.
2024년 1월, "증기선 윌리"에 대한 저작권이 공식적으로 만료되었고, 이제 미키마우스는 자유 이용 저작물이 되었다. 이것은 미국에 있는 누구라도 저작권 침해의 두려움 없이 "증기선 윌리" 버전의 미키마우스 캐릭터를 사용할 수 있다는 것을 의미한다.

release v. (영화를) 개봉하다; (정보·레코드·신간 등을) 공개[발매]하다 groundbreaking a. 신기원을 이룬, 획기적인 synchronize v. 동시성을 갖게 하다, <영화> 음성을 화면과 일치시키다 critically ad. 비평적으로, 비판적으로 acclaim v. 갈채를 보내다, 환호로써 맞이하다 copyright n. 판권, 저작권 extend v. 연장하다; ~의 기한을 연장하다 expiration n. 만료, 만기 due a. 지급 기일이 된, 만기가 된 retain v. 보유하다, 유지하다 the public domain 자유 이용 저작물(저작권이 소멸되었거나 포기된 저작물) infringement n. (법규) 위반, 위배; (특허권 등의) 침해

38 빈칸완성 ②

월트 디즈니사(社)는 만화의 캐릭터에 대한 저작권을 가능한 한 오랫동안 갖고 있기 위해 지속적으로 로비를 하여, 최종적으로 '저자의 사후 70

년까지, 저작권이 있는 자료가 만들어진 때로부터 최대 95년까지' 저작권을 보유할 수 있게 되었는데, "증기선 윌리"는 1928년 11월에 개봉했으므로, 이 작품에 대한 디즈니의 저작권은 95년 동안 지속되어 2023년 말까지 효력이 있고 2024년 시작부터 효력이 없다. 그러므로 빈칸에는 ②가 들어가야 한다.

39 동의어 ①

infringement는 '(법규) 위반', '(특허권 등의) 침해'라는 의미이므로 '위반', '위배'라는 뜻의 violation이 동의어로 적절하다. ② 보호 ③ 탐닉 ④ 일탈, 상이

40 내용일치 ④

"2024년 1월에 "증기선 윌리"에 대한 저작권이 공식적으로 만료되었고, 미키마우스는 자유 이용 저작물이 되었다. 이것은 미국에 있는 누구라도 저작권 침해의 두려움 없이 "증기선 윌리" 버전의 미키마우스 캐릭터를 사용할 수 있다는 것을 의미한다."라고 돼 있으므로 ④가 옳지 않은 진술이다.

다음 중 옳지 않은 진술은?
① "증기선 윌리"에 대한 저작권은 원래 1984년에 만료될 예정이었다.
② "증기선 윌리"는 동시녹음 사운드를 사용한 최초의 애니메이션 중 하나였다.
③ 월트 디즈니사는 "증기선 윌리"에 대한 저작권을 연장하기 위해 노력해 왔다.
④ "증기선 윌리" 버전의 미키마우스 캐릭터를 미국의 모든 사람이 사용할 수 있는 것은 아니다.

41-44

우리는 우리가 생각하는 것만큼 추론을 잘하지 못한다. 우리는 추론을 더 잘 할 수 있는 방법을 배울 필요가 있다. 심리학적 연구들은 또한 왜 우리가 우리의 추론 기술을 개선하기 위해 애써야 하는지를 우리에게 보여준다. 몇몇 실험들에서, 문제는 어떤 주장이 타당한가 하는 것인데, 주장의 전제는 참이면서도 결론이 거짓이 되는 것은 논리적으로 불가능하기 때문이다. 그 결과, 많은 사람들은 어떤 주장이 참이기를 원하기 때문에 그것이 타당하다고 평가한다. '심판들이 불공정하면, 맨체스터 유나이티드가 패배할 것이다. 그러나 심판들은 공정할 것이고, 따라서 맨체스터 유나이티드가 승리할 것이다'라는 주장을 고려해보자. 많은 맨체스터 유나이티드 팬들은 아마도 이 주장이 타당하다고 믿을 것이다. 그러나 이러한 믿음은 올바르지 않은데, 왜냐하면 만약 심판들이 공정한데도 맨체스터 유나이티드가 패배할 경우에 그것의 전제는 참이지만 결론은 거짓이 되기 때문이다. 심판들이 공정하든 그렇지 않든, 맨체스터 유나이티드가 패배하는 일은 일어날 수 있다. 팬들의 실수는 그들이 피하고 싶은, 그들의 팀이 패배할 가능성을 상상하길 꺼려하는 데서 비롯된다. 맨체스터 유나이티드의 라이벌 팀들의 팬들이 이러한 실수를 덜 자주 하는 것은 그런 이유에서다. 그들은 심판들의 공정성과 상관없이 맨체스터 유나이티드가 패배할 가능성을 기꺼이 생각할 것이다. 물론, 그것이 그들이 맨체스터 유나이티드 팬들보다 더 똑똑하거나 더 논리적이라는 것을 의미하진 않는다. 왜냐하면 그들은 자신들이 가장 좋아하는 팀에 대해 같은 실수를 할 것이기 때문이다. 양측 모두 희망적 사고를 하고 있는 것이다.

work on (해결·개선하기 위해) ~에 애쓰다[공들이다] argument n. 논쟁; 주장 valid a. 근거가 확실한, 타당한 logically ad. 논리적으로 premise n. 전제 conclusion n. 결론 assess v. (사람·사물 따위의 성질을[가치를]) 평가[판단]하다 reluctance n. 마음이 내키지 않음

---

41 어법상 적절하지 않은 표현 고르기 ④

'~을 개의치 않고', '~에 관계없이'는 'regardless of'로 표현한다. 그러므로 ⓒ는 of여야 한다.

---

42 부분이해 ③

글의 흐름상 첫 문장에서 언급한 추론 능력을 가리킨다.

---

43 빈칸완성 ①

맨체스터 유나이티드의 팬들은 심판만 공정하다면 자신이 응원하는 팀이 '패배할 수' 없다고 생각하고, 다른 팀의 팬들은 심판의 공정성 여부와 무관하게 맨체스터 유나이티드가 '패배할 수도' 있다고 생각할 것이다. 그러므로 두 빈칸 모두 losing이 들어가야 한다.

---

44 빈칸완성 ①

맨체스터 유나이티드의 팬들이나 다른 팀의 팬들 모두 심판만 공정하면 자신의 팀이 패배할 수 없다는 입장을 보인다는 것이므로, 이는 양측 팬 모두 희망적 사고를 하고 있는 것이라 할 수 있다. 희망적 사고는 '생각하고 싶어 하는 것에 근거하여 신념을 형성하는 것', 즉 바라는 대로 될 것이라고 생각하는 것을 말한다.

다음 중 ⊞에 들어가기에 가장 적절한 문장은?
① 양측 모두 희망적 사고를 한다
② 어느 쪽도 잘못된 추론을 하지 않는다
③ 양측 모두 타당한 논증을 한다
④ 어느 쪽도 비논리적인 과정에 참여하지 않는다

45-47

고대 세계에서 닭은 주로 닭싸움을 위해 길러졌는데, 닭싸움은 닭이 화가 나면 극도로 흥분한다는 것에 의존하는 사악한 도박 경기였다. 승리하여 번식하는 그 새들은 특히 무엇이든 빨간색인 것들을 보면 쉽게 극도로 화가 나게 됐다. 이로부터, 수탉들은 자신에 차 있다는 명성을 얻었다. 그들의 맹렬한 기세는 귀신도 겁을 주어 쫓아낼 수 있을 정도였다. 산업화 이전에 닭이 주로 자명종으로 사용되었던 — 그리스어로는 '깨우는 것'이라는 뜻의 *alektryones*이다 — 반면, 거위는 주로 감시용 동물로 활용되었다. 길들여진 오늘날의 닭은 땅에 사는 비이주성의 텃세가 강한 새였던 야생 닭의 후손이다. 힘은 세지만 멀리 날지 못했던 이들은 밤에는 포식자를 피해 나무에 보금자리를 틀었고, 오늘날의 길들여진 닭도 해가 지면 여전히 급히 보금자리에 들어가야 한다. 이집트 종교에서 닭은 제물로 바쳐지는 새와 시간을 표시해주는 것으로서의 역할을 했다. 닭을 기르는 것에 관한 로마의 지식은 아마도 이집트에서 유래했을 것이다. 기원전 4세기 그리스 기록에 따르면 이집트인들은 가금류 사육과 닭의 인공 부화를 모두 통달했다고 한다. 이집트인들의 부화기는 한 번에 최대 15,000개의 달걀을 부화시킬 수 있었다. 역사적으로, 달걀이 닭보다 먼저 인간의 음식이 되었다는 것은 의심의 여지가 없다. 그러나, 상식적으로 말하자면, 너무 늙어서 알을 낳지 못하는 암탉들이 너무 늙어 제 역할을 하지 못하는 수탉들과 함께 잡아 먹혔다.

rear v. 기르다, 사육하다 cock-fighting n. 닭싸움 vicious a. 사악한 betting n. 내기, 도박 rage n. 격노, 흥분상태 rouse v. 깨우다, 화나게 하다 reproduce v. 번식하다 infuriate v. 격노하게 하다 acquire v. 손에 넣다, 획득하다 reputation n. 평판; 명성 cockiness n. 건방짐, 자만심 ferocity n. 사나움, 잔인성 domestic a. 가정의; 국내의; (동물이) 사육되어 길든 be descended from ~의 자손이다 jungle fowl 야생 닭, 멧닭 territorial a. 영토의; (동물이) 세력권세(勢)의 습성을 갖는 ground-dwelling a. 땅에서 사는 non-migratory a. 비(非)이주성의 roost v. (홰에) 앉다, 보금자리에 들다 predator n. 포식자, 포식동물 urgently ad. 긴급히 sacrificial a. 희생의, 산 제물의 stem from ~에서 유래하다 poultry n. 가금(家禽) husbandry n. (낙농·양계 등을 포함하는) 농업, 경작 artificial a. 인공적인 incubation n. 알을 품음, 부화 hatch v. 알이 깨다, 부화하다

---

45 어법상 적절하지 않은 표현 고르기 ②

접속사 when 뒤에 절의 형태가 와야 한다. 그러므로 ⓑ는 chickens를 받는 대명사 they가 필요하고, 시제는 과거시제가 적절하므로 they were roused가 되어야 한다.

---

46 빈칸완성 ②

앞 문장에서 역사적으로는 '달걀이 닭보다 먼저 인간의 음식이 되었다'는 것이 분명하다고 했는데, 상식적으로는 닭(암탉)도 사람의 음식인 달걀을 낳지 못하게 되면 잡아먹혔던 것이 분명하다는 말이다. 따라서 빈칸에는 ②가 적절하다.

ⓔ에 들어가기에 가장 적절한 표현을 고르시오.
① 시간을 알리다
② 알을 낳다
③ 나무에 보금자리를 틀다
④ 닭싸움에 참가하다

---

47 내용일치 ①

"기원전 4세기 그리스 기록에 따르면 이집트인들은 가금류 사육과 닭의 인공 부화를 모두 통달했다고 한다."라는 내용을 통해 ①이 옳지 않은 진술임을 알 수 있다.

다음 중 옳지 않은 진술은?
① 고대 이집트에서는 닭을 사육하지 않았다.
② 오늘날의 닭의 조상은 이주하지 않았다.
③ 고대에 닭은 사나운 동물로 잘 알려져 있었다.
④ 산업화 시대 이전에 거위는 주로 닭과 다른 용도로 쓰였다.

48-50

자기 통제력은 그것을 잃고 나서야 그 가치를 알게 되는 인지 능력들 중 하나이다. 그것의 원천은 전전두피질(前前頭皮質)이다. 종종 뇌의 실행 중추라 불리는 전전두피질은 당신이 역효과를 내거나 위험한 실수를 하는 것을 막는다.

자기 통제력은 우리에게 도박을 하도록 유혹하는 측좌핵(側坐核), 사막에서 신기루를 보는 시각피질, 그리고 우리에게 어둠 속의 소음에 선뜻 달려들도록 하는 편도체의 명령을 취소시킨다(거역한다). 자기 통제력은 생각과 행동 사이의 공간으로, 건너기 전에 돌다리를 두들겨 보도록 하는 역할을 한다. 만약 자기 통제력이 없다면, 우리 모두는 감옥에 갇혀 있거나 죽었을 것이다.

어떤 사람들은 다른 사람들보다 더 많은 자기 통제력을 가지고 있고, 이러한 차이를 연구함으로써, 연구원들은 이 특성이 우리의 삶 전반에 걸쳐 얼마나 중요한지를 보여주었다. 자기 통제력에 대한 테스트 중 하나는 유명한 마시멜로 실험인데, 이 실험에서 연구원들은 4~6세의 아이들에게 마시멜로를 주고 나서, 곧바로 마시멜로를 먹을 수도 있고 혹은 연구원이 돌아올 때까지 기다려서 더 많은 마시멜로를 받을 수도 있다고 말한다. 어떤 아이들은 곧바로 마시멜로를 먹은 반면, 다른 어떤 아이들은 유혹에 굴복하지 않고 10분, 심지어 15분을 기다렸다. 곧바로 마시멜로를 먹은 아이들은 학교생활을 힘들어하고, 집중하는 것을 어려워하며, 우정을 유지하는 데 곤란을 겪을 가능성이 더 높았다.

cognitive a. 인식[인지]의 appreciate v. 평가하다; 진가를 인정하다 prefrontal cortex 전전두피질(前前頭皮質) counter-productive a. 의도와 반대되는 결과를 초래하는, 역효과를 낳는 countermand v. (명령·주문을) 취소[철회]하다; 반대 명령에 의해 ~에 대한 명령을[요구를] 취소하다 nucleus accumbens 측좌핵(側坐核), 동기 및 보상과 관련된 정보를 처리하는 뇌의 보상체계) visual cortex 시각 피질 mirage n. 신기루 amygdala n. 편도체 jump at ~에 선뜻 달려들다, ~을 덥석 잡다 variation n. (특히 양·정도의) 변화[차이] crucial a. 결정적인, 중대한 trait n. 특색 give in to ~에 굴복하다 temptation n. 유혹

---

48 글의 주제 ①

글의 첫 문장이 주제문이다. 자기 통제력의 중요성과 역할에 대해 주로 이야기하고 있는 글이므로 ①이 주제로 적절하다.

주제로 가장 적절한 것을 고르시오.
① 자기 통제력의 중요성
② 우리 뇌의 다양한 인지적 특징
③ 유년 시절에 자기 통제력을 얻는 방법들
④ 지나친 자기 통제력 행사의 함정

---

49 빈칸완성 ②

빈칸 앞의 '생각과 행동 사이의 공간'은 행동하기에 앞서 생각하게 한다는 의미이므로, 이와 관련된 ②가 빈칸에 들어가기에 적절하다.

Ⓐ에 들어가기에 가장 적절한 표현을 고르시오.
① 추락 전의 상승
② 도약하기 전에 살피기
③ 물질에 앞서는 정신
④ 말 앞의 마차

---

50 내용파악 ③

사막에서 신기루를 보는 것은 '환각' 혹은 '환상'에 해당한다.

다음 중 시각피질이 담당하고 있는 것은?
① 근심
② 불면증
③ 환상
④ 과잉 행동

2024 한양대학교(서울 인문계 A형)

01 ③	**02** ②	**03** ①	**04** ⑤	**05** ③	**06** ②	**07** ①	**08** ②	**09** ③	**10** ③
11 ①	**12** ④	**13** ③	**14** ①	**15** ①	**16** ②	**17** ①	**18** ④	**19** ③	**20** ④
21 ⑤	**22** ⑤	**23** ④	**24** ④	**25** ③	**26** ⑤	**27** ④	**28** ②	**29** ④	**30** ⑤
31 ⑤	**32** ④	**33** ⑤	**34** ②	**35** ①					

01 동의어 ③

unsubstantiated a. 근거 없는 claim n. 주장 meme n. 밈 related to ~와 관련된 psychiatric a. 정신 질환의 visually ad. 시각적으로 aversive a. 혐오의 e.g. 예를 들어 lead to ~을 낳다 exacerbation n. 악화(= aggravation) symptom n. 증상, 증후 abatement n. 감소 alleviation n. 감소 ambivalence n. (상반되는) 감정의 교차; 양면 가치 amelioration n. 개선

정신 질환 증상과 관련된 인터넷 밈들이 혐오 행동(예를 들어, 자해)을 시각적으로 묘사하고 조장하여, 증상을 악화시킨다는 근거 없는 주장이 종종 제기되고 있다.

02 동의어 ②

perspicacity n. 통찰(= sagacity) negotiation n. 협상 compliment v. 칭찬하다 keen a. 예리한 discern v. 식별하다 underlying a. 뒤에 숨어 있는 invaluable a. 매우 유용한[귀중한] secure v. 확보하다 obtuseness n. 무딤 ineptitude n. 무능, 부조리 credence n. 신빙성 verboseness n. 말 많음

복잡한 국제 협상을 헤쳐 나가는 그 외교관의 통찰력은 칭찬받았다. 숨어 있는 의도와 뉘앙스를 파악하는 그의 예리한 통찰은 유리한 합의를 확보하는 데 귀중한 것으로 입증되었다.

03 동의어 ①

evolutionary a. 진화의 intractable a. 억지[고집]스러운, 고집 센, 다루기 힘든(= stubborn) decade n. 10년 adaptation n. 적응 flight n. 비행 elongated a. 길쭉한 scale n. 비늘 empirical a. 경험적인, 실험에 의거한 enervating a. 무기력한 debilitating a. 쇠약하게 만드는 preventable a. 예방할 수 있는 counterproductive a. 역효과를 낳는, 의도와는 반대된

20세기 대부분 동안, 깃털의 진화적 기원은 고전적이지만 다루기 힘든 문제였다. 비행을 위한 적응으로서의 깃털이 길쭉한 비늘에서 파생되었다고 설명하려는 수십 년간의 노력은 그 어떤 의미 있는 경험적 지지도 얻어 내지 못했다.

04 동의어 ⑤

nefarious a. 비도덕적인, 악질적인(= malevolent) eventually ad. 결국 illegal a. 불법적인 under the guise of ~을 가장하여 legitimacy n. 정통성, 합법성 cause harm to ~에 해를 끼치다 mundane a. 일상적인 sedentary a. 앉아 있는 altruistic a. 이타적인 subversive a. 체제 전복적인

회사의 악질적인 활동이 결국 드러나서, 일련의 비윤리적이고 불법적인 관행을 보여주었다. 이러한 행위는 합법성을 가장해서 고객과 환경에 심각한 피해를 입혔다.

05 동의어 ③

impetus n. 동기, 유인, 자극(= inducement) canning n. 통조림 제조 preservative a. 방부제 역할을 하는 quality n. 특징 disclosure n. 폭로, 밝혀진[드러난] 사실 dealbreaker n. (정치·상업에서 일의) 성사 장애 요인 impediment n. 장애물 compromise n. 타협

19세기의 식품 산업화는 인류의 식단에 소금을 도입하게 만든 주요 동기였다. 19세기 말과 20세기 초에 채소 통조림과 과일 통조림 산업이 극적으로 확장되면서 소금과 설탕이 그 보존적 특성 때문에 더욱 많이 사용되었다.

06 동의어 ②

advocate n. 옹호자, 지지자 animal agriculture 유축농업(有畜農業) slaughter n. 도살 pejorative a. 경멸하는, 비난투의(= denigratory) abrogative a. 폐기하는 congenial a. 마음이 맞는 dispassionate a. 감정에 좌우되지 않는 inviolable a. 불가침의

유축농업 감소를 옹호하는 사람들은 '도살 없는', '잔인하지 않은', '동물 없는', '깨끗한 고기'라는 이름들을 제시해왔다. 그러나 전통적인 육류 생산자들은 이러한 명칭이 기존 제품을 비하하는 것이라며 거부해왔다.

07 동의어 ①

be known for ~으로 유명하다 abstruse a. 난해한(= recondite) content n. 내용 delve into 파고들다 subject n. 주제 expertise n. 전문 지식 arcane a. 신비로운, 불가해한 alienate v. 소외시키다

well-versed a. 박식한 malicious a. 악의적인 flamboyant a. 화려한 substantive a. 실질적인 pedagogical a. 교육적인

그 교수의 강의는 난해한 내용으로 유명했고, 종종 일반 학생의 이해를 넘어서는 모호한 주제로 파고들곤 했다. 이러한 불가해한 주제에 대한 그의 전문 지식은 인상적이긴 했지만, 때때로 해당 분야를 잘 모르는 사람들을 소외시켰다.

---

08 동의어　　　　　　　　　　　　　　　　　②

penchant n. 성향 veracity n. 진실(= honesty) standout a. 뛰어난 dedication n. 헌신 unwavering a. 확고한 reliable a. 신뢰할만한 mendacity n. 허위 artifice n. 계략 falsity n. 허위, 거짓 erudition n. 박식

진실을 추구하는 그녀의 성향은 그녀를 뛰어난 저널리스트로 만들었다. 진실에 대한 그녀의 헌신은 확고해서, 그녀의 보도는 언제나 사실적이고 신뢰할 수 있게 되었다.

---

09 논리완성　　　　　　　　　　　　　　　　③

순환 정의의 개념을 설명하고 있다. '물체의 질량은 물체가 포함한 물질의 양이다'라고 정의내리면 '물질이 무엇이냐'라는 질문이 던져지는데, 물질보다 더 근본적인 개념이 없으면 다시 질량이라는 개념으로 정의하게 되어 '물질의 양은 물체가 포함하고 있는 질량이다'와 같은 "순환적" 정의가 된다는 것이다.

define A as B A를 B라고 정의하다 mass n. 질량 quantity n. 양(量), 분량 measure v. 측정하다 in terms of ~에 비추어, ~에 의해 fundamental a. 근본적인 circular definition 순환 정의(정의 내용이 서로 의존하여 무한히 순환하는 정의) operationally ad. 조작적으로 i.e. 다시 말해서 rather than ~보다는 figurative a. 비유의 empirical a. 경험적인 hypothetical a. 가설의 lexical a. 어휘의

아이작 뉴턴은 물체의 질량을 물체가 포함하고 있는 '물질의 양(量)'으로 정의했다. 이는 물질이 무엇인지 또는 그 '양'을 어떻게 측정할 수 있는지 하는 의문을 불러일으킨다. 문제는, 일부 양은 더 근본적인 양에 의해(예를 들어, 속도는 거리와 시간에 의해) 정의할 수 있지만, 일부 개념은 너무나 근본적이어서 그러한 시도는 방금 언급한 것과 같은 순환 정의를 낳는다. 이러한 문제에서 벗어나기 위해 우리는 이러한 양을 '조작적으로' 정의할 수 있다. 이것은 양이 무엇인지가 아니라 양이 무엇을 하는지, 다시 말해, 어떻게 작동하는지를 설명한다는 것을 의미한다.

---

10 논리완성　　　　　　　　　　　　　　　　③

빈칸 다음 문장에서 '요점 하나하나가 거칠고 심각하게 전달되었다'고 했으므로 빈칸에는 ③이 적절하다.

heated a. 열띤 deliver v. 전달하다 harshness n. 불쾌감 severity n. 심각함 biting a. 통렬한 caustic a. 신랄한 frustration n. 불만 irritability n. 짜증 tension n. 긴장 languor n. 나른함 geniality n. 상냥함 asperity n. 거침, 신랄함 subterfuge n. 핑계 contrition n. 회개

열띤 토론에서 그의 주장은 두드러지게 거칠었다. 요점 하나하나가 단순한 의견 불일치를 넘어서서 거칠고 심각하게 전달되었다. 그의 어조는 비판적이었을 뿐 아니라 통렬하고 신랄했으며, 반대 견해에 대한 깊은 불만과 짜증을 드러내어 토론에 긴장감을 더했다.

---

11 논리완성　　　　　　　　　　　　　　　　①

앞에서 '역사의 모든 것이 연대적 순서를 특별히 고려하지 않고 일어난다'라고 한 것은 일어나는 일이 그 시점과 필연적 관련성(relevance)이 없다는 말이다. 음악도 그렇다고 했으므로, 빈칸에는 ①이 적절하다. 음악은 개인의 필요와 욕구에 따라 다양하게 해석되고 소비되며, 그 시간적 흐름도 개인의 내적 욕구에 따라 달라질 수 있다는 말이다.

at hand 가까이 without regard for ~은 고려하지 않고 chronology n. 연대 warehouse n. 창고 shelf n. 선반 shelf life 유통 기한 oblivion n. 망각, 잊혀짐 get down to 착수하다 irrelevant a. 무관한 elucidate v. 설명하다 miscellaneous a. 다양한 circumscribed a. 국한된 self-explanatory a. 자명한

오늘날 우리는 달력을 가까이하고 살지만, 동시에 우리는 역사의 모든 것이 연대적 순서를 특별히 고려하지 않고 일어난다는 느낌을 갖고 살고 있다. 음악조차도 일종의 샘플 창고로, 그 유통 기한 — 상대적 영속성이나 망각, 시간적 배치 — 이 궁극적으로는 아무런 상관이 없다. 왜냐하면 우리가 어떤 음악으로 다가가면 그 음악은 청취자, 연주자, 작곡가로서의 우리의 내면적 필요와 욕망에 따라 이리저리 밀려날 수 있기 때문이다.

---

12 논리완성　　　　　　　　　　　　　　　　④

일종의 'not A but B' 구문으로, 세미콜론이 but의 역할을 대신하고 있다. 따라서 뒤에 언급된 '가장 두드러진 부분을 늘 구성한다'는 말과 반대되는 ④가 빈칸에 가장 적절하다.

Charlie Chan 찰리 찬(작가 얼 데어 비거스(Earl Derr Biggers)가 일련의 미스터리 소설을 위해 만든 가상의 호놀룰루 경찰 탐정) pose v. 제기하다 utilize v. 이용하다 uncover v. 밝히다 photoelectric a. 광전자의 radiograph n. X-레이 ultraviolet a. 자외선의 gadgetry n. 도구 routinely ad. 일상적으로 constitute v. 구성하다 distinctive a. 눈에 확 띄는 intrinsic a. 고유한 conducive a. ~에 도움이 되는 peripheral a. 지엽적인 consequent a. 결과로 일어나는

찰리 찬 영화 시리즈 전체에서 현대 기술이 제기하는 문제와 해결책으로 끊임없이 돌아가는 것이 발견되는데, 예를 들면 영화마다 찬의 미스터리 해결은 현미경, 축음기, 영상 통화, 광전자 셀, 방사선 사진, 실험실 실험, 자외선 필름 투사 등 기술 장치를 활용하는(또는 범죄에 사용되는 것을 밝혀내는) 능력에 의존하고 있다. 여기서 지적해 둘 중요한 점은 이러한 도구가 부각되는 순간들은 내러티브에 지엽적이지 않고, 실제로 각 영화에서 가장 두드러진 부분을 늘 구성한다는 것이다.

---

13 논리완성　　　　　　　　　　　　　　　　③

뒤의 문장을 보면 아무리 지루하고 형편없는 책도 다 읽고야 만다고 했으므로, 책을 꼼꼼히 읽는 사람이다. 그리고 부정적인 맥락이므로 빈칸

에는 ③의 '잘 건너뛰며 읽지 못하는 사람'이 적절하다. ④ '빠르게 읽는 정독자'는 앞의 I read slowly와 모순된다.

bore v. 지루하게 만들다   count v. 수를 세다   choosy a. 까다로운   bibliophile n. 애서가   skipper n. 띄엄띄엄 읽는 사람   peruser n. 꼼꼼히 읽는 사람

나는 책을 많이 읽었지만, 형편없는 독서가이다. 나는 천천히 읽으며, 건너뛰며 읽지 못하고 다 읽는다. 아무리 형편없고 지루한 책이라도 다 읽지 않고 남겨놓는 것은 어려운 일이다. 처음부터 끝까지 읽지 않은 책의 수는 손가락으로 셀 수 있을 정도이다.

14 논리완성   ①

앞에서 재즈는 즉흥 연주를 통해 매번 새로움과 혁신을 추구하고, 다른 여러 장르의 음악을 흡수·통합하며 발전하고 있다고 했으므로 정답은 ①이다.

evolution n. 발전   myriad a. 많은   improvisation n. 즉흥 연주   defining a. 본질적인   spontaneously ad. 즉흥적으로   vary v. 변화를 주다   enduring a. 지속적인   sustain v. 유지하다   explore v. 연구하다   commercial a. 상업적인   retain v. 유지하다   adhere to 고수하다

20세기 초의 뿌리에서부터 수많은 현대적 형태에 이르는 재즈 음악의 발전은 이 장르의 역동적인 성격을 반영하고 있다. 아프리카계 미국인 커뮤니티에서 시작된 재즈는 블루스, 래그타임, 유럽 음악의 요소를 결합하여 독특하고 표현이 풍부한 사운드를 만들어 냈다. 즉흥 연주는 재즈의 가장 큰 특징으로, 뮤지션이 공연 중에 즉흥적으로 멜로디, 하모니, 리듬을 만들고 변화시킬 수 있게 해준다. 이러한 즉흥성 요소로 인해 모든 재즈 공연은 독특한 경험이 된다. 수십 년에 걸쳐 재즈는 펑크, 록, 심지어 클래식 음악과 같은 여러 다른 장르의 영향을 수용하며 발전해 왔다. 재즈의 지속적인 매력은 이러한 다양성과 혁신을 포용하는 능력에 있다.

15 논리완성   ①

빈칸 앞의 that절 내용이 상대방의 견해나 생각을 전혀 인정하지 않는 태도를 나타내는데, 이런 태도라면 이치에 맞는 논리적인 설득이나 논의가 불가능해지고 그러면 갈등을 유발하게 될 것이므로 빈칸에는 ①의 '갈등을 조장하다'가 적절하다. ⑤ 망상은 갈등과 달리 타인과의 관계에 일어나는 것이 아니다.

have a tendency to ~하는 경향이 있다   put v. 말하다   maniac n. 미치광이   propensity n. 경향   benighted a. 무지몽매한   as it is 있는 그대로   incompetent a. 무능한   irrational a. 비이성적인   reason with 설득하다, ~와 논의하다   fuel v. 추진하다   conflict n. 갈등, 충돌   relieve v. 덜다   inspire v. 자극하다   trigger v. 자극하다   delusion n. 망상

우리는 자신과 생각이 같은 사람은 똑똑하고 통찰력이 있다고 생각하고, 자신과 생각이 다른 사람은 현실을 있는 그대로 보는 데 약간의 도움이 필요할 수 있다고 생각하는 경향이 있다. 조지 칼린은 이러한 경향을 가리켜 "당신보다 느리게 운전하는 사람은 바보이고, 당신보다 빨리 가는 사람은 미치광이라고 알아차린 적이 있나요?"라고 말했다. 우리는 세상을 정확하게 보고 있지만, 나와 다른 의견을 가진 사람은 무지몽매하다고 생각하

는 이러한 성향은 갈등을 조장한다. 심리학자 리 로스가 주장했듯이, 내가 세상을 있는 그대로 보는데, 당신이 내 생각에 동의하지 않는다면, 나로서는 당신의 행동에 대해 가능한 해석은 몇 가지밖에 없다. 당신이 무능하거나, 비이성적이거나, 착각하고 있을지도 모른다는 것이다. 어떤 경우이든, 나는 당신을 설득할 수 없다.

16 저자의 심경   ②

마지막 문장만 읽어도 감정이 실패자라는 좌절감에서 깨달음을 얻은 만족감으로 변한 것을 알 수 있다. 따라서 ② '좌절감에서 깨달은 기쁨으로'가 정답이다. impatient는 오래 기다려야 하는 것 때문에 짜증이 난 상태를 의미한다.

meticulous a. 세심한   relentless a. 끈질긴   fieldwork n. 현장 연구   chase v. 쫓다   elude v. 피해 나가다   glare v. 노려보다   bear down on 짓누르다   oppressive a. 답답한   affirmation n. 확증   exploration n. 탐구   make sense 이해가 되다   dissipate v. 흩어지다   flaw n. 결점, 결함   contribute to ~에 이바지하다   sense of defeat 패배감   disillusioned a. 환멸을 느낀   enlightened a. 깨우친   impatient a. 초조한   resigned a. 체념한

수년간 세심한 연구와 끈질긴 현장 조사를 한 후에도 내가 추구하던 발견은 찾아낼 수 없을 것 같았다. 데이터 더미에 둘러싸인 채, 사무실에 앉아서 보니 디지털시계의 빨간 숫자가 나를 노려보며, 또 하루가 지나가고 있음을 상기시켰다. 기대의 무게가 어깨를 짓눌렀고, 나의 야망은 답답한 그림자로 바뀌었다. 호흡이 얕아지고 집중력이 흩어졌다. 대학은 내 연구에 많은 투자를 했는데, 이제 나는 내 이론이 틀렸다고 인정하려던 참이었다. 나는 머리를 맑게 하려고 산책하기로 했다. 텅 빈 캠퍼스를 거닐다 보니 스승님의 말씀이 떠올랐다. "과학은 확증을 추구하는 것이 아니라 미지의 세계를 탐구하는 것이다. 잘못된 길로 접어드는 것은 진실을 향해 한 걸음 내딛는 것이다." 갑자기 모든 것이 이해되었다. 나의 '실패'가 사실은 가치 있는 발견이라는 사실을 깨달으면서 압박감은 사라졌다. 불안은 해방감으로 대체되었다. 새로운 활력을 되찾은 나는 내 이론의 결함을 인정하는 것이 더 큰 지식에 기여할 것이라는 것을 깨달았다. 나는 패배감이 아니라 끊임없이 확장되는 과학이라는 퍼즐에 한 조각을 더했다는 만족감을 안고 연구실로 돌아왔다.

17 글의 요지   ①

'사회는 자체적으로 존재하고 유지되기 위해 노력하며, 스스로 살아남는 상태를 유지하기 위해 완벽한 목표 달성을 추구해서는 안 되고, 불완전한 노동이 필요하다. 왜냐하면 완전한 노동의 결과 어떤 목표의 완성이 이루어지는 순간 그 사회는 쇠퇴하기 마련이기 때문이다.'라는 내용이므로 ①이 글의 요지로 적절하다.

institution n. 제도   along with ~와 더불어   tightly woven 빽빽이 짜인   affective a. 감정의, 정서적인   means n. 수단   exertion n. 노력   project v. 투사하다   vague a. 모호한   dominion n. 지배, 통제   imperial a. 제국주의적인   in that ~라는 점에서   exhaustion n. 소진   inertia n. 무기력   dissipation n. 방탕   mythos n. 가치관   decay v. 썩다   by the same token 마찬가지로   cessation n. 중단   remission n. 감면   aim at 목표로 하다   ongoing a. 지속적인   overexertion n. 과로   burnout n. 소진

조직된 노동과 그것을 지탱하는 관습, 관례 및 제도, 그리고 희망, 두려움, 야망으로 촘촘히 짜인 정서적 조직은 사회가 계속 존재를 유지하기 위한 수단을 제공하고, 사회는 사회를 유지하려는 노력 그 자체를 유지함으로써 사회 자신을 유지한다. 사회는 자연 세계 및 인간 세계에 대한 점점 더 많은 지배를 위한 5개년 계획과 더 막연한 야망을 통해 자신을 위한 목표를 설정할 수도 있지만, 사회 목표의 완성이 소진과 무기력과 낭비를 낳을 것이기 때문에 제국주의적 확장이 사실 여전히 미결정적이고 불완전할 수밖에 없다는 점에서, 이러한 제국주의적인 확장은 실제로는 그대로 구체화되는 것이 아니다. 집단적 노력으로서의 노동이라는 가치관에 묶여 있는 사회는 같은 상태를 유지하기 위해, 혹은 썩어 없어지지 않기 위해서라도 성장해야 한다. 마찬가지로 사회는 노력을 통해 계속 존재한다. 노동은 항상 어떤 종류의 완성, 중단 또는 감면을 목표로 한다. 사회를 노동 계획이 작용하는 방식으로 계속 '작용하게' 하는 것은 지속적인 미완성을 목표로 하거나, 노동을 존재 상태로 유지하는 일만을 목표로 한다.

다음 글의 요지로 가장 적절한 것은?
① 사회는 노동의 미결정적(열린 결말의) 미완성에 의해 유지된다.
② 일과 삶의 균형의 중요성은 아무리 강조해도 지나치지 않다.
③ 문명은 일의 가치에 대한 신화 덕분에 이루어졌다.
④ 과로와 소진을 최소화하기 위해 목표를 현실적으로 설정해야 한다.
⑤ 생산적인 사회는 정책의 장기적인 효과를 고려한다.

18 단락배열 ④

주어진 글이 solid facts로 끝났는데, C에 is equally solid이 있으니 자연스럽게 연결된다. C에서 과거의 능력은 물건을 만드는 손재주처럼 표준화된 측정으로 정량화할 수 있는 객관적이고 확실해 보이는 능력이었다고 한 다음, But으로 연결된 A에서는 지금은 무형적이고 정량화할 수 없는, 어떤 콘텐츠에 특정화되지 않은 능력이 필요하다고 한 다음, B에서 그러한 능력은 무엇보다 새로운 기술을 빠르게 배우고, 변화하는 여러 정보와 실무를 처리하고 해석하는 능력이라고 하는 것이 적절한 순서이다.

craftsmanship n. 손재주 displaced a. 추방된 discarded a. 버려진 legible a. 알아볼 수 있는, 명료한 cast aside 버려지다 manufactured goods 공산품 solid a. 확실한 meritocracy n. 능력주의 machinery n. 장치, 기구, 조직 on-the-job 작업 중 evaluation n. 평가 take the place of 대체하다 objectivity n. 객관성 bureaucratic a. 관료주의적인 intangible a. 무형의, 실체가 없는 autonomous a. 자율적인 cutting-edge a. 첨단의 flexible a. 유연한, 융통성 있는 cling to 고수하다 competency n. 능력 practice n. 실무

업무능력에 있어서, 우리는 어떤 사람이 얼마나 업무를 잘 수행하는지를 그들의 노동의 구체적인 결과를 보고 판단할 수 있다. 일자리에서 쫓겨나거나 버려진 노동자들에게 그러한 결과는 적어도 그들이 왜 버려졌는지를 명료하게 알 수 있게 해준다. 인도 소프트웨어 프로그램의 품질과 중국산 공산품의 품질은 확실한 사실이다.
C 시험과 실무 평가의 능력주의 조직도 마찬가지로 확실한 것 같다. 측정은 결국 표준화되어 있으며, 객관성을 보장하기 위해 시험에서 이름 대신 숫자가 사용되는 경우도 종종 있다.
A 그러나 사실 관료주의적 조직은 매우 무형적인 것을 추구한다. 예를 들어, 자율적인 것 같아 보이는 모든 종류의 업무는 정량화할 수 있지만, 구체적으로 자율적 행위가 무엇인지는 정량화할 수 없다. 업무능력은 특정한 영역의 지식을 숙달하고 소유할 것을 요구한다. 하지만 이 새로운 버전

의 재능은 어떤 콘텐츠에 특정화된 것도 아니고, 어떤 콘텐츠에 의해 결정되는 것도 아니다.
B 첨단 기업과 유연한 조직은 옛 능력을 고수하기보다는 새로운 기술을 배울 수 있는 사람들을 필요로 한다. 역동적인 조직은 변화하는 여러 정보와 실무를 처리하고 해석할 수 있는 능력을 강조한다.

19 글의 제목 ③

이 글은 '무한한 것은 가치 없는 것인데, 죽음은 삶을 유한한 것으로 한정 지어 삶에 형태를 부여하는 것 즉, 삶을 이루어주는 것이다'라고 설명하면서 '죽음에 대한 이러한 시각을 받아들일 때 삶을 더욱 풍부하게 즐길 수 있게 된다'고 하고 있다. 따라서 ③이 제목으로 적절하다. ④ 삶의 무의미가 아니라 죽음에 대한 새로운 시각을 제시한 글이다.

confinement n. 감금 epicurean a. 쾌락주의적인 Epicure n. 에피쿠로스 get through 극복하다 tough times 어려운 시절 shapeliness n. 형태 substantial a. 상당한, 내용이 풍부한 transition n. 이행기 come to terms with 타협하다, (사태 등을) 감수하다 bout n. 한차례 let alone 하물며 equalizer n. 평형추 grim a. 엄숙한 Grim Reaper 저승사자, 죽음 cope with 감당하다

우리는 죽음을 있는 그대로, 즉 우리 삶에 형태를 부여하는 한계로 봐야 한다. 죽음을 감금으로, 우리의 인생사업의 부당한 중단으로 보는 것은 잘못이며 도움이 되지 않는다. 끝없이 계속되는 것은 가치를 잃는다. 어려움을 극복하기 위한 에피쿠로스의 팁(쾌락주의적 비결)은 고통에는 끝이 있다는 것을 기억하는 것이다. 그런데 죽음은 "이 또한 지나가리라"를 그 논리적 결론으로 내리는 것이다. 어려운 시기를 극복하기 위한 또 다른 에피쿠로스의 팁은 우정이나 대화와 같은 삶의 좋은 것들을 기억하는 것이다. 그런데 죽음은 시간에 형태를 부여하여 이러한 즐거움들을 풍부하게 만들어준다. 죽음은 단순한 이행이라는 생각을 빨리 중단하고 죽음을 절대적인 끝으로 빨리 받아들일수록, 그만큼 더 빨리 우리는 일시적인 고통을 견디고 아름다움과의 소중한 만남을 누릴 수 있게 된다. 담을 수 있는 그릇이 없다면 삶은 충만할 수 없고, 하물며 넘쳐흐를 수는 더더욱 없다.

다음 글의 제목으로 가장 적절한 것을 고르시오.
① 죽음은 왜 위대한 평형장치인가
② 죽음에 대한 불안을 줄이기 위한 전략들
③ 죽음의 신을 받아들여라: 죽음은 삶을 향상시킨다
④ 삶의 무의미함에 대처하는 방법
⑤ 에피쿠로스의 교훈: 불확실성의 아름다움

20 글의 제목 ④

인간이 존재하며 사회를 이루고 살아간 시초부터 소유는 인간의 주요한 경험이었지만 이에 대한 데이터는 역사시대부터 시작된 기록뿐이므로 소유권에 대한 논의는 역사 기록에 의해 제한된 것일 뿐이라는 내용이므로 ④가 제목으로 적절하다.

materialistically ad. 물질적으로 be concerned with ~에 관심을 두다 mold v. 형성하다 encompass v. 포괄하다 at best 기껏해야 plunge v. 빠지다 confine v. 한정하다 learned man 학자 deal with 다루다 social order 사회 질서 guideline n. 지침 a welter of 엄청난 양의 warp v. 왜곡하다 story n. 역사 epic n. 서사시(서사시는 대체로 영웅담이다) saga n. 영웅담 interdisciplinary a. 상호 학문적인, 학제적인

소유권을 인간 존재와 경험의 주요 요소 중 하나로 논의하는 데 있어서 어려운 점은 데이터가 거의 없다는 것이다. 철학적 관심으로 인간을 다루었던 물질적 관심으로 재산을 다루었든, 경제학을 연구한 대부분 사람들의 많은 생각은 기록된 역사에 의해 형성되었다. 그러나 기록된 역사는 인간의 경험을 포괄하지 못한다. 기껏해야 잠깐이면 과거로 들어가 버릴 뿐이다. 문서화된 기록은 인간 경험에서 겨우 지난 5천 년 또는 6천 년까지로 국한된다. 학자들이 재산과 재산 관계를 연구하기 시작할 때에는 이미 우리는 (선사시대를 지나) 역사 시대에 들어와 있고, 이 학자들은 역사가들이 발견한 것들이나 뒤지고 있다. 거의 모든 초기 역사가들은 정부와 전쟁을 인간 사회 질서를 형성하는 주요 요소로 보았다. 그들은 이미 오래되고 관습으로 왜곡된 수많은 활동 관계 속에서 기본 지침들이 사라져 가는 시점에서 역사에 발을 들였다.

다음 글의 제목으로 가장 적절한 것을 고르시오.
① 소유물 전쟁의 서사시
② 소유권의 구전 역사: 사회 질서 이야기
③ 소유의 착각: 역사는 어떻게 경제 사상을 형성하나
④ 소유권: 문서화 된 기록으로 제한되는 역사적 관점
⑤ 시대별 소유권에 대한 학제적 접근

---

21 내용일치

마지막 문장에서 '자율 신경계는 심박동수와 혈압, 발한 반응을 조절하고, 감정적 경험에서 뇌와 육체를 연결한다.'라고 했으므로 ⑤가 글의 내용과 일치한다.

have an influence on 영향을 미치다   chirp v. 지저귀다   crap n. 똥   house v. 수용하다   limbic a. 변연계의   disgust n. 혐오감   autonomic nervous system 자율 신경계   behind the scenes 막후에서, 남몰래   tirelessly ad. 끊임없이   heart rate 심박동수

감정은 여러 감각을 통해 들어오는 정보를 처리하는 방식에 큰 영향을 미친다. 우리 모두는 기분이 좋을 때 맑은 하늘과 지저귀는 새를 알아차리고, 기분이 좋지 않을 때는 먹구름과 비둘기 똥이 사방에 널려 있는 것을 알아차린 경험이 있다. 우리의 감정은 우리가 알아차리는 것과 그것을 경험하는 방식에 색을 입힌다. 감정은 뇌 표면 아래 깊숙한 곳에 자리 잡고 있다. 이 영역을 변연계 영역이라고 한다. 변연계는 우리의 기쁨과 두려움, 행복과 슬픔, 즐거움과 혐오감을 담당한다. 변연계는 자율 신경계와 밀접하게 연결되어 있다. 뇌의 이 부분은 우리가 의식하지 못하는 순간에도 은밀하게 끊임없이 그 기능을 하기 때문에 '자율적'이다. 자율 신경계는 심박동수와 혈압, 발한 반응을 조절하고, 감정적 경험에서 뇌와 육체를 연결한다.

다음 글의 내용과 가장 가까운 것을 고르시오.
① 긍정적인 분위기는 사물의 불쾌하고 어두운 측면을 강조한다.
② 발한 반응은 주로 뇌의 의식적인 부분에 의해 제어된다.
③ 뇌의 변연계 영역은 뇌의 바깥층에 위치한다.
④ 뇌의 변연계는 주로 논리적 추론을 담당한다.
⑤ 자율 신경계는 감정적 경험과 관련하여 심박동수와 같은 반응을 조절한다.

---

22 내용일치

공화정이 끝나고 아우구스투스 카이사르로부터 시작된 제국 시대에, 제국이 너무 넓고 복잡해서 새로운 건축 방식이 필요했다고 했으므로 ⑤가 글의 내용과 일치한다. ① 직후가 아니다. ② 평민은 제외한다. ③ 성공적으로 관리하지 못하고 위기가 찾아와서 제국이 등장했다. ④ 황제가 없는 기간이 길었다는 말은 없다. 아우구스투스는 율리우스 카이사르 바로 다음의 황제이다.

senate n. 원로원   magistrate n. 치안 판사   consul n. 집정관   conquer v. 정복하다   populace n. 대중   struggle to ~하려 애쓰다   administer v. 운영하다   patrician n. 귀족   pleb n. 평민   assumption n. 장악   dictatorial a. 독재의   assassinate v. 암살하다   usher in 선도하다, 길을 열다

로마 시는 처음에는 저명한 가문 출신 원로원과 선출 치안판사나 집정관이 통치하는 공화정의 중심 도시가 되었다. 로마 군대가 점점 더 많은 이탈리아와 그 너머를 정복해 나가면서 대중은 효율적으로 통치하고 토지 귀족(귀족)과 일반 자유 시민(평민) 모두를 만족시킬 수 있는 정부 시스템을 유지하려 노력했다. 결국 기원전 1세기에 위기가 닥쳐 군사 지도자 율리우스 카이사르가 독재 권력을 장악하게 되었다. 비록 암살당했지만, 그의 통치는 로마 제국의 길을 열었고, 기원전 27년 아우구스투스 카이사르를 시작으로 연이은 황제들에게 권력이 계승되었다. 제국은 넓고 복잡했으므로 초대형 건물을 비교적 빠르고 경제적으로 지을 수 있는 새로운 건축 방식이 필요했다.

다음 글의 내용과 가장 가까운 것을 고르시오.
① 로마 제국은 로마 도시가 세워진 직후에 시작되었다.
② 로마 공화국은 처음에는 원로원, 선출직 집정관, 일반 평민들이 이끌었다.
③ 로마 공화국은 확장 과정에서 귀족과 평민 모두의 요구를 큰 내부 갈등 없이 성공적으로 관리했다.
④ 율리우스 카이사르가 암살당한 후 로마 제국이 시작되기까지 황제가 없는 기간이 길었다.
⑤ 로마의 건축은 정치 체제가 공화정에서 제국으로 바뀌면서 진화했다.

---

23 내용일치

두 번째 문장에서 '캐리커처는 항상 '표현주의적'이었는데, 캐리커처 화가는 그의 피해자의 초상을 갖고, 그것을 왜곡하여 그의 동료에 대해 그가 느끼는 것을 표현하기 때문이다.'라고 했으므로 ④가 글의 내용과 일치한다. ① 자신이 선택한 방법을 캐리커처 화가의 방법에 비교할 수 있다고 했다. ②, ⑤ 실제로는 걸림돌로 판명되었다고 했다.

caricaturist n. 캐리커처 작가, 풍자만화가   expressionist a. 표현주의적인   likeness n. 비슷함, 닮은 얼굴, 초상   distort v. 왜곡하다   as long as ~하는 한   Art with a capital A 본격 예술   deliberately ad. 의도적으로   superiority n. 우월감, 우세   stumbling block 걸림돌   inconsistent a. 일관성 없는   sober a. 냉정한   skepticism n. 의심

반 고흐는 자신이 선택한 방법을 캐리커처 화가의 방법에 비교할 수 있다고 올바르게 말했다. 캐리커처는 항상 '표현주의적'이었는데, 캐리커처 화가는 그의 피해자의 초상을 갖고, 그것을 왜곡하여 그의 동료에 대해 그가 느끼는 것을 표현하기 때문이다. 이러한 자연의 왜곡이 유머라는 깃발 아래 항해하는(진행되는) 한, 누구도 그런 왜곡을 이해하기 어렵다고 생각하는 것 같지 않았다. 유머러스한 예술은 사람들이 본격 예술을 위해 남겨놓은 편견을 가지고 접근하지 않았기 때문에 모든 것이 허용되는 분야였다. 그러나 우월감이 아니라 사랑이나 존경, 두려움을 표현하려고 의도적으로

사물의 모습을 바꾸는 예술인 진지한 캐리커처라는 개념은 반 고흐가 예측했듯이 실제로는 걸림돌로 판명되었다. 그러나 그 개념에는 모순이란 없다. 사물에 대한 우리의 감정이 그 사물을 보는 방식과, 더 나아가 우리가 기억하는 형태에 영향을 미친다는 것은 냉정한 진실이다. 같은 장소라도 행복할 때와 슬플 때에 따라 얼마나 다르게 보이는지 누구나 경험해 보았을 것이다.

다음 글의 내용과 가장 가까운 것을 고르시오.
① 반 고흐는 자신의 방식이 캐리커처 화가의 방식과 완전히 다르다고 주장했다.
② 반 고흐는 진지한 캐리커처가 큰 의심 없이 쉽게 받아들여질 것이라고 예상했다.
③ 반 고흐에 따르면 캐리커처는 왜곡 없이 사실적인 묘사를 엄격하게 준수한다.
④ 캐리커처가 '표현주의적'이라고 묘사되는 이유는 작가의 감정을 표현하기 위해 초상을 왜곡하기 때문이다.
⑤ 반 고흐는 예술에서 외양을 바꾸어 사랑이나 두려움과 같은 감정을 전달하는 것은 일반적으로 논란 없이 받아들여진다고 믿었다.

---

24 내용일치 　　　　　　　　　　　　　　　④

④가 글의 요지이고, 첫 번째 문장의 재진술이다. ② 현대가 아니라 '과거'이다. ③ 더 크지 않고, 마찬가지다. ⑤ 역사와 과학의 관계이지 다른 학문 분야와는 아무런 관계가 없는 내용이다. 그리고 저자는 역사를 과학으로 분류하는 것에 반대하는 것이 아니라 그런 분류를 거부하는 것에 반대한다.

principal a. 주요한　justify v. 정당화하다　perpetuate v. 영속화하다　rift n. 균열　prejudice n. 편견　class structure 계급 구조　chasm n. 틈새　blind alley 막다른 골목　muddled a. 갈피를 못 잡는　botany n. 식물학

역사를 과학이라고 부르기를 거부하는 것에 내가 반대하는 주된 이유는 그 거부가 소위 '두 문화' 사이의 균열을 정당화하고 영속화하기 때문이다. 그 균열 자체는 오래된 과거에 속한 영국사회의 계급구조에 기반을 둔 이 아주 오래된 편견의 산물이다. 나 자신은 역사학자와 지질학자를 분리하는 틈새가 지질학자와 물리학자를 분리하는 틈새보다 더 깊거나 더 메울 수 없다고 생각하지 않는다. 그러나 내가 보기에 이 균열을 메우는 방법은 역사학자에게 기초 과학을 가르치거나 과학자에게 기초 역사를 가르치는 것이 아니다. 어리석은 생각에 의해 우리는 이 막다른 골목까지 와버렸다. 결국 과학자들은 이런 식으로 행동하지 않는다. 나는 엔지니어가 초급 식물학 수업에 참석하라는 권고를 받는다는 말을 들어본 적이 없다.

다음 글의 내용과 가장 가까운 것을 고르시오.
① 저자가 보기에 역사와 과학 사이의 균열은 역사 교육에 더 많은 과학을 통합함으로써 메워질 수 있다.
② 저자가 말하는 '두 문화'의 구분은 현대 영국 사회의 계급 구조의 산물이다.
③ 저자에 따르면, 역사학자와 지질학자 사이의 격차는 지질학자와 물리학자 사이의 격차보다 훨씬 더 크다.
④ 저자는 역사를 과학으로 인정하지 않는 것이 역사와 과학 사이의 구시대적인 구분을 강화한다고 주장한다.
⑤ 역사를 과학으로 분류하는 것에 저자가 반대하는 주된 이유는 다른 학문 분야들 사이에 더 큰 분열을 초래할 수 있기 때문이다.

---

25 내용일치 　　　　　　　　　　　　　　　③

③은 마지막에서 두 번째 문장의 재진술이다. ① 말도 안 되는 소리라고 했다. ② 미학과 물리학에도 적용했다. ④, ⑤ 피타고라스가 개발했다.

statement n. 진술　interpret v. 해석[설명]하다　arithmetic n. 산술　oblong a. 직사각형의 n. 직사각형　pebble n. 조약돌　presumably ad. 아마　atomic a. 원자의　build up 축적하다　molecule n. 분자　arrange v. 배열하다　aesthetics n. 미학

모두가 알다시피 피타고라스는 "모든 것은 숫자다"라고 말했다. 이 말은 현대적으로 해석하면 논리적으로 말도 안 된다. 그러나 그가 말한 의미는 정확히 말도 안 되는 말은 아니었다. 그는 음악에서 숫자의 중요성을 발견했고, 그가 음악과 산술 사이에 설정한 연관관계는 '조화 평균'과 '조화수열'이라는 수학적 용어로 남아 있다. 그는 숫자를 주사위나 카드 게임에서 나타나는 도형으로 생각했다. 우리는 수의 제곱과 세제곱에 대해 이야기하는데, 이는 그에게 빚진 용어이다. 그는 또한 직사각형 수, 삼각형 수, 피라미드형 수 등에 대해서도 이야기했다. 이것들은 그 문제의 도형을 만드는 데 필요한 조약돌의 수였다. 그는 아마도 세상을 원자적인 것으로, 그리고 인간의 몸을 다양한 형태로 배열된 원자로 구성된 분자들로 만들어진 것으로 생각했을 것이다. 이런 식으로 그는 미학에서와 마찬가지로 물리학에서도 산술을 기초연구로 삼고자 했다.

다음 글의 내용과 가장 가까운 것을 고르시오.
① 피타고라스의 "모든 것은 숫자다"라는 말은 현대의 논리적 해석과 완벽하게 일치한다.
② 피타고라스는 숫자는 그 수학적 속성 외에는 실용적인 용도가 없다고 믿었다.
③ 피타고라스의 세계 원자 구조에 대한 견해는 육체도 다양한 형태로 배열된 분자로 구성되어 있다고 제안했다.
④ 숫자를 직사각형, 삼각형, 피라미드 형태로 만드는 아이디어는 피타고라스 이후 수학자들에 의해 개발되었다.
⑤ 피타고라스의 가르침은 주로 철학 개념을 대상으로 했으며, 산술을 물리학 및 미학에 통합하는 것은 다른 사람들에게 맡겼다.

---

26 내용일치 　　　　　　　　　　　　　　　⑤

본문에서 양자 물리학은 복잡해서 본질적으로 어려운 개념 때문에 어렵다기보다는 낯익은 개념을 새롭게 상상하기가 힘들어서 그 생소함 때문에 어렵다고 했다. 또 우리가 양자 개념을 이해하기 위해서는 일상적인 세계 이해를 버려야 한다고 했다. 따라서 ⑤가 글의 내용과 일치한다. ① 복잡한 수학이 필요 없다. ②, ③ 양자 물리학의 대가들은 일상적인 현상이 아니라 블랙홀과 초기 우주의 강력한 중력 같은 해결되지 않은 문제에 집중한다. ④ 양자 물리학은 지성보다는 상상력과 관계가 있다.

unresolved a. 해결되지 않은　quantum physics 양자 물리학　gravity n. 중력　play a part 역할을 하다　intrinsic a. 본질적인　replace A with B B로 A를 대체하다　quantum mechanics 양자역학　treatment n. 논의

물리학계에서 가장 위대한 지성인은 아마도 블랙홀 내부에 존재한다고 추정되며 우주의 초기 진화에 중요한 역할을 했다고 알려진 극도로 강력한 중력에 양자 물리학을 어떻게 적용할까 하는 해결되지 않은 문제를 연구하는 사람들일 것이다. 하지만, 양자 물리학의 기본적인 개념은 사실 로켓 과학이 아니며, 양자 물리학 개념의 어려움은 그 본질적인 어려움보다는

생소함에 관계된 것이다. 우리는 관찰과 경험을 통해 얻은 세계의 작동 방식에 관한 일부 개념들을 버려야 한다. 그러나 일단 버린 후에는, 양자 물리학을 이해하는 데 필요한 새로운 개념으로 대체하기 위해서는 지성보다는 상상력을 발휘해야 한다. 게다가, 양자역학의 원리가 어떻게 일상적인 많은 현상의 기저에 깔려있는지는 완전한 전문적 논의에 필요한 복잡한 수학적 분석을 사용하지 않고도 충분히 이해할 수 있다.

다음 글의 내용과 가장 가까운 것을 고르시오.
① 양자역학의 원리는 복잡한 수학적 분석 없이는 이해할 수 없다.
② 양자 물리학은 블랙홀과 초기 우주의 강력한 중력과는 거의 관련이 없다.
③ 물리학의 위대한 지성인들은 주로 양자 물리학을 일상적인 현상에 적용하는 데 집중한다.
④ 양자 물리학은 일반적으로 '로켓 과학'과 같은 복잡한 과학 이론과 관련된 지적 도전에 관한 것이다.
⑤ 양자 물리학은 복잡성보다는 익숙한 개념을 재해석하는 데 더 중점을 둔다.

---

27 내용일치

마지막에서 두 번째 문장에서 '과거에는 부자와 가난한 사람, 도시와 시골에 사는 사람들이 완전히 다른 식단을 먹고 살았다'고 했으므로, 계급에 따라 식단이 다른 것은 과거의 일이었다고 할 수 있다. 따라서 ④가 글의 내용과 거리가 멀다.

unify v. 통일하다 people n. 민족 specialty n. 특산물 unification n. 통일 flock v. 모여들다 trait n. 속성 tasty a. 맛있는

이탈리아인 대부분이 마침내 통일을 받아들이고 점차 같은 민족에 속해있다고 느끼게 된 이유 중 하나는 같은 것을 먹기 시작했기 때문이다. 이 과정에서 파스타 — 그리고 어느 정도는 피자 — 가 중심적인 역할을 했다. 1800년대 중반만 해도 파스타와 피자는 대체로 나폴리와 그 주변 지역의 특산품으로, 가난한 사람들의 음식이었다. 이탈리아 통일 이후, 가난한 남부 출신 이민자들은 일자리를 찾아 북부 도시로 몰려들었다. 그들은 자신들이 좋아하는 음식을 가져갔고, 가난한 사람들의 음식은 곧 모든 사람이 좋아하는 음식이 되었다. 존 디키가 그의 책 『기쁨(Delizia)』에 쓴 것처럼, 오늘날 이탈리아 사람들의 음식 사랑에서 가장 주목할 만한 특징 중 하나는 음식 사랑이 정말 민주적이라는 점이다. 과거에는 부자와 가난한 사람, 도시와 시골에 사는 사람들이 완전히 다른 식단을 먹고 살았다. 오늘날에는 그들의 자녀와 손자들이 맛있는 요리에 대해 똑같은 지식과 감상을 공유할 가능성이 크다. 소스는 지역마다 조금씩 다르지만, 모두가 같은 파스타 한 그릇을 꿈꾼다.

다음 글의 내용과 거리가 가장 먼 것은?
① 음식은 이탈리아 국가 정체성 형성에서 중요했다.
② 파스타와 피자는 한때 특정 지역과 연관된 음식이었다.
③ 농촌 노동력이 도시로 이동하면서 파스타는 전국적인 음식이 되었다.
④ 이탈리아에서 식단은 계급을 나타내는 중요한 지표로 남아 있다.
⑤ 파스타 소스의 지역적 차이는 이탈리아 전역에서 여전히 발견될 수 있다.

28-29

균형 감각은 고대의 논문에서뿐 아니라 수십 개에 달하는 르네상스 및 바로크 시대의 감각에 대한 표상과 우화에서도 무시되었다. 수 세기 동안 육체와 세계의 관계는 냄새 맡고, 보고, 듣고, 맛보고, 만지는 능력에 의해서만 매개되는 것으로 여겨졌다. 인간에게는 오감만 있다는 주장은 유럽, 미국, 그리고 아시아의 많은 지역에서 널리 퍼져 있었다. 이는 부분적으로는 상하 구분과 좌우 구분이 우리에게 너무나 분명하다 보니 어지럽거나 넘어질 때만 그 중요성을 인식하기 때문이다. 친구가 죽고 나서야 그에 대해 칭찬을 하는 것처럼, 우리는 통합적인 감각을 잃고 나서야 통합적인 감각의 장점을 인식한다. 우리가 그렇게 인식하는 것은 일시적인 변덕으로가 아니라 체내 나침반의 원리 같은 중요한 시계의 조절 원리가 불협화음의 개입을 통해서만, 다시 말해 불균형적인 육체 현상의 자연적 또는 인공적 생성을 통해서만 인식할 수 있기 때문이다.

19세기 초부터 인식 이론은 고전적인 감각 이외의 감각적 특성을 다루기 시작했다. 예를 들어, 나중에 통각이라고 알려진 고통 감각은 촉각과 연관되었고, 갈증, 배고픔, 배뇨 충동은 내분비학의 주제였다. 의학과 생리학은 외부 세계에 접근하는 방법과 피부 내부에서 일어나는 과정의 인식을 어느 정도 구분하기 시작했다. 하지만 시간 경과와 관련된 감각이나 평형과 관련된 감각에 관해서는, 이러한 감각이 어느 정도 '외부'를 가리키는지 혹은 어느 정도로 '내부'를 가리키는지가 명확하지 않았다. 또한 이러한 감각이 순전히 개인적인 감각인지, 혹은 이러한 감각이 습관이나 관습에 따라 달라질 수 있는 것인지 분명하지 않았다.

sense of balance 균형 감각 treatise n. 논문 antiquity n. 고대 representation n. 표상 mediate v. 매개하다 five senses 오감 prevalent a. 널리 퍼진 be owing to ~때문이다 dizzy a. 현기증을 느끼는 lose ground 넘어지다 as with ~와 마찬가지로 integrative a. 통합적인, 완전하게 하는 on a whim 충동적으로 intervention n. 개입, 간섭 dissonance n. 불협화음 sensory a. 감각의 nociception n. 통각 urge n. 충동, 열망 urinate v. 소변을 보다 subject n. 주제 endocrinology n. 내분비학 physiology n. 생리학 when it comes to ~에 관해 말하자면 equilibrium n. 평형상태

---

28 내용일치

첫 문장에서 균형 감각은 르네상스와 바로크 시대에는 무시되었다고 했으므로 ②가 글의 내용과 거리가 먼 것이다.

윗글의 내용과 가장 거리가 먼 것은?
① 수 세기 동안 인식 이론은 오감에 초점을 맞추었다.
② 균형 감각은 르네상스와 바로크 시대부터 연구 대상이었다.
③ 인식 이론은 19세기 초에 질적으로 발전했다.
④ 19세기 이론가들은 촉각과 통각을 연관 지어 설명했다.
⑤ 19세기 이론가들은 균형 감각과 관련된 감각이 완전히 개인적인 것인지 확신하지 못했다.

---

29 동의어

on a whim은 '그때그때, 변덕스럽게'라는 의미로, 이는 '특별한 원칙 없이 당장 생각나는 대로'라는 뜻이므로, ④가 가장 가까운 의미이다.

밑줄 친 "on a whim"의 뜻과 가장 가까운 것은?
① 근근이 먹고살기 위해
② 생각의 양식으로서
③ 극히 드물게
④ 당장 생각나는 대로
⑤ 아슬아슬하게

30-31

인지 심리학의 매혹적인 주제인 거짓 기억 현상은 인간 기억의 오류 가능성과 가변성을 탐구한다. 엘리자베스 로프터스의 획기적인 연구로 인해 널리 알려진 이 개념은 우리 기억이 항상 현실을 정확하게 반영하지는 않는다는 것을 보여준다. 거짓 기억은 사람들이 사건을 실제 일어난 방식과 다르게 기억하거나, 경우에 따라서는, 전혀 일어나지도 않은 사건을 기억하는 심리학적 사례들을 가리킨다. 로프터스의 실험, 특히 '쇼핑몰에서 길을 잃다' 기법은 기억이 얼마나 피암시성이 강한지(남의 영향을 받기 쉬운지)를 보여주었다. 이 실험에서 실험대상자들은 어렸을 때 쇼핑몰에서 길을 잃었다는 거짓 기억을 주입받았다. 놀랍게도 많은 실험대상자가 이 조작된 사건을 생생한 내용으로 기억했다. 이를 통해 거짓 기억이 얼마나 쉽게 만들어질 수 있는지를 보여주었다. 이 연구는 심오한 영향을 미치는데, 특히 목격자의 증언이 결정적일 수 있는 법률 분야에서 그렇다. 거짓 기억 형성은 복잡한 인지 과정과 관련이 있다. 암시, 사회적 압력, 회상 중의 기억의 가변성 같은 요인들이 이 같은 현상의 원인이 된다. 이러한 기억은 실제 기억만큼이나 상세하고 생생하여 개인의 머릿속에서 실제 경험과 구별할 수 없다. 거짓 기억 연구는 기억의 재구성적인 특성을 강조한다. 기억은 사실을 수동적으로 저장하는 것이 아니라 능동적이고 역동적인 과정으로, 쉽게 왜곡될 수 있다. 이러한 이해는 기억의 신뢰성이 아주 중요한 심리학, 법학, 심지어 역사학 등 다양한 분야에 중요한 영향을 미친다.

captivating a. 매력적인 fallibility n. 오류 가능성 malleability n. 가변성 groundbreaking a. 획기적인 reflection n. 반영 refer to 가리키다 suggestible a. 피암시성이 있는(남의 영향을 받기 쉬운) subject n. 실험 대상 implant v. 심다, 이식하다 lost a. 길을 잃은 fabricated a. 조작된 eyewitness n. 목격자 testimony n. 증언 crucial a. 중요한 suggestion n. 암시 indistinguishable a. 구별할 수 없는 susceptible a. 민감한 distortion n. 왜곡 paramount a. 중요한

---

30 내용일치 ⑤

기억은 조작되고 왜곡될 수 있으므로, 목격자의 증언도 믿을 수 없어 신뢰를 받기 어려울 것이므로 ⑤가 글의 내용과 거리가 멀다.

윗글의 내용과 가장 거리가 먼 것은?
① 거짓 기억 현상은 기억이 왜곡되거나 조작될 가능성을 가리킨다.
② 기억은 암시나 사회적 압박과 같은 요인에 의해 영향을 받을 수 있는 역동적인 과정이다.
③ 거짓 기억은 실제 기억만큼이나 상세하고 생생할 수 있다.
④ 로프터스의 '쇼핑몰에서 길을 잃다' 실험은 사람들에게 어린 시절 사건에 관한 조작된 기억을 심어주는 것을 포함했다.
⑤ 로프터스의 연구는 많은 법적 시나리오에서 목격자 증언의 신뢰성을 확인했다.

---

31 빈칸완성 ⑤

기억은 조작되고 왜곡될 수 있는 역동적이고 능동적인 과정이라 했으므로 ⑤의 '재구성적인'이 빈칸에 가장 적절하다.

빈칸에 들어갈 가장 적절한 것은?
① 안정적인
② 사색적인
③ 순종적인
④ 복제된
⑤ 재구성적인

32-33

세계적으로 8,000종(種)이 넘는 개구리와 두꺼비들이 뛰어다니고 울어댄다. 양서류는 적응의 달인이며, 다양하고 독특한 생존 전략을 보유하고 있다. 하지만 IUCN 적색 목록에 따르면 양서류는 지구상에서 두 번째로 멸종이 우려되는 집단이며, 전체 멸종우려 종의 40.7%를 차지하는 멸종이 가장 크게 우려되는 척추동물 강(綱)인 것은 분명하다. 지속적인 서식지 상실, 기후 변화, 팬데믹 항아리곰팡이 병은 양서류를 위협하는 주요 요인들 중 일부다. 하지만 일부 종이 다른 종보다 더 취약한 이유는 아직 대체로 알려져 있지 않다. 개구리와 두꺼비는 항상 갈색과 초록색만 있는 것은 아니며, 믿을 수 없을 정도로 다양한 색과 무늬를 갖고 있고, 심지어 우연히 생겨나지 않은 질감까지 가지고 있다. 어떤 종은 주변 환경과 완벽히 어울려 눈에 띄지 않지만, 어떤 종은 눈에 띄는 색과 무늬(경계색)를 걸고 신호로 사용하여 "나를 만지지 마, 나는 독이 있고, 먹을 수 없어!"라고 외친다. 그러나 색상은 그들이 보여주듯이 시각적 신호로만 기능하지는 않는다.

위장색과 경계색 외에도 색채와, 특히 밝기로 측정되는 멜라닌화는 체온 조절에 중요한 역할을 한다. 이러한 색채 기반 체온 조절 메커니즘은 무미류처럼 흡수하는 햇빛에 의존하여 체온을 높이고 유지하는 곤충 집단에서 점점 더 많이 지지받고 있다. 색의 밝기, 생리학 및 분포 사이의 관계는 열 멜라니즘 가설로 개념화되는데, 이 가설에 따르면 색이 어두운 생물일수록 더 빨리 가열되므로 추운 지역에서 살기에 유리한 반면, 색이 밝은 생물일수록 따뜻한 지역에서 과열이 방지되는 혜택을 누린다.

toad n. 두꺼비 hop v. 깡충깡충 뛰다 croak v. 개골개골[깍깍]하다 adaptation n. 적응, 순응 amphibian n. 양서류 threatened a. 멸종이 우려되는 undisputedly ad. 당연히 vertebrate n. 척추동물 class n. <생물학> 강(綱) habitat n. 서식지 chytrid n. 항아리곰팡이 vulnerable a. 취약한 incredible a. 믿을 수 없는 texture n. 질감 by chance 우연히 seamlessly ad. 완벽하게 detect v. 탐지하다 conspicuous a. 두드러지는 aposematism n. 경계색 inedible a. 먹을 수 없는, 못 먹는 camouflage n. 위장색 melanisation n. 멜라닌화 thermoregulation n. 체온 조절 anuran n. 무미류 thermal melanism hypothesis 열 멜라닌 가설 prevention n. 예방, 방지 overheating n. 과열 implicit a. 암시된 vague a. 모호한

---

32 동의어 ④

conspicuous는 '눈에 띄는'이라는 의미이므로 ④의 evident가 가장 가깝다.

밑줄 친 "conspicuous"의 뜻과 가장 가까운 것은?
① 암시된
② 눈에 띄지 않는
③ 독특한
④ 분명한, 눈에 띄는
⑤ 모호한

33 내용일치 ⑤

열 멜라닌 가설은 마지막 문단에 나오는데, 이 가설에 인용되고 있는 동물은 곤충과 양서류이다. 글 어디에도 포유류 이야기는 없다. 따라서 ⑤가 글의 내용과 거리가 멀다. ① 두 번째 문장에서 양서류는 지구상에서 두 번째로 멸종 우려가 큰 생물군이고, 척추동물 중에서는 멸종 우려가 가장 크다고 했다.

윗글의 내용과 가장 거리가 먼 것은?
① 양서류는 지구상에서 멸종의 우려가 가장 큰 척추동물 집단이다.
② 개구리와 두꺼비의 색은 단순한 시각적 신호 이상의 역할을 한다.
③ 개구리와 두꺼비는 생존을 위한 다양한 전략을 갖고 있다.
④ 특정 종이 다른 종보다 위협에 더 취약한 이유는 여전히 미스터리로 남아 있다.
⑤ 열 멜라닌 가설은 포유류의 색이 체온 조절 능력에 중요한 역할을 한다는 것을 시사한다.

34-35

기초 모델은 다양한 기계 학습 작업의 기초나 시작점 역할을 하는 규모가 크고, 사전 학습된 모델이다. 이러한 모델은 광범위한 데이터 세트로 훈련을 하여, 다양한 하류 응용에 유용한 패턴, 특징 및 표현을 습득한다. 기술적으로 볼 때, 기초 모델은 수년 전부터 사용되어온 개념인 자기 주도 학습과 심층 신경망에 의존하므로 새로운 것이라고 할 수 없다. 하지만, 최근 몇 년 동안 기초 모델의 규모와 범위가 매우 커지면서 달성 가능한 목표의 경계도 확장되었다. 이 모델의 역량은 컴퓨터 하드웨어의 발전을 요구하고 상당히 더 큰 학습 데이터 풀에 대한 접근성을 요구하는 규모에서 비롯된다. 이를 통해 기초 모델들은 탁월한 수준의 균질화를 이루게 되었다. 실제로 연구자와 개발자는, 전이 학습의 다양한 접근 방식 덕분에, 기초 모델이 습득한 지식을 이용하여, 처음부터 훈련하지 않고도 다양한 작업에 그 지식을 적용할 수 있다. 물론 도메인 이동과 분포를 벗어난(학습할 때 보지 못했던) 데이터에 대한 기초 모델의 견고성은 여전히 의심스러운 상태이다. 기초 모델은 제로 샷 및 퓨샷 일반화 능력을 보여줌으로써 자연어 처리 및 컴퓨터 비전 분야를 혁신하고 있다. 이것은 훈련 과정에서 노출된 작업을 넘어 다른 작업까지 적용 가능성을 확장할 수 있다. 이러한 기초 모델이 확장되고 방대한 텍스트 데이터 세트로 훈련되면, 기초 모델의 제로샷과 퓨샷 성과는 미세 조정된 모델의 성과에 필적하고, 경우에 따라서는, 능가하기까지 한다.

foundation model 기반 모델 pre-trained a. 미리 훈련된 act as ~의 역할을 하다 undergo v. 겪다 extensive a. 광범위한 feature n. 특징 representation n. 표현 downstream application 하류 응용 (특징 생산 공정에서 원료나 중간 제품의 가공, 정제, 분리 등 후속 처리 및 응용) novel a. 새로운 self-supervised a. 자기 감독하는 neural network 신경망 potency n. 역량, 잠재력 stem from ~에서 비롯되다 homogenization n. 균질화 exploit v. 이용하다 from scratch 맨 처음부터 transfer learning 전이학습 robustness n. 견고성, 강건함 zero-shot generalization 제로샷 일반화(모델이 이전에 본 적이 없는 클래스나 작업에 대해 일반화하는 능력) few-shot generalization 퓨샷 일반화(모델이 매우 적은 수의 예제로부터 학습하여 새로운 작업이나 클래스에 대해 일반화하는 능력) capability n. 기능, 역량 be exposed to ~에 노출되다 scale up 규모를 확장하다 fine-tuned a. 미세조정한 unsupervised models 비지도 학습 모델(입력 데이터의 구조나 패턴을 발견하고 이를 이용하여 유용한 정보를 추출하는 모델)

34 내용일치 ②

세 번째 문장에서 기초 모델은 수년 전부터 사용되어온 자기 주도 학습과 심층 신경망에 의존하므로 새로운 것이라고 할 수 없다고 했다. 따라서 ②가 글의 내용과 거리가 멀다. 뒤 부분은 옳다.

윗글의 내용과 가장 거리가 먼 것은?
① 기초 모델은 다양한 기계 학습 작업의 시작점 역할을 한다.
② 기초 모델의 메커니즘은 새로운 것이며, 최근 규모와 범위가 확장되면서 그 기능이 크게 확장되었다.
③ 기초 모델의 효율성은 방대한 데이터 세트에 대한 광범위한 훈련과 컴퓨터 하드웨어의 발전에 기인한다.
④ 기초 모델은 제로샷 및 퓨샷 일반화 기능을 선보이며 자연어 처리를 변화시키고 있다.
⑤ 기초 모델의 규모와 범위가 매우 넓기에 연구자들은 이 모델에서 얻은 지식을 다양한 작업에 적용할 수 있다.

35 글의 제목 ①

이 글은 기초 모델이 기계 학습 분야와 관련하여 어떤 것인가를 설명하고 기초 모델이 자연어 처리 및 컴퓨터 비전 분야를 혁신하는 등, 다른 분야에도 영향을 미치고 있다는 내용이므로 ①이 제목으로 적절하다.

윗글의 제목으로 가장 적절한 것은?
① 기계 학습에서 기초 모델의 진화와 영향력
② 미세 조정된 모델의 영향력 탐색
③ 기존 방식이 기초 모델을 능가할 수 있을까?
④ 고급 기계 학습에서 대규모 데이터 세트의 중요성 감소
⑤ 비지도 모델에서 제로샷 및 퓨샷 성능의 우수성

01 ④	02 ②	03 ③	04 ④	05 ①	06 ④	07 ②	08 ③	09 ④	10 ②
11 ③	12 ①	13 ③	14 ②	15 ③	16 ①	17 ④	18 ①	19 ①	20 ③
21 ①	22 ④	23 ②	24 ①	25 ④	26 ②	27 ①	28 ②	29 ④	30 ③
31 ②	32 ②	33 ①	34 ④	35 ②	36 ③	37 ①	38 ③	39 ③	40 ①

01 동의어 ④

meticulous a. 꼼꼼한 Flaubertian a. 플로베르 풍의 timid a. 소심한 incredible a. 믿을 수 없는, 믿기 힘든 effrontery n. 뻔뻔스러움, 무례함(= insolence) congestion n. 혼잡 circumspection n. 신중함 uncouth a. 예의가 없는, 거칠고 서툰

꼼꼼하고 자의식적인 플로베르 양식의 이 초기 작품들을 설명하면서, 벨로(Bellow)는 자신이 소심했으며 자신을 작가이자 예술가로서 세상에 알린다는 것은 놀라울 정도의 뻔뻔한 일로 느껴졌다고 인정했다.

02 동의어 ②

prophet n. 선지자 fulminate v. 맹렬히 비난하다(= inveigh) laud v. 칭찬하다 mistrust v. 신용하지 않다, 의심하다 console v. 위로하다

선지자들은 성전 예배로 충분하다고 생각한 동시대 사람들을 맹렬히 비난했다.

03 동의어 ③

compound v. 복잡하게 만들다, 악화시키다 farce n. 소극(笑劇), 익살극; 익살 verdict n. 평결 coup n. 쿠데타 magnanimously ad. 관대하게(= chivalrously) outrageous a. 터무니없는 sentence n. 선고 형량 ferociously ad. 맹렬하게 coltishly ad. 미숙하게 callously ad. 냉담하게, 태연히

평결 후에 쿠데타 지도자 민 아웅 흘라잉(Min Aung Hlaing) 장군은 부분 사면을 발표하고, 수찌(Suu Kyi) 여사의 터무니없는 4년 형량을 관대하게 절반으로 줄여 줌으로써, 그러지 않아도 우스꽝스러운 상황을 더욱 우스꽝스럽게 만들었다.

04 동의어 ④

not to say ~라고까지 말하는 것은 아니다 analytically minded philosophers 분석 철학자들 trail off 말꼬리를 흐리다 aporia n. 아포리아(하나의 명제에 대해 증거와 반증이 동시에 존재해서 그 진실성을 확립하기 어려운 상태) prattle v. 떠들어 대다(= blather) in search of ~을 찾아 scrutinize v. 검토하다 implead v. 고소하다 enunciate v. 분명히 말하다

이것은 사람은 결코 조용한 아포리아에 빠져 말꼬리를 흐리거나 올바른 단어를 찾아 계속 지껄이지는 않는다고 일부 분석 철학자처럼 말하는 것은 아니다.

05 동의어 ①

prevailing a. 지배적인 compromise n. 타협 be due to ~때문이다 perfidy n. 배신(= treachery) opportunist a. 기회주의적인 trade union 노동조합 alliance n. 동맹 despotism n. 독재 clique n. 파벌

마르쿠제(Marcuse)는 사회민주주의와 공산주의가 자본주의와 역사적인 타협을 이룬 것은 주로 기회주의 정당과 노동조합 지도부의 배신 때문이라는 반공산주의적 혁명 좌파의 지배적인 정치적 판단을 거부했다.

06 동의어 ④

unintelligible a. 이해할 수 없는 disguised a. 변장한 sedulous a. 정성을 다하는, 공들인, 세심한(= punctilious) unmask v. 가면을 벗기다 enticing a. 유혹하는 condoning a. 용서하는 feculent a. 더러운

일부 철학적 이론이 정말 이해할 수 없다면, 그 무의미함은 심히 위장되어 있어서, 그 가면을 벗기기 위해서는 세심한 논증이 필요함에 틀림없다.

07 동의어 ②

resign v. 사임하다 have an effect 영향을 미치다 disintegrate v. 분해하다, 붕괴하다 putrefy v. 곪다, 썩다(=gangrene) elutriate v. 깨끗이 씻다 configurate v. 모양[형태]을 만들다 recalesce v. 다시 뜨거워지다

1947년 비트겐슈타인(Wittgenstein)은 글을 쓰고 싶었고 또한 자신의 가르침이 좋은 영향을 미치지 못한다고 느꼈기 때문에 케임브리지 교수직을 사임했고, 그래서 그는 해체되고 있고 부패하고 있는 영국 문명에서 벗어나 아일랜드에 가서 살았다.

08 동의어 ③

given a. ~을 감안할 때 opprobrium n. 맹비난(= vilification) deceive v. 속이다 spinning n. 말 바꾸기 decency n. 품위 chastity n. 순결 abidance n. 지속

사실, 대부분의 거짓말에 가해지는 비난을 감안해서, 다른 국가나 자신의 국민을 속일 충분한 이유가 있다고 생각하는 지도자들은 거짓말보다는 말 바꾸기와 은폐를 더 선호한다.

09 동의어 ④

exclusionary a. 배타적인 deconstruction n. 해체 insouciantly ad. 태평하게, 태연하게(= equanimously) transgress v. 위반하다 so much so that ~할 정도로까지 as such 그러한 고로, 그러한 까닭에 staggerily ad. 엄청나게 tremendously ad. 엄청나게 blenchingly ad. 움찔하면서

트린(Trinh)의 작품에서는 배타적인 해체 원칙이 태연하게 위반되고 있으며, 사실, 너무나 그렇게 되고 있어서 『여성, 원주민, 타자(他者)』와 같은 작품은 해체에 적대적인 것으로 간주될 수 있고, 그러한 것으로서 해체의 타자로 간주될 수 있다.

10 동의어 ②

jejune a. 미숙한(= puerile) set theory 집합론 topology n. 위상수학 hermeneutic a. 해석학적인 puerperal a. 출산의 clairaudient a. 먼 곳의 소리를 들을 수 있는 cardiant a. 심장을 강화하는

캔터(Cantor)의 구성과 공식화가 집합론과 위상수학에 익숙한 지금 우리에게는 미숙해 보일 수 있지만, 해석학적 해석을 위해서는 기본적인, 특히 기초적인, 개념과 결과를 얻는 것이 한때 얼마나 어려웠을지 이해하려고 해야 한다.

11 관사 ③

클라우디아 샴과 전직 연방준비제도이사회 연구원은 동격관계이다. 여러 연구원 중 한 명이므로 ③의 정관사 the를 a로 바꿔야 한다.

disgrace n. 수치 Federal Reserve 연방준비제도 identify v. 신원을 확인하다

더 이상 자신을 경제학자라고 밝히지 않기로 한 전직 연방준비제도 연구원인 클라우디아 샴(Claudia Sham)에 따르면, 경제학은 수치스러운 것이다.

12 half of ①

half는 바로 명사를 수식하기보다 of를 명사 앞에 두어 '~중에 절반'의 뜻으로 쓰이므로 ①을 half of Americans로 고쳐야 한다. 다른 명사의 경우 half of the employees, half of the books 등, 'half of the 명사'의 형태로 쓰이는 것처럼 half of the Americans로 나타낼 수 있으나 the가 없는 것이 더 일반적이다.

approximately ad. 대략 file tax returns 세금 신고하다

연방 세금을 신고하기에는 소득이 너무 적은 미국인 중에 약 절반은 컴퓨터가 없다.

13 의문부사 ③

③의 의문대명사 what은 절 안에서 주어나 목적어 역할을 해야 하는데, what 이하가 완결된 절이어서 what이 아무 역할을 할 수 없다. 이렇게 완전한 절이 이어지면 의문부사여야 하므로 what을 적절한 의미의 의문부사 why로 고쳐야 한다. ④의 should have pp는 여기서는 '~했어야 했는데, 하지 않았다'는 의미가 아니라 '도대체 (왜/어떻게) ~했단 말인가'라는 '과거에 대한 강한 의문'을 나타내는 표현이다.

undecidability n. 결정 불가능성 in reality 사실 contradictory a. 모순적인 assessment n. 평가

그러나 이 결정 불가능성은 사실 정치적인 것이라기보다는 심층 구조적인 것이다. 그리고 그것은 유토피아에 대한 그렇게도 많은 평론가들이 도대체 왜 그 문제에 대해 모순적인 평가를 내놓았는지를 설명해준다.

14 연결사 ②

②의 that 이하가 something을 수식하려면 관계절이어야 하는데, 동사가 없어서 관계절이 되지 못한다. that이 아니라 전치사가 있으면 '전치사+명사'구로 something을 수식할 수 있으므로 that을 전치사 like로 고쳐야 한다.

유토피아적 형식과 유토피아적 소망을, 다시 말해 문자 텍스트나 장르와 일상생활에서 감지할 수 있는 유토피아적 충동과 전문 해석학적 또는 해석적 방법에 의한 그 충동의 실천과 같은 것을 구별해야 한다고 흔히들 말해 왔다.

15 수동태 ③

③ bind는 타동사인데, 내용상 모두가 함께 '묶여 있다'는 의미이므로 수동태의 과거분사 bound로 고쳐야 한다. ① "us"를 대명사가 아니라 명사로 보므로 "I"의 경우처럼 앞에 부정관사가 있다. ② us는 선행사이다. ④ 형용사 personal이 아니라 명사 relationships를 수식하므로 부사 subtly가 아니라 형용사 subtle이 맞다.

communal a. 공동체적인 so to speak 말하자면 manifold a. 다양한 variegated a. 다양한 종류로 이뤄진 cosmical a. 우주적인

단 하나의 공동체적 '나'만이 있었지만, 또한 말하자면 매우 다양한 인성을 지닌 채 관찰되는 무리인 '우리들'도 있었는데, 우리들 중 각자는 우주 탐사라는 전체 사업에 대한 자신의 독특한 공헌을 창의적으로 표현했지만, 그와 동시에 모두가 미묘한 대인 관계의 조직 안에서 함께 묶여 있었다.

16 부사 close와 closely의 구별 ①

① closely는 '밀접하게, 친밀히'라는 관계적 의미이므로 여기서는 부적절하다. 공간적으로 '가깝게'라는 의미의 부사 close로 고쳐야 한다.

surface n. 표면

이 시점에서 유토피아적 충동의 표현은 의식적인 유토피아적 프로젝트로 바뀌지 않고 그리고 우리가 유토피아적 프로그램이나 유토피아적 실현이라고 부르는 다른 발전 노선으로 넘어가지 않고 현실의 표면에 가능한 한 가깝게 다가왔다.

---

17 전치사+목적어 ④

become incorporated 다음에 명사가 바로 뒤이어 나올 수 없다. '~에 통합된다'는 말이 되기 위해서는 ④를 incorporated into로 바꿔야 한다.

inasmuch as ~하므로 practice n. 실천 succession n. 연속; 승계 interiorize v. 내면화하다 incorporate v. 통합하다

그 장르의 실천이 필연적으로 모어(More)의 기초적인 텍스트에 대한 일반적인 언급을 포함하므로, 역사와 일련의 이어진 유토피아 세대는 그 자체로 후기 유토피아 안에서 내면화되고 유토피아적 주장에 다양하게 통합된다.

---

18 가정법 ①

두 개의 if절의 동사가 'had+pp'로 가정법 과거완료이다. 따라서 주절의 동사가 '조동사의 과거+have p.p.'가 되도록 ①을 have been으로 고쳐야 한다.

uncanny a. 신비한 elapse v. 시간이 경과하다 exclamation n. 절규 untoward a. 뜻밖의 coincidence n. 우연의 일치

만약 그의 절규와 예기치 못한 사건 사이에 시간이 덜 경과했거나, 그가 수많은 유사한 우연의 일치를 만들어낼 수 있었더라면, 그 불가사의한 인상은 더욱 강했을 것이다.

---

19 논리완성 ①

주절의 의미가 '그 어떤 오점도 대의를 위한 실질적인 업적이 수반되었으면 용서될 수 있었다'인데, 오점이 더럽히는 대상은 오점과 반대로 명예롭고 영광스런 것일 것이므로 빈칸에는 은유적으로 '명예'라는 의미로 사용할 수 있는 '가문의 문장이 그려진 방패'라는 의미의 ① escutcheon이 적절하다.

blemish n. 오점, 흠, 결점 in the service of ~을 위한 cause n. 대의 escutcheon n. 문장이 그려진 방패 escalope n. 에스칼로프(얇게 저민 살코기에 빵가루를 발라 튀긴 요리) escuage n. 군역 대납금 escritoire n. 접는 책상

경력의 명예에 묻은 그 어떤 오점도 대의를 위한 실질적인 업적이 수반되었으면 용서받을 수 있었다.

---

20 논리완성 ③

because 앞에서 최선의 관리가 가능했다고 긍정적으로 말했으므로 because 절에서 사망자가 유럽 수준으로 유지되었다고 한 것과 마찬가

지로 대중의 우려를 '없애다', '줄이다'는 긍정적인 의미가 되게 빈칸에는 ③의 dampening이 들어가야 한다.

impersonate v. 가장하다 deteriorate v. 악화시키다 dampen v. 풀이 죽게 만들다 impassion v. 감동하게 만들다

영국은 코로나바이러스의 존재를 가장 잘 관리하는 방법을 강구하고 있는데, 이는 신속하고 정확한 백신 접종으로 사망자가 미국 수준보다는 유럽 수준으로 유지되어 대중의 우려를 줄여 주었기 때문에 가능했다.

---

21 논리완성 ①

빈칸에 들어갈 동사의 주어는 결국 who의 선행사인 eloquent phrasemakers(미사여구를 늘어놓는 웅변가들)이므로 빈칸에는 ①의 perorate(열변을 토하다)가 적절하다.

droits de l'homme 인권 wordy a. 장황한 eloquent a. 달변의 phrasemaker n. 미사여구를 늘어놓는 사람 be willing to 기꺼이 ~하다 insurgent n. 폭도, 반란자 perorate v. 연설하다 gregarine n. 족충 sporulate v. 변태시키다 excise v. 삭제하다

오히려, 트로츠키주의자인 제임스(James)의 인권에 대한 견해는, 역사의 진정한 경제적 동력에 이끌려 열변을 토했지만, 결국에는 반란군의 총구 앞에서 표면상의 귀족정신을 기꺼이 포기할 수밖에 없었던 웅변가들의 장황한 약속 같은 것이었던 것 같다.

---

22 논리완성 ④

경찰에 신고했다고 했으므로 빈칸에는 취객이 '난폭해졌다'는 뜻으로 ④의 obstreperous가 적절하다.

cop n. 경찰 unflappable a. 동요하지 않는 spruce a. 말쑥한 snazzy a. 세련된 obstreperous a. 정신없이 날뛰는, 난폭한

태비(Tabby)는 핑크색 유니폼을 입고 던킨도너츠에 갔으며, 커피를 마시러 온 취객이 정신없이 날뛰자 경찰에 신고했다.

---

23 논리완성 ②

유명한 작가와 비평가들이 『1984』의 결점을 지적하면서도 중요한 작품이라는 사실은 인정할 수밖에 없었다는 내용이다. but 앞에서 부정적으로 언급했으므로 but 다음은 긍정적인 내용이 되어야 하겠는데, couldn't로 부정했으므로 빈칸에는 ②의 '부인하다'가 적절하다.

dissenting a. 반대하는 allege v. 주장하다; 단언하다 actually ad. 사실은 thin character 얇은 캐릭터(뚜렷한 특징이나 개성이 부족한 캐릭터) humdrum a. 단조로운 implausible a. 설득력 없는; 받아들이기 어려운 acquiesce v. 묵인하다 gainsay v. 부정하다 swoon v. 기절하다 tress v. 다발로 쌓다

밀란 쿤데라(Milan Kundera)와 해롤드 블룸(Harold Bloom) 같은 반대의 목소리들은 『1984』가 빈약한 등장인물, 단조로운 글, 받아들이기 어려운 줄거리로 이루어진 형편없는 소설이라고 주장했지만, 그들도 이 작품의 중요성을 부인할 수는 없었다.

24 논리완성 ①

두 번째 분쟁에서 중심에 있던 사람이 이 선교사라고 했으므로 빈칸에는 분쟁과 비슷한 뜻인 ①의 '곤경'이 적절하다.

come to a head 주목받다 be located in ~에 위치하다 agricultural a. 농업의 Presbyterian a. 장로교의 missionary n. 선교사 plight n. 곤경 pledger n. 서약자 pleonexia n. 탐욕 plinth n. 대좌

1925년에 주목받은 두 번째 분쟁은 농업 분야의 매우 다른 상황에서 일어났고, 샘 히긴보탐(Sam Higginbotham)이라는 장로교 선교사가 이 곤경의 중심에 있었다.

25 논리완성 ④

조롱(ridicule)으로 불붙은 언론인들의 견해는 정부에 대한 조롱 섞인 견해일 것이므로 빈칸에는 ④의 jeering(조롱)이 적절하다.

ridicule n. 조롱 enflame v. 불지르다 whet v. 자극하다 appetite n. 식욕 temblor n. 지진 scrooch v. 옹크리다 froth n. 거품 jeering n. 조롱

이 조롱은 이미 적대적인 자유주의 언론인들의 견해에 불을 붙였고, 이 언론인들의 정부 관료들에 대한 조롱은 더욱 비판적인 정치 뉴스에 대한 욕구를 자극했다.

26 논리완성 ②

빈칸 다음의 voices는 howler monkeys(고함원숭이)의 목소리이므로 빈칸에는 howl(울부짖다)과 의미적으로 가까운 ②의 stentorian(큰 목소리의, 우렁찬)이 적절하다.

trace n. 자취, 흔적 tiny a. 작은 skeleton n. 골격 hollow a. 텅 빈 amplify v. 증폭하다 telltale a. 숨길 수 없는 detect v. 탐지하다 fossil n. 화석 scrummy a. 맛있는 stentorian a. 우렁찬 spiteful a. 악의적인 stately a. 위풍당당한

캠프파이어가 흙에 흔적을 남기듯, 말을 해야 할 필요는 골격에 작은 변화를 불러일으킨다. 남미 숲의 고함원숭이가 우렁찬 목소리를 증폭시키는 목구멍 속 텅 빈 뼈 상자(발성기관)만큼 극적인 것은 몇몇 화석에서 발견될 것으로 기대되는 여전히 숨길 수 없는 흔적을 제외하고는 아무 것도 없다.

27 논리완성 ①

빈칸에 들어갈 동사의 목적어는 자산 구조인데, 프롤레타리아 대중, 즉 무산계급이라면 당연히 자신들에게 아무런 재산도 보장하지 않는 자산 구조를 없애려고 노력할 것이므로 빈칸에는 ①이 적절하다.

proletarianization n. 프롤레타리아화, 무산계급화 fascism n. 파시즘 affect v. 영향을 미치다 property n. 자산 strive to ~하려 노력하다 ingest v. 삼키다 supplant v. 대체하다

현대인의 프롤레타리아화와 대중 형성의 증가는 동일한 과정의 두 가지 측면이다. 파시즘은 프롤레타리아 대중이 철폐하려고 노력하는 자산 구조에 영향을 주지 않으면서, 새롭게 생성된 프롤레타리아 대중을 조직하려고 한다.

28 논리완성 ②

wandered를 단서로 하여 ②를 정답으로 선택할 수 있다. direct가 '길을 가리켜주다'는 뜻이므로 wandered about without being directed는 갈 길을 모른 채 이리저리 헤매고 다녔다는 의미이다. with가 아닌 without이므로 disoriented는 부적절하다.

turning n. 모퉁이 presence n. 존재 disoriented a. 방향 감각을 잃은 directed a. 길안내를 받은 mislaid a. 잘못 놓인 attenuated a. 희석된

나는 다음 모퉁이에서 서둘러 좁은 길을 떠났지만 갈 길을 모른 채 한참을 이리저리 헤맨 후 같은 길에 되돌아와 있는 것을 갑자기 발견했는데, 거기서 나의 존재가 사람들의 관심을 끌기 시작했다.

29-31

일반적인 과학적 의미에서 '모델'이라는 낱말은 논리학에서 사용되는 의미와는 상당히 다르다. 예를 들어, 움직이는 물체에 관한 물리학의 뉴턴 모델은 질량과 힘, 속도와 가속도 개념을 사용하고 이러한 개념 간의 관계를 이상화된 물질적 물체에 적용되는 뉴턴 역학 법칙의 형태로 가정한다. 좀 더 최근의 예로는 DNA와 DNA의 세포 복제 및 기타 생물학적 과정에서의 역할에 관한 왓슨-크릭(Watson-Crick) 이중나선 모델을 들 수 있다. 빅뱅에서 최종 붕괴 또는 끝없는 팽창에 이르기까지 우주의 진화를 설명하는 우주론적 모델이나 지속적으로 분기하는 우주를 가정하는 모델과 같은 일부 과학 모델은 매우 순수 이론적이다. 그래서 대략적으로 말하자면, 과학 모델은 실제 현상을 설명하기 위해 세상의 다양한 종류의 물체와 그 물체들의 (아마도 동적인) 상호 관계를 이상적인 형태로 나타내는 이론이다.

논리학자에게 모델은 기본 개념들을 이런저런 방식으로 해석함으로써 주어지는 공리 체계의 구현이다. 공리 체계의 가장 간단한 예 중 하나는 "x는 y보다 작다"라는 순서 관계를 위한 공리 체계이다. 공리는 '이행성'(임의의 x, y, z에 대해 x가 y보다 작고 y가 z보다 작으면 x는 z보다 작다)과, '비대칭성'(임의의 x와 y에 대해 x가 y보다 작고 y가 x보다 작다는 것은 동시에 참일 수 없다)과, '호환성'(임의의 x와 y에 대해 x가 y와 같지 않으면 x가 y보다 작거나 y가 x보다 작다)이다. 이러한 공리 모델의 예는 일반적인 순서 관계를 가진 정수들과 실수들에 의해 제시된다. 실수들은 또한 '조밀성'(임의의 x와 y에 대해 x가 y보다 작으면, x가 z보다 작고 z가 y보다 작은 그런 z가 있어야 한다) 진술 모델을 형성한다. 이 진술은 정수에 대해서는 거짓이다. 가능한 공리로 간주되는 조밀성에 대한 가정은 "x가 y보다 작다"는 순서 관계의 기본 공리들과는 '일치'하면서도 '독립적'이다.

logic n. 논리학 mass n. 질량 velocity n. 속도 posit v. 설정하다 law of mechanics 역학 법칙 helix n. 나선형 replication n. 복제 speculative a. 사색적인, 순수이론적인 collapse n. 붕괴 expansion n. 팽창 bifurcating a. 두 갈래로 나뉘는 axiom n. 공리 one way or another 이런저런 방식으로 ordering relation 선후행의 순서 transitivity n. 타동성, 이행성 compatibility n. 호환성 integer n. 정수(-3, -2, -1, 0, 1, 2, 3... 과 같이 소수점 이하가 없는 수. 양의 정수와

음의 정수가 모두 포함된다) real numbers 실수(모든 유리수와 무리수를 포함하는 수의 집합으로 정수뿐만 아니라 소수점 이하의 숫자도 포함된다) density n. 밀도, 조밀성 tangible a. 확실한 with respect to ~와 관련하여

29 내용추론 ④

임의의 두 실수는 서로 다르기만 하면 크기에 차이가 있어서 '보다 작다'는 순서 관계에 있게 되므로 ④를 추론할 수 있다. ② 조밀성 공리는 정수에 대해서는 성립하지 않아도 실수에 대해서는 성립한다. 즉 예를 들어 2와 3 사이에 다른 정수는 없어도 2와 3 사이에 다른 실수는 무수히 많아서 2와 3 사이에만이 아니라 모든 서로 다른 두 실수 사이에는 또 다른 실수가 있다. ③ 과학 모델이 추상적 개념을 포함할 수도 있다. 일부 과학 모델은 아주 순수 이론적이라고 했다.

다음 중 이 글에서 추론할 수 있는 것은?
① DNA를 통한 유전과 같은 생물학적 현상은 과학 모델을 통해 이해될 수 없다.
② 정수가 아닌 실수가 '보다 작다' 순서 관계의 모델이 될 수 있는데 왜냐하면 조밀성 공리가 실수에 대해 성립하지 않기 때문이다.
③ 과학 모델은 확실한 증거 없이 추측에 근거한 아이디어를 배제할 수 있을 정도로 구체적이어야 한다.
④ 위에서 언급한 공리와 관련하여, 서로 다른 모든 두 실수는 '보다 작다'는 순서 관계로 정렬할 수 있다.

30 내용파악 ③

글에 따르면 조밀성 공리는 "x가 y보다 작으면, x가 z보다 작고 z가 y보다 작은 그런 z가 있어야 한다."로 정의되는데, 정수가 이 공리를 만족하지 못하는 이유는 예를 들어 1과 2와 같은 두 정수 사이에 다른 정수가 없기 때문이다. 따라서 ③이 정답이다. ①과 ②는 사실에 맞지도 않고 ④는 사실에 맞긴 하지만 문제의 이유가 아니다.

글에 따르면, 조밀성 공리는 어떤 이유로 정수에는 참이 <u>아닌가</u>?
① 정수는 실제 사물들 간의 상호 관계를 나타내는 모델이 될 수 없다
② 실수와 달리 정수만 순서 관계를 만족시킨다
③ 1과 2에서와 같이 두 정수 사이에 세 번째 정수가 때때로 있을 수 없다
④ 모든 서로 다른 두 정수는 '보다 작다'는 관계에 있어야 한다

31 부분이해 ②

글에서 저자는 기본 공리에 이행성과 비대칭성, 호환성을 포함시키고, 조밀성 공리를 별도로 이야기한다. 그리고 이 조밀성 공리를 기본 공리와 일치되면서 독립적이라고 말한다. 다시 말해 조밀성 공리는 기본 공리와 모순되지 않고 일치하여 추가될 수 있으며, 기본 공리 없이도 존재하는 독립성이 있어서 추가되지 않아도 된다는 말이다. 따라서 ②가 정답이다. ① 조밀성 공리는 이행성 공리와 모순되지 않는다. ③ 조밀성 공리에 대한 정의일 뿐 라고 말하는 이유는 아니다. ④ 조밀성 공리와 무관한 내용의 진술이다.

글에 따르면, 저자는 왜 라고 말하는가?
① 조밀성 공리는 이행성 공리와는 모순되지만, 비대칭성 공리와는 모순되지 않기 때문이다.
② 조밀성 공리는 '보다 작다'는 순서 관계를 위한 다른 기본 공리에 추가될 수 있지만 반드시 추가될 필요는 없기 때문이다.
③ 서로 다른 두 숫자가 '보다 작다'는 순서 관계에 있으면 항상 두 숫자 사이에서 숫자를 찾을 수 있기 때문이다.
④ 정수만이 실제 세계의 현상을 기술하고 표현할 수 있기 때문이다.

32-34

미학주의는 예술 작품이 예술가의 내면의 주관적 감정을 구체화하여 그 작품 앞에서 같은 감정을 경험한다고 추정되는 관람자에게 전달한다고 주장하는 표현 사상에 의해 지배된다. 미학주의에서 예술은 담론에서 소외되고, 인식론적 지위를 유지하지 못한다. 현대 예술에서 대체로 이 모델은 비판적인 반미학적 재현주의 전통에 의해 대체되었다(인문학과 사회과학에서 일어나고 있는 '정동적 전환'에 따라 미학주의가 다시 등장하는 징후가 있긴 하지만). 재현주의에 따르면 예술 작품은 진실이나 정치 이데올로기를 전달하는 비필수적인 통로이다. 작품의 메시지가 받아들여지고 나면, 작품의 구체적 물질성은 불필요한 것이 되어 버린다. 재현주의 모델의 핵심은 예술 작품은 항상 작품이 만들어지기 전에 먼저 있는 자의식적인 논리적 논증의 산물이라는 사상이다. 물론 이는 전문화된 현대 예술 담론 분야에서는 거의 빛을 보지 못하는 극단적인 입장이다. 그러나 비전문적인 예술 평론에서는 두 가지 입장이 융합되어, 예술을 예술적 표현의 아름다운 산물이자 메시지 전달자로 보기도 한다. 하지만 보다 전문적인 비판적 예술 담론 분야 안에서도 재현주의와 미학주의는 예술에 대한 사고를 멀리서 지배하는 경향이 있다.

다른 어떤 사상가보다도 마르틴 하이데거(Martin Heidegger)는 이 두 주장이 근본적으로 속해 있는 근대 데카르트적 틀 밖에서 예술 작품을 생각하는 방법을 처음으로 제시하였다. 그는 미학주의의 모호하고 말로 표현할 수 없는 경험이나 재현주의의 도구적 사고에 사로잡히지 않은 예술의 자율적인 힘을 보존하고자 한다. 예술 작품과의 만남에 대한 하이데거의 관념에서는, 아는 것은 의지적인 결심과 비의지적인 방임 모두와 연관된다. 여기서 예술적 창작 행위는 현상들이 나타날 수 있도록 '내버려 두는' 사건이며, 자연발생적이든 계산된 것이든 간에 엄격하게 자발적인 행위가 아니다. 하이데거는 그리스어 'technē(테크네)'와 'poiesis(포이에시스)'를 되살려 예술의 생산을 예술작품에 대한 생산주의적 개념(그리고 존재에 대한 생산주의적 해석)보다 먼저 있는 존재론적-현상학적, 인식론적 양식과 연결한다. 하이데거가 볼 때, 예술은 생산에 관한 형이상학적 사상(정신에서 먼저 생각된 사상이나 이미지에 따라 물질을 형성하는 것)보다 먼저 존재하고 그것과 반대되는 일종의 내버려 둠이다. 이러한 관점에 따르면 예술을 만든다는 것은 '창작'으로 생각되기보다는 이미 존재하는 것을 은폐에서 드러나도록 내버려 두는 것으로 이해된다. 아주 넓은 의미에서 예술에 대한 하이데거의 생각은 자기조절적 생산 양식에 따르는 것으로 보인다.

aestheticism n. 미학주의 hold v. 주장하다 materialize v. 구체화하다 subjective a. 주관적인 alienate v. 소외시키다 discourse n. 담론 epistemological a. 인식론적 status n. 지위 displace v. 대체하다 representationalism n. 재현주의, 표상주의 in line with ~에 의거한 affective turn 정동적 전환 take place 일어나다 conduit n. 도관 redundant a. 잉여의 fabrication n. 생산 fusion n. 융합 from a distance 멀리서 Cartesian a. 데카르트적인, 데카르트 철학의 belong to 속하다 autonomous a. 자율적인 hold hostage to 인질로 잡다 vague a. 모호한 ineffable a. 말로 표현할 수 없는 instrumental

a. 도구적인 resoluteness n. 단호함 voluntary a. 자발적인, 임의의 spontaneous a. 즉흥적인 retrieve v. 회수하다 ontological a. 존재론적인 phenomenological a. 현상학적인 modality n. 양식 counter n. 대응 metaphysical a. 형이상학적인 concealment n. 숨김 be amenable to ~에 따르다 autopoietic a. 자기조절적인

---

32 내용파악   ②

첫 번째 문장에서 '미학주의는 예술 작품이 예술가의 내면의 주관적 감정을 구체화하여 관람자에게 전달한다'고 했으므로 ②가 정답이다.

글에 따르면, 미학주의는 예술 작품을 _____로 본다.
① 예술가와 보는 사람이 참여하는 담론의 영향을 받는 창조물
② 예술가 자신의 내적인 느낌과 감정의 독자적 실현
③ 보는 사람의 인식론적 관점에서 특정한 위치를 차지하는 대상
④ 예술가의 정치 이데올로기를 재현하는 일부 메시지의 전달자

---

33 내용추론   ①

두 번째 문단 첫 번째 문장에서 '하이데거는 미학주의와 재현주의 모두가 속해 있는 근대 데카르트적 틀 밖에서 예술 작품을 생각하는 방법을 제시하였다.'고 했으므로 ①이 정답이다. ② 재현주의가 미학주의를 대체했으며, 정동적 전환에 따른 미학주의의 재등장은 징후일 뿐이다. ③ 비전문적인 평론에서는 두 입장 모두 드러난다고 하였다. 두 입장 중 하나를 명확하게 선택한다는 말은 없다. ④ 무시하지 않는다.

다음 중 이 글에서 추론할 수 있는 것은?
① 미학주의와 재현주의 모두 하이데거가 반대했던 데카르트 사상의 영향을 받고 있다.
② 현대 예술에서 미학주의는 이미 '정동적 전환'에 따라 재현주의를 대체했다.
③ 현대의 비판적인 예술 담론에서 비평가들은 미학주의와 재현주의 사이에서 분명한 선택을 하는 경향이 있다.
④ 재현주의를 옹호하는 비평가들은 일반적으로 예술 작품에 대한 논리적 논증의 중요성을 무시한다.

---

34 내용파악   ④

마지막 세 문장에 의하면, 생산주의적 이해는 예술을 외부의 의도에 따라 만들어지는 생산물로 보고, 자기조절적 이해는 예술을 외부의 영향 없이 스스로 의미를 만들어내는 자율적인 시스템으로 본다. 하이데거는 이 두 가지 관점을 상반된 것으로 본다. 따라서 ④가 정답이다.

글에 따르면, 다음 중 하이데거의 예술에 대한 사상이 <u>아닐</u> 것 같은 것은?
① 예술은 자율적인 힘을 가지고 있으며 주관적인 미적 경험이나 도구적 사고의 지배를 받지 않는다.
② 엄밀히 말하면 예술의 창작은 예술가의 의지에 의한 것이 아니라 일종의 사건이 일어나도록 내버려 두는 것이다.
③ 예술을 만드는 것은 사실 무언가를 만드는 행위가 아니라 숨겨져 있던 것을 드러내는 행위이다.
④ 예술 작품에 대한 생산적 이해는 실제로 예술에 대한 자생적 이해와 상관관계가 있다.

35-37

제러미 벤담(Jeremy Bentham)의 팬옵티콘은 현대 권력의 자동적 기능을 보장하는 건축적 형상이다. 우리는 팬옵티콘이 기반을 두고 있는 원리를 잘 알고 있다. 주변에는 고리 모양의 건물이 있고, 중앙에는 탑이 있으며, 이 탑에는 고리 안쪽을 향해 나있는 넓은 창문이 끼워져 있고, 주변 건물은 작은 감방들로 나뉘며, 각 감방은 건물 전체 폭으로 펼쳐져 있다. 감방에는 두 개의 창문이 있는데, 안쪽 창은 탑의 창문을 마주하고, 바깥쪽으로는 빛이 감방 한쪽 끝에서 다른 끝까지 닿을 수 있는 창이 있다. 따라서 질서 유지를 위해 필요한 것은 중앙 타워에 감독관을 배치하고 각 감방에 광인, 죄수, 환자, 사형수 등을 가두는 것뿐이다. 역광 효과로 인해 탑에서 정확하게 빛을 마주하고 서서 주변 감방에 있는 작은 죄수의 그림자까지 정확히 관찰할 수 있다. 감방들은 마치 그만큼 많은 새장, 각각의 배우가 혼자 있는 소극장처럼 완벽하게 개별화되어 있으며 항상 볼 수 있다. 팬옵티콘 메커니즘은 이러한 방식으로 끊임없이 보고 즉시 인식할 수 있는 공간적 통일성을 배치한다. 요컨대, 지하감옥의 원리를 뒤집어서, 둘러싸고, 빛을 빼앗고, 숨기는 세 가지 기능 중 첫 번째 기능만 보존하고 나머지 두 가지는 제거한다. 완전한 조명과 감독관의 눈은 궁극적으로 그들을 보호해주었던 어둠보다 더 많은 것을 포착한다. 가시성은 함정이다.

먼저, 이러한 감시 시스템은 — 부정적인 효과로 — 고야(Goya)의 그림이나 하워드(Howard)의 묘사에 나오는 무리들인, 감금 장소에서 발견되는 떼로 몰려, 울부짖는 무리를 피할 수 있게 했다. 각 개인은 자신의 감방에 안전하게 감금되어 있으며, 감독관은 정면에서 그를 볼 수 있다. 하지만 옆벽 때문에 그는 동료수감자들과 접촉할 수 없다. 그는 감시당하지만, 볼 수는 없다. 그는 정보의 대상일 뿐, 의사소통의 주체가 아니다. 이러한 중앙 탑 맞은편에 있는 그의 방 배치는 축(軸)의 가시성을 그에게 강요한다. 하지만 고리 구조로 분할된 감방들은 측면 방향의 비가시성을 암시한다. 그리고 이러한 비가시성은 질서를 보장한다. 수감자들이 죄수일 경우에도 공모, 집단 탈출 시도, 미래 범죄 계획, 서로 나쁜 영향을 미칠 위험이 사라진다. 환자라면 전염병 위험이 없어지고, 광인들이라면 서로 폭력을 행사할 위험이 줄어든다. 이러한 밀집된 대중, 다양한 교류의 장소, 개인의 융합, 집단적 효과를 주는 군중은 없어지고 분리된 개인들의 집합으로 대체된다. 감시자 관점에서 보면, 군중은 감시가 가능하고 숫자를 매길 수 있는 다수의 개인으로 대체되고, 수감자의 관점에서 보면 군중은 고립되고 감시되는 혼자로 대체된다. 따라서 팬옵티콘에서의 감시는 지속적인 효과를 가지지만, 실제 감시 행위 자체는 불연속적일 수 있다. 권력의 완성은 곧 권력 행사 자체를 불필요하게 만드는 경향이 있다. 이러한 건축 장치는 권력을 행사하는 사람과 상관없이 권력 관계를 창출하고 유지하는 기계가 되어야 한다. 요컨대, 수감자들은 스스로가 지탱하는 권력 상황에 갇히게 되는 것이다.

automatic a. 자동적인 periphery n. 주변 annular a. 고리 모양의 secure v. 확보하다 convict n. 기결수 condemned a. 유죄 선고를 받은 backlighting n. 역광 spatial a. 공간적인 reverse v. 반전시키다 dungeon n. 지하감옥 enclose v. 둘러싸다 howling a. 울부짖는 confinement n. 감금 come in contact with 접촉하다 subject n. 주체 impose v. 부과하다 axial a. 축을 이루는 lateral a. 측면의 inmate n. 수감자 plot n. 음모 collective a. 집단의 reciprocal a. 상호간의 contagion n. 전염 locus n. 장소 sequestered a. 한적한 surveillance n. 감시 apparatus n. 장치

---

35 빈칸완성   ②

팬옵티콘은 권력이 더 미시적이며 자동적으로 행사되는 환경을 조성하

고, 끊임없는 신체적 개입이나 명시적인 명령이 필요하지 않도록 하는 것을 목표로 한다. 수감자들은 끊임없이 감시되고 있다는 것을 알고 있기에 스스로를 규제하고, 이에 따라 경비원에 대한 의존도가 감소한다. 따라서 권력의 실제 행사는 많은 경우 '불필요하게' 된다. 그러므로 ②가 정답이다.

---

36 내용추론   ③

③이 주제에 가까운 내용이다. ① 완전한 조명은 어둠보다 더 많은 것을 포착한다고 했으므로 폭력도 쉽게 발각되어 폭력의 위험이 낮아질 것이다. ② 팬옵티콘의 목적은 자동적이며 미시적인 권력이지, 조명 박탈이 아니다. ④ 간수의 수가 증가하여 수감자의 권력이 폐지된다는 언급은 없다.

다음 중 이 글에서 추론할 수 있는 것은?
① 팬옵티콘의 완전 조명 시스템은 결국 수감자들이 서로에게 폭력을 행사할 위험을 높인다.
② 벤담의 팬옵티콘은 군집하는 사람들을 에워싸고 빛을 완전히 박탈하는 것을 목표로 한다.
③ 벤담의 팬옵티콘은 건축 공간을 작은 단위로 나누어 현대적 형태의 권력이 보다 자동으로 작동하도록 돕는다.
④ 벤담의 팬옵티콘에서 수감자의 집단적 권력은 간수의 수가 증가하여 폐지될 수 있다.

---

37 글의 목적   ①

팬옵티콘의 특별한 구조로 인해 수감자들을 감시하는 권력이 어떻게 효율적으로 구현되는지를 보여주는 글이므로 ①이 글의 목적으로 적절하다.

다음 중 이 글의 주요 목적이 될 가능성이 가장 큰 것은?
① 팬옵티콘의 공간 메커니즘을 통해 새로운 형태의 권력이 어떻게 구현되었는지를 독자들에게 알리기 위해
② 교도소 감방에서 전염이나 폭력의 위험을 피할 방법을 독자들에게 알리기 위해
③ 근대적 권력과 개성의 개념이 현대에 이르러 집단적 인간의 힘으로 어떻게 대체되었는지를 독자들에게 알리기 위해
④ 현대 권력의 기능이 불연속적이고 비영구적인 감시 시스템에서 어떻게 파생되는지 독자들에게 알리기 위해

38-40

원어민우월주의는 영어 교육(ELT)에 만연한 이념으로 정의되며, '원어민' 교사가 '서구 문화'를 대표하고 그 서구 문화에서 영어와 영어 교육 방법론의 이상이 비롯된다는 믿음을 특징으로 갖고 있다. 이러한 편견은 '원어민'과 '비원어민'이라는 겉으로만 그럴듯하나, 형편없이 정의된 이념적으로 구축된 개념에 기반하고 있으며, '비원어민 교사'로 정의되는 영어 교사에게 수많은 부정적인 결과를 초래해왔다. 이렇게 거짓되고 잘못 정의된 용어를 기반으로 한 그런 이념이 작동하고 있다는 사실은 '비원어민 교사'가 전 세계 영어 교사의 대다수(줄잡아 추산해도 약 80%)를 차지한다는 사실을 고려할 때 특히 문제가 된다.
홀리데이(Holliday)가 '원어민우월주의'라는 용어를 만들었는데, 이 용어

는 ELT에서 문화와 정치 문제를 다루면서 문화주의와 오리엔탈리즘에 대한 논의를 포함함으로써 더 포괄적인 방식으로 다루고자 한다. 컬럼비아 대학의 영문학과 교수 에드워드 사이드(Edward Said)는 그의 저서에서 오리엔탈리즘을 '동양을 다루기 — 동양에 대해 말하고, 동양을 설명하고, 동양을 가르치고, 동양에 이주하고, 동양을 통치함으로써, 동양을 다루기 — 위한 기업적 관례, 요컨대, 동양을 지배하고 동양을 재구성하고 동양에 대한 권위를 갖는 서구적 스타일로서의 오리엔탈리즘'이라고 설명했다. 사이드는 오리엔탈리즘을 그것이 복잡한 시스템, 문화, 집단을 본질화(본질적 요소로만 단순화)하고 뉘앙스가 결여된 간결한 방식으로 설명한다는 점에서 환원주의적이라고 말했다. 하나의 구성체로서의 '오리엔트(동양)'가 이런 점을 반영하는데, 그 용어의 단순성이 담론의 환원적 성격을 강조하고 있다. 서서(Susser)는 ELT에서 작동하고 있는 오리엔탈리즘의 명백한 예를 제공하는데, 이를 위해 그는 일본에 입국하는 외국인 교사에게 조언을 제공하는 자료와 다문화 학습 스타일에 대한 연구를 살펴본다. 서서는 이러한 텍스트가 가정(假定), 고정관념, 상투적 표현, 오류에 근거해 있다는 것을 발견했는데, 이는 현지 교사, 학생, 교육 기관을 '타자화'하고 일본인에 대한 고정관념적인 이미지로부터 저자들이 쌓아온 문제를 해결하려고 시도함으로써 현지의 그들에 대한 서구 교사의 권위를 정당화하려는 의도로 보였다.
서서가 이것에 대해 들고 있는 분명한 예는 일본 학생들에 대한 다두르(Dadour)와 로빈스(Robbins)의 진술인데, 그들은 일본 학생들이 교사가 제공하는 정보를 수동적으로 흡수하기를 더 선호한다고 주장한다. 이것은 일본, 중국 및 기타 동아시아 국가 학생들에 대한 일반적인 고정관념적인 묘사인데, 이런 묘사는 이론적 근거도 의심스러울 뿐만 아니라 학생들의 태도에 대한 연구에서도 잘못된 것으로 드러난 바 있다. 서구 중심적인 편견을 가진 구조와 시스템이 ELT업계를 지배하기 위해 ELT 내의 담론을 사용해온 방식은 '비원어민' 전문가에게 여러 가지 바람직하지 않은 결과를 초래했다.

pervasive a. 널리 퍼진 be characterized by ~라는 특징을 갖고 있다 methodology n. 방법론 bias n. 편견 spurious a. 그럴싸한 at play 작용하고 있는 make up 구성하다 conservative a. 보수적인 coin v. 용어를 만들다 deal with 다루다, 처리하다 overarching a. 포괄적인 corporate a. 기업의 institution n. 제도, 관습, 관례 reductive a. 환원주의적인 construct n. 구성체 at work 작동하는 stereotype n. 고정관념 platitude n. 진부한 의견 legitimize v. 정당화하다, 합법화하다 othering n. 타자화(他者化) preference n. 선호 mediatize v. 매체화하다

---

38 내용추론   ③

원어민우월주의는 오리엔탈리즘과 마찬가지로 편견과 고정관념에서 비롯된 이념으로 사실을 너무 단순화시키는 환원주의적인 성격은 있지만 지나치게 결정론적이라고는 할 수 없고, 교육과 학습의 주체와 비원어민 교사의 선택 문제는 언급되지 않았으므로 ③은 추론할 수 없다. ① 원어민우월주의를 본문에서는 영어교육(ELT)과 관련지어 설명하지만 다른 서양 언어의 경우에도 문화주의와 오리엔탈리즘에 입각해 볼 때 동양의 국가에서는 원어민우월주의가 존재할 것으로 충분히 추론할 수 있고 원어민 교사가 비원어민 교사보다 우월하다는 인식이 만연해 있으면 교사 채용에서도 원어민 교사가 유리할 것이다.

다음 중 이 글에서 추론할 수 없는 것은?
① 원어민우월주의는 특히 영어가 외국어인 환경에 국한되지는 않지만, 고용 관행에 영향을 미쳐 '원어민'에게 유리하게 만드는 경향이 있다.
② ELT는 여전히 서구 '원어민'의 목소리가 지배하는 분야이다.
③ 원어민우월주의 개념은 지나치게 결정론적이며, 주체의 역할과 비원어민 교사가 선택권을 행사하는 방식을 경시한다.
④ 원어민우월주의 개념의 한 측면은 '타자화'를 통해 비서구 문화를 소외시키는 이념적 담론이다.

---

39 글의 목적

원어민우월주의가 ELT 분야에 어떻게 부정적인 영향을 미치는가를 설명하는 글이다. 따라서 ③이 글의 목적으로 적절하다. ④ 원어민우월주의 담론의 예를 제시하기 위한 것은 아니다.

다음 중 이 글의 목적은?
① 원어민우월주의와 오리엔탈리즘의 관계를 설명하기 위해
② 원어민우월주의가 어떻게 일본인에 대한 고정관념을 낳았는지를 설명하기 위해
③ 이념적으로 구성된 원어민우월주의 개념의 부정적인 효과를 독자에게 알리기 위해
④ 일반적으로 서구 중심적 편견을 포함하는 원어민우월주의에 대한 문제 많은 담론의 예를 제시하기 위해

---

40 내용파악

서양식 영어 모델은 부정적인 것은 아니므로 그것을 학생들이 좋아한다고 해서 그것이 여기서 말하는 비원어민 교사에게 바람직하지 않은 결과는 아니다. 따라서 ①이 정답이다. ④ 원어민 교사가 더 우월하다는 담론이 사실을 지나치게 단순화하여 환원주의적 성격을 띠며 주위 사람들에게 전달될 때 비원어민 교사의 사기를 떨어뜨리는 분위기를 조성하게 될 것이다.

다음 중 "비원어민" 전문가에게 바람직하지 않은 결과"의 좋은 예가 될 수 없는 것은?
① 서양식 영어 모델에 대한 학생 선호
② '비원어민' 교사가 진정성이 떨어지는 것으로 그려짐
③ 비원어민 교사보다 '원어민' 교사를 더 긍정적으로 그리는 ELT 교재
④ 원어민우월주의 담론의 환원주의적 성격을 강조하며 전달되는 담론

01 ③	02 ③	03 ②	04 ④	05 ④	06 ②	07 ①	08 ②	09 ②	10 ④
11 ①	12 ③	13 ④	14 ④	15 ③	16 ①	17 ③	18 ②	19 ①	20 ①
21 ④	22 ③	23 ③	24 ②	25 ①					

01 동의어 ③

inhuman a. 비인간적인 narrator n. (소설의) 서술자 gaze upon 살펴보다, 응시하다 theological a. 신학적인 heft n. 무게(= weight) call one's bluff 위선을 드러내다 dystopian a. 디스토피아의, 반이상향의 insignificance n. 무의미 fragility n. 연약함 meagerness n. 빈약함

저자는 자신의 디스토피아 소설에서 비인간적이지만 그럼에도 너무나 인간적인 서술자를 이용하여 인생의 신학적인 무게를 살펴보고 그것의 위선을 드러내었다.

02 동의어 ③

accent n. 어투, 말투 punishing a. 고통을 주는, 심한 blandness n. 단조로움(= dullness) cliché n. (진부한) 판에 박힌 문구 banality n. 진부함; 진부한 말 evasion n. 얼버무리기, (대답을) 모호한 말로 피하기 objectivity n. 객관성 particularity n. 특수성 impartiality n. 공명정대

그의 최근 소설들 중 대부분은 심한 단조로움이 묻어나는 말투로 서술된다. 즉, 그의 소설은 모두 상투적인 표현, 진부한 표현, 그리고 얼버무리는 모호한 표현 같은 기법들을 많이 사용한다.

03 동의어 ②

directive n. 지시문 explicit a. 명확한, 분명한 imperative a. 필수적인(= essential) prescribe v. 처방하다; 규정하다 sequence n. 연속; 순서 preceding a. 이전의 precise a. 정확한 implicit a. 암시된, 내포된 eccentric a. 괴짜인, 별난

잡지에서 사진을 보는 사람들에게 캡션이 제공해주는 지시문들이 사진 하나하나의 의미가 앞선 모든 사진들의 연속에 의해 규정되는 것 같이 여겨지는 영화에서는 훨씬 더 명확해지고 필수적인 것으로 된다.

04 동의어 ④

shrivel v. 쪼글쪼글하게 만들다, 위축되다(= dwindle) artificial a. 인위적인 build-up n. 증가; 증강 personality n. 인간적 매력 cult n. 추종 집단 foster v. 조성하다 preserve v. 보존하다 spell n. 마법; 매력 burgeon v. 갑자기 발전하다[성장하다] bustle v. 분주히 돌아다니다 flush v. (얼굴이) 붉어지다, 상기되다

영화는 아우라의 위축에 대한 대응으로 스튜디오 밖에서 개성을 인위적으로 강화시키고, 영화 산업의 자금으로 양성된 유명배우에 대한 숭배는 그 사람의 고유한 아우라를 보존하는 것이 아니라 개성이라는 마법을 보존한다.

05 동의어 ④

class n. 종류 morbid a. (정신이) 병적인 anxiety n. 불안 no other than 다름 아닌 ~인 uncanny a. 섬뜩한, 기괴한 irrespective of ~와 관계없이(= regardless of) arouse v. 유발하다; 자극하다 dread n. 두려움 affect n. 정서, 감정 impertinent a. 무례한 irreverent a. 불경한 regretful a. 유감스러워하는

이런 종류의 병적인 불안은, 그것이 원래 두려움이나 어떤 다른 감정을 유발했는지와 관계없이, 다름 아닌 섬뜩한 것일 것이다.

06 동의어 ②

take place 일어나다 cast one's shadow on ~에 그림자를 드리우다 modest a. 겸손한; 적당한 presentiment n. (특히 불길한) 예감, 육감(= foreboding) come true (소망 등이) 이루어지다 tranquility n. 평온, 고요 composure n. 침착, 평정 hostility n. 적대감, 적개심

사고나 사망은 거의 항상 그들의 마음에 먼저 그림자를 드리운 후에 일어난다. 그런 이유로 그들은 보통 잘 들어맞는 불길한 예감이 그들한테 있다고 말하면서 이 상황을 가장 겸손한 방식으로 언급하는 습관이 있다.

07 동의어 ①

take the lead 주도하다 maritime a. 해양의 coalition n. 연합체; 연합(= alliance) militant n. 무장단체 summation n. 합계; 요약 arbitration n. 중재, 조정 lien n. 선취특권, 유치권

바이든(Biden) 행정부가 예멘(Yemen) 무장단체들과 맞서기 위한 해양 연합체 구성 발표를 주도하는 상황에서, 후티(Houthis) 무장단체는 미군과 정면으로 맞서는 것을 피했다.

08 동의어 ②

predominant a. 우세한; 주요한 instrumentalism n. 도구주의(인간의 지성은 그 목적·이상에 도달하기 위한 도구라는 설) enrich v. 풍부하게

하다 consolidate v. 강화하다 prowess n. 뛰어난 능력(= capacity) reliance n. 의존 compassion n. 연민, 동정심 diffidence n. 수줍음

오늘날 고등 교육에서 국제화의 주된 이념은 노동력을 풍부하게 하고 국가의 경제적 역량을 강화하는 것을 목표로 하는 도구주의이다.

09 동의어 ②

immigrant n. 이민자, 이주민 tie n. 관계 emigration n. (자국에서 타국으로의) 이민, 이주 transnational n. 초국적자 shuttle v. (두 장소를 자주) 왕래하다 acculturate v. 다른 문화에 성공적으로 동화되다(= assimilate) affirm v. 확인하다 accede v. 동의하다 abbreviate v. (단어·구 등을) 축약하다

이주민들에 대한 다른 연구는 그들이 이주해 떠나온 국가와의 유대관계와, 새로 이민 온 국가의 문화에 동화되는(문화 변용하는) 자들로서가 아니라 초국적자들로서의 그리고 양 국가를 오가는 사람들로서의 새로운 정체성과의 유대관계가 중요하다는 것을 보여준다.

10 동명사의 태 ④

④에서 전치사 of의 목적어로 동명사가 온 것은 맞지만, 수동태인 being constituted 다음에 목적어가 올 수 없으므로 목적어를 취할 수 있도록 ④를 능동태 동명사인 constituting으로 고쳐야 한다. ② 주어는 복수 명사인 procedures이다.

swarm v. 들끓다, 많이 모여들다 far from ~은커녕 proliferate v. 급증하다 unreadable a. 이해하기 어려운 tactics n. 전술 constitute v. ~을 구성하다 regulation n. 규제; 규칙 surreptitious a. 은밀한

정부의 행정집행에 의해 규제되거나 제거되기는커녕 불법행위가 급증하는 가운데 강화되어왔으며, 이해하기 어렵지만 안정적인 전술에 따라 일상적인 규제와 은밀한 창작행위를 구성할 정도로 결합된 이들 절차의 만연한 행위를 사람들은 추구할 수 있다.

11 수동태 ①

effect는 타동사이므로 능동태로 쓰일 경우 반드시 목적어가 있어야 하는데, 주어진 문장에는 목적어가 없다. 따라서 목적어가 필요 없는 수동태가 되도록 ①을 been effected로 고쳐야 한다. ④ 부정문에서 need는 조동사로 쓰이므로 동사원형인 be는 옳은 표현이다.

object-choice n. <정신분석> 대상 선택(사랑의 대상으로 선택된 사람[물건]) effect v. ~을 결과하다, (결과로서) 초래하다 narcissistic a. 자기애의 cathexis n. 정신집중, 심적 부착 regress v. 회귀[역행]하다 identification n. (심리적) 동일시 substitute n. 대체물 erotic a. 연애의

그(사랑의) 대상 선택은 자기애에 기초하여 결과된 것이어서, 이렇게 하는 데 장애가 발생할 때, 대상에 대한 정신집중은 자기애로 회귀할 수 있다. 그러면 그 대상과의 자기애적인 동일시가 연애에의 정신집중을 대체하는 것이 되며, 그 결과, 연인과의 갈등에도 불구하고 애정 관계는 포기되어질 필요가 없게 된다.

12 in such a way as to부정사 ③

'in such a way as to부정사'가 '~하는 (그런) 방식으로'라는 뜻으로 쓰이는 관용표현이므로 ③을 to부정사를 만드는 동사원형 transcribe로 고쳐야 한다.

transcribe v. (생각·말을 글로) 기록하다 trajectory n. 궤도, 궤적 curve n. 곡선 pass by 지나가다

걷기의 실행은 경로와 궤적을 기록하는 방식으로 도시 지도 위에서 추적될 수 있는 것이 사실이지만, 굵든 가늘든 이 곡선들은 말(言)처럼 지나간 것의 부재를 가리킬 뿐이다.

13 자동사 arrive와 호응하는 전치사 ④

자동사 arrive는 그 뒤에 목적어를 취하는 경우 대개 전치사 at과 함께 쓰이므로, ④의 for를 at으로 고쳐야 한다.

be tempted to do ~하고 싶어지다 psychogenic a. 심인성의, 마음[기분]탓인 if it were not for 만약 ~이 없다면 psycho-analytic a. 정신분석의

만약 그 정신분석법이 만족스러운 해결책에 도달하는 데 성공했다는 사실이 없다면, 이 사례들을 비심인성이라고 여기고 싶어질 것이다.

14 타동사 ④

stress는 타동사이므로 전치사 없이 바로 목적어를 취한다. 따라서 ④를 stressing으로 고쳐야 한다.

of concern 중요한 demand n. 수요 economy n. (경제 주체로서의) 국가 stress v. ~을 압박하다

공급 안정은 정치적으로 불안정한 세계에서 중요하며, 중국과 그 밖의 개발도상국들로부터 수입되는 석유에 대한 신규 수요가 시장을 압박하고 있다.

15 관계대명사 ③

'전치사+관계대명사' 다음에는 완전한 절이 오는데, ③ 다음에는 불완전한 절이 왔으므로 전치사가 없어야 한다. ③을 계속적 용법으로 쓰이는 which로 고쳐야 한다.

attendant a. 수반되는, 부수적인 disruption n. 붕괴, 와해; 환경 파괴 ecosystem n. 생태계 extraction n. 추출(어떤 과정을 거쳐 뽑아냄) fossil fuel 화석연료

모든 것은 관련 생태계의 환경 파괴가 수반되는 어떤 형태의 토지 사용이나, 핵연료의 경우에는 덜 그렇지만 화석연료의 경우에는 환경 파괴적일 수 있는 어떤 형태의 추출을 필요로 한다.

16 논리완성 ①

a type of power와 a ~ own exercise까지가 동격이므로, '권력의 유형'이 무엇인지를 부연 설명하는 말이 a ~ own exercise가 되어야 한다. 빈칸에 ①의 modality(형태)가 들어갈 경우 '유형(type)'을 대신해 쓸 수 있으며, 권력의 유형이 '권력 그 자체를 행사하는 방식'이라고 부연설명 할 수 있으므로, ①이 정답이다.

discipline n. 규율, 훈육 identify v. 동일시하다 institution n. 제도 apparatus n. 장치 exercise n. (권력 등의) 행사, 발휘 anatomy n. 해부; 해부학 modality n. 형태, 방식 modicum n. 소량 molt n. 털갈이, 탈피 mood n. 기분; 분위기

푸코(Foucault)의 규율은 어떤 제도나 장치와도 동일시될 수 없는데, 왜냐하면 그것은 권력의 유형, 즉 권력 그 자체의 행사 방식으로, 모든 일련의 도구, 기법, 절차, 그리고 적용 수준을 포함하기 때문이다. 즉, 그것은 권력의 해부학이며, 기술이다.

---

17 부정주어 so … as ~ ③

주어에 부정어 no가 포함되어 있으므로 'not so … as ~'라는 부정의 원급비교 구문이 되어야 한다. 따라서 빈칸에는 ③의 as가 적절하다.

apprehensiveness n. 불안감 in this respect 이런 점에서 dread v. 두려워하다

많은 성인들은 이런 점에서 아직도 불안감을 갖고 있으며, 눈의 부상만큼 그들이 두려워하는 신체 부상은 없다.

---

18 논리완성 ②

금융 위기가 닥쳤을 정도라면, 돈이 심각하게 부족했을 것이다. 따라서 국제통화기금으로부터 구제 금융을 받아야 할 필요성을 '초래했을' 것이므로, ②가 빈칸에 적절하다.

strike v. (재난 등이) 닥치다 bailout n. 구제 금융, 긴급 금융 지원 International Monetary Fund 국제통화기금(IMF) threaten v. 위협하다 precipitate v. (특히 나쁜 일을) 재촉하다, 초래하다 chagrin v. 원통하게 하다 mobilize v. 동원하다

1997년에는 아시아 금융위기가 닥쳐서, 국제통화기금(IMF)으로부터 경제적 구제 금융을 받아야 할 필요성을 초래했다.

---

19 논리완성 ①

조기 유학이 '불리한 점'이 되는 것은 유학을 마치고 돌아온 사람들이 유학에서 배운 영어가 효과를 내지 못하는 경우이고, 그런 일이 생기는 것은 '업무수행'에서일 것이므로 빈칸에는 ①의 performing(업무를 수행하는)이 들어가야 한다.

work v. 작용하다 perform v. (과제 등을) 수행하다 exploit v. 착취하다 explore v. 탐험하다 bring v. 가져오다

'조기유학'(이른 시기의 유학)은 유학을 마치고 돌아온 사람들이 직장에서 영어로 업무를 수행하는 데 엄청난 스트레스를 겪고 있다고 전하므로, 일부 경우에는 불리한 점으로 작용하기까지 했다.

20-22

20세기에 많은 철학자들은 세상에 대한 인간의 지식을 시각적인 인식과 유사하다고 주장할 때 어떤 운명적인 결과가 초래될 것인지에 대해 우려하기 시작했다. 예를 들어, 존 듀이(John Dewey)는 1929년에 플라톤(Plato)과 아리스토텔레스(Aristotle) 이후 서양의 철학은 지식 이론이 시각 행위에서 일어나는 것을 모델로 삼는다는 '관찰자 지식 이론'에 지배받아 왔다고 주장했다. 그리고 그는 지식인 계급의 실용적인 활동에 대한 전통적인 경시를 강화하기 위해, 세상을 명확하게 '보는' 것, 즉 명확한 관찰과 정확한 현실 묘사의 중요성에 대한 철학의 상응하는 주장을 비판했다. 듀이의 판단에 따르면, 관찰자 지식 이론은 철학적 탐구와 과학적 탐구의 목적이, 우리가 시각 행위로 하는 것 같이, 어떤 식으로든 현실에 개입하거나 변경하려 하지 않고 현실을 알아가는 것이라는 서양 철학자들 사이에 만연한 심오한 확신(또는 편견)을 반영한다. 그는 더 나아가 독립적으로 실재하는 것을 정확하고 왜곡되지 않게 표현하기 위한 이런 탐구의 주요 결과가 친숙하지만, 그가 볼 때는 불필요하고 무익한 논쟁이라고 주장하는데, 그 논쟁은 어떤 대상 — 물리적, 수학적, 논리적 대상 — 이 실제로 가장 확실하고 가장 실질적인지를 둘러싼, 그리고 진정한 지식이 어떤 종류의 대상에 부합하려고 노력해야 하는지를 둘러싼, 철학자들 사이의 논쟁이다.

관찰자 지식 이론에 대한 대안으로, 듀이는 실험의 개념에 기초한 실용적이고 참여적인 지식 개념을 제안한다. 이 모델에 따르면, 탐구자는 인간의 활동과 무관하다고 가정되는 현실과 자신의 생각을 일치시키려고 노력함으로써 순전히 이론적인 이해를 추구하는 것이 아니라, 오히려 연구 대상(예를 들어 화학물질을 첨가하거나 식물이 자라는 토양을 변화시킴)에 작용하여 알려진 것들을 생성하는 데 참여한다. 모든 진정한 지식이 이러한 실험 모델에 따라 이해된다면, 지식의 대상은 선험적인 존재나 본질적인 존재에 고정된 것으로 여겨지지 않을 것이며, 물리학이든, 화학이든, 사회학이든, 심리학이든 간에 우리가 일하는 어떤 분야에서건 지시된 행동의 결과에 존재하는 것으로 보일 것이라고 듀이는 주장한다. 그 결과, 지식의 어떠한 단일한 대상도 가장 실재하는 것으로 제시될 수 없는데, 왜냐하면 우리가 알고 있는 모든 것들이 구체적이고 똑같이 긴급한 문제들을 처리하기 위해 설계된 세상에 있는 대상들에 대한 구체적이고 실질적인 운영의 산물로 이해될 것이기 때문이다.

analogous to ~와 유사한 visual a. 시각적인 spectator n. 관객; 목격자 corresponding a. (~에) 상응하는 representation n. 묘사, 표현 depreciation n. 얕봄, 멸시 modify v. 수정하다 undistorted a. 왜곡되지 않은 conform to ~을 따르다 alternative n. 대안 conception n. (계획 등의) 구상 assume v. 추정하다 independent of ~와는 관계없는 antecedental a. 선행의 pressing a. 긴급한

---

20 빈칸완성 ①

빈칸 앞에서 20세기의 수많은 철학자들이 세상에 대한 인간의 지식과 시각적인 인식이 유사하다고 주장할 경우 발생하는 운명적인 결과에 대해 우려한다고 한 다음, 빈칸 다음에 20세기의 수많은 철학자들의 예로 1929년에 말한 존 듀이의 주장이 나왔으므로, ①의 for example이 빈칸에 적절하다.

21 내용파악 ④

첫 단락 마지막 부분의 논쟁은 존 듀이는 불필요하고 무익한 논쟁이라고 생각하지만, 관찰자 지식 이론을 지지하는 전통적인 서양 철학자들 사이에는 중요하고 친숙한 논쟁이었으므로 ④는 존 듀이의 견해일 뿐 관찰자 지식 이론의 특징은 아니다. 따라서 ④가 정답이다. ③ 첫 단락 첫 부분에서 존 듀이가 비판한 철학의 주장이 '지식인 계급의 실용적인 활동에 대한 전통적인 경시를 강화하기 위해, 세상을 명확하게 보는 것, 즉 명확한 관찰과 정확한 현실 묘사가 중요하다'는 주장이므로 관찰자 지식 이론은 '실용적인 활동에 대한 전통적인 경시'와 일치한다고 할 수 있다.

위 글에 의하면, 다음 중 '관찰자 지식 이론'의 특징일 수 있는 것이 아닌 것은?
① 사람들이 지식을 획득하는 방법은 실제 현실을 그들이 보고 관찰하는 방법을 기반으로 모델링되며 모델링 되어야 한다.
② 철학적인 이론들은 현실 세계에서 무엇이 실재하는지를 올바른 방식으로 설명해야 한다.
③ 실용적인 측면은 현실을 이해하는 것과 무관하기 때문에 철학을 하는 데 있어서 무시되는 것이 좋다.
④ 무엇이 확실하고 무엇이 실재하는지에 관한 논쟁들은 우리의 실제 삶에 기여하지 않으므로, 중요하지 않다.

22 내용추론 ③

듀이는 실험의 개념에 기초한 실용적이고 참여적인 지식 개념을 제안했다고 했으며, 지식의 대상이 고정된 것으로 여겨지지 않을 것이라고 했으므로, ③이 정답이다. ① because가 아니라 if이면 플라톤(Plato)과 아리스토텔레스(Aristotle) 이후 서양 철학자들의 경우를 가리킬 수 있다. ② unchanging이 잘못이다.

다음 중 위 글에서 추론할 수 있는 것은?
① 철학자들은 무엇을 어떻게 볼 수 있는지에 기초해 이론을 만들기 때문에 무엇이 실재하는지를 볼 수가 없다.
② 듀이에 따르면, 사람들은 오직 실험에만 기초한 변하지 않은 현실에 대한 지식을 획득할 수 있다고 한다.
③ 듀이의 입장에서 중요한 것은 고정된 현실이 아니라 행동의 결과인데, 행동의 결과를 통해 우리는 지식을 얻는다.
④ 플라톤과 아리스토텔레스는 실용적인 문제들에 대한 작품을 저술했으므로, 그들은 실험적 지식에 존경심을 보이는 것이라고 말할 수 있다.

23-25

실수(實數)는 거리, 각도, 시간, 에너지, 온도 또는 그 밖의 수많은 기하학적·물리적 양을 측정하는 데 필요한 크기를 제공해주는 것처럼 보이기 때문에 '실수'라고 불린다. 그러나 추상적으로 정의된 '실수'와 물리적인 양 사이의 관계는 생각만큼 명확하지 않다. 실수는 실제 물리적으로 객관적인 양이 아니라 수학적인 이상화를 의미한다. 실수 체계는 조밀성 (공리)의 속성을 갖고 있다. 예를 들어 두 개의 수 사이의 거리가 아무리 가까워도 두 개의 수 사이에는 제3의 수가 존재한다는 것이다. 물리적 거리나 시간이 현실적으로 이러한 특성을 가지고 있다고 말할 수 있는지는 분명치 않다. 만일 우리가 두 지점 사이의 물리적 거리를 계속해서 나눈다면, 우리는 결국 그 거리가 일반적으로 의미가 없어지는 너무나 작은 척도에 도달하게 될 것이다. 아원자 입자 크기의 10의 20승분의 1인 '양자 중력' 척도

에서는 이것이 실제로 사실일 것이라고 예상된다. 그러나 실수를 반영하려면 우리는 이보다 훨씬 더 무한히 작은 척도로 가야 한다. 가령 10의 200승분의 1이나 10의 2,000승분의 1 같은 것 말이다. 그렇게 터무니없이 작은 척도가 어떤 물리적인 의미를 갖는지는 명확하지 않다. 이와 상응하는 시간의 아주 작은 간격에도 유사한 의견이 적용될 것이다.

물리학에서 실수 체계는 거리와 시간의 물리적인 개념과 실수 체계가 매우 광범위하게 일치한다는 사실을 비롯해 수학적 유용성, 단순성, 그리고 간결성으로 선택된다. 실수 체계가 모든 방면에서 이런 물리적인 개념들과 일치하는 것으로 알려져 있기 때문에 실수 체계가 선택된 것은 아니다. 사실 아주 작은 거리나 시간의 척도에서 이러한 일치가 없다고 예상하는 것이 당연하다. 간단한 거리를 측정할 때는 자를 사용하는 것이 일반적이지만, 우리가 그것들의 원자 척도로 내려갈 때 알갱이 같은 성질을 띠게 된다. 이것은 그 자체로는 우리가 실수를 정확한 방식으로 계속 사용하는 것을 방해하지 않지만, 훨씬 짧은 거리를 측정하기 위해서는 훨씬 더 정교함이 필요하다. 우리는 결국 가장 작은 척도로 거리를 측정하는 기본 원칙에는 어려움이 있을 수 있는 것으로 적어도 약간은 의심해야 한다. 밝혀진 바에 따르면, 자연은 우리에게 놀라울 정도로 친절하며, 우리가 일상적인 척도나 그 이상의 척도로 사물을 설명하기 위해 우리가 익숙해져 있는 동일한 실수가 원자보다 훨씬 작은 척도, 심지어 예를 들어 전자나 양성자 같은 아원자 입자의 '고전적인' 직경의 100분의 1 이하, 그리고 그런 입자보다 20배나 작은 '양자 중력 척도'에서도 유용성을 유지하는 것으로 보인다. 이것은 경험에서 비롯된 놀라운 추론이다. 실수 거리에 대한 보다 친숙한 개념은 가장 멀리 떨어진 퀘이사나 그 너머까지 적용되는 것으로 보이며, 전체 범위는 최소 10의 42승과 아마도 10의 60승 이상이다. 사실, 실수 체계의 적절성에 대해서는 가끔 의문이 제기된다. 그런 숫자의 타당성에 대한 우리의 초기 경험이 비교적 제한된 범위에 놓여 있는 상황에서, 물리학의 정확한 설명을 위해 이 숫자에 그렇게나 많이 신뢰를 갖는 이유는 무엇인가?

real number 실수(實數, 유리수와 무리수의 총칭) magnitude n. <수학> 크기 angle n. 각도 geometrical a. 기하학의 abstractly ad. 추상적으로 clear-cut a. 명쾌한 objective a. 객관적인 property n. 속성, 특성 density n. 밀도 scale n. 척도 cease to do ~을 하지 않게 되다 quantum gravity 양자 중력 subatomic particle 아원자 입자 this is the case 이것이 사실이다 mirror v. 반영하다 absurdly ad. 터무니없이 utility n. 유용성 accord with ~와 일치하다 may well do ~하는 것은 당연하다 ruler n. (길이 측정에 쓰는) 자 take on (성질을) 띠다 granular a. 알갱이의, 알갱이로 된 get down to 차분히 착수하다 classical a. 고전적인 say ad. 예를 들어 electron n. 전자 proton n. 양성자, 양자 extraordinary a. 놀라운; 대단한 extrapolation n. 추정, 추론 quasar n. <천문> 준항성(準恒星), 퀘이사 confidence n. 신뢰; 확신 relevance n. 타당성; 관련성

23 내용파악 ③

물리학에서 실수 체계는 '수학적 유용성, 단순성, 그리고 간결성'으로 선택된다고 했으므로, ③이 정답이다.

위 글에 의하면, 물리학에서 실수 체계가 왜 사용되는가?
① 실수 체계의 구체성과 직관성 때문에
② 실수 체계의 현실과의 완전하고 전체적인 일치 때문에
③ 실수 체계의 수학적 간결성과 유용성 때문에
④ 실수 체계의 무한히 작은 아원자 척도에 대한 적용가능성 때문에

24 내용추론 ②

실수는 물리적인 양을 측정하는 데 필요한 크기를 제공해주는 것처럼 보이기 때문에 '실수'라고 불리지만, 실수와 물리적인 양 사이의 관계는 생각만큼 명확하지 않다고 했고 '두 지점 사이의 물리적 거리를 계속해서 나누면, 결국 그 거리가 일반적으로 의미가 없어지는 너무나 작은 척도에 도달하게 될 것'이라 했으므로, ②가 정답이다. 그래서 ④는 추론할 수 있다.

다음 중 위 글에서 추론할 수 없는 것은?
① 물리적 현상은 실수를 이용함으로써 수학적으로 이상화될 수 있다.
② 물리적인 양은 항상 의미 있는 방식으로 특정한 실수에 일치한다.
③ 실수는 거대한 양뿐 아니라 무한소의 양도 표현하는데 이용될 수 있다.
④ 실수의 조밀성은 물리적인 양을 측정하는 데 유용하지 않을지도 모른다.

25 뒷내용 추론 ①

본문의 마지막 문장에서 실수의 타당성에 대한 우리의 초기 경험이 제한된 상황에서, 물리학의 정확한 설명을 위해 실수에 그렇게나 많은 신뢰를 갖는 이유가 무엇인가라고 의문을 제기했다. 따라서 이어질 내용으로는 이에 대한 답변인 '실수가 신뢰를 받는 이유'에 대한 내용이 이어지는 것이 가장 자연스러우므로, ①이 정답이다.

다음 중 본문 바로 다음에 이어질 내용으로 가장 적절한 것은?
① 실수 체계가 많은 물리학 영역에서 그렇게 신뢰를 받으며 사용되는 이유
② 실수 체계가 다른 수 체계와 다른 이유
③ 측정하는 데 쓰이는 자가 물리학에서 사용될 수 없는 이유
④ 수학적 유용성, 단순성, 그리고 간결성이 물리학적으로 중요한 이유

편입 합격의 길을 제시하는 김영 로드맵
김영편입 영어 시리즈

| 초심자를 위한 편입영어 지침서 |

문법 이론 　　　　독해 이론 　　　　논리 이론

| 기초 실력 점검을 위한 초급 난이도 단계 |

문법 기출 1단계 　　독해 기출 1단계 　　논리 기출 1단계

문법 워크북 1단계 　독해 워크북 1단계 　논리 워크북 1단계

| 반드시 알아야 할 빈출 중고급 난이도 단계 |

문법 기출 2단계 　　독해 기출 2단계 　　논리 기출 2단계

문법 워크북 2단계 　독해 워크북 2단계 　논리 워크북 2단계

| 대학별 실전대비를 위한 최종 단계 |

영어 기출문제 해설집 　　수학 기출문제 해설집

김영편입 캠퍼스와 **시중 대형서점**에서 구입 가능
(교보문고, 영풍문고, 반디앤루니스, 인터파크, yes24, 알라딘 등)

김영편입 영어 기출문제 해설집 200% 활용법

1. 편입기출 출제경향 및 심층분석 확인!
편입영어 시험의 추세를 가늠해 볼 수 있는 영역별 문제 비율 및 심층분석을 통해 2025학년도 편입
영어 시험 대비 학습목표를 설정할 수 있습니다.

2. 실전 시험과 유사한 환경에서 모의평가!
실제 시험장에서 긴장하지 않고 시험환경에 얼마나 잘 적응할 수 있느냐가 고득점의 필수요건이므로,
수록된 기출문제의 문항 수와 시험시간을 확인하고 실제 시험처럼 제한시간 안에 풀어보면서 실전
감각을 익혀야 합니다.

3. 풀어본 문제는 해설집을 통해 개념정리!
문제를 제대로 이해하지 못하고 정답을 맞힌 경우 비슷한 유형의 문제가 시험에 다시 출제되면 오답을
고를 가능성이 높습니다. 따라서 문제의 해석과 분석뿐만 아니라 오답에 대한 설명을 통해 문제를
완벽하게 이해하고 넘어가야 합니다.